"This is an excellent, refreshing way to study literature. The selections will engage students while at the same time providing them with the necessary tools to critically study, discuss, think, and write about literature. Everything needed to teach an introduction to literature course can be found in the text."

—Judy Davidson, University of Texas, Pan American

"[*Retellings* is] wildly ambitious, insightful, original, creative, fresh, and challenging."

—Lee Campbell, Valdosta State University

"*Retellings* is among the most thorough and enlightening of anthologies I have seen in a long time. . . . [*Retellings* has] the best section on documentation and research I have seen in an anthology devoted primarily to literature."

—Erskine Carter, Black Hawk College

"The concept of 'retellings' is brilliant."

—Donna Bauerly, Loras College

"*Retellings* brings together familiar and unfamiliar materials in original and suggestive ways. . . . The pairings are sometimes clever and always thought-provoking. The book asks students to operate at a high intellectual level but gives them the rhetorical tools to make this possible."

—Christy Desmet, University of Georgia

"Students will find [*Retellings*] both interesting and approachable. I can imagine a wide range of research topics these readings might suggest, including topics across the disciplines and across the arts."

—Lynee Lewis Gaillet, Georgia State University

"Student and instructor friendly, utilitarian as well as philosophically and culturally rich . . . a successful attempt to interconnect themes and ideas across cultural and chronological boundaries."

—Jon G. Bentley, Albuquerque TVI Community College

"The variety of voices retelling cultural stories and myths is an absolute for helping students understand their own stories or the stories of others and all those stories' truths. Students need to hear and read and appreciate how stories are not always from one perspective, one time, one culture. *Retellings* reinforces such a thesis."

—Bill Holbrook, Ball State University

"*Retellings* offers fresh approaches to age-old topics."

—Juanita Butler, Prairie State College

Retellings

∼ *Retellings* ∼

A Thematic Literature Anthology

M. B. Clarke
University of California, Davis

A. G. Clarke
American River College

Boston   Burr Ridge, IL   Dubuque, IA   Madison, WI   New York
San Francisco   St. Louis   Bangkok   Bogotá   Caracas   Kuala Lumpur
Lisbon   London   Madrid   Mexico City   Milan   Montreal   New Delhi
Santiago   Seoul   Singapore   Sydney   Taipei   Toronto

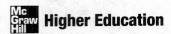
Retellings: A Thematic Literature Anthology

Published by McGraw-Hill, an imprint of The McGraw-Hill Companies, Inc., 1221 Avenue of the Americas, New York, NY 10020. Copyright 2004 by McGraw-Hill. All rights reserved. No part of this publication may be reproduced or distributed in any form or by any means, or stored in a database or retrieval system, without the prior written consent of The McGraw-Hill Companies, Inc., including but not limited to, in any network or other electronic storage or transmission, or broadcast for distance learning.

This book is printed on acid-free paper.

8 9 0 DOC DOC 0

ISBN-13: 978-0-07-241469-1
ISBN-10: 0-07-241469-3

Vice president and editor-in-chief: *Thalia Dorwick;* publisher: *Steve Debow;* sponsoring editor: *Alexis Walker;* developmental editor: *Anne Stameshkin;* marketing manager: *David S. Patterson;* design manager: *Cassandra Chu;* project manager: *Christina Gimlin;* production supervisor: *Tandra Jorgensen;* photo research coordinator: *Natalia Peschiera;* photo researcher: *David Tietz;* art editor: *Cristin Yancey;* supplements producer: *Kate Boylan;* interior design: *Linda Robertson/Michael Remener;* cover design: *Joan Greenfield;* compositor: *Thompson Type;* typeface: *Bembo;* printer: *RR Donnelley, Crawfordsville*

On the cover: Andy Warhol, © Andy Warhol Foundation, Inc./Art Resouce, NY. © 2003 Andy Warhol Foundation for the Visual Arts/Artist Rights Society (ARS), New York; Leonardo Da Vinci, © Réunion des Musées Nationaux/Art Resource, NY.

Because this page cannot legibly accommodate all the copyright notices, credits are listed on page C-1 following the appendixes and constitute an extension of the copyright page.

Library of Congress Cataloging-in-Publication Data
Clarke, Arlene.
    Retellings / Arlene Clarke, Marlene Clarke.—1st ed.
      p. cm.
    Includes index.
    ISBN 0-07-241469-3
      1. Literature, Modern—History and criticism. 2. Literature—Collections. I. Clarke, Marlene. II. Title.

PN 701.C55 2003
809'.03—dc21
                                                                      2003056161
www.mhhe.com

In memory of our parents
Leslie Clarke and Mildred E. Clarke
Whose retellings we are

ABOUT THE AUTHORS

M. B. Clarke and A. G. Clarke were born and raised in San Francisco, twin sisters in a family of five daughters. After attending San Francisco public schools, each earned a B.A. and an M.A. in literature at San Francisco State College and then went on to earn a Ph.D from the University of California at Berkeley, where they also taught their first sections of first-year English and basic composition.

Since 1983, M. B. Clarke has been teaching at one of UC Berkeley's sister campuses, the University of California at Davis. At UC Davis, she has taught a wide range of writing classes, from basic composition and first-year writing courses in the essay and imaginative literature to advanced composition courses in legal writing and technical and professional writing. She has occasionally taught courses in her doctoral specialty of Middle English literature, and she designed and taught for the humanities program a course on narrative built on the idea of "retellings" in art and literature.

Along with Nancy Morrow, M. B. Clarke is the editor of *Currents of Inquiry,* a thematic collection of essays written for use in first- and second-year writing courses.

After receiving her Ph.D in 1983, A. G. Clarke worked for a time as a freelance writer and consultant. Since 1989, she has taught at American River College, a community college in Sacramento, California, that serves a diverse student body with varied career and academic goals. She teaches courses in developmental and college writing and in literature, including introductory courses in her doctoral specialties of the novel and Victorian literature.

The Clarkes have previously collaborated on a number of projects, among them a series of writing workbooks for students in the elementary and middle grades and a series of remedial texts for adult learners.

The earlier collaborations and the collaboration on *Retellings* have come naturally and easily because, as twins, the sisters have shared their earliest memories and experiences. In fact, their identity as twins no doubt has something to do with their interest in *Retellings.* Because they are fraternal (nonidentical) twins, they don't look at each other as one looks into a mirror. At the same time, though, the experience of each twin is so bound in the experience of both twins that there is some way in which each "retells" the other. As in the "retellings" clusters in the anthology that follows, similarity and difference overlap and fuse.

Preface to Instructors

WHY "RETELLINGS"?

The genesis for *Retellings* came years ago, when the two of us were remarking on the number of prequels and sequels that were finding their ways onto movie and television screens and the shelves of popular fiction. Why, we wondered, were our students so drawn to remakes of movies and situation comedies we'd first ourselves seen when we were their age? Why was *Nick at Nite* so popular, given its presentation of television shows that were originally written and performed for audiences of a generation ago? How was it that a whole new generation of students could recite lines from not only *The Brady Bunch* movie but the original *Brady Bunch* television shows or sing the lyrics for the old *Patty Duke Show* or *Gilligan's Island,* situation comedies that had originally been taken off the air decades before? It was as if by watching the television shows of their parents' generations and, at the same time, watching sitcom versions of their parents' lives, they were re-creating those shows and lives a generation later.

The phenomenon extended beyond the airing of old reruns on cable television, though. At the same time, Hollywood was discovering William Shakespeare and Jane Austen, and these pillars of English Department literature curricula were being re-created and reinvented on the screen in rich new productions. For a time we could walk into a classroom and overhear students talking about a Shakespeare or Austen movie they had seen over the weekend, on their own time, for *pleasure.* With the help of these Hollywood retellings, they had discovered quite on their own just how much fun literature and even literary analysis could be, and we wanted to tap into that enthusiasm.

FROM RETELLINGS TO RICHER DISCUSSIONS

The more we talked about the phenomenon of these movie and television retellings of earlier stories, the more we realized that it wasn't a phenomenon at all. We were simply seeing Umberto Eco's belief made manifest that all storytellers (and audiences) retell stories that have already been told; all storytellers pay homage to earlier stories and reinvent them for a new time and audience. Mindful of our students' interest in updated versions of Shakespeare and Jane Austen, we began more and more to move beyond pairings and clusters bound by a common literary theme to pairings of works that more consciously told and retold the same story. Many of the works we taught and considered teaching were longer works, novels and plays, for instance: *Jane Eyre* and *Wide Sargasso Sea; King Lear* and *A Thousand Acres* or Akira Kurosawa's film *Ran; Oedipus Rex* and *The Darker Face of the Earth.* Almost invariably, these pairings led to a richer discussion of both the retelling and the original text, a more complete understanding of how an author's decisions about setting, character, and theme are made and transmitted.

Students were excited to find the comparisons and contrasts and to make meaning out of them. They were excited to move beyond the summaries and statements of story fact that sometimes plagued their essays. They were, in other words, increasingly excited to *think* about the literature and their reasons for responding as they did. As we moved to pairings of shorter works—short stories and poems—we found an equal enthusiasm.

BEYOND CLOSE READING: A COMPARATIVE APPROACH

Like many instructors, we have frequently taught the selections in the "Poems and Paintings" sections of many literature anthologies. In those sections, which are devoted to artistic and literary tellings of the same story, we and our students found the same kind of interest in retellings that prompted our interest in new versions of old tales. In the theories of intertextuality and reader response criticism, we found a theoretical base that allowed us and our students to build further on the close readings we had been asking them to do.

In fact, we have striven in *Retellings* to provide many theoretical and personal entrances into the literature included. The comparative approach is, of course, quite an old one, as a glance at early scholarship on sources and analogues for Shakespeare's and Chaucer's works makes clear. We are not, then, claiming to break new ground. Instead, we are hoping to encourage students to think more deeply along the lines that already inform much of their thinking. All of us often think comparatively. It is impossible not to. And we believe that asking students to compare and contrast stories, and think about how authorial decisions and readers' responses are made, will make them better and more involved readers. At the same time, in the Reflections sections in each literature chapter, we have included many works that haven't yet inspired conscious retellings of their own. In part we have included them because too many well-known and highly teachable works would otherwise have been excluded; in part we have included them because they extend the conversation, inviting students and instructors alike to consider why some stories get told more than others—and provide opportunities for students to try their hands and minds at their own retellings.

STUDENTS AS INTERPRETERS, INTERPRETERS AS RETELLERS

Retellings asks its readers to see similarity in difference and difference in similarity, to consider the cultural, gender, and temporal perspectives that make us unique and the stories that bring us together. In the introductory chapters to *Retellings* we ask students to take a similar look at literary genre itself. In our experience, students often think of poems, short stories, and dramas as very different things. And of course in many ways they are; each of the genres demands a slightly different approach from its readers. While giving students the tools for reading literature written in each of the genres, we have also attempted, however, to show students that all literature—indeed all "texts"—can be opened up through the same kind of interpretation. Whereas many literature anthologies seem to suggest that only poems are highly metaphorical or symbolic, or that only dramas ask us to visualize a scene and the characters' gestures, we want in chapter 2 to alert readers to the qualities that all texts share, to ask of drama or even poetry some of the same questions about character they have been taught to ask of short stories. We want, in other words, to encourage students to see every work of literature as unique and as part of the several traditions—literary, cultural, temporal, philosophical—to which it belongs. We want students to see each poem or short story as a potential play, or each play as the basis for a short story that may not yet have been written. We want them, finally, to see themselves as tellers of the tales they read, to see that with every interpretation—a student interpretation no less than a professional interpretation—a new story begins.

SUPPLEMENTS ACCOMPANYING *RETELLINGS*

Please contact your local McGraw-Hill representative for details concerning policies, prices, and availability of these supplements, as some restrictions may apply.

Supplements for Students

ARIEL (A Resource for the Interactive Exploration of Literature) CD-ROM: ARIEL, McGraw-Hill English's fully interactive CD-ROM, is an exciting new tool that introduces students to the pleasures of studying literature. The CD features nearly thirty casebooks on authors ranging from Sophocles to Rita Dove. Each casebook offers a rich array of resources, including hyperlinked texts, video and audio clips, critical essays, a biography, bibliography, and webliography, essay questions, quizzes, and visuals. General resources include a robust glossary and numerous other resources.

Online Learning Center (www.mhhe.com/clarke): The Online Learning Center (www.mhhe.com/clarke), integrated with the print text through the use of Web icons, offers Featured Author casebooks with biographies, quizzes, hyperlinked texts, a variety of writing assignments, and a secure download of the complete Instructor's Manual for professors.

Trade Books: A number of modern and classic works of fiction, nonfiction, and drama are available at a substantial discount when packaged with *Retellings:*

Abbey, *The Monkey Wrench Gang*
Achebe, *Things Fall Apart*
Alexie, *The Lone Ranger and Tonto Fistfight in Heaven*
Carter, *Integrity*
Cisneros, *The House on Mango Street*
Conrad, *Heart of Darkness*
Dillard, *Pilgrim at Tinker Creek*
Erdrich, *Love Medicine*
Hurston, *Their Eyes Were Watching God*
Kahn, *Boys of Summer*
Kingston, *Woman Warrior*
Marquez, *One Hundred Years of Solitude*
Mason, *Clear Springs*
McCarthy, *All the Pretty Horses*
Momaday, *House Made of Dawn*

Tan, *Joy Luck Club*
White, *Essays of E.B. White*

The iDeal Reader (www.mhhe.com/idealreader) and Selections from *The American Tradition in Literature*: Available through McGraw-Hill's Primis Content Center, these special collections offer an impressive array of works of fiction, poetry, drama, and essays that can be used to supplement *Retellings*. Instructors receive desk copies in 8–10 days, at no obligation; since each instructor-built supplement has a unique ISBN, bookstore orders for student copies are as straightforward as orders for any other print text. For more information, please visit www.mhhe.com/idealreader or www.primiscontentcenter.com.

Poetry to My Ear (0-07-229543-0): This CD-ROM covers the formal components of poetry (rhyme, rhythm, line, and form), defines and illustrates concepts, and enables students to try their own hands at some of the techniques in an interactive studio. By offering students the opportunity to hear a recitation of each anthologized poem, in some cases by the author, this groundbreaking teaching tool engages students with poetry and poetic language. Poetry to My Ear is available at a discount when packaged with *Retellings*.

Supplements for Instructors

Instructor's Manual: This valuable instructor's resource written and developed by the authors is password-protected and available for download at www.mhhe.com/clarke.

Videos and DVDs: Please ask your McGraw-Hill sales representative about videos and DVDs available to adopters for free or at reduced rates.

In Their Own Voices: A Century of Recorded Poetry (0-07-242404-4): This audio CD offers a collection of classic and contemporary poems in the voices of the poets who wrote them.

PageOut, WebCT, and More! The online content of *Retellings* is supported by WebCT, eCollege.com, and Blackboard. Additionally, our PageOut service is available to get you and your course up and running online in a matter of hours—at no cost! To find out more, contact your local McGraw-Hill representative or visit http://www.pageout.net.

ACKNOWLEDGMENTS

Like most such projects, *Retellings* has a history longer than its time of production. We began talking with students and colleagues about the project years ago, and many of them offered suggestions for works that we might include in a *Retellings* course or book. For all of their suggestions and encouragement, and for their willingness to listen to our ideas and pass along student essays, we would like to thank the following: John Boe, Dale Flynn, Pamela Major, Nancy Morrow, and the late Barbara Jane Hotchkiss at UC Davis; Sandra Cleary, Jane de Leon, Mary Higgins, Tom Logan, Dale Metcalfe, Mary Lou Nugent, Judie Rae, Gordon Roadcap, Harold Schneider, and Rod Siegfried from American River College. And, of course, we would like to thank our students—for their advice, their intelligence, and their enthusiasm.

We are grateful as well to the many reviewers who devoted considerable time and professional expertise to *Retellings*, inspiring us to make revisions that, we hope, made the book stronger. Our thanks to

James Armstrong, Virginia Union University
Amy Baldwin, Pulaski Technical College
Donna Marie Bauerly, Loras College
Jon Bentley, Albuquerque Technical Vocational Institute
Juanita P. Butler, Prairie State College
J. Lee Campbell, Valdosta State University
Erskine Carter, Black Hawk College
Callie J. Coy, Triton College
Judy C. Davidson, University of Texas—Pan American
Christy Desmet, University of Georgia
Christiane Farnan, Siena College
Lois Fennelly, Bethune-Cookman College
Michael Flaherty, Triton College
Lynee Lewis Gaillet, Georgia State University
Janet Gardner, University of Massachusetts—Dartmouth
Keith Haynes, Yavapai College
William Holbrook, Ball State University
Karen J. Jacobsen, University of Arkansas
J. Paul Johnson, Winona State University
Mary Ann Klein, Quincy University
Sarah L. Larson, Georgia Perimeter College
Paul Lizotte, Rivier College
Robert Lynch, Longwood College
Robert M. Myers, Lock Haven University
Betsy Nies, University of North Florida
Laura K. Noell, Northern Virginia Community College
Janice Norton, Arizona State University
Lillian Polak, Nassau Community College
Michael W. Punches, Oklahoma City Community College
Randy Rambo, Illinois Valley Community College
Fiona Tolhurst, Alfred University
Maria W. Warren, University of West Florida
Dennis Williams, College of Charleston

We feel fortunate to have worked with an amazing team of editors at McGraw-Hill. Our thanks to Sarah Touborg, who saw the promise in the project even in its early raw form and who never pushed us to abandon the central idea of retellings; to Alexis Walker, who guided us through the entire project with extraordinary tact and good humor, providing us with marketing *and* literary expertise; and to developmental editor Anne Stameshkin and permissions editor Marty Granahan, who took the book so ably through its last stages. We'd also like to thank David Patterson, marketing manager; Todd Vaccaro, media producer; Joshua Feldman (coordinator of ARIEL); Christina Gimlin, project manager; Tandra Jorgensen, production supervisor; Cassandra Chu, designer; Cristin Yancey, art editor; Natalia Peschiera, photo research coordinator; David Tietz, photo researcher; and Kate Boylan, supplements producer.

Finally, we owe a special thanks to those in our family who supplied materials and expertise, encouragement and patience, enduring too many too-short phone calls and delayed plans as we worked on *Retellings;* to Judy Nemzer, Jennifer Nuckles, and Katherine Conrad, our thanks and our love.

Preface to the Student

"Every Story Tells a Story That Has Already Been Told"

Generations of college students in the United States have opened books like this one to discover a preface or introduction with a title something like "Why Read and Study Literature?" The answers to that question are usually both general and simple: literature provides us with entry into others' worlds. It allows us to interact, at least in our imaginations, with people of different times, cultures, socioeconomic groups, genders, and ethnic backgrounds than our own. Those reasons for reading literature are no less true today than they were generations ago.

For all of its apparent simplicity, though, the question "Why read and study literature?" contains within it more questions. Once you begin to examine it closely— to analyze it as you would any text—the question itself begins to unravel. What, finally, does "literature" mean? When we ask, "Why read and study literature?" don't we also need to be asking, "What literature should we read and study?"

In the past two or three decades, students and scholars of literature have provided a number of answers to that last question. It used to be that such experts could easily rattle off a list of the "must reads": every educated person, it was assumed, would read works by such literary luminaries as Shakespeare, Sophocles, Tolstoy, and Wordsworth—all of them well-known literary figures not only in our time but also in their own times. In more recent years, however, readers have debated, sometimes with passionate intensity, the question of who and what belong on the list of "must reads," what is called the **literary canon.** In what have come to be known as the "canon wars," some readers have remarked that the writers of the traditional canon are certainly talented and insightful but that most of them are also white, male, upper class, and European. Where, they wonder, are the voices, the insights, and the perspectives of those who belong to the less privileged segments of society?

Those who have defended the canon have argued that writers such as Shakespeare and Sophocles have stood the test of time, that their writing has truths and evokes emotions that transcend time, culture, socioeconomic status, ethnicity, and gender. They argue further that every culture is enriched when its members share common knowledge and experiences; if we all agree on what belongs to the literary canon—and if we all read some of the works on the list—literature can provide us with some of that shared knowledge and experience.

On the other side of the battle lines are an array of critics who argue that we have too long restricted students' reading to the "canon" and that we need to open up readers' experiences and ears to literature that has too long been overlooked. These critics argue that the writings of "dead white males" have dominated the literature classroom and that the voices of lesser-known, but nevertheless important, writers have consequently been silenced. With the silencing of those voices, the literary canon has, such critics argue, supported the dominant white male culture and given it greater authority. Viewed in this way, literature has become a tool of oppression.

Clearly, then, there is not a quick and easy answer to the question of what literature students should study. Perhaps the best answer is that they should read it all, both the well-known writers and the lesser-known writers, who have important perspectives of their own. That isn't entirely practical, of course. None of us can read it "all." Such, though, is one of the premises behind *Retellings*. It *is* important, we think, for students to read the "greats," to get a sense of the literary traditions that help give all cultures their shape, and to interact, even if only in one's imagination, with some of the great minds of the ages. It *is* important to read what others are reading, to find in literature a place where readers of different backgrounds can come together in community.

At the same time, though, it is important to recognize that there have always been other voices and to hear what those voices have to say for themselves rather than to hear those voices as they are filtered through another's consciousness. For example, realistic as his women characters may be—more than one critic has commented on how vibrant Shakespeare's heroines are—Shakespeare still comes to his understanding of female psychology from the position of an outsider. How, one might ask, would a *woman* write about those same characters as they negotiate the worlds of Shakespeare's plays? Would her representation of their psychology be similar to Shakespeare's? Similarly, would a writer who comes from a relatively privileged social position tell the same story of poverty or discrimination as a writer who has experienced poverty or discrimination firsthand? Would a writer of European descent tell the same story of African colonization that a writer of African descent would tell?

Retellings provides you with the material to begin to answer such questions. We have included in the book pairs and clusters of readings that tell and retell the same stories. The story told by a writer from the traditional literary canon is placed alongside the responses to it, stories (or plays or poems) told by lesser-known writers who come from very different backgrounds. Often one writer's hero becomes another's villain, or one writer's minor character becomes another's major character. Sometimes the male storyteller in one version is answered by a female storyteller in another. In short, we have collected readings that will allow you to examine how stories get changed as they get told and retold from different cultural, socioeconomic, gender, and ethnic perspectives.

Critics call this approach **intertextuality** because texts are intertwined and interacting with one another. Some critics have gone so far as to say that intertextuality is the basis of all reading and writing, all stories. As Umberto Eco, novelist and literary critic, puts it, "I discovered what writers have always known (and have told us again and again): books always speak of other books, and every story tells a story that has already been told" (qtd. in Hutcheon 8). By becoming attuned to the ways in which stories respond to one another, especially by reading two versions of the same story, a reader gains a richer understanding of each and a stronger sense of how all texts are shaped by and reflect the cultures in which they are created and received.

You will find as you read through *Retellings* that we have occasionally introduced "nonliterary" texts: essays, films, advertisements, historical and journalistic pieces, pictures, and even children's stories. These texts, too, form an intertextual

relationship with the literature we present. When a poet writes a poem about a painting, for instance, he is asking us to rethink our response to the painting; we therefore
need the painting to understand the poem and can use the poem to reach one interpretation of the painting. Something similar happens when we watch a film made
from a book. Both offer particular versions of the story's "truths": once you have seen
the film, you may see in the book elements, attitudes, and ideas you had not seen before; once you have read the book, your response to the film may change. Something
similar happens as well when writers of fiction take their material from actual events.
All writing, maybe all thinking, is interpretive, and in the intersection between reality
and writing, a new dimension is created, one that is neither wholly real nor wholly
fictive. In studying that moment of intersection, a reader gets a stronger sense of how
a writer manipulates character and event, whether that writer is a writer of fiction or
a writer who professes to tell only the facts.

As you think about how stories get told and retold and about how texts get
shaped, we encourage you, then, to broaden your definitions of *story* and *text*. Even an
inanimate object can tell a "story," as any child with a favorite toy will tell you, even
long after she has grown up. Even a situation comedy or a horror film or a comic
book or a children's story based on a piece of literature can retell a story in ways that
illuminate both the original story and our responses to it. Indeed, many great writers
would probably encourage us to break down the barriers between "Culture" with a
capital "C" and popular culture, such as that represented by television and film. Many,
including Shakespeare, have been interested in appealing to the broadest possible audience, not just a tiny segment of the upper class. Some have argued, in fact, that, were
Shakespeare alive today, he would be writing not for the stage but for television or
film—or perhaps for advertising. Like what we commonly think of as "literature,"
television shows, movies, and advertisements use the written word in an attempt to
engage their audiences emotionally and to "sell" an idea.

In providing you with pairs and clusters of literary and nonliterary texts that are
told and retold, we thus hope to encourage you to think of literature as part of a larger
world in which many conversations are taking place. Although we sometimes think of
great authors such as Shakespeare or Sophocles or even Robert Louis Stevenson as
telling us things, almost lecturing to us, we would like you instead to think of them as
presenting only one version of the "truth," whatever truth that may be. They may
often start the conversation, creating the characters and laying out the plot situations,
but they are not the only participants in it. *Retellings* gives you the opportunity to
hear what other voices have to say, to listen as they respond to the dominant voices,
adding their own correctives and insights and giving you a chance to add your own.

Work Cited

Hutcheon, Linda. "Historiographic Metafiction: Parody and the Intertextuality
of History." *Intertextuality and Contemporary American Fiction*. Ed. Patrick
O'Donnell and Robert Con Davis. Baltimore: Johns Hopkins UP, 1989.
3–32.

Retellings
A Thematic Literature Anthology

by M. B. Clarke and A. G. Clarke

~ Part 1 ~

Reading Literature

The Big Picture

1 Telling and Retelling Stories
2 Reading across Genres: The Elements of Literature

GUIDED TOUR

Welcome! The following pages will serve as a map of sorts to using this book. Spending a few minutes getting to know the features and organization of the text will help you get the most out of *Retellings*.

Part I of *Retellings* will introduce you to the big picture: reading and thinking critically about **literature across the genres**. **Part II** invites you to explore **literature by genre**, focusing on the key elements of **Fiction**, **Poetry**, **Drama**, and **Nonfiction and Other Nonliterary Texts**.

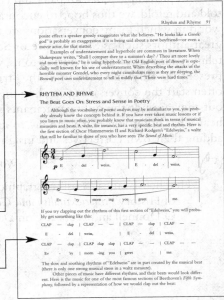

Rhythm and Rhyme 91

posite effect: a speaker grossly exaggerates what she believes. "He looks like a Greek god" is probably an exaggeration if it is being said about a new boyfriend—or even a movie actor, for that matter.

Examples of understatement and hyperbole are common in literature. When Shakespeare writes, "Shall I compare thee to a summer's day? / Thou art more lovely and more temperate," he is using hyperbole. The Old English poet of *Beowulf* is especially well known for his use of understatement. When describing the attacks of the horrible monster Grendel, who every night cannibalizes men as they are sleeping, the *Beowulf* poet uses understatement to tell us mildly that "These were hard times."

RHYTHM AND RHYME
The Beat Goes On: Stress and Sense in Poetry

Although the vocabulary of poetic analysis may be unfamiliar to you, you probably already know the concept behind it. If you have ever taken music lessons or if you listen to music often, you probably know that musicians think in terms of musical measures and beats. A waltz, for instance, has a very specific beat and rhythm. Here is the first section of Oscar Hammerstein II and Richard Rodgers's "Edelweiss," a waltz that will be familiar to those of you who have seen *The Sound of Music*:

If you try clapping out the rhythms of this first section of "Edelweiss," you will probably get something like this:

CLAP — clap | CLAP — — | CLAP — clap | CLAP —
E — del | weiss, | E — del | weiss,
CLAP — clap | CLAP clap clap | CLAP — — | CLAP —
Ev — 'ry | morn -ing you | greet | me.

The slow and soothing rhythms of "Edelweiss" are in part created by the musical beat (there is only one strong musical stress in a waltz measure).

Other pieces of music have different rhythms, and their beats would look different. Here is the music for one of the most famous sections of Beethoven's *Fifth Symphony*, followed by a representation of how we would clap out the beat:

Part III features a step-by-step explanation of **Writing about Literature**—from brainstorming techniques to revising and editing—culminating in a **sample student paper**.

Putting It All Together 173

Johnson 1

Heather Johnson

Professor Clarke

English 3

15 May 2003

"In Thy Marble Vault": Violence and Coercion in Andrew Marvell's "To His Coy Mistress"

In Andrew Marvell's poem "To His Coy Mistress," a man attempts to convince a reluctant lover to engage in more physical forms of affection. The speaker argues that time is the obstacle the couple face and that her way of thinking of time (a way that convinces her to wait) is unrealistic. Death comes for all, he argues, and one never knows when, so best to enjoy the present. Although it may seem that Marvell's speaker uses the fleeting nature of time as his primary persuasive tool, his arguments illuminate a worldview wherein women have no worth outside of their attractiveness to men. Over the course of the poem, the speaker devalues his mistress's wishes and decisions, uses violent language and imagery to threaten her, and makes it clear that his interest in her will cease in a short time regardless of whether or not she has sex with him.

In the first section of the poem, the speaker describes a dreamland of love, a world without the limits of time. He imagines his mistress finding rubies "by the Indian Ganges' side" while he writes love songs by the shores of his hometown's river (5–7). Their "long love's day" would be spent in romantic contemplation, and "should [she] please refuse," he

11

Innocence Lost

Icare
Henri Matisse

CHAPTER INTRODUCTION

After the horrific events of September 11, 2001, we heard again and again from commentator after commentator, "Things will never be the same." We were told, "Americans have lost their innocence. Never again will they feel secure. They are now learning what the rest of the world has long known: the world is a very dangerous place, and there are no safe havens." Paradoxically, such comments seemed at the same time both profoundly true and profoundly simplistic.

Perhaps more than other peoples, many Americans have often assumed that they were a chosen people, living a golden dream of freedom and prosperity. Part of the country's cultural history, part of its cultural myth, is that when situations become intolerable, Americans move on, leaving behind old civilizations and old problems in an attempt to create new American utopias. Because eighteenth-century England did not offer freedoms enough, some of its citizens set sail for a new land. Because British

Each of the four **theme-based chapters** in **Part IV** opens with a **frontispiece** that illustrates the theme, a **chapter introduction,** and a **work or works that represent the overarching theme.** Within each theme, an **Album of Retellings** features numerous sub-themes, each offering retellings of a core story.

858 INNOCENCE LOST

Pieter Breughel The Elder (ca. 1525–1569), *Landscape with the Fall of Icarus*, ca. 1558

from Ovid's *Metamorphoses* ask us to respond to the creative imagination and skill that give the father and son their wings? What is the relationship between creativity and art on the one hand and the earthly and everyday on the other?

2. Although Ovid's story is fundamentally very unrealistic—it is difficult to believe that Daedalus could fashion from wax and birds' feathers the kind of wings that would enable humans to fly—the poet is nevertheless careful to include moments of high realism. Where does the poem seem most realistic? How does the realism influence our response to the relationship between father and son and to the poem's overall themes?
3. Several times in the narrative, Ovid reminds his audience of Icarus's tragic future. Why does the poet undercut the story's suspense? Why do those reminders occur when they do—and how do you respond to them?
4. The story of Perdix seems like an afterthought, but there are some connections between it and the story of Icarus. How is Perdix like and/or unlike Icarus? Does the story of Perdix change your response to Daedalus?

QUESTIONS FOR DISCUSSION AND WRITING

1. Breughel's painting of the fall of Icarus clearly draws its inspiration from the Ovidian story. Compare Breughel's version and Ovid's. How are the two similar? How are they different? If you were to paint Ovid's story, how similar would your painting be to Breughel's? If you were to tell the story behind Breughel's painting, how similar would your version be to Ovid's? Finally, imagine yourself choosing an en-

ALBUM OF RETELLINGS 1: Nearly every **cluster of Retellings (or sub-theme)** opens with the most traditional or oldest version of a story; in "Testing the Limits: The Story of Icarus," for example, the first reading is Ovid's version of the Icarus tale. This is followed by retellings of the story, which, in this cluster, include visual interpretations and poems: Auden's poem "Musée des Beaux Arts," Williams's poem "Landscape with the Fall of Icarus," and Breughel's painting *Landscape with the Fall of Icarus*.

Hayden • O Daedalus, Fly Away Home   863

just spread his arms and
    flew away home.

Drifting night in the windy pines
night is a laughing, night is a longing.
    Pretty Malinda, come to me.

Night is a mourning juju man
weaving a wish and a weariness together
    to make two wings.

    O fly away home fly away

QUESTIONS FOR DISCUSSION AND WRITING

1. Robert Hayden's "O Daedalus, Fly Away Home" may seem at first glance to have very little to do with the classical story, but in its use of the image of a man flying with wings made of "a wish and a weariness" woven together, it takes its cue from the myth. How does a knowledge of the Ovidian story affect your reading of "O Daedalus"?
2. Why does Hayden focus on Daedalus, the father, rather than on Icarus, the son?
3. What finally is the connection between the "wish" and the "weariness"? How possible is it to extricate one from the other?

QUESTIONS FOR CROSS READING: TESTING THE LIMITS:
THE STORY OF ICARUS

1. Even in their retellings of a classical story, several of these poets are clearly influenced by the circumstances of their own times, places, and backgrounds. Consider the poems' dates of composition. How might events and attitudes of their own times have caused the poets to respond to the Daedalus–Icarus story as they do?
2. How would you characterize the tones and rhythms of Auden's and Williams's poems? How do the titles and the first words of the poems influence our response to the Icarus–Daedalus story and the significance the two poets find in it? What is the effect of the poets' using Breughel's retelling of Ovid rather than referring to the Ovidian story directly?
4. Unlike Breughel, Matisse (see 000) concentrates the entire focus of his painting on Icarus—so much so that we see almost none of the boy's surroundings. What do we see? How do the painting's focus and its relative lack of details affect your response to the Icarus story? How does Matisse's image of Icarus compare with those of Breughel and the writers in this section?

ALBUM OF RETELLINGS 2: Questions for Discussion and Writing follow each work in the album. **Questions for Cross Reading** appear at the end of each set of Retellings.

868 INNOCENCE LOST

Braniff 5

Here Auden contrasts suffering with daily tasks like eating and walking, as well as comparing the passionate waiting of the aged with the joyful playing of the young. He continues these contrasts as he discusses the fall of Icarus.

    In Breughel's *Icarus*, for instance: how everything
        turns away
    Quite leisurely from the disaster; the ploughman may
    Have heard the splash, the forsaken cry,
    But for him it was not an important failure . . .
                                            (14–17)
    . . . the expensive delicate ship that must have seen
    Something amazing, a boy falling out of the sky,
    Had somewhere to get to and sailed calmly on.   (19–21)

    Like Williams and Breughel, Auden's theme is in sharp contrast to that of Ovid's message. In the original, Icarus's fall is significantly tragic. In Auden's, the fall was but a small part of the lives of the busy farmer and hurried ship, who, without even thinking about it, knew that life goes quietly on.

    The two poems of Williams and Auden, though different in structure, share the same basic theme; the suffering of life is not any more significant than a spring's day or a farmer's plow. There is little we can do to avoid the suffering and pain of mortality. Whether right or wrong, the real nature of humans is to continue on with the daily tasks of living, often unaware of the sufferings of others.

ALBUM OF RETELLINGS 3: Essays or works of creative writing by students are included in some Retellings sections; the Icarus section includes a paper by student Christopher Braniff called "The Insignificance of Icarus."

1318   A CASEBOOK ON *HAMLET*: MURDER AND MADNESS

From Kenneth Branagh's *Hamlet*, 1997

KENNETH BRANAGH (1960–   )
Two Excerpts from Kenneth Branagh's 1996 Screenplay of Hamlet:
I.ii.42–159 *and* III.i.90–184   1996

I.ii.42–159

    Time now to turn on the charm with the young aristocrats. Also a good show for the ladies, who crane their necks on the balconies to see which of the bright young things around the throne will be indulged with a public favour.

CLAUDIUS: And now, Laertes, what's the news with you?
    You told us of some suit.

    (A darkly handsome young man steps forward. In the uniform of a cadet.)

CLAUDIUS (*continuing*):   What is't, Laertes?
    You cannot speak of reason to the Dane
    And lose your voice. What wouldst thou beg, Laertes,
    That shall not be my offer, not thy asking?
    The head is not more native to the heart,
    The hand more instrumental to the mouth,
    Than is the throne of Denmark to thy father.

    (He turns to POLONIUS, once again letting the court know how the power structure stands. Then on with a smile.)

CASEBOOKS 1: Three Casebooks of Retellings explore retold stories in depth, moving beyond the primary retellings to include critical essays and topics for research. These casebooks also include a number of **visuals.**

C. P. CAVAFY (1863–1933)

Oedipus

Written after reading the description of the painting "Oedipus and the Sphinx" by Gustav Moreau.

The Sphinx is fallen on him,
with teeth and talons outspread
and with all the furor of life.
Oedipus succumbed to her first impulse;
her first appearance terrified him—
such a face, and such talk
till then he had never imagined.
But though the monster rests
her two paws on Oedipus' breast
he has recovered quickly—and now
he no longer fears her for he has
the solution ready and he will win.
And yet he does not rejoice over this victory.
His glance, full of melancholy,
is not on the Sphinx; far off he sees
the narrow path that leads to Thebes
and will end at Colonus.
And his soul clearly forebodes
that there the Sphinx will accost him again
with more difficult and more baffling
enigmas that have no answer.

QUESTIONS FOR DISCUSSION AND WRITING

1. Though this does not literally happen in Sophocles's play, Cavafy believes that at Colonus "the Sphinx will accost [Oedipus] again." How might the Sphinx's riddle

CASEBOOKS 2: "A Casebook on *Oedipus: Living with Fate*" opens with an introduction and moves on to the core text, Sophocles' drama *Oedipus*. This is followed by a variety of retellings, including stills from film versions, poems, Freud's famous psychological analysis of the "Oedipus complex," and critical essays.

why? Is one ending more "conclusive" than the other? To what extent does the change in ending change your response to the characters? The play's themes?

MAKING CONNECTIONS: A CASEBOOK ON *OEDIPUS:* LIVING WITH FATE

1. For modern readers, the story of Oedipus is closely linked to Freud's concept of the Oedipus complex. Which of the modern writers show an awareness of Freud's theory? Are their attitudes toward that theory the same or different? How?
2. Oedipus is guilty of two "sins"—killing his father and sleeping with his mother. Which writers emphasize which? Do the differences in emphasis represent different attitudes toward "sin"?
3. Cavafy, Rukeyser, and Jarrell all focus on the Sphinx and her riddle. Do they envision the Sphinx in the same way? How important to each of them is it that the Sphinx is female? In what ways do they see the answer to the riddle as an important part of the whole myth?
4. Gallaher's and Sheck's poems both focus on Jocasta. Is this the same Jocasta? How do their Jocastas compare with Sophocles's Jocasta or with Dove's Amalia?
5. Many of the modern works draw on images and ideas Sophocles uses. Trace one of these images or ideas (for example, light and dark imagery, plague imagery, or the idea of guilt and innocence) through several of the works. Are the writers creating the same effects with these images and ideas?

TOPICS FOR RESEARCH: A CASEBOOK ON *OEDIPUS:* LIVING WITH FATE

1. Greek ideas about fate and free will may differ from our own, thus making it difficult for us to understand the extent to which Oedipus can choose to disobey the prophecy. Research Greek ideas about the relationship between people and the gods and about the extent to which the Greeks believed in the idea of fate.
2. In using the Oedipus story as the basis for some of his psychological theories, Freud seems to assume that Oedipus is, even if unconsciously, attracted to his mother. But historians often caution us to remember that in Greek times, Oedipus's decision to marry the queen would have been a political one. Research Greek attitudes toward marriage among those of the ruling class. To what extent were marriages seen as political alliances? How did the Greeks view the roles of and relationships between men and women?
3. Oedipus is called a *tyrannus*. Although our word "tyrant" is derived from the Greek *tyrannus*, the Greek word has very different connotations and meanings from those of the modern English word. Research the meaning of *tyrannus* and the nature of the relationships between ancient Greek leaders and those they governed.

CASEBOOKS 3: Each work in the casebooks is followed by **Questions for Discussion and Writing; Making Connections** questions at the end of each casebook ask you to compare, contrast, and draw connections among the various works. Finally, **Topics for Research** prompt you to further exploration of the casebook's content.

A **four-color insert** offers full-color versions of visual retellings of works in the text.

Advertising poster for the movie *Forbidden Planet*, a science-fiction version of *The Tempest*, 1956, MGM.

La Vûe (Sight), from *The Lady and the Unicorn* tapestries, ca. 1500. The Cluny Museum, Paris.

The Unicorn in Captivity, late 15th–early 16th century. Silk, wool, silver, and gilt threads, 145 x 99 in. The Metropolitan Museum of Art, New York.

2

3

1480 A CASEBOOK ON *DR. JEKYLL AND MR. HYDE*: WHAT LIES WITHIN

A Film or Video Recording

Lee, Spike, dir. *4 Little Girls.* Videocassette. HBO, 1998.

Electronic Sources

Increasingly, researchers access journal articles and other information sources online. Electronic sources are still very new, however, and bibliographic methods somewhat fluid. In general, you should give as much information as possible. Dating is especially important because online sources may be modified at any time. As a result, it is very important to give your date of access and the date of the original publication (whether in print or online); the date of access comes just before the address, or URL (Uniform Resource Locator). When you give the URL, break the line only at a slash mark. Do not add a hyphen, as you would for a split word; it may be read as part of the URL. Because URLs and online texts can change at any time, you may want to print out the material you are using; the printout will record the URL and the date of access.

For a scholarly project:

The Little Red Riding Hood Project. Ed. Michael N. Salda. Vers. 1.0. Dec. 1995. De Grummond Children's Literature Research Collection. U. of Southern Mississippi. 18 April 2002 <http://www-dept.usm/;slengdept/lrrh/lrrhhome.htm>.

For a work within a scholarly project:

Very, Lydia L. "Red Riding Hood." Boston: L. Prang, 1863. *The Little Red Riding Hood Project.* Ed. Michael N. Salda. Vers. 1.0. Dec. 1995. De Grummond Children's Literature Research Collection. U. of Southern Mississippi. 18 April 2002 <http://www-dept.usm/~engdept/lrrh/lrrhb.htm>.

For a journal article accessed online:

Burnett, Mark Thornton. "The 'very cunning of the scene': Kenneth Branagh's *Hamlet.*" *Literature-Film Quarterly* 25.2 (1997). EBSCO Publishing Database. 23 March 2002 <www.arc.losrios.cc.ca.us/~library/lib>mdatabases.html.>

In general, for online sources, you are following a form similar to that for the print sources, with the URL and date of access added. For electronic sources especially, however, you may find gaps in the recommendations about documentation form, even if you consult a lengthy resource such as the *MLA Handbook.* You may need to adapt the documentation form to fit your own particular source. Always err on the side of providing additional information.

PUTTING IT ALL TO WORK: A SAMPLE STUDENT PAPER

We have included in the pages that follow a student paper that uses literary criticism in its critical argument. As you read, pay particular attention to the way the student integrates quotations from both the literary text and from the critics who have

Appendixes include **"Breaking the Boundaries" writing assignments** that involve works from different themes; guidelines for using and documenting sources; an introduction to the schools of literary criticism; and brief biographies of selected authors.

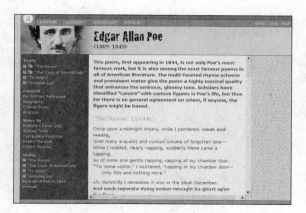

We hope that you will come away from *Retellings* with a greater appreciation of and love for literature, and perhaps with the desire to add your *own* retellings to a timeless story or two.

If you'd like to learn more about selected authors and their works, please visit the Online Learning Center at **www.mhhe.com/clarke** or explore ARIEL, the CD-ROM that accompanies this text.

Contents

Part V   *For Further Study: Three Casebooks of Retellings*   *1057*

12   *A Casebook on* Oedipus: *Living with Fate*   *1060*

13   *A Casebook on* Hamlet: *Murder and Madness*   *1213*

14 *A Casebook on* Dr. Jekyll and Mr. Hyde: *What Lies Within* *1373*

Appendix 1: Writing Assignments *A-1*

Appendix 2: Using and Documenting Sources *A-21*

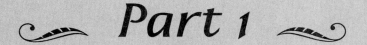

Part 1

Reading Literature
The Big Picture

Telling and Retelling Stories

In the preface, we talked generally about how individuals and cultures retell the same stories. In this chapter, we want to discuss more specifically how the same stories are told, retold, and read. As we said earlier, some literary historians argue that there are, in fact, a limited number of stories. In an age and culture such as our own, which often values the original, even the eccentric, over the traditional and communal, that may seem like a negative comment. In fact, though, an understanding of what different versions of the same story have in common—and, perhaps even more significant, how they differ—can often open a rich and exciting window into time, place, and culture. To read the same story told from a number of different temporal, geographical, and cultural perspectives enables us to isolate what makes each time and place unique and, at the same time, to recognize the kinship between ourselves and those whose cultures or periods in history would otherwise make them seem like strangers.

READING AND INTERPRETATION

The Influence of Culture: Three Tellings of "Cinderella"

Literary critics and anthropologists have been struck by how often the same story is told by many cultures. Many cultures have a Flood story, for instance, and many have strikingly similar stories about the origins of the universe. Whether these stories all hearken back to an unknown **archetype,** or original model story that is the origin of all later stories, or whether there is some more direct means of transmission from one culture to another, a comparison among the versions of a story can tell us much about culture and narrative. To see how cultural influences shape a story, consider what happens to the Cinderella story when it is told by authors from different cultures separated by vast expanses of time and geography. Look first at the following Golden Book adaptation of Walt Disney's *Cinderella,* a version familiar to many children who grow up in the United States:

Adapted by CAMPBELL GRANT

Walt Disney's "Cinderella"

Once upon a time in a far-away land lived a sweet and pretty girl named Cinderella. She made her home with her <u>mean old stepmother</u> and <u>her two stepsister</u>s, and they made her do all the work in the house.

got invited to the ball

Cinderella cooked and baked. She cleaned and scrubbed. She had no time left for parties and fun.

But one day an invitation came from the palace of the king.

A great ball was to be given for the prince of the land. And every young girl in the kingdom was invited.

"How nice!" thought Cinderella. "I am invited, too."

But her mean stepsisters never thought of her. They thought only of themselves, of course. They had all sorts of jobs for Cinderella to do.

"Wash this slip. Press this dress. Curl my hair. Find my fan."

They both kept shouting, as fast as they could speak.

"But I must get ready myself. I'm going, too," said Cinderella.

"You!" they hooted. "The Prince's ball for you?"

And they kept her busy all day long. She worked in the morning, while her stepsisters slept. She worked all afternoon, while they bathed and dressed. And in the evening she had to help them put on the finishing touches for the ball. She had not one minute to think of herself.

Soon the coach was ready at the door. The ugly stepsisters were powdered, pressed, and curled. But there stood Cinderella in her workaday rags.

"Why, Cinderella!" said the stepsisters. "You're not dressed for the ball."

"No," said Cinderella. "I guess I cannot go."

Poor Cinderella sat weeping in the garden.

Suddenly a little old woman with a sweet, kind face stood before her. It was her fairy godmother.

"Hurry, child!" she said. "You are going to the ball!"

her fairy godmother changed all her things

Cinderella could hardly believe her eyes! The fairy godmother turned a fat pumpkin into a splendid coach.

Next her pet mice became horses, and her dog a fine footman. The barn horse was turned into a coachman.

magic →

"There, my dear," said the fairy godmother. "Now into the coach with you, and off to the ball you go."

"But my dress—" said Cinderella.

"Lovely, my dear," the fairy godmother began. Then she really looked at Cinderella's rags.

"Oh, good heavens," she said. "You can never go in that." She waved her magic wand.

"Salaga doola,
Menchicka boola,
Bibbidi-bobbidi-boo!" she said.

There stood Cinderella in the loveliest ball dress that ever was. And on her feet were tiny glass slippers!

"Oh," cried Cinderella. "How can I ever thank you?"

"Just have a wonderful time at the ball, my dear," said her fairy godmother. "But remember, this magic lasts only until midnight. At the stroke of midnight, the spell will be broken. And everything will be as it was before."

"I will remember," said Cinderella. "It is more than I ever dreamed of."

Then into the magic coach she stepped, and was whirled away to the ball.

at midnight the spell ends

And such a ball! The king's palace was ablaze with lights. There was music and laughter. And every lady in the land was dressed in her beautiful best.

But Cinderella was the loveliest of them all. The prince never left her side, all evening long. They danced every dance. They had supper side by side. And they happily smiled into each other's eyes.

But all at once the clock began to strike midnight, Bong Bong Bong—

"Oh!" cried Cinderella. "I almost forgot!"

And without a word, away she ran, out of the ballroom and down the palace stairs. She lost one glass slipper. But she could not stop.

Into her magic coach she stepped, and away it rolled. But as the clock stopped striking, the coach disappeared. And no one knew where she had gone.

Next morning all the kingdom was filled with the news. The Grand Duke was going from house to house, with a small glass slipper in his hand. For the prince had said he would marry no one but the girl who could wear that tiny shoe.

Every girl in the land tried hard to put it on. The ugly stepsisters tried hardest of all. But not a one could wear the glass shoe.

And where was Cinderella? Locked in her room. For the mean old stepmother was taking no chances of letting her try on the slipper. Poor Cinderella! It looked as if the Grand Duke would surely pass her by.

But her little friends the mice got the stepmother's key. And they pushed it under Cinderella's door. So down the long stairs she came, as the Duke was just about to leave.

"Please!" cried Cinderella. "Please let me try."

And of course the slipper fitted, since it was her very own.

That was all the Duke needed. Now his long search was done. And so Cinderella became the prince's bride, and lived happily ever after—and the little pet mice lived in the palace and were happy ever after, too.

In this version of the Cinderella story, the emphasis is on romance and magic, not on violence. Although the stepsisters and stepmother are called "mean," the meanness is more a matter of pettiness and jealousy than of violent aggression. The mean stepfamily is forgotten as soon as Cinderella's life is magically transformed by her fairy godmother and the prince's love.

Now read the nineteenth-century German version of "Cinderella" by the Brothers Grimm:

BROTHERS GRIMM

Cinderella

The wife of a rich man fell ill. When she realized that the end was near, she called her only daughter to her bedside and said: "Dear child, if you are good and say your prayers, our dear Lord will always be with you, and I shall look down on you from heaven and always be with you." Then she shut her eyes and passed away.

Every day the girl went to the grave of her mother and wept. She was always good and said her prayers. When winter came, the snow covered the grave with

[handwritten margin note: Prince is looking for the owner of the slipper]

[handwritten margin note: every girl tried to commit him it was hers]

[handwritten margin note: never talked about that (not real mom)] a white blanket, and when the sun had taken it off again in the spring, the rich man remarried.

His new wife brought with her two daughters, whose features were beautiful and white, but whose hearts were foul and black. This meant the beginning of a hard time for the poor stepchild. "Why should this silly goose be allowed to sit in the parlor with us?" the girls said. "If you want to eat bread, you'll have to earn it. Out with the kitchen maid!" → they're mean to her

They took away her beautiful clothes, dressed her in an old grey smock, and gave her some wooden shoes. "Just look at the proud princess in her finery!" they shouted and laughed, taking her out to the kitchen. From morning until night she had to work hard. Every day, she got up before daybreak to carry water, start the fire, cook, and wash. On top of that the two sisters did everything imaginable to make her miserable. They ridiculed her and threw peas and lentils into the ashes so that she would have to sit down in the ashes and pick them out. In the evening, when she was completely exhausted from work, she didn't have a bed but had to lie down next to the hearth in ashes. She always looked so dusty and dirty that people started to call her Cinderella.

One day, the father was going to the fair and he asked his two stepdaughters what he could bring back for them. "Beautiful dresses," said one.

"Pearls and jewels," said the other.

"But you, Cinderella," he asked, "what do you want?"

"Father," she said, "break off the first branch that brushes against your hat on the way home and bring it to me."

And so he bought beautiful dresses, pearls, and jewels for the two stepsisters. On the way home, when he was riding through a thicket of green bushes, a hazel branch brushed against him and knocked his hat off. When he arrived home, he gave his stepdaughters what they had asked for, and to Cinderella he gave the branch from the hazel bush. Cinderella thanked him, went to her mother's grave, and planted a hazel sprig on it. She wept so hard that her tears fell to the ground and watered it. It grew and became a beautiful tree. Three times a day Cinderella went and sat under it, and wept and prayed. Each time a little white bird would also fly to the tree, and if she made a wish, the little bird would toss down what she had wished for. (like fairy godmother)

It happened that one day the king announced a festival that was to last for three days and to which all the beautiful young ladies of the land were invited from whom his son might choose a bride. When the two stepsisters heard that they too had been asked to attend, they were in fine spirits. They called Cinderella and said: "Comb our hair, brush our shoes, and fasten our buckles. We're going to the wedding at the king's palace."

Cinderella did as she was told, but she wept, for she too would have liked to go to the ball, and she begged her stepmother to let her go.

"Cinderella," she said, "How can you go to a wedding when you're covered with dust and dirt? How can you want to go to a ball when you have neither a dress nor shoes?"

Cinderella kept pleading with her, and so she finally said: "Here, I've dumped a bowlful of lentils into the ashes. If you can pick out the lentils in the next two hours, then you may go."

The girl went out the back door into the garden and called out: "O tame little doves, little turtledoves, and all you little birds in the sky, come and help me put

the good ones into the little pot,
the bad ones into your little crop."

They helped her do her chores (the birds)

Two little white doves came flying in through the kitchen window, followed by little turtle doves. And finally all the birds in the sky came swooping and fluttering and settled down in the ashes. The little doves nodded their heads and began to peck, peck, peck, peck, and then the others began to peck, peck, peck, peck and put all the good lentils into the bowl. Barely an hour had passed when they were finished and flew back out the window.

The girl brought the bowl to her stepmother and was overjoyed because she was sure that she would now be able to go to the wedding. But the stepmother said: "No, Cinderella, you have nothing to wear, and you don't know how to dance. Everybody would just laugh at you."

When Cinderella began to cry, the stepmother said: "If you can pick out two bowlfuls of lentils from the ashes in the next hour, then you can go."

But she thought to herself: "She'll never be able to do it."

After she had dumped the two bowlfuls of lentils into the ashes, the girl went out the back door into the garden and called out: "O tame little doves, little turtle-doves, and all you little birds in the sky, come and help me put

the good ones into the little pot,
the bad ones into your little crop."

Two little white doves came flying in through the kitchen window, followed by little turtle doves. And finally all the birds in the sky came swooping and fluttering and settled down in the ashes. The little doves nodded their heads and began to peck, peck, peck, peck, and then the others began to peck, peck, peck, peck and put all the good lentils into the bowl. Barely a half hour had passed when they were finished and flew back out the window.

The girl brought the bowls back to her stepmother and was overjoyed because she was sure that she would now be able to go to the wedding. But her stepmother said: "It's no use. You can't come along since you have nothing to wear and don't know how to dance. We would be so embarrassed." Turning her back on Cinderella, she hurried off with her two proud daughters.

Now that no one was at home any longer, Cinderella went to her mother's grave under the hazel tree and called:

Stepmother still wouldn't let her go.

"Shake your branches, little tree,
Toss gold and silver down on me."

The bird tossed down a dress of gold and silver, with slippers embroidered with silk and silver. She slipped the dress on hastily and left for the wedding. Her sister and her stepmother had no idea who she was. She looked so beautiful in the dress of gold that they thought she must be the daughter of a foreign king. They never imagined it could be Cinderella for they were sure that she was at home, sitting in the dirt and picking lentils out of the ashes.

The prince approached Cinderella, took her by the hand, and danced with her. He didn't intend to dance with anyone else and never let go of her hand. Whenever anyone else asked her to dance, he would say: "She is my partner."

Cinderella danced until it was night, then she wanted to go home. The prince said: "I will go with you and be your escort," for he wanted to find out about the beautiful girl's family. But she managed to slip away from him and bounded into a dovecote. The prince waited until Cinderella's father arrived and told him that the strange girl had bounded into the dovecote. The old man thought: "Could it be Cinderella?" He sent for an ax and pick and broke into the dovecote, but no one was inside it. And when they went back to the house, there was Cinderella, lying in the ashes in her filthy clothes with a dim little oil lamp burning on the mantel. Cinderella had jumped down from the back of the dovecote and had run over to the little hazel tree, where she slipped out of her beautiful dress and put it on the grave. The bird took the dress back, and Cinderella had slipped into her grey smock and settled back into the ashes in the kitchen.

The next day, when the festivities started up again and the parents had left with the stepsisters, Cinderella went to the hazel tree and said:

"Shake your branches, little tree,
Toss gold and silver down on me."

The bird tossed down a dress that was even more splendid than the previous one. And when she appeared at the wedding in this dress, everyone was dazzled by her beauty. The prince, who had been waiting for her to arrive, took her by the hand and danced with her alone. Whenever anyone came and asked her to dance, he would say: "She is my partner."

At night she wanted to leave, and the prince followed her, hoping to see which house she would enter. But she bounded away and disappeared into the garden behind the house, where there was a beautiful, tall tree from whose branches hung magnificent pears. She climbed up through the branches as nimbly as a squirrel, and the prince had no idea where she was. He waited until her father got there and said to him: "The strange girl has escaped, but I believe that she climbed up into the pear tree."

The father thought: "Could it be Cinderella?" and he sent for an ax and chopped down the tree. But no one was in it. When they went into the kitchen, Cinderella was, as usual, lying in the ashes, for she had jumped down on the other side of the tree, taken the beautiful dress to the bird on the hazel tree, and slipped on her little grey smock again.

On the third day, when the parents and sisters had left, Cinderella went to her mother's grave and said to the little tree:

"Shake your branches, little tree,
Toss gold and silver down on me."

The bird tossed down a dress which was more splendid and radiant than anything she had ever had, and the slippers were covered in gold. When she got to the wedding in that dress, everyone was speechless with amazement. The prince danced with her alone, and if someone asked her to dance, he would say: "She is my partner."

At night, Cinderella wanted to leave, and the prince wanted to escort her, but she slipped away so quickly that he was unable to follow her. The prince had planned a trick. The entire staircase had been coated with pitch, and as the girl went running down the stairs, her left slipper got stuck. The prince lifted it up: it was a dainty little shoe covered with gold.

The next morning he went with it to the father and said to him: "No one else will be my bride but the woman whose foot fits this golden shoe." The two sisters were overjoyed, for they both had beautiful feet. The elder went with her mother into a room to try it on. But the shoe was too small for her, for she couldn't get her big toe into it. Her mother handed her a knife and said: "Cut the toe off. Once you're queen, you won't need to go on foot any more."

The girl sliced off her toe, forced her foot into the shoe, gritted her teeth, and went out to meet the prince. He lifted her up on his horse as his bride, and rode away with her. But they had to pass by the grave, where two little doves were perched in the little hazel tree, calling out:

"Roo coo coo, roo coo coo,
blood's in the shoe:
the shoe's too tight,
the real bride's waiting another night."

When he looked down at her foot, he saw blood spurting from it and turned his horse around. He brought the false bride back home, and said that since she was not the true bride, her sister should try the shoe on. The sister went into her room and succeeded in getting her toes into the shoe, but her heel was too big. Her mother handed her a knife and said: "Cut off part of your heel. Once you're queen, you won't need to go on foot any more."

The girl sliced off a piece of her heel, forced her foot into the shoe, gritted her teeth, and went out to meet the prince. He lifted her up on his horse as his bride, and rode away with her. When they passed by the little hazel tree, two little doves were perched there, calling out:

"Roo coo coo, roo coo coo,
blood's in the shoe:
the shoe's too tight,
the real bride's waiting another night."

When he looked down at her foot, he saw blood spurting from it and staining her white stockings completely red. Then he turned his horse around and brought the false bride back home. "She's not the true bride either," he said. "Don't you have another daughter?"

"No," said the man, "there's only puny little Cinderella, my dead wife's daughter, but she can't possibly be the bride."

The prince asked that she be sent for, but the mother said: "Oh no, she's much too dirty to be seen."

The prince insisted, and Cinderella was summoned. First she washed her hands and face completely clean, then she went and curtsied before the prince, who handed her the golden shoe. She sat down on a stool, took her foot out of the heavy wooden shoe, and put it into the slipper. It fit perfectly. And when she stood up and the prince looked her straight in the face, he recognized the beautiful girl with whom he had danced and exclaimed: "She is the true bride." The stepmother and the two sisters were horrified and turned pale with rage. But the prince lifted Cinderella up on his horse and rode away with her. When they passed by the little hazel tree, the two little white doves called out:

"Roo coo coo, roo coo coo,
no blood in the shoe:
the shoe's not tight,
the real bride's here tonight."

After they had called out these words, the doves both came flying down and perched on Cinderella's shoulders, one on the right, the other on the left, and there they stayed.

On the day of the wedding to the prince, the two false sisters came and tried to ingratiate themselves and share in Cinderella's good fortune. When the couple went to church, the elder sister was on the right, the younger on the left side: the doves pecked one eye from each one. Later, when they left the church, the elder sister was on the left, the younger on the right. The doves pecked the other eye from each one. And so they were punished for their wickedness and malice with blindness for the rest of their lives.

Most readers familiar with the Disney version of *Cinderella* will probably be struck by how different the German version is. Though we know, for instance, that the Disney Cinderella's mother has died and that her father has remarried, in the German version we see more vividly the young girl's grief and her ultimate rejection by her father, for whom she seems only an afterthought. There are other differences as well; the German heroine is much more active and resourceful than the more passive and demure American Cinderella: she calls the birds to her aid, and she runs from the prince and returns to her place in the ashes. She also apparently receives help from her dead mother, rather than from a magical fairy godmother appearing from nowhere. Most obvious, however, are the differences in the atmospheres of the two stories. Nowhere in the Disney version is there the suggestion of violence that permeates the German version, with its broken promises, bloody feet, and blinded eyes.

A comparison of the German and Disney versions may, then, reveal much about the two cultures' ideas of ideal womanhood, justice, magic, and spirituality. It will reveal as well something about each culture's way of looking at childhood. Although the Grimm version was available for telling, most American parents of the mid–twentieth century were more drawn than their earlier German counterparts to images of a sentimental happily-ever-after world in which romance, rather than punishment, dominates. That was the world in which they wanted their children to live.

Perhaps even more interesting, though, is a comparison of these Western versions of the Cinderella story to the Chinese story of Yeh-hsien, which was written over one thousand years ago and is the first known version of "Cinderella." As you read the tale, think about how it compares with the other Cinderella stories printed here.

Yeh-hsien

Among the people of the south there is a tradition that before the Ch'in and Han dynasties there was a cave-master called Wu. The aborigines called the place the Wu cave. He married two wives. One wife died. She had a daughter called Yeh-hsien, who from childhood was intelligent and good at making pottery on the wheel. Her father loved her. After some years the father died, and she was ill-treated by her stepmother, who always made her collect firewood in dangerous places and draw water from deep pools. She once got a fish about two inches long, with red fins and golden eyes. She put it into a bowl of water. It grew bigger every day, and after she had changed the bowl several times she could find no bowl big enough for it, so she threw it into the back pond. Whatever food was left over from meals she put into the water to feed it. When she came to the pond, the fish always exposed its head and pillowed it on the bank; but when anyone else came, it did not come out. The step-mother knew about this, but when she watched for it, it did not once appear. So she tricked the girl, saying, "Haven't you worked hard! I am going to give you a new dress." She then made the girl change out of her tattered clothing. Afterwards she sent her to get water from another spring and reckoning that it was several hundred leagues, the step-mother at her leisure put on her daughter's clothes, hid a sharp blade up her sleeve, and went to the pond. She called to the fish. The fish at once put its head out, and she chopped it off and killed it. The fish was now more than ten feet long. She served it up and it tasted twice as good as an ordinary fish. She hid the bones under the dung-hill. Next day, when the girl came to the pond, no fish appeared. She howled with grief in the open countryside, and suddenly there appeared a man with his hair loose over his shoulders and coarse clothes. He came down from the sky. He consoled her saying, "Don't howl! Your step-mother has killed the fish and its bones are under the dung. You go back, take the fish's bones and hide them in your room. Whatever you want, you have only to pray to them for it. It is bound to be granted." The girl followed his advice, and was able to provide herself with gold, pearls, dresses and food whenever she wanted them.

When the time came for the cave-festival, the step-mother went, leaving the girl to keep watch over the fruit-trees in the garden. She waited till the step-mother was some way off, and then went herself, wearing a cloak of stuff spun from king-fisher feathers and shoes of gold. Her step-sister recognized her and said to the step-mother, "That's very like my sister." The step-mother suspected the same thing. The girl was aware of this and went away in such a hurry that she lost one shoe. It was picked up by one of the people of the cave. When the step-mother got home, she found the girl asleep, with her arms round one of the trees in the garden, and thought no more about it.

This cave was near to an island in the sea. On this island was a kingdom called T'o-han. Its soldiers had subdued twenty or thirty other islands and it had a coast-line of several thousand leagues. The cave-man sold the shoe in T'o-han, and the ruler of T'o-han got it. He told those about him to put it on; but it was an inch too small even for the one among them that had the smallest foot. He ordered all the women in his kingdom to try it on; but there was not one that it fitted. It was light as down and made no noise even when treading on stone. The king of T'o-han thought the cave-man had got it unlawfully. He put him in prison and tortured him, but did not end by finding out where it had come from. So he threw it down at the wayside. Then they went everywhere through all the people's houses and arrested them. If there was a woman's shoe, they arrested them and told the king of T'o-han. He thought it strange, searched the inner-rooms and found Yeh-hsien. He made her put on the shoe, and it was true.

Yeh-hsien then came forward, wearing her cloak spun from halcyon feathers and her shoes. She was as beautiful as a heavenly being. She now began to render service to the king, and he took the fish-bones and Yeh-hsien, and brought them back to his country.

The step-mother and step-sister were shortly afterwards struck by flying stones, and died. The cave people were sorry for them and buried them in a stone-pit, which was called the Tomb of the Distressed Women. The men of the cave made mating-offerings there; any girl they prayed for there, they got. The king of T'o-han, when he got back to his kingdom made Yeh-hsien his chief wife. The first year the king was very greedy and by his prayers to the fish-bones got treasures and jade without limit. Next year, there was no response, so the king buried the fish-bones on the sea-shore. He covered them with a hundred bushels of pearls and bordered them with gold. Later there was a mutiny of some soldiers who had been conscripted and their general opened (the hiding-place) in order to make better provision for his army. One night they (the bones) were washed away by the tide.

EXERCISE: TRYING IT OUT

If you had not been told that this was a "Chinese Cinderella," would you have recognized it as a Cinderella story? Why or why not? Write down the elements of the story that seem most like the Cinderella tale you know and the ones least like it.

You might have noticed some similarities between the Chinese "Cinderella" and the Western ones. For example, all the Cinderellas have an unusually small foot, a characteristic that probably comes from the Chinese original. For the Chinese, a small foot was a sign of femininity, a cultural value supported by the practice of foot binding. We also see in the Chinese tale the wicked stepmother and a hint of the wicked stepsister familiar to those who know the Western versions of "Cinderella."

At the same time, the tale of Yeh-hsien is very different from the two later stories, and we may well wonder if those differences are the result of cultural differences. Most notably, Yeh-hsien seems less central to the story than do the American and German Cinderellas. Is that, perhaps, the result of a culture that valued the communal more than the individual? In the Chinese version, there is also less emphasis on the labor performed by the heroine: most modern readers are used to seeing a Cinderella among the cinders, sweeping the hearth and doing the hardest, dirtiest tasks of the household. Did nineteenth- and twentieth-century Western culture perhaps place a different value on domestic labor than did the China of a thousand years ago? Did the long-ago Chinese storyteller view work differently than do Western Europeans and Americans? Or did the ancient Chinese simply assume that life was difficult for everyone and so find no need to mention the heroine's daily routine?

Other elements emphasized in the two modern versions are also less important in the Chinese original. For example, the stepsister in the Chinese story plays a surprisingly minor role. Is sibling rivalry perhaps a modern invention, something we become more aware of only as life becomes easier? In addition, though Yeh-hsien becomes the "chief wife" of the king, he does not seem a Prince Charming; there is no sense that he provides the completion of the story, the "happily ever after" of the more modern stories. Does that perhaps suggest that romantic love was not as important to the Chinese audience as to German and American ones?

No matter how you view the Cinderellas of the three versions, you will undoubtedly see that the heroine is different in each of the stories. The characterizations of the heroine and those she meets, her actions and reactions, and the atmosphere of the world around her—all tell us something about what each culture values and how it looks at the world.

EXERCISE: TRYING IT OUT

The story of Cinderella you are familiar with probably goes back many years. Write an updated version of the story to make it more contemporary. What changes did you make—and why? How would you preserve the story as a children's story?

The Influence of Time

As we have just seen, different cultures tell the same stories differently. No less important is the fact that different cultures—and different individuals within those cultures—also *read* the same stories differently. Our readings of those stories are sometimes informed by years of personal and cultural history that separate us from the stories' first tellings, and our interpretations of them are a kind of retelling. Consider, for instance, what happens when we read about a hero like Shakespeare's Prospero (the main character of *The Tempest*). Many years before the play starts, Prospero's brother had stolen his dukedom from him and cast Prospero and his daughter adrift. Shipwrecked on an island, Prospero has used magic to rule the island and control its inhabitants, among them the "slave" Caliban and the spirit Ariel. At the end of the play, though, Prospero renounces his magic, leaving the island and returning home. Do we see that ending as fully positive?

In answering that question, we need to think not only about our own twenty-first-century response but also about the response that Shakespeare's original audience would likely have had. Although we can work to immerse ourselves in Renaissance history and literature, try as we might, we cannot fully recapture the sensations that an early-seventeenth-century theater audience must have had when watching Prospero renounce the magic that had allowed him to keep the bestial Caliban in check. Unlike the audiences of earlier times, we no longer believe in monsters. In fact, we have often come to distrust those who seek to dominate or who label as monstrous those who are "different." We may, then, be far less likely than the original audience to find Caliban bestial or Prospero admirable, and we may be far more tempted to brand Prospero's actions as "patriarchal" or "colonial." However knowledgeable about early literature and history we are, we cannot completely shake from our vision the perspectives brought by our living in the twenty-first century.

Rather than lament our inability to recapture the literary response of a time gone by, we ask you here to confront that inability head-on. One way to do that is, of course, to attempt to read the stories as their original audiences would have heard them, to learn about the assumptions and values that they would have brought to their hearing or reading of a piece of literature. When those of us who quite happily and comfortably inhabit the New World read Shakespeare's *Tempest*, it is important that we learn to see it as a drama written partly in response to the tensions experienced by European explorers who, leaving the known world, voyaged into alien territory rumored to be populated by subhuman beasts. Hindsight and an understanding of indigenous cultures have shown us that the New World is hospitable and fertile, a place that is now—and was during Shakespeare's time—home to sophisticated and humane civilizations. But for those traveling to uncharted lands, no such assurances existed, and it is important for us when we read works such as *The Tempest* to attempt to recapture that mixed air of excitement and anxiety that infects all explorers. It is important as well to understand, even if we do not share, the assumptions and biases of an earlier time.

In reading literature from the past, we gain a better understanding of earlier times and begin to understand how our own age shapes our responses to life and literature. An audience fearful of the creature emerging from the wilderness is hardly likely to want to stop to think about how that creature might be looking at things. But, perhaps more comfortable in a modern society's ability to defeat any monster, in 1969 Caribbean author Aimé Césaire did something like that, offering us a version of Shakespeare's play with an articulate "monster." In Césaire's *A Tempest,* Caliban raises questions about the heroism of Prospero, who has, after all, overrun the land of the New World and sought to dominate its inhabitants. In reading Césaire's play, we come to understand how Shakespeare's assumptions about civilization and humanity differ from our own; at the same time, as we reread Shakespeare's play in light of Césaire's later one, we begin to see a complexity that we might not otherwise have noticed. Perhaps Shakespeare meant *The Tempest* to contain a hint of criticism about Prospero's treatment of Caliban and a small bit of sympathy for the natural "savage" who has lost his land and his freedom.

EXERCISES: TRYING IT OUT

1. Think of a story from long ago—a fairy tale, perhaps—that pits a hero against a monster or villain. Usually such stories are sympathetic to the hero. Rewrite that story from the monster's or villain's point of view. How would you get your readers to sympathize with the monster? How would you tailor your story to an audience of children? An audience of teenagers or adults?

2. In a small way, the time-related reactions we have been discussing occur even from one generation to the next. Perhaps parents of most generations have found the popular music of teenagers discordant or shocking, and perhaps most teenagers have been equally dismissive of the music of an earlier generation. Take the lyrics from one of your favorite songs and retell them in the style of your parents' generation; or do the opposite, and take the lyrics from a song of their generation and retell it in the language and beat of today's music.

The Importance of Perspective

All of these different tales and responses to them are, finally, a matter of **perspective,** and in *Retellings* we are asking you to think about the ways in which the perspectives of the teller, the artistic center (the hero, the **protagonist**), and the audience all figure into an interpretation of a work of literature. *Perspective* is, of course, a term that pertains to how we see something. In representing a three-dimensional object on a two-dimensional surface, an artist must think about how large or small something seems when seen from a distance, how the angle from which it is viewed changes what the observer sees, or how the juxtaposition, the placing side by side, of two items causes us to see each differently.

The importance of perspective and the difficulty of keeping in mind two perspectives at once become especially clear at the visual level when we look at optical illusions. Look, for instance, at this familiar optical illusion:

Do you see two lovers? A wine goblet? Both images? Once you have trained your eyes to see both the lovers and the goblet, you can easily move back and forth between the images, and your mind will begin to recognize that the two exist simultaneously. It is a similar kind of mental exercise that we are asking you to perform in your reading of literature. It is not a matter of whether Shakespeare's Prospero is a perfect hero *or* a flawed man; he may well be both, and the reading of alternate versions of his and others' stories will, we think, help you begin to see that works of literature can support these contradictory readings, these opposed perspectives.

Years ago, literary critic Norman Rabkin called this creation of simultaneously opposed, or different, images and ideas *complementarity,* and he said that complementarity is the hallmark of much great literature. It is also, we think, the hallmark of much great reading of literature, and for that reason this focus on multiple perspectives is at the center of our approach in *Retellings.* To be able to see the ideas or events of a piece of literature (or of life, for that matter) from the varied perspectives of its many participants and observers is, we think, to see it whole, in its full complexity. That means, then, seeing the piece from the perspectives of its author and its original audience while at the same time comparing those earlier perspectives to the perspectives of readers who are outside that author's mind and time.

In many ways, what we are asking you to do is to apply to literature a kind of thinking that you are already familiar with. To understand the importance of perspective to interpretation, you need only think about a controversial or highly charged family event, say, a public fight between you and your sister. Would all those who witnessed the event emphasize the same details? Would you, in other words, all tell the same story? Your version may be no more or less true than, say, your mother's or father's version or that of a sibling; it may be no more or less true than that of a friend or stranger who observed the scene. What gets emphasized, though, is both enhanced and limited by the teller's perspective. You know more than anyone else what was going on in your mind; at the same time what you were thinking and feeling is bound to have influenced both what you observed and how you narrate it. In other words, your understanding—and your ability to see and interpret fact—is influenced by your perspective and by your assumptions.

EXERCISE: TRYING IT OUT

Think back to an important event in your life, and interview as many of the participants and observers as you can. How much do their tellings differ from one another? What do the differences tell us about the tellers' needs, values, and beliefs?

Such complexity of thought is already inherent in much of our thinking. When Rabkin wrote about complementarity, he was, in fact, borrowing a term coined by physicists Niels Bohr and J. Robert Oppenheimer to describe the physicist's dilemma in seeing an electron as both a particle and a wave. How can it be both? More important, perhaps, what happens when we need to see it as both, and what can be gained by alternating between apparently opposed theories and trying to hold them in mind simultaneously? We move back and forth between supposedly competing theories in other disciplines as well. Is alcoholism caused by a chemical imbalance? Is it a psychological dependency? A learned behavior? Is the manic depressive the victim of a personality disorder best studied by psychologists or of a physiological process that can be put in check by a neurologist? How the "story" of the alcoholic or the manic depressive is told has far-reaching implications for how that person is treated and perceived, and there is some danger in thinking that a simple cure can come from a single avenue of healing. In physics and medicine, as well as in literature, the perspectives of the teller and observer significantly affect the interpretation of fact.

EXERCISES: TRYING IT OUT

1. At the linguistic level, Rabkin's idea of complementarity can be demonstrated by the use of **oxymorons,** words or phrases that contain within them their opposites. (A San Francisco newspaper columnist once called these "self-canceling phrases.") Examples of oxymorons include "bittersweet," "wise fool," "make haste

slowly," "deceitful truth," and "burned with a cold anger." List five or more oxymorons. Then write a brief (one-page) story or poem that demonstrates the principle behind one of the oxymorons.

2. Think of an area of complex social concern (for example, public art, transportation, poverty, the economy). Write down five or six different "perspectives" on that area, considering how these different perspectives might make consensus difficult. For example, how might an engineer, a social worker, a taxpayer, a senior citizen, and a politician all view the issue?

Riddling: Multiple Perspectives   Literary texts open themselves up to the kind of multiplicity of understanding that we have been discussing even more deliberately than do medical cases or physical phenomena. Indeed, from your earliest experiences with texts, whether oral or written, you were already beginning to play with the importance of multiple perspectives and to understand the ways the same story can be retold. Most riddles and jokes, and many childhood songs, rely on their tellers' ability to play with literary perspective and surprise, to hold simultaneously two contrary, or different, readings of a work. One of the first riddles that many children learn relies on a sound play that allows for two different endings:

What is black and white and red/read all over?

The child who tells this riddle anticipates two different responses, each of which has the potential to be "right," and each of which has the potential to be "wrong." To his listener, there is no difference in sound between "red" and "read," so the teller can easily "fool" his listener. If that listener thinks she knows the answer to the riddle—a newspaper is certainly black and white and read all over—the teller can trick her into believing that she was wrong: the answer isn't "a newspaper" but rather "a blushing zebra," which is black and white and *red* all over. If the savvy listener responds with "a blushing zebra" from the beginning, she, too, will discover that she is "wrong," for the answer this time around is "a newspaper." Finally, of course, neither riddle solver is wrong; both answers exist simultaneously in the riddle, and the joy—for the child learning to riddle and for the adult reading a sophisticated piece of literature—is often in discovering that very fact.

Such riddling is also found in more serious, adult works, sometimes even in pieces of literature that are not technically riddles. Consider, for instance, the poem "you fit into me," by Margaret Atwood. The poem deliberately uses an ambiguity similar to that of the newspaper/blushing zebra riddle. Rather than give you the entire poem at once, we are going to ask you to read it line by line, thinking along with us about how you would "solve" the riddle of the poetic narrative. As we read each line, we will be doing what all readers do: telling ourselves the story of the poem. Each additional line we read will help us tell an increasingly complex story and force us to revise our earlier impressions of emotions and events. As we read, we will, then, be casting our minds forward to what is about to happen and backward to what has already happened; we will be telling and retelling the poem.

The poem begins:

you fit into me

The line asks us to envision a perfect relationship, probably a relationship between a man and a woman perfectly matched to each other. There is in the idea of "fitting" a suggestion both of sexual intimacy and of a oneness that encourages us to believe that the two people have somehow completed each other. We hear not only "you fit *into* me" but also "you fit me," and we believe that this is a perfect and enduring relationship.

Further insinuations of that endurance and of the perfection of that relationship come in the poem's second line:

> like a hook into an eye

The line depends on some knowledge of the relationship between a hook and an eye, a once-common way of fastening garments. A hook fastened to one side of an opening is placed into a loop (or "eye") fastened to the other side, thus bringing the two sides together. (In our experience, students are most familiar with hooks and eyes on women's bras.) This image is in many ways a further illustration of the couple's closeness: the metaphor of the hook and eye helps us to envision them coming closer together, forming a circle of intimacy and closing out the rest of the world.

> you fit into me
> like a hook into an eye

the speaker tells her lover, and we think about the romantic perfection of their love. Then we read the next line:

> a fish hook

Suddenly we need to rethink our earlier reaction, to "retell" the poem to ourselves. The mood has shifted, and we have to start thinking about a different kind of hook. So familiar (at least it was familiar at one time) is the image of the hook and eye that we may have been deceived into seeing a "false" image. It is now not the fastener joining two pieces of cloth—and two people—that the speaker wants us to see: it is the fish hook that ensnares an unsuspecting fish and carries it to its death. It is not that we didn't know about fish hooks when we read the first lines; it is that the speaker's juxtaposition of *hook* and *eye* cleverly led us astray, so that we "wrongly" imagined an innocent calm that has now been rent apart by the image of the fish hook.

The torment of the third line is further intensified in the fourth, which even more fully disrupts our earlier sense of romantic perfection:

> an open eye.

It is no longer the fish that is hooked but rather a human eye. Whatever sympathy we might have felt for the fish hooked by the angler's rod is turned into a more selfish chilling horror when we imagine our own eye being pierced by a fish hook.

In four lines, then, the poem has surprised us into a rejection of our first reading of the poem's situation. What is described is not a perfect relationship filled with joy and romance but rather a hostile one marked by violence and pain. We come to understand and experience the violence and pain all the more strongly for having first experienced the romantic innocence of the first two lines. In other words, the first reading is not "false" so much as incomplete. We don't understand the pain without having first understood the joy. The poem works best when it gets told and retold, when we see the joy of the early love in isolation *and* when we see it in the context of the later bitterness, when we see the pain as a later incarnation of the love that earlier brought uncorrupted happiness. Like the optical illusion discussed previously, "you fit into me" asks us to see two things in isolation from each other and to see them simultaneously; in the process, we come to a richer understanding of the couple and their relationship.

Here is Atwood's short poem in its entirety:

MARGARET ATWOOD (1939–   )

you fit into me _____ *1971*

> you fit into me
> like a hook into an eye
>
> a fish hook
> an open eye

EXERCISES: TRYING IT OUT

1. Although we tend to put riddles in the same category as jokes, there is a long tra-
    dition of literary riddles, designed both to tease the reader and to exhibit the
    writer's craft. Here is one written by Sylvia Plath in 1960:

SYLVIA PLATH (1932–1963)

Metaphors _____ *1960*

> I'm a riddle in nine syllables,
> An elephant, a ponderous house,
> A melon strolling on two tendrils.
> O red fruit, ivory, fine timbers!
> This loaf's big with its yeasty rising.
> Money's new-minted in this fat purse.
> I'm a means, a stage, a cow in calf.
> I've eaten a bag of green apples,
> Boarded the train there's no getting off.

5

What answer(s) can you propose for this riddle? What might you deduce about
the time and culture that gave rise to it?

2. Children love riddles, but riddles are not at all childish. In fact, they are hard to write:
    the writer does not want to give everything away too soon, but he also does not
    want to leave the meaning so obscure that the audience will feel cheated in the end.
    Try your hand at writing a riddle that conveys its answer subtly and poetically
    (though not necessarily in poetic form). After you've written it, test it out on at least
    four or five people. How successfully did you manage to keep your audience in sus-
    pense, surprise them at the end, and capture the essence of the thing being described?

Parody: "Dover Beach" and "The Dover Bitch"

Atwood's "you fit into me," like the riddles and optical illusions discussed earlier, contains within itself its own retellings: the reader or observer sees several stories

at once. Another kind of retelling occurs when one work *consciously* retells another, asking readers to rethink their responses to the events, characters, or mood of an earlier work. Among the most familiar of such conscious retellings are *parodies*. A **parody** is a work that humorously imitates, and sometimes mocks, a more serious work. If you think back to your childhood, you can probably remember several parodies of adult verse that you found humorous. We remember gleefully singing a parody of the Civil War–era song "The Battle Hymn of the Republic," which begins, "Mine eyes have seen the glory of the coming of the Lord"; our version began, "My eyes have seen the glory of the burning of the school" and told of students' raucous celebration of victory over their teachers. College students have devised similar parodies; " 'Twas the Night before Finals," a parodic retelling of " 'Twas the Night before Christmas," makes the rounds in many dorm rooms at the end of each school term, especially when finals occur right before the winter holidays.

Many children (and college students) see parody and joke as a means of debunking what they do not yet understand or value, but these forms also serve important psychological and literary functions. The child who sings of the "glory of the burning of the school" is no doubt testing, or fantasizing about, his control over the teachers and institution that often seem omnipotent; the student who recites a parody of " 'Twas the Night before Christmas" recalls a childhood joy untouched by the pressures that finals bring and, at the same time, gains some mastery over the stresses of the moment. In both cases, the parody also emphasizes the teller's entrance into the literary conversation. By using literary works from the dominant culture, parodists both pay tribute to that culture and assert their independence from it.

EXERCISES: TRYING IT OUT

1. Most of us know parodies from our childhoods. Collect several such parodies and analyze the ways the parodies work. What do they have in common with the thing being parodied? How do they differ from the original? What purpose do they serve?

2. Choose a well-known piece of literature or an excerpt from a piece of literature. Or, instead, choose a well-known traditional song from your childhood. Write a parody of that work. Finally, write a brief analysis of the methods and purpose of your parody, showing how the parody encourages us to think about the original in new ways.

   Some suggestions for works you might parody:
   Shakespeare's "To be or not to be" speech from *Hamlet*
   Emily Dickinson's "Because I could not stop for Death—"
   Brewster Higley's "Home on the Range"
   Katharine Lee Bates's "America the Beautiful"

We turn now to two poems that we think illuminate well the rich complexity of literary retellings. As you read Matthew Arnold's "Dover Beach," think about its content, its rhythms, and its tone. We want you to experience the poem as much as you can, as the speaker and his silent lover experience it. First, read the poem aloud, paying attention to its story:

MATTHEW ARNOLD (1822–1888)

Dover Beach   1867

The sea is calm tonight.
The tide is full, the moon lies fair
Upon the straits; on the French coast the light
Gleams and is gone; the cliffs of England stand,
Glimmering and vast, out in the tranquil bay.   5
Come to the window, sweet is the night-air!
Only, from the long line of spray
Where the sea meets the moon-blanched land,
Listen! you hear the grating roar
Of pebbles which the waves draw back, and fling,   10
At their return, up the high strand,
Begin, and cease, and then again begin,
With tremulous cadence slow, and bring
The eternal note of sadness in.

Sophocles long ago   15
Heard it on the Aegean, and it brought
Into his mind the turbid ebb and flow
Of human misery; we
Find also in the sound a thought,
Hearing it by this distant northern sea.   20

The Sea of Faith
Was once, too, at the full, and round earth's shore
Lay like the folds of a bright girdle furled.
But now I only hear
Its melancholy, long, withdrawing roar,   25
Retreating, to the breath
Of the night-wind, down the vast edges drear
And naked shingles of the world.

Ah, love, let us be true
To one another! for the world, which seems   30
To lie before us like a land of dreams,
So various, so beautiful, so new,
Hath really neither joy, nor love, nor light,
Nor certitude, nor peace, nor help for pain;
And we are here as on a darkling plain   35
Swept with confused alarms of struggle and flight,
Where ignorant armies clash by night.

As you read the poem aloud, you may have noticed that the rhythms and sounds have a kind of calming effect, not unlike the rhythms and sounds of the calm sea to which the first line alludes. "The sea is calm tonight," the speaker tells us, and so too is the speaker himself.

As we read on, we sense something more: a feeling of nostalgia or loss. The light from France "Gleams and is gone"; the waves "bring / The eternal note of sadness in." An awareness of the crisis in faith that shook the nineteenth century gives us some sense of the emotional and intellectual atmosphere that surrounds the couple in the poem: with the mechanization brought by the Industrial Revolution and the newfound interest in the scientific method and scientific exploration (Charles Darwin's theories about evolution were published in *The Origin of the Species* only nine years after "Dover Beach"), religious faith was frequently put to the test. The speaker of "Dover Beach," presumably joined by his beloved, looks from his window out across the English Channel (France is situated across the Channel from Dover); he remembers a time when the Sea of Faith was round and full. What he hears now is only its "melancholy, long, withdrawing roar."

Against that melancholy vision of a lost faith the speaker counterposes the image of his love, a love that seems at first to offer hope but finally is apparently vulnerable and powerless in a world of such pain:

> Ah, love, let us be true
> To one another! for the world, which seems
> To lie before us like a land of dreams,
> So various, so beautiful, so new,
> Hath really neither joy, nor love, nor light,
> Nor certitude, nor peace, nor help for pain;
> And we are here as on a darkling plain
> Swept with confused alarms of struggle and flight,
> Where ignorant armies clash by night.

The opening of the stanza, with its "Ah, love, let us be true," promises a bulwark against the onslaughts of an unromantic and threatening world. But even in the next line, some of that promise is removed; "we" cannot hope to be "true," but only "true / To one another." The faith of a belief in God has necessarily, and with some sense of disappointment, been replaced with a different kind of fidelity: the more immediate, and less universal, love for a woman. And then even that is taken away; only a few lines later we learn that the world, which seems dream-beautiful, "Hath really neither joy, *nor love,* nor light." So even the love that the stanza's opening asked us to envision is perhaps illusory.

What, then, is Arnold's poem *about*? Finally, it is probably less about the couple standing in their room overlooking the beautifully moonlit English Channel than it is about the anxieties that have beset the speaker and the age in which he lives. Perhaps that is why the poem seems as much a monologue as a poem addressed to a nearby lover. You might, in fact, try to imagine that lover more fully present in the poem. That is close to what Anthony Hecht did when composing his modern retelling of "Dover Beach." Hecht's poem is entitled "The Dover Bitch," and it takes a decidedly modern look at the romantic depression of Arnold's poem:

ANTHONY HECHT (1923–   )

The Dover Bitch: A Criticism of Life _____ *1968*

For Andrews Wanning

So there stood Matthew Arnold and this girl
With the cliffs of England crumbling away behind them,
And he said to her, "Try to be true to me,
And I'll do the same for you, for things are bad
All over, etc., etc." 5
Well now, I knew this girl. It's true she had read
Sophocles in a fairly good translation
And caught that bitter allusion to the sea,
But all the time he was talking she had in mind
The notion of what his whiskers would feel like 10
On the back of her neck. She told me later on
That after a while she got to looking out
At the lights across the channel, and really felt sad,
Thinking of all the wine and enormous beds
And blandishments in French and the perfumes. 15
And then she got really angry. To have been brought
All the way down from London, and then be addressed
As a sort of mournful cosmic last resort
Is really tough on a girl, and she was pretty.
Anyway, she watched him pace the room 20
And finger his watch-chain and seem to sweat a bit,
And then she said one or two unprintable things.
But you mustn't judge her by that. What I mean to say is,
She's really all right. I still see her once in a while
And she always treats me right. We have a drink 25
And I give her a good time, and perhaps it's a year
Before I see her again, but there she is,
Running to fat, but dependable as they come.
And sometimes I bring her a bottle of *Nuit d'Amour.*

When we have asked students to read Hecht's poem, they have almost always responded appreciatively, nodding like conspirators at his poking fun at Arnold's speaker and the situation in which he finds himself. They, perhaps like Hecht's speaker, see the speaker in Arnold's poem as whiny and self-indulgent, so caught up in his own anxieties that he cannot take notice of the other human being in the room.

Certainly the tone and diction of Hecht's poem reinforce these responses. The play on "beach" and "bitch" in the title itself seems to give away Hecht's less-than-reverent attitude toward the despair expressed by Arnold's speaker. And the clipped and colloquial slang of Hecht's poem further contrasts with the more elevated diction and conscious literary allusions of Arnold's, perhaps implying an ironic comment by the twentieth-century American about the more reserved—and more snobbish?—Englishman. There are also, of course, the explicit reminders of the earlier speaker's willingness simply to ignore the woman to whom he is supposedly professing his love. Hecht's speaker reminds us of that other's presence, asking us to imagine, as Arnold's does not, the loneliness and purposelessness of the woman who simply stands by while her lover muses about the loss of faith and gives himself over to cosmic despair.

Hecht's speaker further asks us to compare the woman's vision of the "wine and enormous beds / And blandishments in French and the perfumes" with what Arnold's speaker sees from the window: an amorphous vision of the retreating Sea of Faith and of senseless battles between "ignorant" armies. There is in her vision something so much more tangible and life-giving that it is easy to see in his an empty philosophical pomposity. So, readers sometimes reason, Hecht is clearly making fun of Arnold, illuminating the superior realism of our own culture and era and puncturing the false sentimentality of Arnold's.

A closer reading of the two poems will show, however, that this is a case in which a parody does not simply ridicule the earlier work that inspired it. Despite its raw language and tone, despite its willingness to stand back (and ask us to stand back) and laugh at the exaggeration of "Dover Beach," "The Dover Bitch" is in its own way as nostalgic as Arnold's poem. Indeed, rather than undercut the values and assumptions of the earlier work, it may actually affirm them, revealing the extent to which Arnold's speaker prophesied the hollowness of our own time. In this respect, "The Dover Bitch" provides a good example of **irony:** the author wants us to believe the opposite of what is said. In Hecht's "The Dover Bitch," the speaker approves of the woman's behavior; Hecht seems to find it shallow and disappointing.

To see how the irony in "The Dover Bitch" works, examine the ways in which Hecht's language echoes Arnold's and comments upon his words. Do we really want to live in a world in which promises of romantic fidelity (Ah, love, let us be true / To one another!") are replaced by promises to "*Try* to be true to me, / And I'll do the same for you"? Isn't there something depressing in the deliberate understatement of "for things are bad / All over, etc., etc."—something that not only questions the foundations of the earlier speaker's despair but also makes our own ability to understand the reality of that despair seem hollow? When we read Arnold's poem we may believe that love can no longer hold the world together, and we mourn the loss of its power. When we read Hecht's we know that even the idea of love has disappeared: the pure and gentle romance of a night of love has been replaced by sexual promiscuity and the promise of a cheap perfume: "a bottle of *Nuit d'Amour.*"

We cannot understand the depths of the cynicism of Hecht's speaker without at the same time understanding the fullness of the loss described in Arnold's poem. In reading the two together, then, we come to appreciate more fully the loss that Arnold describes and, while appreciating Hecht's humor, to understand more completely that the cynicism of Hecht's poem is simply the underside of Arnold's nostalgic longings. Hecht, too, regrets the loss of romantic love and the ascendancy of modern realism and lust.

EXERCISE: TRYING IT OUT

Although Hecht calls our attention to the point of view of the woman, his speaker is still a man. Now write a third version of the poem, this time from the point of view of the woman herself. What does that third perspective add to our understanding of Arnold's and Hecht's poems?

_____

READING CRITICALLY AND THINKING CRITICALLY: *WHAT* VERSUS *HOW* AND *WHY*

Finally we turn to another work by Margaret Atwood, whose "you fit into me" we discussed earlier in this chapter. This time we ask you to read one of her short stories, "Happy Endings." In it, Atwood makes explicit much of what we are talking about here: she presents several endings to the same story, asking us to envision the same two people living in several different story lines. As you read the story, notice how each ending comments on the ones before it.

MARGARET ATWOOD (1939–   )

Happy Endings _____ *1983*

John and Mary meet.
What happens next?
If you want a happy ending, try A.

A

John and Mary fall in love and get married. They both have worthwhile and re-munerative jobs which they find stimulating and challenging. They buy a charming house. Real estate values go up. Eventually, when they can afford live-in help, they have two children, to whom they are devoted. The children turn out well. John and Mary have a stimulating and challenging sex life and worthwhile friends. They go on fun vacations together. They retire. They both have hobbies which they find stimulating and challenging. Eventually they die. This is the end of the story.

B

Mary falls in love with John but John doesn't fall in love with Mary. He merely uses her body for selfish pleasure and ego gratification of a tepid kind. He comes to her apartment twice a week and she cooks him dinner, you'll notice that he doesn't even consider her worth the price of a dinner out, and after he's eaten the dinner he fucks her and after that he falls asleep, while she does the dishes so he won't think she's untidy, having all those dirty dishes lying around, and puts on fresh lipstick so she'll look good when he wakes up, but when he wakes up he doesn't even notice, he puts on his socks and his shorts and his pants and his shirt and his tie and his shoes, the reverse order from the one in which he took them off. He doesn't take off Mary's clothes, she takes them off herself, she acts as if she's dying for it every time, not because she likes sex exactly, she doesn't, but she wants John to think she does because if they do it often enough surely he'll get used to her, he'll come to depend on her and they will get married, but John goes out the door with hardly so much as a good-night and three days later he turns up at six o'clock and they do the whole thing again.

Mary gets run-down. Crying is bad for your face, everyone knows that and so does Mary but she can't stop. People at work notice. Her friends tell her John is a rat, a pig, a dog, he isn't good enough for her, but she can't believe it. Inside John, she thinks, is another John, who is much nicer. This other John will emerge like a butter-fly from a cocoon, a Jack from a box, a pit from a prune, if the first John is only squeezed enough.

One evening John complains about the food. He has never complained about the food before. Mary is hurt.

Her friends tell her they've seen him in a restaurant with another woman, whose name is Madge. It's not even Madge that finally gets to Mary; it's the restaurant. John has never taken Mary to a restaurant. Mary collects all the sleeping pills and aspirins she can find, and takes them and a half a bottle of sherry. You can see what kind of a woman she is by the fact that it's not even whiskey. She leaves a note for John. She hopes he'll discover her and get her to the hospital in time and repent and then they can get married, but this fails to happen and she dies.

John marries Madge and everything continues as in A.

C

John, who is an older man, falls in love with Mary, and Mary, who is only twenty-two, feels sorry for him because he's worried about his hair falling out. She sleeps with him even though she's not in love with him. She met him at work. She's in love with someone called James, who is twenty-two also and not yet ready to settle down.

John on the contrary settled down long ago: this is what is bothering him. John has a steady, respectable job and is getting ahead in his field, but Mary isn't impressed by him, she's impressed by James, who has a motorcycle and a fabulous record collec-tion. But James is often away on his motorcycle, being free. Freedom isn't the same for girls, so in the meantime Mary spends Thursday evenings with John. Thursdays are the only days John can get away.

John is married to a woman called Madge and they have two children, a charm-ing house which they bought just before the real estate values went up, and hobbies which they find stimulating and challenging, when they have the time. John tells Mary how important she is to him, but of course he can't leave his wife because a commitment is a commitment. He goes on about this more than is necessary and Mary finds it boring, but older men can keep it up longer so on the whole she has a fairly good time.

One day James breezes in on his motorcycle with some top-grade California hybrid and James and Mary get higher than you'd believe possible and they climb into bed. Everything becomes very underwater, but along comes John, who has a key to Mary's apartment. He finds them stoned and entwined. He's hardly in any position to be jealous, considering Madge, but nevertheless he's overcome with despair. Finally he's middle-aged, in two years he'll be bald as an egg and he can't stand it. He pur-chases a handgun, saying he needs it for target practice—this is the thin part of the plot, but it can be dealt with later—and shoots the two of them and himself.

Madge, after a suitable period of mourning, marries an understanding man called Fred and everything continues as in A, but under different names.

D

Fred and Madge have no problems. They get along exceptionally well and are good at working out any little difficulties that may arise. But their charming house is by the seashore and one day a giant tidal wave approaches. Real estate values go down. The rest of the story is about what caused the tidal wave and how they escape from it. They do, though thousands drown, but Fred and Madge are virtuous and lucky. Finally on high ground they clasp each other, wet and dripping and grateful, and continue as in A.

E

Yes, but Fred has a bad heart. The rest of the story is about how kind and understanding they both are until Fred dies. Then Madge devotes herself to charity work until the end of A. If you like, it can be "Madge," "cancer," "guilty and confused," and "bird watching."

F

If you think this is all too bourgeois, make John a revolutionary and Mary a counterespionage agent and see how far that gets you. Remember, this is Canada. You'll still end up with A, though in between you may get a lustful brawling saga of passionate involvement, a chronicle of our times, sort of.

You'll have to face it, the endings are the same however you slice it. Don't be deluded by any other endings, they're all fake, either deliberately fake, with malicious intent to deceive, or just motivated by excessive optimism if not by downright sentimentality.

The only authentic ending is the one provided here:
John and Mary die. John and Mary die. John and Mary die.

So much for endings. Beginnings are always more fun. True connoisseurs, however, are known to favor the stretch in between, since it's the hardest to do anything with.

That's about all that can be said for plots, which anyway are just one thing after another, a what and a what and a what.

Now try How and Why.   •

The story is simple enough; the couple's life together (or apart) simply gets retold in many ways. Not all of the endings are "happy," though the title seems to promise that they will be. Indeed, each of the endings is a comment on the very idea of a happy ending. How happy can we expect an ending to be when, as the speaker tells us at the story's end,

The only authentic ending is the one provided here:
John and Mary die. John and Mary die. John and Mary die.

Even if John and Mary inevitably die, their deaths are just plot details, some of what Atwood calls the *whats* of the story. Those *whats* are the kind of narrative details that make up each of the tellings and retellings in this anthology, and they are, of course, crucial to our understanding of character and meaning. But they are also finally not in themselves enough. It is in the juxtaposition of those details and the comparisons among the "happy endings" of each telling and retelling that meaning gets made. So, like Atwood, we ask you to move beyond the *whats* and "Now try How and Why."

This emphasis on the *how* and *why* and on understanding the importance of perspective is at the foundation of critical thinking and reading. Critical thinking and reading are strongly linked to questioning strategies—and *how* and *why* questions and other questions about perspective are a good place to start because they cannot be answered with simple *yes* or *no* answers. As you read, ask yourself *why* authors have chosen to do what they have done and *how* they have created their stories; think about *how* you as a reader respond to their choices and *why* you respond as you do. Ask questions about the writers' assumptions—perhaps assumptions about society or about people or about accepted beliefs or about what makes a good poem (or piece of fiction or play)— while trying to avoid any assumptions of your own. It may sometimes seem that the more questions you ask, the more you come up with confusing and even contradictory answers. One of the most difficult things to do as a reader (and writer) is to embrace that confusion and ambiguity, but if you allow yourself to accept the messiness of thinking, you will in the end be more likely to think clearly and logically.

The willingness to examine a piece of writing from multiple perspectives is an important strategy for critical thinking and reading. You might ask yourself, for instance, how a work would be changed if the main character were different or if the author's style were altered. You might try turning your own response on its head, attempting to construct an opposing argument. You should not, of course, ignore the *whats* in this process: you will need to collect as many *whats* as possible; they will often form the evidence you use to support your answers to the *how* and *why* questions.

To understand the importance of moving beyond the *whats*, think about the fable of the blind men and the elephant: one blind man, examining its trunk, concluded that the beast was very much like a snake; another, feeling the flapping ears, thought it was like a fan; a third, touching the legs, thought it resembled a tree. Each perspective was quite accurate—except that it was so limited. The moral, of course, is that to see something whole and complete, we must look at it from as many perspectives as possible, gaining as complete a sense of *what* as possible.

Once we have seen the trunk, ears, and legs, however, we still need to put them together into the elephant. The blind men limited themselves to the *whats* of the elephant; they should also have considered the *hows* and *whys*: *how* do the parts fit together, and *why* are they placed where they are? Effective thinking often involves a moving back and forth between the *whats* and the *hows* and the *whys*—between the pieces and the whole, the specifics and the generalities.

To avoid the error that the blind men faced, you will want, then, to do more than collect, or list, the *whats*. Critical thinking also involves an understanding of patterns. In reading a piece of literature, you might, for instance, recognize the patterns in particular characters' behavior, thought, or even dress, or you might notice patterns of imagery designed to evoke particular responses or to illuminate particular themes, as, for example, in the use of doors in Robert Louis Stevenson's *Dr. Jekyll and Mr.*

Hyde. Once you have noticed the pattern, you can try to understand the meaning of the door image, wondering about the feelings of secrecy and of physical and psychological enclosure it creates. As you read, then, you should take in the details and stand back occasionally, seeing if those details form a particular pattern. In the patterns the meaning may be revealed.

The idea behind *Retellings* is to encourage you to think and read critically, to turn a piece of literature around before your eyes, knowing that the more questions you ask of it and the more ideas you try out, the more likely you are to understand its inner workings and appreciate its intellectual and emotional complexity. Approach each piece of literature as you would a riddle or a puzzle; see in it its contrary messages and images. Think about how others have retold the stories. What do their retellings tell us about their own times and cultures? What do the retellings tell us about the time and culture in which the story was first framed? Indeed, think about how *you* would retell the story—and why. In doing so, you will discover just how much fun the serious game of literature can be.

Work Cited

Rabkin, Norman. *Shakespeare and the Common Understanding*. New York: Macmillan, 1967.

2

Reading across Genres

The Elements of Literature

Verbal messages bombard us every day, whether they come from what we read in magazines and books, what we see on television and at the movies, or what we encounter as we surf the Internet or drive down the highway. Some of those messages amuse us, some enlighten us, and still others sell us ideas or products. Whatever their intent, and whatever our reasons for reading them, though, each of these "texts" tells a story, and each creates a sense of a **speaker, character,** and **setting.** All messages also depend to some extent on an **appeal to our senses,** primarily through sound or through visual imagery, and all depend on an **audience.** It is not, after all, only the creator who creates the message. The message is communicated only if we, the audience, hear it and somehow understand it.

TELLING THE TALE: THE ROLE OF THE SPEAKER

From the time that we are children, we learn to distinguish among *speakers.* One might even argue that learning to distinguish among the voices one hears is an important part of learning language and of being socialized. Many parents have been amused—and shocked—at hearing their offspring parrot back to playmates or pets their own warnings, reprimands, and rules, all repeated authoritatively with a childish lisp. The child is learning what voices must be most listened to and how they should be interpreted. Sometimes the strength of the voice is created by the authority behind it, by the authority of a parent or teacher, for example. Sometimes the voice is distinguished by the **tone,** by the playfulness, solemnity, or teasing quality of the voice. In speech, that tone can be created by the loudness or pitch of the voice. In a printed text, the author does not have volume or pitch at his disposal, but the word choice and such things as rhythm and rhyme can still create a strong sense of mood, one that few readers will miss.

As you read a piece of literature (or of any writing, for that matter), you will want to pay particular attention to the speaker who is giving voice to the words on the page. It is what the speaker sees and tells—his **point of view**—that influences our own response. Make special note of your first impressions of the speaker and then of how those impressions change as you read on. For instance, in his poem "Porphyria's Lover," Robert Browning creates a murderous madman whose madness becomes apparent only gradually.

ROBERT BROWNING (1812–1889)

Porphyria's Lover _____ *1834*

<blockquote>

The rain set early in tonight,
  The sullen wind was soon awake,
It tore the elm-tops down for spite,
  And did its worst to vex the lake:
⁵ I listened with heart fit to break.
When glided in Porphyria; straight
  She shut the cold out and the storm,
And kneeled and made the cheerless grate
  Blaze up, and all the cottage warm;
¹⁰ Which done, she rose, and from her form
Withdrew the dripping cloak and shawl,
  And laid her soiled gloves by, untied
Her hat and let the damp hair fall,
  And, last, she sat down by my side
¹⁵ And called me. When no voice replied,
She put my arm about her waist,
  And made her smooth white shoulder bare
And all her yellow hair displaced,
  And stooping, made my cheek lie there,
²⁰ And spread, o'er all, her yellow hair,
Murmuring how she loved me—she
  Too weak, for all her heart's endeavor,
To set its struggling passion free
  From pride, and vainer ties dissever,
²⁵ And give herself to me forever.
But passion sometimes would prevail,
  Nor could tonight's gay feast restrain
A sudden thought of one so pale
  For love of her, and all in vain:
³⁰ So, she was come through wind and rain.
Be sure I looked up at her eyes
  Happy and proud; at last I knew
Porphyria worshiped me; surprise
  Made my heart swell, and still it grew
³⁵ While I debated what to do.
That moment she was mine, mine, fair,
  Perfectly pure and good: I found
A thing to do, and all her hair
  In one long yellow string I wound
⁴⁰ Three times her little throat around,
And strangled her. No pain felt she;
  I am quite sure she felt no pain.
As a shut bud that holds a bee,

</blockquote>

> I warily opened her lids: again
> Laughed the blue eyes without a stain.   45
> And I untightened next the tress
>   About her neck; her cheek once more
> Blushed bright beneath my burning kiss:
>   I propped her head up as before,
> Only, this time my shoulder bore   50
> Her head, which droops upon it still:
>   The smiling rosy little head,
> So glad it has its utmost will,
>   That all it scorned at once is fled,
> And I, its love, am gained instead!   55
> Porphyria's love: she guessed not how
> Her darling one wish would be heard.
> And thus we sit together now,
>   And all night long we have not stirred,
> And yet God has not said a word!   60

The opening of the poem does not reveal that this speaker is mad. Certainly he seems upset: he says his heart was "fit to break." We see that he is sad and perhaps that he projects his own feelings on the scene outside him (obviously the wind is not *literally* "sullen" or acting in "spite," nor is it trying to "vex the lake"). The opening lines of the poem also seem to reveal a speaker in control of his language and his ideas, one who seems observant and reasonable. As we read onward and get to know the speaker better, though, our first impression of him is likely to change, and we may feel a sense of surprise and shock. Speakers, like the people we know in real life, don't always reveal everything about themselves on first meeting.

On the other hand, again as in real life, sometimes we form immediate impressions of a speaker on first meeting, and sometimes those impressions stick. Sometimes, in fact, a few lines are all it takes, as in the opening sentences of Edgar Allan Poe's "The Tell-Tale Heart" (for the full text, see 404–7):

> True!—nervous—very, very dreadfully nervous I had been and am; but why *will* you say that I am mad? The disease had sharpened my senses—not destroyed—not dulled them. Above all was the sense of hearing acute. I heard all things in the heaven and in the earth. I heard many things in hell. How, then, am I mad? Hearken! And observe how healthily—how calmly I can tell you the whole story.

If someone were to sit next to us on the bus and say, "I don't care what they say—I am *not* crazy!" most of us would get up and sit somewhere else. The very insistence on his sanity by Poe's *narrator* probably makes us doubt it. (A **narrator** is a particular kind of speaker; literary critics usually reserve the word *narrator* for those who tell stories, or narratives. For that reason poems, which often do not tell stories so much as express ideas or emotions, usually have "speakers," and stories have "narrators.")

Other details support the doubts we have about Poe's narrator. He himself admits he is "very, very dreadfully nervous," an indication already of some mental instability. The staccato effect created by the dashes contributes to the nervous tone. In addition, the narrator arouses our suspicions by making an odd and irrational equation between "sharp senses" and sanity; despite his claim, we know that many people with failing eyesight or poor hearing are eminently sane—and the reverse is equally true. The narrator goes on to claim he has "heard all things in the heaven and in the earth," as well as "in hell"; unless he has supernatural powers, which seems unlikely, that claim substantiates our impression that he is mentally unstable.

In both "Porphyria's Lover" and "The Tell-Tale Heart," we can draw some very definite conclusions without knowing the speakers' names, their occupations, or even what they look like—things we still do not know by the end of the stories. Through their own words, the speakers tell us about themselves in ways they never intend. In each case, the teller is part of the tale itself.

EXERCISES: TRYING IT OUT

1. We said earlier that Browning's speaker does not immediately reveal his madness and that we discover that madness only gradually. At what point in "Porphyria's Lover" do you *suspect* that the speaker is mad? At what point are you *convinced* of the speaker's madness?

2. Characterize the voice of the speaker in each of the following excerpts. Is the speaker calm and rational? Emotional? Cynical or sarcastic?

   a.   In walks these three girls in nothing but bathing suits. I'm in the third checkout slot, with my back to the door, so I don't see them until they're over by the bread. The one that caught my eye first was the one in the plaid green two-piece. She was a chunky kid, with a good tan and a sweet broad soft-looking can with those two crescents of white just under it, where the sun never seems to hit, at the top of the backs of her legs. I stood there with my hand on a box of HiHo crackers trying to remember if I rang it up or not. I ring it up again and the customer starts giving me hell. She's one of those cash-register-watchers, a witch about fifty with rouge on her cheekbones and no eyebrows, and I know it made her day to trip me up. She'd been watching cash registers for fifty years and probably never seen a mistake before.

   From John Updike, "A & P"

   b.   You do not do, you do not do
   Any more, black shoe
   In which I have lived like a foot
   For thirty years, poor and white,
   Barely daring to breathe or Achoo.

   Daddy, I have had to kill you.
   You died before I had time—
   Marble-heavy, a bag full of God,
   Ghastly statue with one grey toe
   Big as a Frisco seal

And a head in the freakish Atlantic
Where it pours bean green over blue
In the waters off beautiful Nauset.
I used to pray to recover you.
Ach, du.

From Sylvia Plath, "Daddy"

Because the speaker or narrator is central to a work—after all, hers is the lens, the point of view, through which we see everything—it is especially important that we take a moment to consider who she is. Following are some questions that you might ask about any speaker or narrator.

Questions to Ask about the Role of the Speaker

1. What does the work reveal about the speaker?
   A. What is the speaker's name? If the speaker is unnamed, how do you respond to the lack of a name?
   B. Where and when was the speaker born? Where does the speaker live now?
   C. What is the social class of the speaker? (Consider indirect indications of class—where the speaker lives, what vocabulary the speaker uses, what the speaker's clothes and habits are, etc.)
   D. What is the gender of the speaker? Is gender seen as an issue in the work? How do others respond to it?
   E. How old does the speaker seem to be? What implications does the speaker's age have? (For instance, is it associated with frailty, strength, wisdom, or ignorance?)
2. What does the speaker's tone indicate about the speaker's mood? Is it serious? Authoritative? Cynical? Playful? Emotional? Sad? Angry? Innocent? Naïve?
3. Does the speaker seem to respond appropriately to the situation at hand? Why or why not?
4. What are the speaker's values? What does the speaker have to say about morality or about society?

GETTING TO KNOW THE PEOPLE: CHARACTER AND CHARACTERIZATION

At the heart of every narrative are characters who are shaped by and who shape the events. A useful distinction between types of characters was made by E. M. Forster, himself an accomplished novelist. Forster said that there are two types of characters, *flat and round.* **Flat characters** are often static; they remain fixed over time, and there

is little sense that they grow or change throughout the course of the story. Flat characters are, then, not three-dimensional; we do not see them as real people with histories and rich inner lives, and often they function almost symbolically. For example, the narrator of Poe's "The Tell-Tale Heart" is relatively flat. Although we get a strong sense of his mental state, otherwise we learn little about him. We do not know what truly motivates him, only that he hates the old man's "evil eye"—and that hardly seems sufficient motivation for murder. We know next to nothing about his life, cir-cumstances, or beliefs—not his age, his name, his relationship to the old man, or his occupation. So we do not see him as firmly "placed," rooted in a time and place and having a full psychology. He may, for that reason, seem less like us, less lifelike, than a more fully developed character.

In contrast, a **round character** is very much an individual, someone like our-selves with a range of emotional responses and a full history (even if we don't neces-sarily learn all of that history). Unlike the static flat character, a round character is usually dynamic. He *does* grow or change. The round character is also firmly "placed," usually in a community of some sort. A round character has both an inner and an outer life, both reactions and interactions. Leslie Marmon Silko's "Yellow Woman" provides a good example of a round character.

LESLIE SILKO (1948–)

Yellow Woman   1973

1

My thigh clung to his with dampness, and I watched the sun rising up through the tamaracks and willows. The small brown water birds came to the river and hopped across the mud, leaving brown water scratches in the alkali–white crust. They bathed in the river silently. I could hear the water, almost at our feet where the narrow fast channel bubbled and washed green ragged moss and fern leaves. I looked at him beside me, rolled in the red blanket on the white river sand. I cleaned the sand out of the cracks between my toes, squinting because the sun was above the willow trees. I looked at him for the last time, sleeping on the white river sand.

I felt hungry and followed the river south the way we had come the afternoon be-fore, following our footprints that were already blurred by lizard tracks and bug trails. The horses were still lying down, and the black one whinnied when he saw me but he did not get up—maybe it was because the corral was made out of thick cedar branches and the horses had not yet felt the sun like I had. I tried to look beyond the pale red mesas to the pueblo. I knew it was there, even if I could not see it, on the sandrock hill above the river, the same river that moved past me now and had reflected the moon last night.

The horse felt warm underneath me. He shook his head and pawed the sand. The bay whinnied and leaned against the gate trying to follow. I slid off the horse and tied him close to the other horse. I walked north with the river again, and the white sand broke loose in footprints over footprints.

"Wake up."

He moved in the blanket and turned his face to me with his eyes still closed. I knelt down to touch him.

"I'm leaving."

He smiled now, eyes still closed. "You are coming with me, remember?" He sat up now with his bare dark chest and belly in the sun.

"Where?"

"To my place."

"And will I come back?"

He pulled his pants on. I walked away from him, feeling him behind me and smelling the willows.

"Yellow Woman," he said.

I turned to face him. "Who are you?" I asked.

He laughed and knelt on the low, sandy bank, washing his face in the river. "Last night you guessed my name, and you knew why I had come."

I stared past him at the shallow moving water and tried to remember the night, but I could only see the moon in the water and remember his warmth around me.

"But I only said that you were him and that I was Yellow Woman—I'm not really her—I have my own name and I come from the pueblo on the other side of the mesa. Your name is Silva and you are a stranger I met by the river yesterday afternoon."

He laughed softly. "What happened yesterday has nothing to do with what you will do today, Yellow Woman."

"I know—that's what I'm saying—the old stories about the ka'tsina spirit and Yellow Woman can't mean us."

My old grandpa liked to tell those stories best. There is one about Badger and Coyote who went hunting and were gone all day, and when the sun was going down they found a house. There was a girl living there alone, and she had light hair and eyes and she told them that they could sleep with her. Coyote wanted to be with her all night so he sent Badger into a prairie-dog hole, telling him he thought he saw something in it. As soon as Badger crawled in, Coyote blocked up the entrance with rocks and hurried back to Yellow Woman.

"Come here," he said gently.

He touched my neck and I moved close to him to feel his breathing and to hear his heart. I was wondering if Yellow Woman had known who she was—if she knew that she would become part of the stories. Maybe she'd had another name that her husband and relatives called her so that only the ka'tsina from the north and the storytellers would know her as Yellow Woman. But I didn't go on; I felt him all around me, pushing me down into the white river sand.

Yellow Woman went away with the spirit from the north and lived with him and his relatives. She was gone for a long time, but then one day she came back and she brought twin boys.

"Do you know the story?"

"What story?" He smiled and pulled me close to him as he said this. I was afraid lying there on the red blanket. All I could know was the way he felt, warm, damp, his body beside me. This is the way it happens in the stories, I was thinking, with no thought beyond the moment she meets the ka'tsina spirit and they go.

"I don't have to go. What they tell in stories was real only then, back in time immemorial, like they say."

He stood up and pointed at my clothes tangled in the blanket. "Let's go," he said.

I walked beside him, breathing hard because he walked fast, his hand around my wrist. I had stopped trying to pull away from him, because his hand felt cool and the sun was high, drying the river bed into alkali. I will see someone, eventually I will see someone, and then I will be certain that he is only a man—some man from nearby—and I will be sure that I am not Yellow Woman. Because she is from out of time past and I live now and I've been to school and there are highways and pickup trucks that Yellow Woman never saw.

It was an easy ride north on horseback. I watched the change from the cottonwood trees along the river to the junipers that brushed past us in the foothills, and finally there were only piñons, and when I looked up at the rim of the mountain plateau I could see pine trees growing on the edge. Once I stopped to look down, but the pale sandstone had disappeared and the river was gone and the dark lava hills were all around. He touched my hand, not speaking, but always singing softly a mountain song and looking into my eyes.

I felt hungry and wondered what they were doing at home now—my mother, my grandmother, my husband, and the baby. Cooking breakfast, saying, "Where did she go?—maybe kidnapped," and Al going to the tribal police with the details: "She went walking along the river."

The house was made with black lava rock and red mud. It was high above the spreading miles of arroyos and long mesas. I smelled a mountain smell of pitch and buck brush. I stood there beside the black horse, looking down on the small, dim country we had passed, and I shivered.

"Yellow Woman, come inside where it's warm."

2

He lit a fire in the stove. It was an old stove with a round belly and an enamel coffeepot on top. There was only the stove, some faded Navajo blankets, and a bedroll and cardboard box. The floor was made of smooth adobe plaster, and there was one small window facing east. He pointed at the box.

"There's some potatoes and the frying pan." He sat on the floor with his arms around his knees pulling them close to his chest and he watched me fry the potatoes. I didn't mind him watching me because he was always watching me—he had been watching me since I came upon him sitting on the river bank trimming leaves from a willow twig with his knife. We ate from the pan and he wiped the grease from his fingers on his Levis.

"Have you brought women here before?" He smiled and kept chewing, so I said, "Do you always use the same tricks?"

"What tricks?" He looked at me like he didn't understand.

"The story about being a ka'tsina from the mountains. The story about Yellow Woman."

Silva was silent; his face was calm.

"I don't believe it. Those stories couldn't happen now," I said.

He shook his head and said softly, "But someday they will talk about us, and they will say, 'Those two lived long ago when things like that happened.'"

He stood up and went out. I ate the rest of the potatoes and thought about things—about the noise the stove was making and the sound of the mountain wind outside. I remembered yesterday and the day before, and then I went outside.

I walked past the corral to the edge where the narrow trail cut through the black rim rock. I was standing in the sky with nothing around me but the wind that came down from the blue mountain peak behind me. I could see faint mountain images in the distance, miles across the vast spread of mesas and valleys and plains. I wondered who was over there to feel the mountain wind on those sheer blue edges—who walks on the pine needles in those blue mountains.

"Can you see the pueblo?" Silva was standing behind me.

I shook my head. "We're too far away."

"From here I can see the world." He stepped out on the edge. "The Navajo reservation begins over there." He pointed to the east. "The Pueblo boundaries are over here." He looked below us to the south, where the narrow trail seemed to come from. "The Texans have their ranches over there, starting with that valley, the Concho Valley. The Mexicans run some cattle over there too."

"Do you ever work for them?"

"I steal from them," Silva answered. The sun was dropping behind us and shadows were filling the land below. I turned away from the edge that dropped forever into the valleys below.

"I'm cold," I said; "I'm going inside." I started wondering about this man who could speak the Pueblo language so well but who lived on a mountain and rustled cattle. I decided that this man Silva must be Navajo, because Pueblo men didn't do things like that.

"You must be a Navajo."

Silva shook his head gently. "Little Yellow Woman," he said, "you never give up, do you? I have told you who I am. The Navajo people know me, too." He knelt down and unrolled the bedroll and spread the extra blankets out on a piece of canvas. The sun was down, and the only light in the house came from outside—the dim orange light from sundown.

I stood there and waited for him to crawl under the blankets.

"What are you waiting for?" he said, and I lay down beside him. He undressed me slowly like the night before beside the river—kissing my face gently and running his hands up and down my belly and legs. He took off my pants and then he laughed.

"Why are you laughing?"

"You are breathing so hard."

I pulled away from him and turned my back to him.

He pulled me around and pinned me down with his arms and chest. "You don't understand, do you, little Yellow Woman? You will do what I want."

And again he was all around me with his skin slippery against mine, and I was afraid because I understood that his strength could hurt me. I lay underneath him and I knew that he could destroy me. But later, while he slept beside me, I touched his face and I had a feeling—the kind of feeling for him that overcame me that morning along the river. I kissed him on the forehead and he reached out for me.

When I woke up in the morning he was gone. It gave me a strange feeling because for a long time I sat there on the blankets and looked around the little house for some object of his—some proof that he had been there or maybe that he was coming back. Only the blankets and the cardboard box remained. The .30–30 that had been leaning in the corner was gone, and so was the knife I had used the night before. He was gone, and I had my chance to go now. But first I had to eat, because I knew it would be a long walk home.

I found some dried apricots in the cardboard box, and I sat down on a rock at the edge of the plateau rim. There was no wind and the sun warmed me. I was surrounded by silence. I drowsed with apricots in my mouth, and I didn't believe that there were highways or railroads or cattle to steal.

When I woke up, I stared down at my feet in the black mountain dirt. Little black ants were swarming over the pine needles around my foot. They must have smelled the apricots. I thought about my family far below me. They would be wondering about me, because this had never happened to me before. The tribal police would file a report. But if old Grandpa weren't dead he would tell them what happened—he would laugh and say, "Stolen by a ka'tsina, a mountain spirit. She'll come home—they usually do." There are enough of them to handle things. My mother and grandmother will raise the baby like they raised me. Al will find someone else, and they will go on like before, except that there will be a story about the day I disappeared while I was walking along the river. Silva had come for me, he said he had. I did not decide to go. I just went. Moonflowers blossom in the sand hills before dawn, just as I followed him. That's what I was thinking as I wandered along the trail through the pine trees.

It was noon when I got back. When I saw the stone house I remembered that I had meant to go home. But that didn't seem important any more, maybe because there were little blue flowers growing in the meadow behind the stone house and the gray squirrels were playing in the pines next to the house. The horses were standing in the corral, and there was a beef carcass hanging on the shady side of a big pine in front of the house. Flies buzzed around the clotted blood that hung from the carcass. Silva was washing his hands in a bucket full of water. He must have heard me coming because he spoke to me without turning to face me.

"I've been waiting for you."

"I went walking in the big pine trees."

I looked into the bucket full of bloody water with brown-and-white animal hairs floating in it. Silva stood there letting his hands drip, examining me intently.

"Are you coming with me?"

"Where?" I asked him.

"To sell the meat in Marquez."

"If you're sure it's O.K."

"I wouldn't ask you if it wasn't," he answered.

He sloshed the water around in the bucket before he dumped it out and set the bucket upside down near the door. I followed him to the corral and watched him saddle the horses. Even beside the horses he looked tall, and I asked him again if he wasn't Navajo. He didn't say anything; he just shook his head and kept cinching up the saddle.

"But Navajos are tall."

"Get on the horse," he said, "and let's go."

The last thing he did before we started down the steep trail was to grab the .30–30 from the corner. He slid the rifle into the scabbard that hung from his saddle.

"Do they ever try to catch you?" I asked.

"They don't know who I am."

"Then why did you bring the rifle?"

"Because we are going to Marquez where the Mexicans live."

3

The trail leveled out on a narrow ridge that was steep on both sides like an animal spine. On one side I could see where the trail went around the rocky gray hills and disappeared into the southeast where the pale sandrock mesas stood in the distance near my home. On the other side was a trail that went west, and as I looked far into the distance I thought I saw the little town. But Silva said no, that I was looking in the wrong place, that I just thought I saw houses. After that I quit looking off into the distance; it was hot and the wildflowers were closing up their deep-yellow petals. Only the waxy cactus flowers bloomed in the bright sun, and I saw every color that a cactus blossom can be; the white ones and the red ones were still buds, but the purple and the yellow were blossoms, open full and the most beautiful of all.

Silva saw him before I did. The white man was riding a big gray horse, coming up the trail toward us. He was traveling fast and the gray horse's feet sent rocks rolling off the trail into the dry tumbleweeds. Silva motioned for me to stop and we watched the white man. He didn't see us right away, but finally his horse whinnied at our horses and he stopped. He looked at us briefly before he loped the gray horse across the three hundred yards that separated us. He stopped his horse in front of Silva, and his young fat face was shadowed by the brim of his hat. He didn't look mad, but his small, pale eyes moved from the blood-soaked gunny sacks hanging from my saddle to Silva's face and then back to my face.

"Where did you get the fresh meat?" the white man asked.

"I've been hunting," Silva said, and when he shifted his weight in the saddle the leather creaked.

"The hell you have, Indian. You've been rustling cattle. We've been looking for the thief for a long time."

The rancher was fat, and sweat began to soak through his white cowboy shirt and the wet cloth stuck to the thick rolls of belly fat. He almost seemed to be panting from the exertion of talking, and he smelled rancid, maybe because Silva scared him.

Silva turned to me and smiled. "Go back up the mountain, Yellow Woman."

The white man got angry when he heard Silva speak in a language he couldn't understand. "Don't try anything, Indian. Just keep riding to Marquez. We'll call the state police from there."

The rancher must have been unarmed because he was very frightened and if he had a gun he would have pulled it out then. I turned my horse around and the rancher yelled, "Stop!" I looked at Silva for an instant and there was something ancient and dark—something I could feel in my stomach—in his eyes, and when I glanced at his hand I saw his finger on the trigger of the .30–30 that was still in the saddle scabbard. I slapped my horse across the flank and sacks of raw meat swung against my knees as the horse leaped up the trail. It was hard to keep my balance, and once I thought I felt the saddle slipping backward; it was because of this that I could not look back.

I didn't stop until I reached the ridge where the trail forked. The horse was breathing deep gasps and there was a dark film of sweat on its neck. I looked down in the direction I had come from, but I couldn't see the place. I waited. The wind came up and pushed warm air past me. I looked up at the sky, pale blue and full of thin clouds and fading vapor trails left by jets.

I think four shots were fired—I remember hearing four hollow explosions that reminded me of deer hunting. There could have been more shots after that, but I couldn't have heard them because my horse was running again and the loose rocks were making too much noise as they scattered around his feet.

Horses have a hard time running downhill, but I went that way instead of uphill to the mountain because I thought it was safer. I felt better with the horse running southeast past the round gray hills that were covered with cedar trees and black lava rock. When I got to the plain in the distance I could see the dark green patches of tamaracks that grew along the river; and beyond the river I could see the beginning of the pale sandrock mesas. I stopped the horse and looked back to see if anyone was coming; then I got off the horse and turned the horse around, wondering if it would go back to its corral under the pines on the mountain. It looked back at me for a moment and then plucked a mouthful of green tumbleweeds before it trotted back up the trail with its ears pointed forward, carrying its head daintily to one side to avoid stepping on the dragging reins. When the horse disappeared over the last hill, the gunny sacks full of meat were still swinging and bouncing.

4

I walked toward the river on a wood-hauler's road that I knew would eventually lead to the paved road. I was thinking about waiting beside the road for someone to drive by, but by the time I got to the pavement I had decided it wasn't very far to walk if I followed the river back the way Silva and I had come.

The river water tasted good, and I sat in the shade under a cluster of silvery willows. I thought about Silva, and I felt sad at leaving him; still, there was something strange about him, and I tried to figure it out all the way back home.

I came back to the place on the river bank where he had been sitting the first time I saw him. The green willow leaves that he had trimmed from the branch were still lying there, wilted in the sand. I saw the leaves and I wanted to go back to him—to kiss him and to touch him—but the mountains were too far away now. And I told myself, because I believe it, he will come back sometime and be waiting again by the river.

I followed the path up from the river into the village. The sun was getting low, and I could smell supper cooking when I got to the screen door of my house. I could hear their voices inside—my mother was telling my grandmother how to fix the Jell-O and my husband, Al, was playing with the baby. I decided to tell them that some Navajo had kidnapped me, but I was sorry that old Grandpa wasn't alive to hear my story because it was the Yellow Woman stories he liked to tell best.   •

After reading the story, we know some definite things about the main character's background. She is a Pueblo Indian who "comes from the pueblo on the other side of the mesa," where she lives with her mother, grandmother, husband (Al), and baby. She met Silva at the river the day before the story begins and identifies him with the *ka'tsina* spirit from the traditional tales told to her by her grandfather. We know as well that she would like to see herself as Yellow Woman, a mythic character from long ago. Still, despite the traditional background created by the stories of Yellow Woman and the mountain spirit, we know hers is a modern story, describing a time very much like our own: the narrator wonders if her husband will report her disappearance to the tribal police, and she returns home to see her mother teaching her grandmother how to make Jell-O.

Even if she remains somewhat of a mystery to us, we see the Yellow Woman as a rounded individual, with a fully realistic life and a complex emotional state marked by shifts in feeling. It is in many ways her very "roundedness" that creates the "problem" of the story: Can a modern woman who lives in the real world be the Yellow Woman of myth? Is Silva truly a mountain spirit or simply a renegade? Does the narrator see Silva as a brutal rapist or a gentle mountain-spirit lover? Do we share her views or judge them as inadequate? Our answers may be uncertain, for the story creates a dreamlike state that blurs the boundaries between the real and the mythical, between the rounded character who is the narrator and the flat mythic characters of Yellow Woman, Badger, and Coyote. Nevertheless, Yellow Woman is lifelike in a way that Poe's madman is not.

The distinction between flat and round characters is not always a clear-cut one: characters are often somewhat round, somewhat flat. In addition, this is not a distinction between effective and ineffective methods of characterization. Flat characters can be just as effective as round ones. Poe's narrator, for instance, would probably be less effective as a round character. A bogeyman like him is best left shadowy and faceless; what we imagine is often more horrible than what we know. In contrast to Poe's, Silko's story *needs* a round character to create the tensions between the realistic world and the mythic one.

Though we may think of characters as belonging to fictions, poets may also create a vivid sense of character. For example, Anthony Hecht's "The Dover Bitch" retells Matthew Arnold's "Dover Beach" by making Arnold's shadowy characters much more vivid—much more rounded. (The poems are printed on 21, 23.) Whereas Arnold's speaker focuses on the "beach," Hecht's focuses on the "bitch," as the two titles indicate. Hecht's poem fleshes out Arnold's "love," making her very fleshy indeed. We learn that she is at least somewhat educated (she has read Sophocles in translation), that her speech is earthy (she says "one or two unprintable things"), and that she is sensual, thinking of "all the wine and enormous beds / And blandishments in French and the perfumes." In addition, Hecht expands on the character of Matthew Arnold (a character here, not the actual poet). Though in the first poem, the speaker is mostly just a voice, in Hecht's poem Matthew Arnold has a body. We watch him nervously pace and sweat, uncertain about what to do with this girl (significantly, *not* his wife) he has brought to Dover from London. The speaker of Hecht's poem may not be fully sympathetic toward the man in the honeymoon suite nor wholly reliable in his portrayal of the "bitch." Through him Hecht does, however, give both characters a physical presence that they did not have in Arnold's poem. Whereas Arnold's poem conveys a complex sense of nineteenth-century anxiety, Hecht's creates a stronger sense of rounded characters.

Most dramas also depend heavily on character. For example, much of how we read Shakespeare's *Hamlet* depends on how we read the title character. After having killed the king (Hamlet's father), Hamlet's uncle takes the throne, marrying Hamlet's mother. The play asks us to ponder Hamlet's responsibilities as a son and prince. The introspective Hamlet hesitates to act. Are we to see him as cautious or indecisive? What are the implications of his action or inaction for himself, his family, and the state? However we answer these questions, we must attempt to come to terms with them. By puzzling over character, we often unlock the meaning and artistry of the work itself.

EXERCISES: TRYING IT OUT

1. Many poems and short stories written for children deliberately use "flat" characters. In other words, we know very little about the characters. Rewrite a story from your childhood, making the characters more "round." How do the changes affect the atmosphere and themes of the story?

2. Often the details about a character seem insignificant at first, but the significance becomes more clear when we try to imagine a retelling in which a crucial detail is changed. What would be the effect of the changes given below?

    The central character in "Cinderella" is a boy.

    In "Yellow Woman," Silva is a white rancher.

Although we often think of story primarily as a matter of **plot,** of the events that unfold, there are no plots without characters. More important, characters *make* plots. You need only think about how two people set along the same path in life could easily find themselves in different physical and emotional places at life's—or story's—end. In literature, not only what the characters do but what they feel and how they interact create the story line. So as you read, think not only about what happens but about whom it happens to and, finally, about how much character and the conflicts between characters *are* meaning.

Questions to Ask about Characters and Characterization

(Notice that many of these questions are similar to those we asked about the speaker-narrator—a reminder that speakers are characters and that characters can often be reimagined as speakers-narrators.)

1. Who are the most important characters in the work?

2. Which of the characters are flat? Which are round? In other words, do we see the characters as very much like real people?

3. What do we know about the characters? Consider what we are told about their ages, physical appearances, economic and social classes, and family relationships. Do any of the characters change over the course of the story? (Note: Flat characters often will not change, whereas round characters will.)

4. What things seem to be most important to each of the characters? What people do the characters value? What objects?
5. What beliefs does each of the characters hold dear? What beliefs does each reject?
6. What emotions seem most typical for each character? Do we see a range or does one emotion dominate? What typically provokes the strongest emotions?
7. How does each of the characters interact with others? How do others seem to respond to each of the characters?

TIME AND PLACE: LOOKING AT SETTING

The Physical Setting

Most of us are keenly aware of our physical surroundings; we know that in some places we feel comfortable, in other places nervous or even fearful. So important is our sense of place to our sense of comfort that we may follow a whole list of unwritten rules about what to wear and how to behave in certain places. In our shower in the comfort of our home, for example, we may whistle happily or sing off-key. In the doctor's examination room or in the locker room at the gym, however, our nakedness may take on a very different meaning for us, and we will probably behave in a more inhibited way. In literature, too, different places—different physical settings—affect characters' and readers' responses to events. It is no surprise, then, that in retelling stories, writers often change the locales, almost automatically creating very different responses in the audience.

Writers frequently create strong first impressions by describing at the beginning of a work the **setting,** the place and time, in which events occur. That setting can strongly affect the mood of the work, evoking a particular emotional response. Authors may also use **physical setting** to explain characters' motivations and to reflect their inner lives. Look, for instance, at how important the details of Mrs. Wright's life become in Susan Glaspell's *Trifles*.

SUSAN GLASPELL (1882–1948)

Trifles _____ *1916*

Characters
GEORGE HENDERSON, *County Attorney*
HENRY PETERS, *Sheriff*
LEWIS HALE, *A Neighboring Farmer*
MRS. PETERS
MRS. HALE

Scene *The kitchen in the now abandoned farmhouse of* JOHN WRIGHT, *a gloomy kitchen, and left without having been put in order—unwashed pans under the sink, a loaf of bread outside the breadbox, a dish towel on the table—other signs of incompleted work. At the rear* *the outer door opens and the* SHERIFF *comes in followed by the* COUNTY ATTORNEY *and* HALE. *The* SHERIFF *and* HALE *are men in middle life, the* COUNTY ATTORNEY *is a young man; all are much bundled up and go at once to the stove. They are followed by two women—the* SHERIFF'*s wife first; she is a slight wiry woman, a thin nervous face.* MRS. HALE *is larger and would ordinarily be called more comfortable looking, but she is disturbed now and looks fearfully about as she enters. The women have come in slowly, and stand close together near the door.*

COUNTY ATTORNEY [*rubbing his hands*]: This feels good. Come up to the fire, ladies.

MRS. PETERS [*after taking a step forward*]: I'm not—cold.

SHERIFF [*unbuttoning his overcoat and stepping away from the stove as if to mark the beginning of official business*]: Now, Mr. Hale, before we move things about, you explain to Mr. Henderson just what you saw when you came here yesterday morning.

COUNTY ATTORNEY: By the way, has anything been moved? Are things just as you left them yesterday?

5   SHERIFF [*looking about*]: It's just the same. When it dropped below zero last night I thought I'd better send Frank out this morning to make a fire for us—no use getting pneumonia with a big case on, but I told him not to touch anything except the stove—and you know Frank.

COUNTY ATTORNEY: Somebody should have been left here yesterday.

SHERIFF: Oh—yesterday. When I had to send Frank to Morris Center for that man who went crazy—I want you to know I had my hands full yesterday, I knew you could get back from Omaha by today and as long as I went over everything here myself—

COUNTY ATTORNEY: Well, Mr. Hale, tell just what happened when you came here yesterday morning.

HALE: Harry and I had started to town with a load of potatoes. We came along the road from my place and as I got here I said, "I'm going to see if I can't get John Wright to go in with me on a party telephone." I spoke to Wright about it once before and he put me off, saying folks talked too much anyway, and all he asked was peace and quiet—I guess you know about how much he talked himself; but I thought maybe if I went to the house and talked about it before his wife, though I said to Harry that I didn't know as what his wife wanted made much difference to John—

10   COUNTY ATTORNEY: Let's talk about that later, Mr. Hale. I do want to talk about that, but tell now just what happened when you got to the house.

HALE: I didn't hear or see anything; I knocked at the door, and still it was all quiet inside. I knew they must be up, it was past eight o'clock. So I knocked again, and I thought I heard somebody say, "Come in." I wasn't sure, I'm not sure yet, but I opened the door—this door [*Indicating the door by which the two women are still standing*] and there in that rocker—[*Pointing to it*] sat Mrs. Wright.

[*They all look at the rocker.*]

COUNTY ATTORNEY: What—was she doing?

HALE: She was rockin' back and forth. She had her apron in her hand and was kind of—pleating it.

COUNTY ATTORNEY: And how did she—look?

15   HALE: Well, she looked queer.

COUNTY ATTORNEY: How do you mean—queer?

HALE: Well, as if she didn't know what she was going to do next. And kind of done up.

COUNTY ATTORNEY: How did she seem to feel about your coming?

HALE: Why, I don't think she minded—one way or other. She didn't pay much attention. I said, "How do, Mrs. Wright, it's cold, ain't it?" And she said, "Is it?"—and went on kind of pleating at her apron. Well, I was surprised; she didn't ask me to come up to the stove, or to set down, but just sat there, not even looking at me, so I said, "I want to see John." And then she—laughed. I guess you would call it a laugh. I thought of Harry and the team outside, so I said a little sharp: "Can't I see John?" "No," she says, kind o' dull like. "Ain't he home?" says I. "Yes," says she, "he's home." "Then why can't I see him?" I asked her, out of patience. " 'Cause he's dead," says she. "*Dead?*" says I. She just nodded her head, not getting a bit excited, but rockin' back and forth. "Why—where is he?" says I, not knowing what to say. She just pointed upstairs—like that [*Himself pointing to the room above*]. I got up, with the idea of going up there. I walked from there to here—then I says, "Why, what did he die of?" "He died of a rope round his neck," says she, and just went on pleatin' at her apron. Well, I went out and called Harry. I thought I might—need help. We went upstairs and there he was lying'—

COUNTY ATTORNEY: I think I'd rather have you go into that upstairs, where you can point it all out. Just go on now with the rest of the story. 20

HALE: Well, my first thought was to get that rope off. It looked . . . [*Stops, his face twitches.*] . . . but Harry, he went up to him, and he said, "No, he's dead all right, and we'd better not touch anything." So we went back down stairs. She was still sitting that same way. "Has anybody been notified?" I asked. "No," says she, unconcerned. "Who did this, Mrs. Wright?" said Harry. He said it businesslike—and she stopped pleatin' of her apron. "I don't know," she says. "You don't *know?*" says Harry. "No," says she. "Weren't you sleepin' in the bed with him?" says Harry. "Yes," says she, "but I was on the inside." "Somebody slipped a rope round his neck and strangled him and you didn't wake up?" says Harry. "I didn't wake up," she said after him. We must 'a looked as if we didn't see how that could be, for after a minute she said, "I sleep sound." Harry was going to ask her more questions but I said maybe we ought to let her tell her story first to the coroner, or the sheriff, so Harry went fast as he could to Rivers' place, where there's a telephone.

COUNTY ATTORNEY: And what did Mrs. Wright do when she knew that you had gone for the coroner?

HALE: She moved from that chair to this one over here [*Pointing to a small chair in the corner*] and just sat there with her hands held together and looking down. I got a feeling that I ought to make some conversation, so I said I had come in to see if John wanted to put in a telephone, and at that she started to laugh, and then she stopped and looked at me—scared. [*The* COUNTY ATTORNEY, *who has had his notebook out, makes a note.*] I dunno, maybe it wasn't scared. I wouldn't like to say it was. Soon Harry got back, and then Dr. Lloyd came, and you, Mr. Peters, and so I guess that's all I know that you don't.

COUNTY ATTORNEY [*looking around*]: I guess we'll go upstairs first—and then out to the barn and around there. [*To the* SHERIFF] You're convinced that there was nothing important here—nothing that would point to any motive.

SHERIFF: Nothing here but kitchen things. 25

[The COUNTY ATTORNEY, *after again looking around the kitchen, opens the door of a cupboard closet. He gets up on a chair and looks on a shelf. Pulls his hand away, sticky.*]

COUNTY ATTORNEY: Here's a nice mess.

[*The women draw nearer.*]

MRS. PETERS [*to the other woman*]: Oh, her fruit; it did freeze. [*To the* COUNTY AT-
TORNEY] She worried about that when it turned so cold. She said the fire'd go
out and her jars would break.

SHERIFF: Well, can you beat the women! Held for murder and worryin' about her
preserves.

COUNTY ATTORNEY: I guess before we're through she may have something more
serious than preserves to worry about.

30   HALE: Well, women are used to worrying over trifles.

[*The two women move a little closer together.*]

COUNTY ATTORNEY [*with the gallantry of a young politician*]: And yet, for all their
worries, what would we do without the ladies? [*The women do not unbend. He
goes to the sink, takes a dipperful of water from the pail and pouring it into a basin,
washes his hands. Starts to wipe them on the roller towel, turns it for a cleaner place.*]
Dirty towels! [*Kicks his foot against the pans under the sink.*] Not much of a housekeeper, would you say, ladies?

MRS. HALE [*stiffly*]: There's a great deal of work to be done on a farm.

COUNTY ATTORNEY: To be sure. And yet [*With a little bow to her*] I know there are
some Dickson county farmhouses which do not have such roller towels.

[*He gives it a pull to expose its full length again.*]

MRS. HALE: Those towels get dirty awful quick. Men's hands aren't always as clean as
they might be.

35   COUNTY ATTORNEY: Ah, loyal to your sex, I see. But you and Mrs. Wright were
neighbors. I suppose you were friends, too.

MRS. HALE [*shaking her head*]: I've not seen much of her of late years. I've not been in
this house—it's more than a year.

COUNTY ATTORNEY: And why was that? You didn't like her?

MRS. HALE: I liked her all well enough. Farmers' wives have their hands full, Mr.
Henderson. And then—

COUNTY ATTORNEY: Yes—?

40   MRS. HALE [*looking about*]: It never seemed a very cheerful place.

COUNTY ATTORNEY: No—it's not cheerful. I shouldn't say she had the homemak-
ing instinct.

MRS. HALE: Well, I don't know as Wright had, either.

COUNTY ATTORNEY: You mean that they didn't get on very well?

MRS. HALE: No, I don't mean anything. But I don't think a place'd be any cheerfuller
for John Wright's being in it.

45   COUNTY ATTORNEY: I'd like to talk more of that a little later. I want to get the lay
of things upstairs now.

[*He goes to the left, where three steps lead to a stair door.*]

SHERIFF: I suppose anything Mrs. Peters does'll be all right. She was to take in some clothes for her, you know, and a few little things. We left in such a hurry yesterday.

COUNTY ATTORNEY: Yes, but I would like to see what you take, Mrs. Peters, and keep an eye out for anything that might be of use to us.

MRS. PETERS: Yes, Mr. Henderson.

[*The women listen to the men's steps on the stairs, then look about the kitchen.*]

MRS. HALE: I'd hate to have men coming into my kitchen, snooping around and criticizing.

[*She arranges the pans under sink which the* COUNTY ATTORNEY *had shoved out of place.*]

MRS. PETERS: Of course it's no more than their duty.

MRS. HALE: Duty's all right, but I guess that deputy sheriff that came out to make the fire might have got a little of this on. [*Gives the roller towel a pull.*] Wish I'd thought of that sooner. Seems mean to talk about her for not having things slicked up when she had to come away in such a hurry.

MRS. PETERS [*Who has gone to a small table in the left rear corner of the room, and lifted one end of a towel that covers a pan*]: She had bread set.

[*Stands still.*]

MRS. HALE [*eyes fixed on a loaf of bread beside the breadbox, which is on a low shelf at the other side of the room. Moves slowly toward it*]: She was going to put this in there. [*Picks up loaf, then abruptly drops it. In a manner of returning to familiar things.*] It's a shame about her fruit. I wonder if it's all gone. [*Gets up on the chair and looks.*] I think there's some here that's all right, Mrs. Peters. Yes—here; [*Holding it toward the window.*] this is cherries, too. [*Looking again.*] I declare I believe that's the only one. [*Gets down, bottle in her hand. Goes to the sink and wipes it off on the outside.*] She'll feel awful bad after all her hard work in the hot weather. I remember the afternoon I put up my cherries last summer.

[*She puts the bottle on the big kitchen table, center of the room. With a sigh, is about to sit down in the rocking-chair. Before she is seated realizes what chair it is; with a slow look at it, steps back. The chair which she has touched rocks back and forth.*]

MRS. PETERS: Well, I must get those things from the front room closet. [*She goes to the door at the right, but after looking into the other room, steps back.*] You coming with me, Mrs. Hale? You could help me carry them.

[*They go in the other room; reappear,* MRS. PETERS *carrying a dress and skirt,* MRS. HALE *following with a pair of shoes.*]

MRS. PETERS: My, it's cold in there.

[*She puts the clothes on the big table, and hurries to the stove.*]

MRS. HALE [*examining her skirt*]: Wright was close. I think maybe that's why she kept so much to herself. She didn't even belong to the Ladies Aid. I suppose she felt she couldn't do her part, and then you don't enjoy things when you feel shabby. She used to wear pretty clothes and be lively, when she was Minnie Foster, one of the town girls singing in the choir. But that—oh, that was thirty years ago. This all you was to take in?

MRS. PETERS: She said she wanted an apron. Funny thing to want, for there isn't much to get you dirty in jail, goodness knows. But I suppose just to make her feel more natural. She said they was in the top drawer in this cupboard. Yes, here. And then her little shawl that always hung behind the door. [*Opens stair door and looks.*] Yes, here it is.

[*Quickly shuts door leading upstairs.*]

MRS. HALE [*abruptly moving toward her*]: Mrs. Peters?

MRS. PETERS: Yes, Mrs. Hale?

60   MRS. HALE: Do you think she did it?

MRS. PETERS [*in a frightened voice*]: Oh, I don't know.

MRS. HALE: Well, I don't think she did. Asking for an apron and her little shawl. Worrying about her fruit.

MRS. PETERS [*starts to speak, glances up, where footsteps are heard in the room above. In a low voice*]: Mr. Peters says it looks bad for her. Mr. Henderson is awful sarcastic in a speech and he'll make fun of her sayin' she didn't wake up.

MRS. HALE: Well, I guess John Wright didn't wake when they was slipping that rope under his neck.

65   MRS. PETERS: No, it's strange. It must have been done awful crafty and still. They say it was such a—funny way to kill a man, rigging it all up like that.

MRS. HALE: That's just what Mr. Hale said. There was a gun in the house. He says that's what he can't understand.

MRS. PETERS: Mr. Henderson said coming out that what was needed for the case was a motive; something to show anger, or—sudden feeling.

MRS. HALE [*who is standing by the table*]: Well, I don't see any signs of anger around here. [*She puts her hand on the dish towel which lies on the table, stands looking down at table, one half of which is clean, the other half messy.*] It's wiped to here. [*Makes a move as if to finish work, then turns and looks at loaf of bread outside the breadbox. Drops towel. In that voice of coming back to familiar things.*] Wonder how they are finding things upstairs. I hope she had it a little more red-up up there. You know, it seems kind of *sneaking.* Locking her up in town and then coming out here and trying to get her own house to turn against her!

MRS. PETERS: But Mrs. Hale, the law is the law.

70   MRS. HALE: I s'pose 'tis. [*Unbuttoning her coat.*] Better loosen up your things, Mrs. Peters. You won't feel them when you go out.

[MRS. PETERS *takes off her fur tippet, goes to hang it on hook at back of room, stands looking at the under part of the small corner table.*]

MRS. PETERS: She was piecing a quilt.

[*She brings the large sewing basket and they look at the bright pieces.*]

MRS. HALE: It's log cabin pattern. Pretty, isn't it? I wonder if she was goin' to quilt it or just knot it?

[*Footsteps have been heard coming down the stairs. The* SHERIFF *enters followed by* HALE *and the* COUNTY ATTORNEY.]

SHERIFF: They wonder if she was going to quilt it or just knot it!

[*The men laugh; the women look abashed.*]

COUNTY ATTORNEY [*rubbing his hands over the stove*]: Frank's fire didn't do much up there, did it? Well, let's go out to the barn and get that cleared up.

[*The men go outside.*]

MRS. HALE [*resentfully*]: I don't know as there's anything so strange, our takin' up our time with little things while we're waiting for them to get the evidence. [*She sits down at the big table smoothing out a block with decision.*] I don't see as it's anything to laugh about.

MRS. PETERS [*apologetically*]: Of course they've got awful important things on their minds.

[*Pulls up a chair and joins* MRS. HALE *at the table.*]

MRS. HALE [*examining another block*]: Mrs. Peters, look at this one. Here, this is the one she was working on, and look at the sewing! All the rest of it has been so nice and even. And look at this! It's all over the place! Why, it looks as if she didn't know what she was about!

[*After she has said this they look at each other, then start to glance back at the door. After an instant* MRS. HALE *has pulled at a knot and ripped the sewing.*]

MRS. PETERS: Oh, what are you doing, Mrs. Hale?

MRS. HALE [*mildly*]: Just pulling out a stitch or two that's not sewed very good. [*Threading a needle.*] Bad sewing always made me fidgety.

MRS. PETERS [*nervously*]: I don't think we ought to touch things.

MRS. HALE: I'll just finish up this end. [*Suddenly stopping and leaning forward.*] Mrs. Peters?

MRS. PETERS: Yes, Mrs. Hale?

MRS. HALE: What do you suppose she was so nervous about?

MRS. PETERS: Oh—I don't know. I don't know as she was nervous. I sometimes sew awful queer when I'm just tired. [MRS. HALE *starts to say something, looks at* MRS. PETERS, *then goes on sewing.*] Well, I must get these things wrapped up. They may be through sooner than we think. [*Putting apron and other things together.*] I wonder where I can find a piece of paper, and string.

MRS. HALE: In that cupboard, maybe.

MRS. PETERS [*looking in cupboard*]: Why, here's a birdcage. [*Holds it up.*] Did she have a bird, Mrs. Hale?

MRS. HALE: Why, I don't know whether she did or not—I've not been here for so long. There was a man around last year selling canaries cheap, but I don't know as she took one; maybe she did. She used to sing real pretty herself.

MRS. PETERS [*glancing around*]: Seems funny to think of a bird here. But she must have had one, or why would she have a cage? I wonder what happened to it.

MRS. HALE: I s'pose maybe the cat got it.

90   MRS. PETERS: No, she didn't have a cat. She's got that feeling some people have
about cats—being afraid of them. My cat got in her room and she was real upset
and asked me to take it out.

  MRS. HALE: My sister Bessie was like that. Queer, ain't it?

  MRS. PETERS [*examining the cage*]: Why, look at this door. It's broke. One hinge is
pulled apart.

  MRS. HALE [*looking too*]: Looks as if someone must have been rough with it.

  MRS. PETERS: Why, yes.

[*She brings the cage forward and puts it on the table.*]

95   MRS. HALE: I wish if they're going to find any evidence they'd be about it. I don't
like this place.

  MRS. PETERS: But I'm awful glad you came with me, Mrs. Hale. It would be lone-
some for me sitting here alone.

  MRS. HALE: It would, wouldn't it? [*Dropping her sewing.*] But I tell you what I do
wish, Mrs. Peters. I wish I had come over sometimes when *she* was here. I—
[*Looking around the room.*]—wish I had.

  MRS. PETERS: But of course you were awful busy, Mrs. Hale—your house and your
children.

  MRS. HALE: I could've come. I stayed away because it weren't cheerful—and that's
why I ought to have come. I—I've never liked this place. Maybe because it's
down in a hollow and you don't see the road. I dunno what it is but it's a lone-
some place and always was. I wish I had come over to see Minnie Foster sometimes. I can see now—

[*Shakes her head.*]

100   MRS. PETERS: Well, you mustn't reproach yourself, Mrs. Hale. Somehow we just
don't see how it is with other folks until—something comes up.

  MRS. HALE: Not having children makes less work—but it makes a quiet house, and
Wright out to work all day, and no company when he did come in. Did you
know John Wright, Mrs. Peters?

  MRS. PETERS: Not to know him; I've seen him in town. They say he was a good man.

  MRS. HALE: Yes—good; he didn't drink, and kept his word as well as most, I guess,
and paid his debts. But he was a hard man, Mrs. Peters. Just to pass the time of
day with him—[*Shivers.*] Like a raw wind that gets to the bone. [*Pauses, her eye
falling on the cage.*] I should think she would 'a wanted a bird. But what do you
suppose went with it?

  MRS. PETERS: I don't know, unless it got sick and died.

[*She reaches over and swings the broken door, swings it again. Both women watch it.*]

105   MRS. HALE: You weren't raised round here, were you? [MRS. PETERS *shakes her head.*]
You didn't know—her?

  MRS. PETERS: Not till they brought her yesterday.

  MRS. HALE: She—come to think of it, she was kind of like a bird herself—real sweet
and pretty, but kind of timid and—fluttery. How—she—did—change. [*Silence;
then as if struck by a happy thought and relieved to get back to everyday things.*] Tell

you what, Mrs. Peters, why don't you take the quilt in with you? It might take up her mind.

MRS. PETERS: Why, I think that's a real nice idea, Mrs. Hale. There couldn't possibly be any objection to it, could there? Now, just what would I take? I wonder if her patches are in here—and her things.

[*They look in the sewing basket.*]

MRS. HALE: Here's some red. I expect this has got sewing things in it. [*Brings out a fancy box.*] What a pretty box. Looks like something somebody would give you. Maybe her scissors are in here. [*Opens box. Suddenly puts her hand to her nose.*] Why—[MRS. PETERS *bends nearer, then turns her face away.*] There's something wrapped up in this piece of silk.

MRS. PETERS: Why, this isn't her scissors.   110

MRS. HALE [*lifting the silk*]: Oh, Mrs. Peters—it's—

[MRS. PETERS *bends closer.*]

MRS. PETERS: It's the bird.

MRS. HALE [*jumping up*]: But, Mrs. Peters—look at it! Its neck! Look at its neck! It's all—other side *to.*

MRS. PETERS: Somebody—wrung—its—neck.

[*Their eyes meet. A look of growing comprehension, of horror. Steps are heard outside.* MRS. HALE *slips box under quilt pieces, and sinks into her chair. Enter* SHERIFF *and* COUNTY ATTORNEY. MRS. PETERS *rises.*]

COUNTY ATTORNEY [*as one turning from serious things to little pleasantries*]: Well, ladies   115
have you decided whether she was going to quilt it or knot it?

MRS. PETERS: We think she was going to—knot it.

COUNTY ATTORNEY: Well, that's interesting, I'm sure. [*Seeing the birdcage.*] Has the bird flown?

MRS. HALE [*putting more quilt pieces over the box*]: We think the—cat got it.

COUNTY ATTORNEY [*Preoccupied*]: Is there a cat?

[MRS. HALE *glances in a quick covert way at* MRS. PETERS.]

MRS. PETERS: Well, not *now.* They're superstitious, you know. They leave.   120

COUNTY ATTORNEY [*to* SHERIFF PETERS, *continuing an interrupted conversation*]: No sign at all of anyone having come from the outside. Their own rope. Now let's go up again and go over it piece by piece. [*They start upstairs.*] It would have to have been someone who knew just the—

[MRS. PETERS *sits down. The two women sit there not looking at one another, but as if peering into something and at the same time holding back. When they talk now it is in the manner of feeling their way over strange ground, as if afraid of what they are saying, but as if they cannot help saying it.*]

MRS. HALE: She liked the bird. She was going to bury it in that pretty box.

MRS. PETERS [*in a whisper*]: When I was a girl—my kitten—there was a boy took a hatchet, and before my eyes—and before I could get there—[*Covers her face an instant.*] If they hadn't held me back I would have—[*Catches herself, looks upstairs where steps are heard, falters weakly.*]—hurt him.

MRS. HALE [*with a slow look around her*]: I wonder how it would seem never to have had any children around. [*Pause.*] No, Wright wouldn't like the bird—a thing that sang. She used to sing. He killed that, too.

125 MRS. PETERS [*moving uneasily*]: We don't know who killed the bird.

MRS. HALE: I knew John Wright.

MRS. PETERS: It was an awful thing was done in this house that night, Mrs. Hale. Killing a man while he slept, slipping a rope around his neck that choked the life out of him.

MRS. HALE: His neck. Choked the life out of him.

[*Her hand goes out and rests on the birdcage.*]

MRS. PETERS [*with rising voice*]: We don't know who killed him. We don't *know.*

130 MRS. HALE [*her own feeling not interrupted*]: If there'd been years and years of nothing, then a bird to sing to you, it would be awful—still, after the bird was still.

MRS. PETERS [*something within her speaking*]: I know what stillness is. When we homesteaded in Dakota, and my first baby died—after he was two years old, and me with no other then—

MRS. HALE [*moving*]: How soon do you suppose they'll be through, looking for the evidence?

MRS. PETERS: I know what stillness is. [*Pulling herself back.*] The law has got to punish crime, Mrs. Hale.

MRS. HALE [*not as if answering that*]: I wish you'd seen Minnie Foster when she wore a white dress with blue ribbons and stood up there in the choir and sang. [*A look around the room.*] Oh, I *wish* I'd come over here once in a while! That was a crime! That was a crime! Who's going to punish that?

135 MRS. PETERS [*looking upstairs*]: We mustn't—take on.

MRS. HALE: I might have known she needed help! I know how things can be—for women. I tell you, it's queer, Mrs. Peters. We live close together and we live far apart. We all go through the same things—it's all just a different kind of the same thing. [*Brushes her eyes; noticing the bottle of fruit, reaches out for it.*] If I was you I wouldn't tell her her fruit was gone. Tell her it *ain't.* Tell her it's all right. Take this in to prove it to her. She—she may never know whether it was broke or not.

MRS. PETERS [*takes the bottle, looks about for something to wrap it in; takes petticoat from the clothes brought from the other room, very nervously begins winding this around the bottle. In a false voice*]: My, it's a good thing the men couldn't hear us. Wouldn't they just laugh! Getting all stirred up over a little thing like a—dead canary. As if that could have anything to do with—with—wouldn't they *laugh!*

[*The men are heard coming down stairs.*]

MRS. HALE [*under her breath*]: Maybe they would—maybe they wouldn't.

COUNTY ATTORNEY: No, Peters, it's all perfectly clear except a reason for doing it. But you know juries when it comes to women. If there was some definite thing. Something to show—something to make a story about—a thing that would connect up with this strange way of doing it—

[*The women's eyes meet for an instant. Enter* HALE *from outer door.*]

HALE: Well, I've got the team around. Pretty cold out there.   140

COUNTY ATTORNEY: I'm going to stay here a while by myself. [*To the* SHERIFF.]
    You can send Frank out for me, can't you? I want to go over everything. I'm
    not satisfied that we can't do better.

SHERIFF: Do you want to see what Mrs. Peters is going to take in?

[*The* COUNTY ATTORNEY *goes to the table, picks up the apron, laughs.*]

COUNTY ATTORNEY: Oh, I guess they're not very dangerous things the ladies have
    picked out. [*Moves a few things about, disturbing the quilt pieces which cover the box.
    Steps back.*] No, Mrs. Peters doesn't need supervising. For that matter, a sheriff's
    wife is married to the law. Ever think of it that way, Mrs. Peters?

MRS. PETERS: Not—just that way.

SHERIFF [*chuckling*]: Married to the law. [*Moves toward the other room.*] I just want you   145
    to come in here a minute, George. We ought to take a look at these windows.

COUNTY ATTORNEY [*scoffingly*]: Oh, windows!

SHERIFF: We'll be right out, Mr. Hale.

[HALE *goes outside. The* SHERIFF *follows the* COUNTY ATTORNEY *into the other
room. Then* MRS. HALE *rises, hands tight together, looking intensely at* MRS. PETERS,
whose eyes make a slow turn, finally meeting MRS. HALE's. *A moment* MRS. HALE
holds her, then her own eyes point the way to where the box is concealed. Suddenly
MRS. PETERS *throws back quilt pieces and tries to put the box in the bag she is
wearing. It is too big. She opens box, starts to take bird out, cannot touch it, goes to
pieces, stands there helpless. Sound of a knob turning in the other room.* MRS. HALE
snatches the box and puts it in the pocket of her big coat. Enter COUNTY ATTORNEY
and SHERIFF.]

COUNTY ATTORNEY [*facetiously*]: Well, Henry, at least we found out that she was
    not going to quilt it. She was going to—what is it you call it, ladies?

MRS. HALE [*her hand against her pocket*]: We call it—knot it, Mr. Henderson.

Curtain •

As you read *Trifles*, you undoubtedly noticed that the male and female characters interpret the small details—the "trifles"—of the setting differently. The men see
in the disorderly kitchen evidence of Mrs. Wright's failures as a housekeeper; the
women see it as evidence of her unusual mental agitation. Those differences of opinion, the differences in the ways the characters look at setting, give shape to the play's
themes: men and women see things differently, and the failure to recognize women's
needs results in tragedy. But there is more to the setting than that. Consider not only
the details of the setting that we see onstage (the dirty towels, the unbaked bread, the
ruined cherry preserves); consider also the setting that is outside the house and that is
revealed to us (much as in prose fiction) only in the language of the characters. That
setting, too, helps us understand Mrs. Wright's life and her motivations.

EXERCISE: TRYING IT OUT

Think about the descriptions of the Wrights' home, the setting that does *not* appear onstage. What do they tell us about the Wrights' life together and about their emotional and social well-being?

————————

As is true in *Trifles*, in any staged play the importance of setting is often obvious from the very beginning—we are, after all, watching a scene that unfolds in a physical setting onstage; there is no way to create that scene without someone's having envisioned a setting. Poems and short stories also rely on setting for some of their effects. Short story writers will often describe the physical setting of the work in the first few paragraphs. In "Yellow Woman," for example, Silko focuses on the natural scene before she tells us anything about the narrator or the man who lies beside her. Look again at the first three paragraphs of Silko's story (36). The scene is described precisely: we see the tamaracks and the willows, the small brown water birds hopping across the mud, the rushing water, and the rising sun. The attention to the natural details may suggest that people and nature are in harmony, sharing the same rhythms. However, as we read on, the precision blurs and the sense of harmony is disrupted. We learn of another place, a pueblo that the narrator cannot see. We find that the human footsteps from the day before have been obliterated, first by lizard and bug tracks, then by the narrator's own returning footsteps. Those blurred footsteps correspond to an uncertainty of emotion. Does the narrator long for the pueblo she cannot see? Or does a sense of yearning force her to return to the man in the red blanket? The shift in setting, the going forth and the return, corresponds to the narrator's own emotional conflict. In this story, as in most, setting is not, then, fully distinct from characterization or **theme** (the basic ideas of the story). Readers who skip over "mere" description often miss important indications of a work's meanings.

Setting is also linked to character in Robert Louis Stevenson's *Dr. Jekyll and Mr. Hyde*. In that story (see 1374–1413), the proper, respectable Dr. Jekyll is associated with an elegant, well-run mansion. From the first chapter, however, we learn that this house has two doors: one a clean, well-kept door that proudly fronts a public street, the other a dirty, marred door that does not even seem to belong to the house. The first is, of course, the door associated with the seemingly upright Dr. Jekyll, the second the door associated with the nefarious Mr. Hyde. Only by the end of the story will the reader understand the essential meaning imparted by this physical setting: just as we discover that both doors belong to the same place, we find that Dr. Jekyll and Mr. Hyde are closely linked.

The Temporal Setting

It is not only the physical setting that is important. The **temporal setting,** or the time in which the events take place, may also be significant, and often the physical and temporal settings together create a mood. In *Dr. Jekyll and Mr. Hyde,* for instance, the combination of time (night) and a fog-shrouded place underscores the story's suspense and horror. Almost all of the scenes in which the evil Mr. Hyde appears occur at night or during very foggy days, emphasizing both the darkly sinister quality of

Hyde and his essential unknowableness—he is never fully seen, either by the reader or by the other characters.

Edgar Allan Poe makes similar use of temporal setting in "The Tell-Tale Heart." Like Stevenson, Poe recognizes that we do not respond to things in the same way during the day as we do at night; in the sunlight, anxieties and fears tend to diminish, even disappear, but at night they are magnified. Playing on that common response to nighttime fears, Poe tells of a narrator who "every night, about midnight, . . . turned the latch of [the old man's] door and opened it." When the old man awakens after having heard a noise, most of us can relate very strongly to his emotion. His fears are nighttime fears most of us have shared: he has heard a noise and is uncertain whether it is the creaking of the house or something more sinister. Awake for an hour, he listens intently, too fearful to get up to investigate. Were the story set in the daytime, the old man's fears might seem unfounded, perhaps even laughable, to the reader. But the nighttime setting helps create the suspense Poe is after.

EXERCISE: TRYING IT OUT

Read the first two paragraphs of James Joyce's "Araby." What do you deduce about the story's events and themes from the way the physical setting is described?

Retelling Time and Place

Both Stevenson and Poe play on our reactions to night, setting their stories at the time of day that often gives rise to dark terrors. But it is not time of day alone that creates a temporal setting. The year—or even century—may also be important. Such is the case when a movie producer or filmmaker sets a Shakespeare play in a period after Shakespeare's own. For instance, a recent movie of Shakespeare's *Richard III* was set in a 1930s London that had a Nazi-like atmosphere, thereby encouraging its twentieth-century audience to experience more intimately the chaos of a despotic and dissolving state. The Oregon Shakespeare Festival made a similar choice when it chose a twentieth-century setting for its production of Shakespeare's *Henry IV, Part I*. At the center of that play is Prince Hal, a wild and rebellious prince who seems too immature and thoughtless to be the country's next king. Audiences prepared for a more traditional approach to Shakespeare were shocked when, in the first scene of the Oregon production, Prince Hal roared onto stage on a motorcycle, punk rock music blaring. Throughout the play, flashing strobe lights, loud music, and long hair helped reinforce the notion of Hal as a rebellious teenager unsympathetic to the more conservative and "responsible" demeanor of his father's generation. How better to capture the audience's own generational tensions? The setting of the Oregon production thus forced the audience to rethink the relationship between Hal and his father, seeing it in the light of their own relationships with parents and children.

Rita Dove's retelling of Sophocles' *Oedipus*, which is (along with *Oedipus* itself) included in this anthology, similarly takes an old story and alerts us to its modern meanings by setting it in more recent times. Sophocles himself did not set the original play in his own time (the fifth century B.C.); Oedipus and his story are part of Greek legend. As a result, Sophocles' audience would have seen the time setting of the play as that of a distant legendary period when gods and heroes interacted more directly than they did in the audience's own time. When she decided to retell the story in *The Darker Face of the Earth*, Rita Dove, a contemporary American writer, set it in a time period her American audience would likewise have seen as part of an almost legendary past: the era of slavery before the Civil War.

Despite the fact that the time periods of both Sophocles' and Dove's plays are part of "legend" for the audiences, the differences in the time and place of the story result in a very different "feel" and very different possibilities for the two stories. Sophocles' Greek audience, like the characters in *Oedipus*, would have believed strongly in fate and in the possibility that the gods would interfere directly in their lives and create a plague to punish them. The legendary past starkly dramatizes beliefs the audience still held.

For most in Dove's twentieth- and twenty-first-century audiences, however, such beliefs would seem odd, even impenetrable. Instead, Dove substituted *race* for fate, hoping to drive home to her audience the importance of race in determining an individual's future. For a black man born in a white society, she seems to believe, race is as important a determining factor—as important a limitation—as fate was for Sophocles' Oedipus. So she retells the Greek story with American characters in a particularly race-conscious setting: an American slave plantation of the nineteenth century. The two playwrights thus create settings (times and places) that best allow them to explore the concerns most pertinent to the times in which they were writing.

Cultural Setting

Setting finally goes beyond time and place to become a **cultural setting,** a setting that contains within it a set of beliefs and values. Times and places are not neutral. The prevailing attitudes and beliefs in a prison, for instance, are probably rather different from those in a college classroom (though students and teachers might notice some similarities, as well). Two writers may set their stories in the same time and place but among different people—with, perhaps, different economic statuses, different levels of education, different religions, different racial or ethnic heritages, different political views, and different backgrounds (perhaps, say, those of a group of recent immigrants or a group of long-established families). All of these differences add up to differences in culture.

Such a difference in culture can be demonstrated by a comparison of Matthew Arnold's "Dover Beach" and Anthony Hecht's "The Dover Bitch" (see 21 and 23). The physical settings of the two poems are literally the same: both are set at Dover Beach in England. Hecht, though he is a modern poet, also creates the same temporal setting that Arnold did: Hecht's poem refers to Matthew Arnold and the "girl" as if they are alive. Presumably, then, both poems are set at Dover Beach in the mid–nineteenth century (when Matthew Arnold wrote "Dover Beach"). However, there are some important differences in the ways in which the two settings are described. For Arnold, "the cliffs of England stand, / Glimmering and vast, out in the tranquil bay." In contrast, for Hecht, "the cliffs of England [are] crumbling away." Instead of the potentially majestic and dignified setting of Arnold's Dover Beach, we are now invited to see the scene as one of deterioration. The same physical setting thus elicits two very different responses.

Arnold's setting helps us feel the loss that the speaker feels; Hecht's setting shows us that there is no sense of loss—for the speaker, the "crumbling" is so far advanced that he doesn't even know that there is anything to lose.

These differences in physical setting reflect differences in the cultural setting. Arnold's poem mourns the loss of love and certainty in life; it clearly values these things, which is why their loss creates such sadness. The speaker also obviously values education, including literature, and so refers to Sophocles, the Greek playwright. Though the time and place of Hecht's "The Dover Bitch" are the same as Arnold's, the cultural atmosphere is very different. The woman being addressed is no longer "love," but rather a "bitch." The "bitch" is not "true," as Arnold hoped his love would be, but rather—in her sexual availability—"dependable as they come." Instead of valuing a classical education (Sophocles was being read only in a fairly good translation, not in the Greek original, after all) and mourning the loss of love and faith, Hecht's cultural setting is one in which cynicism and sexual promiscuity abound. The people in Hecht's world are not very apt to regret the loss of faith and love—they have never had these things and do not believe they ever existed. Obviously, much has changed culturally between the times of the two poems.

Though it is set in the middle of the nineteenth century, Hecht's poem was written in 1968. There are a hundred years of cultural differences between the time setting of the poem and the time in which it was written. As a result, "The Dover Bitch" helps us to see that setting is created by more than just when and where the author sets the work. In many ways, the full setting—the cultural setting in the broadest sense—is created by the juxtaposition of the time and place in which the piece is written and those in which it is set. Hecht's cultural setting reflects the values and attitudes of 1968 America more than those of mid-nineteenth-century England. Hecht uses the nineteenth-century setting, in part, to show just how far we have come (or fallen) since Matthew Arnold's time.

A similar cultural dislocation is at work in Rita Dove's *The Darker Face of the Earth*. Though the play is set in the South during the time of slavery, surely no real slaves ever talked in the ways in which Dove's slaves talk; few, if any, slave mistresses behaved the way her slave mistress does. In both cases there is a boldness that would probably not have belonged to a slave or a Southern belle of that time period. It is important, though, to remember that the play was written at the end of the twentieth century, not during the early nineteenth century in which it is set. As with Hecht's poem, there is a hundred years' difference between the time in which the poem is set and the time of its writing. Dove's audience comes to the play with firm convictions that slavery was wrong, and she doesn't need to create a realistic plantation to convince the audience of that. In order to explore the conflict between the desire for freedom and the limitations of social circumstances, Dove expands the cultural setting—using the values of her modern audience to help shape the dialog and actions of her nineteenth-century characters in a way that goes beyond realism.

EXERCISE: TRYING IT OUT

Retell a story you know well, altering the physical or temporal setting. You might, for instance, retell a fairy tale so that it takes place in more modern times (as was done in the recent film *Ever After*, which retells the Cinderella story), or you might retell an American story by setting it in another country (or retell a myth from another country by setting it in the United States).

It is easy to think of the time and place of a literary work as a mere backdrop, a stage on which the characters move and the plot unfolds. But, as we said earlier, all of us know from our own lives that setting influences much of what we think and do. What is true for us is equally true for the characters and events of literature.

Questions to Ask about Setting

1. In what time period is the work set? If the time period is not explicitly stated, do details in the work suggest a particular time period? (For instance, are cars or horses the mode of transportation? Is the telephone mentioned? Is the computer? What do the roles of the women or the social interactions among various economic and ethnic groups suggest about the time period?)
2. What time of day seems to dominate in the work? What is the typical weather? (Sunny? Rainy? Foggy?) What moods are associated with the time?
3. Where is the story set physically? In what nation? In what city, town, or rural area? Do events occur inside or outside? Do the settings seem wide and expansive, or narrow and claustrophobic? How might the descriptions of places reflect the events that take place or the characterizations?
4. Do the characters move in a particular circle with established values? For instance, what can you tell about the prevailing economic status? Religion? Education? Family history? Racial or ethnic background?
5. Look at when the story was written. Is the story set in a time and place very different from the author's own? How much have the values and attitudes of the author's own time and place found their way into the work, even if that time and place are very different from the setting?

APPEALS TO THE SENSES: SOUND AND VISUAL IMAGERY

In modern-day America, we have come to expect multimedia extravaganzas that engage as many of our senses as possible. Not only do we listen to the music; we watch a flashing light show or a twenty-foot video backdrop. Sight, sound, and lyrics come together to fully engage us in the artists' meanings.

Similarly, reading literature or watching plays can be a very sensual experience, one involving a number of different senses. Great works often appeal to several senses at once. Not only do we take in the meaning of the words, but we also hear their sounds and watch the word pictures created for us. Sound, then, can be as important to our response to literature as it is to our response to music, and sight can be as important in literature as it is in art, even if the sounds and sights occur only inside our heads.

Sound and Sense

When most of us think about sound in literature, we probably think about poetry, rhyme in particular. Because the use of rhyme and poetic meter is a specialized topic, we will leave it for the discussion of poetry in chapter 4. Here we want to discuss the use of sounds in all types of literature. For example, in "Stopping by Woods on a Snowy Evening," Robert Frost is doing more than simply relying on rhyme to tie sound to meaning:

ROBERT FROST (1874–1963)

Stopping by Woods on a Snowy Evening _____ 1923

Whose woods these are I think I know.
His house is in the village though;
He will not see me stopping here
To watch his woods fill up with snow.

My little horse must think it queer   5
To stop without a farmhouse near
Between the woods and frozen lake
The darkest evening of the year.

He gives his harness bells a shake
To ask if there is some mistake.   10
The only other sound's the sweep
Of easy wind and downy flake.

The woods are lovely, dark and deep,
But I have promises to keep,
And miles to go before I sleep,   15
And miles to go before I sleep.

In the first stanza alone, Frost uses a lot of *w* sounds (*whose, woods, will, watch,* and *woods* again), *s* or *z* sounds (in *whose, woods, house, see, stopping,* and *snow*), and long *o* sounds (*know, though,* and *snow*). The effect is wintry, for the sounds create the soft "windy" sound of falling snow. Frost uses other sounds as well to create different tempos in the poem. The first two lines of each stanza, for instance, depend mostly on consonant sounds; they create a quick rhythm that underscores the speaker's—and his horse's—need to get going. The last two lines of each stanza, however, depend more on long vowel sounds (as in "miles to go before *I* sleep"). These long vowel sounds slow the poem down; as a result, they help create the speaker's feeling of weariness and reluctance to move on. For "Stopping by Woods on a Snowy Evening," sound is not separate from the meaning of the poem: it is *part* of the meaning.

It is not only poets who use sound to convey their ideas. Edgar Allan Poe uses sound to create a very definite sense of the speaker in the opening of "The Tell-Tale Heart." If you read the following passage aloud, you will discover that the exclamation marks, italics, and dashes all create a sense of irritable excitability.

> True!—nervous—very, very dreadfully nervous I had been and am; but why *will* you say that I am mad? The disease had sharpened my senses—not destroyed—not dulled them. Above all was the sense of hearing acute. I heard all things in the heaven and in the earth. I heard many things in hell. How, then, am I mad? Hearken! And observe how healthily—how calmly I can tell you the whole story.

The punctuation marks and italics used here indicate a series of quick stops and starts and moments of intense emphasis that help us to hear the sharpness in the narrator's voice, and the use of short sentences and short words with strong sounds (notice the frequent use of the *d* sound) makes the speaker's words sound frenzied and disconnected. There are here none of the lilting and soothing sounds of "Stopping by Woods."

Playwrights may also depend on sound to create moods and reinforce ideas. We frequently see the deliberate use of sound in Shakespeare's plays. His aristocratic, "serious" characters usually speak in poetry; his clowns, generally lower-class characters, speak in everyday speech, often employing the slang of the day. The *sounds* of their speeches help characterize the speakers, letting the audience know how seriously we are to take them and their pronouncements. Additionally, Shakespeare often uses rhymed lines at the end of a scene as a way of alerting the audience that a shift in the setting will occur; the rhyme is equivalent to lowering the curtain in a modern play (Shakespeare's stage did not have the stage curtains we take for granted today). Whether consciously or not, we are so responsive to the influence of sounds that no sound is fully "meaningless." Sound conveys important things about mood and character—and even about structure.

Sight and Sense

Literature not only appeals to our sense of sound but also appeals strongly to our visual sense. The pattern of pictures that authors create results in the **imagery** of the work. Settings often are a large part of the imagery. For instance, as noted earlier, many of the key scenes in the short novel *Dr. Jekyll and Mr. Hyde* take place at night. The reader pictures the darkness, and the imagery of the night creates a mood of a threatening evil throughout the work. Similarly, Matthew Arnold uses vivid word pictures in "Dover Beach" to help us see very clearly the beach itself:

> The sea is calm tonight.
> The tide is full, the moon lies fair
> Upon the straits; on the French coast the light
> Gleams and is gone; the cliffs of England stand,
> Glimmering and vast, out in the tranquil bay.
> Come to the window, sweet is the night-air!
> Only, from the long line of spray
> Where the sea meets the moon-blanched land,
> Listen! you hear the grating roar
> Of pebbles which the waves draw back, and fling,
> At their return, up the high strand,
> Begin, and cease, and then again begin,

With tremulous cadence slow, and bring
The eternal note of sadness in.

We see the moonlit beach, with the coast of France beyond, and we watch the waves coming and going. The scene also sets up the light/dark imagery of the poem: there is light, but it is the light of the moon rather than of the sun. It is a "glimmering" light that "gleams and is gone." This imagery will reinforce the meaning of the poem: light, and the certainty it represents, cannot be counted on.

As the examples from "Dover Beach" and *Dr. Jekyll and Mr. Hyde* show, a literal—or physical—setting can have a **figurative** meaning: the details of the scene may suggest ideas the writer wants to reinforce. Sometimes, however, what we see never is literal, but only figurative, a turn of speech. The author may create **metaphors,** imagery based on stated or implied comparisons. In her poem "The Fish," for instance, Elizabeth Bishop sometimes explicitly signals to us her use of figurative language: the fish has skin "like brown wallpaper" and a swim-bladder "like a big peony." (The complete poem is printed on 934–36.) These explicit comparisons, with the use of *like* or *as,* are **similes,** a special type of metaphor. The author asks us to visualize one thing as *like* another in order to convey the work's meaning. In the case of "The Fish," for example, the wallpaper simile may suggest that the fish is somehow domestic, perhaps feminine; the peony simile may also suggest femininity, or perhaps it is an image of nature (but of the land rather than the sea).

Elsewhere in the same poem, the speaker describes the eyes of the fish as "tarnished tinfoil." In this case, a different kind of metaphor is created—this one is not a simile (there is no explicit comparison word such as *as* or *like*). The poet has *implied* the comparison. Again, though, the poet creates an image, a picture in the reader's mind that may help convey the writer's ideas. Tinfoil, like wallpaper, may seem domestic to the reader and so suggest that the fish belongs to a familiar home environment. Whether literal or figurative, explicit or implied, imagery is part of the visual texture of a work. What we see helps create the meanings for us.

EXERCISES: TRYING IT OUT

1. Many common expressions rely on imagery and metaphor: "as dead as a doornail," "as honest as the day is long," "time flies," "happy as a clam." Try creating three or four images of your own, perhaps using the following beginnings to get yourself started:
   as lively as a _____
   as unhappy as a _____
   as tired as a _____
2. In a book entitled *De/Compositions,* W. D. Snodgrass retells some famous poems, altering their word choices and structures. In his retellings of Shakespeare's Sonnet 73, he deliberately changes the metaphors of Shakespeare's original. Read Shakespeare's original (printed first) and then Snodgrass's two retellings. How do Snodgrass's changes affect our responses to Shakespeare's poem?

WILLIAM SHAKESPEARE (1564–1616)

That time of year thou may'st in me behold _____ *1609*

> That time of year thou may'st in me behold
> When yellow leaves, or none, or few, do hang
> Upon those boughs which shake against the cold,
> Bare ruined choirs where late the sweet birds sang.
> 5   In me thou see'st the twilight of such day
> As after sunset fadeth in the west,
> Which by-and-by black night doth take away,
> Death's second self that seals up all in rest.
> In me thou see'st the glowing of such fire
> 10   That on the ashes of his youth doth lie,
> As the deathbed whereon it must expire,
> Consumed with that which it was nourished by.
>   This thou perceiv'st, which makes thy love more strong,
>   To love that well which thou must leave ere long.

W. D. SNODGRASS

Sonnet #73

—*de/composed from Shakespeare*

> That time of year thou mayst in me behold
> When foliage takes flight and leaves the tree
> So leafless boughs are subject to the cold
> Where summer birds made music formerly.
> 5   In me thou mayst behold how light can fade
> That once shone brightly all across the sky
> But as time passes turns to deepening shade
> Declining to Death's darkness by and by.
> In me you see how fires burned down may be
> 10   Still bright above the fuel already burned
> Although the fire must go out finally,
> Consumed by getting that for which it yearned.
>   This thou perceivest though not turned cold thereby
>   And love me more though soon I have to die.

W. D. SNODGRASS

Sonnet #73

—*re/de/composed from Shakespeare*

> I've reached an age when everybody sees
> Signs that I'm old, no young growth anymore

Or vigor in my frail extremities—
Ruins that were so full of life before.
In me is seen fading vitality   5
As if now aging powers have declined
Till they will soon have vanished totally
In death which [leaves] no slightest thing behind.
Such remnants of past strengths appear in me
As have used up their former youthful forces   10
And now they wait to give up utterly
Having exhausted all of their resources.
    And yet your love for me grows even stronger
    Knowing I've got to go before much longer.

Although we experience the world largely through our five senses of sight, hearing, touch, taste, and smell, readers often overlook the way that writers appeal to those senses. To do so, though, is to miss much of what helps writers create the world of their characters. It is also to miss the often subtle artistry by which writers encourage us to think and feel along with them.

Questions to Ask about Appeals to the Senses

1. Trying to block out any meanings associated with the words, concentrate on what the words of the piece sound like. Do certain sounds dominate? Are they harsh or soft sounds? Do they create "whooshing" or hissing sounds? Does the rhythm seem flowing or staccato? Quick or slow? What states of mind or emotions are suggested by the sounds?
2. Do certain sounds appear in some parts of the work but not in others? Does their placement cause them to be associated with certain ideas?
3. What pictures do you envision when you read particular words in the work? Are the images "light" or "dark"? Natural or artificial? What moods do you associate with these pictures?
4. Does the writer use *metaphors* (including similes)? If so, what associations do you have with the comparisons that are being made?

THE READER'S ROLE: THE IMPORTANCE OF AUDIENCE

Have you heard the old question, "If a tree falls in the forest and there is no one there to hear it, does it make a sound?" A similar question might be asked about literature: "If there is no one there to read a book, does its message exist?" Can a "message" exist if it is not received? Writing is primarily a form of communication, and communication is a two-way street. It is true that we all sometimes write only for ourselves; we may, for example, create lists of things to do or to remember or write a journal that expresses feelings meant for us alone. More typically, though, we write *to* and *for* someone other than ourselves. The piece of writing, then, must take into account not only what the writer wants to communicate but also what the audience is likely to hear. As we saw in the discussion of cultural setting, the audience is part of the culture assumed by a writer. Good writers (including the writers of nonliterary texts) know that they depend on their audiences to help create their messages, and good writers construct their pieces with the likely responses of their audiences in mind.

Differing Worldviews

Some audience reactions are so typical as to be almost universal, from time to time and culture to culture. We almost invariably, for instance, react positively to loving parents and children and to warm, sunny days; most of us will find violence disturbing and be made uneasy by storms and darkness. At the same time, however, not all audiences *do* react alike to all situations. Differences in audience response may become especially marked if centuries have passed since a work was written. The audience of a play written during the Renaissance—which occurred four hundred years ago—may have had very different values from our own. For example, an English Renaissance playwright might reasonably have assumed that certain religious beliefs were widely held by his audience and that his audience would have an everyday familiarity with Biblical allusions and Christian religious observances and traditions. A modern American audience, in contrast, tends to be more secularized, and it may be made up of people holding many different religious beliefs, many of them based on Judaism and the religions of the East rather than on Christianity. A relatively small proportion of an American audience would have the familiarity with the Bible that a Renaissance writer would have taken for granted among even the most uneducated members of his audience. As a consequence, a modern American audience might misunderstand parts of a Renaissance drama or even become bored through lack of understanding.

Similarly, a nineteenth-century writer would assume in his audience a kind of optimism at odds with the cynicism we often take for granted today; the nineteenth-century writer would also assume a conservatism about sexual behavior and gender roles that many people would not currently accept. On the other hand, today's writers can assume a degree of scientific understanding that would have seemed foreign to writers and audiences of earlier times.

The issue here is not necessarily about which time and culture is "right" about its values or beliefs, though most readers will have own their opinions about that. The point is that, to read literature effectively, readers must imagine themselves as belonging concurrently to two audiences: the original audience of the piece of literature and the contemporary audience to which the readers actually belong. It is hardly fair to criticize a Renaissance writer, for instance, for not sharing our worldview; the world has changed in ways that the writer could never have imagined. To get the most out of literature, then, we need to imagine ourselves in the culture of the writer's time. We do not have to accept the prejudices of an earlier time or even ignore the unwarranted biases that great writers may have, but we do need to acknowledge that definitions of "racism" or "sexism" change with the times.

Because cultural and literary values shift over time and geography, even something as fundamental as the determination of the merit of a piece of work or the understanding of its basic meaning may shift radically. For example, every age has its own favorite Shakespeare plays, and every age (and audience) reads Shakespeare in the light of its own values. Until the twentieth century, for instance, Caliban, the island "savage" in Shakespeare's *The Tempest,* was viewed the way the main character Prospero views him: as a monster with animalistic needs and desires. Prospero, the magician of the play and Caliban's master, was usually seen as wielding power responsibly, attempting to curb Caliban's animal nature for the good of both Caliban himself and the surrounding "civilization." In the mid–twentieth century, however, the view of Caliban and Prospero shifted as the beliefs of the audience shifted. No longer did people accept without question the idea that colonizing "primitive" peoples was a way of bringing progress to them. Some readers now saw Caliban as the rightful owner of the island that Prospero had stolen from him, a native like the Native Americans or Australian aborigines. Prospero began to be viewed as a colonizer, someone using brute force to impose his own beliefs for his own benefit. It is this modern view of Shakespeare's play that underlies Aimé Césaire's retelling in *A Tempest* (343–71). By reading both literary versions of a colonial relationship, perhaps we more fully understand the complexity of the issue and of our own responses to it.

Finding the Evidence

It does not always take centuries for a new reading of a piece of literature to gain ascendancy. Theodore Roethke's "My Papa's Waltz" provides a case in point:

THEODORE ROETHKE (1908–1963)
My Papa's Waltz _____ 1942

> The whiskey on your breath
> Could make a small boy dizzy;
> But I hung on like death:
> Such waltzing was not easy.
>
> We romped until the pans   5
> Slid from the kitchen shelf;
> My mother's countenance
> Could not unfrown itself.
>
> The hand that held my wrist
> Was battered on one knuckle;   10
> At every step you missed
> My right ear scraped a buckle.
>
> You beat time on my head
> With a palm caked hard by dirt,

15   Then waltzed me off to bed
     Still clinging to your shirt.

EXERCISE: TRYING IT OUT

Describe the situation in the poem. What is the relationship between the father and the child? What motivates the two to behave as they do? How does the mother figure in the poem?

Readers often split quite dramatically in their responses to this poem. Some argue that the poem is a description of a little friendly roughhousing between father and son. Others see in the poem a description of a drunken father who, at best, lets his roughhousing get out of hand and, at worst, is guilty of child abuse. Roethke himself expressed surprise at the number of readers who saw the situation as frightening for the boy, especially because he saw the poem as autobiographical. Was Roethke simply unconscious of the hidden tensions in his relationship with his father? Are we much more sensitive to the possibilities of child abuse than were readers when the poem was first published (in 1948)? Are we *too* ready to see the possibility of abuse and so read *into* the poem our own fears? Again, the poem has not changed—but its message seems to have changed because the audience has changed.

Because good literature is usually richly textured, it allows us to interpret it in a variety of ways. What the author intended may or may not be part of the message. We are all aware of situations in which others have misinterpreted our words—and the fault may lie as much in us as in our hearers. We may weakly claim, "That is not what I meant," but it may in fact be what we said. The author does not necessarily have the last word on the meaning of the work: he may not be aware of all that was said, for better or worse. For that reason, though Roethke did not intend his poem to be about child abuse, that doesn't mean it is not. No matter what the intention behind it, the work has a life and meaning of its own.

If the author does not have the last word, though, neither does the audience. The audience can also misinterpret. Because literature can often be interpreted in a number of ways—sometimes even in contradictory ways—it may be tempting to see all opinions as equally valid. However, all opinions are *not* created equal, about literature or life. Before we accept someone else's opinion about what candidate we should vote for, what public policy to support, or what product to buy, we reasonably ask for reasons, evidence to back up our decisions. The same is true for any interpretation of literature: the best opinions are those that are supported by the text.

Again Roethke's "My Papa's Waltz" provides a good example. We might reasonably ask, "What in the poem creates a lighthearted mood that suggests friendly roughhousing?" A reader might point to a number of things. Waltzing is usually viewed positively; it suggests the partners are of one mind, moving together. It may even suggest affection between the partners. In addition, the boy does not seem to be resisting or trying to get away: he is hanging on and clinging to the father (lines 3 and 16). The poem also uses a word we associate with childish play: "romped" (5). The best evidence that the mood of the poem is positive comes from the poem itself, not from the reader's own experience with his father.

However, in the analysis of literature—just as in the analysis of an argument or issue—it is always a good idea to look at both sides. To look at the other argument about Roethke's poem, we might ask, "What in the poem suggests that the scene is grim, perhaps even abusive?" Again, a careful reader should begin with evidence *in* the poem, not outside it. A reader who takes this second position might remark that the boy is hanging on "like death" (3); "death" certainly seems to create a negative mood. The mother is frowning, as if she disapproves of what is happening (7–8). There is some evidence of barely suppressed violence: the father's hand is "battered on one knuckle" (9–10), the boy's ear is scraping the father's belt buckle (12), and the father is beating time on the boy's head (13).

Clearly, there is evidence *in the poem* that supports two very different interpretations. How, then, are we to reach a conclusion about what the poem means? As long as the reader has grounded an interpretation in the text itself, the conclusion is finally up to her. Ideally, the reader considers both the positive and negative language before she reaches an interpretation. A reader might even decide that the poem is finally ambiguous, with perhaps the boy taking a childish view of the roughhousing and an adult reader taking an opposed view of the violence. Different readers—and different audiences—are likely to draw different conclusions, just as they do about all sorts of matters, literary or not. The important thing is that the piece of literature is allowed to speak to us, providing the most important evidence for our conclusions.

EXERCISES: TRYING IT OUT

1. Locate a poem or short story that you loved as a child and reread it. How does your adult perspective alter your response not only to the style but also to the themes and characters?
2. Choose a poem (or song) or short story that seems to you to have particular significance for people of a particular cultural, ethnic, gender, or generational background. Ask people from that background to respond to the work, saying not only whether they like it but also what they see as its essential meaning. Then ask others with very different backgrounds to respond to the same poem or short story. How similar or different are their responses? To what extent did the assumptions and values they brought to the work matter?

Here are some poems and short stories (all printed in this anthology) that might work well:

Roethke's "My Papa's Waltz"
Oates's "Where Are You Going, Where Have You Been?"
Updike's "A & P"
Housman's "To an Athlete Dying Young"
Walker's "Everyday Use"

Questions to Ask about Audience

1. What would the original audience have assumed about the proper role of women, about the structure of the family, about religious beliefs, about economic and social classes, and about the value of education?
2. How much racial, ethnic, and religious diversity would have existed in the original audience? What assumptions would that audience have made about other races, ethnic groups, and religions?
3. Would the author have been like or unlike the original audience reading or viewing the work? To answer this question, you might draw on any information you have about the author's life, as well as on information from the text itself.
4. In what ways would a contemporary audience differ from the original audience? Are we more likely or less likely to share the author's values than the original audience would have been?
5. How might your own individual experiences influence the way you respond to a work? Are these individual experiences common enough to make your response a typical one?

As you read a piece of literature, or any text, you will want to be aware of how your own values and assumptions may influence your response to it. Because literature does not exist without an audience and because readers help create meaning, we need to ask the same kinds of questions about the readers who come *to* the work as we do about the characters who live *in* the work.

Work Cited

Snodgrass, W. D. *De/Compositions*. Saint Paul: Graywolf, 2001.

Part 2

Reading Different Genres

In chapter 2, we looked at elements common to many types of literature. No matter whether a piece is a poem, a work of fiction, or a drama, for instance, it may depend on characters or setting. For all works the reader (or perhaps the viewer of a play) is an important participant in the creation of meaning. At the same time, the different kinds of literature—called the **genres**—have significant differences, and readers respond differently to them. Some readers prefer novels, experiencing them as whole worlds to which they may escape. Others prefer poems, which for them convey intense feeling in an economical package. Still others most enjoy reading or watching plays, believing that the theatrical experience re-creates life most as it is lived, with character and plot seeming to exist without authorial intrusion.

Obviously, no one literary genre is better than another, but the fact that many readers have preferences tells us that there are important distinctions among them and that one genre can do things for us that another cannot. Understanding the conventions, forms, and expectations of a particular genre can help us to appreciate it more, so in the next several chapters we look closely at how each literary genre makes its meaning and creates its effects. We also look at nonliterary genres, such as essays, advertising, and film; they, too, are part of the tapestry of messages we receive.

Reading Short Fiction

People seem to have an inborn need to hear stories. The earliest stories were told through pictures as cave paintings and, later, in poems, such as the Greek *Odyssey* and the Old English *Beowulf,* that were recited orally. Today we tell and hear stories in many media, not only in literature but also in stage performances, movies, television shows, and even some advertisements. Much of what we are going to say about **prose fiction** (short stories and novels) applies to those other forms of storytelling as well, but literary fiction also presents some special considerations. Even in a story as short as Kate Chopin's "The Story of an Hour," we can see the elements of fiction at work.

KATE CHOPIN (1851–1904)

The Story of an Hour _____ 1894

Knowing that Mrs. Mallard was afflicted with a heart trouble, great care was taken to break to her as gently as possible the news of her husband's death.

It was her sister Josephine who told her, in broken sentences, veiled hints that revealed in half concealing. Her husband's friend Richards was there, too, near her. It was he who had been in the newspaper office when intelligence of the railroad disaster was received, with Brently Mallard's name leading the list of "killed." He had only taken the time to assure himself of its truth by a second telegram, and had hastened to forestall any less careful, less tender friend in bearing the sad message.

She did not hear the story as many women have heard the same, with a paralyzed inability to accept its significance. She wept at once, with sudden, wild abandonment, in her sister's arms. When the storm of grief had spent itself she went away to her room alone. She would have no one follow her.

There stood, facing the open window, a comfortable, roomy armchair. Into this she sank, pressed down by a physical exhaustion that haunted her body and seemed to reach into her soul.

She could see in the open square before her house the tops of trees that were all aquiver with the new spring life. The delicious breath of rain was in the air. In the street below a peddler was crying his wares. The notes of a distant song which some one was singing reached her faintly, and countless sparrows were twittering in the eaves.

There were patches of blue sky showing here and there through the clouds that had met and piled above the other in the west facing her window.

She sat with her head thrown back upon the cushion of the chair quite motionless, except when a sob came up into her throat and shook her, as a child who has cried itself to sleep continues to sob in its dreams.

She was young, with a fair, calm face, whose lines bespoke repression and even a certain strength. But now there was a dull stare in her eyes, whose gaze was fixed away off yonder on one of those patches of blue sky. It was not a glance of reflection, but rather indicated a suspension of intelligent thought.

There was something coming to her and she was waiting for it, fearfully. What was it? She did not know; it was too subtle and elusive to name. But she felt it, creeping out of the sky, reaching toward her through the sounds, the scents, the color that filled the air.

Now her bosom rose and fell tumultuously. She was beginning to recognize this thing that was approaching to possess her, and she was striving to beat it back with her will—as powerless as her two white slender hands would have been.

When she abandoned herself a little whispered word escaped her slightly parted lips. She said it over and over under her breath: "Free, free, free!" The vacant stare and the look of terror that had followed it went from her eyes. They stayed keen and bright. Her pulse beat fast, and the coursing blood warmed and relaxed every inch of her body.

She did not stop to ask if it were not a monstrous joy that held her. A clear and exalted perception enabled her to dismiss the suggestion as trivial.

She knew that she would weep again when she saw the kind, tender hands folded in death; the face that had never looked save with love upon her, fixed and gray and dead. But she saw beyond that bitter moment a long procession of years to come that would belong to her absolutely. And she opened and spread her arms out to them in welcome.

There would be no one to live for during those coming years; she would live for herself. There would be no powerful will bending her in that blind persistence with which men and women believe they have a right to impose a private will upon a fellow-creature. A kind intention or a cruel intention made the act seem no less a crime as she looked upon it in that brief moment of illumination.

And yet she had loved him—sometimes. Often she had not. What did it matter! What could love, the unsolved mystery, count for in face of this possession of self-assertion which she suddenly recognized as the strongest impulse of her being!

"Free! Body and soul free!" she kept whispering.

Josephine was kneeling before the closed door with her lips to the keyhole, imploring for admission. "Louise, open the door! I beg; open the door—you will make yourself ill. What are you doing, Louise? For heaven's sake open the door."

"Go away. I am not making myself ill." No; she was drinking in a very elixir of life through that open window.

Her fancy was running riot along those days ahead of her. Spring days, and summer days, and all sorts of days that would be her own. She breathed a quick prayer that life might be long. It was only yesterday she had thought with a shudder that life might be long.

She arose at length and opened the door to her sister's importunities. There was a feverish triumph in her eyes, and she carried herself unwittingly like a goddess of

Victory. She clasped her sister's waist, and together they descended the stairs. Richards stood waiting for them at the bottom.

Some one was opening the front door with a latchkey. It was Brently Mallard who entered, a little travel-stained, composedly carrying his grip-sack and umbrella. He had been far from the scene of accident, and did not even know there had been one. He stood amazed at Josephine's piercing cry; at Richards's quick motion to screen him from the view of his wife.

But Richards was too late.

When the doctors came they said she had died of heart disease—of joy that kills.

Short as this story is, it has many of the same elements of fiction we might examine in a five-hundred-page novel.

ELEMENTS OF FICTION

The Narrator/Point of View

Short stories and novels both depend greatly for their effects on the *point of view* of the tale. That point of view limits what we see and how we respond to it; we see people and events through the eyes of the person telling about them. In the previous discussion of the speaker/narrative voice in chapter 2 (31–35), we looked at the ways in which our responses are often determined by what we think of the *narrator,* the person telling the story. If we do not trust that narrator for some reason—if we see the narrator as an **unreliable narrator**—we need to look beyond the narrator, trying to see the real situation or understand the other characters without the narrator's prejudices obscuring our vision of them. Questions about who is telling us the story thus become vital from the very opening lines of a piece of prose fiction.

Sometimes the narrator is so completely reliable as to be an **omniscient,** or all-knowing, **narrator.** We accept without question what an omniscient narrator tells us about when and where a story takes place; the events are all taken as "true," and we don't need to make allowances for the narrator's human fallibility. We do not, for example, ask whether the narrator might have misremembered the sequence of events or forgotten crucial details. (Think, for example, of how unsatisfying a mystery story would be if the narrator "forgot" to tell us clues we needed to solve the mystery.)

We also take for granted the omniscient narrator's ability to enter the characters' minds and correctly convey to us what the characters think and feel. With god-like powers, the narrator is able to interpret accurately for us the motives and emotions of *all* the characters, without any intervening motives or emotions distorting those interpretations. This narrator exists only to tell the story and plays no part in the story itself. In some cases, the omniscient narrator can become so invisible that we feel as if the story is simply telling itself.

In some works of prose fiction, a **limited omniscient narrator** is created. This narrator seems to be omniscient and to have the omniscient narrator's power to know all about the events and characters. Yet, despite this power, the narrative point of view is limited: the omniscient narrator focuses primarily on one character, giving that character's view of things. Thus, though the narrator may theoretically know all, it conveys the limited perspective of that one character, reporting that character's fallible view of a situation and that character's prejudices.

Consider, for instance, the narrator in Kate Chopin's "The Story of an Hour"; that narrator is clearly limited. Although the narrator occasionally shifts away from Mrs. Mallard's point of view, the emphasis is on her reactions and feelings. We do not, for example, get the point of view of Brently—or even much of the points of view of Richards or Josephine—and we recognize that these other characters might tell different versions of the story than does this limited narrator. Brently, for instance, would probably have a very different perspective on his marriage than does Louise. In recognizing that fact, we also recognize the extent to which Chopin directs our responses to the story's events. In large part, we experience life as Mrs. Mallard does and so experience with her a sense of women's subjugation to even the most loving of husbands. Had the point of view been Brently's, or even Josephine's, that idea about marriage could not have been developed. In other words, though largely reliable, the narrator of "The Story of an Hour" asks us to accept Mrs. Mallard's view of things. As in other stories with a limited narrator, we trust the narrator, but we must also recognize its limitations.

Both of the types of narration we have been considering—omniscient narration and limited omniscient narration—are types of **third-person narration.** In a third-person narration, there is no "I," and all the characters are referred to in the third person, as "he," "she," or "they," or by name or role (as "Mrs. Mallard," or "her sister," or "the maid"). In such narrations, the narrator is outside the story. In other types of stories, the narrator is a part of the story, becoming both teller and character. In such a case, the narration is a **first-person narration,** with an "I" (or very occasionally a "we") telling the story. We are usually made aware of the "I" in the opening lines of the story. For instance, in Tony Eprile's "A True History of the Notorious Mr. Edward Hyde" (1419–26), we learn at the beginning: "'Yde's the name. Edward 'yde . . . or Hyde, as educated folk like yourself would have it." A first-person narrator is, by definition, limited. Like any of us, a first-person narrator is limited by personal experience, values, and beliefs.

Changing the form of narration is sometimes the foundation for a "retelling." For example, in *The Strange Case of Dr. Jekyll and Mr. Hyde,* Robert Louis Stevenson uses a limited omniscient narrator. Much of the story is filtered through the consciousness of Dr. Jekyll's lawyer and longtime friend, Mr. Utterson. As both a friend and a lawyer, Mr. Utterson is privy to many of the details of Dr. Jekyll's life; he cannot, however, know everything. He is presumably somewhat detached and very rational, bringing to the story a concern and sympathy for his friend but also a lawyerly objectivity we feel we can trust. In his retelling, Eprile uses a different narrator, Mr. Hyde. In the process, he also changes our relationship to the tale. We now feel a sympathy for Mr. Hyde that the original is without. Stevenson's story keeps Mr. Hyde at a distance, suggesting that he is the epitome of a finally unknowable evil. By making Mr. Hyde the narrator, Eprile suggests otherwise: "Evil" is a matter of perspective, and flawed humans fall into vice for all too understandable reasons.

How we respond to a narrator thus often determines how we understand a story's meanings. We bring to literature the same kinds of reactions and judgments we apply in real life. When a particular acquaintance tells us about something that has happened, we may hear the story with some skepticism, knowing that this person tends to exaggerate his own virtues and accomplishments; another acquaintance, we know, may allow his own insecurity or anxiety to magnify the fearfulness of a situation. Some tellers use humor to disguise serious issues; others inadvertently treat the most comic events with a lugubrious seriousness. Just as in life, in literature we need to get to know the teller, to learn how reliable the narrative is.

EXERCISES: TRYING IT OUT

1. Retell "The Story of an Hour" from the point of view of one of the other characters—Brently, Richards, or Josephine. How does the change in point of view alter the story?
2. Many opening lines of novels are justly famous for creating a vivid sense of the narrator. Read the following opening lines and consider what they lead you to expect from the narrator. Is the narrator omniscient or limited? Is the narrator credible? What can you infer about the narrator from the language of the narration?

   a.   It is a truth universally acknowledged, that a single man in possession of a good fortune must be in want of a wife.

   However little known the feelings or views of such a man may be on his first entering a neighbourhood, this truth is so well fixed in the minds of the surrounding families, that he is considered as the rightful property of someone or other of their daughters.

   From Jane Austen, *Pride and Prejudice*

   b.   You don't know about me, without you have read a book by the name of "The Adventures of Tom Sawyer," but that ain't no matter. That book was made by Mr. Mark Twain, and he told the truth, mainly. There was things which he stretched, but mainly he told the truth. That is nothing. I never seen anybody but lied, one time or another, without it was Aunt Polly, or the widow, or maybe Mary.

   From Mark Twain, *The Adventures of Huckleberry Finn*

   c.   Whether I shall turn out to be the hero of my own life, or whether that station will be held by anybody else, these pages must show. To begin my life with the beginning of my life, I record that I was born (as I have been informed and believe) on a Friday, at twelve o'clock at night. It must be remarked that the clock began to strike, and I began to cry, simultaneously.

   From Charles Dickens, *David Copperfield*

   d.   If you really want to hear about it, the first thing you'll probably want to know is where I was born, and what my lousy childhood was like, and how my parents were occupied all before they had me, and all that David Copperfield kind of crap, but I don't feel like going into it, if you want to know the truth. In the first place, that stuff bores me, and in the second place, my parents would have about two hemorrhages apiece if I told about anything like that, especially my father. They're *nice* and all—I'm not saying that—but they're touchy as hell.

From J. D. Salinger, *The Catcher in the Rye*

Plot

The *plot* of a piece of fiction is the story line: what happens. If someone were to ask you what a story was about, you would probably respond with a summary of the plot. At the same time, however, plot involves much more than just the events of the story. It involves our understanding of how those events are related, of the causes and effects of what is happening. The novelist E. M. Forster defined plot as follows:

> Let us define a plot. We have defined a story as a narrative of events arranged in their time-sequence. A plot is also a narrative of events, the emphasis falling on causality. "The king died and then the queen died" is a story. "The king died, and then the queen died of grief" is a plot. The time-sequence is preserved, but the sense of causality overshadows it. Or again: "The queen died, no one knew why, until it was discovered that it was through grief at the death of the king." This is a plot with a mystery in it, a form capable of high development. [. . .] Consider the death of the queen. If it is in a story we say "and then?" If it is in a plot we ask "why?"

Think about how what Forster says might apply to "The Story of an Hour." The *story* might be "Louise Mallard was informed of her husband's death in a railroad accident. When he later walked through the door, she died." The *plot,* as Forster defines it, tells us much more: it tells us Louise Mallard's reaction to the news and the reason *why* she died.

It is sometimes helpful to break the plot down into separate elements, particularly those of the **conflict** and the **resolution.** Stories generally depend on some type of "problem," whether that problem is emotional, physical, or social. That problem leads to a conflict, perhaps between characters or within the main character's mind. In "The Story of an Hour," for example, the conflict is internal: Mrs. Mallard is at first torn between grief and joy at the news of her husband's death. Both she and the reader are somewhat shocked to learn that joy is, in fact, the emotion that comes to dominate. At the end of a story, the conflict usually disappears; in the resolution, the problem is "solved." Sometimes a **false resolution** occurs before the real one. In "The Story of an Hour," for instance, we may think we have reached a resolution when we see Louise recognizing and embracing her sense of freedom. The real resolution, however, occurs when Brently returns—and Louise dies. Her death, not her emotional freedom, provides the final end to the emotional conflict.

Our understanding of cause and effect, of conflict and resolution, depends a great deal on our understanding of the **chronology,** or the time sequence, of the plot. It is important to realize, however, that fiction writers sometimes disrupt the chronology of their stories. Often they provide us with **flashbacks,** which look back to and explain events that occurred prior to the story. In "The Story of an Hour," the flashbacks are very brief: we are told, for instance, that Brently had "never looked save with love" upon Louise and that "she had loved him—sometimes." Frequently, fiction writers also look ahead: by using **foreshadowing,** they anticipate what will happen later in the story. Characters may pass a cemetery or discuss death; by this means, the author could be hinting at deaths to come (as happens, for example, in "A Good Man Is Hard to Find" on 393–403). Usually such hints are deliberately subtle and easy to miss; most authors do not want to undermine the **suspense** of the story, the delay of information that fuels our desire to keep reading to find out what happens next. Only at the end of the story—or perhaps only when we reread it—do we understand that foreshadowing has been used.

Because most short stories are short, they usually confine themselves to one plot. Longer works, however, particularly novels, may have more than one plot. Generally, a main plot holds most of our interest, but we may also learn other stories along the way, usually the stories of minor, less prominent characters. These less central plots are called **subplots,** and in long novels there may be quite a few of them. Often, however, by the end of the novel the subplots have flowed into the main plot: the details they provide eventually prove significant to our understanding of the main plot.

EXERCISES: TRYING IT OUT

1. If you were to expand "The Story of an Hour," what flashbacks might you include? What subplots would you develop?
2. Unlike life, stories rarely contain insignificant plot details. The mere fact that a detail is present often means that it is significant. (That is why in a story or novel we rarely see characters engaged in the mundane events of everyday life: they don't usually go grocery shopping or watch television or play computer games unless those activities are significant to our understanding of the story.) Read one of the following stories and imagine how its meanings and moods would be different if you removed from it a minor plot detail.

    "A Rose for Emily": Assume Emily's relatives never came to stay with her.

    "The Yellow Wallpaper": Assume the narrator has not just had a baby.

    "A & P": Assume Queenie walks into the store by herself.

Character

As we saw in chapter 2 (35–45), characters are the people in a work. We may see these characters as highly realistic, with full histories (even if we don't know those full histories) and realistic psychologies. In other words, we might consider them very much like ourselves. As we saw earlier (35–36), these fully developed and lifelike characters are often called *round* characters. Other characters, however, remain shadowy, perhaps intentionally so. These *flat* characters may seem almost like objects, part of the landscape rather than fully functioning human beings. Both kinds of characters can be highly effective, but we do tend to respond to them differently.

EXERCISE: TRYING IT OUT

Mrs. Mallard in "The Story of an Hour" is very much a round character. What are we told about her that makes us see her as a real person?

_____

Characters can also be divided into **major** and **minor characters.** The major characters are those we learn about and care about the most; the minor characters are less central to the story. In "The Story of an Hour" Louise Mallard is the only major character (longer works will usually have more major characters); Richards, Josephine, and Brently are all minor characters. The character at the center of the story—often the hero or heroine, though the character is not always "heroic"—is called the **protagonist.** (Louise Mallard is the protagonist of "The Story of an Hour.") In many stories, the protagonist meets his or her match in an **antagonist,** a character who attempts to thwart the protagonist; perhaps Brently could be considered an unwitting antagonist in Chopin's story, and Mr. Hyde could certainly be considered the antagonist in Stevenson's story (and the protagonist in Eprile's).

We learn about characters in many different ways: by what we are told by the narrator, by what the characters themselves do and say, by what other characters say about them and how they interact with them. Just as in life, much of what we learn may be indirect. For example, in "The Story of an Hour," what we learn about Brently we learn indirectly, from Louise's reaction to the news of his death and perhaps from his friend Richards. Because Richards is such a considerate friend, we might reasonably assume that Brently also is considerate. Because Louise thinks of Brently's "kind, tender hands" and says he "had never looked save with love upon her," we might also decide that he is a loving husband. At the same time, Louise's joy at the news of his death might suggest that he is a controlling husband who does not allow his wife a free expression of her feelings and selfhood. Putting these seemingly contradictory pictures together, we might decide that Brently's control over his wife is unconscious, that his consideration masks deeply held but probably unexamined beliefs about the role of women. We have not been told such things directly, but we might reasonably conclude them from what we are told.

In making inferences about character (or anything else, for that matter), we must stay with what we know, not what we imagine on our own. For example, given Louise's reaction to the news of her husband's apparent death, a reader might imagine that her husband had verbally or physically abused her, but there is nothing in the story to suggest that that is the case. If we say that Brently abused Louise, we are writing our own story, not really responding to Chopin's.

Setting/Atmosphere

In chapter 2, we looked at setting, the time and place of a story, poem, or play (45–60). Descriptions of setting are often especially important in prose fiction. Where and when a story is set can tell us many important things about how we are meant to respond. For instance, a story set in New York in 1850 will display a different set of beliefs and values and lifestyles than a story set in New York in 2004—or 2020. Similarly, stories set in the same year but in very different places—in a small Midwest town, say, or in Paris—will evoke different sets of behaviors from the characters and different responses from the reader. So important is setting to our understanding of the meaning of a story that writers carefully decide how to describe their settings, for the descriptive language they use is an important part of what we as readers see and feel.

Think about what we learn about the setting of "The Story of an Hour." The story is set during a spring day and takes place within a single hour. Presumably it is set in Chopin's own time; the story was written in 1894, a date that seems consistent with details within the short story: the railroad is a major source of transportation and a telegram is sent to verify the report of Brently's death. From what we know of that time period, we may suspect that women had few opportunities to express themselves (at that time, for instance, women of the middle class did not work outside the home, nor could women vote). What we know of the time helps us make sense of Louise's reactions to the news of her husband's death.

EXERCISE: TRYING IT OUT

Imagine "The Story of an Hour" reset in the current year. What changes would you have to make to the story—and why? How well would the story work in a contemporary setting?

No setting is—or can be—described in purely neutral tones. The language that is used helps create our responses. For instance, a warm day may be described in ways that make us feel the sweat trickle uncomfortably down our backs, or the language may suggest a comfortable warmth. How the setting is described may contribute to the **atmosphere** or mood of the work. For example, in "The Story of an Hour," outside Louise's window

> . . . the tops of trees . . . were all aquiver with the new spring life. The delicious breath of rain was in the air. In the street below a peddler was crying his wares. The notes of a distant song which some one was singing reached her faintly, and countless sparrows were twittering in the eaves.
>
> There were patches of blue sky showing here and there through the clouds that had met and piled above the other in the west facing her window.

This is more than mere description; through this description Chopin creates important ideas. We share Louise's point of view, and as we look through the open window and see the spring scene and watch the clouds part, we begin to contrast the freedom of the world outside her bedroom with the claustrophobia she has felt inside her house and inside her marriage. The setting thus helps us understand Louise's joy at seeing the expansive world outside her window. In short, setting underscores what we learn about the character.

EXERCISES: TRYING IT OUT

1. Rewrite the preceding passage from "The Story of an Hour," changing what Louise and we see outside her open window. How does your revision change the atmosphere of the story?

2. Consider the setting of one of the following. How would our responses to the story's characters, events, and moods change if the setting were changed as indicated?

> "Araby" is set in the twenty-first-century United States.
>
> "The Yellow Wallpaper" is set in a big-city apartment.

Theme

The *theme* of a story is its message, the point that the author wants us to understand not only about the characters in the story but also about the people and world outside the story. Although *theme* is sometimes defined as the topic of a work ("Monsters and Heroes" might be called the "theme" of chapter 8, for instance), we would like to encourage you to think about theme as more equivalent to the thesis of an essay. (For a discussion of the thesis of an essay, see 159–60.) Like a thesis, a theme should be able to be expressed in a sentence conveying an opinion. For instance, from what we learn of the plot, characters, and setting—from many of the ideas we have discussed previously—we might conclude that the theme of "The Story of an Hour" is that at the end of the nineteenth century women were so constrained even in loving marriages that only death could set them free. We might reach our conclusion about this theme from the sympathy that the story creates for Louise (which is partly created by the limited omniscient narration), the knowledge we have that Brently is a loving husband, and the resolution of the plot (with Louise's death). Nowhere does Chopin state her theme explicitly—authors of literary works rarely do—but she does nevertheless do more than present us with the topic of nineteenth-century marriage. Through her story she conveys also an attitude toward marriage.

To determine the theme of "The Story of an Hour," then, a reader would need to identify Chopin's attitude toward Louise's marriage. That means moving well beyond the facts of the story and avoiding the trap of falling into summary. The idea that Louise is unhappy in her marriage is not a theme, for instance; it is simply a fact of the story. If all readers would immediately agree with a particular idea, it is probably not the theme, but rather a summary of a basic plot element. In "The Story of an Hour," then, the theme is less *that* Louise is unhappy in her marriage—we would all agree about that—than it is *why* she is unhappy in her marriage (some might see the problem as a problem in all marriages, some in Louise's kind of marriage, some in Louise herself).

Most themes are also more than simple "morals." Because good story writers are usually looking at the complexities of human behaviors and motivations, writers seldom use simplistic moral statements as their themes. For instance, one might say that the moral of "The Story of an Hour" is that husbands need to be considerate of their wives to make them happy. However, although "The Story of an Hour" does convey that idea, the theme goes beyond that moral; after all, by the standards of the day, Brently *was* considerate of his wife. Themes are usually more complicated than morals. Indeed, good literature is so rich that a single work may have more than one theme, and readers may even disagree about exactly what those themes are.

When trying to determine a story's themes, don't overlook the title. Consider, for example, the title of "The Story of an Hour." The story does take place in a single hour, but the title implies much more than that: it implicitly asks us to contrast the events and emotions of that hour with those of Mrs. Mallard's entire marriage. Perhaps the title asks us to believe that Mrs. Mallard has lived more in that hour than in years of marriage. For another example, think about the title of Alice Walker's "Everyday Use" (564–70); it helps us see the story as a comment on the value of the familiar objects we use every day. In many cases, titles gain their significance only by the end of the story; as a result, they deserve a second consideration by the reader, who might easily have missed the implications on first reading the title.

EXERCISE: TRYING IT OUT

Imagine changing one of the key elements of "The Story of an Hour"—perhaps the point of view, the characterization, or key plot details. How would your changes affect the theme of the story?

Fictional Form

Both short stories and novels are forms of prose fiction, the difference between the two being, most simply, a matter of length. A traditional definition of a short story is that it is a piece of prose fiction that can be read at one sitting. Of course, readers vary widely in what they would read at one sitting, but a rough rule of thumb is that a short story does not exceed about 75 pages. Obviously, this is a *very* rough guideline, so much so that sometimes a third category is created: the **novella,** which might be considered a long short story or a short novel. (Again, roughly speaking, a novella is about 75–150 pages long. Robert Louis Stevenson's *The Strange Case of Dr. Jekyll and Mr. Hyde,* contained in this anthology, is an example of a novella.)

Because of the differences in the ways in which short stories and novels are read, they tend to do different things. As a general rule, the short story is closer to poetry than the novel is: both poems (which are usually short) and short stories often depend on an intensity of emotional effect, one that would be disrupted if the work were laid aside several times. Usually, a short story restricts itself to one or two settings and only a handful of characters. The emphasis is often on a single dramatic event and the characters' reactions to it. For example, the events of "The Story of an Hour" literally take place in only one hour.

The focus on a single setting is usually matched by a focus on a single character's reaction to a single event. Thus, in Chopin's story, though we learn a great deal about Mrs. Mallard's current emotional state, we learn little about her life history or even about her marriage. Instead, the story focuses almost exclusively on her reaction to the news of her husband's death and his subsequent return. In this story, as in many short stories, it is the character's psychology that we are interested in. Such an interest in psychology is also evident in stories that examine the deterioration of a character's mental state—Edgar Allan Poe's "The Tell-Tale Heart" or Charlotte Perkins Gilman's "The Yellow Wallpaper," for instance.

If the short story tends to be psychological, the novel tends to be social. Even if there is a single main character in a novel, the minor characters are often fully

Questions to Ask about Fiction

1. How long is the piece of prose fiction? Would it be likely to be read at one sitting or at several? To what extent does the length of the work encourage or inhibit the development of particular kinds of characters? To what extent does length encourage or inhibit particular kinds of themes?
2. If the piece is short, what one "effect" or emotion does it produce? If the piece is long, what kind of world or society is created?
3. What does the reader learn about who is telling the story? If the narrator is omniscient, is that omniscience full or limited? If the narration is a first-person narration, how fully does the narrator participate in the events of the story? Is the narrator an unreliable narrator or a relatively objective observer? How might the narrator's character traits influence how the story is told?
4. How would you summarize the story of the work? How would you summarize the plot?
5. List the major characters in the work. What do we know about them? What can we infer about their values, beliefs, and motivations?
6. How is the setting of the story described? What atmosphere do the words and images create? How does setting reflect theme? Influence the characters' emotions and behaviors? Direct our responses?
7. Consider when and where the story is set. What beliefs and lifestyles are associated with the story's time and place?
8. How would you define the themes of the story?

detailed, given life histories and inner lives of their own. These characters interact with one another and react to events, creating a sense of social complication and complexity. Because of the ability of the novel to mirror these complications and complexities of social life, novels, more often than short stories, comment on issues of social class, money, and gender inequality. They may comment on current social practices (as Charles Dickens does, for example, in his attack on the welfare system in *Oliver Twist,* or as Jane Austen does in her examination of marriage in her novels). Novels are often crowded with the details of everyday life, and from them we may learn about a particular time and country's clothing, typical meals (and the time of day of those meals), transportation, schools, and expected behaviors. Put simply, the novel has the space to contain a world and a lifetime; the short story focuses on a small corner of that world and, often, a short moment in time.

Work Cited

Forster, E. M. *Aspects of the Novel.* New York: Harcourt Harvest, 1955.

4

Reading Poetry

Whatever their current thoughts on the subject, many students loved poetry when they were young children; they loved the sounds of the words and the making of rhyme, and they loved the beat of the rhythms and the sights and moods created by the images. However, when they grow up, some of those same young poetry lovers become wary of poetry, fearful that they won't "get it" or convinced that others are reading into poems meanings that their authors could never have intended. Some of that fear and suspicion comes from a sense that poetry was not meant to be analyzed but simply enjoyed; some of it comes from a lack of familiarity with the poetic tradition and with the language of literary analysis. We do not at all believe, though, that analysis and appreciation are somehow antithetical. In fact, we believe quite the opposite, and we hope to convince you here that a familiarity with the process of literary analysis can help you appreciate poetry as much as you did when you were a child, though of course differently.

The Speaker

If you have read chapters 2 and 3, you know that one of the most important elements of any piece of literature is the speaker and that speakers come in many types. Some reveal themselves as full-blown personalities from the very beginning: we know who they are, where they come from, what motivates their thoughts and actions. Other speakers, however, are considerably less visible. They may, in fact, not seem to reveal themselves at all. The difference between these two kinds of speakers is often the difference between a speaker who speaks in the *first person* (using "I") and one who speaks in the *third person* (never using "I," and referring to all characters by name or role or as "he," "she," or "they"; a third-person speaker may even seem to speak in a kind of disembodied voice).

Although the concept of a first- or third-person narrator is more commonly discussed in analyses of fiction, it can also be applied to the reading of poetry, as we saw in the discussion of Robert Browning's "Porphyria's Lover" in chapter 2 (32–33). The first-person speaker of Browning's poem is, as we saw earlier, a central character in the poem. He is clearly not the poet but rather a fictional murderer speaking of his crime.

Sometimes, however, the first-person speaker of a poem is less clearly fictional, and a poet may seem to be writing about himself and his own experiences. That is the case in

Matthew Arnold's "Dover Beach" (see 21), which is thought to have been written when Arnold was staying at Dover Beach during his honeymoon. When we read "Ah, love, let us be true / To one another!" we may assume that Arnold is the speaker and that he is addressing his new wife. That assumption may be strengthened if we realize that the sadness of the poem and the lament for the ebbing of the "Sea of Faith" correspond to the themes and moods of Arnold's other writings, in which he expresses concern for the loss of religious and social certainties. It would, however, be a mistake to identify the poet and the speaker too closely. Though the poem contains many of Arnold's beliefs and anxieties, it is probably unrealistic to believe that anyone could—or perhaps would want to—express those beliefs and anxieties so articulately and poetically on his honeymoon night. As soon as the reader recognizes that the central event of the poem is at least partly fictionalized, it becomes clear that the speaker himself must be fictionalized as well.

In fact, often the historical evidence outside a work suggests that the writer and speaker *must* be different. For example, the speaker of "The Dover Bitch," Anthony Hecht's parody of Arnold's poem (see 23), *cannot* be Hecht himself. Because Hecht was born long after Arnold died, he could *not* have known the "girl" in Arnold's poem, though the speaker of "The Dover Bitch" does know her. So generally, it is best to assume that the speaker of a poem (as of other types of literature) is not the author unless the reader has specific evidence, perhaps drawn from the author's biography or other writings, demonstrating that the two voices match.

THE LANGUAGE OF POETRY

When most of us think about poetry, we think immediately about the difference between poetic language and the language of everyday talk. Whereas short stories and plays often attempt to imitate everyday speech as closely as possible, poems often use a language of their own. After all, how many of us speak in rhyme or in conscious rhythm? In fact, some of what we associate with poetry has given it a bad name. When we don't trust someone's sentiments, we may accuse that person of being "flowery" in speech or writing and then, with a sneer, we say that the language sounds "too poetic." People sometimes think of poets as cryptic, writing a mysterious kind of secret language understood only by other poets or members of a kind of literature club. It is true that the language of poetry is often different from the language we use elsewhere. It tends to communicate its ideas much less directly than do other forms of writing. But an understanding of the elements of poetic language and structure, what is called the poem's **prosody,** should help you solve the poetic puzzle.

Word Choice

Like any good writer, a poet pays considerable attention to the words he chooses, taking care to consider not only the literal meanings of words, their **denotations,** but also the emotional meanings they convey, their **connotations.** Poets are often especially interested in conveying strong emotion; in fact, in one of the most famous definitions of *poetry,* poet William Wordsworth said that "poetry is the spontaneous overflow of powerful feelings: it takes its origin from emotion recollected in tranquility." When you read a poem, then, you want to pay attention not only to what the words mean but also to how their connotations convey powerful emotion.

Think again about Theodore Roethke's "My Papa's Waltz," which we discussed in chapter 2 (67–68). As we noted there, the poem has elicited contradictory responses from readers, some of whom see it as a poem about child abuse and others of whom see it as a poem about a father and son playing roughly with one another. For those who lean toward the second interpretation, the use of words such as *romped,* with its implications of childhood fun, and *waltz,* with its implications of romance and gentility, makes it difficult to see the poem as anything other than vibrant and lighthearted. On the other hand, for those who see the situation of the poem as a frightening one, the connotations of a word such as *death* cannot be ignored. Any reading of the poem must consider the strong connotations of all of these words and account for the *tone,* or mood, that they help create.

"in Just-" by e. e. cummings is another example of a poem that uses words with powerful connotations:

e. e. cummings (1894–1962)

in Just- _____ *1923*

```
        in Just-
        spring      when the world is mud-
        luscious the little
        lame balloonman

        whistles      far      and wee                              5

        and eddieandbill come
        running from marbles and
        piracies and it's
        spring

        when the world is puddle-wonderful                         10

        the queer
        old balloonman whistles
        far      and      wee
        and bettyandisbel come dancing

        from hop-scotch and jump-rope and                          15

        it's
        spring
        and
            the

                goat-footed                                        20

        balloonMan      whistles
        far
        and
        wee
```

On first reading, this seems almost a nonsense poem. The poet has made up his own words—*puddle-wonderful* and *mud-luscious,* for example—and he has put familiar words, such as *wee,* into unfamiliar contexts. Even before we puzzle over the meanings of the words, though, we begin to get some sense of their power. *Wee* makes us think of "wee" things, childish and small, even precious. There can be nothing threatening in something "wee." Hopscotch, jump rope, marbles, and childhood piracies, even spring itself—all have positive connotations that make us think of a time of youth and innocence, a time of sunny days and childish pleasures. At the same time, though they may simply describe a physical reality, words such as *lame* and *goat-footed* have powerful negative connotations. Compare either to a word such as *handicapped* or *disabled,* and you will see that there is more than physical description involved. (Think, for example, of why we call excuses *lame.*)

Even before we know what the poem means, then, we know that its words evoke some very different, even contrasting, moods. The combination of words with positive and negative connotations gives "in Just-" an ambiguous tone. Is the atmosphere lighthearted or ominous? By determining what tone of voice a reader should use when reading the poem aloud, you would be well on your way to resolving the tensions of the poem and discovering its theme.

EXERCISE: TRYING IT OUT

Rewrite "in Just-" in prose form, using words that have no strong connotations: try to describe the scene that cummings describes, but do so in language that is as neutral as possible. Then write a paragraph or two explaining how your version and his evoke different responses from the reader.

Figurative Language

Linguists tell us that in some ways all language is *figurative language;* that is, all language stands for something. To see that, you need only to think about how disappointed you would be if you ordered "chocolate cake" at a restaurant and someone handed you a piece of paper with the words "chocolate cake" printed nicely on it. Of course, some uses of language are considerably more figurative than others. Among writers, poets are the most apt to use highly figurative language; in other words, poetic language is more likely than other forms to imply something rather than state it directly.

Among the most common kinds of figurative language in all literature, but especially in poetry, is the *metaphor.* As we said in chapter 2 (63), metaphors (and *similes,* which are a special kind of metaphor) involve either an implied or an explicit comparison between two things. They are powerful because they allow the poet—or any writer—to explain the unfamiliar or elusive in terms of the familiar or tangible. When a lover says, for instance, that his beloved's eyes are "like diamonds," he gives us something to picture, helping us see the sparkle and shine more vividly. As with any comparison, a metaphor allows a writer to refer to two things at once, a particularly useful device in poetry, in which lots of meaning gets packed into a small space.

Consider, for instance, Sylvia Plath's riddle poem, "Metaphors" (see exercise on 19). That poem uses an **extended metaphor** (a metaphor of more than a line or two) to invite a comparison between poems and babies. In reading that comparison, we get a new sense of just how similar are the birth of a child and the birth of a poem, and because we are familiar with the love a mother feels for her child, the use of the metaphor may give us new insight into how the "mother" of a poem may feel about her poetic offspring. The metaphor thus helps us to see in the processes of birth and creativity something we have perhaps not seen before.

Metaphors are not always wholly serious, however. They also help us play with language. Look, for instance, at Shakespeare's "My mistress's eyes are nothing like the sun" (425), a poem that uses metaphor to show that even the best poem or metaphor falls short of an intense reality. Poets who have compared their lovers' eyes to the sun (or some other natural wonder) have not seen the sun for what it is, Shakespeare tells us; nor have they understood the full value and richness of their love.

Because they usually create word pictures, metaphors, including similes are often part of the visual patterns, the *imagery,* of a poem. In poetry, images often help to create the meaning of the poem. In "Stopping by Woods" (61), the images of winter and silence combine to create a feeling of melancholy; we know what it is like to feel enveloped by cold, silence, and solitude, all evoked by the images of the snow falling silently on a snow-filled scene populated only by the man and his horse. Or consider the imagery of Langston Hughes's "Harlem" (938). We see so vividly the images of concentrated power that it is difficult not to feel the uneasiness created by the anticipation of an explosion.

Poetic imagery, whether in the form of metaphors or just visual patterns, often functions as a **symbol,** which means that it often functions as a representative of something else, usually some kind of universal concept. Poets, like other writers, frequently use some fairly traditional symbols. For example, because it is associated with fertility and birth in the plant and animal worlds, springtime is often associated with youth and youthful sexuality. That traditional association might prove meaningful in any reading of "in Just-." Similarly, because it is associated with the end of the year, bare trees, and a sterile-looking landscape, winter is often associated with death or an inward-looking solitude. Those associations might be relevant to a reading of Frost's "Stopping by Woods." Other traditional symbolic associations include the association of colors with various emotions (red for passion, green for envy or growth, white for purity, and so forth) and of natural elements with various life forces (air is often associated with the breath of life or an intangible spirituality, and fire is often associated with passion, for instance).

In analyzing poetry for its symbolic meaning, you will want to pay particular attention to what you know about poetic tradition. Although it can be fun and exciting to find a symbolic meaning in a poet's use of a particular image, it can also be dangerous. Tempting as it is to say "X symbolizes Y," you will usually want to be certain that there is some poetic convention or tradition behind your conclusion. You need to think about the writer's own culture and its storehouse of symbolic meanings, remembering that the symbolic associations common in one culture may not be common in another. (For a further discussion of how writers use symbols, read the sections "Psychological Criticism" and "Mythological or Archetypal Criticism" in appendix 3.)

Poets, like other writers, may also include in their writing references to people and events outside their works. Such references are called **allusions,** and they allow a poet to bring to bear on a very short poem a long literary or historical tradition. Look back at cummings's "in Just-." We mentioned earlier the negative connotations of *goat-footed,* but you may also have wondered why cummings used *goat-footed* to describe the balloonman rather than, for instance, *cow-footed.* An understanding of *goat-footed* as an allusion to classical mythology helps solve the puzzle: Pan, a figure from Greek mythology, was also goat-footed.

EXERCISE: TRYING IT OUT

Look up a discussion of Pan in an encyclopedia, in a book on classical mythology, or on the Web. How does what you learn from that discussion help you understand the possible allusion to Pan in cummings's "in Just-"? How does it influence your reading of the poem as a whole?

Because poems are shorter, less sustained works than plays and short stories, they also lend themselves easily to two other kinds of figurative language: **personification** and **paradox.** Personification involves the giving of human characteristics and personality to an inanimate being or even an idea. In "Death, be not proud" (see 95), poet John Donne uses personification when he addresses Death as if it were a person: "Death, thou shalt die," he says. Personification is usually a device that works best in relatively short works. To understand why, you need only to think about our likely response if someone spent a long time assigning human characteristics to something inanimate—as, for instance, the narrator of the short story "The Yellow Wallpaper" does (see 527–38). In part, it is her extensive use of personification that signifies her growing mental instability. Because personification involves the use of highly figurative language, the genres that tend more toward realism—short stories, plays, and essays—are far less likely to use it than is poetry.

For similar reasons, poetry generally makes more use of paradox than do longer works. The line from "Death, be not proud" quoted in the preceding paragraph contains not only personification but also, coincidentally, an instance of paradox. Paradox, which literally means "beyond what is thought," occurs when two contradictory ideas are considered equally believable. (The ideas of *complementarity* and *oxymoron,* which we discussed in chapters 1 and 2, both focus on the paradoxical.) In the line from Donne's poem, it seems unbelievable that death can die, but the paradox is resolved when one realizes that for Donne God resolves all paradoxes and the promise of an afterlife puts to death Death itself.

Closely related to the idea of paradox is the idea of *irony,* which comes into play when words say literally the opposite of what the speaker really means. Sometimes irony occurs with the use of either **understatement** or **hyperbole.** Understatement involves the deliberate and extreme diminishing of a response or idea, as if someone were to say "that was unusual" when he saw an alien creature. Hyperbole has the opposite effect: a speaker grossly exaggerates what she believes. "He looks like a Greek god" is probably an exaggeration if it is being said about a new boyfriend—or even a movie actor, for that matter.

Examples of understatement and hyperbole are common in literature. When Shakespeare writes, "Shall I compare thee to a summer's day? / Thou art more lovely and more temperate," he is using hyperbole. The Old English poet of *Beowulf* is especially well known for his use of understatement. When describing the attacks of the horrible monster Grendel, who every night cannibalizes men as they are sleeping, the *Beowulf* poet uses understatement to tell us mildly that "These were hard times."

RHYTHM AND RHYME

The Beat Goes On: Stress and Sense in Poetry

Although the vocabulary of poetic analysis may be unfamiliar to you, you probably already know the concepts behind it. If you have ever taken music lessons or if you listen to music often, you probably know that musicians think in terms of musical measures and beats. A waltz, for instance, has a very specific beat and rhythm. Here is the first section of Oscar Hammerstein II and Richard Rodgers's "Edelweiss," a waltz that will be familiar to those of you who have seen *The Sound of Music*:

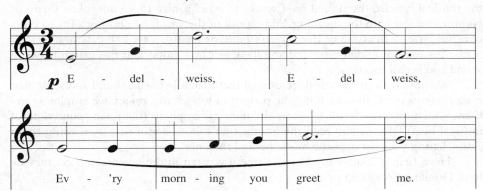

If you try clapping out the rhythms of this first section of "Edelweiss," you will probably get something like this:

CLAP	—	clap		CLAP	—	—		CLAP	—	clap		CLAP	—	—
E	-	del		weiss,				E	-	del		weiss,		

CLAP	—	clap		CLAP	clap	clap		CLAP	—	—		CLAP	—	—
Ev	-	'ry		morn	-ing	you		greet				me.		

The slow and soothing rhythms of "Edelweiss" are in part created by the musical beat (there is only one strong musical stress in a waltz measure).

Other pieces of music have different rhythms, and their beats would look different. Here is the music for one of the most famous sections of Beethoven's *Fifth Symphony,* followed by a representation of how we would clap out the beat:

Clap Clap Clap   CLAP — — | Clap Clap Clap | CLAP — —

The beat pattern is obviously very different from that of "Edelweiss," and the difference in rhythm is partly what gives the two pieces of music such a different feel. "Edelweiss" is lyrical and soothing; Beethoven's *Fifth* is thunderous and ominous. The moods are created by more than the beats, of course; the context of the music surrounding them and the pitch and loudness of the notes all contribute to the way the music asks us to respond. But no one who listens to music—whether that music is classical or current—would be surprised to hear that beat and rhythm are among the most important components of any musical composition.

The same is true for poetry, and we have spent as much time as we have on music to assure you that much of what we are about to say you have known since you first heard the sounds and rhythms of music and the sounds and rhythms of language. Like music, spoken language has a rhythm and a beat that convey meaning, and like the musical lyricist, the skilled poet works to synchronize those unspoken forms of communication with the meanings and moods of the words he chooses. (Try to put a cheerful lyric to the tune of Beethoven's *Fifth,* or try to create a threatening lyric to match the tune of "Edelweiss," and you'll see just how important this match between sound and verbal meaning is.)

We now turn to the consideration of that match between sound and sense that makes poetry work. In examining the pattern of sounds in a poem, we employ **scansion,** which involves deciding where the metrical emphasis (the poetic equivalent of musical beat) falls. As you read the poems that follow, begin first by reading them aloud, letting your ear hear the music behind the lines.

Here, first, is "Batter my heart," a poem written in the seventeenth century by John Donne, an Anglican priest:

JOHN DONNE (1572–1631)

Batter my heart, three-personed God _____ *1633*

Batter my heart, three-personed God; for You
As yet but knock, breathe, shine, and seek to mend;
That I may rise and stand, o'erthrow me, and bend
Your force to break, blow, burn, and make me new.
I, like an usurped town, to another due,
Labor to admit You, but O, to no end;
Reason, Your viceroy in me, me should defend,
But is captíved, and proves weak or untrue.
Yet dearly I love You, and would be lovèd fain,

But am betrothed unto Your enemy.
Divorce me, untie or break that knot again;
Take me to You, imprison me, for I,
Except You enthrall me, never shall be free,
Nor ever chaste, except You ravish me.   •

A first reading of the poem will probably yield at least a vague notion of violence. Many of the poet's word choices—*batter, knock, o'erthrow, break, blow, burn,* and so forth—ask us to envision a violent struggle, in this case a struggle that the speaker welcomes. As much as their meanings, the sounds of the words reinforce the speaker's notion that the struggle is a necessary and life-affirming, even life-giving, one. Here's how we would **scan** (mark the metrical beat of) the first several lines of the poem. (The **accent,** or **stress, mark** over a word or syllable indicates where the emphasis would go; the curved half-circle indicates a word or syllable with little or no stress.)

Batter my heart, three-personed God; for You

As yet but knock, breathe, shine, and seek to mend;

That I may rise and stand, o'erthrow* me, and bend

Your force to break, blow, burn, and make me new.

Notice how many of the words that are stressed are those that pertain to the actions of the "three-personed God" (the Christian Trinity of the Father, Son, and Holy Spirit) to whom the speaker is addressing his poem: *batter, knock, breathe, shine, seek, o'erthrow, break, blow, burn,* and *make* all emphasize the three-personed God's muscular and energetic power, giving His actions more significance and making the speaker seem like the passive recipient of the actions he is describing.

The **meter,** or rhythm, of the poem thus reinforces the speaker's notion that God is the power behind the action and that a person's job is simply to accept with joy the actions directed at him. The significance of the metrical pattern is perhaps made even more striking when one considers that the "typical" poetic pattern in English is that of the alternation between an unstressed and a stressed syllable (˘ ´). Donne often breaks the common pattern by juxtaposing several stressed symbols, thereby calling more attention to the words that get stressed unexpectedly. At the same time, the piling up of stressed syllables and the frequent use of punctuation breaks (called **caesuras**) slow down the movement of the poem. (Like Beethoven's *Fifth,* "Batter my heart" is almost impossible to read quickly and cheerfully.) Thus the repetition of the hard "b" sound, the caesuras, and the metrical beat reinforce the notion that God has waged a violent battle to win the speaker over from his "enemy," the Devil.

Now consider the very different rhythms created by poet Emily Dickinson:

*The apostrophe indicates that a letter has been left out, the *v* in *overthrow.* Donne wants us to pronounce *overthrow* not as "o-ver-throw" but as "or-throw."

EMILY DICKINSON (1830–1886)

Because I could not stop for Death— _____ 1863

Because I could not stop for Death—
He kindly stopped for me—
The Carriage held but just Ourselves—
And Immortality.

5   We slowly drove—He knew no haste
And I had put away
My labor and my leisure too,
For His Civility—

We passed the School, where Children strove
10   At Recess—in the Ring—
We passed the Fields of Gazing Grain—
We passed the Setting Sun—

Or rather—He passed Us—
The Dews drew quivering and chill—
15   For only Gossamer, my Gown—
My Tippet—only Tulle—

We paused before a House that seemed
A Swelling of the Ground—
The Roof was scarcely visible—
20   The Cornice—in the Ground—

Since then—'tis Centuries—and yet
Feels shorter than the Day
I first surmised the Horses' Heads
Were toward Eternity—

Notice that in Dickinson's poem there is none of the clipped language of Donne's "Batter my heart," and the rhythms are much more regular; there are fewer breaks in the conventional pattern alternating between an unstressed syllable and a stressed one (˘ ´). Here is how we would scan the first four lines:

Because I could not stop for Death—

He kindly stopped for me—

The Carriage held but just Ourselves—

And Immortality.

We should point out here that not all readers would scan the poem in the same way; just as any one person's speech patterns are different from another's, one reader may read the metrical patterns of a poem differently than another. Most would, though, see in Emily Dickinson's poem a regularity of pattern, a quiet conversational rhythm, that is not found in John Donne's poems. The differences in the poets' rhythms reflect differences in their perceptions of their subject. Donne's speaker sees Death and the Devil as enemies who must and will be vanquished in a violent struggle, whereas Dickinson's sees Death as a friend, even a kindly courtier, who takes her to immortal life.

EXERCISE: TRYING IT OUT

Following is John Donne's "Death, be not proud." Scan the poem yourself, placing an accent mark over strongly stressed syllables and a half-circle over weakly stressed syllables. Then write a brief analysis of how the metrical stresses help create and reflect the poem's themes and mood.

JOHN DONNE (1572–1631)

Death, be not proud

Death, be not proud, though some have calléd thee
Mighty and dreadful, for thou are not so;
For those whom thou think'st thou dost overthrow
Die not, poor Death, nor yet canst thou kill me.
From rest and sleep, which but thy pictures be,
Much pleasure; then from thee much more must flow,   5
And soonest our best men with thee do go,
Rest of their bones, and soul's delivery.
Thou art slave to fate, chance, kings, and desperate men,
And dost with poison, war, and sickness dwell,
And poppy or charms can make us sleep as well   10
And better than thy stroke; why swell'st thou then?
One short sleep past, we wake eternally
And death shall be no more; Death, thou shalt die.

Traditional Metrical Patterns

The conversational quality of Dickinson's poetry is achieved in part by her use of the rhythmical patterns of everyday English. Many poems use an almost entirely conversational rhythm. Many modern poets write in **free verse,** which has no regular rhythm or rhyme pattern. At the same time, linguists tell us that English has a natural rhythm, and many older and more traditional poets make deliberate use of that natural rhythm, making it the pattern of their poetry. The regular pattern of everyday speech is a pattern of an unstressed syllable followed by a stressed syllable; literary critics call that pairing an **iamb.** That term may be familiar to you if you have previously studied any of Shakespeare's poetry, which relies on what critics call **iambic pentameter:** ten-syllable lines composed of five iambs. (*Penta* is the Greek word for "five.") Look, for instance, at these well-known lines from Shakespeare:

˘ ´ | ˘ ´ | ˘ ´ | ˘ ´ | ˘ ´

A horse! | A horse! | My king | dom for | a horse!   From Shakespeare, *Richard III.*V.iv.7

˘ ´ | ˘ ´ | ˘ ´ | ˘ ´ | ˘ ´

To be | or not | to be, | that is | the ques | tion.   From Shakespeare, *Hamlet.* III.i.56

Some readers would place the stresses differently, perhaps pronouncing "that" and "is" in the line from *Hamlet* with unequal amounts of emphasis, for instance; and you may also have noticed that that same line has an extra syllable. Still, the overall pattern is an iambic one, and the result is a poetry that sounds both poetic and conversational. (In his plays, Shakespeare often uses a particular kind of conversational iambic pentameter: **blank verse.** Blank verse involves unrhymed iambic pentameter lines.)

Like Shakespeare, Donne uses what is basically an iambic pentameter rhythm, though an irregular one. Dickinson uses a different iambic pattern in "Because I could not stop for Death—": critics would analyze it as the alternation of lines of **iambic tetrameter** (with four iambs per line) and **iambic trimeter** (with three iambs per line). *Tetra* comes from the Greek word for "four" and *tri* from the Greek word for "three" (think about tetrahedrons, which have four planes, and of triangles, which have three sides).

Some Common Iambic Forms Illustrated Remember that an iamb is composed of an unstressed syllable followed by a stressed syllable (˘ ´).

iambic pentameter: 5 iambs per line (˘ ´ | ˘ ´ | ˘ ´ | ˘ ´ | ˘ ´)

˘ ´ | ˘ ´ | ˘ ´ | ˘ ´ | ˘ ´

Example: That time | of year | thou may'st | in me | behold

˘ ´ | ˘ ´ | ˘ ´ | ˘ ´ | ˘ ´

When yel | low leaves, | or none, | or few, | do hang

˘ ´ | ˘ ´ | ˘ ´ | ˘ ´ | ˘ ´

Upon | those boughs | which shake | against | the cold,

˘ ´ | ˘ ´ | ˘ ´ | ˘ ´ | ˘ ´

Bare ru | ined choirs | where late | the sweet | birds sang.

From Shakespeare, Sonnet 73

iambic tetrameter: 4 iambs per line (˘ ´ | ˘ ´ | ˘ ´ | ˘ ´)

Example: If all | the world | and love | were young,

And truth | in ev | ery shep | herd's tongue,

These pret | ty plea | sures might | me move,

To live | with thee | and be | thy love.

From Raleigh, "The Nymph's Reply to the Shepherd"

iambic trimeter: 3 iambs per line (˘ ´ | ˘ ´ | ˘ ´) (Few poems use iambic trimeter alone; it appears most often in the **ballad stanza,** which alternates lines of iambic tetrameter and iambic trimeter.)

Example: We romped | until | the pans

Slid from | the kitch | en shelf;

My moth | er's coun | tenance

Could not | unfrown | itself.

From Roethke, "My Papa's Waltz"

As we said earlier, most poems written in English use an iambic pattern (˘ ´), but there are some less common patterns that are also useful for literary critics to know; of these less frequently used patterns, the ones that you are most likely to run into are these:

the **trochee,** which is composed of first a stressed and then an unstressed

syllable ("Tyger! tyger! burning bright" [from Blake's "The Tyger"])

the **dactyl,** which is composed of a stressed syllable followed by two unstressed

syllables ("Slouches towards Bethlehem to be born" [from Yeats's "The Second Coming"]; notice that the last metrical foot is not dactylic)

the anapest, which is composed of two unstressed syllables followed by a stressed syllable ("I remem   ber the gulls   and the waves" [from Rukeyser's "Waiting for Icarus"])

It is probably less important that you know the labels that literary critics use than that you recognize the importance of pattern in poetry. As you read poetry, listen, then, to its sounds as well as its meaning, training your ear to hear what the primary patterns are; once you have done that, you can begin to understand how sound and sense conform *and* to listen for those moments when a poet deliberately breaks an established pattern and calls your attention to an important word or concept.

EXERCISES: TRYING IT OUT

The following exercises ask you to scan some pieces of writing. Remember that for a literary critic, scanning involves analyzing the writing for its meter.

1. Although we don't often do so, prose and speech can be analyzed for their rhythms and patterns, too. In your library or on the World Wide Web, locate a copy of one of the following and scan a paragraph or two from it: Lincoln's Gettysburg Address, the opening of The Declaration of Independence, the Preamble to the U.S. Constitution, Martin Luther King, Jr.'s, "I Have a Dream" speech.
2. Test out the notion that everyday speech and writing in English usually follow an iambic pattern by scanning a piece of writing not meant for poetic analysis. You might, for instance, scan a paragraph from one of your textbooks for another class or scan a news article or even a letter from a friend or a piece of your own writing.
3. Here are some lines from poetry. Scan them and identify their metrical patterns. Do they use iambs? Trochees? Dactyls? Anapests? Are they pentameter lines? Tetrameter lines? Trimeter lines? Something else?

   a. 'Twas brillig, and the slithy toves
          Did gyre and gimble in the wabe:
       All mimsy were the borogoves,
          And the mome raths outgrabe.

   From Carroll, "Jabberwocky"

   b. As the guests arrive at my son's party
       they gather in the living room—
       short men, men in first grade
       with smooth jaws and chins.

   From Olds, "Rites of Passage"

   c. She begins, and my grandmother joins her.
       Mother and daughter sing like young girls.

If my father were alive, he would play
His accordion and sway like a boat.

From Lee, "I Ask My Mother to Sing"

Rhyme

If there is one thing that most of us associate with poetry, it is probably rhyme. Although not all poems rhyme, many do, and critics have devised a kind of shorthand for talking about the rhyme patterns, often called the **rhyme schemes,** of poems; they assign each new rhyme a new letter of the alphabet. So, for instance, the first four lines of "Batter my heart" have a rhyme scheme of *abba*; because *you* in the first line rhymes with *new* in the fourth, they are both assigned the letter *a,* and because *mend* and *bend* use the same new rhyme sound, they are both assigned the next letter of the alphabet, *b:*

Batter my heart, three-personed God; for You	*a*
As yet but knock, breathe, shine, and seek to mend;	*b*
That I may rise and stand, o'erthrow me, and bend	*b*
Your force to break, blow, burn, and make me new.	*a*

As with poetic meter, it is important to notice rhyme scheme because looking at how it works can often help us understand a poet's meaning. Words or lines that rhyme are often meant to be compared or contrasted, as in the **couplet** (the final two rhyming lines) at the end of "Batter my heart":

Except You enthrall me, never shall be free,
Nor ever chaste, except You ravish me.

The couplet invites us to see the paradox of the entire poem: the violent battle and the ravishment are acts of love meant to save the speaker's soul. (Enslavement to God brings freedom of the spirit; true purity—chastity—comes with the soul's ravishment.) A similar function is served by the **internal rhyme** in line 7 of "America the Beautiful"; there a rhyme occurs within the line itself:

And crown thy good with brotherhood

We are meant to see American brotherhood as one of the "goods" that have been bestowed on the country.

Sometimes poets use inexact rhymes, which are called either *eye rhymes* or *near rhymes* or *slant rhymes*. The term **eye rhyme** is used most often to describe what looks like rhyme but isn't quite: "love" and "prove" might be considered eye rhymes, for instance (although at one point in the history of the English language, they were probably exact rhymes). The term **slant rhyme** or **near rhyme** is more often used to describe words that almost rhyme, as, for instance, "bush" and "brush." A poet often uses such rhymes to reinforce meaning or mood; when Theodore Roethke rhymes "dizzy" and "easy" in "My Papa's Waltz," for instance, the slant rhyme reinforces the notion that Papa is a little tipsy.

Alliteration and Assonance

Two other terms used to describe sounds in poetry will also be helpful to use as you analyze poems. **Alliteration** is a term used to describe the repetition of consonant sounds, usually at the beginning of words. The repetition of the hard *b* sounds in "Batter my heart," which we noted previously, is an example of alliteration. Its use slows down the line, making it sound hard and dramatic. (If you doubt the extent to which alliteration slows down a line, try to repeat "break, blow, burn" quickly several times. Or, better yet, think about the effect of the alliteration in a common tongue-twister such as "Peter Piper picked a peck of pickled peppers.")

Similar to alliteration is the poetic device of **assonance.** Whereas alliteration involves the repetition of consonant sounds, assonance involves the repetition of vowel sounds. As we noted in chapter 2, the repetition of the long *o* sound in Frost's "Stopping by Woods" contributes to the poem's soothing tones. William Blake also uses assonance in "The Tyger," in which the repetition of the long *i* sound helps to elongate the lines, expressing the sense of wonderment:

> Tyger! tyger! burning bright
> In the forests of the night,
> What immortal hand or eye
> Could frame thy fearful symmetry?

POETIC STRUCTURE AND GENRE

Like books and essays, poems, even relatively short ones, are often broken into sections that are separated from each other by white space on the page. Each such section in a poem is called a **stanza,** and each stanza typically develops one idea or image (much as a paragraph does in an essay). Look back, for instance, at Emily Dickinson's poem "Because I could not stop for Death—" (94). It is divided into six stanzas, each one creating a separate scene: the first shows Death stopping for the speaker; the second discusses the coach ride; the third shows a schoolyard and field of grain; the fourth describes the speaker's clothing; the fifth presents a "house" (or grave); and the last sums up the poem.

Stanzas are not the only kind of "division" poets use. A pattern of rhyme also gives a poem structure, and an attention to that structure will often yield information about a poem's thematic movement. Here, for instance, is one of Shakespeare's most famous short poems. It is a **sonnet,** which is a fourteen-line poem in iambic pentameter with a particular repeating rhyme scheme; we have indicated the rhyme scheme for you.

> That time of year thou may'st in me behold   *a*
> When yellow leaves, or none, or few, do hang   *b*
> Upon those boughs which shake against the cold,   *a*
> Bare ruined choirs where late the sweet birds sang.   *b*
> In me thou see'st the twilight of such day   *c*
> As after sunset fadeth in the west,   *d*

Which by-and-by black night doth take away,	c
Death's second self that seals up all in rest.	d
In me thou see'st the glowing of such fire	e
That on the ashes of his youth doth lie,	f
As the deathbed whereon it must expire,	e
Consumed with that which it was nourished by.	f
This thou perceiv'st, which makes thy love more strong,	g
To love that well which thou must leave ere long.	g

Notice that the poet begins a new rhyme pattern every four lines; as a result, the poem is composed of three **quatrains** (groups of four lines) and a couplet. Once you've identified the quatrains, you will also have an easier time seeing that each quatrain elaborates on a single image: the first quatrain describes the months when autumn is turning to winter, the second the twilight hours between day and night, and the third the moment before the fire goes out. The poem thus moves through increasingly shorter time spans until it reaches the final couplet, which, as is common in a Shakespearean sonnet, brings the parts of the poem together and suggests a possible theme. The poem's rhyme scheme and its structure help the poet convey his idea: life is short and so we must love well while (and what) we can. (For a more extended discussion of how Sonnet 73 works, see appendix 1, A-4–5.)

The sonnet is only one of many poetic forms. Sonnets themselves can be broken into two types: the Shakespearean sonnet, which has three quatrains and a couplet, and the **Italian** or **Petrarchan sonnet,** which has an **octave** (a unit of eight lines with a repeating rhyme scheme) and a **sestet** (a unit of six lines with a repeating rhyme scheme). Donne's "Batter my heart" and "Death, be not proud" belong to the Italian sonnet tradition.

Another familiar poetic form is the *ballad stanza* (an alternation of iambic tetrameter and iambic trimeter), which we have already seen in Emily Dickinson's poem. As its name implies, the ballad stanza is most familiar in the genre of the **ballad.** Ballads are an old form; they come from an oral tradition of poetry in which the poems were transmitted by song rather than written on the page. They usually take as their subject such universals as love and death, and often, though not always, tell the story with an air of melancholy or tragedy.

Other poetic genres you'll find in *Retellings* include the **dramatic monologue,** a poem meant to be read as the words of someone thinking aloud (Browning's "Porphyria's Lover" and "My Last Duchess" are examples of dramatic monologues) and the **lyric,** which is a verse song, usually composed of short lines of rhyming poetry (see Marlowe's "The Passionate Shepherd to His Love" and Raleigh's "The Nymph's Reply to the Shepherd" in chapter 9).

We have emphasized the importance of poetic patterns largely because those patterns often hint at a poem's meaning. It is easy to rhyme words or to form sentences that alternate stressed and unstressed syllables in a consistent pattern. What is not easy is to use those rhymes and stresses in combination with image patterns and meaning to create a work of art. Most of us have heard something of the long tradition that

Questions to Ask about Poetry

1. How would you characterize the speaker of the poem?
2. What words in the poem have strong connotations? How do the poet's word choices create the tone of the poem? How do they reinforce the meaning?
3. What use of figurative language does the poet make? To what effect?
4. What allusions, if any, does the poem use? How do those allusions work thematically?
5. Does the poem have a regular metrical pattern? If so, what words and images does that metrical pattern emphasize? How does the pattern of emphasis—and any departures from that pattern—connect to the poem's theme?
6. Does the poem have a regular rhyme scheme? How are the rhyming words related to the poem's theme? To what extent does the rhyme scheme encourage us to compare or contrast words and ideas? Look not only at the rhymes themselves but at the way they add significance to the lines in which they occur.
7. How is the poem structured? What thematic significance might the structural units (e.g., couplets, quatrains, stanzas) have?

tells us that poets are simply inspired by dreams and Muses, that words and images come to them unbidden. But most poetry is carefully and thoughtfully shaped; poets, like all writers (and like musicians, painters, and scientists), try out more than one idea, more than one image. In reading poetry, our job is to figure out why, finally, the poet chose one image, sound, or form over another. And by analyzing the inner workings of the poem, its prosody, we can begin to unfold many of its secrets.

5

Reading Drama

When a blockbuster special effects movie comes out, many of us rush to the theaters, knowing that this is not the kind of movie we want to see on video. Some movies just need to be seen on the big screen rather than on the family television. Even less spectacular movies are sometimes better seen in the theater than at home; for instance, comedies always seem funnier in the theater than at home. Hearing an audience laugh provokes our own laughter (which is why many television shows have laugh tracks).

The difference between watching a film in a movie theater and watching a video at home is rather like the difference between seeing a play performed onstage and reading it. Reading is usually a private, internal activity, whereas watching a play is an external one. Even in a darkened theater, we never quite lose the sense that the performance is public and that we are not alone but are members of an audience, experiencing the play communally. Whereas a reader responds only to what the author writes, a member of an audience responds not only to the play onstage but also to those around her.

Even if there were no one else in the audience, though, our relationship to characters on the stage or screen would likely be very different from our relationship to characters on the printed page: the stage or film characters are, of course, external to us, not characters we imagine. Reading a play is, then, a somewhat artificial experience. In a textbook such as this one we obviously cannot produce the play for you, directing real actors to play it out before your eyes. The best advice we can give you is that you should try to produce it for yourself in your imagination. As you read *Los Vendidos,* then, try to imagine the performance of the drama.

LUIS VALDEZ (1940–   )
Los Vendidos _____ *1967*

List of Characters
HONEST SANCHO
SECRETARY
FARM WORKER

JOHNNY

REVOLUCIONARIO

MEXICAN–AMERICAN

Scene. *Honest Sancho's Used Mexican Lot and Mexican Curio Shop. Three models are on display in* HONEST SANCHO's *shop: to the right, there is a* REVOLUCIONARIO, *complete with sombrero, carrilleras and carabina 30–30. At center, on the floor, there is the* FARM WORKER, *under a broad straw sombrero. At stage left is the* PACHUCO, *filero in hand.*

(HONEST SANCHO *is moving among his models, dusting them off and preparing for another day of business.*)

SANCHO: Bueno, bueno, mis monos, vamos a ver a quien vendemos ahora, ¿no? (*To audience.*) ¡Quihubo! I'm Honest Sancho and this is my shop. Antes fui contratista pero ahora logré tener mi negocito. All I need now is a customer. (*A bell rings offstage.*) Ay, a customer!

SECRETARY (*Entering*): Good morning, I'm Miss Jimenez from—

SANCHO: ¡Ah, una chicana! Welcome, welcome Señorita Jiménez.

SECRETARY (*Anglo pronunciation*): JIM-enez.

5   SANCHO: ¿Qué?

SECRETARY: My name is Miss JIM-enez. Don't you speak English? What's wrong with you?

SANCHO: Oh, nothing. Señorita JIM-enez. I'm here to help you.

SECRETARY: That's better. As I was starting to say, I'm a secretary from Governor Reagan's office, and we're looking for a Mexican type for the administration.

SANCHO: Well, you come to the right place, lady. This is Honest Sancho's Used Mexican Lot, and we got all types here. Any particular type you want?

10   SECRETARY: Yes, we were looking for somebody suave—

SANCHO: Suave.

SECRETARY: Debonair.

SANCHO: De buen aire.

SECRETARY: Dark.

15   SANCHO: Prieto.

SECRETARY: But of course not too dark.

SANCHO: No muy prieto.

SECRETARY: Perhaps, beige.

SANCHO: Beige, just the tone. Así como cafecito con leche, ¿no?

20   SECRETARY: One more thing. He must be hard-working.

SANCHO: That could only be one model. Step right over here to the center of the shop, lady. (*They cross to the* FARM WORKER.) This is our standard farm worker model. As you can see, in the words of our beloved Senator George Murphy, he is "built close to the ground." Also take special notice of his four-ply Goodyear huaraches, made from the rain tire. This wide-brimmed sombrero is an extra added feature—keeps off the sun, rain, and dust.

SECRETARY: Yes, it does look durable.

SANCHO: And our farmworker model is friendly. Muy amable. Watch. (*Snaps his fingers.*)

FARM WORKER (*Lifts up head*): Buenos días, señorita. (*His head drops.*)

SECRETARY: My, he's friendly.   25

SANCHO: Didn't I tell you? Loves his patrones! But his most attractive feature is that he's hard-working. Let me show you. (*Snaps fingers.* FARM WORKER *stands.*)

FARM WORKER: ¡El jale! (*He begins to work.*)

SANCHO: As you can see, he is cutting grapes.

SECRETARY: Oh, I wouldn't know.

SANCHO: He also picks cotton. (*Snap.* FARM WORKER *begins to pick cotton.*)   30

SECRETARY: Versatile isn't he?

SANCHO: He also picks melons. (*Snap.* FARM WORKER *picks melons.*) That's his slow speed for late in the season. Here's his fast speed. (*Snap.* FARM WORKER *picks faster.*)

SECRETARY: ¡Chihuahua! . . . I mean, goodness, he sure is a hard worker.

SANCHO (*Pulls the* FARM WORKER *to his feet*): And that isn't the half of it. Do you see these little holes on his arms that appear to be pores? During those hot sluggish days in the field, when the vines or the branches get so entangled, it's almost impossible to move; these holes emit a certain grease that allows our model to slip and slide right through the crop with no trouble at all.

SECRETARY: Wonderful. But is he economical?   35

SANCHO: Economical? Señorita, you are looking at the Volkswagen of Mexicans. Pennies a day is all it takes. One plate of beans and tortillas will keep him going all day. That, and chile. Plenty of chile. Chile jalapenos, chile verde, chile colorado. But, of course, if you do give him chile (*Snap.* FARM WORKER *turns left face. Snap.* FARM WORKER *bends over.*) then you have to change his oil filter once a week.

SECRETARY: What about storage?

SANCHO: No problem. You know these new farm labor camps our Honorable Governor Reagan has built out by Parlier or Raisin City? They were designed with our model in mind. Five, six, seven, even ten in one of those shacks will give you no trouble at all. You can also put him in old barns, old cars, river banks. You can even leave him out in the field overnight with no worry!

SECRETARY: Remarkable.

SANCHO: And here's an added feature: Every year at the end of the season, this model   40
goes back to Mexico and doesn't return, automatically, until next Spring.

SECRETARY: How about that. But tell me: does he speak English?

SANCHO: Another outstanding feature is that last year this model was programmed to go out on STRIKE! (*Snap.*)

FARM WORKER: ¡HUELGA! ¡HUELGA! Hermanos, sálganse de esos files. (*Snap. He stops.*)

SECRETARY: No! Oh no, we can't strike in the State Capitol.

SANCHO: Well, he also scabs. (*Snap.*)   45

FARM WORKER: Me vendo barato, ¿y qué? (*Snap.*)

SECRETARY: That's much better, but you didn't answer my question. Does he speak English?

SANCHO: Bueno . . . no, pero he has other—

SECRETARY: No.

SANCHO: Other features.   50

SECRETARY: NO! He just won't do!

SANCHO: Okay, okay pues. We have other models.

SECRETARY: I hope so. What we need is something a little more sophisticated.

SANCHO: Sophisti—¿qué?

55 SECRETARY: An urban model.

SANCHO: Ah, from the city! Step right back. Over here in this corner of the shop is exactly what you're looking for. Introducing our new 1969 JOHNNY PACHUCO model! This is our fast-back model. Streamlined. Built for speed, low-riding, city life. Take a look at some of these features. Mag shoes, dual exhausts, green chartreuse paint-job, dark-tint windshield, a little poof on top. Let me just turn him on. (*Snap.* JOHNNY *walks to stage center with a pachuco bounce.*)

SECRETARY: What was that?

SANCHO: That, señorita, was the Chicano shuffle.

SECRETARY: Okay, what does he do?

60 SANCHO: Anything and everything necessary for city life. For instance survival: He knife fights. (*Snap.* JOHNNY *pulls out switch blade and swings at* SECRETARY.)

(SECRETARY *screams.*)

SANCHO: He dances. (*Snap.*)

JOHNNY (*Singing*): "Angel Baby, my Angel Baby . . ." (*Snap.*)

SANCHO: And here's a feature no city model can be without. He gets arrested, but not without resisting, of course. (*Snap.*)

JOHNNY: ¡En la madre, la placa! I didn't do it! I didn't do it! (JOHNNY *turns and stands up against an imaginary wall, legs spread out, arms behind his back.*)

65 SECRETARY: Oh no, we can't have arrests! We must maintain law and order.

SANCHO: But he's bilingual!

SECRETARY: Bilingual?

SANCHO: Simón que yes. He speaks English! Johnny, give us some English. (*Snap.*)

JOHNNY (*Comes downstage*): Fuck-you!

70 SECRETARY (*Gasps*): Oh! I've never been so insulted in my whole life!

SANCHO: Well, he learned it in your school.

SECRETARY: I don't care where he learned it.

SANCHO: But he's economical!

SECRETARY: Economical?

75 SANCHO: Nickels and dimes. You can keep Johnny running on hamburgers, Taco Bell tacos, Lucky Lager beer, Thunderbird wine, yesca—

SECRETARY: Yesca?

SANCHO: Mota.

SECRETARY: Mota?

SANCHO: Leños . . . Marijuana. (*Snap;* JOHNNY *inhales on an imaginary joint.*)

80 SECRETARY: That's against the law!

JOHNNY (*Big smile, holding his breath*): Yeah.

SANCHO: He also sniffs glue. (*Snap.* JOHNNY *inhales glue, big smile.*)

JOHNNY: Tha's too much man, ése.

SECRETARY: No, Mr. Sancho, I don't think this—

85 SANCHO: Wait a minute, he has other qualities I know you'll love. For example, an inferiority complex. (*Snap.*)

JOHNNY (*To Sancho*): You think you're better than me, huh ése? (*Swings switch blade.*)

SANCHO: He can also be beaten and he bruises, cut him and he bleeds; kick him and he—(*He beats, bruises and kicks* PACHUCO.) Would you like to try it?

SECRETARY: Oh, I couldn't.

SANCHO: Be my guest. He's a great scapegoat.

SECRETARY: No, really.

SANCHO: Please.

SECRETARY: Well, all right. Just once. (*She kicks* PACHUCO.) Oh, he's so soft.

SANCHO: Wasn't that good? Try again.

SECRETARY (*Kicks* PACHUCO): Oh, he's so wonderful! (*She kicks him again.*)

SANCHO: Okay, that's enough, lady. You ruin the merchandise. Yes, our Johnny Pachuco model can give you many hours of pleasure. Why, the L.A.P.D. just bought twenty of these to train their rookie cops on. And talk about maintenance. Señorita, you are looking at an entirely self-supporting machine. You're never going to find our Johnny Pachuco model on the relief rolls. No, sir, this model knows how to liberate.

SECRETARY: Liberate?

SANCHO: He steals. (*Snap.* JOHNNY *rushes the* SECRETARY *and steals her purse.*)

JOHNNY: ¡Dame esa bolsa, vieja! (*He grabs the purse and runs. Snap by* SANCHO. *He stops.*)

(SECRETARY *runs after* JOHNNY *and grabs purse away from him, kicking him as she goes.*)

SECRETARY: No, no, no! We can't have any *more* thieves in the State Administration. Put him back.

SANCHO: Okay, we still got other models. Come on, Johnny, we'll sell you to some old lady. (SANCHO *takes* JOHNNY *back to his place.*)

SECRETARY: Mr. Sancho, I don't think you quite understand what we need. What we need is something that will attract the women voters. Something more traditional, more romantic.

SANCHO: Ah, a lover. (*He smiles meaningfully.*) Step right over here, señorita. Introducing our standard Revolucionario and/or Early California Bandit type. As you can see he is well-built, sturdy, durable. This is the International Harvester of Mexicans.

SECRETARY: What does he do?

SANCHO: You name it, he does it. He rides horses, stays in the mountains, crosses deserts, plains, rivers, leads revolutions, follows revolutions, kills, can be killed, serves as a martyr, hero, movie star—did I say movie star? Did you ever see *Viva Zapata? Viva Villa? Villa Rides? Pancho Villa Returns? Pancho Villa Goes Back? Pancho Villa Meets Abbott and Costello*—

SECRETARY: I've never seen any of those.

SANCHO: Well, he was in all of them. Listen to this. (*Snap.*)

REVOLUCIONARIO (*Scream*): ¡VIVA VILLAAAAA!

SECRETARY: That's awfully loud.

SANCHO: He has a volume control. (*He adjusts volume. Snap.*)

REVOLUCIONARIO (*Mousey voice*): ¡Viva Villa!

SECRETARY: That's better.

SANCHO: And even if you didn't see him in the movies, perhaps you saw him on TV. He makes commercials. (*Snap.*)

REVOLUCIONARIO: Is there a Frito Bandito in your house?

SECRETARY: Oh yes, I've seen that one!

115   SANCHO: Another feature about this one is that he is economical. He runs on raw horsemeat and tequila!

SECRETARY: Isn't that rather savage?

SANCHO: Al contrario, it makes him a lover. (*Snap.*)

REVOLUCIONARIO (*To* SECRETARY): ¡Ay, mamasota, cochota, ven pa'ca! (*He grabs* SECRETARY *and folds her back—Latin-Lover style.*)

SANCHO (*Snap.* REVOLUCIONARIO *goes back upright*): Now wasn't that nice?

120   SECRETARY: Well, it was rather nice.

SANCHO: And finally, there is one outstanding feature about this model. I KNOW the ladies are going to love: He's a GENUINE antique! He was made in Mexico in 1910!

SECRETARY: Made in Mexico?

SANCHO: That's right. Once in Tijuana, twice in Guadalajara, three times in Cuernavaca.

SECRETARY: Mr. Sancho, I thought he was an American product.

125   SANCHO: No, but—

SECRETARY: No, I'm sorry. We can't buy anything but American-made products. He just won't do.

SANCHO: But he's an antique!

SECRETARY: I don't care. You still don't understand what we need. It's true we need Mexican models such as these, but it's more important that he be *American.*

SANCHO: American?

30   SECRETARY: That's right, and judging from what you've shown me, I don't think you have what we want. Well, my lunch hour's almost over; I better—

SANCHO: Wait a minute! Mexican but American?

SECRETARY: That's correct.

SANCHO: Mexican but . . . (*A sudden flash.*) AMERICAN! Yeah, I think we've got exactly what you want. He just came in today! Give me a minute. (*He exits. Talks from backstage.*) Here he is in the shop. Let me just get some papers off. There. Introducing our new 1970 Mexican-American! Ta-ra-ra-ra-ra-ra-RA-RAAA!

(SANCHO *brings out the Mexican-American model, a clean-shaven middle-class type in a business suit, with glasses.*)

SECRETARY (*Impressed*): Where have you been hiding this one?

35   SANCHO: He just came in this morning. Ain't he a beauty? Feast your eyes on him! Sturdy US STEEL frame, streamlined, modern. As a matter of fact, he is built exactly like our Anglo models except that he comes in a variety of darker shades: naugahyde, leather, or leatherette.

SECRETARY: Naugahyde.

SANCHO: Well, we'll just write that down. Yes, señorita, this model represents the apex of American engineering! He is bilingual, college educated, ambitious! Say the word "acculturate" and he accelerates. He is intelligent, well-mannered, clean—did I say clean? (*Snap.* MEXICAN-AMERICAN *raises his arm.*) Smell.

SECRETARY (*Smells*): Old Sobaco, my favorite.

SANCHO (*Snap.* MEXICAN-AMERICAN *turns toward Sancho*): Eric! (*To Secretary.*) We call him Eric García. (*To* ERIC.) I want you to meet Miss JIM-enez, Eric.

MEXICAN-AMERICAN: Miss JIM-enez, I am delighted to make your acquaintance. *140*
(*He kisses her hand.*)

SECRETARY: Oh, my, how charming!

SANCHO: Did you feel the suction? He has seven especially engineered suction cups right behind his lips. He's a charmer all right!

SECRETARY: How about boards? Does he function on boards?

SANCHO: You name them, he is on them. Parole boards, draft boards, school boards, taco quality control boards, surf boards, two-by-fours.

SECRETARY: Does he function in politics? *145*

SANCHO: Señorita, you are looking at a political MACHINE. Have you ever heard of the OEO, EOC, COD, WAR ON POVERTY? That's our model! Not only that, he makes political speeches.

SECRETARY: May I hear one?

SANCHO: With pleasure. (*Snap.*) Eric, give us a speech.

MEXICAN-AMERICAN: Mr. Congressman, Mr. Chairman, members of the board, honored guests, ladies and gentlemen. (SANCHO *and* SECRETARY *applaud.*) Please, please. I come before you as a Mexican-American to tell you about the problems of the Mexican. The problems of the Mexican stem from one thing and one thing alone: He's stupid. He's uneducated. He needs to stay in school. He needs to be ambitious, forward-looking, harder-working. He needs to think American, American, American, AMERICAN, AMERICAN AMERICAN. GOD BLESS AMERICA! GOD BLESS AMERICA! GOD BLESS AMER-ICA!! (*He goes out of control.*)

(SANCHO *snaps frantically and the* MEXICAN-AMERICAN *finally slumps forward, bending at the waist.*)

SECRETARY: Oh my, he's patriotic too! *150*

SANCHO: Sí, Señorita, he loves his country. Let me just make a little adjustment here. (*Stands* MEXICAN-AMERICAN *up.*)

SECRETARY: What about upkeep? Is he economical?

SANCHO: Well, no, I won't lie to you. The Mexican-American costs a little bit more, but you get what you pay for. He's worth every extra cent. You can keep him running on dry Martinis, Langendorf bread.

SECRETARY: Apple pie?

SANCHO: Only Mom's. Of course, he's also programmed to eat Mexican food on *155*
ceremonial functions, but I must warn you: an overdose of beans will plug up his exhaust.

SECRETARY: Fine! There's just one more question: HOW MUCH DO YOU WANT FOR HIM?

SANCHO: Well, I tell you what I'm gonna do. Today and today only, because you've been so sweet, I'm gonna let you steal this model from me! I'm gonna let you drive him off the lot for the simple price of—let's see taxes and licence included—$15,000.

SECRETARY: Fifteen thousand DOLLARS? For a MEXICAN!

SANCHO: Mexican? What are you talking, lady? This is a Mexican-AMERICAN! We had to melt down two pachucos, a farm worker and three gabachos to make this model! You want quality, but you gotta pay for it! This is no cheap runabout. He's got class!

160 SECRETARY: Okay, I'll take him.

SANCHO: You will?

SECRETARY: Here's your money.

SANCHO: You mind if I count it?

SECRETARY: Go right ahead.

165 SANCHO: Well, you'll get your pink slip in the mail. Oh, do you want me to wrap him up for you? We have a box in the back.

SECRETARY: No, thank you. The Governor is having a luncheon this afternoon, and we need a brown face in the crowd. How do I drive him?

SANCHO: Just snap your fingers. He'll do anything you want.

(SECRETARY snaps. MEXICAN-AMERICAN steps forward.)

MEXICAN-AMERICAN: RAZA QUERIDA, ¡VAMOS LEVANTANDO ARMAS PARA LIBERARNOS DE ESTOS DESGRACIADOS GABACHOS QUE NOS EXPLOTAN! VAMOS.

SECRETARY: What did he say?

170 SANCHO: Something about lifting arms, killing white people, etc.

SECRETARY: But he's not supposed to say that!

SANCHO: Look, lady, don't blame me for bugs from the factory. He's your Mexican-American; you bought him, now drive him off the lot!

SECRETARY: But he's broken!

SANCHO: Try snapping another finger.

(SECRETARY snaps. MEXICAN-AMERICAN comes to life again.)

175 MEXICAN-AMERICAN: ¡ESTA GRAN HUMANIDAD HA DICHO BASTA! Y SE HA PUESTO EN MARCHA! ¡BASTA! ¡BASTA! ¡VIVA LA RAZA! ¡VIVA LA CAUSA! ¡VIVA LA HUELGA! ¡VIVAN LOS BROWN BERETS! ¡VIVAN LOS ESTUDIANTES! ¡CHICANO POWER!

(The MEXICAN-AMERICAN turns toward the SECRETARY, who gasps and backs up. He keeps turning toward the PACHUCO, FARM WORKER, and REVOLUCIONARIO, snapping his fingers and turning each of them on, one by one.)

PACHUCO (Snap. To SECRETARY): I'm going to get you, baby! ¡Viva la Raza!

FARM WORKER (Snap. To SECRETARY): ¡Viva la huelga! ¡Viva la huelga! ¡VIVA LA HUELGA!

REVOLUCIONARIO (Snap. To SECRETARY): ¡Viva la revolución! ¡VIVA LA REVOLUCIÓN!

(The three models join together and advance toward the SECRETARY, who backs up and runs out of the shop screaming. SANCHO is at the other end of the shop holding *his money in his hand. All freeze. After a few seconds of silence, the* PACHUCO *moves and stretches, shaking his arms and loosening up. The* FARM WORKER *and* REVOLUCIONARIO *do the same.* SANCHO *stays where he is, frozen to the spot.)*

JOHNNY: Man, that was a long one, ése. (*Others agree with him.*)

FARM WORKER: How did we do?   180

JOHNNY: Perty good, look at all that lana, man! (*He goes over to* SANCHO *and removes the money from his hand.* SANCHO *stays where he is.*)

REVOLUCIONARIO: En la madre, look at all the money.

JOHNNY: We keep this up, we're going to be rich.

FARM WORKER: They think we're machines.

REVOLUCIONARIO: Burros.   185

JOHNNY: Puppets.

MEXICAN-AMERICAN: The only thing I don't like is—how come I always got to play the godamn Mexican-American?

JOHNNY: That's what you get for finishing high school.

FARM WORKER: How about our wages, ése?

JOHNNY: Here it comes right now. $3,000 for you, $3,000 for you, $3,000 for you,   190
and $3,000 for me. The rest we put back into the business.

MEXICAN-AMERICAN: Too much, man. Heh, where you vatos going tonight?

FARM WORKER: I'm going over to Concha's. There's a party.

JOHNNY: Wait a minute, vatos. What about our salesman? I think he needs an oil job.

REVOLUCIONARIO: Leave him to me.

(*The* PACHUCO, FARMWORKER *and* MEXICAN-AMERICAN *exit, talking loudly about their plans for the night. The* REVOLUCIONARIO *goes over to* SANCHO, *removes his derby hat and cigar, lifts him up and throws him over his shoulder.* SANCHO *hangs loose, lifeless.)*

REVOLUCIONARIO (*To audience*): He's the best model we got! ¡Ajua! (*Exit.*)   195

(*End.*) •

Short as *Los Vendidos* is, it draws its audience in with its use of humor and its political message. Although the setting and characters are obviously not realistic, we accept their truths for the span of the play, especially if we see the play unfold onstage. As we watch from our seats in a theater, we see the stage as a world with its own realities. As a literary critic, however, you will want to do more than observe the world before you: you will want to figure out what makes it work. To do that, you will want to examine the elements that, together, make up a drama.

ELEMENTS OF DRAMA

The Absence of the Narrator

One of the main features of drama, whether that drama is the drama of the stage or the drama of television and movies, is that there is no narrator, only characters. (Even if a play contains a character called the narrator, that person is still just a character. The audience of a drama sees the events for itself, not from the point of view of a single character.) Drama usually presents *many* points of view, without any one necessarily being more authoritative than the others. This absence of a definitive point of view makes drama a very different genre from the others. In *Los Vendidos,* for example, we do not have any narrator guiding our reactions, letting us know what Honest Sancho thinks about the Secretary or how we are supposed to judge her requests. Because there is no narrator in a play, we respond to many of the elements of drama differently than we typically do to the elements of the poem, short story, or novel.

EXERCISES: TRYING IT OUT

1. Rewrite *Los Vendidos* as a short story. What changes do you need to make—and why?
2. In chapter 2 we included Susan Glaspell's play *Trifles.* Glaspell also wrote a short story, titled "A Jury of Her Peers," based on the play. Locate a copy of that short story at your local or campus library or, perhaps, on the Web. What differences do you notice between the two works? To what extent do those differences result from the differences in the two genres?

Plot and Structure

Many of the plot elements we discussed in relation to stories in chapter 3 are also present in plays. For drama, too, it is important to keep Forster's definition of plot in mind: the plot of a play, like that of a story, contains not only what happens but also what we learn about *why* it happens. Plays, like stories, also have a *conflict* (or problem) and a *resolution* (or solution). Just as in stories, the conflict may be internal, as it is, for example, in *Hamlet,* in which we watch the title character debate how—or whether—he ought to avenge the murder of his father. The conflict may also be external, between characters or between a character and his circumstances. In *Los Vendidos,* the conflict is between what the Secretary wishes to buy and what the salesman can sell her. Valdez presents us with the first *false resolution* (see 78) when Honest Sancho sells the Secretary the apparently perfect model of a Mexican American. However, that resolution disappears when Eric proves as dangerous as the other Mexican models. At that point, the Secretary flees, no longer interested in the merchandise she has purchased, and again we expect the play to end. The Secretary's escape seems to be a resolution. The second apparent resolution is also a false one, though. The real resolution occurs shortly after, when we learn that none of the models is actually for sale: the models, we learn to our surprise, are real, whereas the salesman is simply a machine.

Even so short a play as *Los Vendidos,* then, has a kind of plot twist, a change in direction that keeps us attentive and involved. Longer plays are likely to have even more changes in direction. Sometimes those changes in direction are accomplished by means of *subplots* (see 79). In Shakespeare's plays, for instance, there may be two or three subplots in addition to the main plot.

Longer plays are also divided into **acts** and **scenes,** which function much the way that chapter divisions in books or commercial breaks on television do. Often an act or scene ends at a moment when a character has learned a secret or at a moment of unresolved tension or suspense. By breaking the act or scene at such a moment, the playwright (or for older plays sometimes a later editor) contributes to the audience's sense of involvement. Just as we wait impatiently for a commercial to end so that we can see how events play themselves out, the audience at a theatrical production awaits scene or act changes to discover what happens next.

In live performances, scene and act divisions are also practical ones. On television or in the movies, the location of action can shift easily from one filmed setting to another; the director merely needs to put together two pieces of film. For a staged play, however, a change in time or place often has to be accompanied by a change in the actual **stage set,** all of the structures and items that indicate when and where the actions are occurring. At the end of a scene or act, the curtain may come down or the theater may be darkened as stagehands change the background scenery. Any writer writing for the stage must, then, be aware of how many times she can change location and even of how much time stagehands are going to need to accomplish a scene or act change. For these practical and thematic reasons, acts and scenes are important indications of how the playwright sees the structure of the play.

The number of acts in a play varies from play to play. Some short plays—such as *Los Vendidos* and *Trifles*—have only a single act. Shakespeare's plays always have five acts, though the number of scenes in a Shakespeare play varies considerably from act to act and from play to play. Typically in a Shakespeare play, the act divisions correspond to the structure of the plot. The first three acts define the conflict; by the end of the third act, the conflict has been intensified. The last two acts work out the resolution of the conflict. Though Shakespeare's plays always have five acts, most playwrights vary the number of acts in their plays, depending on the action they are representing.

Whether a play is a longer play divided into acts or scenes or a shorter one-act play like *Los Vendidos* and *Trifles,* it is also restricted by the very pragmatic limitations of audience patience. Whereas a story—which may expand into a lengthy novel—can be read in many sittings, a play has to be performed in one sitting. For that reason, most plays (like movies) are about two or three hours long; rarely are audiences willing to sit for a period of time much longer than that. This restriction on length may affect the way a plot is developed. For example, though a play may span a considerable amount of time, it can do so only by leaping over a gap in time (we may move from one scene to a "twenty years later" scene); we learn about the intervening time through what the characters tell us, but we do not see the whole progression of events (as we might in a novel). Similarly, we may learn about crucial prior events through what we are told; we will not usually be shown them. Time and setting thus work differently in a play than in a short story or novel. Although Shakespeare's Jacques may have been right when he said that "All the world's a stage" in *As You Like It,* the world of the stage is usually, by necessity, compact and time bound.

EXERCISE: TRYING IT OUT

Los Vendidos is a short play with only one scene (and one act). If you were going to expand the play, what other scenes might you add? What changes, if any, would you have to make to Valdez's original to support the new material? As you think about these questions, take your cues from what Valdez has already included. Whatever you add should be consistent with the themes, mood, and characters Valdez has included.

―――――――――――

Character

At the beginning of most plays is a list of **dramatis personae,** the people (or characters) in the play. Characterization in a play has much in common with characterization in any work (see 35–45 for a general discussion of character). There is usually a main character, a *protagonist;* sometimes the playwright draws our attention to this protagonist by naming the play after him or her, as Sophocles did with *Antigone* or Shakespeare did with *Hamlet.* Sometimes there is also an *antagonist,* a key figure opposing the protagonist's actions and values. Creon, Antigone's uncle and the ruler of Thebes, is the antagonist in *Antigone* (1006–43), and Claudius, Hamlet's stepfather and the illegitimate king, is the antagonist in *Hamlet.*

Despite the similarities between the characters in plays and short stories, the differences in the two genres' construction mean that dramatic characters operate somewhat differently than do the characters in a short story. Because there is no narrator in a play to tell us what a character is thinking or to give us a character's prior history and because there are no camera tricks that allow for easy flashbacks to a character's earlier life, all this information is usually conveyed through the spoken word, often through **dialog,** what the characters say to each other. Sometimes a playwright may also have a character give a **soliloquy,** a speech spoken when the character is alone, one that purports to give the character's innermost thoughts. Occasionally, we may hear **asides,** brief comments the character supposedly mutters, comments overheard by the audience but not by the other characters. Soliloquies and asides make us privy to the private thoughts of the character.

Because plays are visual creations, we also learn a great deal about character through the costuming, gestures, and tone of voice of the actors. Such elements may be as important as the words on the page in helping us understand the characters. For example, is the tone of the speeches in *Los Vendidos* humorous? Playful? Teasing? Cynical? Bitter? How the actors read the lines would tell us that. Costuming may play an equally important role in showing us what a character is. For instance, a play may tell us that the character wears a "simple dress." How are we to interpret that? Does the "simple dress" seem shabby? Out of date? Classically elegant? The costumes the actors wear, the ways they speak the words, and the gestures they make may radically affect how we see the characters, so much so that different productions of the same play may lead to vastly different responses on the part of the audience. Consider, for instance, the very different responses evoked by these two movie portrayals of Hamlet, his mother, and his new stepfather.

Claudius (Derek Jacobi), Hamlet (Kenneth Branagh), and Gertrude (Julie Christie) from Branagh's *Hamlet* (1996). (See color insert.)

Hamlet (Ethan Hawke), Gertrude (Diane Venora), and Claudius (Kyle MacLachlan). The Mira-max *Hamlet* (2000) is set in present-day New York City. (See color insert.)

Modern playwrights in particular may try to control an audience's responses through the **stage directions,** which are the author's directions about motivation, gesturing, tone of voice, and costuming (and setting as well). In *Los Vendidos,* for example, we are told that the Farm Worker "lifts his head" and that the Secretary "gasps." The playwright may even attempt to convey certain motivations or emotions through the stage directions, as when Valdez indicates:

SECRETARY (*Impressed*): Where have you been hiding this one?

It will be up to the director to decide *how* the Secretary should convey the fact that she is impressed, but Valdez has made it clear *that* she is impressed.

Some authors' stage directions are very elaborate and detailed. However, much is still left to the discretion of the director of the play and to the actors in determining how the play is performed. If you have the opportunity to see two different productions of the same play, you will easily see how much your responses are determined by a director's decisions.

EXERCISES: TRYING IT OUT

1. Compared with many other playwrights, Valdez includes relatively few stage directions in *Los Vendidos*. Add three or four stage directions, indicating the characters' gestures or emotions. Why did you make your additions?
2. Valdez does not tell us how Honest Sancho and the Secretary are dressed. Write stage directions specifying the costuming of the two characters, and defend your choices.
3. Isolate a particular scene in a play other than *Los Vendidos*. If you were going to direct it, what stage directions would you add? What gestures and intonations would you have the actors use—and why? What other stage directions, gestures, and intonations *might* be used—and why would you reject them?

Setting and Staging

Plays are very visual experiences. We *see* them unfold, and much of what we see has to do with the *stage set* of the play, the physical structures built onstage to represent the *setting* (the time and place) of the play. **Props,** movable physical objects such as chairs, glasses, or tools, contribute to our sense of a detailed setting. The set may represent a modern kitchen in a spacious suburban home or, as in *Los Vendidos,* a small curio shop; it may bring us back into ancient times or take us ahead into the future. In constructing sets, the directors of stage plays are confined by certain restrictions. Whereas television shows and movies can be filmed at various locations, the cast of a stage play cannot simply get up and go to another theater that has another set representing a new location. The set of a stage play must physically fit on the stage and, if there are scene changes, the set must be portable enough to be moved quickly or hidden behind curtains. Despite these restrictions, sets often are fully detailed and elaborate. They may be highly realistic or wonderfully fabulous. Because areas under the stage, overhead, and in the wings are at the director's disposal, all sorts of set changes and special effects may be created on the modern stage.

The set that is used may greatly affect how we respond to a play. Consider, for example, Shakespeare's *The Tempest.* The play takes place on a deserted island; that much Shakespeare explicitly tells us. But how are we to imagine that island? A director might make it a fairy-tale kind of island, one that offers a tropical refuge from the pressures of real life. The set may help us see the protagonist Prospero as a wise king, one who benevolently controls the evil spirit of the island, the bestial Caliban, and who seems gently paternal in his dealings with his daughter. The island of this *Tempest* is a life-affirming place. Another director, however, might make very different decisions. Her set might be constructed to make the island itself threatening and inhuman, a nightmarish place the inhabitants (and viewers) wish to leave behind. Her set may underscore a view of Prospero as a tyrannical wizard, using his power to control the lives of others. Significantly, either interpretation of the play might be created without the director's altering a single word of Shakespeare's work.

In addition to sets, directors have other ways in which to create the setting of a play. Just as the music in a horror film or romantic drama signals a moment of terror or of romance, the music of a staged play may be used to enhance a mood, to make a scene seem ominous or lighthearted. Lighting also contributes to our sense of the setting. It, along with sound effects, may create a storm; colored lights may create a pleasant rosy glow or a stark icy scene. Lighting may draw our attention to a particular part of the stage, perhaps to an element of the set or to a character. Taken all together, these elements go beyond creating just a sense of the physical setting; they guide our responses in ways we may not even be aware of. (For more information about the staging and theatrical conventions of drama, see the Introductions to *The Tempest, Antigone,* and *Oleanna,* later in this book.)

EXERCISE: TRYING IT OUT

Valdez tells us very little about the set he has in mind for *Los Vendidos.* Imagine that it is your job to construct that set and to assemble the props. What would the finished set look like? What would your list of props be? How would the stage set reflect your interpretation of the play?

The Audience and Dramatic Irony

Whenever there is a contradiction between what seems to be true and what is true, *irony* is created. In *Los Vendidos,* for instance, the ending is ironic: we thought that Honest Sancho was real and the models were objects; it turns out that the opposite is true. The title of the play *Trifles* also provides an example of irony: the little housekeeping details that the men in the play see as "trifles" are highly significant, so much so that they lead the women to solve the murder the men are investigating.

A special type of irony, **dramatic irony,** sometimes occurs in plays (and sometimes in other kinds of works as well). In this case, the audience is aware of things a character in the play does not know, perhaps because viewers have heard what other characters have said or seen what they did. For instance, as a character exults in his own well-being, we may know that, ironically, a murderer is hiding under the bed, ready to strike at any minute. Sometimes the audience gains its superior understanding from the knowledge it brings to the play. For example, Sophocles' original Greek audience was well aware of the Oedipus legend. That audience knew that Oedipus was wrong in thinking that, by solving an old murder, he would win the admiration of his Theban subjects. The audience knew that his investigation would lead, ironically, to his own downfall. (For a more comic approach to this kind of audience foreknowledge and dramatic irony, think about modern movies and activities, such as *The Rocky Horror Picture Show* and the sing-along productions of *The Sound of Music*. Because the audience knows what will happen before the characters do, audience members are encouraged to shout out words of warning and advice.)

Theme

As is true for any work of literature, the theme of a play is the "message" it conveys, the idea that the author wants to communicate to the reader or audience. (See the discussion of theme in fiction on 82–83.) Themes may be communicated through any—or all—of the elements of a piece of literature. The events and motivations that we discover through the plot; the characters and our sympathies or antipathies for them; the setting and the atmosphere it creates—all these affect our responses to the work, and from those responses we gain our understanding of the work's ideas.

In *Los Vendidos,* for instance, we are immediately struck by the way in which the Mexicans are portrayed. The setting—Honest Sancho's Used Mexican Lot and Mexican Curio Shop—suggests that the Mexicans are objects, like used cars or cheap souvenirs. The Secretary, a Chicana who has Anglicized her name, presumably so that she will "fit in," wants to purchase Mexicans to serve as political tokens: they will contribute to the seeming "diversity" of the government while helping maintain the status quo. When we are introduced to the "models," we see them as stereotypes rather than as fully realized human beings; only the surprise ending tells us otherwise. All these elements of the setting, the plot, and the characterization lead us to one of the themes of the play: Because we have been fooled along with the Secretary, we share some of her culpability; we, too, have reduced the Mexicans to objects, stereotypes, and "tokens" used for political purposes.

As with all literary works, the title of *Los Vendidos* may provide an important indication of the work's theme. *Los Vendidos* means "the sold," and the title operates on several levels. The title seems to refer literally to the selling of the Mexican models. However, after reading the play, we may ask ourselves who has been "sold," or tricked, and who has "sold out." Those questions, we may find, alert us to the theme of the play.

EXERCISE: TRYING IT OUT

Invent two or three alternate titles for *Los Vendidos* (either in English or in Spanish). What themes of the work do they reflect?

DRAMATIC CONVENTIONS: THE FOURTH WALL

Part of the illusion of drama is usually created by the presence of the **fourth wall.** As we look at the stage, it is as if one of the walls, the so-called fourth wall, has become transparent. We look through it into a house, for example, watching the people inside live out their lives. They are utterly unaware of us and act unself-consciously when they are alone, revealing things in front of us that they would reveal to no one. We are "flies on the wall," enjoying an intimate view of the lives before us.

Sometimes the convention of the fourth wall is obeyed rigidly, with no acknowledgment between actor and audience. For centuries, however, playwrights and directors have played with the convention. Because the drama's characters (or at least the actors playing them) and the audience of a stage play occupy the same physical space, more interaction between them is possible than is true for television or movies. In some plays, the characters spill into the audience, and a sword fight, for instance, may take place in the aisles of the theater. In other plays, seemingly innocent members of the audience may suddenly stand up and move toward the stage, becoming part of the action. In still other plays, a character may speak directly to the audience, overtly erasing the line of separation. Though a deliberate undermining of the theatrical illusion can be seen in plays centuries old, an explicitly ironic undermining of conventions is more typical of modern plays than of older plays. Whether the convention is affirmed or undermined, however, how the "fourth wall" is treated can be an important indication of a playwright's view of "reality" and its relationship to art.

TYPES OF DRAMA

Traditionally, there have been two types of drama: tragedies and comedies. Tragedies are, of course, serious and sad; often they end in death. Comedies, in contrast, are humorous and lighthearted; often they end in marriage. Within these broad definitions, however, there are more specific characteristics that help us define each of the types, as well as a third type, tragicomedy, that combines elements of the two.

Tragedy

The characteristics associated with ancient Greek tragedy were so influential that they helped define tragedies for centuries after. For the Greeks, the **tragic hero** was someone of high birth, usually a king (such as Oedipus) or a member of the royal family (such as Antigone). Because ordinary people were too low to "fall" very far, their circumstances did not lead to "tragedy." According to Aristotle, who defined many of the elements of Greek tragedy for us, the tragic hero is guilty of **hamartia,** an error that sets in motion the tragic circumstances. Traditionally, that error has been defined as a **"tragic flaw,"** a moral failing, and often as **hubris,** an excessive pride that leads heroes to believe that they are on the same level as the gods.

The Greek concept of hamartia, however, does not necessarily refer to a moral failing, and the idea of a "tragic flaw" may sometimes lead to an overly simplistic view of the tragic hero. Some commentators, for instance, *do* see Oedipus as "flawed," as too quick to anger or too eager to escape the fate that the gods have preordained for him. Others, however, see him as innocent, a victim of the gods who have doomed him to kill his father and marry his mother; these critics wonder what choice he has but to pursue the tragedy to the end, especially given the fact that, until the truth is discovered, the people of Thebes will continue to be visited by a horrible plague. The "errors" Oedipus makes are, then, subject to interpretation and may result as much from his ignorance as from any character flaw. For those critics who think Oedipus is *not* morally flawed, hamartia involves only an error in judgment and an unhappy fate, not a tragic flaw.

Later playwrights such as Shakespeare generally followed the Greek tradition of tragedy, but with some variations. Like the Greek tragic heroes, Shakespeare's tragic heroes enjoy high positions as the plays begin. All the tragedies end in the heroes' falls; in fact, all end with the protagonists' deaths. Traditionally, Shakespeare's great tragic heroes have also been seen as having "tragic flaws." Hamlet's flaw, for example, has been defined as indecisiveness, Othello's as jealousy, Macbeth's as too great an ambition. As with the Greek tragedies, however, it is often wise to consider the "tragic flaw" as merely a starting point, for such labels may mask the complexities of the tragic heroes' behaviors and motivations. Hamlet may in fact be indecisive, but it is important to go on to ask *why* he hesitates to act and even whether that hesitation may be the result of moral strengths.

Modern tragedies depart considerably from the earlier model of tragedy. Modern tragic heroes seldom enjoy high positions; more typically, they are ordinary people, rather like us. The tragedy of their lives may be created by themselves, but not necessarily by what we would consider spectacular moral failings. Often they are deluded about themselves and how others see them, as John is in David Mamet's *Oleanna* (573–601). Perhaps the social circumstances of their lives trap them as much as their responses to those circumstances do, as is true for Augustus in Rita Dove's *The Darker Face of the Earth*. Their inability to escape the traps of life that many people face, however those traps are defined or whatever their causes, is often what makes their situations tragic to us.

Comedy

Comedies are, by definition, humorous, whether the humor is created by funny situations or verbal wit (or both). Unlike tragedies, comedies have always focused on ordinary people, making it easy for us to identify with the characters and the dilemmas they face. No matter what confusions or entanglements they suffer, we can laugh at the characters (and sometimes even at their suffering). We are usually certain from the beginning that the problems will disappear by the end, and all will be well.

There are two main types of comedy, **romantic comedies** and **satires.** Romantic comedies take love as their subject; we witness the various obstacles placed in the path of true love, whether it be meddling or unsympathetic parents, unrequited love, or unequal social positions. By the end of the romantic comedy, these obstacles have been removed, and the marriage of the couple (perhaps of more than one couple) is celebrated or is impending. Although Shakespeare's *Tempest* is not a pure comedy— it ends with too strong a sense of melancholy and nostalgia for that label to seem appropriate—it has elements of romantic comedy, for the marriage of Miranda and Ferdinand is part of the resolution of the play.

Satires usually do not take love as their subject. Instead, they look at various social ills, using humor to attack the follies of accepted practices or beliefs. In *Los Vendidos,* for example, Valdez satirizes our ethnic stereotypes and political practices. Funny as a satire may be, it is generally less lighthearted than a romantic comedy. The ending, too, is usually less celebratory. Once the obstacles have been removed in a roman-

Questions to Ask about Drama

1. How many acts does the play have? How do the acts correspond to the major plot developments?
2. Make a list of the major characters in the play. Where do their opinions conflict with one another? Whose opinions are we most apt to accept—and why? What motivates the characters? What do we see as their moral and social strengths and weaknesses?
3. Where is the play set (the time and place)? Is there more than one setting? What do the speeches of the characters and the stage directions indicate about how we are supposed to view the setting? If you were creating a stage set for the play, how would you design it—and why?
4. Does the playwright ever break the convention of the "fourth wall"? If he does, what might the purpose be?
5. Would you consider the play realistic? What elements do or do not seem true to life?
6. Is the play a comedy? A tragedy? A tragicomedy? What helps to define its genre?
7. What do the elements of the play suggest about the play's themes?

tic comedy, the couple is integrated into society; we assume that they will take their place as responsible adults, upholding the social values through the accepted institution of marriage. In contrast, satires often maintain a sense of distance from society; even if their endings create a sense of resolution, many of the essential obstacles remain in place. The problems that exist in society have not truly disappeared by the end of the plays—nor do the satiric playwrights want us to emerge from the theater thinking that all is well.

Tragicomedy

Because tragedy and comedy seem so opposite, it might seem strange to think of them as being combined, but in fact playwrights frequently combine the two modes. Modern plays in particular may be full of displays of dazzling wit that we find very funny; at the same time, the vision of the plays may be rather dark, suggesting the difficulties modern people have in finding satisfying relationships to one another, to the community, or to God. (Humor with a tragic message is called **dark humor.**) Susan Glaspell's play *Trifles* might be considered a tragicomedy: there is humor in the contradiction between the men's condescending view of the women and the women's superior understanding; at the same time, the more we understand the hardships of Mrs. Wright's marriage, the more tragic her circumstances seem.

Even earlier plays, such as some of Shakespeare's, have elements of the tragicomedy. *The Tempest,* for instance, is rich with magic, grace, and love, but we know that in the end Prospero must give up his magic and art and look toward the grave.

Such is hardly the spirit of comedy. Others of Shakespeare's plays are even more problematic, perhaps because the playwright seems uncomfortable with the harsh justice meted out to the villains or because we know that on the edges of the happily-ever-after world lie some continuing dangers.

For many readers, drama is the literary genre closest to life. Like us, the characters onstage move about in physical space, they talk aloud to one another, they even make physical contact with other characters, not only in our imaginations but also in the world of tangible reality. It is no wonder that many playwrights have asked us to think of ourselves as actors in our own lives.

6

Reading Nonfiction and Other Nonliterary Texts

READING ESSAYS

In the sixteenth century, when French writer Michel de Montaigne began writing prose pieces that were somewhere between journal entries and opinion pieces, he called his works *Essais.* The French word, which became our word *essays,* refers not simply to the piece of writing but to the mind-set behind it. Montaigne saw his writings as "attempts," "trials." Indeed, he wrote, "Were my mind settled, I would not essay, but resolve myself; it is still a prentice [apprentice]" (Kaiser xiv).

Although today we generally think of **essays** as prose pieces that argue, analyze, or narrate, we would like you to think of them in Montaigne's terms. Even the most polished and emphatic essay is still a "trial." Essays are works of **nonfiction** (they do not narrate made-up events), but they are not works of pure fact; they always include some opinion. If you think about essays in this way, it will be easier for you to think about them as works in progress, as works that you as a reader help to complete. It will, in other words, be easier to read them critically and to apply to them the same kind of analytical skills you would apply to a piece of literature.

It is not only essays, though, that you will want to analyze as literature. To some extent, the line between "literature" and "nonliterature" has always been blurred, as literary writers have often drawn on nonliterary sources, transforming them into works of poetry, fiction, or drama. Today's critics go further, arguing that all texts are shaped by their creators and that, therefore, all texts can profit from literary analysis. According to this way of thinking, no text, not even the most informative and factual, is simply a mirror of reality and fact. All texts, including the "texts" of pictures and other nonverbal media, profitably open themselves up to literary analysis. It is for that reason that we have included in *Retellings* works from genres that were once outside the bounds of "literature." In addition to essays, you will find in this anthology examples from the fields of journalism, film, art, popular culture, and advertising. And we ask you to consider each as a "text" to which you can apply your skills as a literary critic.

Types of Essays

The Narrative Essay Just as there are different genres within the category of "literature," there are different genres within the category of "essay." Perhaps the kind of essay that is closest to literature, and a kind of essay that is often assigned in literature classes, is the **narrative essay,** which takes as its center a story about actual (nonfiction) events. It has largely a chronological organization, moving from one event in time to another, and it focuses on events and the people who live them. Even though it tells a story, though, a narrative essay is still an essay; because events are presented to illustrate an argumentative point (the **thesis**), finally the story takes a backseat to that point.

In *Retellings* we have included several narrative essays. E. B. White's "Once More to the Lake" is a narrative essay, for instance, as is Joan Didion's "Some Dreamers of the Golden Dream." For both White and Didion, the story conveys an argument; in White's case, the argument is largely implicit: as we look at the way his son's experiences do and do not mirror his own, White wants us to see something about the process of aging. Didion similarly uses a story to make a point, though her point is more explicit; by telling of a California murder case, Didion hopes to teach us something important about California itself.

The Descriptive Essay   Like the narrative essay, the **descriptive essay** has much in common with more traditional literary forms. Indeed, hearing the words "descriptive writing," many readers immediately conclude that the subject is creative writing: poetry or short stories, for instance. Of course much literature *is* highly descriptive; through rich and evocative descriptions a writer can create an entire world or arouse strong feelings. It is not only the writer of literature who uses such description, however. A biologist might use a descriptive essay, or part of an essay, to detail an animal's coloring and behavior, or an archeologist might use description to tell readers what an archeological dig looks like at the moment when the archeologists first enter a long-hidden burial site. In other words, although we often think of description and descriptive essays as belonging to fields such as creative writing and literature, a look at the writing you read in all of your classes—and outside school—will tell you otherwise. At the same time, though, it is rare to find an essay that is purely descriptive, just as it is rare to find an essay that is purely narrative. Most essays use a mix of techniques.

The Argumentative or Analytical Essay   Although essays that work primarily by means of narration and description are common in literature classes, most of the essays you read outside literature classes and most of those you write in all of your classes will probably make their arguments more explicitly. Notice, by the way, that "argument" here does not mean that there is an unpleasant or emotional debate going on. Nor does it necessarily mean that a writer is taking sides between a "pro" side of an issue and a "con" side. An argumentative essay simply states a strong thesis—also called a **claim**—about a debatable issue, providing evidence to back up that claim. One kind of argument is called **analysis.** An analysis—or **analytical essay**—focuses on how and why something works or how and why something is true. Most of the essays written about literature are analytical essays that explain how and why we respond to the literary work in the way we do.

Because you will frequently be asked to write and read analytical and argumentative essays, we want to spend some time on a particular example. To illustrate the idea that all "texts" open themselves up to literary analysis and argument, we have chosen an essay by Elayne Rapping that responds to its own nonliterary text: *Roseanne,* a television situation comedy that was popular in the 1990s and that is currently being aired in reruns. As you read the essay, think about the central claim that it is making: What is the primary question, the **thesis question,** the essay is asking, and how can you succinctly summarize the answer to that question? (Note that, although student writers are often encouraged to place a single thesis sentence at the end of the introductory paragraph, not all professional essays do that. You will want to look elsewhere for Rapping's statement of her thesis, and you may discover that it is contained in more than a single sentence.) Rapping has chosen as her subject a topic about which many of us know more than we might care to admit: television. It is partly for that reason that we have included it here.

ELAYNE RAPPING (1938–   )

In Praise of Roseanne

The other night, while flipping among the three nightly network news broadcasts, I stopped—as I often do—to check out the *Roseanne* rerun Fox cleverly schedules during that time slot in New York. And, as often happens, I found myself sticking around longer than I intended, watching the Conners wiggle their way through whatever crisis had hit their Kmart window fan that day.

On the three more respectable networks, the Dow Jones averages rise and fall; Congress and the courts hand down weighty decisions in lofty prose; the official weapons of state are deployed, around the globe and in the inner cities, to preserve democracy and the American way. But in the Conner residence, where most things are either in disrepair or not yet paid for, it is possible to glimpse—as it rarely is on the newscasts themselves—how the fallout from such headlines might actually affect those who are relatively low in the pecking order.

On CBS, NBC, ABC, and CNN, the problems of the women who make headlines are not likely to sound familiar to most of us. Zoë Baird may be struggling with the servant issue. Hillary may have misplaced her capital-gains records. The Queen of England may be embroiled in royal-family dysfunction. But Roseanne, matriarch of the shabby Conner household, will be coping with less glamorous trauma—unemployment, foreclosure, job stress, marital power struggles, unruly and unmotivated kids—in a less dignified but more realistic style.

I am a big fan of Roseanne—Barr, Arnold, Conner, whatever. So are my female and working-class students, who invariably claim her as their own and hang on to her for dear life as they climb the ladder of class and professional achievement—an effort in which their parents have so hopefully invested everything they own. But it recently occurred to me that I have never—in the many years I've regularly analyzed and commented on American popular culture—written a single word about her. Nor have I read many, outside the trashy tabloids, where her personal life and public persona are regularly recorded and described.

In the last year, I've read dozens of academic and popular articles, and two whole books, about *The Cosby Show*. Archie Bunker and *All in the Family* have been praised and analyzed endlessly. Even *Murphy Brown* and *The Mary Tyler Moore Show* are taken seriously in ever-broadening academic and journalistic circles. Not to mention the well-structured, post-structural Madonna, long the darling of feminist critics and academics.

What is it about these other media icons that makes them somehow more "respectable" subjects of intellectual analysis, more suitable to "serious" discourse? What is it about Roseanne that makes her so easy to ignore or write off, despite her (to me) obvious talent, originality, political *chutzpah,* and power? Gender and appearance are surely part of it; but I suspect that class—position as well as attitude—is the major factor. Bill Cosby's Cliff Huxtable, Mary Tyler Moore's Mary Richards, Candice Bergen's Murphy Brown are all well-turned out, well-educated liberal professionals. And the grungy, working-class Archie Bunker, far from scoring points for his class, is always beaten down by the liberal, professional mentality of everyone else on the show. As for Madonna, while she is certainly not respectable, she makes up for it by being blond, chic, and gorgeous, which, in our culture, covers a multitude of social sins.

But Roseanne is a different story, far more unassimilable into mainstream-media iconography than any of these others. Fat, sloppy, foul-mouthed, and bossy, she is just a bit too unrepentantly, combatively proud of her gender and class position and style to be easily molded into the "movin' on up" mode of American mass media. She isn't "movin' up" to anywhere. She is standing pat, week after week on her show—and a lot of the rest of the time in a lot of other places—speaking out for the dignity and the rights of those the media have set out to shame into invisibility or seduce into endless, self-hating efforts at personal transformation. With her bad hair and baggy pants and oversized shirts from the lower level of the mall, with her burned meat loaf and tuna casseroles and Malomars, with her rough language and politically incorrect child-rearing methods, with her dead-end minimum-wage jobs, Roseanne has gone further than Madonna or almost anyone else I can think of at turning the hegemonic norms of the corporate media on their heads. But few of the intellectual writing classes have seen fit to credit, much less celebrate, her for it. So I will.

To appreciate Roseanne's unlikely ascent into prime-time stardom, it's useful to place her within the generic traditions of the family sitcom. Roseanne is not a descendant of the pristine line of virginal wife/mothers who have set the norms for such characters from the days of June Cleaver to the present. No sweetly submissive smiles or politely helpful suggestions to hubby and kids for her. She is one of a rarer breed, the one invented and defined by Lucille Ball in *I Love Lucy,* in which the female protagonist is more Helpmeet from Hell than from Heaven.

The parallels between these two women are interesting, and reveal a lot about what has and hasn't changed for the women—white, working-class, and poor—who make up the female majority in this country (although you'd never know it from watching TV). Both were, and are, popular and powerful beyond the dreams of almost any woman performer of their times. And yet both eschewed the traditional feminine, white, middle-class persona dictated by the norms of their days, preferring to present themselves as wild women, out of bounds, loud, funny, and noisy—all attributes which sexist culture beats out of most of us very early on. In a world in which females are enjoined not to take up too much space, not to make "spectacles" of ourselves, not to "disturb" but to contain "the peace," women like Roseanne and Lucy have always been frightening, repulsive, even indecent. That's why they so appall us even as, consciously or subconsciously, we are drawn to them.

I used to cringe when I watched *I Love Lucy* as a child. She filled me with embarrassment because she was so stereotypically "hysterical," so much a failure in her endless efforts to move out of the confines of traditional femininity and its many indignities (indignities otherwise kept hidden by the Stepford-like types of Donna Reed and June Cleaver).

I was far more comfortable, as a middle-class girl, with the persona created by Mary Tyler Moore—first as the frustrated dancer/wife in *The Dick Van Dyke Show* and later as the first real career woman in her own show. Unlike Lucy, Mary Richards was perfectly groomed and mannered. She was sweetly deferential in her apologetic efforts at assertiveness; embarrassingly grateful for every nod of respect or responsibility from her boss, "Mr. Grant." Ambitious, yes, but never forgetful of the "ladylike" way of moving up the corporate ladder, one dainty, unthreatening step at a time. Where Lucy embarrassed, Mary was soothing. No pratfalls or dumb disguises for her.

But through Roseanne, I've come to see the very improper Lucy differently. For her time, after all, she was a real fighter against those feminine constraints. She tried to *do* things and she tried to do them with other women, against the resistance of every man on the show. She was not well groomed, did not live in tasteful elegance, did not support and help her husband at business and social affairs—far from it. She was full of energy and rebelliousness and, yes, independence—to a point.

But of course she always failed, and lost, and made a fool of herself. Her show was pure slapstick fantasy, because, back then, the things she was trying to achieve were so far from imaginable that someone like her could only exist in a farcical mode. But, as Roseanne's very different way of playing this kind of woman shows, that is no longer true.

Like Lucy, Roseanne is loud, aggressive, messy, and ambitiously bossy. Roseanne, too, has close relationships with other women. And Roseanne, too, is larger than life, excessive, to many frightening and repulsive. But her show is no fantasy. It is the most realistic picture of gender, class, and family relations on television today. And that's because Roseanne herself is so consciously political, so gender- and class-conscious, in every detail of her show.

No more the harried husband rolling his eyes at his wife's antics. Where other sitcoms either ignore feminism and reproduce traditional relations or, perhaps worse, present perfectly harmonious couples—like the Huxtables—for whom gender equity comes as naturally as their good looks, Roseanne and Dan duke it out over gender and power issues as equals who seem really to love, respect, and—not least—get angry at each other.

Nor does Roseanne need to think up crazy schemes for achieving the impossible—a project outside the home. Roseanne, like most of us, needs to work. The jobs she is forced to take—sweeping in a hair salon, waiting tables in malls and diners, working on an assembly line—are very like the ones Lucy nabbed and then messed up, to the wild laughter of the audience. But for Roseanne the humor is different. Roseanne fights with sexist, overbearing bosses, lashes out at her kids because she's stressed out at work, moonlights to get them through the rough days when Dan is out of work. And if these things are funny to watch, they are also deeply revealing of social and emotional truths in the lives of women and working-class families today.

The most touching and impressive thing about this series—and the main reason for its popularity—is its subtle presentation of progressive "messages" in a way that is neither preachy nor condescending to audiences. Much was made of the famous episode in which Roseanne was kissed by a lesbian character. (And it is surely a tribute to Roseanne's integrity and clout that this first lesbian kiss got past Standards and Practices because of her.) But the kiss itself was really no big deal. Lots of shows will be doing this kind of one minute/one scene "Wow, did you see that?" thing soon enough.

Sitcoms are, indeed, informed by liberal values, and they do, indeed, tend to preach to us about tolerance and personal freedom. Lesbianism, as an idea, an abstraction, a new entry on the now very long list of liberal tolerances to which the professional middle classes must pay lip service, was bound to hit prime time soon anyway. What made the Roseanne "lesbian episode" remarkable and radically different from the usual liberal sitcom style of tackling such issues was not the kiss itself but the startlingly honest discussions about homosexuality that followed the kiss, between Dan and his young son D.J.; and then between Dan and Roseanne, in bed.

This segment was politically audacious because it *did not* lecture the vast majority of Americans who are, yes, queasy about homosexuality. It presented them with a mirror image of their own confusion and anxiety, and led them to a position of relative comfort about it all, by sympathizing with their very real concern about radical social and sexual change.

This is how the show attacks all its difficult issues, sensational and mundane. Much has been made of Roseanne's way of yelling at her kids, even hitting them on at least one occasion. Clearly, this is not how parents, since Dr. Spock, have been told to behave, and for obvious and good reason. Nonetheless, we all do these things on occasion. (And those who don't, ever, probably have other serious parenting problems.) To pretend that parents don't do that—as most sitcoms do—is to condescend to viewers who know that this goes on everywhere, and who have, themselves, done it or at least fought the urge.

On *Roseanne,* such behavior is neither denied nor condemned; it is talked about and analyzed. After hitting her son, for example, Roseanne apologizes and confesses, heartbreakingly, that she was herself beaten as a child and that it was wrong then and wrong now. It is this kind of honesty about negative feelings—especially when they are placed in the kind of social and economic context this show never slights—that makes the positive feelings of love and mutual respect within this battered, battling family so very believable.

Which brings me, unavoidably, to the issue of Roseanne Arnold herself, as a public persona—surely the major factor in the public unease about her. There are two "Roseannes"—both media images constructed cleverly and carefully by Arnold herself. "Roseanne Conner" is, as Arnold herself says, "much nicer." She is the sitcom version of how someone overcomes personal and economic difficulty and not only survives but thrives. She comes from a long line of show-business satirists whose humor was based on social and political truth. Like the Marx Brothers and Charlie Chaplin, she is the lovable outsider sneaking into the polite world to expose its hypocrisy and phoniness.

That is the fictional "Roseanne" of sitcom fame. The other persona, "Roseanne Barr Arnold"—the woman who appears in tabloids, talk shows, news shows, and comedy clubs—is far more outrageous, more dangerous. She is the ultimate bad girl, the woman who shouts out to the entire world every angry, nasty, shameful truth and emotion she feels about the lives of women, especially poor women, in America today.

Much of what Roseanne confesses to—about incest, wife abuse, mental illness, obesity, prostitution, lesbianism—makes people uncomfortable. It's tacky, embarrassing, improper, déclassé to discuss these issues in public. But so was much of what we Second Wave feminists and student activists and antiwar protesters and others insisted upon talking about and confessing to and doing in the 1960s. So is what Anita Hill insisted—in much classier style but to no less shock and outrage—on throwing at us from the Senate hearing rooms. So is almost every political statement and action that rocks the reactionary boats of institutionalized power and authority.

And like those other actions and statements, Roseanne's antics are inherently political, radical, salutary. For in speaking out about her hidden demons and ghosts and scars—as a woman, a working-class person, a victim of family and institutional abuse—she speaks *for* the myriad damaged and disempowered souls, mostly still silent and invisible, who also bear the scars of such class, gender, and age abuse.

My timing, as I write this, couldn't be worse, of course. The tabloids are currently ablaze with the latest, and most unfortunate, of Arnold brouhahas. Roseanne, having loudly accused her husband of infidelity and spousal abuse, filed for divorce, then almost immediately rescinded the statements and reconciled with her husband, only to file for divorce again a few weeks later.

I am neither shocked nor disillusioned by this. Every abused woman I have ever known has attempted, unsuccessfully, to leave her destructive relationship many times, before finally finding the strength and support to make the break. This, after all, is the very essence of the abuse syndrome. Only Roseanne, as usual, has chosen to play it out, in all its gory details, in the spotlight.

I'm a Roseanne fan. I like her show and marvel at her compassion and intelligence, at what she manages to get away with. I like her style—even when she offends me and makes me nervous (which she often does)—because the world needs loud-mouthed unattractive women with brains, guts, a social conscience, and a sense of humor. There are few enough of them who make it through puberty with their spirits and energies intact.   •

Even if you are unfamiliar with *Roseanne* and the other television shows Rapping mentions, you have probably watched some situation comedies on television and so have some important background for understanding Rapping's argument. That background will help you analyze Rapping's essay and gain some sense of what all essay writing, including literary analysis, involves: Rapping makes a strong claim—*Roseanne* presents a more realistic portrait of gender roles and expectations than do most television shows—and she provides logically developed arguments and evidence in its support. Equally important is that the claim Rapping presents is one that would surprise many readers, who may well think of *Roseanne* as simply funny or unrealistic and who may consider Roseanne herself simply obnoxious and not the least bit admirable. By highlighting what she sees as the show's realistic feminism and by declaring her admiration for a character and actress who are often denounced or criticized, Rapping does what all successful essayists hope to do: she gives us a new way of looking at things.

Like most analytical or argumentative essays, Rapping's makes its point largely by means of example and evidence. Look, for instance, at the second and third paragraphs of the essay. One of her strategies in praising *Roseanne* is to show that it is more realistic even than news shows that report reality. Rather than simply say that, Rapping tells us about the news stories on the "three more respectable networks," mentioning *particular* stories that they cover: the stock market averages, Congressional and judicial decisions, and political and military actions. Then she goes even further, developing those points with even more detail. To the "three more respectable networks," now identified by name, Rapping adds CNN, and then moves to a brief discussion of their treatment of women's issues. Again, notice that Rapping does more than simply say that the major networks treat women's issues that are irrelevant to most of us. She identifies those issues, naming names: Zoë Baird, Hillary Clinton, and the Queen of England. In these paragraphs, as elsewhere in her essay, then, Rapping does not allow her opinions simply to speak for themselves. Each opinion, each generalization, is developed with a piece of evidence, and that piece of evidence is then developed in some detail.

In developing her point, Rapping employs several strategies. Most dominant, of course, is her use of the details from *Roseanne* and the other situation comedies she discusses. Rapping identifies several key episodes and the events in them. We know, for instance, that Roseanne feels guilty for having hit her son and that she reveals her own history of abuse. We know that she has worked at various blue collar jobs, and, more important, we know what those jobs are. We know that Roseanne is kissed by a gay woman and that that kiss leads to a frank and uncomfortable discussion between Roseanne and Dan. It would be easy to think of these details as just a list of details from Rapping's favorite episodes, but doing so would diminish her argument. Instead of being simply items on a list, each of the details mentioned serves Rapping's argumentative purpose. Each advances her thesis that *Roseanne* takes risks and faces the realities of working-class life head-on.

To strengthen her argument further, Rapping draws on readers' knowledge of television history, comparing *Roseanne* to earlier television shows. In referring to *The Donna Reed Show* and *The Dick Van Dyke Show,* she recalls situation comedies from the early 1960s, a television era that many associate with white middle-class values. Because those shows rarely dealt with social issues or anything other than momentary tensions, they are often easy targets for television critics who think of early television programming as shallow and vapid. One might expect an admirer of *Roseanne* to find *The Donna Reed Show* and *The Dick Van Dyke Show* empty.

Rapping goes further, though. She targets those readers who might find more daring comedies such as *All in the Family* realistic. With its loudmouthed and sometimes offensive depiction of generational conflict and racial bigotry, *All in the Family* seems the height of gritty realism. Rapping argues, though, that *All in the Family* seems more realistic than it is, at least if one is looking at working-class realism. What is important to notice is that Rapping could easily have made her point by referring only to the sugar-coated sitcoms of the 1950s and early 1960s. She strengthens her point considerably by refusing to take the easy way out. As soon as she argues that Madonna, *All in the Family*'s Archie Bunker, and the other media icons she mentions package the same middle-class attitudes and values that early sitcoms did, she has us thinking.

It is this willingness to take chances and look at ideas, events, and people from a new perspective that makes an argumentative essay successful. After all, if a writer says only what we all already know, why would we read what he has to say? If a writer gives opinions but provides no supporting evidence, how can we distinguish between those opinions and simple bias? It is not enough for a writer to say, "Well, that's just my opinion," as if opinion is enough or as if all opinions are equally valid. (To test the assumption that all opinions are equally valid, you need only ask yourself whether you would trust the family doctor or the family lawyer to diagnose a medical ailment. Clearly expertise and training, whether in medicine or law, in popular culture or literature, matter.) As you read essays, and as you write them, you will want to respect the value of expertise and to insist that other readers and writers do the same.

As we said previously, we included Rapping's essay as a model largely because it focuses on a subject, television, that is familiar to most of us. Obviously, not all essays and subjects are so accessible to the average audience. Essays written for more specialized or technical audiences are likely to draw their evidence from more specialized or technical sources. They are likely as well to use more formal language, and they may support their ideas with factual evidence. Whatever the audience or subject of the essay, however, you will want to pay particular attention to the ways in which the evidence is presented and used. Here are some questions you might ask about the evidence presented by any writer:

1. Who or what are the sources of the evidence? Are they reliable and unbiased sources?
2. Can the evidence be verified in some way? In other words, is there more than one single source for the evidence?
3. If the writer is using statistics, what can you determine about how the statistics were gathered? For instance, if the statistics represent responses to survey questions, who was polled? Were the questions phrased in such a way as to avoid bias?
4. If the writer is using scientific data, what was the scientific methodology used in the gathering of the data? If the experiments were to be repeated, would similar results be achieved?
5. If the writer is making analogies or comparisons and contrasts, how valid do the analogies and comparisons seem?
6. If the writer is relying on personal narrative or observation for some of the evidence, how typical do the observations and experiences seem? In other words, are they representative enough to be valid as evidence?
7. When presenting evidence, does the writer consider other ways of interpreting the evidence? In other words, does the writer acknowledge and answer opposing points of view?

Among the analytical essays in *Retellings* are student essays that present a critical thesis about a piece of literature and essays by literary critics E. R. Dodds, P. H. Vellacott, Ernest Jones, Carolyn Heilbrun, Henry James, and Elaine Showalter. Also included are analyses by psychologists Sigmund Freud and Bruno Bettelheim. In each case, the writer makes a claim about a piece of literature or a way of thinking, presents evidence (usually in the form of quotations from the text), and explains to readers how the evidence supports a critical opinion. As you read such essays, pay particular attention to the way writers use quotations, asking yourself whether the writer considers fully the reliability of a speaker and the context of the speaker's words. Make certain, too, that the writer has persuaded you to share his or her foundational assumptions. As is true of any argument, literary criticism based on questionable assumptions will be unpersuasive no matter how many quotations and other forms of evidence the critic supplies.

Elements of Essays

Thesis Essays are often called **expository,** or informative, because they expound on, or elaborate on, a central idea. That central idea is the *thesis,* the single point that all of the other parts of the essay are meant to support and prove. Whether it is stated in an explicit thesis statement or left implied, the thesis is an essential part of any essay. To put it bluntly, if a writer has no thesis, she has no essay.

As we said earlier, students are often encouraged to place their thesis at the end of an essay's first paragraph; that way, both writer and reader can be certain that there *is* a thesis. Professional writers often place their theses at the end of an introduction, too, and for the same reason: the thesis forms a kind of contract between the reader and the writer. It gives them a place over which they might shake hands, agreeing that *this* is what it is all about. Still, keep in mind that professional writers don't always state their theses explicitly, and, if they do, they don't always place them up front. The thesis may be expressed anywhere. A writer may even decide to include a thesis paragraph, as Rapping does toward the end of her essay. In that paragraph (it begins "And like those other actions and statements"), Rapping makes explicit what she has primarily implied elsewhere. She has provided the reader with her evidence beforehand and is now ready to state openly the conclusions she is sure the reader has come to. The thesis paragraph serves the dual purpose of bringing the thesis ideas to the foreground and summing up the essay without Rapping's having to resort to a mechanical and formulaic summary conclusion. (Few readers need a summary conclusion in an essay as short as Rapping's; nor do they need the conclusion signaled to them with a too-obvious "Finally" or "In conclusion.")

EXERCISE: TRYING IT OUT

Reread "In Praise of Roseanne." Is the thesis stated before the thesis paragraph? Is it stated more than once? How would different placements or statements of the thesis alter your response to the essay?

Tone and Style Essays, like all kinds of writing, convey their ideas not only through the words they use but also through their *tones,* the moods they create. Much informational and analytical writing, the kind found in textbooks or in much scholarly writing, strives for a neutral tone. The writer chooses words without strong connotations, hoping to convey a professional and unemotional tone of neutrality. Look, for instance, at these lines from Gary Engle's "What Makes Superman So Darned American?"

> It is impossible to imagine Superman being as popular as he is and speaking as deeply to the American character were he not an immigrant and an orphan. Immigration, of course, is the overwhelming fact in American history. Except for the Indians, all Americans have an immediate sense of their origins elsewhere. . . .

Like the peoples of the nations whose values he defends, Superman is an alien, but not just any alien. He's the consummate and totally uncompromised alien . . .

Although Engle's language seems neutral, even it can profitably be opened to critical analysis. Notice, for instance, Engle's deliberate use of the word *alien,* a word that helps him bridge the gap between the average immigrant's experiences and origins and the extraterrestrial experiences and origins of Superman.

Other kinds of essays may use different tones. A narrative essay, or one written for the audience of a popular magazine, often has a conversational tone, partly because the author wants us to see ourselves in his shoes. "Some Dreamers of the Golden Dream" by Joan Didion, for example, has a somewhat melodramatic tone; Didion chooses words to heighten the emotion and to create a sense of terror and suspense. Here, for instance, is the opening paragraph of "Some Dreamers of the Golden Dream." (The full essay appears on 602–13.)

This is a story about love and death in the golden land, and begins with the country. The San Bernardino Valley lies only an hour east of Los Angeles by the San Bernardino Freeway but is in certain ways an alien place: not the coastal California of the subtropical twilights and the soft westerlies off the Pacific but a harsher California, haunted by the Mojave just beyond the mountains, devastated by the hot dry Santa Ana wind that comes down through the passes at 100 miles an hour and whines through the eucalyptus windbreaks and works on the nerves. October is the bad month for the wind, the month when breathing is difficult and the hills blaze up spontaneously. There has been no rain since April. Every voice seems a scream. It is the season of suicide and divorce and prickly dread, wherever the wind blows.

With carefully chosen language, Didion's opening creates an ominous mood: we are waiting now for something awful to happen.

EXERCISE: TRYING IT OUT

Authors, both professional and student, often convey through their tones something that is not entirely true. Sometimes writers adopt a tone that they hope will convey more confidence than they really feel. Sometimes they try to sound more academic or scholarly, or more neutral and objective, than they really are. Bring in a piece of writing (of your own or of someone else's) with the author's name removed, and ask a classmate to analyze what the tone seems to reveal about the intent and personality of the writer.

The language of an essay is more than a matter of its tone, of course. For essayists, as for writers of imaginative literature, style is partly a matter of tone and word choice, but it is also a matter of how a writer creates images and structures or asks a reader to form logical connections.

Consider this example from "Shooting an Elephant," an essay written by George Orwell (1903–1950), the author of *1984* and *Animal Farm*. In that essay, Orwell tells of his experiences as an Englishman in Burma and argues that those in power often become powerless because they have to keep demonstrating their power. As you read, pay particular attention to Orwell's use of image:

> But at that moment I glanced round at the crowd that had followed me. It was an immense crowd, two thousand at the least and growing every minute. It blocked the road for a long distance on either side. I looked at the sea of yellow faces above the garish clothes—faces all happy and excited over this bit of fun, all certain that the elephant was going to be shot. They were watching me as they would watch a conjurer about to perform a trick. They did not like me, but with the magical rifle in my hands I was momentarily worth watching. And suddenly I realized that I should have to shoot the elephant after all. The people expected it of me and I had got to do it. I could feel their two thousand wills pressing me forward, irresistibly. And it was at this moment, as I stood there with the rifle in my hands, that I first grasped the hollowness, the futility of the white man's dominion in the East. Here was I, the white man with his gun, standing in front of the unarmed native crowd—seemingly the leading actor of the piece, but in reality I was only an absurd puppet pushed to and fro by the will of those yellow faces behind. I perceived in this moment that when the white man turns tyrant, it is his own freedom that he destroys. He becomes a sort of hollow, posing dummy, the conventionalized figure of a sahib. For it is the condition of his rule that he shall spend his life in trying to impress the "natives," and so in every crisis he has got to do what the "natives" expect of him. He wears a mask, and his face grows to fit it. I had got to shoot the elephant. I had committed myself to doing it when I sent for the rifle. A sahib has got to act like a sahib; he has got to appear resolute, to know his own mind and do definite things. To come all that way, rifle in hand, with two thousand people marching at my heels, and then to trail feebly away, having done nothing—no, that was impossible. The crowd would laugh at me. And my whole life, every white man's life in the East, was one long struggle not to be laughed at.

Notice that as the paragraph begins the "natives" are indistinguishable from one another; they all belong to the same "sea of yellow faces," and those faces seem somehow simply to float above the "garish clothes." As the paragraph moves along, the people's *wills* become more important, but the people are still not individuals so much as a force against which the colonial officer must exert his own power. As the imagery implies, the colonial officer—Orwell himself—is even less a full person. Although he begins the paragraph by comparing himself to a "conjurer," he is only "seemingly the leading actor of the piece." He is not the powerful magician who can conjure something (even if only an illusion) out of nothing but rather an actor who speaks the lines and makes the gestures someone else has given him. Even that position is only a "seeming" one, though, for Orwell moves on. He is not a leading actor; he is an "absurd puppet," someone without will and independence, someone who cannot move freely across the stage, and who certainly cannot break free of the strings that bind him to his role and actions. Next, the imagery reveals, that limited amount of movement and life is also illusory; the "absurd puppet" becomes a "hollow, posing dummy," a lifeless, shallow, and empty being without even the appearance of independent thought and movement. In the end, even the illusion of a whole physical body is lost. All that is left is a mask.

For Orwell, then, style tells part of the story and reveals part of the thesis. A careful look at the way he and other essayists manipulate language and image will reward you with a clearer understanding of how they make meaning and how they persuade their audiences to accept their truths.

Like those who write fiction, poetry, and drama, good essay writers craft their essays. As a result, as you read what they have to say, you should pay some attention to the way an author's style moves you along, making you move faster through an essay or slowing you down. Look for places where a series of long sentences is broken by a short, emphatic sentence, calling attention to the idea it contains, or where an author repeats key ideas and phrases to drive them home; pay attention to imagery, just as you would if the work you were reading was a piece of fiction. In the hands of a skilled essayist, style and meaning converge.

EXERCISES: TRYING IT OUT

1. Identify the patterns of imagery in the following. How do the images reinforce each author's meaning?

    a. The dump was our poetry and our history. We took it home with us by the wagonload, bringing back into town the things the town had used and thrown away. Some little part of what we gathered, mainly bottles, we managed to bring back to usefulness, but most of our gleanings we left lying around barn or attic or cellar until in some renewed fury of spring cleaning our families carted them off to the dump again, to be rescued and briefly treasured by some other boy with schemes for making them useful. Occasionally something we really valued with a passion was snatched from us in horror and returned at once. That happened to the mounted head of a white mountain goat, somebody's trophy from old times and the far Rocky Mountains, that I brought home one day in transports of delight. My mother took one look and discovered that his beard was full of moths.

    From Wallace Stegner, "The Town Dump"

    b. In 1926, the O'Banions, still unrepentant despite the loss of their leader, introduced another novelty in gang warfare. In broad daylight, while the streets of Cicero were alive with traffic, they raked Al Capone's headquarters with machine-gun fire from eight touring cars. The cars proceeded down the crowded street outside the Hawthorne Hotel in solemn line, the first one firing blank cartridges to disperse the innocent citizenry and to draw the Capone forces to the doors and windows, while from the succeeding cars, which followed a block behind, flowed a steady rattle of bullets spraying the hotel and the adjoining buildings up and down. One gunman even got out of his car, knelt carefully upon the sidewalk at the door of the Hawthorne, and played one hundred bullets into the lobby—back and forth, as one might play the hose upon one's garden. The casualties were miraculously light, and Scarface Al himself remained in safety, flat on the floor of the Hotel Hawthorne restaurant; nevertheless, the bombardment quite naturally attracted public attention. Even in a day when bullion was transported in armored cars, the transformation of a suburban street into a shooting gallery seemed a little unorthodox.

From Frederick Lewis Allen, *Only Yesterday*

2. Experiment with the effects of tone and style by rewriting a piece of writing that seems highly objective. You might, for instance, take a paragraph from one of your textbooks or the news section of a newspaper. Rewrite the paragraph in a less objective style and tone, using more charged language and more of the techniques we associate with storytelling (narrative, dialog, description, etc.). What is gained with your changes? What is lost?

Structure As with any kind of writing, essays can be structured in a variety of ways. Some essays are primarily narrative; they will move largely by means of a chronological organization: events will unfold in the order in which they occurred. An essay that contains a large amount of description, on the other hand, may be organized spatially; that is, an author will look at the object being described and move, for instance, from right to left or top to bottom, much as a camera might pan across a scene.

The organizations of argumentative and analytical essays are trickier. All of us understand that events unfold in time and that an object or scene becomes clear to us as we move our eyes slowly across its surface. It is less clear how ideas get organized logically; after all, one person's way of looking at an idea may not always be similar to another's way of looking at that same idea.

For that reason, it is sometimes helpful to think in terms of particular modes of organization. Sometimes a writer will organize by means of a cause/effect relationship: the first event not only preceded the second but caused it to happen. Historians often talk in terms of cause and effect when, for instance, they trace the causes of war. So, too, do economists who talk about the causes of an economic downturn or the consequences of a particular business decision. What is important here is that the writer must establish the causal link; she must *show* that X caused Y, not simply say that because X came before Y, it must have caused it. (To see the difference between chronological and cause/effect structures, you need only to think about the kinds of false conclusions that might be drawn about an earthquake. Assume that you are describing the moments before and after the earthquake struck and you know that someone had been planting a tree in her garden right before the earth began shaking. You might say that the earthquake occurred shortly after the woman began digging the hole for the tree, but you almost certainly would not say that the earth shook *because* the woman was digging.)

Another common organizational device is one that guides the reader from the least important idea to the most important one. Writers often choose to move from the least to most important idea to build toward a climax and, at the same time, to encourage their readers to see that an argument is gaining momentum as it moves along. When a writer uses such an organization, he means to persuade you that what he sees as the most important idea *is* the most important idea. You will want to be aware of such persuasive techniques. It is easy to be moved along with the flow of energy and fail to recognize that an author may overstate his case or overemphasize relatively unimportant points.

Finally, a last common organizing principle, one that is at the heart of *Retellings,* is that of **comparison and contrast,** a particularly common mode in the study of literature. Readers of literature are often interested in comparing the behaviors of two characters (a protagonist and an antagonist, for instance) or showing how two authors treat the same theme similarly or differently. In comparing and contrasting, an essay writer might choose one of two structures: a **subject-by-subject structure,** which allows the writer to discuss object (or person, event, or idea) A in the first half of the essay and object (or person, event, or idea) B in the second half, or a **point-by-point structure,** which allows the writer to discuss the first point of comparison or contrast between A and B, then the second point of comparison/contrast, then the third, and so on. (For further information on comparison/contrast structures, see appendix 1.)

We want to emphasize that the simple comparison or contrast of pieces of writing, objects, ideas, people, or events is not enough. Most things can be compared or contrasted in some way; the trick for an essay writer is to use the comparison or contrast to make a valid persuasive point. For example, as we said earlier, when you read Engle's essay on Superman, you will want to ask how (or whether) he persuades you to believe that immigrants and an extraterrestrial being who is shipwrecked on Earth are aliens of the same kind. If you reject the comparison, you are likely to reject the argument that follows; if you accept it, you are likely to be intrigued, and possibly persuaded, by what Engle has to say.

There are many ways to organize an essay—chronologically, spatially, logically. What is most important is that a writer choose clear patterns of organization that will guide the reader from one point to the next. A writer may, in fact, use several patterns of organization—in one section focusing on comparison and contrast, in another on description, and so forth. But each section must have a sense of purpose and organization. A clearly organized essay will reinforce the thesis and make the reader feel as if he is being guided to the same conclusions that the writer reached. An essay that uses no organizational patterns will feel like a jumble, and a reader who is being asked to leap back and forth over logical crevices will worry about losing his footing and falling into a logical abyss.

CRITICAL READING AND NONFICTION: "RETELLING" STORIES OF "FACT"

Most of us bring to the study of literature the knowledge that what we are reading and seeing may need to be interpreted. On the other hand, when we read for information—for instance, when we read the newspaper or a textbook or a scientific document—we generally do not expect to apply analytical skills. We expect to read facts and, unless the writer is expressing an editorial opinion, we often expect those facts to be presented objectively and without embellishment.

How we respond to factual material depends, in part, on what facts are selected and into what context they are placed. As you undoubtedly know from your own experiences, how a fact is told depends on when and where it is told and on who is telling it. Just as you might now give a different account of a childhood event than you would have when it first occurred, historical facts are told differently as time passes. An examination of the tellings and retellings of such events as the bombing of a Birmingham, Alabama, church in 1963 (see chapter 11) will show you that almost thirty years of hindsight result in very different presentations of facts and opinions from the presentations written at the height of the Civil Rights movement. Even two writers looking at a set of facts and events from the same temporal distance may present those facts very differently. It is a fact, for instance, that when Lizzie Borden was put on trial for murdering her father and stepmother she was an unmarried woman living in her wealthy father's household. Some writers, however, see that fact in the light of Lizzie's affectionate dependence on her father. Others see it in the context of the limited opportunities afforded to her by her time, her gender, her social class, and her father's desire to control.

It is not just the selection of facts or the context in which they are placed that may affect our response to informational pieces. The language in which those facts are conveyed is also important. The language of an informative document is likely to be more neutral and less metaphorical than that of an opinion piece or a work of literature; the informative writer usually does not want to elicit an emotional response from us any more than she wants to insert her own emotions. Nevertheless, because language is itself metaphorical and because many words have clear, if subtle, connotations, even many factual documents can be analyzed as literary texts.

To do this kind of analysis means, of course, becoming more alert than usual to the nuances of language in nonliterary prose; it means questioning the objectivity of the language and the implications of structure. When asked to do this kind of analysis, students sometimes tell us that they think we are reading too much into a writer's choice of words or organization, that a writer did not intend the meanings we are finding in his prose. And they may sometimes be right that there was no intention to manipulate or influence the reader's response through the word choices. At the same time, we think such analysis is profitable because it does two important things: it sometimes gets at unintended (perhaps subconscious) meanings, and it makes both readers and writers more alert to the power of language to persuade readers and, indeed, to create (not simply reflect) meaning.

EXERCISES: TRYING IT OUT

1. Write down three or four things you consider absolute "facts." Now pair up with a classmate and examine each other's "facts." Play the role of the skeptic, discussing how and when the "facts" might not be true.
2. Locate two or three children's history books and compare their versions of the same historical event with each other and with a historical account of the event written for adults. In simplifying the event for children, how much do the children's authors have to distort the presentation? What do they have to leave out of their accounts? How might the simplified language lead to a simplified understanding of the event?

Questions to Ask about Nonfiction

1. What is the thesis of the essay? Is the thesis stated explicitly? If so, where?
2. How might the author's background influence the presentation of ideas? Look, for instance, at the author's age, gender, political and moral assumptions, academic discipline, and cultural and social backgrounds.
3. Are there situations in which the facts of the argument might not be seen as facts?
4. Is the author's language meant to be neutral and objective? If so, are there moments when the language is not neutral and objective? (To answer this question, put yourself in the positions of as many different kinds of readers as possible.)
5. What kinds of evidence does the author use? Factual evidence? Anecdotal evidence? Personal experience and observation? How convincing do you find such evidence? How convincing would readers who are somehow different from you find that evidence?
6. How does the author's style reinforce the thesis of the essay? How does it help us recognize which ideas the author wants to emphasize?
7. How does the author organize the material? How effective do you find that organization?

3. Write a narrative about an event fraught with emotion, relating as many of the details as you can remember. Then relate those same facts—retell them—from the point of view of someone very unlike you or even simply from the point of view of a skeptic who is unlikely to believe almost anything he is told. Your goal here is to retain all of the facts included the first time around but to use carefully chosen language to convey a different sense of what happened and to encourage a different response from the reader.

We are not here attempting to call all knowledge into question, only to ask that you consider the ways in which every story—whether told by a poet, a social scientist, a newspaper reporter, or a scientist—is shaped by language and by the values and assumptions that both audience and author bring to it. Even the same story told by two avowedly objective tellers from the same academic discipline or profession can evoke different responses in readers. When the tellers come from different academic disciplines or professions, the divergence in points of view may be even greater.

Not all nonliterary prose is meant to raise such questions, and we are not here suggesting that you pause and puzzle over every word and image in your science or history texts. We are suggesting, though, that all reading and writing involve some interpretation and that as both a reader and a writer, you should tune your mind and ear to the nuances of language and see the work not only from its author's perspective but also from the perspectives of those who may not share the author's values and assumptions. It is in this playing with perspective, this telling and retelling of fact and narrative, that you will be most apt to find yourself reading and writing critically, deeply, and with joy.

"READING" OTHER TEXTS

Buying a Story: Advertising

Although we often think they are not "intellectual" enough to be analyzed, even television programs, films, and advertisements can be looked at as texts worthy of literary analysis. Advertisers and product designers have become particularly adept at selling their products with verbal and nonverbal messages that imply more than they state explicitly. Like the literary artist, the advertiser and product designer often convey their ideas through symbol and innuendo, and by learning to read the texts (the advertisements and products) they present, you will become more adept at understanding how they incite the consumer's thoughts and emotions.

Consider, for instance, some of the slogans for the old Volkswagen Beetle, which became popular as the car of the young during the 1960s:

"Think small."
"It was the only thing to do after the mule died."
"It's ugly, but it gets you there."
"There's no place like car."

Printed in black-and-white advertisements in a no-nonsense plain font, each of these slogans seems almost to denigrate the car, to show how unassuming and unflashy it is. During an era in which youth claimed to despise American consumerism, the slogans were highly effective. Ironically, by seeming to mock consumerism, the ads did a very good job of promoting it.

The advertisers of the New Beetle have drawn on earlier advertising successes, and those successes, too, can be put under the lens of textual analysis. Just as the New Beetle is a kind of re-creation, a retelling, of the old Beetle, some of the New Beetle advertisements ask readers to remember the marketing of the earlier car. Here is what David Kiley, author of *Getting the Bugs Out,* says about the success of early marketing strategies:

Arnold [the advertising firm for the New Beetle] understood the ironic quality of the Beetle that DDB [the advertising firm for the old Beetle] had understood and conveyed so artistically in its advertising until the mid-1970s: *understatement.* The car's magic was that its design did all the talking. . . . Arnold knew it could be original and still tap into what made the original advertising so special and right. One ad that perfectly exemplified how Arnold got it right was a print ad for a lime green New Beetle, with just the word *Lime.* It was brilliant to anyone who remembered the classic "Lemon" ad for the original Beetle. The two ads had nothing to do with one another, yet were connected. The original "Lemon" ad, which was groundbreaking for its use of the word that had become synonymous with poor-quality cars, showed a Beetle that was rejected by quality inspectors in Germany. It looked perfect but was not up to

VW standards. The "Lime" ad, on the other hand, was created just to push a color and celebrate the return of an old friend. (238)

As Kiley demonstrates, the later advertisement cannot be appreciated fully without an understanding of the earlier one. Clearly those responsible for advertising the New Beetle hoped to appeal to consumers' emotions. Among their slogans (qtd. in Kiley 237) were "The engine is in the front, but its heart is in the same place," a reference to the fact that the old Beetle placed its engine in the back but stirred all sorts of emotions. Or another: "If you sold your soul in the '80s, here's your chance to buy it back," equating the car with the youthful idealism—the soul—that the consumer might have lost as he approached middle age and joined the "Establishment."

Products, too, can be read as texts. Look, for instance, at this picture of the VW New Beetle:

Now think about how you would analyze the appeal of the product itself. What moods does the design arouse in you? How would you describe the "personality" of the car? To what age groups would the car most likely appeal, and why? How much do our responses to the New Beetle's "look" depend on our knowledge of the old Beetle?

Here, finally, is how the advertising firm hired to market the New Beetle explains the product design and marketing strategy:

> The research turned up polarizing opinions about the car. Many saw it as a toy. The New Beetle, though, did have its share of fans. Targeting was going to be tough because the interest in the car ranged from the 18- to 34-year-olds that had been the target of "Drivers wanted" on up through baby boomers. It was far more a psychographic than demographic challenge. No matter the age or income, the people who liked the New Beetle and said they would definitely consider buying one, were confident individualists who had a desire to be the center of attention. These people often welled up with emotion when interviewers got them talking about their connection to the Beetle.
>
> "Through the research, we uncovered people's love of round shapes in our world," said [advertising firm Arnold's] Jon Castle. "Circular shapes, sociologists and psychologists told us, represent human forms, such as eyes, faces and heads.

Unlike squares and triangles, circles are inviting and friendly due to the fact that no sharp edges exist."

One sociologist tapped by Arnold for the Beetle launch told them: "In the sixties, it took on added meaning that the Bug was seen as the counter-culture car. One of the things that emerged from that time was 'small is beautiful' and the Beetle was seen as a beautiful car. Today, in American society, on one hand there is this move to standardize everything, and on the other hand you have this quest for individuality. For many drivers, this car will enable them to express themselves. The Beetle is no longer about being the 'people's car,' but rather the 'personal car.'" (Kiley 234)

We have spent so much time on the medium of advertising partly because advertisements form a kind of text with which you are probably very familiar, one that you may well have analyzed on your own. Most of us are well aware that advertisers are out to persuade us to buy their products and that, without careful analysis and some skepticism, we may be susceptible to their subtle persuasions. It would be easy to say that the Beetle, new or old, is "just a car" or that the advertisements are simply clever or cute, just as it would be easy to say that a story is "just a story." In each case, though, the artists who create the product, ad copy, and story are using a mix of linguistic and visual messages to arouse powerful responses. By understanding how they do so, we are more likely both to understand the messages and to appreciate the artistry that went into creating them.

Storytelling in Film and Television

Drawing from The Cave of the Swimmers in *The English Patient*

It is not often that an entirely new art medium is created. The basic literary forms that we have been discussing in this book—poetry, prose fiction, plays, and essays—go back thousands of years. The same thing is true for most of the visual arts—certainly for painting and sculpture. Even advertisements have a long history; although early advertisements are very different from the advertisements we see today, advertisements have probably existed for almost as long as there have been buyers and sellers. Such claims, however, cannot be made for film and television, which were created early in the twentieth century. Going to the movies and watching television are now such popular pastimes that we may forget that the histories of both media are very short, and we may be tempted to dismiss them as simple entertainment. Yet film and television are just as much art forms as any of the others we have been discussing here. For many, in fact, they are the most influential media of our time, and they lend themselves very well to the kind of textual analysis we are discussing. In a book such as this one, with its emphasis on the printed word and the literary material you are likely to be reading in a literature or writing course, we cannot possibly do more than suggest an approach to film study. What follows is necessarily brief, but we hope it provides some hint of the questions you might ask in analyzing a film.

Elements of Film and Television   Film and television have much in common with prose fiction and drama. Narrative (or storytelling) is, of course, the foundation of all of these media, and so for television and film just as for a short story or a play we might look at plot, setting, character, and theme. In fact, we might even ask of television some of the same questions that we ask of novels: Do commercial breaks create the same kind of suspense that chapter divisions in a novel might create, for instance? Do weekly television shows create continuity in the same way that serialized novels, which in the nineteenth century came out in weekly or monthly installments, once did? We might ask whether half-hour or hour-long television shows share some characteristics of narrative with short stories and whether longer, more expansive movies have more in common with novels.

Unlike short stories and novels, however, film and television are visual media, and we also need to consider the elements more specific to film. **Camera angles** may be important. Are we seeing a character head-on or from the side? Is the character in the **foreground** (that is, in the front of the picture) or the **background?** Has the camera **zoomed in,** giving us an extraordinary **close-up** that magnifies faces or objects, making them twenty times the size they are in real life so that they fill the entire screen? Or are we seeing things or people in a **long shot** that pulls away so that a house, say, may appear in the distance, seeming only a few feet high? (**Medium shots** convey a more life-sized impression so that we may see both the people and the background that surrounds them.)

The camera also has the ability to **fade in** and **fade out.** A scene that fades in starts as a blur, with the picture only gradually coming into focus. In a fade-out, the opposite occurs: the scene starts out clear, blurring away, perhaps into a fully black screen. Sometimes as one scene fades out, another fades in, and the two scenes are superimposed so that connections between the two are suggested.

None of these camera techniques occurs in isolation from the story. The **screenplay,** the text from which the play is filmed, will give not only dialog and stage directions but also information about the camera work for the film. When it is based on a novel or play, a screenplay will have much in common with the original literary work. However, the integration of camera work, stage directions, and dialog also creates some significant differences, as you will readily see if you compare Shakespeare's *Hamlet* to Kenneth Branagh's screenplay (excerpted on pages 1318–28).

Film, Television, and Drama Films and television shows also have a great deal in common with plays: for both, the audience is physically present, and there is often a sense of an invisible *fourth wall* (see 118–19). We are using our eyes and ears at once, not only reading (as we might do with novels) or listening (as we might do with oral poetry). The scene is laid before us and we are *almost* there. Films, television shows, and plays are often alike not only in their sense of audience but in the creation of action. Actors use tone and gesture to convey their characters, and sets and costumes play an important part in our interpretation.

At the same time, there are some important differences between films and television shows on the one hand and plays on the other. Anyone who has seen a filmed play is aware that it is just that: a filmed play rather than a film. This difference may, in part, be due to the differences in setting. A theatrical director must use sets that fit on a stage. In contrast, although some television shows are filmed on a stage set, many television shows and most films are filmed on location, in real cities with real buildings and streets, conveying a larger and often more realistic sense of place than a play can. (This realistic use of space was less common in earlier films, for the bulky film equipment of the day was not easily maneuvered into real locations; at the same time, early Hollywood back lots were still *very* large by theatrical standards.) As a general rule, too, a filmed narrative can more easily change scenes than does a play; film editing allows different scenes to be easily spliced together (or juxtaposed digitally), whereas set changes are usually difficult and cumbersome.

Even more important than the differences in the use of sets, however, are the differences in what the viewer sees. A play does not offer a fully selective point of view. As two characters argue onstage, for instance, we may find ourselves focusing on one or the other—perhaps not the same character that the person sitting next to us focuses on. Of course, the dialog and lighting may be used to draw our attention to some facet or another, but to a large extent what we are drawn to is up to us. The same is not true with filmed narratives. The camera itself does a lot of the selecting, creating foregrounds and backgrounds. As the camera closes in, some characters in the scene may be excluded from view. A close-up may even focus on a single face, making it hugely larger than life, showing us every flicker of an eyelash. That close-up will, of course, crowd out all other characters and actions.

Film and Fiction If a film is both like and unlike a play, it is also like and unlike prose fiction. The similarities are often strong because both rely so heavily on story, and the use of the camera can emphasize the subjective point of view often conveyed by a narrator or main character in prose fiction. It is no surprise that, in its infancy, the movie industry looked to classic novels for its first stories. Both classic and modern novels continue to be a rich source for modern screenwriters and filmmakers. For example, there have been close to one hundred movie and television versions of *Dr. Jekyll and Mr. Hyde,* a short novel that we have included in this anthology.

However, though film has much in common with prose fiction and many of the elements are the same, it is less adept than a verbal medium at giving background or historical information directly. Most directors, for example, only sparingly use **voice-overs,** in which an invisible narrator gives background information. Similarly, only rarely in a film are we asked to read printed background information or to read a letter.

Though these techniques, borrowed directly from prose fiction, were used more frequently in the early days of filmmaking, they now usually seem artificial and intrusive.

Today filmmakers are more apt to take advantage of the visual messages imparted by film and to draw on the techniques of color and visual composition that we see in photography and painting. (It is no accident that the early name for film was "moving pictures.") In fact, we often need to focus most on its "pictures" to understand a film's message. The opening of the film of *The English Patient* (based on a novel by Michael Ondaatje) is a case in point. The opening scene contains almost no audible dialog, and yet visually it has a strong impact. As the film opens, we hear a tinkling sound and some inaudible voices; we can't even be sure what language they are speaking. Next we see a brush making strokes on an uneven golden surface. The black strokes are clear, but their significance is not. Are they hieroglyphics or Asian calligraphy?

Gradually, the viewer sees that the strokes are leading to some sort of drawing, but of what is still uncertain. Then the brush (we do not see a human hand) makes a final circular motion, and we see a head being drawn (perhaps), leading us (perhaps) to understand that the drawn figure is human (we will later learn it is a swimmer). Then the golden surface of the paper (or stone) merges into the undulating shapes of sand dunes.

The drawn black figure fades out, and we are left with only the dunes. A shadow of a plane crosses the surface, and we glimpse a woman slumped in the front seat of the plane, her scarf flaring out in the wind; a man is seated in the seat behind her. Soldiers (their voices are not clearly audible, but they seem to be speaking German) shoot at the plane. Next we see the man, clad in sand-colored garments, rise up and out of the plane into a white light. Then the film cuts away; the first scene is over. Before we can understand what we have seen, the pictures shift to a hospital car on a train.

The pictures we have viewed suggest many things, though certainly they raise more questions than they answer. The barely audible voices seem foreign and so suggest an exotic setting (at the very beginning, a female voice singing in a foreign language—perhaps an Arabic language—seems to confirm this). The sand dunes suggest that the setting may be a desert. The images are beautiful, brightly golden, yet not quite happy. The landscape is inhospitable—the only human figures clearly discernible are the hostile soldiers and their victims; the beauty of the scenes is at odds with the guns and the destruction they cause. Even the brush strokes on paper seem oddly detached and nonhuman: we don't see the hand, and we don't easily recognize the human figure being drawn. We are uncertain about what has happened to the occupants of the plane. The male figure ascends into light. Is that ascension meant to suggest life—or death?

The opening scene (which lasts only about three minutes) presents a puzzle. It seems fraught with meaning, perhaps even symbolic meaning. The visual connections among the scenes are clear: the use of color, especially of gold and black, helps us to see them as related. The logical threads are as yet invisible, though. Through the visual components, the filmmaker has thus attempted to convey visually what is done verbally in the novel *The English Patient.* In both novel and film, we see that there are secrets and hidden meanings (and land mines, literal and figurative); as with a jigsaw puzzle, we are trying to see how the pieces fit together and what the big picture represents. At the beginning of the film, no language, no text, helps us. The pictures are

Questions to Ask about Film, Television, and Other Visual Arts

1. What is the overall mood suggested by the visual images (in a picture or film scene, for example)? How do the visual objects create a feeling of sadness, hostility, anxiety, respect, awe, and so forth?
2. As you look at the visual images, what is most noticeable? What creates the strongest impression? Color? Placement? Texture? Size?
3. Look carefully at a single scene or moment on-screen (or in a picture). What is least noticeable—and why? Which objects or figures are large, and which are small? Are the sizes what you would expect? How do close-ups and camera angles reinforce the scene's moods?
4. What colors dominate? What moods are suggested by the colors?
5. Consider the textures of the objects or figures portrayed. How would you describe them? Rough? Smooth? Shaggy? Prickly?
6. Look closely at the shapes and focus. Are the edges sharp? Blurred? Rounded? What might we associate with these shapes? For example, do rounded edges suggest comfort and softness? Does any angularity suggest hostility or nervousness? If some edges seem blurred, are we meant to see the objects as unknowable or unimportant?
7. Which items in the picture seem visually linked (perhaps by color, placement, or size)? What ideas might these visual links suggest?
8. What is the setting of the picture? Urban? Natural? Domestic? Hot? Cold? Lush? Dry? What gets left outside the boundaries of the frame? Why?

"moving," but to understand them, we must interpret them in the same way that we would a painting or photograph, looking at color and composition. Only later in the film will we put these pictures together with the story.

EXERCISE: TRYING IT OUT

Look at the first five or ten minutes of a film with the sound turned off. What do the visual images suggest about the mood, events, and themes of what is to follow?

Works Cited

Kaiser, Walter. Introduction. *Selected Essays of Montaigne*. Trans. John Florio. Boston: Riverside, 1964.

Kiley, David. *Getting the Bugs Out: The Rise, Fall, and Comeback of Volkswagen in America*. New York: Wiley, 2001.

Part 3 ❧

Writing about Literature

7 *Writing from Start to Finish*

7

Writing from Start to Finish

Even professional writers say that on some days there are few things more daunting to a writer than a blank page. Faced with it, many of us find all sorts of more important things to do—clean rooms that we have been content to leave messy for weeks, organize our files, walk the dog. It is not just students who procrastinate when faced with a writing task. Professional writers often share students' painful reluctance to begin. Indeed, many writers have likened the process of writing to bleeding their words onto the page. But writing doesn't have to be so painful. Although we cannot promise to make writing *easy,* we do hope to offer you some tips to make it more manageable, even enjoyable.

Many students uncomfortable with writing have the illusion that "good writers" simply sit down and write: the Muse visits, and the essay (or poem or short story) flows effortlessly forth, as a kind of automatic writing. The manuscripts of well-known writers show that that is seldom the case, however. There may be draft after draft, full of crossings out and changes. The secret to good writing is often a willingness to revise and revise: the Muse visits not once but often, and some of her chatterings will later be ignored or improved on.

The key to good writing is to break writing down into manageable steps. In fact, because it is easier to face small steps than to face large ones, keeping the steps small may help us to resist the tendency to procrastinate. It is *very* tempting to procrastinate if writing a paper means an exhausting all-nighter, staying awake only after countless cups of coffee and with the stress of an impending deadline. It doesn't have to mean that, though. Instead of facing such a nerve-wracking prospect, think about spending a few minutes here and there soon after you have the assignment. At these early stages, you do not need to schedule large blocks of time; just fit in ten or fifteen minutes between classes or while you are waiting for a friend. If you write in small chunks of time, if you allow the ideas to percolate without having to worry about looming deadlines, you may find that writing can be an exciting process of discovery.

GETTING READY TO WRITE

Although we sometimes talk about reading and writing as if they are very different activities, in many ways they are really just opposite sides of the same activity.

For that reason, much of what we have talked about in earlier chapters applies here as well: the questions you ask as a reader will give you material for examination and development when you begin to write. In other words, the prewriting strategies discussed in this section are as much as anything also the habits of any good reader.

Small blocks of time can be very productive for **brainstorming,** the process of generating ideas. This process should not be a stressful one: it doesn't require much time, and the quality of the ideas is not yet at issue. In fact, you should take comfort in the fact that, if you are like most writers, you will at this point probably generate a lot of garbage—that is simply part of the process. Not every idea you come up with will be used, but later is the time to worry about what is or is not useful. (Make procrastination work *for* you for a change.) Early on in the process, you should also not worry about whether the ideas will "go" anywhere or whether the teacher will like them. At this point free yourself from the constraints of logic, organization, and the grade. You can even think of confusion as your ally at this stage—it shows that you are keeping an open mind. Because ideas and meanings are still being teased out, the questions may very well be more important than the answers.

Keeping a Journal and Freewriting

Whether they are students or professionals, many writers find that keeping a writer's journal helps keep them in the mood to write and serves as a source for ideas when they are feeling "dry." A journal is something that is yours alone. You can write anything in it that you want, including your frustrations about writing assignments! Sometimes, in fact, writing about your frustrations can help you get past those frustrations and see your way toward a possible approach to a paper.

A journal can also provide the place for **freewriting,** an activity that requires you to write freely and without pause for a limited amount of time. (You might write for ten to fifteen minutes, for instance.) In freewriting, the idea is to keep writing without stopping, even when the ideas aren't flowing. Even if all you write is "I'm stuck" over and over again, the process of writing the words on the page or the screen—of keeping the pen moving or the fingers typing—will often get your mind working. We know some people who use their writer's journals to create pictures of the paper topics they are writing on or to draw pictures of the situations or characters in a piece of literature. It is amazing how much such a picture can tell you about how you are responding to literary events and characters.

Many writers keep more focused writing journals, though. They write about their responses to what they have read and about interesting things they have heard. They write down quotations or words that strike their fancy, even if they don't know why. Then, when they are about to sit down and work on a paper or other writing task, they read through what they have in their journals, hoping that what they have written there may give birth to new ideas. Sometimes a kind of cross-fertilization process occurs for those who keep writer's journals. For instance, someone faced with an assignment to write about a poem such as Langston Hughes's "Harlem" (see 89) may find helpful his writer's journal entry written in response to a slave narrative he read for his history class. A writer's journal provides a place to store all sorts of apparently miscellaneous ideas and quotations—and to find connections that might otherwise go unnoticed.

EXERCISES: TRYING IT OUT

1. Keep a writer's journal for one week, jotting down in it any interesting observations about or quotations from the week's reading. Let yourself write about anything having to do with your reading, whether that material is assigned for school or done for pleasure. What strikes you about the ideas? The styles? The characters and settings?

   At the end of the week, read one of the poems or stories in *Retellings* and write a paragraph in which you use some of the material in your writer's journal to help you respond to it.

2. Draw a picture that responds to one of the pieces of literature you have been asked to read. You might draw the setting or a character, or you might draw an abstract representation of the mood created by the literary work. Then write a paragraph explaining why you drew the picture as you did and how it helps you (and would help others) to understand the work of literature better.

Annotating a Text

One of the best things you can do to get started on any writing task is to get in the habit of reading critically—and with a pen or pencil in hand. Obviously, if you are reading someone else's book or a library book, you don't want to mark it up; but if you have a copy of your own book, make as many notes while you read as possible. **Annotate** the text, which means comment on those places where you are confused or have questions, those places where you have found significance (even if you do not yet know what the significance is), those places where you notice patterns, and those places to which you want to return. Your comments in the margins do not have to be "intellectual" or even coherent. They simply have to represent your real responses to what you are reading. You might, for instance, write, "What does this mean?" in the margin as a reminder to yourself that you will want to think about that question once you have read the whole work. Or, in response to a character's behavior, you might write something like, "I can't imagine doing that!" or "This doesn't seem very realistic" or even "How would another character in the story respond to that situation?" (If you are reading a book you do not own, keep a tablet nearby, jotting down a few quotations, their page numbers, and your comments.) Most of all, become as fully engaged in your reading as possible. Think of yourself as conversing with the writer and the characters; do not simply stand silently by as the conversation goes on without you.

To demonstrate the process we have in mind, we begin by looking at "To His Coy Mistress" by Andrew Marvell (1621–1678). In our experience, students are often most reluctant to analyze poetry, convinced as they sometimes are that poetry is deliberately obscure, full of "hidden meanings." We doubt that any poet goes to the trouble of "hiding" meaning—after all, most writers want to communicate their ideas and feelings. At the same time, poetry is often subtle and metaphorical, and so its meaning may depend on what is implied rather than on what is said. At this first stage of writing, however, we need most of all to understand what is being said *literally*. We can grapple with the subtleties later. So jot down anything you notice; don't skip over the confusing parts.

Here, then, is how student Heather Johnson annotated "To His Coy Mistress":

Who is the man here? Why doesn't he call her my mistress?

What's Ganges?

What's Humber?

What flood?

Huh?!?!? How is love like vegetables? How do vegetables grow?

Why does her heart come last? And he doesn't praise and adore it the way he does the other parts of her!

"But" makes the poem move in a new direction. And where's the lady?

Vault as in where people keep money and jewelry or vault as in tomb? Sounds like he values her, so maybe it's the safe, but then I don't know why it would be marble.
Her honor's just "quaint"!?!

To His Coy Mistress

Had we but world enough, and time,
This coyness lady, were no crime.
We would sit down, and think which way
To walk, and pass our long love's day.
Thou by the Indian Ganges' side
Shouldst rubies find; I by the tide
Of Humber would complain. I would
Love you ten years before the flood,
And you should, if you please, refuse
Till the conversion of the Jews.
My vegetable love should grow
Vaster than empires and more slow;
An hundred years should go to praise
Thine eyes, and on thy forehead gaze;
Two hundred to adore each breast,
But thirty thousand to the rest;
An age at least to every part,
And the last age should show your heart.
For, lady, you deserve this state,
Nor would I love at lower rate.
But at my back I always hear
Time's wingèd chariot hurrying near;
And yonder all before us lie
Deserts of vast eternity.
Thy beauty shall no more be found;
Nor, in thy marble vault, shall sound
My echoing song; then worms shall try
That long-preserved virginity,
And your quaint honor turn to dust,

(Lines numbered: 5, 10, 15, 20, 25)

Why is the mistress coy? Aren't mistresses usually bold?

Now she seems to be a "lady," not a mistress! And "ladies" don't commit crimes. What kind of crime is she committing? How is coyness even a crime?

When are Jews supposed to be converted? And why do they need to be?

Wow! He is sure going to praise her a long time—especially her breasts!

Very romantic. Is it his picture, or is he just playing to what he thinks is her fantasy? Romance and sex are getting mixed up.

Who'd want to live in a desert for eternity?

She's in the vault and he gets to sing? Where did the worms come from? Are they symbolic? Is he threatening her with death?

I don't think of graves
as "fine"!
Duh! Of course no one
embraces there!

Here's another
indented line.

"Therefore" seems like a
logic word—not the
kind of word I'd use to
get someone to love me.

Vultures are birds of
prey, but I don't know
anything about
"amorous birds of prey."

This tearing doesn't
sound like a good thing!

Another logic word
that sounds too formal
for love-making.

And into ashes all my lust: 30

The grave's a fine and private place,

But none, I think, do there embrace.

Now therefore, while the youthful hue

Sits on thy skin like morning dew

And while thy willing soul transpires   35

At every pore with instant fires,

Now let us sport us while we may,

And now, like amorous birds of prey,

Rather at once our time devour

Than languish in his slow-chapped power. 40

Let us roll all our strength and all

Our sweetness up into one ball,

And tear our pleasures with rough strife

Thorough the iron gates of life:

Thus, though we cannot make our sun   45

Stand still, yet we will make him run.

Dust to dust, ashes to
ashes—sounds like a
funeral. How can lust
turn into ashes? It's
lust he cares about.

Much nicer than dust
and ashes!

What's the soul got to
do with love and lust?

How can someone de-
vour time?

What does "slow-
chapped" mean?

What's "our sweetness"?
If they're in one ball,
where is she?

What are the "iron
gates of life"?

These are, of course, only a few of the annotations a reader of "To His Coy Mistress" might make. Other readers would annotate the poem differently; in fact, the same reader might make different annotations at another time—which is why it is often a good idea to read and annotate a piece of writing several times.

EXERCISE: TRYING IT OUT

Read the text of "To His Coy Mistress" again. Add at least three or four annotations of your own to those already placed in the margins.

Summarizing the Work

The first step in understanding any piece of writing is often simply to summarize its basic meaning. That is especially the case when a work is difficult or unfamiliar. In reading "To His Coy Mistress," for instance, you may be struck by how unfamiliar some of the words are or how much their meanings seem to have shifted; after all, this poem was written more than three hundred years ago. Early on, however, it isn't necessary to understand every word or the purpose of the images. In fact, it may be better at this point not to focus too much on the imagery; you don't want yet to move too far away from the literal specifics of what is being said. By summarizing the poem, by forcing yourself to stick with what it says rather than what it might mean, you can give yourself a strong foundation on which to build later.

In this case, that foundation will be composed of the literal specifics of the poem, which convey a message familiar to us even now, centuries after the poem's composition: the speaker is attempting to get the "coy mistress" to go to bed with him. In the first part of the poem, the speaker tells the mistress that if they had all the time in the world, he could spend years and years courting her. In the second part of the poem, he remarks that life is short and that, after death, they cannot be lovers. In the third part of the poem, he concludes that they should make good use of their time by making love now.

Playing with Word Associations

Once the basic *literal* meaning of the poem is clear, it is time to start thinking a bit more widely about the broader, less literal meanings of the poem. One way to brainstorm is to play with the poem. Don't worry about analyzing it at this point; the idea is to think creatively, not logically. One strategy for generating creative ideas about any subject, including a work of literature, is "random word stimulation," an exercise designed by Edward de Bono. Here's how it works: at random, a writer selects a series of words from a dictionary. (If a dictionary isn't available, almost any book will do; the writer can just randomly point to words until he comes up with a series of words. Ideally, the book should be a general interest book; a specialized book may limit the range of the vocabulary.) De Bono suggests that the words be chosen over the course of several days, perhaps one a day.

These are the words Heather came up with in her brainstorming for "To His Coy Mistress":

chrysanthemum	prattle
device	slimy
share	glass

EXERCISE: TRYING IT OUT

Before reading on, try to make some association, no matter how far-fetched, between each word on the preceding list and "To His Coy Mistress." The idea here is to look at Marvell's poem from a new perspective, a perspective you might not have come up with if you had been concerned solely with being logical. If you feel absolutely stuck, don't worry. (A sense of frustration almost always blocks creative thinking.) Just skip the word or get another from the dictionary. De Bono suggests spending three to five minutes on each word.

Here are some associations Heather made:

Chrysanthemum:
> We might associate love with flowers, but Marvell doesn't seem to use any flowers. Or does "vegetable love" qualify? But vegetables are more "useful"

than flowers; we eat them, not just admire them, and the idea of eating might somehow work with the idea of devouring time. Maybe the speaker is thinking of a "useful" kind of love—a physical love, or lust—rather than a pretty, flowery, and romantic kind of love. But the beginning is flowery. Flowers don't bloom for very long. Maybe that's why they are symbols of love? The speaker doesn't think their love will last long because life doesn't last very long.

Device

I guess you could say the whole poem is a "device," a kind of trick to get the woman into bed. Would this device really convince any woman? Do we know if she is convinced? In other words, does the "device" work?

Share

Share implies two (or more) people having something in common, maybe even helping each other out. Is that true here? Is this love shared? The woman isn't even in the poem. Maybe they're sharing love or sex, but if they're sharing, why isn't she there, especially after the first part?

Prattle

Prattle is kind of meaningless talk. Is this poem just prattle? Is the argument prattle, just chatter meant to seduce the woman? Or is it the opposite of prattle? The poem seems to have a purpose, like an argument, and that doesn't go with prattle.

Slimy

Slime reminds me of the worms in the grave. I see the speaker as sort of slimy, too: he is trying to scare the woman into doing what he wants!

Glass

Glass can be see-through, as in window glass. But it is also an old word for a mirror (or looking glass), so maybe the glass reflects something. The speaker seems transparent, like glass; he just wants to get the woman into bed. Maybe the poem reflects him—it's a mirror that shows who he really is. She doesn't seem to be in the mirror.

There are obviously no right or wrong answers here, and some of these ideas may not prove useful later on. That doesn't matter at this point. The idea is to get the mind to play with the poem, jarring loose any impressions or ideas that might be difficult to get at directly. Looking over the results of the word associations, however, you will see many ideas that *are* useful and worth pursuing.

EXERCISES: TRYING IT OUT

1. Look through the word associations Heather came up with. Find three or four that seem to point you in a promising direction. Then write down two or three new ideas about each, linking them to Marvell's poem.

2. Either individually or in a group, randomly select five more words from the dictionary (or another book). Spend three to five minutes per word writing down associations to "To His Coy Mistress."

3. Either individually or in a group, choose any poem in this anthology to work with. Then select ten words from the dictionary (or a general interest book). Spend three to five minutes per word writing down associations to the poem.

Asking Reporter's Questions

As you may know from other writing classes, one of the traditional ways to get yourself started in thinking about a topic is to ask the kinds of questions that a reporter asks and attempts to answer in the first part of a news story. Those questions are as helpful for a task of literary analysis as they are for any other kind of writing task. The reporter's questions are: Who? What? Where? When? Why? and How? If you have read the earlier chapters, you know that many of these questions overlap with the kinds of questions you would naturally ask as a reader of literature. Here is how Heather applied the reporter's questions to "To His Coy Mistress":

> Who is the speaker?
> Who is the "coy mistress"?
> What is the speaker asking the mistress to do?
> Where are the poem's settings?
> When does the action of the poem take place?
> When and where does the man want to make love to the lady?
> When and where does she want to make love?
> Why does the man seem in such a hurry?
> Why does the mistress want to delay?
> Why doesn't the mistress get to answer the man?
> How is the poem resolved?
> How similar are the two people in the poem?
> How sympathetic are we to the speaker?
> How can the two people make the sun run?

MOVING TOWARD A THESIS
Finding Some Answers

After working with brainstorming questions and activities over the course of several days, a writer is probably ready to move closer to analysis and a more systematic brainstorming approach. At this point, many writers make the mistake of jumping right to a *thesis,* the central idea of a paper. We would advise you against doing that just yet and suggest that, instead, you begin to answer some of the smaller questions you have raised. A writer who tries to answer the big question first will often find that the answers to the smaller questions don't fit, and the temptation is simply to ignore the evidence that contradicts the thesis. If, on the other hand, a writer waits until the smaller questions are answered, she is more likely to arrive at an answer to a thesis question that accounts for more of the evidence. That does not mean that you will end up using all of the answers, only that the conclusions you do draw will be informed by a more complex understanding of the work.

So your first step in writing a trial thesis is to look at some of the questions you asked earlier and to begin to play with answers to those questions. Remember that at this point the annotations and the responses to the questions are meant to be exploratory; the answers may well provide you with further grounds for discussion and investigation. It is still too early for you to feel tied to a permanent thesis. In fact, you will notice that in the following brainstorming responses, Heather has sometimes raised lots of possibilities and even asked new questions without coming to firm conclusions. Eventually a writer will need to draw conclusions; readers want to know more than what the *possible* responses are. But at this point in the writing process, you want to keep your mind open to as many possibilities as you can, and that means leaving some of your responses tentative. Here are Heather's responses to some of her reporter's questions and to some of her annotations in the margins of the poem.

Who is the man in the title? The title says "his," not "my," so the title seems to be being spoken by someone other than the speaker of the poem. Maybe Marvell wants to make it clear that he isn't the same person as the speaker. And maybe that means that Marvell doesn't even agree with the speaker. Maybe the speaker doesn't say "my mistress" because he doesn't feel that he possesses the woman, even though he would like to. Still, he does see her as "his" in some way.

What is the mistress's crime? The speaker seems to think it's a "crime" (against him? against love and human nature?) that the mistress doesn't want to go to bed with him. Is he right? Maybe in Marvell's time it would have been a crime if she had gone to bed with him. What does Marvell want us to think?

Why is the speaker talking about a flood? If he's referring to Noah's flood, that means that he would be talking about a long, long time ago. God was supposed to have sent the flood because the people were sinners, so maybe that brings in a religious element of some kind.

What is "vegetable love"? Vegetables are natural, so maybe this implies that love is natural. Vegetables grow fast, too: they have to get to their full size in a single season. On the other hand, maybe they also die fast because they last only one season.

The speaker is planning to spend a lot of time praising the woman's various body parts. He seems very interested in the woman's breasts—more than in her eyes. It seems much more rude and provocative for a guy to stare at a woman's breasts than it is for him to stare at her eyes. He seems pretty interested in sex here. But then he also says that he saves the heart for last. Maybe he's saving the best for last, or maybe the woman has to reveal her heart herself; that's why it's "shown." When he talks about the heart, the speaker maybe seems less interested in purely physical love.

What are the worms doing here? If the "marble vault" is a tomb, I guess the worms are real worms that live in the dirt in the graveyard. This is a really horrible image. If the worms are "trying" the woman's virginity, does that mean that they are crawling all over and even into her body?

<u>Why does the speaker mention "amorous birds of prey"?</u> Birds are loud and aggressive in their mating, so "amorous birds of prey" doesn't sound very romantic, especially since "birds of prey" are birds that hunt and eat flesh. It sounds as if he's comparing the two of them to vultures, and why would the woman see that as romantic and seductive? And if they are vultures, what are they preying upon and eating?

<u>What does "gates of life" mean?</u> If the lines right before this one are talking about the man and woman making love, then this sounds like pretty rough lovemaking. It sounds almost as if he's forcing himself on the woman (couldn't she be the "iron gates of life" since babies come out of women?) and this seems almost like a rape.

<u>What are "therefore" and "thus" doing in a love poem?</u> I think the speaker is pretending that there's lots of logic here. I don't know whether Marvell thinks that the argument is logical, or whether the woman will think it is logical. I don't think women today would think it was very logical, or at least I don't think they would find it very convincing. Is this love or lust?

<u>How sympathetic are we to the speaker?</u> In some ways, I like the speaker. He wants love and he doesn't want to waste any time because he knows someday they're going to die. He seems fun and funny and realistic and romantic at the same time. But sometimes his language seems a little extreme, even violent, and then I'm not so sure I like him. And I don't think I would want someone to try to get me to bed with him by using such phony logic, by talking about how he wants to stare at my chest, and by being so gross about the worms that are going to go inside my body when I'm dead. Then he seems selfish and disgusting.

<u>Why doesn't the mistress get to answer the man?</u> This poem reminded me a little of "Dover Beach," where the speaker goes on and on about love and faith, but he never really lets the woman answer. So you forget that she's there. You can't forget this woman, though, because the speaker keeps talking about her body and so you can't forget that she has a body. On the other hand, maybe he doesn't see her as a real person because he never lets her talk back. What is she supposed to be doing while he's talking about adoring her eyes and each breast and making the sun run?

As we said earlier, these are just tentative responses to the questions and annotations Heather wrote earlier. We have included them here mostly to give you some sense of how the process of asking and answering questions will lead you closer to a complex and convincing reading of the poem.

EXERCISES: TRYING IT OUT

1. In the earlier annotations and reporter's questions, Heather included many issues and questions that she has not responded to here. Choose two or three of the issues or questions she has *not* addressed and write your own tentative responses to them.

2. Any time you read a piece of literature written more than a hundred years ago, you may want to consider the possibility that the meanings of some of the words have changed. To see whether and how they have changed, critics consult *The Oxford English Dictionary (OED)*, a multivolume dictionary that gives definitions, the history of those definitions, and examples of usage in early works.

   Some of the words in "To His Coy Mistress" have changed in meaning, and the older meanings may be important here. Locate a copy of *The Oxford English Dictionary* (your library may have a print copy or subscribe to the *OED* online), and write down the definitions for the following words:

   coy

   mistress

   quaint

   How did your understanding of the older meanings change your response to the poem?

Formulating the Thesis Question

Now that you have spent some time brainstorming and jotting down tentative answers to the questions you asked earlier, you are ready to write your *thesis question*. At this point it is helpful to think in terms of a question rather than a thesis statement, because if you worry about definitive answers too early in the writing process, you are bound to fall into the trap of pushing aside the moments of confusion or some of your more controversial ideas. Many writers find "right" answers comfort-ing, but if you have answers that are clearly "right" all along, how much are you really likely to be telling your reader? So think about real questions, the kind that you would want answered if *you* were the reader. Finally, as a writer you are also a teacher: be the kind of teacher—interesting and enlightening—who will make your reader want to learn.

Whatever your thesis question, then, it should lead to real insights. That means that a question that can be answered by a clear statement of fact will not work for a thesis. Imagine, for instance, if a writer were to ask as a thesis question, "What does the speaker in 'To His Coy Mistress' want?" Probably the vast majority of readers would answer quickly: he wants the woman to go to bed with him. If everyone (or almost everyone) already knows that answer, what would be the point of writing a paper proving that? So a thesis question must lead to answers and eventually to an essay that will show the reader a new way of looking at things.

A good thesis question will also lead to a complex response, one that can be developed over the course of an essay. For that reason, a question that can be easily answered "yes" or "no" will probably not work very well. Rather than saying, "Do we like the speaker in 'To His Coy Mistress'?" it is probably better to ask, "Why do we find the speaker in 'To His Coy Mistress' admirable (or despicable)?"

But how does one decide on a single thesis question on which to focus? Again, the best strategy here is to return to your prewriting brainstorming activities. If you look at the questions Heather asked, the annotations she wrote, and the tentative answers and word associations she played with, you will undoubtedly discover certain patterns of interest. Notice, for instance, that many of the questions and answers have to do with the question of whether the mistress will, or should, be convinced by the speaker's logic. Notice that many others have to do with the questions of physical love versus emotional love or even religious love. Once you have noticed such patterns—in the poem, in your own responses to the poem—you will have an easier time coming up with a thesis that will not only help you to come to terms with the poem but also interest you as you are writing the essay.

Heather noticed a pattern in her response that focused on the relationship between the mistress and the speaker. As a result, she developed the following thesis question for her paper on "To His Coy Mistress": "How are we meant to respond to the relationship between the speaker and the woman he is addressing?" Once she knew that this was the question she wanted to answer, she was well on her way to writing the first draft of her paper.

MOVING TOWARD THE FIRST DRAFT

At the first-draft stage of the writing process, you should be open to rethinking your thesis and looking for new evidence. We know from talking to students (and from our own experience as writers) that it is very tempting to make the first draft of the paper the final draft of the paper. The paper looks so finished once the words are on the page that it is tempting to think that it is. But in our more realistic moments, we know that that simply cannot be the case. It is just not possible to get all of the ideas on the page, develop them fully, answer opposing points of view, and make everything clear for the reader all in one step. In fact, it is probably not even possible to get all of the ideas down the first time around. As many experts on the writing process tell us, writing is a recursive activity, which means that few writers move constantly forward. Because they are still discovering their ideas, most writers will discover as they move along that they must rework earlier ideas in order to pave the way for the ideas they discovered later in the process. As novelist E. M. Forster put it, "How can I tell what I think till I see what I say?" Until it is all there, you cannot possibly know how it is going to turn out; and until you know how it is all going to turn out, you cannot possibly shape the material to its best advantage. You may as a result find yourself repeatedly returning to what you probably thought of as the "early" stages of writing, returning to those earlier stages in an effort to generate more ideas and to refine the ideas you already have.

Writing Notes and Questions

After deciding to respond to the thesis question raised previously for "To His Coy Mistress," Heather looked at her random jottings, annotations, and questions and decided to brainstorm once again. This time she focused her brainstorming especially on the thesis question: "How are we meant to respond to the relationship between the speaker and the woman he is addressing?" At this point, though, she was still not worried about organizing her essay; she knew that she was still in the process of generating ideas; as a result, she expected to have more questions than definitive answers, and she knew that she could not possibly write a formal outline because she did not yet know fully what she wanted to say. Here is what Heather came up with:

Notes

—"coy"—suggesting that she has a plan? Or is that just how he sees her (not as she means to be seen)?

—the first stanza takes place in a dreamy landscape but is all in the conditional voice. Is he suggesting that this land is attainable (if she has sex with him) or impossible (so she should have sex with him anyway)? I think it's the second.

—he seems to be saying that love itself (outside of the physical) is a fantasy, or at least the possibility of him loving her platonically is.

—does he think his saying that he would love and worship and respect her in the dreamland can count for anything? He says that he would do these things, gaining some romantic pull; at the same time he says they are impossible. Included in the impossible—her refusal (line 9). He's hinting that she doesn't have a choice, that only in fantasy she will be able to "please refuse."

—in line 19 the speaker says that she deserves the treatment he just described, and then in the next line he claims that he wouldn't love "at a lower rate." But he doesn't love her like that and claims that such a situation is impossible—so does that mean he doesn't love her at all?

—the second stanza is very violent and dry, not like the love and water of the first stanza. There are deserts, vaults, worms, dust, ashes, and graves. If he presented the first stanza as fantasy, this must be his vision of reality. I think he is trying to scare her by bringing up death imagery, like he is the one who could be her protector in the face of all of this imminent horror. But death isn't the first thing he mentions—it's the lack of her beauty. We can see where his priorities are.

—he sets up a limited life for her: either she has sex with him or the worms will get her. He can't see a life for her outside of him.

—her decisions are invalidated by his choice of language—"quaint honor." He doesn't think her honor is valuable.

—he even turns the grave into a possible sexual location! "But none, I think, do there embrace." He even leaves room open for the possibility with the "I think." Death and sex all tied up for him.

—final stanza set up as conclusion ("Now therefore")—given what he's presented (her "fantasy" and his harsh "reality"), his conclusion is that she should throw caution and her individual desires to the wind while her "willing soul transpires"—while she's still alive. A little threatening.

—more harsh language, very active and violent (shadowing the sex act?)—her soul breathes with fires, their lovemaking will resemble "birds of prey" "devour[ing]" time, and they'll "tear [their] pleasures with rough strife" (why?).

—odd use of the verb "sport"—sort of playful, more inconsequential than the other verbs (is he implying that the sex part is no big deal?).

—he wants to take her individuality away, "roll" both of them into "one ball," a ball that just happens to be doing what he wanted to do and what she didn't.

—In lecture, the professor said that contemporaries believed that sex shortened your life. Is his urging of her another way to kill her?

—he is arguing that they should throw away time and disregard the way the universe is ruled. But earlier, he ridiculed her for her fantasy world. Isn't this vision just as much a fantasy?

A Rough Outline

Her brainstorming notes gave Heather the confidence to move ahead. Believing that she had sufficient ideas to support a thesis, she now began to look for patterns in her ideas, patterns that would help her refine her thesis and organize her material. Though she was beginning to think about how she would organize the material, she knew that as she wrote the rough draft, new ideas might be generated and her organization might change. Following is Heather's rough outline.

Rough Outline

1. Introduction
   —thesis-like idea—the nature of time seems to be his main argument, but he really claims that women have no worth outside of their value to men. The speaker devalues the lady's desires, frightens her with his language, and threatens her with death and abandonment unless she sleeps with him.

2. Speaker thinks the mistress's values and decisions are fantastic
   —what he presents as her idea of time and the world (the dreamland)
   —his world (and desires) as the opposed reality
   —what she wants of love exists only in fantasy according to him
   —he will never provide her with that sort of devotion
   —irony of the last time image in the poem
   —in the beginning he argues against fantasy, but at the end he proposes fighting real time with her, just in the opposite direction

3. Speaker uses violent imagery and her death as primary arguments
   —he wants to frighten her into surrender with his language
   —lush, moist imagery of the dreamland turns to dry and deathlike imagery
   —conversely, he downplays the actual act by using the verb "sport"
   —language gives away that he doesn't plan to stay with her after she submits
   —she holds nothing for him but her brief beauty
   —contemporary belief that sex would shorten life—he hastens her toward death

4. Mistress (and all women) only valuable to him based on their sexual allure and ability to please him
   —Marvell focuses on speaker's mocking of lady's desires and values
   —all of the romantic stanza is written in the conditional tense
   —he implies that her personal decisions are crushing his love for her
   —third stanza provides the speaker's conclusions
   —he implies that her youth and attractiveness make her valuable
   —mistress only important to him insomuch as she has an effect on him—no independent worth
   —contradicts his statements in first paragraph
   —she is left with no individuality—he subsumes her entirely and she disappears into his vision of sex

5. Conclusion—sum up three main points—he reduces her to just her body, the
   only thing he thinks she can give him
   —how this reflects on his views of women as a whole

Outline/Draft

At this point, Heather had a strong sense of where she was going with her ideas
and a good idea of how she was going to organize them. She was now ready to start
developing her ideas more specifically in terms of the language and argument of Marvell's poem. Even now, though, she knew that what she was writing was "only" a draft,
something to be tinkered with later. To prevent herself from seeing this version as
anything other than a rough draft, Heather decided to develop her ideas as part of a
much more complex outline, something that is really a cross between an outline and a
draft. Here is what she came up with:

OUTLINE/DRAFT

Intro: a brief summary of poem first. Although it may seem
that Marvell's speaker uses the fleeting nature of time as his
primary persuasive tool, his arguments illuminate a worldview
wherein women have no worth outside of their attractiveness
to men. Over the course of the poem, the speaker devalues his
mistress's wishes and decisions, uses violent language and
imagery to threaten her, and makes it clear that his interest
in her will cease in a short time regardless of whether or
not she has sex with him.

1. (two paragraphs? Maybe one with just conclusions he
draws from the fantasy land?) In the first stanza of the poem,
the speaker describes a dreamland of love, a world without
the strictures of time. While he paints a lovely picture, he
makes it clear that he considers such a place fantastic and
unrealistic. He then intimates that this dreamland is his
lady's skewed idea of reality: her desires fit only in a dream
world. The contrast he presents, his viewpoint, is treated as
reality. This assumption implies that eventually they will

---

have sex--if her world (and her choice to wait) is fantasy, then his supposedly practical world (where they consummate the relationship) will triumph over her "delusions." In line 9, he displays this attitude of assured eventual victory. Given all of his fantasy conditions, he assures her that "[she] should if [she] please, refuse," as though her refusal in his world is not valid and not taken seriously. The other conclusion one can draw from the first section is that only in fantasy could he love her for more than she can physically offer him--it would take the impossible end of time for the speaker to love her beyond her "eyes" and "forehead" and "each breast." Ironically, at the end of the poem, he drops his bid for reality as he had defined it and proposes that the couple fight against the nature of time.

2. In contrast to her idea of "long love's day," the speaker details a harsh version of the world meant to frighten her into submission. He uses violent imagery and her death as his primary argument. The rivers and water images of the first section succumb to deserts and dust, fires and graves.

He strays from the serious language once, in his use of the verb "sport" (line 37) to describe their potential consummation, as though to downplay the act itself, present it as a minor thing in contrast to the violence of death. Couched in the language is his admission that he won't be interested after she gives in to him (look at line 39). At the poem's conclusion, he argues that since they can't slow time down (as she wishes), then they should throw it away. If he believes the contemporary idea that sex shortens life, then he hastens her toward death, the very state he is using to persuade her.

3. Given his various arguments and attitudes, the speaker makes it clear that he thinks his mistress (and by extension,

any woman) is only valuable for her youthful sexual allure
and willingness to bend to his wishes. From the first section,
Marvell focuses on the speaker's refusal to take the lady's
requests seriously. The speaker contradicts his sentiments in
the first section with his use of conditional language--he
would/could/should love her the way she desires only if the
universe gave them infinite time (see 20-21). Otherwise, he
cannot (list conditional acts). After thus clarifying that he
is incapable of providing what she desires, he implies that
her values, by not placing him as a priority, are destroying
him and his version of love for her. (See line 29.) Line 33's
"therefore" signals the end of his argument and the beginning
of his conclusions. He comes to the conclusion that her youth
and attractiveness make her valuable, and once those qualities disappear, he will as well. (See 37.) Because her primary draw for him is her attractiveness, the speaker views
the mistress as valuable only in her relationship to him--she
has no independent worth in this life or the afterlife (nor
do her decisions). This contradicts the initial fantasy,
where there is a scenario in which he can love her. The dream
here may not be the issue of infinite time, but instead that
of his potential for real love, respect, and admiration. With
his focus on sex, her individuality is lost. Her soul is only
mentioned in the context of its limited time to engage in
lovemaking (35), and a few lines later he proposes to rid her
of that by merging and his subsuming of her character (rolled
up in one ball).

   Conclusion: During the course of the poem the speaker represents the lady's desires as impossible dreams, threatens
and frightens her, and reduces her total worth to only what
she can wholly give him: her body.

THE PARTS OF THE PAPER: WORKING ON THE INTRODUCTION, BODY, AND CONCLUSION

When we ask students what they have learned about the structure of an essay, they usually say that a paper needs an introduction, body paragraphs, and a conclusion. That much is clear. But once you know that, what do you do next? It is easy enough to say that a paper needs these three main sections, but how do you know what to put in them? And, even more, how do you make the introduction and conclusion sound like the introduction and conclusion?

The Introduction

Many of you have probably learned that a good introduction has to invite the reader into a paper, give the reader a sense of the paper's topic and thesis, and establish the tone of the paper. That is all generally good advice. For literary criticism, though, some of the advice given about introductions for the personal essay does not always work very well. You may, for instance, have learned that one way to begin an introduction is to start with a narrative of some kind, perhaps an experience from your own life. Or you may have learned that a good way to begin is to start with some kind of shocking statement or statistic. Both openings work well for some kinds of essays, but they are very uncommon in literary criticism, mostly because most papers on literature adopt a professional, scholarly tone.

If some of the usual methods do not work, then, what does? Often you will find it easiest to write the introduction for a paper on literature if you begin with a sentence that lets the reader know from the beginning what work you will be talking about. That means that usually the first sentence will contain the author's name (the full name unless the author is very well known) and the full title of the work you will be discussing. Here is the opening paragraph from an article by Christopher Nassaar, a professional critic:

> When Freud in his *Interpretation of Dreams* made his famous observations about *Oedipus the King,* he naturally focused on the main issue: that Oedipus killed his father and married his mother. A further Freudian analysis of the play reveals another issue that came to dominate psychoanalysis: the preference of Oedipus for his daughters. Oedipus's preference for Antigone and Ismene appears only at the very end of the play, but it completes the picture of incest and murder in the family. (Nassar 187)

This introduction may seem to you dauntingly complex. How, you may wonder, could the writer possibly have known all that as he began to write his essay? The answer is that he probably did not. Many writers skip the introduction until the essay is nearly finished, writing it only when they feel they have a good grasp on what they want to say. Others write a sketchy version, filling it out later. Writing processes vary dramatically from writer to writer. If you are stuck when facing the task of writing an introduction, get yourself going by *not* writing it. Write the sections you feel comfortable with and come back to the introduction later. First things don't have to come first.

EXERCISE: TRYING IT OUT

Looking back at Nassaar's introduction, identify its thesis statement. How effective do you think this thesis is likely to be? Why?

The Body Paragraphs: Supplying the Argument and Using Evidence

The real heart of a paper is, of course, what follows the introduction and precedes the conclusion: the parts of the paper that state, argue, and support the thesis. It is in the body paragraphs that a writer makes his case, being certain to make arguable assertions and to support those assertions with clear evidence from the text. It is here that he includes and interprets the kinds of evidence he found when brainstorming about the text. Often novice literary critics do a fine job of making assertions but forget to take the second step and to include in their writing the evidence that led them to their assertions. Or they do the opposite: they provide some intriguing and important details but forget to explain the significance of the evidence. So when you write you will want to make certain that each major assertion is supported by evidence from the text(s) and that each quotation or plot detail is interpreted for the reader. It is often useful to get in the habit of thinking about this process of development as a three-step process: you will want to introduce your idea; include your evidence (and make certain that you let your reader know its context); and then demonstrate how the evidence supports your original assertion. By taking all three steps toward developing the idea, you will guide your reader toward the conclusion you want her to reach.

Using Quotations   Often in a paper that responds to a piece of literature, your evidence will be in the form of references to the text you are discussing, frequently in the form of exact quotations. There are a number of ways to introduce a quotation, but the quotation must be introduced. You will want, then, to avoid allowing a quotation to form a sentence by itself. Instead, give your reader a sense of the context, which would probably include a reminder of who the speaker is and where the quotation occurs. Here are some examples (the number in parentheses is the page number, which a writer includes so that a reader can easily find the quotation in its original context):

> When Mrs. Mallard discovers that her husband is still alive, she has a heart attack and dies "of joy that kills" (75).

> The two women who discover Mrs. Wright's dead bird come to understand why she might have killed her husband. As Mrs. Hale says, "If there'd been years and years of nothing, then a bird to sing to you, it would be awful—still, after the bird was still" (54).

When you are integrating a quotation fully into your own sentence, you may find yourself having to change the wording of the original enough to fit into the grammatical structure of your sentence. To indicate changes—as, for instance, a change of verb tense or pronoun—use **square brackets** ([ ]) around the change. To show where you have omitted words, put three dots (an **ellipsis**) where those words occurred in the original. Here is an example of how a writer might use part of the first paragraph of Poe's "The Tell-Tale Heart" (see 404–7):

> The narrator of "The Tell-Tale Heart" believes that he can "[hear] all things in the heaven and in the earth [and] . . . many things in hell" (404).

Ellipses are useful for omitting material that is not immediately relevant to your point. But use them sparingly and carefully. Readers generally want to see the context in which a quotation appears so that they can be certain the quotation honestly serves the use to which a writer is putting it. You need only to examine the quotation of a critic's opinions to see how the use of ellipses can distort the original meaning.

> The movie is not very good.
> "The movie is . . . good."

OR

> No one would give this movie two thumbs up!
> ". . . two thumbs up!"

Admittedly, few advertisers would be so dishonest as to change a critic's meaning so completely, but it is all too easy to change a meaning unconsciously or accidentally. When you quote, make sure you leave your source's meaning intact.

Finally, the quotation of poetry requires special consideration. When you quote from a poem, you need to remind your reader that it *is* a poem, which means you need to help your reader to see how the poetic structure of the line divisions works. If you are quoting more than three lines, you should simply set the quotation up on the page so that it looks like poetry, putting each line of poetry on its own line in your text. Here, for instance, is how a writer might handle a quotation from "Dover Beach." The numbers in parentheses (as for any poem) refer to line numbers, not page numbers:

> The speaker of Matthew Arnold's "Dover Beach" seems to regret the loss of faith that once helped him make sense of the world:
>
> The Sea of Faith
> Was once, too, at the full, and round earth's shore
> Lay like the folds of a bright girdle furled.
> But now I only hear
> Its melancholy, long, withdrawing roar[.] (21-25)

If you want to quote only two or three lines from a poem, you do not usually set the lines up on the page as poetry. Instead, you indicate the line divisions by means of a **slash mark** (/). Here is another example:

> In the first few lines of "Dover Beach," the speaker paints a soothing, peaceful picture of the seascape outside his window: "The sea is calm tonight. / The tide is full, the moon lies fair / Upon the straits" (1–3).

As is always the case, your goal in quoting from a piece of literature is to give the reader a sense of how your evidence works to prove your assertion and, at the same time, to allow him to see for himself the artistry of the work before him.

Writing a Conclusion

Many writers find conclusions difficult to write. They feel that they have said everything they want to say, and they can't think of any way to wrap it up. You do need to wrap things up, however. To see why it matters, think about how you would feel if a friend simply walked away from you while you were in the middle of a conversation and later explained his rudeness by saying, "Oh, I didn't have anything more to say to you." Your reader may very well feel the same way if you walk away from him in what seems like midthought. So you need to let him know that the essay is coming to an end, that you have said your piece and think you have covered everything. The conclusion is the essay's way of saying "good-bye."

Faced with the end of a paper, many writers are tempted simply to end with "In conclusion" or "Finally," hoping the reader will take that as sufficient evidence that the paper is over. Or they may instead decide to summarize what they have said, a tactic that works better for long papers than for relatively short papers of less than eight to ten pages. (The reader of a short paper has not had time to forget what a writer has said, so he probably does not need to have the ideas summarized.)

So how do you conclude an essay? Although much of the advice is negative—don't bring up an entirely new point, don't leave your reader hanging—there are some tricks to writing a good conclusion. You might, for instance, restate your thesis (but in new words) and then move to a more general point; in this way the conclusion moves in the opposite direction from the introduction, which often moves from a general point to a specific one (the thesis). If you were writing about the blurring of the line between myth and reality in "Yellow Woman," for example, you might end with a statement about how the narrator's real life seems more emotionally empty than the imaginary world offered by Silva. If you were writing about the influence of setting in *Trifles,* you might end by connecting setting, character, and event:

> Isolated from the company of other women, deprived of the one cheerful sound that had interrupted her days of silence, Minnie Wright takes the only path she can: she kills the man who has killed her spirit. Ironically enough, only then does her dreary house open itself to the sounds and life of others. But then—for Minnie and for her husband—it is too late.

Notice, by the way, that both examples have a note of finality to them because both close the door to further discussion: once "Yellow Woman" returns home, her true life seems over; once it is "too late" for the Wrights, there is nothing more to say.

REVISING AND EDITING

Although we have grouped **revising** and **editing** together, in many ways they are very separate processes. Revising involves looking at the paper as a whole, thinking about its ideas and organization, strengthening the evidence and answering more fully the reader's questions and doubts. Editing, on the other hand, involves a careful look at the sentences of the paper, paying particular attention to matters of punctuation, grammar, and usage, and playing with ways to state the ideas more concisely or gracefully. In our experience, students often confuse these two processes, shortchanging the process of revision and worrying too early in the paper-writing process about editorial decisions.

Revising

Students are sometimes surprised when we tell them that professional writers often spend as much time on the revision stage as they do on the first-draft stage of a project. Professional writers know that they are unlikely to have gotten everything "right" during the first-draft stage, when they were still trying to discover what they have to say. Only when they have triumphed over the blank page before them are they now ready to face a new task.

Oddly enough, it doesn't have to feel like a "task" at all. Here, as at the brainstorming stage, you will find yourself having an easier time of it if you begin by allowing yourself to play with your ideas. That does not mean that you are not taking your ideas and the writing task seriously. It means, instead, that you need to give yourself the opportunity to see your ideas from a fresh perspective, moving them around in your head—and on the page or screen. Now, in fact, may be a good time to move back to the annotations and brainstorming you did earlier, using your earlier notes to generate more ideas, thinking some more, too, about your organization. If you read through your essay and are puzzled about how the ideas all fit together (and all of us have had that unsettling experience), don't panic. Instead, ask yourself whether the pieces of your paper might fit together better if you moved some of them around, much as you might move the pieces of a jigsaw puzzle. If you are positive that you are right about something but notice that you have included no evidence, go back and find the evidence to support your firm beliefs. If, on the other hand, you can't find the evidence, now is the time to rethink the idea. The paper isn't, after all, yet finished.

This is also the stage at which to ask yourself whether others might come to a different understanding of the piece of literature on which you are writing. It may well be that other readers believe they have good reasons for their beliefs, and you will want to explain to them why their reasons are not as good as they seem. At this point, it may be helpful to think again about the controlling idea of this book: the idea of "retelling." To help yourself envision what a reader may be thinking, you may want to think about how you could "retell" the piece of literature, or your own paper, from a different sort of reader's perspective. Don't imagine a belligerent reader, simply a reader with a different point of view on the work. What evidence would that reader find to support this different point of view? When you have jotted down possible responses to that opposing point of view, go back and read your own paper and see if you have explained why that crucial opposing view is less solid than your own.

Editing

Only after you have revised your essay to strengthen its ideas and organization should you worry about editing the essay to strengthen its sentence structure. It is not that sentence structure is unimportant—after all, a reader who has trouble with your sentences may find it difficult to understand or appreciate your ideas. Still, you should usually leave editing for the end because there is no point in spending lots of time editing sentences if in the revision stage you are going to either eliminate an idea (and the sentence that conveys it) or shape it in ways that make the original sentence ineffective.

At the same time, this final step warrants your full attention. In these days of computers and spell and grammar checkers, many of us are tempted to "forget" this step, figuring that the computer will have done the job for us. But the spell checker cannot possibly tell us when we have used "there" or "it's" when we meant to say "their" or "its," and it cannot tell us when we have omitted a word altogether. And grammar checkers are still in their infancy; they cannot catch every error, and they often find errors in sentences that are perfectly fine. So it is up to you, the writer, to take final responsibility for making certain that the sentences are correct and will do your ideas justice.

Writers often say that it is difficult to edit their own work because they are so close to the ideas that they do not see their own errors, and we think there is some truth to that. There are a few tricks that can help give you the required distance from your own paper, though. Most helpful, perhaps, is to get the distance of time. If you can put the essay aside for a while—for at least a few hours, but ideally overnight— you may be able to get a fresh perspective on it. Many writers also find it helpful to read the paper aloud. Doing so will give you a chance to hear the errors and the ineffective rhythms that your eyes cannot see. Even better sometimes is reading the paper aloud to someone else or having that other person read it aloud to you. It is amazing what the presence of another set of ears will do to our sense of how our ideas might be received.

Whether you find it easy or difficult to gain objective distance from your own work, you finally want most to keep in mind the fact that you are writing to communicate. An idea that is locked in your own head or trapped in ineffective language cannot change another person's mind or give him new insight, no matter how good that idea is. Many of us struggle so much to get the words on the page that we sometimes almost forget that those words have to serve the reader's needs as well as the writer's.

So frequently do writers forget this basic fact that writing teachers often ask students to move from "writer-based prose" to "reader-based prose": the first refers to prose (writing) that works well for the writer, who already knows the ideas being expressed; the second refers to prose that works well for the reader, who is reading in the hopes of learning something new. If the reader doesn't learn anything, why would he read? And if a writer has no readers, is he really a writer? We encourage you to move beyond even the concept of "writer-based" and "reader-based" prose, though. Instead, think in terms of *idea*-based prose. Value your thinking abilities enough to bring the full weight of your mind to bear on your ideas; value your ideas enough to want others to believe them. If you do, you will find yourself not only writing but becoming a real writer.

A Note on Writing with a Word Processor

Anyone who has moved from writing drafts on paper to writing on a computer screen knows that using a word processing program has had tremendous effects on the way she looks at writing. It is now much easier than it was in the days of pen and paper or even of typewriters to move paragraphs around, making it much easier than it once was to play with several possible methods of organization. Similarly, it is easier to save for another day (and in another file) an idea that catches our interest but can't be made to work in the current paper. What has especially struck us in our own writing is that composing at a keyboard allows us to take more risks. No matter how silly or unformed an idea, we are willing to type it in; after all, it is easy to zap it out of existence if we decide it won't work. That willingness to take chances, to be silly or daring, has, we think, made us enjoy writing more and become better writers.

There are other, less obvious, benefits as well. Writers gain much simply by seeing their own writing on the screen. Even though more and more of us are using computers for almost all of our writing, we may still automatically associate our handwriting with our personalities, so when we see something we have written by hand, it is difficult to see it as anything other than a very personal extension of ourselves. That means that it is also difficult to gain the objectivity necessary to read it as a reader would. Seen on a computer screen or printed out on a page, though, that same writing seems less personally "ours," and we can more easily tinker with it and, if necessary, simply toss out what doesn't work.

Those who struggle over each word they write can also find another benefit in writing with a computer. If you are one of those writers who censors each word or sentence you write, crossing it out or deleting it because it is not "good enough" and crumpling up the paper in disgust, you may find it helpful simply to turn off the computer screen *and keep writing*. After all, if you can't see the words, you can't censor them, and you may be surprised at just how much writing you can get done once you can silence that little voice that tells you it will never be any good.

There are, of course, also dangers in writing on the computer. When you are stuck, there is always the lure of the Internet or a computer game at your fingertips, and it becomes all too easy to get distracted from the actual writing. Although we would not encourage you to give in to those temptations often, you can use them wisely: just reward yourself with a break after you have written a certain number of words, paragraphs, or pages. There is also some danger in the computer's very impressive powers of formatting. Many of us have spent hours trying to make something look right, trying out various font styles and adding charts, graphics, and tables. And all of us know how good a finished paper looks when printed out on a good printer. Don't fall prey to the temptation to value what the paper looks likes over how well it communicates its ideas.

PUTTING IT ALL TOGETHER

Now that we have spent some time examining the prewriting process and discussing the parts of a paper, let us return to student Heather Johnson and look at the finished paper she produced after effectively moving through the processes of brainstorming, outlining, and drafting you saw earlier. As you read the final version of her essay, ask yourself where her argument seems particularly convincing, where you would want more evidence, and where you can advance counterexamples.

Heather Johnson

Professor Clarke

English 3

15 May 2003

"In Thy Marble Vault": Violence and Coercion in Andrew

Marvell's "To His Coy Mistress"

In Andrew Marvell's poem "To His Coy Mistress," a man attempts to convince a reluctant lover to engage in more physical forms of affection. The speaker argues that time is the
obstacle the couple face and that her way of thinking of time
(a way that convinces her to wait) is unrealistic. Death
comes for all, he argues, and one never knows when, so best
to enjoy the present. Although it may seem that Marvell's
speaker uses the fleeting nature of time as his primary persuasive tool, his arguments illuminate a worldview wherein
women have no worth outside of their attractiveness to men.
Over the course of the poem, the speaker devalues his
mistress's wishes and decisions, uses violent language and
imagery to threaten her, and makes it clear that his interest
in her will cease in a short time regardless of whether or
not she has sex with him.

In the first section of the poem, the speaker describes a
dreamland of love, a world without the limits of time. He
imagines his mistress finding rubies "by the Indian Ganges'
side" while he writes love songs by the shores of his hometown's river (5-7). Their "long love's day" would be spent in
romantic contemplation, and "should [she] please refuse," he
would wait until the end of time for her (4, 9). While he

paints a lovely picture, he makes it clear that he considers such a place fantastic and unrealistic by exaggerating the features of the world. The lovers are somehow together even though she is in India and he in England. He vows to love her "ten years before the flood" and continue his affections until they grow "[v]aster than empires" (8, 12). Entire ages would be devoted to praising and admiring her features. Instead of sketching a portrait of a more sympathetic world (where they have fewer obligations or more freedoms), he goes to an impossible extreme.

After describing this world of love, the speaker then intimates that this dreamland is his lady's skewed idea of reality, that her desires fit only in a dream world. For her to act as she does, as though she is living in that world, makes "this coyness" a "crime" (2). The speaker presents the contrasting world (his view of life and love) in the second section as reality. He can "hear / [t]ime's wingèd chariot" at his back; he sees before them "[d]eserts of vast eternity" (22, 24). Unlike the imaginary world of the lady, described in conditional verbs (they could, they would), the second section uses present tense verbs, as though his impressions are immediate recordings of the true world. The speaker does not imagine sitting by a distant river; he actually hears and sees a world of danger and imminent death. The assumption that he is in touch with the real world implies that eventually they will have sex--if her world (and her choice to wait) is fantasy, then his supposedly practical world (where they will consummate the relationship) will triumph over her "delusions." In line 9, he displays this attitude of assured eventual victory. If all of his first-section fantasy conditions were to somehow come true, he assures her that

"[she] should, if [she] please, refuse," as though her
refusal in his world is not valid and not taken seriously.
This line also contains the kernel of a threat: since only in
the dreamworld will her refusal be allowed by him, he will
not allow her to refuse in his vision of reality.

In contrast to her idea of "long love's day," the speaker
details a harsh version of the world meant to frighten her
into submission (line 4). He uses violent imagery and her
death as his primary argument. The rivers and water images
of the first section succumb to deserts and dust, fires and
graves. First, he presents a scene of paranoia and solitude.
The chariot of time "[hurries] near" his back (threatening
to end both of their days) while they stand together in a
wasteland of "vast eternity" (22, 24). She could die at any
moment, he is saying, and the only other person in the world
with her is him. Although he could, at this point, cajole
her with an argument about the two of them being together
forever, fighting the vastness and threat of time, he instead
moves in a much darker direction. Her "beauty shall no more
be found . . . in [her] marble vault," he immediately adds in
lines 25 and 26. He imagines her dead and presents her with
a graphic picture of what her existence in death would consist of: no more of his "echoing song," her body and honor
"[turned] to dust," and most disturbingly, "worms [trying] /
[t]hat long-preserved virginity" (27, 29, 27-28). Implicit in
this description is what he considers to be her only two
choices: sleep with either him or the worms. If she chooses
not to have sex with the speaker, then only the worms (her
death) will have her. He does not present any other options,
and one can assume that this choice constitutes a death-threat
towards her.

The speaker strays from the serious language of the second
and third sections only once, in his use of the verb "sport"
(37) to describe their potential lovemaking, as though to
downplay the act itself, present it as a minor thing in contrast to the violence of death. After the imagery of the
grave and worms, to "sport" with him sounds like a casual
thing indeed, no big deal, certainly not worth the fuss she
is making, especially when contrasted with death. Even then,
the speaker implies in his language that he won't be interested in her after she gives in to him. In line 39 he
proposes that they "at once our time devour," which could be
read as his saying that his one time will be all he needs of
her. After she submits, he will have devoured the time he has
for her; whatever time she has left in her life is none of
his concern. At the poem's conclusion, he argues that since
they can't slow time down (as she wishes), then they should
"make [it] run," throw it away (46). If he believes the contemporary idea that each sex act shortened one's life by a
day, then he hastens her toward death, the very state he used
to persuade her to avoid by having sex with him.

Given his various arguments and attitudes, the speaker
makes it clear that he thinks his mistress (and by extension,
any woman) is valuable only for her youthful sexual allure
and willingness to bend to his wishes. From the first section,
Marvell focuses on the speaker's refusal to take the lady's
requests seriously. The speaker contradicts his sentiments in
the first section with his use of conditional language--he
would/could/should love her the way she desires only if
the universe gave them infinite time. He claims that she
"deserve[s] this state" of respect and dignity and that he
would not "love at [a] lower rate" (19, 20). But the world as

he sees it does not conform to the world of the first section. He does not believe that she deserves respect, and he loves her at a very low rate indeed. The speaker thinks a world that dignifies women and fulfills their wishes is only a fantasy. After thus clarifying that he (and the world) is incapable of providing what she desires, he implies that her values, by both denying the "true" nature of the world and not placing him as a priority, are destroying him and his version of love for her. In line 30, the speaker says that should she die, his lust will turn to ashes. Her "quaint honor," her decision to not submit to him, are killing his affections toward her, he says (29). Her honor is not viewed as a logical decision or value--it is "quaint," and harmful if she wants him to love her. Line 33's "therefore" signals the end of his argument and the beginning of his conclusions. He comes to the conclusion that her youth and attractiveness make her valuable, and once those qualities disappear, he will as well. "While the youthful hue / [s]its on [her] skin" they should make love "while [they] may," he proposes (33–34, 37). As soon as the spark of youth fades, the opportunity for her to be with him will also fade.

Because her primary draw for him is her attractiveness, the speaker views the mistress as valuable only in her relationship to him--she has no independent worth in this life or the afterlife (nor do her decisions). This contradicts the initial fantasy, where there is a scenario (however impossible) in which he can love her. The dream here may not be the issue of infinite time (what he says is needed), but instead that of his potential for real love, respect, and admiration towards women. With his focus on youth and sex, her individuality is lost. Another beautiful young woman could do all that he is asking of her; no mention is made of the mistress's personality outside of her decision not to submit to him. Her soul is mentioned only in the context of its limited time to engage in lovemaking (35), and a few lines later he proposes to rid her of that by subsuming her character: "[l]et us roll all our strength and all / [o]ur sweetness up into one ball," he says. While in some cases this merging could be viewed as a romantic act, the two becoming one, in this scenario the togetherness would exclude her. As she does not want to have sex with him, the "one ball" they would form would be wholly formed of his wishes and his characteristics. He is, in short, proposing to not only take her body, but to take her identity and choices.

During the course of the poem the speaker represents the lady's desires as impossible dreams, threatens and frightens her, and reduces her total worth to only what she can wholly give him: her body. If one attempts to extrapolate the world-view of the speaker, one stumbles onto a frightening but once common world. Men describe and control the lives of women in the world the speaker presents, and only in bending to men's wishes are they able to survive.

Before leaving Heather's paper, we want to note that in writing it, she followed a couple of important conventions of literary analysis:

1. Heather does not summarize the poem, except where some idea is crucial to the point she is making. She assumes, as literary critics generally do, that the reader has read the work. Whether you are writing about a short poem, a play, or a work of fiction, you will want to make sure that the emphasis is on your analysis and interpretation, that any summarizing advances the argument rather than substituting for it.

2. Heather uses the **literary present;** in other words, she writes as if the events and narrative of the poem are occurring at the present moment. You will want to do

the same in your writing about literature, making statements such as "The speaker *says,*" "The Yellow Woman *leaves* her house," and "The 'used Mexican' salesman *makes* his pitch." The idea behind this convention is that the work is eternally present, unfolding before our eyes. The convention also applies to discussions of films and artworks.

Although by convention a writer uses the present tense in analyses of literature, that does not mean that such analyses never contain verbs in other tenses. If your analysis moves away from the scene under discussion to talk about an earlier scene, for instance, you should use the past tense; if you project forward from the scene you are discussing, you should use the future tense. You simply want to use the central scene you are discussing as a temporal reference point, a kind of anchor to help you decide what you want to consider "past" and what you want to consider "future."

One other piece of advice about the literary present: use it to talk about a piece of literature but not to talk about the author as a historical person who actually lived and died. As a result, if you wish to refer to the author as an individual, use the past tense: "Like other people of his time, Marvell probably *believed* . . ." or "Matthew Arnold probably *wrote* 'Dover Beach' to express some of the emotions he was experiencing on his honeymoon." You would, though, use the literary present for both Marvell's speaker and Arnold's, as well as for Marvell and Arnold as "eternal" authors whose works continue to be read long after their deaths. You would say, then, "Arnold *wrote* 'Dover Beach' in the nineteenth century," but "in the poem, Arnold *uses* rhythm to imitate the movement of a calm sea." The historical man who wrote the poem has died, but the author (and his works) lives on.

EXERCISES: TRYING IT OUT

1. Imagine yourself writing a counterargument to Heather's paper. Jot down your notes for such an argument, making certain to refer to particular lines in Marvell's poem. Then develop one of your points in a fully developed paragraph.
2. Although Heather's paper is very good, it was returned to her with the comment that, throughout, the paragraphs need stronger topic sentences and that the last paragraphs in particular tend to be repetitious; they need a tighter organization and focus. What advice would you give Heather about specific problems and about the changes she might make?

As you take on the task of revising Heather Johnson's paper, or even if you only imagine yourself doing so, you complete the circle: Heather's earlier ideas become the foundation for your paper, or at least your version of her paper. In fact, if you were to re-envision her work completely, you would begin to retell it, perhaps making it suit your own purposes. This is, finally, the way good writing always works. One writer builds on the ideas of another, who, in turn, provides the foundation for a third. If you can begin to look at your own writing that way, too, you can begin to think of your earlier ideas as the foundation on which you and your readers will build later ideas and to which you and they will return for more inspiration. Then you will become a writer.

Works Cited

de Bono, Edward. *Lateral Thinking: Creativity Step by Step.* New York: Harper & Row Perennial, 1990.

Nassaar, Christopher S. "Sophocles' *Oedipus the King.*" *Explicator* 55 (1997): 187.

Part 4

Tellings and Retellings

8

Monsters and Heroes

Sir John Tenniel's illustration of "Jabberwocky" for
Lewis Carroll's *Through the Looking-Glass* (1872).

INTRODUCTION

One of our very first experiences in life is the nightmare. No matter how happy
our childhoods, many of us remember being afraid at night. Even as adults, we can recall, often vividly, our childish night terrors, our fears of the monster lurking under
the bed or in the closet. So universal is this experience that it seems deeply embedded
in the human psyche, something felt before it is learned. Many children's books and
poems describe this childhood fear; often telling stories in which the monster is
tamed, they help children conquer their fears. Once the monster becomes the Cookie
Monster, for instance, he seems far less threatening.

Lewis Carroll, the author of *Alice in Wonderland,* gave nineteenth-century children his version of the monster, and the hero who conquers him, in "Jabberwocky."

LEWIS CARROLL
(CHARLES LUTWIDGE DODGSON) (1832–1898)

Jabberwocky _____ *1871*

'Twas brillig, and the slithy toves
    Did gyre and gimble in the wabe:
All mimsy were the borogoves,
    And the mome raths outgrabe.

5   "Beware the Jabberwock, my son!
    The jaws that bite, the claws that catch!
Beware the Jubjub bird, and shun
    The frumious Bandersnatch!"

He took his vorpal sword in hand:
10   Long time the manxome foe he sought—
So rested he by the Tumtum tree,
    And stood awhile in thought.

And, as in uffish thought he stood,
    The Jabberwock, with eyes of flame,
15   Came whiffling through the tulgey wood,
    And burbled as it came!

One, two! One, two! And through and through
    The vorpal blade went snicker-snack!
He left it dead, and with its head
20   He went galumphing back.

"And hast thou slain the Jabberwock?
    Come to my arms, my beamish boy!
O frabjous day! Callooh! Callay!"
    He chortled in his joy.

25   'Twas brillig, and the slithy toves
    Did gyre and gimble in the wabe:
All mimsy were the borogoves,
    And the mome raths outgrabe.

    The poem is a nonsense poem full of nonsense words. Yet unfamiliar as the vocabulary is, we can easily understand the basic meaning of the poem: a terrible monster, the Jabberwock (and its sidekicks the Jubjub bird and the Bandersnatch), must be defeated. The child hero, the "beamish boy," does just that, killing the Jabberwock with his "vorpal sword." All ends happily as good triumphs over evil and the fearsome monster is defeated.

    Though we may outgrow our childish fears, we never do quite outgrow the monster. It continues to loom large in life and literature. Whenever we must face the fearful unknown, we tend to fill it with monsters. Centuries ago, when much of the earth had not yet been explored, maps and travel literature peopled it with mon-

sters and mythical beasts. Even today, we do much the same thing, imaging alien creatures inhabiting the galaxy. The monster may live closer to home as well. Those we
can't—or won't—understand may seem monstrous to us, whether they are those we
see as "crazy," criminals who have committed horrific crimes, or enemies in wartime.

Despite our tendency to project the monster into the world beyond us, the
monster also resides inside. We fear it and yet, ironically, are attracted to it. We find
ourselves avidly following the story of the latest serial killer, or we buy tickets by the
millions to horror films such as the *Friday the 13th* movies or *The Silence of the Lambs*.
Both the attraction and the repulsion are parts of our deepest, most hidden feelings,
what psychologists would call our subconscious. Sometimes the monster acts out for
us not only our fears but also our desires, unleashing the chaotic destructive and sexual energies that we attempt to keep under conscious control. The monster is the gargantuan King Kong, who destroys buildings and airplanes while clutching in his hands
his small human lady love. The monster is Dracula, the fearsome vampire who attacks
and yet also strangely seduces his female victims, or the equally seductive Arnold
Friend, who is at the center of "Where Are You Going, Where Have You Been?," the
first story in this chapter. We abhor King Kong, Dracula, and Arnold Friend, yet perhaps their violence and sexuality tell the secret of our own desires.

Because monsters can be anywhere, inside or outside, the battle to conquer the
monster can never be over. Perhaps we can hope only to control the monster, just as
we learn to control our less civilized impulses. We have learned to control those impulses partly by recognizing their presence and their power, and some have come to
believe that we can control monsters in the same way. Like the alien who kidnaps humans, placing them under a microscope and performing tests on them to understand
their inner workings, we closely examine our monsters, so much so that they may
no longer resemble the monsters of old. This is probably as true in real life as it is in
literature. Even the monsters we read about in the daily newspaper sometimes seem
less monstrous as we read about their unhappy childhoods or their genetic predisposi-
tions or the social and economic conditions that may have led them to commit criminal acts.

Just as we have humanized our monsters, realizing that they are less demonic
than we once thought, we have humanized our heroes, making them more like us
and less like demigods. The heroes of earlier literature were often larger than life—
bigger, smarter, and more powerful than any of us. They were the "beamish boy"
killing the world's Jabberwocks; Odysseus ridding the world of monster after monster
in his ten-year journey home after the Trojan War; or Superman fighting the evils of
the universe. These were the heroes who could defeat any monster and protect the
values of their own cultures and civilizations.

More modern heroes are likely to be more like us, everyday people put in extraordinary situations. That means that they are also more apt than heroes of the past
to have very real human failings. We turn on them the same microscopes we turn
on the monsters and learn about their private indiscretions and their all-too-human
failings. As a result, they can only become less clearly good. For that reason, modern
literature—composed after psychologists and others began to look into our subconscious—has few pure heroes or pure monsters. Indeed, not only are the heroes and
monsters often more like *us* than they once were, but they may also be more like *each
other* than they once were.

The monsters and heroes of childhood have disappeared, only to be replaced by more ambiguous figures. Despite what we may wish to believe, the monster may *not* be an alien creature, an "other," and even the common everyday person may be called on to act heroically. Whether they exist in two bodies or one, the monster and the hero belong to each of us.

An Album of Retellings

THE MODERN MONSTER

JOYCE CAROL OATES (1938–   )

Where Are You Going, Where Have You Been? _____ *1970*
For Bob Dylan

Her name was Connie. She was fifteen and she had a quick nervous giggling habit of craning her neck to glance into mirrors, or checking other people's faces to make sure her own was all right. Her mother, who noticed everything and knew everything and who hadn't much reason any longer to look at her own face, always scolded Connie about it. "Stop gawking at yourself, who are you? You think you're so pretty?" she would say. Connie would raise her eyebrows at these familiar complaints and look right through her mother, into a shadowy vision of herself as she was right at that moment: she knew she was pretty and that was everything. Her mother had been pretty once too, if you could believe those old snapshots in the album, but now her looks were gone and that was why she was always after Connie.

"Why don't you keep your room clean like your sister? How've you got your hair fixed—what the hell stinks? Hair spray? You don't see your sister using that junk."

Her sister June was twenty-four and still lived at home. She was a secretary in the high school Connie attended, and if that wasn't bad enough—with her in the same building—she was so plain and chunky and steady that Connie had to hear her praised all the time by her mother and her mother's sisters. June did this, June did that, she saved money and helped clean the house and cooked and Connie couldn't do a thing, her mind was all filled with trashy daydreams. Their father was away at work most of the time and when he came home he wanted supper and he read the newspaper at supper and after supper he went to bed. He didn't bother talking much to them, but around his bent head Connie's mother kept picking at her until Connie wished her mother was dead and she herself was dead and it was all over. "She makes me want to throw up sometimes," she complained to her friends. She had a high, breathless, amused voice which made everything she said sound a little forced, whether it was sincere or not.

There was one good thing: June went places with girl friends of hers, girls who were just as plain and steady as she, and so when Connie wanted to do that her mother had no objections. The father of Connie's best girl friend drove the girls the three miles to town and left them off at a shopping plaza, so that they could walk through the stores or go to a movie, and when he came to pick them up again at eleven he never bothered to ask what they had done.

They must have been familiar sights, walking around that shopping plaza in their shorts and flat ballerina slippers that always scuffed the sidewalk, with charm bracelets jingling on their thin wrists; they would lean together to whisper and laugh secretly if someone passed by who amused or interested them. Connie had long dark blond hair that drew anyone's eye to it, and she wore part of it pulled up on her head and puffed out and the rest of it she let fall down her back. She wore a pull-over jersey blouse that looked one way when she was at home and another way when she was away from home. Everything about her had two sides to it, one for home and one for anywhere that was not home: her walk that could be childlike and bobbing, or languid enough to make anyone think she was hearing music in her head, her mouth which was pale and smirking most of the time, but bright and pink on these evenings out, her laugh which was cynical and drawling at home—"Ha, ha, very funny"—but high-pitched and nervous anywhere else, like the jingling of the charms on her bracelet.

Sometimes they did go shopping or to a movie, but sometimes they went across the highway, ducking fast across the busy road, to a drive-in restaurant where older kids hung out. The restaurant was shaped like a big bottle, though squatter than a real bottle, and on its cap was a revolving figure of a grinning boy who held a hamburger aloft. One night in mid-summer they ran across, breathless with daring, and right away someone leaned out a car window and invited them over, but it was just a boy from high school they didn't like. It made them feel good to be able to ignore him. They went up through the maze of parked and cruising cars to the bright-lit, fly-infested restaurant, their faces pleased and expectant as if they were entering a sacred building that loomed out of the night to give them what haven and what blessing they yearned for. They sat at the counter and crossed their legs at the ankles, their thin shoulders rigid with excitement, and listened to the music that made everything so good: the music was always in the background like music at a church service, it was something to depend upon.

A boy named Eddie came in to talk with them. He sat backwards on his stool, turning himself jerkily around in semi-circles and then stopping and turning again, and after a while he asked Connie if she would like something to eat. She said she did and so she tapped her friend's arm on her way out—her friend pulled her face up into a brave droll look—and Connie said she would meet her at eleven, across the way. "I just hate to leave her like that," Connie said earnestly, but the boy said that she wouldn't be alone for long. So they went out to his car and on the way Connie couldn't help but let her eyes wander over the windshields and faces all around her, her face gleaming with a joy that had nothing to do with Eddie or even this place; it might have been the music. She drew her shoulders up and sucked in her breath with the pure pleasure of being alive, and just at that moment she happened to glance at a face just a few feet from hers. It was a boy with shaggy black hair, in a convertible jalopy painted gold. He stared at her and then his lips widened into a grin. Connie slit her eyes at him and turned away, but she couldn't help glancing back and there he was still watching her. He wagged a finger and laughed and said, "Gonna get you, baby," and Connie turned away again without Eddie noticing anything.

She spent three hours with him, at the restaurant where they ate hamburgers and drank Cokes in wax cups that were always sweating, and then down an alley a mile or so away, and when he left her off at five to eleven only the movie house was still open at the plaza. Her girl friend was there, talking with a boy. When Connie came up the two girls smiled at each other and Connie said, "How was the movie?" and the girl said, "*You* should know." They rode off with the girl's father, sleepy and pleased, and Connie couldn't help but look at the darkened shopping plaza with its big empty parking lot and its signs that were faded and ghostly now, and over at the drive-in restaurant where cars were still circling tirelessly. She couldn't hear the music at this distance.

Next morning June asked her how the movie was and Connie said, "So-so."

She and that girl and occasionally another girl went out several times a week that way, and the rest of the time Connie spent around the house—it was summer vacation—getting in her mother's way and thinking, dreaming, about the boys she met. But all the boys fell back and dissolved into a single face that was not even a face, but an idea, a feeling, mixed up with the urgent insistent pounding of the music and the humid night air of July. Connie's mother kept dragging her back to the daylight by finding things for her to do or saying, suddenly, "What's this about the Pettinger girl?"

And Connie would say nervously, "Oh, her. That dope." She always drew thick clear lines between herself and such girls, and her mother was simple and kindly enough to believe her. Her mother was so simple, Connie thought, that it was maybe cruel to fool her so much. Her mother went scuffling around the house in old bedroom slippers and complained over the telephone to one sister about the other, then the other called up and the two of them complained about the third one. If June's name was mentioned her mother's tone was approving, and if Connie's name was mentioned it was disapproving. This did not really mean she disliked Connie and actually Connie thought that her mother preferred her to June because she was prettier, but the two of them kept up a pretense of exasperation, a sense that they were tugging and struggling over something of little value to either of them. Sometimes, over coffee, they were almost friends, but something would come up—some vexation that was like a fly buzzing suddenly around their heads—and their faces went hard with contempt.

One Sunday Connie got up at eleven—none of them bothered with church—and washed her hair so that it could dry all day long, in the sun. Her parents and sister were going to a barbecue at an aunt's house and Connie said no, she wasn't interested, rolling her eyes to let her mother know just what she thought of it. "Stay home alone then," her mother said sharply. Connie sat out back in a lawn chair and watched them drive away, her father quiet and bald, hunched around so that he could back the car out, her mother with a look that was still angry and not at all softened through the windshield, and in the back seat poor old June all dressed up as if she didn't know what a barbecue was, with all the running yelling kids and the flies. Connie sat with her eyes closed in the sun, dreaming and dazed with the warmth about her as if this were a kind of love, the caresses of love, and her mind slipped over onto thoughts of the boy she had been with the night before and how nice he had been, how sweet it always was, not the way someone like June would suppose but sweet, gentle, the way it was in movies and promised in songs; and when she opened her eyes she hardly knew where she was, the backyard ran off into weeds and a fence-line of trees and behind it the sky was perfectly blue and still. The asbestos "ranch house" that was now three years old startled her—it looked small. She shook her head as if to get awake.

It was too hot. She went inside the house and turned on the radio to drown out the quiet. She sat on the edge of her bed, barefoot, and listened for an hour and a half to a program called XYZ Sunday Jamboree, record after record of hard, fast, shrieking songs she sang along with, interspersed by exclamations from "Bobby King": "An' look here you girls at Napoleon's—Son and Charley want you to pay real close attention to this song coming up!"

And Connie paid close attention herself, bathed in a glow of slow-pulsed joy that seemed to rise mysteriously out of the music itself and lay languidly about the airless little room, breathed in and breathed out with each gentle rise and fall of her chest.

After a while she heard a car coming up the drive. She sat up at once, startled, because it couldn't be her father so soon. The gravel kept crunching all the way in from the road—the driveway was long—and Connie ran to the window. It was a car she didn't know. It was an open jalopy, painted a bright gold that caught the sunlight opaquely. Her heart began to pound and her fingers snatched at her hair, checking it, and she whispered "Christ, Christ," wondering how bad she looked. The car came to a stop at the side door and the horn sounded four short taps as if this were a signal Connie knew.

She went into the kitchen and approached the door slowly, then hung out the screen door, her bare toes curling down off the step. There were two boys in the car and now she recognized the driver: he had shaggy, shabby black hair that looked crazy as a wig and he was grinning at her.

"I ain't late, am I?" he said.

"Who the hell do you think you are?" Connie said.

"Toldja I'd be out, didn't I?"

"I don't even know who you are."

She spoke sullenly, careful to show no interest or pleasure, and he spoke in a fast bright monotone. Connie looked past him to the other boy, taking her time. He had fair brown hair, with a lock that fell onto his forehead. His sideburns gave him a fierce, embarrassed look, but so far he hadn't even bothered to glance at her. Both boys wore sunglasses. The driver's glasses were metallic and mirrored everything in miniature.

"You wanta come for a ride?" he said.

Connie smirked and let her hair fall loose over one shoulder.

"Don'tcha like my car? New paint job," he said. "Hey."

"What?"

"You're cute."

She pretended to fidget, chasing flies away from the door.

"Don'tcha believe me, or what?" he said.

"Look, I don't even know who you are," Connie said in disgust.

"Hey, Ellie's got a radio, see. Mine's broke down." He lifted his friend's arm and showed her the little transistor the boy was holding, and now Connie began to hear the music. It was the same program that was playing inside the house.

"Bobby King?" she said.

"I listen to him all the time. I think he's great."

"He's kind of great," Connie said reluctantly.

"Listen, that guy's *great*. He knows where the action is."

Connie blushed a little, because the glasses made it impossible for her to see just what this boy was looking at. She couldn't decide if she liked him or if he was just a jerk, and so she dawdled in the doorway and wouldn't come down or go back inside. She said, "What's all that stuff painted on your car?"

"Can'tcha read it?" He opened the door very carefully, as if he was afraid it might fall off. He slid out just as carefully, planting his feet firmly on the ground, the tiny metallic world in his glasses slowing down like gelatine hardening and in the midst of it Connie's bright green blouse. "This here is my name, to begin with," he said. ARNOLD FRIEND was written in tarlike black letters on the side, with a drawing of a round grinning face that reminded Connie of a pumpkin, except it wore sunglasses. "I wanta introduce myself, I'm Arnold Friend and that's my real name and I'm gonna be your friend, honey, and inside the car's Ellie Oscar, he's kinda shy." Ellie brought his transistor radio up to his shoulder and balanced it there. "Now these numbers are a secret code, honey," Arnold Friend explained. He read off the numbers 33, 19, 17 and raised his eyebrows at her to see what she thought of that, but she didn't think much of it. The left rear fender had been smashed and around it was written, on the gleaming gold background: DONE BY CRAZY WOMAN DRIVER. Connie had to laugh at that. Arnold Friend was pleased at her laughter and looked up at her. "Around the other side's a lot more—you wanta come and see them?"

"No."

"Why not?"

"Why should I?"

"Don'tcha wanta see what's on the car? Don'tcha wanta go for a ride?"

"I don't know."

"Why not?"

"I got things to do."

"Like what?"

"Things."

He laughed as if she had said something funny. He slapped his thighs. He was standing in a strange way, leaning back against the car as if he were balancing himself. He wasn't tall, only an inch or so taller than she would be if she came down to him. Connie liked the way he was dressed, which was the way all of them dressed: tight faded jeans stuffed into black, scuffed boots, a belt that pulled his waist in and showed how lean he was, and a white pull-over shirt that was a little soiled and showed the hard small muscles of his arms and shoulders. He looked as if he probably did hard work, lifting and carrying things. Even his neck looked muscular. And his face was a familiar face, somehow: the jaw and chin and cheeks slightly darkened, because he hadn't shaved for a day or two, and the nose long and hawk-like, sniffing as if she were a treat he was going to gobble up and it was all a joke.

"Connie, you ain't telling the truth. This is your day set aside for a ride with me and you know it," he said, still laughing. The way he straightened and recovered from his fit of laughing showed that it had been all fake.

"How do you know what my name is?" she said suspiciously.

"It's Connie."

"Maybe and maybe not."

"I know my Connie," he said, wagging his finger. Now she remembered him even better, back at the restaurant, and her cheeks warmed at the thought of how she sucked in her breath just at the moment she passed him—how she must have looked to him. And he had remembered her. "Ellie and I come out here especially for you," he said. "Ellie can sit in back. How about it?"

"Where?"

"Where what?"

"Where're we going?"

He looked at her. He took off the sunglasses and she saw how pale the skin around his eyes was, like holes that were not in shadow but instead in light. His eyes were chips of broken glass that catch the light in an amiable way. He smiled. It was as if the idea of going for a ride somewhere, to some place, was a new idea to him.

"Just for a ride, Connie sweetheart."

"I never said my name was Connie," she said.

"But I know what it is. I know your name and all about you, lots of things," Arnold Friend said. He had not moved yet but stood still leaning back against the side of his jalopy. "I took a special interest in you, such a pretty girl, and found out all about you like I know your parents and sister are gone somewheres and I know where and how long they're going to be gone, and I know who you were with last night, and your best girl friend's name is Betty. Right?"

He spoke in a simple lilting voice, exactly as if he were reciting the words to a song. His smile assured her that everything was fine. In the car Ellie turned up the volume on his radio and did not bother to look around at them.

"Ellie can sit in the back seat," Arnold Friend said. He indicated his friend with a casual jerk of his chin, as if Ellie did not count and she should not bother with him.

"How'd you find out all that stuff?" Connie said.

"Listen: Betty Schultz and Tony Fitch and Jimmy Pettinger and Nancy Pettinger," he said, in a chant. "Raymond Stanley and Bob Hutter—"

"Do you know all those kids?"

"I know everybody."

"Look, you're kidding. You're not from around here."

"Sure."

"But—how come we never saw you before?"

"Sure you saw me before," he said. He looked down at his boots, as if he were a little offended. "You just don't remember."

"I guess I'd remember you," Connie said.

"Yeah?" He looked up at this, beaming. He was pleased. He began to mark time with the music from Ellie's radio, tapping his fists lightly together. Connie looked away from his smile to the car, which was painted so bright it almost hurt her eyes to look at it. She looked at that name, ARNOLD FRIEND. And up at the front fender was an expression that was familiar—MAN THE FLYING SAUCERS. It was an expression kids had used the year before, but didn't use this year. She looked at it for a while as if the words meant something to her that she did not yet know.

"What're you thinking about? Huh?" Arnold Friend demanded. "Not worried about your hair blowing around in the car, are you?"

"No."

"Think I maybe can't drive good?"

"How do I know?"

"You're a hard girl to handle. How come?" he said. "Don't you know I'm your friend? Didn't you see me put my sign in the air when you walked by?"

"What sign?"

"My sign." And he drew an X in the air, leaning out toward her. They were maybe ten feet apart. After his hand fell back to his side the X was still in the air, almost visible. Connie let the screen door close and stood perfectly still inside it, listening to the music from her radio and the boy's blend together. She stared at Arnold Friend. He stood there so stiffly relaxed, pretending to be relaxed, with one hand idly on the door handle as if he were keeping himself up that way and had no intention of ever moving again. She recognized most things about him, the tight jeans that showed his thighs and buttocks and the greasy leather boots and the tight shirt, and even that slippery friendly smile of his, that sleepy dreamy smile that all the boys used to get across ideas they didn't want to put into words. She recognized all this and also the singsong way he talked, slightly mocking, kidding, but serious and a little melancholy, and she recognized the way he tapped one fist against the other in homage to the perpetual music behind him. But all these things did not come together.

She said suddenly, "Hey, how old are you?"

His smile faded. She could see then that he wasn't a kid, he was much older—thirty, maybe more. At this knowledge her heart began to pound faster.

"That's a crazy thing to ask. Can'tcha see I'm your own age?"

"Like hell you are."

"Or maybe a coupla years older, I'm eighteen."

"Eighteen?" she said doubtfully.

He grinned to reassure her and lines appeared at the corners of his mouth. His teeth were big and white. He grinned so broadly his eyes became slits and she saw how thick the lashes were, thick and black as if painted with a black tarlike material. Then he seemed to become embarrassed, abruptly, and looked over his shoulder at Ellie. "*Him,* he's crazy," he said. "Ain't he a riot, he's a nut, a real character." Ellie was still listening to the music. His sunglasses told nothing about what he was thinking. He wore a bright orange shirt unbuttoned halfway to show his chest, which was a pale, bluish chest and not muscular like Arnold Friend's. His shirt collar was turned up all around and the very tips of the collar pointed out past his chin as if they were protecting him. He was pressing the transistor radio up against his ear and sat there in a kind of daze, right in the sun.

"He's kinda strange," Connie said.

"Hey, she says you're kinda strange! Kinda strange!" Arnold Friend cried. He pounded on the car to get Ellie's attention. Ellie turned for the first time and Connie saw with shock that he wasn't a kid either—he had a fair, hairless face, cheeks reddened slightly as if the veins grew too close to the surface of his skin, the face of a forty-year-old baby. Connie felt a wave of dizziness rise in her at this sight and she stared at him as if waiting for something to change the shock of the moment, make it all right again. Ellie's lips kept shaping words, mumbling along, with the words blasting in his ear.

"Maybe you two better go away," Connie said faintly.

"What? How come?" Arnold Friend cried. "We come out here to take you for a ride. It's Sunday." He had the voice of the man on the radio now. It was the same voice, Connie thought. "Don'tcha know it's Sunday all day and honey, no matter who you were with last night today you're with Arnold Friend and don't you forget it!—Maybe you better step out here," he said, and this last was in a different voice. It was a little flatter, as if the heat was finally getting to him.

"No. I got things to do."

"Hey."

"You two better leave."

"We ain't leaving until you come with us."

"Like hell I am——"

"Connie, don't fool around with me. I mean, I mean, don't fool *around,*" he said, shaking his head. He laughed incredulously. He placed his sunglasses on top of his head, carefully, as if he were indeed wearing a wig, and brought the stems down behind his ears. Connie stared at him, another wave of dizziness and fear rising in her so that for a moment he wasn't even in focus but was just a blur, standing there against his gold car, and she had the idea that he had driven up the driveway all right but had come from nowhere before that and belonged nowhere and that everything about him and even about the music that was so familiar to her was only half real.

"If my father comes and sees you——"

"He ain't coming. He's at the barbecue."

"How do you know that?"

"Aunt Tillie's. Right now they're—uh—they're drinking. Sitting around," he said vaguely, squinting as if he were staring all the way to town and over to Aunt Tillie's backyard. Then the vision seemed to get clear and he nodded energetically. "Yeah. Sitting around. There's your sister in a blue dress, huh? And high heels, the poor sad bitch—nothing like you, sweetheart! And your mother's helping some fat woman with the corn, they're cleaning the corn—husking the corn——"

"What fat woman?" Connie cried.

"How do I know what fat woman. I don't know every goddam fat woman in the world!" Arnold Friend laughed.

"Oh, that's Mrs. Hornby. . . . Who invited her?" Connie said. She felt a little light-headed. Her breath was coming quickly.

"She's too fat. I don't like them fat. I like them the way you are, honey," he said, smiling sleepily at her. They stared at each other for a while, through the screen door. He said softly, "Now what you're going to do is this: you're going to come out that door. You're going to sit up front with me and Ellie's going to sit in the back, the hell with Ellie, right? This isn't Ellie's date. You're my date. I'm your lover, honey."

"What? You're crazy——"

"Yes, I'm your lover. You don't know what that is but you will," he said. "I know that too. I know all about you. But look: it's real nice and you couldn't ask for nobody better than me, or more polite. I always keep my word. I'll tell you how it is, I'm always nice at first, the first time. I'll hold you so tight you won't think you have to try to get away or pretend anything because you'll know you can't. And I'll come inside you where it's all secret and you'll give in to me and you'll love me——"

"Shut up! You're crazy!" Connie said. She backed away from the door. She put her hands against her ears as if she'd heard something terrible, something not meant for her. "People don't talk like that, you're crazy," she muttered. Her heart was almost too big now for her chest and its pumping made sweat break out all over her. She looked out to see Arnold Friend pause and then take a step toward the porch lurching. He almost fell. But, like a clever drunken man, he managed to catch his balance. He wobbled in his high boots and grabbed hold of one of the porch posts.

"Honey?" he said. "You still listening?"

"Get the hell out of here!"

"Be nice, honey. Listen."

"I'm going to call the police——"

He wobbled again and out of the side of his mouth came a fast spat curse, an aside not meant for her to hear. But even this "Christ!" sounded forced. Then he began to smile again. She watched this smile come, awkward as if he were smiling from inside a mask. His whole face was a mask, she thought wildly, tanned down onto his throat but then running out as if he had plastered makeup on his face but had forgotten about his throat.

"Honey—? Listen, here's how it is. I always tell the truth and I promise you this: I ain't coming in that house after you."

"You better not! I'm going to call the police if you—if you don't—"

"Honey," he said, talking right through her voice, "honey, I'm not coming in there but you are coming out here. You know why?"

She was panting. The kitchen looked like a place she had never seen before, some room she had run inside but which wasn't good enough, wasn't going to help her. The kitchen window had never had a curtain, after three years, and there were dishes in the sink for her to do—probably—and if you ran your hand across the table you'd probably feel something sticky there.

"You listening, honey? Hey?"

"—going to call the police—"

"Soon as you touch the phone I don't need to keep my promise and can come inside. You won't want that."

She rushed forward and tried to lock the door. Her fingers were shaking. "But why lock it," Arnold Friend said gently, talking right into her face. "It's just a screen door. It's just nothing." One of his boots was at a strange angle, as if his foot wasn't in it. It pointed out to the left, bent at the ankle. "I mean, anybody can break through a screen door and glass and wood and iron or anything else if he needs to, anybody at all and specially Arnold Friend. If the place got lit up with a fire honey you'd come running out into my arms, right into my arms and safe at home—like you knew I was your lover and'd stopped fooling around. I don't mind a nice shy girl but I don't like no fooling around." Part of those words were spoken with a slight rhythmic lilt, and Connie somehow recognized them—the echo of a song from last year, about a girl rushing into her boyfriend's arms and coming home again—

Connie stood barefoot on the linoleum floor, staring at him. "What do you want?" she whispered.

"I want you," he said.

"What?"

"Seen you that night and thought, that's the one, yes sir. I never needed to look any more."

"But my father's coming back. He's coming to get me. I had to wash my hair first—" She spoke in a dry, rapid voice, hardly raising it for him to hear.

"No, your daddy is not coming and yes, you had to wash your hair and you washed it for me. It's nice and shining and all for me, I thank you, sweetheart," he said, with a mock bow, but again he almost lost his balance. He had to bend and adjust his boots. Evidently his feet did not go all the way down; the boots must have been stuffed with something so that he would seem taller. Connie stared out at him and behind him Ellie in the car, who seemed to be looking off toward Connie's right, into nothing. This Ellie said, pulling the words out of the air one after another as if he were just discovering them, "You want me to pull out the phone?"

"Shut your mouth and keep it shut," Arnold Friend said, his face red from bending over or maybe from embarrassment because Connie had seen his boots. "This ain't none of your business."

"What—what are you doing? What do you want?" Connie said. "If I call the police they'll get you, they'll arrest you—"

"Promise was not to come in unless you touch that phone, and I'll keep that promise," he said. He resumed his erect position and tried to force his shoulders back. He sounded like a hero in a movie, declaring something important. He spoke too loudly and it was as if he were speaking to someone behind Connie. "I ain't made plans for coming in that house where I don't belong but just for you to come out to me, the way you should. Don't you know who I am?"

"You're crazy," she whispered. She backed away from the door but did not want to go into another part of the house, as if this would give him permission to come through the door. "What do you . . . You're crazy, you . . ."

"Huh? What're you saying, honey?"

Her eyes darted everywhere in the kitchen. She could not remember what it was, this room.

"This is how it is, honey: you come out and we'll drive away, have a nice ride. But if you don't come out we're gonna wait till your people come home and then they're all going to get it."

"You want that telephone pulled out?" Ellie said. He held the radio away from his ear and grimaced, as if without the radio the air was too much for him.

"I toldja shut up, Ellie," Arnold Friend said, "you're deaf, get a hearing aid, right? Fix yourself up. This little girl's no trouble and's gonna be nice to me, so Ellie keep to yourself, this ain't your date—right? Don't hem in on me. Don't hog. Don't crush. Don't bird dog. Don't trail me," he said in a rapid meaningless voice, as if he were running through all the expressions he'd learned but was no longer sure which one of them was in style, then rushing on to new ones, making them up with his eyes closed, "Don't crawl under my fence, don't squeeze in my chipmunk hole, don't sniff my glue, suck my popsicle, keep your own greasy fingers on yourself!" He shaded his eyes and peered in at Connie, who was backed against the kitchen table. "Don't mind him honey he's just a creep. He's a dope. Right? I'm the boy for you and like I said you come out here nice like a lady and give me your hand, and nobody else gets hurt, I mean, your nice old bald-headed daddy and your mummy and your sister in her high heels. Because listen: why bring them in this?"

"Leave me alone," Connie whispered.

"Hey, you know that old woman down the road, the one with the chickens and stuff—you know her?"

"She's dead!"

"Dead? What? You know her?" Arnold Friend said.

"She's dead—"

"Don't you like her?"

"She's dead—she's—she isn't here any more—"

"But don't you like her, I mean, you got something against her? Some grudge or something?" Then his voice dipped as if he were conscious of a rudeness. He touched the sunglasses perched on top of his head as if to make sure they were still there. "Now you be a good girl."

"What are you going to do?"

"Just two things, or maybe three," Arnold Friend said. "But I promise it won't last long and you'll like me that way you get to like people you're close to. You will. It's all over for you here, so come on out. You don't want your people in any trouble, do you?"

She turned and bumped against a chair or something, hurting her leg, but she ran into the back room and picked up the telephone. Something roared in her ear, a tiny roaring, and she was so sick with fear that she could do nothing but listen to it—the telephone was clammy and very heavy and her fingers groped down to the dial but were too weak to touch it. She began to scream into the phone, into the roaring. She cried out, she cried for her mother, she felt her breath start jerking back and forth in her lungs as if it were something Arnold Friend were stabbing her with again and again with no tenderness. A noisy sorrowful wailing rose all about her and she was locked inside it the way she was locked inside the house.

After a while she could hear again. She was sitting on the floor with her wet back against the wall.

Arnold Friend was saying from the door, "That's a good girl. Put the phone back."

She kicked the phone away from her.

"No, honey. Pick it up. Put it back right."

She picked it up and put it back. The dial tone stopped.

"That's a good girl. Now come outside."

She was hollow with what had been fear, but what was now just an emptiness. All that screaming had blasted it out of her. She sat, one leg cramped under her, and deep inside her brain was something like a pinpoint of light that kept going and would not let her relax. She thought, I'm not going to see my mother again. She thought, I'm not going to sleep in my bed again. Her bright green blouse was all wet.

Arnold Friend said, in a gentle-loud voice that was like a stage voice, "The place where you came from ain't there any more, and where you had in mind to go is can-celled out. This place you are now—inside your daddy's house—is nothing but a card-board box I can knock down any time. You know that and always did know it. You hear me?"

She thought, I have got to think. I have to know what to do.

"We'll go out to a nice field, out in the country here where it smells so nice and it's sunny," Arnold Friend said. "I'll have my arms around you so you won't need to try to get away and I'll show you what love is like, what it does. The hell with this house! It looks solid all right," he said. He ran a fingernail down the screen and the noise did not make Connie shiver, as it would have the day before. "Now put your hand on your heart, honey. Feel that? That feels solid too but we know better, be nice to me, be sweet like you can because what else is there for a girl like you but to be sweet and pretty and give in?—and get away before her people come back?"

She felt her pounding heart. Her hand seemed to enclose it. She thought for the first time in her life that it was nothing that was hers, that belonged to her, but just a pounding, living thing inside this body that wasn't really hers either.

"You don't want them to get hurt," Arnold Friend went on. "Now get up, honey. Get up all by yourself."

She stood up.

"Now turn this way. That's right. Come over here to me—Ellie, put that away, didn't I tell you? You dope. You miserable creepy dope," Arnold Friend said. His words were not angry but only part of an incantation. The incantation was kindly. "Now come out through the kitchen to me honey and let's see a smile, try it, you're a brave sweet little girl and now they're eating corn and hotdogs cooked to bursting over an outdoor fire, and they don't know one thing about you and never did and honey you're better than them because not a one of them would have done this for you."

Connie felt the linoleum under her feet; it was cool. She brushed her hair back out of her eyes. Arnold Friend let go of the post tentatively and opened his arms for her, his elbows pointing in toward each other and his wrists limp, to show that this was an embarrassed embrace and a little mocking, he didn't want to make her self-conscious.

She put out her hand against the screen. She watched herself push the door slowly open as if she were safe back somewhere in the other doorway, watching this body and this head of long hair moving out into the sunlight where Arnold Friend waited.

"My sweet little blue-eyed girl," he said, in a half-sung sigh that had nothing to do with her brown eyes but was taken up just the same by the vast sunlit reaches of the land behind him and on all sides of him, so much land that Connie had never seen before and did not recognize except to know that she was going to it.

QUESTIONS FOR DISCUSSION AND WRITING

1. Arnold Friend is, of course, at the heart of the story's mystery. How would you characterize Friend? How do the descriptions of his physical appearance, his language, and his behavior toward Connie and her friends and toward his own friend Ellie guide your reading of his character and his function in the story? How do you account for and respond to his knowledge about Connie's family, friends, and neighbors? How much of a monster is Arnold Friend?

2. Connie is clearly attracted to Arnold Friend. Given what you know about Connie's background, personality, and behavior and about Arnold Friend's, why does she find him so appealing, even seductive?

3. When she decides to go with Arnold Friend, Connie seems to be responding to his suggestion that she will be saving her family. How do you respond to her decision and motivation? Is Connie heroic?

4. Although Connie's family fades into the background of the story, they are nevertheless in many ways central to its plot and Connie's character. How do the family dynamics and Connie's attitudes toward her family affect our understanding of who Connie is and wants to be? To what extent do her attitudes toward her parents and her sister shift throughout the story?

5. What is the significance of the story's title? If we are meant to see it as a reflection on Connie's past and future, how would you answer the title's questions?

6. Oates's story ends with Connie leaving her home, but we don't know what happens after she goes off with Arnold Friend. If you were to write a sequel to the story, what would happen next? Why does Oates choose to leave the ending ambiguous?

Laura Dern as Connie in *Smooth Talk,* a film adaptation of "Where Are You Going, Where Have You Been?"

QUESTION FOR DISCUSSION AND WRITING

Consider Connie's appearance, clothing, facial expression, and body language in this movie still from *Smooth Talk.* How much does Laura Dern's representation of Connie match your own sense of how Connie would act when Arnold Friend drives up to her house? What changes, if any, would you make to Connie's appearance and body language? How would those changes reflect your sense of who Connie is?

DON MOSER (1932–   )

The Pied Piper of Tucson   1966

> *Hey, c'mon babe, follow me,*
> *I'm the Pied Piper, follow me,*
> *I'm the Pied Piper,*
> *And I'll show you where it's at.*

—Popular song,
Tucson, winter 1965

At dusk in Tucson, as the stark, yellow-flared mountains begin to blur against the sky, the golden car slowly cruises Speedway. Smoothly it rolls down the long, divided avenue, past the supermarkets, the gas stations and the motels; past the twist joints, the sprawling drive-in restaurants. The car slows for an intersection, stops, then pulls away again. The exhaust mutters against the pavement as the young man driving takes the machine swiftly, expertly through the gears. A car pulls even with him; the teen-age girls in the front seat laugh, wave and call his name. The young man glances toward the rearview mirror, turned always so that he can look at his own reflection, and he appraises himself.

The face is his own creation: the hair dyed raven black, the skin darkened to a deep tan with pancake make-up, the lips whitened, the whole effect heightened by a mole he has painted on one cheek. But the deep-set blue eyes are all his own. Beautiful eyes, the girls say.

Approaching the Hi-Ho, the teen-agers' nightclub, he backs off on the accelerator, then slowly cruises on past Johnie's Drive-in. There the cars are beginning to orbit and accumulate in the parking lot—neat sharp cars with deep-throated mufflers and Maltese-cross decals on the windows. But it's early yet. Not much going on. The driver shifts up again through the gears, and the golden car slides away along the glitter and gimcrack of Speedway. Smitty keeps looking for the action.

Whether the juries in the two trials decide that Charles Howard Schmid Jr. did or did not brutally murder Alleen Rowe, Gretchen Fritz and Wendy Fritz has from the beginning seemed of almost secondary importance to the people of Tucson. They are not indifferent. But what disturbs them far beyond the question of Smitty's guilt or innocence are the revelations about Tucson itself that have followed on the disclosure of the crimes. Starting with the bizarre circumstances of the killings and on through the ugly fragments of the plot—which in turn hint at other murders as yet undiscovered, at teen-age sex, blackmail, even connections with the Cosa Nostra—they have had to view their city in a new and unpleasant light. The fact is that Charles Schmid—who cannot be dismissed as a freak, an aberrant of no consequence—had for years functioned successfully as a member, even a leader, of the yeastiest stratum of Tucson's teen-age society.

As a high school student Smitty had been, as classmates remember, an outsider—but not that far outside. He was small but he was a fine athlete, and in his last year—1960—he was a state gymnastics champion. His grades were poor, but he was in no trouble to speak of until his senior year, when he was suspended for stealing tools from a welding class.

But Smitty never really left the school. After his suspension he hung around waiting to pick up kids in a succession of sharp cars which he drove fast and well. He haunted all the teen-age hangouts along Speedway, including the bowling alleys and the public swimming pool—and he put on spectacular diving exhibitions for girls far younger than he.

At the time of his arrest last November, Charles Schmid was 23 years old. He wore face make-up and dyed his hair. He habitually stuffed three or four inches of old rags and tin cans into the bottoms of his high-topped boots to make himself taller than his five-foot-three and stumbled about so awkwardly while walking that some people thought he had wooden feet. He pursed his lips and let his eyelids droop in order to emulate his idol, Elvis Presley. He bragged to girls that he knew 100 ways to make love, that he ran dope, that he was a Hell's Angel. He talked about being a rough customer in a fight (he was, though he was rarely in one), and he always carried in his pocket tiny bottles of salt and pepper, which he said he used to blind his opponents. He liked to use highfalutin language and had a favorite saying, "I can manifest my neurotical emotions, emancipate an epicureal instinct, and elaborate on my heterosexual tendencies."

He occasionally shocked even those who thought they knew him well. A friend says he once saw Smitty tie a string to the tail of his pet cat, swing it around his head and beat it bloody against a wall. Then he turned calmly and asked, "You feel compassion—why?"

Yet even while Smitty tried to create an exalted, heroic image of himself, he had worked on a pitiable one. "He thrived on feeling sorry for himself," recalls a friend, "and making others feel sorry for him." At various times Smitty told intimates that he had leukemia and didn't have long to live. He claimed that he was adopted, that his real name was Angel Rodriguez, that his father was a "bean" (local slang for Mexican, an inferior race in Smitty's view), and that his mother was a famous lawyer who would have nothing to do with him.

What made Smitty a hero to Tucson's youth?

Isn't Tucson—out there in the Golden West, in the grand setting where the skies are not cloudy all day—supposed to be a flowering of the American Dream? One envisions teen-agers who drink milk, wear crewcuts, go to bed at half past 9, say "Sir" and "Ma'am," and like to go fishing with Dad. Part of Tucson is like this—but the city is not yet Utopia. It is glass and chrome and well-weathered stucco; it is also gimcrack, ersatz and urban sprawl at its worst. Its suburbs stretch for mile after mile—a level sea of bungalows, broken only by mammoth shopping centers, that ultimately peters out among the cholla and saguaro. The city has grown from 85,000 to 300,000 since World War II. Few who live there were born there, and a lot are just passing through. Its superb climate attracts the old and the infirm, many of whom, as one citizen put it, "have come here to retire from their responsibilities to life." Jobs are hard to find and there is little industry to stabilize employment. ("What do people do in Tucson?" the visitor asks. Answer: "They do each other's laundry.")

As for the youngsters, they must compete with the army of semi-retired who are willing to take on part-time work for the minimum wage. Schools are beautiful but overcrowded; and at those with split sessions, the kids are on the loose from noon on, or from 6 p.m. till noon the next day. When they get into trouble, Tucson teenagers are capable of getting into trouble in style: a couple of years ago they shocked the city fathers by throwing a series of beer-drinking parties in the desert, attended by scores of kids. The fests were called "boondockers" and if they were no more sinful than any other kids' drinking parties, they were at least on a magnificent scale. One statistic seems relevant: 50 runaways are reported to the Tucson police department each month.

Of an evening kids with nothing to do wind up on Speedway, looking for action. There is the teen-age nightclub ("Pickup Palace," the kids call it). There are the rock 'n' roll beer joints (the owners check ages meticulously, but young girls can enter if they don't drink; besides, anyone can buy a phony I.D. card for $2.50 around the high schools) where they can Jerk, Swim and Frug away the evening to the room-shaking electronic blare of *Hang On Sloopy*, *The Pied Piper* and a number called *The Bo Diddley Rock*. At the drive-in hamburger and pizza stands their cars circle endlessly, mufflers rumbling, as they check each other over.

Here on Speedway you find Richie and Ronny, out of work and bored and with nothing to do. Here you find Debby and Jabron, from the wrong side of the tracks, aimlessly cruising in their battered old car looking for something—anything—to relieve the tedium of their lives, looking for somebody neat. ("Well if the boys look bitchin', you pull up next to them in your car and you roll down the window and say, 'Hey, how about a dollar for gas?' and if they give you the dollar then maybe you let them take you to Johnie's for a Coke.") Here you find Gretchen, pretty and rich and with problems, bad problems. Of a Saturday night, all of them cruising the long, bright street that seems endlessly in motion with the young. Smitty's people.

He had a nice car. He had plenty of money from his parents, who ran a nursing home, and he was always glad to spend it on anyone who'd listen to him. He had a pad of his own where he threw parties and he had impeccable manners. He was always willing to help a friend and he would send flowers to girls who were ill. He was older and more mature than most of his friends. He knew where the action was, and if he wore make-up—well, at least he was *different*.

Some of the older kids—those who worked, who had something else to do—thought Smitty was a creep. But to the youngsters—to the bored and the lonely, to the dropout and the delinquent, to the young girls with beehive hairdos and tight pants they didn't quite fill out, and to the boys with acne and no jobs—to these people, Smitty was a kind of folk hero. Nutty maybe, but at least more dramatic, more theatrical, more *interesting* than anyone else in their lives: a semi-ludicrous, sexy-eyed pied piper who, stumbling along in his rag-stuffed boots, led them up and down Speedway.

On the evening of May 31, 1964, Alleen Rowe prepared to go to bed early. She had to be in class by 6 a.m., and she had an examination the next day. Alleen was a pretty girl of 15, a better-than-average student who talked about going to college and becoming an oceanographer. She was also a sensitive child—given to reading romantic novels and taking long walks in the desert at night. Recently she had been going through a period of adolescent melancholia, often talking with her mother, a nurse, about death. She would, she hoped, be some day reincarnated as a cat.

On this evening, dressed in a black bathing suit and thongs, her usual costume around the house, she had watched the Beatles on TV and had tried to teach her mother to dance the Frug. Then she took her bath, washed her hair and came out to kiss her mother good night. Norma Rowe, an attractive, womanly divorcee, was somehow moved by the girl's clean fragrance and said, "You smell so good—are you wearing perfume?"

"No, Mom," the girl answered, laughing, "it's just me."

A little later Mrs. Rowe looked in on her daughter, found her apparently sleeping peacefully, and then left for her job as a night nurse in a Tucson hospital. She had no premonition of danger, but she had lately been concerned about Alleen's friendship with a neighbor girl named Mary French.

Mary and Alleen had been spending a good deal of time together, smoking and giggling and talking girl talk in the Rowe backyard. Norma Rowe did not approve. She particularly did not approve of Mary French's friends, a tall, gangling boy of 19 named John Saunders and another named Charles Schmid. She had seen Smitty racing up and down the street in his car and once, when he came to call on Alleen and found her not at home, he had looked at Norma so menacingly with his "pinpoint eyes" that she had been frightened.

Her daughter, on the other hand, seemed to have mixed feelings about Smitty. "He's creepy," she once told her mother, "he just makes me crawl. But he can be nice when he wants to."

At any rate, later that night—according to Mary French's sworn testimony—three friends arrived at Alleen Rowe's house: Smitty, Mary French and Saunders. Smitty had frequently talked with Mary French about killing the Rowe girl by hitting her over the head with a rock. Mary French tapped on Alleen's window and asked her to come out and drink beer with them. Wearing a shift over her bathing suit, she came willingly enough.

Schmid's two accomplices were strange and pitiable creatures. Each of them was afraid of Smitty, yet each was drawn to him. As a baby, John Saunders had been so afflicted with allergies that scabs encrusted his entire body. To keep him from scratching himself his parents had tied his hands and feet to the crib each night, and when eventually he was cured he was so conditioned that he could not go to sleep without being bound hand and foot.

Later, a scrawny boy with poor eyesight ("Just a skinny little body with a big head on it"), he was taunted and bullied by larger children; in turn he bullied those who were smaller. He also suffered badly from asthma and he had few friends. In high school he was a poor student and constantly in minor trouble.

Mary French, 19, was—to put it straight—a frump. Her face, which might have been pretty, seemed somehow lumpy, her body shapeless. She was not dull but she was always a poor student, and she finally had simply stopped going to high school. She was, a friend remembers, "fantastically in love with Smitty. She just sat home and waited while he went out with other girls."

Now, with Smitty at the wheel, the four teen-agers headed for the desert, which begins out Golf Links Road. It is spooky country, dry and empty, the yellow sand clotted with cholla and mesquite and stunted, strangely green palo verde trees, and the great humanoid saguaro that hulk against the sky. Out there at night you can hear the yip and ki-yi of coyotes, the piercing screams of wild creatures—cats, perhaps.

According to Mary French, they got out of the car and walked down into a wash, where they sat on the sand and talked for a while, the four of them. Schmid and Mary then started back to the car. Before they got there, they heard a cry and Schmid turned back toward the wash. Mary went on to the car and sat in it alone. After 45 minutes, Saunders appeared and said Smitty wanted her to come back down. She refused, and Saunders went away. Five or 10 minutes later, Smitty showed up. "He got into the car," says Mary, "and he said, 'We killed her. I love you very much.' He kissed me. He was breathing real hard and seemed excited." Then Schmid got a shovel from the trunk of the car and they returned to the wash. "She was lying on her back and there was blood on her face and head," Mary French testified. Then the three of them dug a shallow grave and put the body in it and covered it up. Afterwards, they wiped Schmid's car clean of Alleen's fingerprints.

More than a year passed. Norma Rowe had reported her daughter missing and the police searched for her—after a fashion. At Mrs. Rowe's insistence they picked up Schmid, but they had no reason to hold him. The police, in fact, assumed that Alleen was just one more of Tucson's runaways.

Norma Rowe, however, had become convinced that Alleen had been killed by Schmid, although she left her kitchen light on every night just in case Alleen did come home. She badgered the police and she badgered the sheriff until the authorities began to dismiss her as a crank. She began to imagine a high-level conspiracy against her. She wrote the state attorney general, the FBI, the U.S. Department of Health, Education and Welfare. She even contacted a New Jersey mystic, who said she could see Alleen's body out in the desert under a big tree.

Ultimately Norma Rowe started her own investigation, questioning Alleen's friends, poking around, dictating her findings to a tape recorder; she even tailed Smitty at night, following him in her car, scared stiff that he might spot her.

Schmid, during this time, acquired a little house of his own. There he held frequent parties, where people sat around amid his stacks of *Playboy* magazines, playing Elvis Presley records and drinking beer.

He read Jules Feiffer's novel, *Harry, the Rat with Women,* and said that his ambition was to be like Harry and have a girl commit suicide over him. Once, according to a friend, he went to see a minister, who gave him a Bible and told him to read the first three chapters of John. Instead Schmid tore the pages out and burned them in the street. "Religion is a farce," he announced. He started an upholstery business with some friends, called himself "founder and president," but then failed to put up the money he'd promised and the venture was short-lived.

He decided he liked blondes best, and took to dyeing the hair of various teen-age girls he went around with. He went out and bought two imitation diamond rings for about $13 apiece and then engaged himself, on the same day, both to Mary French and to a 15-year-old girl named Kathy Morath. His plan, he confided to a friend, was to put each of the girls to work and have them deposit their salaries in a bank account held jointly with him. Mary French did indeed go to work in the convalescent home Smitty's parents operated. When their bank account was fat enough, Smitty withdrew the money and bought a tape recorder.

By this time Smitty also had a girl from a higher social stratum than he usually was involved with. She was Gretchen Fritz, daughter of a prominent Tucson heart surgeon. Gretchen was a pretty, thin, nervous girl of 17 with a knack for trouble. A teacher described her as "erratic, subversive, a psychopathic liar."

At the horsy private school she attended for a time she was a misfit. She not only didn't care about horses, but she shocked her classmates by telling them they were foolish for going out with boys without getting paid for it. Once she even committed the unpardonable social sin of turning up at a formal dance accompanied by boys wearing what was described as beatnik dress. She cut classes, she was suspected of stealing and when, in the summer before her senior year, she got into trouble with juvenile authorities for her role in an attempted theft at a liquor store, the headmaster suggested she not return and then recommended she get psychiatric treatment.

Charles Schmid saw Gretchen for the first time at a public swimming pool in the summer of 1964. He met her by the simple expedient of following her home, knocking on the door and, when she answered, saying, "Don't I know you?" They talked for an hour. Thus began a fierce and stormy relationship. A good deal of what authorities know of the development of this relationship comes from the statements of a spindly scarecrow of a young man who wears pipestem trousers and Beatle boots: Richard Bruns. At the time Smitty was becoming involved with Gretchen, Bruns was 18 years old. He had served two terms in the reformatory at Fort Grant. He had been in and out of trouble all his life, had never fit in anywhere. Yet, although he never went beyond the tenth grade in school and his credibility on many counts is suspect, he is clearly intelligent and even sensitive. He was, for a time, Smitty's closest friend and confidant, and he is today one of the mainstays of the state's case against Smitty. His story:

"He and Gretchen were always fighting," says Bruns. "She didn't want him to drink or go out with the guys or go out with other girls. She wanted him to stay home, call her on the phone, be punctual. First she would get suspicious of him, then he'd get suspicious of her. They were made for each other."

Their mutual jealousy led to sharp and continual arguments. Once she infuriated him by throwing a bottle of shoe polish on his car. Another time she was driving past Smitty's house and saw him there with some other girls. She jumped out of her car and began screaming. Smitty took off into the house, out the back and climbed a tree in his backyard.

His feelings for her were an odd mixture of hate and adoration. He said he was madly in love with her, but he called her a whore. She would let Smitty in her bedroom window at night. Yet he wrote an anonymous letter to the Tucson Health Department accusing her of having venereal disease and spreading it about town. But Smitty also went to enormous lengths to impress Gretchen, once shooting holes through the windows of his car and telling her that thugs, from whom he was protecting her, had fired at him. So Bruns described the relationship.

On the evening of Aug. 16, 1965, Gretchen Fritz left the house with her little sister Wendy, a friendly, lively 13-year-old, to go to a drive-in movie. Neither girl ever came home again. Gretchen's father, like Alleen Rowe's mother, felt sure that Charles Schmid had something to do with his daughters' disappearance, and eventually he hired Bill Heilig, a private detective, to handle the case. One of Heilig's men soon found Gretchen's red compact car parked behind a motel, but the police continued to assume that the girls had joined the ranks of Tucson's runaways.

About a week after Gretchen disappeared, Bruns was at Smitty's home. "We were sitting in the living room," Bruns recalls. "He was sitting on the sofa and I was in the chair by the window and we got on the subject of Gretchen. He said, 'You know I killed her?' I said I didn't, and he said, 'You know where?' I said no. He said, 'I did it here in the living room. First I killed Gretchen, then Wendy was still going "*huh, huh, huh,*" so I . . . [Here Bruns showed how Smitty made a garroting gesture.] Then I took the bodies and put them in the trunk of the car. I put the bodies in the most obvious place I could think of because I just didn't care any more. Then I ditched the car and wiped it clean.'"

Bruns was not particularly upset by Smitty's story. Months before, Smitty had told him of the murder of Alleen Rowe, and nothing had come of that. So he was not certain Smitty was telling the truth about the Fritz girls. Besides, Bruns detested Gretchen himself. But what happened next, still according to Bruns's story, did shake him up.

One night not long after, a couple of tough-looking characters, wearing sharp suits and smoking cigars, came by with Smitty and picked up Bruns. Smitty said they were Mafia, and that someone had hired them to look for Gretchen. Smitty and Bruns were taken to an apartment where several men were present whom Smitty later claimed to have recognized as local Cosa Nostra figures.

They wanted to know what had happened to the girls. They made no threats, but the message, Bruns remembers, came across loud and clear. These were no street-corner punks: these were the real boys. In spite of the intimidating company, Schmid lost none of his insouciance. He said he didn't know where Gretchen was, but if she turned up hurt he wanted these men to help him get whoever was responsible. He added that he thought she might have gone to California.

By the time Smitty and Bruns got back to Smitty's house, they were both a little shaky. Later that night, says Bruns, Smitty did the most unlikely thing imaginable: he called the FBI. First he tried the Tucson office and couldn't raise anyone. Then he called Phoenix and couldn't get an agent there either. Finally he put in a person-to-person call to J. Edgar Hoover in Washington. He didn't get Hoover, of course, but he got someone and told him that the Mafia was harassing him over the disappearance of a girl. The FBI promised to have someone in touch with him soon.

Bruns was scared and said so. It occurred to him now that if Smitty really had killed the Fritz girls and left their bodies in an obvious place, they were in very bad trouble indeed—with the Mafia on the one hand and the FBI on the other. "Let's go bury them," Bruns said.

"Smitty stole the keys to his old man's station wagon," says Bruns, "and then we got a flat shovel—the only one we could find. We went to Johnie's and got a hamburger, and then we drove out to the old drinking spot [in the desert]—that's what Smitty meant when he said the most obvious place. It's where we used to drink beer and make out with girls.

"So we parked the car and got the shovel and walked down there, and we couldn't find anything. Then Smitty said, 'Wait, I smell something.' We went in opposite directions looking, and then I heard Smitty say, 'Come here.' I found him kneeling over Gretchen. There was a white rag tied around her legs. Her blouse was pulled up and she was wearing a white bra and Capris.

"Then he said, 'Wendy's up this way.' I sat there for a minute. Then I followed Smitty to where Wendy was. He'd had the decency to cover her—except for one leg, which was sticking up out of the ground.

"We tried to dig with the flat shovel. We each took turns. He'd dig for a while and then I'd dig for a while, but the ground was hard and we couldn't get anywhere with that flat shovel. We dug for 20 minutes and finally Smitty said we'd better do something because it's going to get light. So he grabbed the rag that was around Gretchen's legs and dragged her down in the wash. It made a noise like dragging a hollow shell. It stunk like hell. Then Smitty said wipe off her shoes, there might be fingerprints, so I wiped them off with my handkerchief and threw it away.

"We went back to Wendy. Her leg was sticking up with a shoe on it. He said take off her tennis shoe and throw it over there. I did, I threw it. Then he said, 'Now you're in this as deep as I am.'" By then, the sisters had been missing for about two weeks.

Early next morning Smitty did see the FBI. Nevertheless—here Bruns's story grows even wilder—that same day Smitty left for California, accompanied by a couple of Mafia types, to look for Gretchen Fritz. While there, he was picked up by the San Diego police on a complaint that he was impersonating an FBI officer. He was detained briefly, released and then returned to Tucson.

But now, it seemed to Richard Bruns, Smitty began acting very strangely. He startled Bruns by saying, "I've killed—not three times, but four. Now it's your turn, Richie." He went berserk in his little house, smashing his fist through a wall, slamming doors, then rushing out into the backyard in nothing but his undershorts, where he ran through the night screaming, "God is going to punish me!" He also decided, suddenly, to get married—to a 15-year-old girl who was a stranger to most of his friends.

If Smitty seemed to Bruns to be losing his grip, Richie Bruns himself was not in much better shape. His particular quirk revolved around Kathy Morath, the thin, pretty, 16-year-old daughter of a Tucson postman. Kathy had once been attracted to Smitty. He had given her one of his two cut-glass engagement rings. But Smitty never really took her seriously, and one day, in a fit of pique and jealousy, she threw the ring back in his face. Richie Bruns comforted her and then started dating her himself. He was soon utterly and irrevocably smitten with goofy adoration.

Kathy accepted Bruns as a suitor, but halfheartedly. She thought him weird (oddly enough, she did not think Smitty in the least weird) and their romance was short-lived. After she broke up with him last July, Bruns went into a blue funk, a nose-dive into romantic melancholy, and then, like some love-swacked Elizabethan poet, he started pouring out his heart to her on paper. He sent her poems, short stories, letters 24 pages long. ("My God, you should have read the stuff," says her perplexed father. "His letters were so romantic it was like 'Next week, East Lynne.'") Bruns even began writing a novel dedicated to "My Darling Kathy."

If Bruns had confined himself to literary catharsis, the murders of the Rowe and Fritz girls might never have been disclosed. But Richie went a little bit around the bend. He became obsessed with the notion that Kathy Morath was the next victim on Smitty's list. Someone had cut the Moraths' screen door, there had been a prowler around her house, and Bruns was sure that it was Smitty. (Kathy and her father, meantime, were sure it was Bruns.)

"I started having this dream," Bruns says. "It was the same dream every night. Smitty would have Kathy out in the desert and he'd be doing all those things to her, and strangling her, and I'd be running across the desert with a gun in my hand, but I could never get there."

If Bruns couldn't save Kathy in his dreams, he could, he figured, stop a walking, breathing Smitty. His scheme for doing so was so wild and so simple that it put the whole Morath family into a state of panic and very nearly landed Bruns in jail.

Bruns undertook to stand guard over Kathy Morath. He kept watch in front of her house, in the alley, and in the street. He patrolled the sidewalk from early in the morning till late at night, seven days a week. If Kathy was home he would be there. If she went out, he would follow her. Kathy's father called the police, and when they told Bruns he couldn't loiter around like that, Bruns fetched his dog and walked the animal up and down the block, hour after hour.

Bruns by now was wallowing in feelings of sacrifice and nobility—all of it un-appreciated by Kathy Morath and her parents. At the end of October, he was finally arrested for harassing the Morath family. The judge, facing the obviously woebegone and smitten young man, told Bruns that he wouldn't be jailed if he'd agree to get out of town until he got over his infatuation.

Bruns agreed and a few days later went to Ohio to stay with his grandmother and to try to get a job. It was hopeless. He couldn't sleep at night, and if he did doze off he had his old nightmare again.

One night he blurted out the whole story to his grandmother in their kitchen. She thought he had had too many beers and didn't believe him. "I hear beer does strange things to a person," she said comfortingly. At her words Bruns exploded, knocked over a chair and shouted, "The one time in my life when I need advice and what do I get?" A few minutes later he was on the phone to the Tucson police.

Things happened swiftly. At Bruns's frantic insistence, the police picked up Kathy Morath and put her in protective custody. They went into the desert and discovered—precisely as Bruns had described them—the grisly, skeletal remains of Gretchen and Wendy Fritz. They started the machinery that resulted in the arrest a week later of John Saunders and Mary French. They found Charles Schmid working in the yard of his little house, his face layered with make-up, his nose covered by a patch of adhesive plaster which he had worn for five months, boasting that his nose was broken in a fight, and his boots packed full of old rags and tin cans. He put up no resistance.

John Saunders and Mary French confessed immediately to their roles in the slaying of Alleen Rowe and were quickly sentenced, Mary French to four to five years, Saunders to life. When Smitty goes on trial for this crime, on March 15, they will be principal witnesses against him.

Meanwhile Richie Bruns, the perpetual misfit, waits apprehensively for the end of the Fritz trial, desperately afraid that Schmid will go free. "If he does," Bruns says glumly, "I'll be the first one he'll kill."

As for Charles Schmid, he has adjusted well to his period of waiting. He is polite and agreeable with all, though at the preliminary hearings he glared menacingly at Richie Bruns. Dressed tastefully, tie neatly knotted, hair carefully combed, his face scrubbed clean of make-up, he is a short, compact, darkly handsome young man with a wide, engaging smile and those deepset eyes.

The people of Tucson wait uneasily for what fresh scandal the two trials may develop. Civic leaders publicly cry that a slur has been cast on their community by an isolated crime. High school students have held rallies and written vehement editorials in the school papers, protesting that they all are being judged by the actions of a few oddballs and misfits. But the city reverberates with stories of organized teen-age crime and vice, in which Smitty is cast in the role of a minor-league underworld boss. None of these later stories has been substantiated.

One disclosure, however, has most disturbing implications: Smitty's boasts may have been heard not just by Bruns and his other intimates, but by other teen-agers as well. How many—and precisely how much they knew—it remains impossible to say. One authoritative source, however, having listened to the admissions of six high school students, says they unquestionably knew enough so that they should have gone to the police—but were either afraid to talk, or didn't want to rock the boat. As for Smitty's friends, the thought of telling the police never entered their minds.

"I didn't know he killed her," said one, "and even if I had, I wouldn't have said anything. I wouldn't want to be a fink."

Out in the respectable Tucson suburbs parents have started to crack down on the youngsters and have declared Speedway hangouts off limits. "I thought my folks were bad before," laments one grounded 16-year-old, "but now they're just impossible."

As for the others—Smitty's people—most don't care very much. Things are duller without Smitty around, but things have always been dull.

"There's nothing to do in this town," says one of his girls, shaking her dyed blond hair. "The only other town I know is Las Vegas and there's nothing to do there either." For her, and for her friends, there's nothing to do in any town.

They are down on Speedway again tonight, cruising, orbiting the drive-ins, stopping by the joints, where the words of *The Bo Diddley Rock* cut through the smoke and the electronic dissonance like some macabre reminder of their fallen hero:

> *All you women stand in line,*
> *And I'll love you all in an hour's time. . . .*
> *I got a cobra snake for a necktie,*
> *I got a brand-new house on the roadside*
> *Covered with rattlesnake hide,*
> *I got a brand-new chimney made on top,*
> *Made out of human skulls.*
> *Come on baby, take a walk with me,*
> *And tell me, who do you love?*
> *Who do you love?*
> *Who do you love?*
> *Who do you love?*

QUESTIONS FOR DISCUSSION AND WRITING

1. Oates tells us that she got her original idea for "Where Are You Going, Where Have You Been?" from the *Life* magazine article included here but that she recalls "deliberately not reading the full article because [she] didn't want to be distracted by too much detail." Compare "Where Are You Going, Where Have You Been?" and "The Pied Piper of Tucson," paying particular attention to what Oates didn't include. Why, for instance, does Mary French have no counterpart in Oates's story? How do Moser's references to Smitty's dealings with the Mafia and the Cosa Nostra cause us to respond to Smitty in ways that we might not respond to Arnold Friend? Is Smitty more or less a monster than Arnold Friend is?

2. At what point did you realize that "The Pied Piper of Tucson" is nonfiction and not a short story? What alerted you to its genre? Finally, what assumptions do you make about the kind of style (word choice, level of description, and characterization) and narrative perspective that are characteristic of and appropriate to nonfiction? To fiction?

3. Schmid's minister tells him to read the first three chapters of John in the Bible's New Testament. "Instead," Moser tells us, "Schmid tore the pages out and burned them in the street. 'Religion is a farce,' he announced" (203). Locate a copy of the Bible and read the first three chapters of John. Why might Schmid have reacted the way he did?

4. Moser's article is an indictment not only of Charles Schmid but also of the teenagers in Tucson who failed to report to police what they knew about Schmid's activities. What makes the teenagers reluctant to go to the police? Had they gone to the police, how does Moser suggest the police would have reacted? Finally, how

similar are Tucson's teenagers to teenagers you know? How do you account for the similarities and/or dissimilarities?

BOB DYLAN (1941–   )

It's All Over Now, Baby Blue _____ 1965

You must leave now, take what you need you think will last
But whatever you wish to keep, you better grab it fast
Yonder stands your orphan with his gun
Crying like a fire in the sun.
Look out, the saints are comin' through   5
And it's all over now, baby blue.

The highway is for gamblers, better use your sins
Take what you have gathered from coincidence
The empty-handed painter from your streets
Is drawing crazy patterns on your sheets   10
This sky too is folding under you
And it's all over now, baby blue.

All your seasick sailors they are rowing home
Your empty-handed army men are going home
The lover who has just walked out your door   15
Has taken all his blankets from the floor
The carpet too is moving under you
And it's all over now, baby blue.

Leave your stepping stones behind, something calls for you
Forget the dead you've left, they will not follow you   20
The vagabond who's rapping at your door
Is standing in the clothes that you once wore
Strike another match, go start anew
And it's all over now, baby blue.

QUESTIONS FOR DISCUSSION AND WRITING

1. Oates wrote her story, she says, when she was intrigued by Bob Dylan's music, especially by "It's All Over Now, Baby Blue," and she dedicates the story to Dylan. What do you see as the connection between her story and Dylan's song?
2. In Oates's story, we learn about the importance of music in Connie's and her friends' lives. How would you describe the kind of music they listen to? What would its themes and values be like? Would the teenagers in Oates's story be listening to songs like this one written by Dylan? Why or why not? How would you compare the themes and motifs of today's popular music to those of the music Connie and her friends would have been listening to?

3. How do Dylan's images of the gun-carrying orphan, the empty-handed painter and army men, and the seasick sailors work? What do the images have in common? How do they help reinforce the song's themes and moods?

Hans Baldung Grien, *Death and the Maiden* (1510).

QUESTION FOR DISCUSSION AND WRITING

In an interview about "Where Are You Going, Where Have You Been?" Oates says that an earlier draft of the story was entitled "Death and the Maiden," after the medieval German engraving that we have included here. What do you see as the relationship between the story and the engraving? How well do you think the title would have worked for the story?

QUESTIONS FOR CROSS READING: THE MODERN MONSTER

1. Oates's story has been retold on film in *Smooth Talk*, and the actual murders formed the basis of two other films: *The Todd Killings* and *The Deadbeat*. Locate one or more of these films and compare the filmed events with those depicted by either Oates or Moser.
2. Moser later coauthored an entire book (also entitled *The Pied Piper of Tucson*) on the Tucson murders, and in more recent years John Gilmore also wrote a book on

the subject: *Cold Blooded: The Saga of Charles Schmid, the Notorious "Pied Piper of Tucson."* Locate a copy of one or both of these books. How do their styles and methods of presentation compare with Oates's fictional account and Moser's *Life* article?
3. Oates's short story, Dylan's song, and Moser's article are all products of the 1960s. In what ways does the time seem to have influenced the events and the writers' ways of writing about them?

MONSTROUS CRIME

ANGELA CARTER (1940–1992)

The Fall River Axe Murders   1986

> *Lizzie Borden with an axe*
> *Gave her father forty whacks*
> *When she saw what she had done*
> *She gave her mother forty one.*

Children's rhyme

Early in the morning of the fourth of August, 1892, in the city of Fall River, Massachusetts.

Hot, hot, hot. Even though it is early in the morning, well before the factory whistle issues its peremptory summons from the dark, satanic mills to which the city owes its present pre-eminence in the cotton trade, the white, furious sun already shimmers and quivers high in the still air.

Nobody could call the New England summer a lovable thing; the inhabitants of New England have never made friends with it. More than the heat, it is the humidity that makes it scarcely tolerable. The weather clings, like a low fever you cannot shake off. The Indians who first lived here had the sense to take off their buckskins as soon as things hotted up and sit, thereafter, up to their necks in ponds. This behaviour is no longer permissible in the "City of Spindles."

However, as in most latitudes with similar summers, everything slows down in these dog days. The blinds are drawn, the shutters closed; all indoors becomes drowsy penumbra in which to nap away the worst heat of the day, and when they venture out again in the refreshed evening, they put on thin clothes loose enough to let cool air circulate refreshingly between the muslin and the skin, so that warm weather, as nature intended, is a sweet, sensual, horizontal thing.

But the descendants of the industrious, self-mortifying saints who imported the Protestant ethic wholesale into a land intended for the siesta are proud of flying in the face of nature. The moment the factory whistle blares—bustle! bustle! bustle! And the stern fathers of Fall River will step briskly forth into the furnace, well wrapped up in flannel underclothes, linen shirts, vests and coats and trousers of good, thick wool, and—final touch—a strangulatory neck tie, as if discomfort were next to godliness.

On this burning morning when, after breakfast and the performance of a few household duties, Lizzie Borden will murder her parents, she will, on rising, don a simple cotton frock that, if worn by itself, might be right for the weather. But, under-neath, has gone a long, starched cotton petticoat; another starched cotton petticoat, a short one; long drawers; woolen stockings; a chemise; and a whalebone corset that takes her viscera in an unkind hand and squeezes them very tightly.

There is also a heavy linen napkin strapped between her legs because she is menstruating.

In all these clothes, out of sorts and nauseous as she is, in this dementing heat, her belly in a vice, she will heat up a flatiron on a stove and press handkerchiefs with the heated iron until it is time for her to go down to the cellar wood-pile to collect the hatchet with which our imagination—"Lizzie Borden with an axe"—always equips her, just as we always visualise Saint Catherine rolling along her wheel, the emblem of her passion.

Soon, in just as many clothes as Miss Lizzie wears, if less fine, Bridget, the ser-vant girl, will slop kerosene on a sheet of last night's newspaper, rumpled up around a stick or two of kindling. When the fire settles down, she will cook breakfast. The fire will keep her company as she washes up afterward, when the mercury pauses briefly at eighty-five before recommencing its giddy ascent upwards.

In a blue serge suit one look at which would be enough to bring you out in prickly heat, old Andrew Borden will perambulate the perspiring town truffling for money like a pig until he will return home mid-morning when he will find his death, unannounced, waiting for him.

In a mean house on Second Street in the smoky city of Fall River, five living creatures are sleeping in the still, warm early morning. They comprise two old men and three women. The first old man owns all the women by either marriage, birth, or contract. His house is narrow as a coffin and that was how he made his fortune—he used to be an undertaker but he has recently branched out in several directions and all his branches bear fruit of the most fiscally gratifying kind.

But you would never think, to look at his house, that he is a successful and pros-perous man. His house is cramped, comfortless—"unpretentious," you might say, if you were sycophantic, while Second Street itself saw better days some time ago. The Borden house—see "Andrew J. Borden" in flowing script on the brass plate next to the door—stands by itself with a few scant feet of yard on either side. On the left is a stable, out of use since he sold the horse. In the back lot grow a few pear trees, laden at this season.

On this particular morning, as luck would have it, only one of the two Borden girls sleeps in their father's house. Emma Lenora, his oldest daughter, has taken herself off to nearby New Bedford for a few days, to catch the ocean breeze.

Few of their social class stay in sweltering Fall River in the sweating months of June, July, and August. But then, few of their social class live on Second Street, in the low part of town where heat gathers like fog. Lizzie was invited away, too, to a sum-mer house by the sea to join a merry band of girls but, as if on purpose to mortify her flesh, as if important business kept her in the exhausted town, as if a wicked fairy spelled her on Second Street, she did not go.

The other old man is some kind of kin of Borden's. He doesn't belong, here; he is a chance bystander, he is irrelevant.

Write him out of the script.

Even though his presence in the doomed house is historically unimpeachable, the colouring of this domestic apocalypse must be crude and the design profoundly simplified for the maximum emblematic effect.

Write John Vinnicum Morse out of the script.

One old man and three of his women sleep in the house on Second Street. These women comprise his second wife, his youngest daughter, and his servant girl.

The City Hall clock whirs and sputters the prolegomena to the first stroke of six and Bridget's alarm clock gives a sympathetic skip and click as the minute hand stutters on the hour; back the little hammer jerks, about to hit the bell on top of her clock, but Bridget's damp eyelids do not shudder with premonition as she lies in her sticking flannel nightgown under one thin sheet on an iron bedstead, lies on her back, as the good nuns taught her in her Irish girlhood, in case she dies during the night, to make less trouble for the one who lays her out.

She is a good girl, on the whole, although her temper is sometimes uncertain and then she will talk back to the missus, sometimes, and will be forced to confess the sin of impatience to the priest. Overcome by heat and nausea—everyone in the house is going to wake up sick today—she will return to this little bed later on in the morning to snatch a few moments' rest. Fateful forty winks! While she indulges in them, the massacre takes place.

A rosary of brown glass beads, a cardboard-backed colour print of the Virgin bought from a Portuguese shop, a flyblown photograph of her solemn mother in Donegal—these lie or are propped on the mantelpiece that, however sharp the Massachusetts winter, has never seen a lit stick. A banged tin trunk at the foot of the bed holds all Bridget's worldly goods.

There is a stiff chair beside the bed with, upon it, a candlestick, matches, the alarm clock that resounds the room with a dyadic, metallic clang for it is a joke between Bridget and her mistress that the girl could sleep through anything, *anything,* and so she needs the alarm clock as well as all the factory whistles that are just about to blast off, just this very second about to blast off. . . .

A splintered pine washstand holds the jug and bowl she never uses; she isn't going to lug water all the way up to the third floor just to wipe herself down, is she? Not when there's water enough in the kitchen, where, in the sink, all will clean their teeth this morning.

Old Borden sees no necessity for baths. He does not believe in total immersion. To lose his natural oils would be to rob his body. Since he does not approve of baths, it goes without saying they do not maintain a bathroom.

A frameless square of mirror reflects in corrugated waves a cracked, dusty soap dish containing a quantity of black metal hair pins.

On bright rectangles of paper blinds move the beautiful shadows of the pear trees.

Although Bridget left the door open a crack in forlorn hopes of coaxing a draught into the room, all the spent heat of the previous day has packed itself tightly into her attic. A dandruff of spent whitewash flakes from the ceiling where a fly drearily whines.

Bridget's lopsided shoes stand together on a hand-braided rug of aged rags. The dress she wears for Mass on Sundays hangs from the hook on the back of the door. The calico dress she will wear for the morning's chores is folded up on the trunk where she left it last night, along with soiled underthings that will do another day.

The house is thickly redolent of sleep, that sweetish smell. Still, all still; in all the house nothing moves except the droning fly and the stillness on the staircase crushes him, he falls still. Stillness pressing against the blinds, stillness, mortal stillness in the room below, where Master and Mistress share the matrimonial bed.

Were the drapes open or the lamp lit, one could better observe the differences between this room and the austerity of the maid's room. Here is a carpet splashed with vigorous flowers even if the carpet is of the cheap and cheerful variety; there are mauve, ochre, and cerise flowers on the wallpaper, even though the wallpaper was old when the Bordens arrived in the house. A dresser with another distorting mirror; no mirror in this house does not take your face and twist it out of shape for you. On the dresser, a runner embroidered with forget-me-nots; on the runner, a bone comb missing three teeth and lightly threaded with grey hairs, a hairbrush backed with ebonised wood, and a number of lace mats underneath small china boxes holding safety pins, hairnets, et cetera. The little hairpiece that Mrs Borden attaches to her balding scalp for daytime wear is curled up like a dead squirrel.

But of Borden's male occupation of this room there is no trace because he has a dressing-room of his own, through *that* door, on the left. . . .

What about the other door, the one next to it?

It leads to the back stairs.

And that yet other door, partially concealed behind the head of the heavy mahogany bed?

If it were not kept securely locked, it would take you into Miss Lizzie's room.

It is a peculiarity of the house, that the rooms are full of doors and—a further peculiarity—all these doors are always kept locked. A house full of locked doors that open only into other rooms with other locked doors. Upstairs and downstairs, all the rooms lead in and out of one another like a maze in a bad dream. It is a house without passages. There is no part of the house that has not been marked out as some inmate's personal territory; it is a house with no shared, no common spaces between one room and the next. It is a house of privacies sealed as close as if they had been sealed with wax on a legal document.

The only way to Emma's room is through Lizzie's. There is no way out of Emma's room. It is a dead end.

The Bordens' custom of locking all the doors, inside and outside, dates from a time, a few years ago, shortly before Bridget came to work for them, when the house was burgled. A person unknown came in through the side door while Borden and his wife had taken one of their rare trips out together. He had loaded her into a trap and set out for a farm they owned outside town, a surprise visit to ensure his tenant, a dour Swede, was not bilking him. The girls stayed at home in their rooms, napping on their beds or repairing ripped hems, or sewing loose buttons more securely, or writing letters, or contemplating acts of charity among the deserving poor, or staring vacantly into space.

I can't imagine what else they might do.

What the girls do when they are on their own is unimaginable to me.

Emma is even more of a mystery than Lizzie because we know less about her. She is a blank space. She has no life. The door from her room leads only into the room of her younger sister.

"Girls" is, of course, a courtesy term. Emma is well into her forties, Lizzie, her thirties, but they did not marry and so live on in their father's house, where they remain in a fictive, protracted childhood, "girls" for good.

In this city of working women, the most visible sign of the status of the Borden girls is that they toil not. "Clickety clack, clickety clack, You've got to work till it breaks your back!" the looms sing to the girls they lured here, the girls fresh from Lancashire, the dark-browed Portuguese, the French Canadian farmers' daughters, the up-country girls, the song whose rhythms now govern the movements of their dexterous fingers. But the Borden girls are deaf to it.

Strange, that endless confinement of these perpetual "girls" who do not labour in the mean house of the rich man. Strange, marginal life that those who lived it believed to be the very printing on the page, to be just exactly why the book was printed in the first place, to be the way all decent folks lived.

While the master and mistress were away and the girls asleep or otherwise occupied, some person or persons unknown tiptoed up the back stairs to the matrimonial bedroom and pocketed Mrs Borden's gold watch and chain, the collar necklace and silver bangle of her remote childhood, and a roll of dollar bills old Borden kept under his clean union suits in the third drawer of the bureau on the left. The intruder attempted to force the lock of the safe, that featureless block of black iron like a slaughtering block or an altar sitting squarely next to the bed on Old Borden's side, but it would have taken a crowbar to adequately penetrate the safe and the intruder tackled it with a pair of nail scissors that were lying handy on the dresser, so *that* didn't come off.

Then the intruder pissed and shitted on the cover of the Bordens' bed, knocked the clutter of this and that on the dresser to the floor, smashing a brace of green and violet porcelain parakeets into a thousand fragments in the process, swept into Old Borden's dressing room, there to maliciously assault his funeral coat as it hung in the moth-balled dark of his closet with the selfsame nail scissors that had been used on the safe, which now split in two and were abandoned on the closet floor, retired to the kitchen, smashed the flour crock and the treacle crock, and then scrawled an obscenity or two on the parlour window with the cake of soap that lived beside the scullery sink.

What a mess! Lizzie stared with vague surprise at the parlor window; she heard the soft bang of the open screen door, swinging idly, although there was no breeze. What was she doing, standing clad only in her corset in the middle of the sitting room? How had she got there? Had she crept down when she heard the screen door rattle? She did not know. She could not remember.

It was well known in polite circles in Fall River that Lizzie suffered from occasional "peculiar spells," as the idiom of the place and time called odd lapses of behaviour, unexpected, involuntary trances, moments of disconnection—those times when the mind misses a beat.

The Indians cursed the land with madness and death.

Even on the sunniest days, you could not say the landscape smiled; the ragged woodland, the ocean beaten out of steel. Not much, here, to cheer the heart, and all beneath the avenging light. The Indians stuck a few flints of their hard-cornered language onto the map, those names like meals of stones—Massachusetts, Pawtuxet, Woonsocket. And there are certain fruits of the region, such as the corn, especially those strange ears of crimson corn—some of the kernels are black, they dry out and rattle, you cannot eat them but people, nowadays, like to hang them on their doors for decoration in the fall—that strange, archaic-looking corn; and various squashes, the long-necked, pale yellow butternut, and the squat, whorled acorn squash, pine-green with a splatter of orange on one flank—squash and pumpkin that look and feel like votive objects carved from wood; you must boil them for hours to make them soft and then they taste flat, insipid, alien. These fruits have the ineradicable somberness of the aborigines.

From puberty, she had been troubled by these curious lapses of consciousness that often, though not always, came at the time of her menses; at these times, everyday things appeared to her with a piercing, appalling clarity that rendered them mysterious beyond words, so that the harsh, serrated leaves knocking against the window were those of a tree whose name she did not know in which sat birds whose names were not yet invented, whirring, clicking, and chucking like no birds known before, while a sputtering radiance emanated from everything. All the familiar things, at those times, seemed to her not only unknown but also unknowable, always unknowable.

So the strangers must have felt after they watched the boat that brought them slide away from them over the horizon and, abandoned, turned their faces inland towards the wilderness with the anguish of the newborn confronted with infinite space.

Time opened in two; suddenly she was not continuous any more.

Dull headaches announced the approaches of these trances, from which she returned as from an electric elsewhere. She would quiver with exhaustion; her sister would bathe her temples with a handkerchief moistened with eau de cologne, she lying on her bedroom sofa.

She had no words with which to describe the over-clarity with which she had seen the everyday things around her, even had she wished to do so. She kept the knowledge she was discontinuous to herself—or, rather, she steadfastly ignored the knowledge that she was discrete because the notion had no meaning to her, or, perhaps, too much meaning for her to assimilate since she believed that either a person was, or else was not. But don't think because she believed this that she believed it *in so many words* . . . she believed it in the same way that she believed she lived in Fall River, Massachusetts, and in the same way that she believed the second Mrs Borden had married her father for his money. She did not believe she believed in these things; she thought she *knew* them for a fact, just as she knew the Portuguese were pigs and God was the Father Almighty.

Therefore these intermittent lapses in day-to-day consciousness, in which she was and was not at the same time, were unaccountable in every way and she did not dare to think of them once she came back to herself. So she remained a stranger to herself.

A trap rattled by in the street outside. A child burst out crying in a house across the way. Lizzie experienced the departure of vision as though it were the clearing of a haze.

"Help! We have been burgled! Help!"

I cannot tell you what effect the burglary had on Borden. It utterly disconcerted him; he was a man stunned. It violated him, even. He was a man raped. It took away his hitherto unshakeable confidence in the integrity inherent in things.

The family broke its habitual silence with one another in order to discuss the burglary, it moved them so. They blamed it on the Portuguese, mostly, but sometimes on the Canucks. If their outrage remained constant and did not diminish with time, the focus of it varied according to their moods, although they always pointed the finger of suspicion at the strangers who lived in the dark ramparts of the company housing a few stinking blocks away. They did not always suspect the dark strangers exclusively; sometimes they thought the culprit might very well have been one of the mill hands fresh from saucy Lancashire across the ocean who did the deed, for a slum landlord has few friends among the criminal classes. Sometimes Lizzie voiced the notion that the lugubrious and monosyllabic Swede out on Old Borden's bit of property at Swansea might have been harbouring a grudge against her father for some reason and, when the old man gruffly reminded her the Swede had the unshakeable alibi of Borden's own presence at the time of the offence, she would fall silent and fix upon the middle distance the large, accusing, blue stare of her pale eyes.

The possibility of a poltergeist occurred to Mrs Borden, although she does not know the word; she knows, however, that her younger stepdaughter could make the plates jump out of sheer spite, if she wanted to. But the old man adores his daughter. Perhaps it is then, after the shock of the burglary, that he decided she needed a change of scene, a dose of sea air, a long voyage.

The only defence against further depredation was to lock everything and then lock it again, to lock and relock everything and then lock it up once more for luck.

After the burglary, the front door and the side door were always locked three times if one of the inhabitants of the house left it for just so long as to go into the yard and pick up a basket of fallen pears when pears were in season, or if the maid went out to hang a bit of washing or Old Borden, after supper, took a piss under a tree.

From this time dated the custom of locking all the bedroom doors on the inside when one was on the inside oneself or on the outside when one was on the outside. Old Borden locked his bedroom door in the morning, when he left it, and put the key in sight of all on the kitchen shelf.

The burglary awakened Old Borden to the evanescent nature of private property. He thereafter undertook an orgy of investment. He would forthwith invest his surplus in good brick and mortar for who can make away with an office block?

A number of leases fell in simultaneously at just this time on a certain street in the downtown area of the city and Borden snapped them up. When he owned the block, he pulled it down. He planned the Borden building, an edifice of shops and offices, dark red brick, deep tan stone, with cast iron detail, from whence, in perpetuity, he might reap a fine harvest of unsaleable rents, and this monument, like that of Ozymandias, would long survive him—indeed, still stands, foursquare and handsome, the Andrew Borden Building on South Main Street.

Not bad for a fish peddler's son, eh? To turn yourself into a solid piece of real estate?

For, although "Borden" is an ancient name in New England and the Borden clan between them owned the better part of Fall River, our Borden, Old Borden, these Bordens, did not spring from a wealthy branch of the family. There were Bordens and Bordens and he was the son of a man who sold fresh fish in a wicker basket from house to house to house. Old Borden's parsimony was bred of poverty but learned to thrive best on prosperity for thrift has a different meaning for the poor; they get no joy of it, it is stark necessity to them. But a penniless miser is a contradiction in terms.

Morose and gaunt, this self-made man is one of few pleasures. His vocation is capital accumulation.

What is his hobby?

Why, grinding the faces of the poor.

First, Andrew Borden was an undertaker and death, recognising an accomplice, did well by him. In the city of spindles, few made old bones; the little children who laboured in the mills died with especial frequency. When he was an undertaker, no!— it was not true he cut the feet of corpses to fit into a job lot of coffins bought cheap as Civil War surplus! That was a rumour put about by his enemies!

With the profits from his coffins, he bought up a tenement or two and made fresh profit from the living. He bought shares in the mills. Then he invested in a brace of banks, so that now he makes a profit on money itself, which is the purest form of profit of all.

Foreclosures and evictions are meat and drink to him. He loves nothing better than a little usury. He is halfway on the road to his first million.

At night, to save the kerosene, he sits in lampless dark. He waters the pear trees with his own urine; waste not, want not. As soon as the daily newspapers are done with, he rips them into squares and stores them in the cellar privy so that they can wipe their arses with them. He mourns the loss of the good organic waste that goes down the privy. He would like to charge the very cockroaches in the kitchen rent. And yet he has not grown fat on all this; the pure flame of his passion has melted off his flesh, his skin sticks to his bones out of sheer parsimony. Perhaps it is from his first profession that he has acquired his bearing, for he walks with the stately dignity of a hearse.

To watch Old Borden bearing down the street toward you was to be filled with an instinctual respect for mortality, whose gaunt ambassador he seemed to be. And it made you think, too, what a triumph over nature it was when we rose up to walk on two legs instead of four, in the first place! For he held himself upright with such ponderous assertion it was a perpetual reminder to all who witnessed his progress how it is not *natural* to be upright, that it is a triumph of the will over gravity, in itself a transcendence of the spirit over matter.

His spine is like an iron rod, forged, not born, impossible to imagine that spine of Old Borden's curled up in the womb in the big C-shape of the fetus; he walks as if his legs had joints at neither knee nor ankle so that his feet strike at the trembling earth like a bailiff pounding a door with an iron bar.

He has a white, chin-strap beard, old-fashioned already in those days. His lips are so thin it looks as if he'd gnawed them off. He is at peace with his god for he has used his talents as the Good Book says he should.

Yet do not think he has no soft spot. Like Old Lear, like Old Goriot, his heart— and, more than that, his cheque book—is putty in his youngest daughter's hands. On his pinky—you cannot see it, it lies under the covers—he wears a gold ring, not a wedding ring but a high school ring, a singular trinket for fabulously misanthropic miser. His youngest daughter gave it to him when she left school and asked him to wear it, always, and so he always does, and will wear it to the grave.

He sleeps fully dressed in a flannel nightshirt over his long-sleeved underwear, and a flannel nightcap, and his back is turned toward his wife of thirty years, as is hers to his.

They are Mr and Mrs Jack Spratt in person, he, tall and gaunt as a hanging judge and she, such a spreading, round little doughball. He is a miser, while she—she is a glutton, a solitary eater, most innocent of vices and yet the shadow or parodic vice of his, for he would like to eat up all the world, or, failing that, since fate has not spread him a sufficiently large table for his ambitions—he is a mute, inglorious Napoleon, he does not know what he might have done because he never had the opportunity—since he has not access to the entire world, he would like to gobble up the city of Fall River. But she, well, she just gently, continuously stuffs herself, doesn't she; she's always nibbling away at something, at the cud, perhaps.

Not that she gets much pleasure from it, either; no gourmet, she, forever meditating the exquisite difference between a mayonnaise sharpened with a few drops of Orleans vinegar or one pointed up with a squeeze of fresh lemon juice. No. Abby never aspired so high, nor would she ever think to do so even if she had the option; she is satisfied to stick to simple gluttony and she eschews all overtones of the sensuality of consumption. Since she relishes not one single mouthful of the food she eats, she knows her ceaseless gluttony is no transgression.

Here they lie in bed together, living embodiments of two of the Seven Deadly Sins, but he knows his avarice is no offence because he never spends any money and she knows she is not greedy because the grub she shovels down gives her dyspepsia. Gives her dyspepsia and worse; in those days, great-grandmother's days, summer and salmonella came in together.

Refrigeration is, perhaps, the only unmitigated blessing that the Age of Technology has brought us, a blessing that has brought no bane in tow, a wholly positive good that can be welcomed without reluctance or qualification. The white-enamelled refrigerator is the genius of every home, the friendly chill of whose breath has banished summer sickness and the runs for good! How often, nowadays, in summer does your milk turn into a sour jelly, or your butter separate itself out into the liquid fat and the corrupt-smelling whey? When did you last see the waxy clusters of the seed-pearl eggs of the blowfly materialise disgustingly on the leftover joint? Perhaps, perfect child of the Frigidaire, you've known none of all this! In those days, however, you took your life in your hands each time you picked up your knife and fork.

On the Saturday preceding the murders, for dinner, at twelve, the Bordens had a big joint of roast mutton, hot. Bridget cooked it. They must have had potatoes with it. Mashed, probably. With flour gravy. I don't know if they had greens or not. The documents don't say. But we know the main items of the Bordens' diet during their last week living because the police thoroughly investigated the rumour that the parents had been poisoned before they had been butchered and so the week's dolorous bill of fare was recorded in full.

On Saturday, they had more mutton, cold, for supper. They ate their roast on Saturdays because they were Sabbatarians and did not believe work should be done on Sundays, so Bridget had Sunday off, to go to church.

Because Bridget had Sundays off, they ate more cold mutton for Sunday dinner, with bread and butter, I dare say, and pickles, perhaps.

On Monday, they had mutton for midday dinner. I don't know how Bridget fixed the mutton; perhaps she warmed it up in left-over gravy, to make a change from having it cold. They had mutton for breakfast on Tuesday, too. It must have been a veritably gargantuan joint of mutton—or did the fault lie with Old Borden; did he carve thin as paper money and lay the slice on the plate with as much disinclination as if he'd been paying back a loan, so the eaters felt he grudged each bite?

There was an ice-box of the old-fashioned, wooden kind, the doors of which must be kept tightly shut at all times or else the ice melts and everything inside goes rotten. Every morning, Bridget put out the pan for the ice-man and filled up the dripping ice-compartment.

In this ice-box, she lodged the remains of the mutton.

In and out of the ice-box went the joint of mutton.

On Tuesday, it was time for a change. They had sword-fish for midday dinner. Bridget bought the thick steaks of sword-fish in a fish-market that smelled like a brothel after a busy night. She put the sword-fish in the ice-box until it was time to grill it. Then the left-over sword-fish went back into the ice-box until supper time, when she warmed it up again. That was the night they vomited again and again.

Bridget kept back the knuckle from the leg of mutton in order to make broth; perhaps the broth was comforting to an upset stomach and perhaps not. They had the broth for Wednesday dinner, followed by mutton, again. Was that warmed over, too? On Wednesday, they had cold mutton for supper, again.

There is nothing quite like cold mutton. The sinewy, grey, lean meat amidst the veined lumps of congealed fat, varicosed with clotted blood; it must be the sheep's Pyrrhic vengeance on the carnivore! Considering that which lay upon her plate, Mrs Borden's habitual gluttony takes on almost an heroic quality. Undeterred by the vileness of the table, still she pigs valiantly away while the girls look on, push their own plates away, wince to see the grease on her chin.

Oh, how she loves to eat! She is Mrs Jack Spratt in person, round as a ball, fat as butter . . . the heavy fare of New England, the chowders, the cornmeal puddings, the boiled dinners, have shaped her, and continue to shape her.

See her rub her bread round her plate. "Is there a little more gravy, Bridget, just to finish up my bread?" She pours cold gravy, lumpy with flour, onto her plate, so much gravy she's forced, in the end, to cut herself just another little corner of bread with which to finish up the gravy.

The sisters think, she eats and eats and eats; she eats everything, she will eat up every single thing, crunch up the plate from which she eats when no more gravy is forthcoming, munch through the greenbacks in father's safe for a salad, for dessert she will polish off the gingerbread house in which they live.

If the old woman thought to deceive them as to her true nature by affecting to confine her voracity only to comestibles, Lizzie knew better; her guzzling stepmother's appetite terrified and appalled her, for it was the only thing within the straight and narrow Borden home that was not kept within confinement.

There had never been any conversation at table; that was not their style. Their stiff lips would part to request the salt, the bread, the butter, yes; but, apart from that, only the raucous squawk of knife on plate and private sounds of chewing and swallowing amplified and publicised and rendered over-intimate, obscene, by the unutterable silence of the narrow dining room. A strip of flypaper hung from a nail over the table, bearing upon it a mourning band of dead flies. A stopped clock of black marble, shaped like a Greek mausoleum, stood on the sideboard, becalmed. Father sat at the head of the table and shaved the meat. Mrs Borden sat at the foot and ate it.

"I won't eat with her; I won't," said Lizzie. "I refuse to sit at the trough with that sow."

After this little explosion of ill temper, Bridget served the meal twice, once for Mr and Mrs Borden, then kept all warm and brought it out again for Lizzie and Emma, since Emma knew it was her duty to take the part of her little sister, her little dearest, the tender and difficult one. After this interruption, calm returned to the household; calm continued to dominate the household.

Saturday, Sunday, Monday, Tuesday, Wednesday. In and out of the ice-box went the slowly dwindling leg of mutton until Thursday dinner was cancelled because corpses and not places were laid out on the table as if the eaters had become the meal.

Back to back they lie. You could rest a sword in the space between the old man and his wife, between the old man's backbone, the only rigid thing he ever offered her, and her soft, warm, enormous bum. Her flannel nightdress is cut on the same lines as his nightshirt except for the limp flannel frill around the neck. She weighs two hundred pounds. She is five feet nothing tall. The bed sags on her side. It is the bed in which his first wife died.

Last night, they dosed themselves with castor oil, due to the indisposition that kept them both awake and vomiting the whole night before that; the copious results of their purges brim the chamberpots beneath the bed.

Their purges flailed them. Their faces show up decomposing green in the dim, curtained room, in which the air is too thick for flies to move.

The youngest daughter dreams behind the locked door.

She threw back the top sheet and her window is wide open but there is no breeze outside this morning to deliciously shiver the screen. Bright sun floods the blinds so that the linen-coloured light shows us how Lizzie has gone to bed as for a levée in a pretty, ruffled nightdress of starched white muslin with ribbons of pastel pink satin threaded through the eyelets of the lace, for is it not the "naughty nineties" everywhere but dour Fall River? Don't the gilded steamships of the Fall River Line signify all the squandered luxury of the Gilded Age within their mahogany and chandeliered interiors? Elsewhere, it is the Belle Epoque. In New York, Paris, London, champagne corks pop and women fall backwards in a crisp meringue of petticoats for fun and profit but not in Fall River. Oh, no. So, in the immutable privacy of her bedroom, for her own delight, Lizzie puts on a rich girl's pretty nightdress, although she lives in a mean house, because she is a rich girl, too.

But she is plain.

The hem of her nightdress is rucked up above her knees because she is a restless sleeper. Her light, dry, reddish hair, crackling with static, slipping loose from the night-time plait, crisps and stutters over the square pillow at which she clutches as she sprawls on her stomach, having rested her cheek on the starched pillowcase for coolness's sake at some earlier hour.

Lizzie was not an affectionate diminutive but the name with which she had been christened. Since she would always be known as "Lizzie," so her father reasoned, why burden her with the effete and fancy prolongation of "Elizabeth"? A miser in everything, he even cropped off half her name before he gave it to her. So "Lizzie" it was, stark and unadorned, and she is a motherless child, orphaned at two years old, poor thing.

Now she is two-and-thirty and yet the memory of that mother whom she cannot remember remains an abiding source of grief: "If mother had lived, everything would have been different."

How? Why? Different in what way? She wouldn't have been able to answer that, lost in a nostalgia for lost affection. Yet how could she have been loved better than by her sister, Emma, who lavished the pent-up treasures of a New England spinster's heart upon the little thing? Different, perhaps, because her natural mother, the first Mrs Borden, subject as she was to fits of sudden, wild, inexplicable rage, might have taken the hatchet to Old Borden on her own account? But Lizzie *loves* her father. All are agreed on that. Lizzie adores the adoring father who, after her mother died, took to himself another wife.

Her bare feet twitch a little, like those of a dog dreaming of rabbits. Her sleep is thin and unsatisfying, full of vague terrors and indeterminate menaces to which she cannot put a name or form once she is awake. Sleep opens within her a disorderly house. But all she knows is, she sleeps badly, and this last, stifling night has been troubled, too, by vague nausea and the gripes of her female pain; her room is harsh with the metallic smell of menstrual blood.

Yesterday evening she slipped out of the house to visit a woman friend. Lizzie was agitated; she kept picking nervously at the shirring on the front of her dress.

"I am afraid . . . that somebody . . . will *do* something," said Lizzie.

"Mrs Borden . . ." and here Lizzie lowered her voice and her eyes looked everywhere in the room except at Miss Russell . . . "Mrs Borden—oh! will you ever believe? Mrs Borden thinks somebody is trying to *poison* us!"

She used to call her stepmother "mother," as duty bade, but after a quarrel about money after her father deeded half a slum property to her stepmother five years before, Lizzie always, with cool scrupulosity, spoke of "Mrs Borden" when she was forced to speak of her and called her "Mrs Borden" to her face, too.

"Last night, Mrs Borden and poor father were so sick! I heard them, through the wall. And, as for me, I haven't felt myself all day, I have felt so strange. So very . . . strange."

Miss Russell hastened to discover an explanation within reason; she was embarrassed to mention the "peculiar spells." Everyone knew there was nothing odd about the Borden girls. It was Lizzie's difficult time of the month, too; her friend could tell by a certain haggard, glazed look on Lizzie's face when it was happening. Yet her gentility forbade her to mention that.

"Something you ate? It must have been something you have eaten. What was yesterday's supper?" solicitously enquired Miss Russell.

"Warmed-over swordfish. We had it hot for dinner though I could not take much. Then Bridget heated up the left-overs for supper but, again, for myself, I could only get down a forkful. Mrs Borden ate up the remains and scoured her plate with her bread. She smacked her lips but then was sick all night." (Note of smugness, here.)

"Oh, Lizzie! In all this heat, this dreadful heat! Twice-cooked fish! You know how quickly fish goes off in this heat! Bridget should have known better than to give you twice-cooked fish!"

"There have been threats," Lizzie pursued remorselessly, keeping her eyes on her nervous fingertips. "So many people, you understand, dislike father."

This cannot be denied. Miss Russell politely remained mute.

"Mrs Borden was so very sick she called the doctor in and Father was abusive toward the doctor and shouted at him and told him he would not pay a doctor's bills whilst we had our own good castor oil in the house. He shouted at the doctor and all the neighbours heard and I was so ashamed. There is a man, you see . . ." and here she ducked her head, while her short, pale eyelashes beat on her cheekbones . . . "such a man, a *dark* man, Portuguese, Italian, I've seen him outside the house at odd, at unexpected hours, early in the morning, late at night, whenever I cannot sleep in this dreadful heat if I raise the blind and peep out, there I see him in the shadows of the pear trees, in the yard . . . perhaps he puts poison in the milk, in the mornings, after the milk-man fills his can.

"Perhaps he poisons the ice, when the ice-man comes."

"How long has he been haunting you?" asked Miss Russell, properly dismayed.

"Since . . . the burglary," said Lizzie and suddenly looked Miss Russell full in the face with a kind of triumph. How large her eyes were, prominent, yet veiled. And her well-manicured fingers went on pecking away at the front of her dress as if she were trying to unpick the shirring.

Miss Russell knew, she just *knew*, this dark man was a figment of Lizzie's imagination. All in a rush, she lost patience with the girl; dark men standing outside her bedroom window, indeed! Yet she was kind and cast about for ways to reassure her.

"But Bridget is up and about when the milk-man and the ice-man call and the whole street is busy and bustling, too; who would dare to put poison in either milk or ice-bucket while half of Second Street looks on? Oh, Lizzie, it is the dreadful summer, the heat, the intolerable heat that's put us all out of sorts, makes us fractious and nervous, makes us sick. So easy to imagine things in this terrible weather, that taints the food and sows worms in the mind. . . . I thought you'd planned to go away, Lizzie, to the ocean. Didn't you plan to take a little holiday, by the sea? Oh, do go! Sea air would blow away all these silly fancies!"

Lizzie neither nods nor shakes her head but continues to worry at her shirring. For does she not have important business in Fall River? Only that morning, had she not been down to the drug-store to try to buy some prussic acid? But how can she tell kind Miss Russell she is gripped by an imperious need to stay in Fall River and murder her parents?

Had all that talk of poison in the vomiting house put her in mind of poison? She went to the drug-store on the corner of Main Street in order to buy prussic acid but nobody would sell it to her so she came home empty-handed. When she asked the corner pharmacist only that morning for a little prussic acid to kill the moth in her seal-skin cape, the man looked at her oddly. "Moth don't breed in seal-skin," he opined. The autopsy will reveal no trace of poison in the stomachs of either parent. She did not try to poison them; she only had it in mind to poison them.

"And this dark man," she pursued to the unwilling Miss Russell, "oh! I have seen the moon glint upon his knife!"

When she wakes up, she can never remember her dreams; she only remembers she slept badly.

Hers is a pleasant room of not ungenerous dimensions, seeing the house is so very small. Besides the bed and the dresser, there is a sofa and a desk; it is her bedroom and also her sitting room and her office, too, for the desk is stacked with account books of the various charitable organisations with which she occupies her ample spare time. The Fruit and Flower Mission, under whose auspices she visits the indigent old in the hospital with gifts; the Women's Christian Temperance Union, for whom she extracts signatures for petitions against the Demon Drink; Christian Endeavour, whatever that is—this is the golden age of good works and she flings herself into committees with a vengeance. What would the daughters of the rich do with themselves if the poor ceased to exist?

Then there is the Newsboys Thanksgiving Dinner Fund; and the Horsetrough Association; and the Chinese Conversion Association—no class nor kind is safe from her merciless charity.

She used to teach a Sunday school class of little Chinese children but they did not like her; they teased her, they played an unpleasant trick on her, one Sunday afternoon they put a dead dog inside her desk, a trick of which one would have thought the Chinese were incapable because they are so impassive and did not even giggle when she shrieked.

First, she shrieked; then she caught hold of the shoulder of the little Chinese boy sitting at the end of the front row—the nearest child she could get at—and started in on hitting him but then the class instantly abandoned its impassivity and let out such a racket the superintendent came before much damage was done. The children were severely punished. They were forbidden to come to Sunday school again.

Bureau; dressing-table; closet; bed; sofa. She spends her days in this room, moving between each of these dull items of furniture in a circumscribed, undeviating, planetary round. She loves her privacy, she loves her room, she locks herself up in it all day. A shelf contains a book or two: *Heroes of the Mission Field, The Romance of Trade.* On the walls, framed photographs of high school friends, sentimentally inscribed, with, tucked inside one frame, a picture postcard showing a black kitten peeking through a horseshoe. A watercolour of a Cape Cod seascape executed with poignant amateur incompetence. A monochrome photograph of two works of art, a Della Robbia madonna and the Mona Lisa; these she bought in the Uffizi and the Louvre, respectively, when she went to Europe.

Europe!

For don't you remember What Katy Did Next? The storybook heroine took the steamship to smoky old London, to elegant, fascinating Paris, to sunny, antique Rome and Florence; the storybook heroine sees Europe reveal itself before her like an interesting series of magic lantern slides on a gigantic screen. All is present and all unreal. The Tower of London; click. Notre Dame; click. The Sistine Chapel; click. Then the lights go out and she is in the dark again.

Of this journey she retained only the most circumspect of souvenirs, that madonna, that Mona Lisa, reproductions of objects of art consecrated by a universal approval of taste. If she came back with a bag full of memories stamped "Never to be Forgotten," she put the bag away under the bed on which she had dreamed of the world before she set out to see it and on which, at home again, she continued to dream, the dream having been transformed not into lived experience but into memory, which is only another kind of dreaming.

Wistfully: "When I was in Florence . . ."

But then, with pleasure, she corrects herself: "When *we* were in Florence . . ."

Because a good deal, in fact, most of the gratification the trip gave her came from having set out from Fall River with a select group of the daughters of respectable and affluent mill owners. Once away from Second Street, she was able to move comfortably in the segment of Fall River society to which she belonged by right of old name and new money but from which, when she was at home, her father's plentiful personal eccentricities excluded her. Sharing bedrooms, sharing staterooms, sharing berths, the girls travelled together in a genteel gaggle that bore its doom already upon it for they were the girls who would not marry, now, and any pleasure they might have obtained from the variety and excitement of the trip was spoiled in advance by the knowledge they were eating up what might have been their own wedding-cake, using up what should have been, if they'd had any luck, their marriage settlements.

All girls pushing thirty, privileged to go out and look at the world before they resigned themselves to the thin condition of New England spinsterhood; but it was a case of look, don't touch. They knew they must not get their hands dirtied or their dresses crushed by the world, while their affectionate companionship en route had a certain steadfast, determined quality about it as they bravely made the best of the second-best.

It was a sour tour, in some ways, and it was a round trip; it ended at the sour place from which it had set out. Home, again, the narrow house, the rooms all locked like those in Bluebeard's Castle, and the fat, white stepmother whom nobody loves sitting in the middle of the spider web; she has not budged a single inch while Lizzie was away but she has grown fatter.

This stepmother oppressed her like a spell. Lizzie will immediately correct the judge at her trial: "She is not my mother, sir; she is my stepmother: my mother died when I was a child." But Old Borden brought his new bride home when his younger girl was five!

Another mystery—how the Bordens contrived to live together for twenty, nearly thirty years without generating amongst themselves a single scrap of the grumbling, irritable, everyday affection without which proximity becomes intolerable; yet their life cannot have been truly intolerable, because they lived it for so long. They bore it. They did not rub along together, somehow; they rubbed each other up the wrong way all the time, and yet they lived in each other's pockets.

Correction: they lived in Old Borden's pocket and all they had in common was the contents of that pocket.

The days open their cramped spaces into other cramped spaces and old furniture and never anything to look forward to, nothing. Empty days. Oppressive afternoons. Nights stalled in calm. Empty days.

When Old Borden dug in his pocket to shell out for Lizzie's trip to Europe, the eye of God on the pyramid blinked to see daylight but no extravagance is too excessive for the miser's younger daughter who is the wild card in this house and, it seems, can have anything she wants, play ducks and drakes with her father's silver dollars if it so pleases her. He pays all her dressmakers' bills on the dot and how she loves to dress up fine! In her unacknowledged, atrocious solitude, she has become addicted to dandyism. He gives her each week in pin money the same as the cook gets for wages and Lizzie gives that which she does not spend on personal adornment to the deserving poor.

He would give his Lizzie anything, anything in the world that lives under the green sign of the dollar.

She would like a pet, a kitten or a puppy; she loves small animals and birds, too, poor, helpless things. She piles high the bird-table all winter. She used to keep some white pouter pigeons in the disused stable, the kind that look like shuttlecocks and go "vroo croo" soft as a cloud.

Surviving photographs of Lizzie Borden show a face it is difficult to look at as if you knew nothing about her; coming events cast their shadow across her face, or else you see the shadows these events have cast—something terrible, something ominous in this face with its jutting, rectangular jaw and those mad eyes of the New England saints, eyes that belong to a person who does not listen . . . fanatic's eyes, you might say, if you knew nothing about her. If you were sorting through a box of old photographs in a junk shop and came across this particular sepia, faded face above the choker collars of the eighteen-nineties, you might murmur when you saw her: "Oh, what big eyes you have!" as Red Riding Hood said to the wolf, but then you might not even pause to pick her out and look at her more closely, for hers is not, in itself, a striking face.

But as soon as the face has a name, once you recognise her, when you know who she is and what it was she did, the face becomes as if of one possessed, and now it haunts you, you look at it again and again, it secretes mystery.

This woman, with her jaw of a concentration camp attendant; and such eyes . . .

In her old age, she wore pince-nez and truly with the years the mad light has departed from those eyes or else is deflected by her glasses—if, indeed, it *was* a mad light, in the first place, for don't we all conceal somewhere photographs of ourselves that make us look like crazed assassins? And, in those early photographs of her young womanhood, she herself does not look so much like a crazed assassin as somebody in extreme solitude, oblivious of that camera in whose direction she obscurely smiles, so that it would not surprise you to learn that she is blind.

There is a mirror on the dresser in which she sometimes looks at those times when time snaps in two and then she sees herself with clairvoyant eyes, as though she were another person.

"Lizzie is not herself, today."

At those times, those irremediable times, she could have raised her muzzle to an aching moon and howled.

At other times, she watches herself doing her hair and trying her clothes on. The distorting mirror reflects her with the queasy fidelity of water. She puts on dresses and then she takes them off. She looks at herself in her corset. She measures herself with the tape measure. She pulls the measure tight. She pats her hair. She tries on a hat, a little hat, a chic little straw toque. She punctures it with a hatpin. She pulls the veil down. She pulls it up. She takes the hat off. She drives the hatpin into it with a vivacious strength she did not know she possessed.

Time goes by and nothing happens.

She traces the outlines of her face with an uncertain hand as if she were thinking of unfastening the bandages on her soul but it isn't time to do that, yet; her new face isn't ready to be seen, yet.

She is a girl of Sargasso calm.

She used to keep her pigeons in the loft above the disused stable and feed them grain out of the palms of her cupped hands. She liked to feel the soft scratch of their little beaks. They murmured "vroo croo" with infinite tenderness. She changed their water every day and cleaned up their leprous messes but Old Borden took a dislike to their cooing, it got on his nerves—who'd have thought he *had* any nerves? But he invented some, they got on them, and one afternoon he took out the hatchet from the wood-pile in the cellar and chopped the pigeons' heads off.

Abby fancied the slaughtered pigeons for a pie but Bridget the servant girl put her foot down, at that; What?!? Make a pie out of Miss Lizzie's beloved turtledoves? JesusMaryandJoseph!!! she exclaimed with characteristic impetuousness; what can they be thinking of! Miss Lizzie so nervy with her funny turns and all! (The maid is the only one in the house with any sense and that's the truth of it.) Lizzie came home from the Fruit and Flowers Mission where she had been reading a tract to an old woman in a poorhouse: "God bless you, Miss Lizzie." At home all was blood and feathers.

She doesn't weep, this one, it isn't her nature, she is still waters, but, when moved, she changes colour, her face flushes, it goes dark, angry, mottled red, marbling up like the marbling on the inner covers of the family Bible. The old man loves his daughter this side of idolatry and pays for everything she wants but all the same he killed her pigeons when his wife wanted to gobble them up.

That is how she sees it. That is how she understands it. Now she cannot bear to watch her stepmother eat. Each bite the woman takes seems to go "vroo croo."

Old Borden cleaned off the hatchet and put it back in the cellar, next to the wood-pile. The red receding from her face, Lizzie went down to inspect the instrument of destruction. She picked it up and weighed it in her hand.

That was a few weeks before, at the beginning of the spring.

Her hands and feet twitch in her sleep; the nerves and muscles of this complicated mechanism won't relax, just won't relax; she is all twang, all tension; she is as taut as the strings of a wind-harp from which random currents of the air pluck out tunes that are not our tunes.

At the first stroke of the City Hall clock, the first factory hooter blares, and then, on another note, another, and another, the Metacomet Mill, the American Mill, the Mechanics Mill . . . until every mill in the entire town sings out aloud in a common anthem of summoning and the hot alleys where the factory folk live blacken with the hurrying throng, hurry! scurry! to loom, to bobbin, to spindle, to dye-shop as to places of worship, men, and women, too, and children, the street blackens, the sky darkens as the chimneys now belch forth, the clang, bang, and clatter of the mills commences.

Bridget's clock leaps and shudders on its chair, about to sound its own alarm. Their day, the Bordens's fatal day, trembles on the brink of beginning.

Outside, above, in the already burning air, see! the angel of death roosts on the roof-tree.

QUESTIONS FOR DISCUSSION AND WRITING

1. Though Lizzie Borden was acquitted, the narrator of Carter's story tells us that Lizzie murdered her stepmother and father. At the same time, the story does not show the murder. What is the effect of leaving the murder scene out? What does the story suggest Lizzie's motives might have been? Do those suggestions of motive make Lizzie seem more or less monstrous? How sympathetic to Lizzie is Carter's story?

2. There are a number of references to fairy tales in the story: to Bluebeard's Castle, to Little Red Riding Hood (a story Carter retold; see 644–50), and to Jack Spratt, for instance. In what ways does "The Fall River Axe Murders" seem like a fairy tale? How well do fairy-tale ideas of heroism, monstrosity, and victimization seem to apply to Carter's story? How is or isn't Mrs. Borden a fairy-tale stepmother? Are the perspectives on morality and psychology offered by the story the same that we get in fairy tales? Why or why not?

3. The story places a great deal of emphasis on eating and meals. What does eating seem to represent in the story? How is it related to the murders?

4. In calling her story "The Fall River Axe Murders," Carter signifies the importance of setting. How do the descriptions of the town and the house help to create and reflect the story's moods and the characters' motives? How do other features of the setting—the descriptions of time and the weather, for instance—function?

Following are three lyrics from Christopher McGovern's musical Lizzie Borden. *In the first song, Lizzie expresses her yearning for a "house on the hill" in the well-to-do part of town.*

CHRISTOPHER MCGOVERN and AMY POWERS
The House on the Hill

Lizzie

The house on the hill
All the trees in a line
So fancy and fine
And the gate . . . so strong, so beautiful

5   Keeping every secret in its halls
Granting every wish within its walls.

From each window sill
You can stand looking down
On the whole of the town
10 Far away from harm
From anyone

Dishes full of strawberries and cream
Featherbeds like some girls only dream
And you never cry
15 No not inside

The house on the hill
I can see that it's near
But it's so far from here
Still it calls to me
20 Especially
Will it turn the darkness into light?
If I wish enough I think I might
See it shining there beneath the moon
Each night it's growing brighter
25 Soon I'll be there
Least I pray each day I will

In the house on the hill

QUESTION FOR DISCUSSION AND WRITING

Certainly the "house on the hill" represents a grandeur Lizzie feels is missing from her home. What else does the house represent to Lizzie?

_____

In the play, Lizzie keeps pet pigeons, pigeons that her father later kills with a hatchet, spattering her with blood. The song is sung alternately by Lizzie and the "girl," a younger version of Lizzie.

Fly Away

Lizzie

Lovely creatures
Loyal friends
I shall keep you safe till daylight ends
I know you'd never mean
To hurt me with goodbye   5
But still the moment that you saw the open sky
You'd fly away

Girl

We'll fly away

Lizzie

Trips of fancy
Foolish flight   10
Wiser not to whet your appetite
For once your eyes have seen
And once your heart has flown
It's harder that the cage
Is all you've ever known   15
Don't fly away

Girl

We'll fly away
I'll keep you safe . . .

Lizzie

Outside the danger lurks
Wherever you may land   20

Girl

From any harms . . .

Lizzie

Outside a stranger waits
To crush you in his hand

Girl

I'll be your friend . . .

Lizzie

25 In here is someone who's devoted just to you

Girl

Come to my arms

Lizzie

Who asks for nothing
But devotion from you too.
Don't fly away

Girl

30 We'll fly away

Lizzie	*Girl*
Stop your dreaming	Don't stop dreaming
Still your wings	Spread your wings

Lizzie/Girl

Close your eyes and think of better things

Lizzie

You know you're all I have

Lizzie/Girl

You'll see . . . I'm all you need   35
And we may both find happiness as long as we

Lizzie

Don't fly away

Girl

Can fly away

Lizzie

Don't fly away.

QUESTIONS FOR DISCUSSION AND WRITING

1. The song alternates between "fly away" and "don't fly away." Why does the adult Lizzie ask the pigeons not to fly away? Why does the girl ask them to fly away?
2. What does "flying away" represent in the song? What is offered by not flying away? What might the song suggest about Lizzie's own reasons for not leaving the "nest"?

The night before the murders, Lizzie sings the following song alone in her room, after having said good-bye to her sister, who is leaving on a short trip. The "girl" is a younger version of Lizzie.

I Cry Alone

Lizzie

I cry alone
When no one else can see
When I am finally sure
No eyes have followed me
Each night I try alone   5
To keep the tears away
They never seem to leave me for too long
So I cry alone
When no one else is near

10 I try to do it quietly
But every wall can hear
I say goodbye alone
To all these memories
I do not see how silence makes me wrong
15 For I was taught that God rewards the strong

Girl

Tears like rain, fall like stars
Gently into my heart
Wind like pain, softly blows
No one hears
20 No one knows

Lizzie

They'll never know my buried dreams
The secret me . . . the me that screams
The painful truth in every single drop
For if I show the me that's real
25 The me that hurts . . . the me that feels
I fear this flood might never stop
Don't know if it would ever stop

For I alone
Know what is really true
30 I'll keep the secret safe
Like I was told to do
So let them try—they'll never see
They'll never get one tear from me
Just let them think my heart has turned to stone

35 Until the day I die
I'll cry . . .

Girl

Tears like blood
Fall like rain
And still I
40 Feel no pain

Lizzie

I cry . . .

Girl

Blood like tears
Pouring down
Clean them up
Make no sound!

Lizzie

Alone.

45

QUESTIONS FOR DISCUSSION AND WRITING

1. What does the song suggest about why Lizzie cries?
2. What in the song might lead us to believe Lizzie is innocent or guilty of the murder?

In a New Light
Lizzie Borden in Jail Awaiting Trial
How She Appeared to a Recent Visitor in Her Cell
Feels Badly Over the Talk that She Shows no Grief

"I know I am innocent, and I have made up my mind that, no matter what happens, I will try to bear it bravely and make the best of it."

The speaker was a woman. The words came slowly, and her eyes filled with tears that did not fall before they were wiped away. The woman was Lizzie Borden, who had been accused of the murder of her father, and personally has been made to appear in the eyes of the public as a monster, lacking in respect for the law, and stolid in her demeanor to such an extent that she never showed emotion at any stage of the tragedy, inquest or trial, and, as far as the Government would allow they knew, had never shown any womanly or human emotion of any sort since the public first crossed the threshold of the Borden house.

I was anxious to see if this girl, with whom I was associated several years ago in the work of the Fall River Fruit and Flower Mission, had changed her character and become a monster since the days when she used to load up the plates of vigorous young newsboys and poor children at the annual turkey dinner provided during the holidays for them and take delight in their healthy appetites.

I sought her in the Taunton Jail and found her unchanged, except that she showed traces of the great trial she has just been through. Her face was thinner, her mouth had a patient look, as if she had been schooling herself to expect and to bear any treatment, however unpleasant, and her eyes were red from the long nights of weeping. A dark shade now protects them from the glaring white light reflected from the walls of her cell.

"How do you get along here, Miss Borden?" I asked her as soon as extra chairs had been secured for the two visitors.

"To tell the truth, I am afraid it is beginning to tell on my health. This lack of fresh air and exercise is hard for me. I have always been out of doors a great deal, and that makes it harder. I cannot sleep nights now, and nothing they give me will produce sleep. If it were not for my friends I should break down, but as long as they stand by me I can bear it. They have been, with few exceptions, true to me all through it, and I appreciate it. If they had not, I don't know how I could have gone through with it. I certainly should have broken down. Some things have been unpleasant, but while every one [has] been so kind to me I ought not to think of those. Marshall Hilliard has been very gentlemanly and kind to me in every way possible.

"The hardest thing for me to stand here is the night, when there is no light. They will not allow me to have even a candle to read by, and to sit in the dark all the evening is very hard; but I do not want any favors that are against the rules. Mr. Wright and his wife are very kind to me, and try to make it easier to bear, but of course, they must do their duty.

"There is one thing that hurts me very much. They say I don't show any grief. Certainly I don't in public. I never did reveal my feelings, and I cannot change my nature now. They say I don't cry. They should see me when I am alone, or sometimes with my friends. It hurts me to think people say so about me. I have tried hard"—and Miss Borden raised her eyes to mine—"to be brave and womanly through it all. I know I am innocent, and I have made up my mind that no matter what comes to me I will try to bear it bravely and make the best of it.

"I read and sew and write. Letters are my greatest comfort and I am allowed to correspond with my friends. I find that I have a great many friends—more than I ever knew I had. I receive a great many letters of sympathy from people whom I don't even know. I try to answer them, but I cannot reply to all. Some of them are anonymous, and are so comforting that I wish the writers would sign them.

"Mrs. Ward—Elizabeth Stuart Phelps—wrote me a very sympathetic letter. Mrs. S. S. Fessenden has been a great comfort to me. She came and has told me that the Boston women were trying to get a petition signed to secure my release on bail. They tell me that is against the laws of the State, and, while I am very, very grateful to all the people who are working for me, I think perhaps it is better to stay here, but their sympathy helps to keep me up.

"I have received a great many letters from members of the W.C.T.U. and Christian Endeavor Society all over the country, and that is another help.

"It is a little thing, I suppose, but it hurt me when they said I was not willing to have my room searched. Why, I had seen so many different men that first day, and had been questioned about everything till my head was confused and in such a whirl that I could not think. I was lying down and Dr. Bowen was just preparing some medicine for me when a man came to my room and began to question me. I knew he was a policeman because he had brass buttons on his clothes. I asked the doctor:

"'Must I see all these people now? It seems as if I cannot think a moment longer, my head pains me so.'

"He went out. When he returned he said I must see them, and then the policeman came back with another man. They spoke about my mother, and that was the time I said, 'She is not my mother, but my stepmother.' I suppose, if it was necessary that I must talk to them just then, I must tell as near as I could what was right.

"As to our not putting on mourning, of which people spoke unfavorably, there was not a moment when I could think of such a thing as a hat or dress. Somebody was talking to me, it seemed, all the time about the murder and asking me questions, and I could not think of anything else. I don't suppose we would have put it on anyway, because my father was very much opposed to the practice, and had always expressed himself to us so.

"If people would only do me justice that is all I ask, but it seems as if every word I have uttered has been distorted and such a false construction placed on it that I am bewildered. I can't understand it."

There was not a trace of anger in her tones—simply a pitiful expression. She recovered herself with an effort, and we said "good-by."

Miss Borden stood in the door of her cell looking after us until we turned the corner of the corridor.

The undertaker came to one of the women in the house and said: "You cannot imagine how natural Mr. Borden looks. I think it would be a comfort to the girls to see him once more."

The lady went in, and, seeing how careful all traces of the wounds had been concealed by the undertaker's art, went to Miss Emma Borden and, explaining the condition, asked her if she cared to go down to see her father and Mrs. Borden. Miss Borden had said good-by to her father when she started on her visit to Fairhaven a week before, and it seemed to her that she preferred to always carry with her the picture of him as she saw him then. Any other would be an added grief to her.

But Miss Lizzie's case was different. Before her would always be the sight of that bloody corpse that appeared to her as she discovered her father lying dead on the sofa. If it could be replaced by some other recollection her friends thought it would be better.

When the house had become a little quiet, Lizzie, accompanied by another lady and the undertaker's assistant, went down stairs to the parlor. In the dark lay the victims of the awful murder. One woman carried a light, whose rays fell on the face of the father. The daughter looked at it earnestly.

"How old father looks," she said.

How many times have other daughters said just the same thing. New England women always think of such things.

The undertaker had washed away the blood, had smoothed out the little curl that always wound about Mr. Borden's ear, and he did look older.

"How much he looks like grandfather."

And then, releasing herself from the supporting arm of the friend, she bent over and kissed her father's cold lips. Then the tears came in a great flood, and the daughter, who had tried to bear up all day and be calm because of her sister, who was not strong and who she feared would be prostrated by the blow, broke down and almost frightened the two women with her grief.

Was that "insensibility?" Was that young woman a "sphinx of coldness?"

The reason the house was without such conveniences was that the girls desired Mr. Borden not to make improvements, because he was talking of moving up "on the hill." Fall River's aristocracy live "on the hill," and Mr. Borden had declared to real estate agents that he was looking for a house in that section and that, although he would just as soon live in the old house, the girls desired to move and he wanted to gratify them.

He said that over a year ago to a well-known real estate agent, who had it in mind and was looking for a bargain for him.

More than that, he had offered $15,000 for a handsome house on Main street, that had just been sold, and found that his namesake, a prominent mill Treasurer, was also trying to buy it for the same sum. He told him if the younger man would get certain land at a bargain he would take half of it, and the two Andrew Bordens would build houses alike and live side by side. This was a few months ago. Naturally any one who contemplated buying a new house and removing to it would not fix up his old house, which was in a district of tenements, as he would if he intended to remain in it.

When Mr. Borden wanted to put in modern improvements, the wife and daughters said they preferred to stand it rather than have the house torn up for piping.

This does not indicate that Lizzie Borden's father was niggardly in his dealings with his family, thereby arousing the girl's indignation and supplying her with a motive for a brutal murder.

They have also tried to urge as a motive that she was kept on a mere pittance, had no spending money nor even enough for necessities, and that she was hard pressed to pay her pew rent sometimes. The fact is that both Emma and Lizzie Borden had more money than they knew how to spend. Their bank books show that they not only had $2500 in cash each, the proceeds of the sale of the old Borden homestead to their father, but Lizzie had mill and other stocks in her own name. The average dividends on mill stocks in Fall River for the past five years was over 8 per cent. Lizzie did not dress poorly. She had handsome cloth gowns and silk dresses and a fine seal sacque. She had just such an outfit as any young woman in her position had who did not try to keep ahead of the fashions. Everything she wore was of fine material. She took trips whenever she pleased. Her father, a few years ago, on the return of his namesake's family from Europe, expressed his regret that he hadn't known of it in time, as the girls wanted to go to Europe and he would have been glad to send them with the Bordens. When Miss Borden did go two years ago she did not have to sell property to secure funds.

In arranging entertainments in the church or for charitable purposes, if there was any especial expense to be borne, it was always assumed by Lizzie Borden. If there was any discrepancy in footing up the results, it was she who made it up. When she bought anything the order was always for the best material and accompanied by the injunction not to spare any cost. She was not extravagant, however.

That she had plenty of money and to spare is shown by the addition she had been making regularly every month to her bank account. It is evident that lack of money could never have supplied a motive in this case.

New York Recorder interview
September 20, 1892

QUESTIONS FOR DISCUSSION AND WRITING

1. Some critics have argued that this news article is fraudulent. Looking at evidence from the article, would you suspect the news story is a fake or based on a real interview? Why?
2. After reading the article, did your sense of Lizzie Borden change? Why or why not? What does the interview suggest about her character? About whether such a person would be likely to commit such a crime?
3. In addition to presenting the interview with Borden, the article answers some of the claims made in the case, particularly about Lizzie's lack of emotion and her father's miserliness. Does the article refute those claims to your satisfaction? How important are those claims to a determination of Lizzie Borden's innocence or guilt?

Will Go to the Jury To-Day

Last Words For Lizzie Borden Spoken by Her Counsel

Ex.-Gov. Robinson Pleads in Her Behalf that the State's Case has Fallen to Pieces—Many Disappointed in His Address, Which Is Almost

Bare of Eloquence—District Attorney Knowlton Started on a Powerful Argument for the Prosecution—He will Finish This Morning.

NEW-BEDFORD, MASS., June 19— In the presence of an audience that so filled the courtroom that it would have been hard to squeeze in another person, ex-Gov. Robinson spoke the last words of the defense to the jury that is trying Lizzie Borden on a charge of murder. He spoke for four hours.

Many who heard him were disappointed. They had expected an eloquent address; what they heard was a calm analysis of the evidence. The argument was that the State had failed to prove its case, and that the defendant had established her innocence.

District Attorney Knowlton began his reply. He will finish it to-morrow morning. So far as he has gone he has spoken with great force and eloquence. It is expected that the case will go to the jury as early as 1 o'clock to-morrow afternoon.

Mr. Robinson began by characterizing the murders as one of the most dastardly and diabolical crimes ever committed in the State.

"A maniac, not a man of senses and heart, a lunatic, a devil.

"They were well directed blows which caused those deaths, not directed by a blunder; none going amiss. Surely we can say at the outset that this was not the careless, untrained doing of one unfamiliar with such work.

"As you begin to contemplate this crime you must say such acts are physically and morally impossible for this young woman. It is a wreck of human morals to say this of her."

Mr. Robinson disclaimed upon the part of the defendant any feelings that she had not been fairly treated by the District Attorney. That officer, he said, was not after blood, but was simply presenting to the jury the case which had been given to him by the Fall River police.

Referring to these men, Mr. Robinson said:

"I have not time to go into sarcasm and denunciation. The blue coat and brass buttons cover up what is inside. The officer is always magnifying this and minimizing that and looking for the one who committed the deed upon which he is at work. The witness stand brings out their weakness when they knock their own heads together, but after all they show themselves to be only men with human weakness."

Urging the jury to confine itself solely to the question of the guilt or innocence of the accused, Mr. Robinson said:

"It is not your business to unravel the mystery, but simply to say whether this woman is guilty—that's all, and, though the real criminal shall never be found, better that than that you should find a wrong verdict. Not who did it, how could it have been done, but did she do it?

"You must not think for a moment that this defendant is set for the finding out of who did it. She is not a detective, and she has been in jail for nine months under constant control from the very day almost of the murders.

"Don't ask her to do impossible things, to do what she can't do; the Commonwealth doesn't want any victims, either; in olden days sacrifices were offered, but in these days we don't even hang witches in Massachusetts. I ask only that you be true to yourselves.

"Under the laws of this State the defendant is permitted to testify on the stand if she desires, but if she does not the statutes say no inference will be drawn as to her action, and the District Attorney will not insult this Court by referring to this in the slightest degree. The law holds that it is too great a strain to put on a defendant to put him on the stand in such cases, and you will not, as you go to your room, depart from this understanding. You must leave out rumors, reports, statements which you heard before the trial commenced, and leave out every single thing which Mr. Moody said he was going to prove unless he did it.

"They were going to prove that this young lady went out to buy poison, but it was not proved. It was not allowed, and I shall expect the District Attorney to get up and say so or I shall be disappointed in him.

"They were going to show you the defendant had contradicted herself, but the court said this was not proper.

"Now, you are not going to say, 'I rather think Messrs. Knowlton and Moody would not have offered this if they had not proof.' That won't do. Decide the case from the evidence on the witness stand and nothing else. So you will leave those things out. No poison, no instrument prepared, no statement made under oath by her that you know anything about, I don't care what you have read.

"It is for us to see whether the defendant or she and accomplices did the deed. There sits the defendant. She comes here under the presumption of innocence, and you must bind her to the axe before you can change this. The chain of direct proof only can show you that she is tied up to this thing.

"There is absolutely no direct evidence against her. Nobody saw, heard, or experienced anything to connect her with the tragedy. No knowledge or use of any instrument has been shown, and it is not shown that she ever touched one, knew of one, or bought one—in fact, the testimony is that she did not know where such things were in the house.

"And the murders told no tale through her. Not a spot on her from her dress to her hair. Yes, there was one on the white skirt—one as big as the head of a pin—and that's every spot of blood that was found on her clothing, and that was on the back of her skirt, although the Government may say she turned her skirt around before she commenced. But nobody claims now that that flyspeck tells any tale.

"Then, there was some talk about a roll of burned paper. That was found by Mr. Harrington, and there were some dark insinuations floating around that Dr. Bowen knew something about it. We thought that the Government was going to claim that the hatchet handle was in that paper, and that the wood had all burned out and left the envelope, and we worried about this until Mullaly and Fleet got here together. Now we know the orphan handle is still flying in the air. For Heaven's sake, get the 125 policemen of Fall River to chase it up and put it where it belongs.

"Now," continued Mr. Robinson, "you are to conceive of the murderer standing over the woman on the floor, and you are to consider how Mr. Borden was slain. Now, what reason is there to consider this defendant guilty? What right have they to say she is?

"Well, first they say she was in the house. Well, that may be the wrong place for her to be, because it is her own home; perhaps it might be better for her to be traveling the streets, but I don't think so. She was in her room when they say Mrs. Borden's body was lying on the floor and that she must have seen the body, but you know you can't stand on the landing and look into the guest chamber.

"Then there is not the slightest evidence that the door was opened at that time, but there is evidence that it was opened later. She had no occasion to go into that spare room. You know that from the habits of the family.

"Now, you know that after the tragedy she told Bridget that Mrs. Borden had a note and had gone out. Now, Mr. Moody said in his opening that Lizzie told a lie about this, but Bridget told the fullest and clearest story about it, and holds it down to herself. There is no doubt she did have a note and she did go out. Now, a person may say, where is the note? We would be glad to see it. They say nobody has come forward to say where it went, but you will find men in the county now who don't know this trial is going on. This note may have been part of a scheme, a foul scheme. We don't know. But that Lizzie lied about it is not so.

"Now, did she go to the barn?" queried Mr. Robinson, coming to his next point. "There comes along an ice cream peddler. Not a distinguished lawyer nor a successful doctor, simply an ice cream peddler, but he knows the nature of an oath, and he saw this woman coming down the yard. He told this story on the 8th of August to the police, and they had it all in their possession. Mr. Mullaly, one of the knights of the handle, you know, says that the peddler said he went down there at 10:30, but Mullaly was contradicted by his own associate."

Mr. Robinson went on from this point to discuss the various allegations of the State as to his client's conduct just before and just after the discovery of the murders. He contended that in these times Miss Borden's behavior was that of an innocent person, and that no inference could be drawn from her acts, her speech, or her appearance favorable to the theory that she committed the murders.

"Then," said Mr. Robinson, "they say she burned the dress. The first thought is that when a person burns up anything in such a case as this an inference is drawn the wrong way as such. But you know the common way now is to burn rags, because you have got to pay the ragman something to take them away. Now the Government says, 'We want the Bedford cord and you have burned it; we want the dress you had on that morning and you have given us another one.'

"Now, there is a difference of opinion among the witnesses about the dress Lizzie wore on that morning. Bridget Sullivan had on a light blue dress that morning and the Government says Lizzie had on a light blue dress, but they were not looking for dress patterns then, and there is likely to have been a difference of opinion. You know that when the people came in at first they saw that she had not a drop of blood on her or about her anywhere.

"Now you start with a dress that every one says there was no blood on it. That dress was in that closet on the shelf, and there it remained until it was burned. Seaver and Fleet say they looked carefully in that place and could find no dress with blood on it. And Emma found that old dress there when she came home, taking up a place she wanted to use.

"But they found another dress and Dr. Dolan discovered the damning evidence, for there was blood on it. But when the dress went into the hands of a man who knew something, Prof. Wood, the dress came back, for there was no blood, and they wanted another one.

"Talk about burning an old dress! Why, it didn't cost altogether over $2. Then the police got everything they could and notified the family that they had got all through, and on Sunday morning, with the windows open, with people about, in broad daylight, she burns this old dress. Couldn't she have disposed of it more easily in a different and more secret manner?

"They will say she changed it, or that she put it under another. If she put on another, then she burned two dresses instead of one, and the Government only wants one. They will go another step in their theory and claim this woman was nude when she committed this crime."

Speaking of the shifting by the State from one hatchet to another, Mr. Robinson said:

"Fall River seems to be prolific of hatchets. If we wait a while we may find another. If we had gone to trial with the cow's hair theory when it was ripe last Fall, the prisoner might have been beyond our reach now. They have had her for ten months in irksome and wearisome and wearing control. She has been in the custody of the State, in a place to which her home was a palace by comparison. You think, gentlemen, you feel the hand of the old Commonwealth guiding you, but you do not; it is a fraud, a theory.

"Murder is bad enough, but murder at the hands of theorizing experts or practicing officers is worse."

Turning to the matter of "exclusive opportunity," Mr. Robinson said:

"They have had all sorts of theories and have abandoned them all. They say they will prove exclusive opportunity. But I say if they can lock up that house to the exclusion of everybody but the two girls, then I am willing to admit that there is strong evidence against the defendant, but it is not so.

"Let us see. The cellar door was locked, sure. The front door is said to have been locked by a bolt, a spring lock, and one other, but we don't know that. The side screen door was not locked—that we are sure of, and there was a perfect entrance to that house by that side screen door. Bridget was outside talking with the Kelley girl and said frankly anybody could have gone in."

Mr. Robinson then took the jury through the house and detailed to them how easily a man could get into the house and secrete himself until such time as he chose to show himself. Admitting such a person was there for murder, there was no reason, he said, why he should allow a second person to interfere with him in his design. He contended that a person could have come in at the front door or the side door at various times that morning.

"The Government says nobody saw any one go in," he added. "That is true, but nobody saw Mr. Borden go out."

Recurring to the matter of the absence of blood from Miss Borden's clothing and person, Mr. Robinson said:

"A significant fact is that there was no blood on her hair, because since there was none found on her the efforts to remove it must have caused a great deal of trouble. It is assumed that she committed that first murder, and what had she to do when her father came in. Why, she must have washed herself and changed her clothes, so as to be all right when her father came, and she undoubtedly was all right when her father came.

"Bridget Sullivan, you remember, does not speak of any changes in dress all the morning, so you must have her come down in the blue dress, get out of it, get in it again, and make several changes in a very brief time.

"She would have to get the bloody dress off a second time, or else use the second bloody dress. But how is the theory of the Government to be accounted for, since there is no other dress missing but the one with the paint on it, and there was no blood on it?

"In order to fit in on the handleless hatchet theory she must go down, wash the handle, break it in two, and go beyond scientific work to get all the blood from the handle. Have I said too much when I say it was a moral and a physical impossibility for her to do all this work of hiding clues in so short a time?"

Mr. Robinson closed with the appeal to the jury to decide the case upon the evidence and deal fairly and justly by his client.

District Attorney Knowlton replied for the State. He said that the jury was trying a crime which would have been believed impossible, and was trying a woman who it would never have been believed would have been charged with the crime.

"But," said Mr. Knowlton, "it was found that these men over in Fall River who went wrong a few years ago were members of a church, and it was demonstrated that those who stand close to the sanctuary are not free from the taint of sin. It is not for me to sneer at Christians; they are all sons of Adam and are but human. They fall all the surer that their reputation has been spotless before. I don't say that because a person has led an honest and upright life therefore he or she is more susceptible to error.

"But she is a woman and it is hard to believe that women can be guilty of crime. It is not a pleasant thing to say, but they are human and no better or no worse than we. They make up for lack of strength in cunning, their hates are more undying, more unyielding, and their passions stronger. The foremost of the murderers of the early ages were women, and they have come down to these times even.

"Over those bodies we stand and we say to ourselves: Can it be possible? This is the most solemn duty of your lives."

Mr. Knowlton said that the distinguishing feature of the case was that the murdered persons did not meet their deaths at the same time.

"That," said he, "is the key of the case. It was the malice against Mrs. Borden that inspired this murder. It was the act of a person who spent the forenoon in that house, and this fact bears on this case from beginning to end."

Having made this premise, Mr. Knowlton coupled with it the assertion, which, he said, was backed by the evidence, that there was ill feeling between Lizzie Borden and her stepmother.

"There was one woman in the world," said he, "who believed that old woman stood between her father and herself. There was nothing in those blows but hatred, and a great strong man would have taken that hatchet and with one blow only would have made an end of it. The arm that wielded that hatchet was strong only in hatred.

"When that woman fell under the blows—the 200-pound woman—the fall must have been heard by whoever was in the house at the time. If Lizzie was down stairs she was in the passageway of the assassin; if she was up stairs she was on the same floor, quite near, and she could not have helped hearing it. No matter how craftily murder is planned there is always some point where the plans fail, and they failed her at a critical time.

"She was alone in the house with that murdered woman. She must have known it, and she knew that by and by there was coming into the house a stern and just man who would have noticed the absence of his beloved wife and who would have asked for her, and that question must be answered.

"He came in and she went to him and said: 'Mother has had a note and has gone out.' When Bridget got through her work Lizzie told her that she was going to lock the screen door, as Mrs. Borden had gone out and she might go out, too. Counsel on the other side said this statement was not a lie, but there was no note. There never was anybody sick, and the note story originated with Lizzie Borden. Bridget Sullivan said she never heard anybody come with a note. She never saw any note, and the first she heard of it was what Lizzie said."

Before Mr. Knowlton could elaborate his theory and connect the killing of Mr. Borden with that of Mrs. Borden court adjourned until to-morrow.

The New York Times
June 20, 1893

QUESTIONS FOR DISCUSSION AND WRITING

1. How convincing is Robinson's defense of Borden? What are the strongest elements in his case? The weakest?
2. The article states near the beginning that many were disappointed by Robinson's statement, feeling it was not "eloquent" enough. Would a more eloquent speech have been more effective? Why or why not? Putting aside the question of the evidence itself, how effective is Robinson's speech rhetorically?
3. In his statement, Knowlton tries to answer the claim that a Christian woman would be incapable of such a murder. How successful is the answer he provides?
4. Before the adjournment, Knowlton began his examination of the evidence. How persuasive is his interpretation of the facts?
5. If you had been a member of the jury, at this point would you have found Robinson's or Knowlton's statement more convincing? Why?

'Guilty—No! No!'
Lizzie Borden's Sister Breaks 20 Year Silence
Tells the Sunday Post of Past and Present Relations With Lizzie

by Edwin J. Maguire

"Queer? Yes, Lizzie was queer, but guilty on that terrible charge made against her—no—emphatically, No. Time and again she has avowed her innocence to me, and I believe her."

Never was the adage "Blood is thicker than water" more strikingly exemplified than in this defence of Lizzie Borden, Fall River's woman of tragedy, uttered by her sister, Emma Borden to the Sunday Post.

Though an estrangement has held a wall of silence between the two sisters for eight years, kinship's ties spurred white-haired, gentle-faced Emma Borden to serve notice on the public at large, through the medium of the Sunday Post, that she believed her sister to be innocent, as declared by a jury in 1893.

And her statement is the first declaration to the outside world that either sister has made regarding that most notable murder mystery—a butchery on which the faintest light is yet to be shed.

For 20 years the Bordens have maintained a sphinx-like attitude toward the treatment accorded the acquitted woman by the world in general and Fall River in particular. Doors of old-time family friends were closed to her following her trial on the charge of murdering Andrew J. Borden, one of the city's wealthiest citizens, and his second wife.

Acquittal Greeted Coolly

A jury's declaration that she was guiltless sent no wave of jubilation over the community where Lizzie Borden was born, where she had been prominent in church and social affairs, and where she had spent her entire life. Congratulations were not showered upon her by those who had been her intimate acquaintances before the trial.

Instead, the frigidity of an Arctic temperature displaced the pleasantries she had formerly known from life-long friends.

Eight years ago, Emma Borden quit the spacious mansion in the French street section of the exclusive "hill district" where she and Lizzie Borden were residing, and established her home with friends. Her seeking, in this way, another home caused the estrangement between the sisters. Since Emma Borden's departure they have never met or communicated with each other. . . .

At first she was disinclined to talk of the subject. Then the Borden blood came into its own, and she cast aside the reserve of 20 years to take up the cudgels for Lizzie Borden.

Difference between Sisters

And her doing so presented a forcible illustration of the contradistinctive natures of the Borden sisters.

Previously, the Sunday Post reporter had visited the splendid 14-room house where Lizzie Borden lives with her four servants, two bull terriers and three cats of the ordinary back-fence variety.

Access to the house was not allowed. The shades were drawn in all of the windows of the stately structure, the massive oak doors both in the front and rear remained securely bolted and the atmosphere of the place was one of decided seclusion. Repeated ringing of front and rear bells and knocking the various doors brought no answer. The caller might as well have tried to gain response from a tomb.

The only signs of life came from two of Lizzie Borden's pet squirrels that were playing havoc with a pile of peanuts she had placed under a tree near the house.

Heads that quickly appeared at the windows of the sightly dwellings of the neighborhood gave indication of the interest taken in happenings in and around the Borden house.

But shortly after leaving the Borden estate, the Post man utilized the telephone. This time there came a response. The maid who answered summoned Lizzie Borden to the telephone.

"Nothing to say," exclaimed Miss Borden in a strong calm voice, after a request for an interview had been made.

On being urged further she fairly shouted: "Nothing, absolutely nothing to say." Then came a decisive "bang" as she slammed the receiver back on the hook. Thus ended the conversation.

But at the residence of the late Rev. E. A. Buck, where Miss Emma Borden is making her home with the Misses Buck, the reception of the Sunday Post man contrasted with the French street visit, just as the characters of the sisters are diametrically opposite.

Lizzie Borden is now 53 years of age and is regarded by some as a woman with iron will, whose apparent disregard for the none too pleasant attention paid her when she ventures abroad is due to her phlegmatic, impassive temperament. There came no sign of emotion from her during the trial. Fall River residents say she has not given any indication of overwrought nerves in the years that have followed.

Gentle-Mannered Sister

But in Emma Borden the writer met a gentle-mannered woman, who unhesitatingly led the way from the front portal of the Buck residence to the quaint parlor at the left. She was courtesy and gentility personified.

Her tranquil face, sweet of expression and enhanced by a pink and white complexion that a debutante might well envy, was crowned with heavy, snow white hair, parted in the center and rippling to the side of the head in curly billows.

There was a look of sadness, even of resignation in Miss Borden's large brown eyes. They seemed to reflect the sorrow and grief that were part of the heritage she received through the untimely death of her father.

A gray dress, rich in material, but unostentatious in style, bespoke the quiet, retiring character of the woman. With its wide flaring skirt and old-fashioned lace trimmings, the costume impressed one as a refined rebuke to the hobble, and other "latest" modes of femininity.

The parlor in which the Post representative interviewed Miss Borden, seemed consecrated to the memory of the Rev. Mr. Buck, who was one of the most beloved clergymen in Fall River, and who, by Emma Borden's own statement, was "my best friend in the world, the one who advised me when matters reached such a pass that I could not stay longer in the same house with Lizzie."

On the walls of the room, which during the Rev. Mr. Buck's lifetime had served as his study, hung framed scriptural texts and religious paintings. One of the latter was "The Last Supper." Another art work dealt with angels and cherubs. On tables and shelves were religious volumes and pamphlets. The chairs and couch were in solid, old-fashioned type, whose faded buff covering did not detract one bit from a comfortable appearance.

Like a Frightful Dream

"The tragedy seems but yesterday, and many times I catch myself wondering whether it is not some frightful dream, after all," said Miss Borden. . . . "Often it had occurred to me how strange is the fact that no one save Lizzie was ever brought to trial for the killing of our father and our mother-in-law. [i.e., stepmother—Eds.]

"Some persons have stated that for years they considered Lizzie's actions decidedly queer.

"But what if she did act queerly? Don't we all do something peculiar at some time or other?

"Queer? Yes, Lizzie is queer. But as for her being guilty, I say 'No,' and decidedly 'No.'

"The day the crime took place I was at Fairhaven on a visit to friends, I hurried home in response to a telegram, and one of the first persons I met was Lizzie. She was very much affected.

"Later, when veiled accusations began to be made, she came to me and said:

"'Emma, it is awful for them to say that I killed poor father and our stepmother. You know that I would not dream of such an awful thing, Emma.'

"Later, after her arrest and during her trial, Lizzie many times reiterated her protest of innocence to me.

"And after her acquittal she declared her guiltlessness during conversations that we had at the French street mansion.

Proof of Innocence

"Here is the strongest thing that has convinced me of Lizzie's innocence. The authorities never found the axe or whatever implement it was that figured in the killing.

"Lizzie, if she had done that deed, could never have hidden the instrument of death so that the police could not find it.

Why, there was no hiding place in the old house that would serve for effectual concealment. Neither did she have the time.

"Another thing to be remembered is Lizzie's affection for dumb animals. She fairly dotes on the dogs, cats and squirrels that are at the French street mansion. She always was fond of pets. Now, any person with a heart like that could never have committed the awful act for which Lizzie was tried and of which she was acquitted.

"I did my duty at the trial when I sat with Lizzie day after day and then testified for her. And despite our estrangement, I am going to do my duty in answering the cruel slanders that have been made against her both in public print and by gossiping persons who seem to take delight in saying cruel things about her.

"The happenings at the French street house that caused me to leave I must refuse to talk about. I did not go until conditions became absolutely unbearable. Then, before taking action, I consulted the Rev. A. E. Buck. . . .

"After carefully listening to my story he said it was imperative that I should make my home elsewhere.

"Before going, I had an agreement drawn up by our lawyer so that no trouble could arise regarding the French street house.

"Although the general public believes that Lizzie owns that house, such is not the case. It is our joint property, and so is the land it stands on. Under the agreement we entered into, Lizzie is to occupy the house as long as she lives, and is to pay me rent for the use of my half of the estate. Lizzie is the sole owner of land she added to the original estate.

"I do not expect ever to set foot on the place while she lives.

Mother's Dying Request

"Perhaps people wondered why I stood so staunchly by Lizzie during the trial. I'll tell them why. Aside from my feeling as a sister, it was because I constantly had in mind our dear mother. She died when Lizzie was only 3 years of age, while I had reached 12 years.

"When my darling mother was on her deathbed she summoned me, and exacted a promise that I would always watch over 'baby Lizzie.'

"From childhood to womanhood and up to the time the murder occurred, I tried to safeguard Lizzie.

"And although it is not generally known, the obligation imposed on me by my mother impelled me to assume as a duty the payment of one-half the costs of that murder trial. Of course, the expenses of such a case were very heavy. I stipulated before the trial was entered upon that I should pay one-half the costs, and I insisted on fulfilling my promise, after everything was over.

"I did my duty at the time of the trial, and I am still going to do it in defending my sister even though circumstances have separated us.

"The vision of my dear mother always is bright in my mind. I want to feel that when Mother and I meet in the hereafter, she will tell me that I was faithful to her trust and that I looked after 'baby Lizzie' to the best of my ability."

At this point of the interview, the emotion which Miss Borden had plainly repressed at times by sheer will power would be denied no longer.

Overcome with Grief

Her soft even tones dropped almost to a moan. Then utterance was checked absolutely. Convulsive sobs shook the form of Lizzie Borden's "little mother."

Abruptly arising from her low rocking chair, Miss Borden slowly paced to and fro, while she pressed a black bordered handkerchief against her face.

For several minutes the paroxysm of grief continued. Then the little figure straightened slowly to dignified posture, the remaining traces of tears were removed by soft dabs of the handkerchief, and Miss Borden became quite herself once more.

"Yes," she resumed slowly, but with clear articulation. "I intend to defend Lizzie against the harsh public so that mother will say I have been faithful to my trust.

"I have been told of the unjust stories that have appeared in print. Right here in Fall River, is a newspaper that year after year, on the anniversary of the crime, publishes what I consider a most uncalled for review of the case. Just what the purpose of this practice is I do not know.

"One of the stories that has been going the rounds in connection with my sister deals with Nance O'Neil, the actress.

"This report is to the effect that Nance O'Neil met my sister in another city, became intimately acquainted with her, and maintained this friendliness until she discovered that the Lizbeth Borden she knew was none other than Lizzie Borden, the woman who had been tried on a charge of murder.

"I know such a tale to be absolutely unfounded. Nance O'Neil has for years been a close friend of Lizzie, and she holds that relation to this very day.

"Another wild rumor has to do with the family fortune. Someone, who knows more about the Borden estate than I and my sister do, has declared that our combined wealth would go over the million mark.

"Now here is the truth in respect to that. If all the property that we own jointly should, through our lawyers, be turned into cash, the total amount of our worldly possessions would not go beyond one-quarter of a million dollars. That is a large amount of money, but is certainly less than a million.

"Some of the neighbors in and around French street who have criticised Lizzie so freely have not treated her as fairly as they might in certain things—matters of business, I mean.

"Some unkind persons have spread the report that my father, despite his great wealth was niggardly and that he refused to even give us sufficient to eat.

"That is a wicked lie. He was a plain-mannered man, but his table was always laden with the best that the market could afford.

"Every Memorial Day I carry flowers to father's grave. And Lizzie does not forget him. But she generally sends her tribute by a florist."

At this juncture, Miss Borden requested to be excused from further conversation.

As she slowly conducted the Post man to the door, she murmured, as if to herself:

"Yes, a jury declared Lizzie to be innocent, but an unkind world has unrelentingly persecuted her. I am still the little mother and though we must live as strangers, I will defend 'Baby Lizzie' against merciless tongues."

Sunday Post
April 13, 1913

QUESTIONS FOR DISCUSSION AND WRITING

1. In this article, we learn a great deal about the homes Emma and Lizzie live in. What do the descriptive details suggest about the sisters and their relationship? How do the author's different receptions at the two houses affect our responses to the sisters?

2. Emma insists that Lizzie is innocent of the murder, yet she also says that she will not visit her in the house they own together. Does that unwillingness to live with Lizzie or to visit her suggest that Emma believes Lizzie to be guilty? Why or why not?

3. Given the language he uses and the selection of details, does the author of the article seem to suggest Lizzie's guilt or innocence? Or is the article neutral? Support your view with details from the article.

FLORENCE KING (1936–   )

A Wasp Looks at Lizzie Borden _____ 1992

The murders of Andrew and Abby Borden on August 4, 1892, are the stuff of doggerel and legend. They also provide a case study of an overcivilized, understated segment of America's gorgeous mosaic.

If you want to understand Anglo-Saxon Americans, study the Lizzie Borden case. No ethnologist could ask for a better control group; except for Bridget Sullivan, the Bordens' maid, the zany tragedy of August 4, 1892, had an all-Wasp cast.

Lizzie was born in Fall River, Massachusetts, on July 19, 1860, and immediately given the Wasp family's favorite substitute for open affection: a nickname. Thirty-two years later at her inquest she stated her full legal name: Lizzie Andrew Borden. "You were so christened?" asked the district attorney.

"I was so christened," she replied.

Lizzie's mother died in 1862. Left with two daughters to raise, her father, Andrew Borden, soon married a chubby spinster of 38 named Abby Durfee Gray. Three-year-old Lizzie obediently called the new wife Mother, but 12-year-old Emma called her Abby.

Andrew Borden was a prosperous but miserly undertaker whose sole interest in life was money. His operations expanded to include banking, cotton mills, and real estate, but no matter how rich he became he never stopped peddling eggs from his farms to his downtown business associates; wicker basket in hand, he would set out for corporate board meetings in anticipation of yet a few more pennies. Although he was worth $500,000 in pre–IRS, gold-standard dollars, he was so tightfisted that he refused to install running water in his home. There was a latrine in the cellar and a pump in the kitchen; the bedrooms were fitted out with water pitchers, wash bowls, chamber pots, and slop pails.

Marriage with this paragon of Yankee thrift evidently drove Abby to seek compensatory emotional satisfaction in eating. Only five feet tall, she ballooned up to more than two hundred pounds and seldom left the house except to visit her half-sister, Mrs. Whitehead.

Emma Borden, Lizzie's older sister, was 42 at the time of the murders. Mouse-like in all respects, she was one of those spinsters who scurry. Other than doing the marketing, she rarely went anywhere except around the corner to visit her friend, another spinster named Alice Russell.

Compared to the rest of her family, Lizzie comes through as a prom queen. Never known to go out with men, at least she went out. A member of Central Congregational, she taught Sunday school, served as secretary-treasurer of the Christian Endeavor Society, and was a card-carrying member of the Women's Christian Temperance Union.

What did she look like? Like everyone else in that inbred Wasp town. *New York Sun* reporter Julian Ralph wrote during the trial:

> By the way, the strangers who are here begin to notice that Lizzie Borden's face is of a type quite common in New Bedford. They meet Lizzie Borden every day and everywhere about town. Some are fairer, some are younger, some are

coarser, but all have the same general cast of features—heavy in the lower face, high in the cheekbones, wide at the eyes, and with heavy lips and a deep line on each side of the mouth.

Plump by our standards, she had what her self-confident era called a good figure. She also had blue eyes, and like all blue-eyed women she had a lot of blue dresses—handy for changing clothes without appearing to have done so. The case is a vortex of dark blue dresses, light blue dresses, blue summer dresses, blue winter dresses, clean blue dresses, paint-stained blue dresses, blood-stained blue dresses, and an all-male jury struggling to tell one from the other.

Five years before the murders, the Bordens had a family fight when Andrew put one of his rental houses in Abby's name. Lizzie and Emma were furious, so they said politely: "What you do for her, you must do for us." That's the Wasp version of a conniption and Andrew knew it, so he took refuge in our cure-all fair play, buying his daughters houses of identical valuation ($1,500) to the one he had given his wife.

Now they were even-steven and everything was settled—except it wasn't. Having failed to clear the air, everyone started smoldering and brooding. Emma and Lizzie stopped eating with the elder Bordens, requiring the maid to set and serve each meal twice. They never reached that pinnacle of Wasp rage called Not Speaking—"We always *spoke*," Emma emphasized at the trial—but she and Lizzie eliminated "Abby" and "Mother" from their respective vocabularies and started calling their stepmother "Mrs. Borden." What a cathartic release that must have been.

Lizzie ticked away for four years until 1891, when she committed a family robbery. Entering the master bedroom through a door in her own room (it was a "shotgun" house with no hallways), she stole her stepmother's jewelry and her father's loose cash.

Andrew and Abby knew that Lizzie was the culprit, and Lizzie knew that they knew, but rather than "have words," Andrew called in the police and let them go through an investigation to catch the person the whole family carefully referred to as "the unknown thief."

The robbery launched a field day of Silent Gestures. Everybody quietly bought lots of locks. To supplement the key locks, there were bolts, hooks, chains, and padlocks. Abby's Silent Gesture consisted of locking and bolting her side of the door that led into Lizzie's room. Lizzie responded with her Silent Gesture, putting a hook on her side of the door and shoving a huge clawfooted secretary in front of it.

The best Silent Gesture was Andrew's. He put the strongest available lock on the master bedroom, but kept the key on the sitting-room mantelpiece in full view of everyone. Lizzie knew she was being tempted to touch it; she also knew that if the key disappeared, she would be suspect. In one fell swoop, Andrew made it clear that he was simultaneously trusting her and distrusting her, and warning her without saying a word. Wasps call this war of nerves the honor system.

Since Emma *was* a Silent Gesture, there was no need for her to do anything except keep on scurrying.

The Borden house must have been a peaceful place. There is nothing on record to show that the Bordens ever raised their voices to one another. "Never a word," Bridget Sullivan testified at the trial, with obvious sincerity and not a little awe.

Bridget, 26 and pretty in a big-boned, countrified way, had been in the Bordens' service for almost three years at the time of the murders. A recent immigrant, she had a brogue so thick that she referred to the Silent Gesture on the mantelpiece as the "kay."

Bridget adored Lizzie. Victoria Lincoln, the late novelist, whose parents were neighbors of the Bordens, wrote in her study of the case: "*De haut en bas*, Lizzie was always kind." Her habit of calling Bridget "Maggie" has been attributed to laziness (Maggie was the name of a former maid), but I think it was an extremity of tact. In that time and place, the name Bridget was synonymous with "Irish maid." Like Rastus in minstrel-show jokes, it was derisory, so Lizzie substituted another.

Anyone who studies the Borden case grows to like Lizzie, or at least admire her, for her rigid sense of herself as a gentlewoman. It would have been so easy for her to cast suspicion on Bridget, or to accuse her outright. Bridget was the only other person in the house when Andrew and Abby were killed. The Irish were disliked in turn-of-the-century Massachusetts; a Yankee jury would have bought the idea of Bridget's guilt. Yet Lizzie never once tried to shift the blame, and she never named Bridget as a suspect.

Scurrying Away

A week before the murders, Emma did something incredible: she went to Fairhaven. Fifteen miles is a long way to scurry but scurry she did, to visit an elderly friend and escape the heat wave that had descended on Fall River.

That same week, Lizzie shared a beach house on Buzzards Bay with five friends. At a press conference after the murders, they showered her with compliments. "She always was self-contained, self-reliant, and very composed. Her conduct since her arrest is exactly what I should have expected. Lizzie and her father were, without being demonstrative, very fond of each other."

They got so caught up in Wasp priorities that they inadvertently sowed a dangerous seed when the reporter asked them if they thought Lizzie was guilty. No, they said firmly, because she had pleaded *not* guilty. "It is more likely that Lizzie would commit a murder than that she would lie about it afterward."

The most puzzling aspect of the case has always been Lizzie's choice of weapons. Ladies don't chop up difficult relatives, but they do poison them. A few days before she was due at the beach house, Lizzie tried to buy prussic acid in her neighborhood drugstore. The druggist's testimony was excluded on a legal technicality, but it establishes her as, in the words of one of her friends, "a monument of straightforwardness."

Picture it: In broad daylight in the middle of a heat wave, she marched into the drugstore carrying a fur cape, announced that there were moths in it, and asked for ten cents' worth of prussic acid to kill them. The druggist was stunned. Even in the casual Nineties, when arsenic was sold over the counter, it was illegal to sell prussic acid. "But I've bought it many times before," Lizzie protested.

The druggist's astonishment mounted in the face of this stouthearted lie. "Well, my good lady, it is something we don't sell except by prescription, as it is a very dangerous thing to handle."

Lizzie left, never dreaming that she might have called attention to herself.

At the beach, her friends noticed that she seemed despondent and preoccupied. They were puzzled when she suddenly cut short her vacation, giving as her excuse some church work, and returned to Fall River.

Back home in the stifling city heat, she sat in her room and brooded. Somehow she had found out that Abby was about to acquire some more real estate; Andrew was planning to put a farm in his wife's name and install his brother-in-law, John Morse, as caretaker. This last was especially infuriating, for Lizzie and Emma were Not Speaking to Uncle John. He had been involved, so they thought, in that other real-estate transfer five years before. Now he was back, plotting to do her and Emma out of their rightful inheritance.

Something had to be done, but what? Lacking ladylike poison, Lizzie did what every overcivilized, understated Wasp is entirely capable of doing once we finally admit we're mad as hell and aren't going to take it any more: She went from Anglo to Saxon in a trice.

Miss Borden Accepts

On the day before the murders, Lizzie joined Abby and Andrew for lunch for the first time in five years—an air-tight alibi, for who would do murder after doing lunch?

That evening, she paid a call on Alice Russell and craftily planted some red herrings. If Machiavelli had witnessed this demonstration of the fine Wasp hand he would have gone into cardiac arrest.

"I have a feeling that something is going to happen," she told Alice. "A feeling that somebody is going to do something." She hammered the point home with stories about her father's "enemies." He was such a ruthless businessman, she said, that "they" all hated him, and she would not put it past "them" to burn down the house.

When she returned home, Uncle John had arrived with plans to spend the night. Since she was Not Speaking to him, she went directly to her room.

The next day, August 4, 1892, the temperature was already in the eighties at sunrise, but that didn't change the Bordens' breakfast menu. Destined to be the most famous breakfast in America, it was printed in newspapers everywhere and discussed by aficionados of the murders for years to come: Alexander Woollcott always claimed it was the motive.

If Lizzie had only waited, Abby and Andrew probably would have died *anyway,* for their breakfast consisted of mutton soup, sliced mutton, pancakes, bananas, pears, cookies, and coffee. Here we recognize the English concept of breakfast-as-weapon designed to overwhelm French tourists and other effete types.

Bridget was the first up, followed by Andrew, who came downstairs with the connubial slop pail and emptied it on the grass in the backyard. That done, he gathered the pears that had fallen to the ground.

After breakfast, Andrew saw Uncle John out and then brushed his teeth at the kitchen sink where Bridget was washing dishes. Moments later, she rushed out to the back yard and vomited. Whether it was the mutton or the toothbrushing or something she had seen clinging to a pear we shall never know, but when she returned to the house, Abby was waiting with an uncharacteristic order. She wanted the windows washed, all of them, inside and out, *now.*

Here is one of the strangest aspects of the case. Victoria Lincoln writes of Abby: "Encased in fat and self-pity, she was the kind who make indifferent housekeepers everywhere." Additionally, the Wasp woman is too socially secure to need accolades like "You could eat off her floor." Why then would Abby order a sick Bridget to wash the windows on a blistering hot day?

Because, says Miss Lincoln, she was getting ready to go to the bank to sign the deed for the farm, and she feared a scene with Lizzie, who, knowing Abby's hermit-like ways, would immediately suspect the truth. The mere thought of "having words" in front of a servant struck horror in Abby's heart, so she invented a task that would take Bridget outside.

That left Lizzie inside.

Around nine o'clock, Abby was tomahawked in the guest room while making Uncle John's bed. Andrew was to meet the same fate around 11. Lizzie's behavior during that two-hour *entr'acte* was a model of Battle-of-Britain calm. She ironed handkerchiefs, sewed a button loop on a blouse, chatted with Bridget about a dress-goods sale, and read *Harper's Weekley*.

Andrew came home at 10:30 and took a nap on the sitting-room sofa. Shortly before 11, Bridget went up to her attic room to rest. At 11:15 she heard Lizzie cry out: "Maggie! Come down quick! Father's dead. Somebody came in and killed him."

Somebody certainly had. The entire left side of his face and head was a bloody pulp; the eye had been severed and hung down his cheek, and one of the blows had bisected a tooth.

Lizzie sent Bridget for Alice Russell and Dr. Bowen, then sat on the back steps. The Bordens' next-door neighbor, Mrs. Adelaide Churchill, called over to her and got a priceless reply: "Oh, Mrs. Churchill, do come over. Someone has killed Father."

Mrs. Churchill came over, took a quick look at Andrew, and asked, "Where is your stepmother, Lizzie?"

The safe thing to say was "I don't know," but the people who invented the honor system are sticklers for the truth. "I don't know but that she's been killed, too, for I thought I heard her come in," Lizzie blurted.

Bridget returned with Miss Russell and Dr. Bowen, who examined Andrew and asked for a sheet to cover the body. Lizzie told Bridget to get it. Whether she said anything else is in dispute; no one present testified to it, but the legend persists that our monument of straightforwardness added, "Better get two."

Bridget and Mrs. Churchill decided to search the house for Abby. They were not gone long. When they returned, a white-faced but contained Mrs. Churchill nodded at Alice Russell.

"There is another?" asked Miss Russell.

"Yes, she is upstairs," said Mrs. Churchill.

The only excited person present was Bridget.

By the Way . . .

By noon, when Uncle John returned for lunch, the cops had come, and a crowd had formed in the street. Knowing of the hatred between Lizzie and Abby, Uncle John must have guessed the truth, but he chose to exhibit so much nonchalance that he became the first suspect. Instead of rushing into the house yelling, "What's the matter?" he ambled into the back yard, picked up some pears, and stood eating them in the shade of the tree.

Meanwhile, the police were questioning Lizzie, who claimed that she had gone to the barn and returned to find her father dead. What had she gone to the barn for? "To get a piece of lead for a fishing sinker."

It was the first thing that popped into her head, less a conscious deception than an ink-blot association triggered by her seaside vacation. She was playing it by ear. It never occurred to her that she could have stalled for time by pretending to faint. Women often fainted in those tightly corseted days, but she even rejected the detective's gallant offer to come back and question her later when she felt better. "No," she said. "I can tell you all I know now as well as at any other time."

A moment later, when the detective referred to Abby as her mother, she drew herself up and said stiffly, "She is not my mother, sir, she is my stepmother. My mother died when I was a child." Before you start diagnosing "self-destructive tendencies," remember that the English novelists' favorite character is the plucky orphan, and she had just become one.

Miss Russell and Dr. Bowen took her upstairs to lie down. Lizzie asked the doctor to send a telegram to Emma in Fairhaven, adding, "Be sure to put it gently, as there is an old person there who might be disturbed." It's all right to disturb your sister as long as you don't disturb strangers; Wasps haven't kithed our kin since the Anglo-Saxon invaders wiped out the Celtic clan system.

Dr. Bowen must have sent the gentlest wire on record, because Emma did not catch the next train, nor the one after that, nor the one after *that*. She didn't return until after seven that night.

When Dr. Bowen returned, Lizzie confided to him that she had torn up a certain note and put the pieces in the kitchen trash can. He hurried downstairs and found them; he was putting them together when a detective walked in. Seeing the name "Emma," he asked Dr. Bowen what it was. "Oh, it is nothing," Dr. Bowen said nonchalantly. "It is something, I think, about my daughter going through somewhere."

Before the detective could react to this bizarre answer, Dr. Bowen, nonchalant as ever, tossed the pieces into the kitchen fire. As he lifted the stove lid, the detective saw a foot-long cylindrical stick lying in the flames. Later, in the cellar, he found a hatchet head that had been washed and rolled while wet in furnace ash to simulate the dust of long disuse.

Lizzie had been in the barn, but not to look for sinkers. The barn contained a vise, blacksmithing tools, and a water pump. Blood can be washed from metal but not from porous wood. She knew she had to separate the hatchet head from the handle and burn the latter. She did all of this in a very brief time, and without giving way to panic.

Victoria Lincoln believes that because she really had been in the barn, her compulsive honesty forced her to admit it to the police. Then she had to think of an innocent reason for going there, and came up with the story about looking for sinkers. "She lied about *why* and *when* she had done things, but she never denied having done them," writes Miss Lincoln.

Alice Russell displayed the same tic: "Alice's conscience forced her to *mention* things at the trial, but not to *stress* them." The Wasp gift for making everything sound trivial, as when we introduce momentous subjects with "Oh, by the way," enabled Alice to testify about a highly incriminating fact in such a way that the prosecution missed its significance entirely.

On one of Alice's trips upstairs on the murder day, she saw Lizzie coming out of *Emma's* room, and a bundled-up blanket on the floor of *Emma's* closet. What was Lizzie doing in Emma's room? What was in the blanket? Victoria Lincoln thinks it contained bloodstained stockings, but the prosecution never tried to find out because Alice made it all sound so matter-of-fact. The same technique worked for Dr. Bowen in the matter of the note; we happy few don't destroy evidence, we just tut-tut it into oblivion.

Everyone who saw Lizzie after the murders testified that there wasn't a drop of blood on her. How did she wash the blood off her skin and hair in a house that had no running water? What trait is cherished by the people who distrust intellectuals? *Common sense* told her to sponge herself off with the diaper-like cloths Victorian women used for sanitary napkins and then put them in her slop pail, which was already full of bloody cloths because she was menstruating that week.

Now we come to the dress she wore when she murdered Abby. Where did she hide it after she changed? Some students of the crime think she committed both murders in the nude, but Victoria Lincoln disagrees and so do I. Murder is one thing, but . . .

Where would any honest Wasp hide a dress? In the dress closet, of course. Like most women, Lizzie had more clothes than hangers, so she knew how easy it is to "lose" a garment by hanging another one on top of it. Victoria Lincoln thinks she hung the blood-stained summer cotton underneath a heavy winter woolen, and then banked on the either–or male mind: the police were looking for a *summer* dress, and men never run out of hangers.

She got no blood at all on the second dress. Her tall father's Prince Albert coat reached to her ankles, and common sense decrees that blood on a *victim's* clothing is only to be expected.

Mistress of Herself

After her arrest Lizzie became America's Wasp Princess. People couldn't say enough nice things about her icy calm, even the Fall River police chief: "She is a remarkable woman and possessed of a wonderful power of fortitude."

A Providence reporter and Civil War veteran: "Most women would faint at seeing her father dead, for I never saw a more horrible sight and I have walked over battlefields where thousands were dead and mangled. She is a woman of remarkable nerve and self-control."

Julian Ralph, *New York Sun:* "It was plain to see that she had complete mastery of herself, and could make her sensations and emotions invisible to an impertinent public."

To ward off a backlash, Lizzie gave an interview to the *New York Recorder* in which she managed to have her bona fides and eat them too: "They say I don't show any grief. Certainly I don't in public. I never did reveal my feelings and I cannot change my nature now."

I find this very refreshing in an age that equates self-control with elitism. If Lizzie were around today she would be reviled as the Phantom of the Oprah.

Wasp emotional repression also gave us the marvelous fight between Lizzie and Emma in Lizzie's jail cell while she was awaiting trial. Described by Mrs. Hannah Reagan, the police matron, it went like this:

"Emma, you have given me away, haven't you?"

"No, Lizzie, I have not."

"You have, and I will let you see I won't give in one inch."

Finis. Lizzie turned over on her cot and lay with her back to Emma, who remained in her chair. They stayed like that for two hours and twenty minutes, until visiting time was up and Emma left.

When Mrs. Reagan spilled this sensational colloquy to the press, Lizzie's lawyers said it was a lie and demanded she sign a retraction. Doubts arose, but Victoria Lincoln believes Mrs. Reagan: "That terse exchange followed by a two-hour-and-twenty-minute sulking silence sounds more like a typical Borden family fight than the sort of quarrel an Irish police matron would dream up from her own experience."

The Last Word

After her acquittal, Lizzie bought a mansion for herself and Emma in Fall River's best neighborhood. Social acceptance was another matter. When she returned to Central Congregational, everyone was very polite, so she took the hint and stopped going.

She lived quietly until 1904, when she got pinched for shoplifting in Providence. This is what really made her an outcast. Murder is one thing, but . . .

In 1913, Emma suddenly moved out and never spoke to Lizzie again. Nobody knows what happened. Maybe Lizzie finally admitted to the murders, but I doubt it; the Protestant conscience is not programmed for pointless confession. It sounds more as if Emma found out that her sister had a sex life.

An enthusiastic theatergoer, Lizzie was a great fan of an actress named Nance O'Neill. They met in a hotel and developed an intense friendship; Lizzie threw lavish parties for Nance and her troupe and paid Nance's legal expenses in contractual disputes with theater owners. Nance was probably the intended recipient of the unmailed letter Lizzie wrote beginning "Dear Friend," and going on to juicier sentiments: "I dreamed of you the other night but I do not dare to put my dreams on paper." If Emma discovered the two were lesbian lovers, it's no wonder she moved out so precipitately. Murder is one thing, but . . .

Lizzie stayed in Fall River, living alone in her mansion, until she died of pneumonia in 1927.

Emma, living in New Hampshire, read of Lizzie's death in the paper but did not attend the funeral or send flowers. Ten days later, Emma died from a bad fall. Both sisters left the bulk of their fortunes to the Animal Rescue League. Nothing could be Waspier, except the explanation little Victoria Lincoln got when she asked her elders why no one ever spoke to their neighbor, Miss Borden. "Well, dear, she was very unkind to her mother and father."

QUESTIONS FOR DISCUSSION AND WRITING

1. In this article, King emphasizes her view that Lizzie and her behavior can be explained by the fact that the Bordens were WASPs (white Anglo-Saxon Protestants).

What characteristics seem typically WASP-like, according to King? Do you agree with this view of what a WASP is? Why or why not?

2. Though King's essay is presented as nonfiction, it often reads like a short story. Where does King report behaviors or motivations that are a matter of conjecture rather than fact? How much does her interpretation rest on such conjectures?

3. Lizzie was acquitted of the murders, but King assumes she was guilty. What evidence does King offer? How convincing is it?

_____

The Borden Home (http://www.lizzie-borden.com)

The Borden Home is a Greek Revival House which has been a city landmark since the infamous ax murders of Andrew and his second wife Abby Borden on August 4, 1892.

Erected in 1845 the home was originally a two family and was later made into a single family by Andrew J. Borden.

Andrew J. Borden bought the house at 92 Second Street to be close to his bank and various downtown businesses. The Bed & Breakfast-Museum is named after Andrew J. Borden's youngest daughter, Lizzie. Although she was tried and acquitted of the crimes she was ostracized by the community of Fall River.

Since the murders on August 4, 1892 the house has been a private residence. Now for the first time the public is allowed not only to view the murder scene, but is given an opportunity to spend a night *(if you dare)* in the actual house where the murders took place.

We offer two two-bedroom suites, Lizzie & Emma's Bedrooms, and Abby & Andrew's Bedrooms (this suite has a private bath); the John Morse Guest Room, Bridget's Attic Room and two additional spacious attic bedrooms (the Jennings & Knowlton Rooms), each of which offer a double bed in a room with Victorian appointments.

Guests are treated to a breakfast similar to the one the Bordens ate on the morning of the murders, which includes bananas, jonny-cakes, sugar cookies and coffee in addition to a delicious meal of breakfast staples.

The interior and exterior of the home have been restored to their original Victorian splendor, with careful attention to making it as close to the Borden home of August 1892 as is possible.

The owners of the home invite all to view their collection of both Fall River and Borden memorabilia in their museum at 92 Second Street.

Located just fifty miles south of Boston, minutes from Providence or Newport, R.I. and the gateway to Cape Cod, this landmark home is accessible from all major highways.

TOUR SCHEDULE

Through October 28, 2001, tours will be available on weekends *only* from 11:00 a.m. to 2:30 p.m. On October 29, public tours will close for the season. Weekend only tours will resume on Memorial Day weekend in May 2002.

QUESTION FOR DISCUSSION AND WRITING

On the face of it, one might not think that a murder scene would make an appealing bed and breakfast, yet obviously the proprietors of the Borden Home disagree. How does their advertisement attempt to appeal to tourists? Would you find it interesting or distasteful to sleep in one of these bedrooms? Why?

QUESTIONS FOR CROSS READING: MONSTROUS CRIME

1. For more than one hundred years, Lizzie Borden has been controversial. Some see her as a coldhearted and monstrous killer, others as a victim of a repressive society. Which attitude seems more prevalent in the readings in this section? Which writers agree with each other, and which disagree?
2. As you read the different selections, you may have been surprised to learn that not all the writers agree about the facts. Which facts are disputed? Are some authors more convincing than others in their presentation of the disputed facts? If so, why?
3. Lizzie is sometimes portrayed as a full human being with an understandable psychology and sometimes reduced to a cartoonish figure. Which of the authors—whether sympathetic or not—treat her as a real human being? What about their portrayals creates a rounded person? If Lizzie is treated as a flat cartoonlike character, how is she drawn? What characteristics are seen as defining her—and why? Are the characterizations of Lizzie as a flat character more likely to portray a monster or a victim? Why?
4. When the writers do see Lizzie as guilty, what do they see as her motives for murder? Do they agree or disagree about those motives? What might their assumptions about motivation tell us about their views of Lizzie, of women in the nineteenth century, of family relationships, of the causes of evil?

THE WANDERING HERO: THE ODYSSEUS STORY

At the end of *The Odyssey,* Homer tells the story of Odysseus's return to his home in Ithaca, where his wife, Penelope, and his son, Telemachos, have awaited his return. Much has changed in the ten years in which Odysseus has been fighting in the Trojan War and wandering in heroic travels homeward. The ever-faithful Penelope has been besieged by suitors wishing to replace her long-overdue husband; the young Telemachos has grown into early manhood and is eager to try to prove his own heroism. The following excerpt from Homer summarizes the scene of Odysseus's homecoming in the words of one of Penelope's dead suitors, whom Odysseus killed when he arrived home.

HOMER (8th–7th C. B.C.?)

from The Odyssey _____   *ca. 8th–7th C. B.C.*

And then the soul of Amphimedon addressed him:
"Glorious son of Atreus, Zeus-nourished Agamemnon,
Lord of men, I do remember all the things you say,
And I shall tell you everything truthfully and well,
5   The evil end of our death, the way it came about.
We wooed the wife of Odysseus, who was gone so long;
She neither refused the hateful wedding nor carried it out,
Contriving for us death and black destiny;
And she devised in her mind this other deceit:
10 She set a great loom in the halls, and on it she wove
A large and delicate fabric. She told us at once:
'Young men, my suitors, since godlike Odysseus is dead,
Wait, though you are eager for this marriage of mine, till I finish
This robe, so that the yarn will not waste in vain,
15 The burial sheet of hero Laertes for the time
When the ruinous fate of long-sorrowful death seizes him,
Lest one of the Achaian women in the district blame me
If he who had won so much lay without covering.'
So she said, and the bold heart was persuaded within us.
20 Then every day she kept weaving there on the great loom,
And in the nights she undid it when she had the torches set up.
So three years she fooled the Achaians and persuaded them.
But when the fourth year came and the seasons came on
Of the waning months and many days came to an end,
25 Right then one of the women who perceived it clearly told it.
And we happened upon her undoing the shining fabric.
Then she finished it, though unwilling and under duress.
And when, having woven the great fabric and washed it,
She showed forth the robe that resembled the sun or the moon,
30 Just then some evil god led Odysseus from someplace
To the verge of the field where the swineherd had his home.
There, too, the beloved son of Odysseus had come
When he went from sandy Pylos in his black ship.
The two of them, contriving an evil death for the suitors,
35 Had arrived at the city of great renown. Odysseus
Was last, and Telemachos led the way ahead of them.
The swineherd brought the man, who wore vile clothes on his skin
And resembled a wretched beggar who was an old man
Walking with a staff. He had sorry clothes on his skin.
40 None of us could recognize that it was he
When he appeared suddenly, not even those who were older,
But we rebuked him with missiles and evil speeches.
Still, he held out all the while with enduring heart
When he was being beaten and rebuked in his own halls.

But when the purpose of aegis-bearing Zeus aroused him   45
He took up the beautiful weapons with Telemachos
And placed them in the chamber and locked the fastenings,
And resourcefully he gave the order to his wife
To set before the suitors the bow and the gray iron,
A contest and start of slaughter for us in our dread fate.   50
No one of us was able to stretch out the string
Of the mighty bow, for we were too weak by far.
But when the great bow came into Odysseus' hands,
Then all of us made a common outcry with speeches,
Not to give him the bow, however much he might say.   55
Telemachos alone urged him on and gave him the order.
Then godly Odysseus, who had endured much, took it in his hand,
Easily strung the bow and shot through the iron.
He went and stood on the threshold, poured the swift arrows out,
Peering round terribly, and hit King Antinoos.   60
And then on the others he let the groan-carrying darts fly,
Taking aim straight across. And they fell thick and fast.
It was known then that one of the gods was their helper for them.
For at once they went on through the house in their rage
And killed them one after another. A sad groaning   65
Rose as their heads were struck. The whole ground ran with blood.
Agamemnon, this is the way we perished, we whose bodies
Are still lying uncared for now in the halls of Odysseus.
For the dear ones in the home of each man do not know it yet,
Those who, when they have washed the black gore from the wounds,   70
May lay us out weeping. For that is the prize of the dead."

QUESTIONS FOR DISCUSSION AND WRITING

1. Penelope keeps her suitors at bay by weaving and unweaving a funeral shroud for her still-living father-in-law, in the process telling her suitors that her still-living husband must be dead. What does the passage ask us to see as the relationship between life and death?
2. What do you learn from the passage about the characters of Odysseus, Penelope, and Telemachos? About their relationships to one another? To what extent is each heroic? To what extent do gender and age define heroism?

ALFRED, LORD TENNYSON (1809–1892)

Ulysses _____ *1833*

It little profits that an idle king,
By this still hearth, among these barren crags,

Matched with an aged wife, I mete and dole
Unequal laws unto a savage race,
5   That hoard, and sleep, and feed, and know not me.
I cannot rest from travel; I will drink
Life to the lees; all times I have enjoyed
Greatly, have suffered greatly, both with those
That loved me, and alone; on shore, and when
10 Through scudding drifts the rainy Hyades
Vexed the dim sea: I am become a name;
For always roaming with a hungry heart
Much have I seen and known; cities of men
And manners, climates, councils, governments,
15 Myself not least, but honored of them all;
And drunk delight of battle with my peers,
Far on the ringing plains of windy Troy.
I am a part of all that I have met;
Yet all experience is an arch wherethrough
20 Gleams that untraveled world, whose margin fades
Forever and forever when I move.
How dull it is to pause, to make an end,
To rust unburnished, not to shine in use!
As though to breathe were life. Life piled on life
25 Were all too little, and of one to me
Little remains; but every hour is saved
From that eternal silence, something more,
A bringer of new things; and vile it were
For some three suns to store and hoard myself,
30 And this gray spirit yearning in desire
To follow knowledge like a sinking star,
Beyond the utmost bound of human thought.
    This is my son, mine own Telemachus
To whom I leave the scepter and the isle—
35 Well-loved of me, discerning to fulfill
This labor, by slow prudence to make mild
A rugged people, and through soft degrees
Subdue them to the useful and the good.
Most blameless is he, centered in the sphere
40 Of common duties, decent not to fail
In offices of tenderness, and pay
Meet adoration to my household gods,
When I am gone. He works his work, I mine.
    There lies the port; the vessel puffs her sail;
45 There gloom the dark broad seas. My mariners,
Souls that have toiled, and wrought, and thought with me—
That ever with a frolic welcome took
The thunder and the sunshine, and opposed
Free hearts, free foreheads—you and I are old;

Old age hath yet his honor and his toil;   50
Death closes all; but something ere the end,
Some work of noble note, may yet be done,
Not unbecoming men that strove with gods.
The lights begin to twinkle from the rocks;
The long day wanes; the slow moon climbs; the deep   55
Moans round with many voices. Come, my friends,
'Tis not too late to seek a newer world.
Push off, and sitting well in order smite
The sounding furrows; for my purpose holds
To sail beyond the sunset, and the baths   60
Of all the western stars, until I die.
It may be that the gulfs will wash us down;
It may be we shall touch the Happy Isles,
And see the great Achilles, whom we knew.
Though much is taken, much abides; and though   65
We are not now that strength which in old days
Moved earth and heaven, that which we are, we are;
One equal temper of heroic hearts,
Made weak by time and fate, but strong in will
To strive, to seek, to find, and not to yield.   70

QUESTIONS FOR DISCUSSION AND WRITING

1. Tennyson's Ulysses ("Ulysses" is another name for "Odysseus") is an old man yearning for his past heroic life. How does Ulysses describe that earlier life? What did it offer that his current life does not?

2. The poem provides a contrast between Ulysses and his "well-loved" son, Telemachus. Why does Ulysses see their "work" as different? Does Ulysses see his own heroic role as superior to or simply different from Telemachus's role? Does the poem suggest that we are meant to see one or the other of the two men as more heroic?

3. The poem makes us very aware of an *aged* Ulysses. What attitude is conveyed toward age? Are we meant to see the link between age and heroism as ironic or to believe that the two are compatible?

C. P. CAVAFY (1863–1933)

Ithaka _____ *1911*

As you set out for Ithaka
hope the voyage is a long one,
full of adventure, full of discovery.

5 Laistrygonians and Cyclops,
angry Poseidon—don't be afraid of them:
you'll never find things like that on your way
as long as you keep your thoughts raised high,
as long as a rare excitement
stirs your spirit and your body.
10 Laistrygonians and Cyclops,
wild Poseidon—you won't encounter them
unless you bring them along inside your soul,
unless your soul sets them up in front of you.

Hope the voyage is a long one.
15 May there be many a summer morning when,
with what pleasure, what joy,
you come into harbors seen for the first time;
may you stop at Phoenician trading stations
to buy fine things,
20 mother of pearl and coral, amber and ebony,
sensual perfume of every kind—
as many sensual perfumes as you can;
and may you visit many Egyptian cities
to gather stores of knowledge from their scholars.

25 Keep Ithaka always in your mind.
Arriving there is what you are destined for.
But do not hurry the journey at all.
Better if it lasts for years,
so you are old by the time you reach the island,
30 wealthy with all you have gained on the way,
not expecting Ithaka to make you rich.

Ithaka gave you the marvelous journey.
Without her you would not have set out.
She has nothing left to give you now.

35 And if you find her poor, Ithaka won't have fooled you.
Wise as you will have become, so full of experience,
you will have understood by then what these Ithakas mean.

QUESTIONS FOR DISCUSSION AND WRITING

1. Ithaka is Odysseus's home, and Cafavy asks us to think about the relationship between heroism and home. How does Cafavy define that relationship? Do you agree with the poem's way of thinking about it?

2. How would you describe the tone of Cafavy's poem? Is it sad? Entreating? Nostalgic? Prayerful? How does your sense of the mood reflect your understanding of the poem's themes?

RICHARD HOWARD (1929–   )

Ithaca: The Palace at Four a.m. _____ 1984

for Katha Pollitt

First Words

No god could make up for the ten years lost
(except by ten years found). Nor would I dream
of trying anything so grandiose
my first night home. Was I trying at all?
Hard to say, when it has taken this long   5
to be in a fitting position ... Still,

your old responses seemed to be intact
before I even touched you. Wasn't it good?
For me it was: all that I waited for
(and I did wait, you know—those episodes   10
with silly what's-her-name were meaningless)
ever since we left those invincible walls

smoking behind us, the islands, the sea
between ... But if you had been satisfied,
would you have left me sleeping behind you?   15
Not of course that *I* could satisfy you,
but the occasion itself? Surely that
afforded a fulfillment sleep might crown!

Just look around you: not one trace of blood
left on the marble, not a sign there was   20
anything like a massacre downstairs
only yesterday morning; then dinner—
wasn't that a nice dinner they gave us?
as if they served a banquet every night!

But all of that—or none of it—would do: 25
the house swept clean of the scum you condoned
(I won't say encouraged, but they did hang on!)
and things back where habit said they belonged:
your own husband lying in your own bed ...
Yet you had to leave it! Without showing   30

much solicitude for a light sleeper
who might, after all, have been easily
disturbed (straw rustles and an old bed creaks,
you know: I've grown accustomed to keeping
my ears open—wandering will do that),   35
you seemed to *drift* over to that corner

where you always kept your loom—it's still there!
and with only one clay lamp to see by

set . . . to work? Penelope, I am here.
40   You don't have to do whatever it was
you told them you were doing any more—
stop picking at that thing, come back to me!

Last Words

What I "have to do" has nothing to do
with what I have—or with doing, either.
45   You tell me I have you. Evidently
you can't imagine what it means to live
inside a legend—scratch a Hero and
you're likely to find almost anything!

Having scratched, I found you. Was I surprised?
50   Once her womb becomes a cave of the winds
which appears to be uninhabited,
there are no surprises for a woman—
she has survived them all. But at the loom
I learned that even you were ignorant,

55   crafty Ulysses! Weaving taught me: our
makeshifts become our mode until there is
no such thing as *meanwhile*. Not craft but art!
So you see, I must ravel the design
all over again: there is no end in sight.
60   Ulysses home? You don't come home at all,

wandering will do that, though I say it
who never left. The loom's my odyssey—
dare I call it my penelopiad?
You think you were asleep just now, don't you,
65   after those homecoming exertions? But
you were never here at all, my husband:

the sea still has you—I heard you insist
you were No-one. No one? How many times
you sighed 'Circle' in that light sleep of yours:
70   she must have had her points, old what's-her-name.
You snored but sirens sang, and when the moon
silvered our bed you seemed to feel the sun

depositing tiny crystals of salt
all over your old skin. You were away.
75   That was your weaving—and my wandering.
The suitors are dead, your bow is a prop,
but neither of *us* is present. Let me
give you some peace at this ungodly hour . . .

Be patient—having found or feigned this much,   80
perhaps the two of us can fool the world
into seeing that famous genre scene:
The King and Queen Restored. It's abstinence
that makes the heart meander: you're at sea,
I worry this web. Lover, welcome home!

QUESTIONS FOR DISCUSSION AND WRITING

1. When Odysseus first returns to Ithaca, there follows a contest of strength and heroism between him and the suitors who have been vying for Penelope. Howard asks
   us to imagine the first moments of privacy and intimacy between Penelope and
   Odysseus. What does his poem tell us about the relationship that is likely to exist
   between the husband and wife who haven't seen each other for ten years?
2. The poem suggests that her weaving has offered Penelope something like what
   the "odyssey" has offered Odysseus. In what sense might that be true? Why does
   she return to her loom?

DOROTHY PARKER (1893–1967)

Penelope _____ *1936*

In the pathway of the sun,
    In the footsteps of the breeze,
Where the world and sky are one,
    He shall ride the silver seas,
        He shall cut the glittering wave.   5
I shall sit at home, and rock;
Rise, to heed a neighbor's knock;
Brew my tea, and snip my thread;
Bleach the linen for my bed.
        They will call him brave.   10

QUESTIONS FOR DISCUSSION AND WRITING

1. The "he" of the poem is Odysseus, and the "I" is Penelope. How does the poem
   characterize Odysseus's actions? How does it characterize Penelope's?
2. The last line of the poem seems ironic, suggesting Penelope may be as brave as
   Odysseus. Why does Parker seem to believe that? To what extent do you agree

with her? Does equating the two kinds of bravery increase Penelope's heroism and/or diminish Odysseus's?

_____

LINDA PASTAN (1932–   )

Rereading The Odyssey in Middle Age _____ 1988

Why was she weaving a shroud for Laertes,
and why have I thought for years
it was a shawl she made, something warm
a man might wrap around her shoulders
5   windy nights—one of the suitors, perhaps,
much younger than she and surely
younger than Odysseus.
Perhaps Laertes kept his eye on her
suspiciously. Did she mean
10   to finish it after all, unweaving
less and less each night, and could that mean
she wished Laertes dead? Yarns dyed the colors
of the sea: greens, purples, and hyacinth.
How can we hope to find the darker threads
15   of her impatience or lust
in the design of that nubby material?
We make our myths from whole cloth anyway
and make ourselves the heroines
of others' imaginings.

20   The shuttle was always moving back
and forth across the loom, as restless
as Odysseus himself, or any man.
I think of the uses of "shroud":
how the night can be shrouded in fog
25   in places like this one, near the sea;
how leaves in summer shroud each mother branch;
and how your husband's father looks at you
with wrinkled lids shrouding
those knowing eyes.
30   What is faithfulness anyway?
Penelope asks. Is the sea faithful
to the shore, whether it beats against it
or withdraws, leaving only a trace
of its commandment on the naked sand?
35   She wonders if Telemachus will find a wife
to weave a shroud for her lost
father-in-law, or would the water
be winding sheet enough for him?

QUESTIONS FOR DISCUSSION AND WRITING

1. Penelope is often considered the epitome of patience and fidelity. But Pastan seems
   to see her otherwise. Which of the two versions of Penelope do you find more
   "realistic" and/or more "true" to human nature? How does the alteration of Penelope's character cause us to rethink Odysseus's character and his heroic mission?
   How does it influence our definition of *heroism*?
2. Pastan's poem is as much about the "I" of the poem as it is about Penelope. How
   would you characterize the speaker?

WILLIAM DICKEY (1928–1994)

Telemachus _____ 1978

1.

> You are grown up, surely it is time for you
> to set off and look for your father, who is missing.
> You have had photographs, but they were taken
> by the family, mostly in black-and-white.
> Those who knew him, women especially,   5
> say: "He was better looking.
> You would have had to see him yourself."
> They flutter their fans.
> Resentfully, they say:
> "There is nothing here that does him justice."   10
>
> You are over six foot yourself, and well set-up.
> Nothing has been lacking in your education.
> But it is not for you they languish and decline
> in their silken reveries, it is not for you
> that their eyes soften, mouths tickle with remembrance.   15
> They think of someone they are jealous of in time.
>
> Up to now, you have hardly been in time.
> For twenty years, the sea has been a bowl,
> still, permanent, in which the island sat.
> The ladies were so many courtesy aunts,   20
> the suitors people who for her own amusement
> your mother entertains. They can be woven
> into her habitual account of day upon day:
> those webs in which you are peripheral, or missing.
>
> Without announcement, you will find yourself   25
> in a small boat, launched into an actual Ocean.
> If you look for hands, there will be only two.
> If you think, you are the mirror of your thinking.

Your skin burns, your hair bleaches from the salt.
30 Any sail you put up has your own name marked upon it.
In the wake you leave, the waves rehearse
and forget you.

The Ocean is empty, but there are always
landfalls. Arriving at evening, no water left,
35 sailing by a difficult strait into the harbor,
you will find, always, your father has been there before you.
In one village they will tell you that they ate him,
but they are not convincing, their eyes shift.
In another port
40 you will find his image in a mud phallic god.
Always the ladies,
holding up the bronze mirror, roughing their nipples,
will say of him: "How could I not remember?"
Out of remembering, they will take you to their beds
45 where he has been before you.
It is hard to imagine a place he has not been.

2.

You must sail into another Ocean, outside
the possible world: a frozen
incumbrance of a place, ice monuments
50 breaking and re-forming, the song of the tall ice.
If there are inhabitants, they do not speak
any of the supple tongues you have picked up, voyaging.
They neither remember you nor remember him.
They sing into your mind: "He is not here."
55 Images flicker and dance in the inhuman sky:
it might be your father, but it is only image.
You have arrived beyond the end of the world.
You have yourself, otherwise there is nothing here.

Even into these waters, Summer comes.
60 A short slackening of the ice
out of which your boat goes free, unguided.
You are interior to the wave, you are yourself.
Being is not a comfort, but an instruction.
As you move north, you civilize
65 the islands: these are people who could be men.
They incline to you, recognizing the change
in your face. They offer their daughters to you,
none of whom has lain with a man. They cry: "Change!"
What they see, looking at you, effects it.
70 Months, perhaps years later, after meeting
with easy indifference women with the feet of birds,

women with dogs barking from their bellies, you return
to the place you set out from, a place
difficult to remember.

Old women come down to the beach. Their fans have rotted. 75
Suitors come down, but they have now no swords.
Your mother comes. She does not know what to say
after all this time. Her eyes have blurred
with the years, even in that place of long-woven calm.
She finds you hard to recognize. "Welcome, Son?" 80
she says with uncertainty. "Welcome, Husband?"

QUESTIONS FOR DISCUSSION AND WRITING

1. Like all sons of heroic fathers, Telemachus is in a difficult position: how can he achieve his own unique heroic identity without constantly being compared to his more famous father or undermined by his father's reputation? How does Dickey's speaker characterize the hero's son? How does Telemachus seem similar to and different from his heroic father, who wandered the world facing and defeating monsters? What is Telemachus's role in the hero's story?

2. At the end of the poem, Penelope confuses her son and her husband. Is the confusion a sign that Telemachus has not succeeded in becoming his own man—or that he *has* succeeded? Why?

LOUISE GLÜCK (1943–   )

Telemachus' Fantasy _____ *1966*

Sometimes I wonder about my father's
years on those islands: why
was he so attractive
to women? He was in straits then, I suppose
desperate. I believe 5
women like to see a man
still whole, still standing, but
about to go to pieces: such
disintegration reminds them
of passion. I think of them as living 10
their whole lives
completely undressed. It must have
dazzled him, I think, women
so much younger than he was
evidently wild for him, ready 15
to do anything he wished. Is it

fortunate to encounter circumstances
so responsive to one's own will, to live
so many years
20   unquestioned, unthwarted? One
would have to believe oneself
entirely good or worthy. I
suppose in time either
one becomes a monster or
25   the beloved sees what one is. I never
wish for my father's life
nor have I any idea
what he sacrificed
to survive that moment. Less dangerous
30   to believe he was drawn to them
and so stayed
to see who they were. I think, though,
as an imaginative man
to some extent he
35   became who they were.

QUESTIONS FOR DISCUSSION AND WRITING

1. In Glück's poem, Telemachus says that he never wished for his father's life. What does he see as the dangers of that life? What do Telemachus's words tell us about the character traits necessary for heroism?
2. Glück's Telemachus suggests that the hero might become a monster. Does he believe that has happened to his father? Do we?

QUESTIONS FOR CROSS READING: THE WANDERING HERO

1. In the works in this cluster, Penelope is shown in a number of ways: as wife, lover, mother, and artist. Think about the selections in which she appears. Do we ever see her whole or only in the fragments of her roles? How are the roles opposed to each other? Which of the roles are most consistent with the idea of heroism? Would you argue that Penelope does or does not achieve the same stature as Odysseus does? Why?
2. Different works take a different view of Odysseus as "wanderer." How do the various poets view his wanderings? Are they part of his heroic mission? A denial of his role as political leader and protector? A repudiation of his family? What are we finally meant to see as his destination?

3. In the works, we catch glimpses of a father, mother, and son: of Odysseus, Penelope, and Telemachus. In which works is the family unit most clearly portrayed? How are the family connections defined?

_____

A BRIEF INTRODUCTION TO SHAKESPEARE'S THEATER

The best known of English Renaissance dramatists, Shakespeare wrote during a time when the theater flourished, giving voice to many of the cultural values of his time. The theater was popular among all classes of people, so much so that it could be called the television of its day. In fact, much like television, in Shakespeare's time the theater was frankly a business, a moneymaking enterprise often seen as disreputable, attracting the rabble of the busy urban center of London. Although we think of Shakespeare's plays as examples of "culture," in his own time the theaters were such raucous places that the Common Council of London licensed the theaters in an attempt to control the mob behavior of the audiences. In response, the builders of the theaters simply avoided government intervention by building their theaters outside London, taking them outside city control. Despite its sometimes problematic reputation, however, the theater did enjoy royal patronage, and its audience ranged from aristocrats to artisans.

Perhaps the outdoor setting of the theater contributed somewhat to its informal atmosphere. Unlike the natural amphitheater that provided the setting for Greek drama (see 1005) and unlike our modern indoor theaters, the Renaissance theater was an elaborate open-air building that closed down in the winter. The stage was raised above ground level, and in front of it as many as 800 spectators might stand, the so-called groundlings, who paid only a penny to attend. Above and behind the groundlings—and on three sides of the stage—were raised galleries, providing about 1,500 covered seats for the more affluent members of the audience, who paid two or three pence for their seats.

Because there was no stage curtain and no artificial lighting, plays had to be performed in the daytime. Without any curtain to hide changes in scenery, the scenery and props were relatively simple, though the Renaissance theater had machinery to lower characters from a raised gallery (called the "heavens"); it also had an understage area (called "hell") from which characters might ascend through a trapdoor. Whereas in the modern theater a curtain comes down at the end of a scene or act, in Shakespeare's plays such endings are often announced by rhymed lines (couplets) or by a procession of characters leaving the stage.

As was true for the Greek stage, Shakespeare's theater had no actresses. Young boys whose voices had not changed played the female roles, adding an extra element of humor to the frequent Shakespearean plot device of young women's disguising themselves as boys. In its focus on the fall of a noble person with a "tragic flaw," Shakespearean tragedy resembles Greek tragedy. In other respects, though, Shakespearean drama departs substantially from Greek assumptions about plays and their staging. The simple costumes and masks of Greek drama were replaced by elaborate costumes, and the story lines also became more elaborate. The "three unities" of time, place, and action (see 1006) are frequently ignored. Time lapses during the play may be considerable; subplots and changes in setting abound. This greater elaboration results in much longer plays than are typical today, so much so that for our modern audiences, the plays must often be cut substantially to fit into a two- to three-hour time frame.

In recent years, Shakespeare's plays have had a resurgence of popularity, primarily in filmed versions. Movies such as Kenneth Branagh's *Hamlet* (of which we give a brief screenplay excerpt later in the anthology) and *Much Ado about Nothing* and Michael Hoffman's *A Midsummer Night's Dream* have made Shakespeare accessible and enjoyable to modern audiences who might otherwise think of his plays as impenetrable. They have also convinced audiences that, as they become more accustomed to it, even the seemingly archaic language of the plays opens itself up to rich and meaningful exploration.

BLURRING THE LINE: *THE TEMPEST*

WILLIAM SHAKESPEARE (1564–1616)

The Tempest _____ *1611*

Names of the Actors

ALONSO, *King of Naples*
SEBASTIAN, *his brother*
PROSPERO, *the right Duke of Milan*
ANTONIO, *his brother, the usurping Duke of Milan*
FERDINAND, *son to the King of Naples*
GONZALO, *an honest old councillor*
ADRIAN *and* ⎫
                  ⎬ *lords*
FRANCISCO, ⎭
CALIBAN, *a savage and deformed slave*
TRINCULO, *a jester*
STEPHANO, *a drunken butler*
MASTER *of a ship*
BOATSWAIN
MARINERS
MIRANDA, *daughter to Prospero*
ARIEL, *an airy spirit*
IRIS, ⎫
CERES, ⎪
JUNO, ⎬ *[presented by] spirits*
NYMPHS, ⎪
REAPERS, ⎭
[OTHER SPIRITS ATTENDING ON PROSPERO]

The scene: *An uninhabited island*

[ACT 1, SCENE 1]

[On board ship, off the island's coast.]

(A tempestuous noise of thunder and lightning heard. Enter a SHIPMASTER and a BOATSWAIN.)

MASTER: Boatswain!

BOATSWAIN: Here, Master. What cheer?

MASTER: Good,° speak to the mariners. Fall to 't yarely,° or we run ourselves aground. Bestir, bestir! *(Exit.)*

(Enter MARINERS.)

BOATSWAIN: Heigh, my hearts! Cheerly, cheerly, my hearts! Yare, yare! Take in the topsail. Tend° to the Master's whistle.—Blow° till thou burst thy wind, if room enough!° 5

(Enter ALONSO, SEBASTIAN, ANTONIO, FERDINAND, GONZALO, and others.)

ALONSO: Good Boatswain, have care. Where's the Master? Play the men.°

BOATSWAIN: I pray now, keep below.

ANTONIO: Where is the Master, Boatswain? 10

BOATSWAIN: Do you not hear him? You mar our labor. Keep° your cabins! You do assist the storm.

GONZALO: Nay, good,° be patient.

BOATSWAIN: When the sea is. Hence! What cares these roarers° for the name of king? To cabin! Silence! Trouble us not. 15

GONZALO: Good, yet remember whom thou hast aboard.

BOATSWAIN: None that I more love than myself. You are a councillor; if you can command these elements to silence and work the peace of the present,° we will not hand° a rope more. Use your authority. If you cannot, give thanks you have lived so long and make yourself ready in your cabin for the mischance of the 20 hours, if it so hap°—Cheerly, good hearts!—Out of our way, I say. *(Exit.)*

GONZALO: I have great comfort from this fellow. Methinks he hath no drowning mark upon him; his complexion is perfect gallows.° Stand fast, good Fate, to his hanging! Make the rope of his destiny our cable, for our own doth little advantage.° If he be not born to be hanged, our case is miserable.° 25

(Exeunt [courtiers].)

(Enter BOATSWAIN.)

ACT 1, SCENE 1. **3 Good:** I.e., it's good you've come, or, my good fellow; **yarely:** Nimbly. **6 Tend:** Attend; **Blow:** (Addressed to the wind.) **6–7 if room enough:** As long as we have sea room enough. **8 Play the men:** Act like men (?) ply, urge the men to exert themselves (?). **11 Keep:** Remain in. **13 good:** Good fellow. **14 roarers:** Waves or winds, or both; spoken to as though they were "bullies" or "blusterers." **18 work . . . present:** Bring calm to our present circumstances. **19 hand:** Handle. **21 hap:** Happen. **23 complexion . . . gallows:** Appearance shows he was born to be hanged (and therefore, according to the proverb, in no danger of drowning). **24–25 our . . . advantage:** Our own cable is of little benefit. **25 case is miserable:** Circumstances are desperate.

BOATSWAIN: Down with the topmast! Yare! Lower, lower! Bring her to try wi' the
main course.° (*A cry within.*) A plague upon this howling! They are louder than
the weather or our office.°

(*Enter* SEBASTIAN, ANTONIO, *and* GONZALO.)

Yet again? What do you hear? Shall we give o'er° and drown? Have you a mind
30   to sink?

SEBASTIAN: A pox o' your throat, you bawling, blasphemous, incharitable dog!

BOATSWAIN: Work you, then.

ANTONIO: Hang, cur! Hang, you whoreson, insolent noisemaker! We are less afraid
to be drowned than thou art.

35   GONZALO: I'll warrant him for drowning,° though the ship were no stronger than a
nutshell and as leaky as an unstanched° wench.

BOATSWAIN: Lay her ahold, ahold!° Set her two courses.° Off to sea again! Lay
her off!

(*Enter* MARINERS, *wet.*)

MARINERS: All lost! To prayers, to prayers! All lost!
[*The* MARINERS *run about in confusion, exiting at random.*]

40   BOATSWAIN: What, must our mouths be cold?°

GONZALO: The King and Prince at prayers! Let's assist them,
For our case is as theirs.

SEBASTIAN: I am out of patience.

ANTONIO: We are merely° cheated of our lives by drunkards.
This wide-chapped° rascal! Would thou mightst lie drowning
The washing of ten tides!°

45   GONZALO: He'll be hanged yet,
Though every drop of water swear against it
And gape at wid'st° to glut° him.
(*A confused noise within:*)   "Mercy on us!"—
"We split, we split!"°—"Farewell my wife and children!"—
"Farewell, brother!"—"We split, we split, we split!"   [*Exit* BOATSWAIN.]

50   ANTONIO: Let's all sink wi' the King.

SEBASTIAN: Let's take leave of him.   (*Exit* [*with* ANTONIO].)

GONZALO: Now would I give a thousand furlongs of sea for an acre of barren
ground: long heath,° brown furze,° anything. The wills above be done! But I
would fain° die a dry death.   (*Exit.*)

26–27 Bring . . . course: Sail her close to the wind by means of the mainsail.   **28 our office:**
I.e., the noise we make at our work.   **29 give o'er:** Give up.   **35 warrant him for drowning:**
Guarantee that he will never be drowned.   **36 unstanched:** Insatiable, loose, unrestrained (suggesting also "incontinent" and "menstrual").   **37 ahold:** Ahull, close to the wind;   **courses:** Sails,
i.e., foresail as well as mainsail, set in an attempt to get the ship back out into open water.   **40
must . . . cold:** I.e., must we drown in the cold sea, or, let us heat up our mouths with liquor.   **43
merely:** Utterly.   **44 wide-chapped:** With mouth wide open.   **44–45 lie . . . tides:** (Pirates
were hanged on the shore and left until three tides had come in.)   **47 at wid'st:** Wide open;
glut: Swallow.   **48 split:** Break apart.   **53 heath:** Heather;   **furze:** Gorse, a weed growing on
wasteland.   **54 fain:** Rather.

[SCENE 2]

[*The island, near Prospero's cell. On the Elizabethan stage, this cell is implicitly at hand throughout the play, although in some scenes the convention of flexible distance allows us to imagine characters in other parts of the island.*]

(*Enter* PROSPERO [*in his magic cloak*] *and* MIRANDA.)

MIRANDA: If by your art,° my dearest father, you have
　　　Put the wild waters in this roar, allay° them.
　　　The sky, it seems, would pour down stinking pitch,
　　　But that the sea, mounting to th' welkin's cheek,°
　　　Dashes the fire out. O, I have suffered   5
　　　With those that I saw suffer! A brave° vessel,
　　　Who had, no doubt, some noble creature in her,
　　　Dashed all to pieces. O, the cry did knock
　　　Against my very heart! Poor souls, they perished.
　　　Had I been any god of power, I would   10
　　　Have sunk the sea within the earth or ere°
　　　It should the good ship so have swallowed and
　　　The freighting° souls within her.
PROSPERO:　　　　　　　　　　　　　Be collected.°
　　　No more amazement.° Tell your piteous° heart
　　　There's no harm done.
MIRANDA:　　　　　　　　　O, woe the day!
PROSPERO:　　　　　　　　　　　　　No harm.   15
　　　I have done nothing but° in care of thee,
　　　Of thee, my dear one, thee, my daughter, who
　　　Art ignorant of what thou art, naught knowing
　　　Of whence I am, nor that I am more better°
　　　Than Prospero, master of a full° poor cell,   20
　　　And thy no greater father.
MIRANDA:　　　　　　　　　　More to know
　　　Did never meddle° with my thoughts.
PROSPERO:　　　　　　　　　　　　　'Tis time
　　　I should inform thee farther. Lend thy hand
　　　And pluck my magic garment from me. So,

　　　　　　　　　　　　　　[*laying down his magic cloak and staff*]

　　　Lie there, my art.—Wipe thou thine eyes. Have comfort.   25
　　　The direful spectacle of the wreck,° which touched
　　　The very virtue° of compassion in thee,
　　　I have with such provision° in mine art
　　　So safely ordered that there is no soul—

SCENE 2. **1 art:** Magic.　**2 allay:** Pacify.　**4 welkin's cheek:** Sky's face.　**6 brave:** Gallant, splendid.　**11 or ere:** Before.　**13 freighting:** Forming the cargo;　**collected:** Calm, composed.　**14 amazement:** Consternation; **piteous:** Pitying.　**16 but:** Except.　**19 more better:** Of higher rank.　**20 full:** Very.　**22 meddle:** Mingle.　**26 wreck:** Shipwreck.　**27 virtue:** Essence.　**28 provision:** Foresight.

30   No, not so much perdition° as an hair
        Betid° to any creature in the vessel
        Which° thou heard'st cry, which thou saw'st sink. Sit down,
        For thou must now know farther.
MIRANDA [*sitting*]:   You have often
        Begun to tell me what I am, but stopped
35   And left me to a bootless inquisition,°
        Concluding, "Stay, not yet."
PROSPERO: The hour's now come;
        The very minute bids thee ope thine ear.
        Obey, and be attentive. Canst thou remember
        A time before we came unto this cell?
40   I do not think thou canst, for then thou wast not
        Out° three years old.
MIRANDA: Certainly, sir, I can.
PROSPERO: By what? By any other house or person?
        Of anything the image, tell me, that
        Hath kept with thy remembrance.
MIRANDA: 'Tis far off,
45   And rather like a dream than an assurance
        That my remembrance warrants.° Had I not
        Four or five women once that tended me?
PROSPERO: Thou hadst, and more, Miranda. But how is it
        That this lives in thy mind? What seest thou else
50   In the dark backward and abysm of time?°
        If thou rememberest aught° ere thou cam'st here,
        How thou cam'st here thou mayst.
MIRANDA: But that I do not.
PROSPERO: Twelve year since, Miranda, twelve year since,
        Thy father was the Duke of Milan and
        A prince of power.
55 MIRANDA: Sir, are not you my father?
PROSPERO: Thy mother was a piece° of virtue, and
        She said thou wast my daughter; and thy father
        Was Duke of Milan, and his only heir
        And princess no worse issued.°
MIRANDA: O the heavens!
60   What foul play had we, that we came from thence?
        Or blessèd was't we did?
PROSPERO: Both, both, my girl.
        By foul play, as thou sayst, were we heaved thence,
        But blessedly holp° hither.

---

30 perdition: Loss.   **31 Betid:** Happened.   **32 Which:** Whom.   **35 bootless inquisition:** Prof-
itless inquiry.   **41 Out:** Fully.   **45–46 assurance . . . warrants:** Certainty that my memory guar-
antees.   **50 backward . . . time:** Abyss of the past.   **51 aught:** Anything.   **56 piece:**
Masterpiece, exemplar.   **59 no worse issued:** No less nobly born, descended.   **63 holp:** Helped.

MIRANDA: O, my heart bleeds
  To think o' the teen that I have turned you to,°
  Which is from° my remembrance! Please you, farther.   65
PROSPERO: My brother and thy uncle, called Antonio—
  I pray thee mark me—that a brother should
  Be so perfidious!—he whom next° thyself
  Of all the world I loved, and to him put
  The manage° of my state, as at that time   70
  Through all the seigniories° it was the first,
  And Prospero the prime° duke, being so reputed
  In dignity, and for the liberal arts
  Without a parallel; those being all my study,
  The government I cast upon my brother   75
  And to my state grew stranger,° being transported°
  And rapt in secret studies. Thy false uncle—
  Dost thou attend me?
MIRANDA: Sir, most heedfully.
PROSPERO: Being once perfected° how to grant suits,
  How to deny them, who t' advance and who   80
  To trash° for overtopping,° new created
  The creatures° that were mine, I say, or changed 'em,
  Or else new formed 'em;° having both the key°
  Of officer and office, set all hearts i' the state
  To what tune pleased his ear, that° now he was   85
  The ivy which had hid my princely trunk
  And sucked my verdure° out on 't.° Thou attend'st not.
MIRANDA: O, good sir, I do.
PROSPERO: I pray thee, mark me.
  I, thus neglecting worldly ends, all dedicated
  To closeness° and the bettering of my mind   90
  With that which, but by being so retired,
  O'erprized all popular rate,° in my false brother
  Awaked an evil nature; and my trust,
  Like a good parent,° did beget of° him
  A falsehood in its contrary as great   95

---

64 teen . . . to: Trouble I've caused you to remember or put you to.   **65 from:** Out of.   **68 next:** Next to.   **70 manage:** Management, administration.   **71 seigniories:** I.e., city-states of northern Italy.   **72 prime:** First in rank and importance.   **76 to . . . stranger:** I.e., withdrew from my responsibilities as duke;   **transported:** Carried away.   **79 perfected:** Grown skillful.   **81 trash:** Check a hound by tying a cord or weight to its neck;   **overtopping:** Running too far ahead of the pack; surmounting, exceeding one's authority.   **82 creatures:** Dependents.   **82–83 or changed . . . formed 'em:** I.e., either changed their loyalties and duties or else created new ones.   **83 key:** (1) Key for unlocking, (2) tool for tuning stringed instruments.   **85 that:** So that.   **87 verdure:** Vitality;   **on 't:** Of it.   **90 closeness:** Retirement, seclusion.   **91–92 but . . . rate:** I.e., were it not that its private nature caused me to neglect my public responsibilities, had a value far beyond what public opinion could appreciate, or, simply because it was done in such seclusion, had a value not appreciated by popular opinion.   **94 good parent:** (Alludes to the proverb that good parents often bear bad children; see also line 119);   **of:** In.

As my trust was, which had indeed no limit,
A confidence sans° bound. He being thus lorded°
Not only with what my revenue yielded
But what my power might else° exact, like one
100   Who, having into° truth by telling of it,
Made such a sinner of his memory
To° credit his own lie,° he did believe
He was indeed the Duke, out o'° the substitution
And executing th' outward face of royalty°
105   With all prerogative. Hence his ambition growing—
Dost thou hear?

MIRANDA: Your tale, sir, would cure deafness.

PROSPERO: To have no screen between this part he played
And him he played it for,° he needs will be°
Absolute Milan.° Me, poor man, my library
110   Was dukedom large enough. Of temporal royalties°
He thinks me now incapable; confederates°—
So dry° he was for sway°—wi' the King of Naples
To give him annual tribute, do him° homage,
Subject his coronet to his° crown, and bend°
115   The dukedom yet° unbowed—alas, poor Milan!—
To most ignoble stooping.

MIRANDA: O the heavens!

PROSPERO: Mark his condition° and th' event,° then tell me
If this might be a brother.

MIRANDA: I should sin
To think but° nobly of my grandmother.
Good wombs have borne bad sons.

120   PROSPERO: Now the condition.
This King of Naples, being an enemy
To me inveterate, hearkens° my brother's suit,
Which was that he,° in lieu o' the premises°
Of homage and I know not how much tribute,
125   Should presently extirpate° me and mine
Out of the dukedom and confer fair Milan,
With all the honors, on my brother. Whereon,

---

97 sans: Without;   **lorded:** Raised to lordship, with power and wealth.   **99 else:** Otherwise, additionally.   **100–102 Who . . . lie:** I.e., who, by repeatedly telling the lie (that he was indeed Duke of Milan), made his memory such a confirmed sinner against truth that he began to believe his own lie.   **100 into:** Unto, against;   **102 To:** So as to.   **103 out o':** As a result of.   **104 And . . . royalty:** And (as a result of) his carrying out all the visible functions of royalty.   **107–108 To have . . . it for:** To have no separation or barrier between his role and himself. (Antonio wanted to act in his own person, not as substitute.)   **108 needs will be:** Insisted on becoming.   **109 Absolute Milan:** Unconditional Duke of Milan.   **110 temporal royalties:** Practical prerogatives and responsibilities of a sovereign.   **111 confederates:** Conspires, allies himself.   **112 dry:** Thirsty; **sway:** Power.   **113 him:** I.e., the King of Naples.   **114 his . . . his:** Antonio's . . . the King of Naples';   **bend:** Make bow down.   **115 yet:** Hitherto.   **117 condition:** Pact;   **event:** Outcome.   **119 but:** Other than.   **122 hearkens:** Listens to.   **123 he:** The King of Naples;   **in . . . premises:** In return for the stipulation.   **125 presently extirpate:** At once remove.

A treacherous army levied, one midnight
Fated to th' purpose did Antonio open
The gates of Milan, and, i' the dead of darkness,   130
The ministers for the purpose° hurried thence°
Me and thy crying self.

MIRANDA: Alack, for pity!
I, not remembering how I cried out then,
Will cry it o'er again. It is a hint°
That wrings° mine eyes to 't.

PROSPERO: Hear a little further,   135
And then I'll bring thee to the present business
Which now's upon's, without the which this story
Were most impertinent.°

MIRANDA: Wherefore° did they not
That hour destroy us?

PROSPERO: Well demanded,° wench.°
My tale provokes that question. Dear, they durst not,   140
So dear the love my people bore me, nor set
A mark so bloody° on the business, but
With colors fairer° painted their foul ends.
In few,° they hurried us aboard a bark,°
Bore us some leagues to sea, where they prepared   145
A rotten carcass of a butt,° not rigged,
Nor tackle,° sail, nor mast; the very rats
Instinctively have quit° it. There they hoist us,
To cry to th' sea that roared to us, to sigh
To th' winds whose pity, sighing back again,   150
Did us but loving wrong.°

MIRANDA: Alack, what trouble
Was I then to you!

PROSPERO: O, a cherubin
Thou wast that did preserve me. Thou didst smile,
Infusèd with a fortitude from heaven,
When I have decked° the sea with drops full salt,   155
Under my burden groaned, which° raised in me
An undergoing stomach,° to bear up
Against what should ensue.

MIRANDA: How came we ashore?

PROSPERO: By Providence divine.   160

---

131 **ministers . . . purpose:** Agents employed to do this; **thence:** From there.   134 **hint:** Occasion.   135 **wrings:** (1) Constrains, (2) wrings tears from.   138 **impertinent:** Irrelevant; **Wherefore:** Why.   139 **demanded:** Asked; **wench:** (Here a term of endearment.)   141–142 **set . . . bloody:** I.e., make obvious their murderous intent (from the practice of marking with the blood of the prey those who have participated in a successful hunt).   143 **fairer:** Apparently more attractive.   144 **few:** Few words; **bark:** Ship.   146 **butt:** Cask, tub.   147 **Nor tackle:** Neither rigging.   148 **quit:** Abandoned.   151 **Did . . . wrong:** (I.e., the winds pitied Prospero and Miranda, though of necessity they blew them from shore.)   155 **decked:** Covered (with salt tears), adorned.   156 **which:** I.e., the smile.   157 **undergoing stomach:** Courage to go on.

Some food we had, and some fresh water, that
A noble Neapolitan, Gonzalo,
Out of his charity, who being then appointed
Master of this design, did give us, with
165   Rich garments, linens, stuffs,° and necessaries,
Which since have steaded much.° So, of° his gentleness,
Knowing I loved my books, he furnished me
From mine own library with volumes that
I prize above my dukedom.

MIRANDA: Would° I might
But ever° see that man!

170   PROSPERO: Now I arise.   [*He puts on his magic cloak.*]
Sit still, and hear the last of our sea sorrow.°
Here in this island we arrived; and here
Have I, thy schoolmaster, made thee more profit°
Than other princess'° can, that have more time
175   For vainer° hours and tutors not so careful.

MIRANDA: Heavens thank you for 't! And now, I pray you, sir—
For still 'tis beating in my mind—your reason
For raising this sea storm?

PROSPERO: Know thus far forth:
By accident most strange, bountiful Fortune,
180   Now my dear lady,° hath mine enemies
Brought to this shore; and by my prescience
I find my zenith° doth depend upon
A most auspicious star, whose influence°
If now I court not, but omit,° my fortunes
185   Will ever after droop. Here cease more questions.
Thou art inclined to sleep. 'Tis a good dullness,°
And give it way.° I know thou canst not choose.   [MIRANDA *sleeps.*]
Come away,° servant, come! I am ready now.
Approach, my Ariel, come.

(*Enter* ARIEL.)

190   ARIEL: All hail, great master, grave sir, hail! I come
To answer thy best pleasure; be 't to fly,
To swim, to dive into the fire, to ride
On the curled clouds, to thy strong bidding task°
Ariel and all his quality.°

PROSPERO: Hast thou, spirit,

---

165 stuffs: Supplies.   **166 steaded much:** Been of much use; **So, of:** Similarly, out of.   **169 Would:** I wish. **170 But ever:** I.e., someday.   **171 sea sorrow:** Sorrowful adventure at sea. **173 more profit:** Profit more.   **174 princess':** Princesses (or the word may be *princes,* referring to royal children both male and female).   **175 vainer:** More foolishly spent.   **180 my dear lady:** (Refers to Fortune, not Miranda).   **182 zenith:** Height of fortune (astrological term).   **183 influence:** Astrological power.   **184 omit:** Ignore.   **186 dullness:** Drowsiness.   **187 give it way:** Let it happen (i.e., don't fight it).   **188 Come away:** Come.   **193 task:** Make demands upon. **194 quality:** (1) Fellow spirits, (2) abilities.

Performed to point° the tempest that I bade thee?   195
ARIEL: To every article.
    I boarded the King's ship. Now on the beak,°
    Now in the waist,° the deck,° in every cabin,
    I flamed amazement.° Sometimes I'd divide
    And burn in many places; on the topmast,   200
    The yards, and bowsprit would I flame distinctly,°
    Then meet and join. Jove's lightning, the precursors
    O' the dreadful thunderclaps, more momentary
    And sight-outrunning° were not.° The fire and cracks
    Of sulfurous roaring the most mighty Neptune°   205
    Seem to besiege and make his bold waves tremble,
    Yea, his dread trident shake.
PROSPERO: My brave spirit!
    Who was so firm, so constant, that this coil°
    Would not infect his reason?
ARIEL: Not a soul
    But felt a fever of the mad° and played   210
    Some tricks of desperation. All but mariners
    Plunged in the foaming brine and quit the vessel,
    Then all afire with me. The King's son, Ferdinand,
    With hair up-staring° —then like reeds, not hair—
    Was the first man that leapt; cried, "Hell is empty,   215
    And all the devils are here!"
PROSPERO: Why, that's my spirit!
    But was not this nigh shore?
ARIEL: Close by, my master.
PROSPERO: But are they, Ariel, safe?
ARIEL: Not a hair perished.
    On their sustaining garments° not a blemish,
    But fresher than before; and, as thou bad'st° me,   220
    In troops° I have dispersed them, 'bout the isle.
    The King's son have I landed by himself,
    Whom I left cooling of° the air with sighs
    In an odd angle° of the isle, and sitting,
    His arms in this sad knot.°   [*He folds his arms.*]
PROSPERO: Of the King's ship,   225
    The mariners, say how thou hast disposed,
    And all the rest o' the fleet.
ARIEL: Safely in harbor

---

195 to point: To the smallest detail.   **197 beak:** Prow.   **198 waist:** Midships;   **deck:** Poop deck at the stern.   **199 flamed amazement:** Struck terror in the guise of fire, i.e., Saint Elmo's fire. **201 distinctly:** In different places.   **204 sight-outrunning:** Swifter than sight;   **were not:** Could not have been.   **205 Neptune:** Roman god of the sea.   **208 coil:** Tumult.   **210 of the mad:** I.e., such as madmen feel.   **214 up-staring:** Standing on end.   **219 sustaining garments:** Garments that buoyed them up in the sea.   **220 bad'st:** Ordered.   **221 troops:** Groups.   **223 cooling of:** Cooling.   **224 angle:** Corner.   **225 sad knot** (Folded arms are indicative of melancholy.)

Is the King's ship; in the deep nook,° where once
Thou called'st me up at midnight to fetch dew°
230   From the still-vexed Bermudas,° there she's hid;
The mariners all under hatches stowed,
Who, with a charm joined to their suffered labor,°
I have left asleep. And for the rest o' the fleet,
Which I dispersed, they all have met again
235   And are upon the Mediterranean float°
Bound sadly home for Naples,
Supposing that they saw the King's ship wrecked
And his great person perish.

PROSPERO: Ariel, thy charge
Exactly is performed. But there's more work.
What is the time o' the day?

240   ARIEL: Past the mid season.°

PROSPERO: At least two glasses.° The time twixt six and now
Must by us both be spent most preciously.

ARIEL: Is there more toil? Since thou dost give me pains,°
Let me remember° thee what thou hast promised,
Which is not yet performed me.

245   PROSPERO: How now? Moody?
What is 't thou canst demand?

ARIEL: My liberty.

PROSPERO: Before the time be out? No more!

ARIEL: I prithee,
Remember I have done thee worthy service,
Told thee no lies, made thee no mistakings, served
250   Without or grudge or grumblings. Thou did promise
To bate° me a full year.

PROSPERO: Dost thou forget
From what a torment I did free thee?

ARIEL: No.

PROSPERO: Thou dost, and think'st it much to tread the ooze
Of the salt deep,
255   To run upon the sharp wind of the north,
To do me° business in the veins° o' the earth
When it is baked° with frost.

ARIEL: I do not, sir.

PROSPERO: Thou liest, malignant thing! Hast thou forgot
The foul witch Sycorax, who with age and envy°
260   Was grown into a hoop?° Hast thou forgot her?

228 nook: Bay.   **229 dew:** (Collected at midnight for magical purposes; compare with line 325.)
230 still-vexed Bermudas: Ever stormy Bermudas.   **232 with . . . labor:** By means of a spell
added to all the labor they have undergone.   **235 float:** Sea.   **240 mid season:** Noon.   **241
glasses:** Hourglasses.   **243 pains:** Labors.   **244 remember:** Remind.   **251 bate:** Remit,
deduct.   **256 do me:** Do for me;   **veins:** Veins of minerals, or, underground streams, thought to
be analogous to the veins of the human body.   **257 baked:** Hardened.   **259 envy:** Malice.   **260
grown into a hoop:** I.e., so bent over with age as to resemble a hoop.

ARIEL: No, sir.

PROSPERO: Thou hast. Where was she born? Speak. Tell me.

ARIEL: Sir, in Argier.°

PROSPERO: O, was she so? I must
  Once in a month recount what thou hast been,
  Which thou forgett'st. This damned witch Sycorax,   265
  For mischiefs manifold and sorceries terrible
  To enter human hearing, from Argier,
  Thou know'st, was banished. For one thing she did°
  They would not take her life. Is not this true?

ARIEL: Ay, sir.   270

PROSPERO: This blue-eyed° hag was hither brought with child°
  And here was left by the sailors. Thou, my slave,
  As thou report'st thyself, was then her servant;
  And, for° thou wast a spirit too delicate
  To act her earthy and abhorred commands,   275
  Refusing her grand hests,° she did confine thee,
  By help of her more potent ministers
  And in her most unmitigable rage,
  Into a cloven pine, within which rift
  Imprisoned thou didst painfully remain   280
  A dozen years; within which space she died
  And left thee there, where thou didst vent thy groans
  As fast as mill wheels strike.° Then was this island—
  Save° for the son that she did litter° here,
  A freckled whelp,° hag-born° —not honored with   285
  A human shape.

ARIEL: Yes, Caliban her son.°

PROSPERO: Dull thing, I say so:° he, that Caliban
  Whom now I keep in service. Thou best know'st
  What torment I did find thee in. Thy groans
  Did make wolves howl, and penetrate the breasts   290
  Of ever-angry bears. It was a torment
  To lay upon the damned, which Sycorax
  Could not gain undo. It was mine art,
  When I arrived and heard thee, that made gape°
  The pine and let thee out.

ARIEL: I thank thee, master.   295

PROSPERO: If thou more murmur'st, I will rend an oak
  And peg thee in his° knotty entrails till

---

263 Argier: Algiers.   **268 one . . . did:** (Perhaps a reference to her pregnancy, for which her life would be spared.)   **271 blue-eyed:** With dark circles under the eyes or with blue eyelids, implying pregnancy; **with child:** Pregnant.   **274 for:** Because.   **276 hests:** Commands.   **283 as mill wheels strike:** As the blades of a mill wheel strike the water.   **284 Save:** Except; **litter:** Give birth to.   **285 whelp:** Offspring (used of animals); **hag-born:** Born of a female demon.   **286 Yes . . . son:** (Ariel is probably concurring with Prospero's comment about a "freckled whelp," not contradicting the point about "A human shape.")   **287 Dull . . . so:** I.e., exactly, that's what I said, you dullard.   **294 gape:** Open wide.   **297 his:** Its.

Thou hast howled away twelve winters.

ARIEL: Pardon, master.
  I will be correspondent° to command
300   And do my spiriting° gently.°
PROSPERO: Do so, and after two days
  I will discharge thee.
ARIEL: That's my noble master!
  What shall I do? Say what? What shall I do?
PROSPERO: Go make thyself like a nymph o' the sea. Be subject
305   To no sight but thine and mine, invisible
  To every eyeball else. Go take this shape
  And hither come in 't. Go, hence with diligence!   (*Exit* [ARIEL].)
  Awake, dear heart, awake! Thou hast slept well.
  Awake!
310   MIRANDA: The strangeness of your story put
  Heaviness° in me.
PROSPERO: Shake it off. Come on,
  We'll visit Caliban, my slave, who never
  Yields us kind answer.
MIRANDA: 'Tis a villain, sir,
  I do not love to look on.
PROSPERO: But, as 'tis,
315   We cannot miss° him. He does make our fire,
  Fetch in our wood, and serves in offices°
  That profit us.—What ho! Slave! Caliban!
  Thou earth, thou! Speak.
CALIBAN (*within*):   There's wood enough within.
PROSPERO: Come forth, I say! There's other business for thee.
320   Come, thou tortoise! When?°

  (*Enter* ARIEL *like a water nymph.*)

  Fine apparition! My quaint° Ariel,
  Hark in thine ear.   [*He whispers.*]
ARIEL: My lord, it shall be done.   (*Exit.*)
PROSPERO: Thou poisonous slave, got° by the devil himself
  Upon thy wicked dam,° come forth!

  (*Enter* CALIBAN.)

325   CALIBAN: As wicked° dew as e'er my mother brushed
  With raven's feather from unwholesome fen°
  Drop on you both! A southwest° blow on ye
  And blister you all o'er!

---

299 correspondent: Responsive, submissive.   **300 spiriting:** Duties as a spirit;   **gently:** Willingly, ungrudgingly.   **311 Heaviness:** Drowsiness.   **315 miss:** Do without.   **316 offices:** Functions, duties.   **320 When:** (An exclamation of impatience.)   **321 quaint:** Ingenious.   **323 got:** Begotten, sired.   **324 dam:** Mother (used of animals).   **325 wicked:** Mischievous, harmful.   **326 fen:** Marsh, bog.   **327 southwest:** I.e., wind thought to bring disease.

PROSPERO: For this, be sure, tonight thou shalt have cramps,
    Side-stitches that shall pen thy breath up. Urchins°   *330*
    Shall forth at vast° of night that they may work
    All exercise on thee. Thou shalt be pinched
    As thick as honeycomb,° each pinch more stinging
    Than bees that made 'em.°
CALIBAN: I must eat my dinner.
    This island's mine, by Sycorax my mother,   *335*
    Which thou tak'st from me. When thou cam'st first,
    Thou strok'st me and made much of me, wouldst give me
    Water with berries in 't, and teach me how
    To name the bigger light, and how the less,°
    That burn by day and night. And then I loved thee   *340*
    And showed thee all the qualities o' th' isle,
    The fresh springs, brine pits, barren place and fertile.
    Cursed be I that did so! All the charms°
    Of Sycorax, toads, beetles, bats, light on you!
    For I am all the subjects that you have,   *345*
    Which first was mine own king; and here you sty° me
    In this hard rock, whiles you do keep from me
    The rest o' th' island.
PROSPERO: Thou most lying slave,
    Whom stripes° may move, not kindness! I have used thee,
    Filth as thou art, with humane° care, and lodged thee   *350*
    In mine own cell, till thou didst seek to violate
    The honor of my child.
CALIBAN: Oho, oho! Would 't had been done!
    Thou didst prevent me; I had peopled else°
    This isle with Calibans.
MIRANDA: Abhorrèd° slave,   *355*
    Which any print° of goodness wilt not take,
    Being capable of all ill! I pitied thee,
    Took pains to make thee speak, taught thee each hour
    One thing or other. When thou didst not, savage,
    Know thine own meaning, but wouldst gabble like   *360*
    A thing most brutish, I endowed thy purposes°
    With words that made them known. But thy vile race,°

---

330 Urchins: Hedgehogs; here, suggesting goblins in the guise of hedgehogs.   **331 vast:** Lengthy, desolate time. (Malignant spirits were thought to be restricted to the hours of darkness.)   **333 As thick as honeycomb:** I.e., all over, with as many pinches as a honeycomb has cells.   **334 'em:** I.e., the honeycomb.   **339 the bigger . . . less:** I.e., the sun and the moon (see Genesis 1:16: "God then made two great lights: the greater light to rule the day, and the less light to rule the night").   **343 charms:** Spells.   **346 sty:** Confine as in a sty.   **349 stripes:** Lashes.   **350 humane:** (Not distinguished as word from *human.*)   **354 peopled else:** Otherwise populated.   **355–366 Abhorrèd . . . prison:** (Sometimes assigned by editors to Prospero.)   **356 print:** Imprint, impression.   **361 purposes:** Meanings, desires.   **362 race:** Natural disposition; species, nature.

Though thou didst learn, had that in 't which good natures
Could not abide to be with; therefore wast thou
365   Deservedly confined into this rock,
Who hadst deserved more than a prison.

CALIBAN: You taught me language, and my profit on 't
Is I know how to curse. The red plague° rid° you
For learning° me your language!

PROSPERO: Hagseed,° hence!
370   Fetch us in fuel, and be quick, thou'rt best,°
To answer other business.° Shrugg'st thou, malice?
If thou neglect'st or dost unwillingly
What I command, I'll rack thee with old° cramps,
Fill all thy bones with aches,° make thee roar
375   That beasts shall tremble at thy din.

CALIBAN: No, pray thee.
[Aside.] I must obey. His art is of such power
It would control my dam's god, Setebos,°
And make a vassal of him.

PROSPERO: So, slave, hence!   (Exit CALIBAN.)

(Enter FERDINAND; and ARIEL, invisible,° playing and singing. [FERDINAND does
not see PROSPERO and MIRANDA.])

(Ariel's Song.)

ARIEL: Come unto these yellow sands,
380   And then take hands;
Curtsied when you have,° and kissed
The wild waves whist,°
Foot it featly° here and there,
And, sweet sprites,° bear
The burden.° Hark, hark!

                                (Burden, dispersedly° [within]. Bow-wow.)
385   The watchdogs bark

                                ([Burden, dispersedly within.] Bow-wow.)
Hark, hark! I hear
The strain of strutting chanticleer
Cry Cock-a-diddle-dow.

---

368 red plague: Plague characterized by red sores and evacuation of blood;   **rid:** Destroy.   **369 learning:** Teaching;   **Hagseed:** Offspring of a female demon.   **370 thou'rt best:** You'd be well advised.   **371 answer other business:** Perform other tasks.   **373 old:** Such as old people suffer, or, plenty of.   **374 aches:** (Pronounced "aitches.")   **377 Setebos:** (A god of the Patagonians, named in Robert Eden's *History of Travel*, 1577.)   **Ariel, invisible:** (Ariel wears a garment that by convention indicates he is invisible to the other characters.)   **381 Curtsied . . . have:** When you have curtsied.   **381–382 kissed . . . whist:** Kissed the waves into silence, or, kissed while the waves are being hushed.   **383 Foot it featly:** Dance nimbly.   **384 sprites:** Spirits.   **385 burden:** Refrain, undersong;   **dispersedly:** I.e., from all directions, not in unison.

FERDINAND: Where should this music be? I' th' air or th' earth?   *390*
    It sounds no more; and sure it waits upon°
    Some god o' th' island. Sitting on a bank,°
    Weeping again the King my father's wreck,
    This music crept by me upon the waters,
    Allaying both their fury and my passion°   *395*
    With its sweet air. Thence° I have followed it,
    Or it hath drawn me rather. But 'tis gone.
    No, it begins again.

(*Ariel's Song.*)

ARIEL: Full fathom five thy father lies.
        Of his bones are coral made.   *400*
    Those are pearls that were his eyes.
        Nothing of him that doth fade
    But doth suffer a sea change
    Into something rich and strange.
    Sea nymphs hourly ring his knell.°   *405*
                (*Burden* [*within*]. Ding dong.)
    Hark, now I hear them, ding dong bell.
FERDINAND: The ditty does remember° my drowned father.
    This is no mortal business, nor no sound
    That the earth owes.° I hear it now above me.
PROSPERO [*to* MIRANDA]: The fringèd curtains of thine eye advance°   *410*
    And say what thou seest yond.
MIRANDA: What is 't? A spirit?
    Lord, how it looks about! Believe me, sir,
    It carries a brave° form. But 'tis a spirit.
PROSPERO: No, wench, it eats and sleeps and hath such senses
    As we have, such. This gallant which thou seest   *415*
    Was in the wreck; and, but° he's something stained°
    With grief, that's beauty's canker,° thou mightst call him
    A goodly person. He hath lost his fellows
    And strays about to find 'em.
MIRANDA: I might call him
    A thing divine, for nothing natural   *420*
    I ever saw so noble.
PROSPERO [*aside*]:   It goes on,° I see,
    As my soul prompts it.—Spirit, fine spirit, I'll free thee
    Within two days for this.

391 waits upon: Serves, attends.   **392 bank:** Sandbank.   **395 passion:** Grief.   **396 Thence:** I.e., from the bank on which I sat.   **405 knell:** Announcement of a death by the tolling of a bell. **407 remember:** Commemorate.   **409 owes:** Owns.   **410 advance:** Raise.   **413 brave:** Excellent.   **416 but:** Except that; **something stained:** Somewhat disfigured.   **417 canker:** Canker-worm (feeding on buds and leaves).   **421 It goes on:** I.e., my plan works.

FERDINAND [*seeing* MIRANDA]: Most sure, the goddess
425   On whom these airs° attend!—Vouchsafe° my prayer
          May know° if you remain° upon this island,
          And that you will some good instruction give
          How I may bear me° here. My prime° request,
          Which I do last pronounce, is—O you wonder!°—
          If you be maid or no?°
430 MIRANDA: No wonder, sir,
          But certainly a maid.
      FERDINAND: My language? Heavens!
          I am the best° of them that speak this speech,
          Were I but where 'tis spoken.
      PROSPERO [*coming forward*]:   How? The best?
          What wert thou if the King of Naples heard thee?
435 FERDINAND: A single° thing, as I am now, that wonders
          To hear thee speak of Naples.° He does hear me,°
          And that he does I weep.° Myself am Naples,°
          Who with mine eyes, never since at ebb,° beheld
          The King my father wrecked.
      MIRANDA: Alack, for mercy!
440 FERDINAND: Yes, faith, and all his lords, the Duke of Milan
          And his brave son° being twain.
      PROSPERO [*aside*]:   The Duke of Milan
          And his more braver° daughter could control° thee,
          If now 'twere fit to do 't. At the first sight
          They have changed eyes.° —Delicate Ariel,
445   I'll set thee free for this. [*To* FERDINAND.] A word, good sir.
          I fear you have done yourself some wrong.° A word!
      MIRANDA [*aside*]: Why speaks my father so urgently? This
          Is the third man that e'er I saw, the first
          That e'er I sighed for. Pity move my father
          To be inclined my way!
450 FERDINAND: O, if a virgin,
          And your affection not gone forth, I'll make you
          The Queen of Naples.
      PROSPERO: Soft, sir! One word more.

---

425 airs: Songs; **Vouchsafe:** Grant. **426 May know:** I.e., that I may know; **remain:** Dwell.
428 bear me: Conduct myself; **prime:** Chief. **429 wonder:** (Miranda's name means "to be
wondered at.") **430 maid or no:** I.e., a human maiden as opposed to a goddess or married
woman. **432 best:** I.e., in birth. **435 single:** (1) Solitary, being at once King of Naples and myself, (2) feeble. **436, 437 Naples:** The King of Naples. **436 He does hear me:** I.e., the King of
Naples does hear my words, for I am King of Naples. **437 And . . . weep:** I.e., and I weep at this
reminder that my father is seemingly dead, leaving me heir. **438 at ebb:** I.e., dry, not weeping.
441 son: (The only reference in the play to a son of Antonio.) **442 more braver:** More splendid; **control:** Refute. **444 changed eyes:** Exchanged amorous glances. **446 done . . .
wrong:** I.e., spoken falsely.

[*Aside.*] They are both in either's° powers; but this swift business
    I must uneasy° make, lest too light winning
    Make the prize light.° [*To* FERDINAND.] One word more: I charge thee   455
    That thou attend° me. Thou dost here usurp
    The name thou ow'st° not, and hast put thyself
    Upon this island as a spy, to win it
    From me, the lord on 't.°
FERDINAND: No, as I am a man.
MIRANDA: There's nothing ill can dwell in such a temple.   460
    If the ill spirit have so fair a house,
    Good things will strive to dwell with 't.°
PROSPERO: Follow me.—
    Speak not you for him; he's a traitor.—Come,
    I'll manacle thy neck and feet together.
    Seawater shalt thou drink; thy food shall be   465
    The fresh-brook mussels, withered roots, and husks
    Wherein the acorn cradled. Follow.
FERDINAND: No!
    I will resist such entertainment° till
    Mine enemy has more power.   (*He draws, and is charmed° from moving.*)
MIRANDA: O dear father,
    Make not too rash° a trial of him, for   470
    He's gentle,° and not fearful.°
PROSPERO: What, I say,
    My foot° my tutor?—Put thy sword up, traitor,
    Who mak'st a show but dar'st not strike, thy conscience
    Is so possessed with guilt. Come, from thy ward,°
    For I can here disarm thee with this stick   475
    And make thy weapon drop.   [*He brandishes his staff.*]
MIRANDA [*trying to hinder him*]: Beseech you, father!
PROSPERO: Hence! Hang not on my garments.
MIRANDA: Sir, have pity!
    I'll be his surety.°
PROSPERO: Silence! One word more
    Shall make me chide thee, if not hate thee. What,   480
    An advocate for an impostor? Hush!
    Thou think'st there is no more such shapes as he,
    Having seen but him and Caliban. Foolish wench,
    To° the most of men this is a Caliban,

---

453 both in either's: Each in the other's.   **454 uneasy:** Difficult.   **454–455 light . . . light:** Easy . . . cheap.   **456 attend:** Follow, obey.   **457 ow'st:** Ownest.   **459 on 't:** Of it.   **462 strive . . . with 't:** I.e., expel the evil and occupy the *temple*, the body.   **468 entertainment:** Treatment. **charmed:** Magically prevented.   **470 rash:** Harsh.   **471 gentle:** Wellborn; **fearful:** Frightening, dangerous, or, perhaps, cowardly.   **472 foot:** Subordinate (Miranda, the foot, presumes to instruct Prospero, the head).   **474 ward:** Defensive posture (in fencing).   **479 surety:** Guarantee. **484 To:** Compared to.

And they to him are angels.

485 MIRANDA: My affections
Are then most humble; I have no ambition
To see a goodlier man.

PROSPERO [*to* FERDINAND]: Come on, obey.
Thy nerves° are in their infancy again
And have no vigor in them.

FERDINAND: So they are.

490 My spirits,° as in a dream, are all bound up.
My father's loss, the weakness which I feel,
The wreck of all my friends, nor this man's threats
To whom I am subdued, are but light° to me,
Might I but through my prison once a day

495 Behold this maid. All corners else° o' th' earth
Let liberty make use of; space enough
Have I in such a prison.

PROSPERO [*aside*]: It works. [*To* FERDINAND.] Come on.—[*To* ARIEL]
Thou hast done well, fine Ariel! [*To* FERDINAND.] Follow me.
[*To Ariel.*] Hark what thou else shalt do me.°

500 MIRANDA [*to* FERDINAND]:   Be of comfort.
My father's of a better nature, sir,
Than he appears by speech. This is unwonted°
Which now came from him.

PROSPERO [*to* ARIEL]:   Thou shalt be as free
As mountain winds; but then° exactly do
All points of my command.

505 ARIEL: To th' syllable.

PROSPERO [*to* FERDINAND]: Come, follow. [*To* MIRANDA.] Speak not for him.

(*Exeunt.*)

[ACT 2, SCENE 1]

[*Another part of the island.*]

(*Enter* ALONSO, SEBASTIAN, ANTONIO, GONZALO, ADRIAN, FRANCISCO, *and others.*)

GONZALO [*to* ALONSO]: Beseech you, sir, be merry. You have cause,
So have we all, of joy, for our escape
Is much beyond our loss. Our hint° of woe
Is common; every day some sailor's wife,

5 The masters of some merchant, and the merchant,°
Have just our theme of woe. But for the miracle,

---

488 nerves: Sinews.   **490 spirits:** Vital powers.   **493 light:** Unimportant.   **495 corners else:** Other corners, regions.   **500 me:** For me.   **502 unwonted:** Unusual.   **504 then:** Until then, or, if that is to be so.   **ACT 2, SCENE 1. 3 hint:** Occasion.   **5 masters . . . the merchant:** Officers of some merchant vessel and the merchant himself, the owner.

I mean our preservation, few in millions
Can speak like us. Then wisely, good sir, weigh
Our sorrow with° our comfort.

ALONSO: Prithee, peace.

SEBASTIAN [*aside to* ANTONIO]: He receives comfort like cold porridge.°   10

ANTONIO [*aside to* SEBASTIAN]: The visitor° will not give him o'er° so.

SEBASTIAN: Look, he's winding up the watch of his wit; by and by it will strike.

GONZALO [*to* ALONSO]: Sir—

SEBASTIAN [*aside to* ANTONIO]: One. Tell.°

GONZALO: When every grief is entertained   15
     That's offered, comes to th' entertainer°—

SEBASTIAN: A dollar.°

GONZALO: Dolor comes to him, indeed. You have spoken truer than you purposed.

SEBASTIAN: You have taken it wiselier than I meant you should.

GONZALO [*to* ALONSO]: Therefore, my lord—   20

ANTONIO: Fie, what a spendthrift is he of his tongue!

ALONSO [*to* GONZALO]: I prithee, spare.°

GONZALO: Well, I have done. But yet—

SEBASTIAN [*aside to* ANTONIO]: He will be talking.

ANTONIO [*aside to* SEBASTIAN]: Which, of he or Adrian, for a good wager, first be-   25
     gins to crow?°

SEBASTIAN: The old cock.°

ANTONIO: The cockerel.°

SEBASTIAN: Done. The wager?

ANTONIO: A laughter.°   30

SEBASTIAN: A match!°

ADRIAN: Though this island seem to be desert°—

ANTONIO: Ha, ha, ha!

SEBASTIAN: So, you're paid.°

ADRIAN: Uninhabitable and almost inaccessible—   35

SEBASTIAN: Yet—

ADRIAN: Yet—

ANTONIO: He could not miss 't.°

ADRIAN: It must needs be° of subtle, tender, and delicate temperance.°

---

9 with: Against.   **10 porridge:** Pun suggested by *peace* for "peas" or "pease," a common ingredient of porridge.   **11 visitor:** One taking nourishment and comfort to the sick, as Gonzalo is doing; **give him o'er:** Abandon him.   **14 Tell:** Keep count.   **15–16 When . . . entertainer:** When every sorrow that presents itself is accepted without resistance, there comes to the recipient.   **17 dollar:** Widely circulated coin, the German thaler and the Spanish piece of eight (Sebastian puns on *entertainer* in the sense of innkeeper; to Gonzalo, *dollar* suggests "dolor," grief).   **22 spare:** Forbear, cease.   **25–26 Which . . . crow:** Which of the two, Gonzalo or Adrian, do you bet will speak (crow) first?   **27 old cock:** I.e., Gonzalo.   **28 cockerel:** I.e., Adrian.   **30 laughter:** (1) Burst of laughter, (2) sitting of eggs. (When Adrian, the *cockerel,* begins to speak two lines later, Sebastian loses the bet. . . .)   **31 A match:** A bargain; agreed.   **32 desert:** Uninhabited.   **34 you're paid:** I.e., you've had your laugh.   **38 miss 't:** (1) Avoid saying "Yet," (2) miss the island.   **39 must needs be:** Has to be;   **temperance:** Mildness of climate.

40   ANTONIO: Temperance° was a delicate° wench.

SEBASTIAN: Ay, and a subtle,° as he most learnedly delivered.°

ADRIAN: The air breathes upon us here most sweetly.

SEBASTIAN: As if it had lungs, and rotten ones.

ANTONIO: Or as 'twere perfumed by a fen.

45   GONZALO: Here is everything advantageous to life.

ANTONIO: True, save° means to live.

SEBASTIAN: Of that there's none, or little.

GONZALO: How lush and lusty° the grass looks! How green!

ANTONIO: The ground indeed is tawny.°

50   SEBASTIAN: With an eye° of green in 't.

ANTONIO: He misses not much.

SEBASTIAN: No. He doth but° mistake the truth totally.

GONZALO: But the rarity of it is—which is indeed almost beyond credit—

SEBASTIAN: As many vouched rarities° are.

55   GONZALO: That our garments, being, as they were, drenched in the sea, hold
        notwithstanding their freshness and glosses, being rather new-dyed than stained
        with salt water.

ANTONIO: If but one of his pockets° could speak, would it not say he lies?

SEBASTIAN: Ay, or very falsely pocket up° his report.°

60   GONZALO: Methinks our garments are now as fresh as when we put them on first in
        Afric, at the marriage of the King's fair daughter Claribel to the King of Tunis.

SEBASTIAN: 'Twas a sweet marriage, and we prosper well in our return.

ADRIAN: Tunis was never graced before with such a paragon to° their queen.

GONZALO: Not since widow Dido's° time.

65   ANTONIO [aside to SEBASTIAN]: Widow? A pox o' that! How came that "widow" in?
        Widow Dido!

SEBASTIAN: What if he had said "widower Aeneas" too? Good Lord, how you take°
        it!

ADRIAN [to GONZALO]: "Widow Dido" said you? You make me study of° that. She
70   was of Carthage, not of Tunis.

GONZALO: This Tunis, sir, was Carthage.

ADRIAN: Carthage?

GONZALO: I assure you, Carthage.

---

40 Temperance: A girl's name;   **delicate:** (Here it means "given to pleasure, voluptuous"; in line
39, "pleasant." Antonio is evidently suggesting that *tender, and delicate temperance* sounds like a Puritan
phrase, which Antonio then mocks by applying the words to a woman rather than an island. He
began this bawdy comparison with a double entendre on *inaccessible,* line 35.)   **41 subtle:** (Here it
means "tricky, sexually crafty"; in line 39, "delicate");   **delivered:** Uttered. (Sebastian joins Antonio
in baiting the Puritans with his use of the pious cant phrase *learnedly delivered.*)   **46 save:** Except.
48 lusty: Healthy.   **49 tawny:** Dull brown, yellowish.   **50 eye:** Tinge, or spot (perhaps with reference to Gonzalo's eye or judgment).   **52 but:** Merely.   **54 vouched rarities:** Allegedly real,
though strange, sights.   **58 pockets:** I.e., because they are muddy.   **59 pocket up:** I.e., conceal,
suppress; often used in the sense of "receive unprotestingly, fail to respond to a challenge";   **his report:** (Sebastian's jest is that the evidence of Gonzalo's soggy and sea-stained pockets would confute
Gonzalo's speech and his reputation for truth telling.)   **63 to:** For.   **64 widow Dido:** Queen of
Carthage, deserted by Aeneas. (She was, in fact, a widow when Aeneas, a widower, met her, but Antonio may be amused at Gonzalo's prudish use of the term *widow* to describe a woman deserted by
her lover.)   **67 take:** Understand, respond to, interpret.   **69 study of:** Think about.

ANTONIO: His word is more than the miraculous harp.°

SEBASTIAN: He hath raised the wall, and houses too.   75

ANTONIO: What impossible matter will he make easy next?

SEBASTIAN: I think he will carry this island home in his pocket and give it his son
    for an apple.

ANTONIO: And, sowing the kernels° of it in the sea, bring forth more islands.

GONZALO: Ay.°   80

ANTONIO: Why, in good time.°

GONZALO [*to* ALONSO]*:* Sir, we were talking° that our garments seem now as fresh
    as when we were at Tunis at the marriage of your daughter, who is now queen.

ANTONIO: And the rarest° that e'er came there.

SEBASTIAN: Bate,° I beseech you, widow Dido.   85

ANTONIO: O, widow Dido! Ay, widow Dido.

GONZALO: Is not, sir, my doublet° as fresh as the first day I wore it? I mean, in a
    sort.°

ANTONIO: That "sort"° was well wished for.

GONZALO: When I wore it at your daughter's marriage.   90

ALONSO: You cram these words into mine ears against
    The stomach of my sense.° Would I had never
    Married° my daughter there! For, coming thence,
    My son is lost and, in my rate,° she too,
    Who is so far from Italy removed   95
    I ne'er again shall see her. O thou mine heir
    Of Naples and of Milan, what strange fish
    Hath made his meal on thee?

FRANCISCO: Sir, he may live.
    I saw him beat the surges° under him
    And ride upon their backs. He trod the water,   100
    Whose enmity he flung aside, and breasted
    The surge most swoll'n that met him. His bold head
    'Bove the contentious waves he kept, and oared
    Himself with his good arms in lusty° stroke
    To th' shore, that o'er his° wave-worn basis bowed,°   105
    As° stooping to relieve him. I not doubt
    He came alive to land.

---

74 miraculous harp: (Alludes to Amphion's harp, with which he raised the walls of Thebes; Gonzalo has exceeded that deed by recreating ancient Carthage—*wall and houses*—mistakenly on the site
of modern-day Tunis. Some Renaissance commentators believed, like Gonzalo, that the two sites
were near each other.)   **79 kernels:** Seeds.   **80 Ay:** (Gonzalo may be reasserting his point about
Carthage, or he may be responding ironically to Antonio, who, in turn, answers sarcastically.)   **81 in
good time:** (An expression of ironical acquiescence or amazement, i.e., "sure, right away.")   **82
talking:** Saying.   **84 rarest:** Most remarkable, beautiful.   **85 Bate:** Abate, except, leave out (Sebastian says sardonically, surely you should allow widow Dido to be an exception).   **87 doublet:**
Close-fitting jacket.   **87–88 in a sort:** In a way.   **89 "sort":** (Antonio plays on the idea of drawing lots and on "fishing" for something to say.)   **92 The stomach . . . sense:** My appetite for
hearing them.   **93 Married:** Given in marriage.   **94 rate:** Estimation, opinion.   **99 surges:**
Waves.   **104 lusty:** Vigorous.   **105 that . . . bowed:** I.e., that projected out over the base of the
cliff that had been eroded by the surf, thus seeming to bend down toward the sea;   **his:** Its.   **106
As:** As if.

ALONSO: No, no, he's gone.

SEBASTIAN [*to* ALONSO]: Sir, you may thank yourself for this great loss,
    That° would not bless our Europe with your daughter,
110   But rather° loose° her to an African,
    Where she at least is banished from your eye,°
    Who hath cause to wet the grief on 't.°

ALONSO: Prithee, peace.

SEBASTIAN: You were kneeled to and importuned° otherwise
    By all of us, and the fair soul herself
115   Weighed between loathness and obedience at
    Which end o' the beam should bow.° We have lost your son,
    I fear, forever. Milan and Naples have
    More widows in them of this business' making°
    Than we bring men to comfort them.
120   The fault's your own.

ALONSO: So is the dear'st° o' the loss.

GONZALO: My lord Sebastian,
    The truth you speak doth lack some gentleness
    And time° to speak it in. You rub the sore
    When you should bring the plaster.°

125 SEBASTIAN: Very well.

ANTONIO: And most chirurgeonly.°

GONZALO [*to* ALONSO]: It is foul weather in us all, good sir,
    When you are cloudy.

SEBASTIAN [*to* ANTONIO]: Fowl° weather?

ANTONIO [*to* SEBASTIAN]:   Very foul.

130 GONZALO: Had I plantation° of this isle, my lord—

ANTONIO [*to* SEBASTIAN]: He'd sow 't with nettle seed.

SEBASTIAN: Or docks, or mallows.°

GONZALO: And were the king on 't, what would I do?

SEBASTIAN: Scape° being drunk for want° of wine.

GONZALO: I' the commonwealth I would by contraries°
135   Execute all things; for no kind of traffic,°
    Would I admit; no name of magistrate,

---

109 That: You who. **110 rather:** Would rather; **loose:** (1) Release, let loose, (2) lose. **111 is banished from your eye:** Is not constantly before your eye to serve as a reproachful reminder of what you have done. **112 Who . . . on 't:** I.e., your eye, which has good reason to weep because of this, or, Claribel, who has good reason to weep for it. **113 importuned:** Urged, implored. **114–116 the fair . . . bow:** Claribel herself was poised uncertainly between unwillingness to marry and obedience to her father as to which end of the scales should sink, which should prevail. **118 of . . . making:** On account of this marriage and subsequent shipwreck. **121 dear'st:** Heaviest, most costly. **124 time:** Appropriate time. **125 plaster:** (A medical application.) **126 chirurgeonly:** Like a skilled surgeon. (Antonio mocks Gonzalo's medical analogy of a *plaster* applied curatively to a wound.) **129 Fowl:** (With a pun on *foul,* returning to the imagery of lines 25–28.) **130 plantation:** Colonization (with subsequent wordplay on the literal meaning, "planting"). **131 docks, mallows:** (Weeds used as antidotes for nettle stings.) **133 Scape:** Escape; **want:** Lack. (Sebastian jokes sarcastically that this hypothetical ruler would be saved from dissipation only by the barrenness of the island.) **134 contraries:** By what is directly opposite to usual custom. **135 traffic:** Trade.

Letters° should not be known; riches, poverty,
And use of service,° none; contract, succession,°
Bourn, bound of land, tilth,° vineyard, none;
No use of metal, corn,° or wine, or oil;   140
No occupation; all men idle, all,
And women too, but innocent and pure;
No sovereignty—

SEBASTIAN: Yet he would be king on 't.

ANTONIO: The latter end of his commonwealth forgets the beginning.

GONZALO: All things in common nature should produce   145
Without sweat or endeavor. Treason, felony,
Sword, pike,° knife, gun, or need of any engine°
Would I not have; but nature should bring forth,
Of its own kind, all foison,° all abundance,
To feed my innocent people.   150

SEBASTIAN: No marrying 'mong his subjects?

ANTONIO: None, man, all idle—whores and knaves.

GONZALO: I would with such perfection govern, sir,
T' excel the Golden Age.°

SEBASTIAN: 'Save° His Majesty!

ANTONIO: Long live Gonzalo!

GONZALO: And—do you mark me, sir?   155

ALONSO: Prithee, no more. Thou dost talk nothing to me.

GONZALO: I do well believe Your Highness, and did it to minister occasion° to these
gentlemen, who are of such sensible° and nimble lungs that they always use° to
laugh at nothing.

ANTONIO: 'Twas you we laughed at.   160

GONZALO: Who in this kind of merry fooling am nothing to you; so you may continue, and laugh at nothing still.

ANTONIO: What a blow was there given!

SEBASTIAN: An° it had not fallen flat-long.°

GONZALO: You are gentlemen of brave mettle;° you would lift the moon out of her   165
sphere° if she would continue in it five weeks without changing.

(*Enter* ARIEL [*invisible*] *playing solemn music.*)

SEBASTIAN: We would so, and then go a-batfowling.°

ANTONIO: Nay, good my lord, be not angry.

---

137 Letters: Learning.   **138 use of service:** Custom of employing servants;   **succession:** Holding of property by right of inheritance.   **139 Bourn . . . tilth:** Boundaries, property limits, tillage
of soil.   **140 corn:** Grain.   **147 pike:** Lance;   **engine:** Instrument of warfare.   **149 foison:**
Plenty.   **154 the Golden Age:** The age, according to Hesiod, when Cronus, or Saturn, ruled the
world; an age of innocence and abundance;   **'Save:** God save.   **157 minister occasion:** Furnish
opportunity.   **158 sensible:** Sensitive;   **use:** Are accustomed.   **164 An:** If;   **flat-long:** With the
flat of the sword, i.e., ineffectually. (Compare with "fallen flat.")   **165 mettle:** Temperament,
courage. (The sense of *metal,* indistinguishable as a form from *mettle,* continues the metaphor of the
sword.)   **166 sphere:** Orbit (literally, one of the concentric zones occupied by planets in Ptolemaic
astronomy).   **167 a-batfowling:** Hunting birds at night with lantern and *bat,* or "stick"; also,
gulling a simpleton (Gonzalo is the simpleton, or fowl, and Sebastian will use the moon as his
lantern).

GONZALO: No, I warrant you, I will not adventure my discretion so weakly.° Will
170   you laugh me asleep? For I am very heavy.°
ANTONIO: Go sleep, and hear us.°

[*All sleep except* ALONSO, SEBASTIAN, *and* ANTONIO.]

ALONSO: What, all so soon asleep? I wish mine eyes
     Would, with themselves, shut up my thoughts.° I find
     They are inclined to do so.
SEBASTIAN: Please you, sir,
175   Do not omit° the heavy° offer of it.
     It seldom visits sorrow; when it doth,
     It is a comforter.
ANTONIO: We two, my lord,
     Will guard your person while you take your rest,
     And watch your safety.
ALONSO: Thank you. Wondrous heavy.

[ALONSO *sleeps. Exit* ARIEL.]

180 SEBASTIAN: What a strange drowsiness possesses them!
ANTONIO: It is the quality o' the climate.
SEBASTIAN: Why
     Doth it not then our eyelids sink? I find not
     Myself disposed to sleep.
ANTONIO: Nor I. My spirits are nimble.
     They° fell together all, as by consent;°
185   They dropped, as by a thunderstroke. What might,
     Worthy Sebastian, O, what might—? No more.
     And yet methinks I see it in thy face,
     What thou shouldst be. Th' occasion speaks thee,° and
     My strong imagination sees a crown
     Dropping upon thy head.
190 SEBASTIAN: What, art thou waking?
ANTONIO: Do you not hear me speak?
SEBASTIAN: I do, and surely
     It is a sleepy° language, and thou speak'st
     Out of thy sleep. What is it thou didst say?
     This is a strange repose, to be asleep
195   With eyes wide open—standing, speaking, moving—
     And yet so fast asleep.
ANTONIO: Noble Sebastian,

---

169 adventure . . . weakly: Risk my reputation for discretion for so trivial a cause (by getting angry at these sarcastic fellows).   **170 heavy:** Sleepy.   **171 Go . . . us:** I.e., get ready for sleep, and we'll do our part by laughing.   **173 Would . . . thoughts:** Would shut off my melancholy brooding when they close themselves in sleep.   **175 omit:** Neglect; **heavy:** Drowsy.   **184 They:** The sleepers; **consent:** Common agreement.   **188 occasion speaks thee:** Opportunity of the moment calls upon you, i.e., proclaims you usurper of Alonso's crown.   **192 sleepy:** Dreamlike, fantastic.

Thou lett'st thy fortune sleep—die, rather; wink'st°
Whiles thou art waking.

SEBASTIAN: Thou dost snore distinctly;°
There's meaning in thy snores.

ANTONIO: I am more serious than my custom. You   200
Must be so too if heed° me, which to do
Trebles thee o'er.°

SEBASTIAN: Well, I am standing water.°

ANTONIO: I'll teach you how to flow.

SEBASTIAN: Do so. To ebb°
Hereditary sloth° instructs me.

ANTONIO: O,
If you but knew how you the purpose cherish   205
Whiles thus you mock it!° How, in stripping it,
You more invest° it!° Ebbing men, indeed,
Most often do so near the bottom° run
By their own fear or sloth.

SEBASTIAN: Prithee, say on.
The setting° of thine eye and cheek proclaim   210
A matter° from thee, and a birth indeed
Which throes° thee much to yield.°

ANTONIO: Thus, sir:
Although this lord° of weak remembrance,° this
Who shall be of as little memory
When he is earthed,° hath here almost persuaded—   215
For he's a spirit of persuasion, only
Professes to persuade°—the King his son's alive,
'Tis as impossible that he's undrowned
As he that sleeps here swims.

SEBASTIAN: I have no hope
That he's undrowned.

ANTONIO: O, out of that "no hope"   220
What great hope have you! No hope that way° is

197 **wink'st:** (You) shut your eyes.   198 **distinctly:** Articulately.   201 **if heed:** If you heed.
202 **Trebles thee o'er:** Makes you three times as great and rich;   **standing water:** Water that
neither ebbs nor flows, at a standstill.   203 **ebb:** Recede, decline.   204 **Hereditary sloth:** Natural laziness and the position of younger brother, one who cannot inherit.   205–206 **If . . . mock
it:** If you only knew how much you really enhance the value of ambition even while your words
mock your purpose.   206–207 **How . . . invest it:** I.e., how the more you speak flippantly of ambition, the more you, in effect, affirm it.   207 **invest:** Clothe (Antonio's paradox is that, by skepti-
cally stripping away illusions, Sebastian can see the essence of a situation and the opportunity it
presents or that, by disclaiming and deriding his purpose, Sebastian shows how valuable it really is).
208 **the bottom:** I.e., on which unadventurous men may go aground and miss the tide of fortune.
210 **setting:** Set expression (of earnestness).   211 **matter:** Matter of importance.   212 **throes:**
Causes pain, as in giving birth;   **yield:** Give forth, speak about.   213 **this lord:** I.e., Gonzalo;
remembrance: (1) Power of remembering, (2) being remembered after his death.   215 **earthed:**
Buried.   216–217 **only . . . persuade:** Whose whole function (as a privy councillor) is to persuade.   221 **that way:** I.e., in regard to Ferdinand's being saved.

Another way so high a hope that even
Ambition cannot pierce a wink° beyond,
But doubt discovery there.° Will you grant with me
225   That Ferdinand is drowned?
SEBASTIAN: He's gone.
ANTONIO: Then tell me,
Who's the next heir of Naples?
SEBASTIAN: Claribel.
ANTONIO: She that is Queen of Tunis; she that dwells
Ten leagues beyond man's life;° she that from Naples
230   Can have no note,° unless the sun were post°—
The Man i' the Moon's too slow—till newborn chins
Be rough and razorable;° she that from° whom
We all were sea-swallowed, though some cast° again,
And by that destiny to perform an act
235   Whereof what's past is prologue, what to come
In yours and my discharge.°
SEBASTIAN: What stuff is this? How say you?
'Tis true my brother's daughter's Queen of Tunis,
So is she heir of Naples, twixt which regions
There is some space.
240   ANTONIO: A space whose every cubit°
Seems to cry out, "How shall that Claribel
Measure us° back to Naples? Keep° in Tunis,
And let Sebastian wake."° Say this were death
That now hath seized them, why, they were no worse
245   Than now they are. There be° that can rule Naples
As well as he that sleeps, lords that can prate°
As amply and unnecessarily
As this Gonzalo. I myself could make
A chough of as deep chat.° O, that you bore
250   The mind that I do! What a sleep were this
For your advancement! Do you understand me?
SEBASTIAN: Methinks I do.
ANTONIO: And how does your content°
Tender° your own good fortune?
SEBASTIAN: I remember

223 wink: Glimpse.   **223–224 Ambition . . . there:** Ambition itself cannot see any further than that hope (of the crown), is unsure of finding anything to achieve beyond it or even there.   **229 Ten . . . life:** I.e., further than the journey of a lifetime.   **230 note:** News, intimation;   **post:** Messenger.   **232 razorable:** Ready for shaving.   **from:** On our voyage from.   **233 cast:** Were disgorged (with a pun on *casting* of parts for a play).   **236 discharge:** Performance.   **240 cubit:** Ancient measure of length of about twenty inches.   **242 Measure us:** I.e., traverse the cubits, find her way;   **Keep:** Stay (addressed to Claribel).   **243 wake:** I.e., to his good fortune.   **245 There be:** There are those.   **246 prate:** Speak foolishly.   **248–249 I . . . chat:** I could teach a jackdaw to talk as wisely, or, be such a garrulous talker myself.   **252 content:** Desire, inclination.   **253 Tender:** Regard, look after.

You did supplant your brother Prospero.

ANTONIO: True.
    And look how well my garments sit upon me,   25
    Much feater° than before. My brother's servants
    Were then my fellows. Now they are my men.

SEBASTIAN: But, for your conscience?

ANTONIO: Ay, sir, where lies that? If 'twere a kibe,°
    'Twould put me to° my slipper; but I feel not   260
    This deity in my bosom. Twenty consciences
    That stand twixt me and Milan,° candied° be they°
    And melt ere they molest!° Here lies your brother,
    No better than the earth he lies upon,
    If he were that which now he's like—that's dead,   265
    Whom I, with this obedient steel, three inches of it,
    Can lay to bed forever; whiles you, doing thus,°
    To the perpetual wink° for aye° might put
    This ancient morsel, this Sir Prudence, who
    Should not° upbraid our course. For all the rest,   270
    They'll take suggestion° as a cat laps milk;
    They'll tell the clock° to any business that
    We say befits the hour.

SEBASTIAN: Thy case, dear friend,
    Shall be my precedent. As thou gott'st Milan,
    I'll come by Naples. Draw thy sword. One stroke   27
    Shall free thee from the tribute° which thou payest,
    And I the king shall love thee.

ANTONIO: Draw together;
    And when I rear my hand, do you the like
    To fall it° on Gonzalo.   [*They draw.*]

SEBASTIAN: O, but one word.   [*They talk apart.*]

(*Enter* ARIEL [*invisible*], *with music and song.*)

ARIEL [*to* GONZALO]: My master through his art foresees the danger   28
    That you, his friend, are in, and sends me forth—
    For else his project dies—to keep them living.   (*Sings in* GONZALO's *ear.*)
       While you here do snoring lie,
       Open-eyed conspiracy
        His time° doth take.   28
       If of life you keep a care,
       Shake off slumber, and beware.

---

256 feater: More becomingly, fittingly. **259 kibe:** Chilblain; here a sore on the heel. **260 put me to:** Oblige me to wear. **262 Milan:** The dukedom of Milan; **candied:** Frozen, congealed in crystalline form; **be they:** May they be. **263 molest:** Interfere. **267 thus:** Similarly. (The actor makes a stabbing gesture.) **268 wink:** Sleep, closing of eyes; **aye:** Ever. **270 Should not:** Would not then be able to. **271 take suggestion:** Respond to prompting. **272 tell the clock:** I.e., agree, answer appropriately, chime. **276 tribute:** (See 1.2.113, 124.) **279 fall it:** Let it fall. **285 time:** Opportunity.

Awake, awake!

ANTONIO: Then let us both be sudden.°

290   GONZALO [*waking*]:   Now, good angels preserve the King!   [*The others wake.*]

ALONSO: Why, how now, ho, awake? Why are you drawn?
          Wherefore this ghastly looking?

GONZALO: What's the matter?

SEBASTIAN: Whiles we stood here securing° your repose,
             Even now, we heard a hollow burst of bellowing

295   Like bulls, or rather lions. Did 't not wake you?
             It struck mine ear most terribly.

ALONSO: I heard nothing.

ANTONIO: O, 'twas a din to fright a monster's ear,
           To make an earthquake! Sure it was the roar
           Of a whole herd of lions.

300   ALONSO: Heard you this, Gonzalo?

GONZALO: Upon mine honor, sir. I heard a humming,
           And that a strange one too, which did awake me.
           I shaked you, sir, and cried.° As mine eyes opened,
           I saw their weapons drawn. There was a noise,

305   That's verily.° 'Tis best we stand upon our guard,
           Or that we quit this place. Let's draw our weapons.

ALONSO: Lead off this ground, and let's make further search
          For my poor son.

GONZALO: Heavens keep him from these beasts!
          For he is, sure, i' th' island.

ALONSO: Lead away.

310   ARIEL [*aside*]:   Prospero my lord shall know what I have done.
           So, King, go safely on to seek thy son.   (*Exeunt [separately].*)

[SCENE 2]

[*Another part of the island.*]

(*Enter* CALIBAN *with a burden of wood. A noise of thunder heard.*)

CALIBAN: All the infections that the sun sucks up
           From bogs, fens, flats,° on Prosper fall, and make him
           By inchmeal° a disease! His spirits hear me,
           And yet I needs must° curse. But they'll nor° pinch,

5   Fright me with urchin shows,° pitch me i' the mire,
           Nor lead me, like a firebrand,° in the dark
           Out of my way, unless he bid 'em. But
           For every trifle are they set upon me,

---

289 sudden: Quick.   **293 securing:** Standing guard over.   **303 cried:** Called out.   **305 verily:**
True.   **SCENE 2. 2 flats:** Swamps.   **3 By inchmeal:** Inch by inch.   **4 needs must:** Have to;
nor: Neither.   **5 urchin shows:** Elvish apparitions shaped like hedgehogs.   **6 like a firebrand:**
They in the guise of a will-o'-the-wisp.

Sometimes like apes, that mow° and chatter at me
And after bite me; then like hedgehogs, which   10
Lie tumbling in my barefoot way and mount
Their pricks at my footfall. Sometimes am I
All wound with° adders, who with cloven tongues
Do hiss me into madness.

(*Enter* TRINCULO.)

                     Lo, now, lo!
Here comes a spirit of his, and to torment me   15
For bringing wood in slowly. I'll fall flat.
Perchance he will not mind° me.   [*He lies down.*]

TRINCULO: Here's neither bush nor shrub to bear off° any weather at all. And another storm brewing; I hear it sing i' the wind. Yond same black cloud, yond
huge one, looks like a foul bombard° that would shed his° liquor. If it should   20
thunder as it did before, I know not where to hide my head. Yond same cloud
cannot choose but fall by pailfuls. [*Seeing* CALIBAN.] What have we here, a man
or a fish? Dead or alive? A fish, he smells like a fish; a very ancient and fishlike
smell; a kind of not-of-the-newest Poor John.° A strange fish! Were I in England now, as once I was, and had but this fish painted,° not a holiday fool there   25
but would give a piece of silver. There would this monster make a man.° Any
strange beast there makes a man. When they will not give a doit° to relieve a
lame beggar, they will lay out ten to see a dead Indian. Legged like a man, and
his fins like arms! Warm, o' my troth!° I do now let loose my opinion, hold it°
no longer: this is no fish, but an islander, that hath lately suffered° by a thunder-   30
bolt. [*Thunder.*] Alas, the storm is come again! My best way is to creep under his
gaberdine.° There is no other shelter hereabout. Misery acquaints a man with
strange bedfellows. I will here shroud° till the dregs° of the storm be past.

                        [*He creeps under* CALIBAN'*s garment.*]

(*Enter* STEPHANO, *singing,* [*a bottle in his hand*].)

STEPHANO: "I shall no more to sea, to sea,
      Here shall I die ashore—"   35
This is a very scurvy tune to sing at a man's funeral.
Well, here's my comfort.   (*Drinks.*)
(*Sings.*)
    "The master, the swabber,° the boatswain, and I,
      The gunner and his mate,
    Loved Mall, Meg, and Marian, and Margery,   40

---

9 mow: Make faces. **13 wound with:** Entwined by. **17 mind:** Notice. **18 bear off:** Keep
off. **20 foul bombard:** Dirty leather jug; **his:** Its. **24 Poor John:** Salted fish, type of poor
fare. **25 painted:** I.e., painted on a sign set up outside a booth or tent at a fair. **26 make a
man:** (1) Make one's fortune, (2) be indistinguishable from an Englishman. **27 doit:** Small coin.
29 o' my troth: By my faith; **hold it:** Hold it in. **30 suffered:** I.e., died. **32 gaberdine:**
Cloak, loose upper garment. **33 shroud:** Take shelter; **dregs:** I.e., last remains (as in a *bombard*
or jug, line 20). **38 swabber:** Crew member whose job is to wash the decks.

> But none of us cared for Kate.
>> For she had a tongue with a tang,°
>> Would cry to a sailor, 'Go hang!'
> She loved not the savor of tar nor of pitch,
45 >> Yet a tailor might scratch her where'er she did itch.°
>> Then to sea, boys, and let her go hang!"
> This is a scurvy tune too. But here's my comfort. (*Drinks.*)

CALIBAN: Do not torment me!° O!

STEPHANO: What's the matter?° Have we devils here? Do you put tricks upon 's°
50 with savages and men of Ind,° ha? I have not scaped drowning to be afeard now
of your four legs. For it hath been said, "As proper° a man as ever went on four
legs° cannot make him give ground"; and it shall be said so again while Stephano
breathes at'° nostrils.

CALIBAN: This spirit torments me! O!

55 STEPHANO: This is some monster of the isle with four legs, who hath got, as I take
it, an ague.° Where the devil should he learn° our language? I will give him
some relief, if it be but for that.° If I can recover° him and keep him tame and
get to Naples with him, he's a present for any emperor that ever trod on neat's
leather.°

60 CALIBAN: Do not torment me, prithee. I'll bring my wood home faster.

STEPHANO: He's in his fit now and does not talk after the wisest.° He shall taste of
my bottle. If he have never drunk wine afore,° it will go near to° remove his fit.
If I can recover° him and keep him tame, I will not take too much° for him. He
shall pay for him that hath° him,° and that soundly.

65 CALIBAN: Thou dost me yet but little hurt; thou wilt anon,° I know it by thy trembling. Now Prosper works upon thee.

STEPHANO: Come on your ways. Open your mouth. Here is that which will give
language to you, cat. Open your mouth.° This will shake your shaking, I can tell
you, and that soundly. [*Giving* CALIBAN *a drink.*] You cannot tell who's your
70 friend. Open your chaps° again.

TRINCULO: I should know that voice. It should be—but he is drowned, and these
are devils. O, defend me!

STEPHANO: Four legs and two voices—a most delicate° monster! His forward voice
now is to speak well of his friend; his backward voice° is to utter foul speeches

---

42 tang: Sting.   **45 tailor . . . itch:** (A dig at tailors for their supposed effeminacy and a bawdy
suggestion of satisfying a sexual craving.)   **48 Do . . . me:** (Caliban assumes that one of Prospero's
spirits has come to punish him.)   **49 What's the matter?:** What's going on here?   **put tricks
upon 's:** Trick us with conjuring shows.   **50 Ind:** India.   **51 proper:** Handsome.   **51–52 four
legs:** (The conventional phrase would supply *two* legs, but the creature Stephano thinks he sees has
four.)   **53 at':** At the.   **56 ague:** Fever. (Probably both Caliban and Trinculo are quaking; see lines
48 and 65–66.);   **should he learn:** Could he have learned.   **57 for that:** I.e., for knowing our
language;   **recover:** Restore.   **58–59 neat's leather:** Cowhide.   **61 after the wisest:** In the
wisest fashion.   **62 afore:** Before;   **go near to:** Be in a fair way to.   **63 I will . . . much:** I.e.,
no sum can be too much.   **63–64 He shall . . . hath him:** I.e., anyone who wants him will have
to pay dearly for him.   **64 hath:** Possesses, receives.   **65 anon:** Presently.   **68 cat . . . mouth:**
(Allusion to the proverb "Good liquor will make a cat speak.")   **70 chaps:** Jaws.   **73 delicate:** Ingenious.   **74 backward voice:** (Trinculo and Caliban are facing in opposite directions. Stephano
supposes the monster to have a rear end that can emit *foul speeches* or foul-smelling wind at the
monster's *other mouth*, line 78.)

and to detract. If all the wine in my bottle will recover him,° I will help° his   75
ague. Come. [*Giving a drink.*] Amen! I will pour some in thy other mouth.

TRINCULO: Stephano!

STEPHANO: Doth thy other mouth call me?° Mercy, mercy! This is a devil, and no
monster. I will leave him. I have no long spoon.°

TRINCULO: Stephano! If thou beest Stephano, touch me and speak to me, for I am   80
Trinculo—be not afeard—thy good friend Trinculo.

STEPHANO: If thou beest Trinculo, come forth. I'll pull thee by the lesser legs. If any
be Trinculo's legs, these are they. [*Pulling him out.*] Thou art very Trinculo indeed! How cam'st thou to be the siege° of this mooncalf?° Can he vent°
Trinculos?   85

TRINCULO: I took him to be killed with a thunderstroke. But art thou not drowned,
Stephano? I hope now thou art not drowned. Is the storm overblown?° I hid
me under the dead mooncalf's gaberdine for fear of the storm. And art thou living, Stephano? O Stephano, two Neapolitans scaped!

[*He capers with* STEPHANO.]

STEPHANO: Prithee, do not turn me about. My stomach is not constant.°   90

CALIBAN: These be fine things, an if° they be not spirits.
That's a brave° god, and bears° celestial liquor.
I will kneel to him.

STEPHANO: How didst thou scape? How cam'st thou hither? Swear by this bottle
how thou cam'st hither. I escaped upon a butt of sack° which the sailors heaved   95
o'erboard—by this bottle,° which I made of the bark of a tree with mine own
hands since° I was cast ashore.

CALIBAN [*kneeling*]: I'll swear upon that bottle to be thy true subject, for the liquor is
not earthly.

STEPHANO: Here. Swear then how thou escapedst.   100

TRINCULO: Swum ashore, man, like a duck. I can swim like a duck, I'll be sworn.

STEPHANO: Here, kiss the book.° Though thou canst swim like a duck, thou art
made like a goose.   [*Giving him a drink.*]

TRINCULO: O Stephano, hast any more of this?

STEPHANO: The whole butt, man. My cellar is in a rock by the seaside, where my   105
wine is hid.—How now, mooncalf? How does thine ague?

CALIBAN: Hast thou not dropped from heaven?

STEPHANO: Out o' the moon, I do assure thee. I was the Man i' the Moon when
time was.°

CALIBAN: I have seen thee in her, and I do adore thee. My mistress showed me thee,   110
and thy dog, and thy bush.°

---

75 If . . . him: Even if it takes all the wine in my bottle to cure him; **help:** Cure. **78 call me:**
I.e., call me by name, know supernaturally who I am. **79 long spoon:** (Allusion to the proverb
"He that sups with the devil has need of a long spoon.") **84 siege:** Excrement; **mooncalf:**
Monstrous or misshapen creature (whose deformity is caused by the malignant influence of the
moon); **vent:** Excrete, defecate. **87 overblown:** Blown over. **90 not constant:** Unsteady.
91 an if: If. **92 brave:** Fine, magnificent; **bears:** He carries. **95 butt of sack:** Barrel of Canary wine. **96 by this bottle:** I.e., I swear by this bottle. **97 since:** After. **102 book:** I.e., bottle (but with ironic reference to the practice of kissing the Bible in swearing an oath; see *I'll be sworn*
in line 101). **108–109 when time was:** Once upon a time. **111 dog . . . bush:** (The Man in
the Moon was popularly imagined to have with him a dog and a bush of thorn.)

STEPHANO: Come, swear to that. Kiss the book. I will furnish it anon with new contents. Swear.   [*Giving him a drink.*]

TRINCULO: By this good light,° this is a very shallow monster! I afeard of him? A
115   very weak monster! The Man i' the Moon? A most poor credulous monster!
Well drawn,° monster, in good sooth!°

CALIBAN [*to* STEPHANO]: I'll show thee every fertile inch o' th' island, And I will
kiss thy foot. I prithee, be my god.

TRINCULO: By this light, a most perfidious and drunken monster! When 's god's
120   asleep, he'll rob his bottle.°

CALIBAN: I'll kiss thy foot. I'll swear myself thy subject.

STEPHANO: Come on then. Down, and swear.   [CALIBAN *kneels.*]

TRINCULO: I shall laugh myself to death at this puppy-headed monster. A most
scurvy monster! I could find in my heart to beat him—

125   STEPHANO: Come, kiss.

TRINCULO: But that the poor monster's in drink.° An abominable monster!

CALIBAN: I'll show thee the best springs. I'll pluck thee berries.
I'll fish for thee and get thee wood enough.
A plague upon the tyrant that I serve!
130   I'll bear him no more sticks, but follow thee,
Thou wondrous man.

TRINCULO: A most ridiculous monster, to make a wonder of a poor drunkard!

CALIBAN: I prithee, let me bring thee where crabs° grow,
And I with my long nails will dig thee pignuts,°
135   Show thee a jay's nest, and instruct thee how
To snare the nimble marmoset.° I'll bring thee
To clustering filberts, and sometimes I'll get thee
Young scamels° from the rock. Wilt thou go with me?

STEPHANO: I prithee now, lead the way without any more talking.—Trinculo, the
140   King and all our company else° being drowned, we will inherit° here.—Here,
bear my bottle.—Fellow Trinculo, we'll fill him by and by again.

CALIBAN (*sings drunkenly*): Farewell, master, farewell, farewell!

TRINCULO: A howling monster; a drunken monster!

CALIBAN: No more dams I'll make for fish,
145   Nor fetch in firing°
At requiring,
Nor scrape trenchering,° nor wash dish.
'Ban, 'Ban, Ca-Caliban
Has a new master. Get a new man!°

---

114 By . . . light: By God's light, by this good light from heaven.   **116 Well drawn:** Well pulled
(on the bottle);   **in good sooth:** Truly, indeed.   **119–120 When . . . bottle:** I.e., Caliban
wouldn't even stop at robbing his god of his bottle if he could catch him asleep.   **126 in drink:**
Drunk.   **133 crabs:** Crab apples, or perhaps crabs.   **134 pignuts:** Earthnuts, edible tuberous
roots.   **136 marmoset:** Small monkey.   **138 scamels:** (Possibly *seamews,* mentioned in Strachey's
letter, or shellfish, or perhaps from *squamelle,* "furnished with little scales." Contemporary French
and Italian travel accounts report that the natives of Patagonia in South America ate small fish described as *fort scameux* and *squame.*)   **140 else:** In addition, besides ourselves;   **inherit:** Take possession.   **145 firing:** Firewood.   **147 trenchering:** Trenchers, wooden plates.   **149 Get a new
man:** (Addressed to Prospero.)

Freedom, high-day!° High-day, freedom! Freedom, high-day, freedom!   150
STEPHANO: O brave monster! Lead the way.   (*Exeunt.*)

[ACT 3, SCENE 1]

[*Before* PROSPERO'*s cell.*]

(*Enter* FERDINAND, *bearing a log.*)

FERDINAND: There be some sports are painful, and their labor
    Delight in them sets off.° Some kinds of baseness°
    Are nobly undergone,° and most poor° matters
    Point to rich ends. This my mean° task
    Would be as heavy to me as odious, but°   5
    The mistress which I serve quickens° what's dead
    And makes my labors pleasures. O, she is
    Ten times more gentle than her father's crabbed,
    And he's composed of harshness. I must remove
    Some thousands of these logs and pile them up,   10
    Upon a sore injunction.° My sweet mistress
    Weeps when she sees me work and says such baseness
    Had never like executor.° I forget;°
    But these sweet thoughts do even refresh my labors,
    Most busy lest when I do it.°

(*Enter* MIRANDA; *and* PROSPERO [*at a distance, unseen*].)

MIRANDA: Alas now, pray you,   15
    Work not so hard. I would the lightning had
    Burnt up those logs that you are enjoined° to pile!
    Pray, set it down and rest you. When this° burns,
    'Twill weep° for having wearied you. My father
    Is hard at study. Pray now, rest yourself.   20
    He's safe for these° three hours.
FERDINAND: O most dear mistress,
    The sun will set before I shall discharge°
    What I must strive to do.
MIRANDA: If you'll sit down,
    I'll bear your logs the while. Pray, give me that.
    I'll carry it to the pile.
FERDINAND: No, precious creature,   25
    I had rather crack my sinews, break my back,

---

150 high-day: Holiday. **ACT 3, SCENE I. 1–2 There . . . sets off:** Some pastimes are laborious, but the pleasure we get from them compensates for the effort. (Pleasure is *set off* by labor as a jewel is set off by its foil.) **2 baseness:** Menial activity. **3 undergone:** Undertaken; **most poor:** Poorest. **4 mean:** Lowly. **5 but:** Were it not that. **6 quickens:** Gives life to. **11 sore injunction:** Severe command. **13 Had . . . executor:** I.e., was never before undertaken by so noble a being; **I forget:** I.e., I forget that I'm supposed to be working, or, I forget my happiness, oppressed by my labor. **15 Most . . . it:** I.e., busy at my labor but with my mind on other things (?) (the line may be in need of emendation). **17 enjoined:** Commanded. **18 this:** I.e., the log. **19 weep:** I.e., exude resin. **21 these:** The next. **22 discharge:** Complete.

Than you should such dishonor undergo
While I sit lazy by.

MIRANDA: It would become me
As well as it does you; and I should do it
30   With much more ease, for my good will is to it,
And yours it is against.

PROSPERO [*aside*]:   Poor worm, thou art infected!
This visitation° shows it.

MIRANDA: You look wearily.

FERDINAND: No, noble mistress, 'tis fresh morning with me
When you are by° at night. I do beseech you—
35   Chiefly that I might set it in my prayers—
What is your name?

MIRANDA: Miranda.—O my father,
I have broke your hest° to say so.

FERDINAND: Admired Miranda!°
Indeed the top of admiration, worth
What's dearest° to the world! Full many a lady
40   I have eyed with best regard,° and many a time
The harmony of their tongues hath into bondage
Brought my too diligent° ear. For several° virtues
Have I liked several women, never any
With so full soul but some defect in her
45   Did quarrel with the noblest grace she owed°
And put it to the foil.° But you, O you,
So perfect and so peerless, are created
Of° every creature's best!

MIRANDA: I do not know
One of my sex; no woman's face remember,
50   Save, from my glass, mine own. Nor have I seen
More that I may call men than you, good friend,
And my dear father. How features are abroad°
I am skilless° of; but, by my modesty,°
The jewel in my dower, I would not wish
55   Any companion in the world but you;
Nor can imagination form a shape,
Besides yourself, to like of.° But I prattle
Something° too wildly, and my father's precepts
I therein do forget.

FERDINAND: I am in my condition°

---

32 visitation: (1) Miranda's visit to Ferdinand, (2) visitation of the plague, i.e., infection of love.
34 by: Nearby.   **37 hest:** Command;   **Admired Miranda:** (Her name means "to be admired or
wondered at.")   **39 dearest:** Most treasured.   **40 best regard:** Thoughtful and approving attention.   **42 diligent:** Attentive;   **several:** Various (also on line 43).   **45 owed:** Owned.   **46 put
. . . foil:** (1) Overthrew it (as in wrestling), (2) served as a *foil*, or "contrast," to set it off.   **48 Of:**
Out of.   **52 How . . . abroad:** What people look like in other places.   **53 skilless:** Ignorant;
modesty: Virginity.   **57 like of:** Be pleased with, be fond of.   **58 Something:** Somewhat.   **59
condition:** Rank.

A prince, Miranda; I do think, a king—   60
I would, not so!—and would° no more endure
This wooden slavery° than to suffer
The flesh-fly° blow° my mouth. Hear my soul speak:
The very instant that I saw you did
My heart fly to your service, there resides   65
To make me slave to it, and for your sake
Am I this patient long-man.
MIRANDA: Do you love me?
FERDINAND: O heaven, O earth, bear witness to this sound,
    And crown what I profess with kind event°
    If I speak true! If hollowly,° invert°   70
    What best is boded° me to mischief!° I
    Beyond all limit of what° else i' the world
    Do love, prize, honor you.
MIRANDA [weeping]:   I am a fool
    To weep at what I am glad of.
PROSPERO [aside]:   Fair encounter
    Of two most rare affections! Heavens rain grace   75
    On that which breeds between 'em!
FERDINAND: Wherefore weep you?
MIRANDA: At mine unworthiness, that dare not offer
    What I desire to give, and much less take
    What I shall die° to want.° But this is trifling,
    And all the more it seeks to hide itself   80
    The bigger bulk it shows. Hence, bashful cunning,°
    And prompt me, plain and holy innocence!
    I am your wife, if you will marry me;
    If not, I'll die your maid.° To be your fellow°
    You may deny me, but I'll be your servant   85
    Whether you will° or no.
FERDINAND: My mistress,° dearest,
    And I thus humble ever.
MIRANDA: My husband, then?
FERDINAND: Ay, with a heart as willing°
    As bondage e'er of freedom. Here's my hand.   90
MIRANDA [clasping his hand]: And mine, with my heart in 't. And now farewell
    Till half an hour hence.
FERDINAND: A thousand thousand!°
                    (Exeunt [FERDINAND and MIRANDA, separately].)

61 would: Wish (it were).   **62 wooden slavery:** Being compelled to carry wood.   **63 flesh-fly:** Insect that deposits its eggs in dead flesh;   **blow:** Befoul with fly eggs.   **69 kind event:** Favorable outcome.   **70 hollowly,** falsely;   **invert:** Turn.   **71 boded:** In store for;   **mischief:** Harm.   **72 what:** Whatever.   **79 die:** (Probably with an unconscious sexual meaning that underlies all of lines 77–81.);   **to want:** Through lacking.   **81 bashful cunning:** Coyness.   **84 maid:** Handmaiden, servant;   **fellow:** Mate, equal.   **86 will:** Desire it;   **My mistress:** I.e., the woman I adore and serve (not an illicit sexual partner).   **89 willing:** Desirous.   **92 A thousand thousand:** I.e., a thousand thousand farewells.

PROSPERO: So glad of this as they I cannot be,
Who are surprised with all;° but my rejoicing
95   At nothing can be more. I'll to my book,
For yet ere suppertime must I perform
Much business appertaining.°   (*Exit.*)

[SCENE 2]

[*Another part of the island.*]

(*Enter* CALIBAN, STEPHANO, *and* TRINCULO.)

STEPHANO: Tell not me. When the butt is out,° we will drink water, not a drop before. Therefore bear up and board 'em.° Servant monster, drink to me.

TRINCULO: Servant monster? The folly of° this island! They say there's but five upon
this isle. We are three of them; if th' other two be brained° like us, the state
5   totters.

STEPHANO: Drink, servant monster, when I bid thee. Thy eyes are almost set° in thy
head.   [*Giving a drink.*]

TRINCULO: Where should they be set° else? He were a brave° monster indeed if
they were set in his tail.

10 STEPHANO: My man-monster hath drowned his tongue in sack. For my part, the sea
cannot drown me. I swam, ere I could recover° the shore, five and thirty leagues°
off and on.° By this light,° thou shalt be my lieutenant, monster, or my
standard.°

TRINCULO: Your lieutenant, if you list;° he's no standard.°

15 STEPHANO: We'll not run,° Monsieur Monster.

TRINCULO: Nor go° neither, but you'll lie° like dogs and yet say nothing neither.

STEPHANO: Mooncalf, speak once in thy life, if thou beest a good mooncalf.

CALIBAN: How does thy honor? Let me lick thy shoe. I'll not serve him. He is not
valiant.

20 TRINCULO: Thou liest, most ignorant monster, I am in case to jostle a constable.°
Why, thou debauched° fish, thou, was there ever man a coward that hath drunk
so much sack° as I today? Wilt thou tell a monstrous lie, being but half a fish
and half a monster?

CALIBAN: Lo, how he mocks me! Wilt thou let him, my lord?

25 TRINCULO: "Lord," quoth he? That a monster should be such a natural!°

---

94 with all: By everything that has happened, or, *withal,* "with it."   **97 appertaining:** Related to
this.   **SCENE 2. 1 out:** Empty.   **2 bear . . . 'em:** (Stephano uses the terminology of maneuver-
ing at sea and boarding a vessel under attack as a way of urging an assault on the liquor supply.)
3 folly of: I.e., stupidity found on.   **4 be brained:** Are endowed with intelligence.   **6 set:** Fixed
in a drunken stare, or, sunk, like the sun.   **8 set:** Placed;   **brave:** Fine, splendid.   **11 recover:**
Gain, reach;   **leagues:** Units of distance, each equaling about three miles.   **12 off and on:** Intermittently;   **By this light:** (An oath: by the light of the sun.)   **13 standard:** Standard-bearer, en-
sign (as distinguished from *lieutenant,* lines 12, 14).   **14 list:** Prefer;   **no standard:** I.e., not able to
stand up.   **15 run:** (1) Retreat, (2) urinate (taking Trinculo's *standard,* line 14, in the old sense of
"conduit").   **16 go:** Walk;   **lie:** (1) Tell lies, (2) lie prostrate, (3) excrete.   **20 in case . . . constable:** I.e., in fit condition, made valiant by drink, to taunt or challenge the police.   **21 debauched:**
(1) Seduced away from proper service and allegiance, (2) depraved.   **22 sack:** Spanish white wine.
25 natural: (1) Idiot, (2) natural as opposed to unnatural, monsterlike.

CALIBAN: Lo, lo, again! Bite him to death, I prithee.
STEPHANO: Trinculo, keep a good tongue in your head. If you prove a mutineer—
the next tree!° The poor monster's my subject, and he shall not suffer indignity.
CALIBAN: I thank my noble lord. Wilt thou be pleased
To hearken once again to the suit I made to thee? 30
STEPHANO: Marry,° will I. Kneel and repeat it. I will stand, and so shall Trinculo.
[CALIBAN *kneels*.]

(*Enter* ARIEL, *invisible*.°)

CALIBAN: As I told thee before, I am subject to a tyrant,
A sorcerer, that by his cunning hath
Cheated me of the island.
ARIEL [*mimicking* TRINCULO]: Thou liest.
CALIBAN: Thou liest, thou jesting monkey, thou!
I would my valiant master would destroy thee. 35
I do not lie.
STEPHANO: Trinculo, if you trouble him any more in 's tale, by this hand, I will sup-
plant° some of your teeth.
TRINCULO: Why, I said nothing.
STEPHANO: Mum, then, and no more.—Proceed. 40
CALIBAN: I say by sorcery he got this isle;
From me he got it. If thy greatness will
Revenge it on him—for I know thou dar'st,
But this thing° dare not—
STEPHANO: That's most certain. 45
CALIBAN: Thou shalt be lord of it, and I'll serve thee.
STEPHANO: How now shall this be compassed?° Canst thou bring me to the party?
CALIBAN: Yea, yea, my lord. I'll yield him thee asleep,
Where thou mayst knock a nail into his head.
ARIEL: Thou liest; thou canst not. 50
CALIBAN: What a pied ninny's° this! Thou scurvy patch!°—
I do beseech thy greatness, give him blows
And take his bottle from him. When that's gone
He shall drink naught but brine, for I'll not show him
Where the quick freshes° are. 55
STEPHANO: Trinculo, run into no further danger. Interrupt the monster one word
further° and, by this hand, I'll turn my mercy out o' doors° and make a stock-
fish° of thee.
TRINCULO: Why, what did I? I did nothing. I'll go farther off.°
STEPHANO: Didst thou not say he lied? 60
ARIEL: Thou liest.

28 the next tree: I.e., you'll hang. **31 Marry:** I.e., indeed (originally an oath, "by the Virgin Mary"). **invisible:** I.e., wearing a garment to connote invisibility, as at 1.2.378. **37–38 supplant:** Uproot, displace. **44 this thing:** I.e., Trinculo. **47 compassed:** Achieved. **51 pied ninny:** Fool in motley; **patch:** Fool. **55 quick freshes:** Running springs. **56–57 one word further:** I.e., one more time. **57 turn . . . doors:** I.e., forget about being merciful. **57–58 stockfish:** Dried cod beaten before cooking. **59 off:** Away.

STEPHANO: Do I so? Take thou that. [*He beats* TRINCULO.] As you like this, give me
    the lie° another time.

TRINCULO: I did not give the lie. Out o' your wits and hearing too? A pox o' your
65   bottle! This can sack and drinking do. A murrain° on your monster, and the
    devil take your fingers!

CALIBAN: Ha, ha, ha!

STEPHANO: Now, forward with your tale. [*To* TRINCULO.] Prithee, stand further
    off.

70 CALIBAN: Beat him enough. After a little time
    I'll beat him too.

STEPHANO: Stand farther.—Come, proceed.

CALIBAN: Why, as I told thee, 'tis a custom with him
    I' th' afternoon to sleep. There thou mayst brain him,
75   Having first seized his books; or with a log
    Batter his skull, or paunch° him with a stake,
    Or cut his weasand° with thy knife. Remember
    First to possess his books, for without them
    He's but a sot,° as I am, nor hath not
80   One spirit to command. They all do hate him
    As rootedly as I. Burn but his books.
    He has brave utensils° —for so he calls them—
    Which, when he has a house, he'll deck withal.°
    And that most deeply to consider is
85   The beauty of his daughter. He himself
    Calls her a nonpareil. I never saw a woman
    But only Sycorax my dam and she;
    But she as far surpasseth Sycorax
    As great'st does least.

90 STEPHANO: Is it so brave° a lass?

CALIBAN: Ay, lord. She will become° thy bed, I warrant,
    And bring thee forth brave brood.

STEPHANO: Monster, I will kill this man. His daughter and I will be king and
    queen—save Our Graces!—and Trinculo and thyself shall be viceroys. Dost thou
95   like the plot, Trinculo?

TRINCULO: Excellent.

STEPHANO: Give me thy hand. I am sorry I beat thee; but, while thou liv'st, keep a
    good tongue in thy head.

CALIBAN: Within this half hour will he be asleep.
100   Wilt thou destroy him then?

STEPHANO: Ay, on mine honor.

ARIEL [*aside*]: This will I tell my master.

CALIBAN: Thou mak'st me merry; I am full of pleasure.

62–63 give me the lie: Call me a liar to my face.   **65 murrain:** Plague (literally, a cattle disease).
76 paunch: Stab in the belly.   **77 weasand:** Windpipe.   **79 sot:** Fool.   **82 brave utensils:** Fine
furnishings.   **83 deck withal:** Furnish it with.   **90 brave:** Splendid, attractive.   **91 become:**
Suit (sexually).

Let us be jocund.° Will you troll the catch°
You taught me but whilere?°   105

STEPHANO: At thy request, monster, I will do reason, any reason.°—Come on,
Trinculo, let us sing.   (Sings.)
"Flout° 'em and scout° 'em
    And scout 'em and flout em!
        Thought is free."   110

CALIBAN: That's not the tune.   (ARIEL plays the tune on a tabor° and pipe.)

STEPHANO: What is this same?

TRINCULO: This is the tune of our catch, played by the picture of Nobody.°

STEPHANO: If thou beest a man, show thyself in thy likeness. If thou beest a devil,
take 't as thou list.°   115

TRINCULO: O, forgive me my sins!

STEPHANO: He that dies pays all debts.° I defy thee. Mercy upon us!

CALIBAN: Art thou afeard?

STEPHANO: No, monster, not I.

CALIBAN: Be not afeard. The isle is full of noises,   120
Sounds, and sweet airs, that give delight and hurt not.
Sometimes a thousand twangling instruments
Will hum about mine ears, and sometimes voices
That, if I then had waked after long sleep,
Will make me sleep again; and then, in dreaming,   125
The clouds methought would open and show riches
Ready to drop upon me, that when I waked
I cried to dream° again.

STEPHANO: This will prove a brave kingdom to me, where I shall have my music for
nothing.   130

CALIBAN: When Prospero is destroyed.

STEPHANO: That shall be by and by.° I remember the story.

TRINCULO: The sound is going away. Let's follow it, and after do our work.

STEPHANO: Lead, monster; we'll follow. I would I could see this taborer! He lays
it on.°   135

TRINCULO: Wilt come? I'll follow, Stephano.   (Exeunt [following ARIEL's music].)

[SCENE 3]

[Another part of the island.]

(Enter ALONSO, SEBASTIAN, ANTONIO, GONZALO, ADRIAN, FRANCISCO, etc.)

GONZALO: By 'r lakin,° I can go no further, sir.

---

104 jocund: Jovial, merry; **troll the catch:** Sing the round. **105 but whilere:** Only a short
time ago. **106 reason, any reason:** Anything reasonable. **108 Flout:** Scoff at; **scout:** Deride.
111 tabor: Small drum. **113 picture of Nobody:** (Refers to a familiar figure with head, arms,
and legs but no trunk.) **115 take 't . . . list:** I.e., take my defiance as you please, as best you can.
117 He . . . debts: I.e., if I have to die, at least that will be the end of all my woes and obligations.
128 to dream: Desirous of dreaming. **132 by and by:** Very soon. **134–135 lays it on:** I.e.,
plays the drum vigorously. **SCENE 3. 1 By 'r lakin:** By our Ladykin, by our Lady.

My old bones aches. Here's a maze trod indeed
Through forthrights and meanders!° By your patience,
I needs must° rest me.

ALONSO: Old lord, I cannot blame thee,
5   Who am myself attached° with weariness,
To th' dulling of my spirits.° Sit down and rest.
Even here I will put off my hope, and keep it
No longer for° my flatterer. He is drowned
Whom thus we stray to find, and the sea mocks
10   Our frustrate° search on land. Well, let him go.   [ALONSO *and* GONZALO *sit.*]

ANTONIO [*aside to* SEBASTIAN]: I am right° glad that he's so out of hope.
Do not, for° one repulse, forgo the purpose
That you resolved t' effect.

SEBASTIAN [*to* ANTONIO]:   The next advantage
Will we take throughly.°

ANTONIO [*to* SEBASTIAN]:   Let it be tonight,
15   For, now° they are oppressed with travel,° they
Will not, nor cannot, use° such vigilance
As when they are fresh.

SEBASTIAN [*to* ANTONIO]:   I say tonight. No more.

(*Solemn and strange music; and* PROSPERO *on the top,*° *invisible.*)

ALONSO: What harmony is this? My good friends, hark!
GONZALO: Marvelous sweet music!

(*Enter several strange shapes, bringing in a banquet, and dance about it with gentle actions of salutations; and, inviting the King, etc., to eat, they depart.*)

20   ALONSO: Give us kind keepers,° heavens! What were these?
SEBASTIAN: A living° drollery.° Now I will believe
That there are unicorns; that in Arabia
There is one tree, the phoenix' throne, one phoenix°
At this hour reigning there.

ANTONIO: I'll believe both;
25   And what does else want credit,° come to me
And I'll be sworn 'tis true. Travelers ne'er did lie,
Though fools at home condemn 'em.

GONZALO: If in Naples
I should report this now, would they believe me

---

3 forthrights and meanders: Paths straight and crooked.   **4 needs must:** Have to.   **5 attached:** Seized.   **6 To . . . spirits:** To the point of being dull- spirited.   **8 for:** As.   **10 frustrate:** Frustrated.   **11 right:** Very.   **12 for:** Because of.   **14 throughly:** Thoroughly.   **15 now:** Now that;   **travel:** Carrying the sense of labor as well as traveling.   **16 use:** Apply;   **on the top:** At some high point of the tiring-house or the theater, on a third level above the gallery.   **20 kind keepers:** Guardian angels.   **21 living:** With live actors;   **drollery:** Comic entertainment, caricature, puppet show.   **23 phoenix:** Mythical bird consumed to ashes every five hundred to six hundred years, only to be renewed into another cycle.   **25 want credit:** Lack credence.

If I should say I saw such islanders?
For, certes,° these are people of the island,   30
Who, though they are of monstrous° shape, yet note,
Their manners are more gentle, kind, than of
Our human generation you shall find
Many, nay, almost any.
PROSPERO [*aside*]:   Honest lord,
Thou hast said well, for some of you there present   35
Are worse than devils.
ALONSO: I cannot too much muse°
Such shapes, such gesture, and such sound, expressing—
Although they want° the use of tongue—a kind
Of excellent dumb discourse.
PROSPERO [*aside*]:   Praise in departing.°
FRANCISCO: They vanished strangely.
SEBASTIAN: No matter, since   40
They have left their viands° behind, for we have stomachs.°
Will 't please you taste of what is here?
ALONSO: Not I.
GONZALO: Faith, sir, you need not fear. When we were boys,
Who would believe that there were mountaineers°
Dewlapped° like bulls, whose throats had hanging at 'em   45
Wallets° of flesh? Or that there were such men
Whose heads stood in their breasts? Which now we find
Each putter-out of five for one° will bring us
Good warrant° of.
ALONSO: I will stand to° and feed,
Although my last°—no matter, since I feel   50
The best° is past. Brother, my lord the Duke,
Stand to, and do as we.   [*They approach the table.*]

(*Thunder and lightning. Enter* ARIEL, *like a harpy,° claps his wings upon the table, and
with a quaint device° the banquet vanishes.°*)

ARIEL: You are three men of sin, whom Destiny—
That hath to instrument this lower world
And what is in 't—the never-surfeited sea   55

---

30 certes: Certainly. **31 monstrous:** Unnatural. **36 muse:** Wonder at. **38 want:** Lack. **39
Praise in departing:** I.e., save your praise until the end of the performance (proverbial). **41
viands:** Provisions; **stomachs:** Appetites. **44 mountaineers:** Mountain dwellers. **45
Dewlapped:** Having a dewlap, or fold of skin hanging from the neck, like cattle. **46 Wallets:**
Pendent folds of skin, wattles. **48 putter-out . . . one:** One who invests money or gambles on
the risks of travel on the condition that the traveler who returns safely is to receive five times the
amount deposited; hence, any traveler. **49 Good warrant:** Assurance; **stand to:** Fall to, take the
risk. **50 Although my last:** Even if this were to be my last meal. **51 best:** Best part of life.
harpy: A fabulous monster with a woman's face and breasts and a vulture's body, supposed to be a
minister of divine vengeance; **quaint device:** Ingenious stage contrivance; **the banquet vanishes:** I.e., the food vanishes; the table remains until line 82.

Hath caused to belch up you,° and on this island
Where man doth not inhabit, you 'mongst men
Being most unfit to life. I have made you mad;
And even with suchlike valor° men hang and drown
Their proper° selves.   [ALONSO, SEBASTIAN, *and* ANTONIO *draw their swords.*]
60   You fools! I and my fellows
Are ministers of Fate. The elements
Of whom° your swords are tempered° may as well
Wound the loud winds, or with bemocked-at° stabs
Kill the still-closing° waters, as diminish
65   One dowl° that's in my plume. My fellow ministers
Are like° invulnerable. If° you could hurt,
Your swords are now too massy° for your strengths
And will not be uplifted. But remember—
For that's my business to you—that you three
70   From Milan did supplant good Prospero;
Exposed unto the sea, which hath requit° it,
Him and his innocent child; for which foul deed
The powers, delaying, not forgetting, have
Incensed the seas and shores, yea, all the creatures,
75   Against your peace. Thee of thy son, Alonso,
They have bereft; and to pronounce by me
Ling'ring perdition,° worse than any death
Can be at once, shall step by step attend
You and your ways; whose° wraths to guard you from—
80   Which here, in this most desolate isle, else° falls
Upon your heads—is nothing° but heart's sorrow
And a clear° life ensuing.

(*He vanishes in thunder; then, to soft music, enter the shapes again, and dance, with
mocks and mows,° and carrying out the table.*)

PROSPERO: Bravely° the figure of this harpy hast thou
Performed, my Ariel; a grace it had devouring.°
85   Of my instruction hast thou nothing bated°
In what thou hadst to say. So,° with good life°

53–56 whom . . . up you: You whom Destiny, controller of the sublunary world as its instrument,
has caused the ever hungry sea to belch up.   **59 suchlike valor:** I.e., the reckless valor derived
from madness.   **60 proper:** Own.   **62 whom:** Which; **tempered:** Composed and hardened.
63 bemocked-at: Scorned.   **64 still-closing:** Always closing again when parted.   **65 dowl:**
Soft, fine feather.   **66 like:** Likewise, similarly; **If:** Even if.   **67 massy:** Heavy.   **71 requit:** Re-
quited, avenged.   **77 perdition:** Ruin, destruction.   **79 whose:** (Refers to the heavenly powers.)
80 else: Otherwise.   **81 is nothing:** There is no way.   **82 clear:** Unspotted, innocent.   **mocks
and mows:** Mocking gestures and grimaces.   **83 Bravely:** Finely, dashingly.   **84 a grace . . .
devouring:** I.e., you gracefully caused the banquet to disappear as if you had consumed it (with
puns on *grace,* meaning "gracefulness" and "a blessing on the meal," and on *devouring,* meaning "a literal eating" and "an all-consuming or ravishing grace").   **85 bated:** Abated, omitted.   **86 So:** In
the same fashion; **good life:** Faithful reproduction.

And observation strange,° my meaner° ministers
Their several kinds° have done. My high charms work,
And these mine enemies are all knit up
In their distractions.° They now are in my power;   90
And in these fits I leave them, while I visit
Young Ferdinand, whom they suppose is drowned,
And his and mine loved darling.   [*Exit above.*]
GONZALO: I' the name of something holy, sir, why° stand you
In this strange stare?
ALONSO: O, it° is monstrous, monstrous!   95
Methought the billows° spoke and told me of it;
The winds did sing it to me, and the thunder,
That deep and dreadful organ pipe, pronounced
The name of Prosper; it did bass my trespass.°
Therefor° my son i' th' ooze is bedded; and   100
I'll seek him deeper than e'er plummet° sounded,°
And with him there lie mudded.   (*Exit.*)
SEBASTIAN: But one fiend at a time,
I'll fight their legions o'er.°
ANTONIO: I'll be thy second.
                    (*Exeunt* [SEBASTIAN *and* ANTONIO].)
GONZALO: All three of them are desperate.° Their great guilt,   105
Like poison given to work a great time after,
Now 'gins to bite the spirits.° I do beseech you,
That are of suppler joints, follow them swiftly
And hinder them from what this ecstasy°
May now provoke them to.
ADRIAN: Follow, I pray you.   (*Exeunt omnes.*)   110

[ACT 4, SCENE 1]

[*Before* PROSPERO'*s cell.*]

(*Enter* PROSPERO, FERDINAND, *and* MIRANDA.)

PROSPERO: If I have too austerely punished you,
Your companion makes amends, for I
Have given you here a third° of mine own life,
Or that for which I live; who once again

---

87 observation strange: Exceptional attention to detail;   **meaner:** I.e., subordinate to Ariel.
88 several kinds: Individual parts.   **90 distractions:** Trancelike state.   **94 why:** (Gonzalo was
not addressed in Ariel's speech to the *three men of sin,* line 53, and is not, as they are, in a maddened
state; see lines 105–107.)   **95 it:** I.e., my sin (also in line 96).   **96 billows:** Waves.   **99 bass my
trespass:** Proclaim my trespass like a bass note in music.   **100 Therefor:** In consequence of that.
101 plummet: A lead weight attached to a line for testing depth;   **sounded:** Probed, tested the
depth of.   **104 o'er:** One after another.   **105 desperate:** Despairing and reckless.   **107 bite the
spirits:** Sap their vital powers through anguish.   **109 ecstasy:** Mad frenzy.   **ACT 4, SCENE 1. 3
a third:** I.e., Miranda, into whose education Prospero has put a third of his life (?) or who represents a large part of what he cares about, along with his dukedom and his learned study (?).

5   I tender° to thy hand. All thy vexations
        Were but my trials of thy love, and thou
        Hast strangely° stood the test. Here, afore heaven,
        I ratify this my rich gift. O Ferdinand,
        Do not smile at me that I boast her off,°
10   For thou shalt find she will outstrip all praise
        And make it halt° behind her.
FERDINAND: I do believe it.
        Against an oracle.°
PROSPERO: Then, as my gift and thine own acquisition
        Worthily purchased, take my daughter. But
15   If thou dost break her virgin-knot before
        All sanctimonious° ceremonies may
        With full and holy rite be ministered,
        No sweet aspersion° shall the heavens let fall
        To make this contract grow; but barren hate,
20   Sour-eyed disdain, and discord shall bestrew
        The union of your bed with weeds° so loathly
        That you shall hate it both. Therefore take heed,
        As Hymen's lamps shall light you.°
FERDINAND: As I hope
        For quiet days, fair issue,° and long life,
25   With such love as 'tis now, the murkiest den,
        The most opportune place, the strong'st suggestion°
        Our worser genius° can,° shall never melt
        Mine honor into lust, to° take away
        The edge° of that day's celebration
30   When I shall think or° Phoebus' steeds are foundered°
        Or Night kept chained below.
PROSPERO: Fairly spoke.
        Sit then and talk with her. She is thine own.

                [FERDINAND *and* MIRANDA *sit and talk together.*]
        What,° Ariel! My industrious servant, Ariel!

        (*Enter* ARIEL.)

ARIEL: What would my potent master? Here I am.

---

5 tender: Offer.   **7 strangely:** Extraordinarily.   **9 boast her off:** I.e., praise her so, or, perhaps an error for "boast of her."   **11 halt:** Limp.   **12 Against an oracle:** Even if an oracle should declare otherwise.   **16 sanctimonious:** Sacred.   **18 aspersion:** Dew, shower.   **21 weeds:** (In place of the flowers customarily strewn on the marriage bed.)   **23 As . . . you:** I.e., as you long for happiness and concord in your marriage. (Hymen was the Greek and Roman god of marriage; his symbolic torches, the wedding torches, were supposed to burn brightly for a happy marriage and smokily for a troubled one.)   **24 issue:** Offspring.   **26 suggestion:** Temptation.   **27 worser genius:** Evil genius, or, evil attendant spirit; **can:** Is capable of.   **28 to:** So as to.   **29 edge:** Keen enjoyment, sexual ardor.   **30 or:** Either; **foundered:** Broken down, made lame. (Ferdinand will wait impatiently for the bridal night.)   **33 What:** Now then.

PROSPERO: Thou and thy meaner fellows° your last service   35
 Did worthily perform, and I must use you
 In such another trick.° Go bring the rabble,°
 O'er whom I give thee power, here to this place.
 Incite them to quick motion, for I must
 Bestow upon the eyes of this young couple   40
 Some vanity° of mine art. It is my promise,
 And they expect it from me.
ARIEL: Presently?°
PROSPERO: Ay, with a twink.°
ARIEL: Before you can say "Come" and "Go,"
 And breathe twice, and cry "So, so,"   45
 Each one, tripping on his toe,
 Will be here with mop and mow.°
 Do you love me, master? No?
PROSPERO: Dearly, my delicate Ariel. Do not approach
 Till thou dost hear me call.
ARIEL: Well; I conceive.°   (*Exit.*) 50
PROSPERO: Look thou be true;° do not give dalliance
 Too much the rein. The strongest oaths are straw
 To the fire i' the blood. Be more abstemious,
 Or else good night° your vow!
FERDINAND: I warrant° you, sir,
 The white cold virgin snow upon my heart°   55
 Abates the ardor of my liver.°
PROSPERO: Well.
 Now come, my Ariel! Bring a corollary,°
 Rather than want° a spirit. Appear, and pertly!° —
 No tongue!° All eyes! Be silent.   (*Soft music.*)

(*Enter* IRIS.)°

IRIS: Ceres,° most bounteous lady, thy rich leas°   60
 Of wheat, rye, barley, vetches,° oats, and peas;
 Thy turfy mountains, where live nibbling sheep,
 And flat meads° thatched with stover,° them to keep;

---

35 meaner fellows: Subordinates.   **37 trick:** Device;   **rabble:** Band, i.e., the *meaner fellows* of line 35.   **41 vanity:** (1) Illusion, (2) trifle, (3) desire for admiration, conceit.   **42 Presently:** Immediately.   **43 with a twink:** In the twinkling of an eye.   **47 mop and mow:** Gestures and grimaces.   **50 conceive:** Understand.   **51 true:** True to your promise.   **54 good night:** I.e., say good-bye to;   **warrant:** Guarantee.   **55 The white . . . heart:** I.e., the ideal of chastity and consciousness of Miranda's chaste innocence enshrined in my heart.   **56 liver:** (As the presumed seat of the passions.)   **57 corollary:** Surplus, extra supply.   **58 want:** Lack;   **pertly:** Briskly.   **59 No tongue:** All the beholders are to be silent (lest the spirits vanish).   **Iris:** Goddess of the rainbow and Juno's messenger.   **60 Ceres:** Goddess of the generative power of nature;   **leas:** Meadows.   **61 vetches:** Plants for forage, fodder.   **63 meads:** Meadows;   **stover:** Winter fodder for cattle.

Thy banks with pionèd and twillèd° brims,
65   Which spongy° April at thy hest° betrims
To make cold nymphs chaste crowns; and thy broom groves,°
Whose shadow the dismissèd bachelor° loves,
Being lass-lorn; thy poll-clipped° vineyard;
And thy sea marge,° sterile and rocky hard,
70   Where thou thyself dost air:° the queen o' the sky,°
Whose watery arch° and messenger am I,
Bids thee leave these, and with her sovereign grace,

(JUNO descends° [slowly in her car].)

Here on this grass plot, in this very place,
To come and sport. Her peacocks° fly amain.°
75   Approach, rich Ceres, her to entertain.°

(Enter CERES.)

CERES: Hail, many-colored messenger, that ne'er
Dost disobey the wife of Jupiter,
Who with thy saffron° wings upon my flowers
Diffusest honeydrops, refreshing showers,
80   And with each end of thy blue bow° dost crown
My bosky° acres and my unshrubbed down,°
Rich scarf° to my proud earth. Why hath thy queen
Summoned me hither to this short-grassed green?
IRIS: A contract of true love to celebrate,
85   And some donation freely to estate°
On the blest lovers.
CERES: Tell me, heavenly bow,
If Venus or her son,° as° thou dost know,
Do now attend the Queen? Since they did plot
The means that° dusky° Dis my daughter got,°
90   Her° and her blind boy's scandaled° company
I have forsworn.
IRIS: Of her society°
Be not afraid. I met her deity°

64 **pionèd and twillèd:** Undercut by the swift current and protected by roots and branches that tangle to form a barricade.   **65 spongy:** Wet;   **hest:** Command.   **66 broom groves:** Clumps of broom, gorse, yellow-flowered shrub.   **67 dismissèd bachelor:** Rejected male lover.   **68 poll-clipped:** Pruned, lopped at the top, or *pole-clipped,* "hedged in with poles."   **69 sea marge:** Shore.   **70 thou . . . air:** You take the air, go for walks;   **queen o' the sky:** I.e., Juno.   **71 watery arch:** Rainbow.   **Juno descends:** I.e., starts her descent from the "heavens" above the stage (?).   **74 peacocks:** Birds sacred to Juno and used to pull her chariot;   **amain:** With full speed.   **75 entertain:** Receive.   **78 saffron:** Yellow.   **80 bow:** I.e., rainbow.   **81 bosky:** Wooded;   **unshrubbed down:** Open upland.   **82 scarf:** (The rainbow is like a colored silk band adorning the earth.)   **85 estate:** Bestow.   **87 son:** I.e., Cupid;   **as:** As far as.   **89 that:** Whereby;   **dusky:** Dark;   **Dis . . . got:** (Pluto, or *Dis,* god of the infernal regions, carried off Proserpina, daughter of Ceres, to be his bride in Hades.)   **90 Her:** I.e., Venus's;   **scandaled:** Scandalous.   **91 society:** Company.   **92 her deity:** I.e., Her Highness.

Cutting the clouds towards Paphos,° and her son
Dove-drawn° with her. Here thought they to have done°
Some wanton charm° upon this man and maid,   95
Whose vows are that no bed-right shall be paid
Till Hymen's torch be lighted; but in vain.
Mars's hot minion° is returned° again;
Her waspish-headed° son has broke his arrows,
Swears he will shoot no more, but play with sparrows°   100
And be a boy right out.°

[JUNO *alights*.]

CERES: Highest Queen of state,°
  Great Juno, comes; I knew her by her gait.°
JUNO: How does my bounteous sister?° Go with me
  To bless this twain, that they may prosperous be,
  And honored in their issue.°   *(They sing:)*   105
JUNO: Honor, riches, marriage blessing,
  Long continuance, and increasing,
  Hourly joys be still° upon you!
  Juno sings her blessings on you.
CERES: Earth's increase, foison plenty,°   110
  Barns and garners° never empty,
  Vines with clustering bunches growing,
  Plants with goodly burden bowing;

  Spring come to you at the farthest
  In the very end of harvest!°   115
  Scarcity and want shall shun you;
  Ceres' blessing so is on you.
FERDINAND: This is a most majestic vision, and
  Harmonious charmingly.° May I be bold
  To think these spirits?
PROSPERO: Spirits, which by mine art   120
  I have from their confines called to enact
  My present fancies.
FERDINAND: Let me live here ever!
  So rare a wondered° father and a wife
  Makes this place Paradise.
                (JUNO *and* CERES *whisper, and send* IRIS *on employment*.)

---

93 Paphos: Place on the island of Cyprus, sacred to Venus.   **94 Dove-drawn:** (Venus's chariot
was drawn by doves); **done:** Placed.   **95 wanton charm:** Lustful spell.   **98 Mars's hot minion:** I.e., Venus, the beloved of Mars;   **returned:** I.e., returned to Paphos.   **99 waspish-headed:**
Hotheaded, peevish.   **100 sparrows:** (Supposed lustful, and sacred to Venus.)   **101 right out:**
Outright.   **Highest . . . state:** Most majestic queen.   **102 gait:** I.e., majestic bearing.   **103 sister:** I.e., fellow goddess (?).   **105 issue:** Offspring.   **108 still:** Always.   **110 foison plenty:**
Plentiful harvest.   **111 garners:** Granaries.   **115 In . . . harvest:** I.e., with no winter in between.
119 charmingly: Enchantingly.   **123 wondered:** Wonder-performing, wondrous.

PROSPERO: Sweet now, silence!
125   Juno and Ceres whisper seriously;
          There's something else to do. Hush and be mute,
          Or else our spell is marred.
IRIS [*calling offstage*]: You nymphs, called naiads,° of the windring° brooks,
          With your sedged° crowns and ever-harmless° looks,
130   Leave your crisp° channels, and on this green land
          Answer your summons; Juno does command.
          Come, temperate° nymphs, and help to celebrate
          A contract of true love. Be not too late.

          (*Enter certain* NYMPHS.)

          You sunburned sicklemen,° of August weary,°
135   Come hither from the furrow° and be merry.
          Make holiday; your rye-straw hats put on,
          And these fresh nymphs encounter° every one
          In country footing.°

          (*Enter certain* REAPERS, *properly*° *habited. They join with the* NYMPHS *in a graceful*
          dance, towards the end whereof PROSPERO *starts suddenly, and speaks; after which, to a*
          strange, hollow, and confused noise, they heavily° *vanish.*)

PROSPERO [*aside*]: I had forgot that foul conspiracy
140   Of the beast Caliban and his confederates
          Against my life. The minute of their plot
          Is almost come. [*To the* SPIRITS.] Well done! Avoid;° no more!
FERDINAND [*to* MIRANDA]: This is strange. Your father's in some passion
          That works° him strongly.
MIRANDA: Never till this day
145   Saw I him touched with anger so distempered.
PROSPERO: You do look, my son, in a moved sort,°
          As if you were dismayed. Be cheerful, sir.
          Our revels° now are ended. These our actors,
          As I foretold you, were all spirits and
150   Are melted into air, into thin air;
          And, like the baseless fabric° of this vision,
          The cloud-capped towers, the gorgeous palaces,
          The solemn temples, the great globe° itself,
          Yea, all which it inherit,° shall dissolve,
155   And, like this insubstantial pageant faded,

---

128 naiads: Nymphs of springs, rivers, or lakes;   **windring:** Wandering, winding (?).   **129**
sedged: Made of reeds;   **ever-harmless:** Ever innocent.   **130 crisp:** Curled, rippled.   **132**
temperate: Chaste.   **134 sicklemen:** Harvesters, field workers who cut down grain and grass;
of August weary: I.e., weary of the hard work of the harvest.   **135 furrow:** I.e., plowed fields.
137 encounter: Join.   **138 country footing:** Country dancing.   **properly:** Suitably;   **heavily:**
Slowly, dejectedly.   **142 Avoid:** Withdraw.   **144 works:** Affects, agitates.   **146 moved sort:**
Troubled state, condition.   **148 revels:** Entertainment, pageant.   **151 baseless fabric:** Unsubstantial theatrical edifice or contrivance.   **153 great globe:** (With a glance at the Globe Theatre.)   **154 which it inherit:** Who subsequently occupy it.

Leave not a rack° behind. We are such stuff
As dreams are made on,° and our little life
Is rounded° with a sleep. Sir, I am vexed.
Bear with my weakness. My old brain is troubled.
Be not disturbed with° my infirmity.   160
If you be pleased, retire° into my cell
And there repose. A turn or two I'll walk
To still my beating° mind.
FERDINAND, MIRANDA: We wish your peace.
                                              (*Exeunt* [FERDINAND *and* MIRANDA].)
PROSPERO: Come with a thought!° I thank thee, Ariel. Come.

(*Enter* ARIEL.)

ARIEL: Thy thoughts I cleave° to. What's thy pleasure?
PROSPERO: Spirit,   165
We must prepare to meet with Caliban.
ARIEL: Ay, my commander. When I presented° Ceres,
I thought to have told thee of it, but I feared
Lest I might anger thee.
PROSPERO: Say again, where didst thou leave these varlets?   170
ARIEL: I told you, sir, they were red-hot with drinking;
So full of valor that they smote the air
For breathing in their faces, beat the ground
For kissing of their feet; yet always bending°
Towards their project. Then I beat my tabor,   175
At which, like unbacked° colts, they pricked their ears,
Advanced° their eyelids, lifted up their noses
As° they smelt music. So I charmed their ears
That calflike they my lowing° followed through
Toothed briers, sharp furzes, pricking gorse,° and thorns,   180
Which entered their frail shins. At last I left them
I' the filthy-mantled° pool beyond your cell,
There dancing up to the chins, that the foul lake
O'erstunk° their feet.
PROSPERO: This was well done, my bird.
Thy shape invisible retain thou still.   185
The trumpery° in my house, go bring it hither,
For stale° to catch these thieves.

---

156 rack: Wisp of cloud.   **157 on:** Of.   **158 rounded:** Surrounded (before birth and after death),
or crowned, rounded off.   **160 with:** By.   **161 retire:** Withdraw, go.   **163 beating:** Agitated.
164 with a thought: I.e., on the instant, or, summoned by my thought, no sooner thought of than
here.   **165 cleave:** Cling, adhere.   **167 presented:** Acted the part of, or, introduced.   **174 bending:** Aiming.   **176 unbacked:** Unbroken, unridden.   **177 Advanced:** Lifted up.   **178 As:** As if.
179 lowing: Mooing.   **180 furzes, gorse:** Prickly shrubs.   **182 filthy-mantled:** Covered with
a slimy coating.   **184 O'erstunk:** Smelled worse than, or, caused to stink terribly.   **186
trumpery:** Cheap goods, the *glistering apparel* mentioned in the following stage direction.   **187
stale:** (1) Decoy, (2) out-of-fashion garments (with possible further suggestions of "horse piss," as in
line 198, and "steal," pronounced like *stale*). *For stale* could also mean "fit for a prostitute."

ARIEL: I go, I go.   (*Exit.*)
PROSPERO: A devil, a born devil, on whose nature
            Nurture can never stick; on whom my pains,
190   Humanely taken, all, all lost, quite lost!
            And as with age his body uglier grows,
            So his mind cankers.° I will plague them all,
            Even to roaring.

(*Enter* ARIEL, *loaden with glistering apparel, etc.*)

                Come, hang them on this line.°

([ARIEL *hangs up the showy finery;* PROSPERO *and* ARIEL *remain,*° *invisible.*] *Enter*
CALIBAN, STEPHANO, *and* TRINCULO, *all wet.*)

CALIBAN: Pray you, tread softly, that the blind mole may
195   Not hear a foot fall. We now are near his cell.
STEPHANO: Monster, your fairy, which you say is a harmless fairy, has done little bet-
            ter than played the jack° with us.
TRINCULO: Monster, I do smell all horse piss, at which my nose is in great indignation.
STEPHANO: So is mine. Do you hear, monster? If I should take a displeasure against
200   you, look you—
TRINCULO: Thou wert but a lost monster.
CALIBAN: Good my lord, give me thy favor still.
            Be patient, for the prize I'll bring thee to
            Shall hoodwink this mischance.° Therefore speak softly.
205   All's hushed as midnight yet.
TRINCULO: Ay, but to lose our bottles in the pool—
STEPHANO: There is not only disgrace and dishonor in that, monster, but an infinite
            loss.
TRINCULO: That's more to me than my wetting. Yet this is your harmless fairy,
210   monster!
STEPHANO: I will fetch off my bottle, though I be o'er ears° for my labor.
CALIBAN: Prithee, my king, be quiet. Seest thou here,
            This is the mouth o' the cell. No noise, and enter.
            Do that good mischief which may make this island
215   Thine own forever, and I thy Caliban
            For aye thy footlicker.
STEPHANO: Give me thy hand. I do begin to have bloody thoughts.
TRINCULO [*seeing the finery*]: O King Stephano! O peer!° O worthy Stephano! Look
            what a wardrobe here is for thee!
220 CALIBAN: Let it alone, thou fool, it is but trash.

---

192 cankers: Festers, grows malignant.   **193 line:** Lime tree or linden.   **Prospero and Ariel
remain:** (The staging is uncertain. They may instead exit here and return with the spirits at line
244.)   **197 jack:** (1) Knave, (2) will-o'-the-wisp.   **204 hoodwink this mischance:** (Misfortune
is to be prevented from doing further harm by being hooded like a hawk and also put out of remembrance.)   **211 o'er ears:** I.e., totally submerged and perhaps drowned.   **218 King . . . peer:**
(Alludes to the old ballad beginning "King Stephen was a worthy peer.")

TRINCULO: Oho, monster! We know what belongs to a frippery.° O King Stephano!
[*He puts on a gown.*]
STEPHANO: Put off° that gown, Trinculo. By this hand, I'll have that gown.
TRINCULO: Thy Grace shall have it.
CALIBAN: The dropsy° drown this fool! What do you mean
    To dote thus on such luggage?° Let 't alone   225
    And do the murder first. If he awake,
    From toe to crown° he'll fill our skins with pinches,
    Make us strange stuff.
STEPHANO: Be you quiet, monster.—Mistress line,° is not this my jerkin?° [*He takes
    it down.*] Now is the jerkin under the line.° Now, jerkin, you are like° to lose   230
    your hair and prove a bald° jerkin.
TRINCULO: Do, do!° We steal by line and level,° an 't like° Your Grace.
STEPHANO: I thank thee for that jest. Here's a garment for 't. [*He gives a garment.*]
    Wit shall not go unrewarded while I am king of this country. "Steal by line and
    level" is an excellent pass of pate.° There's another garment for 't.   235
TRINCULO: Monster, come, put some lime° upon your fingers, and away with the
    rest.
CALIBAN: I will have none on 't. We shall lose our time,
    And all be turned to barnacles,° or to apes
    With foreheads villainous° low.   240
STEPHANO: Monster, lay to° your fingers. Help to bear this° away where my
    hogshead° of wine is, or I'll turn you out of my kingdom. Go to,° carry this.
TRINCULO: And this.
STEPHANO: Ay, and this.   [*They load* CALIBAN *with more and more garments.*]

(*A noise of hunters heard. Enter divers spirits, in shape of dogs and hounds, hunting
them about,* PROSPERO *and* ARIEL *setting them on.*)

PROSPERO: Hey, Mountain, hey!   245
ARIEL: Silver! There it goes, Silver!
PROSPERO: Fury, Fury! There, Tyrant, there! Hark! Hark!
[CALIBAN, STEPHANO, *and* TRINCULO *are driven out.*]

---

221 frippery: Place where cast-off clothes are sold.   **222 Put off:** Put down, or, take off.   **224
dropsy:** Disease characterized by the accumulation of fluid in the connective tissue of the body.
225 luggage: Cumbersome trash.   **227 crown:** Head.   **229 Mistress line:** (Addressed to the
linden or lime tree upon which, at line 193, Ariel hung the *glistering apparel*);   **jerkin:** Jacket made
of leather.   **230 under the line:** Under the lime tree (with punning sense of being south of the
equinoctial line or equator; sailors on long voyages to the southern regions were popularly supposed
to lose their hair from scurvy or other diseases. Stephano also quibbles bawdily on losing hair
through syphilis, and in *Mistress* and *jerkin*);   **like:** Likely.   **231 bald:** (1) Hairless, napless, (2) meager.   **233 Do, do:** I.e., bravo (said in response to the jesting or to the taking of the jerkin, or both);
by line and level: I.e., by means of plumb line and carpenter's level, methodically (with pun on
line, "lime tree," line 230, and *steal,* pronounced like *stale,* i.e., prostitute, continuing Stephano's
bawdy quibble);   **an 't like:** If it please.   **235 pass of pate:** Sally of wit. (The metaphor is from
fencing.)   **236 lime:** Birdlime, sticky substance (to give Caliban sticky fingers).   **239 barnacles:**
Barnacle geese, formerly supposed to be hatched from barnacles attached to trees or to rotting timber; here, evidently used, like *apes,* as types of simpletons.   **240 villainous:** Miserably.   **241 lay
to:** Start using;   **this:** I.e., the *glistering apparel.*   **242 hogshead:** Large cask;   **Go to:** (An expression of exhortation or remonstrance.)

Go, charge my goblins that they grind their joints
With dry° convulsions,° shorten up their sinews
250   With agèd° cramps, and more pinch-spotted make them
Than pard° or cat o' mountain.°
ARIEL: Hark, they roar!
PROSPERO: Let them be hunted soundly.° At this hour
Lies at my mercy all mine enemies.
Shortly shall all my labors end, and thou
255   Shalt have the air at freedom. For a little°
Follow, and do me service.   (*Exeunt.*)

[ACT 5, SCENE 1]

[*Before* PROSPERO'*s cell.*]

(*Enter* PROSPERO *in his magic robes,* [*with his staff,*] *and* ARIEL.)

PROSPERO: Now does my project gather to a head.
My charms crack° not, my spirits obey, and Time
Goes upright with his carriage.° How's the day?
ARIEL: On° the sixth hour, at which time, my lord,
You said our work should cease.
5   PROSPERO: I did say so,
When first I raised the tempest. Say, my spirit,
How fares the King and 's followers?
ARIEL: Confined together
In the same fashion as you gave in charge,
Just as you left them; all prisoners, sir,
10   In the line grove° which weather-fends° your cell.
They cannot budge till your release.° The King,
His brother, and yours abide all three distracted,°
And the remainder mourning over them,
Brim full of sorrow and dismay; but chiefly
15   Him that you termed, sir, the good old lord, Gonzalo.
His tears runs down his beard like winter's drops
From eaves of reeds.° Your charm so strongly works 'em
That if you now beheld them your affections°
Would become tender.
PROSPERO: Dost thou think so, spirit?
ARIEL: Mine would, sir, were I human.°

---

249 dry: Associated with age, arthritic (?);   **convulsions:** Cramps.   **250 agèd:** Characteristic of old age.   **251 pard:** Panther or leopard;   **cat o' mountain:** Wildcat.   **252 soundly:** Thoroughly (and suggesting the sounds of the hunt).   **255 little:** Little while longer.   **ACT 5, SCENE 1. 2 crack:** Collapse, fail. (The metaphor is probably alchemical, as in *project* and *gather to a head,* line 1.) **3 his carriage:** Its burden (time is no longer heavily burdened and so can go *upright,* "standing straight and unimpeded").   **4 On:** Approaching.   **10 line grove:** Grove of lime trees;   **weather-fends:** Protects from the weather.   **11 your release:** You release them.   **12 distracted:** Out of their wits.   **17 eaves of reeds:** Thatched roofs.   **18 affections:** Disposition, feelings.   **20 human:** Humane [as well as human].

PROSPERO: And mine shall.   20
　　Hast thou, which art but air, a touch,° a feeling
　　Of their afflictions, and shall not myself,
　　One of their kind, that relish all as sharply
　　Passion as they,° be kindlier° moved than thou art?
　　Though with their high wrongs I am struck to the quick,   25
　　Yet with my nobler reason 'gainst my fury
　　Do I take part. The rarer° action is
　　In virtue than in vengeance. They being penitent,
　　The sole drift of my purpose doth extend
　　Not a frown further. Go release them, Ariel.   30
　　My charms I'll break, their senses I'll restore,
　　And they shall be themselves.
ARIEL: I'll fetch them, sir.   (*Exit.*)
　　　　　　　　[PROSPERO *traces a charmed circle with his staff.*]
PROSPERO: Ye elves of hills, brooks, standing lakes, and groves,
　　And ye° that on the sands with printless foot
　　Do chase the ebbing Neptune, and do fly him   35
　　When he comes back; you demi-puppets° that
　　By moonshine do the green sour ringlets° make,
　　Whereof the ewe not bites; and you whose pastime
　　Is to make midnight mushrooms,° that rejoice
　　To hear the solemn curfew;° by whose aid,   40
　　Weak masters° though ye be, I have bedimmed
　　The noontide sun, called forth the mutinous winds,
　　And twixt the green sea and the azured vault°
　　Set roaring war; to the dread rattling thunder
　　Have I given fire,° and rifted° Jove's stout oak°   45
　　With his own bolt;° the strong-based promontory
　　Have I made shake, and by the spurs° plucked up
　　The pine and cedar; graves at my command
　　Have waked their sleepers, oped, and let 'em forth
　　By my so potent art. But this rough magic   50
　　I here abjure, and when I have required°
　　Some heavenly music—which even now I do—
　　To work mine end upon their senses that°

---

21 touch: Sense, apprehension.   **23–24 that . . . they:** I who experience human passions as acutely as they.   **24 kindlier:** (1) More sympathetically, (2) more naturally, humanly.   **27 rarer:** Nobler.   **33–50 Ye . . . art:** (This famous passage is an embellished paraphrase of Golding's translation of Ovid's *Metamorphoses,* Book VII, lines 197–219.)   **36 demi-puppets:** Puppets of half size, i.e., elves and fairies.   **37 green sour ringlets:** Fairy rings, circles in grass (actually produced by mushrooms).   **39 midnight mushrooms:** Mushrooms appearing overnight.   **40 curfew:** Evening bell, usually rung at nine o'clock, ushering in the time when spirits are abroad.   **41 Weak masters:** I.e., subordinate spirits, as in 4.1.35 (?).   **43 the azured vault:** I.e., the sky.   **44–45 to . . . fire:** I have discharged the dread rattling thunderbolt.   **45 rifted:** Riven, split;   **oak:** A tree that was sacred to Jove.   **46 bolt:** Lightning bolt.   **47 spurs:** Roots.   **50 rough:** Violent.   **51 required:** Requested.   **53 their senses that:** The senses of those whom.

This airy charm° is for, I'll break my staff,
55   Bury it certain fathoms in the earth,
And deeper than did ever plummet sound
I'll drown my book.   *(Solemn music.)*

(*Here enters* ARIEL *before; then* ALONSO, *with a frantic gesture, attended by*
GONZALO; SEBASTIAN *and* ANTONIO *in like manner, attended by* ADRIAN *and*
FRANCISCO. *They all enter the circle which* PROSPERO *had made, and there stand*
charmed; which PROSPERO *observing, speaks:*)

[*To* ALONSO.] A solemn air,° and° the best comforter
To an unsettled fancy,° cure thy brains,
Now useless, boiled° within thy skull!   [*To* SEBASTIAN *and* ANTONIO.]
60   There stand,
For you are spell-stopped.—
Holy Gonzalo, honorable man,
Mine eyes, e'en sociable° to the show° of thine,
Fall° fellowly drops. [*Aside.*] The charm dissolves apace,
65   And as the morning steals upon the night,
Melting the darkness, so their rising senses
Begin to chase the ignorant fumes° that mantle°
Their clearer° reason.—O good Gonzalo,
My true preserver, and a loyal sir
70   To him thou follow'st! I will pay thy graces°
Home° both in word and deed.—Most cruelly
Didst thou, Alonso, use me and my daughter.
Thy brother was a furtherer° in the act.—
Thou art pinched° for 't now, Sebastian. [*To* ANTONIO.] Flesh and blood,
75   You, brother mine, that entertained ambition,
Expelled remorse° and nature,° whom,° with Sebastian,
Whose inward pinches therefore are most strong,
Would here have killed your king, I do forgive thee,
Unnatural though thou art.—Their understanding
80   Begins to swell, and the approaching tide
Will shortly fill the reasonable shore°
That now lies foul and muddy. Not one of them
That yet looks on me, or would know me.—Ariel,
Fetch me the hat and rapier in my cell.
           [ARIEL *goes to the cell and returns immediately.*]
85   I will discase° me and myself present

---

54 airy charm: I.e., music. **58 air:** Song; **and:** I.e., which is. **59 fancy:** Imagination. **60
boiled:** I.e., extremely agitated. **63 sociable:** Sympathetic; **show:** Appearance. **64 Fall:** Let
fall. **67 ignorant fumes:** Fumes that render them incapable of comprehension; **mantle:** En-
velop. **68 clearer:** Growing clearer. **70 pay thy graces:** Requite your favors and virtues. **71
Home:** Fully. **73 furtherer:** Accomplice. **74 pinched:** Punished, afflicted. **76 remorse:**
Pity; **nature:** Natural feeling; **whom:** I.e., who. **81 reasonable shore:** Shores of reason, i.e.,
minds (their reason returns, like the incoming tide). **85 discase:** Disrobe.

As I was sometime Milan.° Quickly, spirit!
Thou shalt ere long be free.   (ARIEL *sings and helps to attire him.*)
ARIEL: Where the bee sucks, there suck I.
         In a cowslip's bell I lie;
         There I couch° when owls do cry.   90
         On the bat's back I do fly
         After° summer merrily.
         Merrily, merrily shall I live now
         Under the blossom that hangs on the bough.
PROSPERO: Why, that's my dainty Ariel! I shall miss thee,   95
         But yet thou shalt have freedom. So, so, so.°
         To the King's ship, invisible as thou art!
         There shalt thou find the mariners asleep
         Under the hatches. The Master and the Boatswain
         Being awake, enforce them to this place,   100
         And presently,° I prithee.
ARIEL: I drink the air before me and return
         Or ere° your pulse twice beat.   (*Exit.*)
GONZALO: All torment, trouble, wonder, and amazement
         Inhabits here. Some heavenly power guide us   105
         Out of this fearful° country!
PROSPERO: Behold, sir King,
         The wrongèd Duke of Milan, Prospero.
         For more assurance that a living prince
         Does now speak to thee, I embrace thy body;
         And to thee and thy company I bid   110
         A hearty welcome.   [*Embracing him.*]
ALONSO: Whe'er thou be'st he or no,
         Or some enchanted trifle° to abuse° me,
         As late° I have been, I not know. Thy pulse
         Beats as of flesh and blood; and, since I saw thee,
         Th' affliction of my mind amends, with which   115
         I fear a madness held me. This must crave° —
         An if this be at all°—a most strange story.°
         Thy dukedom I resign,° and do entreat
         Thou pardon me my wrongs.° But how should Prospero
         Be living, and be here?
PROSPERO [*to* GONZALO]: First, noble friend,   120
         Let me embrace thine age,° whose honor cannot
         Be measured or confined.   [*Embracing him.*]

---

86 As . . . Milan: In my former appearance as Duke of Milan.   **90 couch:** Lie.   **92 After:** I.e.,
pursuing.   **96 So, so, so:** (Expresses approval of Ariel's help as valet.)   **101 presently:** Immediately.   **103 Or ere:** Before.   **106 fearful:** Frightening.   **112 trifle:** Trick of magic;   **abuse:**
Deceive.   **113 late:** Lately.   **116 crave:** Require.   **117 An . . . all:** If this is actually happening;
story: I.e., explanation.   **118 Thy . . . resign:** (Alonso made arrangements with Antonio at the
time of Prospero's banishment for Milan to pay tribute to Naples; see 1.2.113–127.)   **119 wrongs:**
Wrongdoings.   **121 thine age:** Your venerable self.

GONZALO: Whether this be
    Or be not, I'll not swear.
PROSPERO: You do yet taste
    Some subtleties° o' th' isle, that will not let you
125   Believe things certain. Welcome, my friends all!
    [*Aside to* SEBASTIAN *and* ANTONIO.] But you, my brace° of lords, were I so
       minded,
    I here could pluck His Highness' frown upon you
    And justify you° traitors. At this time
    I will tell no tales.
SEBASTIAN: The devil speaks in him.
PROSPERO: No.
130   [*To* ANTONIO.] For you, most wicked sir, whom to call brother
    Would even infect my mouth, I do forgive
    Thy rankest fault—all of them; and require
    My dukedom of thee, which perforce° I know
    Thou must restore.
ALONSO: If thou be'st Prospero,
135   Give us particulars of thy preservation,
    How thou hast met us here, whom° three hours since
    Were wrecked upon this shore, where I have lost—
    How sharp the point of this remembrance is!—
    My dear son Ferdinand.
PROSPERO: I am woe° for 't, sir.
140 ALONSO: Irreparable is the loss, and Patience
    Says it is past her cure.
PROSPERO: I rather think
    You have not sought her help, of whose soft grace°
    For the like loss I have her sovereign° aid
    And rest myself content.
ALONSO: You the like loss?
145 PROSPERO: As great to me as late,° and supportable
    To make the dear loss, have I° means much weaker
    Than you may call to comfort you; for I
    Have lost my daughter.
ALONSO: A daughter?
150   O heavens, that they were living both in Naples,
    The king and queen there! That° they were, I wish
    Myself were mudded° in that oozy bed
    Where my son lies. When did you lose your daughter?
PROSPERO: In this last tempest. I perceive these lords
155   At this encounter do so much admire°

---

124 subtleties: Illusions, magical powers (playing on the idea of "pastries, concoctions").   **126 brace:** Pair.   **128 justify you:** Prove you to be.   **133 perforce:** Necessarily.   **136 whom:** I.e., who.   **139 woe:** Sorry.   **142 of . . . grace:** By whose mercy.   **143 sovereign:** Efficacious.   **145 late:** Recent.   **145–146 supportable . . . have I:** To make the deeply felt loss bearable, I have.   **151 That:** So that.   **152 mudded:** Buried in the mud.   **155 admire:** Wonder.

That they devour their reason° and scarce think
Their eyes do offices of truth, their words
Are natural breath.° But, howsoever you have
Been jostled from your senses, know for certain
That I am Prospero and that very duke   160
Which was thrust forth of° Milan, who most strangely
Upon this shore, where you were wrecked, was landed
To be the lord on 't. No more yet of this,
For 'tis a chronicle of day by day,°
Not a relation for a breakfast nor   165
Befitting this first meeting. Welcome, sir.
This cell's my court. Here have I few attendants,
And subjects none abroad.° Pray you, look in.
My dukedom since you have given me again,
I will requite° you with as good a thing,   170
At least bring forth a wonder to content ye
As much as me my dukedom.

(*Here* PROSPERO *discovers°* FERDINAND *and* MIRANDA, *playing at chess.*)

MIRANDA: Sweet lord, you play me false.°
FERDINAND: No, my dearest love,
    I would not for the world.   175
MIRANDA: Yes, for a score of kingdoms you should wrangle,
    And I would call it fair play.°
ALONSO: If this prove
    A vision° of the island, one dear son
    Shall I twice lose.
SEBASTIAN: A most high miracle!
FERDINAND [*approaching his father*]:
    Though the seas threaten, they are merciful;   180
    I have cursed them without cause.   [*He kneels.*]
ALONSO: Now all the blessings
    Of a glad father compass° thee about!
    Arise, and say how thou cam'st here.   [FERDINAND *rises.*]
MIRANDA: O, wonder!
    How many goodly creatures are there here!
    How beauteous mankind is! O brave° new world   18.
    That has such people in 't!

---

156 devour their reason: I.e., are openmouthed, dumbfounded.   **156–158 scarce . . . breath:**
Scarcely believe that their eyes inform them accurately as to what they see or that their words are
naturally spoken.   **161 of:** From.   **164 of day by day:** Requiring days to tell.   **168 abroad:**
Away from here, anywhere else.   **170 requite:** Repay;   **discovers:** I.e., by opening a curtain, presumably rearstage.   **173 play me false:** I.e., press your advantage.   **176–177 Yes . . . play:** Yes,
even if we were playing for only twenty kingdoms, you would still press your advantage against me,
and I would lovingly let you do it as though it were fair play, or if you were to play not just for
stakes but literally for kingdoms, my complaint would be out of order in that your "wrangling"
would be proper.   **178 vision:** Illusion.   **182 compass:** Encompass, embrace.   **185 brave:**
Splendid, gorgeously appareled, handsome.

PROSPERO: 'Tis new to thee.
ALONSO: What is this maid with whom thou wast at play?
     Your eld'st° acquaintance cannot be three hours.
     Is she the goddess that hath severed us,
     And brought us thus together?
190   FERDINAND: Sir, she is mortal;
     But by immortal Providence she's mine.
     I chose her when I could not ask my father
     For his advice, nor thought I had one. She
     Is daughter to this famous Duke of Milan,
195   Of whom so often I have heard renown,
     But never saw before; of whom I have
     Received a second life; and second father
     This lady makes him to me.
ALONSO: I am hers.
     But O, how oddly will it sound that I
     Must ask my child forgiveness!
200   PROSPERO: There, sir, stop.
     Let us not burden our remembrances with
     A heaviness° that's gone.
GONZALO: I have inly° wept,
     Or should have spoke ere this. Look down, you gods,
     And on this couple drop a blessèd crown!
205   For it is you that have chalked forth the way°
     Which brought us hither.
ALONSO: I say amen, Gonzalo!
GONZALO: Was Milan° thrust from Milan, that his issue
     Should become kings of Naples? O, rejoice
     Beyond a common joy, and set it down
210   With gold on lasting pillars: In one voyage
     Did Claribel her husband find at Tunis,
     And Ferdinand, her brother, found a wife
     Where he himself was lost; Prospero his dukedom
     In a poor isle; and all of us ourselves
215   When no man was his own.°
ALONSO [*to* FERDINAND *and* MIRANDA]: Give me your hands.
     Let grief and sorrow still° embrace his° heart
     That° doth not wish you joy!
GONZALO: Be it so! Amen!

(*Enter* ARIEL, *with the* MASTER *and* BOATSWAIN *amazedly following.*)

     O, look, sir, look, sir! Here is more of us.
     I prophesied, if a gallows were on land,

---

188 **eld'st:** Longest.   202 **heaviness:** Sadness; **inly:** Inwardly.   205 **chalked . . . way:** Marked as with a piece of chalk the pathway.   207 **Was Milan:** Was the Duke of Milan.   214–215 **all . . . own:** All of us have found ourselves and our sanity when we all had lost our senses.   216 **still:** Always;   **his:** That person's.   217 **That:** Who.

This fellow could not drown.—Now, blasphemy,°   220
That swear'st grace o'erboard,° not an oath° on shore?
Hast thou no mouth by land? What is the news?
BOATSWAIN: The best news is that we have safely found
     Our King and company; the next, our ship—
     Which, but three glasses° since, we gave out° split—   225
     Is tight and yare° and bravely° rigged as when
     We first put out to sea.
ARIEL [aside to PROSPERO]: Sir, all this service
     Have I done since I went.
PROSPERO [aside to ARIEL]:   My tricksy° spirit!
ALONSO: These are not natural events; they strengthen°
     From strange to stranger. Say, how came you hither?   230
BOATSWAIN: If I did think, sir, I were well awake,
     I'd strive to tell you. We were dead of sleep,°
     And—how we know not—all clapped under hatches,
     Where but even now, with strange and several° noises
     Of roaring, shrieking, howling, jingling chains,   235
     And more diversity of sounds, all horrible,
     We were awaked; straightway at liberty;
     Where we, in all her trim, freshly beheld
     Our royal, good, and gallant ship, our Master
     Cap'ring to eye° her. On a trice,° so please you,   240
     Even in a dream, were we divided from them°
     And were brought moping° hither.
ARIEL [aside to PROSPERO]:   Was 't well done?
PROSPERO [aside to ARIEL]: Bravely, my diligence. Thou shalt be free.
ALONSO: This is as strange a maze as e'er men trod,
     And there is in this business more than nature   245
     Was ever conduct° of. Some oracle
     Must rectify our knowledge.
PROSPERO: Sir, my liege,
     Do not infest° your mind with beating on°
     The strangeness of this business. At picked° leisure,
     Which shall be shortly, single° I'll resolve° you,   250
     Which to you shall seem probable,° of every
     These° happened accidents;° till when, be cheerful
     And think of each thing well.° [Aside to ARIEL.] Come hither, spirit.

---

220 blasphemy: I.e., blasphemer.   **221 That swear'st grace o'erboard:** I.e., you who banish heavenly grace from the ship by your blasphemies;   **not an oath:** Aren't you going to swear an oath.   **225 glasses:** I.e., hours;   **gave out:** Reported, professed to be.   **226 yare:** Ready; **bravely:** Splendidly.   **228 tricksy:** Ingenious, sportive.   **229 strengthen:** Increase.   **232 dead of sleep:** Deep in sleep.   **234 several:** Diverse.   **240 Cap'ring to eye:** Dancing for joy to see; **On a trice:** In an instant.   **241 them:** I.e., the other crew members.   **242 moping:** In a daze. **246 conduct:** Guide.   **248 infest:** Harass, disturb;   **beating on:** Worrying about.   **249 picked:** Chosen, convenient.   **250 single:** Privately, by my own human powers;   **resolve:** Satisfy, explain to.   **251 probable:** Plausible.   **251–252 of every These:** About every one of these.   **252 accidents:** Occurrences.   **253 well:** Favorably.

Set Caliban and his companions free.
255   Untie the spell. [*Exit* ARIEL.] How fares my gracious sir?
There are yet missing of your company
Some few odd° lads that you remember not.

(*Enter* ARIEL, *driving in* CALIBAN, STEPHANO, *and* TRINCULO, *in their stolen apparel.*)

STEPHANO: Every man shift° for all the rest,° and let no man take care for himself;
for all is but fortune. Coragio,° bully monster,° coragio!
260   TRINCULO: If these be true spies° which I wear in my head, here's a goodly sight.
CALIBAN: O Setebos, these be brave° spirits indeed!
How fine° my master is! I am afraid
He will chastise me.
SEBASTIAN: Ha, ha!
265   What things are these, my lord Antonio?
Will money buy 'em?
ANTONIO: Very like. One of them
Is a plain fish, and no doubt marketable.
PROSPERO: Mark but the badges° of these men, my lords,
Then say if they be true.° This misshapen knave,
270   His mother was a witch, and one so strong
That could control the moon, make flows and ebbs,
And deal in her command without her power.°
These three have robbed me, and this demidevil—
For he's a bastard° one—had plotted with them
275   To take my life. Two of these fellows you
Must know and own.° This thing of darkness I
Acknowledge mine.
CALIBAN: I shall be pinched to death.
ALONSO: Is not this Stephano, my drunken butler?
SEBASTIAN: He is drunk now. Where had he wine?
280   ALONSO: And Trinculo is reeling ripe.° Where should they
Find this grand liquor that hath gilded° em?
[*To* TRINCULO.] How cam'st thou in this pickle?°
TRINCULO: I have been in such a pickle since I saw you last that, I fear me, will
never out of my bones. I shall not fear flyblowing.°
285   SEBASTIAN: Why, how now, Stephano?

---

257 odd: Unaccounted for. **258 shift:** Provide; **for all the rest:** (Stephano drunkenly gets wrong the saying "Every man for himself.") **259 Coragio:** Courage; **bully monster:** Gallant monster (ironical). **260 true spies:** Accurate observers (i.e., sharp eyes). **261 brave:** Handsome. **262 fine:** Splendidly attired. **268 badges:** Emblems of cloth or silver worn by retainers to indicate whom they serve. (Prospero refers here to the stolen clothes as emblems of their villainy.) **269 true:** Honest. **272 deal . . . power:** Wield the moon's power, either without her authority or beyond her influence, or, even though to do so was beyond Sycorax's own power. **274 bastard:** Counterfeit. **276 own:** Recognize, admit as belonging to you. **280 reeling ripe:** Stumbling drunk. **281 gilded:** (1) Flushed, made drunk, (2) covered with gilt (suggesting the horse urine). **282 pickle:** (1) Fix, predicament, (2) pickling brine (in this case, horse urine). **284 flyblowing:** I.e., being fouled by fly eggs (from which he is saved by being pickled).

STEPHANO: O, touch me not! I am not Stephano, but a cramp.

PROSPERO: You'd be king o' the isle, sirrah?°

STEPHANO: I should have been a sore° one, then.

ALONSO [*pointing to* CALIBAN]: This is a strange thing as e'er I looked on.

PROSPERO: He is as disproportioned in his manners   290
    As in his shape.—Go, sirrah, to my cell.
    Take with you your companions. As you look
    To have my pardon, trim° it handsomely.

CALIBAN: Ay, that I will; and I'll be wise hereafter
    And seek for grace.° What a thrice-double ass   295
    Was I to take this drunkard for a god
    And worship this dull fool!

PROSPERO: Go to. Away!

ALONSO: Hence, and bestow your luggage where you found it.

SEBASTIAN: Or stole it, rather.   [*Exeunt* CALIBAN, STEPHANO, *and* TRINCULO.]

PROSPERO: Sir, I invite Your Highness and your train   300
    To my poor cell, where you shall take your rest
    For this one night; which, part of it, I'll waste°
    With such discourse as, I not doubt, shall make it
    Go quick away: the story of my life,
    And the particular accidents° gone by   305
    Since I came to this isle. And in the morn
    I'll bring you to your ship, and so to Naples,
    Where I have hope to see the nuptial
    Of these our dear-belovèd solemnized;
    And thence retire me° to my Milan, where   310
    Every third thought shall be my grave.

ALONSO: I long
    To hear the story of your life, which must
    Take° the ear strangely.

PROSPERO: I'll deliver° all;
    And promise you calm seas, auspicious gales,
    And sail so expeditious that shall catch   315
    Your royal fleet far off.° [*Aside to* ARIEL.] My Ariel, chick,
    That is thy charge. Then to the elements
    Be free, and fare thou well!—Please you, draw near.°

                  (*Exeunt omnes* [*except* PROSPERO].)

EPILOGUE

(*Spoken by* PROSPERO.)

    Now my charms are all o'erthrown,

---

287 sirrah: (Standard form of address to an inferior, here expressing reprimand.) **288 sore:** (1) Tyrannical, (2) sorry, inept, (3) wracked by pain. **293 trim:** Prepare, decorate. **295 grace:** Pardon, favor. **302 waste:** Spend. **305 accidents:** Occurrences. **310 retire me:** Return. **313 Take:** Take effect upon, enchant; **deliver:** Declare, relate. **315–316 catch . . . far off:** Enable you to catch up with the main part of your royal fleet, now afar off en route to Naples (see 1.2.233–236). **318 draw near:** I.e., enter my cell.

And what strength I have 's mine own,
Which is most faint. Now, 'tis true,
I must be here confined by you
5   Or sent to Naples. Let me not,
Since I have my dukedom got
And pardoned the deceiver, dwell
In this bare island by your spell,
But release me from my bands°
10 With the help of your good hands.°
Gentle breath° of yours my sails
Must fill, or else my project fails,
Which was to please. Now I want°
Spirits to enforce,° art to enchant,
15 And my ending is despair,
Unless I be relieved by prayer,°
Which pierces so that it assaults°
Mercy itself, and frees° all faults.
As you from crimes° would pardoned be,
20 Let your indulgence° set me free.   (*Exit.*)

QUESTIONS FOR DISCUSSION AND WRITING

1. *The Tempest* is sometimes called "Shakespeare's farewell to the stage," partly because it was probably one of his last plays, partly because at the end of the play Prospero—whom some see as a stand-in for the author—abandons his magic and its craft. Look at the character of Prospero. To what extent is he like a playwright, creating the action and manipulating the actors? Do you think we are meant to see his attempts at control as heroic? Is *The Tempest* a celebration and/or a critique of art and the artist?

2. Compare and contrast the characters of Caliban and Ariel, Prospero's two wards. Some readers see in them personifications of the key ideas in the debate about "nature versus nurture." Others see Caliban as the embodiment of people's more sensual nature and Ariel as the embodiment of our more spiritual side. To what extent does the play suggest that Caliban's nature might have been changed had he been nurtured more? Why is it that Prospero treats Ariel so much better than he treats Caliban, even setting Ariel free at the end? How do the characters of Ariel and Caliban help us define the concepts of monstrosity and heroism?

EPILOGUE. **9 bands:** Bonds.   **10 hands:** I.e., applause (the noise of which would break the spell of silence).   **11 Gentle breath:** Favorable breeze (produced by hands clapping or favorable comment).   **13 want:** Lack.   **14 enforce:** Control.   **16 prayer:** I.e., Prospero's petition to the audience.   **17 assaults:** Rightfully gains the attention of.   **18 frees:** Obtains forgiveness for.   **19 crimes:** Sins.   **20 indulgence:** (1) Humoring, lenient approval, (2) remission of punishment for sin.

3. Look at the language of the play. Which characters speak in prose? Which in verse? What do the characters say about the way language works and about its powers? What do their uses of language (metaphors, curses, songs, etc.) tell us about them?

4. *The Tempest* itself contains a number of retellings. In several of his plots, Shakespeare works through the theme of usurpation: in the years before the events of the play, Antonio usurped the dukedom from Prospero; now he and Sebastian plot to overthrow King Alonso; elsewhere on the island, Stephano and Trinculo, aided by Caliban, talk of deposing Prospero. And then there's Prospero himself, who, Caliban says, has stolen the island from him, its rightful lord. The doubling and tripling of plots help us to compare and contrast the various rulers and those they have deposed. What do the comparisons tell us about the leadership qualities of the actual and would-be rulers? Of the ideal ruler? What, moreover, do they tell us about those who were deposed? Did each, in some way, bring upon himself his own overthrow?

5. In part, *The Tempest* is a play about the struggle between innocence and experience. What does it ask us to see as the value of each? The drawbacks of each? In this play that speaks of "sea changes" (see Ariel's song in 1.2), how, if at all, does each of the characters change in the course of the play? What, if anything, does each of them learn? And what (or who) is his or her teacher? (You might here also consider the relationships not only between innocence and experience but among sin, repentance, retribution, and grace.)

6. Caliban and Ariel both seem like characters from another world, neither one quite human. How would you cast these two characters? How magical would you make Ariel? How monstrous Caliban? Why?

7. *The Tempest* is a play rich in images. Look at one of the following image patterns and analyze its significance to the play as a whole: clothing, seeing/sight, sleep/dreams, song/music, speech/muteness/language.

8. What is the function of Gonzalo in the play? Consider his relationships and interactions (both past and present) with Prospero and Alonso *and* with the other members of the royal party.

9. Prospero enslaves not only Caliban and Ariel but, to a certain extent, Ferdinand, whom he accuses of being a traitor and sets to work. What is the function of labor in the play? What do we discover about the characters through their responses to the labors they are assigned?

10. Look at the play's setting. How does the setting influence and reflect the characters' moods, actions, and values? How is the natural setting compared and contrasted to the distant lands from which the characters have come?

QUESTION FOR DISCUSSION AND WRITING

Here is an advertising poster (see also color insert) for the 1956 movie *Forbidden Planet,* a science-fiction takeoff on *The Tempest.* Robby, the Robot, plays a part parallel to Ariel's, and the young woman plays a part parallel to Miranda's. From the picture, what would you expect to be the relationship between Robby and the young woman? What is accomplished and lost by his being cast as a robot? How would you characterize the Miranda figure?

James Condon

Professor Levin

English 117C

16 January 2001

The Usurped Turns Usurper

The tension between Prospero and Caliban is established from the beginning of their first meeting in Act 1, Scene 2, in Shakespeare's *Tempest.* This scene is the reader's first glimpse into the character of Caliban, and through it the reader discovers the nature of Caliban's relationship to

Prospero. The first moment that the pair are onstage together, they curse and insult one another, creating an initial and lasting impression of hostility between the pair. Through Caliban's subsequent speech, the reader learns of his claim to the island through his mother's previous ownership, and of his anger over his current servile role. Prospero's greeting comments and Caliban's account of his history establish the hierarchical relationship between the two and hint at Caliban's necessity in Prospero's rule over their island home.

The exchange between Prospero and Caliban immediately establishes the hierarchical relationship within which the two exist. Key words, uttered by both Prospero and Caliban, set the latter in the role of servant. Prospero initially calls "What ho,! Slave!" (317) and thereby fixes the creature as his servant and inferior; Caliban acknowledges this role when he bitterly admits, "I am all the subjects that you have" (345). The use of the word "subject," one who is under the dominion of a monarch or reigning prince" (OED), associates his master Prospero with monarchy, and at the same time suggests a political undertone to the scene. In this light, the island is a dukedom of sorts, and Prospero is its Duke; indeed, the magician wields the power of such a ruler, and not altogether benevolently, as he confines Caliban in his cell: "here you sty me / In this hard rock, whiles you do keep from me / The rest o' th' island" (346-348). Prospero, then, has established a new dukedom on his island home and lords it over his deformed and hostile servant Caliban. His slave is more than a grumbling dissenter, however; he is a key element to Prospero's continued dominance of the island.

Prospero rules the island absolutely only through his control of Caliban, making the creature extremely important to the magician regardless of the fact that Caliban is his slave. Prospero realizes Caliban's worth, and he points this out to Miranda when he states that Caliban "serves in offices / That profit us" (316–317). Caliban is essentially a creature of the island, possessing a mind-set based in the natural world. Even when Caliban curses Prospero and calls upon his mother's magic, he invokes "toads, beetles, bats" (344), creatures of nature that contrast the airy spirits that Prospero favors. This intimacy with nature is only too apparent to the magician, who calls Caliban "Thou earth, thou" (318) when he hails him from outside his cell. Prospero undoubtedly realized Caliban's natural affinity early on and set out to use it for his own advantage. Once Prospero had earned Caliban's love, the young creature "showed thee all the qualities o' th' isle, / The fresh springs, brine pits, barren place and fertile" (341–342); even at that young age, his knowledge of the island's natural wonders was intimate and extensive. Even against Prospero's magical powers, Caliban is a master of the island in his own right; he knows "all the qualities o' th' isle." By subjugating Caliban, then, Prospero is able to subjugate the entire island and establish his dominion; the magician symbolically controls earth through his sway over Caliban. Prospero could never know the island to the degree that Caliban does, and so he forces Caliban to serve "in offices / That profit us" and use his knowledge to augment Prospero's power.

The irony of the situation is that Prospero has become the very thing that he hates about his brother Antonio. Caliban has a legitimate claim to the island, if only through his previous residency and his intimate knowledge of it, rather than his argument that "This island's mine, by Sycorax

my mother" (335); that line of reasoning seems to be ignored
by the magician throughout the play. Caliban's right to the
island is forgotten as Prospero assumes control and enslaves
he who "first was mine own king" (346). Though Prospero never
gives any sign that he recognizes this role reversal, and
thus one must be hesitant to brand him a hypocrite, the irony
of the situation is still palpable as the usurped Duke
becomes the usurper.

Though Caliban is established in his own speech as Prospero's subordinate, his close association with nature and intimate knowledge of the island lead the magician to use him
as a sort of crutch for his own dominion. The irony of Prospero's conquest of the island may be lost on the characters,
but it is readily apparent to the reader. Still, Prospero is
by no means a villain here, nor is Caliban a simple victim.
In his speech, the creature recounts the early days when he
was united with Prospero and "I loved thee" (340), and then
suddenly turns to cursing and bemoaning his enslavement; he
conveniently leaves out his attempted rape of Miranda, the
act that drove Prospero to withdraw his favor and make Caliban into a servant. Caliban's recollection shades the past
into a version more favorable to his own character, much like
how Prospero's account of his dukedom in Milan glazes over
the fact that he was being an irresponsible ruler. Between
their similar turns of memory and their rival claims to the
same island, both characters are more alike than either would
care to admit. In the end, though, Prospero is completely in
control; Caiban is left only with his impotent plots and
frustrated ambition, "But, as 'tis, / We cannot miss him"
(314-315).

QUESTIONS FOR DISCUSSION AND WRITING

1. What would you identify as Condon's thesis? Where do you find support for that thesis in the paper? How, if at all, would you revise the thesis?

2. In his final paragraph, Condon says that Prospero and Caliban "are more alike than either would care to admit." How well do you think the paper supports that statement? What further supporting evidence can you find from *The Tempest*? What evidence might you advance to counter Condon's claim?

3. Outline the paper, paying particular attention to the topics of each paragraph and to the evidence presented in support of those topics. How might the organization of the paper be sharpened so as to clarify the logical progression of the argument?

4. Although Condon's paper isn't perfect, it is certainly very good. What would you identify as its primary strengths? Why?

MERA MOORE

Miranda Cries, Father's Raping Me and Blaming It on Caliban   *1991*

Stop the canoe—I'm getting ready to vomit. Don't be
stupid—there's land.
Watch out, an iceberg! What? Shut up stupid.
Boom.
5 Dad says my mom is dead and Caliban's mom was a witch.
Witches were burnt: to procure and disseminate birth control
is still criminal.
A patriarchal fiction? Yes, they still believe
a god impregnated Mary with Jesus and stupidity Rosemary's
10 Baby. Who me?
I'm only a woman.
Come impregnate me—isn't that why you've made up the lie
that nobody was ever gassed and cremated in Nazy Germany—
no, not at Dachau, not there so clean and German and Father.

QUESTIONS FOR DISCUSSION AND WRITING

1. Moore's poem draws on Christianity and on *The Tempest*, of course, but in its references to Dachau and Rosemary's Baby (the offspring of the devil from a book and film of the same name), it also draws on modern history and modern popular culture. What is the effect of this mixing of references to such disparate sources? What kinds of monstrosities do the references to Dachau and Rosemary's baby imply?

2. The title of Moore's poem suggests Prospero has raped Miranda. What in Shakespeare's play might suggest incest?

_____

DEBORA GREGER (1949–   )

Miranda on the British Isles _____ 1992

> Were I in England now, as I once was, and had but this fish painted, not a holi-
> day fool there but would give a piece of silver: there would this monster make a
> man; any strange beast there makes a man; when they will not give a doit to re-
> lieve a lame beggar, they will lay out ten to see a dead Indian.
>
> —_The Tempest_

Gray the rabbit pulled from the old hat,
gray the silk handkerchief and the dove.
Gray the rain on the seaside towns
that Prospero and Daughter played,

our magic to be taken with a grain of sand.   5
Still, there were always volunteers,
foreign sailors out of their depth
dying to be sawn in half in front of their mates

or the evening's girls. My father,
Signor Sincerity, dubbed them all Ferdinand.   10
Sometimes, up to his neck in the trick cabinet,
well-worn patter heaped upon his well-lit head,

one winked in semaphore at me.
My father fretted, the old saw threatening to give.
I held the pose I called ship's figurehead,   15
leading with what bosom I had

past the catch lying just ahead.
Gray the tempests pulled from teapots,
gray the mirrors and the smoke.
Below the trapdoor, waves slapped the pier   20

until it shuddered but held on.
A backstage tea kettle shrieked domestically.
An offshore foghorn droned, inharmonious
but constant in its low complaint.

The water-stained curtains were winched shut   25
on the painted smiles of Old Asperity and daughter.
On the shallow waves of applause sailed Caliban,
loutish comedian, trailed by his straight man, Ariel.

30 Gray the backwash of laughter, grayer still
the spray of jokes. A half-full house
of flounder rolled their wandering eyes
toward the wings where chorus girls,

saluting each other for practice,
waited their cue. Gray now the blonde
35 who sang of going no more to sea, to sea,
of dying instead ashore—blue-rinsed

that bleached blonde I was dying to be.
The way sound carried over water,
I'd hear her taking scales like stairs
40 in gray hotels where the lift was always out.

Walls made of paper, walls made of rain—
some nights next door a boat creaked over swells
and muddy from that woozy bed
came birdlike cries, then a beached groan.

45 My father and a chorus girl?
Old Bosporus? Did I want to know?
Like any local fisherman
after the nightly haul, I had net to mend—

my tights. Nightly I played the native,
50 hoisting a cup of Earl Grey's bilge
to the wallpaper's gray roses.
Rain lashed a sea of gray slate roofs.

QUESTIONS FOR DISCUSSION AND WRITING

1. "Miranda on the British Isles" has transformed the characters from *The Tempest* into a carnival act. Who does what in this act? What is Greger saying about each character through his or her role? How does the change to carnival characters ask us to redefine the possibilities of monstrosity and heroism?

2. Greger seems intent on stripping Miranda's story of the ephemeral, magical qualities it has in Shakespeare's romance. How does she make that story seem more mundane? What do Prospero and his magic become? What does Miranda herself become?

3. What is the relationship between the epigraph from *The Tempest* and Greger's poem?

4. Miranda calls Caliban a "loutish comedian" and Ariel his "straight man," suggesting that the two in some way need each other. Where in Shakespeare's play might Greger have found a suggestion for such a relationship? What does the pairing of

the two suggest about the nature of physicality and spirituality? Of monstrosity and spirituality?

ROGER HECHT (1926–   )
Ferdinand To Prospero At Milan   **1970**

I, too, have known the zest to kill, the prompting
To snatch a maiden's clothes away from her
And force her in a thoroughfare to yield
Her body to my pleasure, then to cut
The tongue free of her head and make her serve,   5
On threat of death, as minister and slave
To every whim and winding humor of my will.
Prospero, did I not
Often, how often, whistle the air with arrows
That some sweet beast might gush its blood before me   10
And make me seem commander of the world?
Have I not in pretended play uplifted
This tart dagger that I wear and teased with it
The confluence of veins here at the wrist
While jabbering cries against the maledictions   15
And sometimes negligence of parents and of friends?
Look upon my neck, here where I dug
A little hole after a stripling teacher
Made subject, to awake a drowsing discourse,
My person to the tongue of ridicule.   20
No. These several deeds were not
Calendar incidents to illustrate the boy
In clear distinction from the man you see.
I am a thing of darkness, and I know it:
The shapes may vary, the degrees of dark may seem   25
Here less, here more, but all of man's one stuff
And I am brother in blood to Caliban.
This present world is Milan. Yet on that isle,
On that rough place in an incivil sea,
Since it was strange to us, we lived as strangers,   30
Barbarously to masquerade our doubt,
Furious with loss or, with the cynic creed,
Doted on this and that absurdity,
Believing all action futile and thought the proof
Of nothing other than of vanity.   35

Prospero, suppose
In your imagination, all men live

Forever as we did, forever strangers,
With not a home, a certain friend, a wife;
40 With fowl to feed upon only when mallard, quail,
And honking geese settle awhile nearby;
With not a cloth for clothes but what the weeds
And thick-leaved palms provide; with not a boat
To passage from that foul and muddy shore
45 And a murderous sea to swallow all that dare
Swim from the coast. Imagine years have worn
The patience and the mercy out of us
Until we are made natural and wild
And, in a word, each man's a Caliban
50 Or an Alonso. What would you foresee?
Most solemnly I swear
I see before my eyes much unfleshed bone
Piled like dry sticks to keep a fire live
And one man only left, and that man mad,
55 Shifting on hands and knees, the slack jaws open,
The tongue depending, the squint eyes ravenous,
And, every while, lifting its head to howl
Sounds without syllables till the echoes give it fear
At which it silences and slowly crawls
60 To spit on the noising fire an arm or rib,—
The putrid, insubstantial dregs of its own flesh.

QUESTIONS FOR DISCUSSION AND WRITING

1. Hecht's Ferdinand says that he, like Caliban, is "a thing of darkness" and that he is "brother in blood to Caliban." What similarities does Ferdinand see between himself and Caliban? Do you see these same ties in Shakespeare's play? What does a mirroring of Ferdinand and Caliban tell us about the nature of heroism and monstrosity?
2. Hecht sets Ferdinand's monologue in Milan, presumably after the royal party has returned from the island of *The Tempest* and taken up their former lives. How does Ferdinand compare Milan and the island on which he and his fellows were shipwrecked? Are the conclusions he draws similar to those Shakespeare's play seems to ask us to draw? Are monsters and heroes more likely to be found in one setting than in another?

AIMÉ CÉSAIRE (1913–)

A Tempest _____ *1969*

Characters

As in Shakespeare

Two alterations: ARIEL, *a mulatto slave*
CALIBAN, *a black slave*

An addition: ESHU, *a black devil-god*

(*Ambiance of a psychodrama. The actors enter singly, at random, and each chooses for himself a mask at his leisure.*)

MASTER OF CEREMONIES: Come gentlemen, help yourselves. To each his character, to each character his mask. You, Prospero? Why not? He has reserves of will power he's not even aware of himself. You want Caliban? Well, that's revealing. Ariel? Fine with me. And what about Stephano, Trinculo? No takers? Ah, just in time! It takes all kinds to make a world.   5

    And after all, they aren't the worst characters. No problem about the juvenile leads, Miranda and Ferdinand. You, okay. And there's no problem about the villains either: you, Antonio; you, Alonso, perfect! Oh, Christ! I was forgetting the Gods. Eshu will fit you like a glove. As for the other parts, just take what you want and work it out among yourselves. But make up your minds . . . Now,   10 there's one part I have to pick out myself: you! It's for the part of the Tempest, and I need a storm to end all storms . . . I need a really big guy to do the wind. Will you do that? Fine! And then someone strong for Captain of the ship. Good, now let's go. Ready? Begin. Blow, winds! Rain and lightning *ad lib!*

ACT I
SCENE 1

GONZALO: Of course, we're only straws tossed on the raging sea . . . but all's not lost,   15 Gentlemen. We just have to try to get to the eye of the storm.

ANTONIO: We might have known this old fool would nag us to death!

SEBASTIAN: To the bitter end!

GONZALO: Try to understand what I'm telling you: imagine a huge cylinder like the chimney of a lamp, fast as a galloping horse, but in the center as still and un-   20 moving as a Cyclop's eye. That's what we're talking about when we say "the eye of the storm" and that's were we have to get.

ANTONIO: Oh, great! Do you really mean that the cyclone or Cyclops, if he can't see the beam in his own eye, will let us escape! Oh, that's very illuminating!

GONZALO: It's a clever way of putting it, at any rate. Literally false, but yet quite true.   25 But what's the fuss going on up there? The Captain seems worried. (*Calling.*) Captain!

CAPTAIN (*with a shrug*): Boatswain!

BOATSWAIN: Aye, sir!

30 CAPTAIN: We're coming round windward of the island. At this speed we'll run aground. We've got to turn her around. Heave to! (*Exits.*)

BOATSWAIN: Come on, men! Heave to! To the topsail; man the ropes. Pull! Heave ho, heave ho!

35 ALONSO (*approaching*): Well, Boatswain, how are things going? Where are we?

BOATSWAIN: If you ask me, you'd all be better off below, in your cabins.

ANTONIO: *He* doesn't seem too happy. We'd better ask the Captain. Where's the Captain, Boatswain? He was here just a moment ago, and now he's gone off.

BOATSWAIN: Get back below where you belong! We've got work to do!

GONZALO: My dear fellow, I can quite understand your being nervous, but a man
40 should be able to control himself in any situation, even the most upsetting.

BOATSWAIN: Shove it! If you want to save your skins, you'd better get yourselves back down below to those first-class cabins of yours.

GONZALO: Now, now, my good fellow, you don't seem to know to whom you're speaking. (*Making introductions.*) The King's brother, the King's son and myself,
45 the King's counselor.

BOATSWAIN: King! King! Well, there's someone who doesn't give a fuck more about the king than he does about you or me, and he's called the Gale. His Majesty the Gale! And right now, he's in control and we're all his subjects.

GONZALO: He might just as well be pilot on the ferry to hell . . . his mouth's foul
50 enough!

ANTONIO: In a sense, the fellow *regales* me, as you might say. We'll pull through, you'll see, because he looks to me more like someone who'll end up on the gallows, not beneath the billows.

SEBASTIAN: The end result is the same. The fish will get us and the crows will get him.

55 GONZALO: He did irritate me, rather. However, I take the attenuating circumstances into account . . . and, you must admit, he lacks neither courage nor wit.

BOATSWAIN: (*returning*) Pull in the stud sails. Helmsman, into the wind! Into the wind!

(*Enter* SEBASTIAN, ANTONIO, GONZALO.)

BOATSWAIN: You again! If you keep bothering us and don't get below and say your prayers I'll give up and let you sail the ship! You can't expect me to be the go-
60 between for your souls and Beelzebub!

ANTONIO: It's really too much! The fellow is taking advantage of the situation . . .

BOATSWAIN: Windward! Windward! Heave into the wind!

(*Thunder, lightning.*)

SEBASTIAN: Ho! Ho!

GONZALO: Did you see that? There, at the top of the masts, in the rigging, that glit-
65 ter of blue fire, flashing, flashing? They're right when they call these magic lands, so different from our homes in Europe . . . Look, even the lightning is different!

ANTONIO: Maybe its a foretaste of the hell that awaits us.

GONZALO: You're too pessimistic. Anyway, I've always kept myself in a state of grace, ready to meet my maker.

(SAILORS *enter.*)

70 SAILORS: Shit! We're sinking!

(The passengers can be heard singing "Nearer, my God, to Thee . . .")

BOATSWAIN: To leeward! To leeward!

FERDINAND: *(entering)* Alas! There's no one in hell . . . all the devils are here!

(The ship sinks.)

SCENE 2

MIRANDA: Oh God! Oh God! A sinking ship! Father, help!

PROSPERO: *(enters hurriedly carrying a megaphone.)* Come daughter, calm yourself! It's only a play. There's really nothing wrong. Anyway, everything that happens is for our own good. Trust me, I won't say any more.

MIRANDA: But such a fine ship, and so many fine, brave lives sunk, drowned, laid   5
waste to wrack and ruin . . . A person would have to have a heart of stone not to be moved . . .

PROSPERO: Drowned . . . hmmm. That remains to be seen. But draw near, dear Princess. The time has come.

MIRANDA: You're making fun of me, father. Wild as I am, you know I am happy—   10
like a queen of the wildflowers, of the streams and paths, running barefoot through thorns and flowers, spared by one, caressed by the other.

PROSPERO: But you are a Princess . . . for how else does one address the daughter of a Prince? I cannot leave you in ignorance any longer. Milan is the city of your birth, and the city where for many years I was the Duke.   15

MIRANDA: Then how did we come here? And tell me, too, by what ill fortune did a prince turn into the reclusive hermit you are now, here, on this desert isle? Was it because you found the world distasteful, or through the perfidy of some enemy? Is our island a prison or a hermitage? You've hinted at some mystery so many times and aroused my curiosity, and today you shall tell me all.   20

PROSPERO: In a way, it is because of all the things you mention. First, it is because of political disagreements, because of the intrigues of my ambitious younger brother. Antonio is his name, your uncle, and Alonso the name of the envious King of Naples. How their ambitions were joined, how my brother became the accomplice of my rival, how the latter promised the former his protection and   25
my throne . . . the devil alone knows how all that came about. In any event, when they learned that through my studies and experiments I had managed to discover the exact location of these lands for which many had sought for centuries and that I was making preparations to set forth to take possession of them, they hatched a scheme to steal my as-yet-unborn empire from me. They bribed   30
my people, they stole my charts and documents and, to get rid of me, they denounced me to the Inquisition as a magician and sorcerer. To be brief, one day I saw arriving at the palace men to whom I had never granted audience: the priests of the Holy Office.

(Flashback: Standing before PROSPERO, who is wearing his ducal robes, we see a friar reading from a parchment scroll.)

THE FRIAR: The Holy Inquisition for the preservation and integrity of the Faith   35
and the pursuit of heretical perversion, acting through the special powers

entrusted to it by the Holy Apostolic See, informed of the errors you profess,
insinuate and publish against God and his Creation with regard to the shape of
the Earth and the possibility of discovering other lands, notwithstanding the
40   fact that the Prophet Isaiah stated and taught that the Lord God is seated upon
the circle of the Earth and in its center is Jerusalem and that around the world
lies inaccessible Paradise, convinced that it is through wickedness that to support your heresy you quote Strabus, Ptolemy and the tragic author Seneca,
thereby lending credence to the notion that profane writings can aspire to an
45   authority equal to that of the most profound of the Holy Scriptures, given your
notorious use by both night and day of Arabic calculations and scribblings in
Hebrew, Syrian and other demonic tongues and, lastly, given that you have hitherto escaped punishment owing to your temporal authority and have, if not
usurped, then transformed that authority and made it into a tyranny, doth hereby
50   strip you of your titles, positions and honors in order that it may then proceed
against you according to due process through a full and thorough examination,
under which authority we require that you accompany us.

PROSPERO: (*back in the present*) And yet, the trial they said they were going to hold
never took place. Such creatures of darkness are too much afraid of the light. To
55   be brief: instead of killing me they chose—even worse—to maroon me here
with you on this desert island.

MIRANDA: How terrible, and how wicked the world is! How you must have suffered!

PROSPERO: In all this tale of treason and felony there is but one honorable name:
Gonzalo, counsellor to the King of Naples and fit to serve a better master. By
60   furnishing me with food and clothing, by supplying me with my books and instruments, he has done all in his power to make my exile in this disgusting place
bearable. And now, through a singular turn, Fortune has brought to these shores
the very men involved in the plot against me. My prophetic science had of
course already informed me that they would not be content merely with seiz-
65   ing my lands in Europe and that their greed would win out over their cowardice, that they would confront the sea and set out for those lands my genius
had discovered. I couldn't let them get away with that, and since I was able to
stop them, I did so, with the help of Ariel. We brewed up the storm you have
just witnessed, thereby saving my possessions overseas and bringing the
70   scoundrels into my power at the same time.

(*Enter* ARIEL.)

PROSPERO: Well, Ariel?

ARIEL: Mission accomplished.

PROSPERO: Bravo; good work! But what seems to be the matter? I give you a compliment and you don't seem pleased? Are you tired?

75   ARIEL: Not tired; disgusted. I obeyed you but—well, why not come out with it?—I
did so most unwillingly. It was a real pity to see that great ship go down, so full
of life.

PROSPERO: Oh, so you're upset, are you! It's always like that with you intellectuals!
Who cares! What interests me is not your moods, but your deeds. Let's split: I'll
80   take the zeal and you can keep your doubts. Agreed?

ARIEL: Master, I must beg you to spare me this kind of labour.

PROSPERO: (*shouting*) Listen, and listen good! There's a task to be performed, and I don't care how it gets done!

ARIEL: You've promised me my freedom a thousand times, and I'm still waiting.

PROSPERO: Ingrate! And who freed you from Sycorax, may I ask? Who rent the pine 85 in which you had been imprisoned and brought you forth?

ARIEL: Sometimes I almost regret it . . . After all, I might have turned into a real tree in the end . . . Tree: that's a word that really gives me a thrill! It often springs to mind: palm tree—springing into the sky like a fountain ending in nonchalant, squid-like elegance. The baobab—twisted like the soft entrails of some monster. 90 Ask the calao bird that lives a cloistered season in its branches. Or the Ceiba tree—spread out beneath the proud sun. O bird, o green mansions set in the living earth!

PROSPERO: Stuff it! I don't like talking trees. As for your freedom, you'll have it when I'm good and ready. In the meanwhile, see to the ship. I'm going to have 95 a few words with Master Caliban. I've been keeping my eye on him, and he's getting a little too emancipated. (*Calling*) Caliban! Caliban! (*He sighs.*)

(*Enter* CALIBAN.)

CALIBAN: Uhuru!

PROSPERO: What did you say?

CALIBAN: I said, Uhuru! 100

PROSPERO: Mumbling your native language again! I've already told you, I don't like it. You could be polite, at least; a simple "hello" wouldn't kill you.

CALIBAN: Oh, I forgot . . . But make that as froggy, waspish, pustular and dung-filled "hello" as possible. May today hasten by a decade the day when all the birds of the sky and beasts of the earth will feast upon your corpse! 105

PROSPERO: Gracious as always, you ugly ape! How can anyone be so ugly?

CALIBAN: You think I'm ugly . . . well, I don't think you're so handsome yourself. With that big hooked nose, you look just like some old vulture. (*Laughing*) An old vulture with a scrawny neck!

PROSPERO: Since you're so fond of invective, you could at least thank me for having 110 taught you to speak at all. You, a savage . . . a dumb animal, a beast I educated, trained, dragged up from the bestiality that still clings to you.

CALIBAN: In the first place, that's not true. You didn't teach me a thing! Except to jabber in your own language so that I could understand your orders: chop the wood, wash the dishes, fish for food, plant vegetables, all because you're too lazy 115 to do it yourself. And as for your learning, did you ever impart any of *that* to me? No, you took care not to. All your science you keep for yourself alone, shut up in those big books.

PROSPERO: What would you be without me?

CALIBAN: Without you? I'd be the king, that's what I'd be, the King of the Island. 120 The king of the island given me by my mother, Sycorax.

PROSPERO: There are some family trees it's better not to climb! She's a ghoul! A witch from whom—and may God be praised—death has delivered us.

CALIBAN: Dead or alive, she was my mother, and I won't deny her! Anyhow, you only think she's dead because you think the earth itself is dead . . . It's so much 125 simpler that way! Dead, you can walk on it, pollute it, you can tread upon it

with the steps of a conqueror. I respect the earth, because I know that it is alive,
and I know that Sycorax is alive.
Sycorax. Mother.
130 Serpent, rain, lightning.
And I see thee everywhere!
In the eye of the stagnant pool which stares back at me,
through the rushes,
in the gesture made by twisted root and its awaiting thrust.
135 In the night, the all-seeing blinded night,
the nostril-less all-smelling night!
... Often, in my dreams, she speaks to me and warns me ...
Yesterday, even, when I was lying by the stream on my belly lapping at the
muddy water, when the Beast was about to spring upon me with that huge
140 stone in his hand ...

PROSPERO: If you keep on like that even your magic won't save you from punishment!

CALIBAN: That's right, that's right! In the beginning, the gentleman was all sweet
    talk: dear Caliban here, my little Caliban there! And what do you think you'd
    have done without me in this strange land? Ingrate! I taught you the trees, fruits,
145   birds, the seasons, and now you don't give a damn ... Caliban the animal, Cal-
    iban the slave! I know that story! Once you've squeezed the juice from the or-
    ange, you toss the rind away!

PROSPERO: Oh!

CALIBAN: Do I lie? Isn't it true that you threw me out of your house and made me
150   live in a filthy cave. The ghetto!

PROSPERO: It's easy to say "ghetto"! It wouldn't be such a ghetto if you took the trouble
    to keep it clean! And there's something you forgot, which is that what forced me
    to get rid of you was your lust. Good God, you tried to rape my daughter!

CALIBAN: Rape! Rape! Listen, you old goat, you're the one that put those dirty
155   thoughts in my head. Let me tell you something: I couldn't care less about your
    daughter, or about your cave, for that matter. If I gripe, it's on principle, because
    I didn't like living with you at all, as a matter of fact. Your feet stink!

PROSPERO: I did not summon you here to argue. Out! Back to work! Wood, water,
    and lots of both! I'm expecting company today.

160 CALIBAN: I've had just about enough. There's already a pile of wood that high ...

PROSPERO: Enough! Careful, Caliban! If you keep grumbling you'll be whipped.
    And if you don't step lively, if you keep dragging your feet or try to strike or
    sabotage things, I'll beat you. Beating is the only language you really under-
    stand. So much the worse for you: I'll speak it, loud and clear. Get a move on!

165 CALIBAN: All right, I'm going ... but this is the last time. It's the last time, do you
    hear me? Oh ... I forgot: I've got something important to tell you.

PROSPERO: Important? Well, out with it.

CALIBAN: It's this: I've decided I don't want to be called Caliban any longer.

PROSPERO: What kind of rot is that? I don't understand.

170 CALIBAN: Put it this way: I'm *telling* you that from now on I won't answer to the
    name Caliban.

PROSPERO: Where did you get that idea?

CALIBAN: Well, because Caliban *isn't* my name. It's as simple as that.

PROSPERO: Oh, I suppose it's mine!

CALIBAN: It's the name given me by your hatred, and every time it's spoken it's an   175
insult.

PROSPERO: My, aren't we getting sensitive! All right, suggest something else . . . I've
got to call you something. What will it be? Cannibal would suit you, but I'm
sure you wouldn't like that, would you? Let's see . . . what about Hannibal? That
fits. And why not . . . they all seem to like historical names.   180

CALIBAN: Call me X. That would be best. Like a man without a name. Or, to be
more precise, a man whose name has been stolen. You talk about history . . .
well, that's history, and everyone knows it! Every time you summon me it reminds me of a basic fact, the fact that you've stolen everything from me, even
my identity! Uhuru! (*He exits.*)   185

(*Enter* ARIEL *as a sea-nymph.*)

PROSPERO: My dear Ariel, did you see how he looked at me, that glint in his eye?
That's something new. Well, let me tell you, Caliban is the enemy. As for those
people on the boat, I've changed my mind about them. Give them a scare, but
for God's sake don't touch a hair of their heads! You'll answer to me if you do.

ARIEL: I've suffered too much myself for having made them suffer not to be pleased   190
at your mercy. You can count on me, Master.

PROSPERO: Yes, however great their crimes, if they repent you can assure them of
my forgiveness. They are men of my race, and of high rank. As for me, at my age
one must rise above disputes and quarrels and think about the future. I have a
daughter. Alonso has a son. If they were to fall in love, I would give my consent.   195
Let Ferdinand marry Miranda, and may their marriage bring us harmony and
peace. That is my plan. I want it executed. As for Caliban, does it matter what
that villain plots against me? All the nobility of Italy, Naples and Milan henceforth combined, will protect me bodily. Go!

ARIEL: Yes, Master. Your orders will be fully carried out.   200

(ARIEL *sings:*)

> *Sandy seashore, deep blue sky,*
> *Surf is rising, sea birds fly*
> *Here the lover finds delight,*
> *Sun at noontime, moon at night.*
> *Join hands lovers, join the dance,*   205
> *Find contentment, find romance.*
>
> *Sandy seashore, deep blue sky,*
> *Cares will vanish . . . so can I . . .*

FERDINAND: What is this music? It has led me here and now it stops . . . No, there it
is again . . .   210

ARIEL: (*singing*)

> *Waters move, the ocean flows,*
> *Nothing comes and nothing goes . . .*
> *Strange days are upon us . . .*

> Oysters stare through pearly eyes
215 > Heart-shaped corals gently beat
> In the crystal undersea
>
> Waters move and ocean flows,
> Nothing comes and nothing goes . . .
> Strange days are upon us . . .

220 FERDINAND: What is this that I see before me? A goddess? A mortal?

MIRANDA: I know what *I'm* seeing: a flatterer. Young man, your ability to pay compliments in the situation in which you find yourself at least proves your courage. Who are you?

FERDINAND: As you see, a poor shipwrecked soul.

225 MIRANDA: But one of high degree!

FERDINAND: In other surroundings I might be called "Prince," "son of the King" . . . But, no, I was forgetting . . . not "Prince" but "King," alas . . . "King" because my father has just perished in the shipwreck.

MIRANDA: Poor young man! Here, you'll be received with hospitality and we'll sup-
230 port you in your misfortune.

FERDINAND: Alas, my father . . . Can it be that I am an unnatural son? Your pity would make the greatest of sorrows seem sweet.

MIRANDA: I hope you'll like it here with us. The island is pretty. I'll show you the beaches and the forests, I'll tell you the names of fruits and flowers, I'll intro-
235 duce you to a whole world of insects, of lizards of every hue, of birds . . . Oh, you cannot imagine! The birds! . . .

PROSPERO: That's enough, daughter! I find your chatter irritating . . . and let me assure you, it's not at all fitting. You are doing too much honor to an impostor. Young man, you are a traitor, a spy, and a woman-chaser to boot! No sooner has
240 he escaped the perils of the sea than he's sweet-talking the first girl he meets! You won't get round me that way. Your arrival is convenient, because I need more manpower: you shall be my house servant.

FERDINAND: Seeing the young lady, more beautiful than any wood-nymph, I might have been Ulysses on Nausicaa's isle. But hearing you, Sir, I now understand my
245 fate a little better . . . I see I have come ashore on the Barbary Coast and am in the hands of a cruel pirate. (*Drawing his sword*) However, a gentleman prefers death to dishonor! I shall defend my life with my freedom!

PROSPERO: Poor fool: your arm is growing weak, your knees are trembling! Traitor! I could kill you now . . . but I need the manpower. Follow me.

250 ARIEL: It's no use trying to resist, young man. My master is a sorcerer: neither your passion nor your youth can prevail against him. Your best course would be to follow and obey him.

FERDINAND: Oh God! What sorcery is this? Vanquished, a captive—yet far from rebelling against my fate, I am finding my servitude sweet. Oh, I would be impris-
255 oned for life if only heaven will grant me a glimpse of my sun each day, the face of my own sun. Farewell, Nausicaa.

(*They exit.*)

ACT II
SCENE 1

(CALIBAN's *cave.* CALIBAN *is singing as he works when* ARIEL *enters. He listens to him for a moment.*)

CALIBAN: (*singing*)

> *May he who eats his corn heedless of Shango*
> *Be accursed! May Shango creep beneath*
> *His nails and eat into his flesh!*
> *Shango, Shango ho!*
>
> *Forget to give him room if you dare!*   5
> *He will make himself at home on your nose!*
>
> *Refuse to have him under your roof at your own risk!*
> *He'll tear off your roof and wear it as a hat!*
> *Whoever tries to mislead Shango*
> *Will suffer for it!*   10
> *Shango, Shango ho!*

ARIEL: Greetings, Caliban. I know you don't think much of me, but after all we *are* brothers, brothers in suffering and slavery, but brothers in hope as well. We both want our freedom. We just have different methods.

CALIBAN: Greetings to you. But you didn't come to see me just to make that profes-   15
sion of faith. Come on, Alastor! The old man sent you, didn't he? A great job: carrying out the Master's fine ideas, his great plans.

ARIEL: No, I've come on my own. I came to warn you. Prospero is planning horrible acts of revenge against you. I thought it my duty to alert you.

CALIBAN: I'm ready for him.   20

ARIEL: Poor Caliban, you're doomed. You know that you aren't the stronger, you'll never be the stronger. What good will it do you to struggle?

CALIBAN: And what about you? What good has your obedience done you, your Uncle Tom patience and your sucking up to him. The man's just getting more demanding and despotic day by day.   25

ARIEL: Well, I've at least achieved one thing: he's promised me my freedom. In the distant future, of course, but it's the first time he's actually committed himself.

CALIBAN: Talk's cheap! He'll promise you a thousand times and take it back a thou-sand times. Anyway, tomorrow doesn't interest me. What I want is (*shouting*) "Freedom now!"   30

ARIEL: Okay. But you know you're not going to get it out of him "now," and that he's stronger than you are. I'm in a good position to know just what he's got in his arsenal.

CALIBAN: The stronger? How do you know that? Weakness always has a thousand means and cowardice is all that keeps us from listing them.   35

ARIEL: I don't believe in violence.

CALIBAN: What *do* you believe in, then? In cowardice? In giving up? In kneeling and groveling? That's it, someone strikes you on the right cheek and you offer

the left. Someone kicks you on the left buttock and you turn the right . . . that
way there's no jealousy. Well, that's not Caliban's way . . .

ARIEL: You know very well that that's not what I mean. No violence, no submission
either. Listen to me: Prospero is the one we've got to change. Destroy his serenity
so that he's finally forced to acknowledge his own injustice and put an end to it.

CALIBAN: Oh sure . . . that's a good one! Prospero's conscience! Prospero is an old
scoundrel who has no conscience.

ARIEL: Exactly—that's why it's up to us to give him one. I'm not fighting just for *my*
freedom, for *our* freedom, but for Prospero too, so that Prospero can acquire a
conscience. Help me, Caliban.

CALIBAN: Listen, kid, sometimes I wonder if you aren't a little bit nuts. So that Prospero can acquire a conscience? You might as well ask a stone to grow flowers.

ARIEL: I don't know what to do with you. I've often had this inspiring, uplifting
dream that one day Prospero, you, me, we would all three set out, like brothers,
to build a wonderful world, each one contributing his own special thing: patience, vitality, love, will-power too, and rigor, not to mention the dreams without which mankind would perish.

CALIBAN: You don't understand a thing about Prospero. He's not the collaborating
type. He's a guy who only feels something when he's wiped someone out. A
crusher, a pulveriser, that's what he is! And you talk about brotherhood!

ARIEL: So then what's left? War? And you know that when it comes to that, Prospero
is invincible.

CALIBAN: Better death than humiliation and injustice. Anyhow, I'm going to have
the last word. Unless nothingness has it. The day when I begin to feel that everything's lost, just let me get hold of a few barrels of your infernal powder and as
you fly around up there in your blue skies you'll see this island, my inheritance,
my work, all blown to smithereens . . . and, I trust, Prospero and me with it. I
hope you'll like the fireworks display—it'll be signed Caliban.

ARIEL: Each of us marches to his own drum. You follow yours. I follow the beat of
mine. I wish you courage, brother.

CALIBAN: Farewell, Ariel, my brother, and good luck.

SCENE 2

GONZALO: A magnificent country! Bread hangs from the trees and the apricots are
bigger than a woman's full breast.

SEBASTIAN: A pity that it's so wild and uncultivated . . . here and there.

GONZALO: Oh, that's nothing. If there were anything poisonous, an antidote would
never be far away, for nature is intrinsically harmonious. I've even read somewhere that guano is excellent compost for sterile ground.

SEBASTIAN: Guano? What kind of animal is that? Are you sure you don't mean
iguana?

GONZALO: Young man, if I say guano, I mean guano. Guano is the name for bird-
droppings that build up over centuries, and it is by far the best fertilizer known.
You dig it out of caves . . . If you want my opinion, I think we should investigate
all the caves on this island one by one to see if we find any, and if we do, this island, if wisely exploited, will be richer than Egypt with its Nile.

ANTONIO: Let me understand: your guano cave contains a river of dried bird-shit.

GONZALO: To pick up your image, all we need to do is channel that river, use it to irrigate, if I may use the term, the fields with this wonderful fecal matter, and everything will bloom.

SEBASTIAN: But we'll still need manpower to farm it. Is the island even inhabited?

GONZALO: That's the problem, of course. But if it is, it must be by wonderful people. It's obvious: a wondrous land can only contain wonderful creatures.

ANTONIO: Yes!

> Men whose bodies are wiry and strong
> And women whose eyes are open and frank . . .
> creatures in it! . . .

GONZALO: Something like that! I see you know your literature. But in that case, watch out: it will all mean new responsibilities for us!

SEBASTIAN: How do you get that?

GONZALO: I mean that if the island is inhabited, as I believe, and if we colonize it, as is my hope, then we have to take every precaution not to import our shortcomings, yes, what we call civilization. They must stay as they are: savages, noble and good savages, free, without any complexes or complications. Something like a pool granting eternal youth where we periodically come to restore our aging, citified souls.

ALONSO: Sir Gonzalo, when will you shut up?

GONZALO: Ah, Your Majesty, if I am boring you, I apologize. I was only speaking as I did to distract you and to turn our sad thoughts to something more pleasant. There, I'll be silent. Indeed, these old bones have had it. Oof! Let me sit down . . . with your permission, of course.

ALONSO: Noble Old Man, even though younger than you, we are all in the same fix.

GONZALO: In other words, dead tired and dying of hunger.

ALONSO: I have never pretended to be above the human condition.

(*A strange, solemn music is heard.*)

. . . Listen, listen! Did you hear that?

GONZALO: Yes, it's an odd melody!

(PROSPERO *enters, invisible. Other strange figures enter as well, bearing a laden table. They dance and graciously invite the King and his company to eat, then they disappear.*)

ALONSO: Heaven protect us! Live marionettes!

GONZALO: Such grace! Such music! Hum. The whole thing is most peculiar.

SEBASTIAN: Gone! Faded away! But what does that matter, since they've left their food behind! No meal was ever more welcome. Gentlemen, to table!

ALONSO: Yes, let us partake of this feast, even though it may be our last.

(*They prepare to eat, but Elves enter and, with much grimacing and many contortions, carry off the table.*)

GONZALO: Ah! that's a fine way to behave!

ALONSO: I have the distinct feeling that we have fallen under the sway of powers that are playing at cat and mouse with us. It's a cruel way to make us aware of our dependent status.

GONZALO: The way things have been going it's not surprising, and it will do us no good to protest.

(*The Elves return, bringing the food with them.*)

55 ALONSO: Oh no, this time I won't bite!

SEBASTIAN: I'm so hungry that I don't care, I'll abandon my scruples.

GONZALO: (*to* ALONSO) Why not try? Perhaps the Powers controlling us saw how disappointed we were and took pity on us. After all, even though disappointed a hundred times, Tantalus still tried a hundred times.

60 ALONSO: That was also his torture. I won't touch that food.

PROSPERO: (*invisible*) Ariel, I don't like his refusing. Harass them until they eat.

ARIEL: Why should we go to any trouble for them? If they won't eat, they can die of hunger.

PROSPERO: No, I *want* them to eat.

65 ARIEL: That's despotism. A while ago you made me snatch it away just when they were about to gobble it up, and now that they don't want it you are ready to force feed them.

PROSPERO: Enough hairsplitting! My mood has changed! They insult me by not eating. They must be made to eat out of my hand like chicks. That is a sign of
70 submission I insist they give me.

ARIEL: It's evil to play with their hunger as you do with their anxieties and their hopes.

PROSPERO: That is how power is measured. I am Power.

(ALONSO *and his group eat.*)

ALONSO: Alas, when I think . . .

GONZALO: That's your trouble, Sire: you think too much.

75 ALONSO: And thus I should not even think of my lost son! My throne! My country!

GONZALO: (*eating*) Your son! What's to say we won't find him again! As for the rest of it . . . Look, Sire, this filthy hole is now our entire world. Why seek further? If your thoughts are too vast, cut them down to size.

(*They eat.*)

ALONSO: So be it! But I would prefer to sleep. To sleep and to forget.

80 GONZALO: Good idea! Let's put up our hammocks!

(*They sleep.*)

SCENE 3

ANTONIO: Look at those leeches, those slugs! Wallowing in their slime and their snot: Idiots, slime—they're like beached jellyfish.

SEBASTIAN: Shhh! It's the King. And that old graybeard is his venerable counsellor.

ANTONIO: The King is he who watches over his flock when they sleep. That one
5 isn't watching over anything. Ergo, he's not the King. (*Brusquely*) You're really a bloodless lily-liver if you can see a king asleep without getting certain ideas . . .

SEBASTIAN: I mustn't have any blood, only water.

ANTONIO: Don't insult water. Every time I look at myself I think I'm more handsome, more *there*. My inner juices have always given me my greatness, my true
10 greatness . . . not the greatness men grant me.

SEBASTIAN: All right, so I'm stagnant water.

ANTONIO: Water is never stagnant. It works, it works in us. It is what gives man his dimension, his true one. Believe me, you're mistaken if you don't grab the opportunity when it's offered you. It may never come again.

SEBASTIAN: What are you getting at? I have a feeling I can guess.   15

ANTONIO: Guess, guess! Look at that tree swaying in the wind. It's called a coconut palm. My dear Sebastian, in my opinion it's time to shake the coconut palm.

SEBASTIAN: Now I really don't understand.

ANTONIO: What a dope! Consider my position: I'm Duke of Milan. Well, I wasn't always . . . I had an older brother. That was Duke Prospero. And if I'm now Duke   20
Antonio, it's because I knew when to shake the coconut palm.

SEBASTIAN: And Prospero?

ANTONIO: What do you mean by that? When you shake a tree, someone is bound to fall. And obviously it wasn't me who fell, because here I am: to assist and serve you, Majesty!   25

SEBASTIAN: Enough! He's my brother! My scruples won't allow me to . . . You take care of him while I deal with the old Counsellor.

(*They draw their swords.*)

ARIEL: Stop, ruffians! Resistance is futile: your swords are enchanted and falling from your hands!

ANTONIO, SEBASTIAN: Alas! Alas!   30

ARIEL: Sleepers, awake! Awake, I say! Your life depends on it. With these fine fellows with their long teeth and swords around, anyone who sleeps too soundly risks sleeping forever.

(ALONSO *and* GONZALO *awaken.*)

ALONSO: (*rubbing his eyes*) What's happening? I was asleep, and I was having a terrible dream!   35

ARIEL: No, you were not dreaming. These fine lords here are criminals who were about to perpetrate the most odious of crimes upon you. Yes, Alonso, you may well marvel that a god should fly to your aid. Were to heaven you deserved it more!

ALONSO: I have never been wanting in respect for the divinity . . .

ARIEL: I don't know what effect my next piece of news will have on you: The name   40
of him who has sent me to you is Prospero.

ALONSO: Prospero! God save us! (*He falls to his knees.*)

ARIEL: I understand your feelings. He lives. It is he who reigns over this isle, as he reigns over the spirits of the air you breathe . . . But rise . . . You need fear no longer. He has not saved your lives to destroy them. Your repentance will suffice,   45
for I can see that it is deep and sincere. (*To* ANTONIO *and* SEBASTIAN) As for you, Gentlemen, my master's pardon extends to you as well, on the condition that you renounce your plans, knowing them to be vain.

SEBASTIAN: (*To* ANTONIO) We could have got worse!

ANTONIO: If it were men we were up against, no one could make me withdraw, but   50
when it's demons and magic there's no shame in giving in. (*To* ARIEL) . . . We are the Duke's most humble and obedient servants. Please beg him to accept our thanks.

GONZALO: Oh, how ignoble! How good of you to just wipe the slate clean! No
surface repentance ... not only do you want attrition, you want contrition as
well! Why look at me as though you didn't know what I was talking about? *Attrition:* A selfish regret for offending God, caused by a fear of punishment. *Contrition:* An unselfish regret growing out of sorrow at displeasing God.

ARIEL: Honest Gonzalo, thank you for your clarification. Your eloquence has eased
my mission and your pedagogical skill has abbreviated it, for in a few short words
you have expressed my master's thought. May your words be heard! Therefore,
let us turn the page. To terminate this episode, I need only convoke you all, on
my master's behalf, to the celebrations that this very day will mark the engagement of his daughter, Miranda. Alonso, that's good news for you ...

ALONSO: What—my son?

ARIEL: Correct. Saved by my master from the fury of the waves.

ALONSO: (*falling to his knees*) God be praised for this blessing more than all the rest.
Rank, fortune, throne, I am prepared to forgo all if my son is returned to me ...

ARIEL: Come, Gentlemen, follow me.

ACT III
SCENE 1

FERDINAND: (*hoeing and singing*)

> How life has changed
> Now, hoe in hand
> I work away all day ...
>
> Hoeing all the day,
> I go my weary way ...

CALIBAN: Poor kid! What would he say if he was Caliban! He works night and day,
and when he sings, it's

> Oo-en-day, Oo-en-day, Oo-en-day, Macaya ...

And no pretty girl to console him! (*Sees* MIRANDA *approaching.*) Aha! Let's listen
to this!

FERDINAND: (*singing*)

> How life has changed
> Now, hoe in hand
> I work away all day ...

MIRANDA: Poor young man! Can I help you? You don't look like you were cut out
for this kind of work!

FERDINAND: One word from you would be more help to me than anything in the
world.

MIRANDA: One word? From me? I must say, I ...

FERDINAND: Your name—that's all: What is your name?

MIRANDA: That, I cannot do! It's impossible. My father has expressly forbidden it!

FERDINAND: It is the only thing I long for.

MIRANDA: But I can't, I tell you; it's forbidden!

CALIBAN: (*taking advantage of* MIRANDA's *momentary distraction, he whispers her name to* FERDINAND.) Mi-ran-da!

FERDINAND: All right then, I shall christen you with a name of my own. I will call you Miranda.　25

MIRANDA: That's too much! What a low trick! You must have heard my father calling me . . . Unless it was that awful Caliban who keeps pursuing me and calling out my name in his stupid dreams!

FERDINAND: No, Miranda . . . I had only to allow my eyes to speak, as you your face.　30

MIRANDA: Sssh! My father's coming! He'd better not catch you trying to sweet talk me . . .

FERDINAND: (*Goes back to work, singing.*)

> But times have changed
> Now, hoeing all the day,
> I go my weary way . . .　35

PROSPERO: That's fine, young man! You've managed to accomplish a good deal for a beginning! I see I've misjudged you. But you won't be the loser if you serve me well. Listen, my young friend, there are three things in life: Work, Patience, Continence, and the world is yours . . . Hey, Caliban, I'm taking this boy away with me. He's done enough for one day. But since the job is urgent, see that it gets finished.　40

CALIBAN: Me?

PROSPERO: Yes, you! You've cheated me enough with your loafing and fiddling around, so you can work a double shift for once!

CALIBAN: I don't see why I should do someone else's job!

PROSPERO: Who's the boss here? You or me? Listen, monster: if you don't like work, I'll see to it you change your mind!　45

(PROSPERO *and* FERDINAND *move away.*)

CALIBAN: Go on, go on . . . I'll get you one day, you bastard! (*He sets to work, singing.*)

> "Oo-en-day, Oo-en-day, Oo-en-day, Macaya . . ."

Shit, now it's raining! As if things weren't bad enough . . . (*Suddenly, at the sound of a voice, Caliban stiffens.*) Do you hear that, boy? That voice through the storm. Bah! It's Ariel. No, that's not his voice. Whose, then? With an old coot like Prospero . . . One of his cops, probably. Oh, fine! Now, I'm for it. Men and the elements both against me. Well, the hell with it . . . I'm used to it. Patience! I'll get them yet. In the meantime better make myself scarce! Let Prospero and his storm and his cops go by . . . let the seven maws of Malediction bay!　55

SCENE 2

(*Enter* TRINCULO)

TRINCULO: (*singing*)

> Oh Susannah . . . oh don't you cry for me . . . (*Etc.*)

You can say that again! My dearest Susannah . . . trust Trinculo, we've had all the roaring storms we need, and more! I swear: the whole crew wiped out,

liquidated . . . Nothing! Nothing left . . . ! Nothing but poor wandering and
wailing Trinculo! No question about it, it'll be a while before anyone persuades
me to depart from affectionate women and friendly towns to go off to brave
roaring storms! How it's raining! (*Notices* CALIBAN *underneath the wheelbarrow.*)
Ah, an Indian! Dead or alive? You never know with these tricky races. Yukkk!
Anyhow, this will do me fine. If he's dead, I can use his clothes for shelter, for a
coat, a tent, a covering. If he's alive I'll make him my prisoner and take him
back to Europe and then, by golly, my fortune will be made! I'll sell him to a
carnival. No! I'll show him myself at fairs! What a stroke of luck! I'll just settle
in here where it's warm and let the storm rage! (*He crawls under cover, back to back
with* CALIBAN.)

(*Enter* STEPHANO.)

STEPHANO: (*singing*)

     Blow the man down, hearties,
     Blow the man down . . . (*Etc.*)

(*Takes a swig of his bottle and continues.*)

     Blow, blow, blow the man down . . . (*Etc.*)

Fortunately, there's still a little wine left in this bottle . . . enough to give me
courage! Be of good cheer, Stephano, where there's life there's thirst . . . and vice
versa! (*Suddenly spies* CALIBAN'*s head sticking out of the covers.*) My God, on
Stephano's word, it looks like a Nindian! (*Comes nearer*) And that's just what it is!
A Nindian. That's neat. I really am lucky. There's money to be made from a Nindian like that. If you showed him at a carnival . . . along with the bearded lady
and the flea circus, a real Nindian! An authentic Nindian from the Caribbean!
That means real dough, or I'm the last of the idiots! (*Touching* CALIBAN) But he's
ice cold! I don't know what the body temperature of a Nindian is, but this one
seems pretty cold to me! Let's hope he's not going to croak! How's that for bad
luck: You find a Nindian and he dies on you! A fortune slips through your fingers! But wait, I've got an idea . . . a good swig of this booze between his lips,
that'll warm him up. (*He gives* CALIBAN *a drink.*) Look . . . he's better already. The
little glutton even wants some more! Just a second, just a second! (*He walks around
the wheelbarrow and sees* TRINCULO'*s head sticking out from under the covering.*) Jeez!
I must be seeing things! A Nindian with two heads! Shit! If I have to pour drink
down *two* gullets I won't have much left for myself! Well, never mind. It's incredible . . . your everyday Nindian is already something, but one with two heads . . .
a Siamese-twin Nindian, a Nindian with two heads and eight paws, that's really
something! My fortune is made. Come on, you wonderful monster, you . . . let's
get a look at your other head! (*He draws nearer to* TRINCULO.) Hello! That face
reminds me of something! That nose that shines like a lighthouse . . .

TRINCULO: That gut . . .

STEPHANO: That nose looks familiar . . .

TRINCULO: That gut—there can't be two of them in this lousy world!

STEPHANO: Oh-my-gawd, oh-my-gawd, oh-my-gawd . . . *that's* it . . . it's that crook
Trinculo!

TRINCULO: Good lord! It's Stephano! 45

STEPHANO: So, Trinculo, you were saved too . . . It almost makes you believe God looks after drunks . . .

TRINCULO: Huh! God . . . Bacchus, maybe. As a matter of fact, I reached these welcoming shores by floating on a barrel . . .

STEPHANO: And I by floating on my stomach . . . it's nearly the same thing. But what 50 kind of creature is this? Isn't it a Nindian?

TRINCULO: That's just what I was thinking . . . Yes, by God, it's a Nindian. That's a piece of luck . . . he'll be our guide.

STEPHANO: Judging from the way he can swill it down, he doesn't seem to be stupid. I'll try to civilize him. Oh . . . not too much, of course. But enough so that 55 he can be of some use.

TRINCULO: Civilize him! Shee-it! Does he even know how to talk?

STEPHANO: I couldn't get a word out of him, but I know a way to loosen his tongue. (*He takes a bottle from his pocket.*)

TRINCULO: (*stopping him*) Look here, you're not going to waste that nectar on the 60 first savage that comes along, are you?

STEPHANO: Selfish! Back off! Let me perform my civilizing mission. (*Offering the bottle to* CALIBAN.) Of course, if he was cleaned up a bit he'd be worth more to both of us. Okay? We'll exploit him together? It's a deal? (*To* CALIBAN) Drink up, pal. You. Drink . . . Yum-yum botty botty! (CALIBAN *drinks.*) You, drink more. 65 (CALIBAN *refuses.*) You no more thirsty? (STEPHANO *drinks.*) Me always thirsty! (STEPHANO *and* TRINCULO *drink.*)

STEPHANO: Trinculo, you know I used to be prejudiced against shipwrecks, but I was wrong. They're not bad at all.

TRINCULO: That's true. It seems to make things taste better afterwards . . . 70

STEPHANO: Not to mention the fact that it's got rid of a lot of old farts that were always keeping the world down! May they rest in peace! But then, you liked them, didn't you, all those kings and dukes, all those noblemen! Oh, I served them well enough, you've got to earn your drink somehow . . . But I could never stand them, ever—understand? Never. Trinculo, my friend, I'm a long-time be- 75 liever in the republic . . . you might as well say it: I'm a died-in-the-wool believer in the people first, a republican in my guts! Down with tyrants!

TRINCULO: Which reminds me . . . If, as it would seem, the King and the Duke are dead, there's a crown and a throne up for grabs around here . . .

STEPHANO: By God, you're right! Smart thinking, Trinculo! So, I appoint myself 80 heir . . . I crown myself king of the island.

TRINCULO: (*sarcastically*) Sure you do! And why you, may I ask? I'm the one who thought of it first, that crown!

STEPHANO: Look, Trinculo, don't be silly! I mean, really: just take a look at yourself! What's the first thing a king needs? Bearing. Presence. And if I've got anything, 85 it's that. Which isn't true for everyone. So, I am the King!

CALIBAN: Long live the King!

STEPHANO: It's a miracle . . . he can talk! And what's more, he talks sense! O brave savage! (*He embraces* CALIBAN.) You see, my dear Trinculo, the people has spoken! Vox populi, vox Dei . . . But please, don't be upset. Stephano is magnani- 90 mous and will never abandon his friend Trinculo, the friend who stood by him in his trials. Trinculo, we've eaten rough bread together, we've drunk rot-gut wine together. I want to do something for you. I shall appoint you Marshal. But we're forgetting our brave savage . . . It's a scientific miracle! He can talk!

95 CALIBAN: Yes, Sire. My enthusiasm has restored my speech. Long live the King! But beware the usurper!

STEPHANO: Usurper? Who? Trinculo?

CALIBAN: No, the other one . . . Prospero!

STEPHANO: Prospero? Don't know him.

100 CALIBAN: Well, you see, this island used to belong to me, except that a man named Prospero cheated me of it. I'm perfectly willing to give you my right to it, but the only thing is, you'll have to fight Prospero for it.

STEPHANO: That is of no matter, brave savage. It's a bargain! I'll get rid of this Prospero for you in two shakes.

105 CALIBAN: Watch out, he's powerful.

STEPHANO: My dear savage, I eat a dozen Prosperos like that for breakfast every day. But say no more, say no more! Trinculo, take command of the troops! Let us march upon the foe!

TRINCULO: Yes, forward march! But first, a drink. We will need all our strength and
110   vigor.

CALIBAN: Let's drink, my new-found friends, and let us sing. Let us sing of winning the day and of an end to tyranny.

(Singing)

> Black pecking creature of the savannas
> The quetzal measures out the new day
115 > solid and lively
> in its haughty armor.
> Zing! the determined hummingbird
> revels in the flower's depths,
> going crazy, getting drunk,
120 > a lyrebird gathers up our ravings,
> Freedom hi-day! Freedom hi-day!

STEPHANO and TRINCULO: (Together) Freedom hi-day! Freedom hi-day!

CALIBAN:

> The ringdove dallies amid the trees,
> wandering the islands, here it rests—
125 > The white blossoms of the miconia
> Mingle with the violet blood of ripe berries
> And blood stains your plumage,
> traveller!
> Lying here after a weary day
130 > We listen to it:
> Freedom hi-day! Freedom hi-day!

STEPHANO: Okay, monster . . . enough crooning. Singing makes a man thirsty. Let's drink instead. Here, have some more . . . spirits create higher spirits . . . (Filling a glass.) Lead the way, O bountiful wine! Soldiers, forward march! Or rather . . .

no: At ease! Night is falling, the fireflies twinkle, the crickets chirp, all nature   135
makes its brek-ke-ke-kek! And since night has fallen, let us take advantage of it
to gather our forces and regain our strength, which has been sorely tried by the
unusually . . . copious emotions of the day. And tomorrow, at dawn, with a new
spring in our step, we'll have the tyrant's hide. Good night, gentlemen. (*He falls
asleep and begins to snore.*)   140

SCENE 3

(PROSPERO's *cave*)

PROSPERO: So then, Ariel! Where are the gods and goddesses? They'd better get a
move on! And all of them! I want all of them to take part in the entertainment I
have planned for our dear children. Why do I say "entertainment"? Because
starting today I want to inculcate in them the spectacle of tomorrow's world:
logic, beauty, harmony, the foundations for which I have laid down by my own   5
will-power. Unfortunately, alas, at my age it's time to stop thinking of deeds and
to begin thinking of passing on . . . Enter, then!

(*Gods and Goddesses enter.*)

JUNO: Honor and riches to you! Long continuance and increasing long life and honored issue! Juno sings to you her blessings!

CERES: May scarcity and want shun you! That is Ceres' blessing on you.   10

IRIS: (*beckoning to the Nymphs*) Nymphs, come help to celebrate here a contact of
true love.

(*Nymphs enter and dance.*)

PROSPERO: My thanks, Goddesses, and my thanks to you, Iris. Thank you for your
good wishes.

(*Gods and Goddesses continue their dance.*)

FERDINAND: What a splendid and majestic vision! May I be so bold to think these   15
spirits?

PROSPERO: Yes, spirits which by my art I have from their confines called to greet
you and to bless you.

(*Enter* ESHU.)

MIRANDA: But who is that? He doesn't look very benevolent! If I weren't afraid of
blaspheming, I'd say he was a devil rather than a god.   20

ESHU: (*laughing*) You are not mistaken, fair lady. God to my friends, the Devil to my
enemies! And lots of laughs for all!

PROSPERO: (*softly*) Ariel must have made a mistake. Is my magic getting rusty?
(*Aloud*) What are you doing here? Who invited you? I don't like such loose behavior, even from a god!   25

ESHU: But that's just the point . . . no one invited me . . . And that wasn't very nice!
Nobody remembered poor Eshu! So poor Eshu came anyway. Hihihi! So how
about something to drink? (*Without waiting for a reply, he pours a drink.*) . . . Your
liquor's not bad. However, I must say I prefer dogs! (*Looking at* IRIS) I see that

30   shocks the little lady, but to each his own. Some prefer chickens, others prefer
      goats. I'm not too fond of chickens, myself. But if you're talking about a black
      dog . . . think of poor Eshu!

PROSPERO: Get out! Go away! We will have none of your grimaces and buffoonery
      in this noble assembly. (*He makes a magic sign.*)

35   ESHU: I'm going, boss, I'm going . . . But not without a little song in honor of the
      bride and the noble company, as you say.

> *Eshu can play many tricks,*
> *Give him twenty dogs!*
> *You will see his dirty tricks.*

40
> *Eshu plays a trick on the Queen*
> *And makes her so upset that she runs*
> *Naked into the street*

> *Eshu plays a trick on a bride,*
> *And on the day of the wedding*
45
> *She gets into the wrong bed!*

> *Eshu can throw a stone yesterday*
> *And kill a bird today.*
> *He can make a mess out of order and vice-versa.*
> *Ah, Eshu is a wonderful bad joke.*
50
> *Eshu is not the man to carry a heavy load.*
> *His head comes to a point. When he dances*
> *He doesn't move his shoulders . . .*
> *Oh, Eshu is a merry elf!*

> *Eshu is a merry elf,*
55
> *And he can whip you with his dick,*
> *He can whip you,*
> *He can whip you . . .*

CERES: My dear Iris, don't you find that song quite obscene?

JUNO: It's disgusting! It's quite intolerable . . . if he keeps on, I'm leaving!

60   IRIS: It's like Liber, or Priapus!

JUNO: Don't mention that name in my presence!

ESHU: (*continuing to sing*)

> *. . . with his dick*
> *He can whip you, whip you . . .*

JUNO: Oh! Can't someone get rid of him? I'm not staying here!

65   ESHU: Okay, okay . . . Eshu will go. Farewell, my dear colleagues!

(*Gods and Goddesses exit.*)

PROSPERO: He's gone . . . what a relief! But alas, the harm is done! I am perturbed
      . . . My old brain is confused. Power! Power! Alas! All this will one day fade, like
      foam, like a cloud, like all the world. And what is power, if I cannot calm my
      own fears? But come! My power has gone cold. (*Calling*) Ariel!

ARIEL: (*runs in*) What is it, Sire?   70

PROSPERO: Caliban is alive, he is plotting, he is getting a guerrilla force together and you—you don't say a word! Well, take care of him. Snakes, scorpions, porcupines, all stinging poisonous creatures, he is to be spared nothing! His punishment must be exemplary. Oh, and don't forget the mud and mosquitoes!

ARIEL: Master, let me intercede for him and beg your indulgence. You've got to understand: he's a rebel.   75

PROSPERO: By his insubordination he's calling into question the whole order of the world. Maybe the Divinity can afford to let him get away with it, but I have a sense of responsibility!

ARIEL: Very well, Master.   80

PROSPERO: But a thought: arrange some glass trinkets, some trumpery and some second-hand clothes too . . . but colorful ones . . . by the side of the road along which General Caliban and his troops are travelling. Savages adore loud, gaudy clothes . . .

ARIEL: Master . . .   85

PROSPERO: You're going to make me angry. There's nothing to understand. There is a punishment to be meted out. I will not compromise with evil. Hurry! Unless you want to be the next to feel my wrath.

SCENE 4

(*In the wild; night is drawing to a close; the murmurings of the spirits of the tropical forest are heard.*)

VOICE I: Fly!

VOICE: Here!

VOICE I: Ant!

VOICE II: Here.

VOICE I: Vulture!   5

VOICE II: Here.

VOICE I: Soft-shelled crab, calao, crab, hummingbird!

VOICES: Here. Here. Here.

VOICE I: Cramp, crime, fang, opossum!

VOICE II: Kra. Kra. Kra.   10

VOICE I: Huge hedgehog, you will be our sun today. Shaggy, taloned, stubborn. May it burn! Moon, my fat spider, my big dreamcat, go to sleep, my velvet one.

VOICES: (*singing*)

> *King-ay*
> *King-ay*
> *Von-von*   15
> *Maloto*
> *Vloom-vloom!*

(*The sun rises.* ARIEL'*s band vanishes.* CALIBAN *stands for a moment, rubbing his eyes.*)

CALIBAN: (*rises and searches the bushes*) Have to think about getting going again. Away, snakes, scorpions, porcupines! All stinging, biting, sticking beasts! Sting, fever,

20   venom, away! Or if you really want to lick me, do it with a gentle tongue, like
the toad whose pure drool soothes me with sweet dreams of the future. For it is
for you, for all of us, that I go forth today to face the common enemy. Yes, hereditary and common. Look, a hedgehog! Sweet little thing . . . How can any animal—any natural animal, if I may put it that way—go against me on the day

25   I'm setting forth to conquer Prospero! Unimaginable! Prospero is the Anti-
Nature! And I say, down with Anti-Nature! And does the porcupine bristle his
spines at that? No, he smoothes them down! That's nature! It's kind and gentle,
in a word. You've just got to know how to deal with it. So come on, the way is
clear! Off we go!

(*The band sets out.* CALIBAN *marches forward singing his battle song:*)

30   *Shango carries a big stick,*
          He strikes and money expires!
          He strikes and lies expire!
          He strikes and larceny expires!
          Shango, Shango ho!

35   *Shango is the gatherer of the rain,*
          He passes, wrapped in his fiery cloak,
          His horse's hoofs strike lighting
          On the pavements of the sky!
          Shango is a great knight!
40   *Shango, Shango ho!*

(*The roar of the sea can be heard.*)

STEPHANO: Tell me, brave savage, what is that noise? It sounds like the roaring of a
beast at bay.

CALIBAN: Not at bay . . . more like on the prowl . . . Don't worry, it's a pal of mine.

STEPHANO: You are very closemouthed about the company you keep.

45   CALIBAN: And yet it helps me breathe. That's why I call it a pal. Sometimes it sneezes,
and a drop falls on my forehead and cools me with its salt, or blesses me . . .

STEPHANO: I don't understand. You aren't drunk, are you?

CALIBAN: Come on! It's that howling impatient thing that suddenly appears in a clap
of thunder like some God and hits you in the face, that rises up out of the very
50   depths of the abyss and smites you with its fury! It's the sea!

STEPHANO: Odd country! And an odd baptism!

CALIBAN: But the best is still the wind and the songs it sings . . . its dirty sigh when it
rustles through the bushes, or its triumphant chant when it passes by breaking
trees, remnants of their terror in its beard.

55   STEPHANO: The savage is delirious, he's raving mad! Tough luck, Trinculo, our savage is playing without a full deck!

TRINCULO: I'm kind of shuffling myself . . . In other words, I'm exhausted. I never
knew such hard going! Savage, even your mud is muddier.

CALIBAN: That isn't mud . . . it's something Prospero's dreamed up.

60   TRINCULO: There's a savage for you . . . everything's always caused by someone. The
sun is Prospero's smile. The rain is the tear in Prospero's eye . . . And I suppose

the mud is Prospero's shit. And what about the mosquitoes? What are they, may I ask? Zzzzzz, Zzzzzz . . . do you hear them? My face is being eaten off!

CALIBAN: Those aren't mosquitoes. It's some kind of gas that stings your nose and throat and makes you itch. It's another of Prospero's tricks. It's part of his arsenal. 65

STEPHANO: What do you mean by that?

CALIBAN: I mean his anti-riot arsenal! He's got a lot of gadgets like these . . . gadgets to make you deaf, to blind you, to make you sneeze, to make you cry . . .

TRINCULO: And to make you slip! Shit! This is some fix you've got us in! I can't take anymore . . . I'm going to sit down! 70

STEPHANO: Come on, Trinculo, show a little courage! We're engaged in a mobile ground manoeuvre here, and you know what that means: drive, initiatives, split-second decisions to meet new eventualities, and—above all—mobility. Let's go! Up you get! Mobility!

TRINCULO: But my feet are bleeding! 75

STEPHANO: Get up or I'll knock you down! (TRINCULO *begins to walk again.*) But tell me, my good savage, this usurper of yours seems very well protected. It might be dangerous to attack him!

CALIBAN: You mustn't underestimate him. You mustn't overestimate him, either . . . he's showing his power, but he's doing it mostly to impress us. 80

STEPHANO: No matter. Trinculo, we must take precautions. Axiom: never underestimate the enemy. Here, pass me that bottle. I can always use it as a club.

(*Highly colored clothing is seen, hanging from a rope.*)

TRINCULO: Right, Stephano. On with the battle. Victory means loot. And there's a foretaste of it . . . look at that fine wardrobe! Trinculo, my friend, methinks you are going to put on those britches . . . they'll replace your torn trousers. 85

STEPHANO: Look out, Trinculo . . . one move and I'll knock you down. As your lord and master I have the first pick, and with those britches I'm exercising my feudal rights . . .

TRINCULO: I saw them first!

STEPHANO: The King gets first pick in every country in the world. 90

TRINCULO: That's tyranny, Stephano. I'm not going to let you get away with it.

(*They fight.*)

CALIBAN: Let it alone, fool. I tell you about winning your dignity, and you start fighting over hand-me-downs! (*To himself*) To think I'm stuck with these jokers! What an idiot I am! How could I ever have thought I could create the Revolution with swollen guts and fat faces! Oh well! History won't blame me for not 95 having been able to win my freedom all by myself. It's you and me, Prospero! (*Weapon in hand, he advances on* PROSPERO *who has just appeared.*)

PROSPERO: (*bares his chest to him*) Strike! Go on, strike! Strike your Master, your benefactor! Don't tell me you're going to spare him!

(CALIBAN *raises his arm, but hesitates.*)

Go on! You don't dare! See, you're nothing but an animal . . . you don't know 100 how to kill.

CALIBAN: Defend yourself! I'm not a murderer.

PROSPERO: (*very calm*) The worse for you. You've lost your chance. Stupid as a slave! And now, enough of this farce. (*Calling*) Ariel! (*to* ARIEL) Ariel, take charge of
105   the prisoners!

(CALIBAN, TRINCULO and STEPHANO *are taken prisoners.*)

SCENE 5

(PROSPERO*'s cave.* MIRANDA *and* FERDINAND *are playing chess.*)

MIRANDA: Sir, I think you're cheating.
FERDINAND: And what if I told you that I would not do so for twenty kingdoms?
MIRANDA: I would not believe a word of it, but I would forgive you. Now, be honest . . . you did cheat!
5   FERDINAND: I'm pleased that you were able to tell. (*Laughing*) That makes me less worried at the thought that soon you will be leaving your innocent flowery kingdom for my less-innocent world of men.
MIRANDA: Oh, you know that, hitched to your star, I would brave the demons of hell!

(*The Nobles enter.*)

ALONSO: My son! This marriage! The thrill of it has struck me dumb! The thrill and
10   the joy!
GONZALO: A happy ending to a most opportune shipwreck!
ALONSO: A unique one, indeed, for it can legitimately be described as such.
GONZALO: Look at them! Isn't it wonderful! I've been too choked up to speak, or I would have already told these children all the joy my old heart feels at seeing
15   them living love's young dream and cherishing each other so tenderly.
ALONSO: (*to* FERDINAND *and* MIRANDA) My children, give me your hands. May the Lord bless you.
GONZALO: Amen! Amen!

(*Enter* PROSPERO.)

PROSPERO: Thank you, Gentlemen, for having agreed to join in this little family
20   party. Your presence has brought us comfort and joy. However, you must now think of getting some rest. Tomorrow morning, you will recover your vessels— they are undamaged—and your men, who I can guarantee are safe, hale and hearty. I shall return with you to Europe, and I can promise you—I should say: promise us—a rapid sail and propitious winds.
25   GONZALO: God be praised! We are delighted . . . delighted and overcome! What a happy, what a memorable day! With one voyage Antonio has found a brother, his brother has found a dukedom, his daughter has found a husband. Alonso has regained his son and gained a daughter. And what else? . . . Anyway, I am the only one whose emotion prevents him from knowing what he's saying . . .
30   PROSPERO: The proof of that, my fine Gonzalo, is that you are forgetting someone: Ariel, my loyal servant. (*Turning to* ARIEL) Yes, Ariel, today you will be free. Go, my sweet. I hope you will not be bored.
ARIEL: Bored! I fear that the days will seem all too short!
There, where the Cecropia gloves its impatient hands with silver,
35   Where the ferns free the stubborn black stumps

from their scored bodies with a green cry—
There where the intoxicating berry ripens the visit
of the wild ring-dove
through the throat of that musical bird
I shall let fall   40
one by one,
each more pleasing than the last
four notes so sweet that the last
will give rise to a yearning
in the heart of the most forgetful slaves   45
yearning for freedom!

PROSPERO: Come, come. All the same, you are not going to set my world on fire
with your music, I trust!

ARIEL: (*with intoxication*)
Or on some stony plane
perched on an agave stalk   50
I shall be the thrush that launches
its mocking cry
to the benighted field-hand
"Dig, nigger! Dig, nigger!"
and the lightened agave will   55
straighten from my flight,
a solemn flag.

PROSPERO: That is a very unsettling agenda! Go! Scram! Before I change my mind!

(*Enter* STEPHANO, TRINCULO, CALIBAN.)

GONZALO: Sire, here are your people.

PROSPERO: Oh no, not all of them! Some are yours.   60

ALONSO: True. There's that fool Trinculo and that unspeakable Stephano.

STEPHANO: The very ones, Sire, in person. We throw ourselves at your merciful feet.

ALONSO: What became of you?

STEPHANO: Sire, we were walking in the forest—no, it was in the fields—when we
saw some perfectly respectable clothing blowing in the wind. We thought it   65
only right to collect them and we were returning them to their rightful owner
when a frightful adventure befell us . . .

TRINCULO: Yes, we were mistaken for thieves and treated accordingly.

STEPHANO: Yes, Sire, it is the most dreadful thing that could happen to an honest
man: victims of a judicial error, a miscarriage of justice!   70

PROSPERO: Enough! Today is a day to be benevolent, and it will do no good to try
to talk sense to you in the state you're in . . . Leave us. Go sleep it off, drunkards.
We raise sail tomorrow.

TRINCULO: Raise sail! But that's what we do all the time, Sire, Stephano and I . . . at
least, we raise our glasses, from dawn till dusk till dawn . . . The hard part is   75
putting them down, landing, as you might say.

PROSPERO: Scoundrels! If only life could bring you to the safe harbors of Temperance and Sobriety!

ALONSO: (*indicating* CALIBAN) That is the strangest creature I've ever seen!

PROSPERO: And the most devilish too!   80

GONZALO: What's that? Devilish! You've reprimanded him, preached at him, you've ordered and made him obey and you say he is still indomitable!

PROSPERO: Honest Gonzalo, it is as I have said.

GONZALO: Well—and forgive me, Counsellor, if I give counsel—on the basis of my
85   long experience the only thing left is exorcism. "Begone, unclean spirit, in the name of the Father, of the Son and of the Holy Ghost." That's all there is to it!

(CALIBAN *bursts out laughing.*)

GONZALO: You were absolutely right! And more so than you thought ... He's not just a rebel, he's a real tough customer! (*To* CALIBAN) So much the worse for you, my friend. I have tried to save you. I give up. I leave you to the secular arm!

90   PROSPERO: Come here, Caliban. Have you got anything to say in your own defence? Take advantage of my good humor. I'm in a forgiving mood today.

CALIBAN: I'm not interested in defending myself. My only regret is that I've failed.

PROSPERO: What were you hoping for?

CALIBAN: To get back my island and regain my freedom.

95   PROSPERO: And what would you do all alone here on this island, haunted by the devil, tempest tossed?

CALIBAN: First of all, I'd get rid of you! I'd spit you out, all your works and pomps! Your "white" magic!

PROSPERO: That's a fairly negative program ...

100   CALIBAN: You don't understand it ... I say I'm going to spit you out, and that's very positive ...

PROSPERO: Well, the world is really upside down ... We've seen everything now: Caliban as a dialectician! However, in spite of everything I'm fond of you, Caliban. Come, let's make peace. We've lived together for ten years and worked side
105   by side! Ten years count for something, after all! We've ended up by becoming compatriots!

CALIBAN: You know very well that I'm not interested in peace. I'm interested in being free! Free, you hear?

PROSPERO: It's odd ... no matter what you do, you won't succeed in making me be-
110   lieve that I'm a tyrant!

CALIBAN: Understand what I say, Prospero:
For years I bowed my head
for years I took it, all of it—
your insults, your ingratitude ...
115   and worst of all, more degrading than all the rest,
your condescension.
But now, it's over!
Over, do you hear?
Of course, at the moment
120   You're still stronger than I am.
But I don't give a damn for your power
or for your dogs or your police or your inventions!
And do you know why?
It's because I know I'll get you.
125   I'll impale you! And on a stake that you've sharpened yourself!
You'll have impaled yourself!

Prospero, you're a great magician:
you're an old hand at deception.
And you lied to me so much,
about the world, about myself,   130
that you ended up by imposing on me
an image of myself:
underdeveloped, in your words, undercompetent
that's how you made me see myself!
And I hate that image . . . and it's false!   135
But now I know you, you old cancer,
And I also know myself!
And I know that one day
my bare fist, just that,
will be enough to crush your world!   140
The old world is crumbling down!

Isn't it true? Just look!
It even bores you to death.
And by the way . . . you have a chance to get it over with:
You can pick up and leave.   145
You can go back to Europe.
But the hell you will!
I'm sure you won't leave.
You make me laugh with your "mission"!
Your "vocation"!   150
Your vocation is to hassle me.
And that's why you'll stay,
just like those guys who founded the colonies
and who now can't live anywhere else.
You're just an old addict, that's what you are!   155

PROSPERO: Poor Caliban! You know that you're headed towards your own ruin.
You're sliding towards suicide! You know I will be the stronger, and stronger all
the time. I pity you!

CALIBAN: And I hate you!

PROSPERO: Beware! My generosity has its limits.   160

CALIBAN: (shouting)

> Shango marches with strength
> along his path, the sky!
> Shango is a fire-bearer,
> his steps shake the heavens
> and the earth   165
> Shango, Shango, ho!

PROSPERO: I have uprooted the oak and raised the sea,
I have caused the mountain to tremble and have bared my chest to adversity.
With Jove I have traded thunderbolt for thunderbolt.
Better yet—from a brutish monster I have made man!   170
But ah! To have failed to find the path to man's heart . . .

if that be where man is.
(*to* CALIBAN)
Well, I hate you as well!
For it is you who have made me
175   doubt myself for the first time.
(*to the Nobles*)
... My friends, come near. We must say farewell ... I shall not be going with
you. My fate is here: I shall not run from it.
ANTONIO: What, Sire?
PROSPERO: Hear me well.
180   I am not in any ordinary sense a master,
as this savage thinks,
but rather the conductor of a boundless score:
this isle,
summoning voices, I alone,
185   and mingling them at my pleasure,
arranging out of confusion
one intelligible line.
Without me, who would be able to draw music from all that?
This isle is mute without me.
190   My duty, thus, is here,
and here I shall stay.
GONZALO: Oh day full rich in miracles!
PROSPERO: Do not be distressed. Antonio, be you the lieutenant of my goods and
make use of them as procurator until that time when Ferdinand and Miranda
195   may take effective possession of them, joining them with the Kingdom of Naples.
Nothing of that which has been set for them must be postponed: Let their marriage be celebrated at Naples with all royal splendor. Honest Gonzalo, I place my
trust in your word. You shall stand as father to our princess at this ceremony.
GONZALO: Count on me, Sire.
200   PROSPERO: Gentlemen, farewell.

(*They exit.*)

And now, Caliban, it's you and me!
What I have to tell you will be brief:
Ten times, a hundred times, I've tried to save you,
above all from yourself.
205   But you have always answered me with wrath
and venom,
like the opossum that pulls itself up by its own tail
the better to bite the hand that tears it from the darkness.
Well, my boy, I shall set aside my indulgent nature
210   and henceforth I will answer your violence
with violence!

(*Time passes, symbolized by the curtain's being lowered halfway and reraised. In semi-
darkness* PROSPERO *appears, aged and weary. His gestures are jerky and automatic, his
speech weak, toneless, trite.*)

PROSPERO: Odd, but for some time now we seem to be overrun with opossums. They're everywhere. Peccarys, wild boar, all this unclean nature! But mainly opossums. Those eyes! The vile grins they have! It's as though the jungle was laying siege to the cave . . . But I shall stand firm . . . I shall not let my work per-   215
ish! (*Shouting*) I shall protect civilization! (*He fires in all directions.*) They're done for! Now, this way I'll be able to have some peace and quiet for a while. But it's cold. Odd how the climate's changed. Cold on this island . . . Have to think about making a fire . . . Well, Caliban, old fellow, it's just us two now, here on the island . . . only you and me. You and me. You-me . . . me-you! What in the hell is   220
he up to? (*Shouting*) Caliban!

(*In the distance, above the sound of the surf and the chirping of birds, we hear snatches of* CALIBAN's *song:*)

FREEDOM HI-DAY, FREEDOM HI-DAY!

QUESTIONS FOR DISCUSSION AND WRITING

1. In his introduction to his translation of Césaire's *Une Tempête,* Richard Miller says that "it is essential for the director and the actors to decide what accents, what 'classes,' they wish the various characters to reflect. In my own head, I have heard Ariel's song, for instance, as vaguely calypso; others will have other ideas." If you were directing the play, what accents would you instruct the actors to use? Why? How might your choice of accent reflect a sense of what kinds of people are more likely to be victims and what kinds are more likely to be victimizers?
2. Césaire specifies that the cast of characters is "As in Shakespeare," with the exception of the addition of Eshu and "Two alterations: Ariel, a mulatto slave; Caliban, a black slave." What is the significance of Césaire's instructions here?
3. In the American premiere of *A Tempest,* the characters of Eshu and the Master of Ceremonies were played by the same actor, as were the characters of the Captain and Trinculo. Sometimes an actor will play two roles simply because the acting troupe is short on actors. On the other hand, such doubling can have thematic significance. Which do you think is the case in this instance? Why?
4. *A Tempest* is really a play within a play. The play begins with a Master of Ceremonies assigning parts to an acting troupe, creating what is called a **"frame story."** (A frame story is one that stands outside, and frames, the main action of the play.) Most authors use frame stories to frame the action at the beginning *and* at the end of a work. In *A Tempest,* though, the frame doesn't return at the end of the play. Do you think that was a deliberate decision on Césaire's part, or did he simply forget to return to the acting troupe? If you think the decision was a deliberate one, what thematic significance might it have?
5. Yoruban legend has it that before Shango became the god of the storm, he was a king who ruled with such tyranny that his ministers attempted to depose him, causing Shango to flee the land and, perhaps, kill himself. With this background in mind, what do you see as the significance of the references to Shango in *A Tempest?*
6. Eshu, a trickster god, can bring either misfortune or fortune to those he visits. He is most likely to bring misfortune to those who do not pay proper attention to the

other gods. He is sometimes seen as evil, and he is often seen as one of those most responsible for men's destinies. Why do you think Eshu appears in the wedding scene in *A Tempest*? Why do you think the characters respond to him as they do?

7. At the beginning of Act III, Scene 4, Caliban says Prospero is the Anti-Nature. How is this statement true or untrue? To the extent that it is true, is Caliban a representative of nature? Why or why not? In *The Tempest* and *A Tempest,* is nature more likely to be identified with heroism or monstrosity? Why?

JUSTIN HENDERSON

Enchanted Island _____ **1993**

Shakespeare inspires an award-winning club in Houston

William Shakespeare's last play, *The Tempest,* is the source of imagery for the 4,500-square-foot restaurant and dance club of the same name that Jordan Mozer has designed for a Texas client. The play concerns the magician Prospero, and the wonders he works on an enchanted island between Tunis (Mozer's client is originally from Tunisia) and Naples. The restaurant is Mozer's most restrained creation to date: The interior exhibits the same originality as Mozer's other works, but here the voluptuous forms and cartoonish qualities are toned down in favor of a more refined atmosphere, reflecting the imagery and themes of the play.

"In the space of three hours, Prospero transforms the lives of all around him with his art . . . we suggest his art is comparable to that of a restaurateur," says Mozer. His inspired interpretation of *The Tempest* is launched into the metaphysical realm with this remark. In truth, three hours in a nightclub is not generally the stuff of cathartic transformation, but Tempest's hand-wrought, wind-blown interiors definitely present a promising opening for a dinner date (as a topic for conversation if nothing else). More significant—in an interior which claims such elevated sources of inspiration—is the way the play has been physically realized—how it has been used as a source for design motifs. And Tempest is indeed rich in Shakespearean imagery and ideas. Tempest is circular in plan, like an island, like the magic circle used by Prospero, and magic seems to be woven into every detail. Deriving imagery from the works of John Dee (Queen Elizabeth I's astrologer, Enochian magician, and the model for Prospero), for instance, Mozer created a room-encircling mural of real and imaginary formulas for casting spells. Additionally, mosaic tile medallions incorporate ancient good luck talismans, and the door pull and logo, a three-loop spiral, is derived from a 17th-century etching of an enchanted rope used to raise tempests.

References to the storm—the central act of conjury in the play—are more obvious. Above the pinwheel-patterned hardwood dance floor in the center of the room—the eye of the storm—is a glazed oculus over a pendant light fixture with blown glass elements spinning clockwise. The architectural elements in Tempest, including bars, seats, soffits, shelves, lighting fixtures, and wine cabinets, are located along sixteen lines radiating out from the center; all these elements are sculpted to appear as if whirling, windblown, as is the *tempietto,* or "little temple," a reversed crown with its five legs clothed in baroque black velvet "stockings," which serves as a visual and formal focus within the space.

One might argue that it is an act of hubris to claim William Shakespeare as the source of inspiration for something as mundane as a supperclub, but Mozer has the art to pull it off. Whether or not the people who go to Tempest to dine and dance are aware of the complexity of its sources, they are surely enchanted.

QUESTIONS FOR DISCUSSION AND WRITING

1. Imagine that you have been asked to design a business taking its inspiration from *The Tempest*. (The kind of business is up to you.) How would you "re-create" the play in your design? You will need to think not only about the way the design looks but about the mood it creates. How "enchanted" would you make the scene? How frightening and/or alien?
2. If the Tempest restaurant were, instead, to take its inspiration from Césaire's play, what changes do you suspect it would have to make? What would the final design look like, and how well would that design work for a restaurant?

QUESTIONS FOR CROSS READING:
BLURRING THE LINE: *THE TEMPEST*

1. Look at the characterizations of Ariel, Caliban, Prospero, or Miranda in Césaire's work and Shakespeare's. How are the characterizations similar? How are they different? What do the similarities and/or differences imply about the two plays' themes and the authors' intentions? Who are the heroes of each play? Who are the monsters?
2. In both Shakespeare's play and Césaire's we get alternating views of the island as a kind of paradise and as a kind of hell—or at least a purgatory. (In Césaire's play, for instance, Gonzalo says that the Boatswain of the sinking ship is like a "pilot on the ferry to hell," reminding us of Charon, who ferries the dead to the underworld in classical mythology.) How similar are the islands of the two plays? To what extent does each represent a kind of paradise? A hell? What, finally, is the thematic significance of the island setting?
3. Names have power and significance. What do you see as the significance of the names in Shakespeare's *Tempest*? Why do you suppose Césaire's Caliban wants to change his name? Why does Shakespeare's Prospero forbid Miranda to tell Ferdinand her name, and why is it significant that she disobeys his command? Finally, why do you suppose Césaire has *Caliban,* not Miranda herself, reveal the young heroine's name to Ferdinand?
4. The references to the Inquisition in *A Tempest* bring to mind an era of religious persecution (one which was, in fact, contemporary with Shakespeare). Do you see any such references in Shakespeare's play? How do various kinds of persecution and oppression—religious, political, even sexual—figure in the plays and poems in this cluster?
5. Shakespeare's and Césaire's plays are, at least in part, about the proper relationship between the governor and governed. What does each see as the ideal relationship

between the king and those he rules? How close do the various rulers and would-be rulers come to the plays' definitions of the "ideal king"? If you were a citizen of the plays' worlds, which of the characters would you want for king?

6. Imagine yourself writing sequels to Shakespeare's and Césaire's plays. What would happen in the years after each play's end? Think about the futures of both those who remain on the island kingdom and those who sail back to Naples. Keep in mind that your sequel should be true to the characterizations and themes of the originals.

7. In both Shakespeare's and Césaire's plays and in some of the shorter works in this cluster, there is a clear sexual tension. What do the works see as the danger of uncontrolled sexuality? What do they see as the function of a productive sexuality? Where do the sexual tensions originate, and what do they signify? What is the connection between sexuality and either innocence, villainy, or monstrosity?

8. Goto's poem relies heavily on the passage in *The Tempest* in which Prospero reminds Caliban that he withdrew affection from him when the latter tried to rape Miranda. Look again at that passage and at the comparable passage in Césaire's play. What are the tones and underlying assumptions of each? How does the description of the attempted rape relate to each work's overall themes?

Further Reflections: A Collection of Works on the Theme of Monsters and Heroes

Included in this section are pieces of literature that touch on the theme of Monsters and Heroes. If Umberto Eco is right that "every story tells a story that has already been told," each of the works that follow is in its own way a "retelling." Each asks us to take another look at the ideas of the monster and the hero, and so each may prompt us to rethink—to retell—the stories of the monsters and heroes that we included earlier in this chapter. The works that follow do not, then, have explicit retellings of their own. Instead, they reflect further the issues and images of the monster and the hero.

POETRY

ROBERT BROWNING (1812–1889)

My Last Duchess _____ 1842

Ferrara

> That's my last Duchess painted on the wall,
> Looking as if she were alive. I call
> That piece a wonder, now; Frà Pandolf's hands

Worked busily a day, and there she stands.
Will't please you sit and look at her? I said   5
"Frà Pandolf" by design, for never read
Strangers like you that pictured countenance,
The depth and passion of its earnest glance,
But to myself they turned (since none puts by
The curtain I have drawn for you, but I)   10
And seemed as they would ask me, if they durst,
How such a glance came there; so, not the first
Are you to turn and ask thus. Sir, 'twas not
Her husband's presence only, called that spot
Of joy into the Duchess' cheek; perhaps   15
Frà Pandolf chanced to say, "Her mantle laps
Over my lady's wrist too much," or "Paint
Must never hope to reproduce the faint
Half-flush that dies along her throat." Such stuff
Was courtesy, she thought, and cause enough   20
For calling up that spot of joy. She had
A heart—how shall I say?—too soon made glad,
Too easily impressed; she liked whate'er
She looked on, and her looks went everywhere.
Sir, 'twas all one! My favor at her breast,   25
The dropping of the daylight in the West,
The bough of cherries some officious fool
Broke in the orchard for her, the white mule
She rode with round the terrace—all and each
Would draw from her alike the approving speech,   30
Or blush, at least. She thanked men,—good! but thanked
Somehow—I know not how—as if she ranked
My gift of a nine-hundred-years-old name
With anybody's gift. Who'd stoop to blame
This sort of trifling? Even had you skill   35
In speech—which I have not—to make your will
Quite clear to such an one, and say "Just this
Or that in you disgusts me; here you miss,
Or there exceed the mark"—and if she let
Herself be lessoned so, nor plainly set   40
Her wits to yours, forsooth, and made excuse—
E'en then would be some stooping; and I choose
Never to stoop. Oh sir, she smiled, no doubt,
Whene'er I passed her; but who passed without
Much the same smile? This grew; I gave commands;   45
Then all smiles stopped together. There she stands
As if alive. Will 't please you rise? We'll meet
The company below, then. I repeat,
The Count your master's known munificence
Is ample warrant that no just pretense   50

Of mine for dowry will be disallowed;
Though his fair daughter's self, as I avowed
At starting, is my object. Nay, we'll go
Together down, sir. Notice Neptune, though,
55   Taming a sea-horse, thought a rarity,
Which Claus of Innsbruck cast in bronze for me!

QUESTIONS FOR DISCUSSION AND WRITING

1. Browning's poem is a *dramatic monologue.* The monologue, a speech given by a single person, creates a dramatic story, one of which the speaker is probably only partially aware. The duke is clearly a very controlling person. How does he reveal that? In what ways did he control his late wife? How might he have killed her emotionally as well as physically?
2. Many readers consider the duke a monster not only because he might have had his wife killed but also because he seems cold and distant in his way of looking at the world. To what extent do you think it fair to call the duke a monster?
3. Whom is the duke speaking to and what is the occasion? How does the poem ask us to envision the duke's future?

e. e. cummings (1894–1962)
[Buffalo Bill's]   1925

Buffalo Bill's
defunct
        who used to
        ride a watersmooth-silver
5   stallion
and break onetwothreefourfive pigeonsjustlikethat
                                        Jesus
he was a handsome man
                  and what i want to know is
10   how do you like your blueeyed boy
Mister Death

QUESTIONS FOR DISCUSSION AND WRITING

1. Think about how cummings characterizes Death. Why is death called "Mister Death"? What is the effect of saying "defunct" rather than "dead"? How do these word choices affect our response to the possibility of Buffalo Bill's heroism?

2. The idiosyncratic layout of the poem can be considered part of cummings's poetic structure. What words and ideas does the layout emphasize? How do those words and ideas contribute to the poem's theme?

A. E. HOUSMAN (1859–1936)

To an Athlete Dying Young _____ *1896*

The time you won your town the race
We chaired you through the market-place;
Man and boy stood cheering by,
And home we brought you shoulder-high.

To-day, the road all runners come,   5
Shoulder-high we bring you home,
And set you at your threshold down,
Townsman of a stiller town.

Smart lad, to slip betimes away
From fields where glory does not stay   10
And early though the laurel grows
It withers quicker than the rose.

Eyes the shady night has shut
Cannot see the record cut,
And silence sounds no worse than cheers   15
After earth has stopped the ears:

Now you will not swell the rout
Of lads that wore their honours out,
Runners whom renown outran
And the name died before the man.   20

So set, before its echoes fade,
The fleet foot on the sill of shade,
And hold to the low lintel up
The still-defended challenge-cup.

And round that early-laurelled head   25
Will flock to gaze the strengthless dead
And find unwithered on its curls
The garland briefer than a girl's.

QUESTIONS FOR DISCUSSION AND WRITING

1. Housman's poem superimposes two images: that of the athlete triumphant after a race and that of the athlete's funeral. Which images belong to the athlete's life and

which to his death? How does the juxtaposition affect our responses to each set of images?

2. What is the tone of the poem? What does the tone suggest about its attitude toward life and death?

3. To what extent does Housman's poem view athletic victory as heroic? How would you define athletic heroism in the poem and in today's world?

———————

JOHN KEATS (1795–1821)

La Belle Dame sans Merci ———————————— *1819, 1888*

O what can ail thee, Knight at arms,
    Alone and palely loitering?
The sedge has withered from the Lake
    And no birds sing!

5   O what can ail thee, Knight at arms,
    So haggard, and so woebegone?
The squirrel's granary is full
    And the harvest's done.

I see a lily on thy brow
10   With anguish moist and fever dew,
And on thy cheeks a fading rose
    Fast withereth too.

"I met a Lady in the Meads,
    Full beautiful, a faery's child,
15   Her hair was long, her foot was light
    And her eyes were wild.

"I made a Garland for her head,
    And bracelets too, and fragrant Zone;
She looked at me as she did love
20   And made sweet moan.

"I set her on my pacing steed
    And nothing else saw all day long,
For sidelong would she bend and sing
    A faery's song.

25   "She found me roots of relish sweet,
    And honey wild, and manna dew,
And sure in language strange she said
    'I love thee true.'

"She took me to her elfin grot
30   And there she wept and sighed full sore,

And there I shut her wild wild eyes
   With kisses four.

"And there she lulléd me asleep,
   And there I dreamed, Ah Woe betide!
The latest dream I ever dreamt   35
   On the cold hill side.

"I saw pale Kings, and Princes too,
   Pale warriors, death-pale were they all;
They cried, 'La belle dame sans merci
   Hath thee in thrall!'   40

"I saw their starved lips in the gloam
   With horrid warning gapéd wide,
And I awoke, and found me here
   On the cold hill's side.

"And this is why I sojourn here,   45
   Alone and palely loitering;
Though the sedge is withered from the Lake
   And no birds sing."

QUESTIONS FOR DISCUSSION AND WRITING

1. The poem emphasizes the "belle dame's" alien quality. What words create that emphasis?
2. What makes the "belle dame" attractive to the knight? What makes her frightening? Would you consider her a monster? Why or why not?
3. What is the setting of the poem? What mood does it create?
4. The poem has two speakers. How is our response affected by the change in speaker? How are the voices different?

SYLVIA PLATH (1932–1963)

Daddy _____ *1962, 1965*

You do not do, you do not do
Any more, black shoe
In which I have lived like a foot
For thirty years, poor and white,
Barely daring to breathe or Achoo.   5

Daddy, I have had to kill you.
You died before I had time—
Marble-heavy, a bag full of God,

Ghastly statue with one grey toe
10   Big as a Frisco seal

And a head in the freakish Atlantic
Where it pours bean green over blue
In the waters off beautiful Nauset.
I used to pray to recover you.
15   Ach, du.

In the German tongue, in the Polish town
Scraped flat by the roller
Of wars, wars, wars.
But the name of the town is common.
20   My Polack friend

Says there are a dozen or two.
So I never could tell where you
Put your foot, your root,
I never could talk to you.
25   The tongue stuck in my jaw.

It stuck in a barb wire snare.
Ich, ich, ich, ich,
I could hardly speak.
I thought every German was you.
30   And the language obscene

An engine, an engine
Chuffing me off like a Jew.
A Jew to Dachau, Auschwitz, Belsen.
I began to talk like a Jew.
35   I think I may well be a Jew.

The snows of the Tyrol, the clear beer of Vienna
Are not very pure or true.
With my gypsy ancestress and my weird luck
And my Taroc pack and my Taroc pack
40   I may be a bit of a Jew.

I have always been scared of *you,*
With your Luftwaffe, your gobbledygoo.
And your neat moustache
And your Aryan eye, bright blue.
45   Panzer-man, panzer-man, O You—

Not God but a swastika
So black no sky could squeak through.
Every woman adores a Fascist,
The boot in the face, the brute
50   Brute heart of a brute like you.

You stand at the blackboard, daddy,
In the picture I have of you,
A cleft in your chin instead of your foot
But no less a devil for that, no not
Any less the black man who   55

Bit my pretty red heart in two.
I was ten when they buried you.
At twenty I tried to die
And get back, back, back to you.
I thought even the bones would do.   60

But they pulled me out of the sack,
And they stuck me together with glue.
And then I knew what to do.
I made a model of you,
A man in black with a Meinkampf look   65

And a love of the rack and the screw.
And I said I do, I do.
So daddy, I'm finally through.
The black telephone's off at the root,
The voices just can't worm through.   70

If I've killed one man, I've killed two—
The vampire who said he was you
And drank my blood for a year,
Seven years, if you want to know.
Daddy, you can lie back now.   75

There's a stake in your fat black heart
And the villagers never liked you.
They are dancing and stamping on you.
They always *knew* it was you.
Daddy, daddy, you bastard, I'm through.   80

QUESTIONS FOR DISCUSSION AND WRITING

1. As the poem proceeds, "Daddy" becomes more and more of a monster. What are the images that create that impression?
2. Though the poem is full of bitterness and hatred, there is also a thread that suggests feelings of love and loss. Where does the poem suggest those more positive feelings?
3. Plath's father was not a Nazi, and some readers find the comparison exaggerated. Do you think the images are emotionally true, or are they self-indulgent?
4. The poem ends "Daddy, daddy, you bastard, I'm through," suggesting that some sort of emotional resolution has been reached. *Is* there such a resolution? If so,

what is the nature of that resolution? If not, should there have been a resolution? What kind of resolution could have been reached?

SHORT STORIES

MARGARET ATWOOD (1939–   )

Rape Fantasies _____ 1975

The way they're going on about it in the magazines you'd think it was just invented, and not only that but it's something terrific, like a vaccine for cancer. They put it in capital letters on the front cover, and inside they have these questionnaires like the ones they used to have about whether you were a good enough wife or an endomorph or an ectomorph, remember that? with the scoring upside down on page 73, and then these numbered do-it-yourself dealies, you know? RAPE, TEN THINGS TO DO ABOUT IT, like it was ten new hairdos or something. I mean, what's so new about it?

So at work they all have to talk about it because no matter what magazine you open, there it is, staring you right between the eyes, and they're beginning to have it on the television, too. Personally, I'd prefer a June Allyson movie anytime but they don't make them anymore and they don't even have them that much on the Late Show. For instance, day before yesterday, that would be Wednesday, thank god it's Friday as they say, we were sitting around in the women's lunch room—the *lunch* room, I mean you'd think you could get some peace and quiet in there—and Chrissy closes up the magazine she's been reading and says, "How about it, girls, do you have rape fantasies?"

The four of us were having our game of bridge the way we always do, and I had a bare twelve points counting the singleton with not that much of a bid in anything. So I said one club, hoping Sondra would remember about the one club convention, because the time before when I used that she thought I really meant clubs and she bid us up to three, and all I had was four little ones with nothing higher than a six, and we went down two and on top of that we were vulnerable. She is not the world's best bridge player. I mean, neither am I but there's a limit.

Darlene passed but the damage was done, Sondra's head went round like it was on ball bearings and she said, "*What* fantasies?"

"Rape fantasies," Chrissy said. She's a receptionist and she looks like one; she's pretty but cool as a cucumber, like she's been painted all over with nail polish, if you know what I mean. Varnished. "It says here all women have rape fantasies."

"For Chrissake, I'm eating an egg sandwich," I said, "and I bid one club and Darlene passed."

"You mean, like some guy jumping you in an alley or something," Sondra said. She was eating her lunch, we all eat our lunches during the game, and she bit into a piece of that celery she always brings and started to chew away on it with this thoughtful expression in her eyes and I knew we might as well pack it in as far as the game was concerned.

"Yeah, sort of like that," Chrissy said. She was blushing a little, you could see it even under her makeup.

"I don't think you should go out alone at night," Darlene said, "you put yourself in a position," and I may have been mistaken but she was looking at me. She's the oldest, she's forty-one though you wouldn't know it and neither does she, but I looked it up in the employees' file. I like to guess a person's age and then look it up to see if I'm right. I let myself have an extra pack of cigarettes if I am, though I'm trying to cut down. I figure it's harmless as long as you don't tell. I mean, not everyone has access to that file, it's more or less confidential. But it's all right if I tell you, I don't expect you'll ever meet her, though you never know, it's a small world. Anyway.

"For *heaven's* sake, it's only *Toronto*," Greta said. She worked in Detroit for three years and she never lets you forget it, it's like she thinks she's a war hero or something, we should all admire her just for the fact that she's still walking this earth, though she was really living in Windsor the whole time, she just worked in Detroit. Which for me doesn't really count. It's where you sleep, right?

"Well, do you?" Chrissy said. She was obviously trying to tell us about hers but she wasn't about to go first, she's cautious, that one.

"I certainly don't," Darlene said, and she wrinkled up her nose, like this, and I had to laugh. "I think it's disgusting." She's divorced, I read that in the file too, she never talks about it. It must've been years ago anyway. She got up and went over to the coffee machine and turned her back on us as though she wasn't going to have anything more to do with it.

"Well," Greta said. I could see it was going to be between her and Chrissy. They're both blondes, I don't mean that in a bitchy way but they do try to outdress each other. Greta would like to get out of Filing, she'd like to be a receptionist too so she could meet more people. You don't meet much of anyone in Filing except other people in Filing. Me, I don't mind it so much, I have outside interests.

"Well," Greta said, "I sometimes think about, you know my apartment? It's got this little balcony, I like to sit out there in the summer and I have a few plants out there. I never bother that much about locking the door to the balcony, it's one of those sliding glass ones, I'm on the eighteenth floor for heaven's sake, I've got a good view of the lake and the CN Tower and all. But I'm sitting around one night in my housecoat, watching TV with my shoes off, you know how you do, and I see this guy's feet, coming down past the window, and the next thing you know he's standing on the balcony, he's let himself down by a rope with a hook on the end of it from the floor above, that's the nineteenth, and before I can even get up off the chesterfield he's inside the apartment. He's all dressed in black with black gloves on"—I knew right away what show she got the black gloves off because I saw the same one—"and then he, well, you know."

"You know what?" Chrissy said, but Greta said, "And afterwards he tells me that he goes all over the outside of the apartment building like that, from one floor to another, with his rope and his hook . . . and then he goes out to the balcony and tosses his rope, and he climbs up it and disappears."

"Just like Tarzan," I said, but nobody laughed.

"Is that all?" Chrissy said. "Don't you ever think about, well, I think about being in the bathtub, with no clothes on . . ."

"So who takes a bath in their clothes?" I said, you have to admit it's stupid when you come to think of it, but she just went on, ". . . with lots of bubbles, what I use is

Vitabath, it's more expensive but it's so relaxing, and my hair pinned up, and the door opens and this fellow's standing there . . ."

"How'd he get in?" Greta said.

"Oh, I don't know, through a window or something. Well, I can't very well get out of the bathtub, the bathroom's too small and besides he's blocking the doorway, so I just lie there, and he starts to very slowly take his own clothes off, and then he gets into the bathtub with me."

"Don't you scream or anything?" said Darlene. She'd come back with her cup of coffee, she was getting really interested. "I'd scream like bloody murder."

"Who'd hear me?" Chrissy said. "Besides, all the articles say it's better not to resist, that way you don't get hurt."

"Anyway you might get bubbles up your nose," I said, "from the deep breathing," and I swear all four of them looked at me like I was in bad taste, like I'd insulted the Virgin Mary or something. I mean, I don't see what's wrong with a little joke now and then. Life's too short, right?

"Listen," I said, "those aren't *rape* fantasies. I mean, you aren't getting *raped,* it's just some guy you haven't met formally who happens to be more attractive than Derek Cummins"—he's the Assistant Manager, he wears elevator shoes or at any rate they have these thick soles and he has this funny way of talking, we call him Derek Duck—"and you have a good time. Rape is when they've got a knife or something and you don't want to."

"So what about you, Estelle," Chrissy said, she was miffed because I laughed at her fantasy, she thought I was putting her down. Sondra was miffed too, by this time she'd finished her celery and she wanted to tell about hers, but she hadn't got in fast enough.

"All right, let me tell you one," I said. "I'm walking down this dark street at night and this fellow comes up and grabs my arm. Now it so happens that I have a plastic lemon in my purse, you know how it always says you should carry a plastic lemon in your purse? I don't really do it, I tried it once but the darn thing leaked all over my checkbook, but in this fantasy I have one, and I say to him, 'You're intending to rape me, right?' and he nods, so I open my purse to get the plastic lemon, and I can't find it! My purse is full of all this junk, Kleenex and cigarettes and my change purse and my lipstick and my driver's license, you know the kind of stuff; so I ask him to hold out his hands, like this, and I pile all this junk into them and down at the bottom there's the plastic lemon, and I can't get the top off. So I hand it to him and he's very obliging, he twists the top off and hands it back to me, and I squirt him in the eye."

I hope you don't think that's too vicious. Come to think of it, it is a bit mean, especially when he was so polite and all.

"*That's* your rape fantasy?" Chrissy says. "I don't believe it."

"She's a card," Darlene says, she and I are the ones that've been here the longest and she never will forget the time I got drunk at the office party and insisted I was going to dance under the table instead of on top of it, I did a sort of Cossack number but then I hit my head on the bottom of the table—actually it was a desk—when I went to get up, and I knocked myself out cold. She's decided that's the mark of an original mind and she tells everyone new about it and I'm not sure that's fair. Though I did do it.

"I'm being totally honest," I say. I always am and they know it. There's no point in being anything else, is the way I look at it, and sooner or later the truth will come out so you might as well not waste the time, right? "You should hear the one about the Easy-Off Oven Cleaner."

But that was the end of the lunch hour, with one bridge game shot to hell, and the next day we spent most of the time arguing over whether to start a new game or play out the hands we had left over from the day before, so Sondra never did get a chance to tell about her rape fantasy.

It started me thinking though, about my own rape fantasies. Maybe I'm abnormal or something, I mean I have fantasies about handsome strangers coming in through the window too, like Mr. Clean, I wish one would, please god somebody without flat feet and big sweat marks on his shirt, and over five feet five, believe me being tall is a handicap though it's getting better, tall guys are starting to like someone whose nose reaches higher than their belly button. But if you're being totally honest you can't count those as rape fantasies. In a real rape fantasy, what you should feel is this anxiety, like when you think about your apartment building catching on fire and whether you should use the elevator or the stairs or maybe just stick your head under a wet towel, and you try to remember everything you've read about what to do but you can't decide.

For instance, I'm walking along this dark street at night and this short, ugly fellow comes up and grabs my arm, and not only is he ugly, you know, with a sort of puffy nothing face, like those fellows you have to talk to in the bank when your account's overdrawn—of course I don't mean they're all like that—but he's absolutely covered in pimples. So he gets me pinned against the wall, he's short but he's heavy, and he starts to undo himself and the zipper gets stuck. I mean, one of the most significant moments in a girl's life, it's almost like getting married or having a baby or something, and he sticks the zipper.

So I say, kind of disgusted, "Oh for Chrissake," and he starts to cry. He tells me he's never been able to get anything right in his entire life, and this is the last straw, he's going to jump off a bridge.

"Look," I say, I feel so sorry for him, in my rape fantasies I always end up feeling sorry for the guy, I mean there has to be something *wrong* with them, if it was Clint Eastwood it'd be different but worse luck it never is. I was the kind of little girl who buried dead robins, know what I mean? It used to drive my mother nuts, she didn't like me touching them, because of the germs I guess. So I say, "Listen, I know how you feel. You really should do something about those pimples, if you got rid of them you'd be quite good looking, honest; then you wouldn't have to go around doing stuff like this. I had them myself once," I say, to comfort him, but in fact I did, and it ends up I give him the name of my old dermatologist, the one I had in high school, that was back in Leamington, except I used to go to St. Catharine's for the dermatologist. I'm telling you, I was really lonely when I first came here; I thought it was going to be such a big adventure and all, but it's a lot harder to meet people in a city. But I guess it's different for a guy.

Or I'm lying in bed with this terrible cold, my face is all swollen up, my eyes are red and my nose is dripping like a leaky tap, and this fellow comes in through the window and *he* has a terrible cold too, it's a new kind of flu that's been going around. So he says, "I'b goig do rabe you"—I hope you don't mind me holding my nose like this but that's the way I imagine it—and he lets out this terrific sneeze, which slows him down a bit, also I'm no object of beauty myself, you'd have to be some kind of pervert to want to rape someone with a cold like mine, it'd be like raping a bottle of

LePage's mucilage the way my nose is running. He's looking wildly around the room, and I realize it's because he doesn't have a piece of Kleenex! "Id's ride here," I say, and I pass him the Kleenex, god knows why he even bothered to get out of bed, you'd think if you were going to go around climbing in windows you'd wait till you were healthier, right? I mean, that takes a certain amount of energy. So I ask him why doesn't he let me fix him a Neo-Citran and scotch, that's what I always take, you still have the cold but you don't feel it, so I do and we end up watching the Late Show together. I mean, they aren't all sex maniacs, the rest of the time they must lead a normal life. I figure they enjoy watching the Late Show just like anybody else.

I do have a scarier one though . . . where the fellow says he's hearing angel voices that're telling him he's got to kill me, you know, you read about things like that all the time in the papers. In this one I'm not in the apartment where I live now, I'm back in my mother's house in Leamington and the fellow's been hiding in the cellar, he grabs my arm when I go downstairs to get a jar of jam and he's got hold of the axe too, out of the garage, that one is really scary. I mean, what do you say to a nut like that?

So I start to shake but after a minute I get control of myself and I say, is he sure the angel voices have got the right person, because I hear the same angel voices and they've been telling me for some time that I'm going to give birth to the reincarnation of St. Anne who in turn has the Virgin Mary and right after that comes Jesus Christ and the end of the world, and he wouldn't want to interfere with that, would he? So he gets confused and listens some more, and then he asks for a sign and I show him my vaccination mark, you can see it's sort of an odd-shaped one, it got infected because I scratched the top off and that does it, he apologizes and climbs out the coal chute again, which is how he got in in the first place, and I say to myself there's some advantage in having been brought up a Catholic even though I haven't been to church since they changed the service into English, it just isn't the same, you might as well be a Protestant. I must write to Mother and tell her to nail up that coal chute, it always has bothered me. Funny, I couldn't tell you at all what this man looks like but I know exactly what kind of shoes he's wearing, because that's the last I see of him, his shoes going up the coal chute, and they're the old-fashioned kind that lace up the ankles, even though he's a young fellow. That's strange, isn't it?

Let me tell you though I really sweat until I see him safely out of there and I go upstairs right away and make myself a cup of tea. I don't think about that one much. My mother always said you shouldn't dwell on unpleasant things and I generally agree with that, I mean, dwelling on them doesn't make them go away. Though not dwelling on them doesn't make them go away either, when you come to think of it.

Sometimes I have these short ones where the fellow grabs my arm but I'm really a Kung-Fu expert, can you believe it, in real life I'm sure it would just be a conk on the head and that's that, like getting your tonsils out, you'd wake up and it would be all over except for the sore places, and you'd be lucky if your neck wasn't broken or something, I could never even hit the volleyball in gym and a volleyball is fairly large, you know?—and I just go *zap* with my fingers into his eyes and that's it, he falls over, or I flip him against a wall or something. But I could never really stick my fingers in anyone's eyes, could you? It would feel like hot jello and I don't even like cold jello, just thinking about it gives me the creeps. I feel a bit guilty about that one, I mean how would you like walking around knowing someone's been blinded for life because of you?

But maybe it's different for a guy.

The most touching one I have is when the fellow grabs my arm and I say, sad and kind of dignified, "You'd be raping a corpse." That pulls him up short and I explain that I've just found out I have leukemia and the doctors have only given me a few months to live. That's why I'm out pacing the streets alone at night, I need to think, you know, come to terms with myself. I don't really have leukemia but in the fantasy I do, I guess I chose that particular disease because a girl in my grade four class died of it, the whole class sent her flowers when she was in the hospital. I didn't understand then that she was going to die and I wanted to have leukemia too so I could get flowers. Kids are funny, aren't they? Well, it turns out that he has leukemia himself, and *he* only has a few months to live, that's why he's going around raping people, he's very bitter because he's so young and his life is being taken from him before he's really lived it. So we walk along gently under the street lights, it's spring and sort of misty, and we end up going for coffee, we're happy we've found the only other person in the world who can understand what we're going through, it's almost like fate, and after a while we just sort of look at each other and our hands touch, and he comes back with me and moves into my apartment and we spend our last months together before we die, we just sort of don't wake up in the morning, though I've never decided which one of us gets to die first. If it's him I have to go on and fantasize about the funeral, if it's me I don't have to worry about that, so it just about depends on how tired I am at the time. You may not believe this but sometimes I even start crying. I cry at the ends of movies, even the ones that aren't all that sad, so I guess it's the same thing. My mother's like that too.

The funny thing about these fantasies is that the man is always someone I don't know, and the statistics in the magazines, well, most of them anyway, they say it's often someone you do know, at least a little bit, like your boss or something—I mean, it wouldn't be *my* boss, he's over sixty and I'm sure he couldn't rape his way out of a paper bag, poor old thing, but it might be someone like Derek Duck, in his elevator shoes, perish the thought—or someone you just met, who invites you up for a drink, it's getting so you can hardly be sociable anymore, and how are you supposed to meet people if you can't trust even that basic amount? You can't spend your whole life in the Filing Department or cooped up in your own apartment with all the doors and windows locked and the shades down. I'm not what you would call a drinker but I like to go out now and then for a drink or two in a nice place, even if I am by myself, I'm with Women's Lib on that even though I can't agree with a lot of other things they say. Like here for instance, the waiters all know me and if anyone, you know, bothers me. . . . I don't know why I'm telling you all this, except I think it helps you get to know a person, especially at first, hearing some of the things they think about. At work they call me the office worry wart, but it isn't so much like worrying, it's more like figuring out what you should do in an emergency, like I said before.

Anyway, another thing about it is that there's a lot of conversation, in fact I spend most of my time, in the fantasy that is, wondering what I'm going to say and what he's going to say, I think it would be better if you could get a conversation going. Like, how could a fellow do that to a person he's just had a long conversation with, once you let them know you're human, you have a life too, I don't see how they could go ahead with it, right? I mean, I know it happens but I just don't understand it, that's the part I really don't understand.

1. How would you describe Estelle, the narrator of the story? What do we learn about the circumstances of her life? How does she respond to them?
2. Estelle complains that her coworkers' rape fantasies aren't really *rape* fantasies because no real rapes occur. Are Estelle's fantasies *rape* fantasies? What do her fantasies tell us about her and her view of men? How does she undercut the view of the "rapist" as a monster?
3. Though it is not immediately apparent, the story does have a specific setting, one that we discover only near the end. What is that setting and to whom is Estelle talking? How does our knowledge of that setting change our response to the story?
4. Some readers find "Rape Fantasies" humorous; others find disquieting the attempt to find humor in such a serious subject. How did you respond to the story? How does the humorous treatment of a monstrous subject affect our ideas about what makes something monstrous? How does it affect our ideas about how humor works?

GABRIEL GARCIA MARQUEZ (1928–   )

A Very Old Man with Enormous Wings   1955
A Tale for Children

On the third day of rain they had killed so many crabs inside the house that Pelayo had to cross his drenched courtyard and throw them into the sea, because the newborn child had a temperature all night and they thought it was due to the stench. The world had been sad since Tuesday. Sea and sky were a single ash-gray thing and the sands of the beach, which on March nights glimmered like powdered light, had become a stew of mud and rotten shellfish. The light was so weak at noon that when Pelayo was coming back to the house after throwing away the crabs, it was hard for him to see what it was that was moving and groaning in the rear of the courtyard. He had to go very close to see that it was an old man, a very old man, lying face down in the mud, who, in spite of his tremendous efforts, couldn't get up, impeded by his enormous wings.

Frightened by that nightmare, Pelayo ran to get Elisenda, his wife, who was putting compresses on the sick child, and he took her to the rear of the courtyard. They both looked at the fallen body with mute stupor. He was dressed like a rag-picker. There were only a few faded hairs left on his bald skull and very few teeth in his mouth, and his pitiful condition of a drenched great-grandfather had taken away any sense of grandeur he might have had. His huge buzzard wings, dirty and half-plucked, were forever entangled in the mud. They looked at him so long and so closely that Pelayo and Elisenda very soon overcame their surprise and in the end found him familiar. Then they dared speak to him, and he answered in an incomprehensible dialect with a strong sailor's voice. That was how they skipped over the inconvenience of the wings and quite intelligently concluded that he was a lonely castaway from some foreign ship wrecked by the storm. And yet, they called in a neighbor woman who knew everything about life and death to see him, and all she needed was one look to show them their mistake.

"He's an angel," she told them. "He must have been coming for the child, but the poor fellow is so old that the rain knocked him down."

On the following day everyone knew that a flesh-and-blood angel was held captive in Pelayo's house. Against the judgment of the wise neighbor woman, for whom angels in those times were the fugitive survivors of a celestial conspiracy, they did not have the heart to club him to death. Pelayo watched over him all afternoon from the kitchen, armed with his bailiff's club, and before going to bed he dragged him out of the mud and locked him up with the hens in the wire chicken coop. In the middle of the night, when the rain stopped, Pelayo and Elisenda were still killing crabs. A short time afterward the child woke up without a fever and with a desire to eat. Then they felt magnanimous and decided to put the angel on a raft with fresh water and provisions for three days and leave him to his fate on the high seas. But when they went out into the courtyard with the first light of dawn, they found the whole neighborhood in front of the chicken coop having fun with the angel, without the slightest reverence, tossing him things to eat through the openings in the wire as if he weren't a supernatural creature but a circus animal.

Father Gonzaga arrived before seven o'clock, alarmed at the strange news. By that time onlookers less frivolous than those at dawn had already arrived and they were making all kinds of conjectures concerning the captive's future. The simplest among them thought that he should be named mayor of the world. Others of sterner mind felt that he should be promoted to the rank of five-star general in order to win all wars. Some visionaries hoped that he could be put to stud in order to implant on earth a race of winged wise men who could take charge of the universe. But Father Gonzaga, before becoming a priest, had been a robust woodcutter. Standing by the wire, he reviewed his catechism in an instant and asked them to open the door so that he could take a close look at that pitiful man who looked more like a huge decrepit hen among the fascinated chickens. He was lying in a corner drying his open wings in the sunlight among the fruit peels and breakfast leftovers that the early risers had thrown him. Alien to the impertinences of the world, he only lifted his antiquarian eyes and murmured something in his dialect when Father Gonzaga went into the chicken coop and said good morning to him in Latin. The parish priest had his first suspicion of an imposter when he saw that he did not understand the language of God or know how to greet His ministers. Then he noticed that seen close up he was much too human: he had an unbearable smell of the outdoors, the back side of his wings was strewn with parasites and his main feathers had been mistreated by terrestrial winds, and nothing about him measured up to the proud dignity of angels. Then he came out of the chicken coop and in a brief sermon warned the curious against the risks of being ingenuous. He reminded them that the devil had the bad habit of making use of carnival tricks in order to confuse the unwary. He argued that if wings were not the essential element in determining the difference between a hawk and an airplane, they were even less so in the recognition of angels. Nevertheless, he promised to write a letter to his bishop so that the latter would write to his primate so that the latter would write to the Supreme Pontiff in order to get the final verdict from the highest courts.

His prudence fell on sterile hearts. The news of the captive angel spread with such rapidity that after a few hours the courtyard had the bustle of a marketplace and they had to call in troops with fixed bayonets to disperse the mob that was about to knock the house down. Elisenda, her spine all twisted from sweeping up so much marketplace trash, then got the idea of fencing in the yard and charging five cents admission to see the angel.

The curious came from far away. A traveling carnival arrived with a flying acrobat who buzzed over the crowd several times, but no one paid any attention to him because his wings were not those of an angel but, rather, those of a sidereal bat. The most unfortunate invalids on earth came in search of health: a poor woman who since childhood had been counting her heartbeats and had run out of numbers; a Portuguese man who couldn't sleep because the noise of the stars disturbed him; a sleepwalker who got up at night to undo the things he had done while awake; and many others with less serious ailments. In the midst of that shipwreck disorder that made the earth tremble, Pelayo and Elisenda were happy with fatigue, for in less than a week they had crammed their rooms with money and the line of pilgrims waiting their turn to enter still reached beyond the horizon.

The angel was the only one who took no part in his own act. He spent his time trying to get comfortable in his borrowed nest, befuddled by the hellish heat of the oil lamps and sacramental candles that had been placed along the wire. At first they tried to make him eat some mothballs, which, according to the wisdom of the wise neighbor woman, were the food prescribed for angels. But he turned them down, just as he turned down the papal lunches that the penitents brought him, and they never found out whether it was because he was an angel or because he was an old man that in the end he ate nothing but eggplant mush. His only supernatural virtue seemed to be patience. Especially during the first days, when the hens pecked at him, searching for the stellar parasites that proliferated in his wings, and the cripples pulled out feathers to touch their defective parts with, and even the most merciful threw stones at him, trying to get him to rise so they could see him standing. The only time they succeeded in arousing him was when they burned his side with an iron for branding steers, for he had been motionless for so many hours that they thought he was dead. He awoke with a start, ranting in his hermetic language and with tears in his eyes, and he flapped his wings a couple of times, which brought on a whirlwind of chicken dung and lunar dust and a gale of panic that did not seem to be of this world. Although many thought that his reaction had been one not of rage but of pain, from then on they were careful not to annoy him, because the majority understood that his passivity was not that of a hero taking his ease but that of a cataclysm in repose.

Father Gonzaga held back the crowd's frivolity with formulas of maidservant inspiration while awaiting the arrival of a final judgment on the nature of the captive. But the mail from Rome showed no sense of urgency. They spent their time finding out if the prisoner had a navel, if his dialect had any connection with Aramaic, how many times he could fit on the head of a pin, or whether he wasn't just a Norwegian with wings. Those meager letters might have come and gone until the end of time if a providential event had not put an end to the priest's tribulations.

It so happened that during those days, among so many other carnival attractions, there arrived in town the traveling show of the woman who had been changed into a spider for having disobeyed her parents. The admission to see her was not only less than the admission to see the angel, but people were permitted to ask her all manner of questions about her absurd state and to examine her up and down so that no one would ever doubt the truth of her horror. She was a frightful tarantula the size of a ram and with the head of a sad maiden. What was most heart-rending, however, was not her outlandish shape but the sincere affliction with which she recounted the details of her misfortune. While still practically a child she had sneaked out of her parents' house to go to a dance, and while she was coming back through the woods after having danced all night without permission, a fearful thunderclap rent the sky in two and through the crack came the lightning bolt of brimstone that changed her into a spider. Her only nourishment came from the meatballs that charitable souls chose to toss into her mouth. A spectacle like that, full of so much human truth and with such a fearful lesson, was bound to defeat without even trying that of a haughty angel who scarcely deigned to look at mortals. Besides, the few miracles attributed to the angel showed a certain mental disorder, like the blind man who didn't recover his sight but grew three new teeth, or the paralytic who didn't get to walk but almost won the lottery, and the leper whose sores sprouted sunflowers. Those consolation miracles, which were more like mocking fun, had already ruined the angel's reputation when the woman who had been changed into a spider finally crushed him completely. That was how Father Gonzaga was cured forever of his insomnia and Pelayo's courtyard went back to being as empty as during the time it had rained for three days and crabs walked through the bedrooms.

The owners of the house had no reason to lament. With the money they saved they built a two-story mansion with balconies and gardens and high netting so that crabs wouldn't get in during the winter, and with iron bars on the windows so that angels wouldn't get in. Pelayo also set up a rabbit warren close to town and gave up his job as bailiff for good, and Elisenda bought some satin pumps with high heels and many dresses of iridescent silk, the kind worn on Sunday by the most desirable women in those times. The chicken coop was the only thing that didn't receive any attention. If they washed it down with creolin and burned tears of myrrh inside it every so often, it was not in homage to the angel but to drive away the dungheap stench that still hung everywhere like a ghost and was turning the new house into an old one. At first, when the child learned to walk, they were careful that he not get too close to the chicken coop. But then they began to lose their fears and got used to the smell, and before the child got his second teeth he'd gone inside the chicken coop to play, where the wires were falling apart. The angel was no less standoffish with him than with other mortals, but he tolerated the most ingenious infamies with the patience of a dog who had no illusions. They both came down with chicken pox at the same time. The doctor who took care of the child couldn't resist the temptation to listen to the angel's heart, and he found so much whistling in the heart and so many sounds in his kidneys that it seemed impossible for him to be alive. What surprised him most, however, was the logic of his wings. They seemed so natural on that completely human organism that he couldn't understand why other men didn't have them too.

When the child began school it had been some time since the sun and rain had caused the collapse of the chicken coop. The angel went dragging himself about here and there like a stray dying man. They would drive him out of the bedroom with a broom and a moment later find him in the kitchen. He seemed to be in so many places at the same time that they grew to think that he'd been duplicated, that he was reproducing himself all through the house, and the exasperated and unhinged Elisenda shouted that it was awful living in that hell full of angels. He could scarcely eat and his antiquarian eyes had also become so foggy that he went about bumping into posts. All he had left were the bare cannulae of his last feathers. Pelayo threw a blanket over him and extended him the charity of letting him sleep in the shed, and only then did they notice that he had a temperature at night, and was delirious with the tongue twisters of an old Norwegian. That was one of the few times they became alarmed, for they thought he was going to die and not even the wise neighbor woman had been able to tell them what to do with dead angels.

And yet he not only survived his worst winter, but seemed improved with the first sunny days. He remained motionless for several days in the farthest corner of the courtyard, where no one would see him, and at the beginning of December some large, stiff feathers began to grow on his wings, the feathers of a scarecrow, which looked more like another misfortune of decrepitude. But he must have known the reason for those changes, for he was quite careful that no one should notice them, that no one should hear the sea chanteys that he sometimes sang under the stars. One morning Elisenda was cutting some bunches of onions for lunch when a wind that seemed to come from the high seas blew into the kitchen. Then she went to the window and caught the angel in his first attempts at flight. They were so clumsy that his fingernails opened a furrow in the vegetable patch and he was on the point of knocking the shed down with the ungainly flapping that slipped on the light and couldn't get a grip on the air. But he did manage to gain altitude. Elisenda let out a sigh of relief, for herself and for him, when she saw him pass over the last houses, holding himself up in some way with the risky flapping of a senile vulture. She kept watching him even when she was through cutting the onions and she kept on watching until it was no longer possible for her to see him, because then he was no longer an annoyance in her life but an imaginary dot on the horizon of the sea.

(translated by Gregory Rabassa)

QUESTIONS FOR DISCUSSION AND WRITING

1. The central figure of the story apparently really *is* an angel, despite the villagers' reactions to him and his less-than-clean appearance. Why is it that everyone in the story, including the priest, finds it so difficult to believe that this really is an angel? Is theirs a failure of imagination? Of faith? Does it tell us something about the modern world? About religion? Finally, how do the story's style, descriptions, and title contribute to our sense that this is or isn't a real angel?

2. When Pelayo first comes upon the angel, he is "frightened by that nightmare." Why would he consider it a nightmare, rather than a more pleasant dream or illusion? Why would the wise old neighbor woman consider the angel one of the "fugitive survivors of a celestial conspiracy," in other words, a "fallen angel," or demon? Where do we see the old man viewed as demon/monster and where as a spiritual hero/angel?

3. Look at what happens to Pelayo, Elisenda, and their son after the angel comes to live with them. To what extent do we consider the angel a bringer of good? How do we respond to the family's treatment of the angel?

4. Why, finally, does the angel leave? Why, indeed, does he stay as long as he does?

5. What do we make of the contrast between the angel and the spider woman, whom the villagers find even more intriguing?
6. Is this, as the subtitle indicates, "a tale for children"? In what ways does the subtitle seem appropriate and inappropriate?

FLANNERY O'CONNOR (1925–1964)
A Good Man Is Hard to Find   1955

The grandmother didn't want to go to Florida. She wanted to visit some of her connections in east Tennessee and she was seizing at every chance to change Bailey's mind. Bailey was the son she lived with, her only boy. He was sitting on the edge of his chair at the table, bent over the orange sports section of the *Journal*. "Now look here, Bailey," she said, "see here, read this," and she stood with one hand on her thin hip and the other rattling the newspaper at his bald head. "Here this fellow that calls himself The Misfit is aloose from the Federal Pen and headed toward Florida and you read here what it says he did to these people. Just you read it. I wouldn't take my children in any direction with a criminal like that aloose in it. I couldn't answer to my conscience if I did."

Bailey didn't look up from his reading so she wheeled around then and faced the children's mother, a young woman in slacks, whose face was as broad and innocent as a cabbage and was tied around with a green head-kerchief that had two points on the top like a rabbit's ears. She was sitting on the sofa, feeding the baby his apricots out of a jar. "The children have been to Florida before," the old lady said. "You all ought to take them somewhere else for a change so they would see different parts of the world and be broad. They never have been to east Tennessee."

The children's mother didn't seem to hear her but the eight-year-old boy, John Wesley, a stocky child with glasses, said, "If you don't want to go to Florida, why dontcha stay at home?" He and the little girl, June Star, were reading the funny papers on the floor.

"She wouldn't stay at home to be queen for a day," June Star said without raising her yellow head.

"Yes and what would you do if this fellow, The Misfit, caught you?" the grandmother asked.

"I'd smack his face," John Wesley said.

"She wouldn't stay at home for a million bucks," June Star said. "Afraid she'd miss something. She has to go everywhere we go."

"All right, Miss," the grandmother said. "Just remember that the next time you want me to curl your hair."

June Star said her hair was naturally curly.

The next morning the grandmother was the first one in the car, ready to go. She had her big black valise that looked like the head of a hippopotamus in one corner, and underneath it she was hiding a basket with Pitty Sing, the cat, in it. She didn't intend for the cat to be left alone in the house for three days because he would miss her too much and she was afraid he might brush against one of the gas burners and accidentally asphyxiate himself. Her son, Bailey, didn't like to arrive at a motel with a cat.

She sat in the middle of the back seat with John Wesley and June Star on either side of her. Bailey and the children's mother and the baby sat in front and they left Atlanta at eight forty-five with the mileage on the car at 55890. The grandmother wrote this down because she thought it would be interesting to say how many miles they had been when they got back. It took them twenty minutes to reach the outskirts of the city.

The old lady settled herself comfortably, removing her white cotton gloves and putting them up with her purse on the shelf in front of the back window. The children's mother still had on slacks and still had her head tied up in a green kerchief, but the grandmother had on a navy blue straw sailor hat with a bunch of white violets on the brim and a navy blue dress with a small white dot in the print. Her collars and cuffs were white organdy trimmed with lace and at her neckline she had pinned a purple spray of cloth violets containing a sachet. In case of an accident, anyone seeing her dead on the highway would know at once that she was a lady.

She said she thought it was going to be a good day for driving, neither too hot nor too cold, and she cautioned Bailey that the speed limit was fifty-five miles an hour and that the patrolmen hid themselves behind billboards and small clumps of trees and sped out after you before you had a chance to slow down. She pointed out interesting details of the scenery: Stone Mountain; the blue granite that in some places came up to both sides of the highway; the brilliant red clay banks slightly streaked with purple; and the various crops that made rows of green lace-work on the ground. The trees were full of silver-white sunlight and the meanest of them sparkled. The children were reading comic magazines and their mother had gone back to sleep.

"Let's go through Georgia fast so we won't have to look at it much," John Wesley said.

"If I were a little boy," said the grandmother, "I wouldn't talk about my native state that way. Tennessee has the mountains and Georgia has the hills."

"Tennessee is just a hillbilly dumping ground," John Wesley said, "and Georgia is a lousy state too."

"You said it," June Star said.

"In my time," said the grandmother, folding her thin veined fingers, "children were more respectful of their native states and their parents and everything else. People did right then. Oh look at the cute little pickaninny!" she said and pointed to a Negro child standing in the door of a shack. "Wouldn't that make a picture, now?" she asked and they all turned and looked at the little Negro out of the back window. He waved.

"He didn't have any britches on," June Star said.

"He probably didn't have any," the grandmother explained. "Little niggers in the country don't have things like we do. If I could paint, I'd paint that picture," she said.

The children exchanged comic books.

The grandmother offered to hold the baby and the children's mother passed him over the front seat to her. She set him on her knee and bounced him and told him about the things they were passing. She rolled her eyes and screwed up her mouth and stuck her leathery thin face into his smooth bland one. Occasionally he gave her a faraway smile. They passed a large cotton field with five or six graves fenced in the middle of it, like a small island. "Look at the graveyard!" the grandmother said, pointing it out. "That was the old family burying ground. That belonged to the plantation."

"Where's the plantation?" John Wesley asked.

"Gone With the Wind," said the grandmother. "Ha. Ha."

When the children finished all the comic books they had brought, they opened the lunch and ate it. The grandmother ate a peanut butter sandwich and an olive and would not let the children throw the box and the paper napkins out the window. When there was nothing else to do they played a game by choosing a cloud and making the other two guess what shape it suggested. John Wesley took one of the shape of a cow and June Star guessed a cow and John Wesley said, no, an automobile, and June Star said he didn't play fair and they began to slap each other over the grandmother.

The grandmother said she would tell them a story if they would keep quiet. When she told a story, she rolled her eyes and waved her head and was very dramatic. She said once when she was a maiden lady she had been courted by a Mr. Edgar Atkins Teagarden from Jasper, Georgia. She said he was a very good-looking man and a gentleman and that he brought her a watermelon every Saturday afternoon with his initials cut in it, E. A. T. Well, one Saturday, she said, Mr. Teagarden brought the watermelon and there was nobody at home and he left it on the front porch and returned in his buggy to Jasper, but she never got the watermelon, she said, because a nigger boy ate it when he saw the initials, E. A. T.! This story tickled John Wesley's funny bone and he giggled and giggled but June Star didn't think it was any good. She said she wouldn't marry a man that just brought her a watermelon on Saturday. The grandmother said she would have done well to marry Mr. Teagarden because he was a gentleman and had bought Coca-Cola stock when it first came out and that he had died only a few years ago, a very wealthy man.

They stopped at The Tower for barbecued sandwiches. The Tower was a part stucco and part wood filling station and dance hall set in a clearing outside of Timothy. A fat man named Red Sammy Butts ran it and there were signs stuck here and there on the building and for miles up and down the highway saying, TRY RED SAMMY'S FAMOUS BARBECUE. NONE LIKE FAMOUS RED SAMMY'S! RED SAM! THE FAT BOY WITH THE HAPPY LAUGH! A VETERAN! RED SAMMY'S YOUR MAN!

Red Sammy was lying on the bare ground outside The Tower with his head under a truck while a gray monkey about a foot high, chained to a small chinaberry tree, chattered nearby. The monkey sprang back into the tree and got on the highest limb as soon as he saw the children jump out of the car and run toward him.

Inside, The Tower was a long dark room with a counter at one end and tables at the other and dancing space in the middle. They sat down at a board table next to the nickelodeon and Red Sam's wife, a tall burnt-brown woman with hair and eyes lighter than her skin, came and took their order. The children's mother put a dime in the machine and played "The Tennessee Waltz," and the grandmother said that tune always made her want to dance. She asked Bailey if he would like to dance but he only glared at her. He didn't have a naturally sunny disposition like she did and trips made him nervous. The grandmother's brown eyes were very bright. She swayed her head from side to side and pretended she was dancing in her chair. June Star said play something she could tap to so the children's mother put in another dime and played a fast number and June Star stepped out onto the dance floor and did her tap routine.

"Ain't she cute?" Red Sam's wife said, leaning over the counter. "Would you like to come be my little girl?"

"No I certainly wouldn't," June Star said. "I wouldn't live in a broken-down place like this for a million bucks!" and she ran back to the table.

"Ain't she cute?" the woman repeated, stretching her mouth politely.

"Aren't you ashamed?" hissed the grandmother.

Red Sam came in and told his wife to quit lounging on the counter and hurry up with these people's order. His khaki trousers reached just to his hip bones and his stomach hung over them like a sack of meal swaying under his shirt. He came over and sat down at a table nearby and let out a combination sigh and yodel. "You can't win," he said. "You can't win," and he wiped his sweating red face off with a gray handkerchief. "These days you don't know who to trust," he said. "Ain't that the truth?"

"People are certainly not nice like they used to be," said the grandmother.

"Two fellers come in here last week," Red Sammy said, "driving a Chrysler. It was a old beat-up car but it was a good one and these boys looked all right to me. Said they worked at the mill and you know I let them fellers charge the gas they bought? Now why did I do that?"

"Because you're a good man!" the grandmother said at once.

"Yes'm, I suppose so," Red Sam said as if he were struck with this answer.

His wife brought the orders, carrying the five plates all at once without a tray, two in each hand and one balanced on her arm. "It isn't a soul in this green world of God's that you can trust," she said. "And I don't count nobody out of that, not nobody," she repeated, looking at Red Sammy.

"Did you read about that criminal, The Misfit, that's escaped?" asked the grandmother.

"I wouldn't be a bit surprised if he didn't attact this place right here," said the woman. "If he hears about it being here, I wouldn't be none surprised to see him. If he hears it's two cent in the cash register, I wouldn't be a tall surprised if he . . ."

"That'll do," Red Sam said. "Go bring these people their Co'-Colas," and the woman went off to get the rest of the order.

"A good man is hard to find," Red Sammy said. "Everything is getting terrible. I remember the day you could go off and leave your screen door unlatched. Not no more."

He and the grandmother discussed better times. The old lady said that in her opinion Europe was entirely to blame for the way things were now. She said the way Europe acted you would think we were made of money and Red Sam said it was no use talking about it, she was exactly right. The children ran outside into the white sunlight and looked at the monkey in the lacy chinaberry tree. He was busy catching fleas on himself and biting each one carefully between his teeth as if it were a delicacy.

They drove off again into the hot afternoon. The grandmother took cat naps and woke up every few minutes with her own snoring. Outside of Toombsboro she woke up and recalled an old plantation that she had visited in this neighborhood once when she was a young lady. She said the house had six white columns across the front and that there was an avenue of oaks leading up to it and two little wooden trellis arbors on either side in front where you sat down with your suitor after a stroll in the garden. She recalled exactly which road to turn off to get to it. She knew that Bailey would not be willing to lose any time looking at an old house, but the more she talked about it, the more she wanted to see it once again and find out if the little twin arbors were still standing. "There was a secret panel in this house," she said craftily, not telling the truth but wishing that she were, "and the story went that all the family silver was hidden in it when Sherman came through but it was never found . . ."

"Hey!" John Wesley said. "Let's go see it! We'll find it! We'll poke all the wood-work and find it! Who lives there? Where do you turn off at? Hey Pop, can't we turn off there?"

"We never have seen a house with a secret panel!" June Star shrieked. "Let's go to the house with the secret panel! Hey Pop, can't we go see the house with the se-cret panel!"

"It's not far from here, I know," the grandmother said. "It wouldn't take over twenty minutes."

Bailey was looking straight ahead. His jaw was as rigid as a horseshoe. "No," he said.

The children began to yell and scream that they wanted to see the house with the secret panel. John Wesley kicked the back of the front seat and June Star hung over her mother's shoulder and whined desperately into her ear that they never had any fun even on their vacation, that they could never do what THEY wanted to do. The baby began to scream and John Wesley kicked the back of the seat so hard that his father could feel the blows in his kidney.

"All right!" he shouted and drew the car to a stop at the side of the road. "Will you all shut up? Will you all just shut up for one second? If you don't shut up, we won't go anywhere."

"It would be very educational for them," the grandmother murmured.

"All right," Bailey said, "but get this: this is the only time we're going to stop for anything like this. This is the one and only time."

"The dirt road that you have to turn down is about a mile back," the grand-mother directed. "I marked it when we passed."

"A dirt road," Bailey groaned.

After they had turned around and were headed toward the dirt road, the grand-mother recalled other points about the house, the beautiful glass over the front door-way and the candle-lamp in the hall. John Wesley said that the secret panel was probably in the fireplace.

"You can't go inside this house," Bailey said. "You don't know who lives there."

"While you all talk to the people in front, I'll run around behind and get in a window," John Wesley suggested.

"We'll all stay in the car," his mother said.

They turned onto the dirt road and the car raced roughly along in a swirl of pink dust. The grandmother recalled the times when there were no paved roads and thirty miles was a day's journey. The dirt road was hilly and there were sudden washes in it and sharp curves on dangerous embankments. All at once they would be on a hill, looking down over the blue tops of trees for miles around, then the next minute, they would be in a red depression with the dust-coated trees looking down on them.

"This place had better turn up in a minute," Bailey said, "or I'm going to turn around."

The road looked as if no one had traveled on it in months.

"It's not much farther," the grandmother said and just as she said it, a horrible thought came to her. The thought was so embarrassing that she turned red in the face and her eyes dilated and her feet jumped up, upsetting her valise in the corner. The instant the valise moved, the newspaper top she had over the basket under it rose with a snarl and Pitty Sing, the cat, sprang onto Bailey's shoulder.

The children were thrown to the floor and their mother, clutching the baby, was thrown out the door onto the ground; the old lady was thrown into the front seat. The car turned over once and landed right-side-up in a gulch off the side of the road. Bailey remained in the driver's seat with the cat—gray-striped with a broad white face and an orange nose—clinging to his neck like a caterpillar.

As soon as the children saw they could move their arms and legs, they scrambled out of the car, shouting, "We've had an ACCIDENT!" The grandmother was curled up under the dashboard, hoping she was injured so that Bailey's wrath would not come down on her all at once. The horrible thought she had had before the accident was that the house she had remembered so vividly was not in Georgia but in Tennessee.

Bailey removed the cat from his neck with both hands and flung it out the window against the side of a pine tree. Then he got out of the car and started looking for the children's mother. She was sitting against the side of the red gutted ditch, holding the screaming baby, but she only had a cut down her face and a broken shoulder. "We've had an ACCIDENT!" the children screamed in a frenzy of delight.

"But nobody's killed," June Star said with disappointment as the grandmother limped out of the car, her hat still pinned to her head but the broken front brim standing up at a jaunty angle and the violet spray hanging off the side. They all sat down in the ditch, except the children, to recover from the shock. They were all shaking.

"Maybe a car will come along," said the children's mother hoarsely.

"I believe I have injured an organ," said the grandmother, pressing her side, but no one answered her. Bailey's teeth were clattering. He had on a yellow sport shirt with bright blue parrots designed in it and his face was as yellow as the shirt. The grandmother decided that she would not mention that the house was in Tennessee.

The road was about ten feet above and they could see only the tops of the trees on the other side of it. Behind the ditch they were sitting in there were more woods, tall and dark and deep. In a few minutes they saw a car some distance away on top of a hill, coming slowly as if the occupants were watching them. The grandmother stood up and waved both arms dramatically to attract their attention. The car continued to come on slowly, disappeared around a bend and appeared again, moving even slower, on top of the hill they had gone over. It was a big black battered hearse-like automobile. There were three men in it.

It came to a stop just over them and for some minutes, the driver looked down with a steady expressionless gaze to where they were sitting, and didn't speak. Then he turned his head and muttered something to the other two and they got out. One was a fat boy in black trousers and a red sweat shirt with a silver stallion embossed on the front of it. He moved around on the right side of them and stood staring, his mouth partly open in a kind of loose grin. The other had on khaki pants and a blue striped coat and a gray hat pulled down very low, hiding most of his face. He came around slowly on the left side. Neither spoke.

The driver got out of the car and stood by the side of it, looking down at them. He was an older man than the other two. His hair was just beginning to gray and he wore silver-rimmed spectacles that gave him a scholarly look. He had a long creased face and didn't have on any shirt or undershirt. He had on blue jeans that were too tight for him and was holding a black hat and a gun. The two boys also had guns.

"We've had an ACCIDENT!" the children screamed.

The grandmother had the peculiar feeling that the bespectacled man was someone she knew. His face was as familiar to her as if she had known him all her life but she could not recall who he was. He moved away from the car and began to come down the embankment, placing his feet carefully so that he wouldn't slip. He had on tan and white shoes and no socks, and his ankles were red and thin. "Good afternoon," he said. "I see you all had you a little spill."

"We turned over twice!" said the grandmother.

"Oncet," he corrected. "We seen it happen. Try their car and see will it run, Hiram," he said quietly to the boy with the gray hat.

"What you got that gun for?" John Wesley asked. "Whatcha gonna do with that gun?"

"Lady," the man said to the children's mother, "would you mind calling them children to sit down by you? Children make me nervous. I want all you to sit down right together there where you're at."

"What are you telling US what to do for?" June Star asked.

Behind them the line of woods gaped like a dark open mouth. "Come here," said their mother.

"Look here now," Bailey began suddenly, "we're in a predicament! We're in . . ."

The grandmother shrieked. She scrambled to her feet and stood staring. "You're The Misfit!" she said. "I recognized you at once!"

"Yes'm," the man said, smiling slightly as if he were pleased in spite of himself to be known, "but it would have been better for all of you, lady, if you hadn't of reckernized me."

Bailey turned his head sharply and said something to his mother that shocked even the children. The old lady began to cry and The Misfit reddened.

"Lady," he said, "don't you get upset. Sometimes a man says things he don't mean. I don't reckon he meant to talk to you thataway."

"You wouldn't shoot a lady, would you?" the grandmother said and removed a clean handkerchief from her cuff and began to slap at her eyes with it.

The Misfit pointed the toe of his shoe into the ground and made a little hole and then covered it up again. "I would hate to have to," he said.

"Listen," the grandmother almost screamed, "I know you're a good man. You don't look a bit like you have common blood. I know you must come from nice people!"

"Yes mam," he said, "finest people in the world." When he smiled he showed a row of strong white teeth. "God never made a finer woman than my mother and my daddy's heart was pure gold," he said. The boy with the red sweat shirt had come around behind them and was standing with his gun at his hip. The Misfit squatted down on the ground. "Watch them children, Bobby Lee," he said. "You know they make me nervous." He looked at the six of them huddled together in front of him and he seemed to be embarrassed as if he couldn't think of anything to say. "Ain't a cloud in the sky," he remarked, looking up at it. "Don't see no sun but don't see no cloud neither."

"Yes, it's a beautiful day," said the grandmother. "Listen," she said, "you shouldn't call yourself The Misfit because I know you're a good man at heart. I can just look at you and tell."

"Hush!" Bailey yelled. "Hush! Everybody shut up and let me handle this!" He was squatting in the position of a runner about to sprint forward but he didn't move.

"I pre-chate that, lady," The Misfit said and drew a little circle in the ground with the butt of his gun.

"It'll take a half a hour to fix this here car," Hiram called, looking over the raised hood of it.

"Well, first you and Bobby Lee get him and that little boy to step over yonder with you," The Misfit said, pointing to Bailey and John Wesley. "The boys want to ast you something," he said to Bailey. "Would you mind stepping back in them woods there with them?"

"Listen," Bailey began, "we're in a terrible predicament! Nobody realizes what this is," his voice cracked. His eyes were as blue and intense as the parrots in his shirt and he remained perfectly still.

The grandmother reached up to adjust her hat brim as if she were going to the woods with him but it came off in her hand. She stood staring at it and after a second she let it fall on the ground. Hiram pulled Bailey up by the arm as if he were assisting an old man. John Wesley caught hold of his father's hand and Bobby Lee followed. They went off toward the woods and just as they reached the dark edge, Bailey turned and supporting himself against a gray naked pine trunk, he shouted, "I'll be back in a minute, Mamma, wait on me!"

"Come back this instant!" his mother shrilled but they all disappeared into the woods.

"Bailey Boy!" the grandmother called in a tragic voice but she found she was looking at The Misfit squatting on the ground in front of her. "I just know you're a good man," she said desperately. "You're not a bit common!"

"Nome, I ain't a good man," The Misfit said after a second as if he had considered her statement carefully, "but I ain't the worst in the world neither. My daddy said I was a different breed of dog from my brothers and sisters. 'You know,' Daddy said, 'it's some that can live their whole life out without asking about it and it's others has to know why it is, and this boy is one of the latters. He's going to be into everything!'" He put on his black hat and looked up suddenly and then away deep into the woods as if he were embarrassed again. "I'm sorry I don't have on a shirt before you ladies," he said, hunching his shoulders slightly. "We buried our clothes that we had on when we escaped and we're just making do until we can get better. We borrowed these from some folks we met," he explained.

"That's perfectly all right," the grandmother said. "Maybe Bailey has an extra shirt in his suitcase."

"I'll look and see terrectly," The Misfit said.

"Where are they taking him?" the children's mother screamed.

"Daddy was a card himself," The Misfit said. "You couldn't put anything over on him. He never got in trouble with the Authorities though. Just had the knack of handling them."

"You could be honest too if you'd only try," said the grandmother. "Think how wonderful it would be to settle down and live a comfortable life and not have to think about somebody chasing you all the time."

The Misfit kept scratching in the ground with the butt of his gun as if he were thinking about it. "Yes'm, somebody is always after you," he murmured.

The grandmother noticed how thin his shoulder blades were just behind his hat because she was standing up looking down on him. "Do you ever pray?" she asked.

He shook his head. All she saw was the black hat wiggle between his shoulder blades. "Nome," he said.

There was a pistol shot from the woods, followed closely by another. Then silence. The old lady's head jerked around. She could hear the wind move through the tree tops like a long satisfied insuck of breath. "Bailey Boy!" she called.

"I was a gospel singer for a while," The Misfit said. "I been most everything. Been in the arm service, both land and sea, at home and abroad, been twice married, been an undertaker, been with the railroads, plowed Mother Earth, been in a tornado, seen a man burnt alive oncet," and looked up at the children's mother and the little girl who were sitting close together, their faces white and their eyes glassy; "I even seen a woman flogged," he said.

"Pray, pray," the grandmother began, "pray, pray . . ."

"I never was a bad boy that I remember of," The Misfit said in an almost dreamy voice, "but somewheres along the line I done something wrong and got sent to the penitentiary. I was buried alive," and he looked up and held her attention to him by a steady stare.

"That's when you should have started to pray," she said. "What did you do to get sent to the penitentiary that first time?"

"Turn to the right, it was a wall," The Misfit said, looking up again at the cloudless sky. "Turn to the left, it was a wall. Look up it was a ceiling, look down it was a floor. I forget what I done, lady. I set there and set there, trying to remember what it was I done and I ain't recalled it to this day. Oncet in a while, I would think it was coming to me, but it never come."

"Maybe they put you in by mistake," the old lady said vaguely.

"Nome," he said. "It wasn't no mistake. They had the papers on me."

"You must have stolen something," she said.

The Misfit sneered slightly. "Nobody had nothing I wanted," he said. "It was a head-doctor at the penitentiary said what I had done was kill my daddy but I know that for a lie. My daddy died in nineteen ought nineteen of the epidemic flu and I never had a thing to do with it. He was buried in the Mount Hopewell Baptist churchyard and you can go there and see for yourself."

"If you would pray," the old lady said, "Jesus would help you."

"That's right," The Misfit said.

"Well then, why don't you pray?" she asked trembling with delight suddenly.

"I don't want no hep," he said. "I'm doing all right by myself."

Bobby Lee and Hiram came ambling back from the woods. Bobby Lee was dragging a yellow shirt with bright blue parrots in it.

"Throw me that shirt, Bobby Lee," The Misfit said. The shirt came flying at him and landed on his shoulder and he put it on. The grandmother couldn't name what the shirt reminded her of. "No, lady," The Misfit said while he was buttoning it up, "I found out the crime don't matter. You can do one thing or you can do another, kill a man or take a tire off his car, because sooner or later you're going to forget what it was you done and just be punished for it."

The children's mother had begun to make heaving noises as if she couldn't get her breath. "Lady," he asked, "would you and that little girl like to step off yonder with Bobby Lee and Hiram and join your husband?"

"Yes, thank you," the mother said faintly. Her left arm dangled helplessly and she was holding the baby, who had gone to sleep, in the other. "Hep that lady up, Hiram," The Misfit said as she struggled to climb out of the ditch, "and Bobby Lee, you hold onto that little girl's hand."

"I don't want to hold hands with him," June Star said. "He reminds me of a pig."

The fat boy blushed and laughed and caught her by the arm and pulled her off into the woods after Hiram and her mother.

Alone with The Misfit, the grandmother found that she had lost her voice. There was not a cloud in the sky nor any sun. There was nothing around her but woods. She wanted to tell him that he must pray. She opened and closed her mouth several times before anything came out. Finally she found herself saying, "Jesus, Jesus," meaning, Jesus will help you, but the way she was saying it, it sounded as if she might be cursing.

"Yes'm," The Misfit said as if he agreed. "Jesus thrown everything off balance. It was the same case with Him as with me except He hadn't committed any crime and they could prove I had committed one because they had the papers on me. Of course," he said, "they never shown me my papers. That's why I sign myself now. I said long ago, you get you a signature and sign everything you do and keep a copy of it. Then you'll know what you done and you can hold up the crime to the punishment and see do they match and in the end you'll have something to prove you ain't been treated right. I call myself The Misfit," he said, "because I can't make what all I done wrong fit what all I gone through in punishment."

There was a piercing scream from the woods, followed closely by a pistol report. "Does it seem right to you, lady, that one is punished a heap and another ain't punished at all?"

"Jesus!" the old lady cried. "You've got good blood! I know you wouldn't shoot a lady! I know you come from nice people! Pray! Jesus, you ought not to shoot a lady. I'll give you all the money I've got!"

"Lady," The Misfit said, looking beyond her far into the woods, "there never was a body that give the undertaker a tip."

There were two more pistol reports and the grandmother raised her head like a parched old turkey hen crying for water and called, "Bailey Boy, Bailey Boy!" as if her heart would break.

"Jesus was the only One that ever raised the dead," The Misfit continued, "and He shouldn't have done it. He thrown everything off balance. If He did what He said, then it's nothing for you to do but throw away everything and follow Him, and if He didn't, then it's nothing for you to do but enjoy the few minutes you got left the best way you can—by killing somebody or burning down his house or doing some other meanness to him. No pleasure but meanness," he said and his voice had become almost a snarl.

"Maybe He didn't raise the dead," the old lady mumbled, not knowing what she was saying and feeling so dizzy that she sank down in the ditch with her legs twisted under her.

"I wasn't there so I can't say He didn't," The Misfit said. "I wisht I had of been there," he said, hitting the ground with his fist. "It ain't right I wasn't there because if I had of been there I would of known. Listen lady," he said in a high voice, "if I had of been there I would of known and I wouldn't be like I am now." His voice seemed about to crack and the grandmother's head cleared for an instant. She saw the man's face twisted close to her own as if he were going to cry and she murmured, "Why you're one of my babies. You're one of my own children!" She reached out and touched him on the shoulder. The Misfit sprang back as if a snake had bitten him and shot her three times through the chest. Then he put his gun down on the ground and took off his glasses and began to clean them.

Hiram and Bobby Lee returned from the woods and stood over the ditch, looking down at the grandmother who half sat and half lay in a puddle of blood with her legs crossed under her like a child's and her face smiling up at the cloudless sky.

Without his glasses, The Misfit's eyes were red-rimmed and pale and defenseless looking. "Take her off and throw her where you thrown the others," he said, picking up the cat that was rubbing itself against his leg.

"She was a talker, wasn't she?" Bobby Lee said, sliding down the ditch with a yodel.

"She would have been a good woman," The Misfit said, "if it had been somebody there to shoot her every minute of her life."

"Some fun!" Bobby Lee said.

"Shut up, Bobby Lee," The Misfit said. "It's no real pleasure in life."

QUESTIONS FOR DISCUSSION AND WRITING

1. For the most part, the story stays with the grandmother's point of view. How would you describe the grandmother? Why is such an important character unnamed? Are there ways in which her actions might be seen as heroic? As monstrous?

2. On a second reading, a reader discovers that the ending is foreshadowed. What hints are given that the ending will be horrifying?

3. Flannery O'Connor was a devout Roman Catholic, and she saw her stories as embodying her spiritual values. In the story, the grandmother and The Misfit have a discussion about religion. How would you characterize their religious points of view? What religious point of view does O'Connor seem to be advocating?

4. By calling the murderer "a misfit," the story seems to suggest that he is *not* a monster. Where do you see attempts to make The Misfit understandable, perhaps even sympathetic? How sympathetic did you feel toward him?

5. The title asks us to focus on "a good man." What does the story tell us about "a good man" or "a good woman"? Who in the story might be defined as "good"?

6. Why does the grandmother see The Misfit as one of her own children—and why does The Misfit kill her when she says that?

EDGAR ALLAN POE (1809–1849)

The Tell-Tale Heart _____ *1843, 1850*

True!—nervous—very, very dreadfully nervous I had been and am; but why *will* you say that I am mad? The disease had sharpened my senses—not destroyed—not dulled them. Above all was the sense of hearing acute. I heard all things in the heaven and in the earth. I heard things in hell. How, then, am I mad? Hearken! and observe how healthily—how calmly I can tell you the whole story.

It is impossible to say how first the idea entered my brain; but once conceived, it haunted me day and night. Object there was none. Passion there was none. I loved the old man. He had never wronged me. He had never given me insult. For his gold I had no desire. I think it was his eye! yes, it was this! One of his eyes resembled that of a vulture—a pale blue eye, with a film over it. Whenever it fell upon me, my blood ran cold; and so by degrees—very gradually—I made up my mind to take the life of the old man, and thus rid myself of the eye for ever.

Now this is the point. You fancy me mad. Madmen know nothing. But you should have seen *me*. You should have seen how wisely I proceeded—with what caution—with what foresight—with what dissimulation I went to work! I was never kinder to the old man than during the whole week before I killed him. And every night, about midnight, I turned the latch of his door and opened it—oh, so gently! And then, when I had made an opening sufficient for my head, I put in a dark lantern, all closed, closed, so that no light shone out, and then I thrust in my head. Oh, you would have laughed to see how cunningly I thrust it in! I moved it slowly—very, very slowly, so that I might not disturb the old man's sleep. It took me an hour to place my whole head within the opening so far that I could see him as he lay upon his bed. Ha!—would a madman have been so wise as this? And then, when my head was well in the room, I undid the lantern cautiously—oh, so cautiously—cautiously (for the hinges creaked)—I undid it just so much that a single thin ray fell upon the vulture eye. And this I did for seven long nights—every night just at midnight—but I found the eye always closed; and so it was impossible to do the work; for it was not the old man who vexed me, but his Evil Eye. And every morning, when the day broke, I went boldly into the chamber, and spoke courageously to him, calling him by name in a hearty tone, and inquiring how he had passed the night. So you see he would have been a very profound old man, indeed, to suspect that every night, just at twelve, I looked in upon him while he slept.

Upon the eighth night I was more than usually cautious in opening the door. A watch's minute hand moves more quickly than did mine. Never before that night had I *felt* the extent of my own powers—of my sagacity. I could scarcely contain my feelings of triumph. To think that there I was, opening the door, little by little, and he not even to dream of my secret deeds or thoughts. I fairly chuckled at the idea; and perhaps he heard me; for he moved on the bed suddenly, as if startled. Now you may think that I drew back—but no. His room was as black as pitch with the thick darkness (for the shutters were close fastened, through fear of robbers), and so I knew that he could not see the opening of the door, and I kept pushing it on steadily, steadily.

I had my head in, and was about to open the lantern, when my thumb slipped upon the tin fastening, and the old man sprang up in the bed, crying out—"Who's there?"

I kept quite still and said nothing. For a whole hour I did not move a muscle, and in the meantime I did not hear him lie down. He was still sitting up in the bed, listening—just as I have done, night after night, hearkening to the death watches in the wall.

Presently I heard a slight groan, and I knew it was the groan of mortal terror. It was not a groan of pain or of grief—oh, no!—it was the low stifled sound that arises from the bottom of the soul when overcharged with awe. I knew the sound very well. Many a night, just at midnight, when all the world slept, it has welled up from my own bosom, deepening, with its dreadful echo, the terrors that distracted me. I say I knew it well. I knew what the old man felt, and pitied him, although I chuckled at heart. I knew that he had been lying awake ever since the first slight noise, when he had turned in the bed. His fears had been ever since growing upon him. He had been trying to fancy them causeless, but could not. He had been saying to himself—"It is nothing but the wind in the chimney—it is only a mouse crossing the floor," or "it is merely a cricket which has made a single chirp." Yes, he had been trying to comfort himself with these suppositions; but he had found all in vain. *All in vain;* because Death, in approaching him, had stalked with his black shadow before him, and enveloped the victim. And it was the mournful influence of the unperceived shadow that caused him to feel—although he neither saw nor heard—to *feel* the presence of my head within the room.

When I had waited a long time, very patiently, without hearing him lie down, I resolved to open a little—a very, very little crevice in the lantern. So I opened it—you cannot imagine how stealthily, stealthily—until, at length, a single dim ray, like the thread of the spider, shot from out the crevice and fell upon the vulture eye.

It was open—wide, wide open—and I grew furious as I gazed upon it. I saw it with perfect distinctness—all a dull blue, with a hideous veil over it that chilled the very marrow in my bones; but I could see nothing else of the old man's face or person: for I had directed the ray as if by instinct, precisely upon the damned spot.

And now have I not told you that what you mistake for madness is but over-acuteness of the senses?—now, I say, there came to my ears a low, dull, quick sound, such as a watch makes when enveloped in cotton. I knew *that* sound well, too. It was the beating of the old man's heart. It increased my fury, as the beating of a drum stimulates the soldier into courage.

But even yet I refrained and kept still. I scarcely breathed. I held the lantern motionless. I tried how steadily I could maintain the ray upon the eye. Meantime the hellish tattoo of the heart increased. It grew quicker and quicker, and louder and louder every instant. The old man's terror *must* have been extreme! It grew louder, I say, louder every moment!—do you mark me well? I have told you that I am nervous: so I am. And now at the dead hour of the night, amid the dreadful silence of that old house, so strange a noise as this excited me to uncontrollable terror. Yet, for some minutes longer I refrained and stood still. But the beating grew louder, louder! I thought the heart must burst. And now a new anxiety seized me—the sound would be heard by a neighbor! The old man's hour had come! With a loud yell, I threw open the lantern and leaped into the room. He shrieked once—once only. In an instant I dragged him to the floor, and pulled the heavy bed over him. I then smiled gaily, to find the deed so far done. But, for many minutes, the heart beat on with a muffled sound. This, however, did not vex me; it would not be heard through the wall. At length it ceased. The old man was dead. I removed the bed and examined the corpse. Yes, he was stone, stone dead. I placed my hand upon the heart and held it there many minutes. There was no pulsation. He was stone dead. His eye would trouble me no more.

If still you think me mad, you will think so no longer when I describe the wise precautions I took for the concealment of the body. The night waned, and I worked hastily, but in silence. First of all I dismembered the corpse. I cut off the head and the arms and the legs.

I then took up three planks from the flooring of the chamber, and deposited all between the scantlings. I then replaced the boards so cleverly, so cunningly, that no human eye—not even *his*—could have detected anything wrong. There was nothing to wash out—no stain of any kind—no bloodspot whatever. I had been too wary for that. A tub had caught all—ha! ha!

When I had made an end of these labors, it was four o'clock—still dark as midnight. As the bell sounded the hour, there came a knocking at the street door. I went down to open it with a light heart,—for what had I *now* to fear? There entered three men, who introduced themselves, with perfect suavity, as officers of the police. A shriek had been heard by a neighbor during the night; suspicion of foul play had been aroused; information had been lodged at the police office, and they (the officers) had been deputed to search the premises.

I smiled,—for *what* had I to fear? I bade the gentlemen welcome. The shriek, I said, was my own in a dream. The old man, I mentioned, was absent in the country. I took my visitors all over the house. I bade them search—search *well*. I led them, at length, to *his* chamber. I showed them his treasures, secure, undisturbed. In the enthusiasm of my confidence, I brought chairs into the room, and desired them *here* to rest from their fatigues, while I myself, in the wild audacity of my perfect triumph, placed my own seat upon the very spot beneath which reposed the corpse of the victim.

The officers were satisfied. My *manner* had convinced them. I was singularly at ease. They sat, and while I answered cheerily, they chatted of familiar things. But, ere long, I felt myself getting pale and wished them gone. My head ached, and I fancied a ringing in my ears: but still they sat and still chatted. The ringing became more distinct:—it continued and became more distinct: I talked more freely to get rid of the feeling: but it continued and gained definitiveness—until, at length, I found that the noise was *not* within my ears.

No doubt I now grew *very* pale:—but I talked more fluently, and with a heightened voice. Yet the sound increased—and what could I do? It was *a low, dull, quick sound—much such a sound as a watch makes when enveloped in cotton.* I gasped for breath—and yet the officers heard it not. I talked more quickly—more vehemently; but the noise steadily increased. I arose and argued about trifles, in a high key and with violent gesticulations; but the noise steadily increased. Why *would* they not be gone? I paced the floor to and fro with heavy strides, as if excited to fury by the observations of the men—but the noise steadily increased. Oh God! what *could* I do? I foamed—I raved—I swore! I swung the chair upon which I had been sitting, and grated it upon the boards, but the noise arose over all and continually increased. It grew louder—louder—*louder!* And still the men chatted pleasantly, and smiled. Was it possible they heard not? Almighty God!—no, no! They heard!—they suspected!—they *knew!*— they were making a mockery of my horror!—this I thought, and this I think. But anything was better than this agony! Anything was more tolerable than this derision! I could bear those hypocritical smiles no longer! I felt that I must scream or die!—and now—again!—hark! louder! louder! louder! *louder!*—

"Villains!" I shrieked, "dissemble no more! I admit the deed!—tear up the planks!—here, here!—it is the beating of his hideous heart!"

QUESTIONS FOR DISCUSSION AND WRITING

1. Because "The Tell-Tale Heart" is told from the murderer's perspective, we adopt his point of view. To what extent does that mean that we sympathize more with him than with his victim? Do we reject the narrator as monstrous or understand his point of view? If you were to retell the story from the more objective point of view of an omniscient third-person narrator, what would you gain? What would you lose?

2. The narrator of "The Tell-Tale Heart" insists that he is not mad, but his actions and narrative voice seem to indicate otherwise. What evidence of madness do you find in his behavior? His style? As you are thinking about the latter, you might want to pay special attention to the metaphors he uses and to the sounds and rhythms of his sentences.

3. Because the narrator is unreliable, we may question much of what he tells us, both about what happens and about how we should respond to it. Where in the story do you most doubt what the narrator tells us? Why?

4. In his opening characterization of himself, the narrator tells us that he has had some kind of nervous disease that has sharpened rather than destroyed his senses. Indications of those sharpened senses are apparent throughout the story, not only in his revulsion over the old man's eye but also in his descriptions of the old man and the surrounding scene. How do Poe and his narrator use description to heighten our own sensual responses to the narrative?

5. The story begins with an address to "you": "True!—nervous—very, very dreadfully nervous I had been and am; but why *will* you say that I am mad?" Who is the "you"? What is the effect of having the narrator tell his story to someone else?

6. The beating of the heart at the end of the story becomes unbearable and causes the narrator to confess. What indications, if any, do we have that the police officers suspect him of murder? Whose heart is it that is beating? (In other words, is this a horror story about a victim who refuses to die or is it a psychological horror story about a murderer's inability to escape the guilt of his deed?)

JOHN UPDIKE (1932–   )
A & P   1961

In walks these three girls in nothing but bathing suits. I'm in the third checkout slot, with my back to the door, so I don't see them until they're over by the bread. The one that caught my eye first was the one in the plaid green two-piece. She was a chunky kid, with a good tan and a sweet broad soft-looking can with those two crescents of white just under it, where the sun never seems to hit, at the top of the backs of her legs. I stood there with my hand on a box of HiHo crackers trying to remember if I rang it up or not. I ring it up again and the customer starts giving me hell. She's one of these cash-register-watchers, a witch about fifty with rouge on her cheekbones and no eyebrows, and I know it made her day to trip me up. She'd been watching cash registers for fifty years and probably never seen a mistake before.

By the time I got her feathers smoothed and her goodies into a bag—she gives me a little snort in passing, if she'd been born at the right time they would have burned her over in Salem—by the time I get her on her way the girls had circled around the bread and were coming back, without a pushcart, back my way along the counters, in the aisle between the check-outs and the Special bins. They didn't even have shoes on. There was this chunky one, with the two-piece—it was bright green and the seams on the bra were still sharp and her belly was still pretty pale so I guessed she just got it (the suit)—there was this one, with one of those chubby berry-faces, the lips all bunched together under her nose, this one, and a tall one, with black hair that hadn't quite frizzed right, and one of these sunburns right across under the eyes, and a chin that was too long—you know, the kind of girl other girls think is very "striking" and "attractive" but never quite makes it, as they very well know, which is why they like her so much—and then the third one, that wasn't quite so tall. She was the queen. She kind of led them, the other two peeking around and making their shoulders round. She didn't look around, not this queen, she just walked straight on slowly, on these long white prima donna legs. She came down a little hard on her heels, as if she didn't walk in her bare feet that much, putting down her heels and then letting the weight move along to her toes as if she was testing the floor with every step, putting a little deliberate extra action into it. You never know for sure how girls' minds work (do you really think it's a mind in there or just a little buzz like a bee in a glass jar?) but you got the idea she had talked the other two into coming in here with her, and now she was showing them how to do it, walk slow and hold yourself straight.

She had on a kind of dirty-pink—beige maybe, I don't know—bathing suit with a little nubble all over it and, what got me, the straps were down. They were off her shoulders looped loose around the cool tops of her arms, and I guess as a result the suit had slipped a little on her, so all around the top of the cloth there was this shining rim. If it hadn't been there you wouldn't have known there could have been anything whiter than those shoulders. With the straps pushed off, there was nothing between the top of the suit and the top of her head except just *her,* this clean bare plane of the top of her chest down from the shoulder bones like a dented sheet of metal tilted in the light. I mean, it was more than pretty.

She had sort of oaky hair that the sun and salt had bleached, done up in a bun that was unravelling, and a kind of prim face. Walking into the A & P with your straps down, I suppose it's the only kind of face you *can* have. She held her head so high her neck, coming up out of those white shoulders, looked kind of stretched, but I didn't mind. The longer her neck was, the more of her there was.

She must have felt in the corner of her eye me and over my shoulder Stokesie in the second slot watching, but she didn't tip. Not this queen. She kept her eyes moving across the racks, and stopped, and turned so slow it made my stomach rub the inside of my apron, and buzzed to the other two, who kind of huddled against her for relief, and they all three of them went up the cat-and-dog-food-breakfast-cereal-macaroni-rice-raisins-seasonings-spreads-spaghetti-soft-drinks-crackers-and-cookies aisle. From the third slot I look straight up this aisle to the meat counter, and I watched them all the way. The fat one with the tan sort of fumbled with the cookies, but on second thought she put the packages back. The sheep pushing their carts down the aisle—the girls were walking against the usual traffic (not that we have one-way signs or anything)— were pretty hilarious. You could see them, when Queenie's white shoulders dawned on them, kind of jerk, or hop, or hiccup, but their eyes snapped back to their own baskets and on they pushed. I bet you could set off dynamite in an A & P and the people would by and large keep reaching and checking oatmeal off their lists and muttering "Let me see, there was a third thing, began with A, asparagus, no, ah, yes, applesauce!" or whatever it is they do mutter. But there was no doubt, this jiggled them. A few houseslaves in pin curlers even looked around after pushing their carts past to make sure what they had seen was correct.

You know, it's one thing to have a girl in a bathing suit down on the beach, where what with the glare nobody can look at each other much anyway, and another thing in the cool of the A & P, under the fluorescent lights, against all those stacked packages, with her feet paddling along naked over our checkerboard green-and-cream rubber-tile floor.

"Oh Daddy," Stokesie said beside me. "I feel so faint."

"Darling," I said. "Hold me tight." Stokesie's married, with two babies chalked up on his fuselage already, but as far as I can tell that's the only difference. He's twenty-two, and I was nineteen this April.

"Is it done?" he asks, the responsible married man finding his voice. I forgot to say he thinks he's going to be manager some sunny day, maybe in 1990 when it's called the Great Alexandrov and Petrooshki Tea Company or something.

What he meant was, our town is five miles from a beach, with a big summer colony out on the Point, but we're right in the middle of town, and the women generally put on a shirt or shorts or something before they get out of the car into the street. And anyway these are usually women with six children and varicose veins mapping their legs and nobody, including them, could care less. As I say, we're right in the middle of town, and if you stand at our front doors you can see two banks and the Congregational church and the newspaper store and three real-estate offices and about twenty-seven old freeloaders tearing up Central Street because the sewer broke again. It's not as if we're on the Cape; we're north of Boston and there's people in this town haven't seen the ocean for twenty years.

The girls had reached the meat counter and were asking McMahon something. He pointed, they pointed, and they shuffled out of sight behind a pyramid of Diet Delight peaches. All that was left for us to see was old McMahon patting his mouth and looking after them sizing up their joints. Poor kids, I began to feel sorry for them, they couldn't help it.

Now here comes the sad part of the story, at least my family says it's sad but I don't think it's sad myself. The store's pretty empty, it being Thursday afternoon, so there was nothing much to do except lean on the register and wait for the girls to show up again. The whole store was like a pinball machine and I didn't know which tunnel they'd come out of. After a while they come around out of the far aisle, around the light bulbs, records at discount of the Caribbean Six or Tony Martin Sings or some such gunk you wonder they waste the wax on, sixpacks of candy bars, and plastic toys done up in cellophane that fall apart when a kid looks at them anyway. Around they come, Queenie still leading the way, and holding a little gray jar in her hand. Slots Three through Seven are unmanned and I could see her wondering between Stokes and me, but Stokesie with his usual luck draws an old party in baggy gray pants who stumbles up with four giant cans of pineapple juice (what do these bums *do* with all that pineapple juice? I've often asked myself) so the girls come to me. Queenie puts down the jar and I take it into my fingers icy cold. Kingfish Fancy Herring Snacks in Pure Sour Cream: 49¢. Now her hands are empty, not a ring or a bracelet, bare as God made them, and I wonder where the money's coming from. Still with that prim look she lifts a folded dollar bill out of the hollow at the center of her nubbled pink top. The jar went heavy in my hand. Really, I thought that was so cute.

Then everybody's luck begins to run out. Lengel comes in from haggling with a truck full of cabbages on the lot and is about to scuttle into that door marked MAN-AGER behind which he hides all day when the girls touch his eye. Lengel's pretty dreary, teaches Sunday school and the rest, but he doesn't miss that much. He comes over and says, "Girls, this isn't the beach."

Queenie blushes, though maybe it's just a brush of sunburn I was noticing for the first time, now that she was so close. "My mother asked me to pick up a jar of herring snacks." Her voice kind of startled me, the way voices do when you see the people first, coming out so flat and dumb yet kind of tony, too, the way it ticked over "pick up" and "snacks." All of a sudden I slid right down her voice into her living room. Her father and the other men were standing around in ice-cream coats and bow ties and the women were in sandals picking up herring snacks on toothpicks off a big plate and they were all holding drinks the color of water with olives and sprigs of mint in them. When my parents have somebody over they get lemonade and if it's a real racy affair Schlitz in tall glasses with "They'll Do It Every Time" cartoons stenciled on.

"That's all right," Lengel said. "But this isn't the beach." His repeating this struck me as funny, as if it had just occurred to him, and he had been thinking all these years the A & P was a great big dune and he was the head lifeguard. He didn't like my smiling—as I say he doesn't miss much—but he concentrates on giving the girls that sad Sunday-school-superintendent stare.

Queenie's blush is no sunburn now, and the plump one in plaid, that I liked better from the back—a really sweet can—pipes up, "We weren't doing any shopping. We just came in for the one thing."

"That makes no difference," Lengel tells her, and I could see from the way his eyes went that he hadn't noticed she was wearing a two-piece before. "We want you decently dressed when you come in here."

"We *are* decent," Queenie says suddenly, her lower lip pushing, getting sore now that she remembers her place, a place from which the crowd that runs the A & P must look pretty crummy. Fancy Herring Snacks flashed in her very blue eyes.

"Girls, I don't want to argue with you. After this come in here with your shoulders covered. It's our policy." He turns his back. That's policy for you. Policy is what the kingpins want. What the others want is juvenile delinquency.

All this while, the customers had been showing up with their carts but, you know, sheep, seeing a scene, they had all bunched up on Stokesie, who shook open a paper bag as gently as peeling a peach, not wanting to miss a word. I could feel in the silence everybody getting nervous, most of all Lengel, who asks me, "Sammy, have you rung up this purchase?"

I thought and said "No" but it wasn't about that I was thinking. I go through the punches, 4, 9, GROC, TOT—it's more complicated than you think, and after you do it often enough, it begins to make a little song, that you hear words to, in my case "Hello (*bing*) there, you (*gung*) hap-py *pee-pul* (*splat*)!"—the *splat* being the drawer flying out. I uncrease the bill, tenderly as you may imagine, it just having come from between the two smoothest scoops of vanilla I had ever known were there, and pass a half and a penny into her narrow pink palm, and nestle the herrings in a bag and twist its neck and hand it over, all the time thinking.

The girls, and who'd blame them, are in a hurry to get out, so I say "I quit" to Lengel quick enough for them to hear, hoping they'll stop and watch me, their unsuspected hero. They keep right on going, into the electric eye; the door flies open and they flicker across the lot to their car, Queenie and Plaid and Big Tall Goony-Goony (not that as raw material she was so bad), leaving me with Lengel and a kink in his eyebrow.

"Did you say something, Sammy?"

"I said I quit."

"I thought you did."

"You didn't have to embarrass them."

"It was they who were embarrassing us."

I started to say something that came out "Fiddle-de-doo." It's a saying of my grandmother's, and I know she would have been pleased.

"I don't think you know what you're saying," Lengel said.

"I know you don't," I said. "But I do." I pull the bow at the back of my apron and start shrugging it off my shoulders. A couple customers that had been heading for my slot begin to knock against each other, like scared pigs in a chute.

Lengel sighs and begins to look very patient and old and gray. He's been a friend of my parents for years. "Sammy, you don't want to do this to your Mom and Dad," he tells me. It's true, I don't. But it seems to me that once you begin a gesture it's fatal not to go through with it. I fold the apron, "Sammy" stitched in red on the pocket, and put it on the counter, and drop the bow tie on top of it. The bow tie is theirs, if you've ever wondered. "You'll feel this for the rest of your life," Lengel says, and I know that's true, too, but remembering how he made that pretty girl blush makes me so scrunchy inside I punch the No Sale tab and the machine whirs "pee-pul" and the drawer splats out. One advantage to this scene taking place in summer, I can follow this up with a clean exit, there's no fumbling around getting your coat and galoshes, I just saunter into the electric eye in my white shirt that my mother ironed the night before, and the door heaves itself open, and outside the sunshine is skating around on the asphalt.

I look around for my girls, but they're gone, of course. There wasn't anybody but some young married screaming with her children about some candy they didn't get by the door of a powder-blue Falcon station wagon. Looking back in the big windows, over the bags of peat moss and aluminum lawn furniture stacked on the pavement, I could see Lengel in my place in the slot, checking the sheep through. His face was dark gray and his back stiff, as if he'd just had an injection of iron, and my stomach kind of fell as I felt how hard the world was going to be to me hereafter.

QUESTIONS FOR DISCUSSION AND WRITING

1. At the end of the story, Sammy wants to be a hero. Does he finally see himself as a hero? Do his coworkers and the girls he is trying to protect? Do we? Which, if any, of these opinions does Updike himself seem to share?

2. Readers are often ambivalent about Sammy. Some readers like him a lot, thinking him charming and funny. Others find him shallow and offensive. And still others can't quite decide. Where do you stand on the question of how likable Sammy is? What evidence from the story leads you to your conclusions?

3. As we indicated in question 2 above, not all readers respond to Sammy in the same way. Readers have similarly varied reactions to Queenie and her friends. Poll your classmates and readers outside your class for their responses to the characters and situation in "A&P." To what extent, if any, do those reactions seem influenced by a reader's age or gender?

4. At the end of "A&P" Sammy makes it clear that what he meant as a noble and heroic gesture has gone unnoticed by Queenie and her friends. In that recognition, Sammy realizes as well, perhaps, that the girls look at the world differently than he does. The girls would, then, presumably tell the story differently than Sammy does. Write your own version of "A&P," making Queenie or one of her friends its narrator. Then analyze the ways in which the shift in narrative point of view has changed the story's moods and themes.

5. Although the story focuses on the events of its plot, Updike also frequently describes the setting of the A&P and its shoppers. How does the setting influence Sammy's response to the girls? How do the descriptions of setting influence our response to the story's characters and events?

ESSAY

GARY ENGLE (1947–)

What Makes Superman So Darned American? _____ 1987

When I was young I spent a lot of time arguing with myself about who would win in a fight between John Wayne and Superman. On days when I wore my cowboy hat and cap guns, I knew the Duke would win because of his pronounced superiority in the all-important matter of swagger. There were days, though, when a frayed army blanket tied cape-fashion around my neck signalled a young man's need to believe there could be no end to the potency of his being. Then the Man of Steel was the odds-on favorite to knock the Duke for a cosmic loop. My greatest childhood problem was that the question could never be resolved because no such battle could ever take place. I mean, how would a fight start between the only two Americans who never started anything, who always fought only to defend their rights and the American way?

Now that I'm older and able to look with reason on the mysteries of childhood, I've finally resolved the dilemma. John Wayne was the best older brother any kid could ever hope to have, but he was no Superman.

Superman is *the* great American hero. We are a nation rich with legendary figures. But among the Davy Crocketts and Paul Bunyans and Mike Finks and Pecos Bills and all the rest who speak for various regional identities in the pantheon of American folklore, only Superman achieves truly mythic stature, interweaving a pattern of beliefs, literary conventions, and cultural traditions of the American people more powerfully and more accessibly than any other cultural symbol of the twentieth century, perhaps of any period in our history.

The core of the American myth in *Superman* consists of a few basic facts that remain unchanged throughout the infinitely varied ways in which the myth is told—facts with which everyone is familiar, however marginal their knowledge of the story. Superman is an orphan rocketed to Earth when his native planet Krypton explodes; he lands near Smallville and is adopted by Jonathan and Martha Kent, who inculcate in him their American middle-class ethic; as an adult he migrates to Metropolis where he defends America—no, the world! no, the Universe!—from all evil and harm while playing a romantic game in which, as Clark Kent, he hopelessly pursues Lois Lane, who hopelessly pursues Superman, who remains aloof until such time as Lois proves worthy of him by falling in love with his feigned identity as a weakling. That's it. Every narrative thread in the mythology, each one of the thousands of plots in the fifty-year stream of comics and films and TV shows, all the tales involving the demigods of the Superman pantheon—Superboy, Supergirl, even Krypto the Superdog—every single one reinforces by never contradicting this basic set of facts. That's the myth, and that's where one looks to understand America.

It is impossible to imagine Superman being as popular as he is and speaking as deeply to the American character were he not an immigrant and an orphan. Immigration, of course, is the overwhelming fact in American history. Except for the Indians, all Americans have an immediate sense of their origins elsewhere. No nation on Earth has so deeply embedded in its social consciousness the imagery of passage from one social identity to another: the Mayflower of the New England separatists, the slave ships from Africa and the subsequent underground railroads toward freedom in the North, the sailing ships and steamers running shuttles across two oceans in the nineteenth century, the freedom airlifts in the twentieth. Somehow the picture just isn't complete without Superman's rocketship.

Like the peoples of the nation whose values he defends, Superman is an alien, but not just any alien. He's the consummate and totally uncompromised alien, an immigrant whose visible difference from the norm is underscored by his decision to wear a costume of bold primary colors so tight as to be his very skin. Moreover, Superman the alien is real. He stands out among the hosts of comic book characters (Batman is a good example) for whom the superhero role is like a mask assumed when needed, a costume worn over their real identities as normal Americans. Superman's powers—strength, mobility, x-ray vision and the like—are the comic-book equivalents of ethnic characteristics, and they protect and preserve the vitality of the foster community in which he lives in the same way that immigrant ethnicity has sustained American culture linguistically, artistically, economically, politically, and spiritually.

The myth of Superman asserts with total confidence and a childlike innocence the value of the immigrant in American culture.

From this nation's beginnings Americans have looked for ways of coming to terms with the immigrant experience. This is why, for example, so much of American literature and popular culture deals with the theme of dislocation, generally focused in characters devoted or doomed to constant physical movement. Daniel Boone became an American legend in part as a result of apocryphal stories that he moved every time his neighbors got close enough for him to see the smoke of their cabin fires. James Fenimore Cooper's Natty Bumppo spent the five long novels of the Leather-stocking saga drifting ever westward, like the pioneers who were his spiritual off-spring, from the Mohawk valley of upstate New York to the Great Plains where he died. Huck Finn sailed through the moral heart of America on a raft. Melville's Ishmael, Wister's Virginian, Shane, Gatsby, the entire Lost Generation, Steinbeck's Okies, Little Orphan Annie, a thousand fiddlefooted cowboy heroes of dime novels and films and television—all in motion, searching for the American dream or stubbornly refusing to give up their innocence by growing old, all symptomatic of a national sense of rootlessness stemming from an identity founded on the experience of immigration.

Individual mobility is an integral part of America's dreamwork. Is it any wonder, then, that our greatest hero can take to the air at will? Superman's ability to fly does more than place him in a tradition of mythic figures going back to the Greek messenger god Hermes or Zetes the flying Argonaut. It makes him an exemplar in the American dream. Take away a young man's wheels and you take away his manhood. Jack Kerouac and Charles Kuralt go on the road; William Least Heat Moon looks for himself in a van exploring the veins of America in its system of blue highways; legions of gray-haired retirees turn Air Stream trailers and Winnebagos into proof positive that you can, in the end, take it with you. On a human scale, the American need to keep moving suggests a neurotic aimlessness under the surface of adventure. But take the human restraints off, let Superman fly unencumbered when and wherever he will, and the meaning of mobility in the American consciousness begins to reveal itself. Superman's incredible speed allows him to be as close to everywhere at once as it is physically possible to be. Displacement is, therefore, impossible. His sense of self is not dispersed by his life's migration but rather enhanced by all the universe that he is able to occupy. What American, whether an immigrant in spirit or in fact, could resist the appeal of one with such an ironclad immunity to the anxiety of dislocation?

In America, physical dislocation serves as a symbol of social and psychological movement. When our immigrant ancestors arrived on America's shores they hit the ground running, some to homestead on the Great Plains, others to claw their way up the socioeconomic ladder in coastal ghettos. Upward mobility, westward migration, Sunbelt relocation—the wisdom in America is that people don't, can't, mustn't end up where they begin. This belief has the moral force of religious doctrine. Thus the American identity is ordered around the psychological experience of forsaking or losing the past for the opportunity of reinventing oneself in the future. This makes the orphan a potent symbol of the American character. Orphans aren't merely free to reinvent themselves. They are obliged to do so.

When Superman reinvents himself, he becomes the bumbling Clark Kent, a figure as immobile as Superman is mobile, as weak as his alter ego is strong. Over the years commentators have been fond of stressing how Clark Kent provides an illusory image of wimpiness onto which children can project their insecurities about their own potential (and, hopefully, equally illusory) weaknesses. But I think the role of Clark Kent is far more complex than that.

During my childhood, Kent contributed nothing to my love for the Man of Steel. If left to contemplate him for too long, I found myself changing from cape back into cowboy hat and guns. John Wayne, at least, was no sissy that I could ever see. Of course, in all the Westerns that the Duke came to stand for in my mind, there were elements that left me as confused as the paradox between Kent and Superman. For example, I could never seem to figure out why cowboys so often fell in love when there were obviously better options: horses to ride, guns to shoot, outlaws to chase, and savages to kill. Even on the days when I became John Wayne, I could fall victim to a never-articulated anxiety about the potential for poor judgment in my cowboy heroes. Then, I generally drifted back into a worship of Superman. With him, at least, the mysterious communion of opposites was honest and on the surface of things.

What disturbed me as a child is what I now think makes the myth of Superman so appealing to an immigrant sensibility. The shape-shifting between Clark Kent and Superman is the means by which this mid-twentieth-century, urban story—like the pastoral, nineteenth-century Western before it—addresses in dramatic terms the theme of cultural assimilation.

At its most basic level, the Western was an imaginative record of the American experience of westward migration and settlement. By bringing the forces of civilization and savagery together on a mythical frontier, the Western addressed the problem of conflict between apparently mutually exclusive identities and explored options for negotiating between them. In terms that a boy could comprehend, the myth explored the dilemma of assimilation—marry the school marm and start wearing Eastern clothes or saddle up and drift further westward with the boys.

The Western was never a myth of stark moral simplicity. Pioneers fled civilization by migrating west, but their purpose in the wilderness was to rebuild civilization. So civilization was both good and bad, what Americans fled from and journeyed toward. A similar moral ambiguity rested at the heart of the wilderness. It was an Eden in which innocence could be achieved through spiritual rebirth, but it was also the anarchic force that most directly threatened the civilized values America wanted to impose on the frontier. So the dilemma arose: In negotiating between civilization and the wilderness, between the old order and the new, between the identity the pioneers carried with them from wherever they came and the identity they sought to invent, Americans faced an impossible choice. Either they pushed into the New World wilderness and forsook the ideals that motivated them or they clung to their origins and polluted Eden.

The myth of the Western responded to this dilemma by inventing the idea of the frontier in which civilized ideals embodied in the institutions of family, church, law, and education are revitalized by the virtues of savagery: independence, self-reliance, personal honor, sympathy with nature, and ethical uses of violence. In effect, the mythical frontier represented an attempt to embody the perfect degree of assimilation in which both the old and new identities came together, if not in a single self-image, then at least in idealized relationships, like the symbolic marriage of reformed cowboy and displaced school marm that ended Owen Wister's prototypical *The Virginian*, or the mystical masculine bonding between representatives of an ascendant and a vanishing America—Natty Bumppo and Chingachgook, the Lone Ranger and Tonto. On the Western frontier, both the old and new identities equally mattered.

As powerful a myth as the Western was, however, there were certain limits to its ability to speak directly to an increasingly common twentieth-century immigrant sensibility. First, it was pastoral. Its imagery of dusty frontier towns and breathtaking mountainous desolation spoke most affectingly to those who conceived of the American dream in terms of the nineteenth-century immigrant experience of rural settlement. As the twentieth century wore on, more immigrants were, like Superman, moving from rural or small-town backgrounds to metropolitan environments. Moreover, the Western was historical, often elegiacally so. Underlying the air of celebration in even the most epic and romantic of Westerns—the films of John Ford, say, in which John Wayne stood tall for all that any good American boy could ever want to be—was an awareness that the frontier was less a place than a state of mind represented in historic terms by a fleeting moment glimpsed imperfectly in the rapid wave of westward migration and settlement. Implicitly, then, whatever balance of past and future identities the frontier could offer was itself tenuous or illusory.

Twentieth-century immigrants, particularly the Eastern European Jews who came to America after 1880 and who settled in the industrial and mercantile centers of the Northeast—cities like Cleveland where Jerry Siegel and Joe Shuster grew up and created Superman—could be entertained by the Western, but they developed a separate literary tradition that addressed the theme of assimilation in terms closer to their personal experience. In this tradition issues were clear-cut: Clinging to an Old World identity meant isolation in ghettos, confrontation with a prejudiced mainstream culture, second-class social status, and impoverishment. On the other hand, forsaking the past in favor of total absorption into the mainstream, while it could result in socioeconomic progress, meant a loss of the religious, linguistic, even culinary traditions that provided a foundation for psychological well-being. Such loss was particularly tragic for the Jews because of the fundamental role played by history in Jewish culture.

Writers who worked in this tradition—Abraham Cahan, Daniel Fuchs, Henry Roth, and Delmore Schwartz, among others—generally found little reason to view the experience of assimilation with joy or optimism. Typical of the tradition was Cahan's early novel *Yekl,* on which Joan Micklin Silver's film *Hester Street* was based. A young married couple, Jake and Gitl, clash over his need to be absorbed as quickly as possible into the American mainstream and her obsessive preservation of their Russian-Jewish heritage. In symbolic terms, their confrontation is as simple as their choice of headgear—a derby for him, a babushka for her. That the story ends with their divorce, even in the context of their gradual movement toward mutual understanding of one another's point of view, suggests the divisive nature of the pressures at work in the immigrant communities.

Where the pressures were perhaps most keenly felt was in the schools. Educational theory of the period stressed the benefits of rapid assimilation. In the first decades of this century, for example, New York schools flatly rejected bilingual education—a common response to the plight of non-English-speaking immigrants even today—and there were conscientious efforts to indoctrinate the children of immigrants with American values, often at the expense of traditions within the ethnic community. What resulted was a generational rift in which children were openly embarrassed by and even contemptuous of their parents' values, setting a pattern in American life in which second-generation immigrants migrate psychologically if not physically from their parents, leaving it up to the third generation and beyond to rediscover their ethnic roots.

Under such circumstances, finding a believable and inspiring balance between the old identity and the new, like that implicit in the myth of the frontier, was next to impossible. The images and characters that did emerge from the immigrant communities were often comic. Seen over and over in the fiction and popular theater of the day was the figure of the *yiddische Yankee,* a jingoistic optimist who spoke heavily accented American slang, talked baseball like an addict without understanding the game, and dressed like a Broadway dandy on a budget—in short, one who didn't understand America well enough to distinguish between image and substance and who paid for the mistake by becoming the butt of a style of comedy bordering on pathos. So engrained was this stereotype in popular culture that it echoes today in TV situation comedy.

Throughout American popular culture between 1880 and the Second World War the story was the same. Oxlike Swedish farmers, German brewers, Jewish merchants, corrupt Irish ward healers, Italian gangsters—there was a parade of images that reflected in terms often comic, sometimes tragic, the humiliation, pain, and cultural insecurity of people in a state of transition. Even in the comics, a medium intimately connected with immigrant culture, there simply was no image that presented a blending of identities in the assimilation process in a way that stressed pride, self-confidence, integrity, and psychological well-being. None, that is, until Superman.

The brilliant stroke in the conception of Superman—the sine qua non that makes the whole myth work—is the fact that he has two identities. The myth simply wouldn't work without Clark Kent, mild-mannered newspaper reporter and later, as the myth evolved, bland TV newsman. Adopting the white-bread image of a wimp is first and foremost a moral act for the Man of Steel. He does it to protect his parents from nefarious sorts who might use them to gain an edge over the powerful alien. Moreover, Kent adds to Superman's powers the moral guidance of a Smallville upbringing. It is Jonathan Kent, fans remember, who instructs the alien that his powers must always be used for good. Thus does the myth add a mainstream white Anglo-Saxon Protestant ingredient to the American stew. Clark Kent is the clearest stereotype of a self-effacing, hesitant, doubting, middle-class weakling ever invented. He is the epitome of visible invisibility, someone whose extraordinary ordinariness makes him disappear in a crowd. In a phrase, he is the consummate figure of total cultural assimilation, and significantly, he is not real. Implicit in this is the notion that mainstream cultural norms, however useful, are illusions.

Though a disguise, Kent is necessary for the myth to work. This uniquely American hero has two identities, one based on where he comes from in life's journey, one on where he is going. One is real, one an illusion, and both are necessary for the myth of balance in the assimilation process to be complete. Superman's powers make the hero capable of saving humanity; Kent's total immersion in the American heartland makes him want to do it. The result is an improvement on the Western: an optimistic myth of assimilation but with an urban, technocratic setting.

One must never underestimate the importance to a myth of the most minute elements which do not change over time and by which we recognize the story. Take

Superman's cape, for example. When Joe Shuster inked the first Superman stories, in the early thirties when he was still a student at Cleveland's Glenville High School, Superman was strictly beefcake in tights, looking more like a circus acrobat than the ultimate Man of Steel. By June of 1938 when *Action Comics* no. 1 was issued, the image had been altered to include a cape, ostensibly to make flight easier to render in the pictures. But it wasn't the cape of Victorian melodrama and adventure fiction, the kind worn with a clasp around the neck. In fact, one is hard-pressed to find any precedent in popular culture for the kind of cape Superman wears. His emerges in a seamless line from either side of the front yoke of his tunic. It is a veritable growth from behind his pectorals and hangs, when he stands at ease, in a line that doesn't so much drape his shoulders as stand apart from them and echo their curve, like an angel's wings.

In light of this graphic detail, it seems hardly coincidental that Superman's real, Kryptonic name is Kal-El, an apparent neologism by George Lowther, the author who novelized the comic strip in 1942. In Hebrew, *el* can be both root and affix. As a root, it is the masculine singular word for God. Angels in Hebrew mythology are called *benei Elohim* (literally, sons of the Gods), or *Elyonim* (higher beings). As an affix, *el* is most often translated as "of God," as in the plenitude of Old Testament given names: Ishma-el, Dani-el, Ezeki-el, Samu-el, etc. It is also a common form for named angels in most Semitic mythologies: Israf-el, Aza-el, Uri-el, Yo-el, Rapha-el, Gabri-el and—the one perhaps most like Superman—Micha-el, the warrior angel and Satan's principal adversary.

The morpheme *Kal* bears a linguistic relation to two Hebrew roots. The first, *kal,* means "with lightness" or "swiftness" (faster than a speeding bullet in Hebrew?). It also bears a connection to the root *hal,* where *h* is the guttural *ch* of *chutzpah.* *Hal* translates roughly as "everything" or "all." *Kal-el,* then, can be read as "all that is God," or perhaps more in the spirit of the myth of Superman, "all that God is." And while we're at it, *Kent* is a form of the Hebrew *kana.* In its *k-n-t* form, the word appears in the Bible, meaning "I have found a son."

I'm suggesting that Superman raises the American immigrant experience to the level of religious myth. And why not? He's not just some immigrant from across the waters like all our ancestors, but a real alien, an extraterrestrial, a visitor from heaven if you will, which fact lends an element of the supernatural to the myth. America has no national religious icons nor any pilgrimage shrines. The idea of a patron saint is ludicrous in a nation whose Founding Fathers wrote into the founding documents the fundamental if not eternal separation of church and state. America, though, is pretty much as religious as other industrialized countries. It's just that our tradition of religious diversity precludes the nation's religious character from being embodied in objects or persons recognizably religious, for such are immediately identified by their attachment to specific sectarian traditions and thus contradict the eclecticism of the American religious spirit.

In America, cultural icons that manage to tap the national religious spirit are of necessity secular on the surface and sufficiently generalized to incorporate the diversity of American religious traditions. Superman doesn't have to be seen as an angel to be appreciated, but in the absence of a tradition of national religious iconography, he can serve as a safe, nonsectarian focus for essentially religious sentiments, particularly among the young.

In the last analysis, Superman is like nothing so much as an American boy's fantasy of a messiah. He is the male, heroic match for the Statue of Liberty, come like an immigrant from heaven to deliver humankind by sacrificing himself in the service of others. He protects the weak and defends truth and justice and all the other moral virtues inherent in the Judeo-Christian tradition, remaining ever vigilant and ever chaste. What purer or stronger vision could there possibly be for a child? Now that I put my mind to it, I see that John Wayne never had a chance.

QUESTIONS FOR DISCUSSION AND WRITING

1. Engle claims that "Superman's powers . . . are the comic-book equivalents of ethnic characteristics" (413). Do you agree? In what ways does Superman identify himself as an immigrant and in what ways does he not? In answering your question, you might poll classmates and friends of diverse ethnic and cultural backgrounds. Do they see Superman's experience as an immigrant one? Do people of different ethnic and cultural backgrounds identify with him as fully and easily as Engle does?
2. Like all heroes, Superman has been more popular in some years than in others. How much is he part of the childhoods of today's American children? Do children today look at him the same way that children of the past did? Does he fight the same kinds of monsters and villains that he once did? Has he been replaced by different, or "better," superheroes?
3. If we accept Engle's basic premises, it would seem that the comic book, mythic, movie, and television heroes of our childhoods say much not only about us but also about our cultures. Choose such a hero from your own childhood. How does that hero reflect the values and needs of the culture in which you were raised? How does he or she compare to Superman?
4. Engle mentions a number of heroes who haven't gained the popularity of Superman: Davy Crockett, Paul Bunyan, Mike Fink, and Pecos Bill. Who are these other heroes? Why is it that they haven't gained Superman's popularity?
5. Engle says that Superman's identity as Clark Kent makes him want to fight for middle-class American values. Look at other heroes who have double identities. What do their alter egos tell us about their desires and values? (You might, for instance, think about Spider-Man and Batman.)

MAKING CONNECTIONS: MONSTERS AND HEROES

1. Monsters may be defined in several different ways: they may be defined spiritually, as having a profound sickness of the soul; biologically, as physically deformed; psychologically, as psychotic; socially, as outsiders with no recognized connections to the community; or historically, as war criminals who betray international standards of humanity. Looking back over the selections that you have read, in what categories would you place the monsters? How do the authors create their definitions of the monsters? If you were to retell the stories, how might you alter the perspective to place the monsters in different categories—or, in fact, to not make them monsters at all?

2. A hero might be defined not only as someone who is good or brave but also as someone who embodies the values of the culture to which he or she belongs. Identify the heroes from the selections that you have read. What values are associated with each hero? What do those values tell us about the time and place that gave rise to the hero?

3. From at least the nineteenth century on, the "antihero" has been a popular conception: the antihero is a hero who is a rebel or outsider, often a "bad boy" who defies the recognized authorities and institutions. (In earlier times, the antihero might have been considered a monster.) Think about the antiheroes in the works in this unit: Oates's Arnold Friend/Charles Howard Schmid or perhaps Lizzie Borden. What makes these antiheroes potentially attractive either to the other characters or to us? How do they compare to the antiheroes you may be familiar with from television and movies? Would you consider Caliban an antihero? How might the monsters you have read about be reconceived as antiheroes?

4. Gender is an important part of the way a culture views both the hero and the monster. (Think, for instance, about the differences in our own time of the media treatment of the most horrific male and female killers, particularly mothers and fathers who kill their children.) Taking one or two of the monsters or heroes you have read about, reimagine the story with the gender switched. For instance, could Caliban become Ms. Caliban? Is Lizzie Borden of necessity a different kind of monster than Arnold Friend? If so, why? Could Updike's Sammy become a Samantha defending teenage boys? Could Prospero become Prospera, Miranda's mother? As you consider these questions, consider also how a gender change would change the plot, mood, and themes of any work you consider.

5. What character in the selections you have read would you consider most heroic? How would you defend that choice? What character in the selections would you consider the most monstrous? How would you defend that choice?

6. In even the earliest literature, the line between the hero and the monster is sometimes blurred. The two are, after all, often dependent on each other: a hero may need a monster to defeat. Opposites may in fact be mirror images of each other. Look at some of the hero/monster pairings you have read about: Connie/Arnold Friend, Prospero/Caliban, or the grandmother/The Misfit (in O'Connor's "A Good Man Is Hard to Find"). When do the distinctions between them get blurred? How does that blurring affect our understanding of the nature of good and evil?

7. Sometimes youth and physical vitality are associated with heroism, whereas age and cunning are associated with the monster (or at least the hero's antagonist). One might think, for example, of the young "beamish boy" in "Jabberwocky," of the young Sammy trying so hard to be a hero, or even of Connie, who may think that she is saving her family from the monstrous Arnold Friend. Elsewhere, however, writers suggest that *monstrosity* is young: Arnold Friend, for instance, has a youthful allure (even if he is not truly youthful). Goodness and wisdom may be associated with age, as, for example, is true of Marquez's "Very Old Man with Enormous Wings" or, perhaps, the stories of the elderly Odysseus. How do the authors you have read make the link between youth and age, goodness and evil? Why do they make those links? Why do you think that the associations change from author to author?

8. In this unit, the selections span a great deal of time: from the fifth century BC to our own time. Looking at several works separated by time (and perhaps by country), examine what they may tell us about any cultural and temporal differences in the ideas of the hero and/or the monster.

9. As children, we often have heroes who seem larger than life: perhaps parents or other admired adults, comic book characters (such as Superman), movie and video game heroes. As adolescents and adults, however, we often become skeptical about such heroes, doubting whether "real" heroes actually exist. Similarly, as we grow up, we usually lose our belief in "monsters." How do any of the works you have read reflect a childlike view of the hero or monster? How do any of them reflect an adult view? (Keep in mind that the childlike view does not necessarily suggest that the piece of literature is weaker.)

10. What does a hero do after he stops being a hero? That is the question that Tennyson's "Ulysses" raises. ("Ulysses" is just another name for Odysseus.) It is also a question that we may ask at the end of *The Tempest,* when Prospero is planning to return to Milan. Would you answer the question in the same way that Tennyson suggests it should be answered? (You might go to your library and read other stories in which the young hero becomes older. What happens to that hero—Beowulf, King Arthur—as he ages? Or you might think about popular movies that tell the story of a hero who has grown old and weak: *Hook,* the story of Peter Pan as an adult, or *The Mask of Zorro,* the story of an older Zorro, who must pass his sword—and his mission—on to a younger man.)

11. It has often been argued that we are an age without heroes. Some believe, however, that after September 11, 2001, Americans' view of the possibility of heroism—and perhaps of monstrosity—changed dramatically. In what ways might your response to the selections in this chapter have been influenced by the events of September 11?

9

Love and Friendship

Jean-Léon Gérôme, *Pygmalion and Galatea* (1881).

CHAPTER INTRODUCTION

When Jean-Léon Gérôme painted *Pygmalion and Galatea,* he retold a story that has been told again and again since ancient times. It is the story of an artist who creates a sculpture of a woman so beautiful that he falls in love with the statue. So passionate and sincere is his love for this marble woman whom he calls Galatea that the goddess Aphrodite takes pity on him and brings the statue to life. The artist Pygmalion now has a living woman to love.

In bringing Galatea to life, Aphrodite not only gives Pygmalion a woman to love but also makes manifest important connections among love, art, and self. Galatea is not, after all, a fully independent being: she is Pygmalion's creation. Perhaps he loves her in part for precisely that reason: he creates what he loves so that he can love what he creates. All of this works out well for Pygmalion, of course; having created his ideal woman, he is happy to love her and be loved by her. But what of Galatea's point of view? If we were to retell the story from her point of view, would she be equally satisfied? Certainly Gérôme's painting and many other versions of the story would have us think so. Leaning toward Pygmalion as he reaches up to kiss her, Galatea seems as passionate as he. Still, one might wonder whether Galatea might tell the story differently. After all, Pygmalion gets to create his beloved; Galatea does not. She may well be the ideal woman for him, but is he the ideal man for her? More important, perhaps, does she *want* to be the beloved he has created?

Such are the questions that underlie many love relationships, both in art and in life. Until recently, women were (or were thought to be) flattered by the idea of being put on a pedestal the way that Pygmalion literally puts Galatea on a pedestal. (If you look again at Gérôme's painting, you will see that the sculptor's marble figure is placed atop a pedestal.) In recent years, however, feminists have argued that by putting women on pedestals, men have objectified and dehumanized them; they point to the Pygmalion myth as an example, noting that Galatea is made of marble and brought to life only by a man's love (and a goddess's touch).

The debate about whether women (or men, for that matter) should be flattered or offended by being idealized is, in fact, an old one, one in which many writers have joined. Consider, for instance, this pairing of two poems written centuries ago. The first is by fourteenth-century Italian poet Francis Petrarch, who is immortalizing his beloved Laura:

PETRARCH (1304–1374)
CLIX: Sonnet 126 _____ *ca. 1345*

> In what divine ideal, what lofty sphere
> Is found the pattern from which Nature made
> That face so fair wherein she might parade
> Proof of her heavenly power to mortals here?
> 5   Were ringlets ever loosed of gold more sheer
> To wayward breeze by nymph in pool or glade?
> Was every virtue in one soul displayed
> Ere now?—and how the noblest cost me dear!
> Who knows her not can never realize
> 10   How beauty may the heart of man beguile,
> And who looks not upon my Laura's eyes
> Knows not how love can kill and otherwise
> May heal us; let him hear how soft she sighs
> And gently speaks, oh, let him see her smile!

Although Petrarch assures his readers that Laura is a real woman, his poem springs from a long-standing poetic tradition in which the beloved is admired for her unsurpassed beauty and her almost divine gifts of love and virtue and both admired and feared for her ability to stir powerful passions.

Contrast Petrarch's poem with one written by William Shakespeare two centuries later:

WILLIAM SHAKESPEARE (1564–1616)

My mistress' eyes are nothing like the sun _____ 1609

My mistress' eyes are nothing like the sun;
Coral is far more red than her lips' red;
If snow be white, why then her breasts are dun;
If hairs be wires, black wires grow on her head.
I have seen roses damasked, red and white,   5
But no such roses see I in her cheeks;
And in some perfumes is there more delight
Than in the breath that from my mistress reeks.
I love to hear her speak, yet well I know
That music hath a far more pleasing sound;   10
I grant I never saw a goddess go;
My mistress, when she walks, treads on the ground.
And yet, by heaven, I think my love as rare
As any she belied with false compare.

Shakespeare's sonnet, which also belongs to a long tradition, takes an approach very different from Petrarch's. In this case, it doesn't take divinity and perfection to arouse the speaker's love and passion, nor does the beloved exist only because her lover has created or imagined her. For Shakespeare's speaker, the beloved is a very real, very human person, but one who is nevertheless still rare and wonderful.

Like much literature on the subject, both sonnets indirectly raise questions about how much those we love are figments of our imaginations and how much we recognize their independence from us or see them as ideal (or not-so-ideal) extensions of ourselves. Such questions arise not only in discussions about sexual relationships but also in discussions about love relationships within families and among friends. Psychologists tell us that young children are unable to recognize their parents, particularly their mothers, as anything other than extensions of themselves. Those parents exist as sources of comfort and nourishment, and when they leave the child's field of vision, they leave the world as well. Although we outgrow much of this egocentric insistence on our own centrality and uniqueness, perhaps we do not fully outgrow the belief that parents are parents before they are people. As soon as we call our parents "Mom" and "Dad," we equate them with the roles they play in *our* lives, not quite seeing that they might have lives, needs, and emotions of their own. Poet Robert Hayden plays with this theme in "Those Winter Sundays," in which he describes a moment when he sees beyond his own somewhat sullen self-absorption and recognizes the love and sacrifice inherent in his father's weekly routines.

ROBERT HAYDEN (1913–1980)

Those Winter Sundays _____ *1962*

> Sundays too my father got up early
> and put his clothes on in the blueblack cold,
> then with cracked hands that ached
> from labor in the weekday weather made
> 5   banked fires blaze. No one ever thanked him.
>
> I'd wake and hear the cold splintering, breaking.
> When the rooms were warm, he'd call,
> and slowly I would rise and dress,
> fearing the chronic angers of that house,
>
> 10   Speaking indifferently to him,
> who had driven out the cold
> and polished my good shoes as well.
> What did I know, what did I know
> of love's austere and lonely offices?

To love another, whether a sexual partner, a parent or sibling, or a friend, is, then, both an attempt to break through the self-absorption to which everyone is prone and to extend one's self and imprint one's identity on another and on the world. Perhaps no one is fully human if he or she exists in isolation. In the literature that follows, writers examine the point at which each of us begins and ends. They explore the ways in which we become better through our identification with another and the ways in which a too-close identification, or an imbalance between each person's needs, can destroy one or both of those involved in the relationship. In short, they look at the full complex of emotions built around the idea of love. They ask in literature the same questions each of us asks, almost daily, in life.

An Album of Retellings

IN PRAISE OF THE BELOVED

WILLIAM SHAKESPEARE (1564–1616)

Shall I compare thee to a summer's day? _____ *1609*

> Shall I compare thee to a summer's day?
> Thou art more lovely and more temperate:
> Rough winds do shake the darling buds of May,
> 5   And summer's lease hath all too short a date;
> Sometime too hot the eye of heaven shines,
> And often is his gold complexion dimm'd;

And every fair from fair sometime declines,
By chance or nature's changing course untrimm'd:
But thy eternal summer shall not fade
Nor lose possession of that fair thou ow'st;   10
Nor shall Death brag thou wand'rest in his shade,
When in eternal lines to time thou grow'st;
So long as men can breathe or eyes can see,
So long lives this, and this gives life to thee.

QUESTIONS FOR DISCUSSION AND WRITING

1. The poem begins with a question. How, finally, does the speaker answer that question? *Should* he compare the lover to a summer's day?
2. Like many Shakespearean sonnets, this one is somehow summed up in the couplet, the last two lines of the poem. What do you see as the connection between those lines and the preceding twelve lines?
3. How does time function in the poem? Why is it that "thy eternal summer shall not fade"?

HOWARD MOSS (1922–   )

Shall I Compare Thee to a Summer's Day? _____ 1976

Who says you're like one of the dog days?
You're nicer. And better.
Even in May, the weather can be gray,
And a summer sub-let doesn't last forever.   5
Sometimes the sun's too hot;
Sometimes it is not.
Who can stay young forever?
People break their necks or just drop dead!
But you? Never!   10
If there's just one condensed reader left
Who can figure out the abridged alphabet
    After you're dead and gone,
    In this poem you'll live on!

QUESTIONS FOR DISCUSSION AND WRITING

1. How would you describe the tone and sounds of Moss's poem? What do the tone and sounds indicate about the speaker's relationship with the person being addressed?

2. Moss's poem "translates" Shakespeare's. How do his images and word choices compare with Shakespeare's? Do they lead to a different sense of the relationship among love, poetry, and time?

QUESTIONS FOR CROSS READING: IN PRAISE OF THE BELOVED

1. Although "My mistress' eyes" (425) is not a direct response to a particular sonnet by Petrarch, it is a response to the convention in which Petrarch was writing. Moss's poem, on the other hand, is a direct retelling of Shakespeare's "Shall I compare thee?" Is Moss responding to Shakespeare in the same way that Shakespeare responded to Petrarchan convention?
2. These poems are not only about love; they are about poetry. Do they have the same ideas about poetry's purpose?
3. Moss's poem is a parody of Shakespeare's. Is the purpose of the parody to undercut or reaffirm Shakespeare's ideas? How does Moss's poem achieve its purpose?

The Wooing Game

CHRISTOPHER MARLOWE (1564–1593)

The Passionate Shepherd to His Love _____ *1599*

> Come live with me and be my love,
> And we will all the pleasures prove
> That valleys, groves, hills, and fields,
> Woods, or steepy mountain yields.
>
> 5   And we will sit upon the rocks,
> Seeing the shepherds feed their flocks,
> By shallow rivers to whose falls
> Melodious birds sing madrigals.
>
> And I will make thee beds of roses
> 10   And a thousand fragrant posies,
> A cap of flowers, and a kirtle
> Embroidered all with leaves of myrtle;
>
> A gown made of the finest wool
> Which from our pretty lambs we pull;
> 15   Fair lined slippers for the cold,
> With buckles of the purest gold;
>
> A belt of straw and ivy buds,
> With coral clasps and amber studs:

And if these pleasures may thee move,
Come live with me, and be my love.   20

The shepherds' swains shall dance and sing
For thy delight each May morning:
If these delights thy mind may move,
Then live with me and be my love.   25

SIR WALTER RALEIGH (c. 1552–1618)

The Nymph's Reply to the Shepherd _____ 1599

If all the world and love were young,
And truth in every shepherd's tongue,
These pretty pleasures might me move
To live with thee and be thy love.

Time drives the flocks from field to fold   5
When rivers rage and rocks grow cold,
And Philomel becometh dumb;
The rest complains of cares to come.

The flowers do fade, and wanton fields
To wayward winter reckoning yields;   10
A honey tongue, a heart of gall,
Is fancy's spring, but sorrow's fall.

Thy gowns, thy shoes, thy beds of roses,
Thy cap, thy kirtle, and thy posies
Soon break, soon wither, soon forgotten—   15
In folly ripe, in reason rotten.

Thy belt of straw and ivy buds,
Thy coral clasps and amber studs,
All these in me no means can move
To come to thee and be thy love.   20

But could youth last and love still breed,
Had joys no date nor age no need,
Then these delights my mind might move
To live with thee and be thy love.

QUESTIONS FOR DISCUSSION AND WRITING

1. Marlowe's poem begins with the imperative "Come," Raleigh's with the conditional "If." How do the opening words prepare us for the presentations—the moods and the arguments—that follow?

2. Read Marlowe's and Raleigh's poems aloud. Which of the two moves more quickly? How would you characterize the sounds of each? What, finally, do you see as the relationships between the poems' sounds and their meanings?

3. Marlowe's poem is a **pastoral**: it creates a beautiful, but somewhat unrealistic, view of nature as a setting for love. What imagery in Marlowe's poem contributes to the idea of the pastoral? How does Raleigh undercut the pastoral?

4. Marlowe's poem is spoken by a man, Raleigh's by a woman. How important to the tone, content, and method of each poem is the speaker's gender?

JOHN DONNE (1572–1631)
The Bait   1633

    Come live with me, and be my love,
    And we will some new pleasures prove
    Of golden sands, and crystal brooks,
    With silken lines, and silver hooks.

5   There will the river whispering run
    Warmed by thy eyes, more than the Sun.
    And there th'enamored fish will stay,
    Begging themselves they may betray.

    When thou wilt swim in that live bath,
10   Each fish, which every channel hath,
    Will amorously to thee swim,
    Gladder to catch thee, than thou him.

    If thou, to be so seen, beest loath,
    By Sun, or Moon, thou darknest both,
15   And if my self have leave to see,
    I need not their light, having thee.

    Let others freeze with angling reeds,
    And cut their legs, with shells and weeds,
    Or treacherously poor fish beset,
20   With strangling snare, or windowy net:

    Let coarse bold hands, from slimy nest
    The bedded fish in banks out-wrest,
    Or curious traitors, sleavesilk flies
    Bewitch poor fishes' wandring eyes.

25   For thee, thou needst no such deceit,
    For thou thy self art thine own bait;
    That fish, that is not catched thereby,
    Alas, is wiser far than I.

QUESTIONS FOR DISCUSSION AND WRITING

1. Donne's poem is more realistic than Marlowe's. How does Donne use the images of the natural world to make the lover's plea? Is it the same kind of plea that the speaker of Marlowe's poem is making?
2. Compare the use of rhyme in Marlowe's and Donne's poems. How do the poets pair rhyme words to help them convey their themes?

C. DAY LEWIS (1904–1972)

Song _____ 1935

Come, live with me and be my love,
And we will all the pleasures prove
Of peace and plenty, bed and board,
That chance employment may afford.

I'll handle dainties on the docks   5
And thou shalt read of summer frocks:
At evening by the sour canals
We'll hope to hear some madrigals.

Care on thy maiden brow shall put
A wreath of wrinkles, and thy foot   10
Be shod with pain: not silken dress
But toil shall tire thy loveliness.

Hunger shall make thy modest zone
And cheat fond death of all but bone—
If these delights thy mind may move,   15
Then live with me and be my love.

QUESTIONS FOR DISCUSSION AND WRITING

1. C. Day Lewis wrote his "Song" in 1935. Why might the date of composition be significant?
2. Where is Lewis's "Song" set? How does the poem's setting (temporal and geographical) reflect its mood and theme? How do the mood and theme of Lewis's poem compare with those of Marlowe's?

WILLIAM CARLOS WILLIAMS (1883–1963)

Raleigh Was Right   *1940, 1944*

We cannot go to the country
for the country will bring us no peace
What can the small violets tell us
that grow on furry stems in
5   the long grass among lance shaped leaves?

Though you praise us
and call to mind the poets
who sung of our loveliness
it was long ago!
10   long ago! when country people
would plow and sow with
flowering minds and pockets at ease—
if ever this were true.

Not now, Love itself a flower
15   with roots in a parched ground.
Empty pockets make empty heads.
Cure it if you can but
do not believe that we can live
today in the country
20   for the country will bring us no peace.

QUESTIONS FOR DISCUSSION AND WRITING

1. Williams's title claims that "Raleigh was right." But what does Williams's speaker think Raleigh was right *about*? To what extent do Raleigh's and Williams's poems have the same themes? To what extent do they see love and nature—and the relationship between them—in the same way?
2. Williams wrote his poem in 1940. What about the style and theme suggests this is a modern poem?

OGDEN NASH (1902–1971)

Love under the Republicans (or Democrats)   *1930*

Come live with me and be my love
And we will all the pleasures prove
Of a marriage conducted with economy
In the Twentieth Century Anno Donomy.

We'll live in a dear little walk-up flat   5
With practically room to swing a cat
And a potted cactus to give it hauteur
And a bathtub equipped with dark brown water.
We'll eat, without undue discouragement
Foods low in cost but high in nouragement   10
And quaff with pleasure, while chatting wittily,
The peculiar wine of Little Italy.
We'll remind each other it's smart to be thrifty
And buy our clothes for something-fifty.
We'll stand in line on holidays   15
For seats at unpopular matinees,
And every Sunday we'll have a lark
And take a walk in Central Park.
And one of these days not too remote
I'll probably up and cut your throat.   20

QUESTIONS FOR DISCUSSION AND WRITING

1. Nash's parody of Marlowe's poem sets the lover's proposal in a distinctly *un*pastoral setting, substituting for Marlowe's country setting a city setting over which the Republicans (or Democrats) apparently hold sway. What do you see as the connections between the poem's title and the poem itself? Why do you think Nash chooses to parody Marlowe's poem as a way of commenting on modern-day life?
2. What is the tone of Nash's poem? Sad? Cynical? Humorous? What images and word choices reflect the tone?

QUESTIONS FOR CROSS READING: THE WOOING GAME

1. The pastoral is an old form, one that idealizes nature. From the beginning, however, writers have also cast doubt on the pastoral. What do the poetic responses to Marlowe's poem suggest as the reasons for doubt? Do sixteenth- and seventeenth-century writers such as Raleigh and Donne have the same reasons for doubt as do the modern poets (Lewis, Williams, and Nash)? To what extent can the pastoral coexist with modern life?
2. As this section shows, Marlowe's poem has provoked responses for centuries. Write your own response, poetic or otherwise. What do you see as the possibilities for the pastoral in your own life?

Love and Marriage

LI PO (701–763)

Song of Chang-Kan _____

長干行

When my hair could scarcely cover my forehead,
I used to pluck flowers and play by the door;
You would come, riding on your little bamboo
horse,
And galloping by the couch, you'd toy with
green plums.
5 We both dwelt in Chang-kan town so long ago;
We were just two children so amiable together,
suspecting nothing.

妾髮初覆額
折花門前劇
郎騎竹馬來
遶床弄青梅
同居長干里
兩小無嫌猜

At fourteen I became your wife;
I was so bashful that I'd always hide my face.
Hanging my head and turning to the shadowy
wall,
10 I never looked back once, even you called me a
thousand times.

十四為君婦
羞顏未嘗開
低頭向暗壁
千喚不一回

At fifteen I began to relieve my eyebrows of
shyness,
And we wished to love each other till dust and
ashes.
You would always keep up the faith of
"Bridge-pillar" fidelity,
While I would never dream of vainly climbing
the Hill of Husband-waiting!

十五始展眉
願同塵與灰
常存抱柱信
豈上望夫臺

15 When I was sixteen, you went away on a long
journey,
Voyaging beyond the Chutang Gorge rapids
and the Yanyu Rock.
In May, your boat must never collide against
that deadly rock.
High up the sky on the cliffs, the monkeys
shrieked in wailing!

十六君遠行
瞿塘灩澦堆
五月不可觸
猿鳴天上哀

By our door, do you know that your old
foot-marks
20 Have all been overgrown with green mosses?
The mosses are too deep for me to sweep away,
And the tree leaves are falling in the early
autumn gales.

門前遲行跡
一一生綠苔
苔深不能掃
落葉秋風早

In August here, I gaze at the yellow butterflies,
Fluttering and hovering in pairs over the grass
　in the west garden.
How my heart aches so, when I think of this—
That I must sit here alone in sorrow, my pink
　complexion fading away! . . .

Someday, when you leave the San-pa region
　down the river,
Pray, write me a letter early beforehand.
I will never care for the long distance to
　meeting you.
I'll go as far as the Long Wind Beach!

八月蝴蝶來
雙飛西園草
感此傷妾心   25
坐愁紅顏老

早晚下三巴
預將書報家
相迎不道遠
直至長風沙   30

(translated by Sun Lu)

QUESTIONS FOR DISCUSSION AND WRITING

1. What do we imagine has kept the speaker's husband away from home?
2. Why does the speaker compare the love between herself and her husband to the love of mythical couples? How would the reader's response have been different had she described their love without such comparisons?
3. How would you characterize the tone of the poem? Why?
4. Most of us have to rely on a translation to read Li Po's poem, which means we are relying on another reader to tell—and thus interpret—Li Po's poem for us. If you read Chinese, though, you can tell the story to yourself. How would your translation differ from the one presented here?

EZRA POUND (1885–1972)

The River-Merchant's Wife: A Letter   1916

While my hair was still cut straight across my forehead
Played I about the front gate, pulling flowers.
You came by on bamboo stilts, playing horse,
You walked about my seat, playing with blue plums.
And we went on living in the village of Chōkan: 5
Two small people, without dislike or suspicion.

At fourteen I married My Lord you.
I never laughed, being bashful.
Lowering my head, I looked at the wall.
Called to, a thousand times, I never looked back.   10

At fifteen I stopped scowling,
I desired my dust to be mingled with yours

Forever and forever and forever.
Why should I climb the look out?

15   At sixteen you departed,
You went into far Ku-tō-en, by the river of swirling eddies,
And you have been gone five months.
The monkeys make sorrowful noise overhead.

You dragged your feet when you went out.
20   By the gate now, the moss is grown, the different mosses,
Too deep to clear them away!
The leaves fall early this autumn, in wind.
The paired butterflies are already yellow with August

Over the grass in the West garden;
25   They hurt me. I grow older.
If you are coming down through the narrows of the river Kiang,
Please let me know before hand,
And I will come out to meet you
     As far as Chō-fū-Sa.

QUESTIONS FOR DISCUSSION AND WRITING

1. How would you describe the river merchant's wife's feelings for the boy when she was a small girl? When she was fourteen? Fifteen? Sixteen?
2. The wife tends to express her feelings indirectly. What do her images suggest about her feelings?
3. At the end of the poem, the wife says, "I will come out to meet you." What does this contrast to her earlier timidity tell us about the man, the woman, and their relationship?

EDWARD HIRSCH (1950–   )

The River Merchant: A Letter Home _____ 1981

Sometimes the world seems so large,
You have no idea. Out here at dusk
The barges pull the heaviest cargo, sometimes
They drag whole ships to the sea. Imagine
5   The sound of geese shrieking everywhere,
More geese than you can imagine,
Clustered together and flapping like stars.
Sometimes there are two moons shining at
Once, one clouded in the treetops, one
10   Breaking into shadows on the river.
I don't know what this means.

But from the hill's brow I can see
The lights in every village flickering on,
One by one, but slowly, like this,
Until the whole world gleams   15
Like small coins. Believe me:
There are so many villages like ours,
So many lights all gleaming together
But all separate too, like those moons.
It is too much. I am older now.   20
I want to return to that fateful place
Where the river narrows toward home.

QUESTIONS FOR DISCUSSION AND WRITING

1. Does the river merchant respond to the world beyond his home positively or negatively? How?
2. What sense do you get of the river merchant's feelings for his wife?

QUESTIONS FOR CROSS READING: LOVE AND MARRIAGE

1. Does Sun Yu's or Ezra Pound's translation of Li Po's poem arouse stronger emotions? Why?
2. Consider the ways in which the same image seems to get translated differently by
   Pound and Sun Yu. Look, for instance, at the way the two poets bring in the idea
   of youthful suspicion or at the way they use the image of dust and ashes. Do the
   poets evoke the same responses and emotions with these images? In what other
   instances do you find an apparent difference in interpretation of Li Po's lines?
3. Compare the feelings of the river merchant's wife as they are conveyed in the
   translations of Li Po's poem with those expressed by the speaker of Hirsch's poem.
   Do the husband and wife seem to look at their love and marriage in the same way?
   Are their emotions equally strong? How do their attitudes toward the world outside their home and village compare?

A QUESTION OF FIDELITY

ANTON CHEKHOV (1860–1904)

The Lady with the Pet Dog _____ 1899

I

A new person, it was said, had appeared on the esplanade: a lady with a pet dog.
Dmitry Dmitrich Gurov, who had spent a fortnight at Yalta and had got used to the

place, had also begun to take an interest in new arrivals. As he sat in Vernet's confectionery shop, he saw, walking on the esplanade, a fair-haired young woman of medium height, wearing a beret; a white Pomeranian was trotting behind her.

And afterwards he met her in the public garden and in the square several times a day. She walked alone, always wearing the same beret and always with the white dog; no one knew who she was and everyone called her simply "the lady with the pet dog."

"If she is here alone without husband or friends," Gurov reflected, "it wouldn't be a bad thing to make her acquaintance."

He was under forty, but he already had a daughter twelve years old, and two sons at school. They had found a wife for him when he was very young, a student in his second year, and by now she seemed half as old again as he. She was a tall, erect woman with dark eyebrows, stately and dignified and, as she said of herself, intellectual. She read a great deal, used simplified spelling in her letters, called her husband, not Dmitry, but Dimitry, while he privately considered her of limited intelligence, narrow-minded, dowdy, was afraid of her, and did not like to be at home. He had begun being unfaithful to her long ago—had been unfaithful to her often and, probably for that reason, almost always spoke ill of women, and when they were talked of in his presence used to call them "the inferior race."

It seemed to him that he had been sufficiently tutored by bitter experience to call them what he pleased, and yet he could not have lived without "the inferior race" for two days together. In the company of men he was bored and ill at ease, he was chilly and uncommunicative with them; but when he was among women he felt free, and knew what to speak to them about and how to comport himself; and even to be silent with them was no strain on him. In his appearance, in his character, in his whole make-up there was something attractive and elusive that disposed women in his favor and allured them. He knew that, and some force seemed to draw him to them, too.

Oft-repeated and really bitter experience had taught him long ago that with decent people—particularly Moscow people—who are irresolute and slow to move, every affair which at first seems a light and charming adventure inevitably grows into a whole problem of extreme complexity, and in the end a painful situation is created. But at every new meeting with an interesting woman this lesson of experience seemed to slip from his memory, and he was eager for life, and everything seemed so simple and diverting.

One evening while he was dining in the public garden the lady in the beret walked up without haste to take the next table. Her expression, her gait, her dress, and the way she did her hair told him that she belonged to the upper class, that she was married, that she was in Yalta for the first time and alone, and that she was bored there. The stories told of the immorality in Yalta are to a great extent untrue; he despised them, and knew that such stories were made up for the most part by persons who would have been glad to sin themselves if they had had the chance; but when the lady sat down at the next table three paces from him, he recalled these stories of easy conquests, of trips to the mountains, and the tempting thought of a swift, fleeting liaison, a romance with an unknown woman of whose very name he was ignorant suddenly took hold of him.

He beckoned invitingly to the Pomeranian, and when the dog approached him, shook his finger at it. The Pomeranian growled; Gurov threatened it again.

The lady glanced at him and at once dropped her eyes.

"He doesn't bite," she said and blushed.

"May I give him a bone?" he asked; and when she nodded he inquired affably, "Have you been in Yalta long?"

"About five days."

"And I am dragging out the second week here."

There was a short silence.

"Time passes quickly, and yet it is so dull here!" she said, not looking at him.

"It's only the fashion to say it's dull here. A provincial will live in Belyov or Zhizdra and not be bored, but when he comes here it's 'Oh, the dullness! Oh, the dust!' One would think he came from Granada."

She laughed. Then both continued eating in silence, like strangers, but after dinner they walked together and there sprang up between them the light banter of people who are free and contented, to whom it does not matter where they go or what they talk about. They walked and talked of the strange light on the sea: the water was a soft, warm, lilac color, and there was a golden band of moonlight upon it. They talked of how sultry it was after a hot day. Gurov told her that he was a native of Moscow, that he had studied languages and literature at the university, but had a post in a bank; that at one time he had trained to become an opera singer but had given it up, that he owned two houses in Moscow. And he learned from her that she had grown up in Petersburg, but had lived in S—— since her marriage two years previously, that she was going to stay in Yalta for about another month, and that her husband, who needed a rest, too, might perhaps come to fetch her. She was not certain whether her husband was a member of a Government Board or served on a Zemstvo Council, and this amused her. And Gurov learned that her name was Anna Sergeyevna.

Afterwards in his room at the hotel he thought about her—and was certain that he would meet her the next day. It was bound to happen. Getting into bed he recalled that she had been a schoolgirl only recently, doing lessons like his own daughter; he thought how much timidity and angularity there was still in her laugh and her manner of talking with a stranger. It must have been the first time in her life that she was alone in a setting in which she was followed, looked at, and spoken to for one secret purpose alone, which she could hardly fail to guess. He thought of her slim, delicate throat, her lovely gray eyes.

"There's something pathetic about her, though," he thought, and dropped off.

II

A week had passed since they had struck up an acquaintance. It was a holiday. It was close indoors, while in the street the wind whirled the dust about and blew people's hats off. One was thirsty all day, and Gurov often went into the restaurant and offered Anna Sergeyevna a soft drink or ice cream. One did not know what to do with oneself.

In the evening when the wind had abated they went out on the pier to watch the steamer come in. There were a great many people walking about the dock; they had come to welcome someone and they were carrying bunches of flowers. And two peculiarities of a festive Yalta crowd stood out: the elderly ladies were dressed like young ones and there were many generals.

Owing to the choppy sea, the steamer arrived late, after sunset; and it was a long time tacking about before it put in at the pier. Anna Sergeyevna peered at the steamer and the passengers through her lorgnette as though looking for acquaintances, and whenever she turned to Gurov her eyes were shining. She talked a great deal and asked questions jerkily, forgetting the next moment what she had asked; then she lost her lorgnette in the crush.

The festive crowd began to disperse; it was now too dark to see people's faces; there was no wind any more, but Gurov and Anna Sergeyevna still stood as though waiting to see someone else come off the steamer. Anna Sergeyevna was silent now, and sniffed her flowers without looking at Gurov.

"The weather has improved this evening," he said. "Where shall we go now? Shall we drive somewhere?"

She did not reply.

Then he looked at her intently, and suddenly embraced her and kissed her on the lips, and the moist fragrance of her flowers enveloped him; and at once he looked round him anxiously, wondering if anyone had seen them.

"Let us go to your place," he said softly. And they walked off together rapidly.

The air in her room was close and there was the smell of the perfume she had bought at the Japanese shop. Looking at her, Gurov thought: "What encounters life offers!" From the past he preserved the memory of carefree, good-natured women whom love made gay and who were grateful to him for the happiness he gave them, however brief it might be; and of women like his wife who loved without sincerity, with too many words, affectedly, hysterically, with an expression that it was not love or passion that engaged them but something more significant; and of two or three others, very beautiful, frigid women, across whose faces would suddenly flit a rapacious expression—an obstinate desire to take from life more than it could give, and these were women no longer young, capricious, unreflecting, domineering, unintelligent, and when Gurov grew cold to them their beauty aroused his hatred, and the lace on their lingerie seemed to him to resemble scales.

But here there was the timidity, the angularity of inexperienced youth, a feeling of awkwardness; and there was a sense of embarrassment, as though someone had suddenly knocked at the door. Anna Sergeyevna, "the lady with the pet dog," treated what had happened in a peculiar way, very seriously, as though it were her fall—so it seemed, and this was odd and inappropriate. Her features drooped and faded, and her long hair hung down sadly on either side of her face; she grew pensive and her dejected pose was that of a Magdalene in a picture by an old master.

"It's not right," she said. "You don't respect me now, you first of all."

There was a watermelon on the table. Gurov cut himself a slice and began eating it without haste. They were silent for at least half an hour.

There was something touching about Anna Sergeyevna; she had the purity of a well-bred, naive woman who has seen little of life. The single candle burning on the table barely illuminated her face, yet it was clear that she was unhappy.

"Why should I stop respecting you, darling?" asked Gurov. "You don't know what you're saying."

"God forgive me," she said, and her eyes filled with tears. "It's terrible."

"It's as though you were trying to exonerate yourself."

"How can I exonerate myself? No. I am a bad, low woman; I despise myself and I have no thought of exonerating myself. It's not my husband but myself I have deceived. And not only just now; I have been deceiving myself for a long time. My husband may be a good, honest man, but he is a flunkey! I don't know what he does, what his work is, but I know he is a flunkey! I was twenty when I married him. I was tormented by curiosity; I wanted something better. 'There must be a different sort of life,' I said to myself. I wanted to live! To live, to live! Curiosity kept eating at me—you don't understand, but I swear to God I could no longer control myself; something was going on in me; I could not be held back. I told my husband I was ill, and came here. And here I have been walking about as though in a daze, as though I were mad; and now I have become a vulgar, vile woman whom anyone may despise."

Gurov was already bored with her; he was irritated by her naive tone, by her repentance, so unexpected and so out of place, but for the tears in her eyes he might have thought she was joking or play-acting.

"I don't understand, my dear," he said softly. "What do you want?"

She hid her face on his breast and pressed close to him.

"Believe me, believe me, I beg you," she said, "I love honesty and purity, and sin is loathsome to me; I don't know what I'm doing. Simple people say, 'The Evil One has led me astray.' And I may say of myself now that the Evil One has led me astray."

"Quiet, quiet," he murmured.

He looked into her fixed, frightened eyes, kissed her, spoke to her softly and affectionately, and by degrees she calmed down, and her gaiety returned; both began laughing.

Afterwards when they went out there was not a soul on the esplanade. The town with its cypresses looked quite dead, but the sea was still sounding as it broke upon the beach; a single launch was rocking on the waves and on it a lantern was blinking sleepily.

They found a cab and drove to Oreanda.

"I found out your surname in the hall just now; it was written on the board—von Dideritz," said Gurov. "Is your husband German?"

"No; I believe his grandfather was German, but he is Greek Orthodox himself."

At Oreanda they sat on a bench not far from the church, looked down at the sea, and were silent. Yalta was barely visible through the morning mist; white clouds rested motionlessly on the mountaintops. The leaves did not stir on the trees, cicadas twanged, and the monotonous muffled sound of the sea that rose from below spoke of the peace, the eternal sleep awaiting us. So it rumbled below when there was no Yalta, no Oreanda here; so it rumbles now, and it will rumble as indifferently and as hollowly when we are no more. And in this constancy, in this complete indifference to the life and death of each of us, there lies, perhaps, a pledge of our eternal salvation, of the unceasing advance of life upon earth, of unceasing movement towards perfection. Sitting beside a young woman who in the dawn seemed so lovely, Gurov, soothed and spellbound by these magical surroundings—the sea, the mountains, the clouds, the wide sky—thought how everything is really beautiful in this world when one reflects: everything except what we think or do ourselves when we forget the higher aims of life and our own human dignity.

A man strolled up to them—probably a guard—looked at them and walked away. And this detail, too, seemed so mysterious and beautiful. They saw a steamer arrive from Feodosia, its lights extinguished in the glow of dawn.

"There is dew on the grass," said Anna Sergeyevna, after a silence.

"Yes, it's time to go home."

They returned to the city.

Then they met every day at twelve o'clock on the esplanade, lunched and dined together, took walks, admired the sea. She complained that she slept badly, that she had palpitations, asked the same questions, troubled now by jealousy and now by the fear that he did not respect her sufficiently. And often in the square or the public garden, when there was no one near them, he suddenly drew her to him and kissed her passionately. Complete idleness, these kisses in broad daylight exchanged furtively in dread of someone's seeing them, the heat, the smell of the sea, and the continual flitting before his eyes of idle, well-dressed, well-fed people, worked a complete change in him; he kept telling Anna Sergeyevna how beautiful she was, how seductive, was urgently passionate; he would not move a step away from her, while she was often pensive and continually pressed him to confess that he did not respect her, did not love her in the least, and saw in her nothing but a common woman. Almost every evening rather late they drove somewhere out of town, to Oreanda or to the waterfall; and the excursion was always a success, the scenery invariably impressed them as beautiful and magnificent.

They were expecting her husband, but a letter came from him saying that he had eye-trouble, and begging his wife to return home as soon as possible. Anna Sergeyevna made haste to go.

"It's a good thing I am leaving," she said to Gurov. "It's the hand of Fate!"

She took a carriage to the railway station, and he went with her. They were driving the whole day. When she had taken her place in the express, and when the second bell had rung, she said, "Let me look at you once more—let me look at you again. Like this."

She was not crying but was so sad that she seemed ill and her face was quivering.

"I shall be thinking of you—remembering you," she said. "God bless you; be happy. Don't remember evil against me. We are parting forever—it has to be, for we ought never to have met. Well, God bless you."

The train moved off rapidly, its lights soon vanished, and a minute later there was no sound of it, as though everything had conspired to end as quickly as possible that sweet trance, that madness. Left alone on the platform, and gazing into the dark distance, Gurov listened to the twang of the grasshoppers and the hum of the telegraph wires, feeling as though he had just waked up. And he reflected, musing, that there had now been another episode or adventure in his life, and it, too, was at an end, and nothing was left of it but a memory. He was moved, sad, and slightly remorseful: this young woman whom he would never meet again had not been happy with him; he had been warm and affectionate with her, but yet in his manner, his tone, and his caresses there had been a shade of light irony, the slightly coarse arrogance of a happy male who was, besides, almost twice her age. She had constantly called him kind, exceptional, high-minded; obviously he had seemed to her different from what he really was, so he had involuntarily deceived her.

Here at the station there was already a scent of autumn in the air; it was a chilly evening.

"It is time for me to go north, too," thought Gurov as he left the platform. "High time!"

III

At home in Moscow the winter routine was already established; the stoves were heated, and in the morning it was still dark when the children were having breakfast and getting ready for school, and the nurse would light the lamp for a short time. There were frosts already. When the first snow falls, on the first day the sleighs are out, it is pleasant to see the white earth, the white roofs; one draws easy, delicious breaths, and the season brings back the days of one's youth. The old limes and birches, white with hoar-frost, have a good-natured look; they are closer to one's heart than cypresses and palms, and near them one no longer wants to think of mountains and the sea.

Gurov, a native of Moscow, arrived there on a fine frosty day, and when he put on his fur coat and warm gloves and took a walk along Petrovka, and when on Saturday night he heard the bells ringing, his recent trip and the places he had visited lost all charm for him. Little by little he became immersed in Moscow life, greedily read three newspapers a day, and declared that he did not read the Moscow papers on principle. He already felt a longing for restaurants, clubs, formal dinners, anniversary celebrations, and it flattered him to entertain distinguished lawyers and actors, and to play cards with a professor at the physicians' club. He could eat a whole portion of meat stewed with pickled cabbage and served in a pan, Moscow style.

A month or so would pass and the image of Anna Sergeyevna, it seemed to him, would become misty in his memory, and only from time to time he would dream of her with her touching smile as he dreamed of others. But more than a month went by, winter came into its own, and everything was still clear in his memory as though he had parted from Anna Sergeyevna only yesterday. And his memories glowed more and more vividly. When in the evening stillness the voices of his children preparing their lessons reached his study, or when he listened to a song or to an organ playing in a restaurant, or when the storm howled in the chimney, suddenly everything would rise up in his memory; what had happened on the pier and the early morning with the mist on the mountains, and the steamer coming from Feodosia, and the kisses. He would pace about his room a long time, remembering and smiling; then his memories passed into reveries, and in his imagination the past would mingle with what was to come. He did not dream of Anna Sergeyevna, but she followed him about everywhere and watched him. When he shut his eyes he saw her before him as though she were there in the flesh, and she seemed to him lovelier, younger, tenderer than she had been, and he imagined himself a finer man than he had been in Yalta. Of evenings she peered out at him from the bookcase, from the fireplace, from the corner—he heard her breathing, the caressing rustle of her clothes. In the street he followed the women with his eyes, looking for someone who resembled her.

Already he was tormented by a strong desire to share his memories with someone. But in his home it was impossible to talk of his love, and he had no one to talk to outside; certainly he could not confide in his tenants or in anyone at the bank. And what was there to talk about? He hadn't loved her then, had he? Had there been anything beautiful, poetical, edifying, or simply interesting in his relations with Anna Sergeyevna? And he was forced to talk vaguely of love, of women, and no one guessed what he meant; only his wife would twitch her black eyebrows and say, "The part of a philanderer does not suit you at all, Dimitry."

One evening, coming out of the physicians' club with an official with whom he had been playing cards, he could not resist saying:

"If you only knew what a fascinating woman I became acquainted with at Yalta!"

The official got into his sledge and was driving away, but turned suddenly and shouted:

"Dmitry Dmitrich!"

"What is it?"

"You were right this evening: the sturgeon was a bit high."

These words, so commonplace, for some reason moved Gurov to indignation, and struck him as degrading and unclean. What savage manners, what mugs! What stupid nights, what dull, humdrum days! Frenzied gambling, gluttony, drunkenness, continual talk always about the same thing! Futile pursuits and conversations always about the same topics take up the better part of one's time, the better part of one's strength, and in the end there is left a life clipped and wingless, an absurd mess, and there is no escaping or getting away from it—just as though one were in a madhouse or a prison.

Gurov, boiling with indignation, did not sleep all night. And he had a headache all the next day. And the following nights too he slept badly; he sat up in bed, thinking, or paced up and down his room. He was fed up with his children, fed up with the bank; he had no desire to go anywhere or to talk of anything.

In December during the holidays he prepared to take a trip and told his wife he was going to Petersburg to do what he could for a young friend—and he set off for S——. What for? He did not know, himself. He wanted to see Anna Sergeyevna and talk with her, to arrange a rendezvous if possible.

He arrived at S—— in the morning, and at the hotel took the best room, in which the floor was covered with gray army cloth, and on the table there was an inkstand, gray with dust and topped by a figure on horseback, its hat in its raised hand and its head broken off. The porter gave him the necessary information: von Dideritz lived in a house of his own on Staro-Goncharnaya Street, not far from the hotel: he was rich and lived well and kept his own horses; everyone in the town knew him. The porter pronounced the name: "Dridiritz."

Without haste Gurov made his way to Staro-Goncharnaya Street and found the house. Directly opposite the house stretched a long gray fence studded with nails.

"A fence like that would make one run away," thought Gurov, looking now at the fence, now at the windows of the house.

He reflected: this was a holiday, and the husband was apt to be at home. And in any case, it would be tactless to go into the house and disturb her. If he were to send her a note, it might fall into her husband's hands, and that might spoil everything. The best thing was to rely on chance. And he kept walking up and down the street and along the fence, waiting for the chance. He saw a beggar go in at the gate and heard the dogs attack him; then an hour later he heard a piano, and the sound came to him faintly and indistinctly. Probably it was Anna Sergeyevna playing. The front door opened suddenly, and an old woman came out, followed by the familiar white Pomeranian. Gurov was on the point of calling to the dog, but his heart began beating violently, and in his excitement he could not remember the Pomeranian's name.

He kept walking up and down, and hated the gray fence more and more, and by now he thought irritably that Anna Sergeyevna had forgotten him, and was perhaps already diverting herself with another man, and that that was very natural in a young woman who from morning till night had to look at that damn fence. He went back to his hotel room and sat on the couch for a long while, not knowing what to do, then he had dinner and a long nap.

"How stupid and annoying all this is!" he thought when he woke and looked at the dark windows: it was already evening. "Here I've had a good sleep for some reason. What am I going to do at night?"

He sat on the bed, which was covered with a cheap gray blanket of the kind seen in hospitals, and he twitted himself in his vexation:

"So there's your lady with the pet dog. There's your adventure. A nice place to cool your heels in."

That morning at the station a playbill in large letters had caught his eye. *The Geisha* was to be given for the first time. He thought of this and drove to the theater.

"It's quite possible that she goes to first nights," he thought.

The theater was full. As in all provincial theaters, there was a haze above the chandelier, the gallery was noisy and restless; in the front row, before the beginning of the performance the local dandies were standing with their hands clasped behind their backs; in the Governor's box the Governor's daughter, wearing a boa, occupied the front seat, while the Governor himself hid modestly behind the portiere and only his hands were visible; the curtain swayed; the orchestra was a long time tuning up. While the audience was coming in and taking their seats, Gurov scanned the faces eagerly.

Anna Sergeyevna, too, came in. She sat down in the third row, and when Gurov looked at her his heart contracted, and he understood clearly that in the whole world there was no human being so near, so precious, and so important to him; she, this little, undistinguished woman, lost in a provincial crowd, with a vulgar lorgnette in her hand, filled his whole life now, was his sorrow and his joy, the only happiness that he now desired for himself, and to the sounds of the bad orchestra, of the miserable local violins, he thought how lovely she was. He thought and dreamed.

A young man with small side-whiskers, very tall and stooped, came in with Anna Sergeyevna and sat down beside her; he nodded his head at every step and seemed to be bowing continually. Probably this was the husband whom at Yalta, in an access of bitter feeling, she had called a flunkey. And there really was in his lanky figure, his side-whiskers, his small bald patch, something of a flunkey's retiring manner; his smile was mawkish, and in his buttonhole there was an academic badge like a waiter's number.

During the first intermission the husband went out to have a smoke; she remained in her seat. Gurov, who was also sitting in the orchestra, went up to her and said in a shaky voice, with a forced smile:

"Good evening!"

She glanced at him and turned pale, then looked at him again in horror, unable to believe her eyes, and gripped the fan and the lorgnette tightly together in her hands, evidently trying to keep herself from fainting. Both were silent. She was sitting, he was standing, frightened by her distress and not daring to take a seat beside her. The violins and the flute that were being tuned up sang out. He suddenly felt frightened: it seemed as if all the people in the boxes were looking at them. She got up and went hurriedly to the exit; he followed her, and both of them walked blindly along the corridors and up and down stairs, and figures in the uniforms prescribed for magistrates, teachers, and officials of the Department of Crown Lands, all wearing badges, flitted before their eyes, as did also ladies, and fur coats on hangers; they were conscious of drafts and the smell of stale tobacco. And Gurov, whose heart was beating violently, thought:

"Oh, Lord! Why are these people here and this orchestra!"

And at that instant he suddenly recalled how when he had seen Anna Sergeyevna off at the station he had said to himself that all was over between them and that they would never meet again. But how distant the end still was!

On the narrow, gloomy staircase over which it said "To the Amphitheatre," she stopped.

"How you frightened me!" she said, breathing hard, still pale and stunned. "Oh, how you frightened me! I am barely alive. Why did you come? Why?"

"But do understand, Anna, do understand—" he said hurriedly, under his breath. "I implore you, do understand—"

She looked at him with fear, with entreaty, with love; she looked at him intently, to keep his features more distinctly in her memory.

"I suffer so," she went on, not listening to him. "All this time I have been thinking of nothing but you; I live only by the thought of you. And I wanted to forget, to forget; but why, oh, why have you come?"

On the landing above them two high school boys were looking down and smoking, but it was all the same to Gurov; he drew Anna Sergeyevna to him and began kissing her face and hands.

"What are you doing, what are you doing!" she was saying in horror, pushing him away. "We have lost our senses. Go away today; go away at once—I conjure you by all that is sacred, I implore you—People are coming this way!"

Someone was walking up the stairs.

"You must leave," Anna Sergeyevna went on in a whisper. "Do you hear, Dmitry Dmitrich? I will come and see you in Moscow. I have never been happy; I am unhappy now, and I never, never shall be happy, never! So don't make me suffer still more! I swear I'll come to Moscow. But now let us part. My dear, good, precious one, let us part!"

She pressed his hand and walked rapidly downstairs, turning to look round at him, and from her eyes he could see that she really was unhappy. Gurov stood for a while, listening, then when all grew quiet, he found his coat and left the theater.

IV

And Anna Sergeyevna began coming to see him in Moscow. Once every two or three months she left S—— telling her husband that she was going to consult a doctor about a woman's ailment from which she was suffering—and her husband did and did not believe her. When she arrived in Moscow she would stop at the Slavyansky Bazar Hotel, and at once send a man in a red cap to Gurov. Gurov came to see her, and no one in Moscow knew of it.

Once he was going to see her in this way on a winter morning (the messenger had come the evening before and not found him in). With him walked his daughter, whom he wanted to take to school; it was on the way. Snow was coming down in big wet flakes.

"It's three degrees above zero, and yet it's snowing," Gurov was saying to his daughter. "But this temperature prevails only on the surface of the earth; in the upper layers of the atmosphere there is quite a different temperature."

"And why doesn't it thunder in winter, papa?"

He explained that, too. He talked, thinking all the while that he was on his way to a rendezvous, and no living soul knew of it, and probably no one would ever know. He had two lives, an open one, seen and known by all who needed to know it, full of conventional truth and conventional falsehood, exactly like the lives of his friends and acquaintances; and another life that went on in secret. And through some strange, perhaps accidental, combination of circumstances, everything that was of interest and importance to him, everything that was essential to him, everything about which he felt sincerely and did not deceive himself, everything that constituted the core of his life, was going on concealed from others; while all that was false, the shell in which he hid to cover the truth—his work at the bank, for instance, his discussions at the club, his references to the "inferior race," his appearances at anniversary celebrations with his wife—all that went on in the open. Judging others by himself, he did not believe what he saw, and always fancied that every man led his real, most interesting life under cover of secrecy as under cover of night. The personal life of every individual is based on secrecy, and perhaps it is partly for that reason that civilized man is so nervously anxious that personal privacy should be respected.

Having taken his daughter to school, Gurov went on to the Slavyansky Bazar Hotel. He took off his fur coat in the lobby, went upstairs, and knocked gently at the door. Anna Sergeyevna, wearing his favorite gray dress, exhausted by the journey and by waiting, had been expecting him since the previous evening. She was pale, and looked at him without a smile, and had hardly entered when she flung herself on his breast. That kiss was a long, lingering one, as though they had not seen one another for two years.

"Well, darling, how are you getting on there?" he asked. "What news?"

"Wait; I'll tell you in a moment—I can't speak."

She could not speak; she was crying. She turned away from him, and pressed her handkerchief to her eyes.

"Let her have her cry; meanwhile I'll sit down," he thought, and he seated himself in an armchair.

Then he rang and ordered tea, and while he was having his tea she remained standing at the window with her back to him. She was crying out of sheer agitation, in the sorrowful consciousness that their life was so sad; that they could only see each other in secret and had to hide from people like thieves! Was it not a broken life?

"Come, stop now, dear!" he said.

It was plain to him that this love of theirs would not be over soon, that the end of it was not in sight. Anna Sergeyevna was growing more and more attached to him. She adored him, and it was unthinkable to tell her that their love was bound to come to an end some day; besides, she would not have believed it!

He went up to her and took her by the shoulders, to fondle her and say something diverting, and at that moment he caught sight of himself in the mirror.

His hair was already beginning to turn gray. And it seemed odd to him that he had grown so much older in the last few years, and lost his looks. The shoulders on which his hands rested were warm and heaving. He felt compassion for this life, still so warm and lovely, but probably already about to begin to fade and wither like his own. Why did she love him so much? He always seemed to women different from what he was, and they loved in him not himself, but the man whom their imagination created and whom they had been eagerly seeking all their lives; and afterwards, when they saw their mistake, they loved him nevertheless. And not one of them had been happy with him. In the past he had met women, come together with them, parted from them, but he had never once loved; it was anything you please, but not love. And only now when his head was gray he had fallen in love, really, truly—for the first time in his life.

Anna Sergeyevna and he loved each other as people do who are very close and intimate, like man and wife, like tender friends; it seemed to them that Fate itself had meant them for one another, and they could not understand why he had a wife and she a husband; and it was as though they were a pair of migratory birds, male and female, caught and forced to live in different cages. They forgave each other what they were ashamed of in their past, they forgave everything in the present, and felt that this love of theirs had altered them both.

Formerly in moments of sadness he had soothed himself with whatever logical arguments came into his head, but now he no longer cared for logic; he felt profound compassion, he wanted to be sincere and tender.

"Give it up now, my darling," he said. "You've had your cry; that's enough. Let us have a talk now, we'll think up something."

Then they spent a long time taking counsel together, they talked of how to avoid the necessity for secrecy, for deception, for living in different cities, and not seeing one another for long stretches of time. How could they free themselves from these intolerable fetters?

"How? How?" he asked, clutching his head. "How?"

And it seemed as though in a little while the solution would be found, and then a new and glorious life would begin; and it was clear to both of them that the end was still far off, and that what was to be most complicated and difficult for them was only just beginning.

(translated by Avrahm Yarmolinsky)

QUESTIONS FOR DISCUSSION AND WRITING

1. What is the reader's attitude toward Dmitry? Does that attitude change as the story goes on?
2. How do we finally view the relationship between Dmitry and Anna? Is this a tragic love story? A story of an immoral affair? The story of an obsession?
3. The ending of the story is ambiguous. What are we to imagine the eventual "end" will be? What, exactly, do we surmise will be "complicated and difficult"?
4. Dmitry and Anna both lead double lives: they live public lives with their spouses and friends and private, secret lives with each other. But sometimes it seems as if they also live double lives internally, pretending to emotions they do not feel or remaining unconscious of their real emotions. When and why do the two seem so distant from their inner selves?

JOYCE CAROL OATES (1938–   )

The Lady with the Pet Dog _____ *1972*

I

Strangers parted as if to make way for him.

There he stood. He was there in the aisle, a few yards away, watching her.

She leaned forward at once in her seat, her hand jerked up to her face as if to ward off a blow—but then the crowd in the aisle hid him, he was gone. She pressed both hands against her cheeks. He was not here, she had imagined him.

"My God," she whispered.

She was alone. Her husband had gone out to the foyer to make a telephone call; it was intermission at the concert, a Thursday evening.

Now she saw him again, clearly. He was standing there. He was staring at her. Her blood rocked in her body, draining out of her head . . . she was going to faint . . . They stared at each other. They gave no sign of recognition. Only when he took a step forward did she shake her head *no—no—keep away*. It was not possible.

When her husband returned, she was staring at the place in the aisle where her lover had been standing. Her husband leaned forward to interrupt that stare.

"What's wrong?" he said. "Are you sick?"

Panic rose in her in long shuddering waves. She tried to get to her feet, panicked at the thought of fainting here, and her husband took hold of her. She stood like an aged woman, clutching the seat before her.

At home he helped her up the stairs and she lay down. Her head was like a large piece of crockery that had to be held still, it was so heavy. She was still panicked. She felt it in the shallows of her face, behind her knees, in the pit of her stomach. It sickened her, it made her think of mucus, of something thick and gray congested inside her, stuck to her, that was herself and yet not herself—a poison.

She lay with her knees drawn up toward her chest, her eyes hotly open, while her husband spoke to her. She imagined that other man saying, *Why did you run away from me?* Her husband was saying other words. She tried to listen to them. He was going to call the doctor, he said, and she tried to sit up. "No, I'm all right now," she said quickly. The panic was like lead inside her, so thickly congested. How slow love was to drain out of her, how fluid and sticky it was inside her head!

Her husband believed her. No doctor. No threat. Grateful, she drew her husband down to her. They embraced, not comfortably. For years now they had not been comfortable together, in their intimacy and at a distance, and now they struggled gently as if the paces of this dance were too rigorous for them. It was something they might have known once, but had now outgrown. The panic in her thickened at this double betrayal: she drew her husband to her, she caressed him wildly, she shut her eyes to think about that other man.

A crowd of men and women parting, unexpectedly, and there he stood—there he stood—she kept seeing him, and yet her vision blotched at the memory. It had been finished between them, six months before, but he had come out here . . . and she had escaped him, now she was lying in her husband's arms, in his embrace, her face pressed against his. It was a kind of sleep, this love-making. She felt herself falling asleep, her body falling from her. Her eyes shut.

"I love you," her husband said fiercely, angrily.

She shut her eyes and thought of that other man, as if betraying him would give her life a center.

"Did I hurt you? Are you—?" Her husband whispered.

Always this hot flashing of shame between them, the shame of her husband's near failure, the clumsiness of his love—

"You didn't hurt me," she said.

II

They had said good-by six months before. He drove her from Nantucket, where they had met, to Albany, New York, where she visited her sister. The hours of intimacy in the car had sealed something between them, a vow of silence and impersonality: she recalled the movement of the highways, the passing of other cars, the natural rhythms of the day hypnotizing her toward sleep while he drove. She trusted him, she could sleep in his presence. Yet she could not really fall asleep in spite of her exhaustion, and she kept jerking awake, frightened, to discover that nothing had changed— still the stranger who was driving her to Albany, still the highway, the sky, the antiseptic odor of the rented car, the sense of a rhythm behind the rhythm of the air that might unleash itself at any second. Everywhere on this highway, at this moment, there were men and women driving together, bonded together—what did that mean, to be together? What did it mean to enter into a bond with another person?

No, she did not really trust him; she did not really trust men. He would glance at her with his small cautious smile and she felt a declaration of shame between them.

Shame.

In her head she rehearsed conversations. She said bitterly, "You'll be relieved when we get to Albany. Relieved to get rid of me." They had spent so many days talking, confessing too much, driven to a pitch of childish excitement, laughing together on the beach, breaking into that pose of laughter that seems to eradicate the soul, so many days of this that the silence of the trip was like the silence of a hospital—all these surface noises, these rattles and hums, but an interior silence, a befuddlement. She said to him in her imagination, "One of us should die." Then she leaned over to touch him. She caressed the back of his neck. She said, aloud, "Would you like me to drive for a while?"

They stopped at a picnic area where other cars were stopped—couples, families—and walked together, smiling at their good luck. He put his arm around her shoulders and she sensed how they were in a posture together, a man and a woman forming a posture, a figure, that someone might sketch and show to them. She said slowly, "I don't want to go back. . . ."

Silence. She looked up at him. His face was heavy with her words, as if she had pulled at his skin with her fingers. Children ran nearby and distracted him—yes, he was a father too, his children ran like that, they tugged at his skin with their light, busy fingers.

"Are you so unhappy?" he said.

"I'm not unhappy, back there. I'm nothing. There's nothing to me," she said.

They stared at each other. The sensation between them was intense, exhausting. She thought that this man was her savior, that he had come to her at a time in her life when her life demanded completion, an end, a permanent fixing of all that was troubled and shifting and deadly. And yet it was absurd to think this. No person could save another. So she drew back from him and released him.

A few hours later they stopped at a gas station in a small city. She went to the women's rest room, having to ask the attendant for a key, and when she came back her eye jumped nervously onto the rented car—why? did she think he might have driven off without her?—onto the man, her friend, standing in conversation with the young attendant. Her friend was as old as her husband, over forty, with lanky, sloping shoulders, a full body, his hair thick, a dark, burnished brown, a festive color that made her eye twitch a little—and his hands were always moving, always those rapid conversational circles, going nowhere, gestures that were at once a little aggressive and apologetic.

She put her hand on his arm, a claim. He turned to her and smiled and she felt that she loved him, that everything in her life had forced her to this moment and that she had no choice about it.

They sat in the car for two hours, in Albany, in the parking lot of a Howard Johnson's restaurant, talking, trying to figure out their past. There was no future. They concentrated on the past, the several days behind them, lit up with a hot, dazzling August sun, like explosions that already belonged to other people, to strangers. Her face was faintly reflected in the green-tinted curve of the windshield, but she could not have recognized that face. She began to cry; she told herself: *I am not here, this will pass, this is nothing.* Still, she could not stop crying. The muscles of her face were springy, like a child's, unpredictable muscles. He stroked her arms, her shoulders, trying to comfort her. "This is so hard . . . this is impossible . . ." he said. She felt panic for the world outside this car, all that was not herself and this man, and at the same time she understood that she was free of him, as people are free of other people, she would leave him soon, safely, and within a few days he would have fallen into the past, the impersonal past. . . .

"I'm so ashamed of myself!" she said finally.

She returned to her husband and saw that another woman, a shadow-woman, had taken her place—noiseless and convincing, like a dancer performing certain difficult steps. Her husband folded her in his arms and talked to her of his own loneliness, his worries about his business, his health, his mother, kept tranquilized and mute in a nursing home, and her spirit detached itself from her and drifted about the rooms of the large house she lived in with her husband, a shadow-woman delicate and imprecise. There was no boundary to her, no edge. Alone, she took hot baths and sat exhausted in the steaming water, wondering at her perpetual exhaustion. All that winter she noticed the limp, languid weight of her arms, her veins bulging slightly with the pressure of her extreme weariness. *This is fate,* she thought, to be here and not there, to be one person and not another, a certain man's wife and not the wife of another man. The long, slow pain of this certainty rose in her, but it never became clear, it was baffling and imprecise. She could not be serious about it; she kept congratulating herself on her own good luck, to have escaped so easily, to have freed herself. So much love had gone into the first several years of her marriage that there wasn't much left, now, for another man. . . . She was certain of that. But the bath water made her dizzy, all that perpetual heat, and one day in January she drew a razor blade lightly across the inside of her arm, near the elbow, to see what would happen.

Afterward she wrapped a small towel around it, to stop the bleeding. The towel soaked through. She wrapped a bath towel around that and walked through the empty rooms of her home, lightheaded, hardly aware of the stubborn seeping of blood. There was no boundary to her in this house, no precise limit. She could flow out like her own blood and come to no end.

She sat for a while on a blue love seat, her mind empty. Her husband telephoned her when he would be staying late at the plant. He talked to her always about his plans, his problems, his business friends, his future. It was obvious that he had a future. As he spoke she nodded to encourage him, and her heartbeat quickened with the memory of her own, personal shame, the shame of this man's particular, private wife. One evening at dinner he leaned forward and put his head in his arms and fell asleep, like a child. She sat at the table with him for a while, watching him. His hair had gone gray, almost white, at the temples—no one would guess that he was so quick, so careful a man, still fairly young about the eyes. She put her hand on his head, lightly, as if to prove to herself that he was real. He slept, exhausted.

One evening they went to a concert and she looked up to see her lover there, in the crowded aisle, in this city, watching her. He was standing there, with his overcoat on, watching her. She went cold. That morning the telephone had rung while her husband was still home, and she had heard him answer it, heard him hang up—it must have been a wrong number—and when the telephone rang again, at 9:30, she had been afraid to answer it. She had left home to be out of the range of that ringing, but now, in this public place, in this busy auditorium, she found herself staring at that man, unable to make any sign to him, any gesture of recognition. . . .

He would have come to her but she shook her head. *No. Stay away.*

Her husband helped her out of the row of seats, saying, "Excuse us, please. Excuse us," so that strangers got to their feet, quickly, alarmed, to let them pass. Was that woman about to faint? What was wrong?

At home she felt the blood drain slowly back into her head. Her husband embraced her hips, pressing his face against her, in that silence that belonged to the earliest days of their marriage. She thought, *He will drive it out of me.* He made love to her and she was back in the auditorium again, sitting alone, now that the concert was over. The stage was empty; the heavy velvet curtains had not been drawn; the musicians' chairs were empty, everything was silent and expectant; in the aisle her lover stood and smiled at her—Her husband was impatient. He was apart from her, working on her, operating on her; and then, stricken, he whispered, "Did I hurt you?"

The telephone rang the next morning. Dully, sluggishly, she answered it. She recognized his voice at once—that "Anna?" with its lifting of the second syllable, questioning and apologetic and making its claim—"Yes, what do you want?" she said.

"Just to see you. Please—"

"I can't."

"Anna, I'm sorry, I didn't mean to upset you—"

"I can't see you."

"Just for a few minutes—I have to talk to you—"

"But why, why now? Why now?" she said.

She heard her voice rising, but she could not stop it. He began to talk again, drowning her out. She remembered his rapid conversation. She remembered his gestures, the witty energetic circling of his hands.

"Please don't hang up!" he cried.

"I can't—I don't want to go through it again—"

"I'm not going to hurt you. Just tell me how you are."

"Everything is the same."

"Everything is the same with me."

She looked up at the ceiling, shyly. "Your wife? Your children?"

"The same."

"Your son?"

"He's fine—"

"I'm so glad to hear that. I—"

"Is it still the same with you, your marriage? Tell me what you feel. What are you thinking?"

"I don't know. . . ."

She remembered his intense, eager words, the movement of his hands, that impatient precise fixing of the air by his hands, the jabbing of his fingers.

"Do you love me?" he said.

She could not answer.

"I'll come over to see you," he said.

"No," she said.

What will come next, what will happen?

Flesh hardening on his body, aging. Shrinking. He will grow old, but not soft like her husband. They are two different types: he is nervous, lean, energetic, wise. She will grow thinner, as the tension radiates out from her backbone, wearing down her flesh. Her collarbones will jut out of her skin. Her husband, caressing her in their bed, will discover that she is another woman—she is not there with him—instead she is rising in an elevator in a downtown hotel, carrying a book as a prop, or walking quickly away from that hotel, her head bent and filled with secrets. Love, what to do with it? . . . Useless as moths' wings, as moths' fluttering. . . . She feels the flutterings of silky, crazy wings in her chest.

He flew out to visit her every several weeks, staying at a different hotel each time. He telephoned her, and she drove down to park in an underground garage at the very center of the city.

She lay in his arms while her husband talked to her, miles away, one body fading into another. He will grow old, his body will change, she thought, pressing her cheek against the back of one of these men. If it was her lover, they were in a hotel room: always the propped-up little booklet describing the hotel's many services, with color photographs of its cocktail lounge and dining room and coffee shop. Grow old, leave me, die, go back to your neurotic wife and your sad, ordinary children, she thought, but still her eyes closed gratefully against his skin and she felt how complete their silence was, how they had come to rest in each other.

"Tell me about your life here. The people who love you," he said, as he always did.

One afternoon they lay together for four hours. It was her birthday and she was intoxicated with her good fortune, this prize of the afternoon, this man in her arms! She was a little giddy, she talked too much. She told him about her parents, about her husband. . . . "They were all people I believed in, but it turned out wrong. Now, I believe in you. . . ." He laughed as if shocked by her words. She did not understand. Then she understood. "But I believe truly in you. I can't think of myself without you," she said. . . . He spoke of his wife, her ambitions, her intelligence, her use of the children against him, her use of his younger son's blindness, all of his words gentle and hypnotic and convincing in the late afternoon peace of this hotel room . . . and she felt the terror of laughter, threatening laughter. Their words, like their bodies, were aging.

She dressed quickly in the bathroom, drawing her long hair up around the back of her head, fixing it as always, anxious that everything be the same. Her face was slightly raw, from his face. The rubbing of his skin. Her eyes were too bright, wearily bright. Her hair was blond but not so blond as it had been that summer in the white Nantucket air.

She ran water and splashed it on her face. She blinked at the water. Blind. Drowning. She thought with satisfaction that soon, soon, he would be back home, in that house on Long Island she had never seen, with that woman she had never seen, sitting on the edge of another bed, putting on his shoes. She wanted nothing except to be free of him. Why not be free? *Oh,* she thought suddenly, *I will follow you back and kill you. You and her and the little boy. What is there to stop me?*

She left him. Everyone on the street pitied her, that look of absolute zero.

III

A man and a child, approaching her. The sharp acrid smell of fish. The crashing of waves. Anna pretended not to notice the father with his son—there was something strange about them. That frank, silent intimacy, too gentle, the man's bare feet in the water and the boy a few feet away, leaning away from his father. He was about nine years old and still his father held his hand.

A small yipping dog, a golden dog, bounded near them.

Anna turned shyly back to her reading; she did not want to have to speak to these neighbors. She saw the man's shadow falling over her legs, then over the pages of her book, and she had the idea that he wanted to see what she was reading. The dog nuzzled her; the man called him away.

She watched them walk down the beach. She was relieved that the man had not spoken to her.

She saw them in town later that day, the two of them brown-haired and patient, now wearing sandals, walking with that same look of care. The man's white shorts were soiled and a little baggy. His pullover shirt was a faded green. His face was broad, the cheekbones wide, spaced widely apart, the eyes stark in their sockets, as if they fastened onto objects for no reason, ponderous and edgy. The little boy's face was pale and sharp; his lips were perpetually parted.

Anna realized that the child was blind.

The next morning, early, she caught sight of them again. For some reason she went to the back door of her cottage. She faced the sea breeze eagerly. Her heart hammered. . . . She had been here, in her family's old house, for three days, alone, bitterly satisfied at being alone, and now it was a puzzle to her how her soul strained to fly outward, to meet with another person. She watched the man with his son, his cautious, rather stooped shoulders above the child's small shoulders.

The man was carrying something, it looked like a notebook. He sat on the sand, not far from Anna's spot of the day before, and the dog rushed up to them. The child approached the edge of the ocean, timidly. He moved in short jerky steps, his legs stiff. The dog ran around him. Anna heard the child crying out a word that sounded like "Ty"—it must have been the dog's name—and then the man joined in, his voice heavy and firm.

"Ty—"

Anna tied her hair back with a yellow scarf and went down to the beach.

The man glanced around at her. He smiled. She stared past him at the waves. To talk to him or not to talk—she had the freedom of that choice. For a moment she felt that she had made a mistake, that the child and the dog would not protect her, that behind this man's ordinary, friendly face there was a certain arrogant maleness—then she relented, she smiled shyly.

"A nice house you've got there," the man said.

She nodded her thanks.

The man pushed his sunglasses up on his forehead. Yes, she recognized the eyes of the day before—intelligent and nervous, the sockets pale, untanned.

"Is that your telephone ringing?" he said.

She did not bother to listen. "It's a wrong number," she said.

Her husband calling: she had left home for a few days, to be alone.

But the man, settling himself on the sand, seemed to misinterpret this. He smiled in surprise, one corner of his mouth higher than the other. He said nothing. Anna wondered: *What is he thinking?* The dog was leaping about her, panting against her legs, and she laughed in embarrassment. She bent to pet it, grateful for its busyness. "Don't let him jump up on you," the man said. "He's a nuisance."

The dog was a small golden retriever, a young dog. The blind child, standing now in the water, turned to call the dog to him. His voice was shrill and impatient.

"Our house is the third one down—the white one," the man said.

She turned, startled. "Oh, did you buy it from Dr. Patrick? Did he die?"

"Yes, finally. . . ."

Her eyes wandered nervously over the child and the dog. She felt the nervous beat of her heart out to the very tips of her fingers, the fleshy tips of her fingers: little hearts were there, pulsing. *What is he thinking?* The man had opened his notebook. He had a piece of charcoal and he began to sketch something.

Anna looked down at him. She saw the top of his head, his thick brown hair, the freckles on his shoulders, the quick, deft movement of his hand. Upside down, Anna herself being drawn. She smiled in surprise.

"Let me draw you. Sit down," he said.

She knelt awkwardly a few yards away. He turned the page of the sketch pad. The dog ran to her and she sat, straightening out her skirt beneath her, flinching from the dog's tongue. "Ty!" cried the child. Anna sat, and slowly the pleasure of the moment began to glow in her; her skin flushed with gratitude.

She sat there for nearly an hour. The man did not talk much. Back and forth the dog bounded, shaking itself. The child came to sit near them, in silence. Anna felt that she was drifting into a kind of trance while the man sketched her, half a dozen rapid sketches, the surface of her face given up to him. "Where are you from?" the man asked.

"Ohio. My husband lives in Ohio."

She wore no wedding band.

"Your wife—" Anna began.

"Yes?"

"Is she here?"

"Not right now."

She was silent, ashamed. She had asked an improper question. But the man did not seem to notice. He continued drawing her, bent over the sketch pad. When Anna said she had to go, he showed her the drawings—one after another of her, Anna, recognizably Anna, a woman in her early thirties, her hair smooth and flat across the top of her head, tied behind by a scarf. "Take the one you like best," he said, and she picked one of her with the dog in her lap, sitting very straight, her brows and eyes clearly defined, her lips girlishly pursed, the dog and her dress suggested by a few quick irregular lines.

"Lady with pet dog," the man said.

She spent the rest of that day reading, nearer her cottage. It was not really a cottage—it was a two-story house, large and ungainly and weathered. It was mixed up in her mind with her family, her own childhood, and she glanced up from her book, perplexed, as if waiting for one of her parents or her sister to come up to her. Then she thought of that man, the man with the blind child, the man with the dog, and she could not concentrate on her reading. Someone—probably her father—had marked a passage that must be important, but she kept reading and rereading it: *We try to discover in things, endeared to us on that account, the spiritual glamour which we ourselves have cast upon them; we are disillusioned, and learn that they are in themselves barren and devoid of the charm that they owed, in our minds, to the association of certain ideas. . . .*

She thought again of the man on the beach. She lay the book aside and thought of him: his eyes, his aloneness, his drawings of her.

They began seeing each other after that. He came to her front door in the evening, without the child; he drove her into town for dinner. She was shy and extremely pleased. The darkness of the expensive restaurant released her; she heard herself chatter; she leaned forward and seemed to be offering her face up to him, listening to him. He talked about his work on a Long Island newspaper and she seemed to be listening to him, as she stared at his face, arranging her own face into the expression she had seen in that charcoal drawing. Did he see her like that, then?—girlish and withdrawn and patrician? She felt the weight of his interest in her, a force that fell upon her like a blow. A repeated blow. Of course he was married, he had children—of course she was married, permanently married. This flight from her husband was not important. She had left him before, to be alone, it was not important. Everything in her was slender and delicate and not important.

They walked for hours after dinner, looking at the other strollers, the weekend visitors, the tourists, the couples like themselves. Surely they were mistaken for a couple, a married couple. *This is the hour in which everything is decided,* Anna thought. They had both had several drinks and they talked a great deal. Anna found herself saying too much, stopping and starting giddily. She put her hand to her forehead, feeling faint.

"It's from the sun—you've had too much sun—" he said.

At the door to her cottage, on the front porch, she heard herself asking him if he would like to come in. She allowed him to lead her inside, to close the door. *This is not important,* she thought clearly, *he doesn't mean it, he doesn't love me, nothing will come of it.* She was frightened, yet it seemed to her necessary to give in; she had to leave Nantucket with that act completed, an act of adultery, an accomplishment she would take back to Ohio and to her marriage.

Later, incredibly, she heard herself asking: "Do you . . . do you love me?"

"You're so beautiful!" he said, amazed.

She felt this beauty, shy and glowing and centered in her eyes. He stared at her. In this large, drafty house, alone together, they were like accomplices, conspirators.

She could not think: how old was she? which year was this? They had done something unforgivable together, and the knowledge of it was tugging at their faces. A cloud seemed to pass over her. She felt herself smiling shrilly.

Afterward, a peculiar raspiness, a dryness of breath. He was silent. She felt a strange, idle fear, a sense of the danger outside this room and this old comfortable bed—a danger that would not recognize her as the lady in that drawing, the lady with the pet dog. There was nothing to say to this man, this stranger. She felt the beauty draining out of her face, her eyes fading.

"I've got to be alone," she told him.

He left, and she understood that she would not see him again. She stood by the window of the room, watching the ocean. A sense of shame overpowered her: it was smeared everywhere on her body, the smell of it, the richness of it. She tried to recall him, and his face was confused in her memory: she would have to shout to him across a jumbled space, she would have to wave her arms wildly. *You love me! You must love me!* But she knew he did not love her, and she did not love him; he was a man who drew everything up into himself, like all men, walking away, free to walk away, free to have his own thoughts, free to envision her body, all the secrets of her body. . . . And she lay down again in the bed, feeling how heavy this body had become, her insides heavy with shame, the very backs of her eyelids coated with shame.

"This is the end of one part of my life," she thought.

But in the morning the telephone rang. She answered it. It was her lover: they talked brightly and happily. She could hear the eagerness in his voice, the love in his voice, that same still, sad amazement—she understood how simple life was, there were no problems.

They spent most of their time on the beach, with the child and the dog. He joked and was serious at the same time. He said, once, "You have defined my soul for me," and she laughed to hide her alarm. In a few days it was time for her to leave. He got a sitter for the boy and took the ferry with her to the mainland, then rented a car to drive her up to Albany. She kept thinking: *Now something will happen. It will come to an end.* But most of the drive was silent and hypnotic. She wanted him to joke with her, to say again that she had defined his soul for him, but he drove fast, he was serious, she distrusted the hawkish look of his profile—she did not know him at all. At a gas station she splashed her face with cold water. Alone in the grubby little rest room, shaky and very much alone. In such places are women totally alone with their bodies. The body grows heavier, more evil, in such silence. . . . On the beach everything had been noisy with sunlight and gulls and waves; here, as if run to earth, everything was cramped and silent and dead.

She went outside, squinting. There he was, talking with the station attendant. She could not think as she returned to him whether she wanted to live or not.

She stayed in Albany for a few days, then flew home to her husband. He met her at the airport, near the luggage counter, where her three pieces of pale-brown luggage were brought to him on a conveyer belt, to be claimed by him. He kissed her on the cheek. They shook hands, a little embarrassed. She had come home again.

"How will I live out the rest of my life?" she wondered.

In January her lover spied on her: she glanced up and saw him, in a public place, in the DeRoy Symphony Hall. She was paralyzed with fear. She nearly fainted. In this faint she felt her husband's body, loving her, working its love upon her, and she shut her eyes harder to keep out the certainty of his love—sometimes he failed at loving her, sometimes he succeeded, it had nothing to do with her or her pity or her ten years of love for him, it had nothing to do with a woman at all. It was a private act accomplished by a man, a husband, or a lover, in communion with his own soul, his manhood.

Her husband was forty-two years old now, growing slowly into middle age, getting heavier, softer. Her lover was about the same age, narrower in the shoulders, with a full, solid chest, yet lean, nervous. She thought, in her paralysis, of men and how they love freely and eagerly so long as their bodies are capable of love, love for a woman; and then, as love fades in their bodies, it fades from their souls and they become immune and immortal and ready to die.

Her husband was a little rough with her, as if impatient with himself. "I love you," he said fiercely, angrily. And then, ashamed, he said, "Did I hurt you? . . ."

"You didn't hurt me," she said.

Her voice was too shrill for their embrace.

While he was in the bathroom she went to her closet and took out that drawing of the summer before. There she was, on the beach at Nantucket, a lady with a pet dog, her eyes large and defined, the dog in her lap hardly more than a few snarls, a few coarse soft lines of charcoal . . . her dress smeared, her arms oddly limp . . . her hands not well drawn at all. . . . She tried to think: did she love the man who had drawn this? did he love her? The fever in her husband's body had touched her and driven her temperature up, and now she stared at the drawing with a kind of lust, fearful of seeing an ugly soul in that woman's face, fearful of seeing the face suddenly through her lover's eyes. She breathed quickly and harshly, staring at the drawing.

And so, the next day, she went to him at his hotel. She wept, pressing against him, demanding of him, "What do you want? Why are you here? Why don't you let me alone?" He told her that he wanted nothing. He expected nothing. He would not cause trouble.

"I want to talk about last August," he said.

"Don't—" she said.

She was hypnotized by his gesturing hands, his nervousness, his obvious agitation. He kept saying, "I understand. I'm making no claims upon you."

They became lovers again.

He called room service for something to drink and they sat side by side on his bed, looking through a copy of *The New Yorker,* laughing at the cartoons. It was so peaceful in this room, so complete. They were on a holiday. It was a secret holiday. Four-thirty in the afternoon, on a Friday, an ordinary Friday: a secret holiday.

"I won't bother you again," he said.

He flew back to see her again in March, and in late April. He telephoned her from his hotel—a different hotel each time—and she came down to him at once. She rose to him in various elevators, she knocked on the doors of various rooms, she stepped into his embrace, breathless and guilty and already angry with him, pleading with him. One morning in May, when he telephoned, she pressed her forehead against the doorframe and could not speak. He kept saying, "What's wrong? Can't you talk? Aren't you alone?" She felt that she was going insane. Her head would burst. Why, why did he love her, why did he pursue her? Why did he want her to die?

She went to him in the hotel room. A familiar room: had they been here before? "Everything is repeating itself. Everything is stuck," she said. He framed her face in his hands and said that she looked thinner—was she sick?—what was wrong? She shook herself free. He, her lover, looked about the same. There was a small, angry pimple on his neck. He stared at her, eagerly and suspiciously. Did she bring bad news?

"So you love me? You love me?" she asked.

"Why are you so angry?"

"I want to be free of you. The two of us free of each other."

"That isn't true—you don't want that—"

He embraced her. She was wild with that old, familiar passion for him, her body clinging to his, her arms not strong enough to hold him. Ah, what despair!—what bitter hatred she felt!—she needed this man for her salvation, he was all she had to live for, and yet she could not believe in him. He embraced her thighs, her hips, kissing her, pressing his warm face against her, and yet she could not believe in him, not really. She needed him in order to live, but he was not worth her love, he was not worth her dying. . . . She promised herself this: when she got back home, when she was alone, she would draw the razor more deeply across her arm.

The telephone rang and he answered it: a wrong number.

"Jesus," he said.

They lay together, still. She imagined their posture like this, the two of them one figure, one substance; and outside this room and this bed there was a universe of disjointed, separate things, blank things, that had nothing to do with them. She would not be Anna out there, the lady in the drawing. He would not be her lover.

"I love you so much . . ." she whispered.

"Please don't cry! We have only a few hours, please. . . ."

It was absurd, their clinging together like this. She saw them as a single figure in a drawing, their arms and legs entwined, their heads pressing mutely together. Helpless substance, so heavy and warm and doomed. It was absurd that any human being should be so important to another human being. She wanted to laugh: a laugh might free them both.

She could not laugh.

Sometime later he said, as if they had been arguing, "Look. It's you. You're the one who doesn't want to get married. You lie to me—"

"Lie to you?"

"You love me but you won't marry me, because you want something left over—Something not finished—All your life you can attribute your misery to me, to our not being married—you are using me—"

"Stop it! You'll make me hate you!" she cried.

"You can say to yourself that you're miserable because of *me*. We will never be married, you will never be happy, neither one of us will ever be happy—"

"I don't want to hear this!" she said.

She pressed her hands flatly against her face.

She went to the bathroom to get dressed. She washed her face and part of her body, quickly. The fever was in her, in the pit of her belly. She would rush home and strike a razor across the inside of her arm and free that pressure, that fever.

The impatient bulging of the veins: an ordeal over.

The demand of the telephone's ringing: that ordeal over.

The nuisance of getting the car and driving home in all that five o'clock traffic: an ordeal too much for a woman.

The movement of this stranger's body in hers: over, finished.

Now, dressed, a little calmer, they held hands and talked. They had to talk swiftly, to get all their news in: he did not trust the people who worked for him, he had faith in no one, his wife had moved to a textbook publishing company and was doing well, she had inherited a Ben Shahn painting from her father and wanted to "touch it up a little"—she was crazy!—his blind son was at another school, doing fairly well, in fact his children were all doing fairly well in spite of the stupid mistake of their parents' marriage—and what about her? what about her life? She told him in a rush the one thing he wanted to hear: that she lived with her husband lovelessly, the two of them polite strangers, sharing a bed, lying side by side in the night in that bed, bodies out of which souls had fled. There was no longer even any shame between them.

"And what about me? Do you feel shame with me still?" he asked.

She did not answer. She moved away from him and prepared to leave.

Then, a minute later, she happened to catch sight of his reflection in the bureau mirror—he was glancing down at himself, checking himself mechanically, imperson-ally, preparing also to leave. He too would leave this room: he too was headed some-where else.

She stared at him. It seemed to her that in this instant he was breaking from her, the image of her lover fell free of her, breaking from her . . . and she realized that he existed in a dimension quite apart from her, a mysterious being. And suddenly, joy-fully, she felt a miraculous calm. This man was her husband, truly—they were truly married, here in this room—they had been married haphazardly and accidentally for a long time. In another part of the city she had another husband, a "husband," but she had not betrayed that man, not really. This man, whom she loved above any other per-son in the world, above even her own self-pitying sorrow and her own life, was her truest lover, her destiny. And she did not hate him, she did not hate herself any longer; she did not wish to die; she was flooded with a strange certainty, a sense of gratitude, of pure selfless energy. It was obvious to her that she had, all along, been behaving correctly; out of instinct.

What triumph, to love like this in any room, anywhere, risking even the craziest of accidents!

"Why are you so happy? What's wrong?" he asked, startled. He stared at her. She felt the abrupt concentration in him, the focusing of his vision on her, almost a bitter-ness in his face, as if he feared her. What, was it beginning all over again? Their love beginning again, in spite of them? "How can you look so happy?" he asked. "We don't have any right to it. Is it because . . . ?"

"Yes," she said.

QUESTIONS FOR DISCUSSION AND WRITING

1. Oates's story depends on flashbacks. In fact, it often circles back, retelling the same stories. How do these structures affect the reader's response to the lovers and their affair? When we hear about an event the second or third time, do we respond to it the same way we did the first time around?

2. Anna and her lover keep asking whether they are happy and whether they are truly in love. Are they? To what extent does each seem to have found happiness

and fulfillment in the other? To what extent has the affair made each *less* happy and satisfied?

QUESTIONS FOR CROSS READING: A QUESTION OF FIDELITY

1. Chekhov's story is told from a male point of view, and Oates's is told from a female point of view. How do the two stories reflect these different points of view? Is Oates's story more "feminist" than Chekhov's? Why does Oates leave the male lover unnamed?
2. Chekhov, a Russian writer, sets the story near Moscow and in Yalta, a resort that has a reputation for immorality. Oates, an American writer, sets the story in the United States, at Nantucket, a place of family vacation homes. How do the different settings and descriptions of place provide different contexts for the affairs and contribute to different responses to the characters' behavior?
3. In Chekhov's story the lady owns the pet dog; in Oates's story, the dog belongs to the male lover. How does Oates's change affect the way the reader responds to the characters?
4. How similar are the two stories' views of the affairs? To what extent are Chekhov's and/or Oates's lovers "soul mates"? Is one ending happier than the other?

Janie Charamuga

Professor Logan

English 1B Online

18 September 2001

     The Two Worlds of Gurov

   In Chekov's story, The Lady with the Pet Dog, the charac-

ter of Gurov experiences an escalating conflict between his

outer conventional persona and his inner yearnings. The two

settings of Yalta and Moscow, their physical characteristics

and their associated lifestyles, mirror this divide in

Gurov's personality. Even the season when he arrives in each

place reflects this theme. Yalta is a resort town where he

goes alone during the summer to vacation and enjoy himself.
Moscow is Gurov's home where he returns to for the winter to
be with his wife and children.

When Gurov refers to Yalta he describes a resort town with
festive crowds, diversions, and "the light banter of people
who are free and contented". Though he feels that Yalta
doesn't deserve its immoral reputation he does fantasize a
brief, entertaining affair. He mentions that one peculiarity
of a Yalta crowd is that "the elderly ladies were dressed
like young ones", implying that Yalta is a place to escape
back to the carefree, self-indulgent days of one's youth.
(21) Similarly, Gurov is attracted to Anna who is much
younger than he is. So he too feels drawn to jump backwards
in time to a young or even adolescent state. There is an
abundance of leisure time where "One did not know what to do
with oneself", and the spell of this relaxed atmosphere lends
itself to reflection and easeful musings. (20) "Gurov, soothed
and spellbound by these magical surroundings--the sea, the
mountains, the clouds, the wide sky--thought how everything
is really beautiful in this world when one reflects: everything except what we think or do ourselves when we forget the
higher aims of life and our own human dignity." (47) When he
returns to Moscow however, there is an abrupt change in his
manner and attitude.

Moscow represents formality, convention and history as illustrated by Gurov's arranged marriage and his role as father
to three children. At times he seems content and perhaps reassured by the regularity of Moscow life. When he arrives
home for winter the first snow brings back fond memories
of childhood. (61) He is glad to return to his routine of

reading newspapers, attending dinners and anniversary celebrations, and entertaining distinguished guests. All of these
things paint a picture of a life securely nestled in convention and tradition. (61) Of his relationship with his wife he
says "it was not love or passion that engaged them but something more significant." (27) So even his marriage rests on a
foundation of conventional roles in a conservative society
and he doesn't seem to expect that it should be different
than it is. After getting resettled after his vacation, his
contentment with his life and role in Moscow begins to be
disrupted by memories of his time with Anna.

   What begins as occasional sparks of memory eventually
catch fire as Gurov is consumed with thoughts of Anna. As a
result Moscow and tradition begin to feel confining and bleak.
"Futile pursuits and conversations always about the same topics take up the better part of one's time, the better part of
one's strength, and in the end there is left a life clipped
and wingless, an absurd mess, and there is no escaping or
getting away from it--just as though one were in a madhouse
or a prison." (70) Finally he is compelled to go to Anna's
hometown in search of her.

   When Gurov returns from visiting Anna the conflict he experiences escalates, his symptoms become more acute and his
commentary more intense. ". . . everything that was of interest and importance to him, everything that was essential
to him, everything about which he felt sincerely and did
not deceive himself, everything that constituted the core of
his life, was going on concealed from others; while all that
was false, the shell in which he hid to cover the truth . . .
all that went on in the open." (105) Now our unfortunate

protagonist is in the position of trying to maintain two distinct lives simultaneously. In a sense he has attempted to
bring Yalta home with him, he has let his inner dreams begin
to seep into everyday life. And the disparity between these
elements is torment.

Chekov does an excellent job of illustrating this theme so
common among responsible adults. Speaking from my own
perspective as a middle class American, conventional adult
life brings with it many benefits including a close family, a
variety of job opportunities, a comfortable house, reliable
cars, schools and activities for my children, even a swimming pool. However, along with the fulfillment of this circumstance comes a sometimes staggering load of responsibility
and at times an unending monotony of chores. I imagine it is
very common to occasionally look with longing back to the
years of early adulthood, which represent a more carefree and
self-indulgent lifestyle. Perhaps everyone yearns for a
respite in Yalta. Yet most of us find ways to integrate and
balance these contradictory aspects of life. We set aside
time to relax, time away with our spouse, opportunities to
reflect and redirect our life when we begin to feel too confined. If we don't take these measures we will perhaps find
ourselves in a desperate split as Gurov does. The story ends
with the line ". . . what was to be most complicated and difficult for them was only just beginning." Perhaps Gurov and
Anna sense the unworkable-ness of their duplicity and also
that integration, whatever form it takes, will be an arduous
process.

QUESTIONS FOR DISCUSSION AND WRITING

1. Although Janie Charamuga's paper is generally well written, there are a number of errors, particularly punctuation errors. What punctuation errors did you notice? What other sentence corrections or changes would you make?
2. What is the thesis of Charamuga's essay? As a reader, how satisfactory did you find its placement? What revisions, if any, would you make to the thesis?
3. Does each paragraph discuss a separate idea? Where might the topic sentences be sharpened? How?

BRINGING UP THE PAST

RAYMOND CARVER (1938–1988)
Cathedral _____ *1981*

This blind man, an old friend of my wife's, he was on his way to spend the night. His wife had died. So he was visiting the dead wife's relatives in Connecticut. He called my wife from his in-laws'. Arrangements were made. He would come by train, a five-hour trip, and my wife would meet him at the station. She hadn't seen him since she worked for him one summer in Seattle ten years ago. But she and the blind man had kept in touch. They made tapes and mailed them back and forth. I wasn't enthusiastic about his visit. He was no one I knew. And his being blind bothered me. My idea of blindness came from the movies. In the movies, the blind moved slowly and never laughed. Sometimes they were led by seeing-eye dogs. A blind man in my house was not something I looked forward to.

That summer in Seattle she had needed a job. She didn't have any money. The man she was going to marry at the end of the summer was in officers' training school. He didn't have any money, either. But she was in love with the guy, and he was in love with her, etc. She'd seen something in the paper: HELP WANTED—*Reading to Blind Man,* and a telephone number. She phoned and went over, was hired on the spot. She'd worked with this blind man all summer. She read stuff to him, case studies, reports, that sort of thing. She helped him organize his little office in the county social-service department. They'd become good friends, my wife and the blind man. How do I know these things? She told me. And she told me something else. On her last day in the office, the blind man asked if he could touch her face. She agreed to this. She told me he touched his fingers to every part of her face, her nose—even her neck! She never forgot it. She even tried to write a poem about it. She was always trying to write a poem. She wrote a poem or two every year, usually after something really important had happened to her.

When we first started going out together, she showed me the poem. In the poem, she recalled his fingers and the way they had moved around over her face. In the poem, she talked about what she had felt at the time, about what went through her mind when the blind man touched her nose and lips. I can remember I didn't think much of the poem. Of course, I didn't tell her that. Maybe I just don't understand poetry. I admit it's not the first thing I reach for when I pick up something to read.

Anyway, this man who'd first enjoyed her favors, the officer-to-be, he'd been her childhood sweetheart. So okay. I'm saying that at the end of the summer she let the blind man run his hands over her face, said good-bye to him, married her childhood etc., who was now a commissioned officer, and she moved away from Seattle. But they'd kept in touch, she and the blind man. She made the first contact after a year or so. She called him up one night from an Air Force base in Alabama. She wanted to talk. They talked. He asked her to send him a tape and tell him about her life. She did this. She sent the tape. On the tape, she told the blind man about her husband and about their life together in the military. She told the blind man she loved her husband but she didn't like it where they lived and she didn't like it that he was part of the military-industrial thing. She told the blind man she'd written a poem and he was in it. She told him that she was writing a poem about what it was like to be an Air Force officer's wife. The poem wasn't finished yet. She was still writing it. The blind man made a tape. He sent her the tape. She made a tape. This went on for years. My wife's officer was posted to one base and then another. She sent tapes from Moody AFB, McGuire, McConnell, and finally Travis, near Sacramento, where one night she got to feeling lonely and cut off from people she kept losing in that moving-around life. She got to feeling she couldn't go it another step. She went in and swallowed all the pills and capsules in the medicine chest and washed them down with a bottle of gin. Then she got into a hot bath and passed out.

But instead of dying, she got sick. She threw up. Her officer—why should he have a name? he was the childhood sweetheart, and what more does he want?—came home from somewhere, found her, and called the ambulance. In time, she put it all on a tape and sent the tape to the blind man. Over the years, she put all kinds of stuff on tape and sent the tapes off lickety-split. Next to writing a poem every year, I think it was her chief means of recreation. On one tape, she told the blind man she'd decided to live away from her officer for a time. On another tape, she told him about her divorce. She and I began going out, and of course she told her blind man about it. She told him everything, or so it seemed to me. Once she asked me if I'd like to hear the latest tape from the blind man. This was a year ago. I was on the tape, she said. So I said okay, I'd listen to it. I got us drinks and we settled down in the living room. We made ready to listen. First she inserted the tape into the player and adjusted a couple of dials. Then she pushed a lever. The tape squeaked and someone began to talk in this loud voice. She lowered the volume. After a few minutes of harmless chitchat, I heard my own name in the mouth of this stranger, this blind man I didn't even know! And then this: "From all you've said about him, I can only conclude—" But we were interrupted, a knock at the door, something, and we didn't ever get back to the tape. Maybe it was just as well. I'd heard all I wanted to.

Now this same blind man was coming to sleep in my house.

"Maybe I could take him bowling," I said to my wife. She was at the draining board doing scalloped potatoes. She put down the knife she was using and turned around.

"If you love me," she said, "you can do this for me. If you don't love me, okay. But if you had a friend, any friend, and the friend came to visit, I'd make him feel comfortable." She wiped her hands with the dish towel.

"I don't have any blind friends," I said.

"You don't have *any* friends," she said. "Period. Besides," she said, "goddamn it, his wife's just died! Don't you understand that? The man's lost his wife!"

I didn't answer. She'd told me a little about the blind man's wife. Her name was Beulah. Beulah! That's a name for a colored woman.

"Was his wife a Negro?" I asked.

"Are you crazy?" my wife said. "Have you just flipped or something?" She picked up a potato. I saw it hit the floor, then roll under the stove. "What's wrong with you?" she said. "Are you drunk?"

"I'm just asking," I said.

Right then my wife filled me in with more detail than I cared to know. I made a drink and sat at the kitchen table to listen. Pieces of the story began to fall into place.

Beulah had gone to work for the blind man the summer after my wife had stopped working for him. Pretty soon Beulah and the blind man had themselves a church wedding. It was a little wedding—who'd want to go to such a wedding in the first place?—just the two of them, plus the minister and the minister's wife. But it was a church wedding just the same. It was what Beulah had wanted, he'd said. But even then Beulah must have been carrying the cancer in her glands. After they had been inseparable for eight years—my wife's word, *inseparable*—Beulah's health went into a rapid decline. She died in a Seattle hospital room, the blind man sitting beside the bed and holding on to her hand. They'd married, lived and worked together, slept together—had sex, sure—and then the blind man had to bury her. All this without his having ever seen what the goddamned woman looked like. It was beyond my understanding. Hearing this, I felt sorry for the blind man for a little bit. And then I found myself thinking what a pitiful life this woman must have led. Imagine a woman who could never see herself as she was seen in the eyes of her loved one. A woman who could go on day after day and never receive the smallest compliment from her beloved. A woman whose husband could never read the expression on her face, be it misery or something better. Someone who could wear makeup or not—what difference to him? She could, if she wanted, wear green eye-shadow around one eye, a straight pin in her nostril, yellow slacks and purple shoes, no matter. And then to slip off into death, the blind man's hand on her hand, his blind eyes streaming tears—I'm imagining now—her last thought maybe this: that he never even knew what she looked like, and she on an express to the grave. Robert was left with a small insurance policy and half of a twenty-peso Mexican coin. The other half of the coin went into the box with her. Pathetic.

So when the time rolled around, my wife went to the depot to pick him up. With nothing to do but wait—sure, I blamed him for that—I was having a drink and watching the TV when I heard the car pull into the drive. I got up from the sofa with my drink and went to the window to have a look.

I saw my wife laughing as she parked the car. I saw her get out of the car and shut the door. She was still wearing a smile. Just amazing. She went around to the other side of the car to where the blind man was already starting to get out. This blind man, feature this, he was wearing a full beard! A beard on a blind man! Too much, I say. The blind man reached into the back seat and dragged out a suitcase. My wife took his arm, shut the car door, and, talking all the way, moved him down the drive and then up the steps to the front porch. I turned off the TV. I finished my drink, rinsed the glass, dried my hands. Then I went to the door.

My wife said, "I want you to meet Robert. Robert, this is my husband. I've told you all about him." She was beaming. She had this blind man by his coat sleeve.

The blind man let go of his suitcase and up came his hand.

I took it. He squeezed hard, held my hand, and then he let it go.

"I feel like we've already met," he boomed.

"Likewise," I said. I didn't know what else to say. Then I said, "Welcome. I've heard a lot about you." We began to move then, a little group, from the porch into the living room, my wife guiding him by the arm. The blind man was carrying his suitcase in his other hand. My wife said things like, "To your left here, Robert. That's right. Now watch it, there's a chair. That's it. Sit down right here. This is the sofa. We just bought this sofa two weeks ago."

I started to say something about the old sofa. I'd liked that old sofa. But I didn't say anything. Then I wanted to say something else, small-talk, about the scenic ride along the Hudson. How going *to* New York, you should sit on the right-hand side of the train, and coming *from* New York, the left-hand side.

"Did you have a good train ride?" I said. "Which side of the train did you sit on, by the way?"

"What a question, which side!" my wife said. "What's it matter which side?" she said.

"I just asked," I said.

"Right side," the blind man said. "I hadn't been on a train in nearly forty years. Not since I was a kid. With my folks. That's been a long time. I'd nearly forgotten the sensation. I have winter in my beard now," he said. "So I've been told, anyway. Do I look distinguished, my dear?" the blind man said to my wife.

"You look distinguished, Robert," she said. "Robert," she said. "Robert, it's just so good to see you."

My wife finally took her eyes off the blind man and looked at me. I had the feeling she didn't like what she saw. I shrugged.

I've never met, or personally known, anyone who was blind. This blind man was late forties, a heavy-set, balding man with stooped shoulders, as if he carried a great weight there. He wore brown slacks, brown shoes, a light-brown shirt, a tie, a sports coat. Spiffy. He also had this full beard. But he didn't use a cane and he didn't wear dark glasses. I'd always thought dark glasses were a must for the blind. Fact was, I wished he had a pair. At first glance, his eyes looked like anyone else's eyes. But if you looked close, there was something different about them. Too much white in the iris, for one thing, and the pupils seemed to move around in the sockets without his knowing it or being able to stop it. Creepy. As I stared at his face, I saw the left pupil turn in toward his nose while the other made an effort to keep in one place. But it was only an effort, for that eye was on the roam without his knowing it or wanting it to be.

I said, "Let me get you a drink. What's your pleasure? We have a little of everything. It's one of our pastimes."

"Bub, I'm a Scotch man myself," he said fast enough in this big voice.

"Right," I said. Bub! "Sure you are. I knew it."

He let his fingers touch his suitcase, which was sitting alongside the sofa. He was taking his bearings. I didn't blame him for that.

"I'll move that up to your room," my wife said.

"No, that's fine," the blind man said loudly. "It can go up when I go up."

"A little water with the Scotch?" I said.

"Very little," he said.

"I knew it," I said.

He said, "Just a tad. The Irish actor, Barry Fitzgerald? I'm like that fellow. When I drink water, Fitzgerald said, I drink water. When I drink whiskey, I drink whiskey." My wife laughed. The blind man brought his hand up under his beard. He lifted his beard slowly and let it drop.

I did the drinks, three big glasses of Scotch with a splash of water in each. Then we made ourselves comfortable and talked about Robert's travels. First the long flight from the West Coast to Connecticut, we covered that. Then from Connecticut up here by train. We had another drink concerning that leg of the trip.

I remembered having read somewhere that the blind didn't smoke because, as speculation had it, they couldn't see the smoke they exhaled. I thought I knew that much and that much only about blind people. But this blind man smoked his cigarette down to the nubbin and then lit another one. This blind man filled his ashtray and my wife emptied it.

When we sat down at the table for dinner, we had another drink. My wife heaped Robert's plate with cube steak, scalloped potatoes, green beans. I buttered him up two slices of bread. I said, "Here's bread and butter for you." I swallowed some of my drink. "Now let us pray," I said, and the blind man lowered his head. My wife looked at me, her mouth agape. "Pray the phone won't ring and the food doesn't get cold," I said.

We dug in. We ate everything there was to eat on the table. We ate like there was no tomorrow. We didn't talk. We ate. We scarfed. We grazed that table. We were into serious eating. The blind man had right away located his foods, he knew just where everything was on his plate. I watched with admiration as he used his knife and fork on the meat. He'd cut two pieces of meat, fork the meat into his mouth, and then go all out for the scalloped potatoes, the beans next, and then he'd tear off a hunk of buttered bread and eat that. He'd follow this up with a big drink of milk. It didn't seem to bother him to use his fingers once in a while, either.

We finished everything, including half a strawberry pie. For a few moments, we sat as if stunned. Sweat beaded on our faces. Finally, we got up from the table and left the dirty plates. We didn't look back. We took ourselves into the living room and sank into our places again. Robert and my wife sat on the sofa. I took the big chair. We had us two or three more drinks while they talked about the major things that had come to pass for them in the past ten years. For the most part, I just listened. Now and then I joined in. I didn't want him to think I'd left the room, and I didn't want her to think I was feeling left out. They talked of things that had happened to them—to them!—these past ten years. I waited in vain to hear my name on my wife's sweet lips: "And then my dear husband came into my life"—something like that. But I heard nothing of the sort. More talk of Robert. Robert had done a little of everything, it seemed, a regular blind jack-of-all-trades. But most recently he and his wife had had an Amway distributorship, from which, I gathered, they'd earned their living, such as it was. The blind man was also a ham radio operator. He talked in his loud voice about conversations he'd had with fellow operators in Guam, in the Philippines, in Alaska, and even in Tahiti. He said he'd have a lot of friends there if he ever wanted to go visit those places. From time to time, he'd turn his blind face toward me, put his hand under his beard, ask me something. How long had I been in my present position? (Three years.) Did I like my work? (I didn't.) Was I going to stay with it? (What were the options?) Finally, when I thought he was beginning to run down, I got up and turned on the TV.

My wife looked at me with irritation. She was heading toward a boil. Then she looked at the blind man and said, "Robert, do you have a TV?"

The blind man said, "My dear, I have two TVs. I have a color set and a black-and-white thing, an old relic. It's funny, but if I turn the TV on, and I'm always turning it on, I turn on the color set. It's funny, don't you think?"

I didn't know what to say to that. I had absolutely nothing to say to that. No opinion. So I watched the news program and tried to listen to what the announcer was saying.

"This is a color TV," the blind man said. "Don't ask me how, but I can tell."

"We traded up a while ago," I said.

The blind man had another taste of his drink. He lifted his beard, sniffed it, and let it fall. He leaned forward on the sofa. He positioned his ashtray on the coffee table, then put the lighter to his cigarette. He leaned back on the sofa and crossed his legs at the ankles.

My wife covered her mouth, and then she yawned. She stretched. She said, "I think I'll go upstairs and put on my robe. I think I'll change into something else. Robert, you make yourself comfortable," she said.

"I'm comfortable," the blind man said.

"I want you to feel comfortable in this house," she said.

"I am comfortable," the blind man said.

After she'd left the room, he and I listened to the weather report and then to the sports roundup. By that time, she'd been gone so long I didn't know if she was going to come back. I thought she might have gone to bed. I wished she'd come back downstairs. I didn't want to be left alone with a blind man. I asked him if he wanted another drink, and he said sure. Then I asked if he wanted to smoke some dope with me. I said I'd just rolled a number. I hadn't, but I planned to do so in about two shakes.

"I'll try some with you," he said.

"Damn right," I said. "That's the stuff."

I got our drinks and sat down on the sofa with him. Then I rolled us two fat numbers. I lit one and passed it. I brought it to his fingers. He took it and inhaled.

"Hold it as long as you can," I said. I could tell he didn't know the first thing.

My wife came back downstairs wearing her pink robe and her pink slippers.

"What do I smell?" she said.

"We thought we'd have us some cannabis," I said.

My wife gave me a savage look. Then she looked at the blind man and said, "Robert, I didn't know you smoked."

He said, "I do now, my dear. There's a first time for everything. But I don't feel anything yet."

"This stuff is pretty mellow," I said. "This stuff is mild. It's dope you can reason with," I said. "It doesn't mess you up."

"Not much it doesn't, bub," he said, and laughed.

My wife sat on the sofa between the blind man and me. I passed her the number. She took it and toked and then passed it back to me. "Which way is this going?" she said. Then she said, "I shouldn't be smoking this. I can hardly keep my eyes open as it is. That dinner did me in. I shouldn't have eaten so much."

"It was the strawberry pie," the blind man said. "That's what did it," he said, and he laughed his big laugh. Then he shook his head.

"There's more strawberry pie," I said.

"Do you want some more, Robert?" my wife said.

"Maybe in a little while," he said.

We gave our attention to the TV. My wife yawned again. She said, "Your bed is made up when you feel like going to bed, Robert. I know you must have had a long day. When you're ready to go to bed, say so." She pulled his arm. "Robert?"

He came to and said, "I've had a real nice time. This beats tapes, doesn't it?"

I said, "Coming at you," and I put the number between his fingers. He inhaled, held the smoke, and then let it go. It was like he'd been doing it since he was nine years old.

"Thanks, bub," he said. "But I think this is all for me. I think I'm beginning to feel it," he said. He held the burning roach out for my wife.

"Same here," she said. "Ditto. Me, too." She took the roach and passed it to me. "I may just sit here for a while between you two guys with my eyes closed. But don't let me bother you, okay? Either one of you. If it bothers you, say so. Otherwise, I may just sit here with my eyes closed until you're ready to go to bed," she said. "Your bed's made up, Robert, when you're ready. It's right next to our room at the top of the stairs. We'll show you up when you're ready. You wake me up now, you guys, if I fall asleep." She said that and then she closed her eyes and went to sleep.

The news program ended. I got up and changed the channel. I sat back down on the sofa. I wished my wife hadn't pooped out. Her head lay across the back of the sofa, her mouth open. She'd turned so that her robe slipped away from her legs, exposing a juicy thigh. I reached to draw her robe back over her, and it was then that I glanced at the blind man. What the hell! I flipped the robe open again.

"You say when you want some strawberry pie," I said.

"I will," he said.

I said, "Are you tired? Do you want me to take you up to your bed? Are you ready to hit the hay?"

"Not yet," he said. "No, I'll stay up with you, bub. If that's all right. I'll stay up until you're ready to turn in. We haven't had a chance to talk. Know what I mean? I feel like me and her monopolized the evening." He lifted his beard and he let it fall. He picked up his cigarettes and his lighter.

"That's all right," I said. Then I said, "I'm glad for the company."

And I guess I was. Every night I smoked dope and stayed up as long as I could before I fell asleep. My wife and I hardly ever went to bed at the same time. When I did go to sleep, I had these dreams. Sometimes I'd wake up from one of them, my heart going crazy.

Something about the church and the Middle Ages was on the TV. Not your run-of-the-mill TV fare. I wanted to watch something else. I turned to the other channels. But there was nothing on them, either. So I turned back to the first channel and apologized.

"Bub, it's all right," the blind man said. "It's fine with me. Whatever you want to watch is okay. I'm always learning something. Learning never ends. It won't hurt me to learn something tonight. I got ears," he said.

We didn't say anything for a time. He was leaning forward with his head turned at me, his right ear aimed in the direction of the set. Very disconcerting. Now and then his eyelids drooped and then they snapped open again. Now and then he put his fingers into his beard and tugged, like he was thinking about something he was hearing on the television.

On the screen, a group of men wearing cowls was being set upon and tormented by men dressed in skeleton costumes and men dressed as devils. The men dressed as devils wore devil masks, horns, and long tails. This pageant was part of a procession. The Englishman who was narrating the thing said it took place in Spain once a year. I tried to explain to the blind man what was happening.

"Skeletons," he said. "I know about skeletons," he said, and he nodded.

The TV showed this one cathedral. Then there was a long, slow look at another one. Finally, the picture switched to the famous one in Paris, with its flying buttresses and its spires reaching up to the clouds. The camera pulled away to show the whole of the cathedral rising above the skyline.

There were times when the Englishman who was telling the thing would shut up, would simply let the camera move around over the cathedrals. Or else the camera would tour the countryside, men in fields walking behind oxen. I waited as long as I could. Then I felt I had to say something. I said, "They're showing the outside of this cathedral now. Gargoyles. Little statues carved to look like monsters. Now I guess they're in Italy. Yeah, they're in Italy. There's paintings on the walls of this one church."

"Are those fresco paintings, bub?" he asked, and he sipped from his drink.

I reached for my glass. But it was empty. I tried to remember what I could remember. "You're asking me are those frescoes?" I said. "That's a good question. I don't know."

The camera moved to a cathedral outside Lisbon. The differences in the Portuguese cathedral compared with the French and Italian were not that great. But they were there. Mostly the interior stuff. Then something occurred to me, and I said, "Something has occurred to me. Do you have any idea what a cathedral is? What they look like, that is? Do you follow me? If somebody says cathedral to you, do you have any notion what they're talking about? Do you know the difference between that and a Baptist church, say?"

He let the smoke dribble from his mouth. "I know they took hundreds of workers fifty or a hundred years to build," he said. "I just heard the man say that, of course. I know generations of the same families worked on a cathedral. I heard him say that, too. The men who began their life's work on them, they never lived to see the completion of their work. In that wise, bub, they're no different from the rest of us, right?" He laughed. Then his eyelids drooped again. His head nodded. He seemed to be snoozing. Maybe he was imagining himself in Portugal. The TV was showing another cathedral now. This one was in Germany. The Englishman's voice droned on. "Cathedrals," the blind man said. He sat up and rolled his head back and forth. "If you want the truth, bub, that's about all I know. What I just said. What I heard him say. But maybe you could describe one to me? I wish you'd do it. I'd like that. If you want to know, I really don't have a good idea."

I stared hard at the shot of the cathedral on the TV. How could I even begin to describe it? But say my life depended on it. Say my life was being threatened by an insane guy who said I had to do it or else.

I stared some more at the cathedral before the picture flipped off into the country-side. There was no use. I turned to the blind man and said, "To begin with, they're very tall." I was looking around the room for clues. "They reach way up. Up and up. Toward the sky. They're so big, some of them, they have to have these supports. To help hold them up, so to speak. These supports are called buttresses. They remind me of viaducts, for some reason. But maybe you don't know viaducts, either? Sometimes the cathedrals have devils and such carved into the front. Sometimes lords and ladies. Don't ask me why this is," I said.

He was nodding. The whole upper part of his body seemed to be moving back and forth.

"I'm not doing so good, am I?" I said.

He stopped nodding and leaned forward on the edge of the sofa. As he listened to me, he was running his fingers through his beard. I wasn't getting through to him, I could see that. But he waited for me to go on just the same. He nodded, like he was trying to encourage me. I tried to think what else to say. "They're really big," I said. "They're massive. They're built of stone. Marble, too, sometimes. In those olden days, when they built cathedrals, men wanted to be close to God. In those olden days, God was an important part of everyone's life. You could tell this from their cathedral-building. I'm sorry," I said, "but it looks like that's the best I can do for you. I'm just no good at it."

"That's all right, bub," the blind man said. "Hey, listen. I hope you don't mind my asking you. Can I ask you something? Let me ask you a simple question, yes or no. I'm just curious and there's no offense. You're my host. But let me ask if you are in any way religious? You don't mind my asking?"

I shook my head. He couldn't see that, though. A wink is the same as a nod to a blind man. "I guess I don't believe in it. In anything. Sometimes it's hard. You know what I'm saying?"

"Sure, I do," he said.

"Right," I said.

The Englishman was still holding forth. My wife sighed in her sleep. She drew a long breath and went on with her sleeping.

"You'll have to forgive me," I said. "But I can't tell you what a cathedral looks like. It just isn't in me to do it. I can't do any more than I've done."

The blind man sat very still, his head down, as he listened to me.

I said, "The truth is, cathedrals don't mean anything special to me. Nothing. Cathedrals. They're something to look at on late-night TV. That's all they are."

It was then that the blind man cleared his throat. He brought something up. He took a handkerchief from his back pocket. Then he said, "I get it, bub. It's okay. It happens. Don't worry about it," he said. "Hey, listen to me. Will you do me a favor? I got an idea. Why don't you find us some heavy paper? And a pen. We'll do something. We'll draw one together. Get us a pen and some heavy paper. Go on, bub, get the stuff," he said.

So I went upstairs. My legs felt like they didn't have any strength in them. They felt like they did after I'd done some running. In my wife's room, I looked around. I found some ballpoints in a little basket on her table. And then I tried to think where to look for the kind of paper he was talking about.

Downstairs, in the kitchen, I found a shopping bag with onion skins in the bottom of the bag. I emptied the bag and shook it. I brought it into the living room and sat down with it near his legs. I moved some things, smoothed the wrinkles from the bag, spread it out on the coffee table.

The blind man got down from the sofa and sat next to me on the carpet.

He ran his fingers over the paper. He went up and down the sides of the paper. The edges, even the edges. He fingered the corners.

"All right," he said. "All right, let's do her."

He found my hand, the hand with the pen. He closed his hand over my hand. "Go ahead, bub, draw," he said. "Draw. You'll see. I'll follow along with you. It'll be okay. Just begin now like I'm telling you. You'll see. Draw," the blind man said.

So I began. First I drew a box that looked like a house. It could have been the house I lived in. Then I put a roof on it. At either end of the roof, I drew spires. Crazy.

"Swell," he said. "Terrific. You're doing fine," he said. "Never thought anything like this could happen in your lifetime, did you, bub? Well, it's a strange life, we all know that. Go on now. Keep it up."

I put in windows with arches. I drew flying buttresses. I hung great doors. I couldn't stop. The TV station went off the air. I put down the pen and closed and opened my fingers. The blind man felt around over the paper. He moved the tips of his fingers over the paper, all over what I had drawn, and he nodded.

"Doing fine," the blind man said.

I took up the pen again, and he found my hand. I kept at it. I'm no artist. But I kept drawing just the same.

My wife opened up her eyes and gazed at us. She sat up on the sofa, her robe hanging open. She said, "What are you doing? Tell me, I want to know."

I didn't answer her.

The blind man said, "We're drawing a cathedral. Me and him are working on it. Press hard," he said to me. "That's right. That's good," he said. "Sure. You got it, bub. I can tell. You didn't think you could. But you can, can't you? You're cooking with gas now. You know what I'm saying? We're going to really have us something here in a minute. How's the old arm?" he said. "Put some people in there now. What's a cathedral without people?"

My wife said, "What's going on? Robert, what are you doing? What's going on?"

"It's all right," he said to her. "Close your eyes now," the blind man said to me. I did it. I closed them just like he said.

"Are they closed?" he said. "Don't fudge."

"They're closed," I said.

"Keep them that way," he said. He said, "Don't stop now. Draw."

So we kept on with it. His fingers rode my fingers as my hand went over the paper. It was like nothing else in my life up to now.

Then he said, "I think that's it. I think you got it," he said. "Take a look. What do you think?"

But I had my eyes closed. I thought I'd keep them that way for a little longer. I thought it was something I ought to do.

"Well?" he said. "Are you looking?"

My eyes were still closed. I was in my house. I knew that. But I didn't feel like I was inside anything.

"It's really something," I said.

QUESTIONS FOR DISCUSSION AND WRITING

1. The narrator of Carver's story is not happy about the blind man's visit. *Why* is he so unhappy? To what extent does his opinion of the blind man and his visit change as the story moves along? To what extent does his view of his wife change?
2. For the most part, the narrator and the blind man are very different. In what ways does the story contrast the two characters? Are there any ways in which they are alike? What are the thematic implications of any comparisons and contrasts?
3. Carver's title asks us to focus on the "cathedral." How does the cathedral bring the narrator and the blind man together? Would a different image have brought them together in the same way?
4. Only the blind man in Carver's story is named. Why is he named while the other two characters remain nameless?
5. The blind man and the narrator's wife have had a long-standing friendship. How would you characterize that friendship? What does each seem to get from the relationship?

TESS GALLAGHER (1943–   )

Rain Flooding Your Campfire   *1977*

Mr. G.'s story, the patched-up version I'm about to set straight, starts with a blind man arriving at my house. But the real story begins with my working ten-hour days with Norman Roth, a blind man who hired me because he liked my voice.

My job included typing, running errands, filing, and accompanying the blind man to court. But most of the time was spent reading out loud to him from police reports. We were working Research and Development for the Seattle Police Department.

Those days, before qualified people like Norman got real consideration, a blind man working for the police was definitely rare, not to say bizarre. But they left us alone, those other researchers and developers. They gave us a cubicle with no windows and shut the door. That was okay by Norman. He liked it fine and I guess I did too. It was my job, after all.

Norman was a chain-smoker. He had a little chain he pulled from his vest pocket and rattled the first time he broke the news. Then he laughed and lit up. Sometimes I could barely make out the silo on the State Fair calendar behind him. But we did okay. We listened to each other's stories, tried to make work interesting, even brought treats to share. Frequent breaks made sense, once we realized nobody was keeping tabs on us. What I'm saying is, we edged into friendship during those ten-hour days.

After our work at the SPD wrapped up in the early seventies, Norman and I corresponded by tape, and once in a blue moon we'd telephone. A while later he got married and passed through a series of low-grade jobs for the Feds. Then, with the help of his wife, Caroline, who was sighted, he quit the government and started his own business.

I'd made a few wild swerves and ended up moving back East, working at a gas company and living with Ernest, who, for the most part, understood a woman's life hadn't started the minute he walked through the door. He knew about my ten-year friendship with the blind man I'd known in Seattle. So, when Norman came out East and called from New York City to arrange a visit, Ernest didn't make a big deal. He griped a little, sure. But that's in the nature of things. It probably made things easier that Norman was in mourning after his wife's death, and that his visit to me was part of his journey to see her relatives. Ernest could hardly object under these circumstances.

Norman and I had a saying in our Seattle days when things bummed us out. "Rain flooding your campfire," we'd say to each other, and whatever it was didn't seem so bad. But there was no one to say that to after I read Mr. G.'s version of Norman's visit. All I could think of was the tender, painful things about my friend Mr. G. hadn't known to tell.

Gallivan is Mr. G.'s real name. He and I work graveyard at the gas company. I have a repertoire of sixties songs I hum, two of which will send him flaming from the room—"Maggie May" and "It's All Over Now." I'm also an intermittent whistler. If Mr. G. were doing the work he's paid to, my habits wouldn't be a problem. But most of the time he's hammering at his novels and stories on the secretary's old Selectric. Nothing he writes gets published. Does that stop him? He claims he needs a break-through with the editors. My opinion is, he'll type till kingdom come, inflicting this stuff endlessly on his unfortunate fellow workers.

If Mr. G. were an out-and-out liar I would have more respect for his story-telling. As it is, he can't imagine anything unless he gouges himself with the truth, and that makes it hard for those who know what really happened. The result is the "marble-cake" effect. Aside from this, he's not an altogether bad guy. He did, by default, invite Norman to dinner when he appeared a day earlier than expected.

Ernest and I were just locking the front door, heading to Mr. G.'s, when the phone rang. It was Norman. He was at the train station, wondering where I was.

"I'm here in my house," I said.

"Oh dear," he said. I could picture him touching his watch with the days of the week nubbed into it—a watch he no longer owned, as it turned out.

"It's Friday," I said. "You're a day ahead of me, Norman. No problem," I lied. "I'll be right down to get you." I managed to sound cheerful, practically eager. I phoned Mr. G., who said it would be fine to bring Norman to dinner. Ernest had beefed up a drink, switched on the TV, and stretched out on the couch, so I decided to drive to the station alone.

"Ernest," I said. "Please clear those keepsakes and stack the throw rugs on the porch." I was still worrying about electric cords and faulty railing as I pulled out of the drive.

When Norman married, I'd been grateful for his having Caroline, but I also liked her on her own ground, not just because she was devoted to my friend. I'd been sorry, for both their sakes, that I was so far away when she fell ill. Norman told me in one of his calls before her death more than I could absorb about the cancerous brain tumor that was taking her from him. There'd been months of deterioration. Near the end, we'd recalled better times, one early in their courtship when I'd taken them camping at Mount Angeles. Before she lost her voice, his wife had been looking at the pictures with him, describing them to Norman. The photos of that long-ago trip gave them solace, he said. He used that word, "solace."

"Strange, her losing her voice like that," Norman told me. "Oh, she knew everything. Just couldn't make a peep." He said she would give him little pressure signals on his hand—yeses and noes to questions he formulated. "I had to talk for both of us. 'Want to try some physical therapy?' I'd ask. 'Okay, sure,' I'd say. 'Need that pillow under your shoulders? All right. The window up? Some fresh air?'"

When I arrived at the station, Norman was standing next to a small black valise.

"Norman!" I said, locating myself in front of him. We embraced, then he stepped back, leaned forward and fumbled for my face.

"I'm so humiliated," he said, then planted a kiss hard on my jaw. "A day early! I could evaporate!"

"Now, now," I said. I took his arm and he picked up the valise. "You're here. That's what matters. I just wish I'd had the whole day to look forward to you."

We made our way as far as the taxi stand when he stopped, let go of my arm, set the valise down and took an object the size of a deck of cards from his shirt pocket. "Look at this. My new computerized watch. I guess it was misprogrammed on the day." He pushed a switch activating a voice: "Sat-ur-day: Fi-ive for-ty-ni-en and fif-ty sec-onds." A melodious bell tone sounded.

"That's something," I said. He returned the voice-clock to his pocket, took up his bag and we made our way to the car. I situated him, stowed the valise, then got behind the wheel. "Good to see you, Norm!" I said, and patted him on the arm.

I genuinely liked this man and was very moved by the fact he'd taken the trouble to visit me at this difficult time in his life. "Don't you worry about a thing," I assured him. "Mr. Gallivan says you're welcome to join us for dinner. He's a writer," I told Norman. "He's written six novels and three books of nonfiction. Right now he's suffering writer's block, so he's taking up slack by entertaining people from work."

Norman was fresh from having visited his dead wife's relatives in Vermont. (Mr. G. places them in Connecticut.) Visiting me was his last stop before returning to Seattle. He confessed he didn't miss Caroline as much now as he'd thought he would. "It's a terrible thing," he said. "But true." He was fingering my dashboard, trying to tell the make.

"This isn't the same car you had," he said.

"That one bit the dust long ago," I said. "This is a 1973 Beetle."

Mr. G.'s story begins as we get out of the car at my house and I help Norman up the steps. The narrator sees his wife (that's me!) gripping the arm of the blind man, guiding him toward the house. Here he is, catching a view of the wife in a moment of intimacy with a blind man.

Norman leaned on my arm as we took the steps. "That one nearly got me," he said. On the porch I held back the screen and asked Norman to step inside.

Ernest wasn't around. I set the valise at the end of the couch, moved some newspapers, and Norman sat down. In no time I'd stepped into the kitchen and mixed a couple of Bloody Marys.

Soon we began to reminisce. We sipped our drinks and called up names at the Police Department—Barbara Dukes, a woman officer we'd liked—still and forever, we imagined, in juvenile. Then I mentioned Sergeant Smiley, in the Bad Checks Department.

"Oh, you mean *Chuckles,*" Norman said, arching his chest and leaning back to laugh. "Gee, it's so dark in here I can't *feel* where I'm going," Norman used to say, then purposely bang into a file cabinet. He used to do that a lot, change things from sighted terms to hearing, smelling, or touching. Then he'd laugh his big, booming laugh.

Norman was trying to locate an ashtray on my coffee table. I placed one under his hand. I'd nearly forgotten Ernest when he came down the stairs. Before he could sit down, I motioned him toward us.

"Norman," I said to my friend, "this is Ernest, the man I live with. Ernest, Norman Roth." Norman got to his feet. His hand came up like a pistol, thumb cocked. Ernest looked at the hand, then took it. He was not thrilled to have a blind man in his house. (Mr. G. at least has that much right.)

"Pleased to meet you," Norman said brightly, furrowing his brow as if straining to see. He pumped Ernest's hand like the Tin Man in *The Wizard of Oz,* then reached to relocate his place on the couch before stiffly sitting down again.

"Heard a lot about you," Ernest said.

"Nothing too bad, I hope," Norman said. "I wonder, could I get a light off you, Ernest, if you're still up?"

Ernest fished for his lighter and handed it to me. I flicked it, then touched the flame to the cigarette Norman held between his lips. He inhaled deeply. Smoke issued from his mouth and nose. Once he was satisfied he couldn't be seen, Ernest took a chair near the couch.

"How was the train ride?" he asked. He lifted his bourbon and took a swig.

"Swell, just swell," Norman said. "After I got the porter trained to bring me drinks, it was very pleasant." He put a hand awkwardly inside his jacket lapel and kept it there. He smiled, nodded silently. Suddenly he remembered his cigarette ash. He withdrew the hand and started pinching the air above the coffee table. When he'd located the rim of the ashtray, he knocked his ash expertly and smiled toward the unknown room, obviously enjoying the fact he was on top of things. He lifted his drink and took a long draw.

I should say he's not blond, as Mr. G. describes him. He's bald, except for close-shaven sideburns and a band of hair at the back of his neck. Because his eyes are clouded he's always seemed balder to me than he is. From the start I felt invisible when Norman looked at me. A person could stare back as long as they wanted and not meet the smallest glimmer in those eyes.

"Ever see one of these?" Norman said, offering his voice-watch in Ernest's direction. "Little bugger got me here a day early."

Ernest reached across the coffee table. "Six-twen-ty-four and ni-en seconds," the watch said, then the cherubic bell sounded.

"Great little gadget," Ernest said. "How much did it set you back?"

"Got a deal from the Bureau for the Handicapped," Norman said. He waited for the watch to touch his hand, then slipped it into his pocket.

"Good to see the taxpayers' dollars helping a few needful sorts," Ernest said. I shot him a shut-up-or-I'll-kill-you look, but he just grinned.

"We'd better head to Gallivan's," I announced. Anything to get Ernest's mouth full of food before he started wishing out loud a little federal aid would come his way. We hadn't finished our drinks, so Ernest dropped our glasses into the slots of a carry-out and headed for the car while I helped Norman.

Mr. G. lives in a brick duplex. Shrubs crowd the walkway, but Mr. G. has clipped a little passageway to his door. The whole neighborhood's a mess—cans, bottles, old newspapers, yards knee-high in grass. Naturally Mr. G. does not mention this in his account.

When Mr. G. opens the door he has on what I call his uniform—a yellow shirt, green tie, khaki trousers. He's worn these at the gasworks the three years I've known him. He probably likes not having to interrupt his thoughts with decisions while he dresses every morning.

"Welcome," Mr. G. says to Norman. "Nice you could join us." I stepped to the side so Norman could give Mr. G. one of his pile-driver handshakes.

Ernest squeezed Mr. G.'s arm conspiratorially as he walked past into the living room. Mr. G. positioned my two fellow workers in front of Norman. They each met his grip and stepped back: Sal Fischer—the soft-spoken foreman on swing shift, there with his old Lab, Ripper, and Margaret, a secretary who was dating Sal, pretty in a blue cotton print dress with red tulips along the hem. Ripper nosed Norman's crotch, then grudgingly allowed himself to be petted.

"Smell that food, Norm?" Gallivan said. "We're in the homestretch."

Norman rolled his head toward the kitchen. "I'd know pork roast at fifty paces." He fixed a grin on his face like someone waiting for his picture to be snapped.

"Amazing," Mr. G. said. "You're close. It's back ribs, made with my special Texas barbecue sauce."

I situated Norman on a sturdy chair and went into the kitchen. I knew the dinner had been on hold until we got there, so it was decent of Mr. G. to smooth that over. I could hear Norman's voice above the others. Mr. G. had begun to question him about the free availability of "talking records" for lazy but sighted readers.

"My father *can* read," Mr. G. was saying, "but he doesn't. He might listen, though. If he could just plug in a novel while he shaves or tidies up."

Norman was acting very deaf.

"Ernest," I called into the living room. When he came into the kitchen, drink in hand, I gave him the platter of ribs.

"What're you doing?" he asked. "This isn't your kitchen." His eyes had that glassy look of someone warmed up for a party long before it had started.

"I know," I said. "I'm taking charge." I dished up coleslaw and beans. I filled the water pitcher, then went into the living room to announce we were ready. By the time the others wandered into the dining room, Ernest was seated.

"Here, Norman," Mr. G. offered. "Sit next to me. I want to hear about your Independent Management Enterprises."

"Oh, that's finished," Norman said. "Now that my wife's gone, I don't have the heart for it."

"I'm sorry, I didn't catch that," Mr. G. said and cocked his head. "Gone?" He held his eyes on Norman a moment, then unbuttoned his cuffs, rolled up his sleeves, and forked a side of ribs onto his plate. He raked another portion onto Norman's, then reached across him to serve Margaret, who kept trying to catch my attention, as though I should signal her what to do.

Norman lifted a row of ribs from his plate and began to chew vigorously. He leaned over the table so as not to drop anything onto his lap or the floor. We got into some serious eating. Bones clacked onto our plates. I imagined Norman heard that sound. I'd been enjoying how, without the slightest concession to the sighted world of manners, he licked barbecue sauce from his fingers, when suddenly he pushed his chair back and stood up uncertainly.

"Where's the loo, if you'd be so kind?" The British accent he put on made his question sound refined, almost invisible. He asked it roughly in the direction of the light fixture, then took a jerky step into the table, like one of those TV monsters who can see to kill, but that's about it. Margaret looked alarmed, as if he might stoop and carry her off. I got to my feet and led Norman down a hallway.

"The facility's to your right," I said. "I'll wait for you, Norm." I switched on the light for him, realized what I'd done, then flicked it off.

I heard Norman's watch go off, then the water running. It ran a long time. When he didn't come out, I listened harder. I could hear sobbing. I stood there thinking what to do, then knocked softly and the sobbing stopped. I thought he might really break up if I took his arm when he came out, so I went back to the table and asked Ernest to go get him.

"What'd he do, fall in?" Ernest said. He moved the bones on his plate to one side and helped himself to more ribs. Then he looked wearily at me, pushed his chair back and got up.

In a little while I could hear Ernest and Norman bumping along the hallway. It was then that Ripper broke from under the table. He scrabbled across the hardwood floor and began to tear at Norman's trouser leg. Norman would have been hearing a lot of growling and slavering at his ankles. Sal cursed, rose from his chair, and caught Ripper's collar. He pulled so hard he collided with the table edge. For Norman it was a yowl, then a series of thuds spiced with cursing. He looked strangely disheveled with his trouser cuffs askew.

When things had settled down, I mentioned a TV special I didn't want to miss, thinking to head us home. "It's on the continuing threat of nuclear war," I said. Mr. G. threw down his napkin and said, "I'd love to see that. My TV's on the fritz. We need to face up to the horror of what *could* happen, even if we can't do anything." Mr. G. deftly turned the cleanup over to Margaret and Sal, and followed us through the undergrowth to the car.

"I want to hear about your dreams," Gallivan said to Norman as he slid into the back seat beside him. "Is it true that if someone were throwing, say, a lemon meringue pie at you in a dream—you'd experience the taste of 'lemon pie'; then you'd feel sticky meringue all over your face?"

Norman rocked back and forth against the seat. "That's about it, kiddo."

None of the dinner scene just described or the lemon-pie remark makes it into Mr. G.'s story. He also removes himself entirely from a scene in which, purportedly, a blind man, plus a husband and wife, watch a TV program and the wife falls asleep. One thing is true: I did fall asleep. But not before I'd taken Norman and his bag upstairs to the spare room. I plumped his pillows and helped him locate an ashtray and towels I'd placed on a nightstand. Then he sat on the bedside, tipped his head back and his blind eyes ranged off toward a Mexican vaquero, a velvet wall hanging my brother had bought me in Juárez.

"Caroline's mother," he said. "I think I could have gotten through it okay except for her."

"We'll have a good talk tomorrow, like old times," I said. The vaquero in his spangled sombrero, poised to give a bull the slip, begged me to mention him, but I didn't. Norman could get along without him.

"I just want to tell you this one part," Norman said. He let his head roll back, righted himself and leaned forward. "After the biofeedback petered out, Caroline's mother'd do things like have her refuse drugs for the pain. 'She says she doesn't want those pills,' her mother would say. 'She says she can handle it. Can't you, honey? I mean, imagine me watching someone *else* put words into Caroline's mouth."

I thought about the word "watching," how some of my friends would have tittered at this. But I knew Norman *had* "watched." He gave keen attention to details. I remembered the last time I'd heard him say the word "watched." "I love to *watch* the flames"—he'd said. Our campfire was blazing on that long-ago mountainside and the heat of the flames danced against our faces. We watched.

I stood up and eased my hand under Norman's elbow. I wanted to hear him out, but knew it wasn't the time.

"We'll sit a little, then say good night," I said, as we entered the living room. I coached Norman past my big paradise palm toward the couch. Mr. G. was fine-tuning the set. Ernest had his shoes up on the coffee table. I seated Norman, then told him I was going upstairs to get ready for bed. I glanced at Ernest, who jiggled his eyebrows when he heard me say "bed."

After I'd changed I came downstairs and took a place on the couch near Norman. He'd begun to nod, but I couldn't tell if he was napping or just agreeing to something he was thinking. Mr. G. was banging ice cubes in the kitchen. Ernest lifted his glass in my direction and gave me the old glitter-eye, so I flipped my robe, hoping it would accelerate getting upstairs. But the TV was on and Norman suddenly asked a question.

"What's he mean, 'limited nuclear war'? How limited is it if they obliterate Europe?"

"Next war you're fried, eyeballs and all," Ernest said.

"Or gassed or shot," Norman said. "For once I'm glad I'm not able-bodied."

Mr. G. returned, a drink in each hand. He'd loosened his tie and I could tell he was on the scent of "material." An aircraft carrier as big as three hotels moved heavily across the screen. My eyes were shutting down and I'd be asleep sitting up in no time, but I couldn't seem to move. Ice cubes were clinking in glasses. *Norman hears those ice cubes,* I thought hazily, and felt close to him in the old ways, those times I'd had to think what he needed for an entire day. I also recalled helping him across a log over a river as we'd headed up Mount Angeles, how scared Caroline had been. But Norman had trusted me on the unsteady log, the river rushing and deep ten feet below us. That trust still held a place with me, that's why Norman is here, I thought.

The word "capability" occurred repeatedly in the voice from the TV. Then I heard Norman ask Ernest to find a piece of paper and some scissors. I must have dozed because when I woke up, my robe had fallen open. Ernest, Mr. G., and Norman were bent over the coffee table. Mr. G. had Norman by the hand and was moving his fingers over a piece of paper. "That's the nose right there," Mr. G. was saying. "Feel that?"

"What are you doing?" I asked.

"Helping him *see* a missile," Ernest said. "We cut one out of paper."

"Flash," Norman said. "That means a sudden burst of light."

Ernest laughed. He shook Mr. G.'s arm. "Hey, try cutting out a flash."

"But the word 'light.' What does that really mean to you?" Mr. G. asked Norman. I mean, I could say 'a sudden flash of sagebrush' and it would be all the same, wouldn't it?"

"A nuclear flash would be blinding," Norman said. "In some things, I'm ahead of you."

As Mr. G. tells it, the program was on cancer hot spots in the body, so they weren't examining the cutout of a missile at all, but a drawing of the stomach. Mr. G. ties this in nicely with the death of Norman's wife. The narrator in Mr. G.'s story, an inarticulate sort, experiences blindness through his blind visitor. Mr. G. says he's considering a twist in his rewrite, maybe bringing in Norman's intrusive mother-in-law.

What really happened was that I cinched my robe shut, got up and switched off the TV. "Enough's enough," I said. "Good-bye, world."

I left the three of them sitting there and went upstairs. It was a hot, muggy night. I took off my robe, then my nightgown, and got into bed. I could hear Ernest on the stairs, but he didn't come into the bedroom. Then I heard voices outside on the lawn. It was summer and the screens were on, so whole good-night love scenes from the neighborhood teenagers, or even lovemaking noises from the nearby houses, would drift through the windows.

"Where have you been?" I asked when Ernest finally came into the bedroom.

"Having a cigarette," he said.

"Where's Norman?"

"Nobody ever told your blind man the constellations, so Gallivan's doing it. Out there telling him the stars." He undressed, put on his pajamas, and got into bed. Soon he reached over and began patting my hair the way he does when he wants to get something started. Then he discovered I was naked and his motions took on another eagerness.

"How's Gallivan getting home?" I asked, paying him no mind.

"It's a great night for walking," Ernest said.

I threw back the covers, got up and went over to the open window, raised the shade and looked down. There was Mr. G. holding Norman's arm over his head as if he'd won a prize fight. They were illuminated from above by the street lamp.

"This here, see? That's the Big Dipper." Mr. G. moved Norman's arm in an arc. "The Dipper's handle is along there."

I couldn't see the stars. Nobody could, because the sky was overcast. I'd looked at stars since childhood, but never learned much about constellations. Oh, I knew some bore the names of animals, and Greek gods, and I might have found Orion if my life depended on it, but so far it hadn't.

"What stars?" I asked. "Ernest, take a look at this."

Ernest got out of bed. He stood behind me and leaned over my shoulder. Two men stood in our front yard with their arms raised. Mr. G. was calling out the stars like a stationmaster.

Ernest cupped his hands around my breasts and rested his chin behind my ear. We saw Mr. G. lead Norman into the middle of the street. Then a siren went off somewhere. I began to think how strange it is that stars are silent. What if each star made the smallest noise—say the insistent tone of Norman's watch—what an enormous din would pour down on us!

Mr. G. had turned Norman in another direction entirely. Headlights of a car rose like a strange bloated moon over the hill, beamed on them a moment, then swept precariously down another street. Ernest and I got back into bed, but we could still hear them. It would be just like Gallivan, in some jaunty hail-fellow-well-met good-bye, to forget totally Norman was blind, and simply strike out for home. Which is exactly what he did.

I had wanted to stay awake until Norman was safely inside and in his room—but Ernest's hands began to move over me until my shape seemed to rise and drift from the room. I don't even remember when I closed my eyes.

Somewhere in my uneasy sleep, I saw Norman standing in the front yard. His face was turned skyward and he was holding on to a tree as if he were afraid some force might pull him from the earth. The sky inside his mind must have seemed hugely populated after all the instruction he'd taken.

About then I jerked awake. It was so warm in the house I didn't bother to put on my robe, just made my way downstairs in the dark. My dream had uncannily intersected the real—Norman was there under the trees. I unlatched the screen and went down the porch steps toward him. I didn't speak, but I had a feeling he knew I was there. The houses were dark now and the maples, in a light breeze, made a soft rushing above us which could just as well have belonged to the stars, visible now and blinking calmly down.

I should have been cold outside in the night air, but I wasn't. I heard myself say something consoling as I stood beside Norman. I felt completely unconcerned that I was naked, as if I were somehow still dreaming and protected by the blindness of the world to dreams. It was one of those crossover moments where life overflows, yet somehow keeps its shape. Norman let go of the tree and said, "That you?" "Yes," I said. Then I slipped my hand under his elbow and, as if the entire world were watching and not watching, I guided our beautiful dark heads through a maze of stars, into my sleeping house.

QUESTIONS FOR DISCUSSION AND WRITING

1. Gallagher's narrator mentions several times that she and Norman worked together at a police station. Why do you suppose Gallagher has them work in such a setting?
2. The female narrator of Gallagher's story tells us that Norman is an old friend. How close is that friendship? How does the friendship reflect Norman's and the narrator's personalities, values, and needs?
3. The three men together watch a television show on nuclear war and then draw a nuclear missile. What is the significance of those motifs to their relationships with one another? How do we respond to the narrator's being left out of the interchange?
4. Toward the end of the story, Norman and Mr. G. continue to interact with one another while the narrator and Ernest go up to bed, watch the two men trace the constellations in the sky, and then make love. Why didn't Gallagher have all four people go outside together? Why, in the end, are the narrator and Norman left to reenter the house together?

TESS GALLAGHER

The ending of "The Harvest" (an earlier version of
"Rain Flooding Your Campfire") _____ *1983, 1984*

I threw the covers back, got up and went over to the window. I raised the shade and looked out. There was Mr. G. holding Norman's arm over his head like the poor man had just won a prize fight.

"Now this here, see this? This here's the Big Dipper," I heard Mr. G. say as he moved Norman's arm around. "That's the handle on the Dipper right along there."

I could see them below in the light from the street lamp. They were drawing something in the air. I couldn't see the stars. The sky was overcast. I don't know much of anything about constellations myself, except that some of them bear the names of animals, and Greek gods and heroes.

"What stars?" I said. "Ernest come here and get a look at this."

Ernest slid over to my side of the bed. He stood up behind me and looked over my shoulder at the two men in our front yard with their right arms raised in the air. There was Mr. G. chanting the names of the stars like a station master.

Ernest cupped his hands around my breasts. We watched as Mr. G. led Norman out into the middle of the street. A siren went off somewhere towards town. How silent the stars are, I thought. How silent and far away. If each star were to make just the smallest noise, what a thronging would be over us! The night was as black as any night I've seen. I could see the tops of the houses across the street and that was about it.

Down there in the street, Mr. G. had turned Norman in another direction entirely. The headlights of a car came up over the hill and beamed down on them a moment, then fell away down another street. We got back into bed, but we could still hear them out there. In a minute, Ernest turned into his sleeping position and began to snore. I wanted to stay awake until Norman came in. But I closed my eyes.

Somewhere in my sleep, I thought I saw Norman still out there in the front yard. He was holding onto a tree as if he were afraid he might be pulled off the face of the earth. I went outside and stood a little way from him. I didn't say anything. All the houses were dark. The trees were making a soft rushing sound above us. I should have been cold, but I wasn't. I was asleep as I watched myself say something and go over to him.

I woke up and listened for a few moments. There was no noise from the street. Everything was quiet. I got out of bed. Ernest kept on sleeping. I went into the hall and turned on the light. The door to the guest room stood open. Norman was on his back, asleep, his blind eyes closed, the covers pulled up to his chin. His pants were folded across the back of a chair, but the rest of his clothes were in a heap on the bureau. In his sleep, he sighed. Maybe he was dreaming. If so, I wondered if he had to touch everything in his dream to know where he was.

I left the door open and turned off the hall light. I started to go back to bed. But then I turned and felt my way down the stairs, through the darkened living room and onto the front porch. I stood a moment, staring through the porch screen. The image of Norman and me on the lawn came back. Of course, when I looked, there was no one under the tree. But I pushed the screen door open and moved, as I had in my dream, across the yard. The stars were out. The grass was damp under my bare feet. I stood there and looked into the night. I was wide awake. There was nothing stopping me.

QUESTIONS FOR DISCUSSION AND WRITING

1. The ending of "The Harvest" differs significantly from that of "Rain Flooding Your Campfire." What are some of the differences, and how does a reader respond to them?
2. What does the narrator of "The Harvest" mean by "There was nothing stopping me"?
3. In revising the story, Gallagher also changed the title. The original story is titled "The Harvest," and the image of the harvest is used early in the story, when the narrator says about Mr. G.'s story: "It was like looking out over a field of trampled wheat and knowing that the wheat has still got to be harvested." In "Rain," the narrator tells us, "'Rain flooding your campfire,' we'd say to each other, and whatever it was didn't seem so bad. But there was no one to say that to after I read Mr. G.'s version of Norman's visit." Do these two images convey the same mood and idea? Is one more striking and effective than the other?

QUESTIONS FOR CROSS READING: BRINGING UP THE PAST

1. Throughout "Rain," the narrator refers to "Mr. G.'s story." In what ways is Mr. G.'s story like and unlike Carver's "Cathedral"? How do the differences cause us to respond differently to the two stories?
2. How is the blind man of Carver's story different from Norman Roth? Do the two stories and two narrators view blindness (both physical and metaphorical) the same way?
3. Carver's and Gallagher's stories are different in a number of ways. Examine how each story treats the following. How much does the difference affect our response to the stories and our understanding of their themes?
    Carver uses a male narrator; Gallagher uses a female narrator.
    In Carver's story the couple are married; in Gallagher's story they are not.
    Carver's story tells us less than Gallagher's about the blind man's wife and her death.
    Carver's story tells us less about the early relationship between the blind man and the narrator.
    The subjects of the television programs in Carver's story and Gallagher's two stories are different.
4. The endings of the two stories are very different: Carver's story emphasizes the cathedral and Gallagher's the stars. Does the reader leave the stories with the same "messages"? Are there lessons learned in both stories? If so, who learns them and what exactly is learned?

5. Together, Carver and Gallagher offer us the couple's experience of the visit. Write an essay or short story of your own that conveys instead the blind man's experience of the visit.

THE FAMILY AND BEYOND: THE STORY OF RUTH

רות
Ruth

The Book of Ruth

In the days when the chieftains ruled, there was a famine in the land; and a man of Bethlehem in Judah, with his wife and two sons, went to reside in the country of Moab. ²The man's name was Elimelech, his wife's name was Naomi, and his two sons were named Mahlon and Chilion—Ephrathites of Bethlehem in Judah. They came to the country of Moab and remained there.

³Elimelech, Naomi's husband, died; and she was left with her two sons. ⁴They married Moabite women, one named Orpah and the other Ruth, and they lived there about ten years. ⁵Then those two—Mahlon and Chilion—also died; so the woman was left without her two sons and without her husband.

⁶She started out with her daughters-in-law to return from the country of Moab; for in the country of Moab she had heard that the LORD had taken note of His people and given them food. ⁷Accompanied by her two daughters-in-law, she left the place where she had been living; and they set out on the road back to the land of Judah.

⁸But Naomi said to her two daughters-in-law, "Turn back, each of you to her mother's house. May the LORD deal kindly with you, as you have dealt with the dead and with me! ⁹May the LORD grant that each of you find security in the house of a husband!" And she kissed them farewell. They broke into weeping ¹⁰and said to her, "No, we will return with you to your people."

¹¹But Naomi replied, "Turn back, my daughters! Why should you go with me? Have I

1 וַיְהִ֗י בִּימֵי֙ שְׁפֹ֣ט הַשֹּׁפְטִ֔ים וַיְהִ֥י רָעָ֖ב בָּאָ֑רֶץ וַיֵּ֨לֶךְ אִ֜ישׁ מִבֵּ֧ית לֶ֣חֶם יְהוּדָ֗ה לָגוּר֙ בִּשְׂדֵ֣י מוֹאָ֔ב

2 ה֥וּא וְאִשְׁתּ֖וֹ וּשְׁנֵ֣י בָנָ֑יו וְשֵׁ֣ם הָאִ֣ישׁ אֱלִימֶ֗לֶךְ וְשֵׁ֨ם אִשְׁתּ֜וֹ נׇעֳמִ֗י וְשֵׁ֤ם שְׁנֵֽי־בָנָיו֙ מַחְל֣וֹן וְכִלְי֔וֹן אֶפְרָתִ֖ים מִבֵּ֣ית לֶ֣חֶם יְהוּדָ֑ה וַיָּבֹ֥אוּ שְׂדֵי־מוֹאָ֖ב

3 וַיָּ֥מׇת אֱלִימֶ֖לֶךְ אִ֣ישׁ נׇעֳמִ֑י וַתִּשָּׁאֵ֥ר הִ֖יא וּשְׁנֵ֥י בָנֶֽיהָ׃

4 וַיִּשְׂא֣וּ לָהֶ֗ם נָשִׁים֙ מֹֽאֲבִיּ֔וֹת שֵׁ֤ם הָֽאַחַת֙ עׇרְפָּ֔ה וְשֵׁ֥ם הַשֵּׁנִ֖ית ר֑וּת וַיֵּ֥שְׁבוּ שָׁ֖ם

5 כְּעֶ֣שֶׂר שָׁנִֽים׃ וַיָּמֻ֥תוּ גַם־שְׁנֵיהֶ֖ם מַחְל֣וֹן וְכִלְי֑וֹן וַתִּשָּׁאֵר֙ הָֽאִשָּׁ֔ה מִשְּׁנֵ֥י יְלָדֶ֖יהָ וּמֵאִישָֽׁהּ׃

6 וַתָּ֤קׇם הִיא֙ וְכַלֹּתֶ֔יהָ וַתָּ֖שׇׁב מִשְּׂדֵ֣י מוֹאָ֑ב כִּ֤י שָֽׁמְעָה֙ בִּשְׂדֵ֣ה מוֹאָ֔ב כִּֽי־פָקַ֤ד יְהֹוָה֙ אֶת־

7 עַמּ֔וֹ לָתֵ֥ת לָהֶ֖ם לָ֑חֶם וַתֵּצֵ֗א מִן־הַמָּקוֹם֙ אֲשֶׁ֣ר הָיְתָה־שָּׁ֔מָּה וּשְׁתֵּ֥י כַלֹּתֶ֖יהָ עִמָּ֑הּ וַתֵּלַ֣כְנָה בַדֶּ֔רֶךְ לָשׁ֖וּב אֶל־

8 אֶ֥רֶץ יְהוּדָֽה׃ וַתֹּ֤אמֶר נׇעֳמִי֙ לִשְׁתֵּ֣י כַלֹּתֶ֔יהָ לֵ֣כְנָה שֹּׁ֔בְנָה אִשָּׁ֖ה לְבֵ֣ית אִמָּ֑הּ יַ֣עַשׂ יְהֹוָ֤ה עִמָּכֶם֙ חֶ֔סֶד כַּאֲשֶׁ֧ר עֲשִׂיתֶ֛ם

9 עִם־הַמֵּתִ֖ים וְעִמָּדִֽי׃ יִתֵּ֤ן יְהֹוָה֙ לָכֶ֔ם וּמְצֶ֣אןָ מְנוּחָ֔ה אִשָּׁ֖ה בֵּ֣ית אִישָׁ֑הּ וַתִּשַּׁ֣ק לָהֶ֔ן וַתִּשֶּׂ֥אנָה

10 קוֹלָ֖ן וַתִּבְכֶּֽינָה׃ וַתֹּאמַ֖רְנָה־לָּ֑הּ כִּֽי־אִתָּ֥ךְ נָשׁ֖וּב לְעַמֵּֽךְ׃

11 וַתֹּ֤אמֶר נׇעֳמִי֙ שֹׁ֣בְנָה בְנֹתַ֔י לָ֥מָּה

any more sons in my body, who might be husbands for you? ¹²Turn back, my daughters, for I am too old to be married. Even if I thought there was hope for me, even if I were married tonight and I also bore sons, ¹³should you wait for them to grow up? Should you on their account debar yourselves from marriage? Oh no, my daughters! My lot is far more bitter than yours, for the hand of the LORD has struck out against me."

¹⁴They broke into weeping again, and Orpah kissed her mother-in-law farewell. But Ruth clung to her. ¹⁵So she said, "See, your sister-in-law has returned to her people and her gods. Go follow your sister-in-law." ¹⁶But Ruth replied, "Do not urge me to leave you, to turn back and not follow you. For wherever you go, I will go; wherever you lodge, I will lodge; your people shall be my people, and your God my God. ¹⁷Where you die, I will die, and there I will be buried. Thus and more may the LORD do to me if anything but death parts me from you." ¹⁸When [Naomi] saw how determined she was to go with her, she ceased to argue with her; ¹⁹and the two went on until they reached Bethlehem.

When they arrived in Bethlehem, the whole city buzzed with excitement over them. The women said, "Can this be Naomi?" ²⁰"Do not call me Naomi," she replied. "Call me Mara, for Shaddai has made my lot very bitter. ²¹I went away full, and the LORD has brought me back empty. How can you call me Naomi, when the LORD has dealt harshly with me, when Shaddai has brought misfortune upon me!"

²²Thus Naomi returned from the country of Moab; she returned with her daughter-in-law, Ruth the Moabite. They arrived in Bethlehem at the beginning of the barley harvest.

הֲלָהֵן עִמִּי הַעוֹד־לִי בָנִים
בְּמֵעַי וְהָיוּ לָכֶם לַאֲנָשִׁים:
שֹׁבְנָה בְנֹתַי לֵכְןָ כִּי זָקַנְתִּי ¹²
מִהְיוֹת לְאִישׁ כִּי אָמַרְתִּי יֶשׁ־
לִי תִקְוָה גַּם הָיִיתִי הַלַּיְלָה
לְאִישׁ וְגַם יָלַדְתִּי בָנִים:
הֲלָהֵן ׀ תְּשַׂבֵּרְנָה עַד אֲשֶׁר ¹³
יִגְדָּלוּ הֲלָהֵן תֵּעָגֵנָה לְבִלְתִּי
הֱיוֹת לְאִישׁ אַל בְּנֹתַי כִּי־
מַר־לִי מְאֹד מִכֶּם כִּי־יָצְאָה
בִי יַד־יְהוָה: וַתִּשֶּׂנָה קוֹלָן ¹⁴
וַתִּבְכֶּינָה עוֹד וַתִּשַּׁק עָרְפָּה
לַחֲמוֹתָהּ וְרוּת דָּבְקָה־בָּהּ:
וַתֹּאמֶר הִנֵּה שָׁבָה יְבִמְתֵּךְ ¹⁵
אֶל־עַמָּהּ וְאֶל־אֱלֹהֶיהָ שׁוּבִי
אַחֲרֵי יְבִמְתֵּךְ: וַתֹּאמֶר רוּת ¹⁶
אַל־תִּפְגְּעִי־בִי לְעָזְבֵךְ
לָשׁוּב מֵאַחֲרָיִךְ כִּי אֶל־אֲשֶׁר
תֵּלְכִי אֵלֵךְ וּבַאֲשֶׁר תָּלִינִי
אָלִין עַמֵּךְ עַמִּי וֵאלֹהַיִךְ
אֱלֹהָי: בַּאֲשֶׁר תָּמוּתִי אָמוּת ¹⁷
וְשָׁם אֶקָּבֵר כֹּה יַעֲשֶׂה יְהוָה
לִי וְכֹה יֹסִיף כִּי הַמָּוֶת יַפְרִיד
בֵּינִי וּבֵינֵךְ: וַתֵּרֶא כִּי־ ¹⁸
מִתְאַמֶּצֶת הִיא לָלֶכֶת אִתָּהּ
וַתֶּחְדַּל לְדַבֵּר אֵלֶיהָ:
וַתֵּלַכְנָה שְׁתֵּיהֶם עַד־בֹּאָנָה ¹⁹
בֵּית לָחֶם וַיְהִי כְּבֹאָנָה בֵּית
לֶחֶם וַתֵּהֹם כָּל־הָעִיר עֲלֵיהֶן
וַתֹּאמַרְנָה הֲזֹאת נָעֳמִי:
וַתֹּאמֶר אֲלֵיהֶן אַל־תִּקְרֶאנָה ²⁰
לִי נָעֳמִי קְרֶאןָ לִי מָרָא כִּי־
הֵמַר שַׁדַּי לִי מְאֹד: אֲנִי ²¹
מְלֵאָה הָלַכְתִּי וְרֵיקָם הֱשִׁיבַנִי
יְהוָה לָמָּה תִקְרֶאנָה לִי נָעֳמִי
וַיהוָה עָנָה בִי וְשַׁדַּי הֵרַע־
לִי: וַתָּשָׁב נָעֳמִי וְרוּת ²²
הַמּוֹאֲבִיָּה כַלָּתָהּ עִמָּהּ הַשָּׁבָה
מִשְּׂדֵי מוֹאָב וְהֵמָּה בָּאוּ בֵּית
לֶחֶם בִּתְחִלַּת קְצִיר שְׂעֹרִים:

2 Now Naomi had a kinsman on her husband's side, a man of substance, of the family of Elimelech, whose name was Boaz.

²Ruth the Moabite said to Naomi, "I would like to go to the fields and glean among the ears of grain, behind someone who may show me kindness." "Yes, daughter, go," she replied; ³and off she went. She came and gleaned in a field, behind the reapers; and as luck would have it, it was the piece of land belonging to Boaz, who was of Elimelech's family.

⁴Presently Boaz arrived from Bethlehem. He greeted the reapers, "The LORD be with you!" And they responded, "The LORD bless you!" ⁵Boaz said to the servant who was in charge of the reapers, "Whose girl is that?" ⁶The servant in charge of the reapers replied, "She is a Moabite girl who came back with Naomi from the country of Moab. ⁷She said, 'Please let me glean and gather among the sheaves behind the reapers.' She has been on her feet ever since she came this morning. She has rested but little in the hut."

⁸Boaz said to Ruth, "Listen to me, daughter. Don't go to glean in another field. Don't go elsewhere, but stay here close to my girls. ⁹Keep your eyes on the field they are reaping, and follow them. I have ordered the men not to molest you. And when you are thirsty, go to the jars and drink some of [the water] that the men have drawn."

¹⁰She prostrated herself with her face to the ground, and said to him, "Why are you so kind as to single me out, when I am a foreigner?"

¹¹Boaz said in reply, "I have been told of all that you did for your mother-in-law after the death of your husband, how you left your father and mother and the land of your birth and came to a people you had not known before. ¹²May the LORD reward your deeds. May you have a full recompense from the LORD, the God of Israel, under whose wings you have sought refuge!"

¹³She answered, "You are most kind, my lord, to comfort me and to speak gently to your maidservant—though I am not so much as one of your maidservants."

ב 1 וּלְנָעֳמִי מוֹדָע לְאִישָׁהּ אִישׁ
גִּבּוֹר חַיִל מִמִּשְׁפַּחַת אֱלִימֶלֶךְ
2 וּשְׁמוֹ בֹּעַז: וַתֹּאמֶר רוּת
הַמּוֹאֲבִיָּה אֶל־נָעֳמִי אֵלְכָה־
נָּא הַשָּׂדֶה וַאֲלַקֳטָה בַשִּׁבֳּלִים
אַחַר אֲשֶׁר אֶמְצָא־חֵן בְּעֵינָיו
3 וַתֹּאמֶר לָהּ לְכִי בִתִּי: וַתֵּלֶךְ
וַתָּבוֹא וַתְּלַקֵּט בַּשָּׂדֶה אַחֲרֵי
הַקֹּצְרִים וַיִּקֶר מִקְרֶהָ חֶלְקַת
הַשָּׂדֶה לְבֹעַז אֲשֶׁר מִמִּשְׁפַּחַת
4 אֱלִימֶלֶךְ: וְהִנֵּה־בֹעַז בָּא
מִבֵּית לֶחֶם וַיֹּאמֶר לַקּוֹצְרִים
יְהוָה עִמָּכֶם וַיֹּאמְרוּ לוֹ
5 יְבָרֶכְךָ יְהוָה: וַיֹּאמֶר בֹּעַז
לְנַעֲרוֹ הַנִּצָּב עַל־הַקּוֹצְרִים
6 לְמִי הַנַּעֲרָה הַזֹּאת: וַיַּעַן
הַנַּעַר הַנִּצָּב עַל־הַקּוֹצְרִים
וַיֹּאמַר נַעֲרָה מוֹאֲבִיָּה הִיא
הַשָּׁבָה עִם־נָעֳמִי מִשְּׂדֵי
7 מוֹאָב: וַתֹּאמֶר אֲלַקֳטָה־נָּא
וְאָסַפְתִּי בָעֳמָרִים אַחֲרֵי
הַקּוֹצְרִים וַתָּבוֹא וַתַּעֲמוֹד
מֵאָז הַבֹּקֶר וְעַד־עַתָּה זֶה
8 שִׁבְתָּהּ הַבַּיִת מְעָט: וַיֹּאמֶר
בֹּעַז אֶל־רוּת הֲלוֹא שָׁמַעַתְּ
בִּתִּי אַל־תֵּלְכִי לִלְקֹט בְּשָׂדֶה
אַחֵר וְגַם לֹא תַעֲבוּרִי מִזֶּה
וְכֹה תִדְבָּקִין עִם־נַעֲרֹתָי:
9 עֵינַיִךְ בַּשָּׂדֶה אֲשֶׁר־יִקְצֹרוּן
וְהָלַכְתְּ אַחֲרֵיהֶן הֲלוֹא צִוִּיתִי
אֶת־הַנְּעָרִים לְבִלְתִּי נָגְעֵךְ
וְצָמִת וְהָלַכְתְּ אֶל־הַכֵּלִים
וְשָׁתִית מֵאֲשֶׁר יִשְׁאֲבוּן
10 הַנְּעָרִים: וַתִּפֹּל עַל־פָּנֶיהָ
וַתִּשְׁתַּחוּ אָרְצָה וַתֹּאמֶר אֵלָיו
מַדּוּעַ מָצָאתִי חֵן בְּעֵינֶיךָ
11 לְהַכִּירֵנִי וְאָנֹכִי נָכְרִיָּה: וַיַּעַן
בֹּעַז וַיֹּאמֶר לָהּ הֻגֵּד הֻגַּד לִי
כֹּל אֲשֶׁר־עָשִׂית אֶת־חֲמוֹתֵךְ
אַחֲרֵי מוֹת אִישֵׁךְ וַתַּעַזְבִי

¹⁴At mealtime, Boaz said to her, "Come over here and partake of the meal, and dip your morsel in the vinegar." So she sat down beside the reapers. He handed her roasted grain, and she ate her fill and had some left over.

¹⁵When she got up again to glean, Boaz gave orders to his workers, "You are not only to let her glean among the sheaves, without interference, ¹⁶but you must also pull some [stalks] out of the heaps and leave them for her to glean, and not scold her."

¹⁷She gleaned in the field until evening. Then she beat out what she had gleaned—it was about an *ephah* of barley—¹⁸and carried it back with her to the town. When her mother-in-law saw what she had gleaned, and when she also took out and gave her what she had left over after eating her fill, ¹⁹her mother-in-law asked her, "Where did you glean today? Where did you work? Blessed be he who took such generous notice of you!" So she told her mother-in-law whom she had worked with, saying, "The name of the man with whom I worked today is Boaz."

²⁰Naomi said to her daughter-in-law, "Blessed be he of the LORD, who has not failed in His kindness to the living or to the dead! For," Naomi explained to her daughter-in-law, "the man is related to us; he is one of our redeeming kinsmen." ²¹Ruth the Moabite said, "He even told me, 'Stay close by my workers until all my harvest is finished.'" ²²And Naomi answered her daughter-in-law Ruth, "It is best, daughter, that you go out with his girls, and not be annoyed in some other field." ²³So she stayed close to the maidservants of Boaz, and gleaned until the barley harvest and the wheat harvest were finished. Then she stayed at home with her mother-in-law.

נֶחָמְתָּ֔נִי וְכִ֥י דִבַּ֖רְתָּ עַל־לֵ֣ב
שִׁפְחָתֶ֑ךָ וְאָנֹכִ֕י לֹ֥א אֶהְיֶ֖ה
14 כְּאַחַ֖ת שִׁפְחֹתֶֽיךָ׃ וַיֹּאמֶר֩ לָ֨ה
בֹ֜עַז לְעֵ֣ת הָאֹ֗כֶל גֹּ֤שִֽׁי הֲלֹם֙
וְאָכַ֣לְתְּ מִן־הַלֶּ֔חֶם וְטָבַ֥לְתְּ
פִּתֵּ֖ךְ בַּחֹ֑מֶץ וַתֵּ֙שֶׁב֙ מִצַּ֣ד
הַקֹּֽצְרִ֔ים וַיִּצְבָּט־לָ֣הּ קָלִ֔י
וַתֹּ֥אכַל וַתִּשְׂבַּ֖ע וַתֹּתַֽר׃
15 וַתָּ֖קָם לְלַקֵּ֑ט וַיְצַו֩ בֹּ֨עַז אֶת־
נְעָרָ֜יו לֵאמֹ֗ר גַּ֣ם בֵּ֧ין הָעֳמָרִ֛ים
16 תְּלַקֵּ֖ט וְלֹ֥א תַכְלִימֽוּהָ׃ וְגַ֛ם
שֹׁל־תָּשֹׁ֥לּוּ לָ֖הּ מִן־הַצְּבָתִ֑ים
וַעֲזַבְתֶּ֥ם וְלִקְּטָ֖ה וְלֹ֥א תִגְעֲרוּ־
17 בָֽהּ׃ וַתְּלַקֵּ֥ט בַּשָּׂדֶ֖ה עַד־
הָעָ֑רֶב וַתַּחְבֹּט֙ אֵ֣ת אֲשֶׁר־
לִקֵּ֔טָה וַיְהִ֖י כְּאֵיפָ֥ה שְׂעֹרִֽים׃
18 וַתִּשָּׂ֖א וַתָּב֣וֹא הָעִ֑יר וַתֵּ֥רֶא
חֲמוֹתָ֖הּ אֵ֣ת אֲשֶׁר־לִקֵּ֑טָה
וַתּוֹצֵא֙ וַתִּתֶּן־לָ֔הּ אֵ֥ת אֲשֶׁר־
19 הוֹתִ֖רָה מִשָּׂבְעָֽהּ׃ וַתֹּאמֶר֩ לָ֨הּ
חֲמוֹתָ֜הּ אֵיפֹ֨ה לִקַּ֤טְתְּ הַיּוֹם֙
וְאָ֣נָה עָשִׂ֔ית יְהִ֥י מַכִּירֵ֖ךְ בָּר֑וּךְ
וַתַּגֵּ֣ד לַחֲמוֹתָ֗הּ אֵ֤ת אֲשֶׁר־
עָֽשְׂתָה֙ עִמּ֔וֹ וַתֹּ֗אמֶר שֵׁ֤ם הָאִישׁ֙
אֲשֶׁ֨ר עָשִׂ֧יתִי עִמּ֛וֹ הַיּ֖וֹם בֹּֽעַז׃
20 וַתֹּ֨אמֶר נָעֳמִ֜י לְכַלָּתָ֗הּ בָּר֥וּךְ
הוּא֙ לַֽיהוָ֔ה אֲשֶׁר֙ לֹא־עָזַ֣ב
חַסְדּ֔וֹ אֶת־הַחַיִּ֖ים וְאֶת־
הַמֵּתִ֑ים וַתֹּ֧אמֶר לָ֣הּ נָעֳמִ֗י
קָר֥וֹב לָ֙נוּ֙ הָאִ֔ישׁ מִֽגֹּאֲלֵ֖נוּ
21 הֽוּא׃ וַתֹּ֖אמֶר ר֣וּת הַמּוֹאֲבִיָּ֑ה
גַּ֣ם ׀ כִּי־אָמַ֣ר אֵלַ֗י עִם־
הַנְּעָרִ֤ים אֲשֶׁר־לִי֙ תִּדְבָּקִ֔ין
עַ֣ד אִם־כִּלּ֔וּ אֵ֥ת כָּל־הַקָּצִ֖יר
22 אֲשֶׁר־לִֽי׃ וַתֹּ֥אמֶר נָעֳמִ֖י אֶל־
ר֣וּת כַּלָּתָ֑הּ ט֣וֹב בִּתִּ֗י כִּ֤י תֵֽצְאִי֙
עִם־נַ֣עֲרוֹתָ֔יו וְלֹ֥א יִפְגְּעוּ־בָ֖ךְ
23 בְּשָׂדֶ֥ה אַחֵֽר׃ וַתִּדְבַּ֞ק
בְּנַעֲר֤וֹת בֹּ֙עַז֙ לְלַקֵּ֔ט עַד־
כְּל֥וֹת קְצִֽיר־הַשְּׂעֹרִ֖ים וּקְצִ֣יר
הַֽחִטִּ֑ים וַתֵּ֖שֶׁב אֶת־חֲמוֹתָֽהּ׃

אָבִ֣יךְ וְאִמֵּ֗ךְ וְאֶ֙רֶץ֙ מֽוֹלַדְתֵּ֔ךְ
וַתֵּ֣לְכִ֔י אֶל־עַ֕ם אֲשֶׁ֥ר לֹא־
12 יָדַ֖עַתְּ תְּמ֣וֹל שִׁלְשֹֽׁם׃ יְשַׁלֵּ֥ם
יְהוָ֖ה פָּעֳלֵ֑ךְ וּתְהִ֨י מַשְׂכֻּרְתֵּ֜ךְ
שְׁלֵמָ֗ה מֵעִ֤ם יְהוָה֙ אֱלֹהֵ֣י
יִשְׂרָאֵ֔ל אֲשֶׁר־בָּ֖את לַחֲס֥וֹת
13 תַּ֥חַת־כְּנָפָֽיו׃ וַתֹּ֗אמֶר
אֶמְצָא־חֵ֤ן בְּעֵינֶ֙יךָ֙ אֲדֹנִ֔י כִּ֣י

3 Naomi, her mother-in-law, said to her, "Daughter, I must seek a home for you, where you may be happy. [2]Now there is our kinsman Boaz, whose girls you were close to. He will be winnowing barley on the threshing floor tonight. [3]So bathe, anoint yourself, dress up, and go down to the threshing floor. But do not disclose yourself to the man until he has finished eating and drinking. [4]When he lies down, note the place where he lies down, and go over and uncover his feet and lie down. He will tell you what you are to do." [5]She replied, "I will do everything you tell me."

[6]She went down to the threshing floor and did just as her mother-in-law had instructed her. [7]Boaz ate and drank, and in a cheerful mood went to lie down beside the grainpile. Then she went over stealthily and uncovered his feet and lay down. [8]In the middle of the night, the man gave a start and pulled back—there was a woman lying at his feet!

[9]"Who are you?" he asked. And she replied, "I am your handmaid Ruth. Spread your robe over your handmaid, for you are a redeeming kinsman."

[10]He exclaimed, "Be blessed of the LORD, daughter! Your latest deed of loyalty is greater than the first, in that you have not turned to younger men, whether poor or rich. [11]And now, daughter, have no fear. I will do in your behalf whatever you ask, for all the elders of my town know what a fine woman you are. [12]But while it is true I am a redeeming kinsman, there is another redeemer closer than I. [13]Stay for the night. Then in the morning, if he will act as a redeemer, good! let him redeem. But if he does not want to act as redeemer for you, I will do so myself, as the LORD lives! Lie down until morning."

[14]So she lay at his feet until dawn. She rose before one person could distinguish another, for he thought, "Let it not be known that the woman came to the threshing floor." [15]And he said, "Hold out the shawl you are wearing." She held it while he measured out six measures of barley, and he put it on her back.

When she got back to the town, [16]she came to her mother-in-law, who asked, "How

ג 1 וַתֹּאמֶר לָהּ נָעֳמִי חֲמוֹתָהּ בִּתִּי הֲלֹא אֲבַקֶּשׁ־לָךְ מָנוֹחַ אֲשֶׁר 2 יִיטַב־לָךְ: וְעַתָּה הֲלֹא בֹעַז מֹדַעְתָּנוּ אֲשֶׁר הָיִית אֶת־נַעֲרוֹתָיו הִנֵּה־הוּא זֹרֶה אֶת־גֹּרֶן הַשְּׂעֹרִים הַלָּיְלָה: 3 וְרָחַצְתְּ ׀ וָסַכְתְּ וְשַׂמְתְּ שִׂמְלֹתַיִךְ עָלַיִךְ וְיָרַדְתִּי הַגֹּרֶן אַל־תִּוָּדְעִי לָאִישׁ עַד כַּלֹּתוֹ 4 לֶאֱכֹל וְלִשְׁתּוֹת: וִיהִי בְשָׁכְבוֹ וְיָדַעַתְּ אֶת־הַמָּקוֹם אֲשֶׁר יִשְׁכַּב־שָׁם וּבָאת וְגִלִּית מַרְגְּלֹתָיו וְשָׁכָבְתִּי וְהוּא יַגִּיד 5 לָךְ אֵת אֲשֶׁר תַּעֲשִׂין: וַתֹּאמֶר אֵלֶיהָ כֹּל אֲשֶׁר־תֹּאמְרִי ... 6 אֶעֱשֶׂה: וַתֵּרֶד הַגֹּרֶן וַתַּעַשׂ כְּכֹל אֲשֶׁר־צִוַּתָּה חֲמוֹתָהּ: 7 וַיֹּאכַל בֹּעַז וַיֵּשְׁתְּ וַיִּיטַב לִבּוֹ וַיָּבֹא לִשְׁכַּב בִּקְצֵה הָעֲרֵמָה וַתָּבֹא בַלָּט וַתְּגַל מַרְגְּלֹתָיו 8 וַתִּשְׁכָּב: וַיְהִי בַּחֲצִי הַלַּיְלָה וַיֶּחֱרַד הָאִישׁ וַיִּלָּפֵת וְהִנֵּה 9 אִשָּׁה שֹׁכֶבֶת מַרְגְּלֹתָיו: וַיֹּאמֶר מִי־אָתְּ וַתֹּאמֶר אָנֹכִי רוּת אֲמָתֶךָ וּפָרַשְׂתָּ כְנָפֶךָ עַל־ 10 אֲמָתְךָ כִּי גֹאֵל אָתָּה: וַיֹּאמֶר בְּרוּכָה אַתְּ לַיהוָה בִּתִּי הֵיטַבְתְּ חַסְדֵּךְ הָאַחֲרוֹן מִן־הָרִאשׁוֹן לְבִלְתִּי־לֶכֶת אַחֲרֵי הַבַּחוּרִים אִם־דַּל וְאִם־ 11 עָשִׁיר: וְעַתָּה בִּתִּי אַל־תִּירְאִי כֹּל אֲשֶׁר־תֹּאמְרִי אֶעֱשֶׂה־לָּךְ כִּי יוֹדֵעַ כָּל־שַׁעַר עַמִּי כִּי אֵשֶׁת חַיִל אָתְּ: 12 וְעַתָּה כִּי אָמְנָם כִּי אִם גֹאֵל אָנֹכִי וְגַם יֵשׁ גֹּאֵל קָרוֹב מִמֶּנִּי: 13 לִינִי ׀ הַלַּיְלָה וְהָיָה בַבֹּקֶר אִם־יִגְאָלֵךְ טוֹב יִגְאָל וְאִם־לֹא יַחְפֹּץ לְגָאֳלֵךְ וּגְאַלְתִּיךְ אָנֹכִי חַי־יְהוָה 14 שִׁכְבִי עַד־הַבֹּקֶר: וַתִּשְׁכַּב מַרְגְּלוֹתָו עַד־הַבֹּקֶר וַתָּקָם

is it with you, daughter?" She told her all that the man had done for her; [17]and she added, "He gave me these six measures of barley, saying to me, 'Do not go back to your mother-in-law empty-handed.'" [18]And Naomi said, "Stay here, daughter, till you learn how the matter turns out. For the man will not rest, but will settle the matter today."

4 Meanwhile, Boaz had gone to the gate and sat down there. And now the redeemer whom Boaz had mentioned passed by. He called, "Come over and sit down here, So-and-so!" And he came over and sat down. [2]Then [Boaz] took ten elders of the town and said, "Be seated here"; and they sat down.

[3]He said to the redeemer, "Naomi, now returned from the country of Moab, must sell the piece of land which belonged to our kinsman Elimelech. [4]I thought I should disclose the matter to you and say: Acquire it in the presence of those seated here and in the presence of the elders of my people. If you are willing to redeem it, redeem! But if you will not redeem, tell me, that I may know. For there is no one to redeem but you, and I come after you." "I am willing to redeem it," he replied. [5]Boaz continued, "When you acquire the property from Naomi and from Ruth the Moabite, you must also acquire the wife of the deceased, so as to perpetuate the name of the deceased upon his estate." [6]The redeemer replied, "Then I cannot redeem it for myself, lest I impair my own estate. You take over my right of redemption, for I am unable to exercise it."

[7]Now this was formerly done in Israel in cases of redemption or exchange: to validate any transaction, one man would take off his sandal and hand it to the other. Such was the practice in Israel. [8]So when the redeemer said to Boaz, "Acquire for yourself," he drew off his sandal. [9]And Boaz said to the elders and to the rest of the people, "You are witnesses today that I am acquiring from Naomi all that belonged to Elimelech and all that belonged to Chilion and Mahlon. [10]I am also acquiring Ruth the Moabite, the wife of Mahlon, as my wife, so as to perpetuate the name of the deceased upon his

מַרְגְּלֹתָ֖יו עַד־הַבֹּ֑קֶר וַתָּ֗קָם
בְּטֶ֙רֶם֙ יַכִּ֣יר אִ֣ישׁ אֶת־רֵעֵ֔הוּ
וַיֹּ֕אמֶר אַל־יִוָּדַ֕ע כִּי־בָ֥אָה
15 הָאִשָּׁ֖ה הַגֹּֽרֶן׃ וַיֹּ֙אמֶר֙ הָ֤בִי
הַמִּטְפַּ֙חַת֙ אֲשֶׁר־עָלַ֔יִךְ
וְאֶֽחֳזִי־בָ֖הּ וַתֹּ֣אחֶז בָּ֑הּ וַיָּ֤מָד
שֵׁשׁ־שְׂעֹרִים֙ וַיָּ֣שֶׁת עָלֶ֔יהָ וַיָּבֹ֖א
16 הָעִֽיר׃ וַתָּבוֹא֙ אֶל־חֲמוֹתָ֔הּ
וַתֹּ֖אמֶר מִי־אַ֣תְּ בִּתִּ֑י וַתַּ֨גֶּד־
לָ֕הּ אֵ֛ת כָּל־אֲשֶׁ֥ר עָֽשָׂה־לָ֖הּ
17 הָאִֽישׁ׃ וַתֹּ֕אמֶר שֵׁשׁ־הַשְּׂעֹרִ֥ים
הָאֵ֖לֶּה נָ֣תַן לִ֑י כִּ֤י אָמַר֙ אֵלַ֔י
אַל־תָּב֥וֹאִי רֵיקָ֖ם אֶל־
18 חֲמוֹתֵֽךְ׃ וַתֹּ֙אמֶר֙ שְׁבִ֣י בִתִּ֔י
עַ֚ד אֲשֶׁ֣ר תֵּֽדְעִ֔ין אֵ֖יךְ יִפֹּ֣ל
דָּבָ֑ר כִּ֣י לֹ֤א יִשְׁקֹט֙ הָאִ֔ישׁ כִּֽי־
אִם־כִּלָּ֥ה הַדָּבָ֖ר הַיּֽוֹם׃

1 ד וּבֹ֨עַז עָלָ֣ה הַשַּׁ֗עַר וַיֵּ֣שֶׁב שָׁם֒
וְהִנֵּ֨ה הַגֹּאֵ֤ל עֹבֵר֙ אֲשֶׁ֣ר דִּבֶּר־
בֹּ֔עַז וַיֹּ֛אמֶר ס֥וּרָה שְׁבָה־פֹּ֖ה
2 פְּלֹנִ֣י אַלְמֹנִ֑י וַיָּ֖סַר וַיֵּשֵֽׁב׃ וַיִּקַּ֞ח
עֲשָׂרָ֧ה אֲנָשִׁ֛ים מִזִּקְנֵ֥י הָעִ֖יר
3 וַיֹּ֣אמֶר שְׁבוּ־פֹ֑ה וַיֵּשֵֽׁבוּ׃ וַיֹּ֙אמֶר֙
לַגֹּאֵ֔ל חֶלְקַת֙ הַשָּׂדֶ֔ה אֲשֶׁ֥ר לְאָחִ֖ינוּ
לֶאֱלִימֶ֑לֶךְ מָכְרָ֣ה נׇעֳמִ֔י הַשָּׁ֖בָה מִשְּׂדֵ֥ה
4 מוֹאָֽב׃ וַאֲנִ֨י אָמַ֜רְתִּי אֶגְלֶ֧ה
אׇזְנְךָ֣ לֵאמֹ֗ר קְ֠נֵ֠ה נֶ֥גֶד הַיֹּֽשְׁבִים֮
וְנֶ֣גֶד זִקְנֵ֣י עַמִּי֒ אִם־תִּגְאַל֙ גְּאָ֔ל
וְאִם־לֹ֨א יִגְאַ֜ל הַגִּ֣ידָה לִּ֗י
וְאֵֽדְעָה֙ כִּ֣י אֵ֤ין זֽוּלָתְךָ֙ לִגְא֔וֹל
וְאָנֹכִ֖י אַחֲרֶ֑יךָ וַיֹּ֖אמֶר אָנֹכִ֥י
5 אֶגְאָֽל׃ וַיֹּ֣אמֶר בֹּ֔עַז בְּיוֹם־
קְנוֹתְךָ֥ הַשָּׂדֶ֖ה מִיַּ֣ד נׇעֳמִ֑י וּ֠מֵאֵ֠ת
ר֣וּת הַמּוֹאֲבִיָּ֤ה אֵֽשֶׁת־הַמֵּת֙
קָנִ֔יתִי לְהָקִ֥ים שֵׁם־הַמֵּ֖ת עַל־
6 נַחֲלָתֽוֹ׃ וַיֹּ֣אמֶר הַגֹּאֵ֗ל לֹ֤א
אוּכַל֙ לִגְאׇל־לִ֔י פֶּן־אַשְׁחִ֖ית
אֶת־נַחֲלָתִ֑י גְּאַל־לְךָ֤ אַתָּה֙
אֶת־גְּאֻלָּתִ֔י כִּ֥י לֹא־אוּכַ֖ל
7 לִגְאֹֽל׃ וְזֹאת֩ לְפָנִ֨ים בְּיִשְׂרָאֵ֜ל

estate, that the name of the deceased may not disappear from among his kinsmen and from the gate of his home town. You are witnesses today."

[11] All the people at the gate and the elders answered, "We are. May the LORD make the woman who is coming into your house like Rachel and Leah, both of whom built up the House of Israel! Prosper in Ephrathah and perpetuate your name in Bethlehem! [12] And may your house be like the house of Perez whom Tamar bore to Judah—through the offspring which the LORD will give you by this young woman."

[13] So Boaz married Ruth; she became his wife, and he cohabited with her. The LORD let her conceive, and she bore a son. [14] And the women said to Naomi, "Blessed be the LORD, who has not withheld a redeemer from you today! May his name be perpetuated in Israel! [15] He will renew your life and sustain your old age; for he is born of your daughter-in-law, who loves you and is better to you than seven sons."

[16] Naomi took the child and held it to her bosom. She became its foster mother, [17] and the women neighbors gave him a name, saying, "A son is born to Naomi!" They named him Obed; he was the father of Jesse, father of David.

[18] This is the line of Perez: Perez begot Hezron, [19] Hezron begot Ram, Ram begot Amminadab, [20] Amminadab begot Nahshon, Nahshon begot Salmon, [21] Salmon begot Boaz, Boaz begot Obed, [22] Obed begot Jesse, and Jesse begot David.

עַל־הַגְּאֻלָּה וְעַל־הַתְּמוּרָה
לְקַיֵּם כָּל־דָּבָר שָׁלַף אִישׁ
נַעֲלוֹ וְנָתַן לְרֵעֵהוּ וְזֹאת
8 הַתְּעוּדָה בְּיִשְׂרָאֵל: וַיֹּאמֶר
הַגֹּאֵל לְבֹעַז קְנֵה־לָךְ וַיִּשְׁלֹף
9 נַעֲלוֹ: וַיֹּאמֶר בֹּעַז לַזְּקֵנִים
וְכָל־הָעָם עֵדִים אַתֶּם הַיּוֹם
כִּי קָנִיתִי אֶת־כָּל־אֲשֶׁר
לֶאֱלִימֶלֶךְ וְאֵת כָּל־אֲשֶׁר
לְכִלְיוֹן וּמַחְלוֹן מִיַּד נָעֳמִי:
10 וְגַם אֶת־רוּת הַמֹּאֲבִיָּה אֵשֶׁת

מַחְלוֹן קָנִיתִי לִי לְאִשָּׁה
לְהָקִים שֵׁם־הַמֵּת עַל־
נַחֲלָתוֹ וְלֹא־יִכָּרֵת שֵׁם־הַמֵּת
מֵעִם אֶחָיו וּמִשַּׁעַר מְקוֹמוֹ
11 עֵדִים אַתֶּם הַיּוֹם: וַיֹּאמְרוּ
כָל־הָעָם אֲשֶׁר־בַּשַּׁעַר
וְהַזְּקֵנִים עֵדִים יִתֵּן יְהוָה אֶת־
הָאִשָּׁה הַבָּאָה אֶל־בֵּיתֶךָ
כְּרָחֵל ׀ וּכְלֵאָה אֲשֶׁר בָּנוּ
שְׁתֵּיהֶם אֶת־בֵּית יִשְׂרָאֵל
וַעֲשֵׂה־חַיִל בְּאֶפְרָתָה וּקְרָא
12 שֵׁם בְּבֵית לָחֶם: וִיהִי בֵיתְךָ
כְּבֵית פֶּרֶץ אֲשֶׁר־יָלְדָה תָמָר
לִיהוּדָה מִן־הַזֶּרַע אֲשֶׁר יִתֵּן
יְהוָה לְךָ מִן־הַנַּעֲרָה הַזֹּאת:
13 וַיִּקַּח בֹּעַז אֶת־רוּת וַתְּהִי־לוֹ
לְאִשָּׁה וַיָּבֹא אֵלֶיהָ וַיִּתֵּן יְהוָה
לָהּ הֵרָיוֹן וַתֵּלֶד בֵּן:
14 וַתֹּאמַרְנָה הַנָּשִׁים אֶל־נָעֳמִי
בָּרוּךְ יְהוָה אֲשֶׁר לֹא הִשְׁבִּית
לָךְ גֹּאֵל הַיּוֹם וְיִקָּרֵא שְׁמוֹ
15 בְּיִשְׂרָאֵל: וְהָיָה לָךְ לְמֵשִׁיב
נֶפֶשׁ וּלְכַלְכֵּל אֶת־שֵׂיבָתֵךְ כִּי
כַלָּתֵךְ אֲשֶׁר־אֲהֵבַתֶךְ יְלָדַתּוּ
אֲשֶׁר־הִיא טוֹבָה לָךְ מִשִּׁבְעָה
16 בָּנִים: וַתִּקַּח נָעֳמִי אֶת־הַיֶּלֶד
וַתְּשִׁתֵהוּ בְחֵיקָהּ וַתְּהִי־לוֹ
17 לְאֹמֶנֶת: וַתִּקְרֶאנָה לוֹ
הַשְּׁכֵנוֹת שֵׁם לֵאמֹר יֻלַּד־בֵּן
לְנָעֳמִי וַתִּקְרֶאנָה שְׁמוֹ עוֹבֵד
הוּא אֲבִי־יִשַׁי אֲבִי דָוִד:
18 וְאֵלֶּה תּוֹלְדוֹת פָּרֶץ פֶּרֶץ
19 הוֹלִיד אֶת־חֶצְרוֹן: וְחֶצְרוֹן
הוֹלִיד אֶת־רָם וְרָם הוֹלִיד
20 אֶת־עַמִּינָדָב: וְעַמִּינָדָב
הוֹלִיד אֶת־נַחְשׁוֹן וְנַחְשׁוֹן
21 הוֹלִיד אֶת־שַׂלְמָה: וְשַׂלְמוֹן
הוֹלִיד אֶת־בֹּעַז וּבֹעַז הוֹלִיד
22 אֶת־עוֹבֵד: וְעֹבֵד הוֹלִיד
אֶת־יִשַׁי וְיִשַׁי הוֹלִיד אֶת־
דָּוִד:

QUESTIONS FOR DISCUSSION AND WRITING

1. The relationship between Ruth and Naomi is at the center of the story. What is the nature of the bond between the two women? What strengthens it? Do both women feel the bond equally?

2. Although the relationship between Ruth and Naomi is central to the story, we learn of other relationships as well: for example, the relationships between Naomi and Elimelech; among Orpah and Naomi and Ruth; among Orpah and Ruth and Mahlon and Chilion; and between Ruth and Boaz. How important are these other relationships? How do they influence the relationship between Ruth and Naomi and our understanding of it?

3. *The Book of Ruth* has many strands—themes, for example, of exile, friendship, family, inheritance, and marriage. Where do you see each of these strands in the story? Which are the most important? How is our understanding of each theme influenced by its having been interwoven with the other themes?

4. If you read Hebrew, read the Hebrew original of *The Book of Ruth*. How faithful is the English translation to the original? How do linguistic or cultural differences account for "errors" in the translation?

MARGE PIERCY (1936–   )
The Book of Ruth and Naomi   1992

When you pick up the Tanakh and read
the Book of Ruth, it is a shock
how little it resembles memory.
It's concerned with inheritance,
lands, men's names, how women   5
must wiggle and wobble to live.

Yet women have kept it dear
for the beloved elder who
cherished Ruth, more friend than
daughter. Daughters leave. Ruth   10
brought even the baby she made
with Boaz home as a gift.

Where you go, I will go too,
your people shall be my people,
I will be a Jew for you,   15
for what is yours I will love
as I love you, oh Naomi
my mother, my sister, my heart.

Show me a woman who does not dream
a double, heart's twin, a sister   20

of the mind in whose ear she can whisper,
whose hair she can braid as her life
twists its pleasure and pain and shame.
Show me a woman who does not hide
25   in the locket of bone that deep
eye beam of fiercely gentle love
she had once from mother, daughter,
sister; once like a warm moon
that radiance aligned the tides
30   of her blood into potent order.

At the season of first fruits we recall
those travellers, co-conspirators, scavengers
making do with leftovers and mill ends,
whose friendship was stronger than fear,
35   stronger than hunger, who walked together
the road of shards, hands joined.

QUESTIONS FOR DISCUSSION AND WRITING

1. Why does Piercy title her poem "The Book of Ruth and Naomi" rather than simply "The Book of Ruth"?
2. Piercy says that *The Book of Ruth* is "concerned with inheritance, / lands, men's names, how women / must wiggle and wobble to live." Is this an accurate description of *The Book of Ruth*? Why or why not?
3. "The Book of Ruth and Naomi" says that *The Book of Ruth* reflects a woman's desire for "a double, heart's twin, a sister / of the mind." Does this describe the biblical relationship between Ruth and Naomi? Is Naomi more a mother or a sister to Ruth?

SYLVIA ROTHCHILD (1923–   )

Growing Up and Older with Ruth _____ *1994*

We called it "Shveeis" before it became "Shavuot." It was the most benign and cheerful of the holidays celebrated in my family. Memories of it are stored for me in smells, tastes, textures of fabric and leaf, in the special light of early summer and in some mysterious promise that I don't understand but that lightens my heart. The story of Ruth and Naomi was woven into those memories, a theme with variations that played themselves out in unexpected ways for more than half a century.

I thought of Shveeis as a woman's festival because my father had no visible role in it. It was a holiday my mother made by filling the house with the smell of

The author used *Tanakh: A New Translation of the Holy Scriptures* (Philadelphia, New York, and Jerusalem: Jewish Publication Society, 1985).

caramelized sugar, the juice of huckleberries bursting out of her sweet yeast dough, the pungent smell of onions and farmer cheese in mouth-watering little rolls called *platshintis* and platters of kreplach and blintzes dripping with butter she herself churned. (She didn't trust the grocer's vat of butter, which might have been touched by a knife contaminated by sausage or some forbidden cheese.)

Then there were the long, narrow boxes of greenery and flowers, an annual present from Spitz's florist, bringing aromas from places I'd never seen. My older sister and I would decorate the house. I adorned the places I could reach—the sewing machine, the brass samovar, the bottom of the oak buffet and the china closet. My sister, eight years older, filled the heavy crystal vase and pitcher. She climbed up on a kitchen chair and I handed her the leafy branches one by one, for her to rest on the tops of pictures and mirrors and hang from the Dutch shelves and door lintels. Our walls were covered with pictures. There were the large photographs of grandparents: my father's father who had not come to America, a well-dressed, prosperous-looking burgher with a neatly trimmed beard, wearing a top hat; my mother's father in a skull cap with a beard that fanned out like butterfly wings, a younger version of the grandfather I saw every Sabbath; my gentle-faced grandmother in a wig that made her look older than she was. There were also the pictures my grandfather painted. He was an unusual pious Jew who spent part of his days in prayer and study and the rest painting pictures of the world he left behind. He looked out of his fifth-story tenement on the teeming streets below and painted meadows, orchards in bloom, ducks in a pond, deer in the forest. His pictures filled me with longing for calm, spacious, sweet-smelling rural places, far from the noisy, ugly streets of Williamsburg and the Lower East Side.

My grandfather paid us his annual visit on the afternoon before the holiday began. It was a formal visit to honor his favorite daughter and to enjoy the decorated house and the first fruits from my mother's oven, artfully arranged and presented to him as if he were our surrogate for a Temple priest. I would be dressed up for the occasion in a dress so stiffly starched it hurt to sit down and unbending patent leather shoes that pinched my toes.

When my grandfather had blessed, tasted, and praised everything offered to him, he sat down in the rocking chair next to the piano, filled his pipe, and listened to me play all my pieces. If he asked me to I would sing a few Yiddish songs as well. I wasn't shy. Hungry for praise and attention, it pleased me to entertain him.

On Shveeis, the three small rooms our family of five called home became a magical place, a stage, a bower redolent with the smell of fresh green leaves, roses, and peonies. My pleasure was not only in the transformation we brought about but, even more, in the seasonal discovery that it was possible to alter what was familiar and prosaic, that escape could come not only in daydreams but through physically changing things.

One of my earliest fears was that our lives in those cramped rooms were fixed, that our living arrangements, like our observances, were unalterable. Too young to understand that my parents, in coming to America from villages in Bukovina, had already experienced more change than they could absorb in a lifetime, I knew only that they were content with what they called their "portion" and had no wish for anything new. Even at the age of eight or nine I thought them too easily satisfied, too quick to thank the Almighty for what seemed to me small favors. Spasms of impatience and anger made me feel like a bad daughter. I escaped my bad conscience by losing myself in daydreams in which I was free to be anyone and anywhere I wanted.

In reality, however, I was bound by the restrictions of an observant Jewish home and my parents' fear that I might be led astray by children from families that did not share their sense of what was forbidden and what permitted, what was "edel" (noble) and what "prost" (common). These categories existed not because of what people might say, but because of the "Law" and the "One Above," who was all knowing and all seeing.

I couldn't tell where the law-inspired prohibitions ended and those created by custom and propriety began. Life seemed a minefield of inexplicable "shalt nots" to be negotiated with extreme caution. From the tone of the *mi tur nisht* (one mustn't), I would try to grasp the seriousness of the matter. There seemed, however, to be no hierarchy of prohibitions. I would lie awake at night on the narrow cot I shared with my sister, puzzling over the forbidden things. The dietary rules were no problem. Everything forbidden seemed loathsome and inedible by that time. Sabbath taboos, however, troubled me. Reading was permitted, writing forbidden. Walking was permitted, taking the trolley forbidden, visiting permitted, going to movies forbidden. I knew I must not touch a pencil, a scissors, or a penny. I could not play a note on the piano from sundown to sundown or turn on a light until I had seen three stars, which could be hard to find on a rainy, cloudy Sabbath. I wondered why I, unlike the children of our neighbors, was permitted, even encouraged, to play the piano during the week and not permitted to play in the street where the other children were running, jumping, and shouting. And there were other restrictions: "Have you no one else to befriend?" I heard when I chose Marcella, the Polish janitor's daughter.

Friends my parents approved of were hard to come by. Opportunities for being led astray were minimal. I was enrolled in the Talmud Torah of Williamsburg when I was five, the year I started kindergarten, the year my younger sister was born and I was told that my childhood was over and the time for "acting like a mensch" had arrived. My doll and tea set were packed away in the closet for the baby to play with when she was old enough. From then on I was to devote myself to learning, the opportunity my mother had missed.

I quickly became a small adult with worries, responsibilities, and questions I didn't know how to ask. I watched the adults around me, eavesdropped on their conversations hoping to pick up clues to the mystifying phrases I kept hearing and trying to decode. *Dos redele dreit zich* (the wheel turns) was one. An *ehrlich leben iz a shverlich leben* (an honest life is a hard life) was another, and *shver tzu zein* a Yid (hard to be a Jew) was a kind of refrain that followed the others.

It was at this time that I found the story of Ruth in *The Yiddishe Geshichte,* my Talmud Torah textbook, a collection of legends and stories about events from the time of the Judges till the destruction of the Kingdom of Israel. The stories about Deborah, Samson, and Samuel were interesting but had nothing to do with me. Ruth, however, found a place in my imagination. The illustration that came with the story showed a sweet-faced girl of uncertain age who looked a little like Marcella, the janitor's daughter I was forbidden to play with. Her hair hung to her shoulders and her arms were full of the grain she had gleaned. She was standing in a field my grandfather might have painted.

Reading of the time "when a famine broke out," I imagined it as a variation of the Depression years we were living in. There were no fields to glean in Williamsburg, but it was a time of grave money worries, of pitiful beggars in the streets, of pawning a ring or watch to "make a holiday." One might find a once-prosperous relative selling apples from a little box on the street corner. Reading about Elimelech taking his family to Moab in search of better opportunities, I wondered whether my uncomplaining father, if besieged by famine, would take his family to another place.

That shortened Yiddish version of Ruth's story suggested possibilities I hadn't thought of. For example, the words *shviger* (mother-in-law) and *shneer* (daughter-in-law) sounded ugly to me because I associated them with gossip and family strife. It pleased me to discover a mother- and daughter-in-law who were not each other's enemies. Watching my older sister and her friends searching for husbands made me worry whether anyone would choose me when I grew old enough. In that frame of mind I noted that Ruth didn't wait to be chosen but offered herself. The circumstances of her offer weren't clear in my children's version of the story, nor did it mention that Boaz was an old man, soon to die. It read only as a romance with a happy ending for Ruth, who was "redeemed," for Naomi, who had a grandchild, and for the Jewish people, who would a few generations later have King David, evidence that there was a Father in Heaven looking out for His children, something I desperately wanted to believe.

What amazed me the most was that Ruth and Orpah were Moabites, who were supposed to be forbidden to Jews, just as Marcella the janitor's daughter was forbidden to me. If that were not enough, Ruth's wish to join the Jewish people added another dimension of astonishment.

I had learned early that I had been born into Jewishness and that it couldn't be rejected even if it came with sorrow, difficulties, and disappointments. I was told that our Father in Heaven, who was supposed to be looking out for us, worked in mysterious ways, beyond our understanding. I was expected to live with two contradictory messages. One was *Got iz mit dir* (God is with you), the other, *Vos iz mit dir? Me farlozt zich nisht aufen Rebonosholelem?* (What's wrong with you? Are you expecting God to come down to help you?).

Ruth's choice and Naomi's gratitude made it seem that He might. Their story made the life I was born into seem more worthy and desirable. It was the perfect story to read on Shveeis, when the house smelled of greenery and caramelized sugar.

Almost *twenty years* would pass before I had reason to think of the Book of Ruth again. During that time everything that seemed fixed and unchangeable to me as a child gave way. The structure of our lives had depended on my grandparents' presence. With their deaths the structure collapsed. We moved from Williamsburg to East Flatbush, where Jewish life was more American. English, not Yiddish, was the language of the street. My parents no longer went to an orthodox shul where my grandfather sat in a place of honor on the *bimeh* and my grandmother, surrounded by her daughters, sat in the women's balcony praying loudly, to help the women around her who couldn't read. In the new neighborhood my father joined a large conservative temple and my mother sat beside him.

Studying Hebrew as a modern language in high school, I discovered that "Shveeis" was to be called "Shavuot." I joined a Hebrew Culture Club where we sang about pioneers building "Eretz Yisroel." For Shavuot we danced gestures of gleaning and skipped barefoot on the gym floor with imaginary baskets of *bikurim* on our heads. The Shveeis of my childhood would not be forgotten, but it was relegated to the past. It became my grandfather's holiday, my mother's culinary celebration, not mine.

World War II soon wreaked havoc on all holidays and Sabbaths. They were left to parents to attend to while the children went out to do the work of the world. At eighteen I worked in a defense plant making quartz crystals for the Signal Corps while attending Brooklyn College at night. The administration at that time was trying to free its students from immigrant gestures, accents, and loyalties to prepare us for joining the mainstream without debilitating "defects." Supplying the Signal Corps had a high priority and permitted no time off for holidays. Visible and invisible forces pulled me away from the traditions and prohibitions that had shaped my childhood. It all happened very quickly. At the age of twelve I had expected the Williamsburg Bridge to collapse the first time I took a trolley across it on the Sabbath. At eighteen I rode a nearly empty subway to work on Yom Kippur with impunity, even with some feelings of exhilaration at my liberation.

At twenty-one I married a fellow student, an Air Corps lieutenant, just before he went overseas. It was when he returned and I followed him as an army wife, and later, when I was working while he went to graduate school, that the liberation began to pall, even to feel like a kind of deprivation.

I missed Jewish life and began trying to read myself back into it. In the years of planning my escape from Brooklyn, I read Emerson and Thoreau and imagined myself a writer in a small New England town. Now, in libraries in Texas and Colorado, I read Martin Buber, Maurice Samuel, and Sachar's *History of the Jews.* My search for a way back or forward began with reading.

Two years of teaching elementary Hebrew to rambunctious seven-year-olds in a conservative congregational school added to my confusion. The temple was large and affluent, the rabbi formal and pompous, and the cantor, an opera singer. Services were performances attended as if they were concerts. I could not go back to the world of my parents or grandparents, but I also knew I could find no place for myself in such a congregation.

A few years later, we settled in a small New England town close to Boston, where my husband found work. I was still searching, but less concerned about myself than about how to raise our three young children as Jews. I should have been content in a spacious house of our own, finally surrounded by woods and meadows, the landscape of my grandfather's pictures. I had begun writing and publishing stories. Caring for our two daughters and infant son kept me very busy but didn't assuage a kind of anxiety I couldn't shake off. I suddenly needed to try to bridge the chasm that had developed between my mother's life and my own. I began making Sabbaths and paying attention to holidays. My husband, raised in a secular, nonobservant family, would have been content without my efforts but didn't try to stop me.

I resented having to create holidays without any help but had no choice. The holidays I didn't make, wouldn't happen. Without parents or grandparents close by we were free to live as we pleased and just beginning to understand the weight of that responsibility. The small Jewish community in the town was too new to be of help. It was organized in response to the fact that there were seven churches in the town of four thousand people, each with its Sunday school. Jews, whether or not they'd been members of synagogues before, were expected to create their own "church" and school.

Soon after we arrived, I was recruited to teach a class of twelve-year-old girls. Classes for seven-year-olds were already underway, but there was concern about the older girls, girls going to church dances with their classmates who might be lost to the Jewish community without some special efforts on their behalf.

The parents had modest expectations. They were not interested in studying with their daughters or in observing traditions they had discarded. They were, after all,

American-born and trying to live like their American neighbors. Eastern European Jewish life had no claim on them. It was 1951, only six years after the liberation of Auschwitz, too close to that dreaded time even to speak of it. The state of Israel was only three years old, but of interest only to Zionists—and they were not Zionists. They hoped for what they called "a little bit of Jewishness," for the girls to be able to follow the Hebrew in the prayer book and to learn a little history—"not the sad parts," but enough so they would "know who they are." It was agreed that the girls would be more amenable to a year of intense study if it could conclude with a celebration, a kind of bat mitzvah on Shavuot.

When I began looking for books and making lesson plans, I realized that what I wanted to offer my students would not be found in the books available. I wanted nothing less than to convince them that Judaism was a gift they should not refuse and that they would not want to part with it if they knew what it offered. I wanted to lure them away from what I thought to be trivial American temptations and get them to choose to be Jewish. I decided that the story of Ruth and Naomi and the holiday of Shavuot could provide the focus for our discussions. We could talk about Sinai, about what it meant to "receive" the Torah. We could think about commitment and loyalty, and I could tell them about growing up in a Jewish world.

I would encourage them to write poems and stories, possibly a play based on the Book of Ruth, and see if they could imagine themselves in another time and place. I was excited about leaving my toddlers at home with a baby-sitter three afternoons a week while I spent time with older children. I looked forward to the questions they would ask and planned answers.

I wasn't prepared for the magnitude of their resistance. One or two had come willingly. The others, bribed or nagged, made it clear that they would rather be somewhere else. They learned the Hebrew alphabet in spite of themselves, could read haltingly within a few weeks. We made time lines, played games with history, talked about holidays they didn't celebrate and Sabbaths they didn't keep, but I always felt their distrust and skepticism. They did not want to hear what I had to say.

The questions they asked about the Book of Ruth were not the questions I wanted to answer. That Naomi and Elimelech permitted their sons to marry Moabite women interested them more than Ruth's affection for Naomi. They wondered whether Ruth chose not to return to her people because she was afraid they wouldn't take her back. They fell into fits of giggles about Ruth's coming at night to lie at Boaz's feet and wanted to know what exactly was meant by her being "covered by his blanket." They saw no happy ending in Ruth's marriage to Boaz, who was old enough to be her father, and were outraged to discover that Ruth came with a parcel of land that seemed more valuable than she.

They argued that it wasn't fair for the Jews at Sinai to make a covenant for future generations to keep. They were sure that every generation should be free to choose for itself. I then told them about the rabbi in a little Polish town long ago who on Shavuot absolved his congregation of their Jewishness so that year after year they could choose to accept the Torah and continue to live as Jews.

The girls assured me that would never work in America. Given a choice, they were sure everyone would prefer to be born Christian. Two of the students announced that they'd already decided to marry out of Judaism. The others confessed that they were not yet sure what they wanted or believed, except that they wanted to look, behave, and be accepted as Americans. To be Jewish was to be different and separate, out rather than in. They did not want to be outsiders. Ruth's choice meant nothing to them. The Ruth who had given me a vision of freedom and affection seemed bound, dependent, and manipulated to them.

The year of struggle passed quickly. The celebration at Shavuot took place as planned. There was a brief service led by the cantor, and certificates and prayer books were given out. They read their stories and poems and did the dances I had taught them. The parents were pleased to see how much their daughters had learned. I worried about what they had not learned and wondered how much they'd remember.

Years later one of the students came to see me to tell me what she had done with her life. She confessed that from that year she remembered only the Hebrew letters and the sense of urgency I had created. "What I couldn't forget," she said, "was that you cared so much. Why," she asked, "was it so important to you that we be Jewish and choose Jewish husbands?"

By then I knew that the jousting with my bat mitzvah girls was a preview of and preparation for the struggles I would have with my own children. For a while I had believed that I'd assured their Jewish future. Unlike the girls in my class, they'd grown up with Sabbaths and holidays, with Jewish books and stories and visits to grandparents. They were enrolled in the congregation school when they were seven, had proper bar and bat mitzvot, even visits to Israel.

Saved from the restrictions that had made me rebellious, they were raised to be independent and iconoclastic, Jews who could accept their differences from their peers as we, their parents, accepted ours. They were serious and intelligent. I had trusted them to find their way and believed it would be a Jewish way, not necessarily mine, but Jewish.

I was not prepared to hear "Judaism means nothing to me," as one by one, my young adult children let me know that my "prejudices" were not theirs. My loyalties and compulsions, they said, were not transferable. They were members of a new generation, free to choose their own interests and values, free to live as they pleased, marry as they pleased, and someday raise children as they saw fit. Hadn't I done the same?

An anxious, unsettling time! My husband and I told each other it was a stage that would pass, a trial we would live through as others had before us. We should not have been so sure of ourselves, so arrogantly confident of our power over our children. We should have known it was impossible to impose our loyalties. Why then did we feel so rejected?

We mourned when our children chose non-Jewish mates. In the old days, when intermarriages were rare, the mourning was dramatic and public. In the new time, when intermarriages were common, there was only private, unspoken anguish. "Welcome to the club," whispered friends who had traveled that uncomfortable road before us. No child was cast out, no mirrors were covered, but the feeling of tearing was there. My husband, in spite of the casualness of his Jewish upbringing, had been affected by our years together and felt as keenly as I about the lost Jewish future of our family. We brooded together about what we had done wrong. I began for the first time to wonder how my parents felt when I made choices so different from theirs.

It was in this mood one Shavuot that I read the Book of Ruth again. This time I found myself thinking about Naomi in Moab, wondering if she had feared for her sons in a place where there were no Jewish girls to marry. Had she wept or danced at their weddings? Did she and Elimelech quarrel about the wisdom of living so far from their own people?

There were no clues in the text. I found a midrash that suggested that the misfortunes that befell the family were punishments for choosing Moabite women. In another, however, Elimelech, a man of wealth and power, was himself seen as the cause of the calamities. The marriages to the Moabite women were effects, not causes. His flight from Bethlehem, where he should have accepted responsibility for the poor, was seen as a mark of poor character that deserved punishment.

We hear about Ruth and Orpah only after ten years have gone by. We don't know whether they are typical or unusual Moabite women. We are told nothing about their problems and adjustments when their husbands were alive or how long it took before they were resolved. I thought, of course, of myself and wondered how long it would take before I reconciled myself to what had for so long seemed unacceptable to me. My protracted quarrel with myself was especially painful because I was genuinely fond of the mates my children had chosen. They were not abstract non-Jewish adversaries but good people who had done what I wished my children to do, namely, chosen Jewish mates. Wasn't it unreasonable to hold against them the fact that they hadn't chosen their parents more carefully?

I was, at first, most conscious of what I thought were their un-Jewish qualities. With the passing of time, however, I began to look for aspects of Ruth in each of them. I took comfort from their willingness to share the holiday celebrations I organized. I was grateful for the questions they asked and the respectful way they listened when I tried to answer them. The bonds grew stronger after the births of grandchildren, which gave me and my husband the magical power of grandparents, power we were prepared to exploit and enjoy to the fullest. Unspoken was the hope that our grandchildren would choose the commitments their parents rejected.

Our tension and anxiety began to diminish when we found our children worrying about what to teach their children, asking the same question we had asked at their stage of life. They didn't ask for our advice or help, but watching them begin to search for meaning and structure, it began to seem likely that my people would be theirs after all. The Jewish future of their children would be no more predictable than theirs had been, but they were behaving as if Jewishness was a gift they were finding hard to refuse. I don't know what they would make of the story of Ruth and Naomi or whether they are ready to read it with empathy. I treasure it for the memories and perspectives it brings to life for me and still find in it a promise of hope for the unknowable future—what it has offered since it was first told.

QUESTIONS FOR DISCUSSION AND WRITING

1. Rothchild looks at many different stages of her life and her changing relationship to her Jewish heritage. How does *The Book of Ruth* help her understand these changes—those in her own life as well as those for a younger generation?
2. Rothchild emphasizes different aspects of *The Book of Ruth* over the years. Why does she emphasize different elements at different times? Is one "reading" of *Ruth* more accurate than the others?

3. Rothchild writes of her changing relationship to *The Book of Ruth*. Write an essay in which you similarly examine your own varied responses to a religion or text (religious or secular) that has been an integral part of your life.

___

QUESTIONS FOR CROSS READING:
THE FAMILY AND BEYOND

1. Piercy and Rothchild both examine the meanings of *The Book of Ruth* for modern readers. How are those meanings the same or different for them?
2. Which element of *Ruth* seems most relevant to your own background and circumstances? Why?

___

Immortal Love

MAY SARTON (1912–1995)

The Lady and the Unicorn _____ *1978*

The Cluny Tapestries

> I am the unicorn and bow my head
> You are the lady woven into history
> And here forever we are bound in mystery
> Our wine, Imagination, and our bread,
> 5   And I the unicorn who bows his head.
>
> You are all interwoven in my history
> And you and I have been most strangely wed
> I am the unicorn and bow my head
> And lay my wildness down upon your knee
> 10 You are the lady woven into history.
>
> And here forever we are sweetly wed
> With flowers and rabbits in the tapestry
> You are the lady woven into history
> Imagination is our bridal bed:
> 15 We lie ghostly upon it, no word said.
>
> Among the flowers of the tapestry
> I am the unicorn and by your bed
> Come gently, gently to bow down my head,
> Lay at your side this love, this mystery,
> 20 And call you lady of my tapestry.

La Vue (Sight), from *The Lady and the Unicorn* Tapestries housed at
the Cluny Museum in Paris. This tapestry is one in a series of
tapestries thought to represent the five natural senses of taste,
smell, touch, sight, and hearing. The lady in the tapestry holds a
mirror up to the unicorn, and we see the animal's face reflected
in it. Because the mirror reflects a visual image, this is thought to
be the tapestry that represents the sense of sight. (See color insert.)

I am the unicorn and bow my head
To one so sweetly lost, so strangely wed:

You sit forever under a small formal tree
Where I forever search your eyes to be

Rewarded with this shining tragedy   25
And know your beauty was not cast for me,

Know we are woven all in mystery,
The wound imagined where no one has bled,

My wild love chastened to this history
Where I before your eyes, bow down my head.   30

QUESTIONS FOR DISCUSSION AND WRITING

1. The unicorn says that he and the lady are "wed." In what sense are they wed? How
   would you describe their relationship?
2. The speaker of Sarton's poem is the unicorn himself. How would our responses to
   the poem be different if the woman, or an outsider, were the speaker?

3. The unicorn in Sarton's poem reminds us several times that the lady is "woven into history," but he doesn't say the same about himself. Why?

ANNE MORROW LINDBERGH (1906–2001)

The Unicorn in Captivity _____ *1956*

Here sits the Unicorn
In captivity;
His bright invulnerability
   Captive at last;
5 The chase long past,
Winded and spent,
By the king's spears rent;
Collared and tied
To a pomegranate tree—
10 Here sits the Unicorn
In captivity,
Yet free.

Here sits the Unicorn;
His overtakelessness
15 Bound by a circle small
As a maid's embrace;
Ringed by a round corral;
Pinioned in place
By a fence of scarlet rail,
20 Fragile as a king's crown,
Delicately laid down
Over horn, hoofs, and tail,
As a butterfly net
Is lightly set.

25 He could leap the corral,
If he rose
To his full white height;
He could splinter the fencing light,
With three blows
30 Of his porcelain hoofs in flight—
   If he chose.
He could shatter his prison wall,
Could escape them all—
If he rose,
35 If he chose.

Here sits the Unicorn;
The wounds in his side
Still bleed

The Unicorn in Captivity (housed in the New York Metropolitan Museum of Art), 15th century. This tapestry is thought to be the last in a series of tapestries called *The Hunt of the Unicorn;* the series depicts the hunt, wounding, and capture of the unicorn. (See color insert.)

From the huntsmen's spears,
Yet he takes no heed
Of the blood-red tears
On his milk-white hide,
That spring unsealed,
Like flowers that rise
From the velvet field
In which he lies.
Dream wounds, dream ties
Do not bind him there
In a kingdom where
He is unaware
Of his wounds, of his snare.

Here sits the Unicorn;
Head in a collar cased,
Like a girdle laced
Round a maiden's waist,
Broidered and buckled wide,
Carelessly tied.
He could slip his head
From the jewelled noose
So lightly tied—
If he tried,
As a maid could loose
The belt from her side;
He could slip the bond
So lightly tied—
If he tried.

Here sits the Unicorn;
Leashed by a chain of gold
To the pomegranate tree.
So light a chain to hold
So fierce a beast;
Delicate as a cross at rest
On a maiden's breast.
He could snap the golden chain
With one toss of his mane,
If he chose to move,
If he chose to prove
His liberty.
But he does not choose
What choice would lose.
He stays, the Unicorn,
In captivity.

In captivity,
Flank, hoofs, and mane—

40

45

50

55

60

65

70

75

80

85 Yet look again—
His horn is free,
Rising above Chain, fence, and tree,
Free hymn of love; His horn
Bursts from his tranquil brow
90 Like a comet born;
Cleaves like a galley's prow
Into seas untorn;
Springs like a lily, white
From the Earth below;
95 Spirals, a bird in flight
To a longed-for height;
Or a fountain bright,
Spurting to light
Of early morn—
100 O luminous horn!

Here sits the Unicorn—
In captivity?
In repose.
Forgotten now the blows
105 When the huntsmen rose
With their spears; dread sounds
Of the baying hounds,
With their cry for blood;
And the answering flood
110 In his veins for strife,
Of his rage for life,
In hoofs that plunged,
In horn that lunged.
Forgotten the strife;
115 Now the need to kill
Has died like fire,
And the need to love
Has replaced desire;
Forgotten now the pain
120 Of the wounds, the fence, the chain—
Where he sits so still,
Where he waits Thy will.

Quiet, the Unicorn,
In contemplation stilled,
125 With acceptance filled;
Quiet, save for his horn;
Alive in his horn;
Horizontally,
In captivity;
130 Perpendicularly,

Free.
As prisoners might,
Looking on high at night,
From day-close discipline
Of walls and bars,   135
To night-free infinity
Of sky and stars,
Find here felicity:
So is he free—
The Unicorn.   140
What is liberty?
Here lives the Unicorn,
In captivity,
Free.

QUESTIONS FOR DISCUSSION AND WRITING

1. What characteristics of the unicorn does Lindbergh most focus on? What does her description suggest that the unicorn represents?
2. Lindbergh builds her poem on paradox: the unicorn is captive but free; he could easily escape but he does not. Find the uses of paradox in the poem. How do they illuminate the unicorn's character? The poem's themes?

JAMES THURBER (1894–1961)
The Unicorn in the Garden _____ 1940

Once upon a sunny morning a man who sat in a breakfast nook looked up from his scrambled eggs to see a white unicorn with a gold horn quietly cropping the roses in the garden. The man went up to the bedroom where his wife was still asleep and woke her. "There's a unicorn in the garden," he said. "Eating roses." She opened one unfriendly eye and looked at him. "The unicorn is a mythical beast," she said, and turned her back on him. The man walked slowly downstairs and out into the garden. The unicorn was still there; he was now browsing among the tulips. "Here, unicorn," said the man, and he pulled up a lily and gave it to him. The unicorn ate it gravely. With a high heart, because there was a unicorn in his garden, the man went upstairs and roused his wife again. "The unicorn," he said, "ate a lily." His wife sat up in bed and looked at him, coldly. "You are a booby," she said, "and I am going to have you put in the booby-hatch." The man, who had never liked the words "booby" and "booby-hatch," and who liked them even less on a shining morning when there was a unicorn in the garden, thought for a moment. "We'll see about that," he said. He walked over to the door. "He has a golden horn in the middle of his forehead," he told her. Then he went back to the garden to watch the unicorn; but the unicorn had gone away. The man sat down among the roses and went to sleep.

As soon as the husband had gone out of the house, the wife got up and dressed as fast as she could. She was very excited and there was a gloat in her eye. She telephoned the police and she telephoned a psychiatrist; she told them to hurry to her house and bring a strait-jacket. When the police and the psychiatrist arrived they sat down in chairs and looked at her, with great interest. "My husband," she said, "saw a unicorn this morning." The police looked at the psychiatrist and the psychiatrist looked at the police. "He told me it ate a lily," she said. The psychiatrist looked at the police and the police looked at the psychiatrist. "He told me it had a golden horn in the middle of its forehead," she said. At a solemn signal from the psychiatrist, the police leaped from their chairs and seized the wife. They had a hard time subduing her, for she put up a terrific struggle, but they finally subdued her. Just as they got her into the strait-jacket, the husband came back into the house.

"Did you tell your wife you saw a unicorn?" asked the police. "Of course not," said the husband. "The unicorn is a mythical beast." "That's all I wanted to know," said the psychiatrist. "Take her away. I'm sorry, sir, but your wife is as crazy as a jay bird." So they took her away, cursing and screaming, and shut her up in an institution. The husband lived happily ever after.

Moral: Don't count your boobies until they are hatched.

QUESTIONS FOR DISCUSSION AND WRITING

1. How would you characterize the relationship between the man and his wife? What does their response to the idea of unicorns have to do with their relationship?
2. Thurber's "The Unicorn in the Garden" comically asks us to question whether unicorns are real or imaginary. When you read the story, do you sympathize more with the man or his wife? How would you characterize each person's personality and mental state?

QUESTIONS FOR CROSS READING: IMMORTAL LOVE

1. The two unicorn tapestries included in *Retellings* are among the most famous of medieval tapestries and among the most famous depictions of unicorns in art. Interpretations of the tapestries vary considerably, though. Some see the Cluny tapestry (502) as a representation and an affirmation of the sense of sight and of the love between the lady and her beloved (the unicorn represents the beloved); others see it as a representation of the dangers of vanity and earthly pleasures (the mirror is a common medieval symbol of vanity). "The Unicorn in Captivity" (504) arouses similarly contradictory responses. The unicorn in this tapestry is thought by some to represent the male beloved "captured" by his lady. (According to myth, a unicorn could be captured only by a virgin.) Others think the tapestry is meant to represent the capture and martyrdom of Christ, as unicorns are powerful but

pure creatures who are often sacrificed to fulfill some human need or desire. Which of these interpretations do Lindbergh and Sarton seem most to accept? What images and ideas in their poems lead you to your conclusion?

2. Although very different in mood and form from the other representations of unicorns included here, Thurber's "Unicorn in the Garden" plays on some of the earlier ideas about the relationship between unicorns and humans. Imagine a conversation among the various literary and tapestry artists whose works are represented here. What would each say about the others' ideas about unicorns?

3. For the literary and visual artists represented here, unicorns have a real, if mythical, meaning. Look at several of the representations of unicorns, and perhaps at other stories, poems, songs, and pictures that depict unicorns. What can you deduce about the relationship between unicorns and people? About the unicorns' role in the natural world?

4. Both tapestries represent the natural world as a backdrop to the "stories" they tell. How realistic is the nature that is depicted? What do the tapestries imply about the relationship between the natural world and the people and creatures who inhabit it?

FURTHER REFLECTIONS: A COLLECTION OF WORKS ON THE THEME OF LOVE AND FRIENDSHIP

Included in this section are pieces of literature that touch on the theme of Love and Friendship. If Umberto Eco is right that "every story tells a story that has already been told" (see 000), each of the works that follow is in its own way a "retelling." Each asks us to take another look at the idea and practice of love or at family relationships and friendships. The works that follow do not, then, have explicit retellings of their own. Instead, they reflect further ideas about how and whom we love.

Poetry

WILLIAM BLAKE (1757–1827)

The Sick Rose _____ *1794*

O Rose, thou art sick!
The invisible worm
That flies in the night,
In the howling storm,

Has found out thy bed   5
Of crimson joy,
And his dark secret love
Does thy life destroy.

QUESTIONS FOR DISCUSSION AND WRITING

1. In literature, the rose is often a symbol not only of the natural world but of love. What connections do you see in the poem between love and nature? What is the purpose of such connections?
2. The poem moves in part by means of contrast: we think of roses as beautiful, not sick, for instance. We think of joy as something open and vibrant, not dark and secret. What is the thematic purpose of such contrasts?
3. "Worm" for Blake probably meant something closer to "dragon" than to the earthworm many readers first think of when reading this poem. (The Old English word for dragon is *wyrm*.) How does that knowledge affect your reading of the poem?
4. Read the poem aloud. How do its sounds and rhythms, even its punctuation, establish the poem's moods and themes?

ALLEN GINSBERG (1926–1997)

A Supermarket in California   1956

What thoughts I have of you tonight, Walt Whitman, for I walked down the sidestreets under the trees with a headache self-conscious looking at the full moon.

In my hungry fatigue, and shopping for images, I went into the neon fruit supermarket, dreaming of your enumerations!

What peaches and what penumbras! Whole families shopping at night! Aisles full of husbands! Wives in the avocados, babies in the tomatoes!—and you, García Lorca, what were you doing down by the watermelons?

I saw you, Walt Whitman, childless, lonely old grubber, poking among the meats in the refrigerator and eyeing the grocery boys.

5   I heard you asking questions of each: Who killed the pork chops? What price bananas? Are you my Angel?

I wandered in and out of the brilliant stacks of cans following you, and followed in my imagination by the store detective.

We strode down the open corridors together in our solitary fancy tasting artichokes, possessing every frozen delicacy, and never passing the cashier.

Where are we going, Walt Whitman? The doors close in an hour. Which way does your beard point tonight?

(I touch your book and dream of our odyssey in the supermarket and feel absurd.)

10   Will we walk all night through solitary streets? The trees add shade to shade, lights out in the houses, we'll both be lonely.

Will we stroll dreaming of the lost America of love past blue automobiles in driveways, home to our silent cottage?

Ah, dear father, graybeard, lonely old courage-teacher, what
America did you have when Charon quit poling his ferry and you got
out on a smoking bank and stood watching the boat disappear on the
black waters of Lethe?

QUESTIONS FOR DISCUSSION AND WRITING

1. Both Ginsberg and Whitman were homosexual. What in the poem might suggest their sexual orientation? What does the poem tell us about love?
2. How would you characterize the setting of Ginsberg's poem? What connections does it make between the natural and the artificial?
3. Walt Whitman is a poet known for his suspicion of the material world. How does he seem to figure in this poem?
4. The title tells us not only that the poem is set in a supermarket but that it is set in a supermarket *in California*. Given what you know of the realities and stereotypes of California, why would Ginsberg set his poem there?

NIKKI GIOVANNI (1943–   )

Woman _____ 1978

she wanted to be a blade
of grass amid the fields
but he wouldn't agree
to be the dandelion

she wanted to be a robin singing   5
through the leaves
but he refused to be
her tree

she spun herself into a web
and   looking for a place to rest   10
turned to him
but he stood straight
declining to be her corner

she tried to be a book
but he wouldn't read   15

she turned herself into a bulb
but he wouldn't let her grow

she decided to become
a woman
and though he still refused   20

to be a man
she decided it was all
right

QUESTIONS FOR DISCUSSION AND WRITING

1. The "she" of the poem wanted to be many things: a blade of grass, a singing robin, a web, a book, and a bulb. What do those images of desire suggest to you? And what do the companion masculine images—of the dandelion, the tree, the corner, and the man who doesn't read the book or let the bulb grow—suggest about the man of the poem?

2. At the end of the poem, the woman decides that "it was all / right." What is the tone of those lines? Are we to imagine the woman happy? Reconciled to whatever her situation is?

3. The poem is entitled "Woman," and it ends with the thought that the man "still refused / to be a man." What definitions of *woman* and *man, femininity* and *masculinity* are implied here?

4. Look at the structure of the poem. Is there a thematic purpose to the order of the images? What is the effect of the use of "but" in all the stanzas except the last one, and why does that one stanza break the pattern?

LANGSTON HUGHES (1902–1967)

Mother to Son _____ 1922

Well, son, I'll tell you:
Life for me ain't been no crystal stair.
It's had tacks in it,
And splinters,
5   And boards torn up,
And places with no carpet on the floor—
Bare.
But all the time
I'se been a-climbin' on,
10   And reachin' landin's,
And turnin' corners,
And sometimes goin' in the dark
Where there ain't been no light.
So boy, don't you turn back.
15   Don't you set down on the steps
'Cause you finds it's kinder hard.
Don't you fall now—
For I'se still goin', honey,

I'se still climbin',
And life for me ain't been no crystal stair.   20

QUESTIONS FOR DISCUSSION AND WRITING

1. Most stairs are made of wood, metal, or cement. They are certainly not made of "crystal." So why does the mother in Hughes's poem compare the life that she has had to a "crystal stair"? How is a crystal stair different from the kind of metaphorical staircase the mother has actually had to climb?
2. Look at the poem's line divisions, paying particular attention to the words with which lines begin and end and to the varying lengths of the lines. How do the line breaks help Hughes emphasize particular words and images? How do the line divisions create a poetic rhythm that reinforces the mother's words?
3. The speaker's diction would seem to suggest that she is uneducated and, perhaps, poor. What words convey the mother's economic and educational status? How would the effect of the poem have been different had Hughes chosen to express the mother's ideas and feelings in more "educated" diction?
4. How would you characterize the mother and son's relationship? Is she encouraging her son? Scolding him? Does she sound bitter? Determined?

STEPHEN SHU-NING LIU (1930–   )
My Father's Martial Art _____ *1982*

When he came home Mother said he looked
like a monk and stank of green fungus.
At the fireside he told us about life
at the monastery: his rock pillow,
his cold bath, his steel-bar lifting   5
and his wood-chopping. He didn't see
a woman for three winters, on Mountain O Mei.

"My Master was both light and heavy.
He skipped over treetops like a squirrel.
Once he stood on a chair, one foot tied   10
to a rope. We four pulled; we couldn't
move him a bit. His kicks could split
a cedar's trunk."

I saw Father break into a pumpkin
with his fingers. I saw him drop a hawk   15
with bamboo arrows. He rose before dawn, filled
our backyard with a harsh sound *hah, hah, hah:*
there was his Black Dragon Sweep, his Crane Stand,

his Mantis Walk, his Tiger Leap, his Cobra Coil . . .
20 Infrequently he taught me tricks and made me
fight the best of all the village boys.

From a busy street I brood over high cliffs
on O Mei, where my father and his Master sit:
shadows spread across their faces as the smog
25 between us deepens into a funeral pyre.

But don't retreat into night, my father.
Come down from the cliffs. Come
with a single Black Dragon Sweep and hush
this oncoming traffic with your *hah, hah, hah.*

QUESTIONS FOR DISCUSSION AND WRITING

1. Although the poem contains much about the father's and his Master's skill and power, it begins with a description of how the boy's mother greets her returning husband. How do the opening lines influence your response to the father and his martial arts?
2. How would you describe the boy's relationship with his father? The relationship between the boy's parents? The relationship between the father and his Master? What do you learn about the poem's mood and meaning by comparing the various relationships to one another?
3. At the end of the poem, the boy asks that his father not "retreat into night" and, instead, use his martial arts to "hush / this oncoming traffic with your *hah, hah, hah.*" What is the tone of the boy's silent prayer? What do we think will come of that prayer?
4. Read the poem aloud. How do its sounds and rhythms reinforce what the boy seems to be saying about his father and his practice of martial arts?

JANICE MIRIKITANI (1942–   )
Desert Flowers _____ *1978*

Flowers
faded
in the desert wind.
No flowers grow
5 where dust winds blow
and rain is like
a dry heave moan.

Mama, did you dream about that
beau who would take you
10 away from it all,

who would show you
in his '41 ford
and tell you how soft
your hands
like the silk kimono   15
you folded for the wedding?
Make you forget
about That place,
the back bending
wind that fell like a wall,   20
drowned all your geraniums
and flooded the shed
where you tried to sleep
away hyenas?
And mama,   25
bending in the candlelight,
after lights out in barracks,
an ageless shadow
grows victory flowers
made from crepe paper,   30
shaping those petals
like the tears
your eyes bled.
Your fingers
knotted at knuckles   35
wounded, winding around wire stems
the tiny, sloganed banner:

        "america for americans".

Did you dream
of the shiny ford   40
(only always a dream)
ride your youth
like the wind
in the headless night?

Flowers   45
2 ¢ a dozen,
flowers for American Legions
worn like a badge
on america's lapel
made in post-concentration camps   50
by candlelight.
Flowers
watered
by the spit
of "no japs wanted here",   55

              planted in poverty
              of postwar relocations,
              plucked by
              victory's veterans.

60   Mama, do you dream
                            of the wall of wind
                            that falls
                            on your limbless desert,
                            on stems
65   brimming with petals/crushed
                            crepepaper
                            growing
                            from the crippled
                            mouth of your hand?

70   Your tears, mama,
              have nourished us.
              Your children
              like pollen
              scatter in the wind.

QUESTIONS FOR DISCUSSION AND WRITING

1. How are the mother and children in the poem like the "desert flowers"—real and artificial—the poem describes?
2. Janice Mirikitani was born just before World War II, and her family was moved to a Japanese internment camp during the war. "Desert Flowers" is a response to that experience. What in the poem suggests the mood and surroundings of an internment camp?
3. "Desert Flowers" works in part by means of contrasts. Even its title seems to imply a kind of paradox, as we usually think of flowers as growing in more lush surroundings. What contrasts do you find in the poem? How do they contribute to the poem's meaning?
4. Think about the poem's appearance on the page. Why are some of the stanzas indented so much more than others are?

PAT MORA (1942–   )
Borders _____ *1986*

> *My research suggests that men and women may speak different languages that they assume are the same.* —*Carol Gilligan*

If we're so bright,
why didn't we notice?

I

The side-by-side translations
were the easy ones.
Our tongues tasted *luna*   5
chanting, chanting to the words
it touched; our lips circled
moon sighing its longing.
We knew: similar but different.

II

And we knew of grown-up talk,   10
how even in our own home
like became unlike,
how the child's singsong
                                        I want, I want
burned our mouth   15
when we whispered in the dark.

III

But us? You and I
who've talked for years
tossing words back and forth
                                        success, happiness   20
back and forth
over coffee, over wine
at parties, in bed
and I was sure you heard,
                                        understood,   25
though now I think of it
I can remember screaming
to be sure.
So who can hear
the words we speak   30
you and I, like but unlike,
and translate us to us
side by side?

QUESTIONS FOR DISCUSSION AND WRITING

1. What is the connection between the quotation from Carol Gilligan and the poem
   itself? How are the languages of the speaker and the "you" of the poem similar?
   How are they different? To what extent does the speaker think she and the man
   she is speaking to have been able to bridge the gap between their two languages?

2. Certainly the title refers to the borders between men's and women's languages. What other borders and boundaries do you see in the poem? How do those other borders work thematically?
3. The poem is divided into three parts. What distinguishes each part from the others? Why are the parts of the poem presented in the order in which Mora presents them?
4. "Borders" is composed of many very short poetic lines. Why do the line divisions occur where they do? How does Mora use line divisions to help her emphasize particular words and ideas?

MARGE PIERCY (1936–)

A Work of Artifice _____ 1973

    The bonsai tree
    in the attractive pot
    could have grown eighty feet tall
    on the side of a mountain
5   till split by lightning.
    But a gardener
    carefully pruned it.
    It is nine inches high.
    Every day as he
10   whittles back the branches
    the gardener croons,
    It is your nature
    to be small and cozy,
    domestic and weak;
15   how lucky, little tree,
    to have a pot to grow in.
    With living creatures
    one must begin very early
    to dwarf their growth:
20   the bound feet,
    the crippled brain,
    the hair in curlers,
    the hands you
    love to touch.

QUESTIONS FOR DISCUSSION AND WRITING

1. A bonsai tree is a tree that has been artfully pruned and shaped so that it doesn't grow to anywhere near its full height; it looks, then, like a perfectly formed miniature tree. (The bonsai tree in the poem is only nine inches high, rather than the

eighty feet high it would grow in its natural state.) To what or whom is the bonsai tree implicitly being compared? What makes that comparison apt?

2. Think about the meaning and connotations of the word *artifice*. How would the poem have been different had the title been "A Work of Art"? What does the poem suggest is the appropriate relationship among nature, art, and artifice?

3. The poem has two characters: the bonsai and the gardener. How would you describe the personalities and behaviors of each? What is the relationship between them? As you answer these questions, pay attention not only to what the two characters *do* but also to the connotations of the words used to describe them and their behaviors. What do those connotations tell us about the poem's overall tone and purpose?

4. The "hands you love to touch" is a line from an old hand lotion commercial. What do that allusion and the references to bound feet, crippled brains, and hair in curlers imply about the life of the "living creatures" to whom the poem refers?

CATHY SONG (1955–   )

The Youngest Daughter _____ 1983

> The sky has been dark
> for many years.
> My skin has become as damp
> and pale as rice paper
> and feels the way   5
> mother's used to before the drying sun
> parched it out there in the fields.
>
>   Lately, when I touch my eyelids,
> my hands react as if
> I had just touched something   10
> hot enough to burn.
> My skin, aspirin colored,
> tingles with migraine. Mother
> has been massaging the left side of my face
> especially in the evenings   15
> when the pain flares up.
>
> This morning
> her breathing was graveled,
> her voice gruff with affection
> when I wheeled her into the bath.   20
> She was in a good humor,
> making jokes about her great breasts,
> floating in the milky water
> like two walruses,
> flaccid and whiskered around the nipples.   25

I scrubbed them with a sour taste
in my mouth, thinking:
six children and an old man
have sucked from these brown nipples.

30   I was almost tender
when I came to the blue bruises
that freckle her body,
places where she has been injecting insulin
for thirty years. I soaped her slowly,
35   she sighed deeply, her eyes closed.
It seems it has always
been like this: the two of us
in this sunless room,
the splashing of the bathwater.

40   In the afternoons
when she has rested,
she prepares our ritual of tea and rice,
garnished with a shred of gingered fish,
a slice of pickled turnip,
45   a token for my white body.
We eat in the familiar silence.
She knows I am not to be trusted,
even now planning my escape.
As I toast to her health
50   with the tea she has poured,
a thousand cranes curtain the window,
fly up in a sudden breeze.

QUESTIONS FOR DISCUSSION AND WRITING

1. Describe the relationship between the mother and the daughter in "The Youngest Daughter." Where do the two women seem especially close? Especially distant?
2. Sometimes the daughter seems to be caring for the mother; sometimes the mother seems to be caring for the daughter. When and why do the roles change?
3. Song is particularly good at choosing words and images with powerful connotations. Look at some of those words and images, and analyze their functions in the poem. You might, for instance, think about the image of the breasts that are like walruses, of the "aspirin colored" skin that "tingles with migraine," of the "blue bruises / that freckle [the mother's] body," or of the "thousand cranes [that] curtain the window."
4. Compare and contrast the mother and the daughter in "The Youngest Daughter." In what ways are they alike and different physically? To what extent does a clash of culture or of age and generation influence their relationship?

Short Stories

WILLIAM FAULKNER (1897–1962)

A Rose for Emily   1930

I

When Miss Emily Grierson died, our whole town went to her funeral: the men through a sort of respectful affection for a fallen monument, the women mostly out of curiosity to see the inside of her house, which no one save an old manservant—a combined gardener and cook—had seen in at least ten years.

It was a big, squarish frame house that had once been white, decorated with cupolas and spires and scrolled balconies in the heavily lightsome style of the seventies, set on what had once been our most select street. But garages and cotton gins had encroached and obliterated even the august names of that neighborhood; only Miss Emily's house was left, lifting its stubborn and coquettish decay above the cotton wagons and the gasoline pumps—an eyesore among eyesores. And now Miss Emily had gone to join the representatives of those august names where they lay in the cedar-bemused cemetery among the ranked and anonymous graves of Union and Confederate soldiers who fell at the battle of Jefferson.

Alive, Miss Emily had been a tradition, a duty, and a care; a sort of hereditary obligation upon the town, dating from that day in 1894 when Colonel Sartoris, the mayor—he who fathered the edict that no Negro woman should appear on the streets without an apron—remitted her taxes, the dispensation dating from the death of her father on into perpetuity. Not that Miss Emily would have accepted charity. Colonel Sartoris invented an involved tale to the effect that Miss Emily's father had loaned money to the town, which the town, as a matter of business, preferred this way of re-paying. Only a man of Colonel Sartoris' generation and thought could have invented it, and only a woman could have believed it.

When the next generation, with its more modern ideas, became mayors and al-dermen, this arrangement created some little dissatisfaction. On the first of the year they mailed her a tax notice. February came, and there was no reply. They wrote her a formal letter, asking her to call at the sheriff's office at her convenience. A week later the mayor wrote her himself, offering to call or to send his car for her, and received in reply a note on paper of an archaic shape, in a thin, flowing calligraphy in faded ink, to the effect that she no longer went out at all. The tax notice was also enclosed, with-out comment.

They called a special meeting of the Board of Aldermen. A deputation waited upon her, knocked at the door through which no visitor had passed since she ceased giving china-painting lessons eight or ten years earlier. They were admitted by the old Negro into a dim hall from which a stairway mounted into still more shadow. It smelled of dust and disuse—a close, dank smell. The Negro led them into the parlor. It was furnished in heavy, leather-covered furniture. When the Negro opened the blinds of one window, they could see that the leather was cracked; and when they sat down, a faint dust rose sluggishly about their thighs, spinning with slow motes in the single sun-ray. On a tarnished gilt easel before the fireplace stood a crayon portrait of Miss Emily's father.

They rose when she entered—a small, fat woman in black, with a thin gold chain descending to her waist and vanishing into her belt, leaning on an ebony cane with a tarnished gold head. Her skeleton was small and spare; perhaps that was why what would have been merely plumpness in another was obesity in her. She looked bloated, like a body long submerged in motionless water, and of that pallid hue. Her eyes, lost in the fatty ridges of her face, looked like two small pieces of coal pressed into a lump of dough as they moved from one face to another while the visitors stated their errand.

She did not ask them to sit. She just stood in the door and listened quietly until the spokesman came to a stumbling halt. Then they could hear the invisible watch ticking at the end of the gold chain.

Her voice was dry and cold. "I have no taxes in Jefferson. Colonel Sartoris explained it to me. Perhaps one of you can gain access to the city records and satisfy yourselves."

"But we have. We are the city authorities, Miss Emily. Didn't you get a notice from the sheriff, signed by him?"

"I received a paper, yes," Miss Emily said. "Perhaps he considers himself the sheriff . . . I have no taxes in Jefferson."

"But there is nothing on the books to show that, you see. We must go by the——"

"See Colonel Sartoris. I have no taxes in Jefferson."

"But, Miss Emily——"

"See Colonel Sartoris." (Colonel Sartoris had been dead almost ten years.) "I have no taxes in Jefferson. Tobe!" The Negro appeared. "Show these gentlemen out."

II

So she vanquished them, horse and foot, just as she had vanquished their fathers thirty years before about the smell. That was two years after her father's death and a short time after her sweetheart—the one we believed would marry her—had deserted her. After her father's death she went out very little; after her sweetheart went away, people hardly saw her at all. A few of the ladies had the temerity to call, but were not received, and the only sign of life about the place was the Negro man—a young man then—going in and out with a market basket.

"Just as if a man—any man—could keep a kitchen properly," the ladies said; so they were not surprised when the smell developed. It was another link between the gross, teeming world and the high and mighty Griersons.

A neighbor, a woman, complained to the mayor, Judge Stevens, eighty years old.

"But what will you have me do about it, madam?" he said.

"Why, send her word to stop it," the woman said. "Isn't there a law?"

"I'm sure that won't be necessary," Judge Stevens said. "It's probably just a snake or a rat that nigger of hers killed in the yard. I'll speak to him about it."

The next day he received two more complaints, one from a man who came in diffident deprecation. "We really must do something about it, Judge. I'd be the last one in the world to bother Miss Emily, but we've got to do something." That night the Board of Aldermen met—three graybeards and one younger man, a member of the rising generation.

"It's simple enough," he said. "Send her word to have her place cleaned up. Give her a certain time to do it in, and if she don't. . . ."

"Dammit, sir," Judge Stevens said, "will you accuse a lady to her face of smelling bad?"

So the next night, after midnight, four men crossed Miss Emily's lawn and slunk about the house like burglars, sniffing along the base of the brickwork and at the cellar openings while one of them performed a regular sowing motion with his hand out of a sack slung from his shoulder. They broke open the cellar door and sprinkled lime there, and in all the outbuildings. As they recrossed the lawn, a window that had been dark was lighted and Miss Emily sat in it, the light behind her, and her upright torso motionless as that of an idol. They crept quietly across the lawn and into the shadow of the locusts that lined the street. After a week or two the smell went away.

That was when people had begun to feel really sorry for her. People in our town, remembering how old lady Wyatt, her great-aunt, had gone completely crazy at last, believed that the Griersons held themselves a little too high for what they really were. None of the young men were quite good enough for Miss Emily and such. We had long thought of them as a tableau, Miss Emily a slender figure in white in the background, her father a spraddled silhouette in the foreground, his back to her and clutching a horsewhip, the two of them framed by the back-flung front door. So when she got to be thirty and was still single, we were not pleased exactly, but vindicated; even with insanity in the family she wouldn't have turned down all of her chances if they had really materialized.

When her father died, it got about that the house was all that was left to her; and in a way, people were glad. At last they could pity Miss Emily. Being left alone, and a pauper, she had become humanized. Now she too would know the old thrill and the old despair of a penny more or less.

The day after his death all the ladies prepared to call at the house and offer condolence and aid, as is our custom. Miss Emily met them at the door, dressed as usual and with no trace of grief on her face. She told them that her father was not dead. She did that for three days, with the ministers calling on her, and the doctors, trying to persuade her to let them dispose of the body. Just as they were about to resort to law and force, she broke down, and they buried her father quickly.

We did not say she was crazy then. We believed she had to do that. We remembered all the young men her father had driven away, and we knew that with nothing left, she would have to cling to that which had robbed her, as people will.

III

She was sick for a long time. When we saw her again, her hair was cut short, making her look like a girl, with a vague resemblance to those angels in colored church windows—sort of tragic and serene.

The town had just let the contracts for paving the sidewalks, and in the summer after her father's death they began the work. The construction company came with niggers and mules and machinery, and a foreman named Homer Barron, a Yankee—a big, dark, ready man, with a big voice and eyes lighter than his face. The little boys would follow in groups to hear him cuss the niggers, and the niggers singing in time to the rise and fall of picks. Pretty soon he knew everybody in town. Whenever you heard a lot of laughing anywhere about the square, Homer Barron would be in the center of the group. Presently we began to see him and Miss Emily on Sunday afternoons driving in the yellow-wheeled buggy and the matched team of bays from the livery stable.

At first we were glad that Miss Emily would have an interest, because the ladies all said, "Of course a Grierson would not think seriously of a Northerner, a day laborer." But there were still others, older people, who said that even grief could not cause a real lady to forget *noblesse oblige*—without calling it *noblesse oblige*. They just said, "Poor Emily. Her kinsfolk should come to her." She had some kin in Alabama; but years ago her father had fallen out with them over the estate of old lady Wyatt, the crazy woman, and there was no communication between the two families. They had not even been represented at the funeral.

And as soon as the old people said, "Poor Emily," the whispering began. "Do you suppose it's really so?" they said to one another. "Of course it is. What else could . . . ?" This behind their hands; rustling of craned silk and satin behind jalousies closed upon the sun of Sunday afternoon as the thin, swift clop-clop-clop of the matched team passed: "Poor Emily."

She carried her head high enough—even when we believed that she was fallen. It was as if she demanded more than ever the recognition of her dignity as the last Grierson; as if it had wanted that touch of earthiness to reaffirm her imperviousness. Like when she bought the rat poison, the arsenic. That was over a year after they had begun to say "Poor Emily," and while the two female cousins were visiting her.

"I want some poison," she said to the druggist. She was over thirty then, still a slight woman, though thinner than usual, with cold, haughty black eyes in a face the flesh of which was strained across the temples and about the eye-sockets as you imagine a lighthouse-keeper's face ought to look. "I want some poison," she said.

"Yes, Miss Emily. What kind? For rats and such? I'd recom—"

"I want the best you have. I don't care what kind."

The druggist named several. "They'll kill anything up to an elephant. But what you want is—"

"Arsenic," Miss Emily said. "Is that a good one?"

"Is . . . arsenic? Yes, ma'am. But what you want—"

"I want arsenic."

The druggist looked down at her. She looked back at him, erect, her face like a strained flag. "Why, of course," the druggist said. "If that's what you want. But the law requires you to tell what you are going to use it for."

Miss Emily just stared at him, her head tilted back in order to look him eye for eye, until he looked away and went and got the arsenic and wrapped it up. The Negro delivery boy brought her the package; the druggist didn't come back. When she opened the package at home there was written on the box, under the skull and bones: "For rats."

IV

So the next day we all said, "She will kill herself"; and we said it would be the best thing. When she had first begun to be seen with Homer Barron, we had said, "She will marry him." Then we said, "She will persuade him yet," because Homer himself had remarked—he liked men, and it was known that he drank with the younger men in the Elks' Club—that he was not a marrying man. Later we said, "Poor Emily," behind the jalousies as they passed on Sunday afternoon in the glittering buggy, Miss Emily with her head high and Homer Barron with his hat cocked and a cigar in his teeth, reins and whip in a yellow glove.

Then some of the ladies began to say that it was a disgrace to the town and a bad example to the young people. The men did not want to interfere, but at last the ladies forced the Baptist minister—Miss Emily's people were Episcopal—to call upon her. He would never divulge what happened during that interview, but he refused to go back again. The next Sunday they again drove about the streets, and the following day the minister's wife wrote to Miss Emily's relations in Alabama.

So she had blood-kin under her roof again and we sat back to watch developments. At first nothing happened. Then we were sure that they were to be married. We learned that Miss Emily had been to the jeweler's and ordered a man's toilet set in silver, with the letters H. B. on each piece. Two days later we learned that she had bought a complete outfit of men's clothing, including a nightshirt, and we said, "They are married." We were really glad. We were glad because the two female cousins were even more Grierson than Miss Emily had ever been.

So we were not surprised when Homer Barron—the streets had been finished some time since—was gone. We were a little disappointed that there was not a public blowing-off, but we believed that he had gone on to prepare for Miss Emily's coming, or to give her a chance to get rid of the cousins. (By that time it was a cabal, and we were all Miss Emily's allies to help circumvent the cousins.) Sure enough, after another week they departed. And, as we had expected all along, within three days Homer Barron was back in town. A neighbor saw the Negro man admit him at the kitchen door at dusk one evening.

And that was the last we saw of Homer Barron. And of Miss Emily for some time. The Negro man went in and out with the market basket, but the front door remained closed. Now and then we would see her at a window for a moment, as the men did that night when they sprinkled the lime, but for almost six months she did not appear on the streets. Then we knew that this was to be expected too; as if that quality of her father which had thwarted her woman's life so many times had been too virulent and too furious to die.

When we next saw Miss Emily, she had grown fat and her hair was turning gray. During the next few years it grew grayer and grayer until it attained an even pepper-and-salt iron-gray, when it ceased turning. Up to the day of her death at seventy-four it was still that vigorous iron-gray, like the hair of an active man.

From that time on her front door remained closed, save for a period of six or seven years, when she was about forty, during which she gave lessons in china-painting. She fitted up a studio in one of the downstairs rooms, where the daughters and grand-daughters of Colonel Sartoris' contemporaries were sent to her with the same regularity and in the same spirit that they were sent to church on Sundays with a twenty-five-cent piece for the collection plate. Meanwhile her taxes had been remitted.

Then the newer generation became the backbone and the spirit of the town, and the painting pupils grew up and fell away and did not send their children to her with boxes of color and tedious brushes and pictures cut from the ladies' magazines. The front door closed upon the last one and remained closed for good. When the town got free postal delivery, Miss Emily alone refused to let them fasten the metal numbers above her door and attach a mailbox to it. She would not listen to them.

Daily, monthly, yearly we watched the Negro grow grayer and more stooped, going in and out with the market basket. Each December we sent her a tax notice, which would be returned by the post office a week later, unclaimed. Now and then we would see her in one of the downstairs windows—she had evidently shut up the top floor of the house—like the carven torso of an idol in a niche, looking or not looking at us, we could never tell which. Thus she passed from generation to generation—dear, inescapable, impervious, tranquil, and perverse.

And so she died. Fell ill in the house filled with dust and shadows, with only a doddering Negro man to wait on her. We did not even know she was sick; we had long since given up trying to get any information from the Negro. He talked to no one, probably not even to her, for his voice had grown harsh and rusty, as if from disuse.

She died in one of the downstairs rooms, in a heavy walnut bed with a curtain, her gray head propped on a pillow yellow and moldy with age and lack of sunlight.

V

The Negro met the first of the ladies at the front door and let them in, with their hushed, sibilant voices and their quick, curious glances, and then he disappeared. He walked right through the house and out the back and was not seen again.

The two female cousins came at once. They held the funeral on the second day, with the town coming to look at Miss Emily beneath a mass of bought flowers, with the crayon face of her father musing profoundly above the bier and the ladies sibilant and macabre; and the very old men—some in their brushed Confederate uniforms—on the porch and the lawn, talking of Miss Emily as if she had been a contemporary of theirs, believing that they had danced with her and courted her perhaps, confusing time with its mathematical progression, as the old do, to whom all the past is not a diminishing road but, instead, a huge meadow which no winter ever quite touches, divided from them now by the narrow bottleneck of the most recent decade of years.

Already we knew that there was one room in that region above stairs which no one had seen in forty years, and which would have to be forced. They waited until Miss Emily was decently in the ground before they opened it.

The violence of breaking down the door seemed to fill this room with pervading dust. A thin, acrid pall as of the tomb seemed to lie everywhere upon this room decked and furnished as for a bridal: upon the valance curtains of faded rose color, upon the rose-shaded lights, upon the dressing table, upon the delicate array of crystal and the man's toilet things backed with tarnished silver, silver so tarnished that the monogram was obscured. Among them lay collar and tie, as if they had just been removed, which, lifted, left upon the surface a pale crescent in the dust. Upon a chair hung the suit, carefully folded; beneath it the two mute shoes and the discarded socks.

The man himself lay in the bed.

For a long while we just stood there, looking down at the profound and fleshless grin. The body had apparently once lain in the attitude of an embrace, but now the long sleep that outlasts love, that conquers even the grimace of love, had cuckolded him. What was left of him, rotted beneath what was left of the nightshirt, had become inextricable from the bed in which he lay; and upon him and upon the pillow beside him lay that even coating of the patient and biding dust.

Then we noticed that in the second pillow was the indentation of a head. One of us lifted something from it, and leaning forward, that faint and invisible dust dry and acrid in the nostrils, we saw a long strand of iron-gray hair.

QUESTIONS FOR DISCUSSION AND WRITING

1. Look at the setting of Miss Emily's house. What does it tell us about the differences between Miss Emily and the other townspeople?
2. Who is the narrator of the story? How much do you think he sympathizes with Miss Emily? How much does he share her values? As you think about who the narrator is, think also about how the story would be different if told from a different perspective. How would Miss Emily herself have told her story, do you think? How would Homer Barron have told the story of his courtship of Miss Emily?
3. The story begins "When Miss Emily Grierson died . . . ," so in some ways we know the end of the story even from the start. Why doesn't Faulkner's narrator tell the story in chronological order?
4. Many readers are surprised—even horrified—by the conclusion of "A Rose for Emily." On second and third readings, though, they often realize that the narrator has dropped hints along the way about the circumstances surrounding the discovery of Miss Emily's corpse. Reread the story. Where do you find hints about what the townspeople will discover when Miss Emily dies?
5. Because Miss Emily is dead at the beginning of the story, we learn little about her firsthand. "A Rose for Emily" is nevertheless a keen psychological study of its main character. What in Miss Emily's past motivates her to behave as she does—not only to Homer Barron but also to the townspeople in the story?
6. "A Rose for Emily" is divided into several sections. What holds each of the sections together? In other words, what are the narrative, logical, and thematic purposes behind the divisions?
7. Faulkner himself called this a "ghost story." Who—or what—are the ghosts that haunt Miss Emily and the other characters in the story?

CHARLOTTE PERKINS GILMAN (1860–1935)

The Yellow Wallpaper _____ *1892, 1899*

It is very seldom that mere ordinary people like John and myself secure ancestral halls for the summer.

A colonial mansion, a hereditary estate, I would say a haunted house, and reach the height of romantic felicity—but that would be asking too much of fate!

Still I will proudly declare that there is something queer about it.

Else, why should it be let so cheaply? And why have stood so long untenanted?

John laughs at me, of course, but one expects that in marriage.

John is practical in the extreme. He has no patience with faith, an intense horror of superstition, and he scoffs openly at any talk of things not to be felt and seen and put down in figures.

John is a physician, and *perhaps*—(I would not say it to a living soul, of course, but this is dead paper and a great relief to my mind)—*perhaps* that is one reason I do not get well faster.

You see he does not believe I am sick!

And what can one do?

If a physician of high standing, and one's own husband, assures friends and relatives that there is really nothing the matter with one but temporary nervous depression—a slight hysterical tendency—what is one to do?

My brother is also a physician, and also of high standing, and he says the same thing.

So I take phosphates or phosphites—whichever it is, and tonics, and journeys, and air, and exercise, and am absolutely forbidden to "work" until I am well again.

Personally, I disagree with their ideas.

Personally, I believe that congenial work, with excitement and change, would do me good.

But what is one to do?

I did write for a while in spite of them; but it *does* exhaust me a good deal—having to be so sly about it, or else meet with heavy opposition.

I sometimes fancy that in my condition if I had less opposition and more society and stimulus—but John says the very worst thing I can do is to think about my condition, and I confess it always makes me feel bad.

So I will let it alone and talk about the house.

The most beautiful place! It is quite alone, standing well back from the road, quite three miles from the village. It makes me think of English places that you read about, for there are hedges and walls and gates that lock, and lots of separate little houses for the gardeners and people.

There is a *delicious* garden! I never saw such a garden—large and shady, full of box-bordered paths, and lined with long grape-covered arbors with seats under them.

There were greenhouses, too, but they are all broken now.

There was some legal trouble, I believe, something about the heirs and coheirs; anyhow, the place has been empty for years.

That spoils my ghostliness, I am afraid, but I don't care—there is something strange about the house—I can feel it.

I even said so to John one moonlight evening, but he said what I felt was a *draught,* and shut the window.

I get unreasonably angry with John sometimes. I'm sure I never used to be so sensitive. I think it is due to this nervous condition.

But John says if I feel so, I shall neglect proper self-control; so I take pains to control myself—before him, at least, and that makes me very tired.

I don't like our room a bit. I wanted one downstairs that opened on the piazza and had roses all over the window, and such pretty old-fashioned chintz hangings! But John would not hear of it.

He said there was only one window and not room for two beds, and no near room for him if he took another.

He is very careful and loving, and hardly lets me stir without special direction.

I have a schedule prescription for each hour in the day; he takes all care from me, and so I feel basely ungrateful not to value it more.

He said we came here solely on my account, that I was to have perfect rest and all the air I could get. "Your exercise depends on your strength, my dear," said he, "and your food somewhat on your appetite; but air you can absorb all the time." So we took the nursery at the top of the house.

It is a big, airy room, the whole floor nearly, with windows that look all ways, and air and sunshine galore. It was nursery first and then playroom and gymnasium, I should judge; for the windows are barred for little children, and there are rings and things in the walls.

The paint and paper look as if a boys' school had used it. It is stripped off—the paper—in great patches all around the head of my bed, about as far as I can reach, and in a great place on the other side of the room low down. I never saw a worse paper in my life.

One of those sprawling flamboyant patterns committing every artistic sin.

It is dull enough to confuse the eye in following, pronounced enough to constantly irritate and provoke study, and when you follow the lame uncertain curves for a little distance they suddenly commit suicide—plunge off at outrageous angles, destroy themselves in unheard of contradictions.

The color is repellent, almost revolting: a smouldering unclean yellow, strangely faded by the slow-turning sunlight.

It is a dull yet lurid orange in some places, a sickly sulphur tint in others.

No wonder the children hated it! I should hate it myself if I had to live in this room long.

There comes John, and I must put this away,—he hates to have me write a word.

We have been here two weeks, and I haven't felt like writing before, since that first day.

I am sitting by the window now, up in this atrocious nursery, and there is nothing to hinder my writing as much as I please, save lack of strength.

John is away all day, and even some nights when his cases are serious.

I am glad my case is not serious!

But these nervous troubles are dreadfully depressing.

John does not know how much I really suffer. He knows there is no *reason* to suffer, and that satisfies him.

Of course it is only nervousness. It does weigh on me so not to do my duty in any way!

I meant to be such a help to John, such a real rest and comfort, and here I am a comparative burden already!

Nobody would believe what an effort it is to do what little I am able,—to dress and entertain, and order things.

It is fortunate Mary is so good with the baby. Such a dear baby!

And yet I *cannot* be with him, it makes me so nervous.

I suppose John never was nervous in his life. He laughs at me so about this wall-paper!

At first he meant to repaper the room, but afterwards he said that I was letting it get the better of me, and that nothing was worse for a nervous patient than to give way to such fancies.

He said that after the wall-paper was changed it would be the heavy bedstead, and then the barred windows, and then that gate at the head of the stairs, and so on.

"You know the place is doing you good," he said, "and really, dear, I don't care to renovate the house just for a three months' rental."

"Then do let us go downstairs," I said, "there are such pretty rooms there."

Then he took me in his arms and called me a blessed little goose, and said he would go down to the cellar, if I wished, and have it whitewashed into the bargain.

But he is right enough about the beds and windows and things.

It is as airy and comfortable a room as any one need wish, and, of course, I would not be so silly as to make him uncomfortable just for a whim.

I'm really getting quite fond of the big room, all but that horrid paper.

Out of one window I can see the garden, those mysterious deepshaded arbors, the riotous old fashioned flowers, and bushes and gnarly trees.

Out of another I get a lovely view of the bay and a little private wharf belonging to the estate. There is a beautiful shaded lane that runs down there from the house. I always fancy I see people walking in these numerous paths and arbors, but John has cautioned me not to give way to fancy in the least. He says that with my imaginative power and habit of story-making, a nervous weakness like mine is sure to lead to all manner of excited fancies, and that I ought to use my will and good sense to check the tendency. So I try.

I think sometimes that if I were only well enough to write a little it would relieve the press of ideas and rest me.

But I find I get pretty tired when I try.

It is so discouraging not to have any advice and companionship about my work. When I get really well, John says we will ask Cousin Henry and Julia down for a long visit; but he says he would as soon put fireworks in my pillow case as to let me have those stimulating people about now.

I wish I could get well faster.

But I must not think about that. This paper looks to me as if it *knew* what a vicious influence it had!

There is a recurrent spot where the pattern lolls like a broken neck and two bulbous eyes stare at you upside down.

I get positively angry with the impertinence of it and the everlastingness. Up and down and sideways they crawl, and those absurd, unblinking eyes are everywhere. There is one place where two breadths didn't match, and the eyes go all up and down the line, one a little higher than the other.

I never saw so much expression in an inanimate thing before, and we all know how much expression they have! I used to lie awake as a child and get more entertainment and terror out of blank walls and plain furniture than most children could find in a toy-store.

I remember what a kindly wink the knobs of our big, old bureau used to have, and there was one chair that always seemed like a strong friend.

I used to feel that if any of the other things looked too fierce I could always hop into that chair and be safe.

The furniture in this room is no worse than inharmonious, however, for we had to bring it all from downstairs. I suppose when this was used as a playroom they had to take the nursery things out, and no wonder! I never saw such ravages as the children have made here.

The wall-paper, as I said before, is torn off in spots, and it sticketh closer than a brother—they must have had perseverance as well as hatred.

Then the floor is scratched and gouged and splintered, the plaster itself is dug out here and there, and this great heavy bed, which is all we found in the room, looks as if it had been through the wars.

But I don't mind it a bit—only the paper.

There comes John's sister. Such a dear girl as she is, and so careful of me! I must not let her find me writing.

She is a perfect and enthusiastic housekeeper, and hopes for no better profession. I verily believe she thinks it is the writing which made me sick!

But I can write when she is out, and see her a long way off from these windows.

There is one that commands the road, a lovely shaded winding road, and one that just looks off over the country. A lovely country, too, full of great elms and velvet meadows.

This wall-paper has a kind of sub-pattern in a different shade, a particularly irritating one, for you can only see it in certain lights, and not clearly then.

But in the places where it isn't faded and where the sun is just so I can see a strange, provoking, formless sort of figure, that seems to skulk about behind that silly and conspicuous front design.

There's sister on the stairs!

Well, the Fourth of July is over! The people are all gone and I am tired out. John thought it might do me good to see a little company, so we just had mother and Nellie and the children down for a week.

Of course I didn't do a thing. Jennie sees to everything now.

But it tired me all the same.

John says if I don't pick up faster he shall send me to Weir Mitchell in the fall.

But I don't want to go there at all. I had a friend who was in his hands once, and she says he is just like John and my brother, only more so!

Besides, it is such an undertaking to go so far.

I don't feel as if it was worth while to turn my hand over for anything, and I'm getting dreadfully fretful and querulous.

I cry at nothing, and cry most of the time.

Of course I don't when John is here, or anybody else, but when I am alone.

And I am alone a good deal just now. John is kept in town very often by serious cases, and Jennie is good and lets me alone when I want her to.

So I walk a little in the garden or down that lovely lane, sit on the porch under the roses, and lie down up here a good deal.

I'm getting really fond of the room in spite of the wall-paper. Perhaps *because* of the wall-paper.

It dwells in my mind so!

I lie here on this great immovable bed—it is nailed down, I believe—and follow that pattern about by the hour. It is as good as gymnastics, I assure you. I start, we'll say, at the bottom, down in the corner over there where it has not been touched, and I determine for the thousandth time that I *will* follow that pointless pattern to some sort of a conclusion.

I know a little of the principle of design, and I know this thing was not arranged on any laws of radiation, or alternation, or repetition, or symmetry, or anything else that I ever heard of.

It is repeated, of course, by the breadths, but not otherwise.

Looked at in one way each breadth stands alone, the bloated curves and flourishes—a kind of "debased Romanesque" with *delirium tremens*—go waddling up and down in isolated columns of fatuity.

But, on the other hand, they connect diagonally, and the sprawling outlines run off in great slanting waves of optic horror, like a lot of wallowing seaweeds in full chase.

The whole thing goes horizontally, too, at least it seems so, and I exhaust myself in trying to distinguish the order of its going in that direction.

They have used a horizontal breadth for a frieze, and that adds wonderfully to the confusion.

There is one end of the room where it is almost intact, and there, when the crosslights fade and the low sun shines directly upon it, I can almost fancy radiation after all,—the interminable grotesques seem to form around a common centre and rush off in headlong plunges of equal distraction.

It makes me tired to follow it. I will take a nap I guess.

I don't know why I should write this.

I don't want to.

I don't feel able.

And I know John would think it absurd. But I *must* say what I feel and think in some way—it is such a relief!

But the effort is getting to be greater than the relief.

Half the time now I am awfully lazy, and lie down ever so much.

John says I mustn't lose my strength, and has me take cod liver oil and lots of tonics and things, to say nothing of ale and wine and rare meat.

Dear John! He loves me very dearly, and hates to have me sick. I tried to have a real earnest reasonable talk with him the other day, and tell him how I wish he would let me go and make a visit to Cousin Henry and Julia.

But he said I wasn't able to go, nor able to stand it after I got there; and I did not make out a very good case for myself, for I was crying before I had finished.

It is getting to be a great effort for me to think straight. Just this nervous weakness I suppose.

And dear John gathered me up in his arms, and just carried me upstairs and laid me on the bed, and sat by me and read to me till it tired my head.

He said I was his darling and his comfort and all he had, and that I must take care of myself for his sake, and keep well.

He says no one but myself can help me out of it, that I must use my will and self-control and not let any silly fancies run away with me.

There's one comfort, the baby is well and happy, and does not have to occupy this nursery with the horrid wallpaper.

If we had not used it, that blessed child would have! What a fortunate escape! Why, I wouldn't have a child of mine, an impressionable little thing, live in such a room for worlds.

I never thought of it before, but it is lucky that John kept me here after all; I can stand it so much easier than a baby, you see.

Of course I never mention it to them any more—I am too wise,—but I keep watch of it all the same.

There are things in that wall-paper that nobody knows but me, or ever will.

Behind that outside pattern the dim shapes get clearer every day.

It is always the same shape, only very numerous.

And it is like a woman stooping down and creeping about behind that pattern. I don't like it a bit. I wonder—I begin to think—I wish John would take me away from here!

It is so hard to talk with John about my case, because he is so wise, and because he loves me so.

But I tried it last night.

It was moonlight. The moon shines in all around just as the sun does.

I hate to see it sometimes, it creeps so slowly, and always comes in by one window or another.

John was asleep and I hated to waken him, so I kept still and watched the moonlight on that undulating wall-paper till I felt creepy.

The faint figure behind seemed to shake the pattern, just as if she wanted to get out.

I got up softly and went to feel and see if the paper *did* move, and when I came back John was awake.

"What is it, little girl?" he said. "Don't go walking about like that—you'll get cold."

I thought it was a good time to talk, so I told him that I really was not gaining here, and that I wished he would take me away.

"Why darling!" said he, "our lease will be up in three weeks, and I can't see how to leave before.

"The repairs are not done at home, and I cannot possibly leave town just now. Of course if you were in any danger, I could and would, but you really are better, dear, whether you can see it or not. I am a doctor, dear, and I know. You are gaining flesh and color, your appetite is better, I feel really much easier about you."

"I don't weigh a bit more," said I, "nor as much; and my appetite may be better in the evening when you are here, but it is worse in the morning when you are away!"

"Bless her little heart!" said he with a big hug, "she shall be as sick as she pleases! But now let's improve the shining hours by going to sleep, and talk about it in the morning!"

"And you won't go away?" I asked gloomily.

"Why, how can I, dear? It is only three weeks more and then we will take a nice little trip of a few days while Jennie is getting the house ready. Really, dear, you are better!"

"Better in body perhaps—" I began, and stopped short, for he sat up straight and looked at me with such a stern, reproachful look that I could not say another word.

"My darling," said he, "I beg of you, for my sake and for our child's sake, as well as for your own, that you will never for one instant let that idea enter your mind! There is nothing so dangerous, so fascinating, to a temperament like yours. It is a false and foolish fancy. Can you not trust me as a physician when I tell you so?"

So of course I said no more on that score, and we went to sleep before long. He thought I was asleep first, but I wasn't, and lay there for hours trying to decide whether that front pattern and the back pattern really did move together or separately.

On a pattern like this, by daylight, there is a lack of sequence, a defiance of law, that is a constant irritant to a normal mind.

The color is hideous enough, and unreliable enough, and infuriating enough, but the pattern is torturing.

You think you have mastered it, but just as you get well underway in following, it turns a back somersault and there you are. It slaps you in the face, knocks you down, and tramples upon you. It is like a bad dream.

The outside pattern is a florid arabesque, reminding one of a fungus. If you can imagine a toadstool in joints, an interminable string of toadstools, budding and sprouting in endless convolutions—why, that is something like it.

That is, sometimes!

There is one marked peculiarity about this paper, a thing nobody seems to notice but myself, and that is that it changes as the light changes.

When the sun shoots in through the east window—I always watch for that first long, straight ray—it changes so quickly that I never can quite believe it.

That is why I watch it always.

By moonlight—the moon shines in all night when there is a moon—I wouldn't know it was the same paper.

At night in any kind of light, in twilight, candlelight, lamplight, and worst of all by moonlight, it becomes bars! The outside pattern I mean, and the woman behind it is as plain as can be.

I didn't realize for a long time what the thing was that showed behind, that dim sub-pattern, but now I am quite sure it is a woman.

By daylight she is subdued, quiet. I fancy it is the pattern that keeps her so still. It is so puzzling. It keeps me quiet by the hour.

I lie down ever so much now. John says it is good for me, and to sleep all I can.

Indeed he started the habit by making me lie down for an hour after each meal.

It is a very bad habit I am convinced, for you see I don't sleep.

And that cultivates deceit, for I don't tell them I'm awake—O no!

The fact is I am getting a little afraid of John.

He seems very queer sometimes, and even Jennie has an inexplicable look.

It strikes me occasionally, just as a scientific hypothesis,—that perhaps it is the paper!

I have watched John when he did not know I was looking, and come into the room suddenly on the most innocent excuses, and I've caught him several times *looking at the paper!* And Jennie too. I caught Jennie with her hand on it once.

She didn't know I was in the room, and when I asked her in a quiet, a very quiet voice, with the most restrained manner possible, what she was doing with the paper— she turned around as if she had been caught stealing, and looked quite angry—asked me why I should frighten her so!

Then she said that the paper stained everything it touched, that she had found yellow smooches on all my clothes and John's, and she wished we would be more careful!

Did not that sound innocent? But I know she was studying that pattern, and I am determined that nobody shall find it out but myself!

Life is very much more exciting now than it used to be. You see, I have something more to expect, to look forward to, to watch. I really do eat better, and am more quiet than I was.

John is so pleased to see me improve! He laughed a little the other day, and said I seemed to be flourishing in spite of my wall-paper.

I turned it off with a laugh. I had no intention of telling him it was *because* of the wall-paper—he would make fun of me. He might even want to take me away.

I don't want to leave now until I have found it out. There is a week more, and I think that will be enough.

I'm feeling ever so much better! I don't sleep much at night, for it is so interesting to watch developments; but I sleep a good deal in the daytime.

In the daytime it is tiresome and perplexing.

There are always new shoots on the fungus, and new shades of yellow all over it. I cannot keep count of them, though I have tried conscientiously.

It is the strangest yellow, that wall-paper! It makes me think of all the yellow things I ever saw—not beautiful ones like buttercups, but old, foul, bad yellow things.

But there is something else about that paper—the smell! I noticed it the moment we came into the room, but with so much air and sun it was not bad. Now we have had a week of fog and rain, and whether the windows are open or not, the smell is here.

It creeps all over the house.

I find it hovering in the dining-room, skulking in the parlor, hiding in the hall, lying in wait for me on the stairs.

It gets into my hair.

Even when I go to ride, if I turn my head suddenly and surprise it—there is that smell!

Such a peculiar odor, too! I have spent hours in trying to analyze it, to find what it smelled like.

It is not bad—at first—and very gentle, but quite the subtlest, most enduring odor I ever met.

In this damp weather it is awful. I wake up in the night and find it hanging over me.

It used to disturb me at first. I thought seriously of burning the house—to reach the smell.

But now I am used to it. The only thing I can think of that it is like is the *color* of the paper! A yellow smell.

There is a very funny mark on this wall, low down, near the mopboard. A streak that runs round the room. It goes behind every piece of furniture, except the bed, a long, straight, even *smooch,* as if it had been rubbed over and over.

I wonder how it was done and who did it, and what they did it for. Round and round and round—round and round and round—it makes me dizzy!

I really have discovered something at last.

Through watching so much at night, when it changes so, I have finally found out.

The front pattern *does* move—and no wonder! The woman behind shakes it!

Sometimes I think there are a great many women behind, and sometimes only one, and she crawls around fast, and her crawling shakes it all over.

Then in the very bright spots she keeps still, and in the very shady spots she just takes hold of the bars and shakes them hard.

And she is all the time trying to climb through. But nobody could climb through that pattern—it strangles so; I think that is why it has so many heads.

They get through and then the pattern strangles them off and turns them upside down, and makes their eyes white!

If those heads were covered or taken off it would not be half so bad.

I think that woman gets out in the daytime!

And I'll tell you why—privately—I've seen her!

I can see her out of every one of my windows!

It is the same woman, I know, for she is always creeping, and most women do not creep by daylight.

I see her in that long shaded lane, creeping up and down. I see her in those dark grape arbors, creeping all around the garden.

I see her on that long road under the trees, creeping along, and when a carriage comes she hides under the blackberry vines.

I don't blame her a bit. It must be very humiliating to be caught creeping by daylight!

I always lock the door when I creep by daylight. I can't do it at night, for I know John would suspect something at once.

And John is so queer now, that I don't want to irritate him. I wish he would take another room! Besides, I don't want anybody to get that woman out at night but myself.

I often wonder if I could see her out of all the windows at once.

But, turn as fast as I can, I can only see out of one at one time.

And though I always see her, she *may* be able to creep faster than I can turn!

I have watched her sometimes away off in the open country, creeping as fast as a cloud shadow in a high wind.

If only that top pattern could be gotten off from the under one! I mean to try it, little by little.

I have found out another funny thing, but I shan't tell it this time! It does not do to trust people too much.

There are only two more days to get this paper off, and I believe John is beginning to notice. I don't like the look in his eyes.

And I heard him ask Jennie a lot of professional questions about me. She had a very good report to give.

She said I slept a good deal in the daytime.

John knows I don't sleep very well at night, for all I'm so quiet!

He asked me all sorts of questions, too, and pretended to be very loving and kind. As if I couldn't see through him!

Still, I don't wonder he acts so, sleeping under this paper for three months.

It only interests me, but I feel sure John and Jennie are secretly affected by it.

Hurrah! This is the last day, but it is enough. John is to stay in town over night, and won't be out until this evening.

Jennie wanted to sleep with me—the sly thing! but I told her I should undoubtedly rest better for a night all alone.

That was clever, for really I wasn't alone a bit! As soon as it was moonlight and that poor thing began to crawl and shake the pattern, I got up and ran to help her.

I pulled and she shook, I shook and she pulled, and before morning we had peeled off yards of that paper.

A strip about as high as my head and half around the room.

And then when the sun came and that awful pattern began to laugh at me, I declared I would finish it to-day!

We go away to-morrow, and they are moving all my furniture down again to leave things as they were before.

Jennie looked at the wall in amazement, but I told her merrily that I did it out of pure spite at the vicious thing.

She laughed and said she wouldn't mind doing it herself, but I must not get tired.

How she betrayed herself that time!

But I am here, and no person touches this paper but me,—not *alive!*

She tried to get me out of the room—it was too patent! But I said it was so quiet and empty and clean now that I believed I would lie down again and sleep all I could; and not to wake me even for dinner—I would call when I woke.

So now she is gone, and the servants are gone, and the things are gone, and there is nothing left but that great bedstead nailed down, with the canvas mattress we found on it.

We shall sleep downstairs to-night, and take the boat home to-morrow.

I quite enjoy the room, now it is bare again.

How those children did tear about here!

This bedstead is fairly gnawed!

But I must get to work.

I have locked the door and thrown the key down into the front path.

I don't want to go out, and I don't want to have anybody come in, till John comes.

I want to astonish him.

I've got a rope up here that even Jennie did not find. If that woman does get out, and tries to get away, I can tie her!

But I forgot I could not reach far without anything to stand on!

This bed will *not* move!

I tried to lift and push it until I was lame, and then I got so angry I bit off a little piece at one corner—but it hurt my teeth.

Then I peeled off all the paper I could reach standing on the floor. It sticks horribly and the pattern just enjoys it! All those strangled heads and bulbous eyes and waddling fungus growths just shriek with derision!

I am getting angry enough to do something desperate. To jump out of the window would be admirable exercise, but the bars are too strong even to try.

Besides I wouldn't do it. Of course not. I know well enough that a step like that is improper and might be misconstrued.

I don't like to *look* out of the windows even—there are so many of those creeping women, and they creep so fast.

I wonder if they all come out of that wall-paper as I did?

But I am securely fastened now by my well-hidden rope—you don't get *me* out in the road there!

I suppose I shall have to get back behind the pattern when it comes night, and that is hard!

It is so pleasant to be out in this great room and creep around as I please!

I don't want to go outside. I won't, even if Jennie asks me to.

For outside you have to creep on the ground, and everything is green instead of yellow.

But here I can creep smoothly on the floor, and my shoulder just fits in that long smooch around the wall, so I cannot lose my way.

Why, there's John at the door!

It is no use, young man, you can't open it!

How he does call and pound!

Now he's crying for an axe.

It would be a shame to break down that beautiful door!

"John, dear!" said I in the gentlest voice, "the key is down by the front steps, under a plantain leaf!"

That silenced him for a few moments.

Then he said, very quietly indeed, "Open the door, my darling!"

"I can't," said I. "The key is down by the front door under a plantain leaf!"

And then I said it again, several times, very gently and slowly, and said it so often that he had to go and see, and he got it of course, and came in. He stopped short by the door.

"What is the matter?" he cried. "For God's sake, what are you doing!"

I kept on creeping just the same, but I looked at him over my shoulder.

"I've got out at last," said I, "in spite of you and Jane. And I've pulled off most of the paper, so you can't put me back!"

Now why should that man have fainted? But he did, and right across my path by the wall, so that I had to creep over him every time!

QUESTIONS FOR DISCUSSION AND WRITING

1. Of the narrator of "The Yellow Wallpaper," critic Denise Knight has written: "While some critics have hailed the narrator as a feminist heroine, others have seen in her a maternal failure coupled with a marked fear of female sexuality." How do you see her? How would you answer those who see her differently?

2. "The Yellow Wallpaper" is written in diary form. How would the story have been different had it been written in a more conventional short story form? Had it been written by John or Jennie or the narrator's doctor?

3. Consider what we know about the setting of "The Yellow Wallpaper," including the rooms in the house and the area outside. How does the setting influence the narrator's psychological state? How does it reflect that state?

4. Trace the changes in the narrator's character and her attitudes toward herself, her environment, and her husband. Does she become more or less passive as the story moves along? Does John become more or less active?

5. Horace Scudder, the editor of *The Atlantic Monthly*, refused to publish "The Yellow Wallpaper" because "I could not forgive myself if I made others as miserable as I have made myself!" Many readers, like Scudder, dislike literature that depresses them. Argue against or defend Scudder's idea of what literature should be and his reasons for rejecting "The Yellow Wallpaper."

6. "The Yellow Wallpaper" is a fictional account of Gilman's own mental and emotional collapse, and it gives us some insight into the practices of psychology in the late nineteenth century. Research attitudes toward depression in the late 1800s. How did doctors treat the malady? How would a case of postpartum depression be treated today?

Claudius (Derek Jacobi), Hamlet (Kenneth Branagh), and Gertrude (Julie Christie) in Kenneth Branagh's *Hamlet* (Castle Rock, 1996).

Hamlet (Ethan Hawke), Gertrude (Diane Venora), and Claudius (Kyle MacLachlan). The Miramax *Hamlet* (2000) is set in present-day New York City.

Advertising poster for the movie
Forbidden Planet, a science–fiction
version of *The Tempest*, 1956, MGM.

La Vue (Sight), from *The Lady and the Unicorn* tapestries, ca. 1500. The Cluny Museum, Paris.

The Unicorn in Captivity, late 15th–early 16th century. Silk, wool, silver, and gilt threads, 145 x 99 in. The Metropolitan Museum of Art, New York.

Barbie Doll stamp, from the U.S. Postal Service's series on "The Rebellious Sixties and Man on the Moon," 1999.

Pieter Breughel the Elder, *Landscape with the Fall of Icarus*, ca. 1558. Musee Royaux des Beaux-Arts, Brussels.

Edvard Munch, *The Scream*, 1893.
Tempera and pastels on cardboard,
36 x 29 in. Nasjonalgalleriet, Oslo.

Two parodies of Münch's *The Scream*. Advertising poster for *Home Alone*, 1990, and advertising poster for *Home Alone 2: Lost in New York*, 1992, Twentieth Century Fox.

Lee Teter, *Reflections*, 1988.

Vincent Van Gogh, *The Starry Night*,
1889. Oil on canvas, 29 x 36¼ in.
The Museum of Modern Art, New
York.

ZORA NEALE HURSTON (1891?–1960)

Sweat _____ *1926*

I

It was eleven o'clock of a Spring night in Florida. It was Sunday. Any other night, Delia Jones would have been in bed for two hours by this time. But she was a washwoman, and Monday morning meant a great deal to her. So she collected the soiled clothes on Saturday when she returned the clean things. Sunday night after church, she sorted and put the white things to soak. It saved her almost a half-day's start. A great hamper in the bedroom held the clothes that she brought home. It was so much neater than a number of bundles lying around.

She squatted on the kitchen floor beside the great pile of clothes, sorting them into small heaps according to color, and humming a song in a mournful key, but wondering through it all where Sykes, her husband, had gone with her horse and buckboard.

Just then something long, round, limp, and black fell upon her shoulders and slithered to the floor beside her. A great terror took hold of her. It softened her knees and dried her mouth so that it was a full minute before she could cry out or move. Then she saw that it was the big bull whip her husband liked to carry when he drove.

She lifted her eyes to the door and saw him standing there bent over with laughter at her fright. She screamed at him.

"Sykes, what you throw dat whip on me like dat? You know it would skeer me—looks just like a snake, an' you knows how skeered Ah is of snakes."

"Course Ah knowed it! That's how come Ah done it." He slapped his leg with his hand and almost rolled on the ground in his mirth. "If you such a big fool dat you got to have a fit over a earth worm or a string, Ah don't keer how bad Ah skeer you."

"You ain't got no business doing it. Gawd knows it's a sin. Some day Ah'm goin-tuh drop dead from some of yo' foolishness. 'Nother thing, where you been wid mah rig? Ah feeds dat pony. He ain't fuh you to be drivin' wid no bull whip."

"You sho' is one aggravatin' nigger woman!" he declared and stepped into the room. She resumed her work and did not answer him at once. "Ah done tole you time and again to keep them white folks' clothes outa dis house."

He picked up the whip and glared at her. Delia went on with her work. She went out into the yard and returned with a galvanized tub and set it on the wash-bench. She saw that Sykes had kicked all of the clothes together again, and now stood in her way truculently, his whole manner hoping, *praying,* for an argument. But she walked calmly around him and commenced to re-sort the things.

"Next time, Ah'm gointer kick 'em outdoors," he threatened as he struck a match along the leg of his corduroy breeches.

Delia never looked up from her work, and her thin, stooped shoulders sagged further.

"Ah ain't for no fuss t'night Sykes. Ah just come from taking sacrament at the church house."

He snorted scornfully. "Yeah, you just come from de church house on a Sunday night, but heah you is gone to work on them clothes. You ain't nothing but a hypocrite. One of them amen-corner Christians—sing, whoop, and shout, then come home and wash white folks' clothes on the Sabbath."

He stepped roughly upon the whitest pile of things, kicking them helter-skelter as he crossed the room. His wife gave a little scream of dismay, and quickly gathered them together again.

"Sykes, you quit grindin' dirt into these clothes! How can Ah git through by Sat'day if Ah don't start on Sunday?"

"Ah don't keer if you never git through. Anyhow, Ah done promised Gawd and a couple of other men, Ah ain't gointer have it in mah house. Don't gimme no lip neither, else Ah'll throw 'em out and put mah fist up side yo' head to boot."

Delia's habitual meekness seemed to slip from her shoulders like a blown scarf. She was on her feet; her poor little body, her bare knuckly hands bravely defying the strapping hulk before her.

"Looka heah, Sykes, you done gone too fur. Ah been married to you fur fifteen years, and Ah been takin' in washin' fur fifteen years. Sweat, sweat, sweat! Work and sweat, cry and sweat, pray and sweat!"

"What's that got to do with me?" he asked brutally.

"What's it got to do with you, Sykes? Mah tub of suds is filled yo' belly with vittles more times than yo' hands is filled it. Mah sweat is done paid for this house and Ah reckon Ah kin keep on sweatin' in it."

She seized the iron skillet from the stove and struck a defensive pose, which act surprised him greatly, coming from her. It cowed him and he did not strike her as he usually did.

"Naw you won't," she panted, "that ole snaggle-toothed black woman you runnin' with ain't comin' heah to pile up on *mah* sweat and blood. You ain't paid for nothin' on this place, and Ah'm gointer stay right heah till Ah'm toted out foot foremost."

"Well, you better quit gittin' me riled up, else they'll be totin' you out sooner than you expect. Ah'm so tired of you Ah don't know whut to do. Gawd! How Ah hates skinny wimmen!"

A little awed by this new Delia, he sidled out of the door and slammed the back gate after him. He did not say where he had gone, but she knew too well. She knew very well that he would not return until nearly daybreak also. Her work over, she went on to bed but not to sleep at once. Things had come to a pretty pass!

She lay awake, gazing upon the debris that cluttered their matrimonial trail. Not an image left standing along the way. Anything like flowers had long ago been drowned in the salty stream that had been pressed from her heart. Her tears, her sweat, her blood. She had brought love to the union and he had brought a longing after the flesh. Two months after the wedding, he had given her the first brutal beating. She had the memory of his numerous trips to Orlando with all of his wages when he had returned to her penniless, even before the first year had passed. She was young and soft then, but now she thought of her knotty, muscled limbs, her harsh knuckly hands, and drew herself up into an unhappy little ball in the middle of the big feather bed. Too late now to hope for love, even if it were not Bertha it would be someone else. This case differed from the others only in that she was bolder than the others. Too late for everything except her little home. She had built it for her old days, and planted one by one the trees and flowers there. It was lovely to her, lovely.

Somehow, before sleep came, she found herself saying aloud: "Oh well, whatever goes over the Devil's back, is got to come under his belly. Sometime or ruther,

Sykes, like everybody else, is gointer reap his sowing." After that she was able to build a spiritual earthworks against her husband. His shells could no longer reach her. AMEN. She went to sleep and slept until he announced his presence in bed by kicking her feet and rudely snatching the covers away.

"Gimme some kivah heah, an' git yo' damn foots over on yo' own side! Ah oughter mash you in yo' mouf fuh drawing dat skillet on me."

Delia went clear to the rail without answering him. A triumphant indifference to all that he was or did.

II

The week was full of work for Delia as all other weeks, and Saturday found her behind her little pony, collecting and delivering clothes.

It was a hot, hot day near the end of July. The village men on Joe Clarke's porch even chewed cane listlessly. They did not hurl the cane-knots as usual. They let them dribble over the edge of the porch. Even conversation had collapsed under the heat.

"Heah come Delia Jones," Jim Merchant said, as the shaggy pony came 'round the bend of the road toward them. The rusty buckboard was heaped with baskets of crisp, clean laundry.

"Yep," Joe Lindsay agreed. "Hot or col', rain or shine, jes' ez reg'lar ez de weeks roll roun' Delia carries 'em an' fetches 'em on Sat'day."

"She better if she wanter eat," said Moss. "Syke Jones ain't wuth de shot an' powder hit would tek tuh kill 'em. Not to *huh* he ain't."

"He sho' ain't," Walter Thomas chimed in. "It's too bad, too, cause she wuz a right pretty li'l trick when he got huh. Ah'd uh mah'ied huh mahself if he hadnter beat me to it."

Delia nodded briefly at the men as she drove past.

"Too much knockin' will ruin *any* 'oman. He done beat huh 'nough tuh kill three women, let 'lone change they looks," said Elijah Moseley. "How Syke kin stommuck dat big black greasy Mogul he's layin' roun' wid, gits me. Ah swear dat eight-rock couldn't kiss a sardine can Ah done throwed out de back do' 'way las' yeah."

"Aw, she's fat, thass how come. He's allus been crazy 'bout fat women," put in Merchant. "He'd a' been tied up wid one long time ago if he could a' found one tuh have him. Did Ah tell yuh 'bout him come sidlin' roun' *mah* wife—bringin' her a basket uh peecans outa his yard fuh a present? Yessir, mah wife! She tol' him tuh take 'em right straight back home, 'cause Delia works so hard ovah dat washtub she reckon everything on de place taste lak sweat an' soapsuds. Ah jus' wisht Ah'd a' caught 'im 'roun' dere! Ah'd a' made his hips ketch on fiah down dat shell road."

"Ah know he done it, too. Ah sees 'im grinnin' at every 'oman dat passes," Walter Thomas said. "But even so, he useter eat some mighty big hunks uh humble pie tuh git dat li'l 'oman he got. She wuz ez pritty ez a speckled pup! Dat wuz fifteen years ago. He useter be so skeered uh losin' huh, she could make him do some parts of a husband's duty. Dey never wuz de same in de mind."

"There oughter be a law about him," said Lindsay. "He ain't fit tuh carry guts tuh a bear."

Clarke spoke for the first time. "Tain't no law on earth dat kin make a man be decent if it ain't in 'im. There's plenty men dat takes a wife lak dey do a joint uh sugarcane. It's round, juicy, an' sweet when dey gits it. But dey squeeze an' grind, squeeze an' grind an' wring tell dey wring every drop uh pleasure dat's in 'em out. When dey's satisfied dat dey is wrung dry, dey treats 'em jes' lak dey do a cane-chew. Dey throws 'em away. Dey knows whut dey is doin' while dey is at it, an' hates theirselves fuh it but they keeps on hangin' after huh tell she's empty. Den dey hates huh fuh bein' a cane-chew an' in de way."

"We oughter take Syke an' dat stray 'oman uh his'n down in Lake Howell swamp an' lay on de rawhide till they cain't say Lawd a' mussy. He allus wuz uh ovah-bearin niggah, but since dat white 'oman from up north done teached 'im how to run a automobile, he done got too beggety to live—an' we oughter kill 'im," Old Man Anderson advised.

A grunt of approval went around the porch. But the heat was melting their civic virtue and Elijah Moseley began to bait Joe Clarke.

"Come on, Joe, git a melon outa dere an' slice it up for yo' customers. We'se all sufferin' wid de heat. De bear's done got *me!*"

"Thass right, Joe, a watermelon is jes' whut Ah needs tuh cure de eppizudicks," Walter Thomas joined forces with Moseley. "Come on dere, Joe. We all is steady customers an' you ain't set us up in a long time. Ah chooses dat long, bowlegged Floridy favorite."

"A god, an' be dough. You all gimme twenty cents and slice away," Clarke retorted. "Ah needs a col' slice m'self. Heah, everybody chip in. Ah'll lend y'all mah meat knife."

The money was all quickly subscribed and the huge melon brought forth. At that moment, Sykes and Bertha arrived. A determined silence fell on the porch and the melon was put away again.

Merchant snapped down the blade of his jackknife and moved toward the store door.

"Come on in, Joe, an' gimme a slab uh sow belly an' uh pound uh coffee—almost fuhgot 'twas Sat'day. Got to git on home." Most of the men left also.

Just then Delia drove past on her way home, as Sykes was ordering magnificently for Bertha. It pleased him for Delia to see.

"Git whutsoever yo' heart desires, Honey. Wait a minute, Joe. Give huh two bottles uh strawberry soda-water, uh quart parched ground-peas, an' a block uh chewin' gum."

With all this they left the store, with Sykes reminding Bertha that this was his town and she could have it if she wanted it.

The men returned soon after they left, and held their watermelon feast.

"Where did Syke Jones git da 'oman from nohow?" Lindsay asked.

"Ovah Apopka. Guess dey musta been cleanin' out de town when she lef'. She don't look lak a thing but a hunk uh liver wid hair on it."

"Well, she sho' kin squall," Dave Carter contributed. "When she gits ready tuh laff, she jes' opens huh mouf an' latches it back tuh de las' notch. No ole granpa alligator down in Lake Bell ain't got nothin' on huh."

III

Bertha had been in town three months now. Sykes was still paying her room-rent at Dela Lewis'—the only house in town that would have taken her in. Sykes took her frequently to Winter Park to "stomps." He still assured her that he was the swellest man in the state.

"Sho' you kin have dat li'l ole house soon's Ah git dat 'oman outadere. Everything b'longs tuh me an' you sho' kin have it. Ah sho' 'bominates uh skinny 'oman. Lawdy, you sho' is got one portly shape on you! You kin git *anything* you wants. Dis is *mah* town an' you sho' kin have it."

Delia's work-worn knees crawled over the earth in Gethsemane and up the rocks of Calvary many, many times during these months. She avoided the villagers and meeting places in her efforts to be blind and deaf. But Bertha nullified this to a degree, by coming to Delia's house to call Sykes out to her at the gate.

Delia and Sykes fought all the time now with no peaceful interludes. They slept and ate in silence. Two or three times Delia had attempted a timid friendliness, but she was repulsed each time. It was plain that the breaches must remain agape.

The sun had burned July to August. The heat streamed down like a million hot arrows, smiting all things living upon the earth. Grass withered, leaves browned, snakes went blind in shedding, and men and dogs went mad. Dog days!

Delia came home one day and found Sykes there before her. She wondered, but started to go on into the house without speaking, even though he was standing in the kitchen door and she must either stoop under his arm or ask him to move. He made no room for her. She noticed a soap box beside the steps, but paid no particular attention to it, knowing that he must have brought it there. As she was stooping to pass under his outstretched arm, he suddenly pushed her backward, laughingly.

"Look in de box dere Delia, Ah done brung yuh somethin'!"

She nearly fell upon the box in her stumbling, and when she saw what it held, she all but fainted outright.

"Syke! Syke, mah Gawd! You take dat rattlesnake 'way from heah! You *gottuh*. Oh, Jesus, have mussy!"

"Ah ain't got tuh do nuthin' uh de kin'—fact is Ah ain't got tuh do nothin' but die. Tain't no use uh you puttin' on airs makin' out lak you skeered uh dat snake—he's gointer stay right heah tell he die. He wouldn't bite me cause Ah knows how tuh handle 'im. Nohow he wouldn't risk breakin' out his fangs 'gin yo' skinny laigs."

"Naw, now Syke, don't keep dat thing 'round tryin' tuh skeer me tuh death. You knows Ah'm even feared uh earth worms. Thass de biggest snake Ah evah did see. Kill 'im Syke, please."

"Doan ast me tuh do nothin' fuh yuh. Goin' 'round tryin' tuh be so damn asterperious. Naw, Ah ain't gonna kill it. Ah think uh damn sight mo' uh him dan you! Dat's a nice snake an' anybody doan lak 'im kin jes' hit de grit."

The village soon heard that Sykes had the snake, and came to see and ask questions.

"How de hen-fire did you ketch dat six-foot rattler, Syke?" Thomas asked.

"He's full uh frogs so he cain't hardly move, thass how Ah eased up on 'm. But Ah'm a snake charmer an' knows how tuh handle 'em. Shux, dat aint nothin'. Ah could ketch one eve'y day if Ah so wanted tuh."

"Whut he needs is a heavy hick'ry club leaned real heavy on his head. Dat's de bes' way tuh charm a rattlesnake."

"Naw, Walt, y'all jes' don't understand dese diamon' backs lak Ah do," said Sykes in a superior tone of voice.

The village agreed with Walter, but the snake stayed on. His box remained by the kitchen door with its screen wire covering. Two or three days later it had digested its meal of frogs and literally came to life. It rattled at every movement in the kitchen or the yard. One day as Delia came down the kitchen steps she saw his chalky-white fangs curved like scimitars hung in the wire meshes. This time she did not run away with averted eyes as usual. She stood for a long time in the doorway in a red fury that grew bloodier for every second that she regarded the creature that was her torment.

That night she broached the subject as soon as Sykes sat down to the table.

"Syke, Ah wants you tuh take dat snake 'way fum heah. You done starved me an' Ah put up widcher, you done beat me an Ah took dat, but you done kilt all mah insides bringin' dat varmint heah."

Sykes poured out a saucer full of coffee and drank it deliberately before he answered her.

"A whole lot Ah keer 'bout how you feels inside uh out. Dat snake ain't goin' no damn wheah till Ah gits ready fuh 'im tuh go. So fur as beatin' is concerned, yuh ain't took near all dat you gointer take ef yuh stay 'round me."

Delia pushed back her plate and got up from the table. "Ah hates you, Sykes," she said calmly. "Ah hates you tuh de same degree dat Ah useter love yuh. Ah done took an' took till mah belly is full up tuh mah neck. Dat's de reason Ah got mah letter fum de church an' moved mah membership tuh Woodbridge—so Ah don't haftuh take no sacrament wid yuh. Ah don't wantuh see yuh 'round me atall. Lay 'round wid dat 'oman all yuh wants tuh, but gwan 'way fum me an' mah house. Ah hates yuh lak uh suck-egg dog."

Sykes almost let the huge wad of corn bread and collard greens he was chewing fall out of his mouth in amazement. He had a hard time whipping himself up to the proper fury to try to answer Delia.

"Well, Ah'm glad you does hate me. Ah'm sho' tiahed uh you hangin' ontuh me. Ah don't want yuh. Look at yuh stringey ole neck! Yo' raw-bony laigs an' arms is enough tuh cut uh man tuh death. You looks jes' lak de devvul's doll-baby tuh me. You cain't hate me no worse dan Ah hates you. Ah been hatin' you fuh years."

"Yo' ole black hide don't look lak nothin' tuh me, but uh passle uh wrinkled up rubber, wid yo' big ole yeahs flappin' on each side lak uh paih uh buzzard wings. Don't think Ah'm gointuh be run 'way fum mah house neither. Ah'm goin' tuh de white folks 'bout you, mah young man, de very nex' time you lay yo' han's on me. Mah cup is done run ovah." Delia said this with no signs of fear and Sykes departed from the house, threatening her, but made not the slightest move to carry out any of them.

That night he did not return at all, and the next day being Sunday, Delia was glad she did not have to quarrel before she hitched up her pony and drove the four miles to Woodbridge.

She stayed to the night service—"love feast"—which was very warm and full of spirit. In the emotional winds her domestic trials were borne far and wide so that she sang as she drove homeward,

> Jurden water, black an col'
> Chills de body, not de soul
> An' Ah wantah cross Jurden in uh calm time.

She came from the barn to the kitchen door and stopped.

"Whut's de mattah, ol' Satan, you ain't kickin' up yo' racket?" She addressed the snake's box. Complete silence. She went on into the house with a new hope in its birth struggles. Perhaps her threat to go to the white folks had frightened Sykes! Perhaps he was sorry! Fifteen years of misery and suppression had brought Delia to the place where she would hope *anything* that looked towards a way over or through her wall of inhibitions.

She felt in the match-safe behind the stove at once for a match. There was only one there.

"Dat niggah wouldn't fetch nothin' heah tuh save his rotten neck, but he kin run thew whut Ah brings quick enough. Now he done toted off nigh on tuh haff uh box uh matches. He done had dat 'oman heah in mah house, too."

Nobody but a woman could tell how she knew this even before she struck the match. But she did and it put her into a new fury.

Presently she brought in the tubs to put the white things to soak. This time she decided she need not bring the hamper out of the bedroom; she would go in there and do the sorting. She picked up the pot-bellied lamp and went in. The room was small and the hamper stood hard by the foot of the white iron bed. She could sit and reach through the bedposts—resting as she worked.

"Ah wantah cross Jurden in a calm time." She was singing again. The mood of the "love feast" had returned. She threw back the lid of the basket almost gaily. Then, moved by both horror and terror, she sprang back toward the door. *There lay the snake in the basket!* He moved sluggishly at first, but even as she turned round and round, jumped up and down in an insanity of fear, he began to stir vigorously. She saw him pouring his awful beauty from the basket upon the bed, then she seized the lamp and ran as fast as she could to the kitchen. The wind from the open door blew out the light and the darkness added to her terror. She sped to the darkness of the yard, slamming the door after her before she thought to set down the lamp. She did not feel safe even on the ground, so she climbed up in the hay barn.

There for an hour or more she lay sprawled upon the hay a gibbering wreck.

Finally she grew quiet, and after that came coherent thought. With this stalked through her a cold, bloody rage. Hours of this. A period of introspection, a space of retrospection, then a mixture of both. Out of this an awful calm.

"Well, Ah done de bes' Ah could. If things ain't right, Gawd knows tain't mah fault."

She went to sleep—a twitch sleep—and woke up to a faint gray sky. There was a loud hollow sound below. She peered out. Sykes was at the wood-pile, demolishing a wire-covered box.

He hurried to the kitchen door, but hung outside there some minutes before he entered, and stood some minutes more inside before he closed it after him.

The gray in the sky was spreading. Delia descended without fear now, and crouched beneath the low bedroom window. The drawn shade shut out the dawn, shut in the night. But the thin walls held back no sound.

"Dat ol' scratch is woke up now!" She mused at the tremendous whirr inside, which every woodsman knows, is one of the sound illusions. The rattler is a ventriloquist. His whirr sounds to the right, to the left, straight ahead, behind, close under foot—everywhere but where it is. Woe to him who guesses wrong unless he is prepared to hold up his end of the argument! Sometimes he strikes without rattling at all.

Inside, Sykes heard nothing until he knocked a pot lid off the stove while trying to reach the match-safe in the dark. He had emptied his pockets at Bertha's.

The snake seemed to wake up under the stove and Sykes made a quick leap into the bedroom. In spite of the gin he had had, his head was clearing now.

"Mah Gawd!" he chattered, "ef Ah could on'y strack uh light!"

The rattling ceased for a moment as he stood paralyzed. He waited. It seemed that the snake waited also.

"Oh, fuh de light! Ah thought he'd be too sick"—Sykes was muttering to himself when the whirr began again, closer, right underfoot this time. Long before this, Sykes' ability to think had been flattened down to primitive instinct and he leaped—onto the bed.

Outside Delia heard a cry that might have come from a maddened chimpanzee, a stricken gorilla. All the terror, all the horror, all the rage that man possibly could express, without a recognizable human sound.

A tremendous stir inside there, another series of animal screams, the intermittent whirr of the reptile. The shade torn violently down from the window, letting in the red dawn, a huge brown hand seizing the window stick, great dull blows upon the wooden floor punctuating the gibberish of sound long after the rattle of the snake had abruptly subsided. All this Delia could see and hear from her place beneath the window, and it made her ill. She crept over to the four o'clocks and stretched herself on the cool earth to recover.

She lay there. "Delia, Delia!" She could hear Sykes calling in a most despairing tone as one who expected no answer. The sun crept on up, and he called. Delia could not move—her legs had gone flabby. She never moved, he called, and the sun kept rising.

"Mah Gawd!" She heard him moan, "Mah Gawd fum Heben!" She heard him stumbling about and got up from her flower-bed. The sun was growing warm. As she approached the door she heard him call out hopefully, "Delia, is dat you Ah heah?"

She saw him on his hands and knees as soon as she reached the door. He crept an inch or two toward her—all that he was able, and she saw his horribly swollen neck and his one open eye shining with hope. A surge of pity too strong to support bore her away from that eye that must, could not, fail to see the tubs. He would see the lamp. Orlando with its doctors was too far. She could scarcely reach the chinaberry tree, where she waited in the growing heat while inside she knew the cold river was creeping up and up to extinguish that eye which must know by now that she knew.

QUESTIONS FOR DISCUSSION AND WRITING

1. We are told early in section III that "Delia's work-worn knees crawled over the earth in Gethsemane and up the rocks of Calvary many, many times during these months" (543). Both Gethsemane and Calvary are places mentioned in the Bible. Look these allusions up in a college dictionary, encyclopedia, or other reference tool. What do these allusions tell us about Delia's mood, behavior, and character? How do these and other references to church and religion help us understand the conflict between Delia and Sykes?

2. Delia and Sykes have different ideas about gender and race. How do they and other characters in the story envision the appropriate relationship between men and women? Between people of different races? What point of view does the story as a whole ask us to take?

3. Think about the story's title, which seems to have more to do with Delia's work ethic than it does with the relationship between Sykes and Delia. How does the title connect to the story's theme(s)?
4. What kind of narrator does Hurston use in "Sweat"? How would the story be different had it been told from the point of view of one of the characters in the story?
5. Reread the final paragraph of the story. What is the significance of the tubs? What is it that Sykes "must know by now that she knew"? Does Delia's retreat to the chinaberry tree change our response to her? Why or why not?
6. Delia calls Sykes "ol' scratch," using a folk term for the devil (545). Snakes are also often associated with the devil. Look at the ways in which Sykes, Delia, and the other characters in the story talk about snakes and interact with the snake in the story. How does the snake figure symbolically and thematically in the story?

JAMES JOYCE (1882–1941)

Araby _____ *1905, 1914*

North Richmond Street, being blind, was a quiet street except at the hour when the Christian Brothers' School set the boys free. An uninhabited house of two storeys stood at the blind end, detached from its neighbours in a square ground. The other houses of the street, conscious of decent lives within them, gazed at one another with brown imperturbable faces.

The former tenant of our house, a priest, had died in the back drawing-room. Air, musty from having been long enclosed, hung in all the rooms, and the waste room behind the kitchen was littered with old useless papers. Among these I found a few paper-covered books, the pages of which were curled and damp: *The Abbot,* by Walter Scott, *The Devout Communicant* and *The Memoirs of Vidocq.* I liked the last best because its leaves were yellow. The wild garden behind the house contained a central apple-tree and a few straggling bushes under one of which I found the late tenant's rusty bicycle-pump. He had been a very charitable priest; in his will he had left all his money to institutions and the furniture of his house to his sister.

When the short days of winter came dusk fell before we had well eaten our dinners. When we met in the street the houses had grown sombre. The space of sky above us was the colour of ever-changing violet and towards it the lamps of the street lifted their feeble lanterns. The cold air stung us and we played till our bodies glowed. Our shouts echoed in the silent street. The career of our play brought us through the dark muddy lanes behind the houses where we ran the gantlet of the rough tribes from the cottages, to the back doors of the dark dripping gardens where odours arose from the ashpits, to the dark odorous stables where a coachman smoothed and combed the horse or shook music from the buckled harness. When we returned to the street light from the kitchen windows had filled the areas. If my uncle was seen turning the corner we hid in the shadow until we had seen him safely housed. Or if Mangan's sister came out on the doorstep to call her brother in to his tea we watched her from our shadow peer up and down the street. We waited to see whether she would remain or go in and, if she remained, we left our shadow and walked up to Mangan's steps resignedly. She was waiting for us, her figure defined by the light from the half-opened door. Her brother always teased her before he obeyed and I stood by the railings looking at her. Her dress swung as she moved her body and the soft rope of her hair tossed from side to side.

Every morning I lay on the floor in the front parlour watching her door. The blind was pulled down to within an inch of the sash so that I could not be seen. When she came out on the doorstep my heart leaped. I ran to the hall, seized my books and followed her. I kept her brown figure always in my eye and, when we came near the point at which our ways diverged, I quickened my pace and passed her. This happened morning after morning. I had never spoken to her, except for a few casual words, and yet her name was like a summons to all my foolish blood.

Her image accompanied me even in places the most hostile to romance. On Saturday evenings when my aunt went marketing I had to go to carry some of the parcels. We walked through the flaring streets, jostled by drunken men and bargaining women, amid the curses of labourers, the shrill litanies of shop-boys who stood on guard by the barrels of pigs' cheeks, the nasal chanting of street-singers, who sang a come-all-you about O'Donovan Rossa, or a ballad about the troubles in our native land. These noises converged in a single sensation of life for me: I imagined that I bore my chalice safely through a throng of foes. Her name sprang to my lips at moments in strange prayers and praises which I myself did not understand. My eyes were often full of tears (I could not tell why) and at times a flood from my heart seemed to pour itself out into my bosom. I thought little of the future. I did not know whether I would ever speak to her or not or, if I spoke to her, how I could tell her of my confused adoration. But my body was like a harp and her words and gestures were like fingers running upon the wires.

One evening I went into the back drawing-room in which the priest had died. It was a dark rainy evening and there was no sound in the house. Through one of the broken panes I heard the rain impinge upon the earth, the fine incessant needles of water playing in the sodden beds. Some distant lamp or lighted window gleamed below me. I was thankful that I could see so little. All my senses seemed to desire to veil themselves and, feeling that I was about to slip from them, I pressed the palms of my hands together until they trembled, murmuring: *O love! O love!* many times.

At last she spoke to me. When she addressed the first words to me I was so confused that I did not know what to answer. She asked me was I going to *Araby*. I forget whether I answered yes or no. It would be a splendid bazaar, she said; she would love to go.

—And why can't you? I asked.

While she spoke she turned a silver bracelet round and round her wrist. She could not go, she said, because there would be a retreat that week in her convent. Her brother and two other boys were fighting for their caps and I was alone at the railings. She held one of the spikes, bowing her head towards me. The light from the lamp opposite our door caught the white curve of her neck, lit up her hair that rested there and, falling, lit up the hand upon the railing. It fell over one side of her dress and caught the white border of a petticoat, just visible as she stood at ease.

—It's well for you, she said.

—If I go, I said, I will bring you something.

What innumerable follies laid waste my waking and sleeping thoughts after that evening! I wished to annihilate the tedious intervening days. I chafed against the work of school. At night in my bedroom and by day in the classroom her image came between me and the page I strove to read. The syllables of the word *Araby* were called to me through the silence in which my soul luxuriated and cast an Eastern enchantment over me. I asked for leave to go to the bazaar Saturday night. My aunt was surprised and hoped it was not some Freemason affair. I answered few questions in class. I watched my master's face pass from amiability to sternness; he hoped I was not beginning to idle. I could not call my wandering thoughts together. I had hardly any patience with the serious work of life which, now that it stood between me and my desire, seemed to me child's play, ugly monotonous child's play.

On Saturday morning I reminded my uncle that I wished to go to the bazaar in the evening. He was fussing at the hallstand, looking for the hat-brush, and answered me curtly:

—Yes, boy, I know.

As he was in the hall I could not go into the front parlour and lie at the window. I left the house in bad humour and walked slowly towards the school. The air was pitilessly raw and already my heart misgave me.

When I came home to dinner my uncle had not yet been home. Still it was early. I sat staring at the clock for some time and, when its ticking began to irritate me, I left the room. I mounted the staircase and gained the upper part of the house. The high cold empty gloomy rooms liberated me and I went from room to room singing. From the front window I saw my companions playing below in the street. Their cries reached me weakened and indistinct and, leaning my forehead against the cool glass, I looked over at the dark house where she lived. I may have stood there for an hour, seeing nothing but the brown-clad figure cast by my imagination, touched discreetly by the lamplight at the curved neck, at the hand upon the railings and at the border below the dress.

When I came downstairs again I found Mrs Mercer sitting at the fire. She was an old garrulous woman, a pawnbroker's widow, who collected used stamps for some pious purpose. I had to endure the gossip of the tea-table. The meal was prolonged beyond an hour and still my uncle did not come. Mrs Mercer stood up to go: she was sorry she couldn't wait any longer, but it was after eight o'clock and she did not like to be out late, as the night air was bad for her. When she had gone I began to walk up and down the room, clenching my fists. My aunt said:

—I'm afraid you may put off your bazaar for this night of Our Lord.

At nine o'clock I heard my uncle's latchkey in the halldoor. I heard him talking to himself and heard the hallstand rocking when it had received the weight of his overcoat. I could interpret these signs. When he was midway through his dinner I asked him to give me the money to go to the bazaar. He had forgotten.

—The people are in bed and after their first sleep now, he said.

I did not smile. My aunt said to him energetically:

—Can't you give him the money and let him go? You've kept him late enough as it is.

My uncle said he was very sorry he had forgotten. He said he believed in the old saying: *All work and no play makes Jack a dull boy.* He asked me where I was going and, when I had told him a second time he asked me did I know *The Arab's Farewell to his Steed.* When I left the kitchen he was about to recite the opening lines of the piece to my aunt.

I held a florin tightly in my hand as I strode down Buckingham Street towards the station. The sight of the streets thronged with buyers and glaring with gas recalled to me the purpose of my journey. I took my seat in a third–class carriage of a deserted train. After an intolerable delay the train moved out of the station slowly. It crept on-ward among ruinous houses and over the twinkling river. At Westland Row Station a crowd of people pressed to the carriage doors; but the porters moved them back, say-ing that it was a special train for the bazaar. I remained alone in the bare carriage. In a few minutes the train drew up beside an improvised wooden platform. I passed out on to the road and saw by the lighted dial of a clock that it was ten minutes to ten. In front of me was a large building which displayed the magical name.

I could not find any sixpenny entrance and, fearing that the bazaar would be closed, I passed in quickly through a turnstile, handing a shilling to a weary-looking man. I found myself in a big hall girdled at half its height by a gallery. Nearly all the stalls were closed and the greater part of the hall was in darkness. I recognised a si-lence like that which pervades a church after a service. I walked into the centre of the bazaar timidly. A few people were gathered about the stalls which were still open. Be-fore a curtain, over which the words *Café Chantant* were written in coloured lamps, two men were counting money on a salver. I listened to the fall of the coins.

Remembering with difficulty why I had come I went over to one of the stalls and examined porcelain vases and flowered tea-sets. At the door of the stall a young lady was talking and laughing with two young gentlemen. I remarked their English accents and listened vaguely to their conversation.

—O, I never said such a thing!

—O, but you did!

—O, but I didn't!

—Didn't she say that?

—Yes. I heard her.

—O, there's a . . . fib!

Observing me the young lady came over and asked me did I wish to buy any-thing. The tone of her voice was not encouraging; she seemed to have spoken to me out of a sense of duty. I looked humbly at the great jars that stood like eastern guards at either side of the dark entrance to the stall and murmured:

—No, thank you.

The young lady changed the position of one of the vases and went back to the two young men. They began to talk of the same subject. Once or twice the young lady glanced at me over her shoulder.

I lingered before her stall, though I knew my stay was useless, to make my inter-est in her wares seem the more real. Then I turned away slowly and walked down the middle of the bazaar. I allowed the two pennies to fall against the sixpence in my pocket. I heard a voice call from one end of the gallery that the light was out. The upper part of the hall was now completely dark.

Gazing up into the darkness I saw myself as a creature driven and derided by vanity; and my eyes burned with anguish and anger.

QUESTIONS FOR DISCUSSION AND WRITING

1. "Araby" is set in the boy's house, on his street, and at the bazaar he visits. But it also invokes another setting: the setting of a legendary Arabia. What associations do

you have with Arabia and *The Arabian Nights*? How does the imagined setting of a mythical Araby compare and contrast with the actual settings in which the boy lives and acts? How are the boy's behavior, language, and mood affected by the settings in which he actually and imaginatively finds himself?

2. The characters in "Araby" are unnamed and shadowy figures. Even the boy's love interest is called only "Mangan's sister." Why would Joyce choose to leave the characters unnamed? How would the story have felt different had each of the characters been named? How would it have been different had the other characters been as fully developed as the boy's character is? (Think not only about Mangan and Mangan's sister but also about the priest who once lived and died in the boy's house, about the boy's aunt and uncle, and about those he meets at the bazaar.)

3. How old do you think the boy in "Araby" is? What leads you to your conclusion? How would the story have been different if the boy had been older or younger than you imagine him?

4. Some readers remark that the boy of "Araby" doesn't talk like a boy. Others counter that he doesn't *talk* like a boy but he does *think* and *feel* like a boy. How well does Joyce capture a boy's emotions and an adult's perspective on them?

5. "Araby," like many of Joyce's stories, ends with what is called an *epiphany*, a moment of dramatic realization. There is some debate, however, about exactly what the boy realizes. How do you respond to the boy's final lines? What are the sources of the vanity, anguish, and anger he feels? How much do we sympathize with his feelings?

ALICE MUNRO (1931–   )

The Found Boat   *1974*

At the end of Bell Street, McKay Street, Mayo Street, there was the Flood. It was the Wawanash River, which every spring overflowed its banks. Some springs, say one in every five, it covered the roads on that side of town and washed over the fields, creating a shallow choppy lake. Light reflected off the water made everything bright and cold, as it is in a lakeside town, and woke or revived in people certain vague hopes of disaster. Mostly during the late afternoon and early evening, there were people straggling out to look at it, and discuss whether it was still rising, and whether this time it might invade the town. In general, those under fifteen and over sixty-five were most certain that it would.

Eva and Carol rode out on their bicycles. They left the road—it was the end of Mayo Street, past any houses—and rode right into a field, over a wire fence entirely flattened by the weight of the winter's snow. They coasted a little way before the long grass stopped them, then left their bicycles lying down and went to the water.

"We have to find a log and ride on it," Eva said.

"Jesus, we'll freeze our legs off."

"Jesus, we'll freeze our legs off!" said one of the boys who were there too at the water's edge. He spoke in a sour whine, the way boys imitated girls although it was nothing like the way girls talked. These boys—there were three of them—were all in the same class as Eva and Carol at school and were known to them by name (their names being Frank, Bud and Clayton), but Eva and Carol, who had seen and recognized them from the road, had not spoken to them or looked at them or, even yet, given any sign of knowing they were there. The boys seemed to be trying to make a raft, from lumber they had salvaged from the water.

Eva and Carol took off their shoes and socks and waded in. The water was so cold it sent pain up their legs, like blue electric sparks shooting through their veins, but they went on, pulling their skirts high, tight behind and bunched so they could hold them in front.

"Look at the fat-assed ducks in wading."

"Fat-assed fucks."

Eva and Carol, of course, gave no sign of hearing this. They laid hold of a log and climbed on, taking a couple of boards floating in the water for paddles. There were always things floating around in the Flood—branches, fence-rails, logs, road signs, old lumber; sometimes boilers, washtubs, pots and pans, or even a car seat or stuffed chair, as if somewhere the Flood had got into a dump.

They paddled away from shore, heading out into the cold lake. The water was perfectly clear, they could see the brown grass swimming along the bottom. Suppose it was the sea, thought Eva. She thought of drowned cities and countries. Atlantis. Suppose they were riding in a Viking boat—Viking boats on the Atlantic were more frail and narrow than this log on the Flood—and they had miles of clear sea beneath them, then a spired city, intact as a jewel irretrievable on the ocean floor.

"This is a Viking boat," she said. "I am the carving on the front." She stuck her chest out and stretched her neck, trying to make a curve, and she made a face, putting out her tongue. Then she turned and for the first time took notice of the boys.

"Hey, you sucks!" she yelled at them. "You'd be scared to come out here, this water is ten feet deep!"

"Liar," they answered without interest, and she was.

They steered the log around a row of trees, avoiding floating barbed wire, and got into a little bay created by a natural hollow of the land. Where the bay was now, there would be a pond full of frogs later in the spring, and by the middle of summer there would be no water at all, just a low tangle of reeds and bushes, green, to show that mud was still wet around their roots. Larger bushes, willows, grew around the steep bank of this pond and were still partly out of the water. Eva and Carol let the log ride in. They saw a place where something was caught.

It was a boat, or part of one. An old rowboat with most of one side ripped out, the board that had been the seat just dangling. It was pushed up among the branches, lying on what would have been its side, if it had a side, the prow caught high.

Their idea came to them without consultation, at the same time:

"You guys! Hey, you guys!"

"We found you a boat!"

"Stop building your stupid raft and come and look at the boat!"

What surprised them in the first place was that the boys really did come, scrambling overland, half running, half sliding down the bank, wanting to see.

"Hey, where?"

"Where is it, I don't see no boat."

What surprised them in the second place was that when the boys did actually see what boat was meant, this old flood-smashed wreck held up in the branches, they did not understand that they had been fooled, that a joke had been played on them. They did not show a moment's disappointment, but seemed as pleased at the discovery as if the boat had been whole and new. They were already barefoot, because they had been wading in the water to get lumber, and they waded in here without a stop, surrounding the boat and appraising it and paying no attention even of an insulting kind to Eva and Carol who bobbed up and down on their log. Eva and Carol had to call to them.

"How do you think you're going to get it off?"

"It won't float anyway."

"What makes you think it will float?"

"It'll sink. Glub-blub-blub, you'll all be drownded."

The boys did not answer, because they were too busy walking around the boat, pulling at it in a testing way to see how it could be got off with the least possible damage. Frank, who was the most literate, talkative and inept of the three, began referring to the boat as *she,* an affectation which Eva and Carol acknowledged with fish-mouths of contempt.

"She's caught two places. You got to be careful not to tear a hole in her bottom. She's heavier than you'd think."

It was Clayton who climbed up and freed the boat, and Bud, a tall fat boy, who got the weight of it on his back to turn it into the water so that they could half float, half carry it to shore. All this took some time. Eva and Carol abandoned their log and waded out of the water. They walked overland to get their shoes and socks and bicycles. They did not need to come back this way but they came. They stood at the top of the hill, leaning on their bicycles. They did not go on home, but they did not sit down and frankly watch, either. They stood more or less facing each other, but glancing down at the water and at the boys struggling with the boat, as if they had just halted for a moment out of curiosity, and staying longer than they intended, to see what came of this unpromising project.

About nine o'clock, or when it was nearly dark—dark to people inside the houses, but not quite dark outside—they all returned to town, going along Mayo Street in a sort of procession. Frank and Bud and Clayton came carrying the boat, upside-down, and Eva and Carol walked behind, wheeling their bicycles. The boys' heads were almost hidden in the darkness of the overturned boat, with its smell of soaked wood, cold swampy water. The girls could look ahead and see the street lights in their tin reflectors, a necklace of lights climbing Mayo Street, reaching all the way up to the standpipe. They turned onto Burns Street heading for Clayton's house, the nearest house belonging to any of them. This was not the way home for Eva or for Carol either, but they followed along. The boys were perhaps too busy carrying the boat to tell them to go away. Some younger children were still out playing, playing hopscotch on the sidewalk though they could hardly see. At this time of year the bare sidewalk was still such a novelty and delight. These children cleared out of the way and watched the boat go by with unwilling respect; they shouted questions after it, wanting to know where it came from and what was going to be done with it. No one answered them. Eva and Carol as well as the boys refused to answer or even look at them.

The five of them entered Clayton's yard. The boys shifted weight, as if they were going to put the boat down.

"You better take it round to the back where nobody can see it," Carol said. That was the first thing any of them had said since they came into town.

The boys said nothing but went on, following a mud path between Clayton's house and a leaning board fence. They let the boat down in the back yard.

"It's a stolen boat, you know," said Eva, mainly for the effect. "It must've belonged to somebody. You stole it."

"You was the ones who stole it then," Bud said, short of breath. "It was you seen it first."

"It was you took it."

"It was all of us then. If one of us gets in trouble then all of us does."

"Are you going to tell anybody on them?" said Carol as she and Eva rode home, along the streets which were dark between the lights now and potholed from winter.

"It's up to you. I won't if you won't."

"I won't if you won't."

They rode in silence, relinquishing something, but not discontented.

The board fence in Clayton's back yard had every so often a post which supported it, or tried to, and it was on these posts that Eva and Carol spent several evenings sitting, jauntily but not very comfortably. Or else they just leaned against the fence while the boys worked on the boat. During the first couple of evenings neighborhood children attracted by the sound of hammering tried to get into the yard to see what was going on, but Eva and Carol blocked their way.

"Who said you could come in here?"

"Just us can come in this yard."

These evenings were getting longer, the air milder. Skipping was starting on the sidewalks. Further along the street there was a row of hard maples that had been tapped. Children drank the sap as fast as it could drip into the buckets. The old man and woman who owned the trees, and who hoped to make syrup, came running out of the house making noises as if they were trying to scare away crows. Finally, every spring, the old man would come out on his porch and fire his shotgun into the air, and then the thieving would stop.

None of those working on the boat bothered about stealing sap, though all had done so last year.

The lumber to repair the boat was picked up here and there, along back lanes. At this time of year things were lying around—old boards and branches, sodden mitts, spoons flung out with the dishwater, lids of pudding pots that had been set in the snow to cool, all the debris that can sift through and survive winter. The tools came from Clayton's cellar—left over, presumably, from the time when his father was alive— and though they had nobody to advise them the boys seemed to figure out more or less the manner in which boats are built, or rebuilt. Frank was the one who showed up with diagrams from books and *Popular Mechanics* magazines. Clayton looked at these diagrams and listened to Frank read the instructions and then went ahead and decided in his own way what was to be done. Bud was best at sawing. Eva and Carol watched everything from the fence and offered criticism and thought up names. The names for the boat that they thought of were: Water Lily, Sea Horse, Flood Queen, and Caro-Eve, after them because they had found it. The boys did not say which, if any, of these names they found satisfactory.

The boat had to be tarred. Clayton heated up a pot of tar on the kitchen stove and brought it out and painted slowly, his thorough way, sitting astride the overturned boat. The other boys were sawing a board to make a new seat. As Clayton worked, the tar cooled and thickened so that finally he could not move the brush any more. He turned to Eva and held out the pot and said, "You can go in and heat this on the stove."

Eva took the pot and went up the back steps. The kitchen seemed black after outside, but it must be light enough to see in, because there was Clayton's mother standing at the ironing board, ironing. She did that for a living, took in wash and ironing.

"Please may I put the tar pot on the stove?" said Eva, who had been brought up to talk politely to parents, even wash-and-iron ladies, and who for some reason especially wanted to make a good impression on Clayton's mother.

"You'll have to poke up the fire then," said Clayton's mother, as if she doubted whether Eva would know how to do that. But Eva could see now, and she picked up the lid with the stove-lifter, and took the poker and poked up a flame. She stirred the tar as it softened. She felt privileged. Then and later. Before she went to sleep a picture of Clayton came to her mind; she saw him sitting astride the boat, tarpainting, with such concentration, delicacy, absorption. She thought of him speaking to her, out of his isolation, in such an ordinary peaceful taking-for-granted voice.

On the twenty-fourth of May, a school holiday in the middle of the week, the boat was carried out of town, a long way now, off the road over fields and fences that had been repaired, to where the river flowed between its normal banks. Eva and Carol, as well as the boys, took turns carrying it. It was launched in the water from a cow-trampled spot between willow bushes that were fresh out in leaf. The boys went first. They yelled with triumph when the boat did float, when it rode amazingly down the river current. The boat was painted black, and green inside, with yellow seats, and a strip of yellow all the way around the outside. There was no name on it, after all. The boys could not imagine that it needed any name to keep it separate from the other boats in the world.

Eva and Carol ran along the bank, carrying bags full of peanut butter-and-jam sandwiches, pickles, bananas, chocolate cake, potato chips, graham crackers stuck together with corn syrup and five bottles of pop to be cooled in the river water. The bottles bumped against their legs. They yelled for a turn.

"If they don't let us they're bastards," Carol said, and they yelled together, "We found it! We found it!"

The boys did not answer, but after a while they brought the boat in, and Carol and Eva came crashing, panting down the bank.

"Does it leak?"

"It don't leak yet."

"We forgot a bailing can," wailed Carol, but nevertheless she got in, with Eva, and Frank pushed them off, crying, "Here's to a Watery Grave!"

And the thing about being in a boat was that it was not solidly bobbing, like a log, but was cupped in the water, so that riding in it was not like being on something in the water, but like being in the water itself. Soon they were all going out in the boat in mixed-up turns, two boys and a girl, two girls and a boy, a girl and a boy, until things were so confused it was impossible to tell whose turn came next, and nobody cared anyway. They went down the river—those who weren't riding, running along the bank to keep up. They passed under two bridges, one iron, one cement. Once they saw a big carp just resting, it seemed to smile at them, in the bridge-shaded water. They did not know how far they had gone on the river, but things had changed—the water had got shallower, and the land flatter. Across an open field they saw a building that looked like a house, abandoned. They dragged the boat up on the bank and tied it and set out across the field.

"That's the old station," Frank said. "That's Pedder Station." The others had heard this name but he was the one who knew, because his father was the station agent in town. He said that this was a station on a branch line that had been torn up, and that there had been a sawmill here, but a long time ago.

Inside the station it was dark, cool. All the windows were broken. Glass lay in shards and in fairly big pieces on the floor. They walked around finding the larger pieces of glass and tramping on them, smashing them, it was like cracking ice on puddles. Some partitions were still in place, you could see where the ticket window had been. There was a bench lying on its side. People had been here, it looked as if people came here all the time, though it was so far from anywhere. Beer bottles and pop bottles were lying around, also cigarette packages, gum and candy wrappers, the paper from a loaf of bread. The walls were covered with dim and fresh pencil and chalk writings and carved with knives.

> I LOVE RONNIE COLES
> I WANT TO FUCK
> KILROY WAS HERE
> RONNIE COLES IS AN ASS-HOLE
> WHAT ARE YOU DOING HERE?
> WAITING FOR A TRAIN
> DAWNA MARY-LOU BARBARA JOANNE

It was exciting to be inside this large, dark, empty place, with the loud noise of breaking glass and their voices ringing back from the underside of the roof. They tipped the old beer bottles against their mouths. That reminded them that they were hungry and thirsty and they cleared a place in the middle of the floor and sat down and ate the lunch. They drank the pop just as it was, lukewarm. They ate everything there was and licked the smears of peanut butter and jam off the bread-paper in which the sandwiches had been wrapped.

They played Truth or Dare.

"I dare you to write on the wall, I am a Stupid Ass, and sign your name."

"Tell the truth—what is the worst lie you ever told?"

"Did you ever wet the bed?"

"Did you ever dream you were walking down the street without any clothes on?"

"I dare you to go outside and pee on the railway sign."

It was Frank who had to do that. They could not see him, even his back, but they knew he did it, they heard the hissing sound of his pee. They all sat still, amazed, unable to think of what the next dare would be.

"I dare everybody," said Frank from the doorway, "I dare—Everybody."

"What?"

"Take off all our clothes."

Eva and Carol screamed.

"Anybody who won't do it has to walk—has to *crawl*—around this floor on their hands and knees."

They were all quiet, till Eva said, almost complacently, "What first?"

"Shoes and socks."

"Then we have to go outside, there's too much glass here."

They pulled off their shoes and socks in the doorway, in the sudden blinding sun. The field before them was bright as water. They ran across where the tracks used to go.

"That's enough, that's enough," said Carol. "Watch out for thistles!"

"Tops! Everybody take off their tops!"

"I won't! We won't, will we, Eva?"

But Eva was whirling round and round in the sun where the track used to be. "I don't care, I don't care! Truth or Dare! Truth or Dare!"

She unbuttoned her blouse as she whirled, as if she didn't know what her hand was doing, she flung it off.

Carol took off hers. "I wouldn't have done it, if you hadn't!"

"Bottoms!"

Nobody said a word this time, they all bent and stripped themselves. Eva, naked first, started running across the field, and then all the others ran, all five of them running bare through the knee-high hot grass, running towards the river. Not caring now about being caught but in fact leaping and yelling to call attention to themselves, if there was anybody to hear or see. They felt as if they were going to jump off a cliff and fly. They felt that something was happening to them different from anything that had happened before, and it had to do with the boat, the water, the sunlight, the dark ruined station, and each other. They thought of each other now hardly as names or people, but as echoing shrieks, reflections, all bold and white and loud and scandalous, and as fast as arrows. They went running without a break into the cold water and when it came almost to the tops of their legs they fell on it and swam. It stopped their noise. Silence, amazement, came over them in a rush. They dipped and floated and separated, sleek as mink.

Eva stood up in the water her hair dripping, water running down her face. She was waist deep. She stood on smooth stones, her feet fairly wide apart, water flowing between her legs. About a yard away from her Clayton also stood up, and they were blinking the water out of their eyes, looking at each other. Eva did not turn or try to hide; she was quivering from the cold of the water, but also with pride, shame, boldness, and exhilaration.

Clayton shook his head violently, as if he wanted to bang something out of it, then bent over and took a mouthful of river water. He stood up with his cheeks full and made a tight hole of his mouth and shot the water at her as if it was coming out of a hose, hitting her exactly, first one breast and then the other. Water from his mouth ran down her body. He hooted to see it, a loud self-conscious sound that nobody would have expected, from him. The others looked up from wherever they were in the water and closed in to see.

Eva crouched down and slid into the water, letting her head go right under. She swam, and when she let her head out downstream, Carol was coming after her and the boys were already on the bank, already running into the grass, showing their skinny backs, their white, flat buttocks. They were laughing and saying things to each other but she couldn't hear, for the water in her ears.

"What did he do?" said Carol.

"Nothing."

They crept in to shore. "Let's stay in the bushes till they go," said Eva. "I hate them anyway. I really do. Don't you hate them?"

"Sure," said Carol, and they waited, not very long, until they heard the boys still noisy and excited coming down to the place a bit upriver where they had left the boat. They heard them jump in and start rowing.

"They've got all the hard part, going back," said Eva, hugging herself and shivering violently. "Who cares? Anyway. It never was our boat."

"What if they tell?" said Carol.

"We'll say it's all a lie."

Eva hadn't thought of this solution until she said it, but as soon as she did she felt almost light-hearted again. The ease and scornfulness of it did make them both giggle, and slapping themselves and splashing out of the water they set about developing one of those fits of laughter in which, as soon as one showed signs of exhaustion, the other would snort and start up again, and they would make helpless—soon genuinely helpless—faces at each other and bend over and grab themselves as if they had the worst pain.

QUESTIONS FOR DISCUSSION AND WRITING

1. At the beginning of the story, the boys and girls are mildly antagonistic toward one another. What is the cause of their antagonism? At what point in the story do they seem to change their minds about one another and become less antagonistic? Why?
2. How old are the children in the story? (Think not only about the five main characters but about the unnamed children of the neighborhood as well.) How is age significant to the story's mood and themes?
3. The river and the boat have not only literal meaning but also symbolic value in the story. Why is the river called the Flood? Why does Eva think of the boat as a Viking boat that might carry them out to sea? Why does the boat remain unnamed? How do the children "interact" with water and with the various "boats" they ride?

TILLIE OLSEN (1913–   )
I Stand Here Ironing _____ 1961

I stand here ironing, and what you asked me moves tormented back and forth with the iron.

"I wish you would manage the time to come in and talk with me about your daughter. I'm sure you can help me understand her. She's a youngster who needs help and whom I'm deeply interested in helping."

"Who needs help." . . . Even if I came, what good would it do? You think because I am her mother I have a key, or that in some way you could use me as a key?

She has lived for nineteen years. There is all that life that has happened outside of me, beyond me.

And when is there time to remember, to sift, to weigh, to estimate, to total? I will start and there will be an interruption and I will have to gather it all together again. Or I will become engulfed with all I did or did not do, with what should have been and what cannot be helped.

She was a beautiful baby. The first and only one of our five that was beautiful at birth. You do not guess how new and uneasy her tenancy in her now-loveliness. You did not know her all those years she was thought homely, or see her poring over her baby pictures, making me tell her over and over how beautiful she had been—and would be, I would tell her—and was now, to the seeing eye. But the seeing eyes were few or non-existent. Including mine.

I nursed her. They feel that's important nowadays. I nursed all the children, but with her, with all the fierce rigidity of first motherhood, I did like the books then said. Though her cries battered me to trembling and my breasts ached with swollenness, I waited till the clock decreed.

Why do I put that first? I do not even know if it matters, or if it explains anything.

She was a beautiful baby. She blew shining bubbles of sound. She loved motion, loved light, loved color and music and textures. She would lie on the floor in her blue overalls patting the surface so hard in ecstasy her hands and feet would blur. She was a miracle to me, but when she was eight months old I had to leave her daytimes with the woman downstairs to whom she was no miracle at all, for I worked or looked for work and for Emily's father, who "could no longer endure" (he wrote in his good-bye note) "sharing want with us."

I was nineteen. It was the pre-relief, pre-WPA world of the depression. I would start running as soon as I got off the streetcar, running up the stairs, the place smelling sour, and awake or asleep to startle awake, when she saw me she would break into a clogged weeping that could not be comforted, a weeping I can hear yet.

After a while I found a job hashing at night so I could be with her days, and it was better. But it came to where I had to bring her to his family and leave her.

It took a long time to raise the money for her fare back. Then she got chicken pox and I had to wait longer. When she finally came, I hardly knew her, walking quick and nervous like her father, looking like her father, thin, and dressed in a shoddy red that yellowed her skin and glared at the pockmarks. All the baby loveliness gone.

She was two. Old enough for nursery school they said, and I did not know then what I know now—the fatigue of the long day, and the lacerations of group life in the kinds of nurseries that are only parking places for children.

Except that it would have made no difference if I had known. It was the only place there was. It was the only way we could be together, the only way I could hold a job.

And even without knowing, I knew. I knew the teacher that was evil because all these years it has curdled into my memory, the little boy hunched in the corner, her rasp, "why aren't you outside, because Alvin hits you? that's no reason, go out, scaredy." I knew Emily hated it even if she did not clutch and implore "don't go Mommy" like the other children, mornings.

She always had a reason why we should stay home. Momma, you look sick, Momma. I feel sick. Momma, the teachers aren't there today, they're sick. Momma, we can't go, there was a fire there last night. Momma, it's a holiday today, no school, they told me.

But never a direct protest, never rebellion. I think of our others in their three-, four-year-oldness—the explosions, the tempers, the denunciations, the demands— and I feel suddenly ill. I put the iron down. What in me demanded that goodness in her? And what was the cost, the cost to her of such goodness?

The old man living in the back once said in his gentle way: "You should smile at Emily more when you look at her." What *was* in my face when I looked at her? I loved her. There were all the acts of love.

It was only with the others I remembered what he said, and it was the face of joy, and not of care or tightness or worry I turned to them—too late for Emily. She does not smile easily, let alone almost always as her brothers and sisters do. Her face is closed and somber, but when she wants, how fluid. You must have seen it in her pantomimes, you spoke of her rare gift for comedy on the stage that rouses a laughter out of the audience so dear they applaud and applaud and do not want to let her go.

Where does it come from, that comedy? There was none of it in her when she came back to me that second time, after I had had to send her away again. She had a new daddy now to learn to love, and I think perhaps it was a better time.

Except when we left her alone nights, telling ourselves she was old enough.

"Can't you go some other time, Mommy, like tomorrow?" she would ask. "Will it be just a little while you'll be gone? Do you promise?"

The time we came back, the front door open, the clock on the floor in the hall. She rigid awake. "It wasn't just a little while. I didn't cry. Three times I called you, just three times, and then I ran downstairs to open the door so you could come faster. The clock talked loud. I threw it away, it scared me what it talked."

She said the clock talked loud again that night I went to the hospital to have Susan. She was delirious with the fever that comes before red measles, but she was fully conscious all the week I was gone and the week after we were home when she could not come near the new baby or me.

She did not get well. She stayed skeleton thin, not wanting to eat, and night after night she had nightmares. She would call for me, and I would rouse from exhaustion to sleepily call back: "You're all right, darling, go to sleep, it's just a dream," and if she still called, in a sterner voice, "now go to sleep, Emily, there's nothing to hurt you." Twice, only twice, when I had to get up for Susan anyhow, I went in to sit with her.

Now when it is too late (as if she would let me hold and comfort her like I do the others) I get up and go to her at once at her moan or restless stirring. "Are you awake, Emily? Can I get you something?" And the answer is always the same: "No, I'm all right, go back to sleep, Mother."

They persuaded me at the clinic to send her away to a convalescent home in the country where "she can have the kind of food and care you can't manage for her, and you'll be free to concentrate on the new baby." They still send children to that place. I see pictures on the society page of sleek young women planning affairs to raise money for it, or dancing at the affairs, or decorating Easter eggs or filling Christmas stockings for the children.

They never have a picture of the children so I do not know if the girls still wear those gigantic red bows and the ravaged looks on the every other Sunday when parents can come to visit "unless otherwise notified"—as we were notified the first six weeks.

Oh it is a handsome place, green lawns and tall trees and fluted flower beds. High up on the balconies of each cottage the children stand, the girls in their red bows and white dresses, the boys in white suits and giant red ties. The parents stand below shrieking up to be heard and the children shriek down to be heard, and between them the invisible wall "Not To Be Contaminated by Parental Germs or Physical Affection."

There was a tiny girl who always stood hand in hand with Emily. Her parents never came. One visit she was gone. "They moved her to Rose Cottage," Emily shouted in explanation. "They don't like you to love anybody here."

She wrote once a week, the labored writing of a seven-year-old. "I am fine. How is the baby. If I write my letter nicely I will have a star. Love." There never was a star. We wrote every other day, letters she could never hold or keep but only hear read—once. "We simply do not have room for children to keep any personal possessions," they patiently explained when we pieced one Sunday's shrieking together to plead how much it would mean to Emily, who loved so to keep things, to be allowed to keep her letters and cards.

Each visit she looked frailer. "She isn't eating," they told us.

(They had runny eggs for breakfast or mush with lumps, Emily said later, I'd hold it in my mouth and not swallow. Nothing ever tasted good, just when they had chicken.)

It took us eight months to get her released home, and only the fact that she gained back so little of her seven lost pounds convinced the social worker.

I used to try to hold and love her after she came back, but her body would stay stiff, and after a while she'd push away. She ate little. Food sickened her, and I think much of life too. Oh she had physical lightness and brightness, twinkling by on skates, bouncing like a ball up and down up and down over the jump rope, skimming over the hill; but these were momentary.

She fretted about her appearance, thin and dark and foreign-looking at a time when every little girl was supposed to look or thought she should look a chubby blonde replica of Shirley Temple. The doorbell sometimes rang for her, but no one seemed to come and play in the house or be a best friend. Maybe because we moved so much.

There was a boy she loved painfully through two school semesters. Months later she told me how she had taken pennies from my purse to buy him candy. "Licorice was his favorite and I brought him some every day, but he still liked Jennifer better'n me. Why, Mommy?" The kind of question for which there is no answer.

School was a worry to her. She was not glib or quick in a world where glibness and quickness were easily confused with ability to learn. To her overworked and exasperated teachers she was an overconscientious "slow learner" who kept trying to catch up and was absent entirely too often.

I let her be absent, though sometimes the illness was imaginary. How different from my now-strictness about attendance with the others. I wasn't working. We had a new baby, I was home anyhow. Sometimes, after Susan grew old enough, I would keep her home from school, too, to have them all together.

Mostly Emily had asthma, and her breathing, harsh and labored, would fill the house with a curiously tranquil sound. I would bring the two old dresser mirrors and her boxes of collections to her bed. She would select beads and single earrings, bottle tops and shells, dried flowers and pebbles, old postcards and scraps, all sorts of oddments; then she and Susan would play Kingdom, setting up landscapes and furniture, peopling them with action.

Those were the only times of peaceful companionship between her and Susan. I have edged away from it, that poisonous feeling between them, that terrible balancing of hurts and needs I had to do between the two, and did so badly, those earlier years.

Oh there are conflicts between the others too, each one human, needing, demanding, hurting, taking—but only between Emily and Susan, no, Emily toward Susan that corroding resentment. It seems so obvious on the surface, yet it is not obvious. Susan, the second child, Susan, golden- and curly-haired and chubby, quick and articulate and assured, everything in appearance and manner Emily was not; Susan, not able to resist Emily's precious things, losing or sometimes clumsily breaking them; Susan telling jokes and riddles to company for applause while Emily sat silent (to say to me later: that was *my* riddle, Mother, I told it to Susan); Susan, who for all the five years' difference in age was just a year behind Emily in developing physically.

I am glad for that slow physical development that widened the difference between her and her contemporaries, though she suffered over it. She was too vulnerable for that terrible world of youthful competition, of preening and parading, of constant measuring of yourself against every other, of envy, "If I had that copper hair," "If I had that skin. . . ." She tormented herself enough about not looking like the others, there was enough of the unsureness, the having to be conscious of words before you speak, the constant caring—what are they thinking of me? without having it all magnified by the merciless physical drives.

Ronnie is calling. He is wet and I change him. It is rare there is such a cry now. That time of motherhood is almost behind me when the ear is not one's own but must always be racked and listening for the child cry, the child call. We sit for a while and I hold him, looking out over the city spread in charcoal with its soft aisles of light. "*Shoogily,*" he breathes and curls closer. I carry him back to bed, asleep. *Shoogily.* A funny word, a family word, inherited from Emily, invented by her to say: *comfort.*

In this and other ways she leaves her seal, I say aloud. And startle at my saying it. What do I mean? What did I start to gather together, to try and make coherent? I was at the terrible, growing years. War years. I do not remember them well. I was working, there were four smaller ones now, there was not time for her. She had to help be a mother, and housekeeper, and shopper. She had to set her seal. Mornings of crisis and near hysteria trying to get lunches packed, hair combed, coats and shoes found, everyone to school or Child Care on time, the baby ready for transportation. And always the paper scribbled on by a smaller one, the book looked at by Susan then mislaid, the homework not done. Running out to that huge school where she was one, she was lost, she was a drop; suffering over the unpreparedness, stammering and unsure in her classes.

There was so little time left at night after the kids were bedded down. She would struggle over books, always eating (it was in those years she developed her enormous appetite that is legendary in our family) and I would be ironing, or preparing food for the next day, or writing V-mail to Bill, or tending the baby. Sometimes, to make me laugh, or out of her despair, she would imitate happenings or types at school.

I think I said once: "Why don't you do something like this in the school amateur show?" One morning she phoned me at work, hardly understandable through the weeping: "Mother, I did it. I won, I won; they gave me first prize; they clapped and clapped and wouldn't let me go."

Now suddenly she was Somebody, and as imprisoned in her difference as she had been in anonymity.

She began to be asked to perform at other high schools, even in colleges, then at city and statewide affairs. The first one we went to, I only recognized her that first moment when thin, shy, she almost drowned herself into the curtains. Then: Was this Emily? The control, the command, the convulsing and deadly clowning, the spell, then the roaring, stamping audience, unwilling to let this rare and precious laughter out of their lives.

Afterwards: You ought to do something about her with a gift like that—but without money or knowing how, what does one do? We have left it all to her, and the gift has as often eddied inside, clogged and clotted, as been used and growing.

She is coming. She runs up the stairs two at a time with her light graceful step, and I know she is happy tonight. Whatever it was that occasioned your call did not happen today.

"Aren't you ever going to finish the ironing, Mother? Whistler painted his mother in a rocker. I'd have to paint mine standing over an ironing board." This is one of her communicative nights and she tells me everything and nothing as she fixes herself a plate of food out of the icebox.

She is so lovely. Why did you want me to come in at all? Why were you concerned? She will find her way.

She starts up the stairs to bed. "Don't get me up with the rest in the morning." "But I thought you were having midterms." "Oh, those," she comes back in, kisses me, and says lightly, "in a couple of years when we'll all be atom-dead they won't matter a bit."

She has said it before. She *believes* it. But because I have been dredging the past, and all that compounds a human being is so heavy and meaningful in me, I cannot endure it tonight.

I will never total it all. I will never come in to say: She was a child seldom smiled at. Her father left me before she was a year old. I had to work her first six years when there was work, or I sent her home and to his relatives. There were years she had care she hated. She was dark and thin and foreign-looking in a world where the prestige went to blondeness and curly hair and dimples, she was slow where glibness was prized. She was a child of anxious, not proud, love. We were poor and could not afford for her the soil of easy growth. I was a young mother, I was a distracted mother. There were the other children pushing up, demanding. Her younger sister seemed all that she was not. There were years she did not want me to touch her. She kept too much in herself, her life was such she had to keep too much in herself. My wisdom came too late. She has much to her and probably little will come of it. She is a child of her age, of depression, of war, of fear.

Let her be. So all that is in her will not bloom—but in how many does it? There is still enough left to live by. Only help her to know—help make it so there is cause for her to know—that she is more than this dress on the ironing board, helpless before the iron.

QUESTIONS FOR DISCUSSION AND WRITING

1. By our standards, the mother has made many "mistakes" in raising Emily. What are some of the mistakes and how did they affect Emily? How much are we meant to blame the mother for her treatment of Emily? What circumstances are beyond her control?
2. What is the relationship between Emily's childhood and her talent as a comic?
3. The title, "I Stand Here Ironing," suggests that the mother's ironing is significant to the story. In fact, the story begins and ends with references to the ironing. Why is it important that the mother is ironing as she narrates?

ALICE WALKER (1944–)

Everyday Use

For Your Grandmama

1973

I will wait for her in the yard that Maggie and I made so clean and wavy yesterday afternoon. A yard like this is more comfortable than most people know. It is not just a yard. It is like an extended living room. When the hard clay is swept clean as a floor and the fine sand around the edges lined with tiny, irregular grooves anyone can come and sit and look up into the elm tree and wait for the breezes that never come inside the house.

Maggie will be nervous until after her sister goes: she will stand hopelessly in corners homely and ashamed of the burn scars down her arms and legs, eyeing her sister with a mixture of envy and awe. She thinks her sister has held life always in the palm of one hand, that "no" is a word the world never learned to say to her.

You've no doubt seen those TV shows where the child who has "made it" is confronted, as a surprise, by her own mother and father, tottering in weakly from backstage. (A pleasant surprise, of course: What would they do if parent and child came on the show only to curse out and insult each other?) On TV mother and child embrace and smile into each other's faces. Sometimes the mother and father weep, the child wraps them in her arms and leans across the table to tell how she would not have made it without their help. I have seen these programs.

Sometimes I dream a dream in which Dee and I are suddenly brought together on a TV program of this sort. Out of a dark and soft-seated limousine I am ushered into a bright room filled with many people. There I meet a smiling, gray, sporty man like Johnny Carson who shakes my hand and tells me what a fine girl I have. Then we are on the stage and Dee is embracing me with tears in her eyes. She pins on my dress a large orchid, even though she has told me once that she thinks orchids are tacky flowers.

In real life I am a large, big-boned woman with rough, man-working hands. In the winter I wear flannel nightgowns to bed and overalls during the day. I can kill and clean a hog as mercilessly as a man. My fat keeps me hot in zero weather. I can work outside all day, breaking ice to get water for washing. I can eat pork liver cooked over the open fire minutes after it comes steaming from the hog. One winter I knocked a bull calf straight in the brain between the eyes with a sledge hammer and had the meat hung up to chill before nightfall. But of course all this does not show on television. I am the way my daughter would want me to be: a hundred pounds lighter, my skin like an uncooked barley pancake. My hair glistens in the hot bright lights. Johnny Carson has much to do to keep up with my quick and witty tongue.

But that is a mistake. I know even before I wake up. Who ever knew a Johnson with a quick tongue? Who can even imagine me looking a strange white man in the eye? It seems to me I have talked to them always with one foot raised in flight, with my head turned in whichever way is farthest from them. Dee, though. She would always look anyone in the eye. Hesitation was no part of her nature.

"How do I look, Mama?" Maggie says, showing just enough of her thin body enveloped in pink skirt and red blouse for me to know she's there, almost hidden by the door.

"Come out into the yard," I say.

Have you ever seen a lame animal, perhaps a dog run over by some careless person rich enough to own a car, sidle up to someone who is ignorant enough to be kind to him? That is the way my Maggie walks. She has been like this, chin on chest, eyes on ground, feet in shuffle, ever since the fire that burned the other house to the ground.

Dee is lighter than Maggie, with nicer hair and a fuller figure. She's a woman now, though sometimes I forget. How long ago was it that the other house burned? Ten, twelve years? Sometimes I can still hear the flames and feel Maggie's arms sticking to me, her hair smoking and her dress falling off her in little black papery flakes. Her eyes seemed stretched open, blazed open by the flames reflected in them. And Dee. I see her standing off under the sweet gum tree she used to dig gum out of; a look of concentration on her face as she watched the last dingy gray board of the house fall in toward the red-hot brick chimney. Why don't you do a dance around the ashes? I'd wanted to ask her. She had hated the house that much.

I used to think she hated Maggie, too. But that was before we raised the money, the church and me, to send her to Augusta to school. She used to read to us without pity; forcing words, lies, other folks' habits, whole lives upon us two, sitting trapped and ignorant underneath her voice. She washed us in a river of make-believe, burned us with a lot of knowledge we didn't necessarily need to know. Pressed us to her with the serious way she read, to shove us away at just the moment, like dimwits, we seemed about to understand.

Dee wanted nice things. A yellow organdy dress to wear to her graduation from high school; black pumps to match a green suit she'd made from an old suit somebody gave me. She was determined to stare down any disaster in her efforts. Her eyelids would not flicker for minutes at a time. Often I fought off the temptation to shake her. At sixteen she had a style of her own: and knew what style was.

I never had an education myself. After second grade the school was closed down. Don't ask me why: in 1927 colored asked fewer questions than they do now. Sometimes Maggie reads to me. She stumbles along good-naturedly but can't see well. She knows she is not bright. Like good looks and money, quickness passed her by. She will marry John Thomas (who has mossy teeth in an earnest face) and then I'll be free to sit here and I guess just sing church songs to myself. Although I never was a good singer. Never could carry a tune. I was always better at a man's job. I used to love to milk till I was hoofed in the side in '49. Cows are soothing and slow and don't bother you, unless you try to milk them the wrong way.

I have deliberately turned my back on the house. It is three rooms, just like the one that burned, except the roof is tin; they don't make shingle roofs any more. There are no real windows, just some holes cut in the sides, like the portholes in a ship, but not round and not square, with rawhide holding the shutters up on the outside. This house is in a pasture, too, like the other one. No doubt when Dee sees it she will want to tear it down. She wrote me once that no matter where we "choose" to live, she will manage to come see us. But she will never bring her friends. Maggie and I thought about this and Maggie asked me, "Mama, when did Dee ever *have* any friends?"

She had a few. Furtive boys in pink shirts hanging about on washday after school. Nervous girls who never laughed. Impressed with her they worshiped the well-turned phrase, the cute shape, the scalding humor that erupted like bubbles in lye. She read to them.

When she was courting Jimmy T she didn't have much time to pay to us, but turned all her faultfinding power on him. He *flew* to marry a cheap gal from a family of ignorant flashy people. She hardly had time to recompose herself.

When she comes I will meet—but there they are!

Maggie attempts to make a dash for the house, in her shuffling way, but I stay her with my hand. "Come back here," I say. And she stops and tries to dig a well in the sand with her toe.

It is hard to see them clearly through the strong sun. But even the first glimpse of leg out of the car tells me it is Dee. Her feet were always neat-looking, as if God himself had shaped them with a certain style. From the other side of the car comes a short, stocky man. Hair is all over his head a foot long and hanging from his chin like a kinky mule tail. I hear Maggie suck in her breath. "Uhnnnh," is what it sounds like. Like when you see the wriggling end of a snake just in front of your foot on the road. "Uhnnnh."

Dee next. A dress down to the ground, in this hot weather. A dress so loud it hurts my eyes. There are yellows and oranges enough to throw back the light of the sun. I feel my whole face warming from the heat waves it throws out. Earrings, too, gold and hanging down to her shoulders. Bracelets dangling and making noises when she moves her arm up to shake the folds of the dress out of her armpits. The dress is loose and flows, and as she walks closer, I like it. I hear Maggie go "Uhnnnh" again. It is her sister's hair. It stands straight up like the wool on a sheep. It is black as night and around the edges are two long pigtails that rope about like small lizards disappearing behind her ears.

"Wa-su-zo-Tean-o!" she says, coming on in that gliding way the dress makes her move. The short stocky fellow with the hair to his navel is all grinning and he follows up with "Asalamalakim, my mother and sister!" He moves to hug Maggie but she falls back, right up against the back of my chair. I feel her trembling there and when I look up I see the perspiration falling off her chin.

"Don't get up," says Dee. Since I am stout it takes something of a push. You can see me trying to move a second or two before I make it. She turns, showing white heels through her sandals, and goes back to the car. Out she peeks next with a Polaroid. She stoops down quickly and lines up picture after picture of me sitting there in front of the house with Maggie cowering behind me. She never takes a shot without making sure the house is included. When a cow comes nibbling around the edge of the yard she snaps it and me and Maggie *and* the house. Then she puts the Polaroid in the back seat of the car, and comes up and kisses me on the forehead.

Meanwhile Asalamalakim is going through motions with Maggie's hand. Maggie's hand is as limp as a fish, and probably as cold, despite the sweat, and she keeps trying to pull it back. It looks like Asalamalakim wants to shake hands but wants to do it fancy. Or maybe he don't know how people shake hands. Anyhow, he soon gives up on Maggie.

"Well," I say. "Dee."

"No, Mama," she says. "Not 'Dee,' Wangero Leewanika Kemanjo!"

"What happened to 'Dee'?" I wanted to know.

"She's dead," Wangero said. "I couldn't bear it any longer being named after the people who oppress me."

"You know as well as me you was named after your aunt Dicie," I said. Dicie is my sister. She named Dee. We called her "Big Dee" after Dee was born.

"But who was *she* named after?" asked Wangero.

"I guess after Grandma Dee," I said.

"And who was she named after?" asked Wangero.

"Her mother," I said, and saw Wangero was getting tired. "That's about as far back as I can trace it," I said. Though, in fact, I probably could have carried it back beyond the Civil War through the branches.

"Well," said Asalamalakim, "there you are."

"Uhnnnh," I heard Maggie say.

"There I was not," I said, "before 'Dicie' cropped up in our family, so why should I try to trace it that far back?"

He just stood there grinning, looking down on me like somebody inspecting a Model A car. Every once in a while he and Wangero sent eye signals over my head.

"How do you pronounce this name?" I asked.

"You don't have to call me by it if you don't want to," said Wangero.

"Why shouldn't I?" I asked. "If that's what you want us to call you, we'll call you."

"I know it might sound awkward at first," said Wangero.

"I'll get used to it," I said. "Ream it out again."

Well, soon we got the name out of the way. Asalamalakim had a name twice as long and three times as hard. After I tripped over it two or three times he told me to just call him Hakim-a-barber. I wanted to ask him was he a barber, but I didn't really think he was, so I didn't ask.

"You must belong to those beef-cattle peoples down the road," I said. They said "Asalamalakim" when they met you, too, but they didn't shake hands. Always too busy: feeding the cattle, fixing the fences, putting up salt-lick shelters, throwing down hay. When the white folks poisoned some of the herd the men stayed up all night with rifles in their hands. I walked a mile and a half just to see the sight.

Hakim-a-barber said, "I accept some of their doctrines, but farming and raising cattle is not my style." (They didn't tell me, and I didn't ask, whether Wangero [Dee] had really gone and married him.)

We sat down to eat and right away he said he didn't eat collards and pork was unclean. Wangero, though, went on through the chitlins and corn bread, the greens and everything else. She talked a blue streak over the sweet potatoes. Everything delighted her. Even the fact that we still used the benches her daddy made for the table when we couldn't afford to buy chairs.

"Oh, Mama!" she cried. Then turned to Hakim-a-barber. "I never knew how lovely these benches are. You can feel the rump prints," she said, running her hands underneath her and along the bench. Then she gave a sigh and her hand closed over Grandma Dee's butter dish. "That's it!" she said. "I knew there was something I wanted to ask you if I could have." She jumped up from the table and went over in the corner where the churn stood, the milk in it clabber by now. She looked at the churn and looked at it.

"This churn top is what I need," she said. "Didn't Uncle Buddy whittle it out of a tree you all used to have?"

"Yes," I said.

"Uh huh," she said happily. "And I want the dasher, too."

"Uncle Buddy whittle that, too?" asked the barber.

Dee (Wangero) looked up at me.

"Aunt Dee's first husband whittled the dash," said Maggie so low you almost couldn't hear her. "His name was Henry, but they called him Stash."

"Maggie's brain is like an elephant's," Wangero said, laughing. "I can use the churn top as a centerpiece for the alcove table," she said, sliding a plate over the churn, "and I'll think of something artistic to do with the dasher."

When she finished wrapping the dasher the handle stuck out. I took it for a moment in my hands. You didn't even have to look close to see where hands pushing the dasher up and down to make butter had left a kind of sink in the wood. In fact, there were a lot of small sinks; you could see where thumbs and fingers had sunk into the wood. It was beautiful light yellow wood, from a tree that grew in the yard where Big Dee and Stash had lived.

After dinner Dee (Wangero) went to the trunk at the foot of my bed and started rifling through it. Maggie hung back in the kitchen over the dishpan. Out came Wangero with two quilts. They had been pieced by Grandma Dee and then Big Dee and me had hung them on the quilt frames on the front porch and quilted them. One was in the Lone Star pattern. The other was Walk Around the Mountain. In both of them were scraps of dresses Grandma Dee had worn fifty and more years ago. Bits and pieces of Grandpa Jarrell's Paisley shirts. And one teeny faded blue piece, about the size of a penny matchbox, that was from Great Grandpa Ezra's uniform that he wore in the Civil War.

"Mama," Wangero said sweet as a bird. "Can I have these old quilts?"

I heard something fall in the kitchen, and a minute later the kitchen door slammed.

"Why don't you take one or two of the others?" I asked. "These old things was just done by me and Big Dee from some tops your grandma pieced before she died."

"No," said Wangero. "I don't want those. They are stitched around the borders by machine."

"That'll make them last better," I said.

"That's not the point," said Wangero. "These are all pieces of dresses Grandma used to wear. She did all this stitching by hand. Imagine!" She held the quilts securely in her arms, stroking them.

"Some of the pieces, like those lavender ones, come from old clothes her mother handed down to her," I said, moving up to touch the quilts. Dee (Wangero) moved back just enough so that I couldn't reach the quilts. They already belonged to her.

"Imagine!" she breathed again, clutching them closely to her bosom.

"The truth is," I said, "I promised to give them quilts to Maggie, for when she marries John Thomas."

She gasped like a bee had stung her.

"Maggie can't appreciate these quilts!" she said. "She'd probably be backward enough to put them to everyday use."

"I reckon she would," I said. "God knows I been saving 'em for long enough with nobody using 'em. I hope she will!" I didn't want to bring up how I had offered Dee (Wangero) a quilt when she went away to college. Then she had told me they were old-fashioned, out of style.

"But they're *priceless*!" she was saying now, furiously; for she has a temper. "Maggie would put them on the bed and in five years they'd be in rags. Less than that!"

"She can always make some more," I said. "Maggie knows how to quilt."

Dee (Wangero) looked at me with hatred. "You just will not understand. The point is these quilts, *these* quilts!"

"Well," I said, stumped. "What would *you* do with them?"

"Hang them," she said. As if that was the only thing you *could* do with quilts.

Maggie by now was standing in the door. I could almost hear the sound her feet made as they scraped over each other.

"She can have them, Mama," she said, like somebody used to never winning anything, or having anything reserved for her. "I can 'member Grandma Dee without the quilts."

I looked at her hard. She had filled her bottom lip with checkerberry snuff and it gave her face a kind of dopey, hangdog look. It was Grandma Dee and Big Dee who taught her how to quilt herself. She stood there with her scarred hands hidden in the folds of her skirt. She looked at her sister with something like fear but she wasn't mad at her. This was Maggie's portion. This was the way she knew God to work.

When I looked at her like that something hit me in the top of my head and ran down to the soles of my feet. Just like when I'm in church and the spirit of God touches me and I get happy and shout. I did something I never had done before: hugged Maggie to me, then dragged her on into the room, snatched the quilts out of Miss Wangero's hands and dumped them into Maggie's lap. Maggie just sat there on my bed with her mouth open.

"Take one or two of the others," I said to Dee.

But she turned without a word and went out to Hakim-a-barber.

"You just don't understand," she said, as Maggie and I came out to the car.

"What don't I understand?" I wanted to know.

"Your heritage," she said. And then she turned to Maggie, kissed her, and said, "You ought to try to make something of yourself, too, Maggie. It's really a new day for us. But from the way you and Mama still live you'd never know it."

She put on some sunglasses that hid everything above the tip of her nose and her chin.

Maggie smiled; maybe at the sunglasses. But a real smile, not scared. After we watched the car dust settle I asked Maggie to bring me a dip of snuff. And then the two of us sat there just enjoying, until it was time to go in the house and go to bed.

QUESTIONS FOR DISCUSSION AND WRITING

1. Reread the first two paragraphs of "Everyday Use." What do they tell us about the three women in the story and about their relationships with one another?

2. The narrator tells us about her fantasy of appearing with Dee on a national television show. What does her fantasy reveal about her sense of herself and her relationship with her daughter? What does it tell us about her sense of her heritage and of her place in the world?

3. At the end of the story, Dee tells her mother, "You just don't understand . . . your heritage." Do we agree? What does Dee mean by "heritage"? How would the other women in the story define *heritage*? How would Alice Walker define it?

4. Think about the names in "Everyday Use." According to some critics, the names that Dee and her boyfriend choose are incorrect imitations of African names. What might that tell you about their ties to their African roots? What is the significance of Dee's and Maggie's birth names? Why does Walker choose not to give the narrator a name?

5. Dee would hang the heirloom quilts; Maggie will probably put them to "everyday use." Dee has left the family's impoverished home; Maggie has stayed. Dee has become educated and refined; Maggie is "slow" and unrefined. In many ways, most of Walker's readers are probably more like Dee than like Maggie, but most readers nevertheless sympathize more with Maggie. Think about how you would react to the situations and characters if faced with them in your own life. What would *you* do with the quilts or with a similar family heirloom? Would you be more likely to stay at home or to leave for college? Would you prefer to act, dress, and talk as Dee does or as Maggie does? Once you have answered those questions, ask yourself how the narrator manipulates our sympathies—and to what extent we are meant to think of the narrator's point of view as Walker's point of view. (To help yourself see the importance of the narrative perspective, you might retell the story from an omniscient narrator's point of view or even from Dee's point of view.)

Drama

A Brief Introduction to the Modern Theater When people today go to the theater, they have a very different experience than did people of earlier times. Whereas Greek and Renaissance audiences watched their plays in outdoor theaters, today's theaters are usually indoors, and the plays they stage are lit by artificial light. The movement of the drama from outside to inside, which happened sometime in the late seventeenth century, changed the way plays were viewed and the way they were staged. Plays could now be performed in all weathers and at night, and, because the backstage area was larger, more elaborate stage settings and more frequent changes in setting became possible. During this time, too, actresses first set foot on the stage. Though actresses were not considered quite respectable (their questionable reputation lingered well into the twentieth century), they often gained considerable celebrity.

With the more elaborate settings and the greater use of "special effects" created by artificial lighting, plays often became more realistic. In the nineteenth century, in particular, realism held sway (and it is still influential today). Stage sets and props often create a highly realistic view of a home or workplace. Most important, the characters are less likely to be nobles and peasants and more likely to be members of the middle class, the class to which most of the members of the audiences belong. Their costumes, mannerisms, and speech all suggest they might be our neighbors. Neither heroes nor villains, they live life much as we do. More than earlier playwrights, the dramatists of the modern era put *us* at the center of their works. Whether celebrating the middle class or attacking its hypocrisies, the modern dramatist makes it clear that the characters onstage are not much different from you and me.

Because the dramatist now has a more elaborate staging area to work with than did his Greek and Elizabethan counterparts, the modern playwright often conveys detailed impressions of the settings and the characters. Many also create elaborate stage directions, leaving little for the stage director to interpret. Whereas earlier Greek and Renaissance playwrights included few stage directions (those in modern texts were usually added by later editors), many realistic modern dramatists attempt almost to direct their plays themselves. Fully aware that the author "disappears" once the play is staged, modern playwrights sometimes attempt to control the production as much as possible through the text. They therefore indicate not only what the setting and props should look like but also what the characters are feeling and thinking, creating the specifics we are more used to seeing in a work of prose fiction than in a play.

Here, for example, are George Bernard Shaw's stage directions for Eliza's returning home at the end of the first act of *Pygmalion* (and this is by no means his longest stage direction in the play):

> (*She picks up the basket and trudges up the alley with it to her lodging: a small room with very old wall paper hanging loose in the damp places. A broken pane in the window is mended with paper. A portrait of a popular actor and a fashion plate of ladies' dresses, all wildly beyond poor Eliza's means, both torn from newspapers, are pinned up on the wall. A birdcage hangs in the window; but its tenant died long ago: it remains as a memorial only.*
>
> *These are the only visible luxuries: the rest is the irreducible minimum of poverty's needs: a wretched bed heaped with all sorts of coverings that have any warmth in them, a draped packing case with a basin and jug on it and a little looking glass over it, a chair and table, the refuse of some suburban kitchen, and an American alarum clock on the shelf above the unused fireplace: the whole lighted with a gas lamp with a penny in the slot meter. Rent: four shillings a week.*
>
> *Here Eliza, chronically weary, but too excited to go to bed, sits, counting her new riches and dreaming and planning what to do with them, until the gas goes out, when she enjoys for the first time the sensation of being able to put in another penny without*

grudging it. This prodigal mood does not extinguish her gnawing sense of the need for economy sufficiently to prevent her from calculating that she can dream and plan in bed more cheaply and warmly than sitting up without a fire. So she takes off her shawl and skirt and adds them to the miscellaneous bedclothes. Then she kicks off her shoes and gets into bed without any further change.)

One might wonder just how Shaw expected some of this to be represented on the stage. How, for example, would the audience in the theater know what Eliza's rent is? Or how would it know that this is the first time that she has been able to afford a second penny's worth of gas to heat her room? Modern playwrights, however, are much more interested than earlier playwrights had been in controlling as much of the production as possible, alerting directors and actors (and perhaps readers of the play) to the *playwright's* intentions and interpretations. By noting Eliza's motives and including detailed information about the props in her room, Shaw hopes to add to the realistic texture of the play.

Even when modern playwrights do not include elaborate stage directions, there is often a gritty realism to the events they depict. In David Mamet's *Oleanna,* for instance, the characters' speech so closely mimics the speech of modern life, with its interruptions and its tensions, that the dialogue on the page may look incomplete and confusing. An audience watching and hearing the play is probably less likely to be confused than is a reader, however; to that listening audience, the exchange between Carol and John seems realistically tense. The speech is sharp and disconnected in much the same way that much modern conversation is, and it is punctuated by a raw, and sometimes offensive, language that seems especially modern.

The realistic dialog of *Oleanna* also illustrates another facet of modern literature. In its disconnectedness it has much in common with the equally clipped dialog of a Hemingway short story. In their dialog, Hemingway and Mamet are doing more than mimicking modern speech; they are also drawing attention to a sense of disconnectedness; characters interrupt one another and leave sentences unfinished because there is little sense of continuity and little confidence in universal truths. They miss each other's meanings because meaning itself has been called into question.

In this questioning of truths, in fact, *Oleanna* has something in common with modern plays that belong to a less realistic tradition, that of the Theater of the Absurd. Plays that belong to the absurdist tradition often have little sense of a linear plot with a defined direction, and characters often lack understandable motives and goals. Instead of creating a detailed setting that replicates the inside of a home, such playwrights might create a blighted landscape that is nightmarish but belongs to no particular time or place. Lost, bewildered, in control of nothing, including themselves, the characters may engage in dazzling feats of verbal wit, but wit that seems directionless, satirizing nothing in particular, except perhaps the meaninglessness of life. Through such characters and plots, modernist playwrights attempt to convey the isolation and alienation they feel is typical of our lives today.

Oleanna is part realistic drama, part absurdist drama. Its characters seem very much like us and very much grounded in their positions as teacher and student. At the same time, neither Carol nor John seems quite sure of the rules that govern the games they play. Nor do we. In that sense, *Oleanna* is both realistic and absurd. However we label it, there is no doubt that *Oleanna* is a very modern play.

Carol (Debra Eisenstadt) and John (William H. Macy)
in David Mamet's film version of *Oleanna* (1994).

DAVID MAMET (1947–   )

Oleanna _____ 1991

The want of fresh air does not seem much to affect the happiness of children in a London alley: the greater part of them sing and play as though they were on a moor in Scotland. So the absence of a genial mental atmosphere is not commonly recognized by children who have never known it. Young people have a marvelous faculty of either dying or adapting themselves to circumstances. Even if they are unhappy—very unhappy—it is astonishing how easily they can be prevented from finding it out, or at any rate from attributing it to any other cause than their own sinfulness.

The Way of All Flesh
Samuel Butler

"Oh, to be in *Oleanna,*
That's where I would rather be.
Than be bound in Norway
And drag the chains of slavery."
            —folk song

Characters

CAROL A woman of twenty
JOHN   A man in his forties

The play takes place in John's office.

ONE

> JOHN *is talking on the phone.* CAROL *is seated across the desk from him.*

JOHN (*on phone*): And what about the land. (*Pause*) The land. And what about the
  land? (*Pause*) What about it? (*Pause*) No. I don't understand. Well, yes, I'm
  I'm . . . no, I'm *sure* it's signif . . . I'm sure it's significant. (*Pause*) Because it's significant to mmmmmm . . . did you call Jerry? (*Pause*) Because . . . no, no, no,
  no, no. What did they say . . . ? Did you speak to the *real* estate . . . where *is*
  she . . . ? Well, well, all right. Where are her notes? Where are the notes we took
  with her. (*Pause*) I thought you were? No. No, I'm sorry, I didn't mean that, I
  just thought that I saw you, when we were there . . . what . . . ? I thought I saw
  you with a *pencil*. WHY NOW? is what I'm say . . . well, that's why I say "call
  Jerry." Well, I can't right now, be . . . no, I *didn't* schedule any . . . Grace: I
  didn't . . . I'm well aware . . . Look: Look. Did you call Jerry? Will you call
  Jerry . . . ? Because I can't now. I'll be there, I'm sure I'll be there in fifteen, in
  twenty. I intend to. No, we aren't *going* to lose the, we aren't *going* to lose the
  house. Look: Look, I'm not minimizing it. The "easement." Did she say "easement"? (*Pause*) What did she *say; is* it a "term of art," are we *bound* by it . . . I'm
  sorry . . . (*Pause*) are: we: yes. *Bound* by . . . Look: (*He checks his watch.*) before
  the other side *goes home,* all right? "a term of art." Because: that's right (*Pause*)
  The yard for the boy. Well, that's the whole . . . Look: I'm going to meet you
  there . . . (*He checks his watch.*) Is the realtor there? All right, tell her to show you
  the basement again. Look at the *this* because . . . Bec . . . I'm leaving in, I'm
  leaving in ten or fifteen . . . Yes. No, no, I'll meet you at the new . . . That's a
  good. If he thinks it's necc . . . you tell Jerry to meet . . . All right? We *aren't*
  going to lose the deposit. All right? I'm sure it's going to be . . . (*Pause*) I hope
  so. (*Pause*) I love you, too. (*Pause*) I love you, too. As soon as . . . I will.

  > (*He hangs up.*) (*He bends over the desk and makes a note.*) (*He looks up.*) (*To*
  CAROL:) I'm sorry . . .

CAROL: (*Pause*) What is a "term of art"?
JOHN: (*Pause*) I'm sorry . . . ?
5 CAROL: (*Pause*) What is a "term of art"?
JOHN: Is that what you want to talk about?
CAROL: . . . to talk about . . . ?
JOHN: Let's take the mysticism out of it, shall we? Carol? (*Pause*) Don't you think?
  I'll tell you: when you have some "thing." Which must be broached. (*Pause*)
  Don't you think . . . ? (*Pause*)
CAROL: . . . don't I think . . . ?
10 JOHN: Mmm?
CAROL: . . . did I . . . ?
JOHN: . . . what?

CAROL: Did . . . did I . . . did I say something wr . . .

JOHN: (*Pause*) No. I'm sorry. No. You're right. I'm very sorry. I'm somewhat rushed. As you see. I'm sorry. You're right. (*Pause*) What is a "term of art"? It seems to mean a *term,* which has come, through its use, to mean something *more specific* than the words would, to someone *not acquainted* with them . . . indicate. That, I believe, is what a "term of art," would mean. (*Pause*)

CAROL: You don't know what it means . . . ?   15

JOHN: I'm not sure that I know what it means. It's one of those things, perhaps you've had them, that, you look them up, or have someone explain them to you, and you say "aha," and, you immediately *forget* what . . .

CAROL: You don't do that.

JOHN: . . . I . . . ?

CAROL: You don't do . . .

JOHN: . . . I don't, what . . . ?   20

CAROL: . . . for . . .

JOHN: . . . I don't for . . .

CAROL: . . . no . . .

JOHN: . . . forget things? Everybody does that.

CAROL: No, they don't.   25

JOHN: They don't . . .

CAROL: No.

JOHN: (*Pause*) No. Everybody does that.

CAROL: Why would they do that . . . ?

JOHN: Because. I don't know. Because it doesn't interest them.   30

CAROL: No.

JOHN: I think so, though. (*Pause*) I'm sorry that I was distracted.

CAROL: You don't have to say that to me.

JOHN: You paid me the compliment, or the "obeisance"—all right—of coming in here . . . All right. *Carol.* I find that I am at a *standstill.* I find that I . . .

CAROL: . . . what . . .   35

JOHN: . . . one moment. In regard to your . . . to your . . .

CAROL: Oh, oh. You're buying a new house!

JOHN: No, let's get on with it.

CAROL: "get on"? (*Pause*)

JOHN: I know how . . . *believe* me. I know how . . . potentially *humiliating* these . . . I   40
have no desire to . . . I have no desire other than to help you. But: (*He picks up some papers on his desk.*) I won't even say "but." I'll say that as I go back over the . . .

CAROL: I'm just, I'm just trying to . . .

JOHN: . . . no, it will not do.

CAROL: . . . what? What will . . . ?

JOHN: No. I see, I see what you, it . . . (*He gestures to the papers.*) but your work . . .

CAROL: I'm just: I sit in class I . . . (*She holds up her notebook.*) I take notes . . .   45

JOHN (*simultaneously with* "notes"): Yes. I understand. What I am trying to *tell* you is that some, some basic . . .

CAROL: . . . I . . .

JOHN: . . . one moment: some basic missed communi . . .

CAROL: I'm doing what I'm told. I bought your book, I read your . . .

50 JOHN: No, I'm sure you . . .
    CAROL: No, no, no. I'm doing what I'm told. It's *difficult* for me. It's *difficult* . . .
    JOHN: . . . but . . .
    CAROL: I don't . . . lots of the *language* . . .
    JOHN: . . . please . . .
55 CAROL: The *language,* the "things" that you say . . .
    JOHN: I'm sorry. No. I don't think that that's true.
    CAROL: It *is* true. I . . .
    JOHN: I think . . .
    CAROL: It *is* true.
60 JOHN: . . . I . . .
    CAROL: Why would I . . . ?
    JOHN: I'll tell you why: you're an incredibly bright girl.
    CAROL: . . . I . . .
    JOHN: You're an incredibly . . . you have no problem with the . . . Who's kidding
        who?
65 CAROL: . . . I . . .
    JOHN: No. No. I'll tell you why. I'll tell. . . . I think you're *angry,* I . . .
    CAROL: . . . why would I . . .
    JOHN: . . . wait one moment. I . . .
    CAROL: It *is* true. I have *problems* . . .
70 JOHN: . . . every . . .
    CAROL: . . . I come from a different *social* . . .
    JOHN: . . . ev . . .
    CAROL: a different economic . . .
    JOHN: . . . Look:
75 CAROL: No. I: when I *came* to this school:
    JOHN: Yes. Quite . . . (*Pause*)
    CAROL: . . . does that mean nothing . . . ?
    JOHN: . . . but look: look . . .
    CAROL: . . . I . . .
80 JOHN: (*Picks up paper.*) Here: Please: Sit down. (*Pause*) Sit down. (*Reads from her paper.*)
        "I think that the ideas contained in this work express the author's feelings in a
        way that he intended, based on his results." What can that mean? Do you see?
        What . . .
    CAROL: I, the best that I . . .
    JOHN: I'm saying, that perhaps this course . . .
    CAROL: No, no, no, you can't, you can't . . . I have to . . .
    JOHN: . . . how . . .
85 CAROL: . . . I have to pass it . . .
    JOHN: Carol, I:
    CAROL: I *have* to pass this course, I . . .
    JOHN: Well.
    CAROL: . . . don't you . . .
90 JOHN: Either the . . .
    CAROL: . . . I . . .
    JOHN: . . . either the, I . . . either the *criteria* for judging progress in the class are . . .

CAROL: No, no, no, no, I have to pass it.

JOHN: Now, look: I'm a human being, I . . .

CAROL: I did what you told me. I did, I did everything that, I read your *book,* you told me to buy your book and read it. Everything you *say* I . . . (*She gestures to her notebook.*) (*The phone rings.*) I do. . . . Ev . . .

JOHN: . . . look:

CAROL: . . . everything I'm told . . .

JOHN: Look. Look. I'm not your *father.* (*Pause*)

CAROL: What?

JOHN: I'm.

CAROL: Did I say you were my father?

JOHN: . . . no . . .

CAROL: Why did you say that . . . ?

JOHN: I . . .

CAROL: . . . why . . . ?

JOHN: . . . in class I . . . (*He picks up the phone.*) (*Into phone:*) Hello. I can't talk now. Jerry? Yes? I underst . . . I can't talk now. I know . . . I know . . . Jerry. I can't *talk* now. Yes, I. Call me back in . . . Thank you. (*He hangs up.*) (*To* CAROL:) What do you want me to do? We are two people, all right? Both of whom have subscribed to . . .

CAROL: No, no . . .

JOHN: . . . certain arbitrary . . .

CAROL: No. You have to help me.

JOHN: Certain institutional . . . you tell me what you want me to do. . . . You tell me what you want me to . . .

CAROL: How can I go back and tell them the *grades* that I . . .

JOHN: . . . what can I do . . . ?

CAROL: *Teach* me. *Teach* me.

JOHN: . . . I'm trying to teach you.

CAROL: I read your book. I read it. I don't under . . .

JOHN: . . . you don't understand it.

CAROL: No.

JOHN: Well, perhaps it's not well *written* . . .

CAROL (*simultaneously with* "written"): No. No. No. I want to *understand* it.

JOHN: What don't you understand? (*Pause*)

CAROL: *Any* of it. What you're trying to say. When you talk about . . .

JOHN: . . . yes . . . ? (*She consults her notes.*)

CAROL: "Virtual warehousing of the young" . . .

JOHN: "Virtual warehousing of the young." If we artificially prolong adolescence . . .

CAROL: . . . and about "The Curse of Modern Education."

JOHN: . . . well . . .

CAROL: I don't . . .

JOHN: Look. It's just a *course,* it's just a *book,* it's just a . . .

CAROL: No. No. There are *people* out there. People who came *here.* To know something they didn't *know.* Who *came* here. To be *helped.* To be *helped.* So someone would *help* them. To *do* something. To *know* something. To get, what do they say? "To get on in the world." How can I do that if I don't, if I fail? But I don't *understand.* I don't *understand*. I don't understand what anything means . . . and I walk around. From morning 'til night: with this one thought in my head. I'm *stupid*.

130   JOHN: No one thinks you're stupid.

CAROL: No? What am I . . . ?

JOHN: I . . .

CAROL: . . . what am I, then?

JOHN: I think you're angry. Many people are. I have a *telephone* call that I have to make. And an *appointment,* which is rather *pressing;* though I sympathize with your concerns, and though I wish I had the time, this was not a previously scheduled meeting and I . . .

135   CAROL: . . . you think I'm nothing . . .

JOHN: . . . have an appointment with a *realtor,* and with my wife and . . .

CAROL: You think that I'm stupid.

JOHN: No. I certainly don't.

CAROL: You said it.

140   JOHN: No. I did not.

CAROL: You did.

JOHN: When?

CAROL: . . . you . . .

JOHN: No. I never did, or never would say that to a student, and . . .

145   CAROL: You said, "What can that mean?" (*Pause*) "What can that mean?" . . . (*Pause*)

JOHN: . . . and what did that mean to you . . . ?

CAROL: That meant I'm stupid. And I'll never learn. That's what that meant. And you're right.

JOHN: . . . I . . .

CAROL: But then. But then, what am I doing here . . . ?

150   JOHN: . . . if you thought that I . . .

CAROL: . . . when nobody wants me, and . . .

JOHN: . . . if you interpreted . . .

CAROL: Nobody *tells* me anything. And I *sit* there . . . in the *corner*. In the *back*. And everybody's talking about "this" all the time. And "concepts," and "precepts" and, and, and, and, and, WHAT IN THE WORLD ARE YOU *TALKING* ABOUT? And I read your book. And they said, "Fine, go in that class." Because you talked about responsibility to the young. I DON'T KNOW WHAT IT MEANS AND I'M *FAILING* . . .

JOHN: May . . .

155   CAROL: No, you're right. "Oh, hell." I failed. Flunk me out of it. It's garbage. Everything I do. "The ideas contained in this work express the author's feelings." That's right. That's right. I know I'm stupid. I know what I am. (*Pause*) I know what I am, Professor. You don't have to tell me. (*Pause*) It's pathetic. Isn't it?

JOHN: . . . Aha . . . (*Pause*) Sit down. Sit down. Please. (*Pause*) Please sit down.

CAROL: Why?

JOHN: I want to talk to you.

CAROL: Why?

160   JOHN: Just sit down. (*Pause*) Please. Sit down. Will you, please . . . ? (*Pause. She does so.*) Thank you.

CAROL: What?

JOHN: I want to tell you something.

CAROL: (*Pause*) What?

JOHN: Well, I know what you're talking about.

CAROL: No. You don't.   165

JOHN: I think I do. (*Pause*)

CAROL: How can you?

JOHN: I'll tell you a story about myself. (*Pause*) Do you mind? (*Pause*) I was raised to think myself stupid. That's what I want to tell you. (*Pause*)

CAROL: What do you mean?

JOHN: Just what I said. I was brought up, and my earliest, and most persistent memo-   170
ries are of being told that I was stupid. "You have such *intelligence*. Why must you behave so *stupidly*?" Or, "Can't you *understand*? Can't you *understand*?" And I could *not* understand. I could *not* understand.

CAROL: What?

JOHN: The simplest problem. Was beyond me. It was a mystery.

CAROL: What was a mystery?

JOHN: How people learn. How *I* could learn. Which is what I've been speaking of in class. And of *course* you can't hear it. Carol. Of *course* you can't. (*Pause*) I used to speak of "real people," and wonder what the *real* people did. The *real* people. Who were they? *They* were the people other than myself. The *good* people. The *capable* people. The people who could do the things, *I* could not do: learn, study, retain . . . all that *garbage*—which is what I have been talking of in class, and that's *exactly* what I have been talking of—If you are told. . . . Listen to this. If the young child is told he cannot understand. Then he takes it as a *description* of himself. What am I? I am *that which can not understand*. And I saw you out there, when we were speaking of the concepts of . . .

CAROL: I can't understand any of them.   175

JOHN: Well, then, that's *my* fault. That's not your fault. And that is not verbiage. That's what I firmly hold to be the truth. And I am sorry, and I owe you an apology.

CAROL: Why?

JOHN: And I suppose that I have had some *things* on my mind. . . . We're buying a *house,* and . . .

CAROL: People said that you were stupid . . . ?

JOHN: Yes.   180

CAROL: When?

JOHN: I'll tell you when. Through my life. In my childhood; and, perhaps, they stopped. But I heard them continue.

CAROL: And what did they say?

JOHN: They said I was incompetent. Do you see? And when I'm tested the, the, the *feelings* of my youth about the *very subject of learning* come up. And I . . . I be-come, I feel "unworthy," and "unprepared." . . .

CAROL: . . . yes.   185

JOHN: . . . eh?

CAROL: . . . yes.

JOHN: And I feel that I must fail. (*Pause*)

CAROL: . . . but then you *do* fail. (*Pause*) You have to. (*Pause*) Don't you?

JOHN: A *pilot*. Flying a plane. The pilot is flying the plane. He thinks: Oh, my   190
God, my mind's been drifting! Oh, my God! What kind of a cursed imbecile am I, that I, with this so precious cargo of *Life* in my charge, would allow my

attention to wander. Why was I born? How deluded are those who put their trust in me, . . . et cetera, so on, and he crashes the plane.

CAROL: (*Pause*) He could just . . .

JOHN: That's right.

CAROL: He could say:

JOHN: My attention *wandered* for a moment . . .

195   CAROL: . . . uh huh . . .

JOHN: I had a *thought* I did not like . . . but now:

CAROL: . . . but now it's . . .

JOHN: That's what I'm telling you. It's time to put my attention . . . see: it is not: this is what I learned. It is Not Magic. Yes. Yes. *You*. You are going to be frightened. When faced with what may or may not be but which you are going to perceive as a test. You will become frightened. And you will say: "I am incapable of . . . " and everything *in* you will think these two things. "I must. But I can't." And you will think: Why was I born to be the laughingstock of a world in which everyone is better than I? In which I am entitled to nothing. Where I can not learn.

(*Pause*)

CAROL: Is that . . . (*Pause*) Is that what I have . . . ?

200   JOHN: Well. I don't know if I'd put it that way. Listen: I'm talking to you as I'd talk to my son. Because that's what I'd like him to have that I never had. I'm talking to you the way I wish that someone had talked to me. I don't know how to do it, other than to be *personal*, . . . but . . .

CAROL: Why would you want to be personal with me?

JOHN: Well, you see? That's what I'm saying. We can only interpret the behavior of others through the screen we . . . (*The phone rings.*) Through . . . (*To phone:*) Hello . . . ? (*To* CAROL:) Through the screen we create. (*To phone:*) Hello. (*To* CAROL:) Excuse me a moment. (*To phone:*) Hello? No, I can't talk nnn . . . I know I did. In a few . . . I'm . . . is he coming to the . . . yes. I talked to him. We'll meet you at the No, because I'm with a *student*. It's going to be fff . . . This is important, too. I'm with a *student*, Jerry's going to . . . Listen: the sooner I get off, the sooner I'll be down, all right. I love you. Listen, listen, I said "I love you," it's going to work *out* with the, because I feel that it is, I'll be right down. All right? Well, then it's going to take as long as it takes. (*He hangs up.*) (*To* CAROL:) I'm sorry.

CAROL: What was that?

JOHN: There are some problems, as there usually are, about the final agreements for the new house.

205   CAROL: You're buying a new house.

JOHN: That's right.

CAROL: Because of your promotion.

JOHN: Well, I suppose that that's right.

CAROL: Why did you stay here with me?

210   JOHN: Stay here.

CAROL: Yes. When you should have gone.

JOHN: Because I like you.

CAROL: You like me.

JOHN: Yes.

CAROL: Why?   215

JOHN: Why? Well? Perhaps we're similar. (*Pause*) Yes. (*Pause*)

CAROL: You said "everyone has problems."

JOHN: Everyone has problems.

CAROL: Do they?

JOHN: Certainly.   220

CAROL: You do?

JOHN: Yes.

CAROL: What are they?

JOHN: Well. (*Pause*) Well, you're perfectly right. (*Pause*) If we're going to take off the Artificial *Stricture*, of "Teacher," and "Student," why should *my* problems be any more a mystery than your own? Of *course* I have problems. As you saw.

CAROL: . . . with what?   225

JOHN: With my *wife* . . . with *work* . . .

CAROL: With work?

JOHN: Yes. And, and, perhaps my problems are, do you see? *Similar* to yours.

CAROL: Would you tell me?

JOHN: All right. (*Pause*) I came *late* to teaching. And I found it Artificial. The notion   230
of "I know and you do not"; and I saw an *exploitation* in the education process. I told you. I hated school, I hated teachers. I hated everyone who was in the position of a "boss" because I *knew*—I didn't *think*, mind you, I *knew* I was going to fail. Because I was a fuckup. I was just no goddamned good. When I . . . late in life . . . (*Pause*) When I *got out from under* . . . when I worked my way out of the need to fail. When I . . .

CAROL: How do you do that? (*Pause*)

JOHN: You have to look at what you are, and what you feel, and how you act. And, finally, you have to look at how you act. And say: If that's what I *did,* that must be how I think of myself.

CAROL: I don't understand.

JOHN: If I fail all the time, it must be that I think of myself as a failure. If I do not want to think of myself as a failure, perhaps I should begin by *succeeding* now and again. Look. The tests, you see, which you encounter, in school, in college, in life, were designed, in the most part, for idiots. *By* idiots. There is no need to fail at them. They are not a test of your worth. They are a test of your ability to retain and spout back misinformation. Of *course* you fail them. They're *nonsense*. And I . . .

CAROL: . . . no . . .   235

JOHN: Yes. They're *garbage*. They're a *joke*. Look at me. Look at me. The Tenure Committee. The Tenure Committee. Come to judge me. The Bad Tenure Committee. The "Test." Do you see? They put me to the test. Why, they had people voting on me I wouldn't employ to wax my car. And yet, I go before the Great Tenure Committee, and I have an urge, to *vomit*, to, to, to puke my *badness* on the table, to show them: "I'm no good. Why would you pick *me*?"

CAROL: They granted you tenure.

JOHN: Oh no, they announced it, but they haven't *signed*. Do you see? "At any moment . . ."

240   CAROL: . . . mmm . . .

JOHN: "They might not *sign*" . . . I might not . . . the *house* might not go through . . . Eh? Eh? They'll find out my "dark secret." (*Pause*)

CAROL: . . . what is it . . . ?

JOHN: There *isn't* one. But *they* will find an index of my badness . . .

CAROL: Index?

245   JOHN: A " . . . pointer." A "Pointer." You see? Do you see? I *understand* you. I. Know. That. Feeling. Am I entitled to my job, and my nice *home,* and my *wife,* and my *family,* and so on. This is what I'm saying: That theory of education which, that *theory:*

CAROL: I . . . I . . . (*Pause*)

JOHN: What?

CAROL: I . . .

JOHN: What?

250   CAROL: I want to know about my grade. (*Long pause*)

JOHN: Of course you do.

CAROL: Is that bad?

JOHN: No.

CAROL: Is it bad that I asked you that?

255   JOHN: No.

CAROL: Did I upset you?

JOHN: No. And I apologize. Of *course* you want to know about your grade. And, of course, you can't concentrate on anyth . . . (*The telephone starts to ring.*) Wait a moment.

CAROL: I should go.

JOHN: I'll make you a deal.

260   CAROL: No, you have to . . .

JOHN: Let it ring. I'll make you a deal. You stay here. We'll start the whole course over. I'm going to say it was not you, it was I who was not paying attention. We'll start the whole course over. Your grade is an "A." Your final grade is an "A." (*The phone stops ringing.*)

CAROL: But the class is only half over . . .

JOHN (*simultaneously with* "over"): Your grade for the whole term is an "A." If you will come back and meet with me. A few more times. Your grade's an "A." Forget about the paper. You didn't like it, you didn't like writing it. It's not important. What's important is that I awake your interest, if I can, and that I answer your questions. Let's start over. (*Pause*)

CAROL: Over. With what?

265   JOHN: Say this is the beginning.

CAROL: The beginning.

JOHN: Yes.

CAROL: Of what?

JOHN: Of the class.

270   CAROL: But we can't start over.

JOHN: I say we can. (*Pause*) I say we can.

CAROL: But I don't believe it.

JOHN: Yes, I know that. But it's true. What is The Class but you and me? (*Pause*)

CAROL: There are rules.

JOHN: Well. We'll break them.

CAROL: How can we?

JOHN: We won't tell anybody.

CAROL: Is that all right?

JOHN: I say that it's fine.

CAROL: Why would you do this for me?

JOHN: I like you. Is that so difficult for you to . . .

CAROL: Um . . .

JOHN: There's no one here but you and me. (*Pause*)

CAROL: All right. I did not understand. When you referred . . .

JOHN: All right, yes?

CAROL: When you referred to hazing.

JOHN: Hazing.

CAROL: You wrote, in your book. About the comparative . . . the comparative . . . (*She checks her notes.*)

JOHN: Are you checking your notes . . . ?

CAROL: Yes.

JOHN: Tell me in your own . . .

CAROL: I want to make sure that I have it right.

JOHN: No. Of course. You want to be exact.

CAROL: I want to know everything that went on.

JOHN: . . . that's good.

CAROL: . . . so I . . .

JOHN: That's very good. But I was suggesting, many times, that that which we wish to retain is retained oftentimes, I think, *better* with less expenditure of effort.

CAROL: (*Of notes*) Here it is: you wrote of *hazing*.

JOHN: . . . that's correct. Now: I said "hazing." It means ritualized annoyance. We shove this book at you, we say read it. Now, you say you've read it? I think that you're *lying*. I'll *grill* you, and when I find you've lied, you'll be disgraced, and your life will be ruined. It's a sick game. Why do we do it? Does it educate? In no sense. Well, then, what is higher education? It is something-other-than-useful.

CAROL: What is "something-other-than-useful"?

JOHN: It has become a ritual, it has become an article of faith. That all must be subjected to, or to put it differently, that all are entitled to Higher Education. And my point . . .

CAROL: You disagree with that?

JOHN: Well, let's address that. What do you think?

CAROL: I don't know.

JOHN: What do you think, though? (*Pause*)

CAROL: I don't know.

JOHN: I spoke of it in class. Do you remember my example?

CAROL: Justice.

JOHN: Yes. Can you repeat it to me? (*She looks down at her notebook.*) Without your notes? I ask you as a favor to me, so that I can see if my idea was interesting.

CAROL: You said "justice" . . .

JOHN: Yes?

CAROL: . . . that all are entitled . . . (*Pause*) I . . . I . . . I . . .

JOHN: Yes. To a speedy trial. To a fair trial. But they needn't be given a trial *at all* unless they stand accused. Eh? Justice is their right, should they choose to avail themselves of it, they should have a fair trial. It does not follow, of necessity, a person's life is incomplete without a trial in it. Do you see?

My point is a confusion between equity and *utility* arose. So we confound the *usefulness* of higher education with our, granted, right to equal access to the same. We, in effect, create a *prejudice* toward it, completely independent of . . .

315 CAROL: . . . that it is prejudice that we should go to school?

JOHN: Exactly. (*Pause*)

CAROL: How can you say that? How . . .

JOHN: Good. Good. *Good*. That's right! Speak up! What is a prejudice? An unreasoned belief. We are all subject to it. None of us is not. When it is threatened, or opposed, we feel anger, and feel, do we not? As you do now. Do you not? Good.

CAROL: . . . but how can you . . .

320 JOHN: . . . let us examine. Good.

CAROL: How . . .

JOHN: Good. Good. When . . .

CAROL: I'M SPEAKING . . . (*Pause*)

JOHN: I'm sorry.

325 CAROL: How can you . . .

JOHN: . . . I beg your pardon.

CAROL: That's all right.

JOHN: I beg your pardon.

CAROL: That's all right.

330 JOHN: I'm sorry I interrupted you.

CAROL: That's all right.

JOHN: You were saying?

CAROL: I was saying . . . I was saying . . . . (*She checks her notes.*) How can you say in a class. Say in a college class, that college education is prejudice?

JOHN: I said that our predilection for it . . .

335 CAROL: Predilection . . .

JOHN: . . . you know what that means.

CAROL: Does it mean "liking"?

JOHN: Yes.

CAROL: But how can you say that? That College . . .

340 JOHN: . . . that's my *job,* don't you know.

CAROL: What is?

JOHN: To provoke you.

CAROL: No.

JOHN: Oh. Yes, though.

345 CAROL: To provoke me?

JOHN: That's right.

CAROL: To make me mad?

JOHN: That's right. To force you . . .

CAROL: . . . to make me mad is your job?

JOHN: To force you to . . . listen: (*Pause*) Ah. (*Pause*) When I was young somebody   350
told me, are you ready, the rich copulate less often than the poor. But when
they do, they take more of their clothes off. Years. Years, mind you, I would compare experiences of my own to this dictum, saying, aha, this fits the norm, or ah,
this is a variation from it. What did it mean? Nothing. It was some jerk thing,
some school kid told me that took up room inside my head. (*Pause*)

   Somebody told *you*, and you hold it as an article of faith, that higher education is an unassailable good. This notion is so dear to you that when I question it you become angry. Good. Good, I say. Are not those the very things
which we should question? I say college education, since the war, has become
so a matter of course, and such a fashionable necessity, for those either of or as-
piring *to* to the new vast middle class, that we *espouse* it, as a matter of right, and
have ceased to ask, "What is it good for?" (*Pause*)

   What might be some reasons for pursuit of higher education?
One: A love of learning.
Two: The wish for mastery of a skill.
Three: For economic betterment.
(*Stops. Makes a note.*)
CAROL: I'm keeping you.
JOHN: One moment. I have to make a note . . .
CAROL: It's something that I said?   355
JOHN: No, we're buying a house.
CAROL: You're buying the new house.
JOHN: To go with the tenure. That's right. Nice *house,* close to the *private
school* . . . (*He continues making his note.*) . . . We were talking of economic *better-
ment* (CAROL *writes in her notebook.*) . . . I was thinking of the School Tax. (*He
continues writing.*) (*To himself:*) . . . *where is it written* that I have to send my child
to public school. . . . Is it a law that I have to improve the City Schools at the
expense of my own interest? And, is this not simply *The White Man's Burden?*
Good. And (*Looks up to* CAROL) . . . does this interest you?
CAROL: No. I'm taking notes . . .
JOHN: You don't have to take notes, you know, you can just listen.   360
CAROL: I want to make sure I remember it. (*Pause*)
JOHN: I'm not lecturing you, I'm just trying to tell you some things I think.
CAROL: What do you think?
JOHN: Should all kids go to college? *Why* . . .
CAROL: (*Pause*) To learn.   365
JOHN: But if he does not learn.
CAROL: If the child does not learn?
JOHN: Then why is he in college? Because he was told it was his "right"?
CAROL: Some might find college instructive.
JOHN: I would hope so.   370
CAROL: But how do they feel? Being told they are wasting their time?
JOHN: I don't think I'm telling them that.
CAROL: You said that education was "prolonged and systematic hazing."
JOHN: Yes. It can be so.
CAROL: . . . if education is so *bad,* why do you do it?   375

JOHN: I do it because I love it. (*Pause*) Let's. . . . I suggest you look at the demographics, wage-earning capacity, college- and non-college-educated men and women, 1855 to 1980, and let's see if we can wring some worth from the statistics. Eh? And . . .

CAROL: No.

JOHN: What?

CAROL: I can't understand them.

380   JOHN: . . . you . . . ?

CAROL: . . . the "charts." The *Concepts,* the . . .

JOHN: "Charts" are simply . . .

CAROL: When I leave here . . .

JOHN: Charts, do you see . . .

385   CAROL: No, I can't . . .

JOHN: You can, though.

CAROL: NO, NO—I DON'T UNDERSTAND. DO YOU SEE??? I DON'T *UNDERSTAND* . . .

JOHN: What?

CAROL: *Any* of it. *Any* of it. I'm *smiling* in class, I'm *smiling,* the whole time. What are you *talking* about? What is everyone *talking* about? I don't *understand.* I don't know what it *means.* I don't know what it means to *be* here . . . you tell me I'm intelligent, and then you tell me I should not be *here,* what do you *want* with me? What does it *mean?* Who should I *listen* to . . . I . . .

(*He goes over to her and puts his arm around her shoulder.*)

390   NO! (*She walks away from him.*)

JOHN: Sshhhh.

CAROL: No, I don't under . . .

JOHN: Sshhhhh.

CAROL: I don't know what you're *saying* . . .

395   JOHN: Sshhhhh. It's all right.

CAROL: . . . I have no . . .

JOHN: Sshhhhh. Sshhhhh. Let it go a moment. (*Pause*) Sshhhhh . . . let it go. (*Pause*) Just let it go. (*Pause*) Just let it go. It's all right. (*Pause*) Sshhhhh. (*Pause*) I understand . . . (*Pause*) What do you feel?

CAROL: I feel bad.

JOHN: I know. It's all right.

400   CAROL: I . . . (*Pause*)

JOHN: What?

CAROL: I . . .

JOHN: What? Tell me.

CAROL: I don't understand you.

405   JOHN: I know. It's all right.

CAROL: I . . .

JOHN: What? (*Pause*) What? *Tell* me.

CAROL: I can't tell you.

JOHN: No, you must.

CAROL: I can't. 410

JOHN: No. Tell me. (*Pause*)

CAROL: I'm bad. (*Pause*) Oh, God. (*Pause*)

JOHN: It's all right.

CAROL: I'm . . .

JOHN: It's all right. 415

CAROL: I can't talk about this.

JOHN: It's all right. Tell me.

CAROL: Why do you want to know this?

JOHN: I don't want to know. I want to know whatever you . . .

CAROL: I always . . . 420

JOHN: . . . good . . .

CAROL: I always . . . all my life . . . I have never told anyone this . . .

JOHN: Yes. Go on. (*Pause*) Go on.

CAROL: All of my life . . . (*The phone rings.*) (*Pause.* JOHN *goes to the phone and picks it up.*)

JOHN (*into phone*): I can't talk now. (*Pause*) What? (*Pause*) Hmm. (*Pause*) All right, 425
I . . . I. Can't. Talk. Now. No, no, no, I *Know* I did, but. . . . What? Hello. What? She *what?* She *can't,* she said the agreement is void? How, how is the agreement *void? That's Our House.*

   I have the *paper;* when we come down, next week, with the payment, and the paper, that house is . . . wait, wait, wait, wait, wait, wait, wait: Did Jerry . . . is Jerry there? (*Pause*) Is *she* there . . . ? Does she have a *lawyer* . . . ? How the *hell,* how the *Hell.* That is . . . it's a question, you said, of the *easement.* I don't underst . . . it's not the *whole agreement.* It's just the *easement,* why would she? Put, put, put, *Jerry* on. (*Pause*) Jer, *Jerry:* What the *Hell* . . . that's my *house.* That's . . . Well, I'm, no, no, no, I'm *not* coming ddd . . . List, *Listen, screw* her. You *tell* her. You, listen: I want you to take *Grace,* you take Grace, and get out of that house. You *leave* her there. Her and her lawyer, and you *tell* them, we'll see them in court next . . . no. No. Leave her there, leave her to *stew* in it: You tell her, we're *getting* that house, and we are going to . . . No. I'm *not* coming down. I'll be damned if I'll sit in the same rrr . . . the next, you tell her the next time I *see* her is in court . . . I . . . (*Pause*) What? (*Pause*) What? I don't understand. (*Pause*) Well, what about the house? (*Pause*) There isn't any problem with the hhh . . . (*Pause*) No, no, no, that's all right. All ri . . . All right . . . (*Pause*) Of course. Tha . . . Thank you. No, I will. Right away. (*He hangs up.*) (*Pause*)

CAROL: What is it? (*Pause*)

JOHN: It's a surprise party.

CAROL: It is.

JOHN: Yes. 430

CAROL: A party for you.

JOHN: Yes.

CAROL: Is it your birthday?

JOHN: No.

CAROL: What is it? 435

JOHN: The tenure announcement.

CAROL: The tenure announcement.

JOHN: They're throwing a party for us in our new house.

CAROL: Your new house.

440   JOHN: The house that we're buying.

CAROL: You have to go.

JOHN: It seems that I do.

CAROL: (*Pause*) They're proud of you.

JOHN: Well, there are those who would say it's a form of aggression.

445   CAROL: What is?

JOHN: A surprise.

TWO

JOHN *and* CAROL *seated across the desk from each other.*

JOHN: You see, (*pause*) I love to teach. And flatter myself I am *skilled* at it. And I love the, the aspect of *performance.* I think I must confess that.

When I found I loved to teach I swore that I would not become that cold, rigid automaton of an instructor which I had encountered as a child.

Now, I was not unconscious that it was given me to err upon the other side. And, so, I asked and *ask* myself if I engaged in heterodoxy, I will not say "gratuitously" for I do not care to posit orthodoxy as a given good—but, "to the detriment of, of my students." (*Pause*)

As I said. When the possibility of tenure opened, and, of course, I'd long pursued it, I was, of course *happy,* and *covetous* of it.

5   I asked myself if I was wrong to covet it. And thought about it long, and, I hope, truthfully, and saw in myself several things in, I think, no particular order. (*Pause*)

That I *would* pursue it. That I *desired* it, that I was not pure of longing for security, and that that, perhaps, was not reprehensible in me. That I had duties *beyond* the school, and that my duty to my home, for instance, was, or should be, if it were not, of an equal weight. That tenure, and security, and yes, and *comfort,* were not, of themselves, to be scorned; and were even worthy of honorable pursuit. And that it was given me. Here, in this place, which I enjoy, and in which I find comfort, to assure myself of—as far as it rests in The Material—a continuation of that joy and comfort. In exchange for what? Teaching. Which I love.

What was the price of this security? To obtain *tenure.* Which tenure the committee is in the process of granting me. And on the basis of which I contracted to purchase a house. Now, as you don't have your own family, at this point, you may not know what that means. But to me it is important. A home. A Good Home. To raise my family. Now: The Tenure Committee will meet. This is the process, and a *good* process. Under which the school has functioned for quite a long time. They will meet, and hear your complaint—which you have the right to make; and they will dismiss it. They will *dismiss* your complaint; and, in the intervening period, I will lose my house. I will not be able to close on my house. I will lose my *deposit,* and the home I'd picked out for my wife and son will go by the boards. Now: I see I have angered you. I understand your anger at teachers. I was angry with mine. I felt hurt and humiliated by them. Which is one of the reasons that I went into education.

CAROL: What do you want of me?

JOHN: (*Pause*) I was hurt. When I received the report. Of the tenure committee. I was shocked. And I was hurt. No, I don't mean to subject you to my weak sensibilities. All right. Finally, I didn't understand. Then I thought: is it not always at those points at which we reckon ourselves unassailable that we are most vulnerable and . . . (*Pause*) Yes. All right. You find me pedantic. Yes. I am. By nature, by *birth,* by profession, I don't know . . . I'm always looking for a *paradigm* for . . .

CAROL: I don't know what a paradigm is.   10

JOHN: It's a model.

CAROL: Then why can't you use that word? (*Pause*)

JOHN: If it is important to you. Yes, all right. I was looking for a model. To continue: I feel that one point . . .

CAROL: I . . .

JOHN: One second . . . upon which I am unassailable is my unflinching concern for   15
my students' dignity. I asked you here to . . . in the spirit of *investigation,* to ask you . . . to ask . . . (*Pause*) What have I done to you? (*Pause*) And, and, I suppose, how I can make amends. Can we not settle this now? It's pointless, really, and I want to know.

CAROL: What you can do to force me to retract?

JOHN: That is not what I meant at all.

CAROL: To bribe me, to convince me . . .

JOHN: . . . No.

CAROL: To retract . . .   20

JOHN: That is not what I meant at all. I think that you know it is not.

CAROL: That is not what I know. I *wish* I . . .

JOHN: I do not want to . . . you wish what?

CAROL: No, you said what amends can you make. To force me to retract.

JOHN: That is not what I said.   25

CAROL: I have my notes.

JOHN: Look. Look. The Stoics say . . .

CAROL: The Stoics?

JOHN: The Stoical Philosophers say if you remove the phrase "I have been injured," you have removed the injury. Now: Think: I know that you're upset. Just tell me. Literally. Literally: what wrong have I done you?

CAROL: Whatever you have done to me—to the extent that you've done it to *me,*   30
do you know, rather than to me as a *student,* and, so, to the student body, is contained in my report. To the tenure committee.

JOHN: Well, all right. (*Pause*) Let's see. (*He reads.*) I find that I am sexist. That I am *elitist.* I'm not sure I know what that means, other than it's a derogatory word, meaning "bad." That I . . . That I insist on wasting time, in nonprescribed, in self-aggrandizing and theatrical *diversions* from the prescribed *text* . . . that these have taken both sexist and pornographic forms . . . here we find listed . . . (*Pause*) Here we find listed . . . instances ". . . closeted with a student" . . . "Told a rambling, sexually explicit story, in which the frequency and attitudes of fornication of the poor and rich are, it would seem, the central point . . . moved to *embrace* said student and . . . all part of a pattern . . ." (*Pause*)

(*He reads.*) That I used the phrase "The White Man's Burden" . . . that I told you how I'd asked you to my room because I quote like you. (*Pause*)

(*He reads.*) "He said he 'liked' me. That he 'liked being with me.' He'd let me write my examination paper over, if I could come back oftener to see him in his office." (*Pause*) (*To* CAROL:) It's *ludicrous.* Don't you know that? It's not *necessary.* It's going to *humiliate* you, and it's going to cost me my *house,* and . . .

CAROL: It's "*ludicrous* . . ."?

(JOHN *picks up the report and reads again.*)

35 JOHN: "He told me he had problems with his wife; and that he wanted to take off the artificial stricture of Teacher and Student. He put his arm around me . . ."
CAROL: Do you deny it? Can you deny it . . . ? Do you see? (*Pause*) Don't you see? You don't see, do you?
JOHN: I don't see . . .
CAROL: You think, you think you can deny that these things happened; or, if they *did,* if they *did,* that they meant what you *said* they meant. Don't you see? You drag me in here, you drag us, to listen to you "go on"; and "go on" about this, or that, or we don't "express" ourselves very well. We don't say what we mean. Don't we? Don't we? We *do* say what we mean. And you say that "I don't understand you . . .": Then *you* . . . (*Points.*)
JOHN: "Consult the Report"?
40 CAROL: . . . that's right.
JOHN: You see. You see. Can't you. . . . You see what I'm saying? Can't you tell me in your own words?
CAROL: Those are my own words. (*Pause*)
JOHN: (*He reads.*) "He told me that if I would stay alone with him in his office, he would change my grade to an A." (*To* CAROL:) What have I done to you? Oh. My God, are you so hurt?
CAROL: What I "feel" is irrelevant. (*Pause*)
45 JOHN: Do you know that I tried to help you?
CAROL: What I know I have reported.
JOHN: I would like to help you now. I would. Before this escalates.
CAROL (*simultaneously with* "escalates"): You see. I don't think that I need your help. I don't think I need anything you have.
JOHN: I feel . . .
50 CAROL: I don't *care* what you feel. Do you see? DO YOU SEE? You can't *do* that anymore. You. Do. Not. Have. The. Power. Did you misuse it? *Someone* did. Are you part of that group? *Yes. Yes.* You Are. You've *done* these things. And to say, and to say, "Oh. Let me help you with your problem . . ."
JOHN: Yes. I understand. I understand. You're *hurt.* You're *angry.* Yes. I think your *anger* is *betraying* you. Down a path which helps no one.
CAROL: I don't *care* what you think.

JOHN: You don't? (*Pause*) But you talk of *rights*. Don't you see? *I* have rights too. Do you see? I have a *house* . . . part of the *real* world; and The Tenure Committee, Good Men and True . . .

CAROL: . . . Professor . . .

JOHN: . . . Please: *Also* part of that world: you understand? This is my *life*. I'm not a   55
bogeyman. I don't "stand" for something, I . . .

CAROL: . . . Professor . . .

JOHN: . . . I . . .

CAROL: Professor. I came here as a *favor*. At your personal request. Perhaps I should not have done so. But I did. On my behalf, and on behalf of my group. And you speak of the tenure committee, one of whose members is a woman, as you know. And though you might call it Good Fun, or An Historical Phrase, or An Oversight, or, All of the Above, to refer to the committee as Good Men and True, it is a demeaning remark. It is a sexist remark, and to overlook it is to countenance continuation of that method of thought. It's a remark . . .

JOHN: OH COME ON. Come on. . . . Sufficient to deprive a family of . . .

CAROL: Sufficient? Sufficient? Sufficient? Yes. It is a *fact* . . . and that story, which I   60
quote, is *vile* and *classist,* and *manipulative* and *pornographic.* It . . .

JOHN: . . . it's pornographic . . . ?

CAROL: What gives you the *right*. Yes. To speak to a *woman* in your private . . . Yes. Yes. I'm sorry. I'm sorry. You feel yourself empowered . . . you say so yourself. To *strut*. To *posture*. To "perform." To "Call me in here . . ." Eh? You say that higher education is a joke. And treat it as such, you *treat* it as such. And *confess* to a taste to play the *Patriarch* in your class. To grant *this*. To deny *that*. To embrace your students.

JOHN: How can you assert. How can you stand there and . . .

CAROL: How can you *deny* it. You did it to me. *Here*. You *did*. . . . You *confess*. You love the Power. To *deviate*. To *invent,* to transgress . . . to *transgress* whatever norms have been established for us. And you think it's charming to "question" in yourself this taste to mock and destroy. But you should question it. Professor. And you pick those things which you feel *advance* you: publication, *tenure,* and the steps to get them you call "harmless rituals." And you perform those steps. Although you say it is hypocrisy. But to the aspirations of your students. Of *hardworking students,* who come here, who *slave* to come here—you have no idea what it cost me to come to this school—you *mock* us. You call education "hazing," and from your so-protected, so-elitist seat you hold our confusion as a *joke,* and our hopes and efforts with it. Then you sit there and say "what have I done?" And ask me to understand that *you* have aspirations too. But I tell you. I tell you. That you are vile. And that you are exploitative. And if you possess one ounce of that inner honesty you describe in your book, you can look in yourself and see those things that I see. And you can find revulsion equal to my own. Good day. (*She prepares to leave the room.*)

JOHN: Wait a second, will you, just one moment. (*Pause*) Nice day today.   65

CAROL: What?

JOHN: You said "Good day." I think that it is a nice day today.

CAROL: *Is* it?

JOHN: Yes, I think it is.

70   CAROL: And why is that important?

JOHN: Because it is the essence of all human communication. I say something conventional, you respond, and the information we exchange is not about the "weather," but that we both agree to converse. In effect, we agree that we are both human. (*Pause*)

I'm not a . . . "exploiter," and you're not a . . . "deranged," what? *Revolutionary* . . . that we may, that we may have . . . positions, and that we may have . . . desires, which are in *conflict,* but that we're just human. (*Pause*) That means that sometimes we're *imperfect.* (*Pause*) Often we're in conflict . . . (*Pause*) *Much* of what we do, you're right, in the name of "principles" is *self-serving* . . . much of what we do is *conventional.* (*Pause*) You're right. (*Pause*) You said you came in the class because you wanted to learn about *education.* I don't know that I can teach you about education. But I know that I can tell you what I *think* about education, and then *you* decide. And you don't have to fight with me. *I'm* not the subject. (*Pause*) And where I'm *wrong* . . . perhaps it's not your job to "fix" me. I don't want to fix *you.* I would like to tell you what I *think,* because that *is* my job, conventional as it is, and flawed as I may be. And then, if you can show me some better *form,* then we can proceed from there. But, just like "nice day, isn't it . . . ?" I don't think we can proceed until we accept that each of us is human. (*Pause*) And we still can have difficulties. We *will* have them . . . that's all right too. (*Pause*) Now:

CAROL: . . . wait . . .

JOHN: Yes. I want to hear it.

75   CAROL: . . . the . . .

JOHN: Yes. Tell me frankly.

CAROL: . . . my position . . .

JOHN: I want to hear it. In your own words. What you want. And what you feel.

CAROL: . . . I . . .

80   JOHN: . . . yes . . .

CAROL: My Group.

JOHN: Your "Group" . . . ? (*Pause*)

CAROL: The people I've been talking to . . .

JOHN: There's no shame in that. Everybody needs advisers. Everyone needs to expose themselves. To various points of view. It's not wrong. It's essential. Good. Good. Now: You and I . . . (*The phone rings.*)

85   You and I . . .

(*He hesitates for a moment, and then picks it up.*) (*Into phone*) Hello. (*Pause*) Um . . . no, I know they do. (*Pause*) I know she does. Tell her that I . . . can I call you back? . . . Then tell her that I think it's going to be fine. (*Pause*) Tell her just, just hold on, I'll . . . can I get back to you? . . . Well . . . no, no, no, we're *taking* the house . . . we're . . . no, no, nn . . . no, she will nnn, it's not a *question* of refunding the dep . . . no . . . it's not a *question* of the deposit . . . will you call Jerry? Babe, baby, will you just call Jerry? Tell him, nnn . . . tell him they, well, they're to keep the deposit, because the deal, be . . . because the deal is going to go *through* . . . because I know . . . be . . . will you please? Just *trust* me. Be . . . well, I'm dealing with the complaint. Yes. Right *Now.* Which is why I . . . yes, no, no, it's really, I can't *talk* about it now. Call Jerry, and I can't talk now. Ff . . . fine. Gg . . . good-bye. (*Hangs up.*) (*Pause*) I'm sorry we were interrupted.

CAROL: No . . .

JOHN: I . . . I was saying:

CAROL: You said that we should agree to talk about my complaint.

JOHN: That's correct.   90

CAROL: But we *are* talking about it.

JOHN: Well, that's correct too. You see? This is the *gist* of education.

CAROL: No, no. I mean, we're talking about it at the Tenure Committee Hearing. (*Pause*)

JOHN: Yes, but I'm saying: we can talk about it *now,* as easily as . . .

CAROL: No. I think that we should stick to the process . . .   95

JOHN: . . . wait a . . .

CAROL: . . . the "conventional" process. As you said. (*She gets up.*) And you're right, I'm sorry if I was, um, if I was "discourteous" to you. You're right.

JOHN: Wait, wait a . . .

CAROL: I really should go.

JOHN: Now, look, granted. I have an interest. In the status quo. All right? Everyone   100 does. But what I'm saying is that the *committee* . . .

CAROL: Professor, you're right. Just don't impinge on me. We'll take our differences, and . . .

JOHN: You're going to make a . . . look, look, look, you're going to . . .

CAROL: I shouldn't have come here. They told me . . .

JOHN: One moment. No. No. There are *norms,* here, and there's no reason. Look: I'm trying to *save* you . . .

CAROL: No one *asked* you to . . . you're trying to save *me?* Do me the courtesy to . . .   105

JOHN: I *am* doing you the courtesy. I'm talking *straight* to you. We can settle this *now.* And I want you to sit *down* and . . .

CAROL: You must excuse me . . . . (*She starts to leave the room.*)

JOHN: Sit down, it seems we each have a. . . . Wait one moment. Wait one moment . . . just do me the courtesy to . . .

(*He restrains her from leaving.*)

CAROL: LET ME GO.   110

JOHN: I have no desire to *hold* you, I just want to *talk* to you . . .

CAROL: LET ME GO. LET ME GO. WOULD SOMEBODY *HELP* ME? WOULD SOMEBODY *HELP* ME PLEASE . . . ?

THREE

At rise, CAROL *and* JOHN *are seated.*

JOHN: I have asked you here. (*Pause*) I have asked you here against, against my . . .

CAROL: I was most surprised you asked me.

JOHN: . . . against my better *judgment,* against . . .

CAROL: I was most surprised . . .

JOHN: . . . against the . . . . yes. I'm sure.   5

CAROL: . . . If you would like me to leave, I'll leave. I'll go right now . . . (*She rises.*)

JOHN: Let us begin *correctly,* may we? I feel . . .

CAROL: That is what I wished to do. That's why I came here, but now . . .

JOHN: . . . I feel . . .

10 CAROL: But now perhaps you'd like me to leave . . .

JOHN: I don't want you to leave. I asked you to come . . .

CAROL: I didn't have to come here.

JOHN: No. (*Pause*) Thank you.

CAROL: All right. (*Pause*) (*She sits down.*)

15 JOHN: Although I feel that it *profits,* it would *profit* you something, to . . .

CAROL: . . . what I . . .

JOHN: If you would hear me out, if you would hear me out.

CAROL: I came here to, the court officers told me not to come.

JOHN: . . . the "court" officers . . . ?

20 CAROL: I was shocked that you asked.

JOHN: . . . wait . . .

CAROL: Yes. But I did *not* come here to hear what it "profits" me.

JOHN: The "court" officers . . .

CAROL: . . . no, no, perhaps I should leave . . . (*She gets up.*)

25 JOHN: Wait.

CAROL: No. I shouldn't have . . .

JOHN: . . . wait. Wait. Wait a moment.

CAROL: Yes? What is it you want? (*Pause*) What is it you want?

JOHN: I'd like you to stay.

30 CAROL: You want me to stay.

JOHN: Yes.

CAROL: You do.

JOHN: Yes. (*Pause*) Yes. I would like to have you hear me out. If you would. (*Pause*) Would you please? If you would do that I would be in your debt. (*Pause*) (*She sits.*) Thank You. (*Pause*)

CAROL: What is it you wish to tell me?

35 JOHN: All right. I cannot . . . (*Pause*) I cannot help but feel you are owed an apology. (*Pause*) (*Of papers in his hands*) I have read. (*Pause*) And reread these accusations.

CAROL: What "accusations"?

JOHN: The, the tenure comm . . . what other accusations . . . ?

CAROL: The tenure committee . . . ?

JOHN: Yes.

40 CAROL: Excuse me, but those are not accusations. They have been *proved.* They are facts.

JOHN: . . . I . . .

CAROL: No. Those are not "accusations."

JOHN: . . . those?

CAROL: . . . the committee (*The phone starts to ring.*) the committee has . . .

45 JOHN: . . . All right . . .

CAROL: . . . those are not accusations. The Tenure Committee.

JOHN: ALL RIGHT. ALL RIGHT. ALL RIGHT. (*He picks up the phone.*) Hello. Yes. No. I'm here. Tell Mister . . . No, I can't talk to him now . . . I'm sure he has, but I'm fff . . . I know . . . No, I have no time t . . . tell Mister . . . tell Mist . . . tell Jerry that I'm *fine* and that I'll call him right aw . . . (*Pause*) My wife . . . Yes. I'm sure she has. Yes, thank you. Yes, I'll call her too. I cannot talk to you now. (*He hangs up.*) (*Pause*) All right. It was good of you to come. Thank you. I have studied. I have spent some time studying the indictment.

CAROL: You will have to explain that word to me.

JOHN: An "indictment" . . .

CAROL: Yes.

JOHN: Is a "bill of particulars." A . . .

CAROL: All right. Yes.

JOHN: In which is alleged . . .

CAROL: No. I cannot allow that. I cannot allow that. Nothing is alleged. Everything is proved . . .

JOHN: Please, wait a sec . . .

CAROL: I cannot *come* to allow . . .

JOHN: If I may . . . If I may, from whatever you feel is "established," by . . .

CAROL: The issue here is not what I "feel." It is not my "feelings," but the feelings of women. And men. Your superiors, who've been "polled," do you see? To whom *evidence* has been presented, who have *ruled*, do you see? Who have weighed the testimony and the evidence, and have *ruled*, do you see? That you are *negligent*. That you are *guilty*, that you are found *wanting*, and in *error*; and are *not*, for the reasons so-told, to be given tenure. That you are to be disciplined. For facts. For *facts*. Not "alleged," what is the word? But *proved*. Do you see? *By your own actions.*
    That is what the tenure committee has said. That is what my lawyer said. For what you did in class. For what you did *in this office*.

JOHN: They're going to discharge me.

CAROL: As full well they should. You don't understand? You're angry? What has *led* you to this place? Not your sex. Not your race. Not your class. YOUR OWN ACTIONS. And you're *angry*. You *ask* me here. What *do* you want? You want to "charm" me. You want to "convince" me. You want me to recant. I will *not* recant. Why should I . . . ? What I say is right. You tell me, you are going to tell me that you have a wife and child. You are going to say that you have a career and that you've worked for twenty years for this. Do you know what you've *worked* for? *Power*. For *power*. Do you understand? And you sit there, and you tell me *stories*. About your *house*, about all the private *schools*, and about *privilege*, and how you are entitled. To *buy*, to *spend*, to *mock*, to *summon*. All your stories. All your silly weak *guilt*, it's all about *privilege*; and you won't know it. Don't you see? You worked twenty years for the right to *insult* me. And you feel entitled to be *paid* for it. Your Home. Your Wife . . . Your sweet "deposit" on your house . . .

JOHN: Don't you have feelings?

CAROL: That's my point. You see? Don't you have feelings? Your final argument. What is it that has no feelings. *Animals*. I don't take your side, you question if I'm Human.

JOHN: Don't you have feelings?

CAROL: I have a responsibility. I . . .

JOHN: . . . to . . . ?

CAROL: To? This institution. To the *students*. To my *group*.

JOHN: . . . your "group." . . .

CAROL: Because I speak, yes, not for myself. But for the group; for those who suffer what I suffer. On behalf of whom, even if I, were, inclined, to what, forgive? Forget? What? Overlook your . . .

70 JOHN: . . . my behavior?

CAROL: . . . it would be wrong.

JOHN: Even if you were inclined to "forgive" me.

CAROL: It would be wrong.

JOHN: And what would transpire.

75 CAROL: Transpire?

JOHN: Yes.

CAROL: "Happen?"

JOHN: Yes.

CAROL: Then *say* it. For Christ's sake. Who the *hell* do you think that you are? You want a post. You want unlimited power. To do and to say what you want. As it pleases you—Testing, Questioning, Flirting . . .

80 JOHN: I never . . .

CAROL: Excuse me, one moment, will you?

(*She reads from her notes.*)

The twelfth: "Have a good day, dear."

The fifteenth: "Now, don't *you* look fetching . . ."

April seventeenth: "If you girls would come over here . . ." I saw you. I saw you, Professor. For two semesters sit there, stand there and exploit our, as you thought, "paternal prerogative," and what is that but rape; I swear to God. You asked me in here to explain something to me, as a child, that I did not understand. But I came to explain something to you. You Are Not God. You ask me why I came? I came here to instruct you.

(*She produces his book.*)

85 And your book? You think you're going to show me some "light"? You *"maverick."* Outside of tradition. No, no, (*She reads from the book's liner notes.*) *"of that fine tradition of inquiry. Of Polite skepticism"* . . . and you say you believe in free intellectual discourse. YOU BELIEVE IN NOTHING. YOU BELIEVE IN NOTHING AT ALL.

JOHN: I believe in freedom of thought.

CAROL: Isn't that fine. *Do* you?

JOHN: Yes. I do.

CAROL: Then why do you question, for one moment, the committee's decision refusing your tenure? Why do you question your suspension? You believe in what *you call* freedom of thought. Then, fine. *You* believe in freedom-of-thought *and* a home, and, *and* prerogatives for your kid, *and* tenure. And I'm going to tell you. You believe *not* in "freedom of thought," but in an elitist, in, a protected hierarchy which rewards you. And for whom you are the clown. And you mock and exploit the system which pays your rent. You're wrong. I'm not wrong. You're wrong. You think that I'm full of hatred. I know what you think I am.

JOHN: Do you? 90

CAROL: You think I'm a, of course I do. You think I am a frightened, repressed, confused, I don't know, abandoned young thing of some doubtful sexuality, who wants, power and revenge. (*Pause*) *Don't* you? (*Pause*)

JOHN: Yes. I do. (*Pause*)

CAROL: Isn't that better? And I feel that that is the first moment which you've treated me with respect. For you told me the truth. (*Pause*) I did not come here, as you are assured, to gloat. Why would I want to gloat? I've profited nothing from your, your, as you say, your "misfortune." I came here, as you did me the honor to *ask* me here, I came here to *tell* you something.

(*Pause*) That I think . . . that I think you've been wrong. That I think you've been terribly wrong. Do you hate me now? (*Pause*)

JOHN: Yes. 95

CAROL: Why do you hate me? Because you think me wrong? No. Because I have, you think, *power* over you. Listen to me. Listen to me, Professor. (*Pause*) It is the power that you hate. So deeply that, that any atmosphere of free discussion is impossible. It's not "unlikely." It's *impossible*. Isn't it?

JOHN: Yes.

CAROL: *Isn't* it . . . ?

JOHN: Yes. I suppose.

CAROL: Now. The thing which you find so cruel is the selfsame process of selection 100 I, and my group, go through *every day of our lives.* In admittance to school. In our tests, in our class rankings. . . . Is it unfair? I can't tell you. But, if it is fair. Or even if it is "unfortunate but necessary" for us, then, by God, so must it be for you. (*Pause*) You write of your "responsibility to the young." Treat us with respect, and that will *show* you your responsibility. You write that education is just hazing. (*Pause*) But we worked to get to this school. (*Pause*) And some of us. (*Pause*) Overcame prejudices. Economic, sexual, you cannot begin to imagine. And endured humiliations I *pray* that you and those you love never will encounter. (*Pause*) To gain admittance here. To pursue that same dream of security *you* pursue. We, who, who are, at any moment, in danger of being deprived of it. By . . .

JOHN: . . . by . . . ?

CAROL: By the administration. By the teachers. By *you*. By, say, one low grade, that keeps us out of graduate school; by one, say, one capricious or inventive answer on our parts, which, perhaps, you don't find amusing. Now you *know*, do you see? What it is to be subject to that power. (*Pause*)

JOHN: I don't understand. (*Pause*)

CAROL: My charges are not trivial. You see that in the haste, I think, with which they were accepted. A *joke* you have told, with a sexist tinge. The language you use, a verbal or physical caress, yes, yes, I know, you say that it is meaningless. I understand. I differ from you. To lay a hand on someone's shoulder.

JOHN: It was devoid of sexual content. 105

CAROL: I say it was not. I SAY IT WAS NOT. Don't you begin to *see* . . . ? Don't you begin to understand? IT'S NOT FOR YOU TO SAY.

JOHN: I take your point, and I see there is much good in what you refer to.

CAROL: . . . do you think so . . . ?

JOHN: . . . but, and this is not to say that I cannot change, in those things in which I am deficient . . . But, the . . .

110   CAROL: Do you hold yourself harmless from the charge of sexual exploitativeness . . . ? (*Pause*)

JOHN: Well, I . . . I . . . I . . . You know I, as I said. I . . . think I am not too old to *learn,* and I *can* learn, I . . .

CAROL: Do you hold yourself innocent of the charge of . . .

JOHN: . . . wait, wait, wait . . . All right, let's go back to . . .

CAROL: YOU FOOL. Who do you think I am? To come here and be taken in by a *smile.* You little yapping fool. You think I want "revenge." I don't want revenge. I WANT UNDERSTANDING.

115   JOHN: . . . *do* you?

CAROL: I do. (*Pause*)

JOHN: What's the use. It's over.

CAROL: Is it? What is?

JOHN: My job.

120   CAROL: Oh. Your job. That's what you want to talk about. (*Pause*) (*She starts to leave the room. She steps and turns back to him.*) All right. (*Pause*) What if it were possible that my Group withdraws its complaint. (*Pause*)

JOHN: What?

CAROL: That's right. (*Pause*)

JOHN: Why.

CAROL: Well, let's say as an act of friendship.

125   JOHN: An act of friendship.

CAROL: Yes. (*Pause*)

JOHN: In exchange for what.

CAROL: Yes. But I don't think, "exchange." Not "in exchange." For what do we derive from it? (*Pause*)

JOHN: "Derive."

130   CAROL: Yes.

JOHN: (*Pause*) Nothing. (*Pause*)

CAROL: That's right. We derive nothing. (*Pause*) Do you see that?

JOHN: Yes.

CAROL: That is a little word, Professor. "Yes." "I see that." But you will.

135   JOHN: And you might speak to the committee . . . ?

CAROL: To the committee?

JOHN: Yes.

CAROL: Well. Of course. That's on your mind. We might.

JOHN: "If" what?

140   CAROL: "Given" what. Perhaps. I think that that is more friendly.

JOHN: GIVEN WHAT?

CAROL: And, believe me, I understand your rage. It is not that I don't feel it. But I do not see that it is deserved, so I do not resent it. . . . All right. I have a list.

JOHN: . . . a list.

CAROL: Here is a list of books, which we . . .

145   JOHN: . . . a list of books . . . ?

CAROL: That's right. Which we find questionable.

JOHN: What?

CAROL: Is this so bizarre . . . ?

JOHN: I can't believe . . .

CAROL: It's not necessary you believe it.   150

JOHN: Academic freedom . . .

CAROL: Someone chooses the books. If you can choose them, others can. What are you, "God"?

JOHN: . . . no, no, the "dangerous." . . .

CAROL: You have an agenda, we have an agenda. I am not interested in your feelings or your motivation, but your actions. If you would like me to speak to the Tenure Committee, here is my list. You are a Free Person, you decide. (*Pause*)

JOHN: Give me the list. (*She does so. He reads.*)   155

CAROL: I think you'll find . . .

JOHN: I'm capable of reading it. Thank you.

CAROL: We have a number of *texts* we need re . . .

JOHN: I see that.

CAROL: We're amenable to . . .   160

JOHN: Aha. Well, let me look over the . . . (*He reads.*)

CAROL: I think that . . .

JOHN: LOOK. I'm reading your demands. All right?! (*He reads*) (*Pause*) You want to ban my book?

CAROL: We do not . . .

JOHN (*Of list*): It says here . . .   165

CAROL: . . . We want it removed from inclusion as a representative example of the university.

JOHN: Get out of here.

CAROL: If you put aside the issues of personalities.

JOHN: Get the fuck out of my office.

CAROL: No, I think I would reconsider.   170

JOHN: . . . you think you can.

CAROL: We can and we *will*. Do you want our support? That is the only quest . . .

JOHN: . . . to ban my *book* . . . ?

CAROL: . . . that is correct . . .

JOHN: . . . this . . . this is a *university* . . . we . . .   175

CAROL: . . . and we have a statement . . . which we need you to . . . (*She hands him a sheet of paper.*)

JOHN: No, no. It's out of the question. I'm sorry. I don't know what I was thinking of. I want to tell you something. I'm a teacher. I am a teacher. Eh? It's my *name* on the door, and *I* teach the class, and that's what I do. I've got a book with my name on it. And my son will *see* that *book* someday. And I have a respon . . . No, I'm sorry I have a *responsibility* . . . to *myself,* to my *son,* to my *profession.* . . . I haven't been *home* for two days, do you know that? Thinking this out.

CAROL: . . . you haven't?

JOHN: I've been, no. If it's of interest to you. I've been in a *hotel. Thinking.* (*The phone starts ringing.*) *Thinking* . . .

CAROL: . . . you haven't been home?   180

JOHN: . . . *thinking,* do you see.

CAROL: Oh.

JOHN: And, and, I owe you a debt, I see that now. (*Pause*) You're *dangerous,* you're *wrong* and it's my *job* . . . to say no to you. That's my job. You are absolutely right. You want to ban my book? Go to *hell,* and they can do whatever they want to me.

CAROL: . . . you haven't been home in two days . . .

185   JOHN: I think I told you that.

CAROL: . . . you'd better get that phone. (*Pause*) I think that you should pick up the phone. (*Pause*)

(JOHN *picks up the phone.*)

JOHN (*on phone*): Yes. (*Pause*) Yes. Wh . . . I. I. I had to be away. All ri . . . did they wor . . . did they worry ab . . . No. I'm all right, now, Jerry. I'm f . . . I got a little turned *around,* but I'm *sitting* here and . . . I've got it figured out. I'm fine. I'm fine don't worry about me. I got a little bit mixed up. But I am not sure that it's not a blessing. It cost me my job? Fine. Then the job was not worth having. Tell Grace that I'm coming home and everything is fff . . . (*Pause*) What? (*Pause*) *What?* (*Pause*) What do you *mean?* WHAT? Jerry . . . Jerry. They . . . Who, who, what can they do . . . ? (*Pause*) NO. (*Pause*) NO. They can't do th . . . What do you mean? (*Pause*) But how . . . (*Pause*) She's, she's, she's *here* with me. To . . . Jerry. I don't underst . . . (*Pause*) (*He hangs up.*) (*To* CAROL:) What does this mean?

CAROL: I thought you knew.

JOHN: What. (*Pause*) What does it mean. (*Pause*)

190   CAROL: You tried to rape me. (*Pause*) According to the law. (*Pause*)

JOHN: . . . what . . . ?

CAROL: You tried to rape me. I was leaving this office, you "pressed" yourself into me. You "pressed" your body into me.

JOHN: . . . I . . .

CAROL: My Group has told your lawyer that we may pursue criminal charges.

195   JOHN: . . . no . . .

CAROL: . . . under the statute. I am told. It was battery.

JOHN: . . . no . . .

CAROL: Yes. And attempted rape. That's right (*Pause*)

JOHN: I think that you should go.

200   CAROL: Of course. I thought you knew.

JOHN: I have to talk to my lawyer.

CAROL: Yes. Perhaps you should.

(*The phone rings again.*) (*Pause*)

JOHN: (*Picks up phone. Into phone:*) Hello? I . . . Hello . . . ? I . . . Yes, he just called. No . . . I. I can't talk to you now, Baby. (*To* CAROL:) Get out.

CAROL: . . . your wife . . . ?

205   JOHN: . . . who it is is no concern of yours. Get out. (*To phone:*) No, no, it's going to be all right. I. I can't talk now, Baby. (*To* CAROL:) Get out of here.

CAROL: I'm going.

JOHN: Good.

CAROL (*exciting*): . . . and don't call your wife "baby."

JOHN: What?

CAROL: Don't call your wife baby. You heard what I said.   210

(CAROL *starts to leave the room.* JOHN *grabs her and begins to beat her.*)

JOHN: You vicious little bitch. You think you can come in here with your political correctness and destroy my life?

(*He knocks her to the floor.*)

After how I treated you . . . ? You should be . . . *Rape you* . . . ? Are you kidding me . . . ?

(*He picks up a chair, raises it above his head, and advances on her.*)

I wouldn't touch you with a ten-foot pole. You little *cunt* . . .

(*She cowers on the floor below him. Pause. He looks down at her. He lowers the chair. He moves to his desk, and arranges the papers on it. Pause. He looks over at her.*)

. . . well . . .

(*Pause. She looks at him.*)

CAROL: Yes. That's right.   215

(*She looks away from him, and lowers her head. To herself:*) . . . yes. That's right.

END

QUESTIONS FOR DISCUSSION AND WRITING

1. Although *Oleanna* isn't about love in any traditional sense, it *is* about sexual politics. How much does it matter that John is a man and Carol a woman? Would the play's moods and themes have been different if the teacher and student had both been men or both women? If the teacher had been a woman and the student a man? And to what extent are Carol's and John's uses of language determined by or reflective of their genders?

2. At some theatrical productions of *Oleanna*, theatergoers have been asked to "vote" on whether they sympathize more with Carol or with John. How would you vote and why? Would you vote differently early on in the play than you would as events unfold? Why or why not?

3. *Oleanna* is clearly about conflict—between men and women and between teachers and students. Poll people who have read or seen the play (including your classmates). Do men and women respond differently to the central situation? Do teachers and students?

4. The title of *Oleanna* refers both to a folk song and to a utopian community in Pennsylvania. The Pennsylvania community was started by a Norwegian violinist who, it turned out, bought the land from people who did not themselves own it. The song tells the story of a utopia in which beer runs freely in streams, it rains champagne, crops grow ten feet in a day, and no one has to work. With these facts

in mind, how would you account for the thematic connection between the title of *Oleanna* and the events of the play?

5. At the beginning of the play, Mamet has included a quotation from Samuel Butler's *The Way of All Flesh*. What thematic connections are there between the quotation and the play itself?

6. *Oleanna* contains many threads of meaning. Some audiences think we are meant to see it as a feminist play, others as an antifeminist play. Many think Mamet means for us to see the play as a criticism of what college education has become; but within that group some think the harshest criticisms are directed against teachers, some think they are directed against students, and some think they are directed against administrators. Still others point to the strained dialog and see the play as a play about language and communication. What do *you* think the primary focus of *Oleanna* is? Whatever your answer, you will want not only to consider how the evidence in the play supports your conclusions but also to think about how the other threads of meaning relate to the primary one.

7. Even when viewers and readers agree that the play is at least partly about questions of sexual harassment, they differ over whether sexual harassment has occurred. If your campus has a definition of sexual harassment, how would that definition apply to the actions of John and Carol in *Oleanna*?

8. David Mamet directed the film version of *Oleanna* (1994), which is available on videotape. Locate and watch the film. How much is the film like what you imagined as you read the play? How does the setting in the film match what is described in the text? How is Mamet's view of John's physical encounter with Carol the same or different from what you imagined as you read the play?

JOAN DIDION (1934–   )

Some Dreamers of the Golden Dream 　　　　　　　　　　　　　　 1966

This is a story about love and death in the golden land, and begins with the country. The San Bernardino Valley lies only an hour east of Los Angeles by the San Bernardino Freeway but is in certain ways an alien place: not the coastal California of the subtropical twilights and the soft westerlies off the Pacific but a harsher California, haunted by the Mojave just beyond the mountains, devastated by the hot dry Santa Ana wind that comes down through the passes at 100 miles an hour and whines through the eucalyptus windbreaks and works on the nerves. October is the bad month for the wind, the month when breathing is difficult and the hills blaze up spontaneously. There has been no rain since April. Every voice seems a scream. It is the season of suicide and divorce and prickly dread, wherever the wind blows.

The Mormons settled this ominous country, and then they abandoned it, but by the time they left the first orange tree had been planted and for the next hundred years the San Bernardino Valley would draw a kind of people who imagined they might live among the talismanic fruit and prosper in the dry air, people who brought with them Midwestern ways of building and cooking and praying and who tried to graft those ways upon the land. The graft took in curious ways. This is the California where it is possible to live and die without ever eating an artichoke, without ever meeting a Catholic or a Jew. This is the California where it is easy to Dial-A-Devotion, but hard to buy a book. This is the country in which a belief in the literal interpretation of Genesis has slipped imperceptibly into a belief in the literal interpretation of *Double Indemnity,* the country of the teased hair and the Capris and the girls for whom all life's promise comes down to a waltz-length white wedding dress and the birth of a Kimberly or a Sherry or a Debbi and a Tijuana divorce and a return to hairdressers' school. "We were just crazy kids," they say without regret, and look to the future. The future always looks good in the golden land, because no one remembers the past. Here is where the hot wind blows and the old ways do not seem relevant, where the divorce rate is double the national average and where one person in every thirty-eight lives in a trailer. Here is the last stop for all those who come from somewhere else, for all those who drifted away from the cold and the past and the old ways. Here is where they are trying to find a new life style, trying to find it in the only places they know to look: the movies and the newspapers. The case of Lucille Marie Maxwell Miller is a tabloid monument to that new life style.

Imagine Banyan Street first, because Banyan is where it happened. The way to Banyan is to drive west from San Bernardino out Foothill Boulevard, Route 66: past the Santa Fe switching yards, the Forty Winks Motel. Past the motel that is nineteen stucco tepees: "SLEEP IN A WIGWAM—GET MORE FOR YOUR WAMPUM." Past Fontana Drag City and the Fontana Church of the Nazarene and the Pit Stop A Go-Go; past Kaiser Steel, through Cucamonga, out to the Kapu Kai Restaurant-Bar and Coffee Shop, at the corner of Route 66 and Carnelian Avenue. Up Carnelian Avenue from the Kapu Kai, which means "Forbidden Seas," the subdivision flags whip in the harsh wind. "HALF-ACRE RANCHES! SNACK BARS! TRAVERTINE ENTRIES! $95 DOWN." It is the trail of an intention gone haywire, the flotsam of the New California. But after a while the signs thin out on Carnelian Avenue, and the houses are no longer the bright pastels of the Springtime Home owners but the faded bungalows of the people who grow a few grapes and keep a few chickens out here, and then the hill gets steeper and the road climbs and even the bungalows are few, and here—desolate, roughly surfaced, lined with eucalyptus and lemon groves—is Banyan Street.

Like so much of this country, Banyan suggests something curious and unnatural. The lemon groves are sunken, down a three- or four-foot retaining wall, so that one looks directly into their dense foliage, too lush, unsettlingly glossy, the greenery of nightmare; the fallen eucalyptus bark is too dusty, a place for snakes to breed. The stones look not like natural stones but like the rubble of some unmentioned upheaval. There are smudge pots, and a closed cistern. To one side of Banyan there is the flat valley, and to the other the San Bernardino Mountains, a dark mass looming too high, too fast, nine, ten, eleven thousand feet, right there above the lemon groves. At midnight on Banyan Street there is no light at all, and no sound except the wind in the eucalyptus and a muffled barking of dogs. There may be a kennel somewhere, or the dogs may be coyotes.

Banyan Street was the route Lucille Miller took home from the twenty-four-hour Mayfair Market on the night of October 7, 1964, a night when the moon was dark and the wind was blowing and she was out of milk, and Banyan Street was where, at about 12:30 a.m., her 1964 Volkswagen came to a sudden stop, caught fire, and began to burn. For an hour and fifteen minutes Lucille Miller ran up and down

Banyan calling for help, but no cars passed and no help came. At three o'clock that morning, when the fire had been put out and the California Highway Patrol officers were completing their report, Lucille Miller was still sobbing and incoherent, for her husband had been asleep in the Volkswagen. "What will I tell the children, when there's nothing left, nothing left in the casket," she cried to the friend called to comfort her. "How can I tell them there's nothing left?"

In fact there was something left, and a week later it lay in the Draper Mortuary Chapel in a closed bronze coffin blanketed with pink carnations. Some 200 mourners heard Elder Robert E. Denton of the Seventh-Day Adventist Church of Ontario speak of "the temper of fury that has broken out among us." For Gordon Miller, he said, there would be "no more death, no more heartaches, no more misunderstandings." Elder Ansel Bristol mentioned the "peculiar" grief of the hour. Elder Fred Jensen asked "what shall it profit a man, if he shall gain the whole world, and lose his own soul?" A light rain fell, a blessing in a dry season, and a female vocalist sang "Safe in the Arms of Jesus." A tape recording of the service was made for the widow, who was being held without bail in the San Bernardino County Jail on a charge of first-degree murder.

Of course she came from somewhere else, came off the prairie in search of something she had seen in a movie or heard on the radio, for this is a Southern California story. She was born on January 17, 1930, in Winnipeg, Manitoba, the only child of Gordon and Lily Maxwell, both schoolteachers and both dedicated to the Seventh-Day Adventist Church, whose members observe the Sabbath on Saturday, believe in an apocalyptic Second Coming, have a strong missionary tendency, and, if they are strict, do not smoke, drink, eat meat, use makeup, or wear jewelry, including wedding rings. By the time Lucille Maxwell enrolled at Walla Walla College in College Place, Washington, the Adventist school where her parents then taught, she was an eighteen-year-old possessed of unremarkable good looks and remarkable high spirits. "Lucille wanted to see the world," her father would say in retrospect, "and I guess she found out."

The high spirits did not seem to lend themselves to an extended course of study at Walla Walla College, and in the spring of 1949 Lucille Maxwell met and married Gordon ("Cork") Miller, a twenty-four-year-old graduate of Walla Walla and of the University of Oregon dental school, then stationed at Fort Lewis as a medical officer. "Maybe you could say it was love at first sight," Mr. Maxwell recalls. "Before they were ever formally introduced, he sent Lucille a dozen and a half roses with a card that said even if she didn't come out on a date with him, he hoped she'd find the roses pretty anyway." The Maxwells remember their daughter as a "radiant" bride.

Unhappy marriages so resemble one another that we do not need to know too much about the course of this one. There may or may not have been trouble on Guam, where Cork and Lucille Miller lived while he finished his Army duty. There may or may not have been problems in the small Oregon town where he first set up private practice. There appears to have been some disappointment about their move to California: Cork Miller had told friends that he wanted to become a doctor, that he was unhappy as a dentist and planned to enter the Seventh-Day Adventist College of Medical Evangelists at Loma Linda, a few miles south of San Bernardino. Instead he bought a dental practice in the west end of San Bernardino County, and the family settled there, in a modest house on the kind of street where there are always tricycles and revolving credit and dreams about bigger houses, better streets. That was 1957. By the summer of 1964 they had achieved the bigger house on the better street and the familiar accouterments of a family on its way up: the $30,000 a year, the three children for the Christmas card, the picture window, the family room, the newspaper photographs that showed "Mrs. Gordon Miller, Ontario Heart Fund Chairman. . . ." They were paying the familiar price for it. And they had reached the familiar season of divorce.

It might have been anyone's bad summer, anyone's siege of heat and nerves and migraine and money worries, but this one began particularly early and particularly badly. On April 24 an old friend, Elaine Hayton, died suddenly; Lucille Miller had seen her only the night before. During the month of May, Cork Miller was hospitalized briefly with a bleeding ulcer, and his usual reserve deepened into depression. He told his accountant that he was "sick of looking at open mouths," and threatened suicide. By July 8, the conventional tensions of love and money had reached the conventional impasse in the new house on the acre lot at 8488 Bella Vista, and Lucille Miller filed for divorce. Within a month, however, the Millers seemed reconciled. They saw a marriage counselor. They talked about a fourth child. It seemed that the marriage had reached the traditional truce, the point at which so many resign themselves to cutting both their losses and their hopes.

But the Millers' season of trouble was not to end that easily. October 7 began as a commonplace enough day, one of those days that sets the teeth on edge with its tedium, its small frustrations. The temperature reached 102° in San Bernardino that afternoon, and the Miller children were home from school because of Teachers' Institute. There was ironing to be dropped off. There was a trip to pick up a prescription for Nembutal, a trip to a self-service dry cleaner. In the early evening, an unpleasant accident with the Volkswagen: Cork Miller hit and killed a German shepherd, and afterward said that his head felt "like it had a Mack truck on it." It was something he often said. As of that evening Cork Miller was $63,479 in debt, including the $29,637 mortgage on the new house, a debt load which seemed oppressive to him. He was a man who wore his responsibilities uneasily, and complained of migraine headaches almost constantly.

He ate alone that night, from a TV tray in the living room. Later the Millers watched John Forsythe and Senta Berger in *See How They Run,* and when the movie ended, about eleven, Cork Miller suggested that they go out for milk. He wanted some hot chocolate. He took a blanket and pillow from the couch and climbed into the passenger seat of the Volkswagen. Lucille Miller remembers reaching over to lock his door as she backed down the driveway. By the time she left the Mayfair Market, and long before they reached Banyan Street, Cork Miller appeared to be asleep.

There is some confusion in Lucille Miller's mind about what happened between 12:30 a.m., when the fire broke out, and 1:50 a.m., when it was reported. She says that she was driving east on Banyan Street at about 35 m.p.h. when she felt the Volkswagen pull sharply to the right. The next thing she knew the car was on the embankment, quite near the edge of the retaining wall, and flames were shooting up behind her. She does not remember jumping out. She does remember prying up a stone with which she broke the window next to her husband, and then scrambling down the retaining wall to try to find a stick. "I don't know how I was going to push him out," she says. "I just thought if I had a stick, I'd push him out." She could not, and after a while she ran to the intersection of Banyan and Carnelian Avenue. There are no houses at that corner, and almost no traffic. After one car had passed without stopping, Lucille Miller ran back down Banyan toward the burning Volkswagen. She did not stop, but she slowed down, and in the flames she could see her husband. He was, she said, "just black."

At the first house up Sapphire Avenue, half a mile from the Volkswagen, Lucille Miller finally found help. There Mrs. Robert Swenson called the sheriff, and then, at Lucille Miller's request, she called Harold Lance, the Millers' lawyer and their close friend. When Harold Lance arrived he took Lucille Miller home to his wife, Joan. Twice Harold Lance and Lucille Miller returned to Banyan Street and talked to the Highway Patrol officers. A third time Harold Lance returned alone, and when he came back he said to Lucille Miller, "O.K. . . . you don't talk any more."

When Lucille Miller was arrested the next afternoon, Sandy Slagle was with her. Sandy Slagle was the intense, relentlessly loyal medical student who used to baby-sit for the Millers, and had been living as a member of the family since she graduated from high school in 1959. The Millers took her away from a difficult home situation, and she thinks of Lucille Miller not only as "more or less a mother or a sister" but as "the most wonderful character" she has ever known. On the night of the accident, Sandy Slagle was in her dormitory at Loma Linda University, but Lucille Miller called her early in the morning and asked her to come home. The doctor was there when Sandy Slagle arrived, giving Lucille Miller an injection of Nembutal. "She was crying as she was going under," Sandy Slagle recalls. "Over and over she'd say, 'Sandy, all the hours I spent trying to save him and now what are they trying to *do* to me?'"

At 1:30 that afternoon, Sergeant William Paterson and Detectives Charles Callahan and Joseph Karr of the Central Homicide Division arrived at 8488 Bella Vista. "One of them appeared at the bedroom door," Sandy Slagle remembers, "and said to Lucille, 'You've got ten minutes to get dressed or we'll take you as you are.' She was in her nightgown, you know, so I tried to get her dressed."

Sandy Slagle tells the story now as if by rote, and her eyes do not waver. "So I had her panties and bra on her and they opened the door again, so I got some Capris on her, you know, and a scarf." Her voice drops. "And then they just took her."

The arrest took place just twelve hours after the first report that there had been an accident on Banyan Street, a rapidity which would later prompt Lucille Miller's attorney to say that the entire case was an instance of trying to justify a reckless arrest. Actually what first caused the detectives who arrived on Banyan Street toward dawn that morning to give the accident more than routine attention were certain apparent physical inconsistencies. While Lucille Miller had said that she was driving about 35 m.p.h. when the car swerved to a stop, an examination of the cooling Volkswagen showed that it was in low gear, and that the parking rather than the driving lights were on. The front wheels, moreover, did not seem to be in exactly the position that Lucille Miller's description of the accident would suggest, and the right rear wheel was dug in deep, as if it had been spun in place. It seemed curious to the detectives, too, that a sudden stop from 35 m.p.h.—the same jolt which was presumed to have knocked over a gasoline can in the back seat and somehow started the fire—should have left two milk cartons upright on the back floorboard, and the remains of a Polaroid camera box lying apparently undisturbed on the back seat.

No one, however, could be expected to give a precise account of what did and did not happen in a moment of terror, and none of these inconsistencies seemed in themselves incontrovertible evidence of criminal intent. But they did interest the Sheriff's Office, as did Gordon Miller's apparent unconsciousness at the time of the accident, and the length of time it had taken Lucille Miller to get help. Something, moreover, struck the investigators as wrong about Harold Lance's attitude when he came back to Banyan Street the third time and found the investigation by no means over. "The way Lance was acting," the prosecuting attorney said later, "they thought maybe they'd hit a nerve."

And so it was that on the morning of October 8, even before the doctor had come to give Lucille Miller an injection to calm her, the San Bernardino County Sheriff's Office was trying to construct another version of what might have happened between 12:30 and 1:50 a.m. The hypothesis they would eventually present was based on the somewhat tortuous premise that Lucille Miller had undertaken a plan which failed: a plan to stop the car on the lonely road, spread gasoline over her presumably drugged husband, and, with a stick on the accelerator, gently "walk" the Volkswagen over the embankment, where it would tumble four feet down the retaining wall into the lemon grove and almost certainly explode. If this happened, Lucille Miller might then have somehow negotiated the two miles up Carnelian to Bella Vista in time to be home when the accident was discovered. This plan went awry, according to the Sheriff's Office hypothesis, when the car would not go over the rise of the embankment. Lucille Miller might have panicked then—after she had killed the engine the third or fourth time, say, out there on the dark road with the gasoline already spread and the dogs baying and the wind blowing and the unspeakable apprehension that a pair of headlights would suddenly light up Banyan Street and expose her there—and set the fire herself.

Although this version accounted for some of the physical evidence—the car in low because it had been started from a dead stop, the parking lights on because she could not do what needed doing without some light, a rear wheel spun in repeated attempts to get the car over the embankment, the milk cartons upright because there had been no sudden stop—it did not seem on its own any more or less credible than Lucille Miller's own story. Moreover, some of the physical evidence did seem to support her story: a nail in a front tire, a nine-pound rock found in the car, presumably the one with which she had broken the window in an attempt to save her husband. Within a few days an autopsy had established that Gordon Miller was alive when he burned, which did not particularly help the State's case, and that he had enough Nembutal and Sandoptal in his blood to put the average person to sleep, which did: on the other hand Gordon Miller habitually took both Nembutal and Fiorinal (a common headache prescription which contains Sandoptal), and had been ill besides.

It was a spotty case, and to make it work at all the State was going to have to find a motive. There was talk of unhappiness, talk of another man. That kind of motive, during the next few weeks, was what they set out to establish. They set out to find it in accountants' ledgers and double-indemnity clauses and motel registers, set out to determine what might move a woman who believed in all the promises of the middle class—a woman who had been chairman of the Heart Fund and who always knew a reasonable little dressmaker and who had come out of the bleak wild of prairie fundamentalism to find what she imagined to be the good life—what should drive such a woman to sit on a street called Bella Vista and look out her new picture window into the empty California sun and calculate how to burn her husband alive in a Volkswagen. They found the wedge they wanted closer at hand than they might have at first expected, for, as testimony would reveal later at the trial, it seemed that in December of 1963 Lucille Miller had begun an affair with the husband of one of her friends, a man whose daughter called her "Auntie Lucille," a man who might have seemed to have the gift for people and money and the good life that Cork Miller so noticeably lacked. The man was Arthwell Hayton, a well-known San Bernardino attorney and at one time a member of the district attorney's staff.

In some ways it was the conventional clandestine affair in a place like San Bernardino, a place where little is bright or graceful, where it is routine to misplace the future and easy to start looking for it in bed. Over the seven weeks that it would take to try Lucille Miller for murder, Assistant District Attorney Don A. Turner and defense attorney Edward P. Foley would between them unfold a curiously predictable story. There were the falsified motel registrations. There were the lunch dates, the afternoon drives in Arthwell Hayton's red Cadillac convertible. There were the interminable discussions of the wronged partners. There were the confidantes ("I knew everything," Sandy Slagle would insist fiercely later. "I knew every time, places, everything") and there were the words remembered from bad magazine stories ("Don't kiss me, it will trigger things," Lucille Miller remembered telling Arthwell Hayton in the parking lot of Harold's Club in Fontana after lunch one day) and there were the notes, the sweet exchanges: "Hi Sweetie Pie! You are my cup of tea!! Happy Birthday—you don't look a day over 29!! Your baby, Arthwell."

And, toward the end, there was the acrimony. It was April 24, 1964, when Arthwell Hayton's wife, Elaine, died suddenly, and nothing good happened after that. Arthwell Hayton had taken his cruiser, *Captain's Lady,* over to Catalina that weekend; he called home at nine o'clock Friday night, but did not talk to his wife because Lucille Miller answered the telephone and said that Elaine was showering. The next morning the Haytons' daughter found her mother in bed, dead. The newspapers reported the death as accidental, perhaps the result of an allergy to hair spray. When Arthwell Hayton flew home from Catalina that weekend, Lucille Miller met him at the airport, but the finish had already been written.

It was in the breakup that the affair ceased to be in the conventional mode and began to resemble instead the novels of James M. Cain, the movies of the late 1930's, all the dreams in which violence and threats and blackmail are made to seem commonplaces of middle-class life. What was most startling about the case that the State of California was preparing against Lucille Miller was something that had nothing to do with law at all, something that never appeared in the eight-column afternoon headlines but was always there between them: the revelation that the dream was teaching the dreamers how to live. Here is Lucille Miller talking to her lover sometime in the early summer of 1964, after he had indicated that, on the advice of his minister, he did not intend to see her any more: "First, I'm going to go to that dear pastor of yours and tell him a few things. . . . When I do tell him that, you won't be in the Redlands Church any more. . . . Look, Sonny Boy, if you think your reputation is going to be ruined, your life won't be worth two cents." Here is Arthwell Hayton, to Lucille Miller: "I'll go to Sheriff Frank Bland and tell him some things that I know about you until you'll wish you'd never heard of Arthwell Hayton." For an affair between a Seventh-Day Adventist dentist's wife and a Seventh-Day Adventist personal-injury lawyer, it seems a curious kind of dialogue.

"Boy, I could get that little boy coming and going," Lucille Miller later confided to Erwin Sprengle, a Riverside contractor who was a business partner of Arthwell Hayton's and a friend to both the lovers. (Friend or no, on this occasion he happened to have an induction coil attached to his telephone in order to tape Lucille Miller's call.) "And he hasn't got one thing on me that he can prove. I mean, I've got concrete—he has nothing concrete." In the same taped conversation with Erwin Sprengle, Lucille Miller mentioned a tape that she herself had surreptitiously made, months before, in Arthwell Hayton's car.

"I said to him, I said 'Arthwell, I just feel like I'm being used.' . . . He started sucking his thumb and he said 'I love you. . . . This isn't something that happened yesterday. I'd marry you tomorrow if I could. I don't love Elaine.' He'd love to hear that played back, wouldn't he?"

"Yeah," drawled Sprengle's voice on the tape. "That would be just a little incriminating, wouldn't it?"

"Just a *little* incriminating," Lucille Miller agreed. "It really *is.*"

Later on the tape, Sprengle asked where Cork Miller was.

"He took the children down to the church."

"You didn't go?"

"No."

"You're naughty."

It was all, moreover, in the name of "love"; everyone involved placed a magical faith in the efficacy of the very word. There was the significance that Lucille Miller saw in Arthwell's saying that he "loved" her, that he did not "love" Elaine. There was Arthwell insisting, later, at the trial, that he had never said it, that he may have "whispered sweet nothings in her ear" (as her defense hinted that he had whispered in many ears), but he did not remember bestowing upon her the special seal, saying the word, declaring "love." There was the summer evening when Lucille Miller and Sandy Slagle followed Arthwell Hayton down to his new boat in its mooring at Newport Beach and untied the lines with Arthwell aboard, Arthwell and a girl with whom he later testified he was drinking hot chocolate and watching television. "I did that on purpose," Lucille Miller told Erwin Sprengle later, "to save myself from letting my heart do something crazy."

January 11, 1965, was a bright warm day in Southern California, the kind of day when Catalina floats on the Pacific horizon and the air smells of orange blossoms and it is a long way from the bleak and difficult East, a long way from the cold, a long way from the past. A woman in Hollywood staged an all-night sit-in on the hood of her car to prevent repossession by a finance company. A seventy-year-old pensioner drove his station wagon at five miles an hour past three Gardena poker parlors and emptied three pistols and a twelve-gauge shotgun through their windows, wounding twenty-nine people. "Many young women become prostitutes just to have enough money to play cards," he explained in a note. Mrs. Nick Adams said that she was "not surprised" to hear her husband announce his divorce plans on the Les Crane Show, and, farther north, a sixteen-year-old jumped off the Golden Gate Bridge and lived.

And, in the San Bernardino County Courthouse, the Miller trial opened. The crowds were so bad that the glass courtroom doors were shattered in the crush, and from then on identification disks were issued to the first forty-three spectators in line. The line began forming at 6 a.m., and college girls camped at the courthouse all night, with stores of graham crackers and No-Cal.

All they were doing was picking a jury, those first few days, but the sensational nature of the case had already suggested itself. Early in December there had been an abortive first trial, a trial at which no evidence was ever presented because on the day the jury was seated the San Bernardino *Sun-Telegram* ran an "inside" story quoting Assistant District Attorney Don Turner, the prosecutor, as saying, "We are looking into the circumstances of Mrs. Hayton's death. In view of the current trial concerning the death of Dr. Miller, I do not feel I should comment on Mrs. Hayton's death." It seemed that there had been barbiturates in Elaine Hayton's blood, and there had seemed some irregularity about the way she was dressed on that morning when she was found under the covers, dead. Any doubts about the death at the time, however, had never gotten as far as the Sheriff's Office. "I guess somebody didn't want to rock the boat," Turner said later. "These were prominent people."

Although all of that had not been in the *Sun-Telegram*'s story, an immediate mistrial had been declared. Almost as immediately, there had been another development: Arthwell Hayton had asked newspapermen to an 11 a.m. Sunday morning press conference in his office. There had been television cameras, and flash bulbs popping. "As you gentlemen may know," Hayton had said, striking a note of stiff bonhomie, "there are very often women who become amorous toward their doctor or lawyer. This does not mean on the physician's or lawyer's part that there is any romance toward the patient or client."

"Would you deny that you were having an affair with Mrs. Miller?" a reporter had asked.

"I would deny that there was any romance on my part whatsoever."

It was a distinction he would maintain through all the wearing weeks to come.

So they had come to see Arthwell, these crowds who now milled beneath the dusty palms outside the courthouse, and they had also come to see Lucille, who appeared as a slight, intermittently pretty woman, already pale from lack of sun, a woman who would turn thirty-five before the trial was over and whose tendency toward haggardness was beginning to show, a meticulous woman who insisted, against her lawyer's advice, on coming to court with her hair piled high and lacquered. "I would've been happy if she'd come in with it hanging loose, but Lucille wouldn't do that," her lawyer said. He was Edward P. Foley, a small, emotional Irish Catholic who several times wept in the courtroom. "She has a great honesty, this woman," he added, "but this honesty about her appearance always worked against her."

By the time the trial opened, Lucille Miller's appearance included maternity clothes, for an official examination on December 18 had revealed that she was then three and a half months pregnant, a fact which made picking a jury even more difficult than usual, for Turner was asking the death penalty. "It's unfortunate but there it is," he would say of the pregnancy to each juror in turn, and finally twelve were seated, seven of them women, the youngest forty-one, an assembly of the very peers—housewives, a machinist, a truck driver, a grocery-store manager, a filing clerk—above whom Lucille Miller had wanted so badly to rise.

That was the sin, more than the adultery, which tended to reinforce the one for which she was being tried. It was implicit in both the defense and the prosecution that Lucille Miller was an erring woman, a woman who perhaps wanted too much. But to the prosecution she was not merely a woman who would want a new house and want to go to parties and run up high telephone bills ($1,152 in ten months), but a woman who would go so far as to murder her husband for his $80,000 in insurance, making it appear an accident in order to collect another $40,000 in double indemnity and straight accident policies. To Turner she was a woman who did not want simply her freedom and a reasonable alimony (she could have had that, the defense contended, by going through with her divorce suit), but wanted everything, a woman motivated by "love and greed." She was a "manipulator." She was a "user of people."

To Edward Foley, on the other hand, she was an impulsive woman who "couldn't control her foolish little heart." Where Turner skirted the pregnancy, Foley dwelt upon it, even calling the dead man's mother down from Washington to testify that her son had told her they were going to have another baby because Lucille felt that it would "do much to weld our home again in the pleasant relations that we used to have." Where the prosecution saw a "calculator," the defense saw a "blabbermouth," and in fact Lucille Miller did emerge as an ingenuous conversationalist. Just as, before her husband's death, she had confided in her friends about her love affair, so she chatted about it after his death, with the arresting sergeant. "Of course Cork lived with it for years, you know," her voice was heard to tell Sergeant Paterson on a tape made the morning after her arrest. "After Elaine died, he pushed the panic button one night and just asked me right out, and that, I think, was when he really—the first time he really faced it." When the sergeant asked why she had agreed to talk to him, against the specific instructions of her lawyers, Lucille Miller said airily, "Oh, I've always been basically quite an honest person. . . . I mean I can put a hat in the cupboard and say it cost ten dollars less, but basically I've always kind of just lived my life the way I wanted to, and if you don't like it you can take off."

The prosecution hinted at men other than Arthwell, and even, over Foley's objections, managed to name one. The defense called Miller suicidal. The prosecution produced experts who said that the Volkswagen fire could not have been accidental. Foley produced witnesses who said that it could have been. Lucille's father, now a junior-high-school teacher in Oregon, quoted Isaiah to reporters: *"Every tongue that shall rise against thee in judgment thou shalt condemn."* "Lucille did wrong, her affair," her mother said judiciously. "With her it was love. But with some I guess it's just passion." There was Debbie, the Millers' fourteen-year-old, testifying in a steady voice about how she and her mother had gone to a supermarket to buy the gasoline can the week before the accident. There was Sandy Slagle, in the courtroom every day, declaring that on at least one occasion Lucille Miller had prevented her husband not only from committing suicide but from committing suicide in such a way that it would appear an accident and ensure the double-indemnity payment. There was Wenche Berg, the pretty twenty-seven-year-old Norwegian governess to Arthwell Hayton's children, testifying that Arthwell had instructed her not to allow Lucille Miller to see or talk to the children.

Two months dragged by, and the headlines never stopped. Southern California's crime reporters were headquartered in San Bernardino for the duration: Howard Hertel from the *Times,* Jim Bennett and Eddy Jo Bernal from the *Herald-Examiner.* Two months in which the Miller trial was pushed off the *Examiner's* front page only by the Academy Award nominations and Stan Laurel's death. And finally, on March 2, after Turner had reiterated that it was a case of "love and greed," and Foley had protested that his client was being tried for adultery, the case went to the jury.

They brought in the verdict, guilty of murder in the first degree, at 4:50 p.m. on March 5. "She didn't do it," Debbie Miller cried, jumping up from the spectators' section. "She didn't *do* it." Sandy Slagle collapsed in her seat and began to scream. "Sandy, for God's sake please *don't,*" Lucille Miller said in a voice that carried across the courtroom, and Sandy Slagle was momentarily subdued. But as the jurors left the courtroom she screamed again: "You're murderers. . . . Every last one of you is a *murderer.*" Sheriff's deputies moved in then, each wearing a string tie that read "1965 SHERIFF'S RODEO," and Lucille Miller's father, that sad-faced junior-high-school teacher who believed in the word of Christ and the dangers of wanting to see the world, blew her a kiss off his fingertips.

The California Institution for Women at Frontera, where Lucille Miller is now, lies down where Euclid Avenue turns into country road, not too many miles from where she once lived and shopped and organized the Heart Fund Ball. Cattle graze across the road, and Rainbirds sprinkle the alfalfa. Frontera has a softball field and tennis courts, and looks as if it might be a California junior college, except that the trees are not yet high enough to conceal the concertina wire around the top of the Cyclone fence. On visitors' day there are big cars in the parking area, big Buicks and Pontiacs that belong to grandparents and sisters and fathers (not many of them belong to husbands), and some of them have bumper stickers that say "SUPPORT YOUR LOCAL POLICE."

A lot of California murderesses live here, a lot of girls who somehow misunderstood the promise. Don Turner put Sandra Garner here (and her husband in the gas chamber at San Quentin) after the 1959 desert killings known to crime reporters as "the soda-pop murders." Carole Tregoff is here, and has been ever since she was convicted of conspiring to murder Dr. Finch's wife in West Covina, which is not too far from San Bernardino. Carole Tregoff is in fact a nurse's aide in the prison hospital, and might have attended Lucille Miller had her baby been born at Frontera; Lucille Miller chose instead to have it outside, and paid for the guard who stood outside the delivery room in St. Bernardine's Hospital. Debbie Miller came to take the baby home from the hospital, in a white dress with pink ribbons, and Debbie was allowed to choose a name. She named the baby Kimi Kai. The children live with Harold and Joan Lance now, because Lucille Miller will probably spend ten years at Frontera. Don Turner waived his original request for the death penalty (it was generally agreed that he had demanded it only, in Edward Foley's words, "to get anybody with the slightest trace of human kindness in their veins off the jury"), and settled for life imprisonment with the possibility of parole. Lucille Miller does not like it at Frontera, and has had trouble adjusting. "She's going to have to learn humility," Turner says. "She's going to have to use her ability to charm, to manipulate."

The new house is empty now, the house on the street with the sign that says

PRIVATE ROAD
BELLA VISTA
DEAD END

The Millers never did get it landscaped, and weeds grow up around the fieldstone siding. The television aerial has toppled on the roof, and a trash can is stuffed with the debris of family life: a cheap suitcase, a child's game called "Lie Detector." There is a sign on what would have been the lawn, and the sign reads "ESTATE SALE." Edward Foley is trying to get Lucille Miller's case appealed, but there have been delays. "A trial always comes down to a matter of sympathy," Foley says wearily now. "I couldn't create sympathy for her." Everyone is a little weary now, weary and resigned, everyone except Sandy Slagle, whose bitterness is still raw. She lives in an apartment near the medical school in Loma Linda, and studies reports of the case in *True Police Cases* and *Official Detective Stories.* "I'd much rather we not talk about the Hayton business too much," she tells visitors, and she keeps a tape recorder running. "I'd rather talk about Lucille and what a wonderful person she is and how her rights were violated." Harold Lance does not talk to visitors at all. "We don't want to give away what we can sell," he explains pleasantly; an attempt was made to sell Lucille Miller's personal story to *Life,* but *Life* did not want to buy it. In the district attorney's offices they are prosecuting other murders now, and do not see why the Miller trial attracted so much attention. "It wasn't a very interesting murder as murders go," Don Turner says laconically. Elaine Hayton's death is no longer under investigation. "We know everything we want to know," Turner says.

Arthwell Hayton's office is directly below Edward Foley's. Some people around San Bernardino say that Arthwell Hayton suffered; others say that he did not suffer at all. Perhaps he did not, for time past is not believed to have any bearing upon time present or future, out in the golden land where every day the world is born anew. In any case, on October 17, 1965, Arthwell Hayton married again, married his children's pretty governess, Wenche Berg, at a service in the Chapel of the Roses at a retirement village near Riverside. Later the newlyweds were feted at a reception for seventy-five in the dining room of Rose Garden Village. The bridegroom was in black tie, with a white carnation in his buttonhole. The bride wore a long white *peau de soie* dress and carried a shower bouquet of sweetheart roses with stephanotis streamers. A coronet of seed pearls held her illusion veil.

QUESTIONS FOR DISCUSSION AND WRITING

1. In her preface to *Slouching toward Bethlehem,* a collection that includes "Some Dreamers of the Golden Dream," Didion says, "My only advantage as a reporter is that I am so physically small, so temperamentally unobtrusive, and so neurotically inarticulate that people tend to forget that my presence runs counter to their best interests. And it always does. That is one last thing to remember: *writers are always selling somebody out.*" Who—or what—is she "selling out" in "Some Dreamers of the Golden Dream"?

2. "This is a story about love and death in the golden land." So begins "Some Dreamers of the Golden Dream." Both the first line of the essay and the title imply that the setting itself is an important "character" in the narrative. Look at the descriptions of setting—of Southern California, of the West in general, of Banyan Street. How do those descriptions work thematically? How, in other words, do they help us understand what happened—and why it happened?

3. Didion crafts her prose carefully, often leaving until the end of a sentence a particularly important word or image. Writing of the sound of dogs heard in the night

air, she says, "There may be a kennel somewhere, or the dogs may be coyotes" (603). A little later, writing of Cork Miller's funeral, she ends the paragraph with the surprising information that Lucille Miller has been arrested for his murder: "A tape recording of the service was made for the widow, who was being held without bail in the San Bernardino County Jail on a charge of first-degree murder" (604). Find other such instances in which Didion delays an important piece of information. What are the purpose and effect of this use of suspense? How does the style reinforce the essay's themes and purposes?

4. Throughout "Some Dreamers of the Golden Dream" Didion includes what may seem like extraneous detail irrelevant to the story being told. We hear, for instance, about Mrs. Nick Adams's reaction to her actor-husband's talk-show announcement of his plans for divorce and of the sixteen-year-old who survived his jump from the Golden Gate Bridge (610). We hear that only news of Stan Laurel's death and the Academy Awards drove the Miller case out of the headlines (612) and that Lucille's new baby was named Kimi Kai by her sister. And the essay ends with something not about Lucille Miller but about Arthwell Hayton's marriage and his new bride's wedding dress. Why does Didion include these and other such details? What, if anything, do they have to do with the Millers' story?

MAKING CONNECTIONS: LOVE AND FRIENDSHIP

1. In literature, as in life, the love between parents and children is often complicated by the inability of each to live in the other's shoes or to recognize the need to live separate lives. Compare the family love described in two or three of the following: Hayden's "Those Winter Sundays," Hughes's "Mother to Son," Liu's "My Father's Martial Art," Mirikitani's "Desert Flowers," Song's "The Youngest Daughter," and Olsen's "I Stand Here Ironing." How well do parents and children know and understand each other? What is the source of their misunderstandings?

2. Compare the way sibling relationships are described in Walker's "Everyday Use" and Olsen's "I Stand Here Ironing." How similar are those descriptions to those you have observed and experienced in your own life? Are tensions between siblings in some way inevitable? If so, why?

3. Although they are very different in tone, Joyce's "Araby" and Munro's "The Found Boat" both focus on the nature of adolescent love. How similar are their treatments of the subject? If the boy in "Araby" had found himself on the river with the children in "The Found Boat," would he have joined them in their activities? If they had found themselves on the train to Araby, would they have shared the boy's dreams and passions?

4. Psychologists tell us that love and death are often intertwined in our imaginations and in our experiences, perhaps because both arouse strong emotions, perhaps because we use love in an attempt to ward off death. What are the connections between love and death in Faulkner's "A Rose for Emily," Hurston's "Sweat," and Didion's "Some Dreamers of the Golden Dream"? How strong are the bonds between the two of them? Can they be broken?

5. Look at the love and friendship relationships described in two or three of the works in this chapter. To what extent do people see love and close friendship as a

search for completion? To what extent does finding a second half allow someone to become a new person?

6. Love is satisfying partly because it invites us to lose, or complete, ourselves in another. But in losing ourselves, we may also risk losing our sense of identity, our sense of ourselves as individuals valuable in our own rights. Examine the tensions between love and fulfillment on the one hand and loss of identity on the other in two or three of the works from this chapter.

7. Do men and women think of love and friendship differently? Look at the way men and women characters, narrators, and speakers look at love and friendship in some of the works in this chapter. Do they describe these emotions in similar ways? Do they have the same expectations for them? Do male and female *authors* seem to have the same ideas about love and friendship?

8. How much does setting—one's time and place—affect one's definition of love and friendship and one's ability to love and be loved in return? Look at the significance of setting in two or three of the works in this chapter.

9. Communication between men and women is sometimes complicated by sexual feelings. In addition, some psychologists and linguists argue that men and women look at the world differently and speak different "languages." Looking at two or three works in this chapter, examine how viewpoints or modes of communication that seem distinctly male or female contribute to conflict and miscommunication.

10

Life Passages

CHAPTER INTRODUCTION

People have long noted that our sense of time changes as we grow older. To children, the few short years to adulthood may seem interminably long as they wait seemingly forever for the next birthday or summer vacation or for the time when they will no longer be "too little" to do what they want. Even as adults, we may remember that childhood seemed long, and we marvel at the long stretch of time that was "the fourth grade," when last year passed so quickly. Whereas adults often look nostalgically back at the past, children often look ahead, impatient to grow up. They anticipate adulthood, playing at being Mommy or Daddy, at being teacher or fireman. Yet despite their play, they do not fully believe in their roles. Few children ever really imagine themselves as bald or middle-aged, unable to appreciate the pleasures of roller coasters and mud fights. Even as they anticipate the pleasures and powers of adulthood, children find themselves unable—or unwilling—to grasp the changes that will lead to physical decay or mental stodginess. The child may see him- or herself as the Eternal Child, always playing at adulthood but never actually moving closer toward it.

All this may be just another way of saying that children have no real concept of childhood. They can neither fully appreciate it for what it is nor see it as a stage in a larger lifetime. For that reason, children see a play such as *Peter Pan* very differently than adults do. Like adults, children may very well understand the appeal of Peter, the boy who never grows up. What they may miss in the play, however, is the sadness that tinges Never Land. Peter, finally, can become Eternal Boy only by forgetting—by forgetting those he loves and those he hates. Go to the window as often as he may, he can never fully enter the home and become part of a real family. He is excluded by his exemption from mortality—his exemption from being human. He is Eternal Boy only because he is not really a human boy at all.

Watching real children at play, adults may be both charmed and saddened by the child's eagerness to grow up. Even more intense may be the adult's mixture of nostalgia and dread as the child reaches puberty, that rather precarious border between childhood and adulthood. That very precariousness may, in part, be behind the message of a folktale such as Little Red Riding Hood—a folktale that presents us with a charming little girl but also makes us all too aware of the potential seductions of a "wolf." We see Little Red Riding Hood with the double vision of adulthood, the vision that allows us to see the girl and the potential woman in one. What may seem like a "nursery tale" to a child holds warning implications to the knowing adult.

In addition to the moral complexities that come with sexual maturity, physical maturation carries within it the seeds of mortality. To reproduce—or to have the capability to reproduce—is to perpetuate one's species and one's self in future generations. At the same time, in a sense, it is also to die. If that seems fanciful, think of the many animals who die once offspring have been produced. Similarly, it is no accident that, during the Renaissance, "to die" also meant to have sexual intercourse, for the act of intercourse was thought literally to shorten one's life. The birth of a child is the birth of new life. Inherent in that new life, however, is death itself. Not only do we begin to die as soon as we are born, but with each new generation the older generations find themselves displaced, pushed closer to the grave. Such is the recognition the young father and poet Donald Hall came to on the birth of his son:

DONALD HALL (1928–)

My son, my executioner   1955

My son, my executioner,
   I take you in my arms,
Quiet and small and just astir,
   And whom my body warms.

5   Sweet death, small son, our instrument
      Of immortality,
Your cries and hungers document
      Our bodily decay.

We twenty-five and twenty-two,
10   Who seemed to live forever,
Observe enduring life in you
      And start to die together.

The infant son is both "Sweet death" and "our instrument / Of immortality." The generations march forward into seeming perpetuity, but the cycle of life depends not only on birth but also on death.

The recognition that one will die may be said to be a defining recognition of adulthood. That doesn't mean, however, that death defines life. It is only *part* of the definition. In this chapter, you will be reading works that look at all the stages of life: at childhood, adolescence, adulthood, old age, and death. Often the writers will draw clear demarcations between these stages. The adult may feel the pull of nostalgia, that sweet and sad looking back to the past, especially to the joys of lost childhood. Some great lesson may signal a "coming of age," the coming of emotional maturity. Writers such as Emily Dickinson may even imagine what it feels like to die—whereas other poets look at what they hope will be remembered of them after death.

Though writers often focus on one stage or another, the boundaries between the parts of life are not fully distinct. The child may play at being an adult—but the adult may also play at being a child. One might say, in fact, that the adult still *is* a child, for the child's body and mind have been dissolved into the adult's. We are told that nothing is ever forgotten, that our minds hold all our memories and experiences, if only we could remember to remember them. As adults, we are still the children we once were, for better or worse. Psychologists tell us that many adults continue throughout their lives to act out their childhood patterns, to respond to bosses or other authority figures as they responded to parents, or to seek mates who will help them reenact their parents' marriages, or to interact with peers as the Older Sister or the Little Brother. If at some level we remain the children we were, we also become the adults we knew. Many a middle-aged person has been startled to see staring out of the mirror the face of a parent. We see such child/adult confusion in E. B. White's "Once More to the Lake": as an adult White brings his son to a camp where he had spent his own boyhood summers. As they reenact his childhood summers, White becomes both the child he was and the father he had, child and adult at once.

As each of us passes through the stages of life, the lines between the stages, between child and adult, son or daughter and parent, thus blur. As you look at the chapter's frontispiece, you may see the skull or you may see the young lady looking in the mirror. Once you recognize the optical illusion, however, you will see both, for the skull has always existed in the young lady, just as the young lady exists in the skull.

AN ALBUM OF RETELLINGS

Childhood and Innocence: Little Red Riding Hood

CHARLES PERRAULT (1628–1703)

Little Red Riding Hood _____ *1697*

Once upon a time there was a little village girl, the prettiest that had ever been seen. Her mother doted on her. Her grandmother was even fonder, and made her a little red hood, which became her so well that everywhere she went by the name of Little Red Riding Hood.

One day her mother, who had just made and baked some cakes, said to her:

"Go and see how your grandmother is, for I have been told that she is ill. Take her a cake and this little pot of butter."

Little Red Riding Hood set off at once for the house of her grandmother, who lived in another village.

On her way through a wood she met old Father Wolf. He would have very much liked to eat her, but dared not do so on account of some wood-cutters who were in the forest. He asked her where she was going. The poor child, not knowing that it was dangerous to stop and listen to a wolf, said:

"I am going to see my grandmother, and am taking her a cake and a pot of butter which my mother has sent to her."

"Does she live far away?" asked the Wolf.

"Oh, yes," replied Little Red Riding Hood; "it is yonder by the mill which you can see right below there, and it is the first house in the village."

"Well now," said the Wolf, "I think I shall go and see her too. I will go by this path, and you by that path, and we will see who gets there first."

The Wolf set off running with all his might by the shorter road, and the little girl continued on her way by the longer road. As she went she amused herself by gathering nuts, running after the butterflies, and making nosegays of the wild flowers which she found.

The Wolf was not long in reaching the grandmother's house.

He knocked. *Toc Toc.*

"Who is there?"

"It is your granddaughter, Red Riding Hood," said the Wolf, disguising his voice, "and I bring you a cake and a little pot of butter as a present from my mother."

The worthy grandmother was in bed, not being very well, and cried out to him:

"Pull out the peg and the latch will fall."

The Wolf drew out the peg and the door flew open. Then he sprang upon the poor old lady and ate her up in less than no time, for he had been more than three days without food.

After that he shut the door, lay down in the grandmother's bed, and waited for Little Red Riding Hood.

Presently she came and knocked. *Toc Toc.*

"Who is there?"

Now Little Red Riding Hood on hearing the Wolf's gruff voice was at first frightened, but thinking that her grandmother had a bad cold, she replied:

"It is your granddaughter, Red Riding Hood, and I bring you a cake and a little pot of butter from my mother."

Softening his voice, the Wolf called out to her:

"Pull out the peg and the latch will fall."

Little Red Riding Hood drew out the peg and the door flew open.

When he saw her enter, the Wolf hid himself in the bed beneath the counterpane.

"Put the cake and the little pot of butter on the bin," he said, "and come up on the bed with me."

Little Red Riding Hood took off her clothes and climbed into the bed. She was astonished to see what her grandmother looked like in her nightgown.

"Grandmother," she said, "What big arms you have!"

"The better to hug you with, my child."

"Grandmother, what big legs you have!"

"The better to run with, my child."

"Grandmother, what big ears you have!"

"The better to hear with, my child."

"Grandmother, what big eyes you have!"

"The better to see with, my child."

"Grandmother, what big teeth you have!"

"The better to eat you with!"

Upon saying these words, the wicked wolf threw himself on Little Red Riding Hood and gobbled her up.

Moral

From this story one learns that children,
Especially young girls,
Pretty, well-bred, and genteel,
Are wrong to listen to just anyone,
And it's not at all strange,
If a wolf ends up eating them.
I say a wolf, but not all wolves
Are exactly the same.
Some are perfectly charming,
Not loud, brutal, or angry,
But tame, pleasant, and gentle,
Following young ladies
Right into their homes, into their chambers,
But watch out if you haven't learned that tame wolves
Are the most dangerous of all.

BROTHERS GRIMM
(Jacob 1785–1863; Wilhelm 1786–1859)

Little Red Cap _____ 1812

Once upon a time there was a dear little girl. If you set eyes on her you could not but love her. The person who loved her most of all was her grandmother, and she could never give the child enough. Once she made her a little cap of red velvet. Since it was so becoming and since she wanted to wear it all the time, everyone called her Little Red Cap.

One day her mother said to her: "Look, Little Red Cap. Here's a piece of cake and a bottle of wine. Take them to your grandmother. She is ill and feels weak, and they will give her strength. You'd better start now before it gets too hot, and when you're out in the woods, walk properly and don't stray from the path. Otherwise you'll fall and break the glass, and then there'll be nothing for Grandmother. And when you enter her room, don't forget to say good morning, and don't go peeping in all the corners of the room."

"I'll do just as you say," Little Red Cap promised her mother.

Grandmother lived deep in the woods, half an hour's walk from the village. No sooner had Little Red Cap set foot in the forest than she met the wolf. Little Red Cap had no idea what a wicked beast he was, and so she wasn't in the least afraid of him.

"Good morning, Little Red Cap," he said.

"Thank you kindly, wolf."

"Where are you headed so early in the morning, Little Red Cap?"

"To my grandmother's."

"What's that you've got under your apron?"

"Cake and wine. Yesterday we baked and Grandmother, who is sick and feels weak, needs something to make her feel better."

"Where does your grandmother live, Little Red Cap?"

"It's another quarter of an hour's walk into the woods. Her house is right under three large oaks. You must know the place from the hazel hedges near it," said Little Red Cap.

The wolf thought to himself: "That tender young thing will make a dainty morsel. She'll be even tastier than the old woman. If you're really crafty, you'll get them both."

He walked for a while beside Little Red Cap. Then he said: "Little Red Cap, have you seen the beautiful flowers all about? Why don't you look around for a while? I don't think you've even noticed how sweetly the birds are singing. You are walking along as if you were on the way to school, and yet it's so heavenly out here in the woods."

Little Red Cap opened her eyes wide and saw how the sunbeams were dancing this way and that through the trees and how there were beautiful flowers all about. She thought to herself: "If you bring a fresh bouquet to Grandmother, she will be overjoyed. It's still so early in the morning that I'm sure to get there in plenty of time."

She left the path and ran off into the woods looking for flowers. As soon as she picked one she saw an even more beautiful one somewhere else and went after it, and so she went deeper and deeper into the woods.

The wolf went straight to Grandmother's house and knocked at the door. "Who's there?"

"Little Red Cap, I've brought some cake and wine. Open the door."

"Just raise the latch," Grandmother called out. "I'm too weak to get out of bed."

The wolf raised the latch, and the door swung wide open. Without saying a word, he went straight to Grandmother's bed and gobbled her up. Then he put on her clothes and her nightcap, lay down in her bed, and drew the curtains.

Meanwhile, Little Red Cap had been running around looking for flowers. When she finally had so many that she couldn't carry them all, she suddenly remembered Grandmother and set off again on the path to her house. She was surprised to find the door open, and when she stepped into the house, she had such a strange feeling that she thought to herself: "Oh, my goodness, I'm usually so glad to be at Grandmother's, but today I feel so nervous."

She called out a greeting but there was no answer. Then she went to the bed and drew back the curtains. Grandmother was lying there with her nightcap pulled down over her face. She looked very strange.

"Oh, Grandmother, what big ears you have!"

"The better to hear you with."

"Oh, Grandmother, what big eyes you have!"

"The better to see you with."

"Oh, Grandmother, what big hands you have!"

"The better to grab you with!"

"Oh, Grandmother, what a big, scary mouth you have!"

"The better to eat you with!"

No sooner had the wolf spoken those words than he leaped out of bed and gobbled up poor Little Red Cap.

Once the wolf had satisfied his desires, he lay down again in bed, fell asleep, and began to snore very loudly. A huntsman happened to be passing by the house just then and thought to himself: "How the old woman is snoring! You'd better check to see what's wrong." He walked into the house and when he got to the bed he saw that the wolf was lying in it.

"I've found you at last, you old sinner," he said. "I've been after you for a while now."

He pulled out his musket and was about to take aim when he realized that the wolf might have eaten Grandmother and that she could still be saved. Instead of firing, he took out a pair of scissors and began cutting open the belly of the sleeping wolf. After making a few snips, he could see a red cap faintly. After making a few more cuts, the girl jumped out, crying: "Oh, how terrified I was! It was so dark in the wolf's belly!" And then the old grandmother found her way out alive, though she could hardly breathe. Little Red Cap quickly fetched some large stones and filled the wolf's belly with them. When he awoke, he was about to bound off, but the stones were so heavy that his legs collapsed and he fell down dead.

All three were overjoyed. The huntsman skinned the wolf and went home with the pelt. Grandmother ate the cake and drank the wine Little Red Cap had brought her and recovered her health. Little Red Cap thought to herself: "Never again will you stray from the path and go into the woods, when your mother has forbidden it."

There is also a story about another wolf who met Little Red Cap on the way to Grandmother's, as she was taking her some cakes. The wolf tried to divert her from the path, but Little Red Cap was on her guard and kept right on going. She told her grandmother that she had met the wolf and that he had greeted her. But he had looked at her in such an evil way that "If we hadn't been out in the open, he would have gobbled me right up."

"Well then," said Grandmother. "We'll just lock that door so he can't get in."

Not much later the wolf knocked at the door and called out: "Open the door, Grandmother, it's Little Red Cap. I'm bringing you some cakes."

The two kept quiet and didn't open the door. Then old Grayhead circled the house a few times and finally jumped up on the roof. He was planning on waiting until Little Red Cap went home. Then he was going to creep up after her and gobble her up in the dark. But Grandmother guessed what he had on his mind. There was a big stone trough in front of the house. She said to the child: "Here's a bucket, Little Red Cap. Yesterday I cooked some sausages. Take the water in which they were boiled and pour it into the trough."

Little Red Cap kept carrying water until that big, big trough was completely full. The smell of those sausages reached the wolf's nostrils. His neck was stretched out so long from sniffing and looking around that he lost his balance and began to slide down. He went right down the roof into the trough and was drowned. Little Red Cap walked home cheerfully, and no one did her any harm.

QUESTIONS FOR DISCUSSION AND WRITING

1. Although Perrault and the Grimms tell what is basically the same story, the two versions of "Little Red Riding Hood" contain some important differences. Compare and contrast the two versions' handling of the following elements. How does the comparison illuminate the two stories' themes and characters? Which of the two versions do you find more effective?

     Little Red Riding Hood's leave-taking from her mother
     The function of the woodsman
     The accounts of what finally happens to Little Red Riding Hood and her
        grandmother
2. Perrault's story ends with a poetic moral, the Grimms' version with an epilogue about another encounter with the wolf. How do the epilogues function?
3. In some other versions of the "Little Red Riding Hood" story, the moral has more to do with Little Red Riding Hood's character than it does with the danger presented by strangers. What evidence do you find that Little Red Riding Hood is in some way responsible for her and her grandmother's predicaments? To what extent do we find her behavior blameworthy?
4. In discussing these stories with others, we discovered that many have heard significantly different versions of the "Little Red Riding Hood" tale. If you have heard a different version from the ones presented here, how is your version different? How might your version reflect the needs, desires, and values of those who told you the story (or their sense of your needs and desires)?

TANITH LEE (1947–   )
Wolfland   *1983*

   When the summons arrived from Anna the Matriarch, Lisel did not wish to obey. The twilit winter had already come, and the great snows were down, spreading their aprons of shining ice, turning the trees to crystal candelabra. Lisel wanted to stay in the city, skating fur-clad on the frozen river beneath the torches, dancing till four in the morning, a vivid blonde in the flame-bright ballrooms, breaking hearts and not minding, lying late next day like a cat in her warm, soft bed. She did not want to go traveling several hours into the north to visit Anna the Matriarch.

   Lisel's mother had been dead sixteen years, all Lisel's life. Her father had let her have her own way, in almost everything, for about the same length of time. But Anna the Matriarch, Lisel's maternal grandmother, was exceedingly rich. She lived thirty miles from the city, in a great wild château in the great wild forest.

A portrait of Anna as a young widow hung in the gallery of Lisel's father's house, a wicked-looking, bone-pale person in a black dress, with rubies and diamonds at her throat, and in her ivory yellow hair. Even in her absence, Anna had always had a say in things. A recluse, she had still manipulated like a puppet-master from behind the curtain of the forest. Periodic instructions had been sent, pertaining to Lisel. The girl must be educated by this or that method. She must gain this or that accomplishment, read this or that book, favor this or that cologne or color or jewel. The latter orders were always uncannily apposite and were often complemented by applicable—and sumptuous—gifts. The summons came in company with such. A swirling cloak of scarlet velvet leapt like a fire from its box to Lisel's hands. It was lined with albino fur, all but the hood, which was lined with the finest and heaviest red brocade. A clasp of gold joined the garment at the throat, the two portions, when closed, forming Anna's personal device, a many-petaled flower. Lisel had exclaimed with pleasure, embracing the cloak, picturing herself flying in it across the solid white river like a dangerous blood-red rose. Then the letter fell from its folds.

Lisel had never seen her grandmother, at least, not intelligently, for Anna had been in her proximity on one occasion only: the hour of her birth. Then, one glimpse had apparently sufficed. Anna had snatched it, and sped away from her son-in-law's house and the salubrious city in a demented black carriage. Now, as peremptory as then, she demanded that Lisel come to visit her before the week was out. Over thirty miles, into the uncivilized northern forest, to the strange mansion in the snow.

"Preposterous," said Lisel's father. "The woman is mad, as I've always suspected."

"I shan't go," said Lisel.

They both knew quite well that she would.

One day, every considerable thing her grandmother possessed would pass to Lisel, providing Lisel did not incur Anna's displeasure.

Half a week later, Lisel was on the northern road.

She sat amid cushions and rugs, in a high sled strung with silver bells, and drawn by a single black-satin horse. Before Lisel perched her driver, the whip in his hand, and a pistol at his belt, for the way north was not without its risks. There were, besides, three outriders, also equipped with whips, pistols and knives, and muffled to the brows in fur. No female companion was in evidence. Anna had stipulated that it would be unnecessary and superfluous for her grandchild to burden herself with a maid.

But the whips had cracked, the horses had started off. The runners of the sled had smoothly hissed, sending up lace-like sprays of ice. Once clear of the city, the north road opened like a perfect skating floor of milky glass, dim-lit by the fragile winter sun smoking low on the horizon. The silver bells sang, and the fierce still air through which the horses dashed broke on Lisel's cheeks like the coldest champagne. Ablaze in her scarlet cloak, she was exhilarated and began to forget she had not wanted to come.

After about an hour, the forest marched up out of the ground and swiftly enveloped the road on all sides.

There was presently an insidious, but generally perceptible change. Between the walls of the forest there gathered a new silence, a silence which was, if anything, *alive*, a personality which attended any humanly noisy passage with a cruel and resentful interest. Lisel stared up into the narrow lane of sky above. They might have been moving along the channel of a deep and partly-frozen stream. When the drowned sun flashed through, splinters of light scattered and went out as if in water.

The tall pines in their pelts of snow seemed poised to lurch across the road.

The sled had been driving through the forest for perhaps another hour, when a wolf wailed somewhere amid the trees. Rather than break the silence of the place, the cry seemed born of the silence, a natural expression of the landscape's cold solitude and immensity.

The outriders touched the pistols in their belts, almost religiously, and the nearest of the three leaned to Lisel.

"Madam Anna's house isn't far from here. In any case we have our guns, and these horses could race the wind."

"I'm not afraid," Lisel said haughtily. She glanced at the trees, "I've never seen a wolf. I should be interested to see one."

Made sullen by Lisel's pert reply, the outrider switched tactics. From trying to reassure her, he now ominously said: "Pray you don't, m'mselle. One wolf generally means a pack, and once the snow comes, they're hungry."

"As my father's servant, I would expect you to sacrifice yourself for me, of course," said Lisel. "A fine strong man like you should keep a pack of wolves busy long enough for the rest of us to escape."

The man scowled and spurred away from her.

Lisel smiled to herself. She was not at all afraid, not of the problematical wolves, not even of the eccentric grandmother she had never before seen. In a way, Lisel was looking forward to the meeting, now her annoyance at vacating the city had left her. There had been so many bizarre tales, so much hearsay. Lisel had even caught gossip concerning Anna's husband. He had been a handsome princely man, whose inclinations had not matched his appearance. Lisel's mother had been sent to the city to live with relations to avoid this monster's outbursts of perverse lust and savagery. He had allegedly died one night, mysteriously and luridly murdered on one of the forest tracks. This was not the history Lisel had got from her father, to be sure, but she had always partly credited the more extravagant version. After all, Anna the Matriarch was scarcely commonplace in her mode of life or her attitude to her granddaughter.

Yes, indeed, rather than apprehension, Lisel was beginning to entertain a faintly unholy glee in respect of the visit and the insights it might afford her.

A few minutes after the wolf had howled, the road took a sharp bend, and emerging around it, the party beheld an unexpected obstacle in the way. The driver of the sled cursed softly and drew hard on the reins, bringing the horse to a standstill. The outriders similarly halted. Each peered ahead to where, about twenty yards along the road, a great black carriage blotted the white snow.

A coachman sat immobile on the box of the black carriage, muffled in coal-black furs and almost indistinguishable from them. In forceful contrast, the carriage horses were blonds, and restless, tossing their necks, lifting their feet. A single creature stood on the track between the carriage and the sled. It was too small to be a man, too curiously proportioned to be simply a child.

"What's this?" demanded the third of Lisel's outriders, he who had spoken earlier of the wolves. It was an empty question, but had been a long time in finding a voice for all that.

"I think it is my grandmother's carriage come to meet me," declared Lisel brightly, though, for the first, she had felt a pang of apprehension.

This was not lessened, when the dwarf came loping toward them, like a small, misshapen, furry dog and, reaching the sled, spoke to her, ignoring the others.

"You may leave your escort here and come with us."

Lisel was struck at once by the musical quality of his voice, while out of the shadow of his hood emerged the face of a fair and melancholy angel. As she stared at him, the men about her raised their objections.

"We're to go with m'mselle to her grandmother's house."

"You are not necessary," announced the beautiful dwarf, glancing at them with un-interest. "You are already on the Lady Anna's lands. The coachman and I are all the protection your mistress needs. The Lady Anna does not wish to receive you on her estate."

"What proof," snarled the third outrider, "that you're from Madame's château? Or that she told you to say such a thing. You could have come from anyplace, from Hell itself most likely, and they crushed you in the door as you were coming out."

The riders and the driver laughed brutishly. The dwarf paid no attention to the insult. He drew from his glove one delicate, perfectly formed hand, and in it a folded letter. It was easy to recognize the Matriarch's sanguine wax and the imprint of the petaled flower. The riders brooded, and the dwarf held the letter toward Lisel. She accepted it with an uncanny but pronounced reluctance.

"*Chère,*" it said in its familiar, indeed its unmistakable, characters, "*Why are you delaying the moment when I may look at you? Beautiful has already told you, I think, that your escort may go home. Anna is giving you her own escort, to guide you on the last laps of the journey. Come! Send the men away and step into the carriage.*"

Lisel, reaching the word, or rather the name, Beautiful, had glanced involuntar-ily at the dwarf, oddly frightened at its horrid contrariness and its peculiar truth. A foreboding had clenched around her young heart, and, for a second, inexplicable ter-ror. It was certainly a dreadful dilemma. She could refuse, and refuse thereby the goodwill, the gifts, the ultimate fortune her grandmother could bestow. Or she could brush aside her silly childish fears and walk boldly from the sled to the carriage. Surely, she had always known Madame Anna was an eccentric. Had it not been a source of intrigued curiosity but a few moments ago?

Lisel made her decision.

"Go home," she said regally to her father's servants. "My grandmother is wise and would hardly put me in danger."

The men grumbled, glaring at her, and as they did so, she got out of the sled and moved along the road toward the stationary and funereal carriage. As she came closer, she made out the flower device stamped in gilt on the door. Then the dwarf had darted ahead of her, seized the door, and was holding it wide, bowing to his knees, thus almost into the snow. A lock of pure golden hair spilled across his forehead.

Lisel entered the carriage and sat on the somber cushions. Courageous pru-dence (or greed) had triumphed.

The door was shut. She felt the slight tremor as Beautiful leapt on the box be-side the driver.

Morose and indecisive, the men her father had sent with her were still lingering on the ice between the trees, as she was driven away.

She must have slept, dazed by the continuous rocking of the carriage, but all at once she was wide awake, clutching in alarm at the upholstery. What had roused her was a unique and awful choir. The cries of wolves.

Quite irresistibly she pressed against the window and stared out, impelled to look for what she did not, after all, wish to see. And what she saw was unreassuring.

A horde of wolves was running, not merely in pursuit, but actually alongside the carriage. Pale they were, a pale almost luminous brownish shade, which made them seem phantasmal against the snow. Their small but jewel-like eyes glinted, glowed and burned. As they ran, their tongues lolling sideways from their mouths like those of huge hunting dogs, they seemed to smile up at her, and her heart turned over.

Why was it, she wondered, with panic-stricken anger, that the coach did not go faster and so outrun the pack? Why was it the brutes had been permitted to gain as much distance as they had? Could it be they had already plucked the coachman and the dwarf from the box and devoured them—she tried to recollect if, in her dozing, she had registered masculine shrieks of fear and agony—and that the horses plunged on. Imagination, grown detailed and pessimistic, soon dispensed with these images, replacing them with that of great pepper-colored paws scratching on the frame of the coach, the grisly talons ripping at the door, at last a wolf's savage mask thrust through it, and her own frantic and pointless screaming, in the instants before her throat was silenced by the meeting of narrow yellow fangs.

Having run the gamut of her own premonition, Lisel sank back on the seat and yearned for a pistol, or at least a knife. A malicious streak in her lent her the extraordinary bravery of desiring to inflict as many hurts on her killers as she was able before they finished her. She also took space to curse Anna the Matriarch. How the wretched old woman would grieve and complain when the story reached her. The clean-picked bones of her granddaughter had been found a mere mile or so from her château, in the rags of a blood-red cloak; by the body a golden clasp, rejected as inedible. . . .

A heavy thud caused Lisel to leap to her feet, even in the galloping, bouncing carriage. There at the door, grinning in on her, the huge face of a wolf, which did not fall away. Dimly she realized it must impossibly be balancing itself on the running board of the carriage, its front paws raised and somehow keeping purchase on the door. With one sharp determined effort of its head, it might conceivably smash in the pane of the window. The glass would lacerate, and the scent of its own blood further inflame its starvation. The eyes of it, doused by the carriage's gloom, flared up in two sudden pupilless ovals of fire, like two little portholes into hell.

With a shrill howl, scarcely knowing what she did, Lisel flung herself at the closed door and the wolf the far side of it. Her eyes also blazed, her teeth also were bared, and her nails raised as if to claw. Her horror was such that she appeared ready to attack the wolf in its own primeval mode, and as her hands struck the glass against its face, the wolf shied and dropped away.

In that moment, Lisel heard the musical voice of the dwarf call out from the box, some wordless whoop, and a tall gatepost sprang by.

Lisel understood they had entered the grounds of the Matriarch's château. And, a moment later, learned, though did not understand, that the wolves had not followed them beyond the gateway.

2

The Matriarch sat at the head of the long table. Her chair, like the table, was slender, carved and intensely polished. The rest of the chairs, though similarly high-backed and angular, were plain and dull, including the chair to which Lisel had been conducted. Which increased Lisel's annoyance, the petty annoyance to which her more eloquent emotions of fright and rage had given way, on entering the domestic, if curious, atmosphere of the house. And Lisel must strive to conceal her ill-temper. It was difficult.

The château, ornate and swarthy under its pointings of snow, retained an air of decadent magnificence, which was increased within. Twin stairs flared from an immense great hall. A hearth, large as a room, and crow-hooded by its enormous mantel, roared with muffled firelight. There was scarcely a furnishing that was not at least two hundred years old, and many were much older. The very air seemed tinged by the somber wood, the treacle darkness of the draperies, the old gold gleams of picture frames, gilding and tableware.

At the center of it all sat Madame Anna, in her eighty-first year, a weird apparition of improbable glamour. She appeared, from no more than a yard or so away, to be little over fifty. Her skin, though very dry, had scarcely any lines in it, and none of the pleatings and collapses Lisel generally associated with the elderly. Anna's hair had remained blonde, a fact Lisel was inclined to attribute to some preparation out of a bottle, yet she was not sure. The lady wore black as she had done in the portrait of her youth, a black starred over with astonishing jewels. But her nails were very long and discolored, as were her teeth. These two incontrovertible proofs of old age gave Lisel a perverse satisfaction. Grandmother's eyes, on the other hand, were not so reassuring. Brilliant eyes, clear and very likely sharp-sighted, of a pallid silvery brown. Unnerving eyes, but Lisel did her best to stare them out, though when Anna spoke to her, Lisel now answered softly, ingratiatingly.

There had not, however, been much conversation, after the first clamor at the doorway:

"We were chased by wolves!" Lisel had cried "Scores of them! Your coachman is a dolt who doesn't know enough to carry a pistol. I might have been killed."

"You were not," said Anna, imperiously standing in silhouette against the giant window of the hall, a stained glass of what appeared to be a hunting scene, done in murky reds and staring white.

"No thanks to your servants. You promised me an escort—the only reason I sent my father's men away."

"You had your escort."

Lisel had choked back another flood of sentences: she did not want to get on the wrong side of this strange relative. Nor had she liked the slight emphasis on the word "escort."

The handsome ghastly dwarf had gone forward into the hall, lifted the hem of Anna's long mantle, and kissed it. Anna had smoothed off his hood and caressed the bright hair beneath.

"Beautiful wasn't afraid," said Anna decidedly. "But, then, my people know the wolves will not harm them."

An ancient tale came back to Lisel in that moment. It concerned certain human denizens of the forests, who had power over wild beasts. It occurred to Lisel that mad old Anna liked to fancy herself a sorceress, and Lisel said fawningly: "I should have known I'd be safe. I'm sorry for my outburst, but I don't know the forest as you do. I was afraid."

In her allotted bedroom, a silver ewer and basin stood on a table. The embroideries on the canopied bed were faded but priceless. Antique books stood in a case, catching the firelight, a vast yet random selection of the poetry and prose of many lands. From the bedchamber window, Lisel could look out across the clearing of the park, the white sweep of it occasionally broken by trees in their winter foliage of snow, or by the slash of the track which broke through the high wall. Beyond the wall, the forest pressed close under the heavy twilight of the sky. Lisel pondered with a grim irritation the open gateway. Wolves running, and the way to the château left wide at all times. She visualized mad Anna throwing chunks of raw meat to the wolves as another woman would toss bread to swans.

This unprepossessing notion returned to Lisel during the unusually early dinner, when she realized that Anna was receiving from her silent gliding servants various dishes of raw meats.

"I hope," said Anna, catching Lisel's eye, "my repast won't offend a delicate stomach. I have learned that the best way to keep my health is to eat the fruits of the earth in their intended state—so much goodness is wasted in cooking and garnishing."

Despite the reference to fruit, Anna touched none of the fruit or vegetables on the table. Nor did she drink any wine.

Lisel began again to be amused, if rather dubiously. Her own fare was excellent, and she ate it hungrily, admiring as she did so the crystal goblets and gold-handled knives which one day would be hers.

Presently a celebrated liqueur was served—to Lisel alone—and Anna rose on the black wings of her dress, waving her granddaughter to the fire. Beautiful, meanwhile, had crawled onto the stool of the tall piano and begun to play wildly despairing romances there, his elegant fingers darting over discolored keys so like Anna's strong yet senile teeth.

"Well," said Anna, reseating herself in another carven throne before the cave of the hearth. "What do you think of us?"

"Think, Grandmère? Should I presume?"

"No. But you do."

"I think," said Lisel cautiously, "everything is very fine."

"And you are keenly aware, of course, the finery will eventually belong to you."

"Oh, Grandmère!" exclaimed Lisel, quite genuinely shocked by such frankness.

"Don't trouble yourself," said Anna. Her eyes caught the fire and became like the eyes of the wolf at the carriage window. "You expect to be my heiress. It's quite normal you should be making an inventory. I shan't last forever. Once I'm gone, presumably everything will be yours."

Despite herself, Lisel gave an involuntary shiver. A sudden plan of selling the château to be rid of it flitted through her thoughts, but she quickly put it aside, in case the Matriarch somehow read her mind.

"Don't speak like that, Grandmère. This is the first time I've met you, and you talk of dying."

"Did I? No. I did not. I spoke of *departure*. Nothing dies, it simply transmogrifies." Lisel watched politely this display of apparent piety. "As for my mansion," Anna went on, "you mustn't consider sale, you know." Lisel blanched—as she had feared her mind had been read, or could it merely be that Anna found her predictable? "The château has stood on this land for many centuries. The old name for the spot, do you know that?"

"No, Grandmère."

"This, like the whole of the forest, was called the Wolfland. Because it was the wolves' country before ever men set foot on it with their piffling little roads and tracks, their carriages and foolish frightened walls. Wolfland. Their country then, and when the winter comes, their country once more."

"As I saw, Grandmère," said Lisel tartly.

"As you saw. You'll see and hear more of them while you're in my house. Their voices come and go like the wind, as they do. When that little idiot of a sun slips away and the night rises, you may hear scratching on the lower floor windows. I needn't tell you to stay indoors, need I?"

"Why do you let animals run in your park?" demanded Lisel.

"Because," said Anna, "the land is theirs by right."

The dwarf began to strike a polonaise from the piano. Anna clapped her hands, and the music ended. Anna beckoned, and Beautiful slid off the stool like a precocious child caught stickying the keys. He came to Anna, and she played with his hair. His face remained unreadable, yet his pellucid eyes swam dreamily to Lisel's face. She felt embarrassed by the scene, and at his glance was angered to find herself blushing.

"There was a time," said Anna, "when I did not rule this house. When a man ruled here."

"Grandpère," said Lisel, looking resolutely at the fire.

"*Grandpère*, yes, *Grandpère*." Her voice held the most awful scorn. "Grandpère believed it was a man's pleasure to beat his wife. You're young, but you should know, should be told. Every night, if I was not already sick from a beating, and sometimes when I was, I would hear his heavy drunken feet come stumbling to my door. At first I locked it, but I learned not to. What stood in his way he could always break. He was a strong man. A great legend of strength. I carry scars on my shoulders to this hour. One day I may show you."

Lisel gazed at Anna, caught between fascination and revulsion. "Why do I tell you?" Anna smiled. She had twisted Beautiful's gorgeous hair into a painful knot. Clearly it hurt him, but he made no sound, staring blindly at the ceiling. "I tell you, Lisel, because very soon your father will suggest to you that it is time you were wed. And however handsome or gracious the young man may seem to you that you choose, or that is chosen for you, however noble or marvelous or even docile he may seem, you have no way of being certain he will not turn out to be like your beloved grandpère. Do you know, he brought me peaches on our wedding night, all the way from the hothouses of the city. Then he showed me the whip he had been hiding under the fruit. You see what it is to be a woman, Lisel. Is that what you want? The irrevocable marriage vow that binds you forever to a monster? And even if he is a good man, which is a rare beast indeed, you may die an agonizing death in childbed, just as your mother did."

Lisel swallowed. A number of things went through her head now. A vague acknowledgment that, though she envisaged admiration, she had never wished to marry and therefore never considered it, and a starker awareness that she was being told improper things. She desired to learn more and dreaded to learn it. As she was struggling to find a rejoinder, Anna seemed to notice her own grip on the hair of the dwarf.

"Ah," she said, "forgive me. I did not mean to hurt you."

The words had an oddly sinister ring to them. Lisel suddenly guessed their origin, the brutish man rising from his act of depravity, of necessity still merely sketched by Lisel's innocence, whispering, gloatingly muttering: Forgive me. I did not mean to hurt.

"Beautiful," said Anna, "is the only man of any worth I've ever met. And my servants, of course, but I don't count them as men. Drink your liqueur."

"Yes, Grandmère," said Lisel, as she sipped, and slightly choked.

"Tomorrow," said Anna, "we must serve you something better. A vintage indigenous to the château, made from a flower which grows here in the spring. For now," again she rose on her raven's wings; a hundred gems caught the light and went out, "for now, we keep early hours here, in the country."

"But, Grandmère," said Lisel, astounded, "it's scarcely sunset."

"In my house," said Anna, gently, "you will do as you are told, m'mselle."

And for once, Lisel did as she was told.

At first, of course, Lisel did not entertain a dream of sleep. She was used to staying awake till the early hours of the morning, rising at noon. She entered her bedroom, cast one scathing glance at the bed, and settled herself to read in a chair beside the bedroom fire. Luckily she had found a lurid novel amid the choice of books. By skimming over all passages of meditation, description or philosophy, confining her attention to those portions which contained duels, rapes, black magic and the firing squad, she had soon made great inroads on the work. Occasionally, she would pause, and add another piece of wood to the fire. At such times she knew a medley of doubts concerning her grandmother. That the Matriarch could leave such a novel lying about openly where Lisel could get at it outraged the girl's propriety.

Eventually, two or three hours after the sun had gone and the windows blackened entirely behind the drapes, Lisel did fall asleep. The excitements of the journey and her medley of reactions to Madame Anna had worn her out.

She woke, as she had in the carriage, with a start of alarm. Her reason was the same one. Out in the winter forest of night sounded the awesome choir of the wolves. Their voices rose and fell, swelling, diminishing, resurging, like great icy waves of wind or water, breaking on the silence of the château.

Partly nude, a lovely maiden had been bound to a stake and the first torch applied, but Lisel no longer cared very much for her fate. Setting the book aside, she rose from the chair. The flames were low on the candles and the fire almost out. There was no clock, but it had the feel of midnight. Lisel went to the window and opened the drapes. Stepping through and pulling them fast closed again behind her, she gazed out into the glowing darkness of snow and night.

The wolf cries went on and on, thrilling her with a horrible disquiet, so she wondered how even mad Anna could ever have grown accustomed to them? Was this what had driven her grandfather to brutishness and beatings? And, colder thought, the mysterious violent death he was supposed to have suffered—what more violent than to be torn apart under the pine trees by long pointed teeth?

Lisel quartered the night scene with her eyes, looking for shapes to fit the noises, and, as before, hoping not to find them.

There was decidedly something about wolves. Something beyond their reputation and the stories of the half-eaten bodies of little children with which nurses regularly scared their charges. Something to do with actual appearance, movement; the lean shadow manifesting from between the trunks of trees—the stuff of nightmare. And their howlings! Yet, as it went on and on, Lisel became aware of a bizarre exhilaration, an almost-pleasure in the awful sounds which made the hair lift on her scalp and gooseflesh creep along her arms—the same sort of sensation as biting into a slice of lemon—

And then she saw it, a great pale wolf. It loped by directly beneath the window, and suddenly, to Lisel's horror, it raised its long head, and two fireworks flashed, which were its eyes meeting with hers. A primordial fear, worse even than in the carriage, turned Lisel's bones to liquid. She sank on her knees, and as she knelt there foolishly, as if in prayer, her chin on the sill, she beheld the wolf moving away across the park, seeming to dissolve into the gloom.

Gradually, then, the voices of the other wolves began to dull, eventually falling quiet.

Lisel got up, came back into the room, threw more wood on the fire and crouched there. It seemed odd to her that the wolf had run away from the château, but she was not sure why. Presumably it had ventured near in hopes of food, then, disappointed, withdrawn. That it had come from the spot directly by the hall's doors did not, could not, mean anything in particular. Then Lisel realized what had been so strange. She had seen the wolf in a faint radiance of light—but from where? The moon was almost full, but obscured behind the house. The drapes had been drawn across behind her, the light could not have fallen down from her own window. She was turning back unhappily to the window to investigate when she heard the unmistakable soft thud of a large door being carefully shut below her, in the château.

The wolf had been in the house. Anna's guest.

Lisel was petrified for a few moments, then a sort of fury came to her rescue. How dared the old woman be so mad as all this and expect her civilized granddaughter to endure it? Brought to the wilds, told improper tales, left improper literature to read, made unwilling party to the entertainment of savage beasts. Perhaps as a result of the reading matter, Lisel saw her only course abruptly, and it was escape. (She had already assumed Anna would not allow her grandchild to depart until whatever lunatic game the old beldame was playing was completed.) But if escape, then how? Though there were carriage, horses, even coachman, all were Anna's. Lisel did not have to ponder long, however. Her father's cynicism on the lower classes had convinced her that anyone had his price. She would bribe the coachman—her gold bracelets and her ruby eardrops—both previous gifts of Anna's, in fact. She could assure the man of her father's protection and further valuables when they reached the city. A vile thought came to her at that, that her father might, after all, prove unsympathetic. Was she being stupid? Should she turn a blind eye to Anna's wolfish foibles? If Anna should disinherit her, as surely she would on Lisel's flight—

Assailed by doubts, Lisel paced the room. Soon she had added to them. The coachman might snatch her bribe and still refuse to help her. Or worse, drive her into the forest and violate her. Or—

The night slowed and flowed into the black valleys of early morning. The moon crested the château and sank into the forest. Lisel sat on the edge of the canopied bed, pleating and repleating the folds of the scarlet cloak between her fingers. Her face was pale, her blonde hair untidy and her eyes enlarged. She looked every bit as crazy as her grandmother.

Her decision was sudden, made with an awareness that she had wasted much time. She flung the cloak around herself and started up. She hurried to the bedroom door and softly, softly, opened it a tiny crack.

All was black in the house, neither lamp nor candle visible anywhere. The sight, or rather lack of it, caused Lisel's heart to sink. At the same instant, it indicated that the whole house was abed. Lisel's plan was a simple one. A passage led away from the great hall to the kitchens and servants' quarters and ultimately to a courtyard containing coachhouse and stables. Here the grooms and the coachman would sleep, and here too another gateway opened on the park. These details she had either seen for herself as the carriage was driven off on her arrival or deduced from the apparent structure of the château. Unsure of the hour, yet she felt dawn was approaching. If she could but reach the servants' quarters, she should be able to locate the courtyard. If the coachman proved a villain, she would have to use her wits. Threaten him or cajole him. Knowing very little of physical communion, it seemed better to Lisel in those moments, to lie down with a hairy peasant than to remain the Matriarch's captive. It was that time of night when humans are often prey to ominous or extravagant ideas of all sorts. She took up one of the low-burning candles. Closing the bedroom door behind her, Lisel stole forward into the black nothingness of unfamiliarity.

Even with the feeble light, she could barely see ten inches before her, and felt cautiously about with her free hand, dreading to collide with ornament or furniture and thereby rouse her enemies. The stray gleams, shot back at her from a mirror or a picture frame, misled rather than aided her. At first her total concentration was taken up with her safe progress and her quest to find the head of the double stair. Presently, however, as she pressed on without mishap, secondary considerations began to steal in on her.

If it was difficult to proceed, how much more difficult it might be should she desire to retreat. Hopefully, there would be nothing to retreat from. But the ambiance of the château, inspired by night and the limited candle, was growing more sinister by the second. Arches opened on drapes of black from which anything might spring. All about, the shadow furled, and she was one small target moving in it, lit as if on a stage.

She turned the passage and perceived the curve of the stair ahead and the dim hall below. The great stained window provided a grey illumination which elsewhere was absent. The stars bled on the snow outside and pierced the white panes. Or could it be the initial tinge of dawn?

Lisel paused, confronting once again the silliness of her simple plan of escape. Instinctively, she turned to look the way she had come, and the swiftness of the motion, or some complementary draught, quenched her candle. She stood marooned by this cliché, the phosphorescently discernible space before her, pitch-dark behind, and chose the path into the half-light as preferable.

She went down the stair delicately, as if descending into a ballroom. When she was some twenty steps from the bottom, something moved in the thick drapes beside the outer doors. Lisel froze, feeling a shock like an electric volt passing through her vitals. In another second she knew from the uncanny littleness of the shape that it was Anna's dwarf who scuttled there. But before she divined what it was at, one leaf of the door began to swing heavily inward.

Lisel felt no second shock of fear. She felt instead as if her soul drifted upward from her flesh.

Through the open door soaked the pale ghost-light that heralded sunrise, and with that, a scattering of fresh white snow. Lastly through the door, its long feet crushing both light and snow, glided the wolf she had seen beneath her window. It did not look real, it seemed to waver and to shine, yet, for any who had ever heard the name of wolf, or a single story of them, or the song of their voices, here stood that word, that story, that voice, personified.

The wolf raised its supernatural head and once more it looked at the young girl.

The moment held no reason, no pity, and certainly no longer any hope of escape.

As the wolf began to pad noiselessly up the stair toward Lisel, she fled by the only route now possible to her. Into unconsciousness.

3

She came to herself to find the face of a prince from a romance poised over hers. He was handsome enough to have kissed her awake, except that she knew immediately it was the dwarf.

"Get away from me!" she shrieked, and he moved aside.

She was in the bedchamber, lying on the canopied bed. She was not dead, she had not been eaten or had her throat torn out.

As if in response to her thoughts, the dwarf said musically to her: "You have had a nightmare, m'mselle." But she could tell from a faint expression somewhere between his eyes, that he did not truly expect her to believe such a feeble equivocation.

"There was a wolf," said Lisel, pulling herself into a sitting position, noting that she was still gowned and wearing the scarlet cloak. "A wolf which you let into the house."

"I?" The dwarf elegantly raised an eyebrow.

"You, you frog. Where is my grandmother? I demand to see her at once."

"The Lady Anna is resting. She sleeps late in the mornings."

"Wake her."

"Your pardon, m'mselle, but I take my orders from Madame." The dwarf bowed. "If you are recovered and hungry, a maid will bring *petit déjeuner* at once to your room, and hot water for bathing, when you are ready."

Lisel frowned. Her ordeal past, her anger paramount, she was still very hungry. An absurd notion came to her—*had* it all been a dream? No, she would not so doubt herself. Even though the wolf had not harmed her, it had been real. A household pet, then? She had heard of deranged monarchs who kept lions or tigers like cats. Why not a wolf kept like a dog?

"Bring me my breakfast," she snapped, and the dwarf bowed himself goldenly out.

All avenues of escape seemed closed, yet by day (for it was day, the tawny gloaming of winter) the phenomena of the darkness seemed far removed. Most of their terror had gone with them. With instinctive immature good sense, Lisel acknowledged that no hurt had come to her, that she was indeed being cherished.

She wished she had thought to reprimand the dwarf for his mention of intimate hot water and his presence in her bedroom. Recollections of unseemly novelettes led her to a swift examination of her apparel—unscathed. She rose and stood morosely by the fire, waiting for her breakfast, tapping her foot.

By the hour of noon, Lisel's impatience had reached its zenith with the sun. Of the two, only the sun's zenith was insignificant.

Lisel left the bedroom, flounced along the corridor and came to the stairhead. Eerie memories of the previous night had trouble in remaining with her. Everything seemed to have become rather absurd, but this served only to increase her annoyance. Lisel went down the stair boldly. The fire was lit in the enormous hearth and was blazing cheerfully. Lisel prowled about, gazing at the dubious stained glass, which she now saw did not portray a hunting scene at all, but some pagan subject of men metamorphosing into wolves.

At length a maid appeared. Lisel marched up to her.

"Kindly inform my grandmother that I am awaiting her in the hall." The maid seemed struggling to repress a laugh, but she bobbed a curtsey and darted off. She did not come back, and neither did grandmother.

When a man entered bearing logs for the fire, Lisel said to him, "Put those down and take me at once to the coachman."

The man nodded and gestured her to follow him without a word of acquiescence or disagreement. Lisel, as she let herself be led through the back corridors and by the hub-bub of the huge stone kitchen, was struck by the incongruousness of her actions. No longer afraid, she felt foolish. She was carrying out her "plan" of the night before from sheer pique, nor did she have any greater hope of success. It was more as if some deeply hidden part of herself prompted her to flight, in spite of all resolution, rationality and desire. But it was rather like trying to walk on a numbed foot. She could manage to do it, but without feeling.

The coachhouse and stables bulked gloomily about the courtyard, where the snow had renewed itself in dazzling white drifts. The coachman stood in his black furs beside an iron brazier. One of the blond horses was being shod in an old-fashioned manner, the coachman overseeing the exercise. Seeking to ingratiate herself, Lisel spoke to the coachman in a silky voice.

"I remarked yesterday, how well you controlled the horses when the wolves came after the carriage."

The coachman did not answer, but hearing her voice, the horse sidled a little, rolling its eye at her.

"Suppose," said Lisel to the coachman, "I were to ask you if you would take me back to the city. What would you say?"

Nothing, apparently.

The brazier sizzled and the hammer of the blacksmithing groom smacked the nails home into the horse's hoof. Lisel found the process disconcerting.

"You must understand," she said to the coachman, "my father would give you a great deal of money. He's unwell and wishes me to return. I received word this morning."

The coachman hulked there like a big black bear, and Lisel had the urge to bite him viciously.

"My grandmother," she announced, "would order you to obey me, but she is in bed."

"No, she is not," said the Matriarch at Lisel's back, and Lisel almost screamed. She shot around, and stared at the old woman, who stood about a foot away, imperious in her furs, jewels frostily blistering on her wrists.

"I wish," said Lisel, taking umbrage as her shield, "to go home at once."

"So I gather. But you can't, I regret."

"You mean to keep me prisoner?" blurted Lisel.

Grandmother laughed. The laugh was like fresh ice crackling under a steel skate. "Not at all. The road is snowed under and won't be clear for several days. I'm afraid you'll have to put up with us a while longer."

Lisel, in a turmoil she could not herself altogether fathom, had her attention diverted by the behavior of the horse. It was bristling like a cat, tossing its head, dancing against the rope by which the second groom was holding it.

Anna walked at once out into the yard and began to approach the horse from the front. The horse instantly grew more agitated, kicking up its heels, and neighing croupily. Lisel almost cried an automatic warning, but restrained herself. Let the bel-dame get a kicking, she deserved it. Rather to Lisel's chagrin, Anna reached the horse without actually having her brains dashed out. She showed not a moment's hesitation or doubt, placing her hand on its long nose, eyeing it with an amused tenderness. She looked very cruel and very indomitable.

"There now," said Anna to the horse, which, fallen quiet and still, yet trembled feverishly. "You know you are used to me. You know you were trained to endure me since you were a foal, as your brothers are sometimes trained to endure fire."

The horse hung its head and shivered, cowed but noble.

Anna left it and strolled back through the snow. She came to Lisel and took her arm.

"I'm afraid," said Anna, guiding them toward the château door, "that they're never entirely at peace when I'm in the vicinity, though they are good horses, and well trained. They have borne me long distances in the carriage."

"Do they fear you because you ill-treat them?" Lisel asked impetuously.

"Oh, not at all. They fear me because to them I smell of wolf."

Lisel bridled.

"Then do you think it wise to keep such a pet in the house?" she flared.

Anna chuckled. It was not necessarily a merry sound.

"That's what you think, is it? What a little dunce you are, Lisel. I am the beast you saw last night, and you had better get accustomed to it. Grandmère is a werewolf."

The return walk through the domestic corridors into the hall was notable for its silence. The dreadful Anna, her grip on the girl's arm unabated, smiled thoughtfully to herself. Lisel was obviously also deliberating inwardly. Her conclusions, however, continued to lean to the deranged rather than the occult. Propitiation suggested itself, as formerly, to be the answer. So, as they entered the hall, casting their cloaks to a ser-vant, Lisel brightly exclaimed:

"A werewolf, Grandmère. How interesting!"

"Dear me," said Anna, "what a child." She seated herself by the fire in one of her tall thrones. Beautiful had appeared. "Bring the liqueur and some biscuits," said Anna. "It's past the hour, but why should we be the slaves of custom?"

Lisel perched on a chair across the hearth, watching Anna guardedly.

"You are the interesting one," Anna now declared. "You look sulky rather than intimidated at being mured up here with one whom you wrongly suppose is danger-ously insane. No, *ma chère*, verily I'm not mad, but a transmogrifite. Every evening, once the sun sets, I become a wolf, and duly comport myself as a wolf does."

"You're going to eat me, then," snarled Lisel, irritated out of all attempts to placate.

"Eat you? Hardly necessary. The forest is bursting with game. I won't say I never tasted human meat, but I wouldn't stoop to devouring a blood relation. Enough is enough. Besides, I had the opportunity last night, don't you think, when you swooned away on the stairs not fifty feet from me. Of course, it was almost dawn, and I *had* dined, but to rip out your throat would have been the work only of a moment. There-after we might have stored you in the cold larder against a lean winter."

"*How dare you try to frighten me in this way!*" screamed Lisel in a paroxysm of rage.

Beautiful was coming back with a silver tray. On the tray rested a plate of bis-cuits and a decanter of the finest cut glass containing a golden drink.

"You note, Beautiful," said Madame Anna, "I like this wretched granddaughter of mine. She's very like me."

"Does that dwarf know you are a *werewolf*?" demanded Lisel, with baleful irony.

"Who else lets me in and out at night? But all my servants know, just as my other folk know, in the forest."

"You're disgusting," said Lisel.

"Tut, I shall disinherit you. Don't you want my fortune any more?"

Beautiful set down the tray on a small table between them and began to pour the liqueur, smooth as honey, into two tiny crystal goblets.

Lisel watched. She remembered the nasty dishes of raw meat—part of Anna's game of werewolfery—and the drinking of water, but no wine. Lisel smirked, thinking she had caught the Matriarch out. She kept still and accepted the glass from Beautiful, who, while she remained seated, was a mere inch taller than she.

"I toast you," said Anna, raising her glass to Lisel. "Your health and your joy." She sipped. A strange look came into her strange eyes. "We have," she said, "a brief winter afternoon before us. There is just the time to tell you what you should be told."

"Why bother with me? I'm disinherited."

"Hardly. Taste the liqueur. You will enjoy it."

"I'm surprised that you did, Grandmère."

"Don't be," said Anna with asperity. "This wine is special to this place. We make it from a flower which grows here. A little yellow flower that comes in the spring, or sometimes, even in the winter. There is a difference then, of course. Do you recall the flower of my escutcheon? It is the self-same one."

Lisel sipped the liqueur. She had had a fleeting fancy it might be drugged or tampered with in some way, but both drinks had come from the decanter. Besides, what would be the point? The Matriarch valued an audience. The wine was pleasing, fragrant and, rather than sweet as Lisel had anticipated, tart. The flower which grew in winter was plainly another demented tale.

Relaxed, Lisel leant back in her chair. She gazed at the flames in the wide hearth. Her mad grandmother began to speak to her in a quiet, floating voice, and Lisel saw pictures form in the fire. Pictures of Anna, and of the château, and of darkness itself. . . .

4

How young Anna looked. She was in her twenties. She wore a scarlet gown and a scarlet cloak lined with pale fur and heavy brocade. It resembled Lisel's cloak but had a different clasp. Snow melted on the shoulders of the cloak, and Anna held her slender hands to the fire on the hearth. Free of the hood, her hair, like marvelously tarnished ivory, was piled on her head, and there was a yellow flower in it. She wore ruby eardrops. She looked just like Lisel, or Lisel as she would become in six years or seven.

Someone called. It was more a roar than a call, as if a great beast came trampling into the château. He was a big man, dark, all darkness, his features hidden in a black beard, black hair—more, in a sort of swirling miasmic cloud, a kind of psychic smoke: Anna's hatred and fear. He bellowed for liquor and a servant came running with a jug and cup. The man, Anna's husband, cuffed the servant aside, grabbing the jug as he did so. He strode to Anna, spun her about, grabbed her face in his hand as he had grabbed the jug. He leaned to her as if to kiss her, but he did not kiss, he merely stared. She had steeled herself not to shrink from him, so much was evident. His eyes, roving over her to find some overt trace of distaste or fright, suddenly found instead the yellow flower. He vented a powerful oath. His paw flung up and wrenched the flower free. He slung it in the fire and spat after it.

"You stupid bitch," he growled at her. "Where did you come on that?"

"It's only a flower."

"Not only a flower. Answer me, where? Or do I strike you?"

"Several of them are growing near the gate, beside the wall; and in the forest. I saw them when I was riding."

The man shouted again for his servant. He told him to take a fellow and go out. They must locate the flowers and burn them.

"Another superstition?" Anna asked. Her husband hit her across the head so she staggered and caught the mantel to steady herself.

"*Yes*," he sneered, "another one. Now come upstairs."

Anna said, "Please excuse me, sir, I am not well today."

He said in a low and smiling voice:

"Do as I say, or you'll be worse."

The fire flared on the swirl of her bloody cloak as she moved to obey him.

And the image changed. There was a bedroom, fluttering with lamplight. Anna was perhaps thirty-five or -six, but she looked older. She lay in bed, soaked in sweat, uttering hoarse low cries or sometimes preventing herself from crying. She was in labor. The child was difficult. There were other women about the bed. One muttered to her neighbor that it was beyond her how the master had ever come to sire a child, since he got his pleasure another way, and the poor lady's body gave evidence of how. Then Anna screamed. Someone bent over her. There was a peculiar muttering among the women, as if they attended at some holy ceremony.

And another image came. Anna was seated in a shawl of gilded hair. She held a baby on her lap and was playing with it in an intense, quite silent way. As her hair shifted: traceries became momentarily visible over her bare shoulders and arms, horrible traceries left by a lash.

"Let me take the child," said a voice, and one of the women from the former scene appeared. She lifted the baby from Anna's lap, and Anna let the baby go, only holding her arms and hands in such a way that she touched it to the last second. The other woman was older than Anna, a peasant dressed smartly for service in the château. "You mustn't fret yourself," she said.

"But I can't suckle her," said Anna. "I wanted to."

"There's another can do that," said the woman. "Rest yourself. Rest while he is away." When she said "he" there could be no doubt of the one to whom she referred.

"Then, I'll rest," said Anna. She reclined on pillows, wincing slightly as her back made contact with the fine soft silk. "Tell me about the flowers again. The yellow flowers."

The woman showed her teeth as she rocked the baby. For an instant her face was just like a wolf's.

"You're not afraid," she said. "*He* is. But it's always been here. The wolf-magic. It's part of the Wolfland. Wherever wolves have been, you can find the wolf-magic. Somewhere. In a stream or a cave, or in a patch of ground. The château has it. That's why the flowers grow here. Yes, I'll tell you, then, it's simple. If any eat the flowers, then they receive the gift. It comes from the spirit, the wolfwoman, or maybe she's a goddess, an old goddess left over from the beginning of things, before Christ came to save us all. She has the head of a wolf and yellow hair. You swallow the flowers, and you call her, and she comes, and she gives it you. And then it's yours, till you die."

"And then what? Payment?" said Anna dreamily. "Hell?"

"Maybe."

The image faded gently. Suddenly there was another which was not gentle, a parody of the scene before. Staring light showed the bedchamber. The man, his shadow-face smoldering, clutched Anna's baby in his hands. The baby shrieked; he swung it to and fro as if to smash it on some handy piece of furniture. Anna stood in her nightdress. She held a whip out to him.

"Beat me," she said. "Please beat me. I want you to. Put down the child and beat me. It would be so easy to hurt her, and so soon over, she's so small. But I'm stronger. You can hurt me much more. See how vulnerable and afraid I am. Beat *me.*"

Then, with a snarl he tossed the child onto the bed where it lay wailing. He took the whip and caught Anna by her pale hair—

There was snow blowing like torn paper, everywhere. In the midst of it a servant woman, and a child perhaps a year old with soft dark hair, were seated in a carriage. Anna looked at them, then stepped away. A door slammed, horses broke into a gallop. Anna remained standing in the snow storm.

No picture came. A man's voice thundered: "Where? Where did you send the thing? It's mine, I sired it. My property. *Where?*"

But the only reply he got was moans of pain. She would not tell him, and did not. He nearly killed her that time.

Now it is night, but a black night bleached with whiteness, for a full moon is up above the tops of the winter pines.

Anna is poised, motionless, in a glade of the wild northern forest. She wears the scarlet cloak, but the moon has drained its color. The snow sparkles, the trees are umbrellas of diamond, somber only at their undersides. The moon slaps the world with light. Anna has been singing, or chanting something, and though it can no longer be heard, the dew of it lies heavy over the ground. Something is drawn there, too, in the snow, a circle, and another shape inside it. A fire has been kindled nearby, but now it has burned low and has a curious bluish tinge to it. All at once a wind begins to come through the forest. But it is not wind, not even storm. It is the soul of the forest, the spirit of the Wolfland.

Anna goes to her knees. She is afraid, but it is a new fear, an exulting fear. The stalks of the flowers whose heads she has eaten lie under her knees, and she raises her face like a dish to the moonlight.

The pines groan. They bend. Branches snap and snow showers down from them. The creature of the forest is coming, nearer and nearer. It is a huge single wing, or an enormous engine. Everything breaks and sways before it, even the moonlight, and darkness fills the glade. And out of the darkness Something whirls. It is difficult to see, to be sure—a glimpse of gold, two eyes like dots of lava seven feet in the air, a grey jaw, hung breasts which have hair growing on them, the long hand which is not a hand, lifting— and then every wolf in the forest seems to give tongue, and the darkness ebbs away.

Anna lies on her face. She is weeping. With terror. With—

It is night again, and the man of the house is coming home.

He swaggers, full of local beer and eager to get to his wife. He was angry, a short while since, because his carriage, which was to have waited for him outside the inn, had mysteriously vanished. There will be men to curse and brutalize in the courtyard before he goes up to his beloved Anna, a prelude to his final act with her. He finds her a challenge, his wife. She seems able to withstand so much, looking at him proudly with horror in her eyes. It would bore him to break her. He likes the fact he cannot, or thinks he does. And tonight he has some good news. One of the paid men has brought word of their child. She is discovered at last. She can be brought home to the château to her father's care. She is two years old now. Strong and healthy. Yes, good news indeed.

They had known better in the village than to tell him he should beware on the forest track. He is not anxious about wolves, the distance being less than a mile, and he has his pistol. Besides, he organized a wolf hunt last month and cleared quite a few of the brutes off his land. The area about the château has been silent for many nights. Even Anna went walking without a servant—though he had not approved of that and had taught her a lesson. (Sometimes it occurs to him that she enjoys his lessons as much as he enjoys delivering them, for she seems constantly to seek out new ways to vex him.)

He is about a quarter of a mile from the château now, and here a small clearing opens off on both sides of the track. It is the night after the full moon, and her disc, an almost perfect round, glares down on the clearing from the pine tops. Anna's husband dislikes the clearing. He had forgotten he would have to go through it, for generally he is mounted or in the carriage when he passes the spot. There is some old superstition about the place. He hates it, just as he hates the stinking yellow flowers that grew in it before he burned them out. Why does he hate them? The woman who nursed him told him something and it frightened him, long ago. Well, no matter. He walks more quickly.

How quiet it is, how still. The whole night like a pane of black-white silence. He can hardly hear his own noisy footfalls. There is a disturbance in the snow, over there, a mark like a circle.

Then he realizes something is behind him. He is not sure how he realizes, for it is quite soundless. He stops, and turns, and sees a great and ghostly wolf a few feet from him on the track.

In a way, it is almost a relief to see the wolf. It is alone, and it is a natural thing. Somehow he had half expected something unnatural. He draws his pistol, readies it, points it at the wolf. He is a fine shot. He already visualizes lugging the bloody carcass, a trophy, into the house. He pulls the trigger.

A barren click. He is surprised. He tries again. Another click. It comes to him that his servant has emptied the chamber of bullets. He sees a vision of the park gates a quarter of a mile away, and he turns immediately and runs toward them.

Ten seconds later a warm and living weight crashes against his back, and he falls screaming, screaming before the pain even begins. When the pain does begin, he is unable to scream for very long, but he does his best. The final thing he sees through the haze of his own blood, which has splashed up into his eyes, and the tears of agony and the enclosing of a most atrocious death, are the eyes of the wolf, gleaming coolly back at him. He knows they are the eyes of Anna. And that it is Anna who then tears out his throat.

The small crystal goblet slipped out of Lisel's hand, empty, and broke on the floor. Lisel started. Dazed, she looked away from the fire, to Anna the Matriarch.

Had Lisel been asleep and dreaming? What an unpleasant dream. Or had it been so unpleasant? Lisel became aware her teeth were clenched in spiteful gladness, as if on a bone. If Anna had told her the truth, that man—that *thing*—had deserved it all. To be betrayed by his servants, and by his wife, and to perish in the fangs of a wolf. A werewolf.

Grandmother and granddaughter confronted each other a second, with identical expressions of smiling and abstracted malice. Lisel suddenly flushed, smoothed her face, and looked down. There had been something in the drink after all.

"I don't think this at all nice," said Lisel.

"Nice isn't the word," Anna agreed. Beautiful reclined at her feet, and she stroked his hair. Across the big room, the stained-glass window was thickening richly to opacity. The sun must be near to going down.

"*If* it's the truth," said Lisel primly, "you will go to Hell."

"Oh? Don't you think me justified? He'd have killed your mother at the very least. *You* would never have been born."

Lisel reviewed this hypothetical omission. It carried some weight.

"You should have appealed for help."

"To whom? The marriage vow is a chain that may not be broken. If I had left him, he would have traced me, as he did the child. No law supports a wife. I could only kill him."

"I don't believe you killed him as you say you did."

"Don't you, m'mselle? Well, never mind. Once the sun has set, you'll see it happen before your eyes." Lisel stared and opened her mouth to remonstrate. Anna added gently: "And, I am afraid, not to myself alone."

Aside from all reasoning and the training of a short lifetime, Lisel felt the stranglehold of pure terror fasten on her. She rose and squealed: "What do you mean?"

"I mean," said Anna, "that the liqueur you drank is made from the same yellow flowers I ate to give me the power of transmogrification. I mean that the wolf-magic, once invoked, becomes hereditary, yet dormant. I mean that what the goddess of the Wolfland conveys must indeed be paid for at the hour of death—unless another will take up the gift."

Lisel, not properly understanding, not properly believing, began to shriek wildly. Anna came to her feet. She crossed to Lisel and shook the shrieks out of her, and when she was dumb, thrust her back in the chair.

"Now sit, fool, and be quiet. I've put nothing on you that was not already yours. Look in a mirror. Look at your hair and your eyes and your beautiful teeth. Haven't you always preferred the night to the day, staying up till the morning, lying abed till noon? Don't you love the cold forest? Doesn't the howl of the wolf thrill you through with fearful delight? And why else should the Wolfland accord you an escort, a pack of wolves running by you on the road. Do you think you'd have survived if you'd not been one of their kind, too?"

Lisel wept, stamping her foot. She could not have said at all what she felt. She tried to think of her father and the ballrooms of the city. She tried to consider if she credited magic.

"Now listen to me," snapped Anna, and Lisel muted her sobs just enough to catch the words. "Tonight is full moon, and the anniversary of that night, years ago, when I made my pact with the wolf goddess of the north. I have good cause to suspect I shan't live out this year. Therefore, tonight is the last chance I have to render you in my place into her charge. That frees me from her, do you see? Once you have swallowed the flowers, once she has acknowledged you, you belong to her. At death, I escape her sovereignty, which would otherwise bind me forever to the earth in wolf form, phantom form. A bargain: you save me. But you too can make your escape, when the time comes. Bear a child. You will be mistress here. You can command any man to serve you, and you're tolerable enough the service won't be unwilling. My own child, your mother, was not like me at all. I could not bring her to live with me, once I had the power. I was troubled as to how I should wean her to it. But she died, and in you I saw the mark from the first hour. You are fit to take my place. Your child can take yours."

"You're hateful!" shrieked Lisel. She had the wish to laugh.

But someone was flinging open the doors of the hall. The cinnamon light streamed through and fell into the fire and faded it. Another fire, like antique bronze, was quenching itself among the pines. The dying of the sun.

Anna moved toward the doors and straight out onto the snow. She stood a moment, tall and amazing on the peculiar sky. She seemed a figment of the land itself, and maybe she was.

"Come!" she barked. Then turned and walked away across the park.

All the servants seemed to have gathered like bats in the hall. They were silent, but they looked at Lisel. Her heart struck her over and over. She did not know what she felt or if she believed. Then a wolf sang in the forest. She lifted her head. She suddenly knew frost and running and black stillness, and a platinum moon, red feasts and wild hymnings, lovers with quicksilver eyes and the race of the ice wind and stars smashed under the hard soles of her four feet. A huge white ballroom opened before her, and the champagne of the air filled her mouth.

Beautiful had knelt and was kissing the hem of her red cloak. She patted his head absently, and the gathering of the servants sighed.

Presumably, as Anna's heiress, she might be expected to live on in the forest, in the château which would be hers. She could even visit the city, providing she was home by sunset.

The wolf howled again, filling her veins with light, raising the hair along her scalp.

Lisel tossed her head. Of course, it was all a lot of nonsense.

She hastened out through the doors and over the winter park and followed her grandmother away into the Wolfland.

QUESTIONS FOR DISCUSSION AND WRITING

1. Reread the first three paragraphs. How do they prepare us for what happens to Lisel? Think not only about the descriptions of Lisel's character but about the section's imagery and mood.
2. From the beginning, Anna is called "Anna the Matriarch." What is the thematic significance of the use of *matriarch*? In other words, how does its use hint at the story's themes and attitudes? In what ways is a matriarch the same as or different from a grandmother?

3. Lee's story has some of the markings of a fairy tale. In what ways is "Wolfland" a fairy tale? In what ways do its themes and values differ from those of the fairy tales with which you are familiar?

4. At what point do you realize the truth about Anna's history and her intentions for Lisel? Are there hints early in the story that a rereading would reveal?

5. Consider Lisel's reactions to the wolves she hears and meets throughout the story. What do those reactions tell us about Lisel's character?

6. Lisel's responses to her situation seem in part determined by her reading of romance novels. Why do you think Lee makes romance reading one of Lisel's hobbies?

ANGELA CARTER (1940–1992)

The Company of Wolves _____ 1979

One Beast and only one howls in the woods by night.

The wolf is carnivore incarnate and he's as cunning as he is ferocious; once he's had a taste of flesh, then nothing else will do.

At night, the eyes of wolves shine like candle flames, yellowish, reddish, but that is because the pupils of their eyes fatten on darkness and catch the light from your lantern to flash it back to you—red for danger; if a wolf's eyes reflect only moonlight, then they gleam a cold and unnatural green, a mineral, a piercing color. If the be-nighted traveler spies those luminous, terrible sequins stitched suddenly on the black thickets, then he knows he must run, if fear has not struck him stock-still.

But those eyes are all you will be able to glimpse of the forest assassins as they cluster invisibly round your smell of meat as you go through the wood unwisely late. They will be like shadows, they will be like wraiths, gray members of a congregation of nightmare. Hark! his long, wavering howl . . . an aria of fear made audible.

The wolfsong is the sound of the rending you will suffer, in itself a murdering.

It is winter and cold weather. In this region of mountain and forest, there is now nothing for the wolves to eat. Goats and sheep are locked up in the byre, the deer departed for the remaining pasturage on the southern slopes—wolves grow lean and famished. There is so little flesh on them that you could count the starveling ribs through their pelts, if they gave you time before they pounced. Those slavering jaws; the lolling tongue; the rime of saliva on the grizzled chops—of all the teeming perils of the night and the forest, ghosts, hobgoblins, ogres that grill babies upon gridirons, witches that fatten their captives in cages for cannibal tables, the wolf is worst, for he cannot listen to reason.

You are always in danger in the forest, where no people are. Step between the portals of the great pines where the shaggy branches tangle about you, trapping the unwary traveler in nets as if the vegetation itself were in a plot with the wolves who live there, as though the wicked trees go fishing on behalf of their friends—step between the gateposts of the forest with the greatest trepidation and infinite precautions, for if you stray from the path for one instant, the wolves will eat you. They are gray as famine, they are as unkind as plague.

The grave-eyed children of the sparse villages always carry knives with them when they go out to tend the little flocks of goats that provide the homesteads with acrid milk and rank, maggoty cheeses. Their knives are half as big as they are; the blades are sharpened daily.

But the wolves have ways of arriving at your own hearthside. We try and try but sometimes we cannot keep them out. There is no winter's night the cottager does not fear to see a lean, gray, famished snout questing under the door, and there was a woman once bitten in her own kitchen as she was straining the macaroni.

Fear and flee the wolf; for worst of all, the wolf may be more than he seems.

There was a hunter once, near here, that trapped a wolf in a pit. This wolf had massacred the sheep and goats; eaten up a mad old man who used to live by himself in a hut halfway up the mountain and sing to Jesus all day; pounced on a girl looking after the sheep, but she made such a commotion that men came with rifles and scared him away and tried to track him into the forest but he was cunning and easily gave them the slip. So this hunter dug a pit and put a duck in it, for bait, all alive-oh; and he covered the pit with straw smeared with wolf dung. Quack, quack! went the duck, and a wolf came slinking out of the forest, a big one, a heavy one, he weighed as much as a grown man and the straw gave way beneath him—into the pit he tumbled. The hunter jumped down after him, slit his throat, cut off all his paws for a trophy.

And then no wolf at all lay in front of the hunter but the bloody trunk of a man, headless, footless, dying, dead.

A witch from up the valley once turned an entire wedding party into wolves because the groom had settled on another girl. She used to order them to visit her, at night, from spite, and they would sit and howl around her cottage for her, serenading her with their misery.

Not so very long ago, a young woman in our village married a man who vanished clean away on her wedding night. The bed was made with new sheets and the bride lay down in it; the groom said he was going out to relieve himself, insisted on it, for the sake of decency, and she drew the coverlet up to her chin and she lay there. And she waited and she waited and then she waited again—surely he's been gone a long time? Until she jumps up in bed and shrieks to hear a howling, coming on the wind from the forest.

That long-drawn, wavering howl has, for all its fearful resonance, some inherent sadness in it, as if the beasts would love to be less beastly if only they knew how and never cease to mourn their own condition. There is a vast melancholy in the canticles of the wolves, melancholy infinite as the forest, endless as these long nights of winter, and yet that ghastly sadness, that mourning for their own, irremediable appetites, can never move the heart, for not one phrase in it hints at the possibility of redemption; grace could not come to the wolf from its own despair, only through some external mediator, so that, sometimes, the beast will look as if he half welcomes the knife that dispatches him.

The young woman's brothers searched the outhouses and the haystacks but never found any remains, so the sensible girl dried her eyes and found herself another husband, not too shy to piss into a pot, who spent the nights indoors. She gave him a pair of bonny babies and all went right as a trivet until, one freezing night, the night of the solstice, the hinge of the year when things do not fit together as well as they should, the longest night, her first good man came home again.

A great thump on the door announced him as she was stirring the soup for the father of her children and she knew him the moment she lifted the latch to him although it was years since she'd worn black for him and now he was in rags and his hair hung down his back and never saw a comb, alive with lice.

"Here I am again, missis," he said. "Get me my bowl of cabbage and be quick about it."

Then her second husband came in with wood for the fire and when the first one saw she'd slept with another man and, worse, clapped his red eyes on her little children, who'd crept into the kitchen to see what all the din was about, he shouted: "I wish I were a wolf again, to teach this whore a lesson!" So a wolf he instantly became and tore off the eldest boy's left foot before he was chopped up with the hatchet they used for chopping logs. But when the wolf lay bleeding and gasping its last, the pelt peeled off again and he was just as he had been, years ago, when he ran away from his marriage bed, so that she wept and her second husband beat her.

They say there's an ointment the Devil gives you that turns you into a wolf the minute you rub it on. Or that he was born feet first and had a wolf for his father and his torso is a man's but his legs and genitals are a wolf's. And he has a wolf's heart.

Seven years is a werewolf's natural span, but if you burn his human clothing you condemn him to wolfishness for the rest of his life, so old wives hereabouts think it some protection to throw a hat or an apron at the werewolf, as if clothes made the man. Yet by the eyes, those phosphorescent eyes, you know him in all his shapes; the eyes alone unchanged by metamorphosis.

Before he can become a wolf, the lycanthrope strips stark naked. If you spy a naked man among the pines, you must run as if the Devil were after you.

It is midwinter and the robin, the friend of man, sits on the handle of the gardener's spade and sings. It is the worst time in all the year for wolves, but this strong-minded child insists she will go off through the wood. She is quite sure the wild beasts cannot harm her although, well-warned, she lays a carving knife in the basket her mother has packed with cheeses. There is a bottle of harsh liquor distilled from brambles; a batch of flat oat cakes baked on the hearthstone; a pot or two of jam. The flaxen-haired girl will take these delicious gifts to a reclusive grandmother so old the burden of her years is crushing her to death. Granny lives two hours' trudge through the winter woods; the child wraps herself up in her thick shawl, draws it over her head. She steps into her stout wooden shoes; she is dressed and ready and it is Christmas Eve. The malign door of the solstice still swings upon its hinges, but she has been too much loved ever to feel scared.

Children do not stay young for long in this savage country. There are no toys for them to play with, so they work hard and grow wise, but this one, so pretty and the youngest of her family, a little latecomer, had been indulged by her mother and the grandmother who'd knitted her the red shawl that, today, has the ominous if brilliant look of blood on snow. Her breasts have just begun to swell; her hair is lint, so fair it hardly makes a shadow on her pale forehead; her cheeks are an emblematic scarlet and white and she has just started her woman's bleeding, the clock inside her that will strike, henceforward, once a month.

She stands and moves within the invisible pentacle of her own virginity. She is an unbroken egg; she is a sealed vessel; she has inside her a magic space the entrance to which is shut tight with a plug of membrane; she is a closed system; she does not know how to shiver. She has her knife and she is afraid of nothing.

Her father might forbid her, if he were home, but he is away in the forest, gathering wood, and her mother cannot deny her. The forest closed upon her like a pair of jaws.

There is always something to look at in the forest, even in the middle of winter—the huddled mounds of birds, succumbed to the lethargy of the season, heaped on the creaking boughs and too forlorn to sing; the bright frills of the winter fungi on the blotched trunks of the trees; the cuneiform slots of rabbits and deer, the herringbone tracks of the birds, a hare as lean as a rasher of bacon streaking across the path where the thin sunlight dapples the russet brakes of last year's bracken.

When she heard the freezing howl of a distant wolf, her practiced hand sprang to the handle of her knife, but she saw no sign of a wolf at all, nor of a naked man, neither, but then she heard a clattering among the brushwood and there sprang onto the path a fully clothed one, a very handsome young one, in the green coat and wide-awake hat of a hunter, laden with carcasses of game birds. She had her hand on her knife at the first rustle of twigs, but he laughed with a flash of white teeth when he saw her and made her a comic yet flattering little bow; she'd never seen such a fine fellow before, not among the rustic clowns of her native village. So on they went together, through the thickening light of the afternoon.

Soon they were laughing and joking like old friends. When he offered to carry her basket, she gave it to him although her knife was in it because he told her his rifle would protect them. As the day darkened, it began to snow again; she felt the first flakes settle on her eyelashes, but now there was only half a mile to go and there would be a fire, and hot tea, and a welcome, a warm one, surely, for the dashing huntsman as well as for herself.

This young man had a remarkable object in his pocket. It was a compass. She looked at the little round glass face in the palm of his hand and watched the wavering needle with a vague wonder. He assured her this compass had taken him safely through the wood on his hunting trip because the needle always told him with perfect accuracy where the north was. She did not believe it; she knew she should never leave the path on the way through the wood or else she would be lost instantly. He laughed at her again; gleaming trails of spittle clung to his teeth. He said if he plunged off the path into the forest that surrounded them, he could guarantee to arrive at her grandmother's house a good quarter of an hour before she did, plotting his way through the undergrowth with his compass, while she trudged the long way, along the winding path.

I don't believe you. Besides, aren't you afraid of the wolves? He only tapped the gleaming butt of his rifle and grinned.

Is it a bet? he asked. Shall we make a game of it? What will you give me if I get to your grandmother's house before you? What would you like? she asked disingenuously. A kiss.

Commonplaces of a rustic seduction; she lowered her eyes and blushed. He went through the undergrowth and took her basket with him, but she forgot to be afraid of the beasts, although now the moon was rising, for she wanted to dawdle on her way to make sure the handsome gentleman would win his wager.

Grandmother's house stood by itself a little way out of the village. The freshly falling snow blew in eddies about the kitchen garden and the young man stepped delicately up the snowy path to the door as if he were reluctant to get his feet wet, swinging his bundle of game and the girl's basket and humming a little tune to himself.

There is a faint trace of blood on his chin; he has been snacking on his catch.

He rapped upon the panels with his knuckles.

Aged and frail, granny is three-quarters succumbed to the mortality the ache in her bones promises her and almost ready to give in entirely. A boy came out from the village to build up her hearth for the night an hour ago and the kitchen crackles with busy firelight. She has her Bible for company; she is a pious old woman. She is propped up on several pillows in the bed set into the wall peasant fashion, wrapped up in the patchwork quilt she made before she was married, more years ago than she cares to remember. Two china spaniels with liver-colored blotches on their coats and black noses sit on either side of the fireplace. There is a bright rug of woven rags on the pantiles. The grandfather clock ticks away her eroding time.

We keep the wolves outside by living well.

He rapped upon the panels with his hairy knuckles.

It is your granddaughter, he mimicked in a high soprano. Lift up the latch and walk in, my darling.

You can tell them by their eyes, eyes of a beast of prey, nocturnal, devastating eyes as red as a wound; you can hurl your Bible at him and your apron after, granny; you thought that was a sure prophylactic against these infernal vermin. . . . Now call on Christ and his mother and all the angels in heaven to protect you, but it won't do you any good.

His feral muzzle is sharp as a knife; he drops his golden burden of gnawed pheasant on the table and puts down your dear girl's basket, too. Oh, my God, what have you done with her?

Off with his disguise, that coat of forest-colored cloth, the hat with the feather tucked into the ribbon; his matted hair streams down his white shirt and she can see the lice moving in it. The sticks in the hearth shift and hiss; night and the forest has come into the kitchen with darkness tangled in its hair.

He strips off his shirt. His skin is the color and texture of vellum. A crisp stripe of hair runs down his belly, his nipples are ripe and dark as poison fruit, but he's so thin you could count the ribs under his skin if only he gave you the time. He strips off his trousers and she can see how hairy his legs are. His genitals, huge. Ah! huge.

The last thing the old lady saw in all this world was a young man, eyes like cinders, naked as a stone, approaching her bed. The wolf is carnivore incarnate.

When he had finished with her, he licked his chops and quickly dressed himself again, until he was just as he had been when he came through her door. He burned the inedible hair in the fireplace and wrapped the bones up in a napkin that he hid away under the bed in the wooden chest in which he found a clean pair of sheets. These he carefully put on the bed instead of the telltale stained ones he stowed away in the laundry basket. He plumped up the pillows and shook out the patchwork quilt, he picked up the Bible from the floor, closed it and laid it on the table. All was as it had been before except that grandmother was gone. The sticks twitched in the grate, the clock ticked and the young man sat patiently, deceitfully beside the bed in granny's nightcap. Rat-a-tap-tap.

Who's there, he quavers in granny's antique falsetto. Only your granddaughter.

So she came in, bringing with her a flurry of snow that melted in tears on the tiles, and perhaps she was a little disappointed to see only her grandmother sitting beside the fire. But then he flung off the blanket and sprang to the door, pressing his back against it so that she could not get out again.

The girl looked round the room and saw there was not even the indentation of a head on the smooth cheek of the pillow and how, for the first time she'd seen it so, the Bible lay closed on the table. The tick of the clock cracked like a whip. She wanted her knife from her basket but she did not dare reach for it because his eyes were fixed upon her—huge eyes that now seemed to shine with a unique, interior light, eyes the size of saucers, saucers full of Greek fire, diabolic phosphorescence. What big eyes you have.

All the better to see you with.

No trace at all of the old woman except for a tuft of white hair that had caught in the bark of an unburned log. When the girl saw that, she knew she was in danger of death.

Where is my grandmother?

There's nobody here but we two, my darling.

Now a great howling rose up all around them, near, very near, as close as the kitchen garden, the howling of a multitude of wolves, she knew the worst wolves are hairy on the inside and she shivered, in spite of the scarlet shawl she pulled more closely round herself as if it could protect her, although it was as red as the blood she must spill. Who has come to sing us carols? she said.

Those are the voices of my brothers, darling; I love the company of wolves. Look out of the window and you'll see them.

Snow half-caked the lattice and she opened it to look into the garden. It was a white night of moon and snow; the blizzard whirled round the gaunt, gray beasts who squatted on their haunches among the rows of winter cabbage, pointing their sharp snouts to the moon and howling as if their hearts would break. Ten wolves; twenty wolves—so many wolves she could not count them, howling in concert as if demented or deranged. Their eyes reflected the light from the kitchen and shone like a hundred candles.

It is very cold, poor things, she said; no wonder they howl so.

She closed the window on the wolves' threnody and took off her scarlet shawl, the color of poppies, the color of sacrifices, the color of her menses, and since her fear did her no good, she ceased to be afraid. What shall I do with my shawl?

Throw it on the fire, dear one. You won't need it again.

She bundled up her shawl and threw it on the blaze, which instantly consumed it. Then she drew her blouse over her head; her small breasts gleamed as if the snow had invaded the room. What shall I do with my blouse? Into the fire with it, too, my pet.

The thin muslin went flaring up the chimney like a magic bird and now off came her skirt, her woolen stockings, her shoes, and onto the fire they went, too, and were gone for good. The firelight shone through the edges of her skin; now she was clothed only in her untouched integument of flesh. Thus dazzling, naked, she combed out her hair with her fingers; her hair looked white as the snow outside. Then went directly to the man with red eyes in whose unkempt mane the lice moved; she stood up on tiptoe and unbuttoned the collar of his shirt. What big arms you have.

All the better to hug you with.

Every wolf in the world now howled a prothalamion outside the window as she freely gave the kiss she owed him.

What big teeth you have!

She saw how his jaws began to slaver and the room was full of the clamor of the forest's *Liebestod*, but the wise child never flinched, even when he answered:

All the better to eat you with.

The girl burst out laughing; she knew she was nobody's meat. She laughed at him full in the face, she ripped off his shirt for him and flung it into the fire, in the fiery wake of her own discarded clothing. The flames danced like dead souls on Walpurgisnacht and the old bones under the bed set up a terrible clattering, but she did not pay them any heed. Carnivore incarnate, only immaculate flesh appeases him.

She will lay his fearful head on her lap and she will pick out the lice from his pelt and perhaps she will put the lice into her mouth and eat them, as he will bid her, as she would do in a savage marriage ceremony. The blizzard will die down.

The blizzard dies down, leaving the mountains as randomly covered with snow as if a blind woman had thrown a sheet over them, the upper branches of the forest pines limed, creaking, swollen with the fall. Snowlight, moonlight, a confusion of pawprints. All silent, all still.

Midnight; and the clock strikes. It is Christmas Day, the werewolves' birthday; the door of the solstice stands wide open; let them all slink through.

See! Sweet and sound she sleeps in granny's bed, between the paws of the tender wolf.

QUESTIONS FOR DISCUSSION AND WRITING

1. "The Company of Wolves" has several apparently disconnected sections, among them the opening discussion of the nature of wolves, the story of the hunter who trapped the wolf in the pit, the story of the young woman who remarries after her werewolf husband disappears, and the final story of the young girl who reenacts the story of Little Red Riding Hood, only to find herself cuddled in the wolf's arms at the end of the story. How fully are these various threads intertwined? Do you see a common theme connecting them?
2. The story ends with Little Red Riding Hood sleeping "Sweet and sound . . . in granny's bed." What are we to make of the final relationship between Little Red Riding Hood and the wolf? In what ways has she become wolflike and the wolf human?
3. "The Company of Wolves" opens with some vivid descriptions of wolves and their behavior. Much of the description plays on our stereotypes of wolves. How do wolves figure in literature and myth? What aphorisms or clichés do you know that refer to wolves (e.g., "He's a wolf in sheep's clothing" or "He gave her a wolf whistle")? Finally, do a little research on wolves. How accurate are these literary representations of them?

RONALD BLACKWELL
Li'l Red Riding Hood _____ *1966*

Owoooooooo!
Who's that I see walkin' in these woods?

Why, it's Little Red Riding Hood.
Hey there Little Red Riding Hood,
You sure are looking good.
You're everything a big bad wolf could want.   5
Listen to me.

Little Red Riding Hood
I don't think little big girls should
Go walking in these spooky old woods alone.   10
Owoooooooo!

What big eyes you have,
The kind of eyes that drive wolves mad.
So just to see that you don't get chased
I think I ought to walk with you for a ways.   15

What full lips you have.
They're sure to lure someone bad.
So until you get to grandma's place
I think you ought to walk with me and be safe.

I'm gonna keep my sheep suit on   20
Until I'm sure that you've been shown
That I can be trusted walking with you alone.
Owoooooooo!

Little Red Riding Hood
I'd like to hold you if I could   25
But you might think I'm a big bad wolf so I won't.
Owoooooooo!

What a big heart I have—the better to love you with.
Little Red Riding Hood
Even bad wolves can be good.   30
I'll try to be satisfied just to walk close by your side.
Maybe you'll see things my way before we get to grandma's place.

Little Red Riding Hood
You sure are looking good
You're everything that a big bad wolf could want.   35
Owoooooooo! I mean baaaaaa! Baaa?

QUESTIONS FOR DISCUSSION AND WRITING

1. What kind of wolf is the wolf in Blackwell's song? Threatening? Seductive? What indications do we have of how Little Red Riding Hood responds?
2. Locate a copy of Sam the Sham and the Pharaoh's version of Blackwell's "Li'l Red Riding Hood." How does hearing the song alter your response to its lyrics?

ROALD DAHL (1916–1990)

Little Red Riding Hood and the Wolf _____ 1982

As soon as Wolf began to feel
That he would like a decent meal,
He went and knocked on Grandma's door.
When Grandma opened it, she saw
5   The sharp white teeth, the horrid grin,
And Wolfie said, 'May I come in?'
Poor Grandmamma was terrified,
'He's going to eat me up!' she cried.
And she was absolutely right.
10   He ate her up in one big bite.
But Grandmamma was small and tough,
And Wolfie wailed, "That's not enough!
'I haven't yet begun to feel
'That I have had a decent meal!'
15   He ran around the kitchen yelping,
'I've *got* to have another helping!'
Then added with a frightful leer,
'I'm therefore going to wait right here
'Till Little Miss Red Riding Hood
20   'Comes home from walking in the wood.'
He quickly put on Grandma's clothes,
(Of course he hadn't eaten those.)
He dressed himself in coat and hat.
He put on shoes and after that
25   He even brushed and curled his hair,
Then sat himself in Grandma's chair.
In came the little girl in red.
She stopped. She stared. And then she said,

'What great big ears you have, Grandma.'
30   *'All the better to hear you with,'* the Wolf replied.
'What great big eyes you have, Grandma,'
said Little Red Riding Hood.
'All the better to see you with,' the Wolf replied.

He sat there watching her and smiled.
35   He thought, I'm going to eat this child.
Compared with her old Grandmamma
She's going to taste like caviare.

Then Little Red Riding Hood said, *'But Grandma,*
what a lovely great big furry coat you have on.'
40   'That's wrong!' cried Wolf. 'Have you forgot
'To tell me what BIG TEETH I've got?
'Ah well, no matter what you say,

'I'm going to eat you anyway.'
The small girl smiles. One eyelid flickers.
She whips a pistol from her knickers.   45
She aims it at the creature's head
And *bang bang bang*, she shoots him dead.
A few weeks later, in the wood,
I came across Miss Riding Hood.
But what a change! No cloak of red,   50
No silly hood upon her head.
She said, 'Hello, and do please note
'My lovely furry WOLFSKIN COAT.'

QUESTIONS FOR DISCUSSION AND WRITING

1. In Dahl's version of the Little Red Riding Hood story, the young girl is not a victim but a hero. How old is Dahl's heroine? At what point do you realize that Dahl
   is going to alter the story's ending? What leads you to your realization?
2. Read Dahl's poem aloud. How do the rhymes and meter make it impossible for
   you to see this as a potential tragedy?
3. Dahl omits the first sections of the Little Red Riding Hood story, those in which
   the young girl's mother gives her the basket to take to the grandmother and in
   which Little Red Riding Hood meets the wolf in the woods. How do the omis-
   sions of these details affect our response to the story and its characters?

OLGA BROUMAS (1949–   )

Little Red Riding Hood _____ *1977*

I grow old, old
without you, Mother, landscape
of my heart.   No child, no daughter between my bones
has moved, and passed
out screaming, dressed in her mantle of blood   5

as I did
once through your pelvic scaffold, stretching it
like a wishbone, your tenderest skin
strung on its bow and tightened
against the pain.   I slipped out like an arrow, but not before   10

the midwife
plunged to her wrist and guided
my baffled head to its first mark.   High forceps
might, in that one instant, have accomplished

15   what you and that good woman failed
      in all these years to do: cramp
      me between the temples, hobble
      my baby feet.   Dressed in my red hood, howling, I went—

      evading
20   the white-clad doctor and his fancy claims: microscope,
      stethoscope, scalpel, all
      the better to see with, to hear,
      and to eat—straight from your hollowed basket
      into the midwife's skirts.   I grew up
25   good at evading, and when you said,
      "Stick to the road and forget the flowers, there's
      wolves in those bushes, mind
      where you got to go, mind
      you get there," I
30   minded.   I kept

      to the road, kept
      the hood secret, kept what it sheathed more
      secret still.   I opened
      it only at night, and with other women
35   who might be walking the same road to their own
      grandma's house, each with her basket of gifts, her small hood
      safe in the same part.   I minded well.   I have no daughter

      to trace that road, back to your lap with my laden
      basket of love.   I'm growing
40   old, old
      without you.   Mother, landscape
      of my heart, architect of my body, what other gesture
      can I conceive

      to make with it
45   that would reach you, alone
      in your house and waiting, across this improbable forest
      peopled with wolves and our lost, flower-gathering
      sisters they feed on.

QUESTIONS FOR DISCUSSION AND WRITING

1. Look at Broumas's descriptions of the red hood. What do you think the hood is?
   How does it help define the narrator's sense of herself?

2. Why is it significant that the Little Red Riding Hood of Broumas's poem has
   given birth to no children? Why is it significant that she has always "minded"?
   That she has grown old?

3. The poem is addressed to the speaker's mother, who is waiting alone. What is she waiting *for*?

Gustav Doré, illustration for an 1861 edition of Perrault's *Histoires ou Contes du temps passé avec des Moralités (Tales of Past Times with Morals)*

BRUNO BETTELHEIM (1903–1990)
Little Red Riding Hood   *1976*

A charming, "innocent" young girl swallowed by a wolf is an image which impresses itself indelibly on the mind. In "Hansel and Gretel" the witch only planned to devour the children; in "Little Red Riding Hood" both grandmother and child are actually swallowed up by the wolf. Like most fairy tales, "Little Red Riding Hood" exists in many different versions. The most popular is the Brothers Grimm's story, in which Little Red Cap and the grandmother are reborn and the wolf is meted out a well-deserved punishment.

But the literary history of this story begins with Perrault. It is by his title, "Little Red Riding Hood," that the tale is best known in English, though the title it was given by the Brothers Grimm, "Little Red Cap," is more appropriate. However, Andrew Lang, one of the most erudite and astute students of fairy tales, remarks that if all variants of "Little Red Riding Hood" ended the way Perrault concluded his, we might as well dismiss it. This would probably have been its fate if the Brothers Grimm's version had not made it into one of the most popular fairy tales. But since this story's known history starts with Perrault, we shall consider—and dismiss—his rendering first.

Perrault's story begins like all other well-known versions, telling how the grandmother had made her granddaughter a little red riding hood (or cap), which led to the girl's being known by that name. One day her mother sent Little Red Riding Hood to take goodies to her grandmother, who was sick. The girl's way led her through a forest, where she met up with the wolf. The wolf did not dare to eat her up then because there were woodcutters in the forest, so he asked Little Red Riding Hood where she was going, and she told him. The wolf asked exactly where Grandmother lived, and the girl gave the information. Then the wolf said that he would go visit Grandmother too, and he took off at great speed, while the girl dallied along the way.

The wolf gained entrance at the grandmother's home by pretending to be Little Red Riding Hood, and immediately swallowed up the old woman. In Perrault's story the wolf does not dress up as Grandmother, but simply lies down in her bed. When Little Red Riding Hood arrived, the wolf asked her to join him in bed. Little Red Riding Hood undressed and got into bed, at which moment, astonished at how Grandmother looked naked, she exclaimed, "Grandmother, what big arms you have!" to which the wolf answered: "To better embrace you!" Then Little Red Riding Hood said: "Grandmother, what big legs you have!" and received the reply: "To be better able to run." These two exchanges, which do not occur in the Brothers Grimm's version, are then followed by the well-known questions about Grandmother's big ears, eyes, and teeth. To the last question the wolf answers, "To better eat you." "And, in saying these words, the bad wolf threw himself on Little Red Riding Hood and ate her up."

There Lang's translation ends, as do many others. But Perrault's original rendering continues with a little poem setting forth the moral to be drawn from the story: that nice girls ought not to listen to all sorts of people. If they do, it is not surprising that the wolf will get them and eat them up. As for wolves, these come in all variations; and among them the gentle wolves are the most dangerous of all, particularly those who follow young girls into the streets, even into their homes. Perrault wanted not only to entertain his audience, but to teach a specific moral lesson with each of his tales. So it is understandable that he changed them accordingly. Unfortunately, in doing so, he robbed his fairy stories of much of their meaning. As he tells the story, nobody warned Little Red Riding Hood not to dally on the way to Grandmother's house, or not to stray off the proper road. Also, in Perrault's version it does not make sense that the grandmother, who has done nothing wrong at all, should end up destroyed.

Perrault's "Little Red Riding Hood" loses much of its appeal because it is so obvious that his wolf is not a rapacious beast but a metaphor, which leaves little to the imagination of the hearer. Such simplifications and a directly stated moral turn this potential fairy tale into a cautionary tale which spells everything out completely. Thus the hearer's imagination cannot become active in giving the story a personal meaning. Captive to a rationalistic interpretation of the story's purpose, Perrault makes everything as explicit as possible. For example, when the girl undresses and joins the wolf in bed and the wolf tells her that his strong arms are for embracing her better, nothing is left to the imagination. Since in response to such direct and obvious seduction Little Red Riding Hood makes no move to escape or fight back, either she is stupid or she wants to be seduced. In neither case is she a suitable figure to identify with. With these details Little Red Riding Hood is changed from a naïve, attractive young girl, who is induced to neglect Mother's warnings and enjoy herself in what she consciously believes to be innocent ways, into nothing but a fallen woman.

It destroys the value of a fairy tale for the child if someone details its meaning for him; Perrault does worse—he belabors it. All good fairy tales have meaning on many levels; only the child can know which meanings are of significance to him at the moment. As he grows up, the child discovers new aspects of these well-known tales, and this gives him the conviction that he has indeed matured in understanding, since the same story now reveals so much more to him. This can happen only if the child has not been told didactically what the story is supposed to be about. Only when discovery of the previously hidden meanings of a fairy tale is the child's spontaneous and intuitive achievement does it attain full significance for him. This discovery changes a story from something the child is being given into something he partially creates for himself.

The Brothers Grimm recount two versions of this story, which is very unusual for them. In both, the story and the heroine are called "Little Red Cap" because of the "little cap of red velvet which suited her so well that she would not wear anything else."

The threat of being devoured is the central theme of "Little Red Riding Hood," as it is of "Hansel and Gretel." The same basic psychological constellations which recur in every person's development can lead to the most diverse human fates and personalities, depending on what the individual's other experiences are and how he interprets them to himself. Similarly, a limited number of basic themes depict in fairy stories quite different aspects of the human experience; all depends on how such a motif is elaborated and in what context events happen. "Hansel and Gretel" deals with the difficulties and anxieties of the child who is forced to give up his dependent attachment to the mother and free himself of his oral fixation. "Little Red Cap" takes up some crucial problems the school-age girl has to solve if oedipal attachments linger on in the unconscious, which may drive her to expose herself dangerously to the possibility of seduction.

In both these fairy tales the house in the woods and the parental home are the same place, experienced quite differently because of a change in the psychological situation. In her own home Little Red Cap, protected by her parents, is the untroubled pubertal child who is quite competent to cope. At the home of her grandmother, who is herself infirm, the same girl is helplessly incapacitated by the consequences of her encounter with the wolf.

Hansel and Gretel, subjects of their oral fixation, think nothing of eating the house that symbolically stands for the bad mother who has deserted them (forced them to leave home), and they do not hesitate to burn the witch to death in an oven as if she were food to be cooked for eating. Little Red Cap, who has outgrown her oral fixation, no longer has any destructive oral desires. Psychologically, the distance is enormous between oral fixation symbolically turned into cannibalism, which is the central theme of "Hansel and Gretel," and how Little Red Cap punishes the wolf. The wolf in "Little Red Cap" is the seducer, but as far as the overt content of the story goes, the wolf doesn't do anything that does not come naturally—namely, it devours to feed itself. And it is common for man to kill a wolf, although the method used in this story is unusual.

Little Red Cap's home is one of abundance, which, since she is way beyond oral anxiety, she gladly shares with her grandmother by bringing her food. To Little Red Cap the world beyond the parental home is not a threatening wilderness through which the child cannot find a path. Outside Red Cap's home there is a well-known road, from which, her mother warns, one must not stray.

While Hansel and Gretel have to be pushed out into the world, Little Red Cap leaves her home willingly. She is not afraid of the outside world, but recognizes its beauty, and therein lies a danger. If this world beyond home and duty becomes too attractive, it may induce a return to proceeding according to the pleasure principle—which, we assume, Little Red Cap had relinquished due to her parents' teachings in favor of the reality principle—and then destructive encounters may occur.

This quandary of standing between reality principle and pleasure principle is explicitly stated when the wolf says to Little Red Cap: "See how pretty the flowers are which are all around you. Why don't you look about? I believe you don't even hear how beautifully the little birds are singing. You walk along with singlemindedness and concentration as if you were going to school, while everything out here in the woods is merry." This is the same conflict between doing what one likes to do and what one ought to do which Red Cap's mother had warned her about at the outset, as she admonished her daughter to "walk properly and don't run off the road. . . . And when you come to Grandmother's place, do not forget to wish her a 'Good morning,' and don't look into all the corners as soon as you arrive." So her mother is aware of Little Red Cap's proclivity for straying off the beaten path, and for spying into corners to discover the secrets of adults.

The idea that "Little Red Cap" deals with the child's ambivalence about whether to live by the pleasure principle or the reality principle is borne out by the fact that Red Cap stops gathering flowers only "when she had collected so many that she could not carry any more." At that moment Little Red Cap "once more remembered Grandmother and set out on the way to her." That is, only when picking flowers is no longer enjoyable does the pleasure-seeking id recede and Red Cap become aware of her obligations.

Little Red Cap is very much a child already struggling with pubertal problems for which she is not yet ready emotionally because she has not mastered her oedipal conflicts. That Little Red Cap is more mature than Hansel and Gretel is shown by her questioning attitude toward what she encounters in the world. Hansel and Gretel do not wonder about the gingerbread house, or explore what the witch is all about. Little Red Cap wishes to find out things, as her mother's cautioning her not to peek indicates. She observes that something is wrong when she finds her grandmother "looking very strange," but is confused by the wolf's having disguised himself in the old woman's attire. Little Red Cap tries to understand, when she asks Grandmother about her big ears, observes the big eyes, wonders about the large hands, the horrible mouth. Here is an enumeration of the four senses: hearing, seeing, touching, and tasting; the pubertal child uses them all to comprehend the world.

"Little Red Cap" in symbolic form projects the girl into the dangers of her oedipal conflicts during puberty, and then saves her from them, so that she will be able to mature conflict-free. The maternal figures of mother and witch which were all-important in "Hansel and Gretel" have shrunk to insignificance in "Little Red Cap," where neither mother nor grandmother can do anything—neither threaten nor protect. The male, by contrast, is all-important, split into two opposite forms: the dangerous seducer who, if given in to, turns into the destroyer of the good grandmother and the girl; and the hunter, the responsible, strong, and rescuing father figure.

It is as if Little Red Cap is trying to understand the contradictory nature of the male by experiencing all aspects of his personality: the selfish, asocial, violent, potentially destructive tendencies of the id (the wolf); the unselfish, social, thoughtful, and protective propensities of the ego (the hunter).

Little Red Cap is universally loved because, although she is virtuous, she is tempted; and because her fate tells us that trusting everybody's good intentions, which seems so nice, is really leaving oneself open to pitfalls. If there were not something in us that likes the big bad wolf, he would have no power over us. Therefore, it is important to understand his nature, but even more important to learn what makes him attractive to us. Appealing as naïveté is, it is dangerous to remain naïve all one's life.

But the wolf is not just the male seducer, he also represents all the asocial, animalistic tendencies within ourselves. By giving up the school-age child's virtues of "walking singlemindedly," as her task demands, Little Red Cap reverts to the pleasure-seeking oedipal child. By falling in with the wolf's suggestions, she has also given the wolf the opportunity to devour her grandmother. Here the story speaks to some of the oedipal difficulties which remained unresolved in the girl, and the wolf's swallowing Little Red Cap is the merited punishment for her arranging things so that the wolf can do away with a mother figure. Even a four-year-old cannot help wondering what Little Red Cap is up to when, answering the wolf's question, she gives the wolf specific directions on how to get to her grandmother's house. What is the purpose of such detailed information, the child wonders to himself, if not to make sure that the wolf will find the way? Only adults who are convinced that fairy tales do not make sense can fail to see that Little Red Cap's unconscious is working overtime to give Grandmother away.

Grandmother, too, is not free of blame. A young girl needs a strong mother figure for her own protection, and as a model to imitate. But Red Cap's grandmother is carried away by her own needs beyond what is good for the child, as we are told: "There was nothing she would not have given the child." It would not have been the first or last time that a child so spoiled by a grandmother runs into trouble in real life. Whether it is Mother or Grandmother—this mother once removed—it is fatal for the young girl if this older woman abdicates her own attractiveness to males and transfers it to the daughter by giving her a too attractive red cloak.

All through "Little Red Cap," in the title as in the girl's name, the emphasis is on the color red, which she openly wears. Red is the color symbolizing violent emotions, very much including sexual ones. The red velvet cap given by Grandmother to Little Red Cap thus can be viewed as a symbol of a premature transfer of sexual attractiveness, which is further accentuated by the grandmother's being old and sick, too weak even to open a door. The name "Little Red Cap" indicates the key importance of this feature of the heroine in the story. It suggests that not only is the red cap little, but also the girl. She is too little, not for wearing the cap, but for managing what this red cap symbolizes, and what her wearing it invites.

Little Red Cap's danger is her budding sexuality, for which she is not yet emotionally mature enough. The person who is psychologically ready to have sexual experiences can master them, and grow because of it. But a premature sexuality is a regressive experience, arousing all that is still primitive within us and that threatens to swallow us up. The immature person who is not yet ready for sex but is exposed to an experience which arouses strong sexual feelings falls back on oedipal ways for dealing with it. The only way such a person believes he can win out in sex is by getting rid of the more experienced competitors—hence Little Red Cap's giving specific instructions to the wolf on how to get to Grandmother's house. In doing this, however, she also shows her ambivalence. In directing the wolf to Grandmother, she acts as if she were telling the wolf, "Leave me alone; go to Grandmother, who is a mature woman; she should be able to cope with what you represent; I am not."

This struggle between her conscious desire to do the right thing and the unconscious wish to win out over her (grand)mother is what endears the girl and the story to us and makes her so supremely human. Like many of us when we were children and caught in inner ambivalences that, despite our best efforts, we could not master, she tries to push the problem onto somebody else: an older person, a parent or parent substitute. But by thus trying to evade a threatening situation, she nearly gets destroyed by it.

As mentioned before, the Brothers Grimm also present an important variation of "Little Red Riding Hood," which essentially consists of only an addition to the basic story. In the variation, we are told that at a later time, when Little Red Cap is again taking cakes to her grandmother, another wolf tries to entice her to stray from the direct path (of virtue). This time the girl hurries to Grandmother and tells her all about it. Together they secure the door so that the wolf cannot enter. In the end, the wolf slips from the roof into a trough filled with water and drowns. The story ends, "But Little Red Cap went gaily home, and nobody did any harm to her."

This variation elaborates on what the hearer of the story feels convinced of— that after her bad experience the girl realizes that she is by no means mature enough to deal with the wolf (the seducer), and she is ready to settle down to a good working alliance with her mother. This is symbolically expressed by her rushing to Grandmother as soon as danger threatens, rather than her thinking nothing of it, as she did in her first encounter with the wolf. Little Red Cap works with her (grand)mother and follows her advice—in the continuation, Grandmother tells Red Cap to fill the trough with water that smells of sausages which had been cooked in it, and the smell attracts the wolf so that he falls into the water—and together the two easily overcome the wolf. The child thus needs to form a strong working alliance with the parent of the same sex, so that through identification with the parent and conscious learning from him, the child will grow successfully into an adult.

Fairy stories speak to our conscious and our unconscious, and therefore do not need to avoid contradictions, since these easily coexist in our unconscious. On a quite different level of meaning, what happens with and to Grandmother may be seen in a very different light. The hearer of the story rightly wonders why the wolf does not devour Little Red Cap as soon as he meets her—that is, at the first opportunity. Typically for Perrault, he offers a seemingly rational explanation: the wolf would have done so were it not afraid of some woodcutters who were close by. Since in Perrault's story the wolf is all along a male seducer, it makes sense that an older man might be afraid to seduce a little girl in the sight and hearing of other men.

Things are quite different in the Brothers Grimm's tale, where we are given to understand that the wolf's excessive greed accounts for the delay: "The wolf thought to itself, "That young tender thing, what a fat mouthful, it'll taste much better than the old one: you have to proceed craftily so that you catch both.'" But this explanation does not make sense, because the wolf could have gotten hold of Little Red Cap right then and there, and later tricked the grandmother just as it happens in the story.

The wolf's behavior begins to make sense in the Brothers Grimm's version if we assume that to get Little Red Cap, the wolf first has to do away with Grandmother. As long as the (grand)mother is around, Little Red Cap will not become his. But once the (grand)mother is out of the way, the road seems open for acting on one's desires, which had to remain repressed as long as Mother was around. The story on this level deals with the daughter's unconscious wish to be seduced by her father (the wolf).

With the reactivation in puberty of early oedipal longings, the girl's wish for her father, her inclination to seduce him, and her desire to be seduced by him, also become reactivated. Then the girl feels she deserves to be punished terribly by the mother, if not the father also, for her desire to take him away from Mother. Adolescent reawakening of early emotions which were relatively dormant is not restricted to oedipal feelings, but includes even earlier anxieties and desires which reappear during this period.

On a different level of interpretation, one could say that the wolf does not devour Little Red Cap immediately upon meeting her because he wants to get her into bed with him first: a sexual meeting of the two has to precede her being "eaten up." While most children do not know about those animals of which one dies during the sex act, these destructive connotations are quite vivid in the child's conscious and unconscious mind—so much so that most children view the sexual act primarily as an act of violence which one partner commits on the other. I believe it is the child's unconscious equation of sexual excitement, violence, and anxiety which Djuna Barnes alludes to when she writes: "Children know something they can't tell; they like Red Riding Hood and the wolf in bed!" Because this strange coincidence of opposite emotions characterizing the child's sexual knowledge is given body in "Little Red Riding Hood," the story holds a great unconscious attraction to children, and to adults who are vaguely reminded by it of their own childish fascination with sex.

Another artist has given expression to these same underlying feelings. Gustave Doré, in one of his famous illustrations to fairy tales, shows Little Red Riding Hood and the wolf in bed together. The wolf is depicted as rather placid. But the girl appears to be beset by powerful ambivalent feelings as she looks at the wolf resting beside her. She makes no move to leave. She seems most intrigued by the situation, attracted and repelled at the same time. The combination of feelings her face and body suggest can best be described as fascination. It is the same fascination which sex, and everything surrounding it, exercises over the child's mind. This, to return to Djuna Barnes's statement, is what children feel about Red Riding Hood and the wolf and their relation, but can't tell—and is what makes the story so captivating.

It is this "deathly" fascination with sex—which is experienced as simultaneously the greatest excitement and the greatest anxiety—that is bound up with the little girl's oedipal longings for her father, and with the reactivation of these same feelings in different form during puberty. Whenever these emotions reappear, they evoke memories of the little girl's propensity for seducing her father, and with it other memories of her desire to be seduced by him also.

While in Perrault's rendering the emphasis is on sexual seduction, the opposite is true for the Brothers Grimm's story. In it, no sexuality is directly or indirectly mentioned; it may be subtly implied, but essentially, the hearer has to supply the idea to help his understanding of the story. To the child's mind, the sexual implications remain preconscious, as they should. Consciously a child knows that there is nothing wrong with picking flowers; what is wrong is disobeying Mother when one has to carry out an important mission serving the legitimate interest of the (grand)parent. The main conflict is between what seem justified interests to the child and what he knows his parent wants him to do. The story implies that the child doesn't know how dangerous it may be to give in to what he considers his innocuous desires, so he must learn of this danger. Or rather, as the story warns, life will teach it to him, at his expense.

"Little Red Cap" externalizes the inner processes of the pubertal child: the wolf is the externalization of the badness the child feels when he goes contrary to the admonitions of his parents and permits himself to tempt, or to be tempted, sexually. When he strays from the path the parent has outlined for him, he encounters "badness," and he fears that it will swallow up him and the parent whose confidence he betrayed. But there can be resurrection from "badness," as the story proceeds to tell.

Very different from Little Red Cap, who gives in to the temptations of her id and in doing so betrays mother and grandmother, the hunter does not permit his emotions to run away with him. His first reaction on finding the wolf sleeping in the grandmother's bed is, "Do I find you here, you old sinner? I have been looking for you for a long time"—and his immediate inclination is to shoot the wolf. But his ego (or reason) asserts itself despite the proddings of the id (anger at the wolf), and the hunter realizes that it is more important to try to rescue Grandmother than to give in to anger by shooting the wolf outright. The hunter restrains himself, and instead of shooting the animal dead, he carefully cuts open the wolf's belly with scissors, rescuing Little Red Cap and her grandmother.

The hunter is a most attractive figure, to boys as well as girls, because he rescues the good and punishes the bad. All children encounter difficulties in obeying the reality principle, and they easily recognize in the opposite figures of wolf and hunter the conflict between the id and the ego-superego aspects of their personality. In the hunter's action, violence (cutting open the belly) is made to serve the highest social purpose (rescuing the two females). The child feels that nobody appreciates that his violent tendencies seem constructive to him, but the story shows that they can be.

Little Red Cap has to be cut out of the wolf's stomach as if through a Caesarean operation; thus the idea of pregnancy and birth is intimated. With it, associations of a sexual relation are evoked in the child's unconscious. How does a fetus get into the mother's womb? wonders the child, and decides that it can happen only through the mother having swallowed something, as the wolf did.

Why does the hunter speak of the wolf as an "old sinner" and say that he has been trying to find him for a long time? As the seducer is called a wolf in the story, so the person who seduces, particularly when his target is a young girl, is popularly referred to as an "old sinner" today as in olden times. On a different level, the wolf also represents the unacceptable tendencies within the hunter; we all refer on occasion to the animal within us, as a simile for our propensity for acting violently or irresponsibly to gain our goals.

While the hunter is all-important for the denouement, we do not know where he comes from, nor does he interact with Little Red Cap—he rescues her, that's all. All through "Little Red Cap" no father is mentioned, which is most unusual for a fairy story of this kind. This suggests that the father is present, but in hidden form. The girl certainly expects her father to rescue her from all difficulties, and particularly those emotional ones which are the consequence of her wish to seduce him and to be seduced by him. What is meant here by "seduction" is the girl's desire and efforts to induce her father to love her more than anybody else, and her wish that he should make all efforts to induce her to love him more than anybody else. Then we may see that the father is indeed present in "Little Red Cap" in two opposite forms: as the wolf, which is an externalization of the dangers of overwhelming oedipal feelings, and as the hunter in his protective and rescuing function.

Despite the hunter's immediate inclination to shoot the wolf dead, he does not do so. After her rescue, it is Little Red Cap's own idea to fill the wolf's belly with stones, "and as it woke up, it tried to jump away, but the stones were so heavy that it collapsed and fell to its death." It has to be Little Red Cap who spontaneously plans what to do about the wolf and goes about doing it. If she is to be safe in the future, she must be able to do away with the seducer, be rid of him. If the father-hunter did this for her, Red Cap could never feel that she had really overcome her weakness, because she had not rid herself of it.

It is fairy-tale justice that the wolf should die of what he tried to do: his oral greediness is his own undoing. Since he tried to put something into his stomach nefariously, the same is done to him.

There is another excellent reason why the wolf should not die from having his belly cut open to free those he swallowed up. The fairy tale protects the child from unnecessary anxiety. If the wolf should die when his belly is opened up as in a Caesarean operation, those hearing the story might come to fear that a child coming out of the mother's body kills her. But if the wolf survives the opening up of his belly and dies only because heavy stones were sewn into it, then there is no reason for anxiety about childbirth.

Little Red Cap and her grandmother do not really die, but they are certainly reborn. If there is a central theme to the wide variety of fairy tales, it is that of a rebirth to a higher plane. Children (and adults, too) must be able to believe that reaching a higher form of existence is possible if they master the developmental steps this requires. Stories which tell that this is not only possible but likely have a tremendous appeal to children, because such tales combat the ever-present fear that they won't be able to make this transition, or that they'll lose too much in the process. That is why, for example, in "Brother and Sister" the two do not lose each other after their transformation but have a better life together; why Little Red Cap is a happier girl after her rescue; why Hansel and Gretel are so much better off after their return home.

Many adults today tend to take literally the things said in fairy tales, whereas they should be viewed as symbolic renderings of crucial life experiences. The child understands this intuitively, though he does not "know" it explicitly. An adult's reassurance to a child that Little Red Cap did not "really" die when the wolf swallowed her is experienced by the child as a condescending talking down. This is just the same as if a person is told that in the Bible story Jonah's being swallowed by the big fish was not "really" his end. Everybody who hears this story knows intuitively that Jonah's stay in the fish's belly was for a purpose—namely, so that he would return to life a better man.

The child knows intuitively that Little Red Cap's being swallowed by the wolf—much like the various deaths other fairy-tale heroes experience for a time—is by no means the end of the story, but a necessary part of it. The child also understands that Little Red Cap really "died" as the girl who permitted herself to be tempted by the wolf; and that when the story says "the little girl sprang out" of the wolf's belly, she came to life a different person. This device is necessary because, while the child can readily understand one thing being replaced by another (the good mother by the evil stepmother), he cannot yet comprehend inner transformations. So among the great merits of fairy tales is that through hearing them, the child comes to believe that such transformations are possible.

The child whose conscious and unconscious mind has become deeply involved in the story understands that what is meant by the wolf's swallowing grandmother and girl is that because of what happened, the two were temporarily lost to the world—they lost the ability to be in contact and to influence what goes on. Therefore somebody from the outside must come to their rescue; and where a mother and child are concerned, who could that be but a father?

Little Red Cap, when she fell in with the wolf's seduction to act on the basis of the pleasure principle instead of the reality principle, implicitly returned to a more primitive, earlier form of existence. In typical fairy-story fashion, her return to a more primitive level of life is impressively exaggerated as going all the way to the prebirth existence in the womb, as the child thinks in extremes.

But why must the grandmother experience the same fate as the girl? Why is she both "dead" and reduced to a lower state of existence? This detail is in line with the way the child conceives of what death means—that this person is no longer available, is no longer of any use. Grandparents must be of use to the child—they must be able to protect him, teach him, feed him; if they are not, then they are reduced to a lower form of existence. As unable to cope with the wolf as Little Red Cap is, the grandmother is reduced to the same fate as the girl.

The story makes it quite clear that the two have not died by being swallowed. This is made obvious by Little Red Cap's behavior when liberated. "The little girl sprang out crying: 'Ah, how frightened I have been; how dark it was inside the wolf's body!'" To have been frightened means that one has been very much alive, and signifies a state opposite to death, when one no longer thinks or feels. Little Red Cap's fear was of the darkness, because through her behavior she had lost her higher consciousness, which had shed light on her world. Or as the child who knows he has done wrong, or who no longer feels well protected by his parents, feels the darkness of night with its terrors settle on him.

Not just in "Little Red Cap" but throughout the fairy-tale literature, death of the hero—different from death of old age, after life's fulfillment—symbolizes his failure. Death of the unsuccessful—such as those who tried to get to Sleeping Beauty before the time was ripe and perished in the thorns—symbolizes that this person was not mature enough to master the demanding task which he foolishly (prematurely) undertook. Such persons must undergo further growth experiences, which will enable them to succeed. Those predecessors of the hero who die in fairy stories are nothing but the hero's earlier immature incarnations.

Little Red Cap, having been projected into inner darkness (the darkness inside the wolf), becomes ready and appreciative of a new light, a better understanding of the emotional experiences she has to master, and those others which she has to avoid because as yet they overwhelm her. Through stories such as "Little Red Cap" the child begins to understand—at least on a preconscious level—that only those experiences which overwhelm us arouse in us corresponding inner feelings with which we cannot deal. Once we have mastered those, we need not fear any longer the encounter with the wolf.

This is reinforced by the story's concluding sentence, which does not have Little Red Cap say that she will never again risk encountering the wolf, or go alone in the woods. On the contrary, the ending implicitly warns the child that withdrawal from all problematic situations would be the wrong solution. The story ends: "But Little Red Cap thought 'as long as you live, you won't run off the path into the woods all by yourself when mother has forbidden you to do so.'" With such inner dialogue, backed up by a most upsetting experience, Little Red Cap's encounter with her own sexuality will have a very different outcome, when she is ready—at which time her mother will approve of it.

Deviating from the straight path in defiance of mother and superego was temporarily necessary for the young girl, to gain a higher state of personality organization. Her experience convinced her of the dangers of giving in to her oedipal desires. It is much better, she learns, not to rebel against the mother, nor try to seduce or permit herself to be seduced by the as yet dangerous aspects of the male. Much better, despite one's ambivalent desires, to settle for a while longer for the protection the father provides when he is not seen in his seductive aspects. She has learned that it is better to build father and mother, and their values, deeper and in more adult ways into one's superego, to become able to deal with life's dangers.

There are many modern counterparts to "Little Red Cap." The profundity of fairy tales when compared to much of today's children's literature becomes apparent when one parallels them. David Riesman, for example, has compared "Little Red Riding Hood" with a modern children's story, *Tootle the Engine*, a Little Golden Book which some twenty years ago sold in the millions. In it, an anthropomorphically depicted little engine goes to engine school to learn to become a big streamliner. Like Little Red Riding Hood, Tootle has been told to move only on the tracks. It, too, is tempted to stray off them, since the little engine delights in playing among the pretty flowers in the fields. To stop Tootle from going astray, the townspeople get together and conceive of a clever plan, in which they all participate. Next time Tootle leaves the tracks to wander in its beloved meadows, it is stopped by a red flag wherever it turns, until it promises never to leave the tracks again.

Today we could view this as a story which exemplifies behavior modification through adverse stimuli: the red flags. Tootle reforms, and the story ends with Tootle having mended its ways and indeed going to grow up to be a big streamliner. *Tootle* seems to be essentially a cautionary tale, warning the child to stay on the narrow road of virtue. But how shallow it is when compared with the fairy tale.

"Little Red Cap" speaks of human passions, oral greediness, aggression, and pubertal sexual desires. It opposes the cultured orality of the maturing child (the nice food taken to Grandmother) to its earlier cannibalistic form (the wolf swallowing up Grandmother and the girl. With its violence, including that which saves the two females and destroys the wolf by cutting open its belly and then putting stones into it, the fairy tale does not show the world in a rosy light. The story ends as all figures—girl, mother, grandmother, hunter, and wolf—"do their own thing": the wolf tries to run away and falls to its death, after which the hunter skins the wolf and takes its pelt home; Grandmother eats what Little Red Cap has brought her; and the girl has learned her lesson. There is no conspiracy of adults which forces the story's hero to mend her way as society demands—a process which denies the value of inner-directedness. Far from others doing it for her, Little Red Cap's experience moves her to change herself, as she promises herself that "as long as you live, you won't run off the path into the woods. . . ."

How much truer both to the reality of life and to our inner experiences is the fairy tale when compared with *Tootle*, which uses realistic elements as stage props: trains running on tracks, red flags stopping them. The trappings are real enough, but everything essential is unreal, since the entire population of a town does not stop what it is doing, to help a child mend his ways. Also, there was never any real danger to Tootle's existence. Yes, Tootle is helped to mend its ways but all that is involved in the growth experience is to become a bigger and faster train—that is, an externally more successful and useful adult. There is no recognition of inner anxieties, nor of the dangers of temptation to our very existence. To quote Riesman, "there is none of the grimness of Little Red Riding Hood," which has been replaced by "a fake which the citizens put on for Tootle's benefit." Nowhere in *Tootle* is there an externalization onto story characters of inner processes and emotional problems pertaining to growing up, so that the child may be able to face the first and thus solve the latter.

We can fully believe it when at the end of *Tootle* we are told that Tootle has forgotten it ever did like flowers. Nobody with the widest stretch of imagination can believe that Little Red Riding Hood could ever forget her encounter with the wolf, or will stop liking flowers or the beauty of the world. Tootle's story, not creating any inner conviction in the hearer's mind, needs to rub in its lesson and predict the outcome: the engine will stay on the tracks and become a streamliner. No initiative, no freedom there.

The fairy tale carries within itself the conviction of its message; therefore it has no need to peg the hero to a specific way of life. There is no need to tell what Little Red Riding Hood will do, or what her future will be. Due to her experience, she will be well able to decide this herself. The wisdom about life, and about the dangers which her desires may bring about, is gained by every listener.

Little Red Riding Hood lost her childish innocence as she encountered the dangers residing in herself and the world, and exchanged it for wisdom that only the "twice born" can possess: those who not only master an existential crisis, but also become conscious that it was their own nature which projected them into it. Little Red Riding Hood's childish innocence dies as the wolf reveals itself as such and swallows her. When she is cut out of the wolf's belly, she is reborn on a higher plane of existence; relating positively to both her parents, no longer a child, she returns to life a young maiden.

QUESTIONS FOR DISCUSSION AND WRITING

1. Bettelheim makes a number of controversial assertions. Look at his arguments about one of the following claims. How convincing do you find his logic and his use of evidence? Why?

> In Perrault's story, Little Red Riding Hood is reduced to the status of a fallen woman.
>
> In the fairy tale, Little Red Riding Hood is working out her oedipal conflicts.
>
> The fairy tale is a story about the need to control the pleasure principle.
>
> The wolf represents the primitive id, and the hunter represents the superego.

2. Consider Bettelheim's analysis of Doré's illustration. Are you convinced by it? How else might the illustration be interpreted?

3. Bettelheim tells us that one of the pleasures of fairy tales is that as we grow older we find new meanings in them or that we find meanings that in our younger days we recognized only dimly or unconsciously. What instances in your own experience would support Bettelheim's claim that fairy tales take on different meanings as we grow older?

4. Bettelheim compares *Little Red Riding Hood* and other fairy tales to modern children's stories and finds the modern stories shallow and unimaginative. Find a modern story from your own childhood or one that today's children are reading. Would you agree with Bettelheim's claim? Why or why not?

QUESTIONS FOR CROSS READING:
CHILDHOOD AND INNOCENCE

1. At the end of "Wolfland," Lisel finds that she and her grandmother have much in common with the wolves. Could the same be said about Little Red Riding Hood, her grandmother, and the Wolf in Perrault's and the Grimms' versions? Look back at those earlier tales, comparing the principal characters' behavior, motivations, and dialogue.

2. Both Anna and Lisel wear the scarlet cloak that gives them kinship with Little Red Riding Hood. In what ways is "Wolfland" a retelling of the Little Red Riding Hood story?

3. The story with which "The Company of Wolves" concludes is a coming-of-age story insofar as the young woman is clearly attracted to the wolf-man and, in the end, welcomes his embrace. Where do you find similar suggestions of sexual tension in the other versions of the Little Red Riding Hood story? How are we meant to respond to that sexual tension?

4. Bettelheim interprets the Little Red Riding Hood story as a story of oedipal conflict, seduction, and the onset of puberty. How would you compare his interpretation to the interpretations implied in "Wolfland," "The Company of Wolves," Broumas's "Little Red Riding Hood," and the song by Ronald Blackwell?

Two Reader Response Journals on Little Red Riding Hood

April Munroe Perez
May 29, 2002

   Michael and the Wolf

   We were in the car and my son Michael, who is 4½ years
old, started getting restless. So I decided to tell him the
story of Little Red Riding Hood. I told him from memory and I
kind of mixed up versions. Basically it was the Brothers
Grimm version. After I told him the part about the wolf, trying to run away but since Little Red Riding Hood had sewn
rocks in his belly he was unable to run but instead fell down
dead, he got really sad for the wolf. He didn't want him to
die. I started to wonder if maybe he was too young or too
sensitive for this story. I think he was worried about the
wolf because everything turned out fine in the end. Little Red
Riding Hood and her grandmother are not even hurt by the
wolf. Maybe I made the wolf seem neutral and not scary. I
guess being eaten by a wolf is not so scary if everything
turns out fine in the end.

   Next, I read Michael a 1968, Brothers Grimm version of
Little Red Riding Hood. This time he was scared that the wolf
was going to eat Little Red Riding Hood right from the beginning. A part of that was because after the first time I told
him the story and he was so sympathetic toward the wolf I explained how the wolf was the bad guy. The other reason was
that he could see Little Red Riding Hood right on the cover.

There is a picture of her and she looks very young, only about 4 or 5. I asked him where Little Red Riding Hood was in the picture and he pointed to her with a puzzled look on his face. I said, "That's right," and he said, "Oh, I thought that was a little boy." So maybe he identified with Little Red Riding Hood this time because she looked like a boy about his age.

This time he really didn't like the wolf. He said, "I don't like wolves. They're a little bit scary and sometimes they're a lot scary." I asked him what he thought the wolf might do, and he said, "They'll kill you and eat you and gobble you up." At the end of this version Little Red Riding Hood says that she will always do what her mother tells her. I tried to ask Michael what he learned from the story, but he never mentioned being good or listening to your mother. He said he learned that wolves will eat you.

I asked Michael if he likes this story and he said he does. He was happy that the wolf was killed at the end because he was bad. He was really happy that Little Red Riding Hood was able to have treats with her grandmother. I think this is because Michael is really close to his great-grandmother. He said that this is not one of his favorite stories even though he liked it. I know it has a lot to do with the pictures because they are drawn in that popular 60's style where it's drawn in black and very sketchy. So, everything looks kind of scary. He said that Little Red Riding Hood looks scary at certain points in the story. I wonder how his reactions may have been different if I had chosen a version where Little Red Riding Hood looked older and more feminine and with softer pictures.

QUESTIONS FOR DISCUSSION AND WRITING

1. Michael's responses change as he hears the story the second time. What might have caused the changes?
2. Michael is a 4½-year-old boy. Would an older child's reactions have been different? A younger child's? A girl's?
3. This is a reader response journal entry rather than a polished paper. As a result, the writing is sometimes flawed, and the ideas are not fully developed. Which ideas here seem most worth pursuing for an essay? What would the student need to do to develop the strongest ideas?

Franece Faustman

From the Belly of the Wolf

What am I to make of Little Red Riding Hood as she emerges from the shadows of the wolf? The tales of her journey are many, but they all share a common theme: an innocent is tempted and seduced by a wolf (a little like Eve with the serpent), and then transformed by her experience. This resulting transformation leaves me in a quandary; who exactly does Little Red Riding Hood become? Who, really, is she?

In Perrault's archaic, moralistic version of Little Red Riding Hood, she becomes nothing at all. As penance for her disobedience and seduction by the wolf, she is abruptly de-voured without any magical rebirth, or rescue. Her development is stillborn; her small, sharp baby teeth have been neatly defanged, and her curiosity snuffed out in the belly of the wolf. She is not allowed to live and learn; a stern lesson, indeed, to any other infant rebel listening to Per-rault's tale.

The Brothers Grimm's version, "Little Red Riding Hood," is more generous. Here, Red Riding Hood survives, in spite of her disobedience. Rescued, she springs from the belly of the wolf, free (hopefully) to occasionally stray from the path of duty as she grows up. I sense her quivering, childish curiosity; her world is exquisitely attuned to her newly discovered, infantile senses. She is drawn by the flowers off the beaten path, and fascinated with the big eyes, ears, and teeth of the threatening, seductive wolf. Her sexual identity is young and raw, too, implicit in the little red hood that crowns her head, and her sexual curiosity while in the wolf's bed.

But there is also implicit in the tale a cautionary lesson: if Little Red Riding Hood cannot learn to control her infantile desire to seize, devour, and satisfy herself without consciousness, she will, ultimately, fall prey to her inner wolf, and end up devouring herself.

This painful lesson is serenely ignored by the maiden (Red Riding Hood) of Angela Carter's tale, "The Company of Wolves." This pubescent virgin, described as an "unbroken egg," a "sealed vessel" who is "afraid of nothing," gently seduces the clever, sexy, predatory wolf into lying down with the lamb that she is, sweetly defanging him in the process: "Sweet and sound she sleeps in granny's bed, between the paws of the tender wolf." A feast of the flesh becomes a feast of the heart, and a union of opposites.

In Tanith Lee's darker tale, "Wolfland," Red Riding Hood's quest is not for self-fulfillment, but for power. The savage fangs of the wolf now belong to a woman, heir to a goddess werewolf. Red Riding Hood has come full circle, and is now one with her wolf. His traditionally male powers are now her own: the power to exact retribution and justice; and the power to cause death, all of which run counter to the female ideal of a self-sacrificing giver of life. Lisel (Red Riding Hood) renounces society and becomes a society of one, a law

unto herself. She begins to shed her sheep's clothing, a
haughty sense of conventional propriety that is no more than
skin deep. Her metamorphosis reverses the experience of
Little Red Riding Hood, who is devoured by her wolf; in
"Wolfland," Lisel devours *him*, in effect, digesting lupine
qualities that are portrayed as essentially female. Lisel is
a fitting, if formidable, heir to the Little Red Riding Hood
of the simple nursery tale.

I, myself, see no contradiction between the various transformations undergone by Little Red Riding Hood in the different tales. Whatever else the story is, it is still the
magical tale of a maid and a wolf, journey together through
eternity. I, too, have experienced Little Red Riding Hood's
innocence, her longing for experience and self-fulfillment,
and her struggle for power. The drama of the maid and the
wolf entrances me; it is my struggle, my journey, too.

QUESTION FOR DISCUSSION AND WRITING

Franece Faustman's journal covers a lot of territory. Because it is so wide-ranging,
the entry provides an excellent way of exploring different issues, but it is probably too
scattered for an essay. If you were to turn the entry into an essay, what ideas would
you retain? Why? What might your thesis be?

Childhood Lost and Found: Peter Pan

J. M. BARRIE (1860–1937)

Peter Pan _____ *1904*

ACT I
THE NURSERY

> *The night nursery of the Darling family, which is the scene of our opening Act, is
> at the top of a rather depressed street in Bloomsbury. We have a right to place it where we*

will, and the reason Bloomsbury is chosen is that Mr. Roget once lived there. So did we in days when his Thesaurus was our only companion in London; and we whom he has helped to wend our way through life have always wanted to pay him a little compliment. The Darlings therefore lived in Bloomsbury.

It is a corner house whose top window, the important one, looks upon a leafy square from which Peter used to fly up to it, to the delight of three children and no doubt the irritation of passers-by. The street is still there, though the steaming sausage shop has gone; and apparently the same cards perch now as then over the doors, inviting homeless ones to come and stay with the hospitable inhabitants. Since the days of the Darlings, however, a lick of paint has been applied; and our corner house in particular, which has swallowed its neighbour, blooms with awful freshness as if the colours had been discharged upon it through a hose. Its card now says 'No children,' meaning maybe that the goings-on of Wendy and her brothers have given the house a bad name. As for ourselves, we have not been in it since we went back to reclaim our old Thesaurus.

That is what we call the Darling house, but you may dump it down anywhere you like, and if you think it was your house you are very probably right. It wanders about London looking for anybody in need of it, like the little house in the Never Land.

The blind (which is what PETER would have called the theatre curtain if he had ever seen one) rises on that top room, a shabby little room if MRS. DARLING had not made it the hub of creation by her certainty that such it was, and adorned it to match with a loving heart and all the scrapings of her purse. The door on the right leads into the day nursery, which she has no right to have, but she made it herself with nails in her mouth and a pastepot in her hand. This is the door the children will come in by. There are three beds and (rather oddly) a large dog-kennel; two of these beds, with the kennel, being on the left and the other on the right. The coverlets of the beds (if visitors are expected) are made out of MRS. DARLING's wedding-gown, which was such a grand affair that it still keeps them pinched. Over each bed is a china house, the size of a linnet's nest, containing a night-light. The fire, which is on our right, is burning as discreetly as if it were in custody, which in a sense it is, for supporting the mantelshelf are two wooden soldiers, home-made, begun by MR. DARLING, finished by MRS. DARLING, repainted (unfortunately) by JOHN DARLING. On the fire-guard hang incomplete parts of children's night attire. The door the parents will come in by is on the left. At the back is the bathroom door, with a cuckoo clock over it; and in the centre is the window, which is at present ever so staid and respectable, but half an hour hence (namely at 6.30 p.m.) will be able to tell a very strange tale to the police.

The only occupant of the room at present is NANA the nurse, reclining, not as you might expect on the one soft chair, but on the floor. She is a Newfoundland dog, and though this may shock the grandiose, the not exactly affluent will make allowances. The Darlings could not afford to have a nurse, they could not afford indeed to have children; and now you are beginning to understand how they did it. Of course NANA has been trained by MRS. DARLING, but like all treasures she was born to it. In this play we shall see her chiefly inside the house, but she was just as exemplary outside, escorting the two elders to school with an umbrella in her mouth, for instance, and butting them back into line if they strayed.

The cuckoo clock strikes six, and NANA springs into life. This first moment in the play is tremendously important, for if the actor playing NANA does not spring properly we are undone. She will probably be played by a boy, if one clever enough can be found, and must never be on two legs except on those rare occasions when an ordinary nurse *would be on four. This* NANA *must go about all her duties in a most ordinary manner, so that you know in your bones that she performs them just so every evening at six; naturalness must be her passion; indeed, it should be the aim of every one in the play, for which she is now setting the pace. All the characters, whether grown-ups or babes, must wear a child's outlook on life as their only important adornment. If they cannot help being funny they are begged to go away. A good motto for all would be 'The little less, and how much it is.'*

NANA, *making much use of her mouth, 'turns down' the beds, and carries the various articles on the fire-guard across to them. Then pushing the bathroom door open, she is seen at work on the taps preparing* MICHAEL'S *bath; after which she enters from the day nursery with the youngest of the family on her back.*

MICHAEL (*obstreperous*): I won't go to bed, I won't, I won't. Nana, it isn't six o'clock yet. Two minutes more, please, one minute more? Nana, I won't be bathed, I tell you I will not be bathed.

(*Here the bathroom door closes on them, and* MRS. DARLING, *who has perhaps heard his cry, enters the nursery. She is the loveliest lady in Bloomsbury, with a sweet mocking mouth, and as she is going out to dinner to-night she is already wearing her evening gown because she knows her children like to see her in it. It is a delicious confection made by herself out of nothing and other people's mistakes. She does not often go out to dinner, preferring when the children are in bed to sit beside them tidying up their minds, just as if they were drawers. If* WENDY *and the boys could keep awake they might see her repacking into their proper places the many articles of the mind that have strayed during the day, lingering humorously over some of their contents, wondering where on earth they picked this thing up, making discoveries sweet and not so sweet, pressing this to her cheek and hurriedly stowing that out of sight. When they wake in the morning the naughtinesses with which they went to bed are not, alas, blown away, but they are placed at the bottom of the drawer; and on the top, beautifully aired, are their prettier thoughts ready for the new day.*

As she enters the room she is startled to see a strange little face outside the window and a hand groping as if it wanted to come in.)

MRS. DARLING: Who are you? (*The unknown disappears; she hurries to the window.*) No one there. And yet I feel sure I saw a face. My children! (*She throws open the bathroom door and* MICHAEL'S *head appears gaily over the bath. He splashes; she throws kisses to him and closes the door. 'Wendy, John,' she cries, and gets reassuring answers from the day nursery. She sits down, relieved, on* WENDY'S *bed; and* WENDY *and* JOHN *come in, looking their smallest size, as children tend to do to a mother suddenly in fear for them.*)

JOHN (*histrionically*): We are doing an act; we are playing at being you and father. (*He imitates the only father who has come under his special notice.*) A little less noise there.

WENDY: Now let us pretend we have a baby.

5 JOHN (*good-naturedly*): I am happy to inform you, Mrs. Darling, that you are now a mother. (WENDY *gives way to ecstasy.*) You have missed the chief thing; you haven't asked, 'boy or girl?'

WENDY: I am so glad to have one at all, I don't care which it is.

JOHN (*crushingly*): That is just the difference between gentlemen and ladies. Now
   you tell me.

WENDY: I am happy to acquaint you, Mr. Darling, you are now a father.

JOHN: Boy or girl?

WENDY (*presenting herself*): Girl.   10

JOHN: Tuts.

WENDY: You horrid.

JOHN: Go on.

WENDY: I am happy to acquaint you, Mr. Darling, you are again a father.

JOHN: Boy or girl?   15

WENDY: Boy. (JOHN *beams.*) Mummy, it's hateful of him.

>   (MICHAEL *emerges from the bathroom in* JOHN'*s old pyjamas and giving his face a last
>   wipe with the towel.*)

MICHAEL (*expanding*): Now, John, have me.

JOHN: We don't want any more.

MICHAEL (*contracting*): Am I not to be born at all?

JOHN: Two is enough.   20

MICHAEL (*wheedling*): Come, John; boy, John. (*Appalled*) Nobody wants me!

MRS. DARLING: I do.

MICHAEL (*with a glimmer of hope*): Boy or girl?

MRS. DARLING (*with one of those happy thoughts of hers*): Boy.

>   (*Triumph of* MICHAEL; *discomfiture of* JOHN. MR. DARLING *arrives, in no mood
>   unfortunately to gloat over this domestic scene. He is really a good man as breadwinners
>   go, and it is hard luck for him to be propelled into the room now, when if we had brought
>   him in a few minutes earlier or later he might have made a fairer impression. In the city
>   where he sits on a stool all day, as fixed as a postage stamp, he is so like all the others on
>   stools that you recognise him not by his face but by his stool, but at home the way to
>   gratify him is to say that he has a distinct personality. He is very conscientious, and in
>   the days when* MRS. DARLING *gave up keeping the house books correctly and drew
>   pictures instead (which he called her guesses), he did all the totting up for her, holding her
>   hand while he calculated whether they could have Wendy or not, and coming down on
>   the right side. It is with regret, therefore, that we introduce him as a tornado, rushing into
>   the nursery in evening dress, but without his coat, and brandishing in his hand a
>   recalcitrant white tie.*)

MR. DARLING (*implying that he has searched for her everywhere and that the nursery is a   25
   strange place in which to find her*): Oh, here you are, Mary.

MRS. DARLING (*knowing at once what is the matter*): What is the matter, George dear?

MR. DARLING (*as if the word were monstrous*): Matter! This tie, it will not tie. (*He waxes
   sarcastic.*) Not round my neck. Round the bed-post, oh yes; twenty times have
   I made it up round the bed-post, but round my neck, oh dear no; begs to be
   excused.

MICHAEL (*in a joyous transport*): Say it again, father, say it again!

MR. DARLING (*witheringly*): Thank you. (*Goaded by a suspiciously crooked smile on* MRS.
   DARLING'*s face*) I warn you, Mary, that unless this tie is round my neck we don't
   go out to dinner to-night, and if I don't go out to dinner to-night I never go to

the office again, and if I don't go to the office again you and I starve, and our children will be thrown into the streets.

(*The children blanch as they grasp the gravity of the situation.*)

30   MRS. DARLING: Let me try, dear.

(*In a terrible silence their progeny cluster round them. Will she succeed? Their fate depends on it. She fails—no, she succeeds. In another moment they are wildly gay, romping round the room on each other's shoulders. Father is even a better horse than mother.* MICHAEL *is dropped upon his bed,* WENDY *retires to prepare for hers,* JOHN *runs from* NANA, *who has reappeared with the bath towel.*)

JOHN (*rebellious*): I won't be bathed. You needn't think it.
MR. DARLING (*in the grand manner*): Go and be bathed at once, sir.

(*With bent head* JOHN *follows* NANA *into the bathroom.* MR. DARLING *swells.*)

MICHAEL (*as he is put between the sheets*): Mother, how did you get to know me?
MR. DARLING: A little less noise there.
35   MICHAEL (*growing solemn*): At what time was I born, mother?
MRS. DARLING: At two o'clock in the night-time, dearest.
MICHAEL: Oh, mother, I hope I didn't wake you.
MRS. DARLING: They are rather sweet, don't you think, George?
MR. DARLING (*doting*): There is not their equal on earth, and they are ours, ours!

(*Unfortunately* NANA *has come from the bathroom for a sponge and she collides with his trousers, the first pair he has ever had with braid on them.*)

40   MR. DARLING: Mary, it is too bad; just look at this; covered with hairs. Clumsy, clumsy!

(NANA *goes, a drooping figure.*)

MRS. DARLING: Let me brush you, dear.

(*Once more she is successful. They are now by the fire, and* MICHAEL *is in bed doing idiotic things with a teddy bear.*)

MR. DARLING (*depressed*): I sometimes think, Mary, that it is a mistake to have a dog for a nurse.
MRS. DARLING: George, Nana is a treasure.
MR. DARLING: No doubt; but I have an uneasy feeling at times that she looks upon the children as puppies.
45   MRS. DARLING (*rather faintly*): Oh no, dear one, I am sure she knows they have souls.
MR. DARLING (*profoundly*): I wonder, I wonder.

(*The opportunity has come for her to tell him of something that is on her mind.*)

MRS. DARLING: George, we must keep Nana, I will tell you why. (*Her seriousness impresses him.*) My dear, when I came into this room to-night I saw a face at the window.
MR. DARLING (*incredulous*): A face at the window, three floors up? Pooh!

MRS. DARLING: It was the face of a little boy; he was trying to get in. George, this is not the first time I have seen that boy.

MR. DARLING (*beginning to think that this may be a man's job*): Oho!   50

MRS. DARLING (*making sure that* MICHAEL *does not hear*): The first time was a week ago. It was Nana's night out, and I had been drowsing here by the fire when suddenly I felt a draught, as if the window were open. I looked round and I saw that boy—in the room.

MR. DARLING: In the room?

MRS. DARLING: I screamed. Just then Nana came back and she at once sprang at him. The boy leapt for the window. She pulled down the sash quickly, but was too late to catch him.

MR. DARLING (*who knows he would not have been too late*): I thought so!

MRS. DARLING: Wait. The boy escaped, but his shadow had not time to get out;   55
down came the window and cut it clean off.

MR. DARLING (*heavily*): Mary, Mary, why didn't you keep that shadow?

MRS. DARLING (*scoring*): I did. I rolled it up, George; and here it is.

(*She produces it from a drawer. They unroll and examine the flimsy thing, which is not more material than a puff of smoke, and if let go would probably float into the ceiling without discolouring it. Yet it has human shape. As they nod their heads over it they present the most satisfying picture on earth, two happy parents conspiring cosily by the fire for the good of their children.*)

MR DARLING: It is nobody I know, but he does look a scoundrel.

MRS. DARLING: I think he comes back to get his shadow, George.

MR. DARLING (*meaning that the miscreant has now a father to deal with*): I dare say. (*He*   60
sees himself telling the story to the other stools at the office.) There is money in this, my love. I shall take it to the British Museum to-morrow and have it priced.

(*The shadow is rolled up and replaced in the drawer.*)

MRS. DARLING (*like a guilty person*): George, I have not told you all; I am afraid to.

MR. DARLING (*who knows exactly the right moment to treat a woman as a beloved child*): Cowardy, cowardy custard.

MRS. DARLING (*pouting*): No, I'm not.

MR. DARLING: Oh yes, you are.

MRS. DARLING: George, I'm not.   65

MR. DARLING: Then why not tell? (*Thus cleverly soothed she goes on.*)

MRS. DARLING: The boy was not alone that first time. He was accompanied by—I don't know how to describe it; by a ball of light, not as big as my fist, but it darted about the room like a living thing.

MR. DARLING (*though open-minded*): That is very unusual. It escaped with the boy?

MRS. DARLING: Yes. (*Sliding her hand into his.*) George, what can all this mean?

MR. DARLING (*ever ready*): What indeed!   70

(*This intimate scene is broken by the return of* NANA *with a bottle in her mouth.*)

MRS. DARLING (*at once dissembling*): What is that, Nana? Ah, of course; Michael, it is your medicine.

MICHAEL (*promptly*): Won't take it.

MR. DARLING (*recalling his youth*): Be a man, Michael.

MICHAEL: Won't.

75 MRS. DARLING (*weakly*): I'll get you a lovely chocky to take after it. (*She leaves the room, though her husband calls after her.*)

MR. DARLING: Mary, don't pamper him. When I was your age, Michael, I took medicine without a murmur. I said 'Thank you, kind parents, for giving me bottles to make me well.'

(WENDY, *who has appeared in her night-gown, hears this and believes.*)

WENDY: That medicine you sometimes take is much nastier, isn't it, father?

MR. DARLING (*valuing her support*): Ever so much nastier. And as an example to you, Michael, I would take it now (*thankfully*) if I hadn't lost the bottle.

WENDY (*always glad to be of service*): I know where it is, father. I'll fetch it.

(*She is gone before he can stop her. He turns for help to* JOHN, *who has come from the bathroom attired for bed.*)

80 MR. DARLING: John, it is the most beastly stuff. It is that sticky sweet kind.

JOHN (*who is perhaps still playing at parents*): Never mind, father, it will soon be over.

(*A spasm of ill-will to* JOHN *cuts through* MR. DARLING, *and is gone.* WENDY *returns panting.*)

WENDY: Here it is, father; I have been as quick as I could.

MR. DARLING (*with a sarcasm that is completely thrown away on her*): You have been wonderfully quick, precious quick!

(*He is now at the foot of* MICHAEL'*s bed,* NANA *is by its side, holding the medicine spoon insinuatingly in her mouth.*)

WENDY (*proudly, as she pours out* MR. DARLING'*s medicine*): Michael, now you will see how father takes it.

85 MR. DARLING (*hedging*): Michael first.

MICHAEL (*full of unworthy suspicions*): Father first.

MR. DARLING: It will make me sick, you know.

JOHN (*lightly*): Come on, father.

MR. DARLING: Hold your tongue, sir.

90 WENDY (*disturbed*): I thought you took it quite easily, father, saying 'Thank you, kind parents, for—'

MR. DARLING: That is not the point; the point is that there is more in my glass than in Michael's spoon. It isn't fair, I swear though it were with my last breath, it is not fair.

MICHAEL (*coldly*): Father, I'm waiting.

MR. DARLING: It's all very well to say you are waiting; so am I waiting.

MICHAEL: Father's a cowardy custard.

95 MR. DARLING: So are you a cowardy custard.

(*They are now glaring at each other.*)

MICHAEL: I am not frightened.

MR. DARLING: Neither am I frightened.

MICHAEL: Well, then, take it.

MR. DARLING: Well, then, you take it.

WENDY (*butting in again*): Why not take it at the same time?   *100*

MR. DARLING (*haughtily*): Certainly. Are you ready, Michael?

WENDY (*as nothing has happened*): One—two—three.

(MICHAEL *partakes, but* MR. DARLING *resorts to hanky-panky.*)

JOHN: Father hasn't taken his!

(MICHAEL *howls.*)

WENDY (*inexpressibly pained*): Oh father!

MR. DARLING (*who has been hiding the glass behind him*): What do you mean by 'oh   *105*
father'? Stop that row, Michael. I meant to take mine but I—missed it. (NANA
*shakes her head sadly over him, and goes into the bathroom. They are all looking as if
they did not admire him, and nothing so dashes a temperamental man.*) I say, I have
just thought of a splendid joke. (*They brighten.*) I shall pour my medicine into
Nana's bowl, and she will drink it thinking it is milk! (*The pleasantry does not appeal, but he prepares the joke, listening for appreciation.*)

WENDY: Poor darling Nana!

MR. DARLING: You silly little things; to your beds every one of you; I am ashamed
of you.

(*They steal to their beds as* MRS. DARLING *returns with the chocolate.*)

MRS. DARLING: Well, is it all over?

MICHAEL: Father didn't— (*Father glares.*)

MR. DARLING: All over, dear, quite satisfactorily. (NANA *comes back.*) Nana, good   *110*
dog, good girl; I have put a little milk into your bowl. (*The bowl is by the kennel,
and* NANA *begins to lap, only begins. She retreats into the kennel.*)

MRS. DARLING: What is the matter, Nana?

MR. DARLING (*uneasily*): Nothing, nothing.

MRS. DARLING (*smelling the bowl*): George, it is your medicine!

(*The children break into lamentation. He gives his wife an imploring look; he is begging
for one smile, but does not get it. In consequence he goes from bad to worse.*)

MR. DARLING: It was only a joke. Much good my wearing myself to the bone trying
to be funny in this house.

WENDY (*on her knees by the kennel*): Father, Nana is crying.   *115*

MR. DARLING: Coddle her; nobody coddles me. Oh dear no. I am only the bread-
winner, why should I be coddled? Why, why, why?

MRS. DARLING: George, not so loud; the servants will hear you.

(*There is only one maid, absurdly small too, but they have got into the way of calling her
the servants.*)

MR. DARLING (*defiant*): Let them hear me; bring in the whole world. (*The desperate
man, who has not been in fresh air for days, has now lost all self-control.*) I refuse to
allow that dog to lord it in my nursery for one hour longer. (NANA *supplicates*

him.) In vain, in vain, the proper place for you is the yard, and there you go to be tied up this instant.

(NANA *again retreats into the kennel, and the children add their prayers to hers.*)

MRS. DARLING (*who knows how contrite he will be for this presently*): George, George, remember what I told you about that boy.

120 MR. DARLING: Am I master in this house or is she? (*To* NANA *fiercely*) Come along. (*He thunders at her, but she indicates that she has reasons not worth troubling him with for remaining where she is. He resorts to a false bonhomie.*) There, there, did she think he was angry with her, poor Nana? (*She wriggles a response in the affirmative.*) Good Nana, pretty Nana. (*She has seldom been called pretty, and it has the old effect. She plays rub-a-dub with her paws, which is how a dog blushes.*) She will come to her kind master, won't she? won't she? (*She advances, retreats, waggles her head, her tail, and eventually goes to him. He seizes her collar in an iron grip and amid the cries of his progeny drags her from the room. They listen, for her remonstrances are not inaudible.*)

MRS. DARLING: Be brave, my dears.

WENDY: He is chaining Nana up!

(*This unfortunately is what he is doing, though we cannot see him. Let us hope that he then retires to his study, looks up the word 'temper' in his* Thesaurus, *and under the influence of those benign pages becomes a better man. In the meantime the children have been put to bed in unwonted silence, and* MRS. DARLING *lights the night-lights over the beds.*)

JOHN (*as the barking below goes on*): She is awfully unhappy.

WENDY: That is not Nana's unhappy bark. That is her bark when she smells danger.

125 MRS. DARLING (*remembering that boy*): Danger! Are you sure, Wendy?

WENDY (*the one of the family, for there is one in every family, who can be trusted to know or not to know*): Oh yes.

(*Her mother looks this way and that from the window.*)

JOHN: Is anything there?

MRS. DARLING: All quite quiet and still. Oh, how I wish I was not going out to dinner to-night.

MICHAEL: Can anything harm us, mother, after the night-lights are lit?

130 MRS. DARLING: Nothing, precious. They are the eyes a mother leaves behind her to guard her children.

(*Nevertheless we may be sure she means to tell* LIZA, *the little maid, to look in on them frequently till she comes home. She goes from bed to bed, after her custom, tucking them in and crooning a lullaby.*)

MICHAEL (*drowsily*): Mother, I'm glad of you.

MRS. DARLING (*with a last look round, her hand on the switch*): Dear night-lights that protect my sleeping babes, burn clear and steadfast to-night.

(*The nursery darkens and she is gone, intentionally leaving the door ajar. Something uncanny is going to happen, we expect, for a quiver has passed through the room, just sufficient to touch the night-lights. They blink three times one after the other and go out, precisely as children (whom familiarity has made them resemble) fall asleep. There is another light in the room now, no larger than* MRS. DARLING's *fist, and in the time we have taken to say this it has been into the drawers and wardrobe and searched pockets, as it darts about looking for a certain shadow. Then the window is blown open, probably by the smallest and therefore most mischievous star, and* PETER PAN *flies into the room. In so far as he is dressed at all it is in autumn leaves and cobwebs.)*

PETER (*in a whisper*): Tinker Bell, Tink, are you there? (*A jug lights up.*) Oh, do come out of that jug. (TINK *flashes hither and thither.*) Do you know where they put it? (*The answer comes as of a tinkle of bells; it is the fairy language.* PETER *can speak it, but it bores him.*) Which big box? This one? But which drawer? Yes, do show me. (TINK *pops into the drawer where the shadow is, but before* PETER *can reach it,* WENDY *moves in her sleep. He flies on to the mantelshelf as a hiding-place. Then, as she has not waked, he flutters over the beds as an easy way to observe the occupants, closes the window softly, wafts himself to the drawer and scatters its contents to the floor, as kings on their wedding day toss ha'pence to the crowd. In his joy at finding his shadow he forgets that he has shut up* TINK *in the drawer. He sits on the floor with the shadow, confident that he and it will join like drops of water. Then he tries to stick it on with soap from the bathroom, and this failing also, he subsides dejectedly on the floor. This wakens* WENDY, *who sits up, and is pleasantly interested to see a stranger.*)

WENDY (*courteously*): Boy, why are you crying?

(*He jumps up, and crossing to the foot of the bed bows to her in the fairy way.* WENDY, *impressed, bows to him from the bed.*)

PETER: What is your name?   *135*
WENDY (*well satisfied*): Wendy Moira Angela Darling. What is yours?
PETER (*finding it lamentably brief*): Peter Pan.
WENDY: Is that all?
PETER (*biting his lip*): Yes.
WENDY (*politely*): I am so sorry.   *140*
PETER: It doesn't matter.
WENDY: Where do you live?
PETER: Second to the right and then straight on till morning.
WENDY: What a funny address!
PETER: No, it isn't.   *145*
WENDY: I mean, is that what they put on the letters?
PETER: Don't get any letters.
WENDY: But your mother gets letters?
PETER: Don't have a mother.
WENDY: Peter!   *150*

(*She leaps out of bed to put her arms round him, but he draws back; he does not know why, but he knows he must draw back*)

PETER: You mustn't touch me.
WENDY: Why?
PETER: No one must ever touch me.
WENDY: Why?

155   PETER: I don't know.

    (*He is never touched by any one in the play.*)

  WENDY: No wonder you were crying.

  PETER: I wasn't crying. But I can't get my shadow to stick on.

  WENDY: It has come off! How awful. (*Looking at the spot where he had lain.*) Peter, you have been trying to stick it on with soap!

  PETER (*snappily*): Well then?

160   WENDY: It must be sewn on.

  PETER: What is 'sewn'?

  WENDY: You are dreadfully ignorant.

  PETER: No, I'm not.

  WENDY: I will sew it on for you, my little man. But we must have more light. (*She touches something, and to his astonishment the room is illuminated.*) Sit here. I dare say it will hurt a little.

165   PETER (*a recent remark of hers rankling*): I never cry. (*She seems to attach the shadow. He tests the combination.*) It isn't quite itself yet.

  WENDY: Perhaps I should have ironed it. (*It awakes and is as glad to be back with him as he to have it. He and his shadow dance together. He is showing off now. He crows like a cock. He would fly in order to impress Wendy further if he knew that there is anything unusual in that.*)

  PETER: Wendy, look, look; oh the cleverness of me!

  WENDY: You conceit; of course I did nothing!

  PETER: You did a little.

170   WENDY (*wounded*): A little! If I am no use I can at least withdraw.

    (*With one haughty leap she is again in bed with the sheet over her face. Popping on to the end of the bed the artful one appeals.*)

  PETER: Wendy, don't withdraw. I can't help crowing, Wendy, when I'm pleased with myself. Wendy, one girl is worth more than twenty boys.

  WENDY (*peeping over the sheet*): You really think so, Peter?

  PETER: Yes, I do.

  WENDY: I think it's perfectly sweet of you, and I shall get up again. (*They sit together on the side of the bed.*) I shall give you a kiss if you like.

175   PETER: Thank you. (*He holds out his hand.*)

  WENDY: (*aghast*): Don't you know what a kiss is?

  PETER: I shall know when you give it me. (*Not to hurt his feelings she gives him her thimble.*) Now shall I give you a kiss?

  WENDY (*primly*): If you please. (*He pulls an acorn button off his person and bestows it on her. She is shocked but considerate.*) I will wear it on this chain round my neck. Peter, how old are you?

  PETER (*blithely*): I don't know, but quite young, Wendy. I ran away the day I was born.

180   WENDY: Ran away, why?

  PETER: Because I heard father and mother talking of what I was to be when I became a man. I want always to be a little boy and to have fun; so I ran away to Kensington Gardens and lived a long time among the fairies.

  WENDY (*with great eyes*): You know fairies, Peter!

PETER (*surprised that this should be a recommendation*): Yes, but they are nearly all dead
      now. (*Baldly*) You see, Wendy, when the first baby laughed for the first time, the
      laugh broke into a thousand pieces and they all went skipping about, and that
      was the beginning of fairies. And now when every new baby is born its first
      laugh becomes a fairy. So there ought to be one fairy for every boy or girl.

WENDY (*breathlessly*): Ought to be? Isn't there?

PETER: Oh no. Children know such a lot now. Soon they don't believe in fairies, and   *185*
      every time a child says 'I don't believe in fairies' there is a fairy somewhere that
      falls down dead. (*He skips about heartlessly.*)

WENDY: Poor things!

PETER (*to whom this statement recalls a forgotten friend*): I can't think where she has
      gone. Tinker Bell, Tink, where are you?

WENDY (*thrilling*): Peter, you don't mean to tell me that there is a fairy in this room!

PETER (*flitting about in search*): She came with me. You don't hear anything, do you?

WENDY: I hear—the only sound I hear is like a tinkle of bells.   *190*

PETER: That is the fairy language. I hear it too.

WENDY: It seems to come from over there.

PETER (*with shameless glee*): Wendy, I believe I shut her up in that drawer!

> (*He releases* TINK*, who darts about in a fury using language it is perhaps as well we*
> *don't understand.*)

> You needn't say that; I'm very sorry, but how could I know you were in the
> drawer?

WENDY (*her eyes dancing in pursuit of the delicious creature*): Oh, Peter, if only she would   *195*
      stand still and let me see her!

PETER (*indifferently*): They hardly ever stand still.

> (*To show that she can do even this* TINK *pauses between two ticks of the cuckoo clock.*)

WENDY: I see her, the lovely! where is she now?

PETER: She is behind the clock. Tink, this lady wishes you were her fairy. (*The answer*
      comes immediately.)

WENDY: What does she say?

PETER: She is not very polite. She says you are a great ugly girl, and that she is my   *200*
      fairy. You know, Tink, you can't be my fairy because I am a gentleman and you
      are a lady.

> (TINK *replies.*)

WENDY: What did she say?

PETER: She said 'You silly ass.' She is quite a common girl, you know. She is called
      Tinker Bell because she mends the fairy pots and kettles.

> (*They have reached a chair,* WENDY *in the ordinary way and* PETER *through a hole in*
> *the back.*)

WENDY: Where do you live now?

PETER: With the lost boys.

WENDY: Who are they?   *205*

PETER: They are the children who fall out of their prams when the nurse is looking the other way. If they are not claimed in seven days they are sent far away to the Never Land. I'm captain.

WENDY: What fun it must be.

PETER (*craftily*): Yes, but we are rather lonely. You see, Wendy, we have no female companionship.

WENDY: Are none of the other children girls?

210 PETER: Oh no; girls, you know, are much too clever to fall out of their prams.

WENDY: Peter, it is perfectly lovely the way you talk about girls. John there just despises us.

(PETER, *for the first time, has a good look at* JOHN. *He then neatly tumbles him out of bed*.)

You wicked! you are not captain here. (*She bends over her brother who is prone on the floor*.) After all he hasn't wakened, and you meant to be kind. (*Having now done her duty she forgets* JOHN, *who blissfully sleeps on*.) Peter, you may give me a kiss.

PETER (*cynically*): I thought you would want it back.

(*He offers her the thimble*.)

WENDY (*artfully*): Oh dear, I didn't mean a kiss, Peter. I meant a thimble.

215 PETER (*only half placated*): What is that?

WENDY: It is like this. (*She leans forward to give a demonstration, but something prevents the meeting of their faces*.)

PETER (*satisfied*): Now shall I give you a thimble?

WENDY: If you please. (*Before he can even draw near she screams*.)

PETER: What is it?

220 WENDY: It was exactly as if some one were pulling my hair!

PETER: That must have been Tink. I never knew her so naughty before.

(TINK *speaks. She is in the jug again*.)

WENDY: What does she say?

PETER: She says she will do that every time I give you a thimble.

WENDY: But why?

225 PETER (*equally nonplussed*): Why, Tink? (*He has to translate the answer*.) She said 'You silly ass' again.

WENDY: She is very impertinent. (*They are sitting on the floor now*.) Peter, why did you come to our nursery window?

PETER: To try to hear stories. None of us knows any stories.

WENDY: How perfectly awful!

PETER: Do you know why swallows build in the eaves of houses? It is to listen to the stories. Wendy, your mother was telling you such a lovely story.

230 WENDY: Which story was it?

PETER: About the prince, and he couldn't find the lady who wore the glass slipper.

WENDY: That was Cinderella. Peter, he found her and they were happy ever after.

PETER: I am glad. (*They have worked their way along the floor close to each other, but he now jumps up*.)

WENDY: Where are you going?

PETER (*already on his way to the window*): To tell the other boys.   235
WENDY: Don't go, Peter. I know lots of stories. The stories I could tell to the boys!
PETER (*gleaming*): Come on! We'll fly.
WENDY: Fly? You can fly!

(*How he would like to rip those stories out of her; he is dangerous now.*)

PETER: Wendy, come with me.
WENDY: Oh dear, I mustn't. Think of mother. Besides, I can't fly.   240
PETER: I'll teach you.
WENDY: How lovely to fly!
PETER: I'll teach you how to jump on the wind's back and then away we go. Wendy,
    when you are sleeping in your silly bed you might be flying about with me, say-
    ing funny things to the stars. There are mermaids, Wendy, with long tails. (*She just
    succeeds in remaining on the nursery floor.*) Wendy, how we should all respect you.

(*At this she strikes her colours.*)

WENDY: Of course it's awfully fas-cin-a-ting! Would you teach John and Michael to
    fly too?
PETER (*indifferently*): If you like.   245
WENDY (*playing rum-tum on* JOHN): John, wake up; there is a boy here who is to
    teach us to fly.
JOHN: Is there? Then I shall get up. (*He raises his head from the floor.*) Hullo, I am up!
WENDY: Michael, open your eyes. This boy is to teach us to fly.

(*The sleepers are at once as awake as their father's razor; but before a question can be
asked* NANA'*s bark is heard.*)

JOHN: Out with the light, quick, hide!

(*When the maid* LIZA, *who is so small that when she says she will never see ten again
one can scarcely believe her, enters with a firm hand on the troubled* NANA'*s chain the
room is in comparative darkness.*)

LIZA: There, you suspicious brute, they are perfectly safe, aren't they? Every one of   250
    the little angels sound asleep in bed. Listen to their gentle breathing. (NANA'*s
    sense of smell here helps to her undoing instead of hindering it. She knows that they are
    in the room.* MICHAEL, *who is behind the curtain window, is so encouraged by* LIZA'*s
    last remark that he breathes too loudly,* NANA *knows that kind of breathing and tries to
    break from her keeper's control.*) No more of it, Nana. (*Wagging a finger at her*) I
    warn you if you bark again I shall go straight for master and missus and bring
    them home from the party, and then won't master whip you just! Come along,
    you naughty dog.

(*The unhappy* NANA *is led away. The children emerge exulting from their various
hiding-places. In their brief absence from the scene strange things have been done to
them; but it is not for us to reveal a mysterious secret of the stage. They look just the
same.*)

JOHN: I say, can you really fly?
PETER: Look! (*He is now over their heads.*)

WENDY: Oh, how sweet!

PETER: I'm sweet, oh, I am sweet!

(*It looks so easy that they try it first from the floor and then from their beds, without encouraging results.*)

255 JOHN (*rubbing his knees*): How do you do it?

PETER (*descending*): You just think lovely wonderful thoughts and they lift you up in the air. (*He is off again.*)

JOHN: You are so nippy at it; couldn't you do it very slowly once? (PETER *does it slowly.*) I've got it now, Wendy. (*He tries; no, he has not got it, poor stay-at-home, though he knows the names of all the counties in England and* PETER *does not know one.*)

PETER: I must blow the fairy dust on you first. (*Fortunately his garments are smeared with it and he blows some dust on each.*) Now, try; try from the bed. Just wriggle your shoulders this way, and then let go.

(*The gallant* MICHAEL *is the first to let go, and is borne across the room.*)

MICHAEL (*with a yell that should have disturbed* LIZA): I flewed!

(JOHN *lets go, and meets* WENDY *near the bathroom door though they had both aimed in an opposite direction.*)

260 WENDY: Oh, lovely!

JOHN (*tending to be upside down*): How ripping!

MICHAEL (*playing whack on a chair*): I do like it!

THE THREE: Look at me, look at me, look at me!

(*They are not nearly so elegant in the air as* PETER, *but their heads have bumped the ceiling, and there is nothing more delicious than that.*)

JOHN (*who can even go backwards*): I say, why shouldn't we go out?

265 PETER: There are pirates.

JOHN: Pirates! (*He grabs his tall Sunday hat.*) Let us go at once!

(TINK *does not like it. She darts at their hair. From down below in the street the lighted window must present an unwonted spectacle; the shadows of children revolving in the room like a merry-go-round. This is perhaps what* MR. *and* MRS. DARLING *see as they come hurrying home from the party, brought by* NANA *who, you may be sure, has broken her chain.* PETER's *accomplice, the little star, has seen them coming, and again the window blows open.*)

PETER (*as if he had heard the star whisper 'Cave'*): Now come!

(*Breaking the circle he flies out of the window over the trees of the square and over the house-tops, and the others follow like a flight of birds. The broken-hearted father and mother arrive just in time to get a nip from* TINK *as she too sets out for the Never Land.*)

ACT II
THE NEVER LAND

When the blind goes up all is so dark that you scarcely know it has gone up. This is because if you were to see the island bang (as PETER would say) the wonders of it *might hurt your eyes. If you all came in spectacles perhaps you could see it bang, but to make a rule of that kind would be a pity. The first thing seen is merely some whitish dots trudging along the sward, and you can guess from their tinkling that they are probably fairies of the commoner sort going home afoot from some party and having a cheery tiff by the way. Then* PETER'*s star wakes up, and in the blink of it, which is much stronger than in our stars, you can make out masses of trees, and you think you see wild beasts stealing past to drink, though what you see is not the beasts themselves but only the shadows of them. They are really out pictorially to greet* PETER *in the way they think he would like them to greet him; and for the same reason the mermaids basking in the lagoon beyond the trees are carefully combing their hair; and for the same reason the pirates are landing invisibly from the longboat, invisibly to you but not to the redskins, whom none can see or hear because they are on the war-path. The whole island, in short, which has been having a slack time in* PETER'*s absence, is now in a ferment because the tidings has leaked out that he is on his way back; and everybody and everything know that they will catch it from him if they don't give satisfaction. While you have been told this the sun (another of his servants) has been bestirring himself. Those of you who may have thought it wiser after all to begin this Act in spectacles may now take them off.*

What you see is the Never Land. You have often half seen it before, or even three-quarters, after the night-lights were lit, and you might then have beached your coracle on it if you had not always at the great moment fallen asleep. I dare say you have chucked things on to it, the things you can't find in the morning. In the daytime you think the Never Land is only make-believe, and so it is to the likes of you, but this is the Never Land come true. It is an open-air scene, a forest, with a beautiful lagoon beyond but not really far away, for the Never Land is very compact, not large and sprawly with tedious distances between one adventure and another, but nicely crammed. It is summer time on the trees and on the lagoon but winter on the river, which is not remarkable on PETER'*s island where all the four seasons may pass while you are filling a jug at the well.* PETER'*s home is at this very spot, but you could not point out the way into it even if you were told which is the entrance, not even if you were told that there are seven of them. You know now because you have just seen one of the lost boys emerge. The holes in these seven great hollow trees are the 'doors' down to* PETER'*s home, and he made seven because, despite his cleverness, he thought seven boys must need seven doors.*

The boy who has emerged from his tree is SLIGHTLY, *who has perhaps been driven from the abode below by companions less musical than himself. Quite possibly a genius,* SLIGHTLY *has with him his home-made whistle to which he capers entrancingly, with no audience save a Never ostrich which is also musically inclined. Unable to imitate* SLIGHTLY'*s graces the bird falls so low as to burlesque them and is driven from the entertainment. Other lost boys climb up the trunks or drop from branches, and now we see the six of them, all in the skins of animals they think they have shot, and so round and furry in them that if they fall they roll.* TOOTLES *is not the least brave though the most unfortunate of this gallant band. He has been in fewer adventures than any of them because the big things constantly happen while he has stepped round the corner; he will go off, for instance, in some quiet hour to gather firewood, and then when he returns the others will be sweeping up the blood. Instead of souring his nature this has sweetened it and he is the humblest of the band.* NIBS *is more gay and debonair,* SLIGHTLY *more conceited.* SLIGHTLY *thinks he remembers the days before he was lost, with their manners and customs.* CURLY *is a pickle, and so often has he had to deliver up his person when*

PETER *said sternly, 'Stand forth the one who did this thing,' that now he stands forth whether he has done it or not. The other two are* FIRST TWIN *and* SECOND TWIN, *who cannot be described because we should probably be describing the wrong one. Hunkering on the ground or peeping out of their holes, the six are not unlike village gossips gathered round the pump.*

TOOTLES: Has Peter come back yet, Slightly?

SLIGHTLY (*with a solemnity that he thinks suits the occasion*): No, Tootles, no.

(*They are like dogs waiting for the master to tell them that the day has begun.*)

CURLY (*as if Peter might be listening*): I do wish he would come back.

TOOTLES: I am always afraid of the pirates when Peter is not here to protect us.

5   SLIGHTLY: I am not afraid of pirates. Nothing frightens me. But I do wish Peter would come back and tell us whether he has heard anything more about Cinderella.

SECOND TWIN (*with diffidence*): Slightly, I dreamt last night that the prince found Cinderella.

FIRST TWIN (*who is intellectually the superior of the two*): Twin, I think you should not have dreamt that, for I didn't, and Peter may say we oughtn't to dream differently, being twins, you know.

TOOTLES: I am awfully anxious about Cinderella. You see, not knowing anything about my own mother I am fond of thinking that she was rather like Cinderella.

(*This is received with derision.*)

NIBS: All I remember about my mother is that she often said to father, 'Oh, how I wish I had a cheque book of my own.' I don't know what a cheque book is, but I should just love to give my mother one.

10 SLIGHTLY (*as usual*): My mother was fonder of me than your mothers were of you. (*Uproar.*) Oh yes, she was. Peter had to make up names for you, but my mother had wrote my name on the pinafore I was lost in. 'Slightly Soiled'; that's my name.

(*They fall upon him pugnaciously; not that they are really worrying about their mothers, who are now as important to them as a piece of string, but because any excuse is good enough for a shindy. Not for long is he belaboured, for a sound is heard that sends them scurrying down their holes; in a second of time the scene is bereft of human life. What they have heard from near-by is a verse of the dreadful song with which on the Never Land the pirates stealthily trumpet their approach—*)

Yo ho, yo ho, the pirate life,
The flag of skull and bones,
A merry hour, a hempen rope,
And hey for Davy Jones!

The pirates appear upon the frozen river dragging a raft, on which reclines among cushions that dark and fearful man, CAPTAIN JAS HOOK. *A more villainous-looking brotherhood of men never hung in a row on Execution dock. Here, his great arms bare, pieces of eight in his ears as ornaments, is the handsome* CECCO, *who cut his name on the back of the governor of the prison at Gao. Heavier in the pull is the gigantic black who has had many names since the first one terrified dusky children on the banks of the Guidjo-mo.* BILL JUKES *comes next, every inch of him tattooed, the same* JUKES *who got six dozen on the* Walrus *from Flint. Following these are* COOKSON, *said to be* BLACK MURPHY's *brother (but this was never proved); and* GENTLEMAN STARKEY, *once an usher in a school; and* SKYLIGHTS *(Morgan's Skylights); and* NOODLER, *whose hands are fixed on backwards; and the spectacled boatswain,* SMEE, *the only Nonconformist in* HOOK's *crew; and other ruffians long known and feared on the Spanish main.*

Cruelest jewel in that dark setting is HOOK *himself, cadaverous and blackavised, his hair dressed in long curls which look like black candles about to melt, his eyes blue as the forget-me-not and of a profound insensibility, save when he claws, at which time a red spot appears in them. He has an iron hook instead of a right hand, and it is with this he claws. He is never more sinister than when he is most polite, and the elegance of his diction, the distinction of his demeanour, show him one of a different class from his crew, a solitary among uncultured companions. This courtliness impresses even his victims on the high seas, who note that he always says 'Sorry' when prodding them along the plank. A man of indomitable courage, the only thing at which he flinches is the sight of his own blood, which is thick and of an unusual colour. At his public school they said of him that he 'bled yellow.' In dress he apes the dandiacal associated with Charles II, having heard it said in an earlier period of his career that he bore a strange resemblance to the ill-fated Stuarts. A holder of his own contrivance is in his mouth enabling him to smoke two cigars at once. Those, however, who have seen him in the flesh, which is an inadequate term for his earthly tenement, agree that the grimmest part of him is his iron claw.*

They continue their distasteful singing as they disembark—

Avast, belay, yo ho, heave to,
A-pirating we go,
And if we're parted by a shot
We're sure to meet below!

NIBS, *the only one of the boys who has not sought safety in his tree, is seen for a moment near the lagoon, and* STARKEY's *pistol is at once upraised. The captain twists his hook in him.)*

STARKEY (*abject*): Captain, let go!

HOOK: Put back that pistol, first.

STARKEY: 'Twas one of those boys you hate; I could have shot him dead.

HOOK: Ay, and the sound would have brought Tiger Lily's redskins on us. Do you want to lose your scalp?

SMEE (*wriggling his cutlass pleasantly*): That is true. Shall I after him, Captain, and tickle him with Johnny Corkscrew? Johnny is a silent fellow.

HOOK: Not now. He is only one, and I want to mischief all the seven. Scatter and look for them. (*The boatswain whistles his instructions, and the men disperse on their frightful errand. With none to hear save* SMEE, HOOK *becomes confidential.*) Most of all I want their captain, Peter Pan. 'Twas he cut off my arm. I have waited long to shake his hand with this. (*Luxuriating*) Oh, I'll tear him!

SMEE (*always ready for a chat*): Yet I have oft heard you say your hook was worth a score of hands, for combing the hair and other homely uses.

HOOK: If I was a mother I would pray to have my children born with this instead of
that (*his left arm creeps nervously behind him. He has a galling remembrance*). Smee,
Pan flung my arm to a crocodile that happened to be passing by.

SMEE: I have often noticed your strange dread of crocodiles.

20 HOOK (*pettishly*): Not of crocodiles but of that one crocodile. (*He lays bare a lacerated
heart.*) The brute liked my arm so much, Smee, that he has followed me ever
since, from sea to sea, and from land to land, licking his lips for the rest of me.

SMEE (*looking for the bright side*): In a way it is a sort of compliment.

HOOK (*with dignity*): I want no such compliments; I want Peter Pan, who first gave
the brute his taste for me. Smee, that crocodile would have had me before now,
but by a lucky chance he swallowed a clock, and it goes tick, tick, tick, tick inside him; and so before he can reach me I hear the tick and bolt. (*He emits a hollow rumble.*) Once I heard it strike six within him.

SMEE (*sombrely*): Some day the clock will run down, and then he'll get you.

HOOK (*a broken man*): Ay, that is the fear that haunts me. (*He rises.*) Smee, this seat is
hot; odds, bobs, hammer and tongs, I am burning.

(*He has been sitting, he thinks, on one of the island mushrooms, which are of enormous
size. But this is a hand-painted one placed here in times of danger to conceal a chimney.
They remove it, and tell-tale smoke issues; also, alas, the sound of children's voices.*)

25 SMEE: A chimney!

HOOK (*avidly*): Listen! Smee, 'tis plain they live here, beneath the ground. (*He replaces
the mushroom. His brain works tortuously.*)

SMEE (*hopefully*): Unrip your plan, Captain.

HOOK: To return to the boat and cook a large rich cake of jolly thickness with sugar
on it, green sugar. There can be but one room below, for there is but one chimney. The silly moles had not the sense to see that they did not need a door apiece.
We must leave the cake on the shore of the mermaids' lagoon. These boys are
always swimming about there, trying to catch the mermaids. They will find the
cake and gobble it up, because, having no mother, they don't know how dangerous 'tis to eat rich damp cake. They will die!

SMEE (*fascinated*): It is the wickedest, prettiest policy ever I heard of.

30 HOOK (*meaning well*): Shake hands on 't.

SMEE: No, Captain, no.

(*He has to link with the hook, but he does not join in the song.*)

HOOK: Yo ho, yo ho, when I say 'paw,'
By fear they're overtook,
Naught's left upon your bones when you
Have shaken hands with Hook!

(*Frightened by a tug at his hand, SMEE is joining in the chorus when another sound
stills them both. It is a tick, tick as of a clock, whose significance HOOK is, naturally, the
first to recognise. 'The crocodile!' he cries, and totters from the scene. SMEE follows. A
huge crocodile, of one thought compact, passes across, ticking, and oozes after them. The
wood is now so silent that you may be sure it is full of redskins. TIGER LILY comes
first. She is the belle of the Piccaninny tribe, whose braves would all have her to wife, but*)

she wards them off with a hatchet. She puts her ear to the ground and listens, then beckons, and GREAT BIG LITTLE PANTHER *and the tribe are around her, carpeting the ground. Far away some one treads on a dry leaf.*)

TIGER LILY: Pirates! (*They do not draw their knives; the knives slip into their hands.*) Have um scalps? What you say?

PANTHER: Scalp um, oho, velly quick.

THE BRAVES (*in corroboration*): Ugh, ugh, wah.

(*A fire is lit and they dance round and over it till they seem part of the leaping flames.* TIGER LILY *invokes Manitou; the pipe of peace is broken; and they crawl off like a long snake that has not fed for many moons.* TOOTLES *peers after the tail and summons the other boys, who issue from their holes.*)

TOOTLES: They are gone.

SLIGHTLY (*almost losing confidence in himself*): I do wish Peter was here.

FIRST TWIN: H'sh! What is that? (*He is gazing at the lagoon and shrinks back.*) It is wolves, and they are chasing Nibs!

(*The baying wolves are upon them quicker than any boy can scuttle down his tree.*)

NIBS (*falling among his comrades*): Save me, save me!

TOOTLES: What should we do?

SECOND TWIN: What would Peter do?

SLIGHTLY: Peter would look at them through his legs; let us do what Peter would do.

(*The boys advance backwards, looking between their legs at the snarling red-eyed enemy, who trot away foiled.*)

FIRST TWIN (*swaggering*): We have saved you, Nibs. Did you see the pirates?

NIBS (*sitting up, and agreeably aware that the centre of interest is now to pass to him*): No, but I saw a wonderfuller thing, Twin. (*All mouths open for the information to be dropped into them.*) High over the lagoon I saw the loveliest great white bird. It is flying this way. (*They search the firmament.*)

TOOTLES: What kind of a bird, do you think?

NIBS (*awed*): I don't know; but it looked so weary, and as it flies it moans 'Poor Wendy.'

SLIGHTLY (*instantly*): I remember now there are birds called Wendies.

FIRST TWIN (*who has flown to a high branch*): See, it comes, the Wendy! (*They all see it now.*) How white it is! (*A dot of light is pursuing the bird malignantly.*)

TOOTLES: That is Tinker Bell. Tink is trying to hurt the Wendy. (*He makes a cup of his hands and calls*) Hullo, Tink! (*A response comes down in the fairy language.*) She says Peter wants us to shoot the Wendy.

NIBS: Let us do what Peter wishes.

SLIGHTLY: Ay, shoot it; quick, bows and arrows.

TOOTLES (*first with his bow*): Out of the way, Tink; I'll shoot it. (*His bolt goes home, and* WENDY, *who has been fluttering among the tree-tops in her white nightgown, falls straight to earth. No one could be more proud than* TOOTLES.) I have shot the Wendy; Peter will be so pleased. (*From some tree on which* TINK *is roosting comes the tinkle we can now translate, 'You silly ass.'* TOOTLES *falters.*) Why do you say that? (*The others feel that he may have blundered, and draw away from* TOOTLES.)

SLIGHTLY (*examining the fallen one more minutely*): This is no bird; I think it must be a lady.

NIBS (*who would have preferred it to be a bird*): And Tootles has killed her.

55 CURLY: Now I see, Peter was bringing her to us. (*They wonder for what object.*)

SECOND TWIN: To take care of us? (*Undoubtedly for some diverting purpose.*)

OMNES (*though every one of them had wanted to have a shot at her*): Oh, Tootles!

TOOTLES (*gulping*): I did it. When ladies used to come to me in dreams I said 'Pretty mother,' but when she really came I shot her! (*He perceives the necessity of a solitary life for him.*) Friends, good-bye.

SEVERAL (*not very enthusiastic*): Don't go.

60 TOOTLES: I must; I am so afraid of Peter.

(*He has gone but a step toward oblivion when he is stopped by a crowing as of some victorious cock.*)

OMNES: Peter!

(*They make a paling of themselves in front of* WENDY *as* PETER *skims round the tree-tops and reaches earth.*)

PETER: Greeting, boys! (*Their silence chafes him.*) I am back; why do you not cheer? Great news, boys, I have brought at last a mother for us all.

SLIGHTLY (*vaguely*): Ay, ay.

PETER: She flew this way; have you not seen her?

65 SECOND TWIN (*as* PETER *evidently thinks her important*): Oh mournful day!

TOOTLES (*making a break in the paling*): Peter, I will show her to you.

THE OTHERS (*closing the gap*): No, no.

TOOTLES (*majestically*): Stand back all, and let Peter see.

(*The paling dissolves, and* PETER *sees* WENDY *prone on the ground.*)

PETER: Wendy, with an arrow in her heart! (*He plucks it out.*) Wendy is dead. (*He is not so much pained as puzzled.*)

70 CURLY: I thought it was only flowers that die.

PETER: Perhaps she is frightened at being dead? (*None of them can say as to that.*) Whose arrow? (*Not one of them looks at* TOOTLES.)

TOOTLES: Mine, Peter.

PETER (*raising it as a dagger*): Oh dastard hand!

TOOTLES (*kneeling and baring his breast*): Strike, Peter; strike true.

75 PETER (*undergoing a singular experience*): I cannot strike; there is something stays my hand.

(*In fact* WENDY's *arm has risen.*)

NIBS: 'Tis she, the Wendy lady. See, her arm. (*To help a friend*) I think she said 'Poor Tootles.'

PETER (*investigating*): She lives!

SLIGHTLY (*authoritatively*): The Wendy lady lives.

(*The delightful feeling that they have been cleverer than they thought comes over them and they applaud themselves.*)

PETER (*holding up a button that is attached to her chain*): See, the arrow struck against this. It is a kiss I gave her; it has saved her life.

SLIGHTLY: I remember kisses; let me see it. (*He takes it in his hand.*) Ay, that is a kiss.   80

PETER: Wendy, get better quickly and I'll take you to see the mermaids. She is aw-fully anxious to see a mermaid.

(TINKER BELL, *who may have been off visiting her relations, returns to the wood and, under the impression that* WENDY *has been got rid of, is whistling as gaily as a canary. She is not wholly heartless, but is so small that she has only room for one feeling at a time.*)

CURLY: Listen to Tink rejoicing because she thinks the Wendy is dead! (*Regardless of spoiling another's pleasure*) Tink, the Wendy lives.

(TINK *gives expression to fury.*)

SECOND TWIN (*tell-tale*): It was she who said that you wanted us to shoot the Wendy.

PETER: She said that? Then listen, Tink, I am your friend no more. (*There is a note of acerbity in* TINK's *reply; it may mean 'Who wants you?'*) Begone from me for ever. (*Now it is a very wet tinkle.*)

CURLY: She is crying.   85

TOOTLES: She says she is your fairy.

PETER (*who knows they are not worth worrying about*): Oh well, not for ever, but for a whole week.

(TINK *goes off sulking, no doubt with the intention of giving all her friends an entirely false impression of* WENDY's *appearance.*)

Now what shall we do with Wendy?

CURLY: Let us carry her down into the house.

SLIGHTLY: Ay, that is what one does with ladies.   90

PETER: No, you must not touch her; it wouldn't be sufficiently respectful.

SLIGHTLY: That is what I was thinking.

TOOTLES: But if she lies there she will die.

SLIGHTLY: Ay, she will die. It is a pity, but there is no way out.

PETER: Yes, there is. Let us build a house around her! (*Cheers again, meaning that no difficulty baffles* PETER.) Leave all to me. Bring the best of what we have. Gut our house. Be sharp. (*They race down their trees.*)   95

(*While* PETER *is engrossed in measuring* WENDY *so that the house may fit her,* JOHN *and* MICHAEL, *who have probably landed on the island with a bump, wander forward, so draggled and tired that if you were to ask* MICHAEL *whether he is awake or asleep he would probably answer 'I haven't tried yet.'*)

MICHAEL (*bewildered*): John, John, wake up. Where is Nana, John?

JOHN (*with the help of one eye but not always the same eye*): It is true, we did fly! (*Thankfully*) And here is Peter. Peter, is this the place?

(PETER, *alas, has already forgotten them, as soon maybe as he will forget* WENDY. *The first thing she should do now that she is here is to sew a handkerchief for him, and knot it as a jog to his memory.*)

PETER (*curtly*): Yes.

MICHAEL: Where is Wendy? (PETER *points.*)

100 JOHN (*who still wears his hat*): She is asleep.

MICHAEL: John, let us wake her and get her to make supper for us.

(*Some of the boys emerge, and he pinches one.*)

John, look at them!

PETER (*still house-building*): Curly, see that these boys help in the building of the house.

JOHN: Build a house?

105 CURLY: For the Wendy.

JOHN (*feeling that there must be some mistake here*): For Wendy? Why, she is only a girl.

CURLY: That is why we are her servants.

JOHN (*dazed*): Are you Wendy's servants?

PETER: Yes, and you also. Away with them. (*In another moment they are woodsmen hacking at trees, with CURLY as overseer.*) Slightly, fetch a doctor. (SLIGHTLY *reels and goes. He returns professionally in JOHN's hat.*) Please, sir, are you a doctor?

110 SLIGHTLY (*trembling in his desire to give satisfaction*): Yes, my little man.

PETER: Please, sir, a lady lies very ill.

SLIGHTLY (*taking care not to fall over her*): Tut, tut, where does she lie?

PETER: In yonder glade. (*It is a variation of a game they play.*)

SLIGHTLY: I will put a glass thing in her mouth. (*He inserts an imaginary thermometer in WENDY's mouth and gives it a moment to record its verdict. He shakes it and then consults it.*)

115 PETER (*anxiously*): How is she?

SLIGHTLY: Tut, tut, this has cured her.

PETER (*leaping joyously*): I am glad.

SLIGHTLY: I will call again in the evening. Give her beef tea out of a cup with a spout to it, tut, tut.

(*The boys are running up with odd articles of furniture.*)

PETER (*with an already fading recollection of the Darling nursery*): These are not good enough for Wendy. How I wish I knew the kind of house she would prefer!

120 FIRST TWIN: Peter, she is moving in her sleep.

TOOTLES (*opening WENDY's mouth and gazing down into the depths*): Lovely!

PETER: Oh, Wendy, if you could sing the kind of house you would like to have.

(*It is as if she had heard him.*)

WENDY (*without opening her eyes*):

I wish I had a woodland house,
The littlest ever seen,
With funny little red walls
And roof of mossy green.

(*In the time she sings this and two other verses, such is the urgency of PETER's silent orders that they have knocked down trees, laid a foundation and put up the walls and roof, so that she is now hidden from view. 'Windows,' cries* PETER, *and* CURLY *rushes them in, 'Roses,' and* TOOTLES *arrives breathless with a festoon for the door. Thus springs into existence the most delicious little house for beginners.*)

FIRST TWIN: I think it is finished.

PETER: There is no knocker on the door. (TOOTLES *hangs up the sole of his shoe.*)   125
There is no chimney; we must have a chimney. (*They await his deliberations anxiously.*)

JOHN (*unwisely critical*): It certainly does need a chimney.

(*He is again wearing his hat, which* PETER *seizes, knocks the top off it and places on the roof. In the friendliest way smoke begins to come out of the hat.*)

PETER (*with his hand on the knocker*): All look your best; the first impression is awfully important. (*He knocks, and after a dreadful moment of suspense, in which they cannot help wondering if any one is inside, the door opens and who should come out but* WENDY! *She has evidently been tidying a little. She is quite surprised to find that she has nine children.*)

WENDY (*genteelly*): Where am I?

SLIGHTLY: Wendy lady, for you we built this house.

NIBS *and* TOOTLES: Oh, say you are pleased.   130

WENDY (*stroking the pretty thing*): Lovely, darling house!

FIRST TWIN: And we are your children.

WENDY (*affecting surprise*): Oh?

OMNES (*kneeling, with outstretched arms*): Wendy lady, be our mother! (*Now that they know it is pretend they acclaim her greedily.*)

WENDY (*not to make herself too cheap*): Ought I? Of course it is frightfully fascinating;   135
but you see I am only a little girl; I have no real experience.

OMNES: That doesn't matter. What we need is just a nice motherly person.

WENDY: Oh dear, I feel that is just exactly what I am.

OMNES: It is, it is, we saw it at once.

WENDY: Very well then, I will do my best. (*In their glee they go dancing obstreperously round the little house, and she sees she must be firm with them as well as kind.*) Come inside at once, you naughty children, I am sure your feet are damp. And before I put you to bed I have just time to finish the story of Cinderella.

(*They all troop into the enchanting house, whose not least remarkable feature is that it holds them. A vision of* LIZA *passes, not perhaps because she has any right to be there; but she has so few pleasures and is so young that we just let her have a peep at the little house. By and by* PETER *comes out and marches up and down with drawn sword, for the pirates can be heard carousing far away on the lagoon, and the wolves are on the prowl. The little house, its walls so red and its roof so mossy, looks very cosy and safe, with a bright light showing through the blind, the chimney smoking beautifully, and* PETER *on guard. On our last sight of him it is so dark that we just guess he is the little figure who has fallen asleep by the door. Dots of light come and go. They are inquisitive fairies having a look at the house. Any other child in their way they would mischief, but they just tweak* PETER's *nose and pass on. Fairies, you see, can touch him.*)

ACT III
THE MERMAIDS' LAGOON

It is the end of a long playful day on the lagoon. The sun's rays have persuaded him to give them another five minutes, for one more race over the waters before he gathers them up and lets in the moon. There are many mermaids here, going plop-plop, and one might attempt to count the tails did they not flash and disappear so quickly. At times a lovely girl leaps in the air seeking to get rid of her excess of scales, which fall in a silver shower as she shakes them off. From the coral grottoes beneath the lagoon, where are the mermaids' bed-chambers, comes fitful music.

One of the most bewitching of these blue-eyed creatures is lying lazily on Marooners' Rock, combing her long tresses and noting effects in a transparent shell. PETER *and his band are in the water unseen behind the rock, whither they have tracked her as if she were a trout, and at a signal ten pairs of arms come whack upon the mermaid to enclose her. Alas, this is only what was meant to happen, for she hears the signal (which is the crow of a cock) and slips through their arms into the water. It has been such a near thing that there are scales on some of their hands. They climb on to the rock crestfallen.*

WENDY (*preserving her scales as carefully as if they were rare postage stamps*): I did so want to catch a mermaid.

PETER (*getting rid of his*): It is awfully difficult to catch a mermaid.

(*The mermaids at times find it just as difficult to catch him, though he sometimes joins them in their one game, which consists in lazily blowing their bubbles into the air and seeing who can catch them. The number of bubbles* PETER *has flown away with! When the weather grows cold mermaids migrate to the other side of the world, and he once went with a great shoal of them half the way.*)

They are such cruel creatures, Wendy, that they try to pull boys and girls like you into the water and drown them.

WENDY (*too guarded by this time to ask what he means precisely by 'like you,' though she is very desirous of knowing*): How hateful!

(*She is slightly different in appearance now, rather rounder, while* JOHN *and* MICHAEL *are not quite so round. The reason is that when new lost children arrive at his underground home* PETER *finds new trees for them to go up and down by, and instead of fitting the tree to them he makes them fit the tree. Sometimes it can be done by adding or removing garments, but if you are bumpy, or the tree is an odd shape, he has things done to you with a roller, and after that you fit.*

The other boys are now playing King of the Castle, throwing each other into the water, taking headers and so on; but these two continue to talk.)

5   PETER: Wendy, this is a fearfully important rock. It is called Marooners' Rock. Sailors are marooned, you know, when their captain leaves them on a rock and sails away.

WENDY: Leaves them on this little rock to drown?

PETER (*lightly*): Oh, they don't live long. Their hands are tied, so that they can't swim. When the tide is full this rock is covered with water, and then the sailor drowns.

(WENDY *is uneasy as she surveys the rock, which is the only one in the lagoon and no larger than a table. Since she last looked around a threatening change has come over the scene. The sun has gone, but the moon has not come. What has come is a cold shiver across the waters which has sent all the wiser mermaids to their coral recesses. They know that evil is creeping over the lagoon. Of the boys* PETER *is of course the first to scent it, and he has leapt to his feet before the words strike the rock—*

'And if we're parted by a shot
We're sure to meet below.'

The games on the rock and around it end so abruptly that several divers are checked in the air. There they hang waiting for the word of command from PETER. *When they get it they strike the water simultaneously, and the rock is at once as bare as if suddenly they had been blown off it. Thus the pirates find it deserted when their dinghy strikes the rock and is nearly stove in by the concussion.*)

SMEE: Luff, you spalpeen, luff! (*They are* SMEE *and* STARKEY, *with* TIGER LILY, *their captive, bound hand and foot.*) What we have got to do is to hoist the redskin on to the rock and leave her there to drown.

(*To one of her race this is an end darker than death by fire or torture, for it is written in the laws of the Piccaninnies that there is no path through water to the happy hunting ground. Yet her face is impassive; she is the daughter of a chief and must die as a chief's daughter; it is enough.*)

STARKEY (*chagrined because she does not mewl*): No mewling. This is your reward for prowling round the ship with a knife in your mouth.

TIGER LILY (*stoically*): Enough said.   10

SMEE (*who would have preferred a farewell palaver*): So that's it! On to the rock with her, mate.

STARKEY (*experiencing for perhaps the last time the stirrings of a man*): Not so rough, Smee; roughish, but not so rough.

SMEE (*dragging her on to the rock*): It is the captain's orders.

(*A stave has in some past time been driven into the rock, probably to mark the burial place of hidden treasure, and to this they moor the dinghy.*)

WENDY (*in the water*): Poor Tiger Lily!

STARKEY: What was that? (*The children bob.*)   15

PETER (*who can imitate the captain's voice so perfectly that even the author has a dizzy feeling that at times he was really* HOOK): Ahoy there, you lubbers!

STARKEY: It is the captain; he must be swimming out to us.

SMEE (*calling*): We have put the redskin on the rock, Captain.

PETER: Set her free.

SMEE: But, Captain—   20

PETER: Cut her bonds, or I'll plunge my hook in you.

SMEE: This is queer!

STARKEY (*unmanned*): Let us follow the captain's orders.

(*They undo the thongs and* TIGER LILY *slides between their legs into the lagoon, forgetting in her haste to utter her war-cry, but* PETER *utters it for her, so naturally that even the lost boys are deceived. It is at this moment that the voice of the true* HOOK *is heard.*)

HOOK: Boat ahoy!

25 SMEE (*relieved*): It is the captain.

(HOOK *is swimming, and they help him to scale the rock. He is in gloomy mood.*)

STARKEY: Captain, is all well?

SMEE: He sighs.

STARKEY: He sighs again.

SMEE (*counting*): And yet a third time he sighs. (*With foreboding*) What's up, Captain?

30 HOOK (*who has perhaps found the large rich damp cake untouched*): The game is up. Those boys have found a mother!

STARKEY: Oh evil day!

SMEE: What is a mother?

WENDY (*horrified*): He doesn't know!

HOOK (*sharply*): What was that?

(PETER *makes the splash of a mermaid's tail.*)

35 STARKEY: One of them mermaids.

HOOK: Dost not know, Smee? A mother is— (*He finds it more difficult to explain than he had expected, and looks about him for an illustration. He finds one in a great bird which drifts past in a nest as large as the roomiest basin.*) There is a lesson in mothers for you! The nest must have fallen into the water, but would the bird desert her eggs? (PETER, *who is now more or less off his head, makes the sound of a bird answering in the negative. The nest is borne out of sight.*)

STARKEY: Maybe she is hanging about here to protect Peter?

(HOOK'*s face clouds still further and* PETER *just manages not to call out that he needs no protection.*)

SMEE (*not usually a man of ideas*): Captain, could we not kidnap these boys' mother and make her our mother?

HOOK: Obesity and bunions, 'tis a princely scheme. We will seize the children, make them walk the plank, and Wendy shall be our mother!

40 WENDY: Never! (*Another splash from* PETER.)

HOOK: What say you, bullies?

SMEE: There is my hand on't.

STARKEY: And mine.

HOOK: And there is my hook. Swear. (*All swear.*) But I had forgot; where is the redskin?

45 SMEE (*shaken*): That is all right, Captain; we let her go.

HOOK (*terrible*): Let her go?

SMEE: 'Twas your own orders, Captain.

STARKEY (*whimpering*): You called over the water to us to let her go.

HOOK: Brimstone and gall, what cozening is here? (*Disturbed by their faithful faces*) Lads, I gave no such order.

50 SMEE: 'Tis passing queer.

HOOK (*addressing the immensities*): Spirit that haunts this dark lagoon to-night, dost hear me?

PETER (*in the same voice*): Odds, bobs, hammer and tongs, I hear you.

HOOK (*gripping the stave for support*): Who are you, stranger, speak.

PETER (*who is only too ready to speak*): I am Jas Hook, Captain of the *Jolly Roger*.

HOOK (*now white to the gills*): No, no, you are not.   55

PETER: Brimstone and gall, say that again and I'll cast anchor in you.

HOOK: If you are Hook, come tell me, who am I?

PETER: A codfish, only a codfish.

HOOK (*aghast*): A codfish?

SMEE (*drawing back from him*): Have we been captained all this time by a codfish?   60

STARKEY: It's lowering to our pride.

HOOK (*feeling that his ego is slipping from him*): Don't desert me, bullies.

PETER (*top-heavy*): Paw, fish, paw!

(*There is a touch of the feminine in* HOOK, *as in all the greatest pirates, and it prompts him to try the guessing game.*)

HOOK: Have you another name?

PETER (*falling to the lure*): Ay, ay.   65

HOOK (*thirstily*): Vegetable?

PETER: No.

HOOK: Mineral?

PETER: No.

HOOK: Animal?   70

PETER (*after a hurried consultation with* TOOTLES): Yes.

HOOK: Man?

PETER (*with scorn*): No.

HOOK: Boy?

PETER: Yes.   75

HOOK: Ordinary boy?

PETER: No!

HOOK: Wonderful boy?

PETER (*to* WENDY's *distress*): Yes!

HOOK: Are you in England?   80

PETER: No.

HOOK: Are you here?

PETER: Yes.

HOOK (*beaten, though he feels he has very nearly got it*): Smee, you ask him some questions.

SMEE (*rummaging his brains*): I can't think of a thing.   85

PETER: Can't guess, can't guess! (*Foundering in his cockiness*) Do you give it up?

HOOK (*eagerly*): Yes.

PETER: All of you?

SMEE *and* STARKEY: Yes.

PETER (*crowing*): Well, then, I am Peter Pan!   90

(*Now they have him.*)

HOOK: Pan! Into the water, Smee. Starkey, mind the boat. Take him dead or alive!

PETER (*who still has all his baby teeth*): Boys, lam into the pirates!

(*For a moment the only two we can see are in the dinghy, where* JOHN *throws himself on* STARKEY. STARKEY *wriggles into the lagoon and* JOHN *leaps so quickly after him that he reaches it first. The impression left on* STARKEY *is that he is being attacked by the* TWINS. *The water becomes stained. The dinghy drifts away. Here and there a head shows in the water, and once it is the head of the crocodile. In the growing gloom some strike at their friends,* SLIGHTLY *getting* TOOTLES *in the fourth rib while he himself is pinked by* CURLY. *It looks as if the boys were getting the worse of it, which is perhaps just as well at this point, because* PETER, *who will be the determining factor in the end, has a perplexing way of changing sides if he is winning too easily.* HOOK'*s iron claw makes a circle of black water round him from which opponents flee like fishes. There is only one prepared to enter that dreadful circle. His name is* PAN. *Strangely, it is not in the water that they meet.* HOOK *has risen to the rock to breathe, and at the same moment* PETER *scales it on the opposite side. The rock is now wet and as slippery as a ball, and they have to crawl rather than climb. Suddenly they are face to face.* PETER *gnashes his pretty teeth with joy, and is gathering himself for the spring when he sees he is higher up the rock than his foe. Courteously he waits;* HOOK *sees his intention, and taking advantage of it claws twice.* PETER *is untouched, but unfairness is what he never can get used to, and in his bewilderment he rolls off the rock. The crocodile, whose tick has been drowned in the strife, rears its jaws, and* HOOK, *who has almost stepped into them, is pursued by it to land. All is quiet on the lagoon now, not a sound save little waves nibbling at the rock, which is smaller than when we last looked at it. Two boys appear with the dinghy, and the others despite their wounds climb into it. They send the cry 'Peter—Wendy' across the waters, but no answer comes.*)

NIBS: They must be swimming home.

JOHN: Or flying.

95 FIRST TWIN: Yes, that is it. Let us be off and call to them as we go.

(*The dinghy disappears with its load, whose hearts would sink it if they knew of the peril of* WENDY *and her captain. From near and far away come the cries 'Peter—Wendy' till we no longer hear them.*

Two small figures are now on the rock, but they have fainted. A mermaid who has dared to come back in the stillness stretches up her arms and is slowly pulling WENDY *into the water to drown her.* WENDY *starts up just in time.*)

WENDY: Peter!

(*He rouses himself and looks around him.*)

Where are we, Peter?

PETER: We are on the rock, but it is getting smaller. Soon the water will be over it. Listen!

(*They can hear the wash of the relentless little waves.*)

WENDY: We must go.

100 PETER: Yes.

WENDY: Shall we swim or fly?

PETER: Wendy, do you think you could swim or fly to the island without me?

WENDY: You know I couldn't, Peter; I am just a beginner.

PETER: Hook wounded me twice. (*He believes it; he is so good at pretend that he feels the pain, his arms hang limp.*) I can neither swim nor fly.

WENDY: Do you mean we shall both be drowned?

105

PETER: Look how the water is rising!

(*They cover their faces with their hands. Something touches* WENDY *as lightly as a kiss.*)

PETER (*with little interest*): It must be the tail of the kite we made for Michael; you remember it tore itself out of his hands and floated away. (*He looks up and sees the kite sailing overhead.*) The kite! Why shouldn't it carry you? (*He grips the tail and pulls, and the kite responds.*)

WENDY: Both of us!

PETER: It can't lift two. Michael and Curly tried.

(*She knows very well that if it can lift her it can lift him also, for she has been told by the boys as a deadly secret that one of the queer things about him is that he is no weight at all. But it is a forbidden subject.*)

WENDY: I won't go without you. Let us draw lots which is to stay behind.

110

PETER: And you a lady, never! (*The tail is in her hands, and the kite is tugging hard. She holds out her mouth to* PETER, *but he knows they cannot do that.*) Ready, Wendy!

(*The kite draws her out of sight across the lagoon.*

The waters are lapping over the rock now, and PETER *knows that it will soon be submerged. Pale rays of light mingle with the moving clouds, and from the coral grottoes is to be heard a sound, at once the most musical and the most melancholy in the Never Land, the mermaids calling to the moon to rise.* PETER *is afraid at last, and a tremor runs through him, like a shudder passing over the lagoon; but on the lagoon one shudder follows another till there are hundreds of them, and he feels just the one.*)

PETER (*with a drum beating in his breast as if he were a real boy at last*): To die will be an awfully big adventure.

(*The blind rises again, and the lagoon is now suffused with moonlight. He is on the rock still, but the water is over his feet. The nest is borne nearer, and the bird, after cooing a message to him, leaves it and wings her way upwards.* PETER, *who knows the bird language, slips into the nest, first removing the two eggs and placing them in* STARKEY'S *hat, which has been left on the stave. The hat drifts away from the rock, but he uses the stave as a mast. The wind is driving him toward the open sea. He takes off his shirt, which he had forgotten to remove while bathing, and unfurls it as a sail. His vessel tacks, and he passes from sight, naked and victorious. The bird returns and sits on the hat.*)

ACT IV
THE HOME UNDER THE GROUND

We see simultaneously the home under the ground with the children in it and the wood above ground with the redskins on it. Below, the children are gobbling their evening *meal; above, the redskins are squatting in their blankets near the little house guarding the children from the pirates. The only way of communicating between these two parties is by means of the hollow trees.*

The home has an earthen floor, which is handy for digging in if you want to go fishing; and owing to there being so many entrances there is not much wall space. The table at which the lost ones are sitting is a board on top of a live tree trunk, which has been cut flat but has such growing pains that the board rises as they eat, and they have sometimes to pause in their meals to cut a bit more off the trunk. Their seats are pumpkins or the large gay mushrooms of which we have seen an imitation one concealing the chimney. There is an enormous fireplace which is in almost any part of the room where you care to light it, and across this WENDY *has stretched strings, made of fibre, from which she hangs her washing. There are also various tomfool things in the room of no use whatever.*

MICHAEL*'s basket bed is nailed high up on the wall as if to protect him from the cat, but there is no indication at present of where the others sleep. At the back between two of the tree trunks is a grindstone, and near it is a lovely hole, the size of a band-box, with a gay curtain drawn across so that you cannot see what is inside. This is* TINK*'s withdrawing-room and bed-chamber, and it is just as well that you cannot see inside, for it is so exquisite in its decoration and in the personal apparel spread out on the bed that you could scarcely resist making off with something.* TINK *is within at present, as one can guess from a glow showing through the chinks. It is her own glow, for though she has a chandelier for the look of the thing, of course she lights her residence herself. She is probably wasting valuable time just now wondering whether to put on the smoky blue or the apple-blossom.*

All the boys except PETER *are here, and* WENDY *has the head of the table, smiling complacently at their captivating ways, but doing her best at the same time to see that they keep the rules about hands-off-the-table, no-two-to-speak-at-once, and so on. She is wearing romantic woodland garments, sewn by herself, with red berries in her hair which go charmingly with her complexion, as she knows; indeed she searched for red berries the morning after she reached the island. The boys are in picturesque attire of her contrivance, and if these don't always fit well the fault is not hers but the wearers', for they constantly put on each other's things when they put on anything at all.* MICHAEL *is in his cradle on the wall.* FIRST TWIN *is apart on a high stool and wears a dunce's cap, another invention of* WENDY*'s, but not wholly successful because everybody wants to be dunce.*

It is a pretend meal this evening, with nothing whatever on the table, not a mug, nor a crust, nor a spoon. They often have these suppers and like them on occasions as well as the other kind, which consist chiefly of bread-fruit, tappa rolls, yams, mammee apples and banana splash, washed down with calabashes of poe-poe. The pretend meals are not WENDY*'s idea; indeed she was rather startled to find, on arriving, that* PETER *knew of no other kind, and she is not absolutely certain even now that he does eat the other kind, though no one appears to do it more heartily. He insists that the pretend meals should be partaken of with gusto, and we see his band doing their best to obey orders.*

WENDY (*her fingers to her ears, for their chatter and clatter are deafening*): Si-lence! Is your mug empty, Slightly?

SLIGHTLY (*who would not say this if he had a mug*): Not quite empty, thank you.

NIBS: Mummy, he has not even begun to drink his poe-poe.

SLIGHTLY (*seizing his chance, for this is tale-bearing*): I complain of Nibs!

(JOHN *holds up his hand.*)

WENDY: Well, John?   5
JOHN: May I sit in Peter's chair as he is not here?
WENDY: In your father's chair? Certainly not.
JOHN: He is not really our father. He did not even know how to be a father till I
    showed him.

(*This is insubordination.*)

SECOND TWIN: I complain of John!

(*The gentle* TOOTLES *raises his hand.*)

TOOTLES (*who has the poorest opinion of himself*): I don't suppose Michael would let   10
    me be baby?
MICHAEL: No, I won't.
TOOTLES: May I be dunce?
FIRST TWIN (*from his perch*): No. It's awfully difficult to be dunce.
TOOTLES: As I can't be anything important would any of you like to see me do a
    trick?
OMNES: No.   15
TOOTLES (*subsiding*): I hadn't really any hope.

(*The tale-telling breaks out again.*)

NIBS: Slightly is coughing on the table.
CURLY: The twins began with tappa rolls.
SLIGHTLY: I complain of Nibs!
NIBS: I complain of Slightly!   20
WENDY: Oh dear, I am sure I sometimes think that spinsters are to be envied.
MICHAEL: Wendy, I am too big for a cradle.
WENDY: You are the littlest, and a cradle is such a nice homely thing to have about a
    house. You others can clear away now. (*She sits down on a pumpkin near the fire to
    her usual evening occupation, darning.*) Every heel with a hole in it!

(*The boys clear away with dispatch, washing dishes they don't have in a non-existent
sink and stowing them in a cupboard that isn't there. Instead of sawing the table-leg
to-night they crush it into the ground like a concertina, and are now ready for play, in
which they indulge hilariously.*
    *A movement of the Indians draws our attention to the scene above. Hitherto, with
the exception of* PANTHER, *who sits on guard on top of the little house, they have been
hunkering in their blankets, mute but picturesque; now all rise and prostrate themselves
before the majestic figure of* PETER, *who approaches through the forest carrying a gun
and game bag. It is not exactly a gun. He often wanders away alone with this weapon,
and when he comes back you are never absolutely certain whether he has had an adventure or not. He may have forgotten it so completely that he says nothing about it; and
then when you go out you find the body. On the other hand he may say a great deal
about it, and yet you never find the body. Sometimes he comes home with his face
scratched, and tells* WENDY, *as a thing of no importance, that he got these marks from
the little people for cheeking them at a fairy wedding, and she listens politely, but she is*

never quite sure, you know; indeed the only one who is sure about anything on the island is PETER.)

PETER: The Great White Father is glad to see the Piccaninny braves protecting his wigwam from the pirates.

25   TIGER LILY: The Great White Father save me from pirates. Me his velly nice friend now; no let pirates hurt him.

BRAVES: Ugh, ugh, wah!

TIGER LILY: Tiger Lily has spoken.

PANTHER: Loola, loola! Great Big Little Panther has spoken.

PETER: It is well. The Great White Father has spoken.

(*This has a note of finality about it, with the implied 'And now shut up,' which is never far from the courteous receptions of well-meaning inferiors by born leaders of men. He descends his tree, not unheard by* WENDY.)

30   WENDY: Children, I hear your father's step. He likes you to meet him at the door.
(PETER *scatters pretend nuts among them and watches sharply to see that they crunch with relish.*) Peter, you just spoil them, you know!

JOHN (*who would be incredulous if he dare*): Any sport, Peter?

PETER: Two tigers and a pirate.

JOHN (*boldly*): Where are their heads?

PETER (*contracting his little brows*): In the bag.

35   JOHN: (*No, he doesn't say it. He backs away.*)

WENDY (*peeping into the bag*): They are beauties! (*She has learned her lesson.*)

FIRST TWIN: Mummy, we all want to dance.

WENDY: The mother of such an armful dance!

SLIGHTLY: As it is Saturday night?

(*They have long lost count of the days, but always if they want to do anything special they say this is Saturday night, and then they do it.*)

40   WENDY: Of course it is Saturday night, Peter? (*He shrugs an indifferent assent.*) On with your nighties first.

(*They disappear into various recesses, and* PETER *and* WENDY *with her darning are left by the fire to dodder parentally. She emphasises it by humming a verse of 'John Anderson my Jo,' which has not the desired effect on* PETER. *She is too loving to be ignorant that he is not loving enough, and she hesitates like one who knows the answer to her question.*)

What is wrong, Peter?

PETER (*scared*): It is only pretend, isn't it, that I am their father?

WENDY (*drooping*): Oh yes.

(*His sigh of relief is without consideration for her feelings.*)

But they are ours, Peter, yours and mine.

45   PETER (*determined to get at facts, the only things that puzzle him*): But not really?

WENDY: Not if you don't wish it.

PETER: I don't.

WENDY (*knowing she ought not to probe but driven to it by something within*): What are
    your exact feelings for me, Peter?
PETER (*in the class-room*): Those of a devoted son, Wendy.
WENDY (*turning away*): I thought so.   50
PETER: You are so puzzling. Tiger Lily is just the same; there is something or other
    she wants to be to me, but she says it is not my mother.
WENDY (*with spirit*): No, indeed it isn't.
PETER: Then what is it?
WENDY: It isn't for a lady to tell.

    (*The curtain of the fairy chamber opens slightly, and* TINK, *who has doubtless been
    eavesdropping, tinkles a laugh of scorn.*)

PETER (*badgered*): I suppose she means that she wants to be my mother.   55

    (TINK'*s comment is* 'You silly ass.')

WENDY (*who has picked up some of the fairy words*): I almost agree with her!

    (*The arrival of the boys in their nightgowns turns* WENDY'*s mind to practical matters,
    for the children have to be arranged in line and passed or not passed for cleanliness.*
    SLIGHTLY *is the worst. At last we see how they sleep, for in a babel the great bed which
    stands on end by day against the wall is unloosed from custody and lowered to the floor.
    Though large, it is a tight fit for so many boys, and* WENDY *has made a rule that there
    is to be no turning round until one gives the signal, when all turn at once.*
        FIRST TWIN *is the best dancer and performs mightily on the bed and in it and
    out of it and over it to an accompaniment of pillow fights by the less agile; and then there
    is a rush at* WENDY.)

NIBS: Now the story you promised to tell us as soon as we were in bed!
WENDY (*severely*): As far as I can see you are not in bed yet.

    (*They scramble into the bed, and the effect is as of a boxful of sardines.*)

WENDY (*drawing up her stool*): Well, there was once a gentleman—
CURLY: I wish he had been a lady.   60
NIBS: I wish he had been a white rat.
WENDY: Quiet! There was a lady also. The gentleman's name was Mr. Darling and
    the lady's name was Mrs. Darling—
JOHN: I knew them!
MICHAEL (*who has been allowed to join the circle*): I think I knew them.
WENDY: They were married, you know; and what do you think they had?   65
NIBS: White rats?
WENDY: No, they had three descendants. White rats are descendants also. Almost
    everything is a descendant. Now these three children had a faithful nurse called
    Nana.
MICHAEL (*alas*): What a funny name!
WENDY: But Mr. Darling—(*faltering*) or was it Mrs. Darling?—was angry with her
    and chained her up in the yard; so all the children flew away. They flew away to
    the Never Land, where the lost boys are.
CURLY: I just thought they did; I don't know how it is, but I just thought they did.   70

TOOTLES: Oh, Wendy, was one of the lost boys called Tootles?

WENDY: Yes, he was.

TOOTLES (*dazzled*): Am I in a story? Nibs, I am in a story!

PETER (*who is by the fire making Pan's pipes with his knife, and is determined that* WENDY *shall have fair play, however beastly a story he may think it*): A little less noise there.

75 WENDY (*melting over the beauty of her present performance, but without any real qualms*): Now I want you to consider the feelings of the unhappy parents with all their children flown away. Think, oh think, of the empty beds. (*The heartless ones think of them with glee.*)

FIRST TWIN (*cheerfully*): It's awfully sad.

WENDY: But our heroine knew that her mother would always leave the window open for her progeny to fly back by; so they stayed away for years and had a lovely time.

(PETER *is interested at last.*)

FIRST TWIN: Did they ever go back?

WENDY (*comfortably*): Let us now take a peep into the future. Years have rolled by, and who is this elegant lady of uncertain age alighting at London station?

(*The tension is unbearable.*)

80 NIBS: Oh, Wendy, who is she?

WENDY (*swelling*): Can it be—yes—no—yes, it is the fair Wendy!

TOOTLES: I am glad.

WENDY: Who are the two noble portly figures accompanying her? Can they be John and Michael? They are. (*Pride of* MICHAEL.) 'See, dear brothers,' says Wendy, pointing upward, 'there is the window standing open.' So up they flew to their loving parents, and pen cannot inscribe the happy scene over which we draw a veil. (*Her triumph is spoilt by a groan from* PETER *and she hurries to him.*) Peter, what is it? (*Thinking he is ill, and looking lower than his chest*) Where is it?

PETER: It isn't that kind of pain. Wendy, you are wrong about mothers. I thought like you about the window, so I stayed away for moons and moons, and then I flew back, but the window was barred, for my mother had forgotten all about me and there was another little boy sleeping in my bed.

(*This is a general damper.*)

85 JOHN: Wendy, let us go back!

WENDY: Are you sure mothers are like that?

PETER: Yes.

WENDY: John, Michael! (*She clasps them to her.*)

FIRST TWIN (*alarmed*): You are not to leave us, Wendy?

90 WENDY: I must.

NIBS: Not to-night?

WENDY: At once. Perhaps mother is in half-mourning by this time! Peter, will you make the necessary arrangements?

(*She asks it in the steely tones women adopt when they are prepared secretly for opposition.*)

PETER (*coolly*): If you wish it.

(*He ascends his tree to give the redskins their instructions. The lost boys gather threateningly round* WENDY.)

CURLY: We won't let you go!

WENDY (*with one of those inspirations women have, in an emergency, to make use of some male who need otherwise have no hope*): Tootles, I appeal to you.

TOOTLES (*leaping to his death if necessary*): I am just Tootles and nobody minds me, but the first who does not behave to Wendy I will blood him severely. (PETER *returns.*)

PETER (*with awful serenity*): Wendy, I told the braves to guide you through the wood as flying tires you so. Then Tinker Bell will take you across the sea. (*A shrill tinkle from the boudoir probably means 'and drop her into it.'*)

NIBS (*fingering the curtain which he is not allowed to open*): Tink, you are to get up and take Wendy on a journey. (*Star-eyed*) She says she won't!

PETER (*taking a step toward that chamber*): If you don't get up, Tink, and dress at once— She is getting up!

WENDY (*quivering now that the time to depart has come*): Dear ones, if you will all come with me I feel almost sure I can get my father and mother to adopt you.

(*There is joy at this, not that they want parents, but novelty is their religion.*)

NIBS: But won't they think us rather a handful?

WENDY (*a swift reckoner*): Oh no, it will only mean having a few beds in the drawing-room; they can be hidden behind screens on first Thursdays.

(*Everything depends on* PETER.)

OMNES: Peter, may we go?

PETER (*carelessly through the pipes to which he is giving a finishing touch*): All right.

(*They scurry off to dress for the adventure.*)

WENDY (*insinuatingly*): Get your clothes, Peter.

PETER (*skipping about and playing fairy music on his pipes, the only music he knows*): I am not going with you, Wendy.

WENDY: Yes, Peter!

PETER: No.

(*The lost ones run back gaily, each carrying a stick with a bundle on the end of it.*)

WENDY: Peter isn't coming!

(*All the faces go blank.*)

JOHN (*even* JOHN): Peter not coming!

TOOTLES (*overthrown*): Why, Peter?

PETER (*his pipes more riotous than ever*): I just want always to be a little boy and to have fun.

(*There is a general fear that they are perhaps making the mistake of their lives.*)

Now then, no fuss, no blubbering. (*With dreadful cynicism*) I hope you will like your mothers! Are you ready, Tink! Then lead the way.

(TINK *darts up any tree, but she is the only one. The air above is suddenly rent with shrieks and the clash of steel. Though they cannot see, the boys know that* HOOK *and his crew are upon the Indians. Mouths open and remain open, all in mute appeal to* PETER. *He is the only boy on his feet now, a sword in his hand, the same he slew Barbicue with; and in his eye is the lust of battle.*

We can watch the carnage that is invisible to the children. HOOK *has basely broken the two laws of Indian warfare, which are that the redskins should attack first, and that it should be at dawn. They have known the pirate whereabouts since, early in the night, one of* SMEE'*s fingers crackled. The brushwood has closed behind their scouts as silently as the sand on the mole; for hours they have imitated the lonely call of the coyote; no stratagem has been overlooked, but alas, they have trusted to the pale-face's honour to await an attack at dawn, when his courage is known to be at the lowest ebb.* HOOK *falls upon them pell-mell, and one cannot withhold a reluctant admiration for the wit that conceived so subtle a scheme and the fell genius with which it is carried out. If the braves would rise quickly they might still have time to scalp, but this they are forbidden to do by the traditions of their race, for it is written that they must never express surprise in the presence of the pale-face. For a brief space they remain recumbent, not a muscle moving, as if the foe were here by invitation. Thus perish the flower of the Piccaninnies, though not unavenged, for with* LEAN WOLF *fall* ALF MASON *and* CANARY ROBB, *while other pirates to bite dust are* BLACK GILMOUR *and* ALAN HERB, *that same* HERB *who is still remembered at Manaos for playing skittles with the mate of the Switch for each other's heads.* CHAY TURLEY, *who laughed with the wrong side of his mouth (having no other), is tomahawked by* PANTHER, *who eventually cuts a way through the shambles with* TIGER LILY *and a remnant of the tribe.*

This onslaught passes and is gone like a fierce wind. The victors wipe their cutlasses, and squint, ferret-eyed, at their leader. He remains, as ever, aloof in spirit and in substance. He signs to them to descend the trees, for he is convinced that PAN *is down there, and though he has smoked the bees it is the honey he wants. There is something in* PETER *that at all times goads this extraordinary man to frenzy; it is the boy's cockiness, which disturbs* HOOK *like an insect. If you have seen a lion in a cage futilely pursuing a sparrow you will know what is meant. The pirates try to do their captain's bidding, but the apertures prove to be not wide enough for them; he cannot even ram them down with a pole. He steals to the mouth of a tree and listens.*)

PETER (*prematurely*): All is over!

115 WENDY: But who has won?

PETER: Hst! If the Indians have won they will beat the tom-tom; it is always their signal of victory.

(HOOK *licks his lips at this and signs to* SMEE, *who is sitting on it, to hold up the tom-tom. He beats upon it with his claw, and listens for results.*)

TOOTLES: The tom-tom!

PETER (*sheathing his sword*): An Indian victory!

(*The cheers from below are music to the black hearts above.*)

You are quite safe now, Wendy. Boys, good-bye. (*He resumes his pipes.*)

120 WENDY: Peter, you will remember about changing your flannels, won't you?

PETER: Oh, all right!

WENDY: And this is your medicine.

(She puts something into a shell and leaves it on a ledge between two of the trees. It is only water, but she measures it out in drops.)

PETER: I won't forget.

WENDY: Peter, what are you to me?

PETER *(through the pipes)*: Your son, Wendy.

WENDY: Oh, good-bye!

125

(The travellers start upon their journey, little witting that HOOK has issued his silent orders: a man to the mouth of each tree, and a row of men between the trees and the little house. As the children squeeze up they are plucked from their trees, trussed, thrown like bales of cotton from one pirate to another, and so piled up in the little house. The only one treated differently is WENDY, whom HOOK escorts to the house on his arm with hateful politeness. He signs to his dogs to be gone, and they depart through the wood, carrying the little house with its strange merchandise and singing their ribald song. The chimney of the little house emits a jet of smoke fitfully, as if not sure what it ought to do just now.

HOOK and PETER are now, as it were, alone on the island. Below, PETER is on the bed, asleep, no weapon near him; above, HOOK, armed to the teeth, is searching noiselessly for some tree down which the nastiness of him can descend. Don't be too much alarmed by this; it is precisely the situation PETER would have chosen; indeed if the whole thing were pretend—. One of his arms droops over the edge of the bed, a leg is arched, and the mouth is not so tightly closed that we cannot see the little pearls. He is dreaming, and in his dreams he is always in pursuit of a boy who was never here, nor anywhere: the only boy who could beat him.

HOOK finds the tree. It is the one set apart for SLIGHTLY who being addicted when hot to the drinking of water has swelled in consequence and surreptitiously scooped his tree for easier descent and egress. Down this the pirate wriggles a passage. In the aperture below his face emerges and goes green as he glares at the sleeping child. Does no feeling of compassion disturb his sombre breast? The man is not wholly evil: he has a Thesaurus in his cabin, and is no mean performer on the flute. What really warps him is a presentiment that he is about to fail. This is not unconnected with a beatific smile on the face of the sleeper, whom he cannot reach owing to being stuck at the foot of the tree. He, however, sees the medicine shell within easy reach, and to WENDY's draught he adds from a bottle five drops of poison distilled when he was weeping from the red in his eye. The expression on PETER's face merely implies that something heavenly is going on. HOOK worms his way upwards, and winding his cloak around him, as if to conceal his person from the night of which he is the blackest part, he stalks moodily toward the lagoon.

A dot of light flashes past him and darts down the nearest tree, looking for PETER, only for PETER, quite indifferent about the others when she finds him safe.)

PETER *(stirring)*: Who is that? *(TINK has to tell her tale, in one long ungrammatical sentence.)* The redskins were defeated? Wendy and the boys captured by the pirates! I'll rescue her, I'll rescue her! *(He leaps first at his dagger, and then at his grindstone, to sharpen it. TINK alights near the shell, and rings out a warning cry.)* Oh, that is just my medicine. Poisoned? Who could have poisoned it? I promised Wendy to take it, and I will as soon as I have sharpened my dagger. (TINK, *who sees its red colour and remembers the red in the pirate's eye, nobly swallows the draught as* PETER's *hand is reaching for it.*) Why, Tink, you have drunk my medicine! (*She flutters strangely about the room, answering him now in a very thin tinkle.*) It was poisoned and you drank it to save my life! Tink, dear Tink, are you dying? (*He has never called her dear Tink before, and for a moment she is gay; she alights on his shoulder, gives his chin a loving bite, whispers 'You silly ass,' and falls on her tiny bed. The boudoir, which is lit by her, flickers ominously. He is on his knees by the opening.*)

Her light is growing faint, and if it goes out, that means she is dead! Her voice is so low I can scarcely tell what she is saying. She says—she says she thinks she could get well again if children believed in fairies! (*He rises and throws out his arms he knows not to whom, perhaps to the boys and girls of whom he is not one.*) Do you believe in fairies? Say quick that you believe! If you believe, clap your hands! (*Many clap, some don't, a few hiss. Then perhaps there is a rush of Nanas to the nurseries to see what on earth is happening. But* TINK *is saved.*) Oh, thank you, thank you, thank you! And now to rescue Wendy!

(TINK *is already as merry and impudent as a grig, with not a thought for those who have saved her.* PETER *ascends his tree as if he were shot up it. What he is feeling is 'Hook or me this time!' He is frightfully happy. He soon hits the trail, for the smoke from the little house has lingered here and there to guide him. He takes wing.*)

ACT V
SCENE I
THE PIRATE SHIP

The stage directions for the opening of this scene are as follows:—1 Circuit Amber checked to 80. Battens, all Amber checked, 3 ship's lanterns alight, Arcs: prompt perch 1. Open dark Amber flooding back, O.P. perch open dark Amber flooding upper deck. Arc on tall steps at back of cabin to flood back cloth. Open dark Amber. Warning for slide. Plank ready. Call HOOK.

In the strange light thus described we see what is happening on the deck of the Jolly Roger, *which is flying the skull and crossbones and lies low in the water. There is no need to call* HOOK, *for he is here already, and indeed there is not a pirate aboard who would dare to call him. Most of them are at present carousing in the bowels of the vessel, but on the poop Mullins is visible, in the only great-coat on the ship, raking with his glass the monstrous rocks within which the lagoon is cooped. Such a look-out is supererogatory, for the pirate craft floats immune in the horror of her name.*

From HOOK's *cabin at the back* STARKEY *appears and leans over the bulwark, silently surveying the sullen waters. He is bare-headed and is perhaps thinking with bitterness of his hat, which he sometimes sees still drifting past him with the Never bird sitting on it. The black pirate is asleep on deck, yet even in his dreams rolling mechanically out of the way when* HOOK *draws near. The only sound to be heard is made by* SMEE *at his sewing-machine, which lends a touch of domesticity to the night.*

HOOK *is now leaning against the mast, now prowling the deck, the double cigar in his mouth. With* PETER *surely at last removed from his path we, who know how vain a tabernacle is man, would not be surprised to find him bellied out by the winds of his success, but it is not so; he is still uneasy, looking long and meaninglessly at familiar objects, such as the ship's bell or the Long Tom, like one who may shortly be a stranger to them. It is as if* PAN*'s terrible oath 'Hook or me this time!' had already boarded the ship.*

HOOK (*communing with his ego*): How still the night is; nothing sounds alive. Now is the hour when children in their homes are a-bed; their lips bright-browned with the good-night chocolate, and their tongues drowsily searching for belated crumbs housed insecurely on their shining cheeks. Compare with them the children on this boat about to walk the plank. Split my infinitives, but 'tis my hour of triumph! (*Clinging to this fair prospect he dances a few jubilant steps, but they fall below his usual form.*) And yet some disky spirit compels me now to make my dying speech, lest when dying there may be no time for it. All mortals envy me, yet better perhaps for Hook to have had less ambition! O fame, fame, thou glittering bauble, what if the very— (SMEE, *engrossed in his labours at the sewing-machine, tears a piece of calico with a rending sound which makes the Solitary think for a moment that the untoward has happened to his garments.*) No little children love me. I am told they play at Peter Pan, and that the strongest always chooses to be Peter. They would rather be a Twin than Hook; they force the baby to be Hook. The baby! that is where the canker gnaws. (*He contemplates his industrious boatswain.*) 'Tis said they find Smee lovable. But an hour agone I found him letting the youngest of them try on his spectacles. Pathetic Smee, the Nonconformist pirate, a happy smile upon his face because he thinks they fear him! How can I break it to him that they think him lovable? No, bi-carbonate of Soda, no, not even— (*Another rending of the calico disturbs him, and he has a private consultation with* STARKEY, *who turns him round and evidently assures him that all is well. The peroration of his speech is nevertheless for ever lost, as eight bells strikes and his crew pour forth in bacchanalian orgy. From the poop he watches their dance till it frets him beyond bearing.*) Quiet, you dogs, or I'll cast anchor in you! (*He descends to a barrel on which there are playing-cards, and his crew stand waiting, as ever, like whipped curs.*) Are all the prisoners chained, so that they can't fly away?

JUKES: Ay, ay, Captain.

HOOK: Then hoist them up.

STARKEY (*raising the door of the hold*): Tumble up, you ungentlemanly lubbers.

(*The terrified boys are prodded up and tossed about the deck.* HOOK *seems to have forgotten them; he is sitting by the barrel with his cards.*)

HOOK (*suddenly*): So! Now then, you bullies, six of you walk the plank to-night, but I have room for two cabin-boys. Which of you is it to be? (*He returns to his cards.*)   5

TOOTLES (*hoping to soothe him by putting the blame on the only person, vaguely remembered, who is always willing to act as a buffer*): You see, sir, I don't think my mother would like me to be a pirate. Would your mother like you to be a pirate, Slightly?

SLIGHTLY (*implying that otherwise it would be a pleasure to him to oblige*): I don't think so. Twin, would your mother like—

HOOK: Stow this gab. (*To* JOHN) You boy, you look as if you had a little pluck in you. Didst never want to be a pirate, my hearty?

JOHN (*dazzled by being singled out*): When I was at school I—what do you think, Michael?

MICHAEL (*stepping into prominence*): What would you call me if I joined?   10

HOOK: Blackbeard Joe.

MICHAEL: John, what do you think?

JOHN: Stop, should we still be respectful subjects of King George?

HOOK: You would have to swear 'Down with King George.'

15   JOHN (*grandly*): Then I refuse!

MICHAEL: And I refuse.

HOOK: That seals your doom. Bring up their mother.

(WENDY *is driven up from the hold and thrown to him. She sees at the first glance that the deck has not been scrubbed for years.*)

So, my beauty, you are to see your children walk the plank.

WENDY (*with noble calmness*): Are they to die?

20   HOOK: They are. Silence all, for a mother's last words to her children.

WENDY: These are my last words. Dear boys, I feel that I have a message to you from your real mothers, and it is this, 'We hope our sons will die like English gentlemen.'

(*The boys go on fire.*)

TOOTLES: I am going to do what my mother hopes. What are you to do, Twin?

FIRST TWIN: What my mother hopes. John, what are—

HOOK: Tie her up! Get the plank ready.

(WENDY *is roped to the mast; but no one regards her, for all eyes are fixed upon the plank now protruding from the poop over the ship's side. A great change, however, occurs in the time* HOOK *takes to raise his claw and point to this deadly engine. No one is now looking at the plank: for the tick, tick of the crocodile is heard. Yet it is not to bear on the crocodile that all eyes slew round, it is that they may bear on* HOOK. *Otherwise prisoners and captors are equally inert, like actors in some play who have found themselves 'on' in a scene in which they are not personally concerned. Even the iron claw hangs inactive, as if aware that the crocodile is not coming for it. Affection for their captain, now cowering from view, is not what has given* HOOK *his dominance over the crew, but as the menacing sound draws nearer they close their eyes respectfully.*

There is no crocodile. It is PETER, *who has been circling the pirate ship, ticking as he flies far more superbly than any clock. He drops into the water and climbs aboard, warning the captives with upraised finger (but still ticking) not for the moment to give audible expression to their natural admiration. Only one pirate sees him,* WHIBBLES *of the eye patch, who comes up from below.* JOHN *claps a hand on* WHIBBLES'S *mouth to stifle the groan; four boys hold him to prevent the thud;* PETER *delivers the blow, and the carrion is thrown overboard. 'One!' says* SLIGHTLY, *beginning to count.*

STARKEY *is the first pirate to open his eyes. The ship seems to him to be precisely as when he closed them. He cannot interpret the sparkle that has come into the faces of the captives, who are cleverly pretending to be as afraid as ever. He little knows that the door of the dark cabin has just closed on one more boy. Indeed it is for* HOOK *alone he looks, and he is a little surprised to see him.*)

25   STARKEY (*hoarsely*): It is gone, Captain! There is not a sound.

(*The tenement that is* HOOK *heaves tumultuously and he is himself again.*)

HOOK (*now convinced that some fair spirit watches over him*): Then here is to Johnny
Plank—

> Avast, belay, the English brig
> We took and quickly sank,
> And for a warning to the crew
> We made them walk the plank!

(*As he sings he capers detestably along an imaginary plank and his copy-cats do
likewise, joining in the chorus.*)

> Yo ho, yo ho, the frisky cat,
> You walks along it so,
> Till it goes down and you goes down
> To tooral looral lo!

(*The brave children try to stem this monstrous torrent by breaking into the National
Anthem.*)

STARKEY (*paling*): I don't like it, messmates!

HOOK: Stow that, Starkey. Do you boys want a touch of the cat before you walk the
plank? (*He is more pitiless than ever now that he believes he has a charmed life.*) Fetch
the cat, Jukes; it is in the cabin.

JUKES: Ay, ay, sir. (*It is one of his commonest remarks, and it is only recorded now because he
never makes another. The stage direction 'Exit JUKES' has in this case a special significance. But only the children know that some one is awaiting this unfortunate in the cabin,
and HOOK tramples them down as he resumes his ditty:*)

> Yo ho, yo ho, the scratching cat
> Its tails are nine you know,
> And when they're writ upon your back,
> You're fit to—

(*The last words will ever remain a matter of conjecture, for from the dark cabin comes a
curdling screech which wails through the ship and dies away. It is followed by a sound,
almost more eerie in the circumstances, that can only be likened to the crowing of a cock.*)

HOOK: What was that?

SLIGHTLY (*solemnly*): Two!

(*CECCO swings into the cabin, and in a moment returns, livid.*)

HOOK (*with an effort*): What is the matter with Bill Jukes, you dog?

CECCO: The matter with him is he is dead—stabbed.

PIRATES: Bill Jukes dead!

CECCO: The cabin is as black as a pit, but there is something terrible in there: the
thing you heard a-crowing.

HOOK (*slowly*): Cecco, go back and fetch me out that doodle-doo.

CECCO (*unstrung*): No, Captain, no. (*He supplicates on his knees, but his master advances
on him implacably.*)

HOOK (*in his most syrupy voice*): Did you say you would go, Cecco?

(*CECCO goes. All listen. There is one screech, one crow.*)

30

35

SLIGHTLY (*as if he were a bell tolling*): Three!

40 HOOK: 'Sdeath and oddsfish, who is to bring me out that doodle-doo?

(*No one steps forward.*)

STARKEY (*injudiciously*): Wait till Cecco comes out.

(*The black looks of some others encourage him.*)

HOOK: I think I heard you volunteer, Starkey.

STARKEY (*emphatically*): No, by thunder!

HOOK (*in that syrupy voice which might be more engaging when accompanied by his flute*): My hook thinks you did. I wonder if it would not be advisable, Starkey, to humour the hook?

45 STARKEY: I'll swing before I go in there.

HOOK (*gleaming*): Is it mutiny? Starkey is ringleader. Shake hands, Starkey.

(STARKEY *recoils from the claw. It follows him till he leaps overboard.*)

Did any other gentleman say mutiny?

(*They indicate that they did not even know the late* STARKEY.)

SLIGHTLY: Four!

HOOK: I will bring out that doodle-doo myself.

(*He raises a blunderbuss but casts it from him with a menacing gesture which means that he has more faith in the claw. With a lighted lantern in his hand he enters the cabin. Not a sound is to be heard now on the ship, unless it be* SLIGHTLY *wetting his lips to say 'Five.'* HOOK *staggers out.*)

50 HOOK (*unsteadily*): Something blew out the light.

MULLINS (*with dark meaning*): Some—thing?

NOODLER: What of Cecco?

HOOK: He is as dead as Jukes.

(*They are superstitious like all sailors, and* MULLINS *has planted a dire conception in their minds.*)

COOKSON: They do say as the surest sign a ship's accurst is when there is one aboard more than can be accounted for.

55 NOODLER: I've heard he allus boards the pirate craft at last. (*With dreadful significance*) Has he a tail, Captain?

MULLINS: They say that when he comes it is in the likeness of the wickedest man aboard.

COOKSON (*clinching it*): Has he a hook, Captain?

(*Knives and pistols come to hand, and there is a general cry 'The ship is doomed!' But it is not his dogs that can frighten* JAS HOOK. *Hearing something like a cheer from the boys he wheels round, and his face brings them to their knees.*)

HOOK: So you like it, do you! By Caius and Balbus, bullies, here is a notion: open the cabin door and drive them in. Let them fight the doodle-doo for their lives.

If they kill him we are so much the better; if he kills them we are none the worse.

(*This masterly stroke restores their confidence; and the boys, affecting fear, are driven into the cabin. Desperadoes though the pirates are, some of them have been boys themselves, and all turn their backs to the cabin and listen, with arms outstretched to it as if to ward off the horrors that are being enacted there.*

Relieved by Peter of their manacles, and armed with such weapons as they can lay their hands on, the boys steal out softly as snowflakes, and under their captain's hushed order find hiding-places on the poop. He releases WENDY; *and now it would be easy for them all to fly away, but it is to be* HOOK *or him this time. He signs to her to join the others, and with awful grimness folding her cloak around him, the hood over his head, he takes her place by the mast, and crows.*)

MULLINS: The doodle-doo has killed them all!
SEVERAL: The ship's bewitched.   60

(*They are snapping at* HOOK *again.*)

HOOK: I've thought it out, lads; there is a Jonah aboard.
SEVERAL (*advancing upon him*): Ay, a man with a hook.

(*If he were to withdraw one step their knives would be in him, but he does not flinch.*)

HOOK (*temporising*): No, lads, no, it is the girl. Never was luck on a pirate ship wi' a woman aboard. We'll right the ship when she has gone.
MULLINS (*lowering his cutlass*): It's worth trying.
HOOK: Throw the girl overboard.   65
MULLINS (*jeering*): There is none can save you now, missy.
PETER: There is one.
MULLINS: Who is that?
PETER (*casting off the cloak*): Peter Pan, the avenger!

(*He continues standing there to let the effect sink in.*)

HOOK (*throwing out a suggestion*): Cleave him to the brisket.   70

(*But he has a sinking that this boy has no brisket.*)

NOODLER: The ship's accurst!
PETER: Down, boys, and at them!

(*The boys leap from their concealment and the clash of arms resounds through the vessel. Man to man the pirates are the stronger, but they are unnerved by the suddenness of the onslaught and they scatter, thus enabling their opponents to hunt in couples and choose their quarry. Some are hurled into the lagoon; others are dragged from dark recesses. There is no boy whose weapon is not reeking save* SLIGHTLY, *who runs about with a lantern, counting, ever counting.*)

WENDY (*meeting* MICHAEL *in a moment's lull*): Oh, Michael, stay with me, protect me!
MICHAEL (*reeling*): Wendy, I've killed a pirate!
WENDY: It's awful, awful.   75
MICHAEL: No, it isn't, I like it, I like it.

(He casts himself into the group of boys who are encircling HOOK. *Again and again they close upon him and again and again he hews a clear space.)*

HOOK: Back, back, you mice. It's Hook; do you like him? *(He lifts up* MICHAEL *with his claw and uses him as a buckler. A terrible voice breaks in.)*

PETER: Put up your swords, boys. This man is mine.

*(*HOOK *shakes* MICHAEL *off his claw as if he were a drop of water, and these two antagonists face each other for their final bout. They measure swords at arms' length, make a sweeping motion with them, and bringing the points to the deck rest their hands upon the hilts.)*

HOOK *(with curling lip)*: So, Pan, this is all your doing!

80 PETER: Ay, Jas Hook, it is all my doing.

HOOK: Proud and insolent youth, prepare to meet thy doom.

PETER: Dark and sinister man, have at thee.

(Some say that he had to ask TOOTLES *whether the word was sinister or canister.*
* HOOK or PETER this time! They fall to without another word.* PETER *is a rare swordsman, and parries with dazzling rapidity, sometimes before the other can make his stroke.* HOOK, *if not quite so nimble in wrist play, has the advantage of a yard or two in reach, but though they close he cannot give the quietus with his claw, which seems to find nothing to tear at. He does not, especially in the most heated moments, quite see* PETER, *who to his eyes, now blurred or opened clearly for the first time, is less like a boy than a mote of dust dancing in the sun. By some impalpable stroke* HOOK's *sword is whipped from his grasp, and when he stoops to raise it a little foot is on its blade. There is no deep gash on* HOOK, *but he is suffering torment as from innumerable jags.)*

BOYS *(exulting)*: Now, Peter, now!

*(*PETER *raises the sword by its blade, and with an inclination of the head that is perhaps slightly overdone, presents the hilt to his enemy.)*

HOOK: 'Tis some fiend fighting me! Pan, who and what art thou?

(The children listen eagerly for the answer, none quite so eagerly as WENDY.*)*

85 PETER *(at a venture)*: I'm youth, I'm joy, I'm a little bird that has broken out of the egg.

HOOK: To 't again!

(He has now a damp feeling that this boy is the weapon which is to strike him from the lists of man; but the grandeur of his mind still holds and, true to the traditions of his flag, he fights on like a human flail. PETER *flutters round and through and over these gyrations as if the wind of them blew him out of the danger zone, and again and again he darts in and jags.)*

HOOK *(stung to madness)*: I'll fire the powder magazine. *(He disappears they know not where.)*

CHILDREN: Peter, save us!

*(*PETER, *alas, goes the wrong way and* HOOK *returns.)*

HOOK (*sitting on the hold with gloomy satisfaction*): In two minutes the ship will be blown to pieces.

(*They cast themselves before him in entreaty.*)

CHILDREN: Mercy, mercy!

HOOK: Back, you pewling spawn. I'll show you now the road to dusty death. A holocaust of children, there is something grand in the idea!

(PETER *appears with a smoking bomb in his hand and tosses it overboard.* HOOK *has not really had much hope, and he rushes at his other persecutors with his head down like some exasperated bull in the ring; but with bantering cries they easily elude him by flying among the rigging.*

Where is PETER*? The incredible boy has apparently forgotten the recent doings, and is sitting on a barrel playing upon his pipes. This may surprise others but does not surprise* HOOK. *Lifting a blunderbuss he strikes forlornly not at the boy but at the barrel, which is hurled across the deck.* PETER *remains sitting in the air still playing upon his pipes. At this sight the great heart of* HOOK *breaks. That not wholly unheroic figure climbs the bulwarks murmuring 'Floreat Etona,' and prostrates himself into the water, where the crocodile is waiting for him open-mouthed.* HOOK *knows the purpose of this yawning cavity, but after what he has gone through he enters it like one greeting a friend.*

The curtain rises to show PETER *a very Napoleon on his ship. It must not rise again lest we see him on the poop in* HOOK'*s hat and cigars, and with a small iron claw.*)

SCENE 2
THE NURSERY AND THE TREE-TOPS

The old nursery appears again with everything just as it was at the beginning of the play, except that the kennel has gone and that the window is standing open. So PETER *was wrong about mothers; indeed there is no subject on which he is so likely to be wrong.*

MRS. DARLING *is asleep on a chair near the window, her eyes tired with searching the heavens.* NANA *is stretched out listless on the floor. She is the cynical one, and though custom has made her hang the children's night things on the fire-guard for an airing, she surveys them not hopefully but with some self-contempt.*

MRS. DARLING (*starting up as if we had whispered to her that her brats are coming back*): Wendy, John, Michael! (NANA *lifts a sympathetic paw to the poor soul's lap.*) I see you have put their night things out again, Nana! It touches my heart to watch you do that night after night. But they will never come back.

(*In trouble the difference of station can be completely ignored, and it is not strange to see these two using the same handkerchief. Enter* LIZA, *who in the gentleness with which the house has been run of late is perhaps a little more masterful than of yore.*)

LIZA (*feeling herself degraded by the announcement*): Nana's dinner is served.

(NANA, *who quite understands what are* LIZA'*s feelings, departs for the dining-room with our exasperating leisureliness, instead of running, as we would all do if we followed our instincts.*)

LIZA: To think I have a master as have changed places with his dog!

MRS. DARLING (*gently*): Out of remorse, Liza.

5   LIZA (*surely exaggerating*): I am a married woman myself. I don't think it's respectable to go to his office in a kennel, with the street boys running alongside cheering. (*Even this does not rouse her mistress, which may have been the honourable intention.*) There, that is the cab fetching him back! (*Amid interested cheers from the street the kennel is conveyed to its old place by a cabby and friend, and* MR. DARLING *scrambles out of it in his office clothes.*)

MR. DARLING (*giving her his hat loftily*): If you will be so good, Liza. (*The cheering is resumed.*) It is very gratifying!

LIZA (*contemptuous*): Lot of little boys.

MR. DARLING (*with the new sweetness of one who has sworn never to lose his temper again*): There were several adults to-day.

(*She goes off scornfully with the hat and the two men, but he has not a word of reproach for her. It ought to melt us when we see how humbly grateful he is for a kiss from his wife, so much more than he feels he deserves. One may think he is wrong to exchange into the kennel, but sorrow has taught him that he is the kind of man who whatever he does contritely he must do to excess; otherwise he soon abandons doing it.*)

MRS. DARLING (*who has known this for quite a long time*): What sort of a day have you had, George?

(*He is sitting on the floor by the kennel.*)

10   MR. DARLING: There were never less than a hundred running round the cab cheering, and when we passed the Stock Exchange the members came out and waved.

(*He is exultant but uncertain of himself, and with a word she could dispirit him utterly.*)

MRS. DARLING (*bravely*): I am so proud, George.

MR. DARLING (*commendation from the dearest quarter ever going to his head*): I have been put on a picture postcard, dear.

MRS. DARLING (*nobly*): Never!

MR. DARLING (*thoughtlessly*): Ah, Mary, we should not be such celebrities if the children hadn't flown away.

15   MRS. DARLING (*startled*): George, you are sure you are not enjoying it?

MR. DARLING (*anxiously*): Enjoying it! See my punishment: living in a kennel.

MRS. DARLING: Forgive me, dear one.

MR. DARLING: It is I who need forgiveness, always I, never you. And now I feel drowsy. (*He retires into the kennel.*) Won't you play me to sleep on the nursery piano? And shut that window, Mary dearest; I feel a draught.

MRS. DARLING: Oh, George, never ask me to do that. The window must always be left open for them, always, always.

(*She goes into the day nursery, from which we presently hear her playing the sad song of Margaret. She little knows that her last remark has been overheard by a boy crouching at the window. He steals into the room accompanied by a ball of light.*)

20   PETER: Tink, where are you? Quick, close the window. (*It closes.*) Bar it. (*The bar slams down.*) Now when Wendy comes she will think her mother has barred her

out, and she will have to come back to me! (TINKER BELL *sulks.*) Now, Tink, you and I must go out by the door. (*Doors, however, are confusing things to those who are used to windows, and he is puzzled when he finds that this one does not open on to the firmament. He tries the other, and sees the piano player.*) It is Wendy's mother! (TINK *pops on to his shoulder and they peep together.*) She is a pretty lady, but not so pretty as my mother. (*This is a pure guess.*) She is making the box say 'Come home, Wendy.' You will never see Wendy again, lady, for the window is barred! (*He flutters about the room joyously like a bird, but has to return to that door.*) She has laid her head down on the box. There are two wet things sitting on her eyes. As soon as they go away another two come and sit on her eyes. (*She is heard moaning 'Wendy, Wendy, Wendy.'*) She wants me to unbar the window. I won't! She is awfully fond of Wendy. I am fond of her too. We can't both have her, lady! (*A funny feeling comes over him.*) Come on, Tink; we don't want any silly mothers.

(*He opens the window and they fly out.*
    It is thus that the truants find entrance easy when they alight on the sill, JOHN *to his credit having the tired* MICHAEL *on his shoulders. They have nothing else to their credit; no compunction for what they have done, not the tiniest fear that any just person may be awaiting them with a stick. The youngest is in a daze, but the two others are shining virtuously like holy people who are about to give two other people a treat.*)

MICHAEL (*looking about him*): I think I have been here before.
JOHN: It's your home, you stupid.
WENDY: There is your old bed, Michael.
MICHAEL: I had nearly forgotten.
JOHN: I say, the kennel!   25
WENDY: Perhaps Nana is in it.
JOHN (*peering*): There is a man asleep in it.
WENDY (*remembering him by the bald patch*): It's father!
JOHN: So it is!
MICHAEL: Let me see father. (*Disappointed*) He is not as big as the pirate I killed.   30
JOHN (*perplexed*): Wendy, surely father didn't use to sleep in the kennel?
WENDY (*with misgivings*): Perhaps we don't remember the old life as well as we
    thought we did.
JOHN (*chilled*): It is very careless of mother not to be here when we come back.

(*The piano is heard again.*)

WENDY: H'sh! (*She goes to the door and peeps.*) That is her playing! (*They all have a
    peep.*)
MICHAEL: Who is that lady?   35
JOHN: H'sh! It's mother.
MICHAEL: Then are you not really our mother, Wendy?
WENDY (*with conviction*): Oh dear, it is quite time to be back!
JOHN: Let us creep in and put our hands over her eyes.
WENDY (*more considerate*): No, let us break it to her gently.   40

(*She slips between the sheets of her bed; and the others, seeing the idea at once, get into their beds. Then when the music stops they cover their heads. There are now three distinct bumps in the beds.* MRS. DARLING *sees the bumps as soon as she comes in, but she does not believe she sees them.*)

MRS. DARLING: I see them in their beds so often in my dreams that I seem still to see them when I am awake! I'll not look again. (*She sits down and turns away her face from the bumps, though of course they are still reflected in her mind.*) So often their silver voices call me, my little children whom I'll see no more.

(*Silver voices is a good one, especially about* JOHN; *but the heads pop up.*)

WENDY (*perhaps rather silvery*): Mother!
MRS. DARLING (*without moving*): That is Wendy.
JOHN (*quite gruff*): Mother!
45 MRS. DARLING: Now it is John.
MICHAEL (*no better than a squeak*): Mother!
MRS. DARLING: Now Michael. And when they call I stretch out my arms to them, but they never come, they never come!

(*This time, however, they come, and there is joy once more in the Darling household. The little boy who is crouching at the window sees the joke of the bumps in the beds, but cannot understand what all the rest of the fuss is about.*

The scene changes from the inside of the house to the outside, and we see MR. DARLING *romping in at the door, with the lost boys hanging gaily to his coat-tails. So we may conclude that* WENDY *has told them to wait outside until she explains the situation to her mother, who has then sent* MR. DARLING *down to tell them that they are adopted. Of course they could have flown in by the window like a covey of birds, but they think it better fun to enter by a door. There is a moment's trouble about* SLIGHTLY, *who somehow gets shut out. Fortunately* LIZA *finds him.*)

LIZA: What is the matter, boy?
SLIGHTLY: They have all got a mother except me.
50 LIZA (*starting back*): Is your name Slightly?
SLIGHTLY: Yes'm.
LIZA: Then I am your mother.
SLIGHTLY: How do you know?
LIZA (*the good-natured creature*): I feel it in my bones.

(*They go into the house and there is none happier now than* SLIGHTLY, *unless it be* NANA *as she passes with the importance of a nurse who will never have another day off.* WENDY *looks out at the nursery window and sees a friend below, who is hovering in the air knocking off tall hats with his feet. The wearers don't see him. They are too old. You can't see* PETER *if you are old. They think he is a draught at the corner.*)

55 WENDY: Peter!
PETER (*looking up casually*): Hullo, Wendy.

(*She flies down to him, to the horror of her mother, who rushes to the window.*)

WENDY (*making a last attempt*): You don't feel you would like to say anything to my parents, Peter, about a very sweet subject?
PETER: No, Wendy.

WENDY: About me, Peter?

PETER: No. (*He gets out his pipes, which she knows is a very bad sign. She appeals with her*   60
arms to MRS. DARLING, *who is probably thinking that these children will all need to be tied to their beds at night.*)

MRS. DARLING (*from the window*): Peter, where are you? Let me adopt you too.

(*She is the loveliest age for a woman, but too old to see* PETER *clearly.*)

PETER: Would you send me to school?

MRS. DARLING (*obligingly*): Yes.

PETER: And then to an office?

MRS. DARLING: I suppose so.   65

PETER: Soon I should be a man?

MRS. DARLING: Very soon.

PETER (*passionately*): I don't want to go to school and learn solemn things. No one is going to catch me, lady, and make me a man. I want always to be a little boy and to have fun.

(*So perhaps he thinks, but it is only his greatest pretend.*)

MRS. DARLING (*shivering every time* WENDY *pursues him in the air*): Where are you to live, Peter?

PETER: In the house we built for Wendy. The fairies are to put it high up among the   70
tree-tops where they sleep at night.

WENDY (*rapturously*): To think of it!

MRS. DARLING: I thought all the fairies were dead.

WENDY (*almost reprovingly*): No indeed! Their mothers drop the babies into the Never birds' nests, all mixed up with the eggs, and the mauve fairies are boys and the white ones are girls, and there are some colours who don't know what they are. The row the children and the birds make at bath time is positively deafening.

PETER: I throw things at them.

WENDY: You will be rather lonely in the evenings, Peter.   75

PETER: I shall have Tink.

WENDY (*flying up to the window*): Mother, may I go?

MRS. DARLING (*gripping her for ever*): Certainly not. I have got you home again, and I mean to keep you.

WENDY: But he does so need a mother.

MRS. DARLING: So do you, my love.   80

PETER: Oh, all right.

MRS. DARLING (*magnanimously*): But, Peter, I shall let her go to you once a year for a week to do your spring cleaning.

(WENDY *revels in this, but* PETER, *who has no notion what a spring cleaning is, waves a rather careless thanks.*)

MRS. DARLING: Say good-night, Wendy.

WENDY: I couldn't go down just for a minute?

MRS. DARLING: No.   85

WENDY: Good-night, Peter!

PETER: Good-night, Wendy!

WENDY: Peter, you won't forget me, will you, before spring-cleaning time comes?

(*There is no answer, for he is already soaring high. For a moment after he is gone we still hear the pipes.* MRS. DARLING *closes and bars the window.*)

    We are dreaming now of the Never Land a year later. It is bed-time on the island, and the blind goes up to the whispers of the lovely Never music. The blue haze that makes the wood below magical by day comes up to the tree-tops to sleep, and through it we see numberless nests all lit up, fairies and birds quarrelling for possession, others flying around just for the fun of the thing and perhaps making bets about where the little house will appear to-night. It always comes and snuggles on some tree-top, but you can never be sure which; here it is again, you see JOHN's *hat first as up comes the house so softly that it knocks some gossips off their perch. When it has settled comfortably it lights up, and out come* PETER *and* WENDY.

    WENDY *looks a little older, but* PETER *is just the same. She is cloaked for a journey, and a sad confession must be made about her; she flies so badly now that she has to use a broomstick.*

WENDY (*who knows better this time than to be demonstrative at partings*): Well, good-bye, Peter; and remember not to bite your nails.

90 PETER: Good-bye, Wendy.

WENDY: I'll tell mother all about the spring cleaning and the house.

PETER (*who sometimes forgets that she has been here before*): You do like the house?

WENDY: Of course it is small. But most people of our size wouldn't have a house at all. (*She should not have mentioned size, for he has already expressed displeasure at her growth. Another thing, one he has scarcely noticed, though it disturbs her, is that she does not see him quite so clearly now as she used to do.*) When you come for me next year, Peter—you will come, won't you?

PETER: Yes. (*Gloating*) To hear stories about me!

95 WENDY: It is so queer that the stories you like best should be the ones about yourself.

PETER (*touchy*): Well, then?

WENDY: Fancy your forgetting the lost boys, and even Captain Hook!

PETER: Well, then?

WENDY: I haven't seen Tink this time.

100 PETER: Who?

WENDY: Oh dear! I suppose it is because you have so many adventures.

PETER (*relieved*): 'Course it is.

WENDY: If another little girl—if one younger than I am— (*She can't go on.*) Oh, Peter, how I wish I could take you up and squdge you! (*He draws back.*) Yes, I know. (*She gets astride her broomstick.*) Home! (*It carries her from him over the tree-tops.*

    In a sort of way he understands what she means by 'Yes, I know,' but in most sorts of ways he doesn't. It has something to do with the riddle of his being. If he could get the hang of the thing his cry might become 'To live would be an awfully big adventure!' but he can never quite get the hang of it, and so no one is as gay as he. With rapturous face he produces his pipes, and the Never birds and the fairies gather closer, till the roof of the

little house is so thick with his admirers that some of them fall down the chimney. He
plays on and on till we wake up.)

QUESTIONS FOR DISCUSSION AND WRITING

1. The play opens with Wendy and John pretending to be their parents, and later Wendy pretends that she and Peter are the parents of the lost boys. How do these childish re-creations reflect the roles of the real parents, Mr. and Mrs. Darling? What does the play suggest throughout that a "mother" is? What is a "father"?
2. We learn early in the play that the Darling family is poor, yet they seem well off to many modern American readers. What evidence do you see for a particular financial status? What social/financial class works best with the theme of not growing up?
3. Peter refuses to grow up, yet Wendy takes on adult roles throughout the play (and returns home to grow up at the end). What does the play suggest about "growing up" and its relationship to gender? What is gained and what is lost with maturity? Does this theme hold more power for the adult or the child members of the audience? Why?
4. Captain Hook is obviously the villain of the play. What makes him villainous? How seriously do we take his villainy? In theatrical productions, Hook is traditionally played by the same actor who plays Mr. Darling. What similarities do you see between the two characters? What are the thematic implications of such a casting decision?
5. In the play, we learn that Peter will not be touched and that he seldom remembers things for long. What do these characteristics tell us about Peter?
6. Wendy is sometimes viewed as Peter's mother, sometimes as his mate. Similarly, John and Michael are actually her siblings, but they act like her children in Never Land. What does this confusion suggest about family roles? What does it suggest about the place of sexuality and gender in the family?
7. Throughout the play, there are several subtle comparisons that suggest Peter and Hook are more like one another than we might think. Where do you find such comparisons? What is their effect on your understanding of the two characters?

J. M. BARRIE (1860–1937)
From The Little White Bird   *1902*

Chapter XIV
Peter Pan

If you ask your mother whether she knew about Peter Pan when she was a little girl, she will say, "Why, of course, I did, child," and if you ask her whether he rode on a goat in those days, she will say, "What a foolish question to ask; certainly he did." Then if you ask your grandmother whether she knew about Peter Pan when she was a girl, she also says, "Why, of course, I did, child," but if you ask her whether he rode on a goat in those days, she says she never heard of his having a goat. Perhaps she has forgotten, just as she sometimes forgets your name and calls you Mildred, which is your mother's name. Still, she could hardly forget such an important thing as the goat. Therefore there was no goat when your grandmother was a little girl. This shows that, in telling the story of Peter Pan, to begin with the goat (as most people do) is as silly as to put on your jacket before your vest.

Of course, it also shows that Peter is ever so old, but he is really always the same age, so that does not matter in the least. His age is one week, and though he was born so long ago he has never had a birthday, nor is there the slightest chance of his ever having one. The reason is that he escaped from being a human when he was seven days old; he escaped by the window and flew back to the Kensington Gardens.

If you think he was the only baby who ever wanted to escape, it shows how completely you have forgotten your own young days. When David heard this story first he was quite certain that he had never tried to escape, but I told him to think back hard, pressing his hands to his temples, and when he had done this hard, and even harder, he distinctly remembered a youthful desire to return to the tree-tops, and with that memory came others, as that he had lain in bed planning to escape as soon as his mother was asleep, and how she had once caught him half-way up the chimney. All children could have such recollections if they would press their hands hard to their temples, for, having been birds before they were human, they are naturally a little wild during the first few weeks, and very itchy at the shoulders, where their wings used to be. So David tells me.

I ought to mention here that the following is our way with a story: First, I tell it to him, and then he tells it to me, the understanding being that it is quite a different story; and then I retell it with his additions, and so we go on until no one could say whether it is more his story or mine. In this story of Peter Pan, for instance, the bald narrative and most of the moral reflections are mine, though not all, for this boy can be a stern moralist, but the interesting bits about the ways and customs of babies in the bird-stage are mostly reminiscences of David's, recalled by pressing his hands to his temples and thinking hard.

Well, Peter Pan got out by the window, which had no bars. Standing on the ledge he could see trees far away, which were doubtless the Kensington Gardens, and the moment he saw them he entirely forgot that he was now a little boy in a night-gown, and away he flew, right over the houses to the Gardens. It is wonderful that he could fly without wings, but the place itched tremendously, and perhaps we could all fly if we were as dead-confident-sure of our capacity to do it as was bold Peter Pan that evening.

He alighted gaily on the open sward, between the Baby's Palace and the Serpentine, and the first thing he did was to lie on his back and kick. He was quite unaware already that he had ever been human, and thought he was a bird, even in appearance, just the same as in his early days, and when he tried to catch a fly he did not understand that the reason he missed it was because he had attempted to seize it with his hand, which, of course, a bird never does. He saw, however, that it must be past Lock-out Time, for there were a good many fairies about, all too busy to notice him; they were getting breakfast ready, milking their cows, drawing water, and so on, and the sight of the water-pails made him thirsty, so he flew over to the Round Pond to have a drink. He stooped, and dipped his beak in the pond; he thought it was his beak, but, of course, it was only his nose, and, therefore, very little water came up, and that not so refreshing as usual, so next he tried a puddle, and he fell flop into it. When a real bird falls in flop, he spreads out his feathers and pecks them dry, but Peter could not remember what was the thing to do, and he decided, rather sulkily, to go to sleep on the weeping beech in the Baby Walk.

At first he found some difficulty in balancing himself on a branch, but presently he remembered the way, and fell asleep. He awoke long before morning, shivering, and saying to himself, "I never was out in such a cold night"; he had really been out in colder nights when he was a bird, but, of course, as everybody knows, what seems a warm night to a bird is a cold night to a boy in a night-gown. Peter also felt strangely uncomfortable, as if his head was stuffy; he heard loud noises that made him look round sharply, though they were really himself sneezing. There was something he wanted very much, but, though he knew he wanted it, he could not think what it was. What he wanted so much was his mother to blow his nose, but that never struck him, so he decided to appeal to the fairies for enlightenment. They are reputed to know a good deal.

There were two of them strolling along the Baby Walk, with their arms round each other's waists, and he hopped down to address them. The fairies have their tiffs with the birds, but they usually give a civil answer to a civil question, and he was quite angry when these two ran away the moment they saw him. Another was lolling on a garden-chair, reading a postage-stamp which some human had let fall, and when he heard Peter's voice he popped in alarm behind a tulip.

To Peter's bewilderment he discovered that every fairy he met fled from him. A band of workmen, who were sawing down a toadstool, rushed away, leaving their tools behind them. A milkmaid turned her pail upside down and hid in it. Soon the Gardens were in an uproar. Crowds of fairies were running this way and that, asking each other stoutly, who was afraid; lights were extinguished, doors barricaded, and from the grounds of Queen Mab's palace came the rubadub of drums, showing that the royal guard had been called out. A regiment of Lancers came charging down the Broad Walk, armed with holly-leaves, with which they jog the enemy horribly in passing. Peter heard the little people crying everywhere that there was a human in the Gardens after Lock-out Time, but he never thought for a moment that he was the human. He was feeling stuffier and stuffier, and more and more wistful to learn what he wanted done to his nose, but he pursued them with the vital question in vain; the timid creatures ran from him, and even the Lancers, when he approached them up the Hump, turned swiftly into a side-walk, on the pretence that they saw him there.

Despairing of the fairies, he resolved to consult the birds, but now he remembered, as an odd thing, that all the birds on the weeping beech had flown away when he alighted on it, and though that had not troubled him at the time, he saw its meaning now. Every living thing was shunning him. Poor little Peter Pan, he sat down and cried, and even then he did not know that, for a bird, he was sitting on his wrong part. It is a blessing that he did not know, for otherwise he would have lost faith in his power to fly, and the moment you doubt whether you can fly, you cease for ever to be able to do it. The reason birds can fly and we can't is simply that they have perfect faith, for to have faith is to have wings.

Now, except by flying, no one can reach the island in the Serpentine, for the boats of humans are forbidden to land there, and there are stakes round it, standing up in the water, on each of which a bird-sentinel sits by day and night. It was to the island that Peter now flew to put his strange case before old Solomon Caw, and he alighted on it with relief, much heartened to find himself at last at home, as the birds call the island. All of them were asleep, including the sentinels, except Solomon, who was wide awake on one side, and he listened quietly to Peter's adventures, and then told him their true meaning.

"Look at your night-gown, if you don't believe me," Solomon said, and with staring eyes Peter looked at his night-gown, and then at the sleeping birds. Not one of them wore anything.

"How many of your toes are thumbs?" said Solomon a little cruelly, and Peter saw, to his consternation, that all his toes were fingers. The shock was so great that it drove away his cold.

"Ruffle your feathers," said that gim old Solomon, and Peter tried most desperately hard to ruffle his feathers, but he had none. Then he rose up, quaking, and for the first time since he stood on the window-ledge, he remembered a lady who had been very fond of him.

"I think I shall go back to mother," he said timidly.

"Good-bye," replied Solomon Caw with a queer look.

But Peter hesitated. "Why don't you go?" the old one asked politely.

"I suppose," said Peter huskily, "I suppose I can still fly?"

You see, he had lost faith.

"Poor little half-and-half," said Solomon, who was not really hard-hearted, "you will never be able to fly again, not even on windy days. You must live here on the island always."

"And never even go to the Kensington Gardens?" Peter asked tragically.

"How could you get across?" said Solomon. He promised very kindly, however, to teach Peter as many of the bird ways as could be learned by one of such an awkward shape.

"Then I sha'n't be exactly a human?" Peter asked.

"No."

"Nor exactly a bird?"

"No."

"What shall I be?"

"You will be a Betwixt-and-Between," Solomon said, and certainly he was a wise old fellow, for that is exactly how it turned out.

The birds on the island never got used to him. His oddities tickled them every day, as if they were quite new, though it was really the birds that were new. They came out of the eggs daily, and laughed at him at once, then off they soon flew to be humans, and other birds came out of other eggs, and so it went on for ever. The crafty mother-birds, when they tired of sitting on their eggs, used to get the young ones to break their shells a day before the right time by whispering to them that now was their chance to see Peter washing or drinking or eating. Thousands gathered round him daily to watch him do these things, just as you watch the peacocks, and they screamed with delight when he lifted the crusts they flung him with his hands instead of in the usual way with the mouth. All his food was brought to him from the Gardens at Solomon's orders by the birds. He could not eat worms or insects (which they thought very silly of him), so they brought him bread in their beaks. Thus, when you cry out, "Greedy! Greedy!" to the bird that flies away with the big crust, you know now that you ought not to do this, for he is very likely taking it to Peter Pan.

Peter wore no night-gown now. You see, the birds were always begging him for bits of it to line their nests with, and, being very good-natured, he could not refuse, so by Solomon's advice he had hidden what was left of it. But though he was now quite naked, you must not think that he was cold or unhappy. He was usually very happy and gay, and the reason was that Solomon had kept his promise and taught him many of the bird ways. To be easily pleased, for instance, and always to be really doing something, and to think that whatever he was doing was a thing of vast importance. Peter became very clever at helping the birds to build their nests; soon he could build better than a wood-pigeon, and nearly as well as a blackbird, though never did he satisfy the finches, and he made nice little water-troughs near the nests and dug up worms for the young ones with his fingers. He also became very learned in bird-lore, and knew an east-wind from a west-wind by its smell, and he could see the grass growing and hear the insects walking about inside the tree-trunks. But the best thing Solomon had done was to teach him to have a glad heart. All birds have glad hearts unless you rob their nests, and so as they were the only kind of heart Solomon knew about, it was easy to him to teach Peter how to have one.

Peter's heart was so glad that he felt he must sing all day long, just as the birds sing for joy, but, being partly human, he needed an instrument, so he made a pipe of reeds, and he used to sit by the shore of the island of an evening, practising the sough of the wind and the ripple of the water, and catching handfuls of the shine of the moon, and he put them all in his pipe and played them so beautifully that even the birds were deceived, and they would say to each other, "Was that a fish leaping in the water or was it Peter playing leaping fish on his pipe?" and sometimes he played the birth of birds, and then the mothers would turn round in their nests to see whether they had laid an egg. If you are a child of the Gardens you must know the chestnut-tree near the bridge, which comes out in flower first of all the chestnuts, but perhaps you have not heard why this tree leads the way. It is because Peter wearies for summer and plays that it has come, and the chestnut, being so near, hears him and is cheated.

But as Peter sat by the shore tootling divinely on his pipe he sometimes fell into sad thoughts, and then the music became sad also, and the reason of all this sadness was that he could not reach the Gardens, though he could see them through the arch of the bridge. He knew he could never be a real human again, and scarcely wanted to be one, but oh, how he longed to play as other children play, and of course there is no such lovely place to play in as the Gardens. The birds brought him news of how boys and girls play, and wistful tears started in Peter's eyes.

Perhaps you wonder why he did not swim across. The reason was that he could not swim. He wanted to know how to swim, but no one on the island knew the way except the ducks, and they are so stupid. They were quite willing to teach him, but all they could say about it was, "You sit down on the top of the water in this way, and then you kick out like that." Peter tried it often, but always before he could kick out he sank. What he really needed to know was how you sit on the water without sinking, and they said it was quite impossible to explain such an easy thing as that. Occasionally swans touched on the island, and he would give them all his day's food and then ask them how they sat on the water, but as soon as he had no more to give them the hateful things hissed at him and sailed away.

Once he really thought he had discovered a way of reaching the Gardens. A wonderful white thing, like a runaway newspaper, floated high over the island and then tumbled, rolling over and over after the manner of a bird that has broken its wing. Peter was so frightened that he hid, but the birds told him it was only a kite, and what a kite is, and that it must have tugged its string out of a boy's hand, and soared away. After that they laughed at Peter for being so fond of the kite; he loved it so much that he even slept with one hand on it, and I think this was pathetic and pretty, for the reason he loved it was because it had belonged to a real boy.

To the birds this was a very poor reason, but the older ones felt grateful to him at this time because he had nursed a number of fledglings through the German measles, and they offered to show him how birds fly a kite. So six of them took the end of the string in their beaks and flew away with it; and to his amazement it flew after them and went even higher than they.

Peter screamed out, "Do it again!" and with great good-nature they did it several times, and always instead of thanking them he cried, "Do it again!" which shows that even now he had not quite forgotten what it was to be a boy.

At last, with a grand design burning within his brave heart, he begged them to do it once more with him clinging to the tail, and now a hundred flew off with the string, and Peter clung to the tail, meaning to drop off when he was over the Gardens. But the kite broke to pieces in the air, and he would have drowned in the Serpentine had he not caught hold of two indignant swans and made them carry him to the island. After this the birds said that they would help him no more in his mad enterprise.

[Peter eventually makes it over to Kensington Gardens, where he plays with the fairies each night.]

For, as you know without my telling you, Peter Pan is the fairies' orchestra. He sits in the middle of the ring, and they would never dream of having a smart dance nowadays without him. "P. P." is written on the corner of the invitation-cards sent out by all really good families. They are grateful little people, too, and at the princess's coming-of-age ball (they come of age on their second birthday and have a birthday every month) they gave him the wish of his heart.

The way it was done was this. The Queen ordered him to kneel, and then said that for playing so beautifully she would give him the wish of his heart. Then they all gathered round Peter to hear what was the wish of his heart, but for a long time he hesitated, not being certain what it was himself.

"If I chose to go back to mother," he asked at last, "could you give me that wish?"

Now this question vexed them, for were he to return to his mother they should lose his music, so the Queen tilted her nose contemptuously and said, "Pooh, ask for a much bigger wish than that."

"Is that quite a little wish?" he inquired.

"As little as this," the Queen answered, putting her hands near each other.

"What size is a big wish?" he asked.

She measured it off on her skirt and it was a very handsome length.

Then Peter reflected and said, "Well, then, I think I shall have two little wishes instead of one big one."

Of course, the fairies had to agree, though his cleverness rather shocked them, and he said that his first wish was to go to his mother, but with the right to return to the Gardens if he found her disappointing. His second wish he would hold in reserve.

They tried to dissuade him, and even put obstacles in the way.

"I can give you the power to fly to her house," the Queen said, "but I can't open the door for you."

"The window I flew out at will be open," Peter said confidently. "Mother always keeps it open in the hope that I may fly back."

"How do you know?" they asked, quite surprised, and, really, Peter could not explain how he knew.

"I just do know," he said.

So as he persisted in his wish, they had to grant it. The way they gave him power to fly was this: They all tickled him on the shoulder, and soon he felt a funny itching in that part, and then up he rose higher and higher and flew away out of the Gardens and over the house-tops.

It was so delicious that instead of flying straight to his old home he skimmed away over St. Paul's on the Crystal Palace and back by the river and Regent's Park, and by the time he reached his mother's window he had quite made up his mind that his second wish should be to become a bird.

The window was wide open, just as he knew it would be, and in he fluttered, and there was his mother lying asleep. Peter alighted softly on the wooden rail at the foot of the bed and had a good look at her. She lay with her head on her hand, and the hollow in the pillow was like a nest lined with her brown wavy hair. He remembered, though he had long forgotten it, that she always gave her hair a holiday at night. How sweet the frills of her night-gown were. He was very glad she was such a pretty mother.

But she looked sad, and he knew why she looked sad. One of her arms moved as if it wanted to go round something, and he knew what it wanted to go round.

"Oh, mother," said Peter to himself, "if you just knew who is sitting on the rail at the foot of the bed."

Very gently he patted the little mound that her feet made, and he could see by her face that she liked it. He knew he had but to say "Mother" ever so softly, and she would wake up. They always wake up at once if it is you that says their name. Then she would give such a joyous cry and squeeze him tight. How nice that would be to him, but oh, how exquisitely delicious it would be to her! That I am afraid is how Peter regarded it. In returning to his mother he never doubted that he was giving her the greatest treat a woman can have. Nothing can be more splendid, he thought, than to have a little boy of your own. How proud of him they are; and very right and proper, too.

But why does Peter sit so long on the rail, why does he not tell his mother that he has come back?

I quite shrink from the truth, which is that he sat there in two minds. Sometimes he looked longingly at his mother, and sometimes he looked longingly at the window. Certainly it would be pleasant to be her boy again, but, on the other hand, what times those had been in the Gardens! Was he so sure that he would enjoy wearing clothes again? He popped off the bed and opened some drawers to have a look at his old garments. They were still there, but he could not remember how you put them on. The socks, for instance, were they worn on the hands or on the feet? He was about to try one of them on his hand, when he had a great adventure. Perhaps the drawer had creaked; at any rate, his mother woke up, for he heard her say "Peter," as if it was the most lovely word in the language. He remained sitting on the floor and held his breath, wondering how she knew that he had come back. If she said "Peter" again, he meant to cry "Mother" and run to her. But she spoke no more, she made little moans only, and when next he peeped at her she was once more asleep, with tears on her face.

It made Peter very miserable, and what do you think was the first thing he did? Sitting on the rail at the foot of the bed, he played a beautiful lullaby to his mother on his pipe. He had made it up himself out of the way she said "Peter," and he never stopped playing until she looked happy.

He thought this so clever of him that he could scarcely resist wakening her to hear her say, "Oh, Peter, how exquisitely you play." However, as she now seemed comfortable, he again cast looks at the window. You must not think that he meditated flying away and never coming back. He had quite decided to be his mother's boy, but hesitated about beginning to-night. It was the second wish which troubled him. He no longer meant to make it a wish to be a bird, but not to ask for a second wish seemed wasteful, and, of course, he could not ask for it without returning to the fairies. Also, if he put off asking for his wish too long it might go bad. He asked himself if he had not been hard-hearted to fly away without saying good-bye to Solomon. "I should like awfully to sail in my boat just once more," he said wistfully to his sleeping mother. He quite argued with her as if she could hear him. "It would be so splendid to tell the birds of this adventure," he said coaxingly. "I promise to come back," he said solemnly and meant it, too.

And in the end, you know, he flew away. Twice he came back from the window, wanting to kiss his mother, but he feared the delight of it might waken her, so at last he played her a lovely kiss on his pipe, and then he flew back to the Gardens.

Many nights and even months passed before he asked the fairies for his second wish; and I am not sure that I quite know why he delayed so long. One reason was that he had so many good-byes to say, not only to his particular friends, but to a hundred favourite spots. Then he had his last sail, and his very last sail, and his last sail of all, and so on. Again, a number of farewell feasts were given in his honour; and another comfortable reason was that, after all, there was no hurry, for his mother would never weary of waiting for him. This last reason displeased old Solomon, for it was an encouragement to the birds to procrastinate. Solomon had several excellent mottoes for keeping them at their work, such as "Never put off laying to-day because you can lay tomorrow," and "In this world there are no second chances," and yet here was Peter gaily putting off and none the worse for it. The birds pointed this out to each other, and fell into lazy habits.

But, mind you, though Peter was so slow in going back to his mother, he was quite decided to go back. The best proof of this was his caution with the fairies. They were most anxious that he should remain in the Gardens to play to them, and to bring this to pass they tried to trick him into making such a remark as "I wish the grass was not so wet," and some of them danced out of time in the hope that he might cry, "I do wish you would keep time!" Then they would have said that this was his second wish. But he smoked their design, and though on occasions he began, "I wish—" he always stopped in time. So when at last he said to them bravely, "I wish now to go back to mother for ever and always," they had to tickle his shoulders and let him go.

He went in a hurry in the end because he had dreamt that his mother was crying, and he knew what was the great thing she cried for, and that a hug from her splendid Peter would quickly make her to smile. Oh, he felt sure of it, and so eager was he to be nestling in her arms that this time he flew straight to the window, which was always to be open for him.

But the window was closed, and there were iron bars on it, and peering inside he saw his mother sleeping peacefully with her arm round another little boy.

Peter called, "Mother! mother!" but she heard him not; in vain he beat his little limbs against the iron bars. He had to fly back, sobbing, to the Gardens, and he never saw his dear again. What a glorious boy he had meant to be to her. Ah, Peter, we who have made the great mistake, how differently we should all act at the second chance. But Solomon was right; there is no second chance, not for most of us. When we reach the window it is Lock-out Time. The iron bars are up for life.

QUESTIONS FOR DISCUSSION AND WRITING

1. Barrie sets this earlier version of the Peter Pan story in the real Kensington Gardens, not the imaginary Never Land of the play. How does Barrie's use of a real setting that would have been familiar to his audience change our response to the story of Peter?
2. This version of the story alternates between Peter's desire to escape from the "normal" life of a human boy and his desire to return home to his mother. Which desire seems stronger—and why? What did you as a reader hope that Peter would do?
3. Peter is displaced by a second son. How are we meant to respond to this displacement? Do we see it as the result of Peter's self-absorption—or of his mother's insensitivity?

J. M. BARRIE (1860–1937)

From "When Wendy Grew Up," in Peter and Wendy   1911

Michael believed longer than the other boys, though they jeered at him; so he was with Wendy when Peter came for her at the end of the first year. She flew away with Peter in the frock she had woven from leaves and berries in the Neverland, and her one fear was that he might notice how short it had become, but he never noticed, he had so much to say about himself.

She had looked forward to thrilling talks with him about old times, but new adventures had crowded the old ones from his mind.

"Who is Captain Hook?" he asked with interest when she spoke of the arch enemy.

"Don't you remember," she asked, amazed, "how you killed him and saved all our lives?"

"I forget them after I kill them," he replied carelessly.

When she expressed a doubtful hope that Tinker Bell would be glad to see her he said, "Who is Tinker Bell?"

"O Peter!" she said, shocked; but even when she explained he could not remember.

"There are such a lot of them," he said. "I expect she is no more."

I expect he was right, for fairies don't live long, but they are so little that a short time seems a good while to them.

Wendy was pained too to find that the past year was but as yesterday to Peter; it had seemed such a long year of waiting to her. But he was exactly as fascinating as ever, and they had a lovely spring cleaning in the little house on the tree tops.

Next year he did not come for her. She waited in a new frock because the old one simply would not meet, but he never came.

"Perhaps he is ill," Michael said.

"You know he is never ill."

Michael came close to her and whispered, with a shiver, "Perhaps there is no such person, Wendy!" and then Wendy would have cried if Michael had not been crying.

Peter came next spring cleaning; and the strange thing was that he never knew he had missed a year.

That was the last time the girl Wendy ever saw him. For a little longer she tried for his sake not to have growing pains; and she felt she was untrue to him when she got a prize for general knowledge. But the years came and went without bringing the careless boy; and when they met again Wendy was a married woman, and Peter was no more to her than a little dust in the box in which she had kept her toys. Wendy was grown up. You need not be sorry for her. She was one of the kind that likes to grow up. In the end she grew up of her own free will a day quicker than other girls.

All the boys were grown up and done for by this time; so it is scarcely worth while saying anything more about them. You may see the twins and Nibs and Curly any day going to an office, each carrying a little bag and an umbrella. Michael is an engine-driver. Slightly married a lady of title, and so he became a lord. You see that judge in a wig coming out at the iron door? That used to be Tootles. The bearded man who doesn't know any story to tell his children was once John.

Wendy was married in white with a pink sash. It is strange to think that Peter did not alight in the church and forbid the banns.

Years rolled on again, and Wendy had a daughter. This ought not to be written in ink but in a golden splash.

She was called Jane, and always had an odd inquiring look, as if from the moment she arrived on the mainland she wanted to ask questions. When she was old enough to ask them they were mostly about Peter Pan. She loved to hear of Peter, and Wendy told her all she could remember in the very nursery from which the famous flight had taken place. It was Jane's nursery now, for her father had bought it at the three per cents from Wendy's father, who was no longer fond of stairs. Mrs. Darling was now dead and forgotten.

There were only two beds in the nursery now, Jane's and her nurse's; and there was no kennel, for Nana also had passed away. She died of old age, and at the end she had been rather difficult to get on with, being very firmly convinced that no one knew how to look after children except herself.

Once a week Jane's nurse had her evening off, and then it was Wendy's part to put Jane to bed. That was the time for stories. It was Jane's invention to raise the sheet over her mother's head and her own, thus making a tent, and in the awful darkness to whisper:—

"What do we see now?"

"I don't think I see anything to-night," says Wendy, with a feeling that if Nana were here she would object to further conversation.

"Yes, you do," says Jane, "you see when you were a little girl."

"That is a long time ago, sweetheart," says Wendy. "Ah me, how time flies!"

"Does it fly," asks the artful child, "the way you flew when you were a little girl?"

"The way I flew! Do you know, Jane, I sometimes wonder whether I ever did really fly."

"Yes, you did."

"The dear old days when I could fly!"

"Why can't you fly now, mother?"

"Because I am grown up, dearest. When people grow up they forget the way."

"Why do they forget the way?"

"Because they are no longer gay and innocent and heartless. It is only the gay and innocent and heartless who can fly."

"What is gay and innocent and heartless? I do wish I was gay and innocent and heartless."

Or perhaps Wendy admits she does see something. "I do believe," she says, "that it is this nursery!"

"I do believe it is!" says Jane. "Go on."

They are now embarked on the great adventure of the night when Peter flew in looking for his shadow.

"The foolish fellow," says Wendy, "tried to stick it on with soap, and when he could not he cried, and that woke me, and I sewed it on for him."

"You have missed a bit," interrupts Jane, who now knows the story better than her mother. "When you saw him sitting on the floor crying what did you say?"

"I sat up in bed and I said, 'Boy, why are you crying?'"

"Yes, that was it," says Jane, with a big breath.

"And then he flew us all away to the Neverland and the fairies and the pirates and the redskins and the mermaids' lagoon, and the home under the ground, and the little house."

"Yes! which did you like best of all?"

"I think I liked the home under the ground best of all."

"Yes, so do I. What was the last thing Peter ever said to you?"

"The last thing he ever said to me was, 'Just always be waiting for me, and then some night you will hear me crowing.'"

"Yes!"

"But, alas, he forgot all about me." Wendy said it with a smile. She was as grown up as that.

"What did his crow sound like?" Jane asked one evening.

"It was like this," Wendy said, trying to imitate Peter's crow.

"No, it wasn't," Jane said gravely, "it was like this"; and she did it ever so much better than her mother.

Wendy was a little startled. "My darling, how can you know?"

"I often hear it when I am sleeping," Jane said.

"Ah yes, many girls hear it when they are sleeping, but I was the only one who heard it awake."

"Lucky you!" said Jane.

And then one night came the tragedy. It was the spring of the year, and the story had been told for the night, and Jane was now asleep in her bed. Wendy was sitting on the floor, very close to the fire so as to see to darn, for there was no other light in the nursery; and while she sat darning she heard a crow. Then the window blew open as of old, and Peter dropped on the floor.

He was exactly the same as ever, and Wendy saw at once that he still had all his first teeth.

He was a little boy, and she was grown up. She huddled by the fire not daring to move, helpless and guilty, a big woman.

"Hullo, Wendy," he said, not noticing any difference, for he was thinking chiefly of himself; and in the dim light her white dress might have been the nightgown in which he had seen her first.

"Hullo, Peter," she replied faintly, squeezing herself as small as possible. Something inside her was crying "Woman, woman, let go of me."

"Hullo, where is John?" he asked, suddenly missing the third bed.

"John is not here now," she gasped.

"Is Michael asleep?" he asked, with a careless glance at Jane.

"Yes," she answered; and now she felt that she was untrue to Jane as well as to Peter.

"That is not Michael," she said quickly, lest a judgment should fall on her.

Peter looked. "Hullo, is it a new one?"

"Yes."

"Boy or girl?"

"Girl."

Now surely he would understand; but not a bit of it.

"Peter," she said, faltering, "are you expecting me to fly away with you?"

"Of course; that is why I have come." He added a little sternly, "Have you forgotten that this is spring-cleaning time?"

She knew it was useless to say that he had let many spring-cleaning times pass.

"I can't come," she said apologetically, "I have forgotten how to fly."

"I'll soon teach you again."

"O, Peter, don't waste the fairy dust on me."

She had risen, and now at last a fear assailed him. "What is it?" he cried, shrinking.

"I will turn up the light," she said, "and then you can see for yourself."

For almost the only time in his life that I know of, Peter was afraid. "Don't turn up the light," he cried.

She let her hands play in the hair of the tragic boy. She was not a little girl heartbroken about him; she was a grown woman smiling at it all, but they were wet smiles.

Then she turned up the light, and Peter saw. He gave a cry of pain; and when the tall beautiful creature stooped to lift him in her arms he drew back sharply.

"What is it?" he cried again.

She had to tell him.

"I am old, Peter. I am ever so much more than twenty. I grew up long ago."

"You promised not to!"

"I couldn't help it. I am a married woman, Peter."

"No, you're not."

"Yes, and the little girl in the bed is my baby."

"No, she's not."

But he supposed she was; and he took a step towards the sleeping child with his fist upraised. Of course he did not strike her. He sat down on the floor and sobbed, and Wendy did not know how to comfort him, though she could have done it so easily once. She was only a woman now, and she ran out of the room to try to think.

Peter continued to cry, and soon his sobs woke Jane. She sat up in bed, and was interested at once.

"Boy," she said, "why are you crying?"

Peter rose and bowed to her, and she bowed to him from the bed.

"Hullo," he said.

"Hullo," said Jane.

"My name is Peter Pan," he told her.

"Yes, I know."

"I came back for my mother," he explained, "to take her to the Neverland."

"Yes, I know," Jane said, "I been waiting for you."

When Wendy returned diffidently she found Peter sitting on the bed-post crowing gloriously, while Jane in her nighty was flying round the room in solemn ecstasy.

"She is my mother," Peter explained; and Jane descended and stood by his side, with the look on her face that he liked to see on ladies when they gazed at him.

"He does so need a mother," Jane said.

"Yes, I know," Wendy admitted, rather forlornly; "no one knows it so well as I."

"Good-bye," said Peter to Wendy; and he rose in the air, and the shameless Jane rose with him; it was already her easiest way of moving about.

Wendy rushed to the window.

"No, no!" she cried.

"It is just for spring-cleaning time," Jane said; "he wants me always to do his spring cleaning."

"If only I could go with you!" Wendy sighed.

"You see you can't fly," said Jane.

Of course in the end Wendy let them fly away together. Our last glimpse of her shows her at the window, watching them receding into the sky until they were as small as stars.

As you look at Wendy you may see her hair becoming white, and her figure little again, for all this happened long ago. Jane is now a common grown-up, with a daughter called Margaret; and every spring-cleaning time, except when he forgets, Peter comes for Margaret and takes her to the Neverland, where she tells him stories about himself, to which he listens eagerly. When Margaret grows up she will have a daughter, who is to be Peter's mother in turn; and so it will go on, so long as children are gay and innocent and heartless.

QUESTIONS FOR DISCUSSION AND WRITING

1. Barrie introduces the long-awaited return of Peter with "And then one night came the tragedy." How is the story that follows a tragedy? Whose tragedy is it—Peter's or Wendy's? Why? Does reading the story of the grown-up Wendy and her daughter Jane change your response to the mood or meaning of the original play?
2. The story emphasizes that "children are gay and innocent and heartless." How does the story criticize children and how does it idealize them?
3. The story ends with a look into the future when Jane's own daughter and granddaughter will go off with Peter. What is the effect of this look into a future when each aging woman is replaced in Peter's life and affections by her young daughter?

QUESTION FOR DISCUSSION AND WRITING

Sculpted by George Frampton, the statue of Peter Pan in Kensington Gardens was commissioned by J. M. Barrie. Barrie kept the project secret, and the statue "magi-

cally" appeared on May 1, 1912. How does or doesn't the statue correspond to the impressions of Peter you get in Barrie's works? Does the Peter of the statue seem the same age as the Peter of the play and stories? Why or why not?

CAROLYN LEIGH (1926–1983)

I Won't Grow Up _____ 1954

I won't grow up.
(I won't grow up.)
I don't want to go to school.
(I don't want to go to school.)
Just to learn to be a parrot,   5
(Just to learn to be a parrot,)
And recite a silly rule.
(And recite a silly rule.)

If growing up means it would be
Beneath my dignity to climb a tree,   10
I'll never grow up, never grow up, never grow up,
Not me!
Not I!
Not me!
Not me!   15

I won't grow up.
(I won't grow up.)
I don't want to wear a tie.
(I don't want to wear a tie.)
And a serious expression,   20
(And a serious expression,)
In the middle of July.
(In the middle of July.)

And if it means I must prepare
To shoulder burdens with a worried air,   25
I'll never grow up, never grow up, never grow up,
So there!
Not I!
Not me!
So there!   30
Never gonna be a man, I won't!
Like to see somebody try and make me.
Anyone who wants to try and make me
Turn into a man,
Catch me if you can.   35

I won't grow up.
(I won't grow up.)
Not a penny will I pinch.
(Not a penny will I pinch.)
40   I will never grow a mustache,
(I will never grow a mustache,)
Or a fraction of an inch.
(Or a fraction of an inch.)
'Cause growing up is awfuller
45   Than all the awful things that ever were.
I'll never grow up, never grow up, never grow up,
No sir!
Not I!
Not me!
50   No sir!

QUESTION FOR DISCUSSION AND WRITING

In this song, Peter and the boys enthusiastically declare that they won't grow up. What do they associate with being grown up? Are their views of adulthood those of adults or children? Why?

LYNNE MCMAHON (1951–   )
Peter Pan _____ *1994*

Even after every room's been lit
    and every creak softened
into explanation, and speech itself trails
    its diminuendo
5   into the undifferentiated air which particle
    by molecule
minutely suspires;
    Even after the rocking stops
and the last of the water
10   stills in a ring
on the dribbled wood and the branch
    unknuckles from the pane;
Even after that vast sponge the cranium houses
    releases its sodden cargo
15   and restores to each pock
    and fibrous hollow
the scoured emptiness of coral, the polished

corridors of stone;
Even then
    at the bottom of the bottom
of the untrawled world
    the sharp hook-like thing flashes
and begins to rise.

20

QUESTIONS FOR DISCUSSION AND WRITING

1. What setting does McMahon create with the series of "even after" details?
2. The poem tells us that the "sharp hook-like thing" is "at the bottom of the bottom." "The bottom of the bottom" of what? How does this "sharp hook-like thing" seem like or unlike Captain Hook?
3. The poem is entitled "Peter Pan," but it does not include any direct references to Barrie's story. What, though, does the poem suggest about the meaning of that story?

QUESTIONS FOR CROSS READING: CHILDHOOD LOST AND FOUND

1. The story of Peter Pan has become a cultural myth of Western culture; it is a story known throughout American and European cultures even by those who have not read the stories or seen the play. Why does the story speak to Western culture? What psychological needs and/or fears does it express? Do some of Barrie's versions of the story make those needs and/or fears more apparent than others? How? Do you think the story has the same appeal to people from Asian, Middle Eastern, and African cultures?
2. In the original story in *The White Bird*, Peter is a solitary figure, playing with birds and fairies but not with other children. How does the addition of the Lost Boys change our view of Peter and our understanding of the stories' themes?
3. The earliest version of the story (from *The White Bird*) emphasizes Peter's relationship to his mother; the play and the novel (*Peter and Wendy*) deemphasize that element but add the Darling family. In what ways does the new emphasis on the Darling family (and particularly Wendy) change the original material? How satisfactory a substitute is Wendy for Peter's mother? Is Mrs. Darling seen as a potential mother for Peter?
4. In some respects, the Peter Pan stories are male centered; they work to exclude female influences. On the other hand, the female figures are often idealized. Where do you see evidence of these tensions in the stories? Are the tensions ever satisfactorily resolved? What are we finally to make of Barrie's view of the proper relationships between the genders?

Modeling and Play: The World of Barbie

QUESTIONS FOR DISCUSSION AND WRITING

1. The Barbie stamp (see also color insert) is part of the U.S. Postal Service's series on "The Rebellious Sixties and Man on the Moon." How appropriate does Barbie—and the stamp's depiction of her—seem to that theme?
2. Is the Barbie on the stamp the Barbie that you are most familiar with? Why or why not? What do the clothing and accessories of the postal Barbie suggest about her?

MARGE PIERCY (1936–   )

Barbie Doll   *1969*

This girlchild was born as usual
and presented dolls that did pee-pee
and miniature GE stoves and irons
and wee lipsticks the color of cherry candy.
5   Then in the magic of puberty, a classmate said:
You have a great big nose and fat legs.

She was healthy, tested intelligent,
possessed strong arms and back,
abundant sexual drive and manual dexterity.
10   She went to and fro apologizing.
Everyone saw a fat nose on thick legs.

She was advised to play coy,
exhorted to come on hearty,

exercise, diet, smile and wheedle.
Her good nature wore out   15
like a fan belt.
So she cut off her nose and her legs
and offered them up.
In the casket displayed on satin she lay
with the undertaker's cosmetics painted on,   20
a turned-up putty nose,
dressed in a pink and white nightie.
Doesn't she look pretty? everyone said.
Consummation at last.
To every woman a happy ending.   25

QUESTIONS FOR DISCUSSION AND WRITING

1. Which imagery in Piercy's poem would you consider masculine? Which imagery
   is feminine? What does the imagery suggest about the poem's view of gender roles?
   About the way boys and girls grow up?
2. In the last stanza, why is death presented as a "consummation" and "happy ending"?
3. What is the tone of the poem? Playful and humorous? Angry and bitter?
4. Though Barbie is part of the title, she is never mentioned in the poem itself.
   Why not?

LYNNE MCMAHON (1951–   )

Barbie's Ferrari   *1989*

Nothing is quite alien or quite recognizable at this speed,
Though there is the suggestion of curve, a mutant
Curvature designed, I suppose, to soften or offset
The stiletto toes and karate arms that were too
Angular for her last car, a Corvette as knifed as Barbie   5
Herself, and not the bloodred of Italian Renaissance.
This is Attention. This is detail fitted to sheer
Velocity. For her knees, after all, are locked—
Once fitted into the driving pit, she can only accelerate
Into a future that becomes hauntingly like the past: 10
Nancy Drew in her yellow roadster, a convertible,
I always imagined, the means to an end
Almost criminal in its freedom, its motherlessness.
For Barbie, too, is innocent of parents, pressing
Her unloved breasts to the masculine wheel, gunning   15
The turn into the hallway and out over the maiming stairs,

Every jolt slamming her uterus into uselessness, sealed,
Sealed up and preserved, everything about her becoming
Pure Abstraction and the vehicle for Desire: to be Nancy,
20   To be Barbie, to feel the heaven of Imagination
Breathe its ether on your cheeks, rosying in the slipstream
As the speedster/roadster/Ferrari plummets over the rail
Into the ocean of waxed hardwood below. To crash and burn
And be retrieved. To unriddle the crime. To be
25   Barbie with a plot! That's the soulful beauty of it.
That's the dreaming child.
Not the dawn of Capital, the factories of Hong Kong
Reversing the currency in Beijing. Not the ovarian
Moon in eclipse. Just the dreaming child, the orphan,
30   Turning in slow motion in the air above the bannister,
For whom ideas of gender and marketplace are nothings
Less than nothing. It's the car she was born for.
It's Barbie you mourn for.

QUESTIONS FOR DISCUSSION AND WRITING

1. Though the poem imagines Barbie's Ferrari and the dreams it represents, it also makes us aware of the house in which the child is playing with the toy car. How? What is the effect on the reader of those references?
2. The poem tells us that for the child "ideas of gender and marketplace are nothings." Does the poem ask us to share that view of gender and marketplace or reject it?
3. The Ferrari is identified with the feminine Barbie and with Nancy Drew (the teenaged heroine of a series of mystery novels popular in the 1950s), and yet it has a "masculine wheel" and jolts Barbie's uterus "into uselessness." Are we finally meant to see the Ferrari as feminine or masculine? What does the car represent to the child and to us?

ALLISON JOSEPH (1967–   )

Barbie's Little Sister _____ 1996

How terrible it would be
to be Barbie's little sister,
suspended in perpetual pre-adolescence
while Barbie, hair flying behind her
5   in a tousled blond mane, dashed
from adventure to adventure,
ready for space travel or calf roping
or roller disco in campy, flashy clothes

that defied good taste and reason.
Stuck with the awful nickname Skipper,   10
Barbie's little sis never got out much,
a mere boarder in Barbie's three-story
hot-pink Dream House, too young
to wear the thousands of outfits
stashed in the bedroom closets: 15
purple-beaded Armani evening gowns,
knit sweater dresses by Donna Karan,
specially commissioned tennis togs
sewn personally by Oleg Cassini.
Skipper had to buy off the rack   20
at Kmart, condemned to wear
floral sunsuits with Peter Pan collars.
Unlike her bosomy sister,
Skipper had no chest
for the boys to ogle,   25
until some bright toymaker
gave us "Growing Up Skipper":
with a twist of her right arm,
she grew taller, breasts sprouting
where there once were none,   30
a thick rubber band inside her
pushing her chest up and out
until the band snapped
and Skipper was stuck at age 15,
never the same again.   35
For consolation, she turned to
Barbie's black friend Christie—
who was just figuring out
all the fuss about equal rights—
and Barbie's best pal Midge,   40
who was tired of hearing
about spats with Ken, knowing
he was cheating on America's sweetheart
with every new celebrity doll on the market—
Brooke Shields, Cher, Dorothy Hamill.   45
Together, those three decided
they'd had enough of Toyland—
so they pooled their cash,
swiped Barbie's camper,
and tore out of California   50
for Las Vegas, where they bought
a little establishment not too far
from the gaming houses,
a restaurant for all of us
without thick manes of hair   55

or upturned noses, without
impossibly slender ankles
and tiny feet, without
perfectly molded breasts.

QUESTIONS FOR DISCUSSION AND WRITING

1. The title of the poem suggests that the focus is on Skipper, "Barbie's little sister." What view does the poem provide of Skipper? Of "perpetual pre-adolescence"?
2. Though the poem seems to be about Skipper, it frequently refers to Barbie (and Skipper is identified as *Barbie's* little sister). Trace the references to Barbie throughout the poem. What is its attitude toward Barbie?
3. Skipper, Christie, and Midge all desert Barbie at the end of the poem. Why? Why is Las Vegas a fitting location for their restaurant?

M. G. LORD (1955–   )
Who Is Barbie, Anyway? _____ *1994*

The theme of the convention was "Wedding Dreams," and appropriately it was held in Niagara Falls, the honeymoon capital, a setting of fierce natural beauty pimpled with fast-food joints and tawdry motels. The delegates were not newlyweds who had come to cuddle aboard the *Maid of the Mist*, poignantly hopeful that their union, unlike half of all American marriages, would last. They were not children, who had come to goggle at the cataract over which dozens of cartoon characters had plunged in barrels and miraculously survived. Nor were they shoppers attracted by Niagara's other big draw—the Factory Outlet Mall—where such brand names as Danskin and Benetton, Reebok and Burberrys, Mikasa and Revere Ware could be purchased for as much as 70 percent off retail.

They were, however, consumers, many of whom had been taught a style of consumption by the very object they were convening to celebrate. They had fled the turquoise sky and the outdoor pageantry for the dim, cramped ballroom of the Radisson Hotel. There were hundreds of them: southern ladies in creaseless pant suits dragging befuddled Rotary Club–member husbands; women in T-shirts from Saskatoon and Pittsburgh; stylish young men from Manhattan and West Hollywood. There were housewives and professional women; single people, married people, severely corpulent people, and bony, gangling people. A thirtysomething female from Tyler, Texas, volunteered that she had the same measurements as Twiggy, except that she was one inch wider in the hips. There were people from Austria and Guadeloupe and Scotland. Considering the purpose of the gathering, there were surprisingly few blond people.

These were delegates to the 1992 Barbie-doll collectors' convention, a celebration of the ultimate American girl-thing, an entity too perfect to be made of flesh but rather forged out of mole-free, blemish-resistant, nonbiodegradable plastic. Narrow of waist, slender of hip, and generous of bosom, she was the ideal of postwar feminine beauty when Mattel, Inc., introduced her in 1959—one year before the founding of Overeaters Anonymous, two years before Weight Watchers, and many years before Carol Doda pioneered a new use for silicone. (Unless I am discussing the doll as a sculpture, I will use "she" to refer to Barbie; Barbie is made up of two distinct components: the doll-as-physical-object and the doll-as-invented-personality.) At other collector events, I have witnessed ambivalence toward the doll—T-shirts, for instance, emblazoned with: "I wanna be like Barbie. The bitch has everything." But this crowd took its polyvinyl heroine seriously.

Of course, people tend to take things seriously when money is involved, and Barbie-collecting, particularly for dealers, has become a big business. The earliest version of the doll, a so-called Number One, distinguished by a tiny hole in each foot, has fetched as much as $4,000. The "Side-part American Girl," which features a variation on a pageboy haircut, has brought in $3,000. And because children tend to have a destructive effect on tiny accessories, the compact from Barbie's "Roman Holiday" ensemble, an object no bigger than a baby's thumbnail, has gone for $800. While Barbie-collecting has not replaced baseball as the national pastime, it has, in the fourteen years since the first Barbie convention in Queens, New York, moved from the margins to the mainstream. Over twenty thousand readers buy *Barbie Bazaar*, a glossy bimonthly magazine with full-color, seductively styled photos of old Barbie paraphernalia. And twenty thousand is not an insignificant number of disciples. Christianity, after all, started out with only eleven.

In the shadowy salesroom, amid vinyl cases and cardboard dreamhouses, thousands of Barbies and Barbie's friends were strewn atop one another—naked—suggesting some disturbing hybrid of Woodstock and a Calvin Klein Obsession ad. Others stood bravely—clothed—held up by wire stands. Some were in their original cartons; "NRFB" is collector code for "never removed from box." Still others were limbless, headless, or missing a hand. "Good for parts," a dealer explained. Buyers, wary of deceitful dealers, ran weathered fingers over each small, hard torso, probing for scratches, tooth marks, or, worst of all, for an undeclared spruce-up. Even a skillful application of fresh paint can devalue a doll, as does hair that has been rerooted.

Emotions ran high as deals were cut. A stocky woman in jeans haggled furiously over Barbie's 1963 roadster; I later saw her in the lobby, cradling the car as if it were her firstborn child. Others schmoozed with reliable, well-known dealers—Los Angeles–based Joe Blitman, author of *Vive La Francie*, an homage to Francie, Barbie's small-breasted cousin who was born in 1966 and lasted until 1975; and Sarah Sink Eames, from Boones Mill, Virginia, author of *Barbie Fashion*, a photographic record of the doll's wardrobe. I learned the value of established dealers when I bought "Queen of the Prom," the 1961 Barbie board game, from a shifty-eyed woman who was not a convention regular. "The set's kind of beat-up," she told me, "but all the pieces are authentic." Right, lady. Barbie's allowance, I discovered when I played the game, was five dollars. The smallest denomination in the set she sold me was $100. (The bills were from another game.)

Selling was not the only action at the convention. There was a fashion show in which collectors arranged their not-especially-Barbie-esque bodies into life-size versions of their favorite Barbie outfits. There was a competition of dioramas illustrating the theme "Wedding Dreams"; one, which did not strike me as lighthearted, featured a male doll (not Ken) recoiling in fear and horror from Barbie and, implicitly, Woman, on his wedding night. (His face had been whitened and his eyes widened into circles.) Employees of Mattel were treated like rock stars. Early on the second night of the convention, veteran costume designer Carol Spencer, who has been dressing Barbie since 1963, settled down in the hotel lobby to autograph boxes of "Benefit Ball Barbie," one of her creations in Mattel's Classique Collection, a series promoting its in-house designers. At eleven, she was still signing.

Intense feelings about Barbie do not run exclusively toward love. For every mother who embraces Barbie as a traditional toy and eagerly introduces her daughter to the doll, there is another mother who tries to banish Barbie from the house. For every fluffy blond cheerleader who leaps breast-forward into an exaggerated gender role, there is a recovering bulimic who refuses to wear dresses and blames Barbie for her ordeal. For every collector to whom the amassing of Barbie objects is a language more exquisite than words, there is a fiction writer or poet or visual artist for whom Barbie is muse and metaphor—and whose message concerns class inequities or the dark evanescence of childhood sexuality.

Barbie may be the most potent icon of American popular culture in the late twentieth century. She was a subject of the late pop artist Andy Warhol, and when I read Arthur C. Danto's review of Warhol's 1989 retrospective at the Museum of Modern Art, I thought of her. Danto wrote that pop art's goal was elevating the commonplace; but what, he wondered, would happen when the commonplace ceased to be commonplace? How would future generations interpret Warhol's paintings—generations for which Brillo boxes, Campbell soup labels, and famous faces from the 1960s and '70s would not be instantly identifiable?

Danto's meditations got me thinking about the impermanence of living icons. What, for instance, is Valentino to us today? A shadow jerking across a black-and-white screen, campy at best, no more an image of smoldering sex appeal than, say, Lassie. What is Dietrich? To the millions who read her daughter's vindictive, best-selling biography, she is an amphetamine-ridden drunk with disgusting gynecological problems, so leery of hospitals that she let a wound in her thigh fester until her leg was threatened with amputation. What is Marilyn? A caricature, a corpse, the subject of tedious documentaries linking her to RFK and JFK. And what is Elvis? To anyone over forty, he's probably still the sexy crooner from Tupelo; but younger people recall him as a bloated junkie encrusted with more rhinestones than Liberace.

Barbie has an advantage over all of them. She can never bloat. She has no children to betray her. Nor can she rot, wrinkle, overdose, or go out of style. Mattel has hundreds of people—designers, marketers, market researchers—whose full-time job it is continually to reinvent her. In 1993, fresh versions of the doll did a billion dollars' worth of business. Based on its unit sales, Mattel calculates that every second, somewhere in the world, two Barbies are sold.

Given the emergence of the doll as a symbol in literature and art—not to mention as a merchandising phenomenon—it's time to take a closer look at how Barbie developed and what her ascendancy might signify, even though it's impossible to calculate the doll's influence in any sort of clinical study. By the time children play with Barbie, they have too many other factors in their environment to be able to link a specific behavior trait with a particular toy. But because Barbie has both shaped and responded to the marketplace, it's possible to study her as a reflection of American popular cultural values and notions about femininity. Her houses and friends and clothes provide a window onto the often contradictory demands that the culture has placed upon women.

Barbie was knocked off from the "*Bild* Lilli" doll, a lascivious plaything for adult men that was based on a postwar comic character in the *Bild Zeitung*, a downscale German newspaper similar to America's *National Enquirer*. The doll, sold principally in tobacco shops, was marketed as a sort of three-dimensional pinup. In her cartoon incarnation, Lilli was not merely a doxie, she was a *German* doxie—an ice-blond, pixie-nosed specimen of an Aryan ideal—who may have known hardship during the war, but as long as there were men with checkbooks, was not going to suffer again.

Significantly, the Barbie doll was invented by a woman, Mattel cofounder Ruth Handler, who later established and ran "Nearly Me," a firm that designed and marketed mastectomy prostheses. (As she herself has put it, "My life has been spent going from breasts to breasts.") After Ruth and her husband Elliot, with whom she founded Mattel, left the company in 1975, women have continued to be the key decision makers on the Barbie line; the company's current COO, a fortyish ex–cosmetics marketer given to wearing Chanel suits, has been so involved with the doll that the *Los Angeles Times* dubbed her "Barbie's Doting Sister." In many ways, this makes Barbie a toy designed by women for women to teach women what—for better or worse—is expected of them by society.

Through the efforts of an overzealous publicist, Mattel engineer Jack Ryan, a former husband of Zsa Zsa Gabor, received credit for Barbie in his obituary. Actually, he merely held patents on the waist and knee joints in a later version of the doll; he had little to do with the original. If anyone should share recognition for inventing Barbie it is Charlotte Johnson, Barbie's first dress designer, whom Handler plucked from a teaching job and installed in Tokyo for a year to supervise the production of the doll's original twenty-two outfits.

Handler tries to downplay Barbie's resemblance to Lilli, but I think she should flaunt it. Physically the two are virtually identical; in terms of ethos, they couldn't be more dissimilar. In creating Barbie, Handler credits herself with having fleshed out a two-dimensional paper doll. This does not, however, do justice to her genius. She took Lilli, whom Ryan described as a "hooker or an actress between performances," and recast her as the wholesome all-American girl. Handler knew her market; if any one character trait distinguishes the American middle class, both today and in 1959, it is an obsession with respectability. This is not to say the middle class is indifferent to sex, but that it defines itself in contrast to the classes below it by its display of public propriety. Pornography targeted to the middle class, for example, must have a veneer of artistic or literary pretense—hence *Playboy*, the picture book men can also buy "for the articles."

Barbie and Lilli symbolize the link between the Old World and the New. America is a nation colonized by riffraff; the *Mayflower* was filled with petty criminals and the down-and-out. When Moll Flanders, to cite an emblematic floozy, took off for our shores, she was running from the law. Consequently, what could be more American than being an unimpeachable citizen with a sordid, embarrassing forebear in Europe?

To first-generation Barbie owners, of which I was one, Barbie was a revelation. She didn't teach us to nurture, like our clinging, dependent Betsy Wetsys and Chatty Cathys. She taught us independence. Barbie was her own woman. She could invent herself with a costume change: sing a solo in the spotlight one minute, pilot a starship the next. She was Grace Slick and Sally Ride, Marie Osmond and Marie Curie. She was all that we could be and—if you calculate what at human scale would translate to a thirty-nine-inch bust—more than we could be. And certainly more than we were . . . at six and seven and eight when she appeared and sank her jungle-red talons into our inner lives.

Or into my inner life, anyway. After I begged my mother for a Barbie, she reluctantly gave me a Midge—Barbie's ugly sidekick, who was named for an insect and had blemishes painted on her face. When I complained, she compounded the error by simultaneously giving me a Barbie and a Ken. I still remember Midge's anguish—her sense of isolation—at having to tag along after a couple. In my subsequent doll play, Ken rejected Barbie and forged a tight platonic bond with Midge. He did not, however, reject Barbie's clothes—and the more girlish the better.

To study Barbie, one sometimes has to hold seemingly contradictory ideas in one's head at the same time—which, as F. Scott Fitzgerald has said, is "the test of a first-rate intelligence." The doll functions like a Rorschach test; people project wildly dissimilar and often opposing fantasies on it. Barbie may be a universally recognized image, but what she represents in a child's inner life can be as personal as a fingerprint. It was once fashionable to tar Barbie as a materialistic dumbbell, and for some older feminists it still is; columnists Anna Quindlen and Ellen Goodman seem to be competing to chalk up the greatest number of attacks. Those of us young enough to have played with Barbie, however, realize the case is far from open and shut. In part, this is because imaginative little girls rarely play with products the way manufacturers expect them to. But it also has to do with the products themselves: at worst, Barbie projected an anomalous message; at best, she was a sort of feminist pioneer. And her meaning, like her face, has not been static over time.

Before the divorce epidemic that swept America in the late sixties, Barbie's universe and that of the suburban nuclear family were light years apart. There were no parents or husbands or offspring in Barbie's world; she didn't define herself through relationships of responsibility to men or to her family. Nor was Barbie a numb, frustrated *Hausfrau* out of *The Feminine Mystique*. In the doll's early years, Handler turned down a vacuum company's offer to make a Barbie-sized vacuum because Barbie didn't do what Charlotte Johnson termed "rough housework." When Thorstein Veblen formulated his *Theory of the Leisure Class*, women were expected to perform vicarious leisure and vicarious consumption to show that their husbands were prosperous. But Barbie had no husband. Based on the career outfits in her first wardrobe, she earned her keep modeling and designing clothes. Her leisure and consumption were a testimony to herself.

True, she had a boyfriend, but he was a lackluster fellow, a mere accessory. Mattel, in fact, never wanted to produce Ken; male figure dolls had traditionally been losers in the marketplace. But consumers so pushed for a boyfriend doll that Mattel finally released Ken in 1961. The reason for their demand was obvious. Barbie taught girls what was expected of women, and a woman in the fifties would have been a failure without a male consort, even a drip with seriously abridged genitalia who wasn't very important in her life.

Feminism notwithstanding, the same appears true today, though many of my young friends who own Barbies have embraced a weirdly polygamous approach to marriage, in which an average of eight female dolls share a single overextended Ken. Some mothers facetiously speculate that they are acting out the so-called "man short-age," still referred to by dinner-party hostesses despite its having been discredited by Susan Faludi in *Backlash*. My theory, however, is that smart little girls were made un-easy by the late-eighties version of Ken. Unlike the bright-eyed, innocent Ken with whom I grew up, the later model bears a troubling resemblance to William Kennedy Smith: His brow is low, his neck thick, and his eyes too close together.

With its 1993 "Earring Magic Ken," Mattel perhaps overdid his retreat from heterosexual virility. True, the doll has a smarter-looking face, but between his ear-ring, lavender vest, and what newspapers euphemized as a "ring pendant" ("cock ring" wouldn't, presumably, play to a family audience), he would have fit right in on Christopher Street. Watching my jaw drop at the sight of the doll at Toy Fair, Mattel publicist Donna Gibbs assured me that an earring in one's left ear was innocuous. "Of course," I said feebly, "the same ear in which Joey Buttafuoco wears his."

Barbie, too, has changed her look more than once through the years, though her body has remained essentially unaltered. From an art history standpoint—and Barbie, significantly, has been copyrighted as a work of art—her most radical change came in 1971, and was a direct reflection of the sexual revolution. Until then, Barbie's eyes had been cast down and to one side—the averted, submissive gaze that character-ized female nudes, particularly those of a pornographic nature, from the Renaissance until the nineteenth century. What had been so shocking about Manet's *Olympia* (1865) was that the model was both naked and unabashedly staring at the viewer. By 1971, however, when America had begun to accept the idea that a woman could be both sexual and unashamed, Barbie, in her "Malibu" incarnation, was allowed to have that body and look straight ahead.

The Barbie doll had its first overhaul and face change in 1967, when it acquired eyelashes and a rotating waist. Although the new "Twist 'N Turn" Barbie was not that different from the rigid old one—its gaze was still sidelong—the way it was promoted was not. Girls who traded in their old, beloved Barbies were given a discount on the new model. Twist 'N Turn introduced car designer Harley Earl's idea of "dynamic ob-solescence" to doll bodies. Where once only doll fashions had changed, now the doll itself changed; each year until the eighties, the doll's body would be engineered to perform some new trick—clutch a telephone, hit a tennis ball, even tilt its head back and smooch. Taste was not a big factor in devising the new dolls; in 1975, Mattel came out with "Growing Up Skipper," a preteen doll that, when you shoved its arm back-ward, sprouted breasts.

Fans of conspiracy theories will be disappointed to learn that Barbie's propor-tions were not the result of some misogynistic plot. They were dictated by the me-chanics of clothing construction. The doll is one-sixth the size of a person, but the fabrics she wears are scaled for people. Barbie's middle, her first designer explained, had to be disproportionately narrow to look proportional in clothes. The inner seam on the waistband of a skirt involves four layers of cloth—and four thicknesses of human-scale fabric on a one-sixth-human-scale doll would cause the doll's waist to appear dramatically larger than her hips.

It is one thing for a sexually initiated adult to snicker over the doll's anatomi-cally inaccurate body, quite another to recall how she looked to us when we were children: terrifying yet beguiling; as charged and puzzling as sexuality itself. In the late fifties and early sixties, there was no talk of condoms in the schools, *National Geographic* was a kid's idea of a racy magazine, and the nearest thing to a sexually explicit music video was Annette Funicello bouncing around with the Mouseketeers. Barbie, with her shocking torpedo orbs, and Ken with his mysterious genital bulge, were the extent of our exposure to the secrets of adulthood. Sex is less shrouded now than it was thirty years ago, but today's young Barbie owners are still using the doll to unravel the mystery of gender differences.

Of course, these days, kids have a great deal more to puzzle out. One used to wake up in the morning confident of certain things—among them that there were two genders, masculine and feminine, and that "masculine" was attached to males, "feminine" to females. But on the frontiers of medicine and philosophy, this certainty has been questioned. Geneticists recognize the existence of at least five genders; prenatal hormonal irregularities can, for instance, cause fetuses that are chromosomally female to develop as anatomical males and fetuses that are chromosomally male to develop as anatomical females. Then there are feminist theorists such as Judith Butler who argue that there is no gender at all. *"Gender is a kind of imitation for which there is no original,"* Butler has written. It is something performed, artificial, a "phantasmic ideal of heterosexual identity." All gendering, consequently, is drag, "a kind of impersonation and approximation."

No one disputes that from a young age boys and girls behave differently, but the jury is still out on why. Is such behavior rooted in biology or social conditioning? I think it's possible to look at femininity as a performance—or "womanliness as a masquerade," to borrow from Joan Rivière, a female Freudian who labeled the phenomenon in 1929—without chucking the possibility of biological differences.

Indeed, some of Barbie's most ardent imitators are probably not what Carole King had in mind when she wrote "Natural Woman." Many drag queens proudly cite Barbie's influence; as a child, singer Ru-Paul not only collected Barbies but cut off their breasts. Barbie has, in fact, a drag queen's body: broad shoulders and narrow hips, which are quintessentially male, and exaggerated breasts, which aren't. Then there are biological women whose emulation of Barbie has relied heavily on artifice: the Barbi Twins, identical *Playboy* covergirls who maintain their wasp waists through a diet of Beech-Nut strained veal; and Cindy Jackson, the London-based cosmetic surgery maven who has had more than twenty operations to make her resemble the doll.

When Ella King Torrey, a friend of mine . . . , began researching Barbie at Yale University in 1979, her work was considered cutting-edge and controversial. But these days everybody's deconstructing the doll. Barbie has been the subject of papers presented at the Modern Language Association's 1992 convention and the Ninth Berkshire Conference on the History of Women; rarely does a pop culture conference pass without some mention of the postmodern female fetish figure. Gilles Brougère, a French sociologist, has conducted an exhaustive study of French women and children to determine how different age groups perceive the doll. When scholars deal with Barbie, however, they often take a single aspect of the doll and construct an argument around it. I have resisted that approach. What fascinates me is the whole, ragged, contradictory story—its intrigues, its inconsistencies, and the personalities of its players.

I've tried to pin down exactly what happened in Barbie's first years. Mattel's focus on the future, which may be the secret of its success, has been at the expense of its past. The company has no archive. This may help conceal its embarrassments, but it has also buried its achievements—such as subsidizing Shindana Toys in response to the 1965 Watts riots. The African-American–run, South Central Los Angeles–based company produced ethnically correct playthings long before they were fashionable.

Although Barbie's sales have never substantially flagged, Mattel has been a financial roller coaster. It nearly went broke in 1974, when the imaginative accounting practices of Ruth Handler and some of her top executives led to indictments against them for falsifying SEC information, and again in 1984, when the company shifted its focus from toys to electronic games that nobody wanted to buy. The second time, Michael Milken galloped to the rescue. "I believed in Barbie," Milken told Barbara Walters in 1993. "I called up the head of Mattel and I told him that I personally would be willing to invest two hundred million dollars in his company. There's more Barbie dolls in this country than there are people."

The Barbie story is filled with loose ends and loose screws, but unfortunately very few loose lips. In a world as small as the toy industry, people are discreet about former colleagues because they may have to work with them again. As for welcoming outsiders, the company has much in common with the Kremlin at the height of the Cold War. To a degree, secrecy is vital in the toy business: if a rival learns in August of a clever new toy, he or she can steal the idea and have a knock-off in the stores by Christmas.

Nor am I what Mattel had in mind as its Boswell. Inspired perhaps by Quindlen and Goodman, or, more likely, by fear and a deadline, I had owned up in my weekly *Newsday* column to having cross-dressed Ken because of antipathy toward his girlfriend. This was years before I gave serious thought to Barbie's iconic import, but it was not sufficiently far in the past to have escaped the attention of Mattel publicist Donna Gibbs, who, when I first called her, did not treat me warmly. Miraculously, after a few months, Donna and her colleagues became gracious, charming, and remarkably accommodating. I was baffled, but took it as a sign to keep—like the entity I was studying—on my toes. Still, it was hard not to be seduced by the company, especially by its elves—the designers and sculptors, the "rooters and groomers," as the hair people are called—who really did seem to have a great time playing with their eleven-and-a-half-inch pals.

Toys have always said a lot about the culture that produced them, and especially about how that culture viewed its children. The ancient Greeks, for instance, left behind few playthings. Their custom of exposing weak babies on mountainsides to die does not suggest a concern for the very young. Ghoulish though it may sound, until the eighteenth century, childhood didn't count for much because few people survived it. Children were even dressed like little adults. Although in 1959, much fuss was made over Mattel's "adult" doll, the fact was that until 1820 all dolls were adults. Baby dolls came into existence in the early decades of the nineteenth century along with, significantly, special clothing for children.

Published in 1762, Rousseau's *Émile*, a treatise on education, began to focus attention on the concerns of youngsters, but the cult of childhood didn't take root until Queen Victoria ascended the throne in 1837. "Childhood was invented in the eighteenth century in response to dehumanizing trends of the industrial revolution," psychoanalyst Louise J. Kaplan has observed. "By the nineteenth century, when artists began to see themselves as alienated beings trapped in a dehumanizing social world, the child became the savior of mankind, the symbol of free imagination and natural goodness."

The child was also a consumer of toys, the making of which, by the late nineteenth century, had become an industry. Until World War I, Germany dominated the marketplace; but when German troops began shooting at U.S. soldiers, Americans lost their taste for enemy playthings. This burst of patriotism gave the U.S. toy industry its first rapid growth spurt; its second came after World War II, with the revolution in plastics.

Just as children were "discovered" in the eighteenth century, they were again "discovered" in post–World War II America—this time by marketers. The evolution of the child-as-consumer was indispensable to Barbie's success. Mattel not only pioneered advertising on television, but through that medium it pitched Barbie directly to kids.

It is with an eye toward using objects to understand ourselves that I beg Barbie's knee-jerk defenders and knee-jerk revilers to cease temporarily their defending and reviling. Barbie is too complicated for either an encomium or an indictment. But we will not refrain from looking under rocks.

For women under forty, the implications of such an investigation are obvious. Barbie is a direct reflection of the cultural impulses that formed us. Barbie is our reality. And unsettling though the concept may be, I don't think it's hyperbolic to say: Barbie is us.

QUESTIONS FOR DISCUSSION AND WRITING

1. Lord sees Barbie as representative of middle-class values and respectability. Considering the Barbie outfits and possessions you are familiar with, how would you argue that that statement is or is not true?
2. According to Lord, Barbie does not define herself in terms of a man or family. What, then, does define Barbie? What role does Mattel seem to suggest Ken should have, given the packaging and accessories that accompany him?
3. Lord opens her article with a description of a Barbie convention. What might motivate people to attend such conventions? Why would Barbie be such a desirable object to collect? How do collectible Barbies differ from those actually played with?

QUESTIONS FOR CROSS READING: MODELING AND PLAY

1. Lord remarks that critics of Barbie sometimes see her as a reflection of sexist values and sometimes see her as a feminist pioneer. Which view seems more common in this section? How do the writers communicate their views?
2. Many of the writers in this section find Barbie's sexuality ambiguous; for example, both Piercy and McMahon include masculine automobile images in their poems, and Lord mentions that she enjoyed cross-dressing Ken. What do the different

writers believe that Barbie, her doll companions, and the Barbie accessories tell us about female gender roles?

3. Ken is a part of the Barbie fantasy, but some writers in this section argue that he is not a very important part. What roles do they think Ken plays in the fantasy? What roles do *you* think Ken plays?

4. Write a "retelling" of your own—a short story or poem—that reveals some important part of the Barbie fantasy. You may want to focus on Barbie or Ken or some other member of Barbie's "entourage" or on some of the accessories available.

5. Analyze some of the Web sites devoted to Barbie. What items seem most collectible at this time? What seem to be the intended audiences of the Web sites? What do the Web sites tell you about why Barbie is valued by adults?

6. Visit a large toy store and survey the different Barbies and accessories that are available. Using this information, analyze the fantasies Barbie is currently helping to create. You may want to compare these Barbie fantasies to those you remember from your own childhood or those suggested in the readings.

7. G. I. Joe might be considered the boy's equivalent of Barbie. What do G. I. Joe and the accessories sold with him tell you about the kinds of messages the toy sends to young boys?

Venturing out into the World

KATHERINE MANSFIELD (1888–1923)

Her First Ball _____ *1921*

Exactly when the ball began Leila would have found it hard to say. Perhaps her first real partner was the cab. It did not matter that she shared the cab with the Sheridan girls and their brother. She sat back in her own little corner of it, and the bolster on which her hand rested felt like the sleeve of an unknown young man's dress suit; and away they bowled, past waltzing lampposts and houses and fences and trees.

"Have you really never been to a ball before, Leila? But, my child, how too weird—" cried the Sheridan girls.

"Our nearest neighbor was fifteen miles," said Leila softly, gently opening and shutting her fan.

Oh, dear, how hard it was to be indifferent like the others! She tried not to smile too much; she tried not to care. But every single thing was so new and exciting . . . Meg's tuberoses, Jose's long loop of amber, Laura's little dark head, pushing above her white fur like a flower through snow. She would remember for ever. It even gave her a pang to see her cousin Laurie throw away the wisps of tissue paper he pulled from the fastening of his new gloves. She would like to have kept those wisps as a keepsake, as a remembrance. Laurie leaned forward and put his hand on Laura's knee.

"Look here, darling," he said. "The third and the ninth as usual. Twig?"

Oh, how marvellous to have a brother! In her excitement Leila felt that if there had been time, if it hadn't been impossible, she couldn't have helped crying because she was an only child, and no brother had ever said "Twig?" to her; no sister would ever say, as Meg said to Jose that moment, "I've never known your hair go up more successfully than it has tonight!"

But, of course, there was no time. They were at the drill hall already; there were cabs in front of them and cabs behind. The road was bright on either side with moving fan-like lights, and on the pavement gay couples seemed to float through the air; little satin shoes chased each other like birds.

"Hold on to me, Leila; you'll get lost," said Laura.

"Come on, girls, let's make a dash for it," said Laurie.

Leila put two fingers on Laura's pink velvet cloak, and they were somehow lifted past the big gold lantern, carried along the passage, and pushed into the little room marked "Ladies." Here the crowd was so great there was hardly space to take off their things; the noise was deafening. Two benches on either side were stacked high with wraps. Two old women in white aprons ran up and down tossing fresh armfuls. And everybody was pressing forward trying to get at the little dressing table and mirror at the far end.

A great quivering jet of gas lighted the ladies' room. It couldn't wait; it was dancing already. When the door opened again and there came a burst of tuning from the drill hall, it leaped almost to the ceiling.

Dark girls, fair girls were patting their hair, tying ribbons again, tucking handkerchiefs down the front of their bodices, smoothing marble-white gloves. And because they were all laughing it seemed to Leila that they were all lovely.

"Aren't there any invisible hairpins?" cried a voice. "How most extraordinary! I can't see a single invisible hairpin."

"Powder my back, there's a darling," cried some one else.

"But I must have a needle and cotton. I've torn simply miles and miles of the frill," wailed a third.

Then, "Pass them along, pass them along!" The straw basket of programs was tossed from arm to arm. Darling little pink-and-silver programs, with pink pencils and fluffy tassels. Leila's fingers shook as she took one out of the basket. She wanted to ask someone, "Am I meant to have one too?" but she had just time to read: "Waltz 3. *Two, Two in a Canoe.* Polka 4. *Making the Feathers Fly,*" when Meg cried, "Ready, Leila?" and they pressed their way through the crush in the passage towards the big double doors of the drill hall.

Dancing had not begun yet, but the band had stopped tuning, and the noise was so great it seemed that when it did begin to play it would never be heard. Leila, pressing close to Meg, looking over Meg's shoulder, felt that even the little quivering colored flags strung across the ceiling were talking. She quite forgot to be shy; she forgot how in the middle of dressing she had sat down on the bed with one shoe off and one shoe on and begged her mother to ring up her cousins and say she couldn't go after all. And the rush of longing she had had to be sitting on the veranda of their forsaken upcountry home, listening to the baby owls crying "More pork" in the moonlight, was changed to a rush of joy so sweet that it was hard to bear alone. She clutched her fan, and, gazing at the gleaming, golden floor, the azaleas, the lanterns, the stage at one end with its red carpet and gilt chairs and the band in a corner, she thought breathlessly. "How heavenly; how simply heavenly!"

All the girls stood grouped together at one side of the doors, the men at the other, and the chaperones in dark dresses, smiling rather foolishly, walked with little careful steps over the polished floor towards the stage.

"This is my little country cousin Leila. Be nice to her. Find her partners; she's under my wing," said Meg, going up to one girl after another.

Strange faces smiled at Leila—sweetly, vaguely. Strange voices answered, "Of course, my dear." But Leila felt the girls didn't really see her. They were looking towards the men. Why didn't the men begin? What were they waiting for? There they stood, smoothing their gloves, patting their glossy hair and smiling among themselves. Then, quite suddenly, as if they had only just made up their minds that that was what they had to do, the men came gliding over the parquet. There was a joyful flutter among the girls. A tall, fair man flew up to Meg, seized her program, scribbled something; Meg passed him on to Leila. "May I have the pleasure?" He ducked and smiled. There came a dark man wearing an eyeglass, then cousin Laurie with a friend, and Laura with a little freckled fellow whose tie was crooked. Then quite an old man— fat, with a big bald patch on his head—took her program and murmured, "Let me see, let me see!" And he was a long time comparing his program, which looked black with names, with hers. It seemed to give him so much trouble that Leila was ashamed. "Oh, please don't bother," she said eagerly. But instead of replying the fat man wrote something, glanced at her again. "Do I remember this bright little face?" he said softly. "Is it known to me of yore?" At that moment the band began playing; the fat man disappeared. He was tossed away on a great wave of music that came flying over the gleaming floor, breaking the groups up into couples, scattering them, sending them spinning. . . .

Leila had learned to dance at boarding school. Every Saturday afternoon the boarders were hurried off to a little corrugated iron mission hall where Miss Eccles (of London) held her "select" classes. But the difference between that dusty-smelling hall—with calico texts on the walls, the poor terrified little woman in a brown velvet toque with rabbit's ears thumping the cold piano, Miss Eccles poking the girls' feet with her long white wand—and this was so tremendous that Leila was sure if her partner didn't come and she had to listen to that marvelous music and to watch the others sliding, gliding over the golden floor, she would die at least, or faint, or lift her arms and fly out of one of those dark windows that showed the stars.

"Ours, I think—" Some one bowed, smiled, and offered her his arm; she hadn't to die after all. Some one's hand pressed her waist, and she floated away like a flower that is tossed into a pool.

"Quite a good floor, isn't it?" drawled a faint voice close to her ear.

"I think it's most beautifully slippery," said Leila.

"Pardon!" The faint voice sounded surprised. Leila said it again. And there was a tiny pause before the voice echoed, "Oh, quite!" and she was swung round again.

He steered so beautifully. That was the great difference between dancing with girls and men, Leila decided. Girls banged into each other, and stamped on each other's feet; the girl who was gentleman always clutched you so.

The azaleas were separate flowers no longer, they were pink and white flags streaming by.

"Were you at the Bells' last week?" the voice came again. It sounded tired. Leila wondered whether she ought to ask him if he would like to stop.

"No, this is my first dance," said she.

Her partner gave a little gasping laugh. "Oh, I say," he protested.

"Yes, it is really the first dance I've ever been to." Leila was most fervent. It was such a relief to be able to tell somebody. "You see, I've lived in the country all my life up until now. . . ."

At that moment the music stopped, and they went to sit on two chairs against the wall. Leila tucked her pink satin feet under and fanned herself, while she blissfully watched the other couples passing and disappearing through the swing doors.

"Enjoying yourself, Leila?" asked Jose, nodding her golden head.

Laura passed and gave her the faintest little wink; it made Leila wonder for a moment whether she was quite grown up after all. Certainly her partner did not say very much. He coughed, tucked his handkerchief away, pulled down his waistcoat, took a minute thread off his sleeve. But it didn't matter. Almost immediately the band started, and her second partner seemed to spring from the ceiling.

"Floor's not bad," said the new voice. Did one always begin with the floor? And then, "Were you at the Neaves' on Tuesday?" And again Leila explained. Perhaps it was a little strange that her partners were not more interested. For it was thrilling. Her first ball! She was only at the beginning of everything. It seemed to her that she had never known what the night was like before. Up till now it had been dark, silent, beautiful very often—oh, yes—but mournful somehow. Solemn. And now it would never be like that again—it had opened dazzling bright.

"Care for an ice?" said her partner. And they went through the swing doors, down the passage, to the supper room. Her cheeks burned, she was fearfully thirsty. How sweet the ices looked on little glass plates, and how cold the frosted spoon was, iced too! And when they came back to the hall there was the fat man waiting for her by the door. It gave her quite a shock again to see how old he was; he ought to have been on the stage with the fathers and mothers. And when Leila compared him with her other partners he looked shabby. His waistcoat was creased, there was a button off his glove, his coat looked as if it was dusty with French chalk.

"Come along, little lady," said the fat man. He scarcely troubled to clasp her, and they moved away so gently, it was more like walking than dancing. But he said not a word about the floor. "Your first dance, isn't it?" he murmured.

"How *did* you know?"

"Ah," said the fat man, "that's what it is to be old!" He wheezed faintly as he steered her past an awkward couple. "You see, I've been doing this kind of thing for the last thirty years."

"Thirty years?" cried Leila. Twelve years before she was born!

"It hardly bears thinking about, does it?" said the fat man gloomily. Leila looked at his bald head, and she felt quite sorry for him.

"I think it's marvelous to be still going on," she said kindly.

"Kind little lady," said the fat man, and he pressed her a little closer, and hummed a bar of the waltz. "Of course," he said, "you can't hope to last anything like as long as that. No-o," said the fat man, "long before that you'll be sitting up there on the stage, looking on, in your nice black velvet. And these pretty arms will have turned into little short fat ones, and you'll beat time with such a different kind of fan—a black bony one." The fat man seemed to shudder. "And you'll smile away like the poor old dears up there, and point to your daughter, and tell the elderly lady next to you how some dreadful man tried to kiss her at the club ball. And your heart will ache, ache"— the fat man squeezed her closer still, as if he really was sorry for that poor heart— "because no one wants to kiss you now. And you'll say how unpleasant these polished floors are to walk on, how dangerous they are. Eh, Mademoiselle Twinkletoes?" said the fat man softly.

Leila gave a light little laugh, but she did not feel like laughing. Was it—could it all be true? It sounded terribly true. Was this first ball only the beginning of her last ball after all? At that the music seemed to change; it sounded sad, sad it rose upon a great sigh. Oh, how quickly things changed! Why didn't happiness last for ever? For ever wasn't a bit too long.

"I want to stop," she said in a breathless voice. The fat man led her to the door.

"No," she said, "I won't go outside. I won't sit down. I'll just stand here, thank you." She leaned against the wall, tapping with her foot, pulling up her gloves and trying to smile. But deep inside her a little girl threw her pinafore over her head and sobbed. Why had he spoiled it all?

"I say, you know," said the fat man, "you mustn't take me seriously, little lady."

"As if I should!" said Leila, tossing her small dark head and sucking her underlip. . . .

Again the couples paraded. The swing doors opened and shut. Now new music was given out by the bandmaster. But Leila didn't want to dance any more. She wanted to be home, or sitting on the veranda listening to those baby owls. When she looked through the dark windows at the stars, they had long beams like wings. . . .

But presently a soft, melting, ravishing tune began, and a young man with curly hair bowed before her. She would have to dance, out of politeness, until she could find Meg. Very stiffly she walked into the middle; very haughtily she put her hand on his sleeve. But in one minute, in one turn, her feet glided, glided. The lights, the azaleas, the dresses, the pink faces, the velvet chairs, all became one beautiful flying wheel. And when her next partner bumped her into the fat man and he said, "Par*don*," she smiled at him more radiantly than ever. She didn't even recognize him again.

QUESTIONS FOR DISCUSSION AND WRITING

1. The beginning of the story suggests that for Leila the whole world is dancing before the ball has begun. What does her projection of the ball onto the outer world tell us about her and her view of the ball?

2. The fat man gives Leila a vision of her future that she finds disturbing. Why? How realistic is that vision?

3. At the end of the story Leila is dancing with a young man, and we are told that she doesn't even recognize the fat man. What does her lack of recognition suggest? Do you think she has forgotten the future he has foretold?

WITI IHIMAERA (1944–   )

His First Ball _____ *1989*

Just why it was that he, Tuta Wharepapa, should receive the invitation was a mystery to him. Indeed, when it came, in an envelope bearing a very imposing crest, his mother mistook it for something entirely different—notice of a traffic misdemeanour, a summons perhaps, or even worse, an overdue account. She fingered it gingerly, holding it as far away from her body as possible—just in case a pair of hands came out to grab her fortnightly cheque—and said, 'Here, Tuta. It must be a bill.' She thrust it quickly at her son before he could get away and, wriggling her fingers to get rid of the taint, waited for him to open it.

'Hey—' Tuta said as he stared down at the card. His face dropped such a long way that his mother—her name was Coral—became alarmed. Visions of pleading in court on his behalf flashed through her mind. 'Oh, Tuta, how bad is it?' she said as she prepared to defend her son against all-comers. But Tuta remained speechless and Coral had to grab the card from his hands. 'What's this?' she asked. The card was edged with gold:

> The Aide-de-Camp in Waiting
> Is Desired By Their Excellencies

'Oh, Tuta, what have you done?' Coral said. But Tuta was still in a state of shock. Then, 'Read on, Mum,' he said.

> To Invite Mr Tuta Wharepapa
> To A Dance At Government House

Coral's voice drifted away into speechlessness like her son's. Then she compressed her lips and jabbed Tuta with an elbow. 'I'm tired of your jokes,' she said. 'It's not my joke, Mum,' Tuta responded. 'I know you, Tuta,' Coral continued. 'True, Mum, honest. One of the boys must be having me on.' Coral looked at Tuta, unconvinced. 'Who'd want to have *you* at their flash party?' she asked. 'Just wait till I get the joker who sent this,' Tuta swore to himself. Then Coral began to laugh. 'You? Go to Government House? You don't even know how to bow!' And she laughed and laughed so much at the idea that Tuta couldn't take it. 'Where are you going, Your Highness?' Coral asked. 'To find out who sent this,' Tuta replied, waving the offending invitation in her face. 'By the time I finish with him—or her'—because he suddenly realised Coral herself might have sent it '—they'll be laughing on the other side of their face.' With that, he strode out of the kitchen. 'Oh, Tuta?' he heard Coral call, all la-di-da, 'If you ore gooing pahst Government Howse please convay may regahrds to—' and she burst out laughing again.

Tuta leapt on to his motorbike and, over the rest of the day, roared around the city calling on his mates from the factory. 'It wasn't me, Tuta,' Crazy-Joe said as he sank a red ball in the billiard saloon, 'but I tell you, man, you'll look great in a suit.' Nor was it Blackjack over at the garage, who said, 'But listen, mate, when you go grab some of those Diplo number plates for me, ay?' And neither was it Des, who moonlighted as Desirée Dawn at the strip club, or Sheree, who worked part time at the pinball parlour. 'You couldn't take a partner, could you?' Desirée Dawn breathed hopefully. 'Nah, you wouldn't be able to fit on my bike,' Tuta said—apart from which he didn't think a six-foot transvestite with a passion for pink boas and slit satin dresses would enjoy it all that much. By the end of the day Tuta was no wiser, and when he arrived at Bigfoot's house and found his mate waiting for him in a tiara, he knew that word was getting around. Then it came to him that perhaps the invitation was real after all. Gloria Simmons would know—she was the boss's secretary and knew some lords.

'Oh,' Mrs Simmons whispered reverently as Tuta handed her the crested envelope. She led Tuta into the sitting-room. 'It looks real,' she said as she held it to the light. Then she opened the envelope and, incredulous, asked, '*You* received this?' Tuta nodded. 'You didn't just pick it up on the street,' Mrs Simmons continued, 'and put your name on it?' Offended, Tuta shook his head, saying 'You don't think I want to go, do you?' Mrs Simmons pursed her lips and said, 'Perhaps there's another Tuta Wharepapa, and you got his invitation in error.' And Mrs Simmons's teeth smiled and said, 'In that case, let me ring Government House and let them know.' With that, Mrs Simmons went into another room, where Tuta heard her dialling. Then *her* voice went all la-di-da too as she trilled, 'Ooo, Gahverment Howse? May ay speak to the Aide-de-Camp? Ooo, har do yoo do. So sorry to trouble you but ay am ringing to advayse you—' Tuta rolled his eyes—how come everybody he told about the invitation got infected by some kind of disease! Then he became acutely aware that Mrs Simmons had stopped talking. He heard her gasp. He heard her say in her own lingo, 'You mean to tell me that this is for real? That you people actually sent an invite to a—a—boy who packs batteries in a factory?' She put down the telephone and returned to the sitting-room. She was pale but calm as she said, 'Tuta dear, difficult though this may be, can you remember the woman who came to look at the factory about two months ago?' Tuta knitted his eyebrows. 'Yeah, I think so. That must have been when we opened the new extension.' Mrs Simmons closed her eyes. 'The woman, Tuta. The woman.' Tuta thought again. 'Oh yeah, there *was* a lady, come to think of it, a horsey-looking lady who—' Mrs Simmons interrupted him. 'Tuta, dear, that lady was the wife of the Governor-General.'

Dazed, Tuta said, 'But she didn't say who she was.' And he listened as Mrs Simmons explained that Mrs Governor-General had been very impressed by the workers at the factory and that Tuta was being invited to represent them. 'Of course you will have to go,' Mrs Simmons said. 'One does not say "No" to the Crown.' Then Mrs Simmons got up and telephoned Tuta's mother. 'Coral? Gloria here. Listen, about Tuta, you and I should talk about what is required. What for? Why, when he goes to the ball of course! Now—' *Me? Go to a ball?* Tuta thought. *With all those flash people, all those flash ladies with their crowns and diamonds and emeralds? Not bloody likely—Bigfoot can go, he's already got a tiara, yeah. Not me. They'll have to drag me there. I'm not going. Not me. No fear. No WAY.* But he knew, when he saw the neighbours waiting for him at home that, of course, his mother had already flapped her mouth to everybody. 'Oh yes,' she was telling the neighbours when Tuta walked in, 'it was delivered by special messenger. This dirty big black car came and a man, must have been a flunkey, knocked on the door and—' Then Coral saw Tuta and, 'Oh Tuta,' she cried, opening her arms to him as if she hadn't seen him for days.

After that, of course, there was no turning back. The boss from the factory called to put the hard word on Tuta. Mrs Simmons RSVPeed by telephone and—'Just in case, Tuta dear'—by letter and, once that was done, he had to go. The rest of his mates at the factory got into the act, also, cancelling the airline booking he made to get out of town and, from thereon in, followed him everywhere. 'Giz a break, fellas,' Tuta pleaded as he tried to get out, cajole or bribe himself out of the predicament. But Crazy-Joe only said, 'Lissen, if you don't get there then I'm—' and he drew a finger across his throat, and Blackjack said, 'Hey, man, I know a man who knows a man who can get us a Rolls for the night—' and Bigfoot just handed him the tiara. And boy, did Coral ever turn out to be the walking compendium of What To Do And How To Do It At A Ball. 'Gloria says that we have to take you to a tailor so you can hire a suit. Not just any suit and none of your purple numbers either. A black *conservative* suit. And then we have to get you a bowtie and you have to wear black shoes—so I reckon a paint job on your brown ones will do. You've got a white shirt, thank goodness, but we'll have to get some new socks—calf length so that when you sit down people won't see your hairy legs. Now, what else? Oh yes, I've already made an appointment for you to go to have your hair cut, no buts, Tuta, and the boys are taking you there, so don't think you're going to wriggle out of it. By the time that dance comes around we'll have you decked out like the Prince of Wales—' which was just what Tuta was afraid of.

But that was only the beginning. Not only did his appearance have to be radically altered, but his manners had to be brushed up also—and Mrs Simmons was the first to have a go. 'Tuta dear,' she said when he knocked on her door, 'Do come in. Yes, take your boots off but on THE NIGHT, the shoes stay *on*. Please, come this way. No, Tuta, *after* me, just a few steps behind. Never barge, Tuta and don't shamble along. Be PROUD, Tuta, be HAUGHTY'—and she showed him how to put his nose in the air. Tuta followed her, his nose so high that he almost tripped, into the dining-room. 'Voila!' she said. 'Ay?' Tuta answered. Mrs Simmons then realised that this was going to be very difficult. 'I said, "Ta ra!"' She had set the table with a beautiful cloth—and it appeared to be laid with thousands of knives, forks and spoons. 'This is what it will be like at the ball,' she explained. 'Oh boy,' Tuta said. 'Now, because I'm a lady you must escort me to my seat,' Mrs Simmons said. 'Huh? Can't you walk there yourself?' Tuta asked. 'Just *do* it,' Mrs Simmons responded dangerously, 'and *don't* push me all the way under the table, Tuta, just to the edge will do—' and then, under her breath '—Patience, Gloria dear, *patienza*.' Once seated, she motioned Tuta to a chair opposite her. 'Gee, thanks,' he said. Mrs Simmons paused, thoughtfully, and said, 'Tuta dear, when in doubt don't say *anything*. Just shut your mouth.' She shivered, but really, the boy would only understand common language, '—and keep it shut.' Then she smiled. 'Now follow every action that I make.' Exaggerating the movements for Tuta's benefit, Mrs Simmons said, 'First, take up the spoon. No, not that one, *that* one. That's for your soup, that's for the second course, that's for the third course, that's for the fourth—' Tuta looked helplessly at her. 'Can't I use the same knives and things all the time?' he asked. '*Never*,' Mrs Simmons shivered. 'Well, what's all these courses for?' Tuta objected. 'Why don't they just stick all the kai on the table at once?' Mrs Simmons deigned not to answer. Instead she motioned to the glasses, saying, 'Now *this* is for white wine, this for red wine, this for champagne and this for cognac.' Tuta sighed, saying 'No beer? Thought as much.' Refusing to hear him, Mrs Simmons proceeded, 'You sip your wine just like you sip the soup. Like *so*,' and she showed him. 'No, Tuta, not too fast.

And leave the bowl *on* the table, *don't* put it to your lips. No, *don't* slurp. Oh my goodness. Very GOOD, Tuta! Now wipe your lips with the napkin.' Tuta looked puzzled. 'Ay?' he asked. 'The paper napkin on your lap,' Mrs Simmons said. 'This hanky thing?' Tuta responded. 'Why, Tuta!' Mrs Simmons's teeth said, 'How clever of you to work that out. Shall we proceed to the second course? Good!' Mrs Simmons felt quite sure that Professor Higgins didn't have it *this* bad.

Then, of course, there was the matter of learning how to dance—not hot rock but slow *slow* dancing, holding a girl, 'You know,' Mrs Simmons said, *'together,'* adding, 'and young ladies at the ball are never allowed to decline.' So Tuta made a date with Desirée Dawn after hours at the club. Desirée was just overwhelmed to be asked for advice and told her friends Alexis Dynamite and Chantelle Derrier to help her. 'Lissun, honey,' Desirée said as she cracked her gum. 'No matter what the dance is, there's always a basic rhythm.' Chantelle giggled and said, 'Yeah, very basic.' Ignoring her, Desirée hauled Tuta on to the floor, did a few jeté's and, once she had limbered up, said, 'Now *you* lead,' and 'Oo, honey, I didn't know you were so masterful.' Alexis fluttered her false eyelashes and, 'You two don't need music at *all*,' she whispered. Nevertheless, Alexis ran the tape and the music boomed across the club floor. 'This isn't ball music,' Tuta said as he heard the raunch scream out of the saxes. 'How do *you* know?' Chantelle responded. And Tuta had the feeling that he wasn't going to learn how to dance in any way except improperly. 'Lissun,' Desirée said, 'Alexis and I will show you. Move your butt over here, Lexie. Now, Tuta honey, just watch. Can ya hear the rhythum? Well you go *boom* and a *boom* and a *boom boom boom*.' And Alexis screamed and yelled, 'Desirée, he wants to dance with the girl, not *make* her in the middle of the floor.' And Chantelle only made matters worse by laughing, 'Yeah, you stupid slut, you want him to end up in prison like you?' At which Desirée gasped, walked over to Chantelle, peeled off both Chantelle's false eyelashes, said, 'Can you see better? Good,' and lammed her one in the mouth. As he exited, Tuta knew he would have better luck with Sheree at the pinball parlour—she used to be good at roller skating and could even do the splits in mid-air.

So it went on. The fitting at the tailor's was duly accomplished ('Hmmmmnnnn,' the tailor said as he measured Tuta up. 'Your shoulders are too wide, your hips too large, you have shorter legs than you should have but—Hmmmmnnnn'), his hair was trimmed to within an inch of propriety, and he painted his brown shoes black. His lessons continued with Mrs Simmons, Tuta's mother, the workers from the factory— even the boss—all pitching in to assist Tuta in the etiquette required. For instance: 'If you're talking you ask about the weather. This is called polite conversation. You say "Isn't it lovely?" to everything, even if it isn't. You always say "Yes" if you're offered something, even if you don't want it. The man with the medals is *not* the waiter. He is His Excellency. The lady who looks like a horse is not in drag and you should *not* ask if her tiara fell off the same truck as Bigfoot's.'

Then, suddenly it was time for Tuta to go to the ball. 'Yes, Mum,' he said to Coral as she fussed around him with a clothes brush, 'I've got a hanky, I've brushed my teeth three times already, the invite is in my pocket—' And when Tuta stepped out the door the whole world was there—the boss, Mrs Simmons, Crazy-Joe, Blackjack, Bigfoot and others from the factory, Desirée Dawn and the neighbours. 'Don't let us down,' the boss said. 'Not too much food on the fork,' Mrs Simmons instructed. 'The third boom is the one that does it,' Desirée Dawn called. 'Don't forget the Diplo plates,' Blackjack whispered. 'And don't drink too much of the beer,' Coral said. Then, there was the car, a Jaguar festooned with white ribbons and two small dolls on the bonnet. 'It's a ball I'm off to,' Tuta said sarcastically, 'not a wedding.' Blackjack shrugged his shoulders. 'Best I could do, mate, and this beauty was just sitting there outside the church and—' He got in and started the motor. Tuta sat in the back and, suddenly, Bigfoot and Crazy-Joe were in either side. 'The boss's orders,' they said. 'We deliver you to the door or else—' Outside, Tuta saw the boss draw a line across their necks. The car drew away and as it did so, Mrs Simmons gave a small scream. 'Oh my goodness, I forgot to tell Tuta that if Nature calls he should not use the bushes,' she said.

Looking back, Tuta never quite understood how he ever survived that journey. At one point a police car drew level on the motorway, but when they looked over at the Jaguar and saw Tuta he could just imagine their disbelief, *Nah. Couldn't possibly . . . Nah.* His head was whirling with all the etiquette he had learnt and all the instructions he had to remember. He trembled, squirmed, palpitated and sweated all over the seat. Then he was there, and Blackjack was showing the invitation, and the officer at the gate was looking doubtfully at the wedding decorations, and then 'Proceed ahead, sir,' the officer said. *What a long drive,* Tuta thought. *What a big palace. And look at all those flash people. And they're all going in.* 'Well, mate,' Blackjack said, 'Good luck. Look for us in the car park.' And Crazy-Joe said, 'Hey, give the missus a whirl for me, ay?' and with that, and a squeal of tires (Blackjack was always such a show-off), they were gone.

He was alone. Him. Tuta Wharepapa. Standing there. At the entrance way. Inside he heard music and the laughter of the guests. Then someone grabbed his arm and said, 'Come along!' and before he knew it he was inside and being propelled along a long hallway. And the young woman who had grabbed him was suddenly pulled away by her companion, and Tuta was alone again. *Oh boy,* he thought. *Look at this red carpet.* He felt quite sure that the paint was running off his shoes and that there were great big black footmarks all the way to where he was now standing. Then a voice BOOMED ahead, and Tuta saw that there was a line of people in front and they were handing their invitations in to the bouncer. Tuta joined them. The bouncer was very old and very dignified—he looked, though, as if he should have been retired from the job years ago. *Nah,* Tuta thought. *He couldn't be a bouncer. Must be a toff.* The toff looked Tuta up and down and thrust out his white-gloved hand. 'I got an invitation,' Tuta said. 'True. I got one.' The toff read the card and his eyebrows arched. 'Your name?' he BOOMED. 'Tuta.' Couldn't he read? Then the toff turned away in the direction of a huge ballroom that stretched right to the end of the world. The room seemed to be hung with hundreds of chandeliers and *thousands* of people were either dancing or standing around the perimeter. There were steps leading down to the ballroom and, at the bottom, was a man wearing medals and a woman whose tiara wasn't as sparkly as Bigfoot's—*them.* And Tuta felt *sure,* when the Major-Domo—for that was who the toff was—stepped forward and opened his mouth to announce him, that *everybody* must have heard him BOOM—

'Your Excellencies, Mr Tutae Tockypocka.'

Tuta looked for a hole to disappear into. He tried to backpedal down the hallway but there were people behind him. 'No, you got it wrong,' he said between clenched teeth to the Major-Domo. 'Tutae's a rude word.' But the Major-Domo simply sniffed, handed back the invitation, and motioned Tuta down the stairs. Had *they* heard? In trembling anticipation Tuta approached the Governor-General. 'Mr Horrynotta?' the Governor-General smiled. 'Splendid that you were able to come along. Dear? Here's Mr Tutae.' And in front of him was Mrs Governor-General. 'Mr Forrimoppa, how kind of you to come. May I call you Tutae? Please let me introduce you to Lord Wells.' And Lord Wells, too. 'Mr Mopperuppa, quite a mouth ful, what. Not so with Tutae, what?' *You don't know the half of it*, Tuta thought gloomily. And then Mrs Governor-General just *had* to, didn't she, giggle and pronounce to all and sundry, 'Everybody, you must meet Mr Tutae.' And that's who Tuta became all that evening. 'Have you met Mr Tutae yet? No? Mr Tutae, this is Mr—' And Tuta would either shake hands or do a stiff little bow and look around for that hole in the floor. He once made an attempt to explain what 'tutae' was but heard Mrs Simmons's voice: 'If in doubt, Tuta, *don't*.' So instead he would draw attention away from that word by asking about the weather. 'Do you think it will rain?' he would ask. 'Oh, not inside, Mr Tutae!'—and the word got around that Mr Tutae was such a wit, so funny, so quaint, that he soon found himself exactly where he didn't want to be—at the centre of attention. In desperation, he asked every woman to dance. 'Why, certainly, Mr Tutae!' they said, because ladies never said no. So he danced with them all—a fat lady, a slim lady, a lady whose bones cracked all the time—and, because he was nervous, he went *boom* at every third step, and *that* word got around too. And as the Governor-General waltzed past he shouted, 'Well done, Tutae, jolly good show.'

No matter what he tried to do Tuta could never get away from being at the centre of the crowd or at the centre of attention. Instead of being gratified, however, Tuta became more embarrassed. Everybody seemed to laugh at his every word, even when it wasn't funny, or to accept his way of dancing because it was so *daring*. It seemed as if he could get away with anything. At the same time, Tuta suddenly realised that he was the only Maori there and that perhaps people were mocking him. He wasn't a real person to them, but rather an Entertainment. Even when buffet dinner was served, the crowd still seemed to mock him, pressing in upon him with 'Have some hors-d'oeuvres, Mr Tutae. Some *escalope* of veal, perhaps? You must try the pâté de foie gras! A slice of *jambon*? What about some langouste? Oh, the raspberry gâteau is just divine!' It was as if the crowd knew very well his ignorance of such delicacies and, by referring to them, was putting him down. In desperation Tuta tried some caviar. 'Oh, Mr Tutae, we can see that you just love caviar!' Tuta gave a quiet, almost dangerous, smile. 'Yes,' he said. 'I think it's just divine.'

So it went on. But then, just after the buffet, a Very Important Person arrived and, relieved, Tuta found himself deserted. Interested, he watched as the one who had just arrived became the centre of attention. 'It always happens this way,' a voice said behind Tuta. 'I wouldn't worry about it.' Startled, Tuta turned around and saw a huge fern. 'Before you,' the fern continued, 'it was me.' Then Tuta saw that a young woman was sitting behind the fern. 'I'm not worried,' he said to her, 'I'm glad.' The woman sniffed and said, 'You certainly looked as if you were enjoying it.' Tuta parted the fronds to get a good look at the woman's face—it was a pleasant face, one which could be pretty if it didn't frown so much. 'Shift over,' Tuta said. 'I'm coming to join you.' He sidled around the plant and sat beside her. 'My name is—' he began. 'Yes, I know,' the woman said quickly, 'Mr Tutae.' Tuta shook his head vigorously, 'No, not Tutae. Tuta.' The woman looked at him curiously and, 'Is there a difference?' she asked. 'You better believe it,' Tuta said. 'Oh—' the woman sniffed. 'I'm Joyce.'

The music started to play again. Joyce squinted her eyes and Tuta sighed, 'Why don't you put on your glasses?' Joyce squealed, 'How did you know?' before popping them on and parting the fronds. 'I'm a sociology student,' Joyce muttered. 'Don't you think people's behaviour is just amazing? I mean ay-mayzing?' Tuta shrugged his shoulders and wondered if Joyce was looking at something he couldn't see. 'I mean,' Joyce continued, 'look at them out there, just look at them. This could be India under the Raj. All this British Imperial graciousness and yet the carpet is being pulled from right beneath their feet.' Puzzled, Tuta tried to see the ball through Joyce's eyes, but failed. 'Ah well,' Joyce sighed. Then she put her hand out to Tuta so that he could shake it, saying 'Goodbye, Mr Tuta.' Tuta looked at her and, 'Are you going?' he asked. 'Oh no,' Joyce said, 'I'm staying here until everybody leaves. But you must go out and reclaim attention.' Tuta laughed. 'That new guy's welcome,' he said. 'But don't you want to fulfill their expectations?' Joyce asked. Tuta paused, and 'If that means what I think it means, no,' he said. 'Good,' Joyce responded, 'You are perfectly capable of beating them at their own game. Good luck.'

Then, curious, Tuta asked, 'What did you mean when you said that before me it had been you?' Joyce shifted uneasily, took off her glasses and said, 'Well, I'm not a Maori, but I thought it would have been obvious—' Oh, Tuta thought, she's a plain Jane and people have been making fun of her. 'But that doesn't matter to me,' Tuta said gallantly. 'Really?' Joyce asked. 'I'll prove it,' Tuta said. 'How about having the next dance.' Joyce gasped, 'Are you sure?' Taken aback, Tuta said, 'Of course, I'm sure.' And Joyce said, 'But are you sure you're sure!' To show her, Tuta stood up and took her hand. Joyce sighed and shook her head. 'Well, don't say I didn't warn you.' Then she stood up . . . and up . . . and UP.

'Oh,' Tuta said as he parted the fronds to look up at Joyce's face. She must have been six feet six at least. He and Joyce regarded each other miserably. Joyce bit her lip. Well you asked for it, Tuta thought. 'Come on,' he said, 'let's have a good time.' He reached up, grabbed her waist, put his face against her chest, and they waltzed into the middle of the floor. There, Tuta stood as high on his toes as possible. Oh, why did I come? he thought. Then the music ended and he took Joyce back to the fern. 'I'm sorry I'm such a bad dancer,' she apologised. 'I always took the man's part at school.' Tuta smiled at her, 'That's no sweat. Well—' And he was just about to leave her when he suddenly realised that after all he and Joyce were both outsiders really. And it came to him that, bloody hell, if you could not join them—as if he would really want to do that—then, yes, he could beat them if he wanted to. Not by giving in to them, but by being strong enough to stand up to them. Dance, perhaps, but using his own steps. Listen, also, not to the music of the band but to the music in his head. He owed it, after all, to generous but silly wonderful mixed-up Mum, Mrs Simmons, Desirée Dawn, and the boys—Crazy-Joe, Blackjack and Bigfoot—who were out there but wanting to know enough to get in. But they needed to come in on their own terms—that's what they would have to learn—as the real people they were and not as carbon copies of the people already on the inside. Once they learnt that, oh, world, watch out, for your walls will come down in a flash, like Jericho.

'Look,' Tuta said, 'how about another dance!' Joyce looked at him in disbelief. 'You're a sucker for punishment, aren't you!' she muttered. 'Why?' Tuta bowed, mockingly. 'Well, for one thing, it would be just divine.' At that, Joyce let out a peal of laughter. She stood up again. 'Thank you,' Joyce whispered. Then, 'You know, this is my first ball.' And Tuta smiled and 'It's *my* first ball too,' he said. 'From now on, balls like these will never be the same again.' He took her hand and the band began to wail a sweet but *oh-so-mean* saxophone solo as he led her on to the floor.

QUESTIONS FOR DISCUSSION AND WRITING

1. Indirectly, we learn a great deal about Tuta's social class. What information do we infer about him and his role in society?
2. Tuta's mother and friends invest much time preparing him for the ball. Why? What does the ball represent to them?
3. Joyce considers herself an outsider, just as Tuta is. How do their feelings of discomfort compare? Which one would be more likely to "fit in"—and why?

QUESTIONS FOR CROSS READING: VENTURING OUT INTO THE WORLD

1. "Her First Ball" focuses on the point of view of a young woman, and "His First Ball" focuses on the point of view of a young man. What is the significance of the gender difference in the telling of the stories?
2. Leila belongs to the upper class, whereas Tuta belongs to the working class. How does their class status affect their responses to the balls and others' responses to them? Do the two stories view class in the same way?
3. As a country cousin, Leila is unfamiliar with the experience provided by the ball. In what ways is her status as an outsider like and unlike that of Tuta?
4. Mansfield's fat old man and Ihimaera's Joyce single out the main characters, offering them a new point of view about the ball. Do the two characters have similar lessons to teach the young protagonists? Are we meant to take their lessons seriously?
5. Both Mansfield and Ihimaera are New Zealanders writing about New Zealand, and Ihimaera wrote "His First Ball" as a kind of response to Mansfield's story. Mansfield, however, is a European New Zealander, and Ihimaera is a Maori. What is the nature of Ihimaera's response to Mansfield? Do the two stories share similar themes, or is Ihimaera criticizing Mansfield's message?

Death and Beyond

DYLAN THOMAS (1914–1953)

Do not go gentle into that good night _____ *1951*

> Do not go gentle into that good night,
> Old age should burn and rave at close of day
> Rage, rage against the dying of the light.
>
> Though wise men at their end know dark is right,
> 5 Because their words had forked no lightning they
> Do not go gentle into that good night.
>
> Good men, the last wave by, crying how bright
> Their frail deeds might have danced in a green bay,
> Rage, rage against the dying of the light.
>
> 10 Wild men who caught and sang the sun in flight,
> And learn, too late, they grieved it on its way,
> Do not go gentle into that good night.
>
> Grave men, near death, who see with blinding sight
> Blind eyes could blaze like meteors and be gay,
> 15 Rage, rage against the dying of the light.
>
> And you, my father, there on the sad height,
> Curse, bless, me now with your fierce tears, I pray.
> Do not go gentle into that good night.
> Rage, rage against the dying of the light.

QUESTIONS FOR DISCUSSION AND WRITING

1. How does each stanza of the poem present a different image of those who must die? What do these images suggest about death itself and how the dying approach it?
2. Thomas uses light imagery throughout the poem. What does he associate with light? Is there any suggestion of dark imagery?

LINDA PASTAN (1932–   )

Go Gentle _____ *1982*

> You have grown wings of pain
> and flap around the bed like a wounded gull

calling for water, calling for tea, for grapes
whose skins you cannot penetrate.
Remember when you taught me   5
how to swim? Let go, you said,
the lake will hold you up.
I long to say, Father let go
and death will hold you up.
Outside the fall goes on without us.   10
How easily the leaves give in,
I hear them on the last breath of wind,
passing this disappearing place.

QUESTIONS FOR DISCUSSION AND WRITING

1. How does the speaker describe the dying father?
2. What images does the poem associate with death? What do these images suggest
   about the act of dying and death itself?

EMILY DICKINSON (1830–1886)

I heard a Fly buzz—when I died— _____ *1862, 1896*

I heard a Fly buzz—when I died—
The Stillness in the Room
Was like the Stillness in the Air—
Between the Heaves of Storm—

The Eyes around—had wrung them dry—   5
And Breaths were gathering firm
For that last Onset—when the King
Be witnessed—in the Room—

I willed my Keepsakes—Signed away
What portion of me be   10
Assignable—and then it was
There interposed a Fly—

With Blue—uncertain stumbling Buzz—
Between the light—and me—
And then the Windows failed—and then   15
I could not see to see—

QUESTIONS FOR DISCUSSION AND WRITING

1. Why might a person who is dying think of the "Stillness in the Room" as like the stillness "Between the Heaves of Storm"?
2. The speaker of the poem refers to those gathered around the deathbed as "Eyes" and "Breaths" rather than as people. Why?
3. Dickinson uses dashes rather than commas and periods, and she capitalizes nouns. How does her use of punctuation and capitalization affect the way we read the poem?
4. The speaker focuses on the fly in the room. What associations do we have with flies—and how do those associations work in terms of the poem?

MARILYN NELSON WANIEK (1946–)

Emily Dickinson's Defunct   *1978*

```
       She used to
       pack poems
       in her hip pocket.
       Under all the
   5   gray old lady
       clothes she was
       dressed for action.
       She had hair,
       imagine,
  10   in certain places, and
       believe me
       she smelled human
       on a hot summer day.
       Stalking snakes
  15   or counting
       the thousand motes
       in sunlight
       she walked just
       like an Indian.
  20   She was New England's
       favorite daughter,
       she could pray
       like the devil.
       She was a
  25   two-fisted woman,
       this babe.
       All the flies
       just stood around
```

and buzzed
when she died.

QUESTIONS FOR DISCUSSION AND WRITING

1. How does Waniek's poem suggest that Emily Dickinson is less detached from humanity than Dickinson's life and poems might indicate? What vision of humanity does Waniek's poem offer?
2. Waniek says that Dickinson is "defunct" rather than dead. What are the implications of "defunct"?
3. The last lines of Waniek's poem refer to Dickinson's poem "I heard a Fly buzz." What do the flies mean in Waniek's poem? Do they mean the same thing in Dickinson's poem?

QUESTIONS FOR CROSS READING: DEATH AND BEYOND

1. The poems in this section present opposing views about dying. What do the differences tell us about the speakers' views of death—and of life?
2. Which of the poems are you most sympathetic to? In other words, which poems most accurately express your idea of what you would hope death to be like for yourself or your loved ones?
3. One could argue that a nineteenth-century poet such as Dickinson was more familiar with death than we are: the death of young people was more common in earlier times, and deaths often occurred at home rather than in hospitals. Does Dickinson seem more comfortable with the idea of death than the modern poets do? Why or why not?

FURTHER REFLECTIONS: A COLLECTION OF WORKS ON THE THEME OF LIFE PASSAGES

Included in this section are pieces of literature that touch on the theme of Life Passages. If Umberto Eco is right that "every story tells a story that has already been told," each of the works that follow is in its own way a "retelling." Each asks us to take another look at the times of our own and others' lives, at the moments of youth, age, and death that give our lives structure and meaning. The works that follow do not, then, have explicit retellings of their own. Instead, they reflect further the issues and images of the life passages we all encounter.

Poetry

ELIZABETH BISHOP (1911–1979)

Sestina _____ 1965

       September rain falls on the house.
       In the failing light, the old grandmother
       sits in the kitchen with the child
       beside the Little Marvel Stove,
5   reading the jokes from the almanac,
       laughing and talking to hide her tears.

       She thinks that her equinoctial tears
       and the rain that beats on the roof of the house
       were both foretold by the almanac,
10   but only known to a grandmother.
       The iron kettle sings on the stove.
       She cuts some bread and says to the child,

       It's time for tea now; but the child
       is watching the teakettle's small hard tears
15   dance like mad on the hot black stove,
       the way the rain must dance on the house.
       Tidying up, the old grandmother
       hangs up the clever almanac

       on its string. Birdlike, the almanac
20   hovers half open above the child,
       hovers above the old grandmother
       and her teacup full of dark brown tears.
       She shivers and says she thinks the house
       feels chilly, and puts more wood in the stove.

25   *It was to be,* says the Marvel Stove.
       I know what I know, says the almanac.
       With crayons the child draws a rigid house
       and a winding pathway. Then the child
       puts in a man with buttons like tears
30   and shows it proudly to the grandmother.

       But secretly, while the grandmother
       busies herself about the stove,
       the little moons fall down like tears
       from between the pages of the almanac
35   into the flower bed the child
       has carefully placed in the front of the house.

Time to plant tears, says the almanac.
The grandmother sings to the marvelous stove
and the child draws another inscrutable house.

QUESTIONS FOR DISCUSSION AND WRITING

1. How would you summarize the "story" of the poem? Why do you think the grand-mother is crying?

2. As the title says, the poem is a **sestina:** a poem with six stanzas of six lines each, with the last word of each line being repeated in a different order in each of the stanzas. This form leads to the repetition of six key words: "house," "grandmother," "child," "stove," "almanac," and "tears." What ideas does the poem associate with each of the words? Do their meanings shift as the poem progresses?

WILLIAM BLAKE (1757–1827)
The Lamb _____ *1789*

    Little Lamb, who made thee?
      Dost thou know who made thee?
   Gave thee life, and bid thee feed

By the stream and o'er the mead;
5   Gave thee clothing of delight,
Softest clothing, wooly, bright;
Gave thee such a tender voice,
Making all the vales rejoice?
    Little Lamb, who made thee?
10   Dost thou know who made thee?

    Little Lamb, I'll tell thee,
    Little Lamb, I'll tell thee:
He is callèd by thy name,
For he calls himself a Lamb.
15   He is meek, and he is mild;
He became a little child.
I a child, and thou a lamb,
We are callèd by his name.
    Little Lamb, God bless thee!
20   Little Lamb, God bless thee!

QUESTIONS FOR DISCUSSION AND WRITING

1. The speaker of the poem is a child. How do the language of the poem and the vision it offers seem childlike?
2. Who does the child believe has made the lamb? How are the creator, the child, and the lamb linked?
3. Look at Blake's illustration for the poem. In what ways does it reflect the perspective offered by the poem?

The Tyger   *1794*

Tyger! Tyger! burning bright
In the forests of the night,
What immortal hand or eye
Could frame thy fearful symmetry?

5   In what distant deeps or skies
Burnt the fire of thine eyes?
On what wings dare he aspire?
What the hand, dare seize the fire?

And what shoulder, & what art,
10   Could twist the sinews of thy heart?
And when thy heart began to beat,
What dread hand? & what dread feet?

What the hammer? what the chain?
In what furnace was thy brain?
What the anvil? what dread grasp   15
Dare its deadly terrors clasp?

When the stars threw down their spears,
And water'd heaven with their tears,
Did he smile his work to see?
Did he who made the Lamb make thee?   20

Tyger! Tyger! burning bright
In the forests of the night,
What immortal hand or eye
Dare frame thy fearful symmetry?

QUESTIONS FOR DISCUSSION AND WRITING

1. "The Tyger" was included in Blake's *Songs of Experience*, a series of poems representing adult experience; "The Lamb" was included in Blake's *Songs of Innocence*, a

series representing childlike innocence. In what ways does "The Tyger" provide more of an adult perspective than "The Lamb" does?

2. "The Tyger" does not answer the questions it asks. Why are those questions left open? What does the poem suggest about the tiger's creator and the method of creation?

3. The poem asks us to see the "tiger" as "fearful." Does Blake's illustration show a fearful beast? Why or why not?

4. The poem asks, "Did he who made the Lamb make thee?" How would you answer that question?

GWENDOLYN BROOKS (1917–2000)

We Real Cool _____ 1950

The Pool Players. Seven at the Golden Shovel.

> We real cool. We
> Left school. We
>
> Lurk late. We
> Strike straight. We
>
> Sing sin. We
> Thin gin. We
>
> Jazz June. We
> Die soon.

5

QUESTIONS FOR DISCUSSION AND WRITING

1. What do the details in the poem suggest about the speakers?

2. The poem is set up in such a way that "We" ends all lines but the last. What is the effect of putting "We" at the ends of the lines rather than at the beginnings?

3. The Golden Shovel is presumably the name of the pool parlor. What does the name suggest about the pool players?

ROBERT FROST (1874–1963)

Birches _____ 1916

> When I see birches bend to left and right
> Across the lines of straighter darker trees,
> I like to think some boy's been swinging them.

But swinging doesn't bend them down to stay
As ice-storms do. Often you must have seen them   5
Loaded with ice a sunny winter morning
After a rain. They click upon themselves
As the breeze rises, and turn many-colored
As the stir cracks and crazes their enamel.
Soon the sun's warmth makes them shed crystal shells   10
Shattering and avalanching on the snow-crust—
Such heaps of broken glass to sweep away
You'd think the inner dome of heaven had fallen.
They are dragged to the withered bracken by the load,
And they seem not to break; though once they are bowed   15
So low for long, they never right themselves:
You may see their trunks arching in the woods
Years afterwards, trailing their leaves on the ground
Like girls on hands and knees that throw their hair
Before them over their heads to dry in the sun.   20
But I was going to say when Truth broke in
With all her matter-of-fact about the ice-storm,
I should prefer to have some boy bend them
As he went out and in to fetch the cows—
Some boy too far from town to learn baseball,   25
Whose only play was what he found himself,
Summer or winter, and could play alone.
One by one he subdued his father's trees
By riding them down over and over again
Until he took the stiffness out of them,   30
And not one but hung limp, not one was left
For him to conquer. He learned all there was
To learn about not launching out too soon
And so not carrying the tree away
Clear to the ground. He always kept his poise   35
To the top branches, climbing carefully
With the same pains you use to fill a cup
Up to the brim, and even above the brim.
Then he flung outward, feet first, with a swish,
Kicking his way down through the air to the ground.   40
So was I once myself a swinger of birches.
And so I dream of going back to be.
It's when I'm weary of considerations,
And life is too much like a pathless wood
Where your face burns and tickles with the cobwebs   45
Broken across it, and one eye is weeping
From a twig's having lashed across it open.
I'd like to get away from earth awhile
And then come back to it and begin over.
May no fate willfully misunderstand me   50

And half grant what I wish and snatch me away
Not to return. Earth's the right place for love:
I don't know where it's likely to go better.
I'd like to go by climbing a birch tree,
55   And climb black branches up a snow-white trunk
Toward heaven, till the tree could bear no more,
But dipped its top and set me down again.
That would be good both going and coming back.
One could do worse than be a swinger of birches.

QUESTIONS FOR DISCUSSION AND WRITING

1. According to the speaker, what does it mean to be "a swinger of birches"?
2. At several points in the poem, the speaker refers to heaven. What connections does the poem ask us to make among heaven, earth, and birches? Among birches, childhood, and later life?
3. The poem seems to repudiate Truth "With all her matter-of-fact." Does that mean that the poem is neither truthful nor matter-of-fact? If the poem isn't expressing Truth, what *is* it expressing?
4. Read the poem aloud, paying particular attention to its sounds and rhythms. How do those sounds and rhythms reinforce the poem's mood and the actions it describes?

SEAMUS HEANEY (1939–   )

Mid-Term Break   1966

I sat all morning in the college sick bay
Counting bells knelling classes to a close.
At two o'clock our neighbors drove me home.

In the porch I met my father crying—
5   He had always taken funerals in his stride—
And Big Jim Evans saying it was a hard blow.

The baby cooed and laughed and rocked the pram
When I came in, and I was embarrassed
By old men standing up to shake my hand

10   And tell me they were "sorry for my trouble."
Whispers informed strangers I was the eldest,
Away at school, as my mother held my hand

In hers and coughed out angry tearless sighs.
At ten o'clock the ambulance arrived
15   With the corpse, stanched and bandaged by the nurses.

Next morning I went up into the room. Snowdrops
And candles soothed the bedside; I saw him
For the first time in six weeks. Paler now,

Wearing a poppy bruise on his left temple,
He lay in the four foot box as in his cot.   20
No gaudy scars, the bumper knocked him clear.

A four foot box, a foot for every year.

QUESTIONS FOR DISCUSSION AND WRITING

1. It is not until the end of the poem that we learn that the speaker's four-year-old brother has died. How does the poem prepare us for this revelation? Or is it a surprise? How does the delaying of that information affect our perception of it?
2. How does the poem contrast adulthood and childhood? To what end?
3. The title of the poem emphasizes the "mid-term break" rather than the death. Why?

D. H. LAWRENCE (1885–1930)

Piano _____ *1918*

Softly, in the dusk, a woman is singing to me;
Taking me back down the vista of years, till I see
A child sitting under the piano, in the boom of the tingling strings
And pressing the small, poised feet of a mother who smiles as she sings.

In spite of myself, the insidious mastery of song   5
Betrays me back, till the heart of me weeps to belong
To the old Sunday evenings at home, with winter outside
And hymns in the cozy parlour, the tinkling piano our guide.

So now it is vain for the singer to burst into clamour
With the great black piano appassionato. The glamour   10
Of childish days is upon me, my manhood is cast
Down in the flood of remembrance, I weep like a child for the past.

QUESTIONS FOR DISCUSSION AND WRITING

1. The woman's song brings the speaker back to his childhood. What do we learn about that childhood? How would you describe the speaker's relationship to his mother?

2. Why does the speaker resist "the insidious mastery of song"? Why does he "weep like a child for the past"?
3. How is the singer like the mother and how is she different?
4. Read the poem aloud. How do its sounds and rhythms create its moods? How do they reinforce the themes?

LI-YOUNG LEE (1957–   )

I Ask My Mother to Sing _____ 1986

> She begins, and my grandmother joins her.
> Mother and daughter sing like young girls.
> If my father were alive, he would play
> his accordion and sway like a boat.
>
> 5   I've never been in Peking, or the Summer Palace,
> nor stood on the great Stone Boat to watch
> the rain begin on Kuen Ming Lake, the picnickers
> running away in the grass.
>
> But I love to hear it sung;
> 10   how the waterlilies fill with rain until
> they overturn, spilling water into water,
> then rock back, and fill with more.
>
> Both women have begun to cry.
> But neither stops her song.

QUESTIONS FOR DISCUSSION AND WRITING

1. The poem tells us about three generations: the grandmother, the mother, and the speaker. What does the poem suggest about the relationships among the three generations?
2. Most of the poem focuses on what the mother and grandmother sing about. What vision is created by their song? What is the mood of the song?
3. Why do the mother and grandmother cry as they sing?

SHARON OLDS (1942–   )

Rites of Passage _____ 1983

> As the guests arrive at my son's party
> They gather in the living room—

short men, men in first grade
with smooth jaws and chins.
Hands in pockets, they stand around   5
jostling, jockeying for place, small fights
breaking out and calming. One says to another
How old are you? Six. I'm seven. So?
They eye each other, seeing themselves
tiny in the other's pupils. They clear their   10
throats a lot, a room of small bankers,
they fold their arms and frown. *I could beat you
up,* a seven says to a six,
the dark cake, round and heavy as a
turret, behind them on the table. My son,   15
freckles like specks of nutmeg on his cheeks,
chest narrow as the balsa keel of a
model boat, long hands
cool and thin as the day they guided him
out of me, speaks up as a host   20
for the sake of the group.
We could easily kill a two-year-old,
he says in his clear voice. The other
men agree, they clear their throats
like Generals, they relax and get down to   25
playing war, celebrating my son's life.

QUESTIONS FOR DISCUSSION AND WRITING

1. Several times the speaker refers to the boys as "men." In what ways are they like men? In what ways are they like boys?
2. The speaker's son says, "We could easily kill a two-year-old." Why does he say that? How do we respond to the statement? With amusement? Horror?
3. The poem is titled "Rites of Passage." In what ways does it describe "rites of passage"? What are the rites, or ceremonies? Passage to what?
4. How does the speaker of the poem respond to the boys' conversation? Do you think the birthday child's father would have responded the same way? Why or why not?

PERCY BYSSHE SHELLEY (1792–1822)

Ozymandias _____ *1818*

I met a traveler from an antique land
Who said: "Two vast and trunkless legs of stone

Stand in the desert . . . Near them on the sand,
Half-sunk, a shattered visage lies, whose frown,
5   And wrinkled lip, and sneer of cold command,
Tell that its sculptor well those passions read
Which yet survive, stamped on these lifeless things,
The hand that mocked them, and the heart that fed:
And on the pedestal these words appear:
10   'My name is Ozymandias, king of kings:
Look on my works, ye Mighty, and despair.'
Nothing beside remains. Round the decay
Of that colossal wreck, boundless and bare
The lone and level sands stretch far away."

QUESTIONS FOR DISCUSSION AND WRITING

1. What does the reader learn about Ozymandias? How do we respond to him?
2. When the reader looks at the "shattered visage," *does* he despair? Why or why not?
3. What does the poem seem to be saying about the mighty Ozymandias, about the sculptor, and about the sculpture? Are all three destroyed by time? Why or why not? What connections does the poem suggest between death and art?
4. Who is the "I"? Who is the "traveler"? Does it matter that these two voices/characters tell us the story?

Short Stories

SHERMAN ALEXIE (1966–   )

A Good Story   *1993*

The Quilting

A quiet Saturday reservation afternoon and I pretend sleep on the couch while my mother pieces together another quilt on the living room floor.

"You know," she says. "Those stories you tell, they're kind of sad, enit?"

I keep my eyes closed.

"Junior," she says. "Don't you think your stories are too sad?"

My efforts to ignore her are useless.

"What do you mean?" I ask.

She puts down her scissors and fabric, looks at me so straight that I have to sit up and open my eyes.

"Well," she says. "Ain't nobody cries that much, you know?"

I pretend to rub the sleep from my eyes, stretch my arms and legs, make small noises of irritation.

"I guess," I say. "But ain't nobody laughs as much as the people in my stories, either."

"That's true," she says.

I stand up, shake my pants loose, and walk to the kitchen to grab a Diet Pepsi with cold, cold ice.

Mom quilts silently for a while. Then she whistles.

"What?" I ask her, knowing these signals for attention.

"You know what you should do? You should write a story about something good, a real good story."

"Why?"

"Because people should know that good things always happen to Indians, too."

I take a big drink of Diet Pepsi, search the cupboards for potato chips, peanuts, anything.

"Good things happen," she says and goes back to her quilting.

I think for a moment, put my Diet Pepsi down on the counter.

"Okay," I say. "If you want to hear a good story, you have to listen."

The Story

Uncle Moses sat in his sandwich chair eating a sandwich. Between bites, he hummed an it-is-a-good-day song. He sat in front of the house he built himself fifty years before. The house sat down at random angles to the ground. The front room leaned to the west, the bedroom to the east, and the bathroom simply folded in on itself.

There was no foundation, no hidden closet, nothing built into the thin walls. On the whole, it was the kind of house that would stand even years after Moses died, held up by the tribal imagination. Driving by, the Indians would look across the field toward the house and hold it upright with their eyes, remembering *Moses lived there*.

It would be just enough to ensure survival.

Uncle Moses gave no thought to his passing on most days. Instead, he usually finished his sandwich, held the last bite of bread and meat in his mouth like the last word of a good story.

"Ya-hey," he called out to the movement of air, the unseen. A summer before, Uncle Moses listened to his nephew, John-John, talking a story. John-John was back from college and told Moses that 99 percent of the matter in the universe is invisible to the human eye. Ever since, Moses made sure to greet what he could not see.

Uncle Moses stood, put his hands on his hips, arched his back. More and more, he heard his spine playing stickgame through his skin, singing old dusty words, the words of all his years. He looked at the position of the sun to determine the time, checked his watch to be sure, and looked across the field for the children who would soon come.

The Indian children would come with half-braids, curiosity endless and essential. The children would come from throwing stones into water, from basketball and basketry, from the arms of their mothers and fathers, from the very beginning. This was the generation of HUD house, of car wreck and cancer, of commodity cheese and beef. These were the children who carried dreams in the back pockets of their blue jeans, pulled them out easily, traded back and forth.

"Dreams like baseball cards," Uncle Moses said to himself, smiled hard when he saw the first child running across the field. It was Arnold, of course, pale-skinned boy who was always teased by the other children.

Arnold ran slowly, his great belly shaking with the effort, eyes narrowed in concentration. A full-blood Spokane, Arnold was somehow born with pale, pretty skin and eyes with color continually changing from gray to brown. He liked to sit in the sandwich chair and wait for Uncle Moses to make him a good sandwich.

It took Arnold five minutes to run across the field, and all the while Moses watched him, studied his movements, the way Arnold's hair reached out in all directions, uncombed, so close to electricity, closer to lightning. He did not wear braids, could not sit long enough for his mother.

Be still, be still, she would say between her teeth, but Arnold loved his body too much to remain still.

Big as he was, Arnold was still graceful in his movements, in his hands when he touched his face listening to a good story. He was also the best basketball player in the reservation grade school. Uncle Moses sometimes walked to the playground just to watch Arnold play and wonder at the strange, often improbable gifts a person can receive.

We are all given something to compensate for what we have lost. Moses felt those words even though he did not say them.

Arnold arrived, breathing hard.

"Ya-hey, Little Man," Uncle Moses said.

"Hello, Uncle," Arnold replied, extending his hand in a half-shy, half-adult way, a child's greeting, the affirmation of friendship.

"Where are the others?" Uncle Moses asked, taking Arnold's hand in his own.

"There was a field trip," Arnold answered. "All the others went to a baseball game in Spokane. I hid until they left."

"Why?"

"Because I wanted to see you."

Moses smiled at Arnold's unplanned kindness. He held the child's hand a little tighter and pulled him up close.

"Little Man," he said. "You have done a good thing."

Arnold smiled, pulled his hand away from Moses, and covered his smile, smiling even harder.

"Uncle Moses," he said through his fingers. "Tell me a good story."

Uncle Moses sat down in the story chair and told this very story.

The Finishing

My mother sits quietly, rips a seam, begins to hum a slow song through her skinny lips.

"What you singing?" I ask.

"I'm singing an it-is-a-good-day song."

She smiles and I have to smile with her.

"Did you like the story?" I ask.

She keeps singing, sings a little louder and stronger as I take my Diet Pepsi outside and wait in the sun. It is warm, soon to be cold, but that's in the future, maybe tomorrow, probably the next day and all the days after that. Today, now, I drink what I have, will eat what is left in the cupboard, while my mother finishes her quilt, piece by piece.

Believe me, there is just barely enough goodness in all of this.

QUESTIONS FOR DISCUSSION AND WRITING

1. The narrator tells his mother "a good story." What in the story is "good"?
2. Look at the description of Moses's house. How does the house reflect Moses himself? Does it matter that the house is on a reservation?
3. There are three stories in "A Good Story": the story of the narrator and his mother, the story the narrator tells to his mother, and the story Uncle Moses tells. What themes do these three stories have in common? What is the effect on the reader of telling stories inside stories?
4. "A Good Story" is an intergenerational story. What does it suggest about the relationships between the generations?

TONI CADE BAMBARA (1939–1995)
The Lesson _____ 1972

Back in the days when everyone was old and stupid or young and foolish me and Sugar were the only ones just right, this lady moved on our block with nappy hair and proper speech and no makeup. And quite naturally we laughed at her, laughed the way we did at the junk man who went about his business like he was some big-time president and his sorry-ass horse his secretary. And we kinda hated her too, hated the way we did the winos who cluttered up our parks and pissed on our handball walls and stank up our hallways and stairs so you couldn't halfway play hide-and-seek without a goddamn gas mask. Miss Moore was her name. The only woman on the block with no first name. And she was black as hell, cept for her feet, which were fish-white and spooky. And she was always planning these boring-ass things for us to do, us being my cousin, mostly, who lived on the block cause we all moved North the same time and to the same apartment then spread out gradual to breathe. And our parents would yank our heads into some kinda shape and crisp up our clothes so we'd be presentable for travel with Miss Moore, who always looked like she was going to church, though she never did. Which is just one of the things the grownups talked about when they talked behind her back like a dog. But when she came calling with some sachet she'd sewed up or some gingerbread she'd made or some book, why then they'd all be too embarrassed to turn her down and we'd get handed over all spruced up. She'd been to college and said it was only right that she should take responsibility for the young ones' education, and she not even related by marriage or blood. So they'd go for it. Specially Aunt Gretchen. She was the main gofer in the family. You got some ole dumb shit foolishness you want somebody to go for, you send for Aunt Gretchen. She been screwed into the go-along for so long, it's a blood-deep natural thing with her. Which is how she got saddled with me and Sugar and Junior in the first place while our mothers were in a la-de-da apartment up the block having a good ole time.

So this one day Miss Moore rounds us all up at the mailbox and it's puredee hot and she's knockin herself out about arithmetic. And school suppose to let up in summer I heard, but she don't never let up. And the starch in my pinafore scratching the shit outta me and I'm really hating this nappy-head bitch and her goddamn college degree. I'd much rather go to the pool or to the show where it's cool. So me and Sugar leaning on the mailbox being surly, which is a Miss Moore word. And Flyboy checking out what everybody brought for lunch. And Fat Butt already wasting his peanut-butter-and-jelly sandwich like the pig he is. And Junebug punchin on Q.T.'s arm for potato chips. And Rosie Giraffe shifting from one hip to the other waiting for somebody to step on her foot or ask her if she from Georgia so she can kick ass, preferably Mercedes'. And Miss Moore asking us do we know what money is, like we a bunch of retards. I mean real money, she say, like it's only poker chips or monopoly papers we lay on the grocer. So right away I'm tired of this and say so. And would much rather snatch Sugar and go to the Sunset and terrorize the West Indian kids and take their hair ribbons and their money too. And Miss Moore files that remark away for next week's lesson on brotherhood, I can tell. And finally I say we oughta get to the subway cause it's cooler and besides we might meet some cute boys. Sugar done swiped her mama's lipstick, so we ready.

So we heading down the street and she's boring us silly about what things cost and what our parents make and how much goes for rent and how money ain't divided up right in this country. And then she gets to the part about we all poor and live in the slums, which I don't feature. And I'm ready to speak on that, but she steps out in the street and hails two cabs just like that. Then she hustles half the crew in with her and hands me a five-dollar bill and tells me to calculate 10 percent tip for the driver. And we're off. Me and Sugar and Junebug and Flyboy hangin out the window and hollering to everybody, putting lipstick on each other cause Flyboy a faggot anyway, and making farts with our sweaty armpits. But I'm mostly trying to figure how to spend this money. But they all fascinated with the meter ticking and Junebug starts laying bets as to how much it'll read when Flyboy can't hold his breath no more. Then Sugar lays bets as to how much it'll be when we get there. So I'm stuck. Don't nobody want to go for my plan, which is to jump out at the next light and run off to the first bar-b-que we can find. Then the driver tells us to get the hell out cause we there already. And the meter reads eighty-five cents. And I'm stalling to figure out the tip and Sugar say give him a dime. And I decide he don't need it bad as I do, so later for him. But then he tries to take off with Junebug foot still in the door so we talk about his mama something ferocious. Then we check out that we on Fifth Avenue and everybody dressed up in stockings. One lady in a fur coat, hot as it is. White folks crazy.

"This is the place," Miss Moore say, presenting it to us in the voice she uses at the museum. "Let's look in the windows before we go in."

"Can we steal?" Sugar asks very serious like she's getting the ground rules squared away before she plays. "I beg your pardon," say Miss Moore, and we fall out. So she leads us around the windows of the toy store and me and Sugar screamin, "This is mine, that's mine, I gotta have that; that was made for me, I was born for that," till Big Butt drowns us out.

"Hey, I'm going to buy that there."

"That there? You don't even know what it is, stupid."

"I do so," he say punchin on Rosie Giraffe. "It's a microscope."

"Whatcha gonna do with a microscope, fool?"

"Look at things."

"Like what, Ronald?" ask Miss Moore. And Big Butt ain't got the first notion. So here go Miss Moore gabbing about the thousands of bacteria in a drop of water and the somethinorother in a speck of blood and the million and one living things in the air around us is invisible to the naked eye. And what she say that for? Junebug go to town on that "naked" and we rolling. Then Miss Moore ask what it cost. So we all jam into the window smudgin it up and the price tag say $300. So then she ask how long'd take for Big Butt and Junebug to save up their allowances. "Too long," I say. "Yeh," adds Sugar, "outgrown it by that time." And Miss Moore say no, you never outgrow learning instruments. "Why, even medical students and interns and," blah, blah, blah. And we ready to choke Big Butt for bringing it up in the first damn place.

"This here costs four hundred eighty dollars," say Rosie Giraffe. So we pile up all over her to see what she pointin out. My eyes tell me it's a chunk of glass cracked with something heavy, and different-color inks dripped into the splits, and then the whole thing put into a oven or something. But for $480 if don't make sense.

"That's a paperweight made of semi-precious stones fused together under tremendous pressure," she explains slowly, with her hands doing the mining and all the factory work.

"So what's a paperweight?" asks Rosie Giraffe.

"To weigh paper with, dumbbell," say Flyboy, the wise man from the East.

"Not exactly," says Miss Moore, which is what she say when you warm or way off too. "It's to weigh paper down so it won't scatter and make your desk untidy." So right away me and Sugar curtsy to each other and then to Mercedes who is more the tidy type.

"We don't keep paper on top of the desk in my class," say Junebug, figuring Miss Moore crazy or lyin one.

"At home, then," she say. "Don't you have a calendar and a pencil case and a blotter and a letter-opener on your desk at home where you do your homework?" And she know damn well what our homes look like cause she nosys around in them every chance she gets.

"I don't even have a desk," say Junebug. "Do we?"

"No. And I don't get no homework neither," says Big Butt.

"And I don't even have a home," says Flyboy like he do at school to keep the white folks off his back and sorry for him. Send this poor kid to camp posters, is his specialty.

"I do," says Mercedes. "I have a box of stationery on my desk and a picture of my cat. My godmother bought the stationery and the desk. There's a big rose on each sheet and the envelopes smell like roses."

"Who wants to know about your smelly-ass stationery," say Rosie Giraffe fore I can get my two cents in.

"It's important to have a work area all your own so that . . ."

"Will you look at this sailboat, please," say Flyboy, cuttin her off and pointin to the thing like it was his. So once again we tumble all over each other to gaze at this magnificent thing in the toy store which is just big enough to maybe sail two kittens across the pond if you strap them to the posts right. We all start reciting the price tag like we in assembly. "Handcrafted sailboat of fiberglass at one thousand one hundred ninety-five dollars."

"Unbelievable," I hear myself say and am really stunned. I read it again for myself just in case the group recitation put me in a trance. Same thing. For some reason this pisses me off. We look at Miss Moore and she lookin at us, waiting for I dunno what.

"Who'd pay all that when you can buy a sailboat set for a quarter at Pop's, a tube of glue for a dime, and a ball of string for eight cents? It must have a motor and a whole lot else besides," I say. "My sailboat cost me about fifty cents."

"But will it take water?" say Mercedes with her smart ass.

"Took mine to Alley Pond Park once," say Flyboy. "String broke. Lost it. Pity."

"Sailed mine in Central Park and it keeled over and sank. Had to ask my father for another dollar."

"And you got the strap," laughed Big Butt. "The jerk didn't even have a string on it. My old man wailed on his behind."

Little Q.T. was staring hard at the sailboat and you could see he wanted it bad. But he too little and somebody'd just take it from him. So what the hell. "This boat for kids, Miss Moore?"

"Parents silly to buy something like that just to get all broke up," say Rosie Giraffe.

"That much money it should last forever," I figure.

"My father'd buy it for me if I wanted it."

"Your father, my ass," say Rosie Giraffe getting a chance to finally push Mercedes.

"Must be rich people shop here," say Q.T.

"You are a very bright boy," say Flyboy. "What was your first clue?" And he rap him on the head with the back of his knuckles, since Q.T. the only one he could get away with. Though Q.T. liable to come up behind you years later and get his licks in when you half expect it.

"What I want to know is," I says to Miss Moore though I never talk to her, I wouldn't give the bitch the satisfaction, "is how much a real boat costs? I figure a thousand'd get you a yacht any day."

"Why don't you check that out," she says, "and report back to the group?" Which really pains my ass. If you gonna mess up a perfectly good swim day least you could do is have some answers. "Let's go in," she say like she got something up her sleeve. Only she don't lead the way. So me and Sugar turn the corner to where the entrance is, but when we get there I kinda hang back. Not that I'm scared, what's there to be afraid of, just a toy store. But I feel funny, shame. But what I got to be shamed about? Got as much right to go in as anybody. But somehow I can't seem to get hold of the door, so I step away from Sugar to lead. But she hangs back too. And I look at her and she looks at me and this is ridiculous. I mean, damn, I have never ever been shy about doing nothing or going nowhere. But then Mercedes steps up and then Rosie Giraffe and Big Butt crowd in behind and shove, and next thing we all stuffed into the doorway with only Mercedes squeezing past us, smoothing out her jumper and walking right down the aisle. Then the rest of us tumble in like a glued-together jigsaw done all wrong. And people lookin at us. And it's like the time me and Sugar crashed into the Catholic church on a dare. But once we got in there and everything so hushed and holy and the candles and the bowin and the handkerchiefs on all the drooping heads, I just couldn't go through with the plan. Which was for me to run up to the altar and do a tap dance while Sugar played the nose flute and messed around in the holy water. And Sugar kept givin me the elbow. Then later teased me so bad I tied her up in the shower and turned it on and locked her in. And she'd be there till this day if Aunt Gretchen hadn't finally figured I was lyin about the boarder takin a shower.

Same thing in the store. We all walkin on tiptoe and hardly touchin the games and puzzles and things. And I watched Miss Moore who is steady watchin us like she waitin for a sign. Like Mama Drewery watches the sky and sniffs the air and takes note of just how much slant is in the bird formation. Then me and Sugar bump smack into each other, so busy gazing at the toys, 'specially the sailboat. But we don't laugh and go into our fat-lady bump-stomach routine. We just stare at that price tag. Then Sugar run a finger over the whole boat. And I'm jealous and want to hit her. Maybe not her, but I sure want to punch somebody in the mouth.

"Watcha bring us here for, Miss Moore?"

"You sound angry, Sylvia. Are you mad about something?" Givin me one of them grins like she tellin a grown-up joke that never turns out to be funny. And she's lookin very closely at me like maybe she plannin to do my portrait from memory. I'm mad, but I won't give her that satisfaction. So I slouch around the store bein very bored and say, "Let's go."

Me and Sugar at the back of the train watchin the tracks whizzin by large then small then gettin gobbled up in the dark. I'm thinkin about this tricky toy I saw in the store. A clown that somersaults on a bar then does chin-ups just cause you yank lightly at his leg. Cost $35. I could see me askin my mother for a $35 birthday clown. "You wanna who that costs what?" she'd say, cocking her head to the side to get a better view of the hole in my head. Thirty-five dollars could buy new bunk beds for Junior and Gretchen's boy. Thirty-five dollars and the whole household could go visit Granddaddy Nelson in the country. Thirty-five dollars would pay for the rent and the piano bill too. Who are these people that spend that much for performing clowns and $1000 for toy sailboats? What kinda work they do and how they live and how come we ain't in on it? Where we are is who we are, Miss Moore always pointin out. But it don't necessarily have to be that way, she always adds then waits for somebody to say that poor people have to wake up and demand their share of the pie and don't none of us know what kind of pie she talking about in the first damn place. But she ain't so smart cause I still got her four dollars from the taxi and she sure ain't getting it. Messin up my day with this shit. Sugar nudges me in my pocket and winks.

Miss Moore lines us up in front of the mailbox where we started from, seem like years ago, and I got a headache for thinkin so hard. And we lean all over each other so we can hold up under the draggy-ass lecture she always finishes us off with at the end before we thank her for borin us to tears. But she just looks at us like she readin tea leaves. Finally she say, "Well, what did you think of F.A.O. Schwarz?"

Rosie Giraffe mumbles, "White folks crazy."

"I'd like to go there again when I get my birthday money," says Mercedes, and we shove her out the pack so she has to lean on the mailbox by herself.

"I'd like a shower. Tiring day," say Flyboy.

Then Sugar surprises me by sayin, "You know, Miss Moore, I don't think all of us here put together eat in a year what that sailboat costs." And Miss Moore lights up like somebody goosed her. "And?" she say, urging Sugar on. Only I'm standin on her foot so she don't continue.

"Imagine for a minute what kind of society it is in which some people can spend on a toy what it would cost to feed a family of six or seven. What do you think?"

"I think," say Sugar pushing me off her feet like she never done before, cause I whip her ass in a minute, "that this is not much of a democracy if you ask me. Equal chance to pursue happiness means an equal crack at the dough, don't it?" Miss Moore is beside herself and I am disgusted with Sugar's treachery. So I stand on her foot one more time to see if she'll shove me. She shuts up, and Miss Moore looks at me, sorrowfully I'm thinkin. And somethin weird is goin on, I can feel it in my chest.

"Anybody else learn anything today?" lookin dead at me. I walk away and Sugar has to run to catch up and don't even seem to notice when I shrug her arm off my shoulder.

"Well, we got four dollars anyway," she says.

"Uh hunh."

"We could go to Hascombs and get half a chocolate layer and then go to the Sunset and still have plenty of money for potato chips and ice cream sodas."

"Uh hunh."

"Race you to Hascombs," she say.

We start down the block and she gets ahead which is O.K. by me cause I'm going to the West End and then over to the Drive to think this day through. She can run if she want to and even run faster. But ain't nobody gonna beat me at nuthin.

QUESTIONS FOR DISCUSSION AND WRITING

1. The story opens with Sylvia, the narrator, recalling "the days when everyone was old and stupid or young and foolish." How do we see this view of people reflected in the story itself?
2. What is the "lesson" that Miss Moore wants to teach? How does she teach it? Is it the same lesson that Sylvia learns?
3. Why is Sylvia reluctant to enter the toy store? Why does she compare that reluctance to her reluctance to go into a Catholic church "on a dare"?
4. Sylvia recalls that Miss Moore is always telling the children "Where we are is who we are." In what sense is that true? Do you agree with that statement?
5. What does Sylvia mean at the end of the story when she says "ain't nobody gonna beat me at nuthin"?

WILLA CATHER (1873–1947)

Paul's Case _____ 1905

It was Paul's afternoon to appear before the faculty of the Pittsburgh High School to account for his various misdemeanors. He had been suspended a week ago, and his father had called at the Principal's office and confessed his perplexity about his son. Paul entered the faculty room suave and smiling. His clothes were a trifle out-grown, and the tan velvet on the collar of his open overcoat was frayed and worn; but for all that there was something of the dandy about him, and he wore an opal pin in his neatly knotted black four-in-hand, and a red carnation in his buttonhole. This latter adornment the faculty somehow felt was not properly significant of the contrite spirit befitting a boy under the ban of suspension.

Paul was tall for his age and very thin, with high, cramped shoulders and a narrow chest. His eyes were remarkable for a certain hysterical brilliancy and he continually used them in a conscious, theatrical sort of way, peculiarly offensive in a boy. The pupils were abnormally large, as though he were addicted to belladonna, but there was a glassy glitter about them which that drug does not produce.

When questioned by the Principal as to why he was there, Paul stated, politely enough, that he wanted to come back to school. This was a lie, but Paul was quite accustomed to lying; found it, indeed, indispensable for overcoming friction. His teachers were asked to state their respective charges against him, which they did with such a rancor and aggrievedness as evinced that this was not a usual case. Disorder and impertinence were among the offenses named, yet each of his instructors felt that it was scarcely possible to put into words the real cause of the trouble, which lay in a sort of hysterically defiant manner of the boy's; in the contempt which they all knew he felt for them, and which he seemingly made not the least effort to conceal. Once, when he had been making a synopsis of a paragraph at the blackboard, his English teacher had stepped to his side and attempted to guide his hand. Paul had started back with a shudder and thrust his hands violently behind him. The astonished woman could scarcely have been more hurt and embarrassed had he struck at her. The insult was so involuntary and definitely personal as to be unforgettable. In one way and another he had made all his teachers, men and women alike, conscious of the same feeling of physical aversion. In one class he habitually sat with his hand shading his eyes; in another he always looked out of the window during the recitation; in another he made a running commentary on the lecture, with humorous intention.

His teachers felt this afternoon that his whole attitude was symbolized by his shrug and his flippantly red carnation flower, and they fell upon him without mercy, his English teacher leading the pack. He stood through it smiling, his pale lips parted over his white teeth. (His lips were continually twitching, and he had a habit of raising his eyebrows that was contemptuous and irritating to the last degree.) Older boys than Paul had broken down and shed tears under that baptism of fire, but his set smile did not once desert him, and his only sign of discomfort was the nervous trembling of the fingers that toyed with the buttons of his overcoat, and an occasional jerking of the other hand that held his hat. Paul was always smiling, always glancing about him, seeming to feel that people might be watching him and trying to detect something. This conscious expression, since it was as far as possible from boyish mirthfulness, was usually attributed to insolence or "smartness."

As the inquisition proceeded, one of his instructors repeated an impertinent remark of the boy's, and the Principal asked him whether he thought that a courteous speech to have made a woman. Paul shrugged his shoulders slightly and his eyebrows twitched.

"I don't know," he replied. "I didn't mean to be polite or impolite, either. I guess it's a sort of way I have of saying things regardless."

The Principal, who was a sympathetic man, asked him whether he didn't think that a way it would be well to get rid of. Paul grinned and said he guessed so. When he was told that he could go, he bowed gracefully and went out. His bow was but a repetition of the scandalous red carnation.

His teachers were in despair, and his drawing master voiced the feeling of them all when he declared there was something about the boy which none of them understood. He added: "I don't really believe that smile of his comes altogether from insolence; there's something sort of haunted about it. The boy is not strong, for one thing. I happen to know that he was born in Colorado, only a few months before his mother died out there of a long illness. There is something wrong about the fellow."

The drawing master had come to realize that, in looking at Paul, one saw only his white teeth and the forced animation of his eyes. One warm afternoon the boy had gone to sleep at his drawing-board, and his master had noted with amazement what a white, blue-veined face it was; drawn and wrinkled like an old man's about the eyes, the lips twitching even in his sleep, and stiff with a nervous tension that drew them back from his teeth.

His teachers left the building dissatisfied and unhappy; humiliated to have felt so vindictive toward a mere boy, to have uttered this feeling in cutting terms, and to have set each other on, as it were, in the gruesome game of intemperate reproach. Some of them remembered having seen a miserable street cat set at bay by a ring of tormentors.

As for Paul, he ran down the hill whistling the Soldiers' Chorus from *Faust,* looking wildly behind him now and then to see whether some of his teachers were not there to writhe under his light-heartedness. As it was now late in the afternoon and Paul was on duty that evening as usher at Carnegie Hall, he decided that he would not go home to supper. When he reached the concert hall the doors were not yet open and, as it was chilly outside, he decided to go up into the picture gallery—always deserted at this hour—where there were some of Raffaelli's gay studies of Paris streets and an airy blue Venetian scene or two that always exhilarated him. He was delighted to find no one in the gallery but the old guard, who sat in one corner, a newspaper on his knee, a black patch over one eye and the other closed. Paul possessed himself of the place and walked confidently up and down, whistling under his breath. After a while he sat down before a blue Rico and lost himself. When he bethought him to look at his watch, it was after seven o'clock, and he rose with a start and ran downstairs, making a face at Augustus, peering out from the cast-room, and an evil gesture at the Venus of Milo as he passed her on the stairway.

When Paul reached the ushers' dressing-room half-a-dozen boys were there already, and he began excitedly to tumble into his uniform. It was one of the few that at all approached fitting, and Paul thought it very becoming—though he knew that the tight, straight coat accentuated his narrow chest, about which he was exceedingly sensitive. He was always considerably excited while he dressed, twanging all over to the tuning of the strings and the preliminary flourishes of the horns in the music-room; but tonight he seemed quite beside himself, and he teased and plagued the boys until, telling him that he was crazy, they put him down on the floor and sat on him.

Somewhat calmed by his suppression, Paul dashed out to the front of the house to seat the early comers. He was a model usher; gracious and smiling he ran up and down the aisles; nothing was too much trouble for him; he carried messages and brought programmes as though it were his greatest pleasure in life, and all the people in his section thought him a charming boy, feeling that he remembered and admired them. As the house filled, he grew more and more vivacious and animated, and the color came to his cheeks and lips. It was very much as though this were a great reception and Paul were the host. Just as the musicians came out to take their places, his English teacher arrived with checks for the seats which a prominent manufacturer had taken for the season. She betrayed some embarrassment when she handed Paul the tickets, and a hauteur which subsequently made her feel very foolish. Paul was startled for a moment, and had the feeling of wanting to put her out; what business had she here among all these fine people and gay colors? He looked her over and decided that she was not appropriately dressed and must be a fool to sit downstairs in such togs. The tickets had probably been sent her out of kindness, he reflected as he put down a seat for her, and she had about as much right to sit there as he had.

When the symphony began Paul sank into one of the rear seats with a long sigh of relief, and lost himself as he had done before the Rico. It was not that symphonies, as such, meant anything in particular to Paul, but the first sigh of the instruments seemed to free some hilarious and potent spirit within him; something that struggled there like the Genius in the bottle found by the Arab fisherman. He felt a sudden zest of life; the lights danced before his eyes and the concert hall blazed into unimaginable splendor. When the soprano soloist came on, Paul forgot even the nastiness of his teacher's being there and gave himself up to the peculiar stimulus such personages always had for him. The soloist chanced to be a German woman, by no means in her first youth, and the mother of many children; but she wore an elaborate gown and a tiara, and above all she had that indefinable air of achievement, that world-shine upon her, which, in Paul's eyes, made her a veritable queen of Romance.

After a concert was over Paul was always irritable and wretched until he got to sleep, and tonight he was even more than usually restless. He had the feeling of not being able to let down, of its being impossible to give up this delicious excitement which was the only thing that could be called living at all. During the last number he withdrew and, after hastily changing his clothes in the dressing-room, slipped out to the side door where the soprano's carriage stood. Here he began pacing rapidly up and down the walk, waiting to see her come out.

Over yonder the Schenley, in its vacant stretch, loomed big and square through the fine rain, the windows of its twelve stories glowing like those of a lighted cardboard house under a Christmas tree. All the actors and singers of the better class stayed there when they were in the city, and a number of the big manufacturers of the place lived there in the winter. Paul had often hung about the hotel, watching the people go in and out, longing to enter and leave school-masters and dull care behind him forever.

At last the singer came out, accompanied by the conductor, who helped her into her carriage and closed the door with a cordial *auf wiedersehen* which set Paul to wondering whether she were not an old sweetheart of his. Paul followed the carriage over to the hotel, walking so rapidly as not to be far from the entrance when the singer alighted, and disappeared behind the swinging glass doors that were opened by a negro in a tall hat and a long coat. In the moment that the door was ajar it seemed to Paul that he, too, entered. He seemed to feel himself go after her up the steps, into the warm, lighted building, into an exotic, a tropical world of shiny, glistening surfaces and basking ease. He reflected upon the mysterious dishes that were brought into the dining-room, the green bottles in buckets of ice, as he had seen them in the supper party pictures of the *Sunday World* supplement. A quick gust of wind brought the rain down with sudden vehemence, and Paul was startled to find that he was still outside in the slush of the gravel driveway; that his boots were letting in the water and his scanty overcoat was clinging wet about him; that the lights in front of the concert hall were out, and that the rain was driving in sheets between him and the orange glow of the windows above him. There it was, what he wanted—tangibly before him, like the fairy world of a Christmas pantomime, but mocking spirits stood guard at the doors, and, as the rain beat in his face, Paul wondered whether he were destined always to shiver in the black night outside, looking up at it.

He turned and walked reluctantly toward the car tracks. The end had to come sometime; his father in his night-clothes at the top of the stairs, explanations that did not explain, hastily improvised fictions that were forever tripping him up, his upstairs room and its horrible yellow wall-paper, the creaking bureau with the greasy plush collar-box, and over his painted wooden bed the pictures of George Washington and John Calvin, and the framed motto, "Feed my Lambs," which had been worked in red worsted by his mother.

Half an hour later, Paul alighted from his car and went slowly down one of the side streets off the main thoroughfare. It was a highly respectable street, where all the houses were exactly alike, and where businessmen of moderate means begot and reared large families of children, all of whom went to Sabbath-school and learned the shorter catechism, and were interested in arithmetic; all of whom were as exactly alike as their homes, and of a piece with the monotony in which they lived. Paul never went up Cordelia Street without a shudder of loathing. His home was next to the house of the Cumberland minister. He approached it tonight with the nerveless sense of defeat, the hopeless feeling of sinking back forever into ugliness and commonness that he had always had when he came home. The moment he turned into Cordelia Street he felt the waters close above his head. After each of these orgies of living, he experienced all the physical depression which follows a debauch; the loathing of respectable beds, of common food, of a house penetrated by kitchen odors; a shuddering repulsion for the flavorless, colorless mass of every-day existence; a morbid desire for cool things and soft lights and fresh flowers.

The nearer he approached the house, the more absolutely unequal Paul felt to the sight of it all; his ugly sleeping chamber; the cold bath-room with the grimy zinc tub, the cracked mirror, the dripping spigots; his father, at the top of the stairs, his hairy legs sticking out from his night-shirt, his feet thrust into carpet slippers. He was so much later than usual that there would certainly be inquiries and reproaches. Paul stopped short before the door. He felt that he could not be accosted by his father tonight; that he could not toss again on that miserable bed. He would not go in. He would tell his father that he had no car fare, and it was raining so hard he had gone home with one of the boys and stayed all night.

Meanwhile, he was wet and cold. He went around to the back of the house and tried one of the basement windows, found it open, raised it cautiously, and scrambled down the cellar wall to the floor. There he stood, holding his breath, terrified by the noise he had made, but the floor above him was silent, and there was no creak on the stairs. He found a soap-box, and carried it over to the soft ring of light that streamed from the furnace door, and sat down. He was horribly afraid of rats, so he did not try to sleep, but sat looking distrustfully at the dark, still terrified lest he might have awakened his father. In such reactions, after one of the experiences which made days and nights out of the dreary blanks of the calendar, when his senses were deadened, Paul's head was always singularly clear. Suppose his father had heard him getting in at the window and had come down and shot him for a burglar? Then, again, suppose his father had come down, pistol in hand, and he had cried out in time to save himself, and his father had been horrified to think how nearly he had killed him? Then, again, suppose a day should come when his father would remember that night, and wish there had been no warning cry to stay his hand? With this last supposition Paul entertained himself until daybreak.

The following Sunday was fine; the sodden November chill was broken by the last flash of autumnal summer. In the morning Paul had to go to church and Sabbath-school, as always. On seasonable Sunday afternoons the burghers of Cordelia Street always sat out on their front "stoops," and talked to their neighbors on the next stoop, or called to those across the street in neighborly fashion. The men usually sat on gay cushions placed upon the steps that led down to the sidewalk, while the women, in their Sunday "waists," sat in rockers on the cramped porches, pretending to be greatly at their ease. The children played in the streets; there were so many of them that the place resembled the recreation grounds of a kindergarten. The men on the steps—all in their shirt sleeves, their vests unbuttoned—sat with their legs well apart, their stomachs comfortably protruding, and talked of the prices of things, or told anecdotes of the sagacity of their various chiefs and overlords. They occasionally looked over the multitude of squabbling children, listened affectionately to their high-pitched, nasal voices, smiling to see their own proclivities reproduced in their offspring, and interspersed their legends of the iron kings with remarks about their sons' progress at school, their grades in arithmetic, and the amounts they had saved in their toy banks.

On this last Sunday of November, Paul sat all the afternoon on the lowest step of his "stoop," staring into the street, while his sisters, in their rockers, were talking to the minister's daughters next door about how many shirt-waists they had made in the last week, and how many waffles some one had eaten at the last church supper. When the weather was warm, and his father was in a particularly jovial frame of mind, the girls made lemonade, which was always brought out in a red-glass pitcher, ornamented with forget-me-nots in blue enamel. This the girls thought very fine, and the neighbors always joked about the suspicious color of the pitcher.

Today Paul's father sat on the top step, talking to a young man who shifted a restless baby from knee to knee. He happened to be the young man who was daily held up to Paul as a model, and after whom it was his father's dearest hope that he would pattern. This young man was of a ruddy complexion, with a compressed, red mouth, and faded, nearsighted eyes, over which he wore thick spectacles, with gold bows that curved about his ears. He was clerk to one of the magnates of a great steel corporation, and was looked upon in Cordelia Street as a young man with a future. There was a story that, some five years ago—he was now barely twenty-six—he had been a trifle dissipated, but in order to curb his appetites and save the loss of time and strength that a sowing of wild oats might have entailed, he had taken his chief's advice, oft reiterated to his employees, and at twenty-one had married the first woman whom he could persuade to share his fortunes. She happened to be an angular school-mistress, much older than he, who also wore thick glasses, and who had now borne him four children, all nearsighted, like herself.

The young man was relating how his chief, now cruising in the Mediterranean, kept in touch with all the details of the business, arranging his office hours on his yacht just as though he were at home, and "knocking off work enough to keep two stenographers busy." His father told, in turn, the plan his corporation was considering, of putting in an electric railway plant at Cairo. Paul snapped his teeth; he had an awful apprehension that they might spoil it all before he got there. Yet he rather liked to hear these legends of the iron kings that were told and retold on Sundays and holidays; these stories of palaces in Venice, yachts on the Mediterranean, and high play at Monte Carlo appealed to his fancy, and he was interested in the triumphs of these cash boys who had become famous, though he had no mind for the cash-boy stage.

After supper was over, and he had helped to dry the dishes, Paul nervously asked his father whether he could go to George's to get some help in his geometry, and still more nervously asked for car fare. This latter request he had to repeat, as his father, on principle, did not like to hear requests for money, whether much or little. He asked Paul whether he could not go to some boy who lived nearer, and told him that he ought not to leave his school work until Sunday; but he gave him the dime. He was not a poor man, but he had a worthy ambition to come up in the world. His only reason for allowing Paul to usher was that he thought a boy ought to be earning a little.

Paul bounded upstairs, scrubbed the greasy odor of the dish-water from his hands with the ill-smelling soap he hated, and then shook over his fingers a few drops of violet water from the bottle he kept hidden in his drawer. He left the house with his geometry conspicuously under his arm, and the moment he got out of Cordelia Street and boarded a downtown car, he shook off the lethargy of two deadening days, and began to live again.

The leading juvenile of the permanent stock company which played at one of the downtown theatres was an acquaintance of Paul's, and the boy had been invited to drop in at the Sunday-night rehearsals whenever he could. For more than a year Paul had spent every available moment loitering about Charley Edwards's dressing-room. He had won a place among Edwards's following not only because the young actor, who could not afford to employ a dresser, often found him useful, but because he recognized in Paul something akin to what churchmen term "vocation."

It was at the theatre and at Carnegie Hall that Paul really lived; the rest was but a sleep and a forgetting. This was Paul's fairy tale, and it had for him all the allurement of a secret love. The moment he inhaled the gassy, painty, dusty odor behind the scenes, he breathed like a prisoner set free, and felt within him the possibility of doing or saying splendid, brilliant, poetic things. The moment the cracked orchestra beat out the overture from *Martha*, or jerked at the serenade from *Rigoletto*, all stupid and ugly things slid from him, and his senses were deliciously, yet delicately, fired.

Perhaps it was because, in Paul's world, the natural nearly always wore the guise of ugliness, that a certain element of artificiality seemed to him necessary in beauty. Perhaps it was because his experience of life elsewhere was so full of Sabbath-school picnics, petty economies, wholesome advice as to how to succeed in life, and the unescapable odors of cooking, that he found this existence so alluring, these smartly-clad men and women so attractive, that he was so moved by these starry apple orchards that bloomed perennially under the limelight.

It would be difficult to put it strongly enough how convincingly the stage entrance of that theatre was for Paul the actual portal of Romance. Certainly none of the company ever suspected it, least of all Charley Edwards. It was very like the old stories that used to float about London of fabulously rich Jews, who had subterranean halls there, with palms, and fountains, and soft lamps and richly apparelled women who never saw the disenchanting light of London day. So, in the midst of that smoke-palled city, enamored of figures and grimy toil, Paul had his secret temple, his wishing carpet, his bit of blue-and-white Mediterranean shore bathed in perpetual sunshine.

Several of Paul's teachers had a theory that his imagination had been perverted by garish fiction, but the truth was that he scarcely ever read at all. The books at home were not such as would either tempt or corrupt a youthful mind, and as for reading the novels that some of his friends urged upon him—well, he got what he wanted much more quickly from music; any sort of music, from an orchestra to a barrel organ. He needed only the spark, the indescribable thrill that made his imagination master of his senses, and he could make plots and pictures enough of his own. It was equally true that he was not stage struck—not, at any rate, in the usual acceptation of that expression. He had no desire to become an actor, any more than he had to become a musician. He felt no necessity to do any of these things; what he wanted was to see, to be in the atmosphere, float on the wave of it, to be carried out, blue league after blue league, away from everything.

After a night behind the scenes, Paul found the school-room more than ever repulsive; the bare floors and naked walls; the prosy men who never wore frock coats, or violets in their buttonholes; the women with their dull gowns, shrill voices, and pitiful seriousness about prepositions that govern the dative. He could not bear to have the other pupils think, for a moment, that he took these people seriously; he must convey to them that he considered it all trivial, and was there only by way of a jest, anyway. He had autographed pictures of all the members of the stock company which he showed his classmates, telling them the most incredible stories of his familiarity with these people, of his acquaintance with the soloists who came to Carnegie Hall, his suppers with them and the flowers he sent them. When these stories lost their effect, and his audience grew listless, he became desperate and would bid all the boys good-bye, announcing that he was going to travel for a while; going to Naples, to Venice, to Egypt. Then, next Monday, he would slip back, conscious and nervously smiling; his sister was ill, and he should have to defer his voyage until spring.

Matters went steadily worse with Paul at school. In the itch to let his instructors know how heartily he despised them and their homilies, and how thoroughly he was appreciated elsewhere, he mentioned once or twice that he had no time to fool with theorems; adding—with a twitch of the eyebrows and a touch of that nervous bravado which so perplexed them—that he was helping the people down at the stock company; they were old friends of his.

The upshot of the matter was that the Principal went to Paul's father, and Paul was taken out of school and put to work. The manager at Carnegie Hall was told to get another usher in his stead; the door-keeper at the theatre was warned not to admit him to the house; and Charley Edwards remorsefully promised the boy's father not to see him again.

The members of the stock company were vastly amused when some of Paul's stories reached them—especially the women. They were hardworking women, most of them supporting indigent husbands or brothers, and they laughed rather bitterly at having stirred the boy to such fervid and florid inventions. They agreed with the faculty and with his father that Paul's was a bad case.

The east-bound train was ploughing through a January snow-storm; the dull dawn was beginning to show grey when the engine whistled a mile out of Newark. Paul started up from the seat where he had lain curled in uneasy slumber, rubbed the breath-misted window glass with his hand, and peered out. The snow was whirling in curling eddies above the white bottom lands, and the drifts lay already deep in the fields and along the fences, while here and there the long dead grass and dried weed stalks protruded black above it. Lights shone from the scattered houses, and a gang of laborers who stood beside the track waved their lanterns.

Paul had slept very little, and he felt grimy and uncomfortable. He had made the all-night journey in a day coach, partly because he was ashamed, dressed as he was, to go into a Pullman, and partly because he was afraid of being seen there by some Pittsburgh businessman, who might have noticed him in Denny & Carson's office. When the whistle awoke him, he clutched quickly at his breast pocket, glancing about him with an uncertain smile. But the little, clay-bespattered Italians were still sleeping, the slatternly women across the aisle were in open-mouthed oblivion, and even the crumby, crying babies were for the nonce stilled. Paul settled back to struggle with his impatience as best as he could.

When he arrived at the Jersey City station, he hurried through his breakfast, manifestly ill at ease and keeping a sharp eye about him. After he reached the Twenty-third Street station, he consulted a cabman, and had himself driven to a men's furnishing establishment that was just opening for the day. He spent upward of two hours there, buying with endless reconsidering and great care. His new street suit he put on in the fitting-room; the frock coat and dress clothes he had bundled into the cab with his linen. Then he drove to a hatter's and a shoe house. His next errand was at Tiffany's, where he selected his silver and a new scarf-pin. He would not wait to have his silver marked, he said. Lastly, he stopped at a trunk shop on Broadway, and had his purchases packed into various travelling bags.

It was a little after one o'clock when he drove up to the Waldorf, and after settling with the cabman, went into the office. He registered from Washington; said his mother and father had been abroad, and that he had come down to await the arrival of their steamer. He told his story plausibly and had no trouble, since he volunteered to pay for them in advance, in engaging his rooms; a sleeping-room, sitting-room and bath.

Not once, but a hundred times Paul had planned this entry into New York. He had gone over every detail of it with Charley Edwards, and in his scrap book at home there were pages of description about New York hotels, cut from the Sunday papers. When he was shown to his sitting-room on the eighth floor, he saw at a glance that everything was as it should be; there was but one detail in his mental picture that the place did not realize, so he rang for the bell boy and sent him down for flowers. He moved about nervously until the boy returned, putting away his new linen and fingering it delightedly as he did so. When the flowers came, he put them hastily into water, and then tumbled into a hot bath. Presently he came out of his white bathroom, resplendent in his new silk underwear, and playing with the tassels of his red robe. The snow was whirling so fiercely outside his windows that he could scarcely see across the street, but within the air was deliciously soft and fragrant. He put the violets and jonquils on the taboret beside the couch, and threw himself down, with a long sigh, covering himself with a Roman blanket. He was thoroughly tired; he had been in such haste, he had stood up to such a strain, covered so much ground in the last twenty-four hours, that he wanted to think how it had all come about. Lulled by the sound of the wind, the warm air, and the cool fragrance of the flowers, he sank into deep, drowsy retrospection.

It had been wonderfully simple; when they had shut him out of the theatre and concert hall, when they had taken away his bone, the whole thing was virtually determined. The rest was a mere matter of opportunity. The only thing that at all surprised him was his own courage—for he realized well enough that he had always been tormented by fear, a sort of apprehensive dread that, of late years, as the meshes of the lies he had told closed about him, had been pulling the muscles of his body tighter and tighter. Until now, he could not remember the time when he had not been dreading something. Even when he was a little boy, it was always there—behind him, or before, or on either side. There had always been the shadowed corner, the dark place into which he dared not look, but from which something seemed always to be watching him—and Paul had done things that were not pretty to watch, he knew.

But now he had a curious sense of relief, as though he had at last thrown down the gauntlet to the thing in the corner.

Yet it was but a day since he had been sulking in the traces; but yesterday afternoon that he had been sent to the bank with Denny & Carson's deposit, as usual—but this time he was instructed to leave the book to be balanced. There was above two thousand dollars in checks, and nearly a thousand in the bank notes which he had taken from the book and quietly transferred to his pocket. At the bank he had made out a new deposit slip. His nerves had been steady enough to permit of his returning to the office, where he had finished his work and asked for a full day's holiday tomorrow, Saturday, giving a perfectly reasonable pretext. The bank book, he knew, would not be returned before Monday or Tuesday, and his father would be out of town for the next week. From the time he slipped the bank notes into his pocket until he boarded the night train for New York, he had not known a moment's hesitation. It was not the first time Paul had steered through treacherous waters.

How astonishingly easy it had all been; here he was, the thing done; and this time there would be no awakening, no figure at the top of the stairs. He watched the snow flakes whirling by his window until he fell asleep.

When he awoke, it was three o'clock in the afternoon. He bounded up with a start; half of one of his precious days gone already! He spent more than an hour in dressing, watching every stage of his toilet carefully in the mirror. Everything was quite perfect; he was exactly the kind of boy he had always wanted to be.

When he went downstairs, Paul took a carriage and drove up Fifth Avenue toward the Park. The snow had somewhat abated; carriages and tradesmen's wagons were hurrying soundlessly to and fro in the winter twilight; boys in woollen mufflers were shovelling off the doorsteps; the avenue stages made fine spots of color against the white street. Here and there on the corners were stands, with whole flower gardens blooming under glass cases, against the sides of which the snow flakes stuck and melted; violets, roses, carnations, lilies of the valley—somehow vastly more lovely and alluring that they blossomed thus unnaturally in the snow. The Park itself was a wonderful stage winterpiece.

When he returned, the pause of the twilight had ceased, and the tune of the streets had changed. The snow was falling faster, lights streamed from the hotels that reared their dozen stories fearlessly up into the storm, defying the raging Atlantic winds. A long, black stream of carriages poured down the avenue, intersected here and there by other streams, tending horizontally. There were a score of cabs about the entrance of his hotel, and his driver had to wait. Boys in livery were running in and out of the awning stretched across the sidewalk, up and down the red velvet carpet laid from the door to the street. Above, about, within it all was the rumble and roar, the hurry and toss of thousands of human beings as hot for pleasure as himself, and on every side of him towered the glaring affirmation of the omnipotence of wealth.

The boy set his teeth and drew his shoulders together in a spasm of realization: the plot of all dramas, the text of all romances, the nerve-stuff of all sensations was whirling about him like the snow flakes. He burnt like a faggot in a tempest.

When Paul went down to dinner, the music of the orchestra came floating up the elevator shaft to greet him. His head whirled as he stepped into the thronged corridor, and he sank back into one of the chairs against the wall to get his breath. The lights, the chatter, the perfumes, the bewildering medley of color—he had, for a moment, the feeling of not being able to stand it. But only for a moment; these were his own people, he told himself. He went slowly about the corridors, through the writing-rooms, smoking-rooms, reception-rooms, as though he were exploring the chambers of an enchanted palace, built and peopled for him alone.

When he reached the dining-room he sat down at a table near a window. The flowers, the white linen, the many-colored wine glasses, the gay toilettes of the women, the low popping of corks, the undulating repetitions of the *Blue Danube* from the orchestra, all flooded Paul's dream with bewildering radiance. When the roseate tinge of his champagne was added—that cold, precious, bubbling stuff that creamed and foamed in his glass—Paul wondered that there were honest men in the world at all. This was what all the world was fighting for, he reflected; this was what all the struggle was about. He doubted the reality of his past. Had he ever known a place called Cordelia Street, a place where fagged-looking businessmen got on the early car; mere rivets in a machine they seemed to Paul—sickening men, with combings of children's hair always hanging to their coats, and the smell of cooking in their clothes. Cordelia Street—Ah! that belonged to another time and country; had he not always been thus, had he not sat here night after night, from as far back as he could remember, looking pensively over just such shimmering textures, and slowly twirling the stem of a glass like this one between his thumb and middle finger? He rather thought he had.

He was not in the least abashed or lonely. He had no especial desire to meet or to know any of these people; all he demanded was the right to look on and conjecture, to watch the pageant. The mere stage properties were all he contended for. Nor was he lonely later in the evening, in his loge at the Metropolitan. He was now entirely rid of his nervous misgivings, of his forced aggressiveness, of the imperative desire to show himself different from his surroundings. He felt now that his surroundings explained him. Nobody questioned the purple; he had only to wear it passively. He had only to glance down at his attire to reassure himself that here it would be impossible for anyone to humiliate him.

He found it hard to leave his beautiful sitting-room to go to bed that night, and sat long watching the raging storm from his turret window. When he went to sleep it was with the lights turned on in his bedroom; partly because of his old timidity, and partly so that, if he should wake in the night, there would be no wretched moment of doubt, no horrible suspicion of yellow wall-paper, or of Washington and Calvin above his bed.

Sunday morning the city was practically snow-bound. Paul breakfasted late, and in the afternoon he fell in with a wild San Francisco boy, a freshman at Yale, who said he had run down for a "little flyer" over Sunday. The young man offered to show Paul the night side of the town, and the two boys went out together after dinner, not returning to the hotel until seven o'clock the next morning. They had started out in the confiding warmth of a champagne friendship, but their parting in the elevator was singularly cool. The freshman pulled himself together to make his train, and Paul went to bed. He awoke at two o'clock in the afternoon, very thirsty and dizzy, and rang for ice-water, coffee, and the Pittsburgh papers.

On the part of the hotel management, Paul excited no suspicion. There was this to be said for him, that he wore his spoils with dignity and in no way made himself conspicuous. Even under the glow of his wine he was never boisterous, though he found the stuff like a magician's wand for wonder-building. His chief greediness lay in his ears and eyes, and his excesses were not offensive ones. His dearest pleasures were the grey winter twilights in his sitting-room; his quiet enjoyment of his flowers, his clothes, his wide divan, his cigarette, and his sense of power. He could not remember a time when he had felt so at peace with himself. The mere release from the necessity of petty lying, lying every day and every day, restored his self-respect. He had never lied for pleasure, even at school; but to be noticed and admired, to assert his difference from other Cordelia Street boys; and he felt a good deal more manly, more honest, even, now that he had no need for boastful pretensions, now that he could, as his actor friends used to say, "dress the part." It was characteristic that remorse did not occur to him. His golden days went by without a shadow, and he made each as perfect as he could.

On the the eighth day after his arrival in New York, he found the whole affair exploited in the Pittsburgh papers, exploited with a wealth of detail which indicated that local news of a sensational nature was at a low ebb. The firm of Denny & Carson announced that the boy's father had refunded the full amount of the theft, and that they had no intention of prosecuting. The Cumberland minister had been interviewed, and expressed his hope of yet reclaiming the motherless lad, and his Sabbath-school teacher declared that she would spare no effort to that end. The rumor had reached Pittsburgh that the boy had been seen in a New York hotel, and his father had gone East to find him and bring him home.

Paul had just come in to dress for dinner; he sank into a chair, weak to the knees, and clasped his head in his hands. It was to be worse than jail, even; the tepid waters of Cordelia Street were to close over him finally and forever. The grey monotony stretched before him in hopeless, unrelieved years; Sabbath-school, Young People's Meeting, the yellow-papered room, the damp dishtowels; it all rushed back upon him with a sickening vividness. He had the old feeling that the orchestra had suddenly stopped, the sinking sensation that the play was over. The sweat broke out on his face, and he sprang to his feet, looked about him with his white, conscious smile, and winked at himself in the mirror. With something of the old childish belief in miracles with which he had so often gone to class, all his lessons unlearned, Paul dressed and dashed whistling down the corridor to the elevator.

He had no sooner entered the dining-room and caught the measure of the music than his remembrance was lightened by his old elastic power of claiming the moment, mounting with it, and finding it all-sufficient. The glare and glitter about him, the mere scenic accessories had again, and for the last time, their old potency. He would show himself that he was game, he would finish the thing splendidly. He doubted, more than ever, the existence of Cordelia Street, and for the first time he drank his wine recklessly. Was he not, after all, one of those fortunate beings born to the purple, was he not still himself and in his own place? He drummed a nervous accompaniment to the Pagliacci music and looked about him, telling himself over and over that it had paid.

He reflected drowsily, to the swell of the music and the chill sweetness of his wine, that he might have done it more wisely. He might have caught an outboard steamer and been well out of their clutches before now. But the other side of the world had seemed too far away and too uncertain then; he could not have waited for it; his need had been too sharp. If he had to choose over again, he would do the same thing tomorrow. He looked affectionately about the dining-room, now gilded with a soft mist. Ah, it had paid indeed!

Paul was awakened next morning by a painful throbbing in his head and feet. He had thrown himself across the bed without undressing, and had slept with his shoes on. His limbs and hands were lead heavy, and his tongue and throat were parched and burnt. There came upon him one of those fateful attacks of clear-headedness that never occurred except when he was physically exhausted and his nerves hung loose. He lay still and closed his eyes and let the tide of things wash over him.

His father was in New York; "stopping at some joint or other," he told himself. The memory of successive summers on the front stoop fell upon him like a weight of black water. He had not a hundred dollars left; and he knew now, more than ever, that money was everything, the wall that stood between all he loathed and all he wanted. The thing was winding itself up; he had thought of that on his first glorious day in New York, and had even provided a way to snap the thread. It lay on his dressing-table now; he had got it out last night when he came blindly up from dinner, but the shiny metal hurt his eyes, and he disliked the looks of it.

He rose and moved about with a painful effort, succumbing now and again to attacks of nausea. It was the old depression exaggerated; all the world had become Cordelia Street. Yet somehow he was not afraid of anything, was absolutely calm; perhaps because he had looked into the dark corner at last and knew. It was bad enough, what he saw there, but somehow not so bad as his long fear of it had been. He saw everything clearly now. He had a feeling that he had made the best of it, that he had lived the sort of life he was meant to live, and for half an hour he sat staring at the revolver. But he told himself that was not the way, so he went downstairs and took a cab to the ferry.

When Paul arrived at Newark, he got off the train and took another cab, directing the driver to follow the Pennsylvania tracks out of the town. The snow lay heavy on the roadways and had drifted deep in the open fields. Only here and there the dead grass or dried weed stalks projected, singularly black, above it. Once well into the country, Paul dismissed the carriage and walked, floundering along the tracks, his mind a medley of irrelevant things. He seemed to hold in his brain an actual picture of everything he had seen that morning. He remembered every feature of both his drivers, of the toothless old woman from whom he had bought the red flowers in his coat, the agent from whom he had got his ticket, and all of his fellow-passengers on the ferry. His mind, unable to cope with vital matters near at hand, worked feverishly and deftly at sorting and grouping these images. They made for him a part of the ugliness of the world, of the ache in his head, and the bitter burning on his tongue. He stooped and put a handful of snow into his mouth as he walked, but that, too, seemed hot. When he reached a little hillside, where the tracks ran through a cut some twenty feet below him, he stopped and sat down.

The carnations in his coat were drooping with the cold, he noticed; their red glory all over. It occurred to him that all the flowers he had seen in the glass cases that first night must have gone the same way, long before this. It was only one splendid breath they had, in spite of their brave mockery at the winter outside the glass; and it was a losing game in the end, it seemed, this revolt against the homilies by which the world is run. Paul took one of the blossoms carefully from his coat and scooped a little hole in the snow, where he covered it up. Then he dozed a while, from his weak condition, seemingly insensible to the cold.

The sound of an approaching train awoke him, and he started to his feet, remembering only his resolution, and afraid lest he should be too late. He stood watching the approaching locomotive, his teeth chattering, his lips drawn away from them in a frightened smile; once or twice he glanced nervously sidewise, as though he were being watched. When the right moment came, he jumped. As he fell, the folly of his haste occurred to him with merciless clearness, the vastness of what he had left undone. There flashed through his brain, clearer than ever before, the blue of Adriatic water, the yellow of Algerian sands.

He felt something strike his chest, and that his body was being thrown swiftly through the air, on and on, immeasurably far and fast, while his limbs were gently relaxed. Then, because the picture-making mechanism was crushed, the disturbing visions flashed into black, and Paul dropped back into the immense design of things.

QUESTIONS FOR DISCUSSION AND WRITING

1. Paul feels that he is an outsider—and his father and teachers also see him as a misfit. What is it about him that makes it difficult for him to fit in? In what ways are his feelings typically adolescent, and in what ways are they individual?

2. The story contrasts two worlds: the mundane world of home and school and the exciting world of the theater and hotel. What qualities are associated with each? Do we fully accept Paul's view of the two worlds? Why or why not?

3. Paul is certain that his rightful place is in the glamorous world of the New York well-to-do. Do you agree that that is where he really "belongs"?

4. Who is to blame for "Paul's case"? Paul himself? Society? His family? The school system? If Paul had lived into adulthood, do you believe that he would have found his own happiness?

RALPH ELLISON (1914–1994)

Battle Royal _____ 1947

It goes a long way back, some twenty years. All my life I had been looking for something, and everywhere I turned someone tried to tell me what it was. I accepted their answers too, though they were often in contradiction and even self-contradictory. I was naive. I was looking for myself and asking everyone except myself questions which I, and only I, could answer. It took me a long time and much painful boomeranging of my expectations to achieve a realization everyone else appears to have been born with: That I am nobody but myself. But first I had to discover that I am an invisible man!

And yet I am no freak of nature, nor of history. I was in the cards, other things having been equal (or unequal) eighty-five years ago. I am not ashamed of my grandparents for having been slaves. I am only ashamed of myself for having at one time been ashamed. About eighty-five years ago they were told that they were free, united with others of our country in everything pertaining to the common good, and, in everything social, separate like the fingers of the hand. And they believed it. They exulted in it. They stayed in their place, worked hard, and brought up my father to do the same. But my grandfather is the one. He was an odd old guy, my grandfather, and I am told I take after him. It was he who caused the trouble. On his deathbed he called my father to him and said, "Son, after I'm gone I want you to keep up the good fight. I never told you, but our life is a war and I have been a traitor all my born days, a spy in the enemy's country ever since I give up my gun back in the Reconstruction. Live with your head in the lion's mouth. I want you to overcome 'em with yeses, undermine 'em with grins, agree 'em to death and destruction, let 'em swoller you till they vomit or bust wide open." They thought the old man had gone out of his mind. He had been the meekest of men. The younger children were rushed from the room, the shades drawn and the flame of the lamp turned so low that it sputtered on the wick like the old man's breathing. "Learn it to the younguns," he whispered fiercely; then he died.

But my folks were more alarmed over his last words than over his dying. It was as though he had not died at all, his words caused so much anxiety. I was warned emphatically to forget what he had said and, indeed, this is the first time it has been mentioned outside the family circle. It had a tremendous effect upon me, however. I could never be sure of what he meant. Grandfather had been a quiet old man who never made any trouble, yet on his deathbed he had called himself a traitor and a spy, and he had spoken of his meekness as a dangerous activity. It became a constant puzzle which lay unanswered in the back of my mind. And whenever things went well for me I remembered my grandfather and felt guilty and uncomfortable. It was as though I was carrying out his advice in spite of myself. And to make it worse, everyone loved me for it. I was praised by the most lily-white men of the town. I was considered an example of desirable conduct—just as my grandfather had been. And what puzzled me was that the old man had defined it as *treachery.* When I was praised for my conduct I felt a guilt that in some way I was doing something that was really against the wishes of the white folks, that if they had understood they would have desired me to act just the opposite, that I should have been sulky and mean, and that that really would have been what they wanted, even though they were fooled and thought they wanted me to act as I did. It made me afraid that some day they would look upon me as a traitor and I would be lost. Still I was more afraid to act any other way because they didn't like that at all. The old man's words were like a curse. On my graduation day I delivered an oration in which I showed that humility was the secret, indeed, the very essence of progress. (Not that I believed this—how could I, remembering my grandfather?—I only believed that it worked.) It was a great success. Everyone praised me and I was invited to give the speech at a gathering of the town's leading white citizens. It was a triumph for our whole community.

It was in the main ballroom of the leading hotel. When I got there I discovered that it was on the occasion of a smoker, and I was told that since I was to be there anyway I might as well take part in the battle royal to be fought by some of my schoolmates as part of the entertainment. The battle royal came first.

All of the town's big shots were there in their tuxedoes, wolfing down the buffet foods, drinking beer and whiskey and smoking black cigars. It was a large room with a high ceiling. Chairs were arranged in neat rows around three sides of a portable boxing ring. The fourth side was clear, revealing a gleaming space of polished floor. I had some misgivings over the battle royal, by the way. Not from a distaste for fighting, but because I didn't care too much for the other fellows who were to take part. They were tough guys who seemed to have no grandfather's curse worrying their minds. No one could mistake their toughness. And besides, I suspected that fighting a battle royal might detract from the dignity of my speech. In those pre-invisible days I visualized myself as a potential Booker T. Washington. But the other fellows didn't care too much for me either, and there were nine of them. I felt superior to them in my way, and I didn't like the manner in which we were all crowded together into the servants' elevator. Nor did they like my being there. In fact, as the warmly lighted floors flashed past the elevator we had words over the fact that I, by taking part in the fight, had knocked one of their friends out of a night's work.

We were led out of the elevator through a rococo hall into an anteroom and told to get into our fighting togs. Each of us was issued a pair of boxing gloves and ushered out into the big mirrored hall, which we entered looking cautiously about us and whispering, lest we might accidentally be heard above the noise of the room. It was foggy with cigar smoke. And already the whiskey was taking effect. I was shocked to see some of the most important men of the town quite tipsy. They were all there— bankers, lawyers, judges, doctors, fire chiefs, teachers, merchants. Even one of the more fashionable pastors. Something we could not see was going on up front. A clarinet was vibrating sensuously and the men were standing up and moving eagerly forward. We were a small tight group, clustered together, our bare upper bodies touching and shining with anticipatory sweat, while up front the big shots were becoming increasingly excited over something we still could not see. Suddenly I heard the school superintendent, who had told me to come, yell, "Bring up the shines, gentlemen! Bring up the little shines!"

We were rushed up to the front of the ballroom, where it smelled even more strongly of tobacco and whiskey. Then we were pushed into place. I almost wet my pants. A sea of faces, some hostile, some amused, ringed around us, and in the center, facing us, stood a magnificent blonde—stark naked. There was dead silence. I felt a blast of cold air chill me. I tried to back away, but they were behind me and around me. Some of the boys stood with lowered heads, trembling. I felt a wave of irrational guilt and fear. My teeth chattered, my skin turned to goose flesh, my knees knocked. Yet I was strongly attracted and looked in spite of myself. Had the price of looking been blindness, I would have looked. The hair was yellow like that of a circus kewpie doll, the face heavily powdered and rouged, as though to form an abstract mask, the eyes hollow and smeared a cool blue, the color of a baboon's butt. I felt a desire to spit upon her as my eyes brushed slowly over her body. Her breasts were firm and round as the domes of East Indian temples, and I stood so close as to see the fine skin tex-ture and beads of pearly perspiration glistening like dew around the pink and erected buds of her nipples. I wanted at one and the same time to run from the room, to sink through the floor, or go to her and cover her from my eyes and the eyes of the others with my body; to feel the soft thighs, to caress her and destroy her, to love her and murder her, to hide from her, and yet to stroke where below the small American flag tattooed upon her belly her thighs formed a capital V. I had a notion that of all in the room she saw only me with her impersonal eyes.

And then she began to dance, a slow sensuous movement; the smoke of a hun-dred cigars clinging to her like the thinnest of veils. She seemed like a fair bird-girl girdled in veils calling to me from the angry surface of some gray and threatening sea. I was transported. Then I became aware of the clarinet playing and the big shots yelling at us. Some threatened us if we looked and others if we did not. On my right I saw one boy faint. And now a man grabbed a silver pitcher from a table and stepped close as he dashed ice water upon him and stood him up and forced two of us to sup-port him as his head hung and moans issued from his thick bluish lips. Another boy began to plead to go home. He was the largest of the group, wearing dark red fighting trunks much too small to conceal the erection which projected from him as though in answer to the insinuating low-registered moaning of the clarinet. He tried to hide himself with his boxing gloves.

And all the while the blonde continued dancing, smiling faintly at the big shots who watched her with fascination, and faintly smiling at our fear. I noticed a certain merchant who followed her hungrily, his lips loose and drooling. He was a large man who wore diamond studs in a shirtfront which swelled with the ample paunch un-derneath, and each time the blonde swayed her undulating hips he ran his hand through the thin hair of his bald head and, with his arms upheld, his posture clumsy like that of an intoxicated panda, wound his belly in a slow and obscene grind. This creature was completely hypnotized. The music had quickened. As the dancer flung herself about with a detached expression on her face, the men began reaching out to touch her. I could see their beefy fingers sink into the soft flesh. Some of the others tried to stop them as she began to move around the floor in graceful circles, as they gave chase, slipping and sliding over the polished floor. It was mad. Chairs went crash-ing, drinks were spilt, as they ran laughing and howling after her. They caught her just as she reached a door, raised her from the floor, and tossed her as college boys are tossed at a hazing, and above her red, fixed-smiling lips I saw the terror and disgust in her eyes, almost like my own terror and that which I saw in some of the other boys. As I watched, they tossed her twice and her soft breasts seemed to flatten against the air and her legs flung wildly as she spun. Some of the more sober ones helped her to escape. And I started off the floor, heading for the anteroom with the rest of the boys.

Some were still crying in hysteria. But as we tried to leave we were stopped and ordered to get into the ring. There was nothing to do but what we were told. All ten of us climbed under the ropes and allowed ourselves to be blindfolded with broad bands of white cloth. One of the men seemed to feel a bit sympathetic and tried to cheer us up as we stood with our backs against the ropes. Some of us tried to grin. "See that boy over there?" one of the men said. "I want you to run across at the bell and give it to him right in the belly. If you don't get him, I'm going to get you. I don't like his looks." Each of us was told the same. The blindfolds were put on. Yet even then I had been going over my speech. In my mind each word was as bright as flame. I felt the cloth pressed into place, and frowned so that it would be loosened when I relaxed.

But now I felt a sudden fit of blind terror. I was unused to darkness. It was as though I had suddenly found myself in a dark room filled with poisonous cotton-mouths. I could hear the bleary voices yelling insistently for the battle royal to begin.

"Get going in there!"

"Let me at that big nigger!"

I strained to pick up the school superintendent's voice, as though to squeeze some security out of that slightly more familiar sound.

"Let me at those black sonsabitches!" someone yelled.

"No, Jackson, no!" another voice yelled. "Here, somebody, help me hold Jack."

"I want to get at that ginger-colored nigger. Tear him limb from limb," the first voice yelled.

I stood against the ropes trembling. For in those days I was what they called ginger-colored, and he sounded as though he might crunch me between his teeth like a crisp ginger cookie.

Quite a struggle was going on. Chairs were being kicked about and I could hear voices grunting as with a terrific effort. I wanted to see, to see more desperately than ever before. But the blindfold was tight as a thick skin-puckering scab and when I raised my gloved hands to push the layers of white aside a voice yelled, "Oh, no you don't, black bastard! Leave that alone!"

"Ring the bell before Jackson kills him a coon!" someone boomed in the sudden silence. And I heard the bell clang and the sound of the feet scuffling forward.

A glove smacked against my head. I pivoted, striking out stiffy as someone went past, and felt the jar ripple along the length of my arm to my shoulder. Then it seemed as though all nine of the boys had turned upon me at once. Blows pounded me from all sides while I struck out as best I could. So many blows landed upon me that I wondered if I were not the only blindfolded fighter in the ring, or if the man called Jackson hadn't succeeded in getting me after all.

Blindfolded, I could no longer control my motions. I had no dignity. I stumbled about like a baby or a drunken man. The smoke had become thicker and with each new blow it seemed to sear and further restrict my lungs. My saliva became like hot bitter glue. A glove connected with my head, filling my mouth with warm blood. It was everywhere. I could not tell if the moisture I felt upon my body was sweat or blood. A blow landed hard against the nape of my neck. I felt myself going over, my head hitting the floor. Streaks of blue light filled the black world behind the blindfold. I lay prone, pretending that I was knocked out, but felt myself seized by hands and yanked to my feet. "Get going, black boy! Mix it up!" My arms were like lead, my head smarting from blows. I managed to feel my way to the ropes and held on, trying to catch my breath. A glove landed in my mid-section and I went over again, feeling as though the smoke had become a knife jabbed into my guts. Pushed this way and that by the legs milling around me, I finally pulled erect and discovered that I could see the black, sweat-washed forms weaving in the smoky-blue atmosphere like drunken dancers weaving to the rapid drumlike thuds of blows.

Everyone fought hysterically. It was complete anarchy. Everybody fought everybody else. No group fought together for long. Two, three, four, fought one, then turned to fight each other, were themselves attacked. Blows landed below the belt and in the kidney, with the gloves open as well as closed, and with my eye partly opened now there was not so much terror. I moved carefully, avoiding blows, although not too many to attract attention, fighting from group to group. The boys groped about like blind, cautious crabs crouching to protect their mid-sections, their heads pulled in short against their shoulders, their arms stretched nervously before them, with their fists testing the smoke-filled air like the knobbed feelers of hypersensitive snails. In one corner I glimpsed a boy violently punching the air and heard him scream in pain as he smashed his hand against a ring post. For a second I saw him bent over holding his hand, then going down as a blow caught his unprotected head. I played one group against the other, slipping in and throwing a punch then stepping out of range while pushing the others into the melee to take the blows blindly aimed at me. The smoke was agonizing and there were no rounds, no bells at three minute intervals to relieve our exhaustion. The room spun round me, a swirl of lights, smoke, sweating bodies surrounded by tense white faces. I bled from both nose and mouth, the blood spattering upon my chest.

The men kept yelling, "Slug him, black boy! Knock his guts out!"

"Uppercut him! Kill him! Kill that big boy!"

Taking a fake fall, I saw a boy going down heavily beside me as though we were felled by a single blow, saw a sneaker-clad foot shoot into his groin as the two who had knocked him down stumbled upon him. I rolled out of range, feeling a twinge of nausea.

The harder we fought the more threatening the men became. And yet, I had begun to worry about my speech again. How would it go? Would they recognize my ability? What would they give me?

I was fighting automatically when suddenly I noticed that one after another of the boys was leaving the ring. I was surprised, filled with panic, as though I had been left alone with an unknown danger. Then I understood. The boys had arranged it among themselves. It was the custom for the two men left in the ring to slug it out for the winner's prize. I discovered this too late. When the bell sounded two men in tuxedoes leaped into the ring and removed the blindfold. I found myself facing Tatlock, the biggest of the gang. I felt sick at my stomach. Hardly had the bell stopped ringing in my ears than it clanged again and I saw him moving swiftly toward me.

Thinking of nothing else to do I hit him smash on the nose. He kept coming, bringing the rank sharp violence of stale sweat. His face was a black blank of a face, only his eyes alive—with hate of me and aglow with a feverish terror from what had happened to us all. I became anxious. I wanted to deliver my speech and he came at me as though he meant to beat it out of me. I smashed him again and again, taking his blows as they came. Then on a sudden impulse I struck him lightly and as we clinched, I whispered, "Fake like I knocked you out, you can have the prize."

"I'll break your behind," he whispered hoarsely.

"For *them*?"

"For *me*, sonofabitch!"

They were yelling for us to break it up and Tatlock spun me half around with a blow, and as a joggled camera sweeps in a reeling scene, I saw the howling red faces crouching tense beneath the cloud of blue-gray smoke. For a moment the world wavered, unraveled, flowed, then my head cleared and Tatlock bounced before me. That fluttering shadow before my eyes was his jabbing left hand. Then falling forward, my head against his damp shoulder, I whispered,

"I'll make it five dollars more."

"Go to hell!"

But his muscles relaxed a trifle beneath my pressure and I breathed, "Seven?"

"Give it to your ma," he said, ripping me beneath the heart.

And while I still held him I butted him and moved away. I felt myself bombarded with punches. I fought back with hopeless desperation. I wanted to deliver my speech more than anything else in the world, because I felt that only these men could judge truly my ability, and now this stupid clown was ruining my chances. I began fighting carefully now, moving in to punch him and out again with my greater speed. A lucky blow to his chin and I had him going too—until I heard a loud voice yell, "I got my money on the big boy."

Hearing this, I almost dropped my guard. I was confused: Should I try to win against the voice out there? Would not this go against my speech, and was not this a moment for humility, for nonresistance? A blow to my head as I danced about sent my right eye popping like a jack-in-the-box and settled my dilemma. The room went red as I fell. It was a dream fall, my body languid and fastidious as to where to land, until the floor became impatient and smashed up to meet me. A moment later I came to. An hypnotic voice said FIVE emphatically. And I lay there, hazily watching a dark red spot of my own blood shaping itself into a butterfly, glistening and soaking into the soiled gray world of the canvas.

When the voice drawled TEN I was lifted up and dragged to a chair. I sat dazed. My eye pained and swelled with each throb of my pounding heart and I wondered if now I would be allowed to speak. I was wringing wet, my mouth still bleeding. We were grouped along the wall now. The other boys ignored me as they congratulated Tatlock and speculated as to how much they would be paid. One boy whimpered over his smashed hand. Looking up front, I saw attendants in white jackets rolling the portable ring away and placing a small square rug in the vacant space surrounded by chairs. Perhaps, I thought, I will stand on the rug to deliver my speech.

Then the M.C. called to us, "Come on up here boys and get your money." We ran forward to where the men laughed and talked in their chairs, waiting. Everyone seemed friendly now.

"There it is on the rug," the man said. I saw the rug covered with coins of all dimensions and a few crumpled bills. But what excited me, scattered here and there, were the gold pieces.

"Boys, it's all yours," the man said. "You get all you grab."

"That's right, Sambo," a blond man said, winking at me confidentially.

I trembled with excitement, forgetting my pain. I would get the gold and the bills, I thought. I would use both hands. I would throw my body against the boys nearest me to block them from the gold.

"Get down around the rug now," the man commanded, "and don't anyone touch it until I give the signal."

"This ought to be good," I heard.

As told, we got around the square rug on our knees. Slowly the man raised his freckled hand as we followed it upward with our eyes.

I heard, "These niggers look like they're about to pray!"

Then, "Ready," the man said. "Go!"

I lunged for a yellow coin lying on the blue design of the carpet, touching it and sending a surprised shriek to join those rising around me. I tried frantically to remove my hand but could not let go. A hot, violent force tore through my body, shaking me like a wet rat. The rug was electrified. The hair bristled up on my head as I shook myself free. My muscles jumped, my nerves jangled, writhed. But I saw that this was not stopping the other boys. Laughing in fear and embarrassment, some were holding back and scooping up the coins knocked off by the painful contortions of the others. The men roared above us as we struggled.

"Pick it up, goddamnit, pick it up!" someone called like a bass-voiced parrot. "Go on, get it!"

I crawled rapidly around the floor, picking up the coins, trying to avoid the coppers and to get greenbacks and the gold. Ignoring the shock by laughing, as I brushed the coins off quickly, I discovered that I could contain the electricity—a contradiction, but it works. Then the men began to push us onto the rug. Laughing embarrassedly, we struggled out of their hands and kept after the coins. We were all wet and slippery and hard to hold. Suddenly I saw a boy lifted into the air, glistening with sweat like a circus seal, and dropped, his wet back landing flush upon the charged rug, heard him yell and saw him literally dance upon his back, his elbows beating a frenzied tattoo upon the floor, his muscles twitching like the flesh of a horse stung by many flies. When he finally rolled off, his face was gray and no one stopped him when he ran from the floor amid booming laughter.

"Get the money," the M.C. called. "That's good hard American cash!"

And we snatched and grabbed, snatched and grabbed. I was careful not to come too close to the rug now, and when I felt the hot whiskey breath descend upon me like a cloud of foul air I reached out and grabbed the leg of a chair. It was occupied and I held on desperately.

"Leggo, nigger! Leggo!"

The huge face wavered down to mine as he tried to push me free. But my body was slippery and he was too drunk. It was Mr. Colcord, who owned a chain of movie houses and "entertainment palaces." Each time he grabbed me I slipped out of his hands. It became a real struggle. I feared the rug more than I did the drunk, so I held on, surprising myself for a moment by trying to topple *him* upon the rug. It was such an enormous idea that I found myself actually carrying it out. I tried not to be obvious, yet when I grabbed his leg, trying to tumble him out of the chair, he raised up roaring with laughter, and, looking at me with soberness dead in the eye, kicked me viciously in the chest. The chair leg flew out of my hand and I felt myself going and rolled. It was as though I had rolled through a bed of hot coals. It seemed a whole century would pass before I would roll free, a century in which I was seared through the deepest levels of my body to the fearful breath within me and the breath seared and heated to the point of explosion. It'll all be over in a flash, I thought as I rolled clear. It'll all be over in a flash.

But not yet, the men on the other side were waiting, red faces swollen as though from apoplexy as they bent forward in their chairs. Seeing their fingers coming toward me I rolled away as a fumbled football rolls off the receiver's fingertips, back into the coals. That time I luckily sent the rug sliding out of place and heard the coins ringing against the floor and the boys scuffling to pick them up and the M.C. calling, "All right, boys, that's all. Go get dressed and get your money."

I was limp as a dish rag. My back felt as though it had been beaten with wires.

When we had dressed the M.C. came in and gave us each five dollars, except Tatlock, who got ten for being last in the ring. Then he told us to leave. I was not to get a chance to deliver my speech, I thought. I was going out into the dim alley in despair when I was stopped and told to go back. I returned to the ballroom, where the men were pushing back their chairs and gathering in groups to talk.

The M.C. knocked on a table for quiet. "Gentlemen," he said, "we almost forgot an important part of the program. A most serious part, gentlemen. This boy was brought here to deliver a speech which he made at his graduation yesterday . . ."

"Bravo!"

"I'm told that he is the smartest boy we've got out there in Greenwood. I'm told that he knows more big words than a pocket-sized dictionary."

Much applause and laughter.

"So now, gentlemen, I want you to give him your attention."

There was still laughter as I faced them, my mouth dry, my eye throbbing. I began slowly, but evidently my throat was tense, because they began shouting, "Louder! Louder!"

"We of the younger generation extol the wisdom of that great leader and educator," I shouted, "who first spoke these flaming words of wisdom: 'A ship lost at sea for many days suddenly sighted a friendly vessel. From the mast of the unfortunate vessel was seen a signal: "Water, water; we die of thirst!" The answer from the friendly vessel came back: "Cast down your bucket where you are." The captain of the distressed vessel, at last heeding the injunction, cast down his bucket, and it came up full of fresh sparkling water from the mouth of the Amazon River.' And like him I say, and in his words, "To those of my race who depend upon bettering their condition in a foreign land, or who underestimate the importance of cultivating friendly relations with the Southern white man, who is his next-door neighbor, I would say: "Cast down your bucket where you are"—cast it down in making friends in every manly way of the people of all races by whom we are surrounded . . .'"

I spoke automatically and with such fervor that I did not realize that the men were still talking and laughing until my dry mouth, filling up with blood from the cut, almost strangled me. I coughed, wanting to stop and go to one of the tall brass,

sand-filled spittoons to relieve myself, but a few of the men, especially the superintendent, were listening and I was afraid. So I gulped it down, blood, saliva, and all, and continued. (What powers of endurance I had during those days! What enthusiasm! What a
belief in the rightness of things!) I spoke even louder in spite of the pain. But still they
talked and still they laughed, as though deaf with cotton in dirty ears. So I spoke with
greater emotional emphasis. I closed my ears and swallowed blood until I was nause-
ated. The speech seemed a hundred times as long as before, but I could not leave out a
single word. All had to be said, each memorized nuance considered, rendered. Nor was
that all. Whenever I uttered a word of three or more syllables a group of voices would
yell for me to repeat it. I used the phrase "social responsibility" and they yelled:

"What's that word you say, boy?"

"Social responsibility," I said.

"What?"

"Social . . ."

"Louder."

". . . responsibility."

"More!"

"Respon—"

"Repeat!"

"—sibility."

The room filled with the uproar of laughter until, no doubt, distracted by having to gulp down my blood, I made a mistake and yelled a phrase I had often seen denounced in newspaper editorials, heard debated in private.

"Social . . ."

"What?" they yelled.

". . . equality—"

The laughter hung smokelike in the sudden stillness. I opened my eyes, puzzled.
Sounds of displeasure filled the room. The M.C. rushed forward. They shouted hostile
phrases at me. But I did not understand.

A small dry mustached man in the front row blared out, "Say that slowly, son!"

"What, sir?"

"What you just said!"

"Social responsibility, sir," I said.

"You weren't being smart, were you, boy?" he said, not unkindly.

"No, sir!"

"You sure that about 'equality' was a mistake?"

"Oh, yes, sir," I said. "I was swallowing blood."

"Well, you had better speak more slowly so we can understand. We mean to do
right by you, but you've got to know your place at all times. All right, now, go on
with your speech."

I was afraid. I wanted to leave but I wanted also to speak and I was afraid they'd
snatch me down.

"Thank you, sir," I said, beginning where I had left off, and having them ignore
me as before.

Yet when I finished there was a thunderous applause. I was surprised to see the
superintendent come forth with a package wrapped in white tissue paper, and, gesturing for quiet, address the men.

"Gentlemen, you see that I did not overpraise this boy. He makes a good speech and some day he'll lead his people in the proper paths. And I don't have to tell you that that is important in these days and times. This is a good, smart boy, and so to encourage him in the right direction, in the name of the Board of Education I wish to present him a prize in the form of this . . ."

He paused, removing the tissue paper and revealing a gleaming calfskin brief case.

". . . in the form of this first-class article from Shad Whitmore's shop."

"Boy," he said, addressing me, "take this prize and keep it well. Consider it a badge of office. Prize it. Keep developing as you are and some day it will be filled with important papers that will help shape the destiny of your people."

I was so moved that I could hardly express my thanks. A rope of bloody saliva forming a shape like an undiscovered continent drooled upon the leather and I wiped it quickly away. I felt an importance that I had never dreamed.

"Open it and see what's inside," I was told.

My fingers a-tremble, I complied, smelling the fresh leather and finding an official-looking document inside. It was a scholarship to the state college for Negroes. My eyes filled with tears and I ran awkwardly off the floor.

I was overjoyed; I did not even mind when I discovered that the gold pieces I had scrambled for were brass pocket tokens advertising a certain make of automobile.

When I reached home everyone was excited. Next day the neighbors came to congratulate me. I even felt safe from grandfather, whose deathbed curse usually spoiled my triumphs. I stood beneath his photograph with my brief case in hand and smiled triumphantly into his stolid black peasant's face. It was a face that fascinated me. The eyes seemed to follow everywhere I went.

That night I dreamed I was at a circus with him and that he refused to laugh at the clowns no matter what they did. Then later he told me to open my brief case and read what was inside and I did, finding an official envelope stamped with the state seal; and inside the envelope I found another and another, endlessly, and I thought I would fall of weariness. "Them's years," he said. "Now open that one." And I did and in it I found an engraved document containing a short message in letters of gold. "Read it," my grandfather said. "Out loud!"

"To Whom It May Concern," I intoned. "Keep This Nigger-Boy Running."

I awoke with the old man's laughter ringing in my ears.

(It was a dream I was to remember and dream again for many years after. But at that time I had no insight into its meaning. First, I had to attend college.)

QUESTIONS FOR DISCUSSION AND WRITING

1. The story is framed by the memory of the speaker's grandfather and the words he spoke on his deathbed. Has the narrator been a spy and a traitor without realizing it? Why or why not?
2. How do the white men taunt the black boys with the presence of the stripper? How is her presence at the dinner like and unlike that of the boys?

3. How do the white men reconcile the different events of the evening—the striptease, the fight, the electrified rug and coins, the narrator's speech, and the presentation of the briefcase and scholarship? How does the narrator? How does the reader?
4. The story "Battle Royal" is from Ellison's novel *The Invisible Man*. How does the story suggest the theme of invisibility?
5. How old is the narrator when the events of the story occur? How would the story have been different if he had been younger or older?

LOUISE ERDRICH (1954–)

The Red Convertible _____ 1984

Lyman Lamartine

I was the first one to drive a convertible on my reservation. And of course it was red, a red Olds. I owned that car along with my brother Henry Junior. We owned it together until his boots filled with water on a windy night and he bought out my share. Now Henry owns the whole car, and his younger brother Lyman (that's myself), Lyman walks everywhere he goes.

How did I earn enough money to buy my share in the first place? My one talent was I could always make money. I had a touch for it, unusual in a Chippewa. From the first I was different that way, and everyone recognized it. I was the only kid they let in the American Legion Hall to shine shoes, for example, and one Christmas I sold spiritual bouquets for the mission door to door. The nuns let me keep a percentage. Once I started, it seemed the more money I made the easier the money came. Everyone encouraged it. When I was fifteen I got a job washing dishes at the Joliet Café, and that was where my first big break happened.

It wasn't long before I was promoted to busing tables, and then the short-order cook quit and I was hired to take her place. No sooner than you know it I was managing the Joliet. The rest is history. I went on managing. I soon became part owner, and of course there was no stopping me then. It wasn't long before the whole thing was mine.

After I'd owned the Joliet for one year, it blew over in the worst tornado ever seen around here. The whole operation was smashed to bits. A total loss. The fryalator was up in a tree, the grill torn in half like it was paper. I was only sixteen. I had it all in my mother's name, and I lost it quick, but before I lost it I had every one of my relatives, and their relatives, to dinner, and I also bought that red Olds I mentioned, along with Henry.

The first time we saw it! I'll tell you when we first saw it. We had gotten a ride up to Winnipeg, and both of us had money. Don't ask me why, because we never mentioned a car or anything, we just had all our money. Mine was cash, a big bankroll from the Joliet's insurance. Henry had two checks—a week's extra pay for being laid off, and his regular check from the Jewel Bearing Plant.

We were walking down Portage anyway, seeing the sights, when we saw it. There it was, parked, large as life. Really as *if* it was alive. I thought of the word *repose,* because the car wasn't simply stopped, parked, or whatever. That car reposed, calm and gleaming, a FOR SALE sign in its left front window. Then, before we had thought it over at all, the car belonged to us and our pockets were empty. We had just enough money for gas back home.

We went places in that car, me and Henry. We took off driving all one whole summer. We started off toward the Little Knife River and Mandaree in Fort Berthold and then we found ourselves down in Wakpala somehow, and then suddenly we were over in Montana on the Rocky Boys, and yet the summer was not even half over. Some people hang on to details when they travel, but we didn't let them bother us and just lived our everyday lives here to there.

I do remember this one place with willows. I remember I laid under those trees and it was comfortable. So comfortable. The branches bent down all around me like a tent or a stable. And quiet, it was quiet, even though there was a powwow close enough so I could see it going on. The air was not too still, not too windy either. When the dust rises up and hangs in the air around the dancers like that, I feel good. Henry was asleep with his arms thrown wide. Later on, he woke up and we started driving again. We were somewhere in Montana, or maybe on the Blood Reserve—it could have been anywhere. Anyway it was where we met the girl.

All her hair was in buns around her ears, that's the first thing I noticed about her. She was posed alongside the road with her arm out, so we stopped. That girl was short, so short her lumber shirt looked comical on her, like a nightgown. She had jeans on and fancy moccasins and she carried a little suitcase.

"Hop on in," says Henry. So she climbs in between us.

"We'll take you home," I says. "Where do you live?"

"Chicken," she says.

"Where the hell's that?" I ask her.

"Alaska."

"Okay," says Henry, and we drive.

We got up there and never wanted to leave. The sun doesn't truly set there in summer, and the night is more a soft dusk. You might doze off, sometimes, but before you know it you're up again, like an animal in nature. You never feel like you have to sleep hard or put away the world. And things would grow up there. One day just dirt or moss, the next day flowers and long grass. The girl's name was Susy. Her family really took to us. They fed us and put us up. We had our own tent to live in by their house, and the kids would be in and out of there all day and night. They couldn't get over me and Henry being brothers, we looked so different. We told them we knew we had the same mother, anyway.

One night Susy came in to visit us. We sat around in the tent talking of this thing and that. The season was changing. It was getting darker by that time, and the cold was even getting just a little mean. I told her it was time for us to go. She stood up on a chair.

"You never seen my hair," Susy said.

That was true. She was standing on a chair, but still, when she unclipped her buns the hair reached all the way to the ground. Our eyes opened. You couldn't tell how much hair she had when it was rolled up so neatly. Then my brother Henry did something funny. He went up to the chair and said, "Jump on my shoulders." So she did that, and her hair reached down past his waist, and he started twirling, this way and that, so her hair was flung out from side to side.

"I always wondered what it was like to have long pretty hair," Henry says. Well we laughed. It was a funny sight, the way he did it. The next morning we got up and took leave of those people.

On to greener pastures, as they say. It was down through Spokane and across Idaho then Montana and very soon we were racing the weather right along under the Canadian border through Columbus, Des Lacs, and then we were in Bottineau County and soon home. We'd made most of the trip, that summer, without putting up the car hood at all. We got home just in time, it turned out, for the army to remember Henry had signed up to join it.

I don't wonder that the army was so glad to get my brother that they turned him into a Marine. He was built like a brick outhouse anyway. We liked to tease him that they really wanted him for his Indian nose. He had a nose big and sharp as a hatchet, like the nose on Red Tomahawk, the Indian who killed Sitting Bull, whose profile is on signs all along the North Dakota highways. Henry went off to training camp, came home once during Christmas, then the next thing you know we got an overseas letter from him. It was 1970, and he said he was stationed up in the northern hill country. Whereabouts I did not know. He wasn't such a hot letter writer, and only got off two before the enemy caught him. I could never keep it straight, which direction those good Vietnam soldiers were from.

I wrote him back several times, even though I didn't know if those letters would get through. I kept him informed all about the car. Most of the time I had it up on blocks in the yard or half taken apart, because that long trip did a hard job on it under the hood.

I always had good luck with numbers, and never worried about the draft myself. I never even had to think about what my number was. But Henry was never lucky in the same way as me. It was at least three years before Henry came home. By then I guess the whole war was solved in the government's mind, but for him it would keep on going. In those years I'd put his car into almost perfect shape. I always thought of it as his car while he was gone, even though when he left he said, "Now it's yours," and threw me his key.

"Thanks for the extra key," I'd said. "I'll put it up in your drawer just in case I need it." He laughed.

When he came home, though, Henry was very different, and I'll say this: the change was no good. You could hardly expect him to change for the better, I know. But he was quiet, so quiet, and never comfortable sitting still anywhere but always up and moving around. I thought back to times we'd sat still for whole afternoons, never moving a muscle, just shifting our weight along the ground, talking to whoever sat with us, watching things. He'd always had a joke, then, too, and now you couldn't get him to laugh, or when he did it was more the sound of a man choking, a sound that stopped up the throats of other people around him. They got to leaving him alone most of the time, and I didn't blame them. It was a fact: Henry was jumpy and mean.

I'd bought a color TV set for my mom and the rest of us while Henry was away. Money still came very easy. I was sorry I'd ever bought it though, because of Henry. I was also sorry I'd bought color, because with black-and-white the pictures seem older and farther away. But what are you going to do? He sat in front of it, watching it, and that was the only time he was completely still. But it was the kind of stillness that you see in a rabbit when it freezes and before it will bolt. He was not easy. He sat in his chair gripping the armrests with all his might, as if the chair itself was moving at a high speed and if he let go at all he would rocket forward and maybe crash right through the set.

Once I was in the room watching TV with Henry and I heard his teeth click at something. I looked over, and he'd bitten through his lip. Blood was going down his chin. I tell you right then I wanted to smash that tube to pieces. I went over to it but Henry must have known what I was up to. He rushed from his chair and shoved me out of the way, against the wall. I told myself he didn't know what he was doing.

My mom came in, turned the set off real quiet, and told us she had made something for supper. So we went and sat down. There was still blood going down Henry's chin, but he didn't notice it and no one said anything, even though every time he took a bite of his bread his blood fell onto it until he was eating his own blood mixed in with the food.

While Henry was not around we talked about what was going to happen to him. There were no Indian doctors on the reservation, and my mom couldn't come around to trusting the old man, Moses Pillager, because he courted her long ago and was jealous of her husbands. He might take revenge through her son. We were afraid that if we brought Henry to a regular hospital they would keep him.

"They don't fix them in those places," Mom said; "they just give them drugs."

"We wouldn't get him there in the first place," I agreed, "so let's just forget about it."

Then I thought about the car.

Henry had not even looked at the car since he'd gotten home, though like I said, it was in tip-top condition and ready to drive. I thought the car might bring the old Henry back somehow. So I bided my time and waited for my chance to interest him in the vehicle.

One night Henry was off somewhere. I took myself a hammer. I went out to that car and I did a number on its underside. Whacked it up. Bent the tail pipe double. Ripped the muffler loose. By the time I was done with the car it looked worse than any typical Indian car that has been driven all its life on reservation roads, which they always say are like government promises—full of holes. It just about hurt me, I'll tell you that! I threw dirt in the carburetor and I ripped all the electric tape off the seats. I made it look just as beat up as I could. Then I sat back and waited for Henry to find it.

Still, it took him over a month. That was all right, because it was just getting warm enough, not melting, but warm enough to work outside.

"Lyman," he says, walking in one day, "that red car looks like shit."

"Well it's old," I says. "You got to expect that."

"No way!" says Henry. "That car's a classic! But you went and ran the piss right out of it, Lyman, and you know it don't deserve that. I kept that car in A-one shape.

You don't remember. You're too young. But when I left, that car was running like a watch. Now I don't even know if I can get it to start again, let alone get it anywhere near its old condition."

"Well you try," I said, like I was getting mad, "but I say it's a piece of junk."

Then I walked out before he could realize I knew he'd strung together more than six words at once.

After that I thought he'd freeze himself to death working on that car. He was out there all day, and at night he rigged up a little lamp, ran a cord out the window, and had himself some light to see by while he worked. He was better than he had been before, but that's still not saying much. It was easier for him to do the things the rest of us did. He ate more slowly and didn't jump up and down during the meal to get this or that or look out the window. I put my hand in the back of the TV set, I admit, and fiddled around with it good, so that it was almost impossible now to get a clear picture. He didn't look at it very often anyway. He was always out with that car or going off to get parts for it. By the time it was really melting outside, he had it fixed.

I had been feeling down in the dumps about Henry around this time. We had always been together before. Henry and Lyman. But he was such a loner now that I didn't know how to take it. So I jumped at the chance one day when Henry seemed friendly. It's not that he smiled or anything. He just said, "Let's take that old shitbox for a spin." Just the way he said it made me think he could be coming around.

We went out to the car. It was spring. The sun was shining very bright. My only sister, Bonita, who was just eleven years old, came out and made us stand together for a picture. Henry leaned his elbow on the red car's windshield, and he took his other arm and put it over my shoulder, very carefully, as though it was heavy for him to lift and he didn't want to bring the weight down all at once.

"Smile," Bonita said, and he did.

That picture. I never look at it anymore. A few months ago, I don't know why, I got his picture out and tacked it on the wall. I felt good about Henry at the time, close to him. I felt good having his picture on the wall, until one night when I was looking at television. I was a little drunk and stoned. I looked up at the wall and Henry was staring at me. I don't know what it was, but his smile had changed, or maybe it was gone. All I know is I couldn't stay in the same room with that picture. I was shaking. I got up, closed the door, and went into the kitchen. A little later my friend Ray came over and we both went back into that room. We put the picture in a brown bag, folded the bag over and over tightly, then put it way back in a closet.

I still see that picture now, as if it tugs at me, whenever I pass that closet door. The picture is very clear in my mind. It was so sunny that day Henry had to squint against the glare. Or maybe the camera Bonita held flashed like a mirror, blinding him, before she snapped the picture. My face is right out in the sun, big and round. But he might have drawn back, because the shadows on his face are deep as holes. There are two shadows curved like little hooks around the ends of his smile, as if to frame it and try to keep it there—that one, first smile that looked like it might have hurt his face. He has his field jacket on and the worn-in clothes he'd come back in and kept wearing ever since. After Bonita took the picture, she went into the house and we got into the car. There was a full cooler in the trunk. We started off, east, toward Pembina and the Red River because Henry said he wanted to see the high water.

The trip over there was beautiful. When everything starts changing, drying up, clearing off, you feel like your whole life is starting. Henry felt it, too. The top was down and the car hummed like a top. He'd really put it back in shape, even the tape on the seats was very carefully put down and glued back in layers. It's not that he smiled again or even joked, but his face looked to me as if it was clear, more peaceful. It looked as though he wasn't thinking of anything in particular except the bare fields and windbreaks and houses we were passing.

The river was high and full of winter trash when we got there. The sun was still out, but it was colder by the river. There were still little clumps of dirty snow here and there on the banks. The water hadn't gone over the banks yet, but it would, you could tell. It was just at its limit, hard swollen, glossy like an old gray scar. We made ourselves a fire, and we sat down and watched the current go. As I watched it I felt something squeezing inside me and tightening and trying to let go all at the same time. I knew I was not just feeling it myself; I knew I was feeling what Henry was going through at that moment. Except that I couldn't stand it, the closing and opening. I jumped to my feet. I took Henry by the shoulders and I started shaking him. "Wake up," I says, "wake up, wake up, wake up!" I didn't know what had come over me. I sat down beside him again.

His face was totally white and hard. Then it broke, like stones break all of a sudden when water boils up inside them.

"I know it," he says. "I know it. I can't help it. It's no use."

We start talking. He said he knew what I'd done with the car. It was obvious it had been whacked out of shape and not just neglected. He said he wanted to give the car to me for good now, it was no use. He said he'd fixed it just to give it back and I should take it.

"No way," I says, "I don't want it."

"That's okay," he says, "you take it."

"I don't want it, though," I says back to him, and then to emphasize, just to emphasize, you understand, I touch his shoulder. He slaps my hand off.

"Take that car," he says.

"No," I say. "Make me," I say, and then he grabs my jacket and rips the arm loose. That jacket is a class act, suede with tags and zippers. I push Henry backwards, off the log. He jumps up and bowls me over. We go down in a clinch and come up swinging hard, for all we're worth, with our fists. He socks my jaw so hard I feel like it swings loose. Then I'm at his rib cage and land a good one under his chin so his head snaps back. He's dazzled. He looks at me and I look at him and then his eyes are full of tears and blood and at first I think he's crying. But no, he's laughing. "Ha! Ha!" he says. "Ha! Ha! Take good care of it."

"Okay," I say. "Okay, no problem. Ha! Ha!"

I can't help it, and I start laughing, too. My face feels fat and strange, and after a while I get a beer from the cooler in the trunk, and when I hand it to Henry he takes his shirt and wipes my germs off. "Hoof-and-mouth disease," he says. For some reason this cracks me up, and so we're really laughing for a while, and then we drink all the rest of the beers one by one and throw them in the river and see how far, how fast, the current takes them before they fill up and sink.

"You want to go on back?" I ask after a while. "Maybe we could snag a couple nice Kashpaw girls."

He says nothing. But I can tell his mood is turning again.

"They're all crazy, the girls up here, every damn one of them."

"You're crazy too," I say, to jolly him up. "Crazy Lamartine boys!"

He looks as though he will take this wrong at first. His face twists, then clears, and he jumps up on his feet. "That's right!" he says. "Crazier 'n hell. Crazy Indians!"

I think it's the old Henry again. He throws off his jacket and starts swinging his legs out from the knees like a fancy dancer. He's down doing something between a grouse dance and a bunny hop, no kind of dance I ever saw before, but neither has anyone else on all this green growing earth. He's wild. He wants to pitch whoopee! He's up and at me and all over. All this time I'm laughing so hard, so hard my belly is getting tied up in a knot.

"Got to cool me off!" he shouts all of a sudden. Then he runs over to the river and jumps in.

There's boards and other things in the current. It's so high. No sound comes from the river after the splash he makes, so I run right over. I look around. It's getting dark. I see he's halfway across the water already, and I know he didn't swim there but the current took him. It's far. I hear his voice, though, very clearly across it.

"My boots are filling," he says.

He says this in a normal voice, like he just noticed and he doesn't know what to think of it. Then he's gone. A branch comes by. Another branch. And I go in.

By the time I get out of the river, off the snag I pulled myself onto, the sun is down. I walk back to the car, turn on the high beams, and drive it up the bank. I put it in first gear and then I take my foot off the clutch. I get out, close the door, and watch it plow softly into the water. The headlights reach in as they go down, searching, still lighted even after the water swirls over the back end. I wait. The wires short out. It is all finally dark. And then there is only the water, the sound of it going and running and going and running and running.

QUESTIONS FOR DISCUSSION AND WRITING

1. The story centers on the relationship between Lyman and Henry. In what ways are the brothers similar and in what ways are they different? How would you describe their sibling bond?

2. The red convertible is clearly very important to the two brothers. What does it represent to each of them? Why does Lyman drive it into the river after his brother drowns?

3. Henry says he is jumping into the river to cool off. Does the story suggest the drowning is an accident or a suicide? If it is a suicide, why did Henry decide to end his life?

4. The opening of the story tells us that Henry's boots filled with water and that Henry bought out his brother's share in the car. That information hints at the ending but doesn't fully disclose it. How is the story strengthened or weakened by this enigmatic opening?

5. We learn that Henry was changed by his experience in Vietnam, but we don't learn any details about that experience. How would the story be more or less effective if we were given those details?

JAMAICA KINCAID (1949–   )
Girl _____ *1978*

Wash the white clothes on Monday and put them on the stone heap; wash the color clothes on Tuesday and put them on the clothesline to dry; don't walk barehead in the hot sun; cook pumpkin fritters in very hot sweet oil; soak your little cloths right after you take them off; when buying cotton to make yourself a nice blouse, be sure that it doesn't have gum on it, because that way it won't hold up well after a wash; soak salt fish overnight before you cook it; is it true that you sing benna in Sunday school?; always eat your food in such a way that it won't turn someone else's stomach; on Sundays try to walk like a lady and not like the slut you are so bent on becoming; don't sing benna in Sunday school; you musn't speak to wharf-rat boys, not even to give directions; don't eat fruits on the street—flies will follow you; *but I don't sing benna on Sundays at all and never in Sunday school;* this is how to sew on a button; this is how to make a buttonhole for the button you have just sewed on; this is how to hem a dress when you see the hem coming down and so to prevent yourself from looking like the slut I know you are so bent on becoming; this is how you iron your father's khaki shirt so that it doesn't have a crease; this is how you iron your father's khaki pants so that they don't have a crease; this is how you grow okra—far from the house, because okra tree harbors red ants; when you are growing dasheen, make sure it gets plenty of water or else it makes your throat itch when you are eating it; this is how you sweep a corner; this is how you sweep a whole house; this is how you sweep a yard; this is how you smile to someone you don't like too much; this is how you smile to someone you don't like at all; this is how you smile to someone you like completely; this is how you set a table for tea; this is how you set a table for dinner; this is how you set a table for dinner with an important guest; this is how you set a table for lunch; this is how you set a table for breakfast; this is how to behave in the presence of men who don't know you very well, and this way they won't recognize immediately the slut I have warned you against becoming; be sure to wash every day, even if it is with your own spit; don't squat down to play marbles—you are not a boy, you know; don't pick people's flowers—you might catch something; don't throw stones at blackbirds, because it might not be a blackbird at all; this is how to make a bread pudding; this is how to make doukona; this is how to make pepper pot; this is how to make a good medicine for a cold; this is how to make a good medicine to throw away a child before it even becomes a child; this is how to catch a fish; this is how to throw back a fish you don't like, and that way something bad won't fall on you; this is how to bully a man; this is how a man bullies you; this is how to love a man, and if this doesn't work there are other ways, and if they don't work don't feel too bad about giving up; this is how to spit up in the air if you feel like it, and this is how to move quick so that it doesn't fall on you; this is how to make ends meet; always squeeze bread to make sure it's fresh; *but what if the baker won't let me feel the bread?;* you mean to say that after all you are really going to be the kind of woman who the baker won't let near the bread?

QUESTIONS FOR DISCUSSION AND WRITING

1. How would you describe the mother who is speaking? How does she view her daughter? How does her daughter view her?
2. The story is probably set in Antigua, where Jamaica Kincaid was raised. What can you infer from the story itself about the setting?
3. The story is written in one sentence. How would it change if it were broken into many sentences?
4. If you were to write a story called "Girl" that reflected your own culture, what sort of instructions would you include? What would you include for a story titled "Boy"?

MARY MCCARTHY (1912–1989)

A Tin Butterfly   1946

The man we had to call Uncle Myers was no relation to us. This was a point on which we four orphan children were very firm. He had married our great-aunt Margaret shortly before the death of our parents and so became our guardian while still a benedict—not perhaps a very nice eventuality for a fat man of forty-two who has just married an old maid with a little income to find himself summoned overnight from his home in Indiana to be the hired parent of four children, all under seven years old.

When Myers and Margaret got us, my three brothers and me, we were a handful; on this there were no two opinions in the McCarthy branch of the family. The famous flu epidemic of 1918, which had stricken our little household en route from Seattle to Minneapolis and carried off our parents within a day of each other, had, like all God's devices, a meritorious aspect, soon discovered by my grandmother Mc-Carthy: a merciful end had been put to a regimen of spoiling and coddling, to Japanese houseboys, iced cakes, picnics, upset stomachs, diamond rings (imagine!), an ermine muff and neckpiece, furred hats and coats. My grandmother thanked her stars that Myers and her sister Margaret were available to step into the breach. Otherwise, we might have had to be separated, an idea that moistened her hooded grey eyes, or been taken over by "the Protestants"—thus she grimly designated my grandfather Preston, a respectable Seattle lawyer of New England antecedents who, she many times declared with awful emphasis, had refused to receive a Catholic priest in his house! But our Seattle grandparents, coming on to Minneapolis for the funeral, were too broken up, she perceived, by our young mother's death to protest the McCarthy arrangements. Weeping, my Jewish grandmother (Preston, born Morganstern), still a beauty, like her lost daughter, acquiesced in the wisdom of keeping us together in the religion my mother had espoused. In my sickbed, recovering from the flu in my grandmother McCarthy's Minneapolis house, I, the eldest and the only girl, sat up and watched the other grandmother cry, dampening her exquisite black veil. I did not know that our parents were dead or that my sobbing grandmother—whose green Seattle terraces I remembered as delightful to roll down on Sundays—had just now, downstairs in my grandmother McCarthy's well-heated sun parlor, met the middle-aged pair who had come on from Indiana to undo her daughter's mistakes. I was only six years old and had just started school in a Sacred Heart convent on a leafy boulevard in Seattle before the fatal November trek back east, but I was sharp enough to see that Grandmother Preston did not belong here, in this dour sickroom, and vain enough to pride myself on drawing the inference that something had gone awry.

We four children and our keepers were soon installed in the yellow house at 2427 Blaisdell Avenue that had been bought for us by my grandfather McCarthy. It was situated two blocks away from his own prosperous dwelling, with its grandfather clock, tapestries, and Italian paintings, in a block that some time before had begun to "run down." Flanked by two-family houses, it was simply a crude box in which to stow furniture, and lives, like a warehouse; the rooms were small and brownish and for some reason dark, though I cannot think why, since the house was graced by no ornamental planting; a straight cement driveway ran up one side; in the back, there was an alley. Downstairs, there were a living room, a "den," a dining room, a kitchen, and a lavatory; upstairs, there were four bedrooms and a bathroom. The dingy wallpaper of the rooms in which we children slept was promptly defaced by us; bored without our usual toys, we amused ourselves by making figures on the walls with our wet tongues. This was our first crime, and I remember it because the violence of the whipping we got surprised us; we had not known we were doing wrong. The splotches on the walls remained through the years to fix this first whipping and the idea of badness in our minds; they stared at us in the evenings when, still bored but mute and tamed, we learned to make shadow figures on the wall—the swan, the rabbit with its ears wiggling—to while away the time.

It was this first crime, perhaps, that set Myers in his punitive mold. He saw that it was no sinecure he had slipped into. Childless, middle-aged, he may have felt in his slow-turning mind that his inexperience had been taken advantage of by his wife's grandiloquent sister, that the vexations outweighed the perquisites; in short, that he had been sold. This, no doubt, was how it must have really looked from where he sat—in a brown leather armchair in the den, wearing a blue work shirt, stained with sweat, open at the neck to show an undershirt and lion-blond, glinting hair on his chest. Below this were workmen's trousers of a brownish-gray material, straining at the buttons and always gaping slightly, just below the belt, to show another glimpse of underwear, of a yellowish white. On his fat head, frequently, with its crest of bronze curly hair, were the earphones of a crystal radio set, which he sometimes, briefly, in a generous mood, fitted over the grateful ears of one of my little brothers.

A second excuse for Myers' behavior is manifest in this description. He had to contend with Irish social snobbery, which looked upon him dispassionately from four sets of green eyes and set him down as "not a gentleman." "My father was a gentleman and you're not"—what I meant by these categorical words I no longer know precisely, except that my father had had a romantic temperament and was a spendthrift; but I suppose there was also included some notion of courtesy. Our family, like many Irish Catholic new-rich families, was filled with aristocratic delusions; we children were always being told that we were descended from the kings of Ireland and that we were related to General "Phil" Sheridan, a dream of my great-aunt's. More precisely, my great-grandfather on this side had been a streetcar conductor in Chicago.

But at any rate Myers (or Meyers) Shriver (or Schreiber—the name had apparently been Americanized) was felt to be beneath us socially. Another count against him in our childish score was that he was a German, or, rather, of German descent, which made us glance at him fearfully in 1918, just after the armistice. In Minneapolis at that time, there was great prejudice among the Irish Catholics, not only against the Protestant Germans, but against all the northern bloods and their hateful Lutheran heresy. Lutheranism to us children was, first of all, a religion for servant girls and, secondly, a sort of yellow corruption associated with original sin and with Martin Luther's tongue rotting in his mouth as God's punishment. Bavarian Catholics, on the other hand, were singled out for a special regard; we saw them in an Early Christian light, brunette and ringleted, like the Apostles. This was due in part to the fame of Oberammergau and the Passion Play, and in part to the fact that many of the clergy in our diocese were Bavarians; all through this period I confided my sins of disobedience to a handsome, dark, young Father Elderbush. Uncle Myers, however, was a Protestant, although, being too indolent, he did not go to church; he was not one of us. And the discovery that we could take refuge from him at school, with the nuns, at church, in the sacraments, seemed to verify the ban that was on him; he was truly outside grace. Having been impressed with the idea that our religion was a sort of logical contagion, spread by holy books and good example, I could never understand why Uncle Myers, bad as he was, had not caught it; and his obduracy in remaining at home in his den on Sundays, like a somnolent brute in its lair, seemed to me to go against nature.

Indeed, in the whole situation there was something unnatural and inexplicable. His marriage to Margaret, in the first place: he was younger than his wife by three years, and much was made of this difference by my grandmother McCarthy, his wealthy sister-in-law, as though it explained everything in a slightly obscene way. Aunt Margaret, née Sheridan, was a well-aged quince of forty-five, with iron-gray hair shading into black, a stiff carriage, high-necked dresses, unfashionable hats, a copy of *Our Sunday Visitor* always under her arm—folded, like a flail—a tough dry skin with soft colorless hairs on it, like dust, and furrowed and corrugated, like the prunes we ate every day for breakfast. It could be said of her that she meant well, and she meant especially well by Myers, all two hundred and five pounds, dimpled double chin, and small, glinting, gross blue eyes of him. She called him "Honeybunch," pursued him with attentions, special foods, kisses, to which he responded with tolerance, as though his swollen passivity had the character of a male thrust or assertion. It was clear that he did not dislike her, and that poor Margaret, as her sister said, was head over heels in love with him. To us children, this honeymoon rankness was incomprehensible; we could not see it on either side for, quite apart from everything else, both parties seemed to us very old, as indeed they were, compared to our parents, who had been young and handsome. That he had married her for her money occurred to us inevitably, though it may not have been so; very likely it was his power over her that he loved, and the power he had to make her punish us was perhaps her strongest appeal to him. They slept in a bare, ugly bedroom with a tall, cheap pine chiffonier on which Myers' black wallet and his nickels and dimes lay spread out when he was at home—did he think to arouse our cupidity or did he suppose that this stronghold of his virility was impregnable to our weak desires? Yet, as it happened, we did steal from him, my brother Kevin and I—rightfully, as we felt, for we were allowed no pocket money (two pennies were given us on Sunday morning to put into the collection plate) and we guessed that the money paid by our grandfather for the household found its way into Myers' wallet.

And here was another strange thing about Myers. He not only did nothing for a living but he appeared to have no history. He came from Elkhart, Indiana, but beyond this fact nobody seemed to know anything about him—not even how he had met my aunt Margaret. Reconstructed from his conversation, a picture of Elkhart emerged for us that showed it as a flat place consisting chiefly of ball parks, poolrooms, and hardware stores. Aunt Margaret came from Chicago, which consisted of the Loop, Marshall Field's, assorted priests and monsignors, and the black-and-white problem. How had these two worlds impinged? Where our family spoke freely of its relations, real and imaginary, Myers spoke of no one, not even a parent. At the very beginning, when my father's old touring car, which had been shipped on, still remained in our garage, Myers had certain seedy cronies whom he took riding in it or who simply sat in it in our driveway, as if anchored in a houseboat; but when the car went, they went or were banished. Uncle Myers and Aunt Margaret had no friends, no couples with whom they exchanged visits—only a middle-aged, black-haired, small, emaciated woman with a German name and a yellowed skin whom we were taken to see one afternoon because she was dying of cancer. This protracted death had the aspect of a public execution, which was doubtless why Myers took us to it; that is, it was a spectacle and it was free, and it inspired restlessness and depression. Myers was the perfect type of rootless municipalized man who finds his pleasures in the handouts or overflow of an industrial civilization. He enjoyed standing on a curbstone, watching parades, the more nondescript the better, the Labor Day parade being his favorite, and next to that a military parade, followed by the commercial parades with floats and girls dressed in costumes; he would even go to Lake Calhoun or Lake Harriet for doll-carriage parades and competitions of children dressed as Indians. He liked bandstands, band concerts, public parks devoid of grass; skywriting attracted him; he was quick to hear of a department-store demonstration where colored bubbles were blown, advertising a soap, to the tune of "I'm Forever Blowing Bubbles," sung by a mellifluous soprano. He collected coupons and tinfoil, bundles of newspaper for the old rag-and-bone man (thus interfering seriously with our school paper drives), free samples of cheese at Donaldson's, free tickets given out by a neighborhood movie house to the first installment of a serial—in all the years we lived with him, we never saw a full-length movie but only those truncated beginnings. He was also fond of streetcar rides (could the system have been municipally owned?), soldiers' monuments, cemeteries, big, coarse flowers like cannas and cockscombs set in beds by city gardeners. Museums did not appeal to him, though we did go one night with a large crowd to see Marshal Foch on the steps of the Art Institute. He was always weighing himself on penny weighing machines. He seldom left the house except on one of these purposeless errands, or else to go to a ball game, by himself. In the winter, he spent the days at home in the den, or in the kitchen, making candy. He often had enormous tin trays of decorated fondants cooling in the cellar, which leads my brother Kevin to think today that at one time in Myers' life he must have been a pastry cook or a confectioner. He also liked to fashion those little figures made of pipe cleaners that were just then coming in as favors in the better candy shops, but Myers used *old* pipe cleaners, stained yellow and brown. The bonbons, with their pecan or almond topping, that he laid out in such perfect rows were for his own use; we were permitted to watch him set them out, but never—and my brother Kevin confirms this—did we taste a single one.

In the five years we spent with Myers, the only candy I ever had was bought with stolen money and then hidden in the bottom layer of my paper-doll set; the idea of stealing to buy candy and the hiding place were both lifted from Kevin. Opening my paper-doll box one day, I found it full of pink and white soft-sugar candies, which it seemed to me God or the fairies had sent me in response to my wishes and prayers, until I realized that Kevin was stealing, and using my paper-doll box for a cache; we had so few possessions that he had no place of his own to hide things in. Underneath the mattress was too chancy, as I myself found when I tried to secrete magazines of Catholic fiction there; my aunt, I learned, was always tearing up the bed and turning the mattress to find out whether you had wet it and attempted to hide your crime by turning it over. Reading was forbidden us, except for schoolbooks and, for some reason, the funny papers and magazine section of the Sunday Hearst papers, where one read about leprosy, the affairs of Count Boni de Castellane, and a strange disease that turned people to stone creepingly from the feet up.

This prohibition against reading was a source of scandal to the nuns who taught me in the parochial school, and I think it was due to their intervention with my grandmother that finally, toward the end, I was allowed to read openly the Camp Fire Girls series, *Fabiola,* and other books I have forgotten. Myers did not read; before the days of the crystal set, he passed his evenings listening to the phonograph in the living room: Caruso, Harry Lauder, "Keep the Home Fires Burning," "There's a Sweet Little Nest," and "Listen to the Mocking Bird." It was his pleasure to make the four of us stand up in a line and sing to him the same tunes he had just heard on the phonograph, while he laughed at my performance, for I tried to reproduce the staccato phrasing of the sopranos, very loudly and off key. Also, he hated long words, or, rather, words that he regarded as long. One summer day, in the kitchen, when I had been ordered to swat flies, I said, "They disappear so strangely," a remark that he mimicked for years whenever he wished to humiliate me, and the worst of this torture was that I could not understand what was peculiar about the sentence, which seemed to me plain ordinary English, and, not understanding, I knew that I was in perpetual danger of exposing myself to him again.

So far as we knew, he had never been in any army, but he liked to keep smart military discipline. We had frequently to stand in line, facing him, and shout answers to his questions in chorus. "Forward *march!*" he barked after every order he gave us. The Fourth of July was the only holiday he threw himself into with geniality. Anything that smacked to him of affectation or being "stuck-up" was subject to the harshest reprisals from him, and I, being the oldest, and the one who remembered my parents and the old life best, was the chief sinner, sometimes on purpose, sometimes unintentionally.

When I was eight, I began writing poetry in school: "Father Gaughan is our dear parish priest / And he is loved from west to east." And "Alas, Pope Benedict is dead, / The sorrowing people said." Pope Benedict at that time was living, and, as far as I know, in good health; I had written this opening couplet for the rhyme and the sad idea; but then, very conveniently for me, about a year later he died, which gave me a feeling of fearsome power, stronger than a priest's power of loosing and binding. I came forward with my poem and it was beautifully copied out by our teacher and served as the school's elegy at a memorial service for the Pontiff. I dared not tell that I had had it ready in my desk. Not long afterward, when I was ten, I wrote an essay for a children's contest on "The Irish in American History," which won first the city and then the state prize. Most of my facts I had cribbed from a series on Catholics in American history that was running in *Our Sunday Visitor.* I worked on the assumption that anybody who was Catholic must be Irish, and then, for good measure, I went over the signers of the Declaration of Independence and added any name that sounded Irish to my ears. All this was clothed in rhetoric invoking "the lilies of France"—God knows why, except that I was in love with France and somehow, through Marshal MacMahon, had made Lafayette out an Irishman. I believe that even Kosciusko figured as an Irishman *de coeur.* At any rate, there was a school ceremony, at which I was presented with the city prize (twenty-five dollars, I think, or perhaps that was the state prize); my aunt was in the audience in her best mallard-feathered hat, looking, for once, proud and happy. She spoke kindly to me as we walked home, but when we came to our ugly house, my uncle silently rose from his chair, led me into the dark downstairs lavatory, which always smelled of shaving cream, and furiously beat me with the razor strop—to teach me a lesson, he said, lest I become stuck-up. Aunt Margaret did not intervene. After her first look of discomfiture, her face settled into folds of approval; she had been too soft. This was the usual tribute she paid Myers' greater discernment—she was afraid of losing his love by weakness. The money was taken, "to keep for me," and that, of course, was the end of it. Such was the fate of anything considered "much too good for her," a category that was rivaled only by its pendant, "plenty good enough."

We were beaten all the time, as a matter of course, with the hairbrush across the bare legs for ordinary occasions, and with the razor strop across the bare bottom for special occasions, like the prize-winning. It was as though these ignorant people, at sea with four frightened children, had taken a Dickens novel—*Oliver Twist,* perhaps, or *Nicholas Nickleby*—for a navigation chart. Sometimes our punishments were earned, sometimes not; they were administered gratuitously, often, as preventive medicine. I was whipped more frequently than my brothers, simply by virtue of seniority; that is, every time one of them was whipped, I was whipped also, for not having set a better example, and this was true for all four of us in a descending line. Kevin was whipped for Preston's misdeeds and for Sheridan's, and Preston was whipped for Sheridan's, while Sheridan, the baby and the favorite, was whipped only for his own. This naturally made us fear and distrust each other, and only between Kevin and myself was there a kind of uneasy alliance. When Kevin ran away, as he did on one famous occasion, I had a feeling of joy and defiance, mixed with the fear of punishment for myself, mixed with something worse, a vengeful anticipation of the whipping *he* would surely get. I suppose that the two times I ran away, his feelings were much the same— envy, awe, fear, admiration, and a certain evil thrill, collusive with my uncle, at the thought of the strop ahead. Yet, strange to say, nobody was beaten on these historic days. The culprit, when found, took refuge at my grandmother's, and a fearful hush lay over the house on Blaisdell Avenue at the thought of the monstrous daring and deceitfulness of the runaway; Uncle Myers, doubtless, was shaking in his boots at the prospect of explanations to the McCarthy family council. The three who remained at home were sentenced to spend the day upstairs, in strict silence. But if my uncle's impartial application of punishment served to make us each other's enemies very often, it did nothing to establish discipline, since we had no incentive to behave well, not knowing when we might be punished for something we had not done or even for something that by ordinary standards would be considered good. We knew not when we would offend, and what I learned from this, in the main, was a policy of lying and concealment; for several years after we were finally liberated, I was a problem liar.

Despite Myers' quite justified hatred of the intellect, of reading and education (for he was right—it *was* an escape from him), my uncle, like all dictators, had one book that he enjoyed. It was *Uncle Remus,* in a red cover—a book I detested—which he read aloud to us in his den over and over again in the evenings. It seemed to me that this reduction of human life to the level of talking animals and this corruption of language to dialect gave my uncle some very personal relish. He knew I hated it and he rubbed it in, trotting my brother Sheridan on his knee as he dwelt on some exploit of Br'er Fox's with many chuckles and repetitions. In *Uncle Remus,* he had his hour, and to this day I cannot read anything in dialect or any fable without some degree of repugnance.

A distinction must be made between my uncle's capricious brutality and my aunt's punishments and repressions, which seem to have been dictated to her by her conscience. My aunt was not a bad woman; she was only a believer in method. Since it was the family theory that we had been spoiled, she undertook energetically to remedy this by quasi-scientific means. Everything we did proceeded according to schedule and in line with an over-all plan. She was very strong, naturally, on toilet-training, and everything in our life was directed toward the after-breakfast session on "the throne." Our whole diet—not to speak of the morning orange juice with castor oil in it that was brought to us on the slightest pretext of "paleness"—was centered around this levee. We had prunes every day for breakfast, and corn-meal mush, Wheatena, or farina, which I had to eat plain, since by some medical whim it had been decided that milk was bad for me. The rest of our day's menu consisted of parsnips, turnips, rutabagas, carrots, boiled potatoes, boiled cabbage, onions, Swiss chard, kale, and so on; most green vegetables, apparently, were too dear to be appropriate for us, though I think that, beyond this, the family had a sort of moral affinity for the root vegetable, stemming, perhaps, from everything fibrous, tenacious, watery, and knobby in the Irish peasant stock. Our desserts were rice pudding, farina pudding, overcooked custard with little air holes in it, prunes, stewed red plums, rhubarb, stewed pears, stewed dried peaches. We must have had meat, but I have only the most indistinct recollection of pale lamb stews in which the carrots outnumbered the pieces of white, fatty meat and bone and gristle; certainly we did not have steak or roasts or turkey or fried chicken, but perhaps an occasional boiled fowl was served to us with its vegetables (for I do remember the neck, shrunken in its collar of puckered skin, coming to me as my portion, and the fact that if you sucked on it, you could draw out an edible white cord), and doubtless there was meat loaf and beef stew. There was no ice cream, cake, pie, or butter, but on rare mornings we had johnnycake or large woolly pan-cakes with Karo syrup.

We were not allowed to leave the table until every morsel was finished, and I used to sit through half a dark winter afternoon staring at the cold carrots on my plate, until, during one short snowy period, I found that I could throw them out the back window if I raised it very quietly. (Unfortunately, they landed on the tar roofing of a sort of shed next to the back porch, and when the snow finally melted, I met a terrible punishment.) From time to time, we had a maid, but the food was so wretched that we could not keep "girls," and my aunt took over the cooking, with sour enthu-siasm, assisted by her sister, Aunt Mary, an arthritic, white-haired, wan, devout old lady who had silently joined our household and earned her keep by helping with the sewing and dusting and who tried to stay out of Myers' way. With her gentle help, Aunt Margaret managed to approximate, on a small scale, the conditions prevailing in the orphan asylums we four children were always dreaming of being let into.

Myers did not share our diet. He sat at the head of the table, with a napkin around his neck, eating the special dishes that Aunt Margaret prepared for him and sometimes putting a spoonful on the plate of my youngest brother, who sat next to him in a high chair. At breakfast, he had corn flakes or shredded wheat with bananas or fresh sliced peaches, thought by us to be a Lucullan treat. At dinner, he had pigs' feet and other delicacies I cannot remember. I only know that he shared them with Sheridan, who was called Herdie, as my middle brother was called Pomps, or Pomp-sie—childish affectionate nicknames inherited from our dead parents that sounded damp as gravemold in my aunt Margaret's flannelly voice, which reminded one of a chest rag dipped in asafetida to ward off winter throat ailments.

In addition to such poultices, and mustard plasters, and iron pills to fortify our already redoubtable diet, we were subject to other health fads of the period and of my great-aunt's youth. I have told elsewhere of how we were put to bed at night with our mouths sealed with adhesive tape to prevent mouth-breathing; ether, which made me sick, was used to help pull the tape off in the morning, but a grimy, gray, rubbery remainder was usually left on our upper lips and in the identations of our pointed chins when we set off for school in our heavy outer clothes, long underwear, black stockings, and high shoes. Our pillows were taken away from us; we were given a sulphur-and-molasses spring tonic, and in the winter, on Saturdays and Sundays, we were made to stay out three hours in the morning and three in the afternoon, regard-less of the temperature. We had come from a mild climate, in Seattle, and at fifteen, twenty, or twenty-four below zero we could not play, even if we had had something to play with, and used simply to stand in the snow, crying, and beating sometimes on the window with our frozen mittens, till my aunt's angry face would appear there and drive us away.

No attempt was made to teach us a sport, winter or summer; we were forbid-den to slide in Fairoaks Park nearby, where in winter the poorer children made a track of ice down a hill, which they flashed down sitting or standing, but I loved this daring sport and did it anyway, on the way home from school, until one day I tore my shabby coat on the ice and was afraid to go home. A kind woman named Mrs. Corkerey, who kept a neighborhood candy store across from our school, mended it for me, very skill-fully, so that my aunt never knew; nevertheless, sliding lost its lure for me, for I could not risk a second rip.

The neighbors were often kind, surreptitiously, and sometimes they "spoke" to the sisters at the parochial school, but everyone, I think, was afraid of offending my grandparents, who diffused an air of wealth and pomp when they entered their pew at St. Stephen's Church on Sunday. Mrs. Corkerey, in fact, got herself and me in trouble by feeding me in the mornings in her kitchen above the candy store when I stopped to pick up her daughter, Clarazita, who was in my class. I used to lie to Mrs. Corkerey and say that I had had no breakfast (when the truth was that I was merely hungry), and she went to the nuns finally in a state of indignation. The story was checked with my aunt, and I was obliged to admit that I had lied and that they did feed me, which must have disillusioned Mrs. Corkerey forever with the pathos of orphaned childhood. It was impossible for me to explain to her then that what I needed was her pity and her fierce choleric heart. Another neighbor, Mr. Harrison, a well-to-do old bachelor or widower who lived in the corner house, used sometimes to take us bathing, and it was thanks to his lessons that I learned to swim—a strange antiquated breast stroke—copied from an old man with a high-necked bathing suit and a beard. In general, we were not supposed to have anything to do with the neighbors or with other children. It was a rule that other children were not allowed to come into our yard or we to go into theirs, nor were we permitted to walk to school with another boy or girl. But since we were in school most of the day, five days a week, our guardians could not prevent us from making friends despite them; other children were, in fact, very much attracted to us, pitying us for our woebegone condition and respecting us because we were thought to be rich. Our grandmother's chauffeur, Frank, in her winter Pierce-Arrow and summer Locomobile, was well known in the neighborhood, waiting outside church on Sunday to take her home from Mass. Sometimes we were taken, too, and thus our miserable clothes and underfed bodies were associated with high financial status and became a sort of dubious privilege in the eyes of our classmates.

We both had enviable possessions and did not have them. In the closet in my bedroom, high on the top shelf, beyond my reach even standing on a chair, was a stack of cardboard doll boxes, containing wonderful French dolls, dressed by my Seattle grandmother in silks, laces, and satins, with crepe-de-Chine underwear and shoes with high heels. These and other things were sent us every year at Christmastime, but my aunt had decreed that they were all too good for us, so they remained in their boxes and wrappings, *verboten*, except on the rare afternoon, perhaps once in a twelve-month or so, when a relation or a friend of the family would come through from the West, and then down would come the dolls, out would come the baseball gloves and catchers' masks and the watches and the shiny cars and the doll houses, and we would be set to playing with these things on the floor of the living room while the visitor tenderly looked on. As soon as the visitor left, bearing a good report of our household, the dolls and watches and cars would be whisked away, to come out again for the next emergency. If we had been clever, we would have refused this bait and paraded our misery, but we were too simple to do anything but seize the moment and play out a whole year's playtime in this gala hour and a half. Such techniques, of course, are common in concentration camps and penal institutions, where the same sound calculation of human nature is made. The prisoners snatch at their holiday; they trust their guards and the motto *"Carpe diem"* more than they do the strangers who have come to make the inspection. Like all people who have been mistreated, we were wary of being taken in; we felt uneasy about these visitors—Protestants from Seattle—who might be much worse than our uncle and aunt. The latter's faults, at any rate, we knew. Moreover, we had been subjected to propaganda: we had been threatened with the Seattle faction, time and again, by our uncle, who used to jeer and say to us, "*They*'d make you toe the chalk line."

The basis, I think, of my aunt's program for us was in truth totalitarian: she was idealistically bent on destroying our privacy. She imagined herself as enlightened in comparison with our parents, and a super-ideal of health, cleanliness, and discipline softened in her own eyes the measures she applied to attain it. A nature not unkindly was warped by bureaucratic zeal and by her subservience to her husband, whose masterful autocratic hand cut through our nonsense like a cleaver. The fact that our way of life resembled that of an orphan asylum was not a mere coincidence; Aunt Margaret strove purposefully toward a corporate goal. Like most heads of institutions, she longed for the eyes of Argus. To the best of her ability, she saw to it that nothing was hidden from her. Even her health measures had this purpose. The aperients we were continually dosed with guaranteed that our daily processes were open to her inspection, and the monthly medical checkup assured her, by means of stethoscope and searchlight and tongue depressor, that nothing was happening inside us to which she was not privy. Our letters to Seattle were written under her eye, and she scrutinized our homework sharply, though her arithmetic, spelling, and grammar were all very imperfect. We prayed, under supervision, for a prescribed list of people. And if we were forbidden companions, candy, most toys, pocket money, sports, reading, entertainment, the aim was not to make us suffer but to achieve efficiency. It was simpler to interdict other children than to inspect all the children with whom we might want to play. From the standpoint of efficiency, our lives, in order to be open, had to be empty; the books we might perhaps read, the toys we might play with figured in my aunt's mind, no doubt, as what the housewife calls "dust catchers"—around these distractions, dirt might accumulate. The inmost folds of consciousness, like the belly button, were regarded by her as unsanitary. Thus; in her spiritual outlook, my aunt was an early functionalist.

Like all systems, my aunt's was, of course, imperfect. Forbidden to read, we told stories, and if we were kept apart, we told them to ourselves in bed. We made romances out of our schoolbooks, even out of the dictionary, and read digests of novels in the *Book of Knowledge* at school. My uncle's partiality for my youngest brother was a weakness in him, as was my aunt Mary's partiality for me. She was supposed to keep me in her room, sewing on squares of cheap cotton, making handkerchiefs with big, crude, ugly hems, and ripping them out and making them over again, but though she had no feeling for art or visual beauty (she would not even teach me to darn, which is an art, or to do embroidery, as the nuns did later on, in the convent), she liked to talk of the old days in Chicago and to read sensational religious fiction in a magazine called the *Extension,* which sometimes she let me take to my room, with a caution against being caught. And on the Sunday walks that my uncle headed, at the end of an interminable streetcar ride, during which my bigger brothers had to scrunch down to pass for under six, there were occasions on which he took us (in military order) along a wooded path, high above the Mississippi River, and we saw late-spring harebells and, once, a coral-pink snake. In Minnehaha Park, a favorite resort, we were allowed to play on the swings and to examine the other children riding on the ponies or on a little scenic railway. Uncle Myers always bought himself a box of Cracker Jack, which we watched him eat and delve into, to find the little favor at the bottom—a ritual we deeply envied, for, though we sometimes had popcorn at home (Myers enjoyed popping it) and even, once or twice, homemade popcorn balls with molasses, we had never had more than a taste of this commercial Cracker Jack, with peanuts in it, which seemed to us the more valuable because *he* valued it and would often come home eating a box he had bought at a ball game. But one Sunday, Uncle Myers, in full, midsummer mood, wearing his new pedometer, bought my brother Sheridan a whole box for himself.

Naturally, we envied Sheridan—the only blond among us, with fair red-gold curls, while the rest of us were all pronounced brunets, with thick black brows and lashes—as we watched him, the lucky one, munch the sticky stuff and fish out a painted tin butterfly with a little pin on it at the bottom. My brothers clamored around him, but I was too proud to show my feelings. Sheridan was then about six years old, and this butterfly immediately became his most cherished possession—indeed, one of the few he had. He carried it about the house with him all the next week, clutched in his hand or pinned to his shirt, and my two other brothers followed him, begging him to be allowed to play with it, which slightly disgusted me, at the age of ten, for I knew that I was too sophisticated to care for tin butterflies and I felt in this whole affair the instigation of my uncle. He was relishing my brothers' performance and saw to it, strictly, that Sheridan clung to his rights in the butterfly and did not permit anybody to touch it. The point about this painted tin butterfly was not its intrinsic value; it was the fact that it was virtually the only toy in the house that had not been, so to speak, socialized, but belonged privately to one individual. Our other playthings—a broken-down wooden swing, an old wagon, a dirty sandbox, and perhaps a fire engine or so and some defaced blocks and twisted second-hand train tracks in the attic—were held by us all in common, the velocipedes we had brought with us from Seattle having long ago foundered, and the skipping rope, the jacks, the few marbles, and the pair of rusty roller skates that were given us being decreed to be the property of all. Hence, for a full week this butterfly excited passionate emotions, from which I held myself stubbornly apart, refusing even to notice it, until one afternoon, at about four o'clock, while I was doing my weekly chore of dusting the woodwork, my white-haired aunt Mary hurried softly into my room and, closing the door behind her, asked whether I had seen Sheridan's butterfly.

The topic wearied me so much that I scarcely lifted my head, answering no, shortly, and going on with my dusting. But Aunt Mary was gently persistent: Did I know that he had lost it? Would I help her look for it? This project did not appeal to me, but in response to some faint agitation in her manner, something almost pleading, I put down my dustcloth and helped her. We went all over the house, raising carpets, looking behind curtains, in the kitchen cupboards, in the Victrola, everywhere but in the den, which was closed, and in my aunt's and uncle's bedroom. Somehow—I do not know why—I did not expect to find the butterfly, partly, I imagine, because I was indifferent to it and partly out of the fatalism that all children have toward lost objects, regarding them as irretrievable, vanished into the flux of things. At any rate I was right: we did not find it and I went back to my dusting, vindicated. Why should *I* have to look for Sheridan's stupid butterfly, which he ought to have taken better care of? "Myers is upset," said Aunt Mary, still hovering, uneasy and diffident, in the door-way. I made a slight face, and she went out, plaintive, remonstrant, and sighing, in her pale, high necked, tight-buttoned dress.

It did not occur to me that I was suspected of stealing this toy, even when Aunt Margaret, five minutes later, burst into my room and ordered me to come and look for Sheridan's butterfly. I protested that I had already done so, but she paid my objections no heed and seized me roughly by the arm. "Then do it again, Miss, and mind that you find it." Her voice was rather hoarse and her whole furrowed iron-gray aspect somewhat tense and disarrayed, yet I had the impression that she was not angry with me but with something in outer reality—what one would now call fate or contingency. When I had searched again, lackadaisically, and again found nothing, she joined in with vigor, turning everything upside down. We even went into the den, where Myers was sitting, and searched all around him, while he watched us with an ironical expression, filling his pipe from a Bull Durham sack. We found nothing, and Aunt Margaret led me upstairs to my room, which I ransacked while she stood and watched me. All at once, when we had finished with my bureau drawers and my closet, she appeared to give up. She sighed and bit her lips. The door cautiously opened and Aunt Mary came in. The two sisters looked at each other and at me. Margaret shrugged her shoulders. "She hasn't got it, I do believe," she said.

She regarded me then with a certain relaxing of her thick wrinkles, and her heavy-skinned hand, with its wedding ring, came down on my shoulder. "Uncle Myers thinks you took it," she said in a rusty whisper, like a spy or a scout. The consciousness of my own innocence, combined with a sense of being let into the confederacy of the two sisters, filled me with excitement and self-importance. "But I didn't, Aunt Margaret," I began proclaiming, making the most of my moment. "What would I want with his silly old butterfly?" The two sisters exchanged a look. "That's what I said, Margaret!" exclaimed old Aunt Mary sententiously. Aunt Margaret frowned; she adjusted a bone hairpin in the coiled rings of her unbecoming coiffure. "Mary Therese," she said to me, solemnly, "if you know anything about the butterfly, if one of your brothers took it, tell me now. If we don't find it, I'm afraid Uncle Myers will have to punish you." "He *can't* punish me, Aunt Margaret," I insisted, full of righteousness. "Not if I didn't do it and *you* don't think I did it." I looked up at her, stagily trustful, resting gingerly on this solidarity that had suddenly appeared between us. Aunt Mary's pale old eyes watered. "You mustn't let Myers punish her, Margaret, if you don't think she's done wrong." They both glanced up at the Murillo Madonna that was hanging on my stained wall. Intelligence passed between them and I was sure that, thanks to our Holy Mother, Aunt Margaret would save me. "Go along, Mary Therese," she said hoarsely. "Get yourself ready for dinner. And don't you say a word of this to your uncle when you come downstairs."

When I went down to dinner, I was exultant, but I tried to hide it. Throughout the meal, everyone was restrained; Herdie was in the dumps about his butterfly, and Preston and Kevin were silent, casting covert looks at me. My brothers, apparently, were wondering how I had avoided punishment, as the eldest, if for no other reason. Aunt Margaret was rather flushed, which improved her appearance slightly. Uncle Myers had a cunning look, as though events would prove him right. He patted Sheridan's golden head from time to time and urged him to eat. After dinner, the boys filed into the den behind Uncle Myers, and I helped Aunt Margaret clear the table. We did not have to do the dishes, for at this time there was a "girl" in the kitchen. As we were lifting the white tablecloth and the silence pad, we found the butterfly—pinned to the silence pad, right by my place.

My hash was settled then, though I did not know it. I did not catch the significance of its being found at *my* place. To Margaret, however, this was grimly conclusive. She had been too "easy," said her expression; once again Myers had been right. Myers went through the formality of interrogating each of the boys in turn ("No, sir," "No, sir," "No, sir") and even, at my insistence, of calling in the Swedish girl from the kitchen. Nobody knew how the butterfly had got there. It had not been there before dinner, when the girl set the table. My judges therefore concluded that I had had it hidden on my person and had slipped it under the tablecloth at dinner, when nobody was looking. This unanimous verdict maddened me, at first simply as an indication of stupidity—how could they be so dense as to imagine that I would hide it by my own place, where it was sure to be discovered? I did not really believe that I was going to be punished on such ridiculous evidence, yet even I could form no theory of how the butterfly had come there. My first base impulse to accuse the maid was scoffed out of my head by reason. What would a grownup want with a silly six-year-old's toy? And the very unfairness of the condemnation that rested on me made me reluctant to transfer it to one of my brothers. I kept supposing that the truth somehow would out, but the interrogation suddenly ended and every eye avoided mine.

Aunt Mary's dragging step went up the stairs, the boys were ordered to bed, and then, in the lavatory, the whipping began. Myers beat me with the strop, until his lazy arm tired; whipping is hard work for a fat man, out of condition, with a screaming, kicking, wriggling ten-year-old in his grasp. He went out and heaved himself, panting, into his favorite chair and I presumed that the whipping was over. But Aunt Margaret took his place, striking harder than he, with a hairbrush, in a businesslike, joyless way, repeating, "Say you did it, Mary Therese, say you did it." As the blows fell and I did not give in, this formula took on an intercessory note, like a prayer. It was clear to me that she was begging me to surrender and give Myers his satisfaction, for my own sake, so that the whipping could stop. When I finally cried out "All right!" she dropped the hairbrush with a sigh of relief; a new doubt of my guilt must have been visiting her, and my confession set everything square. She led me in to my uncle, and we both stood facing him, as Aunt Margaret, with a firm but not ungentle hand on my shoulder, whispered, "Just tell him, 'Uncle Myers, I did it,' and you can go to bed." But the sight of him, sprawling in his leather chair, complacently waiting for this, was too much for me. The words froze on my tongue. I could not utter them to *him*. Aunt Margaret urged me on, reproachfully, as though I were breaking our compact, but as I looked straight at him and assessed his ugly nature, I burst into yells. "I didn't! I didn't!" I gasped, between screams. Uncle Myers shot a vindictive look at his wife, as though he well understood that there had been collusion between us. He ordered me back to the dark lavatory and symbolically rolled up his sleeve. He laid on the strop decisively, but this time I was beside myself, and when Aunt Margaret hurried in and tried to reason with me, I could only answer with wild cries as Uncle Myers, gasping also, put the strop back on its hook. "You take her," he articulated, but Aunt Margaret's hairbrush this time was perfunctory, after the first few angry blows that punished me for having disobeyed her. Myers did not take up the strop again; the whipping ended, whether from fear of the neighbors or of Aunt Mary's frail presence upstairs or sudden guilty terror, I do not know; perhaps simply because it was past my bedtime.

I finally limped up to bed, with a crazy sense of inner victory, like a saint's, for I had not recanted, despite all they had done or could do to me. It did not occur to me that I had been unchristian in refusing to answer a plea from Aunt Margaret's heart and conscience. Indeed, I rejoiced in the knowledge that I had *made* her continue to beat me long after she must have known that I was innocent; this was her punishment for her condonation of Myers. The next morning, when I opened my eyes on the Murillo Madonna and the Baby Stuart, my feeling of triumph abated; I was afraid of what I had done. But throughout that day and the next, they did not touch me. I walked on air, incredulously and, no doubt, somewhat pompously, seeing myself as a figure from legend: my strength was *as* the strength of ten because my *heart* was pure! Afterward, I was beaten, in the normal routine way, but the question of the butterfly was closed forever in that house.

In my mind, there was, and still is, a connection between the butterfly and our rescue, by our Protestant grandfather, which took place the following year, in the fall or early winter. Already defeated, in their own view, or having ceased to care what became of us, our guardians, for the first time, permitted two of us, my brother Kevin and me, to be alone with this strict, kindly lawyer, as we walked the two blocks between our house and our grandfather McCarthy's. In the course of our walk, between the walls of an early snow, we told Grandpa Preston everything, overcoming our fears and fixing our minds on the dolls, the baseball gloves, and the watches. Yet, as it happened, curiously enough, albeit with a certain aptness, it was not the tale of the butterfly or the other atrocities that chiefly impressed him as he followed our narration with precise legal eyes but the fact that I was not wearing my glasses. I was being punished for breaking them in a fall on the school playground by having to go without; and I could not see why my account of this should make him flush up with anger—to me it was a great relief to be free of those disfiguring things. But he shifted his long, lantern jaw and, settling our hands in his, went straight as a writ up my grandfather McCarthy's front walk. Hence it was on a question of health that this good American's alarms finally alighted; the rest of what we poured out to him he either did not believe or feared to think of, lest he have to deal with the problem of evil.

On health grounds, then, we were separated from Uncle Myers, who disappeared back into Elkhart with his wife and Aunt Mary. My brothers were sent off to the sisters in a Catholic boarding school, with the exception of Sheridan, whom Myers was permitted to bear away with him, like a golden trophy. Sheridan's stay, however, was of short duration. Very soon, Aunt Mary died, followed by Aunt Margaret, followed by Uncle Myers; within five years, still in the prime of life, they were all gone, one, two, three, like ninepins. For me, a new life began, under a happier star. Within a few weeks after my Protestant grandfather's visit, I was sitting in a compartment with him on the train, watching the Missouri River go westward to its source, wearing my white-gold wrist watch and a garish new red hat, a highly nervous child, fanatical against Protestants, who, I explained to Grandpa Preston, all deserved to be burned at the stake. In the dining car, I ordered greedily, lamb chops, pancakes, sausages, and then sat, unable to eat them. "Her eyes," observed the waiter, "are bigger than her stomach."

Six or seven years later, on one of my trips east to college, I stopped in Minneapolis to see my brothers, who were all together now, under the roof of a new and more indulgent guardian, my uncle Louis, the handsomest and youngest of the McCarthy uncles. All the old people were dead; my grandmother McCarthy, but recently passed away, had left a fund to erect a chapel in her name in Texas, a state with which she had no known connection. Sitting in the twilight of my uncle Louis' screened porch, we sought a common ground for our reunion and found it in Uncle Myers. It was then that my brother Preston told me that on the famous night of the butterfly, he had seen Uncle Myers steal into the dining room from the den and lift the tablecloth, with the tin butterfly in his hand.

Uncle Harry tells me that twice in my father's diary, on February 28 and November 7, 1916, the single word, "butterfly," is written over a whole page. Like most of Uncle Harry's contributions, this gave me quite a jar. Inexplicable, I thought, until I remembered that my father, as a boy, collected butterflies. My grandmother had a case of his specimens. That is the only light I can throw on the notation.

As for Uncle Myers, Uncle Harry writes that this "mountain of blubber" claimed to have been a pickle-buyer around Terre Haute, Indiana. I never heard of his being a pickle-buyer, but it goes with him, certainly. On the other hand, those trays of candy did have a professional look. My feeling is that he had not worked at anything since marrying my aunt. According to Uncle Harry, the family firm gave Uncle Myers a job, soliciting grain shipments on the road, with a salary of $250 a month, mileage books, and an expense account. The job was supposed to keep him in western South Dakota, North Dakota, and eastern Montana, where living was cheap. His expense accounts—lunch checks of three and four dollars on transcontinental trains—were a stunner to Uncle Harry, who had thought up the idea of sending him into this semi-arid territory.

If he was on the road, how can he have been at home all the time? I cannot reconcile this, and Uncle Harry's suggestion—that there might have been two of him—does not really help. He was at home all the time; my brother Kevin agrees. The only exception was a short period when he had jury duty; he used to leave the house in the mornings then, wearing a black bowler hat. I like to think of Uncle Myers as a juror. Kevin believes he may have gone away once on a brief trip—to Elkhart, we would have thought. But this may have represented the time of his employment with the Capital Elevator Company, for I cannot suppose that the firm kept him on very long.

Kevin adds a note about Uncle Myers and ball games. With my little brothers, Uncle Myers used to stand outside the ball park until the seventh-inning stretch, when the bleachers were thrown open and anyone could come in, free. Thus they saw only the ends of ball games, as we saw only the beginnings of movies. There was a superb consistency in our life, like that of a work of art. That is why even I find it sometimes incredible. A small correction, however, is necessary: I did once see a full-length feature. It was in the church basement or school auditorium, and the name of the film was The Seal of the Confessional. *I recall a scene in which an atheist who defied God was struck by lightning. Naturally, it was free.*

About the tin butterfly episode, I must make a more serious correction or at least express a doubt. An awful suspicion occurred to me as I was reading it over the other day. I suddenly remembered that in college I had started writing a play on this subject. Could the idea that Uncle Myers put the butterfly at my place have been suggested to me by my teacher? I can almost hear her voice saying to me, excitedly: "Your uncle must have done it!" (She was Mrs. Hallie Flanagan, later head of the Federal Theatre.) And I can visualize a stage scene, with Uncle Myers tip-

toeing in and pinning the butterfly to the silence pad. After a struggle with my conscience (the first Communion again), I sent for Kevin and consulted him about my doubts. He remembers the butterfly episode itself and the terrible whipping; he remembers the scene on Uncle Louis' screened porch when we four, reunited, talked about Uncle Myers. But he does not remember Preston's saying that Uncle Myers put the butterfly there. Preston, consulted by long-distance telephone, does not remember either saying it or seeing it. (He cannot have been more than seven when the incident happened and would be unlikely, therefore, to have preserved such a clear and dramatic recollection.) It still seems to me certain that we at least discussed the butterfly affair on Uncle Louis' porch, and I may have put forward Mrs. Flanagan's theory, to which Preston may have agreed, warmly. He may even, says Kevin, have thought, for the moment, he remembered, once the idea was suggested to him. But this is all conjecture; I do not know, really, whether I took the course in Playwriting before or after the night on Uncle Louis' porch. The most likely thing, I fear, is that I fused two memories. Mea culpa. The play, by the way, was never finished. I did not get beyond the first act, which was set in my grandmother's sun parlor and showed our first meeting with our guardians. It was thinking about that meeting, obviously, that nagged me into remembering Mrs. Flanagan and the play. But who did put the butterfly by my place? It may have been Uncle Myers after all. Even if no one saw him, he remains a suspect: he had motive and opportunity. "I'll bet your uncle did it!"—was that what she said?

It was fall or early winter, I wrote, when my grandfather Preston arrived from Seattle and listened to our tale. Kevin thinks it was spring. We both remember the snow. Probably he is right, for he recalls a sequel to this story that took place in summer, after I had gone and the household had been broken up. He and Preston were taken, temporarily, to stay at my grandmother McCarthy's house. For the first time, they enjoyed the freedom of the streets; up to then, we had all been kept behind our iron fence. He and Preston borrowed a wagon from a neighbor girl named Nancy and rode up and down Blaisdell Avenue, past the house we had lived in. To their surprise, Uncle Myers was still there, sitting on the front porch with Sheridan on his lap. The two little boys rode the borrowed wagon along the sidewalk on the other side of the street, screaming names and taunts at Uncle Myers, reveling like demons in their freedom and his powerlessness to harm them: "Yah, yah, yah!" Uncle Myers made no response; he simply sat there, a passive target, with Sheridan on his knee. No doubt, all the neighbors were watching. For Kevin, as he tells it, Uncle Myers' helplessness slowly took the pleasure out of this victory parade; he felt embarrassed for the motionless fat man and drove the wagon away.

A few days later, they went past the house again. It was empty. Something tempted them to try to get in, and they climbed through a basement window that was open. The house looked very strange; all the furniture had been removed. Suddenly, a fury seized them; they began ripping off the wallpaper—the wallpaper we had been punished for spoiling. They tore it off in strips and then they flung open the medicine cabinet. Someone had forgotten to empty it, and all the family medicines were there, together with an empty jar of Aunt Mary's beef tea. They threw the medicine bottles at the walls, smashing them; a horrible orange color—the prevailing tone of the medicines—was splattered over everything. They were revenging themselves on the house. After they had wrecked it to the limit of their powers, they climbed out through the basement window.

When what they had done was discovered, my grandmother undertook to punish Kevin. She spanked him, in her bathroom, with her hairbrush, pulling him firmly over her knee. It interested him to find that her spanking did not hurt. Prone in her grasp, he howled dutifully, but inwardly he was smiling at her efforts. He thought of Aunt Margaret's hairbrush and Uncle

Myers' razor strop and felt a tenderness for my grandmother—the tenderness of experience toward innocence. That fall, he and Preston were sent to St. Benedict's Academy, after a summer stay at Captain Billy Fawcett's Breezy Point.

A final note on Aunt Margaret's health regimen. I have a perfect digestion and very good health; I suppose I owe it to Aunt Margaret. It is true that we children were sick a great deal before we came to her; and no doubt she hardened us with her prunes and parsnips and no pillow and five-mile hikes. Kevin used to have two snapshots, one taken by Aunt Margaret and one by Uncle Myers; they were inscribed "Before the Five Mile Hike" and "After the Five Mile Hike." The one showing Uncle Myers, in a cap, has mysteriously disappeared during the last year or so. My brother Preston thought he had a photo of him, but that, too, is gone. It is as if Uncle Myers himself had contrived to filch away the proof that he had existed corporeally.

One of the family photographs that has recently come to light shows the four of us children, looking very happy, with a pony on which Preston and Sheridan are sitting. We are all dressed up; I am not wearing my glasses, and my straight hair is softly curled. That pony was a stage prop. He used to be led up and down our street by an itinerant photographer, soliciting trade. The photograph, of course, was sent out west to the Preston family, who were in no position to know that this was the only time we had ever been close to a pony. It was found among my grandmother Preston's effects.

I should have supposed that Uncle Myers and Aunt Margaret were unusual, even unique people. But I had a letter from a reader in Chicago who told me that Myers was so like his father that he was tempted to believe in reincarnation. And Aunt Margaret's regimen was almost precisely that followed in this reader's household fifteen years later: the same menus, with the addition of codfish balls, the same prolonged sessions on "the throne," the same turning over of the mattress to make sure it had not been wet, the same putting away of presents on the grounds that they were "much too good." There was the razor strop, too, and the dream of being admitted to an orphan asylum, and the threat that some other members of the family (possibly Protestants) would "make you toe the chalk line." This man and his sister had lost only their mother; the neighbors used to feed them, too.

Even more curious was a letter from Australia from a woman of sixty, telling me that reading "Yonder Peasant" had been "probably the most uncanny experience" of her life. She and her four brothers and sisters had lost both their parents, and their childhood, she said, was an almost complete replica of mine. "Had I your gift of writing . . . I should have written long ago, and written a story that would have been disbelieved, because it would have been so unbelievable—and yet every word of it would have been starkly true. That was why I read and reread your article which . . . was so like our experience . . . that it seemed I was writing and not you."

This woman had been born a Catholic, like the man in Chicago. Her father had married a Protestant.

QUESTIONS FOR DISCUSSION AND WRITING

1. Some readers are intrigued by McCarthy's inability to distinguish between the facts of her childhood and her possibly false memories of events. Others find the ambiguity frustrating, even annoying. How do you respond? Would you character-

ize McCarthy's "taking it all back" as a mark of her honesty? Her willingness to manipulate the reader? An artistic desire to have something "both ways"?

2. Although this chapter from *Memories of a Catholic Girlhood* is entitled "A Tin Butterfly," the tin butterfly episode takes up very little of the chapter's space. Why does McCarthy apportion her space as she does? What is the effect of her using the chapter's title to refer to the one event about which she is the *least* certain? What is the effect of her titling the chapter "*A* Tin Butterfly" rather than "*The* Tin Butterfly"?

3. Examine the descriptions and characterizations of Uncle Myers and Aunt Margaret. How do the physical descriptions of the two guardians contribute to our responses to them? (You will want to consider not only the literal meanings of the descriptions but also the connotations of the words McCarthy chooses.) How would you retell the story from the point of view of either Aunt Margaret or Uncle Myers?

4. McCarthy's narrative is a "retelling" in a couple of ways: in retracting her accusation against Myers, she asks us to retell the story of the tin butterfly and rethink its implications. But one could also say that her way of telling the story of her own life is itself a kind of retelling of the fictions she was so drawn to. Look, for instance, at the ways she compares and contrasts her parents and her guardians and at the ways in which she characterizes herself as a kind of martyr. How might her life be read as a kind of saint's life or as a fairy tale? How do her choices of words and images reinforce that reading?

5. Most of us have had the experience that Mary McCarthy has had: we remember a childhood event vividly but, when we check with other family members, we discover that our memories and theirs are different in crucial ways. Sometimes what we *know* happened *could not* have happened. Examine such a memory from your own life. How are your memories different from those of others? How do you explain those differences? (Think in terms not only of the reason that one person's memory faculties might be superior to another's but also of each person's emotional and psychological needs to envision and "remember" a particular truth.)

E. B. WHITE (1899–1985)

Once More to the Lake _____ 1941

August 1941

One summer, along about 1904, my father rented a camp on a lake in Maine and took us all there for the month of August. We all got ringworm from some kittens and had to rub Pond's Extract on our arms and legs night and morning, and my father rolled over in a canoe with all his clothes on; but outside of that the vacation was a success and from then on none of us ever thought there was any place in the world like that lake in Maine. We returned summer after summer—always on August 1st for one month. I have since become a salt-water man, but sometimes in summer there are days when the restlessness of the tides and the fearful cold of the sea water and the incessant wind which blows across the afternoon and into the evening make me wish for the placidity of a lake in the woods. A few weeks ago this feeling got so strong I bought myself a couple of bass hooks and a spinner and returned to the lake where we used to go, for a week's fishing and to revisit old haunts.

I took along my son, who had never had any fresh water up his nose and who had seen lily pads only from train windows. On the journey over to the lake I began to wonder what it would be like. I wondered how time would have marred this unique, this holy spot—the coves and streams, the hills that the sun set behind, the camps and the paths behind the camps. I was sure that the tarred road would have found it out and I wondered in what other ways it would be desolated. It is strange how much you can remember about places like that once you allow your mind to re-turn into the grooves which lead back. You remember one thing, and that suddenly reminds you of another thing. I guess I remembered clearest of all the early mornings, when the lake was cool and motionless, remembered how the bedroom smelled of the lumber it was made of and of the wet woods whose scent entered through the screen. The partitions in the camp were thin and did not extend clear to the top of the rooms, and as I was always the first up I would dress softly so as not to wake the others, and sneak out into the sweet outdoors and start out in the canoe, keeping close along the shore in the long shadows of the pines. I remembered being very care-ful never to rub my paddle against the gunwale for fear of disturbing the stillness of the cathedral.

The lake had never been what you would call a wild lake. There were cottages sprinkled around the shores, and it was in farming country although the shores of the lake were quite heavily wooded. Some of the cottages were owned by nearby farm-ers, and you would live at the shore and eat your meals at the farmhouse. That's what our family did. But although it wasn't wild, it was a fairly large and undisturbed lake and there were places in it which, to a child at least, seemed infinitely remote and primeval.

I was right about the tar: it led to within half a mile of the shore. But when I got back there, with my boy, and we settled into a camp near a farmhouse and into the kind of summertime I had known, I could tell that it was going to be pretty much the same as it had been before—I knew it, lying in bed the first morning, smelling the bedroom, and hearing the boy sneak quietly out and go off along the shore in a boat. I began to sustain the illusion that he was I, and therefore, by simple transposition, that I was my father. This sensation persisted, kept cropping up all the time we were there. It was not an entirely new feeling, but in this setting it grew much stronger. I seemed to be living a dual existence. I would be in the middle of some simple act, I would be picking up a bait box or laying down a table fork, or I would be saying something, and suddenly it would be not I but my father who was saying the words or making the gesture. It gave me a creepy sensation.

We went fishing the first morning. I felt the same damp moss covering the worms in the bait can, and saw the dragonfly alight on the tip of my rod as it hovered a few inches from the surface of the water. It was the arrival of this fly that convinced me beyond any doubt that everything was as it always had been, that the years were a mirage and there had been no years. The small waves were the same, chucking the rowboat under the chin as we fished at anchor, and the boat was the same boat, the same color green and the ribs broken in the same places, and under the floor-boards the same fresh-water leavings and débris—the dead helgramite, the wisps of moss, the rusty discarded fishhook, the dried blood from yesterday's catch. We stared silently at the tips of our rods, at the dragonflies that came and went. I lowered the tip of mine into the water, tentatively, pensively dislodging the fly, which darted two feet away, poised, darted two feet back, and came to rest again a little farther up the rod. There had been no years between the ducking of this dragonfly and the other one—the one that was part of memory. I looked at the boy, who was silently watching his fly, and it was my hands that held his rod, my eyes watching. I felt dizzy and didn't know which rod I was at the end of.

We caught two bass, hauling them in briskly as though they were mackerel, pulling them over the side of the boat in a businesslike manner without any landing net, and stunning them with a blow on the back of the head. When we got back for a swim before lunch, the lake was exactly where we had left it, the same number of inches from the dock, and there was only the merest suggestion of a breeze. This seemed an utterly enchanted sea, this lake you could leave to its own devices for a few hours and come back to, and find that it had not stirred, this constant and trustworthy body of water. In the shallows, the dark, water-soaked sticks and twigs, smooth and old, were undulating in clusters on the bottom against the clean ribbed sand, and the track of the mussel was plain. A school of minnows swam by, each minnow with its small individual shadow, doubling the attendance, so clear and sharp in the sunlight. Some of the other campers were in swimming, along the shore, one of them with a cake of soap, and the water felt thin and clear and unsubstantial. Over the years there had been this person with the cake of soap, this cultist, and here he was. There had been no years.

Up to the farmhouse to dinner through the teeming, dusty field, the road under our sneakers was only a two-track road. The middle track was missing, the one with the marks of the hooves and the splotches of dried, flaky manure. There had always been three tracks to choose from in choosing which track to walk in; now the choice was narrowed down to two. For a moment I missed terribly the middle alternative. But the way led past the tennis court, and something about the way it lay there in the sun reassured me; the tape had loosened along the backline, the alleys were green with plantains and other weeds, and the net (installed in June and removed in September) sagged in the dry noon, and the whole place steamed with midday heat and hunger and emptiness. There was a choice of pie for dessert, and one was blueberry and one was apple, and the waitresses were the same country girls, there having been no passage of time, only the illusion of it as in a dropped curtain—the waitresses were still fifteen; their hair had been washed, that was the only difference—they had been to the movies and seen the pretty girls with the clean hair.

Summertime, oh summertime, pattern of life indelible, the fadeproof lake, the woods unshatterable, the pasture with the sweetfern and the juniper forever and ever, summer without end; this was the background, and the life along the shore was the design, the cottagers with their innocent and tranquil design, their tiny docks with the flagpole and the American flag floating against the white clouds in the blue sky, the little paths over the roots of the trees leading from camp to camp and the paths leading back to the outhouses and the can of lime for sprinkling, and at the souvenir counters at the store the miniature birch-bark canoes and the post cards that showed things looking a little better than they looked. This was the American family at play, escaping the city heat, wondering whether the newcomers in the camp at the head of the cove were "common" or "nice," wondering whether it was true that the people who drove up for Sunday dinner at the farmhouse were turned away because there wasn't enough chicken.

It seemed to me, as I kept remembering all this, that those times and those summers had been infinitely precious and worth saving. There had been jollity and peace and goodness. The arriving (at the beginning of August) had been so big a business in itself, at the railway station the farm wagon drawn up, the first smell of the pine-laden air, the first glimpse of the smiling farmer, and the great importance of the trunks and your father's enormous authority in such matters, and the feel of the wagon under you for the long ten-mile haul, and at the top of the last long hill catching the first view of the lake after eleven months of not seeing this cherished body of water. The shouts and cries of the other campers when they saw you, and the trunks to be unpacked, to give up their rich burden. (Arriving was less exciting nowadays, when you sneaked up in your car and parked it under a tree near the camp and took out the bags and in five minutes it was all over, no fuss, no loud wonderful fuss about trunks.)

Peace and goodness and jollity. The only thing that was wrong now, really, was the sound of the place, an unfamiliar nervous sound of the outboard motors. This was the note that jarred, the one thing that would sometimes break the illusion and set the years moving. In those other summertimes all motors were inboard; and when they were at a little distance, the noise they made was a sedative, an ingredient of summer sleep. They were one-cylinder and two-cylinder engines, and some were make-and-break and some were jump-spark, but they all made a sleepy sound across the lake. The one-lungers throbbed and fluttered, and the twin-cylinder ones purred and purred, and that was a quiet sound too. But now the campers all had outboards. In the daytime, in the hot mornings, these motors made a petulant, irritable sound; at night, in the still evening when the afterglow lit the water, they whined about one's ears like mosquitoes. My boy loved our rented outboard, and his great desire was to achieve singlehanded mastery over it, and authority, and he soon learned the trick of choking it a little (but not too much), and the adjustment of the needle valve. Watching him I would remember the things you could do with the old one-cylinder engine with the heavy flywheel, how you could have it eating out of your hand if you got really close to it spiritually. Motor boats in those days didn't have clutches, and you would make a landing by shutting off the motor at the proper time and coasting in with a dead rudder. But there was a way of reversing them, if you learned the trick, by cutting the switch and putting it on again exactly on the final dying revolution of the flywheel, so that it would kick back against compression and begin reversing. Approaching a dock in a strong following breeze, it was difficult to slow up sufficiently by the ordinary coasting method, and if a boy felt he had complete mastery over his motor, he was tempted to keep it running beyond its time and then reverse it a few feet from the dock. It took a cool nerve, because if you threw the switch a twentieth of a second too soon you could catch the flywheel when it still had speed enough to go up past center, and the boat would leap ahead, charging bull-fashion at the dock.

We had a good week at the camp. The bass were biting well and the sun shone endlessly, day after day. We would be tired at night and lie down in the accumulated heat of the little bedrooms after the long hot day and the breeze would stir almost imperceptibly outside and the smell of the swamp drift in through the rusty screens. Sleep would come easily and in the morning the red squirrel would be on the roof, tapping out his gay routine. I kept remembering everything, lying in bed in the mornings—the small steamboat that had a long rounded stern like the lip of a Ubangi, and how quietly she ran on the moonlight sails, when the older boys played their mandolins and the girls sang and we ate doughnuts dipped in sugar, and how sweet the music was on the water in the shining night, and what it had felt like to think about girls then. After breakfast we would go up to the store and the things were in the same place—the minnows in a bottle, the plugs and spinners disarranged and pawed over by the youngsters from the boys' camp, the fig newtons and the Beeman's gum. Outside, the road was tarred and cars stood in front of the store. Inside, all was just as it had always been, except there was more Coca Cola and not so much Moxie and root beer and birch beer and sarsaparilla. We would walk out with a bottle of pop apiece and sometimes the pop would backfire up our noses and hurt. We explored the streams, quietly, where the turtles slid off the sunny logs and dug their way into the soft bottom; and we lay on the town wharf and fed worms to the tame bass. Everywhere we went I had trouble making out which was I, the one walking at my side, the one walking in my pants.

One afternoon while we were there at that lake a thunderstorm came up. It was like the revival of an old melodrama that I had seen long ago with childish awe. The second-act climax of the drama of the electrical disturbance over a lake in America had not changed in any important respect. This was the big scene, still the big scene. The whole thing was so familiar, the first feeling of oppression and heat and a general air around camp of not wanting to go very far away. In midafternoon (it was all the same) a curious darkening of the sky, and a lull in everything that had made life tick; and then the way the boats suddenly swung the other way at their moorings with the coming of a breeze out of the new quarter, and the premonitory rumble. Then the kettle drum, then the snare, then the bass drum and cymbals, then crackling light against the dark, and the gods grinning and licking their chops in the hills. Afterward the calm, the rain steadily rustling in the calm lake, the return of light and hope and spirits, and the campers running out in joy and relief to go swimming in the rain, their bright cries perpetuating the deathless joke about how they were getting simply drenched, and the children screaming with delight at the new sensation of bathing in the rain, and the joke about getting drenched linking the generations in a strong indestructible chain. And the comedian who waded in carrying an umbrella.

When the others went swimming my son said he was going in too. He pulled his dripping trunks from the line where they had hung all through the shower, and wrung them out. Languidly, and with no thought of going in, I watched him, his hard little body, skinny and bare, saw him wince slightly as he pulled up around his vitals the small, soggy, icy garment. As he buckled the swollen belt suddenly my groin felt the chill of death.

QUESTIONS FOR DISCUSSION AND WRITING

1. White's essay describes some significant differences between his past experience and the present one. What types of things have changed and what types have stayed

the same? Did the essay make you more aware of the similarities between the two camp experiences or of the differences?

2. At the end of the story, White feels "the chill of death" as his son pulls on the cold, wet swimming trunks. Why?

3. Analyze White's style. When does it seem exaggerated and romantic? When does it seem matter-of-fact? Consider not only word choices but also sentence lengths and rhythms. How does White's style reflect the moods and meanings he is trying to convey?

MAKING CONNECTIONS: LIFE PASSAGES

1. "Little Red Riding Hood" and *Peter Pan* are both widely known children's stories, the first a folktale created by "the folk" over many generations and the second written by J. M. Barrie in the nineteenth century. How do the stories view childhood? What threatens childhood in these stories? Do adults and children respond to the stories in the same or different ways? How do their differing processes of creation affect the stories and their themes?

2. Some of the works in this chapter are "coming-of-age" stories, stories that represent a character's crossing of the threshold to adult awareness. Which stories fit this category? How do the moments of awareness compare? In what ways might the Peter Pan stories be viewed as *anti*-coming-of-age stories?

3. Death is an overwhelming fact of life, and writers throughout the ages have tried to come to terms with it. Looking at some of the works that deal with death, consider how the writers view the great fact of mortality. What consolations, if any, are offered? How is death presented—as something fearful, or something natural, or something leading to an afterlife?

4. Several of the works in this chapter (for instance, "Her First Ball," the Little Red Riding Hood stories, and the Peter Pan stories) deal with the dawning of sexual awareness. Sometimes that awareness is presented directly and sometimes indirectly. How do various authors view adolescence and sexual maturity? How do the cultural backgrounds of the authors affect their portrayals?

5. Nostalgia is a very adult emotion, one that is often bittersweet. Which of the works in this chapter would you consider nostalgic? How do the authors view the past? Realistically or sentimentally? In what ways does their view of the past influence their (or their characters') relationship to the present?

6. In both "Paul's Case" and "The Red Convertible" we witness the death, possibly suicide, of a young man. Why do these young men find life intolerable? To what extent is their unhappiness caused by forces outside their control?

7. One might view adulthood as maturity, as the coming to full physical, emotional, and mental powers. On the other hand, it might be viewed as a loss of the freshness and innocence of childhood. Which of the works in this chapter see childhood and adulthood as opposed? Which stage of life is seen as "better"—and why?

Innocence Lost

Henri Matisse, *Icaire*.

CHAPTER INTRODUCTION

After the horrific events of September 11, 2001, we heard again and again from commentator after commentator, "Things will never be the same." We were told, "Americans have lost their innocence. Never again will they feel secure. They are now learning what the rest of the world has long known: the world is a very dangerous place, and there are no safe havens." Paradoxically, such comments seemed at the same time both profoundly true and profoundly simplistic.

Perhaps more than other peoples, many Americans have often assumed that they were a chosen people, living a golden dream of freedom and prosperity. Part of the country's cultural history, part of its cultural myth, is that when situations become intolerable, Americans move on, leaving behind old civilizations and old problems in an attempt to create new American utopias. Because eighteenth-century England did not offer freedoms enough, some of its citizens set sail for a new land. Because these new immigrants chafed at British colonial restraints, they freed themselves from them, creating a new nation. Because East Coast traditions seemed confining, many immigrants set out for the West, looking to the western horizon for a new frontier. Even in the twentieth and twenty-first centuries, many would say that the American dream of expansion is alive and well. Although America no longer has any geographical horizon left, many Americans look to the future, creating visions out of expanding technologies and economies; they may even look to the infinities of outer space, called the "final frontier" on a popular television series. If things are not yet perfect, maybe they soon will be.

History and geography have often seemed to work together to make these visions of an ideal society seem possible. Whereas elsewhere in the world, nations jostle against each other, eyeing each other uneasily across their borders, Americans have had almost a full continent to stretch out in. Despite America's superpower status, its citizens have often felt comfortably separate from the rest of the world. Even the wars in which they have participated have sometimes seemed remote to Americans at home. World War I and World War II were both, in the words of an old song, "over there." While America's allies (and enemies) suffered the devastation and terrors of repeated bombings, the homeland was safe. No shots were fired on U.S. continental soil. More recent wars were even farther "over there," in faraway locales, such as Korea and Vietnam, which seemed distant even to well-traveled or well-read Americans.

For many Americans, September 11 changed all this. For the first time in American history, the war was on U.S. continental soil; the casualties were American civilians going about their everyday lives. Suddenly, the world seemed smaller and the dangers closer than they had ever seemed before. Government officials repeatedly told Americans to stay on "high alert," validating people's anxiety rather than offering the reassurance they hoped for. Truly, Americans' experience of their place in the world seemed profoundly changed after September 11.

At the same time, many also knew that in important ways nothing had really changed. One of the lessons of maturity is that the seemingly absolute comforts and reassurances of home belong only to children, not adults; adults know that life is inherently dangerous and that our securities and prosperities can be attacked and undermined by forces outside our control. We know that truth as individuals and we know it as nations, for it is a lesson taught again and again by history. Repeatedly—not just on September 11—Americans have lost their illusions. Some may have thought of America as a "melting pot," with people of all races and ethnicities living harmoniously together, but of course others knew differently, and the Civil Rights movement of the 1960s showed everyone the racial divisions beneath the surface. Americans lost their illusions then, too. In 1963, when racial tensions led to the bombing of a church in Birmingham, Alabama, and the deaths of four little girls, *Newsweek* headlined, "My God, You're Not Even Safe in Church" (see 891). With horror Americans reacted to the idea that one more sanctuary was gone. They lost their illusions again during the Vietnam War, a war that called into question the apparent truths of previous wars, with their goals of going "over there" to "make the world safe for democracy." Unlike earlier international wars, the Vietnam War—or at least the verbal war about it—*was* fought on American soil, as Americans watched news footage of the death and devastation from their comfortable living rooms and as protest marches filled American streets. The war came home, as those same living rooms became battlefields for arguments between parents and children who had profoundly different ideas about how—or whether—the United States should be engaged in Vietnam.

Americans lost their innocence then, too, as well as their sense of youthful invincibil-ity. This, after all, was a war America could not win. So deep were the divisions cre-ated by that war that, as two of the articles included in this chapter make clear, even years after the war's end, controversy raged over how best to memorialize the Ameri-can soldiers who died in Vietnam.

Perhaps every generation must lose its innocence, coming to adulthood with the recognition that security belongs to no place and no time, to no society ever known. Though the shock of recognition may be particularly strong in a young na-tion that seems to offer boundless opportunities and possibilities, that shock of recog-nition is not, of course, only American. The double vision—the need to create an ideal world and the recognition of the brutalities of the real world—is apparent in "Naming of Parts," a poem written in 1946 by the British poet Henry Reed.

HENRY REED (1914–1986)
Naming of Parts _____ 1946

Today we have naming of parts. Yesterday,
We had daily cleaning. And tomorrow morning,
We shall have what to do after firing. But today,
Today we have naming of parts. Japonica
Glistens like coral in all of the neighboring gardens,   5
    And today we have naming of parts.

This is the lower sling swivel. And this
Is the upper sling swivel, whose use you will see,
When you are given your slings. And this is the piling swivel,
Which in your case you have not got. The branches   10
Hold in the gardens their silent, eloquent gestures,
    Which in our case we have not got.

This is the safety-catch, which is always released
With an easy flick of the thumb. And please do not let me
See anyone using his finger. You can do it quite easy   15
If you have any strength in your thumb. The blossoms
Are fragile and motionless, never letting anyone see
    Any of them using their finger.

And this you can see is the bolt. The purpose of this
Is to open the breech, as you see. We can slide it   20
Rapidly backwards and forwards: we call this
Easing the spring. And rapidly backwards and forwards
The early bees are assaulting and fumbling the flowers:
    They call it easing the Spring.

They call it easing the Spring: it is perfectly easy   25
If you have any strength in your thumb: like the bolt,
And the breech, and the cocking-piece, and the point of balance,

Which in our case we have not got; and the almond-blossom
Silent in all of the gardens and the bees going backwards and forwards,
30　　　　　For today we have naming of parts.

The detached voice of the instructor takes for granted the lethal purpose of the weapon. We are told, "And tomorrow morning, / We shall have what to do after firing." The emphasis of tomorrow's lesson, we suspect, will continue to be on the gun; the human casualties are simply accepted, taken for granted. At the same time, however, the attention of the novice soldier listening to the lesson constantly wanders away from the gun to the "neighboring gardens," with their fragile blossoms and fumbling bees and the life-giving process of pollination. There is no "point of balance," we are told near the end of the poem, no way to reconcile the deadly horror of war and the vision of an Edenic garden. And so the poem shifts abruptly between the two, just as for individuals and nations the cycle of hope and disillusionment is always renewed.

After September 11, things will never be the same—but they never are, no matter what happens. As you read the selections that follow, you will see repeatedly the need to look for havens, whether in the past, the present, or the future, whether at home or abroad. Writers of all times and cultures have searched for those havens, no matter how many times they have witnessed defeat, no matter how many times innocence has been lost. In the selections that follow, you will see too how often writers give voice to their sadness, disillusionment, and outrage with the imperfections of the social world—passions that are often, however, only the other side of their hopes.

The story of Icarus, one of the stories featured in this chapter, captures that intermingling of hope and disillusionment. Imprisoned by a monster, Icarus and his father, Daedalus, fashion waxen wings with which to fly away. As they reach toward the heavens, Icarus flies too close to the sun, melting his wings and falling to his death. Henri Matisse's painting *Icaire* (at the opening of this chapter) catches the ambiguity of the story. With birdlike wings, Icarus is flying in the heavens. Does the picture show him in the moment of ascent or fall? Perhaps it does not matter, for ascent implies descent, just as disillusionment feeds on hope. As the poet Robert Hayden says of Icarus and Daedalus (and perhaps of us all), life is

weaving a wish and a weariness together
to make two wings.

An Album of Retellings

TRANSGRESSIONS: LOT'S WIFE

Genesis 19

And there came two angels to Sodom at even: and Lot sat in the gate of Sodom: and Lot seeing them rose up to meet them; and he bowed himself with his face toward the ground;

2　And he said, Behold now, my lords, turn in, I pray you, into your servant's house, and tarry all night, and wash your feet, and ye shall rise up early, and go on your ways. And they said, Nay; but we will abide in the street all night.

3 And he pressed upon them greatly; and they turned in unto him, and entered into his house; and he made them a feast, and did bake unleavened bread, and they did eat.

4 But before they lay down, the men of the city, even the men of Sodom, compassed the house round, both old and young, all the people from every quarter:

5 And they called unto Lot, and said unto him, Where are the men which came in to thee this night? bring them out unto us, that we may know them.

6 And Lot went out at the door unto them, and shut the door after him,

7 And said, I pray you, brethren, do not so wickedly.

8 Behold now, I have two daughters which have not known man; let me, I pray you, bring them out unto you, and do ye to them as is good in your eyes: only unto these men do nothing; for therefore came they under the shadow of my roof.

9 And they said, Stand back. And they said again, This one fellow came in to sojourn, and he will needs be a judge: now will we deal worse with thee, than with them. And they pressed sore upon the man, even Lot, and came near to break the door.

10 But the men put forth their hand, and pulled Lot into the house to them, and shut to the door.

11 And they smote the men that were at the door of the house with blindness, both small and great: so that they wearied themselves to find the door.

12 And the men said unto Lot, Hast thou here any besides? son in law, and thy sons, and thy daughters, and whatsoever thou hast in the city, bring them out of this place:

13 For we will destroy this place, because the cry of them is waxen great before the face of the LORD; and the LORD hath sent us to destroy it.

14 And Lot went out, and spake unto his sons in law, which married his daughters, and said, Up, get you out of this place; for the LORD will destroy this city. But he seemed as one that mocked unto his sons in law.

15 And when the morning arose, then the angels hastened Lot, saying, Arise, take thy wife, and thy two daughters, which are here; lest thou be consumed in the iniquity of the city.

16 And while he lingered, the men laid hold upon his hand, and upon the hand of his wife, and upon the hand of his two daughters; the LORD being merciful unto him: and they brought him forth, and set him without the city.

17 And it came to pass, when they had brought them forth abroad, that he said, Escape for thy life; look not behind thee, neither stay thou in all the plain; escape to the mountain, lest thou be consumed.

18 And Lot said unto them, Oh, not so, my Lord:

19 Behold now, thy servant hath found grace in thy sight, and thou hast magnified thy mercy, which thou hast shewed unto me in saving my life; and I cannot escape to the mountain, lest some evil take me, and I die:

20 Behold now, this city is near to flee unto, and it is a little one: Oh, let me escape thither, (is it not a little one?) and my soul shall live.

21 And he said unto him, See, I have accepted thee concerning this thing also, that I will not overthrow this city, for the which thou hast spoken.

22 Haste thee, escape thither; for I cannot do any thing till thou be come thither. Therefore the name of the city was called Zoar.

23 The sun was risen upon the earth when Lot entered into Zoar.

24 Then the LORD rained upon Sodom and upon Gō-mŏr'-răh brimstone and fire from the LORD out of heaven;

25 And he overthrew those cities, and all the plain, and all the inhabitants of the cities, and that which grew upon the ground.

26 But his wife looked back from behind him, and she became a pillar of salt.

27 And Abraham gat up early in the morning to the place where he stood before the LORD:

28 And he looked toward Sodom and Gō-mŏr'-răh, and toward all the land of the plain, and beheld, and, lo, the smoke of the country went up as the smoke of a furnace.

29 And it came to pass, when God destroyed the cities of the plain, that God remembered Abraham, and sent Lot out of the midst of the overthrow, when he overthrew the cities in the which Lot dwelt.

30 And Lot went up out of Zoar, and dwelt in the mountain, and his two daughters with him; for he feared to dwell in Zoar: and he dwelt in a cave, he and his two daughters.

31 And the firstborn said unto the younger, Our father is old, and there is not a man in the earth to come in unto us after the manner of all the earth:

32 Come, let us make our father drink wine, and we will lie with him, that we may preserve seed of our father.

33 And they made their father drink wine that night: and the firstborn went in, and lay with her father; and he perceived not when she lay down, nor when she arose.

34 And it came to pass on the morrow, that the firstborn said unto the younger, Behold, I lay yesternight with my father: let us make him drink wine this night also; and go thou in, and lie with him, that we may preserve seed of our father.

35 And they made their father drink wine that night also: and the younger arose, and lay with him; and he perceived not when she lay down, nor when she arose.

36 Thus were both the daughters of Lot with child by their father.

37 And the firstborn bare a son, and called his name Moab: the same is the father of the Moabites unto this day.

38 And the younger, she also bare a son, and called his name Bĕn-ăm'-mī: the same is the father of the children of Ammon unto this day.

QUESTIONS FOR DISCUSSION AND WRITING

1. Though God decides to destroy Sodom and Gomorrah, He spares Lot. What in the story suggests Lot is worthy of a special deliverance? How would you describe Lot's character? (Think not only about the character traits that might cause him to be delivered but also about those traits you may find less admirable.)

2. We learn very little about Lot's wife in this story. Why do you think Lot was told not to look back? Why might his wife have disobeyed the injunction when Lot did not?

ANNA AKHMATOVA (1889–1966)

Lot's Wife _____ before 1940

The just man followed then his angel guide
Where he strode on the black highway, hulking and bright;
But a wild grief in his wife's bosom cried,
Look back, it is not too late for a last sight

Of the red towers of your native Sodom, the square   5
Where once you sang, the gardens you shall mourn,
And the tall house with empty windows where
You loved your husband and your babes were born.

She turned, and looking on the bitter view
Her eyes were welded shut by mortal pain;   10
Into transparent salt her body grew,
And her quick feet were rooted in the plain.

Who would waste tears upon her? Is she not
The least of our losses, this unhappy wife?
Yet in my heart she will not be forgot   15
Who, for a single glance, gave up her life.

                    (Translated by Richard Wilbur)

QUESTIONS FOR DISCUSSION AND WRITING

1. What reason does the poem give for the backward glance of Lot's wife?
2. What is the speaker's attitude toward Lot's wife and her transgression? To what extent do you share that attitude?

STEVIE SMITH (1902–1971)

Lot's Wife _____ 1972

"In that rich, oil-bearing region, it is probable that Lot's wife was turned into a pillar of asphalt—not salt."

—Sir William Whitebait, Member of the Institute of Mining Engineers

I long for the desolate valleys,
Where the rivers of asphalt flow,
For here in the streets of the living,
Where my footsteps run to and fro,

5   Though my smile be never so friendly,
     I offend wherever I go.

     Yes, here in the land of the living,
     Though a marriage be fairly sprung,
     And the heart be loving and giving,
10   In the end it is sure to go wrong.

     Then take me to the valley of asphalt,
     And turn me to a river of stone,
     That no tree may shift to my sighing,
     Or breezes convey my moan.

QUESTIONS FOR DISCUSSION AND WRITING

1. Lot's wife seems to be the speaker of the poem. Why is she unhappy?
2. In the original biblical story, Lot's wife is turned into a pillar of salt because she looks back to Sodom. Why does Smith have her change into "a river of stone" in a "valley of asphalt" instead of a "pillar of salt"? Do we respond differently to Smith's image than to that of the biblical original?

KRISTINE BATEY (1951–   )

Lot's Wife _____ *1978*

     While Lot, the conscience of a nation,
     struggles with the Lord,
     she struggles with the housework.
     The City of Sin is where
5   she raises the children.
     Ba'al or Adonai—
     Whoever is God—
     the bread must still be made
     and the doorsill swept.
10   The Lord may kill the children tomorrow,
     but today they must be bathed and fed.
     Well and good to condemn your neighbors' religion;
     but weren't they there
     when the baby was born,
15   and when the well collapsed?
     While her husband communes with God
     she tucks the children into bed.
     In the morning, when he tells her of the judgment,
     she puts down the lamp she is cleaning

and calmly begins to pack.   20
In between bundling up the children
and deciding what will go,
she runs for a moment
to say goodbye to the herd,
gently patting each soft head   25
with tears in her eyes for the animals that will not understand.
She smiles blindly to the woman
who held her hand at childbed.
It is easy for eyes that have always turned to heaven
not to look back;   30
those that have been—by necessity—drawn to earth
cannot forget that life is lived from day to day.
Good, to a God, and good in human terms
are two different things.
On the breast of the hill, she chooses to be human,   35
and turns, in farewell—
and never regrets
the sacrifice.

QUESTIONS FOR DISCUSSION AND WRITING

1. In characterizing Lot's wife, how much does Batey modernize her? To what extent
   are the tasks performed by Lot's wife timeless?
2. The poem opposes Lot's heavenly vision with his wife's earthbound one. Which of
   the two perspectives does the poem support more? Is it sacrilegious to say that
   "good" is different for God and for humans?

CHRISTINE HOLBO

Gomorrah   *1992*

Also, in Gomorrah, there were plays,
a life of the mind;
there were the schools
and the quiet temples; Sodom
and "the new theatre"   5
were conveniently located,
just an hour's ride away. There
the wife of Lot held her
gatherings, "my *petites
soirées*," for the priests   10
and the politicians
and the intellectual élite.

> *And in the hills the wild dogs cried*
> *And the sand shifted on the desert stones.*

15 But Gomorrah was mostly as you will have heard:
    litigious, polyglot, city of worlds; a scene
    from a favorite story frequently told.
    There was the traffic, the market banter—
    merchants crying catalogues of marvels: uncut
20 rubies, silver mirrors, porcelain,
    parrots, olives at discount, clocks and
    sea salt, carbuncles, pearls—the streets
    full of crowds, the dirty gypsies,
    the quick brown-ankled girls,
25 the old men smoking on the temple
    stoop, the smells of hashish and tanneries,
    the bellowing herds.

> *And in the hills the wild dogs cried*
> *And the desert gods shifted sand across the stones.*

30 The wife of Lot
    was not *so* young anymore.
    She didn't laugh like
    the brown-ankled girls;
    the wife of Lot wore a veil in public,
35 and held her tongue.
    And she kept the books
    in the family establishment,
    was quick with an abacus
    or a bon mot or advice about money;
40 knew how to cook
    wild duck with rice, how to
    pack a camel—and the best caterers
    in town "just like old friends,"
    and most of the city councilmen.
45 The wife of Lot
    did what she thought
    fitting and appropriate
    for the wife of a public figure
    and a pillar of the community.

> *And the gods ran along the desert*
> *And a voice echoed across the stones.*

    Also, the forenamed woman kept
    the books from "my schoolgirl days"
    at the Temple. She remembered
55 learning how to pray,
    and the philosophers, taught

by an old and frightening priest
at the gilded knees of an idol.
"Someday I'll get back to
them," she would say.   60

The wife of Lot
had two pretty daughters,
"the very image of their mother";
they were sent, like the mother,
to the Temple school, the very best,   65
and were taught French
and the philosophers, and could
quite intelligently discuss
"the name of God" or, alternatively,
"the common good."   70
        They were only young girls,
of course; they liked best to laugh
and they were beautifully dressed
and were like all girls silly.
        She asked, "Who am I   75
thus to be blessed?"

    And a spirit cried, "Atone, atone,"
    And the wind ran along the desert stone.

Once in a generation or so,
a war or an epiphany occurs,   80
or a transformation, or a revolution,
or a waiting God stirs; a name
comes into a city, a word
is passed down—an Idea seeks
ten righteous men to save,   85
the rest, the evidently lost, to reap;
to separate those who have kept
their faith from the too far gone,
and from those who have lost
what they'd sought to keep.   90
Once in a generation
a warning is heard—

    Flee, flee to the hills, flee to the valleys,
    The cities. Abandon. Atone.

Lot consulted his in-laws,   95
And the two daughters wept,
And the wife of Lot packed, asking
herself, "How much should we keep?
How much can be kept?"
        They made   100
the abandoning leap—

but you know the rest: how
Lot and his daughters fled
from that place, how they passed
105 the test. And how
a moment's recollection,
a sudden grief, a backward
glance revealed what she
had quietly foreseen: a pocky
110 and astringent silent thing.

QUESTIONS FOR DISCUSSION AND WRITING

1. In the Bible, Sodom and Gomorrah are so wicked that God destroys them. How wicked are Sodom and Gomorrah in Holbo's poem?
2. How are Lot's wife and her life described? How do the descriptions work thematically?
3. The italicized words in the poem seem to be spoken in a different, more ponderous voice than the rest of the poem. What do those italicized lines tell us? How does their meaning progress and change through the poem? How would you characterize the speaker of those lines?
4. In the poem, why does Lot's wife look back? How is it that her "backward / glance revealed what she / had quietly foreseen"?

MURIEL RUKEYSER (1913–1980)

Ms. Lot   *1976*

Well, if he treats me like a young girl still,
That father of mine, and here's my sister
And we're still traveling into the hills—
But everyone on the road knows he offered us
5 To the Strangers when all they wanted was men,
And the cloud of smoke still over the twin cities
And mother a salt lick the animals come to—
Who's going to want me now?
Mother did not even know
10 She was not to turn around and look.
God spoke to Lot, my father.
She was hard of hearing. He knew that.
I don't believe he told her, anyway.
What kind of father is that, or husband?
15 He offered us to those men. They didn't want women.
Mother always used to say:
Some normal man will come along and need you.

QUESTIONS FOR DISCUSSION AND WRITING

1. Compare Rukeyser's poem to the biblical story. What details has Rukeyser used? What has she added or changed? How do her additions and changes reinforce her poem's mood and theme(s)?
2. In the poem, the daughter of Lot blames him for his treatment of his wife and daughters. In what ways does the biblical story suggest that Lot's behavior is blameworthy?
3. The use of "Ms." is clearly very modern. How does the poem apply modern feminist values to the biblical story? Would you argue that the modern perspective leads to a greater understanding of the Biblical story or a distortion of it? Why?

QUESTIONS FOR CROSS READING: TRANSGRESSIONS

1. In the biblical story and poems, we get very different perspectives of Lot. In which do we learn the most about him? How do the various writers change our sense of who he is and how he lives? Which is the most sympathetic to Lot and which the least sympathetic? Why?
2. In the biblical story, we learn very little about Lot's wife. What details have the modern poets added about her? How is she characterized? What is her life like? In which poems is her backward glance treated as a sign of weakness and in which as a sign of strength?
3. Compare and contrast the different treatments of the wicked cities of Sodom and Gomorrah. In which works do they seem wicked and in which not? How do the changes in setting change the meaning of the story of Lot and his wife?
4. Consider the role of gender in each of the works presented here. Which seem to present a feminist view? A patriarchal view? How would the story and its themes change if God had spoken to Lot's wife and if Lot were the one who transgressed by looking back?
5. The story of Lot is the story of a man rescued by God. It would seem, then, to be a happy story insofar as sin and evil are destroyed and the good man triumphs. Is it a happy story? Is it, in other words, a story of salvation, or is it something else?

TESTING THE LIMITS: THE STORY OF ICARUS

OVID (43 B.C.–A.D. 17?)

The Story of Daedalus and Icarus _____ *ca. A.D. 8*

> Homesick for homeland, Daedalus hated Crete
> And his long exile there, but the sea held him.
> "Though Minos blocks escape by land or water,"

Daedalus said, "surely the sky is open,
And that's the way we'll go. Minos' dominion
Does not include the air." He turned his thinking
Toward unknown arts, changing the laws of nature.
He laid out feathers in order, first the smallest,
A little larger next it, and so continued,
The way that pan-pipes rise in gradual sequence.
He fastened them with twine and wax, at middle,
At bottom, so, and bent them, gently curving,
So that they looked like wings of birds, most surely.
And Icarus, his son, stood by and watched him,
Not knowing he was dealing with his downfall,
Stood by and watched, and raised his shiny face
To let a feather, light as down, fall on it,
Or stuck his thumb into the yellow wax,
Fooling around, the way a boy will, always,
Whenever a father tries to get some work done.
Still, it was done at last, and the father hovered,
Poised, in the moving air, and taught his son:
"I warn you, Icarus, fly a middle course:
Don't go too low, or water will weigh the wings down;
Don't go too high, or the sun's fire will burn them.
Keep to the middle way. And one more thing,
No fancy steering by star or constellation,
Follow my lead!" That was the flying lesson,
And now to fit the wings to the boy's shoulders.
Between the work and warning the father found
His cheeks were wet with tears, and his hands trembled.
He kissed his son (*Good-bye,* if he had known it),
Rose on his wings, flew on ahead, as fearful
As any bird launching the little nestlings
Out of high nest into thin air. *Keep on,*
Keep on, he signals, *follow me!* He guides him
In flight—O fatal art!—and the wings move
And the father looks back to see the son's wings moving.
Far off, far down, some fisherman is watching
As the rod dips and trembles over the water,
Some shepherd rests his weight upon his crook,
Some ploughman on the handles of the ploughshare,
And all look up, in absolute amazement,
At those air-borne above. They must be gods!
They were over Samos, Juno's sacred island,
Delos and Paros toward the left, Lebinthus
Visible to the right, and another island,
Calymne, rich in honey. And the boy
Thought *This is wonderful!* and left his father,
Soared higher, higher, drawn to the vast heaven,

Nearer the sun, and the wax that held the wings
Melted in that fierce heat, and the bare arms
Beat up and down in air, and lacking oarage
Took hold of nothing. *Father!* he cried, and *Father!*
Until the blue sea hushed him, the dark water   55
Men call the Icarian now. And Daedalus,
Father no more, called "Icarus, where are you!
Where are you, Icarus? Tell me where to find you!"
And saw the wings on the waves, and cursed his talents,
Buried the body in a tomb, and the land   60
Was named for Icarus.
                        During the burial
A noisy partridge, from a muddy ditch,
Looked out, drummed with her wings in loud approval.
No other bird, those days, was like the partridge,
Newcomer to the ranks of birds; the story   65
Reflects no credit on Daedalus. His sister,
Ignorant of the fates, had sent her son
To Daedalus as apprentice, only a youngster,
Hardly much more than twelve years old, but clever,
With an inventive turn of mind. For instance,   70
Studying a fish's backbone for a model,
He had notched a row of teeth in a strip of iron,
Thus making the first saw, and he had bound
Two arms of iron together with a joint
To keep them both together and apart,   75
One standing still, the other traversing
In a circle, so men came to have the compass.
And Daedalus, in envy, hurled the boy
Headlong from the high temple of Minerva,
And lied about it, saying he had fallen   80
Through accident, but Minerva, kind protectress
Of all inventive wits, stayed him in air,
Clothed him with plumage; he still retained his aptness
In feet and wings, and kept his old name, Perdix,
But in the new bird-form, Perdix, the partridge,   85
Never flies high, nor nests in trees, but flutters
Close to the ground, and the eggs are laid in hedgerows.
The bird, it seems, remembers, and is fearful
Of all high places.

QUESTIONS FOR DISCUSSION AND WRITING

1. Daedalus and Icarus achieve a dream many men have had: they fly like birds and
   thus achieve a freedom unknown to earthbound man. How does the selection

from Ovid's *Metamorphoses* ask us to respond to the creative imagination and skill that give the father and son their wings? What is the relationship between creativity and art on the one hand and the earthly and everyday on the other?

2. Although Ovid's story is fundamentally very unrealistic—it is difficult to believe that Daedalus could fashion from wax and birds' feathers the kind of wings that would enable humans to fly—the poet is nevertheless careful to include moments of high realism. Where does the poem seem most realistic? How does the realism influence our response to the relationship between father and son and to the poem's overall themes?

3. Several times in the narrative, Ovid reminds his audience of Icarus's tragic future. Why does the poet undercut the story's suspense? Why do those reminders occur when they do—and how do you respond to them?

4. The story of Perdix seems like an afterthought, but there are some connections between it and the story of Icarus. How is Perdix like and/or unlike Icarus? Does the story of Perdix change your response to Daedalus?

Pieter Breughel the Elder, *Landscape with the Fall of Icarus* (ca. 1558). (See color insert.)

QUESTIONS FOR DISCUSSION AND WRITING

1. Breughel's painting of the fall of Icarus clearly draws its inspiration from the Ovidian story. Compare Breughel's version and Ovid's. How are the two similar? How are they different? If you were to paint Ovid's story, how similar would your painting be to Breughel's? If you were to tell the story behind Breughel's painting, how similar would your version be to Ovid's? Finally, imagine yourself choosing an en-

tirely different medium for telling the Daedalus and Icarus story. If you were, for instance, to write music (with or without lyrics), how would that music sound?

2. What does the painting seem to be saying about the connection between the everyday and people's dreams and aspirations? Given that those in the foreground of the picture clearly go about their everyday lives, could the picture be seen as an affirmation of the everyday? If so, does that affirmation come at the expense of dreamers and their dreams? Why or why not?

W. H. AUDEN (1907–1973)

Musée des Beaux Arts _____ *1940*

About suffering they were never wrong,
The old Masters: how well they understood
Its human position: how it takes place
While someone else is eating or opening a window or just walking dully along;
How, when the aged are reverently, passionately waiting   5
For the miraculous birth, there always must be
Children who did not specially want it to happen, skating
On a pond at the edge of the wood:
They never forgot
That even the dreadful martyrdom must run its course   10
Anyhow in a corner, some untidy spot
Where the dogs go on with their doggy life and the torturer's horse
Scratches its innocent behind on a tree.

In Breughel's *Icarus,* for instance: how everything turns away
Quite leisurely from the disaster; the ploughman may   15
Have heard the splash, the forsaken cry,
But for him it was not an important failure; the sun shone
As it had to on the white legs disappearing into the green
Water, and the expensive delicate ship that must have seen
Something amazing, a boy falling out of the sky,   20
Had somewhere to get to and sailed calmly on.

QUESTIONS FOR DISCUSSION AND WRITING

1. Auden's poem works in part by means of contrasts. How do these contrasts help Auden convey his themes and influence our responses to the fall of Icarus and the idea of heroism?

2. When you read Auden's poem aloud and look at the way it is set up on the page, you may notice that its lines are of very different lengths: some are much longer and "slower" than others are. What thematic significance do you find in the way

Auden structures his poem? Think in particular about how the lineation may cause us to emphasize or deemphasize certain ideas and images.

WILLIAM CARLOS WILLIAMS (1883–1963)

Landscape with the Fall of Icarus   1963

According to Breughel
when Icarus fell
it was spring

5   a farmer was ploughing
his field
the whole pageantry

of the year was
awake tingling
near

10 the edge of the sea
concerned
with itself

sweating in the sun
that melted
15 the wings' wax

unsignificantly
off the coast
there was

a splash quite unnoticed
20 this was
Icarus drowning

QUESTIONS FOR DISCUSSION AND WRITING

1. The first stanza tells us that "Icarus fell," but we don't learn until the last stanza that Icarus drowned. What is the effect of delaying the information about Icarus's fate?
2. Williams uses almost no capitalization and punctuation in his poem. Does the absence of punctuation make the poem harder to read? What purposes might the omission of capitalization and punctuation serve?

ANNE SEXTON (1928–1974)

To a Friend Whose Work Has Come to Triumph _____ 1962

Consider Icarus, pasting those sticky wings on,
testing that strange little tug at his shoulder blade,
and think of that first flawless moment over the lawn
of the labyrinth. Think of the difference it made!
There below are the trees, as awkward as camels;   5
and here are the shocked starlings pumping past
and think of innocent Icarus who is doing quite well:
larger than a sail, over the fog and the blast
of the plushy ocean, he goes. Admire his wings!
Feel the fire at his neck and see how casually   10
he glances up and is caught, wondrously tunneling
into that hot eye. Who cares that he fell back to the sea?
See him acclaiming the sun and come plunging down
while his sensible daddy goes straight into town.

QUESTIONS FOR DISCUSSION AND WRITING

1. How would you characterize the Icarus of Sexton's poem? Is he heroic? Tragic? Foolish?
2. Why is the Icarus story appropriate for "a friend whose work has come to triumph"?

MURIEL RUKEYSER (1913–1980)

Waiting for Icarus _____ 1973

He said he would be back and we'd drink wine together
He said that everything would be better than before
He said we were on the edge of a new relation
He said he would never again cringe before his father
He said that he was going to invent full-time   5
He said he loved me that going into me
He said was going into the world and the sky
He said all the buckles were very firm
He said the wax was the best wax
He said Wait for me here on the beach   10
He said Just don't cry

I remember the gulls and the waves
I remember the islands going dark on the sea
I remember the girls laughing

15   I remember they said he only wanted to get away from me
I remember mother saying: Inventors are like poets,
a trashy lot
I remember she told me those who try out inventions are worse
I remember she added: Women who love such are the worst of all

20   I have been waiting all day, or perhaps longer.
I would have liked to try those wings myself.
It would have been better than this.

QUESTIONS FOR DISCUSSION AND WRITING

1. Rukeyser's poem creates a new character in the Icarus story: a woman waiting for a lover who will never return. Her Icarus is, then, a grown man, not a boy. How does that fact affect your response to him and his story?
2. What is the effect of the repetitions of "He said" and "I remember" in Rukeyser's poem? Why does Rukeyser break the pattern of repetition in the poem's last three lines?
3. Icarus and the speaker of the poem must clearly have different dreams for themselves. How would you characterize those dreams? How much do those dreams depend on the dreamer's gender?

ROBERT HAYDEN (1913–1980)

O Daedalus, Fly Away Home _____ 1966

(For Maia and Julie)

Drifting night in the Georgia pines,
coonskin drum and jubilee banjo.
    Pretty Malinda, dance with me.

Night is juba, night is conjo.
5   Pretty Malinda, dance with me.

Night is an African juju man
weaving a wish and a weariness together
    to make two wings.

    O fly away home fly away

10 Do you remember Africa?

    O cleave the air fly away home

My gran, he flew back to Africa,
just spread his arms and
    flew away home.

Drifting night in the windy pines;
night is a laughing, night is a longing.
   Pretty Malinda, come to me.

Night is a mourning juju man
weaving a wish and a weariness together
   to make two wings.

   O fly away home fly away

QUESTIONS FOR DISCUSSION AND WRITING

1. Robert Hayden's "O Daedalus, Fly Away Home" may seem at first glance to have
   very little to do with the classical story, but in its use of the image of a man flying
   with wings made of "a wish and a weariness" woven together, it takes its cue from
   the myth. How does a knowledge of the Ovidian story affect your reading of
   "O Daedalus"?
2. Why does Hayden focus on Daedalus, the father, rather than on Icarus, the son?
3. What finally is the connection between the "wish" and the "weariness"? How
   possible is it to extricate one from the other?

QUESTIONS FOR CROSS READING: TESTING THE LIMITS

1. Even in their retellings of a classical story, several of these poets are clearly influenced by the circumstances of their own times, places, and backgrounds. Consider the poems' dates of composition. How might events and attitudes of their
   own times have caused the poets to respond to the Daedalus–Icarus story as
   they do?
2. How would you characterize the tones and rhythms of Auden's and Williams's
   poems? How do the titles and the first words of the poems influence our response
   to the Icarus–Daedalus story and the significance the two poets find in it? What is
   the effect of the poets' using Breughel's retelling of Ovid rather than referring to
   the Ovidian story directly?
3. Unlike Breughel, Matisse (see 843) concentrates the entire focus of his painting on
   Icarus—so much so that we see almost none of the boy's surroundings. What *do*
   we see? How do the painting's focus and its relative lack of details affect your response to the Icarus story? How does Matisse's image of Icarus compare with those
   of Breughel and the writers in this section?

Christopher Braniff

Professor Clarke

English 1B

26 February 2002

        The Insignificance of Icarus

    The ancient Greeks, like many others before and since
them, have told countless stories of heroes who rose to great
heights only to fall into disaster. Ovid's "Icarus" is a perfect example of such a tale. For Ovid, Icarus's fall was an
impressive tragedy, significant for everyone to know and
learn. Others, like poets William Carlos Williams and W. H.
Auden, offer a different view regarding the suffering and
tragedy of Icarus. Both Williams and Auden use the structure
and theme of their poems "Landscape with the Fall of Icarus"
and "Musée des Beaux Arts" to reflect the idea portrayed by
Peter Breughel's painting "Landscape with the Fall of Icarus";
that individual human suffering is rather insignificant when
compared to the grander scheme of daily life.

    In the story of Icarus, Ovid tells of Daedalus, a wise in-
ventor, his son, Icarus, and their desire to escape from
Crete, the island where they live in exile. Daedalus creates
wings made of feathers and held together by wax so that he
and his son can fly away home. "Don't go too low, or water
will weigh the wings down; / Don't go too high, or the sun's
fire will burn them" (24–25), Daedalus tells his son as they
prepare to leave. Shepherds and plowmen watch as the two fly
high above, so amazed by the feat that they proclaim, "They
must be gods!" (44). Icarus, leaving his father, flies higher
and higher, "drawn to the vast heaven" (50), only to have his

wings burn up in the heat of the sun and his body fall helplessly to the sea below. A fall so tragic, so appalling, that
the sea he fell into is called the Icarian and the land where
his father buried him is named for Icarus.

Peter Breughel portrays this tragic story in a painting
entitled "Landscape with the Fall of Icarus." In the painting, one can see the ordinary activities of springtime: a man
plowing his field, a shepherd herding sheep, ships setting off
to sea. Icarus falling to his demise in the background seems
like more of an afterthought than the subject of the painting. It seems like Brueghel is commenting on how apathetic
people are to individual suffering.

It is this idea of apathy that Williams and Auden
demonstrate in their poems. These poets use both the theme
and the structure of their poems to illustrate their point.
William Carlos Williams's poem "Landscape with the Fall of
Icarus" shares the same title as Breughel's painting. What
one first notices is its form and structure. It's a short poem
made up of seven stanzas of three lines each. The lines are
short, often only one or two words. As one reads the poem,
there is almost a feeling of playfulness due to its short
lines and stanzas. The lack of punctuation and capital letters adds to this feeling. There is no rigid rhyming pattern,
but one notices internal rhymes like "year" and "near" in the
following lines:

> the whole pageantry
>
> of the year was
> awake tingling
> near   (6–9)

These short lines and free rhymes give the poem a feeling of
lightness, almost like a lazy springtime morning.

   What one notices next is the theme Williams portrays. The
poem starts off almost leisurely. It describes a farmer plowing his field. Williams uses words like "tingling" (8) and
"sweating" (13) to remind us of a spring day. He describes
the sea as "concerned / with itself" (11–12), implying that
everyone and every thing has its own tasks to deal with. It's
not until the end of the poem that we hear of Icarus.

> unsignificantly
>
> off the coast
>
> there was
>
> a splash quite unnoticed
>
> this was
>
> Icarus drowning   (16–21)

The drowning of Icarus seems to contrast sharply with the
light mood of the poem. It's interesting that Williams uses
the coinage "unsignificantly" (16) as opposed to "insignifi-
cantly" in this closing part. The misspelling draws our attention to this idea that Icarus's death had little meaning,
that the suffering of the individual is often quite trivial
to the lives of others. This is in sharp contrast with Ovid's
message of how the fall of Icarus was quite significant to the
lives of those around who had called Icarus god-like and had
named the sea that took his life after him. Like Breughel's
painting, Williams portrays the death of Icarus as an afterthought to the springtime day and the lives of those around.

   W. H. Auden's "Musée des Beaux Arts" touches upon the same
themes as Williams's poem, but seems to have a much more serious and grave tone. Its starting line, "About suffering they

were never wrong" (1), signifies its more serious tone. The structure of "Musée des Beaux Arts" seems to be somewhat fragmented and quite different from the structure of Williams's poem. Some of the lines are rather long and some are short. There is rhyming, but the rhyming pattern seems to be ever changing. For example, the first line ends with "wrong" and rhymes with "along" in the fourth line. There is space between the rhymes. Later in the poem, the rhymes come more quickly. The rhymes "away" (14) and "may" (15) as well as "green" (18) and "seen" (19) are right next to each other. This gives the poem a more hurried feeling toward the end. This rhyming pattern along with the long and short lines give the reader a slight feeling of uneasiness. As we read, we try to find a sense of beat or rhythm but cannot. This feeling is very different from Williams's playfulness. The rhythm in Auden's poem seems to imply a mild sense of frustration.

Auden uses this feeling of frustration to touch upon the same theme that Breughel and Williams express, that individual suffering is often trivial compared to the lives of others. Auden does this by contrasting images of suffering with images of day to day life. Two such contrasts are in the following passage:

About suffering . . .

. . . how well they understood

Its human position: how it takes place

While someone else is eating or opening a window or just

    walking dully along;

How, when the aged are reverently, passionately waiting

For the miraculous birth, there always must be

Children who did not specially want it to happen, skating

On a pond at the edge of the wood: (1–8)

Here Auden contrasts suffering with daily tasks like eating
and walking, as well as comparing the passionate waiting of
the aged with the joyful playing of the young. He continues
these contrasts as he discusses the fall of Icarus.

> In Breughels's *Icarus,* for instance: how everything
>> turns away
> Quite leisurely from the disaster; the ploughman may
> Have heard the splash, the forsaken cry,
> But for him it was not an important failure . . .
>
> (14-17)

> . . . the expensive delicate ship that must have seen
> Something amazing, a boy falling out of the sky,
> Had somewhere to get to and sailed calmly on.   (19-21)

Like Williams and Breughel, Auden's theme is in sharp contrast to that of Ovid's message. In the original, Icarus's
fall is significantly tragic. In Auden's, the fall was but a
small part of the lives of the busy farmer and hurried ship,
who, without even thinking about it, knew that life goes
quietly on.

The two poems of Williams and Auden, though different in
structure, share the same basic theme; the suffering of life
is not any more significant than a spring's day or a farmer's
plow. There is little we can do to avoid the suffering and
pain of mortality. Whether right or wrong, the real nature of
humans is to continue on with the daily tasks of living,
often unaware of the sufferings of others.

QUESTIONS FOR DISCUSSION AND WRITING

1. What is Braniff's thesis, and where is it stated? To what extent do you agree with the thesis?
2. Braniff makes a number of important observations about the poems' rhymes and line lengths, but he does not always develop his observations as fully as he might, or at least he does not always make his conclusions explicit. Find two or three such instances of insufficient development in the paper and develop the ideas yourself, keeping in mind that you must be true to Braniff's thesis.
3. Braniff's paper is a comparison/contrast paper. Does it primarily use a point-by-point structure or a subject-by-subject structure (see 137)? What revisions, if any, would you suggest Braniff make to the paper's organization?

A WORLD OF HORROR

Edvard Munch, *The Scream,* 1893. (See color insert.)

QUESTIONS FOR DISCUSSION AND WRITING

1. Like all paintings, Munch's "The Scream" works visually rather than verbally. So, although it may implicitly tell a story, it is up to the viewer to fill in the gaps of

that story. What is the story that the painting tells you? Is your story similar to the stories others "read" in the painting? What is lost in a verbal translation of the painting? What is gained? In other words, to what extent do you agree with the old proverb that "a picture is worth a thousand words"?

2. Many of those who see Munch's painting or representations of it are surprised to learn that it was painted at the end of the nineteenth century. If you were surprised, why? What seems particularly "modern" about it? If you weren't surprised, why not?

QUESTIONS FOR DISCUSSION AND WRITING

1. Whether intentionally or not, these two pictures from *Home Alone* movie advertisements (see also color insert) seem to parody Munch's painting, which has become a popular image on items as varied as mugs, t-shirts, inflatable dolls, and checks. How well do you think the parodies here work? After seeing these parodies, do you respond differently to Munch's painting than you did the first time you saw it? If you have seen the *Home Alone* movies, do you in any way respond differently to them than you did before seeing Munch's painting?

2. After the 9/11/01 terrorist attack on the World Trade Center in New York City, many worried that the Statue of Liberty and other symbols of American history and democracy were vulnerable to attack. Given people's concerns and the symbolic importance of the Statue of Liberty, are people likely to find a parody like the one above as funny as they might once have found it? Why or why not?

DONALD HALL (1928–   )

The Scream _____ 1990

1. Observe. Ridged, raised, tactile, the horror
    of the skinned head is there. It is skinned
    which had a covering-up before,
    and now is nude, and is determined

    by what it perceives. The blood not Christ's,   5
    blood of death without resurrection,
    winds flatly in the air. Habit foists
    conventional surrender to one

    response in vision, but it fails here,
    where the partaking viewer is freed   10
    into the under-skin of his fear.
    Existence is laid bare, and married

    to a movement of caught perception
    where the unknown will become the known
    as one piece of the rolling mountain   15
    becomes another beneath the stone

    which shifts now toward the happy valley
    which is not prepared, as it could not
    be, for the achieved catastrophe
    which produces no moral upshot,   20

    no curtain, epilogue, nor applause,
    no Dame to return purged to the Manse
    (the Manse is wrecked)—not even the pause,
    the repose of art that has distance.

2. We, unlike Munch, observe his The Scream   25
    making words, since perhaps we too know
    the head's "experience of extreme
    disorder." We have made our bravo,

    but such, of course, will never equal
    the painting. What is the relation?   30
    A word, which is at once richly full
    of attributes: thinginess, reason,

    reference, time, noise, among others;
    bounces off the firm brightness of paint
    as if it had no substance, and errs   35
    toward verbalism, naturally. Mayn't

    we say that time cannot represent
    space in art? "The fascination of

40 what's impossible" may be present,
motivating the artist to move.

So the poet, the talker, aims his
words at the object, and his words go
faster and faster, and now he is
like a cyclotron, breaking into

45 the structure of things by repeated
speed and force in order to lay bare
in words, naturally, unworded
insides of things, the things that are there.

QUESTIONS FOR DISCUSSION AND WRITING

1. Hall tells us that the "partaking viewer is freed / into the under-skin of his fear."
   Examine his word choices here. In what way are we "partaking" viewers rather
   than simply "viewers"? What are the implications of "under-skin"?
2. Hall's poem moves between images of hope and life on the one hand and those of
   horror and death on the other. What is the thematic significance of these contrasts?

QUESTIONS FOR CROSS READING: A WORLD OF HORROR

1. In his poem, Hall suggests that "the poet, the talker," tries to "lay bare / in words,
   naturally, unworded / insides of things, the things that are there." Considering the
   painting and poem together, how do you think the poem helps illuminate the
   painting? How does it fall short of representing the "unworded / insides of things"?
   Can Hall's statement be applied to all poems? What can paintings do that poems
   cannot (and vice versa)?
2. Compare Donald Hall's response to Munch's painting and your own. How are
   they similar? How do they differ? Which conveys a stronger sense of modern horror or anxiety?

Everyman and Every Day

W. H. AUDEN (1907–1973)
The Unknown Citizen   *1940*
(To JS/07/M/378 This Marble Monument Is Erected by the State)

He was found by the Bureau of Statistics to be
One against whom there was no official complaint,
And all the reports on his conduct agree

That, in the modern sense of an old-fashioned word, he was a saint,
For in everything he did he served the Greater Community.   5
Except for the War till the day he retired
He worked in a factory and never got fired
But satisfied his employers, Fudge Motors Inc.
Yet he wasn't a scab or odd in his views,
For his Union reports that he paid his dues,   10
(Our report on his Union shows it was sound)
And our Social Psychology workers found
That he was popular with his mates and liked a drink.
The Press are convinced that he bought a paper every day
And that his reactions to advertisements were normal in every way.   15
Policies taken out in his name prove that he was fully insured,
And his Health-card shows he was once in hospital but left it cured.
Both Producers Research and High-Grade Living declare
He was fully sensible to the advantages of the Installment Plan
And had everything necessary to the Modern Man,   20
A phonograph, a radio, a car and a frigidaire.
Our researchers into Public Opinion are content
That he held the proper opinions for the time of year;
When there was peace, he was for peace; when there was war, he went.
He was married and added five children to the population,   25
Which our Eugenist says was the right number for a parent of his generation.
And our teachers report that he never interfered with their education.

Was he free? Was he happy? The question is absurd:
Had anything been wrong, we should certainly have heard.

QUESTIONS FOR DISCUSSION AND WRITING

1. Auden's "unknown citizen" is a *citizen,* and his monument is erected by the state.
   In what ways does the poem view him as a member of a society? How does the
   poem seem to be characterizing the society in which the citizen lives?
2. Although we learn little about the man himself, we learn lots of details about what
   the unknown citizen did and with whom he interacted. Why does Auden choose
   to focus on the particular details he includes? What do the details reveal about the
   man's emotional state?

HOWARD NEMEROV (1920–1991)
Life Cycle of Common Man _____ 1960

Roughly figured, this man of moderate habits,
This average consumer of the middle class,

Consumed in the course of his average life span
Just under half a million cigarettes,
5   Four thousand fifths of gin and about
A quarter as much vermouth; he drank
Maybe a hundred thousand cups of coffee,
And counting his parents' share it cost
Something like half a million dollars
10   To put him through life. How many beasts
Died to provide him with meat, belt and shoes
Cannot be certainly be said.
                But anyhow,
It is in this way that a man travels through time,
Leaving behind him a lengthening trail
15   Of empty bottles and bones, of broken shoes,
Frayed collars and worn out or outgrown
Diapers and dinnerjackets, silk ties and slickers.

Given the energy and security thus achieved,
He did . . . ? What? The usual things, of course,
20   The eating, dreaming, drinking and begetting,
And he worked for the money which was to pay
For the eating, et cetera, which were necessary
If he were to go on working for the money, et cetera,
But chiefly he talked. As the bottles and bones
25   Accumulated behind him, the words proceeded
Steadily from the front of his face as he
Advanced into the silence and made it verbal.
Who can tally the tale of his words? A lifetime
Would barely suffice for their repetition;
30   If you merely printed all his commas the result
Would be a very large volume, and the number of times
He said "thank you" or "very little sugar, please,"
Would stagger the imagination. There were also
Witticisms, platitudes, and statements beginning
35   "It seems to me" or "As I always say."
Consider the courage in all that, and behold the man
Walking into deep silence, with the ectoplastic
Cartoon's balloon of speech proceeding
Steadily out of the front of his face, the words
40   Borne along on the breath which is his spirit
Telling the numberless tale of his untold Word
Which makes the world his apple, and forces him to eat.

QUESTIONS FOR DISCUSSION AND WRITING

1. Nemerov's "common man" is introduced as a "consumer." What does that focus
tell us about Nemerov's attitude toward modern society and its values?

2. Nemerov emphasizes the common man as a speaker of many words. What do these words tell us about the "common man" and who he is?
3. At the end of the poem, Nemerov says the world was the man's "apple," referring perhaps to the story of Eden. In what ways is the world an apple like the apple eaten by Adam and Eve?

WILLIAM WORDSWORTH (1770–1850)

The world is too much with us ————————————————————— *1807*

> The world is too much with us; late and soon,
> Getting and spending, we lay waste our powers;
> Little we see in Nature that is ours;
> We have given our hearts away, a sordid boon!
> This Sea that bares her bosom to the moon, 5
> The winds that will be howling at all hours,
> And are up-gathered now like sleeping flowers,
> For this, for everything, we are out of tune;
> It moves us not.—Great God! I'd rather be
> A Pagan suckled in a creed outworn; 10
> So might I, standing on this pleasant lea,
> Have glimpses that would make me less forlorn;
> Have sight of Proteus rising from the sea;
> Or hear old Triton blow his wreathéd horn.

QUESTIONS FOR DISCUSSION AND WRITING

1. What does Wordsworth mean by "the world is too much with us"? What would a world that is not so much "with us" look and feel like?
2. Why might the speaker want to be "a Pagan suckled in a creed outworn"? What does that statement suggest about the speaker's attitude toward Christianity?
3. Wordsworth's poem is a *sonnet,* a form that is very controlled and defined. How does that sense of poetic control contribute to or undermine the theme of the poem?

DENISE LEVERTOV (1923–1997)

O Taste and See ————————————————————— *1964*

> The world is
> not with us enough.
> O taste and see
>
> the subway Bible poster said,
> meaning The Lord, meaning 5

if anything all that lives
to the imagination's tongue,

grief, mercy, language,
tangerine, weather, to
10 breathe them, bite,
savor, chew, swallow, transform

into our flesh our
deaths, crossing the street, plum, quince,
living in the orchard and being

15 hungry, and plucking
the fruit.

QUESTIONS FOR DISCUSSION AND WRITING

1. Levertov's poem is a response to William Wordsworth's "The world is too much with us," and her opening seems to repudiate Wordsworth's opening. Why does Levertov feel that we need the world "with us"? How does she define the "world"? How does Wordsworth?

2. Levertov refers to a "subway Bible poster," and her use of "flesh," death, and "pluck-ing / the fruit" evokes Garden of Eden scenes. Is she rejecting or embracing the biblical point of view? How does her religious stance compare with Wordsworth's?

QUESTIONS FOR CROSS READING:
EVERYMAN AND EVERY DAY

1. To what extent are Auden's "unknown citizen" and Nemerov's "common man" the same person? What are the differences between the two?

2. Wordsworth's poem was written in the nineteenth century, whereas Auden's, Nemerov's, and Levertov's are all twentieth-century poems. In what ways do the modern poets' poems seem more modern in their concerns? In what ways are the concerns of the four poets similar? Do the four view the "world" in similar or different ways?

MODERN DISILLUSIONMENT

WALLACE STEVENS (1879–1955)

Disillusionment of Ten O'Clock _____ 1923

The houses are haunted
By white night-gowns.
None are green,
Or purple with green rings,

Or green with yellow rings,   5
Or yellow with blue rings.
None of them are strange,
With socks of lace
And beaded ceintures.
People are not going   10
To dream of baboons and periwinkles.
Only, here and there, an old sailor,
Drunk and asleep in his boots,
Catches tigers
In red weather.   15

QUESTIONS FOR DISCUSSION AND WRITING

1. Why does Stevens provide so many details about what the nightgowns do *not* look like? Why does the poem focus more on the nightgowns than on the people wearing them?
2. Why are the houses "haunted"? What does it mean to be haunted by nightgowns?
3. The poem suggests that the drunken old sailor is different from the inhabitants of the houses. What does the contrast suggest about Stevens's attitude toward the inhabitants and the sailor?
4. What in the poem suggests "disillusionment of ten o'clock"? In other words, what is suggested both by the emotion and by the time of day? What is the source of the disillusionment?

SUZANNE CLEMINSHAW (1964–   )
Disillusionment of Ten O'Clock _____ *1995*

The houses are haunted
By white night-gowns.
None are green,
Or purple with green rings,
Or green with yellow rings,   5
Or yellow with blue rings.
None of them are strange,
With socks of lace
And beaded ceintures.
People are not going   10
To dream of baboons and periwinkles.
Only, here and there, an old sailor,
Drunk and asleep in his boots,
Catches tigers
In red weather.   15

Wallace Stevens

Memories are like viruses. They infect whole families. I should know. I have been earning money as a bartender at weddings at the country club this summer. My friend Casey and I do it. We had to provide our own tuxedos and wear them, but the girls really go for them. And around one in the morning, it never fails, some red-faced uncle comes up and says he wants to take over the bar and that we should go dance with his nieces. There are always nieces. They all go to Mount Holyoke or Bryn Mawr and they have pinkish indentations across the bridges of their noses from the glasses they removed just before the wedding. Glabella is the word for it—the space between your eyebrows. It sounds sort of sexual and sort of like an isle off the coast of Italy. Just knowing this word makes these spectacle-less girls somewhat charming—knowing that they are probably more aware of their glabellas than girls with twenty-twenty vision.

I'm studying the classics at college. When I tell parents this at the weddings they look at me kind of strange, but also as if it's noble, like I joined the Peace Corps or something. Like it's something they're glad someone is doing but relieved it's not their kids.

I have to finish a paper for Modern Poetry this summer. It's on 'Disillusionment of Ten O'Clock' by Wallace Stevens. I got an incomplete for the course and the professor said he wouldn't flunk me if I get the paper into him by the end of July. I haven't written a word yet and this weekend is the fourth of July. My parents said they wouldn't ground me for the incomplete if I go to the library for a few hours a day to work on it. I sit in the reference section, thinking of the nieces and what they would look like sans taffetta skirts, sans glasses, perched on the dusty lectern that holds a mammoth Random House Dictionary, opened to the letter V. I never realized how interesting the reference section could be. I've been looking up the etymologies of words today. Virgin means man-trap.

There are always stories being told at weddings. After a few glasses of wine everybody remembers stories. Families have their own Greek tragedies but they usually run along the lines of family accidents. The time Matthew got his hand smashed in the car door on the family vacation, the time the McKnights' poodle scratched Missy's cornea, the time Uncle Bob got a suction-cup dart stuck to his forehead at Jenny's birthday party, the time Peter stuck an unstrung pearl up his nose. I guess this is the only common ground for all these cousins who haven't seen each other for a couple of decades. One of these wedding planner books was left on the bar one night. The first line of the page it was opened to said, 'Place distant cousins further away at tables in the nearest row on the far left or right.' Second cousins are a lot like Greek characters. They are the ones that send your family these long tragic mimeographed letters at Christmas-time telling you about cousin William's operation and cousin Bette's imprisonment. There are a lot of Hecuba-types amongst second cousins.

Where Streetsboro Road begins, at the exit off of Highway 77, there is a Moo Shu Chinese Restaurant with a plastic pagoda out front, the Atomic Bar that looks like a set from a sixties motorcycle movie and the No-Tell Motel with a flashing pink and black neon sign of a winking cat. Then there's a trailer park, with all these rusty trailers sitting on the pavement. You never see anyone outside of them and it makes me think of those places up north where whales go to die. Then there's a stretch of road that's just marshes on either side that developers always want to landfill and build on but environmentalists protest because there's some musk-rat that will go extinct if they do. After a few miles of these marshes the road gets all windy and overhung with huge trees that stand at the edge of the road like obedient dogs. There's a stoplight at the end of all these trees and this is where Ridgewood starts. Past the stoplight are eighteenth-century houses with plaques in front of them telling you how old they are. They are all painted white and have black shutters and there is a brick pavement out in front of them. Further along are shops contained within more eighteenth-century houses—there is Haddie H. Halpern's, a women's dress shop where there are huge stuffed pigs with gold rings in their noses under all the dress racks and velvet cushion seats in the dressing rooms. My mom used to take me in there before my voice changed. Once I saw Mrs Cutter run out of Haddie H. Halpern's in just her slip to talk to her husband who was standing on the pavement. She's very pretty. Further on there are lots of gift shops with things made out of glass and wood in the windows and antique shops with Amish quilts and old clocks. There are also a ton of real estate offices, and the women who work in them are always marching up and down the pavement wearing suits of red or green or yellow depending on which real estate company they work for. They look like brand new items in a hardware store. You take a right just past the gazebo where there are band concerts and ice cream socials in the summer and you're on Ogilby Drive. You go past Ms Dimmer's house, who has hair the colour of flat champagne and wears silk robes all day out in her grape arbour and is pretty crazy—for instance, she can't stand the word 'succulence' and as kids we used to hide under her bushes and chant 'succulence, succulence' until she banged open her shutters and flung wineglasses of water out at us. I've felt pretty bad about this lately. The houses get bigger as you drive further down Ogilby—there is Mr Mastrioni's house that has gates and everyone says he works for the Mafia and his son told our class that they bury their victims face down so they can't haunt the killers, but he might have said this just to get popular. Further on is Mr Huxley's, he owns sports cars that sit in the driveway with grimacing grills and back ends that lift up in the air like the rear ends of mating baboons. You turn left at Mr Huxley's and then you are on Treelawn Avenue. Here the houses are large and sunken in among big elms and maples—the houses and trees on Treelawn seem to have some sort of communion, there is something pachydermish about them. If they were alive, they would be slow-moving and powerful and unaware of what is scurrying about at their feet. If you turn right into the driveway of 154 Treelawn, you are at my house. It is large and white with green-and-white-striped awnings over the windows. I used to eat pears under the Oriental plum tree in the front yard and pretend I was in China.

Casey is majoring in pre-med at Columbia. I grew up with him here in Ridgewood. He's always been into obscure diseases of the mind and body. Like in sixth grade we both pretended we were missing our left arms, which made lunch and scooter dodge ball in gym difficult. Then in tenth grade he put on that he had 'Tourette's Syndrome' and screamed 'Fuck you cunt' at the principal's secretary. He got ten consecutive Saturday detentions, but the teachers still liked him because he's so brilliant and all. Like he could probably figure out this poem in one hour and write twenty pages about it in the next but I'm basically pretty ethical about these things. In fact, I think I'd like to be a poet. I'd never tell Casey that, he'd think it's 'fruity' and not lucrative enough. You can be sure all the uncles know how lucrative Casey's profession will be—the nieces are marched up to him in an unending procession. Casey's goal is to have some obscure tropical disease named after him.

Why do the words in poetry sound so different than words on billboards, in advertisements or coming out of the mouths of people you know? The word purple in this poem sounds different from purple in everyday life. Purple in real life is a Crayola crayon, my father's deep purple leather chair, the ink they stamp on fresh meat. Purple in the poem sounds like it comes from some other place, far away from crayons or grapes, somewhere where it exists on its own, purely purple, without having to inhabit an object.

The uncles all hang out at the bar. Most of them are large with shoulders like bridges but there's always a little one stuck in among them like a sneeze. They are at that obscure stage in life—in between yelling 'Hey Dude' to their friends and wearing black socks and brown shoes down to the beach. They all bore each other like mad, choking back yawns like snakes swallowing mice, but they try to rise above it by acting boisterous and describing the hips on a new secretary with hand motions in the air.

Around twelve I was dancing with one of the nieces. There were all these little kids running in and out amongst the dancing couples like stinging nettles, and then I saw Mrs Cutter. I hadn't seen her since I saw her in her slip outside Haddie H. Halpern's. She wore this dress with purple and yellow flowers on it, but the fabric was kind of see-throughish and when she moved, the flowers seemed to go from solid to liquid and back again—like they were freezing and melting and then freezing again. I've read that the Greeks got their idea for the shape of their vases from the shadows of women dancing on a sunlit wall. 'What are you majoring in?' the niece asked. I watched Mrs Cutter as she disappeared behind a row of black tuxedos. A little kid ran by and nearly knocked us over. 'What are you majoring in?' the niece asked again once we got our balance. She had this brand new notebook feel to her. I caught sight of purple and yellow in between black suits. 'Huh?' I asked. *What are you majoring in?* I couldn't get sex off my mind for the rest of the night. All the big vases in the room started looking like Venuses of Willendorf.

It's hard to think poetic thoughts in Ridgewood. I'm not just procrastinating. I think you need a clean fall of vertical light on everything—clean blue, clean white, clean curves, clean angles. In Ridgewood there is too much bric-a-brac. There are cupolas and shutters and door wreaths and flowers. Tons of flowers. Did the Greeks have flower-beds? I can't imagine it. Geraniums are like caged animals. Geraniums are a hindrance to the mind.

I remember seeing Mrs Cutter one winter. She was in front of me at the traffic light in a blue convertible. Its top was down. And it was snowing. Just a light snow. There was a pinkish glow to the flakes from the red light. The snow was falling gently upon Mrs Cutter's bare head—almost as if someone was placing each flake there in some sort of arrangement.

At the Ridgewood Public Library there are glass cases full of objects at the entranceway. There are Indian head nickels and Mrs Maddie Cohasset's widow's ring, which is onyx and opened part way to show the piece of hair off her husband's head who was killed in the Civil War, and also an indentured servant's contract with the red seal of the King that looks like melted red licorice. And there's this big soup tureen, with painted Chinese pagodas and trees and little people moving over bridges and a typewritten card under it that says, 'This soup tureen was used in the service of luncheon to Mrs Mamie Eisenhower when she visited Ridgewood in 1965.' It's kind of creepy and Egyptian—all these artefacts of Ridgewood. It's like no one is sure the past actually ever occurred so they have to prove it by displaying all these things in these glass coffins. All these commemorative plaques and historical items in Ridgewood get on your nerves after a while—you start to feel like you're living in one big sunken Spanish galleon.

Later on that night, the night Mrs Cutter was at the wedding, I saw her out by the pool. It was drained, I guess because they were going to clean it, and the lawn chairs were sitting aimlessly around it like bison panting around an empty watering hole. I went up to her and said hello. 'Don't you love aquamarine?' she said, looking down into the pool. 'Yeah, I guess so.' I didn't really know what to say. 'Not just the colour. The word. Aquamarine.' She sat down at the edge of the pool and let her feet dangle into it. 'Aquamarine,' she said into the pool, and it echoed a bit. Her voice sounded like a clear stream running over smooth pebbles. I sat down next to her. I tried it. 'Aquamarine.' It sounded great. I realized it must be my favourite word. When you say it, you can feel yourself submerging into its complex turquoise depths, bubbles rising at each consonant. And I wasn't even drunk. Mrs Cutter must have been reading my mind because she looked at me and said, 'I'm not drunk.' 'I didn't think so,' I said, even though I guess I did. She kicked her feet against the pool wall and the flowers on her dress danced around. I wanted to ask her something but I couldn't think of a question. Someone called my name and I remembered I was supposed to be working.

'None are green, / Or purple with green rings, / Or green with yellow rings, / Or yellow with blue rings.' I used to picture blue rings coming out of President Nixon's mouth whenever he spoke. Watergate was on television all the time one summer when I was little. It was on all day long and then at night too. I'd be in bed and I could hear President Nixon's voice on the television downstairs. I'd picture the blue rings rolling outwards from the television set. They never seemed to dissipate, like smoke, but wheeled behind the furniture and up the stairs to spin like tops in the corner of my bedroom. It's funny how language can be a force like electricity or gravity—the way it pulls on you, how it can cause chemical changes, blushes, yawns, shivers.

Mrs Dawson came up to me tonight. She used to babysit for me when I was little. She got stuck on the subject of how I used to suck my thumb. About how I was eight years old and still sucked my thumb. How I put my left thumb in my mouth and then rubbed my nose with my left index finger. She demonstrated this. All the uncles laughed. Then Mrs Dawson wanted me to demonstrate how I used to do it. She said she tried to put oil of cloves on my thumb to get me to stop, but nothing, absolutely nothing could stop me. She reminded me of my sister's music box that played 'Blue Danube' over and over unless you closed its lid. She plants rows of geraniums in front of her house.

'From whence hast thou come and whither thou goest?' Socrates reminds me of the uncles at the weddings. He is always nosing into other people's business, wanting to dredge up their pasts and corner them about their futures. I wouldn't want to get into a conversation with Socrates. People at weddings are always asking you, 'What are you going to do?' It is a terrible question. It gives you this unsettled vertigo feeling. I wanted to be a Pony Express rider when I was little. I remember seeing an old ad for riders in a history book. It said you had to be willing to risk death daily, that you needed to be young, skinny and an expert rider, and that orphans were preferred. Who could resist this? But I guess as you get older you start worrying about breaking your legs and stuff. Heraclitus saw organisms as storms of fire, but everyone seems to simmer down after a while. There's some guy, Boris Ulla or Olla, who is a fish-frightener. He frightens salmon. It's true. These domesticated salmon don't learn fear in the laboratory they are raised in so Boris has to teach them to be frightened before he releases them into a natural stream. This is what Boris 'does.' I wonder what the uncles are afraid of. They don't seem to be frightened of anything—they have the same elephant attitude as their trees and houses. But I don't think they would be Pony Express riders.

'The houses are haunted by white nightgowns.' I have looked up haunted in the dictionary. It means to visit often or continually, to recur repeatedly, supposedly frequented by ghosts. There is an upright Steinway in the corner of the library that I think is haunted. It bears the inscription: 'Played by Sir Robert Winston on his visit to the United States, April, 1940.' It is made of cherry wood and depending on the light, I can see different figures traced in the grain: first Oriental men pulling carts, then plum trees with laughing branches. They have the motility of clouds. Because it is humid, the piano gives off a deep brown smell, the smell of shadows. Plants communicate through smell; they can warn each other of poisons and insects. I wonder if inanimate objects can do the same, hot rocks in summer, the insides of old pianos, suitcases in closets, books packed together tight. I wonder if everything is haunted, if everything is talking behind our backs.

Around two in the morning the parents leave the reception. They are slightly drunk and swaying in front of their newly-polished cars shining under the streetlamp like huge metallic June-bugs. This desolate look sometimes flashes across their faces, like they have arrived after a week's train journey only to find an empty station with a broken timetable. But then I guess they think 'tomorrow' and they put their car keys in the lock. I sometimes try to picture the bride and groom in the hotel room later that night. I never completely imagine the ACT, but I see her on the bed, cocooned in her white stockings and him, lit by the supermarket light of the bathroom, his tuxedo tie undone and hanging around his neck like two black goldfish, his mind thinking the Far Eastern thoughts of a new husband.

The library has the smell of old school buildings. You wonder if learning gives off a smell. The librarian is this man with long fingernails. You can hear him flipping through books. Clip, clip, clip. He has an unnatural skin colour because he is never out in the sun. He reminds me of those phosphorescent jelly-like things you find under old piers at night that no one knows the name of. But I like him. There is something foreign about him, even though he's American. It is interesting to watch him move— the cuffs of his trousers lift up to cling to his socks for a moment and then drop down against his shoes. It is funny how a detail like that can make you feel for a person.

This poem makes you notice colours more. Purple grapes, purple nights, blue towels, blue gardens, yellow skies, yellow eyes, green celery, green salamanders, red stop signs, red nail polish, white houses, white tennis shorts, white lawn chairs, white cake, white wedding dresses. Casey once told me that there is nothing perfectly white in nature.

I keep thinking about Mrs Cutter out on that pavement in front of Haddie H. Halpern's in her white slip. The mica in the pavement was sparkling and it made it look like her feet were sparkling too. She was angry. You could tell by the way she was standing that she was angry. It was a very sunny day. I could see the shadows of her legs under her slip. The ancients thought that anger could be a form of art.

I went walking through the neighbourhood last night. It was late and all the lights were out. Everyone was asleep. You wonder what these people dream about. That line about baboons and periwinkles has really gotten to me. It's been running through my mind all week. It's been like a mosquito buzzing in my ear. 'People are not going to dream of baboons and periwinkles. People are not going to dream of baboons and periwinkles.' These lines are like checkmates in chess or something. They just leave you stranded. All the lights were out down our street. I thought of all these people turning their pillows over to the cool side. My mother used to tell me to turn my pillow over whenever I had a nightmare, because then I'd get the good side. I still do it sometimes, although I don't have nightmares much anymore. It was so quiet on the street. It's strange to think of everyone going into their own private trance every night. It's like everyone's diving into a private grotto and then they resurface in the morning and have their coffee and get in their cars and go to their offices without a thought about the strange place they just came from. I read that under the Sahara desert are all these small seas and rivers, where all these multi-coloured and unknown fish live and swim.

One of the uncles got extremely drunk last night. Casey and I found him in the hallway leading to the kitchen. He was walking as though the hallway had stairs. Casey got a hold of his shoulders and led him over to a chair. 'Come on sugar shoes,' he said real gently. Casey and I are used to dealing with drunks. 'Life is a series of endless yellow hills young man,' the uncle mumbled at Casey's fly. Uncles start to talk in proverbs by the end of the night. Casey and I call them the 'Unclilian Dialogues.' One of them stayed in my mind though. 'The man who asks many questions may seem stupid for a moment, but the man who asks no questions stays stupid all his life.' The thing was, the uncle who said this said it in such an exclamatory way—you could tell in the way he said it that he thought in exclamation points rather than question marks.

Your body is always lagging behind your thoughts. I sit in the library and my thoughts go zooming, but pretty soon my body drags them back down to the hard yellow wooden chair I always sit in. Casey is always saying we should get back to our limbic system, the ancient reptile brain, and think fierce wild animal thoughts. He usually makes this point in reference to one of the nicer-looking nieces, but I think it would be a good idea all around. Casey is also into how our bodies are full of memories. He's always pointing out aspects of people that he feels fell behind in evolution. Some uncle has a gibbon hand (an elongated palm and short fingers), another orangutang arms. He says there are vestiges of evolution all over our bodies—the third eyelid at the corner of our eyes, the muscles used for smiling being once the muscles used for snarling. They seem like price tags left on clothing. Most of these people at the wedding are Protestant, but most of them would say they believe in evolution. I don't think they really believe in it though. I don't think they believe that they are animals.

Weddings are like painting a scenic background for LOVE. The background really starts to overshadow the original intention if you ask me. I can't believe how thick these wedding planner books are. We used to have a print of Fragonard's 'Progress of Love' in our bathroom. I used to think this was what 'love' was—bluegrey trees in the background haunting roses in the foreground. Everything gets so concrete as you get older. When I was eleven Casey told me that having an orgasm was like a dozen great sneezes all at once. It ruined it a little.

Mrs Cutter was in the library today. She knows the librarian. He was looking something up for her in the card catalogue. Click, click, click. I could see the parting in his hair as he leaned over the file. It was all crazy and jagged and meandering like a South American river. He said something to Mrs Cutter and blushed and she laughed. Her laugh sounds all shiny and new like patent-leather shoes. He helped her get all these books and then she sat down at one of the long yellow tables and looked at them. I don't see many married women in the library. Or men. Usually just students and children. I was going to go up and talk to her, but she seemed so absorbed. She had a little notebook and a pencil and she was writing a lot. After a few hours she left and I went over to the table she was sitting at. I could smell her perfume. The books were all about gardening. 'Horticulture and You.' 'Basic Pruning for the Beginner.' I closed the one that was still open on the table and looked at its cover. 'Petunias and Geraniums: Happy Bed-fellows.'

I have decided to look up each word of the first line of the poem—'The houses are haunted by white nightgowns'—in the dictionary. If I can just make the words concrete then maybe the meaning will follow. But it just ends up making a new poem:

> A particular person or thing
> By how much,
>
> Or a building to live in, a shelter
> To cover
> and exist,
>
> and visit often or continually,
> repeatedly occurring and
> supposedly frequented by ghosts.
> Near
>
> and following in a series
> in another dimension.
> Having the color of pure snow or milk
>
> A light colored part,
>
> Pale, wan, like a loose gown
> worn to bed by women or girls.

You realize, though, that you could look up all the words in the first line and get all their definitions, and then look up the definitions of those words in the new line and then look up those definitions, ad infinitum. It gets you dizzy just thinking about it. There is no end. It's like a mirror facing a mirror. I drove by Mrs Cutter's house today. She was out in the front garden. She was out there talking to her house-maid. She had white gardening gloves on and a white skirt. But you couldn't see her legs through it. All around them were cartons of red geraniums.

QUESTIONS FOR DISCUSSION AND WRITING

1. What do we learn about the narrator of the story? How do we respond to him?
2. Throughout the story, the narrator notices the colors of things and mentions exotic places. What are some of these references? What do they convey about the narrator and his view of life? About the world in which he lives?
3. The narrator frequently compares people and objects to animals. Trace some of these metaphors. How do they make us respond to the characters and objects— and to the narrator?

4. At one point, the narrator tells us, "Geraniums are like caged animals. Geraniums are a hindrance to the mind" (880). He also says that Mrs. Dawson, his old babysitter, grows geraniums, and at the end of the story we learn that Mrs. Cutter has referred to a book on geraniums and is now planting red geraniums. What finally does the story seem to suggest geraniums represent?

QUESTIONS FOR CROSS READING: MODERN DISILLUSIONMENT

1. What in the story might correspond to Stevens's residents in white nightgowns? What suggests the drunken old sailor? Are the messages of the poem and short story the same or different?
2. Write a poem, short story, or essay titled "(some emotion) of _____ O'Clock." What images and/or ideas do you associate with this time and emotion?

Warring Within: Birmingham and the Struggle for Civil Rights

DUDLEY RANDALL (1914–2000)

Ballad of Birmingham _____ *1966*

(On the Bombing of a Church in Birmingham, Alabama, 1963)

"Mother dear, may I go downtown
Instead of out to play,
And march the streets of Birmingham
In a Freedom March today?"

"No, baby, no, you may not go,   5
For the dogs are fierce and wild,
And clubs and hoses, guns and jail
Aren't good for a little child."

"But, mother, I won't be alone.
Other children will go with me,   10
And march the streets of Birmingham
To make our country free."

"No, baby, no, you may not go,
For I fear those guns will fire.
But you may go to church instead   15
And sing in the children's choir."

She has combed and brushed her night-dark hair,
And bathed rose petal sweet,

And drawn white gloves on her small brown hands,
20   And white shoes on her feet.

The mother smiled to know her child
Was in the sacred place,
But that smile was the last smile
To come upon her face.

25   For when she heard the explosion,
Her eyes grew wet and wild.
She raced through the streets of Birmingham
Calling for her child.

She clawed through bits of glass and brick,
30   Then lifted out a shoe.
"O here's the shoe my baby wore,
But, baby, where are you?"

QUESTIONS FOR DISCUSSION AND WRITING

1. Randall's poem derives its power from the strong contrast between the child's innocence and her fate—as well as between the mother's expectations of what is safe and what in fact is dangerous. Where do you see some of these contrasts in the poem? How do they work thematically?
2. Randall's poem sets up a well-defined rhythm and rhyme pattern. How do these patterns reflect the themes of the poem?

RAYMOND L. PATTERSON (1929–2001)
Birmingham 1963

Sunday morning and her mother's hands
Weaving the two thick braids of her springing hair,
Pulling her sharply by one bell-rope when she would
Not sit still, setting her ringing,
5   While the radio church choir prophesied the hour
With theme and commercials, while the whole house tingled;
And she could not stand still in that awkward air;
Her dark face shining, her mother now moving the tiny buttons,
Blue against blue, the dress which took all night making,
10   That refused to stay fastened;
There was some pull which hurried her out to Sunday School
Toward the lesson and the parable's good news,
The quiet escape from the warring country of her feelings,
The confused landscape of grave issues and people.

But now we see   15
Now we see through the glass of her mother's wide screaming
Eyes into the room where the homemade bomb
Blew the room down where her daughter had gone:
Under the leaves of hymnals, the plaster and stone,
The blue dress, all undone—   20
The day undone to the bone—
Her still, dull face, her quiet hair;
Alone amid the rubble, amid the people
Who perish, being innocent.

QUESTIONS FOR DISCUSSION AND WRITING

1. The poem sets up a strong contrast between the girl's restlessness at home and the complete rest created by her death. What language in the poem reinforces this contrast? What is the speaker's attitude toward the contrasts? What does it say about the possibility of peacefulness in life?
2. How does Patterson's poem prepare us for the death of the little girl—or does the murder come as a surprise?

RICHARD FARINA (1936–1966)

Birmingham Sunday _____ 1964

Come round by my side and I'll sing you a song
I'll sing it so softly, it'll do no one wrong
On Birmingham Sunday, the blood ran like wine
And the choir kept singing of freedom

That cold autumn morning no eyes saw the sun   5
And Addie Mae Collins, her number was one
At an old Baptist church, there was no need to run
And the choir kept singing of freedom

The clouds they were gray and the autumn winds blew
And Denise McNair brought the number to two   10
The falcon of Death was a creature they knew
And the choir kept singing of freedom

The church it was crowded but no one could see
That Cynthia Wesley's dark number was three
Her prayers and her feelings would shame you and me   15
And the choir kept singing of freedom

Young Carol Robertson entered the door
And the number her killers had given was four

20   She asked for a blessing, but asked for no more
        And the choir kept singing of freedom

        On Birmingham Sunday the noise shook the ground
        And people all over the earth turned around
        For no one recalled a more cowardly sound
        And the choir kept singing of freedom

25   The men in the forest, they asked it of me
        How many blackberries grew in the blue sea
        And I asked them right with a tear in my eye
        How many dark ships in the forest

        The Sunday has come and the Sunday has gone
30   And I can't do much more than to sing you this song
        I'll sing it so softly, it'll do no one wrong
        And the choirs keep singing of freedom

QUESTIONS FOR DISCUSSION AND WRITING

1. Like many folk songs and ballads, "Birmingham Sunday" has a refrain, in this case a single line that, with some modifications, keeps getting repeated. Consider the contexts of "And the choir kept singing of freedom." Do those contexts change the way we hear and respond to the words? What do the minor changes in wording signify?

2. The poem lists the four victims of the bombing. What is the effect of the listlike numbering? How distinct are the girls from one another? What is the effect of making them distinct individuals and/or deemphasizing their individuality?

LANGSTON HUGHES (1902–1967)

Birmingham Sunday   *1967*
(September 15, 1963)

        Four little girls
        Who went to Sunday School that day
        And never came back home at all
        But left instead
5   Their blood upon the wall
        With spattered flesh
        And bloodied Sunday dresses
        Torn to shreds by dynamite
        That China made aeons ago—
10   Did not know
        That what China made

Before China was ever Red at all
Would redden with their blood
This Birmingham-on-Sunday wall.

 Four tiny girls   15
Who left their blood upon that wall,
In little graves today await
The dynamite that might ignite
The fuse of centuries of Dragon Kings
Whose tomorrow sings a hymn   20
The missionaries never taught Chinese
In Christian Sunday School
To implement the Golden Rule.

 Four little girls
Might be awakened someday soon   25
By songs upon the breeze
As yet unfelt among magnolia trees.

QUESTIONS FOR DISCUSSION AND WRITING

1. Hughes places the bombing and the deaths of the little girls in the context of the Chinese invention of dynamite. What is the effect for the reader of that context? Does it reinforce the magnitude of the bombing or does it undercut our sense of the specific event? Why? How does the implied comparison affect our belief in the possibility of peace?
2. In the last line, Hughes says that the songs are "yet unfelt among magnolia trees." What do the magnolia trees represent? Why are the songs "yet unfelt"?

MICHAEL HARPER (1938–)

American History   *1970*

For John Callahan

Those four black girls blown up
in that Alabama church
remind me of five hundred
middle passage blacks,
in a net, under water   5
in Charleston harbor
so *redcoats* wouldn't find them.
Can't find what you can't see
can you?

QUESTIONS FOR DISCUSSION AND WRITING

1. Harper says that the four little girls remind him of the 500 black slaves who drowned. In what ways might the four little girls be like the drowned slaves? What does the comparison imply about equality and freedom and about race relations in the United States?
2. How would you characterize the speaker of the last sentence of Harper's poem? What is the meaning of his statement?

THOMAS MERTON (1915–1968)

And the Children of Birmingham

And the children of Birmingham
Walked into the story
Of Grandma's pointed teeth
("Better to love you with")
5   Reasonable citizens
Rose to exhort them all:
"Return at once to schools of friendship.
Buy in stores of love and law."

(And tales were told
10   Of man's best friend, the Law.)

And the children of Birmingham
Walked in the shadow
Of Grandma's devil
Smack up against
15   The singing wall.
Fire and water
Poured over everyone:
"Hymns were extreme,
So there could be no pardon!"

20   And old Grandma
Began the lesson
Of everybody's skin,
Everybody's fun:
"Liberty may bite
25   An irresponsible race
Forever singing,"
Grandma said,
"Forever making love:
Look at all the children!"

30   (And tales were told
Of man's best friend, the Law.)

And the children of Birmingham
Walked into the fury
Of Grandma's hug:
Her friendly cells   35
("Better to love you with.")
Her friendly officers
And "dooms of love."

Laws had a very long day
And all were weary.   40

But what the children did that time
Gave their town
A name to be remembered!

(And tales were told
Of man's best friend, the Law.)   45

QUESTIONS FOR DISCUSSION AND WRITING

1. Merton's poem is not about the Birmingham bombing itself but about the "children's crusade" that led up to it. In Birmingham, children participated in the Civil Rights marches and boycotts; fire hoses were turned on them, and the protesters were jailed. How does the poem allude to these events?
2. Merton seems to be alluding to the Little Red Riding Hood story. How do the allusions affect the reader? What do they imply about childhood and innocence?
3. Is Grandma seen as affectionate or malevolent? What does she seem to represent in the poem?
4. How does the poem view the Law? What laws are being referred to?

Newsweek: "My God, You're Not Even Safe in Church" _____ 1963

Spring came menacingly to Birmingham as the Negro revolution budded, then blossomed violently amid the police dogs and fire hoses. And summer came, a sweaty season of tension and dwindling hope that the new city administration would fulfill spring's agreement to ease the rigid barriers against the Negro. Now summer gave way to a time of darkening fears. Would autumn and the court-ordered desegregation of Birmingham's public schools bring a new harvest of violence?

Schools opened. The Negroes entered. And the first week passed, disrupted only by noisy protests—little violence. But there was still Saturday, a dangerous day when the rednecks, with nothing much to do, would tank up in their jook joints. Anything could happen on Saturday night.

But nothing did. And Sunday dawned quietly, a day of unvarying routine for most of Birmingham's 340,887 people: best clothes, shiny shoes, Sunday school, church, chicken dinner, family visiting. Birmingham has 680 churches (425 white and 255 Negro), and city fathers are given to boasting that they are well attended. So they were as this Sunday came, a chilly overcast day full of the special quiet hustle that goes with getting the kids to Sunday school.

Because his wife was ailing, Claude A. Wesley, 54, gray-haired principal of a Negro school, oversaw the Sunday morning routine for his daughter, a bubbly bright-eyed 14-year-old named Cynthia. Together they did the dishes after a breakfast of bacon, eggs, and coffee before she got into her Sunday best—a ruffled white dress. Cynthia draped a red sweater over her shoulders, and quickly fed her cocker spaniel, Toots. Then she was ready.

"Go In": After pausing under the sugarberry trees before their brick-front home to wave good-by to Mrs. Wesley, father and daughter climbed in the family's black Mercury and drove to the 16th Street Baptist Church.

Wesley let Cynthia out at the curb and gently shooed her toward the buff brick church. "You go on in, honey," he said. "I'm going to get some gas and I'll be back in a minute."

At 9:22 a.m. Claude Wesley stood by his car at a service station two blocks from the church, watching the attendant fill the tank. Suddenly Sunday blew up. Rocks and glass rattled through the trees. Wesley heard screams and broke into a run toward the church. Someone had dynamited the Sunday school.

Within hours, the explosion sent a shock wave of horror and outrage through-out the South, across the land, around the world. The blast had killed four little Negro girls. There was every sign it would add new intensity to the seething racial turmoil of Birmingham—where bombings have been a commonplace—new fervor to the Negro revolt, new impetus to lagging Federal civil-rights legislation.

The first effect of the bombing, in Birmingham, was a fast-moving phantas-magoria of grief, terror, and hysteria. Pouring out of the church into the chilly street, women and children shrieked amid the debris. Men shouted. A young girl, Sarah Collins, staggered blindly out of the hole ripped by the explosion, her face spewing blood. She stretched her arms in front of her, unseeing, and screamed incoherently.

Negroes by the hundreds swarmed to the scene. Many flung rocks at police cars as they arrived, sirens whining. Half a dozen ambulances and a fire truck raced up into the pandemonium. A Negro woman, heel-deep in glass in the street, screamed: "In church! My God, you're not even safe in church." A slender Negro man with eyes wild with hate shrieked repeatedly: "Let me at the bastards. I'll kill them! I'll kill them!" "Murderers! Murderers!" a Negro woman echoed.

Inside the gutted church, workmen found—in addition to the four horribly battered bodies—blood-splattered copies of kindergarten leaflets bearing the day's prayer ("Dear God, we are sorry for the times when we were unkind") and pages from a religious coloring book. One youngster had been coloring an outline of a girl praying and, with a rough crayon scrawl, had rendered the face black. The main force of the dynamite had struck a dozen girls in a rest room by the downstairs auditorium.

Outside the church, Claude Wesley had been walking around and around look-ing for Cynthia. Someone finally suggested that Claude Wesley should go to the hos-pital. There he met his slender wife and they were taken to a room where the dead girls lay covered. "They asked me if my daughter was wearing a ring," the father said. "I said yes, she was, and they pulled her little hand out and the little ring was there."

"She's Dead, Baby": So went the melancholy business of identifying the other three victims—Denise McNair, age 11, Carol Robertson, age 14, and Addie Mae Collins, age 14. The blast decapitated one of them, left an apple-size hole in the back of another's head. Mrs. McNair, herself one of the 400 persons in the church when the bomb went off, had also searched desperately for her daughter. Finally, she reported sadly to her father, M.W. Pippen. "Daddy, I can't find Denise." "She's dead, baby," he sobbed. "I've got one of her shoes in here. I'd like to blow the whole town up."

For hours, as the families tended their dead, the city threatened to blow up. Birmingham Negroes had endured many bombings. The latest had been two different blasts within the last month at the home of Arthur D. Shores, an attorney; the best known—until Sunday—the explosion in the A.G. Gaston Motel while Martin Luther King Jr. was a guest last May 11. In all, there have been 50 bombings since World War II and so many in one Negro residential section that it is known as Dynamite Hill. But this time, the aftermath was almost as bloody as the blast itself.

Police and sheriff's deputies armed themselves with shotguns, carbines, rifles, and pistols. They fired over the heads of surging Negro crowds at the church, driving them into adjacent streets and alleys. Back came an answering hail of rocks and glass fragments.

As word of the bombing spread, rock fights between Negroes and whites broke out at street corners. One ended around 4:30 p.m. only when cops arrived. White youths, waving Confederate flags, remained behind, but the Negroes fled down an alley. An officer yelled for one of them, Johnny Robinson, 16, to halt. When he didn't, the cop shotgunned him in the back. Robinson pitched forward, face down under a clothesline, blood pouring from his mouth. He was dead when they got him to University Hospital.

A Last Ride: In the Northwest corner of the city, James Ware, a 16-year-old Negro, was bicycling homeward with his brother Virgil, 13, on the handle bars. On Docena Road a red motorbike, decorated with Confederate stickers and carrying two white youths, approached them. The boy riding double pulled out a pistol, fired twice. Virgil pitched off the handle bars. "Jim, I'm shot," he cried on the ground. "No, you ain't. You ain't shot. Get up, Virg," James said. Virgil, .22-caliber bullets in his head and chest, then died. The next day, two 16-year-old white boys, Michael Lee Farley and Larry Joe Sims, confessed. Farley drove the motorbike. Sims fired the shots. Earlier Sunday they had attended Sunday school. In the afternoon they attended a segregationist rally at a Go Kart track in nearby Midfield. Both were Eagle Scouts and neighbors considered them "model" Birmingham youths. They didn't know Virgil Ware. Why did they kill him? "They didn't give any reason," said the sheriff's office.

Birmingham's bloody Sunday passed, at length, after an anguished night lit by widespread arson and shattered by the crash of rock, glass, and gunfire. Whites shot and wounded two more Negroes during the night, and many whites—including a honeymoon couple going home to Chicago from Florida—were stoned by Negroes. When Monday finally came, nobody around could provide any clear reason for anything that had happened.

The reasons were not far to seek—in the long-steeping racism of Birmingham's whole seamy past; in the failure of the city's officials to implement the agreement ending last spring's bitter Negro demonstrations, in the ugly climate created by Gov. George C. Wallace through his latest defiance of the law and courts.

Moderate Mayor: The city's Mayor Albert Boutwell, an affable lawyer touted as a "moderate," had been moderate indeed about meeting the demands presumably won by the Negroes in their negotiations. So far, desegregation, Birmingham-style, meant Negroes could eat at two white lunch counters; one municipal job had been upgraded.

Boutwell's response to the bombing now seemed characteristic. Graying and thin-mouthed, he wept real tears, but his words were self-exonerating: "All of us are victims," he said, "and most of us are innocent victims." His action only incensed the Negroes further. He called for assistance from Gov. George C. Wallace who promptly dispatched tough, head-knocking Col. Al Lingo and a company of state troopers to the city. "Sending Lingo in here was like spitting in our face," said one Negro.

For days before the bombing, Birmingham's temperament, already inflamed, had been raised to fever pitch by Governor Wallace himself through his illegal efforts to block school desegregation. President Kennedy, expressing a "deep sense of outrage and grief" over the bombing, pinned the responsibility on Wallace without naming him. "It is regrettable," the President said, "that public disparagement of law and order has encouraged violence which has fallen upon the innocent."

Vigilante Patrols: News of the bombing and the ensuing terror in Birmingham had hardly broken before the Kennedy Administration's chief racial trouble shooter, Assistant Attorney General Burke Marshall, flew to the scene. What he found was worse than he had imagined. Fear gripped the whole community—white as well as black. The police force's self-appointed job, he discovered, was to protect the whites against the Negroes. Negroes, Marshall found, were patrolling their own neighborhoods as armed vigilantes. Negro children attending newly desegregated schools couldn't get police protection; they had to call on U.S. marshals.

The city's Negro leadership was planning a massive protest march on the capitol in Montgomery. And soon, it was plain, massive demonstrations could well erupt again on Birmingham's streets. "There is a breakdown of law and order in Birmingham and we need Federal troops," a passionately gesturing Rev. Fred R. Shuttlesworth shouted to a Negro rally the day after Bloody Sunday.

Other Negro leaders, such as the Rev. Martin Luther King Jr., who flew in from Atlanta, took up the plea for the President to send in Federal troops. At least, they said, he could attend the funeral himself—or proclaim a day of national mourning for the four dead children.

No Communication: But the basic urgent need in Birmingham, as Burke Marshall saw it, was to open communications between the races; they had completely broken down. "The police chief or Mayor Boutwell would have fainted if we had even suggested they confer with the Negro leaders," said a Justice Department official. The city, Marshall found, was unwilling even to go along with the suggestion that Negro police be added to the force to restore the Negro community's confidence in local law enforcement.

After Marshall reported the grim picture to Washington, the President agreed to see a delegation of seven Birmingham Negro leaders. Underscoring the Administration's cautious approach to the touchy crisis, the President also arranged to receive a delegation of white leaders from the city this week, and later a group of its white ministers.

Mr. Kennedy announced he was naming a two-man committee as his personal representatives to work for a conciliation of the races in Birmingham. The appointees: former Army football coach Earl H. (Red) Blaik, who has no special ties with the

South, and former Army Secretary Kenneth C. Royall, a North Carolinian with an anti-Dixiecrat record.

Retired Officers: To many, the naming of a committee seemed a feeble gesture; and there was some groping to understand the special qualifications of its two members. But Administration aides insisted this was a course both practical and indispensable. Marshall's own usefulness as a mediator had become hampered by rising antipathy to the Justice Department in Birmingham. And mediation was a necessity. It was the President's hope that Blaik and Royall, both respected, both men with military backgrounds, could reopen the dialogue between the deadlocked Negroes and whites. The Rev. Martin Luther King Jr., spokesman for the seven-man delegation that visited the White House, agreed it was a crucial objective. But others criticized the President for doing too little.

"We ask for Federal troops," said a Washington Negro bitterly, "and we get two retired officers." Author James Baldwin told an angry Manhattan rally that the appointment of a committee was an "insult to the Negro race." While protests flared, the search for the bombers went quietly and intensively on.

It wouldn't be an easy investigation. Birmingham police, despite their vast experience with bombings, have never solved one. But this time, a special force of fifteen FBI agents was on the scene, and a Justice Department spokesman said it would be the most rigorous manhunt since John Dillinger was bagged.

The reverberations of the crime pursued President Kennedy to New York City, where his appearance before the United Nations General Assembly drew bitter civil-rights pickets into nearby streets. Unaware they were outside, the President put the bombing in a world context in his address to the U.N., urging the organization to safeguard all human rights. "Those rights are not respected," he said, "when a Buddhist priest is driven from his pagoda, when a synagogue is shut down, when a Protestant church cannot open a mission, when a cardinal is forced into hiding, or when a crowded church is bombed."

But it was left to two Southerners to read the portents of Bloody Sunday most eloquently.

Mute Leaders: One, Charles Longstreet Weltner, a young congressman from Atlanta, Ga., took the bombing as a signal for Southern moderates to begin speaking out. "There was a time when silence amid the denunciations of others was a positive virtue," he said. "But, in face of the events on Sunday, who can remain silent? . . . I know why it happened. It happened because those chosen to lead have failed to lead. Those whose task it is to speak have stood mute. And in so doing, we have permitted the voice of the South to preach defiance and disorder. We have stood by, leaving the field to reckless and violent men. For all our hand-wringing . . . we will never put down violence until we can raise a higher standard."

The other Southerner, Martin Luther King Jr., spoke a moving epitaph for Cynthia Wesley, Denise McNair, Carol Robertson, and Addie Mae Collins. "They are the martyred heroines of a holy crusade for freedom and human dignity," he said. ". . . They have something to say to each of us in their death . . . to every minister of the gospel who has remained silent behind the safe security of stained-glass windows . . . to every politician who has fed his constituents with the stale bread of hatred and the spoiled meat of racism . . . They say to us that we must be concerned not merely about who murdered them but about the system, the way of life, the philosophy which produced the murderers. Their death says to us that we must work passionately and unrelentingly for the realization of the American dream. And so, my friends, they did not die in vain . . ."

FRANK SIKORA (1936–   )
From Until Justice Rolls Down _____ *1991*

1

The Victims
Addie Mae Collins   Cynthia Wesley
Carole Robertson   Denise McNair
Sunday, September 15, 1963. Birmingham, Alabama

When they had first started walking to church that day, their behavior had been proper, befitting young girls on their way to praise the Lord. Addie Mae Collins, age fourteen, often walked the sixteen blocks to the Sixteenth Street Baptist Church with her older sister Janie and younger sister Sarah. But this time, before they had gone more than two blocks, they began playing football, using Addie's purse as the football and giggling and laughing as they ran for passes and dodged about. The route to church was along streets lined with dogwood, oak, and mimosa; the near northwest side of the city was a lower-middle-class, mostly black neighborhood, where frame houses mingled with small stores and other businesses. A number of girls at the church, including Addie, were to be ushers that day. All were wearing white dresses.

At her house, fourteen-year-old Cynthia Wesley was ready to go out the door with her father, Claude, when she was stopped by her mother. "Young lady, your slip is hanging below your dress," said Gertrude Wesley. "You just don't put your clothes on any way when you're going to church, because you never know how you're coming back." Cynthia had hurriedly made the necessary adjustments before running out the door. She and her father would arrive before the start of Sunday school, 9:30 A.M. Her mother would never see her again.

Meanwhile, Cynthia's closest friend, Carole Robertson, also fourteen, had already arrived at church, driven by her father, Alvin C. Robertson.

The last of the four to arrive was eleven-year-old Carol Denise McNair, who was known to her family and friends as Denise. The day before, Denise and a friend from across the street, Barbara Nunn, and some other children had been playing kickball and a game they called four-square. "It was just a game we made up, I guess," Miss Nunn would say in later times. "Denise was just a kid, just a girl who liked to have fun and play, like all kids. She had a dog she called Whitey. She really loved that dog."

On that Sunday morning Denise was going to go to church early and planned to ride with her father, Chris McNair, a photographer. But he was a member of another church and was running late that morning. So she had told him, "That's okay, Daddy, go ahead." She waited and rode with her mother, saying goodbye to her dog before leaving.

After the hot summer, the day was refreshingly cool, with morning temperatures in the low sixties. Behind a cloud bank, the sun was a silver blur as it edged up above the hump of high hills along the eastern edge of this industrial city of 340,000.

The year 1963 had not been kind to Birmingham; racial discord had projected the city onto the front pages of newspapers around the world, as well as in the eye of TV cameras. City authorities had used dogs and fire hoses to dispel crowds of blacks, and the homes of some black leaders had been bombed.

Martin Luther King, Jr., had announced early in the year that he had selected Birmingham as a target of the Southern Christian Leadership Conference's effort to overcome racial barriers. He called it the most segregated city in the South.

Birmingham had undergone political upheaval in late 1962 and early 1963, changing its form of government from a three-member commission—one of the commissioners had been Eugene "Bull" Connor—to a mayor-council system. Connor, a hard-line segregationist, had fought the change, but after he failed to block it he entered the race to be the city's new mayor. The election was held March 5; Connor and another candidate, Albert Boutwell, got the most votes but neither received a majority. They faced each other in a runoff on April 2. Boutwell, a soft-spoken racial moderate, won the runoff by more than eight thousand votes, but Connor refused to leave office, filing a court challenge.

Against this backdrop, King came to town. "He was not welcome," recalled *The Birmingham News,* in a commemorative story twenty years later. *The News* had blasted Connor's police department in 1961 for its mishandling of the Freedom Riders who were beaten by klansmen, and in 1963 it also blasted King in an editorial: "His very presence will be upsetting to whites familiar with his Albany [Georgia] record. King has made shocking statements in the past, of personal unwillingness to say in advance whether he would accept court orders—even though he expects whites to do so. His 'non-violent' policy is violated every time he promotes demonstrations or turmoil not related to achievement of justice under the law. . . . He should stay out of Birmingham."

King and the local leader of the Birmingham drive, the Reverend Fred Shuttlesworth, who headed the Alabama Christian Movement, waited until April 3, the day after the runoff, to begin their challenge to the city's laws and customs embracing segregation. On that bright, warm Wednesday, *The News* carried a story on the front page that captured the mood of the day for many people: "This, happily, is a new day for Birmingham. There's a new feeling in the air. There's a new spirit of optimism." The story was signed by the mayor-elect, Albert Boutwell.

On that same day, King and Shuttlesworth sent a group of blacks to obtain service at Britling's Restaurant; fourteen were arrested. Simultaneously, other groups went to lunch counters at some of the city's larger department stores—Pizitz, Loveman's, Kress, and Woolworth's. The blacks found "Closed" signs at each of them, but Birmingham's new day had begun.

This was a city where blacks found little in the way of steady employment, other than cleaning up offices or homes, cooking in restaurants, or toiling in the iron and steel foundries; the few black professionals were teachers or preachers. There were no black store clerks, secretaries, police officers, librarians, or firefighters. This was the Birmingham that still posted "White only" signs over water fountains and restrooms; black people could not sit at lunch counters or in the main sections of theaters.

King brought his Southern Christian Leadership Conference to Birmingham to marshal a challenge to legal segregation. Although he held rallies at several churches in the black community, the chief rallying spot was the Sixteenth Street Baptist

Church, chosen for its size, its history, and its location. The church, a yellow-brown structure built in the Byzantine style, had a membership of more than four hundred, including many prominent black citizens: lawyers, teachers, dentists. It sat cater-corner from Kelly Ingram Park, a one-square-block area of trees and grass that was an ideal place to mobilize an army of marchers and send them down Fifth Avenue to the downtown, just four blocks away. At the church King preached harmony: "I don't like the way Mr. Bull Connor acts, but I love him, because Jesus said love is greater than hate." It was here in Birmingham that the civil rights movement adopted its anthem, "We Shall Overcome."

Marches began in April and resulted in thousands of arrests; "Never have so many gone to jail in the cause of freedom," said King. Fire hoses and snarling police dogs were used against large groups of spectators who gathered to watch the marches.

On May 9 King and his top aides, Shuttlesworth and Ralph Abernathy, reached an agreement with Birmingham business leaders to desegregate lunch counters, drinking fountains, and restrooms, and to begin hiring blacks as sales clerks. King hailed it as "the most significant victory for justice that we have seen in the Deep South." The agreement was announced on May 10, and on the next day Bull Connor angrily denounced it as King's "lyingest, face-saving" act. That night bombs exploded at the black-owned Gaston Motel and at the home of King's brother, A. D. King. The bombings triggered a riot by twenty-five hundred blacks; fifty persons were injured. President John F. Kennedy sent federal troops to Alabama, staging them at Fort McClellan, near Anniston, and at Maxwell Air Force Base in Montgomery. But the troops never moved into Birmingham, and a strained calm settled over the city. On May 20 Bull Connor, having lost his court challenges of the elections, left office.

The church rallies began to dwindle, and blacks and whites alike tried to return to a more normal life. Then, as autumn approached, the city was again jolted by racial turmoil. Federal judges in Alabama had ordered twenty-four blacks enrolled at previously all-white schools. Five of those black students were in Birmingham. Alabama Governor George C. Wallace, who had made his stand in the schoolhouse door at The University of Alabama in June, vowed to fight the desegregation of the state's public schools.

On the night of August 20, 1963, the home of black attorney Arthur Shores was bombed, but no one was hurt. Shores had been involved in the desegregation of The University of Alabama and in efforts to invalidate Birmingham's ordinances maintaining residential segregation. As the opening day of school neared, white resistance mounted. Crowds of whites waving Confederate flags protested desegregation orders and rode motorcades through the city. On the night of September 4 another bomb exploded at Shores's home, this time slightly injuring his wife, Theodora. Blacks reacted in anger, boiling out into Center Street near the Shores home, in the city's near west side. Police hurried to the scene; shots were fired. A black man was shot and killed as he reportedly ran from a house firing a gun. That night, twenty-one persons were injured, including some officers who were struck by bricks, rocks, and bottles.

But on this Sunday morning of September 15, 1963, the din of the desegregation effort had been stilled. At the church, the lesson for the day was "The Love That Forgives."

At 9:10 A.M. church members William and Mamie Grier, both schoolteachers, neared the church in their new blue and white Buick Electra. About two blocks from the church Mrs. Grier pointed at another car and said, "Look at that." What had caught

her attention was the Confederate flag that fluttered from the car's whiplike radio an-
tenna. Mrs. Grier would later tell the FBI that the car appeared to be a 1955 Chevro-
let, greenish in color. It had been driven by a lone white man, she said. Confederate
flags had been common on cars during the early 1960s, and many blacks viewed them
as a symbol of the bad old days, when whites went to war for the right to keep blacks
in slavery. The Griers had followed the car; it turned on Sixteenth Street, passed the
church, then continued on. They watched until it passed from view. Then they turned
into the church parking lot. There had been some anxiety among church members
because of the rash of bombings in Birmingham in recent weeks, and only the Sunday before, the church secretary, Mary Buycks, had received a phone call from a man
who said, "This is the KKK. Your church will be bombed tonight." It had turned out
to be a hoax.

2

As the Collins sisters had strolled along playing football, Bennie H. Wilson, deacon in charge of custodial services, was walking up the concrete steps leading to the
side entrance of the church. Had he looked under the steps he would have seen it—a
box packed with thick sticks of dynamite, each of them wrapped in brownish-green
paper. The box had been placed there during the night. But Wilson didn't look, and
neither did anyone else. At least a dozen church members would walk up the steps
that morning.

Most of the adults gathered upstairs in the main sanctuary, while the children
and teenagers went downstairs to the assembly area, a large room with light brown
walls that had served the church as a sanctuary until the upstairs was completed in
1911. Some of the Sunday school classes were held in the assembly area, but others
were housed in the small rooms that fringed it. In the northeast corner of the basement, almost directly behind the side steps, was the women's lounge.

Ella C. Demand began her class at 9:30; after a discussion of the lesson, some of
the teenage girls began talking about their duties as ushers. At about 10:10, Cynthia
Wesley and Carole Robertson asked permission to go to the lounge so they could
freshen up for the service. They would have to be upstairs by 10:30.

Also at about 10:10 A.M. Maxine McNair and her daughter Denise arrived.
Mrs. McNair went to the adult class on the main floor, while Denise hurried down to
the small basement room where Mrs. Clevon Phillips was conducting class. A few
minutes after she entered the room, Denise raised her hand and asked permission to
go to the lounge. The teacher nodded. Out in the assembly area, Denise paused. To
her right, about forty feet away, she saw Rosetta Young, one of the sponsors of the
youth ushers. Denise ran across the room to her.

"My, don't you look pretty," said Mrs. Young.

The girl smiled. "Thank you, ma'am."

She whirled then, and went to the lounge. Her words to Mrs. Young were probably her last.

In the meantime, the Collins girls were giggling their way along, throwing
Addie's purse about and running so hard that they began to perspire.

"This is the best time we've ever had coming to church," said Janie, the oldest at
sixteen. Sarah, thirteen, was the youngest; Addie was fourteen. When they finally arrived
at the church it was well past 10 A.M. and the Sunday school classes were about over.

"Now come on, y'all," chided Janie. "We can't go into church looking like this. We got all messed up. Come on, we're going down to the lounge to straighten up." They went to the women's lounge in the basement. In a few minutes Janie was ready. "Now y'all hurry and come on up," she called as she left the lounge and went upstairs.

Denise McNair entered the lounge where the other girls were freshening up for the service. A twelve-year-old girl named Marsha Stollenwerck had just left. Still in the room were Cynthia Wesley, Carole Robertson, and Addie Mae and Sarah Collins.

There was little being said. The girls were checking themselves out in the mirror, straightening dresses, running a hand over their hair. Sarah had just turned on the water to wash her hands and glanced to her right, watching her sister Addie fussing with the sash of Denise's dress, which had come undone; she was retying the bow in it.

Suddenly, there was a sharp blast, and Sarah saw the outside wall crumbling. She caught just a glimpse of it—bricks and mortar and glass and wire gauge flying through the air. The exterior wall of the church was thirty inches thick, composed of stone and brick. The force of the blast blew out the section under the window and fragmented the stone and brick, as well as the limestone sills of the double window. A huge gaping hole appeared.

But Sarah didn't see that. She had already fallen blinded and bleeding and was screaming hysterically for her sister: "Addie! Addie! Addie!"

But there was no sound from Addie . . . or from Carole or Cynthia or Denise.

Upstairs, in the sanctuary, the sound of the blast brought a moment of stunned silence. Then: "We've been bombed!" someone screamed. The clock in the sanctuary stopped at 10:22.

To some it had sounded like a loud crack of thunder, almost ear-splitting. To others it seemed like a dull thud, like someone thumping a big washtub. And to some there was no sound at all, just things flying and falling wildly through the air, glass breaking, doors flipping open—a sudden wave of heat riding silently through their church.

Marsha Stollenwerck, who had been in the lounge until a few minutes before the blast, told the FBI that she had heard "a big noise" and had tried to run out the back door of the church—but she was pushed back, she had said, as if by some invisible force. Then she ran to the main entrance, located on the Sixth Avenue side, and went out.

Mrs. Young, who had moments before been talking with Denise McNair, was talking to some other children when the explosion occurred. She grabbed those nearby and fell to the floor. In the moment of panic that followed, she saw smoke billowing from the lounge area and feared the worst. She took the hands of the children near her and led them up the stairs and out the Sixth Avenue entrance. As they departed, they shot hasty glances about the church interior. Most of the large, stained-glass windows were broken; in one, the body of Jesus on the cross remained intact, but the head had been blown away.

Mamie Grier, the teacher who had been suspicious of the green Chevy with the Confederate flag on it, was conducting an adult Sunday school class in the choir loft. Attending were Earline Tankersley, Ida Freeman, Maggie Webb, and Maxine McNair, Denise's mother, who was the last to arrive. The class was ending when the bomb went off; the sound seemed to come from the basement, on the Sixteenth Street side. Maxine McNair began to scream. She jumped up and ran out and circled behind the church, running up the alley to the Sixth Avenue side of the church, the main entrance. Mrs. Tankersley followed, later recalling that she was in such shock she couldn't remember exactly what had happened, only that they were outside, running.

In Ella Demand's classroom, from which Carole and Cynthia had been excused so they could go to the lounge, the explosion was not heard at all, said the instructor. She was suddenly aware of glass breaking and felt a surge of air move through the room. Then she saw smoke billowing in the hallways and heard screams.

In Mrs. Clevon Phillips's class, the four girls who remained there after Denise left for the ladies' lounge were unhurt. Their teacher led them up the stairs to the main sanctuary, then out the Sixth Avenue door.

In the lounge area, which had taken the brunt of the explosion, girls were screaming and crying, groping their way through the dust and smoke. The Reverend John Cross, the pastor, appeared in the hallway to help search for victims; he was bleeding from the head. As the adult church members began calling out names, it became clear that there were people who had been in the part of the building that was now reduced to rubble.

By then medical rescue units were on the scene, and police urged church members and bystanders to back away. Someone spotted a shoe, and a woman cried out that it belonged to Denise McNair. Her sobs mingled with the endless wail of ambulances.

One by one, the girls were pulled from the debris. Three were apparently dead on the spot, witnesses said. One man told the FBI later that although he heard one girl moan he felt she was near death. A fifth girl, badly injured and later identified as Sarah Collins, was alive, and an ambulance driver said he heard her mutter something. According to him, the girl said, "I saw two white men run through and then the wall fell down. I thought they were reporters. God will save me."

The weeks of threats and hoaxes had finally crashed down upon the church and its people, taking the lives of four innocent victims, girls who had not directly taken part in the civil rights marches or the attempt to desegregate the schools.

They had come to praise the Lord. Now they were dead.

3

In the moments following the explosion, scores of angry blacks gathered at the intersection of Sixteenth Street and Seventh Avenue North. Police, wearing helmets and holding shotguns, kept the crowd away from the church, but some young men in the crowd threw rocks and bricks. Cars driven by whites were pelted; some were overturned. Several vacant houses and a small shop were torched.

Before the day was over, racial violence had claimed the lives of two other black youths. Sixteen-year-old James Robinson was shot in the back by police as he ran down an alley near the church, after a rock fight between black and white teenagers. Police said Robinson had been part of a group of teenagers that threw rocks at police. In a suburb of Birmingham about ten miles from the church, thirteen-year-old Virgil Ware was killed by a white teenager who had spent the afternoon at a segregationist rally. Ware was riding on the handlebars of a bicycle being pedaled by his brother when a red motorbike approached, decorated with Confederate insignia; witnesses reported no exchange of words or other provocation before a boy on the motorbike—a sixteen-year-old Eagle scout—pulled out a pistol and shot twice at Ware, killing him.

The Reverend Cross, still bewildered by the tragedy that had struck his parishioners, told the Associated Press, "We've been expecting this all along, waiting for it, knowing it would come, wondering when." Later, he added, "I've received half a dozen bomb threats since last April. We've searched the church several times. We've called off nighttime meetings, because we felt it would be just too dangerous to gather, even if only to pray. We haven't underestimated the extremists. We've known right along there were people in this town capable of anything. Even this."

Hundreds of persons, meanwhile, had hurried to University Hospital to find out the fate of those rushed there earlier by ambulance. Guards kept the crowd back from the door. "Anguish was a living nightmare," wrote Lou Isaacson, a reporter for *The Birmingham News,* as he witnessed the fathers and mothers who came in sobbing to identify the girls, "victim by victim, scream by scream."

The only survivor in the women's lounge was Sarah Collins. She had screamed for her sister in the hellish moment after the explosion; then, blinded, lay in the rubble crying softly. "I didn't know what had happened," she said later. "I was calling for Addie because I thought she and the others had run out of there and I wanted her to come help me. I never went unconscious. I just couldn't see and I wanted to get out of there."

She had twenty-one pieces of glass in her face and eyes, and more in the chest and legs. A deep cut on her right leg would leave a scar for the rest of her life. She was taken by ambulance to University Hospital, where doctors felt she would lose sight in the right eye but could retain vision in the left. For days she would lie in the hospital room with bandages across both eyes, wondering what had happened. Family members did not immediately tell her about Addie or the three other girls who had been in the lounge with her, but Sarah would later say that she knew something bad had happened to her sister. And one day she overheard the nurses talking in hushed tones, and she knew Addie was dead.

She would remain in the hospital for two months. When she was released, she could see from one eye but had a glass right eye.

Gertrude Wesley, Cynthia's mother, was in shock when she heard of the bombing and the death of her daughter, whom she and her husband, Claude, had adopted at the age of six. Later, she would recall:

I remembered the Saturday night before. Cynthia was at home and she was reading the newspaper and she came across a story in the obituary column about a little baby dying. And she came to me and showed me the paper. She said, "I didn't know babies died like that. I just thought old people died." And I said to her, "Well, when you go into a flower garden you don't always get something in bloom. Sometimes you pick a bud. See, the Lord wanted a bud this time, and he took that baby." And Cynthia thought about it and said, "Oh."

Next morning she was getting ready to go to church. And I told her about her slip showing and telling her to be careful about your appearance, because you never know how you're coming home. And she never did come home again. It really got to me. I kept thinking about her talking about the baby dying and me saying something about the Lord taking a bud, and about never knowing how you're coming back. She never came back. I didn't see her anymore. And I didn't want to see her that way.

Alpha Robertson, Carole's mother, was a member of the church but had not attended Sunday school. She had been at home getting ready for the main service when the telephone rang; someone called to tell her a bomb had exploded. She rushed to the church. Her husband, Alvin, who attended St. John AME Church, was already there with other relatives.

"I didn't know at the time about Carole," Mrs. Robertson would recall later. "I was there and everybody was rolling around trying to find out something, and my husband came up and told me to go home. He asked Lorenzo 'Piper' Davis, a friend of ours, to take me home. He stopped by Sardis Church for his wife and she came to my house to wait with me."

It was a short time later that another call came—this time announcing that Carole had been killed. In the shock and grief that followed, Mrs. Robertson would recall the last hours of Carole's life:

> She was wearing medium high-heeled shoes, the first time she had ever worn them. We had bought them the day before. She and I had gone shopping and we found the shoes, which were shiny black ones. She liked them. We went to Odom, Bowers, and White, which was a department store in the downtown. And we also picked her out a winter coat and put it on layaway. Before we left, Carole also found this necklace which she liked, so we bought it, too. And on that Sunday morning she wore the new shoes and her necklace. After the bombing, I think some weeks after, Mrs. Lillian S. Moore of the Davenport and Harris Funeral Home, came and brought me the shoes. There wasn't a scratch on them. Not one mark. I kept them for years and years, but finally I gave them to my other daughter, but she couldn't wear them because they were not the right size. But she still has them. About a week after it happened, I had a friend call the store and told them to take Carole's winter coat off layaway, that we wouldn't be getting it.

The next day, Monday, September 16, the Robertsons had the crushing duty of planning their daughter's funeral. They decided to have it quickly, at St. John, where Mr. Robertson was a member. Meanwhile, plans were being made for a mass funeral with the Reverend Martin Luther King, Jr., presiding. "We didn't know at first about that," Mrs. Robertson said, "and we had just made our own plans for Carole."

That Monday night King and several ministers came to the Robertson home to ask them to delay Carole's funeral for a day and have it included with the other three victims. Mrs. Robertson declined. Carole's funeral was held that Tuesday, September 17, at St. John AME Church, with the Reverend Cross officiating; nearly two thousand persons crammed inside the church and stood in the street outside. Gazing down on the flower-banked casket, Cross spoke somberly: "This atrocious act was committed not against race, but against all freedom-loving persons in the world. Somehow, out of this dastardly act, we have been brought together again as never before. May we not seek revenge against those who are guilty, but find our refuge in love and the words of Paul, who said, 'All things work together for good for those who love God.'"

The Reverend C. E. Thomas, pastor of St. John, told the gathering: "I want to speak to all who are here, people of both races and many creeds. I am speaking for the ministers of this city. Keep cool heads. We cannot win freedom with violence." Several hundred people were waiting outside the church as the casket was carried out and placed in a hearse to be taken to Shadow Lawn Cemetery.

On Wednesday, September 18, a crowd estimated at seven thousand gathered in and around the Sixth Avenue Baptist Church, about a mile from the bombed church. Most stood out in the streets. King led the services for Cynthia Wesley, Addie Mae Collins, and Carol Denise McNair, calling them "the modern heroines of a holy crusade." As many as two thousand may have jammed into the church itself, straining to hear King's words above the shouts of agony that punctuated the service; many in the church wept.

"We must not harbor the desire to retaliate with violence," King declared. "The deaths may well serve as the redemptive force that brings light to this dark city."

Several times during the service, members of the family or girls in the choir broke down, crying; three women collapsed and were helped from the church. Then it was over, and the pallbearers took the caskets, one by one, and edged them out into the afternoon sunlight. As they appeared at the church entrance the crowd outside reacted: some moaned and wailed; some cried out hysterically. The caskets were put in the waiting hearses then, and the journey to two cemeteries began. As the processional left the church some of the young men in the crowd began to shout insults at white spectators and police; Captain James Lay, a black civil defense official, with police officers standing behind him, quieted them down, and they finally dispersed.

The funeral entourage for Denise McNair wended its way through the southwest section of the city and into the rolling, wooded Shadow Lawn Cemetery. Flowers were still piled freshly on Carole Robertson's grave. The procession for Cynthia Wesley and Addie Collins moved slowly to Woodlawn Cemetery in the city's east side, on a slope near the airport.

4

On the afternoon of the bombing about two thousand whites had gathered in the suburb of Midfield to hold a rally protesting the desegregation of West End High School, which had been ordered by federal court. But the planned cavalcade into Birmingham was called off because of the racially tense situation. At the rally, the Reverend Ferrell Griswold condemned the bombers and said he hoped they would be quickly apprehended. The crowd applauded him. Then, a white teenager was cheered when he strung up an effigy labeled "Kennedy."

The FBI sent dozens of agents into Birmingham for the most intense probe since the search for gangland figure John Dillinger in the 1930s. In the aftermath of the bombing there were shock and rage among the black leadership of Birmingham and Alabama. President Kennedy, who had ordered the Justice Department to send the FBI, expressed grief for the families of the four victims and also sent former Army football coach Earl "Red" Blaik and former secretary of the army Kenneth Royall to Birmingham to meet with both black and white leaders. Kennedy invited a group of city leaders to come to the White House and meet with him. Blacks asked the president to send federal troops into the city, but he declined.

Governor George Wallace, meanwhile, was targeted with an injunction by the state's five federal judges, led by U.S. District Judge Frank M. Johnson, Jr., to stand aside in his efforts to block school desegregation in the state. Wallace reacted in character. He told reporters, "The federal courts—through the Kennedys—have laid the predicate that they will allow the Justice Department to jail the governor of Alabama without benefit of trial or jury, and I resent it." The bombing that took four lives, the governor said, was a "dastardly act by a demented fool . . . who has universal hate in his heart."

On Monday at the weekly noon meeting of the Young Men's Business Club, attorney Charles Morgan, Jr., obtained permission to read a statement. He began by asking, "Who did it?" and proceeded to lay the blame for the bombing on all Alabama residents who had remained silent on the issue of desegregation or who had vowed to maintain the racial status quo. "We are a mass of intolerance and bigotry and stand indicted before our young," he read. "We are cursed by the failure of each of us to accept responsibility, by our defense of an already dead institution." He concluded, "Every person in this community who has in any way contributed to the popularity of hatred is at least as guilty, or more so, as the demented fool who threw that bomb."

The reaction of the state press was mixed. "May God Forgive Us," lamented an editorial in the Talladega *Daily Home:* "This should be Alabama's universal cry in the wake of our blackest day. May God forgive this newspaper and all others for any mishandling of news, any editorial comments which may have helped to sow the seeds of violence. May God forgive the bombers who put a bloody 'amen' to the hour of worship." Later, it added, "The shame will be ours forever."

In its September 16 edition, *The Birmingham News*'s editorial, entitled "The Shock and Shame," read: "Not one word or a million makes up for the deaths of four innocent children in the Sunday School bombing yesterday morning." It added, "It is yet possible, despite the host of unsolved bombings, that what must be a small band of men will be arrested and tried for what must be called outright murder wholly premeditated and carried out. Every white man certainly should be asking himself how he would feel if for years the unidentified had made his wife, his children, his home, his church, the object of such hatred." It concluded, "May God grant us a strength of leadership and a wisdom we have yet to attain. Beyond this prayer nothing now makes much sense."

The Cullman Times blamed national leaders for the bombing. "Blood is on the hands of those persons who have promoted racism for their own selfish interests. There is no doubt the Kennedys and Martin Luther King and numerous others have promoted the issues for their own personal gain."

The Valley Voice, a northwest Alabama weekly, said that "Birmingham, shocked and shamed and knocked to its knees by 10 sticks of dynamite, is to be pitied. What more, we may ask, can happen?"

The Selma Times-Journal pondered, "It is difficult for decent, civilized people to express what is in their hearts."

The Birmingham News carried a letter from a "G. Jones" of Huntsville, who wrote to the editor: "I wonder if the Negroes of Birmingham have stopped long enough to try to figure out who is at the root of all their troubles. Two men—John and Bobby Kennedy. If the thought has not occurred to them, they should think it over."

The week of the bombing, U.S. District Judge Clarence Allgood convened a federal grand jury to deal with what he said was a band of citizens who were making a mockery of federal law. He had originally notified the jurors to be there because of the wave of violence that was sweeping Birmingham in reaction to federal court orders regarding school desegregation. "In recent weeks we have witnessed what amounts to mockery of our laws, a mockery by those who would cut the very roots of our American system of justice," he said, "who in doing so would starve the growth of our way of life and snuff out human life with insane fury and irrationality. Sunday's bombing of a Negro church—a place of worship—where the lives of four children were taken, is a hideous example. I can think of no greater heresy or a more blackening sin against humanity."

QUESTIONS FOR DISCUSSION AND WRITING

1. In the *Newsweek* article and the excerpt from Sikora's book, what personal information do we get about the girls and their families? What information are we given about the wider historical context? Which element—the personal or historical—dominates in each piece? In what ways are the elements woven together effectively or ineffectively?

2. Almost thirty years separate the writing of the *Newsweek* article and Sikora's book. What elements from the *Newsweek* article show that it was written shortly after the event? What elements in the Sikora piece show that almost thirty years have passed since the bombing? What is gained or lost by the immediacy of the *Newsweek* article and by the more distant perspective of the Sikora piece?

3. When the *Newsweek* article was written, the Civil Rights movement was highly controversial. What in the article suggests sympathy or lack of sympathy for the movement?

QUESTIONS FOR CROSS READING: WARRING WITHIN

1. Imaginative works based on historical events sometimes take liberties with the historical facts. What in the poems is historically accurate, and what is fictionalized? Why do the writers seem to make the choices they do?

2. Three of the girls who died in the bombing were fourteen years old, and one was eleven. Though we usually think of fourteen-year-olds as teenagers on their way to becoming young adults, many of the works emphasize that the girls are "little." Which works juvenilize the girls—and how? What is the effect on the reader of making the girls seem younger than they are?

3. In 1998, Spike Lee produced a moving documentary on the Birmingham bombing titled *4 Little Girls*. The documentary interweaves family photographs with the accounts of parents, siblings, and friends of the four girls; it also includes footage from the Civil Rights protests. Locate and watch Lee's film. (The documentary is available on videotape.) What does it add to what you had already learned about the girls and the bombing? In what ways are the techniques of the film—for instance, the weaving of historical and personal information or the emphasis on the "littleness" of the girls—the same as or different from the techniques used in the prose pieces and the poetry?

4. In 1977 Robert Chambliss was convicted of the bombing and sentenced to life imprisonment. (He died in prison in 1985.) In 2001 and 2002, Thomas Blanton and Bobby Frank Cherry were also convicted and sentenced to life imprisonment. Research the legal cases of these three men. What evidence was brought against them? How did the cases change with the passage of so much time between the bombing and the trials? To what extent do the convictions of these men restore a sense of justice to the situation?

MEMORIALIZING VIETNAM

ROBERT SOUTHWELL (1561–1595)

The Burning Babe _____   *1602*

As I in hoary winter's night stood shivering in the snow,
Surprised I was with sudden heat which made my heart to glow;
And lifting up a fearful eye to view what fire was near,
A pretty babe all burning bright did in the air appear;
Who, scorchèd with excessive heat, such floods of tears did shed   5
As though his floods should quench his flames which with his tears were fed.
"Alas," quoth he, "but newly born in fiery heats I fry,
Yet none approach to warm their hearts or feel my fire but I!
My faultless breast the furnace is, the fuel wounding thorns,
Love is the fire, and sighs the smoke, the ashes shame and scorns;   10
The fuel justice layeth on, and mercy blows the coals,
The metal in this furnace wrought are men's defilèd souls,
For which, as now on fire I am to work them to their good,
So will I melt into a bath to wash them in my blood."
With this he vanished out of sight and swiftly shrunk away,   15
And straight I callèd unto mind that it was Christmas day.

QUESTIONS FOR DISCUSSION AND WRITING

1. At the end of the poem, the speaker tells us "it was Christmas day." Why is the day significant? Why does Southwell leave this information to the end?
2. "The Burning Babe" has evoked very different responses from readers. Some find its images fresh and effective; others find them grotesque and forced. How do *you* respond? As you think about your response, you will want to think about both the literal and the metaphorical levels on which the images function and about how they create images of promise and/or destruction.

DENISE LEVERTOV (1923–1997)

Advent 1966 —————————————————————————— *1970*

Because in Vietnam the vision of a Burning Babe
is multiplied, multiplied,
     the flesh on fire
not Christ's, as Southwell saw it, prefiguring
the Passion upon the Eve of Christmas,

5 but wholly human and repeated, repeated,
infant after infant, their names forgotten,
their sex unknown in the ashes,
set alight, flaming but not vanishing,
not vanishing as his vision but lingering,

10 cinders upon the earth or living on
moaning and stinking in hospitals three abed;

because of this my strong sight,
my clear caressive sight, my poet's sight I was given
that it might stir me to song,
is blurred.
15   There is a cataract filming over
my inner eyes. Or else a monstrous insect
has entered my head, and looks out
from my sockets with multiple vision,

seeing not the unique Holy Infant
20 burning sublimely, an imagination of redemption,
furnace in which souls are wrought into new life,
but, as off a beltline, more, more senseless figures aflame.

And this insect (who is not there—
it is my own eyes do my seeing, the insect
25 is not there, what I see is there)
will not permit me to look elsewhere,

or if I look, to see except dulled and unfocused
the delicate, firm, whole flesh of the still unburned.

QUESTIONS FOR DISCUSSION AND WRITING

1. In her poem, Levertov not only alludes to Southwell's "The Burning Babe" but
   retells his story in the light of the horror she sees in the Vietnam War. So the
   promise of Southwell's poem is turned on its head, replaced by the horror of a
   promise destroyed. Compare the two poems. How are the two "babes" similar?

How does Southwell's poem provide an ironic backdrop for (or commentary on) Levertov's?

2. Compare the poems' meters, rhythms, and structures. Do you find them equally effective? Do they seem equally appropriate to their subject matters?

3. Look at the ways the speakers talk of themselves, their bodies, and their experiences. How similar are these self-reflections and self-discoveries? How do the poets' ways of speaking of themselves reflect the themes they are hoping to convey?

The picture, poems, and articles that follow "retell" the story of the Vietnam War through their depiction of the Vietnam Memorial in Washington, D.C. Because they return to the same images, we have appended all questions at the end of the cluster.

Lee Teter, *Reflections* (1988). (See color insert.)

ROBERT DANA (1929–   )

At the Vietnam War Memorial, Washington, D.C.   _____ 1985

Today, everything takes
the color of the sun. The air
is filled and fine with it;
the dead leaves, lumped
and molten; flattened grass
taking it like platinum;
the mall, the simple, bare

5

plan of a tree standing
clothed and sudden in its
10   clean, explicable light.

And across the muddy
grounds of Constitution
Gardens, we've come to find
your brother's name, etched
15   in the long black muster
of sixteen years of war—
the earth walked raw
this morning by workmen still
gravelling paths, and people
20   brought here by dreams
more solemn than grief.

A kid in a sweater hurries
past us, face clenched
against tears. And couples,
25   grey-haired, touching hands,
their midwestern faces calm,
plain as the stencilled names
ranked on the black marble
in order of casualty.
30   The 57,939 dead. Soldiers,
bag-boys, lost insurance
salesmen, low riders
to nowhere gone no place—
file after broken file
35   of this army standing at rest.

Were there roses? I can't
remember. I remember
your son playing in the sun,
light as a seed. Beside
40   him, the names of the dead
afloat in the darker light
of polished stone. Reo
Owens. Willie Lee Baker.
Your brother. The names
45   of those who believed and
those who didn't, who died
with a curse on their lips
for the mud, the pitiless sea,
mists of gasoline and rain.

50   In your photograph, it's
1967. June. On the pad

of a carrier, Donald squats
in fatigues, smoking, beside
a rescue chopper, a man
loneliness kept lean;   55
the sea behind him slurs
like waste metal. He looks
directly at the camera, and
his eyes offer the serious
light of one who's folded   60
the empty hands of his
life once too often.
Before nightfall, his bird
will go down aslant God's
gaze like a shattered   65
grasshopper, and the moons
in the rice-paddies cry
out in burning tongues.

All words are obscene
beside these names. In the   70
morning the polished stone
gives back, we see ourselves—
two men, a woman, a boy,
reflected in grey light,
a dying world among the dead,   75
the dead among the living.
Down the poisoned Chesapeake,
leaking freighters haul
salt or chemicals. In a grey
room, a child rises in her   80
soiled slip and pops the
shade on another day; blue,
streaked with high cloud.

These lives once theirs
are now ours. The silver   85
air whistles into our lungs.
And underfoot, the world
lurches toward noon and
anarchy,—a future bright
with the vision of that   90
inconceivable, final fire-storm,
in which, for one dead second,
we shout our names, cut
them, like these, into air
deeper than any natural   95
shadow, darker than avenues
memoried in hidden trees.

RAY A. YOUNG BEAR (1950–)

Wadasa Nakamoon, Vietnam Memorial _____ *1984*

Last night when the yellow moon
of November broke through the last line
of turbulent Midwestern clouds,
a lone frog, the same one
5   who probably announced
the premature spring floods,
attempted to sing.
Veterans' Day, and it was
sore-throat weather.
10   In reality the invisible musician
reminded me of my own doubt.
The knowledge that my grandfathers
were singers as well as composers—
one of whom felt the simple utterance
15   of a vowel made for the start
of a melody—did not produce
the necessary memory or feeling
to make a Wadasa Nakamoon,
Veterans' Song.
20   All I could think of
was the absence of my name
on a distant black rock.
Without this monument
I felt I would not be here.
25   For a moment, I questioned
why I had to immerse myself
in country, controversy and guilt,
but I wanted to honor them.
Surely, the song they presently
30   listened to along with my grandfathers
was the ethereal kind which did not stop.

W. D. EHRHART (1948–)

Midnight at the Vietnam Veterans Memorial _____ *1984*

Fifty-eight thousand American dead,
average age: nineteen years, six months.
Get a driver's license,
graduate from high school,
5   die.
All that's left of them

we've turned to stone.
What they never got to do
grows dimmer by the year.

But in the moon's dim light   10
when no one's here,
the names rise up, step down
and start the long procession home
to what they left undone,
to what they loved, to anywhere   15
that's not this silent wall of kids,
this smell of death
and dreams.

WALTER MCDONALD (1934–   )

Black Granite Burns Like Ice _____ *1993*

Watching the world from above,
all fallen friends applaud
in blisters on our backs.
Wherever I go, there's fire.

My dreams are napalm.   5
I've been to the wall
and placed my fingers on their names.
Black granite burns like ice

no lips can taste. Sad music's
on my mind, a war on every channel.   10
After the madness of Saigon
I flew back through California

to the plains, hardscrabble fields
with cactus and the ghosts of rattlers.
I feed the hawks field mice and rabbits.   15
I'm no Saint Francis,

but even the buzzards circle,
hoping whatever I own keeps dying.
My wife's green eyes count cattle
all week long, saving each calf,   20

each wounded goat ripped open
by barbed wire. After dark
we rock on the porch
and watch the stars,

wondering how many owls dive   25
silently per acre, how many snakes

per grandchild, how many wars
before all dreams are fire.

ROBERT SCHULTZ

Vietnam War Memorial, Night _____ *1992*

To the left the spotlit Washington Monument
Jabs the air, progenitive, white;
Beyond trees, to the right, the stonework glows
Where Lincoln broods in his marble seat;

5   And here, between, in the humid dark,
Where curving pathways lead and branch,
Sally and I step forward carefully
Somewhere near the open trench.

Choppers shuttle across the sky
10   With jets for National crying down,
But we've lost our way. The intricate dark
In the center of town moves all around.

There are others here: white T-shirts drift
In heavy air. Then three bronze soldiers
15   Caught in floodlights across the field
Stare hard at where we want to go.

From above we find the wall's far end
And begin to descend. Ahead of us
Soft footlights brush the lustered stone,
20   Dim figures trace their hands across

The rows of letters, and others, hushed,
File past in the dark. At first we are only
Ankle deep in the names of the dead,
But the path slopes down. Quietly,

25   We wade on in. In the depths beside
The lit inscription, men and women
Hold each other, mortal, drowning.
Many have stopped at a chosen station

To touch an absence carved away.
30   From deep inside the chiselled panels
Particular deaths rush out at them.
The minds of veterans gape like tunnels

To burning huts. We are over our heads.
Now Sally turns, sobs hard, and stops.
35   We cling to each other like all the rest
And climb away with altered steps.

YUSEF KOMUNYAKAA (1947–   )

Facing It _____ *1988*

My black face fades,
hiding inside the black granite.
I said I wouldn't,
dammit: No tears.
I'm stone. I'm flesh.   5
My clouded reflection eyes me
like a bird of prey, the profile of night
slanted against morning. I turn
this way—the stone lets me go.
I turn that way—I'm inside   10
the Vietnam Veterans Memorial
again, depending on the light
to make a difference.
I go down the 58,022 names,
half-expecting to find   15
my own in letters like smoke.
I touch the name Andrew Johnson;
I see the booby trap's white flash.
Names shimmer on a woman's blouse
but when she walks away   20
the names stay on the wall.
Brushstrokes flash, a red bird's
wings cutting across my stare.
The sky. A plane in the sky.
A white vet's image floats   25
closer to me, then his pale eyes
look through mine. I'm a window.
He's lost his right arm
inside the stone. In the black mirror
a woman's trying to erase names: 30
No, she's brushing a boy's hair.

PAMELA REIDHAMMER-BASURTO

The Crowd on the Wall _____

Your father wouldn't come.
He stopped and turned away
when he saw this Black Wall
saying your name.

They have an index here,   5
like a telephone book,

and I found you right away,
although I was in no hurry.

As others huddle in whispers,
10   I walk alone and listen
to a wall saturated
with endings.

There, there is your name.
The lettering is precise.
15   The spelling,
                accurate.

You are placed exactly
when you died,
between these thousands
of others.

20   Excellent records were kept
for those of us here,
as if this proves
this war was correct after all.

I still worry. Your father
25   shakes his head when I say
I pray our son
was not a virgin.

The crowd on the Wall
speaks, their voices roar
30   into a war cry
that only I hear.

Their words
can't be distinguished
no matter how hard I listen
35   for just your voice.

Do all parents come here
to hang by their fingertips
from the chiseled names
they had chosen at birth?

LESLIE ALLEN (1935–   )

Offerings at the Wall _____   **1995**

"The Faces of the American Dead in Vietnam" was *Life* magazine's cover story on June 27, 1969. Photographs and brief biographies of the 242 Americans killed in action during one week, from May 28 to June 3, marched on for pages. When the issue appeared, American troop strength in Vietnam was at an all-time high; President Richard M. Nixon had begun the secret bombing of Cambodia in March, and just days before press time he had announced plans to withdraw twenty-five thousand troops from Southeast Asia.

The article both tapped and fueled a surge in antiwar sentiment that culminated in that fall's massive antiwar demonstrations. Exactly a quarter-century later a copy of that *Life* was left at the Vietnam Veterans Memorial. No explanation was attached. But in some way that yellowed issue spoke more than adequately for the continuing effect of the war on whoever left it.

The issue joined nearly forty thousand other offerings that have been left at the memorial since its dedication in 1982. Service medals, candles, combat boots, letters to dead lovers, dog tags, poems, unopened sardine cans, insignia, newspaper obituaries, prom pictures, wedding rings, birthday cards, Desert Storm memorabilia—it is a collection of writings and objects at once highly personal and yet so emblematic that it calls to mind the groupings of things that have been buried in time capsules.

Instead these items all go to MARS, a drab brick behemoth down the road from NASA's Goddard Space Flight Center, in Glenn Dale, Maryland. MARS—for Museum and Archaeological Regional Storage—houses more than forty collections of objects from local parks and historic buildings in the National Park Service's purview. Most of the twenty-five-thousand-square-foot warehouse, however, is taken up by the rows upon rows of steel cases, white acid-free Hollinger boxes, and rolling carts that hold the Vietnam Veterans Memorial Collection.

The collection is an anomaly worthy of the experience it reflects. Everything left at the memorial—which includes the black granite wall and two newer statues—has been picked up and preserved by the Park Service, save for live plant matter, which is thrown away, and unaltered flags, which go to civic groups. Splintering Popsicle sticks with illegible inscriptions are logged in alongside expert stained-glass likenesses of combat insignia. Yet the National Park Service has defined MARS as a storage facility and keeps it closed to the general public.

The sheer volume of new accessions has meant an unending backlog of uncatalogued items for the collection's curator, Duery Felton, Jr., himself a seriously wounded Vietnam combat veteran, and his lone assistant. Since the Park Service formally began accumulating things from the Vietnam Veterans Memorial in 1984, their numbers have steadily increased to an average of nearly a thousand a month.

That this flood tide of artifacts and documents shows no sign of ebbing even as the war itself recedes into the past testifies to the insistent role Vietnam continues to play in the national imagination. As that role has evolved, the memorial itself has become a combination of holy shrine and secular bulletin board.

Even before it was built, the designer Maya Ying Lin's sunken granite chevron, conceived as a project for a Yale seminar in funerary architecture, inspired comparisons with a grave site. Its multitudinous detractors sometimes went much further: The veteran and author James Webb predicted the memorial would become "a wailing wall for future anti-draft and anti-nuclear demonstrators."

It was initially so controversial that most political leaders, including President Ronald Reagan, refused to attend its dedication, in November 1982. But the emotional outpouring that accompanied that event was unprecedented for a public ribbon cutting; Washington absorbed the greatest influx of veterans since a Grand Army of the Republic encampment ninety years earlier. When the last speech ended, a hundred and fifty thousand people surged over the crowd-control fences and into the memorial's embrace, weeping, searching, reaching, stroking the names engraved on its black granite arms. Thousands stayed on through the night.

Dozens of unusual mementos were left that weekend. Jan Scruggs, who first propounded the idea for the memorial, particularly recalls "a very haunting pair of cowboy boots. No note, no nothing. You could read your own story into it." A couple of days later Tony Migliaccio, a National Park Service grounds supervisor, found a teddy bear, the earliest of at least forty stuffed bears left at the wall. It later became known simply as "the first bear." No policy existed for dealing with boots, bears, letters, and other such things, so Migliaccio mentally labeled them lost and found, put them in a cardboard box beside the lawn mowers and lime sacks in his storage area, and figured the phenomenon would pass. It didn't.

Most of the early offerings came from veterans or their close relatives. More often than not they were notes, letters, and cards that spoke directly to one of the 58,191 men and women named on the wall.

On notepaper from a Washington hotel:

> My dearest Paul
>   I finally got here—a beautiful monument for you.
>   I miss you—and I know you're watching over me.
>   I love you.
>   Your wife

From a mother's letter on Memorial Day 1983: "I see your name on a black wall. A name I gave you as I held you so close after you were born, never dreaming of the too few years I was to have with you."

From the beginning the memorial has been a place where the living commune with the dead. Maya Lin herself described her creation as "an interface between the sunny world and the quiet, dark world beyond, that we can't enter." The granite's mirrorlike polish, a crucial detail in her design specifications, adds to the effect; it lets visitors see their own reflections hovering over the names of their dead and merging with them.

Lydia Fish, director of the Vietnam Veterans Oral History and Folklore Project, calls the wall the "strangest of all sacred places," describing it as a liminal site, or sensory or psychological threshold. A professor of folklore at the State University College at Buffalo, she has conducted fieldwork at many shrines and points out that the Vietnam Veterans Memorial is one of them, a place of pilgrimage, of moral quests.

By the time the Vietnam Veterans Memorial Fund passed control of the memorial to the National Park Service, in 1984, the pilgrimage was well established. Hawaiian veterans arrived bearing a chain of orchids that stretched the entire length of the wall. Native American veterans have held tribal rituals there, bringing beaded eagle feathers, ceremonial war shields, and medicine bundles.

For the majority of Vietnam veterans who go to the memorial alone, however, the journey has offered a release from a sense of isolation. Some have left notes that speak of their arrival as a homecoming. Others have sought the expiation of guilt, another traditional impetus to pilgrimage. What has come to be called survivor guilt underpins thousands of apologies left for dead comrades.

"We did what we could but it was not enough because I found you here," reads one. "You are not just a name on this wall. You are alive. You are blood on my hands. You are screams in my ears. You are eyes in my soul.

"I told you you'd be all right, but I lied, and please forgive me."

As the memorial became a place for pilgrimage, its creator's intentions were, on various levels, borne out. "I didn't want a static object that people would just look at," Lin has written, "but something they could relate to as on a journey, or passage, that would bring each to his own conclusions." The descent toward the wall's vertex, where the names tower overhead, symbolized that journey. The arrangement of those names is even more suggestive.

During the wall's construction, some veterans demanded that the dead be listed alphabetically; hundreds of Smiths and Joneses, and some identical names, would have appeared telephone-directory-style, one after another. Lin stuck to her demand that the names be listed in chronological order of death and alphabetized within each day. As the war progressed, every day held its own story. The wall would repeat those stories. Here were the nurses who died with their patients when a field hospital came under attack; there, a son's name among those of buddies he had mentioned in letters home.

Each day's casualties would be threads in the narrative of an epic poem. But by its very design the memorial presented a broken narrative: The 58,196 names begin at the vertex on the east wall, under the date 1959, continue panel by panel eastward, in the direction of the Washington Monument, and then stop before the sequence resumes at the far end of the west wall and moves east toward the vertex and the last panel, above the date 1975. That broken circle, Lin envisioned, would be completed by each visitor.

The arrangement seemed fitting for a war that had had no conventional narrative structure—a war without a clear beginning or end, without well-articulated goals, fought sometimes with scant regard for geographic boundaries and, indeed, remaining undeclared, technically not a war at all. Circumstances had conspired to isolate the GI from nearly everything beyond a concern for his own survival during the usual 365-day tour. Soldiers in Vietnam rarely fought in the units they had trained with, nor, when it was over, did they come home with comrades. The World War II troopship with its slow, gradual communal return to a world beyond war gave way to a swift, solitary plane ride to a country filled with people who knew little of the GI's sacrifice.

Suddenness also marked the removal, by strangers, of dead or wounded comrades from the battlefield. Medevac usually came so quickly that many GIs never knew until they searched the wall whether a friend had lived or died. "How angry I was to find you here," wrote one vet to his dead comrades.

Maya Lin's wall offered the veterans a place not only to mourn but also to add bits of their own fragmented experience to the collective narrative. *This is what happened,* many of the messages seem to say. A four-page letter addressed to the soldiers of the 101st Airborne begins: "The worst memory for me is the day I sent the 76 men out of your 85 to their deaths. I have to explain and I pray to God you will understand." And the plain truth needn't be verbal: The shell that had killed a comrade was both an obituary and a tribute.

Particular kinds of offerings that tend to show up repeatedly say specific things about how GIs experienced the war. Food and drink—whiskey, canned ravioli, peanuts—often appear at the wall. The donors are usually veterans, who remember vividly the lack of these things. Tins of sardines and bottles of beer, transformed into votives, replace those borrowed or purloined years ago in Asia. Army-issue can openers show up by the dozens. Bags of M&Ms appear without explanation; Felton believes they pay tribute to the underequipped medics who administered them as placebos when the morphine ran out.

Along with their dog tags come parts of GIs' uniforms: headgear, fatigues, dozens of pairs of combat boots, flak jackets, patches. The sheer variety suggests the vast web of service units that operated in Vietnam, as well as the war's long duration. Boots, for instance, progress from old-style Army footwear, brittle from storage since Korea, to Panama-soled ones that resisted booby traps and punji sticks.

Families and friends offer civilian mementos of the men and women they knew: a golfer's clubs, a musician's trumpet, a hobbyist's model car. A canvas bag recalls a paper route. "Floyd, you get one free throw," wrote "Lil' Sis" on an All Star basketball. High school varsity letters and pennants echo the fact that the average age of the American soldier in Vietnam was nineteen—seven years younger than his World War II counterpart.

No shrine or war memorial has ever before attracted such unconventional and eclectic offerings. But no other war was fought in the context of the 1960s, when appearances and objects both acquired heightened symbolic meanings. The draft card, the black armband, and the white armband became icons; "in country," GIs routinely individualized their uniforms and gear to denote affiliation—as in the slashed combat boots of a 1st Cavalry unit—or allegiance—as in peace symbols drawn across the backs of utility shirts.

Now the era's cultural detritus appears at the wall like things washed ashore after years at sea. A working television set is left off one day, perhaps to signify the nation's first televised war or perhaps just the property of some luckless draftee who never came home to watch it again. Like more than two-thirds of the objects left at the memorial, it arrived without explanation. "Everything is left for a reason, but unless you have a real understanding, it's dangerous to interpret the objects," Duery Felton says. He welcomes explanatory letters, and he seeks out help with unusual insignia, patches, and other military markings. He has learned the stories behind everything from Pan American "kiddie wings" to British sterling shaving kits.

But sometimes meaning remains in the eye of the beholder. In 1991 Felton teamed up with Jennifer Locke of the Smithsonian Institution, a child during the Vietnam War, to select items for a small exhibit at the Museum of American History. Felton, as Locke tells it, wanted to include a parking ticket, speculating that it bespoke the Vietnam veteran's continuing problems with impersonal authority; Locke saw something that had fallen out of someone's pocket. In the end the ticket didn't make the final cut, but a pacifier did. "It could have been dropped by accident," Locke says, "or it could have belonged to the child of someone who was killed in Vietnam."

Before about 1985, when word began to spread that the things left at the memorial were being saved, most of what turned up was what Felton calls "pocketables"—a beaded necklace or a swizzle stick—or "field expedients"—two cigarettes made into a cross. Subsequently, many of the offerings began to look more elaborate and premeditated. The word processor took over from the scrawled note, the prepared work from the found object. Donors often alerted the National Park Service before relinquishing objects of value at the memorial.

Leaving something behind began to be a standard ritual for a visit to the wall. At the same time, there came to be more participation by visitors who had no close connection to anyone named on the wall. Boy Scout troops left wreaths for hometown heroes; a German sailor penned an antiwar message on his white cap. Offerings unrelated to the war accumulated. A twisted scrap of gray metal appeared one day; the donor explained that it was wreckage from a B-52 that had crashed in Kentucky in 1959, killing his father. Someone else left two large crystals wrapped in blue velvet—a "psychic guide" for the collection's keepers.

Donors who came neither to mourn nor to commune with their own dead were helping to turn the memorial into a bulletin board, and like all bulletin boards, the memorial began to attract its share of advertising. The director of the radical antiabortion group Operation Rescue has left his business card, and so have politicians, psychotherapists, and business owners.

As a public forum the wall began early on to attract social and political discourse beyond the war's immediate range. A Medal of Honor, the nation's highest military service award, was returned by a Vietnam veteran with a letter that began:

> Dear President Reagan,
>
> The enclosed statement of my renunciation of the Congressional Medal of Honor and its associated benefits represents my strongest public expression of opposition to U.S. military policies in Central America. You have been the champion of these brutal policies. I hold you most responsible for their origin and implementation.

For their part, Ronald and Nancy Reagan weighed in with a handwritten message at the wall:

> Our young friends:
>
> Yes young friends, for in our hearts you will always be young, full of the love that is youth, love of life, love of joy, love of country. You fought for your country and for its safety and for the freedom of others with strength and courage. . . .

More recently Operation Desert Storm yielded, among other things, a crop of yellow ribbons, a few signs that said NO BLOOD FOR OIL, and one that read GUYS, THIS TIME WE WON. Since then the tokens of major marches—pro-choice, pro-life, gay rights—have regularly lined the wall.

On Memorial Day 1993 the wreath that President Clinton laid at the wall had to be removed as soon as he finished his speech to escape destruction by hostile spectators. That Clinton's behavior as a college student could still provoke such animus nearly a quarter-century later underscores the truism that Vietnam endures in extremely powerful ways. A great number of notes and tributes at the wall refer to veterans whose names do not appear there because they died not in action but years later, from the aftereffects of the herbicide Agent Orange or from posttraumatic stress disorder, both the subject of tireless veterans' rights campaigns.

By far the most potent and enduring issue for some visitors to the wall has been the fate of those servicemen they believe are still held captive in Vietnam. Some thirteen hundred men are designated on the wall as unaccounted for, their names signaled by crosses. An unofficial, round-the-clock vigil for the missing, kept since Christmas Eve 1982, functions like a volunteer priesthood at the memorial.

Hundreds and hundreds of letters have been left at the wall. This one carries a date that almost certainly is the day the event that haunts the writer took place.

17 September 1973

John,

The things that I am going to say in this letter are about twenty years and a whole lifetime late, but maybe that won't matter once they've been said.

I've taken the entire responsibility for your death on myself for this whole time. Even now, I intellectually know that there were many mistakes that led to your dying, some of them yours, too. I just have a hard time feeling like it's not my fault.

We trusted each other, implicitly. We depended on each other. We supported each other. We shared a whole lot in the time that we knew each other: pain, hunger, sickness, triumph, laughter, and more than a little excitement. We even shared a lover, Death. Both of us wooed the bitch, but you won her. What a deal for you. You know, I've never forgiven you for leaving me alone. I've been alone and lonely ever since.

Actually, it's probably better that you won. The way things have been back here in the world . . . you'd have had a hard time. Hell, I've had a hard time and I was always the stable one. You'd have wound up dead or jailed.

I never thanked you for the times that you saved my life. Any more than you thanked me for the times that I saved yours. I kind of thought that it was understood, and didn't matter. I mean, even if one of us had said thanks, the answer would have been "F— it. It don't mean nothin'." It does seem to mean something now. It's important. Thanks.

It's just that you've got to know that what happened was done for the best for all of us. We couldn't help you; not without risking us all. We sure as hell weren't going to leave you. It fell to me 'cause I was your partner, I guess. After all, a *man* shoots his own dog, right? God help me. I can still smell your blood and that damned Wyler's lemonade all over me.

I've been looking for forgiveness for twenty years, now. You can't forgive me, now, even if you thought there was a need to. So, lately, I've been trying to forgive myself. You know, I feel like I got punished for doing what we all knew was the right thing. Nobody would talk about it (not like I would have wanted to); when I got back from R&R they gave me an FNG partner. I felt like it was a death sentence. Even that poor bastard paid for your death by way of my treatment of him.

I want you to know that I avenged your death many times over, that day. The bread that those dinks cast upon the waters was returned to them tenfold. That sounds kind of silly, but I know the vindictive kind of person you were and it would have been important to you. I guess it must have been important to me, but I think that I was trying to die, too. The incompetent bastards just couldn't do me.

A lot of the guys who were there say they feel like they lost something in country. I know what I lost. I've always said that when you died, it was like killing the other half of myself. Maybe that's not necessarily true. What I did lose was youth . . . all of the idealism, trust, self-confidence, and personal power that we had, either inside or drilled into us. I'm scared, now, most of the time, and I hurt a lot.

What happened to us has cost me a life as much as it cost you yours. I've never been able to get close to anyone since you died. My wife, my step-daughter, my son. I live in the past, 'cause today hurts too much. I want out of the past. The war is over. I need my war to be over, too.

I never got to say goodbye. So I've come to this monument to have a little memorial service and to say goodbye and to let you go. I'll never forget you, don't worry about that. Hell, I'm a living testimony that you were good at what we did.

Goodbye, John. If there is a caring, Christian God, I hope that he has forgiven both of us and taken you with all of our brother warriors to a peaceful final reward.

Your partner,
J.C.

POW/MIA bracelets accumulate by the thousands, the objects most commonly left at the memorial.

The POW issue has been a powerful stimulant to the imagination. The redemption of the film hero John Rambo, a misfit veteran turned POW rescuer, has proved so resonant that the family of a real-life Rambo listed on the wall, Arthur John Rambo of Montana, had to appeal to the Park Service for help in halting all the rubbings being made of his name. More recently dog tags purportedly belonging to MIAs have been sold in Vietnam to veterans who later deposited them at the wall.

Wherever pilgrimages become popular, industries proliferate to make and sell devotional trinkets, and Duery Felton has lately seen the same process at work at the wall. The cause, he believes, is the newfound prestige of the Vietnam veteran; the result, a boom in ersatz insignia, patches, uniforms, and other accouterments of the Vietnam grunt, including Zippo lighters newly "antiqued" in Vietnam. So the multitude of Vietnam experiences contained in the collection's objects and words has come to include the pseudo-experience. But that makes sense. Pilgrimage sites are, in the words of the anthropologist Victor Turner, "cultural magnets, attracting symbols of many kinds." They lie outside the normal bounds of society, where the real and the unreal can flourish side by side. Along with the pre-aged Zippos and the Rambo name rubbings, the wall has begun to attract fortyish nonveterans who arrive for holiday weekends fully arrayed in the uniforms of Vietnam service. Nearby the POW/MIA vigil draws clusters of fatigue-clad youths who never knew anyone listed as missing. Just beyond the memorial are trucks run by Vietnamese immigrants who sell hot dogs to former GIs. One senses, in all this, an attempt to close a circle around a reality still as elusive as Vietnam's ever was.

For most people who regularly come to the memorial, the annual cycle of birthdays, holidays, and anniversaries defines an unrelenting reality: more than fifty-eight thousand deaths. (Vietnam puts its own dead at one million; its missing at three hundred thousand.) News of marriages, divorces, births, and deaths takes up the thread of narratives broken off a generation ago. On Father's Day 1994 rangers picked up a double brass picture frame. One side held two blurry sonogram images; the other, a handwritten note:

Happy Father's Day, Daddy.
　　Here are the first two images of your first grandchild. . . . Dad—this child will know you—just how I have grown to know and love you—even though the last time I saw you I was only four months old. . . .

Another letter accompanied a small hand-tinted photograph of a Vietnamese man and young girl:

Dear Sir,
　　For twenty two years I have carried your picture in my wallet. I was only eighteen years old that day we faced one another on that trail in Chu Lai, Vietnam. . . . So many times over the years I have stared at your picture and your daughter, I suspect. Each time my heart and gutts [sic] would burn with the pain of guilt. I have two daughters myself now. One is twenty. The other one is twenty-two, and has blessed me with two granddaughters. . . . Forgive me Sir, I

shall try to live my life to the fullest, an opportunity that you and many others were denied."

As curator of the Vietnam Veterans Memorial Collection, Duery Felton tries to keep his professional distance from the emotional content of the letters and mementos. He has, however, observed in them a tone of deepening continuity, as the Vietnam generation gives way to multiple generations. And they in turn show every sign of remaining part of a larger, ongoing Vietnam experience.

GRANT F. SCOTT (1961–   )

Meditations in Black: The Vietnam Veterans Memorial _____ 1990

The conclusion of Bobbie Ann Mason's *In Country* turns on a subtle anachronism. As the main character stands before the Vietnam Veterans Memorial, we expect that she will find her father's name, touch it, and experience a familiar type of catharsis or reconciliation. Surprisingly, she can make no mystical connection with the wall or her father's name; her reaction is in fact anything but revelatory. As Mason points out, "She feels funny touching it. A scratching on a rock. Writing."[1] Sensing that something is missing, Samantha returns to the directory looking for her father there. When she finally does locate him, however, it is not his name, but her own that startles her into discovery:

SAM ALAN HUGHES PFC AR 02 MAR
49 02 FEB 67 HOUSTON TX 14E 104

It is the first on a line. It is down low enough to touch. She touches her own name. How odd it feels, as though all the names in America have been used to decorate this wall (245).

By placing Samantha in the monument, and symbolically in the Vietnam war itself (where she has tried to imagine herself throughout the novel), Mason not only conflates past and present, but also temporarily erases the boundaries between viewer and art object, male and female, Vietnam and America, and most importantly for our purposes, the living and the dead. Among other things, the end of the novel cleverly completes Sam's imaginative experience in the war by making her one of its casualties; the passage suggests, then, that the wall works anachronistically, as memory does, as identity does, prompting the viewer to suspend conventional categories of time and place.

In the very middle of another book, written much earlier and from an entirely different cultural vantage point, the protagonist makes a similar trip to a kind of war memorial:

He set all his strength to the journey assigned to him. They were now nearing the most distant and secluded fields thronged by those glorious in war. Here Daniel Lee, here James Stevenson of illustrious arms, and here the pallid wraith of Robert Runge all met him, and Gregory Scott too, who had fallen in war

[1] Bobbie Ann Mason, *In Country* (New York: Harper and Row, 1985), 244.

and had been lamented grievously in the world above. Bitterly he sighed as he saw all the long line of them: Craig McCorkle, Marco Baruzzi, Thomas Van Houten, Gerald Brown, Alan Garcia, and Terrence O'Boyle. The souls gathered crowding around him on his right hand and on his left. They were not contented with a single view; they liked to hold him in conversation, to walk close beside him, and to hear from him why he had come.[2]

As you may or may not have guessed, the narrator here is Virgil, the protagonist Aeneas, though the warriors he encounters in his descent to the underworld have been replaced by names from a war that will take place over 2000 years later. This anachronism is my own, and, as I will try to show, it is not merely gratuitous. What I hope to reveal is that the experience of visiting (and writing) the Vietnam Veterans Memorial bears striking affinities with mythical journeys to the underworld, where the living are permitted a brief communication with the dead; the wall itself figuratively disrupts time in a way that encourages this strange kind of rendezvous. As one observer has said, "Through an uncanny reversal, the names of the dead appear more real, more substantial than we do; here it is the living reflected in the black granite who are only appearances."[3]

One of the ways that the VVM makes this analogy as well as Samantha's response possible is by positing its own essential difference from the genre of conventional war memorials, particularly as it is embodied on or near Washington's mall. Maya Lin, the student who designed the VVM, has said that in the class where she first mulled over the project, they had "been questioning what a war memorial is, its purpose, its responsibility. Many earlier war memorials were propagandized statements about the victor, the issues, the politics, and not about the people who served and died . . . I didn't want a static object that people would just look at."[4]

Indeed, as Lin well knew, Washington is full of such objects—memorials to the Marine Corps, the Seabees, the Second Division, to Jefferson and Lincoln and Grant, and of course most famously, to Washington. Where these edifices thrust exuberantly towards the sky, the VVM's predominant movement is downwards into the earth, so that instead of dominating the landscape, it modestly harmonizes with its natural surroundings, and in fact doubles them in its reflective surface. Further, where traditional memorials make use of the classical triangular composition to force the viewer's eye upwards, the VVM wittily turns this inverted "V" on its side, so that it embraces us and our gaze, if not always on the level, is predominantly horizontal rather than vertical.[5] This is not a monument, like the Jefferson Memorial, at which we are for ever craning our necks.

Where the other memorials are primarily hewn out of white marble or fashioned from bronze, the VVM is composed of black granite, "a fact," as one guide I

[2] *The Aeneid*, W.F. Jackson Knight, trans. (Middlesex, England: Penguin Books, 1975), 161.

[3] Arthur C. Danto, "The Vietnam Veterans Memorial," 241 *Nation* (31 Aug. '85), 153.

[4] Cited in Wilbur E. Garrett, "Vietnam Veterans Memorial: America Remembers," 167 *National Geographic* (My '85), 557.

[5] Peter Larson, in a letter responding to criticisms of the Wall's inverted "V", alludes to another more egalitarian and perhaps more appropriate meaning: "As for the design, it does resemble, as one descends the steps, an inverted V, and I can understand why the notion of 'reversed victory' might annoy some people, but that same symbol is the one that Pfcs. wore, often proudly, on their arms or collars as they struggled in the mud," *The Los Angeles Times* (6 Feb. 1982), Part II, 2.

spoke with confessed, "we can hardly overlook in a city of white monuments and buildings, a city run by white men." Where the other memorials pin the spectator to one spot, effectually inducing stasis, the VVM promotes action, gently urging its viewer to walk down into its space and to read its names. And what we cannot avoid seeing here is our own reflection, and the way that we are almost casually inserted among the names of the dead, as well as, I think, symbolically implicated in the actions that generated this "grim roster."[6]

Like the war that it memorializes, this monument will not tolerate indifference. Neither can its geometry be said to be apolitical, as the design committee specified and most commentators have subsequently argued; for it gestures towards the Washington monument in the east, the Lincoln memorial in the west. It is naive to assume, as one critic has, that these gestures represent its harmonizing impulse and its effort to include the nation's past in its own design.[7] Rather, as anyone who has been impressed by the VVM's *difference* from these other structures will tell you, the wings of the memorial point rather than encompass, indict rather than include or meliorate. Coming out of the shallow dark cleft in the landscape, it is impossible not to sense the Washington Monument's arrogance, or the tomb-like stolidity of the Lincoln Memorial. It seems impossible not to relate the semantics of these structures to the sobering grammar of the VVM's names.

Finally, and most interestingly, where Washington's other memorials are primarily icons, powerful images of soldiers and horses and war, the VVM is first and foremost a text, an idea that is subtly underscored in its overall form which suggests an open book. What we are overwhelmed by here is not the glorious and heroic feats of courageous soldiers, not victories and battles and bravery, but the long list of the dead; this wall unrolls precisely that final script of war that other memorials try to conceal. Although the black granite panels are beautiful, as one observer has said, we are ultimately "inundated by the flood of names" (Zahn, 212).

If most conventional memorials employ a patriotic rhetoric of images designed to make us emulate the fallen hero, this one urges us to remember the dead and avoid repeating their actions. This is its vital link to the present and to the future. The simple *tour de force* of the names persuades us to reflect on the sadness and the waste of war, the immense loss, not the heroism. In this way it is a most unchivalrous monument, for it implicitly criticizes the presiding ideology of memorials that would glorify war in order to seduce an entirely new generation of young men into battle. The fact that it offers no overt visual symbols of glory or patriotism (except the ones people leave at the grave site) enhances this affect and reinforces the contemplative nature of the memorial.

Unlike the most famous monuments on the Mall, then, the VVM cannot be described with words like "sublime," "awesome," "magnificent," "grand," or "imposing." It is not a monument that makes us aware of how small we are, how awkward and feeble in comparison to the grandeur of the past. Rather, as many observers will at-

---

[6]Gordon C. Zahn, "Memories in Stone," 149 *America* (15 Oct. '83), 212.

[7]See Charles L. Griswold, "The Vietnam Veterans Memorial and the Washington Mall: Philosophical Thoughts on Political Iconography," 12 *Critical Inquiry* (Summer, '86), 712–713. Although I am greatly indebted to this essay, I wonder about the rosy optimism of its conclusions. On closer scrutiny many of Griswold's assumptions seem to issue from the emotionally charged atmosphere of the Memorial's dedication; his desire to celebrate the Wall's patriotic and therapeutic function thus seems to cloud his discussion of its fundamentally "interrogative" character.

test, there is something about the scale that puts it directly within our ken. Instead of diminishing or paralyzing us, it embraces and welcomes, drawing us inexorably downward and inward. This memorial quietly involves us in its space and with its names in a way that both humbles and humanizes us.

Thus, rather than being immediate and overwhelming—as, for instance, in the Washington Monument—the impact of the VVM is gradual and grows the longer we remain and drift along its walkway. This is perhaps why veterans linger here sometimes for hours, and why they keep coming back. It may also explain why the first impulse of every visitor is to touch the wall, whether he or she knows somebody who died in the war or not. There is a magnetism about the memorial that cannot be accounted for solely by the absorptive nature of its color. " 'I don't know what it is,' said Kenneth Young, a Vietnam vet who stood for two hours, staring at the wall, stepping away to think, stepping back to touch again the names he knew. 'You have to touch it. There's something about touching it.' "[8] To be sure, this response is one we are always rebuked for in traditional museums, or are subconsciously persuaded against in the cool bright whiteness of the Washington or Lincoln monuments. These we must bow before and worship, not touch. Like the jar in Wallace Steven's little allegory of monuments, "(they do) not give of bird or bush," but take "dominion everywhere."[9]

In many ways, then, the VVM is a profoundly human memorial, one which does not resist so much as encourage human imprint. Visitors are constantly seen not only making rubbings of names, but leaving mementos—notes, flags, flowers, photographs—as if the men that seem to lie buried behind those names were still warm and alive. And this is why the critics of the memorial—men as diverse as H. Ross Perot, Tom Wolfe, and Henry Hyde—were and are essentially wrong in calling it "abstract, minimalist, and elitest," or, in the phrase that came to epitomize the response of the opposition: "a black gash of shame."[10] The fundamental error of these assessments is not so much that they are hasty or inaccurate (for all their misguided animosity and insensitivity, they in fact have a kind of intuitive rightness), but that they assume the Vietnam war was really no different in kind from the other wars and that it deserves to be remembered with a traditional realist memorial.

Certainly the memorial is not elitist, as the hundreds of thousands who have by now visited it would testify, nor is it a "perverse prank" or a source of general befuddlement to the public, as Tom Wolfe early on predicted it would become. One of the things that prevents these labels from obtaining is precisely the participatory nature of the wall. Unlike its neighboring cousins, the Veterans memorial does not just encourage us to touch its surface, but absolutely mandates it. Whereas the other monuments are eerily self-sufficient, boasting forms that are clearly closed, the VVM necessitates

[8]Cited from *The New York Times* (11 Nov. 1982), B15.
[9]Wallace Stevens, *The Collected Poems* (New York: Vintage Books, 1982), 76.
[10]The complaints over the Memorial's color finally subsided after General George Price, who was attending a debate over the newly proposed monument, fumed in exasperation: "I am sick and tired of hearing black called a color of shame." *Time* (22 Feb. 1982), 19. A close look at the descriptions of the opposition reveals their tendency to conceive of the wall as a subversive "other," whether feminine ("Tribute to Jane Fonda," "wailing wall," "degrading ditch") or black. The goal, in the words of one senator, was "to neutralize this apolitical statement" by offsetting it with a more traditional sculpture and a conspicuous flag—an idea that was exactly realized two years later by Frederick Hart's piece. For more on the controversy, see Elizabeth Hess, "A Tale of Two Memorials," 71 *Art in America* (Ap. '83), 120–127, and C.T. Buckley, "The Wall," 104 *Esquire* (Sept. '85), 61–73.

our existence and our gaze for the completion of its aesthetic. Its form is wonderfully open and unfinished, which means that what we bring to it is as important as what it offers. The criticism that the Wall only honors those who died or are missing rather than all those who served is therefore misleading. Since the monument needs us to complete its conception, it honors both the living and the dead; a fact, as Charles Griswold has noted, that is reinforced in the work's name—the *Veterans* memorial.

In the end, the Wall remains as profoundly about the viewer as about the war and the soldiers who died in that war. In these terms, it is a mortal monument, if that is possible, and we get this sense from the startling fragility of its edges, where its form tapers into the landscape. Here the thin black marble seems almost tentatively propped up against the earth, as if any day the memorial will be dismantled and driven away to another site. This strange sense of impermanence defies all our expectations of monuments and their imperial ambitions of outlasting time.

The VVM is fundamentally different from other monuments in one other crucial aspect as well, and this will bring us back to my initial meditation on the mythical nature of its experience. Instead of prompting and then figuring our own passivity, the VVM makes us work to obtain its full affect. What one critic of the memorial called its "random scattering of names" is really a brilliant arrangement which radically personalizes the chronology of war.[11] Rather than listing by battalion, regiment, or letter, the VVM presents its soldiers in the order in which they died, further disrupting this sequence by beginning and ending *in medias res.* It is only when we reach the middle of the memorial and are standing in its delta, that we confront the war's official beginning and end. And though we may not initially realize it, upon first approaching the VVM from the Lincoln Memorial, we encounter only the illusion of beginning, as well as the illusion of alphabetical order, since the first name is John Anderson.

The important thing to note here is not so much the ingenuity of the layout, but its affect on the viewer. The monument's choreography makes it impossible to find a name without either asking a park guide or looking it up in voluminous directories that are provided at the entrance. Hence, the monument effectively turns the viewer into an active seeker who must search out the name or names of the dead. (The numerous pilgrimages to the memorial by veterans and others have been well-documented and further suggest the VVM's special status.) Metaphorically, we are placed in a battlefield, and forced to identify the bodies of our fallen comrades. As is the case with Odysseus or Aeneas, the search for the dead is difficult and must be undertaken with the aid of ritual. In *The Odyssey* and *The Aeneid,* for instance, the entrance to Hades is so notoriously hard to locate that both heroes must at last resort to divine assistance. Similarly, many accounts of visiting the VVM emphasize the memorial's elusiveness. As Jerome Chandler says, "It's not an easy place to find."[12] Several of the first reporters, in fact, had to ask groundsmen—those mundane modern Virgils—for directions. This seems to me entirely fitting, as does the parallel between the hero's ritual sacrifice of animals in the underworld and the modern visitor's personal offerings at the VVM. No other memorial encourages people to leave valuable mementos and artifacts in quite this way, or to honor the dead with a hush that is usually reserved for churches.

---

[11] Tom Carhart, cited in Hess.
[12] Cited in David A. Hoekema, "A Wall for Remembering," *Commonweal* (15 July 1983), 398.

Finally, as Aeneas and Odysseus come to the underworld expressly to offer proper burial to lost crew members, so too do we approach the Veterans Memorial intent on burying somebody. By moving through the ritual of locating and touching the name we symbolically reenact a burial that the nation as a whole neglected to perform. From the Wall we resurrect and then bury our loved one or our friend, but properly this time and with the kind of private ceremony that this monument uniquely fosters and that seems only appropriate for the kind of war Vietnam was.

It is significant, of course, that the mythical hero ventures into the underworld because he has lost his navigator, has himself gone astray (this is true of *The Inferno* as well, only Dante's wayward helmsman is internal). Summoning the shade and carrying out the forgotten codes of burial is an attempt to right the course of the hero's ship, as well as the ship of state. It is an act that momentarily halts the progress of narrative time in order to heal a past wound. Standing before the VVM, we are placed at a similar threshold, where we attempt to reconcile our world with the world of the dead; as we stare into the reflective surface we cannot help thinking as well that Vietnam was our Troy and that this Homeric list of names represents all of America and that our identity, eerily inscribed by these names, is on some level inseparable from our nation's. Itself a rift or scar in the earth, like a seam in time, the memorial is the place where we come not only to read the war and bury the dead, but to stare at the wound in the nation's body and to participate in its healing.[13]

QUESTIONS FOR CROSS READING: MEMORIALIZING VIETNAM

1. Many of the poems included here comment on some of the central features of the memorial—its reflective quality, the black granite, and the listing of the dead and missing. How do they respond to these features? To what extent do the poets find similar meanings in the memorial? How similar are the emotions the memorial evokes in those who write about it?

2. In "Offerings at the Wall," Allen says that the wall has been viewed as a wailing wall, a gravestone, a holy shrine, and a secular bulletin board. To that list, Scott, in "Meditations in Black," adds the image of an open book inscribed with the names of the dead. How are these complementary or opposing views of the memorial? Which image seems to you most fitting and most powerful?

3. What feelings motivate the "offerings at the wall"? Are similar or different feelings conveyed in the poems and in Teter's "Reflections"?

4. Which poems emphasize the perspective of the war dead? Which emphasize the views of the survivors? How are these perspectives similar, and how are they opposed?

---

[13] The metaphor of a scar or cut is in fact Maya Lin's, who used it suggestively in recalling her initial inspiration for the project: "I had an impulse to cut open the earth . . . an initial violence that in time would heal. The grass would grow back, but the cut would remain, a pure flat surface, like a geode when you cut into it and polish the edge" (Garrett, 557).

5. One of the initial objections to Maya Lin's design of the Vietnam Veterans Memorial was that its modernist features were too abstract; some people felt that the memorial would not "tell a story" viewers could respond to. However, as the various responses included here show, many find a very powerful story in the memorial. What is that story? How does it compare with the stories told by traditional war memorials that represent the human form? Which kind of story do you find more powerful? Why?

6. Research the controversy that surrounded the selection of Maya Lin's design and the subsequent decision to add Frederick Hart's more traditional war statue nearby. What values and beliefs lie behind the controversy? To what extent was this a disagreement about art? To what extent did this controversy reflect the national debate about the Vietnam War itself?

7. Visit a variety of war memorials in your area (memorializing, for instance, the Civil War, the Spanish American War, World War I, World War II, the Korean War, the Vietnam War, and the Gulf War). What do these memorials tell us about the artists' (and perhaps the community's) attitudes toward these wars and the sacrifices made by those who fought in them?

PEACE IN THE NIGHT SKY

Vincent Van Gogh, *Starry Night,* (1889). (See color insert.)

QUESTION FOR DISCUSSION AND WRITING

Before reading the poetic retellings of Van Gogh's "Starry Night," write your own response to it. How do Van Gogh's uses of color, perspective, and proportion affect your response? What do you see as the mood of the town? If you were to write a story about the night that Van Gogh is painting, what events would that story tell? What would it imply about the possibilities of peace and hope?

ANNE SEXTON (1928–1974)

The Starry Night _____ *1962*

That does not keep me from having a terrible need of—shall I say the word—religion.
Then I go out at night to paint the stars.

—Vincent van Gogh in a letter to his brother

The town does not exist
except where one black-haired tree slips
up like a drowned woman into the hot sky.
The town is silent. The night boils with eleven stars
Oh starry starry night! This is how   5
I want to die.

It moves. They are all alive.
Even the moon bulges in its orange irons
to push children, like a god, from its eye.
The old unseen serpent swallows up the stars.   10
Oh starry starry night! This is how
I want to die:

into that rushing beast of the night,
sucked up by that great dragon, to split
from my life with no flag,   15
no belly,
no cry.

QUESTIONS FOR DISCUSSION AND WRITING

1. Consider the images and word choices of Sexton's poem—the reference to a town that does not exist, the comparison of the tree to a drowned woman, the images of the boiling night and bulging moon, and so forth. How do they contribute to the poem's mood and meaning? How do they convey a sense of what dreams are possible?

2. Two of Sexton's stanzas end with the words "This is how / I want to die." How would you define "this"? What in the poem leads you to that definition?

DON MCLEAN (1945–   )

Vincent _____ *1971*

Starry, starry night
Paint your palette blue and gray.
Look out on a summer's day
With eyes that know the darkness in my soul.

5   Shadows on the hills
Sketch the trees and the daffodils,
Catch the breeze and the winter chills,
In colors on the snowy linen land.

Now I understand
10   What you tried to say to me,
How you suffered for your sanity,
And how you tried to set them free.

They would not listen.
They did not know how.
15   Perhaps they'll listen now.

Starry, starry night,
Flaming flowers that brightly blaze,
Swirling clouds in violet haze
Reflect in Vincent's eyes of china blue.

20   Colors changing hue
Morning fields of amber grain,
Weathered faces lined in pain
Are soothed beneath the artist's loving hand.

Now I understand
25   What you tried to say to me,
And how you suffered for your sanity
And how you tried to set them free.

They would not listen.
They did not know how.
30   Perhaps they'll listen now.

For they could not love you,
But still your love was true.
And when no hope was left in sight

On that starry, starry night,
You took your life as lovers often do.   35

But I could have told you, Vincent,
This world was never meant
For one as beautiful as you.

Starry, starry night
Portraits hung in empty halls,   40
Frameless heads on nameless walls,
With eyes that watch the world and can't forget.

Like the strangers that you've met
The ragged men in ragged clothes,
The silver thorn of bloody rose   45
Lie crushed and broken on the virgin snow.

Now I think I know
What you tried to say to me,
And how you suffered for your sanity
And how you tried to set them free.   50

They would not listen.
They're not listening still.
Perhaps they never will.

QUESTIONS FOR DISCUSSION AND WRITING

1. Stanzas 4 and 8 end "Perhaps they'll listen now"; the final stanza ends "Perhaps
   they never will [listen]." What leads to the speaker's greater pessimism towards the
   poem's end?
2. Don McLean's lyrics refer to several of Van Gogh's paintings. Locate pictures of
   some of those paintings and compare them both with McLean's descriptions of them
   and with each other. What similarities do these other paintings have to *Starry Night*?
3. Locate a copy of McLean's song so that you can hear it. How does the music affect
   your understanding of and response to the lyrics? Do the moods suggested by the
   words and music match? If so, how? If not, where and why do they not match?

QUESTIONS FOR CROSS READING: PEACE IN THE NIGHT SKY

1. Sexton's poem begins with an epigraph, a quotation from a letter Van Gogh wrote
   his brother. How does Van Gogh's painting fulfill a "terrible need of . . . religion"?
2. Both Sexton and McLean see something in "Starry Night" that reminds them of
   death (their own and Van Gogh's) and the line between sanity and insanity. To what
   extent does the painting evoke such thoughts? How do the poets use the meanings,

connotations, and sounds of words to convey such thoughts in their poems? How much do the poets believe in the possibility of tranquility?

FURTHER REFLECTIONS: A COLLECTION OF WORKS ON THE THEME OF INNOCENCE LOST

Included in this section are pieces of literature that touch on the ideas of a lost innocence, of a corrupt civilization, and of modern disillusionment. If Umberto Eco is right that "every story tells a story that has already been told," each of the works that follow is in its own way a "retelling." Each asks us to take another look at humankind's attempts to fashion a civilization and at the losses that result from the failure of a utopian ideal. The works that follow do not, then, have retellings of their own. Instead they reflect further the issues and images of the civilized world.

Poetry

ELIZABETH BISHOP (1911–1979)

The Fish   1946

I caught a tremendous fish
and held him beside the boat
half out of water, with my hook
fast in a corner of his mouth.
5   He didn't fight.
He hadn't fought at all.
He hung a grunting weight,
battered and venerable
and homely. Here and there
10   his brown skin hung in strips
like ancient wall-paper,
and its pattern of darker brown
was like wall-paper:
shapes like full-blown roses
15   stained and lost through age.
He was speckled with barnacles,
fine rosettes of lime,
and infested
with tiny white sea-lice,
20   and underneath two or three
rags of green weed hung down.
While his gills were breathing in
the terrible oxygen
—the frightening gills,

fresh and crisp with blood,
that can cut so badly—
I thought of the coarse white flesh
packed in like feathers,
the big bones and the little bones,
the dramatic reds and blacks
of his shiny entrails,
and the pink swim-bladder
like a big peony.
I looked into his eyes
which were far larger than mine
but shallower, and yellowed,
the irises backed and packed
with tarnished tinfoil
seen through the lenses
of old scratched isinglass.
They shifted a little, but not
to return my stare.
—It was more like the tipping
of an object toward the light.
I admired his sullen face,
the mechanism of his jaw,
and then I saw
that from his lower lip
—if you could call it a lip—
grim, wet, and weapon-like,
hung five old pieces of fish-line,
or four and a wire leader
with the swivel still attached,
with all their five big hooks
grown firmly in his mouth.
A green line, frayed at the end
where he broke it, two heavier lines,
and a fine black thread
still crimped from the strain and snap
when it broke and he got away.
Like medals with their ribbons
frayed and wavering,
a five-haired beard of wisdom
trailing from his aching jaw.
I stared and stared
and victory filled up
the little rented boat,
from the pool of bilge
where oil had spread a rainbow
around the rusted engine
to the bailer rusted orange,

25

30

35

40

45

50

55

60

65

70

the sun-cracked thwarts,
the oarlocks on their strings,
the gunnels—until everything
75 was rainbow, rainbow, rainbow!
And I let the fish go.

QUESTIONS FOR DISCUSSION AND WRITING

1. Bishop's descriptions of the fish are detailed and vivid. They are also perhaps a little unusual insofar as she often uses language that we don't associate with fish. Look at the word choices and images Bishop uses. How do they capture the fish's essence? How do they help the speaker bridge the gap between the fish and the human?
2. How would you describe the relationship between the speaker and the fish? At what point do you realize that the speaker is going to let the fish go? *Why* does the speaker release the fish?
3. What is the victory that "fill[s] up / the little rented boat"? Why is it that the speaker emphasizes that "everything / was rainbow, rainbow, rainbow!"? How hopeful is the poem's conclusion?
4. Although "The Fish" is shaped like a poem, readers sometimes have trouble seeing it as a poem. How would you defend it as a poem? In other words, aside from the typographical setup on the page, what makes it seem like a poem? What makes it seem like something other than a poem?

WILLIAM BLAKE (1757–1827)

London _____ *1794*

I wander thro' each charter'd street,
Near where the charter'd Thames does flow,
And mark in every face I meet
Marks of weakness, marks of woe.

5 In every cry of every Man,
In every Infant's cry of fear,
In every voice, in every ban,
The mind-forg'd manacles I hear.

How the Chimney-sweeper's cry
10 Every black'ning Church appalls;
And the hapless Soldier's sigh
Runs in blood down Palace walls.

But most thro' midnight streets I hear
How the youthful Harlot's curse

Blasts the new born Infant's tear,   15
And blights with plagues the Marriage hearse.

QUESTIONS FOR DISCUSSION AND WRITING

1. For most of the eighteenth century, London was a center of learning, political energy, and culture. For William Blake, it is clearly something else: a city constrained by rules and inhabited by citizens whom its boundaries confine. As you read the poem, what images of imprisonment do you find? Where does Blake seem deliberately to be calling into question the more typical views of London?
2. "London" refers to several important institutions: the government, the church, and the rite of marriage. Does it convey similar attitudes toward those institutions? Are the institutions in some ways intertwined?
3. Consider the poem's structure and its use of repetition. Why are the images ordered as they are? Would a rearrangement of the poem's stanzas alter your perception of its themes? What is the effect of the repetition?
4. The final stanza of the poem combines images of birth and death, infant innocence and adult sexuality (and disease). How do those images lead you to an understanding of the poem as a whole?

PAUL LAURENCE DUNBAR (1872–1906)

We wear the mask   1896

We wear the mask that grins and lies,
It hides our cheeks and shades our eyes—
This debt we pay to human guile;
With torn and bleeding hearts we smile,
And mouth with myriad subtleties.   5

Why should the world be over-wise,
In counting all our tears and sighs?
Nay, let them only see us, while
    We wear the mask.

We smile, but, O great Christ, our cries   10
To thee from tortured souls arise.
We sing, but oh the clay is vile
Beneath our feet, and long the mile;
But let the world dream otherwise,
    We wear the mask!   15

QUESTIONS FOR DISCUSSION AND WRITING

1. What does the "mask" consist of? Why does it need to be worn? What is being hidden—and from whom?
2. Dunbar is an African American poet. To what extent does the poem refer directly to the African American experience, and to what extent is the message universal?

LANGSTON HUGHES (1902–1967)

Harlem   *1951*

> What happens to a dream deferred?
>
> > Does it dry up
> > like a raisin in the sun?
> > Or fester like a sore—
> 5 And then run?
> > Does it stink like rotten meat?
> > Or crust and sugar over—
> > like a syrupy sweet?
>
> > Maybe it just sags
> 10 like a heavy load.
>
> > *Or does it explode?*

QUESTIONS FOR DISCUSSION AND WRITING

1. In this short poem, Hughes presents us with five images: a raisin in the sun, a sore, rotten meat, a syrupy sweet, and a heavy load. Which of these images are positive and which are negative? How do the images compare with one another, and how are they connected to the idea of "a dream deferred"? Which suggest a potential to "explode"? Is the order of the images significant?
2. The poem asks a series of questions, with only one direct statement (and that is stated as a "maybe"). What is the effect of asking questions without providing answers?
3. The poem is titled "Harlem," but Harlem is not mentioned anywhere in the poem. What do the images suggest about Harlem? Why might Hughes have chosen to present his ideas about Harlem so indirectly through imagery?

RANDALL JARRELL (1914–1965)

The Death of the Ball Turret Gunner   *1945*

> From my mother's sleep I fell into the State
> And I hunched in its belly till my wet fur froze.

Six miles from earth, loosed from its dream of life,
I woke to black flak and the nightmare fighters.
When I died they washed me out of the turret with a hose.   *5*

QUESTIONS FOR DISCUSSION AND WRITING

1. The ball turret gunner is firing a gun from the belly of an airplane. How does he characterize the airplane and his position in it?
2. What does the speaker mean when he says, "From my mother's sleep I fell into the State"?
3. The poem links birth and death images. What in the language suggests birth, possibly a failed birth? What suggests death? Does the joining of the seemingly opposed images suggest hope or despair?

WILFRED OWEN (1893–1918)

Dulce et Decorum Est   *1920*

Bent double, like old beggars under sacks,
Knock-kneed, coughing like hags, we cursed through sludge,
Till on the haunting flares we turned our backs
And towards our distant rest began to trudge.
Men marched asleep. Many had lost their boots   *5*
But limped on, blood-shod. All went lame; all blind;
Drunk with fatigue; deaf even to the hoots
Of tired, outstripped Five-Nines that dropped behind.

Gas! GAS! Quick, boys!—An ecstasy of fumbling,
Fitting the clumsy helmets just in time;   *10*
But someone still was yelling out and stumbling
And flound'ring like a man in fire or lime . . .
Dim, through the misty panes and thick green light,
As under a green sea, I saw him drowning.

In all my dreams, before my helpless sight,   *15*
He plunges at me, guttering, choking, drowning.
If in some smothering dreams you too could pace
Behind the wagon that we flung him in,
And watch the white eyes writhing in his face,
His hanging face, like a devil's sick of sin;   *20*
If you could hear, at every jolt, the blood
Come gargling from the froth-corrupted lungs,
Obscene as cancer, bitter as the cud
Of vile, incurable sores on innocent tongues,—
My friend, you would not tell with such high zest   *25*
To children ardent for some desperate glory,

The old Lie: *Dulce et decorum est*
Pro patria mori.

QUESTIONS FOR DISCUSSION AND WRITING

1. A young soldier during World War I, Wilfred Owen tells here the story of the death and horror experienced during one march. With its graphic details, the poem is a horrible retelling of the "old Lie" with which it ends: "Dulce et decorum est / Pro patria mori" ("How sweet it is to die for one's country"). How do the poem's title and the old lie, on the one hand, and the poem's graphic details, on the other, comment ironically upon one another?
2. Owen puts words in unusual ironic juxtaposition with one another. Think, for instance, of "drunk with fatigue," or "blood-shod," or "an ecstasy of fumbling." Where else does the poem use words normally associated with something quite different from war? How does the diction help to reinforce Owen's ultimate point?
3. Read the poem aloud, paying particular attention to its sounds. How do the rhythms of the lines and the sounds of the individual words—even the use of punctuation—contribute to our ability to imagine the poem's atmosphere and the speaker's feelings?

THEODORE ROETHKE (1908–1963)

Dolor _____ *1943, 1948*

I have known the inexorable sadness of pencils,
Neat in their boxes, dolor of pad and paper-weight,
All the misery of manila folders and mucilage,
Desolation in immaculate public places,
5 Lonely reception room, lavatory, switchboard,
The unalterable pathos of basin and pitcher,
Ritual of multigraph, paper-clip, comma,
Endless duplication of lives and objects.
And I have seen dust from the walls of institutions,
10 Finer than flour, alive, more dangerous than silica,
Sift, almost invisible, through long afternoons of tedium,
Dropping a fine film on nails and delicate eyebrows,
Glazing the pale hair, the duplicate grey standard faces.

QUESTIONS FOR DISCUSSION AND WRITING

1. Why does the speaker associate office supplies with "inexorable sadness"?
2. The poem moves between supplies and offices, concluding with the "dust from the walls of institutions." What holds all these images together to create the mood of the poem?

3. How does the poem describe the inhabitants of the offices? What do the descriptions tell us about Roethke's theme(s)? About modern life?

DYLAN THOMAS (1914–1953)

The Hand That Signed the Paper _____ 1936

The hand that signed the paper felled a city
Five sovereign fingers taxed the breath,
Doubled the globe of dead and halved a country;
These five kings did a king to death.

The mighty hand leads to a sloping shoulder,   5
The finger joints are cramped with chalk;
A goose's quill has put an end to murder
That put an end to talk.

The hand that signed the treaty bred a fever,
And famine grew, and locusts came;   10
Great is the hand that holds dominion over
Man by a scribbled name.

The five kings count the dead but do not soften
The crusted wound nor stroke the brow;
A hand rules pity as a hand rules heaven;   15
Hands have no tears to flow.

QUESTIONS FOR DISCUSSION AND WRITING

1. Why does the speaker talk about the "hand that signed the paper" rather than the person who made the decisions? What does the poem imply about the relationship between the governor and the governed?
2. Look at the ways in which the hand is described. How do the descriptions work thematically?
3. Words that imply size or amount occur frequently in this poem. To what effect?

WILLIAM BUTLER YEATS (1865–1939)

The Lake Isle of Innisfree _____ 1892

I will arise and go now, and go to Innisfree,
And a small cabin build there, of clay and wattles made:
Nine bean-rows will I have there, a hive for the honey-bee,
And live alone in the bee-loud glade.

5 And I shall have some peace there, for peace comes dropping slow,
   Dropping from the veils of the morning to where the cricket sings;
   There midnight's all a glimmer, and noon a purple glow,
   And evening full of the linnet's wings.

   I will arise and go now, for always night and day
10 I hear lake water lapping with low sounds by the shore;
   While I stand on the roadway, or on the pavements gray,
   I hear it in the deep heart's core.

QUESTIONS FOR DISCUSSION AND WRITING

1. Read "The Lake Isle of Innisfree" aloud. How do its sounds contribute to its meaning?
2. Compare and contrast the poem's images of nature and of the city. What does the natural world offer the speaker that the city cannot? In which setting is man most likely to find freedom and hope?
3. In his autobiography, Yeats tells us that he wanted to live a Thoreau-like existence on the Isle of Innisfree. Locate a copy of Henry David Thoreau's *Walden,* and compare Thoreau's and Yeats's descriptions of the natural world and of man's place in it.

WILLIAM BUTLER YEATS (1865–1939)

The Second Coming _____ *1921*

   Turning and turning in the widening gyre
   The falcon cannot hear the falconer;
   Things fall apart; the center cannot hold;
   Mere anarchy is loosed upon the world,
5 The blood-dimmed tide is loosed, and everywhere
   The ceremony of innocence is drowned;
   The best lack all conviction, while the worst
   Are full of passionate intensity.

   Surely some revelation is at hand;
10 Surely the Second Coming is at hand;
   The Second Coming! Hardly are those words out
   When a vast image out of *Spiritus Mundi*
   Troubles my sight: somewhere in sands of the desert
   A shape with lion body and the head of a man,
15 A gaze blank and pitiless as the sun,
   Is moving its slow thighs, while all about it
   Reel shadows of the indignant desert birds.
   The darkness drops again; but now I know
   That twenty centuries of stony sleep

Were vexed to nightmare by a rocking cradle,
And what rough beast, its hour come round at last,
Slouches towards Bethlehem to be born?

20

QUESTIONS FOR DISCUSSION AND WRITING

1. Yeats believed in historical cycles, and he felt that a new cycle was beginning. What signs in the poem suggest that a new era is about to begin? Are those signs positive or negative?
2. The second stanza mentions the "Second Coming," which usually refers to the return of Christ. Does the poem envision a messiah, or savior? If so, how would you characterize that messiah? If not, what kind of birth does the poem describe?

SHORT STORIES

STEPHEN CRANE (1871–1900)

The Bride Comes to Yellow Sky _____ *1898*

I

The great Pullman was whirling onward with such dignity of motion that a glance from the window seemed simply to prove that the plains of Texas were pouring eastward. Vast flats of green grass, dull-hued spaces of mesquite and cactus, little groups of frame houses, woods of light and tender trees, all were sweeping into the east, sweeping over the horizon, a precipice.

A newly married pair had boarded this coach at San Antonio. The man's face was reddened from many days in the wind and sun, and a direct result of his new black clothes was that his brick-colored hands were constantly performing in a most conscious fashion. From time to time he looked down respectfully at his attire. He sat with a hand on each knee, like a man waiting in a barber's shop. The glances he devoted to other passengers were furtive and shy.

The bride was not pretty, nor was she very young. She wore a dress of blue cashmere, with small reservations of velvet here and there and with steel buttons abounding. She continually twisted her head to regard her puff sleeves, very stiff, straight, and high. They embarrassed her. It was quite apparent that she had cooked, and that she expected to cook, dutifully. The blushes caused by the careless scrutiny of some passengers as she had entered the car were strange to see upon this plain, under-class countenance, which was drawn in placid, almost emotionless lines.

They were evidently very happy. "Ever been in a parlor-car before?" he asked, smiling with delight.

"No," she answered; "I never was. It's fine, ain't it?"

"Great! And then after a while we'll go forward to the diner and get a big layout. Finest meal in the world. Charge a dollar."

"Oh, do they?" cried the bride. "Charge a dollar? Why, that's too much—for us—ain't it, Jack?"

"Not this trip, anyhow," he answered bravely. "We're going to go the whole thing."

Later he explained to her about the trains. "You see, it's a thousand miles from one end of Texas to the other, and this train runs right across it and never stops but four times." He had the pride of an owner. He pointed out to her the dazzling fittings of the coach, and in truth her eyes opened wider as she contemplated the sea-green figured velvet, the shining brass, silver, and glass, the wood that gleamed as darkly brilliant as the surface of a pool of oil. At one end a bronze figure sturdily held a support for a separated chamber, and at convenient places on the ceiling were frescoes in olive and silver.

To the minds of the pair, their surroundings reflected the glory of their marriage that morning in San Antonio. This was the environment of their new estate, and the man's face in particular beamed with an elation that made him appear ridiculous to the negro porter. This individual at times surveyed them from afar with an amused and superior grin. On other occasions he bullied them with skill in ways that did not make it exactly plain to them that they were being bullied. He subtly used all the manners of the most unconquerable kind of snobbery. He oppressed them, but of this oppression they had small knowledge, and they speedily forgot that infrequently a number of travelers covered them with stares of derisive enjoyment. Historically there was supposed to be something infinitely humorous in their situation.

"We are due in Yellow Sky at 3:42," he said, looking tenderly into her eyes.

"Oh, are we?" she said, as if she had not been aware of it. To evince surprise at her husband's statement was part of her wifely amiability. She took from a pocket a little silver watch, and as she held it before her and stared at it with a frown of attention, the new husband's face shone.

"I bought it in San Anton' from a friend of mine," he told her gleefully.

"It's seventeen minutes past twelve," she said, looking up at him with a kind of shy and clumsy coquetry. A passenger, noting this play, grew excessively sardonic, and winked at himself in one of the numerous mirrors.

At last they went to the dining-car. Two rows of negro waiters, in glowing white suits, surveyed their entrance with the interest and also the equanimity of men who had been forewarned. The pair fell to the lot of a waiter who happened to feel pleasure in steering them through their meal. He viewed them with the manner of a fatherly pilot, his countenance radiant with benevolence. The patronage, entwined with the ordinary deference, was not plain to them. And yet, as they returned to their coach, they showed in their faces a sense of escape.

To the left, miles down a long purple slope, was a little ribbon of mist where moved the keening Rio Grande. The train was approaching it at an angle, and the apex was Yellow Sky. Presently it was apparent that, as the distance from Yellow Sky grew shorter, the husband became commensurately restless. His brick-red hands were more insistent in their prominence. Occasionally he was even rather absent-minded and far-away when the bride leaned forward and addressed him.

As a matter of truth, Jack Potter was beginning to find the shadow of a deed weigh upon him like a leaden slab. He, the town marshal of Yellow Sky, a man known, liked, and feared in his corner, a prominent person, had gone to San Antonio to meet a girl he believed he loved, and there, after the usual prayers, had actually induced her to marry him, without consulting Yellow Sky for any part of the transaction. He was now bringing his bride before an innocent and unsuspecting community.

Of course, people in Yellow Sky married as it pleased them, in accordance with a general custom; but such was Potter's thought of his duty to his friends, or of their idea of his duty, or of an unspoken form which does not control men in these matters, that he felt he was heinous. He had committed an extraordinary crime. Face to face with this girl in San Antonio, and spurred by his sharp impulse, he had gone headlong over all the social hedges. At San Antonio he was like a man hidden in the dark. A knife to sever any friendly duty, any form, was easy to his hand in that remote city. But the hour of Yellow Sky, the hour of daylight, was approaching.

He knew full well that his marriage was an important thing to his town. It could only be exceeded by the burning of the new hotel. His friends could not forgive him. Frequently he had reflected on the advisability of telling them by telegraph, but a new cowardice had been upon him. He feared to do it. And now the train was hurrying him toward a scene of amazement, glee, and reproach. He glanced out of the window at the line of haze swinging slowly in towards the train.

Yellow Sky had a kind of brass band, which played painfully, to the delight of the populace. He laughed without heart as he thought of it. If the citizens could dream of his prospective arrival with his bride, they would parade the band at the station and escort them, amid cheers and laughing congratulations, to his adobe home.

He resolved that he would use all the devices of speed and plains-craft in making the journey from the station to his house. Once within that safe citadel he could issue some sort of a vocal bulletin, and then not go among the citizens until they had time to wear off a little of their enthusiasm.

The bride looked anxiously at him. "What's worrying you, Jack?"

He laughed again. "I'm not worrying, girl. I'm only thinking of Yellow Sky."

She flushed in comprehension.

A sense of mutual guilt invaded their minds and developed a finer tenderness. They looked at each other with eyes softly aglow. But Potter often laughed the same nervous laugh. The flush upon the bride's face seemed quite permanent.

The traitor to the feelings of Yellow Sky narrowly watched the speeding landscape. "We're nearly there," he said.

Presently the porter came and announced the proximity of Potter's home. He held a brush in his hand and, with all his airy superiority gone, he brushed Potter's new clothes as the latter slowly turned this way and that way. Potter fumbled out a coin and gave it to the porter, as he had seen others do. It was a heavy and muscle-bound business, as that of a man shoeing his first horse.

The porter took their bag, and as the train began to slow they moved forward to the hooded platform of the car. Presently the two engines and their long string of coaches rushed into the station of Yellow Sky.

"They have to take water here," said Potter, from a constricted throat and in mournful cadence, as one announcing death. Before the train stopped, his eye had swept the length of the platform, and he was glad and astonished to see there was none upon it but the station-agent, who, with a slightly hurried and anxious air, was walking toward the water-tanks. When the train had halted, the porter alighted first and placed in position a little temporary step.

"Come on, girl," said Potter, hoarsely. As he helped her down they each laughed on a false note. He took the bag from the negro, and bade his wife cling to his arm. As they slunk rapidly away, his hang-dog glance perceived that they were unloading the two trunks, and also that the station-agent far ahead near the baggage-car had turned and was running toward him, making gestures. He laughed, and groaned as he laughed, when he noted the first effect of his marital bliss upon Yellow Sky. He gripped his wife's arm firmly to his side, and they fled. Behind them the porter stood chuckling fatuously.

II

The California express on the Southern Railway was due at Yellow Sky in twenty-one minutes. There were six men at the bar of the "Weary Gentleman" saloon. One was a drummer who talked a great deal and rapidly; three were Texans who did not care to talk at that time; and two were Mexican sheep-herders who did not talk as a general practice in the "Weary Gentleman" saloon. The barkeeper's dog lay on the board walk that crossed in front of the door. His head was on his paws, and he glanced drowsily here and there with the constant vigilance of a dog that is kicked on occasion. Across the sandy street were some vivid green grass plots, so wonderful in appearance amid the sands that burned near them in a blazing sun that they caused a doubt in the mind. They exactly resembled the grass mats used to represent lawns on the stage. At the cooler end of the railway station a man without a coat sat in a tilted chair and smoked his pipe. The fresh-cut bank of the Rio Grande circled near the town, and there could be seen beyond it a great, plum-coloured plain of mesquite.

Save for the busy drummer and his companions in the saloon, Yellow Sky was dozing. The new-comer leaned gracefully upon the bar, and recited many tales with the confidence of a bard who has come upon a new field.

"—and at the moment that the old man fell down stairs with the bureau in his arms, the old woman was coming up with two scuttles of coal, and, of course—"

The drummer's tale was interrupted by a young man who suddenly appeared in the open door. He cried: "Scratchy Wilson's drunk, and has turned loose with both hands." The two Mexicans at once set down their glasses and faded out of the rear entrance of the saloon.

The drummer, innocent and jocular, answered: "All right, old man. S'pose he has. Come in and have a drink, anyhow."

But the information had made such an obvious cleft in every skull in the room that the drummer was obliged to see its importance. All had become instantly solemn. "Say," said he, mystified, "what is this?" His three companions made the introductory gesture of eloquent speech, but the young man at the door forestalled them.

"It means, my friend," he answered, as he came into the saloon, "that for the next two hours this town won't be a health resort."

The barkeeper went to the door and locked and barred it. Reaching out of the window, he pulled in heavy wooden shutters, and barred them. Immediately a solemn, chapel-like gloom was upon the place. The drummer was looking from one to another.

"But, say," he cried, "what is this, anyhow? You don't mean there is going to be a gun-fight?"

"Don't know whether there'll be a fight or not," answered one man grimly. "But there'll be some shootin'—some good shootin'."

The young man who had warned them waved his hand. "Oh, there'll be a fight fast enough if any one wants it. Anybody can get a fight out there in the street. There's a fight just waiting."

The drummer seemed to be swayed between the interest of a foreigner and a perception of personal danger.

"What did you say his name was?" he asked.

"Scratchy Wilson," they answered in chorus.

"And will he kill anybody? What are you going to do? Does this happen often? Does he rampage around like this once a week or so? Can he break in that door?"

"No, he can't break down that door," replied the barkeeper. "He's tried it three times. But when he comes you'd better lay down on the floor, stranger. He's dead sure to shoot at it, and a bullet may come through."

Thereafter the drummer kept a strict eye upon the door. The time had not yet been called for him to hug the floor, but, as a minor precaution, he sidled near to the wall. "Will he kill anybody?" he said again.

The men laughed low and scornfully at the question.

"He's out to shoot, and he's out for trouble. Don't see any good in experimentin' with him."

"But what do you do in a case like this? What do you do?"

A man responded: "Why, he and Jack Potter—"

"But," in chorus, the other men interrupted, "Jack Potter's in San Anton'."

"Well, who is he? What's he got to do with it?"

"Oh, he's the town marshal. He goes out and fights Scratchy when he gets on one of these tears."

"Wow," said the drummer, mopping his brow. "Nice job he's got."

The voices had toned away to mere whisperings. The drummer wished to ask further questions which were born of an increasing anxiety and bewilderment; but when he attempted them, the men merely looked at him in irritation and motioned him to remain silent. A tense waiting hush was upon them. In the deep shadows of the room their eyes shone as they listened for sounds from the street. One man made three gestures at the barkeeper, and the latter, moving like a ghost, handed him a glass and a bottle. The man poured a full glass of whisky, and set down the bottle noiselessly. He gulped the whisky in a swallow, and turned again toward the door in immovable silence. The drummer saw that the barkeeper, without a sound, had taken a Winchester from beneath the bar. Later he saw this individual beckoning to him, so he tiptoed across the room.

"You better come with me back of the bar."

"No, thanks," said the drummer, perspiring. "I'd rather be where I can make a break for the back door."

Whereupon the man of bottles made a kindly but peremptory gesture. The drummer obeyed it, and finding himself seated on a box with his head below the level of the bar, balm was laid upon his soul at sight of various zinc and copper fittings that bore a resemblance to armorplate. The barkeeper took a seat comfortably upon an adjacent box.

"You see," he whispered, "this here Scratchy Wilson is a wonder with a gun—a perfect wonder—and when he goes on the war trail, we hunt our holes—naturally. He's about the last one of the old gang that used to hang out along the river here. He's a terror when he's drunk. When he's sober he's all right—kind of simple—wouldn't hurt a fly—nicest fellow in town. But when he's drunk—whoo!"

There were periods of stillness. "I wish Jack Potter was back from San Anton'," said the barkeeper. "He shot Wilson up once—in the leg—and he would sail in and pull out the kinks in this thing."

Presently they heard from a distance the sound of a shot, followed by three wild yowls. It instantly removed a bond from the men in the darkened saloon. There was a shuffling of feet. They looked at each other. "Here he comes," they said.

III

A man in a maroon-colored flannel shirt, which had been purchased for purposes of decoration and made, principally, by some Jewish women on the east side of New York, rounded a corner and walked into the middle of the main street of Yellow Sky. In either hand the man held a long, heavy, blue-black revolver. Often he yelled, and these cries rang through a semblance of a deserted village, shrilly flying over the roofs in a volume that seemed to have no relation to the ordinary vocal strength of a man. It was as if the surrounding stillness formed the arch of a tomb over him. These cries of ferocious challenge rang against walls of silence. And his boots had red tops with gilded imprints, of the kind beloved in winter by little sledding boys on the hill-sides of New England.

The man's face flamed in a rage begot of whisky. His eyes, rolling and yet keen for ambush, hunted the still doorways and windows. He walked with the creeping movement of the midnight cat. As it occurred to him, he roared menacing information. The long revolvers in his hands were as easy as straws; they were moved with an electric swiftness. The little fingers of each hand played sometimes in a musician's way. Plain from the low collar of the shirt, the cords of his neck straightened and sank, straightened and sank, as passion moved him. The only sounds were his terrible invitations. The calm adobes preserved their demeanor at the passing of this small thing in the middle of the street.

There was no offer of fight; no offer of fight. The man called to the sky. There were no attractions. He bellowed and fumed and swayed his revolvers here and everywhere.

The dog of the barkeeper of the "Weary Gentleman" saloon had not appreciated the advance of events. He yet lay dozing in front of his master's door. At sight of the dog, the man paused and raised his revolver humorously. At sight of the man, the dog sprang up and walked diagonally away, with a sullen head, and growling. The man yelled, and the dog broke into a gallop. As it was about to enter an alley, there was a loud noise, a whistling, and something spat the ground directly before it. The dog screamed, and, wheeling in terror, galloped headlong in a new direction. Again there was a noise, a whistling, and sand was kicked viciously before it. Fear-stricken, the dog turned and flurried like an animal in a pen. The man stood laughing, his weapons at his hips.

Ultimately the man was attracted by the closed door of the "Weary Gentleman" saloon. He went to it, and hammering with a revolver, demanded drink.

The door remaining imperturbable, he picked a bit of paper from the walk and nailed it to the framework with a knife. He then turned his back contemptuously upon this popular resort, and walking to the opposite side of the street, and spinning there on his heel quickly and lithely, fired at the bit of paper. He missed it by a half inch. He swore at himself, and went away. Later he comfortably fusilladed the windows of his most intimate friend. The man was playing with this town. It was a toy for him.

But still there was no offer of fight. The name of Jack Potter, his ancient antagonist, entered his mind, and he concluded that it would be a glad thing if he should go to Potter's house and by bombardment induce him to come out and fight. He moved in the direction of his desire, chanting Apache scalp-music.

When he arrived at it, Potter's house presented the same still front as had the other adobes. Taking up a strategic position, the man howled a challenge. But this house regarded him as might a great stone god. It gave no sign. After a decent wait, the man howled further challenges, mingling with them wonderful epithets.

Presently there came the spectacle of a man churning himself into deepest rage over the immobility of a house. He fumed at it as the winter wind attacks a prairie cabin in the North. To the distance there should have gone the sound of a tumult like the fighting of 200 Mexicans. As necessity bade him, he paused for breath or to reload his revolvers.

IV

Potter and his bride walked sheepishly and with speed. Sometimes they laughed together shamefacedly and low.

"Next corner, dear," he said finally.

They put forth the efforts of a pair walking bowed against a strong wind. Potter was about to raise a finger to point the first appearance of the new home when, as they circled the corner, they came face to face with a man in a maroon-colored shirt who was feverishly pushing cartridges into a large revolver. Upon the instant the man dropped his revolver to the ground, and, like lightning, whipped another from its holster. The second weapon was aimed at the bridegroom's chest.

There was silence. Potter's mouth seemed to be merely a grave for his tongue. He exhibited an instinct to at once loosen his arm from the woman's grip, and he dropped the bag to the sand. As for the bride, her face had gone as yellow as old cloth. She was a slave to hideous rites gazing at the apparitional snake.

The two men faced each other at a distance of three paces. He of the revolver smiled with a new and quiet ferocity.

"Tried to sneak up on me," he said. "Tried to sneak up on me!" His eyes grew more baleful. As Potter made a slight movement, the man thrust his revolver venomously forward. "No, don't you do it, Jack Potter. Don't you move a finger toward a gun just yet. Don't you move an eyelash. The time has come for me to settle with you, and I'm goin' to do it my own way and loaf along with no interferin'. So if you don't want a gun bent on you, just mind what I tell you."

Potter looked at his enemy. "I ain't got a gun on me, Scratchy," he said. "Honest, I ain't." He was stiffening and steadying, but yet somewhere at the back of his mind a vision of the Pullman floated, the sea-green figured velvet, the shining brass, silver, and glass, the wood that gleamed as darkly brilliant as the surface of a pool of oil—all the glory of the marriage, the environment of the new estate. "You know I fight when it comes to fighting, Scratchy Wilson, but I ain't got a gun on me. You'll have to do all the shootin' yourself."

His enemy's face went livid. He stepped forward and lashed his weapon to and fro before Potter's chest. "Don't you tell me you ain't got no gun on you, you whelp. Don't tell me no lie like that. There ain't a man in Texas ever seen you without no gun. Don't take me for no kid." His eyes blazed with light, and his throat worked like a pump.

"I ain't takin' you for no kid," answered Potter. His heels had not moved an inch backward. "I'm takin' you for a ———— fool. I tell you I ain't got a gun, and I ain't. If you're goin' to shoot me up, you better begin now. You'll never get a chance like this again."

So much enforced reasoning had told on Wilson's rage. He was calmer. "If you ain't got a gun, why ain't you got a gun?" he sneered. "Been to Sunday-school?"

"I ain't got a gun because I've just come from San Anton' with my wife. I'm married," said Potter. "And if I'd thought there was going to be any galoots like you prowling around when I brought my wife home, I'd had a gun, and don't you forget it."

"Married!" said Scratchy, not at all comprehending.

"Yes, married. I'm married," said Potter, distinctly.

"Married?" said Scratchy. Seemingly for the first time he saw the drooping, drowning woman at the other man's side. "No!" he said. He was like a creature allowed a glimpse of another world. He moved a pace backward, and his arm with the revolver dropped to his side. "Is this the lady?" he asked.

"Yes, this is the lady," answered Potter.

There was another period of silence.

"Well," said Wilson at last, slowly, "I s'pose it's all off now."

"It's all off if you say so, Scratchy. You know I didn't make the trouble." Potter lifted his valise.

"Well, I 'low it's off, Jack," said Wilson. He was looking at the ground. "Married!" He was not a student of chivalry; it was merely that in the presence of this foreign condition he was a simple child of the earlier plains. He picked up his starboard revolver, and placing both weapons in their holsters, he went away. His feet made funnel-shaped tracks in the heavy sand.

QUESTIONS FOR DISCUSSION AND WRITING

1. At one point in the story we are told that Jack Potter is Scratchy Wilson's "ancient antagonist." What does each man seem to represent? Why are they opposed?
2. Yellow Sky appears to be a typical town of the Old West, the kind of town we know from stories and movies. In what ways does the town seem to belong to Western lore? What in the story suggests that the Old West is ceasing to exist? Is the disappearance of the Old West seen as a loss or a gain?
3. Potter and his new wife are nervous as they approach Yellow Sky, and Potter had not told the town that he planned to marry. Why are they nervous and secretive?

To what extent are we sympathetic to their anxiety and guilt? To what extent are we amused by their feelings?

4. When Scratchy learns that Potter is married, he is "like a creature allowed a glimpse of another world," and he decides "it's all off." What is this new world? Why does Scratchy think it is "all off"?

5. In the last line of the story, we are told that Scratchy's "feet made funnel-shaped tracks in the heavy sand." What does the image suggest? How might it be appropriate to the theme of the story?

NATHANIEL HAWTHORNE (1804–1864)

Young Goodman Brown _____ *1828*

Young Goodman Brown came forth at sunset, into the street of Salem village, but put his head back, after crossing the threshold, to exchange a parting kiss with his young wife. And Faith, as the wife was aptly named, thrust her own pretty head into the street, letting the wind play with the pink ribbons of her cap, while she called to Goodman Brown.

"Dearest heart," whispered she, softly and rather sadly, when her lips were close to his ear, "prithee, put off your journey until sunrise, and sleep in your own bed to-night. A lone woman is troubled with such dreams and such thoughts, that she's afeard of herself, sometimes. Pray, tarry with me this night, dear husband, of all nights in the year!"

"My love and my Faith," replied young Goodman Brown, "of all nights in the year, this one night must I tarry away from thee. My journey, as thou callest it, forth and back again, must needs be done 'twixt now and sunrise. What, my sweet, pretty wife, dost thou doubt me already, and we but three months married!"

"Then God bless you!" said Faith with the pink ribbons, "and may you find all well, when you come back."

"Amen!" cried Goodman Brown. "Say thy prayers, dear Faith, and go to bed at dusk, and no harm will come to thee."

So they parted; and the young man pursued his way, until, being about to turn the corner by the meeting-house, he looked back and saw the head of Faith still peeping after him, with a melancholy air, in spite of her pink ribbons.

"Poor little Faith!" thought he, for his heart smote him. "What a wretch am I, to leave her on such an errand! She talks of dreams, too. Methought, as she spoke, there was trouble in her face, as if a dream had warned her what work is to be done to-night. But no, no! 't would kill her to think it. Well; she's a blessed angel on earth; and after this one night, I'll cling to her skirts and follow her to Heaven."

With this excellent resolve for the future, Goodman Brown felt himself justified in making more haste on his present evil purpose. He had taken a dreary road, darkened by all the gloomiest trees of the forest, which barely stood aside to let the narrow path creep through, and closed immediately behind. It was as lonely as could be; and there is this peculiarity in such a solitude, that the traveller knows not who may be concealed by the innumerable trunks and the thick boughs overhead; so that, with lonely footsteps, he may yet be passing through an unseen multitude.

"There may be a devilish Indian behind every tree," said Goodman Brown to himself; and he glanced fearfully behind him, as he added, "What if the devil himself should be at my very elbow!"

His head being turned back, he passed a crook of the road, and looking forward again, beheld the figure of a man, in grave and decent attire, seated at the foot of an old tree. He arose at Goodman Brown's approach, and walked onward, side by side with him.

"You are late, Goodman Brown," said he. "The clock of the Old South was striking, as I came through Boston; and that is full fifteen minutes agone."

"Faith kept me back awhile," replied the young man, with a tremor in his voice, caused by the sudden appearance of his companion, though not wholly unexpected.

It was now deep dusk in the forest, and deepest in that part of it where these two were journeying. As nearly as could be discerned, the second traveller was about fifty years old, apparently in the same rank of life as Goodman Brown, and bearing a considerable resemblance to him, though perhaps more in expression than features. Still, they might have been taken for father and son. And yet, though the elder person was as simply clad as the younger, and as simple in manner too, he had an indescribable air of one who knew the world, and would not have felt abashed at the governor's dinner-table, or in King William's court, were it possible that his affairs should call him thither. But the only thing about him that could be fixed upon as remarkable, was his staff, which bore the likeness of a great black snake, so curiously wrought, that it might almost be seen to twist and wriggle itself like a living serpent. This, of course, must have been an ocular deception, assisted by the uncertain light.

"Come, Goodman Brown!" cried his fellow-traveller, "this is a dull pace for the beginning of a journey. Take my staff, if you are so soon weary."

"Friend," said the other, exchanging his slow pace for a full stop, "having kept covenant by meeting thee here, it is my purpose now to return whence I came. I have scruples, touching the matter thou wot'st of."

"Sayest thou so?" replied he of the serpent, smiling apart. "Let us walk on, nevertheless, reasoning as we go, and if I convince thee not, thou shalt turn back. We are but a little way in the forest, yet."

"Too far, too far!" exclaimed the goodman, unconsciously resuming his walk. "My father never went into the woods on such an errand, nor his father before him. We have been a race of honest men and good Christians, since the days of the martyrs. And shall I be the first of the name of Brown that ever took this path and kept—"

"Such company, thou wouldst say," observed the elder person, interrupting his pause. "Well said, Goodman Brown! I have been as well acquainted with your family as with ever a one among the Puritans; and that's no trifle to say. I helped your grandfather, the constable, when he lashed the Quaker woman so smartly through the streets of Salem. And it was I that brought your father a pitch-pine knot, kindled at my own hearth, to set fire to an Indian village, in King Philip's war. They were my good friends, both; and many a pleasant walk have we had along this path, and returned merrily after midnight. I would fain be friends with you, for their sake."

"If it be as thou sayest," replied Goodman Brown, "I marvel they never spoke of these matters. Or, verily, I marvel not, seeing that the least rumor of the sort would have driven them from New England. We are a people of prayer and good works to boot, and abide no such wickedness."

"Wickedness or not," said the traveller with the twisted staff, "I have a very general acquaintance here in New England. The deacons of many a church have drunk the communion wine with me; the selectmen, of divers towns, make me their chairman; and a majority of the Great and General Court are firm supporters of my interest. The governor and I, too—but these are state secrets."

"Can this be so!" cried Goodman Brown, with a stare of amazement at his undisturbed companion. "Howbeit, I have nothing to do with the governor and council; they have their own ways, and are no rule for a simple husbandman like me. But, were I to go on with thee, how should I meet the eye of that good old man, our minister, at Salem village? Oh, his voice would make me tremble, both Sabbath-day and lecture-day!"

Thus far, the elder traveller had listened with due gravity, but now burst into a fit of irrepressible mirth, shaking himself so violently, that his snakelike staff actually seemed to wriggle in sympathy.

"Ha, ha, ha!" shouted he, again and again; then composing himself, "Well, go on, Goodman Brown, go on; but, prithee, don't kill me with laughing!"

"Well, then, to end the matter at once," said Goodman Brown, considerably nettled, "there is my wife, Faith. It would break her dear little heart; and I'd rather break my own!"

"Nay, if that be the case," answered the other, "e'en go thy ways, Goodman Brown. I would not, for twenty old women like the one hobbling before us, that Faith should come to any harm."

As he spoke, he pointed his staff at a female figure on the path, in whom Goodman Brown recognized a very pious and exemplary dame, who had taught him his catechism in youth, and was still his moral and spiritual adviser, jointly with the minister and Deacon Gookin.

"A marvel, truly, that Goody Cloyse should be so far in the wilderness, at nightfall!" said he. "But, with your leave, friend, I shall take a cut through the woods, until we have left this Christian woman behind. Being a stranger to you, she might ask whom I was consorting with, and whither I was going."

"Be it so," said his fellow-traveller. "Betake you to the woods, and let me keep the path."

Accordingly, the young man turned aside, but took care to watch his companion, who advanced softly along the road, until he had come within a staff's length of the old dame. She, meanwhile, was making the best of her way, with singular speed for so aged a woman, and mumbling some indistinct words, a prayer, doubtless, as she went. The traveller put forth his staff, and touched her withered neck with what seemed the serpent's tail.

"The devil!" screamed the pious old lady.

"Then Goody Cloyse knows her old friend?" observed the traveller, confronting her, and leaning on his writhing stick.

"Ah, forsooth, and is it your worship, indeed?" cried the good dame. "Yea, truly is it, and in the very image of my old gossip, Goodman Brown, the grandfather of the silly fellow that now is. But, would your worship believe it? my broomstick hath strangely disappeared, stolen, as I suspect, by that unhanged witch, Goody Cory, and that, too, when I was all anointed with the juice of smallage and cinque-foil and wolf's-bane—"

"Mingled with fine wheat and the fat of a new-born babe," said the shape of old Goodman Brown.

"Ah, your worship knows the recipe," cried the old lady, cackling aloud. "So, as I was saying, being all ready for the meeting, and no horse to ride on, I made up my mind to foot it; for they tell me there is a nice young man to be taken into communion tonight. But now your good worship will lend me your arm, and we shall be there in a twinkling."

"That can hardly be," answered her friend. "I may not spare you my arm, Goody Cloyse, but here is my staff, if you will."

So saying, he threw it down at her feet, where, perhaps, it assumed life, being one of the rods which its owner had formerly lent to the Egyptian Magi. Of this fact, however, Goodman Brown could not take cognizance. He had cast his eyes in astonishment, and looking down again, beheld neither Goody Cloyse nor the serpentine staff, but his fellow-traveller alone, who waited for him as calmly as if nothing had happened.

"That old woman taught me my catechism!" said the young man; and there was a world of meaning in this simple comment.

They continued to walk onward, while the elder traveller exhorted his companion to make good speed and persevere in the path, discoursing so aptly, that his arguments seemed rather to spring up in the bosom of his auditor, than to be suggested by himself. As they went he plucked a branch of maple, to serve for a walking-stick, and began to strip it of the twigs and little boughs, which were wet with evening dew. The moment his fingers touched them, they became strangely withered and dried up, as with a week's sunshine. Thus the pair proceeded, at a good free pace, until suddenly, in a gloomy hollow of the road, Goodman Brown sat himself down on the stump of a tree, and refused to go any farther.

"Friend," said he, stubbornly, "my mind is made up. Not another step will I budge on this errand. What if a wretched old woman do choose to go to the devil, when I thought she was going to Heaven! Is that any reason why I should quit my dear Faith, and go after her?"

"You will think better of this by and by," said his acquaintance, composedly. "Sit here and rest yourself awhile; and when you feel like moving again, there is my staff to help you along."

Without more words, he threw his companion the maple stick, and was as speedily out of sight as if he had vanished into the deepening gloom. The young man sat a few moments by the roadside, applauding himself greatly, and thinking with how clear a conscience he should meet the minister, in his morning walk, nor shrink from the eye of good old Deacon Gookin. And what calm sleep would be his, that very night, which was to have been spent so wickedly, but purely and sweetly now, in the arms of Faith! Amidst these pleasant and praiseworthy meditations, Goodman Brown heard the tramp of horses along the road, and deemed it advisable to conceal himself within the verge of the forest, conscious of the guilty purpose that had brought him thither, though now so happily turned from it.

On came the hoof-tramps and the voices of the riders, two grave old voices, conversing soberly, as they drew near. These mingled sounds appeared to pass along the road, within a few yards of the young man's hiding-place; but owing, doubtless, to the depth of the gloom, at that particular spot, neither the travellers nor their steeds were visible. Though their figures brushed the small boughs by the wayside, it could not be seen that they intercepted, even for a moment, the faint gleam from the strip of bright sky, athwart which they must have passed. Goodman Brown alternately crouched and stood on tiptoe, pulling aside the branches, and thrusting forth his head as far as he durst, without discerning so much as a shadow. It vexed him the more, because he could have sworn, were such a thing possible, that he recognized the voices of the minister and Deacon Gookin, jogging along quietly, as they were wont to do, when bound to some ordination or ecclesiastical council. While yet within hearing, one of the riders stopped to pluck a switch.

"Of the two, reverend Sir," said the voice like the deacon's, "I had rather miss an ordination dinner than to-night's meeting. They tell me that some of our community are to be here from Falmouth and beyond, and others from Connecticut and Rhode Island; besides several of the Indian powwows, who, after their fashion, know almost as much deviltry as the best of us. Moreover, there is a goodly young woman to be taken into communion."

"Mighty well, Deacon Gookin!" replied the solemn old tones of the minister. "Spur up, or we shall be late. Nothing can be done, you know, until I get on the ground."

The hoofs clattered again, and the voices, talking so strangely in the empty air, passed on through the forest, where no church had ever been gathered, nor solitary Christian prayed. Whither, then, could these holy men be journeying, so deep into the heathen wilderness? Young Goodman Brown caught hold of a tree, for support, being ready to sink down on the ground, faint and over-burthened with the heavy sickness of his heart. He looked up to the sky, doubting whether there really was a Heaven above him. Yet, there was the blue arch, and the stars brightening in it.

"With Heaven above, and Faith below, I will yet stand firm against the devil!" cried Goodman Brown.

While he still gazed upward, into the deep arch of the firmament, and had lifted his hands to pray, a cloud, though no wind was stirring, hurried across the zenith, and hid the brightening stars. The blue sky was still visible, except directly overhead, where this black mass of cloud was sweeping swiftly northward. Aloft in the air, as if from the depths of the cloud, came a confused and doubtful sound of voices. Once, the listener fancied that he could distinguish the accents of townspeople of his own, men and women, both pious and ungodly, many of whom he had met at the communion-table, and had seen others rioting at the tavern. The next moment, so indistinct were the sounds, he doubted whether he had heard aught but the murmur of the old forest, whispering without a wind. Then came a stronger swell of those familiar tones, heard daily in the sunshine, at Salem village, but never, until now, from a cloud at night. There was one voice, of a young woman, tittering lamentations, yet with an uncertain sorrow, and entreating for some favor, which, perhaps, it would grieve her to obtain. And all the unseen multitude, both saints and sinners, seemed to encourage her onward.

"Faith!" shouted Goodman Brown, in a voice of agony and desperation; and the echoes of the forest mocked him, crying—"Faith! Faith!" as if bewildered wretches were seeking her, all through the wilderness.

The cry of grief, rage, and terror was yet piercing the night, when the unhappy husband held his breath for a response. There was a scream, drowned immediately in a louder murmur of voices fading into far-off laughter, as the dark cloud swept away, leaving the clear and silent sky above Goodman Brown. But something fluttered lightly down through the air, and caught on the branch of a tree. The young man seized it and beheld a pink ribbon.

"My Faith is gone!" cried he, after one stupefied moment. "There is no good on earth, and sin is but a name. Come, devil! for to thee is this world given."

And maddened with despair, so that he laughed loud and long, did Goodman Brown grasp his staff and set forth again, at such a rate, that he seemed to fly along the forest path, rather than to walk or run. The road grew wilder and drearier, and more faintly traced, and vanished at length, leaving him in the heart of the dark wilderness, still rushing onward, with the instinct that guides mortal man to evil. The whole forest was peopled with frightful sounds: the creaking of the trees, the howling of wild beasts, and the yell of Indians; while, sometimes, the wind tolled like a distant church bell, and sometimes gave a broad roar around the traveller, as if all Nature was laughing him to scorn. But he was himself the chief horror of the scene, and shrank not from its other horrors.

"Ha! ha! ha!" roared Goodman Brown, when the wind laughed at him. "Let us hear which will laugh loudest! Think not to frighten me with your deviltry! Come witch, come wizard, come Indian powwow, come devil himself! and here comes Goodman Brown. You may as well fear him as he fear you!"

In truth, all through the haunted forest, there could be nothing more frightful than the figure of Goodman Brown. On he flew, among the black pines, brandishing his staff with frenzied gestures, now giving vent to an inspiration of horrid blasphemy, and now shouting forth such laughter, as set all the echoes of the forest laughing like demons around him. The fiend in his own shape is less hideous, than when he rages in the breast of man. Thus sped the demoniac on his course, until, quivering among the trees, he saw a red light before him, as when the felled trunks and branches of a clearing have been set on fire, and throw up their lurid blaze against the sky, at the hour of midnight. He paused, in a lull of the tempest that had driven him onward, and heard the swell of what seemed a hymn, rolling solemnly from a distance, with the weight of many voices. He knew the tune. It was a familiar one in the choir of the village meeting-house. The verse died heavily away, and was lengthened by a chorus, not of human voices, but of all the sounds of the benighted wilderness, pealing in awful harmony together. Goodman Brown cried out; and his cry was lost to his own ear, by its unison with the cry of the desert.

In the interval of silence, he stole forward, until the light glared full upon his eyes. At one extremity of an open space, hemmed in by the dark wall of the forest, arose a rock, bearing some rude, natural resemblance either to an altar or a pulpit, and surrounded by four blazing pines, their tops aflame, their stems untouched, like candles at an evening meeting. The mass of foliage, that had overgrown the summit of the rock, was all on fire, blazing high into the night, and fitfully illuminating the whole field. Each pendent twig and leafy festoon was in a blaze. As the red light arose and fell, a numerous congregation alternately shone forth, then disappeared in shadow, and again grew, as it were, out of the darkness, peopling the heart of the solitary woods at once.

"A grave and dark-clad company!" quoth Goodman Brown.

In truth, they were such. Among them, quivering to-and-fro, between gloom and splendor, appeared faces that would be seen, next day, at the council-board of the province, and others which, Sabbath after Sabbath, looked devoutly heavenward, and benignantly over the crowded pews, from the holiest pulpits in the land. Some affirm, that the lady of the governor was there. At least, there were high dames well known to her, and wives of honored husbands, and widows a great multitude, and ancient maidens, all of excellent repute, and fair young girls, who trembled lest their mothers should espy them. Either the sudden gleams of light, flashing over the obscure field, bedazzled Goodman Brown, or he recognized a score of the church members of Salem village, famous for their especial sanctity. Good old Deacon Gookin had arrived, and waited at the skirts of that venerable saint, his reverend pastor. But, irreverently consorting with these grave, reputable, and pious people, these elders of the church, these chaste dames and dewy virgins, there were men of dissolute lives and women of spotted fame, wretches given over to all mean and filthy vice, and suspected even of horrid crimes. It was strange to see, that the good shrank not from the wicked, nor were the sinners abashed by the saints. Scattered, also, among their pale-faced enemies, were the Indian priests, or powwows, who had often scared their native forest with more hideous incantations than any known to English witchcraft.

"But, where is Faith?" thought Goodman Brown; and, as hope came into his heart, he trembled.

Another verse of the hymn arose, a slow and mournful strain, such as the pious love, but joined to words which expressed all that our nature can conceive of sin, and darkly hinted at far more. Unfathomable to mere mortals is the lore of fiends. Verse after verse was sung, and still the chorus of the desert swelled between, like the deepest tone of a mighty organ. And, with the final peal of that dreadful anthem, there came a sound, as if the roaring wind, the rushing streams, the howling beasts, and every other voice of the unconverted wilderness were mingling and according with the voice of guilty man, in homage to the prince of all. The four blazing pines threw up a loftier flame, and obscurely discovered shapes and visages of horror on the smoke-wreaths, above the impious assembly. At the same moment, the fire on the rock shot redly forth, and formed a glowing arch above its base, where now appeared a figure. With reverence be it spoken, the apparition bore no slight similitude, both in garb and manner, to some grave divine of the New England churches.

"Bring forth the converts!" cried a voice, that echoed through the field and rolled into the forest.

At the word, Goodman Brown stepped forth from the shadow of the trees, and approached the congregation, with whom he felt a loathful brotherhood, by the sympathy of all that was wicked in his heart. He could have well-nigh sworn, that the shape of his own dead father beckoned him to advance, looking downward from a smoke-wreath, while a woman, with dim features of despair, threw out her hand to warn him back. Was it his mother? But he had no power to retreat one step, nor to resist, even in thought, when the minister and good old Deacon Gookin seized his arms, and led him to the blazing rock. Thither came also the slender form of a veiled female, led between Goody Cloyse, that pious teacher of the catechism, and Martha Carrier, who had received the devil's promise to be queen of hell. A rampant hag was she! And there stood the proselytes, beneath the canopy of fire.

"Welcome, my children," said the dark figure, "to the communion of your race! Ye have found, thus young, your nature and your destiny. My children, look behind you!"

They turned; and flashing forth, as it were, in a sheet of flame, the fiend-worshippers were seen; the smile of welcome gleamed darkly on every visage.

"There," resumed the sable form, "are all whom ye have reverenced from youth. Ye deemed them holier than yourselves, and shrank from your own sin, contrasting it with their lives of righteousness and prayerful aspirations heavenward. Yet, here are they all, in my worshipping assembly! This night it shall be granted you to know their secret deeds; how hoary-bearded elders of the church have whispered wanton words to the young maids of their households; how many a woman, eager for widow's weeds, has given her husband a drink at bedtime, and let him sleep his last sleep in her bosom; how beardless youths have made haste to inherit their father's wealth; and how fair damsels—blush not, sweet ones!—have dug little graves in the garden, and bidden me, the sole guest, to an infant's funeral. By the sympathy of your human hearts for sin, ye shall scent out all the places—whether in church, bed-chamber, street, field, or forest— where crime has been committed, and shall exult to behold the whole earth one stain of guilt, one mighty blood-spot. Far more than this! It shall be yours to penetrate, in every bosom, the deep mystery of sin, the fountain of all wicked arts, and which inexhaustibly supplies more evil impulses than human power—than my power, at its utmost!—can make manifest in deeds. And now, my children, look upon each other."

They did so; and, by the blaze of the hell-kindled torches, the wretched man beheld his Faith, and the wife her husband, trembling before that unhallowed altar.

"Lo! there ye stand, my children," said the figure, in a deep and solemn tone, almost sad, with its despairing awfulness, as if his once angelic nature could yet mourn for our miserable race. "Depending upon one another's hearts, ye had still hoped that virtue were not all a dream! Now are ye undeceived!—Evil is the nature of mankind. Evil must be your only happiness. Welcome, again, my children, to the communion of your race!"

"Welcome!" repeated the fiend-worshippers, in one cry of despair and triumph.

And there they stood, the only pair, as it seemed, who were yet hesitating on the verge of wickedness, in this dark world. A basin was hollowed, naturally, in the rock. Did it contain water, reddened by the lurid light? or was it blood? or, perchance, a liquid flame? Herein did the Shape of Evil dip his hand, and prepare to lay the mark of baptism upon their foreheads, that they might be partakers of the mystery of sin, more conscious of the secret guilt of others, both in deed and thought, than they could now be of their own. The husband cast one look at his pale wife, and Faith at him. What polluted wretches would the next glance show them to each other, shuddering alike at what they disclosed and what they saw!

"Faith! Faith!" cried the husband. "Look up to Heaven, and resist the Wicked One!"

Whether Faith obeyed, he knew not. Hardly had he spoken, when he found himself amid calm night and solitude, listening to a roar of the wind, which died heavily away through the forest. He staggered against the rock, and felt it chill and damp, while a hanging twig, that had been all on fire, besprinkled his cheek with the coldest dew.

The next morning, young Goodman Brown came slowly into the street of Salem village staring around him like a bewildered man. The good old minister was taking a walk along the grave-yard, to get an appetite for breakfast and meditate his sermon, and bestowed a blessing, as he passed, on Goodman Brown. He shrank from the venerable saint, as if to avoid an anathema. Old Deacon Gookin was at domestic worship, and the holy words of his prayer were heard through the open window. "What God doth the wizard pray to?" quoth Goodman Brown. Goody Cloyse, that excellent old Christian, stood in the early sunshine, at her own lattice, catechizing a little girl, who had brought her a pint of morning's milk. Goodman Brown snatched away the child, as from the grasp of the fiend himself. Turning the corner by the meeting-house, he spied the head of Faith, with the pink ribbons, gazing anxiously forth, and bursting into such joy at sight of him that she skipt along the street, and almost kissed her husband before the whole village. But Goodman Brown looked sternly and sadly into her face, and passed on without a greeting.

Had Goodman Brown fallen asleep in the forest, and only dreamed a wild dream of a witch-meeting?

Be it so, if you will. But, alas! it was a dream of evil omen for young Goodman Brown. A stern, a sad, a darkly meditative, a distrustful, if not a desperate man did he become, from the night of that fearful dream. On the Sabbath day, when the congregation were singing a holy psalm, he could not listen, because an anthem of sin rushed loudly upon his ear, and drowned all the blessed strain. When the minister spoke from the pulpit, with power and fervid eloquence, and with his hand on the open Bible, of the sacred truths of our religion, and of saint-like lives and triumphant deaths, and of future bliss or misery unutterable, then did Goodman Brown turn pale, dreading lest the roof should thunder down upon the gray blasphemer and his hearers. Often, awaking suddenly at midnight, he shrank from the bosom of Faith, and at morning or eventide, when the family knelt down at prayer, he scowled, and muttered to himself, and gazed sternly at his wife, and turned away. And when he had lived long, and was borne to his grave, a hoary corpse, followed by Faith, an aged woman, and children and grand-children, a goodly procession, besides neighbors not a few, they carved no hopeful verse upon his tombstone; for his dying hour was gloom.

QUESTIONS FOR DISCUSSION AND WRITING

1. How would you describe the mood of the opening scene, in which young Goodman Brown takes his leave of Faith? What contributes to your definition of the mood?

2. Whatever happens in the woods, we have a sense that Goodman Brown has lost something important. How do you envision his life before his journey into the woods? What is it that he has lost?

3. Hawthorne leaves it up to his readers to decide whether Goodman Brown dreamt his experiences or actually lived them. Do you think the experiences in the woods were a dream or reality? Why might Hawthorne have left the answer up to us, and to what extent does your answer influence your understanding of the story's themes?

4. Brown seems to come to some understanding of what evil and sin are. How would he define these terms? Is his definition the same as the definitions of the old man who leads him into the woods? Are they the same as Hawthorne's and ours?

5. "Young Goodman Brown" is often considered an **allegory,** that is, a story in which characters stand for virtues, vices, or emotions and in which many of the details of the setting function symbolically. What allegorical characteristics do you see in the story? How effective do you find the use of allegory? If you were to retell the story

in a less allegorical, more realistic way, what changes would you have to make? What would you gain and lose by choosing this other manner of presentation?

ERNEST HEMINGWAY (1899–1961)

A Clean, Well-Lighted Place   1933

It was late and everyone had left the café except an old man who sat in the shadow the leaves of the tree made against the electric light. In the day time the street was dusty, but at night the dew settled the dust and the old man liked to sit late because he was deaf and now at night it was quiet and he felt the difference. The two waiters inside the café knew that the old man was a little drunk, and while he was a good client they knew that if he became too drunk he would leave without paying, so they kept watch on him.

"Last week he tried to commit suicide," one waiter said.

"Why?"

"He was in despair."

"What about?"

"Nothing."

"How do you know it was nothing?"

"He has plenty of money."

They sat together at a table that was close against the wall near the door of the café and looked at the terrace where the tables were all empty except where the old man sat in the shadow of the leaves of the tree that moved slightly in the wind. A girl and a soldier went by in the street. The street light shone on the brass number on his collar. The girl wore no head covering and hurried beside him.

"The guard will pick him up," one waiter said.

"What does it matter if he gets what he's after?"

"He had better get off the street now. The guard will get him. They went by five minutes ago."

The old man sitting in the shadow rapped on his saucer with his glass. The younger waiter went over to him.

"What do you want?"

The old man looked at him. "Another brandy," he said.

"You'll be drunk," the waiter said. The old man looked at him. The waiter went away.

"He'll stay all night," he said to his colleague. "I'm sleepy now. I never get into bed before three o'clock. He should have killed himself last week."

The waiter took the brandy bottle and another saucer from the counter inside the café and marched out to the old man's table. He put down the saucer and poured the glass full of brandy.

"You should have killed yourself last week," he said to the deaf man. The old man motioned with his finger. "A little more," he said. The waiter poured on into the glass so that the brandy slopped over and ran down the stem into the top saucer of the pile. "Thank you," the old man said. The waiter took the bottle back inside the café. He sat down at the table with his colleague again.

"He's drunk now," he said.

"He's drunk every night."

"What did he want to kill himself for?"

"How should I know."

"How did he do it?"

"He hung himself with a rope."

"Who cut him down?"

"His niece."

"Why did they do it?"

"Fear for his soul."

"How much money has he got?"

"He's got plenty."

"He must be eighty years old."

"Anyway I should say he was eighty."

"I wish he would go home. I never get to bed before three o'clock. What kind of hour is that to go to bed?"

"He stays up because he likes it."

"He's lonely. I'm not lonely. I have a wife waiting in bed for me."

"He had a wife once too."

"A wife would be no good to him now."

"You can't tell. He might be better with a wife."

"His niece looks after him."

"I know. You said she cut him down."

"I wouldn't want to be that old. An old man is a nasty thing."

"Not always. This old man is clean. He drinks without spilling. Even now, drunk. Look at him."

"I don't want to look at him. I wish he would go home. He has no regard for those who must work."

The old man looked from his glass across the square, then over at the waiters.

"Another brandy," he said, pointing to his glass. The waiter who was in a hurry came over.

"Finished," he said, speaking with that omission of syntax stupid people employ when talking to drunken people or foreigners. "No more tonight. Close now."

"Another," said the old man.

"No. Finished." The waiter wiped the edge of the table with a towel and shook his head.

The old man stood up, slowly counted the saucers, took a leather coin purse from his pocket and paid for the drinks, leaving half a peseta tip.

The waiter watched him go down the street, a very old man walking unsteadily but with dignity.

"Why didn't you let him stay and drink?" the unhurried waiter asked. They were putting up the shutters. "It is not half-past two."

"I want to go home to bed."

"What is an hour?"

"More to me than to him."

"An hour is the same."

"You talk like an old man yourself. He can buy a bottle and drink at home."

"It's not the same."

"No, it is not," agreed the waiter with a wife. He did not wish to be unjust. He was only in a hurry.

"And you? You have no fear of going home before your usual hour?"

"Are you trying to insult me?"

"No, hombre, only to make a joke."

"No," the waiter who was in a hurry said, rising from pulling down the metal shutters. "I have confidence. I am all confidence."

"You have youth, confidence, and a job," the older waiter said. "You have everything."

"And what do you lack?"

"Everything but work."

"You have everything I have."

"No. I have never had confidence and I am not young."

"Come on. Stop talking nonsense and lock up."

"I am of those who like to stay late at the café," the older waiter said. "With all those who do not want to go to bed. With all those who need a light for the night."

"I want to go home and into bed."

"We are of two different kinds," the older waiter said. He was now dressed to go home. "It is not only a question of youth and confidence although those things are very beautiful. Each night I am reluctant to close up because there may be some one who needs the café."

"Hombre, there are bodegas open all night long."

"You do not understand. This is a clean and pleasant café. It is well lighted. The light is very good and also, now, there are shadows of the leaves."

"Good night," said the younger waiter.

"Good night," the other said. Turning off the electric light he continued the conversation with himself. It is the light of course but it is necessary that the place be clean and pleasant. You do not want music. Certainly you do not want music. Nor can you stand before a bar with dignity although that is all that is provided for these hours. What did he fear? It was not fear or dread. It was a nothing that he knew too well. It was all a nothing and a man was nothing too. It was only that and light was all it needed and a certain cleanness and order. Some lived in it and never felt it but he knew it was nada y pues nada y pues nada. Our nada who art in nada, nada be thy name thy kingdom nada thy will be nada in nada as it is in nada. Give us this nada our daily nada and nada us our nada as we nada our nadas and nada us not into nada but deliver us from nada; pues nada. Hail nothing full of nothing, nothing is with thee. He smiled and stood before a bar with a shining steam pressure coffee machine.

"What's yours?" asked the barman.

"Nada."

"Otro loco mas," said the barman and turned away.

"A little cup," said the waiter.

The barman poured it for him.

"The light is very bright and pleasant but the bar is unpolished," the waiter said.

The barman looked at him but did not answer. It was too late at night for conversation.

"You want another copita?" the barman asked.

"No, thank you," said the waiter and went out. He disliked bars and bodegas. A clean, well-lighted café was a very different thing. Now, without thinking further, he would go home to his room. He would lie in the bed and finally, with daylight, he would go to sleep. After all, he said to himself, it is probably only insomnia. Many must have it.

QUESTIONS FOR DISCUSSION AND WRITING

1. For the deaf old customer and the middle-aged waiter, there is a big difference between a bar and a "clean, well-lighted café." What is that difference? Why do they see a difference that neither the young waiter nor the bartender sees?

2. In many ways, we know very little about the characters in this story. We don't know much about what they look like, for instance. In fact, we don't even know their names. Why does Hemingway choose to tell us so little?

3. Given what you know about his situation and the world in which he lives, why did the old man try to kill himself?

4. Hemingway is known for a style that relies heavily on simple and compound sentences (sentences with no subordinate clauses). Rewrite a passage from the story, including more subordinate clauses—more clauses that make logical and temporal connections. How does a different style change the reader's response to the story and its themes?

5. After the customer leaves, the middle-aged waiter talks to himself, reciting a bitter retelling of the Lord's Prayer. How does his "prayer" figure in the story's themes? What significance do you see in the substitution of *nada* ("nothing") for particular words in the Lord's Prayer?

SHIRLEY JACKSON (1919–1965)
The Lottery _____ *(1948)*

The morning of June 27th was clear and sunny, with the fresh warmth of a full-summer day; the flowers were blossoming profusely and the grass was richly green. The people of the village began to gather in the square, between the post office and the bank, around ten o'clock; in some towns there were so many people that the lottery took two days and had to be started on June 26th, but in this village, where there were only about three hundred people, the whole lottery took less than two hours, so it could begin at ten o'clock in the morning and still be through in time to allow the villagers to get home for noon dinner.

The children assembled first, of course. School was recently over for the summer, and the feeling of liberty sat uneasily on most of them; they tended to gather together quietly for a while before they broke into boisterous play, and their talk was still of the classroom and the teacher, of books and reprimands. Bobby Martin had already stuffed his pockets full of stones, and the other boys soon followed his example, selecting the smoothest and roundest stones; Bobby and Harry Jones and Dickie Delacroix—the villagers pronounced this name "Dellacroy"—eventually made a great pile of stones in one corner of the square and guarded it against the raids of the other boys. The girls stood aside, talking among themselves, looking over their shoulders at the boys, and the very small children rolled in the dust or clung to the hands of their older brothers or sisters.

Soon the men began to gather, surveying their own children, speaking of planting and rain, tractors and taxes. They stood together, away from the pile of stones in the corner, and their jokes were quiet and they smiled rather than laughed. The women, wearing faded house dresses and sweaters, came shortly after their menfolk. They greeted one another and exchanged bits of gossip as they went to join their husbands. Soon the women, standing by their husbands, began to call to their children, and the children came reluctantly, having to be called four or five times. Bobby Martin ducked under his mother's grasping hand and ran, laughing, back to the pile of stones. His father spoke up sharply, and Bobby came quickly and took his place between his father and his oldest brother.

The lottery was conducted—as were the square dances, the teenage club, the Halloween program—by Mr. Summers, who had time and energy to devote to civic activities. He was a roundfaced, jovial man and he ran the coal business, and people were sorry for him, because he had no children and his wife was a scold. When he arrived in the square, carrying the black wooden box, there was a murmur of conversation among the villagers and he waved and called, "Little late today, folks." The postmaster, Mr. Graves, followed him, carrying a three-legged stool, and the stool was put in the center of the square and Mr. Summers set the black box down on it. The villagers kept their distance, leaving a space between themselves and the stool, and when Mr. Summers said, "Some of you fellows want to give me a hand?" there was a hesitation before two men, Mr. Martin and his oldest son, Baxter, came forward to hold the box steady on the stool while Mr. Summers stirred up the papers inside it.

The original paraphernalia for the lottery had been lost long ago, and the black box now resting on the stool had been put into use even before Old Man Warner, the oldest man in town, was born. Mr. Summers spoke frequently to the villagers about making a new box, but no one liked to upset even as much tradition as was represented by the black box. There was a story that the present box had been made with some pieces of the box that had preceded it, the one that had been constructed when the first people settled down to make a village here. Every year, after the lottery, Mr. Summers began talking again about a new box, but every year the subject was allowed to fade off without anything's being done. The black box grew shabbier each year; by now it was no longer completely black but splintered badly along one side to show the original wood color, and in some places faded or stained.

Mr. Martin and his oldest son, Baxter, held the black box securely on the stool until Mr. Summers had stirred the papers thoroughly with his hand. Because so much of the ritual had been forgotten or discarded, Mr. Summers had been successful in having slips of paper substituted for the chips of wood that had been used for generations. Chips of wood, Mr. Summers had argued, had been all very well when the village was tiny, but now that the population was more than three hundred and likely to keep on growing, it was necessary to use something that would fit more easily into the black box. The night before the lottery, Mr. Summers and Mr. Graves made up the slips of paper and put them in the box, and it was then taken to the safe of Mr. Summers's coal company and locked up until Mr. Summers was ready to take it to the square next morning. The rest of the year, the box was put away, sometimes one place, sometimes another; it had spent one year in Mr. Graves's barn and another year underfoot in the post office, and sometimes it was set on a shelf in the Martin grocery and left there.

There was a great deal of fussing to be done before Mr. Summers declared the lottery open. There were lists to make up—of heads of families, heads of households in each family, members of each household in each family. There was the proper swearing-in of Mr. Summers by the postmaster, as the official of the lottery; at one time, some people remembered, there had been a recital of some sort, performed by the official of the lottery, a perfunctory, tuneless chant that had been rattled off duly each year; some people believed that the official of the lottery used to stand just so when he said or sang it, others believed that he was supposed to walk among the people, but years and years ago this part of the ritual had been allowed to lapse. There had been, also, a ritual salute, which the official of the lottery had had to use in addressing each person who came up to draw from the box, but this also had changed with time, until now it was felt necessary only for the official to speak to each person approaching. Mr. Summers was very good at all this; in his clean white shirt and blue jeans, with one hand resting carelessly on the black box, he seemed very proper and important as he talked interminably to Mr. Graves and the Martins.

Just as Mr. Summers finally left off talking and turned to the assembled villagers, Mrs. Hutchinson came hurriedly along the path to the square, her sweater thrown over her shoulders, and slid into place in the back of the crowd. "Clean forgot what day it was," she said to Mrs. Delacroix, who stood next to her, and they both laughed softly. "Thought my old man was out back stacking wood," Mrs. Hutchinson went on, "and then I looked out the window and the kids were gone, and then I remembered it was the twenty-seventh and came a-running." She dried her hands on her apron, and Mrs. Delacroix said, "You're in time, though. They're still talking away up there."

Mrs. Hutchinson craned her neck to see through the crowd and found her husband and children standing near the front. She tapped Mrs. Delacroix on the arm as a farewell and began to make her way through the crowd. The people separated good-humoredly to let her through; two or three people said, in voices just loud enough to be heard across the crowd, "Here comes your Missus, Hutchinson," and "Bill, she made it after all." Mrs. Hutchinson reached her husband, and Mr. Summers, who had been waiting, said cheerfully, "Thought we were going to have to get on without you, Tessie." Mrs. Hutchinson said, grinning, "Wouldn't have me leave m'dishes in the sink, now would you, Joe?" and soft laughter ran through the crowd as the people stirred back into position after Mrs. Hutchinson's arrival.

"Well, now," Mr. Summers said soberly, "guess we better get started, get this over with, so's we can go back to work. Anybody ain't here?"

"Dunbar," several people said. "Dunbar, Dunbar."

Mr. Summers consulted his list. "Clyde Dunbar," he said. "That's right. He's broke his leg, hasn't he? Who's drawing for him?"

"Me, I guess," a woman said, and Mr. Summers turned to look at her. "Wife draws for her husband," Mr. Summers said. "Don't you have a grown boy to do it for you, Janey?" Although Mr. Summers and everyone else in the village knew the answer perfectly well, it was the business of the official of the lottery to ask such questions formally. Mr. Summers waited with an expression of polite interest while Mrs. Dunbar answered.

"Horace's not but sixteen yet," Mrs. Dunbar said regretfully. "Guess I gotta fill in for the old man this year."

"Right," Mr. Summers said. He made a note on the list he was holding. Then he asked, "Watson boy drawing this year?"

A tall boy in the crowd raised his hand. "Here," he said. "I'm drawing for m'mother and me." He blinked his eyes nervously and ducked his head as several voices in the crowd said things like "Good fellow, Jack," and "Glad to see your mother's got a man to do it."

"Well," Mr. Summers said, "guess that's everyone. Old Man Warner make it?"

"Here," a voice said, and Mr. Summers nodded.

A sudden hush fell on the crowd as Mr. Summers cleared his throat and looked at the list. "All ready?" he called. "Now, I'll read the names—heads of families first—and the men come up and take a paper out of the box. Keep the paper folded in your hand without looking at it until everyone has had a turn. Everything clear?"

The people had done it so many times that they only half listened to the directions; most of them were quiet, wetting their lips, not looking around. Then Mr. Summers raised one hand high and said, "Adams." A man disengaged himself from the crowd and came forward. "Hi, Steve," Mr. Summers said, and Mr. Adams said, "Hi, Joe." They grinned at one another humorlessly and nervously. Then Mr. Adams reached into the black box and took out a folded paper. He held it firmly by one corner as he turned and went hastily back to his place in the crowd, where he stood a little apart from his family, not looking down at his hand.

"Allen," Mr. Summers said. "Anderson. . . . Bentham."

"Seems like there's no time at all between lotteries any more," Mrs. Delacroix said to Mrs. Graves in the back row. "Seems like we got through with the last one only last week."

"Time sure goes fast," Mrs. Graves said.

"Clark. . . . Delacroix."

"There goes my old man," Mrs. Delacroix said. She held her breath while her husband went forward.

"Dunbar," Mr. Summers said, and Mrs. Dunbar went steadily to the box while one of the women said, "Go on, Janey," and another said, "There she goes."

"We're next," Mrs. Graves said. She watched while Mr. Graves came around from the side of the box, greeted Mr. Summers gravely, and selected a slip of paper from the box. By now, all through the crowd there were men holding the small folded papers in their large hands, turning them over and over nervously. Mrs. Dunbar and her two sons stood together, Mrs. Dunbar holding the slip of paper.

"Harburt. . . . Hutchinson."

"Get up there, Bill," Mrs. Hutchinson said, and the people near her laughed.

"Jones."

"They do say," Mr. Adams said to Old Man Warner, who stood next to him, "that over in the north village they're talking of giving up the lottery."

Old Man Warner snorted. "Pack of crazy fools," he said. "Listening to the young folks, nothing's good enough for *them*. Next thing you know, they'll be wanting to go back to living in caves, nobody work any more, live *that* way for a while. Used to be a saying about 'Lottery in June, corn be heavy soon.' First thing you know, we'd all be eating stewed chickweed and acorns. There's *always* been a lottery," he added petulantly. "Bad enough to see young Joe Summers up there joking with everybody."

"Some places have already quit lotteries," Mrs. Adams said.

"Nothing but trouble in *that*," Old Man Warner said stoutly. "Pack of young fools."

"Martin." And Bobby Martin watched his father go forward. "Overdyke. . . . Percy."

"I wish they'd hurry," Mrs. Dunbar said to her older son. "I wish they'd hurry."

"They're almost through," her son said.

"You get ready to run tell Dad," Mrs. Dunbar said.

Mr. Summers called his own name and then stepped forward precisely and selected a slip from the box. Then he called, "Warner."

"Seventy-seventh year I been in the lottery," Old Man Warner said as he went through the crowd. "Seventy-seventh time."

"Watson." The tall boy came awkwardly through the crowd. Someone said, "Don't be nervous, Jack," and Mr. Summers said, "Take your time, son."

"Zanini."

After that, there was a long pause, a breathless pause, until Mr. Summers, holding his slip of paper in the air, said, "All right, fellows." For a minute, no one moved, and then all the slips of paper were opened. Suddenly, all women began to speak at once, saying, "Who is it?" "Who's got it?" "Is it the Dunbars?" "Is it the Watsons?" Then the voices began to say, "It's Hutchinson. It's Bill." "Bill Hutchinson's got it."

"Go tell your father," Mrs. Dunbar said to her older son.

People began to look around to see the Hutchinsons. Bill Hutchinson was standing quiet, staring down at the paper in his hand. Suddenly, Tessie Hutchinson shouted to Mr. Summers, "You didn't give him time enough to take any paper he wanted. I saw you. It wasn't fair!"

"Be a good sport, Tessie," Mrs. Delacroix called, and Mrs. Graves said, "All of us took the same chance."

"Shut up, Tessie," Bill Hutchinson said.

"Well, everyone," Mr. Summers said, "that was done pretty fast, and now we've got to be hurrying a little more to get done in time." He consulted his next list. "Bill," he said, "you draw for the Hutchinson family. You got any other households in the Hutchinsons?"

"There's Don and Eva," Mrs. Hutchinson yelled. "Make them take their chance!"

"Daughters draw with their husbands' families, Tessie," Mr. Summers said gently. "You know that as well as anyone else."

"It wasn't fair," Tessie said.

"I guess not, Joe," Bill Hutchinson said regretfully. "My daughter draws with her husband's family, that's only fair. And I've got no other family except the kids."

"Then, as far as drawing for families is concerned, it's you," Mr. Summers said in explanation, "and as far as drawing for households is concerned, that's you, too. Right?"

"Right," Bill Hutchinson said.

"How many kids, Bill?" Mr. Summers asked formally.

"Three," Bill Hutchinson said. "There's Bill, Jr., and Nancy, and little Dave. And Tessie and me."

"All right, then," Mr. Summers said. "Harry, you got their tickets back?"

Mr. Graves nodded and held up the slips of paper. "Put them in the box, then," Mr. Summers directed. "Take Bill's and put it in."

"I think we ought to start over," Mrs. Hutchinson said, as quietly as she could. "I tell you it wasn't *fair*. You didn't give him time enough to choose. *Every*body saw that."

Mr. Graves had selected the five slips and put them in the box, and he dropped all the papers but those onto the ground, where the breeze caught them and lifted them off.

"Listen, everybody," Mrs. Hutchinson was saying to the people around her.

"Ready, Bill?" Mr. Summers asked, and Bill Hutchinson, with one quick glance around at his wife and children, nodded.

"Remember," Mr. Summers said, "take the slips and keep them folded until each person has taken one. Harry, you help little Dave." Mr. Graves took the hand of the little boy, who came willingly with him up to the box. "Take a paper out of the box, Davy," Mr. Summers said. Davy put his hand into the box and laughed. "Take just *one* paper," Mr. Summers said. "Harry, you hold it for him." Mr. Graves took the child's hand and removed the folded paper from the tight fist and held it while little Dave stood next to him and looked up at him wonderingly.

"Nancy next," Mr. Summers said. Nancy was twelve, and her school friends breathed heavily as she went forward, switching her skirt, and took a slip daintily from the box. "Bill, Jr.," Mr. Summers said, and Billy, his face red and his feet over-large, nearly knocked the box over as he got a paper out. "Tessie," Mr. Summers said. She hesitated for a minute, looking around defiantly, and then set her lips and went up to the box. She snatched a paper out and held it behind her.

"Bill," Mr. Summers said, and Bill Hutchinson reached into the box and felt around, bringing his hand out at last with the slip of paper in it.

The crowd was quiet. A girl whispered, "I hope it's not Nancy," and the sound of the whisper reached the edges of the crowd.

"It's not the way it used to be," Old Man Warner said clearly. "People ain't the way they used to be."

"All right," Mr. Summers said. "Open the papers. Harry, you open little Dave's."

Mr. Graves opened the slip of paper and there was a general sigh through the crowd as he held it up and everyone could see that it was blank. Nancy and Bill, Jr., opened theirs at the same time, and both beamed and laughed, turning around to the crowd and holding their slips of paper above their heads.

"Tessie," Mr. Summers said. There was a pause, and then Mr. Summers looked at Bill Hutchinson, and Bill unfolded his paper and showed it. It was blank.

"It's Tessie," Mr. Summers said, and his voice was hushed. "Show us her paper, Bill."

Bill Hutchinson went over to his wife and forced the slip of paper out of her hand. It had a black spot on it, the black spot Mr. Summers had made the night before with the heavy pencil in the coal-company office. Bill Hutchinson held it up, and there was a stir in the crowd.

"All right, folks," Mr. Summers said, "let's finish quickly."

Although the villagers had forgotten the ritual and lost the original black box, they still remembered to use stones. The pile of stones the boys had made earlier was ready; there were stones on the ground with the blowing scraps of paper that had come out of the box. Mrs. Delacroix selected a stone so large she had to pick it up with both hands and turned to Mrs. Dunbar. "Come on," she said. "Hurry up."

Mrs. Dunbar had small stones in both hands, and she said, gasping for breath, "I can't run at all. You'll have to go ahead and I'll catch up with you."

The children had stones already, and someone gave little Davy Hutchinson a few pebbles.

Tessie Hutchinson was in the center of a cleared space by now, and she held her hands out desperately as the villagers moved in on her. "It isn't fair," she said. A stone hit her on the side of the head.

Old Man Warner was saying, "Come on, come on, everyone." Steve Adams was in the front of the crowd of villagers, with Mrs. Graves beside him.

"It isn't fair, it isn't right," Mrs. Hutchinson screamed, and then they were upon her.

QUESTIONS FOR DISCUSSION AND WRITING

1. What associations are created by the title of the story? How would the reader's expectations be different if Jackson had used a different title with similar meanings but different connotations? (Think, for instance, of such titles as "The Prize" and "The Gamble.")
2. For most first-time readers, the horrifying conclusion comes as a surprise. However, those who have read the story before see that there are many foreshadowings. What ominous signs appear early on in the story? How does Jackson keep us off balance, undercutting those ominous signs so that we might dismiss them?
3. The exact setting of the story is undefined. What does the reader assume about where and when the story takes place? How does the setting help explain why the townspeople continue the lottery?
4. Because "The Lottery" was written shortly after the end of World War II, some readers have seen it as warning of the danger of simply following "orders," whether given by leaders or by one's neighbors. Does this seem a legitimate reading of the story? Do the townspeople succumb to natural aggressions or to cultural imperatives?

GISH JEN (1956–   )

In the American Society _____ 1986

1. His Own Society

When my father took over the pancake house, it was to send my little sister Mona and me to college. We were only in junior high at the time, but my father believed in getting a jump on things. "Those Americans always saying it," he told us. "Smart guys thinking in advance." My mother elaborated, explaining that businesses took bringing up, like children. They could take years to get going, she said, years.

In this case, though, we got rich right away. At two months we were breaking even, and at four, those same hotcakes that could barely withstand the weight of butter and syrup were supporting our family with ease. My mother bought a station wagon with air conditioning, my father an oversized, red vinyl recliner for the back room; and as time went on and the business continued to thrive, my father started to talk about his grandfather and the village he had reigned over in China—things my father had never talked about when he worked for other people. He told us about the bags of rice his family would give out to the poor at New Year's, and about the people who came to beg, on their hands and knees, for his grandfather to intercede for the more wayward of their relatives. "Like that Godfather in the movie," he would tell us as, his feet up, he distributed paychecks. Sometimes an employee would get two green envelopes instead of one, which meant that Jimmy needed a tooth pulled, say, or that Tiffany's husband was in the clinker again.

"It's nothing, nothing," he would insist, sinking back into his chair. "Who else is going to take care of you people?"

My mother would mostly just sigh about it. "Your father thinks this is China," she would say, and then she would go back to her mending. Once in a while, though, when my father had given away a particularly large sum, she would exclaim, outraged, "But this here is the U-S-of-A!"—this apparently having been what she used to tell immigrant stock boys when they came in late.

She didn't work at the supermarket anymore; but she had made it to the rank of manager before she left, and this had given her not only new words and phrases, but new ideas about herself, and about America, and about what was what in general. She had opinions, now, on how downtown should be zoned; she could pump her own gas and check her own oil; and for all she used to chide Mona and me for being "copycats," she herself was now interested in espadrilles, and wallpaper, and most recently, the town country club.

"So join already," said Mona, flicking a fly off her knee.

My mother enumerated the problems as she sliced up a quarter round of watermelon: there was the cost. There was the waiting list. There was the fact that no one in our family played either tennis or golf.

"So what?" said Mona.

"It would be waste," said my mother.

"Me and Callie can swim in the pool."

"Plus you need that recommendation letter from a member."

"Come *on,*" said Mona. "Annie's mom'd write you a letter in a *sec.*"

My mother's knife glinted in the early summer sun. I spread some more newspaper on the picnic table.

"*Plus* you have to eat there twice a month. You know what that means." My mother cut another, enormous slice of fruit.

"No, I *don't* know what that means," said Mona.

"It means Dad would have to wear a jacket, dummy," I said.

"Oh! Oh! Oh!" said Mona, clasping her hand to her breast. "Oh! Oh! Oh! Oh! Oh!"

We all laughed: my father had no use for nice clothes, and would wear only ten-year-old shirts, with grease-spotted pants, to show how little he cared what anyone thought.

"Your father doesn't believe in joining the American society," said my mother. "He wants to have his own society."

"So go to dinner without him." Mona shot her seeds out in long arcs over the lawn. "Who cares what he thinks?"

But of course we all did care, and knew my mother could not simply up and do as she pleased. For in my father's mind, a family owed its head a degree of loyalty that left no room for dissent. To embrace what he embraced was to love; and to embrace something else was to betray him.

He demanded a similar sort of loyalty of his workers, whom he treated more like servants than employees. Not in the beginning, of course. In the beginning all he wanted was for them to keep on doing what they used to do, and to that end he concentrated mostly on leaving them alone. As the months passed, though, he expected more and more of them, with the result that for all his largesse, he began to have trouble keeping help. The cooks and busboys complained that he asked them to fix radiators and trim hedges, not only at the restaurant, but at our house; the waitresses that he sent them on errands and made them chauffeur him around. Our head waitress, Gertrude, claimed that he once even asked her to scratch his back.

"It's not just the blacks don't believe in slavery," she said when she quit.

My father never quite registered her complaint, though, nor those of the others who left. Even after Eleanor quit, then Tiffany, then Gerald, and Jimmy, and even his best cook, Eureka Andy, for whom he had bought new glasses, he remained mostly convinced that the fault lay with them.

"All they understand is that assembly line," he lamented. "Robots, they are. They want to be robots."

There *were* occasions when the clear running truth seemed to eddy, when he would pinch the vinyl of his chair up into little peaks and wonder if he were doing things right. But with time he would always smooth the peaks back down; and when business started to slide in the spring, he kept on like a horse in his ways.

By the summer our dishboy was overwhelmed with scraping. It was no longer just the hashbrowns that people were leaving for trash, and the service was as bad as the food. The waitresses served up French pancakes instead of German, apple juice instead of orange, spilt things on laps, on coats. On the Fourth of July some greenhorn sent an entire side of fries slaloming down a lady's *massif centrale*. Meanwhile in the back room, my father labored through articles on the economy.

"What is housing starts?" he puzzled. "What is GNP?"

Mona and I did what we could, filling in as busgirls and bookkeepers and, one afternoon, stuffing the comments box that hung by the cashier's desk. That was Mona's idea. We rustled up a variety of pens and pencils, checked boxes for an hour, smeared the cards up with coffee and grease, and waited. It took a few days for my father to notice that the box was full, and he didn't say anything about it for a few days more. Finally, though, he started to complain of fatigue; and then he began to complain that the staff was not what it could be. We encouraged him in this—pointing out, for instance, how many dishes got chipped—but in the end all that happened was that, for the first time since we took over the restaurant, my father got it into his head to fire someone.

Skip, a skinny busboy who was saving up for a sports car, said nothing as my father mumbled on about the price of dishes. My father's hands shook as he wrote out the severance check; and he spent the rest of the day napping in his chair once it was over.

As it was going on midsummer, Skip wasn't easy to replace. We hung a sign in the window and advertised in the paper, but no one called the first week, and the person who called the second didn't show up for his interview. The third week, my father phoned Skip to see if he would come back, but a friend of his had already sold him a Corvette for cheap.

Finally a Chinese guy named Booker turned up. He couldn't have been more than thirty, and was wearing a lighthearted seersucker suit, but he looked as though life had him pinned: his eyes were bloodshot and his chest sunken, and the muscles of his neck seemed to strain with the effort of holding his head up. In a single dry breath he told us that he had never bussed tables but was willing to learn, and that he was on the lam from the deportation authorities.

"I do not want to lie to you," he kept saying. He had come to the United States on a student visa, had run out of money, and was now in a bind. He was loath to go back to Taiwan, as it happened—he looked up at this point, to be sure my father wasn't pro-KMT—but all he had was a phony social security card and a willingness to absorb all blame, should anything untoward come to pass.

"I do not think, anyway, that it is against law to hire me, only to be me," he said, smiling faintly.

Anyone else would have examined him on this, but my father conceived of laws as speed bumps rather than curbs. He wiped the counter with his sleeve, and told Booker to report the next morning.

"I will be good worker," said Booker.

"Good," said my father.

"Anything you want me to do, I will do."

My father nodded.

Booker seemed to sink into himself for a moment. "Thank you," he said finally. "I am appreciate your help. I am very, very appreciate for everything." He reached out to shake my father's hand.

My father looked at him. "Did you eat today?" he asked in Mandarin.

Booker pulled at the hem of his jacket.

"Sit down," said my father. "Please, have a seat."

My father didn't tell my mother about Booker, and my mother didn't tell my father about the country club. She would never have applied, except that Mona, while over at Annie's, had let it drop that our mother wanted to join. Mrs. Lardner came by the very next day.

"Why, I'd be honored and delighted to write you people a letter," she said. Her skirt billowed around her.

"Thank you so much," said my mother. "But it's too much trouble for you, and also my husband is . . ."

"Oh, it's no trouble at all, no trouble at all. I tell you." She leaned forward so that her chest freckles showed. "I know just how it is. It's a secret of course, but you know, my natural father was Jewish. Can you see it? Just look at my skin."

"My husband," said my mother.

"I'd be honored and delighted," said Mrs. Lardner with a little wave of her hands. "Just honored and delighted."

Mona was triumphant. "See, Mom," she said, waltzing around the kitchen when Mrs. Lardner left. "What did I tell you? 'I'm just honored and delighted, just honored and delighted.'" She waved her hands in the air.

"You know, the Chinese have a saying," said my mother. "To do nothing is better than to overdo. You mean well, but you tell me now what will happen."

"I'll talk Dad into it," said Mona, still waltzing. "Or I bet Callie can. He'll do anything Callie says."

"I can try, anyway," I said.

"Did you hear what I said?" said my mother. Mona bumped into the broom closet door. "You're not going to talk anything; you've already made enough trouble." She started on the dishes with a clatter.

Mona poked diffidently at a mop.

I sponged off the counter. "Anyway," I ventured, "I bet our name'll never even come up."

"That's if we're lucky," said my mother.

"There's all these people waiting," I said.

"Good," she said. She started on a pot.

I looked over at Mona, who was still cowering in the broom closet. "In fact, there's some black family's been waiting so long, they're going to sue," I said.

My mother turned off the water. "Where'd you hear that?"

"Patty told me."

She turned the water back on, started to wash a dish, then put it back down and shut the faucet.

"I'm sorry," said Mona.

"Forget it," said my mother. "Just forget it."

Booker turned out to be a model worker, whose boundless gratitude translated into a willingness to do anything. As he also learned quickly, he soon knew not only how to bus, but how to cook, and how to wait table, and how to keep the books. He fixed the walk-in door so that it stayed shut, reupholstered the torn seats in the dining room, and devised a system for tracking inventory. The only stone in the rice was that he tended to be sickly; but, reliable even in illness, he would always send a friend to take his place. In this way we got to know Ronald, Lynn, Dirk, and Cedric, all of whom, like Booker, had problems with their legal status and were anxious to please. They weren't all as capable as Booker, though, with the exception of Cedric, whom my father often hired even when Booker was well. A round wag of a man who called Mona and me *shou hou*—skinny monkeys—he was a professed nonsmoker who was nevertheless always begging drags off of other people's cigarettes. This last habit drove our head cook, Fernando, crazy, especially since, when refused a hit, Cedric would occasionally snitch one. Winking impishly at Mona and me, he would steal up to an ashtray, take a quick puff, and then break out laughing so that the smoke came rolling out of his mouth in a great incriminatory cloud. Fernando accused him of stealing fresh cigarettes too, even whole packs.

"Why else do you think he's weaseling around in the back of the store all the time," he said. His face was blotchy with anger. "The man is a frigging thief."

Other members of the staff supported him in this contention and joined in on an "Operation Identification," which involved numbering and initialing their cigarettes—even though what they seemed to fear for wasn't so much their cigarettes as their jobs. Then one of the cooks quit; and rather than promote someone, my father hired Cedric for the position. Rumors flew that he was taking only half the normal salary, that Alex had been pressured to resign, and that my father was looking for a position with which to placate Booker, who had been bypassed because of his health.

The result was that Fernando categorically refused to work with Cedric.

"The only way I'll cook with that piece of slime," he said, shaking his huge tattooed fist, "is if it's his ass frying on the grill."

My father cajoled and cajoled, to no avail, and in the end was simply forced to put them on different schedules.

The next week Fernando got caught stealing a carton of minute steaks. My father would not tell even Mona and me how he knew to be standing by the back door when Fernando was on his way out, but everyone suspected Booker. Everyone but Fernando, that is, who was sure Cedric had been the tip-off. My father held a staff meeting in which he tried to reassure everyone that Alex had left on his own, and that he had no intention of firing anyone. But though he was careful not to mention Fernando, everyone was so amazed that he was being allowed to stay that Fernando was incensed nonetheless.

"Don't you all be putting your bug eyes on me," he said. "*He's* the frigging crook." He grabbed Cedric by the collar.

Cedric raised an eyebrow. "Cook, you mean," he said.

At this Fernando punched Cedric in the mouth; and the words he had just uttered notwithstanding, my father fired him on the spot.

With everything that was happening, Mona and I were ready to be getting out of the restaurant. It was almost time: the days were still stuffy with summer, but our window shade had started flapping in the evening as if gearing up to go out. That year the breezes were full of salt, as they sometimes were when they came in from the East, and they blew anchors and docks through my mind like so many tumbleweeds, filling my dreams with wherries and lobsters and grainy-faced men who squinted, day in and day out, at the sky.

It was time for a change, you could feel it; and yet the pancake house was the same as ever. The day before school started my father came home with bad news.

"Fernando called police," he said, wiping his hand on his pant leg.

My mother naturally wanted to know what police; and so with much coughing and hawing, the long story began, the latest installment of which had the police calling immigration, and immigration sending an investigator. My mother sat stiff as whalebone as my father described how the man summarily refused lunch on the house and how my father had admitted, under pressure, that he knew there were "things" about his workers.

"So now what happens?"

My father didn't know. "Booker and Cedric went with him to the jail," he said. "But me, here I am." He laughed uncomfortably.

The next day my father posted bail for "his boys" and waited apprehensively for something to happen. The day after that he waited again, and the day after that he called our neighbor's law student son, who suggested my father call the immigration department under an alias. My father took his advice; and it was thus that he discovered that Booker was right: it was illegal for aliens to work, but it wasn't to hire them.

In the happy interval that ensued, my father apologized to my mother, who in turn confessed about the country club, for which my father had no choice but to forgive her. Then he turned his attention back to "his boys."

My mother didn't see that there was anything to do.

"I like to talking to the judge," said my father.

"This is not China," said my mother.

"I'm only talking to him. I'm not give him money unless he wants it."

"You're going to land up in jail."

"So what else I should do?" My father threw up his hands. "Those are my boys."

"Your boys!" exploded my mother. "What about your family? What about your wife?"

My father took a long sip of tea. "You know," he said finally. "In the war my father sent our cook to the soldiers to use. He always said it—the province comes before the town, the town comes before the family."

"A restaurant is not a town," said my mother.

My father sipped at his tea again. "You know, when I first come to the United States, I also had to hide-and-seek with those deportation guys. If people did not helping me, I'm not here today."

My mother scrutinized her hem.

After a minute I volunteered that before seeing a judge, he might try a lawyer.

He turned. "Since when did you become so afraid like your mother?"

I started to say that it wasn't a matter of fear, but he cut me off.

"What I need today," he said, "is a son."

My father and I spent the better part of the next day standing in lines at the immigration office. He did not get to speak to a judge, but with much persistence he managed to speak to a judge's clerk, who tried to persuade him that it was not her place to extend him advice. My father, though, shamelessly plied her with compliments and offers of free pancakes until she finally conceded that she personally doubted anything would happen to either Cedric or Booker.

"Especially if they're 'needed workers,'" she said, rubbing at the red marks her glasses left on her nose. She yawned. "Have you thought about sponsoring them to become permanent residents?"

Could he do that? My father was overjoyed. And what if he saw to it right away? Would she perhaps put in a good word with the judge?

She yawned again, her nostrils flaring. "Don't worry," she said. "They'll get a fair hearing."

My father returned jubilant. Booker and Cedric hailed him as their savior, their Buddha incarnate. He was like a father to them, they said; and laughing and clapping, they made him tell the story over and over, sorting over the details like jewels. And how old was the assistant judge? And what did she say?

That evening my father tipped the paperboy a dollar and bought a pot of mums for my mother, who suffered them to be placed on the dining room table. The next night he took us all out to dinner. Then on Saturday, Mona found a letter on my father's chair at the restaurant.

Dear Mr. Chang,

You are the grat boss. But, we do not like to trial, so will runing away now. Plese to excus us. People saying the law in America is fears like dragon. Here is only $140. We hope some day we can pay back the rest bale. You will getting interest, as you diserving, so grat a boss you are. Thank you for every thing. In next life you will be burn in rich family, with no more pancaks.

Yours truley,
Booker + Cedric

In the weeks that followed my father went to the pancake house for crises, but otherwise hung around our house, fiddling idly with the sump pump and boiler in an effort, he said, to get ready for winter. It was as though he had gone into retirement, except that instead of moving South, he had moved to the basement. He even took to showering my mother with little attentions, and to calling her "old girl," and when we finally heard that the club had entertained all the applications it could for the year, he was so sympathetic that he seemed more disappointed than my mother.

2. In the American Society

Mrs. Lardner tempered the bad news with an invitation to a bon voyage "bash" she was throwing for a friend of hers who was going to Greece for six months.

"Do come," she urged. "You'll meet everyone, and then, you know, if things open up in the spring . . ." She waved her hands.

My mother wondered if it would be appropriate to show up at a party for someone they didn't know, but "the honest truth" was that this was an annual affair. "If it's not Greece, it's Antibes," sighed Mrs. Lardner. "We really just do it because his wife left him and his daughter doesn't speak to him, and poor Jeremy just feels so *unloved*."

She also invited Mona and me to the goings-on, as "*demi*-guests" to keep Annie out of the champagne. I wasn't too keen on the idea, but before I could say anything, she had already thanked us for so generously agreeing to honor her with our presence.

"A pair of little princesses, you are!" she told us. "A pair of princesses!"

The party was that Sunday. On Saturday, my mother took my father out shopping for a suit. As it was the end of September, she insisted that he buy a worsted rather than a seersucker, even though it was only ten, rather than fifty percent off. My father protested that it was as hot out as ever, which was true—a thick Indian summer had cozied murderously up to us—but to no avail. Summer clothes, said my mother, were not properly worn after Labor Day.

The suit was unfortunately as extravagant in length as it was in price, which posed an additional quandary, since the tailor wouldn't be in until Monday. The salesgirl, though, found a way of tacking it up temporarily.

"Maybe this suit not fit me," fretted my father.

"Just don't take your jacket off," said the salesgirl.

He gave her a tip before they left, but when he got home refused to remove the price tag.

"I like to asking the tailor about the size," he insisted.

"You mean you're going to *wear* it and then return it?" Mona rolled her eyes.

"I didn't say I'm return it," said my father stiffly. "I like to asking the tailor, that's all."

The party started off swimmingly, except that most people were wearing bermudas or wrap skirts. Still, my parents carried on, sharing with great feeling the complaints about the heat. Of course my father tried to eat a cracker full of shallots and burnt himself in an attempt to help Mr. Lardner turn the coals of the barbeque; but on the whole he seemed to be doing all right. Not nearly so well as my mother, though, who had accepted an entire cupful of Mrs. Lardner's magic punch, and seemed indeed to be under some spell. As Mona and Annie skirmished over whether some boy in their class inhaled when he smoked, I watched my mother take off her shoes, laughing and laughing as a man with a beard regaled her with Navy stories by the pool. Apparently he had been stationed in the Orient and remembered a few words of Chinese, which made my mother laugh still more. My father excused himself to go to the men's room then drifted back and weighed anchor at the hors d'oeuvres table, while my mother sailed on to a group of women, who tinkled at length over the clarity of her complexion. I dug out a book I had brought.

Just when I'd cracked the spine, though, Mrs. Lardner came by to bewail her shortage of servers. Her caterers were criminals, I agreed; and the next thing I knew I was handing out bits of marine life, making the rounds as amicably as I could.

"Here you go, Dad," I said when I got to the hors d'oeuvres table.

"Everything is fine," he said.

I hesitated to leave him alone; but then the man with the beard zeroed in on him, and though he talked of nothing but my mother, I thought it would be okay to get back to work. Just that moment, though, Jeremy Brothers lurched our way, an empty, albeit corked, wine bottle in hand. He was a slim, well-proportioned man, with a Roman nose and small eyes and a nice manly jaw that he allowed to hang agape.

"Hello," he said drunkenly. "Pleased to meet you."

"Pleased to meeting you," said my father.

"Right," said Jeremy. "Right. Listen. I have this bottle here, this most recalcitrant bottle. You see that it refuses to do my bidding. I bid it open sesame, please, and it does nothing." He pulled the cork out with his teeth, then turned the bottle upside down.

My father nodded.

"Would you have a word with it please?" said Jeremy. The man with the beard excused himself. "Would you please have a goddamned word with it?"

My father laughed uncomfortably.

"Ah!" Jeremy bowed a little. "Excuse me, excuse me, excuse me. You are not my man, not my man at all." He bowed again and started to leave, but then circled back. "Viticulture is not your forte, yes I can see that, see that plainly. But may I trouble you on another matter? Forget the damned bottle." He threw it into the pool, and winked at the people he splashed. "I have another matter. Do you speak Chinese?"

My father said he did not, but Jeremy pulled out a handkerchief with some characters on it anyway, saying that his daughter had sent it from Hong Kong and that he thought the characters might be some secret message.

"Long life," said my father.

"But you haven't looked at it yet."

"I know what it says without looking." My father winked at me.

"You do?"

"Yes, I do."

"You're making fun of me, aren't you?"

"No, no, no," said my father, winking again.

"Who are you anyway?" said Jeremy.

His smile fading, my father shrugged.

"Who are you?"

My father shrugged again.

Jeremy began to roar. "This is my party, *my party,* and I've never seen you before in my life." My father backed up as Jeremy came toward him. "*Who are you?* WHO ARE YOU?"

Just as my father was going to step back into the pool, Mrs. Lardner came running up. Jeremy informed her that there was a man crashing his party.

"Nonsense," said Mrs. Lardner. "This is Ralph Chang, who I invited extra especially so he could meet you." She straightened the collar of Jeremy's peach-colored polo shirt for him.

"Yes, well we've had a chance to chat," said Jeremy.

She whispered in his ear; he mumbled something; she whispered something more.

"I do apologize," he said finally.

My father didn't say anything.

"I do." Jeremy seemed genuinely contrite. "Doubtless you've seen drunks before, haven't you? You must have them in China."

"Okay," said my father.

As Mrs. Lardner glided off, Jeremy clapped his arm over my father's shoulders. "You know, I really am quite sorry, quite sorry."

My father nodded.

"What can I do, how can I make it up to you?"

"No thank you."

"No, tell me, tell me," wheedled Jeremy. "Tickets to casino night?" My father shook his head. "You don't gamble. Dinner at Bartholomew's?" My father shook his head again. "You don't eat." Jeremy scratched his chin. "You know, my wife was like you. Old Annabelle could never let me make things up—never, never, never, never, never."

My father wriggled out from under his arm.

"How about sport clothes? You are rather overdressed, you know, excuse me for saying so. But here." He took off his polo shirt and folded it up. "You can have this with my most profound apologies." He ruffled his chest hairs with his free hand.

"No thank you," said my father.

"No, take it, take it. Accept my apologies." He thrust the shirt into my father's arms. "I'm so very sorry, so very sorry. Please, try it on."

Helplessly holding the shirt, my father searched the crowd for my mother.

"Here, I'll help you off with your coat."

My father froze.

Jeremy reached over and took his jacket off. "Milton's, one hundred twenty-five dollars reduced to one hundred twelve-fifty," he read. "What a bargain, what a bargain!"

"Please give it back," pleaded my father. "Please."

"Now for your shirt," ordered Jeremy.

Heads began to turn.

"Take off your shirt."

"I do not take orders like a servant," announced my father.

"Take off your shirt, or I'm going to throw this jacket right into the pool, just right into this little pool here." Jeremy held it over the water.

"Go ahead."

"One hundred twelve–fifty," taunted Jeremy. "One hundred twelve . . ."

My father flung the polo shirt into the water with such force that part of it bounced back up into the air like a fluorescent fountain. Then it settled into a soft heap on top of the water. My mother hurried up.

"You're a sport!" said Jeremy, suddenly breaking into a smile and slapping my father on the back. "You're a sport! I like that. A man with spirit, that's what you are. A man with panache. Allow me to return to you your jacket." He handed it back to my father. "Good value you got on that, good value."

My father hurled the coat into the pool too. "We're leaving," he said grimly. "Leaving!"

"Now, Ralphie," said Mrs. Lardner, bustling up; but my father was already stomping off.

"Get your sister," he told me. To my mother: "Get your shoes."

"That was *great*, Dad," said Mona as we walked down to the car. "You were *stupendous*."

"Way to show 'em," I said.

"What?" said my father offhandedly.

Although it was only just dusk, we were in a gulch, which made it hard to see anything except the gleam of his white shirt moving up the hill ahead of us.

"It was all my fault," began my mother.

"Forget it," said my father grandly. Then he said, "The only trouble is I left those keys in my jacket pocket."

"Oh *no*," said Mona.

"Oh no is right," said my mother.

"So we'll walk home," I said.

"But how're we going to get into the *house*," said Mona.

The noise of the party churned through the silence.

"Someone has to going back," said my father.

"Let's go to the pancake house first," suggested my mother. "We can wait there until the party is finished, and then call Mrs. Lardner."

Having all agreed that that was a good plan, we started walking again.

"God, just think," said Mona. "We're going to have to *dive* for them."

My father stopped a moment. We waited.

"You girls are good swimmers," he said finally. "Not like me."

Then his shirt started moving again, and we trooped up the hill after it, into the dark.

QUESTIONS FOR DISCUSSION AND WRITING

1. The first part of the story is called "His Own Society," presumably referring to the society that Ralph Chang creates and "owns" and in which he lives. How would you describe Ralph's relationships with his employees and his family? How is our view of his society influenced by the fact that we view it through the eyes of Ralph's daughter?

2. The second part of the story is called "In the American Society." How does the second part relate to the first part? The story as a whole is also called "In the American Society," which might give added weight to the second half. Why are the title and subtitle the same?

3. Callie and Mona are clearly more Americanized than their parents. How do the two generations look at things differently?

4. In what ways is the Chang family living the American dream? In what ways are they outsiders not fully assimilated into (accepted by or accepting of) American society?

D. H. LAWRENCE (1885–1930)

The Rocking-Horse Winner 1926

There was a woman who was beautiful, who started with all the advantages, yet she had no luck. She married for love, and the love turned to dust. She had bonny children, yet she felt they had been thrust upon her, and she could not love them. They looked at her coldly, as if they were finding fault with her. And hurriedly she felt she must cover up some fault in herself. Yet what it was that she must cover up she never knew. Nevertheless, when her children were present, she always felt the center of her heart go hard. This troubled her, and in her manner she was all the more gentle and anxious for her children, as if she loved them very much. Only she herself knew that at the center of her heart was a hard little place that could not feel love, no, not for anybody. Everybody else said of her: "She is such a good mother. She adores her children." Only she herself, and her children themselves, knew it was not so. They read it in each other's eyes.

There were a boy and two little girls. They lived in a pleasant house, with a garden, and they had discreet servants, and felt themselves superior to anyone in the neighborhood.

Although they lived in style, they felt always an anxiety in the house. There was never enough money. The mother had a small income, and the father had a small income, but not nearly enough for the social position which they had to keep up. The father went into town to some office. But though he had good prospects, these prospects never materialized. There was always the grinding sense of the shortage of money, though the style was always kept up.

At last the mother said: "I will see if *I* can't make something." But she did not know where to begin. She racked her brains, and tried this thing and the other, but could not find anything successful. The failure made deep lines come into her face. Her children were growing up, they would have to go to school. There must be more money, there must be more money. The father, who was always very handsome and expensive in his tastes, seemed as if he never *would* be able to do anything worth doing. And the mother, who had a great belief in herself, did not succeed any better, and her tastes were just as expensive.

And so the house came to be haunted by the unspoken phrase: *There must be more money! There must be more money!* The children could hear it all the time though nobody said it aloud. They heard it at Christmas, when the expensive and splendid toys filled the nursery. Behind the shining modern rocking horse, behind the smart doll's house, a voice would start whispering: "There *must* be more money! There *must* be more money!" And the children would stop playing, to listen for a moment. They would look into each other's eyes, to see if they had all heard. And each one saw in the eyes of the other two that they too had heard. "There *must* be more money! There *must* be more money!"

It came whispering from the springs of the still-swaying rocking horse, and even the horse, bending his wooden, champing head, heard it. The big doll, sitting so pink and smirking in her new pram, could hear it quite plainly, and seemed to be smirking all the more self-consciously because of it. The foolish puppy, too, that took the place of the teddy bear, he was looking so extraordinarily foolish for no other reason but that he heard the secret whisper all over the house: "There *must* be more money!"

Yet nobody ever said it aloud. The whisper was everywhere, and therefore no one spoke it. Just as no one ever says: "We are breathing!" in spite of the fact that breath is coming and going all the time.

"Mother," said the boy Paul one day, "why don't we keep a car of our own? Why do we always use Uncle's, or else a taxi?"

"Because we're the poor members of the family," said the mother.

"But why *are* we, Mother?"

"Well—I suppose," she said slowly and bitterly, "it's because your father has no luck."

The boy was silent for some time.

"Is luck money, Mother?" he asked rather timidly.

"No, Paul. Not quite. It's what causes you to have money."

"Oh!" said Paul vaguely. "I thought when Uncle Oscar said *filthy lucker,* it meant money."

"*Filthy lucre* does mean money," said the mother. "But it's lucre, not luck."

"Oh!" said the boy. "Then what *is* luck, Mother?"

"It's what causes you to have money. If you're lucky you have money. That's why it's better to be born lucky than rich. If you're rich, you may lose your money. But if you're lucky, you will always get more money."

"Oh! Will you? And is Father not lucky?"

"Very unlucky, I should say," she said bitterly.

The boy watched her with unsure eyes.

"Why?" he asked.

"I don't know. Nobody ever knows why one person is lucky and another unlucky."

"Don't they? Nobody at all? Does *nobody* know?"

"Perhaps God. But He never tells."

"He ought to, then. And aren't you lucky either, Mother?"

"I can't be, if I married an unlucky husband."

"But by yourself, aren't you?"

"I used to think I was, before I married. Now I think I am very unlucky indeed."

"Why?"

"Well—never mind! Perhaps I'm not really," she said.

The child looked at her, to see if she meant it. But he saw, by the lines of her mouth, that she was only trying to hide something from him.

"Well, anyhow," he said stoutly, "I'm a lucky person."

"Why?" said his mother, with a sudden laugh.

He stared at her. He didn't even know why he had said it.

"God told me," he asserted, brazening it out.

"I hope He did, dear!" she said, again with a laugh, but rather bitter.

"He did, Mother!"

"Excellent!" said the mother.

The boy saw she did not believe him; or, rather, that she paid no attention to his assertion. This angered him somewhat, and made him want to compel her attention.

He went off by himself, vaguely, in a childish way, seeking for the clue to "luck." Absorbed, taking no heed of other people, he went about with a sort of stealth, seeking inwardly for luck. He wanted luck, he wanted it, he wanted it. When the two girls were playing dolls in the nursery, he would sit on his big rocking horse, charging madly into space, with a frenzy that made the little girls peer at him uneasily. Wildly the horse careered, the waving dark hair of the boy tossed, his eyes had a strange glare in them. The little girls dared not speak to him.

When he had ridden to the end of his mad little journey, he climbed down and stood in front of his rocking horse, staring fixedly into its lowered face. Its red mouth was slightly open, its big eye was wide and glassy-bright.

Now! he could silently command the snorting steed. Now, take me to where there is luck! Now take me!

And he would slash the horse on the neck with the little whip he had asked Uncle Oscar for. He *knew* the horse could take him to where there was luck, if only he forced it. So he would mount again, and start on his furious ride, hoping at last to get there. He knew he could get there.

"You'll break your horse, Paul!" said the nurse.

"He's always riding like that! I wish he'd leave off!" said his elder sister Joan.

But he only glared down on them in silence. Nurse gave him up. She could make nothing of him. Anyhow he was growing beyond her.

One day his mother and his uncle Oscar came in when he was on one of his furious rides. He did not speak to them.

"Hallo, you young jockey! Riding a winner?" said his uncle.

"Aren't you growing too big for a rocking horse? You're not a very little boy any longer, you know," said his mother.

But Paul only gave a blue glare from his big, rather close-set eyes. He would speak to nobody when he was in full tilt. His mother watched him with an anxious expression on her face.

At last he suddenly stopped forcing his horse into the mechanical gallop, and slid down.

"Well, I got there!" he announced fiercely, his blue eyes still flaring, and his sturdy long legs straddling apart.

"Where did you get to?" asked his mother.

"Where I wanted to go," he flared back at her.

"That's right, son!" said Uncle Oscar. "Don't you stop till you get there. What's the horse's name?"

"He doesn't have a name," said the boy.

"Gets on without all right?" asked the uncle.

"Well, he has different names. He was called Sansovino last week."

"Sansovino, eh? Won the Ascot. How did you know his name?"

"He always talks about horse races with Bassett," said Joan.

The uncle was delighted to find that his small nephew was posted with all the racing news. Bassett, the young gardener, who had been wounded in the left foot in the war and had got his present job through Oscar Cresswell, whose batman he had been, was a perfect blade of the "turf." He lived in the racing events, and the small boy lived with him.

Oscar Cresswell got it all from Bassett.

"Master Paul comes and asks me, so I can't do more than tell him, sir," said Bassett, his face terribly serious, as if he were speaking of religious matters.

"And does he ever put anything on a horse he fancies?"

"Well—I don't want to give him away—he's a young sport, a fine sport, sir. Would you mind asking him himself? He sort of takes a pleasure in it, and perhaps he'd feel I was giving him away, sir, if you don't mind."

Bassett was serious as a church.

The uncle went back to his nephew and took him off for a ride in the car.

"Say, Paul, old man, do you ever put anything on a horse?" the uncle asked.

The boy watched the handsome man closely.

"Why, do you think I oughtn't to?" he parried.

"Not a bit of it! I thought perhaps you might give me a tip for the Lincoln."

The car sped on into the country, going down to Uncle Oscar's place in Hampshire.

"Honor bright?" said the nephew.

"Honor bright, son!" said the uncle.

"Well, then, Daffodil."

"Daffodil! I doubt it, sonny. What about Mirza?"

"I only know the winner," said the boy. "That's Daffodil."

"Daffodil, eh?"

There was a pause. Daffodil was an obscure horse comparatively.

"Uncle!"

"Yes, son?"

"You won't let it go any further, will you? I promised Bassett."

"Bassett be damned, old man! What's he got to do with it?"

"We're partners. We've been partners from the first. Uncle, he lent me my first five shillings, which I lost. I promised him, honor bright, it was only between me and him; only you gave me that ten-shilling note I started winning with, so I thought you were lucky. You won't let it go any further, will you?"

The boy gazed at his uncle from those big, hot, blue eyes, set rather close together. The uncle stirred and laughed uneasily.

"Right you are, son! I'll keep your tip private. Daffodil, eh? How much are you putting on him?"

"All except twenty pounds," said the boy. "I keep that in reserve."

The uncle thought it a good joke.

"You keep twenty pounds in reserve, do you, you young romancer? What are you betting, then?"

"I'm betting three hundred," said the boy gravely. "But it's between you and me, Uncle Oscar! Honor bright?"

The uncle burst into a roar of laughter.

"It's between you and me all right, you young Nat Gould," he said, laughing. "But where's your three hundred?"

"Bassett keeps it for me. We're partners."

"You are, are you! And what is Bassett putting on Daffodil?"

"He won't go quite as high as I do, I expect. Perhaps he'll go a hundred and fifty."

"What, pennies?" laughed the uncle.

"Pounds," said the child, with a surprised look at his uncle. "Bassett keeps a bigger reserve than I do."

Between wonder and amusement Uncle Oscar was silent. He pursued the matter no further, but he determined to take his nephew with him to the Lincoln races.

"Now, son," he said, "I'm putting twenty on Mirza, and I'll put five for you on any horse you fancy. What's your pick?"

"Daffodil, Uncle."

"No, not the fiver on Daffodil!"

"I should if it was my own fiver," said the child.

"Good! Good! Right you are! A fiver for me and a fiver for you on Daffodil."

The child had never been to a race meeting before, and his eyes were blue fire. He pursed his mouth tight, and watched. A Frenchman just in front had put his money on Lancelot. Wild with excitement, he flailed his arms up and down, yelling *Lancelot! Lancelot!* in his French accent.

Daffodil came in first, Lancelot second, Mirza third. The child, flushed and with eyes blazing, was curiously serene. His uncle brought him four five-pound notes, four to one.

"What am I to do with these?" he cried, waving them before the boy's eyes.

"I suppose we'll talk to Bassett," said the boy. "I expect I have fifteen hundred now; and twenty in reserve; and this twenty."

His uncle studied him for some moments.

"Look here, son!" he said. "You're not serious about Bassett and that fifteen hundred, are you?"

"Yes, I am. But it's between you and me, Uncle. Honor bright!"

"Honor bright all right, son! But I must talk to Bassett."

"If you'd like to be a partner, Uncle, with Bassett and me, we could all be partners. Only, you'd have to promise, honor bright, Uncle, not to let it go beyond us three. Bassett and I are lucky, and you must be lucky, because it was your ten shillings I started winning with . . ."

Uncle Oscar took both Bassett and Paul into Richmond Park for an afternoon, and there they talked.

"It's like this, you see, sir," Bassett said. "Master Paul would get me talking about racing events, spinning yarns, you know, sir. And he was always keen on knowing if I'd made or if I'd lost. It's about a year since, now, that I put five shillings on Blush of Dawn for him—and we lost. Then the luck turned, with that ten shillings he had from you, that we put on Singhalese. And since then, it's been pretty steady, all things considering. What do you say, Master Paul?"

"We're all right when we're sure," said Paul. "It's when we're not quite sure that we go down."

"Oh, but we're careful then," said Bassett.

"But when are you *sure*?" Uncle Oscar smiled.

"It's Master Paul, sir," said Bassett, in a secret, religious voice. "It's as if he had it from heaven. Like Daffodil, now, for the Lincoln. That was as sure as eggs."

"Did you put anything on Daffodil?" asked Oscar Cresswell.

"Yes, sir. I made my bit."

"And my nephew?"

Bassett was obstinately silent, looking at Paul.

"I made twelve hundred, didn't I, Bassett? I told Uncle I was putting three hundred on Daffodil."

"That's right," said Bassett, nodding.

"But where's the money?" asked the uncle.

"I keep it safe locked up, sir. Master Paul he can have it any minute he likes to ask for it."

"What, fifteen hundred pounds?"

"And twenty! And *forty*, that is, with the twenty he made on the course."

"It's amazing!" said the uncle.

"If Master Paul offers you to be partners, sir, I would, if I were you; if you'll excuse me," said Bassett.

Oscar Cresswell thought about it.

"I'll see the money," he said.

They drove home again, and sure enough, Bassett came round to the garden house with fifteen hundred pounds in notes. The twenty pounds reserve was left with Joe Glee, in the Turf Commission deposit.

"You see, it's all right, Uncle, when I'm *sure!* Then we go strong, for all we're worth. Don't we, Bassett?"

"We do that, Master Paul."

"And when are you sure?" said the uncle, laughing.

"Oh, well, sometimes I'm *absolutely* sure, like about Daffodil," said the boy; "and sometimes I have an idea; and sometimes I haven't even an idea, have I, Bassett? Then we're careful, because we mostly go down."

"You do, do you! And when you're sure, like about Daffodil, what makes you sure, sonny?"

"Oh, well, I don't know," said the boy uneasily. "I'm sure, you know, Uncle; that's all."

"It's as if he had it from heaven, sir," Bassett reiterated.

"I should say so!" said the uncle.

But he became a partner. And when the Leger was coming on, Paul was "sure" about Lively Spark, which was a quite inconsiderable horse. The boy insisted on putting a thousand on the horse, Bassett went for five hundred, and Oscar Cresswell two hundred. Lively Spark came in first, and the betting had been ten to one against him. Paul had made ten thousand.

"You see," he said, "I was absolutely sure of him."

Even Oscar Cresswell had cleared two thousand.

"Look here, son," he said, "this sort of thing makes me nervous."

"It needn't Uncle! Perhaps I shan't be sure again for a long time."

"But what are you going to do with your money?" asked the uncle.

"Of course," said the boy. "I started it for Mother. She said she had no luck, because Father is unlucky, so I thought if *I* was lucky, it might stop whispering."

"What might stop whispering?"

"Our house. I *hate* our house for whispering."

"What does it whisper?"

"Why—why"—the boy fidgeted—"why, I don't know. But it's always short of money, you know, Uncle."

"I know it, son, I know it."

"You know people send Mother writs, don't you, Uncle?"

"I'm afraid I do," said the uncle.

"And then the house whispers, like people laughing at you behind your back. It's awful, that is! I thought if I was lucky . . ."

"You might stop it," added the uncle.

The boy watched him with big blue eyes, that had an uncanny cold fire in them, and he said never a word.

"Well, then!" said the uncle. "What are we doing?"

"I shouldn't like Mother to know I was lucky," said the boy.

"Why not, son?"

"She'd stop me."

"I don't think she would."

"Oh!"—and the boy writhed in an odd way—"I *don't* want her to know, Uncle."

"All right, son! We'll manage it without her knowing."

They managed it very easily. Paul, at the other's suggestion, handed over five thousand pounds to his uncle, who deposited it with the family lawyer, who was then to inform Paul's mother that a relative had put five thousand pounds into his hands, which sum was to be paid out a thousand pounds at a time, on the mother's birthday, for the next five years.

"So she'll have a birthday present of a thousand pounds for five successive years," said Uncle Oscar. "I hope it won't make it all the harder for her later."

Paul's mother had her birthday in November. The house had been "whispering" worse than ever lately, and, even in spite of his luck, Paul could not bear up against it. He was very anxious to see the effect of the birthday letter, telling his mother about the thousand pounds.

When there were no visitors, Paul now took his meals with his parents, as he was beyond the nursery control. His mother went into town nearly every day. She had discovered that she had an odd knack of sketching furs and dress materials, so she worked secretly in the studio of a friend who was the chief artist for the leading drapers. She drew the figures of ladies in furs and ladies in silk and sequins for the newspaper advertisements. This young woman artist earned several thousand pounds a year, but Paul's mother only made several hundreds, and she was again dissatisfied. She so wanted to be first in something, and she did not succeed, even in making sketches for drapery advertisements.

She was down to breakfast on the morning of her birthday. Paul watched her face as she read her letters. He knew the lawyer's letter. As his mother read it, her face hardened and became more expressionless. Then a cold, determined look came on her mouth. She hid the letter under the pile of others, and said not a word about it.

"Didn't you have anything nice in the post for your birthday, Mother?" said Paul.

"Quite moderately nice," she said, her voice cold and absent.

She went away to town without saying more.

But in the afternoon Uncle Oscar appeared. He said Paul's mother had had a long interview with the lawyer, asking if the whole five thousand could not be advanced at once, as she was in debt.

"What do you think, Uncle?" said the boy.

"I leave it to you, son."

"Oh, let her have it, then! We can get some more with the other," said the boy.

"A bird in the hand is worth two in the bush, laddie!" said Uncle Oscar.

"But I'm sure to *know* for the Grand National; or the Lincolnshire; or else the Derby. I'm sure to know for *one* of them," said Paul.

So Uncle Oscar signed the agreement, and Paul's mother touched the whole five thousand. Then something very curious happened. The voices in the house suddenly went mad, like a chorus of frogs on a spring evening. There were certain new furnishings, and Paul had a tutor. He was *really* going to Eton, his father's school, in the following autumn. There were flowers in the winter, and a blossoming of the luxury Paul's mother had been used to. And yet the voices in the house, behind the sprays of mimosa and almond blossom, and from under the piles of iridescent cushions, simply trilled and screamed in a sort of ecstasy: "There *must* be more money! Oh-h-h; there *must* be more money. Oh, now, now-w! Now-w-w—there *must* be more money!—more than ever! More than ever!"

It frightened Paul terribly. He studied away at his Latin and Greek. But his intense hours were spent with Bassett. The Grand National had gone by; he had not "known," and had lost a hundred pounds. Summer was at hand. He was in agony for the Lincoln. But even for the Lincoln he didn't "know," and he lost fifty pounds. He became wild-eyed and strange, as if something were going to explode in him.

"Let it alone, son! Don't you bother about it!" urged Uncle Oscar. But it was as if the boy couldn't really hear what his uncle was saying.

"I've got to know for the Derby! I've got to know for the Derby!" the child reiterated, his big blue eyes blazing with a sort of madness.

His mother noticed how overwrought he was.

"You'd better go to the seaside. Wouldn't you like to go now to the seaside, instead of waiting? I think you'd better," she said, looking down at him anxiously, her heart curiously heavy because of him.

But the child lifted his uncanny blue eyes. "I couldn't possibly go before the Derby, Mother!" he said. "I couldn't possibly!"

"Why not?" she said, her voice becoming heavy when she was opposed. "Why not? You can still go from the seaside to see the Derby with your uncle Oscar, if that's what you wish. No need for you to wait here. Besides, I think you care too much about these races. It's a bad sign. My family has been a gambling family, and you won't know till you grow up how much damage it has done. But it has done damage. I shall have to send Bassett away, and ask Uncle Oscar not to talk racing to you, unless you promise to be reasonable about it; go away to the seaside and forget it. You're all nerves!"

"I'll do what you like, Mother, so long as you don't send me away till after the Derby," the boy said.

"Send you away from where? Just from this house?"

"Yes," he said, gazing at her.

"Why, you curious child, what makes you care about this house so much, suddenly? I never knew you loved it."

He gazed at her without speaking. He had a secret within a secret, something he had not divulged, even to Bassett or to his uncle Oscar.

But his mother, after standing undecided and a little bit sullen for some moments, said:

"Very well, then! Don't go to the seaside till after the Derby, if you don't wish it. But promise me you won't let your nerves go to pieces. Promise you won't think so much about horse racing and *events,* as you call them!"

"Oh, no," said the boy casually. "I won't think much about them, Mother. You needn't worry. I wouldn't worry, Mother, if I were you."

"If you were me and I were you," said his mother, "I wonder what we *should* do!"

"But you know you needn't worry, Mother, don't you?" the boy repeated.

"I should be awfully glad to know it," she said wearily.

"Oh, well you *can,* you know. I mean, you *ought* to know you needn't worry," he insisted.

"Ought I? Then I'll see about it," she said.

Paul's secret of secrets was his wooden horse, that which had no name. Since he was emancipated from a nurse and a nursery governess, he had had his rocking horse removed to his own bedroom at the top of the house.

"Surely, you're too big for a rocking horse!" his mother had remonstrated.

"Well, you see, Mother, till I can have a *real* horse, I like to have *some* sort of animal about," had been his quaint answer.

"Do you feel he keeps you company?" She laughed.

"Oh, yes! He's very good, he always keeps me company, when I'm there," said Paul. So the horse, rather shabby, stood in an arrested prance in the boy's bedroom.

The Derby was drawing near, and the boy grew more and more tense. He hardly heard what was spoken to him, he was very frail, and his eyes were really uncanny. His mother had sudden strange seizures of uneasiness about him. Sometimes, for half an hour, she would feel a sudden anxiety about him that was almost anguish. She wanted to rush to him at once, and know he was safe.

Two nights before the Derby, she was at a big party in town, when one of her rushes of anxiety about her boy, her firstborn, gripped her heart till she could hardly speak. She fought with the feeling, might and main, for she believed in common sense. But it was too strong. She had to leave the dance and go downstairs to telephone to the country. The children's nursery governess was terribly surprised and startled at being rung up in the night.

"Are the children all right, Miss Wilmot?"

"Oh, yes, they are quite all right."

"Master Paul? Is he all right?"

"He went to bed as right as a trivet. Shall I run up and look at him?"

"No," said Paul's mother reluctantly. "No! Don't trouble. It's all right. Don't sit up. We shall be home fairly soon." She did not want her son's privacy intruded upon.

"Very good," said the governess.

It was about one o'clock when Paul's mother and father drove up to their house. All was still. Paul's mother went to her room and slipped off her white fur cloak. She had told her maid not to wait up for her. She heard her husband downstairs, mixing a whisky and soda.

And then, because of the strange anxiety at her heart, she stole upstairs to her son's room. Noiselessly she went along the upper corridor. Was there a faint noise? What was it?

She stood, with arrested muscles, outside his door, listening. There was a strange, heavy, and yet not loud noise. Her heart stood still. It was a soundless noise, yet rushing and powerful. Something huge, in violent, hushed motion. What was it? What in God's name was it? She ought to know. She felt that she knew the noise. She knew what it was.

Yet she could not place it. She couldn't say what it was. And on and on it went, like a madness.

Softly, frozen with anxiety and fear, she turned the door handle.

The room was dark. Yet in the space near the window, she heard and saw something plunging to and fro. She gazed in fear and amazement.

Then suddenly she switched on the light, and saw her son, in his green pajamas, madly surging on the rocking horse. The blaze of light suddenly lit him up, as he urged the wooden horse, and lit her up, as she stood, blonde, in her dress of pale green and crystal, in the doorway.

"Paul!" she cried. "Whatever are you doing?"

"It's Malabar!" he screamed, in a powerful, strange voice. "It's Malabar!"

His eyes blazed at her for one strange and senseless second, as he ceased urging his wooden horse. Then he fell with a crash to the ground, and she, all her tormented motherhood flooding upon her, rushed to gather him up.

But he was unconscious, and unconscious he remained, with some brain fever. He talked and tossed, and his mother sat stonily by his side.

"Malabar! It's Malabar! Bassett, Bassett, I *know*! It's Malabar!"

So the child cried, trying to get up and urge the rocking horse that gave him his inspiration.

"What does he mean by Malabar?" asked the heart-frozen mother.

"I don't know," said the father stonily.

"What does he mean by Malabar?" she asked her brother Oscar.

"It's one of the horses running for the Derby," was the answer.

And, in spite of himself, Oscar Cresswell spoke to Bassett, and himself put a thousand on Malabar: at fourteen to one.

The third day of the illness was critical: they were waiting for a change. The boy, with his rather long, curly hair, was tossing ceaselessly on the pillow. He never slept nor regained consciousness, and his eyes were like blue stones. His mother sat, feeling her heart had gone, turned actually into a stone.

In the evening, Oscar Cresswell did not come, but Bassett sent a message, saying could he come up for one moment, just one moment? Paul's mother was very angry at the intrusion, but on second thought she agreed. The boy was the same. Perhaps Bassett might bring him to consciousness.

The gardener, a shortish fellow with a little brown mustache, and sharp little brown eyes, tiptoed into the room, touched his imaginary cap to Paul's mother, and stole to the bedside, staring with glittering, smallish eyes at the tossing, dying child.

"Master Paul!" he whispered. "Master Paul! Malabar came in first all right, a clean win. I did as you told me. You've made over seventy thousand pounds, you have; you've got over eighty thousand. Malabar came in all right, Master Paul."

"Malabar! Malabar! Did I say Malabar, Mother? Did I say Malabar? Do you think I'm lucky, Mother? I knew Malabar, didn't I? Over eighty thousand pounds! I call that lucky, don't you, Mother? Over eighty thousand pounds! I knew, didn't I know I knew? Malabar came in all right. If I ride my horse till I'm sure, then I tell you, Bassett, you can go as high as you like. Did you go for all you were worth, Bassett?"

"I went a thousand on it, Master Paul."

"I never told you, Mother, that if I can ride my horse, and *get there,* then I'm absolutely sure—oh, absolutely! Mother, did I ever tell you? I *am* lucky!"

"No, you never did," said the mother.

But the boy died in the night.

And even as he lay dead, his mother heard her brother's voice saying to her: "My God, Hester, you're eighty-odd thousand to the good, and a poor devil of a son to the bad. But, poor devil, poor devil, he's best gone out of a life where he rides his rocking horse to find a winner."

QUESTIONS FOR DISCUSSION AND WRITING

1. Both Paul and his mother are very concerned with "luck." What ideas do they associate with "luck"? How much are we meant to value the same "lucky" things and ideas that they value? To what extent do we share their conclusions about how lucky and unlucky they are?
2. Does Paul's mother love him? Does he think she loves him? Why or why not?
3. Why is it so important to Paul to pick the winning horses?
4. The rocking horse is called "modern." In what ways is this a modern family with modern values and problems? How does Lawrence want us to respond to those values and problems?

TIM O'BRIEN (1947–   )
The Things They Carried _____ *1986*

First Lieutenant Jimmy Cross carried letters from a girl named Martha, a junior at Mount Sebastian College in New Jersey. They were not love letters, but Lieutenant Cross was hoping, so he kept them folded in plastic at the bottom of his rucksack. In the late afternoon, after a day's march, he would dig his foxhole, wash his hands under a canteen, unwrap the letters, hold them with the tips of his fingers, and spend the last hour of light pretending. He would imagine romantic camping trips into the White Mountains in New Hampshire. He would sometimes taste the envelope flaps, knowing her tongue had been there. More than anything, he wanted Martha to love him as he loved her, but the letters were mostly chatty, elusive on the matter of love. She was a virgin, he was almost sure. She was an English major at Mount Sebastian, and she wrote beautifully about her professors and roommates and midterm exams, about her respect for Chaucer and her great affection for Virginia Woolf. She often quoted lines of poetry; she never mentioned the war, except to say, Jimmy, take care of yourself. The letters weighed ten ounces. They were signed "Love, Martha," but Lieutenant Cross understood that "Love" was only a way of signing and did not mean what he sometimes pretended it meant. At dusk, he would carefully return the letters to his rucksack. Slowly, a bit distracted, he would get up and move among his men, checking the perimeter, then at full dark he would return to his hole and watch the night and wonder if Martha was a virgin.

The things they carried were largely determined by necessity. Among the necessities or near necessities were P-38 can openers, pocket knives, heat tabs, wrist watches, dog tags, mosquito repellant, chewing gum, candy, cigarettes, salt tablets, packets of Kool-Aid, lighters, matches, sewing kits, Military Payment Certificates, C rations, and two or three canteens of water. Together, these items weighed between fifteen and twenty pounds, depending upon a man's habits or rate of metabolism. Henry Dobbins, who was a big man, carried extra rations; he was especially fond of canned peaches in heavy syrup over pound cake. Dave Jensen, who practiced field hygiene, carried a toothbrush, dental floss, and several hotel-size bars of soap he'd stolen on R&R in Sydney, Australia. Ted Lavender, who was scared, carried tranquilizers until he was shot in the head outside the village of Than Khe in mid-April. By necessity, and because it was SOP, they all carried steel helmets that weighed five pounds including the liner and camouflage cover. They carried the standard fatigue jackets and trousers. Very few carried underwear. On their feet they carried jungle boots— 2.1 pounds—and Dave Jensen carried three pairs of socks and a can of Dr. Scholl's foot powder as a precaution against trench foot. Until he was shot, Ted Lavender carried six or seven ounces of premium dope, which for him was a necessity. Mitchell Sanders, the RTO, carried condoms. Norman Bowker carried a diary. Rat Kiley carried comic books. Kiowa, a devout Baptist, carried an illustrated New Testament that had been presented to him by his father, who taught Sunday school in Oklahoma City, Oklahoma. As a hedge against bad times, however, Kiowa also carried his grandmother's distrust of the white man, his grandfather's old hunting hatchet. Necessity dictated. Because the land was mined and booby-trapped, it was SOP for each man to carry a steel-centered, nylon-covered flak jacket, which weighed 6.7 pounds, but which on hot days seemed much heavier. Because you could die so quickly, each man carried at least one large compress bandage, usually in the helmet band for easy access. Because the nights were cold, and because the monsoons were wet, each carried a green plastic poncho that could be used as a raincoat or ground sheet or makeshift tent. With its quilted liner, the poncho weighed almost two pounds, but it was worth every ounce. In April, for instance, when Ted Lavender was shot, they used his poncho to wrap him up, then to carry him across the paddy, then to lift him into the chopper that took him away.

They were called legs or grunts.

To carry something was to "hump" it, as when Lieutenant Jimmy Cross humped his love for Martha up the hills and through the swamps. In its intransitive form, "to hump" meant "to walk," or "to march," but it implied burdens far beyond the intransitive.

Almost everyone humped photographs. In his wallet, Lieutenant Cross carried two photographs of Martha. The first was a Kodachrome snapshot signed "Love," though he knew better. She stood against a brick wall. Her eyes were gray and neutral, her lips slightly open as she stared straight-on at the camera. At night, sometimes, Lieutenant Cross wondered who had taken the picture, because he knew she had boyfriends, because he loved her so much, and because he could see the shadow of the picture taker spreading out against the brick wall. The second photograph had been clipped from the 1968 Mount Sebastian yearbook. It was an action shot—women's volleyball—and Martha was bent horizontal to the floor, reaching, the palms of her hands in sharp focus, the tongue taut, the expression frank and competitive. There was no visible sweat. She wore white gym shorts. Her legs, he thought, were almost certainly the legs of a virgin, dry and without hair, the left knee cocked and carrying her entire weight, which was just over one hundred pounds. Lieutenant Cross remembered touching that left knee. A dark theater, he remembered, and the movie was *Bonnie and Clyde,* and Martha wore a tweed skirt, and during the final scene, when he touched her knee, she turned and looked at him in a sad, sober way that made him pull his hand back, but he would always remember the feel of the tweed skirt and the knee beneath it and the sound of the gunfire that killed Bonnie and Clyde, how embarrassing it was, how slow and oppressive. He remembered kissing her good night at the dorm door. Right then, he thought, he should've done something brave. He should've carried her up the stairs to her room and tied her to the bed and touched that left knee all night long. He should've risked it. Whenever he looked at the photographs, he thought of new things he should've done.

What they carried was partly a function of rank, partly of field specialty.

As a first lieutenant and platoon leader, Jimmy Cross carried a compass, maps, code books, binoculars, and a .45-caliber pistol that weighed 2.9 pounds fully loaded. He carried a strobe light and the responsibility for the lives of his men.

As an RTO, Mitchell Sanders carried the PRC-25 radio, a killer, twenty-six pounds with its battery.

As a medic, Rat Kiley carried a canvas satchel filled with morphine and plasma and malaria tablets and surgical tape and comic books and all the things a medic must carry, including M&M's for especially bad wounds, for a total weight of nearly twenty pounds.

As a big man, therefore a machine gunner, Henry Dobbins carried the M-60, which weighed twenty-three pounds unloaded, but which was almost always loaded. In addition, Dobbins carried between ten and fifteen pounds of ammunition draped in belts across his chest and shoulders.

As PFCs or Spec 4s, most of them were common grunts and carried the standard M-16 gas-operated assault rifle. The weapon weighed 7.5 pounds unloaded, 8.2 pounds with its full twenty-round magazine. Depending on numerous factors, such as topography and psychology, the riflemen carried anywhere from twelve to twenty magazines, usually in cloth bandoliers, adding on another 8.4 pounds at minimum, fourteen pounds at maximum. When it was available, they also carried M-16 maintenance gear—rods and steel brushes and swabs and tubes of LSA oil—all of which weighed about a pound. Among the grunts, some carried the M-79 grenade launcher, 5.9 pounds unloaded, a reasonably light weapon except for the ammunition, which was heavy. A single round weighed ten ounces. The typical load was twenty-five rounds. But Ted Lavender, who was scared, carried thirty-four rounds when he was shot and killed outside Than Khe, and he went down under an exceptional burden, more than twenty pounds of ammunition, plus the flak jacket and helmet and rations and water and toilet paper and tranquilizers and all the rest, plus the unweighed fear. He was dead weight. There was no twitching or flopping. Kiowa, who saw it happen, said it was like watching a rock fall, or a big sandbag or something—just boom, then down—not like the movies where the dead guy rolls around and does fancy spins and goes ass over teakettle—not like that, Kiowa said, the poor bastard just flat-fuck fell. Boom. Down. Nothing else. It was a bright morning in mid-April. Lieutenant Cross felt the pain. He blamed himself. They stripped off Lavender's canteens and ammo, all the heavy things, and Rat Kiley said the obvious, the guy's dead, and Mitchell Sanders used his radio to report one U.S. KIA and to request a chopper. Then they wrapped Lavender in his poncho. They carried him out to a dry paddy, established security, and sat smoking the dead man's dope until the chopper came. Lieutenant Cross kept to himself. He pictured Martha's smooth young face, thinking he loved her more than anything, more than his men, and now Ted Lavender was dead because he loved her so much and could not stop thinking about her. When the dust-off arrived, they carried Lavender aboard. Afterward they burned Than Khe. They marched until dusk, then dug their holes, and that night Kiowa kept explaining how you had to be there, how fast it was, how the poor guy just dropped like so much concrete. Boom-down, he said. Like cement.

In addition to the three standard weapons—the M-60, M-16, and M-79—they carried whatever presented itself, or whatever seemed appropriate as a means of killing or staying alive. They carried catch-as-catch-can. At various times, in various situations, they carried M-14s and CAR-15s and Swedish Ks and grease guns and captured AK-47s and Chi-Coms and RPGs and Simonov carbines and black-market Uzis and .38-caliber Smith & Wesson handguns and 66 mm LAWs and shotguns and silencers and blackjacks and bayonets and C-4 plastic explosives. Lee Strunk carried a slingshot; a weapon of last resort, he called it. Mitchell Sanders carried brass knuckles. Kiowa carried his grandfather's feathered hatchet. Every third or fourth man carried a Claymore antipersonnel mine—3.5 pounds with its firing device. They all carried fragmentation grenades—fourteen ounces each. They all carried at least one M-18 colored smoke grenade—twenty-four ounces. Some carried CS or tear-gas grenades. Some carried white-phosphorus grenades. They carried all they could bear, and then some, including a silent awe for the terrible power of the things they carried.

In the first week of April, before Lavender died, Lieutenant Jimmy Cross received a good-luck charm from Martha. It was a simple pebble, an ounce at most. Smooth to the touch, it was a milky-white color with flecks of orange and violet, oval-shaped, like a miniature egg. In the accompanying letter, Martha wrote that she had found the pebble on the Jersey shoreline, precisely where the land touched water at high tide, where things came together but also separated. It was this separate-but-together quality, she wrote, that had inspired her to pick up the pebble and to carry it in her breast pocket for several days, where it seemed weightless, and then to send it through the mail, by air, as a token of her truest feelings for him. Lieutenant Cross found this romantic. But he wondered what her truest feelings were, exactly, and what she meant by separate-but-together. He wondered how the tides and waves had come into play on that afternoon along the Jersey shoreline when Martha saw the pebble and bent down to rescue it from geology. He imagined bare feet. Martha was a poet, with the poet's sensibilities, and her feet would be brown and bare, the toenails unpainted, the eyes chilly and somber like the ocean in March, and though it was painful, he wondered who had been with her that afternoon. He imagined a pair of shadows moving along the strip of sand where things came together but also separated. It was phantom jealousy, he knew, but he couldn't help himself. He loved her so much. On the march, through the hot days of early April, he carried the pebble in his mouth, turning it with his tongue, tasting sea salts and moisture. His mind wandered. He had difficulty keeping his attention on the war. On occasion he would yell at his men to spread out the column, to keep their eyes open, but then he would slip away into daydreams, just pretending, walking barefoot along the Jersey shore, with Martha, carrying nothing. He would feel himself rising. Sun and waves and gentle winds, all love and lightness.

What they carried varied by mission.

When a mission took them to the mountains, they carried mosquito netting, machetes, canvas tarps, and extra bug juice.

If a mission seemed especially hazardous, or if it involved a place they knew to be bad, they carried everything they could. In certain heavily mined AOs, where the land was dense with Toe Poppers and Bouncing Betties, they took turns humping a twenty-eight-pound mine detector. With its headphones and big sensing plate, the equipment was a stress on the lower back and shoulders, awkward to handle, often useless because of the shrapnel in the earth, but they carried it anyway, partly for safety, partly for the illusion of safety.

On ambush, or other night missions, they carried peculiar little odds and ends. Kiowa always took along his New Testament and a pair of moccasins for silence. Dave Jensen carried night-sight vitamins high in carotin. Lee Strunk carried his slingshot; ammo, he claimed, would never be a problem. Rat Kiley carried brandy and M&M's. Until he was shot, Ted Lavender carried the starlight scope, which weighed 6.3 pounds with its aluminum carrying case. Henry Dobbins carried his girlfriend's pantyhose wrapped around his neck as a comforter. They all carried ghosts. When dark came, they would move out single file across the meadows and paddies to their ambush coordinates, where they would quietly set up the Claymores and lie down and spend the night waiting.

Other missions were more complicated and required special equipment. In mid-April, it was their mission to search out and destroy the elaborate tunnel complexes in the Than Khe area south of Chu Lai. To blow the tunnels, they carried one-pound blocks of pentrite high explosives, four blocks to a man, sixty-eight pounds in all. They carried wiring, detonators, and battery-powered clackers. Dave Jensen carried earplugs. Most often, before blowing the tunnels, they were ordered by higher command to search them, which was considered bad news, but by and large they just shrugged and carried out orders. Because he was a big man, Henry Dobbins was excused from tunnel duty. The others would draw numbers. Before Lavender died there were seventeen men in the platoon, and whoever drew the number seventeen would strip off his gear and crawl in head first with a flashlight and Lieutenant Cross's .45-caliber pistol. The rest of them would fan out as security. They would sit down or kneel, not facing the hole, listening to the ground beneath them, imagining cobwebs and ghosts, whatever was down there—the tunnel walls squeezing in—how the flashlight seemed impossibly heavy in the hand and how it was tunnel vision in the very strictest sense, compression in all ways, even time, and how you had to wiggle in—ass and elbows—a swallowed-up feeling—and how you found yourself worrying about odd things—will your flashlight go dead? Do rats carry rabies? If you screamed, how far would the sound carry? Would your buddies hear it? Would they have the courage to drag you out? In some respects, though not many, the waiting was worse than the tunnel itself. Imagination was a killer.

On April 16, when Lee Strunk drew the number seventeen, he laughed and muttered something and went down quickly. The morning was hot and very still. Not good, Kiowa said. He looked at the tunnel opening, then out across a dry paddy toward the village of Than Khe. Nothing moved. No clouds or birds or people. As they waited, the men smoked and drank Kool-Aid, not talking much, feeling sympathy for Lee Strunk but also feeling the luck of the draw. You win some, you lose some, said Mitchell Sanders, and sometimes you settle for a rain check. It was a tired line and no one laughed.

Henry Dobbins ate a tropical chocolate bar. Ted Lavender popped a tranquilizer and went off to pee.

After five minutes, Lieutenant Jimmy Cross moved to the tunnel, leaned down, and examined the darkness. Trouble, he thought—a cave-in maybe. And then suddenly, without willing it, he was thinking about Martha. The stresses and fractures, the quick collapse, the two of them buried alive under all that weight. Dense, crushing love. Kneeling, watching the hole, he tried to concentrate on Lee Strunk and the war, all the dangers, but his love was too much for him, he felt paralyzed, he wanted to sleep inside her lungs and breathe her blood and be smothered. He wanted her to be a virgin and not a virgin, all at once. He wanted to know her. Intimate secrets—why poetry? Why so sad? Why the grayness in her eyes? Why so alone? Not lonely, just alone—riding her bike across campus or sitting off by herself in the cafeteria. Even dancing, she danced alone—and it was the aloneness that filled him with love. He remembered telling her that one evening. How she nodded and looked away. And how, later, when he kissed her, she received the kiss without returning it, her eyes wide open, not afraid, not a virgin's eyes, just flat and uninvolved.

Lieutenant Cross gazed at the tunnel. But he was not there. He was buried with Martha under the white sand at the Jersey shore. They were pressed together, and the pebble in his mouth was her tongue. He was smiling. Vaguely, he was aware of how quiet the day was, the sullen paddies, yet he could not bring himself to worry about matters of security. He was beyond that. He was just a kid at war, in love. He was twenty-two years old. He couldn't help it.

A few moments later Lee Strunk crawled out of the tunnel. He came up grinning, filthy but alive. Lieutenant Cross nodded and closed his eyes while the others clapped Strunk on the back and made jokes about rising from the dead.

Worms, Rat Kiley said. Right out of the grave. Fuckin' zombie.

The men laughed. They all felt great relief.

Spook City, said Mitchell Sanders.

Lee Strunk made a funny ghost sound, a kind of moaning, yet very happy, and right then, when Strunk made that high happy moaning sound, when he want *Ahhooooo*, right then Ted Lavender was shot in the head on his way back from peeing.

He lay with his mouth open. The teeth were broken. There was a swollen black bruise under his left eye. The cheekbone was gone. Oh shit, Rat Kiley said, the guy's dead. The guy's dead, he kept saying, which seemed profound—the guy's dead. I mean really.

The things they carried were determined to some extent by superstition. Lieutenant Cross carried his good-luck pebble. Dave Jensen carried a rabbit's foot. Norman Bowker, otherwise a very gentle person, carried a thumb that had been presented to him as a gift by Mitchell Sanders. The thumb was dark brown, rubbery to the touch, and weighed four ounces at most. It had been cut from a VC corpse, a boy of fifteen or sixteen. They'd found him at the bottom of an irrigation ditch, badly burned, flies in his mouth and eyes. The boy wore black shorts and sandals. At the time of his death he had been carrying a pouch of rice, a rifle, and three magazines of ammunition.

You want my opinion, Mitchell Sanders said, there's a definite moral here.

He put his hand on the dead boy's wrist. He was quiet for a time, as if counting a pulse, then he patted the stomach, almost affectionately, and used Kiowa's hunting hatchet to remove the thumb.

Henry Dobbins asked what the moral was.

Moral?

You know. *Moral*.

Sanders wrapped the thumb in toilet paper and handed it across to Norman Bowker. There was no blood. Smiling, he kicked the boy's head, watched the flies scatter, and said, It's like that old TV show—Paladin. Have gun, will travel.

Henry Dobbins thought about it.

Yeah, well, he finally said. I don't see no moral.

There it *is*, man.

Fuck off.

They carried USO stationery and pencils and pens. They carried Sterno, safety pins, trip flares, signal flares, spools of wire, razor blades, chewing tobacco, liberated joss sticks and statuettes of the smiling Buddha, candles, grease pencils, *The Stars and Stripes*, fingernail clippers, Psy Ops leaflets, bush hats, bolos, and much more. Twice a week, when the resupply choppers came in, they carried hot chow in green Mermite cans and large canvas bags filled with iced beer and soda pop. They carried plastic water containers, each with a two-gallon capacity. Mitchell Sanders carried a set of starched tiger fatigues for special occasions. Henry Dobbins carried Black Flag insecticide. Dave Jensen carried empty sandbags that could be filled at night for added protection. Lee Strunk carried tanning lotion. Some things they carried in common. Taking turns, they carried the big PRC-77 scrambler radio, which weighed thirty pounds with its battery. They shared the weight of memory. They took up what others could no longer bear. Often, they carried each other, the wounded or weak. They carried infections. They carried chess sets, basketballs, Vietnamese-English dictionaries, insignia of rank, Bronze Stars and Purple Hearts, plastic cards imprinted with the Code of Conduct. They carried diseases, among them malaria and dysentery. They carried lice and ringworm and leeches and paddy algae and various rots and molds. They carried the land itself—Vietnam, the place, the soil—a powdery orange-red dust that covered their boots and fatigues and faces. They carried the sky. The whole atmosphere, they carried it, the humidity, the monsoons, the stink of fungus and decay, all of it, they carried gravity. They moved like mules. By daylight they took sniper fire, at night they were mortared, but it was not battle, it was just the endless march, village to village, without purpose, nothing won or lost. They marched for the sake of the march. They plodded along slowly, dumbly, leaning forward against the heat, unthinking, all blood and bone, simple grunts, soldiering with their legs, toiling up the hills and down into the paddies and across the rivers and up again and down, just humping, one step and then the next and then another, but no volition, no will, because it was automatic, it was anatomy, and the war was entirely a matter of posture and carriage, the hump was everything, a kind of inertia, a kind of emptiness, a dullness of desire and intellect and conscience and hope and human sensibility. Their principles were in their feet. Their calculations were biological. They had no sense of strategy or mission. They searched the villages without knowing what to look for, not caring, kicking over jars of rice, frisking children and old men, blowing tunnels, sometimes setting fires and sometimes not, then forming up and moving on to the next village, then other villages, where it would always be the same. They carried their own lives. The pressures were enormous. In the heat of early afternoon, they would remove their helmets and flak jackets, walking bare, which was dangerous but which helped ease the strain. They would often discard things along the route of march. Purely for comfort, they would throw away rations, blow their Claymores and grenades, no matter, because by nightfall the resupply choppers would arrive with more of the same, then a day or two later still more, fresh watermelons and crates of ammunition and sunglasses and woolen sweaters—the resources were stunning—sparklers for the Fourth of July, colored eggs for Easter. It was the great American war chest—the fruits of science, the smokestacks, the canneries, the arsenals at Hartford, the Minnesota forests, the machine shops, the vast fields of corn and wheat—they carried like freight trains; they carried it on their backs and shoulders—and for all the ambiguities of Vietnam, all the mysteries and unknowns, there was at least the single abiding certainty that they would never be at a loss for things to carry.

After the chopper took Lavender away, Lieutenant Jimmy Cross led his men into the village of Than Khe. They burned everything. They shot chickens and dogs, they trashed the village well, they called in artillery and watched the wreckage, then they marched for several hours through the hot afternoon, and then at dusk, while Kiowa explained how Lavender died, Lieutenant Cross found himself trembling.

He tried not to cry. With his entrenching tool, which weighed five pounds, he began digging a hole in the earth.

He felt shame. He hated himself. He had loved Martha more than his men, and as a consequence Lavender was now dead, and this was something he would have to carry like a stone in his stomach for the rest of the war.

All he could do was dig. He used his entrenching tool like an ax, slashing, feeling both love and hate, and then later, when it was full dark, he sat at the bottom of his foxhole and wept. It went on for a long while. In part, he was grieving for Ted Lavender, but mostly it was for Martha, and for himself, because she belonged to another world, which was not quite real, and because she was a junior at Mount Sebastian College in New Jersey, a poet and a virgin and uninvolved, and because he realized she did not love him and never would.

Like cement, Kiowa whispered in the dark. I swear to God—boom-down. Not a word.

I've heard this, said Norman Bowker.

A pisser, you know? Still zipping himself up. Zapped while zipping.

All right, fine. That's enough.

Yeah, but you had to see it, the guy just—

I *heard,* man. Cement. So why not shut the fuck *up?*

Kiowa shook his head sadly and glanced over at the hole where Lieutenant Jimmy Cross sat watching the night. The air was thick and wet. A warm, dense fog had settled over the paddies and there was the stillness that precedes rain.

After a time Kiowa sighed.

One thing for sure, he said. The Lieutenant's in some deep hurt. I mean that crying jag—the way he was carrying on—it wasn't fake or anything, it was real heavy-duty hurt. The man cares.

Sure, Norman Bowker said.

Say what you want, the man does care.

We all got problems.

Not Lavender.

No, I guess not, Bowker said. Do me a favor, though.

Shut up?

That's a smart Indian. Shut up.

Shrugging, Kiowa pulled off his boots. He wanted to say more, just to lighten up his sleep, but instead he opened his New Testament and arranged it beneath his head as a pillow. The fog made things seem hollow and unattached. He tried not to think about Ted Lavender, but then he was thinking how fast it was, no drama, down and dead, and how it was hard to feel anything except surprise. It seemed un-Christian. He wished he could find some great sadness, or even anger, but the emotion wasn't there and he couldn't make it happen. Mostly he felt pleased to be alive. He liked the smell of the New Testament under his cheek, the leather and ink and paper and glue, whatever the chemicals were. He liked hearing the sounds of night. Even his fatigue, it felt fine, the stiff muscles and the prickly awareness of his own body, a floating feeling. He enjoyed not being dead. Lying there, Kiowa admired Lieutenant Jimmy Cross's capacity for grief. He wanted to share the man's pain, he wanted to care as Jimmy Cross cared. And yet when he closed his eyes, all he could think was Boom-down, and all he could feel was the pleasure of having his boots off and the fog curling in around him and the damp soil and the Bible smells and the plush comfort of night.

After a moment Norman Bowker sat up in the dark.

What the hell, he said. You want to talk, *talk.* Tell it to me.

Forget it.

No, man, go on. One thing I hate, it's a silent Indian.

For the most part they carried themselves with poise, a kind of dignity. Now and then, however, there were times of panic, when they squealed or wanted to squeal but couldn't, when they twitched and made moaning sounds and covered their heads and said Dear Jesus and flopped around on the earth and fired their weapons blindly and cringed and sobbed and begged for the noise to stop and went wild and made stupid promises to themselves and to God and to their mothers and fathers, hoping not to die. In different ways, it happened to all of them. Afterward, when the firing ended, they would blink and peek up. They would touch their bodies, feeling shame, then quickly hiding it. They would force themselves to stand. As if in slow motion, frame by frame, the world would take on the old logic—absolute silence, then the wind, then sunlight, then voices. It was the burden of being alive. Awkwardly, the men would reassemble themselves, first in private, then in groups, becoming soldiers again. They would repair the leaks in their eyes. They would check for casualties, call in dust-offs, light cigarettes, try to smile, clear their throats and spit and begin cleaning their weapons. After a time someone would shake his head and say, No lie, I almost shit my pants, and someone else would laugh, which meant it was bad, yes, but the guy had obviously not shit his pants, it wasn't that bad, and in any case nobody would ever do such a thing and then go ahead and talk about it. They would squint into the dense, oppressive sunlight. For a few moments, perhaps, they would fall silent, lighting a joint and tracking its passage from man to man, inhaling, holding in the humiliation. Scary stuff, one of them might say. But then someone else would grin or flick his eyebrows and say, Roger-dodger, almost cut me a new asshole, *almost*.

There were numerous such poses. Some carried themselves with a sort of wistful resignation, others with pride or stiff soldierly discipline or good humor or macho zeal. They were afraid of dying but they were even more afraid to show it.

They found jokes to tell.

They used a hard vocabulary to contain the terrible softness. *Greased,* they'd say. *Offed, lit up, zapped while zipping.* It wasn't cruelty, just stage presence. They were actors and the war came at them in 3-D. When someone died, it wasn't quite dying, because in a curious way it seemed scripted, and because they had their lines mostly memorized, irony mixed with tragedy, and because they called it by other names, as if to encyst and destroy the reality of death itself. They kicked corpses. They cut off thumbs. They talked grunt lingo. They told stories about Ted Lavender's supply of tranquilizers, how the poor guy didn't feel a thing, how incredibly tranquil he was.

There's a moral here, said Mitchell Sanders.

They were waiting for Lavender's chopper, smoking the dead man's dope.

The moral's pretty obvious, Sanders said, and winked. Stay away from drugs. No joke, they'll ruin your day every time.

Cute, said Henry Dobbins.

Mind-blower, get it? Talk about wiggy—nothing left, just blood and brains.

They made themselves laugh.

There it is, they'd say, over and over, as if the repetition itself were an act of poise, a balance between crazy and almost crazy, knowing without going. There it is, which meant be cool, let it ride, because oh yeah, man, you can't change what can't be changed, there it is, there it absolutely and positively and fucking well *is*.

They were tough.

They carried all the emotional baggage of men who might die. Grief, terror, love, longing—these were intangibles, but the intangibles had their own mass and specific gravity, they had tangible weight. They carried shameful memories. They carried the common secret of cowardice barely restrained, the instinct to run or freeze or hide, and in many respects this was the heaviest burden of all, for it could never be put down, it required perfect balance and perfect posture. They carried their reputations. They carried the soldier's greatest fear, which was the fear of blushing. Men killed, and died, because they were embarrassed not to. It was what had brought them to the war in the first place, nothing positive, no dreams of glory or honor, just to avoid the blush of dishonor. They died so as not to die of embarrassment. They crawled into tunnels and walked point and advanced under fire. Each morning, despite the unknowns, they made their legs move. They endured. They kept humming. They did not submit to the obvious alternative, which was simply to close the eyes and fall. So easy, really. Go limp and tumble to the ground and let the muscles unwind and not speak and not budge until your buddies picked you up and lifted you into the chopper that would roar and dip its nose and carry you off to the world. A mere matter of falling, yet no one ever fell. It was not courage, exactly; the object was not valor. Rather, they were too frightened to be cowards.

By and large they carried these things inside, maintaining the masks of composure. They sneered at sick call. They spoke bitterly about guys who had found release by shooting off their own toes or fingers. Pussies, they'd say. Candyasses. It was fierce, mocking talk, with only a trace of envy or awe, but even so, the image played itself out behind their eyes.

They imagined the muzzle against flesh. They imagined the quick, sweet pain, then the evacuation to Japan, then a hospital with warm beds and cute geisha nurses.

They dreamed of freedom birds.

At night, on guard, staring into the dark, they were carried away by jumbo jets. They felt the rush of takeoff. *Gone!* they yelled. And then velocity, wings and engines, a smiling stewardess—but it was more than a plane, it was a real bird, a big sleek silver bird with feathers and talons and high screeching. They were flying. The weights fell off, there was nothing to bear. They laughed and held on tight, feeling the cold slap of wind and altitude, soaring, thinking *It's over, I'm gone!*—they were naked, they were light and free—it was all lightness, bright and fast and bouyant, light as light, a helium buzz in the brain, a giddy bubbling in the lungs as they were taken up over the clouds and the war, beyond duty, beyond gravity and mortification and global entanglements—*Sin loi!* they yelled, *I'm sorry, motherfuckers, but I'm out of it, I'm goofed, I'm on a space cruise, I'm gone!*—and it was a restful, disencumbered sensation, just riding the light waves, sailing that big silver freedom bird over the mountains and oceans, over America, over the farms and great sleeping cities and cemeteries and highways and the golden arches of McDonald's. It was flight, a kind of fleeing, a kind of falling, falling higher and higher, spinning off the edge of the earth and beyond the sun and through the vast, silent vacuum where there were no burdens and where everything weighed exactly nothing. *Gone!* they screamed, *I'm sorry but I'm gone!* And so at night, not quite dreaming, they gave themselves over to lightness, they were carried, they were purely borne.

On the morning after Ted Lavender died, First Lieutenant Jimmy Cross crouched at the bottom of his foxhole and burned Martha's letters. Then he burned the two photographs. There was a steady rain falling, which made it difficult, but he used heat tabs and Sterno to build a small fire, screening it with his body, holding the photographs over the tight blue flame with the tips of his fingers.

He realized it was only a gesture. Stupid, he thought. Sentimental, too, but mostly just stupid.

Lavender was dead. You couldn't burn the blame.

Besides, the letters were in his head. And even now, without photographs, Lieutenant Cross could see Martha playing volleyball in her white gym shorts and yellow T-shirt. He could see her moving in the rain.

When the fire died out, Lieutenant Cross pulled his poncho over his shoulders and ate breakfast from a can.

There was no great mystery, he decided.

In those burned letters Martha had never mentioned the war, except to say, Jimmy, take care of yourself. She wasn't involved. She signed the letters "Love," but it wasn't love, and all the fine lines and technicalities did not matter.

The morning came up wet and blurry. Everything seemed part of everything else, the fog and Martha and the deepening rain.

It was a war, after all.

Half smiling, Lieutenant Jimmy Cross took out his maps. He shook his head hard, as if to clear it, then bent forward and began planning the day's march. In ten minutes, or maybe twenty, he would rouse the men and they would pack up and head west, where the maps showed the country to be green and inviting. They would do what they had always done. The rain might add some weight, but otherwise it would be one more day layered upon all the other days.

He was realistic about it. There was that new hardness in his stomach.

No more fantasies, he told himself.

Henceforth, when he thought about Martha, it would be only to think that she belonged elsewhere. He would shut down the daydreams. This was not Mount Sebastian, it was another world, where there were no pretty poems or midterm exams, a place where men died because of carelessness and gross stupidity. Kiowa was right. Boom-down, and you were dead, never partly dead.

Briefly, in the rain, Lieutenant Cross saw Martha's gray eyes gazing back at him.

He understood.

It was very sad, he thought. The things men carried inside. The things men did or felt they had to do.

He almost nodded at her, but didn't.

Instead he went back to his maps. He was now determined to perform his duties firmly and without negligence. It wouldn't help Lavender, he knew that, but from this point on he would comport himself as a soldier. He would dispose of his good-luck pebble. Swallow it, maybe, or use Lee Strunk's slingshot, or just drop it along the trail. On the march he would impose strict field discipline. He would be careful to send out flank security, to prevent straggling or bunching up, to keep his troops moving at the proper pace and at the proper interval. He would insist on clean weapons. He would confiscate the remainder of Lavender's dope. Later in the day, perhaps, he would call the men together and speak to them plainly. He would accept the blame for what had happened to Ted Lavender. He would be a man about it. He would look them in the eyes, keeping his chin level, and he would issue the new SOPs in a calm, impersonal tone of voice, an officer's voice, leaving no room for argument or discussion. Commencing immediately, he'd tell them, they would no longer abandon equipment along the route of march. They would police up their acts. They would get their shit together, and keep it together, and maintain it neatly and in good working order.

He would not tolerate laxity. He would show strength, distancing himself.

Among the men there would be grumbling, of course, and maybe worse, because their days would seem longer and their loads heavier, but Lieutenant Cross reminded himself that his obligation was not to be loved but to lead. He would dispense with love; it was not now a factor. And if anyone quarreled or complained, he would simply tighten his lips and arrange his shoulders in the correct command posture. He might give a curt little nod. Or he might not. He might just shrug and say Carry on, then they would saddle up and form into a column and move out toward the villages of Than Khe.

QUESTIONS FOR DISCUSSION AND WRITING

1. Make a list of the tangible objects carried by each of the characters. What does each list tell you about each soldier, both about his military function and about what he values as an individual? How do the things carried—both tangible and intangible items—link the men to the war? To Vietnam? To home?
2. The first part of the story often consists of lists, whereas the second part moves away from actual items carried. How does the second, more narrative, part of the story relate to the lists of the first part?
3. At the end of the story Cross burns Martha's letters and photographs. By doing so, does he lighten his burden or add to it? How?
4. Though most of the story concerns itself with "the things they carried," we also get images of the soldiers *being* carried. What does being carried suggest? How are the two images linked?

WILLIAM CARLOS WILLIAMS (1883–1963)
The Use of Force _____ 1938

They were new patients to me, all I had was the name, Olson. Please come down as soon as you can, my daughter is very sick.

When I arrived I was met by the mother, a big startled looking woman, very clean and apologetic who merely said, Is this the doctor? and let me in. In the back, she added. You must excuse us, doctor, we have her in the kitchen where it is warm. It is very damp here sometimes.

The child was fully dressed and sitting on her father's lap near the kitchen table. He tried to get up, but I motioned for him not to bother, took off my overcoat and started to look things over. I could see that they were all very nervous, eyeing me up and down distrustfully. As often, in such cases, they weren't telling me more than they had to, it was up to me to tell them; that's why they were spending three dollars on me.

The child was fairly eating me up with her cold, steady eyes, and no expression to her face whatever. She did not move and seemed, inwardly, quiet; an unusually attractive little thing, and as strong as a heifer in appearance. But her face was flushed, she was breathing rapidly, and I realized that she had a high fever. She had magnificent blonde hair, in profusion. One of those picture children often reproduced in advertising leaflets and the photogravure sections of the Sunday papers.

She's had a fever for three days, began the father and we don't know what it comes from. My wife has given her things, you know, like people do, but it don't do no good. And there's been a lot of sickness around. So we tho't you'd better look her over and tell us what is the matter.

As doctors often do I took a trial shot at it as a point of departure. Has she had a sore throat?

Both parents answered me together, No . . . No, she says her throat don't hurt her.

Does your throat hurt you? added the mother to the child. But the little girl's expression didn't change nor did she move her eyes from my face.

Have you looked?

I tried to, said the mother, but I couldn't see.

As it happens we had been having a number of cases of diphtheria in the school to which this child went during that month and we were all, quite apparently, thinking of that, though no one had as yet spoken of the thing.

Well, I said, suppose we take a look at the throat first. I smiled in my best professional manner and asking for the child's first name I said, come on, Mathilda, open your mouth and let's take a look at your throat.

Nothing doing.

Aw, come on, I coaxed, just open your mouth wide and let me take a look. Look, I said opening both hands wide, I haven't anything in my hands. Just open up and let me see.

Such a nice man, put in the mother. Look how kind he is to you. Come on, do what he tells you to. He won't hurt you.

At that I ground my teeth in disgust. If only they wouldn't use the word "hurt" I might be able to get somewhere. But I did not allow myself to be hurried or disturbed but speaking quietly and slowly I approached the child again.

As I moved my chair a little nearer suddenly with one cat-like movement both her hands clawed instinctively for my eyes and she almost reached them too. In fact she knocked my glasses flying and they fell, though unbroken, several feet away from me on the kitchen floor.

Both the mother and father almost turned themselves inside out in embarrassment and apology. You bad girl, said the mother, taking her and shaking her by one arm. Look what you've done. The nice man . . .

For heaven's sake, I broke in. Don't call me a nice man to her. I'm here to look at her throat on the chance that she might have diphtheria and possibly die of it. But that's nothing to her. Look here, I said to the child, we're going to look at your throat. You're old enough to understand what I'm saying. Will you open it now by yourself or shall we have to open it for you?

Not a move. Even her expression hadn't changed. Her breaths however were coming faster and faster. Then the battle began. I had to do it. I had to have a throat culture for her own protection. But first I told the parents that it was entirely up to them. I explained the danger but said that I would not insist on a throat examination so long as they would take the responsibility.

If you don't do what the doctor says you'll have to go to the hospital, the mother admonished her severely.

Oh yeah? I had to smile to myself. After all, I had already fallen in love with the savage brat, the parents were contemptible to me. In the ensuing struggle they grew more and more abject, crushed, exhausted while she surely rose to magnificent heights of insane fury of effort bred of her terror of me.

The father tried his best, and he was a big man but the fact that she was his daughter, his shame at her behavior and his dread of hurting her made him release her just at the critical moment several times when I had almost achieved success, till I wanted to kill him. But his dread also that she might have diphtheria made him tell me to go on, go on though he himself was almost fainting, while the mother moved back and forth behind us raising and lowering her hands in an agony of apprehension.

Put her in front of you on your lap, I ordered, and hold both her wrists.

But as soon as he did the child let out a scream. Don't, you're hurting me. Let go of my hands. Let them go I tell you. Then she shrieked terrifyingly, hysterically. Stop it! Stop it! You're killing me!

Do you think she can stand it, doctor! said the mother.

You get out, said the husband to his wife. Do you want her to die of diphtheria?

Come on now, hold her, I said.

Then I grasped the child's head with my left hand and tried to get the wooden tongue depressor between her teeth. She fought, with clenched teeth, desperately! But now I also had grown furious—at a child. I tried to hold myself down but I couldn't. I know how to expose a throat for inspection. And I did my best. When finally I got the wooden spatula behind the last teeth and just the point of it into the mouth cavity, she opened up for an instant but before I could see anything she came down again and gripping the wooden blade between her molars she reduced it to splinters before I could get it out again.

Aren't you ashamed, the mother yelled at her. Aren't you ashamed to act like that in front of the doctor?

Get me a smooth-handled spoon of some sort, I told the mother. We're going through with this. The child's mouth was already bleeding. Her tongue was cut and she was screaming in wild hysterical shrieks. Perhaps I should have desisted and come back in an hour or more. No doubt it would have been better. But I have seen at least two children lying dead in bed of neglect in such cases, and feeling that I must get a diagnosis now or never I went at it again. But the worst of it was that I too had got beyond reason. I could have torn the child apart in my own fury and enjoyed it. It was a pleasure to attack her. My face was burning with it.

The damned little brat must be protected against her own idiocy, one says to one's self at such times. Others must be protected against her. It is social necessity. And all these things are true. But a blind fury, a feeling of adult shame, bred of a longing for muscular release are the operatives. One goes on to the end.

In a final unreasoning assault I overpowered the child's neck and jaws. I forced the heavy silver spoon back of her teeth and down her throat till she gagged. And there it was—both tonsils covered with membrane. She had fought valiantly to keep me from knowing her secret. She had been hiding that sore throat for three days at least and lying to her parents in order to escape just such an outcome as this.

Now truly she *was* furious. She had been on the defensive before but now she attacked. Tried to get off her father's lap and fly at me while tears of defeat blinded her eyes.

QUESTIONS FOR DISCUSSION AND WRITING

1. How necessary do you think the use of force is in the doctor's examination of the child's throat? In other words, do you see the doctor's actions as civilized? Savage?

Both? To what extent do you think your own attitude toward and experience with doctors might influence your response to the events of the story?

2. Look at the doctor's relationship with the young girl's parents. Why does it matter that these are new patients about whom he knows little more than their name? How does each of the parents respond to the doctor? How does he respond to each of them?

3. About midway through the story, the doctor tells us that he has "fallen in love with the savage brat"; later he tells us, "I could have torn the child apart in my own fury and enjoyed it. It was a pleasure to attack her." How do you reconcile these two attitudes toward the child and her resistance to the doctor's attempts to minister to her?

4. William Carlos Williams was himself a doctor; in fact, he was a pediatrician. How does that knowledge affect your response to the doctor in the story?

Drama

A Brief Introduction to Greek Drama   Much of what we take for granted in the theater today would have been unknown in past centuries. For example, we probably expect a curtain to come down at the end of the play, and we probably associate staged plays with closed theaters we can attend any time of year, day or night. However, audiences of other times would have had very different expectations about the theater, the actors, and the plays themselves.

Having originated in the sixth century B.C., Greek drama had its greatest flourishing a century later. The plays were part of religious–civic festivals held in honor of Dionysus, a god of fertility and wine, and at each festival three playwrights competed in a contest for the best tragedy sequence. (A separate competition for comedies was added later.) Each of the playwrights produced three tragedies and a satyr (an erotic comedy), and at the end of the festival a jury of ten citizens selected a winning playwright. The prizes were not awarded on the basis of the best "new" story; Greek audiences would not have expected to see "new" stories at all. Instead, they would have judged the plays on how well the playwrights retold well-known legends and myths and used their skill to convey spiritual or political truths.

Greek plays were performed outside, in a natural amphitheater, with the audience sitting on a grassy hillside above the performance area (later, benches were built into the hillside). As many as fifteen thousand spectators attended the performances, and although the audience consisted mostly of male citizens, a cross section of the population would probably have been present, including some women and slaves.

Many of the theatrical conventions and methods that we are used to now would have been unfamiliar to the Greeks. Costumes were probably relatively simple, and there would have been little in the way of scenery. The actors (all male) wore platform shoes and masks representing the characters they played (a bearded old man or a young woman, for instance). The shoes and masks would have helped those far away from the performance area take in the essentials of the roles. The actors moved about in a relatively bare acting space. It was only an open area (the orchestra) with a small building set in the background; that building served as both a changing room and a stage backdrop representing any structures in the play. There would also have been a "mechane," or machine (in this case, a crane), sometimes used to introduce a god from the heavens at the end of a play. (The use of such a machine gave rise to the Latin expression *deus ex machina,* or "god from the machine," to refer to a sudden, usually illogical, means of resolving dramatic conflict.)

By modern standards, the Greek plays are short, though it is important to remember that audiences would have been viewing four plays in a single day. By our standards, there are also few actors. Originally, the plays were probably performed by the Chorus alone, a group of male actors who would have danced and sung in unison. A single actor was added by the playwright Thespis (from whose name we get the word *thespian,* to refer to an actor). The playwright Aeschylus added a second actor, and Sophocles added a third. That does not mean, however, that there were only three roles. As Sophocles's *Oedipus* and *Antigone* show, there were more than three characters—actors took on more than one role each, a practice simplified by the use of masks. Even after the introduction of actors, the Chorus still remained onstage throughout the entire play and retained an important role. It continued to help define for the audience the reactions of the common people, with whom the audience would have identified.

The Greeks would also have expected their plays to follow what Aristotle and his later commentators called the **three unities—the unity of action, time, and place.** To be unified by action, a play had to focus on a single action; Greek plays seldom have subplots. In addition, because they are seldom set in more than one time and place, they are considered unified by time and place. In other words, a Greek play would not usually have a "five years later" scene, nor would one scene be succeeded by another geographically distant. The time is real time: the action generally takes place during the same amount of time that it takes to perform the play, or at least not in a substantially longer amount of time. Often, too, the entire play is set in one location, perhaps in front of the palace, as in the case of *Oedipus* and *Antigone.*

Different as the Greek theatrical conventions may be from those we are used to, the essentials of human nature have not changed. In *Oedipus* we see a king's struggle to face an unwanted destiny and put the public good above his private will; in *Antigone,* we see a conflict between a young woman's devotion to her family and a king's sense of the needs of the state. Although the plays belong to a distant time and place, these conflicts between the individual good and the public welfare continue to echo across the centuries.

SOPHOCLES (496?–406 B.C.)

Antigone _____ *ca. 441 B.C.*

Characters

ANTIGONE, *daughter of Oedipus and Jocasta*
ISMENE, *sister of Antigone*
A CHORUS *of old Theban citizens and their* LEADER
CREON, *king of Thebes, uncle of Antigone and Ismene*
A SENTRY
HAEMON, *son of Creon and Eurydice*

TIRESIAS, *a blind prophet*
A MESSENGER
EURYDICE, *wife of Creon*
GUARDS, ATTENDANTS, AND A BOY

Time and Scene *The royal house of Thebes. It is still night, and the invading armies of Argos have just been driven from the city. Fighting on opposite sides, the sons of* OEDIPUS, ETEOCLES *and* POLYNICES, *have killed each other in combat. Their uncle,* CREON, *is now king of Thebes.*

Enter ANTIGONE, *slipping through the central doors of the palace. She motions to her sister,* ISMENE, *who follows her cautiously toward an altar at the center of the stage.*

ANTIGONE: My own flesh and blood—dear sister, dear Ismene,
　　　how many griefs our father Oedipus handed down!
　　　Do you know one, I ask you, one grief
　　　that Zeus will not perfect for the two of us
　　　while we still live and breathe? There's nothing,　　　　　　　　5
　　　no pain—our lives are pain—no private shame,
　　　no public disgrace, nothing I haven't seen
　　　in your griefs and mine. And now this:
　　　an emergency decree, they say, the Commander
　　　has just declared for all of Thebes.　　　　　　　　　　　　　10
　　　What, haven't you heard? Don't you see?
　　　The doom reserved for enemies
　　　marches on the ones we love the most.
ISMENE: Not I, I haven't heard a word, Antigone.
　　　Nothing of loved ones,　　　　　　　　　　　　　　　　　15
　　　no joy or pain has come my way, not since
　　　the two of us were robbed of our two brothers,
　　　both gone in a day, a double blow—
　　　not since the armies of Argos vanished,
　　　just this very night. I know nothing more,　　　　　　　　　20
　　　whether our luck's improved or ruin's still to come.
ANTIGONE: I thought so. That's why I brought you out here,
　　　past the gates, so you could hear in private.
ISMENE: What's the matter? Trouble, clearly . . .
　　　you sound so dark, so grim.　　　　　　　　　　　　　　25
ANTIGONE: Why not? Our own brothers' burial!
　　　Hasn't Creon graced one with all the rites,
　　　disgraced the other? Eteocles, they say,
　　　has been given full military honors,
　　　rightly so—Creon's laid him in the earth　　　　　　　　　30
　　　and he goes with glory down among the dead.
　　　But the body of Polynices, who died miserably—
　　　why, a city-wide proclamation, rumor has it,
　　　forbids anyone to bury him, even mourn him.
　　　He's to be left unwept, unburied, a lovely treasure　　　　　35

for birds that scan the field and feast to their heart's content.

Such, I hear, is the martial law our good Creon
lays down for you and me—yes, me, I tell you—
and he's coming here to alert the uninformed
40   in no uncertain terms,
and he won't treat the matter lightly. Whoever
disobeys in the least will die, his doom is sealed:
stoning to death inside the city walls!

There you have it. You'll soon show what you are,
45   worth your breeding, Ismene, or a coward—
for all your royal blood.
ISMENE: My poor sister, if things have come to this,
who am I to make or mend them, tell me,
what good am I to you?
ANTIGONE: Decide.
50   Will you share the labor, share the work?
ISMENE: What work, what's the risk? What do you mean?
ANTIGONE (*Raising her hands*): Will you lift up his body with these bare hands
and lower it with me?
ISMENE: What? You'd bury him—
when a law forbids the city?
ANTIGONE: Yes!
55   He is my brother and—deny it as you will—
your brother too.
No one will ever convict me for a traitor.
ISMENE: So desperate, and Creon has expressly—
ANTIGONE: No,
he has no right to keep me from my own.
60 ISMENE: Oh my sister, think—
think how our own father died, hated,
his reputation in ruins, driven on
by the crimes he brought to light himself
to gouge out his eyes with his own hands—
65   then mother . . . his mother and wife, both in one,
mutilating her life in the twisted noose—
and last, our two brothers dead in a single day,
both shedding their own blood, poor suffering boys,
battling out their common destiny hand-to-hand.

70   Now look at the two of us, left so alone . . .
think what a death we'll die, the worst of all
if we violate the laws and override
the fixed decree of the throne, its power—
we must be sensible. Remember we are women,
75   we're not born to contend with men. Then too,
we're underlings, ruled by much stronger hands,
so we must submit in this, and things still worse.

I, for one, I'll beg the dead to forgive me—
I'm forced, I have no choice—I must obey
the ones who stand in power. Why rush to extremes?   80
It's madness, madness.

ANTIGONE: I won't insist,
    no, even if you should have a change of heart,
    I'd never welcome you in the labor, not with me.
    So, do as you like, whatever suits you best—
    I'll bury him myself.   85
    And even if I die in the act, that death will be a glory.
    I'll lie with the one I love and loved by him—
    an outrage sacred to the gods! I have longer
    to please the dead than please the living here:
    in the kingdom down below I'll lie forever.   90
    Do as you like, dishonor the laws
    the gods hold in honor.

ISMENE: I'd do them no dishonor . . .
    but defy the city? I have no strength for that.

ANTIGONE: You have your excuses. I am on my way,
    I'll raise a mound for him, for my dear brother.   95

ISMENE: Oh Antigone, you're so rash—I'm so afraid for you!

ANTIGONE: Don't fear for me. Set your own life in order.

ISMENE: Then don't, at least, blurt this out to anyone.
    Keep it a secret. I'll join you in that, I promise.

ANTIGONE: Dear god, shout it from the rooftops. I'll hate you   100
    all the more for silence—tell the world!

ISMENE: So fiery—and it ought to chill your heart.

ANTIGONE: I know I please where I must please the most.

ISMENE: Yes, if you can, but you're in love with impossibility.

ANTIGONE: Very well then, once my strength gives out   105
    I will be done at last.

ISMENE: You're wrong from the start,
    you're off on a hopeless quest.

ANTIGONE: If you say so, you will make me hate you,
    and the hatred of the dead, by all rights,
    will haunt you night and day.   110
    But leave me to my own absurdity, leave me
    to suffer this—dreadful thing. I'll suffer
    nothing as great as death without glory.

    (*Exit to the side.*)

ISMENE: Then go if you must, but rest assured,
    wild, irrational as you are, my sister,   115
    you are truly dear to the ones who love you.

    (*Withdrawing to the palace. Enter a* CHORUS, *the old citizens of Thebes, chanting as the sun begins to rise.*)

CHORUS: Glory!—great beam of sun, brightest of all

that ever rose on the seven gates of Thebes,
   you burn through night at last!
120   Great eye of the golden day,
mounting the Dirce's banks you throw him back—
the enemy out of Argos, the white shield, the man of bronze—
he's flying headlong now
          the bridle of fate stampeding him with pain!

125   And he had driven against our borders,
      launched by the warring claims of Polynices—
      like an eagle screaming, winging havoc
      over the land, wings of armor
      shielded white as snow,
130   a huge army massing,
      crested helmets bristling for assault.

He hovered above our roofs, his vast maw gaping
closing down around our seven gates,
      his spears thirsting for the kill
135   but now he's gone, look,
before he could glut his jaws with Theban blood
or the god of fire put our crown of towers to the torch.
He grappled the Dragon none can master—Thebes—
      the clang of our arms like thunder at his back!

140   Zeus hates with a vengeance all bravado,
      the mighty boasts of men. He watched them
      coming on in a rising flood, the pride
      of their golden armor ringing shrill—
      and brandishing his lightning
145   blasted the fighter just at the goal,
      rushing to shout his triumph from our walls.

Down from the heights he crashed, pounding down on the earth!
And a moment ago, blazing torch in hand—
          mad for attack, ecstatic
150   he breathed his rage, the storm
      of his fury hurling at our heads!
But now his high hopes have laid him low
and down the enemy ranks the iron god of war
      deals his rewards, his stunning blows—Ares
155   rapture of battle, our right arm in the crisis.

      Seven captains marshaled at seven gates
      seven against their equals, gave
      their brazen trophies up to Zeus,
      god of the breaking rout of battle,
160   all but two: those blood brothers,
      one father, one mother—matched in rage,

spears matched for the twin conquest—
clashed and won the common prize of death.

But now for Victory! Glorious in the morning,
joy in her eyes to meet our joy   165
     she is winging down to Thebes,
our fleets of chariots wheeling in her wake—
    Now let us win oblivion from the wars,
thronging the temples of the gods
in singing, dancing choirs through the night!   170
    Lord Dionysus, god of the dance
    that shakes the land of Thebes, now lead the way!

(*Enter* CREON *from the palace, attended by his guard.*)

    But look, the king of the realm is coming,
    Creon, the new man for the new day,
    whatever the gods are sending now . . .   175
    what new plan will he launch?
    Why this, this special session?
    Why this sudden call to the old men
    summoned at one command?

CREON: My countrymen,
the ship of state is safe. The gods who rocked her,   180
after a long, merciless pounding in the storm,
have righted her once more.
                Out of the whole city
I have called you here alone. Well I know,
first, your undeviating respect
for the throne and royal power of King Laius.   185
Next, while Oedipus steered the land of Thebes,
and even after he died, your loyalty was unshakable,
you still stood by their children. Now then,
since the two sons are dead—two blows of fate
in the same day, cut down by each other's hands,   190
both killers, both brothers stained with blood—
as I am next in kin to the dead,
I now possess the throne and all its powers.

Of course you cannot know a man completely,
his character, his principles, sense of judgment,   195
not till he's shown his colors, ruling the people,
making laws. Experience, there's the test.
As I see it, whoever assumes the task,
the awesome task of setting the city's course,
and refuses to adopt the soundest policies   200
but fearing someone, keeps his lips locked tight,
he's utterly worthless. So I rate him now,
I always have. And whoever places a friend

above the good of his own country, he is nothing:

205   I have no use for him. Zeus my witness,
Zeus who sees all things, always—
I could never stand by silent, watching destruction
march against our city, putting safety to rout,
nor could I ever make that man a friend of mine

210   who menaces our country. Remember this:
our country *is* our safety.
Only while she voyages true on course
can we establish friendships, truer than blood itself.
Such are my standards. They make our city great.

215   Closely akin to them I have proclaimed,
just now, the following decree to our people
concerning the two sons of Oedipus.
Eteocles, who died fighting for Thebes,
excelling all in arms: he shall be buried,

220   crowned with a hero's honors, the cups we pour
to soak the earth and reach the famous dead.

But as for his blood brother, Polynices,
who returned from exile, home to his father-city
and the gods of his race, consumed with one desire—

225   to burn them roof to roots—who thirsted to drink
his kinsmen's blood and sell the rest to slavery:
that man—a proclamation has forbidden the city
to dignify him with burial, mourn him at all.
No, he must be left unburied, his corpse

230   carrion for the birds and dogs to tear,
an obscenity for the citizens to behold!

These are my principles. Never at my hands
will the traitor be honored above the patriot.
But whoever proves his loyalty to the state:

235   I'll prize that man in death as well as life.
LEADER: If this is your pleasure, Creon, treating
our city's enemy and our friend this way . . .
The power is yours, I suppose, to enforce it
with the laws, both for the dead and all of us,
the living.

240   CREON: Follow my orders closely then,
be on your guard.
LEADER: We're too old.
Lay that burden on younger shoulders.
CREON: No, no,
I don't mean the body—I've posted guards already.
LEADER: What commands for us then? What other service?

245   CREON: See that you never side with those who break my orders.

LEADER: Never. Only a fool could be in love with death.

CREON: Death is the price—you're right. But all too often
    the mere hope of money has ruined many men.

(*A* SENTRY *enters from the side.*)

SENTRY: My lord,
    I can't say I'm winded from running, or set out
    with any spring in my legs either—no sir,   250
    I was lost in thought, and it made me stop, often,
    dead in my tracks, wheeling, turning back,
    and all the time a voice inside me muttering,
    "Idiot, why? You're going straight to your death."
    Then muttering, "Stopped again, poor fool?   255
    If somebody gets the news to Creon first,
    what's to save your neck?"
                     And so,
    mulling it over, on I trudged, dragging my feet,
    you can make a short road take forever . . .
    but at last, look, common sense won out,   260
    I'm here, and I'm all yours,
    and even though I come empty-handed
    I'll tell my story just the same, because
    I've come with a good grip on one hope,
    what will come will come, whatever fate—   265

CREON: Come to the point!
    What's wrong—why so afraid?

SENTRY: First, myself, I've got to tell you,
    I didn't do it, didn't see who did—
    Be fair, don't take it out on me.   270

CREON: You're playing it safe, soldier,
    barricading yourself from any trouble.
    It's obvious, you've something strange to tell.

SENTRY: Dangerous too, and danger makes you delay
    for all you're worth.   275

CREON: Out with it—then dismiss!

SENTRY: All right, here it comes. The body—
    someone's just buried it, then run off . . .
    sprinkled some dry dust on the flesh,
    given it proper rites.

CREON: What?   280
    What man alive would dare—

SENTRY: I've no idea, I swear it.
    There was no mark of a spade, no pickaxe there,
    no earth turned up, the ground packed hard and dry,
    unbroken, no tracks, no wheelruts, nothing,
    the workman left no trace. Just at sunup   285
    the first watch of the day points it out—

it was a wonder! We were stunned . . .
a terrific burden too, for all of us, listen:
you can't see the corpse, not that it's buried,
290   really, just a light cover of road-dust on it,
as if someone meant to lay the dead to rest
and keep from getting cursed.
Not a sign in sight that dogs or wild beasts
had worried the body, even torn the skin.

295   But what came next! Rough talk flew thick and fast,
guard grilling guard—we'd have come to blows
at last, nothing to stop it; each man for himself
and each the culprit, no one caught red-handed,
all of us pleading ignorance, dodging the charges,
300   ready to take up red-hot iron in our fists,
go through fire, swear oaths to the gods—
"I didn't do it, I had no hand in it either,
not in the plotting, not in the work itself!"

Finally, after all this wrangling came to nothing,
305   one man spoke out and made us stare at the ground,
hanging our heads in fear. No way to counter him,
no way to take his advice and come through
safe and sound. Here's what he said:
"Look, we've got to report the facts to Creon,
310   we can't keep this hidden." Well, that won out,
and the lot fell on me, condemned me,
unlucky as ever, I got the prize. So here I am,
against my will and yours too, well I know—
no one wants the man who brings bad news.

LEADER: My king,
315   ever since he began I've been debating in my mind,
could this possibly be the work of the gods?

CREON: Stop—
before you make me choke with anger—the gods!
You, you're senile, must you be insane?
You say—why it's intolerable—say the gods
320   could have the slightest concern for that corpse?
Tell me, was it for meritorious service
they proceeded to bury him, prized him so? The hero
who came to burn their temples ringed with pillars,
their golden treasures—scorch their hallowed earth
325   and fling their laws to the winds.
Exactly when did you last see the gods
celebrating traitors? Inconceivable!

No, from the first there were certain citizens
who could hardly stand the spirit of my regime,

grumbling against me in the dark, heads together,   330
tossing wildly, never keeping their necks beneath
the yoke, loyally submitting to their king.
These are the instigators, I'm convinced—
they've perverted my own guard, bribed them
to do their work.

                Money! Nothing worse   335
in our lives, so current, rampant, so corrupting.
Money—you demolish cities, root men from their homes,
you train and twist good minds and set them on
to the most atrocious schemes. No limit,
you make them adept at every kind of outrage,   340
every godless crime—money!

                Everyone—
the whole crew bribed to commit this crime,
they've made one thing sure at least:
sooner or later they will pay the price.

(*Wheeling on the* SENTRY.)

                You—
I swear to Zeus as I still believe in Zeus,   345
if you don't find the man who buried that corpse,
the very man, and produce him before my eyes,
simple death won't be enough for you,
not till we string you up alive
and wring the immorality out of you.   350
Then you can steal the rest of your days,
better informed about where to make a killing.
You'll have learned, at last, it doesn't pay
to itch for rewards from every hand that beckons.
Filthy profits wreck most men, you'll see—   355
they'll never save your life.
SENTRY: Please,
    may I say a word or two, or just turn and go?
CREON: Can't you tell? Everything you say offends me.
SENTRY: Where does it hurt you, in the ears or in the heart?
CREON: And who are you to pinpoint my displeasure?   360
SENTRY: The culprit grates on your feelings,
    I just annoy your ears.
CREON: Still talking?
    You talk too much! A born nuisance—
SENTRY: Maybe so,
    but I never did this thing, so help me!
CREON: Yes you did—
    what's more, you squandered your life for silver!   365
SENTRY: Oh it's terrible when the one who does the judging
    judges things all wrong.

CREON: Well now,
        you just be clever about your judgments—
        if you fail to produce the criminals for me,
370   you'll swear your dirty money brought you pain.

(*Turning sharply, reentering the palace.*)

SENTRY: I hope he's found. Best thing by far.
        But caught or not, that's in the lap of fortune;
        I'll never come back, you've seen the last of me.
        I'm saved, even now, and I never thought,
375   I never hoped—
        dear gods, I owe you all my thanks!

(*Rushing out.*)

CHORUS: Numberless wonders
        terrible wonders walk the world but none the match for man—
        that great wonder crossing the heaving gray sea,
                        driven on by the blasts of winter
380   on through breakers crashing left and right,
                holds his steady course
        and the oldest of the gods he wears away—
        the Earth, the immortal, the inexhaustible—
        as his plows go back and forth, year in, year out
385   with the breed of stallions turning up the furrows.

        And the blithe, lightheaded race of birds he snares,
        the tribes of savage beasts, the life that swarms the depths—
                        with one fling of his nets
        woven and coiled tight, he takes them all,
390   man the skilled, the brilliant!
        He conquers all, taming with his techniques
        the prey that roams the cliffs and wild lairs,
        training the stallion, clamping the yoke across
                his shaggy neck, and the tireless mountain bull.

395 And speech and thought, quick as the wind
                and the mood and mind for law that rules the city—
                all these he has taught himself
        and shelter from the arrows of the frost
        when there's rough lodging under the cold clear sky
400   and the shafts of lashing rain—
                        ready, resourceful man!
                        Never without resources
        never an impasse as he marches on the future—
        only Death, from Death alone he will find no rescue
405   but from desperate plagues he has plotted his escapes.

Man the master, ingenious past all measure

past all dreams, the skills within his grasp—
    he forges on, now to destruction
now again to greatness. When he weaves in
the laws of the land, and the justice of the gods   410
that binds his oaths together
           he and his city rise high—
                    but the city casts out
that man who weds himself to inhumanity
thanks to reckless daring. Never share my hearth   415
never think my thoughts, whoever does such things.

(*Enter* ANTIGONE *from the side, accompanied by the* SENTRY.)

    Here is a dark sign from the gods—
    what to make of this? I know her,
    how can I deny it? That young girl's Antigone!
    Wretched, child of a wretched father,   420
    Oedipus. Look, is it possible?
    They bring you in like a prisoner—
    why? did you break the king's laws?
    Did they take you in some act of mad defiance?
SENTRY: She's the one, she did it single-handed—   425
    we caught her burying the body. Where's Creon?

(*Enter* CREON *from the palace.*)

LEADER: Back again, just in time when you need him.
CREON: In time for what? What is it?
SENTRY: My king,
    there's nothing you can swear you'll never do—
    second thoughts make liars of us all.   430
    I could have sworn I wouldn't hurry back
    (what with your threats, the buffeting I just took),
    but a stroke of luck beyond our wildest hopes,
    what a joy, there's nothing like it. So,
    back I've come, breaking my oath, who cares?   435
    I'm bringing in our prisoner—this young girl—
    we took her giving the dead the last rites.
    But no casting lots this time; this is *my* luck,
    my prize, no one else's.
                    Now, my lord,
    here she is. Take her, question her,   440
    cross-examine her to your heart's content.
    But set me free, it's only right—
    I'm rid of this dreadful business once for all.
CREON: Prisoner! Her? You took her—where, doing what?
SENTRY: Burying the man. That's the whole story.
CREON: What?   445
    You mean what you say, you're telling me the truth?

SENTRY: She's the one. With my own eyes I saw her
    bury the body, just what you've forbidden.
    There. Is that plain and clear?

450   CREON: What did you see? Did you catch her in the act?

SENTRY: Here's what happened. We went back to our post,
    those threats of yours breathing down our necks—
    we brushed the corpse clean of the dust that covered it,
    stripped it bare . . . it was slimy, going soft,

455   and we took to high ground, backs to the wind
    so the stink of him couldn't hit us;
    jostling, baiting each other to keep awake,
    shouting back and forth—no napping on the job,
    not this time. And so the hours dragged by

460   until the sun stood dead above our heads,
    a huge white ball in the noon sky, beating,
    blazing down, and then it happened—
    suddenly, a whirlwind!
    Twisting a great dust-storm up from the earth,

465   a black plague of the heavens, filling the plain,
    ripping the leaves off every tree in sight,
    choking the air and sky. We squinted hard
    and took our whipping from the gods.

    And after the storm passed—it seemed endless—

470   there, we saw the girl!
    And she cried out a sharp, piercing cry,
    like a bird come back to an empty nest,
    peering into its bed, and all the babies gone . . .
    Just so, when she sees the corpse bare

475   she bursts into a long, shattering wail
    and calls down withering curses on the heads
    of all who did the work. And she scoops up dry dust,
    handfuls, quickly, and lifting a fine bronze urn,
    lifting it high and pouring, she crowns the dead
    with three full libations.

480   Soon as we saw
    we rushed her, closed on the kill like hunters,
    and she, she didn't flinch. We interrogated her,
    charging her with offenses past and present—
    she stood up to it all, denied nothing. I tell you,

485   it made me ache and laugh in the same breath.
    It's pure joy to escape the worst yourself,
    it hurts a man to bring down his friends.
    But all that, I'm afraid, means less to me
    than my own skin. That's the way I'm made.

CREON (*Wheeling on* ANTIGONE):   You,

490   with your eyes fixed on the ground—speak up.

Do you deny you did this, yes or no?
ANTIGONE: I did it. I don't deny a thing.
CREON (*To the* SENTRY): You, get out, wherever you please—
  you're clear of a very heavy charge.

(*He leaves;* CREON *turns back to* ANTIGONE.)

You, tell me briefly, no long speeches—   495
  were you aware a decree had forbidden this?
ANTIGONE: Well aware. How could I avoid it? It was public.
CREON: And still you had the gall to break this law?
ANTIGONE: Of course I did. It wasn't Zeus, not in the least,
  who made this proclamation—not to me.   500
  Nor did that Justice, dwelling with the gods
  beneath the earth, ordain such laws for men.
  Nor did I think your edict had such force
  that you, a mere mortal, could override the gods,
  the great unwritten, unshakable traditions.   505
  They are alive, not just today or yesterday:
  they live forever, from the first of time,
  and no one knows when they first saw the light.

  These laws—I was not about to break them,
  not out of fear of some man's wounded pride,   510
  and face the retribution of the gods.
  Die I must, I've known it all my life—
  how could I keep from knowing?—even without
  your death-sentence ringing in my ears.
  And if I am to die before my time   515
  I consider that a gain. Who on earth,
  alive in the midst of so much grief as I,
  could fail to find his death a rich reward?
  So for me, at least, to meet this doom of yours
  is precious little pain. But if I had allowed   520
  my own mother's son to rot, an unburied corpse—
  that would have been an agony! This is nothing.
  And if my present actions strike you as foolish,
  let's just say I've been accused of folly
  by a fool.
LEADER: Like father like daughter,   525
  passionate, wild . . .
  she hasn't learned to bend before adversity.
CREON: No? Believe me, the stiffest stubborn wills
  fall the hardest; the toughest iron,
  tempered strong in the white-hot fire,   530
  you'll see it crack and shatter first of all.
  And I've known spirited horses you can break
  with a light bit—proud, rebellious horses.

535   There's no room for pride, not in a slave,
not with the lord and master standing by.

This girl was an old hand at insolence
when she overrode the edicts we made public.
But once she'd done it—the insolence,
540   twice over—to glory in it, laughing,
mocking us to our face with what she'd done.
I'm not the man, not now: she is the man
if this victory goes to her and she goes free.

Never! Sister's child or closer in blood
than all my family clustered at my altar
545   worshiping Guardian Zeus—she'll never escape,
she and her blood sister, the most barbaric death.
Yes, I accuse her sister of an equal part
in scheming this, this burial.

(*To his attendants.*)

                        Bring her here!
I just saw her inside, hysterical, gone to pieces.
550   It never fails: the mind convicts itself
in advance, when scoundrels are up to no good,
plotting in the dark. Oh but I hate it more
when a traitor, caught red-handed,
tries to glorify his crimes.

555 ANTIGONE: Creon, what more do you want
than my arrest and execution?

CREON: Nothing. Then I have it all.

ANTIGONE: Then why delay? Your moralizing repels me,
every word you say—pray god it always will.
So naturally all I say repels you too.

560   Enough.
Give me glory! What greater glory could I win
than to give my own brother decent burial?
These citizens here would all agree,

(*To the* CHORUS.)

                they'd praise me too
565 if their lips weren't locked in fear.

(*Pointing to* CREON.)

Lucky tyrants—the perquisites of power!
Ruthless power to do and say whatever pleases *them*.

CREON: You alone, of all the people in Thebes,
see things that way.

ANTIGONE: They see it just that way
570 but defer to you and keep their tongues in leash.

CREON: And you, aren't you ashamed to differ so from them?
　　So disloyal!
ANTIGONE:　　　Not ashamed for a moment,
　　not to honor my brother, my own flesh and blood.
CREON: Wasn't Eteocles a brother too—cut down, facing him?
ANTIGONE: Brother, yes, by the same mother, the same father.　　　575
CREON: Then how can you render his enemy such honors,
　　such impieties in his eyes?
ANTIGONE: He'll never testify to that,
　　Eteocles dead and buried.
CREON:　　　　　　　　He will—
　　if you honor the traitor just as much as him.　　　580
ANTIGONE: But it was his brother, not some slave that died—
CREON: Ravaging our country!—
　　but Eteocles died fighting in our behalf.
ANTIGONE: No matter—Death longs for the same rites for all.
CREON: Never the same for the patriot and the traitor.　　　585
ANTIGONE: Who, Creon, who on earth can say the ones below
　　don't find this pure and uncorrupt?
CREON: Never. Once an enemy, never a friend,
　　not even after death.
ANTIGONE: I was born to join in love, not hate—　　　590
　　that is my nature.
CREON:　　　　　　Go down below and love,
　　if love you must—love the dead! While I'm alive,
　　no woman is going to lord it over me.

(Enter ISMENE from the palace, under guard.)

CHORUS:　　　　　　　　　　　Look,
　　Ismene's coming, weeping a sister's tears,
　　loving sister, under a cloud . . .　　　595
　　her face is flushed, her cheeks streaming.
　　Sorrow puts her lovely radiance in the dark.
CREON:　　　　　　　　　　　You—
　　in my house, you viper, slinking undetected,
　　sucking my life-blood! I never knew
　　I was breeding twin disasters, the two of you　　　600
　　rising up against my throne. Come, tell me,
　　will you confess your part in the crime or not?
　　Answer me. Swear to me.
ISMENE:　　　　　　　I did it, yes—
　　if only she consents—I share the guilt,
　　the consequences too.
ANTIGONE:　　　　　　No,　　　605
　　Justice will never suffer that—not you,
　　you were unwilling. I never brought you in.
ISMENE: But now you face such dangers . . . I'm not ashamed

> to sail through trouble with you,
> make your troubles mine.

610 ANTIGONE: Who did the work?
> Let the dead and the god of death bear witness!
> I've no love for a friend who loves in words alone.

ISMENE: Oh no, my sister, don't reject me, please,
> let me die beside you, consecrating
> the dead together.

615 ANTIGONE: Never share my dying,
> don't lay claim to what you never touched.
> My death will be enough.

ISMENE: What do I care for life, cut off from you?

ANTIGONE: Ask Creon. Your concern is all for him.

ISMENE: Why abuse me so? It doesn't help you now.

620 ANTIGONE: You're right—
> if I mock you, I get no pleasure from it,
> only pain.

ISMENE: Tell me, dear one,
> what can I do to help you, even now?

ANTIGONE: Save yourself. I don't grudge you your survival.

625 ISMENE: Oh no, no, denied my portion in your death?

ANTIGONE: You chose to live, I chose to die.

ISMENE: Not, at least,
> without every kind of caution I could voice.

ANTIGONE: Your wisdom appealed to one world—mine, another.

ISMENE: But look, we're both guilty, both condemned to death.

630 ANTIGONE: Courage! Live your life. I gave myself to death,
> long ago, so I might serve the dead.

CREON: They're both mad, I tell you, the two of them.
> One's just shown it, the other's been that way
> since she was born.

ISMENE: True, my king,
635 the sense we were born with cannot last forever . . .
> commit cruelty on a person long enough
> and the mind begins to go.

CREON: Yours did,
> when you chose to commit your crimes with her.

ISMENE: How can I live alone, without her?

CREON: Her?
640 Don't even mention her—she no longer exists.

ISMENE: What? You'd kill your own son's bride?

CREON: Absolutely:
> there are other fields for him to plow.

ISMENE: Perhaps,
> but never as true, as close a bond as theirs.

CREON: A worthless woman for my son? It repels me.

645 ISMENE: Dearest Haemon, your father wrongs you so!

CREON: Enough, enough—you and your talk of marriage!
ISMENE: Creon—you're really going to rob your son of Antigone?
CREON: Death will do it for me—break their marriage off.
LEADER: So, it's settled then? Antigone must die?
CREON: Settled, yes—we both know that.   650

(*To the guards.*)

Stop wasting time. Take them in.
From now on they'll act like women.
Tie them up, no more running loose;
even the bravest will cut and run,
once they see Death coming for their lives.   655

(*The guards escort* ANTIGONE *and* ISMENE *into the palace.* CREON *remains while
the old citizens form their chorus.*)

CHORUS: Blest, they are the truly blest who all their lives
have never tasted devastation. For others, once
the gods have rocked a house to its foundations
the ruin will never cease, cresting on and on
from one generation on throughout the race—   660
like a great mounting tide
driven on by savage northern gales,
        surging over the dead black depths
roiling up from the bottom dark heaves of sand
and the headlands, taking the storm's onslaught full-force,   665
roar, and the low moaning
                        echoes on and on
                                    and now
as in ancient times I see the sorrows of the house,
the living heirs of the old ancestral kings,
piling on the sorrows of the dead
        and one generation cannot free the next—   670
some god will bring them crashing down,
the race finds no release.
And now the light, the hope
        springing up from the late last root
in the house of Oedipus, that hope's cut down in turn   675
by the long, bloody knife swung by the gods of death
by a senseless word
                        by fury at the heart.
                                Zeus,
yours is the power, Zeus, what man on earth
can override it, who can hold it back?
Power that neither Sleep, the all-ensnaring   680
        no, nor the tireless months of heaven
can ever overmaster—young through all time,
mighty lord of power, you hold fast

the dazzling crystal mansions of Olympus.
685   And throughout the future, late and soon
as through the past, your law prevails:
no towering form of greatness
enters into the lives of mortals
free and clear of ruin.
True,
690   our dreams, our high hopes voyaging far and wide
bring sheer delight to many, to many others
delusion, blithe, mindless lusts
and the fraud steals on one slowly . . . unaware
till he trips and puts his foot into the fire.
695   He was a wise old man who coined
the famous saying: "Sooner or later
foul is fair, fair is foul
to the man the gods will ruin"—
He goes his way for a moment only
700   free of blinding ruin.

(*Enter* HAEMON *from the palace.*)

Here's Haemon now, the last of all your sons.
Does he come in tears for his bride,
his doomed bride, Antigone—
bitter at being cheated of their marriage?

705   CREON: We'll soon know, better than seers could tell us.

(*Turning to* HAEMON.)

Son, you've heard the final verdict on your bride?
Are you coming now, raving against your father?
Or do you love me, no matter what I do?

HAEMON: Father, I'm your *son* . . . you in your wisdom
710   set my bearings for me—I obey you.
No marriage could ever mean more to me than you,
whatever good direction you may offer.

CREON: Fine, Haemon.
That's how you ought to feel within your heart,
subordinate to your father's will in every way.
715   That's what a man prays for: to produce good sons—
households full of them, dutiful and attentive,
so they can pay his enemy back with interest
and match the respect their father shows his friend.
But the man who rears a brood of useless children,
720   what has he brought into the world, I ask you?
Nothing but trouble for himself, and mockery
from his enemies laughing in his face.
Oh Haemon,
never lose your sense of judgment over a woman.

The warmth, the rush of pleasure, it all goes cold
in your arms, I warn you . . . a worthless woman   725
in your house, a misery in your bed.
What wound cuts deeper than a loved one
turned against you? Spit her out,
like a mortal enemy—let the girl go.
Let her find a husband down among the dead.   730

Imagine it: I caught her in naked rebellion,
the traitor, the only one in the whole city.
I'm not about to prove myself a liar,
not to my people, no, I'm going to kill her!
That's right—so let her cry for mercy, sing her hymns   735
to Zeus who defends all bonds of kindred blood.
Why, if I bring up my own kin to be rebels,
think what I'd suffer from the world at large.
Show me the man who rules his household well:
I'll show you someone fit to rule the state.   740
That good man, my son,
I have every confidence he and he alone
can give commands and take them too. Staunch
in the storm of spears he'll stand his ground,
a loyal, unflinching comrade at your side.   745

But whoever steps out of line, violates the laws
or presumes to hand out orders to his superiors,
he'll win no praise from me. But that man
the city places in authority, his orders
must be obeyed, large and small,   750
right and wrong.
              Anarchy—
show me a greater crime in all the earth!
She, she destroys cities, rips up houses,
breaks the ranks of spearmen into headlong rout.
But the ones who last it out, the great mass of them   755
owe their lives to discipline. Therefore
we must defend the men who live by law,
never let some woman triumph over us.
Better to fall from power, if fall we must,
at the hands of a man—never be rated   760
inferior to a woman, never.

LEADER: To us,
    unless old age has robbed us of our wits,
    you seem to say what you have to say with sense.

HAEMON: Father, only the gods endow a man with reason,
    the finest of all their gifts, a treasure.   765
    Far be it from me—I haven't the skill,
    and certainly no desire, to tell you when,

if ever, you make a slip in speech . . . though
someone else might have a good suggestion.

770   Of course it's not for you,
in the normal run of things, to watch
whatever men say or do, or find to criticize.
The man in the street, you know, dreads your glance,
he'd never say anything displeasing to your face.
775   But it's for me to catch the murmurs in the dark,
the way the city mourns for this young girl.
"No woman," they say, "ever deserved death less,
and such a brutal death for such a glorious action.
She, with her own dear brother lying in his blood—
780   she couldn't bear to leave him dead, unburied,
food for the wild dogs or wheeling vultures.
Death? She deserves a glowing crown of gold!"
So they say, and the rumor spreads in secret,
darkly . . .
              I rejoice in your success, father—
785   nothing more precious to me in the world.
What medal of honor brighter to his children
than a father's growing glory? Or a child's
to his proud father? Now don't, please,
be quite so single-minded, self-involved,
790   or assume the world is wrong and you are right.
Whoever thinks that he alone possesses intelligence,
the gift of eloquence, he and no one else,
and character too . . . such men, I tell you,
spread them open—you will find them empty.
                                        No,
795   it's no disgrace for a man, even a wise man,
to learn many things and not to be too rigid.
You've seen trees by a raging winter torrent,
how many sway with the flood and salvage every twig,
but not the stubborn—they're ripped out, roots and all.
800   Bend or break. The same when a man is sailing:
haul your sheets too taut, never give an inch,
you'll capsize, go the rest of the voyage
keel up and the rowing-benches under.

Oh give way. Relax your anger—change!
805   I'm young, I know, but let me offer this:
it would be best by far, I admit,
if a man were born infallible, right by nature.
If not—and things don't often go that way,
it's best to learn from those with good advice.

810   LEADER: You'd do well, my lord, if he's speaking to the point,

to learn from him,

(*Turning to* HAEMON.)

         and you, my boy, from him.
    You both are talking sense.
CREON: So,
    men our age, we're to be lectured, are we?—
    schooled by a boy his age?
HAEMON: Only in what is right. But if I seem young,   *815*
    look less to my years and more to what I do.
CREON: Do? Is admiring rebels an achievement?
HAEMON: I'd never suggest that you admire treason.
CREON: Oh?—
    isn't that just the sickness that's attacked her?
HAEMON: The whole city of Thebes denies it, to a man.   *820*
CREON: And is Thebes about to tell me how to rule?
HAEMON: Now, you see? Who's talking like a child?
CREON: Am I to rule this land for others—or myself?
HAEMON: It's no city at all, owned by one man alone.
CREON: What? The city *is* the king's—that's the law!   *825*
HAEMON: What a splendid king you'd make of a desert island—
    you and you alone.
CREON (*To the* CHORUS): This boy, I do believe,
    is fighting on her side, the woman's side.
HAEMON: If you are a woman, yes;
    my concern is all for you.   *830*
CREON: Why, you degenerate—bandying accusations,
    threatening me with justice, your own father!
HAEMON: I see my father offending justice—wrong.
CREON: Wrong?
    To protect my royal rights?
HAEMON: Protect your rights?
    When you trample down the honors of the gods?   *835*
CREON: You, you soul of corruption, rotten through—
    woman's accomplice!
HAEMON: That may be,
    but you'll never find me accomplice to a criminal.
CREON: That's what *she* is,
    and every word you say is a blatant appeal for her—   *840*
HAEMON: And you, and me, and the gods beneath the earth.
CREON: You'll never marry her, not while she's alive.
HAEMON: Then she'll die . . . but her death will kill another.
CREON: What, brazen threats? You go too far!
HAEMON: What threat?
    Combating your empty, mindless judgments with a word?   *84*
CREON: You'll suffer for your sermons, you and your empty wisdom!

HAEMON: If you weren't my father, I'd say you were insane.

CREON: Don't flatter me with Father—you woman's slave!

HAEMON: You really expect to fling abuse at me
    and not receive the same?

850 CREON: Is that so!
    Now, by heaven, I promise you, you'll pay—
    taunting, insulting me! Bring her out,
    that hateful—she'll die now, here,
    in front of his eyes, beside her groom!

855 HAEMON: No, no, she will never die beside me—
    don't delude yourself. And you will never
    see me, never set eyes on my face again.
    Rage your heart out, rage with friends
    who can stand the sight of you.

    (Rushing out.)

860 LEADER: Gone, my king, in a burst of anger.
    A temper young as his . . . hurt him once,
    he may do something violent.

CREON: Let him do—
    dream up something desperate, past all human limit!
    Good riddance. Rest assured,

865   he'll never save those two young girls from death.

LEADER: Both of them, you really intend to kill them both?

CREON: No, not her, the one whose hands are clean;
    you're quite right.

LEADER: But Antigone—
    what sort of death do you have in mind for her?

870 CREON: I'll take her down some wild, desolate path
    never trod by men, and wall her up alive
    in a rocky vault, and set out short rations,
    just a gesture of piety
    to keep the entire city free of defilement.

875   There let her pray to the one god she worships:
    Death—who knows?—may just reprieve her from death.
    Or she may learn at last, better late than never,
    what a waste of breath it is to worship Death.

    (Exit to the palace.)

CHORUS: Love, never conquered in battle
880   Love the plunderer laying waste the rich!
    Love standing the night-watch
             guarding a girl's soft cheek,
    you range the seas, the shepherds' steadings off in the wilds—
    not even the deathless gods can flee your onset,
885   nothing human born for a day—
    whoever feels your grip is driven mad.

Love

you wrench the minds of the righteous into outrage,
swerve them to their ruin—you have ignited this,
this kindred strife, father and son at war
            and Love alone the victor— 890
warm glance of the bride triumphant, burning with desire!
Throned in power, side-by-side with the mighty laws!
Irresistible Aphrodite, never conquered—
Love, you mock us for your sport.

(ANTIGONE *is brought from the palace under guard.*)

      But now, even I'd rebel against the king, 895
      I'd break all bounds when I see this—
      I fill with tears, can't hold them back,
      not any more . . . I see Antigone make her way
      to the bridal vault where all are laid to rest.

ANTIGONE: Look at me, men of my fatherland, 900
      setting out on the last road
looking into the last light of day
the last I'll ever see . . .
the god of death who puts us all to bed
takes me down to the banks of Acheron alive— 905
      denied my part in the wedding-songs,
no wedding-song in the dusk has crowned my marriage—
I go to wed the lord of the dark waters.

CHORUS: Not crowned with glory, crowned with a dirge,
      you leave for the deep pit of the dead. 910
      No withering illness laid you low,
      no strokes of the sword—a law to yourself,
      alone, no mortal like you, ever, you go down
      to the halls of Death alive and breathing.

ANTIGONE: But think of Niobe—well I know her story— 915
      think what a living death she died,
Tantalus' daughter, stranger queen from the east:
there on the mountain heights, growing stone
binding as ivy, slowly walled her round
and the rains will never cease, the legends say 920
the snows will never leave her . . .
      wasting away, under her brows the tears
showering down her breasting ridge and slopes—
a rocky death like hers puts me to sleep.

CHORUS: But she was a god, born of gods, 925
      and we are only mortals born to die.
      And yet, of course, it's a great thing
      for a dying girl to hear, just hear
      she shares a destiny equal to the gods,
      during life and later, once she's dead.

930   ANTIGONE: O you mock me!
     Why, in the name of all my fathers' gods
     why can't you wait till I am gone—
         must you abuse me to my face?
     O my city, all your fine rich sons!
935   And you, you springs of the Dirce,
     holy grove of Thebes where the chariots gather,
         you at least, you'll bear me witness, look,
     unmourned by friends and forced by such crude laws
     I go to my rockbound prison, strange new tomb—
940   always a stranger, O dear god,
     I have no home on earth and none below,
       not with the living, not with the breathless dead.
CHORUS: You went too far, the last limits of daring—
     smashing against the high throne of Justice!
945   Your life's in ruins, child—I wonder . . .
     do you pay for your father's terrible ordeal?
ANTIGONE: There—at last you've touched it, the worst pain
     the worst anguish! Raking up the grief for father
     three times over, for all the doom
950   that's struck us down, the brilliant house of Laius.
     O mother, your marriage-bed
     the coiling horrors, the coupling there—
     you with your own son, my father—doomstruck mother!
     Such, such were my parents, and I their wretched child.
955   I go to them now, cursed, unwed, to share their home—
     I am a stranger! O dear brother, doomed
     in your marriage—your marriage murders mine,
     your dying drags me down to death alive!

(*Enter* CREON.)

CHORUS: Reverence asks some reverence in return—
960   but attacks on power never go unchecked,
     not by the man who holds the reins of power.
     Your own blind will, your passion has destroyed you.
ANTIGONE: No one to weep for me, my friends,
     no wedding-song—they take me away
965   in all my pain . . . the road lies open, waiting.
     Never again, the law forbids me to see
     the sacred eye of day. I am agony!
     No tears for the destiny that's mine,
     no loved one mourns my death.
CREON: Can't you see?
970   If a man could wail his own dirge *before* he dies,
     he'd never finish.

(*To the guards.*)

Take her away, quickly!
Wall her up in the tomb, you have your orders.
Abandon her there, alone, and let her choose—
death or a buried life with a good roof for shelter.
As for myself, my hands are clean. This young girl—   975
dead or alive, she will be stripped of her rights,
her stranger's rights, here in the world above.
ANTIGONE: O tomb, my bridal-bed—my house, my prison
cut in the hollow rock, my everlasting watch!
I'll soon be there, soon embrace my own,   980
the great growing family of our dead
Persephone has received among her ghosts.

                                      I,
the last of them all, the most reviled by far,
go down before my destined time's run out.
But still I go, cherishing one good hope: 985
my arrival may be dear to father,
dear to you, my mother,
dear to you, my loving brother, Eteocles—
When you died I washed you with my hands,
I dressed you all, I poured the cups   990
across your tombs. But now, Polynices,
because I laid your body out as well,
this, this is my reward. Nevertheless
I honored you—the decent will admit it—
well and wisely too.

                         Never, I tell you,   995
if I had been the mother of children
or if my husband died, exposed and rotting—
I'd never have taken this ordeal upon myself,
never defied our people's will. What law,
you ask, do I satisfy with what I say?   1000
A husband dead, there might have been another.
A child by another too, if I had lost the first.
But mother and father both lost in the halls of Death,
no brother could ever spring to light again.

For this law alone I held you first in honor.   1005
For this, Creon, the king, judges me a criminal
guilty of dreadful outrage, my dear brother!
And now he leads me off, a captive in his hands,
with no part in the bridal-song, the bridal-bed,
denied all joy of marriage, raising children—   1010
deserted so by loved ones, struck by fate,
I descend alive to the caverns of the dead.

What law of the mighty gods have I transgressed?
Why look to the heavens any more, tormented as I am?

1015   Whom to call, what comrades now? Just think,
       my reverence only brands me for irreverence!
       Very well: if this is the pleasure of the gods,
       once I suffer I will know that I was wrong.
       But if these men are wrong, let them suffer
1020   nothing worse than they mete out to me—
       these masters of injustice!
LEADER: Still the same rough winds, the wild passion
       raging through the girl.
CREON (*To the guards*):   Take her away.
       You're wasting time—you'll pay for it too.
1025   ANTIGONE: Oh god, the voice of death. It's come, it's here.
CREON: True. Not a word of hope—your doom is sealed.
ANTIGONE: Land of Thebes, city of all my fathers—
       O you gods, the first gods of the race!
       They drag me away, now, no more delay.
1030   Look on me, you noble sons of Thebes—
       the last of a great line of kings,
       I alone, see what I suffer now
       at the hands of what breed of men—
       all for reverence, my reverence for the gods!

(*She leaves under guard; the* CHORUS *gathers.*)

1035   CHORUS: Danaë, Danaë—
       even she endured a fate like yours,
       in all her lovely strength she traded
       the light of day for the bolted brazen vault—
       buried within her tomb, her bridal-chamber,
1040   wed to the yoke and broken.
             But she was of glorious birth
                   my child, my child
       and treasured the seed of Zeus within her womb,
       the cloudburst streaming gold!
1045   The power of fate is a wonder,
             dark, terrible wonder—
             neither wealth nor armies
             towered walls nor ships
             black hulls lashed by the salt
1050   can save us from that force.

       The yoke tamed him too
             young Lycurgus flaming in anger
       king of Edonia, all for his mad taunts
       Dionysus clamped him down, encased
1055   in the chain-mail of rock
             and there his rage

his terrible flowering rage burst—
sobbing, dying away . . . at last that madman
came to know his god—
    the power he mocked, the power
    he taunted in all his frenzy
    trying to stamp out
    the women strong with the god—
    the torch, the raving sacred cries—
    enraging the Muses who adore the flute.

And far north where the Black Rocks
    cut the sea in half
and murderous straits
split the coast of Thrace
    a forbidding city stands
where once, hard by the walls
the savage Ares thrilled to watch
a king's new queen, a Fury rearing in rage
    against his two royal sons—
    her bloody hands, her dagger-shuttle
stabbing out their eyes—cursed, blinding wounds—
their eyes blind sockets screaming for revenge!

They wailed in agony, cries echoing cries
    the princes doomed at birth . . .
and their mother doomed to chains,
walled off in a tomb of stone—
    but she traced her own birth back
to a proud Athenian line and the high gods
and off in caverns half the world away,
born of the wild North Wind
    she sprang on her father's gales,
    racing stallions up the leaping cliffs—
child of the heavens. But even on her the Fates
the gray everlasting Fates rode hard
my child, my child.

(*Enter* TIRESIAS, *the blind prophet, led by a boy.*)

TIRESIAS: Lords of Thebes,
    I and the boy have come together,
    hand in hand. Two see with the eyes of one . . .
    so the blind must go, with a guide to lead the way.
CREON: What is it, old Tiresias? What news now?
TIRESIAS: I will teach you. And you obey the seer.
CREON: I will,
    I've never wavered from your advice before.
TIRESIAS: And so you kept the city straight on course.

CREON: I owe you a great deal, I swear to that.

TIRESIAS: Then reflect, my son: you are poised,

1100   once more, on the razor-edge of fate.

CREON: What is it? I shudder to hear you.

TIRESIAS: You will learn

    when you listen to the warnings of my craft.

    As I sat on the ancient seat of augury,

    in the sanctuary where every bird I know

1105   will hover at my hands—suddenly I heard it,

    a strange voice in the wingbeats, unintelligible,

    barbaric, a mad scream! Talons flashing, ripping,

    they were killing each other—that much I knew—

    the murderous fury whirring in those wings

    made that much clear!

1110   I was afraid,

    I turned quickly, tested the burnt-sacrifice,

    ignited the altar at all points—but no fire,

    the god in the fire never blazed.

    Not from those offerings . . . over the embers

1115   slid a heavy ooze from the long thighbones,

    smoking, sputtering out, and the bladder

    puffed and burst—spraying gall into the air—

    and the fat wrapping the bones slithered off

    and left them glistening white. No fire!

1120   The rites failed that might have blazed the future

    with a sign. So I learned from the boy here;

    he is my guide, as I am guide to others.

                   And it's you—

    your high resolve that sets this plague on Thebes.

    The public altars and sacred hearths are fouled,

125   one and all, by the birds and dogs with carrion

    torn from the corpse, the doomstruck son of Oedipus!

    And so the gods are deaf to our prayers, they spurn

    the offerings in our hands, the flame of holy flesh.

    No birds cry out an omen clear and true—

130   they're gorged with the murdered victim's blood and fat.

    Take these things to heart, my son, I warn you.

    All men make mistakes, it is only human.

    But once the wrong is done, a man

    can turn his back on folly, misfortune too,

135   if he tries to make amends, however low he's fallen,

    and stops his bullnecked ways. Stubbornness

    brands you for stupidity—pride is a crime.

    No, yield to the dead!

    Never stab the fighter when he's down.

140   Where's the glory, killing the dead twice over?

I mean you well. I give you sound advice.
It's best to learn from a good adviser
when he speaks for your own good:
it's pure gain.
CREON: Old man—all of you! So,   114.
you shoot your arrows at my head like archers at the target—
I even have *him* loosed on me, this fortune-teller.
Oh his ilk has tried to sell me short
and ship me off for years. Well,
drive your bargains, traffic—much as you like—
in the gold of India, silver-gold of Sardis.   115.
You'll never bury that body in the grave,
not even if Zeus's eagles rip the corpse
and wing their rotten pickings off to the throne of god!
Never, not even in fear of such defilement
will I tolerate his burial, that traitor.   115
Well I know, we can't defile the gods—
no mortal has the power.
                              No,
reverend old Tiresias, all men fall,
it's only human, but the wisest fall obscenely
when they glorify obscene advice with rhetoric—   116
all for their own gain.
TIRESIAS: Oh god, is there a man alive
who knows, who actually believes . . .
CREON: What now?
What earth-shattering truth are you about to utter?
TIRESIAS: . . . just how much a sense of judgment, wisdom   116
is the greatest gift we have?
CREON: Just as much, I'd say,
as a twisted mind is the worst affliction going.
TIRESIAS: You are the one who's sick, Creon, sick to death.
CREON: I am in no mood to trade insults with a seer.
TIRESIAS: You have already, calling my prophecies a lie.
CREON: Why not?   117
You and the whole breed of seers are mad for money!
TIRESIAS: And the whole race of tyrants lusts to rake it in.
CREON: This slander of yours—
are you aware you're speaking to the king?
TIRESIAS: Well aware. Who helped you save the city?
CREON: You—   117
you have your skills, old seer, but you lust for injustice!
TIRESIAS: You will drive me to utter the dreadful secret in my heart.
CREON: Spit it out! Just don't speak it out for profit.
TIRESIAS: Profit? No, not a bit of profit, not for you.
CREON: Know full well, you'll never buy off my resolve.   118

TIRESIAS: Then know this too, learn this by heart!
The chariot of the sun will not race through
so many circuits more, before you have surrendered
one born of your own loins, your own flesh and blood,
185   a corpse for corpses given in return, since you have thrust
to the world below a child sprung for the world above,
ruthlessly lodged a living soul within the grave—
then you've robbed the gods below the earth,
keeping a dead body here in the bright air,
190   unburied, unsung, unhallowed by the rites.

You, you have no business with the dead,
nor do the gods above—this is violence
you have forced upon the heavens.
And so the avengers, the dark destroyers late
195   but true to the mark, now lie in wait for you,
the Furies sent by the gods and the god of death
to strike you down with the pains that you perfected!

There. Reflect on that, tell me I've been bribed.
The day comes soon, no long test of time, not now,
200   that wakes the wails for men and women in your halls.
Great hatred rises against you—
cities in tumult, all whose mutilated sons
the dogs have graced with burial, or the wild beasts,
some wheeling crow that wings the ungodly stench of carrion
205   back to each city, each warrior's hearth and home.

These arrows for your heart! Since you've raked me
I loose them like an archer in my anger,
arrows deadly true. You'll never escape
their burning, searing force.

(*Motioning to his escort.*)

210   Come, boy, take me home.
So he can vent his rage on younger men,
and learn to keep a gentler tongue in his head
and better sense than what he carries now.

(*Exit to the side.*)

LEADER: The old man's gone, my king—
215   terrible prophecies. Well I know,
since the hair on this old head went gray,
he's never lied to Thebes.
CREON: I know it myself—I'm shaken, torn.
It's a dreadful thing to yield . . . but resist now?
220   Lay my pride bare to the blows of ruin?
That's dreadful too.

LEADER: But good advice,
     Creon, take it now, you must.
CREON: What should I do? Tell me . . . I'll obey.
LEADER: Go! Free the girl from the rocky vault
     and raise a mound for the body you exposed.   122.
CREON: That's your advice? You think I should give in?
LEADER: Yes, my king, quickly. Disasters sent by the gods
     cut short our follies in a flash.
CREON: Oh it's hard,
     giving up the heart's desire . . . but I will do it—
     no more fighting a losing battle with necessity.   123
LEADER: Do it now, go, don't leave it to others.
CREON: Now—I'm on my way! Come, each of you,
     take up axes, make for the high ground,
     over there, quickly! I and my better judgment
     have come round to this—I shackled her,   123
     I'll set her free myself. I am afraid . . .
     it's best to keep the established laws
     to the very day we die.

     (*Rushing out, followed by his entourage. The* CHORUS *clusters around the altar.*)

CHORUS: God of a hundred names!
                    Great Dionysus—
          Son and glory of Semele! Pride of Thebes—
Child of Zeus whose thunder rocks the clouds—
Lord of the famous lands of evening—
King of the Mysteries!
                    King of Eleusis, Demeter's plain
her breasting hills that welcome in the world—
Great Dionysus!
               Bacchus, living in Thebes   124
the mother-city of all your frenzied women—
                              Bacchus
          living along the Ismenus' rippling waters
standing over the field sown with the Dragon's teeth!

You—we have seen you through the flaring smoky fires,
     your torches blazing over the twin peaks   125
where nymphs of the hallowed cave climb onward
               fired with you, your sacred rage—
we have seen you at Castalia's running spring
and down from the heights of Nysa crowned with ivy
the greening shore rioting vines and grapes   125
          down you come in your storm of wild women
          ecstatic, mystic cries—
                         Dionysus—
down to watch and ward the roads of Thebes!

First of all cities, Thebes you honor first
1260   you and your mother, bride of the lightning—
come, Dionysus! now your people lie
in the iron grip of plague,
come in your racing, healing stride
               down Parnassus' slopes
or across the moaning straits.
265   Lord of the dancing—
dance, dance the constellations breathing fire!
Great master of the voices of the night!
Child of Zeus, God's offspring, come, come forth!
Lord, king, dance with your nymphs, swirling, raving
270   arm-in-arm in frenzy through the night
          they dance you, Iacchus—
                    Dance, Dionysus
giver of all good things!

(*Enter a* MESSENGER *from the side.*)

MESSENGER: Neighbors,
friends of the house of Cadmus and the kings,
there's not a thing in this life of ours
275   I'd praise or blame as settled once for all.
Fortune lifts and Fortune fells the lucky
and unlucky every day. No prophet on earth
can tell a man his fate. Take Creon:
there was a man to rouse your envy once,
280   as I see it. He saved the realm from enemies;
taking power, he alone, the lord of the fatherland,
he set us true on course—flourished like a tree
with the noble line of sons he bred and reared . . .
and now it's lost, all gone.
                  Believe me,
285   when a man has squandered his true joys,
he's good as dead, I tell you, a living corpse.
Pile up riches in your house, as much as you like—
live like a king with a huge show of pomp,
but if real delight is missing from the lot,
290   I wouldn't give you a wisp of smoke for it,
not compared with joy.
LEADER: What now?
What new grief do you bring the house of kings?
MESSENGER: Dead, dead—and the living are guilty of their death!
LEADER: Who's the murderer? Who is dead? Tell us.
295   MESSENGER: Haemon's gone, his blood spilled by the very hand—
LEADER: His father's or his own?
MESSENGER: His own . . .
raging mad with his father for the death—

LEADER: Oh great seer,
    you saw it all, you brought your word to birth!
MESSENGER: Those are the facts. Deal with them as you will.

    (*As he turns to go,* EURYDICE *enters from the palace.*)

LEADER: Look, Eurydice. Poor woman, Creon's wife,   1300
    so close at hand. By chance perhaps,
    unless she's heard the news about her son.
EURYDICE: My countrymen,
    all of you—I caught the sound of your words
    as I was leaving to do my part,
    to appeal to queen Athena with my prayers.   1305
    I was just loosing the bolts, opening the doors,
    when a voice filled with sorrow, family sorrow,
    struck my ears, and I fell back, terrified,
    into the women's arms—everything went black.
    Tell me the news, again, whatever it is . . .   1310
    sorrow and I are hardly strangers;
    I can bear the worst.
MESSENGER: I—dear lady,
    I'll speak as an eye-witness. I was there.
    And I won't pass over one word of the truth.
    Why should I try to soothe you with a story,   1315
    only to prove a liar in a moment?
    Truth is always best.
             So,
    I escorted your lord, I guided him
    to the edge of the plain where the body lay,
    Polynices, torn by the dogs and still unmourned.   1320
    And saying a prayer to Hecate of the Crossroads,
    Pluto too, to hold their anger and be kind,
    we washed the dead in a bath of holy water
    and plucking some fresh branches, gathering . . .
    what was left of him, we burned them all together   1325
    and raised a high mound of native earth, and then
    we turned and made for that rocky vault of hers,
    the hollow, empty bed of the bride of Death.
    And far off, one of us heard a voice,
    a long wail rising, echoing   1330
    out of that unhallowed wedding-chamber;
    he ran to alert the master and Creon pressed on,
    closer—the strange, inscrutable cry came sharper,
    throbbing around him now, and he let loose
    a cry of his own, enough to wrench the heart,   1335
    "Oh god, am I the prophet now? going down
    the darkest road I've ever gone? My son—
    it's *his* dear voice, he greets me! Go, men,

closer, quickly! Go through the gap,
1340   the rocks are dragged back—
right to the tomb's very mouth—and look,
see if it's Haemon's voice I think I hear,
or the gods have robbed me of my senses."

The king was shattered. We took his orders,
1345   went and searched, and there in the deepest,
dark recesses of the tomb we found her . . .
hanged by the neck in a fine linen noose,
strangled in her veils—and the boy,
his arms flung around her waist,
1350   clinging to her, wailing for his bride,
dead and down below, for his father's crimes
and the bed of his marriage blighted by misfortune.
When Creon saw him, he gave a deep sob,
he ran in, shouting, crying out to him,
1355   "Oh my child—what have you done? what seized you,
what insanity? what disaster drove you mad?
Come out, my son! I beg you on my knees!"
But the boy gave him a wild burning glance,
spat in his face, not a word in reply,
1360   he drew his sword—his father rushed out,
running as Haemon lunged and missed!—
and then, doomed, desperate with himself,
suddenly leaning his full weight on the blade,
he buried it in his body, halfway to the hilt.
1365   And still in his senses, pouring his arms around her,
he embraced the girl and breathing hard,
released a quick rush of blood,
bright red on her cheek glistening white.
And there he lies, body enfolding body . . .
1370   he has won his bride at last, poor boy,
not here but in the houses of the dead.

Creon shows the world that of all the ills
afflicting men the worst is lack of judgment.

(EURYDICE *turns and reenters the palace.*)

LEADER: What do you make of that? The lady's gone,
without a word, good or bad.

375   MESSENGER: I'm alarmed too
but here's my hope—faced with her son's death,
she finds it unbecoming to mourn in public.
Inside, under her roof, she'll set her women
to the task and wail the sorrow of the house.
380   She's too discreet. She won't do something rash.

LEADER: I'm not so sure. To me, at least,

a long heavy silence promises danger,
just as much as a lot of empty outcries.
MESSENGER: We'll see if she's holding something back,
hiding some passion in her heart.   1385
I'm going in. You may be right—who knows?
Even too much silence has its dangers.

(*Exit to the palace. Enter* CREON *from the side, escorted by attendants carrying* HAEMON'*s body on a bier.*)

LEADER: The king himself! Coming toward us,
look, holding the boy's head in his hands.
Clear, damning proof, if it's right to say so—   1390
proof of his own madness, no one else's,
no, his own blind wrongs.
CREON: Ohhh,
so senseless, so insane . . . my crimes,
my stubborn, deadly—
Look at us, the killer, the killed,   1395
father and son, the same blood—the misery!
My plans, my mad fanatic heart,
my son, cut off so young!
Ai, dead, lost to the world,
not through your stupidity, no, my own.
LEADER: Too late,   1400
too late, you see what justice means.
CREON: Oh I've learned
through blood and tears! Then, it was then,
when the god came down and struck me—a great weight
shattering, driving me down that wild savage path,
ruining, trampling down my joy. Oh the agony,   1405
the heartbreaking agonies of our lives.

(*Enter the* MESSENGER *from the palace.*)

MESSENGER: Master,
what a hoard of grief you have, and you'll have more.
The grief that lies to hand you've brought yourself—

(*Pointing to* HAEMON'*s body.*)

the rest, in the house, you'll see it all too soon.
CREON: What now? What's worse than this?
MESSENGER: The queen is dead.   1410
The mother of this dead boy . . . mother to the end—
poor thing, her wounds are fresh.
CREON: No, no,
harbor of Death, so choked, so hard to cleanse!—
why me? why are you killing me?
Herald of pain, more words, more grief?   1415

I died once, you kill me again and again!
What's the report, boy . . . some news for me?
My wife dead? O dear god!
Slaughter heaped on slaughter?

(*The doors open; the body of* EURYDICE *is brought out on her bier.*)

MESSENGER: See for yourself:
now they bring her body from the palace.
1420 CREON: Oh no,
another, a second loss to break the heart.
What next, what fate still waits for me?
I just held my son in my arms and now,
look, a new corpse rising before my eyes—
1425   wretched, helpless mother—O my son!
MESSENGER: She stabbed herself at the altar,
then her eyes went dark, after she'd raised
a cry for the noble fate of Megareus, the hero
killed in the first assault, then for Haemon,
1430 then with her dying breath she called down
torments on your head—you killed her sons.
CREON: Oh the dread,
I shudder with dread! Why not kill me too?—
run me through with a good sharp sword?
Oh god, the misery, anguish—
1435 I, I'm churning with it, going under.
MESSENGER: Yes, and the dead, the woman lying there,
piles the guilt of all their deaths on you.
CREON: How did she end her life, what bloody stroke?
MESSENGER: She drove home to the heart with her own hand,
1440 once she learned her son was dead . . . that agony.
CREON: And the guilt is all mine—
can never be fixed on another man,
no escape for me. I killed you,
I, god help me, I admit it all!

(*To his attendants.*)

1445 Take me away, quickly, out of sight.
I don't even exist—I'm no one. Nothing.
LEADER: Good advice, if there's any good in suffering.
Quickest is best when troubles block the way.
CREON: (*Kneeling in prayer*) Come, let it come!—that best of fates for me
1450 that brings the final day, best fate of all.
Oh quickly, now—
so I never have to see another sunrise.
LEADER: That will come when it comes;
we must deal with all that lies before us.
1455 The future rests with the ones who tend the future.

CREON: That prayer—I poured my heart into that prayer!
LEADER: No more prayers now. For mortal men
    there is no escape from the doom we must endure.
CREON: Take me away, I beg you, out of sight.   1460
    A rash, indiscriminate fool!
    I murdered you, my son, against my will—
    you too, my wife . . .
                Wailing wreck of a man,
    whom to look to? where to lean for support?

(Desperately turning from HAEMON *to* EURYDICE *on their biers.)*

    Whatever I touch goes wrong—once more
    a crushing fate's come down upon my head.   1465

(The MESSENGER *and attendants lead* CREON *into the palace.)*

CHORUS: Wisdom is by far the greatest part of joy,
    and reverence toward the gods must be safeguarded.
    The mighty words of the proud are paid in full
    with mighty blows of fate, and at long last
        those blows will teach us wisdom.   1470

(The old citizens exit to the side.)

(translated by Robert Fagles)

QUESTIONS FOR DISCUSSION AND WRITING

1. Early on in the play, Antigone tells Ismene: "You'll soon show what you are, / worth your breeding, Ismene, or a coward— / for all your royal blood" (44–46). In his first speech in the play, Creon takes a very different view, proclaiming, "As I see it, whoever assumes the task, / the awesome task of setting the city's course, / and refuses to adopt the soundest policies / but fearing someone, keeps his lips locked tight, / he's utterly worthless" (198–202). The two central characters thus make clear that they come to the central issue of the play with very different assumptions about the relative importance of private and public good. Examine that opposition. To what extent do other characters in the play share Antigone's and Creon's worldviews? To what extent does each of the central characters recognize the value of the other's moral system?

2. Antigone believes herself to be motivated by loyalty to family; Creon believes himself to be motivated by his desire to put the public good first. But each may have unspoken, or unrecognized, motivations. And each, perhaps wrongly, ascribes to others in the play a number of motives for their actions. Consider the following characters. What motivates them to act as they do? To what extent are we meant to sympathize with their motives and/or to find them faulty?

Antigone	Creon
Haemon	Ismene
the Sentry	

3. Antigone goes to her death upholding a moral principle, and for that action many see her as a hero. Other readers, though, find less to admire in her character. Where do you stand? Do you *like* Antigone? Do you find her words and actions heroic? Why or why not? Similarly, do you like Creon? Find him heroic? Why or why not?

4. Although Creon and Antigone are clearly in conflict, and clearly hold different values, it might also be said that they are more similar than either would care to admit. What similarities do you see in their characters? In their modes of behavior? In their attitudes about themselves and others?

5. When he first learns that someone has illegally buried Polynices, Creon immediately assumes that that someone is a man, and, throughout the play, he and others exhibit surprise, and perhaps disgust, at Antigone's unfeminine behavior. What role does gender play in *Antigone*? Think not only about how men and women behave and speak but also about how various characters speak of gender throughout the drama. To what extent are we meant to think of the clash between Creon and Antigone as a clash not only between the state and the family but also between men and women? How much is the play about the clash between generations?

6. Look at the role of the Chorus in *Antigone*. With whom does the Chorus seem to identify and sympathize throughout the play? When, and how and why, does the Chorus's point of view shift?

JONATHAN SWIFT (1667–1745)

A Modest Proposal   1729

For Preventing the Children of Poor People in Ireland from Being a Burden to Their Parents or Country, and for Making Them Beneficial to the Public

It is a melancholy object to those who walk through this great town or travel in the country, when they see the streets, the roads, and cabin doors, crowded with beggars of the female-sex, followed by three, four, or six children, all in rags and importuning every passenger for an alms. These mothers, instead of being able to work for their honest livelihood, are forced to employ all their time in strolling to beg sustenance for their helpless infants, who, as they grow up, either turn thieves for want of work, or leave their dear native country to fight for the Pretender in Spain, or sell themselves to the Barbadoes.

I think it is agreed by all parties that this prodigious number of children in the arms, or on the backs, or at the heels of their mothers, and frequently of their fathers, is in the present deplorable state of the kingdom a very great additional grievance; and therefore whoever could find out a fair, cheap, and easy method of making these children sound, useful members of the commonwealth would deserve so well of the public as to have his statue set up for a preserver of the nation.

But my intention is very far from being confined to provide only for the children of professed beggars; it is of a much greater extent, and shall take in the whole number of infants at a certain age who are born of parents in effect as little able to support them as those who demand our charity in the streets.

As to my own part, having turned my thoughts for many years upon this important subject, and maturely weighed the several schemes of other projectors, I have always found them grossly mistaken in their computation. It is true, a child just dropped from its dam may be supported by her milk for a solar year, with little other nourishment; at most not above the value of two shillings, which the mother may certainly get, or the value in scraps, by her lawful occupation of begging; and it is exactly at one year old that I propose to provide for them in such a manner as instead of being a charge upon their parents or the parish, or wanting food and raiment for the rest of their lives, they shall on the contrary contribute to the feeding, and partly to the clothing, of many thousands.

There is likewise another great advantage in my scheme, that it will prevent those voluntary abortions, and that horrid practice of women murdering their bastard children, alas, too frequent among us, sacrificing the poor innocent babes, I doubt, more to avoid the expense than the shame, which would move tears and pity in the most savage and inhuman breast.

The number of souls in this kingdom being usually reckoned one million and a half, of these I calculate there may be about two hundred thousand couple whose wives are breeders; from which number I subtract thirty thousand couples who are able to maintain their own children, although I apprehend there cannot be so many under the present distresses of the kingdom; but this being granted, there will remain an hundred and seventy thousand breeders. I again subtract fifty thousand for those women who miscarry, or whose children die by accident or disease within the year. There only remain an hundred and twenty thousand children of poor parents annually born. The question therefore is, how this number shall be reared and provided for, which, as I have already said, under the present situation of affairs, is utterly impossible by all the methods hitherto proposed. For we can neither employ them in handicraft or agriculture; we neither build houses (I mean in the country) nor cultivate land. They can very seldom pick up a livelihood by stealing till they arrive at six years old, except where they are of towardly parts; although I confess they learn the rudiments much earlier, during which time they can however be looked upon only as probationers, as I have been informed by a principal gentleman in the county of Cavan, who protested to me that he never knew above one or two instances under the age of six, even in a part of the kingdom so renowned for the quickest proficiency in that art.

I am assured by our merchants that a boy or a girl before twelve years old is no salable commodity; and even when they come to this age they will not yield above three pounds, or three pounds and half a crown at most on the Exchange; which cannot turn to account either to the parents or the kingdom, the charge of nutriment and rags having been at least four times that value.

I shall now therefore humbly propose my own thoughts, which I hope will not be liable to the least objection.

I have been assured by a very knowing American of my acquaintance in London, that a young healthy child well nursed is at a year old a most delicious, nourishing, and wholesome food, whether stewed, roasted, baked, or boiled; and I make no doubt that it will equally serve in a fricassee or a ragout.

I do therefore humbly offer it to public consideration that of the hundred and twenty thousand children, already computed, twenty thousand may be reserved for breed, whereof only one fourth part to be males, which is more than we allow to sheep, black cattle, or swine; and my reason is that these children are seldom the fruits of marriage, a circumstance not much regarded by our savages, therefore one male will be sufficient to serve four females. That the remaining hundred thousand may at a year old be offered in sale to the persons of quality and fortune through the kingdom, always advising the mother to let them suck plentifully in the last month, so as to render them plump and fat for a good table. A child will make two dishes at an entertainment for friends; and when the family dines alone, the fore or hind quarter will make a reasonable dish, and seasoned with a little pepper or salt will be very good boiled on the fourth day, especially in winter.

I have reckoned upon a medium that a child just born will weigh twelve pounds, and in a solar year if tolerably nursed increaseth to twenty-eight pounds.

I grant this food will be somewhat dear, and therefore very proper for landlords, who, as they have already devoured most of the parents, seem to have the best title to the children.

Infant's flesh will be in season throughout the year, but more plentiful in March, and a little before and after. For we are told by a grave author, an eminent French physician, that fish being a prolific diet, there are more children born in Roman Catholic countries about nine months after Lent than at any other season; therefore, reckoning a year after Lent, the markets will be more glutted than usual, because the number of popish infants is at least three to one in this kingdom; and therefore it will have one other collateral advantage, by lessening the number of Papists among us.

I have already computed the charge of nursing a beggar's child (in which list I reckon all cottagers, laborers, and four fifths of the farmers) to be about two shillings per annum, rags included; and I believe no gentleman would repine to give ten shillings for the carcass of a good fat child, which, as I have said, will make four dishes of excellent nutritive meat, when he hath only some particular friend or his own family to dine with him. Thus the squire will learn to be a good landlord, and grow popular among the tenants; the mother will have eight shillings net profit, and be fit for work till she produces another child.

Those who are more thrifty (as I must confess the times require) may flay the carcass; the skin of which artificially dressed will make admirable gloves for ladies, and summer boots for fine gentlemen.

As to our city of Dublin, shambles may be appointed for this purpose in the most convenient parts of it, and butchers we may be assured will not be wanting; although I rather recommend buying the children alive, and dressing them hot from the knife as we do roasting pigs.

A very worthy person, a true lover of his country, and whose virtues I highly esteem, was lately pleased in discoursing on this matter to offer a refinement upon my scheme. He said that many gentlemen of this kingdom, having of late destroyed their deer, he conceived that the want of venison might be well supplied by the bodies of young lads and maidens, not exceeding fourteen years of age nor under twelve, so great a number of both sexes in every county being now ready to starve for want of work and service; and these to be disposed of by their parents, if alive, or otherwise by their nearest relations. But with due deference to so excellent a friend and so deserving a patriot, I cannot be altogether in his sentiments; for as to the males, my American acquaintance assured me from frequent experience that their flesh was generally tough and lean, like that of our schoolboys, by continual exercise, and their taste disagreeable; and to fatten them would not answer the charge. Then as to the females, it would, I think with humble submission, be a loss to the public, because they soon would become breeders themselves: and besides, it is not improbable that some scrupulous people might be apt to censure such a practice (although indeed very unjustly) as a little bordering upon cruelty; which, I confess, hath always been with me the strongest objection against any project, how well soever intended.

But in order to justify my friend, he confessed that this expedient was put into his head by the famous Psalmanazar, a native of the island Formosa, who came from thence to London above twenty years ago, and in conversation told my friend that in his country when any young person happened to be put to death, the executioner sold the carcass to persons of quality as a prime dainty; and that in his time the body of a plump girl of fifteen, who was crucified for an attempt to poison the emperor, was sold to his Imperial Majesty's prime minister of state, and other great mandarins of the court, in joints from the gibbet, at four hundred crowns. Neither indeed can I deny that if the same use were made of several plump young girls in this town, who without one single groat to their fortunes cannot stir abroad without a chair, and appear at the playhouse and assemblies in foreign fineries which they never will pay for, the kingdom would not be the worse.

Some persons of a desponding spirit are in great concern about that vast number of poor people who are aged, diseased, or maimed, and I have been desired to employ my thoughts what course may be taken to ease the nation of so grievous an encumbrance. But I am not in the least pain upon that matter, because it is very well known that they are every day dying and rotting by cold and famine, and filth and vermin, as fast as can be reasonably expected. And as to the younger laborers, they are now in almost as hopeful a condition. They cannot get work, and consequently pine away for want of nourishment to a degree that if at any time they are accidentally hired to common labor, they have not strength to perform it; and thus the country and themselves are happily delivered from the evils to come.

I have too long digressed, and therefore shall return to my subject. I think the advantages by the proposal which I have made are obvious and many, as well as of the highest importance.

For first, as I have already observed, it would greatly lessen the number of Papists, with whom we are yearly overrun, being the principal breeders of the nation as well as our most dangerous enemies; and who stay at home on purpose to deliver the kingdom to the Pretender, hoping to take their advantage by the absence of so many good Protestants, who have chosen rather to leave their country than to stay at home and pay tithes against their conscience to an Episcopal curate.

Secondly, the poorer tenants will have something valuable of their own, which by law may be made liable to distress, and help to pay their landlord's rent, their corn and cattle being already seized and money a thing unknown.

Thirdly, whereas the maintenance of an hundred thousand children, from two years old and upwards, cannot be computed at less than ten shillings a piece per annum, the nation's stock will be thereby increased fifty thousand pounds per annum, besides the profit of a new dish introduced to the tables of all gentlemen of fortune in the kingdom who have any refinement in taste. And the money will circulate among ourselves, the goods being entirely of our own growth and manufacture.

Fourthly, the constant breeders, besides the gain of eight shillings sterling per annum by the sale of their children, will be rid of the charge of maintaining them after the first year.

Fifthly, this food would likewise bring great custom to taverns, where the vintners will certainly be so prudent as to procure the best receipts for dressing it to perfection, and consequently have their houses frequented by all the fine gentlemen, who justly value themselves upon their knowledge in good eating; and a skillful cook, who understands how to oblige his guests, will contrive to make it as expensive as they please.

Sixthly, this would be a great inducement to marriage, which all wise nations have either encouraged by rewards or enforced by laws and penalties. It would increase the care and tenderness of mothers toward their children, when they were sure of a settlement for life to the poor babes, provided in some sort by the public, to their annual profit instead of expense. We should see an honest emulation among the married women, which of them could bring the fattest child to the market. Men would become as fond of their wives during the time of their pregnancy as they are now of their mares in foal, their cows in calf, or sows when they are ready to farrow; nor offer to beat or kick them (as is too frequent a practice) for fear of a miscarriage.

Many other advantages might be enumerated. For instance, the addition of some thousand carcasses in our exportation of barreled beef, the propagation of swine's flesh, and improvement in the art of making good bacon, so much wanted among us by the great destruction of pigs, too frequent at our tables, which are no way comparable in taste or magnificence to a well-grown, fat, yearling child, which roasted whole will make a considerable figure at a lord mayor's feast or any other public entertainment. But this and many others I omit, being studious of brevity.

Supposing that one thousand families in this city would be constant customers for infants' flesh, besides others who might have it at merry meetings, particularly weddings and christenings, I compute that Dublin would take off annually about twenty thousand carcasses, and the rest of the kingdom (where probably they will be sold somewhat cheaper) the remaining eighty thousand.

I can think of no one objection that will possibly be raised against this proposal, unless it should be urged that the number of people will be thereby much lessened in the kingdom. This I freely own, and it was indeed one principal design in offering it to the world. I desire the reader will observe, that I calculate my remedy for this one individual kingdom of Ireland and for no other that ever was, is, or I think ever can be upon earth. Therefore let no man talk to me of other expedients: of taxing our absentees at five shillings a pound: of using neither clothes nor household furniture except what is of our own growth and manufacture: of utterly rejecting the materials and instruments that promote foreign luxury: of curing the expensiveness of pride, vanity, idleness, and gaming in our women: of introducing a vein of parsimony, prudence, and temperance: of learning to love our country, in the want of which we differ even from Laplanders and the inhabitants of Topinamboo: of quitting our animosities and factions, nor acting any longer like the Jews, who were murdering one another at the very moment their city was taken: of being a little cautious not to sell our country and conscience for nothing: of teaching landlords to have at least one degree of mercy toward their tenants: lastly, of putting a spirit of honesty, industry, and skill into our shopkeepers; who, if a resolution could now be taken to buy only our native goods, would immediately unite to cheat and exact upon us in the price, the measure, and the goodness, nor could ever yet be brought to make one fair proposal of just dealing, though often and earnestly invited to it.

Therefore I repeat, let no man talk to me of these and the like expedients, till he hath at least some glimpse of hope that there will ever be some hearty and sincere attempt to put them in practice.

But as to myself, having been wearied out for many years with offering vain, idle, visionary thoughts, and at length utterly despairing of success, I fortunately fell upon this proposal, which, as it is wholly new, so it hath something solid and real, of no expense and little trouble, full in our own power, and whereby we can incur no danger in disobliging England. For this kind of commodity will not bear exportation, the flesh being of too tender a consistence to admit a long continuance in salt, although perhaps I could name a country which would be glad to eat up our whole nation without it.

After all, I am not so violently bent upon my own opinion as to reject any offer proposed by wise men, which shall be found equally innocent, cheap, easy, and effectual. But before something of that kind shall be advanced in contradiction to my scheme, and offering a better, I desire the author or authors will be pleased maturely to consider two points. First, as things now stand, how they will be able to find food and raiment for an hundred thousand useless mouths and backs. And secondly, there being a round million of creatures in human figure throughout this kingdom, whose sole subsistence put into a common stock would leave them in debt two millions of pounds sterling, adding those who are beggars by profession to the bulk of farmers, cottagers, and laborers, with their wives and children who are beggars in effect; I desire those politicians who dislike my overture, and may perhaps be so bold to attempt an answer, that they will first ask the parents of these mortals whether they would not at this day think it a great happiness to have been sold for food at a year old in the manner I prescribe, and thereby have avoided such a perpetual scene of misfortunes as they have since gone through by the oppression of landlords, the impossibility of paying rent without money or trade, the want of common sustenance, with neither house nor clothes to cover them from the inclemencies of the weather, and the most inevitable prospect of entailing the like or greater miseries upon their breed forever.

I profess, in the sincerity of my heart, that I have not the least personal interest in endeavoring to promote this necessary work, having no other motive than the public good of my country, by advancing our trade, providing for infants, relieving the poor, and giving some pleasure to the rich. I have no children by which I can propose to get a single penny; the youngest being nine years old, and my wife past childbearing.

QUESTIONS FOR DISCUSSION AND WRITING

1. One of the most famous essays in English, "A Modest Proposal" caused quite a stir when it was first published. Many of Swift's original readers—and many readers today—did not understand that Swift was being *ironic,* that he was not actually proposing the cannibalistic practices he outlines here. Those readers' failure to understand Swift's intentions rests in large part on a failure to distinguish between

Swift and his speaker. Analyze the character of the speaker in "A Modest Proposal." What values, skills, and assumptions does he hold dear? What values, skills, and assumptions does Swift seem to hold dear?

2. Aside from the obvious moral problem with the "modest proposal," it makes perfect sense insofar as it would have solved the problems of overpopulation and poverty that beset Ireland during Swift's time. Look at the logic in "A Modest Proposal." What kinds of arguments does the speaker make? How well does he refute opposing points of view and show the deficiencies of other, less modest, proposals?

3. Throughout "A Modest Proposal," the speaker uses for people language we usually consider appropriate for discussions of nonhuman animals. Find some of the uses of such language. How do they reinforce Swift's purpose?

4. The speaker delays the actual proposal until well into the essay. What is the effect of the delay? When the proposal was made, were you shocked by the speaker's solution to Ireland's problems? Why might Swift have chosen to shock us rather than to write a more straightforward essay?

5. Swift's essay is a *satire,* a somewhat bitter but humorous piece meant to attack current social conditions. The essay does suggest some pragmatic reforms, however. Where are they discussed in the essay? How do we respond to them?

GEORGE ORWELL (1903–1950)

Marrakech   *1939*

As the corpse went past the flies left the restaurant table in a cloud and rushed after it, but they came back a few minutes later.

The little crowd of mourners—all men and boys, no women—threaded their way across the market-place between the piles of pomegranates and the taxis and the camels, wailing a short chant over and over again. What really appeals to the flies is that the corpses here are never put into coffins, they are merely wrapped in a piece of rag and carried on a rough wooden bier on the shoulders of four friends. When the friends get to the burying-ground they hack an oblong hole a foot or two deep, dump the body in it and fling over it a little of the dried-up, lumpy earth, which is like broken brick. No gravestone, no name, no identifying mark of any kind. The burying-ground is merely a huge waste of hummocky earth, like a derelict building-lot. After a month or two no one can even be certain where his own relatives are buried.

When you walk through a town like this—two hundred thousand inhabitants, of whom at least twenty thousand own literally nothing except the rags they stand up in—when you see how the people live, and still more how easily they die, it is always difficult to believe that you are walking among human beings. All colonial empires are in reality founded upon that fact. The people have brown faces—besides, there are so many of them! Are they really the same flesh as yourself? Do they even have names? Or are they merely a kind of undifferentiated brown stuff, about as individual as bees or coral insects? They rise out of the earth, they sweat and starve for a few years, and then they sink back into the nameless mounds of the graveyard and nobody notices that they are gone. And even the graves themselves soon fade back into the soil. Sometimes, out for a walk, as you break your way through the prickly pear, you notice that it is rather bumpy underfoot, and only a certain regularity in the bumps tells you that you are walking over skeletons.

I was feeding one of the gazelles in the public gardens.

Gazelles are almost the only animals that look good to eat when they are still alive, in fact, one can hardly look at their hindquarters without thinking of mint sauce. The gazelle I was feeding seemed to know that this thought was in my mind, for though it took the piece of bread I was holding out it obviously did not like me. It nibbled rapidly at the bread, then lowered its head and tried to butt me, then took another nibble and then butted again. Probably its idea was that if it could drive me away the bread would somehow remain hanging in mid-air.

An Arab navvy working on the path nearby lowered his heavy hoe and sidled towards us. He looked from the gazelle to the bread and from the bread to the gazelle, with a sort of quiet amazement, as though he had never seen anything quite like this before. Finally he said shyly in French:

"*I* could eat some of that bread."

I tore off a piece and he stowed it gratefully in some secret place under his rags. This man is an employee of the Municipality.

When you go through the Jewish quarters you gather some idea of what the medieval ghettoes were probably like. Under their Moorish rulers the Jews were only allowed to own land in certain restricted areas, and after centuries of this kind of treatment they have ceased to bother about overcrowding. Many of the streets are a good deal less than six feet wide, the houses are completely windowless, and sore-eyed children cluster everywhere in unbelievable numbers, like clouds of flies. Down the centre of the street there is generally running a little river of urine.

In the bazaar huge families of Jews, all dressed in the long black robe and little black skull-cap, are working in dark fly-infested booths that look like caves. A carpenter sits cross-legged at a prehistoric lathe, turning chair-legs at lightning speed. He works the lathe with a bow in his right hand and guides the chisel with his left foot, and thanks to a lifetime of sitting in this position his left leg is warped out of shape. At his side his grandson, aged six, is already starting on the simpler parts of the job.

I was just passing the coppersmiths' booths when somebody noticed that I was lighting a cigarette. Instantly, from the dark holes all round, there was a frenzied rush of Jews, many of them old grandfathers with flowing grey beards, all clamouring for a cigarette. Even a blind man somewhere at the back of one of the booths heard a rumour of cigarettes and came crawling out, groping in the air with his hand. In about a minute I had used up the whole packet. None of these people, I suppose, works less than twelve hours a day, and every one of them looks on a cigarette as a more or less impossible luxury.

As the Jews live in self-contained communities they follow the same trades as the Arabs, except for agriculture. Fruitsellers, potters, silversmiths, blacksmiths, butchers, leatherworkers, tailors, water-carriers, beggars, porters—whichever way you look you see nothing but Jews. As a matter of fact there are thirteen thousand of them, all living in the space of a few acres. A good job Hitler isn't here. Perhaps he is on his way, however. You hear the usual dark rumours about the Jews, not only from the Arabs but from the poorer Europeans.

"Yes, *mon vieux,* they took my job away from me and gave it to a Jew. The Jews! They're the real rulers of this country, you know. They've got all the money. They control the banks, finance—everything."

"But," I said, "isn't it a fact that the average Jew is a labourer working for about a penny an hour?"

"Ah, that's only for show! They're all moneylenders really. They're cunning, the Jews."

In just the same way, a couple of hundred years ago, poor old women used to be burned for witchcraft when they could not even work enough magic to get themselves a square meal.

All people who work with their hands are partly invisible, and the more important the work they do, the less visible they are. Still, a white skin is always fairly conspicuous. In northern Europe, when you see a labourer ploughing a field, you probably give him a second glance. In a hot country, anywhere south of Gibraltar or east of Suez, the chances are that you don't even see him. I have noticed this again and again. In a tropical landscape one's eye takes in everything except the human beings. It takes in the dried-up soil, the prickly pear, the palm-tree and the distant mountain, but it always misses the peasant hoeing at his patch. He is the same colour as the earth, and a great deal less interesting to look at.

It is only because of this that the starved countries of Asia and Africa are accepted as tourist resorts. No one would think of running cheap trips to the Distressed Areas. But where the human beings have brown skins their poverty is simply not noticed. What does Morocco mean to a Frenchman? An orange-grove or a job in government service. Or to an Englishman? Camels, castles, palm-trees, Foreign Legionnaires, brass trays and bandits. One could probably live here for years without noticing that for nine-tenths of the people the reality of life is an endless, back-breaking struggle to wring a little food out of an eroded soil.

Most of Morocco is so desolate that no wild animal bigger than a hare can live on it. Huge areas which were once covered with forest have turned into a treeless waste where the soil is exactly like broken-up brick. Nevertheless a good deal of it is cultivated, with frightful labour. Everything is done by hand. Long lines of women, bent double like inverted capital Ls, work their way slowly across the field, tearing up the prickly weeds with their hands, and the peasant gathering lucerne for fodder pulls it up stalk by stalk instead of reaping it, thus saving an inch or two on each stalk. The plough is a wretched wooden thing, so frail that one can easily carry it on one's shoulder, and fitted underneath with a rough iron spike which stirs the soil to a depth of about four inches. This is as much as the strength of the animals is equal to. It is usual to plough with a cow and a donkey yoked together. Two donkeys would not be quite strong enough, but on the other hand two cows would cost a little more to feed. The peasants possess no harrows, they merely plough the soil several times over in different directions, finally leaving it in rough furrows, after which the whole field has to be shaped with hoes into small oblong patches, to conserve water. Except for a day or two after the rare rainstorms there is never enough water. Along the edges of the fields channels are hacked out to a depth of thirty or forty feet to get at the tiny trickles which run through the subsoil.

Every afternoon a file of very old women passes down the road outside my house, each carrying a load of firewood. All of them are mummified with age and the sun, and all of them are tiny. It seems to be generally the case in primitive communities that the women, when they get beyond a certain age, shrink to the size of children. One day a poor old creature who could not have been more than four feet tall crept past me under a vast load of wood. I stopped her and put a five-sou piece (a little more than a farthing) into her hand. She answered with a shrill wail, almost a scream, which was partly gratitude but mainly surprise. I suppose that from her point of view, by taking any notice of her, I seemed almost to be violating a law of nature. She accepted her status as an old woman, that is to say as a beast of burden. When a family is travelling it is quite usual to see a father and a grown-up son riding ahead on donkeys, and an old woman following on foot, carrying the baggage.

But what is strange about these people is their invisibility. For several weeks, always at about the same time of day, the file of old women had hobbled past the house with their firewood, and though they had registered themselves on my eyeballs I cannot truly say that I had seen them. Firewood was passing—that was how I saw it. It was only that one day I happened to be walking behind them, and the curious up-and-down motion of a load of wood drew my attention to the human being underneath it. Then for the first time I noticed the poor old earth-coloured bodies, bodies reduced to bones and leathery skin, bent double under the crushing weight. Yet I suppose I had not been five minutes on Moroccan soil before I noticed the overloading of the donkeys and was infuriated by it. There is no question that the donkeys are damnably treated. The Moroccan donkey is hardly bigger than a St. Bernard dog, it carries a load which in the British army would be considered too much for a fifteen-hands mule, and very often its pack-saddle is not taken off its back for weeks together. But what is peculiarly pitiful is that it is the most willing creature on earth, it follows its master like a dog and does not need either bridle or halter. After a dozen years of devoted work it suddenly drops dead, whereupon its master tips it into the ditch and the village dogs have torn its guts out before it is cold.

This kind of thing makes one's blood boil, whereas—on the whole—the plight of the human beings does not. I am not commenting, merely pointing to a fact. People with brown skins are next door to invisible. Anyone can be sorry for the donkey with its galled back, but it is generally owing to some kind of accident if one even notices the old woman under her load of sticks.

As the storks flew northward the Negroes were marching southward—a long, dusty column, infantry, screw-gun batteries and then more infantry, four or five thousand men in all, winding up the road with a clumping of boots and a clatter of iron wheels.

They were Senegalese, the blackest Negroes in Africa, so black that sometimes it is difficult to see whereabouts on their necks the hair begins. Their splendid bodies were hidden in reach-me-down khaki uniforms, their feet squashed into boots that looked like blocks of wood, and every tin hat seemed to be a couple of sizes too small. It was very hot and the men had marched a long way. They slumped under the weight of their packs and the curiously sensitive black faces were glistening with sweat.

As they went past a tall, very young Negro turned and caught my eye. But the look he gave me was not in the least the kind of look you might expect. Not hostile, not contemptuous, not sullen, not even inquisitive. It was the shy, wide-eyed Negro look, which actually is a look of profound respect. I saw how it was. This wretched boy, who is a French citizen and has therefore been dragged from the forest to scrub floors and catch syphilis in garrison towns, actually has feelings of reverence before a white skin. He has been taught that the white race are his masters, and he still believes it.

But there is one thought which every white man (and in this connection it doesn't matter twopence if he calls himself a Socialist) thinks when he sees a black army marching past. "How much longer can we go on kidding these people? How long before they turn their guns in the other direction?"

It was curious, really. Every white man there has this thought stowed somewhere or other in his mind. I had it, so had the other onlookers, so had the officers on their sweating chargers and the white NCOs marching in the ranks. It was a kind of secret which we all knew and were too clever to tell; only the Negroes didn't know it. And really it was almost like watching a flock of cattle to see the long column, a mile or two miles of armed men, flowing peacefully up the road, while the great white birds drifted over them in the opposite direction, glittering like scraps of paper.

QUESTIONS FOR DISCUSSION AND WRITING

1. "Marrakech" is composed of a series of vignettes, of short scenes that seem distinct from one another. Why do you suppose Orwell chose to use such vignettes rather than a more traditional essay structure? Why does he present the vignettes in the order given here? How do the vignettes lead to a thesis? What is that thesis?
2. One of the principles behind "Marrakech" is that the people have become almost invisible and their lives apparently insignificant. How does Orwell's language—his word choices, his imagery, even his sentence structure—convey those notions?
3. Orwell comments almost as frequently on the animals and insects of Marrakech as he does on the people, inviting a comparison between animals and insects on the one hand and people on the other. Why?
4. Many readers are puzzled by the image with which the essay ends: "And really it was almost like watching a flock of cattle to see the long column, a mile or two miles of armed men, flowing peacefully up the road, while the great white birds drifted over them in the opposite direction, glittering like scraps of paper." How effective and meaningful do you find the image? What do you see as its significance?
5. In many ways, "Marrakech" is an observation essay. Orwell piles up his observations, often with little comment, and asks us to draw conclusions from the juxtapositions of ideas. (He even says at one point "I am not commenting, merely pointing to a fact" [1053].) But clearly the juxtaposition of particular kinds of images points us to particular kinds of conclusions. Write a similar observation essay of your own in which, through the careful juxtaposition of the details you have observed, you invite your reader to reach the conclusions you have not stated explicitly.

MAKING CONNECTIONS: INNOCENCE LOST

1. Some of the writers and artists in this chapter are looking not so much at particular events as at the general conditions of modern civilization. Choose two or three writers who deal with this subject. Do they share similar visions of modern life?

What values and feelings do they focus on? What do they see as the sources of modern discontents? What sources of joy do they see? To what extent can the differences in perspective be attributed to the times in which the authors were writing?

2. Many of the writers in this chapter look at what it means to be a member of a racial minority in the United States. Do these writers see themselves as inevitably outside the American mainstream? Do they wish to "assimilate" or remain separate? How much does the stance of the writer depend on his or her race or ethnicity? How much does it depend on when the work was written?

3. In some of the works in this chapter, characters are attempting to escape what seems to be an "evil" situation or civilization. Looking at *The Scream*—art and poem—the stories of Lot's wife, and the Icarus legends, consider what it is that the characters are escaping. How well defined are the "evils"? To what extent is society to blame for them? How successful are the escapes?

4. Art and literature have long concerned themselves with war, whether they have glorified victories, memorialized the dead, or agonized about the waste of life. This chapter contains literary and artistic responses to World War I, World War II, and the Vietnam War. Which of the works would you characterize as supporting a particular war, which as opposing it? How do the various works represent different perspectives—those of the citizens at home, those of grieving family members, those of the soldiers themselves? Are the works responding to a particular time and war—or are they timeless?

5. Our first experiences of society are greatly influenced by our attitudes toward our homes, and for many, "home" represents the most secure haven from the pressures and anxieties of the society outside. How do works in this chapter create a sense of "home"? What is the relationship between the home and the larger society?

6. Traditionally, men have been considered responsible for building civilizations, whereas women's spheres have been domestic. As a result, many aspects of civilization—its institutions and laws, for instance—have been considered "male." Recently, however, female voices have challenged that assumption. Looking at both male and female writers in this chapter, where do you see "male" versions of civilization and society, and where do you see "female" views? If particular works had instead been written by members of the other gender, how might they have been different?

7. The works in this chapter often swing between hope and disillusionment (though in modern works disillusionment seems more dominant). Which of the works would you consider to be the most hopeful? Which the least hopeful? Why?

8. Many of the works in this chapter focus on social injustices. What do the writers see as unjust? What are the sources of the injustice? Human nature? Social imperfections? How hopeful are the writers that the injustices can be corrected? What must be done to correct them?

9. Most discussions of social injustice concern themselves as well with the nature of Law: moral law, religious law, and civil law. How does Law come to be defined in the works in this chapter? What happens when the various kinds of law clash with one another? Which law does each of the writers think should prevail? Which law do you think should prevail?

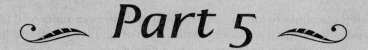

Part 5

For Further Study

Three Casebooks of Retellings

The following casebooks focus on three stories that have been influential in Western literature and culture: the stories of Oedipus, Hamlet, and Dr. Jekyll and Mr. Hyde. The three central works are products of very different times and societies, *Oedipus* of fifth-century B.C. Greece, *Hamlet* of sixteenth-century England, and *Dr. Jekyll and Mr. Hyde* of nineteenth-century England. Different as their times and the prevailing beliefs were, however, the three authors do have something in common. All ask us to look deeply into ourselves, to determine what makes us who we are and who we want to be. Of the three, only *Dr. Jekyll* was written at a time when psychologists were making a scientific study of the human mind, but all three speak to the psyches of each of us. It is partly for that reason that they have been so enormously influential. Few among us have not heard the names of Oedipus, Hamlet, Dr. Jekyll, and Mr. Hyde, even if we have not read their stories. They have earned a place in the popular imagination, as well as in the pages of literature.

Such works of literature have much to show us about ourselves and about how the people of other times and places answered profound and timeless questions about people's behavior, thoughts, and feelings. They have begun a conversation in which we all can take part and have provided us, even those of us who are living lives very different from those of these authors or their characters, a place to gather together to join that conversation. Still, as we said in the preface to *Retellings,* in recent years, students and professors alike have sometimes questioned the privileged status that we give such authors, arguing that they have earned their place in the literary canon partly by virtue of their place as white males who enjoyed a high status in their societies; it is in part that status, perhaps, that allows them to speak with such authority. Their title characters—Oedipus, Hamlet, and Dr. Jekyll—enjoy a similarly high status: Oedipus, the prince of Corinth, becomes King of Thebes; Hamlet is prince of Denmark; Dr. Jekyll is a well-to-do and highly respected physician. It may be true that all these works ask universal questions about identity and the nature of good and evil, but they ask those questions from positions of dominance and privilege.

Those of us who do not enjoy such privileged positions—after all, few of us are kings or princes—may sometimes be tempted to look in these works for characters who are more like us. In doing so, we may find ourselves looking at those who live in the margins and shadows of the works and wondering about characters and values that almost disappear from view when the focus remains on the rich and powerful. The retellings in the casebooks (and throughout this anthology) are often based on just that sort of wondering. They make central the marginalized and give voice to those who might otherwise remain silent or unheard.

Think, for instance, about the story of Oedipus and how it might be retold. Horrible as it must have been for Oedipus to discover that he had killed his father and married his mother, we may be struck by the fact that we hear little about Jocasta, his wife and mother. After all, she, too, must face the horror of learning that she has committed incest. Although Sophocles keeps his focus tightly on Oedipus, two later tellers, poets Laurie Sheck and Edwin Gallaher, remind us that this is Jocasta's story, too. From dramatist Rita Dove we get a reimagining of the story in which Oedipus is no longer a king who is the son of a king but rather a black slave chained to his destiny in the pre–Civil War American South.

Similarly, though *Hamlet* often dwells on Hamlet's feelings as a son and prince whose mother has married his father's murderer and usurper, perhaps Hamlet's mother,

Gertrude, may have a different version of what has happened, a version like that imagined by Margaret Atwood or retrieved from the background by Carolyn Heilbrun in her literary analysis of the play. Caught sometimes between her son, the prince, and the two kings who have married her, Gertrude nevertheless has a voice of her own.

To Robert Louis Stevenson, as to many in nineteenth-century England, it may have seemed only natural that the monstrous Hyde would appear lower class, easily identified as "not a gentleman" no matter how fine his clothes. To the twentieth-century writer Tony Eprile, however, such class distinctions no longer seem valid, and his story, told from the point of view of Hyde, celebrates the vitality of the working class while considering upper-class refinements suspect. Elaine Showalter, in her critical examination of Stevenson's novella, asks us to see even the circle of wealthy bachelors in a new light. Though these respected and privileged professionals may appear to represent established values, she wonders if in fact they are at the margin of society, a group of homosexuals the truth of whose lives can never quite be spoken.

In retelling the works included in the casebooks, the retellers do more than add a corrective to the originals, providing us with another point of view; they also pay homage to them, showing us that the works of Sophocles, Shakespeare, and Stevenson are not irrelevant to our current social concerns and questions but part of the conversation about those concerns and questions. Writers such as Sophocles, Shakespeare, and Stevenson have through their artistry raised important questions, told important truths, and created rich worlds that have earned them well-deserved places in the world of literature. Theirs are rich and important voices for us to hear. The retellers do, however, ask us to hear voices other than those of the "dead white males" of the literary canon, other than those who often represent privilege and power; they ask us to hear voices that in the context of the original works are perhaps whispers not easily heard. As we hope these casebooks will remind you, every one of these voices is well worth listening to.

12

A Casebook on Oedipus:
Living with Fate

CHAPTER INTRODUCTION

For centuries, the name "Oedipus" has evoked horror in those who have heard it. Who among us does not shudder at the hero's tragic discovery that he has accidentally killed his own father and had an incestuous relationship with his mother? So universal are the taboos of patricide and incest that, even millennia after it was first written, the play continues to spark terror—and debate—among theater audiences.

Just what makes the play strike such a chord in its audiences? According to psychologist Sigmund Freud, whose brief analysis we have included in this chapter, we respond so powerfully to the play because we all recognize ourselves in Oedipus, because the play gives dramatic reality to our shadowy desires to kill the same-gender parent who has displaced us in our opposite-gender parent's affections. In short, according to Freud, young boys see in Oedipus their own unspoken desires to eliminate the father who keeps them from the mother's bed—and they see in Oedipus's terrible fate the recognition of what goes wrong if they give in to those desires. (Freud argued that young girls have a similar desire to displace their mothers in their fathers' affections. This he called the Electra complex, after another figure of Greek myth.)

In developing his ideas about the Oedipus complex, Freud not only attempted to explain developmental psychology but also began to explain just why the play and its hero have become so much a part of us that even those who have never read or seen Sophocles' play often know the story. The play has, in other words, passed from literature to life—it has become part of who we are and how we see ourselves.

As influential in psychology and literary criticism as Freud's interpretation has been, however, it is not the only interpretation possible. Many readers point to the fact that Oedipus commits patricide and incest accidentally; he doesn't know the identities of the man he kills or the woman he marries. Historians go even further, reminding us that Oedipus undoubtedly marries Jocasta to solidify his political strength when he arrives in Thebes. How better to establish the authority of one's kingship than to marry the woman everyone recognizes as queen?

Whether one accepts Freud's psychological interpretation or more historical interpretations, one thing is clear. Oedipus himself is horrified by the knowledge he achieves at the play's end; he views parricide and incest much as we do: as crimes against family and humanity. That recognition, more than the murder or marriage itself, is at the heart of the play's tragedy.

Seen in this light, *Oedipus the King* (or *Oedipus Rex*) is a play about coming to understanding and self-knowledge. In modern terms, it is a play about identity, about who Oedipus's parents are and about what kind of man he is. The literary artists and the critics whose works we have included here reflect that theme of identity in their retellings of Sophocles' story. (Sophocles was himself retelling an earlier version of the myth, as some of the critics here remind us.) In the tellings and retellings, questions of identity, of self-knowledge, and of individual will and moral obligation constantly surface. If Oedipus's search for truth is a search to fulfill the Greek dictum "know thyself," what are we to make of the knowledge he achieves? Would it have been better had he *not* known himself? After all, had he not known of his parentage, he could have died happy in his ignorance of the parricide and incest in which he had engaged.

Or are we *really* meant to see that ignorance as true happiness? Maybe, instead, we are meant to believe that knowledge and truth are in themselves to be valued even at the expense of human suffering. Perhaps Oedipus is heroic because he comes to know himself despite the inevitable destruction that knowledge will bring. Perhaps, in fact, self-knowledge *always* brings suffering of a kind to those who know themselves, for even the most heroic among us is doomed to bear some form of "pollution" within. *Oedipus* thus invites a dual reaction: although we may admire Oedipus for the persistence with which he seems to pursue the answer to the puzzle before him, we must also recognize that he *is* the pollution that has brought withering crops and death to the people of Thebes.

For modern readers, it is difficult to avoid questions about whether Oedipus *deserves* the fate into which he was born. After all, the gods have always known that he will kill his father and marry his mother. The idea of fate is foreign to us, perhaps most especially in America, a country seemingly founded on the idea that each of us can break free of the constraints of birth, ethnicity, gender, and economic status and become "all that we can be." But we need look only into our own history to recognize that Oedipus is more akin to us than we might at first think. It is not simply that we may all in our subconsciouses play out the Oedipus story, as Freud said. It may be that even in more public ways we live the Oedipus story.

Such is the assumption behind Rita Dove's *The Darker Face of the Earth*. Even if we do not believe that the gods guide our actions (or even simply predict those actions), we often do recognize the extent to which we are sometimes constrained by factors of birth or genetics. Perhaps the gods have not directed or limited our actions, but the government or social institutions or genetics may. Imagine yourself a black man on a nineteenth-century slave plantation, desirous of living the life of a free man but prevented from doing so by the color of your skin and your status as "property." How would you forge an identity separate from the one that had been imposed on you by the social institution of slavery? How much would your actions and reactions be determined by your position as a slave? And what would happen if you discovered that you were not, after all, the man that you had always thought you were? Could you shake free of the identity with which you had always lived?

Oedipus and its retellings invite us, then, to look into ourselves and our society. It is not only a story about a man who commits unspeakable acts but a story about a man whose sense of self and place are shaken so profoundly that he can no longer live in the world. It is a story that asks us to reach beyond sympathy and horror and to recognize a truth that is at once both exhilarating and terrible: We *are* Oedipus.

For a discussion of the history and staging of Greek drama, see 1005–6.

SOPHOCLES (496? B.C.–406 B.C.)

Oedipus the King _____ ca. 430 B.C.

Characters

OEDIPUS, *king of Thebes*
A PRIEST *of Zeus*
CREON, *brother of Jocasta*
A CHORUS *of Theban citizens and their* LEADER
TIRESIAS, *a blind prophet*
JOCASTA, *the queen, wife of Oedipus*
A MESSENGER *from Corinth*
A SHEPHERD
A MESSENGER *from inside the palace*
ANTIGONE, ISMENE: *daughters of Oedipus and Jocasta*
GUARDS AND ATTENDANTS
PRIESTS *of Thebes*

> **Time and Scene** *The royal house of Thebes. Double doors dominate the façade; a stone altar stands at the center of the stage.*
>
> *Many years have passed since* OEDIPUS *solved the riddle of the Sphinx and ascended the throne of Thebes, and now a plague has struck the city. A procession of priests enters; suppliants, broken and despondent, they carry branches wound in wool and lay them on the altar.*
>
> *The doors open. Guards assemble.* OEDIPUS *comes forward, majestic but for a telltale limp, and slowly views the condition of his people.*

OEDIPUS: Oh my children, the new blood of ancient Thebes,
    why are you here? Huddling at my altar,
    praying before me, your branches wound in wool.
    Our city reeks with the smoke of burning incense,
5   rings with cries for the Healer and wailing for the dead.
    I thought it wrong, my children, to hear the truth
    from others, messengers. Here I am myself—
    you all know me, the world knows my fame:
    I am Oedipus.

(*Helping a priest to his feet.*)

              Speak up, old man. Your years,
10   your dignity—you should speak for the others.
    Why here and kneeling, what preys upon you so?

Some sudden fear? some strong desire?
You can trust me. I am ready to help,
I'll do anything. I would be blind to misery
not to pity my people kneeling at my feet.   15
PRIEST: Oh Oedipus, king of the land, our greatest power!
You see us before you now, men of all ages
clinging to your altars. Here are boys,
still too weak to fly from the nest,
and here the old, bowed down with the years,   20
the holy ones—a priest of Zeus myself—and here
the picked, unmarried men, the young hope of Thebes.
And all the rest, your great family gathers now,
branches wreathed, massing in the squares,
kneeling before the two temples of queen Athena   25
or the river-shrine where the embers glow and die
and Apollo sees the future in the ashes.
                                        Our city—
look around you, see with your own eyes—
our ship pitches wildly, cannot lift her head
from the depths, the red waves of death . . .   30
Thebes is dying. A blight on the fresh crops
and the rich pastures, cattle sicken and die,
and the women die in labor, children stillborn,
and the plague, the fiery god of fever hurls down
on the city, his lightning slashing through us—   35
raging plague in all its vengeance, devastating
the house of Cadmus! And black Death luxuriates
in the raw, wailing miseries of Thebes.
Now we pray to you. You cannot equal the gods,
your children know that, bending at your altar.   40
But we do rate you first of men,
both in the common crises of our lives
and face-to-face encounters with the gods.
You freed us from the Sphinx, you came to Thebes
and cut us loose from the bloody tribute we had paid   45
that harsh, brutal singer. We taught you nothing,
no skill, no extra knowledge, still you triumphed.
A god was with you, so they say, and we believe it—
you lifted up our lives.
                                So now again,
Oedipus, king, we bend to you, your power—   50
we implore you, all of us on our knees:
find us strength, rescue! Perhaps you've heard
the voice of a god or something from other men,
Oedipus . . . what do you know?
The man of experience—you see it every day—   55
his plans will work in a crisis, his first of all.

Act now—we beg you, best of men, raise up our city!
Act, defend yourself, your former glory!
Your country calls you savior now
60   for your zeal, your action years ago.
Never let us remember of your reign:
you helped us stand, only to fall once more.
Oh raise up our city, set us on our feet.
The omens were good that day you brought us joy—
65   be the same man today!
Rule our land, you know you have the power,
but rule a land of the living, not a wasteland.
Ship and towered city are nothing, stripped of men
alive within it, living all as one.

OEDIPUS: My children,
70   I pity you. I see—how could I fail to see
what longings bring you here? Well I know
you are sick to death, all of you,
but sick as you are, not one is sick as I.
Your pain strikes each of you alone, each
75   in the confines of himself, no other. But my spirit
grieves for the city, for myself and all of you.
I wasn't asleep, dreaming. You haven't wakened me—
I have wept through the nights, you must know that,
groping, laboring over many paths of thought.
80   After a painful search I found one cure:
I acted at once. I sent Creon,
my wife's own brother, to Delphi—
Apollo the Prophet's oracle—to learn
what I might do or say to save our city.

85   Today's the day. When I count the days gone by
it torments me . . . what is he doing?
Strange, he's late, he's gone too long.
But once he returns, then, then I'll be a traitor
if I do not do all the god makes clear.
90 PRIEST: Timely words. The men over there
are signaling—Creon's just arriving.
OEDIPUS (*Sighting* CREON, *then turning to the altar*): Lord Apollo,
let him come with a lucky word of rescue,
shining like his eyes!
PRIEST: Welcome news, I think—he's crowned, look,
95   and the laurel wreath is bright with berries.
OEDIPUS: We'll soon see. He's close enough to hear—

(*Enter* CREON *from the side; his face is shaded with a wreath.*)

Creon, prince, my kinsman, what do you bring us?
What message from the god?

CREON: Good news.
    I tell you even the hardest things to bear,
    if they should turn out well, all would be well.   100

OEDIPUS: Of course, but what were the god's *words*? There's no hope
    and nothing to fear in what you've said so far.

CREON: If you want my report in the presence of these people . . .

(*Pointing to the priests while drawing* OEDIPUS *toward the palace.*)

    I'm ready now, or we might go inside.

OEDIPUS: Speak out,
    speak to us all. I grieve for these, my people,   105
    far more than I fear for my own life.

CREON: Very well,
    I will tell you what I heard from the god.
    Apollo commands us—he was quite clear—
    "Drive the corruption from the land,
    don't harbor it any longer, past all cure,   110
    don't nurse it in your soil—root it out!"

OEDIPUS: How can we cleanse ourselves—what rites?
    What's the source of the trouble?

CREON: Banish the man, or pay back blood with blood.
    Murder sets the plague-storm on the city.

OEDIPUS: Whose murder?   11
    Whose fate does Apollo bring to light?

CREON: Our leader,
    my lord, was once a man named Laius,
    before you came and put us straight on course.

OEDIPUS: I know—
    or so I've heard. I never saw the man myself.

CREON: Well, he was killed, and Apollo commands us now—   120
    he could not be more clear,
    "Pay the killers back—whoever is responsible."

OEDIPUS: Where on earth are they? Where to find it now,
    the trail of the ancient guilt so hard to trace?

CREON: "Here in Thebes," he said.   12
    Whatever is sought for can be caught, you know,
    whatever is neglected slips away.

OEDIPUS: But where,
    in the palace, the fields or foreign soil,
    where did Laius meet his bloody death?

CREON: He went to consult an oracle, Apollo said,   13
    and he set out and never came home again.

OEDIPUS: No messenger, no fellow-traveler saw what happened?
    Someone to cross-examine?

CREON: No,
    they were all killed but one. He escaped,
    terrified, he could tell us nothing clearly,   13

nothing of what he saw—just one thing.

OEDIPUS: What's that?
One thing could hold the key to it all,
a small beginning give us grounds for hope.

CREON: He said thieves attacked them—a whole band,
not single-handed, cut King Laius down.

140 OEDIPUS: A thief,
so daring, so wild, he'd kill a king? Impossible,
unless conspirators paid him off in Thebes.

CREON: We suspected as much. But with Laius dead
no leader appeared to help us in our troubles.

145 OEDIPUS: Trouble? Your *king* was murdered—royal blood!
What stopped you from tracking down the killer
then and there?

CREON: The singing, riddling Sphinx.
She . . . persuaded us to let the mystery go
and concentrate on what lay at our feet.

OEDIPUS: No,
150 I'll start again—I'll bring it all to light myself!
Apollo is right, and so are you, Creon,
to turn our attention back to the murdered man.
Now you have *me* to fight for you, you'll see:
I am the land's avenger by all rights,
155 and Apollo's champion too.
But not to assist some distant kinsman, no,
for my own sake I'll rid us of this corruption.
Whoever killed the king may decide to kill me too,
with the same violent hand—by avenging Laius
I defend myself.

(*To the priests.*)

160   Quickly, my children.
Up from the steps, take up your branches now.

(*To the guards.*)

One of you summon the city here before us,
tell them I'll do everything. God help us,
we will see our triumph—or our fall.

(OEDIPUS *and* CREON *enter the palace, followed by the guards.*)

165 PRIEST: Rise, my sons. The kindness we came for
Oedipus volunteers himself.
Apollo has sent his word, his oracle—
Come down. Apollo, save us, stop the plague.

(*The priests rise, remove their branches and exit to the side.*)

(Enter a CHORUS, *the citizens of Thebes, who have not heard the news that* CREON *brings. They march around the altar, chanting.*)

CHORUS: Zeus!
    Great welcome voice of Zeus, what do you bring?
    What word from the gold vaults of Delphi   170
    comes to brilliant Thebes? Racked with terror—
                    terror shakes my heart
    and I cry your wild cries, Apollo, Healer of Delos
    I worship you in dread . . . what now, what is your price?
    some new sacrifice? some ancient rite from the past   175
    come round again each spring?—
        what will you bring to birth?
    Tell me, child of golden Hope
        warm voice that never dies!

    You are the first I call, daughter of Zeus   180
    deathless Athena—I call your sister Artemis,
    heart of the market place enthroned in glory,
                guardian of our earth—
    I call Apollo, Archer astride the thunderheads of heaven—
    O triple shield against death, shine before me now!   185
    If ever, once in the past, you stopped some ruin
    launched against our walls
        you hurled the flame of pain
    far, far from Thebes—you gods
        come now, come down once more!
                    No, no   190
    the miseries numberless, grief on grief, no end—
    too much to bear, we are all dying
    O my people . . .
        Thebes like a great army dying
    and there is no sword of thought to save us, no   195
    and the fruits of our famous earth, they will not ripen
    no and the women cannot scream their pangs to birth—
    screams for the Healer, children dead in the womb
        and life on life goes down
                you can watch them go   200
    like seabirds winging west, outracing the day's fire
    down the horizon, irresistibly
        streaking on to the shores of Evening
                  Death
    so many deaths, numberless deaths on deaths, no end—
    Thebes is dying, look, her children   205
    stripped of pity . . .
        generations strewn on the ground
    unburied, unwept, the dead spreading death
    and the young wives and gray-haired mothers with them

210   cling to the altars, trailing in from all over the city—
           Thebes, city of death, one long cortege
                   and the suffering rises
                           wails for mercy rise
                   and the wild hymn for the Healer blazes out
215   clashing with our sobs our cries of mourning—
               O golden daughter of god, send rescue
               radiant as the kindness in your eyes!
           Drive him back!—the fever, the god of death
                           that raging god of war
220   not armored in bronze, not shielded now, he burns me,
           battle cries in the onslaught burning on—
           O rout him from our borders!
           Sail him, blast him out to the Sea-queen's chamber
                           the black Atlantic gulfs
225   or the northern harbor, death to all
           where the Thracian surf comes crashing.
           Now what the night spares he comes by day and kills—
           the god of death.

                       O lord of the stormcloud,
           you who twirl the lightning, Zeus, Father,
230   thunder Death to nothing!

           Apollo, lord of the light, I beg you—
               whip your longbow's golden cord
           showering arrows on our enemies—shafts of power
           champions strong before us rushing on!

235   Artemis, Huntress,
           torches flaring over the eastern ridges—
                           ride Death down in pain!

           God of the headdress gleaming gold, I cry to you—
           your name and ours are one, Dionysus—
240   come with your face aflame with wine
                           your raving women's cries
               your army on the march! Come with the lightning
           come with torches blazing, eyes ablaze with glory!
           Burn that god of death that all gods hate!

           (OEDIPUS *enters from the palace to address the* CHORUS, *as if addressing the entire city of Thebes.*)

245   OEDIPUS: You pray to the gods? Let me grant your prayers.
           Come, listen to me—do what the plague demands:
           you'll find relief and lift your head from the depths.

           I will speak out now as a stranger to the story,
           a stranger to the crime. If I'd been present then,
250   there would have been no mystery, no long hunt

without a clue in hand. So now, counted
a native Theban years after the murder,
to all of Thebes I make this proclamation:
if any one of you knows who murdered Laius,
the son of Labdacus, I order him to reveal 255
the whole truth to me. Nothing to fear,
even if he must denounce himself,
let him speak up
and so escape the brunt of the charge—
he will suffer no unbearable punishment, 260
nothing worse than exile, totally unharmed.

(OEDIPUS *pauses, waiting for a reply.*)

Next,
if anyone knows the murderer is a stranger,
a man from alien soil, come, speak up.
I will give him a handsome reward, and lay up
gratitude in my heart for him besides. 265

(*Silence again, no reply.*)

But if you keep silent, if anyone panicking,
trying to shield himself or friend or kin,
rejects my offer, then hear what I will do.
I order you, every citizen of the state
where I hold throne and power: banish this man— 270
whoever he may be—never shelter him, never
speak a word to him, never make him partner
to your prayers, your victims burned to the gods.
Never let the holy water touch his hands.
Drive him out, each of you, from every home. 275
He is the plague, the heart of our corruption,
as Apollo's oracle has just revealed to me.
So I honor my obligations:
I fight for the god and for the murdered man.

Now my curse on the murderer. Whoever he is, 280
a lone man unknown in his crime
or one among many, let that man drag out
his life in agony, step by painful step—
I curse myself as well . . . if by any chance
he proves to be an intimate of our house, 285
here at my hearth, with my full knowledge,
may the curse I just called down on him strike me!
These are your orders: perform them to the last.
I command you, for my sake, for Apollo's, for this country
blasted root and branch by the angry heavens. 290
Even if god had never urged you on to act,
how could you leave the crime uncleansed so long?
A man so noble—your king, brought down in blood—

you should have searched. But I am the king now,
295   I hold the throne that he held then, possess his bed
and a wife who shares our seed . . . why, our seed
might be the same, children born of the same mother
might have created blood-bonds between us
if his hope of offspring had not met disaster—
300   but fate swooped at his head and cut him short.
So I will fight for him as if he were my father,
stop at nothing, search the world
to lay my hands on the man who shed his blood,
the son of Labdacus descended of Polydorus,
305   Cadmus of old and Agenor, founder of the line:
their power and mine are one.

                      Oh dear gods,
my curse on those who disobey these orders!
Let no crops grow out of the earth for them—
shrivel their women, kill their sons,
310   burn them to nothing in this plague
that hits us now, or something even worse.
But you, loyal men of Thebes who approve my actions,
may our champion, Justice, may all the gods
be with us, fight beside us to the end!

315   LEADER: In the grip of your curse, my king, I swear
I'm not the murderer, I cannot point him out.
As for the search, Apollo pressed it on us—
he should name the killer.

OEDIPUS: Quite right,
but to force the gods to act against their will—
no man has the power.

320   LEADER: Then if I might mention
the next best thing . . .

OEDIPUS: The third best too—
don't hold back, say it.

LEADER: I still believe . . .
Lord Tiresias sees with the eyes of Lord Apollo.
Anyone searching for the truth, my king,
325   might learn it from the prophet, clear as day.

OEDIPUS: I've not been slow with that. On Creon's cue
I sent the escorts, twice, within the hour.
I'm surprised he isn't here.

LEADER: We need him—
without him we have nothing but old, useless rumors.

330   OEDIPUS: Which rumors? I'll search out every word.

LEADER: Laius was killed, they say, by certain travelers.

OEDIPUS: I know—but no one can find the murderer.

LEADER: If the man has a trace of fear in him
he won't stay silent long,
335   not with your curses ringing in his ears.

OEDIPUS: He didn't flinch at murder,
    he'll never flinch at words.

(*Enter* TIRESIAS, *the blind prophet, led by a boy with escorts in attendance. He remains at a distance.*)

LEADER: Here is the one who will convict him, look,
    they bring him on at last, the seer, the man of god.
    The truth lives inside him, him alone.

OEDIPUS: O Tiresias,   340
    master of all the mysteries of our life,
    all you teach and all you dare not tell,
    signs in the heavens, signs that walk the earth!
    Blind as you are, you can feel all the more
    what sickness haunts our city. You, my lord,   345
    are the one shield, the one savior we can find.

    We asked Apollo—perhaps the messengers
    haven't told you—he sent his answer back:
    "Relief from the plague can only come one way.
    Uncover the murderers of Laius,   350
    put them to death or drive them into exile."
    So I beg you, grudge us nothing now, no voice,
    no message plucked from the birds, the embers
    or the other mantic ways within your grasp.
    Rescue yourself, your city, rescue me—   355
    rescue everything infected by the dead.
    We are in your hands. For a man to help others
    with all his gifts and native strength:
    that is the noblest work.

TIRESIAS: How terrible—to see the truth
    when the truth is only pain to him who sees!   360
    I knew it well, but I put it from my mind,
    else I never would have come.

OEDIPUS: What's this? Why so grim, so dire?

TIRESIAS: Just send me home. You bear your burdens,
    I'll bear mine. It's better that way,   365
    please believe me.

OEDIPUS: Strange response . . . unlawful,
    unfriendly too to the state that bred and reared you—
    you withhold the word of god.

TIRESIAS: I fail to see
    that your own words are so well-timed.
    I'd rather not have the same thing said of me . . .   370

OEDIPUS: For the love of god, don't turn away,
    not if you know something. We beg you,
    all of us on our knees.

TIRESIAS: None of you knows—
    and I will never reveal my dreadful secrets,

375 not to say your own.

OEDIPUS: What? You know and you won't tell?
You're bent on betraying us, destroying Thebes?

TIRESIAS: I'd rather not cause pain for you or me.
So why this . . . useless interrogation?
You'll get nothing from me.

380 OEDIPUS: Nothing! You,
you scum of the earth, you'd enrage a heart of stone!
You won't talk? Nothing moves you?
Out with it, once and for all!

TIRESIAS: You criticize my temper . . . unaware
385 of the one *you* live with, you revile me.

OEDIPUS: Who could restrain his anger hearing you?
What outrage—you spurn the city!

TIRESIAS: What will come will come.
Even if I shroud it all in silence.

390 OEDIPUS: What will come? You're bound to *tell* me that.

TIRESIAS: I will say no more. Do as you like, build your anger
to whatever pitch you please, rage your worst—

OEDIPUS: Oh I'll let loose, I have such fury in me—
now I see it all. You helped hatch the plot,
395 you did the work, yes, short of killing him
with your own hands—and given eyes I'd say
you did the killing single-handed!

TIRESIAS: Is that so!
I charge you, then, submit to that decree
you just laid down: from this day onward
400 speak to no one, not these citizens, not myself.
You are the curse, the corruption of the land!

OEDIPUS: You, shameless—
aren't you appalled to start up such a story?
You think you can get away with this?

TIRESIAS: I have already.
405 The truth with all its power lives inside me.

OEDIPUS: Who primed you for this? Not your prophet's trade.

TIRESIAS: You did, you forced me, twisted it out of me.

OEDIPUS: What? Say it again—I'll understand it better.

TIRESIAS: Didn't you understand, just now?
410 Or are you tempting me to talk?

OEDIPUS: No, I can't say I grasped your meaning.
Out with it, again!

TIRESIAS: I say you are the murderer you hunt.

OEDIPUS: That obscenity, twice—by god, you'll pay.

415 TIRESIAS: Shall I say more, so you can really rage?

OEDIPUS: Much as you want. Your words are nothing—
futile.

TIRESIAS: You cannot imagine . . . I tell you,
you and your loved ones live together in infamy,

you cannot see how far you've gone in guilt.

OEDIPUS: You think you can keep this up and never suffer?   420

TIRESIAS: Indeed, if the truth has any power.

OEDIPUS: It does
but not for you, old man. You've lost your power,
stone-blind, stone-deaf—senses, eyes blind as stone!

TIRESIAS: I pity you, flinging at me the very insults
each man here will fling at you so soon.

OEDIPUS: Blind,   425
lost in the night, endless night that nursed you!
You can't hurt me or anyone else who sees the light—
you can never touch me.

TIRESIAS: True, it is not your fate
to fall at my hands. Apollo is quite enough,
and he will take some pains to work this out.   430

OEDIPUS: Creon! Is this conspiracy his or yours?

TIRESIAS: Creon is not your downfall, no, you are your own.

OEDIPUS: O power—
wealth and empire, skill outstripping skill
in the heady rivalries of life,
what envy lurks inside you! Just for this,   435
the crown the city gave me—I never sought it,
they laid it in my hands—for this alone, Creon,
the soul of trust, my loyal friend from the start
steals against me . . . so hungry to overthrow me
he sets this wizard on me, this scheming quack,   440
this fortune-teller peddling lies, eyes peeled
for his own profit—seer blind in his craft!

Come here, you pious fraud. Tell me,
when did you ever prove yourself a prophet?
When the Sphinx, that chanting Fury kept her deathwatch here,   445
why silent then, not a word to set our people free?
There was a riddle, not for some passer-by to solve—
it cried out for a prophet. Where were you?
Did you rise to the crisis? Not a word,
you and your birds, your gods—nothing.   450
No, but I came by, Oedipus the ignorant,
I stopped the Sphinx! With no help from the birds,
the flight of my own intelligence hit the mark.

And this is the man you'd try to overthrow?
You think you'll stand by Creon when he's king?   455
You and the great mastermind—
you'll pay in tears, I promise you, for this,
this witch-hunt. If you didn't look so senile
the lash would teach you what your scheming means!

LEADER: I would suggest his words were spoken in anger,   460
Oedipus . . . yours too, and it isn't what we need.

The best solution to the oracle, the riddle
posed by god—we should look for that.
TIRESIAS: You are the king no doubt, but in one respect,
465   at least, I am your equal: the right to reply.
I claim that privilege too.
I am not your slave. I serve Apollo.
I don't need Creon to speak for me in public.
                                        So,
you mock my blindness? Let me tell you this.
470   You with your precious eyes,
you're blind to the corruption of your life,
to the house you live in, those you live with—
who *are* your parents? Do you know? All unknowing
you are the scourge of your own flesh and blood,
475   the dead below the earth and the living here above,
and the double lash of your mother and your father's curse
will whip you from this land one day, their footfall
treading you down in terror, darkness shrouding
your eyes that now can see the light!
                                        Soon, soon
480   you'll scream aloud—what haven won't reverberate?
What rock of Cithaeron won't scream back in echo?
That day you learn the truth about your marriage,
the wedding-march that sang you into your halls,
the lusty voyage home to the fatal harbor!
485   And a crowd of other horrors you'd never dream
will level you with yourself and all your children.

There. Now smear us with insults—Creon, myself
and every word I've said. No man will ever
be rooted from the earth as brutally as you.
490   OEDIPUS: Enough! Such filth from him? Insufferable—
what, still alive? Get out—
faster, back where you came from—vanish!
TIRESIAS: I would never have come if you hadn't called me here.
OEDIPUS: If I thought you would blurt out such absurdities,
495   you'd have died waiting before I'd had you summoned.
TIRESIAS: Absurd, am I! To you, not to your parents:
the ones who bore you found me sane enough.
OEDIPUS: Parents—who? Wait . . . who is my father?
TIRESIAS: This day will bring your birth and your destruction.
500   OEDIPUS: Riddles—all you can say are riddles, murk and darkness.
TIRESIAS: Ah, but aren't you the best man alive at solving riddles?
OEDIPUS: Mock me for that, go on, and you'll reveal my greatness.
TIRESIAS: Your great good fortune, true, it was your ruin.
OEDIPUS: Not if I saved the city—what do I care?
TIRESIAS: Well then, I'll be going.

(*To his attendant.*)

505

Take me home, boy.

OEDIPUS: Yes, take him away. You're a nuisance here.
Out of the way, the irritation's gone.

(*Turning his back on* TIRESIAS, *moving toward the palace.*)

TIRESIAS: I will go,
once I have said what I came here to say.
I will never shrink from the anger in your eyes—
you can't destroy me. Listen to me closely: 510
the man you've sought so long, proclaiming,
cursing up and down, the murderer of Laius—
he is here. A stranger,
you may think, who lives among you,
he soon will be revealed a native Theban   515
but he will take no joy in the revelation.
Blind who now has eyes, beggar who now is rich,
he will grope his way toward a foreign soil,
a stick tapping before him step by step.

(OEDIPUS *enters the palace.*)

Revealed at last, brother and father both   520
to the children he embraces, to his mother
son and husband both—he sowed the loins
his father sowed, he spilled his father's blood!

Go in and reflect on that, solve that.
And if you find I've lied   525
from this day onward call the prophet blind.

(TIRESIAS *and the boy exit to the side.*)

CHORUS: Who—
who is the man the voice of god denounces
resounding out of the rocky gorge of Delphi?
The horror too dark to tell,
whose ruthless bloody hands have done the work?   530
His time has come to fly
to outrace the stallions of the storm
his feet a streak of speed—
Cased in armor, Apollo son of the Father
lunges on him, lightning-bolts afire!   535
And the grim unerring Furies
closing for the kill.
Look,
the word of god has just come blazing
flashing off Parnassus' snowy heights!
That man who left no trace—   540
after him, hunt him down with all our strength!
Now under bristling timber

          up through rocks and caves he stalks
              like the wild mountain bull—
545   cut off from men, each step an agony, frenzied, racing blind
        but he cannot outrace the dread voices of Delphi
        ringing out of the heart of Earth,
          the dark wings beating around him shrieking doom
              the doom that never dies, the terror—
550   The skilled prophet scans the birds and shatters me with terror!
        I can't accept him, can't deny him, don't know what to say,
        I'm lost, and the wings of dark foreboding beating—
        I cannot see what's come, what's still to come . . .
        and what could breed a blood feud between
555   Laius' house and the son of Polybus?
        I know of nothing, not in the past and not now,
        no charge to bring against our king, no cause
        to attack his fame that rings throughout Thebes—
          not without proof—not for the ghost of Laius,
560   not to avenge a murder gone without a trace.

        Zeus and Apollo know, they know, the great masters
          of all the dark and depth of human life.
        But whether a mere man can know the truth,
        whether a seer can fathom more than I—
565   there is no test, no certain proof
          though matching skill for skill
        a man can outstrip a rival. No, not till I see
        these charges proved will I side with his accusers.
        We saw him then, when the she-hawk swept against him,
570   saw with our own eyes his skill, his brilliant triumph—
          there was the test—he was the joy of Thebes!
          Never will I convict my king, never in my heart.

    (*Enter* CREON *from the side.*)

CREON: My fellow-citizens, I hear King Oedipus
        levels terrible charges at me. I had to come.
575   I resent it deeply. If, in the present crisis,
        he thinks he suffers any abuse from me,
        anything I've done or said that offers him
        the slightest injury, why, I've no desire
        to linger out this life, my reputation in ruins.
580   The damage I'd face from such an accusation
        is nothing simple. No, there's nothing worse:
        branded a traitor in the city, a traitor
        to all of you and my good friends.
LEADER: True,
        but a slur might have been forced out of him,
585   by anger perhaps, not any firm conviction.
CREON: The charge was made in public, wasn't it?

I put the prophet up to spreading lies?

LEADER: Such things were said . . .
    I don't know with what intent, if any.

CREON: Was his glance steady, his mind right   590
    when the charge was brought against me?

LEADER: I really couldn't say. I never look
    to judge the ones in power.

    (*The doors open.* OEDIPUS *enters.*)

             Wait,
  here's Oedipus now.

OEDIPUS: You—here? You have the gall
  to show your face before the palace gates?   595
  You, plotting to kill me, kill the king—
  I see it all, the marauding thief himself
  scheming to steal my crown and power!

                   Tell me,
  in god's name, what did you take me for,
  coward or fool, when you spun out your plot?   600
  Your treachery—you think I'd never detect it
  creeping against me in the dark? Or sensing it,
  not defend myself? Aren't you the fool,
  you and your high adventure. Lacking numbers,
  powerful friends, out for the big game of empire—   605
  you need riches, armies to bring that quarry down!

CREON: Are you quite finished? It's your turn to listen
  for just as long as you've . . . instructed me.
  Hear me out, then judge me on the facts.

OEDIPUS: You've a wicked way with words, Creon,   610
  but I'll be slow to learn—from you.
  I find you a menace, a great burden to me.

CREON: Just one thing, hear me out in this.

OEDIPUS: Just one thing,
  don't tell *me* you're not the enemy, the traitor.

CREON: Look, if you think crude, mindless stubbornness   61
  such a gift, you've lost your sense of balance.

OEDIPUS: If you think you can abuse a kinsman,
  then escape the penalty, you're insane.

CREON: Fair enough, I grant you. But this injury   62
  you say I've done you, what is it?

OEDIPUS: Did you induce me, yes or no,
  to send for that sanctimonious prophet?

CREON: I did. And I'd do the same again.

OEDIPUS: All right then, tell me, how long is it now
  since Laius . . .

CREON: Laius—what did *he* do?

OEDIPUS: Vanished,   62
  swept from sight, murdered in his tracks.

CREON: The count of the years would run you far back . . .

OEDIPUS: And that far back, was the prophet at his trade?

CREON: Skilled as he is today, and just as honored.

OEDIPUS: Did he ever refer to me then, at that time?

630 CREON: No,
    never, at least, when I was in his presence.

OEDIPUS: But you did investigate the murder, didn't you?

CREON: We did our best, of course, discovered nothing.

OEDIPUS: But the great seer never accused me then—why not?

635 CREON: I don't know. And when I don't, *I* keep quiet.

OEDIPUS: You do know this, you'd tell it too—
    if you had a shred of decency.

CREON: What?
    If I know, I won't hold back.

OEDIPUS: Simply this:
    if the two of you had never put heads together,

640   we would never have heard about *my* killing Laius.

CREON: If that's what he says . . . well, you know best.
But now I have a right to learn from you
as you just learned from me.

OEDIPUS: Learn your fill,
    you never will convict me of the murder.

645 CREON: Tell me, you're married to my sister, aren't you?

OEDIPUS: A genuine discovery—there's no denying that.

CREON: And you rule the land with her, with equal power?

OEDIPUS: She receives from me whatever she desires.

CREON: And I am the third, all of us are equals?

650 OEDIPUS: Yes, and it's there you show your stripes—
    you betray a kinsman.

CREON: Not at all.
    Not if you see things calmly, rationally,
    as I do. Look at it this way first:
    who in his right mind would rather rule

655   and live in anxiety than sleep in peace?
    Particularly if he enjoys the same authority.
    Not I, I'm not the man to yearn for kingship,
    not with a king's power in my hands. Who would?
    No one with any sense of self-control.

660   Now, as it is, you offer me all I need,
    not a fear in the world. But if I wore the crown . . .
    there'd be many painful duties to perform,
    hardly to my taste.

                How could kingship
    please me more than influence, power

665   without a qualm? I'm not that deluded yet,
    to reach for anything but privilege outright,
    profit free and clear.
    Now all men sing my praises, all salute me,

now all who request your favors curry mine.
I am their best hope: success rests in me.   670
Why give up that, I ask you, and borrow trouble?
A man of sense, someone who sees things clearly
would never resort to treason.
No, I have no lust for conspiracy in me,
nor could I ever suffer one who does.   675

Do you want proof? Go to Delphi yourself,
examine the oracle and see if I've reported
the message word-for-word. This too:
if you detect that I and the clairvoyant
have plotted anything in common, arrest me,   680
execute me. Not on the strength of one vote,
two in this case, mine as well as yours.
But don't convict me on sheer unverified surmise.
How wrong it is to take the good for bad,
purely at random, or take the bad for good.   685
But reject a friend, a kinsman? I would as soon
tear out the life within us, priceless life itself.
You'll learn this well, without fail, in time.
Time alone can bring the just man to light—
the criminal you can spot in one short day.
LEADER: Good advice,   690
    my lord, for anyone who wants to avoid disaster.
    Those who jump to conclusions may go wrong.
OEDIPUS: When my enemy moves against me quickly,
    plots in secret, I move quickly too, I must,
    I plot and pay him back. Relax my guard a moment,   695
    waiting his next move—he wins his objective,
    I lose mine.
CREON: What do you want?
    You want me banished?
OEDIPUS: No, I want you dead.
CREON: Just to show how ugly a grudge can . . .
OEDIPUS: So,
    still stubborn? you don't think I'm serious?   700
CREON: I think you're insane.
OEDIPUS: Quite sane—in my behalf.
CREON: Not just as much in mine?
OEDIPUS: You—my mortal enemy?
CREON: What if you're wholly wrong?
OEDIPUS: No matter—I must rule.
CREON: Not if you rule unjustly.
OEDIPUS: Hear him, Thebes, my city!
CREON: My city too, not yours alone!   70
LEADER: Please, my lords.

    (Enter JOCASTA from the palace.)

Look, Jocasta's coming,
and just in time too. With her help
you must put this fighting of yours to rest.

JOCASTA: Have you no sense? Poor misguided men,
710   such shouting—why this public outburst?
Aren't you ashamed, with the land so sick,
to stir up private quarrels?

(*To* OEDIPUS.)

Into the palace now. And Creon, you go home.
Why make such a furor over nothing?

715   CREON: My sister, it's dreadful . . . Oedipus, your husband,
he's bent on a choice of punishments for me,
banishment from the fatherland or death.

OEDIPUS: Precisely. I caught him in the act, Jocasta,
plotting, about to stab me in the back.

720   CREON: Never—curse me, let me die and be damned
if I've done you any wrong you charge me with.

JOCASTA: Oh god, believe it, Oedipus,
honor the solemn oath he swears to heaven.
Do it for me, for the sake of all your people.

(*The* CHORUS *begins to chant.*)

725   CHORUS: Believe it, be sensible
give way, my king, I beg you!

OEDIPUS: What do you want from me, concessions?

CHORUS: Respect him—he's been no fool in the past
and now he's strong with the oath he swears to god.

OEDIPUS: You know what you're asking?

CHORUS: I do.

730   OEDIPUS: Then out with it!

CHORUS: The man's your friend, your kin, he's under oath—
don't cast him out, disgraced
branded with guilt on the strength of hearsay only.

OEDIPUS: Know full well, if that is what you want
you want me dead or banished from the land.

735   CHORUS: Never—
no, by the blazing Sun, first god of the heavens!
Stripped of the gods, stripped of loved ones,
let me die by inches if that ever crossed my mind.
But the heart inside me sickens, dies as the land dies
740   and now on top of the old griefs you pile this,
your fury—both of you!

OEDIPUS: Then let him go,
even if it does lead to my ruin, my death
or my disgrace, driven from Thebes for life.
It's you, not him I pity—your words move me.
745   He, wherever he goes, my hate goes with him.

CREON: Look at you, sullen in yielding, brutal in your rage—
    you will go too far. It's perfect justice:
    natures like yours are hardest on themselves.
OEDIPUS: Then leave me alone—get out!
CREON: I'm going.   750
    You're wrong, so wrong. These men know I'm right.

(*Exit to the side. The* CHORUS *turns to* JOCASTA.)

CHORUS: Why do you hesitate, my lady
    why not help him in?
JOCASTA: Tell me what's happened first.
CHORUS: Loose, ignorant talk started dark suspicions
    and a sense of injustice cut deeply too.   755
JOCASTA: On both sides?
CHORUS: Oh yes.
JOCASTA: What did they say?
CHORUS: Enough, please, enough! The land's so racked already
    or so it seems to me . . .
    End the trouble here, just where they left it.
OEDIPUS: You see what comes of your good intentions now?   760
    And all because you tried to blunt my anger.
CHORUS: My king,
    I've said it once, I'll say it time and again—
      I'd be insane, you know it,
    senseless, ever to turn my back on you.
    You who set our beloved land—storm-tossed, shattered—   765
    straight on course. Now again, good helmsman,
    steer us through the storm!

(*The* CHORUS *draws away, leaving* OEDIPUS *and* JOCASTA *side by side.*)

JOCASTA: For the love of god,
    Oedipus, tell me too, what is it?
    Why this rage? You're so unbending.
OEDIPUS: I will tell you. I respect you, Jocasta,   770
    much more than these men here . . .

(*Glancing at the* CHORUS.)

    Creon's to blame, Creon schemes against me.
JOCASTA: Tell me clearly, how did the quarrel start?
OEDIPUS: He says *I* murdered Laius—I am guilty.
JOCASTA: How does he know? Some secret knowledge   775
    or simple hearsay?
OEDIPUS: Oh, he sent his prophet in
    to do his dirty work. You know Creon,
    Creon keeps his own lips clean.
JOCASTA: A prophet?
    Well then, free yourself of every charge!
    Listen to me and learn some peace of mind: 780

no skill in the world,
nothing human can penetrate the future.
Here is proof, quick and to the point.

An oracle came to Laius one fine day
785 (I won't say from Apollo himself
but his underlings, his priests) and it declared
that doom would strike him down at the hands of a son,
our son, to be born of our own flesh and blood. But Laius,
so the report goes at least, was killed by strangers,
790 thieves, at a place where three roads meet . . . my son—
he wasn't three days old and the boy's father
fastened his ankles, had a henchman fling him away
on a barren, trackless mountain.
                                        There, you see?
Apollo brought neither thing to pass. My baby
795 no more murdered his father than Laius suffered—
his wildest fear—death at his own son's hands.
That's how the seers and all their revelations
mapped out the future. Brush them from your mind.
Whatever the god needs and seeks
he'll bring to light himself, with ease.

800 OEDIPUS: Strange,
hearing you just now . . . my mind wandered,
my thoughts racing back and forth.
JOCASTA: What do you mean? Why so anxious, startled?
OEDIPUS: I thought I heard you say that Laius
805 was cut down at a place where three roads meet.
JOCASTA: That was the story. It hasn't died out yet.
OEDIPUS: Where did this thing happen? Be precise.
JOCASTA: A place called Phocis, where two branching roads,
one from Daulia, one from Delphi,
810 come together—a crossroads.
OEDIPUS: When? How long ago?
JOCASTA: The heralds no sooner reported Laius dead
than you appeared and they hailed you king of Thebes.
OEDIPUS: My god, my god—what have you planned to do to me?
JOCASTA: What, Oedipus? What haunts you so?
815 OEDIPUS: Not yet.
Laius—how did he look? Describe him.
Had he reached his prime?
JOCASTA: He was swarthy,
and the gray had just begun to streak his temples,
and his build . . . wasn't far from yours.
OEDIPUS: Oh no no,
820 I think I've just called down a dreadful curse
upon myself—I simply didn't know!
JOCASTA: What are you saying? I shudder to look at you.

OEDIPUS: I have a terrible fear the blind seer can see.
    I'll know in a moment. One thing more—
JOCASTA: Anything,
    afraid as I am—ask, I'll answer, all I can.   825
OEDIPUS: Did he go with a light or heavy escort,
    several men-at-arms, like a lord, a king?
JOCASTA: There were five in the party, a herald among them,
    and a single wagon carrying Laius.
OEDIPUS: Ai—
    now I can see it all, clear as day.   830
    Who told you all this at the time, Jocasta?
JOCASTA: A servant who reached home, the lone survivor.
OEDIPUS: So, could he still be in the palace—even now?
JOCASTA: No indeed. Soon as he returned from the scene
    and saw you on the throne with Laius dead and gone,   835
    he knelt and clutched my hand, pleading with me
    to send him into the hinterlands, to pasture,
    far as possible, out of sight of Thebes.
    I sent him away. Slave though he was,
    he'd earned that favor—and much more.   840
OEDIPUS: Can we bring him back, quickly?
JOCASTA: Easily. Why do you want him so?
OEDIPUS: I am afraid,
    Jocasta, I have said too much already.
    That man—I've got to see him.
JOCASTA: Then he'll come.
    But even I have a right, I'd like to think,   845
    to know what's torturing you, my lord.
OEDIPUS: And so you shall—I can hold nothing back from you,
    now I've reached this pitch of dark foreboding.
    Who means more to me than you? Tell me,
    whom would I turn toward but you   850
    as I go through all this?

    My father was Polybus, king of Corinth.
    My mother, a Dorian, Merope. And I was held
    the prince of the realm among the people there,
    till something struck me out of nowhere,   855
    something strange . . . worth remarking perhaps,
    hardly worth the anxiety I gave it.
    Some man at a banquet who had drunk too much
    shouted out—he was far gone, mind you—
    that I am not my father's son. Fighting words!   860
    I barely restrained myself that day
    but early the next I went to mother and father,
    questioned them closely, and they were enraged
    at the accusation and the fool who let it fly.
    So as for my parents I was satisfied,   86

but still this thing kept gnawing at me,
the slander spread—I had to make my move.
                                                And so,
unknown to mother and father I set out for Delphi,
and the god Apollo spurned me, sent me away
870   denied the facts I came for,
but first he flashed before my eyes a future
great with pain, terror, disaster—I can hear him cry,
"You are fated to couple with your mother, you will bring
a breed of children into the light no man can bear to see—
875   you will kill your father, the one who gave you life!"
I heard all that and ran. I abandoned Corinth,
from that day on I gauged its landfall only
by the stars, running, always running
toward some place where I would never see
880   the shame of all those oracles come true.
And as I fled I reached that very spot
where the great king, you say, met his death.
Now, Jocasta, I will tell you all.
Making my way toward this triple crossroad
885   I began to see a herald, then a brace of colts
drawing a wagon, and mounted on the bench . . . a man,
just as you've described him, coming face-to-face,
and the one in the lead and the old man himself
were about to thrust me off the road—brute force—
890   and the one shouldering me aside, the driver,
I strike him in anger!—and the old man, watching me
coming up along his wheels—he brings down
his prod, two prongs straight at my head!
I paid him back with interest!
895   Short work, by god—with one blow of the staff
in this right hand I knock him out of his high seat,
roll him out of the wagon, sprawling headlong—
I killed them all—every mother's son!

Oh, but if there is any blood-tie
900   between Laius and this stranger . . .
what man alive more miserable than I?
More hated by the gods? *I* am the man
no alien, no citizen welcomes to his house,
law forbids it—not a word to me in public,
905   driven out of every hearth and home.
And all these curses I—no one but I
brought down these piling curses on myself!
And you, his wife, I've touched your body with these,
the hands that killed your husband cover you with blood.

910   Wasn't I born for torment? Look me in the eyes!

I am abomination—heart and soul!
I must be exiled, and even in exile
never see my parents, never set foot
on native ground again. Else I am doomed
to couple with my mother and cut my father down . . .   *915*
Polybus who reared me, gave me life.
                              But why, why?
Wouldn't a man of judgment say—and wouldn't he be right—
some savage power has brought this down upon my head?

Oh no, not that, you pure and awesome gods,
never let me see that day! Let me slip   *920*
from the world of men, vanish without a trace
before I see myself stained with such corruption,
stained to the heart.
LEADER: My lord, you fill our hearts with fear.
     But at least until you question the witness,   *925*
     do take hope.
OEDIPUS: Exactly. He is my last hope—
     I am waiting for the shepherd. He is crucial.
JOCASTA: And once he appears, what then? Why so urgent?
OEDIPUS: I will tell you. If it turns out that his story
     matches yours, I've escaped the worst.   *930*
JOCASTA: What did I say? What struck you so?
OEDIPUS: You said *thieves*—
     he told you a whole band of them murdered Laius.
     So, if he still holds to the same number,
     I cannot be the killer. One can't equal many.
     But if he refers to one man, one alone,   *935*
     clearly the scales come down on me:
     I am guilty.
JOCASTA: Impossible. Trust me,
     I told you precisely what he said,
     and he can't retract it now
     the whole city heard it, not just I.   *940*
     And even if he should vary his first report
     by one man more or less, still, my lord,
     he could never make the murder of Laius
     truly fit the prophecy. Apollo was explicit:
     my son was doomed to kill my husband . . . my son,   *945*
     poor defenseless thing, he never had a chance
     to kill his father. They destroyed him first.

     So much for prophecy. It's neither here nor there.
     From this day on, I wouldn't look right or left.
OEDIPUS: True, true. Still, that shepherd,   *950*
     someone fetch him—now!
JOCASTA: I'll send at once. But do let's go inside.

I'd never displease you, least of all in this.

(OEDIPUS *and* JOCASTA *enter the palace.*)

CHORUS: Destiny guide me always
955   Destiny find me filled with reverence
               pure in word and deed.
         Great laws tower above us, reared on high
         born for the brilliant vault of heaven—
               Olympian Sky their only father,
960   nothing mortal, no man gave them birth,
         their memory deathless, never lost in sleep:
         within them lives a mighty god, the god does not
               grow old.

         Pride breeds the tyrant
         violent pride, gorging, crammed to bursting
965   with all that is overripe and rich with ruin—
         clawing up to the heights, headlong pride
         crashes down the abyss—sheer doom!
               No footing helps, all foothold lost and gone.
         But the healthy strife that makes the city strong—
970   I pray that god will never end that wrestling:
         god, my champion, I will never let you go.
         But if any man comes striding, high and mighty
               in all he says and does,
         no fear of justice, no reverence
975   for the temples of the gods—
               let a rough doom tear him down,
         repay his pride, breakneck, ruinous pride!
         If he cannot reap his profits fairly
               cannot restrain himself from outrage—
980   mad, laying hands on the holy things untouchable!

               Can such a man, so desperate, still boast
                  he can save his life from the flashing bolts of god?
                     If all such violence goes with honor now
                        why join the sacred dance?

985   Never again will I go reverent to Delphi,
               the inviolate heart of Earth
         or Apollo's ancient oracle at Abae
         or Olympia of the fires—
               unless these prophecies all come true
990   for all mankind to point toward in wonder.
         King of kings, if you deserve your titles
               Zeus, remember, never forget!
         You and your deathless, everlasting reign.

               They are dying, the old oracles sent to Laius,

now our masters strike them off the rolls.
    Nowhere Apollo's golden glory now—
      the gods, the gods go down.   995

(*Enter* JOCASTA *from the palace, carrying a suppliant's branch wound in wool.*)

JOCASTA: Lords of the realm, it occurred to me,
    just now, to visit the temples of the gods,
    so I have my branch in hand and incense too.   1000

    Oedipus is beside himself. Racked with anguish,
    no longer a man of sense, he won't admit
    the latest prophecies are hollow as the old—
    he's at the mercy of every passing voice
    if the voice tells of terror.   100
    I urge him gently, nothing seems to help,
    so I turn to you, Apollo, you are nearest.

(*Placing her branch on the altar, while an old herdsman enters from the side, not the one just summoned by the King but an unexpected* MESSENGER *from Corinth.*)

    I come with prayers and offerings . . . I beg you,
    cleanse us, set us free of defilement!
    Look at us, passengers in the grip of fear,   101
    watching the pilot of the vessel go to pieces.
MESSENGER (*Approaching* JOCASTA *and the* CHORUS):
    Strangers, please, I wonder if you could lead us
    to the palace of the king . . . I think it's Oedipus.
    Better, the man himself—you know where he is?
LEADER: This is his palace, stranger. He's inside.   101
    But here is his queen, his wife and mother
    of his children.
MESSENGER: Blessings on you, noble queen,
    queen of Oedipus crowned with all your family—
    blessings on you always!
JOCASTA: And the same to you, stranger, you deserve it . . .   102
    such a greeting. But what have you come for?
    Have you brought us news?
MESSENGER: Wonderful news—
    for the house, my lady, for your husband too.
JOCASTA: Really, what? Who sent you?
MESSENGER: Corinth.
    I'll give you the message in a moment.   102
    You'll be glad of it—how could you help it?—
    though it costs a little sorrow in the bargain.
JOCASTA: What can it be, with such a double edge?
MESSENGER: The people there, they want to make your Oedipus
    king of Corinth, so they're saying now.   10
JOCASTA: Why? Isn't old Polybus still in power?

MESSENGER: No more. Death has got him in the tomb.

JOCASTA: What are you saying? Polybus, dead?—dead?

MESSENGER: If not,
if I'm not telling the truth, strike me dead too.

1035 JOCASTA (*To a servant*): Quickly, go to your master, tell him this!

You prophecies of the gods, where are you now?
This is the man that Oedipus feared for years,
he fled him, not to kill him—and now he's dead,
quite by chance, a normal, natural death,
not murdered by his son.

1040 OEDIPUS (*Emerging from the palace*): Dearest,
what now? Why call me from the palace?

JOCASTA (*Bringing the* MESSENGER *closer*): Listen to *him,* see for yourself what all
those awful prophecies of god have come to.

OEDIPUS: And who is he? What can he have for me?

1045 JOCASTA: He's from Corinth, he's come to tell you
your father is no more—Polybus—he's dead!

OEDIPUS (*Wheeling on the* MESSENGER): What? Let me have it from your lips.

MESSENGER: Well,
if that's what you want first, then here it is:
make no mistake, Polybus is dead and gone.

1050 OEDIPUS: How—murder? sickness?—what? what killed him?

MESSENGER: A light tip of the scales can put old bones to rest.

OEDIPUS: Sickness then—poor man, it wore him down.

MESSENGER: That,
and the long count of years he'd measured out.

OEDIPUS: So!
Jocasta, why, why look to the Prophet's hearth,
1055 the fires of the future? Why scan the birds
that scream above our heads? They winged me on
to the murder of my father, did they? That was my doom?
Well look, he's dead and buried, hidden under the earth,
and here I am in Thebes, I never put hand to sword—
1060 unless some longing for me wasted him away,
then in a sense you'd say I caused his death.
But now, all those prophecies I feared—Polybus
packs them off to sleep with him in hell!
They're nothing, worthless.

JOCASTA: There.
1065 Didn't I tell you from the start?

OEDIPUS: So you did. I was lost in fear.

JOCASTA: No more, sweep it from your mind forever.

OEDIPUS: But my mother's bed, surely I must fear—

JOCASTA: Fear?
What should a man fear? It's all chance,
1070 chance rules our lives. Not a man on earth

can see a day ahead, groping through the dark.
Better to live at random, best we can.
And as for this marriage with your mother—
have no fear. Many a man before you,
in his dreams, has shared his mother's bed.   1075
Take such things for shadows, nothing at all—
Live, Oedipus,
as if there's no tomorrow!

OEDIPUS: Brave words,
and you'd persuade me if mother weren't alive.
But mother lives, so for all your reassurances   1080
I live in fear, I must.

JOCASTA: But your father's death,
that, at least, is a great blessing, joy to the eyes!

OEDIPUS: Great, I know . . . but I fear *her*—she's still alive.

MESSENGER: Wait, who is this woman, makes you so afraid?

OEDIPUS: Merope, old man. The wife of Polybus.   1085

MESSENGER: The queen? What's there to fear in her?

OEDIPUS: A dreadful prophecy, stranger, sent by the gods.

MESSENGER: Tell me, could you? Unless it's forbidden
other ears to hear.

OEDIPUS: Not at all.
Apollo told me once—it is my fate—   1090
I must make love with my own mother,
shed my father's blood with my own hands.
So for years I've given Corinth a wide berth,
and it's been my good fortune too. But still,
to see one's parents and look into their eyes   1095
is the greatest joy I know.

MESSENGER: You're afraid of that?
That kept you out of Corinth?

OEDIPUS: My *father*, old man—
so I wouldn't kill my father.

MESSENGER: So that's it.
Well then, seeing I came with such good will, my king,
why don't I rid you of that old worry now?   1100

OEDIPUS: What a rich reward you'd have for that!

MESSENGER: What do you think I came for, majesty?
So you'd come home and I'd be better off.

OEDIPUS: Never, I will never go near my parents.

MESSENGER: My boy, it's clear, you don't know what you're doing.   1105

OEDIPUS: What do you mean, old man? For god's sake, explain.

MESSENGER: If you ran from *them,* always dodging home . . .

OEDIPUS: Always, terrified Apollo's oracle might come true—

MESSENGER: And you'd be covered with guilt, from both your parents.

OEDIPUS: That's right, old man, that fear is always with me.   1110

MESSENGER: Don't you know? You've really nothing to fear.

OEDIPUS: But why? If I'm their son—Merope, Polybus?

MESSENGER: Polybus was nothing to you, that's why, not in blood.

OEDIPUS: What are you saying—Polybus was not my father?

MESSENGER: No more than I am. He and I are equals.

1115 OEDIPUS: My father—

how can my father equal nothing? You're nothing to me!

MESSENGER: Neither was he, no more your father than I am.

OEDIPUS: Then why did he call me his son?

MESSENGER: You were a gift,

years ago—know for a fact he took you

from my hands.

1120 OEDIPUS: No, from another's hands?

Then how could he love me so? He loved me, deeply . . .

MESSENGER: True, and his early years without a child

made him love you all the more.

OEDIPUS: And you, did you . . .

buy me? find me by accident?

MESSENGER: I stumbled on you,

down the woody flanks of Mount Cithaeron.

125 OEDIPUS: So close,

what were you doing here, just passing through?

MESSENGER: Watching over my flocks, grazing them on the slopes.

OEDIPUS: A herdsman, were you? A vagabond, scraping for wages?

MESSENGER: Your savior too, my son, in your worst hour.

OEDIPUS: Oh—

130 when you picked me up, was I in pain? What exactly?

MESSENGER: Your ankles . . . they tell the story. Look at them.

OEDIPUS: Why remind me of that, that old affliction?

MESSENGER: Your ankles were pinned together. I set you free.

OEDIPUS: That dreadful mark—I've had it from the cradle.

135 MESSENGER: And you got your name from that misfortune too,

the name's still with you.

OEDIPUS: Dear god, who did it?—

mother? father? Tell me.

MESSENGER: I don't know.

The one who gave you to me, he'd know more.

OEDIPUS: What? You took me from someone else?

You didn't find me yourself?

140 MESSENGER: No sir,

another shepherd passed you on to me.

OEDIPUS: Who? Do you know? Describe him.

MESSENGER: He called himself a servant of . . .

if I remember rightly—Laius.

(JOCASTA *turns sharply.*)

145 OEDIPUS: The king of the land who ruled here long ago?

MESSENGER: That's the one. That herdsman was *his* man.

OEDIPUS: Is he still alive? Can I see him?

MESSENGER: They'd know best, the people of these parts.

(OEDIPUS *and the* MESSENGER *turn to the* CHORUS.)

OEDIPUS: Does anyone know that herdsman,
    the one he mentioned? Anyone seen him   1150
    in the fields, here in the city? Out with it!
    The time has come to reveal this once for all.

LEADER: I think he's the very shepherd you wanted to see,
    a moment ago. But the queen, Jocasta,
    she's the one to say.

OEDIPUS: Jocasta,   1155
    you remember the man we just sent for?
    Is *that* the one he means?

JOCASTA: That man . . .
    why ask? Old shepherd, talk, empty nonsense,
    don't give it another thought, don't even think—

OEDIPUS: What—give up now, with a clue like this?   1160
    Fail to solve the mystery of my birth?
    Not for all the world!

JOCASTA: Stop—in the name of god,
    if you love your own life, call off this search!
    My suffering is enough.

OEDIPUS: Courage!
    Even if my mother turns out to be a slave,   1165
    and I a slave, three generations back,
    you would not seem common.

JOCASTA: Oh no,
    listen to me, I beg you, don't do this.

OEDIPUS: Listen to you? No more. I must know it all,
    must see the truth at last.

JOCASTA: No, please—   1170
    for your sake—I want the best for you!

OEDIPUS: Your best is more than I can bear.

JOCASTA: You're doomed—
    may you never fathom who you are!

OEDIPUS (*To a servant*): Hurry, fetch me the herdsman, now!
    Leave her to glory in her royal birth.   1175

JOCASTA: Aieeeeee—
          man of agony—
    that is the only name I have for you,
    that, no other—ever, ever, ever!

(*Flinging through the palace doors. A long, tense silence follows.*)

LEADER: Where's she gone, Oedipus?
    Rushing off, such wild grief . . .   1180
    I'm afraid that from this silence

something monstrous may come bursting forth.

OEDIPUS: Let it burst! Whatever will, whatever must!
   I must know my birth, no matter how common
1185   it may be—I must see my origins face-to-face.
   She perhaps, she with her woman's pride
   may well be mortified by my birth,
   but I, I count myself the son of Chance,
   the great goddess, giver of all good things—
1190   I'll never see myself disgraced. She is my mother!
   And the moons have marked me out, my blood-brothers,
   one moon on the wane, the next moon great with power.
   That is my blood, my nature—I will never betray it,
   never fail to search and learn my birth!

1195   CHORUS: Yes—if I am a true prophet
         if I can grasp the truth,
      by the boundless skies of Olympus,
   at the full moon of tomorrow, Mount Cithaeron
1200   you will know how Oedipus glories in you—
   you, his birthplace, nurse, his mountain-mother!
   And we will sing you, dancing out your praise—
   you lift our monarch's heart!
      Apollo, Apollo, god of the wild cry
         may our dancing please you!
                              Oedipus—
1205   son, dear child, who bore you?
   Who of the nymphs who seem to live forever
   mated with Pan, the mountain-striding Father?
   Who was your mother? who, some bride of Apollo
   the god who loves the pastures spreading toward the sun?
1210   Or was it Hermes, king of the lightning ridges?
   Or Dionysus, lord of frenzy, lord of the barren peaks—
   did he seize you in his hands, dearest of all his lucky finds?—
      found by the nymphs, their warm eyes dancing, gift
   to the lord who loves them dancing out his joy!

(OEDIPUS *strains to see a figure coming from the distance. Attended by palace guards, an* *old* SHEPHERD *enters slowly, reluctant to approach the king.*)

1215   OEDIPUS: I never met the man, my friends . . . still,
   if I had to guess, I'd say that's the shepherd,
   the very one we've looked for all along.
   Brothers in old age, two of a kind,
   he and our guest here. At any rate
1220   the ones who bring him in are my own men,
   I recognize them.

(*Turning to the* LEADER.)

      But you know more than I,

you should, you've seen the man before.

LEADER: I know him, definitely. One of Laius' men,
a trusty shepherd, if there ever was one.

OEDIPUS: You, I ask you first, stranger,
you from Corinth—is this the one you mean?

MESSENGER: You're looking at him. He's your man.

OEDIPUS (*To the* SHEPHERD): You, old man, come over here—
look at me. Answer all my questions.
Did you ever serve King Laius?

SHEPHERD: So I did . . .
a slave, not bought on the block though,
born and reared in the palace.

OEDIPUS: Your duties, your kind of work?

SHEPHERD: Herding the flocks, the better part of my life.

OEDIPUS: Where, mostly? Where did you do your grazing?

SHEPHERD: Well,
Cithaeron sometimes, or the foothills round about.

OEDIPUS: This man—you know him? ever see him there?

SHEPHERD (*Confused, glancing from the* MESSENGER *to the King*):
Doing what?—what man do you mean?

OEDIPUS (*Pointing to the* MESSENGER): This one here—ever have dealings with him?

SHEPHERD: Not so I could say, but give me a chance,
my memory's bad . . .

MESSENGER: No wonder he doesn't know me, master.
But let me refresh his memory for him.
I'm sure he recalls old times we had
on the slopes of Mount Cithaeron;
he and I, grazing our flocks, he with two
and I with one—we both struck up together,
three whole seasons, six months at a stretch
from spring to the rising of Arcturus in the fall,
then with winter coming on I'd drive my herds
to my own pens, and back he'd go with his
to Laius' folds.

(*To the* SHEPHERD.)

                    Now that's how it was,
wasn't it—yes or no?

SHEPHERD: Yes, I suppose . . .
it's all so long ago.

MESSENGER: Come, tell me,
you gave me a child back then, a boy, remember?
A little fellow to rear, my very own.

SHEPHERD: What? Why rake up that again?

MESSENGER: Look, here he is, my fine old friend—
the same man who was just a baby then.

SHEPHERD: Damn you, shut your mouth—quiet!

OEDIPUS: Don't lash out at him, old man—
  you need lashing more than he does.
SHEPHERD: Why,
  master, majesty—what have I done wrong?
OEDIPUS: You won't answer his question about the boy.
1265 SHEPHERD: He's talking nonsense, wasting his breath.
OEDIPUS: So, you won't talk willingly—
  then you'll talk with pain.

  (*The guards seize the* SHEPHERD.)

SHEPHERD: No, dear god, don't torture an old man!
OEDIPUS: Twist his arms back, quickly!
SHEPHERD: God help us, why?—
1270 what more do you need to know?
OEDIPUS: Did you give him that child? He's asking.
SHEPHERD: I did . . . I wish to god I'd died that day.
OEDIPUS: You've got your wish if you don't tell the truth.
SHEPHERD: The more I tell, the worse the death I'll die.
1275 OEDIPUS: Our friend here wants to stretch things out, does he?

  (*Motioning to his men for torture.*)

SHEPHERD: No, no, I gave it to him—I just said so.
OEDIPUS: Where did you get it? Your house? Someone else's?
SHEPHERD: It wasn't mine, no, I got it from . . . someone.
OEDIPUS: Which one of them?

  (*Looking at the citizens.*)

        Whose house?
SHEPHERD: No—
1280 god's sake, master, no more questions!
OEDIPUS: You're a dead man if I have to ask again.
SHEPHERD: Then—the child came from the house . . .
  of Laius.
OEDIPUS: A slave? or born of his own blood?
SHEPHERD: Oh no,
  I'm right at the edge, the horrible truth—I've got to say it!
1285 OEDIPUS: And I'm at the edge of hearing horrors, yes, but I must hear!
SHEPHERD: All right! His son, they said it was—his son!
  But the one inside, your wife,
  she'd tell it best.
OEDIPUS: My wife—
1290 *she* gave it to you?
SHEPHERD: Yes, yes, my king.
OEDIPUS: Why, what for?
SHEPHERD: To kill it.
OEDIPUS: Her own child,
1295 how could she?

SHEPHERD: She was afraid—
    frightening prophecies.
OEDIPUS: What?
SHEPHERD: They said—
    he'd kill his parents.
OEDIPUS: But you gave him to this old man—why?   1300
SHEPHERD: I pitied the little baby, master,
    hoped he'd take him off to his own country,
    far away, but he saved him for this, this fate.
    If you are the man he says you are, believe me,
    you were born for pain.
OEDIPUS: O god—   1305
    all come true, all burst to light!
    O light—now let me look my last on you!
    I stand revealed at last—
    cursed in my birth, cursed in marriage,
    cursed in the lives I cut down with these hands!   1310

(*Rushing through the doors with a great cry. The Corinthian* MESSENGER, *the*
SHEPHERD *and attendants exit slowly to the side.*)

CHORUS: O the generations of men
    the dying generations—adding the total
    of all your lives I find they come to nothing . . .
        does there exist, is there a man on earth
    who seizes more joy than just a dream, a vision?   1315
    And the vision no sooner dawns than dies
    blazing into oblivion.

    You are my great example, you, your life
    your destiny, Oedipus, man of misery—
    I count no man blest.

            You outranged all men!   1320
        Bending your bow to the breaking-point
    you captured priceless glory, O dear god,
    and the Sphinx came crashing down,
            the virgin, claws hooked
    like a bird of omen singing, shrieking death—   1325
    like a fortress reared in the face of death
    you rose and saved our land.

    From that day on we called you king
    we crowned you with honors, Oedipus, towering over all—
    mighty king of the seven gates of Thebes.   1330
    But now to hear your story—is there a man more agonized?
    More wed to pain and frenzy? Not a man on earth,
    the joy of your life ground down to nothing
    O Oedipus, name for the ages—

1335   one and the same wide harbor served you
                               son and father both
        son and father came to rest in the same bridal chamber.
        How, how could the furrows your father plowed
        bear you, your agony, harrowing on
        in silence O so long?

1340   But now for all your power
        Time, all-seeing Time has dragged you to the light,
        judged your marriage monstrous from the start—
        the son and the father tangling, both one—
        O child of Laius, would to god
1345   I'd never seen you, never never!
            Now I weep like a man who wails the dead
        and the dirge comes pouring forth with all my heart!
        I tell you the truth, you gave me life
        my breath leapt up in you
1350   and now you bring down night upon my eyes.

(*Enter a* MESSENGER *from the palace.*)

MESSENGER: Men of Thebes, always first in honor,
        what horrors you will hear, what you will see,
        what a heavy weight of sorrow you will shoulder . . .
        if you are true to your birth, if you still have
1355   some feeling for the royal house of Thebes.
        I tell you neither the waters of the Danube
        nor the Nile can wash this palace clean.
        Such things it hides, it soon will bring to light—
        terrible things, and none done blindly now,
1360   all done with a will. The pains
        we inflict upon ourselves hurt most of all.
LEADER: God knows we have pains enough already.
        What can you add to them?
MESSENGER: The queen is dead.
LEADER: Poor lady—how?
1365 MESSENGER: By her own hand. But you are spared the worst,
        you never had to watch . . . I saw it all,
        and with all the memory that's in me
        you will learn what that poor woman suffered.

        Once she'd broken in through the gates,
1370   dashing past us, frantic, whipped to fury,
        ripping her hair out with both hands—
        straight to her rooms she rushed, flinging herself
        across the bridal-bed, doors slamming behind her—
        once inside, she wailed for Laius, dead so long,
1375   remembering how she bore his child long ago,
        the life that rose up to destroy him, leaving

its mother to mother living creatures
with the very son she'd borne.
Oh how she wept, mourning the marriage-bed
where she let loose that double brood—monsters—   138
husband by her husband, children by her child.
                                    And then—
but how she died is more than I can say. Suddenly
Oedipus burst in, screaming, he stunned us so
we couldn't watch her agony to the end,
our eyes were fixed on him. Circling   138
like a maddened beast, stalking, here, there,
crying out to us—
                    Give him a sword! His wife,
no wife, his mother, where can he find the mother earth
that cropped two crops at once, himself and all his children?
He was raging—one of the dark powers pointing the way,   139
none of us mortals crowding around him, no,
with a great shattering cry—someone, something leading him on—
he hurled at the twin doors and bending the bolts back
out of their sockets, crashed through the chamber.
And there we saw the woman hanging by the neck,   139
cradled high in a woven noose, spinning,
swinging back and forth. And when he saw her,
giving a low, wrenching sob that broke our hearts,
slipping the halter from her throat, he eased her down,
in a slow embrace he laid her down, poor thing . . .   14(
then, what came next, what horror we beheld!

He rips off her brooches, the long gold pins
holding her robes—and lifting them high,
looking straight up into the points,
he digs them down the sockets of his eyes, crying, "You,   14(
you'll see no more the pain I suffered, all the pain I caused!
Too long you looked on the ones you never should have seen,
blind to the ones you longed to see, to know! Blind
from this hour on! Blind in the darkness—blind!"
His voice like a dirge, rising, over and over   14
raising the pins, raking them down his eyes.
And at each stroke blood spurts from the roots,
splashing his beard, a swirl of it, nerves and clots—
black hail of blood pulsing, gushing down.

These are the griefs that burst upon them both,   14
coupling man and woman. The joy they had so lately,
the fortune of their old ancestral house
was deep joy indeed. Now, in this one day,
wailing, madness and doom, death, disgrace,
all the griefs in the world that you can name,   14

all are theirs forever.

LEADER: Oh poor man, the misery—
has he any rest from pain now?

(*A voice within, in torment.*)

MESSENGER: He's shouting,
"Loose the bolts, someone, show me to all of Thebes!
My father's murderer, my mother's—"
425   No, I can't repeat it, it's unholy.
Now he'll tear himself from his native earth,
not linger, curse the house with his own curse.
But he needs strength, and a guide to lead him on.
This is sickness more than he can bear.

(*The palace doors open.*)

                                   Look,
430   he'll show you himself. The great doors are opening—
you are about to see a sight, a horror
even his mortal enemy would pity.

(*Enter* OEDIPUS, *blinded, led by a boy. He stands at the palace steps, as if surveying his people once again.*)

CHORUS: O the terror—
the suffering, for all the world to see,
the worst terror that ever met my eyes.
435   What madness swept over you? What god,
what dark power leapt beyond all bounds,
beyond belief, to crush your wretched life?—
godforsaken, cursed by the gods!
I pity you but I can't bear to look.
440   I've much to ask, so much to learn,
so much fascinates my eyes,
but you . . . I shudder at the sight.

OEDIPUS: Oh, Ohh—
the agony! I am agony—
where am I going? where on earth?
445   where does all this agony hurl me?
where's my voice?—
           winging, swept away on a dark tide—
My destiny, my dark power, what a leap you made!

CHORUS: To the depths of terror, too dark to hear, to see.
450 OEDIPUS: Dark, horror of darkness
           my darkness, drowning, swirling around me
           crashing wave on wave—unspeakable, irresistible
                   headwind, fatal harbor! Oh again,
           the misery, all at once, over and over
455   the stabbing daggers, stab of memory

raking me insane.

CHORUS: No wonder you suffer
    twice over, the pain of your wounds,
    the lasting grief of pain.

OEDIPUS: Dear friend, still here?
    Standing by me, still with a care for me,
    the blind man? Such compassion,   1460
        loyal to the last. Oh it's you,
    I know you're here, dark as it is
    I'd know you anywhere, your voice—
    it's yours, clearly yours.

CHORUS: Dreadful, what you've done . . .
    how could you bear it, gouging out your eyes?   1465
    What superhuman power drove you on?

OEDIPUS: Apollo, friends, Apollo—
    he ordained my agonies—these, my pains on pains!
    But the hand that struck my eyes was mine,
    mine alone—no one else—   1470
        I did it all myself!
    What good were eyes to me?
    Nothing I could see could bring me joy.

CHORUS: No, no, exactly as you say.

OEDIPUS: What can I ever see?
    What love, what call of the heart   1475
    can touch my ears with joy? Nothing, friends.
        Take me away, far, far from Thebes,
        quickly, cast me away, my friends—
    this great murderous ruin, this man cursed to heaven,
    the man the deathless gods hate most of all!   1480

CHORUS: Pitiful, you suffer so, you understand so much . . .
    I wish you had never known.

OEDIPUS: Die, die—
    whoever he was that day in the wilds
    who cut my ankles free of the ruthless pins,
    he pulled me clear of death, he saved my life   1485
    for this, this kindness—
                    Curse him, kill him!
    If I'd died then, I'd never have dragged myself,
    my loved ones through such hell.

CHORUS: Oh if only . . . would to god.

OEDIPUS: I'd never have come to this,   1490
    my father's murderer—never been branded
    mother's husband, all men see me now! Now,
        loathed by the gods, son of the mother I defiled
        coupling in my father's bed, spawning lives in the loins
    that spawned my wretched life. What grief can crown this grief?   1495
        It's mine alone, my destiny—I am Oedipus!

CHORUS: How can I say you've chosen for the best?
        Better to die than be alive and blind.
OEDIPUS: What I did was best—don't lecture me,
1500   no more advice. I, with *my* eyes,
        how could I look my father in the eyes
        when I go down to death? Or mother, so abused . . .
        I have done such things to the two of them,
        crimes too huge for hanging.
                                Worse yet,
1505   the sight of my children, born as they were born,
        how could I long to look into their eyes?
        No, not with these eyes of mine, never.
        Not this city either, her high towers,
        the sacred glittering images of her gods—
1510   I am misery! I, her best son, reared,
        as no other son of Thebes was ever reared,
        I've stripped myself, I gave the command myself.
        All men must cast away the great blasphemer,
        the curse now brought to light by the gods,
1515   the son of Laius—I, my father's son!

        Now I've exposed my guilt, horrendous guilt,
        could I train a level glance on you, my countrymen?
        Impossible! No, if I could just block off my ears,
        the springs of hearing, I would stop at nothing—
1520   I'd wall up my loathsome body like a prison,
        blind to the sound of life, not just the sight.
        Oblivion—what a blessing . . .
        for the mind to dwell a world away from pain.

        O Cithaeron, why did you give me shelter?
1525   Why didn't you take me, crush my life out on the spot?
        I'd never have revealed my birth to all mankind.

        O Polybus, Corinth, the old house of my fathers,
        so I believed—what a handsome prince you raised—
        under the skin, what sickness to the core.
1530   Look at me! Born of outrage, outrage to the core.

        O triple roads—it all comes back, the secret,
        dark ravine, and the oaks closing in
        where the three roads join . . .
        You drank my father's blood, my own blood
1535   spilled by my own hands—you still remember me?
        What things you saw me do? Then I came here
        and did them all once more!
                         Marriages! O marriage,
        you gave me birth, and once you brought me into the world
        you brought my sperm rising back, springing to light

fathers, brothers, sons—one murderous breed—
brides, wives, mothers. The blackest things
a man can do, I have done them all!   154

                    No more—
it's wrong to name what's wrong to do. Quickly,
for the love of god, hide me somewhere,
kill me, hurl me into the sea   154
where you can never look on me again.

(*Beckoning to the* CHORUS *as they shrink away.*)

                              Closer,
it's all right. Touch the man of grief.
Do. Don't be afraid. My troubles are mine
and I am the only man alive who can sustain them.

(*Enter* CREON *from the palace, attended by palace guards.*)

LEADER: Put your requests to Creon. Here he is,   155
    just when we need him. He'll have a plan, he'll act.
    Now that he's the sole defense of the country
    in your place.
OEDIPUS: Oh no, what can I say to him?
    How can I ever hope to win his trust?
    I wronged him so, just now, in every way.   155
    You must see that—I was so wrong, so wrong.
CREON: I haven't come to mock you, Oedipus,
    or to criticize your former failings.

(*Turning to the guards.*)

                              You there,
    have you lost all respect for human feelings?
    At least revere the Sun, the holy fire   156
    that keeps us all alive. Never expose a thing
    of guilt and holy dread so great it appalls
    the earth, the rain from heaven, the light of day!
    Get him into the halls—quickly as you can.
    Piety demands no less. Kindred alone   156
    should see a kinsman's shame. This is obscene.
OEDIPUS: Please, in god's name . . . you wipe my fears away,
    coming so generously to me, the worst of men.
    Do one thing more, for your sake, not mine.
CREON: What do you want? Why so insistent?   157
OEDIPUS: Drive me out of the land at once, far from sight,
    where I can never hear a human voice.
CREON: I'd have done that already, I promise you.
    First I wanted the god to clarify my duties.
OEDIPUS: The god? His command was clear, every word: 157
    death for the father-killer, the curse—

he said destroy me!

CREON: So he did. Still, in such a crisis
it's better to ask precisely what to do.

OEDIPUS: So miserable—
580   you would consult the god about a man like me?

CREON: By all means. And this time, I assume,
even you will obey the god's decrees.

OEDIPUS: I will,
I will. And you, I command you—I beg you . . .
the woman inside, bury her as you see fit.
585   It's the only decent thing,
to give your own the last rites. As for me,
never condemn the city of my fathers
to house my body, not while I'm alive, no,
let me live on the mountains, on Cithaeron,
590   my favorite haunt, I have made it famous.
Mother and father marked out that rock
to be my everlasting tomb—buried alive.
Let me die there, where they tried to kill me.

Oh but this I know: no sickness can destroy me,
595   nothing can. I would never have been saved
from death—I have been saved
for something great and terrible, something strange.
Well let my destiny come and take me on its way!
About my children, Creon, the boys at least,
600   don't burden yourself. They're men,
wherever they go, they'll find the means to live.
But my two daughters, my poor helpless girls,
clustering at our table, never without me
hovering near them . . . whatever I touched,
605   they always had their share. Take care of them,
I beg you. Wait, better—permit me, would you?
Just to touch them with my hands and take
our fill of tears. Please . . . my king.
Grant it, with all your noble heart.
610   If I could hold them, just once, I'd think
I had them with me, like the early days
when I could see their eyes.

(ANTIGONE *and* ISMENE, *two small children, are led in from the palace by a nurse.*)

                              What's that?
O god! Do I really hear you sobbing?—
my two children. Creon, you've pitied me?
615   Sent me my darling girls, my own flesh and blood!
Am I right?

CREON: Yes, it's my doing.

I know the joy they gave you all these years,
the joy you must feel now.

OEDIPUS: Bless you, Creon!
May god watch over you for this kindness,
better than he ever guarded me.

                              Children, where are you?   162
Here, come quickly—

(*Groping for* ANTIGONE *and* ISMENE, *who approach their father cautiously, then embrace him.*)

                    Come to these hands of mine,
your brother's hands, your own father's hands
that served his once bright eyes so well—
that made them blind. Seeing nothing, children,   162
knowing nothing, I became your father,
I fathered you in the soil that gave me life.

How I weep for you—I cannot see you now . . .
just thinking of all your days to come, the bitterness,
the life that rough mankind will thrust upon you.
Where are the public gatherings you can join,   163
the banquets of the clans? Home you'll come,
in tears, cut off from the sight of it all,
the brilliant rites unfinished.
And when you reach perfection, ripe for marriage,
who will he be, my dear ones? Risking all   163
to shoulder the curse that weighs down my parents,
yes and you too—that wounds us all together.
What more misery could you want?
Your father killed his father, sowed his mother,
one, one and the selfsame womb sprang you—   164
he cropped the very roots of his existence.

Such disgrace, and you must bear it all!
Who will marry you then? Not a man on earth.
Your doom is clear: you'll wither away to nothing,
single, without a child.

(*Turning to* CREON)

                    Oh Creon,   164
you are the only father they have now . . .
we who brought them into the world
are gone, both gone at a stroke—
Don't let them go begging, abandoned,
women without men. Your own flesh and blood!   16!
Never bring them down to the level of my pains.
Pity them. Look at them, so young, so vulnerable,

shorn of everything—you're their only hope.
Promise me, noble Creon, touch my hand!

(*Reaching toward* CREON, *who draws back.*)

1655   You, little ones, if you were old enough
to understand, there is much I'd tell you.
Now, as it is, I'd have you say a prayer.
Pray for life, my children,
live where you are free to grow and season.
1660   Pray god you find a better life than mine,
the father who begot you.

CREON: Enough.
       You've wept enough. Into the palace now.

OEDIPUS: I must, but I find it very hard.

CREON: Time is the great healer, you will see.

1665   OEDIPUS: I am going—you know on what condition?

CREON: Tell me. I'm listening.

OEDIPUS: Drive me out of Thebes, in exile.

CREON: Not I. Only the gods can give you that.

OEDIPUS: Surely the gods hate me so much—

CREON: You'll get your wish at once.

1670   OEDIPUS: You consent?

CREON: I try to say what I mean; it's my habit.

OEDIPUS: Then take me away. It's time.

CREON: Come along, let go of the children.

OEDIPUS: No—
       don't take them away from me, not now! No no no!

(*Clutching his daughters as the guards wrench them loose and take them through the palace doors.*)

1675   CREON: Still the king, the master of all things?
       No more: here your power ends.
       None of your power follows you through life.

(*Exit* OEDIPUS *and* CREON *to the palace. The* CHORUS *comes forward to address the audience directly.*)

CHORUS: People of Thebes, my countrymen, look on Oedipus.
       He solved the famous riddle with his brilliance,
1680   he rose to power, a man beyond all power.
       Who could behold his greatness without envy?
       Now what a black sea of terror has overwhelmed him.
       Now as we keep our watch and wait the final day,
       count no man happy till he dies, free of pain at last.

(*Exit in procession.*)

QUESTIONS FOR DISCUSSION AND WRITING

1. When we are first introduced to Oedipus, he is at the height of his powers. How do the Thebans view their king? How does he view his subjects?

2. Several characters, including Tiresias and Jocasta, warn Oedipus to discontinue his search for answers. Why does Oedipus ignore these warnings? How does the audience react to them? Do we consider Oedipus wise or foolish for continuing his search?

3. The gods are mentioned throughout the play, but they do not take an active role in it. How do the characters in the play view the gods? How do we?

4. At what point does Oedipus realize he has killed his father and married his mother? Should he have come to the realization before he does? If so, when should he have understood the truth?

5. The play focuses on Oedipus's growing knowledge of his patricide and incest, but Jocasta also comes to that knowledge. How would you compare Oedipus's and her reactions to the dawning knowledge of their incestuous relationship?

6. For centuries readers have debated Oedipus's guilt or innocence. Some readers feel that Oedipus is guiltless and so undeserving of his fate. Others see Oedipus as flawed, arguing that he is guilty of *hubris,* or excessive pride, in attempting to avoid his fate. Where do you stand regarding Oedipus's guilt or innocence? What is the evidence for both points of view?

7. The function that the Chorus serves in *Oedipus* is unclear. It may provide a kind of narrative voice, giving us the playwright's point of view; it may offer us a "man-in-the-street" response to the events; it may suggest a link to the gods. What role do you think the Chorus plays? Do you respond to its pronouncements in different ways at different points in the play?

8. Focusing on a single image pattern in *Oedipus* (for example, the blindness or plague/contamination images), consider how this pattern affects our view of the characters and/or themes of the play. Does the meaning of the image change as the play proceeds?

9. Both Jocasta's suicide and Oedipus's blinding take place offstage. What does the play gain and/or lose by having these horrific events reported rather than shown? How would the play feel different if the suicide and blinding happened onstage?

10. Imagine that you have been asked to produce and direct a performance of *Oedipus.* You are more concerned with bringing to life the play's themes, concerns, and atmosphere than in reproducing the kind of drama that would have been presented in Sophocles' time. Given the fact that some of the play's methods and concerns—the use of the Chorus, the belief in Fate, and so forth—might seem alien to an audience of today, how would you produce and direct the play so that it had the kind of effect on a modern audience that it must have had on its original Greek audience? How and why would your changes affect our responses to the play?

QUESTION FOR DISCUSSION AND WRITING

The picture is from a 1968 movie of *Oedipus*, starring Christopher Plummer as Oedipus and Lilli Palmer as Jocasta. What does the picture suggest about the relationship between Oedipus and Jocasta? At what point in the play would you expect such a moment to occur?

C. P. CAVAFY (1863–1933)

Oedipus

> *Written after reading the description of the painting "Oedipus and the Sphinx" by Gustav Moreau.*

The Sphinx is fallen on him,
with teeth and talons outspread
and with all the furor of life.
Oedipus succumbed to her first impulse;
5   her first appearance terrified him—
such a face, and such talk
till then he had never imagined.
But though the monster rests
her two paws on Oedipus' breast
10   he has recovered quickly—and now
he no longer fears her for he has
the solution ready and he will win.
And yet he does not rejoice over this victory.
His glance, full of melancholy,
15   is not on the Sphinx; far off he sees
the narrow path that leads to Thebes
and will end at Colonus.
And his soul clearly forebodes

that there the Sphinx will accost him again
with more difficult and more baffling   20
enigmas that have no answer.

QUESTIONS FOR DISCUSSION AND WRITING

1. Though this does not literally happen in Sophocles' play, Cavafy believes that at
   Colonus "the Sphinx will accost [Oedipus] again." How might the Sphinx's riddle
   be related to the "enigmas" Oedipus faces as he searches for the truth and punishes
   himself for containing the pollution that has brought the plague to Thebes?
2. Cavafy alludes to Oedipus's courage (he is not afraid), his intelligence (he can answer the riddle), and his soul (he forebodes the future). Which of these parts of
   Oedipus's character seems most important to Cavafy? To Sophocles?

EDWIN MUIR (1887–1959)

Oedipus

I, Oedipus, the club-foot, made to stumble,
Who long in the light have walked the world in darkness,
And once in the darkness did that which the light
Found and disowned—too well I have loved the light,
Too dearly have rued the darkness. I am one   5
Who as in innocent play sought out his guilt,
And now through guilt seeks other innocence,
Beset by evil thoughts, led by the gods.

There was a room, a bed of darkness, once
Known to me, now to all. Yet in that darkness,   10
Before the light struck, she and I who lay
There without thought of sin and knew each other
Too well, yet were to each other quite unknown
Though fastened mouth to mouth and breast to breast—
Strangers laid on one bed, as children blind,   15
Clear-eyed and blind as children—did we sin
Then on that bed before the light came on us,
Desiring good to each other, bringing, we thought,
Great good to each other? But neither guilt nor death.

Yet if that darkness had been darker yet,   20
Buried in endless dark past reach of light
Or eye of the gods, a kingdom of solid darkness
Impregnable and immortal, would we have sinned,
Or lived like the gods in deathless innocence?

25   For sin is born in the light; therefore we cower
    Before the face of the light that none can meet
    And all must seek. And when in memory now,
    Woven of light and darkness, a stifling web,
    I call her back, dear, dreaded, who lay with me,
30   I see guilt, only guilt, my nostrils choke
    With the smell of guilt, and I can scarcely breathe
    Here in the guiltless guilt-evoking sun.

    And when young Oedipus—for it was Oedipus
    And not another—on that long vanished night
35   Far in my night, at that predestined point
    Where three paths like three fates crossed one another,
    Tracing the evil figure—when I met
    The stranger who menaced me, and flung the stone
    That brought him death and me this that I carry,
40   It was not him but fear I sought to kill,
    Fear that, the wise men say, is father of evil,
    And was my father in flesh and blood, yet fear,
    Fear only, father and fear in one dense body,
    So that there was no division, no way past:
45   Did I sin then, by the gods admonished to sin,
    By men enjoined to sin? For it is duty
    Of god and man to kill the shapes of fear.

    These thoughts recur, vain thoughts. The gods see all,
    And will what must be willed, which guards us here.
50   Their will in them was anger, in me was terror
    Long since, but now is peace. For I am led
    By them in darkness; light is all about me;
    My way lies in the light; they know it; I
    Am theirs to guide and hold. And I have learned,
55   Though blind, to see with something of their sight,
    Can look into that other world and watch
    King Oedipus the just, crowned and discrowned,
    As one may see oneself rise in a dream,
    Distant and strange. Even so I see
60   The meeting at the place where three roads crossed,
    And who was there and why, and what was done
    That had to be done and paid for. Innocent
    The deed that brought the guilt of father-murder. Pure

    The embrace on the bed of darkness. Innocent
65   And guilty. I have wrought and thought in darkness,
    And stand here now, an innocent mark of shame,
    That so men's guilt might be made manifest
    In such a walking riddle—their guilt and mine,
    For I've but acted out this fable. I have judged

Myself, obedient to the gods' high judgment,   70
And seen myself with their pure eyes, have learnt
That all must bear a portion of the wrong
That is driven deep into our fathomless hearts
Past sight or thought; that bearing it we may ease
The immortal burden of the gods who keep   75
Our natural steps and the earth and skies from harm.

QUESTIONS FOR DISCUSSION AND WRITING

1. In Muir's poem, Oedipus explores his guilt and innocence. Does he finally see himself as guilty or innocent? Does the reader reach the same conclusion he does?
2. There is light and dark imagery throughout the poem. What is associated with light? What is associated with darkness? How does the imagery reinforce the poem's themes and its characterization of Oedipus?
3. What is the tone of the poem? Is Oedipus bemoaning his fate? Offering excuses? Expressing repentance or repugnance?

RANDALL JARRELL (1914–1965)

The Sphinx's Riddle to Oedipus

Not to have guessed is better: what is, ends,
But among fellows, with reluctance,
Clasped by the Woman-Breasted, Lion-Pawed.

To have clasped in one's own arms a mother,
To have killed with one's own hands a father   5
—Is not this, Lame One, to have been alone?

The seer is doomed for seeing; and to understand
Is to pluck out one's own eyes with one's own hands.
But speak: what has a woman's breasts, a lion's paws?

You stand at midday in the marketplace   10
Before your life: to see is to have spoken.
—Yet to see, Blind One, is to be alone.

QUESTIONS FOR DISCUSSION AND WRITING

1. What qualities about Oedipus does Jarrell's poem emphasize? Is Jarrell drawing on Sophocles' play or adding to it?

2. "The Sphinx's Riddle to Oedipus" suggests that Oedipus would have been better off not guessing the answer to the Sphinx's riddle. What would have happened had he not guessed the answer? Do you think that would have been better than what actually happens to him?

CARL DENNIS (1939–   )

Oedipus the King _____ *1990*

Hard to forgive Freud, the exposer of fictions,
When he borrows the name of a great mythical king
To cover our common wish not to share mom
With anyone, not even with dad.

5   Oedipus, solver of riddles too hard for us,
Freud's inspiration and mentor,
Teacher and pupil of one mind with the sphinx
That man is the mystery,
Three people at least in one.

10 But even Freud, with all his interpreting,
Didn't manage to save a city, as Oedipus did.
Vienna could have done without him,
He knew, and would go on as before,
Winning and wasting.

15 We never imagine Oedipus one of us
Except for a moment, just after the plague arrives,
When he vows to rid the city of its pollution,
To root the murderer out, no matter where.
We too could have made a mistake like that.

20 But when the question changes slowly
To who exactly his parents are
We would have stopped, as the prophet advises.
While the King, suspecting the worst, presses on.

Freud may have taken the facts, however painful,
25 As evidence he was only human,
Alive and desiring.
But Oedipus chooses to be guilty,
To blind himself, to banish himself
And go the gods one better, the father gods
30 Who didn't love him as a father should.

As for his mother, if he has one then,
It's the earth, who feels him tapping
Her breast with his cane
As he hobbles along outside the walls.
35 "Where are you going, dear Son?" she calls.

"For you the door to my dark house stands open.
No other house will take you in."

QUESTIONS FOR DISCUSSION AND WRITING

1. What is the poem's attitude toward Freud's use of the Oedipus legend?
2. Do you agree with Dennis that "Oedipus chooses to be guilty" and that "we would have stopped" seeking the answers that Oedipus persists in seeking? If Oedipus chooses to be guilty, what is he guilty of? Why would we have made a different decision?
3. Why does Dennis say that Oedipus's mother is the Earth? Why doesn't he acknowledge Jocasta as Oedipus's mother?

TOM LEHRER (1928–   )

Oedipus Rex _____ 1959

From the Bible to the popular song,
There's one theme that we find right along,
Of all ideals they hold as good,
The most sublime is motherhood.
There was a man, who, so it seems,   5
Once carried this ideal to extremes,
He loved his mother and she loved him,
And yet his story is rather grim.

There once lived a man named Oedipus Rex,
You may have heard about his odd complex,   10
His name appears in Freud's index,
'Cos he *loved* his mother!

His rivals used to say quite a bit
That as a monarch he was most unfit,
But still and all, they had to admit   15
That he *loved* his mother!

Yes he loved his mother like no other,
His daughter was his sister
And his son was his brother,
One thing on which you can depend is,   20
He sure knew who a boy's best friend is!

When he found what he had done,
He tore his eyes out one by one,
A tragic end to a loyal son,
Who *loved* his mother!   25

So be sweet and kind to mother,
Now and then have a chat,
Buy her candy or some flowers,
Or a brand-new hat—
30   But maybe you'd better let it go that . . .
Or you might find yourself with a quite complex complex,
And you may end up like Oedipus,
I'd rather marry a duck-billed platypus,
Then end up like old Oedipus Rex!

QUESTIONS FOR DISCUSSION AND WRITING

1. Does Lehrer seem to be drawing more on Sophocles or on Freud (1114–16)? What elements of the Oedipus story does he most emphasize, and why?
2. We see very readily that Lehrer's intent is humorous. What indicates that? Does the humor indicate contempt or admiration for the Oedipus legend?
3. Lehrer's piece is really a song. Locate a copy of the song. Is your response different when you hear the "poem" with the music?

MURIEL RUKEYSER (1913–1980)
Myth _____ 1973

Long afterward, Oedipus, old and blinded, walked the
roads. He smelled a familiar smell. It was
the Sphinx. Oedipus said, "I want to ask one question.
Why didn't I recognize my mother?" "You gave the
5   wrong answer," said the Sphinx. "But that was what
made everything possible," said Oedipus. "No," she said.
"When I asked, What walks on four legs in the morning,
two at noon, and three in the evening, you answered,
Man. You didn't say anything about woman."
10   "When you say Man," said Oedipus, "you include women
too. Everyone knows that." She said, "That's what
you think."

QUESTIONS FOR DISCUSSION AND WRITING

1. Rukeyser suggests that Oedipus's fatal mistake was that he didn't take "woman" into account. Can Sophocles' play be read to support that interpretation? If so, where? If not, why not?
2. What "myths" might Rukeyser be alluding to in her title?

LAURIE SHECK

Filming Jocasta _____ 1992

You must not show her face. Only the hands
where each granite planetary knuckle
slowly pales as if submerged in water, stripped down as after seizure,
those hands that now hold nothing.

And the rope; umbilical, predatory,   5
how it hangs so strictly from the ceiling
while her robes waft with such softness against the backdrop
of the palace walls, harsh walls. As if to say, But once
she was a child, once swaddled, innocent, even she,
the long ago and ever after faintly beating in each cell.   10

Then bring the camera closer, closer in,
it is important not to lie. And show how the robes are crevices
of riddled light, how innocence is touched
by fraudulence; there is no other story, other text.
No music to accompany her body. Only the slow turning of the rope.   15
Only that score that is no score, how silence is the voice
of damage, its taped mouth.

And her shadow on the wall, freakish curtain oddly beating
in the wind, blurred inscription of some lost intention;
let the camera hold it for a moment, then move on.   20
Here is the empty room, how large it is, how drafty.

And her smallness, for a moment, so pitiful within it;
the room like a mouth that can't speak, like the silence her body
has become, her body like a severed tongue.
And then let her body and the room become a city   25
where the hollowed laws are quiet, the gated storefronts quiet.
And all throughout the city's central district
there are rows of display cases, necklaces glittering
on velvet covered cardboard shaped like collarbones and necks.
Blue velvet, diamonds, gold. And rings lined up in rows,   30
hat pins poised like silver birds, white gloves
on plaster hands. City that turns and turns
on its invisible cold rope, and the shadows of the awful tapered hands.

No one has found her yet,
her body white as streetglare, the cold glow of the unbought   35
still poised there, waiting to be bought. Her hands frozen
as if molded, waiting. But still there is the question of her face,
the horrible purple, the messiness of crime.
The way the eyes bulge out like vats of half-spilled
paint, innards churning in the wind.   40
Not even eyes now, really, but the aftermath of eyes,

exploded. At least the frozen hands are whole,
as if some innocence remained within them even to the end.
But there was no innocence in the eyes.
45   And the hands cannot cover them.

QUESTIONS FOR DISCUSSION AND WRITING

1. What does Sheck's "filming" of Jocasta tell us about how she views her?
2. The poem emphasizes the image of hands. What do the hands represent?
3. If you were filming Jocasta's death, what exactly would you show? How would you film Oedipus's blinding?

EDWIN GALLAHER

Jocasta _____ 1993

Loving that man was a way of hating God:
useless, and no sense of privacy.
The fates fell, like cats tumbling
down the palace stairs, and soon I fell—
5   we all fell—so many dry men in Thebes.
Piece by piece was miscast, dissembled:
the crossroads at midnight, men's bones
shattered against fire-creased iron.
Crowned triumphant, he solved riddles,
10   told lies, made much of love and daughters.
He of course will spare them the knife.
Yet he never told me how the history
of man and woman was a kind of amnesia,
a handsome riddle unanswered and unasked.
15   Imagine the fury and fireworks of stories
told by men who can't see. Imagine
an army and war. Imagine two lovers
who make both bed and grave together.
I am alone, and these bright threads
20   tangle in their deadliness. Hanging
from the beam, I wish the stars were blind.

QUESTIONS FOR DISCUSSION AND WRITING

1. Gallaher's Jocasta says that loving Oedipus was "a way of hating God." In what sense might that be true? Does Gallaher's Jocasta finally blame or absolve Oedipus? For what crimes?

2. Why does Jocasta see herself as alone? How do the images and structure of the poem reinforce her sense of aloneness?

SIGMUND FREUD (1856–1939)

The Oedipus Complex _____ 1900

In my experience, which is already extensive, the chief part in the mental lives of all children who later become psychoneurotics is played by their parents. Being in love with the one parent and hating the other are among the essential constituents of the stock of psychical impulses which is formed at that time and which is of such importance in determining the symptoms of the later neurosis. It is not my belief, however, that psychoneurotics differ sharply in this respect from other human beings who remain normal—that they are able, that is, to create something absolutely new and peculiar to themselves. It is far more probable—and this is confirmed by occasional observations on normal children—that they are only distinguished by exhibiting on a magnified scale feelings of love and hatred to their parents which occur less obviously and less intensely in the minds of most children.

This discovery is confirmed by a legend that has come down to us from classical antiquity: a legend whose profound and universal power to move can only be understood if the hypothesis I have put forward in regard to the psychology of children has an equally universal validity. What I have in mind is the legend of King Oedipus and Sophocles' drama which bears his name.

Oedipus, son of Laïus, King of Thebes, and of Jocasta, was exposed as an infant because an oracle had warned Laïus that the still unborn child would be his father's murderer. The child was rescued, and grew up as a prince in an alien court, until, in doubts as to his origin, he too questioned the oracle and was warned to avoid his home since he was destined to murder his father and take his mother in marriage. On the road leading away from what he believed was his home, he met King Laïus and slew him in a sudden quarrel. He came next to Thebes and solved the riddle set him by the Sphinx who barred his way. Out of gratitude the Thebans made him their king and gave him Jocasta's hand in marriage. He reigned long in peace and honour, and she who, unknown to him, was his mother bore him two sons and two daughters. Then at last a plague broke out and the Thebans made enquiry once more of the oracle. It is at this point that Sophocles' tragedy opens. The messengers bring back the reply that the plague will cease when the murderer of Laïus has been driven from the land.

> But he, where is he? Where shall now be read
> The fading record of this ancient guilt?

The action of the play consists in nothing other than the process of revealing, with cunning delays and ever-mounting excitement—a process that can be likened to the work of a psychoanalysis—that Oedipus himself is the murderer of Laïus, but further that he is the son of the murdered man and of Jocasta. Appalled at the abomination which he has unwittingly perpetrated, Oedipus blinds himself and forsakes his home. The oracle has been fulfilled.

Oedipus Rex is what is known as a tragedy of destiny. Its tragic effect is said to lie in the contrast between the supreme will of the gods and the vain attempts of mankind to escape the evil that threatens them. The lesson which, it is said, the deeply moved spectator should learn from the tragedy is submission to the divine will and realization of his own impotence. Modern dramatists have accordingly tried to achieve a similar tragic effect by weaving the same contrast into a plot invented by themselves. But the spectators have looked on unmoved while a curse or an oracle was fulfilled in spite of all the efforts of some innocent man: later tragedies of destiny have failed in their effect.

If *Oedipus Rex* moves a modern audience no less than it did the contemporary Greek one, the explanation can only be that its effect does not lie in the contrast between destiny and human will, but is to be looked for in the particular nature of the material on which that contrast is exemplified. There must be something which makes a voice within us ready to recognize the compelling force of destiny in the *Oedipus,* while we can dismiss as merely arbitrary such dispositions as are laid down in [Grillparzer's] *Die Ahnfrau* or other modern tragedies of destiny. And a factor of this kind is in fact involved in the story of King Oedipus. His destiny moves us only because it might have been ours—because the oracle laid the same curse upon us before our birth as upon him. It is the fate of all of us, perhaps, to direct our first sexual impulse towards our mother and our first hatred and our first murderous wish against our father. Our dreams convince us that that is so. King Oedipus, who slew his father Laïus and married his mother Jocasta, merely shows us the fulfilment of our own childhood wishes. But, more fortunate than he, we have meanwhile succeeded, in so far as we have not become psychoneurotics, in detaching our sexual impulses from our mothers and in forgetting our jealousy of our fathers. Here is one in whom these primaeval wishes of our childhood have been fulfilled, and we shrink back from him with the whole force of the repression by which those wishes have since that time been held down within us. While the poet, as he unravels the past, brings to light the guilt of Oedipus, he is at the same time compelling us to recognize our own inner minds, in which those same impulses, though suppressed, are still to be found. The contrast with which the closing Chorus leaves us confronted—

> . . . Fix on Oedipus your eyes,
> Who resolved the dark enigma, noblest champion and most wise.
> Like a star his envied fortune mounted beaming far and wide:
> Now he sinks in seas of anguish, whelmed beneath a raging tide . . .

—strikes as a warning at ourselves and our pride, at us who since our childhood have grown so wise and so mighty in our own eyes. Like Oedipus, we live in ignorance of these wishes, repugnant to morality, which have been forced upon us by Nature, and after their revelation we may all of us well seek to close our eyes to the scenes of our childhood.

There is an unmistakable indication in the text of Sophocles' tragedy itself that the legend of Oedipus sprang from some primaeval dream-material which had as its content the distressing disturbance of a child's relation to his parents owing to the first stirrings of sexuality. At a point when Oedipus, though he is not yet enlightened, has begun to feel troubled by his recollection of the oracle, Jocasta consoles him by referring to a dream which many people dream, though, as she thinks, it has no meaning:

> Many a man ere now in dreams hath lain
> With her who bare him. He hath least annoy
> Who with such omens troubleth not his mind.

Today, just as then, many men dream of having sexual relations with their mothers, and speak of the fact with indignation and astonishment. It is clearly the key to the tragedy and the complement to the dream of the dreamer's father being dead. The story of Oedipus is the reaction of the imagination to these two typical dreams. And just as these dreams, when dreamt by adults, are accompanied by feelings of repulsion, so too the legend must include horror and self-punishment.

QUESTIONS FOR DISCUSSION AND WRITING

1. Oedipus himself does not know that Laius is his father or that Jocasta is his mother. Had he known, he would undoubtedly have acted differently toward them. To what extent does that invalidate Freud's conclusions about the Oedipus legend? Why?
2. Freud's theories have always been controversial. To what extent do you think children exhibit signs of an "Oedipus complex"? Is the response toward the mother and father different for boys and girls? Could Sophocles have written a play about a female "Oedipus"? What would it have looked like?

P. H. VELLACOTT
The Guilt of Oedipus*   1964

In this paper I propose to deal with some difficulties in Sophocles' *Oedipus Tyrannus,* of which some have been noticed before, others I think have not. I am going to propose an unorthodox explanation, not through any love of unorthodoxy, but in the spirit of Oedipus himself, who when faced with a puzzle could not resist following a fact to its logical conclusion. The Sphinx's riddle was not, after all, a very hard one; and Oedipus doubtless grew tired of being praised for ingenuity. My thesis too disclaims that dubious quality. Ingenuity is what many of us have been using all our lives to explain difficulties in this play which may after all be insoluble.

The story, as it existed in Sophocles' time, before he wrote his play, seems to have been as follows: Laios king of Thebes was told by the Delphic oracle that if he married Iocasta his son would kill him. He ignored the oracle and married Iocasta. When the child was born Laios pierced and bound his ankles and exposed him on Kithairon, where he was found by a shepherd who took him to Corinth; there he was brought up as the son of King Polybos. The Delphic oracle later told Oedipus that he was fated to kill his father and marry his mother. He set out towards Thebes, and on

---

*Vellacott's quotations and line numbers do not correspond to the text of Oedipus included in this anthology. He has used a different translation of the play.

the way killed Laios, not knowing who he was. Arrived at Thebes, he vanquished the Sphinx by guessing her riddle, and for reward became king of Thebes and married Iocasta. Sixteen or more years later, when Thebes was visited by plague, Oedipus investigated the murder of Laios and discovered his own double guilt; whereupon Iocasta hanged herself and Oedipus blinded himself.

Now this story, in its elaboration of detail and in the vividness of its characters, compares with the greatest of the Greek legend-cycles—with those of Herakles, Theseus, the war at Troy; in particular, because of the way it shows a family curse descending through three generations, it invites comparison with the myth of the House of Atreus. It has the same splendour of setting, the same extremes of emotion, the same concern with both sexual relationship and dynastic power, the same close link with the supernatural as evidenced in the Delphic oracle and the utterances of prophets, the same sense of inescapable Fate. Yet there is one point of difference between the two myths; and it is a central point.

The story of the House of Atreus shows from beginning to end the actions of men and women as being carried out under the eye of gods in a universe where cause and effect have a moral significance. The central figure, Agamemnon, is shown faced with a desperate dilemma, but there is no doubt that the decision he made was the wrong one, and that his sin incurred the retribution which followed. The central figure of the Theban legend, Oedipus, is by contrast apparently innocent. The worst he is usually accused of by students of Sophocles' play is hasty temper—and this itself is Sophocles' own invention rather than part of the basic myth. As a result the whole sequence of events is barren of any significant moral or religious content. There is an inherited curse, but no real sin to justify it; so that the only lesson to be drawn is one of total pessimism, and the only attitude encouraged is that of uncomprehending resignation. What is more disturbing, the story appears to show two crimes of the most heinous and polluting kind actually brought about by divine guidance—a circumstance which can only be regarded as a direct blow at the concept of a coherent world in which Zeus upholds a moral standard.

Let us try to picture Sophocles, with the example of the *Oresteia* to challenge his consciousness of his own poetic power, contemplating the Oedipus-myth as dramatic material. When a dramatist begins to write a play about characters whose story is already fixed in outline, before he can compose any dialogue, he must collect all the material he intends either to use or to assume as part of the story, and in imagination live it all through, dramatizing in his own mind many scenes which will never find a place in his play, but which will clarify for him a character's state of mind at a given moment, or fill in decorative or poetic background. There is a great deal of this in *Agamemnon,* where Aeschylus pictures for us such inessential details as the distress of the forsaken Menelaus, the scene in Troy on Helen's arrival; besides the essential details given in the long sequence about Iphigenia in the first great Ode. In Sophocles' *Oedipus,* however, the unfolding of the plot depends closely on a long string of events stretching back thirty-five years, all narrated at various points in the dialogue, and beginning the story at the time when Laios consulted Apollo as to whether he should marry Iocasta, and was told that, if he did, his son would kill him. The birth of Oedipus, the maiming of his feet, the exposure, the deception, the childhood in Corinth, the visit to Delphi, the encounter by the road-junction, the Sphinx and her riddle, the deliverance of Thebes from the first plague—all these events Sophocles pieces together, every one of them necessary to his story. Yet in none of these do we find what we are looking for—what Sophocles must surely have looked for—some sin, some fault in Oedipus' character which would justify to men the seemingly cruel and immoral ways of Zeus or of Apollo or of Fate. There is no question here of an individual god being arraigned, as Euripides arraigns Aphrodite or Apollo, while the concept of justice itself remains secure in the hand of Zeus. The terrible destiny of Oedipus is shown as one put upon him by supernatural powers in general, by that comprehensive Fate which governs every man's life.

We do, however, glean from these narratives which Sophocles gives us one detail which makes moral as well as dramatic sense. Laios, after receiving divine warning that if he married Iocasta his son would kill him, clearly committed two sins: he ignored the warning and married Iocasta; and then, having begotten a son, he was morally guilty of that son's death; though the formula of exposure on the mountain, being designed to give the infant a one percent chance of survival, cleared Laios from ritual pollution. Here, then, is a sin in the previous generation; but when we look for its repetition in Oedipus (as Agamemnon repeated his father's guilt) we find nothing. How can there be a true tragedy without a sin? Where is the dignity, the awe, of *nemesis* without *hybris*? True, in line 873 the Chorus seem to rebuke Oedipus for *hybris,* alluding apparently to his extraordinary and groundless accusations against Teiresias and Kreon; but this bad behaviour of Oedipus, besides being inexplicable in view of the character established for him in the opening scene, does not belong to the main stream of the story at all. Usually the best that can be said for it is that Sophocles inserted it to provide Oedipus with a sin to justify his downfall; and to some this explanation will seem unworthy of Sophocles.

I have given above a list of the past events in the story which Sophocles has included as narrative in his dialogue in order to provide us with the essential background of his drama—the birth of Oedipus, the journey to Delphi, and so on. Perhaps you observed that I omitted from my list one detail; one which is more significant than any other. The details I mentioned are all essential to the usual version of the story; but Sophocles added one detail which is *not* essential to the usual version: the incident of the man who got drunk at a banquet and told Oedipus he was not the son of Polybos. Sophocles could have invented a dozen reasons why Oedipus should visit Delphi; but he used this one. Now see how Oedipus continues his story to Iocasta: 'At Delphi I was not given the knowledge which I came to seek, but was told that I was fated to marry my mother and kill my father. When I heard this, I turned my back on Corinth, to go towards any place where I might never see the fulfilment of this shameful oracle.'

That statement would make sense, if Oedipus had gone to Delphi on some state mission for King Polybos. But Oedipus went to Delphi, says Sophocles, because he had been led to doubt that Polybos was his father. It has generally been assumed that the horror of the new prophecy drove clean out of Oedipus' mind the question about his parentage which he had come to ask. That might have been so, had the question and the prophecy been unconnected. In fact they were so obviously and frighteningly connected that I do not believe Sophocles could imagine that Oedipus would fail to connect them. The doubt about his parentage doubled the menace of the prophecy. He would have been thankful indeed, could he have believed that by turning his back on Corinth he could face the rest of the world without apprehension. That was now impossible: he knew that he might meet his true father or his true mother anywhere in Greece; no place was safe.

We must leave for the moment the question why Oedipus apparently expected Iocasta to accept this curious *non sequitur*; and turn instead to ask, what did Sophocles intend us to picture as Oedipus' state of mind when he left the Delphic oracle? He had come there convinced that there was a mystery connected with his birth; the oracle plainly confirmed this. So now, if he was to avoid heinous pollution, he must make for himself two unbreakable rules: never to kill an older man; and never to marry an older woman. The incident at the banquet makes it clear that these two rules, and not the resolve to keep away from Corinth, would be the probable preoccupation of Oedipus' thoughts as he left Delphi. Then, twenty-four hours later, in the midst of an angry scuffle, his head singing from a vicious blow, he looks up and sees before his eyes a furious middle-aged face with greying hair. For a fraction of a second comes the thought of the oracle's warning—this is the man I must not strike. But his blood is boiling; the man has struck him first. The grey hair lies in the dust, near four other bodies. Oedipus has, at the first opportunity, ignored a divine warning. That this man could be his father would be a coincidence so incredible as to be impossible; but this was the risk he ought not to have taken. He is guilty. Sophocles, by inventing and introducing the incident at the banquet, has entirely changed the moral situation of Oedipus in the story. He is no longer the innocent victim of malevolent powers. *Dike,* Justice, daughter of Zeus, a goddess forgotten in the version of the myth which had been current for centuries, reappears, resuscitated by a single subtle creation of the poet.

We shall soon need to look again at the long central scene where Oedipus tells his story to Iocasta. But this scene can only be understood if first we are clearly aware of what happened in the previous scene, where Oedipus confronts Teiresias. Here is a summary of the information which Teiresias gives Oedipus: (1) line 337, a hint: 'You have not seen that your own kinswoman is living with you.' (2) line 353, a plain statement: 'You are the defiler of the land.' (3) this is repeated in line 362: 'You killed Laios.' (4) line 366: 'You are living in shameful union with your nearest kin, and do not know it.' (5) line 373: 'You call me blind, deaf, and dull-witted—soon everyone will hurl those reproaches at you.' (6) line 414: 'You do not see what a terrible situation you are in, or whom you are living with.' (7) line 415: 'Do you know whose son you are? And you are an enemy to your own kin both dead and living.' (8) line 420: 'You will shriek aloud when you learn the truth about your marriage—a truth which shall make you level with yourself and with your children.' (9) lines 437–9: 'The mystery of your birth shall be revealed today.' (10) lines 450 ff.: 'The killer of Laios is here, passing as a foreigner, but in truth a Theban; brother and father of his children, son and husband of his mother.'

Now look at the man to whom all this is said. First, he is a famous solver of riddles. Second, he had been told at Delphi that he would kill his father and marry his mother. Third, even before that he had doubted if he was the son of Polybos. Fourth, he remembered only too well killing a man—an older man—on the road from Thebes to Delphi, at a time and place corresponding with the murder of Laios, as Kreon has just reminded him. Fifth, Kreon has also told him that only one man escaped—another point which Oedipus can hardly have forgotten. Sixth, if Oedipus had misgivings about having killed an older man, he must certainly have had more misgivings about having married an older woman. Now, how could a man bearing all that in his memory listen to the repeated and repeated words of Teiresias and not recognize the truth?

One more point before we move on to the central scene. Let us look at our hero's name. He announces it himself in line 8: ὁ πᾶσι κλεινὸς Οἰδίπους καλούμενος. 'Called by all men Oedipus.' 'Oedipus' means 'swollen-footed'. Let us look into a later scene, that with the Messenger from Corinth, lines 1031 ff.

> OED. What pain had I when you took me in your arms?
> MESS. Your ankles could bear witness to that.
> OED. *Oimoi,* why do you mention that ancient injury?
> MESS. Your feet were pierced, and I'm the man who freed you.
> OED. That terrible disgrace (δεινὸν ὄνειδος) I bore from the cradle.

Nothing could show more clearly that Sophocles thought of the maimed feet as something of which Oedipus was bitterly and constantly conscious.

Now we are ready for the central scene, where everything becomes even more astonishing. Here is Oedipus, remembering the oracle, remembering his encounter by the cross-roads; and a few minutes ago he was told by Teiresias again and again, 'You killed Laios; Laios was your father: Iocasta is your mother.' To him Iocasta now says, 'Laios was once told by an oracle of Apollo that his son and mine would kill him. So as soon as the child was born Laios pinned its ankles together and exposed it on a mountain. Subsequently Laios was killed by robbers near a road-junction.'

Each of these statements connects at once with a thought seething on the surface of Oedipus' mind. The oracle given to Laios corresponds with the oracle given to Oedipus. Iocasta's mention of the road-junction reminds Oedipus of his encounter at that spot. But the third is by far the most significant: the maimed ankles, added to everything that has been said already, *must* identify Oedipus, to his own perception, as Iocasta's son. Yet Oedipus in his reply passes over the unique clue of the maimed ankles, and takes up the commonplace clue of the road-junction—though Iocasta has not even said that it was the road to Delphi. What was Sophocles' purpose in making Iocasta mention the maimed ankles at this point? It was quite unnecessary. Are we to say he didn't know what he was doing? We must also remember another point. The close connexion of so many strands of evidence might well be missed by a modern English theatre-audience; but Sophocles wrote this play for an audience whose minds were trained by constant practice in law-courts to follow arguments and weave evidence together. What then was he trying to do in this play?

So far I have drawn your attention to certain facts of the text. When we come to draw inferences, perhaps the only indisputable one is, that Sophocles' intention in this play is something beyond what we have hitherto understood. A second inference, which may be called probable rather than certain, is that Sophocles intended, by the incident at the banquet, to present Oedipus to us as consciously guilty. This idea is strengthened by the fact that it makes the sin of Oedipus the same as that of Laios, and so gives poetic as well as moral meaning to the hereditary curse. The next step in our inquiry, then, is to follow up the implications of this idea.

Let us assume that Sophocles, steeping his imagination in the story, and pondering its characters and their experiences as a dramatist inevitably does, finds himself examining the possibility that Oedipus really was guilty. He has killed this man—an older man; he had been warned that he was fated to kill his father; and he is far from certain that his father is Polybos. That this dead man should be his father would be an incredible coincidence; nevertheless Oedipus, conscious that he had acted rashly, can hardly fail to look at the dead man's face to see if it bears any resemblance to his own.

Also, knowing that one servant escaped back to Thebes, Oedipus, on entering Thebes himself, can hardly fail to keep his ears open for any talk of a man lately murdered on the Delphi road. Indeed he could not fail, even if he had been innocent, to be told by every Theban he met that the king had been murdered, with the time, the place, and details of the carriage, horses, and servants. Greeks talk all the time about everything. If we are speaking factually about the myth, rather than critically about the play, it is certain that within an hour of entering Thebes Oedipus knew that he had killed Laios. Then he volunteered to interview the Sphinx, knowing that the prize was Laios' widow. Therefore—again speaking factually—it is certain that Oedipus said to himself: 'If the man I killed was my father, and if I overcome the Sphinx and marry the queen, the oracle will be exactly fulfilled, and I shall have only myself to blame.' A horrible thought. What could he do to reassure himself? He could try to clear his mind of the suspicion of a likeness between himself and the dead man. He could inquire how old the queen was, and if she had had a son eighteen years ago. Suppose he was told she had? Then the risk was too appalling, and he must give up all idea of becoming king of Thebes. And yet, *why* was he now forced into this frustrating position? Because a drunkard had shouted 'Bastard' at him. The thing was ridiculous; but for that one drunken word, his course and his conscience would have been clear. Was a drunkard's shout to rob him of a throne? Finally, is it surprising that Iocasta, whose adolescent beauty had inspired the cautious Laios to defy Apollo, should in her maturity, at thirty-five, prove irresistible to Laios' son?

If Sophocles, in order to add moral and religious content to this marvellous story which so curiously lacked it, ever conceived and explored the possibility that Oedipus was in fact guilty, he could hardly fail to reason as I have reasoned, and so to see just how it came about that a good man like Oedipus could, in extraordinary circumstances, make this fatal decision to run a ninety-nine per cent risk, and stake his life on a one per cent possibility that he was after all the son of Polybos. He still had two more bridges to cross: first, the moment when he would meet the queen and scan her face to tell how old she was, and to discern any possible likeness to his own; second—and here we come to the central feature of the whole story, embodied in the name—the moment when his wife would see the scars on his feet. It was clear that if Iocasta was in fact a mother who eighteen years ago had lost a son with scarred feet, she would not be likely to forget his eighteenth birthday. The news that her husband had been killed by an unknown assailant would certainly suggest to her that the Delphic oracle nineteen years ago had told Laios the truth, and that her son was perhaps not far off; so that now, meeting a wandering foreigner aged eighteen she would look in his face for a likeness to her late husband, and at his feet for the scars.

The final stage of this course of reasoning presents us with the picture of Oedipus and Iocasta living together in mutual love, each having chosen to believe as truth the one per cent possibility that their marriage was lawful; building up for themselves a version of past events which was satisfactory and painless, even if it involved some dangerous corners; and pushing the terrible probability further and further into the recesses of forgetfulness—which in busy lives can be very deep; while his guilt retains for Oedipus just enough reality to act as a constant spur to make amends for the frightful wrong he may have inflicted on Iocasta and on Thebes, by devoting himself tirelessly to the tasks of a loving father of his family and of his people. This is the character so emphatically established for him in the opening scene of the play. Then at last, after sixteen or seventeen years, came the return of the plague; and Oedipus knew that the gods, who neither forget nor forgive, were at work, his respite was at an end and his ordeal before him. If Sophocles once set foot on the path of reasoning which supposes the gods to be just and Oedipus to be guilty, I see no point at which he could have turned aside before reaching the situation I have just described.

Take the words of the Priest of Zeus in lines 31 ff. 'We regard you, Oedipus, as the first of men, both in the ordinary chances of life and in dealings with the gods. Now help us, either by some utterance you have heard from a god, or perhaps a word from some man has given you knowledge. For with men of experience I observe this, that the results of their decisions live. You brought us good fortune before: now be the same as you were then.' 'Be the same' . . . Oedipus, resolute to be now utterly different from the man he was then, replies: 'There is not one of you whose sickness is as grievous as mine. I assure you, I have shed many tears, and paced many paths in the wanderings of anxious thought.'

The outcome of those pacing thoughts was now clear in his mind. There were three points. First, he must submit himself to public exposure of the two facts that he killed his father Laios and that Iocasta is his mother. Second: after the exposure, the choice would appear to be suicide or banishment—but suicide would admit defeat at the hands of Fate, and Oedipus would not admit defeat. He had sinned, and he would pay; but he had a right, even though guilty, to live. Third: there was one thing which was his own private concern, which Thebes—which even his children—need never know; and that was, the fact that his guilt had been knowingly incurred, that he had been aware of his own pollution from the beginning. That was between himself and Iocasta, and the gods. The city could be delivered, and that ultimate truth could remain his secret and hers, to carry silent to the grave.

Now, supposing Sophocles to have perceived—and I believe he did perceive it—that the story was capable of being developed along these lines, what did he in fact do with this potential material? To begin with, it was obvious that the story, so developed, acquired a moral and religious seriousness which it did not have before. On the other hand, to present such a story on the Attic stage involved insuperable difficulties. The whole drama now took place within one man's consciousness; Oedipus could speak no unveiled word to Iocasta, nor she to him, nor either to anyone else; so how could the true situation be conveyed to an audience? In fact, my own guess would be that the story as I have outlined it was something like what actually happened to Oedipus, but that the central truth of the matter dropped out after one generation of popular telling, and never reappeared until the dramatic imagination of Sophocles looked below the surface of the folk-tale and found it. But having found it he saw that such a conception was impossible to express in the conventional forms of tragedy, and even if the attempt were made it would be missed or rejected by most of the audience. Yet this conception was so exciting as drama, and morally and theologically so moving, that to abandon it entirely in favour of the popular, and morally nihilistic, version seemed like an abdication from the poet's prophetic task. Then this possibility is to be considered: that Sophocles in the end decided to write his play on the basis of the popular concept of an innocent Oedipus lured by Fate into a disastrous trap; but that, in order to record for ever his own deeper perception, he embodied in the play certain features, notably the incident at the banquet, which, if rationally examined, would suggest what the real story of Oedipus was. The play, of course, on a prima-facie interpretation makes good enough sense—almost good enough, though there are anomalies and contradictions which may prove disturbing even in a good performance. The dramatic power of a gradual revelation conceals the moral poverty of the theme. But all the serious difficulties of the plot vanish once they are seen as subtle contributions towards this other view of the character and situation of Oedipus.

First, the statement that he had believed that in avoiding Corinth he was avoiding parricide and incest now appears as an essential element in the make-believe world which Oedipus had to construct to protect his own sanity, and in which he lived safely for sixteen years. (This statement appears again in lines 990–7.) Secondly, his ignoring of Iocasta's reference to the maimed ankles is also explained: the disclosure must be carried out one stage at a time, and the killer of Laios revealed before the son of Iocasta was identified. The third point, which I have already mentioned briefly, is more important. It is the behaviour of Oedipus to Teiresias and Kreon, which evinces a lack of stability and common sense excusable perhaps in an adolescent, but entirely destructive of the godlike character given to Oedipus in the first scene. But Oedipus' wild and angry accusations make sense if Sophocles had in mind the situation I have suggested. On this view Oedipus, being willing himself to give his life for Thebes ('The king must die' was a familiar formula), and hoping for the help of the omniscient Teiresias in his desperately difficult task, is met with a blank refusal. As his own anger swells, he realizes that anger is the one thing which will make Teiresias speak. So he goads Teiresias with extravagant charges, whereupon Teiresias utters the whole truth. Even then the Chorus appear hardly to have heard it—the truth is not only incredible but inaudible to respectable old men. Then if they will not listen to Teiresias, perhaps Kreon will help—he may well have guessed who Oedipus is, he knew Laios, and is likely to have seen the scars. So Oedipus attacks him too. But Kreon gives nothing away. His scene, however, serves to give another dimension to Iocasta, as well as to prepare the audience for his important role in the last scene.

The play *Oedipus Tyrannus,* then, was written to tell the simple story which is familiar to us and was familiar to the contemporaries of Sophocles; that was the only story which he could expect to be understood and accepted. But I believe, on the evidence I have put before you, that as he wrote it the poet had also in mind another story, which may even have been the true story of Oedipus; and that his consciousness of this story and of its importance made him include certain elements which cannot be properly accounted for on the basis of the popular version; and made him, moreover, at numerous points in the dialogue use a double irony whose significance only appears when the possibility is considered that Oedipus at the beginning of the action has known for sixteen years in what a terrible position he is, and is now engaged in an act of voluntary atonement which will save his city at the price of destroying his own life.

This view makes the final scene, if possible, even more poignant. Iocasta, who has suppressed knowledge of the truth more completely than Oedipus, sees the end coming as early as line 765, where Oedipus asks for the old slave to be sent for; Iocasta knows, though Oedipus does not yet know, that this is the same man who took her infant son to the mountain and did not kill him. From that point on, Oedipus knows that both he and Iocasta know where they are going; but he must lead, and she must follow, without a word. When she has finally rushed out in despair, Oedipus, aware that he has sent her to her death, finds the only refuge from his anguish in taunting Iocasta with pride of birth. He cannot afford to weaken yet with tears, for he has still the last lap to run—the interview with the Theban shepherd. When that is over, he will no longer need to hold back anything.

From the old shepherd Oedipus forces the last drop of truth. Only then does he stand at the point where he had so often imagined himself standing—but imagination was feeble and useless and had given him barely a faint taste of the agony and horror into which his instinctive honour and courage had now led him. He suddenly sees the utmost depth. 'I should never have been born. What I am is now brought to light; and this light shall be my last.' He goes in, finds Iocasta as he knew he would find her; and reaches his own terrible fulfilment.

Much has been written about the pessimism of the ancient Greeks; and this play is usually included in the evidence—a play which shows a man guilty of hasty temper and a woman guilty of disparaging remarks about prophecy (both very common faults) but otherwise innocent—shows them both subjected to the most dreadful agony and humiliation by blind Chance or cruel Fate. There were, of course, many Greeks who would have called that a fair picture of human life. But such a picture implies a universe in which there is no place for *Dike,* Justice, as a divinity. I believe that Sophocles saw the myth of Oedipus as containing a deeper message, as illustrating a universe where *Dike* is the daughter of Zeus. He suggests that the sin of Oedipus was not a mere matter of hasty temper, but an obstinate neglect of divine warning in the pursuit of his passions and his ambitions; the taking of a risk he had no right to take, one which put a whole city in peril. Therefore his punishment is not a blind cruelty of Fate, but one more assurance that the world is ruled by *Dike,* that cause produces effect, that Nature pays every debt. Furthermore, the central figure of this drama now appears potentially in a different light, as being no longer a pitiful, helpless plaything of circumstance, a broken man acknowledging transcendent Powers whose purpose is at best mysterious, at worst gratuitously malevolent. He is a man capable both of evil and of good, a man conscious of *Dike* as a force in the universe which he honours, and which, in its operation against himself, he will obey with dedicated courage, acknowledging his own debt. That is a picture which defies pessimism, and gives both to man and to the gods an honourable part in the development even of the most painful and terrible events.

The question which I have raised in this paper may well have other aspects; but it is the dramatic aspect which opens the inquiry; and I think it likely, having stuck my spade into the well-raked flower-bed of Sophoclean Tragedy, that it will be found I am not so much sowing a seed of uneasiness and doubt, as watering a well-rooted plant which conscientious gardeners have for many years guiltily regarded as a weed.

E. R. DODDS (1893–1979)

On Misunderstanding the Oedipus Rex*   1966

On the last occasion when I had the misfortune to examine in Honour Moderations at Oxford I set a question on the *Oedipus Rex,* which was among the books

---

*Dodds's quotations and line numbers do not correspond to the text of *Oedipus* included in this anthology. He has used a different translation of the play.

prescribed for general reading. My question was 'In what sense, if in any, does the *Oedipus Rex* attempt to justify the ways of God to man?' It was an optional question; there were plenty of alternatives. But the candidates evidently considered it a gift: nearly all of them attempted it. When I came to sort out the answers I found that they fell into three groups.

The first and biggest group held that the play justifies the gods by showing—or, as many of them said, 'proving'—that we get what we deserve. The arguments of this group turned upon the character of Oedipus. Some considered that Oedipus was a bad man: look how he treated Creon—naturally the gods punished him. Others said 'No, not altogether bad, even in some ways rather noble; but he had one of those fatal ἁμαρτίαι that all tragic heroes have, as we know from Aristotle. And since he had a ἁμαρτία he could of course expect no mercy: the gods had read the *Poetics*.' Well over half the candidates held views of this general type.

A second substantial group held that the *Oedipus Rex* is 'a tragedy of destiny.' What the play 'proves,' they said, is that man has no free will but is a puppet in the hands of the gods who pull the strings that make him dance. Whether Sophocles thought the gods justified in treating their puppet as they did was not always clear from their answers. Most of those who took this view evidently disliked the play; some of them were honest enough to say so.

The third group was much smaller, but included some of the more thoughtful candidates. In their opinion Sophocles was 'a pure artist' and was therefore not interested in justifying the gods. He took the story of Oedipus as he found it, and used it to make an exciting play. The gods are simply part of the machinery of the plot.

Ninety per cent of the answers fell into one or the other of these three groups. The remaining ten per cent had either failed to make up their minds or failed to express themselves intelligibly.

It was a shock to me to discover that all these young persons, supposedly trained in the study of classical literature, could read this great and moving play and so completely miss the point. For all the views I have just summarized are in fact demonstrably false (though some of them, and some ways of stating them, are more crudely and vulgarly false than others). It is true that each of them has been defended by some scholars in the past, but I had hoped that all of them were by now dead and buried. Wilamowitz thought he had killed the lot in an article published in *Hermes* (34 [1899], 55 ff.) more than half a century ago; and they have repeatedly been killed since. Yet their unquiet ghosts still haunt the examination-rooms of universities—and also, I would add, the pages of popular handbooks on the history of European drama. Surely that means that we have somehow failed in our duty as teachers?

It was this sense of failure which prompted me to attempt once more to clear up some of these ancient confusions. If the reader feels—as he very well may—that in this paper I am flogging a dead horse, I can only reply that on the evidence I have quoted the animal is unaccountably still alive.

I

I shall take Aristotle as my starting point, since he is claimed as the primary witness for the first of the views I have described. From the thirteenth chapter of the *Poetics* we learn that the best sort of tragic hero is a man highly esteemed and prosperous who falls into misfortune because of some serious (μεγάλη) ἁμαρτία: examples,

Oedipus and Thyestes. In Aristotle's view, then, Oedipus' misfortune was directly occasioned by some serious ἁμαρτία; and since Aristotle was known to be infallible, Victorian critics proceeded at once to look for this ἁμαρτία, And so, it appears, do the majority of present-day undergraduates.

What do they find? It depends on what they expect to find. As we all know, the word ἁμαρτία is ambiguous: in ordinary usage it is sometimes applied to false moral judgements, sometimes to purely intellectual error—the average Greek did not make our sharp distinction between the two. Since *Poetics* 13 is in general concerned with the moral character of the tragic hero, many scholars have thought in the past (and many undergraduates still think) that the ἁμαρτία of Oedipus must in Aristotle's view be a moral fault. They have accordingly gone over the play with a microscope looking for moral faults in Oedipus, and have duly found them—for neither here nor anywhere else did Sophocles portray that insipid and unlikely character, the man of perfect virtue. Oedipus, they point out, is proud and over-confident; he harbours unjustified suspicions against Teiresias and Creon; in one place (lines 964 ff.) he goes so far as to express some uncertainty about the truth of oracles. One may doubt whether this adds up to what Aristotle would consider μεγάλη ἁμαρτία. But even if it did, it would have no direct relevance to the question at issue. Years before the action of the play begins, Oedipus was already an incestuous parricide; if that was a punishment for his unkind treatment of Creon, then the punishment preceded the crime—which is surely an odd kind of justice.

'Ah,' says the traditionalist critic, 'but Oedipus' behaviour on the stage reveals the man he always was: he was punished for his basically unsound character.' In that case, however, someone on the stage ought to tell us so: Oedipus should repent, as Creon repents in the *Antigone;* or else another speaker should draw the moral. To ask about a character in fiction 'Was he a good man?' is to ask a strictly meaningless question: since Oedipus never lived we can answer neither 'Yes' nor 'No.' The legitimate question is 'Did Sophocles intend us to think of Oedipus as a good man?' This *can* be answered—not by applying some ethical yardstick of our own, but by looking at what the characters in the play say about him. And by that test the answer is 'Yes.' In the eyes of the Priest in the opening scene he is the greatest and noblest of men, the saviour of Thebes who with divine aid rescued the city from the Sphinx. The Chorus has the same view of him: he has proved his wisdom, he is the darling of the city, and never will they believe ill of him (504 ff.). And when the catastrophe comes, no one turns round and remarks 'Well, but it was your own fault: it must have been; Aristotle says so.'

In my opinion, and in that of nearly all Aristotelian scholars since Bywater, Aristotle does *not* say so; it is only the perversity of moralizing critics that has misrepresented him as saying so. It is almost certain that Aristotle was using ἁμαρτία here as he uses ἁμάρτημα in the *Nicomachean Ethics* (1135[b] 12) and in the *Rhetoric* (1374[b] 6), to mean an offence committed in ignorance of some material fact and therefore free from πονηρία or κακία. These parallels seem decisive; and they are confirmed by Aristotle's second example—Thyestes, the man who ate the flesh of his own children in the belief that it was butcher's meat, and who subsequently begat a child on his own daughter, not knowing who she was. His story has clearly much in common with that of Oedipus, and Plato as well as Aristotle couples the two names as examples of the gravest ἁμαρτία (*Laws* 838 c). Thyestes and Oedipus are both of them men who violated the most sacred of Nature's laws and thus incurred the most horrible of all pollutions; but they both did so without πονηρία, for they knew not what they did—in Aristotle's quasi-legal terminology, it was a ἁμάρτημα, not an ἀδίκημα. That is why they were in his view especially suitable subjects for tragedy. Had they acted knowingly, they would have been inhuman monsters, and we could not have felt for them that pity which tragedy ought to produce. As it is, we feel both pity, for the fragile estate of man, and terror, for a world whose laws we do not understand. The ἁμαρτία of Oedipus did not lie in losing his temper with Teiresias; it lay quite simply in parricide and incest—a μεγάλη ἁμαρτία indeed, the greatest a man can commit.

The theory that the tragic hero must have a grave moral flaw, and its mistaken ascription to Aristotle, has had a long and disastrous history. It was gratifying to Victorian critics, since it appeared to fit certain plays of Shakespeare. But it goes back much further, to the seventeenth-century French critic Dacier, who influenced the practice of the French classical dramatists, especially Corneille, and was himself influenced by the still older nonsense about 'poetic justice'—the notion that the poet has a moral duty to represent the world as a place where the good are always rewarded and the bad are always punished. I need not say that this puerile idea is completely foreign to Aristotle and to the practice of the Greek dramatists; I only mention it because on the evidence of those Honour Mods. papers it would appear that it still lingers on in some youthful minds like a cobweb in an unswept room.

To return to the *Oedipus Rex,* the moralist has still one last card to play. Could not Oedipus, he asks, have escaped his doom if he had been more careful? Knowing that he was in danger of committing parricide and incest, would not a really prudent man have avoided quarrelling, even in self-defence, with men older than himself, and also love-relations with women older than himself? Would he not, in Waldock's ironic phrase, have compiled a handlist of all the things he must not do? In real life I suppose he might. But we are not entitled to blame Oedipus either for carelessness in failing to compile a handlist or for lack of self-control in failing to obey its injunctions. For no such possibilities are mentioned in the play, or even hinted at; and it is an essential critical principle that *what is not mentioned in the play does not exist.* These considerations would be in place if we were examining the conduct of a real person. But we are not: we are examining the intentions of a dramatist, and we are not entitled to ask questions that the dramatist did not intend us to ask. There is only one branch of literature where we are entitled to ask such questions about τὰ ἐκτὸς, τοῦ δράματος, namely the modern detective story. And despite certain similarities the *Oedipus Rex* is not a detective story but a dramatized folktale. If we insist on reading it as if it were a law report we must expect to miss the point.[1]

---

1. The danger is exemplified by Mr. P. H. Vellacott's article, 'The Guilt of Oedipus,' which appeared shortly after my talk was delivered. By treating Oedipus as an historical personage and examining his career from the 'common-sense' standpoint of a prosecuting counsel Mr. Vellacott has no difficulty in showing that Oedipus must have guessed the true story of his birth long before the point at which the play opens—and guiltily done nothing about it. Sophocles, according to Mr. Vellacott, realized this, but unfortunately could not present the situation in these terms because 'such a conception was impossible to express in the conventional forms of tragedy'; so for most of the time he reluctantly fell back on 'the popular concept of an innocent Oedipus lured by Fate into a disastrous trap.' We are left to conclude either that the play is a botched compromise or else that the common sense of the law-courts is not after all the best yardstick by which to measure myth.

In any case, Sophocles has provided a conclusive answer to those who suggest that Oedipus could, and therefore should, have avoided his fate. The oracle was *unconditional* (line 790): it did not say 'If you do so-and-so you will kill your father'; it simply said 'You will kill your father, you will sleep with your mother.' And what an oracle predicts is bound to happen. Oedipus does what he can to evade his destiny: he resolves never to see his supposed parents again. But it is quite certain from the first that his best efforts will be unavailing. Equally unconditional was the original oracle given to Laius (711 ff.): Apollo said that he *must* (χρῆναι) die at the hand of Jocasta's child; there is no saving clause. Here there is a significant difference between Sophocles and Aeschylus. Of Aeschylus' trilogy on the House of Laius only the last play, the *Septem,* survives. Little is known of the others, but we do know, from *Septem* 742 ff., that according to Aeschylus the oracle given to Laius *was* conditional: 'Do not beget a child; for *if* you do, that child will kill you.' In Aeschylus the disaster *could* have been avoided, but Laius sinfully disobeyed and his sin brought ruin to his descendants. In Aeschylus the story was, like the *Oresteia,* a tale of crime and punishment; but Sophocles chose otherwise—that is why he altered the form of the oracle. There is no suggestion in the *Oedipus Rex* that Laius sinned or that Oedipus was the victim of an hereditary curse, and the critic must not assume what the poet has abstained from suggesting. Nor should we leap to the conclusion that Sophocles left out the hereditary curse because he thought the doctrine immoral; apparently he did not think so, since he used it both in the *Antigone* (585 ff.) and in the *Oedipus at Colonus* (964 ff.). What his motive may have been for ignoring it in the *Oedipus Rex* we shall see in a moment.

I hope I have now disposed of the moralizing interpretation, which has been rightly abandoned by the great majority of contemporary scholars. To mention only recent works in English, the books of Whitman, Waldock, Letters, Ehrenberg, Knox, and Kirkwood, however much they differ on other points, all agree about the essential moral innocence of Oedipus.

II

But what is the alternative? If Oedipus is the innocent victim of a doom which he cannot avoid, does this not reduce him to a mere puppet? Is not the whole play a 'tragedy of destiny' which denies human freedom? This is the second of the heresies which I set out to refute. Many readers have fallen into it, Sigmund Freud among them; and you can find it confidently asserted in various popular handbooks, some of which even extend the assertion to Greek tragedy in general—thus providing themselves with a convenient label for distinguishing Greek from 'Christian' tragedy. But the whole notion is in fact anachronistic. The modern reader slips into it easily because *we* think of two clear-cut alternative views—either we believe in free will or else we are determinists. But fifth-century Greeks did not think in these terms any more than Homer did: the debate about determinism is a creation of Hellenistic thought. Homeric heroes have their predetermined 'portion of life' (μοῖρα), they must die on their 'appointed day' (αἴσιμον ἦμαρ,) but it never occurs to the poet or his audience that this prevents them from being free agents. Nor did Sophocles intend that it should occur to readers of the *Oedipus Rex.* Neither in Homer nor in Sophocles does divine foreknowledge of certain events imply that all human actions are predetermined. If explicit confirmation of this is required, we have only to turn to lines 1230 ff., where the Messenger emphatically distinguishes Oedipus' self-blinding as 'voluntary' and 'self-chosen' from the 'involuntary' parricide and incest. Certain of Oedipus' past actions were fate-bound; but everything that he does on the stage from first to last he does as a free agent.

Even in calling the parricide and the incest 'fate-bound' I have perhaps implied more than the average Athenian of Sophocles' day would have recognized. As A. W. Gomme put it, 'the gods know the future, but they do not order it: they know who will win the next Scotland and England football match, but that does not alter the fact that the victory will depend on the skill, the determination, the fitness of the players, and a little on luck.' That may not satisfy the analytical philosopher, but it seems to have satisfied the ordinary man at all periods. Bernard Knox aptly quotes the prophecy of Jesus to St. Peter, 'Before the cock crow, thou shalt deny me thrice.' The Evangelists clearly did not intend to imply that Peter's subsequent action was 'fate-bound' in the sense that he could not have chosen otherwise; Peter fulfilled the prediction, but he did so by an act of free choice.

In any case I cannot understand Sir Maurice Bowra's idea that the gods *force* on Oedipus the knowledge of what he has done. They do nothing of the kind; on the contrary, what fascinates us is the spectacle of a man freely choosing, from the highest motives, a series of actions which lead to his own ruin. Oedipus might have left the plague to take its course; but pity for the sufferings of his people compelled him to consult Delphi. When Apollo's word came back, he might still have left the murder of Laius uninvestigated; but piety and justice required him to act. He need not have forced the truth from the reluctant Theban herdsman; but because he cannot rest content with a lie, he must tear away the last veil from the illusion in which he has lived so long. Teiresias, Jocasta, the herdsman, each in turn tries to stop him, but in vain: he must read the last riddle, the riddle of his own life. The immediate cause of Oedipus' ruin is not 'Fate' or 'the gods'—no oracle said that he must discover the truth—and still less does it lie in his own weakness; what causes his ruin is his own strength and courage, his loyalty to Thebes, and his loyalty to the truth. In all this we are to see him as a free agent: hence the suppression of the hereditary curse. And his self-mutilation and self-banishment are equally free acts of choice.

Why does Oedipus blind himself? He tells us the reason (1369 ff.): he has done it in order to cut himself off from all contact with humanity; if he could choke the channels of his other senses he would do so. Suicide would not serve his purpose: in the next world he would have to meet his dead parents. Oedipus mutilates himself because he can face neither the living nor the dead. But why, if he is morally innocent? Once again, we must look at the play through Greek eyes. The doctrine that nothing matters except the agent's intention is a peculiarity of Christian and especially of post-Kantian thought. It is true that the Athenian law courts took account of intention: they distinguished as ours do between murder and accidental homicide or homicide committed in the course of self-defence. If Oedipus had been tried before an Athenian court he would have been acquitted—of murdering his father. But no human court could acquit him of pollution; for pollution inhered in the act itself, irrespective of motive. Of that burden Thebes could not acquit Oedipus, and least of all could its bearer acquit himself.

The nearest parallel to the situation of Oedipus is in the tale which Herodotus tells about Adrastus, son of Gordies. Adrastus was the involuntary slayer of his own brother, and then of Atys, the son of his benefactor Croesus; the latter act, like the killing of Laius, fulfilled an oracle. Croesus forgave Adrastus because the killing was unintended (ἀέκων), and because the oracle showed that it was the will of 'some god.' But Adrastus did not forgive himself: he committed suicide, 'conscious' says Herodotus, 'that of all men known to him he bore the heaviest burden of disaster.' It is for the same reason that Oedipus blinds himself. Morally innocent though he is and knows himself to be, the objective horror of his actions remains with him and he feels that he has no longer any place in human society. Is that simply archaic superstition? I think it is something more. Suppose a motorist runs down a man and kills him, I think he *ought* to feel that he has done a terrible thing, even if the accident is no fault of his: he has destroyed a human life, which nothing can restore. In the objective order it is acts that count, not intentions. A man who has violated that order may well feel a sense of guilt, however blameless his driving.

But my analogy is very imperfect, and even the case of Adrastus is not fully comparable. Oedipus is no ordinary homicide: he has committed the two crimes which above all others fill us with instinctive horror. Sophocles had not read Freud, but he knew how people *feel* about these things—better than some of his critics appear to do. And in the strongly patriarchal society of ancient Greece the revulsion would be even more intense than it is in our own. We have only to read Plato's prescription for the treatment to be given to parricides (*Laws* 872 c ff.). For this deed, he says, there can be no purification: the parricide shall be killed, his body shall be laid naked at a cross-roads outside the city, each officer of the State shall cast a stone upon it, and then the bloody remnant shall be flung outside the city's territory and left unburied. In all this he is probably following actual Greek practice. And if that is how Greek justice treated parricides, is it surprising that Oedipus treats himself as he does, when the great king, 'the first of men,' the man whose intuitive genius had saved Thebes, is suddenly revealed to himself as a thing so unclean that 'neither the earth can receive it, nor the holy rain nor the sunshine endure its presence' (1426)?

III

At this point I am brought back to the original question I asked the undergraduates: does Sophocles in this play attempt to justify the ways of God to man? If 'to justify' means 'to explain in terms of *human* justice,' the answer is surely 'No.' If human justice is the standard, then, as Waldock bluntly expressed it, 'Nothing can excuse the gods, and Sophocles knew it perfectly well.' Waldock does not, however, suggest that the poet intended any attack on the gods. He goes on to say that it is futile to look for any 'message' or 'meaning' in this play: 'there is no meaning,' he tells us, 'in the *Oedipus Rex;* there is merely the terror of coincidence.' Kirkwood seems to take a rather similar line: 'Sophocles,' he says, 'has no theological pronouncements to make and no points of criticism to score.' These opinions come rather close to, if they do not actually involve, the view adopted by my third and last group of undergraduates—the view that the gods are merely agents in a traditional story which Sophocles, a 'pure artist,' exploits for dramatic purposes without raising the religious issue or drawing any moral whatever.

This account seems to me insufficient; but I have more sympathy with it than I have with either of the other heresies. It reflects a healthy reaction against the old moralizing school of critics; and the text of the play appears at first sight to support it.

It is a striking fact that after the catastrophe no one on the stage says a word either in justification of the gods or in criticism of them. Oedipus says 'These things were Apollo'—and that is all. If the poet has charged him with a 'message' about divine justice or injustice, he fails to deliver it. And I fully agree that there is no reason at all why we should require a dramatist—even a Greek dramatist—to be for ever running about delivering banal 'messages.' It is true that when a Greek dramatic poet had something he passionately wanted to say to his fellow citizens he felt entitled to say it. Aeschylus in the *Oresteia,* Aristophanes in the *Frogs,* had something to say to their people and used the opportunity of saying it on the stage. But these are exceptional cases—both these works were produced at a time of grave crisis in public affairs—and even here the 'message' appears to me to be incidental to the true function of the artist, which I should be disposed to define, with Dr. Johnson, as 'the enlargement of our sensibility.' It is unwise to generalize from special cases. (And, incidentally, I wish undergraduates would stop writing essays which begin with the words 'This play *proves* that . . . .' Surely no work of art can ever 'prove' anything: what value could there be in a 'proof' whose premises are manufactured by the artist?)

Nevertheless, I cannot accept the view that the *Oedipus Rex* conveys *no* intelligible meaning and that Sophocles' plays tell us nothing of his opinions concerning the gods. Certainly it is always dangerous to use dramatic works as evidence of their author's opinions, and especially of their religious convictions: we can legitimately discuss religion *in* Shakespeare, but do we know anything at all about the religion *of* Shakespeare? Still, I think I should venture to assert two things about Sophocles' opinions:

First, he did not believe (or did not always believe) that the gods are in any human sense 'just';

Secondly, he did always believe that the gods exist and that man should revere them.

The first of these propositions is supported not only by the implicit evidence of the *Oedipus Rex* but by the explicit evidence of another play which is generally thought to be close in date to it. The closing lines of the *Trachiniae* contain a denunciation in violent terms of divine injustice. No one answers it. I can only suppose that the poet had no answer to give.

For the second of my two propositions we have quite strong *external* evidence—which is important, since it is independent of our subjective impressions. We know that Sophocles held various priesthoods; that when the cult of Asclepius was introduced to Athens he acted as the god's host and wrote a hymn in his honour; and that he was himself worshipped as a 'hero' after his death, which seems to imply that he accepted the religion of the State and was accepted by it. But the external evidence does not stand alone: it is strongly supported by at least one passage in the *Oedipus Rex*. The celebrated choral ode about the decline of prophecy and the threat to religion (lines 863–910) was of course suggested by the scene with Creon which precedes it; but it contains generalizations which have little apparent relevance either to Oedipus or to Creon. Is the piety of this ode purely conventional, as Whitman maintained in a vigorous but sometimes perverse book? One phrase in particular seems to forbid this interpretation. If men are to lose all respect for the gods, in that case, the Chorus asks, τί δεῖ με χορεύειν (895). If by this they mean merely 'Why should I, Theban elder, dance?,' the question is irrelevant and even slightly ludicrous; the meaning is surely 'Why should I, an Athenian citizen, continue to serve in a chorus?' In speaking of themselves as a chorus they step out of the play into the contemporary world, as Aristophanes' choruses do in the *parabasis*. And in effect the question they are asking seems to be this: 'If Athens loses faith in religion, if the views of the Enlightenment prevail, what significance is there in tragic drama, which exists as part of the service of the gods?' To that question the rapid decay of tragedy in the fourth century may be said to have provided an answer.

In saying this, I am not suggesting with Ehrenberg that the character of Oedipus reflects that of Pericles, or with Knox that he is intended to be a symbol of Athens: allegory of that sort seems to me wholly alien to Greek tragedy. I am only claiming that at one point in this play Sophocles took occasion to say to his fellow citizens something which he felt to be important. And it *was* important, particularly in the period of the Archidamian War, to which the *Oedipus Rex* probably belongs. Delphi was known to be pro-Spartan: that is why Euripides was given a free hand to criticize Apollo. But if Delphi could not be trusted, the whole fabric of traditional belief was threatened with collapse. In our society religious faith is no longer tied up with belief in prophecy; but for the ancient world, both pagan and Christian, it was. And in the years of the Archidamian War belief in prophecy was at a low ebb; Thucydides is our witness to that.

I take it, then, as reasonably certain that while Sophocles did not pretend that the gods are in any human sense just he nevertheless held that they are entitled to our worship. Are those two opinions incompatible? Here once more we cannot hope to understand Greek literature if we persist in looking at it through Christian spectacles. To the Christian it is a necessary part of piety to believe that God is just. And so it was to Plato and to the Stoics. But the older world saw no such necessity. If you doubt this, take down the *Iliad* and read Achilles' opinion of what divine justice amounts to (xxiv. 525–33); or take down the Bible and read the Book of Job. Disbelief in divine justice as measured by human yardsticks can perfectly well be associated with deep religious feeling. 'Men,' said Heraclitus, 'find some things unjust, other things just; but in the eyes of God all things are beautiful and good and just.' I think that Sophocles would have agreed. For him, as for Heraclitus, there is an objective world-order which man must respect, but which he cannot hope fully to understand.

IV

Some readers of the *Oedipus Rex* have told me that they find its atmosphere stifling and oppressive: they miss the tragic exaltation that one gets from the *Antigone* or the *Prometheus Vinctus*. And I fear that what I have said here has done nothing to remove that feeling. Yet it is not a feeling which I share myself. Certainly the *Oedipus Rex* is a play about the blindness of man and the desperate insecurity of the human condition: in a sense every man must grope in the dark as Oedipus gropes, not knowing who he is or what he has to suffer; we all live in a world of appearance which hides from us who-knows-what dreadful reality. But surely the *Oedipus Rex* is also a play about human greatness. Oedipus is great, not in virtue of a great worldly position—for his worldly position is an illusion which will vanish like a dream—but in virtue of his inner strength: strength to pursue the truth at whatever personal cost, and strength to accept and endure it when found. 'This horror is mine,' he cries, 'and none but I is *strong* enough to bear it' (1414). Oedipus is great because he accepts the responsibility for *all* his acts, including those which are objectively most horrible, though subjectively innocent.

To me personally Oedipus is a kind of symbol of the human intelligence which cannot rest until it has solved all the riddles—even the last riddle, to which the answer is that human happiness is built on an illusion. I do not know how far Sophocles intended that. But certainly in the last lines of the play (which I firmly believe to be genuine) he does generalize the case, does appear to suggest that in some sense Oedipus is every man and every man is potentially Oedipus. Freud felt this (he was not insensitive to poetry), but as we all know he understood it in a specific psychological sense. 'Oedipus' fate,' he says, 'moves us only because it might have been our own, because the oracle laid upon us before birth the very curse which rested upon him. It may be that we were all destined to direct our first sexual impulses towards our mothers, and our first impulses of hatred and violence towards our fathers; our dreams convince us that we were.' Perhaps they do; but Freud did not ascribe his interpretation of the myth to Sophocles, and it is not the interpretation I have in mind. Is there not in the poet's view a much wider sense in which every man is Oedipus? If every man could tear away the last veils of illusion, if he could see human life as time and the gods see it, would he not see that against that tremendous background all the generations of men are as if they had not been, ἴσα καὶ τὸ μηδὲν ζώσας (1187)? That was how Odysseus saw it when he had conversed with Athena, the embodiment of divine wisdom. 'In Ajax' condition,' he says, 'I recognize my own: I perceive that all men living are but appearance or unsubstantial shadow.'

> ὁρῶ γὰρ ἡμᾶς οὐδὲν ὄντας ἄλλο πλὴν
> εἴδωλ, ὅσοιπερ ζῶμεν, ἢ κούφην σκιάν.

So far as I can judge, on this matter Sophocles' deepest feelings did not change. The same view of the human condition which is made explicit in his earliest extant play is implicit not only in the *Oedipus Rex* but in the *Oedipus Coloneus,* in the great speech where Oedipus draws the bitter conclusion from his life's experience and in the famous ode on old age. Whether this vision of man's estate is true or false I do not know, but it ought to be comprehensible to a generation which relishes the plays of Samuel Beckett. I do not wish to describe it as a 'message.' But I find in it an enlargement of sensibility. And that is all I ask of any dramatist.

QUESTIONS FOR DISCUSSION AND WRITING

1. Vellacott and Dodds obviously have the same evidence before them—they are both interpreting Sophocles' *Oedipus*—but they come to very different conclusions about the central character's moral culpability. Which of the two critics presents the more convincing case? Why?

2. In looking at *Oedipus,* Vellacott and Dodds both pay some attention to each of the following events and ideas. Compare and contrast their ways of dealing with each.
   Oedipus's anger
   The idea of moral pollution
   Attitudes toward the gods
   Determinism versus free will

3. Dodds says that "it is an essential critical principle that *what is not mentioned in the play does not exist*" (1128). How does Vellacott violate this principle? How reason-

able do you consider the principle? Does it extend to discussions of characters'
motivations and thoughts—or only to discussions of their actions?

RITA DOVE (1952–   )

The Darker Face of the Earth _____ 2000

Cast

Female slaves:

> PHEBE
> PSYCHE, *in her mid teens*
> SCYLLA, *pronounced "Skilla"*
> TICEY, *a house slave*
> DIANA, *a young girl about 12 years old*
> SLAVE WOMAN/NARRATOR

Male slaves:

> HECTOR, *an African*
> ALEXANDER
> SCIPIO, *pronounced "Sippio"*
> AUGUSTUS NEWCASTLE, *a mulatto*

The whites:

> AMALIA JENNINGS LAFARGE
> LOUIS LAFARGE, *Amalia's husband*
> DOCTOR, *in his fifties*
> JONES, *the overseer, in his thirties*

The black conspirators:

> LEADER
> BENJAMIN SKEENE
> HENRY BLAKE

Other slaves and conspirators

Time

> Prologue: *about 1820.*
> Acts I and II: *twenty years later.*

Place

> The action takes place in antebellum *South Carolina, on the Jennings Plantation and in
> its environs.*

> The characters of Psyche and Diana, as well as the Doctor and Jones, can be played by
> the same actors, as long as it is made clear to the audience that they are different people.

> On occasion, the slaves comment upon the play somewhat in the manner of a Greek cho-
> rus. Individual characters are bound by time and circumstance; the chorus of slaves is more
> detached and omnipresent. By moving and speaking in a ritualized manner, they provide

vocal and percussive counterpoint to the action. The slave woman who occasionally steps forward as the narrator, is quietly present in all slave scenes.

PROLOGUE

Lights rise on the big house, revealing the porch, AMALIA'*s bedroom,* LOUIS' *study and the hallway.*

HECTOR, *a slave in his early twenties, is standing on the porch, looking up at a second-story window.* PHEBE, *a slave girl in her early teens, runs onstage; she is coming from the basement kitchen. Skinny and electric, she is chuckling to herself.*

PHEBE: What some people won't do
        for attention! Shore,
        he's alright-looking—
        but that ain't qualification enough
5   for the big white bed
        in the big white house!

(*Laughs at her own wit; then, skipping in a circle, sings.*)

        Stepped on a pin, the pin bent,
        and that's the way the story went!
PSYCHE (*Offstage*): Phebe! Phebe! You up there?
10 PHEBE: Here I am, Psyche!

        (PSYCHE *enters. She is petite, shy; though not much older than* PHEBE, *she treats her like a little sister.*)

PSYCHE: You shouldn't go running off
         by yourself, chile.
PHEBE: Look: Hector on the porch.

        (*She giggles and points to* HECTOR.)

PSYCHE: Leave him be, poor soul.
15 PHEBE: Aw, Psyche! Anybody crazy enough
         to be standing there, thinking he—
PSYCHE: Shush now, chile!

        (PHEBE *shrugs, hums and skips again. The other* SLAVES *straggle in, tired from the day's work, whispering among themselves, a suppressed excitement in their manner.*)

PHEBE: What took you all so long?
        Slower than a pack of lame turtles.
20 ALEXANDER (*A dignified man in his forties*): We all ain't quite
        so spry as you, gal.
PHEBE: Shh!

        (*Everyone freezes.*)

        I thought I heard something.

PSYCHE: Aw, girl—

SCYLLA (*A tall dark woman in her twenties*): Must be a hard birthin'.   25

PSYCHE: I sure hope she makes it. Her mama—

SCYLLA: Her mama was the weakest excuse for a woman
    ever dropped on this earth. But this one—

(*With a significant look to the window.*)

this one got her daddy in her.

ALEXANDER: Nothing but trouble, I tell you.   30
    Nothing but trouble.

(*Lights up on* AMALIA'*s bedroom.* AMALIA JENNINGS LAFARGE *lies in a canopy
bed, a thickly swaddled babe in her arms. She is an attractive white woman, close to 20
years old, who exhibits more intelligence and backbone than is generally credited to a
Southern belle. The* DOCTOR, *an older whiskered gentleman, is pacing the floor.*
AMALIA, *though exhausted, appears amused.*)

AMALIA: Well, Doctor, isn't he beautiful?

DOCTOR: This is serious, Amalia!
    If the niggers get wind of this—

(AMALIA *begins humming a lullaby to the baby.*)

AMALIA: Don't get melodramatic, Doctor;   35
    you'll frighten my son. See?

(*Baby raises a cry;* AMALIA *continues to hum while the* DOCTOR *keeps pacing.
Among the* SLAVES, SCYLLA *stands up, clutching her stomach.*)

SCYLLA: Oh! Oh!

OTHERS: What is it, Scylla? What is it?

SCYLLA: It's out in the world.

(*The* SLAVES *look at her in fear.*)

ALEXANDER: Lord have mercy.   40

(*The* SLAVES *gather around* SCYLLA *as she tries to straighten up but cannot.*
HECTOR'*s gaze is still fixed on the window.* AMALIA'*s husband rushes into the
bedroom.* LOUIS LAFARGE *is a handsome man in his twenties. The* DOCTOR *holds
him back.*)

LOUIS: Doctor—

DOCTOR: Everything's fine. Just go on back outside.

LOUIS: Can't a man see his own child?

(*Tears himself free and rushes over to the bed.*)

AMALIA: What, Louis—struck dumb?

LOUIS: My God!   45

AMALIA: Isn't he a fine strapping boy?

DOCTOR: This is unnatural.

LOUIS: Who did this to you?
    I'll have him whipped to a pulp—
50 AMALIA (*Hissing*): So it's alright for you
    to stroll out by the cabins
    any fine night you please? Ha—
    the Big White Hunter with his scrawny whip!
LOUIS: That tears it!
55 DOCTOR: Quiet! They might hear.
LOUIS: I'll kill her!

    (LOUIS *lunges at* AMALIA; *the* DOCTOR *restrains him.*)

DOCTOR: Hold it, sir! Calm yourself!
AMALIA (*To the* DOCTOR): Daddy tried to keep me from
    marrying him—but I was in love
60   with riding boots and the smell
    of shaving cream and bourbon.
    I was in love with a cavalryman
    and nothing could stop me,
    not even Daddy!

    (*To* LOUIS, *who is being forced into an armchair by the* DOCTOR.)

65   But not even Daddy
    suspected where you would seek
    your satisfaction.
    It was your right
    to pull on those riding boots
70   and stalk little slave girls.
    God knows what you do to them
    in the name of ownership.

    (*Depleted from the bravado she has mustered,* AMALIA *bends over the baby so they won't see her exhaustion.* LOUIS, *still sitting in the armchair, grabs the* DOCTOR *by the shirt and pulls him down to his level.*)

LOUIS: Get rid of it! Destroy the bastard!
DOCTOR: My charge is to preserve life,
75   Mr LaFarge, not to destroy it.
LOUIS: What's the matter? Aren't you a man?
DOCTOR (*Scathingly; a fierce whisper*): My manhood isn't the question here.
    Do you want your business
    smeared across the whole county?
80   Think for a minute: What have we got
    here? A fresh slave. New property.
    And you're in need of a little spare change,
    aren't you? I understand the cards
    haven't been much in your favor lately.
85 LOUIS: What are you trying to say, Doctor?
AMALIA: Stop your whispering, gentlemen.

No one's going to touch this baby!
LOUIS: You can be sure I'll never
    touch you again!
AMALIA: That's one blessing.   90
DOCTOR: Is this baby worth destroying your life?

(*Pulling* LOUIS *aside.*)

Give me a minute alone with her.
I'll make her see reason. Go on, now.

(*He shoves the reluctant* LOUIS *out of the door, then moves quickly to the window to
peek out on the* SLAVES *below. Among the* SLAVES, *excitement reigns as* SCYLLA
hobbles over to HECTOR, *whose eyes are still fixed on the bedroom window.*)

PHEBE (*To* PSYCHE): Scylla gonna be alright?   95
PSYCHE (*Sees the curtains move*): Hush chile!

(*Pointing to the window.*)

Something's stirring.

(*The* SLAVES *look up to the window and freeze. The* DOCTOR *returns to* AMALIA,
who is singing to the baby.)

DOCTOR: You can cease your motherly blandishments,
    Amalia. He's gone.
AMALIA: I knew you were good for something besides
    tonics and botched surgeries, Doctor!   100
DOCTOR: Oh, you're mighty clever, Miss Jennings—
    no wonder your marriage is a disappointment.
    Hell, your daddy saw it coming;
    he worried about you. How many times
    did he have to haul you back from the fields,   105
    kicking and scratching like a she-cat?
AMALIA: And just who was I supposed to
    play with—the pigs and the chickens?
    Daddy could run a plantation
    but he didn't know the first thing   110
    about raising a daughter. All morning
    he'd teach me to calculate inventory,
    but he expected his slippers darned come evening!
    And when I refused, off I went—
    to finishing school and the Charleston society balls.   11.

(*Lights up on* LOUIS, *sitting on the bed in his room, head in hands.*)

LOUIS: Spare change. Spare change!
    How they all smirk! I know what they're thinking.
    "Louis sure slipped into a silk-lined purse!"

(*Takes a swig from a flask in his jacket.*)

Damn his blasted Hippocratic oath!

(*Paces, agitated; then stops, an idea dawning.*)

120   That's it! Of course.
           Doctor, I'll save you the trouble.

(*He rummages in drawers; lights up on* AMALIA's *room.*)

AMALIA: When I came home from Charleston
           with my brand new dashing husband,
           Daddy had the slaves line the path
125   from the gate to the front porch;
           and as we walked through the ranks
           each one stepped up with
           the nosegays they had picked—
           awkward bunches of wildflowers.
130   I was laughing, gathering up bouquets
           and tossing them to Louis.

           We were almost to the porch
           when suddenly there appeared this . . .
           this rose. One red rose,
135   thrust right into the path so we had to stop.
           I recognised him right away.
           We hadn't seen each other
           since Daddy sent him to the fields.
           We used to sneak out to Mama's
140   old cutting garden; it was overgrown
           and the roses had run particularly wild!

(*Softly, remembering.*)

           One day he covered me in rose petals,
           then blew them off, one by one.
           He'd never seen anything like them
145   back in Africa.

(*In wonder.*)

           And there he stood, all grown up,
           with one red rose held out
           like it was a piece of him
           growing straight from his fist.
150   "What a lovely tribute to the bride!" I said—

(*Shaking off the spell of the memory.*)

           then passed it to Louis to tuck in with the rest.
DOCTOR: I suppose there's no sense in talking about
           your duty to the institution of marriage.
AMALIA: I made one mistake—Louis.

I don't have to go on living it.   155
DOCTOR: Oh, there's where you're wrong.
    Amalia Jennings. Some mistakes
    don't right themselves that easy.
    Some mistakes you live with until you die.

(*Lights up on* LOUIS *in his bedroom as he emerges from the back of the wardrobe with a
pair of spurs, still trailing red ribbons.*)

LOUIS (*Sneering*): There they are!   160
    Amalia's Christmas present—
    fancy new riding spurs!
    Won't they make a special
    "christening" present
    for the little bitty baby   165
    to tuck in with its blanket!

(LOUIS *chuckles as he pockets the spurs and leaves the room. Lights up on* SLAVES.
HECTOR *stretches his hand toward the window and speaks, as if trying to remember.*)

HECTOR: Eshu Elewa . . .
PHEBE: What's he saying?
PSYCHE: Something surely gone wrong.

(*Lights up on* AMALIA *and* DOCTOR.)

DOCTOR: How long do you think it will take   170
    before your slaves begin to speak back?
    To botch the work and fall ill
    with mysterious ailments? Then
    who will help you—Louis?
    An overseer who knows his mistress   175
    is tainted with slave funk? In a bad year,
    how much will you have to beg
    to get a tab at the store?
    Who will you invite to tea, Amalia—
    your dashing blackamoor?   180
AMALIA: What a convenient morality, Doctor.
DOCTOR: I'm just trying to save
    your daddy's good name.
    As for your precious little bundle—
    how long do you think he'll last   185
    with Louis feeling as he does?
    How long before your child
    accidentally drowns
    or stumbles under a horse's hooves?
    You can't keep him, Amalia;   190
    if you truly love him,
    you cannot keep him.

(AMALIA *buries her face in the pillow and begins to weep.*)

DOCTOR: I know a family who handles
these . . . delicate matters.

195   They'll raise him and arrange for sale
when it's time.

(AMALIA *clutches the baby to her.*)

He'll be treated well. I'll make sure of that.

(*Silence.* AMALIA *stares at the baby.*)

AMALIA: Give me a little more time!
DOCTOR: You had nine months.

(*The baby makes a noise; she lays him on her breast.*)

200   AMALIA: There's no way back, is there?

(HECTOR *falls to his knee and cries out;* SCYLLA *tries to restrain him.*)

HECTOR: Eshu Elewa ogo gbogbo!
SCYLLA: No, Hector.
ALEXANDER: Lord help him.
PSYCHE: Lord help us all.

(*Lights up on* AMALIA's *bedroom; there's a knock at the door.*)

205   DOCTOR: There he is. Now:
I'll take the baby to Charleston tonight.
You must play the wronged wife.
No matter the truth—whatever the truth—
this affair was an act of revenge,

210   your retaliation to Louis' philandering.
But you won't keep the child
to taunt him, oh, no! Instead,
you'll forgive and forget . . . and show him
how to turn a profit besides.

(AMALIA *stares at the* DOCTOR *with disgust. The* DOCTOR *opens the door.*)

215   Come in, sir.

(LOUIS *enters, glaring.*)

This is a damned tricky situation,
but I think I've sorted it out.

(*Warming up to his role as the arbiter of responsibility and morality; pacing self-
importantly.*)

Out of rage and sorrow over
your philandering behaviour, Louis,

220   Amalia has responded in kind.
An extreme vindication, true,
and utterly reprehensible—unless

we remember what prompted it
in the first place. Are we agreed?

(*Both* LOUIS *and* AMALIA *are silent.*)

As for the bastard child . . .   225

(*Pauses for effect.*)

Amalia has agreed to let it go.
I have a friend in Charleston
who likes raising slaves
from the ground up. He's familiar
with the story of the distraught wife   230
confronted with the evidence
of a husband's wandering lust.

LOUIS: No! I won't take the blame!

DOCTOR: No one need know it's come
from the Jennings Plantation.   235

LOUIS: What about the niggers? They're out
on the lawn, waiting for news.

DOCTOR: We'll say the poor soul expired
directly after birth, took one breath
and died. I've taken the body away.   240

LOUIS: No funeral? Niggers love funerals.

DOCTOR: No—Amalia didn't want a funeral.
They'll believe it. They have no choice.

(*To* AMALIA.)

You better make sure the father
keeps his mouth shut.   245

AMALIA (*Haunted*): Who would believe him?

LOUIS: I must say, your ingenuity is impressive,
Doctor. It's what I'd call a "master" plan.

(*Pointing to the sideboard where* AMALIA *keeps an oblong wicker sewing basket,
trimmed with red velvet rosettes and lined in blue silk.*)

That basket—surely you'd donate
your sewing basket to the cause,   250
Amalia? It would fit so nicely
behind the good doctor's saddle.

DOCTOR (*Examines the basket*): Yes, that will do.

(LOUIS *places the basket next to the bed.*)

AMALIA: Go tell them.
Spread the sad tidings.   255

(*She says this with difficulty.* DOCTOR *and* LOUIS *exit as* AMALIA *carefully unwraps
the baby and inspects him, top to toe. Lights up on the* DOCTOR *and* LOUIS *in the
hall;* TICEY, *a house slave in her forties, approaches them.*)

TICEY: How's Miss Jennings, suh?
    The baby sure sounds like a big one!
DOCTOR (*Harshly*): The baby's dead.
TICEY: Dead? But I heard it cry!
260   DOCTOR: He cried out once. Poor little thing
    had no more breath left.
TICEY: Now, if that ain't the strangest thing . . .
LOUIS (*Sharply*): What's so strange about it?
    The baby just up and died.
265   Happens all the time.
DOCTOR: Look at you, standing here arguing
    like a fool hen, while your mistress
    is in there crying her eyes out!

(*Shaking his head.*)

    Now go on out to those niggers—
270   I know you got them waiting by the porch.
    Tell them there'll be no wailing and moaning,
    no singing or mighty sorry, Ma'am.
    Miss Jennings wants no funeral.
    Miss Jennings wants to forget.
275   Go on now, scat!
TICEY: Yassuh. Sorry suh.

(TICEY *exits. During the following scene she approaches* PSYCHE, *takes her aside, whispering. At* PSYCHE'*s shocked reaction, the* SLAVES, *except for* HECTOR *and* SCYLLA, *crowd around.* TICEY *retreats back into the house while the other* SLAVES *lower their heads, softly humming in a frozen tableau.* HECTOR *falls to his knees;* SCYLLA *stands over him, severely bent.*)

(*In the bedroom,* AMALIA *embraces the baby one last time.*)

AMALIA: This basket will be your cradle now.
    Blue silk for my prince, and a canopy of roses!
    Don't be afraid: it's warm inside.

(*Places first a small blanket, then the baby inside, takes one last look, nearly breaking down.*)

280   I dreamed you before you came;
    now I must remember you before you go.

(*Collects herself as she wraps the blanket around the baby and closes the lid.*)

DOCTOR: Let's get this over with.
LOUIS: Go ahead. Doctor, I—I'll wait here.

(*The* DOCTOR *enters the bedroom.*)

DOCTOR: Ready?

(AMALIA *averts her head, thrusts the basket at him.*)

I wasn't sure you had it in you,   285
but I'll say one thing, Amalia Jennings—
you are your father's daughter.

(DOCTOR *exits with the basket.* AMALIA *buries her face in the pillows.*)

DOCTOR: I best be on my way.
LOUIS: You have a hard ride ahead of you, Doctor.
Would you care for a bit of bourbon   290
to warm your way?
DOCTOR (*Slightly surprised*): Why yes, that would do nicely.
Just put it with my things.

(*As the* DOCTOR *turns to get his coat and hat,* LOUIS *slips the spurs in the sewing basket, under the blanket, then puts the flask into the* DOCTOR's *bag.*)

LOUIS: There, you're all set—
best medicine made by man!   295
DOCTOR: It's over, Louis. Nothing left but to forget.
LOUIS: Have a pleasant journey, Doctor.
DOCTOR: I will try.

(*Lights go out as the* DOCTOR *exits. The* SLAVE WOMAN/NARRATOR *steps forward. During the* NARRATOR's *speech, the* SLAVES *go about their tasks, humming as the lights slowly warm to sunrise and the stage begins to transmogrify, simulating the passing of 20 years: a tree growing, the big house being enlarged, etc.*)

NARRATOR: Take a little seed,   300
put it in the ground;
the seed takes root,
sends its tendrils down

till the sapling shoots
its branches high—
roots piercing ground,   305
limbs touching sky.

Now the mighty tree
is twenty years tall;
seed become king,
and the king takes all.   310

ACT ONE
SCENE 1

The cotton fields, DIANA, *a slave girl, collapses.* SCIPIO, *a young slave working nearby, hesitates.*

SCIPIO: Move it gal, or
you'll feel it later!
PHEBE (*Helping her up*): Lift in your knees, Diana;

try not to think about your blood.
5   Tomorrow's Sunday—
tomorrow you can rest.
DIANA (*Derisively*): Blessed be the Sabbath!
PHEBE: The child's too young to tote that sack.
She should be helping in the kitchen,
10   like we was raised.
ALEXANDER: You was raised with Massa Jennings,
Phebe—and he been gone these twenty-some years.
You know his daughter got other ideas.
PHEBE: She grow eviller year for year.
15   ALEXANDER: Ain't right, a woman
running a plantation like that.
SCIPIO: Woman? She's more man than woman.
PHEBE: And more devil than man.
ALEXANDER: Ever since she lost that child.
20   PHEBE: Oh, Alexander!
ALEXANDER: White folks feel a loss
as much as we do—
it's just that they ain't
used to losing. I tell you,
25   Miss Amalia went crazy in the head
the day she lost that baby boy.
SCYLLA: That's not the way Ticey told it.

(SCYLLA *is severely bent over and walks with a limp. Her gaze is fearful.*)

ALEXANDER (*To* DIANA): Nowadays old Ticey don't tell us
field niggers nothing. But that night
30   she come from the Big House
and say to Psyche . . .
PHEBE: That's enough, Alexander.
DIANA: Phebe, what was my mama like?
PHEBE: Chile, you heard that story
35   a hundred times. Ain't no different now,
just 'cause you turned to a woman yourself.
DIANA: Please, Phebe.
PHEBE (*Tenderly, as she resumes picking cotton*): Psyche was the sister I never had.
Why, she pulled me offa trouble
40   so many times, I thought her hand
had growed to my shoulder!
DIANA (*Begins to cry*): I wish I'd a known her.
PHEBE: Childbirth can kill the strongest woman.
ALEXANDER: Or kill the child.
45   SCYLLA: You still believe the white folks?
That baby weren't born dead.
Ticey heard it cry. I seen the doctor
carry it off in a basket, but

it weren't dead. I felt it kick.

DIANA (*Wiping her tears*): The baby kicked?   50

ALEXANDER: Scylla got her powers that night.

SCYLLA (*Staring at* DIANA, *who shrinks back*): The child was born alive!
    I know. I felt it.

PHEBE: Scylla . . .

SCYLLA: The veil was snatched from my eyes—   55
    and over the hill I saw
    bad times a-coming. Bad times
    coming over the hill on mighty horses,
    horses snorting as they galloped
    through slave cabin and pillared mansion,   60
    horses whinnying as they trampled
    everything in their path.
    Like a thin black net
    the curse settled over the land.

DIANA: What curse?   65

PHEBE: Don't pay her no mind.

SCYLLA: The curse touched four people.

DIANA (*Getting scared*): Who were they?
    Who were the four people?

SLAVES: Black woman, black man,   70
    white woman, white man.

SCYLLA: When the curse came I stood up
    to meet it, and it knocked me
    to the ground.

SLAVES: Black woman.   75

SCYLLA: My womb dried up,
    but the power churned in me.

PHEBE: We best get back to pickin'.
    No tellin' where Jones got off to—

SCIPIO: Same place he always "gets off to"   80
    —that clump of timothy at the spring
    where he's tucked his whiskey!

(SCYLLA *appears to be in a trance;* SLAVES *accompany her in a syncopated whisper.*)

SCYLLA: Hector, son of Africa—
    stolen from his father's hut,
    sold on the auction block!   85

SLAVES: Black man.

SCYLLA: Hector was a slave in the fields
    until Miss Amalia took him up
    to the house. He followed her
    like her own right shoe.   90
    When she felt faint,
    he brought her iced lemon water;
    when she started to show,

        he helped her up the stairs;
95   when the baby kicked,
        he soothed her.
        But when her time came
        he had to stand out by the porch
        like the rest of us.
100   And when Ticey brought the news
        Hector fell to his knees
        and ate dirt like a worm.
        Now he lives alone
        and catches snakes in the swamp.
105 SLAVES: Black woman, black man—
        both were twisted
        when the curse came over the hill.
    SCYLLA: While the slave turned to grief,
        the master turned to business.
110   Miss Amalia hiked up her skirts
        and pulled on man's boots.
    SLAVES: White woman.
    SCYLLA: And Massa Louis . . . Massa Louis
        took off his riding breeches—
115 SLAVES: White man.
    SCYLLA: —and shut himself upstairs.
        Some nights you can see him out
        on the balcony, staring at the sky:
        he has machines to measure the stars.
120 SLAVES: Black woman, black man;
        white woman, white man!
    SCYLLA: Four people touched by the curse:
        but the curse is not complete.
    DIANA: I'm scared.
125 PHEBE (*In spite of herself*): Did you have to tell her so much,
        Scylla? She's just a child.
    SCYLLA: She's old enough to know,
        and you're old enough to know better.
    PHEBE: I was there, too. I didn't see
130   no horses comin' over the hill.
        You just crumpled up like a leaf.

        (AMALIA *enters unseen in riding clothes, whip in hand*.)

    SCYLLA: I can strike you down like lightning,
        Phebe. I can send demons mightier—
    AMALIA: What's this?
135 PHEBE: How—how de do, Miss Amalia!
        We was just trying to figure out
        what to do with Diana here.
    AMALIA: She seems healthy enough to me—

good stock, young and fresh.

PHEBE (*Motioning for* DIANA *to look sicker*): She fell out something awful.   140
    It don't look like she feel too good—

AMALIA: You aren't here to play doctor, Phebe.
    Where is that Jones? Jones!

(JONES *is nowhere to be seen. Impatient,* AMALIA *prods* DIANA *with the whip stock.*)

Lazy pack! I swear I've seen cows
    smarter than you! Jones!   145

JONES (*Rushes in, wiping his mouth with his sleeve*): Yes, Miss Jennings?

AMALIA: Get these niggers in line!
    Drink on your own time.

JONES: Yes'm.

AMALIA: I'll see you this evening   150
    up at the house.

JONES: Yes, Ma'am. I'll be there, Ma'am!

(*She strides off;* JONES *mops his brow with a huge handkerchief.*)

Goddamn niggers, gotta watch you
    every second! Get that gal back on her feet!

(*Cracking his whip.*)

Keep your mouths shut and your hands picking   155
    or you'll feel my lash, sick or not!

(*Watches them resume work; then exits.*)

SCYLLA: I believe it's about time for you
    to pay me a little visit, Phebe.
    Tomorrow evening—
    after the moon's set.   160

PHEBE: Aw, Scylla, I didn't mean nothing—

SCYLLA: It'll be pitch dark. Take care
    you don't trip on the way.

(*Blackout.*)

SCENE 2

The big house, the parlor and LOUIS' *study.*

LOUIS *is visible at the window of his study, peering through a telescope at the stars; he occasionally takes notes or sips his brandy.*

AMALIA *sits at the desk in the parlor;* JONES *stands in front of her.*

JONES: Sorry about this afternoon, Ma'am.
    That little gal seemed real sick, you know.

AMALIA: Mr. Jones, I am aware you come fresh
      from the well-groomed slave holdings
5   of Dawson's Plantation. And I was not
      so naïve, upon hiring you, to believe
      Dawson's high-minded economic philosophy
      had not rubbed off on you.
      But that's not what I called you for.
10   I bought a new buck yesterday:
      here are his papers.
JONES (*Glancing through the documents*): Miss Jennings! You can't be serious!
AMALIA: Something wrong, Jones?
JONES: Augustus Newcastle? That slave's
15   the most talked-about nigger
      along the Southern seaboard!
AMALIA: Good! We'll be famous.
JONES: Story goes he belonged to a British sea captain
      who treated him like his own son,
20   and promised him his freedom when he died.
      But the brother who executed the estate
      sold the boy to pay off the debts.
      After that, the nigger went wild.
      They lost count of how many times he ran off,
25   how many times they caught him—

      (*Frantically leafs through the papers.*)

      here it is: "Twenty-two
      acts of aggression and rebellion."
      Twenty-two separate acts!
AMALIA: That's why I got him so cheaply.
30 JONES: But Miss Jennings! They say
      his back's so laced with scars
      it's as rutted as a country road.
      Rumor has it he can read and write.
      If you don't mind my saying so,
35   Ma'am, an educated nigger
      brings nothing but trouble.
      Sure as I'm standing here,
      he'll stir up the others.
AMALIA: I wonder just how smart he is.
40 JONES: It's a miracle no one ever killed him.
AMALIA (*Sharply*): I own Augustus Newcastle,
      and I'll make him serve up.
      Any objections?
JONES: No, Ma'am. Sorry, Ma'am.
45 AMALIA: They're bringing him over tonight;
      put him in the barn and chain him down.
      You can show him around tomorrow.

If he's as smart as they say,
he could help you oversee the ginning.
You may go.   50

(*This last is a jab at* JONES, *who looks at her for a moment, then turns on his heel and exits.*)

(*Blackout.*)

SCENE 3

In the fields.

Sunday. The slaves have been "let out in the fields" to occupy themselves as they please. They have settled into two groups—some joke, tell stories, and dance, while others are quieter, chanting and praying. As the lights come up, the groups are rivaling each other in melody, the quieter ones humming in a minor key while the others counterpoint in a jauntier tune.

SCIPIO: Have you seen the new man?
Mister Jones been showing him around.
ALEXANDER: I saw 'em down
by the gin house.
That's one wild nigger.   5
PHEBE: He spent last night
chained in the barn.
Chained!
SCIPIO: Must be mighty tough.
Heard tell he's sailed the seas!   10
DIANA: Did he sail the seas to Canada?

(*Shocked silence; everybody looks at her.*)

ALEXANDER: Gal, don't let nobody
hear you say that word;
Miss Amalia'll have your head on a stick.
As far as you concerned   15
there's nothing in this world
but South Carolina and this here plantation.

(AUGUSTUS *enters in leg chains, followed by a watchful* JONES. AUGUSTUS *is a tall, handsome young man with caramel-toned skin and piercing eyes. His righteous anger is thinly concealed behind his slave mannerisms.* JONES *bluffs his way with a squeaky bravado.*)

JONES: Here's the new buck you all
been whispering about!

(*Removes the leg chains; then, to* AUGUSTUS.)

You're lucky it's Sunday. Tomorrow   20

you'll get a taste of how things run
around here. First horn at day-clean!

(JONES *exits. There is a moment's awkward silence as* AUGUSTUS *rubs his ankles where the chains have chafed. He looks up, calmly surveying the two groups.*)

SCIPIO: Welcome, stranger, welcome.
They call me Scipio.
25   What do you go by?
AUGUSTUS: Augustus.
SCIPIO (*Stretching the name out, trying to make it fit his tongue*): Au-gus-tus?
Ain't never heard that one before.
What kind of name is that?
30   AUGUSTUS: The name of a king.

(*Uneasy silence.*)

PHEBE: Don't pay Scipio no mind.
He's always joking.
I'm Phebe. And this is Alexander.

(ALEXANDER *nods, warily.*)

Alexander been here longer than anyone, I reckon.
35   ALEXANDER: How do.

(SCYLLA *enters with a water gourd and watches the introductions with a hard eye.*
PHEBE *rushes to introduce them.*)

PHEBE: And this here's Scylla. Scylla,
he's the new one, go by the name of—
AUGUSTUS: Augustus Newcastle.
SCYLLA: Newcastle. Is that your captain's name?
40   AUGUSTUS: Scylla was the rock,
Charybdis the whirlpool,
that pulled the sailors down.

(*General astonishment.*)

PHEBE: Now this little girl—

(*Pushes* DIANA *over to* AUGUSTUS.)

was born and raised
45   right here on this plantation.
AUGUSTUS: What's your name, child?
DIANA (*Shyly*): Diana.
AUGUSTUS: My, my. The sun and the moon
all in one morning!

(*The* SLAVES *look bewildered. He laughs softly.*)

50   Don't mind me. I'm just glad to meet you all.

(*Some* SLAVES *take up their chant again.* AUGUSTUS *walks upstage and stands looking into the distance. Although they are curious, the other* SLAVES *let him be. Only* DIANA *stares after him.*)

PHEBE: Come on, Scipio, give us a story.
SCIPIO: You always wanting a story!
    How many stories you think I got?
PHEBE: I think you grow them in your sleep.
SCIPIO: Well, I ain't got a story this time.   55
PHEBE: Aw, Scipio! You dog!
SCIPIO: But I got a song:

(*Accompanies himself on a handmade string instrument while his friends clap, pat their bodies, etc.*)

    The possum said, don't hurt me,
    I'm harmless if you please!
    The nigger said, I'm harmless, too,   60
    And got down on his knees.

    The possum cocked his little head
    And contemplated long;
    You're running just like me, he said
    And joined into the song.   65

    Old Mr Coon just happened by
    Where the two sang merrily;
    I don't trust you, cried Mr. Coon,
    Why, you just as black as me!

    You're just as black as me, Coon said,   70
    but your tail ain't quite so long!
    The Mr Coon ran in the woods
    And wouldn't join their song.

(*Laughter.* DIANA *walks over to* AUGUSTUS.)

DIANA: What you looking at?
AUGUSTUS: Just looking.   75
DIANA: Ain't nothing out there but the swamp.
AUGUSTUS: Do you know what's beyond that swamp?
DIANA: What?
AUGUSTUS: The world.
PHEBE (*To* SCIPIO): Is that all?   80
SCIPIO: No, there's more:

(*Singing.*)

    The nigger wrapped his fingers
    Around the possum's throat.
    The possum didn't have the time
    To sing another note.   85

That night the nigger had himself
A pot of possum stew.
That harmless meat is just the thing
To warm your innards through!

90 DIANA: What did you mean by
the sun and the moon?
AUGUSTUS: Beg pardon?
DIANA: The sun and the moon—you asked
my name and then you said you had
95 the sun and the moon all in one day.
AUGUSTUS: You're a curious one, aren't you?
DIANA: Uh-huh.
AUGUSTUS: Well—a long time ago there were
gods to look after the earth and the sky.
100 Phoebus was the god of the sun;
your friend's name is Phebe.
And your name stood for the moon.
People wrote poems to Diana,
goddess of the moon.
105 DIANA: What's poems?
AUGUSTUS: A poem is . . .

(*Looking over at* SCIPIO.)

. . . a song without music.

(*Looks off towards the swamp.*)

Who's that old man?
DIANA: Phebe, Hector's coming up from the swamp!
110 PHEBE: Don't fret, chile.
Hector talk kind of crazy sometimes,
but he don't hurt nobody.
AUGUSTUS: His name is Hector?
PHEBE: Yeah. Massa Jennings give it to him
115 straight off the boat. He used to talk
African—but he forgot most of it.
AUGUSTUS: What does he do in the swamp?
PHEBE (*Catching a warning look from* SCYLLA): He lives there.
AUGUSTUS: Hector, mighty warrior,
120 abandoned by the gods.
DIANA: You know a lot of things.
AUGUSTUS: Nothing you couldn't learn
if you had the chance.

(*Enter* HECTOR, *now middle-aged, dressed in muddy rags. He carries a dead snake in a net and looks around with wild, piercing eyes, then wanders up to* DIANA.)

HECTOR (*Tenderly*): Eshu Elewa ogo gbogbo!

(DIANA *shrinks back.* HECTOR *taps* AUGUSTUS *on the shoulder, holding out the net.*)

I catch snakes: big ones, little ones.   125
I'm going to catch all the snakes in the swamp.
AUGUSTUS: I don't know much about snakes,
     my friend.
HECTOR: I'm gonna catch all the snakes in the swamp!
They grow and grow, so many of them.   130
But I'll kill them! I'll kill them all!
SCYLLA: Shh, Hector!
Don't let the snakes hear!

(*She puts her arm around* HECTOR *and pats him gently on the back, all the while staring at* AUGUSTUS, *as the lights dim and go out.*)

SCENE 4

SCYLLA's *cabin and the area outside of the slave cabins.*

Night. SCYLLA *sits in her cabin behind a crude table strewn with an assortment of bones, twisted roots, beads, and dried corncobs. Three candles light up her face from below.* AUGUSTUS, *in ankle chains, squats outside the slave cabins. In the distance can be heard the rhythmic ecstasy of the Sunday night "shout."* PHEBE *at the door with a small cloth bundle. She looks behind her.*

SCYLLA: Come in, child. Sit.

(PHEBE *sits.*)

I know your heart, Phebe.
You have made the spirits angry!
PHEBE: I never meant no harm—
SCYLLA: Shh!   5

(*Picks out a forked branch and arranges the candles in a half-circle around the branch.*)

The body moves through the world.

(*Places a round white stone in the fork of the branch.*)

The mind rests in the body.

(*Sprinkles green powder from a vial onto branch and stone.*)

The soul is bright
as a jewel, lighter than air.

(*Blows the powder away; the candles flare,* PHEBE *coughs.*)

There is a curse on the land.   10
The net draws closer.
What have you brought?

PHEBE: Here!

(*Shoves her bundle across the table.* SCYLLA *pulls out a pink ribbon and drapes it over the branch.*)

SCYLLA: "Eshu Elewa ogo gbogbo . . .

(*Sprinkling powder on the first candle.*)

15   . . . oki kosi eyo!"

(*The candle flares and goes out.*)

You have tried to make the earth
give up her dead.
PHEBE: Oh!
SCYLLA (*Pulling out a shell necklace, draping it over the branch*): "Kosi eyo,
20   kosi iku . . .

(*Sprinkling powder on the second candle.*)

. . . kosi ano!"

(*The second candle goes out.*)

PHEBE: Have mercy . . .
SCYLLA: You have tried to snatch words
back from the air. The wind is angry.
25   It will take more than these—

(*Indicating* PHEBE'*s offerings.*)

to satisfy him.
PHEBE (*Pulls a white handkerchief out of her pocket*):
Here's . . . a hankie from my mama.
There's a little lace on it—see?

(SCYLLA *snatches the handkerchief, places it on the branch and repeats the procedure with powder and incantation.*)

SCYLLA: "Ni oru ko mi gbogbo
30   omonile fu kuikuo
modupue—
baba mi Elewa!"

(*The third candle flickers but stays lit.*)

Ah!
PHEBE: What is it?
35 SCYLLA: Are you prepared to hear
what the spirits have to say?
PHEBE (*Gathering courage*): If there's something I need to know,
I want to know it.
SCYLLA: I give you two warnings.
40   One: guard your footsteps;

they are your mark on the earth.
If a sharp stone or piece of glass
falls into the path you have walked,
you will go lame.
Two: guard your breath;   45
do not throw with words.
Whenever the wind blows,
if your mouth is open,
your soul could be snatched away.
That is all.   50
PHEBE: Scylla . . .
SCYLLA: Go now!

(SCYLLA *mutters over the candles as* PHEBE *hurries off, shuffling her feet to blur her
footprints as she flees. On the way she passes* AUGUSTUS. *In the distance the* SLAVES
can be heard humming during the "shout.")

AUGUSTUS: Evening.
PHEBE (*Caught in the act of obliterating her steps; embarrassed*): Evening.
AUGUSTUS: Back from the shout?   55
PHEBE (*Trying not to speak*): Uh-uh.
AUGUSTUS: What's your hurry? Why don't
     you keep me company for a spell?
     Unless you're scared of me, that is.
PHEBE: Scared of you? Why should   60
     I be scared of you?
AUGUSTUS: I can't think of a reason in the world.
     Come on, rest yourself.

(PHEBE *sits down beside him carefully.*)

AUGUSTUS: Sure is a fine night.

(PHEBE *nods.*)

     You're trembling.   65
PHEBE: I am?

(*Claps her hand over her mouth.*)

AUGUSTUS: And I don't believe
     it's entirely my doing.

(*He says this in a mildly flirtatious manner, then looks off, unaware of the effect this has
on* PHEBE, *who has stopped thinking about* SCYLLA *and is now acutely aware of*
AUGUSTUS *as a man.* AUGUSTUS *continues speaking, preoccupied once again with his
hatred.*)

Fear! Fear eats out the heart.
It'll cause kings and field niggers alike   70
to crawl in their own piss. Listen
to them sing!

What kind of god preaches such misery?

(*Gesturing in the direction of the "shout."*)

       White-fearing niggers.
75   Death-fearing slaves.
PHEBE: Ain't you ever scared?
AUGUSTUS: Of what? White folks?
       They're more afraid of me. Pain?
       Every whipping's got to come to an end.
80 PHEBE: I heard you've been whipped
       so many times, they lost count.
AUGUSTUS: They think they can beat me to my senses.
       Then they look into my eyes
       and see I'm not afraid.
85 PHEBE: It'd be something, not to be afraid.
AUGUSTUS: You have to have a purpose.
       Something bigger than anything
       they can do to you.
PHEBE (*Suppressing a shudder*): And ain't nobody ever tried to kill you?
90 AUGUSTUS: Oh, yes. First time,
       I was hardly alive.
       They ripped me from my mother
       the night I was born
       and threw me out like trash.
95   I didn't walk until I was three.
PHEBE: Lord have mercy.
AUGUSTUS: Mercy had nothing to do with it!
       Missy couldn't stand the sight of me.
       Just look at me! It's an old story.

100   You've stopped trembling.
       Now why don't you tell me
       what made you quake that way
       in the first place?

(PHEBE *shakes her head.*)

       Conjuration, I imagine?
105   Mumble-jumble from that hateful woman.
PHEBE: Her name's Scylla.
AUGUSTUS: Women like her, hah!
       They get a chill one morning,
       hear an owl or two, and snap!—
110   they've received their "powers"!
       Then they collect a few old bones,
       dry some herbs, and they're in business.
PHEBE: She told me to watch my footsteps—
AUGUSTUS: —or you'd fall lame.

PHEBE: And to keep my mouth shut   115
　　　when the wind blowed—
AUGUSTUS: —or else the wind spirit
　　　would steal your soul.
PHEBE: How'd you know?
AUGUSTUS: You think she's the only conjure-woman   120
　　　in the world? Why, your Scylla's a baby
　　　compared to the voodoo chiefs in the islands.
　　　They can kill you with a puff of smoke
　　　from their pipes—if you believe in them.
　　　Take me: I've been cursed enough times   125
　　　to bring down a whole fleet of ships
　　　around me—but here I sit, high and dry.
　　　So I guess they must be saving me
　　　for something special.

(PHEBE *looks at* AUGUSTUS *in wonder; the lights dim as the other* SLAVES *slowly come on stage, singing as they take their places in the fields. The song sung during the "shout" has modulated into a percussive piece with no words—clapping, sighs, whispered exclamations and grunts punctuate what becomes a work song.*)

SLAVES: No way out, gotta keep on—   130
　　　No way but to see it through.
NARRATOR: Don't sass, don't fight!
　　　Lay low, grin bright!
NARRATOR/SLAVES: No way but to see it through.

SCENE 5

The cotton fields. The light brightens: high noon. JONES *enters, looks at the sun and cracks his whip as he calls out.*

JONES: Noon!

(*He exits, wiping his brow with a huge handkerchief. The* SLAVES *groan and sigh as they settle down with their provisions—cornpone and salt pork and gourds of water.*)

ALEXANDER (*Making sure that* JONES *is out of earshot*): I swear on all my years
　　　there's nothing I hate so much as cotton.
　　　Picking, toting, weighing, tramping:
　　　the work keeps coming.   5
SCIPIO: No end in sight, and that's the truth!

(*Leans back, hands under head.*)

Now what I'd fancy is a life at sea.
Sun and sky and blue water,
with just a sip of rum
every once in a while.   10
You been to sea, Augustus.

What's it like?

AUGUSTUS: It ain't the easy life.

SCIPIO: But what's it like, man?

15 The closest I been to the sea
was when the cotton gin came in
to Charleston port. All those fine
flapping sails and tall masts,
cotton bales stacked to heaven . . .

20 Did you visit lots of strange places?

AUGUSTUS: We sailed the West Indies route.
Stocked up rum, tobacco, beads—

SCYLLA (*Scathingly*): —and traded them for slaves.
Did you have to ride cargo?

25 AUGUSTUS (*With a sharp look, sarcastically*): Cap'n Newcastle was a generous master.

(*Resuming his story.*)

But those ports! Sand so white,
from far off it looked like
spilled cream. Palm trees taller
than our masts, loaded with coconuts.

30 DIANA: What's a coconut?

AUGUSTUS: It's a big brown gourd
with hair on it like a dog,
and when you break it open
sweet milk pours out.

35 DIANA: What does it taste like?

AUGUSTUS: It tastes like . . .
just coconut. There's nothing like it.

SCYLLA: Your stories stir up trouble,
young man.

(PHEBE *moves as if to stop him; he motions her back.*)

40 AUGUSTUS: Seems you're the only one
who's riled up, Scylla.

SCYLLA: You're what we call an uppity nigger.
And uppity niggers always trip themselves up.

AUGUSTUS: Are you going to put a curse on me, too,

45 Scylla? Cross your eyes
and wave a few roots in the air
until I fall on my knees?

SCYLLA: No need to curse you;
you have been cursed already.

50 AUGUSTUS: You feed on ignorance
and call it magic. What kind of prophet
works against her own people?

(*The* SLAVES *murmur.* SCYLLA *stands up.*)

SCYLLA: Oh, you may dance now,
    but you will fall.
    The evil inside you
    will cut you down to your knees,   *55*
    and you will crawl—crawl in front of us all!

(Lights dim, then grow mottled and swamp-green as all exit.)

SCENE 6

The swamp. Lights remain mottled and swamp-green. Night sounds filter in as
HECTOR *enters.*

HECTOR: Easy, easy: don't tell the cook
    the meat's gone bad.

(Slashes at the underbrush.)

We got to cut it out.
Ya! Ya!

(Hacks in rhythm for a moment.)

I can smell it. Pah!   *5*

(Sniffs, then peers.)

But there's a rose in the gravy, oh yes—
a rose shining through the mists, a red smell.
Red and mean.

But how sweet she smelled!
Cottons and flowers.   *10*
And lemons that bite back
when you touch them to the tongue.

Shh! Don't tell the cook.
Black folks fiddle, the white folks stare.

(There is a bird call; HECTOR *conceals himself.* AUGUSTUS *enters; he appears to be*
following the sound. He gives out a matching call, then bursts into a clearing in the
swamp where a group of black men sit in a circle around a small fire, chanting softly. The
LEADER *of the group rises.)*

LEADER: There you are!   *15*
    We've called two nights.
AUGUSTUS: Who are you?
LEADER: Patience, Augustus Newcastle.
    Oh yes, we know all about you.
AUGUSTUS: What do you want?   *20*
LEADER: Your courage has been a beacon—
CONSPIRATORS: Amen! Selah!

(*The* CONSPIRATORS *surround the* LEADER; *they react to his words in a call-and-response fashion; their movements are vaguely ritualistic and creepy, as if they were under a spell; this effect can be enhanced with dance and pantomime.* AUGUSTUS *stands still as the* CONSPIRATORS *swarm around him, occasionally trying to pull him among them.*)

LEADER: —and we need men willing to fight
for freedom! Tell me, Augustus Newcastle:
25 are you prepared to sign your name
with the revolutionary forces?
AUGUSTUS: First tell me who you are.
LEADER: So cautious? We expected a bit more daring
from someone of your reputation.
30 AUGUSTUS: I am many things, but I'm not a fool.
LEADER (*Laughs*): Shall we show him, brothers?
CONSPIRATORS: Selah!
LEADER: Each of us has been called forth
as a warrior of righteousness.
35 Each wandered in darkness
until he found the light of brotherhood!
Take young Benjamin Skeene:

(BENJAMIN *squares his shoulders as he steps forward; he is a trim young man who, judging from his clothes, must be either a house slave or a freeman.*)

As a skilled carpenter, he enjoys
a fair amount of freedom.
40 BENJAMIN: The boss man's glad
I can make his deliveries.
LEADER: So we've arranged a few
deposits of our own.
Benjamin, can you find a way
45 to fasten this blade to a pole?
BENJAMIN: Easy.
LEADER: Every man who can wield a stick
shall have a bayonet!
CONSPIRATORS: Selah!
50 LEADER: A few were more reluctant . . .
or shall I say cautious?
Henry Blake, for instance:

(HENRY, *a dark, middle-aged man, steps forward hesitantly.*)

Fear had made him grateful
for every crumb his master dropped him.

(*The two act out the following exchange.*)

55 HENRY: I don't want no part of this!
LEADER: You followed the sign;

you have been called!

HENRY: Any fool knows a mockingbird
    when he hears one—and that
    weren't no mockingbird!   60

LEADER (*Threatening*): Are you prepared to slay
    our oppressors, male and female,
    when it is deemed time, according
    to the plans of insurrection drawn up
    and approved by members present?   65

HENRY: I'm against the white man
    much as all of you—but murder?
    "Thou shalt not kill," saith the
    Commandments.

LEADER: Who made your master?   70

HENRY: God.

LEADER: And who made you?

HENRY: God.

LEADER: Then aren't you as good as your master
    if God made you both?   75

HENRY: I'm not a vengeful man.

LEADER: But our Lord is a vengeful God.
    "Whoever steals a man," He says,
    "whether he sells him or
    is found in possession of him,   80
    shall be put to death."

    Who is not with us
    is against us.
    You answered the call.
    If you turn back now . . .   85

(HENRY *slowly lifts his head, squares his shoulders, and remains frozen in the spotlight while the* LEADER *speaks to* AUGUSTUS.)

LEADER: He was brought to reason.

CONSPIRATORS: Selah.

LEADER: So the one becomes many
    and the many, one.
    Hence our password: 90
    "May Fate be with you—

CONSPIRATORS: And with us all!"

AUGUSTUS: Now I see who you are.

LEADER: Augustus Newcastle: are you prepared
    to slay our oppressors,   95
    male and female,
    when it is deemed time, according
    to the plans of insurrection
    drawn up and approved by members present?

100   AUGUSTUS: I am.
LEADER: Enter your name in the Book of Redemption!

(AUGUSTUS *signs the book*.)

CONSPIRATORS: Selah! Selah!
AUGUSTUS: Tell me what to do.
LEADER: You'll need a second-in-command.
105   Report your choice to us;
           we will send out the sign.

(*Turning to the group*.)

           My brothers, it is time to be free!
           Maps are being prepared
           of the city and its surroundings
110   along with the chief points of attack.
           Bullets wait in kegs under the dock.
           Destiny calls!
CONSPIRATORS: Amen!
LEADER: There are barrels of gun powder
115   stacked in a cave outside Dawson's Plantation.
           Our Toby has been busy—

(CONSPIRATORS *nod and laugh in consent*.)

           but he cannot risk further expeditions.
           Henry Blake!

(HENRY *steps forward*.)

           Your owner praised you in the marketplace
120   as the most trustworthy nigger
           he ever had the fortune of owning.
           Now it is up to you
           to put your master's trust to the test.

(HENRY *bows his head in assent, steps back into the group*.)

           Destiny calls us! The reckoning is nigh!
125   But remember: trust no-one.
           All those who are not with us
           are against us, blacks as well
           as whites. Oh, do not falter!
           Bolster your heart with the memory
130   of the atrocities committed upon your mothers.
           Gird your loins with vengeance,
           strap on the shining sword of freedom!
CONSPIRATORS: Selah!
LEADER: Brothers, are you with me?
135   CONSPIRATORS: Right behind you!
LEADER: Then nothing can stop us now!

AUGUSTUS (*Blurting out*): My orders! What are my orders?
LEADER (*A little taken aback, but decides on the role of the amused patriarch*):
    Patience, my son! Patience and cunning.
    Sow discontent among your brethren,
    inspire them to fury.   140
AUGUSTUS: I can do more. Read maps, write passes—
LEADER: That is all for now.
    Is that clear?

    (*Strained silence; the* LEADER *speaks reassuringly.*)

    You will recognize the signal.

    (*The* CONSPIRATORS *begin humming "Steal Away."*)

LEADER: Go to your people and test their minds;   145
    so when the fires of redemption
    lick the skies of Charleston,
    they will rise up, up—
    a mighty army
    marching into battle!   150
CONSPIRATORS: Steal away, steal away,
    Steal away to Jesus!
    Steal away, steal away home,
    I ain't got long to stay here.

    (*The* CONSPIRATORS *continue singing as they exchange farewells and slip off.*
    HECTOR *appears at the edge of the undergrowth, a dead snake in his outstretched*
    arms.)

    (*Blackout.*)

SCENE 7

    The cotton fields.

NARRATOR: A sniff of freedom's all it takes
    to feel history's sting;
    there's danger by-and-by
    when the slaves won't sing.

    (JONES *supervises the picking, which transpires without singing; the silence is eerie.*
    JONES' *appearance is slovenly, as if he's already been drinking.*)

JONES: Move it, nigger! Faster!   5
    What you glaring at? Faster!

    (*The* SLAVES *continue picking at the same rate.* JONES *looks at the sun, then cracks his*
    whip.)

    Aw, the hell with ya! Noon!

(*He stumbles offstage. The* SLAVES *divide into two groups: some hum spirituals while the others gather around* AUGUSTUS.)

SCIPIO: Come on, Augustus, what else?

AUGUSTUS: Did you know there are slaves
10   who have set themselves free?

SCIPIO (*Almost afraid to ask*): How'd they do that?

AUGUSTUS: Santo Domingo, San Domingue, Hispaniola—
         three names for an island
         rising like a fortress
15   from the waters of the Caribbean.
         An island of sun and forest,
         wild fruit and mosquitoes—
         and slaves, many slaves—half a million.
         Slaves to chop sugar, slaves
20   to pick coffee beans, slaves to do
         their French masters' every bidding.

         Then one summer, news came
         from the old country: Revolution!
         Plantation owners broke into a sweat;
25   their slaves served cool drinks
         while the masters rocked on their verandas,
         discussing each outrage:
         people marching against the king,
         crowds pouring into the streets,
30   shouting three words:
         Liberté!

SLAVES: We shall be free!

AUGUSTUS: *Égalité!*

SLAVES: Master and slave.

35 AUGUSTUS: *Fraternité!*

SLAVES: Brothers and sisters!

AUGUSTUS: *Liberté, Égalité, Fraternité*—three words
         were all the island masters talked about
         that summer, while their slaves
40   served carefully and listened.

SLAVES: *Liberté, Égalité, Fraternité!*

(*During the following speech, a smouldering growl among the* SLAVES *grows louder and louder, until it explodes in a shout.*)

AUGUSTUS: Black men meeting in the forest:
         Eight days, they whispered,
         and we'll be free. For eight days
45   bonfires flashed in the hills:
         Equality. For eight days
         tom-toms spoke in the mountains:
         Liberty. For eight days

the tom-toms sang: Brothers and sisters.
And on the eighth day, swift as lightning,   50
the slaves attacked.

SLAVES: Yah!

(AMALIA *enters, unseen, and stands listening.*)

AUGUSTUS: They came down the mountains
to the sound of tambourines and conch shells.
With torches they swept onto the plantations,   55
with the long harvest knives
they chopped white men down
like sugar cane. For three weeks
the flames raged; then the sun
broke through the smoke and shone   60
upon a new nation, a black nation—
Haiti!

SLAVES: Haiti!

AUGUSTUS (*Looking intently at the faces around him*): Now do you see
why they've kept this from us,   65
brothers and sisters?

AMALIA: A lovely speech.

(*The* SLAVES *are horrified.* AUGUSTUS *stands impassive.*)

I see you're a poet
as well as a rebel.

(JONES *rushes in.*)

JONES: Anything wrong, Miss Jennings?   70

AMALIA: Not a thing, Jones. Just passing
the time of day with my happy flock—
which is more than I see you doing.

JONES: But it's noon, Miss Jennings!
They need nourishment   75
if we're going to get this crop in.

AMALIA: It appears they've been getting
a different sort of sustenance.

JONES (*Uncomprehending*): Beg pardon, Ma'am?

AMALIA (*Impatient with* JONES): See that they work an extra hour tonight.   80
I don't care if they have to pick by moonlight!

(*To* AUGUSTUS.)

As for you: I'll see you
up at the house. Come at sunset—
the view over the fields
is most enchanting then.   85

(*She strides off. Blackout.*)

SCENE 8

The big house, LOUIS' *study and the parlor.*

Twilight filters through the curtains; the frogs have started up in the swamp.

LOUIS *paces back and forth in his room, holding a chart; he stops to stare at it for a moment, then waves it in disgust and paces once more.*

LOUIS: Something's out there: I can feel it!
    What a discovery it would be.
    But no—

(*Grabs his brandy.*)

5   No new coin shines
    for Louis LaFarge
    among the stars!

(*He stops at the window and stares out.*)

(AMALIA *sits in the parlor reading, a decanter of sherry and a tea service on the table next to the sofa. The evening song of the* SLAVES *floats in from the fields—a plaintive air with a compelling affirmation of life, a strange melody with no distinct beat or tune.* TICEY, *the old house slave, enters.*)

TICEY: Miss Amalia?
AMALIA (*Without turning*): Yes?
TICEY: That new slave, Ma'am—
10   he's standing at the front porch!
AMALIA (*Amused*): The front porch? Well, show him in, Ticey!

(TICEY *exits;* AMALIA *rises and goes to the window. She is looking out toward the fields when* AUGUSTUS *appears in the doorway. Although she knows he is there, she does not turn around.*)

AMALIA: What are they singing?
AUGUSTUS: No words you'd understand.
    No tune you'd recognise.
15 AMALIA: And how is it they all sing together?
AUGUSTUS: It's the sorrow songs.
    They don't need a psalm book.
AMALIA (*Resumes her imperious manner*): "Personal servant to Captain Newcastle
    of the schooner Victoria. Ports of call:
20   St Thomas, Tobago, St Croix,
    Martinique"—in other words,
    a slave ship.
AUGUSTUS: Yes.
AMALIA: And what did you learn
25   under your captain's tutelage?

AUGUSTUS: Reading. Writing. Figures.

AMALIA: What did you read?

AUGUSTUS: Milton. The Bible.
And the Tales of the Greeks.

AMALIA (*Thrusting the book she's been reading at him*):
See the blue ribbon sticking out?   30
You may start there.

(AUGUSTUS *turns the book over to read the title, then looks at her for a moment before returning it. She snatches the book.*)

AMALIA: Too difficult? No doubt you'd do better
with the Greek original—

(*Slyly.*)

but we are not that cultured a household.

(*Circling him.*)

I wondered could there be a nigger alive   35
smart as this one's claimed to be?
Of course, if there were, he might
be smart enough to pretend
he wasn't smart at all.

AUGUSTUS: No pretense. I've read that one already.   40
In my opinion, the Greeks
were a bit too predictable.

AMALIA: A slave has no opinion!

(*Regaining her composure.*)

I could have you flogged to your bones
for what you did today.   45

AUGUSTUS: Why didn't you?

(*The* SLAVES *stop singing.*)

AMALIA: Daddy said a master knows his slaves
better than they know themselves.
And he never flogged a slave—
he said it was a poor businessman   50
who damaged his own merchandise.

AUGUSTUS (*Sarcastically*): An enlightened man, your father.

AMALIA: He let me run wild until
it was time to put on crinolines.
My playmates were sent to the fields,   55
and I was sent to the parlor with needlework—
a scented, dutiful daughter.

AUGUSTUS: Most men find intelligence troubling
in a woman—even fathers.

AMALIA: Then, off I went to finishing school: Miss Peeters'   60

Academy for Elocution and Deportment!
"The art of conversation," she used to say—
please, sit down!—"is to make
the passing of time agreeable."

(*Arranging her dress as she sits on the sofa.*)

65   "suitable subjects are—"
Sit down, I said!

(*Softer, but with an edge.*)

One does not conduct conversation
while standing.

(*She indicates a chair, upholstered in champagne-colored tufted damask.* AUGUSTUS *moves toward it but swiftly and gracefully drops cross-legged to the floor, daringly close to* AMALIA's *slippered feet. She starts to pull away—then slowly extends her feet again.*)

"Suitable subjects for
70   genteel conversation are:

(*Ticking them off on her fingers.*)

"Nature. Travel. History.
And above all, culture—
painting, music, and books."

Well, we're done with books!
75   Tell me, Mr Newcastle—
was the weather in the Indies
very different from here?
AUGUSTUS: Warmer.
AMALIA: Is that all?
80   AUGUSTUS: There was always a breeze.
AMALIA: And an abundance of exotic
foods, I'm sure.
AUGUSTUS: We had our share of papaya.

(*The slaves start up a new song, more African in rhythm and harmonies.*)

AMALIA: Imagine that. Subject number two:
85   Travel. So many ports!

(*Shaking her head charmingly.*)

Did Captain Newcastle
allow you to go ashore
at St Thomas, Tobago, Martinique?
AUGUSTUS (*On guard*): No.
90   AMALIA: Charleston has welcomed a fair share
of immigrants to her shores.

(*Laughs delicately.*)

There was that Haiti business around the time
I was born. Over five hundred French plantation owners
fled here. The whole city was in panic.
Why, my dear husband—hear him pacing   95
up there, wearing out the floorboards?—
little Louis showed up in Charleston harbor
that year, with his blue blood *maman* and *papa*.
Liberté, Égalité, Fraternité!

(*Looking directly at* AUGUSTUS.)

It was a brilliant revolution.   100
I've often wondered why our niggers
don't revolt. I've said to myself:
"Amalia, if you had been a slave,
you most certainly would have plotted
an insurrection by now."   105

(*Turns away from* AUGUSTUS.)

But we say all sorts of things
to ourselves, don't we?
There's no telling what we'd do
if the moment were there for the taking.

(*Lights up on* LOUIS, *still staring out the window*.)

LOUIS: You can't hide forever.   110
There's a hole in the heavens,
and you're throbbing right behind it.

(*Whispers.*)

I can feel you.
AMALIA: Have you ever heard of the *Amistad*?
AUGUSTUS: Why?   115
AMALIA: The *Amistad*: a slave ship.
Three days off the port of Principe
the Africans freed themselves
and attacked with machetes and harpoons.
Cinque, their leader, spared two sailors   120
to steer them back to Africa.
But Cinque was unfamiliar with the stars
in our hemisphere. Each morning
he set course east by the sun;
each night the sailors turned the ship   125
and steered west—until they managed
to land on our coast and deliver
Cinque and his followers to execution.
AUGUSTUS: A bit of a storybook ending, isn't it?
AMALIA: What's that supposed to mean?   130

AUGUSTUS: It's just so perfect a lesson.
AMALIA: You don't believe me?
    It was in the newspapers.

    (*Significantly.*)

135   You followed your precious captain
    everywhere; you were there when
    he loaded slave cargo into the hold
    or plotted a new course.
    What an admirable science, navigation!
    It must be terribly complicated,
140   even for you.
AUGUSTUS (*Getting up from the floor*): Now I have a story for you.
    Once there was a preacher slave
    went by the name of Isaac.
    When God called him
145   he was a boy, out hunting rice birds.
    Killing rice birds is easy—
    just pinch off their heads.

    (*Indicating the sherry.*)

    May I?

    (AMALIA *flinches, nods. He pours the sherry expertly.*)

    But one day, halfway up the tree
150   where a nest of babies chirped,
    a voice called out: "Don't do it, Isaac."
    It was an angel, shining
    in the crook of a branch.
    Massa let him preach.
155   What harm could it do?

    (*Sitting down in the damask chair.*)

    Then a slave uprising in Virginia
    had all the white folks
    watching their own niggers
    for signs of treachery.
160   No more prayer meetings, Isaac!
    But God would not wait,
    so Isaac kept on preaching
    at night, in the woods.

    Of course he was caught.
165   Three of his congregation
    were shot on the spot, three others branded
    and their feet pierced.
    But what to do about Isaac,

gentle Isaac who had turned traitor?

AMALIA: Is there a point to this?   170

AUGUSTUS: I'm just passing the time of evening
    with . . . conversation.

(*Upstairs,* LOUIS *positions his telescope at the window and searches the heavens.*)

LOUIS: There it is . . . no, wait!
    Gone.

(*Shakes his head in despair.*)

Sometimes I catch   175
a glimmer, a hot blue flash—
then it disappears.
Show yourself, demon!

(*In the parlor,* AUGUSTUS *takes a sip of sherry and continues.*)

AUGUSTUS: First they flogged him. Then
    they pickled the wounds with salt water,   180
    and when they were nearly healed,
    he was flogged again, and the wounds
    pickled again, and on and on for weeks
    while Massa sold off Isaac's children
    one by one. They took him to see   185
    his wife on the auction block,
    baby at her breast.
    A week later it was his turn.
    His back had finally healed;
    but as his new owner led him   190
    from the auction block,
    Isaac dropped down dead.

(*Pause; more to himself than to* AMALIA.)

They couldn't break his spirit,
so they broke his heart.

(*They stare at each other for a moment; then* AMALIA *rises and walks to the window. It has gotten dark outside.*)

AMALIA: They're still singing.   19[ ]
    How can they have songs left?

AUGUSTUS (*Joining her at the window*): As many songs as sorrows.

AMALIA: And you, Augustus? Were you ever happy?

AUGUSTUS: Happy? No.

AMALIA: Never? Not even on the ship   20[ ]
    with the whole sea around you?

AUGUSTUS: I was a boy. I felt lucky, not happy.

AMALIA: I was happy once.
    I traded it for luck.

205   AUGUSTUS: Luck's a dangerous master.
      AMALIA: Half my life I spent dreaming,
            the other half burying dreams.

            (*Bitter laugh, turns to* AUGUSTUS.)

            Funny, isn't it?
      AUGUSTUS (*Turns away from her with difficulty, stares out the window*):
            One soft spring night
210   when the pear blossoms
            cast their pale faces
            on the darker face of the earth,
            Massa stood up from the porch swing
            and said to himself, "I think
215   I'll make me another bright-eyed pickaninny."
            Then he stretched and headed
            for my mother's cabin. And now—
            that pickaninny, who started out
            no more than the twinkle in a white man's eye
220   and the shame between his mama's legs—
            now he stands in the parlor of
            another massa, entertaining the pretty mistress
            with stories of whippings and heartbreak.
      AMALIA (*Half to herself*): Pretty? Am I pretty?
225   AUGUSTUS (*Answers in spite of himself*): You can put a rose in a vase
            with a bunch of other flowers;
            but when you walk into the room
            the rose is the only thing you see.

            (AMALIA *touches his wrist, then traces the vein up his arm, as if remembering.*)

      AMALIA: Imagine! A life without even
230   a smidgen of happiness . . .
      AUGUSTUS (*Wrestling with desire*): I'm not one of your dreams.
      AMALIA: No? Perhaps not. What a pity.

            (*She touches his cheek; he holds her hand there. They lean towards each other slowly, as
            the* SLAVES' *sorrow song surges—but before their lips touch, there is a blackout.*)

ACT TWO
SCENE 1

Dream sequence.

Dimly lit, the light rather blue. Each group is in its appointed "place" on stage—
AMALIA *in her parlour with* TICEY *standing impassively in the background;* LOUIS
above, in his study; most SLAVES *going about their chores;* SCYLLA *isolated, with her
herbs and potions. In the swamp,* HECTOR *searches for snakes; the* CONSPIRATORS
huddle, occasionally lifting a fist into the circle. AUGUSTUS *stands front and centre, back*

to the audience, gazing at AMALIA. *Mostly silhouettes are seen, except when a single voice rises out of the chanting, which will grow to cacophony at the end of the sequence.*

SLAVES: They have bowed our heads,
    they have bent our backs.
    Mercy, mercy,
    Lord above, mercy.
AMALIA: I slept, but my heart was awake.
    How beautiful he is!
SLAVES: Lord have mercy.
    They have bowed our heads . . .
SCYLLA: There's a curse on the land.
    The net draws closer.
HECTOR: Under rocks, 'twixt reeds and roots . . .
SLAVES: They have bent our backs,
    they have snatched our songs . . .
AUGUSTUS (*Singing*): Sometimes I feel like a motherless child . . .
SLAVES (*Joining in*): A motherless child, a motherless child,
    sometimes I feel like a motherless child—

    (*Continue humming through most of the scene.*)

LOUIS (*In a scientific voice, detached, as if reciting*):
    Every night at the same hour, each star appears
    slightly to the west of its previous position.
    Scientists calculate that the 12 houses of the zodiac
    have shifted so radically since ancient times,
    their relation to each other
    may now signify completely different portents.
HECTOR: So many, so many.
SLAVES (*Singing*): A long way from home.
AUGUSTUS: One soft night, Massa stood up—
CONSPIRATORS: Selah.
AUGUSTUS: —and laughed to himself.
CONSPIRATORS: It is time.
SCYLLA: The net draws tighter.
CONSPIRATORS: Selah!
AUGUSTUS: One darkening evening, I stood up—

    (SLAVES *humming,* CONSPIRATORS *chanting "Selah" in a barely audible whisper.*)

    —and she was mine,
    mine all night, until
    the day breathed fire
    and the shadows fled.
AMALIA: Look, how beautiful he is!
CONSPIRATORS: Rise up!
SLAVES (*Simultaneously*): Mercy, mercy.
AMALIA: His eyes, his brow, his cheeks—

5

10

15

20

25

30

35

40 CONSPIRATORS: Rise up!
AMALIA: —his lips . . .
AUGUSTUS: . . . until the day breathed fire . . .
HECTOR: Eshu Elewa . . . ogo . . . gbogbo.
SLAVES: They have bowed our heads,
45   they have bent our backs.
SCYLLA: Closer . . .

(PHEBE *dashes to center-stage, hands outstretched as if to hold back a flood.*)

PHEBE: Stop it! Stop!!!

(*Everyone freezes.*)

SCENE 2

The tableau remains.

PHEBE *drops her arms and moves slightly stage-left.* AUGUSTUS, *with his back still to the audience, backs downstage, towards the slave cabins, looking alternately at* AMALIA *and the* CONSPIRATORS *until the tableau disintegrates.* PHEBE *taps him on the shoulder, and he whirls around.*

PHEBE: Evenin'.
AUGUSTUS: Oh! Phebe. Evening.
PHEBE: You're trembling.
AUGUSTUS: I am?

(*Laughs.*)

5   Cold spell coming on, I imagine.
PHEBE: No, that's what you said to me!

(AUGUSTUS *looks at her, uncomprehending.*)

That time I was coming back from Scylla's,
scared to open my mouth, you said:
"What's your hurry?" And then you said,
10   "You're trembling," and I said, "I am?"
—just like you did now.
AUGUSTUS: Oh.
PHEBE: What's your hurry?
Heading up to the House again?
15 AUGUSTUS: I got a moment.
PHEBE: Sit yourself down, then.
Rest a spell.

(*They sit side by side;* PHEBE *embarrassed,* AUGUSTUS *nervous.*)

PHEBE: You sure be up there a long time.
At the Big House, I mean.

AUGUSTUS (*Tersely*): Missy's orders.   20
PHEBE: What else she have you doing?
AUGUSTUS: We practice the fine art of conversation.
PHEBE: Quit fooling!
AUGUSTUS: Oh, yes, we talk about everything—
  weather and the science of navigation,   25
  recent history and ancient literature.
PHEBE: What's that she-fox up to now?
AUGUSTUS: It's simple: she wants to tame me.
  And if I get better treatment
  than the rest of you,   30
  all my talk about Haiti
  won't hold much water.
PHEBE: So she think she can get us
  to fighting amongst ourselves!
AUGUSTUS: Seems plenty folks want things   35
  just the way they are.
  Alexander keeps his distance, lately.
PHEBE: Alexander's seen his share of sorrow.
  He just wants to live in peace.
AUGUSTUS: And die in peace?   40
PHEBE (*Not catching his drift*): I 'spect so. Who doesn't?
  Oh, that's right—
  you and Death gonna walk outta here
  hand and hand!

(PHEBE *laughs;* AUGUSTUS *is spooked.*)

  Alexander don't mean you no spite.   45
  And Scipio—Scipio say
  you his man, any time, any place!
  You shoulda seen him the other day,
  putting voodoo spells on the chickens!
  Then he pick up the milk bucket   50
  and pranced around, serving up
  revolution lemonade! Now there's
  a body need of some occupation!
AUGUSTUS (*Aside*): Maybe I can help him find it.
PHEBE: 'Course, you got Diana's heart.   55
  She thinks the sun and the moon
  set in your face.
AUGUSTUS: Then there's Scylla.
PHEBE: Hmmpf! Woman had me nearly crazy,
  clamping my mouth and wiping my
  footsteps   60
  so I ended up getting nowhere.
  As far as I'm concerned,
  Scylla can roll her eye and talk conjuration

65   till the summer go cold and the cotton pick itself!
AUGUSTUS: Now, that's the fire I saw!
PHEBE: Huh?
AUGUSTUS: The first time I saw you,
        I thought to myself:
70   "That's not the spirit of a slave.
        That's a pure flame."

(PHEBE *tucks her head.*)

PHEBE (*Flattered*): Go on.
AUGUSTUS: Tell me—how did you land
        on the Jennings Plantation?
75 PHEBE: I didn't land at all. I was borned here.
AUGUSTUS: So this is your home.
PHEBE: Much as any of us got
        a home on this earth.
AUGUSTUS: And your folks?
80 PHEBE: My father was sold before I was borned.
        Mama . . . it's a long story.
AUGUSTUS: I got time.

(PHEBE *stares down at the ground as if she's conjuring the memory out of the dust; then
she begins.*)

PHEBE: Mama worked in the kitchen until
        I was about five; that's when
85   fever broke out in the quarters.
        She used to set table scraps out
        for the field hands, and I
        stuck wildflowers in the baskets
        to pretty 'em up. Mama said
90   you never know what a flower can mean
        to somebody in misery.

        That fever tore through the cabins like wildfire.
        Massa Jennings said the field hands
        spread contamination and forbid them
95   to come up to the house, but
        Mama couldn't stand watching them
        just wasting away—so she started
        sneaking food to the quarters at night.

        Then the fever caught her too.
100   She couldn't hide it long.
        And Massa Jennings found out.

(*Gulps a deep breath for strength, reliving the scene.*)

        Mama started wailing right there at the stove.
        Hadn't she been a good servant?

Who stayed up three nights straight
to keep Massa's baby girl among the living   *105*
when her own mother done left this world?
Who did he call when the fire
needed lighting? Who mended the pinafores
Miss Amalia was forever snagging on bushes?

Mama dropped to her knees   *110*
and stretched out her arms along the floor.
She didn't have nowheres to go;
she'd always been at the Big House.
"Where am I gonna lay
my poor sick head?" she asked.   *115*

He stood there, staring
like she was a rut in the road,
and he was trying to figure out
how to get round it.

Then he straightened his waistcoat   *120*
and said: "You have put me and my child
in the path of mortal danger,
and you dare ask me what to do
with your nappy black head?"
He didn't even look at her—   *125*
just spoke off into the air
like she was already a ghost.

(*Woodenly.*)

She died soon after.

(AUGUSTUS *takes* PHEBE *into his arms.*)

AUGUSTUS (*A bit helplessly*): Lord have mercy.
PHEBE: Mercy had nothing to do with it.   *130*
    Ain't that what you said?
AUGUSTUS: Phebe, how far would you go
    to avenge your mother's death?
PHEBE: There you go again
    with your revolution talk.   *135*
AUGUSTUS: How far?
PHEBE: We ain't got no tom-toms
    like them slaves in Haiti!
AUGUSTUS: You don't need tom-toms.
    Just a bird call.   *140*

(PHEBE *looks at him, uncomprehending.* AUGUSTUS *stares off.*)

(*Stage dims to black: a single spot on the* NARRATOR.)

NARRATOR: What is it about him, girl—

the book-learning, his acquaintance with the world?
He can stand up to a glare,
but he doesn't know his heart.
145   Look around you, child: It's growing dark.

SCENE 3

The cotton house.

Almost sundown: JONES *is in the field supervising the bringing in of the cotton, which has been weighed and now must be tramped down in order to be stored. There is the steady beat of stomping feet throughout the scene.* PHEBE *and* AUGUSTUS *are outside the cotton house.*

PHEBE: Any news?
AUGUSTUS: I expect another signal
any day now. Then I'll know more.
PHEBE: What are they waiting for?
5   You reckon something's gone wrong—
AUGUSTUS (*Calming her*): Shh. They have their reasons.
Patience.

(PHEBE *catches him looking at the sky.*)

PHEBE (*With a mixture of jealousy and trepidation*): You better get on up there—
sun's almost touching.

(PHEBE *scoots inside the cotton house.* AUGUSTUS *studies the horizon, his expression inexplicable, then exits as* JONES *enters from the fields, urging along the next group bearing cotton. The* SLAVES *are sweaty and tired.* JONES *looks after* AUGUSTUS; *it's clear he's been told not to interfere.*)

10   JONES: Keep it moving!
Don't be looking at the sun;
you got a whole long while
before your day is over!

(JONES *exits. The scene opens to the inside of the cotton house;* SCIPIO *dumps the sacks of cotton onto the floor while the other* SLAVES *tramp it down. The dull thud of stomping feet punctuates the dialogue; changes in pace and rhythm signal changes in mood and tension. On his way for the next sack of cotton,* SCIPIO *looks out the one small window.*)

SCIPIO: There he goes.
15   ALEXANDER: Every evening, same time.
SCYLLA: It's the devil's work afoot, for sure.
SCIPIO: It *is* peculiar! I wonder—
PHEBE: It ain't your task to wonder.
SCIPIO: What's the matter with you, gal?
20   Most times you're the one speculating

about other folks' doings.
Maybe you're sweet on him.

(*General laughter.*)

PHEBE: If you ain't finding fault with someone,
you all laughing at them! We all been
called up to the house one time or another.   25
Ain't nothing special in that.

SCYLLA: For weeks on end? As soon as
the sun eases into the sycamores,
there ain't a hair of his to be seen
till daylight.   30

(*Significant pause.*)

Except maybe on his lady's pillow.

PHEBE: What are you trying to say, Scylla?

SCYLLA: I ain't *trying* to say nothing.

ALEXANDER: He's certainly the boldest nigger
I've ever seen.   35

SCIPIO (*Shaking his head in admiration*): That's the truth there!
The way he handles Massa Jones—
no bowing or scraping for him.
That eye of his could cut
through stone. Jones don't know   40
what to do with that nigger!
He's plain scared, and that's a fact.

PHEBE: Maybe they're just talking.

DIANA: Augustus is nice.

ALEXANDER: Nice as the devil was to Eve.   45

SCYLLA: A slave and his missus
ain't got nothing to talk about.
Oh, he might have bold ideas,
but he'll never put them to work.
She'll see to that.   50

PHEBE: What do you mean?

SCYLLA: That first master of his kept him in style.
That's why he ran away so much afterwards—
he ain't used to being treated like a regular slave.
A whip can't make him behave: 55
Miss Amalia knows that.
So she's trying another way—
and it appears to be working.

SCIPIO: Well, I'll be.

DIANA: What 'pears to be working?   60

SCYLLA: What's the only thing
white folks think
a nigger buck's good for?

It wouldn't be the first time.

65 ALEXANDER (*Slowly*): If that's what he's doing,
    he's headed for big trouble.

PHEBE: I don't believe it!
    And even if it's true, it's 'cause
    he ain't got no choice!

70 SCYLLA: You been mighty contrary lately, Phebe.

PHEBE: I ain't afraid of every shadow!

SCIPIO (*Trying to avert disaster*): Scylla, don't mind her.
    She's feeling the weather.

SCYLLA: I'm warning you, Phebe.

75 PHEBE: I already got a pack of curses
    on my head. A few more won't hurt.

ALEXANDER: Phebe! Don't talk to Scylla like that!

PHEBE: Should have done it a long time ago.
    Woman had me nearly crazy!

80   If anyone around here's putting
    sharp stones in my path,
    it ain't no earth spirit.
    If there's a curse here,
    Scylla, it's you.

(*Everyone stops stamping.*)

85 DIANA: Phebe . . .

PHEBE: Yes, Scylla, you're the curse—
    with all your roots and potions.
    Tell me: How come you never put a spell
    on Miss Amalia? Why didn't you
90   sprinkle some powder over a candle
    to make her house go up in flames
    one night? That would have been some magic.

(*Timid murmurs from the others.*)

SCYLLA: I do what the spirits tell me.

PHEBE: Then those slaves in Haiti
95   must have known some better spirits.

SCYLLA: Some nigger comes in here with
    a few pretty stories,
    and you think he's the Savior!

ALEXANDER: Dear Lord!

100 PHEBE: The Savior was never
    to your liking, Scylla.
    He took too much attention
    away from you.

ALEXANDER: Have mercy!

105 SCYLLA (*Drawing herself into her full "conjurer" posture*): There's a vine in the woods
    with a leaf like a saw blade.

One side of the leaf is shiny dark
and pocked like skin;
the other side is dusty gray.
Touch the gray side to a wound,   110
the sore will shut and heal.
But touch it with the shiny side,
and the wound will boil up
and burst open.

PHEBE: Always talking in riddles!   115
Why don't you come right out and
say what you mean for a change?

(*Agreeing murmurs;* SCYLLA *looks darkly around until everyone grows silent.*)

SCYLLA: Alright, I'll tell you direct.
Your Augustus is pretty clever—
been lots of places and knows   120
the meanings of words and things like that.
But something's foul in his blood,
and what's festering inside him
nothing this side of the living
can heal. A body hurting that bad   125
will do anything to get relief—anything.

(*Looking around at all of them.*)

So keep talking about Haiti
and sharpening your sticks!
But know one thing:
that nigger's headed for destruction,   130
and you're all headed there with him.

(*They stare at her as the lights dim to blackout.*)

SCENE 4

The swamp.

Night: mottled light. Strangely twisted branches, replete with Spanish moss and vines; huge gnarled roots slick with wet. The whole resembles abstract gargoyles in a gothic cathedral. There's a gigantic tree trunk. At some remove—in front of the proscenium, or silhouetted against the backdrop—the SLAVES *pantomime the motions of evening chores: mending tools, shelling beans, stirring the stew.*

When the lights come up, HECTOR *is puttering around the perimeter of the swamp, muttering to himself; he finds a snake and lifts it up triumphantly before whacking off the head.*

HECTOR: Hah! So many—under rocks, 'twixt reeds,

they lie and breed, breed, breed.
The wicked never rest.

(*Stops, listens.*)

What's that? Someone coming!

(*He scrambles for cover as* HENRY *and* AUGUSTUS *enter, stop, and shake hands.*)

5   HENRY: Good night, friend.
           We will be victorious.
    AUGUSTUS: May Fate be with us, brother.
    HENRY: Oh she is, brother, she is.
            It was a golden day
10   when Fate brought you to us.

(*They exchange the secret handshake;* HENRY *exits.* AUGUSTUS *looks after him; then, as soon as he thinks he's alone, he sinks down on a fallen log, burying his face in his hands.* HECTOR—*well hidden from* AUGUSTUS *but visible to the audience—looks on with keen interest; he recognizes this kind of despair.* AUGUSTUS's *soliloquy is more an agitated outpouring than a reflective speech.*)

    AUGUSTUS: Compass and sextant. Ropes thick as my wrist,
               coiled like greased snakes. A cutlass.
               The rough caress of the anchor line slithering
               between my boy palms. The hourglass tipped,
15   surrendering sand in a thin stream of sighs.
               Clouded belly of the oil lamp dangling from a chain.
               And everything rocking, rocking.

(*Hums a lullaby.*)

Dark green pillows, salve for my wounds.
"Who did this to you, boy?"
20   "It was the sun, Father; see its spokes?"
     "Child of midnight, the sun can't hurt you!"

(*Sings softly.*)

"Jesus Savior pilot me
over life's tempestuous sea . . ."

(*Speaks.*)

And when she looks at me—
25   such a cool sweet look—
     each scar weeps like an open wound.

(*Softer.*)

If fear eats out the heart,
what does love do?

(HECTOR *springs out of hiding;* AUGUSTUS *jumps up.*)

HECTOR: You! I've seen you before.

AUGUSTUS (*Relieved*): That you have, my friend. 30
  I'm from the Jennings Plantation, like you.

HECTOR (*Stares at him suspiciously*): Like me? Like me you say?
  We'll see about that.

  (*Circles him, inspecting.*)

  What are you doing in my swamp?

AUGUSTUS: Taking a walk. Breathing the night air. 35

HECTOR: Wrong! You were with someone.
  I saw you!

AUGUSTUS: Just a friend, Hector. Don't you have friends?

HECTOR: I saw you. I heard you!
  How do you know my name? 40

AUGUSTUS: We met before, don't you remember?
  I'm the new slave on the Jennings Plantation.

HECTOR: You're the one who came in leg irons,
  along the road—

  (*Circling him very closely, so that* AUGUSTUS *must back up.*)

  I never heard of leg irons on this plantation before. 45

  (*Crowds* AUGUSTUS, *who trips on a root and falls.*)

  You must be dangerous.

AUGUSTUS: I was sold in chains and spent my first night
  in the barn. The overseer
  didn't have enough sense to take them off
  until Amalia gave the order— 50

HECTOR: Amalia? Amalia!
  You are plotting some evil.

AUGUSTUS: You've got swamp fever, old man.
  I plan no evil.

HECTOR: I heard you! 55
  Men come and go in wagons.
  They whisper and shake hands.
  They come out at night
  when the innocent sleep.

AUGUSTUS: These men—what do they look like? 60

HECTOR: They have the devil's eye.

AUGUSTUS: Are they black men, or white?

HECTOR: You are one of them!

AUGUSTUS: If they are black, black like
  me and you, how can they be evil? 65

HECTOR (*Vehemently*): No, no—the world's not right, don't you see?
  I took the curse as far away as I could.

AUGUSTUS: There is no curse!

HECTOR (*Draping moss and vines over the tree trunk to make a "throne"*):

Ah, but the little mother's gone.
70   And I came here where evil
bubbles out of the ground.
Once I didn't watch out;
I got lost in the smell of a rose
and snap!—the snake bit down.
75   Little mother was mother no more.
AUGUSTUS: I'm no snake, Hector.
HECTOR: Evil isn't the snake, little man.
Evil is what grows the snake.

(*Gazing into the distance.*)

Such a cool sweet look . . .

(*Cuts a piercing glance at* AUGUSTUS, *who recognizes his own words and is on guard—though against what, he's not sure.*)

80   AUGUSTUS: You *are* crazy.
HECTOR: Once we had a garden to hide in,
but we were children.

(*Taking his seat on the throne; with a full sweep of his arm.*)

This is my home now.
I am king here.

(*Regarding him suspiciously.*)

85   Every man has his place.
AUGUSTUS: And you are fortunate to have found yours.
They've left you in peace.
But what of your brothers and sisters?
They cry out in their bondage.
90   They have no place in this world
to lay their heads.
HECTOR (*In a low growl*): You are planning a great evil.
You come out at night
when the innocent sleep—

(*Raising his voice.*)

95   but I won't let you harm her!
AUGUSTUS: Shh! Someone might hear.
HECTOR: I won't let you harm her!

(*Screaming.*)

Danger! Wake up, children!

(*The* SLAVES *wake up and stumble out of their cabins, in a bewildered pantomime. The* CONSPIRATORS *also appear and consult each other.*)

AUGUSTUS (*Grabbing* HECTOR *to silence him*): Quiet! Do you want to bring the whole pack down on us?   100

HECTOR (*Hits* AUGUSTUS *in the chest; crazed*): Wake up! Wake up!
    Mother, Father!
    They're coming for us!

(HECTOR *tries to run out of the swamp.* AUGUSTUS *tackles him from behind.*)

AUGUSTUS: Crazy fool! You'll spoil everything!
    I've . . . come . . . to . . . save you!   105

(*A fierce struggle ensues.*)

HECTOR (*In a vision from his childhood in Africa*): Fire! Fire!
    The huts . . . the boats . . .
    blood in the water.
    Run, children, run!

(AUGUSTUS *gains control and kneels over* HECTOR, *choking him;* HECTOR *gasps and is finally still. When* AUGUSTUS *realizes* HECTOR *is dead, he collapses on the lifeless body.*)

AUGUSTUS: Damn you, old man! I came to save you.   110

(*After a moment, he collects himself and stands up, his voice breaking, more pitiful than angry.*)

Who is not with us, is against us.
HENRY: Selah.

(*The* SLAVES *begin humming as* AUGUSTUS *kneels and wraps the body in vines, then rolls it under a clump of moss and exposed roots.*)

AUGUSTUS: Let these vines be your shroud,
    this moss a pillow for your head.
    These roots will be your coffin,   115
    this dark water your grave.
SLAVES: Selah.
AUGUSTUS: Sleep, Hector. Sleep and be free.

(*The* SLAVES *look at* SCYLLA, *who lifts her hand slowly.*)

SCYLLA: Eshu Elewa ogo gbogbo.

(*Blackout.*)

SCENE 5

Lights rise on the NARRATOR.

NARRATOR: Sweet whispers can leave a bitter taste
    when a body's supposed to be freedom bound.
    Every day as the sun comes easing down,
    our man climbs the stairs to sherry and lace.

(*Lights rise on the big house,* LOUIS' *study and the parlour. Early evening.* LOUIS *sits hunched over his charts. He is excited.*)

5 LOUIS: Nothing in the books.
Empty sky in all the charts.
And yet I've seen it, with my own eyes!
Last night it was the brightest.

(*Draws a few lines with his compass, looks up wistfully.*)

What once was a void
10 fills with feverish matter.

(LOUIS *continues to fiddle with his papers throughout the scene, occasionally jumping up to peer through the telescope.*)

(AMALIA *stands by the fireplace, reading aloud from a book.*)

AMALIA: The princess said to her father, "Bring me
strawberries, I am hungry for strawberries."

(*She shuts the book.*)

He came back with a husband instead.

(*Kneels before the fireplace, trying to start it.*)

"I'm getting too old to tend the garden,"
15 the king said. "Here is a husband for you—
he will fetch your strawberries."
The princess stomped her foot and replied
if she must have a husband,
she would rather marry the fox,
20 who at least knew where the sweetest berries grew.

And so she ran out of the palace
and into the woods, on and on
until a pebble in her shoe forced her to stop.
But it was not a pebble at all—
25 it was the king's head, shrunk to the size
of a pea.
"Put me in your pocket,"
the king pleaded, "and take me away with you."
Horrified, the princess threw the king's head down
30 and ran on. But she had not gone far
before she had to stop again,
and this time when she shook out her shoe,
it was the head of her husband that said:
"Please put me in your pocket
35 so that I may love you wherever you go."
The princess threw his head down, too,
and ran faster; but before long her shoe stopped her

for the third time. And this time
it was her own head she held in her hands.

(*She burns her hand, curses softly. There is a knock at the door. An agitated* JONES *steps into the room, leaving the door open.*)

JONES: Beg pardon for the disturbance, Ma'am,   40
   but the matter's urgent.

(AMALIA *rises, pulling her shawl tighter in exasperation, and takes a seat behind the desk, glaring.*)

AMALIA: Since you've barged in, Mr. Jones,
   the least you can do is close the door.
   There's a chill; I believe I've caught it.
JONES (*Closes the door, steps up to the desk*): Just what I wanted to talk to you about,   45
   Miss Jennings. This cold spell—
   it'll kill the last of the crops
   if we don't get them in soon.

(AMALIA *doesn't respond.*)
   Ma'am, you let the niggers
   leave the fields early.   50
AMALIA: I thought you'd be happy, Mr. Jones.
   Aren't such measures part of
   your economic philosophy?
JONES: Not when there's cotton to be picked.
AMALIA: An hour more or less can hardly matter.   55
   Now—this cold spell is unusual,
   but not as threatening
   as you make it out to be.
JONES: Well, the niggers sure are spooked.
   They're just sitting around or looking off   60
   in the sky. Matter of fact, they ain't even
   been tending their own gardens.
AMALIA: This late in the season
   I don't imagine there's much left to tend.
JONES: And that crazy slave, the one's   65
   got the shack out in the swamp—
AMALIA: Hector?
JONES: Yes'm, that's the one I mean.
   No one's seen hide nor hair of him.
AMALIA: Hector's in the habit of appearing   70
   whenever he has snakes to parade.
JONES: But it's been three days, Ma'am!
AMALIA: Cold weather makes the snakes scarce.
   Is that all, Jones?
JONES: Yes, Ma'am, as you please.   75
   Good evening, Miss Jennings.

(JONES *exits, closing the door behind him.* AMALIA *shakes herself once, briskly, as if trying to restore some measure of reason or calm.*)

AMALIA: He's just waiting till the cold clears.
He'll be alright.

(*Starts toward the window, stops to look in the mirror.*)

80
She looked down at her own head,
cradling it in her cupped palms,
and cried and cried herself to sleep
beneath a giant oak tree.
No one heard her. No one came.
85
And so she perished,
and her body was never found,
even to this day.

(*Listening.*)

Augustus?

(AUGUSTUS *enters, looking worn and preoccupied.* AMALIA *runs to embrace him.*)

AMALIA: So you've come after all!

(*Reaching out to stroke his chest.*)

You look tired.
90
AUGUSTUS (*Uncomfortable*): I nearly collided with Jones,
barrelling full steam across the porch.
AMALIA: Did he see you?
AUGUSTUS: Shadows are kind to niggers.
AMALIA: You're not a nigger!
95
AUGUSTUS (*Catching her hand by the wrist*): Yes I am, Amalia.
Best not forget that.
AMALIA (*Leading him to the fire*): Come and get warm.
AUGUSTUS (*Hanging back*): What did Jones want?
AMALIA: Oh, he was complaining about the weather.
100
AUGUSTUS: The cold's hard on the crops.
They should be picked fast.
AMALIA (*Lightly*): Scylla says the weather will break tomorrow.
AUGUSTUS: Since when have you taken to consulting Scylla?
AMALIA: I didn't "consult" her.
105
She came up today and said,
"If it please the Mistress,
the cold has run its course.
Morn will break warm, no worry."
AUGUSTUS: Why should you risk your profit
110
on Scylla's words?
AMALIA: Look at us, squabbling about agriculture!
Forget about the weather!

Who cares what happens out there?
AUGUSTUS: Someone's got to care, Missy.
AMALIA: Don't call me that.   115
AUGUSTUS: That's what you are. And I'm your slave.
    Nothing has changed that.
AMALIA (*Putting her hand to his mouth;* AUGUSTUS *withdraws, but only slightly*):
    Shh! If this is all the world they've left us,
    then it's ours to make over.
    From time to time we can step out   120
    to show ourselves to the people
    so they will have someone to blame.
AUGUSTUS: It's too late.
AMALIA: Don't you think I see the suffering?
    Don't you think I know I'm the cause?   125

    (*With sarcasm and self-loathing.*)

    But a master cannot allow himself
    the privilege of sorrow. A master
    must rule, or die.
AUGUSTUS (*Pained, thinking of* HECTOR): Dying used to be such
    a simple business. Easy—   130

    (*Caresses her neck.*)

    as long as there was
    nothing to live for.

    (*Tightening his grip;* AMALIA *shows no fear.*)

    And murder simply a matter of being
    on the right side of the knife.
AMALIA (*Caressing him, pulling his shirt up*): Have you ever used a knife?   135
    Have you ever killed someone?
AUGUSTUS (*Haunted, evasive*): Now where would I get a knife?

    (*Turns abruptly away; from outside, barely audible, come the opening strains of "Steal Away."*)

AMALIA (*Touching each scar on his back as she talks*): Your back is like a book
    no-one can bear to read to the end—
    each angry gash, each proud welt . . .   140
    But these scars on your side are different.

    (*Touching them gently.*)

    They couldn't have come from a whipping.
    They're more like—more like
    markings that turn up in fairy tales
    of princes and paupers exchanged at birth.   145
AUGUSTUS: I've had them since birth.
AMALIA (*Caressing him*): So they are magical!

AUGUSTUS: Hardly—unless the art of survival
    is in your magician's bag of tricks.

(AUGUSTUS *begins to return* AMALIA's *attentions.*)

150 AMALIA: They even look like crowns.
    Or suns—exploding suns!
    How did you come by them?
AUGUSTUS (*Abrupt*): No more stories.
AMALIA: Please?
155 AUGUSTUS: Another time.
    There's enough sorrow on earth tonight.

(*Embracing her.*)

And what's the harm in borrowing
a little happiness?
AMALIA: Take this, then—

(*Kisses him.*)

160 and this—

(*He pulls her down on the sofa as the strains of "Steal Away" grow ever more urgent.*
AUGUSTUS *appears not to hear. He and* AMALIA *embrace passionately as the light*
dims.)

SCENE 6

In the slave cemetery.

HECTOR's *funeral.* HECTOR's *body is lying in state on a crude platform, covered with*
a rough blanket. The SLAVES *march around the bier as they sing. After a little while*
JONES *enters and stands uncertainly in the background;* AMALIA *watches from her bed-*
room window.

LOUIS *sits at his window but has turned his back. He stares into nothingness, brandy*
glass in hand.

SLAVES: Oh Deat' him is a little man,
    And him goes from do' to do',
    Him kill some souls and him cripple up,
    And him lef' some souls to pray.

5   Do Lord, remember me,
    Do Lord, remember me.
    I cry to the Lord as de year roll aroun',
    Lord, remember me.
ALEXANDER: No children, and his kinfolk
10   scattered around this world.
PHEBE: We were all his friends, Alexander.

ALEXANDER: But his youngest child's
    got to pass over and under!
    Who's going to do it?
PHEBE: Every child on this plantation   15
    was like his child, Alexander.
    Don't you worry.
ALEXANDER (*Breaking down*): To die like that, swoll up
    and burst open like a—
PHEBE: He's at rest now. He don't feel it.   20

    (*The* SLAVES *stop marching to prepare for the ritual of the "passing." In this rite, the youngest child of the deceased is passed under and over the coffin to signify the continuity of life.*)

SLAVES: My fader's done wid de trouble o' de world,
    Wid de trouble o' de world,
    Wid de trouble o' de world,
    My fader's done wid de trouble o' de world,
    Outshine de sun.   25

    (AUGUSTUS *appears and he stands at a distance;* PHEBE *goes over to him.*)

ALEXANDER: Here he come, stopping by
    when he's good and ready.
    Too busy to pay proper respect to the dead.
SCIPIO: Each soul grieves in its own way.
PHEBE: Where were you?   30
AUGUSTUS: I came as soon as I heard—
PHEBE (*Secretive*): Not here, man. There.

    (*Gestures toward the swamp.*)

    They were calling for you last night.
    Didn't you hear that "Steal Away"?
    They sang till I thought the dead   35
    would rise out of their graves and follow!
    I was crazy with worry.
    Finally I went and told them
    you couldn't get away.

    (AUGUSTUS *glances up at the house, locks gazes with* AMALIA.)

    On the way back I tripped   40
    over what I thought was an old root,
    and there he was—
AUGUSTUS: *You* found him?
PHEBE: Under the crook of a mangrove,
    wrapped in vines. Poor Hector!   45
    All those years folks thought
    he was crazy—

    (*Looking up at* AMALIA's *window.*)

when he was just sick at heart.

ALEXANDER: Hector took a liking to you,
50   Diana. You should be the one.

(PHEBE *joins the mourners as* ALEXANDER *and* SCIPIO *pass* DIANA *under and over
the coffin.*)

SLAVES: Lift him high, Lord,
         Take him by the arm.
         Wrap him in glory,
         Dip him in balm.

(AUGUSTUS *kneels wearily.* SCYLLA, *ravaged with grief and more stooped than ever,
approaches.*)

55 SCYLLA: He thought evil could be caught.
AUGUSTUS: Yes.
SCYLLA: But evil breeds inside, in the dark.
         I can smell its sour breath.
AUGUSTUS: Don't come around me, then.
60 SCYLLA: You believe you can cure the spirit
         just by riling it. What will
         these people do with your hate
         after you free them—as you promise?
AUGUSTUS: I got better things to do
65   than argue with you, Scylla.
SCYLLA: Oh yes, you're a busy man;
         you got to watch for people waiting
         to trip you up; you think
         danger's on the outside.
70   But do you know what's inside
         you, Augustus Newcastle?
         The seeds of the future; they'll have their way.
         You can't escape.
         You are in your skin wherever you go.

(*Turns to the mourners, who have just completed the ritual of the passing, and calls out.*)

75   Eshu Elewa ogo gbogbo!
ALEXANDER: He's gone over. He's flown on the wind.
SCYLLA: He came with no mother to soothe him.
         He came with no father to teach him.
         He came with no names for his gods.
80 PHEBE: No way but to see it through.
SCYLLA: Who can I talk to about his journey?
         He stood tall, so they bent his back.
         He found love, so they ate his heart.
         Eshu Elewa ogo gbogbo!
85 SCIPIO: This is what a man comes to.
SCYLLA: Who will remember him,

without a father, without a mother?

PHEBE: Poor people, you've lost your wings.

SCYLLA: Eshu Elewa ogo gbogbo!
    Where are the old words now?   *90*
    Scattered by the wind.

ALEXANDER: The body a feather, the spirit a flame.

SCYLLA: And now the sun
    has come out to warm him.

SCIPIO: Too late! He's flown.   *95*

SCYLLA: But the wind won't carry me!

(*The* SLAVES *hum and chant as they disperse, their song becoming gradually less mournful and more urgent as we segue into the next scene.*)

NARRATOR: Sunday evening;
    New moon, skies clear.
    The wheel's stopped turning:
    Redemption's here.   *100*

SCENE 7

Near the slave cabins.

Early evening, shortly before sunset: PHEBE *and* AUGUSTUS *come from the shadows. In the background the* SLAVES *go about evening chores while singing, a mixture of militant spirituals and African chants, with whispered phrases such as "Rise up!" or "Mean to be free!" occasionally audible.*

AUGUSTUS: Everything's ready.

PHEBE: Yes.

AUGUSTUS: We've been careful.

PHEBE: Oh, yes.

AUGUSTUS (*Pacing*): Any day now. Any time!   *5*

PHEBE: It's been three days, Augustus—
    three days since you heard the call
    and didn't answer.

AUGUSTUS: Tonight's new moon; skies are clear.
    Destiny calls!   *10*

PHEBE: Are you sure it's not just your destiny?

AUGUSTUS: What do you mean?

PHEBE: Every time you talk about
    victory and vengeance,
    it's as if you're saying   *15*
    my victory, my vengeance.
    As if you didn't care about
    anyone's pain but yours.

AUGUSTUS: Are you with us, or against us?

PHEBE: Ain't nothing wrong with feelings,   *20*

Augustus—just where they lead you.
Now when it comes to hating,
you and Miss Amalia are a lot alike.

(AUGUSTUS *whirls, but she stands her ground.*)

25   She used to be different—high-minded,
but always ready to laugh.
When she married Massa Louis
she began to sour.
Seemed like disappointment killed her.

(*Hesitates, then hurries through.*)

And now you've brought her back to life.
30   No wonder you're mixed up!
AUGUSTUS: Why are you telling me this?
PHEBE: Because I care what happens to you
more than revolution or freedom.
Those may be traitor's words, but
35   I don't care. 'Cause maybe—
maybe if you hadn't let hate
take over your life, you might have
had some love left over for me.

(*She runs off.* AUGUSTUS *slowly sits down, as if a new and treacherous path had opened before him.* BENJAMIN *and* HENRY *enter unseen.* AUGUSTUS *buries his face in his hands.*)

BENJAMIN (*Whispering*): There he is. Don't look
40   so fearful now, does he?

(*Makes a bird call.*)

AUGUSTUS: Who's there?

(*He leaps to his feet; the* CONSPIRATORS *approach.*)

BENJAMIN: May Fate be with you.
AUGUSTUS: You've brought news?
BENJAMIN: Most of the news is old, brother.
45   AUGUSTUS: It couldn't be helped;
I was under constant guard.
BENJAMIN: Constant guard? Constant companionship
would be closer to the truth.
AUGUSTUS: Talk straight!
50   BENJAMIN: Straight as a bullet, brother.
You sent word that you were "being watched"—
naturally, we sent someone to see about
your difficulties. What a surprise
to find out who your guard was
55   and how tenderly

she watched over you!

AUGUSTUS: Missy needed a buck—what of it?

BENJAMIN: Sound mighty proud, buck.

AUGUSTUS: Just the facts, brother, just the facts.
Should I knock her hand away   60
to prove my loyalty to the cause?
Why not charm her instead?

BENJAMIN: That never used to be your style.

AUGUSTUS: I've never been so close to freedom.

BENJAMIN: All the more reason to see   65
you don't spoil it.

(*Looks skyward.*)

The night's perfect:
clear skies, new moon.

AUGUSTUS: Tonight? I knew it!
I'll assemble my forces.   70

BENJAMIN: Hold on. You'll be coming with us.

AUGUSTUS: But—

BENJAMIN: You told us what you wanted us to believe.
We've got orders to bring you to headquarters.
They'll decide what's to be done.   75

AUGUSTUS: I can't leave. My people need me!

BENJAMIN: This is death's business, brother.
Even a nigger as famous as you
can't be given the benefit of the doubt!
Your second-in-command—   80

AUGUSTUS: Phebe?

BENJAMIN: —will organize things here.

(*Takes* AUGUSTUS *by the arm.*)

Henry will deliver her orders.
We'll wait in the wagon. Come on!

(*All exit; blackout. The chanting of the* SLAVES *grows louder, with snatches of spirituals in high descant, but the lyrics of the spirituals are volatile. The percussive, more African-based chants prevail, with key phrases like "Freedom, children, freedom!" emerging ever stronger through the next scene.*)

SCENE 8

The big house: AMALIA'*s bedroom,* LOUIS' *study and the hallway.*

Evening: LOUIS *stands at the open window of his study, looking through the telescope, alternately at the night sky and down over the plantation grounds.*

AMALIA *sits on the window seat in her bedroom.* PHEBE *enters.*

PHEBE: You wanted me, Ma'am?

AMALIA: Good evening, Phebe!
I was sitting at the window,
catching the last rays of sunlight,
5   when I happened to see you
darting from group to group,
talking to this slave and that,
and I said to myself: "Perhaps
Phebe would like to talk to me, too."

10   PHEBE (*On her guard*): I'm pleased to talk conversation
whenever you like, Miss Amalia.

AMALIA (*Slightly sarcastic*): It seems you're mighty pleased
with other people's conversations
these days.

15   PHEBE: I don't follow your meaning, Ma'am.

AMALIA: Oh, really? I notice
you and Augustus have no problem
following each other's meaning.

PHEBE: Augustus ain't nothing
20   but a friend, Ma'am.
I don't recollect talking to him
any more than anyone else.

(*Laughs nervously.*)

Me and my big mouth always be
yakking at somebody or another.

25   AMALIA: Don't talk yourself
into trouble, Phebe.

PHEBE: Beg pardon, Ma'am.
I didn't mean nothing by it.

AMALIA: Everyone can see
30   you're making a fool of yourself
over him! Have you spoken
to Augustus today?

PHEBE: I can't rightly say, Ma'am.

(*At a warning look from* AMALIA.)

That is—I talked to a lot of people
35   and he was amongst them, but
we didn't say more than a how-de-do.

AMALIA: Tell Augustus I want to see him.

PHEBE (*Thrown into panic*): I don't know—I mean—

AMALIA: What's the matter, Phebe?

40   PHEBE: Nothing, Ma'am.
It might take a while, is all.

AMALIA (*Sarcastic*): And why is that?

PHEBE: It's just—well, Augustus been keeping

to himself lately. I seen him
going off in the direction of the swamp;   45
he's got some crazy idea
about fixing up Hector's shack.
AMALIA (*Haunted*): Oh.
When he returns, send him up.
PHEBE: Yes, Ma'am.   50

(PHEBE *exits. In the hallway she runs into* AUGUSTUS. *He is very agitated.*)

PHEBE: (*Whispering*): You! Here?
AUGUSTUS: Yes. They sent me back.
PHEBE: I thought for sure they was going to do
something awful to you.
AUGUSTUS: The sun travels its appointed track,   55
a knot of fire, day in day out—
what could be more awful?
PHEBE: Augustus, what is it?
Can I help?
AUGUSTUS: This job I do alone.   60
PHEBE: But surely you can take a minute
to go in there and smooth
that she-hawk's feathers down
so's the rest of us can—

(AMALIA *steps out and peers into the dim hall.* AUGUSTUS *shrinks into the shadows.*)

AMALIA: Is that you, Phebe?   65
PHEBE: Yes'm. I was just on my way downstairs.
AMALIA: I heard voices.
PHEBE: That was me, Ma'am.
I twisted my foot in the dark—
guess I was talking to it.   70

(*Laughs nervously.*)

My mama used to say it helps
to talk the hurt out.
AMALIA: Well, do your talking
elsewhere. Go on!

(PHEBE *hesitates, then exits.* AMALIA *stands looking into the darkness for a moment,
then goes back into her room.* AUGUSTUS *steps out of hiding, holding a knife. The*
CONSPIRATORS *can be heard in the background.*)

LEADER: Prove you haven't betrayed the cause!   75
BENJAMIN: Kill them both—
HENRY: —your mistress
and her foolish husband.
AUGUSTUS: That's fate for you, Amalia.

(*Looks at the knife.*)

80   That white throat, bared for kisses . . .
        one quick pass, and it will flow
        redder than a thousand roses.

        Everything was so simple before!
        Hate and be hated.
85   But this—love or freedom—
        is the devil's choice.

(Steeling himself, he heads for LOUIS' *room. Lights up on* LOUIS, *who is sitting with his right hand tucked nervously in the lap of his dressing gown. His back is to* AUGUSTUS, *who enters stealthily.)*

LOUIS (*Startling* AUGUSTUS, *who stops in his tracks*):
        No-one has come through that door
        for years. You're the new one, aren't you?

(Unseen by AUGUSTUS, *he pulls a pistol out of his lap.)*

        A wild nigger, I hear. Amalia's latest indulgence.
90 AUGUSTUS: So this is the great white master,
        trembling in his dressing gown!
    LOUIS: Beware of the Moon in the house of Mars!

(Stands up and turns, hiding the pistol as he and AUGUSTUS *face off.)*

        The stars can tell you everything—
        war and pestilence, love and betrayal.
95 AUGUSTUS: War? Yes, this is war. Say your prayers,
        Massa—you have a hard ride ahead of you.
    LOUIS: A hard ride, me? I don't think so.

(Aims his pistol at AUGUSTUS.)

        A man should be able to kill
        when he has to, don't you agree?

(Startled by this unexpected turn of events, AUGUSTUS *freezes.* LOUIS *reaches for the bottle on the table with his other hand.)*

100   Perhaps you'd care for a bit of bourbon
        to warm your way?
    AUGUSTUS (*Trying to compose himself*): You can't stop what's coming
        over the hill.
    LOUIS (*Shakes his pistol at* AUGUSTUS, *shouting*):
        This time I won't leave things up to chance!

(Muttering.)

05   What a fool I was!
        I should have smothered the bastard
        right there in the basket.
        That's the man's way.

AUGUSTUS: Basket? What basket?

LOUIS: Amalia's of course. Amalia's basket.   110

It was—

(*Slight pause; distracted.*)

The doctor refused to kill it.
What else was there to do?

(AUGUSTUS *lunges, knocking the gun from* LOUIS' *hand and overpowering him.*)

AUGUSTUS: There goes your last chance, fool!

(*Drags* LOUIS *by the collar toward center-stage.*)

This basket—what did it look like?   115

LOUIS: What do you care?

AUGUSTUS (*Holds the knife to* LOUIS' *throat*): Enough to slit your throat.

LOUIS (*Whimpering*): Oh, it was beautiful! White wicker,
lined in blue satin, tiny red rosettes
marching along the rim . . .   120

AUGUSTUS (*Slowly lets go of* LOUIS' *collar*): And your spurs slipped right inside.

LOUIS: Amalia's Christmas present.
Oh, was the good doctor relieved!
"It's a miracle," he said,
"but the child's still alive!"   125

AUGUSTUS: And still lives to this day.
Spurs bite into a horse's belly—
think what they can do
to a newborn child!

(*Rips open his shirt.*)

LOUIS: You?   130

AUGUSTUS: All my life I tried to imagine
what you would look like.
Would you be tall or stooped over?
Blue eyes, or brown?
Would you dress in white linen   135
or dash around in a dusty greatcoat?
to think that your blood flows
through my veins—

(*Advances on* LOUIS, *who staggers back into the chair.*)

LOUIS: My blood?

AUGUSTUS: When I think of you forcing   140
your wretched seed into my mother,
I want to rip you—

LOUIS: Me, your father?
You think I'm your father?

AUGUSTUS: I heard it from your own lips.   145

LOUIS (*Bursts into laughter*): Of course! Of course!
    The stars said it all:
    who is born into violence
    shall live to fulfill it.
150   Who shuns violence
    will die by the sword.
AUGUSTUS (*Pulls* LOUIS *from the chair, knife at his throat*):
    What happened to my mother?
    What did you do to her?
LOUIS (*In a crafty voice*): I haven't touched her since.
155   Ask Amalia—
    she runs this plantation.
    She knows your mother better than anyone!
AUGUSTUS: Amalia? Of course!
    Missy wanted the bastard child dead.
160   Now I understand: It's an old story.
LOUIS: You understand nothing.

    (*A sudden shout outside; the revolt has begun. Both men freeze, listening.*)

AUGUSTUS: It's time!

    (*Stabs* LOUIS *as the sounds of the revolt grow.*)

LOUIS: You were there . . . all along . . .
AUGUSTUS (*Letting* LOUIS' *body drop*): So, Amalia—and to think
165   I tried to bargain for your life!
SLAVES: Freedom! Freedom! Selah! Selah!

    (AUGUSTUS *heads for* AMALIA's *room; lights come up on* AMALIA, *who has stepped into the hall.*)

AMALIA: Augustus, there you are! What's happening?
    I called Ticey, but she won't come!
AUGUSTUS (*Backing her into the room*): I thought you didn't care
170   what happened out there.
AMALIA: Why are they shouting?
    Why doesn't Jones make them stop?
AUGUSTUS: I reckon the dead don't make good overseers.
    Your slaves are rebelling, Missy.
175   *Liberté, Égalité, Fraternité!*
AMALIA (*Stares at him uncomprehendingly, then runs to the window*):
    Rebelling? My slaves?
    Augustus, make them stop!
    They'll listen to you!
AUGUSTUS: Like I listened to you?
180   You led me into your parlour
    like a dog on a leash. Sit, dog!
    Heel! Care for a sherry? A fairy tale?
AMALIA: No, you were different!

You were—
AUGUSTUS (*Grabs her*): No more conversation!   185
    Where is my mother?
AMALIA: Your mother? How would I know a thing like that?
AUGUSTUS: Your husband confessed.
AMALIA (*Aware of danger on all sides, seeking escape*):
    What could Louis have to confess?
AUGUSTUS: A shrewd piece of planning,   190
    to destroy him with his own son
    after you had failed to destroy
    the son himself!
    But you had to be patient.
    Twenty years you had to wait   195
    before you could buy me back.
AMALIA: Louis, your father? You must be joking!
AUGUSTUS: Shall I help you remember?
    You supplied the basket yourself—
AMALIA: Basket?   200
AUGUSTUS: —lined in blue satin, trimmed with rosettes—
AMALIA: *Red* rosettes?
AUGUSTUS: Monsieur LaFarge agreed
    to sell his own baby—but that wasn't enough,
    was it? You wanted the child dead.   205
    So you slipped a pair of riding spurs
    into the sewing basket.
    And you know the kind of scars
    spurs leave, Missy. Like crowns . . .
    or exploding suns.   210
AMALIA: My God.
AUGUSTUS: The woman who patched me up
    kept that basket as a reminder.
AMALIA: No . . .
AUGUSTUS (*Shakes her*): What did you do with my mother?   215
    Who is she?

(*Slaps her.*)

    Tell me!
AMALIA (*Wrenches free to face him; her voice trembling*):
    So you want to know who your mother is?
    You think, if I tell you,
    the sad tale of your life   220
    will find its storybook ending?
    Well then, this will be my last story—
    and when I have finished,
    you will wish you had never
    stroked my hair or kissed my mouth.   225
    You will wish you had no eyes to see

or ears to hear. You will wish
you had never been born.
AUGUSTUS: I've heard grown men scream,
230   watched as the branding iron
sank into their flesh. I've seen
pregnant women slit open like melon,
runaways staked to the ground
and whipped until
235   they floated in their own blood and piss.
Don't think you can frighten me, Missy:
Nothing your lips can tell
can be worse than what
these eyes have seen.
240 AMALIA: Bravo! What a speech!
But you've seen nothing.

(*Backs up to appraise him, smiling, slightly delirious.*)

That same expression! How could I forget?
My lover then stood as tall as you now.
AUGUSTUS: Your lover?

(PHEBE *bursts in.*)

245 PHEBE: They're coming, Augustus!
They're coming to see if you did
what you were told! Oh, Augustus—
you were supposed to kill her!
AUGUSTUS (*Shaking himself into action, threatening* AMALIA):
My mother, who is my mother?
250   Out with it!
AMALIA: Phebe, you tell him.
You were there.
Everyone was there—
under my window,
255   waiting for news . . .
PHEBE: That . . . was the night
we all came to wait out the birth.
AUGUSTUS: What birth?
AMALIA: Hector on the porch.
260 AUGUSTUS: What about Hector?

(*More shouts outside; compelled by the urgency of the growing revolution,* PHEBE *tries to distract* AUGUSTUS.)

PHEBE: There's no time!
AUGUSTUS (*Grabs* AMALIA *as if to slit her throat*): What about Hector?
AMALIA: Chick in a basket, going to market!
They said you died, poor thing.

That's why Hector went to the swamp.   265

(AUGUSTUS *stares desperately at her.* PHEBE *turns, thunderstruck.*)

AUGUSTUS: Hector?
AMALIA: But you didn't die. You're here . . .

(*Reaches for him; he draws back.*)

PHEBE (*Looks from* AMALIA *to* AUGUSTUS, *horror growing, recites tonelessly*):
    Stepped on a pin, the pin bent,
    and that's the way the story went.
AMALIA (*Sadly, in a small voice*): Silk for my prince, and a canopy of roses!   270
    You were so tiny—so sweet and tiny.
    I didn't know about the spurs.
PHEBE: You sold your own child.
    Hector's child.
AUGUSTUS: Hector . . .   275

(*The knife slips from his fingers.*)

AMALIA: I was trying to save you!
AUGUSTUS: Save me?
AMALIA (*Extremely agitated*): I felt like they had hacked out my heart.
    But I wouldn't let them see me cry.
AUGUSTUS (*Wrestling with the horror*): You? My mother?   280
AMALIA (*Clutching herself*): It was like missing an arm or a leg
    that pains and throbs, even though
    you can look right where it was
    and see there's nothing left.

(*She stops abruptly.*)

AUGUSTUS: My own mother gave me away.   285
    But I found my way back . . .
    a worm crawling into its hole.
AMALIA: For weeks afterwards
    my breasts ached with milk.
AUGUSTUS (*Sinking to his knees*): Better I had bled to death in that basket.   290

(*A great shout goes up as the insurrectionists gain entry to the main house.* AMALIA
takes advantage of the ensuing distraction to pick up the knife.)

PHEBE: Augustus!
AUGUSTUS (*Passive*): The Day of Redemption is here.
PHEBE: They'll kill you, Augustus!
AUGUSTUS: Time to be free.
AMALIA: Poor baby! I thought   29.
    I could keep you from harm—
    and here you are,
    right in harm's way.

(PHEBE *gasps;* AMALIA *stabs herself as* AUGUSTUS, *alerted by* PHEBE's *gasp, jumps up, too late to stop her. The room turns red as the out-buildings go up in flames.*)

AUGUSTUS: Amalia!

(*Catching her as she falls.*)

300   No . . .

(*Calling out in anguish.*)

Eshu Elewa ogo gbogbo!

(*The chanting of the rebelling* SLAVES *grows louder.*)

PHEBE: Oh, Augustus . . .
AUGUSTUS (*Lays* AMALIA's *body down, gently*): I had the sun and the moon
          once. And the stars
305   with their cool gaze.
          Now it's dark.
PHEBE: It's alright. You'll be alright now.
AUGUSTUS (*Staring as if trying to make out something in the distance*):
          Who's there? How she stares,
          like a cat at midnight!
310   PHEBE: Nobody's there, Augustus.
AUGUSTUS: Don't you see her?

(PHEBE *shakes her head, terrified.*)

          Look, she's hidden behind a tree.
PHEBE: Oh, Augus—
AUGUSTUS: Shh! You'll frighten her. There's another one—
315   he's been flogged and pickled in brine.
          That skinny boy ate dirt; that's why he staggers.
          So many of them, limping, with brands
          on their cheeks! Oh, I can't bear it!
PHEBE: Come along, now.
320   AUGUSTUS (*Calling out to the "ghosts"*): I came to save you!

(*The* SLAVES *burst in, brandishing bayonets and torches.*)

BENJAMIN: He did it.
SLAVES: Selah! We're free!

(*The* SLAVES *lift* AUGUSTUS *onto their shoulders. The* SLAVE WOMAN/
NARRATOR *stands at the door, holding a torch, taking in the scene.*)

SLAVES: Freedom, freedom, freedom . . .

(*The "Freedom!" chant grows louder and more persistent as the* SLAVES *parade out of the room,* AUGUSTUS *on their shoulders;* PHEBE *follows them, sobbing.* SCYLLA *takes the torch from the* SLAVE WOMAN/NARRATOR *and sets fire to the window's billowing curtains as she slowly straightens up to her full height.*)

(*Blackout.*)

(*The End.*)

QUESTIONS FOR DISCUSSION AND WRITING

1. Both Amalia and Augustus are problematic characters. How much do you sympathize with each of them? Does your opinion change as the play progresses?
2. Scylla speaks of the "curse" early on in the play, yet Augustus sees her voodoo as mere superstition. What is the curse? Are events in the play determined by it?
3. Dove shows some key scenes that Sophocles merely reports—the birth and maiming of the infant and the killing of the father(s). How do these differences in dramatic technique affect the audience's response to the material?
4. Sophocles' Thebes is presented as a homogeneous society, while Dove's plantation is divided along racial lines. How do those differences affect the ways in which the characters act and the audiences respond?
5. In Dove's play, the slaves seem to function as a chorus. How is their role the same as or different from that of the Chorus in Sophocles' play?
6. Dove uses star, sun, and moon imagery throughout the play. How does the audience respond to these various references?
7. Because *The Darker Face of the Earth* is a modern retelling of the Oedipus story, each of the characters in Dove's play *might* be comparable to a character in Sophocles' play. Compare and contrast one or two characters in Dove's play to the parallel character(s) in *Oedipus*. To what extent are the characters similar in their personalities and in their roles? How do the differences reflect differences in the two dramatists' themes and concerns and in their audience's expectations and assumptions?
8. Compare and contrast a single event as it is played out in Dove's drama to the parallel event in *Oedipus*. How do Dove's changes and reinterpretations of the event affect our understanding of her play's themes and concerns?
9. Although *The Darker Face of the Earth* is a relatively new play—it is only a few years old—Dove sets the action in the pre–Civil War South. Imagine that you have decided to write a new version of *Oedipus* or *The Darker Face of the Earth* set in the twenty-first century. Consider the changes that you would need to make in the story for it to work in this new time setting. Why would you make the changes?
10. Modern audiences do not believe in Fate in the same way that Greek audiences did. How does *The Darker Face of the Earth* update the Greek concept of Fate to account for its characters' beliefs, personalities, and/or actions?
11. *Oedipus* is, as its title suggests, clearly a play about one man; *The Darker Face of the Earth* focuses less fully on a single character. What is the effect of Dove's broader focus? How does it reflect her themes and concerns and/or her audience's expectations and assumptions?
12. Amalia is more central to Dove's play than Jocasta is to Sophocles'. How does the difference in focus influence our reactions to the situations in which the characters find themselves? To the plays' themes?

RITA DOVE (1952–   )

The recognition scene from the first edition of The Darker Face of the Earth

AUGUSTUS (*shakes her*): He said you know who my mother is.
    Tell me! Tell me!

    (*slaps her*)

    Come on, bitch—
    who is my mother?

AMALIA (*wrenching free, her voice trembling with horror, toneless and shrill at the same time*):
5   So you want to know, do you?
    You want to know your mother?
    I have one more story for you—
    and when I have finished
    you will wish
10   you had never set your man's foot
    on this plantation.
    You will wish
    you had not stroked my hair
    or touched my breasts or
15   lain with me in that bed.
    You will wish
    you had no eyes to see
    or ears to hear
    or mouth to kiss.
20   You will wish
    you had never been born.

AUGUSTUS: Out with it!

AMALIA: I was the one
    who put you in that basket.
25   Yes, I was the one
    who sold you—but
    it's not like you think.
    I wanted to save you.
    Save you!
30   I didn't know about the spurs.
    You were so tiny . . .

    (*breaks into laughter*)

    My God! My lover then
    stood as tall as you.

AUGUSTUS: Your lover . . .

35 AMALIA: Haven't you figured it out yet?
    Yes, Louis did take to slave girls;
    ask any of them. Diana has his eyes.
    But you—

AUGUSTUS: Diana my sister?

AMALIA: —you are not his son!   40
    Hector knew;
    that's why he went to the swamp.
    And I never touched him again.

    (AUGUSTUS *looks slowly, desperately at her.*)

    Now do you understand?
    I—am—your—mother!   45

    (*bursts into wild laughter*)

    Your mother!

    (*begins to reel through the room, laughing incessantly*)

    Your mother!

AUGUSTUS: NO!

    (*falls to his knees, wild-eyed*)

    The snakes. So many snakes.

    (*in a little voice*)

    The sun and the moon at once.   50
    And the stars.
    Don't forget the stars.

PHEBE (*runs in*): Augustus! Augustus, they're coming!

    (*sees* AMALIA, *hesitates*)

    They're coming to see if you did
    what you were told.   55
    Oh, Augustus, you were supposed to kill her!
    You've got to run!

AUGUSTUS: Don't cry, girl.
    I'll be alright.

PHEBE (*in tears*): They'll kill you, Augustus.   60
    Run!

    (*With a choked cry,* AMALIA *dashes toward the door. Still on his knees,* AUGUSTUS
    reaches out to stop her.*)

AUGUSTUS: Stay!

    (AUGUSTUS *clutches* AMALIA's *knees; she stares down at him, tenderly pulling his
    head against her.* NED *and* BENJAMIN *rush in, pistols drawn.*)

NED: Bloody traitor!

    (*shoots;* AMALIA *falls*)

AUGUSTUS: Mother . . .

    (BENJAMIN *shoots;* AUGUSTUS *sinks on top of* AMALIA's *body*)

65 PHEBE: Augustus!

> (*She kneels beside him.* NED *and* BENJAMIN *turn on their heels and leave. The revolting slaves pour in, brandishing sticks and torches.*)

SLAVES: We're free! We're free!

> (SCYLLA *is the last to enter. As* PHEBE *sobs,* SCYLLA *takes in the scene, staring at the bodies as she slowly straightens up to her full height. Blackout.*)

QUESTION FOR DISCUSSION AND WRITING

As a comparison of the two versions of *The Darker Face of the Earth* play shows, Dove made a major revision to the ending of the play. Which ending do you prefer— and why? Is one ending more "conclusive" than the other? To what extent does the change in ending change your response to the characters? The play's themes?

MAKING CONNECTIONS: A CASEBOOK ON *OEDIPUS*

1. For modern readers, the story of Oedipus is closely linked to Freud's concept of the Oedipus complex. Which of the modern writers show an awareness of Freud's theory? Are their attitudes toward that theory the same or different? How?
2. Oedipus is guilty of two "sins"—killing his father and sleeping with his mother. Which writers emphasize which? Do the differences in emphasis represent different attitudes toward "sin"?
3. Cavafy, Rukeyser, and Jarrell all focus on the Sphinx and her riddle. Do they envision the Sphinx in the same way? How important to each of them is it that the Sphinx is female? In what ways do they see the answer to the riddle as an important part of the whole myth?
4. Gallaher's and Sheck's poems both focus on Jocasta. Is this the same Jocasta? How do their Jocastas compare with Sophocles' Jocasta or with Dove's Amalia?
5. Many of the modern works draw on images and ideas Sophocles uses. Trace one of these images or ideas (for example, light and dark imagery, plague imagery, or the idea of guilt and innocence) through several of the works. Are the writers creating the same effects with these images and ideas?

TOPICS FOR RESEARCH: A CASEBOOK ON *OEDIPUS*

1. Greek ideas about fate and free will may differ from our own, thus making it difficult for us to understand the extent to which Oedipus can choose to disobey the prophecy. Research Greek ideas about the relationship between people and the gods and about the extent to which the Greeks believed in the idea of fate.
2. In using the Oedipus story as the basis for some of his psychological theories, Freud seems to assume that Oedipus is, even if unconsciously, attracted to his

mother. But historians often caution us to remember that in Greek times, Oedipus's decision to marry the queen would have been a political one. Research Greek attitudes toward marriage among those of the ruling class. To what extent were marriages seen as political alliances? How did the Greeks view the roles of and relationships between men and women?

3. Oedipus is called a *tyrannus*. Although our word *tyrant* is derived from the Greek *tyrannus*, the Greek word has very different connotations and meanings from those of the modern English word. Research the meaning of *tyrannus* and the nature of the relationships between ancient Greek leaders and those they governed.

4. In their critical responses to *Oedipus*, Vellacott and Dodds both consider Greek ideas about patricide, incest, and moral "pollution." Do some research of your own on how Greek society would have viewed a man who had—knowingly or not—committed such actions against family. How would he have been punished? How much would a person's *intention* to commit a moral or legal crime figure in Greek society's response to the crime? How much would it figure in our own time?

5. *Oedipus* is sometimes compared to *The Book of Job* in the Bible because both concern themselves with the suffering of what may be viewed as innocent men. Locate a copy of *Job* and compare and contrast the Judeo-Christian view of the suffering of an innocent man with the Greek view offered in *Oedipus*. Are the Judeo-Christian God and the Greek gods seen as moral entities? How is such suffering justified in the religious contexts of the two cultures?

6. Looking at two or three translations of *Oedipus*, compare their renderings of a few speeches or a scene or two. How do the different translations influence our understanding of the characters and/or themes of the play?

7. Locate two or three reviews of different *Oedipus* film or stage productions. Compare and contrast the reviews. What do the reviews suggest about how the productions have interpreted the play? What do they suggest about how the reviewers themselves see the play?

8. In *The Darker Face of the Earth*, Amalia asks Augustus if he has ever heard of the *Amistad*. Do some research on the *Amistad*. How does Amalia's question help us understand her concerns about the slave rebellions of the nineteenth century?

9. *The Darker Face of the Earth* tells the story of love affairs between a white mistress and two black slaves (Augustus and his father, Hector). Do some research to find out how common such affairs were. Does your research suggest any historical basis for this element in Dove's play? If so, what would have been the likely social and personal outcomes of such an affair?

10. *The Darker Face of the Earth* ends with a slave revolt. We do not learn whether the revolt is successful, however. Research the history of such revolts. How did they typically end?

11. Augustus is highly educated and somewhat contemptuous of the other slaves' folk ways and beliefs. Research the state of education among slaves during the nineteenth century. What kinds and levels of education did most slaves have? What was the status of and attitude toward an educated slave?

12. Voodoo clearly plays some part in *The Darker Face of the Earth*. Do some research on voodoo and on its prevalence among slaves in nineteenth-century America. How does a knowledge of voodoo inform your reading of the slaves' characters and the play's themes?

13

A Casebook on Hamlet

Murder and Madness

For many of Shakespeare's admirers, *Hamlet* is his best play. Actors beg to play the part of the central character, hoping to demonstrate their command of the range and depth of emotion, the quick changes of mood, and the soaring poetry that make him one of the greatest characters of literature. And the language of the play has become so much a part of our culture that even those who don't admire the play—even those who have not read or seen it—can parrot some of its more famous lines: "To be, or not to be, that is the question" and "But this above all, to thine own self be true." These are the kinds of lines that not only shape people's poetic sensibilities but give them a sense of themselves.

Still, though, students sometimes tell us that they find the play difficult or, worse, unexciting. *Hamlet* is, some of our students tell us, a play with little action. Nothing *happens* in it, they say; Hamlet just stands around talking . . . and talking . . . and talking—sometimes to others, but often to himself. And yet, no matter how accurate this response, it also strikes us as absolutely wrong.

Nothing happens? Imagine yourself in Hamlet's position: your father, the king, has recently died. He was a man whom you loved and admired, a man who cannot easily be replaced either in your heart or in the kingship. In mourning, you grieve over your loss and prepare yourself to assume your role as the next king. And then, while you are away at college, your mother, only recently widowed, remarries, and her new husband—your uncle!—takes upon himself the role of king. Your mother, it seems, is no longer grieving her loss, and she has replaced your much-loved and admired father with a man who seems base and ignoble in comparison. How easy would it be for you to love and honor your new stepfather, as your mother wishes you to do? How easy would it be for you to accept his ascension to the throne that you believe is rightfully yours?

Although he is a prince and a man supposedly born centuries before our time, Hamlet faces a particularly modern predicament. His mother wants him to accept his new stepfather and to keep the peace in the household. Like many a woman who re-marries, she wants her new husband and her son to get along. And like many a child whose parent has remarried—much too quickly, the child often believes—Hamlet wants nothing to do with his new parent. He faces more serious complications than the average person: his uncle has murdered his father, his girlfriend has gone over to the enemy, and he has accidentally killed his girlfriend's meddling father. Still, al-though his circumstances are more extreme than those faced by the modern child of a ruptured family, Hamlet shares much of the family trauma and inner turmoil of a child of the twenty-first century.

To make things more difficult for Hamlet, all of this family turmoil is played out in public, on the grand stage of the royal court. The father Hamlet's uncle murdered was, after all, also the king, the leader of his people and God's representative. This is not just an individual family's tragedy; it is a tragedy that threatens the foundations of the kingdom. Even if as a son Hamlet were able to forgive his uncle for the murder of his father and forgive his mother for her overhasty marriage, as a citizen and prince, can he simply ignore crimes against the kingdom and against God?

In facing questions about the obligations he owes to God, to his dead father, to his kingdom, and to himself, Hamlet dissects the very nature of existence. Here, too, the play has a modern appeal. The lines we quoted above appeal to many readers because they are beautiful poetry and because they reverberate through the ages. To those familiar with the existentialist movement of the twentieth century, "To be or not to be" will sound a familiar chord; like the existentialist of a later era, Hamlet contemplates the meaning, or meaninglessness, of his own existence. What does it mean to *be*? What does it mean to heed the advice "to thine own self be true"? How, indeed, is the self defined? If it is defined by one's parentage, what happens when that parentage is denied or the foundations on which it is built are shaken? After all, in recognizing his uncle's treachery, Hamlet also recognizes his mother's disloyalty to him and to his father. In many ways, the play describes his coming to terms not only with the loss of his father but also with the loss of his mother. Once orphaned, who does the child, perhaps even the adult child who no longer "needs" his parents, become? Even when we know ourselves, how can we be true to those selves if in our action we betray our moral principles and in our inaction we betray our fathers?

Finally, what makes *Hamlet* a particularly poignant play is that it is a play about enforced solitude, about the loss of the standards by which one measures oneself and gains stability. Partly through circumstance, partly through villainy, and partly through his own doing, Hamlet is stripped of his parents, his college friends, and his beloved. No longer a son or a college student or a lover or the clear heir to the throne, he stands alone, the image of an oddly modern man who fears that he has nothing to give shape and purpose to his being.

This is clearly Hamlet's play. He gives the play its name, and he speaks more lines than any other character. Though a drama has no clear point of view—there is no narrator to tell us what to think or to read the characters' minds for us—this is so clearly Hamlet's play that his mood becomes the play's mood, and his tragedy the play's tragedy. But it is important to notice as well that not all audiences and critics see Hamlet as entirely sympathetic. Several of the works included in this chapter imply that his actions and moods are both immature and petulant, the behaviors and moods of a small child who cannot have his mother's full attention and who cannot sustain a mature love relationship with a woman. In the retellings of the play there are, indeed, hints that this is *too* much Hamlet's play. What of Gertrude's point of view? Surely she is entitled to a mature love relationship—even one filled with sexual pleasure—after her first husband's death. What of the other losses that are tragedies in their own rights? After all, Ophelia, too, has lost not only her father and her lover but herself, and Laertes has lost a father and a sister.

Hamlet's is not the only tragedy, but it is the tragedy around which all the others revolve. It is the tragedy that gives the play its shape and its meaning. And it is the tragedy that all of us fear: the tragedy of losing our sense of self and purpose, our place in the world. Although the play is centuries old, then, its tragedy is the tragedy of modern life.

WILLIAM SHAKESPEARE (1564–1616)

Hamlet, Prince of Denmark _____ 1600

Characters

CLAUDIUS, *King of Denmark*
HAMLET, *son to the late and nephew to the present king*
POLONIUS, *lord chamberlain*
HORATIO, *friend to Hamlet*
LAERTES, *son to Polonius*
VOLTIMAND
CORNELIUS
ROSENCRANTZ   } *courtiers*
GUILDENSTERN
OSRIC
A GENTLEMAN
A PRIEST
MARCELLUS } *officers*
BERNARDO
FRANCISCO, *a soldier*
REYNALDO, *servant to Polonius*
PLAYERS
TWO CLOWNS, *grave-diggers*
FORTINBRAS, *Prince of Norway*
A CAPTAIN
ENGLISH AMBASSADORS
GERTRUDE, *Queen of Denmark, and mother to Hamlet*
OPHELIA, *daughter to Polonius*
GHOST *of Hamlet's father*
(LORDS, LADIES, OFFICERS, SOLDIERS, SAILORS, MESSENGERS, *and* OTHER ATTENDANTS)

Scene. *Denmark.*

ACT I
SCENE I [*Elsinore. A platform° before the castle.*]

(*Enter* BERNARDO *and* FRANCISCO, *two sentinels.*)

I.i. s.d. platform a level space on the battlements of the royal castle at Elsinore, a Danish seaport; now Helsingör.

BERNARDO: Who's there?

FRANCISCO: Nay, answer me:° stand, and unfold yourself.

BERNARDO: Long live the king!°

FRANCISCO: Bernardo?

5 BERNARDO: He.

FRANCISCO: You come most carefully upon your hour.

BERNARDO: 'Tis now struck twelve; get thee to bed, Francisco.

FRANCISCO: For this relief much thanks: 'tis bitter cold,
    And I am sick at heart.

BERNARDO: Have you had quiet guard?

10 FRANCISCO: Not a mouse stirring.

BERNARDO: Well, good night.
    If you do meet Horatio and Marcellus,
    The rivals° of my watch, bid them make haste.

(*Enter* HORATIO *and* MARCELLUS.)

FRANCISCO: I think I hear them. Stand, ho! Who is there?

HORATIO: Friends to this ground.

15 MARCELLUS: And liegemen to the Dane.

FRANCISCO: Give you° good night.

MARCELLUS: O, farewell, honest soldier:
    Who hath reliev'd you?

FRANCISCO: Bernardo hath my place.
    Give you good night.   (*Exit* FRANCISCO.)

MARCELLUS: Holla! Bernardo!

BERNARDO: Say,
    What, is Horatio there?

HORATIO: A piece of him.

20 BERNARDO: Welcome, Horatio. Welcome, good Marcellus.

MARCELLUS: What, has this thing appear'd again to-night?

BERNARDO: I have seen nothing.

MARCELLUS: Horatio says 'tis but our fantasy,
    And will not let belief take hold of him.

25 Touching this dreaded sight, twice seen of us:
    Therefore I have entreated him along
    With us to watch the minutes of this night;
    That if again this apparition come,
    He may approve° our eyes and speak to it.

HORATIO: Tush, tush, 'twill not appear.

30 BERNARDO: Sit down awhile;
    And let us once again assail your ears,
    That are so fortified against our story
    What we have two nights seen.

---

2 me this is emphatic, since Francisco is the sentry.   **3 Long live the king!** either a password or greeting: Horatio and Marcellus use a different one in line 15.   **13 rivals** partners.   **16 Give you** God give you.   **29 approve** corroborate.

HORATIO: Well, sit we down,
   And let us hear Bernardo speak of this.
BERNARDO: Last night of all,   35
   When yond same star that's westward from the pole°
   Had made his course t' illume that part of heaven
   Where now it burns, Marcellus and myself,
   The bell then beating one,—

(*Enter* GHOST.)

MARCELLUS: Peace, break thee off; look, where it comes again!   40
BERNARDO: In the same figure, like the king that's dead.
MARCELLUS: Thou art a scholar;° speak to it, Horatio.
BERNARDO: Looks 'a not like the king? mark it, Horatio.
HORATIO: Most like: it harrows° me with fear and wonder.
BERNARDO: It would be spoke to.°
MARCELLUS: Speak to it, Horatio.   45
HORATIO: What art thou that usurp'st this time of night,
   Together with that fair and warlike form
   In which the majesty of buried Denmark°
   Did sometimes march? by heaven I charge thee, speak!
MARCELLUS: It is offended.
BERNARDO: See it stalks away!   50
HORATIO: Stay! speak, speak! I charge thee, speak!   (*Exit* GHOST.)
MARCELLUS: 'Tis gone, and will not answer.
BERNARDO: How now, Horatio! you tremble and look pale:
   Is not this something more than fantasy?
   What think you on 't?   55
HORATIO: Before my God, I might not this believe
   Without the sensible and true avouch
   Of mine own eyes.
MARCELLUS: Is it not like the king?
HORATIO: As thou art to thyself:
   Such was the very armour he had on   60
   When he the ambitious Norway combated;
   So frown'd he once, when, in an angry parle,
   He smote° the sledded Polacks° on the ice.
   'Tis strange.
MARCELLUS: Thus twice before, and jump° at this dead hour,   65
   With martial stalk hath he gone by our watch.
HORATIO: In what particular thought to work I know not;
   But in the gross and scope° of my opinion,

---

36 pole polestar.   **42 scholar** exorcisms were performed in Latin, which Horatio as an educated man would be able to speak.   **44 harrows** lacerates the feelings.   **45 It . . . to** a ghost could not speak until spoken to.   **48 buried Denmark** the buried king of Denmark.   **63 smote** defeated. **63 sledded Polacks** Polanders using sledges.   **65 jump** exactly.   **68 gross and scope** general drift.

This bodes some strange eruption to our state.

70 MARCELLUS: Good now,° sit down, and tell me, he that knows,
     Why this same strict and most observant watch
     So nightly toils° the subject° of the land,
     And why such daily cast° of brazen cannon,
     And foreign mart° for implements of war;
75   Why such impress° of shipwrights, whose sore task
     Does not divide the Sunday from the week;
     What might be toward, that this sweaty haste
     Doth make the night joint-laborer with the day:
     Who is't that can inform me?

     HORATIO: That can I;
80   At least, the whisper goes so. Our last king,
     Whose image even but now appear'd to us,
     Was, as you know, by Fortinbras of Norway,
     Thereto prick'd on° by a most emulate° pride,
     Dar'd to the combat; in which our valiant Hamlet—
85   For so this side of our known world esteem'd him—
     Did slay this Fortinbras; who, by a seal'd compact,
     Well ratified by law and heraldry,°
     Did forfeit, with his life, all those his lands
     Which he stood seiz'd° of, to the conqueror:
90   Against the which, a moiety competent°
     Was gaged by our king; which had return'd
     To the inheritance of Fortinbras,
     Had he been vanquisher; as, by the same comart,°
     And carriage° of the article design'd,
95   His fell to Hamlet. Now, sir, young Fortinbras,
     Of unimproved° mettle hot and full,°
     Hath in the skirts of Norway here and there
     Shark'd up° a list of lawless resolutes,°
     For food and diet,° to some enterprise
100 That hath a stomach in't; which is no other—
     As it doth well appear unto our state—
     But to recover of us, by strong hand
     And terms compulsatory, those foresaid lands
     So by his father lost: and this, I take it,
105 Is the main motive of our preparations,
     The source of this our watch and the chief head
     Of this post-haste and romage° in the land.

---

70 Good now an expression denoting entreaty or expostulation.   **72 toils** causes or makes to toil.
72 subject people, subjects.   **73 cast** casting, founding.   **74 mart** buying and selling, traffic.   **75
impress** impressment.   **83 prick'd on** incited.   **83 emulate** rivaling.   **87 law and heraldry**
heraldic law, governing combat.   **89 seiz'd** possessed.   **90 moiety competent** adequate or sufficient portion.   **93 comart** joint bargain.   **94 carriage** import, bearing.   **96 unimproved** not
turned to account.   **96 hot and full** full of fight.   **98 Shark'd up** got together in haphazard
fashion.   **98 resolutes** desperadoes.   **99 food and diet** no pay but their keep.   **107 romage**
bustle, commotion.

BERNARDO: I think it be no other but e'en so:
　　Well may it sort° that this portentous figure
　　Comes armed through our watch; so like the king　　　　110
　　That was and is the question of these wars.
HORATIO: A mote° it is to trouble the mind's eye.
　　In the most high and palmy state° of Rome,
　　A little ere the mightiest Julius fell,
　　The graves stood tenantless and the sheeted dead　　　115
　　Did squeak and gibber in the Roman streets:
　　As stars with trains of fire° and dews of blood,
　　Disasters° in the sun; and the moist star°
　　Upon whose influence Neptune's empire° stands
　　Was sick almost to doomsday with eclipse:　　　　　120
　　And even the like precurse° of fear'd events,
　　As harbingers preceding still the fates
　　And prologue to the omen coming on,
　　Have heaven and earth together demonstrated
　　Unto our climatures and countrymen.—　　　　　125

(*Enter* GHOST.)

　　But soft, behold! lo, where it comes again!
　　I'll cross° it, though it blast me. Stay, illusion!
　　If thou hast any sound, or use of voice,
　　Speak to me!　　　　　　　　　　　(*It*° *spreads his arms.*)
　　If there be any good thing to be done,　　　　　130
　　That may to thee do ease and grace to me,
　　Speak to me!
　　If° thou art privy to thy country's fate,
　　Which, happily, foreknowing may avoid,
　　O, speak!　　　　　　　　　　　　　　135
　　Or if thou hast uphoarded in thy life
　　Extorted treasure in the womb of earth,
　　For which, they say, you spirits oft walk in death,　　(*The cock crows.*)
　　Speak of it: stay, and speak! Stop it, Marcellus.
MARCELLUS: Shall I strike at it with my partisan?°　　　140
HORATIO: Do, if it will not stand.
BERNARDO:　　　　　　　'Tis here!
HORATIO:　　　　　　　　　　'Tis here!
MARCELLUS: 'Tis gone!　　　　　　　　　　　[*Exit* GHOST.]
　　We do it wrong, being so majestical,
　　To offer it the show of violence;
　　For it is, as the air, invulnerable,　　　　　　145

109 sort suit.　**112 mote** speck of dust.　**113 palmy state** triumphant sovereignty.　**117 stars . . . fire** i.e., comets.　**118 Disasters** unfavorable aspects.　**118 moist star** the moon, governing tides.
119 Neptune's empire the sea.　**121 precurse** heralding.　**127 cross** meet, face, thus bringing down the evil influence on the person who crosses it.　**s.d. It** the Ghost, or perhaps Horatio.
133–139 If . . . in the following seven lines, Horatio recites the traditional reasons why ghosts might walk.　**140 partisan** long-handled spear with a blade having lateral projections.

And our vain blows malicious mockery.

BERNARDO: It was about to speak, when the cock crew.°

HORATIO: And then it started like a guilty thing
    Upon a fearful summons. I have heard,
150   The cock, that is the trumpet to the morn,
    Doth with his lofty and shrill-sounding throat
    Awake the god of day; and, at his warning,
    Whether in sea or fire, in earth or air,
    Th' extravagant and erring° spirit hies
155   To his confine:° and of the truth herein
    This present object made probation.°

MARCELLUS: It faded on the crowing of the cock.
    Some say that ever 'gainst° that season comes
    Wherein our Saviour's birth is celebrated,
160   The bird of dawning singeth all night long:
    And then, they say, no spirit dare stir abroad;
    The nights are wholesome; then no planets strike,°
    No fairy takes, nor witch hath power to charm,
    So hallow'd and so gracious° is that time.

165 HORATIO: So have I heard and do in part believe it.
    But, look, the morn, in russet mantle clad,
    Walks o'er the dew of yon high eastward hill:
    Break we our watch up; and by my advice,
    Let us impart what we have seen to-night
170   Unto young Hamlet; for, upon my life,
    This spirit, dumb to us, will speak to him.
    Do you consent we shall acquaint him with it,
    As needful in our loves, fitting our duty?

MARCELLUS: Let's do 't, I pray; and I this morning know
175   Where we shall find him most conveniently.   *(Exeunt.)*

SCENE II [*A room of state in the castle.*]

Flourish. Enter CLAUDIUS, *King of Denmark,* GERTRUDE *the Queen,*
COUNCILORS, POLONIUS *and his Son* LAERTES, HAMLET, *cum aliis*° [*including*
VOLTIMAND *and* CORNELIUS].

KING: Though yet of Hamlet our dear brother's death
    The memory be green, and that it us befitted
    To bear our hearts in grief and our whole kingdom
    To be contracted in one brow of woe,

---

147 cock crew according to traditional ghost lore, spirits returned to their confines at cockcrow.
154 extravagant and erring wandering. Both words mean the same thing.   **155 confine** place
of confinement.   **156 probation** proof, trial.   **158 'gainst** just before.   **162 planets strike** it
was thought that planets were malignant and might strike travelers by night.   **164 gracious** full of
goodness.   **I.ii. s.d. cum aliis** with others.

Yet so far hath discretion fought with nature   5
That we with wisest sorrow think on him,
Together with remembrance of ourselves.
Therefore our sometime sister, now our queen,
Th' imperial jointress° to this warlike state,
Have we, as 'twere with a defeated joy,—   10
With an auspicious and a dropping eye,
With mirth in funeral and with dirge in marriage,
In equal scale weighing delight and dole,—
Taken to wife: nor have we herein barr'd
Your better wisdoms, which have freely gone   15
With this affair along. For all, our thanks.
Now follows, that° you know, young Fortinbras,
Holding a weak supposal° of our worth,
Or thinking by our late dear brother's death
Our state to be disjoint° and out of frame,°   20
Colleagued° with this dream of his advantage,°
He hath not fail'd to pester us with message,
Importing° the surrender of those lands
Lost by his father, with all bands of law,
To our most valiant brother. So much for him.   25
Now for ourself and for this time of meeting:
Thus much the business is: we have here writ
To Norway, uncle of young Fortinbras,—
Who, impotent and bed-rid, scarcely hears
Of this his nephew's purpose,—to suppress   30
His further gait° herein; in that the levies,
The lists and full proportions, are all made
Out of his subject:° and we here dispatch
You, good Cornelius, and you, Voltimand,
For bearers of this greeting to old Norway;   35
Giving to you no further personal power
To business with the king, more than the scope
Of these delated° articles allow.
Farewell, and let your haste commend your duty.

CORNELIUS: }
VOLTIMAND: } In that and all things will we show our duty.   40

KING: We doubt it nothing: heartily farewell.

[*Exeunt* VOLTIMAND *and* CORNELIUS.]

And now, Laertes, what's the news with you?

9 **jointress** woman possessed of a jointure, or, joint tenancy of an estate.   17 **that** that which.   18 **weak supposal** low estimate.   20 **disjoint** distracted, out of joint.   20 **frame** order.   21 **Colleagued** added to.   21 **dream . . . advantage** visionary hope of success.   23 **Importing** purporting, pertaining to.   31 **gait** proceeding.   33 **Out of his subject** at the expense of Norway's subjects (collectively).   38 **delated** expressly stated.

You told us of some suit; what is't, Laertes?
You cannot speak of reason to the Dane,°
45   And lose your voice:° what wouldst thou beg, Laertes,
That shall not be my offer, not thy asking?
The head is not more native° to the heart,
The hand more instrumental° to the mouth,
Than is the throne of Denmark to thy father.
What wouldst thou have, Laertes?
50   LAERTES: My dread lord,
Your leave and favor to return to France;
From whence though willingly I came to Denmark,
To show my duty in your coronation,
Yet now, I must confess, that duty done,
55   My thoughts and wishes bend again toward France
And bow them to your gracious leave and pardon.°
KING: Have you your father's leave? What says Polonius?
POLONIUS: He hath, my lord, wrung from me my slow leave
By laborsome petition, and at last
60   Upon his will I seal'd my hard consent:
I do beseech you, give him leave to go.
KING: Take thy fair hour, Laertes; time be thine,
And thy best graces spend it at thy will!
But now, my cousin° Hamlet, and my son,—
65   HAMLET [*aside*]: A little more than kin, and less than kind!°
KING: How is it that the clouds still hang on you?
HAMLET: Not so, my lord; I am too much in the sun.°
QUEEN: Good Hamlet, cast thy nighted color off,
And let thine eye look like a friend on Denmark.
70   Do not for ever with thy vailed lids
Seek for thy noble father in the dust:
Thou know'st 'tis common; all that lives must die,
Passing through nature to eternity.
HAMLET: Ay, madam, it is common.°
QUEEN: If it be,
75   Why seems it so particular with thee?
HAMLET: Seems, madam! nay, it is; I know not "seems."
'Tis not alone my inky cloak, good mother,
Nor customary suits° of solemn black,

---

44 the Dane Danish king.   **45 lose your voice** speak in vain.   **47 native** closely connected, related.   **48 instrumental** serviceable.   **56 leave and pardon** permission to depart.   **64 cousin** any kin not of the immediate family.   **65 A little . . . kind!** i.e., my relation to you has become more than kinship warrants; it has also become unnatural.   **67 I am . . . sun** the senses seem to be: I am too much out of doors, I am too much in the sun of your grace (ironical), I am too much of a son to you. Possibly an allusion to the proverb "Out of heaven's blessing into the warm sun"; i.e., Hamlet is out of house and home in being deprived of the kingship.   **74 Ay . . . common** i.e., it is common, but it hurts nevertheless; possibly a reference to the commonplace quality of the queen's remark.   **78 customary suits** suits prescribed by custom for mourning.

Nor windy suspiration° of forc'd breath,
No, nor the fruitful river in the eye, 80
Nor the dejected 'haviour of the visage,
Together with all forms, moods, shapes of grief,
That can denote me truly: these indeed seem,
For they are actions that a man might play:
But I have that within which passeth show; 85
These but the trappings and the suits of woe.

KING: 'Tis sweet and commendable in your nature, Hamlet,
To give these mourning duties to your father:
But, you must know, your father lost a father;
That father lost, lost his, and the survivor bound 90
In filial obligation for some term
To do obsequious° sorrow: but to persever
In obstinate condolement° is a course
Of impious stubbornness; 'tis unmanly grief;
It shows a will most incorrect° to heaven, 95
A heart unfortified, a mind impatient,
An understanding simple and unschool'd:
For what we know must be and is as common
As any the most vulgar thing° to sense,
Why should we in our peevish opposition 100
Take it to heart? Fie! 'tis a fault to heaven,
A fault against the dead, a fault to nature,
To reason most absurd; whose common theme
Is death of fathers, and who still hath cried,
From the first corse till he that died to-day, 105
"This must be so." We pray you, throw to earth
This unprevailing° woe, and think of us
As of a father: for let the world take note,
You are the most immediate° to our throne:
And with no less nobility° of love 110
Than that which dearest father bears his son,
Do I impart° toward you. For your intent
In going back to school in Wittenberg,°
It is most retrograde° to our desire:
And we beseech you, bend you° to remain 115
Here, in the cheer and comfort of our eye,
Our chiefest courtier, cousin, and our son.

QUEEN: Let not thy mother lose her prayers, Hamlet:
I pray thee, stay with us; go not to Wittenberg.

---

79 windy suspiration heavy sighing. **92 obsequious** dutiful. **93 condolement** sorrowing.
95 incorrect untrained, uncorrected. **99 vulgar thing** common experience. **107 unprevailing** unavailing. **109 most immediate** next in succession. **110 nobility** high degree. **112 impart** the object is apparently love (1.110). **113 Wittenberg** famous German university founded in 1502. **114 retrograde** contrary. **115 bend you** incline yourself; imperative.

120   HAMLET: I shall in all my best obey you, madam.

KING: Why, 'tis a loving and a fair reply:
Be as ourself in Denmark. Madam, come;
This gentle and unforc'd accord of Hamlet
Sits smiling to my heart: in grace whereof,
125   No jocund health that Denmark drinks to-day,
But the great cannon to the clouds shall tell,
And the king's rouse° the heaven shall bruit again,°
Re-speaking earthly thunder. Come away.

(*Flourish. Exeunt all but* HAMLET.)

HAMLET: O, that this too too sullied flesh would melt,
130   Thaw and resolve itself into a dew!
Or that the Everlasting had not fix'd
His canon 'gainst self-slaughter! O God! God!
How weary, stale, flat and unprofitable,
Seem to me all the uses of this world!
135   Fie on't! ah fie! 'tis an unweeded garden,
That grows to seed; things rank and gross in nature
Possess it merely.° That it should come to this!
But two months dead: nay, not so much, not two:
So excellent a king; that was, to this,
140   Hyperion° to a satyr; so loving to my mother
That he might not beteem° the winds of heaven
Visit her face too roughly. Heaven and earth!
Must I remember? why, she would hang on him,
As if increase of appetite had grown
145   By what it fed on: and yet, within a month—
Let me not think on't—Frailty, thy name is woman!—
A little month, or ere those shoes were old
With which she followed my poor father's body,
Like Niobe,° all tears:—why she, even she—
150   O God! a beast, that wants discourse of reason,°
Would have mourn'd longer—married with my uncle,
My father's brother, but no more like my father
Than I to Hercules: within a month:
Ere yet the salt of most unrighteous tears
155   Had left the flushing in her galled° eyes.
She married. O, most wicked speed, to post
With such dexterity° to incestuous sheets!
It is not nor it cannot come to good:

127 rouse draft of liquor.   **127 bruit again** echo.   **137 merely** completely, entirely.   **140 Hyperion** God of the sun in the older regime of ancient gods.   **141 beteem** allow.   **149 Niobe** Tantalus's daughter, who boasted that she had more sons and daughters than Leto; for this Apollo and Artemis slew her children. She was turned into stone by Zeus on Mount Sipylus.   **150 discourse of reason** process or faculty of reason.   **155 galled** irritated.   **157 dexterity** facility.

But break, my heart; for I must hold my tongue.

(*Enter* HORATIO, MARCELLUS, *and* BERNARDO.)

HORATIO: Hail to your lordship!   160
HAMLET: I am glad to see you well:
    Horatio!—or I do forget myself.
HORATIO: The same, my lord, and your poor servant ever.
HAMLET: Sir, my good friend; I'll change that name with you:°
And what make you from Wittenberg, Horatio?   165
    Marcellus?
MARCELLUS: My good lord—
HAMLET: I am very glad to see you. Good even, sir.
    But what, in faith, make you from Wittenberg?
HORATIO: A truant disposition, good my lord.   170
HAMLET: I would not hear your enemy say so,
    Nor shall you do my ear that violence,
    To make it truster of your own report
    Against yourself: I know you are no truant.
    But what is your affair in Elsinore?   175
    We'll teach you to drink deep ere you depart.
HORATIO: My lord, I came to see your father's funeral.
HAMLET: I prithee, do not mock me, fellow-student;
    I think it was to see my mother's wedding.
HORATIO: Indeed, my lord, it follow'd hard° upon.   180
HAMLET: Thrift, thrift, Horatio! the funeral bak'd meats°
    Did coldly furnish forth the marriage tables.
    Would I had met my dearest° foe in heaven
    Or ever I had seen that day, Horatio!
    My father!—methinks I see my father.   185
HORATIO: Where, my lord!
HAMLET: In my mind's eye, Horatio.
HORATIO: I saw him once; 'a° was a goodly king.
HAMLET: 'A was a man, take him for all in all,
    I shall not look upon his like again.
HORATIO: My lord, I think I saw him yesternight.   190
HAMLET: Saw? who?
HORATIO: My lord, the king your father.
HAMLET: The king my father!
HORATIO: Season your admiration° for a while
    With an attent ear, till I may deliver,
    Upon the witness of these gentlemen,   195

---

164 I'll . . . you I'll be your servant, you shall be my friend; also explained as "I'll exchange the
name of friend with you." **180 hard** close. **181 bak'd meats** meat pies. **183 dearest** direst;
the adjective *dear* in Shakespeare has two different origins; O.E. *deore*, "beloved," and O.E. *deore*,
"fierce." *Dearest* is the superlative of the second. **187 'a** he. **193 Season your admiration** restrain your astonishment.

This marvel to you.

HAMLET: For God's love, let me hear.

HORATIO: Two nights together had these gentlemen,
    Marcellus and Bernardo, on their watch,
    In the dead waste and middle of the night,
200   Been thus encount'red. A figure like your father,
    Armed at point exactly, cap-a-pe,°
    Appears before them, and with solemn march
    Goes slow and stately by them: thrice he walk'd
    By their oppress'd° and fear-surprised eyes,
205   Within his truncheon's° length; whilst they, distill'd°
    Almost to jelly with the act° of fear,
    Stand dumb and speak not to him. This to me
    In dreadful secrecy impart they did;
    And I with them the third night kept the watch:
210   Where, as they had deliver'd, both in time,
    Form of the thing, each word made true and good,
    The apparition comes: I knew your father;
    These hands are not more like.

HAMLET: But where was this?

MARCELLUS: My lord, upon the platform where we watch'd.

HAMLET: Did you not speak to it?

215 HORATIO: My lord, I did;
    But answer made it none: yet once methought
    It lifted up it° head and did address
    Itself to motion, like as it would speak;
    But even then the morning cock crew loud,
220   And at the sound it shrunk in haste away,
    And vanish'd from our sight.

HAMLET: 'Tis very strange.

HORATIO: As I do live, my honor'd lord, 'tis true;
    And we did think it writ down in our duty
    To let you know of it.

225 HAMLET: Indeed, indeed, sirs, but this troubles me.
    Hold you the watch to-night?

MARCELLUS: ⎫
BERNARDO: ⎬   We do, my lord.

HAMLET: Arm'd, say you?

MARCELLUS: ⎫
BERNARDO: ⎬ Arm'd, my lord.

HAMLET: From top to toe?

MARCELLUS: ⎫
BERNARDO: ⎬   My lord, from head to foot.

230 HAMLET: Then saw you not his face?

---

201 cap-a-pe from head to foot.   **204 oppress'd** distressed.   **205 truncheon** officer's staff.
205 disill'd softened, weakened.   **206 act** action.   **217 it** its.

HORATIO: O, yes, my lord; he wore his beaver° up.

HAMLET: What, look'd he frowningly?

HORATIO: A countenance more
    In sorrow than in anger.

HAMLET: Pale or red?

HORATIO: Nay, very pale.

HAMLET: And fix'd his eyes upon you?

HORATIO: Most constantly.

HAMLET: I would I had been there.   235

HORATIO: It would have much amaz'd you.

HAMLET: Very like, very like. Stay'd it long?

HORATIO: While one with moderate haste might tell a hundred.

MARCELLUS: ⎫
BERNARDO: ⎬ Longer, longer.

HORATIO: Not when I saw't.

HAMLET: His beard was grizzled,—no?   240

HORATIO: It was, as I have seen it in his life,
    A sable° silver'd.

HAMLET: I will watch to-night;
    Perchance 'twill walk again.

HORATIO: I warr'nt it will.

HAMLET: If it assume my noble father's person,
    I'll speak to it, though hell itself should gape   245
    And bid me hold my peace. I pray you all,
    If you have hitherto conceal'd this sight,
    Let it be tenable in your silence still;
    And whatsoever else shall hap to-night,
    Give it an understanding, but no tongue;   250
    I will requite your loves. So, fare you well:
    Upon the platform, 'twixt eleven and twelve,
    I'll visit you.

ALL: Our duty to your honor.

HAMLET: Your loves, as mine to you: farewell.   (*Exeunt [all but* HAMLET].)
    My father's spirit in arms! all is not well;   255
    I doubt° some foul play: would the night were come!
    Till then sit still, my soul: foul deeds will rise,
    Though all the earth o'erwhelm them, to men's eyes.   (*Exit.*)

SCENE III [*A room in Polonius's house.*]

(*Enter* LAERTES *and* OPHELIA, *his Sister.*)

LAERTES: My necessaries are embark'd: farewell:
    And, sister, as the winds give benefit
    And convoy is assistant,° do not sleep,

---

231 beaver visor on the helmet.   **242 sable** black color.   **256 doubt** fear.   **I.iii. 3 convoy is assistant** means of conveyance are available.

But let me hear from you.

OPHELIA: Do you doubt that?

5 LAERTES: For Hamlet and the trifling of his favor,
　　　　　Hold it a fashion° and a toy in blood,°
　　　　　A violet in the youth of primy° nature,
　　　　　Forward,° not permanent, sweet, not lasting,
　　　　　The perfume and suppliance of a minute;°
　　　　　No more.

OPHELIA: No more but so?

10 LAERTES: Think it no more:
　　　　　For nature, crescent,° does not grow alone
　　　　　In thews° and bulk, but, as this temple° waxes,
　　　　　The inward service of the mind and soul
　　　　　Grows wide withal. Perhaps he loves you now,
15　　　　And now no soil° nor cautel° doth besmirch
　　　　　The virtue of his will: but you must fear,
　　　　　His greatness weigh'd,° his will is not his own;
　　　　　For he himself is subject to his birth:
　　　　　He may not, as unvalued persons do,
20　　　　Carve for himself; for on his choice depends
　　　　　The safety and health of this whole state;
　　　　　And therefore must his choice be circumscrib'd
　　　　　Unto the voice and yielding° of that body
　　　　　Whereof he is the head. Then if he says he loves you,
25　　　　It fits your wisdom so far to believe it
　　　　　As he in his particular act and place
　　　　　May give his saying deed;° which is no further
　　　　　Than the main voice of Denmark goes withal.
　　　　　Then weigh what loss your honor may sustain,
30　　　　If with too credent° ear you list his songs,
　　　　　Or lose your heart, or your chaste treasure open
　　　　　To his unmast'red° importunity.
　　　　　Fear it, Ophelia, fear it, my dear sister,
　　　　　And keep you in the rear of your affection,
35　　　　Out of the shot and danger of desire.
　　　　　The chariest° maid is prodigal enough,
　　　　　If she unmask her beauty to the moon:
　　　　　Virtue itself 'scapes not calumnious strokes:
　　　　　The canker galls the infants of the spring,°
40　　　　Too oft before their buttons° be disclos'd,°

6 **fashion** custom, prevailing usage.　6 **toy in blood** passing amorous fancy.　7 **primy** in its prime.　8 **Forward** precocious.　9 **suppliance of a minute** diversion to fill up a minute.　11 **crescent** growing, waxing.　12 **thews** bodily strength.　12 **temple** body.　15 **soil** blemish.　15 **cautel** crafty device.　17 **greatness weigh'd** high position considered.　23 **voice and yielding** assent, approval.　27 **deed** effect.　30 **credent** credulous.　32 **unmast'red** unrestrained.　36 **chariest** most scrupulously modest.　39 **The canker . . . spring** the cankerworm destroys the young plants of spring.　40 **buttons** buds.　40 **disclos'd** opened.

And in the morn and liquid dew° of youth
Contagious blastments° are most imminent.
Be wary then; best safety lies in fear:
Youth to itself rebels, though none else near.

OPHELIA: I shall the effect of this good lesson keep,   45
As watchman to my heart. But, good my brother,
Do not, as some ungracious° pastors do,
Show me the steep and thorny way to heaven;
Whiles, like a puff'd° and reckless libertine,
Himself the primrose path of dalliance treads,   50
And recks° not his own rede.°

(*Enter* POLONIUS.)

LAERTES: O, fear me not.
I stay too long: but here my father comes.
A double° blessing is a double grace;
Occasion° smiles upon a second leave.   55

POLONIUS: Yet here, Laertes? aboard, aboard, for shame!
The wind sits in the shoulder of your sail,
And you are stay'd for. There; my blessing with thee!
And these few precepts° in thy memory
Look thou character.° Give thy thoughts no tongue,   60
Nor any unproportion'd° thought his act.
Be thou familiar, but by no means vulgar.°
Those friends thou hast, and their adoption tried,
Grapple them to thy soul with hoops of steel;
But do not dull thy palm with entertainment   65
Of each new-hatch'd, unfledg'd° comrade. Beware
Of entrance to a quarrel, but being in,
Bear't that th' opposed may beware of thee.
Give every man thy ear, but few thy voice;
Take each man's censure, but reserve thy judgement.   70
Costly thy habit as thy purse can buy,
But not express'd in fancy;° rich, not gaudy;
For the apparel oft proclaims the man,
And they in France of the best rank and station
Are of a most select and generous chief in that.°   75
Neither a borrower nor a lender be;
For loan oft loses both itself and friend,
And borrowing dulleth edge of husbandry.°

41 liquid dew i.e., time when dew is fresh.   **42 blastments** blights.   **47 ungracious** graceless.
49 puff'd bloated.   **51 recks** heeds.   **51 rede** counsel.   **54 double** i.e., Laertes has already bade
his father good-bye.   **55 Occasion** opportunity.   **59 precepts** many parallels have been found to
the series of maxims which follows, one of the closer being that in Lyly's Euphues.   **60 character**
inscribe.   **61 unproportion'd** inordinate.   **62 vulgar** common.   **66 unfledg'd** immature.   **72
express'd in fancy** fantastical in design.   **75 Are . . . that** *chief* is usually taken as a substantive
meaning "head," "eminence."   **78 husbandry** thrift.

This above all: to thine own self be true,
80   And it must follow, as the night the day,
          Thou canst not then be false to any man.
          Farewell: my blessing season° this in thee!
     LAERTES: Most humbly do I take my leave, my lord.
     POLONIUS: The time invites you; go; your servants tend.
85   LAERTES: Farewell, Ophelia; and remember well
          What I have said to you.
     OPHELIA: 'Tis in my memory lock'd,
          And you yourself shall keep the key of it.
     LAERTES: Farewell.   (*Exit* LAERTES.)
     POLONIUS: What is 't, Ophelia, he hath said to you?
90   OPHELIA: So please you, something touching the Lord Hamlet.
     POLONIUS: Marry, well bethought:
          'Tis told me, he hath very oft of late
          Given private time to you; and you yourself
          Have of your audience been most free and bounteous:
95   If it be so, as so't is put on° me,
          And that in way of caution, I must tell you,
          You do not understand yourself so clearly
          As it behooves my daughter and your honor.
          What is between you? give me up the truth.
100 OPHELIA: He hath, my lord, of late made many tenders°
          Of his affection to me.
     POLONIUS: Affection! pooh! you speak like a green girl,
          Unsifted° in such perilous circumstance.
          Do you believe his tenders, as you call them?
105 OPHELIA: I do not know, my lord, what I should think.
     POLONIUS: Marry, I will teach you: think yourself a baby;
          That you have ta'en these tenders° for true pay,
          Which are not sterling.° Tender° yourself more dearly;
          Or—not to crack the wind° of the poor phrase,
110   Running it thus—you'll tender me a fool.°
     OPHELIA: My lord, he hath importun'd me with love
          In honorable fashion.
     POLONIUS: Ay, fashion° you may call it; go to, go to.
     OPHELIA: And hath given countenance° to his speech, my lord,
115   With almost all the holy vows of heaven.
     POLONIUS: Ay, springes° to catch woodcocks.° I do know,
          When the blood burns, how prodigal the soul
          Lends the tongue vows: these blazes, daughter,

---

82 season mature.   **95 put on** impressed on.   **100, 104 tenders** offers.   **103 Unsifted** untried.
107 tenders promises to pay.   **108 sterling** legal currency.   **108 Tender** hold.   **109 crack the
wind** i.e., run it until it is broken-winded.   **110 tender . . . fool** show me a fool (for a daughter).
113 fashion mere form, pretense.   **114 countenance** credit, support.   **116 springes** snares.
116 woodcocks birds easily caught, type of stupidity.

Giving more light than heat, extinct in both,
Even in their promise, as it is a-making,   12•
You must not take for fire. From this time
Be somewhat scanter of your maiden presence;
Set your entreatments° at a higher rate
Than a command to parley.° For Lord Hamlet,
Believe so much in him,° that he is young,   12:
And with a larger tether may he walk
Than may be given you: in few,° Ophelia,
Do not believe his vows; for they are brokers;°
Not of that dye° which their investments° show,
But mere implorators of° unholy suits,   13•
Breathing° like sanctified and pious bawds,
The better to beguile. This is for all:
I would not, in plain terms, from this time forth,
Have you so slander° any moment leisure,
As to give words or talk with the Lord Hamlet.   13.
Look to 't, I charge you: come your ways.
OPHELIA: I shall obey, my lord.   (*Exeunt.*)

SCENE IV [*The platform.*]

(*Enter* HAMLET, HORATIO, *and* MARCELLUS.)

HAMLET: The air bites shrewdly; it is very cold.
HORATIO: It is a nipping and an eager air.
HAMLET: What hour now?
HORATIO: I think it lacks of twelve.
MARCELLUS: No, it is struck.
HORATIO: Indeed? I heard it not: then it draws near the season   5
    Wherein the spirit held his wont to walk.

(*A flourish of trumpets, and two pieces go off.*)

    What does this mean, my lord?
HAMLET: The king doth wake° to-night and takes his rouse,°
    Keeps wassail,° and the swagg'ring up-spring° reels;°
    And, as he drains his draughts of Rhenish° down,   10
    The kettle-drum and trumpet thus bray out
    The triumph of his pledge.°
HORATIO: Is it a custom?
HAMLET: Ay, marry, is 't:

123 **entreatments** conversations, interviews. 124 **command to parley** mere invitation to talk.
125 **so . . . him** this much concerning him. 127 **in few** briefly. 128 **brokers** go-betweens,
procurers. 129 **dye** color or sort. 129 **investments** clothes. 130 **implorators of** solicitors
of. 131 **Breathing** speaking. 134 **slander** bring disgrace or reproach upon. I.iv. 8 **wake** stay
awake, hold revel. 8 **rouse** carouse, drinking bout. 9 **wassail** carousal. 9 **up-spring** last and
wildest dance at German merry-makings. 9 **reels** reels through. 10 **Rhenish** Rhine wine. 12
Triumph . . . pledge his glorious achievement as a drinker.

But to my mind, though I am native here
15 And to the manner born,° it is a custom
More honor'd in the breach than the observance.
This heavy-headed revel east and west
Makes us traduc'd and tax'd of other nations:
They clepe° us drunkards, and with swinish phrase°
20 Soil our addition;° and indeed it takes
From our achievements, though perform'd at height,
The pith and marrow of our attribute.°
So, oft it chances in particular men,
That for some vicious mole of nature° in them,
25 As, in their birth—wherein they are not guilty,
Since nature cannot choose his origin—
By the o'ergrowth of some complexion,
Oft breaking down the pales° and forts of reason,
Or by some habit that too much o'er-leavens°
30 The form of plausive° manners, that these men,
Carrying, I say, the stamp of one defect,
Being nature's livery,° or fortune's star,°—
Their virtues else—be they as pure as grace,
As infinite as man may undergo—
35 Shall in the general censure take corruption
From that particular fault: the dram of eale°
Doth all the noble substance of a doubt
To his own scandal.°

(*Enter* GHOST.)

HORATIO: Look, my lord, it comes!
HAMLET: Angels and ministers of grace° defend us!
40 Be thou a spirit of health or goblin damn'd,
Bring with thee airs from heaven or blasts from hell,
Be thy intents wicked or charitable,
Thou com'st in such a questionable° shape
That I will speak to thee: I'll call thee Hamlet,
45 King, father, royal Dane: O, answer me!
Let me not burst in ignorance; but tell
Why thy canoniz'd° bones, hearsed° in death,

15 to . . . born destined by birth to be subject to the custom in question.   **19 clepe** call.   **19 with swinish phrase** by calling us swine.   **20 addition** reputation.   **22 attribute** reputation.   **24 mole of nature** natural blemish in one's constitution.   **28 pales** palings (as of a fortification).   **29 o'er-leavens** induces a change throughout (as yeast works in bread).   **30 plausive** pleasing.   **32 nature's livery** endowment from nature.   **32 fortune's star** the position in which one is placed by fortune, a reference to astrology. The two phrases are aspects of the same thing.   **36 dram of eale** has had various interpretations, the preferred one being probably, "a dram of evil."   **36–38 the dram . . . scandal** a famous crux.   **39 ministers of grace** messengers of God.   **43 questionable** inviting question or conversation.   **47 canoniz'd** buried according to the canons of the church.   **47 hearsed** coffined.

Have burst their cerements;° why the sepulchre,
Wherein we saw thee quietly interr'd,
Hath op'd his ponderous and marble jaws,   50
To cast thee up again. What may this mean,
That thou, dead corse, again in complete steel
Revisits thus the glimpses of the moon,°
Making night hideous; and we fools of nature°
So horridly to shake our disposition   55
With thoughts beyond the reaches of our souls?
Say, why is this? wherefore? what should we do?

([GHOST] *beckons* [HAMLET].)

HORATIO: It beckons you to go away with it,
     As if it some impartment° did desire
     To you alone.
MARCELLUS: Look, with what courteous action   60
     It waves you to a more removed° ground:
     But do not go with it.
HORATIO: No, by no means.
HAMLET: It will not speak; then I will follow it.
HORATIO: Do not, my lord!
HAMLET: Why, what should be the fear?
     I do not set my life at a pin's fee;   65
     And for my soul, what can it do to that,
     Being a thing immortal as itself?
     It waves me forth again: I'll follow it.
HORATIO: What if it tempt you toward the flood, my lord,
     Or to the dreadful summit of the cliff   70
     That beetles o'er° his base into the sea,
     And there assume some other horrible form,
     Which might deprive your sovereignty of reason°
     And draw you into madness? think of it:
     The very place puts toys of desperation,°   75
     Without more motive, into every brain
     That looks so many fathoms to the sea
     And hears it roar beneath.
HAMLET: It waves me still.
     Go on; I'll follow thee.
MARCELLUS: You shall not go, my lord.
HAMLET: Hold off your hands!   80
HORATIO: Be rul'd; you shall not go.

48 cerements grave-clothes. **53 glimpses of the moon** the earth by night. **54 fools of na-**
ture mere men, limited to natural knowledge. **59 impartment** communication. **61 removed**
remote. **71 beetles o'er** overhangs threateningly. **73 deprive . . . reason** take away the sovereignty of your reason. It was thought that evil spirits would sometimes assume the form of departed
spirits in order to work madness in a human creature. **75 toys of desperation** freakish notions of
suicide.

HAMLET: My fate cries out,
    And makes each petty artere° in this body
    As hardy as the Nemean lion's° nerve.°
    Still am I call'd. Unhand me, gentlemen.
85   By heaven, I'll make a ghost of him that lets° me!
    I say, away! Go on; I'll follow thee.   (*Exeunt* GHOST *and* HAMLET.)
HORATIO: He waxes desperate with imagination.
MARCELLUS: Let's follow; 'tis not fit thus to obey him.
HORATIO: Have after. To what issue° will this come?
90 MARCELLUS: Something is rotten in the state of Denmark.
HORATIO: Heaven will direct it.°
MARCELLUS: Nay, let's follow him.   (*Exeunt.*)

SCENE V [*Another part of the platform.*]

(*Enter* GHOST *and* HAMLET.)

HAMLET: Whither wilt thou lead me? speak; I'll go no further.
GHOST: Mark me.
HAMLET: I will.
GHOST: My hour is almost come,
    When I to sulphurous and tormenting flames
    Must render up myself.
HAMLET: Alas, poor ghost!
5 GHOST: Pity me not, but lend thy serious hearing
    To what I shall unfold.
HAMLET: Speak; I am bound to hear.
GHOST: So art thou to revenge, when thou shalt hear.
HAMLET: What?
GHOST: I am thy father's spirit,
10   Doom'd for a certain term to walk the night,
    And for the day confin'd to fast° in fires,
    Till the foul crimes done in my days of nature
    Are burnt and purg'd away. But that I am forbid
    To tell the secrets of my prison-house,
15   I could a tale unfold whose lightest word
    Would harrow up thy soul, freeze thy young blood,
    Make thy two eyes, like stars, start from their spheres,°
    Thy knotted° and combined° locks to part
    And each particular hair to stand an end,
20   Like quills upon the fretful porpentine:°

82 artere artery.   **83 Nemean lion's** Nemean lion was one of the monsters slain by Hercules.
83 nerve sinew, tendon. The point is that the arteries which were carrying the spirits out into the
body were functioning and were as stiff and hard as the sinews of the lion.   **85 lets** hinders.   **89
issue** outcome.   **91 it** i.e., the outcome.   **I.v. 11 fast** probably, do without food. It has been
sometimes taken in the sense of doing general penance.   **17 spheres** orbits.   **18 knotted** perhaps
intricately arranged.   **18 combined** tied, bound.   **20 porpentine** porcupine.

But this eternal blazon° must not be
To ears of flesh and blood. List, list, O, list!
If thou didst ever thy dear father love—
HAMLET: O God!
GHOST: Revenge his foul and most unnatural° murder.   25
HAMLET: Murder!
GHOST: Murder most foul, as in the best it is;
   But this most foul, strange and unnatural.
HAMLET: Haste me to know't, that I, with wings as swift
   As meditation or the thoughts of love,   30
   May sweep to my revenge.
GHOST: I find thee apt;
   And duller shouldst thou be than the fat weed°
   That roots itself in ease on Lethe wharf,°
   Wouldst thou not stir in this. Now, Hamlet, hear:
   'Tis given out that, sleeping in my orchard,   35
   A serpent stung me; so the whole ear of Denmark
   Is by a forged process of my death
   Rankly abus'd: but know, thou noble youth,
   The serpent that did sting thy father's life
   Now wears his crown.
HAMLET: O my prophetic soul!   40
   My uncle!
GHOST: Ay, that incestuous, that adulterate° beast,
   With witchcraft of his wit, with traitorous gifts,—
   O wicked wit and gifts, that have the power
   So to seduce!—won to his shameful lust   45
   The will of my most seeming-virtuous queen:
   O Hamlet, what a falling-off was there!
   From me, whose love was of that dignity
   That it went hand in hand even with the vow
   I made to her in marriage, and to decline   50
   Upon a wretch whose natural gifts were poor
   To those of mine!
   But virtue, as it never will be moved,
   Though lewdness court it in a shape of heaven,
   So lust, though to a radiant angel link'd,   55
   Will sate itself in a celestial bed,
   And prey on garbage.
   But, soft! methinks I scent the morning air;
   Brief let me be. Sleeping within my orchard,

---

21 **eternal blazon** promulgation or proclamation of eternity, revelation of the hereafter.   25 **unnatural** i.e., pertaining to fratricide.   32 **fat weed** many suggestions have been offered as to the particular plant intended, including asphodel; probably a general figure for plants growing along rotting wharves and piles.   33 **Lethe wharf** bank of the river of forgetfulness in Hades.   42 **adulterate** adulterous.

60   My custom always of the afternoon,
    Upon my secure° hour thy uncle stole,
    With juice of cursed hebona° in a vial,
    And in the porches of my ears did pour
    The leperous° distilment; whose effect
65   Holds such an enmity with blood of man
    That swift as quicksilver it courses through
    The natural gates and alleys of the body,
    And with a sudden vigor it doth posset°
    And curd, like eager° droppings into milk,
70   The thin and wholesome blood: so did it mine;
    And a most instant tetter bark'd about,
    Most lazar-like,° with vile and loathsome crust,
    All my smooth body.
    Thus was I, sleeping, by a brother's hand
75   Of life, of crown, of queen, at once dispatch'd:°
    Cut off even in the blossoms of my sin,
    Unhous'led,° disappointed,° unanel'd,°
    No reck'ning made, but sent to my account
    With all my imperfections on my head:
80   O, horrible! O, horrible! most horrible!°
    If thou hast nature in thee, bear it not;
    Let not the royal bed of Denmark be
    A couch for luxury° and damned incest.
    But, howsomever thou pursues this act,
85   Taint not thy mind,° nor let thy soul contrive
    Against thy mother aught: leave her to heaven
    And to those thorns that in her bosom lodge,
    To prick and sting her. Fare thee well at once!
    The glow-worm shows the matin° to be near,
90   And 'gins to pale his uneffectual fire:°
    Adieu, adieu, adieu! remember me.   [*Exit.*]
HAMLET: O all you host of heaven! O earth! what else?
    And shall I couple° hell? O, fie! Hold, hold, my heart;
    And you, my sinews, grow not instant old,
95   But bear me stiffly up. Remember thee!
    Ay, thou poor ghost, whiles memory holds a seat
    In this distracted globe.° Remember thee!

---

61 secure confident, unsuspicious.   **62 hebona** generally supposed to mean henbane, conjectured hemlock; *ebenus,* meaning "yew."   **64 leperous** causing leprosy.   **68 posset** coagulate, curdle.   **69 eager** sour, acid.   **72 lazar-like** leperlike.   **75 dispatch'd** suddenly bereft.   **77 Unhous'led** without having received the sacrament.   **77 disappointed** unready, without equipment for the last journey.   **77 unanel'd** without having received extreme unction.   **80 O . . . horrible** many editors give this line to Hamlet: Garrick and Sir Henry Irving spoke it in that part.   **83 luxury** lechery.   **85 Taint . . . mind** probably, deprave not thy character, do nothing except in the pursuit of a natural revenge.   **89 matin** morning.   **90 uneffectual fire** cold light.   **93 couple** add.   **97 distracted globe** confused head.

Yea, from the table of my memory
I'll wipe away all trivial fond records,
All saws° of books, all forms, all pressures° past,   100
That youth and observation copied there;
And thy commandment all alone shall live
Within the book and volume of my brain,
Unmix'd with baser matter: yes, by heaven!
O most pernicious woman!   105
O villain, villain, smiling, damned villain!
My tables,°—meet it is I set it down,
That one may smile, and smile, and be a villain;
At least I am sure it may be so in Denmark: [*Writing.*]
So, uncle, there you are. Now to my word;°   110
It is "Adieu, adieu! remember me,"
I have sworn't.

(*Enter* HORATIO *and* MARCELLUS.)

HORATIO: My lord, my lord—
MARCELLUS: Lord Hamlet,—
HORATIO: Heavens secure him!
HAMLET: So be it!
MARCELLUS: Hillo, ho, ho,° my lord!   115
HAMLET: Hillo, ho, ho, boy! come, bird, come.
MARCELLUS: How is't, my noble lord?
HORATIO: What news, my lord?
HAMLET: O, wonderful!
HORATIO: Good my lord, tell it.
HAMLET: No; you will reveal it.   120
HORATIO: Not I, my lord, by heaven.
MARCELLUS: Nor I, my lord.
HAMLET: How say you, then; would heart of man once think it?
    But you'll be secret?
HORATIO: }
MARCELLUS: }   Ay, by heaven, my lord.
HAMLET: There's ne'er a villain dwelling in all Denmark
    But he's an arrant° knave.   125
HORATIO: There needs no ghost, my lord, come from the grave
    To tell us this.
HAMLET: Why, right; you are in the right;
    And so, without more circumstance at all,
    I hold it fit that we shake hands and part:
    You, as your business and desire shall point you;   130
    For every man has business and desire,

---

100 saws wise sayings.   **100 pressures** impressions stamped.   **107 tables** probably a small portable writing-tablet carried at the belt.   **110 word** watchword.   **115 Hillo, ho, ho** a falconer's call to a hawk in air.   **125 arrant** thoroughgoing.

>   Such as it is; and for my own poor part,
>   Look you, I'll go pray.
> HORATIO: These are but wild and whirling words, my lord.
> 35 HAMLET: I am sorry they offend you, heartily;
>   Yes, 'faith, heartily.
> HORATIO: There's no offence, my lord.
> HAMLET: Yes, by Saint Patrick,° but there is, Horatio,
>   And much offence too. Touching this vision here,
>   It is an honest° ghost, that let me tell you:
> 40   For your desire to know what is between us,
>   O'ermaster 't as you may. And now, good friends,
>   As you are friends, scholars and soldiers,
>   Give me one poor request.
> HORATIO: What is 't, my lord? we will.
> 45 HAMLET: Never make known what you have seen to-night.
> HORATIO: }
> MARCELLUS: } My lord, we will not.
> HAMLET: Nay, but swear 't.
> HORATIO: In faith,
>   My lord, not I.
> MARCELLUS: Nor I, my lord, in faith.
> HAMLET: Upon my sword.°
> MARCELLUS: We have sworn, my lord, already.
> 50 HAMLET: Indeed, upon my sword, indeed.   (GHOST *cries under the stage.*)
> GHOST: Swear.
> HAMLET: Ah, ha, boy! say'st thou so? art thou there, truepenny?°
>   Come on—you hear this fellow in the cellarage—
>   Consent to swear.
> HORATIO: Propose the oath, my lord.
> 55 HAMLET: Never to speak of this that you have seen,
>   Swear by my sword.
> GHOST [*beneath*]: Swear.
> HAMLET: Hic et ubique?° then we'll shift our ground.
>   Come hither, gentlemen,
> 60   And lay your hands again upon my sword:
>   Swear by my sword,
>   Never to speak of this that you have heard.
> GHOST [*beneath*]: Swear by his sword.
> HAMLET: Well said, old mole! canst work i' th' earth so fast?
> 65   A worthy pioner!° Once more remove, good friends.
> HORATIO: O day and night, but this is wondrous strange!
> HAMLET: And therefore as a stranger give it welcome.

---

137 Saint Patrick St. Patrick was the keeper of Purgatory and patron saint of all blunders and confusion.   **139 honest** i.e., a real ghost and not an evil spirit.   **149 sword** i.e., the hilt in the form of a cross.   **152 truepenny** good old boy, or the like.   **158 Hic et ubique?** here and everywhere?   **165 pioner** digger, miner.

There are more things in heaven and earth, Horatio,
Than are dreamt of in your philosophy.
But come;   170
Here, as before, never, so help you mercy,
How strange or odd soe'er I bear myself,
As I perchance hereafter shall think meet
To put an antic° disposition on,
That you, at such times seeing me, never shall,   175
With arms encumb'red° thus, or this head-shake,
Or by pronouncing of some doubtful phrase,
As "Well, well, we know," or "We could, an if we would,"
Or "If we list to speak," or "There be, an if they might,"
Or such ambiguous giving out,° to note°   180
That you know aught of me: this not to do,
So grace and mercy at your most need help you,
Swear.
GHOST [beneath]: Swear.
HAMLET: Rest, rest, perturbed spirit! [They swear.] So, gentlemen,   185
With all my love I do commend me to you:
And what so poor a man as Hamlet is
May do, t' express his love and friending° to you,
God willing, shall not lack. Let us go in together;
And still your fingers on your lips, I pray.   190
The time is out of joint: O cursed spite,
That ever I was born to set it right!
Nay, come, let's go together.   (Exeunt.)

ACT II
SCENE I [A room in Polonius's house.]

(Enter old POLONIUS with his man [REYNALDO].)

POLONIUS: Give him this money and these notes. Reynaldo.
REYNALDO: I will, my lord.
POLONIUS: You shall do marvellous wisely, good Reynaldo,
Before you visit him, to make inquire
Of his behavior.
REYNALDO: My lord, I did intend it.   5
POLONIUS: Marry, well said; very well said. Look you, sir,
Inquire me first what Danskers° are in Paris;
And how, and who, what means, and where they keep,°
What company, at what expense; and finding
By this encompassment° and drift° of question   10

---

174 antic fantastic.   **176 encumb'red** folded or entwined.   **180 giving out** profession of
knowledge.   **180 to note** to give a sign.   **188 friending** friendliness.   **II.i. 7 Danskers** *Danke*
was a common variant for *Denmark*; hence *Dane*.   **8 keep** dwell.   **10 encompassment** round-
about talking.   **10 drift** gradual approach or course.

That they do know my son, come you more nearer
Than your particular demands will touch it:°
Take° you as 'twere, some distant knowledge of him;
As thus, "I know his father and his friends;
15 And in part him": do you mark this, Reynaldo?
REYNALDO: Ay, very well, my lord.
POLONIUS: "And in part him; but" you may say "not well:
But, if't be he I mean, he's very wild;
Addicted so and so": and there put on° him
20 What forgeries° you please; marry, none so rank
As may dishonor him; take heed of that;
But, sir, such wanton,° wild and usual slips
As are companions noted and most known
To youth and liberty.
REYNALDO: As gaming, my lord.
25 POLONIUS: Ay, or drinking, fencing,° swearing, quarrelling,
Drabbing;° you may go so far.
REYNALDO: My lord, that would dishonor him.
POLONIUS: 'Faith, no; as you may season it in the charge.
You must not put another scandal on him,
30 That he is open to incontinency;°
That's not my meaning: but breathe his faults so quaintly°
That they may seem the taints of liberty,°
The flash and outbreak of a fiery mind,
A savageness in unreclaimed° blood,
Of general assault.°
35 REYNALDO: But, my good lord,—
POLONIUS: Wherefore should you do this?
REYNALDO: Ay, my lord,
I would know that.
POLONIUS: Marry, sir, here's my drift;
And, I believe, it is a fetch of wit:°
You laying these slight sullies on my son,
40 As 'twere a thing a little soil'd i' th' working,
Mark you,
Your party in converse, him you would sound,
Having ever° seen in the prenominate° crimes
The youth you breathe of guilty, be assur'd
45 He closes with you in this consequence;°

11–12 come . . . it i.e., you will find out more this way than by asking pointed questions.   **13 Take** assume, pretend.   **19 put on** impute to.   **20 forgeries** invented tales.   **22 wanton** sportive, unrestrained.   **25 fencing** indicative of the ill repute of professional fencers and fencing schools in Elizabethan times.   **26 Drabbing** associated with immoral women.   **30 incontinency** habitual loose behavior.   **31 quaintly** delicately, ingeniously.   **32 taints of liberty** blemishes due to freedom.   **34 unreclaimed** untamed.   **35 general assault** tendency that assails all untrained youth.   **38 fetch of wit** clever trick.   **43 ever** at any time.   **43 prenominate** before-mentioned.   **45 closes . . . consequence** agrees with you in this conclusion.

"Good sir," or so, or "friend," or "gentleman,"
According to the phrase or the addition
Of man and country.
REYNALDO: Very good, my lord.
POLONIUS: And then, sir, does 'a this—'a does—what was I about to say?
By the mass, I was about to say something: where did I leave?   50
REYNALDO: At "closes in the consequence," at "friend or so," and "gentleman."
POLONIUS: At "closes in the consequence," ay, marry;
He closes thus: "I know the gentleman;
I saw him yesterday, or t' other day,
Or then, or then; with such, or such; and, as you say,   55
There was 'a gaming; there o'ertook in's rouse;°
There falling out at tennis": or perchance,
"I saw him enter such a house of sale,"
Videlicet,° a brothel, or so forth.
See you now;   60
Your bait of falsehood takes this carp of truth:
And thus do we of wisdom and of reach,°
With windlasses° and with assays of bias,°
By indirections° find directions° out:
So by my former lecture° and advice,   65
Shall you my son. You have me, have you not?
REYNALDO: My lord, I have.
POLONIUS: God bye ye;° fare ye well.
REYNALDO: Good my lord!
POLONIUS: Observe his inclination in yourself.°
REYNALDO: I shall, my lord.   70
POLONIUS: And let him ply his music.°
REYNALDO: Well, my lord.
POLONIUS: Farewell!   (*Exit* REYNALDO.)

(*Enter* OPHELIA.)

                    How now, Ophelia! what's the matter?
OPHELIA: O, my lord, my lord, I have been so affrighted!
POLONIUS: With what, i' th' name of God?
OPHELIA: My lord, as I was sewing in my closet,°   75
Lord Hamlet, with his doublet° all unbrac'd;°
No hat upon his head; his stockings foul'd,
Ungart'red, and down-gyved° to his ankle;

---

56 o'ertook in's rouse overcome by drink.   **59 Videlicet** namely.   **62 reach** capacity, ability.
63 windlasses i.e., circuitous paths.   **63 assays of bias** attempts that resemble the course of the
bowl, which, being weighted on one side, has a curving motion.   **64 indirections** devious courses.
64 directions straight courses, i.e., the truth.   **65 lecture** admonition.   **67 bye ye** be with you.
69 Observe . . . yourself in your own person, not by spies; or conform your own conduct to his
inclination; or test him by studying yourself.   **71 ply his music** probably to be taken literally.   **75
closet** private chamber.   **76 doublet** close-fitting coat.   **76 unbrac'd** unfastened.   **78 down-
gyved** fallen to the ankles (like gyves or fetters).

Pale as his shirt; his knees knocking each other;
80 And with a look so piteous in purport
As if he had been loosed out of hell
To speak of horrors,—he comes before me.
POLONIUS: Mad for thy love?
OPHELIA: My lord, I do not know;
But truly, I do fear it.
POLONIUS: What said he?
85 OPHELIA: He took me by the wrist and held me hard;
Then goes he to the length of all his arm;
And, with his other hand thus o'er his brow,
He falls to such perusal of my face
As 'a would draw it. Long stay'd he so;
90 At last, a little shaking of mine arm
And thrice his head thus waving up and down,
He rais'd a sigh so piteous and profound
As it did seem to shatter all his bulk°
And end his being: that done, he lets me go:
95 And, with his head over his shoulder turn'd,
He seem'd to find his way without his eyes;
For out o'doors he went without their helps,
And, to the last, bended their light on me.
POLONIUS: Come, go with me: I will go seek the king.
100 This is the very ecstasy of love,
Whose violent property° fordoes° itself
And leads the will to desperate undertakings
As oft as any passion under heaven
That does afflict our natures. I am sorry.
105 What, have you given him any hard words of late?
OPHELIA: No, my good lord, but, as you did command,
I did repel his letters and denied
His access to me.
POLONIUS: That hath made him mad.
I am sorry that with better heed and judgement
110 I had not quoted° him: I fear'd he did but trifle,
And meant to wrack thee; but, beshrew my jealousy!°
By heaven, it is as proper to our age
To cast beyond° ourselves in our opinions
As it is common for the younger sort
115 To lack discretion. Come, go we to the King:
This must be known; which, being kept close, might move
More grief to hide than hate to utter love.°
Come.   (*Exeunt.*)

93 bulk body.   **101 property** nature.   **101 fordoes** destroys.   **110 quoted** observed.   **111
beshrew my jealousy** curse my suspicions.   **113 cast beyond** overshoot, miscalculate.   **116–117
might . . . love** i.e., I might cause more grief to others by hiding the knowledge of Hamlet's love
for Ophelia than hatred to me and mine by telling of it.

SCENE II [*A room in the castle.*]

(*Flourish. Enter* KING *and* QUEEN, ROSENCRANTZ, *and* GUILDENSTERN [*with others*].)

KING: Welcome, dear Rosencrantz and Guildenstern!
Moreover that° we much did long to see you,
The need we have to use you did provoke
Our hasty sending. Something have you heard
Of Hamlet's transformation; so call it,   5
Sith° nor th' exterior nor the inward man
Resembles that it was. What it should be,
More than his father's death, that thus hath put him
So much from th' understanding of himself,
I cannot dream of: I entreat you both,   10
That, being of so young days° brought up with him,
And sith so neighbor'd to his youth and havior,
That you vouchsafe your rest° here in our court
Some little time: so by your companies
To draw him on to pleasures, and to gather,   15
So much as from occasion you may glean,
Whether aught, to us unknown, afflicts him thus,
That, open'd, lies within our remedy.
QUEEN: Good gentlemen, he hath much talk'd of you;
And sure I am two men there are not living   20
To whom he more adheres. If it will please you
To show us so much gentry° and good will
As to expend your time with us awhile.
For the supply and profit° of our hope,
Your visitation shall receive such thanks   25
As fits a king's remembrance.
ROSENCRANTZ: Both your majesties
Might, by the sovereign power you have of us,
Put your dread pleasures more into command
Than to entreaty.
GUILDENSTERN: But we both obey,   30
And here give up ourselves, in the full bent°
To lay our service freely at your feet,
To be commanded.
KING: Thanks, Rosencrantz and gentle Guildenstern.
QUEEN: Thanks, Guildenstern and gentle Rosencrantz: 35
And I beseech you instantly to visit
My too much changed son. Go, some of you,
And bring these gentlemen where Hamlet is.
GUILDENSTERN: Heavens make our presence and our practices

II.ii. 2 Moreover that besides the fact that. **6 Sith** since. **11 of . . . days** from such early youth. **13 vouchsafe your rest** please to stay. **22 gentry** courtesy. **24 supply and profit** aid and successful outcome. **31 in . . . bent** to the utmost degree of our mental capacity.

Pleasant and helpful to him!

40   QUEEN: Ay, amen!

(*Exeunt* ROSENCRANTZ *and* GUILDENSTERN [*with some* ATTENDANTS].)

(*Enter* POLONIUS.)

POLONIUS: Th' ambassadors from Norway, my good lord,
    Are joyfully return'd.
KING: Thou still hast been the father of good news.
POLONIUS: Have I, my lord? I assure my good liege,
45   I hold my duty, as I hold my soul,
    Both to my God and to my gracious king:
    And I do think, or else this brain of mine
    Hunts not the trail of policy so sure
    As it hath us'd to do, that I have found
50   The very cause of Hamlet's lunacy.
KING: O, speak of that; that do I long to hear.
POLONIUS: Give first admittance to th' ambassadors;
    My news shall be the fruit to that great feast.
KING: Thyself do grace to them, and bring them in.   [*Exit* POLONIUS.]
55   He tells me, my dear Gertrude, he hath found
    The head and source of all your son's distemper.
QUEEN: I doubt° it is no other but the main;°
    His father's death, and our o'erhasty marriage.
KING: Well, we shall sift him.

(*Enter* AMBASSADORS [VOLTIMAND *and* CORNELIUS, *with* POLONIUS].)

                    Welcome, my good friends!
60   Say, Voltimand, what from our brother Norway?
VOLTIMAND: Most fair return of greetings and desires.
    Upon our first, he sent out to suppress
    His nephew's levies; which to him appear'd
    To be a preparation 'gainst the Polack;
65   But, better look'd into, he truly found
    It was against your highness: whereat griev'd,
    That so his sickness, age and impotence
    Was falsely borne in hand,° sends out arrests
    On Fortinbras; which he, in brief, obeys;
70   Receives rebuke from Norway, and in fine°
    Makes vow before his uncle never more
    To give th' assay° of arms against your majesty.
    Whereon old Norway, overcome with joy,
    Gives him three score thousand crowns in annual fee,
75   And his commission to employ those soldiers,

---

57 doubt fear.   **57 main** chief point, principal concern.   **68 borne in hand** deluded.   **70 in fine** in the end.   **72 assay** assault, trial (of arms).

So levied as before, against the Polack:
With an entreaty, herein further shown, [*giving a paper.*]
That it might please you to give quiet pass
Through your dominions for this enterprise,
On such regards of safety and allowance°   80
As therein are set down.

KING: It likes° us well;
And at our more consider'd° time we'll read,
Answer, and think upon this business.
Meantime we thank you for your well-took labor:
Go to your rest; at night we'll feast together: 85
Most welcome home!   (*Exeunt* AMBASSADORS.)

POLONIUS: This business is well ended.
My liege, and madam, to expostulate
What majesty should be, what duty is,
Why day is day, night night, and time is time,
Were nothing but to waste night, day and time.   90
Therefore, since brevity is the soul of wit,°
And tediousness the limbs and outward flourishes,°
I will be brief: your noble son is mad:
Mad call I it; for, to define true madness
What is 't but to be nothing else but mad?   95
But let that go.

QUEEN: More matter, with less art.

POLONIUS: Madam, I swear I use no art at all.
That he is mad, 'tis true: 'tis true 'tis pity;
And pity 'tis 'tis true: a foolish figure;°
But farewell it, for I will use no art.   100
Mad let us grant him, then: and now remains
That we find out the cause of this effect,
Or rather say, the cause of this defect,
For this effect defective comes by cause:
Thus it remains, and the remainder thus.   105
Perpend.°
I have a daughter—have while she is mine—
Who, in her duty and obedience, mark,
Hath given me this: now gather, and surmise.   [*Reads the letter*]
"To the celestial and my soul's idol, the most beautified Ophelia,"—   110
That's an ill phrase, a vile phrase; "beautified" is a vile phrase: but you shall
hear.   [*Reads.*]
Thus:
"In her excellent white bosom, these, & c."

---

80 safety and allowance pledges of safety to the country and terms of permission for the troops
to pass.   **81 likes** pleases.   **82 consider'd** suitable for deliberation.   **91 wit** sound sense or judgment.   **92 flourishes** ostentation, embellishments.   **99 figure** figure of speech.   **106 Perpend**
consider.

115   QUEEN: Came this from Hamlet to her?
        POLONIUS: Good madam, stay awhile; I will be faithful.   [*Reads.*]
                        "Doubt thou the stars are fire;
                            Doubt that the sun doth move;
                            Doubt truth to be a liar;
120   But never doubt I love.
            "O dear Ophelia, I am ill at these numbers;° I have not art to reckon° my
            groans: but that I love thee best, O most best, believe it. Adieu.
            "Thine evermore, most dear lady, whilst this machine° is to him,

                                                                        HAMLET"

125   This, in obedience, hath my daughter shown me,
        And more above,° hath his solicitings,
        As they fell out° by time, by means° and place,
        All given to mine ear.
    KING: But how hath she
        Receiv'd his love?
    POLONIUS: What do you think of me?
130 KING: As of a man faithful and honorable.
    POLONIUS: I would fain prove so. But what might you think,
        When I had seen this hot love on the wing—
        As I perceiv'd it, I must tell you that,
        Before my daughter told me—what might you,
135   Or my dear majesty your queen here, think,
        If I had play'd the desk or table-book,°
        Or given my heart a winking,° mute and dumb,
        Or look'd upon this love with idle sight;
        What might you think? No, I went round to work,
140   And my young mistress thus I did bespeak:°
        "Lord Hamlet is a prince, out of thy star;°
        This must not be": and then I prescripts gave her,
        That she should lock herself from his resort,
        Admit no messengers, receive no tokens.
145   Which done, she took the fruits of my advice;
        And he, repelled—a short tale to make—
        Fell into a sadness, then into a fast,
        Thence to a watch,° thence into a weakness,
        Thence to a lightness,° and, by this declension,°
150   Into the madness wherein now he raves,
        And all we mourn for.

---

121 ill . . . numbers unskilled at writing verses.   **121 reckon** number metrically, scan.   **123 machine** bodily frame.   **126 more above** moreover.   **127 fell out** occurred.   **127 means** opportunities (of access).   **136 play'd . . . table-book** i.e., remained shut up, concealed this information.   **137 given . . . winking** given my heart a signal to keep silent.   **140 bespeak** address.   **141 out . . . star** above thee in position.   **148 watch** state of sleeplessness.   **149 lightness** lightheartedness.   **149 declension** decline, deterioration.

KING: Do you think 'tis this?

QUEEN: It may be, very like.

POLONIUS: Hath there been such a time—I would fain know that—
    That I have positively said "'Tis so,"
    When it prov'd otherwise?

KING: Not that I know.   155

POLONIUS [*pointing to his head and shoulder*]: Take this from this, if this be otherwise:
    If circumstances lead me, I will find
    Where truth is hid, though it were hid indeed
    Within the centre.°

KING: How may we try it further?

POLONIUS: You know, sometimes he walks four hours together   160
    Here in the lobby.

QUEEN: So he does indeed.

POLONIUS: At such a time I'll loose my daughter to him:
    Be you and I behind an arras° then;
    Mark the encounter: if he love her not
    And be not from his reason fall'n thereon,°   165
    Let me be no assistant for a state,
    But keep a farm and carters.

KING: We will try it.

(*Enter* HAMLET [*reading on a book*].)

QUEEN: But, look, where sadly the poor wretch comes reading.

POLONIUS: Away, I do beseech you both, away:

(*Exeunt* KING *and* QUEEN [*with* ATTENDANTS].)

    I'll board° him presently. O, give me leave.   170
    How does my good Lord Hamlet?

HAMLET: Well, God-a-mercy.

POLONIUS: Do you know me, my lord?

HAMLET: Excellent well; you are a fishmonger.°

POLONIUS: Not I, my lord.   175

HAMLET: Then I would you were so honest a man.

POLONIUS: Honest, my lord!

HAMLET: Ay, sir; to be honest, as this world goes, is to be one man picked out of ten
    thousand.

POLONIUS: That's very true, my lord.   180

HAMLET: For if the sun breed maggots in a dead dog, being a good kissing
    carrion,°—Have you a daughter?

POLONIUS: I have, my lord.

---

159 centre middle point of the earth.   **163 arras** hanging, tapestry.   **165 thereon** on that account.   **170 board** accost.   **174 fishmonger** an opprobrious expression meaning "bawd," "procurer."   **181–182 good kissing carrion** i.e., a good piece of flesh for kissing (?).

HAMLET: Let her not walk i' the sun:° conception° is a blessing: but as your daughter
185   may conceive—Friend, look to 't.

POLONIUS [*aside*]: How say you by° that? Still harping on my daughter: yet he knew
       me not at first; 'a said I was a fishmonger: 'a is far gone, far gone: and truly in
       my youth I suffered much extremity for love; very near this. I'll speak to him
       again. What do you read, my lord?

190   HAMLET: Words, words, words.

POLONIUS: What is the matter,° my lord?

HAMLET: Between who?°

POLONIUS: I mean, the matter that you read, my lord.

HAMLET: Slanders, sir: for the satirical rogue says here that old men have grey beards,
195   that their faces are wrinkled, their eyes purging° thick amber and plum-tree gum
       and that they have a plentiful lack of wit, together with most weak hams: all
       which, sir, though I most powerfully and potently believe, yet I hold it not hon-
       esty° to have it thus set down, for yourself, sir, should be old as I am, if like a
       crab you could go backward.

200   POLONIUS [*aside*]: Though this be madness, yet there is method in 't.—Will you
       walk out of the air, my lord?

HAMLET: Into my grave.

POLONIUS: Indeed, that's out of the air. [*Aside.*] How pregnant sometimes his replies
       are! a happiness° that often madness hits on, which reason and sanity could not
205   so prosperously° be delivered of. I will leave him, and suddenly contrive the
       means of meeting between him and my daughter.—My honorable lord, I will
       most humbly take my leave of you.

HAMLET: You cannot, sir, take from me any thing that I will more willingly part
       withal: except my life, except my life, except my life.

(*Enter* GUILDENSTERN *and* ROSENCRANTZ.)

210   POLONIUS: Fare you well, my lord.

HAMLET: These tedious old fools!

POLONIUS: You go to seek the Lord Hamlet; there he is.

ROSENCRANTZ [*to* POLONIUS]: God save you, sir!   [*Exit* POLONIUS.]

GUILDENSTERN: My honored lord!

215   ROSENCRANTZ: My most dear lord!

HAMLET: My excellent good friends! How dost thou, Guildenstern? Ah, Rosen-
       crantz! Good lads, how do ye both?

ROSENCRANTZ: As the indifferent° children of the earth.

GUILDENSTERN: Happy, in that we are not over-happy;
220   On Fortune's cap we are not the very button.

HAMLET: Nor the soles of her shoe?

ROSENCRANTZ: Neither, my lord.

---

184 i' the sun in the sunshine of princely favors.   **184 conception** quibble on "understanding"
and "pregnancy."   **186 by** concerning.   **191 matter** substance.   **192 Between who?** Hamlet
deliberately takes *matter* as meaning "basis of dispute."   **195 purging** discharging.   **197–198 honesty** decency.   **204 happiness** felicity of expression.   **205 prosperously** successfully.   **218 indifferent** ordinary.

HAMLET: Then you live about her waist, or in the middle of her favors?

GUILDENSTERN: 'Faith, her privates° we.

HAMLET: In the secret parts of Fortune? O, most true; she is a strumpet. What's the news?   225

ROSENCRANTZ: None, my lord, but that the world's grown honest.

HAMLET: Then is doomsday near: but your news is not true. Let me question more in particular: what have you, my good friends, deserved at the hands of Fortune, that she sends you to prison hither?   230

GUILDENSTERN: Prison, my lord!

HAMLET: Denmark's a prison.

ROSENCRANTZ: Then is the world one.

HAMLET: A goodly one; in which there are many confines,° wards and dungeons, Denmark being one o' the worst.   235

ROSENCRANTZ: We think not so, my lord.

HAMLET: Why, then, 'tis none to you; for there is nothing either good or bad, but thinking makes it so: to me it is a prison.

ROSENCRANTZ: Why then, your ambition makes it one; 'tis too narrow for your mind.   240

HAMLET: O God, I could be bounded in a nutshell and count myself a king of infinite space, were it not that I have bad dreams.

GUILDENSTERN: Which dreams indeed are ambition, for the very substance of the ambitious° is merely the shadow of a dream.

HAMLET: A dream itself is but a shadow.   245

ROSENCRANTZ: Truly, and I hold ambition of so airy and light a quality that it is but a shadow's shadow.

HAMLET: Then are our beggars bodies, and our monarchs and outstretched heroes the beggars' shadows. Shall we to the court? for, by my fay,° I cannot reason.°

ROSENCRANTZ: ⎫
GUILDENSTERN: ⎬ We'll wait upon° you.   250

HAMLET: No such matter: I will not sort° you with the rest of my servants, for, to speak to you like an honest man, I am most dreadfully attended.° But, in the beaten way of friendship,° what make you at Elsinore?

ROSENCRANTZ: To visit you, my Lord; no other occasion.

HAMLET: Beggar that I am, I am ever poor in thanks; but I thank you: and sure, dear friends, my thanks are too dear a° halfpenny. Were you not sent for? Is it your own inclining? Is it a free visitation? Come, come, deal justly with me: come, come; nay, speak.   255

GUILDENSTERN: What should we say, my lord?

HAMLET: Why, any thing, but to the purpose. You were sent for; and there is a kind of confession in your looks which your modesties have not craft enough to color: I know the good king and queen have sent for you.   260

---

224 privates i.e., ordinary men (sexual pun on private parts).   **234 confines** places of confinement.   **243–244 very . . . ambitious** that seemingly most substantial thing which the ambitious pursue.   **249 fay** faith.   **249 reason** argue.   **250 wait upon** accompany.   **251 sort** class.   **252 dreadfully attended** poorly provided with servants.   **252–253 in the . . . friendship** as a matter of course among friends.   **256 a** i.e., at a.

ROSENCRANTZ: To what end, my lord?

HAMLET: That you must teach me. But let me conjure° you, by the rights of our fel-
265 lowship, by the consonancy of our youth,° by the obligation of our ever-
preserved love, and by what more dear a better proposer° could charge you
withal, be even and direct with me, whether you were sent for, or no?

ROSENCRANTZ [*aside to* GUILDENSTERN]: What say you?

HAMLET [*aside*]: Nay, then, I have an eye of you.—If you love me, hold not off.

270 GUILDENSTERN: My lord, we were sent for.

HAMLET: I will tell you why; so shall my anticipation prevent your discovery,° and
your secrecy to the king and queen moult no feather. I have of late—but wherefore I know not—lost all my mirth, forgone all custom of exercises; and indeed
it goes so heavily with my disposition that this goodly frame, the earth, seems to
275 me a sterile promontory, this most excellent canopy, the air, look you, this brave
o'erhanging firmament, this majestical roof fretted° with golden fire, why, it ap-
peareth nothing to me but a foul and pestilent congregation of vapors. What a
piece of work is a man! how noble in reason! how infinite in faculties!° in form
and moving how express° and admirable! in action how like an angel! in appre-
280 hension° how like a god! the beauty of the world! The paragon of animals! And
yet, to me, what is this quintessence° of dust? man delights not me: no, nor
woman neither, though by your smiling you seem to say so.

ROSENCRANTZ: My lord, there was no such stuff in my thoughts.

HAMLET: Why did you laugh then, when I said "man delights not me"?

285 ROSENCRANTZ: To think, my lord, if you delight not in man, what lenten° entertainment the players shall receive from you: we coted° them on the way; and
hither are they coming, to offer you service.

HAMLET: He that plays the king shall be welcome; his majesty shall have tribute of
me; the adventurous knight shall use his foil and target;° the lover shall not sigh
290 gratis; the humorous man° shall end his part in peace; the clown shall make
those laugh whose lungs are tickle o' the sere;° and the lady shall say her mind
freely, or the blank verse shall halt for 't.° What players are they?

ROSENCRANTZ: Even those you were wont to take delight in, the tragedians of the
city.

295 HAMLET: How chances it they travel? their residence,° both in reputation and profit,
was better both ways.

ROSENCRANTZ: I think their inhibition° comes by the means of the late innovation.°

---

264 conjure adjure, entreat.   **265 consonancy of our youth** the fact that we are of the same
age.   **266 better proposer** one more skillful in finding proposals.   **271 prevent your discovery**
forestall your disclosure.   **276 fretted** adorned.   **278 faculties** capacity.   **279 express** well-
framed (?), exact (?).   **279–280 apprehension** understanding.   **281 quintessence** the fifth
essence of ancient philosophy, supposed to be the substance of the heavenly bodies and to be latent
in all things.   **285 lenten** meager.   **286 coted** overtook and passed beyond.   **289 foil and target** sword and shield.   **290 humorous man** actor who takes the part of the humor characters.
291 tickle o' the sere easy on the trigger.   **291–292 the lady . . . for 't** the lady (fond of talking) shall have opportunity to talk, blank verse or no blank verse.   **295 residence** remaining in
one place.   **297 inhibition** formal prohibition (from acting plays in the city or, possibly, at court).
297 innovation the new fashion in satirical plays performed by boy actors in the "private" theaters.

HAMLET: Do they hold the same estimation they did when I was in the city? are they so followed?

ROSENCRANTZ: No, indeed, are they not.   300

HAMLET: How° comes it? do they grow rusty?

ROSENCRANTZ: Nay, their endeavor keeps in the wonted pace: but there is, sir, an aery° of children, little eyases,° that cry out on the top of question,° and are most tyrannically° clapped for 't: these are now the fashion, and so berattle° the common stages°—so they call them—that many wearing rapiers° are afraid of   305
goose-quills° and dare scarce come thither.

HAMLET: What, are they children? who maintains 'em? how are they escoted?° Will they pursue the quality° no longer than they can sing?° will they not say afterwards, if they should grow themselves to common° players—as it is most like, if their means are no better—their writers do them wrong, to make them exclaim   310
against their own succession?°

ROSENCRANTZ: 'Faith, there has been much to do on both sides; and the nation holds it no sin to tarre° them to controversy: there was, for a while, no money bid for argument,° unless the poet and the players went to cuffs° in the question.°

HAMLET: Is 't possible?   315

GUILDENSTERN: O, there has been much throwing about of brains.

HAMLET: Do the boys carry it away?°

ROSENCRANTZ: Ay, that they do, my lord; Hercules and his load° too.

HAMLET: It is not very strange; for my uncle is king of Denmark, and those that would make mows° at him while my father lived, give twenty, forty, fifty, a hun-   320
dred ducats° a-piece for his picture in little.° 'Sblood, there is something in this more than natural, if philosophy could find it out.

(*A flourish [of trumpets within].*)

GUILDENSTERN: There are the players.

HAMLET: Gentlemen, you are welcome to Elsinore. Your hands, come then: the appurtenance of welcome is fashion and ceremony; let me comply° with you in   325
this garb,° lest my extent° to the players, which, I tell you, must show fairly out-

---

301–318 How . . . load too the passage is the famous one dealing with the War of the Theaters (1599–1602); namely, the rivalry between the children's companies and the adult actors. **303 aery** nest. **303 eyases** young hawks. **303 cry . . . question** speak in a high key dominating conversation; clamor forth the height of controversy; probably "excel"; perhaps intended to decry leaders of the dramatic profession. **304 tyrannically** outrageously. **304 berattle** berate. **305 common stages** public theaters. **305 many wearing rapiers** many men of fashion, who were afraid to patronize the common players for fear of being satirized by the poets who wrote for the children. **306 goose-quills** i.e., pens of satirists. **307 escoted** maintained. **308 quality** acting profession. **308 no longer . . . sing** i.e., until their voices change. **309 common** regular, adult. **311 succession** future careers. **313 tarre** set on (as dogs). **314 argument** probably, plot for a play. **314 went to cuffs** came to blows. **314 question** controversy. **317 carry it away** win the day. **318 Hercules . . . load** regarded as an allusion to the sign of the Globe Theatre, which was Hercules bearing the world on his shoulder. **320 mows** grimaces. **321 ducats** gold coins worth 9s. 4d. **321 in little** in miniature. **325 comply** observe the formalities of courtesy. **326 garb** manner. **326 extent** showing of kindness.

wards, should more appear like entertainment than yours. You are welcome: but my uncle-father and aunt-mother are deceived.

GUILDENSTERN: In what, my dear lord?

330   HAMLET: I am but mad north-north-west:° when the wind is southerly I know a hawk from a handsaw.°

(*Enter* POLONIUS.)

POLONIUS: Well be with you, gentlemen!

HAMLET: Hark you, Guildenstern; and you too: at each ear a hearer: that great baby you see there is not yet out of his swaddling-clouts.°

335   ROSENCRANTZ: Happily he is the second time come to them; for they say an old man is twice a child.

HAMLET: I will prophesy he comes to tell me of the players; mark it.—You say right, sir: o' Monday morning;° 'twas then indeed.

POLONIUS: My lord, I have news to tell you.

340   HAMLET: My lord, I have news to tell you. When Roscius° was an actor in Rome,—

POLONIUS: The actors are come hither, my lord.

HAMLET: Buz, buz!°

POLONIUS: Upon my honor,—

HAMLET: Then came each actor on his ass,—

345   POLONIUS: The best actors in the world, either for tragedy, comedy, history, pastoral, pastoral-comical, historical-pastoral, tragical-historical, tragical-comical-historical-pastoral, scene individable,° or poem unlimited:° Seneca° cannot be too heavy, nor Plautus° too light. For the law of writ and the liberty,° these are the only men.

350   HAMLET: O Jephthah, judge of Israel,° what a treasure hadst thou!

POLONIUS: What a treasure had he, my lord?

HAMLET: Why,
　　　　"One fair daughter, and no more,
　　　　The which he loved passing well."

355   POLONIUS [*aside*]: Still on my daughter.

HAMLET: Am I not i' the right, old Jephthah?

POLONIUS: If you call me Jephthah, my lord, I have a daughter that I love passing° well.

HAMLET: Nay, that follows not.

360   POLONIUS: What follows, then, my lord?

330 I am . . . north-north-west I am only partly mad, i.e., in only one point of the compass. **331 handsaw** a proposed reading of *hernshaw* would mean "heron"; *handsaw* may be an early corruption of *hernshaw*. Another view regards hawk as the variant of *hack*, a tool of the pickax type, and *handsaw* as a saw operated by hand.   **334 swaddling-clouts** clothes in which to wrap a newborn baby.   **338 o' Monday morning** said to mislead Polonius.   **340 Roscius** a famous Roman actor.   **342 Buz, buz** an interjection used at Oxford to denote stale news.   **347 scene individable** a play observing the unity of place.   **347 poem unlimited** a play disregarding the unities of time and place.   **347 Seneca** writer of Latin tragedies, model of early Elizabethan writers of tragedy.   **348 Plautus** writer of Latin comedy.   **348 law . . . liberty** pieces written according to rules and without rules, i.e., "classical" and "romantic" dramas.   **350 Jephthah . . . Israel** Jephthah had to sacrifice his daughter; see Judges 11.   **357 passing** surpassingly.

HAMLET: Why,
            "As by lot, God wot,"
        and then, you know,
            "It came to pass, as most like° it was,"—
        the first row° of the pious chanson° will show you more; for look, where my   365
        abridgement comes.°

(*Enter the* PLAYERS.)

        You are welcome, masters; welcome, all. I am glad to see thee well. Welcome,
        good friends. O, old friend! why, thy face is valanced ° since I saw thee last:
        comest thou to beard me in Denmark? What, my young lady and mistress! By'r
        lady, your ladyship is nearer to heaven than when I saw you last, by the altitude   370
        of a chopine.° Pray God, your voice, like a piece of uncurrent° gold, be not
        cracked within the ring.° Masters, you are all welcome. We'll e'en to 't like
        French falconers, fly at any thing we see: we'll have a speech straight: come, give
        us a taste of your quality; come, a passionate speech.

FIRST PLAYER: What speech, my good lord?   375

HAMLET: I heard thee speak me a speech once, but it was never acted; or, if it was,
        not above once; for the play, I remember, pleased not the million; 'twas caviary
        to the general:° but it was—as I received it, and others, whose judgements in
        such matters cried in the top of° mine—an excellent play, well digested in the
        scenes, set down with as much modesty as cunning.° I remember, one said there   380
        were no sallets° in the lines to make the matter savory, nor no matter in the
        phrase that might indict° the author of affectation; but called it an honest
        method, as wholesome as sweet, and by very much more handsome than fine.°
        One speech in 't I chiefly loved: 'twas Æneas' tale to Dido;° and thereabout of it
        especially, where he speaks of Priam's slaughter: if it live in your memory, begin   385
        at this line: let me see, let me see—
            "The rugged Pyrrhus,° like th' Hyrcanian beast,"°—
        'tis not so:—it begins with Pyrrhus:—
            "The rugged Pyrrhus, he whose sable arms,
        Black as his purpose, did the night resemble   390
        When he lay couched in the ominous horse,°
        Hath now this dread and black complexion smear'd
        With heraldry more dismal; head to foot

---

364 like probable.   **365 row** stanza.   **365 chanson** ballad.   **366 abridgement comes** opportunity comes for cutting short the conversation.   **368 valanced** fringed (with a beard).   **371
chopine** kind of shoe raised by the thickness of the heel; worn in Italy, particularly in Venice.   **371
uncurrent** not passable as lawful coinage.   **371–372 cracked within the ring** in the center of
coins were rings enclosing the sovereign's head; if the coin was cracked within this ring, it was unfit
for currency.   **377–378 caviary to the general** not relished by the multitude.   **379 cried in
the top of** spoke with greater authority than.   **380 cunning** skill.   **381 sallets** salads: here, spicy
improprieties.   **382 indict** convict.   **383 as wholesome . . . fine** its beauty was not that of
elaborate ornament, but that of order and proportion.   **384 Æneas' tale to Dido** the lines recited
by the player are imitated from Marlowe and Nashe's Dido Queen of Carthage (II.i. 214 ff.). They
are written in such a way that the conventionality of the play within a play is raised above that of
ordinary drama.   **387 Pyrrhus** a Greek hero in the Trojan War.   **387 Hyrcanian beast** the tiger;
see Virgil, Aeneid, IV. 266.   **391 ominous horse** Trojan horse.

Now is he total gules;° horridly trick'd°
395 With blood of fathers, mothers, daughters, sons,
Bak'd and impasted° with the parching streets,
That lend a tyrannous and a damned light
To their lord's murder: roasted in wrath and fire,
And thus o'er-sized° with coagulate gore,
400 With eyes like carbuncles, the hellish Pyrrhus
Old grandsire Priam seeks."
So, proceed you.
POLONIUS: 'Fore God, my lord, well spoken, with good accent and good discretion.
FIRST PLAYER: "Anon he finds him
405 Striking too short at Greeks; his antique sword,
Rebellious to his arm, lies where it falls,
Repugnant° to command: unequal match'd,
Pyrrhus at Priam drives; in rage strikes wide;
But with the whiff and wind of his fell sword
410 Th' unnerved father falls. Then senseless Ilium,°
Seeming to feel this blow, with flaming top
Stoops to his base, and with a hideous crash
Takes prisoner Pyrrhus' ear: for, lo! his sword
Which was declining on the milky head
415 Of reverend Priam, seem'd i' th' air to stick:
So, as a painted tyrant,° Pyrrhus stood,
And like a neutral to his will and matter,°
Did nothing.
But, as we often see, against° some storm,
420 A silence in the heavens, the rack° stand still,
The bold winds speechless and the orb below
As hush as death, anon the dreadful thunder
Doth rend the region,° so, after Pyrrhus' pause,
Aroused vengeance sets him new a-work;
425 And never did the Cyclops' hammers fall
On Mars's armor forg'd for proof eterne°
With less remorse than Pyrrhus' bleeding sword
Now falls on Priam.
Out, out, thou strumpet, Fortune! All you gods,
430 In general synod,° take away her power;
Break all the spokes and fellies° from her wheel,
And bowl the round nave° down the hill of heaven,
As low as to the fiends!"
POLONIUS: This is too long.

394 gules red, a heraldic term.   **394 trick'd** spotted, smeared.   **396 impasted** made into a paste.
399 o'er-sized covered as with size or glue.   **407 Repugnant** disobedient.   **410 Then senseless Ilium** insensate Troy.   **416 painted tyrant** tyrant in a picture.   **417 matter** task.   **419
against** before.   **420 rack** mass of clouds.   **423 region** assembly.   **426 proof eterne** external
resistance to assault.   **430 synod** assembly.   **431 fellies** pieces of wood forming the rim of a
wheel.   **432 nave** hub.

HAMLET: It shall to the barber's, with your beard. Prithee, say on: he's for a jig° or a   *435*
    tale of bawdry,° or he sleeps: say on: come to Hecuba.°

FIRST PLAYER: "But who, ah woe! had seen the mobled° queen—"

HAMLET: "The mobled queen"?

POLONIUS: That's good; "mobled queen" is good.

FIRST PLAYER: "Run barefoot up and down, threat'ning the flames   *440*
    With bisson rheum;° a clout° upon that head
    Where late the diadem stood, and for a robe,
    About her lank and all o'er-teemed° loins,
    A blanket, in the alarm of fear caught up;
    Who this had seen, with tongue in venom steep'd,   *445*
    'Gainst Fortune's state would treason have pronounc'd:°
    But if the gods themselves did see her then
    When she saw Pyrrhus make malicious sport
    In mincing with his sword her husband's limbs,
    The instant burst of clamor that she made,   *450*
    Unless things mortal move them not at all,
    Would have made milch° the burning eyes of heaven,
    And passion in the gods."

POLONIUS: Look, whe'r he has not turned° his color and has tears in 's eyes.
    Prithee, no more.   *455*

HAMLET: 'Tis well; I'll have thee speak out the rest soon. Good my lord, will you see
    the players well bestowed? Do you hear, let them be well used; for they are the
    abstract° and brief chronicles of the time: after your death you were better have
    a bad epitaph than their ill report while you live.

POLONIUS: My lord, I will use them according to their desert.   *460*

HAMLET: God's bodykins,° man, much better: use every man after his desert, and
    who shall 'scape whipping? Use them after your own honor and dignity: the less
    they deserve, the more merit is in your bounty. Take them in.

POLONIUS: Come, sirs.

HAMLET: Follow him, friends: we'll hear a play tomorrow. [*Aside to* FIRST PLAYER.]   *465*
    Dost thou hear me, old friend; can you play the Murder of Gonzago?

FIRST PLAYER: Ay, my lord.

HAMLET: We'll ha 't to-morrow night. You could, for a need, study a speech of some
    dozen or sixteen lines,° which I would set down and insert in 't, could you not?

FIRST PLAYER: Ay, my lord.   *470*

HAMLET: Very well. Follow that lord; and look you mock him not.—My good
    friends, I'll leave you till night: you are welcome to Elsinore.

    (*Exeunt* POLONIUS *and* PLAYERS.)

ROSENCRANTZ: Good my lord!   (*Exeunt* [ROSENCRANTZ *and* GUILDENSTERN.])

---

435 jig comic performance given at the end or in an interval of a play.   **436 bawdry** indecency.
436 Hecuba wife of Priam, king of Troy.   **437 mobled** muffled.   **441 bisson rheum** blinding
tears.   **441 clout** piece of cloth.   **443 o'er-teemed** worn out with bearing children.   **446 pro-
nounc'd** proclaimed.   **452 milch** moist with tears.   **454 turned** changed.   **458 abstract** summary account.   **461 bodykins** diminutive form of the oath "by God's body."   **469 dozen or
sixteen lines** critics have amused themselves by trying to locate Hamlet's lines.

HAMLET: Ay, so, God bye to you.—Now I am alone.

475   O, what a rogue and peasant° slave am I!
    Is it not monstrous that this player here,
    But in a fiction, in a dream of passion,
    Could force his soul so to his own conceit
    That from her working all his visage wann'd,°
480   Tears in his eyes, distraction in 's aspect.
    A broken voice, and his whole function suiting
    With forms to his conceit?° and all for nothing!
    For Hecuba!
    What's Hecuba to him, or he to Hecuba,
485   That he should weep for her? What would he do,
    Had he the motive and the cue for passion
    That I have? He would drown the stage with tears
    And cleave the general ear with horrid speech,
    Make mad the guilty and appall the free,
490   Confound the ignorant, and amaze indeed
    The very faculties of eyes and ears.
    Yet I,
    A dull and muddy-mettled° rascal, peak,°
    Like John-a-dreams,° unpregnant of° my cause,
495   And can say nothing; no, not for a king.
    Upon whose property° and most dear life
    A damn'd defeat was made. Am I a coward?
    Who calls me villain? breaks my pate across?
    Plucks off my beard, and blows it in my face?
500   Tweaks me by the nose? gives me the lie i' th' throat,
    As deep as to the lungs? who does me this?
    Ha!
    'Swounds, I should take it: for it cannot be
    But I am pigeon-liver'd° and lack gall
505   To make oppression bitter, or ere this
    I should have fatted all the region kites°
    With this slave's offal: bloody, bawdy villain!
    Remorseless, treacherous, lecherous, kindless° villain!
    O, vengeance!
510   Why, what an ass am I! This is most brave,
    That I, the son of a dear father murder'd,
    Prompted to my revenge by heaven and hell,
    Must, like a whore, unpack my heart with words,

---

475 peasant base.   **479 wann'd** grew pale.   **481–82 his whole . . . conceit** his whole being responded with forms to suit his thought.   **493 muddy-mettled** dull-spirited.   **493 peak** mope, pine.   **494 John-a-dreams** an expression occurring elsewhere in Elizabethan literature to indicate a dreamer.   **494 unpregnant of** not quickened by.   **496 property** proprietorship (of crown and life).   **504 pigeon-liver'd** the pigeon was supposed to secrete no gall; if Hamlet, so he says, had had gall, he would have felt the bitterness of oppression, and avenged it.   **506 region kites** kites of the air.   **508 kindless** unnatural.

And fall a-cursing, like a very drab,°
A stallion!°   515
Fie upon 't! foh! About,° my brains! Hum, I have heard
That guilty creatures sitting at a play
Have by the very cunning of the scene
Been struck so to the soul that presently
They have proclaim'd their malefactions;   520
For murder, though it have no tongue, will speak
With most miraculous organ. I'll have these players
Play something like the murder of my father
Before mine uncle: I'll observe his looks:
I'll tent° him to the quick: if 'a do blench,°   525
I know my course. The spirit that I have seen
May be the devil:° and the devil hath power
T' assume a pleasing shape; yea, and perhaps
Out of my weakness and my melancholy,
As he is very potent with such spirits,°   530
Abuses me to damn me: I'll have grounds
More relative° than this:° the play's the thing
Wherein I'll catch the conscience of the king.

ACT III
SCENE I [*A room in the castle.*]

(*Enter* KING, QUEEN, POLONIUS, OPHELIA, ROSENCRANTZ,
GUILDENSTERN, LORDS.)

KING: And can you, by no drift of conference,°
    Get from him why he puts on this confusion,
    Grating so harshly all his days of quiet
    With turbulent and dangerous lunacy?
ROSENCRANTZ: He does confess he feels himself distracted;   5
    But from what cause 'a will by no means speak.
GUILDENSTERN: Nor do we find him forward° to be sounded,
    But, with a crafty madness, keeps aloof,
    When we would bring him on to some confession
    Of his true state.
QUEEN: Did he receive you well?   10
ROSENCRANTZ: Most like a gentleman.
GUILDENSTERN: But with much forcing of his disposition.°
ROSENCRANTZ: Niggard of question;° but, of our demands,
    Most free in his reply.

---

514 drab prostitute.   **515 stallion** prostitute (male or female).   **516 About** about it, or turn
thou right about.   **525 tent** probe.   **525 blench** quail, flinch.   **527 May be the devil** Hamlet's
suspicion is properly grounded in the belief of the time.   **530 spirits** humors.   **532 relative**
closely related, definite.   **532 this** i.e., the ghost's story.   **III.i. 1 drift of conference** device of
conversation.   **7 forward** willing.   **12 forcing of his disposition** i.e., against his will.   **13
Niggard of question** sparing of conversation.

QUEEN: Did you assay° him
15   To any pastime?
ROSENCRANTZ: Madam, it so fell out, that certain players
        We o'er-raught° on the way: of these we told him;
        And there did seem in him a kind of joy
        To hear of it: they are here about the court,
20   And, as I think, they have already order
        This night to play before him.
POLONIUS: 'Tis most true:
        And he beseech'd me to entreat your majesties
        To hear and see the matter.
KING: With all my heart; and it doth much content me
25   To hear him so inclin'd.
        Good gentlemen, give him a further edge,°
        And drive his purpose into these delights.
ROSENCRANTZ: We shall, my lord. (*Exeunt* ROSENCRANTZ *and* GUILDENSTERN.)
KING: Sweet Gertrude, leave us too;
        For we have closely° sent for Hamlet hither,
30   That he, as 'twere by accident, may here
        Affront° Ophelia:
        Her father and myself, lawful espials,°
        Will so bestow ourselves that, seeing, unseen,
        We may of their encounter frankly judge,
35   And gather by him, as he is behav'd,
        If 't be th' affliction of his love or no
        That thus he suffers for.
QUEEN: I shall obey you.
        And for your part, Ophelia, I do wish
        That your good beauties be the happy cause
40   Of Hamlet's wildness:° so shall I hope your virtues
        Will bring him to his wonted way again,
        To both your honors.
OPHELIA: Madam, I wish it may.   [*Exit* QUEEN.]
POLONIUS: Ophelia, walk you here. Gracious,° so please you,
        We will bestow ourselves. [*To* OPHELIA.] Read on this book;
45   That show of such an exercise° may color°
        Your loneliness. We are oft to blame in this,—
        'Tis too much prov'd—that with devotion's visage
        And pious action we do sugar o'er
        The devil himself.
KING [*Aside*]:   O, 'tis too true!

---

14 assay try to win.   **17 o'er-raught** overtook.   **26 edge** incitement.   **29 closely** secretly.
31 Affront confront.   **32 lawful espials** legitimate spies.   **40 wildness** madness.   **43 Gracious**
your grace (addressed to the king).   **45 exercise** act of devotion (the book she reads is one of devotion).   **45 color** give a plausible appearance to.

How smart a lash that speech doth give my conscience!   50
The harlot's cheek, beautied with plast'ring art,
Is not more ugly to° the thing° that helps it
Than is my deed to my most painted word:
O heavy burthen!

POLONIUS: I hear him coming: let's withdraw, my lord.   55

[*Exeunt* KING *and* POLONIUS.]

(*Enter* HAMLET.)

HAMLET: To be, or not to be: that is the question:
Whether 'tis nobler in the mind to suffer
The slings and arrows of outrageous fortune,
Or to take arms against a sea° of troubles,
And by opposing end them? To die: to sleep;   60
No more; and by a sleep to say we end
The heart-ache and the thousand natural shocks
That flesh is heir to, 'tis a consummation
Devoutly to be wish'd. To die, to sleep;
To sleep: perchance to dream: ay, there's the rub;   65
For in that sleep of death what dreams may come
When we have shuffled° off this mortal coil,°
Must give us pause: there's the respect°
That makes calamity of so long life;°
For who would bear the whips and scorns of time,°   70
Th' oppressor's wrong, the proud man's contumely,
The pangs of despis'd° love, the law's delay,
The insolence of office° and the spurns°
That patient merit of th' unworthy takes,
When he himself might his quietus° make   75
With a bare bodkin?° who would fardels° bear,
To grunt and sweat under a weary life,
But that the dread of something after death,
The undiscover'd country from whose bourn°
No traveller returns, puzzles the will   80
And makes us rather bear those ills we have
Than fly to others that we know not of?
Thus conscience° does make cowards of us all;

---

52 to compared to.   **52 thing** i.e., the cosmetic.   **59 sea** the mixed metaphor of this speech has often been commented on; a later emendation *siege* has sometimes been spoken on the stage.   **67 shuffled** sloughed, cast.   **67 coil** usually means "turmoil"; here, possibly "body" (conceived of as wound about the soul like rope); *clay, soil, veil,* have been suggested as emendations.   **68 respect** consideration.   **69 of . . . life** so long-lived.   **70 time** the world.   **72 despis'd** rejected.   **73 office** office-holders.   **73 spurns** insults.   **75 quietus** acquittance; here, death.   **76 bare bodkin** mere dagger; *bare* is sometimes understood as "unsheathed."   **76 fardels** burdens.   **79 bourn** boundary.   **83 conscience** probably, inhibition by the faculty of reason restraining the will from doing wrong.

And thus the native hue° of resolution
85   Is sicklied o'er° with the pale cast° of thought,
And enterprises of great pitch° and moment°
With this regard° their currents° turn awry,
And lose the name of action—Soft you now!
The fair Ophelia! Nymph, in thy orisons°
Be all my sins rememb'red.

90   OPHELIA: Good my lord,
How does your honor for this many a day?

HAMLET: I humbly thank you; well, well, well.

OPHELIA: My lord, I have remembrances of yours,
That I have longed long to re-deliver;
I pray you, now receive them.

95   HAMLET: No, not I;
I never gave you aught.

OPHELIA: My honor'd lord, you know right well you did;
And, with them, words of so sweet breath compos'd
As made the things more rich: their perfume lost,
100   Take these again; for to the noble mind
Rich gifts wax poor when givers prove unkind.
There, my lord.

HAMLET: Ha, ha! are you honest?°

OPHELIA: My lord?

105   HAMLET: Are you fair?

OPHELIA: What means your lordship?

HAMLET: That if you be honest and fair, your honesty° should admit no discourse
to° your beauty.

OPHELIA: Could beauty, my lord, have better commerce° than with honesty?

110   HAMLET: Ay, truly; for the power of beauty will sooner transform honesty from what
it is to a bawd than the force of honesty can translate beauty into his likeness:
this was sometime a paradox, but now the time° gives it proof. I did love you
once.

OPHELIA: Indeed, my lord, you made me believe so.

115   HAMLET: You should not have believed me; for virtue cannot so inoculate° our old
stock but we shall relish of it:° I loved you not.

OPHELIA: I was the more deceived.

HAMLET: Get thee to a nunnery: why wouldst thou be a breeder of sinners? I am
myself indifferent honest;° but yet I could accuse me of such things that it were

---

84 native hue natural color; metaphor derived from the color of the face.   **85 sicklied o'er** given
a sickly tinge.   **85 cast** shade of color.   **86 pitch** height (as of falcon's flight).   **86 moment** importance.   **87 regard** respect, consideration.   **87 currents** courses.   **89 orisons** prayers.
103–108 are you honest . . . beauty *honest* meaning "truthful" and "chaste" and *fair* meaning
"just, honorable" (line 105) and "beautiful" (line 107) are not mere quibbles; the speech has the
irony of a double entendre.   **107 your honesty** your chastity.   **107–108 discourse to** familiar
intercourse with.   **109 commerce** intercourse.   **112 the time** the present age.   **115 inoculate**
graft (metaphorical).   **116 but . . . it** i.e., that we do not still have about us a taste of the old
stock, i.e., retain our sinfulness.   **119 indifferent honest** moderately virtuous.

better my mother had not borne me: I am very proud, revengeful, ambitious, 120
with more offences at my beck° than I have thoughts to put them in, imagination to give them shape, or time to act them in. What should such fellows as I
do crawling between earth and heaven? We are arrant knaves, all; believe none
of us. Go thy ways to a nunnery. Where's your father?

OPHELIA: At home, my lord.   125

HAMLET: Let the doors be shut upon him, that he may play the fool no where but in
's own house. Farewell.

OPHELIA: O, help him, you sweet heavens!

HAMLET: If thou dost marry, I'll give thee this plague for thy dowry: be thou as
chaste as ice, as pure as snow, thou shalt not escape calumny. Get thee to a nun- 130
nery, go: farewell. Or, if thou wilt needs marry, marry a fool; for wise men know
well enough what monsters° you make of them. To a nunnery, go, and quickly
too. Farewell.

OPHELIA: O heavenly powers, restore him!

HAMLET: I have heard of your° paintings too, well enough; God hath given you one 135
face, and you make yourselves another: you jig,° you amble, and you lisp; you
nick-name God's creatures, and make your wantonness your ignorance.° Go to,
I'll no more on 't; it hath made me mad. I say, we will have no more marriage:
those that are married already, all but one,° shall live; the rest shall keep as they
are. To a nunnery, go.   (*Exit.*)   140

OPHELIA: O, what a noble mind is here o'er-thrown!
    The courtier's, soldier's, scholar's, eye, tongue, sword;
    Th' expectancy and rose° of the fair state,
    The glass of fashion and the mould of form,°
    Th' observ'd of all observers,° quite, quite down!   145
    And I, of ladies most deject and wretched,
    That suck'd the honey of his music vows,
    Now see that noble and most sovereign reason,
    Like sweet bells jangled, out of time and harsh;
    That unmatch'd form and feature of blown° youth   150
    Blasted with ecstasy:° O, woe is me,
    T' have seen what I have seen, see what I see!

(*Enter* KING *and* POLONIUS.)

KING: Love! his affections do not that way tend;
    Nor what he spake, though it lack'd form a little,
    Was not like madness. There's something in his soul,   155
    O'er which his melancholy sits on brood;
    And I do doubt° the hatch and the disclose°

---

121 **beck** command.   132 **monsters** an allusion to the horns of a cuckold.   135 **your** indefinite
use.   136 **jig** move with jerky motion; probably allusion to the jig, or song and dance, of the current stage.   137 **make . . . ignorance** i.e., excuse your wantonness on the ground of your ignorance.   139 **one** i.e., the king.   143 **expectancy and rose** source of hope.   144 **The
glass . . . form** the mirror of fashion and the pattern of courtly behavior.   145 **observ'd . . . observers** i.e., the center of attention in the court.   150 **blown** blooming.   151 **ecstasy** madness.
157 **doubt** fear.   157 **disclose** disclosure or revelation (by chipping of the shell).

Will be some danger: which for to prevent,
I have in quick determination
160 Thus set it down: he shall with speed to England,
For the demand of our neglected tribute:
Haply the seas and countries different
With variable° objects shall expel
This something-settled° matter in his heart,
165 Whereon his brains still beating puts him thus
From fashion of himself.° What think you on 't?
POLONIUS: It shall do well: but yet do I believe
The origin and commencement of his grief
Sprung from neglected love. How now, Ophelia!
170 You need not tell us what Lord Hamlet said;
We heard it all. My lord, do as you please;
But, if you hold it fit, after the play
Let his queen mother all alone entreat him
To show his grief: let her be round° with him;
175 And I'll be plac'd, so please you, in the ear
Of all their conference. If she find him not,
To England send him, or confine him where
Your wisdom best shall think.
KING: It shall be so:
Madness in great ones must not unwatch'd go.   (*Exeunt.*)

SCENE II [*A hall in the castle.*]

(*Enter* HAMLET *and three of the* PLAYERS.)

HAMLET: Speak the speech, I pray you, as I pronounced it to you, trippingly on the
tongue: but if you mouth it, as many of your° players do, I had as lief the town-
crier spoke my lines. Nor do not saw the air too much with your hand, thus,
but use all gently; for in the very torrent, tempest, and, as I may say, whirlwind
5 of your passion, you must acquire and beget a temperance that may give it
smoothness. O, it offends me to the soul to hear a robustious° periwig-pated°
fellow tear a passion to tatters, to very rags, to split the ears of the groundlings,°
who for the most part are capable of° nothing but inexplicable° dumb-shows
and noise: I would have such a fellow whipped for o'er-doing Termagant;° it
10 out-herods Herod:° pray you, avoid it.
FIRST PLAYER: I warrant your honor.

---

163 variable various. **164 something-settled** somewhat settled. **166 From . . . himself** out
of his natural manner. **174 round** blunt. III.ii. **2 your** indefinite use. **6 robustious** violent,
boisterous. **6 periwig-pated** wearing a wig. **7 groundlings** those who stood in the yard of
the theater. **8 capable of** susceptible to being influenced by. **8 inexplicable** of no significance
worth explaining. **9 Termagant** a god of the Saracens; a character in the St. Nicholas play, where
one of his worshipers, leaving him in charge of goods, returns to find them stolen whereupon he
beats the god (or idol), which howls vociferously. **10 Herod** Herod of Jewry; a character in "The
Slaughter of the Innocents" and other cycle plays. The part was played with great noise and fury.

HAMLET: Be not too tame neither, but let your own discretion be your tutor: suit the action to the word, the word to the action; with this special observance, that you o'er-step not the modesty of nature: for any thing so overdone is from the purpose of playing, whose end, both at the first and now, was and is, to hold, as 't were, the mirror up to nature; to show virtue her own feature, scorn her own image, and the very age and body of the time his form and pressure.° Now this overdone, or come tardy off,° though it make the unskilful laugh, cannot but make the judicious grieve; the censure of the which one° must in your allowance o'erweigh a whole theatre of others. O, there be players that I have seen play, and heard others praise, and that highly, not to speak it profanely, that, neither having the accent of Christians nor the gait of Christian, pagan, nor man, have so strutted and bellowed that I have thought some of nature's journeymen° had made men and not made them well, they imitated humanity so abominably.

FIRST PLAYER: I hope we have reformed that indifferently° with us, sir.

HAMLET: O, reform it altogether. And let those that play your clowns speak no more than is set down for them; for there be of° them that will themselves laugh, to set on some quantity of barren° spectators to laugh too; though, in the mean time, some necessary question of the play be then to be considered: that's villanous, and shows a most pitiful ambition in the fool that uses it. Go, make you ready.

[*Exeunt* PLAYERS.]

(*Enter* POLONIUS, GUILDENSTERN, *and* ROSENCRANTZ.)

How now, my lord! will the king hear this piece of work?

POLONIUS: And the queen too, and that presently.

HAMLET: Bid the players make haste.   [*Exit* POLONIUS.]

Will you two help to hasten them?

ROSENCRANTZ: ⎱
⎰ We will, my lord.
GUILDENSTERN: ⎰   (*Exeunt the two.*)

HAMLET: What ho! Horatio!

(*Enter* HORATIO.)

HORATIO: Here, sweet lord, at your service.

HAMLET: Horatio, thou art e'en as just° a man

As e'er my conversation cop'd withal.

HORATIO: O, my dear lord,—

HAMLET: Nay, do not think I flatter;

For what advancement may I hope from thee

That no revenue hast but thy good spirits,

To feed and clothe thee? Why should the poor be flatter'd?

No, let the candied tongue lick absurd pomp,

15

20

25

30

35

40

45

---

17 pressure stamp, impressed character. **18 come tardy off** inadequately done. **19 the censure . . . one** the judgment of even one of whom. **23–24 journeymen** laborers not yet masters in their trade. **26 indifferently** fairly, tolerably. **28 of** i.e., some among them. **29 barren** i.e., of wit. **40 just** honest, honorable.

And crook the pregnant° hinges of the knee
Where thrift° may follow fawning. Dost thou hear?
Since my dear soul was mistress of her choice
50 And could of men distinguish her election,
S'hath seal'd thee for herself: for thou hast been
As one, in suff'ring all, that suffers nothing,
A man that fortune's buffets and rewards
Hast ta'en with equal thanks: and blest are those
55 Whose blood and judgement are so well commeddled,
That they are not a pipe for fortune's finger
To sound what stop° she please. Give me that man
That is not passion's slave, and I will wear him
In my heart's core, ay, in my heart of heart,
60 As I do thee.—Something too much of this.—
There is a play to-night before the king;
One scene of it comes near the circumstance
Which I have told thee of my father's death:
I prithee, when thou seest that act afoot,
65 Even with the very comment of thy soul°
Observe my uncle: if his occulted° guilt
Do not itself unkennel in one speech,
It is a damned° ghost that we have seen,
And my imaginations are as foul
70 As Vulcan's stithy.° Give him heedful note;
For I mine eyes will rivet to his face,
And after we will both our judgements join
In censure of his seeming.°
HORATIO: Well, my Lord:
If 'a steal aught the whilst this play is playing,
75 And 'scape detecting, I will pay the theft.

(*Enter trumpets and kettledrums*, KING, QUEEN, POLONIUS, OPHELIA,
[ROSENCRANTZ, GUILDENSTERN, *and* OTHERS].)

HAMLET: They are coming to the play; I must be idle:° Get you a place.
KING: How fares our cousin Hamlet?
HAMLET: Excellent, i' faith; of the chameleon's dish:° I eat the air, promise-crammed:
you cannot feed capons so.
80 KING: I have nothing with° this answer, Hamlet; these words are not mine.°
HAMLET: No, nor mine now. [*To* POLONIUS.] My lord, you played once i' the university, you say?

---

47 pregnant pliant.   **48 thrift** profit.   **57 stop** hole in a wind instrument for controlling the
sound.   **65 very . . . soul** inward and sagacious criticism.   **66 occulted** hidden.   **68 damned**
in league with Satan.   **70 stithy** smithy, place of stiths (anvils).   **73 censure . . . seeming** judgment of his appearance or behavior.   **76 idle** crazy, or not attending to anything serious.   **78
chameleon's dish** chameleons were supposed to feed on air. (Hamlet deliberately misinterprets the
king's "fares" as "feeds.")   **80 have . . . with** make nothing of.   **80 are not mine** do not respond to what I ask.

POLONIUS: That did I, my lord; and was accounted a good actor.

HAMLET: What did you enact?

POLONIUS: I did enact Julius Cæsar: I was killed i' the Capitol; Brutus killed me.   85

HAMLET: It was a brute part of him to kill so capital a calf there. Be the players ready?

ROSENCRANTZ: Ay, my lord; they stay upon your patience.

QUEEN: Come hither, my dear Hamlet, sit by me.

HAMLET: No, good mother, here's metal more attractive.

POLONIUS [to the king]: O, ho! do you mark that?   90

HAMLET: Lady, shall I lie in your lap?   [Lying down at OPHELIA's feet.]

OPHELIA: No, my lord.

HAMLET: I mean, my head upon your lap?

OPHELIA: Ay, my lord.

HAMLET: Do you think I meant country° matters?   95

OPHELIA: I think nothing, my lord.

HAMLET: That's a fair thought to lie between maids' legs.

OPHELIA: What is, my lord?

HAMLET: Nothing.

OPHELIA: You are merry, my lord.   100

HAMLET: Who, I?

OPHELIA: Ay, my lord.

HAMLET: O God, your only° jig-maker.° What should a man do but be merry? for, look you, how cheerfully my mother looks, and my father died within's two hours.   105

OPHELIA: Nay, 'tis twice two months, my lord.

HAMLET: So long? Nay then, let the devil wear black, for I'll have a suit of sables.° O heavens! die two months ago, and not forgotten yet? Then there's hope a great man's memory may outlive his life half a year: but, by 'r lady, 'a must build churches, then; or else shall 'a suffer not thinking on,° with the hobbyhorse,   110 whose epitaph is "For, O, for, O, the hobbyhorse is forgot."°

(The trumpets sound. Dumb show follows.)

(Enter a KING and a QUEEN [very lovingly]; the QUEEN embracing him, and he her. [She kneels, and makes show of protestation unto him.] He takes her up, and declines his head upon her neck: he lies him down upon a bank of flowers: she, seeing him asleep, leaves him. Anon comes in another man, takes off his crown, kisses it, pours poison in the sleeper's ears, and leaves him. The QUEEN returns; finds the KING dead, makes passionate action. The POISONER, with some three or four come in again, seem to condole with her. The dead body is carried away. The POISONER woos the QUEEN with gifts: she seems harsh awhile, but in the end accepts love.   [Exeunt.])

OPHELIA: What means this, my lord?

HAMLET: Marry, this is miching mallecho;° it means mischief.

95 **country** with a bawdy pun.   103 **your only** only your.   103 **jig-maker** composer of jigs (song and dance).   107 **suit of sables** garments trimmed with the fur of the sable, with a quibble on *sable* meaning "black."   110 **suffer . . . on** undergo oblivion.   111 **"For . . . forgot"** verse of a song occurring also in "Love's Labour's Lost," III.i.30; the hobbyhorse was a character in the Morris Dance.   113 **miching mallecho** sneaking mischief.

OPHELIA: Belike this show imports the argument of the play.

(*Enter* PROLOGUE.)

115 HAMLET: We shall know by this fellow: the players cannot keep counsel; they'll tell all.

OPHELIA: Will 'a tell us what this show meant?

HAMLET: Ay, or any show that you'll show him: be not you ashamed to show, he'll not shame to tell you what it means.

120 OPHELIA: You are naught, you are naught:° I'll mark the play.

PROLOGUE: For us, and for our tragedy,
　　　Here stooping° to your clemency,
　　　We beg your hearing patiently.   [*Exit.*]

HAMLET: Is this a prologue, or the posy° of a ring?

125 OPHELIA: 'Tis brief, my lord.

HAMLET: As woman's love.

(*Enter* [*two Players as*] KING *and* QUEEN.)

PLAYER KING: Full thirty times hath Phoebus' cart gone round
　　　Neptune's salt wash° and Tellus'° orbed ground,
　　　And thirty dozen moons with borrowed° sheen
130　　　About the world have times twelve thirties been,
　　　Since love our hearts and Hymen° did our hands
　　　Unite commutual° in most sacred bands.

PLAYER QUEEN: So many journeys may the sun and moon
　　　Make us again count o'er ere love be done!
135　　　But, woe is me, you are so sick of late,
　　　So far from cheer and from your former state,
　　　That I distrust° you. Yet, though I distrust,
　　　Discomfort you, my lord, it nothing must:
　　　For women's fear and love holds quantity;°
140　　　In neither aught, or in extremity.
　　　Now, what my love is, proof hath made you know;
　　　And as my love is siz'd, my fear is so:
　　　Where love is great, the littlest doubts are fear;
　　　Where little fears grow great, great love grows there.

145 PLAYER KING: 'Faith, I must leave thee, love, and shortly too;
　　　My operant° powers their functions leave° to do:
　　　And thou shalt live in this fair world behind,
　　　Honor'd, belov'd; and haply one as kind
　　　For husband shalt thou—

PLAYER QUEEN:　　　　　　O, confound the rest!
150　　　Such love must needs be treason in my breast:

---

120 naught indecent.　**122 stooping** bowing.　**124 posy** motto.　**128 salt wash** the sea.　**128 Tellus** goddess of the earth (*orbed ground*).　**129 borrowed** i.e., reflected.　**131 Hymen** god of matrimony.　**132 commutual** mutually.　**137 distrust** am anxious about.　**139 holds quantity** keeps proportion between.　**146 operant** active.　**146 leave** cease.

In second husband let me be accurst!
None wed the second but who kill'd the first.
HAMLET (*aside*): Wormwood, wormwood.
PLAYER QUEEN: The instances that second marriage move
    Are base respects of thrift, but none of love: 155
    A second time I kill my husband dead,
    When second husband kisses me in bed.
PLAYER KING: I do believe you think what now you speak;
    But what we do determine oft we break.
    Purpose is but the slave to memory,   160
    Of violent birth, but poor validity:
    Which now, like fruit unripe, sticks on the tree;
    But fall, unshaken, when they mellow be.
    Most necessary 'tis that we forget
    To pay ourselves what to ourselves is debt: 165
    What to ourselves in passion we propose,
    The passion ending, doth the purpose lose.
    The violence of either grief or joy
    Their own enactures° with themselves destroy:
    Where joy most revels, grief doth most lament;   170
    Grief joys, joy grieves, on slender accident.
    This world is not for aye,° nor 'tis not strange
    That even our loves should with our fortunes change;
    For 'tis a question left us yet to prove,
    Whether love lead fortune, or else fortune love.   175
    The great man down, you mark his favorite flies;
    The poor advanc'd makes friends of enemies.
    And hitherto doth love on fortune tend;
    For who° not needs shall never lack a friend,
    And who in want a hollow friend doth try,   180
    Directly seasons° him his enemy.
    But, orderly to end where I begun,
    Our wills and fates do so contrary run
    That our devices still are overthrown;
    Our thoughts are ours, their ends° none of our own: 185
    So think thou wilt no second husband wed;
    But die thy thoughts when thy first lord is dead.
PLAYER QUEEN: Nor earth to me give food, nor heaven light!
    Sport and repose lock from me day and night!
    To desperation turn my trust and hope!   190
    An anchor's° cheer° in prison be my scope!
    Each opposite° that blanks° the face of joy
    Meet what I would have well and it destroy!

---

169 enactures fulfillments. **172 aye** ever. **179 who** whoever. **181 seasons** matures, ripens.
185 ends results. **191 An anchor's** an anchorite's. **191 cheer** fare; sometimes printed as *chair*.
192 opposite adverse thing. **192 blanks** causes to blanch or grow pale.

Both here and hence pursue me lasting strife,
195   If, once a widow, ever I be wife!
HAMLET: If she should break it now!
PLAYER KING: 'Tis deeply sworn. Sweet, leave me here awhile;
      My spirits grow dull, and fain I would beguile
      The tedious day with sleep.   [*Sleeps.*]
PLAYER QUEEN: Sleep rock thy brain;
200   And never come mischance between us twain!   (*Exit.*)
HAMLET: Madam, how like you this play?
QUEEN: The lady doth protest too much, methinks.
HAMLET: O, but she'll keep her word.
KING: Have you heard the argument? Is there no offence in 't?
205   HAMLET: No, no, they do but jest, poison in jest; no offence i' the world.
KING: What do you call the play?
HAMLET: The Mouse-trap. Marry, how? Tropically.° This play is the image of a mur-
      der done in Vienna: Gonzago° is the duke's name; his wife, Baptista: you shall
      see anon; 't is a knavish piece of work: but what o' that? your majesty and we
210   that have free souls, it touches us not: let the galled jade° winch,° our withers°
      are unwrung.°

(*Enter* LUCIANUS.)

      This is one Lucianus, nephew to the king.
OPHELIA: You are as good as a chorus,° my lord.
HAMLET: I could interpret between you and your love, if I could see the puppets
215   dallying.°
OPHELIA: You are keen, my lord, you are keen.
HAMLET: It would cost you a groaning to take off my edge.
OPHELIA: Still better, and worse.°
HAMLET: So you mistake° your husbands. Begin, murderer; pox,° leave thy damnable
220   faces, and begin. Come: the croaking raven doth bellow for revenge.
LUCIANUS: Thoughts black, hands apt, drugs fit, and time agreeing;
      Confederate° season, else no creature seeing;
      Thou mixture rank, of midnight weeds collected,
      With Hecate's° ban° thrice blasted, thrice infected,
225   Thy natural magic and dire property,
      On wholesome life usurp immediately.

                              [*Pours the poison into the sleeper's ears.*]

207 Tropically figuratively, *tropically* suggests a pun on *trap* in Mouse-trap (1.211).   **208 Gonzago** in 1538 Luigi Gonzago murdered the Duke of Urbano by pouring poisoned lotion in his ears. **210 galled jade** horse whose hide is rubbed by saddle or harness.   **210 winch** wince.   **210 withers** the part between the horse's shoulder blades.   **211 unwrung** not wrung or twisted.   **213 chorus** in many Elizabethan plays the action was explained by an actor known as the "chorus"; at a puppet show the actor who explained the action was known as an "interpreter," as indicated by the lines following.   **215–217 dallying** with sexual suggestion, continued in **keen** (sexually aroused), **groaning** (i.e., in pregnancy), and **edge** (i.e., sexual desire or impetuosity).   **218 Still . . . worse** more keen, less decorous.   **219 mistake** err in taking.   **219 pox** an imprecation.   **222 Confederate** conspiring (to assist the murderer).   **224 Hecate** the goddess of witchcraft.   **224 ban** curse.

HAMLET: 'A poisons him i' the garden for his estate. His name's Gonzago: the story is extant, and written in very choice Italian: you shall see anon how the murderer gets the love of Gonzago's wife.

OPHELIA: The king rises.   230

HAMLET: What, frighted with false fire!°

QUEEN: How fares my lord?

POLONIUS: Give o'er the play.

KING: Give me some light away!

POLONIUS: Lights, lights, lights!   (*Exeunt all but* HAMLET *and* HORATIO.)   235

HAMLET: Why,° let the strucken deer go weep,

    The hart ungalled play;

    For some must watch, while some must sleep:

        Thus runs the world away.

    Would not this,° sir, and a forest of feathers°—if the rest of my fortunes turn   240

    Turk with° me—with two Provincial roses° on my razed° shoes, get me a fel-

    lowship in a cry° of players,° sir?

HORATIO: Half a share.°

HAMLET: A whole one, I.

    For thou dost know, O Damon dear,   245

        This realm dismantled° was

    Of Jove himself; and now reigns here

        A very, very°—pajock.°

HORATIO: You might have rhymed.

HAMLET: O good Horatio, I'll take the ghost's word for a thousand pound.   250

    Didst perceive?

HORATIO: Very well, my lord.

HAMLET: Upon the talk of the poisoning?

HORATIO: I did very well note him.

HAMLET: Ah, ha! Come, some music! come, the recorders!°   255

    For if the king like not the comedy,

    Why then, belike, he likes it not, perdy.°

    Come, some music!

(*Enter* ROSENCRANTZ *and* GUILDENSTERN.)

GUILDENSTERN: Good my lord, vouchsafe me a word with you.

HAMLET: Sir, a whole history.   260

---

231 false fire fireworks, or a blank discharge.   **236–239 Why . . . away** probably from an old ballad, with allusion to the popular belief that a wounded deer retires to weep and die. Cf. "As You Like It," II.i.66.   **240 this** i.e., the play.   **240 feathers** allusion to the plumes which Elizabethan actors were fond of wearing.   **240–241 turn Turk with** go back on.   **241 two Provincial roses** rosettes of ribbon like the roses of Provins near Paris, or else the roses of Provence.   **241 razed** cut, slashed (by way of ornament).   **242 cry** pack (as of hounds).   **241–242 fellowship . . . players** partnership in a theatrical company.   **243 Half a share** allusion to the custom in dramatic companies of dividing the ownership into a number of shares among the householders.   **246 dismantled** stripped, divested.   **245–248 For . . . very** probably from an old ballad having to do with Damon and Pythias.   **248 pajock** peacock (a bird with a bad reputation). Possibly the word was *patchock,* diminutive of *patch,* clown.   **255 recorders** wind instruments of the flute kind.   **257 perdy** corruption of *par dieu.*

GUILDENSTERN: The king, sir,—

HAMLET: Ay, sir, what of him?

GUILDENSTERN: Is in his retirement marvellous distempered.

HAMLET: With drink, sir?

265 GUILDENSTERN: No, my lord, rather with choler.°

HAMLET: Your wisdom should show itself more richer to signify this to his doctor;
for, for me to put him to his purgation would perhaps plunge him into far more
choler.

GUILDENSTERN: Good my lord, put your discourse into some frame° and start not

270   so wildly from my affair.

HAMLET: I am tame, sir: pronounce.

GUILDENSTERN: The queen, your mother, in most great affliction of spirit, hath
sent me to you.

HAMLET: You are welcome.

275 GUILDENSTERN: Nay, good my lord, this courtesy is not of the right breed. If it shall
please you to make me a wholesome° answer, I will do your mother's commandment; if not, your pardon and my return shall be the end of my business.

HAMLET: Sir, I cannot.

GUILDENSTERN: What, my lord?

280 HAMLET: Make you a wholesome answer; my wit's diseased: but, sir, such answer as I
can make, you shall command; or, rather, as you say, my mother: therefore no
more, but to the matter:° my mother, you say,—

ROSENCRANTZ: Then thus she says; your behavior hath struck her into amazement
and admiration.

285 HAMLET: O wonderful son, that can so 'stonish a mother! But is there no sequel at
the heels of this mother's admiration? Impart.

ROSENCRANTZ: She desires to speak with you in her closet, ere you go to bed.

HAMLET: We shall obey, were she ten times our mother. Have you any further trade
with us?

290 ROSENCRANTZ: My lord, you once did love me.

HAMLET: And do still, by these pickers and stealers.°

ROSENCRANTZ: Good my lord, what is your cause of distemper? you do, surely, bar
the door upon your own liberty, if you deny your griefs to your friend.

HAMLET: Sir, I lack advancement.

295 ROSENCRANTZ: How can that be, when you have the voice° of the king himself for
your succession in Denmark?

HAMLET: Ay, sir, but "While the grass grows,"°—the proverb is something musty.

(*Enter the* PLAYERS *with recorders.*)

O, the recorders! let me see one. To withdraw° with you:—why do you go about
to recover the wind° of me, as if you would drive me into a toil?°

---

265 choler bilious disorder, with quibble on the sense "anger."   **269 frame** order.   **276 wholesome** sensible.   **282 matter** matter in hand.   **291 pickers and stealers** hands, so called from
the catechism "to keep my hands from picking and stealing."   **295 voice** support.   **297
"While . . . grows"** the rest of the proverb is "the silly horse starves." Hamlet may be destroyed
while he is waiting for the succession to the kingdom.   **298 withdraw** speak in private.   **299 recover the wind** get to the windward side.   **299 toil** snare.

GUILDENSTERN: O, my lord, if my duty be too bold, my love is too unmannerly.° 300

HAMLET: I do not well understand that. Will you play upon this pipe?

GUILDENSTERN: My lord, I cannot.

HAMLET: I pray you.

GUILDENSTERN: Believe me. I cannot.

HAMLET: I beseech you. 305

GUILDENSTERN: I know no touch of it, my lord.

HAMLET: 'Tis as easy as lying: govern these ventages° with your fingers and thumb, give it breath with your mouth, and it will discourse most eloquent music. Look you, these are the stops.

GUILDENSTERN: But these cannot I command to any utterance of harmony; I have 310 not the skill.

HAMLET: Why, look you now, how unworthy a thing you make of me! You would play upon me; you would seem to know my stops; you would pluck out the heart of my mystery; you would sound me from my lowest note to the top of my compass:° and there is much music, excellent voice, in this little organ;° yet 315 cannot you make it speak. 'Sblood, do you think I am easier to be played on than a pipe? Call me what instrument you will, though you can fret° me, you cannot play upon me.

(*Enter* POLONIUS.)

God bless you, sir!

POLONIUS: My lord, the queen would speak with you, and presently. 320

HAMLET: Do you see yonder cloud that 's almost in shape of a camel?

POLONIUS: By the mass, and 'tis like a camel, indeed.

HAMLET: Methinks it is like a weasel.

POLONIUS: It is backed like a weasel.

HAMLET: Or like a whale? 325

POLONIUS: Very like a whale.

HAMLET: Then I will come to my mother by and by. [*Aside.*] They fool me to the top of my bent.°—I will come by and by.°

POLONIUS: I will say so.   [*Exit.*]

HAMLET: By and by is easily said. 330

Leave me, friends.   [*Exeunt all but* HAMLET.]

'Tis now the very witching time° of night,

When churchyards yawn and hell itself breathes out

Contagion to this world: now could I drink hot blood,

And do such bitter business as the day 335

Would quake to look on. Soft! now to my mother.

O heart, lose not thy nature; let not ever

The soul of Nero° enter this firm bosom:

---

300 if . . . unmannerly if I am using an unmannerly boldness, it is my love which occasions it.
307 ventages stops of the recorder.   315 compass range of voice.   315 organ musical instrument, i.e., the pipe.   317 fret quibble on meaning "irritate" and the piece of wood, gut, or metal which regulates the fingering.   328 top of my bent limit of endurance, i.e., extent to which a bow may be bent.   328 by and by immediately.   332 witching time i.e., time when spells are cast.   338 Nero murderer of his mother, Agrippina.

340
Let me be cruel, not unnatural:
I will speak daggers to her, but use none;
My tongue and soul in this be hypocrites;
How in my words somever she be shent,°
To give them seals° never, my soul, consent!   (*Exit.*)

SCENE III [*A room in the castle.*]

(*Enter* KING, ROSENCRANTZ, *and* GUILDENSTERN.)

KING: I like him not, nor stands it safe with us
To let his madness range. Therefore prepare you;
I your commission will forthwith dispatch,°
And he to England shall along with you:
5
The terms° of our estate° may not endure
Hazard so near us as doth hourly grow
Out of his brows.°
GUILDENSTERN: We will ourselves provide:
Most holy and religious fear it is
To keep those many many bodies safe
10
That live and feed upon your majesty.
ROSENCRANTZ: The single and peculiar° life is bound,
With all the strength and armor of the mind,
To keep itself from noyance;° but much more
That spirit upon whose weal depend and rest
15
The lives of many. The cess° of majesty
Dies not alone; but, like a gulf,° doth draw
What's near it with it: it is a massy wheel,
Fix'd on the summit of the highest mount,
To whose huge spokes ten thousand lesser things
20
Are mortis'd and adjoin'd; which, when it falls,
Each small annexment, petty consequence,
Attends° the boist'rous ruin. Never alone
Did the king sigh, but with a general groan.
KING: Arm° you, I pray you, to this speedy voyage;
25
For we will fetters put about this fear,
Which now goes too free-footed.
ROSENCRANTZ: We will haste us.

(*Exeunt* GENTLEMEN [ROSENCRANTZ *and* GUILDENSTERN].)

(*Enter* POLONIUS.)

POLONIUS: My lord, he's going to his mother's closet:

342 **shent** rebuked.   343 **give them seals** confirm with deeds.   **III.iii. 3 dispatch** prepare.
5 terms condition, circumstances.   **5 estate** state.   **7 brows** effronteries.   **11 single and peculiar** individual and private.   **13 noyance** harm.   **15 cess** decease.   **16 gulf** whirlpool.   **22 Attends** participates in.   **24 Arm** prepare.

Behind the arras° I'll convey° myself,
To hear the process;° I'll warrant she'll tax him home:°
And, as you said, and wisely was it said,   30
'Tis meet that some more audience than a mother,
Since nature makes them partial, should o'erhear
The speech, of vantage.° Fare you well, my liege:
I'll call upon you ere you go to bed,
And tell you what I know.

KING: Thanks, dear my lord.   (*Exit* [POLONIUS].)   35
O, my offence is rank, it smells to heaven;
It hath the primal eldest curse° upon't,
A brother's murder. Pray can I not,
Though inclination be as sharp as will:°
My stronger guilt defeats my strong intent;   40
And, like a man to double business bound,
I stand in pause where I shall first begin,
And both neglect. What if this cursed hand
Were thicker than itself with brother's blood,
Is there not rain enough in the sweet heavens   45
To wash it white as snow? Whereto serves mercy
But to confront° the visage of offence?
And what's in prayer but this two-fold force,
To be forestalled° ere we come to fall,
Or pardon'd being down? Then I'll look up;   50
My fault is past. But, O, what form of prayer
Can serve my turn? "Forgive me my foul murder"?
That cannot be: since I am still possess'd
Of those effects for which I did the murder,
My crown, mine own ambition° and my queen.   55
May one be pardon'd and retain th' offence?°
In the corrupted currents° of this world
Offence's gilded hand° may shove by justice,
And oft 'tis seen the wicked prize° itself
Buys out the law: but 'tis not so above;   60
There is no shuffling,° there the action lies°
In his true nature; and we ourselves compell'd,
Even to the teeth and forehead° of our faults,
To give in evidence. What then? what rests?°

---

28 arras screen of tapestry placed around the walls of household apartments.   **28 convey** implication of secrecy; *convey* was often used to mean "steal."   **29 process** proceedings.   **29 tax him home** reprove him severely.   **33 of vantage** from an advantageous place.   **37 primal eldest curse** the curse of Cain, the first to kill his brother.   **39 sharp as will** i.e., his desire is as strong as his determination.   **47 confront** oppose directly.   **49 forestalled** prevented.   **55 ambition** i.e., realization of ambition.   **56 offence** benefit accruing from offense.   **57 currents** courses.   **58 gilded hand** hand offering gold as a bribe.   **59 wicked prize** prize won by wickedness.   **61 shuffling** escape by trickery.   **61 lies** is sustainable.   **63 teeth and forehead** very face.   **64 rests** remains.

65   Try what repentance can: what can it not?
    Yet what can it when one can not repent?
    O wretched state! O bosom black as death!
    O limed° soul, that, struggling to be free,
    Art more engag'd!° Help, angels! Make assay!°
70   Bow, stubborn knees; and, heart with strings of steel,
    Be soft as sinews of the new-born babe!
    All may be well.   *[He kneels.]*

    (*Enter* HAMLET.)

HAMLET: Now might I do it pat,° now he is praying;
    And now I'll do't. And so 'a goes to heaven;
75   And so am I reveng'd. That would be scann'd:°
    A villain kills my father; and for that,
    I, his sole son, do this same villain send
    To heaven.
    Why, this is hire and salary, not revenge.
80   'A took my father grossly, full of bread;°
    With all his crimes broad blown,° as flush° as May;
    And how his audit stands who knows save heaven?
    But in our circumstance and course° of thought,
    'Tis heavy with him: and am I then reveng'd,
85   To take him in the purging of his soul,
    When he is fit and season'd for his passage?°
    No!
    Up, sword; and know thou a more horrid hent:°
    When he is drunk asleep,° or in his rage,
90   Or in th' incestuous pleasure of his bed;
    At game, a-swearing, or about some act
    That has no relish of salvation in't;
    Then trip him, that his heels may kick at heaven,
    And that his soul may be as damn'd and black
95   As hell, whereto it goes. My mother stays:
    This physic° but prolongs thy sickly days.   (*Exit.*)

KING [*Rising*]: My words fly up, my thoughts remain below:
    Words without thoughts never to heaven go.   (*Exit.*)

SCENE IV [*The Queen's closet.*]

    (*Enter* [QUEEN] GERTRUDE *and* POLONIUS.)

POLONIUS: 'A will come straight. Look you lay° home to him:

---

68 limed caught as with birdlime.   **69 engag'd** embedded.   **69 assay** trial.   **73 pat** opportunely.   **75 would be scann'd** needs to be looked into.   **80 full of bread** enjoying his worldly pleasures (see Ezekiel 16:49).   **81 broad blown** in full bloom.   **81 flush** lusty.   **83 in . . . course** as we see it in our mortal situation.   **86 fit . . . passage** i.e., reconciled to heaven by forgiveness of his sins.   **88 hent** seizing; or more probably, occasion of seizure.   **89 drunk asleep** in a drunken sleep.   **96 physic** purging (by prayer).   **III.iv. 1 lay** thrust.

Tell him his pranks have been too broad° to bear with,
And that your grace hath screen'd and stood between
Much heat° and him. I'll sconce° me even here.
Pray you, be round° with him.   5
HAMLET (*within*): Mother, mother, mother!
QUEEN: I'll warrant you,
Fear me not: withdraw, I hear him coming.

                              [POLONIUS *hides behind the arras.*]

(*Enter* HAMLET.)

HAMLET: Now, mother, what's the matter?
QUEEN: Hamlet, thou hast thy father much offended.
HAMLET: Mother, you have my father° much offended.   10
QUEEN: Come, come, you answer with an idle tongue.
HAMLET: Go, go, you question with a wicked tongue.
QUEEN: Why, how now, Hamlet!
HAMLET: What's the matter now?
QUEEN: Have you forgot me?
HAMLET: No, by the rood,° not so:
You are the queen, your husband's brother's wife;   15
And—would it were not so!—you are my mother.
QUEEN: Nay, then, I'll set those to you that can speak.
HAMLET: Come, come, and sit you down; you shall not budge;
You go not till I set you up a glass
Where you may see the inmost part of you.   20
QUEEN: What wilt thou do? thou wilt not murder me?
Help, help, ho!
POLONIUS [*behind*]: What, ho! help, help; help!
HAMLET [*drawing*]: How now! a rat? Dead, for a ducat, dead!
                              [*Makes a pass through the arras.*]
POLONIUS [*behind*]: O, I am slain!   [*Falls and dies.*]   25
QUEEN: O me, what hast thou done?
HAMLET: Nay, I know not:
Is it the king?
QUEEN: O, what a rash and bloody deed is this!
HAMLET: A bloody deed! almost as bad, good mother,
As kill a king, and marry with his brother.   30
QUEEN: As kill a king!
HAMLET: Ay, lady, it was my word.
                              [*Lifts up the arras and discovers* POLONIUS.]
Thou wretched, rash, intruding fool, farewell!
I took thee for thy better: take thy fortune;
Thou find'st to be too busy is some danger.
Leave wringing of your hands: peace! sit you down,   35

2 **broad** unrestrained.   4 **Much heat** i.e., the king's anger.   5 **round** blunt.
9–10 **thy father . . . my father** i.e., Claudius, the elder Hamlet.   14 **rood** cross.

And let me wring your heart; for so I shall,
If it be made of penetrable stuff,
If damned custom have not braz'd° it so
That it be proof and bulwark against sense.

40   QUEEN: What have I done, that thou dar'st wag thy tongue
In noise so rude against me?

HAMLET: Such an act
That blurs the grace and blush of modesty,
Calls virtue hypocrite, takes off the rose
From the fair forehead of an innocent love

45   And sets a blister° there, makes marriage-vows
As false as dicers' oaths: O, such a deed
As from the body of contraction° plucks
The very soul, and sweet religion° makes
A rhapsody° of words: heaven's face does glow

50   O'er this solidity and compound mass
With heated visage, as against the doom
Is thought-sick at the act.°

QUEEN: Ay me, what act,
That roars so loud, and thunders in the index?°

HAMLET: Look here, upon this picture, and on this.

55   The counterfeit presentment° of two brothers.
See, what a grace was seated on this brow;
Hyperion's° curls; the front° of Jove himself;
An eye Mars, to threaten and command;
A station° like the herald Mercury

60   New-lighted on a heaven-kissing hill;
A combination and form indeed,
Where every god did seem to set his seal,
To give the world assurance° of a man:
This was your husband. Look you now, what follows:

65   Here is your husband; like a mildew'd ear,°
Blasting his wholesome brother. Have you eyes?
Could you on this fair mountain leave to feed,
And batten° on this moor?° Ha! have you eyes?
You cannot call it love; for at your age

70   The hey-day° in the blood is tame, it's humble,
And waits upon the judgement: and what judgement
Would step from this to this? Sense, sure, you have,

---

38 braz'd brazened, hardened.   45 sets a blister brands as a harlot.   47 contraction the marriage contract.   48 religion religious vows.   49 rhapsody senseless string.   49–52
heaven's . . . act heaven's face blushes to look down upon this world, compounded of the four elements, with hot face as though the day of doom were near, and thought-sick at the deed (i.e.,
Gertrude's marriage).   53 index prelude or preface.   55 counterfeit presentment portrayed
representation.   57 Hyperion's the sun god's.   57 front brow.   59 station manner of standing.
63 assurance pledge, guarantee.   65 mildew'd ear see Genesis 41:5–7.   68 batten grow fat.
68 moor barren upland.   70 hey-day state of excitement.

Else could you not have motion,° but sure, that sense
Is apoplex'd° for madness would not err.
Nor sense to ecstasy was ne'er so thrall'd°   75
But it reserv'd some quality of choice,°
To serve in such a difference. What devil was't
Tha' thus hath cozen'd° you at hoodman-blind?°
Eyes without feeling, feeling without sight,
Ears without hands or eyes, smelling sans° all,   80
Or but a sickly part of one true sense
Could not so mope.°
O shame! where is thy blush? Rebellious hell,
If thou canst mutine° in a matron's bones,
To flaming youth let virtue be as wax,   85
And melt in her own fire: proclaim no shame
When the compulsive ardor gives the charge,°
Since frost itself as actively doth burn
And reason panders will°

QUEEN: O Hamlet, speak no more:
Thou turn'st mine eyes into my very soul;   90
And there I see such black and grained° spots
As will not leave their tinct.

HAMLET: Nay, but to live
In the rank sweat of an enseamed° bed,
Stew'd in corruption, honeying and making love
Over the nasty sty,—

QUEEN: O, speak to me no more;   95
These words, like daggers, enter in mine ears;
No more, sweet Hamlet!

HAMLET: A murderer and a villain;
A slave that is not twentieth part the tithe
Of your precedent lord;° a vice of kings;°
A cutpurse of the empire and the rule,   100
That from a shelf the precious diadem stole,
And put it in his pocket!

QUEEN: No more!

(*Enter* GHOST.)

HAMLET: A king of shreds and patches,°—
    Save me, and hover o'er me with your wings,
105   You heavenly guards! What would your gracious figure?
QUEEN: Alas, he's mad!
HAMLET: Do you not come your tardy son to chide,
    That, laps'd in time and passion,° lets go by
    Th' important° acting of your dread command?
110   O, say!
GHOST: Do not forget: this visitation
    Is but to whet thy almost blunted purpose.
    But, look, amazement° on thy mother sits:
    O, step between her and her fighting soul:
115   Conceit in weakest bodies strongest works:
    Speak to her, Hamlet.
HAMLET: How is it with you, lady?
QUEEN: Alas, how is 't with you,
    That you do bend your eye on vacancy
    And with th' incorporal° air do hold discourse?
120   Forth at your eyes your spirits wildly peep;
    And, as the sleeping soldiers in th' alarm,
    Your bedded° hair, like life in excrements,°
    Start up, and stand an° end. O gentle son,
    Upon the heat and flame of thy distemper
125   Sprinkle cool patience. Whereon do you look?
HAMLET: On him, on him! Look you, how pale he glares!
    His form and cause conjoin'd,° preaching to stones,
    Would make them capable.—Do not look upon me;
    Lest with this piteous action you convert
130   My stern effects:° then what I have to do
    Will want true color;° tears perchance for blood.
QUEEN: To whom do you speak this?
HAMLET: Do you see nothing there?
QUEEN: Nothing at all; yet all that is I see.
HAMLET: Nor did you nothing hear?
QUEEN: No, nothing but ourselves.
135 HAMLET: Why, look you there! look, how it steals away!
    My father, in his habit as he liv'd!
    Look, where he goes, even now, out at the portal!   (*Exit* GHOST.)
QUEEN: This is the very coinage of your brain:

---

103 shreds and patches i.e., motley, the traditional costume of the Vice. **108 laps'd . . . passion** having suffered time to slip and passion to cool; also explained as "engrossed in casual events and lapsed into mere fruitless passion, so that he no longer entertains a rational purpose." **109 important** urgent. **113 amazement** frenzy, distraction. **119 incorporal** immaterial. **122 bedded** laid in smooth layers. **122 excrements** the hair was considered an excrement or voided part of the body. **123 an** on. **127 conjoin'd** united. **129–130 convert . . . effects** divert me from my stern duty. For *effects*, possibly *affects* (affections of the mind). **131 want true color** lack good reason so that (with a play on the normal sense of color) I shall shed tears instead of blood.

> This bodiless creation ecstasy
> Is very cunning in.

HAMLET: Ecstasy!   140
> My pulse, as yours, doth temperately keep time,
> And makes as healthful music: it is not madness
> That I have utt'red: bring me to the test,
> And I the matter will re-word,° which madness
> Would gambol° from. Mother, for love of grace,   145
> Lay not that flattering unction° to your soul,
> That not your trespass, but my madness speaks:
> It will but skin and film the ulcerous place,
> Whiles rank corruption, mining° all within,
> Infects unseen. Confess yourself to heaven;   150
> Repent what's past; avoid what is to come;°
> And do not spread the compost° on the weeds,
> To make them ranker. Forgive me this my virtue;°
> For in the fatness° of these pursy° times
> Virtue itself of vice must pardon beg,   155
> Yea, curb° and woo for leave to do him good.

QUEEN: O Hamlet, thou hast cleft my heart in twain.

HAMLET: O, throw away the worser part of it,
> And live the purer with the other half.
> Good night: but go not to my uncle's bed;   160
> Assume a virtue, if you have it not.
> That monster, custom, who all sense doth eat,
> Of habits devil, is angel yet in this,
> That to the use of actions fair and good
> He likewise gives a frock or livery,   165
> That aptly is put on. Refrain to-night,
> And that shall lend a kind of easiness
> To the next abstinence: the next more easy;
> For use almost can change the stamp of nature,
> And either . . . the devil, or throw him out°   170
> With wondrous potency. Once more, good night:
> And when you are desirous to be bless'd,°
> I'll blessing beg of you. For this same lord,   _[Pointing to POLONIUS.]_
> I do repent: but heaven hath pleas'd it so,
> To punish me with this and this with me,   175
> That I must be their scourge and minister.
> I will bestow him, and will answer well
> The death I gave him. So, again, good night.

144 **re-word** repeat in words.   145 **gambol** skip away.   146 **unction** ointment used medicinally or as a rite; suggestion that forgiveness for sin may not be so easily achieved.   149 **mining** working under the surface.   151 **what is to come** i.e., the sins of the future.   152 **compost** manure.   153 **this my virtue** my virtuous talk in reproving you.   154 **fatness** grossness.   154 **pursy** short-winded, corpulent.   156 **curb** bow, bend the knee.   170 defective line usually emended by inserting *master* after *either*.   172 **be bless'd** become blessed, i.e., repentant.

I must be cruel, only to be kind:

180   Thus bad begins and worse remains behind.

One word more, good lady.

QUEEN: What shall I do?

HAMLET: Not this, by no means, that I bid you do:

Let the bloat° king tempt you again to bed;

Pinch wanton on your cheek; call you his mouse;

185   And let him, for a pair of reechy° kisses,

Or paddling in your neck with his damn'd fingers,

Make you to ravel all this matter out,

That I essentially° am not in madness,

But mad in craft. 'Twere good you let him know;

190   For who, that's but a queen, fair, sober, wise,

Would from a paddock,° from a bat, a gib,°

Such dear concernings° hide? who would do so?

No, in despite of sense and secrecy,

Unpeg the basket on the house's top,

195   Let the birds fly, and, like the famous ape,°

To try conclusions,° in the basket creep,

And break your own neck down.

QUEEN: Be thou assur'd, if words be made of breath,

And breath of life, I have no life to breathe

200   What thou hast said to me.

HAMLET: I must to England; you know that?

QUEEN: Alack,

I had forgot: 'tis so concluded on.

HAMLET: There's letters seal'd: and my two schoolfellows,

Whom I will trust as I will adders fang'd,

205   They bear the mandate; they must sweep my way,°

And marshal me to knavery. Let it work;

For 'tis the sport to have the enginer°

Hoist° with his own petar:° and 't shall go hard

But I will delve one yard below their mines,

210   And blow them at the moon: O, 'tis most sweet,

When in one line two crafts° directly meet.

This man shall set me packing:°

I'll lug the guts into the neighbor room.

---

183 bloat bloated.   **185 reechy** dirty, filthy.   **188 essentially** in my essential nature.   **191 paddock** toad.   **191 gib** tomcat.   **192 dear concernings** important affairs.   **195 the famous ape** a letter from Sir John Suckling seems to supply other details of the story, otherwise not identified: "It is the story of the jackanapes and the partridges; thou starest after a beauty till it be lost to thee, then let'st out another, and starest after that till it is gone too."   **196 conclusions** experiments. **205 sweep my way** clear my path.   **207 enginer** constructor of military works, or possibly, artilleryman.   **208 Hoist** blown up.   **208 petar** defined as a small engine of war used to blow in a door or make a breach, and as a case filled with explosive materials.   **211 two crafts** two acts of guile, with quibble on the sense of "two ships."   **212 set me packing** set me to making schemes, and set me to lugging (him), and, also, send me off in a hurry.

Mother, good night. Indeed this counsellor
Is now most still, most secret and most grave,   215
Who was in life a foolish prating knave.
Come, sir, to draw° toward an end with you.
Good night, mother.

> (*Exeunt* [*severally;* HAMLET *dragging in* POLONIUS.])

ACT IV
SCENE I [*A room in the castle.*]

> (*Enter* KING *and* QUEEN, *with* ROSENCRANTZ *and* GUILDENSTERN.)

KING: There's matter in these sighs, these profound heaves:
  You must translate: 'tis fit we understand them.
  Where is your son?
QUEEN: Bestow this place on us a little while.

> [*Exeunt* ROSENCRANTZ *and* GUILDENSTERN.]

  Ah, mine own lord, what have I seen to-night!   5
KING: What, Gertrude? How does Hamlet?
QUEEN: Mad as the sea and wind, when both contend
  Which is the mightier: in his lawless fit,
  Behind the arras hearing something stir,
  Whips out his rapier, cries, "A rat, a rat!"   10
  And, in this brainish° apprehension,° kills
  The unseen good old man.
KING: O heavy deed!
  It had been so with us, had we been there:
  His liberty is full of threats to all;
  To you yourself, to us, to every one.   15
  Alas, how shall this bloody deed be answer'd?
  It will be laid to us, whose providence°
  Should have kept short,° restrain'd and out of haunt,°
  This mad young man: but so much was our love,
  We would not understand what was most fit;   20
  But, like the owner of a foul disease,
  To keep it from divulging,° let it feed
  Even on the pith of life. Where is he gone?
QUEEN: To draw apart the body he hath kill'd:
  O'er whom his very madness, like some ore   25
  Among a mineral° of metals base,
  Shows itself pure; 'a weeps for what is done.
KING: O Gertrude, come away!
  The sun no sooner shall the mountains touch,

---

217 draw come, with quibble on literal sense. **IV.i. 11 brainish** headstrong, passionate. **11 apprehension** conception, imagination. **17 providence** foresight. **18 short** i.e., on a short tether. **18 out of haunt** secluded. **22 divulging** becoming evident. **26 mineral** mine.

30   But we will ship him hence: and this vile deed
      We must, with all our majesty and skill,
      Both countenance and excuse. Ho, Guildenstern!

      (*Enter* ROSENCRANTZ *and* GUILDENSTERN.)

      Friends both, go join you with some further aid:
      Hamlet in madness hath Polonius slain,
35   And from his mother's closet hath he dragg'd him:
      Go seek him out; speak fair, and bring the body
      Into the chapel. I pray you, haste in this.

      [*Exeunt* ROSENCRANTZ *and* GUILDENSTERN.]

      Come, Gertrude, we'll call up our wisest friends;
      And let them know, both what we mean to do,
40   And what's untimely done . . . °
      Whose whisper o'er the world's diameter,°
      As level° as the cannon to his blank,°
      Transports his pois'ned shot, may miss our name,
      And hit the woundless° air. O, come away!
45   My soul is full of discord and dismay.   (*Exeunt.*)

SCENE II [*Another room in the castle.*]

      (*Enter* HAMLET.)

HAMLET: Safely stowed.
ROSENCRANTZ:
GUILDENSTERN: } [*within*] Hamlet! Lord Hamlet!
HAMLET: But soft, what noise? Who calls on Hamlet? O, here they come.

      (*Enter* ROSENCRANTZ *and* GUILDENSTERN.)

ROSENCRANTZ: What have you done, my lord, with the dead body?
5   HAMLET: Compounded it with dust, whereto 'tis kin.
ROSENCRANTZ: Tell us where 'tis, that we may take it thence
      And bear it to the chapel.
HAMLET: Do not believe it.
ROSENCRANTZ: Believe what?
10 HAMLET: That I can keep your counsel° and not mine own. Besides, to be demanded
      of a sponge! What replication° should be made by the son of a king?
ROSENCRANTZ: Take you me for a sponge, my lord?
HAMLET: Ay, sir, that soaks up the king's countenance, his rewards, his authorities.°
      But such officers do the king best service in the end: he keeps them, like an ape
15   an apple, in the corner of his jaw; first mouthed, to be last swallowed: when he

---

40 defective line; some editors add: *so haply, slander;* others add: *for, haply, slander;* other conjectures.
41 diameter extent from side to side.   **42 level** straight.   **42 blank** white spot in the center of a
target.   **44 woundless** invulnerable.   **IV.ii. 10 keep your counsel** Hamlet is aware of their
treachery but says nothing about it.   **11 replication** reply.   **13 authorities** authoritative backing.

needs what you have gleaned, it is but squeezing you, and, sponge, you shall be
dry again.

ROSENCRANTZ: I understand you not, my lord.

HAMLET: I am glad of it: a knavish speech sleeps in a foolish ear.

ROSENCRANTZ: My lord, you must tell us where the body is, and go with us to the   20
king.

HAMLET: The body is with the king, but the king is not with the body.° The king is
a thing—

GUILDENSTERN: A thing, my lord!

HAMLET: Of nothing: bring me to him. Hide fox, and all after.°   (*Exeunt.*)   25

SCENE III [*Another room in the castle.*]

(*Enter* KING, *and two or three.*)

KING: I have sent to seek him, and to find the body.
How dangerous is it that this man goes loose!
Yet must not we put the strong law on him:
He's lov'd of the distracted° multitude,
Who like not in their judgement, but their eyes;   5
And where 'tis so, th' offender's scourge° is weigh'd,°
But never the offence. To bear all smooth and even,
This sudden sending him away must seem
Deliberate pause:° diseases desperate grown
By desperate appliance are reliev'd,   10
Or not at all.

(*Enter* ROSENCRANTZ, [GUILDENSTERN,] *and all the rest.*)

            How now! what hath befall'n?

ROSENCRANTZ: Where the dead body is bestow'd, my lord,
We cannot get from him.

KING: But where is he?

ROSENCRANTZ: Without, my lord; guarded, to know your pleasure.

KING: Bring him before us.   15

ROSENCRANTZ: Ho! bring in the lord.

(*They enter* [*with* HAMLET].)

KING: Now, Hamlet, where's Polonius?

HAMLET: At supper.

KING: At supper! where?

HAMLET: Not where he eats, but where 'a is eaten: a certain convocation of politic°   20
worms° are e'en at him. Your worm is your only emperor for diet: we fat all

---

22 The body . . . body there are many interpretations; possibly, "The body lies in death with the
king, my father; but my father walks disembodied"; or "Claudius has the bodily possession of kingship, but kingliness, or justice of inheritance, is not with him."   **25 Hide . . . after** an old signal
cry in the game of hide-and-seek.   **IV.iii. 4 distracted** i.e., without power of forming logical
judgments.   **6 scourge** punishment.   **6 weigh'd** taken into consideration.   **9 Deliberate pause**
considered action.   **20–21 convocation . . . worms** allusion to the Diet of Worms (1521).   **20
politic** crafty.

creatures else to fat us, and we fat ourselves for maggots: your fat king and your
lean beggar is but variable service,° two dishes, but to one table: that's the end.

KING: Alas, alas!

25   HAMLET: A man may fish with the worm that hath eat of a king, and eat of the fish
that hath fed of that worm.

KING: What dost thou mean by this?

HAMLET: Nothing but to show you how a king may go a progress° through the guts
of a beggar.

30   KING: Where is Polonius?

HAMLET: In heaven; send thither to see: if your messenger find him not there, seek
him i' the other place yourself. But if indeed you find him not within this
month, you shall nose him as you go up the stairs into the lobby.

KING [*to some* ATTENDANTS]: Go seek him there.

35   HAMLET: 'A will stay till you come.   [*Exeunt* ATTENDANTS.]

KING: Hamlet, this deed, for thine especial safety,—
Which we do tender,° as we dearly grieve
For that which thou hast done,—must send thee hence
With fiery quickness: therefore prepare thyself;

40   The bark is ready, and the wind at help,
Th' associates tend, and everything is bent
For England.

HAMLET: For England!

KING: Ay, Hamlet.

HAMLET: Good.

KING: So is it, if thou knew'st our purposes.

HAMLET: I see a cherub° that sees them. But, come; for England! Farewell, dear

45   mother.

KING: Thy loving father, Hamlet.

HAMLET: My mother: father and mother is man and wife; man and wife is one flesh;
and so, my mother. Come, for England!   (*Exit.*)

KING: Follow him at foot;° tempt him with speed aboard;

50   Delay it not; I'll have him hence to-night:
Away! for every thing is seal'd and done
That else leans on th' affair: pray you, make haste.

                                        [*Exeunt all but the* KING.]

And, England, if my love thou hold'st at aught—
As my great power thereof may give thee sense,

55   Since yet thy cicatrice° looks raw and red
After the Danish sword, and thy free awe°
Pays homage to us—thou mayst not coldly set
Our sovereign process; which imports at full,
By letters congruing to that effect,

60   The present death of Hamlet. Do it, England;

---

23 variable service a variety of dishes.   **28 progress** royal journey of state.   **37 tender** regard,
hold dear.   **44 cherub** cherubim are angels of knowledge.   **49 at foot** close behind, at heel.   **55
cicatrice** scar.   **56 free awe** voluntary show of respect.

For like the hectic° in my blood he rages,
And thou must cure me: till I know 'tis done,
Howe'er my haps,° my joys were ne'er begun.   (*Exit.*)

SCENE IV [*A plain in Denmark.*]

(*Enter* FORTINBRAS *with his Army over the stage.*)

FORTINBRAS: Go, captain, from me greet the Danish king;
　Tell him that, by his license,° Fortinbras
　Craves the conveyance° of a promis'd march
　Over his kingdom. You know the rendezvous.
　If that his majesty would aught with us,   5
　We shall express our duty in his eye;°
　And let him know so.
CAPTAIN:　　　　　　　　I will do't, my lord.
FORTINBRAS: Go softly° on.   [*Exeunt all but* CAPTAIN.]

(*Enter* HAMLET, ROSENCRANTZ, [GUILDENSTERN,] &c.)

HAMLET: Good sir, whose powers are these?
CAPTAIN: They are of Norway, sir.   10
HAMLET: How purpos'd, sir, I pray you?
CAPTAIN: Against some part of Poland.
HAMLET: Who commands them, sir?
CAPTAIN: The nephew to old Norway, Fortinbras.
HAMLET: Goes it against the main° of Poland, sir,   15
　Or for some frontier?
CAPTAIN: Truly to speak, and with no addition,
　We go to gain a little patch of ground
　That hath in it no profit but the name.
　To pay five ducats, five, I would not farm it;°   20
　Nor will it yield to Norway or the Pole
　A ranker rate, should it be sold in fee.°
HAMLET: Why, then the Polack never will defend it.
CAPTAIN: Yes, it is already garrison'd.
HAMLET: Two thousand souls and twenty thousand ducats   25
　Will not debate the question of this straw;°
　This is th' imposthume° of much wealth and peace,
　That inward breaks, and shows no cause without
　Why the man dies. I humbly thank you, sir.
CAPTAIN: God be wi' you, sir.   [*Exit.*]
ROSENCRANTZ:　　　　　　Will 't please you go, my lord?   30
HAMLET: I'll be with you straight. Go a little before.

---

61 hectic fever.　**63 haps** fortunes.　**IV.iv. 2 license** leave.　**3 conveyance** escort, convey.　**6 in his eye** in his presence.　**8 softly** slowly.　**15 main** country itself.　**20 farm it** take a lease of it.　**22 fee** fee simple.　**26 debate . . . straw** settle this trifling matter.　**27 imposthume** purulent abscess or swelling.

[*Exeunt all except* HAMLET.]

How all occasions° do inform against° me,
And spur my dull revenge! What is a man,
If his chief good and market of his time°
35   Be but to sleep and feed? a beast, no more.
Sure, he that made us with such large discourse,
Looking before and after, gave us not
That capability and god-like reason
To fust° in us unus'd. Now, whether it be
40   Bestial oblivion, or some craven scruple
Of thinking too precisely on th' event,
A thought which, quarter'd, hath but one part wisdom
And ever three parts coward, I do not know
Why yet I live to say "This thing's to do";
45   Sith I have cause and will and strength and means
To do 't. Examples gross as earth exhort me:
Witness this army of such mass and charge
Led by a delicate and tender prince,
Whose spirit with divine ambition puff'd
50   Makes mouths at the invisible event,
Exposing what is mortal and unsure
To all that fortune, death and danger dare,
Even for an egg-shell. Rightly to be great
Is not to stir without great argument,
55   But greatly to find quarrel in a straw
When honor's at the stake. How stand I then,
That have a father kill'd, a mother stain'd,
Excitements of° my reason and my blood,
And let all sleep? while, to my shame, I see
60   The imminent death of twenty thousand men,
That, for a fantasy and trick° of fame,
Go to their graves like beds, fight for a plot°
Whereon the numbers cannot try the cause,
Which is not tomb enough and continent
65   To hide the slain? O, from this time forth,
My thoughts be bloody, or be nothing worth!   (*Exit.*)

SCENE V [*Elsinore. A room in the castle.*]

(*Enter* HORATIO, [QUEEN] GERTRUDE, *and a* GENTLEMAN.)

QUEEN: I will not speak with her.
GENTLEMAN: She is importunate, indeed distract:

---

32 occasions incidents, events.   **32 inform against** generally defined as "show," "betray" (i.e., his tardiness); more probably inform means "take shape," as in Macbeth, II.i.48.   **34 market of his time** the best use he makes of his time, or, that for which he sells his time.   **39 fust** grow moldy.   **58 Excitements of** incentives to.   **61 trick** toy, trifle.   **62 plot** i.e., of ground.

Her mood will needs be pitied.

QUEEN: What would she have?

GENTLEMAN: She speaks much of her father; says she hears
    There's tricks° i' th' world; and hems, and beats her heart;°   5
    Spurns enviously at straws;° speaks things in doubt,
    That carry but half sense: her speech is nothing,
    Yet the unshaped° use of it doth move
    The hearers to collection;° they yawn° at it,
    And botch° the words up fit to their own thoughts;   10
    Which, as her winks, and nods, and gestures yield° them,
    Indeed would make one think there might be thought,
    Though nothing sure, yet much unhappily.°

HORATIO: 'Twere good she were spoken with: for she may strew
    Dangerous conjectures in ill-breeding minds.°   15

QUEEN: Let her come in.   [*Exit* GENTLEMAN.]
    [*Aside.*] To my sick soul, as sin's true nature is,
    Each toy seems prologue to some great amiss:°
    So full of artless jealousy is guilt,
    It spills itself in fearing to be spilt.°   20

(*Enter* OPHELIA [*distracted*].)

OPHELIA: Where is the beauteous majesty of Denmark?

QUEEN: How now, Ophelia!

OPHELIA (*she sings*): How should I your true love know
        From another one?
    By his cockle hat° and staff,   25
        And his sandal shoon.°

QUEEN: Alas, sweet lady, what imports this song?

OPHELIA: Say you? nay, pray you mark.
    (*Song*) He is dead and gone, lady,
        He is dead and gone;   30
    At his head a grass-green turf,
        At his heels a stone.
    O, ho!

QUEEN: Nay, but, Ophelia—

OPHELIA: Pray you, mark   35
    [*Sings.*] White his shroud as the mountain snow,—

(*Enter* KING.)

IV.v. 5 tricks deceptions. **5 heart** i.e., breast. **6 Spurns . . . straws** kicks spitefully at small objects in her path. **8 unshaped** unformed, artless. **9 collection** inference, a guess at some sort of meaning. **9 yawn** wonder. **10 botch** patch. **11 yield** deliver, bring forth (her words). **13 much unhappily** expressive of much unhappiness. **15 ill-breeding minds** minds bent on mischief. **18 great amiss** calamity, disaster. **19–20 So . . . spilt** guilt is so full of suspicion that it unskillfully betrays itself in fearing to be betrayed. **25 cockle hat** hat with cockleshell stuck in it as a sign that the wearer has been a pilgrim to the shrine of St. James of Compostella; the pilgrim's garb was a conventional disguise for lovers. **26 shoon** shoes.

QUEEN: Alas, look here, my lord.

OPHELIA (*Song*): Larded° all with flowers;

   Which bewept to the grave did not go

40   With true-love showers.

KING: How do you, pretty lady?

OPHELIA: Well, God 'ild° you! They say the owl° was a baker's daughter. Lord, we know what we are, but know not what we may be. God be at your table!

KING: Conceit upon her father.

45 OPHELIA: Pray let's have no words of this; but when they ask you what it means, say you this:

   (*Song*) To-morrow is Saint Valentine's day,

     All in the morning betime,

   And I a maid at your window,

50   To be your Valentine.°

   Then up he rose, and donn'd his clothes,

     And dupp'd° the chamber-door;

   Let in the maid, that out a maid

     Never departed more.

55 KING: Pretty Ophelia!

OPHELIA: Indeed, la, without an oath, I'll make an end on 't:

   [*Sings.*] By Gis° and by Saint Charity,

     Alack, and fie for shame!

   Young men will do 't, if they come to 't;

60   By cock,° they are to blame.

   Quoth she, before you tumbled me,

     You promis'd me to wed.

   So would I ha' done, by yonder sun,

     An thou hadst not come to my bed.

65 KING: How long hath she been thus?

OPHELIA: I hope all will be well. We must be patient: but I cannot choose but weep, to think they would lay him i' the cold ground. My brother shall know of it: and so I thank you for your good counsel. Come, my coach! Good night, ladies; good night, sweet ladies; good night, good night. [*Exit.*]

70 KING: Follow her close; give her good watch, I pray you.   [*Exit* HORATIO.]

   O, this is the poison of deep grief; it springs

   All from her father's death. O Gertrude, Gertrude,

   When sorrows come, they come not single spies,

   But in battalions. First, her father slain:

75   Next your son gone; and he most violent author

   Of his own just remove: the people muddied,

   Thick and unwholesome in their thoughts and whispers,

   For good Polonius' death; and we have done but greenly,°

---

38 Larded decorated.   **42 God 'ild** god yield or reward.   **42 owl** reference to a monkish legend that a baker's daughter was turned into an owl for refusing bread to the Savior.   **50 Valentine** this song alludes to the belief that the first girl seen by a man on the morning of this day was his valentine, or true love.   **52 dupp'd** opened.   **57 Gis** Jesus.   **60 cock** perversion of "God" in oaths. **78 greenly** foolishly.

In hugger-mugger° to inter him: poor Ophelia
Divided from herself and her fair judgement,   80
Without the which we are pictures, or mere beasts:
Last, and as much containing as all these,
Her brother is in secret come from France;
Feeds on his wonder, keeps himself in clouds,°
And wants not buzzers° to infect his ear   85
With pestilent speeches of his father's death;
Wherein necessity, of matter beggar'd,°
Will nothing stick° our person to arraign
In ear and ear.° O my dear Gertrude, this,
Like to a murd'ring-piece,° in many places   90
Gives me superfluous death.   (A noise within.)

QUEEN: Alack, what noise is this?
KING: Where are my Switzers?° Let them guard the door.

(Enter a MESSENGER.)

What is the matter?
MESSENGER: Save yourself, my Lord:
The ocean, overpeering° of his list,°
Eats not the flats with more impiteous haste   95
Than young Laertes, in a riotous head,
O'erbears your officers. The rabble call him lord;
And, as the world were now but to begin,
Antiquity forgot, custom not known,
The ratifiers and props of every word,°   100
They cry "Choose we: Laertes shall be king":
Caps, hands, and tongues, applaud it to the clouds:
"Laertes shall be king, Laertes king!"   (A noise within.)

QUEEN: How cheerfully on the false trail they cry!
O, this is counter,° you false Danish dogs!   105
KING: The doors are broke.

(Enter LAERTES with others.)

LAERTES: Where is this king? Sirs, stand you all without.
DANES: No, let's come in.
LAERTES: I pray you, give me leave.
DANES: We will, we will.   [They retire without the door.]

LAERTES: I thank you: keep the door. O thou vile king,   110
    Give me my father!
QUEEN: Calmly, good Laertes.

---

79 hugger-mugger secret haste. **84 in clouds** invisible. **85 buzzers** gossipers. **87 of matter beggar'd** unprovided with facts. **88 nothing stick** not hesitate. **89 In ear and ear** in everybody's ears. **90 murd'ring-piece** small cannon or mortar; suggestion of numerous missiles fired. **92 Switzers** Swiss guards, mercenaries. **94 overpeering** overflowing. **94 list** shore. **100 word** promise. **105 counter** a hunting term meaning to follow the trail in a direction opposite to that which the game has taken.

LAERTES: That drop of blood that's calm proclaims me bastard,
    Cries cuckold to my father, brands the harlot
    Even here, between the chaste unsmirched brow
    Of my true mother.

115 KING: What is the cause, Laertes,
    That thy rebellion looks so giant-like?
    Let him go, Gertrude; do not fear our person:
    There's such divinity doth hedge a king,
    That treason can but peep to° what it would,°
120   Acts little of his will. Tell me, Laertes,
    Why thou art thus incens'd. Let him go, Gertrude.
    Speak, man.

LAERTES: Where is my father?

KING: Dead.

QUEEN: But not by him.

KING: Let him demand his fill.

125 LAERTES: How came he dead? I'll not be juggled with:
    To hell, allegiance! vows, to the blackest devil!
    Conscience and grace, to the profoundest pit!
    I dare damnation. To this point I stand,
    That both the worlds I give to negligence,°
130   Let come what comes; only I'll be reveng'd
    Most thoroughly° for my father.

KING: Who shall stay you?

LAERTES: My will,° not all the world's:
    And for my means, I'll husband them so well,
    They shall go far with little.

KING: Good Laertes,
135   If you desire to know the certainty
    Of your dear father, is 't writ in your revenge,
    That, swoopstake,° you will draw both friend and foe,
    Winner and loser?

LAERTES: None but his enemies.

KING: Will you know them then?

140 LAERTES: To his good friends thus wide I'll ope my arms;
    And like the kind life-rend'ring pelican,°
    Repast° them with my blood.

KING: Why, now you speak
    Like a good child and a true gentleman.
    That I am guiltless of your father's death,
145   And am most sensibly in grief for it,

---

119 peep to i.e., look at from afar off.   **119 would** wishes to do.   **129 give to negligence** he despises both the here and the hereafter.   **131 throughly** thoroughly.   **132 My will** he will not be stopped except by his own will.   **137 swoopstake** literally, drawing the whole stake at once, i.e., indiscriminately.   **141 pelican** reference to the belief that the pelican feeds its young with its own blood.   **142 Repast** feed.

It shall as level to your judgement 'pear
As day does to your eye.

(*A noise within: "Let her come in."*)

LAERTES: How now! what noise is that?

(*Enter* OPHELIA.)

O heat,° dry up my brains! tears seven times salt,
Burn out the sense and virtue of mine eye!   *150*
By heaven, thy madness shall be paid with weight,
Till our scale turn the beam. O rose of May!
Dear maid, kind sister, sweet Ophelia!
O heavens! is 't possible, a young maid's wits
Should be as mortal as an old man's life?   *155*
Nature is fine in love, and where 'tis fine,
It sends some precious instance of itself
After the thing it loves.

OPHELIA (*Song*): They bore him barefac'd on the bier;
        Hey non nonny, nonny, hey nonny;   *160*
        And in his grave rain'd many a tear:—
        Fare you well, my dove!

LAERTES: Hadst thou thy wits, and didst persuade revenge,
        It could not move thus.

OPHELIA [*sings*]: You must sing a–down a–down,   *165*
        An you call him a–down–a.
        O, how the wheel° becomes it! It is the false steward,° that stole his master's
        daughter.

LAERTES: This nothing's more than matter.

OPHELIA: There's rosemary,° that's for remembrance; pray you, love, remember: and   *170*
        there is pansies,° that's for thoughts.

LAERTES: A document° in madness, thoughts and remembrance fitted.

OPHELIA: There's fennel° for you, and columbines:° there's rue° for you; and here's
        some for me: we may call it herb of grace o' Sundays: O, you must wear your
        rue with a difference. There's a daisy:° I would give you some violets,° but they   *175*
        withered all when my father died: they say 'a made a good end,—
        [*Sings.*] For bonny sweet Robin is all my joy.°

LAERTES: Thought° and affliction, passion, hell itself,

---

149 heat probably the heat generated by the passion of grief. **167 wheel** spinning wheel as accompaniment to the song refrain. **167–168 false steward . . . daughter** the story is unknown. **170 rosemary** used as a symbol of remembrance both at weddings and at funerals. **171 pansies** emblems of love and courtship. Cf. French *penseés*. **172 document** piece of instruction or lesson. **173 fennel** emblem of flattery. **173 columbines** emblem of unchastity (?) or ingratitude (?). **173 rue** emblem of repentance. It was usually mingled with holy water and then known as herb of grace. Ophelia is probably playing on the two meanings of *rue*, "repentant" and "even for Ruth (pity)"; the former signification is for the queen, the latter for herself. **175 daisy** emblem of dissembling, faithlessness. **175 violets** emblems of faithfulness. **177 For . . . joy** probably a line from a Robin Hood ballad. **178 Thought** melancholy thought.

She turns to favor and to prettiness.

180 OPHELIA (*Song*): And will 'a not come again?°
And will 'a not come again?
No, no, he is dead:
Go to thy death-bed:
He never will come again.

185 His beard was as white as snow,
All flaxen was his poll:°
He is gone, he is gone,
And we cast away° moan:
God ha' mercy on his soul!

190 And of all Christian souls, I pray God. God be wi' you.   [*Exit.*]
LAERTES: Do you see this, O God?
KING: Laertes, I must commune with your grief,
Or you deny me right.° Go but apart,
Make choice of whom your wisest friends you will,

195 And they shall hear and judge 'twixt you and me:
If by direct or by collateral° hand
They find us touch'd,° we will our kingdom give,
Our crown, our life, and all that we call ours,
To you in satisfaction; but if not,

200 Be you content to lend your patience to us,
And we shall jointly labor with your soul
To give it due content.
LAERTES: Let this be so;
His means of death, his obscure funeral—
No trophy, sword, nor hatchment° o'er his bones,

205 No noble rite nor formal ostentation—
Cry to be heard, as 'twere from heaven to earth,
That I must call 't in question.
KING: So you shall;
And where th' offence is let the great axe fall.
I pray you, go with me.   (*Exeunt.*)

SCENE VI [*Another room in the castle.*]

(*Enter* HORATIO *and others.*)

HORATIO: What are they that would speak with me?
GENTLEMAN: Sea-faring men, sir: they say they have letters for you.
HORATIO: Let them come in.   [*Exit* GENTLEMAN.]
I do not know from what part of the world
5   I should be greeted, if not from lord Hamlet.

---

180 And . . . again this song appeared in the songbooks as "The Merry Milkmaids' Dumps."
186 poll head.   **188 cast away** shipwrecked.   **193 right** my rights.   **196 collateral** indirect.
197 touch'd implicated.   **204 hatchment** tablet displaying the armorial bearings of a deceased person.

(*Enter* SAILORS.)

FIRST SAILOR: God bless you, sir.

HORATIO: Let him bless thee too.

FIRST SAILOR: 'A shall sir, an 't please him. There's a letter for you, sir; it comes from
the ambassador that was bound for England; if your name be Horatio, as I am
let to know it is.   10

HORATIO [*reads*]: "Horatio, when thou shalt have overlooked this, give these fellows
some means° to the King: they have letters for him. Ere we were two days old
at sea, a pirate of very warlike appointment gave us chase. Finding ourselves too
slow of sail, we put on a compelled valor, and in the grapple I boarded them: on
the instant they got clear of our ship; so I alone became their prisoner. They   15
have dealt with me like thieves of mercy:° but they knew what they did; I am
to do a good turn for them. Let the king have the letters I have sent; and repair
thou to me with as much speed as thou wouldst fly death. I have words to speak
in thine ear will make thee dumb; yet are they much too light for the bore° of
the matter. These good fellows will bring thee where I am. Rosencrantz and   20
Guildenstern hold their course for England: of them I have much to tell thee.
Farewell.   "He that thou knowest thine, HAMLET."

Come, I will give you way for these your letters;
And do 't the speedier, that you may direct me
To him from whom you brought them.   (*Exeunt.*)   25

SCENE VII [*Another room in the castle.*]

(*Enter* KING *and* LAERTES.)

KING: Now must your conscience° my acquittance seal,
And you must put me in your heart for friend,
Sith you have heard, and with a knowing ear,
That he which hath your noble father slain
Pursued my life.

LAERTES: It well appears: but tell me   5
Why you proceeded not against these feats,
So criminal and so capital° in nature,
As by your safety, wisdom, all things else,
You mainly° were stirr'd up.

KING: O, for two special reasons;
Which may to you, perhaps, seem much unsinew'd,°   10
But yet to me th' are strong. The queen his mother
Lives almost by his looks; and for myself—
My virtue or my plague, be it either which—
She's so conjunctive° to my life and soul,

IV.vi. 12 **means** means of access.   16 **thieves of mercy** merciful thieves.   19 **bore** caliber, importance.   IV.vii. 1 **conscience** knowledge that this is true.   7 **capital** punishable by death.
9 **mainly** greatly.   10 **unsinew'd** weak.   14 **conjunctive** conformable (the next line suggesting
planetary conjunction).

15   That, as the star moves not but in his sphere,°
        I could not but by her. The other motive,
        Why to a public count° I might not go,
        Is the great love the general gender° bear him;
        Who, dipping all his faults in their affection,
20   Would, like the spring° that turneth wood to stone,
        Convert his gyves° to graces; so that my arrows,
        Too slightly timber'd° for so loud° a wind,
        Would have reverted to my bow again,
        And not where I had aim'd them.

25 LAERTES: And so have I a noble father lost;
        A sister driven into desp'rate terms,°
        Whose worth, if praises may go back° again,
        Stood challenger on mount° of all the age°
        For her perfections: but my revenge will come.

30 KING: Break not your sleeps for that: you must not think
        That we are made of stuff so flat and dull
        That we can let our beard be shook with danger
        And think it pastime. You shortly shall hear more:
        I lov'd your father, and we love ourself;
35   And that, I hope, will teach you to imagine—

        (*Enter a* MESSENGER *with letters.*)

        How now! what news?

MESSENGER: Letters, my lord, from Hamlet:
        These to your majesty; this to the queen.°

KING: From Hamlet! who brought them?

MESSENGER: Sailors, my lord, they say; I saw them not:
40   They were given me by Claudio;° he receiv'd them
        Of him that brought them.

KING: Laertes, you shall hear them.
        Leave us.   [*Exit* MESSENGER.]
        [*Reads.*] "High and mighty, You shall know I am set naked° on your kingdom.
        To-morrow shall I beg leave to see your kingly eyes: when I shall, first asking
45   your pardon thereunto, recount the occasion of my sudden and more strange
        return.   HAMLET."
        What should this mean? Are all the rest come back?
        Or is it some abuse, and no such thing?

LAERTES: Know you the hand?

---

15 sphere the hollow sphere in which, according to Ptolemaic astronomy, the planets were supposed to move.   **17 count** account, reckoning.   **18 general gender** common people.   **20
spring** i.e., one heavily charged with lime.   **21 gyves** fetters; here, faults, or possibly, punishments
inflicted (on him).   **22 slightly timber'd** light.   **22 loud** strong.   **26 terms** state, condition.
27 go back i.e., to Ophelia's former virtues.   **28 on mount** set up on high, mounted (on horseback).   **28 of all the age** qualifies *challenger* and not *mount*.   **37 to the queen** one hears no
more of the letter to the queen.   **40 Claudio** this character does not appear in the play.   **43
naked** unprovided (with retinue).

KING: 'Tis Hamlet's character. "Naked!"
   And in a postscript here, he says "alone."   50
   Can you devise° me?
LAERTES: I'm lost in it, my lord. But let him come;
   It warms the very sickness in my heart,
   That I shall live and tell him to his teeth,
   "Thus didst thou."
KING: If it be so, Laertes—   55
   As how should it be so? how otherwise?°—
   Will you be rul'd by me?
LAERTES: Ay, my lord;
   So you will not o'errule me to a peace.
KING: To thine own peace. If he be now return'd,
   As checking at° his voyage, and that he means   60
   No more to undertake it, I will work him
   To an exploit, now ripe in my device,
   Under the which he shall not choose but fall:
   And for his death no wind of blame shall breathe,
   But even his mother shall uncharge the practice°   65
   And call it accident.
LAERTES: My lord, I will be rul'd;
   The rather, if you could devise it so
   That I might be the organ.°
KING: It falls right.
   You have been talk'd of since your travel much,
   And that in Hamlet's hearing, for a quality   70
   Wherein, they say, you shine: your sum of parts
   Did not together pluck such envy from him
   As did that one, and that, in my regard,
   Of the unworthiest siege.°
LAERTES: What part is that, my lord?
KING: A very riband in the cap of youth,   75
   Yet needful too; for youth no less becomes
   The light and careless livery that it wears
   Than settled age his sables° and his weeds,
   Importing health and graveness. Two months since,
   Here was a gentleman of Normandy:—   80
   I have seen myself, and serv'd against, the French,
   And they can well° on horseback: but this gallant
   Had witchcraft in 't; he grew unto his seat;
   And to such wondrous doing brought his horse,

51 devise explain to.   **56 As . . . otherwise?** how can this (Hamlet's return) be true? (yet) how otherwise than true (since we have the evidence of his letter)? Some editors read "How should it not be so," etc., making the words refer to Laertes's desire to meet with Hamlet.   **60 checking at** used in falconry of a hawk's leaving the quarry to fly at a chance bird, turn aside.   **65 uncharge the practice** acquit the stratagem of being a plot.   **68 organ** agent, instrument.   **74 siege** rank. **78 sables** rich garments.   **82 can well** are skilled.

85   As had he been incorps'd and demi-natur'd°
                With the brave beast: so far he topp'd° my thought,
                That I, in forgery° of shapes and tricks,
                Come short of what he did.
      LAERTES: A Norman was 't?
      KING: A Norman.
      LAERTES: Upon my life, Lamord.°
90   KING: The very same.
      LAERTES: I know him well: he is the brooch indeed
                And gem of all the nation.
      KING: He made confession° of you,
                And gave you such a masterly report
95   For art and exercise° in your defence°
                And for your rapier most especial,
                That he cried out, 'twould be a sight indeed,
                If one could match you: the scrimers° of their nation,
                He swore, had neither motion, guard, nor eye,
100   If you oppos'd them. Sir, this report of his
                Did Hamlet so envenom with his envy
                That he could nothing do but wish and beg
                Your sudden coming o'er, to play° with you.
                Now, out of this,—
      LAERTES: What out of this, my lord?
105   KING: Laertes, was your father dear to you?
                Or are you like the painting of a sorrow,
                A face without a heart?
      LAERTES: Why ask you this?
      KING: Not that I think you did not love your father;
                But that I know love is begun by time;
110   And that I see, in passages of proof,°
                Time qualifies the spark and fire of it.
                There lives within the very flame of love
                A kind of wick or snuff that will abate it;
                And nothing is at a like goodness still;
115   For goodness, growing to a plurisy,°
                Dies in his own too much:° that we would do,
                We should do when we would; for this "would" changes
                And hath abatements° and delays as many
                As there are tongues, are hands, are accidents;°

85 incorps'd and demi-natur'd of one body and nearly of one nature (like the centaur). **86 topp'd** surpassed. **87 forgery** invention. **90 Lamord** this refers possibly to Pietro Monte, instructor to Louis XII's master of the horse. **93 confession** grudging admission of superiority. **95 art and exercise** skillful exercise. **95 defence** science of defense in sword practice. **98 scrimers** fencers. **103 play** fence. **110 passages of proof** proved instances. **115 plurisy** excess, plethora. **116 in his own too much** of its own excess. **118 abatements** diminutions. **119 accidents** occurrences, incidents.

And then this "should" is like a spendthrift° sigh,   120
That hurts by easing. But, to the quick o' th' ulcer:°—
Hamlet comes back: what would you undertake,
To show yourself your father's son in deed
More than in words?

LAERTES: To cut his throat i' th' church.

KING: No place, indeed, should murder sanctuarize;°   125
Revenge should have no bounds. But, good Laertes,
Will you do this, keep close within your chamber.
Hamlet return'd shall know you are come home:
We'll put on those shall praise your excellence
And set a double varnish on the fame   130
The Frenchman gave you, bring you in fine together
And wager on your heads: he, being remiss,
Most generous and free from all contriving,
Will not peruse the foils; so that, with ease,
Or with a little shuffling, you may choose   135
A sword unbated,° and in a pass of practice°
Requite him for your father.

LAERTES: I will do 't:
And, for that purpose, I'll anoint my sword.
I bought an unction of a mountebank,°
So mortal that, but dip a knife in it,   140
Where it draws blood no cataplasm° so rare,
Collected from all simples° that have virtue
Under the moon,° can save the thing from death
That is but scratch'd withal: I'll touch my point
With this contagion, that, if I gall° him slightly,   145
It may be death.

KING: Let's further think of this;
Weigh what convenience both of time and means
May fit us to our shape:° if this should fail,
And that our drift look through our bad performance,°
'Twere better not assay'd: therefore this project   150
Should have a back or second, that might hold,
If this should blast in proof.° Soft! let me see:
We'll make a solemn wager on your cunnings:°
I ha 't:

---

120 **spendthrift** an allusion to the belief that each sigh cost the heart a drop of blood.   121 **quick o' th' ulcer** heart of the difficulty.   125 **sanctuarize** protect from punishment; allusion to the right of sanctuary with which certain religious places were invested.   136 **unbated** not blunted, having no button.   136 **pass of practice** treacherous thrust.   139 **mountebank** quack doctor.   141 **cataplasm** plaster or poultice.   142 **simples** herbs.   143 **Under the moon** i.e., when collected by moonlight to add to their medicinal value.   145 **gall** graze, wound.   148 **shape** part we propose to act.   149 **drift . . . performance** intention be disclosed by our bungling.   152 **blast in proof** burst in the test (like a cannon).   153 **cunnings** skills.

155   When in your motion you are hot and dry—
      As make your bouts more violent to that end—
      And that he calls for drink, I'll have prepar'd him
      A chalice° for the nonce, whereon but sipping,
      If he by chance escape your venom'd stuck,°
160   Our purpose may hold there. But stay, what noise?

      (*Enter* QUEEN.)

QUEEN: One woe doth tread upon another's heel,
        So fast they follow: your sister's drown'd, Laertes.
LAERTES: Drown'd! O, where?
QUEEN: There is a willow° grows askant° the brook,
165   That shows his hoar° leaves in the glassy stream;
        There with fantastic garlands did she make
        Of crow-flowers,° nettles, daisies, and long purples°
        That liberal° shepherds give a grosser name,
        But our cold maids do dead men's fingers call them:
170   There, on the pendent boughs her crownet° weeds
        Clamb'ring to hang, an envious sliver° broke;
        When down her weedy° trophies and herself
        Fell in the weeping brook. Her clothes spread wide;
        And, mermaid-like, awhile they bore her up:
175   Which time she chanted snatches of old lauds;°
        As one incapable° of her own distress,
        Or like a creature native and indued°
        Upon that element: but long it could not be
        Till that her garments, heavy with their drink,
180   Pull'd the poor wretch from her melodious lay
        To muddy death.
LAERTES: Alas, then, she is drown'd?
QUEEN: Drown'd, drown'd.
LAERTES: Too much of water hast thou, poor Ophelia,
        And therefore I forbid my tears: but yet
185   It is our trick;° nature her custom holds,
        Let shame say what it will: when these are gone,
        The woman will be out.° Adieu, my Lord:
        I have a speech of fire, that fain would blaze,
        But that this folly drowns it.
                                                        (*Exit.*)
KING: Let's follow, Gertrude:
190   How much I had to do to calm his rage!

158 chalice cup.   **159 stuck** thrust (from stoccado).   **164 willow** for its significance of forsaken love.   **164 askant** aslant.   **165 hoar** white (i.e., on the underside).   **167 crow-flowers** butter-cups.   **167 long purples** early purple orchids.   **168 liberal** probably, free-spoken.   **170 crownet** coronet; made into a chaplet.   **171 sliver** branch.   **172 weedy** i.e., of plants.   **175 lauds** hymns.   **176 incapable** lacking capacity to apprehend.   **177 indued** endowed with qualities fitting her for living in water.   **185 trick** way.   **186–187 when . . . out** when my tears are all shed, the woman in me will be satisfied.

Now fear I this will give it start again;
Therefore let 's follow.   (*Exeunt.*)

ACT V
SCENE I [*A churchyard*.]

(*Enter two* CLOWNS° [*with spades, &c.*].)

FIRST CLOWN: Is she to be buried in Christian burial when she wilfully seeks her
     own salvation?

SECOND CLOWN: I tell thee she is; therefore make her grave straight:° the crowner°
     hath sat on her, and finds it Christian burial.

FIRST CLOWN: How can that be, unless she drowned herself in her own defence?   5

SECOND CLOWN: Why, 'tis found so.

FIRST CLOWN: It must be "se offendendo";° it cannot be else. For here lies the point:
     if I drown myself wittingly,° it argues an act: and an act hath three branches;° it
     is, to act, to do, and to perform: argal,° she drowned herself wittingly.

SECOND CLOWN: Nay, but hear you, goodman delver,°—   10

FIRST CLOWN: Give me leave. Here lies the water; good: here stands the man; good:
     if the man go to this water, and drown himself, it is, will he, nill he, he goes,—
     mark you that; but if the water come to him and drown him, he drowns not
     himself: argal, he that is not guilty of his own death shortens not his own life.

SECOND CLOWN: But is this law?   15

FIRST CLOWN: Ay, marry, is 't; crowner's quest° law.

SECOND CLOWN: Will you ha' the truth on 't? If this had not been a gentlewoman,
     she should have been buried out o' Christian burial.

FIRST CLOWN: Why, there thou say'st:° and the more pity that great folk should
     have countenance° in this world to drown or hang themselves, more than their   20
     even° Christian. Come, my spade. There is no ancient gentlemen but gardeners,
     ditchers, and grave-makers: they hold up° Adam's profession.

SECOND CLOWN: Was he a gentleman?

FIRST CLOWN: 'A was the first that ever bore arms.

SECOND CLOWN: Why, he had none.   25

FIRST CLOWN: What, art a heathen? How dost thou understand the Scripture? The
     Scripture says "Adam digged": could he dig without arms? I'll put another ques-
     tion to thee: if thou answerest me not to the purpose, confess thyself°—

SECOND CLOWN: Go to.°

FIRST CLOWN: What is he that builds stronger than either the mason, the ship-   30
     wright, or the carpenter?

SECOND CLOWN: The gallows-maker; for that frame outlives a thousand tenants.

V.i. s.d. clowns the word *clown* was used to denote peasants as well as humorous characters; here
applied to the rustic type of clown.   **3 straight** straightway, immediately; some interpret "from east
to west in a direct line, parallel with the church."   **3 crowner** coroner.   **7 "se offendendo"** for
se defendendo, term used in verdicts of justifiable homicide.   **8 wittingly** intentionally.   **8 three
branches** parody of legal phraseology.   **9 argal** corruption of ergo, therefore.   **10 delver** digger.
16 quest inquest.   **19 there thou say'st** that's right.   **20 countenance** privilege.   **21 even** fellow.   **22 hold up** maintain, continue.   **28 confess thyself** "and be hanged" completes the
proverb.   **29 Go to** perhaps, "begin," or some other form of concession.

FIRST CLOWN: I like thy wit well, in good faith: the gallows does well; but how does
    it well? it does well to those that do ill: now thou dost ill to say the gallows is
35   built stronger than the church: argal, the gallows may do well to thee. To 't again,
    come.

SECOND CLOWN: Who builds stronger than a mason, a shipwright, or a carpenter?

FIRST CLOWN: Ay, tell me that, and unyoke.°

SECOND CLOWN: Marry, now I can tell.

40 FIRST CLOWN: To 't.

SECOND CLOWN: Mass,° I cannot tell.

(*Enter* HAMLET *and* HORATIO [*at a distance*].)

FIRST CLOWN: Cudgel thy brains no more about it, for your dull ass will not mend
    his pace with beating; and, when you are asked this question next, say "a grave-
    maker": the houses he makes lasts till doomsday. Go, get thee in, and fetch me a
45   stoup° of liquor.

([*Exit* SECOND CLOWN.] *Song.* [*He digs.*])

    In youth, when I did love, did love,
        Methought it was very sweet,
    To contract—O—the time, for—a—my behove,°
        O, methought, there—a—was nothing—a—meet.

50 HAMLET: Has this fellow no feeling of his business, that 'a sings at gravemaking?

HORATIO: Custom hath made it in him a property of easiness.°

HAMLET: 'Tis e'en so: the hand of little employment hath the daintier sense.

FIRST CLOWN: (*Song.*) But age, with his stealing steps,
        Hath claw'd me in his clutch,
55   And hath shipped me into the land
        As if I had never been such.   [*Throws up a skull.*]

HAMLET: That skull had a tongue in it, and could sing once: how the knave jowls° it
    to the ground, as if 'twere Cain's jaw-bone,° that did the first murder! This might
    be the pate of a politician,° which this ass now o'er-reaches;° one that would
60   circumvent God, might it not?

HORATIO: It might, my lord.

HAMLET: Or of a courtier; which could say "Good morrow, sweet lord! How dost
    thou, sweet lord?" This might be my lord such-a-one, that praised my lord such-
    a-one's horse, when he meant to beg it; might it not?

65 HORATIO: Ay, my lord.

HAMLET: Why, e'en so: and now my Lady Worm's; chapless,° and knocked about the
    mazzard° with a sexton's spade: here's fine revolution, an we had the trick to see
    't. Did these bones cost no more the breeding, but to play at loggats° with 'em?
    mine ache to think on 't.

---

38 unyoke after this great effort you may unharness the team of your wits.   **41 Mass** by the Mass.
45 stoup two-quart measure.   **48 behove** benefit.   **51 property of easiness** a peculiarity that
now is easy.   **57 jowls** dashes.   **58 Cain's jaw-bone** allusion to the old tradition that Cain slew
Abel with the jawbone of an ass.   **59 politician** schemer, plotter.   **59 o'er-reaches** quibble on
the literal sense and the sense "circumvent."   **66 chapless** having no lower jaw.   **67 mazzard**
head.   **68 loggats** a game in which six sticks are thrown to lie as near as possible to a stake fixed in
the ground, or block of wood on a floor.

FIRST CLOWN: (*Song.*) A pick-axe, and a spade, a spade,   70
  For and° a shrouding sheet:
O, a pit of clay for to be made
  For such a guest is meet.   [*Throws up another skull.*]

HAMLET: There's another: why may not that be the skull of a lawyer? Where be his
  quiddities° now, his quillities,° his cases, his tenures,° and his tricks? why does   75
  he suffer this mad knave now to knock him about the sconce° with a dirty
  shovel, and will not tell him of his action of battery? Hum! This fellow might be
  in 's time a great buyer of land, with his statutes, his recognizances,° his fines, his
  double vouchers,° his recoveries:° is this the fine° of his fines, and the recovery
  of his recoveries, to have his fine pate full of fine dirt? Will his vouchers vouch   80
  him no more of his purchases, and double ones too, than the length and breadth
  of a pair of indentures?° The very conveyances of his lands will scarcely lie in
  this box; and must the inheritor° himself have no more, ha?

HORATIO: Not a jot more, my lord.

HAMLET: Is not parchment made of sheep-skins?   85

HORATIO: Ay, my lord, and of calf-skins° too.

HAMLET: They are sheep and calves which seek out assurance in that.° I will speak
  to this fellow. Whose grave's this, sirrah?

FIRST CLOWN: Mine, sir.

  [*Sings.*] O, a pit of clay for to be made   90
  For such a guest is meet.

HAMLET: I think it be thine, indeed; for thou liest in 't.

FIRST CLOWN: You lie out on't, sir, and therefore 't is not yours: for my part, I do
  not lie in 't, yet it is mine.

HAMLET: Thou dost lie in 't, to be in 't and say it is thine: 'tis for the dead, not for   95
  the quick; therefore thou liest.

FIRST CLOWN: 'Tis a quick lie, sir; 'twill away again, from me to you.

HAMLET: What man dost thou dig it for?

FIRST CLOWN: For no man, sir.

HAMLET: What woman, then?   100

FIRST CLOWN: For none, neither.

HAMLET: Who is to be buried in 't?

FIRST CLOWN: One that was a woman, sir; but, rest her soul, she's dead.

HAMLET: How absolute° the knave is! we must speak by the card,° or equivocation°
  will undo us. By the Lord, Horatio, these three years I have taken note of it; the   105
  age is grown so picked° that the toe of the peasant comes so near the heel of
  the courtier, he galls° his kibe.° How long hast thou been a gravemaker?

---

71 For and and moreover.   **75 quiddities** subtleties, quibbles.   **75 quillities** verbal niceties,
subtle distinctions.   **75 tenures** the holding of a piece of property or office or the conditions or
period of such holding.   **76 sconce** head.   **78 statutes, recognizances** legal terms connected
with the transfer of land.   **79 vouchers** persons called on to warrant a tenant's title.   **79 recoveries** process for transfer of entailed estate.   **79 fine** the four uses of this word are as follows: (1) end,
(2) legal process, (3) elegant, (4) small.   **82 indentures** conveyances or contracts.   **83 inheritor**
possessor, owner.   **86 calf-skins** parchments.   **87 assurance in that** safety in legal parchments.
104 absolute positive, decided.   **104 by the card** with precision, i.e., by the mariner's card on
which the points of the compass were marked.   **104 equivocation** ambiguity in the use of terms.
106 picked refined, fastidious.   **107 galls** chafes.   **107 kibe** chilblain.

FIRST CLOWN: Of all the day i' the year, I came to 't that day that our last king Hamlet overcame Fortinbras.

110 HAMLET: How long is that since?

FIRST CLOWN: Cannot you tell that? Every fool can tell that: It was the very day that young Hamlet was born; he that is mad, and sent into England.

HAMLET: Ay, marry, why was he sent into England?

FIRST CLOWN: Why, because 'a was mad: 'a shall recover his wits there; or, if 'a do

115   not, 'tis no great matter there.

HAMLET: Why?

FIRST CLOWN: 'Twill not be seen in him there; there the men are as mad as he.

HAMLET: How came he mad?

FIRST CLOWN: Very strangely, they say.

120 HAMLET: How strangely?

FIRST CLOWN: Faith, e'en with losing his wits.

HAMLET: Upon what ground?

FIRST CLOWN: Why, here in Denmark: I have been sexton here, man and boy, thirty years.°

125 HAMLET: How long will a man lie i' the earth ere he rot?

FIRST CLOWN: Faith, if 'a be not rotten before 'a die—as we have many pocky° corses now-a-days, that will scarce hold the laying in—'a will last you some eight year or nine year: a tanner will last you nine year.

HAMLET: Why he more than another?

130 FIRST CLOWN: Why, sir, his hide is so tanned with his trade, that 'a will keep out water a great while; and your water is a sore decayer of your whoreson dead body. Here's a skull now hath lain you i' th' earth three and twenty years.

HAMLET: Whose was it?

FIRST CLOWN: A whoreson mad fellow's it was: whose do you think it was?

135 HAMLET: Nay, I know not.

FIRST CLOWN: A pestilence on him for a mad rogue! 'a poured a flagon of Rhenish on my head once. This same skull, sir, was Yorick's skull, the king's jester.

HAMLET: This?

FIRST CLOWN: E'en that.

140 HAMLET: Let me see. [*Takes the skull.*] Alas, poor Yorick! I knew him, Horatio: a fellow of infinite jest, of most excellent fancy: he hath borne me on his back a thousand times; and now, how abhorred in my imagination it is! My gorge rises at it. Here hung those lips that I have kissed I know not how oft. Where be your gibes now? your gambols? your songs? your flashes of merriment, that were

145   wont to set the table on a roar? Not one now, to mock your own grinning? Quite chap-fallen? Now get you to my lady's chamber, and tell her, let her paint an inch thick, to this favor she must come; make her laugh at that. Prithee, Horatio, tell me one thing.

HORATIO: What's that, my lord?

150 HAMLET: Dost thou think Alexander looked o' this fashion i' the earth?

HORATIO: E'en so.

123–124 thirty years this statement with that in lines 111–112 shows Hamlet's age to be thirty years.   **126 pocky** rotten, diseased.

HAMLET: And smelt so? pah!   [*Puts down the skull.*]

HORATIO: E'en so, my lord.

HAMLET: To what base uses we may return, Horatio! Why may not imagination trace
the noble dust of Alexander, till'a find it stopping a bunghole?   155

HORATIO: 'Twere to consider too curiously,° to consider so.

HAMLET: No, faith, not a jot; but to follow him thither with modesty enough, and
likelihood to lead it: as thus: Alexander died, Alexander was buried, Alexander
returneth into dust; the dust is earth; of earth we make loam;° and why of that
loam, whereto he was converted, might they not stop a beer-barrel?   160

    Imperious° Cæsar, dead and turn'd to clay,
    Might stop a hole to keep the wind away:
    O, that that earth, which kept the world in awe,
    Should patch a wall t'expel the winter's flaw!°

But soft! but soft awhile! here comes the king,   165

(*Enter* KING, QUEEN, LAERTES, *and the Corse of* [OPHELIA, *in procession, with*
PRIEST, LORDS, *etc.*].)

    The queen, the courtiers: who is this they follow?
    And with such maimed rites? This doth betoken
    The corse they follow did with desp'rate hand
    Fordo° it° own life: 'twas of some estate.
    Couch° we awhile, and mark.   [*Retiring with* HORATIO.]   170

LAERTES: What ceremony else?

HAMLET: That is Laertes,
    A very noble youth: mark.

LAERTES: What ceremony else?

FIRST PRIEST: Her obsequies have been as far enlarg'd°   175
    As we have warranty: her death was doubtful;
    And, but that great command o'ersways the order,
    She should in ground unsanctified have lodg'd
    Till the last trumpet; for charitable prayers,
    Shards,° flints and pebbles should be thrown on her: 180
    Yet here she is allow'd her virgin crants,°
    Her maiden strewments° and the bringing home
    Of bell and burial.°

LAERTES: Must there no more be done?

FIRST PRIEST: No more be done:
    We should profane the service of the dead   185
    To sing a requiem and such rest to her
    As to peace-parted° souls.

---

156 curiously minutely.   **159 loam** clay paste for brickmaking.   **161 Imperious** imperial.   **164
flaw** gust of wind.   **169 Fordo** destroy.   **169 it** its.   **170 Couch** hide, lurk.   **175 enlarg'd** extended, referring to the fact that suicides are not given full burial rites.   **180 Shards** broken bits of
pottery.   **181 crants** garlands customarily hung upon the biers of unmarried women.   **182 strew-
ments** traditional strewing of flowers.   **182–183 bringing . . . burial** the laying to rest of the
body, to the sound of the bell.   **188 peace-parted** allusion to the text "Lord, now lettest thy servant depart in peace."

LAERTES: Lay her i' th' earth:
          And from her fair and unpolluted flesh
190   May violets spring! I tell thee, churlish priest,
          A minist'ring angel shall my sister be,
          When thou liest howling.°
HAMLET: What, the fair Ophelia!
QUEEN: Sweets to the sweet: farewell!   [*Scattering flowers.*]
        I hop'd thou shouldst have been my Hamlet's wife;
195   I thought thy bride-bed to have deck'd, sweet maid,
        And not have strew'd thy grave.
LAERTES: O, treble woe
        Fall ten times treble on that cursed head,
        Whose wicked deed thy most ingenious sense°
        Depriv'd thee of! Hold off the earth awhile,
200   Till I have caught her once more in mine arms: [*Leaps into the grave.*]
        Now pile your dust upon the quick and dead,
        Till of this flat a mountain you have made,
        T' o'ertop old Pelion,° or the skyish head
        Of blue Olympus.
205 HAMLET [*Advancing*]: What is he whose grief
        Bears such an emphasis? whose phrase of sorrow
        Conjures the wand'ring stars,° and makes them stand
        Like wonder-wounded hearers? This is I,
        Hamlet the Dane.   [*Leaps into the grave.*]
LAERTES: The devil take thy soul!   [*Grappling with him.*]
210 HAMLET: Thou pray'st not well.
        I prithee, take thy fingers from my throat;
        For, though I am not splenitive° and rash,
        Yet have I in me something dangerous,
        Which let thy wisdom fear: hold off thy hand.
KING: Pluck them asunder.
215 QUEEN: Hamlet, Hamlet!
ALL: Gentlemen,—
HORATIO: Good my lord, be quiet.

        [*The* ATTENDANTS *part them, and they come out of the grave.*]

HAMLET: Why, I will fight with him upon this theme
        Until my eyelids will no longer wag.°
QUEEN: O my son, what theme?
220 HAMLET: I lov'd Ophelia: forty thousand brothers
        Could not, with all their quantity° of love,
        Make up my sum. What wilt thou do for her?

---

192 howling i.e., in hell.   **198 ingenious sense** mind endowed with finest qualities.   **203 Pelion** Olympus, Pelion, and Ossa are mountains in the north of Thessaly.   **207 wand'ring stars** planets.   **212 splenitive** quick-tempered.   **218 wag** move (not used ludicrously).   **221 quantity** some suggest that the word is used in a deprecatory sense (little bits, fragments).

KING: O, he is mad, Laertes.

QUEEN: For love of God, forbear° him.

HAMLET: 'Swounds,° show me what thou 'lt do: 225
 Woo 't° weep? woo 't fight? woo 't fast? woo 't tear thyself?
 Woo 't drink up eisel?° eat a crocodile?
 I'll do 't. Dost thou come here to whine?
 To outface me with leaping in her grave?
 Be buried quick with her, and so will I: 230
 And, if thou prate of mountains, let them throw
 Millions of acres on us, till our ground,
 Singeing his pate against the burning zone,°
 Make Ossa like a wart! Nay, an thou 'lt mouth,
 I'll rant as well as thou.

QUEEN: This is mere madness: 235
 And thus awhile the fit will work on him;
 Anon, as patient as the female dove.
 When that her golden couplets° are disclos'd,
 His silence will sit drooping.

HAMLET: Hear you, sir;
 What is the reason that you use me thus?   240
 I lov'd you ever: but it is no matter;
 Let Hercules himself do what he may,
 The cat will mew and dog will have his day.

KING: I pray thee, good Horatio, wait upon him. (*Exit* HAMLET *and* HORATIO.)
 [*To* LAERTES.] Strengthen your patience in° our last night's speech;   245
 We'll put the matter to the present push.°
 Good Gertrude, set some watch over your son.
 This grave shall have a living° monument:
 An hour of quiet shortly shall we see;
 Till then, in patience our proceeding be. (*Exeunt.*)   250

SCENE II [*A hall in the castle.*]

(*Enter* HAMLET *and* HORATIO.)

HAMLET: So much for this, sir: now shall you see the other;
 You do remember all the circumstance?

HORATIO: Remember it, my lord!

HAMLET: Sir, in my heart there was a kind of fighting,
 That would not let me sleep: methought I lay   5
 Worse than the mutines° in the bilboes.° Rashly,°
 And prais'd be rashness for it, let us know,

224 forbear leave alone. **225 'Swounds** oath, "God's wounds." **226 Woo 't** wilt thou. **227 eisel** vinegar. Some editors have taken this to be the name of a river, such as the Yssel, the Weissel, and the Nile. **233 burning zone** sun's orbit. **238 golden couplets** the pigeon lays two eggs; the young when hatched are covered with golden down. **245 in** by recalling. **246 present push** immediate test. **248 living** lasting; also refers (for Laertes's benefit) to the plot against Hamlet. **V.ii. 6 mutines** mutineers. **6 bilboes** shackles. **6 Rashly** goes with line 12.

Our indiscretion sometime serves us well,
When our deep plots do pall:° and that should learn us
10   There's a divinity that shapes our ends,
Rough-hew° them how we will,—
HORATIO: That is most certain.
HAMLET: Up from my cabin,
My sea-gown° scarf'd about me, in the dark
Grop'd I to find out them; had my desire,
15   Finger'd° their packet, and in fine° withdrew
To mine own room again; making so bold,
My fears forgetting manners, to unseal
Their grand commission; where I found, Horatio,—
O royal knavery!—an exact command,
20   Larded° with many several sorts of reasons
Importing Denmark's health and England's too,
With, ho! such bugs° and goblins in my life,°
That, on the supervise,° no leisure bated,°
No, not to stay the grinding of the axe,
My head should be struck off.
25   HORATIO: Is 't possible?
HAMLET: Here's the commission: read it at more leisure.
But wilt thou hear me how I did proceed?
HORATIO: I beseech you.
HAMLET: Being thus be-netted round with villanies,—
30   Ere I could make a prologue to my brains,
They had begun the play°—I sat me down,
Devis'd a new commission, wrote it fair:
I once did hold it, as our statists° do,
A baseness to write fair° and labor'd much
35   How to forget that learning, but, sir, now
It did me yeoman's° service: wilt thou know
Th' effect of what I wrote?
HORATIO: Ay, good my lord.
HAMLET: An earnest conjuration from the king,
As England was his faithful tributary,
40   As love between them like the palm might flourish,
As peace should still her wheaten garland° wear
And stand a comma° 'tween their amities,

---

9 pall fail.   **11 Rough-hew** shape roughly; it may mean "bungle."   **13 sea-gown** "A sea-gown, or a corase, high-collered, and short-sleeved gowne, reaching down to the mid-leg, and used most by seamen and saylors" (Cotgrave, quoted by Singer).   **15 Finger'd** pilfered, filched.   **15 in fine** finally.   **20 Larded** enriched.   **22 bugs** bug-bears.   **22 such . . . life** such imaginary dangers if I were allowed to live.   **23 supervise** perusal.   **23 leisure bated** delay allowed.   **30–31 prologue . . . play** i.e., before I could begin to think, my mind had made its decision.   **33 statists** statesmen.   **34 fair** in a clear hand.   **36 yeoman's** i.e., faithful.   **41 wheaten garland** symbol of peace.   **42 comma** smallest break or separation. Here amity begins and amity ends the period, and peace stands between like a dependent clause. The comma indicates continuity, link.

And many such-like 'As'es° of great charge,°
That, on the view and knowing of these contents,
Without debatement further, more or less,   45
He should the bearers put to sudden death,
Not shriving-time° allow'd.

HORATIO: How was this seal'd?

HAMLET: Why, even in that was heaven ordinant.°
   I had my father's signet in my purse,
   Which was the model of that Danish seal;   50
   Folded the writ up in the form of th' other,
   Subscrib'd it, gave 't th' impression, plac'd it safely,
   The changeling never known. Now, the next day
   Was our sea-fight; and what to this was sequent°
   Thou know'st already.   55

HORATIO: So Guildenstern and Rosencrantz go to 't.

HAMLET: Why, man, they did make love to this employment;
   They are not near my conscience; their defeat
   Does by their own insinuation° grow:
   'Tis dangerous when the baser nature comes   60
   Between the pass° and fell incensed° points
   Of mighty opposites.

HORATIO: Why, what a king is this!

HAMLET: Does it not, think thee, stand° me now upon—
   He that hath kill'd my king and whor'd my mother,
   Popp'd in between th' election° and my hopes,   65
   Thrown out his angle° for my proper life,
   And with such coz'nage° —is 't not perfect conscience,
   To quit° him with this arm? and is 't not to be damn'd,
   To let this canker° of our nature come
   In further evil?   70

HORATIO: It must be shortly known to him from England
   What is the issue of the business there.

HAMLET: It will be short: the interim is mine;
   And a man's life's no more than to say "One."
   But I am very sorry, good Horatio,   75
   That to Laertes I forgot myself;
   For, by the image of my cause, I see
   The portraiture of his: I'll court his favors:
   But, sure, the bravery° of his grief did put me
   Into a tow'ring passion.   80

HORATIO: Peace! who comes here?

---

43 'As'es the "whereases" of a formal document, with play on the word *ass*.   **43 charge** import, and burden.   **47 shriving-time** time for absolution.   **48 ordinant** directing.   **54 sequent** subsequent.   **59 insinuation** interference.   **61 pass** thrust.   **61 fell incensed** fiercely angered.   **63 stand** become incumbent.   **65 election** the Danish throne was filled by election.   **66 angle** fishing line.   **67 coz'nage** trickery.   **68 quit** repay.   **69 canker** ulcer, or possibly the worm which destroys buds and leaves.   **79 bravery** bravado.

(*Enter a* COURTIER [OSRIC].)

OSRIC: Your lordship is right welcome back to Denmark.

HAMLET: I humbly thank you, sir. [*To* HORATIO.] Dost know this water-fly?°

HORATIO: No, my good lord.

HAMLET: Thy state is the more gracious; for 'tis a vice to know him. He hath much
85   land, and fertile: let a beast be lord of beasts,° and his crib shall stand at the king's
     mess:° 'tis a chough;° but, as I say, spacious in the possession of dirt.

OSRIC: Sweet lord, if your lordship were at leisure, I should impart a thing to you
     from his majesty.

HAMLET: I will receive it, sir, with all diligence of spirit. Put your bonnet to his right
90   use; 'tis for the head.

OSRIC: I thank you lordship, it is very hot.

HAMLET: No, believe me, 'tis very cold; the wind is northerly.

OSRIC: It is indifferent° cold, my lord, indeed.

HAMLET: But yet methinks it is very sultry and hot for my complexion.

95   OSRIC: Exceedingly, my lord; it is very sultry,—as 'twere,—I cannot tell how.
     But, my lord, his majesty bade me signify to you that 'a has laid a great wager
     on your head: sir, this is the matter,—

HAMLET: I beseech you, remember°—   [HAMLET *moves him to put on his hat.*]

OSRIC: Nay, good my lord; for mine ease,° in good faith. Sir, here is newly come to
100 court Laertes; believe me, an absolute gentleman, full of most excellent differ-
     ences, of very soft° society and great showing:° indeed, to speak feelingly° of
     him, he is the card° or calendar of gentry,° for you shall find in him the conti-
     nent of what part a gentleman would see.

HAMLET: Sir, his definement° suffers no perdition° in you; though, I know, to divide
105 him inventorially° would dozy° the arithmetic of memory, and yet but yaw°
     neither, in respect of his quick sail. But, in the verity of extolment, I take him to
     be a soul of great article;° and his infusion° of such dearth and rareness,° as, to
     make true diction of him, his semblable° is his mirror; and who else would
     trace° him, his umbrage,° nothing more.

110 OSRIC: Your lordship speaks most infallibly of him.

HAMLET: The concernancy,° sir? why do we wrap the gentleman in our more rawer
     breath?°

82 water-fly vain or busily idle person.   **85 lord of beasts** cf. Genesis 1:26, 28.   **85–86 his
crib . . . mess** he shall eat at the king's table, i.e., be one of the group of persons (usually four)
constituting a mess at a banquet.   **86 chough** probably, chattering jackdaw; also explained as chuff,
provincial boor or churl.   **93 indifferent** somewhat.   **98 remember** i.e., remember thy courtesy; conventional phrase for "Be covered."   **99 mine ease** conventional reply declining the invitation of "Remember thy courtesy."   **101 soft** gentle.   **101 showing** distinguished appearance.
101 feelingly with just perception.   **102 card** chart, map.   **102 gentry** good breeding.   **104
definement** definition.   **104 perdition** loss, diminution.   **104–105 divide him inventorially**
i.e., enumerate his graces.   **105 dozy** dizzy.   **105 yaw** to move unsteadily (of a ship).   **107 article** moment or importance.   **107 infusion** infused temperament, character imparted by nature.
107 dearth and rareness rarity.   **108 semblable** true likeness.   **109 trace** follow.   **109 umbrage** shadow.   **111 concernancy** import.   **112 breath** speech.

OSRIC: Sir?

HORATIO [*aside to* HAMLET]: Is 't not possible to understand in another tongue?° You will do 't, sir, really.   115

HAMLET: What imports the nomination° of this gentleman?

OSRIC: Of Laertes?

HORATIO [*aside to* HAMLET]: His purse is empty already; all 's golden words are spent.

HAMLET: Of him, sir.

OSRIC: I know you are not ignorant—   120

HAMLET: I would you did, sir; yet, in faith, if you did, it would not much approve° me. Well, sir?

OSRIC: You are not ignorant of what excellence Laertes is—

HAMLET: I dare not confess that, lest I should compare with him in excellence; but, to know a man well, were to know himself.°   125

OSRIC: I mean, sir, for his weapon; but in the imputation° laid on him by them, in his meed° he's unfellowed.

HAMLET: What's his weapon?

OSRIC: Rapier and dagger.

HAMLET: That's two of his weapons; but, well.   130

OSRIC: The king, sir, hath wagered with him six Barbary horses: against the which he has impawned,° as I take it, six French rapiers and poniards, with their assigns, as girdle, hangers,° and so: three of the carriages, in faith, are very dear to fancy,° very responsive° to the hilts, most delicate° carriages, and of very liberal conceit.°   135

HAMLET: That call you the carriages?

HORATIO [*aside to* HAMLET]: I knew you must be edified by the margent° ere you had done.

OSRIC: The carriages, sir, are the hangers.

HAMLET: The phrase would be more german° to the matter, if we could carry cannon by our sides: I would it might be hangers till then. But, on: six Barbary horses against six French swords, their assigns, and three liberal-conceited carriages; that's the French bet against the Danish. Why is this "impawned," as you call it?   140

OSRIC: The king, sir, hath laid, that in a dozen passes between yourself and him, he shall not exceed you three hits: he hath laid on twelve for nine; and it would come to immediate trial, if your lordship would vouchsafe the answer.   145

HAMLET: How if I answer "no"?

OSRIC: I mean, my lord, the opposition of your person in trial.

HAMLET: Sir, I will walk here in the hall: if it please his majesty, it is the breathing time° of day with me; let the foils be brought, the gentleman willing, and the   150

---

114 Is 't . . . tongue? i.e., can one converse with Osric only in this outlandish jargon?   **116 nomination** naming.   **121 approve** command.   **124–125 but . . . himself** but to know a man as excellent were to know Laertes.   **126 imputation** reputation.   **127 meed** merit.   **132 he has impawned** he has wagered.   **133 hangers** straps on the sword belt from which the sword hung.   **133–134 dear to fancy** fancifully made.   **134 responsive** probably, well balanced, corresponding closely.   **134 delicate** i.e., in workmanship.   **134–135 liberal conceit** elaborate design.   **137 margent** margin of a book, place for explanatory notes.   **140 german** germane; appropriate.   **150–151 breathing time** exercise period.

king hold his purpose, I will win for him as I can; if not, I will gain nothing but my shame and the odd hits.

OSRIC: Shall I re-deliver you e'en so?

155 HAMLET: To this effect, sir; after what flourish your nature will.

OSRIC: I commend my duty to your lordship.

HAMLET: Yours, yours. [*Exit* OSRIC.] He does well to commend it himself; there are no tongues else for 's turn.

HORATIO: This lapwing° runs away with the shell on his head.

160 HAMLET: 'A did comply, sir, with his dug,° before 'a sucked it. Thus has hey—and many more of the same breed that I know the drossy° age dotes on—only got the tune° of the time and out of an habit of encounter;° a kind of yesty° collection, which carries them through and through the most fann'd and winnowed° opinions; and do but blow them to their trial, the bubbles are out.°

165 LORD: My lord, his majesty commended him to you by young Osric, who brings back to him, that you attend him in the hall: he sends to know if your pleasure hold to play with Laertes, or that you will take longer time.

HAMLET: I am constant to my purposes; they follow the king's pleasure: if his fitness speaks, mine is ready; now or whensoever, provided I be so able as now.

170 LORD: The king and queen and all are coming down.

HAMLET: In happy time.°

LORD: The queen desires you to use some gentle entertainment to Laertes before you fall to play.

HAMLET: She well instructs me.   [*Exit* LORD.]

175 HORATIO: You will lose this wager, my lord.

HAMLET: I do not think so; since he went into France, I have been in continual practice; I shall win at the odds. But thou wouldst not think how ill all 's here about my heart: but it is no matter.

HORATIO: Nay, good my lord,—

180 HAMLET: It is but foolery; but it is such a kind of gain-giving,° as would perhaps trouble a woman.

HORATIO: If your mind dislike any thing, obey it: I will forestall their repair hither, and say you are not fit.

HAMLET: Not a whit, we defy augury: there's a special providence in the fall of a

185 sparrow. If it be now, 'tis not to come; if it be not to come, it will be now; if it be not now, yet it will come: the readiness is all:° since no man of aught he leaves knows, what is 't to leave betimes? Let be.

(*A table prepared.* [*Enter*] *Trumpets, Drums, and Officers with cushions;* KING, QUEEN, [OSRIC,] *and all the State; foils, daggers,* [*and wine borne in;*] *and* LAERTES.)

---

159 lapwing peewit; noted for its wiliness in drawing a visitor away from its nest and its supposed habit of running about when newly hatched with its head in the shell; possibly an allusion to Osric's hat. **160 did comply . . . dug** paid compliments to his mother's breast. **161 drossy** frivolous. **162 tune** temper, mood. **162 habit of encounter** demeanor of social intercourse. **162 yesty** frothy. **163 fann'd and winnowed** select and refined. **164 blow . . . out** i.e., put them to the test, and their ignorance is exposed. **171 in happy time** a phrase of courtesy. **180 gain-giving** misgiving. **186 all** all that matters.

KING: Come, Hamlet, come, and take this hand from me.

[*The king puts* LAERTES*'s hand into* HAMLET*'s.*]

HAMLET: Give me your pardon, sir: I have done you wrong;
But pardon 't as you are a gentleman.   190
This presence° knows,
And you must needs have heard, how I am punish'd
With a sore distraction. What I have done,
That might your nature, honor and exception°
Roughly awake, I here proclaim was madness.   195
Was 't Hamlet wrong'd Laertes? Never Hamlet:
If Hamlet from himself be ta'en away,
And when he's not himself does wrong Laertes,
Then Hamlet does it not, Hamlet denies it.
Who does it, then? His madness: if 't be so,   200
Hamlet is of the faction that is wrong'd;
His madness is poor Hamlet's enemy.
Sir, in this audience,
Let my disclaiming from a purpos'd evil
Free me so far in your most generous thoughts,   205
That I have shot mine arrow o'er the house,
And hurt my brother.

LAERTES: I am satisfied in nature,°
Whose motive, in this case, should stir me most
To my revenge: but in my terms of honor
I stand aloof; and will no reconcilement,   210
Till by some elder masters, of known honor,
I have a voice° and precedent of peace,
To keep my name ungor'd. But till that time,
I do receive your offer'd love like love,
And will not wrong it.

HAMLET: I embrace it freely;   215
And will this brother's wager frankly play.
Give us the foils. Come on.

LAERTES: Come, one for me.

HAMLET: I'll be your foil,° Laertes: in mine ignorance
Your skill shall, like a star i' th' darkest night,
Stick fiery off° indeed.

LAERTES: You mock me, sir.   220

HAMLET: No, by this hand.

KING: Give them the foils, young Osric. Cousin Hamlet,
You know the wager?

---

191 presence royal assembly.   **194 exception** disapproval.   **207 nature** i.e., he is personally satisfied, but his honor must be satisfied by the rules of the code of honor.   **212 voice** authoritative
pronouncement.   **218 foil** quibble on the two senses: "background which sets something off," and
"blunted rapier for fencing."   **220 Stick fiery off** stand out brilliantly.

HAMLET: Very well, my lord;
     Your grace has laid the odds o' th' weaker side.

225   KING: I do not fear it; I have seen you both:
     But since he is better'd, we have therefore odds.

LAERTES: This is too heavy, let me see another.

HAMLET: This likes me well. These foils have all a length?

     [*They prepare to play.*]

OSRIC: Ay, my good lord.

230   KING: Set me the stoups of wine upon that table.
     If Hamlet give the first or second hit,
     Or quit in answer of the third exchange,
     Let all the battlements their ordnance fire;
     The king shall drink to Hamlet's better breath;

235   And in the cup an union° shall he throw,
     Richer than that which four successive kings
     In Denmark's crown have worn. Give me the cups;
     And let the kettle° to the trumpet speak,
     The trumpet to the cannoneer without,

240   The cannons to the heavens, the heavens to earth,
     "Now the king drinks to Hamlet." Come begin: (*Trumpets the while.*)

     And you, the judges, bear a wary eye.

HAMLET: Come on, sir.

LAERTES: Come, my lord.   [*They play.*]

HAMLET: One.

LAERTES: No.

HAMLET: Judgement.

OSRIC: A hit, a very palpable hit.

     (*Drums, trumpets, and shot. Flourish. A piece goes off.*)

LAERTES: Well; again.

245   KING: Stay; give me drink. Hamlet, this pearl° is thine;
     Here's to thy health. Give him the cup.

HAMLET: I'll play this bout first; set it by awhile.
     Come. [*They play.*] Another hit; what say you?

LAERTES: A touch, a touch, I do confess 't.

KING: Our son shall win.

250   QUEEN: He's fat,° and scant of breath.
     Here, Hamlet, take my napkin, rub thy brows:
     The queen carouses° to thy fortune, Hamlet.

HAMLET: Good madam!

KING: Gertrude, do not drink.

---

235 union pearl.   **238 kettle** kettledrum.   **245 pearl** i.e., the poison.   **250 fat** not physically fit, out of training. Some earlier editors speculated that the term applied to the corpulence of Richard Burbage, who originally played the part, but the allusion now appears unlikely. "Fat" may also suggest "sweaty."   **252 carouses** drinks a toast.

QUEEN: I will, my lord; I pray you, pardon me.   [*Drinks.*]

KING [*aside*]: It is the poison'd cup: it is too late.   255

HAMLET: I dare not drink yet, madam; by and by.

QUEEN: Come, let me wipe thy face.

LAERTES: My lord, I'll hit him now.

KING: I do not think 't.

LAERTES [*aside*]: And yet 'tis almost 'gainst my conscience.

HAMLET: Come, for the third, Laertes: you but dally;   260
    I pray you, pass with your best violence;
    I am afeard you make a wanton° of me.

LAERTES: Say you so? come on.   [*They play.*]

OSRIC: Nothing, neither way.

LAERTES: Have at you now!

[LAERTES *wounds* HAMLET; *then, in scuffling, they change rapiers,*° *and* HAMLET
    wounds LAERTES.]

KING: Part them; they are incens'd.   265

HAMLET: Nay, come again.   [*The* QUEEN *falls.*]

OSRIC: Look to the queen there, ho!

HORATIO: They bleed on both sides. How is it, my lord?

OSRIC: How is 't, Laertes?

LAERTES: Why, as a woodcock° to mine own springe,° Osric;
    I am justly kill'd with mine own treachery.   270

HAMLET: How does the queen?

KING: She swounds° to see them bleed.

QUEEN: No, no, the drink, the drink,—O my dear Hamlet,—
    The drink, the drink! I am poison'd.   [*Dies.*]

HAMLET: O villany! Ho! let the door be lock'd:
    Treachery! Seek it out.   [LAERTES *falls.*]   27.

LAERTES: It is here, Hamlet: Hamlet, thou art slain;
    No med'cine in the world can do thee good;
    In thee there is not half an hour of life;
    The treacherous instrument is in thy hand,
    Unbated° and envenom'd: the foul practice   280
    Hath turn'd itself on me; lo, here I lie,
    Never to rise again: thy mother's poison'd:
    I can no more: the king, the king's to blame.

HAMLET: The point envenom'd too!
    Then, venom, to thy work.   [*Stabs the* KING.]   28

ALL: Treason! treason!

KING: O, yet defend me, friends; I am but hurt.

HAMLET: Here, thou incestuous, murd'rous, damned Dane.

---

262 wanton spoiled child. **s.d. in scuffling, they change rapiers** according to a widespread
stage tradition, Hamlet receives a scratch, realizes that Laertes's sword is unbated (not blunted), and
accordingly forces an exchange. **269 woodcock** as type of stupidity or as decoy. **269 springe**
trap, snare. **271 swounds** swoons. **280 Unbated** Not blunted with a button.

Drink off this potion. Is thy union here?
Follow my mother.   [KING *dies.*]

290   LAERTES: He is justly serv'd;
        It is a poison temper'd° by himself.
        Exchange forgiveness with me, noble Hamlet:
        Mine and my father's death come not upon thee,
        Nor thine on me!   [*Dies.*]

295   HAMLET: Heaven make thee free of it! I follow thee.
        I am dead, Horatio. Wretched queen, adieu!
        You that look pale and tremble at this chance,
        That are but mutes° or audience to this act,
        Had I but time—as this fell sergeant,° Death,
300   Is strict in his arrest—O, I could tell you—
        But let it be. Horatio, I am dead;
        Thou livest; report me and my cause aright
        To the unsatisfied.

        HORATIO: Never believe it:
        I am more an antique Roman° than a Dane:
        Here's yet some liquor left.

305   HAMLET: As th' art a man,
        Give me the cup: let go, by heaven, I'll ha 't.
        O God! Horatio, what a wounded name,
        Things standing thus unknown, shall live behind me!
        If thou didst ever hold me in thy heart,
310   Absent thee from felicity awhile,
        And in this harsh world draw thy breath in pain,
        To tell my story.   (*A march afar off.*)
                        What warlike noise is this?

        OSRIC: Young Fortinbras, with conquest come from Poland,
        To the ambassadors of England gives
        This warlike volley.

315   HAMLET: O, I die, Horatio;
        The potent poison quite o'er-crows° my spirit:
        I cannot live to hear the news from England;
        But I do prophesy th' election lights
        On Fortinbras: he has my dying voice;
320   So tell him, with th' occurrents,° more and less,
        Which have solicited.° The rest is silence.   [*Dies.*]

        HORATIO: Now cracks a noble heart. Good night, sweet prince;
        And flights of angels sing thee to thy rest!
        Why does the drum come hither?   [*March within.*]

        (*Enter* FORTINBRAS, *with the* [English] AMBASSADORS [*and others*].)

---

291 temper'd mixed.   **298 mutes** performers in a play who speak no words.   **299 sergeant** sheriff's officer.   **304 Roman** it was the Roman custom to follow masters in death.   **316 o'er-crows** triumphs over.   **320 occurrents** events, incidents.   **321 solicited** moved, urged.

FORTINBRAS: Where is this sight?

HORATIO: What is it you would see?   *325*
    If aught of woe or wonder, cease your search.

FORTINBRAS: This quarry° cries on havoc.° O proud Death,
    What feast is toward in thine eternal cell,
    That thou so many princes at a shot
    So bloodily hast struck?

FIRST AMBASSADOR: The sight is dismal;   *330*
    And our affairs from England come too late:
    The ears are senseless that should give us hearing,
    To tell him his commandment is fulfill'd,
    That Rosencrantz and Guildenstern are dead:
    Where should we have our thanks?

HORATIO: Not from his mouth,°   *335*
    Had it th' ability of life to thank you:
    He never gave commandment for their death.
    But since, so jump° upon this bloody question,°
    You from the Polack wars, and you from England,
    Are here arriv'd, give order that these bodies   *340*
    High on a stage° be placed to the view;
    And let me speak to th' yet unknowing world
    How these things came about: so shall you hear
    Of carnal, bloody, and unnatural acts,
    Of accidental judgements, casual slaughters,   *345*
    Of deaths put on by cunning and forc'd cause,
    And, in this upshot, purposes mistook
    Fall'n on th' inventors' heads: all this can I
    Truly deliver.

FORTINBRAS: Let us haste to hear it,
    And call the noblest to the audience.   *350*
    For me, with sorrow I embrace my fortune:
    I have some rights of memory° in this kingdom,
    Which now to claim my vantage doth invite me.

HORATIO: Of that I shall have also cause to speak,
    And from his mouth whose voice will draw on more:°   *355*
    But let this same be presently perform'd,
    Even while men's minds are wild; lest more mischance,
    On° plots and errors, happen.

FORTINBRAS: Let four captains
    Bear Hamlet, like a soldier, to the stage;
    For he was likely, had he been put on,   *360*
    To have prov'd most royal: and, for his passage,°

---

327 quarry heap of dead.   **327 cries on havoc** proclaims a general slaughter.   **335 his mouth**
i.e., the king's.   **338 jump** precisely.   **338 question** dispute.   **341 stage** platform.   **352 of
memory** traditional, remembered.   **355 voice . . . more** vote will influence still others.   **358
On** on account of, or possibly, on top of, in addition to.   **361 passage** death.

The soldiers' music and the rites of war
Speak loudly for him.
Take up the bodies: such a sight as this
Becomes the field,° but here shows much amiss.
Go, bid the soldiers shoot.

365

(*Exeunt* [*marching, bearing off the dead bodies; after which a peal of ordnance is shot off*].)

QUESTIONS FOR DISCUSSION AND WRITING

1. In part, *Hamlet* is a play about parent–child relationships. We learn about the relationships between Hamlet and his stepfather, Claudius, between Hamlet and his dead father, between Hamlet and his mother, between Polonius and each of his children (Ophelia and Laertes), and even between Fortinbras and his dead father. How do these various relationships compare with one another? What do they tell us about the appropriate relationships between parent and child?

2. Hamlet says that he is avenging his father's murder, but some critics have claimed that he is at least as concerned about what he sees as his mother's lust as he is about his father's death. Look at how Hamlet talks about his mother and about Gertrude's relationships with the elder Hamlet, Claudius, and her son. To what extent do you agree with critics who think Hamlet is most worried about the way his uncle has displaced *him* in his mother's affections?

3. In the last speech of the play, Fortinbras says that Hamlet would have made a good king had he been given the chance. To what extent to you agree with that assessment of Hamlet's character? Why?

4. Look at the first scene of the play. How does it prepare us for the characterizations and themes to come?

5. Ophelia is driven mad, and Hamlet at least pretends to be mad. What causes each to lose grasp of reality? How does the play seem to define madness?

6. *Hamlet* has several image patterns that would seem to illuminate and reinforce Shakespeare's themes. Look at one of the following, and analyze the way it works thematically:

    Metaphors of melting and insubstantiality and their opposites (including shadows, questions about how solid something is, etc.)
    The use of flowers
    Military images

7. There is much in the play about duty and obligation, as they are owed to one's parent(s), friends, and king. What, finally, does the play tell us about what we each owe to others?

8. How much do we sympathize with Hamlet, not only with his motives, but also with his action and inaction? Think, for instance, about his decision not to kill Claudius while Claudius is praying, or about the way he talks to and about

---

365 field i.e., of battle.

his mother, about his treatment of Ophelia, about his attitudes toward and killing of Polonius.

9. In one of the most famous speeches from *Hamlet,* Polonius tells his son, Laertes, "to thine own self be true." That advice assumes both that one knows oneself and that one should and can be true to oneself. Who in the play is true to him- or herself? How do we respond to the fact that it is Polonius who delivers this advice?

10. Claudius is clearly the villain of the play. But even he has moments when he does not seem fully villainous. Where does he seem least villainous? If he were to tell the story of *Hamlet,* how might Claudius be more sympathetic to us?

11. In addition to Hamlet, we see several other young men in the play: Laertes, Fortinbras, and Horatio. How does Hamlet compare with each of them?

12. Love, sex, and death are somehow mixed together in this play. It is not just that those whom one loves die; it is also that talk of love often leads to talk of death and vice versa. Locate some such moments when the conversation turns from talk of love and sex to talk of death or when talk of death leads to talk of love and sex. What connections does the play ask us to see among the three? Why?

13. It is a critical commonplace to see Hamlet's "tragic flaw" as his inability to act, but not all readers agree with this sentiment. Would you agree that he is to be faulted for failing to act more quickly? Is he equally slow to act throughout the entire play?

14. We know that the ghost Hamlet has seen is real and that Hamlet has good reason to believe in his uncle's treachery and his mother's immorality. We also know that he is feigning madness. We know all this, though, because we are privy to scenes and speeches that many in the play do not see and hear. Imagine yourself a member of Claudius's court or a common person in Denmark. If you had not heard and seen what Hamlet has heard and seen, and if you had not heard Hamlet's speeches about his thoughts and motivations, how would you tell the story of *Hamlet?*

15. In many ways, *Hamlet* is a play about acting: Hamlet takes on the role of a madman, players who visit the court act out "The Murder of Gonzago," and many characters pretend to have emotions or motives that we know they do not really have. What does the play suggest is the appropriate relationship between playacting and reality?

From Kenneth Branagh's *Hamlet*, 1996.

QUESTION FOR DISCUSSION AND WRITING

In his filmed production of *Hamlet,* Kenneth Branagh makes frequent use of mirrors and other doubling devices to reflect some of the play's themes. How do the layout, setting, and costuming in this scene from *Hamlet* reflect Branagh's interest in doubling? What in Shakespeare's play gives rise to Branagh's use of doubling?

KENNETH BRANAGH (1960–   )

Two excerpts from Kenneth Branagh's 1996 screenplay of Hamlet*: I.ii.42–159 and III.i.90–184*   *1996*

I.ii.42–159

(*Time now to turn on the charm with the young aristocrats. Also a good show for the ladies, who crane their necks on the balconies to see which of the bright young things around the throne will be indulged with a public favour.*)

CLAUDIUS: And now, Laertes, what's the news with you?
You told us of some suit.

(*A darkly handsome young man steps forward. In the uniform of a cadet.*)

CLAUDIUS (*continuing*):   What is't, Laertes?
You cannot speak of reason to the Dane

And lose your voice. What wouldst thou beg, Laertes,
That shall not be my offer, not thy asking? 5
The head is not more native to the heart,
The hand more instrumental to the mouth,
Than is the throne of Denmark to thy father.

(*He turns to* POLONIUS, *once again letting the court know how the power structure stands. Then on with a smile.*)

CLAUDIUS (*continuing*): What wouldst thou have, Laertes?
LAERTES (*nervous*):   My dread lord,
Your leave and favour to return to France, 10

(*Knowing looks from around the court. The phrase 'sowing wild oats' comes to people's minds.* LAERTES *responds quickly.*)

LAERTES: From whence, though willingly I came to Denmark
To show my duty in your coronation,
Yet now I must confess, that duty done,
My thoughts and wishes bend again towards France
And bow them to your gracious leave and pardon. 15

(*The King teases it out for a moment.*)

CLAUDIUS: Have you your father's leave? What says Polonius?

(*Dad joins in with the gentle ribbing.*)

POLONIUS: He hath, my lord, wrung from me my slow leave
By laboursome petition and at last
Upon his will I sealed my hard consent.
I do beseech you give him leave to go. 20

(CLAUDIUS *steps down to* LAERTES.)

CLAUDIUS: Take thy fair hour, Laertes. Time be thine,
And thy best graces spend it at thy will.

(*As the* AUDIENCE *applauds, the Camera tracks slowly past them and comes to a halt under the right hand balcony. There at the other end of the hall is a black silhouette of a man. We make an abrupt Cut. The humorous applause that has greeted* LAERTES'*s departure is stopped by a big Close-up on* CLAUDIUS *and his firm tone.*)

CLAUDIUS (*continuing*): But now, my cousin Hamlet, and my son—

(*We make another an abrupt cut back to the lonely figure behind the bleachers.*)

HAMLET: A little more than kin, and less than kind.
CLAUDIUS: How is it that the clouds still hang on you? 25

(*From* CLAUDIUS'*s POV we see* HAMLET *move forward and sit down.*)

HAMLET: Not so, my lord, I am too much in the sun.

(*We see reaction on the* AUDIENCE'*s faces. This is embarrassing. The* QUEEN *moves away from the throne and we see her and her son in profile 2-shot. She attempts intimacy. This should not be public.*)

GERTRUDE: Good Hamlet, cast thy nighted colour off,
    And let thine eye look like a friend on Denmark.
    Do not for ever with thy vailèd lids
30   Seek for thy noble father in the dust.
    Thou know'st 'tis common—all that lives must die,
    Passing through nature to eternity.
HAMLET: Ay, madam, it is common.
GERTRUDE: If it be,
    Why seems it so particular with thee?

(In his shocked reaction he raises his voice, so that the CROWD *can almost hear the hissed reproaches that he shoots at her grief-free demeanour.)*

35   HAMLET: Seems, madam? Nay, it is. I know not 'seems.'
    'Tis not alone my inky cloak, good mother
    Nor customary suits of solemn black,
    Nor windy suspiration of forced breath,
    No, nor the fruitful river in the eye,
40   Nor the dejected haviour of the visage,
    Together with all forms, moods, shapes of grief
    That can denote me truly. These indeed 'seem,'
    For they are actions that a man might play;
    But I have that within which passeth show—
45   These but the trappings and the suits of woe.

(There are whispers now through the CROWD. *They're witnessing a scene that should take place behind closed doors.* CLAUDIUS *has had enough. Time for action.)*

CLAUDIUS: 'Tis sweet and commendable in your nature, Hamlet,

(He goes towards the Prince bringing in the CROWD *with his voice. This will now be a very public conversation.)*

CLAUDIUS *(continuing)*: To give these mourning duties to your father;
    But you must know your father lost a father;
    That father lost, lost his; and the survivor bound
50   In filial obligation for some term
    To do obsequious sorrow. But to persever
    In obstinate condolement is a course
    Of impious stubbornness, 'tis unmanly grief,
    It shows a will most incorrect to heaven,

(As CLAUDIUS *gives this rough lecture, he directs his injunctions to the physically immobile Prince. The great gallery of Courtiers behind, packed to the rafters. The power and strength of the King's position chillingly clear.)*

55   CLAUDIUS *(continuing)*: A heart unfortified, a mind impatient,
    An understanding simple and unschooled;
    For what we know must be, and is as common
    As any the most vulgar thing to sense,
    Why should we in our peevish opposition

Take it to heart? Fie, 'tis a fault to heaven, 60
A fault against the dead, a fault to nature,
To reason most absurd, whose common theme
Is death of fathers, and who still hath cried
From the first corpse till he that died today,
'This must be so.'

(CLAUDIUS *puts his arm around* HAMLET. *An invasion of intimacy.*)

CLAUDIUS (*continuing*): We pray you throw to earth 65
This unprevailing woe, and think of us
As of a father; for let the world take note

(*He drags* HAMLET *out onto the dais and produces the next information with a great Churchillian flourish.* HAMLET *eventually will be King—*CLAUDIUS *has nominated him here and now—all is well. The* CROWD *respond.*)

CLAUDIUS (*continuing*): You are the most immediate to our throne,

(*Huge applause from the* CROWD.)

CLAUDIUS (*continuing*): And with no less nobility of love
Than that which dearest father bears his son 70
Do I impart towards you.

(*Now, the atmosphere changes.*)

CLAUDIUS (*continuing*):   For your intent
In going back to school in Wittenberg,

(*The great issue comes up.* LAERTES, OPHELIA, GERTRUDE *all wanting to see* HAMLET *take his rightful place.*)

CLAUDIUS (*continuing*): It is most retrograde to our desire,
And we beseech you bend you to remain
Here in the cheer and comfort of our eye, 75
Our chiefest courtier, cousin, and our son.

(*Quiet again. The* AUDIENCE *straining to overhear.*)

GERTRUDE: Let not thy mother lose her prayers, Hamlet.
I pray thee stay with us, go not to Wittenberg.

(*We see* HAMLET's *crushed body language. The sense of a head bowed. Nevertheless he is a Prince and this is clear in the manner of his reply.*)

HAMLET: I shall in all my best obey you, madam.
CLAUDIUS: Why, 'tis a loving and a fair reply. 80
Be as ourself in Denmark.
                    (*To* GERTRUDE) Madam, come.

(*He takes her hand and moves to the front of the Dais. They effectively mask* HAMLET *from the Court. Peace is restored. Finally neither foreign upstarts nor truculent nephews have thrown this new King off balance, at this formal opening of his new parliament. He is intimate with her now. Happily letting the Court share their obvious intoxication with each other.)*

CLAUDIUS: This gentle and unforced accord of Hamlet
        Sits smiling to my heart; in grace whereof,
        No jocund health that Denmark drinks today
85   But the great cannon to the clouds shall tell,
        And the King's rouse the heavens shall bruit again,
        Re-speaking earthly thunder.

(Confetti begins to fall.)

CLAUDIUS: Come, away.

(Cheers, trumpets. The Royal Couple race out like the hungry newlyweds they are. The happy CROWD *chase them like a drunken wedding party. The huge hall empties almost by magic. We see the end doors shut and then we see* HAMLET *still standing at the throne. His body collapses, leaning on the arms of the thrones as we hear him start to speak we move slowly around him.)*

HAMLET: O that this too too solid flesh would melt,
90   Thaw and resolve itself into a dew,
        Or that the Everlasting had not fixed
        His canon 'gainst self-slaughter! O God, O God,
        How weary, stale, flat, and unprofitable
        Seem to me all the uses of this world!
95   Fie on't, ah fie, fie! 'Tis an unweeded garden
        That grows to seed; things rank and gross in nature
        Possess it merely. That it should come to this—

(The Camera moves with HAMLET *down the hall.)*

HAMLET *(continuing)*: But two months dead—nay, not so much, not two—
        So excellent a King, that was to this
100   Hyperion to a satyr, so loving to my mother
        That he might not beteem the winds of heaven
        Visit her face too roughly! Heaven and earth,
        Must I remember? Why, she would hang on him
        As if increase of appetite had grown
105   By what it fed on, and yet within a month—
        Let me not think on't; frailty, thy name is woman—

(He turns to face away from the door.)

HAMLET *(continuing)*: A little month, or ere those shoes were old
        With which she followed my poor father's body,
        Like Niobe, all tears, why she, even she—
110   O God, a beast that wants discourse of reason
        Would have mourned longer!—married with mine uncle,
        My father's brother, but no more like my father
        Than I to Hercules, within a month,

Ere yet the salt of most unrighteous tears
Had left the flushing in her gallèd eyes,
She married. O most wicked speed, to post
With such dexterity to incestuous sheets!

115

(*He looks back down the almost empty state hall. We see the melancholic profile of a young man in black military cadet uniform, flaxen hair and a single tear trailing down a face more used to smiles.*)

HAMLET (*continuing*): It is not, nor it cannot come to good.
But break, my heart, for I must hold my tongue.

(*His eyes close as he hears a door open and readies himself for one more invasion of his non-existent privacy; a princely sigh.*)

QUESTIONS FOR DISCUSSION AND WRITING

1. What is Branagh's sense of the king's and court's attitudes toward Laertes at the beginning of the scene? How does Branagh change the mood when the camera's and king's attention shifts to Hamlet? What do the stage directions imply about how we should compare and contrast Laertes and Hamlet?

2. Branagh's stage directions tell us that the exchange between Hamlet and his parents is embarrassing and somewhat out of place. Do you agree that the exchange would be better left for a private moment? Why might Claudius want the moment to be public?

3. In many ways, Branagh encourages us to see things from Claudius's literal and figurative point of view in this scene. How do the stage directions—the camera movements and the audience's reactions—encourage us to identify with Claudius? What is the effect of that identification? Would you have encouraged a similar identification with the king had you been directing the play?

4. How does Branagh want us to see the relationship between Claudius and Gertrude? To what extent do the stage directions help us understand Hamlet's view of the relationship? To what extent does Branagh seem to think we should share Hamlet's view of his mother and her new husband?

III.i.90–184

OPHELIA: Good my lord,
How does your honour for this many a day?

(*It's a huge relief to see her. But this is a very formal greeting. Strange, even despite recent events.*)

HAMLET: I humbly thank you; well, well, well.

(*He moves to her and they embrace and kiss, a moment of bliss but then she breaks away. She is still cool, trying to hold herself together.*)

OPHELIA: My lord, I have remembrances of yours
5   That I have longèd long to redeliver.

(She hands him a package of his love letters and poems.)

OPHELIA *(continuing)*: I pray you now receive them.

(This is not like her. Or if it is, he won't play this adolescent game. He is petulant.)

HAMLET: No, not I, I never gave you aught.

(Starting to have more of a conversation with him now, instead of worrying about the listeners. She lowers her voice, she is annoyed and hurt by him in her own right. She wants him to know the truth of her feelings. Not what she's been told to do.)

OPHELIA: My honoured lord, you know right well you did,
    And with them words of so sweet breath compos'd
    As made the things more rich.

(She tries to be hard.)

10 OPHELIA *(continuing)*:   Their perfume lost,
    Take these again; for to the noble mind
    Rich gifts wax poor when givers prove unkind.
    There, my lord.

(He lashes out at the letters, sending them flying from her hand across the hall.)

HAMLET: Ha, ha? Are you honest?
OPHELIA: My lord.

(Come on.)

15 HAMLET: Are you fair?
OPHELIA: What means your lordship?

(Oh, really.)

HAMLET: That if you be honest and fair, your honesty should admit no discourse to
    your beauty.

(She tries to give as good as she gets but she is still brittle, on her dignity, and never unaware of being watched.)

OPHELIA: Could beauty, my lord, have better commerce
20   than with honesty?

(He replies fiercely and with a heart-rending disillusion.)

HAMLET: Ay, truly, for the power of beauty will sooner transform honesty from what
    it is to a bawd than the force of honesty can translate beauty into his likeness.
    This was sometime a paradox, but now the time gives it proof.

*(Don't you **realize** what was between us?)*

HAMLET *(continuing)*: I did love you once.

(I don't know any more. I hoped so. I hope so.)

OPHELIA: Indeed, my lord, you made me believe so.   25

(*He seems to understand her confusion and berates himself. She is right. He **is** unworthy. He ought to end it now.*)

HAMLET: You should not have believed me, for virtue cannot so inoculate our old stock but we shall relish of it. I loved you not.

(*Ah, the truth at last.*)

OPHELIA: I was the more deceived.

(*But of course it isn't the truth. It's much more complex than that. He can't tell her why it has ended, of his terrible personal situation, but he can warn someone he loves to beware of* CLAUDIUS, POLONIUS, *and even him, a man unworthy of her love. He wants her to be safe. To escape.*)

HAMLET: Get thee to a nunnery. Why wouldst thou be a breeder of sinners? I am myself indifferent honest, but yet I could accuse me of such things that it were   30
better my mother had not borne me. I am very proud, revengeful, ambitious, with more offences at my beck than I have thoughts to put them in, imagination to give them shape, or time to act them in. What should such fellows as I do crawling between earth and heaven? We are arrant knaves, all. Believe none of us. Go thy ways to a nunnery.   35

(*A tiny noise! She glances across the room. And then it dawns. The Hall is empty. As never before. It's a trap. She has been unable to be purely honest—almost an impossibility with her—surely she is not part of a trap? Not her . . . not her . . .*)

HAMLET (*continuing*): Where's your father?

(*The most agonizing decision of her young life.*)

OPHELIA: At home, my lord.

(*And with that phrase their love is dead. We seem to see both their hearts break before us. Both their hearts and, apparently, his mind.*)

HAMLET: Let the doors be shut upon him, that he may
play the fool nowhere but in's own house. Farewell.

(*We are Close on her agonized face.*)

OPHELIA: O help him, you sweet heavens!   40

(*He explodes with fury. He picks her up by the arm with great force. He then starts to drag her down the opposite side of the Hall to the spying pair. As he does so he flings open each mirrored door. We track with them and see many pairs of* HAMLETs *and* OPHELIAs *as the inner and outer mirrors add visual chaos to the already savage race around the Hall.*)

HAMLET: If thou dost marry, I'll give thee this plague for thy dowry: be thou as chaste as ice, as pure as snow, thou shalt not escape calumny. Get thee to a nunnery, go, farewell. Or if thou wilt needs marry, marry a fool; for wise men know

well enough what monsters you make of them. To a nunnery, go, and quickly,
45 too. Farewell.

(He has run off for a moment, leaving her sobbing.)

OPHELIA: Heavenly powers, restore him.

(He rushes back to her and drags her to the other side of the hall.)

HAMLET: I have heard of your paintings, too, well enough.
God hath given you one face,

(He flings her around like a rag doll.)

HAMLET *(continuing):*   and you make yourselves another.
You jig, you amble, and you lisp, and nickname God's creatures,

(He shoves her hard against the mirrored door behind which her father stands.)

(Cut to: Interior/ANTE–ROOM Day)

(POLONIUS inside is appalled. CLAUDIUS stops him opening the door.)

50 HAMLET *(continuing):* and make your wantonness your ignorance.

*(All passion almost spent. We see from inside the two faces against the mirror. Hers
contorted against the glass.)*

HAMLET *(continuing):* Go to, I'll no more on't. It hath made me mad.
I say we will have no more marriages. Those that are married already—all but
one—shall live. The rest shall keep as they are.

*(He flings open the door and drags OPHELIA into the room and pushes her to the floor.
He catches sight of one of the hidden doors just before it snaps shut!)*

(Interior/ANTE–ROOM Day)

*(He moves back to OPHELIA. He speaks quietly to her now. Their heads very close to-
gether. It's over.)*

HAMLET *(continuing):* To a nunnery, go.

(HAMLET goes back into the State Hall and away.)

(OPHELIA stays where he has pushed her, wrecked in every sense.)

55 OPHELIA: O what a noble mind is here o'erthrown!
The courtier's, soldier's, scholar's eye, tongue, sword,
Th' expectancy and rose of the fair state,
The glass of fashion and the mould of form,
Th' observed of all observers, quite, quite, down!

(She is in a state of utter shock.)

60 OPHELIA *(continuing):* And I, of ladies most deject and wretched,
That sucked the honey of his music vows,
Now see that noble and most sovereign reason

Like sweet bells jangled out of tune and harsh;
That unmatched form and feature of blown youth
Blasted with ecstasy. O woe is me,   65
T' have seen what I have seen, see what I see!

(*From the other hidden door enter* CLAUDIUS *and* POLONIUS. *The national crisis
steps up a gear. This man is dangerous.* POLONIUS *goes to the prostrate* OPHELIA *and
cradles her in his arms. He is severely shaken.*)

CLAUDIUS: Love? His affections do not that way tend,
Nor what he spake, though it lacked form a little,
Was not like madness. There's something in his soul
O'er which his melancholy sits on brood,   70
And I do doubt the hatch and the disclose
Will be some danger; which to prevent
I have in quick determination
Thus set it down: he shall with speed to England
For the demand of our neglected tribute.   75

(*He calms down a little after this outburst. Rationalizes.*)

CLAUDIUS (*continuing*): Haply the seas and countries different,
With variable objects, shall expel
This something-settled matter in his heart,
Whereon his brains still beating puts him thus
From fashion of himself. What think you on't?   80
POLONIUS (*strangely quiet*): It shall do well. But yet do I believe
The origin and commencement of this grief
Sprung from neglected love.

(*He continues to stroke her head like a parent singing a lullaby to a baby.*)

POLONIUS (*continuing*):   How now, Ophelia?
You need not tell us what Lord Hamlet said;
We heard it all.   85

(*He quietly offers the following advice.*)

POLONIUS (*continuing*): My lord, do as you please,
But, if you hold it fit, after the play
Let his queen mother all alone entreat him
To show his griefs. Let her be round with him,
And I'll be placed, so please you, in the ear   90
Of all their conference. If she find him not,
To England send him, or confine him where
Your wisdom best shall think.
CLAUDIUS: It shall be so.
Madness in great ones must not unwatch'd go.

(*He closes his eyes for a moment, behind him we see the father's and daughter's silent
distress.*)

QUESTIONS FOR DISCUSSION AND WRITING

1. In staging this scene, Branagh asks us to think about the relationship between Hamlet and Ophelia *before* the play begins. How does he seem to see that relationship? How do his stage directions reveal his sense of who Hamlet and Ophelia are and of what their love has been like?

2. Branagh's stage directions tell us that Hamlet advises Ophelia to "get thee to a nunnery" because he wants her to be safe. But not all critics and audiences think of the advice as so kindly. Why do *you* think Hamlet tells Ophelia to go live in a convent, away from the world and away from men? (In answering this question, you might also want to look "nunnery" up in the *OED* [see 1325]; in Renaissance times, the word was sometimes used to describe something other than a convent.)

3. Were you surprised at the violence and chaos that Branagh brings to his direction of the scene? By striking out at Ophelia physically, does Branagh's Hamlet lose our sympathy and understanding? Is this characterization of Hamlet consistent with your interpretation of his character?

4. Branagh's direction of the scene makes it impossible for us to forget that Claudius and Polonius are watching the lovers quarrel. How do we respond to their spying? To their inaction when things turn violent?

MARK THORNTON BURNETT

The 'Very Cunning of the Scene': Kenneth Branagh's Hamlet   1996

On 21 January 1997, Kenneth Branagh's film version of *Hamlet* received its United Kingdom premiere at the newly opened Waterfront Hall in Belfast. It was an important event, as the audience was able to appreciate Branagh's four-hour realization of Shakespeare's play in a spectacular chrome and glass environment, a manifestation of the prosperity that has come to Belfast in the wake of the peace process. But the occasion also provided an opportunity to reflect upon the achievement of this extraordinary actor and director. If, in Britain, Branagh has been maligned for his "populist" readings of Shakespeare, film critics in the United States have praised him for his reworking of Renaissance theatrical traditions and acute cinematic intelligence.[1] In this essay, I will discuss the numerous virtues and isolated infelicities of Branagh's *Hamlet* in an attempt to discriminate between these judgments. While paying close attention to the film's textual sensitivity, I will also concentrate upon the "cunning" (or "art") of its "scene" (or representational devices).

I

Perhaps the most impressive element of the film is Branagh's performance as Hamlet, played in such a way as to bring out the multiple dimensions of a tortured psyche. Thus, from a grieving son lurking in the shadows at the start, Branagh moves to an explosive "man of action" in the later scenes, a knowing impersonator of madness and a theatrically dynamic presence. While Branagh clearly points up a personality-based and romantic reading of Shakespeare's play, the film is arguably more obviously dominated by its political resonances. For this *Hamlet* constructs Denmark as a militaristic state. Already in the opening scenes, there are glimpses of preparations for war; Hamlet strides through an arsenal on his way to encounter the ghost; and displays of fencing practice punctuate the narrative, foreshadowing the catastrophic conclusion. It is to Branagh's credit that he has restored to *Hamlet* its military subtexts, and the film does not hesitate to demonstrate the extent to which Denmark's power is dependent upon the cooperation of a gallery of soldierly underlings—Rosencrantz (Timothy Spall) and Guildenstern (Reece Dinsdale) wear regimental sashes; guards invade Ophelia's chamber; and the grave digger (Billy Crystal) arranges skulls side-by-side with all the precision of a campaigning general. Nor is this merely an extraneous interpretation. The play abounds in marital rhetoric, as when Claudius enjoins the "kettle to the trumpet speak, / The trumpet to the cannoneer without, / The cannons to the heavens" (V.ii.242–44). Branagh takes his cue from the specific orientation of Shakespeare's text in a persuasive reconsideration of the material bases upon which Elsinore's preeminence is founded.

It is part of the versatility of the film's representational scheme that Branagh also develops the Fortinbras sub-plot, which is so often omitted from modern productions. Frequent use is made of parallel montage whereby the "scene" cuts between unfolding wrangles at Elsinore and the relentless advances of Fortinbras's army. At one point, newspaper headlines are deployed to highlight the threat of the Norwegian commander, played with an icy implacability by Rufus Sewell. As the film progresses, it would seem as if there is every justification for the nervousness of the sentry who patrols the castle's gates.

The "cunning" of the film's representational devices can be apprehended no less forcibly in set design and staging procedures. Joel Fineman's work on fratricide and cuckoldry has established the importance of Hamlet's "doubling" structures and assessment and mirrored arrangements. Branagh's Hamlet fits well with this assessment, since its interior scenes take place in a state hall lined with windows and mirrored doors. In such a setting, Hamlet is forced to confront reflections of himself, such as Claudius (Derek Jacobi), who, with his blonde hair and clipped beard, bears an uncanny resemblance to Branagh's Dane. The points of contact between the characters are also incestuously underlined when Hamlet pushes Ophelia (Kate Winslet) against one of the hall's mirrors, not realizing that Claudius and Polonius are hidden behind it. Branagh himself has observed that the set was intended to suggest "a vain world . . . looking in on itself . . . that seems confident and open but conceals corruption" (qtd. in LoMonico 6). It is a bold and critically current view, and one for which there is considerable textual support. Once again, Branagh is keen to place a visual slant upon the concerns of the text, and this imperative is ably demonstrated in the presentation of a court, which, as it contemplates its own self image, faces only an inevitable decline.

To the broad brush strokes of the design can be added the nuanced local effects with which the film abounds. As the "cunning" of the film is displayed in its overall montage, so is it revealed in a spectrum of more specialized scenic details and connections. First, several fresh areas of meaning come into play in images of domestic intimacy. After an assignation with a prostitute, Polonius (Richard Briers) dresses himself to tutor Reynaldo (Gerard Depardieu) in the art of surveillance, which makes an intriguing link with the following scene where Ophelia describes Hamlet's appearance before her "with all his doublet all unbrac'd" (II.i.76). As she recovers upon her father's bed, it is implied that Ophelia has been abused by Hamlet and will be prostituted by her brothel-frequenting father. Second, the density of scenic business reinforces the narrative continuum and creates unexpected poetic correspondences. Claudius and Laertes (Michael Maloney) quaff brandy together as they plot Hamlet's downfall. Their conspiratorial drinking is immediately overtaken by the description of Ophelia's drowning, and subsequently by the grave digger's observation that a tanner's hide "is so tanned with his trade that a will keep out water a great while, and your water is a sore decayer of your whoreson dead body" (V.i.139–41). Through such networks of "liquid" allusion, visual stimuli in the film enrich the play's textual fabric, exposing reductive, consuming systems in which a woman's innocence is at the mercy of paternalistic hypocrisy.

By concentrating key scenes of the play in particular locations, the film pushes to their furthest extent the areas of overlap between visual messages and verbal utterances. Notably the chapel, a dimly lit but ornate interior, serves as a suggestive site for the prompting of confessional revelations. Toward the beginning of the film, Polonius thrusts Ophelia into a confession box to quiz her about the "very ecstasy" of Hamlet's "love" (II.i.100). A more unsettling use of the box occurs when Claudius creeps into it to lament his "rank" (III.iii.36) offence. Lighting upon Claudius, Hamlet forces his knife through the grill, becoming an unpunctual but unconsoling father confessor. As well as enhancing the impression of a world suffering from the effects of withholding secrets, these locational moments complicate the implications of the play's rhetoric. When Hamlet urges Gertrude (Julie Christie) to "Confess [herself] to heaven" and "Repent what's past" (III.iv.150–51), for instance, one is reminded of a developing intrigue that finds its expression in parodic gestures toward absolution. As confessional textual details are taken up in the film's confessional sequences, a lively sense of escalating frustrations is elaborated.

The partnership shared between the verbal and the visual is demonstrated most eloquently in the scenes involving the ghost. Played by Brian Blessed and shot from a high angle perspective, the ghost is discovered as a militant spectre of colossal proportions. As the ghost confesses its secrets, bursts of flame break through the forest floor and smoke billows about the trees, apt metaphors for the opening of the sepulcher's "ponderous and marble jaws" (I.iv.50) and for the "blasts from hell" with which the supernatural visitation is associated. Similarly, when the ghost appears in Gertrude's chamber, an eerie music sounds, stressing again the possibility that Hamlet senior may be a demon in disguise. True to the infernal suggestions of Shakespeare's text, the film imagines the ghost as a force whose motives are questionable in the extreme.

Characteristic of both the general representational strategies and the local colouring is the productively restless camera work. Often, repeated camera movements illuminate psychological connections. In the opening scene, the camera zooms outward to show the disappearing ghost, a trajectory followed again for Hamlet's "How all occasions do inform against me" (IV.iv.32) speech: the comparable tracking shots hint at a revitalized paternal and filial alliance. More striking, it might be suggested, are the ways in which the camera prowls around groups of characters, often exploiting 360-degree pans. When Claudius and Polonius agree to spy upon the prince, they are circled by the camera, as is Hamlet on confronting his mother in her "closet." In this scene, in fact, the voyeuristic impression created is reinforced by the chamber's Tiepolo-like wall paintings of eavesdroppers leaning over balustrades to watch an event of clearly spellbinding significance. This innovative use of the camera has several effects. At once, it adds to the sense of a court dominated by dark secrets and political espionage. In the same moment, it sharpens an awareness of the ever in-creasing danger of Fortinbras's army, a force which will eventually encircle the castle itself. The closer Fortinbras draws, the more exactly does he seem to represent the eye that subjects all of Elsinore to an uncompromising, comprehensive scrutiny.

II

Despite the obvious felicities of Branagh's interpretation, there are moments when the film suffers from a textually unwarrantable amount of scenic business. Such is the enthusiasm to illustrate the action, that the film occasionally provides the audi-ence with a surplus of informational materials. Admittedly, some of these additions are superficially attractive, as when Hamlet senior is presented sleeping in his orchard, only to be retrospectively upstaged by the Player King who appears in an identical colorful costume. At other points, however, ambiguities in the text are flattened by the assumption that the spectators are incapable of imagining for themselves. Jump cuts, flashbacks, and spliced narratives—such as images of Claudius's hand untying Gertrude's bodice, of Claudius keeping "wassail" (I.iv.9), and of Hamlet and Ophelia making love—take away from the plural meanings that the verse alone is able to gen-erate. In this way, although the urge to fill in the spaces that the text leaves open makes for a clear story line, it also reduces the "heart" of the play's "mystery" (III.ii.321), substituting a one-dimensional reading for irresolution and elusive uncertainty.

Equally troubling is the recourse to sentimentality in scenes where a much harder or even ironic sensibility would seem to be at work. The score is generally ex-citedly august, but several musical themes seem inappropriate. As an example, one can cite the scene in which Laertes takes leave of Polonius, which provides the politician with an opportunity to bully his son into filial subservience. Yet in Branagh's *Hamlet*, romantic organ music (in conjunction with soft focus camera work) is instrumental in subordinating the text's ironic potential to a bonding between father and son that can be dramatically supported only with difficulty.

In the same mold are those moments when Hamlet views "man" (II.ii.280) as a "quintessence of dust" (II.ii.283), and when Ophelia laments the disruption to his "noble mind" (III.i.141): a romantic theme sounds precisely at the point where the text calls for a bitter or dissonant musical accompaniment. With such romantic musi-cal evocations, the film runs the risk of papering over some of the more unpalatable dimensions of the text—including Hamlet's participation in the victimization of Ophelia—and comes close to putting a rose-tinted view of the Dane in the place of a more all-embracing political critique.

III

Notwithstanding individual shortcomings, Branagh's *Hamlet* most often capti-vates with its blend of sumptuous internal scenes and sweeping exterior visuals. If, moreover, the film caters to the postmodern viewer in piecing out textual gaps, it also manages to find new preoccupations in an all too familiar narrative. The film is perhaps at its freshest, and at its most absorbing, after the "Intermission," when the break-up of Elsinore is an urgent prospect. Clearly apparent in the film's latter stages is the shrunken character of the court: only a handful of attendants are present at Ophelia's funeral, a stark contrast with the swelling numbers flocking to enjoy the play-within-the-play and an indicator of Claudius's waning control. Even before Fortinbras makes his spectacular final entrance, monarchical authority is wavering, as Gertrude's increasingly sour expressions indicate. When the climax arrives, Fortinbras's troops crash through the state hall's windows and mirrored doors, a timely lesson for a court that has been incapable of recognizing its own fragile illusions. Hamlet is given a soldier's funeral, a move which identifies him with Fortinbras, the commander whose superior military prowess allows him to declare himself the state's inheritor.

But Branagh's *Hamlet* goes beyond a simple dichotomy between military technology and political supremacy. In many respects, it probes deeper levels of meaning, which lie outside the merely filmic and textual relationship. Above all, this *Hamlet* is intertextual in that it repeatedly articulates its connections to a host of other texts and histories. Faithful to the 1623 First Folio version of the play, the film is suitably bookish, and a favourite retreat for Hamlet is his book-lined study: it is here, not accidentally, that he consults a treatise on demons before setting out to confront the ghost. Branagh, it seems, is concerned to authenticate himself as a leading Shakespearean by stressing the decision to realize the entire play, an undertaking unique in the theatrical record. In this endeavour, he is aided by many of the luminaries of the Shakespearean establishment. There is more than a passing intertextuality involved in casting Derek Jacobi as Claudius, for the actor played Hamlet in 1979 at the Old Vic, took the part in a BBC version of the play in 1980, and directed Branagh in the title role for the 1988 Renaissance Theatre Company production (Branagh vi–vii.175). If Jacobi is Branagh's filmic father, then Branagh is Jacobi's theatrical son. A legitimating imperative would also appear to lie behind the casting of John Gielgud (Priam) and Judi Dench (Hecuba) in non-speaking appearances, and an intertextual dimension is certainly detectable in Charlton Heston's cameo role as the Player King. By drawing upon the pooled resources of Stratford-upon-Avon dignitaries, and of Hollywood "epic" veterans, Branagh, with typical audacity, sets himself up as another epic filmmaker, as a bardic interpreter with impeccable credentials.

Yet the film's intertextuality does not end with casting associations. Part of the grandeur of the film depends upon the numerous exterior views of Blenheim Palace (masquerading as the castle of Elsinore), which is shot in a wide-screen 70mm format. From this "scene" of epic architectural magnificence a number of intertextual resonances can be inferred. Following the defeat of the French at Blenheim in 1704, the palace was constructed for the Duke of Marlborough as thanks for a landmark victory. Sir Winston Churchill was born at Blenheim in 1874, and members of the family still live at the palace. With these contexts in mind, it can be argued that Branagh's *Hamlet* operates as a metaphor for historical conflicts between England and France, between England and Germany, and even between the English royal family and a more powerful political entity. The film is too complex to be straightjacketed within a simple allegory, however, and equally invests in provoking contrary readings that go against its more obvious contextual correspondences. At the close, the imposing statue of Hamlet senior is toppled to the ground, and any spectator attuned to the recent collapse of the communist countries will not miss the parallel. Branagh's *Hamlet* is an eloquent disquisition on the perils of aristocratic and royal authority; it is also a "cunning" celebration of the plebeian forces that contest the ownership of power and privilege.

What, finally, of the "scene" of the premiere itself? By staging the premiere in Belfast, Branagh, poised between two cultures in that he was born in Belfast but brought up in England, is bringing Shakespeare back to an adopted Irish homeland. Something of this was hinted at in the promotional material about the charity that the screening of the film supports: "First Run Belfast" sponsors local thespians to stage theatrical ventures or to study drama outside Northern Ireland. *Hamlet,* one might suggest, represents Branagh's attempt to negotiate, like Hamlet himself, a tricky trajectory (and a narrative of exile and return) between London, Hollywood, and Belfast, just as the Danish prince follows a similar journey from Wittenberg to England and finally to Denmark. When Julie Christie introduced the film at the premiere, she too made use of the "homecoming" motif, describing Branagh, strangely Gertrude-like, as "your boy." Branagh, however, was not present. Away in the United States filming *The Gingerbread Man,* he was available only as a simulacrum on a videotaped message, transformed into a ghostly echo of his cinematic counterpart.

Notes

1 See Christopher Goodwin. "Love Him, Loathe Him: Ken Divides Us All," *The Sunday Times* (19 January 1997): 8–9; and Geoffrey O'Brien. "The Ghosts at the Feast," *The New York Review of Books* (6 February 1997): 15–16.

Works Cited

Branagh, Kenneth. *"Hamlet" by William Shakespeare: Screenplay and Introduction.* London: Chatto and Windus, 1996.

Fineman, Joel. "Fratricide and Cuckoldry: Shakespeare's Doubles." *Representing Shakespeare: New Psychoanalytic Essays.* Ed. Murray M. Schwartz and Coppelia Khan. Baltimore and London: Johns Hopkins UP, 1980. 70–109.

LoMonico, Michael. "Branagh's Hamlet—Power and Opulence." *Shakespeare* 1.1 (1996).

Shakespeare, William. *Hamlet.* Ed. Harold Jenkins. London and New York: Methuen, 1987.

QUESTIONS FOR DISCUSSION AND WRITING

1. Burnett notes that many directors cut the Fortinbras scenes, but Branagh emphasizes the military context of the play. To what extent do you think that the military element is crucial to our understanding of *Hamlet*? Why?

2. Burnett comments on Branagh's use of visual images: the use of mirrors, the chapel scenes, and the demon imagery, for example. How do these images underscore ideas in the play itself?

3. Burnett admires Branagh's "intertextuality" in casting both well-known Shakespearean actors and Hollywood stars in the film. How successful do you think such casting choices are? What is gained or lost by such a mixing?

4. Burnett criticizes a few of Branagh's decisions. For instance, he does not like the loss of the ambiguity and irony of Shakespeare's play, and he thinks that Branagh tends to

sentimentalize Hamlet. Given your reading of the play, how important are ambiguity and irony in it? How much do you think Hamlet should be sentimentalized?

5. If you have seen Branagh's film, which of Burnett's points do you agree or disagree with? What elements in the film that Burnett did not comment on did you admire or dislike?

MARGARET ATWOOD (1939–)

Gertrude Talks Back   1994

I always thought it was a mistake, calling you Hamlet. I mean, what kind of a name is that for a young boy? It was your father's idea. Nothing would do but that you had to be called after him. Selfish. The other kids at school used to tease the life out of you. The nicknames! And those terrible jokes about pork.

I wanted to call you George.

I am *not* wringing my hands. I'm drying my nails.

Darling, please stop fidgeting with my mirror. That'll be the third one you've broken.

Yes, I've seen those pictures, thank you very much.

I *know* your father was handsomer than Claudius. High brow, aquiline nose and so on, looked great in uniform. But handsome isn't everything, especially in a man, and far be it from me to speak ill of the dead, but I think it's about time I pointed out to you that your dad just wasn't a whole lot of fun. Noble, sure, I grant you. But Claudius, well, he likes a drink now and then. He appreciates a decent meal. He enjoys a laugh, know what I mean? You don't always have to be tiptoeing around because of some holier-than-thou principle or something.

By the way, darling, I wish you wouldn't call your stepdad *the bloat king.* He does have a slight weight problem, and it hurts his feelings.

The rank sweat of a *what*? My bed is certainly not *enseamed,* whatever that might be! A nasty sty, indeed! Not that it's any of your business, but I change those sheets twice a week, which is more than you do, judging from that student slum pigpen in Wittenberg. I'll certainly never visit you *there* again without prior warning! I see that laundry of yours when you bring it home, and not often enough either, by a long shot! Only when you run out of black socks.

And let me tell you, everyone sweats at a time like that, as you'd find out very soon if you ever gave it a try. A real girlfriend would do you a heap of good. Not like that pasty-faced what's-her-name, all trussed up like a prize turkey in those touch-me-not corsets of hers. If you ask me, there's something off about that girl. Border-line. Any little shock could push her right over the edge.

Go get yourself someone more down-to-earth. Have a nice roll in the hay. Then you can talk to me about nasty sties.

No, darling, I am not *mad* at you. But I must say you're an awful prig sometimes. Just like your Dad. *The Flesh,* he'd say. You'd think it was dog dirt. You can excuse that in a young person, they are always so intolerant, but in someone his age it was getting, well, very hard to live with, and that's the understatement of the year.

Some days I think it would have been better for both of us if you hadn't been an only child. But you realize who you have to thank for *that*. You have no idea what I used to put up with. And every time I felt like a little, you know, just to warm up my aging bones, it was like I'd suggested murder.

You think *what*? You think Claudius murdered your Dad? Well, no wonder you've been so rude to him at the dinner table!

If I'd known *that*, I could have put you straight in no time flat.

It wasn't Claudius, darling.

It was me.

QUESTIONS FOR DISCUSSION AND WRITING

1. How would you characterize Gertrude in Atwood's story? What do her tone and her characterizations of her son and husbands tell us about who she is and what she values? How similar is Atwood's Gertrude to Shakespeare's?
2. Gertrude seems not to like her son very much. How does the Hamlet of Atwood's story compare to the Hamlet of Shakespeare's play?
3. What motivates Atwood's Gertrude to kill her first husband? How much do we sympathize with her for doing so?

LOUIS MACNEICE   (1907–1963)

Rites of war _____ *1958*

So, Fortinbras; Alas is now the keyword here.
A waste you say? Yet graced with swagged and canopied verse,
All tragedies of kings having wings to raise their gloom

(Even as the lights go down the crowns come up) but you, sir,
Have seen far more of gore without this pomp, have heard   5
Your dying soldiers cry though not in iambics, not
In any manner of speech to reach the future's ear,
Their death being merely breath that ceased and flesh that slumped
As both, it is true, must do ten years, ten centuries, hence,
On a cutprice night, not a flight of angels near to sing   10
Their souls to whatever rest were best if souls they had.
Still, at this stage and age before, if ever, we read
The story, the glory, in full of your Polack wars and the long
List of your dead—you said a waste, did you not?—we also
Trust for the future's sake you will take your immediate cue,   15
That curtain, that certain line—and the last chance to boot
For Fortinbras to pass. Go, bid the soldiers shoot.

QUESTIONS FOR DISCUSSION AND WRITING

1. MacNeice's poem is apparently set at the moment when Fortinbras comes from the battlefield to find Hamlet, Laertes, Claudius, and Gertrude dead. What comparisons does the poem ask us to make between Fortinbras's (and his soldiers') experience of war and the tragedy that has befallen the royal court? What is the significance of those comparisons?

2. The poem alludes both to Horatio's prayer that angels speed Hamlet to his final resting place and to the last words of Shakespeare's play. What effect do those allusions have on our understanding of war and of Fortinbras's proper role?

3. What is the significance of the poem's title? What are the "rites" to which the title refers? How much do those rites, or war itself, seem to come to the forefront of our experience of Shakespeare's *Hamlet*?

JOHN CIARDI (1916–1986)

Hamlet in the Wings   1961

(*Spoken as he waits to make his entrance for the final scene*)

My father died, my mother married.
I can say, in general, I disapproved
Of the lengths to which things had been carried
Even before Ophelia was removed.

5   There's the king-my-father, and my own sweet chick,
And her father to boot, and my good old drinking
Stinking school pals. I could feel sick
If I thought about it, and I *am* thinking.

Two were the best, and two were measly,
10 And one a fool, and that makes five.
God, I could swallow my bodkin easily.
Mother, what are we doing alive?

Let spooks, I say, do their own killing.
Do you hear, Horatio? Well, all's not lost:
15 My uncle's breathing, but God willing,
The fashion in kings is to turn ghost.

It's the rage in Denmark all this season:
The best, the measly, the in-between,
And the worst—right down to the worm of treason—
20 Are spooking out on my lady the Queen.

Mother, Mother, bring me a cup.
My throat is cut as any pig's.

I'll bleed until I fill it up,
And you must drink while my uncle jigs.

Denmark's dead and the world is dying.   25
Horatio, run away and live.
A man could get to the moon with trying,
Or cross the sea in a sieve.

There are spooks in the cellarage. Mothers in the hay.
Worms in the crown. And school's recessed.   30
My girl and her daddy are stinking up the clay.
And I'm very carelessly dressed,

Like my girl and her daddy and my daddy too.
It's hard, Horatio, being quality folks.
I could be as simple and as loyal as you   35
If the egg of our making had a choice of yolks.

I'd choose the smallest yolk of all:
No royalty, no loyalty, but all sincerity.
I'd be no prince and I'd live in no hall.
I'd be born an actor and just play at being me.   40

Then every time I cried, and every time I died,
I'd listen for applause, and I'd damn them all
If they coughed, or whispered, or sat dry-eyed,
Or didn't have me up for a curtain call.

I'd be me, do you see, but all the me I'd be   45
Would be seven turns a week, with the Wednesday matinee.
And both kings, in street clothes, would drink with me.
And I'd have a turn at bouncing in the hay

With the chick that plays Ophelia, and now and then
With the wench that plays the queen to bust a gusset.   50
And the passions we'd tatter, m'lords and gentlemen,
Would be art, were you competent to discuss it.

Ready, Horatio? Let's get that duel done with.
Is it art or life that piles the corpses high?
You've had luck enough: you've had a prince to run with.   55
Come in now and watch me try to die.

My father and my chick and her father are dead.
Rosencrantz and Guildenstern are done for.
And the wench that plays my mother's fast to bed,
But not to the bed she got a son for.   60

Born and done for, dead and married.
I must say again, in general, that I disapprove
Of the lengths to which I feel things have been carried.
And there's still a cord of corpses to remove.

65   To it, Horatio. It's time again to go.
     But is it art or life comes next? And I—
     I've rehearsed it all so often I don't know—
     Am I Hamlet, or *a* Hamlet? When I die

     Will it be in blood, Horatio, or merely in the script?
70   All a-thump or in a nicely practiced fall?
     My shirt is slit already. Will my soul get ripped?
     And shall I rise to judgment or a curtain call?

QUESTIONS FOR DISCUSSION AND WRITING

1. Who is the speaker of the poem: Hamlet or an actor playing Hamlet? Why does it matter?
2. How would you characterize the tone and diction of the poem? How do the tone and diction affect our response to the events being described?
3. In describing Hamlet as "in the wings," the poem makes it sound as if he is an actor in his own life—and that maybe all of us are actors in our lives. How does the poem compare acting and living? To what end?
4. In Ciardi's poem, Hamlet says that, given the choice, he would choose a different role in life. How do his given role and his desired role compare? What are the advantages and disadvantages of each? Would Hamlet *be* Hamlet if he were to take on the new role that he envisions for himself?

LOUIS SIMPSON (1923–   )

Laertes in Paris

   I

   Decades of disaster, a deluge . . .
   Helmets glimpsed in battle on the plain . . .
   Back to Paris for a kindly refuge
   You come, demoralized and drenched again,
5 With your poetic soul like a black dog.

   The old cathedrals, comfortably huge,
   Loom up looking brighter for the rain;
   Around them history swirls like a fog.
   You swear you never mean to leave again
   For Denmark.
10   For here's wine to make you laugh,
   And crowds that shout and hurry out of breath
   To see the Queen, or a two-headed calf,
   And jugglers with a sudden cure for death.

Don't think your sins are a prerogative.
In Paris there is nothing to forgive.   15

II

You love, you're loved: she's pretty and she's clever,
A girl with black hair fitting at your throat
Like a violin: it seems she never
Under your fingers gives out one false note.
You talk the smallest matter three times over.   20
Sure, if you didn't, all the world would love her.

You have her heart, and that's a kind of pledge.
Still, so much sweetness sets your teeth on edge,
And I can see you on the sunny days
Fishing for a siren off the quais.   25
Your argument: beauty's to be admired
Unless you're blind. What then, and not desired?

III

"Dear Sir,
         You have been absent from your classes
At the Sorbonne . . ."   30
                    l'œuvre, l'homme, le milieu
Bray all the cacaphonic little asses.
It all depends upon the point of view.

And then, you've been too credulous in a way,
Read Villon, Ronsard, Du Bellay.   35
Let them send warnings written in such rhyme
To pick no roses—and you'll not waste time.

IV

The day was misty, then at once was spring,
She was a dancing girl, no icicle;
No sooner had she set your young heart beating   40
Than she turned maudlin, cursed and fickle,
And all her tears were running down your face.

You sit like a successful thief, spendthrift,
Letting her jewels trickle through your hands.
You only got what you had eyes to lift,   45
Her sapphire moon, the stars like diamonds.

This life, if you continue, means disgrace.

V

A night sky like the passion of a saint,
That clears to let the sudden moon look through.

50 It seems the very gods come here to paint
And hang their pictures up for public view.

Not like that sullen city in the West
Blazing in a romantic solitude,
Where each American's a self-made artist
55 Who knows his masterpiece will not be viewed.

VI

A letter in the morning . . . it's your father.
You hold it to the light . . . probably words
Of good advice, when you had rather
Have his signature to buy new swords.

60 What's this! It's not your father's hand at all:
The Government . . . eggs must be going bad.
The pages with official seals out-bawl
Their meaning, and you gather

Your father's killed, your sister has gone mad.

VII

65 Each man has his Hamlet, that dark other
Self who is the conscience left behind,
Who should be cherished dearly as a brother
But is a sort of madness of the mind:
A serious dark-dressed entire shape
70 From which no slightest duty can escape.

And every man his Denmark, that dark country,
Familiar, incestuous, to which
He must return, in his turn to stand sentry
Until his blood has filled the Castle ditch,
75 And clear his father's honor with his life,
And take a perfect ignorance to wife.

To Denmark, then. To face the breaking storm,
The ghosts, the duty, the ingratitude.
God knows you wished that thinking man no harm
80 And Paris seemed a lasting interlude.
But that the stream of life may be renewed
One man must die, the other may sleep warm.

QUESTIONS FOR DISCUSSION AND WRITING

1. How does the poem characterize Laertes? How is he spending his time in Paris,
   and how are we meant to respond to his behavior? Think especially about how he

views women and his studies. What does the speaker mean when he says, "This life, if you continue, means disgrace" (stanza IV)? Where in Shakespeare's play do you find hints of similar characterizations of Laertes?

2. Look at the poem's division into stanzas. How do the mood and tone change as we move from one stanza to another?

3. Although Polonius doesn't appear in the poem, we get some sense of his relationship with Laertes. What is it? How similar is it to the father–son relationship that we see in Shakespeare's *Hamlet*?

4. Toward the end of the poem, Laertes gets word of the bad state of affairs in Denmark, and we are invited to compare him and Hamlet: "Each man has his Hamlet, that dark other / Self who is the conscience left behind." What comparisons between the two men do you see? What are the thematic implications—for Simpson and for Shakespeare—of that comparison?

THE ASSOCIATION OF THE BAR OF THE CITY OF NEW YORK

Excerpts from The Elsinore Appeal: People v. Hamlet _____ 1996

In October of 1994, the Association of the Bar of the City of New York staged a mock court hearing at which lawyers held a trial of Hamlet, who was charged with the murders of six people (Polonius, Ophelia, Rosencrantz, Guildenstern, Claudius, and Laertes). As part of their mock proceedings, the prosecution and defense attorneys prepared legal briefs arguing for or against each of the legal charges. We excerpt here some of the arguments from those briefs.

Royal Danish Court of Appeals
for the Elsinore Circuit

State of Denmark,
Appellee,
against
Hamlet, Prince of Denmark,
Appellant

Daniel J. Kornstein
Attorney for Appellant

Introductory Statement

Only rarely—once every four hundred years or so—does a criminal case come along so riddled with interesting error as this one. This is an appeal from six homicide convictions: five for second-degree murder (Laertes, Claudius, Polonius, and Rosencrantz, and Guildenstern), *N.Y. Penal L.* § 125.25, and one for second-degree manslaughter (Ophelia). *N.Y. Penal L.* § 125.15. On reexamining the judgment below, the Court, like one of the gravediggers who testified at trial, should ask, "But is this law?" (*Hamlet*, 5.1.21). The answer is "no," and each conviction should be reversed.

I.

Since Hamlet suffered from diminished mental capacity, such lack of culpability requires reversal on all counts

At trial, appellant proved two defenses involving lack of culpability. First, he showed that at the time of the conduct alleged, as a result of mental disease or defect, he lacked substantial capacity to know or appreciate either (a) the nature and consequences of such conduct, or (b) that such conduct was wrong. *See N.Y. Penal L.* § 30.05. Second, defendant at the very least met the lesser standard of proving that he acted under the influence of extreme emotional disturbance for which there was a reasonable explanation or excuse from the defendant's point of view. *N.Y. Penal L.* § 125.25. Mental disease or defect is a complete defense to all charges, and emotional disturbance is a defense to second-degree murder and a mitigating factor for lesser offenses.

Appellant's mind was so disturbed and delusional that, as many witnesses observed, he talked irrationally, believed he saw and spoke to a ghost, and even explained that it was the ghost who told him to kill Claudius. Long referred to by the press as "the melancholy Dane," appellant, who testified at trial that he was at home recovering from a difficult and stressful year of studying law at Wittenberg University, was thrown further off balance and indeed was grief-stricken and severely depressed by his father's murder, his mother's quick marriage to the murderer—appellant's own uncle—and Ophelia's neglect of appellant's love. His emotional strain caused him to swing wildly between paralytic inaction and manic action. He even became suicidal.

The irrationality of such behavior hardly went unnoticed. Several of the decedents themselves had on a number of occasions called appellant "mad" and his actions "lunacy." Even Hamlet knew he was beset "with a sore distraction" (5.2.228). "What I have done," Hamlet says, referring to his killing of Polonius, "I here proclaim was madness. / Was't Hamlet wronged Laertes? Never Hamlet. / . . . His madness is poor Hamlet's enemy" (5.2.228–37).

In the trial court, the government tried to minimize this evidence by arguing that appellant's madness was feigned, that appellant himself at one point said he intended to put "an antic disposition on" (1.5.181). But for the government to stress that one, isolated utterance is not only to overlook appellant's entire psychological profile, but also to fail to distinguish between Hamlet's feigned madness and his real madness. When Hamlet chose, as in certain obvious encounters with Polonius, Claudius, Gertrude, and others, he brilliantly pretended to be irrational. At other times, also equally obvious, appellant's genuine grief, clinical depression and delusional thinking seriously impaired his mental capacity.

* * *

VI.

Since Hamlet, more victim than wrongdoer, acted properly in bringing a murderer to justice, and fought to resist revenge, the indictment should be dismissed "in the interest of justice"

This peculiar case is, in more senses than one, a tragedy that cries out for dismissal "in the interest of justice." *N.Y. Crim. Proc. L.* § 210.40. In addition to all the obvious mitigating factors surrounding Hamlet's lack of culpability, the history, character, and condition of appellant as himself a victim of a severely dysfunctional family and a disastrous first year at law school, other compelling considerations clearly demonstrate that appellant's conviction, a first offense, results in injustice.

Almost everyone assumes appellant had a duty to seek revenge, that he should have killed Claudius—a murderer, a regicide, and usurper of the throne—much sooner than he did. It is precisely appellant's delay in avenging his father's death that is often considered his basic weakness and that led to disaster. From this perspective, Hamlet did nothing wrong and everything right by killing Claudius. For doing so, for upholding the law, he should be praised not punished.

But this Court should also explore the thesis that Hamlet's delay does him credit as well, that appellant's indecision was an effort not to yield to the passion for revenge. Appellant's inner struggle then becomes an effort to transcend the lower morality of his time and environment and move beyond a rule of force and private vengeance to a modern rule of law. Appellant represents humanity's effort, faced with forces that would drag it backward, to ascend to a higher level. Hamlet reflects this civilizing function of law by struggling to resist the primitive call for revenge.

★ ★ ★

Conclusion

Appellant himself should have the final say on his own appeal. After four long centuries without an appeal, appellant was right to complain bitterly of "the law's delay." (3.1.73). After reviewing the prosecutor's sophistry, we respond, as appellant did to Polonius: "Words. Words. Words." (2.2.193). And, having exposed the "rotten" State's case, we ask of the State's counsel, as did appellant of another lawyer on another occasion: "Where be his quiddits now, his quillets, his cases, his tenures, and his tricks?" (5.1.99–100).

For the reasons given, the conviction below should be reversed.

Respectfully submitted,

DANIEL J. KORNSTEIN
Attorney for Appellant

Royal Danish Court of Appeals
for the Elsinore Circuit

State of Denmark,
Appellee,
against
Hamlet, formerly Prince of Denmark,
Appellant

Stephen Gillers
Attorney for Appellee

OF COUNSEL: Hayley Baruk, Davida H. Isaacs, Christopher M. Locke, Linda A. Shashoua, Jonathan Wayne (admitted under the Elsinore Student Practice Rule)

Introductory Statement

Hamlet, a serial killer, was unable to persuade the jury that madness or justification should excuse his bloody deeds. His own words betray his claim of madness. His justification defense fails on the facts. His immunity arguments are wrong on the law. His life sentence should be affirmed.

I.

The jury properly concluded that Hamlet did not meet his burden of proving insanity

Hamlet would have this Court recognize an entirely new defense to homicide: The Abused Prince Syndrome. It should not.

Penal Law § 40.15 gave Hamlet an "affirmative defense" if he suffered from a "mental disease or defect" that caused him to lack "substantial capacity to know or appreciate either [1] the nature and consequences of [his] conduct; or [2] that such conduct was wrong." The jury did not believe Hamlet or his paid experts.

Not only did Hamlet tell his friends that "I perchance hereafter shall think meet to put an antic disposition on" (1.5.180–81), he did so, and turned it on and off as it suited him.

When the king, queen, and others arrived for *The Murder of Gonzago,* Hamlet told Horatio, with whom he had been conversing in blank verse, "I must be idle. Get you a place." (3.2.89–90). Hamlet then "maneuvers a quick change into prose," as Harry Levin testified to the jury. (The Question of Hamlet, at 116.) Similar abrupt shifts occur when Hamlet encounters Ophelia (3.1.94) and when Osric approaches Hamlet and Horatio (5.2.82). These sudden changes from poetry to prose—accompanied by changes in the clarity of his language—prove that Hamlet did indeed "put an antic disposition on" as he predicted he would.

Following *The Murder of Gonzago,* when the queen exclaimed that Hamlet was suffering from "ecstasy" the defendant replied: "It is not madness / That I have uttered. Bring me to the test, And I the matter will reword which madness / Would gambol from." (3.4.148–51). Moments later, the defendant cautioned his mother against letting Claudius know "That I essentially am not in madness, But mad in craft." (3.4.194–95).

Hamlet's "madness" appeared only in the presence of persons he distrusted (the king, Rosencrantz and Guildenstern, Ophelia, Polonius). Even then, as others noted, "[t]hough this be madness, yet there is method in't" (Polonius) (2.2.205–06). Guildenstern recognized Hamlet's behavior as a "crafty madness" that "keeps [him] aloof." (3.1.8.). Hamlet was in fact quite reasonable in conversation with his schoolmates until he asked "Were you not sent for?" (2.2.275) and realized they were.

Hamlet's "antic disposition" protected him from Claudius while he tried to discover whether the "spirit that I have seen" is "the devil," who "hath power / T'assume a pleasing shape." (2.2.600–601). Harry Levin testified that Hamlet was "clearly thoughtsick rather than brainsick" (p. 113), and explained Hamlet's time-buying strategy as having successfully "forced" Claudius "against his habit, to continue more or less in Hamlet's medium." (p. 117).

Like the jury, Claudius also doubted Hamlet's madness: "Nor what he spake, though it lack'd form a little, / Was not like madness. There's something in his soul /

O'er which his melancholy sits on brood, / And I do not doubt the hatch and the disclose / Will be some danger." (3.1.166–70). Claudius used each of Polonius and Ophelia, and Rosencrantz and Guildenstern, to "pluck out the heart of [Hamlet's] mystery" (3.2.364–65), but to no avail.

Meanwhile, Hamlet crafted a brilliant and rational strategy to "catch the conscience of the King" (2.2.606) with evidence of his demeanor during *The Murder of Gonzago*. The jury could well have found that a man who could devise this plan and would not act on the Ghost's directive until he could ascertain its authenticity ("I'll have grounds / More relative than this") (2.2.604–5) knew that murder is wrong.

The jury rejected Hamlet's self-serving statement to Laertes. As the State argued, law student Hamlet was already planning his defense. He knew that his speech would be reported in *The Elsinore Bugle,* which was covering the fencing match, and hoped the pretrial publicity would influence the jury. It didn't. Hamlet's excuse to Laertes was "disingenuous" (Levin at 113). Hamlet's own expert, Samuel Johnson, admitted the "falsehood" of this apology on cross-examination and wished that "Hamlet had made some other defence." *The Plays of William Shakespeare* (1775) (vol. 8).

What we have said here applies equally well to Hamlet's effort to avoid responsibility under Penal Law § 125.25 (extreme emotional disturbance), an affirmative defense that the jury rejected and which is not satisfied by evidence of "stress." *People v. LaSalle,* 105 A.D.2d 756, 481 N.Y.S.2d 408 (2d Dept. 1984) (stress not amounting to loss of control inadequate). We discuss this issue further at Point III.

Appellant argues that he must be insane because he saw and conversed with the ghost of King Hamlet. This Court need not decide whether the ghost is real, although we can't help adding that three others also saw it, on three separate evenings, that they heard it order them to "swear" an oath, and that the ghost's specific information about King Hamlet's death turned out to be correct. Be that as it may, having seen and talked to the ghost, Hamlet rationally and, as his counsel admitted in summation, in a "lawyerly" fashion (Daniel Kornstein, *Kill All the Lawyers? Shakespeare's Legal Appeal* at 97), pursued "grounds / More relative than this" before murdering Claudius. Even on appeal, contradicting himself, the defendant takes "credit" for this caution, citing its "civilizing dimension," while also proclaiming his insanity. See Point VI infra.

* * *

VI.

This Court should not dismiss the indictment "in the interest of justice," for a serial killer who shows no contrition

What we have so far shown amply demonstrates how monstrous it would be for this Court to relieve the defendant of his criminal responsibility in the interest of justice. We pause only to note the blatant contradiction between Hamlet's assertion under this Point—that his "delay does him credit" and "reflects [the] civilizing function of law"—with his earlier argument that he was suffering from a "mental disease or defect" that rendered him unable to know that his acts were wrong.

Hamlet's "interest of justice" defense is the only nonjurisdictional defense he offers for his murder of Claudius. Yet when Hamlet slew Claudius, with a "point" he knew was "envenomed" (5.2.324), he could safely have retreated and won vindication in law. He had proof of Claudius's scheme on his own life—the king's letter to the

English monarch. Because, as next explained, Denmark is an elective monarchy, this letter could have been used to depose Claudius. Hamlet may or may not have been able to convince a law court that Claudius killed his father, based on the demeanor evidence at *The Murder of Gonzago,* but Laertes's dying declaration, Fed.R.Ev. 804(b)(2) (5.2.316–23), together with the physical evidence, would have established Claudius's legal guilt for the death of Gertrude.

★ ★ ★

Conclusion

The defendant's homicides have resulted in the deaths of six people, including an entire family of three. The convictions should be affirmed.

Respectfully submitted,

STEPHEN GILLERS
Attorney for Appellee

OF COUNSEL: Hayley Baruk, Davida H. Isaacs, Christopher M. Locke, Linda A. Shashoua, Jonathan Wayne (admitted under the Elsinore Student Practice Rule)

**Royal Danish Court of Appeals
for the Elsinore Circuit**

**State of Denmark,
Appellee,**
against
**Hamlet, Prince (and Future King) of Denmark,
Appellant**

**Daniel J. Kornstein
Attorney for Appellant**

The government's brief is full of legalistic "quiddits" (*i.e.,* subtleties) and "quillets" (*i.e.,* evasions) (5.1.99–100). It has the novel, odd, and revisionist distinction of quickly dispatching one of the greatest heroes in Western civilization, a most thoughtful figure, an "idealist" with exquisite "moral" sensibility (A. C. Bradley, *Shakespearean Tragedy* 111–13 (Penguin 1991)), as no more than a remorseless, psychopathic "serial killer." The government's brief equates appellant with Ted Bundy. But the equation is false, the government's quillets easily exposed, and a sinister abuse of legal process unmasked.

Quillet No. 1: Although the government scoffs at appellant's argument based on lack of mental capacity, Hamlet's "madness is surely the most interesting and most challenging" aspect of this case, as one expert testified. K. R. Eissler, *Discourse on Hamlet and HAMLET* 400 (1971). But expert testimony can be found to support either side of the question. An expert cited by the government has testified, "Hamlet's state of mind is one of those questions upon which all of the doctors have disagreed." Harry Levin, *The Question of Hamlet* 111 (1959).

The record itself, rather than the divided experts' testimony, is a better guide. While stressing appellant's sometimes pretended madness, the government turns a blind eye to all proof of Hamlet's genuine emotional disturbance. The evidence will simply not support a finding that appellant was *always* faking his unbalanced mental state. Nor does it help the government to imply that talking ghosts, like UFOs, are real if seen by more than one person. The government ignores the dual character of appellant's madness, one part feigned, one part real.

What the government sarcastically dubs the "Abused Prince Syndrome" was a mental condition no different from the battered-wife syndrome, post-traumatic stress disorder, or the child-abuse accommodation syndrome in that, in conjunction with mental illness, it gave rise to terrible acts of violence for which Hamlet was not responsible.

★ ★ ★

Quillet No. 6: The government's opposition to dismissal "in the interest of justice" should shock the Court's conscience. As one expert testified, "Nearly all readers, commentators, and critics are agreed in thinking that it was Hamlet's duty to kill." Harold Goddard, *The Meaning of Shakespeare* 333 (1951). Indeed, two of the government's own experts—A. C. Bradley and John Dover Wilson—testified that Hamlet had such a "sacred duty." It is paradoxical to punish someone for carrying out what "nearly all" think was a sacred duty.

★ ★ ★

Conclusion

The government's argument against sovereign immunity unwittingly reveals the sinister motive behind this prosecution. It is a common story of the corrupting influence of power. Fortinbras, having seized the throne in Denmark without any lawful claim, now refuses to step down. His attorney general seeks to keep Prince Hamlet, Fortinbras's only rival, in prison for life because Hamlet is "loved" by the "multitude" (4.3.4 and 4.7.19) and poses a genuine threat to Fortinbras's naked power grab. *Cf.* Richard III and the Princes in the Tower; Elizabeth I and Mary Queen of Scots.

We appeal to the integrity and the independence of this Court not to be cowed by the trappings of authority as represented by the illegal Fortinbras regime, but to do the right thing. *Cf. United States v. Nixon,* 418 U.S. 683 (1974); *N.Y. Times Co. v. United States,* 403 U.S. 713 (1971).

For the reasons given, the conviction below should be reversed.

Respectfully submitted,

DANIEL J. KORNSTEIN
Attorney for Appellant

QUESTIONS FOR DISCUSSION AND WRITING

1. Are you more convinced by the defense attorney's arguments or the prosecuting attorney's arguments? Why? Which of the two attorneys seems to have the better understanding of the facts of Shakespeare's play? Which seems to understand Hamlet's character better?

2. In arguing *People v. Hamlet,* both attorneys rely not only on Shakespeare's play but also on their understanding of modern American law. To what extent do their assumptions and attitudes about the law, about human behavior, and about morality differ from those that Shakespeare was conveying in *Hamlet?*

LAURA BOHANNAN
Shakespeare in the Bush _____ 1966

Just before I left Oxford for the Tiv in West Africa, conversation turned to the season at Stratford. "You Americans," said a friend, "often have difficulty with Shakespeare. He was, after all, a very English poet, and one can easily misinterpret the universal by misunderstanding the particular."

I protested that human nature is pretty much the same the whole world over; at least the general plot and motivation of the greater tragedies would always be clear—everywhere—although some details of custom might have to be explained and difficulties of translation might produce other slight changes. To end an argument we could not conclude, my friend gave me a copy of *Hamlet* to study in the African bush: it would, he hoped, lift my mind above its primitive surroundings, and possibly I might, by prolonged meditation, achieve the grace of correct interpretation.

It was my second field trip to that African tribe, and I thought myself ready to live in one of its remote sections—an area difficult to cross even on foot. I eventually settled on the hillock of a very knowledgeable old man, the head of a homestead of some hundred and forty people, all of whom were either his close relatives or their wives and children. Like the other elders of the vicinity, the old man spent most of his time performing ceremonies seldom seen these days in the more accessible parts of the tribe. I was delighted. Soon there would be three months of enforced isolation and leisure, between the harvest that takes place just before the rising of the swamps and the clearing of new farms when the water goes down. Then, I thought, they would have even more time to perform ceremonies and explain them to me.

I was quite mistaken. Most of the ceremonies demanded the presence of elders from several homesteads. As the swamps rose, the old men found it too difficult to walk from one homestead to the next, and the ceremonies gradually ceased. As the swamps rose even higher, all activities but one came to an end. The women brewed beer from maize and millet. Men, women, and children sat on their hillocks and drank it.

People began to drink at dawn. By midmorning the whole homestead was singing, dancing, and drumming. When it rained, people had to sit inside their huts: there they drank and sang or they drank and told stories. In any case, by noon or before, I either had to join the party or retire to my own hut and my books. "One does not discuss serious matters when there is beer. Come, drink with us." Since I lacked their capacity for the thick native beer, I spent more and more time with *Hamlet.* Before the end of the second month, grace descended on me. I was quite sure that *Hamlet* had only one possible interpretation, and that one universally obvious.

Early every morning, in the hope of having some serious talk before the beer party, I used to call on the old man at his reception hut—a circle of posts supporting a thatched roof above a low mud wall to keep out wind and rain. One day I crawled through the low doorway and found most of the men of the homestead sitting huddled in their ragged cloths on stools, low plank beds, and reclining chairs, warming themselves against the chill of the rain around a smoky fire. In the center were three pots of beer. The party had started.

The old man greeted me cordially. "Sit down and drink." I accepted a large calabash[1] full of beer, poured some into a small drinking gourd, and tossed it down. Then I poured some more into the same gourd for the man second in seniority to my host before I handed my calabash over to a young man for further distribution. Important people shouldn't ladle beer themselves.

"It is better like this," the old man said, looking at me approvingly and plucking at the thatch that had caught in my hair. "You should sit and drink with us more often. Your servants tell me that when you are not with us, you sit inside your hut looking at a paper."

The old man was acquainted with four kinds of "papers": tax receipts, bride price receipts, court fee receipts, and letters. The messenger who brought him letters from the chief used them mainly as a badge of office, for he always knew what was in them and told the old man. Personal letters for the few who had relatives in the government or mission stations were kept until someone went to a large market where there was a letter writer and reader. Since my arrival, letters were brought to me to be read. A few men also brought me bride price receipts, privately, with requests to change the figures to a higher sum. I found moral arguments were of no avail, since in-laws are fair game, and the technical hazards of forgery difficult to explain to an illiterate people. I did not wish them to think me silly enough to look at any such papers for days on end, and I hastily explained that my "paper" was one of the "things of long ago" of my country.

"Ah," said the old man. "Tell us."

I protested that I was not a storyteller. Storytelling is a skilled art among them; their standards are high, and the audiences critical—and vocal in their criticism. I protested in vain. This morning they wanted to hear a story while they drank. They threatened to tell me no more stories until I told them one of mine. Finally, the old man promised that no one would criticize my style "for we know you are struggling with our language." "But," put in one of the elders, "you must explain what we do not understand, as we do when we tell you our stories." Realizing that here was my chance to prove *Hamlet* universally intelligible, I agreed.

The old man handed me some more beer to help me on with my storytelling. Men filled their long wooden pipes and knocked coals from the fire to place in the pipe bowls; then, puffing contentedly, they sat back to listen. I began in the proper style, "Not yesterday, not yesterday, but long ago, a thing occurred. One night three men were keeping watch outside the homestead of the great chief, when suddenly they saw the former chief approach them."

"Why was he no longer their chief?"

"He was dead," I explained. "That is why they were troubled and afraid when they saw him."

"Impossible," began one of the elders, handing his pipe on to his neighbor, who interrupted, "Of course it wasn't the dead chief. It was an omen sent by a witch. Go on."

---

[1]calabash—a gourd used as a bowl or pitcher.

Slightly shaken, I continued. "One of these three was a man who knew things"—the closest translation for scholar, but unfortunately it also meant witch. The second elder looked triumphantly at the first. "So he spoke to the dead chief saying, 'Tell us what we must do so you may rest in your grave,' but the dead chief did not answer. He vanished, and they could see him no more. Then the man who knew things—his name was Horatio—said this event was the affair of the dead chief's son, Hamlet."

There was a general shaking of heads round the circle. "Had the dead chief no living brothers? Or was this son the chief?"

"No," I replied. "That is, he had one living brother who became the chief when the elder brother died."

The old man muttered: such omens were matters for chiefs and elders, not for youngsters; no good could come of going behind a chief's back; clearly Horatio was not a man who knew things.

"Yes, he was," I insisted, shooing a chicken away from my beer. "In our country the son is next to the father. The dead chief's younger brother had become the great chief. He had also married his elder brother's widow only about a month after the funeral."

"He did well," the old man beamed and announced to the others, "I told you that if we knew more about Europeans, we would find they really were very like us. In our country also," he added to me, "the younger brother marries the elder brother's widow and becomes the father of his children. Now, if your uncle, who married your widowed mother, is your father's full brother, then he will be a real father to you. Did Hamlet's father and uncle have one mother?"

His question barely penetrated my mind; I was too upset and thrown too far off balance by having one of the most important elements of *Hamlet* knocked straight out of the picture. Rather uncertainly I said that I thought they had the same mother, but I wasn't sure—the story didn't say. The old man told me severely that these genealogical details made all the difference and that when I got home I must ask the elders about it. He shouted out the door to one of his younger wives to bring his goatskin bag.

Determined to save what I could of the mother motif, I took a deep breath and began again. "The son Hamlet was very sad because his mother had married again so quickly. There was no need for her to do so, and it is our custom for a widow not to go to her next husband until she has mourned for two years."

"Two years is too long," objected the wife, who had appeared with the old man's battered goatskin bag. "Who will hoe your farms for you while you have no husband?"

"Hamlet," I retorted without thinking, "was old enough to hoe his mother's farms himself. There was no need for her to remarry." No one looked convinced. I gave up. "His mother and the great chief told Hamlet not to be sad, for the great chief himself would be a father to Hamlet. Furthermore, Hamlet would be the next chief: therefore he must stay to learn the things of a chief. Hamlet agreed to remain, and all the rest went off to drink beer."

While I paused, perplexed at how to render Hamlet's disgusted soliloquy to an audience convinced that Claudius and Gertrude had behaved in the best possible manner, one of the younger men asked me who had married the other wives of the dead chief.

"He had no other wives," I told him.

"But a chief must have many wives! How else can he brew beer and prepare food for all his guests?"

I said firmly that in our country even chiefs had only one wife, that they had servants to do their work, and that they paid them from tax money.

It was better, they returned, for a chief to have many wives and sons who would help him hoe his farms and feed his people; then everyone loved the chief who gave much and took nothing—taxes were a bad thing.

I agreed with the last comment, but for the rest fell back on their favorite way of fobbing off my questions: "That is the way it is done, so that is how we do it."

I decided to skip the soliloquy. Even if Claudius was here thought quite right to marry his brother's widow, there remained the poison motif, and I knew they would disapprove of fratricide. More hopefully I resumed, "That night Hamlet kept watch with the three who had seen his dead father. The dead chief again appeared, and although the others were afraid, Hamlet followed his dead father off to one side. When they were alone, Hamlet's dead father spoke."

"Omens can't talk!" The old man was emphatic.

"Hamlet's dead father wasn't an omen. Seeing him might have been an omen, but he was not." My audience looked as confused as I sounded. "It *was* Hamlet's dead father. It was a thing we call a 'ghost.'" I had to use the English word, for unlike many of the neighboring tribes, these people didn't believe in the survival after death of any individuating part of the personality.

"What is a 'ghost'? An omen?"

"No, a 'ghost' is someone who is dead but who walks around and can talk, and people can hear him and see him but not touch him."

They objected. "One can touch zombis."

"No, no! It was not a dead body the witches had animated to sacrifice and eat. No one else made Hamlet's dead father walk. He did it himself."

"Dead men can't walk," protested my audience as one man.

I was quite willing to compromise. "A 'ghost' is the dead man's shadow."

But again they objected. "Dead men cast no shadows."

"They do in my country," I snapped.

The old man quelled the babble of disbelief that arose immediately and told me with that insincere, but courteous, agreement one extends to the fancies of the young, ignorant, and superstitious, "No doubt in your country the dead can also walk without being zombis." From the depths of his bag he produced a withered fragment of kola nut, bit off one end to show it wasn't poisoned, and handed me the rest as a peace offering.

"Anyhow," I resumed, "Hamlet's dead father said that his own brother, the one who became chief, had poisoned him. He wanted Hamlet to avenge him. Hamlet believed this in his heart, for he did not like his father's brother." I took another swallow of beer. "In the country of the great chief, living in the same homestead, for it was a very large one, was an important elder who was often with the chief to advise and help him. His name was Polonius. Hamlet was courting his daughter, but her father and her brother . . . [I cast hastily about for some tribal analogy] warned her not to let Hamlet visit her when she was alone on her farm, for he would be a great chief and so could not marry her."

"Why not?" asked the wife, who had settled down on the edge of the old man's chair. He frowned at her for asking stupid questions and growled, "They lived in the same homestead."

"That was not the reason," I informed them. "Polonius was a stranger who lived in the homestead because he helped the chief, not because he was a relative."

"Then why couldn't Hamlet marry her?"

"He could have," I explained, "but Polonius didn't think he would. After all, Hamlet was a man of great importance who ought to marry a chief's daughter, for in his country a man could have only one wife. Polonius was afraid that if Hamlet made love to his daughter, then no one else would give a high price for her."

"That might be true," remarked one of the shrewder elders, "but a chief's son would give his mistress's father enough presents and patronage to more than make up the difference. Polonius sounds like a fool to me."

"Many people think he was," I agreed. "Meanwhile Polonius sent his son Laertes off to Paris to learn the things of that country, for it was the homestead of a very great chief indeed. Because he was afraid that Laertes might waste a lot of money on beer and women and gambling, or get into trouble by fighting, he sent one of his servants to Paris secretly, to spy out what Laertes was doing. One day Hamlet came upon Polonius's daughter Ophelia. He behaved so oddly he frightened her. Indeed"—I was fumbling for words to express the dubious quality of Hamlet's madness—"the chief and many others had also noticed that when Hamlet talked one could understand the words but not what they meant. Many people thought that he had become mad." My audience suddenly became much more attentive. "The great chief wanted to know what was wrong with Hamlet, so he sent for two of Hamlet's age mates [school friends would have taken long explanation] to talk to Hamlet and find out what troubled his heart. Hamlet, seeing that they had been bribed by the chief to betray him, told them nothing. Polonius, however, insisted that Hamlet was mad because he had been forbidden to see Ophelia, whom he loved."

"Why," inquired a bewildered voice, "should anyone bewitch Hamlet on that account?"

"Bewitch him?"

"Yes, only witchcraft can make anyone mad, unless, of course, one sees the beings that lurk in the forest."

I stopped being a storyteller, took out my notebook and demanded to be told more about these two causes of madness. Even while they spoke and I jotted notes, I tried to calculate the effect of this new factor on the plot. Hamlet had not been exposed to the beings that lurk in the forests. Only his relatives in the male line could bewitch him. Barring relatives not mentioned by Shakespeare, it had to be Claudius who was attempting to harm him. And, of course, it was.

For the moment I staved off questions by saying that the great chief also refused to believe that Hamlet was mad for the love of Ophelia and nothing else. "He was sure that something much more important was troubling Hamlet's heart."

"Now Hamlet's age mates," I continued, "had brought with them a famous storyteller. Hamlet decided to have this man tell the chief and all his homestead a story about a man who had poisoned his brother because he desired his brother's wife and wished to be chief himself. Hamlet was sure the great chief could not hear the story without making a sign if he was indeed guilty, and then he would discover whether his dead father had told him the truth."

The old man interrupted, with deep cunning, "Why should a father lie to his son?" he asked.

I hedged: "Hamlet wasn't sure that it really was his dead father." It was impossible to say anything, in that language, about devil-inspired visions.

"You mean," he said, "it actually was an omen, and he knew witches sometimes send false ones. Hamlet was a fool not to go to one skilled in reading omens and divining the truth in the first place. A man-who-sees-the-truth could have told him how his father died, if he really had been poisoned, and if there was witchcraft in it; then Hamlet could have called the elders to settle the matter."

The shrewd elder ventured to disagree. "Because his father's brother was a great chief, one-who-sees-the-truth might therefore have been afraid to tell it. I think it was for that reason that a friend of Hamlet's father—a witch and an elder—sent an omen so his friend's son would know. Was the omen true?"

"Yes," I said, abandoning ghosts and the devil; a witch-sent omen it would have to be. "It was true, for when the storyteller was telling his tale before all the homestead, the great chief rose in fear. Afraid that Hamlet knew his secret he planned to have him killed."

The stage set of the next bit presented some difficulties of translation. I began cautiously. "The great chief told Hamlet's mother to find out from her son what he knew. But because a woman's children are always first in her heart, he had the important elder Polonius hide behind a cloth that hung against the wall of Hamlet's mother's sleeping hut. Hamlet started to scold his mother for what she had done."

There was a shocked murmur from everyone. A man should never scold his mother.

"She called out in fear, and Polonius moved behind the cloth. Shouting, 'A rat!' Hamlet took his machete and slashed through the cloth." I paused for dramatic effect. "He had killed Polonius!"

The old men looked at each other in supreme disgust. "That Polonius truly was a fool and a man who knew nothing! What child would not know enough to shout, 'It's me!'" With a pang, I remembered that these people are ardent hunters, always armed with bow, arrow, and machete; at the first rustle in the grass an arrow is aimed and ready, and the hunter shouts "Game!" If no human voice answers immediately, the arrow speeds on its way. Like a good hunter Hamlet had shouted, "A rat!"

I rushed in to save Polonius's reputation. "Polonius did speak. Hamlet heard him. But he thought it was the chief and wished to kill him to avenge his father. He had meant to kill him earlier that evening. . . ." I broke down, unable to describe to these pagans, who had no belief in individual afterlife, the difference between dying at one's prayers and dying "unhousell'd, disappointed, unaneled."[2]

This time I had shocked my audience seriously. "For a man to raise his hand against his father's brother and the one who has become his father—that is a terrible thing. The elders ought to let such a man be bewitched."

I nibbled at my kola nut in some perplexity, then pointed out that after all the man had killed Hamlet's father.

"No," pronounced the old man, speaking less to me than to the young men sitting behind the elders. "If your father's brother has killed your father, you must appeal to your father's age mates; *they* may avenge him. No man may use violence against his

___

[2] unhousell'd, disappointed, unaneled—without last rites.

senior relatives." Another thought struck him. "But if his father's brother had indeed been wicked enough to bewitch Hamlet and make him mad that would be a good story indeed, for it would be his fault that Hamlet, being mad, no longer had any sense and thus was ready to kill his father's brother."

There was a murmur of applause. *Hamlet* was again a good story to them, but it no longer seemed quite the same story to me. As I thought over the coming complications of plot and motive, I lost courage and decided to skim over dangerous ground quickly.

"The great chief," I went on, "was not sorry that Hamlet had killed Polonius. It gave him a reason to send Hamlet away, with his two treacherous age mates, with letters to a chief of a far country, saying that Hamlet should be killed. But Hamlet changed the writing on their papers, so that the chief killed his age mates instead." I encountered a reproachful glare from one of the men whom I had told undetectable forgery was not merely immoral but beyond human skill. I looked the other way.

"Before Hamlet could return, Laertes came back for his father's funeral. The great chief told him Hamlet had killed Polonius. Laertes swore to kill Hamlet because of this, and because his sister Ophelia, hearing her father had been killed by the man she loved, went mad and drowned in the river."

"Have you already forgotten what we told you?" The old man was reproachful. "One cannot take vengeance on a madman; Hamlet killed Polonius in his madness. As for the girl, she not only went mad, she was drowned. Only witches can make people drown. Water itself can't hurt anything. It is merely something one drinks and bathes in."

I began to get cross. "If you don't like the story, I'll stop."

The old man made soothing noises and himself poured me some more beer. "You tell the story well, and we are listening. But it is clear that the elders of your country have never told you what the story really means. No, don't interrupt! We believe you when you say your marriage customs are different, or your clothes and weapons. But people are the same everywhere; therefore, there are always witches and it is we, the elders, who know how witches work. We told you it was the great chief who wished to kill Hamlet, and now your own words have proved us right. Who were Ophelia's male relatives?"

"There were only her father and her brother." Hamlet was clearly out of my hands.

"There must have been many more; this also you must ask of your elders when you get back to your country. From what you tell us, since Polonius was dead, it must have been Laertes who killed Ophelia, although I do not see the reason for it."

We had emptied one pot of beer, and the old men argued the point with slightly tipsy interest. Finally one of them demanded of me, "What did the servant of Polonius say on his return?"

With difficulty I recollected Reynaldo and his mission. "I don't think he did return before Polonius was killed."

"Listen," said the elder, "and I will tell you how it was and how your story will go, then you may tell me if I am right. Polonius knew his son would get into trouble, and so he did. He had many fines to pay for fighting, and debts from gambling. But he had only two ways of getting money quickly. One was to marry off his sister at once, but it is difficult to find a man who will marry a woman desired by the son of a chief. For if the chief's heir commits adultery with your wife, what can you do? Only a fool calls a case against a man who will someday be his judge. Therefore Laertes had to take the second way: he killed his sister by witchcraft, drowning her so he could secretly sell her body to the witches."

I raised an objection. "They found her body and buried it. Indeed, Laertes jumped into the grave to see his sister once more—so, you see, the body was truly there. Hamlet, who had just come back, jumped in after him."

"What did I tell you?" The elder appealed to the others. "Laertes was up to no good with his sister's body. Hamlet prevented him, because the chief's heir, like a chief, does not wish any other man to grow rich and powerful. Laertes would be angry, because he would have killed his sister without benefit to himself. In our country he would try to kill Hamlet for that reason. Is this not what happened?"

"More or less," I admitted. "When the great chief found Hamlet was still alive, he encouraged Laertes to try to kill Hamlet and arranged a fight with machetes between them. In the fight both the young men were wounded to death. Hamlet's mother drank the poisoned beer that the chief meant for Hamlet in case he won the fight. When he saw his mother die of poison, Hamlet, dying, managed to kill his father's brother with his machete."

"You see, I was right!" exclaimed the elder.

"That was a very good story," added the old man, "and you told it with very few mistakes. There was just one more error, at the very end. The poison Hamlet's mother drank was obviously meant for the survivor of the fight, whichever it was. If Laertes had won, the great chief would have poisoned him, for no one would know that he arranged Hamlet's death. Then, too, he need not fear Laertes' witchcraft; it takes a strong heart to kill one's only sister by witchcraft.

"Sometime," concluded the old man, gathering his ragged toga about him, "you must tell us some more stories of your country. We, who are elders, will instruct you in their true meaning, so that when you return to your own land your elders will see that you have not been sitting in the bush, but among those who know things and who have taught you wisdom."

QUESTIONS FOR DISCUSSION AND WRITING

1. In telling the story of *Hamlet* to the tribespeople in the bush, Bohannan finds herself having to make many changes. The story becomes as much their telling as hers and Shakespeare's. What gets changed in this new telling? How do the changes affect the play's characterizations and themes?

2. Bohannan starts her essay assuming that *Hamlet* is a universal story, one whose basic meaning will be understood by people of differing cultures. How much does her experience undercut that assumption? Are the changes made to the story simply a way of translating it into different cultural terms—or do the changes alter the basic meanings and values of the play?

3. If you know a non-Western culture well, tell the story of *Hamlet* as you would tell it to people from that culture. How similar are Shakespeare's assumptions about vengeance, parent–child relationships, ghosts, and spirituality to the assumptions

your new audience would hold? How would you have to alter the story to make it comprehensible to them?

4. In some ways all of us now reading (or watching) the play are in a position analogous to the position of the tribespeople: Shakespeare's culture is not our own. In retelling the story of *Hamlet* to a modern audience, what changes would you have to make? What might get lost in the translation from one temporal culture to another?

ADRIENNE MILLER and ANDREW GOLDBLATT

"Defining the Hamlet Syndrome," from The Hamlet Syndrome: Overthinkers Who Underachieve   1989

The Hamlet Syndrome is characterized by an inability to decide between the heart and the dollar. To Hamlet, the heart represents principle, conscience, consideration for others—all those intangibles that make someone morally good; the dollar represents wealth, power, and inclusion in the mainstream—the standards by which we measure ourselves against others. Hamlets are bright, sensitive, well-educated, middle-class young people aged twenty-one to forty. More than anything else they want to preserve their purity of heart, but they also feel the need to succeed and earn lots of money and esteem. Torn between their dual desires, they can't decide what to do, and so they do nothing. While inaction effectively preserves their purity of heart, it puts the dollar further and further out of reach. As the years roll by and Hamlets grow tired of making just enough money to survive, their bitterness toward themselves and the system increases, leading to frustration, cynicism, and a dramatic loss of self-esteem.

Almost every Hamlet has at least one personality trait that predisposes him to the syndrome. He may never have developed the taste for risk required for success in a free market economy. He may have been humiliated by defeat once too often to engage in competition. He may have little patience for details or knotty problems. He may lack self-confidence. He may hate work. He may be a procrastinator, figuring that he'll get around to a career sometime in the future. Or he may be passive by nature, counting himself a victim of forces beyond his control. Whatever the personality trait, it provides psychological underpinning for the Hamlet Syndrome and makes the heart-or-dollar conflict more than just a philosophical conundrum.

The Hamlet Syndrome is named after William Shakespeare's most famous character. Hamlet, the prince of Denmark, is known to all as the speaker of the immortal line "To be or not to be." He's witty, well-educated, from one of the best families in Europe—and, for a thirty-year-old, pathetically indecisive. When an uncle murders Hamlet's father and marries Hamlet's mother, in the process usurping Hamlet's throne, the brooding prince simply *has* to act. After all, if that's no cause for action, nothing is! Yet Hamlet protests, procrastinates, and intellectually perambulates through the entire play before he finally makes the move he was supposed to make at the beginning. For all his insight he simply cannot take control, and so over the years his name has become synonymous with indecision and inaction.

QUESTIONS FOR DISCUSSION AND WRITING

1. Miller and Goldblatt argue that Hamlets are "characterized by an inability to decide between the heart and the dollar." If that is the case for Shakespeare's Hamlet, what is his heart telling him to do, and how does the dollar figure into the play?

2. In the second paragraph of the excerpt, Miller and Goldblatt list the personality traits characteristic of Hamlets. Which of those traits would you argue characterize Shakespeare's Hamlet, and why?

3. Would you agree with Miller and Goldblatt that at the end of the play Hamlet "finally makes the move he was supposed to make at the beginning"? How would we have responded differently to Hamlet had he moved more quickly?

MARY PIPHER (1947–   )

From Reviving Ophelia _____ *1994*

The story of Ophelia, from Shakespeare's *Hamlet,* shows the destructive forces that affect young women. As a girl, Ophelia is happy and free, but with adolescence she loses herself. When she falls in love with Hamlet, she lives only for his approval. She has no inner direction; rather she struggles to meet the demands of Hamlet and her father. Her value is determined utterly by their approval. Ophelia is torn apart by her efforts to please. When Hamlet spurns her because she is an obedient daughter, she goes mad with grief. Dressed in elegant clothes that weigh her down, she drowns in a stream filled with flowers.

Girls know they are losing themselves. One girl said, "Everything good in me died in junior high." Wholeness is shattered by the chaos of adolescence. Girls become fragmented, their selves split into mysterious contradictions. They are sensitive and tenderhearted, mean and competitive, superficial and idealistic. They are confident in the morning and overwhelmed with anxiety by nightfall. They rush through their days with wild energy and then collapse into lethargy. They try on new roles every week—this week the good student, next week the delinquent and the next, the artist. And they expect their families to keep up with these changes.

QUESTIONS FOR DISCUSSION AND WRITING

1. Where do you find evidence in Shakespeare's play to support Pipher's claim that Ophelia loses her sense of identity and joy when she falls in love with Hamlet?

2. Would you agree with Pipher that Hamlet spurns Ophelia "because she is an obedient daughter"?

3. In her book, Pipher argues that young adolescent women are much like Ophelia. Would you agree? Do you think the characteristics Pipher identifies are more

likely to be the characteristics of young women than of young men? Why? Are young adolescent men very much like Hamlet?

ERNEST JONES (1879–1958)

Tragedy and the Mind of the Infant _____ 1949

As a child Hamlet had experienced the warmest affection for his mother, and this, as is always so, had contained elements of a disguised erotic quality, still more so in infancy. The presence of two traits in the Queen's character accord with this assumption, namely her markedly sensual nature and her passionate fondness for her son. The former is indicated in too many places in the play to need specific reference, and is generally recognized. The latter is also manifest: Claudius says, for instance (79), "The Queen his mother lives almost by his looks." Nevertheless Hamlet appears to have with more or less success weaned himself from her and to have fallen in love with Ophelia. The precise nature of his original feeling for Ophelia is a little obscure. We may assume that at least in part it was composed of a normal love for a prospective bride, though the extravagance of the language used (the passionate need for absolute certainty, etc.) suggests a somewhat morbid frame of mind. There are indications that even here the influence of the old attraction for the mother is still exerting itself. Although some writers, following Goethe, see in Ophelia many traits of resemblance to the Queen, perhaps just as striking are the traits contrasting with those of the Queen. Whatever truths there may be in the many German conceptions of Ophelia as a sensual wanton . . . still the very fact that it needed what Goethe happily called the "innocence of insanity" to reveal the presence of any such libidinous thoughts demonstrates in itself the modesty and chasteness of her habitual demeanour. Her naïve piety, her obedient resignation, and her unreflecting simplicity sharply contrast with the Queen's character, and seem to indicate that Hamlet by a characteristic reaction towards the opposite extreme had unknowingly been impelled to choose a woman who should least remind him of his mother. A case might even be made out for the view that part of his courtship originated not so much in direct attraction for Ophelia as in an unconscious desire to play her off against his mother, just as a disappointed and piqued lover so often has resort to the arms of a more willing rival. It would not be easy otherwise to understand the readiness with which he later throws himself into this part. When, for instance, in the play scene he replies to his mother's request to sit by her with the words "No, good mother, here's metal more attractive" and proceeds to lie at Ophelia's feet, we seem to have a direct indication of his attitude; and his coarse familiarity and bandying of ambiguous jests with the woman he has recently so ruthlessly jilted are hardly intelligible unless we bear in mind that they were carried out under the heedful gaze of the Queen. It is as if his unconscious were trying to convey to her the following thought: "You give yourself to other men whom you prefer to me. Let me assure you that I can dispense with your favours and even prefer those of a woman whom I no longer love." His extraordinary outburst of bawdiness on this occasion, so unexpected in a man of obviously fine feeling, points unequivocally to the sexual nature of the underlying turmoil.

Now comes the father's death and the mother's second marriage. The association of the idea of sexuality with his mother, buried since infancy, can no longer be concealed from his consciousness. As Bradley well says: "Her son was forced to see in her action not only an astounding shallowness of feeling, but an eruption of coarse sensuality, 'rank and gross,' speeding post-haste to its horrible delight." Feelings which once, in the infancy of long ago, were pleasurable desires can now, because of his repressions, only fill him with repulsion. The long "repressed" desire to take his father's place in his mother's affection is stimulated to unconscious activity by the sight of someone usurping this place exactly as he himself had once longed to do. More, this someone was a member of the same family, so that the actual usurpation further resembled the imaginary one in being incestuous. Without his being in the least aware of it these ancient desires are ringing in his mind, are once more struggling to find conscious expression, and need such an expenditure of energy again to "repress" them that he is reduced to the deplorable mental state he himself so vividly depicts.

There follows the Ghost's announcement that the father's death was a willed one, was due to murder. Hamlet, having at the moment his mind filled with natural indignation at the news, answers normally enough with the cry (21):

> Haste me to know't, that I with wings as swift
> As meditation or the thoughts of love,
> May sweep to my revenge.

The momentous words follow revealing who was the guilty person, namely a relative who had committed the deed at the bidding of lust.[1] Hamlet's second guilty wish had thus also been realized by his uncle, namely to procure the fulfilment of the first—the possession of the mother—by a personal deed, in fact by murder of the father. The two recent events, the father's death and the mother's second marriage, seemed to the world to have no inner causal relation to each other, but they represented ideas which in Hamlet's unconscious fantasy had always been closely associated. These ideas now in a moment forced their way to conscious recognition in spite of all "repressing forces," and found immediate expression in his almost reflex cry: "O my prophetic soul! My uncle?" The frightful truth his unconscious had already intuitively divined, his consciousness had now to assimilate as best it could. For the rest of the interview Hamlet is stunned by the effect of the internal conflict thus re-awakened, which from now on never ceases, and into the essential nature of which he never penetrates.

One of the first manifestations of the awakening of the old conflict in Hamlet's mind is his reaction against Ophelia. This is doubly conditioned by the two opposing attitudes in his own mind. In the first place, there is a complex reaction in regard to his mother. As was explained above, the being forced to connect the thought of his mother with sensuality leads to an intense sexual revulsion, one that is only temporarily broken down by the coarse outburst discussed above. Combined with this is a fierce jealousy, unconscious because of its forbidden origin, at the sight of her giving herself to another man, a man whom he had no reason whatever either to love or to respect. Consciously this is allowed to express itself, for instance after the prayer scene, only in the form of extreme resentment and bitter reproaches against her. His resentment against

---

[1] It is not maintained that this was by any means Claudius' whole motive, but it was evidently a powerful one and the one that most impressed Hamlet.

women is still further inflamed by the hypocritical prudishness with which Ophelia
follows her father and brother in seeing evil in his natural affection, an attitude which
poisons his love in exactly the same way that the love of his childhood, like that of all
children, must have been poisoned. He can forgive a woman neither her rejection of
his sexual advances nor, still less, her alliance with another man. Most intolerable of all
to him, as Bradley well remarks, is the sight of sensuality in a quarter from which he
had trained himself ever since infancy rigorously to exclude it. The total reaction cul-
minates in the bitter misogyny of his outburst against Ophelia, who is devastated at
having to bear a reaction so wholly out of proportion to her own offence and has no
idea that in reviling her Hamlet is really expressing his bitter resentment against his
mother.[2] "I have heard of your paintings too, well enough; God has given you one
face, and you make yourselves another; you jig, you amble, and you lisp, and nickname
God's creatures, and make your wantonness your ignorance. Go to, I'll no more on't;
it hath made me mad" (47). On only one occasion does he for a moment escape from
the sordid implication with which his love has been impregnated and achieve a healthier attitude towards Ophelia, namely at the open grave when in remorse he breaks
out at Laertes for presuming to pretend that his feeling for her could ever equal that
of her lover. Even here, however, as Dover Wilson has suggested, the remorse behind
his exaggerated behaviour springs not so much from grief at Ophelia's death as from
his distress at his bad conscience that had killed his love—he acts the lover he fain
would have been.

Hamlet's attitude towards Ophelia is still more complex. Dover Wilson has ad-
duced good evidence for thinking that Hamlet is supposed to have overheard the intrigue in which Polonius "looses" his daughter to test her erstwhile lover, a suggestion
which had previously been made by Quincy Adams. This is probably an echo of the
old (Saxo) saga in which the girl is employed by the king to test his capacity for sexual love and so decide whether he is an imbecile or a cunning enemy. It certainly
helps to explain the violence with which he attacks her feminine charms and treats
her worse than a paid prostitute. He feels she is sent to lure him on and then, like his
mother, to betray him at the behest of another man. The words "Get thee to a nunnery"[3] thus have a more sinister connotation, for in Elizabethan, and indeed in later,
times this was also a term for a brothel; the name "Covent Garden" will elucidate the
point to any student of the history of London.

The underlying theme relates ultimately to the splitting of the mother image
which the infantile unconscious effects into two opposite pictures: one of a virginal
Madonna, an inaccessible saint towards whom all sensual approaches are unthinkable,
and the other of a sensual creature accessible to everyone. Indications of this dichotomy between love and lust (Titian's Sacred and Profane Love) are to be found
later in most men's sexual experiences. When sexual repression is highly pronounced,

---

[2] His similar tone and advice to the two women show plainly how closely they are identified in his
mind. Cp. "Get thee to a nunnery: why wouldst thou be a breeder of sinners?" (46–47) with "Refrain to-night; And that shall lend a kind of easiness To the next abstinence" (65).

The identification is further demonstrated in the course of the play by Hamlet's killing the
men who stand between him and these women (Claudius and Polonius).

[3] This exhortation (with its usual connotation of chastity) may be equated with the one addressed
later to his mother, "Go not to my uncle's bed," indicating Hamlet's identification of the two women
in his feelings.

as with Hamlet, then both types of women are felt to be hostile: the pure one out of resentment at her repulses, the sensual one out of the temptation she offers to plunge into guiltiness. Misogyny, as in the play, is the inevitable result.

The intensity of Hamlet's repulsion against woman in general, and Ophelia in particular, is a measure of the powerful "repression" to which his sexual feelings are being subjected. The outlet for those feelings in the direction of his mother has always been firmly dammed, and now that the narrower channel in Ophelia's direction has also been closed the increase in the original direction consequent on the awakening of early memories tasks all his energy to maintain the "repression." His pent-up feelings find a partial vent in other directions. The petulant irascibility and explosive outbursts called forth by his vexation at the hands of Guildenstern and Rosencrantz, and especially of Polonius, are evidently to be interpreted in this way, as also is in part the burning nature of his reproaches to his mother. Indeed, towards the end of his interview with his mother the thought of her misconduct expresses itself in that almost physical disgust which is so characteristic a manifestation of intensely "repressed" sexual feeling.

> Let the bloat king tempt you again to bed,
> Pinch wanton on your cheek, call you his mouse,
> And let him for a pair of reechy kisses,
> Or paddling in your neck with his damn'd fingers,
> Make you to ravel all this matter out (65)

Hamlet's attitude towards Polonius is highly instructive. Here the absence of family tie and of other similar influences enables him to indulge to a relatively unrestrained extent his hostility towards what he regards as a prating and sententious dotard.[4] The analogy he effects between Polonius and Jephthah is in this connection especially pointed. It is here that we see his fundamental attitude towards moralizing elders who use their power to thwart the happiness of the young, and not in the overdrawn and melodramatic portrait in which he delineates his father: "A combination and a form indeed, where every god did seem to set his seal to give the world assurance of a man."

It will be seen from the foregoing that Hamlet's attitude towards his uncle-father is far more complex than is generally supposed. He of course detests him, but it is the jealous detestation of one evil-doer towards his successful fellow. Much as he hates him, he can never denounce him with the ardent indignation that boils straight from his blood when he reproaches his mother, for the more vigorously he denounces his uncle the more powerfully does he stimulate to activity his own unconscious and "repressed" complexes. He is therefore in a dilemma between on the one hand allowing his natural detestation of his uncle to have free play, a consummation which would stir still further his own horrible wishes, and on the other hand ignoring the imperative call for the vengeance that his obvious duty demands. His own "evil" prevents

---

[4]It is noteworthy how many producers and actors seem to accept Hamlet's distorted estimate of Polonius, his garrulity being presumably an excuse for overlooking the shrewdness and soundness of his worldly wisdom. After all, his diagnosis of Hamlet's madness as being due to unrequited love for Ophelia was not so far from the mark, and he certainly recognized that his distressful condition was of sexual origin.

him from completely denouncing his uncle's, and in continuing to "repress" the former he must strive to ignore, to condone, and if possible even to forget the latter; *his moral fate is bound up with his uncle's for good or ill.* In reality his uncle incorporates the deepest and most buried part of his own personality, so that he cannot kill him without also killing himself. This solution, one closely akin to what Freud has shown to be the motive of suicide in melancholia, is actually the one that Hamlet finally adopts. The course of alternate action and inaction that he embarks on, and the provocations he gives to his suspicious uncle, can lead to no other end than to his own ruin and, incidentally, to that of his uncle. Only when he has made the final sacrifice and brought himself to the door of death is he free to fulfil his duty, to avenge his father, and to slay his other self—his uncle.

There are two moments in the play when he is nearest to murder, and it is noteworthy that in both the impulse has been dissociated from the unbearable idea of incest. The second is of course when he actually kills the King, when the Queen is already dead and lost to him for ever, so that his conscience is free of an ulterior motive for the murder. The first is more interesting. It is clear that Hamlet is a creature of highly charged imagination; Vischer, for instance, quite rightly termed him a "Phantasiemensch." As is known, the danger then is that phantasy may on occasion replace reality. Now Otto Rank, who uses the same term, has plausibly suggested that the emotionally charged play scene, where a nephew kills his uncle(!), and when there is no talk of adultery or incest, is in Hamlet's imagination an equivalent for fulfilling his task.[5] It is easier to kill the King when there is no ulterior motive behind it, no talk of mother or incest. When the play is over he is carried away in exultation as if he had really killed the King himself, whereas all he has actually done is to warn him and so impel him to sign a death warrant. That his pretext for arranging the play—to satisfy himself about Claudius' guilt and the Ghost's honesty—is specious is plain from the fact that *before* it he had been convinced of both and was reproaching himself for his neglect. When he then comes on the King praying, and so to speak finds him surprisingly still alive, he realizes that his task is still in front of him, but can only say "Now *might* I do it" (not "will"). He then expresses openly the unconscious thoughts of his infancy—the wish to kill the man who is lying with his mother ("in th' incestuous pleasure of his bed")—but he knows only too well that his own guilty motive for doing so would always prevent him. So there is no way out of the dilemma, and he blunders on to destruction.

The call of duty to kill his stepfather cannot be obeyed because it links itself with the unconscious call of his nature to kill his mother's husband, whether this is the first or the second; the absolute "repression" of the former impulse involves the inner prohibition of the latter also. It is no chance that Hamlet says of himself that he is prompted to his revenge "by heaven and hell."

In this discussion of the motives that move or restrain Hamlet we have purposely depreciated the subsidiary ones—such as his exclusion from the throne where Claudius

---

[5]There is a delicate point here which may appeal only to psychoanalysts. It is known that the occurrence of a dream within a dream (when one dreams that one is dreaming) is always found when analysed to refer to a theme which the person wishes were "only a dream," i.e. not true. I would suggest that a similar meaning attaches to a "play within a play," as in "Hamlet." So Hamlet (as nephew) can kill the King in his imagination since it is "only a play" or "only in play."

has blocked the normal solution of the Oedipus complex (to succeed the father in due course)—which also play a part, so as to bring out in greater relief the deeper and effective ones that are of preponderating importance. These, as we have seen, spring from sources of which he is quite unaware, and we might summarize the internal conflict of which he is the victim as consisting in a struggle of the "repressed" mental processes to become conscious. The call of duty, which automatically arouses to activity these unconscious processes, conflicts with the necessity of "repressing" them still more strongly; for the more urgent is the need for external action the greater is the effort demanded of the "repressing" forces. It is his moral duty, to which his father exhorts him, to put an end to the incestuous activities of his mother (by killing Claudius), but his unconscious does not want to put an end to them (he being identified with Claudius in the situation), and so he cannot. His lashings of self-reproach and remorse are ultimately because of this very failure, i.e. the refusal of his guilty wishes to undo the sin. By refusing to abandon his own incestuous wishes he perpetuates the sin and so must endure the stings of torturing conscience. And yet killing his mother's husband would be equivalent to committing the original sin himself, which would if anything be even more guilty. So of the two impossible alternatives he adopts the passive solution of letting the incest continue vicariously, but at the same time provoking destruction at the King's hand. Was ever a tragic figure so torn and tortured!

Action is paralysed at its very inception, and there is thus produced the picture of apparently causeless inhibition which is so inexplicable both to Hamlet and to readers of the play. This paralysis arises, however, not from physical or moral cowardice, but from that intellectual cowardice, that reluctance to dare the exploration of his inmost soul, which Hamlet shares with the rest of the human race. "Thus conscience does make cowards of us all."

QUESTIONS FOR DISCUSSION AND WRITING

1. Readers of Jones's essay typically respond either very positively or very negatively. How do you respond? Why?
2. Jones asks us to think about the extent to which Gertrude and Ophelia can and should be compared and contrasted. What similarities do you see in the two women's behaviors? What differences? To what extent is Hamlet's reaction to one determined by his relationship with the other?
3. Jones writes as a Freudian; he sees in *Hamlet* a literary depiction of the Oedipus complex (the young boy's desire to kill his father so that he might sleep with his mother and have her for himself). He argues further that Hamlet sees in Claudius the fulfillment of his own oedipal desires: Claudius *has* killed Hamlet's father and married Hamlet's mother. What evidence does Jones bring to his belief that Hamlet has an Oedipus complex? How convincing do you find that evidence?
4. In his argument, Jones says that Hamlet and Claudius share some personality traits. What evidence does he provide? How convincing do you find that evidence? How would you substantiate or refute Jones's claims with further evidence from the play?

CAROLYN HEILBRUN (1926–   )

The Character of Hamlet's Mother _____ *1990*

The character of Hamlet's mother has not received the specific critical attention it deserves. Moreover, the traditional account of her personality as rendered by the critics will not stand up under close scrutiny of Shakespeare's play.

None of the critics of course has failed to see Gertrude as vital to the action of the play; not only is she the mother of the hero, the widow of the Ghost, and the wife of the current King of Denmark, but the fact of her hasty and, to the Elizabethans, incestuous marriage, the whole question of her "falling off," occupies a position of barely secondary importance in the mind of her son, and of the Ghost. Indeed, Freud and Jones see her, the object of Hamlet's Oedipus complex, as central to the motivation of the play.[1] But the critics, with no exception that I have been able to find, have accepted Hamlet's word "frailty" as applying to her whole personality, and have seen in her not one weakness, or passion in the Elizabethan sense, but a character of which weakness and lack of depth and vigorous intelligence are the entire explanation. Of her can it truly be said that carrying the "stamp of one defect," she did "in the general censure take corruption from that particular fault" (I.iv.35–36).

The critics are agreed that Gertrude was not a party to the late King's murder and indeed knew nothing of it, a point which on the clear evidence of the play, is indisputable. They have also discussed whether or not Gertrude, guilty of more than an "o'er-hasty marriage," had committed adultery with Claudius before her husband's death. I will return to this point later on. Beyond discussing these two points, those critics who have dealth specifically with the Queen have traditionally seen her as well-meaning but shallow and feminine, in the pejorative sense of the word: incapable of any sustained rational process, superficial and flighty. It is this tradition which a closer reading of the play will show to be erroneous.

Professor Bradley describes the traditional Gertrude thus:

> The Queen was not a bad-hearted woman, not at all the woman to think little of murder. But she had a soft animal nature and was very dull and very shallow. She loved to be happy, like a sheep in the sun, and to do her justice, it pleased her to see others happy, like more sheep in the sun. . . . It was pleasant to sit upon her throne and see smiling faces around her, and foolish and unkind in Hamlet to persist in grieving for his father instead of marrying Ophelia and making everything comfortable. . . . The belief at the bottom of her heart was that the world is a place constructed simply that people may be happy in it in a good-humored sensual fashion.[2]

Later on, Bradley says of her that when affliction comes to her "the good in her nature struggles to the surface through the heavy mass of sloth."

Granville-Barker is not quite so extreme. Shakespeare, he says,

> gives us in Gertrude the woman who does not mature, who clings to her youth and all that belongs to it, whose charm will not change but at last fade and

---

[1] William Shakespeare, *Hamlet,* with a psycholoanalytical study by Ernest Jones, M.D. (London: Vision Press, 1947), pp. 7–42.

[2] A. C. Bradley, *Shakespearean Tragedy* (New York: Macmillan, 1949), p. 167.

wither, a pretty creature, as we see her, desperately refusing to grow old. . . . She is drawn for us with unemphatic strokes, and she has but a passive part in the play's action. She moves throughout in Claudius' shadow; he holds her as he won her, by the witchcraft of his wit.[3]

Elsewhere Granville-Barker says "Gertrude who will certainly never see forty-five again, might better be 'old.' [That is, portrayed by an older, mature actress.] But that would make her relations with Claudius—and *their* likelihood is vital to the play—quite incredible" (p. 226). Granville-Barker is saying here that a woman about forty-five years of age cannot feel any sexual passion nor arouse it. This is one of the mistakes which lie at the heart of the misunderstanding about Gertrude.

Professor Dover Wilson sees Gertrude as more forceful than either of these two critics will admit, but even he finds the Ghost's unwillingness to shock her with knowledge of his murder to be one of the basic motivations of the play, and he says of her "Gertrude is always hoping for the best."[4]

Now whether Claudius won Gertrude before or after her husband's death, it was certainly not, as Granville-Barker implies, with "the witchcraft of his wit" alone. Granville-Barker would have us believe that Claudius won her simply by the force of his persuasive tongue. "It is plain," he writes, that the Queen "does little except echo his [Claudius'] wishes; sometimes—as in the welcome to Rosencrantz and Guilden-stern—she repeats his very words" (p. 227), though Wilson must admit later that Gertrude does not tell Claudius everything. Without dwelling here on the psychol-ogy of the Ghost, or the greater burden borne by the Elizabethan words "witchcraft" and "wit," we can plainly see, for the Ghost tells us, how Claudius won the Queen: the Ghost considers his brother to be garbage, and "lust," the Ghost says, "will sate it-self in a celestial bed and prey on garbage" (I.v.54–55). "Lust"—in a woman of forty-five or more—is the key word here. Bradley, Granville-Barker, and to a lesser extent Professor Dover Wilson, misunderstand Gertrude largely because they are unable to see lust, the desire for sexual relations, as the passion, in the Elizabethan sense of the word, the flaw, the weakness which drives Gertrude to an incestuous marriage, appalls her son, and keeps him from the throne. Unable to explain her marriage to Claudius as the act of any but a weak-minded vacillating woman, they fail to see Gertrude for the strong-minded, intelligent, succinct, and, apart from this passion, sensible woman that she is.

To understand Gertrude properly, it is only necessary to examine the lines Shakespeare has chosen for her to say. She is, except for her description of Ophelia's death, concise and pithy in speech, with a talent for seeing the essence of every situa-tion presented before her eyes. If she is not profound, she is certainly never silly. We first hear her asking Hamlet to stop wearing black, to stop walking about with his eyes downcast, and to realize that death is an inevitable part of life. She is, in short, asking him not to give way to the passion of grief, a passion of whose force and dan-gers the Elizabethans are aware, as Miss Campbell has shown.[5] Claudius echoes her with a well-reasoned argument against grief which was, in its philosophy if not in its language, a piece of commonplace Elizabethan lore. After Claudius' speech, Gertrude

[3]Harley Granville-Barker, *Prefaces to Shakespeare* (Princeton: Princeton University Press, 1946), 1:227.
[4]J. Dover Wilson, *What Happens in Hamlet* (Cambridge: Cambridge University Press, 1951), p. 125.
[5]Lily B. Campbell, *Shakespeare's Tragic Heroes* (New York: Barnes & Noble, 1952), pp. 112–113.

asks Hamlet to remain in Denmark, where he is rightly loved. Her speeches have been short, however warm and loving, and conciseness of statement is not the mark of a dull and shallow woman.

We next hear her, as Queen and gracious hostess, welcoming Rosencrantz and Guildenstern to the court, hoping, with the King, that they may cheer Hamlet and discover what is depressing him. Claudius then tells Gertrude, when they are alone, that Polonius believes he knows what is upsetting Hamlet. The Queen answers:

> I doubt it is no other than the main,
> His father's death and our o'er-hasty marriage. (II.ii.56–57)

This statement is concise, remarkably to the point, and not a little courageous. It is not the statement of a dull, slothful woman who can only echo her husband's words. Next, Polonius enters with his most unbrief apotheosis to brevity. The Queen interrupts him with five words: "More matter with less art" (II.ii.95). It would be difficult to find a phrase more applicable to Polonius. When this gentleman, in no way deterred from his loquacity, after purveying the startling news that he has a daughter, begins to read a letter, the Queen asks pointedly "Came this from Hamlet to her?" (II.ii.114).

We see Gertrude next in Act III, asking Rosencrantz and Guildenstern, with her usual directness, if Hamlet received them well, and if they were able to tempt him to any pastime. But before leaving the room, she stops for a word of kindness to Ophelia. It is a humane gesture, for she is unwilling to leave Ophelia, the unhappy tool of the King and Polonius, without some kindly and intelligent appreciation of her help:

> And for your part, Ophelia, I do wish
> That your good beauties be the happy cause
> Of Hamlet's wildness. So shall I hope your virtues
> Will bring him to his wonted way again,
> To both your honors. (III.i.38–42)

It is difficult to see in this speech, as Bradley apparently does, the gushing shallow wish of a sentimental woman that class distinctions shall not stand in the way of true love.

At the play, the Queen asks Hamlet to sit near her. She is clearly trying to make him feel he has a place in the court of Denmark. She does not speak again until Hamlet asks her how she likes the play. "The lady doth protest too much, methinks" (III.ii.240) is her immortal comment on the player queen. The scene gives her four more words: when Claudius leaps to his feet, she asks "How fares my Lord?" (III.ii.278).

I will for the moment pass over the scene in the Queen's closet, to follow her quickly through the remainder of the play. After the closet scene, the Queen comes to speak to Claudius. She tells him, as Hamlet has asked her to, that he, Hamlet, is mad, and has killed Polonius. She adds, however, that he now weeps for what he has done. She does not wish Claudius to know what she now knows, how wild and fearsome Hamlet has become. Later, she does not wish to see Ophelia, but hearing how distracted she is, consents. When Laertes bursts in ready to attack Claudius, she immediately steps between Claudius and Laertes to protect the King, and tells Laertes it is not Claudius who has killed his father. Laertes will of course soon learn this, but it is Gertrude who manages to tell him before he can do any meaningless damage. She leaves Laertes and the King together, and then returns to tell Laertes that his sister is drowned. She gives her news directly, realizing that suspense will increase the pain of it, but this is the one time in the play when her usual pointed conciseness would be the mark neither of intelligence nor kindness, and so, gently, and at some length, she tells Laertes of his sister's death, giving him time to recover from the shock of grief, and to absorb the meaning of her words. At Ophelia's funeral the Queen scatters flowers over the grave:

> Sweets to the sweet; farewell!
> I hop'd thou shouldst have been my Hamlet's wife.
> I thought thy bride-bed to have deck'd, sweet maid,
> And not t' have strew'd thy grave. (V.i.266–269)

She is the only one present decently mourning the death of someone young, and not heated in the fire of some personal passion.

At the match between Hamlet and Laertes, the Queen believes that Hamlet is out of training, but glad to see him at some sport, she gives him her handkerchief to wipe his brow, and drinks to his success. The drink is poisoned and she dies. But before she dies she does not waste time on vituperation; she warns Hamlet that the drink is poisoned to prevent his drinking it. They are her last words. Those critics who have thought her stupid admire her death; they call it uncharacteristic.

In Act III, when Hamlet goes to his mother in her closet his nerves are pitched at the very height of tension; he is on the edge of hysteria. The possibility of murdering his mother has in fact entered his mind, and he has just met and refused an opportunity to kill Claudius. His mother, meanwhile, waiting for him, has told Polonius not to fear for her, but she knows when she sees Hamlet that he may be violently mad. Hamlet quips with her, insults her, tells her he wishes she were not his mother, and when she, still retaining dignity, attempts to end the interview, Hamlet seizes her and she cries for help. The important thing to note is that the Queen's cry "Thou wilt not murder me" (III.iv.21) is not foolish. She has seen from Hamlet's demeanor that he is capable of murder, as indeed in the next instant he proves himself to be.

We next learn from the Queen's startled "As kill a king" (III.iv.30) that she has no knowledge of the murder, though of course this is only confirmation here of what we already know. Then the Queen asks Hamlet why he is so hysterical:

> What have I done, that thou dar'st wag thy tongue
> In noise so rude against me? (III.iv.39–40)

Hamlet tells her: it is her lust, the need of sexual passion, which has driven her from the arms and memory of her husband to the incomparably cruder charms of his brother. He cries out that she has not even the excuse of youth for her lust:

> O Shame! where is thy blush? Rebellious hell,
> If thou canst mutine in a matron's bones,
> To flaming youth let virtue be as wax
> And melt in her own fire. Proclaim no shame
> When the compulsive ardor gives the charge,
> Since frost itself as actively doth burn,
> And reason panders will. (III.iv.82–87)

This is not only a lust, but a lust which throws out of joint all the structure of human morality and relationships. And the Queen admits it. If there is one quality that has characterized, and will characterize, every speech of Gertrude's in the play, it is the ability to see reality clearly, and to express it. This talent is not lost when turned upon herself:

> O Hamlet, speak no more!
> Thou turn'st mine eyes into my very soul,
> And there I see such black and grained spots
> As will not leave their tinct. (III.iv.88–91)

She knows that lust has driven her, that this is her sin, and she admits it. Not that she wishes to linger in the contemplation of her sin. No more, she cries, no more. And then the Ghost appears to Hamlet. The Queen thinks him mad again—as well she might—but she promises Hamlet that she will not betray him—and she does not.

Where, in all that we have seen of Gertrude, is there the picture of "a soft animal nature, very dull and very shallow"? She may indeed be "animal" in the sense of "lustful." But it does not follow that because she wishes to continue a life of sexual experience, her brain is soft or her wit unperceptive.

Some critics, having accepted Gertrude as a weak and vacillating woman, see no reason to suppose that she did not fall victim to Claudius' charms before the death of her husband and commit adultery with him. These critics, Professor Bradley among them (p. 166), claim that the elder Hamlet clearly tells his son that Gertrude has committed adultery with Claudius in the speech beginning "Ay that incestuous, that adulterate beast" (I.v.41ff). Professor Dover Wilson presents the argument:

> Is the Ghost speaking here of the o'er-hasty marriage of Claudius and Gertrude? Assuredly not. His "certain term" is drawing rapidly to an end, and he is already beginning to "scent the morning air." Hamlet knew of the marriage, and his whole soul was filled with nausea at the thought of the speedy hasting to "incestuous sheets." Why then should the Ghost waste precious moments in telling Hamlet what he was fully cognisant of before? . . . Moreover, though the word "incestuous" was applicable to the marriage, the rest of the passage is entirely inapplicable to it. Expressions like "witchcraft," "traitorous gifts," "seduce," "shameful lust," and "seeming virtuous" may be noted in passing. But the rest of the quotation leaves no doubt upon the matter. (p. 293)

Professor Dover Wilson and other critics have accepted the Ghost's word "adulterate" in its modern meaning. The Elizabethan word "adultery," however, was not restricted to its modern meaning, but was used to define any sexual relationship which could be called unchaste, including of course an incestuous one.[6] Certainly the elder Hamlet considered the marriage of Claudius and Gertrude to be unchaste and unseemly, and while his use of the word "adulterate" indicates his very strong feelings about the marriage, it would not to an Elizabethan audience necessarily mean that he believed Gertrude to have been false to him before his death. It is important to notice, too, that the Ghost does not apply the term "adulterate" to Gertrude, and he may well have considered the term a just description of Claudius' entire sexual life.

---

[6]See Bertram Joseph, *Conscience and the King* (London: Chatto and Windus, 1953), pp. 16–19.

But even if the Ghost used the word "adulterate" in full awareness of its modern restricted meaning, it is not necessary to assume on the basis of this single speech (and it is the only shadow of evidence we have for such a conclusion) that Gertrude was unfaithful to him while he lived. It is quite probable that the elder Hamlet still considered himself married to Gertrude, and he is moreover revolted that her lust for him ("why she would hang on him as if increase of appetite had grown by what it fed on") should have so easily transferred itself to another. This is why he uses the expressions "seduce," "shameful lust," and others. Professor Dover Wilson has himself said "Hamlet knew of the marriage, and his whole soul was filled with nausea at the thought of the speedy hasting to incestuous sheets"; the soul of the elder Hamlet was undoubtedly filled with nausea too, and this could well explain his using such strong language, as well as his taking the time to mention the matter at all. It is not necessary to consider Gertrude an adulteress to account for the speech of the Ghost.

Gertrude's lust was, of course, more important to the plot than we may at first perceive. Charlton Lewis, among others, has shown how Shakespeare kept many of the facts of the plots from which he borrowed without maintaining the structures which explained them. In the original Belleforest story, Gertrude (substituting Shakespeare's more familiar names) was daughter of the king; to become king, it was necessary to marry her. The elder Hamlet, in marrying Gertrude, ousted Claudius from the throne.[7] Shakespeare retained the shell of this in his play. When she no longer has a husband, the form of election would be followed to declare the next king, in this case undoubtedly her son Hamlet. By marrying Gertrude, Claudius "popp'd in between th' election and my hopes" (V.ii.65), that is, kept young Hamlet from the throne. Gertrude's flaw of lust made Claudius' ambition possible, for without taking advantage of the Queen's desire still to be married, he could not have been king.

But Gertrude, if she is lustful, is also intelligent, penetrating, and gifted with a remarkable talent for concise and pithy speech. In all the play, the person whose language hers most closely resembles is Horatio. "Sweets to the sweet," she has said at Ophelia's grave. "Good night sweet prince," Horatio says at the end. They are neither of them dull, or shallow, or slothful, though one of them is passion's slave.

QUESTIONS FOR DISCUSSION AND WRITING

1. Heilbrun argues that Gertrude has been misunderstood by earlier, largely male, critics. What are the crucial differences between her interpretation of Gertrude's character and the interpretations of the critics she cites? How convincing do you find her evidence?

2. In assessing Gertrude's behavior and character, Heilbrun quotes many of the Queen's more important speeches and lays them next to one another to give us a complete picture. Some readers argue, however, that in removing the speeches from their contexts in the play, Heilbrun makes Gertrude a more prominent character

---

[7] Charlton M. Lewis, *The Genesis of Hamlet* (New York: Henry Holt, 1907), p. 36.

than she is and also somewhat misrepresents her motivations and personality. How would you respond to such criticism of Heilbrun's method? Why?

MAKING CONNECTIONS: *HAMLET*

1. The writers represented in this chapter have very different attitudes toward Hamlet. Some see him as too much the thinker, paralyzed and weak. Others see him as a man victimized by circumstance and by others' treachery. Which of the writers sympathize with Hamlet the most? Why? How would they answer the hero's critics? Where do you stand on the question of Hamlet's character?

2. Both Branagh and Heilbrun clearly feel some sympathy for Gertrude, who, they think, loves both her new husband and her son. How do the other writers in the chapter, including Shakespeare himself, want us to respond to Gertrude's character? Is she weak and "womanly"? Caught in an inescapable dilemma? Where would you place yourself in the debate?

3. Simpson and MacNeice both write of some of the "other" young men in Shakespeare's play. In the works in this chapter, how do Laertes and Fortinbras compare with Hamlet? With one another? If Simpson, MacNiece, and Shakespeare were to find themselves talking about youth and the process of maturation, would they have similar points of view?

4. At the heart of *Hamlet* are questions of the strength and nature of various kinds of love: sexual love, parent–child love, love between siblings, and love between friends. How similar are the descriptions of and attitudes toward love expressed in the works in this chapter? How is love best achieved and maintained? How does it get polluted and corrupted? How much does each writer believe in its possibility?

5. Audiences over the centuries have responded very differently to Shakespeare's depiction of women. Some have applauded him for his deft handling of female characters; others have criticized him and his male heroes for what they see as misogyny. Where do you see evidence in *Hamlet* for both points of view? How would Pipher and Heilbrun respond to the critics' assessment of Shakespeare's characterization of women?

6. Shakespeare, Branagh, and Ciardi all have something to say about acting. How do their views about actors and the roles they play compare?

7. The two film stills on page 115 show very different versions of Hamlet, Claudius, and Gertrude. What sorts of characters and relationships do the two pictures seem to reflect? Which picture is closer to your own interpretation of the characters?

TOPICS FOR RESEARCH: A CASEBOOK ON *HAMLET*

1. When talking about Hamlet's madness—real or feigned—many modern readers want to talk about the fact that he claims to see his father's ghost. Clearly Gertrude, who does not see her late husband's ghost, believes Hamlet to be delusional when

he says he does. But beliefs about ghosts and demons were different in Shakespeare's time than they are in our own. Do some research into the way people of the Renaissance viewed ghosts and their hauntings.

2. Many modern critics, including Ernest Jones (and Sigmund Freud), have seen in Hamlet an Elizabethan re-creation of the Oedipus theme, and ideas about sexuality and sexual relations are mentioned frequently in the play itself. Do some research into Renaissance ideas about appropriate courtships and sexual behaviors for young single people and into expected sexual and marriage behaviors among middle-aged couples. See, too, if you can discover how the Renaissance would have viewed the marriage between a sister- and brother-in-law. How does your research help you respond to the various situations in which Shakespeare's characters find themselves?

3. *Hamlet* is open to a variety of different, sometimes conflicting, interpretations, and anyone who decides to stage or film the play is bound to find himself having to make decisions about theme and character. View two or three different versions of the play (either staged or filmed) and compare and contrast their treatments of one of the following:

> Hamlet's relationship with Ophelia
> Hamlet's relationship with Gertrude
> Claudius
> The relationship between Claudius and Gertrude
> The relationship between Polonius and Laertes or Polonius and Ophelia
> Hamlet's madness

4. So tormented is Hamlet by his personal problems that it is sometimes easy to forget that this is also a play about kingship and succession. What can you discover about English and Danish ideas of kingship? How would the people of Shakespeare's time have defined a "good king"? How were kings chosen in England and Denmark during the Renaissance? How likely was it that Shakespeare knew about the details of Danish kingship?

5. Ophelia and Hamlet both descend into madness (or, in Hamlet's case, perhaps into feigned madness), and both also at least flirt with the idea of suicide. Research Renaissance attitudes toward madness. What did the Renaissance believe drove people mad? What was the possibility for treatment and cure? How was suicide viewed during Shakespeare's time?

6. Hamlet decides against killing Claudius while Claudius is praying because he doesn't want Claudius to die at a moment at which he is cleansed of his sins. Research Renaissance beliefs about sin and absolution. How would the people of Shakespeare's time have looked at Claudius's moment of prayer? Would they have regarded it as sinful for Hamlet to kill Claudius while Claudius was praying? Would they have regarded it as sinful for Hamlet to kill Claudius under any circumstances? Would they have considered it sinful for him to send his friends Rosencrantz and Guildenstern to their deaths?

7. *Hamlet* belongs to a genre of literature called revenge plays (or revenge tragedies). Locate information about the genre, and/or read one or two other revenge plays. What are the defining characteristics of such plays?

A Casebook on Dr. Jekyll and Mr. Hyde

What Lies Within

Any fan of modern suspense movies knows that much turns upon who the killer is. Is he the long-haired, disheveled transient with wild eyes and a sinister smile? Or, more frighteningly, is he the clean-cut young man wearing a suit and carrying a briefcase? Whatever the movie answer to such questions, we know from our everyday lives that our answers rely on certain preconceptions. As we nervously assess the odd passenger in the elevator or the person huddled in a city doorway, we may ask ourselves whether the stranger is harmless or dangerous. How, in such everyday circumstances, do we decide whether to get on the elevator with the stranger or to cross the street to avoid a particular doorway? In our heads, we all have pictures of "the criminal" that help us make such decisions within seconds.

Rationally, of course, we know that our assumptions about criminality are dubious. We have learned again and again that the glowering dark figure may be harmless, whereas the boy-next-door may be a serial killer. Yet appearance is often all we have to go by in our quick brushes with each other in the elbow-to-elbow life of many communities. Our attempt to use appearance as a guide to moral character is hardly a new one. Centuries ago, people believed, or at least the literature of earlier time often implied, that the outside truly reflected the inside, as we often see in Shakespeare. In *The Tempest,* for example, Caliban the "monster" seems monstrous both within and without, whereas Ariel the beautiful spirit apparently represents all that is good. We think we have only to look at them to know what they are.

By the end of the nineteenth century, when Robert Louis Stevenson was writing *Dr. Jekyll and Mr. Hyde,* this belief in the correspondence between the outer and the inner had seemed to gain scientific validity. Scientists measured foreheads and eye sizes; they examined physical characteristics they thought were indicators of criminality. By our standards, the early science of criminology was not very scientific, and theories about what a criminal looked like were often determined as much by racism and other prejudices as by any scientific measurements. In the context of the science of the day, however, Stevenson's Mr. Hyde *looks* like a criminal: he is dark, hairy, and muscular. Though the characters of the novel are puzzled by their inability to describe him specifically, they know at once that he is ugly, lower class, and repulsive. In other words, he is the opposite of the good Dr. Jekyll, who is handsome and gentlemanly.

Opposite as Jekyll and Hyde seem, however, the mirror in Dr. Jekyll's lab gives away the secret. Dr. Jekyll and Mr. Hyde are opposites only in the sense that mirror images are opposites; perhaps Hyde cannot be described because finally he looks too much like Dr. Jekyll to be recognized for what he is. The question of "what does a criminal look like" is exploded by the end of Stevenson's novella. The more accurate question may be "Who is a criminal?" The answer to that question is a shocking one: maybe we *all* are, or at least we all have the capability to become criminals.

That recognition anticipates modern psychology. Though *Dr. Jekyll and Mr. Hyde* was written before Freud's theories of the psyche were known in England, Hyde is very much like Freud's id—the unrestrained part of the psyche capable of violence and uncontrolled sexuality. Hyde, like the id, is all impulse—impulse that recognizes only its own desires.

The fundamental psychological truths of the novel may explain why the story has endured for more than one hundred years. Like that other great monster novel, *Frankenstein,* Stevenson's *Dr. Jekyll and Mr. Hyde* was conceived in a dream, that taproot to our hidden desires. Perhaps because it taps into all of our psyches, *Dr. Jekyll and Mr. Hyde* has become a cultural myth, known to many who have never read it, and it has persisted in many forms. Even though the story poses seemingly adult questions about sexuality, violence, and the human attraction to evil, it has at the same time become popular among young children; children's versions abound. Film and television adaptations have also proliferated; *Dr. Jekyll and Mr. Hyde* has formed the basis of nearly one hundred film and television adaptations, as well as numerous stage productions. New York City even has a Jekyll and Hyde restaurant. Clearly this is a work that says much to us.

In its exploration of our own potential for criminality, Stevenson's novella creates the world of nightmare, for Hyde often emerges from the dark, fog-shrouded streets of London. He has, we are told, behaved more disreputably than Dr. Jekyll did before the monster was unleashed—but how? What exactly are his crimes? Are they sexual? If so, what form do they take, and why would they have been so shocking to a Victorian society that, for all its outward respectability, did a thriving business in prostitution and pornography? Or is Hyde's debauchery largely a matter of uncontrollable violence? Again, although we have glimpses into his violent actions, the answer to those questions remains elusive—which is why retellings, whether in film or prose, often fill in the gaps with lurid details, with rapes and bloodshed. Perhaps part of Stevenson's artistry is that he left untold the acting out of Jekyll's secret desires. Hyde acts out those unspeakable desires we all have but will never tell. In this way he is, as much as Oedipus or Hamlet, representative of us all.

ROBERT LOUIS STEVENSON (1850–1894)

The Strange Case of Dr. Jekyll and Mr. Hyde _____ 1886

To Katharine de Mattos

It's ill to loose the bands that God decreed to bind;
Still will we be the children of the heather and the wind;

Far away from home, O it's still for you and me
That the broom is blowing bonnie in the north countrie.

Story of the Door

Mr Utterson the lawyer was a man of a rugged countenance, that was never lighted by a smile; cold, scanty and embarrassed in discourse; backward in sentiment; lean, long, dusty, dreary, and yet somehow lovable. At friendly meetings, and when the wine was to his taste, something eminently human beaconed from his eye; something indeed which never found its way into his talk, but which spoke not only in these silent symbols of the after-dinner face, but more often and loudly in the acts of his life. He was austere with himself; drank gin when he was alone, to mortify a taste for vintages; and though he enjoyed the theatre, had not crossed the doors of one for twenty years. But he had an approved tolerance for others; sometimes wondering, almost with envy, at the high pressure of spirits involved in their misdeeds; and in any extremity inclined to help rather than to reprove. 'I incline to Cain's heresy,' he used to say quaintly: 'I let my brother go to the devil in his own way.' In this character it was frequently his fortune to be the last reputable acquaintance and the last good influence in the lives of down-going men. And to such as these, so long as they came about his chambers, he never marked a shade of change in his demeanour.

No doubt the feat was easy to Mr Utterson; for he was undemonstrative at the best, and even his friendships seemed to be founded in a similar catholicity of good-nature. It is the mark of a modest man to accept his friendly circle ready made from the hands of opportunity; and that was the lawyer's way. His friends were those of his own blood, or those whom he had known the longest; his affections, like ivy, were the growth of time, they implied no aptness in the object. Hence, no doubt, the bond that united him to Mr Richard Enfield, his distant kinsman, the well-known man about town. It was a nut to crack for many, what these two could see in each other, or what subject they could find in common. It was reported by those who encountered them in their Sunday walks, that they said nothing, looked singularly dull, and would hail with obvious relief the appearance of a friend. For all that, the two men put the greatest store by these excursions, counted them the chief jewel of each week, and not only set aside occasions of pleasure, but even resisted the calls of business, that they might enjoy them uninterrupted.

It chanced on one of these rambles that their way led them down a by street in a busy quarter of London. The street was small and what is called quiet, but it drove a thriving trade on the week-days. The inhabitants were all doing well, it seemed, and all emulously hoping to do better still, and laying out the surplus of their gains in coquetry; so that the shop fronts stood along that thoroughfare with an air of invitation, like rows of smiling saleswomen. Even on Sunday, when it veiled its more florid charms and lay comparatively empty of passage, the street shone out in contrast to its dingy neighbourhood, like a fire in a forest; and with its freshly painted shutters, well-polished brasses, and general cleanliness and gaiety of note, instantly caught and pleased the eye of the passenger.

Two doors from one corner, on the left hand going east, the line was broken by the entry of a court; and just at that point, a certain sinister block of building thrust forward its gable on the street. It was two storeys high; showed no window, nothing but a

door on the lower storey and a blind forehead of discoloured wall on the upper; and
bore in every feature the marks of prolonged and sordid negligence. The door, which
was equipped with neither bell nor knocker, was blistered and distained. Tramps
slouched into the recess and struck matches on the panels; children kept shop upon the
steps; the schoolboy had tried his knife on the mouldings; and for close on a generation
no one had appeared to drive away these random visitors or to repair their ravages.

Mr Enfield and the lawyer were on the other side of the by street; but when
they came abreast of the entry, the former lifted up his cane and pointed.

'Did you ever remark that door?' he asked; and when his companion had replied
in the affirmative, 'It is connected in my mind,' added he, 'with a very odd story.'

'Indeed!' said Mr Utterson, with a slight change of voice, 'and what was that?'

'Well, it was this way,' returned Mr Enfield: 'I was coming home from some
place at the end of the world, about three o'clock of a black winter morning, and my
way lay through a part of town where there was literally nothing to be seen but lamps.
Street after street, and all the folks asleep—street after street, all lighted up as if for a
procession, and all as empty as a church—till at last I got into that state of mind when
a man listens and listens and begins to long for the sight of a policeman. All at once, I
saw two figures: one a little man who was stumping along eastward at a good walk,
and the other a girl of maybe eight or ten who was running as hard as she was able
down a cross-street. Well, sir, the two ran into one another naturally enough at the
corner; and then came the horrible part of the thing; for the man trampled calmly
over the child's body and left her screaming on the ground. It sounds nothing to hear,
but it was hellish to see. It wasn't like a man; it was like some damned Juggernaut. I
gave a view halloa, took to my heels, collared my gentleman, and brought him back
to where there was already quite a group about the screaming child. He was perfectly
cool and made no resistance, but gave me one look, so ugly that it brought out the
sweat on me like running. The people who had turned out were the girl's own family; and pretty soon the doctor, for whom she had been sent, put in his appearance.
Well, the child was not much the worse, more frightened, according to the Sawbones;
and there you might have supposed would be an end to it. But there was one curious
circumstance. I had taken a loathing to my gentleman at first sight. So had the child's
family, which was only natural. But the doctor's case was what struck me. He was the
usual cut-and-dry apothecary, of no particular age and colour, with a strong Edinburgh accent, and about as emotional as a bagpipe. Well, sir, he was like the rest of us:
every time he looked at my prisoner, I saw that Sawbones turned sick and white with
the desire to kill him. I knew what was in his mind, just as he knew what was in mine;
and killing being out of the question, we did the next best. We told the man we could
and would make such a scandal out of this, as should make his name stink from one
end of London to the other. If he had any friends or any credit, we undertook that he
should lose them. And all the time, as we were pitching it in red hot, we were keeping
the women off him as best we could, for they were as wild as harpies. I never saw a
circle of such hateful faces; and there was the man in the middle, with a kind of black
sneering coolness—frightened too, I could see that—but carrying it off, sir, really like
Satan. "If you choose to make capital out of this accident," said he, "I am naturally
helpless. No gentleman but wishes to avoid a scene," says he. "Name your figure."
Well, we screwed him up to a hundred pounds for the child's family; he would have

clearly liked to stick out; but there was something about the lot of us that meant mischief, and at last he struck. The next thing was to get the money; and where do you think he carried us but to that place with the door?—whipped out a key, went in, and presently came back with the matter of ten pounds in gold and a cheque for the balance on Coutts's, drawn payable to bearer, and signed with a name that I can't mention, though it's one of the points of my story, but it was a name at least very well known and often printed. The figure was stiff; but the signature was good for more than that, if it was only genuine. I took the liberty of pointing out to my gentleman that the whole business looked apocryphal; and that a man does not, in real life, walk into a cellar door at four in the morning and come out of it with another man's cheque for close upon a hundred pounds. But he was quite easy and sneering. "Set your mind at rest," says he; "I will stay with you till the banks open, and cash the cheque myself." So we all set off, the doctor, and the child's father, and our friend and myself, and passed the rest of the night in my chambers; and next day, when we had breakfasted, went in a body to the bank. I gave in the cheque myself, and said I had every reason to believe it was a forgery. Not a bit of it. The cheque was genuine.'

'Tut-tut!' said Mr Utterson.

'I see you feel as I do,' said Mr Enfield. 'Yes, it's a bad story. For my man was a fellow that nobody could have to do with, a really damnable man; and the person that drew the cheque is the very pink of the proprieties, celebrated too, and (what makes it worse) one of your fellows who do what they call good. Blackmail, I suppose; an honest man paying through the nose for some of the capers of his youth. Blackmail House is what I call that place with the door, in consequence. Though even that, you know, is far from explaining all,' he added; and with the words fell into a vein of musing.

From this he was recalled by Mr Utterson asking rather suddenly: 'And you don't know if the drawer of the cheque lives there?'

'A likely place, isn't it?' returned Mr Enfield. 'But I happen to have noticed his address; he lives in some square or other.'

'And you never asked about—the place with the door?' said Mr Utterson.

'No, sir: I had a delicacy,' was the reply. 'I feel very strongly about putting questions; it partakes too much of the style of the day of judgment. You start a question, and it's like starting a stone. You sit quietly on the top of a hill; and away the stone goes, starting others; and presently some bland old bird (the last you would have thought of) is knocked on the head in his own back garden, and the family have to change their name. No, sir, I make it a rule of mine: the more it looks like Queer Street, the less I ask.'

'A very good rule, too,' said the lawyer.

'But I have studied the place for myself,' continued Mr Enfield. 'It seems scarcely a house. There is no other door, and nobody goes in or out of that one, but, once in a great while, the gentleman of my adventure. There are three windows looking on the court on the first floor; none below; the windows are always shut, but they're clean. And then there is a chimney, which is generally smoking; so somebody must live there. And yet it's not so sure; for the buildings are so packed together about that court, that it's hard to say where one ends and another begins.'

The pair walked on again for a while in silence; and then—'Enfield,' said Mr Utterson, 'that's a good rule of yours.'

'Yes, I think it is,' returned Enfield.

'But for all that,' continued the lawyer, 'there's one point I want to ask: I want to ask the name of that man who walked over the child.'

'Well,' said Mr Enfield, 'I can't see what harm it would do. It was a man of the name of Hyde.'

'Hm,' said Mr Utterson. 'What sort of a man is he to see?'

'He is not easy to describe. There is something wrong with his appearance; something displeasing, something downright detestable. I never saw a man I so disliked, and yet I scarce know why. He must be deformed somewhere; he gives a strong feeling of deformity, although I couldn't specify the point. He's an extraordinary-looking man, and yet I really can name nothing out of the way. No, sir; I can make no hand of it; I can't describe him. And it's not want of memory; for I declare I can see him this moment.'

Mr Utterson again walked some way in silence, and obviously under a weight of consideration. 'You are sure he used a key?' he inquired at last.

'My dear sir . . .' began Enfield, surprised out of himself.

'Yes, I know,' said Utterson; 'I know it must seem strange. The fact is, if I do not ask you the name of the other party, it is because I know it already. You see, Richard, your tale has gone home. If you have been inexact in any point, you had better correct it.'

'I think you might have warned me,' returned the other, with a touch of sullenness. 'But I have been pedantically exact, as you call it. The fellow had a key; and, what's more, he has it still. I saw him use it, not a week ago.'

Mr Utterson sighed deeply, but said never a word; and the young man presently resumed. 'Here is another lesson to say nothing,' said he. 'I am ashamed of my long tongue. Let us make a bargain never to refer to this again.'

'With all my heart,' said the lawyer. 'I shake hands on that, Richard.'

Search for Mr Hyde

That evening Mr Utterson came home to his bachelor house in sombre spirits, and sat down to dinner without relish. It was his custom of a Sunday, when this meal was over, to sit close by the fire, a volume of some dry divinity on his reading-desk, until the clock of the neighbouring church rang out the hour of twelve, when he would go soberly and gratefully to bed. On this night, however, as soon as the cloth was taken away, he took up a candle and went into his business room. There he opened his safe, took from the most private part of it a document endorsed on the envelope as Dr Jekyll's Will, and sat down with a clouded brow to study its contents. The will was holograph; for Mr Utterson, though he took charge of it now that it was made, had refused to lend the least assistance in the making of it; it provided not only that, in case of the decease of Henry Jekyll, M.D., D.C.L., LL.D., F.R.S., &c., all his possessions were to pass into the hands of his 'friend and benefactor Edward Hyde'; but that in case of Dr Jekyll's 'disappearance or unexplained absence for any period exceeding three calendar months,' the said Edward Hyde should step into the said Henry Jekyll's shoes without further delay, and free from any burthen or obligation, beyond the payment of a few small sums to the members of the doctor's household. This document had long been the lawyer's eyesore. It offended him both as a lawyer and as a lover of the sane and customary sides of life, to whom the fanciful was the immodest. And hitherto it was his ignorance of Mr Hyde that had swelled his indignation; now, by a sudden turn, it was his knowledge. It was already bad enough when the name was but a name of which he could learn no more. It was worse when it began to be clothed upon with detestable attributes; and out of the shifting, insubstantial mists that had so long baffled his eye, there leaped up the sudden, definite presentment of a fiend.

'I thought it was madness,' he said, as he replaced the obnoxious paper in the safe; 'and now I begin to fear it is disgrace.'

With that he blew out his candle, put on a great coat, and set forth in the direction of Cavendish Square, that citadel of medicine, where his friend the great Dr Lanyon, had his house and received his crowding patients. 'If any one knows, it will be Lanyon,' he had thought.

The solemn butler knew and welcomed him; he was subjected to no stage of delay, but ushered direct from the door to the dining room, where Dr Lanyon sat alone over his wine. This was a hearty, healthy, dapper, red-faced gentleman, with a shock of hair prematurely white, and a boisterous and decided manner. At sight of Mr Utterson, he sprang up from his chair and welcomed him with both hands. The geniality, as was the way of the man, was somewhat theatrical to the eye; but it reposed on genuine feeling. For these two were old friends, old mates both at school and college, both thorough respecters of themselves and of each other, and, what does not always follow, men who thoroughly enjoyed each other's company.

After a little rambling talk, the lawyer led up to the subject which so disagreeably preoccupied his mind.

'I suppose, Lanyon,' he said, 'you and I must be the two oldest friends that Henry Jekyll has?'

'I wish the friends were younger,' chuckled Dr Lanyon. 'But I suppose we are. And what of that? I see little of him now.'

'Indeed!' said Utterson. 'I thought you had a bond of common interest.'

'We had,' was his reply. 'But it is more than ten years since Henry Jekyll became too fanciful for me. He began to go wrong, wrong in mind; and though, of course, I continue to take an interest in him for old sake's sake as they say, I see and I have seen devilish little of the man. Such unscientific balderdash,' added the doctor, flushing suddenly purple, 'would have estranged Damon and Pythias.'

This little spirit of temper was somewhat of a relief to Mr Utterson. 'They have only differed on some point of science,' he thought; and being a man of no scientific passions (except in the matter of conveyancing), he even added: 'It is nothing worse than that!' He gave his friend a few seconds to recover his composure, and then approached the question he had come to put.

'Did you ever come across a *protégé* of his—one Hyde?' he asked.

'Hyde?' repeated Lanyon. 'No. Never heard of him. Since my time.'

That was the amount of information that the lawyer carried back with him to the great, dark bed on which he tossed to and fro until the small hours of the morning began to grow large. It was a night of little ease to his toiling mind, toiling in mere darkness and besieged by questions.

Six o'clock struck on the bells of the church that was so conveniently near to Mr Utterson's dwelling, and still he was digging at the problem. Hitherto it had touched him on the intellectual side alone; but now his imagination also was engaged, or rather enslaved; and as he lay and tossed in the gross darkness of the night and the curtained room, Mr Enfield's tale went by before his mind in a scroll of lighted pictures. He would be aware of the great field of lamps of a nocturnal city; then of the figure of a man walking swiftly; then of a child running from the doctor's; and then these met, and that human Juggernaut trod the child down and passed on regardless of her screams. Or else he would see a room in a rich house, where his friend lay asleep, dreaming and smiling at his dreams; and then the door of that room would be opened, the curtains of the bed plucked apart, the sleeper recalled, and, lo! there would stand by his side a figure to whom power was given, and even at that dead hour he must rise and do its bidding. The figure in these two phases haunted the lawyer all night; and if at any time he dozed over, it was but to see it glide more stealthily through sleeping houses, or move the more swiftly, and still the more swiftly, even to dizziness, through wider labyrinths of lamp-lighted city, and at every street corner crush a child and leave her screaming. And still the figure had no face by which he might know it; even in his dreams it had no face, or one that baffled him and melted before his eyes; and thus it was that there sprang up and grew apace in the lawyer's mind a singularly strong, almost an inordinate, curiosity to behold the features of the real Mr Hyde. If he could but once set eyes on him, he thought the mystery would lighten and perhaps roll altogether away, as was the habit of mysterious things when well examined. He might see a reason for his friend's strange preference or bondage (call it which you please), and even for the startling clauses of the will. And at least it would be a face worth seeing: the face of a man who was without bowels of mercy: a face which had but to show itself to raise up, in the mind of the unimpressionable Enfield, a spirit of enduring hatred.

From that time forward, Mr Utterson began to haunt the door in the by street of shops. In the morning before office hours, at noon when business was plenty and time scarce, at night under the face of the fogged city moon, by all lights and at all hours of solitude or concourse, the lawyer was to be found on his chosen post.

'If he be Mr Hyde,' he had thought, 'I shall be Mr Seek.'

And at last his patience was rewarded. It was a fine dry night; frost in the air; the streets as clean as a ball-room floor; the lamps, unshaken by any wind, drawing a regular pattern of light and shadow. By ten o'clock, when the shops were closed, the by street was very solitary, and, in spite of the low growl of London from all around, very silent. Small sounds carried far; domestic sounds out of the houses were clearly audible on either side of the roadway; and the rumour of the approach of any passenger preceded him by a long time. Mr Utterson had been some minutes at his post when he was aware of an odd light footstep drawing near. In the course of his nightly patrols he had long grown accustomed to the quaint effect with which the footfalls of a single person, while he is still a great way off, suddenly spring out distinct from the vast hum and clatter of the city. Yet his attention had never before been so sharply and decisively arrested; and it was with a strong, superstitious prevision of success that he withdrew into the entry of the court.

The steps drew swiftly nearer, and swelled out suddenly louder as they turned the end of the street. The lawyer, looking forth from the entry, could soon see what manner of man he had to deal with. He was small, and very plainly dressed; and the look of him, even at that distance, went somehow strongly against the watcher's inclination. But he made straight for the door, crossing the roadway to save time; and as he came, he drew a key from his pocket, like one approaching home.

Mr Utterson stepped out and touched him on the shoulder as he passed. 'Mr Hyde, I think?'

Mr Hyde shrank back with a hissing intake of the breath. But his fear was only momentary; and though he did not look the lawyer in the face, he answered coolly enough: 'That is my name. What do you want?'

'I see you are going in,' returned the lawyer. 'I am an old friend of Dr Jekyll's— Mr Utterson, of Gaunt Street—you must have heard my name; and meeting you so conveniently, I thought you might admit me.'

'You will not find Dr Jekyll; he is from home,' replied Mr Hyde, blowing in the key. And then suddenly, but still without looking up, 'How did you know me?' he asked.

'On your side,' said Mr Utterson, 'will you do me a favour?'

'With pleasure,' replied the other. 'What shall it be?'

'Will you let me see your face?' asked the lawyer.

Mr Hyde appeared to hesitate; and then, as if upon some sudden reflection, fronted about with an air of defiance; and the pair stared at each other pretty fixedly for a few seconds. 'Now I shall know you again,' said Mr Utterson. 'It may be useful.'

'Yes,' returned Mr Hyde, 'it is as well we have met; and *à propos,* you should have my address.' And he gave a number of a street in Soho.

'Good God!' thought Mr Utterson, 'can he too have been thinking of the will?' But he kept his feelings to himself, and only grunted in acknowledgment of the address.

'And now,' said the other, 'how did you know me?'

'By description,' was the reply.

'Whose description?'

'We have common friends,' said Mr Utterson.

'Common friends!' echoed Mr Hyde, a little hoarsely. 'Who are they?'

'Jekyll, for instance,' said the lawyer.

'He never told you,' cried Mr Hyde, with a flush of anger. 'I did not think you would have lied.'

'Come,' said Mr Utterson, 'that is not fitting language.'

The other snarled aloud into a savage laugh; and the next moment, with extraordinary quickness, he had unlocked the door and disappeared into the house.

The lawyer stood awhile when Mr Hyde had left him, the picture of disquietude. Then he began slowly to mount the street, pausing every step or two, and putting his hand to his brow like a man in mental perplexity. The problem he was thus debating as he walked was one of a class that is rarely solved. Mr Hyde was pale and dwarfish; he gave an impression of deformity without any namable malformation, he had a displeasing smile, he had borne himself to the lawyer with a sort of murderous mixture of timidity and boldness, and he spoke with a husky, whispering and somewhat broken voice,—all these were points against him; but not all of these together could explain the hitherto unknown disgust, loathing and fear with which Mr Utterson regarded him. 'There must be something else,' said the perplexed gentleman. 'There *is* something more, if I could find a name for it. God bless me, the man seems hardly human! Something troglodytic, shall we say? or can it be the old story of Dr Fell? or is it the mere radiance of a foul soul that thus transpires through, and transfigures, its clay continent? The last, I think; for, O my poor old Harry Jekyll, if ever I read Satan's signature upon a face, it is on that of your new friend!'

Round the corner from the by street there was a square of ancient, handsome houses, now for the most part decayed from their high estate, and let in flats and chambers to all sorts and conditions of men: map-engravers, architects, shady lawyers, and the agents of obscure enterprises. One house, however, second from the corner, was still occupied entire; and at the door of this, which wore a great air of wealth and comfort, though it was now plunged in darkness except for the fan-light, Mr Utterson stopped and knocked. A well-dressed, elderly servant opened the door.

'Is Dr Jekyll at home, Poole?' asked the lawyer.

'I will see, Mr Utterson,' said Poole, admitting the visitor, as he spoke, into a large, low-roofed, comfortable hall, paved with flags, warmed (after the fashion of a country house) by a bright, open fire, and furnished with costly cabinets of oak. 'Will you wait here by the fire, sir? or shall I give you a light in the dining-room?'

'Here, thank you,' said the lawyer; and he drew near and leaned on the tall fender. This hall, in which he was now left alone, was a pet fancy of his friend the doctor's; and Utterson himself was wont to speak of it as the pleasantest room in London. But to-night there was a shudder in his blood; the face of Hyde sat heavy on his memory; he felt (what was rare in him) a nausea and distaste of life; and in the gloom of his spirits, he seemed to read a menace in the flickering of the firelight on the polished cabinets and the uneasy starting of the shadow on the roof. He was ashamed of his relief when Poole presently returned to announce that Dr Jekyll was gone out.

'I saw Mr Hyde go in by the old dissecting-room door, Poole,' he said. 'Is that right, when Dr Jekyll is from home?'

'Quite right, Mr Utterson, sir,' replied the servant. 'Mr Hyde has a key.'

'Your master seems to repose a great deal of trust in that young man, Poole,' resumed the other, musingly.

'Yes, sir, he do indeed,' said Poole. 'We have all orders to obey him.'

'I do not think I ever met Mr Hyde?' asked Utterson.

'O dear no, sir. He never *dines* here,' replied the butler. 'Indeed, we see very little of him on this side of the house; he mostly comes and goes by the laboratory.'

'Well, good-night, Poole.'

'Good-night, Mr Utterson.'

And the lawyer set out homeward with a very heavy heart. 'Poor Harry Jekyll,' he thought, 'my mind misgives me he is in deep waters! He was wild when he was young; a long while ago, to be sure; but in the law of God there is no statute of limitations. Ah, it must be that; the ghost of some old sin, the cancer of some concealed disgrace; punishment coming, *pede claudo*, years after memory has forgotten and self-love condoned the fault.' And the lawyer, scared by the thought, brooded awhile on his own past, groping in all the corners of memory, lest by chance some Jack-in-the-Box of an old iniquity should leap to light there. His past was fairly blameless; few men could read the rolls of their life with less apprehension; yet he was humbled to the dust by the many ill things he had done, and raised up again into a sober and fearful gratitude by the many that he had come so near to doing, yet avoided. And then by a return on his former subject, he conceived a spark of hope. 'This Master Hyde, if he were studied,' thought he, 'must have secrets of his own: black secrets, by the look of him; secrets compared to which poor Jekyll's worst would be like sunshine. Things cannot continue as they are. It turns me quite cold to think of this creature stealing like a thief to Harry's bedside; poor Harry, what a wakening! And the danger of it! for if this Hyde suspects the existence of the will, he may grow impatient to inherit. Ay, I must put my shoulder to the wheel—if Jekyll will but let me,' he added, 'if Jekyll will only let me.' For once more he saw before his mind's eye, as clear as a transparency, the strange clauses of the will.

Dr Jekyll Was Quite at Ease

A fortnight later, by excellent good fortune, the doctor gave one of his pleasant dinners to some five or six old cronies, all intelligent reputable men, and all judges of good wine; and Mr Utterson so contrived that he remained behind after the others had departed. This was no new arrangement, but a thing that had befallen many scores of times. Where Utterson was liked, he was liked well. Hosts loved to detain the dry lawyer, when the light-hearted and the loose-tongued had already their foot on the threshold; they liked to sit awhile in his unobtrusive company, practising for solitude, sobering their minds in the man's rich silence, after the expense and strain of gaiety. To this rule Dr Jekyll was no exception; and as he now sat on the opposite side of the fire—a large, well-made, smooth-faced man of fifty, with something of a slyish cast perhaps, but every mark of capacity and kindness—you could see by his looks that he cherished for Mr Utterson a sincere and warm affection.

'I have been wanting to speak to you, Jekyll,' began the latter. 'You know that will of yours?'

A close observer might have gathered that the topic was distasteful; but the doctor carried it off gaily. 'My poor Utterson,' said he, 'you are unfortunate in such a client. I never saw a man so distressed as you were by my will; unless it were that hide-bound pedant, Lanyon, at what he called my scientific heresies. O, I know he's a good fellow—you needn't frown—an excellent fellow, and I always mean to see more of him; but a hide-bound pedant for all that; an ignorant, blatant pedant. I was never more disappointed in any man than Lanyon.'

'You know I never approved of it,' pursued Utterson, ruthlessly disregarding the fresh topic.

'My will? Yes, certainly, I know that,' said the doctor, a trifle sharply. 'You have told me so.'

'Well, I tell you so again,' continued the lawyer. 'I have been learning something of young Hyde.'

The large handsome face of Dr Jekyll grew pale to the very lips, and there came a blackness about his eyes. 'I do not care to hear more,' said he. 'This is a matter I thought we had agreed to drop.'

'What I heard was abominable,' said Utterson.

'It can make no change. You do not understand my position,' returned the doctor, with a certain incoherency of manner. 'I am painfully situated, Utterson; my position is a very strange—a very strange one. It is one of those affairs that cannot be mended by talking.'

'Jekyll,' said Utterson, 'you know me: I am a man to be trusted. Make a clean breast of this in confidence; and I make no doubt I can get you out of it.'

'My good Utterson,' said the doctor, 'this is very good of you, this is downright good of you, and I cannot find words to thank you in. I believe you fully; I would trust you before any man alive, ay, before myself, if I could make the choice; but indeed it isn't what you fancy; it is not so bad as that; and just to put your good heart at rest, I will tell you one thing: the moment I choose, I can be rid of Mr Hyde. I give you my hand upon that; and I thank you again and again; and I will just add one little word, Utterson, that I'm sure you'll take in good part: this is a private matter, and I beg of you to let it sleep.'

Utterson reflected a little, looking in the fire.

'I have no doubt you are perfectly right,' he said at last, getting to his feet.

'Well, but since we have touched upon this business, and for the last time, I hope,' continued the doctor, 'there is one point I should like you to understand. I have really a very great interest in poor Hyde. I know you have seen him; he told me so; and I fear he was rude. But I do sincerely take a great, a very great interest in that young man; and if I am taken away, Utterson, I wish you to promise me that you will bear with him and get his rights for him. I think you would, if you knew all; and it would be a weight off my mind if you would promise.'

'I can't pretend that I shall ever like him,' said the lawyer.

'I don't ask that,' pleaded Jekyll, laying his hand upon the other's arm; 'I only ask for justice; I only ask you to help him for my sake, when I am no longer here.'

Utterson heaved an irrepressible sigh. 'Well,' said he, 'I promise.'

The Carew Murder Case

Nearly a year later, in the month of October, 18——, London was startled by a crime of singular ferocity, and rendered all the more notable by the high position of the victim. The details were few and startling. A maid-servant living alone in a house not far from the river had gone upstairs to bed about eleven. Although a fog rolled over the city in the small hours, the early part of the night was cloudless, and the lane, which the maid's window overlooked, was brilliantly lit by the full moon. It seems she was romantically given; for she sat down upon her box, which stood immediately under the window, and fell into a dream of musing. Never (she used to say, with streaming tears, when she narrated that experience), never had she felt more at peace with all men or thought more kindly of the world. And as she so sat she became aware of an aged and beautiful gentleman with white hair drawing near along the lane; and advancing to meet him, another and very small gentleman, to whom at first she paid less attention. When they had come within speech (which was just under the maid's eyes) the older man bowed and accosted the other with a very pretty manner of politeness. It did not seem as if the subject of his address were of great importance; indeed, from his pointing, it sometimes appeared as if he were only inquiring his way; but the moon shone on his face as he spoke, and the girl was pleased to watch it, it seemed to breathe such an innocent and old-world kindness of disposition, yet with something high too, as of a well-founded self-content. Presently her eye wandered to the other, and she was surprised to recognise in him a certain Mr Hyde, who had once visited her master and for whom she had conceived a dislike. He had in his hand a heavy cane, with which he was trifling; but he answered never a word, and seemed to listen with an ill-contained impatience. And then all of a sudden he broke out in a great flame of anger, stamping with his foot, brandishing the cane, and carrying on (as the maid described it) like a madman. The old gentleman took a step back, with the air of one very much surprised and a trifle hurt; and at that Mr Hyde broke out of all bounds, and clubbed him to the earth. And next moment, with ape-like fury, he was trampling his victim under foot, and hailing down a storm of blows, under which the bones were audibly shattered and the body jumped upon the roadway. At the horror of these sights and sounds, the maid fainted.

It was two o'clock when she came to herself and called for the police. The murderer was gone long ago; but there lay his victim in the middle of the lane, incredibly mangled. The stick with which the deed had been done, although it was of some rare and very tough and heavy wood, had broken in the middle under the stress of this insensate cruelty; and one splintered half had rolled in the neighbouring gutter—the other, without doubt, had been carried away by the murderer. A purse and a gold watch were found upon the victim; but, no cards or papers, except a sealed and stamped envelope, which he had been probably carrying to the post, and which bore the name and address of Mr Utterson.

This was brought to the lawyer the next morning, before he was out of bed; and he had no sooner seen it, and been told the circumstances, than he shot out a solemn lip. 'I shall say nothing till I have seen the body,' said he; 'this may be very serious. Have the kindness to wait while I dress.' And with the same grave countenance, he hurried through his breakfast and drove to the police station, whither the body had been carried. As soon as he came into the cell, he nodded.

'Yes,' said he, 'I recognise him. I am sorry to say that this is Sir Danvers Carew.'

'Good God, sir!' exclaimed the officer, 'is it possible?' And the next moment his eye lighted up with professional ambition. 'This will make a deal of noise,' he said. 'And perhaps you can help us to the man.' And he briefly narrated what the maid had seen, and showed the broken stick.

Mr Utterson had already quailed at the name of Hyde; but when the stick was laid before him, he could doubt no longer: broken and battered as it was, he recognised it for one that he had himself presented many years before to Henry Jekyll.

'Is this Mr Hyde a person of small stature?' he inquired.

'Particularly small and particularly wicked-looking, is what the maid calls him,' said the officer.

Mr Utterson reflected; and then, raising his head, 'If you will come with me in my cab,' he said, 'I think I can take you to his house.'

It was by this time about nine in the morning, and the first fog of the season. A great chocolate-coloured pall lowered over heaven, but the wind was continually charging and routing these embattled vapours; so that as the cab crawled from street to street, Mr Utterson beheld a marvellous number of degrees and hues of twilight; for here it would be dark like the back-end of evening; and there would be a glow of a rich, lurid brown, like the light of some strange conflagration; and here, for a moment, the fog would be quite broken up, and a haggard shaft of daylight would glance in between the swirling wreaths. The dismal quarter of Soho seen under these changing glimpses, with its muddy ways, and slatternly passengers, and its lamps, which had never been extinguished or had been kindled afresh to combat this mournful reinvasion of darkness, seemed, in the lawyer's eyes, like a district of some city in a nightmare. The thoughts of his mind, besides, were of the gloomiest dye; and when he glanced at the companion of his drive, he was conscious of some touch of that terror of the law and the law's officers which may at times assail the most honest.

As the cab drew up before the address indicated, the fog lifted a little and showed him a dingy street, a gin palace, a low French eating-house, a shop for the retail of penny numbers and two-penny salads, many ragged children huddled in the doorways, and many women of many different nationalities passing out, key in hand, to have a morning glass; and the next moment the fog settled down again upon that part, as brown as umber, and cut him off from his blackguardly surroundings. This was the home of Henry Jekyll's favourite; of a man who was heir to a quarter of a million sterling.

An ivory-faced and silvery-haired old woman opened the door. She had an evil face, smoothed by hypocrisy; but her manners were excellent. Yes, she said, this was Mr Hyde's, but he was not at home; he had been in that night very late, but had gone away again in less than an hour: there was nothing strange in that; his habits were very irregular, and he was often absent; for instance, it was nearly two months since she had seen him till yesterday.

'Very well then, we wish to see his rooms,' said the lawyer; and when the woman began to declare it was impossible, 'I had better tell you who this person is,' he added. 'This is Inspector Newcomen of Scotland Yard.'

A flash of odious joy appeared upon the woman's face. 'Ah!' said she, 'he is in trouble! What has he done?'

Mr Utterson and the inspector exchanged glances. 'He don't seem a very popular character,' observed the latter. 'And now, my good woman, just let me and this gentleman have a look about us.'

In the whole extent of the house, which but for the old woman remained otherwise empty, Mr Hyde had only used a couple of rooms; but these were furnished with luxury and good taste. A closet was filled with wine; the plate was of silver, the napery elegant; a good picture hung upon the walls, a gift (as Utterson supposed) from Henry Jekyll, who was much of a connoisseur; and the carpets were of many plies and agreeable in colour. At this moment, however, the rooms bore every mark of having been recently and hurriedly ransacked; clothes lay about the floor, with their pockets inside out; lockfast drawers stood open; and on the hearth there lay a pile of grey ashes, as though many papers had been burned. From these embers the inspector disinterred the butt end of a green cheque book, which had resisted the action of the fire; the other half of the stick was found behind the door; and as this clinched his suspicions, the officer declared himself delighted. A visit to the bank, where several thousand pounds were found to be lying to the murderer's credit, completed his gratification.

'You may depend upon it, sir,' he told Mr Utterson. 'I have him in my hand. He must have lost his head, or he never would have left the stick or, above all, burned the cheque book. Why, money's life to the man. We have nothing to do but wait for him at the bank, and get out the handbills.'

This last, however, was not so easy of accomplishment; for Mr Hyde had numbered few familiars—even the master of the servant-maid had only seen him twice; his family could nowhere be traced; he had never been photographed; and the few who could describe him differed widely, as common observers will. Only on one point were they agreed; and that was the haunting sense of unexpressed deformity with which the fugitive impressed his beholders.

Incident of the Letter

It was late in the afternoon when Mr Utterson found his way to Dr Jekyll's door, where he was at once admitted by Poole, and carried down by the kitchen offices and across a yard which had once been a garden, to the building which was indifferently known as the laboratory or the dissecting-rooms. The doctor had bought the house from the heirs of a celebrated surgeon; and his own tastes being rather chemical than anatomical, had changed the destination of the block at the bottom of the garden. It was the first time that the lawyer had been received in that part of his friend's quarters; and he eyed the dingy windowless structure with curiosity, and gazed round with a distasteful sense of strangeness as he crossed the theatre, once crowded with eager students and now lying gaunt and silent, the tables laden with chemical apparatus, the floor strewn with crates and littered with packing straw, and the light falling dimly through the foggy cupola. At the further end, a flight of stairs mounted to a door covered with red baize; and through this Mr Utterson was at last received into the doctor's cabinet. It was a large room, fitted round with glass presses, furnished, among other things, with a cheval-glass and a business table, and looking out upon the court by three dusty windows barred with iron. The fire burned in the grate; a lamp was set lighted on the chimney-shelf, for even in the houses the fog began to lie thickly; and there, close up to the warmth, sat Dr Jekyll, looking deadly sick. He did not rise to meet his visitor, but held out a cold hand and bade him welcome in a changed voice.

'And now,' said Mr Utterson, as soon as Poole had left them, 'you have heard the news?'

The doctor shuddered. 'They were crying it in the square,' he said. 'I heard them in my dining room.'

'One word,' said the lawyer. 'Carew was my client, but so are you; and I want to know what I am doing. You have not been mad enough to hide this fellow?'

'Utterson, I swear to God,' cried the doctor, 'I swear to God I will never set eyes on him again. I bind my honour to you that I am done with him in this world. It is all at an end. And indeed he does not want my help; you do not know him as I do; he is safe, he is quite safe; mark my words, he will never more be heard of.'

The lawyer listened gloomily; he did not like his friend's feverish manner. 'You seem pretty sure of him,' said he; 'and for your sake, I hope you may be right. If it came to a trial, your name might appear.'

'I am quite sure of him,' replied Jekyll; 'I have grounds for certainty that I cannot share with any one. But there is one thing on which you may advise me. I have— I have received a letter; and I am at a loss whether I should show it to the police. I should like to leave it in your hands, Utterson; you would judge wisely, I am sure; I have so great a trust in you.'

'You fear, I suppose, that it might lead to his detection?' asked the lawyer.

'No,' said the other. 'I cannot say that I care what becomes of Hyde; I am quite done with him. I was thinking of my own character, which this hateful business has rather exposed.'

Utterson ruminated awhile; he was surprised at his friend's selfishness, and yet relieved by it. 'Well,' said he, at last, 'let me see the letter.'

The letter was written in an odd, upright hand, and signed 'Edward Hyde': and it signified, briefly enough, that the writer's benefactor, Dr Jekyll, whom he had long so unworthily repaid for a thousand generosities, need labour under no alarm for his safety as he had means of escape on which he placed a sure dependence. The lawyer liked this letter well enough; it put a better colour on the intimacy than he had looked for, and he blamed himself for some of his past suspicions.

'Have you the envelope?' he asked.

'I burned it,' replied Jekyll, 'before I thought what I was about. But it bore no postmark. The note was handed in.'

'Shall I keep this and sleep upon it?' asked Utterson.

'I wish you to judge for me entirely,' was the reply. 'I have lost confidence in myself.'

'Well, I shall consider,' returned the lawyer. 'And now one word more: it was Hyde who dictated the terms in your will about that disappearance?'

The doctor seemed seized with a qualm of faintness; he shut his mouth tight and nodded.

'I knew it,' said Utterson. 'He meant to murder you. You have had a fine escape.'

'I have had what is far more to the purpose,' returned the doctor solemnly: 'I have had a lesson—O God, Utterson, what a lesson I have had!' And he covered his face for a moment with his hands.

On his way out, the lawyer stopped and had a word or two with Poole. 'By the by,' said he, 'there was a letter handed in today: what was the messenger like?' But Poole was positive nothing had come except by post; 'and only circulars by that,' he added.

This news sent off the visitor with his fears renewed. Plainly the letter had come by the laboratory door; possibly, indeed, it had been written in the cabinet; and, if that were so, it must be differently judged, and handled with the more caution. The news boys, as he went, were crying themselves hoarse along the footways: 'Special edition. Shocking murder of an M.P.' That was the funeral oration of one friend and client; and he could not help a certain apprehension lest the good name of another should be sucked down in the eddy of the scandal. It was, at least, a ticklish decision that he had to make; and, self-reliant as he was by habit, he began to cherish a longing for advice. It was not to be had directly; but perhaps, he thought, it might be fished for.

Presently after, he sat on one side of his own hearth, with Mr Guest, his head clerk, upon the other, and midway between, at a nicely calculated distance from the fire, a bottle of a particular old wine that had long dwelt unsunned in the foundations of his house. The fog still slept on the wing above the drowned city, where the lamps glimmered like carbuncles; and through the muffle and smother of these fallen clouds, the procession of the town's life was still rolling in through the great arteries with a sound as of a mighty wind. But the room was gay with firelight. In the bottle the acids were long ago resolved; the imperial dye had softened with time, as the colour grows richer in stained windows; and the glow of hot autumn afternoons on hillside vineyards was ready to be set free and to disperse the fogs of London. Insensibly the lawyer melted. There was no man from whom he kept fewer secrets than Mr Guest; and he was not always sure that he kept as many as he meant. Guest had often been on business to the doctor's; he knew Poole; he could scarce have failed to hear of Mr Hyde's familiarity about the house; he might draw conclusions: was it not as well, then, that he should see a letter which put that mystery to rights? and above all, since Guest, being a great student and critic of handwriting, would consider the step natural and obliging? The clerk, besides, was a man of counsel; he would scarce read so strange a document without dropping a remark; and by that remark Mr Utterson might shape his future course.

'This is a sad business about Sir Danvers,' he said.

'Yes, sir, indeed. It has elicited a great deal of public feeling,' returned Guest. 'The man, of course, was mad.'

'I should like to hear your views on that,' replied Utterson. 'I have a document here in his handwriting; it is between ourselves, for I scarce know what to do about it; it is an ugly business at the best. But there it is; quite in your way: a murderer's autograph.'

Guest's eyes brightened, and he sat down at once and studied it with passion. 'No, sir,' he said; 'not mad; but it is an odd hand.'

'And by all accounts a very odd writer,' added the lawyer.

Just then the servant entered with a note.

'Is that from Dr Jekyll, sir?' inquired the clerk. 'I thought I knew the writing. Anything private, Mr Utterson?'

'Only an invitation to dinner. Why? Do you want to see it?'

'One moment. I thank you, sir'; and the clerk laid the two sheets of paper alongside and sedulously compared their contents. 'Thank you, sir,' he said at last, returning both; 'it's a very interesting autograph.'

There was a pause, during which Mr Utterson struggled with himself. 'Why did you compare them, Guest?' he inquired suddenly.

'Well, sir,' returned the clerk, 'there's a rather singular resemblance; the two hands are in many points identical; only differently sloped.'

'Rather quaint,' said Utterson.

'It is, as you say, rather quaint,' returned Guest.

'I wouldn't speak of this note, you know,' said the master.

'No, sir,' said the clerk. 'I understand.'

But no sooner was Mr Utterson alone that night than he locked the note into his safe, where it reposed from that time forward. 'What!' he thought. 'Henry Jekyll forge for a murderer!' And his blood ran cold in his veins.

Remarkable Incident of Dr Lanyon

Time ran on; thousands of pounds were offered in reward, for the death of Sir Danvers was resented as a public injury; but Mr Hyde had disappeared out of the ken of the police as though he had never existed. Much of his past was unearthed, indeed, and all disreputable: tales came out of the man's cruelty, at once so callous and violent, of his vile life, of his strange associates, of the hatred that seemed to have surrounded his career; but of his present whereabouts, not a whisper. From the time he had left the house in Soho on the morning of the murder, he was simply blotted out; and gradually, as time drew on, Mr Utterson began to recover from the hotness of his alarm, and to grow more at quiet with himself. The death of Sir Danvers was, to his way of thinking, more than paid for by the disappearance of Mr Hyde. Now that that evil influence had been withdrawn, a new life began for Dr Jekyll. He came out of his seclusion, renewed relations with his friends, became once more their familiar guest and entertainer; and whilst he had always been known for charities, he was now no less distinguished for religion. He was busy, he was much in the open air, he did good; his face seemed to open and brighten, as if with an inward consciousness of service; and for more than two months the doctor was at peace.

On the 8th of January Utterson had dined at the doctor's with a small party; Lanyon had been there; and the face of the host had looked from one to the other as in the old days when the trio were inseparable friends. On the 12th, and again on the 14th, the door was shut against the lawyer. 'The doctor was confined to the house,'

Poole said, 'and saw no one.' On the 15th he tried again, and was again refused; and having now been used for the last two months to see his friend almost daily, he found this return of solitude to weigh upon his spirits. The fifth night he had in Guest to dine with him; and the sixth he betook himself to Dr Lanyon's.

There at least he was not denied admittance; but when he came in, he was shocked at the change which had taken place in the doctor's appearance. He had his death-warrant written legibly upon his face. The rosy man had grown pale; his flesh had fallen away; he was visibly balder and older; and yet it was not so much these to-kens of a swift physical decay that arrested the lawyer's notice, as a look in the eye and quality of manner that seemed to testify to some deep-seated terror of the mind. It was unlikely that the doctor should fear death; and yet that was what Utterson was tempted to suspect. 'Yes,' he thought; 'he is a doctor, he must know his own state and that his days are counted; and the knowledge is more than he can bear.' And yet when Utterson remarked on his ill looks, it was with an air of great firmness that Lanyon declared himself a doomed man.

'I have had a shock,' he said, 'and I shall never recover. It is a question of weeks. Well, life has been pleasant; I liked it; yes, sir, I used to like it. I sometimes think if we knew all, we should be more glad to get away.'

'Jekyll is ill, too,' observed Utterson. 'Have you seen him?'

But Lanyon's face changed, and he held up a trembling hand. 'I wish to see or hear no more of Dr Jekyll,' he said, in a loud, unsteady voice. 'I am quite done with that person; and I beg that you will spare me any allusion to one whom I regard as dead.'

'Tut, tut,' said Mr Utterson; and then, after a considerable pause, 'Can't I do any-thing?' he inquired. 'We are three very old friends, Lanyon; we shall not live to make others.'

'Nothing can be done,' returned Lanyon; 'ask himself.'

'He will not see me,' said the lawyer.

'I am not surprised at that,' was the reply. 'Some day, Utterson, after I am dead, you may perhaps come to learn the right and wrong of this. I cannot tell you. And in the meantime, if you can sit and talk with me of other things, for God's sake, stay and do so; but if you cannot keep clear of this accursed topic, then, in God's name, go, for I cannot bear it.'

As soon as he got home, Utterson sat down and wrote to Jekyll, complaining of his exclusion from the house, and asking the cause of this unhappy break with Lanyon; and the next day brought him a long answer, often very pathetically worded, and sometimes darkly mysterious in drift. The quarrel with Lanyon was incurable. 'I do not blame our old friend,' Jekyll wrote, 'but I share his view that we must never meet. I mean from henceforth to lead a life of extreme seclusion; you must not be surprised, nor must you doubt my friendship, if my door is often shut even to you. You must suffer me to go my own dark way. I have brought on myself a punishment and a dan-ger that I cannot name. If I am the chief of sinners, I am the chief of sufferers also. I could not think that this earth contained a place for sufferings and terrors so unman-ning; and you can do but one thing, Utterson, to lighten this destiny, and that is to re-spect my silence.' Utterson was amazed; the dark influence of Hyde had been withdrawn, the doctor had returned to his old tasks and amities; a week ago, the prospect had smiled with every promise of a cheerful and an honoured age; and now in a moment, friendship and peace of mind and the whole tenor of his life were wrecked. So great and unprepared a change pointed to madness; but in view of Lanyon's manner and words, there must lie for it some deeper ground.

A week afterwards Dr Lanyon took to his bed, and in something less than a fortnight he was dead. The night after the funeral, at which he had been sadly affected, Utterson locked the door of his business room, and sitting there by the light of a melancholy candle, drew out and set before him an envelope addressed by the hand and sealed with the seal of his dead friend. 'PRIVATE: for the hands of J. G. Utterson ALONE, and in case of his predecease *to be destroyed unread*,' so it was emphatically superscribed; and the lawyer dreaded to behold the contents. 'I have buried one friend to-day,' he thought: 'what if this should cost me another?' And then he condemned the fear as a disloyalty, and broke the seal. Within there was another enclosure, likewise sealed, and marked upon the cover as 'not to be opened till the death or disappearance of Dr Henry Jekyll.' Utterson could not trust his eyes. Yes, it was disappearance; here again, as in the mad will, which he had long ago restored to its author, here again were the idea of a disappearance and the name of Henry Jekyll bracketed. But in the will, that idea had sprung from the sinister suggestion of the man Hyde; it was set there with a purpose all too plain and horrible. Written by the hand of Lanyon, what should it mean? A great curiosity came to the trustee, to disregard the prohibition and dive at once to the bottom of these mysteries; but professional honour and faith to his dead friend were stringent obligations; and the packet slept in the inmost corner of his private safe.

It is one thing to mortify curiosity, another to conquer it; and it may be doubted if, from that day forth, Utterson desired the society of his surviving friend with the same eagerness. He thought of him kindly; but his thoughts were disquieted and fearful. He went to call indeed; but he was perhaps relieved to be denied admittance; perhaps, in his heart, he preferred to speak with Poole upon the doorstep, and surrounded by the air and sounds of the open city, rather than to be admitted into that house of voluntary bondage, and to sit and speak with its inscrutable recluse. Poole had, indeed, no very pleasant news to communicate. The doctor, it appeared, now more than ever confined himself to the cabinet over the laboratory, where he would sometimes even sleep; he was out of spirits, he had grown very silent, he did not read; it seemed as if he had something on his mind. Utterson became so used to the unvarying character of these reports, that he fell off little by little in the frequency of his visits.

Incident at the Window

It chanced on Sunday, when Mr Utterson was on his usual walk with Mr Enfield, that their way lay once again through the by street; and that when they came in front of the door, both stopped to gaze on it.

'Well,' said Enfield, 'that story's at an end, at least. We shall never see more of Mr Hyde.'

'I hope not,' said Utterson. 'Did I ever tell you that I once saw him, and shared your feeling of repulsion?'

'It was impossible to do the one without the other,' returned Enfield. 'And, by the way, what an ass you must have thought me, not to know that this was a back way to Dr Jekyll's! It was partly your own fault that I found it out, even when I did.'

'So you found it out, did you?' said Utterson. 'But if that be so, we may step into the court and take a look at the windows. To tell you the truth, I am uneasy about poor Jekyll; and even outside, I feel as if the presence of a friend might do him good.'

The court was very cool and a little damp, and full of premature twilight, although the sky, high up overhead, was still bright with sunset. The middle one of the three windows was half way open; and sitting close beside it, taking the air with an infinite sadness of mien, like some disconsolate prisoner, Utterson saw Dr Jekyll.

'What! Jekyll!' he cried. 'I trust you are better.'

'I am very low, Utterson,' replied the doctor drearily; 'very low. It will not last long, thank God.'

'You stay too much indoors,' said the lawyer. 'You should be out, whipping up the circulation like Mr Enfield and me. (This is my cousin—Mr Enfield—Dr Jekyll.) Come, now; get your hat and take a quick turn with us.'

'You are very good,' sighed the other. 'I should like to very much; but no, no, no, it is quite impossible; I dare not. But indeed, Utterson, I am very glad to see you; this is really a great pleasure. I would ask you and Mr Enfield up, but the place is really not fit.'

'Why then,' said the lawyer, good-naturedly, 'the best thing we can do is to stay down here, and speak with you from where we are.'

'That is just what I was about to venture to propose,' returned the doctor, with a smile. But the words were hardly uttered, before the smile was struck out of his face and succeeded by an expression of such abject terror and despair, as froze the very blood of the two gentlemen below. They saw it but for a glimpse, for the window was instantly thrust down; but that glimpse had been sufficient, and they turned and left the court without a word. In silence, too, they traversed the by street; and it was not until they had come into a neighbouring thoroughfare, where even upon a Sunday there were still some stirrings of life, that Mr Utterson at last turned and looked at his companion. They were both pale; and there was an answering horror in their eyes.

'God forgive us! God forgive us!' said Mr Utterson.

But Mr Enfield only nodded his head very seriously, and walked on once more in silence.

The Last Night

Mr Utterson was sitting by his fireside one evening after dinner, when he was surprised to receive a visit from Poole.

'Bless me, Poole, what brings you here?' he cried; and then, taking a second look at him, 'What ails you?' he added; 'is the doctor ill?'

'Mr Utterson,' said the man, 'there is something wrong.'

'Take a seat, and here is a glass of wine for you,' said the lawyer. 'Now, take your time, and tell me plainly what you want.'

'You know the doctor's ways, sir,' replied Poole, 'and how he shuts himself up. Well, he's shut up again in the cabinet; and I don't like it, sir—I wish I may die if I like it. Mr Utterson, sir, I'm afraid.'

'Now, my good man,' said the lawyer, 'be explicit. What are you afraid of?'

'I've been afraid for about a week,' returned Poole, doggedly disregarding the question, 'and I can bear it no more.'

The man's appearance amply bore out his words; his manner was altered for the worse; and except for the moment when he had first announced his terror, he had not once looked the lawyer in the face. Even now, he sat with the glass of wine untasted on his knee, and his eyes directed to a corner of the floor. 'I can bear it no more,' he repeated.

'Come,' said the lawyer, 'I see you have some good reason, Poole; I see there is something seriously amiss. Try to tell me what it is.'

'I think there's been foul play,' said Poole, hoarsely.

'Foul play!' cried the lawyer, a good deal frightened, and rather inclined to be irritated in consequence. 'What foul play? What does the man mean?'

'I daren't say, sir,' was the answer; 'but will you come along with me and see for yourself?'

Mr Utterson's only answer was to rise and get his hat and great coat; but he observed with wonder the greatness of the relief that appeared upon the butler's face, and perhaps with no less, that the wine was still untasted when he set it down to follow.

It was a wild, cold, seasonable night of March, with a pale moon, lying on her back as though the wind had tilted her, and a flying wrack of the most diaphanous and lawny texture. The wind made talking difficult, and flecked the blood into the face. It seemed to have swept the streets unusually bare of passengers, besides; for Mr Utterson thought he had never seen that part of London so deserted. He could have wished it otherwise; never in his life had he been conscious of so sharp a wish to see and touch his fellow-creatures; for, struggle as he might, there was borne in upon his mind a crushing anticipation of calamity. The square, when they got there, was all full of wind and dust, and the thin trees in the garden were lashing themselves along the railing. Poole, who had kept all the way a pace or two ahead, now pulled up in the middle of the pavement, and in spite of the biting weather, took off his hat and mopped his brow with a red pocket-handkerchief. But for all the hurry of his coming, these were not the dews of exertion that he wiped away, but the moisture of some strangling anguish; for his face was white, and his voice, when he spoke, harsh and broken.

'Well, sir,' he said, 'here we are, and God grant there be nothing wrong.'

'Amen, Poole,' said the lawyer.

Thereupon the servant knocked in a very guarded manner; the door was opened on the chain; and a voice asked from within, 'Is that you, Poole?'

'It's all right,' said Poole. 'Open the door.'

The hall, when they entered it, was brightly lighted up; the fire was built high; and about the hearth the whole of the servants, men and women, stood huddled together like a flock of sheep. At the sight of Mr Utterson, the housemaid broke into hysterical whimpering; and the cook, crying out, 'Bless God! it's Mr Utterson,' ran forward as if to take him in her arms.

'What, what? Are you all here?' said the lawyer, peevishly. 'Very irregular, very unseemly: your master would be far from pleased.'

'They're all afraid,' said Poole.

Blank silence followed, no one protesting; only the maid lifted up her voice and now wept loudly.

'Hold your tongue!' Poole said to her, with a ferocity of accent that testified to his own jangled nerves; and indeed when the girl had so suddenly raised the note of her lamentation, they had all started and turned towards the inner door with faces of dreadful expectation. 'And now,' continued the butler, addressing the knife-boy, 'reach me a candle, and we'll get this through hands at once.' And then he begged Mr Utterson to follow him, and led the way to the back garden.

'Now, sir,' said he, 'you come as gently as you can. I want you to hear, and I don't want you to be heard. And see here, sir, if by any chance he was to ask you in, don't go.'

Mr Utterson's nerves, at this unlooked-for termination, gave a jerk that nearly threw him from his balance; but he recollected his courage, and followed the butler into the laboratory building and through the surgical theatre, with its lumber of crates and bottles, to the foot of the stair. Here Poole motioned him to stand on one side and listen; while he himself, setting down the candle and making a great and obvious call on his resolution, mounted the steps, and knocked with a somewhat uncertain hand on the red baize of the cabinet door.

'Mr Utterson, sir, asking to see you,' he called; and even as he did so, once more violently signed to the lawyer to give ear.

A voice answered from within: 'Tell him I cannot see any one,' it said, complainingly.

'Thank you, sir,' said Poole, with a note of something like triumph in his voice; and taking up his candle, he led Mr Utterson back across the yard and into the great kitchen, where the fire was out and the beetles were leaping on the floor.

'Sir,' he said, looking Mr Utterson in the eyes, 'was that my master's voice?'

'It seems much changed,' replied the lawyer, very pale, but giving look for look.

'Changed? Well, yes, I think so,' said the butler. 'Have I been twenty years in this man's house, to be deceived about his voice? No, sir; master's made away with; he was made away with eight days ago, when we heard him cry out upon the name of God; and *who's* in there instead of him, and *why* it stays there, is a thing that cries to Heaven, Mr Utterson!'

'This is a very strange tale, Poole; this is rather a wild tale, my man,' said Mr Utterson, biting his finger. 'Suppose it were as you suppose, supposing Dr Jekyll to have been—well, murdered, what could induce the murderer to stay? That won't hold water; it doesn't commend itself to reason.'

'Well, Mr Utterson, you are a hard man to satisfy, but I'll do it yet,' said Poole. 'All this last week (you must know) him, or it, or whatever it is that lives in that cabinet, has been crying night and day for some sort of medicine and cannot get it to his mind. It was sometimes his way—the master's, that is—to write his orders on a sheet of paper and throw it on the stair. We've had nothing else this week back; nothing but papers, and a closed door, and the very meals left there to be smuggled in when nobody was looking. Well, sir, every day, ay, and twice and thrice in the same day, there have been orders and complaints, and I have been sent flying to all the wholesale chemists in town. Every time I brought the stuff back, there would be another paper telling me to return it, because it was not pure, and another order to a different firm. This drug is wanted bitter bad, sir, whatever for.'

'Have you any of these papers?' asked Mr Utterson.

Poole felt in his pocket and handed out a crumpled note, which the lawyer, bending nearer to the candle, carefully examined. Its contents ran thus: 'Dr Jekyll presents his compliments to Messrs Maw. He assures them that their last sample is impure and quite useless for his present purpose. In the year 18——, Dr J. purchased a somewhat large quantity from Messrs M. He now begs them to search with the most sedulous care, and should any of the same quality be left, to forward it to him at once. Expense is no consideration. The importance of this to Dr J. can hardly be exaggerated.' So far the letter had run composedly enough; but here, with a sudden splutter of the pen, the writer's emotion had broken loose. 'For God's sake,' he had added, 'find me some of the old.'

'This is a strange note,' said Mr Utterson; and then sharply, 'How do you come to have it open?'

'The man at Maw's was main angry, sir, and he threw it back to me like so much dirt,' returned Poole.

This is unquestionably the doctor's hand, do you know?' resumed the lawyer.

'I thought it looked like it,' said the servant, rather sulkily; and then, with another voice, 'But what matters hand of write?' he said. 'I've seen him!'

'Seen him?' repeated Mr Utterson. 'Well?'

'That's it!' said Poole. 'It was this way. I came suddenly into the theatre from the garden. It seems he had slipped out to look for this drug, or whatever it is; for the cabinet door was open, and there he was at the far end of the room digging among the crates. He looked up when I came in, gave a kind of cry, and whipped upstairs into the cabinet. It was but for one minute that I saw him, but the hair stood upon my head like quills. Sir, if that was my master, why had he a mask upon his face? If it was my master, why did he cry out like a rat and run from me? I have served him long enough. And then . . .' the man paused and passed his hand over his face.

'These are all very strange circumstances,' said Mr Utterson, 'but I think I begin to see daylight. Your master, Poole, is plainly seized with one of those maladies that both torture and deform the sufferer; hence, for aught I know, the alteration of his voice; hence the mask and his avoidance of his friends; hence his eagerness to find this drug, by means of which the poor soul retains some hope of ultimate recovery—God grant that he be not deceived! There is my explanation; it is sad enough, Poole, ay, and appalling to consider; but it is plain and natural, hangs well together and delivers us from all exorbitant alarms.'

'Sir,' said the butler, turning to a sort of mottled pallor, 'that thing was not my master, and there's the truth. My master'—here he looked round him, and began to whisper—'is a tall fine build of a man, and this was more of a dwarf.' Utterson attempted to protest. 'O, sir,' cried Poole, 'do you think I do not know my master after twenty years? do you think I do not know where his head comes to in the cabinet door, where I saw him every morning of my life? No, sir, that thing in the mask was never Dr Jekyll—God knows what it was, but it was never Dr Jekyll; and it is the belief of my heart that there was murder done.'

'Poole,' replied the lawyer, 'if you say that, it will become my duty to make certain. Much as I desire to spare your master's feelings, much as I am puzzled about this note, which seems to prove him to be still alive, I shall consider it my duty to break in that door.'

'Ah, Mr Utterson, that's talking!' cried the butler.

'And now comes the second question,' resumed Utterson: 'Who is going to do it?'

'Why, you and me, sir,' was the undaunted reply.

'That is very well said,' returned the lawyer; 'and whatever comes of it, I shall make it my business to see you are no loser.'

'There is an axe in the theatre,' continued Poole; 'and you might take the kitchen poker for yourself.'

The lawyer took that rude but weighty instrument into his hand, and balanced it. 'Do you know, Poole,' he said, looking up, 'that you and I are about to place our-selves in a position of some peril?'

'You may say so, sir, indeed,' returned the butler.

'It is well, then, that we should be frank,' said the other. 'We both think more than we have said; let us make a clean breast. This masked figure that you saw, did you recognise it?'

'Well, sir, it went so quick, and the creature was so doubled up, that I could hardly swear to that,' was the answer. 'But if you mean, was it Mr Hyde?—why, yes, I think it was! You see, it was much of the same bigness; and it had the same quick light way with it; and then who else could have got in by the laboratory door? You have not forgot, sir, that at the time of the murder he had still the key with him? But that's not all. I don't know, Mr Utterson, if ever you met this Mr Hyde?'

'Yes,' said the lawyer, 'I once spoke with him.'

'Then you must know, as well as the rest of us, that there was something queer about that gentleman—something that gave a man a turn—I don't know rightly how to say it, sir, beyond this: that you felt in your marrow—kind of cold and thin.'

'I own I felt something of what you describe,' said Mr Utterson.

'Quite so, sir,' returned Poole. 'Well, when that masked thing like a monkey jumped up from among the chemicals and whipped into the cabinet, it went down my spine like ice. O, I know it's not evidence, Mr Utterson; I'm book-learned enough for that; but a man has his feelings; and I give you my bible-word it was Mr Hyde!'

'Ay, ay,' said the lawyer. 'My fears incline to the same point. Evil, I fear, founded—evil was sure to come—of that connection. Ay, truly, I believe you; I believe poor Harry is killed; and I believe his murderer (for what purpose, God alone can tell) is still lurking in his victim's room. Well, let our name be vengeance. Call Bradshaw.'

The footman came at the summons, very white and nervous.

'Pull yourself together, Bradshaw,' said the lawyer. 'This suspense, I know, is telling upon all of you; but it is now our intention to make an end of it. Poole, here, and I are going to force our way into the cabinet. If all is well, my shoulders are broad enough to bear the blame. Meanwhile, lest anything should really be amiss, or any malefactor seek to escape by the back, you and the boy must go round the corner with a pair of good sticks, and take your post at the laboratory door. We give you ten minutes, to get to your stations.'

As Bradshaw left, the lawyer looked at his watch. 'And now, Poole, let us get to ours,' he said; and taking the poker under his arm, he led the way into the yard. The scud had banked over the moon, and it was now quite dark. The wind, which only broke in puffs and draughts into that deep well of building, tossed the light of the candle to and fro about their steps, until they came into the shelter of the theatre, where they sat down silently to wait. London hummed solemnly all around; but nearer at hand, the stillness was only broken by the sound of a footfall moving to and fro along the cabinet floor.

'So it will walk all day, sir,' whispered Poole; 'ay, and the better part of the night. Only when a new sample comes from the chemist, there's a bit of a break. Ah, it's an ill conscience that's such an enemy to rest! Ah, sir, there's blood foully shed in every step of it! But hark again, a little closer—put your heart in your ears Mr Utterson, and tell me, is that the doctor's foot?'

The steps fell lightly and oddly, with a certain swing, for all they went so slowly; it was different indeed from the heavy creaking tread of Henry Jekyll. Utterson sighed. 'Is there never anything else?' he asked.

Poole nodded. 'Once,' he said. 'Once I heard it weeping!'

'Weeping? how that?' said the lawyer, conscious of a sudden chill of horror.

'Weeping like a woman or a lost soul,' said the butler. 'I came away with that upon my heart, that I could have wept too.'

But now the ten minutes drew to an end. Poole disinterred the axe from under a stack of packing straw; the candle was set upon the nearest table to light them to the attack; and they drew near with bated breath to where the patient foot was still going up and down, up and down in the quiet of the night.

'Jekyll,' cried Utterson, with a loud voice, 'I demand to see you.' He paused a moment, but there came no reply. 'I give you fair warning, our suspicions are aroused, and I must and shall see you,' he resumed; 'if not by fair means, then by foul—if not of your consent, then by brute force!'

'Utterson,' said the voice, 'for God's sake, have mercy!'

'Ah, that's not Jekyll's voice—it's Hyde's!' cried Utterson. 'Down with the door, Poole!'

Poole swung the axe over his shoulder; the blow shook the building, and the red baize door leaped against the lock and hinges. A dismal screech, as of mere animal terror, rang from the cabinet. Up went the axe again, and again the panels crashed and the frame bounded; four times the blow fell; but the wood was tough and the fittings were of excellent workmanship; and it was not until the fifth that the lock burst in sunder, and the wreck of the door fell inwards on the carpet.

The besiegers, appalled by their own riot and the stillness that had succeeded, stood back a little and peered in. There lay the cabinet before their eyes in the quiet lamplight, a good fire glowing and chattering on the hearth, the kettle singing its thin strain, a drawer or two open, papers neatly set forth on the business table, and nearer the fire, the things laid out for tea; the quietest room, you would have said, and, but for the glazed presses full of chemicals, the most commonplace that night in London.

Right in the midst there lay the body of a man sorely contorted and still twitching. They drew near on tiptoe, turned it on its back, and beheld the face of Edward Hyde. He was dressed in clothes far too large for him, clothes of the doctor's bigness; the cords of his face still moved with a semblance of life, but life was quite gone; and by the crushed phial in the hand and the strong smell of kernels that hung upon the air, Utterson knew that he was looking on the body of a self-destroyer.

'We have come too late,' he said sternly, 'whether to save or punish. Hyde is gone to his account; and it only remains for us to find the body of your master.'

The far greater proportion of the building was occupied by the theatre, which filled almost the whole ground storey, and was lighted from above, and by the cabinet, which formed an upper storey at one end and looked upon the court. A corridor joined the theatre to the door on the by street; and with this, the cabinet communicated separately by a second flight of stairs. There were besides a few dark closets and a spacious cellar. All these they now thoroughly examined. Each closet needed but a glance, for all they were empty and all, by the dust that fell from their doors, had stood long unopened. The cellar, indeed, was filled with crazy lumber, mostly dating from the times of the surgeon who was Jekyll's predecessor; but even as they opened the door, they were advertised of the uselessness of further search by the fall of a perfect mat of cobweb which had for years sealed up the entrance. Nowhere was there any trace of Henry Jekyll, dead or alive.

Poole stamped on the flags of the corridor. 'He must be buried here,' he said, hearkening to the sound.

'Or he may have fled,' said Utterson, and he turned to examine the door in the by street. It was locked; and lying near by on the flags, they found the key, already stained with rust.

'This does not look like use,' observed the lawyer.

'Use!' echoed Poole. 'Do you not see, sir, it is broken? much as if a man had stamped on it.'

'Ah,' continued Utterson, 'and the fractures, too, are rusty.' The two men looked at each other with a scare. 'This is beyond me, Poole,' said the lawyer. 'Let us go back to the cabinet.'

They mounted the stair in silence, and still, with an occasional awestruck glance at the dead body, proceeded more thoroughly to examine the contents of the cabinet. At one table, there were traces of chemical work, various measured heaps of some white salt being laid on glass saucers, as though for an experiment in which the unhappy man had been prevented.

'That is the same drug that I was always bringing him,' said Poole; and even as he spoke, the kettle with a startling noise boiled over.

This brought them to the fireside, where the easy chair was drawn cosily up, and the tea things stood ready to the sitter's elbow, the very sugar in the cup. There were several books on a shelf; one lay beside the tea things open, and Utterson was amazed to find it a copy of a pious work for which Jekyll had several times expressed a great esteem, annotated, in his own hand, with startling blasphemies.

Next, in the course of their review of the chamber, the searchers came to the cheval-glass, into whose depth they looked with an involuntary horror. But it was so turned as to show them nothing but the rosy glow playing on the roof, the fire sparkling in a hundred repetitions along the glazed front of the presses, and their own pale and fearful countenances stooping to look in.

'This glass has seen some strange things, sir,' whispered Poole.

'And surely none stranger than itself,' echoed the lawyer, in the same tone. 'For what did Jekyll'—he caught himself up at the word with a start, and then conquering the weakness: 'what could Jekyll want with it?' he said.

'You may say that!' said Poole.

Next they turned to the business table. On the desk, among the neat array of papers, a large envelope was uppermost, and bore, in the doctor's hand, the name of Mr Utterson. The lawyer unsealed it, and several enclosures fell to the floor. The first was a will, drawn in the same eccentric terms as the one which he had returned six months before, to serve as a testament in case of death and as a deed of gift in case of disappearance; but in place of the name of Edward Hyde, the lawyer, with indescribable amazement, read the name of Gabriel John Utterson. He looked at Poole, and then back at the papers, and last of all at the dead malefactor stretched upon the carpet.

'My head goes round,' he said. 'He has been all these days in possession; he had no cause to like me; he must have raged to see himself displaced; and he has not destroyed this document.'

He caught the next paper; it was a brief note in the doctor's hand and dated at the top. 'O Poole!' the lawyer cried, 'he was alive and here this day. He cannot have been disposed of in so short a space; he must be still alive, he must have fled! And then, why fled? and how? and in that case can we venture to declare this suicide? O, we must be careful. I foresee that we may yet involve your master in some dire catastrophe.'

'Why don't you read it, sir?' asked Poole.

'Because I fear,' replied the lawyer, solemnly. 'God grant I have no cause for it!' And with that he brought the paper to his eyes, and read as follows:

> My dear Utterson,—When this shall fall into your hands, I shall have disappeared, under what circumstances I have not the penetration to foresee, but my instinct and all the circumstances of my nameless situation tell me that the end is sure and must be early. Go then, and first read the narrative which Lanyon warned me he was to place in your hands; and if you care to hear more, turn to the confession of
>
> Your unworthy and unhappy friend,
>
> Henry Jekyll

'There was a third enclosure,' asked Utterson.

'Here, sir,' said Poole, and gave into his hands a considerable packet sealed in several places.

The lawyer put it in his pocket. 'I would say nothing of this paper. If your master has fled or is dead, we may at least save his credit. It is now ten; I must go home and read these documents in quiet; but I shall be back before midnight, when we shall send for the police.'

They went out, locking the door of the theatre behind them; and Utterson, once more leaving the servants gathered about the fire in the hall, trudged back to his office to read the two narratives in which this mystery was now to be explained.

Dr Lanyon's Narrative

On the ninth of January, now four days ago, I received by the evening delivery a registered envelope, addressed in the hand of my colleague and old school-companion, Henry Jekyll. I was a good deal surprised by this; for we were by no means in the habit of correspondence; I had seen the man, dined with him, indeed, the night before; and I could imagine nothing in our intercourse that should justify the formality of registration. The contents increased my wonder; for this is how the letter ran:

> *10th December 18———*
>
> Dear Lanyon,—You are one of my oldest friends; and although we may have differed at times on scientific questions, I cannot remember, at least on my side, any break in our affection. There was never a day when, if you had said to me, "Jekyll, my life, my honour, my reason, depend upon you," I would not have sacrificed my fortune or my left hand to help you. Lanyon, my life, my honour, my reason, are all at your mercy; if you fail me to-night, I am lost. You might suppose, after this preface, that I am going to ask you for something dishonourable to grant. Judge for yourself.

I want you to postpone all other engagements for to-night—ay, even if you were summoned to the bedside of an emperor; to take a cab, unless your carriage should be actually at the door; and, with this letter in your hand for consultation, to drive straight to my house. Poole, my butler, has his orders; you will find him waiting your arrival with a locksmith. The door of my cabinet is then to be forced; and you are to go in alone; to open the glazed press (letter E) on the left hand, breaking the lock if it be shut; and to draw out, *with all its contents as they stand,* the fourth drawer from the top or (which is the same thing) the third from the bottom. In my extreme distress of mind, I have a morbid fear of misdirecting you; but even if I am in error, you may know the right drawer by its contents: some powders, a phial, and a paper book. This drawer I beg of you to carry back with you to Cavendish Square exactly as it stands.

That is the first part of the service: now for the second. You should be back, if you set out at once on the receipt of this, long before midnight; but I will leave you that amount of margin, not only in the fear of one of those obstacles that can neither be prevented nor foreseen, but because an hour when your servants are in bed is to be preferred for what will then remain to do. At midnight, then, I have to ask you to be alone in your consulting-room, to admit with your own hand into the house a man who will present himself in my name, and to place in his hands the drawer that you will have brought with you from my cabinet. Then you will have played your part and earned my gratitude completely. Five minutes afterwards, if you insist upon an explanation, you will have understood that these arrangements are of capital importance; and that by the neglect of one of them, fantastic as they must appear, you might have charged your conscience with my death or the shipwreck of my reason.

Confident as I am that you will not trifle with this appeal, my heart sinks and my hand trembles at the bare thought of such a possibility. Think of me at this hour, in a strange place, labouring under a blackness of distress that no fancy can exaggerate, and yet well aware that, if you will but punctually serve me, my troubles will roll away like a story that is told. Serve me, my dear Lanyon, and save

Your friend,

H. J.

PS.—I had already sealed this up when a fresh terror struck upon my soul. It is possible that the post office may fail me, and this letter not come into your hands until to-morrow morning. In that case, dear Lanyon, do my errand when it shall be most convenient for you in the course of the day; and once more expect my messenger at midnight. It may then already be too late; and if that night passes without event, you will know that you have seen the last of Henry Jekyll.

Upon the reading of this letter, I made sure my colleague was insane; but till that was proved beyond the possibility of doubt, I felt bound to do as he requested. The less I understood of this farrago, the less I was in a position to judge of its importance; and an appeal so worded could not be set aside without a grave responsibility. I rose accordingly from table, got into a hansom, and drove straight to Jekyll's house. The butler was awaiting my arrival; he had received by the same post as mine a registered letter of instruction, and had sent at once for a locksmith and a carpenter. The tradesmen came while we were yet speaking; and we moved in a body to old Dr Denman's surgical theatre, from which (as you are doubtless aware) Jekyll's private cabinet is most conveniently entered. The door was very strong, the lock excellent; the carpenter avowed he would have great trouble, and have to do much damage, if force were to be used; and the locksmith was near despair. But this last was a handy fellow, and after two hours' work, the door stood open. The press marked E was unlocked; and I took out the drawer, had it filled up with straw and tied in a sheet, and returned with it to Cavendish Square.

Here I proceeded to examine its contents. The powders were neatly enough made up, but not with the nicety of the dispensing chemist; so that it was plain they were of Jekyll's private manufacture; and when I opened one of the wrappers, I found what seemed to me a simple crystalline salt of a white colour. The phial, to which I next turned my attention, might have been about half-full of a blood-red liquor, which was highly pungent to the sense of smell, and seemed to me to contain phosphorus and some volatile ether. At the other ingredients I could make no guess. The book was an ordinary version book, and contained little but a series of dates. These covered a period of many years, but I observed that the entries ceased nearly a year ago and quite abruptly. Here and there a brief remark was appended to a date, usually no more than a single word: 'double' occurring perhaps six times in a total of several hundred entries; and once very early in the list and followed by several marks of exclamation, 'total failure!!!' All this, though it whetted my curiosity, told me little that was definite. Here were a phial of some tincture, a paper of some salt, and the record of a series of experiments that had led (like too many of Jekyll's investigations) to no end of practical usefulness. How could the presence of these articles in my house affect either the honour, the sanity, or the life of my flighty colleague? If his messenger could go to one place, why could he not go to another? And even granting some impediment, why was this gentleman to be received by me in secret? The more I reflected, the more convinced I grew that I was dealing with a case of cerebral disease; and though I dismissed my servants to bed, I loaded an old revolver, that I might be found in some posture of self-defence.

Twelve o'clock had scarce rung out over London, ere the knocker sounded very gently on the door. I went myself at the summons, and found a small man crouching against the pillars of the portico.

'Are you come from Dr Jekyll?' I asked.

He told me 'yes' by a constrained gesture; and when I had bidden him enter, he did not obey me without a searching backward glance into the darkness of the square. There was a policeman not far off, advancing with his bull's eye open; and at the sight, I thought my visitor started and made greater haste.

These particulars struck me, I confess, disagreeably; and as I followed him into the bright light of the consulting-room, I kept my hand ready on my weapon. Here, at last, I had a chance of clearly seeing him. I had never set eyes on him before, so much was certain. He was small, as I have said: I was struck besides with the shocking expression of his face, with his remarkable combination of great muscular activity and great apparent debility of constitution, and—last but not least—with the odd, subjective disturbance caused by his neighbourhood. This bore some resemblance to incipient rigor, and was accompanied by a marked sinking of the pulse. At the time, I set it down to some idiosyncratic, personal distaste, and merely wondered at the acuteness of the symptoms; but I have since had reason to believe the cause to lie much deeper in the nature of man, and to turn on some nobler hinge than the principle of hatred.

This person (who had thus, from the first moment of his entrance, struck in me what I can only describe as a disgustful curiosity) was dressed in a fashion that would have made an ordinary person laughable; his clothes, that is to say, although they were of rich and sober fabric, were enormously too large for him in every measurement— the trousers hanging on his legs and rolled up to keep them from the ground, the waist of the coat below his haunches, and the collar sprawling wide upon his shoulders. Strange to relate, this ludicrous accoutrement was far from moving me to laughter. Rather, as there was something abnormal and misbegotten in the very essence of the creature that now faced me—something seizing, surprising and revolting—this fresh disparity seemed but to fit in with and to reinforce it; so that to my interest in the man's nature and character there was added a curiosity as to his origin, his life, his fortune and status in the world.

These observations, though they have taken so great a space to be set down in, were yet the work of a few seconds. My visitor was, indeed, on fire with sombre excitement.

'Have you got it?' he cried. 'Have you got it?' And so lively was his impatience that he even laid his hand upon my arm and sought to shake me.

I put him back conscious at his touch of a certain icy pang along my blood. 'Come, sir,' said I. 'You forget that I have not yet the pleasure of your acquaintance. Be seated, if you please.' And I showed him an example, and sat down myself in my customary seat and with as fair an imitation of my ordinary manner to a patient, as the lateness of the hour, the nature of my pre-occupations, and the horror I had of my visitor would suffer me to muster.

'I beg your pardon, Dr Lanyon,' he replied, civilly enough. 'What you say is very well founded; and my impatience has shown its heels to my politeness. I come here at the instance of your colleague, Dr Henry Jekyll, on a piece of business of some moment; and I understood . . .' he paused and put his hand to his throat, and I could see, in spite of his collected manner, that he was wrestling against the approaches of the hysteria—'I understood, a drawer . . .'

But here I took pity on my visitor's suspense, and some perhaps on my own growing curiosity.

'There it is, sir,' said I, pointing to the drawer where it lay on the floor behind a table, and still covered with the sheet.

He sprang to it, and then paused, and laid his hand upon his heart; I could hear his teeth grate with the convulsive action of his jaws; and his face was so ghastly to see that I grew alarmed both for his life and reason.

'Compose yourself,' said I.

He turned a dreadful smile to me, and, as if with the decision of despair, plucked away the sheet. At sight of the contents, he uttered one loud sob of such immense relief that I sat petrified. And the next moment, in a voice that was already fairly well under control, 'Have you a graduated glass?' he asked.

I rose from my place with something of an effort, and gave him what he asked.

He thanked me with a smiling nod, measured out a few minims of the red tincture and added one of the powders. The mixture, which was at first of a reddish hue, began, in proportion as the crystals melted, to brighten in colour, to effervesce audibly, and to throw off small fumes of vapour. Suddenly, and at the same moment, the ebullition ceased, and the compound changed to a dark purple, which faded again more slowly to a watery green. My visitor, who had watched these metamorphoses with a keen eye, smiled, set down the glass upon the table, and then turned and looked upon me with an air of scrutiny.

'And now,' said he, 'to settle what remains. Will you be wise? will you be guided? will you suffer me to take this glass in my hand, and to go forth from your house without further parley? or has the greed of curiosity too much command of you? Think before you answer, for it shall be done as you decide. As you decide, you shall be left as you were before, and neither richer nor wiser, unless the sense of service rendered to a man in mortal distress may be counted as a kind of riches of the soul. Or, if you shall so prefer to choose, a new province of knowledge and new avenues to fame and power shall be laid open to you, here, in this room, upon the instant; and your sight shall be blasted by a prodigy to stagger the unbelief of Satan.'

'Sir,' said I, affecting a coolness that I was far from truly possessing, 'you speak enigmas, and you will perhaps not wonder that I hear you with no very strong impression of belief. But I have gone too far in the way of inexplicable services to pause before I see the end.'

'It is well,' replied my visitor. 'Lanyon, you remember your vows: what follows is under the seal of our profession. And now, you who have so long been bound to the most narrow and material views, you who have denied the virtue of transcendental medicine, you who have derided your superiors—behold!'

He put the glass to his lips, and drank at one gulp. A cry followed; he reeled, staggered, clutched at the table and held on, staring with injected eyes, gasping with open mouth; and as I looked, there came, I thought, a change—he seemed to swell—his face became suddenly black, and the features seemed to melt and alter—and the next moment I had sprung to my feet and leaped back against the wall, my arm raised to shield me from that prodigy, my mind submerged in terror.

'O God!' I screamed, and 'O God!' again and again; for there before my eyes—pale and shaken, and half fainting, and groping before him with his hands, like a man restored from death—there stood Henry Jekyll!

What he told me in the next hour I cannot bring my mind to set on paper. I saw what I saw, I heard what I heard, and my soul sickened at it; and yet, now when that sight has faded from my eyes, I ask myself if I believe it, and I cannot answer. My life is shaken to its roots; sleep has left me; the deadliest terror sits by me at all hours of the day and night; I feel that my days are numbered, and that I must die; and yet I shall die incredulous. As for the moral turpitude that man unveiled to me, even with tears of penitence, I cannot, even in memory, dwell on it without a start of horror. I will say but one thing, Utterson, and that (if you can bring your mind to credit it) will be more than enough. The creature who crept into my house that night was, on Jekyll's own confession, known by the name of Hyde and hunted for in every corner of the land as the murderer of Carew.

HASTIE LANYON

Henry Jekyll's Full Statement of the Case

I was born in the year 18—— to a large fortune, endowed besides with excellent parts, inclined by nature to industry, fond of the respect of the wise and good among my fellow-men, and thus, as might have been supposed, with every guarantee of an honourable and distinguished future. And indeed, the worst of my faults was a certain impatient gaiety of disposition, such as has made the happiness of many, but such as I found it hard to reconcile with my imperious desire to carry my head high, and wear a more than commonly grave countenance before the public. Hence it came about that I concealed my pleasures; and that when I reached years of reflection, and began to look round me and take stock of my progress and position in the world, I stood already committed to a profound duplicity of life. Many a man would have even blazoned such irregularities as I was guilty of; but from the high views that I had set before me, I regarded and hid them with an almost morbid sense of shame. It was thus rather the exacting nature of my aspirations, than any particular degradation in my faults, that made me what I was and, with even a deeper trench than in the majority of men, severed in me those provinces of good and ill which divide and compound man's dual nature. In this case, I was driven to reflect deeply and inveterately on that hard law of life which lies at the root of religion, and is one of the most plentiful springs of distress. Though so profound a double-dealer, I was in no sense a hypocrite; both sides of me were in dead earnest; I was no more myself when I laid aside restraint and plunged in shame, than when I laboured, in the eye of day, at the furtherance of knowledge or the relief of sorrow and suffering. And it chanced that the direction of my scientific studies, which led wholly towards the mystic and the transcendental, reacted and shed a strong light on this consciousness of the perennial war among my members. With every day, and from both sides of my intelligence, the moral and the intellectual, I thus drew steadily nearer to that truth by whose partial discovery I have been doomed to such a dreadful shipwreck: that man is not truly one, but truly two. I say two, because the state of my own knowledge does not pass beyond that point. Others will follow, others will outstrip me on the same lines; and I hazard the guess that man will be ultimately known for a mere polity of multifarious, incongruous and independent denizens. I, for my part, from the nature of my life, advanced infallibly in one direction and in one direction only. It was on the moral side, and in my own person, that I learned to recognise the thorough and primitive duality of man; I saw that, of the two natures that contended in the field of my consciousness, even if I could rightly be said to be either, it was only because I was radically both; and from an early date, even before the course of my scientific discoveries had begun to suggest the most naked possibility of such a miracle, I had learned to dwell with pleasure, as a beloved daydream, on the thought of the separation of these elements. If each, I told myself, could but be housed in separate identities, life would be relieved of all that was unbearable; the unjust might go his way, delivered from the aspirations and remorse of his more upright twin; and the just could walk steadfastly and securely on his upward path, doing the good things in which he found his pleasure, and no longer exposed to disgrace and penitence by the hands of this extraneous evil. It was the curse of mankind that these incongruous faggots were thus bound together—that in the agonised womb of consciousness these polar twins should be continuously struggling. How, then, were they dissociated?

I was so far in my reflections when, as I have said, a side light began to shine upon the subject from the laboratory table. I began to perceive more deeply than it has ever yet been stated, the trembling immateriality, the mist-like transience, of this seemingly so solid body in which we walk attired. Certain agents I found to have the power to shake and to pluck back that fleshly vestment, even as a wind might toss the curtains of a pavilion. For two good reasons, I will not enter deeply into this scientific branch of my confession. First, because I have been made to learn that the doom and burthen of our life is bound for ever on man's shoulders; and when the attempt is made to cast it off, it but returns upon us with more unfamiliar and more awful pressure. Second, because, as my narrative will make, alas! too evident, my discoveries were incomplete. Enough, then, that I not only recognised my natural body for the mere aura and effulgence of certain of the powers that made up my spirit, but managed to compound a drug by which these powers should be dethroned from their supremacy, and a second form and countenance substituted, none the less natural to me because they were the expression, and bore the stamp, of lower elements in my soul.

I hesitated long before I put this theory to the test of practice. I knew well that I risked death; for any drug that so potently controlled and shook the very fortress of identity, might by the least scruple of an overdose or at the least inopportunity in the moment of exhibition, utterly blot out that immaterial tabernacle which I looked to it to change. But the temptation of a discovery so singular and profound at last overcame the suggestions of alarm. I had long since prepared my tincture; I purchased at once, from a firm of wholesale chemists, a large quantity of a particular salt, which I knew, from my experiments, to be the last ingredient required; and, late one accursed night, I compounded the elements, watched them boil and smoke together in the glass, and when the ebullition had subsided, with a strong glow of courage, drank off the potion.

The most racking pangs succeeded: a grinding in the bones, deadly nausea, and a horror of the spirit that cannot be exceeded at the hour of birth or death. Then these agonies began swiftly to subside, and I came to myself as if out of a great sickness. There was something strange in my sensations, something indescribably new and, from its very novelty, incredibly sweet. I felt younger, lighter, happier in body; within I was conscious of a heady recklessness, a current of disordered sensual images running like a mill race in my fancy, a solution of the bonds of obligation, an unknown but not an innocent freedom of the soul. I knew myself, at the first breath of this new life, to be more wicked, tenfold more wicked, sold a slave to my original evil; and the thought, in that moment, braced and delighted me like wine. I stretched out my hands, exulting in the freshness of these sensations; and in the act, I was suddenly aware that I had lost in stature.

There was no mirror, at that date, in my room; that which stands beside me as I write was brought there later on, and for the very purpose of those transformations. The night, however, was far gone into the morning—the morning, black as it was, was nearly ripe for the conception of the day—the inmates of my house were locked in the most rigorous hours of slumber; and I determined, flushed as I was with hope and triumph, to venture in my new shape as far as to my bedroom. I crossed the yard, wherein the constellations looked down upon me, I could have thought, with wonder, the first creature of that sort that their unsleeping vigilance had yet disclosed to them; I stole through the corridors, a stranger in my own house; and coming to my room, I saw for the first time the appearance of Edward Hyde.

I must here speak by theory alone, saying not that which I know, but that which I suppose to be most probable. The evil side of my nature, to which I had now transferred the stamping efficacy, was less robust and less developed than the good which I had just deposed. Again, in the course of my life, which had been, after all, nine-tenths a life of effort, virtue and control, it had been much less exercised and much less exhausted. And hence, as I think, it came about that Edward Hyde was so much smaller, slighter, and younger than Henry Jekyll. Even as good shone upon the countenance of the one, evil was written broadly and plainly on the face of the other. Evil besides (which I must still believe to be the lethal side of man) had left on that body an imprint of deformity and decay. And yet when I looked upon that ugly idol in the glass, I was conscious of no repugnance, rather of a leap of welcome. This, too, was myself. It seemed natural and human. In my eyes it bore a livelier image of the spirit, it seemed more express and single, than the imperfect and divided countenance, I had been hitherto accustomed to call mine. And in so far I was doubtless right. I have observed that when I wore the semblance of Edward Hyde, none could come near to me at first without a visible misgiving of the flesh. This, as I take it, was because all human beings, as we meet them, are commingled out of good and evil: and Edward Hyde, alone, in the ranks of mankind, was pure evil.

I lingered but a moment at the mirror: the second and conclusive experiment had yet to be attempted; it yet remained to be seen if I had lost my identity beyond redemption and must flee before daylight from a house that was no longer mine; and hurrying back to my cabinet, I once more prepared and drank the cup, once more suffered the pangs of dissolution, and came to myself once more with the character, the stature, and the face of Henry Jekyll.

That night I had come to the fatal cross roads. Had I approached my discovery in a more noble spirit, had I risked the experiment while under the empire of generous or pious aspirations, all must have been otherwise, and from these agonies of death and birth I had come forth an angel instead of a fiend. The drug had no discriminating action; it was neither diabolical nor divine; it but shook the doors of the prison-house of my disposition; and, like the captives of Philippi, that which stood within ran forth. At that time my virtue slumbered; my evil, kept awake by ambition, was alert and swift to seize the occasion; and the thing that was projected was Edward Hyde. Hence, although I had now two characters as well as two appearances, one was wholly evil, and the other was still the old Henry Jekyll, that incongruous compound of whose reformation and improvement I had already learned to despair. The movement was thus wholly toward the worse.

Even at that time, I had not yet conquered my aversion to the dryness of a life of study. I would still be merrily disposed at times; and as my pleasures were (to say the least) undignified, and I was not only well known and highly considered, but growing towards the elderly man, this incoherency of my life was daily growing more unwelcome. It was on this side that my new power tempted me until I fell in slavery. I had but to drink the cup, to doff at once the body of the noted professor, and to assume, like a thick cloak, that of Edward Hyde. I smiled at the notion; it seemed to me at the time to be humorous; and I made my preparations with the most studious care. I took and furnished that house in Soho to which Hyde was tracked by the police; and engaged as housekeeper a creature whom I well knew to be silent and unscrupulous. On the other side, I announced to my servants that a Mr Hyde (whom I described) was to have full liberty and power about my house in the square; and, to parry mishaps, I even called and made myself a familiar object in my second character. I next drew up that will to which you so much objected; so that if anything befell me in the person of Dr Jekyll, I could enter on that of Edward Hyde without pecuniary loss. And thus fortified, as I supposed, on every side, I began to profit by the strange immunities of my position.

Men have before hired bravos to transact their crimes, while their own person and reputation sat under shelter. I was the first that ever did so for his pleasures. I was the first that could thus plod in the public eye with a load of genial respectability, and in a moment, like a schoolboy, strip off these lendings and spring headlong into the sea of liberty. But for me, in my impenetrable mantle, the safety was complete. Think of it—I did not even exist! Let me but escape into my laboratory door, give me but a second or two to mix and swallow the draught that I had always standing ready; and, whatever he had done, Edward Hyde would pass away like the stain of breath upon a mirror; and there in his stead, quietly at home, trimming the midnight lamp in his study, a man who could afford to laugh at suspicion, would be Henry Jekyll.

The pleasures which I made haste to seek in my disguise were, as I have said, undignified; I would scarce use a harder term. But in the hands of Edward Hyde they soon began to turn towards the monstrous. When I would come back from these excursions, I was often plunged into a kind of wonder at my vicarious depravity. This familiar that I called out of my own soul, and sent forth alone to do his good pleasure, was a being inherently malign and villainous; his every act and thought centred on self; drinking pleasure with bestial avidity from any degree of torture to another; relentless like a man of stone. Henry Jekyll stood at times aghast before the acts of Edward Hyde; but the situation was apart from ordinary laws, and insidiously relaxed the grasp of conscience. It was Hyde, after all, and Hyde alone, that was guilty. Jekyll was no worse; he woke again to his good qualities seemingly unimpaired; he would even make haste, where it was possible, to undo the evil done by Hyde. And thus his conscience slumbered.

Into the details of the infamy at which I thus connived (for even now I can scarce grant that I committed it) I have no design of entering. I mean but to point out the warnings and the successive steps with which my chastisement approached. I met with one accident which, as it brought on no consequence, I shall no more than mention. An act of cruelty to a child aroused against me the anger of a passerby, whom I recognised the other day in the person of your kinsman; the doctor and the child's family joined him; there were moments when I feared for my life; and at last, in order to pacify their too just resentment, Edward Hyde had to bring them to the door, and pay them in a cheque drawn in the name of Henry Jekyll. But this danger was easily eliminated from the future by opening an account at another bank in the name of Edward Hyde himself; and when, by sloping my own hand backwards, I had supplied my double with a signature, I thought I sat beyond the reach of fate.

Some two months before the murder of Sir Danvers, I had been out for one of my adventures, had returned at a late hour, and woke the next day in bed with somewhat odd sensations. It was in vain I looked about me; in vain I saw the decent furniture and tall proportions of my room in the square; in vain that I recognised the pattern of the bed curtains and the design of the mahogany frame; something still kept insisting that I was not where I was, that I had not wakened where I seemed to be, but in the little room in Soho where I was accustomed to sleep in the body of Edward Hyde. I smiled to myself, and, in my psychological way, began lazily to inquire into the elements of this illusion, occasionally, even as I did so, dropping back into a comfortable morning doze. I was still so engaged when, in one of my more wakeful moments, my eye fell upon my hand. Now, the hand of Henry Jekyll (as you have often remarked) was professional in shape and size; it was large, firm, white and comely. But the hand which I now saw, clearly enough in the yellow light of a mid-London morning, lying half shut on the bed-clothes, was lean, corded, knuckly, of a dusky pallor, and thickly shaded with a swart growth of hair. It was the hand of Edward Hyde.

I must have stared upon it for near half a minute, sunk as I was in the mere stupidity of wonder, before terror woke up in my breast as sudden and startling as the crash of cymbals; and bounding from my bed, I rushed to the mirror. At the sight that met my eyes, my blood was changed into something exquisitely thin and icy. Yes, I had gone to bed Henry Jekyll, I had awakened Edward Hyde. How was this to be explained? I asked myself; and then, with another bound of terror—how was it to be remedied? It was well on in the morning; the servants were up; all my drugs were in the cabinet—a long journey, down two pairs of stairs, through the back passage, across the open court and through the anatomical theatre, from where I was then standing horror-struck. It might indeed be possible to cover my face; but of what use was that, when I was unable to conceal the alteration in my stature? And then, with an over-powering sweetness of relief, it came back upon my mind that the servants were already used to the coming and going of my second self. I had soon dressed, as well as I was able, in clothes of my own size; had soon passed through the house, where Bradshaw stared and drew back at seeing Mr Hyde at such an hour and in such a strange array; and ten minutes later, Dr Jekyll had returned to his own shape and was sitting down, with a darkened brow, to make a feint of breakfasting.

Small indeed was my appetite. This inexplicable incident, this reversal of my previous experience, seemed, like the Babylonian finger on the wall, to be spelling out the letters of my judgment; and I began to reflect more seriously than ever before on the issues and possibilities of my double existence. That part of me which I had the power of projecting had lately been much exercised and nourished; it had seemed to me of late as though the body of Edward Hyde had grown in stature, as though (when I wore that form) I were conscious of a more generous tide of blood; and I began to spy a danger that, if this were much prolonged, the balance of my nature might be permanently overthrown, the power of voluntary change be forfeited, and the character of Edward Hyde become irrevocably mine. The power of the drug had not been always equally displayed. Once, very early in my career, it had totally failed me; since then I had been obliged on more than one occasion to double, and once, with infinite risk of death, to treble the amount; and these rare uncertainties had cast hitherto the sole shadow on my contentment. Now, however, and in the light of that morning's accident, I was led to remark that whereas, in the beginning, the difficulty had been to throw off the body of Jekyll, it had of late gradually but decidedly transferred itself to the other side. All things therefore seemed to point to this: that I was slowly losing hold of my original and better self, and becoming slowly incorporated with my second and worse.

Between these two I now felt I had to choose. My two natures had memory in common, but all other faculties were most unequally shared between them. Jekyll (who was a composite) now with the most sensitive apprehensions, now with a greedy gusto, projected and shared in the pleasures and adventures of Hyde; but Hyde was indifferent to Jekyll, or but remembered him as the mountain bandit remembers the cavern in which he conceals himself from pursuit. Jekyll had more than a father's interest; Hyde had more than a son's indifference. To cast in my lot with Jekyll was to die to those appetites which I had long secretly indulged and had of late begun to pamper. To cast it in with Hyde was to die to a thousand interests and aspirations, and to become, at a blow and for ever, despised and friendless. The bargain might appear unequal; but there was still another consideration in the scales; for while Jekyll would suffer smartingly in the fires of abstinence, Hyde would be not even conscious of all that he had lost. Strange as my circumstances were, the terms of this debate are as old and commonplace as man; much the same inducements and alarms cast the die for any tempted and trembling sinner; and it fell out with me, as it falls with so vast a majority of my fellows, that I chose the better part and was found wanting in the strength to keep to it.

Yes, I preferred the elderly and discontented doctor, surrounded by friends and cherishing honest hopes; and bade a resolute farewell to the liberty, the comparative youth, the light step, leaping pulses and secret pleasures, that I had enjoyed in the disguise of Hyde. I made this choice perhaps with some unconscious reservation, for I neither gave up the house in Soho, nor destroyed the clothes of Edward Hyde, which still lay ready in my cabinet. For two months, however, I was true to my determination; for two months I led a life of such severity as I had never before attained to, and enjoyed the compensations of an approving conscience. But time began at last to obliterate the freshness of my alarm; the praises of conscience began to grow into a thing of course; I began to be tortured with throes and longings, as of Hyde struggling after freedom; and at last, in an hour of moral weakness, I once again compounded and swallowed the transforming draught.

I do not suppose that when a drunkard reasons with himself upon his vice, he is once out of five hundred times affected by the dangers that he runs through his brutish physical insensibility; neither had I, long as I had considered my position, made enough allowance for the complete moral insensibility and insensate readiness to evil which were the leading characters of Edward Hyde. Yet it was by these that I was punished. My devil had been long caged, he came out roaring. I was conscious, even when I took the draught, of a more unbridled, a more furious propensity to ill. It must have been this, I suppose, that stirred in my soul that tempest of impatience with which I listened to the civilities of my unhappy victim; I declare at least, before God, no man morally sane could have been guilty of that crime upon so pitiful a provocation; and that I struck in no more reasonable spirit than that in which a sick child may break a plaything. But I had voluntarily stripped myself of all those balancing instincts by which even the worst of us continues to walk with some degree of steadiness among temptations; and in my case, to be tempted, however slightly, was to fall.

Instantly the spirit of hell awoke in me and raged. With a transport of glee, I mauled the unresisting body, tasting delight from every blow; and it was not till weariness had begun to succeed that I was suddenly, in the top fit of my delirium, struck through the heart by a cold thrill of terror. A mist dispersed; I saw my life to be forfeit; and fled from the scene of these excesses, at once glorying and trembling, my lust of evil gratified and stimulated, my love of life screwed to the topmost peg. I ran to the house in Soho, and (to make assurance doubly sure) destroyed my papers; thence I set out through the lamplit streets, in the same divided ecstasy of mind, gloating on my crime, light-headedly devising others in the future, and yet still hastening and still harkening in my wake for the steps of the avenger. Hyde had a song upon his lips as he compounded the draught, and as he drank it pledged the dead man. The pangs of transformation had not done tearing him, before Henry Jekyll, with streaming tears of gratitude and remorse, had fallen upon his knees and lifted his clasped hand to God. The veil of self-indulgence was rent from head to foot, I saw my life as a whole: I followed it up from the days of childhood, when I had walked with my father's hand, and through the self-denying toils of my professional life, to arrive again and again, with the same sense of unreality, at the damned horrors of the evening. I could have screamed aloud; I sought with tears and prayers to smother down the crowd of hideous images and sounds with which my memory swarmed against me; and still, between the petitions, the ugly face of my inquity stared into my soul. As the acuteness of this remorse began to die away, it was succeeded by a sense of joy. The problem of my conduct was solved. Hyde was henceforth impossible; whether I would or not, I was now confined to the better part of my existence; and, oh, how I rejoiced to think it! with what willing humility I embraced anew the restrictions of natural life! with what sincere renunciation I locked the door by which I had so often gone and come, and ground the key under my heel!

The next day came the news that the murder had been overlooked, that the guilt of Hyde was patent to the world, and that the victim was a man high in public estimation. It was not only a crime, it had been a tragic folly. I think I was glad to know it; I think I was glad to have my better impulses thus buttressed and guarded by the terrors of the scaffold. Jekyll was now my city of refuge; let but Hyde peep out an instant, and the hands of all men would be raised to take and slay him.

I resolved in my future conduct to redeem the past; and I can say with honesty that my resolve was fruitful of some good. You know yourself how earnestly in the last months of last year I laboured to relieve suffering; you know that much was done for others, and that the days passed quietly, almost happily for myself. Nor can I truly say that I wearied of this beneficent and innocent life; I think instead that I daily enjoyed it more completely; but I was still cursed with my duality of purpose; and as the first edge of my penitence wore off, the lower side of me, so long indulged, so recently chained down, began to growl for licence. Not that I dreamed of resuscitating Hyde; the bare idea of that would startle me to frenzy: no, it was in my own person that I was once more tempted to trifle with my conscience; and it was as an ordinary secret sinner that I at last fell before the assaults of temptation.

There comes an end to all things; the most capacious measure is filled at last; and this brief condescension to my evil finally destroyed the balance of my soul. And yet I was not alarmed; the fall seemed natural, like a return to the old days before I had made my discovery. It was a fine, clear January day, wet under foot where the frost had melted, but cloudless overhead; and the Regent's Park was full of winter chirrupings and sweet with Spring odours. I sat in the sun on a bench; the animal within me licking the chops of memory; the spiritual side a little drowsed, promising subsequent penitence, but not yet moved to begin. After all, I reflected, I was like my neighbours; and then I smiled, comparing myself with other men, comparing my active goodwill with the lazy cruelty of their neglect. And at the very moment of that vainglorious thought, a qualm came over me, a horrid nausea and the most deadly shuddering. These passed away, and left me faint; and then as in its turn the faintness subsided, I began to be aware of a change in the temper of my thoughts, a greater boldness, a contempt of danger, a solution of the bonds of obligation. I looked down; my clothes hung formlessly on my shrunken limbs; the hand that lay on my knee was corded and hairy. I was once more Edward Hyde. A moment before I had been safe of all men's respect, wealthy, beloved—the cloth laying for me in the dining-room at home; and now I was the common quarry of mankind, hunted, houseless, a known murderer, thrall to the gallows.

My reason wavered, but it did not fail me utterly. I have more than once observed that, in my second character, my faculties seemed sharpened to a point and my spirits more tensely elastic; thus it came about that, where Jekyll perhaps might have succumbed, Hyde rose to the importance of the moment. My drugs were in one of the presses of my cabinet: how was I to reach them? That was the problem that (crushing my temples in my hands) I set myself to solve. The laboratory door I had closed. If I sought to enter by the house, my own servants would consign me to the gallows. I saw I must employ another hand, and thought of Lanyon. How was he to be reached? how persuaded? Supposing that I escaped capture in the streets, how was I to make my way into his presence? and how should I, an unknown and displeasing visitor, prevail on the famous physician to rifle the study of his colleague, Dr Jekyll? Then I remembered that of my original character, one part remained to me: I could write my own hand; and once I had conceived that kindling spark, the way that I must follow became lighted up from end to end.

Thereupon, I arranged my clothes as best I could, and summoning a passing hansom, drove to an hotel in Portland Street, the name of which I chanced to remember. At my appearance (which was indeed comical enough, however tragic a fate these garments covered) the driver could not conceal his mirth. I gnashed my teeth upon him with a gust of devilish fury; and the smile withered from his face—happily for him— yet more happily for myself, for in another instant I had certainly dragged him from his perch. At the inn, as I entered, I looked about me with so black a countenance as made the attendants tremble; not a look did they exchange in my presence; but obsequiously took my orders, led me to a private room, and brought me wherewithal to write. Hyde in danger of his life was a creature new to me: shaken with inordinate anger, strung to the pitch of murder, lusting to inflict pain. Yet the creature was astute; mastered his fury with a great effort of the will; composed his two important letters, one to Lanyon and one to Poole, and, that he might receive actual evidence of their being posted, sent them out with directions that they should be registered.

Thenceforward, he sat all day over the fire in the private room, gnawing his nails; there he dined, sitting alone with his fears, the waiter visibly quailing before his eye; and thence, when the night was fully come, he set forth in the corner of a closed cab, and was driven to and fro about the streets of the city. He, I say—I cannot say, I. That child of Hell had nothing human; nothing lived in him but fear and hatred. And when at last, thinking the driver had begun to grow suspicious, he discharged the cab and ventured on foot, attired in his misfitting clothes, an object marked out for observation, into the midst of the nocturnal passengers, these two base passions raged within him like a tempest. He walked fast, hunted by his fears, chattering to himself, skulking through the less frequented thoroughfares, counting the minutes that still divided him from midnight. Once a woman spoke to him, offering, I think, a box of lights. He smote her in the face, and she fled.

When I came to myself at Lanyon's, the horror of my old friend perhaps affected me somewhat: I do not know; it was at least but a drop in the sea to the abhorrence with which I looked back upon these hours. A change had come over me. It was no longer the fear of the gallows, it was the horror of being Hyde that racked me. I received Lanyon's condemnation partly in a dream; it was partly in a dream that I came home to my own house and got into bed. I slept after the prostration of the day, with a stringent and profound slumber which not even the nightmares that wrung me could avail to break. I awoke in the morning shaken, weakened, but refreshed. I still hated and feared the thought of the brute that slept within me, and I had not of course forgotten the appalling dangers of the day before; but I was once more at home, in my own house and close to my drugs; and gratitude for my escape shone so strong in my soul that it almost rivalled the brightness of hope.

I was stepping leisurely across the court after breakfast, drinking the chill of the air with pleasure, when I was seized again with those indescribable sensations that heralded the change; and I had but the time to gain the shelter of my cabinet, before I was once again raging and freezing with the passions of Hyde. It took on this occasion a double dose to recall me to myself; and alas, six hours after, as I sat looking sadly in the fire, the pangs returned, and the drug had to be re-administered. In short, from that day forth it seemed only by a great effort as of gymnastics, and only under the immediate stimulation of the drug, that I was able to wear the countenance of Jekyll. At all hours of the day and night I would be taken with the premonitory shudder; above all, if I slept, or even dozed for a moment in my chair, it was always as Hyde that I awakened. Under the strain of this continually impending doom and by the sleeplessness to which I now condemned myself, ay, even beyond what I had thought possible to man, I became, in my own person, a creature eaten up and emptied by fever, languidly weak both in body and mind, and solely occupied by one thought: the horror of my other self. But when I slept, or when the virtue of the medicine wore off, I would leap almost without transition (for the pangs of transformation grew daily less marked) into the possession of a fancy brimming with images of terror, a soul boiling with causeless hatreds, and a body that seemed not strong enough to contain the raging energies of life. The powers of Hyde seemed to have grown with the sickliness of Jekyll. And certainly the hate that now divided them was equal on each side. With Jekyll, it was a thing of vital instinct. He had now seen the full deformity of that creature that shared with him some of the phenomena of consciousness, and was co-heir with him to death: and beyond these links of community, which in themselves made the most poignant part of his distress, he thought of Hyde, for all his energy of life, as of something not only hellish but inorganic. This was the shocking thing; that the slime of the pit seemed to utter cries and voices; that the amorphous dust gesticulated and sinned; that what was dead, and had no shape, should usurp the offices of life. And this again, that that insurgent horror was knit to him closer than a wife, closer than an eye; lay caged in his flesh, where he heard it mutter and felt it struggle to be born; and at every hour of weakness, and in the confidences of slumber, prevailed against him, and deposed him out of life. The hatred of Hyde for Jekyll was of a different order. His terror of the gallows drove him continually to commit temporary suicide, and return to his subordinate station of a part instead of a person; but he loathed the necessity, he loathed the despondency into which Jekyll was now fallen, and he resented the dislike with which he was himself regarded. Hence the ape-like tricks that he would play me, scrawling in my own hand blasphemies on the pages of my books, burning the letters and destroying the portrait of my father; and indeed, had it not been for his fear of death, he would long ago have ruined himself in order to involve me in the ruin. But his love of life is wonderful; I go further: I, who sicken and freeze at the mere thought of him, when I recall the abjection and passion of this attachment, and when I know how he fears my power to cut him off by suicide, I find it in my heart to pity him.

It is useless, and the time awfully fails me, to prolong this description; no one has ever suffered such torments, let that suffice; and yet even to these, habit brought—no, not alleviation—but a certain callousness of soul, a certain acquiescence of despair; and my punishment might have gone on for years, but for the last calamity which has now fallen, and which has finally severed me from my own face and nature. My provision of the salt, which had never been renewed since the date of the first experiment, began to run low. I sent out for a fresh supply, and mixed the draught; the ebullition followed, and the first change of colour, not the second; I drank it, and it was without efficiency. You will learn from Poole how I have had London ransacked; it was in vain; and I am now persuaded that my first supply was impure, and that it was that unknown impurity which lent efficacy to the draught.

About a week has passed, and I am now finishing this statement under the influence of the last of the old powders. This, then, is the last time, short of a miracle, that Henry Jekyll can think his own thoughts or see his own face (now how sadly altered!) in the glass. Nor must I delay too long to bring my writing to an end; for if my narrative has hitherto escaped destruction, it has been by a combination of great prudence and great good luck. Should the throes of change take me in the act of writing it, Hyde will tear it in pieces; but if some time shall have elapsed after I have laid it by, his wonderful selfishness and circumscription to the moment will probably save it once again from the action of his ape-like spite. And indeed the doom that is closing on us both has already changed and crushed him. Half an hour from now, when I shall again and for ever reindue that hated personality, I know how I shall sit shuddering and weeping in my chair, or continue, with the most strained and fearstruck ecstasy of listening, to pace up and down this room (my last earthly refuge) and give ear to every sound of menace. Will Hyde die upon the scaffold? or will he find the courage to release himself at the last moment? God knows; I am careless; this is my true hour of death, and what is to follow concerns another than myself. Here, then, as I lay down the pen, and proceed to seal up my confession, I bring the life of that unhappy Henry Jekyll to an end.

QUESTIONS FOR DISCUSSION AND WRITING

1. As Jekyll's alter ego, Hyde seems both different from and similar to Jekyll. In what ways does the story see them as alike? In what ways different?

2. The effect of Stevenson's story depends in part on its atmosphere. What do we know about the setting of the story? How do we respond to it?

3. Like many authors, Stevenson may be creating his characters' names with an eye to the effect they will have on the reader. What associations do the names of Jekyll, Hyde, and Utterson have for you? Think not only about what the characters do but about how their names sound and what the names seem to suggest.

4. The society we see in Stevenson's story is composed exclusively of bachelors, usually middle-aged or elderly ones. How is the story affected by the exclusion of female voices and influences?

5. Stevenson's story concerns itself with the nature of good and evil, and we may be tempted to see Jekyll as good and Hyde as evil. It is important, though, to remember that Hyde is, in fact, a part of Jekyll. What does the story tell us about good and evil?

The Strange Case of Dr. T. and Mr. H.   1886

Or Two Single Gentlemen rolled into one. (Parody in Punch.)

Chapter I.—Story of the Bore.

Mr. STUTTERSON, the lawyer, was a man of a rugged countenance, that was never lighted by a smile, not even when he saw a little old creature in clothes much too large for him, come round the corner of a street and trample a small boy nearly to death. The little old creature would have rushed away, when an angry crowd surrounded him, and tried to kill him. But he suddenly disappeared into a house that did not belong to him, and gave the crowd a cheque with a name upon it that cannot be divulged until the very last chapter of this interesting narrative. Then the crowd allowed the little old creature to go away.

"Let us never refer to the subject again," said Mr. STUTTERSON.

"With all my heart," replied the entire human race, escaping from his button-holding propensities.

Chapter II.—Mr. Hidanseek is found in the Vague Murder Case.

Mr. STUTTERSON thought he would look up his medical friends. He was not only a bore, but a stingy one. He called upon the Surgeons when they were dining, and generally managed to obtain an entrance with the soup. "You here!" cried Dr. ONION, chuckling. "Don't speak to me about TREKYL—he is a fool, an ass, a dolt, a humbug, and my oldest friend."

"You think he is too scientific, and makes very many extraordinary experiments," said STUTTERSON, disposing of the fish, two entrees and the joint.

"Precisely," replied ONION, chuckling more than ever—"as you will find out in the last Chapter. And now, as you have cleared the table, hadn't you better go?"

"Certainly," returned the Lawyer, departing (by the way, *not* returning), and he went to visit Mr. HIDANSEEK. He found that individual, and asked to see his face.

"Why not?" answered the little old creature in the baggy clothes, defiantly. "Don't you recognize me?"

"Mr. R. L. STEVENSON says I mustn't," was the wary response; "for, if I did, I should spoil the last chapter."

Shortly after this Mr. HIDANSEEK, being asked the way by a Baronet out for a midnight stroll, immediately hacked his interrogator to pieces with a heavy umbrella. Mr. STUTTERSON therefore called upon Dr. TREKYL, to ask for an explanation.

"Wait a moment," said that eminent physician, retiring to an inner apartment, where he wrote the following note:—

"Please, Sir, I didn't do it."

"TREKYL forge for a murderer!" exclaimed STUTTERSON; and his blood ran cold in his veins.

Chapter III.—And any quantity of Chapters to make your flesh creep.

And so it turned out that TREKYL made a will, which contained a strange provision that, if he disappeared, HIDANSEEK was to have all his property. Then Dr. ONION went mad with terror, because, after some whiskey-and-water, he fancied that his old friend TREKYL had turned into the tracked and hunted murderer, HIDANSEEK.

"Was it the whiskey?" asked STUTTERSON.

"Wait until the end!" cried the poor medical man, and, with a loud shriek, he slipped out of his coat, leaving the button-hole in the bore's hand, and died!

Chapter the last.—The wind-up.

I am writing this—I, TREKYL, the man who signed the cheque for HIDANSEEK in Chapter I., and wrote the forged letter a little later on. I hope you are all puzzled. I had no fixed idea how it would end when I began, and I trust you will see your way clearer through the mystery than I do, when you have come to the imprint.

As you may have gathered from ONION's calling me "a humbug, &c., &c.," I was very fond of scientific experiments. I was. And I found one day, that I, TREKYL, had a great deal of sugar in my composition. By using powdered acidulated drops I discovered that I could change myself into somebody else. It was very sweet!

So I divided myself into two, and thought of a number of things. I thought how pleasant it would be to have no conscience, and be a regular bad one, or, as the vulgar call it, bad 'un. I swallowed the acidulated drops, and in a moment I became a little old creature, with an acquired taste for trampling out children's brains, and hacking to death (with an umbrella) midnight Baronets who had lost their way. I had a grand time of it! It was all the grander, because I found that by substituting sugar for the drops I could again become the famous doctor, whose chief employment was to give Mr. STUTTERSON all my dinner. So much bad had been divided into the acidulated HIDANSEEK that I hadn't enough left in the sugary TREKYL to protest against the bore's importunities.

Well, that acidulated fool HIDANSEEK got into serious trouble, and I wanted to cut him. But I couldn't; when I had divided myself into him one day, I found it impossible to get the right sort of sugar to bring me back again. For the right sort of sugar was adulterated, and adulterated sugar cannot be obtained in London!

And now, after piecing all this together, if you can't see the whole thing at a glance, I am very sorry for you, and can help you no further. The fact is, I have got to the end of my "141 pages for a shilling." I might have made myself into four or five people instead of two,—who are quite enough for the money.

QUESTIONS FOR DISCUSSION AND WRITING

1. Written just about a month after the publication of *Dr. Jekyll and Mr. Hyde,* the *Punch* parody would have been read by many who had not yet read Stevenson's novella. Would they have found the parody funny? Why or why not? How might the parody have made them more or less likely to read Stevenson's work?

2. The parody has changed many of the incidents of the original work. What changes have been made? How might the changes affect our response to the events?

3. The parody has changed the names of the original characters, but the new names are more than amusing "sound-alikes." What characteristics do the names suggest about the characters? How are or aren't those characteristics like those suggested in Stevenson's work?

4. The parody insists that Utterson is a bore. Is that a fair assessment of the way that Stevenson characterizes the lawyer? How might Stevenson's work have been changed if the lawyer had been less of a "bore"?

5. The parody comments on the way that information in Stevenson's work is withheld until the end. How important is that as a criticism of the original novella?

6. Although the parody isn't a traditional review, its writer clearly has an opinion about Stevenson's work. How would you characterize that opinion? To what extent do you think it is justified?

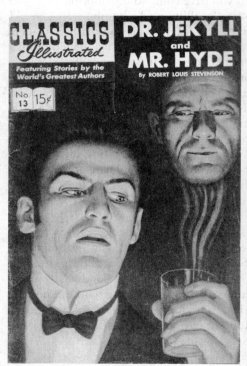

1953   Two covers for comic book retellings of *Dr. Jekyll and Mr. Hyde.*   1976

QUESTIONS FOR DISCUSSION AND WRITING

1. Examine the *Classics Illustrated* cover closely. What is the effect of putting Dr. Jekyll in evening dress? How sinister does Mr. Hyde seem? Does he seem like or unlike Jekyll? What do the two figures seem to be looking at?

2. Examine the *Marvel Classics Comics* cover closely. How do we respond to the scientific apparatus? The skull on the bookshelf? How do the Hyde faces compare with Dr. Jekyll's? Why are there three faces on the cover when the story is about only two personalities?
3. Compare and contrast the two comic book covers. Do they create the same impressions of Dr. Jekyll? Of Mr. Hyde? Of the scientific experiment? What do the two covers suggest about the mood of the story and how we are likely to respond to it? Which seems more true to your reading of Stevenson's story?

KATE MCMULLAN (1947–   )
Dr. Jekyll and Mr. Hyde _____ *1984*

No one has ever suffered as I have. No one! This is the last time that I, Dr. Henry Jekyll, can think my own thoughts. Or see my own face in the mirror.

Soon I will turn into Edward Hyde again. And that will be the end of Henry Jekyll. Forever!

So I must hurry. I must write down my story while I still can. I do not know if anyone will ever read it. What if Hyde finds my writing? He will tear it to bits. But I must tell my story. And so, let me begin.

Chapter 1

I remember everything about the night I first took the drug. The magic drug that changed me into Edward Hyde.

I was a well-known doctor. One of the best in London. Many sick people came to me. And I helped them all.

On this day I was just showing a young woman to the door. In her arms she held a baby. She looked up at me with tears in her eyes.

"Doctor," she began, "I thank you. With all my heart. I was so afraid that my baby was not going to live. If only . . . if only I had some money. . . ."

"Do not think about paying me," I told her. "Seeing your little girl smile is enough for me. See that she gets a lot of rest now."

"Thank you," she said again. And she went out.

As I closed the door I noticed my butler, Poole. He had been watching me.

"You look tired, sir," he said. "You should get some rest too."

I looked at the clock. It *had* been a long day.

"You are right, Poole," I said. "You may get dinner ready now. I need to eat. I have a long night before me. In my lab."

"Yes, sir," said Poole. He turned to go. But he turned back again.

"You do so much good, sir," he said. "So much good."

With that, he left.

I shook my head.

"If he only knew," I thought. "If he only knew that there is another side to me. A side that I hide. A side that is not good at all!"

★ ★ ★

When Utterson was gone, I went to my lab. I got out the clothes I had bought that day. And then I made the drug. I swallowed every drop. The shaking came on me as before. It was horrible. Horrible! But at last it stopped. And again I had turned into Edward Hyde.

I wasted no time. I changed into my new clothes. I took my cane. Then I headed out the back door of the lab and into the street.

Oh! How free I felt! I walked down streets I had walked all my life. I saw people I knew well. But they had no idea who I was! The good doctor had been left behind.

At a corner I spotted a horse and carriage. Quickly I climbed in.

"Take me to Soho!" I shouted to the driver. "And hurry up about it!"

"Yes, sir!" answered the driver. He looked at me strangely. I saw that he had no liking for me.

The carriage started rolling. Soho was a dark and dangerous part of London that I loved well. I had gone there before a few times as Henry Jekyll. But I was always afraid that someone would know me. But now that fear was gone. I was Edward Hyde. Going out for a night on the town.

The carriage stopped.

"Here we are, sir," the driver said. "Soho."

I jumped out of the carriage. I threw a few coins onto the ground and laughed. "You want your money? Then dig for it!" And off I went into the night.

What a time I had! I drank and drank. I got into fights. I could see in people's eyes that they were afraid of me. They backed off when I came near. This just excited me! I laughed in their scared faces.

★ ★ ★

For two months I had kept this evil animal caged inside me. Now he was out! Out with the anger of a hundred howling monsters. I got out Hyde's clothes and threw them on. They were not so loose now. In these two months Hyde had grown bigger. And stronger. I burst out into the quiet London night.

As I raced down the street, I saw someone coming toward me. It was an old man. His white hair looked like a halo in the moonlight. He came closer. And I saw that it was Sir Danvers Carew. Going, I guessed, to meet Utterson.

The old man smiled at me. And then he stopped. I looked into his eyes. Such kind eyes. He asked me directions, smiling as he spoke. Here was a man as good and trusting as a child. His goodness made me even more angry. I don't know why, but it did. As he talked I raised my cane and hit him full in the face. The look in his eyes filled me with a twisted joy! Again I hit him. And again and again. With every blow, I grew more excited. I kept hitting the old man until there was no life left in him. And even then I did not stop. The thrill of killing had me in its hold.

Then suddenly I heard a loud scream. I looked back at my house. At one of the windows I saw my maid, Amanda. She had been watching! She had seen it all!

"Police!" she cried. "Help! Someone! Help! A murder! A most terrible murder!"

With one last blow that broke my cane, I left Carew. I looked up at the window again. My maid was still there. Screaming! Lights were going on in other houses. Soon there would be many people on the street.

"There is the killer!" Amanda screamed. "There! Stop him! Stop that man! I know him! It is Edward Hyde!"

QUESTIONS FOR DISCUSSION AND WRITING

1. The children's version of *Dr. Jekyll and Mr. Hyde* opens differently than Stevenson's. What are some of the differences? How do they affect our response to Dr. Jekyll and his experiment?
2. Both Stevenson and McMullan are somewhat vague about the crimes Hyde commits. What are the reasons for their reticence? Do the two versions of the story lead the reader to similar or different conclusions about the nature of Hyde's evildoing?
3. The children's adaptation of *Dr. Jekyll and Mr. Hyde* is told in the first person by Dr. Jekyll, whereas Stevenson's novella is told in the third person, though from the perspective of Utterson. How do the differences in narration affect the way we look at the characters and events of the story?
4. McMullan adds some details that are not in Stevenson's story: about the taunting of the coachman and about the encounter with Sir Danvers Carew, for instance. How effective do you find the inclusion of such details? How do they influence our reactions to Mr. Hyde and the themes of the story?
5. Though it was written for adults, *Dr. Jekyll and Mr. Hyde* has long been adapted for children. Why would the story appeal to children? What lessons might adults hope children would learn from it?

TONY EPRILE

A True History of the Notorious Mr. Edward Hyde   *1995*

'Yde's the name. Edward 'yde . . . or Hyde, as educated folk like yourself would have it. That's my real name, although for the past fifty years, Hyde has stayed hidden under the moniker of Edward Layman. To the good people here in the West Midlands, I'm just Layman or Ed, no different from nobody else, a stand-up bloke, a hardworker but no boss's tool, fond of his pint of bitter and mild and always ready for a joke or sing-along. Only my cousin Vic—and now *you*—knows my real name, the one that sends chills up the world's spine. As Hyde, I've been called a deformed and depraved creature of Hell, a vicious human Juggernaut. "Edward Hyde, alone in the ranks of mankind, was pure evil." Nice words, I must say. Courtesy of none other than the ultimate toffee nose, Dr. Jekyll, Harley Street specialist and a man noted for his good works. Where's the charity in such talk? I ask. And yet, because he went to the right schools and said things in such a reasonable, sophisticated way, you believe him. Funny, how people can be educated but not smart, i'n' it?

Jekyll. Even today I can't hear his name without the hair on my neck rising in pure animal rage. And to think I used to admire the man. I wanted to be like him, to talk posh and live in a house filled with elegant appurtenances instead of mere furniture. Even when it finally penetrated the great Roman wall of my thick prole's head that I was hopelessly trapped in Dr. Jekyll's rotten web (while *he* grew bloated and fat on my helpless struggles), I still wanted what he had. You see, Jekyll—let him rot in Hell, appurtenances and all—had class. And that, as Cousin Vic would say, is what it's all about.

I was just recently turned twenty when I met the illustrious Dr. Jekyll, and of all the days in my life, that one stands out clearest in memory. It was a spring morning of sharp brightness, sunlight pouring in like newly minted sovereigns. Not at all the usual pewter-gray skies of London, and I was cocksure and full of myself that day. My luck was up, or so I thought. There's something about being young that makes you feel un-defeatable: I had a nice chunk of money weighing down my pockets and raw pleasure in the unfettered, wiry roll of my youthful muscles as I strolled the streets of London. The evening before, I had landed an unexpected five guineas. I'd gone with some of my mates to one of Jimmy Wilshire's fighting cellars. This was not one of your Marquis of Queensbury bouts of fisticuffs, but the aptly called "Big Knuckle"—where it's bare knuckles and bare feet and you fight on until you or your opponent are knocked sense-less. It was strictly out of the bounds of The Law, of course, but any night of the week, if you knew where to look, you could find yourself in a small ill-lit room in which two brawny boyos were laying into each other on the roped-off mats in the center to the cheers of a crowd of red-faced men yelling themselves hoarse. And it wasn't just commoners who frequented Jimmy Wilshire's cellars, but toffs putting down pound bets on their favorites and standing close enough to the action to get blood on their evening jackets or to catch the occasional flying molar for a souvenir.

Hard Anthony had just knocked his opponent cold in mere minutes of combat, and the barker was now offering a purse of five guineas to anyone in the audience game enough to spend ten minutes in the ring with him. I had been an occasional stevedore on the London docks and taken part in my share of pub brawls, where the stake was your own skin and the weapons included knives, if you had one, and any-thing else that came to hand if you did not. So, with my friends' raucous encourage-ment, I took on the bet. Hard Anthony came up to me with a friendly grin and a hand extended for a gentlemanly shake. I'd been caught by just such a bit of com-monplace treachery in one of the few street tussles I'd lost, so I pretended to let my-self be pulled off-balance but quickly ducked under the flying fist that was following up fast behind the handshake. It was Hard Anthony's turn to be off-guard, and I took the wind out of his sails with a lightning-quick knee to the groin, the good old Ringsend uppercut. He was knackered good and proper, and though he was a tough berk, practiced in a range of dirty tricks—like greasing himself all over with oil so you couldn't get a purchase—I'm no sluggard when it comes to a barney, and it didn't take all that long before I tossed his unconscious carcass into a pile of chairs that seemed to have been placed there for just that purpose. My only injuries were a few scratches—Hard Anthony clawed like a woman—and a bruise under my eye from a vicious head butt.

That is how on a bright morning, with my head still cottony from the rounds of Jimmy Wilshire's home-brewed gin and porter that I had treated and been treated to, I happened to be walking along Harley Street and paused for a moment next to a brass shingle announcing the name Henry Jekyll, M.D., D.C.L., LL.D., F.R.S., and enough other initials to show that the inhabitant could split himself in half and open two medical practices. It recalled to me a condition which was a cause of some em-barrassment, the results of a few moments of friendliness with a comely scullery maid. Just thinking about it brought on the discomfort, a burning exaggerated by the quan-tity of liquor I had consumed the night before. Jingling the still half-full purse in my trouser pocket, I clambered up the stairs and pounded the fateful knocker.

I found myself quite humbled by my surroundings: grim Poole the manservant in his somber duds, the unobtrusively expensive furnishings, and the resounding church-like quiet of the high-ceilinged chambers. Jekyll, a tall man with wispy hair combed back from his forehead, was equally imposing in his fine-tailored clothing, but he knew what he was about and had me quickly stripped and diagnosed . . . a salve administered and injunctions to use more salve at regular intervals and to drink large quantities of water, only water. "For the next two weeks, you will just have to be satisfied with the fact that the City of London rocks gently upon an artesian well and not a brewery," he said with mocking seriousness. "And, of course, abstinence of another kind for the same period is a definite must."

All this was something I could easily live with, and I was relieved to have taken care of the problem so easily. A quite different shock was in store for me. The bill Jekyll presented me with was for five guineas. I now eyed the gracious furniture with bitterness, having seen how it came to be purchased. This was more than I earned in two weeks of stevedoring and, unfortunately, more than remained to me in the little purse that I now emptied onto the tabletop. Three pounds six was all that was left after the previous night's generosity.

"That's all I've got, governor. And for me that's a tidy sum of money."

"I've no doubt. But I'm not so sure the police would see it in that light." Jekyll looked at me thoughtfully, murmuring to himself: "A fine example of the unconscious brute side of human nature. Enters here without a thought to payment and consequences . . . a certain animal magnetism . . . the beast happy in its ignorant cavern . . ."

He grew contemplative, studying me for a while. Then he began to question me closely as to how I had come about the bruise under my eye and other particulars. When I balked at telling him at length of the source of my little illness, he gazed at me coldly and offered to dispatch Poole to seek out the nearest policeman. But when I told him the details of my rendezvous with the scullion in the small alcove behind the coal shuttle of her employers' house, his friendliness returned, and he smiled delightedly while he drank in the details like a navvy confronted with his first pint of shoretime ale.

"Marvelous," he said, examining his own plump, manicured hand with manifest satisfaction. "It's an ill wind that brings no good, Mr. Hyde. I think we can come to an arrangement that will be of benefit to both of us.

"You see before you," he continued, "a man who is known and respected throughout all London—a doer of good deeds, a pillar of society. My stature, nay, my very upbringing . . . the air I breathe in these luxurious chambers constrains me to act always in a civilized manner. Not for me the brute spontaneity of a quick dalliance behind the coal scuttle, the thump on the head for the fool who dares look at me cross-eyed. No, I *must* comport myself with decency at all times, fettered by my higher place in the scale of evolution as surely as the gallows thief is prevented from fleeing to freedom by his leg irons . . ."

Jekyll continued in this manner for some time. I did not understand all of what he was saying at that instant, but I gathered that I was to be his proxy. My work was to indulge in my animal lusts, and all I had to do was report my doings to Dr. Jekyll in order to be forgiven my debt and receive a handsome retainer besides.

"Go forth and be *wicked,* Hyde," Jekyll intoned as he let me out the back door of his building, the entrance I was to use from now on in any communication with him.

At first, I thought that Dr. Jekyll was either cracked or just plain having me on, but the following Friday—the date he had set for our next encounter—curiosity took my feet down the back lane on the far side of Harley Street. On my way there, an odd incident occurred. A small girl dressed in a striped pinafore was so intent on chasing a child's hoop, which she kept balanced by tapping it with a light cane, that she ran full-tilt into me. I lifted her up, helped her retrieve the hoop, and gave her a halfpenny to bring back the smile to her limpid, innocent face.

Approaching the cellar door, I rapped once on its thick oak paneling, thinking that if there was no response, I could chalk the whole thing off to a moment's eccentricity on the doctor's part. To my surprise, the door swung open immediately, and Jekyll ushered me inside with every sign of having eagerly been awaiting my arrival.

"So, my good Hyde, what acts of gross turpitude have you committed since last we met?" he demanded.

Since I had been obeying his orders to stay clear of intoxicating beverages, my time had passed slowly and with little opportunity for mischief. Racking my brains, I thought of a little trick I had played some months before on a certain fishmonger in the Haymarket. The man was a fussy sort, always checking the balance of his weighing scales to make quite sure some poor old missis wasn't getting away with a free sliver of fin or tail. While my best butty, Townsend, distracted the man—"What's this, then? A grouper? Never heard of it. Got any eels? I could go for a nice eel"—I quickly nicked a couple of the weights that served to balance out the scale in graded half ounces. Pretending it had happened just days before, I narrated this history, much to Dr. Jekyll's delight.

"Capital, Hyde, capital. A little rough justice, if you will. And what else? What other means has Satan found to tempt you?"

I was forced to plunder my memory's storehouse—surely I had not done only good deeds in the interval?—when, suddenly, inspiration struck. I told Jekyll the story of the child and her hoop . . . only, this time there was no stopping to help her up and dust her off. Instead, I joyously trod the helpless infant into the ground with my heavy work boots, indifferent to her terrified screams. Jekyll shivered as I described how the little hoop cracked underfoot like a chicken bone.

"And you didn't look back at all, Hyde?" he asked, rubbing his hands with glee.

"Not even once, Dr. Jekyll. Not once."

Jekyll gave me ten pounds and said he looked forward to our meeting the following week. As I was leaving, he called me back. "It's almost noon now. If you walk towards Cavendish Square, you'll be sure to encounter a stout gentleman dressed in a finely tailored charcoal-gray overcoat complete with beaver-skin top hat. In all likelihood, he'll have in his hands an ebony cane that is the very twin of this one. The man's name is Utterson, and he has an appointment with me. Spatter some mud on him for me—hey, Hyde? Or, better yet, smear some chalk on the back of his overcoat."

For all his sophistication, Dr. Jekyll's notion of evil-doing was still that of a schoolboy.

For about six months, the arrangement between Jekyll and myself was useful for us both. For Jekyll, it was a chance to experience vicariously a lifestyle at complete odds with his habitual one. For me, it was a steady source of good money . . . but more than that, it was an opportunity to live outside the limits of my ilk and income. I valued the time spent with Jekyll, and I even borrowed some of his books to go through afterwards in my own time. Jekyll had a command of the Queen's English that I frankly envied, and I would find myself assuming some of his mannerisms and using some of his more eloquent locutions. See?—"locutions," that's a Jekyll word. His influence is with me even now.

Of course, there were difficulties. One day, I wore to our cellar meeting a fancy singlet modeled on Jekyll's own that I had bought with some of the money I had saved up. When he saw me in it, far from being flattered, he was furious.

"I pay you because you bring me the stink of the gutter, Hyde, not the scent of Savile Row," he railed. "Don't try to turn yourself into a gentleman, my boy. It would be a ridiculous sight: like a bullock laying eggs!"

He softened a little under my injured glare. "Come now, don't look at me like that. I suppose we all have a right to play at being what we're not—I, to be a brute, and you, to be a fine gentleman—but we need to keep some perspective, not let it go to our heads."

I suppose if that had been the only problem, I could have borne with it without too much complaint. What did it matter if Jekyll mocked at my lack of education, and even more so at my desire to make up for it? Let him be superior and condescending. It didn't stop me from learning what I wanted to learn. As Vic says about me, I can talk management, and I can talk mates.

No, the real problem was a certain universal fact of human nature: yesterday's vice is worth about as much as yesterday's daily paper. The wine of *my* evil deeds soon stopped intoxicating Jekyll; he must have stronger stuff! From being content to hear about my misdeeds, he went to being an observer . . . then observer became participant, and the downfall of us both was assured.

It started off with Jekyll having me stage a bare-fist bout in his capacious cellar. The audience was "a select few" of Jekyll's friends, men whom he trusted, classmates and old boys from Jekyll's public school. Among them was Utterson, who chose not to recognize in me the churl who had befouled his greatcoat with a hearty slap on the back. Another was a spry, white-haired gentleman named Sir Danvers Carew, an MP and a peer of the realm, no less. We put on a good show for the fine gentlemen. Too good a show, in fact, for I got carried away one day and beat my opponent, a young ruffian I'd known from the docks, into an insensate pulp.

You see, as Jekyll became more depraved in his desires, so I became more corrupt. I came to revel in the role into which he had cast me, like a music hall performer who forgets that it's all a mickey-take. With the money Jekyll gave me, I found I could buy the downtrodden, attractive youth of London. There was not a young household maid or messenger lad that I could not entice into Jekyll's cellar, where the practice of vice had achieved a rare pitch of refinement. These are memories I prefer not to call to mind, the times I spent swaggering around the city bullying my peers with my own physical strength and Jekyll's pecuniary wherewithal. My encounters with women ceased to be a jolly lark, a moment's warm reprieve from the cares of daily life. Instead, they were a transaction.

Things began to heat up for me, dangers that were the result of my new life. Jimmy Wilshire was out to get me for intruding on his territory, or so it was rumored. Hard Anthony himself was supposed to be waiting for me in some dark lane or courtyard, armed with cosh and shiv. At first I didn't care. I borrowed Jekyll's tough ebony cane and let it be known on the street that Hard Anthony had better stay out of *my* way. But there were other things that did begin to bother me: the way my former mates avoided me or only sought me out when the need for lucre grew overpowering. The hard-edged way the girls now looked at me . . . how they let me debauch them with my five- and ten-pound notes. People had become afraid of me. The drubbing I'd given to my youthful sparring partner (it had cost me a tidy sum to mollify him while he recovered from his injuries) had become part of city lore and was much exaggerated in the telling. Even Townsend, the jokester who had grown up just two houses away from me and who as long as I knew him was always up for a lark . . . he only came to me when he needed money, acted sullen and fearful, let me push him around without answering back. I was coming to know Jekyll's loneliness, the knowledge that no one gives a hoot for you yourself but only for the bit of silver that might fall their way. Not to say I didn't take pride in my newfound power—in the very independence Jekyll's money bought me—but it was slowly, much too slowly, beginning to sink in that all this was playacting. I had given up my own soul to become another man's thrall.

I will not bore you, dear Reader, with a lengthy account of my downward spiral in the ensuing months. Jekyll himself berated me for "opening the gates of Hell" to him, while simultaneously charging me with the arrangement of ever more wanton acts of dissipation. One moment he would threaten to bring in The Law on the grounds that I was extorting money from him, the next moment he would beg me not to disrupt his only true moments of pleasure. Many times I thought of simply disappearing, of leaving without a word, but always the lure of Jekyll's fascinating character—along with the sense of invincibility brought on by a steady supply of cash and the protecting shield of the doctor's reputation—brought me back. The truth is that I, too, was addicted to the heady fumes of unbridled wickedness, the gratifying crunch of cartilage beneath knuckle, the wild debauches in the cellar. And yet I was racked by the twin goads of conscience and fear. As Jekyll one day said, we were "like man's twin demons of good and evil locked in mortal embrace while our worldly bark teeters on the edge of the waterfall."

Late one night, as all things must, the whole charade came to an end. It was one of those dark, brooding nights when all but the friendless are home in a warm bed beside the pale embers of a dying fire. Patches of mist floated hither and yon like untethered wraiths, and I wandered alone like them, lost in embittered reflection. All of a sudden, a slender, white-haired figure appeared in front of me. It was Sir Danvers Carew, who seemed both surprised and delighted to see me here. Carew was a quiet sort, with the distinguished air of a man who knows his own importance. He kept himself aloof during our mad carousals, but he was always there to the last minute, smiling to himself, sitting a little to one side.

"Ah, it's Henry Jekyll's hired bravo," Carew remarked in his melodious voice, and began to inquire earnestly and sympathetically after my health. In the next moment, he made a proposal to me of such audacious indecency that my mind reeled. Suddenly, the Spirit of Justice, of right and wrong, that had been until now bottled up inside me as in a pressure boiler, rose up with irresistible force. With a shout, I sprang upon Carew and knocked him to the ground, where I dealt out my answer to his disgusting suggestion with Jekyll's ebony cane. A moment later I came to my senses, and tossing the shattered cudgel aside, I fled.

I wandered away from the city on foot, my mind cast loose from its moorings. For several days I walked, stopping only occasionally to rest or buy some food, and eventually I found myself in the West Midlands, the industrial heart of our fabled isle. It was late afternoon, but it might as well have been night, the way the clouds of factory smoke blotted out the pallid sun. The clang of machinery was almost deafening, and here and there flames shot out to silhouette a human figure as a boiler door was opened to feed the mechanical beast. The place uncannily resembled an oil painting of Hell that had hung in Jekyll's office, but for me it was an honest spot, one where I could preserve my anonymity in the midst of other rough, working folks like myself. I remembered that a favorite cousin lived here, Vic Goodston, and by dint of asking in various local pubs, I was soon able to locate him. Vic helped me get a job at a local foundry, where the softened pads of my fingers and palms soon acquired the callouses of forthright toil. It was work that brought me back to myself. No thought was required, none of the fancy words I had learned while hanging about with the upper crust . . . just a steady hand and muscles that could endure a full day of shoveling coal into a giant, blasting furnace.

As my mind healed itself, the fear that I would be discovered and hauled off to the gallows became ever stronger. Vic's discreet inquiries helped allay my fears as we gradually pieced together the story of why Scotland Yard was no longer searching for the violent madman and killer, Edward Hyde. The first shock was that Dr. Henry Jekyll himself was dead, and by his own hand. Before downing the deadly draught of prussic acid, he had written out a lengthy manuscript, detailing the fiction you all know so well.

Don't believe for a moment that Jekyll was motivated by any desire to aid the man he had so grievously injured. No, Jekyll was simply being true to his race—avoiding the scandal that would bring down not only himself, but his friend Utterson and the rest of the select crowd who frequented Jekyll's cellar. The world could not be allowed to think that its most elite denizens harbored tastes that can charitably be called unsavory. No, far better if society should think that by taking a few salt compounds, the noble Jekyll was turned into a beast, a mere day laborer, a stinking, odious hand-for-hire controlled not by his brain but his brute instincts. It was a fabrication that would not have taken in a child, but the bonded word of aristocrats like Utterson and of the police detectives, whose nests were feathered by a limitless supply of pound notes, was enough to convince a gullible public. I suppose I should be grateful to Jekyll for providing me with a way out, a substantial grant on my lease in this vale of tears, but I'm not. There's no reason to believe he did it for me. There's no reason to believe he ever saw me as his fellow. He took no more notice of the man who carried out the whims of his lowest self than he would have of the bootblack who put shine to his shoes.

There have been many times, though, when I've lain sleepless at night harried by the knowledge that my safety was illusory . . . that perhaps I didn't disappear into the anonymity of the working world, but my whereabouts were known to Jekyll's friends, to be revealed or not as it suited them. Lately, it has come to me that I'd been gulled more than I knew. All those learned treatises about the duality of man and the thin veneer of civilization that appeared after Jekyll's "revelations" came to light, they're all a load of bollocks. I sense Jekyll's hand in this somewhere, his love of deceit and subterfuge. How can we be sure it was his body in that casket borne by grim procession to Highgate Cemetery? London's morgue is full of happy dossers who have shucked off this mortal coil without friend or relation to mourn or identify them. Would it not be like Dr. Henry Jekyll to get another—some unknown, some anonymous roustabout, whose passing has left not a ripple on the surface of the London "that matters"—to take his place on that final journey while he sequesters himself at a friend's country estate or sojourns on the continent? It amazes me that I did not consider this possibility before, but blithely and blindly pursued my rounds of honest toil while Jekyll—my tormentor, my gilded double—remained alive, chuckling to himself at the stupidity of the inferior classes. How easily we are fooled. How unfailingly we accept even the most obvious fictions. How avidly we seize on the story that confirms our prejudice while the unpalatable truth goes begging. Dupes, all of us. And you, too, Reader. Wot'cher.

QUESTIONS FOR DISCUSSION AND WRITING

1. In telling his own story, Hyde explains and perhaps rationalizes his behavior. How sympathetic are you to Eprile's Hyde? Do you consider him a reliable narrator? Why or why not?

2. Eprile's story is set in nineteenth-century London. What kind of place is the London of the story? What mood does the setting create?

3. Eprile's story ends with "Dupes, all of us. And you, too, Reader. Wot'cher." (*Wot'cher* means "what cheer," and, according to author Tony Eprile, has the force of "celebration and of the pleasure of life.") How is the reader a dupe? What does Hyde's cheery ending tell us about him and his attitudes toward both the story he has told and the reader?

HENRY JAMES (1843–1916)
Partial Portraits
1894

Is *Doctor Jekyll and Mr. Hyde* a work of high philosophic intention, or simply the most ingenious and irresponsible of fictions? It has the stamp of a really imaginative production, that we may take it in different ways; but I suppose it would generally be called the most serious of the author's tales. It deals with the relation of the baser parts of man to his nobler, of the capacity for evil that exists in the most generous natures; and it expresses these things in a fable which is a wonderfully happy invention. The subject is endlessly interesting, and rich in all sorts of provocation, and Mr. Stevenson is to be congratulated on having touched the core of it. I may do him injustice, but it is, however, here, not the profundity of the idea which strikes me so much as the art of the presentation—the extremely successful form. There is a genuine feeling for the perpetual moral question, a fresh sense of the difficulty of being good and the brutishness of being bad; but what there is above all is a singular ability in holding the interest. I confess that that, to my sense, is the most edifying thing in the short, rapid, concentrated story, which is really a masterpiece of concision. There is some thing almost impertinent in the way, as I have noticed, in which Mr. Stevenson achieves his best effects without the aid of the ladies, and *Doctor Jekyll* is a capital example of his heartless independence. It is usually supposed that a truly poignant impression cannot be made without them, but in the drama of Mr. Hyde's fatal ascendancy they remain altogether in the wing. It is very obvious—I do not say it cynically—that they must have played an important part in his development. The gruesome tone of the tale is, no doubt, deepened by their absence: it is like the late afternoon light of a foggy winter Sunday, when even inanimate objects have a kind of wicked look. I remember few situations in the pages of mystifying fiction more to the purpose than the episode of Mr. Utterson's going to Doctor Jekyll's to confer with the butler when the Doctor is locked up in his laboratory, and the old servant, whose sagacity has hitherto encountered successfully the problems of the sideboard and the pantry, confesses that this time he is utterly baffled. The way the two men, at the door of the laboratory, discuss the identity of the mysterious personage inside, who has revealed himself in two or three inhuman glimpses to Poole, has those touches of which irresistible shudders are made. The butler's theory is that his master has been murdered, and that the murderer is in the room, personating him with a sort of clumsy diabolism. "Well, when that masked thing like a monkey jumped from among the chemicals and whipped into the cabinet, it went down my spine like ice." That is the effect upon the reader of most of the story. I say of most rather than of all, because the ice rather melts in the sequel, and I have some difficulty in accepting the business of the powders, which seems to me too explicit and explanatory. The powders constitute the machinery of the transformation, and it will probably have struck many readers that this uncanny process would be more conceivable (so far as one may speak of the conceivable in such a case), if the author had not made it so definite.

QUESTIONS FOR DISCUSSION AND WRITING

1. James says that Stevenson's novella gives us "a fresh sense of the difficulty of being good and the brutishness of being bad." Do you agree with James's assessment? Why or why not?
2. James was one of the first commentators to remark on the absence of women in *Dr. Jekyll and Mr. Hyde.* Yet James also says women "must have played an important part in his [Hyde's] development." What in the novel supports that suggestion?
3. Himself a novelist, James believes that the explanations regarding the "powders" weaken the novella. How might you argue that James is right or wrong? What would be gained or lost by making the transformation process less definite?

ELAINE SHOWALTER (1941–   )

Dr. Jekyll's Closet _____ 1990

In January 1886, the same month that Robert Louis Stevenson published *The Strange Case of Dr. Jekyll and Mr. Hyde,* another strange case of "multiple personality" was introduced to English readers in the pages of *The Journal of Mental Science.* It involved a male hysteric named "Louis V.," a patient at Rochefort Asylum in France whose case of "morbid disintegration" had fascinated French doctors. Louis V.'s hysterical attacks had begun in adolescence, when he underwent a startling metamorphosis. Having been a "quiet, well-behaved, and obedient" street urchin, he abruptly became "violent, greedy, and quarrelsome," a heavy drinker, a political radical, and an atheist. So far his "symptoms" might be those of any teenage boy; but what seems to have upset his doctors particularly was that he tried to caress them. The French physicians attributed his condition to a shock he had received from being frightened by a viper, and they cured him through hypnosis so effectively that he could not even remember what he had done.[1] Stevenson (called "Louis" by his friends), may well have read the case of Louis V. It had been written up earlier in the *Archives de Neurologie,* and his wife recalled that he had been "deeply impressed" by a "paper he read in a French journal on subconsciousness" while he was writing *Jekyll and Hyde.*[2] He was also a friend of Frederic W. H. Myers, who discussed the case for English specialists. But male hysteria was a topic of considerable scientific interest in 1886. Berjon in France published his book, *La grande hystérie chez l'homme,* and in Austria Freud made his debut at the Vienna Medical Society with a controversial paper about male hysteria. While it was recognized in men, hysteria carried the stigma of being a humiliatingly female affliction. Another scholar of male hysteria, Charcot's disciple Emile Batault, observed that hysterical men in the Salpetriere's special ward were "timid and fearful men, whose gaze is neither lively nor piercing, but rather soft, poetic, and languorous. Coquettish and eccentric, they prefer ribbons and scarves to hard manual labor."[3] Later this view of the hysterical man as effeminate would be carried into psychoanalytic theory, where the male hysteric is seen as repressing his bisexuality or homosexuality through the language of the body. Homosexuality was also a topic of considerable scientific and legal interest in 1886. In January, just as Stevenson published his novel, the Labouchere Amendment criminalizing homosexual acts went into effect, and Krafft-Ebing's *Psychopathia Sexualis* offered some of the first case studies of homosexual men.[4] By the 1880s, such scholars as Jeffrey Weeks and Richard Dellamora have shown, the Victorian homosexual world had evolved into a secret but active subculture, with its own language, styles, practices, and meeting places. For most middle-class inhabitants of this world, homosexuality represented a double life in which a respectable daytime world, often involving marriage and family, existed alongside a night world of homoeroticism. Indeed, the fin de siecle was the golden age of literary and sexual doubles. "Late Victorian duality," writes Karl Miller in *Doubles,* "may be identified with the dilemmas, for males, of a choice between male and female roles, or of a possible union of such opposites. The 'Nineties School of Duality' framed a dialect and a dialectic, for the love that dared not speak its name, for the vexed question of homosexuality and bisexuality."[5] J. A. Symonds wrote poignantly in his journals of "the dual life . . . which had been habitual."[6] In Oscar Wilde's *The Importance of Being Earnest,* leading a double life is called "Bunburying" and represents, as one critic notes, "the 'posing' and 'double lives' to which homosexuals were accustomed."[7]

Stevenson was the fin de siecle laureate of the double life. In an essay on dreams, he described his passionate aim to "find a body, a vehicle for that strong sense of man's double being" which he had felt as a student in Edinburgh when he dreamed of leading "a double life: one of the day, one of the night."[8] The double life of the day and the night is also the double life of the writer, the split between reality and the imagination. Nonetheless, biographers have long hinted that Stevenson's own double life was more than the standard round of brothels and nighttime bohemia, and have rattled such skeletons in Stevenson's closet as "homosexuality, impotence, a passionate feeling for his stepson, submission to a wilful and predatory wife."[9] In particular, Stevenson was the object of extraordinary passion on the part of other men. According to Andrew Lang, he "possessed, more than any man I ever met, the power of making other men fall in love with him."[10] Among the group of friends, both homosexual and heterosexual, in Stevenson's large literary and bohemian circle, "male appreciation of Stevenson was often intensely physical."[11] Some of this appreciation and sexual ambiguity is vividly conveyed in the portrait *Robert Louis Stevenson and His Wife* (1885) by one of the artists in Stevenson's circle who led his own double life, John Singer Sargent. In the foreground, a slender and anxious looking Stevenson stares out at the painter, elongated fingers nervously stroking his droopy mustache. On the right, on the very margins of the painting, her body cut off by the picture frame, is the shadowy figure of his wife Fanny reclining on a velvet sofa, wrapped from head to toe in a gilded veil. Between the two is a door in the background wall, opening into a dark closet. For Stevenson himself, the painting was "too eccentric to be exhibited. I am at one extreme corner; my wife, in this wild dress, and looking like a ghost, is at the extreme other end. . . . All this is touched in a lovely witty touch of Sargent's; but of course, it looks dam queer as a whole." For Sargent, the painting showed Stevenson trapped by domesticity and femininity; it is, he said, "the caged animal lecturing about the foreign specimen in the corner."[12] In his marriage to Fanny, Stevenson wrote to W. E. Henley, he had come out "as limp as a lady's novel . . . the embers of the once gay R. L. S."[13]

Stevenson's real sexuality is much less the issue in *Jekyll and Hyde,* however, than his sense of the fantasies beneath the surface of daylight decorum, the shadow of homosexuality that surrounded Clubland and the nearly hysterical terror of revealing forbidden emotions between men that constituted the dark side of patriarchy. In many respects, *The Strange Case of Dr. Jekyll and Mr. Hyde* is a case study of male hysteria, not only that of Henry but also of the men in the community around him. It can most persuasively be read as a fable of fin de siecle homosexual panic, the discovery and resistance of the homosexual self.[14] In contrast to the way it has been represented in film and popular culture, *Jekyll and Hyde* is a story about communities of men. From the moment of its publication, many critics have remarked on the "maleness," even the monasticism, of the story.[15]

The characters are all middle-aged bachelors who have no relationships with women except as servants. Furthermore, they are celibates whose major emotional contacts are with each other and with Henry Jekyll. A female reviewer of the book expressed her surprise that "no woman's name occurs in the book, no romance is even suggested in it." Mr. Stevenson, wrote the critic Alice Brown, "is a boy who has no mind to play with girls."[16] The romance of Jekyll and Hyde is conveyed instead through men's names, men's bodies, and men's psyches. Henry Jekyll is in a sense the odd man of fin de siecle literature.

Unable to pair off with either a woman or another man, Jekyll divides himself and finds his only mate in his double, Edward Hyde. Jekyll is thus both odd and even, both single and double. "Man is not truly one, but truly two," he observes, and his need to pursue illicit sexual pleasure and yet to live up to the exacting moral standards of his bleak professional community has committed him to "a profound duplicity of life," accompanied by "an almost morbid sense of shame." Coming to acknowledge his unutterable desires, Jekyll longs to separate his mind and his body: "If each, I told myself, could be housed in separable identities, life would be relieved of all that was unbearable."

Not only the personality of Jekyll but everything else about the book seems divided and split; Stevenson wrote two drafts of the novel: the notebook draft and the printer's copy; the fragments or "fractions" of the manuscript are scattered among four libraries (two would obviously be more poetically just, but I cannot tell a lie); and Longmans published two Jekyll-and-Hyde-like simultaneous editions, a paperback shilling shocker and a more respectable cloth-bound volume.[17] In it Stevenson alludes obliquely to the composition process in the novel itself when Dr. Lanyon discovers the notebook in which Jekyll had recorded his experiments: "Here and there a brief remark was appended to a date, usually no more than a single word: 'double' occurring perhaps six times in a total of several hundred entries; and once very early in the list and followed by several marks of exclamation, 'total failure!'" Just as Jekyll searches for the proper dose to fight decomposition, Stevenson hints at his own frustration in composing the narrative of doubles.

Like the stories hysterical women told Freud, full of gaps, inconsistencies, and contradictions, Dr. Jekyll's story is composed of fragments and fractions, told through a series of narratives that the reader must organize into a coherent case history. The central narrator of the story is Gabriel John Utterson, who utters the tale and eventually inherits Jekyll's estate. More than the others in their social circle, Utterson is a "Jekyll manqué."[18] Like many narrators in late Victorian fiction, he is a lawyer, a spokesman for the Law of the Father and the social order, and "a lover of the sane and customary sides of life." His demeanor is muted and sober: "scanty and embarrassed in discourse," "undemonstrative" and "backward in sentiment," austere and self-denying, he spends evenings alone drinking gin "to mortify a taste for vintages" or reading "a volume of some dry divinity." Although he likes the theater, he has not "crossed the doors of one for twenty years." He has almost a dread of the fanciful, a fear of the realm of the anarchic imagination.

Yet like Jekyll, Utterson also has an unconventional side to keep down; indeed, his self-mortification seems like an effort to stay within the boundaries of masculine propriety. Utterson's fantasies take the form of vicarious identification with the high spirits and bad fortune of "down-going men," for whom he is often the last respectable friend. "I incline to Cain's heresy," he is wont to say; "I let my brother go to the devil in his own way." Utterson, too, has a particular male friend, the younger "man about town" Richard Enfield, whom he sees every Sunday for an excursion that is the "chief jewel of every week," although "it was a nut to crack for many, what these two could see in each other." In another scene, he shares an intimate evening with his clerk Mr. Guest, his own confidant; at least "there was no man from whom he kept fewer secrets." Perhaps because his own life is so involved with repression and fantasy, Utterson becomes "enslaved" to the mystery of Hyde: "If he be Mr. Hyde . . . I shall be Mr. Seek." He begins to haunt the "by street" near Jekyll's house and to have rape fantasies of a faceless figure who opens the door to the room where Jekyll lies sleeping, pulls back the curtains of the bed, and forces Jekyll to rise and do his bidding.

Fin de siecle images of forced penetration through locked doors into private cabinets, rooms, and closets permeate Utterson's narrative; as Stephen Heath notes, "the organizing image for this narrative is the breaking down of doors, learning the secret behind them."[19] The narrators of Jekyll's secret attempt to open up the mystery of another man, not by understanding or secret sharing, but by force. "Make a clean breast of this [to me] in confidence," Utterson pleads with Jekyll, who rebuffs him: "it isn't what you fancy; it is not so bad as that." Jekyll cannot open his heart or his breast even to his dearest male friends. Thus they must spy on him to enter his mind, to get to the bottom of his secrets. The first chapter is called "The Story of the Door," and while Hyde, as the text repeatedly draws to our attention, has a key to Jekyll's house, Utterson makes violent entries, finally breaking down the door of Jekyll's private closet with an axe, as if into what Jekyll calls "the very fortress of identity."

One of the secrets behind these doors is that Jekyll has a mirror in his cabinet, a discovery almost as shocking to Utterson and the butler Poole as the existence of Hyde. "This glass has seen some queer doings," Poole exclaims in the manuscript (changed to "strange things" in the text).[20] The mirror testifies not only to Jekyll's scandalously unmanly narcissism but also to the sense of the mask and the Other that has made the mirror an obsessive symbol in homosexual literature. Behind Jekyll's red baize door, Utterson sees his own mirrored face, the image of the painfully repressed desires that the cane and the axe cannot wholly shatter and destroy. The agitation and anxiety felt by the bachelor friends of Jekyll's circle reflects their mutual, if tacit and unspoken, understanding of Jekyll's "strange preference" for Edward Hyde. Utterson, Enfield, and Lanyon initially think that Jekyll is keeping Hyde. What they see is that their rich friend Harry Jekyll has willed his very considerable estate to a loutish younger man, who comes and goes as he pleases, has expensive paintings and other gifts from Jekyll in his Soho apartment, gives orders to the servants, and cashes large checks Jekyll has signed. However unsuitable, this young man is Jekyll's "favorite," a term that, as Vladimir Nabokov noted in his lecture on the novel, "sounds almost like *minion*."[21] Jekyll's apparent infatuation with Hyde reflects the late-nineteenth-century upper-middle-class eroticizing of working-class men as the ideal homosexual objects. "The moving across the class barrier," Weeks points out, "on the one hand the search for 'rough trade,' and on the other the reconciling effect of sex across class lines, was an important and recurrent theme in the homosexual world."[22] Edward Carpenter dreamed of being loved by "the thick-thighed hot coarse fleshed young bricklayer with the strap round his waist," while E. M. Forster fantasized about "a strong young man of the working-class."[23] Furthermore, prostitution was "an indispensable part of the male homosexual life . . . with participants beginning usually in their midteens and generally leaving the trade by their mid-twenties." The "kept boy" was as common as the rough trade picked up on the streets. When Hyde is "accosted" by the "aged and beautiful" M. P., Sir Danvers Carew, late at night in the dark streets by the river and beats him to death, Hyde both strikes at a father figure and suggests a male prostitute mugging a client on the docks. Furthermore, Enfield calls Jekyll's abode "Blackmail House" on "Queer Street" and speculates that Jekyll is "an honest man paying through the nose for some of the capers of his youth." While Enfield explicitly does not want to pursue these implications, "the more it looks like Queer Street, the less I ask," the butler Poole has also noted "something queer" about Hyde. As a number of scholars have noted, the homosexual significance of "queer" had entered English slang by 1900.[24] "'Odd,' 'queer,' 'dark,' 'fit,' 'nervous,'" notes Karl Miller, "these are the bricks which had built the house of the double."[25]

For contemporary readers of Stevenson's novel, moreover, the term "blackmail" would have immediately suggested homosexual liaisons. Originating in sixteenth-century Scotland, it was generally associated with accusations of buggery.[26] Furthermore, the vision of blackmail as the penalty for homosexual sin was intensified by the Labouchere Amendment. While homosexual men had long been vulnerable to blackmail, the new law, as Edward Carpenter noted, "opened wider than ever before the door to a real, most serious social evil and crime, that of blackmailing."[27] Popularly known as the "Blackmailer's Charter," the Labouchere Amendment put closeted homosexual men like Oscar Wilde and J. A. Symonds at particular risk. It made a major contribution to that "blackmailability" that Sedgwick sees as a crucial component of the "leverage of homophobia."[28] In his original draft of the manuscript, Stevenson was more explicit about the sexual practices that had driven Jekyll to a double life. Jekyll has become "from an early age . . . the slave of certain appetites," vices which are "at once criminal in the sight of the law and abhorrent in themselves. They cut me off from the sympathy of those whom I otherwise respected."[29] While these passages were omitted in the published version, Stevenson retained the sense of abhorrence and dread that surrounds Hyde. The metaphors associated with Hyde are those of abnormality, criminality, disease, contagion, and death. The reaction of the male characters to Hyde is uniformly that of "disgust, loathing, and fear," suggestive of the almost hysterical homophobia of the late nineteenth century. In the most famous code word of Victorian homosexuality, they find something unspeakable about Hyde "that gave a man a turn," something "surprising and revolting." Indeed, the language surrounding Hyde is almost uniformly negative, although when Jekyll first takes the drug, he feels "younger, lighter, happier in the body." Hyde is represented as ape-like, pale, and inexpressibly deformed, echoing the imagery of syphilitic afflictions in nineteenth-century medical texts, and Utterson speculates that Jekyll may have contracted a disease from Hyde, "one of those maladies that both torture and deform the sufferer," for which he is seeking the drug as an antidote. Meditating on Jekyll's possible youthful crime, Utterson fears "the cancer of some concealed disgrace; punishment coming, *pede claudo.*"

Along with the imagery of disease and retribution, the Latin phrase (literally "on halting foot") suggests a bilingual pun on "pederasty." The male homosexual body is also represented in the narrative in a series of images suggestive of anality and anal intercourse. Hyde travels in the "chocolate brown fog" that beats about the "back-end of the evening," while the streets he traverses are invariably "muddy" and "dark." Jekyll's house, with its two entrances, is the most vivid representation of the male body. Hyde always enters it through the blistered back door, which, in Stevenson's words, is "equipped with neither bell nor knocker" and bears the "marks of prolonged and sordid negligence." Finally, the suicide which ends Jekyll's narrative is the only form of narrative closure thought appropriate to the Gay Gothic, where the protagonist's death is both martyrdom and retribution. To learn Jekyll/Hyde's secret leads to death; it destroys Dr. Lanyon, for example, as later, Dorian Gray also causes the suicide of a number of young men and then kills himself. While Jekyll tries to convince himself that his desire is merely an addiction, a bad habit that he can overcome whenever he wants, he gradually comes to understand that Hyde is indeed part of him. In a final spasm of homophobic guilt, Jekyll slays his other "hated personality." Death is the only solution to the "illness" of homosexuality. As A. E. Houseman would write in *A Shropshire Lad*:

> Shot? So quick, so clean an ending?
> Oh that was right, lad, that was brave:
> Yours was not an ill for mending,
> 'Twas best to take it to the grave.

Jekyll is a "self-destroyer," Utterson concludes, not only because he has killed himself but because it is self-destructive to violate the sexual codes of one's society.[30] In the multiplication of narrative viewpoints that makes up the story, however, one voice is missing: that of Hyde himself. We never hear his account of the events, his memories of his strange birth, his pleasure and fear. Hyde's story would disturb the sexual economy of the text, the sense of panic at having liberated an uncontrollable desire. Hyde's hysterical narrative comes to us in two ways: in the representation of his feminine behavior and in the body language of hysterical discourse. As William Veeder points out, "despite all his 'masculine' traits of preternatural strength and animal agility, Hyde is prey to what the nineteenth century associated primarily with women."[31] He is seen "wrestling against the approaches of hysteria" and is heard "weeping like a woman." Hyde's reality breaks through Jekyll's body in the shape of his hand, the timber of his voice, and the quality of his gait. In representing the effects of splitting upon the male body, Stevenson drew upon the advanced medical science of his day. In the 1860s, the French neuroanatomist Paul Broca had first established the concept of the double brain and of left cerebral dominance. Observing that language disorders resulted from left-brain injuries, he hypothesized that the left frontal brain lobes, which controlled the right side of the body, were the seat of the intellectual and motor skills. Thus the left brain was more important than the right and virtually defined the distinction between the animal and the human. The right frontal brain lobes, which controlled the left side of the body, were subordinate; they were the seat of lesser, nonverbal traits. Individuals in whom the right hemisphere predominated had to be low on the human evolutionary scale. In describing or imagining the operations of the double brain, European scientists were influenced by their cultural assumptions about duality, including gender, race, and class. They characterized one side of the brain and body as masculine, rational, civilized, European, and highly evolved, and the other as feminine, irrational, primitive, and backward. Many scientists argued that the intellectual inferiority and social subordination of women and blacks could be attributed to their weak left brains. Furthermore, when mental disturbances occurred, as one physician noted in 1887, there must be a terrible struggle "between the left personality and the right personality, or in other more familiar terms, between the good and the bad side."[32]

These ideas about the brain were strongly related to late-nineteenth-century ideas about handedness, since handedness was usually inversely related to brain dominance and considerable effort was made to get left-handed children to change. Freud's close friend Wilhelm Fliess, however, argued that all human beings were bisexual, with the dominant side of the brain representing the dominant gender, and the other the repressed gender. Thus Fliess believed that normal, heterosexual people would be right-handed, while "effeminate men and masculine women are entirely or partly left-handed."[33]

The imagery of hands is conspicuous in the text of *Jekyll and Hyde* and has also been dramatically put to use in the various film versions, where Hyde's hands seem almost to have a life of their own. It draws upon ideas of the double brain and hand, as well as upon other social and sexual meanings. As a child, Jekyll recalls, he had "walked with my father's hand," suggesting that he had taken on the bodily symbols of the "right" proper hand of patriarchal respectability and constraint. Hyde seems to be the sinister left hand of Jekyll, the hand of the rebellious and immoral son. Suddenly Jekyll discovers that he cannot control the metamorphosis; he wakes up to find that his own hand, the hand of the father, the "large firm, white and comely" hand of the successful professional, has turned into the "lean, corded knuckly," and hairy hand of Hyde. The implied phallic images here also suggest the difference between the properly socialized sexual desires of the dominant society and the twisted, sadistic, and animal desires of the other side. Jekyll's "hand" also means his handwriting and signature, which Hyde can forge, although his own writing looks like Jekyll's with a different slant. As Frederic W. H. Myers wrote to Stevenson, "Hyde's writing might look like Jekyll's, done with the left *hand*."[34] Finally, the image draws upon the Victorian homosexual trope of the left hand of illicit sexuality. Jekyll tells Lanyon that in the days of their Damon and Pythias friendship, he would have sacrificed "my left hand to help you." In his secret memoirs, Symonds, too, uses the figure of the useless hand "clenched in the grip of an unconquerable love" to express his double life and the sublimation of his homosexual desires.[35]

Some men, like Symonds and Wilde, may have read the book as a signing to the male community. "Viewed as an allegory," Symonds wrote to Stevenson, "it touches upon one too closely. Most of us at some epoch of our lives have been upon the verge of developing a Mr. Hyde."[36] Wilde included an anecdote in "The Decay of Lying" about "a friend of mine, called Mr. Hyde" who finds himself eerily reliving the events in Stevenson's story. But most Victorian and modern readers ignored such messages or evaded them. While there have been over seventy film and television versions of *Dr. Jekyll and Mr. Hyde,* not one tells the story as Stevenson wrote it, that is, as a story about men. All of the versions add women to the story and either eliminate the homoerotic elements or suggest them indirectly through imagery and structural elements. When Stevenson's friends Andrew Lang and Rider Haggard claimed to have written a version of the story in their collaborative novel *The World's Desire,* they thought the most improbable part was when "the hero having gone to bed with Mrs. Jekyll wakes up with Mrs. Hyde."[37] Thomas Sullivan's 1887 stage adaptation of the story, starring the American actor Richard Masefield, invented a good girl wooed by Jekyll. Hollywood expanded upon this by giving Hyde a "bad" girl barmaid or a woman of the lower classes, although she is never a wholly unsympathetic character. The John Barrymore film in 1920 created an amalgamation of Stevenson's story and Wilde's *The Picture of Dorian Gray.* The high-minded and idealistic Jekyll is in love with the girlish Millicent, the daughter of a Wildean Sir George Carew. But the rakish Carew taunts Jekyll with his innocence, and, in lines taken from Lord Henry Wotton in Wilde's text, urges him to taste temptation. Carew takes Jekyll to a music hall and introduces him to "Miss Gina," an exotic Italian dancer. Lust then becomes Jekyll's motive for the experiment, and his Hyde embarks on a career of debauchery that first leads him to destroy Gina, then takes him to opium dens and brothels, and ends with his vengeful murder of the tempter Carew. Here most explicitly, the "gentlemen," in their silk hats and capes, move easily from the drawing rooms of Mayfair to the alleys of Soho and the East End, while the women's positions are fixed. Millicent and Miss Gina never meet; and we cannot imagine that Millicent would trade places with the dance-hall girl. By grafting the Wilde plot onto the story of Jekyll and Hyde, moreover, the film suggests the seduction of Jekyll by Carew and constructs the triangle of father, daughter, and suitor as the bisexual rivalry of father and daughter for Jekyll's love. Jekyll kills himself by drinking poison, since at the deeper level of the film he is implicated in the unspeakable.

But in films where the homoerotic has been completely suppressed, Jekyll does not have to commit suicide. The question of Jekyll's motives was given a more Freudian cast in the 1941 MGM version directed by Victor Fleming and starring Spencer Tracy, Lana Turner, and Ingrid Bergman. Turner plays Beatrix Emery, Jekyll's innocent, upper-class, blond fiancee, while Ingrid Bergman plays Ivy, the barmaid. When Bea's father breaks off their engagement because of Jekyll's blasphemous experiments and takes his daughter away for a trip to the Continent, Jekyll's bottled-up sexual frustration, as well as the absence of the father and fiancee, causes Hyde to emerge and drives him toward Ivy. In a decade when Hollywood was fascinated by psychoanalysis, Jekyll's fantasies are represented in heavy-handed Freudian dream sequences, in which Jekyll becomes a champagne bottle popping its cork and then drives and lashes Bea and Ivy like a team of horses. Jekyll's sexuality is improper both within the bounds of patriarchal Victorian society and within the bounds of American values of the 1940s. Male sexuality is clearly limited to the spheres of either marriage or prostitution. Jekyll's profession itself is ambiguous in its sexuality. At their first meeting, he saves Ivy from a rapist and then examines her for injuries; since she does not know he is a doctor, the scene is full of double entendre. But the point is that "Jekyll has adopted a professional ethic by which available flesh is divested (as it were) of its erotic potential."[38] Yet Bea and Ivy are not simply "good" and "bad" women; Bea also feels desire for Jekyll, while Ivy feels love and their moral complexity (complicated by the off-screen media identities of Turner and Bergman) deconstructs the simple dualism of Jekyll and Hyde as well. Moreover, the daylight Victorian world of patriarchy, in which Bea is an accepted object of exchange between her father and Jekyll, corresponds to the nighttime world in which Hyde is a sexual sadist who buys and then tyrannizes a working-class woman, whom he keeps imprisoned and finally kills. Women are property in either case. What is particularly interesting is that Hyde never goes after the virginal, "good" woman; his sexuality is clearly seen as bad and thus must be taken to low haunts and lower-class women.

In this film, then, the complex problems of male identity and male sexuality are translated into stereotypical problems of women, and the bisexual elements the text attributes to its male protagonists are made the exclusive property of the female characters. The oedipal relationship in which Bea is a substitute for her dead mother and subject to her father's incestuous jealousy substitutes for the text's hints that Jekyll is in rebellion against his own father and the fathers of society. Ivy, rather than Hyde, is represented as an emotional hysteric. The film even makes Jekyll a kindly psychiatrist, whom Ivy visits by day in search of treatment for her nervous illness caused by his visits as Hyde by night. (In Rouben Mamoulian's 1932 film version of the story, with

Frederic March, Jekyll voices a keen interest in psychoanalysis.) In short, the *women* are sick rather than the uncontrollably mutating Jekyll, who is seen as only the guilt-less victim of his altruistic scientific ambitions. Since his desires are acceptably hetero-sexual, Jekyll feels no guilt and does not commit suicide; he is arrested by Lanyon and the police and taken into custody as he mutates into Hyde while insisting, "I'm Henry Jekyll. I've done nothing."

A particularly interesting film version of Stevenson's story is *Dr. Jekyll and Sister Hyde* (Hammer Studios, 1971). Here the motive is the classic one of the male scientist trying to find the female secrets of creating life. Searching for a means to prolong life, the woman-hating Dr. Jekyll uses the morgue as the source of female reproductive organs for his elixir. When he takes the potion, he becomes a beautiful woman, his own female double, and ecstatically explores his new breasts. Soon the female person-ality is taking over, first overwhelming the professional Jekyll with a sudden and irre-sistible desire to shop but quickly becoming a murderous rival for the single body. In order to prevent her from taking over, Jekyll has to kill women to keep up his supply of the potion. In a nice twist on the idea of the secret identity, he gets his female per-sona to become Jack the Ripper, since the police are not looking for a woman. Fi-nally, as he runs from the police after a killing, Jekyll is trapped on a rooftop. In a clever version of the text's transformation scene, Jekyll helplessly becomes Sister Hyde; the camera cuts "to a close-up of those strong, hairy hands; we watch them elongate and become hairless."[39] As the weaker sex, Sister Hyde cannot hold on and drops into the hands of the police. The film's mingling of themes of duality and bisexuality, science and religion, is a closer reading of Stevenson's story than the more celebrated Hollywood versions.

With Jekyll and Hyde in mind, we think of the late nineteenth century as the age of split personalities who solve their social and sexual problems by neatly separat-ing mind and body, good and evil, upstairs and downstairs. But is the divided self of the fin de siecle narrative everybody's fantasy? Can women as well as men have double lives? Can there be a woman in Dr. Jekyll's closet? We could certainly not rewrite Stevenson's novel as the story of Dr. Jekyll's sister, Dr. Henrietta Jekyll (M.D., Zurich 1880), even if she were born, like her brother, with an "impatient gaiety of disposition" that left her "discontented" and unfulfilled. While Victorian gentlemen had the prerogative of moving freely through the zones of the city, Victorian ladies were not permitted to cross urban, class, and sexual boundaries, let alone have access to a nighttime world of sexual anarchy in bars, clubs, brothels, and illicit sexuality as an alternative to their public life of decorum and restraint. In the 1880s, a "lady was simply not supposed to be seen aimlessly wandering the streets in the evening or eat-ing alone."[40] As Virginia Woolf wrote about the 1880s in her novel *The Pargiters* (later, *The Years*), young women could not visit friends, walk in the dark, or go to the theater unaccompanied. "To be seen alone in Piccadilly was equivalent to walking up Aber-com Terrace in a dressing gown carrying a sponge."[41] Indeed, at the universities, women students were not permitted to attend lectures at the men's colleges unchap-eroned, and even visits from brothers were carefully supervised.[42]

Nor would an Edie Hyde have fared much better. In 1886, the year that Steven-son wrote his story, Eleanor Marx protested that the effects of Victorian sexual repres-sion were far worse for unmarried women of all social classes than for men. "Society provides [for men] the means of gratifying the sex instinct. In the eyes of that same society an unmarried woman who acts after the fashion habitual to her unmarried brothers and the men who dance with her at balls or work with her in the shop, is a pariah."[43] A working-class Edie Hyde wandering around the docks alone in the early hours of morning would have been taken for a prostitute or killed by Jack the Ripper. Furthermore, a lesbian double life for women was not part of cultural mythology in the 1800s. While, as Jeffrey Weeks has explained, "by the end of the nineteenth century a recognizably 'modern' male homosexual identity was beginning to emerge, . . . it would be another generation before female homosexuality reached a corresponding level of articulacy. The lesbian identity was much less clearly defined and the lesbian subculture was minimal in comparison with the male and even more overwhelmingly upper class or literary."[44] In 1920, Vita Sackville-West described herself as a "Dr. Jekyll and Mr. Hyde personality," torn between her love for her husband and her "perverted lesbian" attachment to women.[45] But in 1921, British legislators refused to include women in the Labouchere Amendment because lesbianism was too deeply disturbing even to forbid: "To adopt a clause of this kind," one M.P. proclaimed, "would harm by introducing into the minds of perfectly innocent people the most revolting thoughts."[46]

But the impossibility of actualized double lives for women did not mean that women were not as divided by fantasies, longings, and unrealized desires as men. Women as well as men were "truly two," as the celebrated Boston physician Morton Prince eloquently explained when he wrote at the turn of the century about the repressed sexuality of women: "The multiform sides of a woman's nature differ from man's only in form and their conventional expressions. The contrasting sides, however, of the gentler sex are much less conspicuous to the world than men's and are more easily overlooked. In women, as every woman knows but few men, one or more sides of the character are by the necessity of social customs camouflaged. From childhood she is taught by the conventions of society, by the social taboo, to restrain and repress, often even from herself, many impulses and cravings which are born within her, as well as many thoughts and sentiments which she has acquired by experience, by contact with the world and therefore by riper knowledge. The repression under the social codes of these natural expressions of a part of her personality has belied nature which has been confined for centuries in a café hung with opaque curtains, like unto the spiritualistic dark cabinets. But within her social cabinet, all sorts of orgies of human nature have been seething."[47] Moreover, as the new science of psychoanalysis was demonstrating, transgressive desires in women seem to have led to guilt, inner conflict, and neurotic self-punishment, rather than to fantasies or realities of criminal acting out. In "Civilized Sexual Morality and Modern Nervous Illness," Freud named neurosis as the opposite of what he called "perversion." While neurotics, according to Freud, negatively repress their instincts, leading to nervous illness and hysteria, perverts more energetically put their desires into practice. These differences, furthermore, are gendered. As Freud concludes,

> the discovery that perversions and neuroses stand in the relation of positive and negative is often unmistakably confirmed by observations made on the members of one generation of a family. Quite frequently a brother is a sexual pervert, while his sister, who, being a woman, possesses a weaker sexual instinct, is a neurotic whose symptoms express the same inclinations as the perversions of her more sexually active brother. And correspondingly, in many families, the men are healthy, but from a social point of view immoral to an undesirable degree, while the women are high-minded and over-refined, but severely neurotic.

According to Freud's theory, we cannot recast Jekyll and Hyde with female protagonists because a female Dr. Jekyll with a repressed Sister Hyde is more likely to be agoraphobic than to be picking up (or beating up) men in the street. The brother acting out *his* instincts in East London will be Jack the Ripper, while his sister will be Jill the Weeper, home with her migraines, depressions, and breakdowns.

Yet medical literature of the fin de siecle reveals that observed clinical cases of multiple personality were predominantly female and that in life rather than art, hysterical self-fragmentation was more likely to be a feminine than a masculine response to social pressures. Putting Stevenson's "strange case" in the contexts of late Victorian sexual culture and contrasting it to medical narratives of the period that described strange cases of *female* split personality reveals both some of the dualistic fantasies of the fin de siecle and the ways that they were constructed in terms of gender, sexuality, homophobia, and patriarchy. Dr. Morton Prince of Boston was the leading American medical expert on multiple personality at the fin de siecle and treated two of the most famous female cases, "Miss Beauchamp" and "B.C.A." in the 1890s. The "multiple personalities" of Miss Beauchamp and B.C.A. were all too clearly facets of female repression and rebellion, attempts to live by a different set of values and norms, particularly those having to do with women's restrictive roles. While Victorian men could get through the week on a mere two personalities, Victorian women seemed to need at least three. In the United States especially, duality always seemed insufficient to accommodate the competitive and contradictory ambitions of an expanding nation and to cope with the conflicts in women's roles that were a major factor in the American phenomenon of multiple personality. But despite their parallels to Stevenson's strange case, these female cases were much less adventurous than Jekyll and Hyde. "Miss Beauchamp" was really Clara Norton Fowler, a twenty-five-year-old "bibliophile," who was "never so happy as when allowed to delve amongst books." In 1898 she came to Prince with neurasthenic symptoms, which he traced to a traumatic shock at the age of eighteen: a male voyeur had spied on her through a window and "she saw his excited manner and heard his voice between the peals of thunder."[48] Under hypnosis, she developed three personalities, which he called BII, BIII, and BIV, and thought of as the Saint, the Woman, and the Devil. While BII was anxious, rigid, and neurotic, BII (who first called herself "She," after Rider Haggard's heroine but then chose the name "Sally Beauchamp") was vivacious, high-spirited, and amoral. Sally was also openly and passionately enamored of Dr. Prince: "I love you always, you know *always,* but best when you are strong and splendid, when you are tired and people are not nice to you . . ." she wrote to him. "Please forgive me again . . . and let me stay with you. *Please* please please." Prince's daughter recalled that when Sally "was too obstreperous, odors of ether would emerge from the office," as he attempted to "subjugate this mischievous nature." These multiple personalities were created during the therapy, and on the whole did not appear outside of it. Despite Sally's wishes, Prince would not allow her to become the dominant personality. She went "back to where she came from," "imprisoned" and "squeezed" into the body of a unified "Miss Beauchamp," and after her treatment with Prince, she attended Radcliffe College and married another prominent Boston neurologist. Her story was turned into a Broadway play by David Belasco, *The Case of Becky,* in which the neurologist, renamed "Dr. Emerson," declares, "Dorothy is Dr. Jekyll; Becky, her other self, is Mr. Hyde." The case of B.C.A. is even more compelling and more like the story of Jekyll and Hyde. At Dr. Prince's request, Nellie Bean, or "B.C.A," wrote a fascinating study called "My Life

As a Dissociated Personality" (1909), which has two narrative sections, one written by the Hyde personality, "B," and the other by the cured personality, "C," looking back on her experience. "A" was a forty-year-old widow in 1898 when she first came to Prince suffering from depression, insomnia, headaches, and odd behaviors. A was morbid, helpless, prudish, and terrified of living without a man. Like Fowler, she was intellectual, literary, and frustrated by the pressures toward domestic submission enjoined by her society. One of her symptoms was the emergence of another self, B, who was daring and independent. B had named herself "Bertha Amory" after the feminist heroine of a novel by Frances Hodgson Burnett. She wore white instead of widow's weeds, enjoyed "fun and gay time," smoked, danced, and flirted with men, and allowed one Mr. Hopkins to kiss her. B was alarmed by A's anxiety and by her schemes to remarry: "Why, if she got married I would be married too I suppose, and I won't. I *can't.*" She thought that A should sell her house instead and use the money to start a new life. Among B's interests was the field of psychology, toward which she felt "full of enthusiasm." Like Hyde, B felt youthfully liberated from A: "As B, I was lighthearted and happy and life seemed good to me; I wanted to live; my pulses beat fuller, my blood ran warmer through my veins than it ever had done before. I seemed more alive . . . I felt much younger, and looked so, for the lines of care, anxiety, sorrow and fatigue had faded from my face . . . I neglected my family and friends shamefully . . . my tastes, ideals and points of view were completely changed." Furthermore, B felt no guilt over her new behavior: "The only emotion that I remember to have experienced is one of pleasure and happiness. I know nothing of remorse, reproach, and despair."

Prince called B "a psychological impossibility," and his goal in the therapy was to get rid of her. B, for her part, was bewildered by Prince's preference for the straitlaced and neurotic A: "I cannot see why Dr. Prince would rather have that emotional, hysterical set than to have me! It passes comprehension." In notes left on tables and dressers, B pleaded with A not to tell Dr. Prince everything she was doing and finally planned to run away: "There are lots of things in the world to do and I am going to do some of them if I have half a chance." As Prince constructed a sober compromise figure, C, under hypnosis, B became increasingly alarmed. She begged Prince to let her be the dominant personality: "I am afraid I am going to be a woman just like A & C. I don't want to, Dr. Prince . . . I want to be just what I have always been just 'B,' free as the wind, no body, no soul, no heart. I don't want to love people because if one loves one must suffer; that is what it means to be a woman, to love and suffer." But the wild, Bronteish B, with her longings for exploration and freedom, her lack of guilt, and her independence from men, could not survive in Prince's Boston at the turn of the century. In his terms, she was indeed a monster who had to die. Under hypnotic treatment, Prince finally managed to suppress both the A and B personalities, and the C personality took over. As C, Mrs. Bean spent the remaining years of her life as Prince's devoted research assistant and typist. She did not remarry. It seems a convenient resolution for Prince and a prosaic fate for the rebellious B, who had pleaded not to be cured into feminine "normalcy."

> It's fantastic, she said.
> Since becoming a single, I've really
> Gotten into myself.
> (Sandra Gilbert, "Singles")

Even in the late twentieth century, the age of the single, the story of Jekyll and Hyde does not seem to have lost its appeal. In 1989 and 1990, Michael Caine, Anthony Perkins, Everett Quinton, and Robert Goulet all appeared in adaptations. And fascination with fin de siecle male doubling persists, especially in the work of collaborative artists such as Gilbert and George, McDermott and McGough, and the Starn Twins; David McDermott and Peter McGough, particularly, produce work that alludes to fin de siecle homosexual themes, such as *Queer—1885,* or *Green Carnations—1887.*[49] On the screen, the Jekyll-Hyde story has become the dark-side film (*Something Wild, After Hours*), in which an innocent or upright young man meets a femme fatale who takes him to the dark side of himself: a violent, sadistic, and sexually perverse man. The most successful of these films, David Lynch's *Blue Velvet* (1986), uses Isabella Rossellini in a striking homage to her mother, Ingrid Bergman, while Dennis Hopper is a psychopathic version of Spencer Tracy's sadistic Hyde.

Can we imagine a female Dr. Jekyll today? Susan Sontag's short story *Doctor Jekyll* (1978) is a clever postmodernist version set in contemporary Manhattan. Jekyll is a successful surgeon, Hyde is a delinquent addict. Hyde finally persuades Jekyll to try some violence in his own right, and Jekyll goes to prison for the attempted murder of Hyde. But Sontag does not attempt to imagine the story from a woman's perspective. Similarly, Joyce Carol Oates, in the series of novels about twins and doubling she published under the pseudonym Rosamund Smith, projects the heroine's split psyche onto twinned or doubled male characters.[50] And Fay Weldon, in *Lives and Loves of a She-Devil,* has a Hyde heroine who makes herself over into a beautiful Jekyll.

The Scottish novelist Emma Tennant, however, has written a brilliant feminist version of Stevenson's novel called *Two Women of London: The Strange Case of Ms. Jekyll and Mrs. Hyde* (1989). Tennant has suggested that the double story is particularly meaningful both for women and for Scottish writers who invented it and who grew up within a bilingual and double culture; her earlier novel, *The Bad Sister,* also deals with the theme of the split female psyche.[51] Set in the Notting Hill district of London, *Two Women of London* incorporated the true story of a modern Ripper, the Notting Hill Rapist, with a reimagining of the double theme. The beautiful and fashionable art dealer Eliza Jekyll is really the aging welfare mother Mrs. Hyde, abandoned with her three children by her husband and first tranquilized and then transmogrified by drugs. When she reverts to being Mrs. Hyde, Eliza Jekyll becomes a feminist avenger, murdering the rapist and also the man who has abandoned her. In Eliza Jekyll's statement of the case in Tennant's modernized version of Stevenson's multiple narrative, a message on her answering machine explains: "I am as I am: I was brought up to believe in happiness and my parents and school teachers gave me nothing but love and encouragement. I had no idea of the reality of life, of the pain and suffering which once was considered an integral part of it." There could obviously be an American version of Tennant's novel, but the American urban narrative that suggests itself to me is far more violent. Henrietta Jekyll, a distinguished woman scientist in her mid-fifties, unmarried, admired by all the other single and successful career women in her social circle, longs for another identity, another body, in which to live out her repressed desires. She takes a potion and is transformed into a young, tough, sexy, streetwise babe with a lot of makeup, tight leather clothes, and no inhibitions. So far, so good. But then the story pulls up short. Where does Edie Hyde go once she's all dressed up? To look for Mr. Goodbar? To walk in Central Park? To the porn shops and sex shows in

Times Square? All these roles are dangerous and victimizing for women, not empowering as they might be for men. Henrietta Jekyll would soon become a rape or homicide statistic, a gory headline in the *Daily News,* or a lurid cover story in *People* magazine.

The Jekyll-Hyde story, however, has taken a weird realistic turn in the United States where, in the last few decades, there has been an epidemic among women of what is now called multiple personality disorder, or MPD. In the MPD movement, according to Nicholas Humphrey and Daniel Dennett, "women outnumber men by at least four to one, and there is reason to believe that the vast majority—perhaps 95 percent—have been sexually or physically abused as children."[52] The theory is that the sexually abused child shuts off a part of itself in denial, which then undergoes further splittings. (From this point of view, we might speculate that Jekyll's problem was that he had been abused by a relative, teacher, or servant.) The "host" personality thus generates several "alters," and the number of alters is increasing. While the fin de siecle fiction of doubles involves two personalities, and the modern medical literature on split personality, as in the symbolically named *Three Faces of Eve* (1957), usually involves three personae, the median number of alters for patients described in the current medical literature is eleven. We might say that as the roles demanded of American women increase, female personalities do as well. By 1975, for example, when her identity became public, Eve's selves had "multiplied like rabbits," reaching a grand total of twenty-two and beating Sybil's previous record of sixteen.[53] Furthermore, some of these selves are now masculine; in order for the Jekyll-Hyde fantasy of liberation to be fully imagined for a woman, Henrietta Jekyll had to turn into a man. In a fin de siecle postfeminist America where there is so much from which to dissociate oneself, women are going to need both a Sister Hyde and a Mister Hyde.

Notes

1. Frederic W. H. Myers, "Multiplex Personality," *The Nineteenth Century* (November 1886): 648–66.
2. Mrs. R. L. Stevenson, "Note," in *Works of Robert Louis Stevenson: Skerryvore Edition* (London: Heinemann, 1924), 4:xvii.
3. Emile Batault, *Contribution à l'étude de l'hystérie chez l'homme* (Paris, 1885), author's translation.
4. See Wayne Koestenbaum, "The Shadow Under the Bed: Dr. Jekyll, Mr. Hyde, and the Labouchère Amendment," *Critical Matrix* 1 (Spring 1988): 31–55.
5. Miller, *Doubles,* p. 216.
6. Phyllis Grosskurth, ed., *The Memoirs of John Addington Symonds: The Secret Homosexual Life of a Leading Nineteenth-Century Man of Letters* (Chicago: University of Chicago Press, 1984), p. 122.
7. Regenia Gagnier, *Idylls of the Marketplace,* p. 158.
8. "A Chapter on Dreams," in *The Works of Robert Louis Stevenson* (London, 1922), p. 247.
9. Miller, *Doubles,* p. 213. For discussions of Stevenson's homosociality/homosexuality, see William Veeder's brilliant essay, "Children of the Night: Stevenson and Patriarchy," in *Dr. Jekyll and Mr. Hyde after One Hundred Years* (Chicago: University of Chicago Press, 1988), William Veeder and Gordon Hirsch, eds., especially pp.

159–60; and Wayne Koestenbaum, *Double Talk: The Erotics of Male Literary Collaboration* (New York and London: Routledge, 1989), pp. 145–51.

10. Andrew Lang, "Recollections of Robert Louis Stevenson," *Adventures Among Books* (London: Longmans, Green, and Co., 1903), p. 51.

11. Jenni Calder, *Robert Louis Stevenson: A Life Study* (New York: Oxford University Press, 1980), p. 65.

12. Quoted in Stanley Olson, *John Singer Sargent* (New York: St. Martin's Press, 1986), pp. 115, 114.

13. Malcolm Elwin, *The Strange Case of Robert Louis Stevenson* (London: Macdonald, 1950), p. 198; quoted in Koestenbaum, *Double Talk,* p. 150.

14. Eve Kosofsky Sedgwick has called the genre to which Stevenson's novel belongs "the paranoid Gothic." According to Sedgwick, "the Gothic novel crystallized for English audiences the terms of a dialectic between male homosexuality and homophobia, in which homophobia appeared thematically in paranoid plots" (*Between Men,* p. 92). Such texts involved doubled male figures, one of whom feels obsessed by or persecuted by the other; and the central image of the unspeakable secret. I am indebted also to Paul Zablocki, and to John Perry's unpublished senior thesis, "Novel as Homotext: A Gay Critical Approach to Narrative," Princeton University, 1987.

15. See, for example, the excellent essay by Stephen Heath, "Psychopathia sexualis: Stevenson's *Strange Case,*" *Critical Quarterly* 28 (1986), p. 28.

16. Julia Wedgwood, *Contemporary Review* 49 (April 1886): 594–95; and Alice Brown, *Study of Stevenson* (Boston: Copeland and Day, 1895); quoted in Koestenbaum, *Double Talk,* p. 145.

17. For the manuscripts and publishing history of the novel, see William Veeder, "The Texts in Question," and Veeder and Hirsch, eds., "Collated Fragments of the Manuscript Drafts of *Strange Case of Dr. Jekyll and Mr. Hyde,*" in *Dr. Jekyll and Mr. Hyde,* pp. 3–58.

18. James Twitchell, *Dreadful Pleasures: An Anatomy of Modern Horror* (New York: Oxford University Press, 1985), p. 236.

19. Heath, "Psychopathia sexualis," p. 95.

20. Veeder and Hirsch, *Dr. Jekyll and Mr. Hyde,* p. 55.

21. Vladimir Nabokov, "The Strange Case of Dr. Jekyll and Mr. Hyde," in *Lectures on Literature,* ed. Fredson Bowers (New York: Harcourt Brace Jovanovich, 1980), p. 194.

22. Weeks, *Sex, Politics, and Society,* p. 113.

23. Weeks, *Sex, Politics, and Society,* p. 113.

24. See Veeder, "Children of the Night," in *Dr. Jekyll and Mr. Hyde,* p. 159.

25. Miller, *Doubles,* p. 241.

26. Alexander Welsh, *George Eliot and Blackmail* (Cambridge: Harvard University Press, 1985), p. 9.

27. Edward Carpenter, *The Intermediate Sex,* p. 79; quoted in Weeks, *Coming Out,* p. 21.

28. Sedgwick, *Between Men,* p. 88.

29. Veeder, "Collated Fragments," pp. 34–35.

30. Thanks to Paul Zablocki and Gary Sunshine, students in my course on the fin de siecle, for their comments on "homotextuality" and suicide.

31. Veeder, "Children of the Night," p. 149. Thanks to Phil Pearson.

32. Anne Harrington, *Medicine, Mind, and the Double Brain* (Princeton: Princeton University Press, 1987), p. 170.

33. Harrington, *Medicine, Mind, and the Double Brain,* p. 94.
34. Paul Maixner, *Robert Louis Stevenson: The Critical Heritage* (London: Routledge Kegan Paul, 1981), p. 215.
35. See Christopher Craft, "'Descend and Touch and Enter': Tennyson's Strange Manner of Address," *Genders* 1 (Spring 1988): 91–92.
36. J. A. Symonds to Stevenson, 3 March 1886, in *Letters of J. A. Symonds,* eds. Herbert M. Schueller and Robert L. Peters (Detroit: Wayne State University Press, 1968), pp. 120–21.
37. Quoted in Jenni Calder, *Robert Louis Stevenson,* p. 118.
38. I am indebted for this observation to Daniel Jaeger-Mendelsohn in the Classics Department at Princeton.
39. Twitchell, *Dreadful Pleasures,* p. 256.
40. Vicinus, *Independent Women,* p. 297.
41. Virginia Woolf, *The Pargiters,* ed. Mitchell Leaska (London: Harcourt Brace Jovanovich, 1977), p. 37.
42. Vicinus, *Independent Women,* p. 146.
43. Marx and Aveling, *The Woman Question,* p. 9.
44. Weeks, *Sex, Politics, and Society,* p. 115.
45. Nigel Nicholson, *Portrait of a Marriage* (London: Athenaeum, 1973), p. 35.
46. *Parliamentary Debates,* Commons, 1921, vol. 145, p. 1805.
47. Morton Prince, *Psychotherapy and Multiple Personality: Selected Essays,* ed. Nathan G. Hale, Jr. (Cambridge: Harvard University Press, 1975), p. 195.
48. Prince, *Psychotherapy and Multiple Personalty,* p. 151.
49. Roberta Smith, "Singular Artists Who Work in the First Person Plural," *New York Times,* Sunday, 10 May 1987. Thanks to Wayne Koestenbaum for this reference.
50. See Rosamond Smith, *Lives of the Twins* (New York: Simon and Schuster, 1987), and *Soul/Mate* (New York: E. P. Dutton, 1989).
51. Sue Roe and Emma Tennant, "Women Talking About Writing," in *Women's Writing: A Challenge to Theory,* ed. Moira Monteith (New York: St. Martin's Press, 1986).
52. Humphrey and Dennett, "Speaking for Ourselves: An Assessment of Multiple Personality Disorder," *Raritan* 9 (Summer 1989): 68.
53. See Michael G. Kenny, *The Passion of Ansel Bourne: Multiple Personality in American Culture* (Washington: Smithsonian Institution Press, 1986), pp. 161–82.

QUESTIONS FOR DISCUSSION AND WRITING

1. Showalter's essay covers a lot of territory. She looks at nineteenth-century attitudes toward homosexuality and female/male hysteria, at film versions of the Stevenson story, at multiple personality disorder, and at whether Jekyll or Hyde could be a woman. What connects these ideas?

2. Showalter suggests that *Dr. Jekyll and Mr. Hyde* is coded to represent homosexual behaviors. How convincing did you find her argument?

3. Showalter draws upon evidence from a variety of sources: film, literary criticism, psychological treatises, Stevenson's biography, and so forth. How convincing do

you find her uses of such evidence? Would you credit some kinds of evidence more than others? If so, why?

MAKING CONNECTIONS: *DR. JEKYLL AND MR. HYDE*

1. Eprile's story and the children's version obviously draw on Stevenson's, but there are significant differences between them. How are Jekyll's and Hyde's backgrounds, personalities, and needs different in the stories?
2. *Dr. Jekyll and Mr. Hyde* is set in the London of Stevenson's time, a setting that would have been familiar to many of his readers. That setting may seem historically (and perhaps geographically) remote to many modern readers, however. How do McMullan's and Eprile's Londons compare to Stevenson's?
3. *Dr. Jekyll and Mr. Hyde* is a moral fable, one obviously concerned with the nature of good and evil. What it has to say about morality is not entirely clear, however. Does the novella suggest that repression leads to the creation of Mr. Hyde? Or is lack of self-restraint responsible? Do later versions of the story—Eprile's and the children's version, for instance—reach the same conclusions that Stevenson's story does?
4. The *Punch* parody and James's commentary were written shortly after the publication of Stevenson's novella, whereas Showalter's essay was written a hundred years later. How does the difference in time affect the critical focus on the novella? Are the parody and James's criticism more "male" than Showalter's essay?
5. Henry James objected to Stevenson's use of the "powders" as a means of transformation, and Eprile dispenses with the "powders" entirely. How are our responses to Stevenson's and Eprile's stories affected by the differing explanations of the connections between Jekyll and Hyde?
6. Both McMullan's adaptation of Stevenson's story and the comic books were created with children in mind. Given the comic book covers, would you suspect the comic books would be like or unlike McMullan's version? How?

TOPICS FOR RESEARCH: *DR. JEKYLL AND MR. HYDE*

1. *Dr. Jekyll and Mr. Hyde* has become a cultural story, one familiar even to people who have never read the novella. Interview at least ten people who have not read the story, getting their impressions of what the story is about. What do those interviewed include and what do they omit in their renderings? What do their versions tell you about our culture's understanding of the story's meaning?
2. Because *Dr. Jekyll and Mr. Hyde* is such a popular story, it has been retold in many ways: in films (including *Mary Reilly,* a version told from the point of view of Jekyll's housemaid), in many children's books, in comic books, in a stage musical, and even in a restaurant (the Jekyll and Hyde Club in New York; see www.eerie.com). Looking at one or more of these "retellings," analyze what it has to tell us about the story. What is included, omitted, or distorted by the new version? Why?

3. Oscar Wilde's novel *The Picture of Dorian Gray* was published in 1890, just four years after Stevenson's *Dr. Jekyll and Mr. Hyde*. The two works are similar in that both deal with a splitting of personality, one that allows a seemingly virtuous character to mask his misdeeds. Read Wilde's novel, comparing it with Stevenson's story. Are the splits that occur similar or different? How do the moral perspectives of the two works compare?

4. Stevenson's depiction of Hyde seems to have been influenced by nineteenth-century ideas about criminality. Research the ideas of late-nineteenth-century criminologists, particularly Cesare Lombroso. How might those ideas have influenced Stevenson's portrayal of Hyde and the crimes he commits?

5. As created by Stevenson, Jekyll is both a scientist and physician, though he does not seem to treat patients. The perception of medicine and science has shifted considerably over the years. Research late-nineteenth-century attitudes toward doctors and research scientists. Were scientific discoveries generally viewed with suspicion or optimism? Who held a higher social status, physicians or research scientists? How would Jekyll's not practicing medicine have been judged?

6. Commentators have often remarked that the world of *Dr. Jekyll and Mr. Hyde* is a world of middle-aged bachelors. During the late nineteenth century, marriage was a topic of frequent public discussion, though usually in terms of marriage prospects for women. Research attitudes toward unmarried men. Were they viewed as shirking their public duties? Were they the butt of jokes, as spinsters often were?

7. *Dr. Jekyll and Mr. Hyde* was a runaway bestseller, though even Stevenson himself thought the book was more popular than good. Locate reviews written when the book was first published. What do the critics see as the book's strengths and weaknesses?

APPENDIX 1
Writing Assignments

BREAKING THE BOUNDARIES:
WRITING TOPICS THAT MOVE ACROSS THEMES

1. Many of the works in *Retellings* describe parent–child relationships. How do they envision the joys and tensions of such relationships? How much do you think Freud's theories about oedipal feelings apply to the parent–child relationships described in literature? To what extent are we meant to think of children and parents as extensions of one another, more alike than different? To what extent are we meant to think that the relationship is torn by generational differences? How does the portrayal of parent–child relationships reinforce the works' themes? (As you consider these questions, think not only about parents and children but also about surrogate parents and children.)

2. Villains and monsters populate the literature of all ages. What do the villains and monsters across the ages have in common? To what extent have later authors redefined "monstrosity" and evil? How do definitions of monstrosity reflect concerns about the relationship between the individual and the larger society? About the relationship between the "other" and the dominant culture? How do they reflect a writer's sense of the ties that hold a culture together?

3. Compare works that are considered tragic or that have an element of the tragic. Do they define "tragedy" in the same way? If definitions of tragedy differ according to time, place, and culture, what do those differences in definition tell us about a people's values and assumptions?

4. Heraclitus, an ancient Greek author from the sixth century B.C., is thought to have said that "character is destiny." To what extent is that true in the works you have been reading? Where does an individual's responsibility for his or her destiny begin and end? To what extent are an individual's behaviors, actions, and circumstances determined by forces outside of him- or herself? If outside forces *do* determine events and actions, what is the individual's appropriate response to those forces? When outside forces seem to control an individual's ideas and behaviors, what are those forces? How do they contribute to our sense of a culture's primary values and concerns?

5. The definition of a "good king" (or "good leader") is at the center of many literary works. Compare and contrast the definitions in two or more of the works included in *Retellings*. What is the ideal relationship between the leader and those he or she governs? What values and beliefs should guide the leader's thoughts and actions? How should he or she find the appropriate balance between conflicting goals? How do the qualities of a good leader change across time and place? What do those qualities tell us about each culture's values?

6. Several works in *Retellings* focus on the colonial experience of both the colonizer and the colonized. To what extent do they come to the same conclusions about the morality and practicality of colonial rule? How does point of view—individual, temporal, and/or cultural—influence the conclusions?

7. Compare the ways in which two or three of the works in *Retellings* characterize woman and womanhood or man and manhood. Are women and men motivated by different emotions and circumstances? To what extent are women and men defined by their relationships with each other? As far as you can tell, how much does an author's gender influence his or her characterizations of women and men?

8. Some readers say that Hamlet's problem is that he is too passive: he thinks too much and does too little. Some readers say that Oedipus's problem is the opposite: he acts before he thinks. What other heroes in *Retellings* might be characterized as active or passive? How are we meant to respond to their activity or passivity? What does a comparison tell us about how activity and passivity are defined and valued across the boundaries of time, gender, ethnicity, and/or culture?

9. Compare and contrast the ways in which two or three authors envision the process of growing up. How pleasant or painful is the process? How do the authors convey the differences between adolescents—their behaviors and their emotions—and children or adults? In literature, do young men and women experience and respond to adolescence in the same way? Do authors of different times and cultures represent the process of growth in similar ways?

10. Literature often concerns itself either overtly or implicitly with the issue of social justice. Compare the ways in which several of the authors in *Retellings* define the relationship between the citizen and the government and the ways they look at the reasons for social injustice and the prospects for justice. According to the literature you have read, how are ideas about social justice most likely to be formed? What is most likely to happen when the principles of social justice are violated?

11. It is often said that we no longer believe in heroes or in hope. To what extent do modern works of literature (those written in the second half of the twentieth century) seem to bear out this notion that we do not believe in meaningful heroic action or in the possibility of a better future? Are the heroes of older works more "heroic"? Are the older literary works apparently more optimistic?

12. Look at two or three works that describe crimes. How do they define "criminal behavior"? What motivates the criminals to commit their crimes? How much does a knowledge of a criminal's psychology tempt us to excuse the crimes? How much does it encourage us to see ourselves in the criminal's position? Are the authors whose works you are analyzing equally horrified by the crimes they describe? Are the readers? Do we see the criminals more as people or as monsters? How does a comparison of the works help us refine our definitions of criminality?

13. It is sometimes said that Western countries are too often defined by their consumerism—that we value products over ideas and ideals. Choose two or three authors represented in *Retellings* and compare and contrast their apparent attitudes toward consumer culture. How are readers meant to respond to material culture? According to the authors whose works you are analyzing, how fully does materialism describe and define American values?

14. Literature often depends on the use of suspense. Compare and contrast the methods by which several works create a feeling of suspense. To what extent do second and third readings alert readers to the ways in which an author has prepared

them for the ending? Think not only about works that surprise you with their endings but about works in which we *know* the likely ending but nevertheless feel ourselves becoming more anxious as we read. How do the authors of such works create the sense of impending doom? Which of the methods of creating suspense do you find most effective? Why?

15. It is a critical commonplace that older works of literature focus on the wealthy and powerful and modern works focus on the common person. In your reading of the literature in *Retellings,* how valid does that statement seem? How does the focus on a particular socioeconomic group of individuals affect our response to a piece of literature?

16. Look at the roles of memory and the past in two or three works. Are past events considered realistically? Nostalgically? Is the past a country to which we wish we could once again travel, or is it a land better left behind us? In the literature, how does a character's personal, cultural, or familial past influence and reflect his or her present?

17. Irony depends in part on the juxtaposition of something that is true with something that is not true (or seems not to be true) or on the use of language that would seem to be inappropriate in some way. Compare and contrast the way several authors use irony to make their points. Are they using irony to the same end? Does the use of irony reflect particular social, cultural, or temporal concerns and attitudes? Do some cultures or ages seem more likely than others to be "ironic"? Why?

18. In American culture, mothers-in-law have often been viewed contemptuously, and some readers have remarked that, in an American cultural context, *The Book of Ruth's* positive portrayal of the daughter-in-law–mother-in-law bond is striking. Looking at some portrayals of mothers-in-law (for instance, in literature, films, and jokes), examine *why* mothers-in-law are viewed negatively in our culture. If you are familiar with another culture, you may want to compare and contrast its view to the American one.

19. Consider the treatment of stepfathers and stepmothers in literature. How do Hamlet and Lizzie Borden respond to their new parents, for instance? How does the stepmother in the Cinderella stories respond to her new child? Now compare and contrast the stepparent–stepchild relationships as depicted in these works with the same relationships in works seen outside of *Retellings.* You might consider not only other pieces of literature (fairy tales, for instance) but also works of popular culture in which the relationship is explored (think, for instance, of the television show and movies of *The Brady Bunch* or the movies *The Sound of Music* and *The Parent Trap* or any number of others). Finally, what do psychologists tell us about the relationship between a stepparent and stepchild?

20. Look at several literary depictions of the immigrant experience or of the experience of a member of an ethnic minority living in the United States. How much do the characters seem to desire acculturation and assimilation? How much do they regret the loss of a unique cultural identity? How similar are the experiences from one ethnic group to another? How does the cultural background of the author influence the way the immigrant experience is portrayed?

21. Some readers believe that writers write best about what they know firsthand and that it is difficult, even impossible, for authors to convey realistically the thoughts, feelings, and behaviors of someone who is fundamentally different from themselves.

Look at the works of two women writers and two men writers in *Retellings*. Do their styles and characterizations somehow mark the authors' genders? In other words, do women writers write better about women's experiences than men do? Do men writers write better about men's experiences than women do? How might the answers to such questions influence a reader's attitude toward the literary canon?

22. Look at the treatment of adolescence or old age in two or three works. How important to the characterizations are the ages of the authors when they were writing about adolescence or old age?

23. Readers sometimes claim that they can identify a piece as the work of a woman or a man simply by means of style and content or that they can distinguish between an older work and a more modern work by considering the mood and characterizations of the work. Test out this notion by asking people outside your class to look at some short poems or excerpts from short stories or plays and to identify anonymous authors' times or genders. Choose a range of authors—a mix of men and women or a mix of authors from different time periods. For each author, remove the name and any features that *clearly* identify the writer's time or gender. Do not, in other words, choose passages that use language that seems archaic or that seem to present things so clearly from a feminist point of view that we cannot help but think the authors are women. What do your findings show you about whether there is such a thing as a male or female style or whether people of earlier times came to their works with different values and assumptions than we do?

24. Look at the treatment of home in several works. How are characters shaped by their ideas about what home should be and what it is? Do different time periods seem to define home differently?

25. Like all of us, writers often turn the lens on themselves, examining the purpose and value of what they do. In other words, their writing sometimes focuses on the subject of writing, literature, and art. What conclusions do the writers and artists in *Retellings* draw about the nature and purpose of art and literature? About the connections between verbal and visual art on the one hand and reality on the other? How do these conclusions compare with those of the average reader?

26. What gives rise to hope and fear in the works included in *Retellings*? Have the sources of hope and fear changed over time? Do the characters in later works respond to hope and fear in ways similar to or different from the ways characters in earlier works respond? What do the sources of and responses to hope and fear reveal about an author's values and attitudes?

27. Look at the treatment of education in several works. What does a formal education offer? What are the limitations of a formal education? What kinds and sources of education are valued more than others? How does the treatment of education reflect a character's and/or an author's values? How much is education linked to questions of individuality? Social justice? Economic prosperity? Self-knowledge and self-worth?

28. What might the literature included here imply about how ideas of love and love relationships have changed over time? Consider descriptions of courtship, love fantasies, jealousies, and actual relationships.

29. In the literature you have read, what gives a character a sense of self and self-worth? To what extent do others and external forces define a person? To what extent does someone shape his or her own self? What happens when one's sense of self is not reinforced by outside people or forces?

SOME COMMON ASSIGNMENTS

The kind of paper you write in response to a piece of literature will, of course, often depend on the kind of assignment you have been given. You may be responding to a topic given to you by your instructor and will, of course, want to follow the guidelines laid out in the topic. There are, however, several common writing tasks, and having a general idea of what each entails may help you get started on your paper.

Explication

The word **explicate** comes from the Latin word for "*unfold*." An explication is a line-by-line unfolding of the meaning in a poem. (Poems open themselves up to explication because they are relatively short; *explicate* is not used for short stories, plays, novels, or essays.) When a writer is asked to explicate a poem, he is being asked to move systematically through the poem, line by line, looking at what the words mean literally and at what their connotations might tell us about their function in the poem. A systematic annotation of the poem being discussed will usually be enormously helpful if you are being asked to explicate a poem because it forces you to consider the poem in all of its details. That doesn't mean, however, that an explication mechanically lists the lines and comments on them. Clearly such a structure would bore the reader (and probably the writer as well). Here is a sample explication of Shakespeare's "That Time of Year," a poem that we discussed in chapter 4 (100–101). Notice as you read how the line-by-line analysis is integrated into the larger examination of the poem.

David Lee

Professor Clarke

English 3

6 February 2002

    Time and Structure in "That Time of Year": An Explication

    In Sonnet 73 ("That time of year"), Shakespeare traces the inevitable progress towards decay and death. Although we don't know who the "me" of line one is, we do know that that "me" contains within itself a "time of year" when trees are dropping their leaves or are already bare. It is a season with little warmth and life--even the trees are "shaking," presumably from the winds, though there is also a feeling of bone-chilling cold. The birds have left: the trees are "bare ruined choirs, where late the sweet birds sang." Spring will, of course, one day return, but for the moment, the image the poet offers is of a season of cold and silence with little sense of a life-affirming warmth or joy. "Time"--which, not coincidentally, is the first word in the poem to receive metrical stress--exerts some pressure.

The second quatrain begins with a reference to a shorter span of time. Now the "me" of the poem has been reduced to "the twilight of such day / As after sunset fadeth in the west." The shorter time period is matched by a bleaker outlook: the yellow (in the leaves) of the first quatrain has given way to the sunset that is swallowed up by "black night." Significantly, that night is also called "Death's second self that seals up all in rest" (8), and the poet emphasizes the significance of the mention of death by departing from his usually very regular iambic pentameter pattern. If he had stayed with the normal metrical pattern, the first syllable of the line would not have received metrical stress, but surely no reader can read line 8 without emphasizing its first word, "Death's." As a result, even though the poet is talking about sleep, which is only "death's second self" not death itself, the reader cannot help but see a connection between death and sleep, death and twilight.

The reference to death in line 8 closes out the second quatrain with an image both of death itself and a sleep that mimics death. When we read "Death's second self that seals up all in rest," we almost read "death's second self that *seals up all the rest*." There is, then, a hint that death is inevitable and that all of us will come too soon to the moment of death. Still, there is here, as there was in the first quatrain, some feeling that death isn't inevitable or final.

Just as winter is followed by spring, sunset is followed by sunrise and sleep by waking. This quatrain, like the first, reinforces a cyclical notion of death *and* rebirth.

With the third quatrain, beginning in line 9, the poem moves to a third image: "In me thou see'st the glowing of such fire / That on the ashes of his youth doth lie" (9–10). The first line in the pair seems to offer some hope with "the glowing of such fire"; we envision a fire warming us, or the speaker, against the cold twilight of the preceding lines. At the same time, the fire is nourished by its own ashes, and youth is gone. In the two lines that follow we learn that fire consumes itself, nourishing itself with the very fuel that, once expended in the form of ashes, will smother it. Just as youth and passion die in age, so, too, do the flames of the fire burn brightly for only a short span of time.

This quatrain, like the ones before it, seems to prefigure a movement toward the moment of death. The span of months of the first quatrain has given way first to the span of hours in the second and then to the span of moments in the third. As the fire feeds upon itself, we know that it will in only moments be extinguished. We may now see that extinguishing as final. Though spring follows winter and sunrise follows sunset, once the fire is out, it is out for good.

As is frequently true of the Shakespearean sonnet, the final couplet of the poem encapsulates the whole and comments upon it. Although there may be some confusion over whether the "that" in line 14 refers to life itself or to a particular beloved, this much is clear: the speaker is advising his hearer to recognize the movement of time and the approach of death and to appreciate and embrace what his life has offered.

Notice that the explication takes all of its evidence from within the poem. There is nothing here about Shakespeare's life or other writings or about the sonnet tradition. The writer has focused on unfolding this one poem, in the process helping us see how it works and what it means.

Analysis

Closely related to the idea of explication is the idea of *analysis*. An analysis, too, involves an examination of how a work's style and structure, characters, speakers, and setting contribute to its art and its themes. When you are asked to write an analytical paper, you are being asked to take a work apart and put it back together. You will have the most success in writing an analytical paper if you remember what we said earlier about *thesis* (125). An analytical paper usually expresses an opinion that answers a *how* or *why* question. Think back, for instance, to the thesis question Heather Johnson asked and answered in her paper on "To His Coy Mistress": "How are we meant to respond to the relationship between the speaker and the woman he is addressing?" (see chapter 7). Other *how* questions for an analytical paper might ask, "How does the final couplet in 'That Time of Year' complete the poem's theme?" or "How are love, faith, and war related in 'Dover Beach'?" *Why* questions will similarly lead to analytical papers: "Why does Silko blur the line between myth and reality in 'Yellow Woman'?" or "Why do Mrs. Hale and Mrs. Peters hide the evidence in *Trifles*?"

Whereas an explication is a response to a short piece of literature that can be examined line by line, an analysis often takes a more global approach and is organized logically rather than chronologically. For an example of an analytical paper, look again at Heather Johnson's paper on "To His Coy Mistress" (see chapter 7). You will notice that her key ideas, rather than the chronological order of the poem, are used to organize the essay.

Comparison and Contrast

Comparison and contrast papers are very common in literature classes and in literary criticism. Often the process of comparing and contrasting two things—two stories, two authors, two characters, two themes, and so forth—will give a writer and her reader a more solid insight into how each of those things works. That is, in fact, the reasoning behind *Retellings*. As we said earlier, we believe that a reader can often come to a richer understanding of a work of literature by reading a retelling of it and then comparing the two versions.

Think back, for instance, to your first response to "To His Coy Mistress" and then to Heather Johnson's paper on the poem. Both your response and Heather's were shaped by a close reading of Marvell's poem, and both you and Heather "retold" the story in your own terms because you highlighted some of Marvell's ideas and thrust others into the background. Now think about how your reading of "To His Coy Mistress" might be affected by your reading of the "updated" versions that follow.

ARCHIBALD MACLEISH (1892–1982)

You, Andrew Marvell   1930

And here face down beneath the sun
And here upon earth's noonward height
To feel the always coming on
The always rising of the night:

5   To feel creep up the curving east
The earthy chill of dusk and slow
Upon those under lands the vast
And ever climbing shadow grow

And strange at Ecbatan the trees
10   Take leaf by leaf the evening strange
The flooding dark about their knees
The mountains over Persia change

And now at Kermanshah the gate
Dark empty and the withered grass
15   And through the twilight now the late
Few travelers in the westward pass

And Baghdad darken and the bridge
Across the silent river gone
And through Arabia the edge
20   Of evening widen and steal on

And deepen on Palmyra's street
The wheel rut in the ruined stone
And Lebanon fade out and Crete
High through the clouds and overblown

25   And over Sicily the air
Still flashing with the landward gulls
And loom and slowly disappear
The sails above the shadowy hulls

And Spain go under and the shore
30   Of Africa the gilded sand
And evening vanish and no more
The low pale light across that land

Nor now the long light on the sea:

And here face downward in the sun
35   To feel how swift how secretly
The shadow of the night comes on . . .

DIANE ACKERMAN (1948–   )

A Fine, a Private Place _____ 1983

He took her one day
under the blue horizon
where long sea fingers
parted like beads
hitched in the doorway   5
of an opium den,
and canyons mazed the deep
reef with hollows,
cul-de-sacs, and narrow boudoirs,
and had to ask twice   10
before she understood
his stroking her arm
with a marine feather
slobbery as aloe pulp
was wooing, or saw the octopus   15
in his swimsuit
stretch one tentacle
and ripple its silky bag.

While bubbles rose
like globs of mercury,   20
they made love
mask to mask, floating
with oceans of air between them,
she his sea-geisha
in an orange kimono   25
of belts and vests,
her lacquered hair waving,
as Indigo Hamlets
tattooed the vista,
and sunlight   30
cut through the water,
twisting its knives
into corridors of light.

His sandy hair
and sea-blue eyes,   35
his kelp-thin waist
and chest ribbed wider
than a sandbar
where muscles domed
clear and taut as shells   40
(freckled cowries,
flat, brawny scallops

the color of dawn),
his sea-battered hands
45   gripping her thighs
like tawny starfish
and drawing her close
as a pirate vessel
to let her board:
50   who was this she loved?

Overhead, sponges
sweating raw color
jutted from a coral arch,
Clown Wrasses
55   hovered like fireworks,
and somewhere an abalone opened
its silver wings.
Part of a lusty dream
under aspic, her hips rolled
60   like a Spanish galleon,
her eyes swam
and chest began to heave.
Gasps melted on the tide.
Knowing she would soon be
65   breathless as her tank,
he pumped his brine
deep within her,
letting sea water drive it
through petals
70   delicate as anemone veils
to the dark purpose
of a conch-shaped womb.
An ear to her loins
would have heard the sea roar.

75   When panting ebbed,
and he signaled *Okay?*
as lovers have asked,
land or waterbound
since time heaved ho,
80   he led her to safety:
shallower realms,
heading back toward
the boat's even keel,
though ocean still petted her
85   cell by cell, murmuring
along her legs and neck,
caressing her
with pale, endless arms.

Later, she thought often
of that blue boudoir,
pillow-soft and filled
with cascading light,   90
where together
they'd made a bell
that dumbly clanged   95
beneath the waves
and minutes lurched
like mountain goats.
She could still see
the quilted mosaics   100
that were fish
twitching spangles overhead,
still feel the ocean
inside and out, turning her
evolution around.   105

She thought of it miles
and fathoms away, often,
at odd moments: watching
the minnow snowflakes
dip against the windowframe,   110
holding a sponge
idly under tap-gush,
sinking her teeth
into the cleft
of a voluptuous peach.   115

J. PETER MEINKE (1932–   )

To His Coy Mistress, 1966   *1966*

My dear, the problem is the same: time
is of the essence, worlds fall apart;
you perpetrate an ancient crime
by holding heart away from heart.
I want to praise your beauty, but the age   5
is one of the understatement, with emotions
suspect; at low tide, the ancient rage
for beauty ebbs with other oceans,
and we find ourselves embarrassed on the beach.

But let me sing to you my timeless song—   10
don't turn away—I want our love to reach
around the world's impediments, the long
separations and the dry sands,

the iron gates and the relentless pull
15   of nervous moons and nerveless hands.
These plastic days, insensate, dull,
and fearful, can be redeemed by those
who listen to the singing of the vein,
who disregard the thorn to pluck the rose,
20   who love the sun, and understand the rain.

Now therefore, come with me and be my love
without consulting counselor or graph.
Let us wing naked as the birds above
and not consider who has the last dry laugh;
25   for remember, they who love first, love best:
decorum and statistics rule the rest.

To understand a "retelling," a reader must keep two (or more) works in mind. As the retellings throughout this book demonstrate, the reteller almost always depends on the reader's knowledge of the original (or most famous) version of the work. Without that knowledge, the point of the retelling may very well be lost. These later poems, then, are best understood in the context of Marvell's: a reader needs to see how the modern poets are using and changing the original to create meanings of their own. Any discussion of them lends itself naturally to a comparison/contrast structure.

EXERCISES: TRYING IT OUT

1. In chapter 7, you read about Edward de Bono's "random word stimulation" exercises. Using his method, individually or in groups randomly select ten words from the dictionary. Brainstorm associations between the words and one of the retellings of "To His Coy Mistress." Then associate those same words with Marvell's poem. How similar are the associations? How might the ease or difficulty with which you can associate the same words with the two different poems illuminate the similarities and differences between Marvell's themes and the second poet's?

2. Compare and contrast the speaker in Marvell's poem with the speaker in one of the retellings. How similar do their backgrounds seem? Their attitudes toward the women and the worlds in which they live? Their tones? What, finally, do the similarities and differences tell us about the artistry and purposes of the two poems?

Many writers find comparison/contrast papers difficult to write because they involve juggling two things at once. You will probably find it easier to keep things ordered if from the beginning you have a clear idea of the criteria that form the basis of the comparison and contrast. You might, for instance, choose to compare Marvell's poem and one of the retellings on the basis of the following: their speakers' personalities, their tones, their uses of imagery and setting, and their treatments of women. If you think from the beginning of having to talk about two poems and four elements for each, the task may seem overwhelming and confusing. So writers of comparison/

contrast papers have commonly used one of two structures to give their papers shape: the *point-by-point* structure and the *subject-by-subject* structure.

In a comparison of Marvell's poem and one of the retellings, for example, a writer might choose a point-by-point structure and write about the speaker's personality in each, then discuss each poem's tone, then move on to an analysis of how both writers use imagery and setting, and finally write about the treatment of women. Or a writer might choose a subject-by-subject structure and first discuss Marvell's poem thoroughly (writing about all the points mentioned above: the speaker, the tone, the imagery and setting, and the treatment of women) and then follow that up with a discussion of all of these same points as they apply to the retelling. Note, by the way, that any one of these smaller subjects may be complex enough to require more than a paragraph for development; in other words, you may find yourself devoting several paragraphs to the discussion of imagery and setting if each writer uses more than one kind of image or if each image has more than one purpose behind it.

Whatever organizational pattern the writer chooses, however, it is important that the comparison/contrast structure support a clear thesis. Comparisons and contrasts are meaningless unless they serve a greater purpose. *Any* two things are comparable or different in some striking ways. It is your job to help your reader see the *significance* of those similarities or differences. For literature, that significance will almost always involve a discussion of the themes of the works. Remember that the question you want to answer is still an analytical one, and the comparison/contrast is a means toward an analytical end, not simply a mechanical listing of similarities and differences.

Following is a comparison/contrast essay by student James Rallis, who chose to write his own poetic retelling of Marvell's poem and then went on to compare and contrast his new version and Marvell's original.

JAMES RALLIS

To His Coy Mister

> Had we but world enough, and time,
> This closet, fair sir, were no crime.
> You'd long deny your inner self,
> And leave true love upon a shelf.
> You'd sit beside the Key West dunes,[1]
> And long to touch those daylight moons.
> In Frisco I'd beneath a pall,
> Love you ten years before Stonewall.[2]
> And even if the truth you'd fight,
> 'Til our acceptance by the right.
> Fruity love I'd grow and nourish,
> And in old age it would flourish.
> Twenty-one years should I exalt,
> Your chest and abs are without fault.

5

10

1 Key West dunes: Gay nude beach area in Key West, Florida.   **2 Stonewall:** 1969, New York City riots that many see as the birth of the modern gay rights movement.

15   Forty-two to cherish your face,
    At sixty-three we'd just embrace.
    When eighty years had come and gone,
    We'd Marvell that we've loved so long.
    We must have love's consummation,
20   As that future love's foundation.
       The clock that ticks inside my ear,
    Time's running out; the end is near,
    Death's vault a closet for all time.
    You must decide while in your prime.
25   Alone and old, a joyless fate
    For you is certain if you wait.
    A belly large, a hairless head,
    Then you may wish that you were dead.
    You mustn't wait too long to seize
30   The gay man who wants you to please.
    The lust of youth will soon be changed
    Into a love that's rearranged.
       Now my advances do not mock
    Before the crow of morning cock
35   Take your place here within my bed
    Give up on going straight ahead.
    Stop tearing through the hellish gate
    But fall at once for me prostrate.
    So hurry now it is the hour
40   Before it wilts give me your flower.
    Let healing come from our embrace
    Let us caduceus[3] replace.
    Let pleasure now become our game
    Extinguish not this ball of flame.
45   Let's make time fly by having fun
    It will stand still if I you shun.

James Rallis

Prof. A. Clarke

English 1B

14 February 2002

    "To His Coy Mister"

    A Seize the Gay Poem

3 Caduceus: The symbol of medicine with two intertwined snakes on a winged staff.

The first time I read Andrew Marvell's "To His Coy Mistress," I longed to read a similar poem from the perspective of a gay man; unable to find one, I decided that I needed to write that poem. I took apart Marvell's poem piece by piece. I explored the structure and patterns in the original work. I looked for themes and symbols that I could use or change in my poem. I then embarked on a journey through the mind of a gay man who was courting someone who was not responding favorably to advances that were being made. The new poem then came easily; it seemed to write itself at times. "To His Coy Mister" is a poem that mimics the message, structure, patterns, and tone that Marvell uses in "To His Coy Mistress," while restructuring the themes and symbols to reflect a modern gay perspective.

The suitor in "To His Coy Mister" is pursuing a man who he believes is gay, but there is little evidence present in the poem to support his assertion. Like the woman in Marvell's poem there is no way to know what the "mister" feels for his wooer. In each poem it is clear that the person speaking feels that he can be the only hope for his target's future sexual, romantic and spiritual future. As my speaker relentlessly pursues the object of his lust, he uses flattery and romance to entice his love. He follows this romantic speech with threats. Unlike the man in Marvell's poem, my speaker uses only a quick reference to the grave in the second stanza but follows with threats that have an even greater sting when they are spoken to many young gay males: the threat of becoming old, fat, and bald. Many men within the gay community view youth and beauty as the measure of one's worth; as youth fades so does one's desirability. Finally, in the third stanza, my speaker uses strong sexual references and symbols to get his "mister" into bed.

Using "To His Coy Mistress" as a template, I followed the rhythm and structure exactly. I used the paragraph stanzas employed by Marvell in his work to highlight the differing themes of romance, death, and sex. I followed the eight beats per line seen in the original poem and kept the exact number of lines. Using couplets for the rhyme structure, I followed Marvell's poem with only a few exceptions. Today's English creates approximate rhymes within the lines of two couplets in Marvell's poem; each line in the couplets rhymes exactly, though, to the corresponding line in the other. This is seen when Marvell says:

And yonder all before us *lie*
Deserts of vast *eternity.* (23–24)

and,

My echoing song; then worms shall *try*
That long-preserved *virginity.* (27–28) (My emphasis)

I used only one rhyme approximation in my poem when I rhyme "consummation" (19) to "foundation" (20). Because the words I picked best reflected my views, I chose not to follow the above pattern for any of my lines. I could not find lines that both fit Marvell's pattern and said what I wanted them to say, so I chose to deviate. Other deviations became necessary as I attempted to write this new poem.

Writing in a time of strong religious belief, Marvell chose to set his time frame for love between "the flood" (8) and the end of time; I chose rather to set my speaker's love between the "Stonewall" (8) riots and the ". . . . acceptance by the right" (10), a day that may or may not come, to reflect a gay time line. Marvell goes for the eternal in his time line, while I give the hope of only one lifetime. Marvell's world view gives hope of a life after this; my view gives the reader a sense of finality within this life. I, like Marvell, increase the amount of time as the first stanza goes on, but unlike his unrealistic praising of the woman's beauty, I chose to set up the hope of a relationship that will change over time. This changes the theme slightly, but still reflects the need to act quickly. The only allusions to the eternal made in my poem are when I call "Death's vault a closet for all time" (23), and when I bring the lovers to the end of their lives together. I used the words "we'd Marvell that we've loved so long" (18). This use of Marvell's name suggests that the lovers may look to the time line that was put forth in the original poem to hope that their love will last even after their deaths. Other references to time shared by the poems are seen by frequent usage of words like "now" (Marvell 32 and 36; Rallis 33, 39 and 43) to show the urgency the speakers want to convey.

Britain was an empire that stretched far and wide. Marvell, in his poem, places the principals at the farthest reaches of the British Empire. The mistress is placed in India (5) and her suitor is in England (7). For gay Americans, the places that offer freedom and acceptance are difficult to find. I placed my two speakers in Key West (5) and San Francisco (7), as they are at opposite ends of what many view as the American gay empire. These uses of locations are just part of the imagery that is used in these poems; they are placed so far apart to show the distance between the speakers that must be crossed before their love can be made whole.

Sexuality plays an important role in both Marvell's poem and mine. While there are blatant requests for sex in both poems, other demands are hidden within the imagery used. Symbols of both sexes' genitalia can be found in both poems. Marvell says:

Let us roll all our strength, and all
Our sweetness, up into one ball;
And tear our pleasures with rough strife
Through the iron gates of life. (41-44)

The "ball," of course, symbolizes the male and the female is symbolized by the "gates of life." I too used symbols to portray both gay and heterosexual sex. The lines that best illustrate this point are:

Before the crow of morning cock
Take your place here within my bed
Give up on going straight ahead.
Stop tearing through the hellish gate . . . (34-37)

The "morning cock" is an unabashed reference to male genitalia and the use of the phrase "hellish gate" for the feminine is the suitor's attempt to disparage females and his lover's contact with them, while echoing the gate image used by Marvell.

One major difference between the poems is my use of imagery that is chosen to symbolize gay love and lust; Marvell, of course, used none in his poem. The closet references (2 and 23) are clear references to those who live life closeted, or who are secretly gay. The reference to "fruity love" (11) is used to echo much of the straight world's view of gay love; the word "fruit" is often used as a disparaging name for gay men. The word "prostrate" (38) was chosen as a reference to the desire of the speaker to see his love face down in a position of submission and worship. The intertwining serpents in the "caduceus" (42) symbolize the double phallus found in a gay male relationship. The identification of gay men as "flaming" has been a part of the English language for hundreds of years. Gay men had been used as kindling, or faggots, for the blazes used to burn suspected witches throughout Europe. I chose "ball of flame" (44) to reference this gay term and joined with a clear image of the male genitalia. Changing some of the representational language was important to highlight the gay male themes, yet these changes barely made an impact on the tone used by Marvell. Living in the moment is essential to happiness.

Seize the day; a message that has been echoing for generations endures. "To His Coy Mistress" differs from my poem "To His Coy Mister" on many levels. The times, places, images and even some of the themes are changed in my poem; the message remains the same. Both suitors use every tool in their arsenals to convince the objects of their lust that the time for sexual gratification is now. My suitor may be gay, but his desires to be loved and wanted are the same as those voiced by the speaker in the poem by Marvell over three hundred years ago. My wooer asserts that it is better to make time speed along by experiencing everything life has to offer than to sit back and watch it pass at a snail's pace when he says:

Let's make time fly by having fun
It will stand still if I you shun. (45–46)

The man in Marvell's original poem reflects the same sentiment

when Marvell writes:

Thus, though we cannot make our sun

Stand still, yet we will make him run. (45-46)

Both suitors assert that a life of love and sexual fulfilment

are the only remedy for a long and lonely existence.

Review

One other assignment is common in literature classes: the review. You may be familiar with this kind of writing if you have ever read a review of a book, movie, or play in the newspaper. For literature, essentially a review seeks to answer a question such as the following: "How effective is this piece of writing?" A reviewer evaluates the work by considering how well it does the job it has set out to do. Some questions a reviewer might answer:

How realistically does the work portray its characters and setting?

How well do style and meaning reinforce one another?

For what kind of audience is the work most likely to be effective?

The goal of a review is less to show *how* a piece of literature works than it is to show *how well* it works.

The last piece of advice we can give you about responding to assignments is that you should work to make the assignment your own. That doesn't mean that you should simply discard the topic or ignore the parts that you don't understand or that don't immediately appeal to you. It does mean, though, that you should turn it around in your mind, looking at it, as you look at all writing, from as many perspectives as possible. Few teachers have a specific paper in mind that they want you to match; the best essays offer original insights, ones the teacher may well not have thought of. Find an entrance into the topic that will arouse your own interest and make you feel at home with it. That way you are sure to find more, and more interesting, things to say. And if *you* are interested and enthusiastic, your reader will be, too.

APPENDIX 2
Using and Documenting Sources

DOING THE RESEARCH

In your literature class, you may be required to write a research paper. Traditionally, such research has required an examination of literary criticism, the kind of scholarly articles in which professional critics (usually professors) advance their interpretations of a piece of literature. Reading what professional literary critics have to say about a work may help you refine your own ideas and strengthen your own argument. It is especially important, however, to remember that your own research essay should not simply be a report; your job is not merely to summarize what others have said but rather to build upon their ideas and/or to show where their analyses are incomplete or faulty. Finally, you should be presenting *your* ideas; *your* ideas and *your* voice should dominate.

Student critics sometimes find themselves intimidated by the words and ideas of professional critics and scholars. They read what a famous critic has said and reason that his is a brilliant interpretation expressed perfectly. How can they possibly compete? They may very well feel that they cannot—and so they may end up quoting extensively or summarizing what the critic has to say. Do not let the professional critics intimidate you. Although they have the advantage of many years of education and experience reading literature, your essay belongs to you, not them. So prevent your ideas from being overrun by theirs by generating your ideas and tentative thesis *before* you look to other sources. Rather than go to other literary critics for ideas, decide what you have to say *before* you consult them. Let other critics agree or disagree with *you,* not the other way around.

Literary research may also involve looking at material other than the interpretations offered by literary critics. Throughout this book, in fact, we have asked you to take an *intertextual* approach, to enrich your readings by examining the retellings of and responses to stories provided by many different sources, not all of them from the field of literature or from the journals of literary criticism. Those sources have included, then, not only other literary renderings of the same story—other retellings and critical interpretations—but also material from other disciplines. Literature is fundamentally an interdisciplinary study. It is not created in a vacuum. As a result, it is sometimes useful to find out about an author's personal history or about the times in which the author lived. For example, if you were writing a paper on Shakespeare's *The Tempest,* you might want to find out about what parts of the known world English explorers of the time had "discovered" and what the prevailing ideas were about the unknown parts of the world. As part of an examination of early love poetry, you might want to research courtship behaviors, attitudes toward premarital sex, and expectations about dowries. Depending on the nature of the assignment made, there may be scope for research in all sorts of disciplines that interest you: certainly in history and psychology, and often in the sciences.

In years past, students who needed to do research set off for the library, and the library is still a useful place to start. Even before you leave for the library, though, you may want to do some preliminary searches online. Most academic libraries have now discarded their card catalogs, but online library catalogs will often help you locate books and articles on your subject. The advantage of such online searches is that they allow you to refine your search terms so that you can search for author's name AND title AND subject matter, all at once. They also make it much easier to search not only book titles but also periodical indices. The latter can be especially valuable to the writer looking for more specialized material. In our experience, students sometimes limit themselves to their library's catalog of books. You will find much valuable material, and often more helpful material, if you look as well in your library's catalogs of periodicals. Whereas books may contain extended arguments about a large subject, the articles in journals will be more narrowly defined, and the subject matter may, as a result, prove more useful to you. Because they come out frequently ("periodically"), periodicals are also often more up-to-date than books.

Don't overlook one of the most useful reference sources of all: the reference librarian. We can offer some general advice here, but long hours spent in libraries have taught us that many libraries have their own quirks. What might take you hours to find through the online catalog, the librarians may find in minutes. Some sources (such as pamphlet files or special collections) may not even be entered in the catalog. If your school offers general library orientations, attending one would be a good investment of your time, one that will repay you handsomely in the time it will save. At these orientations, librarians typically point out many of the general and specific reference books available and offer an overview of the databases to which your particular library subscribes. Reference librarians are also usually available for specific questions about specific research projects. It will be up to you to do the reading and gathering of information you will need, but librarians can offer important insights into the research process and specialized sources.

For literary criticism, one of the most useful sources is the *MLA International Bibliography,* published in print form in two volumes annually by the Modern Language Association. The annual volumes provide a listing of all the articles on literature (English and foreign) and related topics that have been published in scholarly journals that year. The *MLA International Bibliography* is also available in a CD-ROM version, which contains all the information from the annual volumes from 1963 on. Other useful computerized databases for literary studies include Infotrac, JSTOR, and EBSCO, all of which contain abstracts (summaries of articles) and some full-text articles from scholarly journals. As part of Infotrac, you may also have access to gale.net, which provides biographical information and links to literary criticism.

Through such databases, full-text articles can be downloaded from the computer, vastly expanding the resources available to you. If your library subscribes to these kinds of databases, it becomes much less important to you what periodicals the library actually holds. Because you can often access these databases from computers outside the library, you may even find it much more convenient to do your research from home. And, of course, with this kind of research, you do not need to worry about when the library is open; you can usually access the databases day or night, seven days a week.

Computer research is *very* convenient and it often gives you access to high-quality materials. Keep in mind, though, that those trips to the library may still be necessary. Not everything is on the computer. If you limit yourself only to computer research, you will limit what you can find out. (The reverse is also true; if you do not use the computer, you may also miss some valuable sources.)

In both online catalogs and databases, you can usually search for items by author, title, or key word (or subject). Many also allow you to limit your searches in various ways, perhaps by year of publication, to English-only items, to items held only in particular libraries, or to specified periodicals. If, for instance, your subject is such that only very recent articles are useful to you, you may be able to limit the search to works published in the past five years. If you are using an online catalog and need to be able to access items immediately—in other words, you do not have time to use interlibrary loan—you may want to limit your search to your own campus library. Maybe you are looking for an article you came across before and cannot remember the author or title, but you do remember the subject and which journal it is in. You may be able to limit the search in such a way that you can quickly find the article again.

Many catalogs and databases use Boolean logic (named after a nineteenth-century mathematician, George Boole). Some familiarity with this logic may help you limit your searches effectively. For the most part, the key word searches can be limited by the use of *and, or,* and *not.* Say, for example, you are looking for works dealing with Charles Dickens's visit to the United States. You might enter

"Charles Dickens" and "United States"

to include both subjects. (This search command can also be represented as +Charles Dickens +United States.) If you want to narrow the topic to exclude information about his visit to Boston, you might enter

"Charles Dickens" and "United States" not Boston
(+Charles Dickens +United States −Boston)

If you want to include Canada, you might enter

"Charles Dickens" and ("United States" or Canada)

That command would allow you to access articles on both subjects, even if some of the particular items discussed only the United States or only Canada. (With symbols, this would become +Charles Dickens +United States Canada; the absence of a symbol between *United States* and *Canada* implies the use of *or.*) You may also be able to restrict your searches by doing phrase searching. If, for example, you are looking for information on the Volkswagen Beetle, you might enter "Volkswagen Beetle." If you entered the items separately, you would get information on Volkswagens and information on Beetles (probably including the insect, because many online searches do not respond to capitalization). Keep in mind that the information we are giving here is very general; if you want specific help, online catalogs and databases usually have links to "help" or "search definitions" that further explain the particularities of the individual search systems.

Online catalogs and library databases often yield high-quality materials that are useful for academic papers. You do need to consider the nature of your research project, however. How scholarly is it? For some classes and some topics, it might be fine to go to general interest materials, such as encyclopedias and popular magazines. For other classes, your instructor may expect you to go to more academic work, particularly to journals.

Periodicals are often a good source for up-to-date information and ideas. Two types of periodicals, magazines and newspapers, come out very frequently—daily, weekly, or monthly. The articles in them are often written by journalists for the general public. In contrast, journals are scholarly periodicals that usually come out only a few times a year, often four times. (Their titles will often contain the word *Journal* or *Quarterly*.) They are written for and by scholars in the field. Some databases will allow you to limit your search to such scholarly journals. There may be a box for you to check that indicates that you want to limit your search to articles that have been *peer reviewed*. That means that the articles in such periodicals are reviewed by other experts in the field before they are accepted for publication. Such a peer review will usually ensure that the article is a reliable academic or professional source.

In addition to that found in library online catalogs and databases, information is also available on the World Wide Web. General search engines such as Yahoo, Google, and AltaVista may yield a lot of information. Here, however, extra caution is advisable. Anyone (or anyone with access to a computer and a little computer savvy) now has a printing press. That is the beauty of the Web and also the danger. Because we are used to according respect to printed works, anything printed may seem almost automatically true to us. There is some validity to this gut feeling; traditionally, it has not been easy to get works published, so presumably only the best works have found publishers. The Internet, on the other hand, makes it easy for anyone to "publish" anything, no matter how few its merits. When you access a Web site, you may be reading the words of a well-respected expert in the field or the words of the next-door neighbor whose opinions you have learned to distrust. You do not always know; on the Web, the next-door neighbor may be claiming to be an expert.

So how do you make sense of what you come up with from general Web searches? Look carefully at the computer address (the **URL**, or uniform resource locator) and any identifying marks on the site. A "dot edu" (**.edu**) address may mean the writer is a professor at a college or university. A "dot gov" (**.gov**) address means the source is the government. A "dot org" (**.org**) address means the source is a nonprofit organization. But caution is still called for in all these cases. Not all professors are experts in all fields, and not all people with .edu addresses are scholars. (Many students have .edu addresses, for instance.) In addition, what may be useful in the context of a class as a handout or study guide may not have the authoritative weight of a peer-reviewed journal article. We have all learned over the years that the government does not have the last word on what we should think, and government officials may not be experts in particular fields. Similarly, though an organization may be nonprofit, that does not mean that it does not have its own agenda. Most nonprofit organizations, in fact, are established to *pursue* a particular agenda.

Though Internet sources may call for an extra degree of caution, in the case of literary studies (probably in the case of most studies), it is wise to view *all* your sources with a degree of skepticism. You will find that the experts do not all agree, that they read lines of poetry in very different ways or use some parts of a short story to bolster their cases while ignoring others. Keep an open mind, but keep your own mind.

Taking Notes

Once you have discovered material that you wish to use, you will need to take notes on it. In the past many researchers used index cards (sometimes called note cards). Some even set up two systems of note cards, one set recording bibliographic information on the book or article used and the other set recording the main ideas from the work. Other researchers set up only one set of cards, recording bibliographic information at the top of the summary. What can be done on index cards can also be done in other ways. Some researchers prefer to use regular sheets of paper; some prefer to underline and annotate photocopies of relevant articles or books or downloaded copies. An increasing number of researchers take their notes directly on the computer, even copying and pasting relevant material directly to their own files.

Most people who have done research soon hit on a method or combination of methods with which they are comfortable. Whatever method you choose, however, some general pieces of advice (or warning) apply. You need, for instance, to distinguish in your notes between summaries (which record only the main ideas), paraphrases (which record all the ideas, but in the note taker's own words), and quotations. (For a fuller discussion of summary, paraphrase, and quotation, see the next section.) It is especially important for you to know when you are using your own words and when you are recording the author's. It is very easy to get into the bad habit of taking notes that are partially your words and partially the author's or to download another writer's words and paste them directly into your note file or draft without attribution. It may even seem efficient to do this—until later, when you have no idea which words are whose. Such "borrowings," even inadvertent ones, are a form of plagiarism. If you are later unsure whether the words on the page are yours or another author's, you should plan to reword your notes. Be equally careful in distinguishing between your own ideas and the original author's. If you have a comment of your own to make, record it differently than you record your summary or paraphrase; you might, for instance, switch colors or bracket your own comments. That way, you will keep track of where your ideas begin and others' end.

As you are writing down quotations you hope to include in your final paper, you need to take some extra precautions. Be particularly careful to check the wording, especially if there is any doubt about whether you will be able to access the source again. (Remember, books are checked out, library periodicals may be misshelved, Web sites change.) It is also helpful to indicate in the quotations you copy where page breaks occur. You may need that information for your parenthetical citations.

Quotations, Summary, and Paraphrase

No matter how a writer uses outside sources, it is important that she acknowledge her debt to those other writers fully. To fail to do so is to commit the academic crime of plagiarism. Acknowledging sources will, in fact, make the writer's own case look better: she has gone to the trouble of seeing what others think and of representing their points of view fairly. A writer can use others' ideas and words in several ways, and each way requires its own method of acknowledgment.

When a writer uses another's words exactly—word for word—he is quoting directly from the writer and must enclose the quotation in quotation marks (" ") and let the reader know who wrote the words quoted. There are several ways to include the author's name in the text. A writer might, for instance, simply say something like the following:

> According to critic Bernard Duyfhuizen, "a female reader of 'To His Coy Mistress' might have trouble identifying with the poem's speaker; therefore, her first response would be to identify with the listener-in-the-poem, the eternally silent Coy Mistress" (415).

The full source for the quotation would then be included in a list of Works Cited at the end of the paper. Or a writer might write instead something like this:

> There is no doubt that men and women respond differently to literature with strong gender implications. As one critic has put it, "a female reader of 'To His Coy Mistress' might have trouble identifying with the poem's speaker; therefore, her first response would be to identify with the listener-in-the-poem, the eternally silent Coy Mistress" (Duyfhuizen 415).

Because the original author is not mentioned in the writer's own sentence, the author's name has to be included in the parenthetical reference following the quotation.

In both of these examples, the writer is quoting from her source; all of the words (and even the punctuation) between the quotation marks are exactly as they appear in Duyfhuizen's original article. Often, though, a writer does not need to quote exactly because she is interested less in the exact wording her source used than in the idea itself. In that case, a writer has two choices: she can **paraphrase** the source, using her own words to convey the whole of the writer's message, or she can **summarize** the source, paring the source's message down into a much shorter space. Because neither a summary nor a paraphrase uses the author's original words, quotation marks are not used.

One might paraphrase the quotation from Duyfhuizen's paragraph as follows:

> Duyfhuizen believes that women who read "To His Coy Mistress" are more likely than men to think about the poem's events from the mistress's point of view, despite the fact that she never speaks (415).

Notice that the idea is Duyfhuizen's but completely different words and a different sentence structure are used. Students sometimes make the mistake of paraphrasing quotations very closely, substituting their own words here and there and making it hard for a reader to know where their words begin and the words of the original sources end. To avoid that kind of confusion (and charges of plagiarism), it is best to make certain that a paraphrase captures the original writer's ideas in all new words and structures.

When a writer is interested primarily in the general idea that his source conveys, he will usually decide neither to quote nor to paraphrase but, instead, to summarize. In that case he might take five or six sentences to convey the idea of a five- to ten-page article or story.

What is important to realize is that whether a writer is quoting, paraphrasing, or summarizing, he still owes it to his source and to his reader to acknowledge the borrowing. As you know from your own writing, writers work hard to think through their ideas and explain them to other people; they deserve to have their hard work acknowledged—and a reader deserves to be told where he can go to get more information from your source should he choose to look for it.

Avoiding Plagiarism

Some plagiarism (the use of others' words *or* ideas) is the result of sloppy note taking or research techniques. Other plagiarism may be more deliberate, an unethical shortcut. The truth is, though, that college teachers and college disciplinary boards may not care very much about the difference as they discipline offenders. They are not necessarily able, after all, to determine motivation, to distinguish between what is accidental and what is purposeful. Many teachers and disciplinary officers assume, with some justification, that college students should already know enough about documentation to avoid plagiarism. Depending on the teacher and on a particular college's own policies, the penalties for plagiarism can be very severe. Offenders may receive a failing grade on the paper or in the course or be suspended from the college for a year or two; in some cases, they may be permanently expelled. Often, whatever other punishments are meted out, the plagiarism becomes part of the student's college record.

Some teachers feel they have witnessed a new wave of plagiarism with the increasing use of the Internet. Students used to go to the library and copy from books or copy from study aids such as *Cliff's Notes;* now they may simply download passages or even whole papers from the Internet. In some cases, they may download professional essays; in other cases, they may take papers from Internet sites that make papers available either free or for a charge. Most of these cases of dishonesty are flagrant; they are clearly not the result of ignorance or even sloppiness.

Students who buy papers on the Internet should be aware that such papers are often of very low quality. Many Internet paper mills are happy to "publish" anyone's paper, whether the writer is an A student or a C or D student, a college student or a high school student. Many students unhappily discover that, with very little effort, they could easily have written a better paper on their own.

Cases of plagiarism may also be easier to track than some students realize. Just as the Internet may make it easy to download a paper, it often makes it easy to catch such cheating. By entering a few sentences into a search engine, a teacher can sometimes reach the student's source in only a few minutes. Many colleges and universities are also now subscribing to special databases that allow teachers to access many of the Internet sources that sell student papers; sometimes, the major publishers offer free or reduced-cost subscriptions to such databases to teachers who order their textbooks. If only as a deterrent, students should be aware of these resources available to teachers who suspect plagiarism.

To avoid charges of plagiarism, you need to be scrupulous in your dealings with other writers' material. Changing a word here and there does not make ideas your own. Consider, for example, a passage from Mark Thornton Burnett's essay on Kenneth Branagh's film of *Hamlet*. (The full essay is included on 1328–1333.)

For this *Hamlet* constructs Denmark as a militaristic state. Already in the opening scenes, there are glimpses of preparations for war; Hamlet strides through an arsenal on his way to encounter the ghost; and displays of fencing practice punctuate the narrative, foreshadowing the catastrophic conclusion. It is to Branagh's credit that he has restored to *Hamlet* its military subtexts, and the film does not hesitate to demonstrate the extent to which Denmark's power is dependent upon the cooperation of a gallery of soldierly underlings—Rosencrantz (Timothy Spall) and Guildenstern (Reece Dinsdale) wear regimental sashes; guards invade Ophelia's chamber; and the grave digger (Billy Crystal) arranges skulls side-by-side with all the precision of a campaigning general.

Suppose a writer were to make the following use of this passage:

> Mark Thornton Burnett says that Branagh makes Denmark a military state. From the very beginning of the play, we see preparations for war. For example, Hamlet walks through an arsenal before he sees the ghost. There are displays of fencing practice throughout the story, which foreshadows the tragic ending. To Branagh's credit, he has brought back to *Hamlet* its military subtexts, and the film demonstrates the way in which Denmark's power depends on soldiers—Rosencrantz and Guildenstern wear military sashes; guards enter Ophelia's room; and the grave digger places skulls in precise lines as if he were a general.

This is clearly plagiarism. Though Burnett is credited at the beginning, the writer does not indicate the extent of the borrowings. It should be made clear *throughout* the paragraph that these are Burnett's ideas. The wording, sentence structure, and organization are also *much* too close to Burnett's.

Compare this use of Burnett's essay:

> Mark Thornton Burnett admires Branagh's emphasis of the military subplot, noting that throughout the film there are visual reminders that Denmark is at war. For example, Burnett comments on the frequent use of fencing matches in the film and the frequent presence of soldiers, with even Rosencrantz and Guildenstern wearing military insignia.

Not all of Burnett's examples are included in this summary, but it is made clear that the examples are Burnett's and not the writer's. The writing and organization are also the writer's own.

It is true that not *all* sources need to be cited and documented. As a general rule, matters of common knowledge do not have to be cited and documented. This rule can be somewhat tricky to apply, however. You would not, for example, need to cite the fact that William Faulkner's story "A Rose for Emily" was published in 1930, even though most people (including many professors of literature) could not give you that date offhand. The date, however, would be considered "common knowledge" because it could easily be found in many reference books—literature reference books, encyclopedias, any Faulkner biography, literary histories of the period, and so forth. Easily available dates are usually considered "common knowledge." Statistics, however, usually are *not* common knowledge. Statistic gathering is an imprecise science; to trust statistics we need to know when and how they were gathered and perhaps by whom. As a result, you usually need a source for statistics. Scholarly ideas are also *not* "common knowledge." An idea about an author from a famous critic may seem very authoritative to you, but the idea still belongs to the critic and so should be cited. Because there are many gray areas in terms of what is "common knowledge," it is best to err on the side of caution. When it doubt, cite.

CITATION AND DOCUMENTATION

In the previous section, we have discussed the importance of citation. In this section, we will discuss *how* to cite. For many years, the method of citation was the footnote, and some disciplines still depend on the footnote. (Your teacher may also prefer a footnote if only a single source has been used.) The footnote is very convenient for the reader: all the pertinent information is available at the bottom of the page, and the citation doesn't "clutter" the text itself, interrupting the flow of the argument. In the days before computers, however, footnotes were *very* inconvenient for typists and publishers: the need for the footnote had to be anticipated and room left at the bottom of the page. That was more difficult than it sounds, especially when it was uncertain just how much space a quotation would take and so which page it would end on.

Because of the inconvenience to the preparers of the documents, gradually many writers moved to the *endnote.* Notes with bibliographic citations were placed at the ends of articles or chapters. Now there was no inconvenience to the preparer of the manuscript, but the notes were much less useful to readers, who had to keep flipping back and forth between the text and the endnotes.

Though some writers and publishers continue to use both footnotes and endnotes—and though both are made easier by today's word processing software—the Modern Language Association (MLA), which "regulates" bibliographic matters for the literature and language disciplines, changed its citation method about fifteen years ago to a combination of the parenthetical citation and the bibliography. This system has many of the advantages of both the footnote and endnote systems. Key information is placed in the text in parenthetical citations, where readers can find it without having to look away from the text, and more complete bibliographic information is placed at the end so readers who want to explore an argument further can get the information necessary for their search. Most English classes employ this MLA system of documentation.

Parenthetical Citations

Whether you have quoted, summarized, or paraphrased someone else's work, a source must be credited, and you usually should give credit within a parenthetical citation. There are two different methods for quotations, depending on whether the quotation is integrated into the text or set off from it. The MLA rule is that prose more than four lines in length is set off, poetry of more than three lines is set off. (For additional information on quoting, see 167–168.)

The following is an example of a quotation that is set off:

In his analysis of Kenneth Branagh's film of *Hamlet,* Mark Thornton Burnett remarks:

> For this *Hamlet* constructs Denmark as a militaristic state. Already in the opening scenes, there are glimpses of preparations for war; Hamlet strides through an arsenal on his way to encounter the ghost; and displays of fencing practice punctuate the narrative, foreshadowing the catastrophic conclusion. It is to Branagh's credit that he has restored to *Hamlet* its military subtexts, and the film does not hesitate to demonstrate the extent to which Denmark's power is dependent

> upon the cooperation of a gallery of soldierly underlings—
> Rosencrantz (Timothy Spall) and Guildenstern (Reece Dinsdale)
> wear regimental sashes; guards invade Ophelia's chamber; and the
> grave digger (Billy Crystal) arranges skulls side-by-side with all the
> precision of a campaigning general. (1328–1329)

The quotation is inset ten spaces, or an inch. Notice that no quotation marks are added; the original quotation is reproduced exactly as it was in the original (if the original had had quotation marks within it, they would, of course, have been retained).

The in-text parenthetical citation includes page numbers only, without the addition of *p.* or *pg.* or *pp.* For an inset quotation, no period comes after the parenthetical citation; the parenthetical citation simply hangs "loose" at the end. (In cases in which the last line of the quotation is so long that there is no room for the parenthetical citation, the citation is dropped to the next line but kept flush with the right margin.) To find more complete information about the source of the article, the reader would go to the Works Cited page and look under Burnett for full bibliographic information.

The use of the parenthetical citation varies slightly for an integrated quotation:

> In his analysis of Kenneth Branagh's film of *Hamlet,* Mark Thornton Burnett
> says that Branagh "constructs Denmark as a militaristic state" (1328).

The primary difference between the parenthetical citation for an integrated quotation and one that is set off is that for the integrated quotation, the citation is made part of the sentence: notice that the end quotation marks come at the end of the quotation and *before* the page citation and that the period comes *after* the citation. Similarly, any punctuation that the original author used at the end is dropped to make way for the writer's own sentence structure. Thus, in the example given, Burnett's period at the end of the word "state" is omitted, because it does not make sense in the context of the new sentence structure. (The exception here would be an exclamation point or a question mark; those marks would be retained.)

Typically, for both integrated and offset quotations, the quotation is introduced with the author's name, as is done in the examples. Occasionally, however, that is not the case. Then, the author's name needs to be added to the parenthetical citation so that the reader knows where to look for the source in the Works Cited list (see next section). Occasionally, you may even need to include a shortened version of the title in the parenthetical citation. That might be necessary, for instance, if you had listed two works by Burnett on your Works Cited page; without the shortened version of the title, the reader would not know which one was being referred to in the parenthetical citation. Here is an example of a quotation with a parenthetical citation that includes author's name, shortened title, and page number:

> The Elsinore of Shakespeare's *Hamlet* can be created in various ways. It may be
> a brooding, moody place suitable for Hamlet's introspection. Conversely, as in
> Branagh's film, it may be created as "a militaristic state" with constant "glimpses
> of preparations for war" (Burnett, "Cunning" 1329).

In this case, there is a comma between the author's name and the key word of the title, but none before the page number. This last parenthetical citation is a bit cluttered, however. Long parenthetical citations may disrupt the reader's sense of what you are saying. So include only what is necessary. When it is at all possible, put the author's name and, if necessary, the title of the work in your own text. (But do *not* include page numbers in your text; they *always* belong in the parenthetical citations.)

Documentation

Though many of the basics of bibliographic form have been the same for decades, some changes have occurred in recent years. In fact, MLA is still struggling to keep up with the challenges created by the increasing use of different kinds of electronic sources. The authoritative guide for student use of MLA bibliographic forms is the *MLA Handbook for Writers of Research Papers*. At more than three hundred pages, this book examines virtually every situation you will be faced with, so it can provide you with more guidance about unusual situations than can a brief introduction such as this one.

In the past, researchers included a *bibliography* at the end of their articles or books. However, *bibliography* refers literally to a listing of books or other printed material. Today, researchers often draw on nonprint sources such as videotapes and electronic sources. As a result, instead of providing a bibliography, researchers now usually include a Works Cited page (or pages) at the end of their papers. The Works Cited page includes every work for which a parenthetical citation has been supplied within the paper. Alternatively, a researcher might include a Works Consulted list; this is potentially a larger list than the Works Cited list. The Works Consulted list includes all works that were consulted during the project, even those that have not been used directly enough to call for a parenthetical citation. It is often a good idea to include a Works Consulted list if you have consulted works that have provided general background information that seems to fall under "common knowledge" or that may have influenced your thinking in a general way.

The organization of the Works Cited and Works Consulted lists is alphabetical, making it easy for readers to find the authors' names included near or within the parenthetical citations. After the first line, all lines of each citation are indented five spaces to highlight the alphabetical nature of the listings. The key information within each citation is separated by periods.

Books and Parts of Books

For books and parts of books, the order of the information is as follows, though not every entry will include all of this information:

1. Author's name, last name first for a single author. Give the name as the author gives it, including middle name or initial. Additional authors' names are provided first name first.
2. Title of a section of a book (the title of an essay, short story, or poem included in an anthology, for instance). Enclose this title in quotation marks.
3. Title of the book. Include any subtitle, preceded by a colon. Underline the title, including any marks of punctuation.
4. Name of editor or translator, first name first. Indicate editor by "Ed." and translator by "Trans." The abbreviation comes before the editor's or translator's name.
5. Number of the edition used (unless it is a first edition).
6. Number of the volume used (in a multivolume work).

7. Name of the series.
8. Place of publication, followed by a colon, then the name of the publishing company, followed by a comma, then the date of publication.
9. Page numbers (only if the title of the section of the book has been given).

A Book with a Single Author

Dove, Rita. *The Darker Face of the Earth.* 3rd ed. Ashland, OR: Storyline, 2000.
Kidder, Tracy. *Hometown.* New York: Random House, 1999.

For Dove's play, notice that the state abbreviation (OR) is given for the place of publication, because many readers would not know where Ashland is. Because this is not the first edition of Dove's play, the edition is given in numerical form (2nd, 3rd, 4th, etc.).

A Book with More Than One Author

Robinson, John P., and Geoffrey Godbey. *Time for Life: The Surprising Ways Americans Use Their Time.* University Park, PA: Penn. State UP, 1997.

Note that the second author is given first name first. For the publisher's name, abbreviations are acceptable; UP is the accepted abbreviation for "University Press."

An Anthology or Collection of Works

Kates, Judith A., and Gail Twersky Reimer, eds. *Reading Ruth: Contemporary Women Reclaim a Sacred Story.* New York: Ballantine-Random House, 1994.

Kates and Reimer are identified here as editors because they are not the authors of the material in the book. Many publishers also have "imprints," or special names for a certain group of books (often their paperbacks). In this case, Ballantine is an "imprint" put out by Random House. Other imprints are Anchor Books (by Doubleday), Riverside (by Houghton Mifflin), and Bedford (by St. Martin's Press). When you are using an imprint, include the names of both the imprint and the publisher.

A Work Included in an Anthology

Hirsch, Marianne. "Reading Ruth with Naomi." *Reading Ruth: Contemporary Women Reclaim a Sacred Story.* Ed. Judith A. Kates and Gail Twersky Reimer. New York: Ballantine-Random House, 1994. 309–15.

Because a work in the anthology and not the anthology itself is being cited, the editors' names are given after the title of the book. In addition, the page numbers of the selection are included. Notice that for three-digit numbers that share the same hundred marker (in this case the 300s), only the last two digits of the second number need to be given.

Cross-References

Sometimes you may be using more than one work from an anthology. In that case you would cite the anthology itself and then include shortened versions for the individual works in the anthology.

Hirsch, Marianne. "Reading Ruth with Naomi." Kates and Reimer 309–15.

For this example, the reader would look under Kates and Reimer to get the full bibliographic information.

Periodicals

Unlike books, periodicals (which include newspapers, magazines, and journals) come out at intervals, usually fairly regular intervals. How they are cited depends in part on how often they come out. The periodical citation includes less information than does the citation for books. For example, it does not include the name of the publisher or the place of publication. Omit *The, A,* and *An* from the titles of periodicals. For newspapers and magazines, do not give the volume number, even if that information is supplied. Do give volume numbers for scholarly journals, however.

An Article in a Newspaper

Hume, Elizabeth. "Student filmmakers get noticed—for reel." *Sacramento Bee* 15 April 2002, final ed.: E1+.

Give the edition (late edition, final edition, etc.) if it is named on the front page, as different editions of the same daily newspaper may be different. The + indicates that the article is continued on another page.

An Article in a Magazine

If the magazine is published every one or two weeks, give the complete date of publication. For a magazine published every month or two, give the month or months.

Goldberger, Paul. "Bug Love." *New Yorker* 20 April 1998: 66.

Pachetti, Nick. "The Best Advice Money Can Buy." *Money* August 2001: 69–80.

The New Yorker is published weekly, whereas *Money* is published monthly.

An Article in a Scholarly Journal

Skorczewski, Dawn. " 'Everybody Has Their Own Ideas': Responding to Cliché in Student Writing." *CCC* 52 (2000): 220–39.

You should include all of the page numbers of the complete article, not just the portion you may have used. It is also acceptable to use well-known abbreviations for journal titles. In this case, *CCC* stands for *The Journal of the Conference on College Composition and Communication*. The "52" after the title refers to the volume number.

Nonprint Sources

Personal Interview

Jorgensen, Samuel. Personal Interview. 18 Sept. 2002.

Sound Recording

McGovern, Christopher, and Amy Powers. "The House on the Hill." *Lizzie Borden: Original Cast Recording.* Original Cast Records, 1999.

A Film or Video Recording

Lee, Spike, dir. *4 Little Girls.* Videocassette. HBO, 1998.

Electronic Sources

Increasingly, researchers access journal articles and other information sources online. Electronic sources are still very new, however, and bibliographic methods somewhat fluid. In general, you should give as much information as possible. Dating is especially important because online sources may be modified at any time. As a result, it is very important to give your date of access and the date of the original publication (whether in print or online); the date of access comes just before the address, or URL (uniform resource locator). When you give the URL, break the line only at a slash mark. Do not add a hyphen, as you would for a split word; it may be read as part of the URL. Because URLs and online texts can change at any time, you may want to print out the material you are using; the printout will record the URL and the date of access.

For a Scholarly Project

The Little Red Riding Hood Project. Ed. Michael N. Salda. Vers. 1.0. Dec. 1995. De Grummond Children's Literature Research Collection. U. of Southern Mississippi. 18 April 2002 <http://www-dept.usm/~engdept/lrrh/lrrhhome.htm>.

For a Work within a Scholarly Project

Very, Lydia L. "Red Riding Hood." Boston: L. Prang, 1863. *The Little Red Riding Hood Project.* Ed. Michael N. Salda. Vers. 1.0. Dec. 1995. De Grummond Children's Literature Research Collection. U. of Southern Mississippi. 18 April 2002 <http://www-dept.usm/~engdept/lrrh/lrrhb.htm>.

For a Journal Article Accessed Online

Burnett, Mark Thornton. "The 'very cunning of the scene': Kenneth Branagh's *Hamlet.*" *Literature Film Quarterly* 25.2 (1997). EBSCO Publishing Database. 23 March 2002 <www.arc.losrios.cc.ca.us/~library/lib_databases.html.>

In general, for online sources, you are following a form similar to that for the print sources, with the URL and date of access added. For electronic sources especially, however, you may find gaps in the recommendations about documentation form, even if you consult a lengthy resource such as the *MLA Handbook.* You may need to adapt the documentation form to fit your own particular source. Always err on the side of providing additional information.

PUTTING IT ALL TO WORK: A SAMPLE STUDENT PAPER

We have included in the pages that follow a student paper that uses literary criticism in its critical argument. As you read, pay particular attention to the way the student integrates quotations from both the literary text and from the critics who have written on it and the way she cites others' ideas and words in her own text. Notice, too, that the writer synthesizes others' arguments with her own; she uses them to bolster her own argument and to show the weaknesses of opposing points of view. This is a critical essay, not simply a report of what others have had to say. Finally, notice that at the end of her essay, the student has included a Works Cited page, with full bibliographic citations.

Karen Di Filippo

Professor Nugent

English 1B

16 April 2002

"Paul's Case" and the Greed for Pleasure

Willa Cather's "Paul's Case" is a story about a youth who shuns everyday life for the call of a more pleasurable, yet more debased existence. Paul is a young man who is irreconcilably alienated from the world he knows. He considers his home and school ugly, prosaic, and full of "dull care." Conversely, he idolizes the life of pleasure that he imagines can be found in the world of theater and art and wealth. That world, however, is unhealthy for him. And, although he mocks the values of his schoolteachers, father, and neighbors, he has in fact adopted some of those values.

Paul's home is on Cordelia Street, a "highly respectable street" that he considers a pit of "ugliness and commonness" (Cather 136). Sharon O'Brien sees Cordelia Street as a microcosm of the "emotionally and aesthetically bankrupt middle class world" and emphasizes its ugliness as the impetus that pushes Paul to excess in the alternate world of art and pleasure (O'Brien 282). Conversely, Marilyn Arnold points out that Paul has a "warped perception" of Cordelia Street. In reality,

Cordelia Street is a place of fairly affluent and pleasant living. The important point, however, is not whether Paul's hatred of Cordelia Street is justified. The important point is
that Paul feels that he does not belong in the Cordelia Street
world. His impertinent attitude toward his teachers, his endless lying, his self-conscious mannerisms, and his manner of
dress all reflect Paul's attempts to defy that world, while his
visits to the art gallery, his job as an usher at Carnegie
Hall, and his evenings at the theater all reflect his attempts
to escape that world. He both defies and escapes from this
world when he steals money from his employers and goes to New
York, but ultimate escape comes only in his death.

Paul is not an artist, nor is he interested in art primarily for its own sake. He values art because of the "indescribable thrill that made his imagination master of his
senses" (Cather 140). What he gets from art is sensual pleasure. Later, he uses stolen money to achieve the same thing,
in the form of fine clothes, champagne, flowers, and warm,
scented air. Although Paul concludes that money is
everything, it is not money he wants but rather things that
money can buy. Loretta Wasserman argues that Paul's desires
are a kind of "call."

> The call that Paul heeds, the call to the soul's
> life, is--not to put too fine a point on it--the
> call of Beauty. Paul is that most familiar of Ro-
> mantic figures--the yearner for an ineffable world,
> beauty in this one as the promise of the truth of
> the other. We may say that Paul is on the first rung
> of Plato's ladder--rather, considering where and
> who he is, reaching desperately for the rung.
> (Wasserman 125)

Although Paul does indeed desire beautiful things, and deplores ugliness, it is not purely beauty that Paul desires. He wants glitter and glamour and artificial beauty. For example, cut flowers seem all the more "lovely and alluring that they blossomed thus unnaturally in the snow" (Cather 144). Furthermore, art and, later, money don't just provide beauty; they also give him a sense of power. When he is backstage at the theater, he senses "within him the possibility of doing or saying splendid, brilliant, poetic things" (Cather 139). Later, when he is in New York, his "sense of power" is one of his "dearest pleasures," along with cigarettes and fine clothes (Cather 146). It seems clear that Paul cannot be considered a high-minded, philosophic pursuer of "Beauty." The world he desires to be part of is not the world of art and beauty, but rather that of pleasure.

Sharon O'Brien draws connections between "Paul's Case" and the other stories in *The Troll Garden*, the volume in which the short story first appeared. The troll garden refers to Charles Kingsley's parable about the Romans and Germanic tribes, in which the Romans' "corrupt civilization" lures and entices the "forest children" Germans (O'Brien 272). A quotation from Kingsley's work formed one of two epigraphs in the book, the other being from "Goblin Market" by Christina Rossetti. In the "Goblin Market" story, a little girl eats the goblin men's tempting but forbidden fruits and is subsequently ruined by desire for more (O'Brien 273). Also, a connection is made to Cather's conceptions of Presbyteria, a dull, repressive environment, and Bohemia, a glittering, beautiful world.

Cordelia Street, his dreary home where the ugliness of petty-bourgeoise life is symbolized by the 'horrible yellow wallpaper,' the bathroom's grimy

zinc tub and dripping spigots, and his father's
hairy legs and carpet slippers, is Cather's Presbyteria. Paul's alternative world of fairy-tale
allure--his troll garden--is the concert hall and
theater where he feasts on delicious sensations, a
version of Cather's Bohemia. (O'Brien 282-83)

Paul rejects Presbyteria and tries to assert his citizenship
in Bohemia. However, the fruit which is offered in this world
is forbidden and unhealthy, and leads him into endless desire
for still more pleasure. The more time he spends at the theater or Carnegie Hall, the more his ordinary life inspires
revulsion. When his desire is thwarted, he takes drastic measures to obtain the forbidden fruit. However, the desire for
the fruit can never be satisfied (O'Brien 273).

Paul believes that he belongs in the world of shine and
luxury, Bohemia, instead of in the world of drabness and monotony, Presbyteria. At school he feels he "must convey to
them [the other pupils] that he considered it all trivial,
and was only there by way of a jest" (Cather 140). He considers the time he spends at home and at school "a sleep and a
forgetting" (Cather 139). In contrast, when he reaches New
York with the stolen money, he believes he is where he
belongs. "These were his own people," and he feels that "his
surroundings [explain] him." It seems as if he has always
lived in this world; "Cordelia Street . . . belonged to another time and country" (Cather 145). Paul, however, is
wrong. As Marilyn Arnold points out, he has, to some extent,
a citizenship in Cordelia Street.

Paul wants to believe that Cordelia Street and his
high school represent the very antithesis of the

world for which he was made, the world of wealth

and glamour. What he fails to perceive is that the

ideals of Cordelia Street are identical with his

own. . . . Cordelia Street, like Paul, worships

glamour and money and the things money can buy.

Indeed, Paul has partially internalized some of the Calvinis-
tic values with which he has been surrounded; they are represented by the "shadowed corner . . . from which something
seemed always to be watching him" (Cather 143). This thing,
which causes him constant dread, is only vanquished when Paul
completely breaks away from the code of acceptable behavior
by stealing his employer's money. Even so, his goal, wealth,
is proper; only his means are unacceptable by Cordelia Street
standards. Ultimately, this principle of blurring between
Paul's two worlds works in the other direction, and "all the
world [becomes] Cordelia Street" (Cather 148). He is alienated from all of society, which freezes him like the snow
freezes his red carnation. At that point, he has no place
in the world, and death becomes his only alternative
(Arnold 183).

   "Paul's Case" is a story about a boy who cannot find his
niche in society. He doesn't believe he belongs in the bourgeois world of his family, but he can't survive in the world
of pleasure that he thinks he was born to inhabit. In part,
this is because that world exists partially in Paul's imagination; in part, it's because that world is poisonously unhealthy; and, in part, it's because Paul is prevented from
inhabiting that world by a cold society. Like his symbols,
the flowers, Paul has "one splendid breath" before he is
"crushed" (Cather 149). He does not regret the life he has
chosen. "If he had to choose it over again, he would do the

same thing tomorrow," he decides during his last indulgent evening (Cather 147). Later, he expresses the feeling that "he had lived the sort of life he was meant to live" (Cather 148). Paul's overriding passion is for pleasure. Denied that, he chooses to kill himself rather than be suffocated by an existence he cannot appreciate.

Works Cited

Arnold, Marilyn. "Two of the Lost." <u>Modern Critical Views: Willa Cather</u>. Ed. Harold Bloom. New York: Chelsea, 1985. 177–83.

Cather, Willa. "Paul's Case." <u>Forty Short Stories: A Portable Anthology</u>. Ed. Beverly Lawn. Boston: Bedford/St. Martin's, 2001. 131–49.

O'Brien, Sharon. <u>Willa Cather: The Emerging Voice</u>. New York: Oxford UP, 1987.

Wasserman, Loretta. "Is Cather's Paul a Case?" <u>Modern Fiction Studies</u> 36 (1990): 121–29.

Work Cited

Duyfhuizen, Bernard. "Textual Harassment of Marvell's Coy Mistress: The Institutionalization of Masculine Criticism." *College English* 50 (1988): 415.

APPENDIX 3
Schools of Literary Criticism

Throughout *Retellings,* we have included stories that have been told and retold and have asked you to consider how the changes from one version to another help highlight different authors' themes and interests and provoke different responses from readers. It is not just poems, short stories, and dramas that retell other pieces of literature, however. Readers do that, too. When we read, we emphasize some parts of a story, play, or poem and thrust others into the background. In the process, we alter the original somewhat, interpreting it for ourselves. That interpretation is itself one kind of retelling.

In choosing (even subconsciously) what to emphasize and what to ascribe less importance to—even in choosing the questions to ask about a work—literary critics place themselves in a particular **school of literary criticism.** Although most critics borrow from several different critical schools (you will find as you read on that the various schools sometimes ask similar questions), most also associate themselves primarily with a single school, with a particular group of critics who tend to look at pieces of literature in similar ways. If this concept seems unfamiliar, think about the ways in which political parties or religions or cultural groups or even generations help people define their ideas. The group, or school, to which one belongs often not only gives one an identity but also gives one a way of looking at the world. Just as a Republican and a Democrat or a teenager and a senior citizen may look at the same event differently, so too do literary critics look at the same work differently.

GENDER STUDIES

In responding to "To His Coy Mistress," student Heather Johnson, whose paper appears in chapter 7, focused on questions about the woman's relationship with the man. Although the man is the speaker of the poem, Heather was as interested in the role of the silent woman as in the role of the man, and her paper focuses much of its attention on the power relationship between the man and the woman. Heather thus places herself in the role of a *feminist critic,* a reader who considers the extent to which the speaker's gender influences his or her perspective on events and characters.

A feminist critic would ask, then, how the poem would be different if told from the seduced woman's point of view or whether a female poet would write a seduction poem differently than a male poet would if, for instance, the seducer were female and the listener male. In short, for such a critic, questions about gender predominate. Are male and female writers equally successful in creating male and female characters? Do they use similar language and similar images to describe male and female roles and psychologies? Do they, in fact, define "male" and "female" in similar ways?

In "To His Coy Mistress," for instance, how much are the characters' behaviors determined by their gender? Is the woman's "coyness" an innate mark of her femininity, a socially constructed (or expected) behavior, or something individual that she can and does control? Is the man's use of reason a mark of his masculinity? Is his interest in sex and seduction typically male? Gender critics also consider how much the *reader's* gender influences his or her response to a work. Do men and women read "To His Coy Mistress" in the same way? In particular, do they respond to the idea of seduction, the speaker's methods of seduction, and the images of sex and sexuality in the same ways? Should they? Can they?

Feminist criticism is one type of **gender criticism** and **gender studies.** Another group of gender critics are those who focus on **gay and lesbian studies.** According to this group of critics, too, gender is a defining part of one's identity. However, for critics interested in gay and lesbian studies, issues of sexual orientation are even more important than gender itself. That is true even when the love relationship described is a heterosexual one. For instance, "To His Coy Mistress" is clearly a poem about the speaker's desire for a heterosexual relationship: the title refers to a man (it uses "his") and a woman (it refers to her as "mistress"). At the same time, though, the kinds of questions asked by critics of gay and lesbian studies may help us to see the poem in provocative ways.

Although the speaker and mistress of the poem are almost certainly man and woman, are they *necessarily* heterosexual? Just as a feminist critic might argue that there is in the speaker's aggressiveness a masculine domination, even perhaps a fantasy of rape, a critic interested in gay and lesbian studies might take note of the fact that the woman is unresponsive—or at least the speaker implies that she is unresponsive. Does her "coyness" indicate a lack of interest in the particular man or a lack of interest in a heterosexual relationship? In fact, a gender critic might ask us to consider why we *assume* that both the pursuer and the pursued are heterosexual. Finally, such a critic might question how much the language of the poem depends on the two lovers' being of different sexes. In other words, how would the language have to change if one man were seducing another? Such are the questions that are at the heart of student James Rallis's reconstruction of "To His Coy Mistress" (see 1459–60). In "To His Coy Mister," James asks us to envision the poem as a seduction poem spoken by a gay speaker, and in his analysis James invites us to examine the ways in which critics and readers sensitive to the issue of sexual orientation might rethink cultural and literary assumptions about heterosexuality and homosexuality. In the process of such an inquiry, a reader would again have to confront the question of whether male and female psychologies and modes of behavior are genetically or socially and culturally determined.

SOCIOHISTORICAL CRITICISM

Criticism that focuses primarily on issues of gender is relatively new, the product of sociopolitical movements of the mid–twentieth century, particularly the sexual revolution and the women's and gay rights movements. Although seen as a separate school of criticism, gender studies has much in common with **sociohistorical criticism,** which, as its name implies, focuses largely on issues related to the social movements and beliefs prevalent when a piece of literature was written.

A sociohistorical critic might ask, for instance, how political and social events of the writer's time have influenced the way the writer presents characters, themes, and settings. It might be important to consider whether a major event such as a war or an economic depression was occurring during an author's lifetime or to know that a major philosophical or cultural change was taking place. Such revolutionary rethinking of worldviews occurred, for instance, when Europeans first came upon the peoples of the New World in the early Renaissance and when the advent of the Industrial Revolution changed people's ideas about the nature of work and the relationship between man (or woman) and machine. A knowledge of such historical movements and events is certain to help us respond more fully to works written during their times. Knowing that *The Tempest* was written during an age of intense exploration, we are led to ask questions about how typical Shakespeare's attitude toward the New World and its inhabitants was. Knowing that William Blake wrote "London" during the early days of the Industrial Revolution, we are more able to see in it a criticism of the new relationship between people and their natural and urban environments.

In addition to looking at historical events and movements, a sociohistorical critic might also want to know something about prevalent attitudes toward economic classes and about the possibility of movement from one economic class to another or about the status and roles of men and women. In short, a sociohistorical critic is interested in anything that has to do with the social and cultural environment in which a literary work was composed and read.

New Historicism

Within the general category of sociohistorical criticism are more specialized critical movements. Several relatively recent kinds of criticism have moved sociohistorical criticism in new directions. **New historicism** includes much of what traditional sociohistorical criticism has included, but it widens the scope of study to include the kinds of documents that were once associated largely with fields other than literary studies. Whereas the traditional sociohistorical critic would probably have limited his or her research primarily to the study of the historical and literary documents surrounding a particular work's composition, a new historicist critic might link economic documents or scientific treatises to the study of a literary work. The critic might look at medical records or documents from anthropology to explain the behavior or attitudes of fictional characters. A new historicist critic is also more likely than were earlier sociohistorical critics to consider the differences between the present-day reading of a work and the likely reception of a work during the author's own time. If attitudes and beliefs have changed since the time of a work's composition—and for all but the most recent of works they are likely to have done so—a new historicist critic is interested in showing us how the readings of the two times (the author's time and our own) might compete with or augment one another.

Postcolonial Criticism

Closely connected to the new historicism movement is another form of sociohistorical criticism: **postcolonial criticism.** Postcolonial critics are largely interested in a particular cultural/political relationship: that between the colonizer and the colonized. Postcolonial critics are, then, most likely to focus on works of literature written by and about those who have lived under colonial rule. Sometimes they focus on literary works that overtly discuss the relationship between the colonizer and the colonized, works such as Joseph Conrad's *Heart of Darkness* and Aimé Césaire's *A Tempest*. (Césaire's play is included in this anthology, on 343–71). But their interest also extends to those works that deal, more or less unconsciously, with the power relationship that is an integral part of colonialism. Such is the case, for instance, with the postcolonial criticism of Shakespeare's *The Tempest,* a play that is also included in this anthology. Shakespeare may not have been fully aware that he was writing from the position of a member of the colonial, or dominant, culture, but postcolonial critics ask us nevertheless to consider the extent to which that perspective influences Shakespeare's treatment of the indigenous peoples who inhabit the New World.

For the postcolonial critic a number of questions arise: What *is* the power relationship between colonizer and colonized? How does that relationship affect the psychology and behavior of both parties? What are the personal and political ethics involved in such a situation? Some readers argue that postcolonial critics, like feminist critics, take a modern political sensibility and apply it unfairly to works of earlier times, and there can be no doubt that the authors and audiences of earlier times would have found some twenty-first-century beliefs and attitudes foreign, even horrifying. At the same time, though, new historicism and postcolonial and gender criticism encourage us to become more aware of the nuances of a literary work—and to ask ourselves whether the author of an early work *necessarily* subscribes to the sociopolitical or gender beliefs popular during his or her time. Such criticism also asks us to consider the ethical value of literature: Can we admire a literary work that fosters values we find outdated or repugnant?

Marxist Criticism

Postcolonial criticism has at its foundation a belief that the relationship between the colonizing power and the colony is a defining one that affects all aspects of people's behaviors, values, and attitudes. A similar assumption underlies **Marxist criticism.** Based on the theories of Karl Marx, Marxist criticism relies on the belief that class struggles and the antipathy between the individual and the state underlie human behavior. A Marxist critic is likely to ask questions about the characters' socioeconomic status, about their ability to move from one class to another, and about the power relationships among various segments of society, whether those segments are defined by economic status, culture, or ethnicity. Such a critic is likely to ask whether the society envisioned in a literary work is a just one and whether all segments of society are equally and fairly represented in the work.

Cultural Studies

Until recently, sociohistorical critics have primarily been interested in large questions about political, social, and cultural movements, the kind of movements and events that are written about in history books. In more recent years, though, a group of critics interested in popular culture have come to examine the extent to which the daily activities and interests of the common person may have an influence on and be reflected in literature. Part of a field called **cultural studies,** this kind of criticism asks readers to think about how media—such as television, cartoons, popular music, and video games—can be viewed as kinds of literary texts and about how our interest in such forms has influenced the way we create and respond to literature.

Obviously, earlier ages did not have the electronic media that we now have, but they nevertheless had their own popular culture, and an understanding of how everyday people lived their lives—how they amused themselves, what they read and thought—can sometimes enhance our understanding of the worlds that literary authors create. Consider, for instance, the fact that Shakespeare's audiences were composed of common people as well as nobles and royalty. To keep the common people interested, he needed to appeal to their tastes as well as to the tastes of the more wealthy and educated in the audience. Much of the humor in Shakespeare's plays is designed, then, to entice the "lower" classes. Remembering this appeal to "low culture," you can more easily understand why cultural critics find so interesting and exciting the current trend to film plays and novels with settings and stage props that make similar appeals to popular culture. (We are thinking here of a musical such as *Les Misérables,* which sets Hugo's tragic novel to modern music; of the Baz Luhrmann *Romeo and Juliet,* which sets Shakespeare's story at Verona Beach and uses punk music and an MTV style; and of *10 Things I Hate about You,* a popular retelling of Shakespeare's *Taming of the Shrew* set in a high school.)

A belief in the value of cultural criticism also underlies some of the choices we have made in this anthology. Cultural critics have, for instance, spent time examining some of the cultural icons and myths we have included in this anthology: Lizzie Borden, Barbie, and Superman, for instance. Lizzie Borden, Barbie, and Superman clearly do not belong to the same tradition of "high culture" that Shakespeare and Marvell do. When seen as texts in their own right, they do, nevertheless, lend themselves to a kind of literary analysis.

Biographical Criticism

Whereas the kinds of sociohistorical criticism discussed earlier concentrate on the influences of the larger society, **biographical critics** pay particular attention to the ways in which an author's life might have influenced his or her creations. We know from James Joyce's own writings and from his biographers, for example, that Joyce felt both deeply rooted in the Irish culture and entrapped by it; knowing that may help us understand the importance of setting in Joyce's short story "Araby" (see 547–50). We know from Charlotte Perkins Gilman's autobiographical writing that she herself experienced the kind of depression—and was victimized by the kind of medical treatment—described in "The Yellow Wallpaper" (see 527–38), and that knowledge may help us understand better the narrator's descent into madness and the realism that is at the story's core.

By knowing a little about an author's own life, a reader can often, then, gain insight into that author's characters, themes, and attitudes. At the same time, of course, it is important to recognize that all literary works are fictional creations. No matter how much Joyce and Gilman draw on their own experiences and emotions, their stories remain fictions.

PSYCHOLOGICAL CRITICISM

As we have seen, sociohistorical criticism looks at the ways in which external social, political, and cultural events and movements shape an author's approach and the world he or she creates. In contrast, **psychological criticism** looks at internal influences on an author's creation and our reception of it. (In determining those internal influences, the psychological critic often relies on biographical criticism.) Of particular interest to psychological critics are Sigmund Freud's theories about the relationship between children and their parents, about sexuality, and about dreams.

Freud himself borrowed the terminology of his theories from the world of literature. His ideas about the **Oedipus complex** (the theory that very young boys move through a stage in which they are attracted to their mothers and want to displace their fathers) found a literary predecessor in the Greek story of Oedipus. (Sophocles' dramatic version of that story is included in this anthology, on 1060–1105; Freud's comments on the play are on 1114–16.) Freud's parallel theory for girls, called the **Electra complex,** similarly took its name from a character in Greek myth. (According to Freud, girls are attracted to their fathers and want to displace their mothers.) These Freudian theories have been enormously influential in the creation and study of literature. Works as varied as Shakespeare's *Hamlet,* D. H. Lawrence's short stories and novels, and fairy tales about evil stepmothers have all been interpreted as stories about a child's desire to remove a parental rival from his or her world so that he or she may have the opposite-sex parent all to him- or herself.

Much of Freud's work depends on the idea that our attitudes and behaviors are often influenced by subconscious thoughts and emotions, and psychological critics apply the idea of the subconscious to their interpretations of literary works. When analyzing a work of literature, a psychological critic is careful to distinguish between an author's *intention* and his or her *meaning,* arguing that the author may not always be fully conscious of the meaning his or her subconscious has prompted him or her to create. A psychological critic would, therefore, be interested in the possibility that Theodore Roethke was not entirely conscious of his feelings toward his father when he wrote "My Papa's Waltz" (see 67–69).

A psychological critic may also ask whether the words and images can be read symbolically. In such a system of analysis, many everyday objects are seen as evocative of sexual fantasies and desires or of maleness and femaleness. For instance, a key being fit into a lock can sometimes be seen as emblematic of a union between a man and a woman. (Although such an interpretation may at first seem forced, it is interesting to note that this kind of attribution of "maleness" and "femaleness" to everyday objects extends well beyond the realm of literary criticism. Plumbers talk of "male" and "female" pipe couplings, for instance.) Similarly, a psychological critic might argue that water imagery in literature is sometimes used to create a sense of womblike comfort. Psychological critics thus ask us to see in a literary work the inner and hidden workings of the human mind and heart. They ask us to look beyond the literal and into the symbolic.

MYTHOLOGICAL OR ARCHETYPAL CRITICISM

Mythological or archetypal criticism, heavily influenced by psychologist Carl Jung, has much in common with psychological criticism. Mythological critics, like psychological critics, believe that much of literature (and life) has its roots in subconscious stories and fantasies about which we are often only dimly aware. For the mythological critic, though, those stories and fantasies are less individual than they are universal. According to such critics, all peoples—no matter their culture, gender, or personal history—share certain stories, called archetypes.

One common archetypal story is the story of a cataclysmic flood that destroys all of civilization; the story of Noah belongs to this story class, as do stories from ancient Sumeria and Native American myth. Some other archetypal stories are those of the suitor who has to please a young woman's father by accomplishing an impossible task; of the poor, mistreated, and sometimes orphaned child who discovers that he or she is really a prince or princess; of the man or woman who descends into the underworld, often in search of a lost love. According to many mythological critics, there are a limited number of myths, and each piece of literature involves the retelling of an old myth or combination of myths. Some tellings are more sophisticated or more complex than others, but all are, finally, retellings of works told earlier.

Like psychological criticism, mythological criticism relies heavily on an author's and reader's ability to read the world symbolically. For such a critic, there are powerful and universal archetypes that evoke a whole constellation of meanings. Water, earth, air, and fire—the four elements of nature—all have archetypal meanings, for instance. Water purifies and cleanses; it gives life. Both of these meanings are present in the story of the Flood, which is seen as a story about how the waters overtake the earth so as to cleanse it of its impurities and bring new life. According to Christian theology, the same story is retold in miniature in an individual's life through the process of baptism, whereby water is again used to cleanse an individual of all sins and bring eternal life. Earth has similar archetypal properties, but as a more physically tangible thing it can represent not only the life-giving power of the soil but also the dust to which all of us will return. Similarly, fire and air also may have archetypal meaning: fire as an agent of destruction and purification, air as an element of the spirit.

Colors, too, can be used as archetypes. Green is often seen as the color of growth and rebirth, red as the color of passion and love, white as the color of purity and virginity, black the color of death and evil. Archetypal critics argue that such archetypes are universal—and it is clear that many of the same symbols are used from one culture or time to another, even when those cultures would have been unaware of one another. We would, though, caution you against ignoring some of the cultural influences that might throw such interpretations into doubt. Cultural anthropologists tell us, for instance, that in some cultures white is associated more with death than it is with purity and that red is the color of luck, not of passion. So in applying the methods of the archetypal critic, you may also want to consider whether the archetypes you are examining are likely to be archetypes that are particular to a specific culture or are more universal.

Although students are sometimes rightfully suspicious of what they consider unnecessary and strained symbol hunting, both psychological and archetypal critics often make a powerful case for seeing in everyday things something more significant. Both, for instance, have argued that snakes, worms, and dragons are creatures of the night, the dark side, and the subconscious. For that reason, they are also often emblematic of a negative sexual energy. For many readers, that is the case in both "To His Coy Mistress" and Blake's "The Sick Rose" (see 152–53 and 509). By recognizing the archetype of the snake's and worm's (dragon's) association with negative passion, readers will, then, recognize a very important reading of both Marvell's and Blake's poems.

NEW CRITICISM, OR FORMALISM

The forms of criticism we have discussed so far rely largely on a knowledge of events, ideas, and environments external to the piece of literature being studied. They are concerned primarily with questions of content rather than issues of form. Critics who are more interested in the structure of a work are called **New Critics** (the emphasis on form was considered new when new criticism emerged in the middle of the twentieth century) or **formalists.** Poet Archibald MacLeish put the New Critic's approach well when he wrote in "Ars Poetica" that "A poem should not mean / But be." The "being" of a poem, or any work of literature—the artistic way it is put together—is what is of primary interest to the formalist critic. Such a critic is likely to ask questions about imagery, poetic meter, sound, and rhyme; about how stanza, chapter, or act and scene divisions create meaning. Do they, for instance, encourage a feeling of suspense? How does the author's choice of narrative voice influence our understanding of events and characters? What use of irony does the writer make—and to what end? How do the connotations, not just the denotations, of words create meaning? How do image patterns create and reinforce thematic meaning?

For an example of a New Critic's approach, you might look back at the brainstorming questions for "To His Coy Mistress" in chapter 7. As you reread those questions, notice how many of them focus on the structure of the poem and the specific word choices—all matters of particular interest to the New Critic.

READER-RESPONSE CRITICISM AND DECONSTRUCTIONISM

In the past twenty years or so, two other schools of criticism have also gained some prominence. **Reader-response critics** combine many of the approaches we have discussed in this chapter, noting that each reader responds to a text with a unique set of assumptions and expectations, that there are as many different versions of a text as there are readers, and that authors and readers create meaning together. A reader-response critic asks questions about how a work was received by its original audience and by every audience since then, comparing the readers and their readings, as well as looking at the original piece of literature. In the process, readers themselves become "texts" worthy of study and interpretation. A reader-response critic looking at "To His Coy Mistress" might, for instance, trace the history of responses from the Renaissance to today or compare the responses of male and female readers, showing how each grounds his or her interpretation in the language of the text.

The past few decades have given rise also to **deconstructionism.** Like reader-response critics, *deconstructionists* argue that no work of literature has a single fixed meaning. Whereas reader-response critics revel in the possibility of multiple meanings, however, deconstructionists argue that any search for such meaning is futile. Whenever one finds oneself closing in on the meaning of a work, the work begins to deconstruct itself, falling apart in ambiguity and contradiction. Deconstructionists do not, however, simply throw up their hands at the impossibility of interpretation; instead, they delight in it, finding multiple meanings and accepting—and rejecting—all of them.

As you read this section, you may have been overwhelmed, and a little frustrated, by the multiplicity of critical approaches. Most of us want to believe that a close analysis of something will lead to a "right" answer, and it is clear that different critics with different critical approaches may arrive at different, maybe even contradictory, answers. We do not want to leave you with the impression, though, that anything goes when it comes to reading literature, that one person's interpretation is always as good as another's. The best interpretations are those that most take into account the words on the page and that consider the extent to which one's interpretation is idiosyncratic. By thinking in terms of a variety of critical approaches, you are more likely to find one that most suits your understanding of how literature works, and you are also more likely to open your mind to the full range of possibilities.

Finally, we would like to borrow a little from reader-response criticism. If it is true that each reader creates his or her own unique version of a text, then it is also true that each reader and critic is retelling the stories he or she reads. As you read the literature in *Retellings,* and as you read what other critics have had to say about it, think of how each of those readings and retellings might itself be open to analysis. Compare those retellings to the other retellings you have before you. In the process, we believe, you will come to appreciate more fully the way literature and our responses to it enrich our sense of ourselves and the world in which we live.

APPENDIX 4
Brief Biographies of Selected Authors

SHERMAN ALEXIE (1966–   ). Alexie is a Spokane/Coeur d'Alene Indian who grew up on the Spokane Indian Reservation. College educated, Alexie considers his reservation experiences an important part of his identity and a major source of his writing; he continues to live on the reservation. With firsthand experience of the despair, poverty, and alcoholism of reservation life, Alexie frequently draws on these realities in his stories. At the same time, the stories often contain a dark humor that expresses the richness of Native American traditions and values.

MARGARET ATWOOD (1939–   ). Born in Ottawa, Atwood is one of Canada's best-known writers. She is a prolific writer—of poetry, short stories, novels, and essays—and her work has been both critically acclaimed and popular with the general public. A feminist, Atwood often focuses on women who have been unwillingly victimized. Atwood herself sees motifs of isolation and survival as extending beyond feminist concerns; she believes these themes are typical of Canadian literature, in part because Canada has large wilderness territories and in part because it neighbors a superpower. Atwood currently lives in Toronto.

W. H. AUDEN (1907–1973). One of the major literary figures of the twentieth century, Auden was born in York, England, and educated at Oxford. At Oxford he became the center of the "Auden Generation," a group of influential poets. Influenced by both Marx and Freud, Auden's early work often expresses his social and psychological interests. Though political and psychological concerns remained important to him, Auden became increasingly religious. In whatever form they are expressed, moral concerns dominate his work. His poems are often a study of contrasts, both formal and colloquial, both serious and whimsical. In 1946, Auden became an American citizen. In his last years, however, he returned to live in Europe.

TONI CADE BAMBARA (1939–1995). Bambara was born in New York City. She earned a BA in 1959 from Queens College and an MA in 1964 from City College of the City University of New York. An African American writer who often took African American urban life as her subject, Bambara is noted for her ability to capture authentic speech and for her realistic examination of ordinary people and their concerns. Bambara wrote short stories, novels, and screenplays. She taught at a number of colleges but also remained a social activist. Born Toni Cade, she adopted the surname Bambara, taking it from a signature she found among her great-grandmother's possessions.

J. M. BARRIE (1860–1937). Barrie was born in Scotland and educated at Edinburgh University. When his older brother, David, died at age thirteen, their mother was plunged into a permanent invalid state. Some critics believe that David is the psychological source for Peter Pan, the lost child who yearns for a mother but cannot find her, the boy who will never grow up. Barrie married an actress in 1894, but the marriage, which was childless, was an unhappy one and ended in divorce in 1909. During the marriage, Barrie befriended the five Davies boys, and when the boys' parents died, Barrie became their guardian. The Davies boys provided Barrie with another model for Peter Pan. The play of *Peter Pan* opened in London in 1904 and was an immediate success. Though Barrie wrote many other plays, none was as successful as *Peter Pan.*

BRUNO BETTELHEIM (1903–1990). Born in Vienna, Austria, Bettelheim studied under Sigmund Freud. Shortly after he earned his PhD at the University of Vienna, he was sent to Dachau and Buchenwald, Nazi concentration camps. Released after a year, he came to the United States, and in 1944 he became a citizen. From 1944 to 1973, he headed the Sonia Shankman Orthogenic School of the University of Chicago, a school for emotionally disturbed children. Both his concentration camp experiences and his work with disturbed children form the foundation of much of Bettelheim's work. He wrote on the psychological pressures exerted by the terrifying existence in the camps, examining the ways in which his own knowledge of psychology allowed him to resist those pressures. His humane treatment of mentally ill children helped create an unusually high success rate in their treatment. Bettelheim's *The Uses of Enchantment* (1976), a Freudian analysis of fairy tales, explores the ways in which the tales help children understand and resolve their often unconscious desires and fears.

ELIZABETH BISHOP (1911–1979). Bishop was born in Worcester, Massachusetts. Because her father died when she was only a few months old and her mother had a nervous breakdown and was eventually institutionalized, Bishop was raised by her grandparents and one of her aunts and moved among their houses. As a child, she was often ill, so she occupied herself with reading and writing; when she went to college at Vassar, it was natural for her to become part of the same circle of future writers that included Mary McCarthy. After her graduation, Bishop traveled frequently, and her observations as a traveler inform much of her work. "The Fish," one of her best-known poems, exhibits her interest in detail and her ability to see the extraordinary in the ordinary. Bishop won the Pulitzer Prize for poetry for *Poems: North & South [and] A Cold Spring.*

WILLIAM BLAKE (1757–1827). Blake was born in London and received formal training in art. He earned an often meager living as an artist, primarily as an engraver who illustrated his own and other poets' works. A visionary who wrote a series of prophetic books loosely based on the biblical Fall and Redemption, Blake was in his own time sometimes considered insane. Though relatively unknown as both an artist and poet during his lifetime, he became much admired in the early twentieth century. Many of his most famous short poems are from *Songs of Innocence,* which provides a naive, childlike view of the world. Companion poems were included in *Songs of Experience,* which looks at the same situations from a cynical adult perspective. In this volume are the companion poems "The Lamb" (from *Songs of Innocence*) and "The Tyger" (from *Songs of Experience*). Blake's illustrations for the poems are also included.

KENNETH BRANAGH (1960–   ). Born in Belfast, Ireland, into a working-class family, Branagh moved with his family to England in 1969. That move made the young Branagh, Irish accent and all, into something of an outsider; that experience of distance and alienation has frequently influenced Branagh's work. Branagh has become well known as an actor, director, and screenwriter. In addition to acting in and directing *Hamlet,* he has directed and taken leading roles in *Henry V, Much Ado about Nothing* (playing Benedick), and *Othello* (playing Iago). In 1989, Branagh married the actress Emma Thompson; they were divorced in 1995.

ROBERT BROWNING (1812–1889). Born in a suburb near London and educated primarily at home, Browning read omnivorously in his father's extensive library. He continued to live with his parents until the age of thirty-four, when he eloped to Italy with the poet Elizabeth Barrett. Their fifteen-year marriage ended with Elizabeth Barrett Browning's death in 1861, and Browning returned to London. Though during the marriage Browning was often best known as Elizabeth Barrett Browning's husband, after her death his reputation grew; in the twentieth century his poetic reputation far outstripped hers. Browning's creation of dramatic monologues (including "Prophyria's Lover" and "My Last Duchess") represented a bold departure from the poetry of the time. Set in a distant past, these poems explore issues of good and evil that are timeless. Revealing more than they know, the speakers often provide complex studies of human psychology.

ANGELA CARTER (1940–1992). Carter was born and died in London, and, aside from the two years she spent in Japan, she lived her entire life in England. Educated at the University of Bristol, she studied medieval literature, elements of which often find their way into her work. Carter wrote fairy tales for both children and adults. Her adult fairy tales are often a mix of familiar fairy-tale motifs and violence and eroticism, creating Freudian fantasylands that are part nightmare and part wish fulfillment. Often considered a feminist writer, Carter blended her interest in the woman's perspective and in fantasy/nightmare in works such as "The Company of Wolves" and "The Fall River Ax Murders."

RAYMOND CARVER (1938–1988). Born in Oregon to a working-class family, Carver often wrote stories about working-class life in the Pacific Northwest. Married and the father of two children by the time he was twenty, he went from one low-paying job to another. Hoping to write, Carver entered college and graduated from Humboldt State College in 1963. His working-class background and life experiences are often presented in his stories, in which we see strained relationships, the constant struggle to make ends meet, and the use of alcohol and marijuana to deaden the pain of unsatisfying relationships and jobs. After having divorced his first wife, Carver met poet Tess Gallagher. They lived together beginning in 1979 and were married in 1988, less than two months before Carver's death from lung cancer.

WILLA CATHER (1873–1947). Although she was born in Virginia, Cather moved as a child to Nebraska, the state with which she is most often identified. She graduated from the University of Nebraska in 1895, and after that she worked as a journalist, editor, and teacher, writing on the side until she felt financially ready to devote herself to the full-time writing of fiction. Uncomfortable with the realities of modern experience, she often looks back longingly in her stories to prairie farms worked by immigrant farmers of the type she knew from her childhood. Another common theme represented in her works is the difficulty that those with artistic temperaments have in adapting to the sordid nature of material life, a theme we see in one of her best short stories, "Paul's Case," which was published in 1905.

C. P. CAVAFY (1863–1933). Cavafy was born in Alexandria, Egypt, to Greek parents. After his father's death in 1870, the family moved to England, where Cavafy learned English. Financial difficulties led to a return to Alexandria and then a move to Greece. As an adult, Cavafy returned to Alexandria, and he spent most of his working life employed at the Ministry of Public Works. Though Cavafy is now considered one of the best Greek poets of the twentieth century, his work was seldom published during his lifetime, perhaps because much of his poetry consists of erotic homosexual love poems. His other major subject is historical—both "Ithaka" and "Oedipus" fall into this category, reflecting his interest in ancient Greek legends.

AIMÉ CÉSAIRE (1913–   ). Césaire was born on Martinique and educated in Paris at the Sorbonne. He has had a successful political career in Martinique, serving as mayor of Fort-de-France since 1945 and as a member of the French National Assembly. Originally a Communist, he is now a member of a leftist political group. Césaire advocates "negritude," the abandonment of French colonial influences and the promotion of black culture. These values, often expressed in Césaire's poetry and plays, have been very influential in both Africa and the Caribbean. Though he was originally influenced by surrealism, since the 1950s Césaire has adopted more realistic forms, which he believes better express his political ideals.

ANTON CHEKHOV (1860–1909). Born in Russia, Chekhov is often considered a major influence in the development of the modern short story and play. The grandson of a serf who purchased his family's freedom, Chekhov was well aware of the realities of peasant and working-class life. Chekhov earned an MD from Moscow University in 1884 and worked many years as a physician. Initially, he wrote short comic pieces as a way of supplementing his family's income. The first symptoms of tuberculosis appeared in 1884, and Chekhov struggled with the disease until his death. In 1901, he reluctantly married his mistress at her insistence, and the marriage was generally not a happy one; the two often lived apart. Chekhov's works are noted for an ironic, bare style that often emphasizes character and atmosphere over plot, creating psychological interest.

KATE CHOPIN (1851–1904). Chopin was born in St. Louis, Missouri. When she was a child, her father died in a train accident, an event that is the basis for "The Story of an Hour." In 1870 she married Oscar Chopin, and the couple moved to the New Orleans area, where Chopin became familiar with the Creole life that she frequently depicts in her stories and novels. After her husband's death in 1883, Chopin turned to writing. Her works often portray women who feel limited sexually and emotionally in their marriages and who seek independence and sexual satisfaction outside of marriage.

Because Chopin's work explores the plight and psychology of such women without making moral judgments about their desires or behavior, it was often considered scandalous at the time. In recent years, however, it has been lauded for its portraits of repression and oppression.

SUZANNE CLEMINSHAW (1964–   ). Cleminshaw was born in Boston, Massachusetts, but grew up in Ohio. In 1990, she moved to England to live. Her story "Disillusionment of Ten O'Clock" was published in *First Fictions 12* in 1995. Cleminshaw has recently published her first novel, *Las Grande Ideas,* the coming-of-age story of a girl about to turn thirteen, the age at which her sister had died before Cleminshaw was born.

STEPHEN CRANE (1871–1900). The youngest of fourteen children, Crane was born in Newark, New Jersey. He left college to work as a journalist, work that brought him into contact with the most desperate New York slums. In 1897, he left with his common-law wife for England, where he continued to work as a reporter. Crane died at the age of 28 from tuberculosis. His background and experiences as a reporter often inform his fiction writing. Highly realistic, his stories mark the beginning of modern American Naturalism. Crane is also a master ironist, as we see in "The Bride Comes to Yellow Sky," in which our expectations of a Western gunfight are deflated by the realities of everyday life.

E. E. CUMMINGS (1894–1962). Cummings was born in Cambridge, Massachusetts. His father was a professor at Harvard University, and cummings earned both his BA and MA at Harvard. From early childhood, cummings wanted to be a poet, and for many years he wrote a poem a day. After college, cummings went to France to serve as an ambulance driver during World War I. When he and a friend wrote provocative comments in letters, trying to get as much past French censors as possible, they were detained for treason for a few months. Writing of the experience later in *The Enormous Room,* cummings cheerfully viewed it as having contributed to his growth. After the war, cummings moved back and forth between New York and Paris, devoting himself to both poetry and painting. Cummings is considered one of the most innovative of twentieth-century poets. His use of idiosyncratic punctuation and syntax, his word coinages, and the unusual placements of his poetic lines all contribute to his celebration of individuality.

EMILY DICKINSON (1830–1886). Dickinson was born and died in Amherst, Massachusetts. Though she led a conventional life until her late twenties or early thirties, an unknown traumatic event occurred then that caused her to withdraw almost completely from society. During the last seventeen years of her life, she remained in her home, even avoiding visitors. Though Dickinson sought to have her poems published during her own lifetime, she met with little encouragement. Her poems, unsentimental and experimental, offered little to satisfy the tastes of her time. Dickinson wrote over fifteen hundred poems, only seven of which were published in her lifetime, and those anonymously. Dickinson is now generally considered one of the most important American poets. Her most common topic is death, though she also explores nature and solitude.

JOAN DIDION (1934–   ). Born in Sacramento, California, Didion for many years was known primarily as a California essayist and novelist. After having graduated from the University of California, Berkeley, in 1956, Didion went to New York, where she became an editor for *Vogue* magazine. In 1964, she married fellow writer John Gregory Dunne, and the two returned to California. The California of the 1960s became her primary subject in her collection of essays *Slouching towards Bethlehem* (1968), from which "Some Dreamers of the Golden Dream" is taken. California is, however, in many respects a metaphor for the social collapse and fragmentation Didion saw in the larger American society. Didion's later writings have moved beyond California to explore other regions of the United States and the world. A distinctive prose stylist, Didion depends very much on the particular detail; it is in those details that she sees evidence for her wider themes.

JOHN DONNE (1572–1631). Donne was born in London to a devout Roman Catholic family at a time when Catholics were subject to extreme prejudice and even violence. In the 1590s, Donne became an Anglican after a period of religious searching. His public career flourished, and he became secretary to Sir Thomas Egerton, Lord Keeper of the Great Seal. When Egerton learned of Donne's secret marriage to his niece, however, he withdrew his support. With a growing family (he had twelve children) to support, Donne struggled financially. In 1615, at the urging of King James, Donne took Anglican orders. He soon became dean of St. Paul's, enjoying a public career as one of the great preachers of his age. Donne's life has sometimes been divided into halves: that of Jack the Rake, who wrote love poetry, and that of Donne the Divine, who wrote religious poems and sermons. Though the composition dates of many of his works are uncertain, that split now seems too simplistic. Donne probably concerned himself with both religious questions and love poetry throughout his life. In his love poetry, Donne often expresses the need to create a private lovers' world. All of his work is marked by the use of paradoxes and the joining of strikingly dissimilar images.

RITA DOVE (1952–   ). Born in Akron, Ohio, to well-educated parents, Dove was a distinguished high school and college student; she earned her BA from Miami University (Ohio) in 1973. From 1993 to 1995, she served as the U.S. Poet Laureate, the first African American and the youngest poet to hold that office. Best known as a poet, Dove has also written a novel, short stories, and a play (*The Darker Face of the Earth*, 1994). Though racial issues sometimes find their way into her works, her treatment of those issues often transcends race, providing wider historical and more universal human perspectives. We see that balancing act in *The Darker Face of the Earth*. Set in the pre–Civil War South, it examines a love affair between a white mistress and a black slave and so of necessity has much to do with race. However, by using the Oedipus legend, Dove asks us to look at issues of identity and fate that are also timeless.

RALPH ELLISON (1914–1994). Ellison was born in Oklahoma City, Oklahoma, a frontier state that Ellison felt helped him understand the shifting nature of racial relationships and identities. From 1933 to 1936, he attended the Tuskegee Institute in Alabama, where he studied music. Leaving college, he went to New York City, where he met such influential African American writers as Langston Hughes and Richard Wright. In part because he did not write the more sociological protest-style novel identified with novelists such as Wright, Ellison became a somewhat controversial figure, though few would now doubt that his contribution to twentieth-century fiction has been an important one. It took Ellison seven years to write *Invisible Man,* his only completed novel, published in 1952. Though "Battle Royal" had originally appeared on its own as a short story, it was incorporated into *Invisible Man.* As "Battle Royal" shows, the novel is concerned with matters of racial identity and strife. However, the novel moves beyond purely racial concerns, examining the nature of selfhood in wider terms.

TONY EPRILE. Eprile grew up in South Africa, the son of German Jewish parents. After a police raid on their home, the family voluntarily left the country, an experience that Eprile says gave him an understanding of the nature of exile. His experiences in South Africa are reflected in his book *Temporary Sojourner and Other South African Stories* (1989). Eprile has taught at a number of American colleges and universities; he currently resides in Bennington, Vermont. "A True History of the Notorious Mr. Edward Hyde" was published in the journal *Ploughshares* in 1995.

LOUISE ERDRICH (1954–   ). Born to a Chippewa Indian mother and a German American father and the oldest of seven children, Erdrich was raised in North Dakota. She became familiar with her Native American heritage through her parents, who worked at a Bureau of Indian Affairs boarding school, and her grandparents, who resided on an Indian reservation. Erdrich received her BA from Dartmouth College and her MA from Johns Hopkins University. In 1981 she married fellow writer Michael Dorris. The two frequently collaborated, even on works published under the name of one or the other. By the time of Dorris's suicide in 1997, however, the two had separated. Erdrich's poetry and fiction often reflect her Native American heritage, showing the tensions between traditional and modern values and behaviors. Her plots are frequently nonlinear, even circular, as in "The Red Convertible," which provides its ending in the introductory paragraph.

WILLIAM FAULKNER (1897–1962). Faulkner was born in Mississippi, the state in which he spent most of his life and the state that forms the setting for most of his works. A high school dropout, Faulkner attended the University of Mississippi from 1919 to 1920 as a special student. *The Sound and the Fury* (1929) was his first great novel, the first in a series that was to establish him as one of the most important American novelists of the twentieth century. Much of Faulkner's fiction is set in the imaginary Yoknapatawpha County, Mississippi. In his works, he explores issues tied to the Deep South, issues such as race and illusions of antebellum grandeur. Important as the Southern setting is to his fiction, these issues transcend that setting, as Faulkner examines ways in which ties to the past fetter the present. His experimentation with point of view was also a bold departure from the fiction of the day. In 1949, Faulkner won the Nobel Prize for Literature.

SIGMUND FREUD (1856–1939). Freud, who is usually considered the father of psychoanalysis, was born in Moravia (now Czechoslovakia). When he was a small child, his family moved to Vienna, Austria, where Freud was to spend most of his life. He earned his MD in 1886 from the University of Vienna. Initially interested in neurology, Freud's discovery that neurological symptoms could be psychological in origin led him to an examination of the psyche. He believed that much behavior is motivated by unconscious desires, often sexual in nature. Arrested sexual development in childhood, he thought, might lead to adult neuroses. Formulating his theory of the oedipal complex, according to which boys desire to kill their fathers and marry their mothers, Freud believed that boys need to learn to resolve these conflicts in order to form healthy adult sexual relationships. (He thought girls are motivated by the similar Electra complex.) As Jews, Freud and his family were in danger from the Nazis during World War II. With the intervention of President Franklin D. Roosevelt, they were able to escape to London, where Freud spent the last year of his life.

ROBERT FROST (1874–1963). Although he is very definitely a New England poet, Frost was born in San Francisco, California. After his father's death, the family moved to New England, which was Frost's ancestral home. He began writing poetry in high school and went on to attend Dartmouth College and Harvard University, though he never earned a degree. After college, he worked as a teacher and a farmer. Because he was unable to find acceptance as a poet in the United States, he left for England in 1912, where he established his literary reputation. By the time he returned to New England in 1915, he had become well known, and he remained a popular poet until his death. Compared with the work of many of his contemporaries, his poems were considered conversational and readable; they employed traditional rhythms and rhymes. At the same time, Frost's message is often very modern. Beneath the scenes of rural calmness are often undertones of alienation and death.

TESS GALLAGHER (1943–   ). Gallagher was born in Port Angeles, Washington, the eldest of five children. Her father was a logger, longshoreman, and fisherman, and her mother often helped her father with his logging work. Gallagher entered the University of Washington with the intention of studying to become a journalist. While there, she took a poetry class from poet Theodore Roethke and decided to become a poet. Her poetry is often autobiographical, focusing on her father and the Washington settings of her childhood. After two failed marriages, Gallagher began living with story writer Raymond Carver, whom she married shortly before his death in 1988. Her sense of loss and grief forms the subject of her poems in *Moon Crossing Bridge* (1992). Though she has written short stories for years, Gallagher, perhaps because of her involvement with Carver's work, has turned increasingly to fiction. "Rain Flooding Your Campfire," a retelling of one of Carver's stories, was published in *At the Owl Woman Saloon* in 1997.

CHARLOTTE PERKINS GILMAN (1860–1935). Gilman was born in Hartford, Connecticut. Her father abandoned the family when she was an infant, and her mother deliberately withheld affection from her daughter, hoping to make her strong enough to resist any emotional dependence on others. In 1884, Gilman married Charles Walter Stetson. After a year of marriage and the birth of a daughter, Gilman fell into a profound depression. She was treated by S. Weir Mitchell, who advocated the "rest cure," minimizing stimulation of any kind; the treatment, Gilman believed, made her worse. The experience forms the basis of Gilman's most famous story, "The Yellow Wallpaper," published in 1899. Believing that her marriage contributed to her depression, Gilman separated from her husband and went to California. After divorcing her first husband, Gilman married her cousin, George Houghton Gilman, in 1900. In 1935, suffering from cancer, she committed suicide. Gilman wrote extensively on women's issues, advocating women's equality. Gilman's ideas about independence and equality were influenced by her great-aunt, Harriet Beecher Stowe, the abolitionist author of *Uncle Tom's Cabin.*

SUSAN GLASPELL (1882?–1948). Born in either 1876 or 1882 in Davenport, Iowa, Glaspell graduated from Drake University in 1899. Over the course of her life, she wrote nine novels, including several bestsellers. Her reputation has diminished, however, and none of those novels is currently in print. In addition to writing fiction, Glaspell and her husband established the Provincetown (Massachusetts) Players, a theater group that gave many young playwrights their start. Glaspell's own one-act play *Trifles* was produced by the group in 1916; she later turned it into a short story, "A Jury of Her Peers."

BROTHERS GRIMM Jacob (1785–1863) and Wilhelm (1786–1859) Grimm were born in Hanau, Germany, to a prominent family. On the death of their father in 1796, however, the family circumstances became more modest, and the two brothers often struggled financially when they were sent to the university. Both brothers were noted for their studious habits; both studied law; both held positions as librarians and professors that allowed them to pursue their scholarly interests. The two collaborated on collecting and writing German folktales, as well as on a German dictionary. Their contributions to German literature and linguistics are impressive and established for them international reputations.

DONALD HALL (1928–   ). Hall was born in New Haven, Connecticut. His childhood was immersed in poetry; both his mother and grandfather frequently recited poems to him. Educated at Harvard University and Oxford University, Hall studied for a year under the poet Archibald MacLeish. Most of Hall's career was spent teaching at the University of Michigan. In 1975 he bought his grandparents' farm in New Hampshire and retired there to write full time. Hall's poetry is sometimes formal and structured, sometimes conversational and fluid; often it combines both qualities. As "My Son, My Executioner" shows, Hall is frequently concerned with autobiographical subjects. His poems (and essays) center on family and history, on reminiscence, the passage of time, and aging.

NATHANIEL HAWTHORNE (1804–1864). Hawthorne was born in Salem, Massachusetts, on Independence Day, and his life is bound up with American history. His ancestors arrived in New England in 1630 and became prominent in New England history, including the Salem witch trials. That colonial past, as well as issues of guilt and sin, was to figure prominently in Hawthorne's fiction. After studying at Bowdoin College in Maine, he returned home to live with his mother, spending years in literary obscurity as he learned his craft. His work in time became critically acclaimed, and he is one of the first great American fiction writers. As is true of "Young Goodman Brown," Hawthorne's fiction is often highly symbolic, and the boundaries between good and evil, love and destructive obsession are often blurred.

ROBERT HAYDEN (1913–1980). Hayden was born Asa Bundy Sheffey in Detroit, Michigan. Though he remained in contact with both his biological parents, Hayden was raised by foster parents who renamed him. After graduating from college, Hayden became a professor, first at Fisk University (Tennessee) and then at his alma mater, the University of Michigan. Hayden, however, considered himself primarily a poet. Though he was relatively unknown as a poet during his own lifetime, Hayden's poetry is now well received. His work often reflects racial themes, but Hayden refused to identify himself as an African American poet, preferring instead to see himself and his poetry as belonging to a wider literary tradition.

ERNEST HEMINGWAY (1899–1961). The son of a physician, Hemingway was born in Oak Park, Illinois, and raised in an upper-class family. When he graduated from high school, Hemingway became a reporter. In 1918, he volunteered as a Red Cross ambulance driver and was sent to the Italian front. A few weeks later, he was sent home, a decorated hero, having been seriously wounded. After recuperating from his wounds, Hemingway returned to writing, as both a reporter and a fiction writer. Much of the 1920s and 1930s he spent abroad, and Paris cafés, Spanish bullfights, and African game hunting became a part of both his life and his fiction. Hemingway served as a war correspondent during the Spanish Civil War and World War II. In 1954, he was awarded the Nobel Prize in Literature. Seven years later, suffering from depression, he committed suicide. Hemingway is noted for his terse, almost telegraphic style. The economy of words often reflects a sense of the loss of traditional values and certainties. "A Clean, Well-Lighted Place" depicts the typical world of Hemingway's fiction, in which the highest ideal is frequently stoicism, a brave endurance of disillusionment and the fear of "nada."

LANGSTON HUGHES (1902–1967). Although he was born in Joplin, Missouri, Hughes grew up in the Midwest. A prolific writer of more than 60 books, Hughes published his first book of poems in 1926, before he had even graduated from Lincoln University (1929). Before establishing himself as a writer, Hughes held many jobs, including jobs as a sailor on voyages to Africa and Europe. He settled in New York City and became a leading member of the Harlem Renaissance, an African American artistic and literary movement of the 1920s centered in New York City's Harlem. Hughes's poetry is often influenced by jazz and blues rhythms, and his speakers are generally plain-spoken, working-class African Americans. Though Hughes's work certainly shows a deep awareness of the costs of racial discrimination, it is nevertheless often characterized by a gentle humor and dignified wisdom.

ZORA NEALE HURSTON (1891–1960). Hurston was born and raised in Eatonville, Florida, the first all-black incorporated town. After doing graduate work with the famous anthropologist Franz Boas at Columbia University, Hurston collected African American folktales, tales which often appear in her fiction. She lived intermittently in New York City, where she became associated with Langston Hughes and other members of the Harlem Renaissance, a loosely associated group of African American poets and novelists. Perhaps because of her childhood in a town governed by black people Hurston refused to see racial discrimination as a defining element of her life. That refusal, coming as it did at a time of increasing awareness of racial injustices, may in r explain the relative obscurity of Hurston's work during her own lifetime. Hurston died penniless and was buried in an unmarked grave. In recent years, however, her work has gained in popularity, and she is now recognized as an important female African American voice, one that speaks of the individuality and rich cultural life of African Americans.

WITI IHIMAERA (1944–   ). Born in Gisborne, New Zealand, to a Maori farmer, Ihimaera graduated from the Victoria University of Wellington in 1970 and worked for a few years as a journalist. From 1973 on, he has been a diplomatic officer at the Ministry of Foreign Affairs in Wellington, New Zealand. Ihimaera believes that there are two New Zealands, that of the Maori and that of the Pakeha (Europeans). In both his writing and his career, he is devoted to making others aware of the Maori New Zealand. "His First Ball" was published in *Dear Miss Mansfield: A Tribute to Kathleen Mansfield Beauchamp* (1989). In that story, Ihimaera nods to the Pakeha vision of a fellow New Zealander (represented in Mansfield's "Her First Ball") while also emphasizing his own Maori vision.

SHIRLEY JACKSON (1919–1965). Born in San Francisco to an affluent family, at the age of fourteen Jackson moved with her family to New York. After graduation from Syracuse University, Jackson married, and she and her husband settled in Vermont, where she was to spend most of the rest of her life. Jackson's writing falls into two very different categories: humorous stories of domestic life (she was the mother of four children) and modern gothic stories. "The Lottery," Jackson's most famous work, clearly falls into the second category. When it was published in *The New Yorker* on June 26, 1948, the magazine received hundreds of letters in response, more than it had received for any other piece it had ever published. Many readers found the story disturbing. By making evil part of an everyday setting, Jackson asks her reader to reexamine the moral, social, and psychological realities we take for granted.

RANDALL JARRELL (1914–1965). Jarrell was born in Nashville, Tennessee, but spent part of his childhood in southern California. At Vanderbilt University, he majored in psychology; there he also studied and wrote poetry. After earning a master's degree, Jarrell became a college instructor. With the start of World War II, he enlisted in the air force. When he was unable to become a pilot, he became first a flight instructor and then a celestial navigation instructor. Though he returned to his career as a college professor after the war, the war and its soldiers continued to haunt his imagination. In many of his poems, as in "The Death of the Ball Turret Gunner" (1945), he takes the perspective of a dead soldier for whom the circumstances of both his life and death are a dreamlike blur.

GISH JEN (1956–   ). Jen grew up in Scarsdale, New York, the daughter of immigrant Chinese parents. She graduated in 1977 with a BA from Harvard University and earned an MFA from the University of Iowa in 1983. Though Jen sees her stories as representing universal human situations, they often deal with the cultural confusions and difficulties of Asian American immigrants. Jen usually treats the process of assimilation humorously and hopefully. Ralph and Helen Chang and their daughters

Mona and Callie are featured not only in "In the American Society" but also in Jen's novels *Typical American* (1991) and *Mona in the Promised Land* (1996).

JAMES JOYCE (1882–1941). Joyce was born and raised in Dublin, the son of a talented father who tried his hand at many things but was seldom financially successful. Joyce's education was a Catholic one. After graduating from University College, Dublin, Joyce went to Paris, and he was to live abroad in Paris and Switzerland for most of the rest of his life. Disenchanted by middle-class Dublin society, Joyce rebelled against its values. However, though the adult Joyce did not live in Dublin, it was the setting for all of his fiction, including *Dubliners* (1914), a collection of short stories that contains "Araby." Joyce's work did not find much of an audience during his own lifetime, and his financial situation was usually precarious. His experiments with point of view (with "stream of consciousness") created a style that was too challenging to be popular. The sexual nature of his work also led to controversy. His novel *Ulysses* was banned as obscene; it took a court ruling to allow it to be distributed.

JAMAICA KINCAID (1949–   ). Kincaid was born in St. Johns, Antigua, a Caribbean island; her father was a carpenter and cabinet maker. At the age of seventeen, she left for New York to work as an au pair. Her writing came to the attention of *The New Yorker,* and she was hired as a staff writer, working in that capacity from 1978 to 1995. "Girl" was part of her first collection of short stories, *At the Bottom of the River* (1983). Kincaid has become a naturalized U.S. citizen and currently lives in Vermont. Her prose is noted for its evocative, poetic style. As is true of "Girl," her fiction is often autobiographical; in it she frequently portrays a struggle between mother and daughter. In addition to stories and novels, Kincaid has written *My Brother* (1997), a memoir of her brother, who died from AIDS, as well as two books on gardening.

D. H. LAWRENCE (1885–1930). Lawrence was born in Eastwood, Nottinghamshire, England. His father was a miner, but his mother, who had more education, aspired to better things for her children. Lawrence was close to his mother and often sided with her, rejecting the kind of life and the values represented by his father. After earning a teacher's certificate, Lawrence taught school. When he fell in love with Frieda von Richthofen, the wife of a colleague, they left for Germany together. The start of World War I brought them back to England, but Lawrence's opposition to the war soon brought him into conflict with the authorities. After the war, he generally lived abroad, in Italy, Australia, Mexico, and France. Lawrence's fiction was often controversial at the time, largely because of its honest sexuality. Like his parents' marriage, his own was sometimes stormy, and we often see marital tensions represented in his works. As Lawrence grew older, he came to view the conventional gentility represented by his mother with more suspicion, and he came to appreciate the vitality represented by his miner father.

TANITH LEE (1947–   ). Lee was born in London, England, where she went to secondary school and studied art. She writes children's literature, fantasy, and science fiction, and her writings frequently reflect her interest in past civilizations and in psychic powers. She counts among her works many retellings of classic fairy tales, many of which, like "Wolfland," take a dark and erotic turn; in many of the retellings, the hero or heroine familiar to us from classic fairy tales becomes the villain.

DENISE LEVERTOV (1923–1997). Born in Ilfex, England, Levertov received no formal education as a child; instead, she was introduced to the great poetry and fiction of the nineteenth century by her Welsh mother, who read aloud to Levertov and her sister. Some critics credit this informal schooling for the smooth conversational diction of much of Levertov's writing. During World War II, Levertov served as a nurse, giving her a sense of the realities of war; years later, after moving to the United States and becoming an American citizen, she would actively protest U.S. involvement in Vietnam and participate in demonstrations for nuclear disarmament. Levertov's political pieces have often been received less favorably than her other works, and Levertov herself acknowledged that they blur the line between poetry and prose. Nevertheless, critics have generally responded very favorably to Levertov's work, and she has taken her place as a major poet of the twentieth century.

DAVID MAMET (1947–   ). Born in Chicago, Mamet attended the Neighborhood Playhouse School of the Theater and Goddard College. The author of numerous essays, poems, and plays, David Mamet is perhaps best known for *Oleanna,* for *Glengarry Glen Ross* (for which he won a Pulitzer Prize), and for a number of Hollywood screenplays and television shows. In addition to writing the screenplays for his own plays, Mamet wrote the screenplays for two well-known Hollywood films, *The Verdict* and *Wag the Dog.* Mamet has also written for television, including for *L.A. Law* and *Hill Street Blues.* His works are characterized by language play and by a kind of cryptic quality—he has said that people love a mystery, and he sometimes seems intent on leaving the mystery mysterious. He once described *Oleanna,* which was first produced in 1991, as a classically structured tragedy that invites questions about whose tragedy the play describes.

KATHERINE MANSFIELD (1888–1923). Born into a wealthy family in New Zealand, Mansfield was educated in London, where she majored in music and continued with the writing she had begun as a young child. Away from her family and the quiet New Zealand town where she had grown up, Mansfield embarked on a bohemian life that would later provide her with some of the material for her stories; indeed, she is said to have married her first husband simply so that she could gain the necessary experiences for a book she was writing. Intent on experiencing life to the fullest, Mansfield wrote primarily about the events she witnessed every day. Like "Her First Ball," her stories are usually stories of character, exuberant in their rich detail and imagery, and a bit cynical in tone and mood.

GABRIEL (JOSE) GARCIA MARQUEZ (1928–   ). Born in Colombia, Marquez is a Nobel Prize laureate whose writings have earned him not only critical praise but also popularity. His *One Hundred Years of Solitude* was so popular in Latin America that its first printing sold out in the first week. Later printings, both in Spanish and in translation, sold out almost as quickly. Meanwhile, critics gave the highest praise to Marquez; one called him the greatest Spanish writer since Cervantes (the author of *Don Quixote*), and another said he thought *One Hundred Years of Solitude* was the first piece of writing since Genesis that should be required reading for every living person. Many of Marquez's writings, including "A Very Old Man with Enormous Wings," belong to a genre that has been called "magical realism," but he is not a pure fantasy writer. A journalist by training and interest, Marquez combines fact and fiction, and his writings often reflect the political and social beliefs that have sometimes made his politics unpopular—so much so that he has even had some difficulty gaining entry into the United States.

MARY MCCARTHY (1912–1989). Born in Seattle and orphaned at age six, McCarthy was a prolific novelist and essay writer and one of the central figures of the New York intellectual movement of the twentieth century. Among her friends were dramatist Lillian Hellman and political essayist Hannah Arendt, and she was married for a time to Edmund Wilson, a major literary critic. Noted for her political moralism and her sometimes blunt dislike for anything hypocritical or untruthful, McCarthy became involved in a number of important causes. Among her writings are *Vietnam, Hanoi,* and *Medina,* three collections of essays about her travels to Vietnam and America's involvement in the Vietnam War. Her best-selling novel *The Group* was made into a popular movie. McCarthy's autobiographical *Memories of a Catholic Girlhood* tells of the time from her earliest memories, through her years as an orphan in the abusive household of an aunt and uncle to her time as a college student at Vassar. In it McCarthy also reveals her interest in exploring the lines between fact and fiction.

LYNNE MCMAHON (1951–   ). Born in Marshalltown, Iowa, McMahon grew up in Texas and Louisiana. She received her PhD at the University of Utah in 1982 and now teaches poetry and literature seminars at the University of Missouri. Her books of poetry include *Faith, Devolution of the Nude, The House of Entertaining Science,* and *Sentimental Standards.* She has also published essays in such places as *The New York Times Book Review, New Virginia Review, The Atlantic Review,* and *The Southern Review.* McMahon regularly gives poetry readings throughout the United States and Britain and has received several awards for her work.

ALICE MUNRO (1931–   ). Born in Wingham, Canada, Alice Munro grew up on a silver fox farm located outside the town. A good student, she earned a scholarship to the University of Western Ontario. After a divorce and remarriage, she moved back to a home near her childhood home and there continues to write her stories. Like "The Found Boat," most of her short stories and television plays are set in the everyday world of rural Canada, and her characters, often young women, live through common events. Those events seem, though, to take on a kind of magical importance. Often Munro's stories have little sense of resolution: there are no neat endings or moral meanings to her stories. Instead, Munro writes in conversational tones about the commonplace mysteries of life; she doesn't solve the mysteries so much as imbue them with interest and magic, leaving it up to her readers to understand and enjoy them.

JOYCE CAROL OATES (1938–   ). A prolific writer of poems, short stories, novels, plays, and essays, Oates was born in Lockport, New York. She graduated from Syracuse University and received an MA from the University of Wisconsin. She began writing early in life; at fifteen, she sent a completed novel to a publisher for his consideration.

Because she did not think she could made a career out of her writing, she planned to earn a PhD in literature and changed her mind only when she saw that one of her stories had been given an honorable mention in a collection of "best" American stories. Since becoming a writer, Oates has averaged an amazing two books a year. Best known for her short stories, she writes not only in a variety of genres but in a variety of styles. In "Where Are You Going, Where Have You Been?" (1966) Oates examines everyday events that take a horrible and violent turn for a middle-class adolescent, but in other pieces she has written about poverty and race relations, on the one hand, and about the American upper class, on the other. Throughout her work, there runs a strain of moral realism; all art is, Oates believes, moral and instructional.

TIM O'BRIEN (1946–   ). Born William Timothy O'Brien in Austin, Minnesota, O'Brien was drafted into the Army immediately after his graduation from Macalester College in 1968. For two years, he served in Vietnam, where he was wounded and awarded the Purple Heart. O'Brien's experiences in Vietnam provided him with the material for much of his fiction, including "The Things They Carried," and his fiction has earned him a reputation as one of the premier war writers of our time. His fiction often mixes the grittiness of war realism with a kind of dream quality that makes for a psychological and spiritual realism. O'Brien has said that one tells lies in fiction to capture a spiritual truth.

FLANNERY O'CONNOR (1925–1964). Born Mary Flannery O'Connor in Savannah, Georgia, O'Connor attended the Women's College of Georgia before going on to receive her master's in fine arts from the State University of Iowa. One of the most important short story writers of the twentieth century, O'Connor belongs to a rich Southern tradition of writers. Nevertheless, she established a voice and approach all her own. By her own accounts, at the heart of her writing is a deep belief in the tenets of Roman Catholicism, but her writing is not overtly religious. The worlds of her stories, including that of "A Good Man Is Hard to Find" (1955), are peopled by grotesque characters who behave in ways that are at once odd, humorous, and poignant. Although they often commit acts of physical or psychological violence, even the least sympathetic among them usually come to recognize the gift of salvation offered by the Christian God.

TILLIE OLSEN (1912–   ). The daughter of immigrant Russian Jews who had fled Russia after participating in a failed political revolution, Olsen didn't establish herself as a writer until she had reached middle age, having spent the first part of her adulthood raising four children, working at various jobs, and working for a number of political causes. For a time Olsen was a member of the Young People's Socialist League and the Young Communist League and a union activist. When she did begin to write, her fiction and essays revealed her political and personal experiences. "I Stand Here Ironing" (originally published as "Help Her to Believe" in 1956) includes many of the themes common in her writing; the story tells of a mother who, burdened by poverty and too little time, finds herself reflecting on her relationship with her eldest daughter, who has grown into a young woman she loves but barely knows.

GEORGE ORWELL (1903–1950). Orwell was born Eric Arthur Blair in Bengal, India, where his father was a civil servant, but he was raised in England in what he called "shabby" gentility. He left Eton College in 1921 to return to India as a member of the Indian Imperial Police. There he began to examine his beliefs about the destructiveness of colonial power. Both in his fiction and in his essays, including "Marrakech," Orwell frequently writes about the corrupting influence of power. He is best known for *Animal Farm,* a political allegory about the Communist Revolution in Russia, and for *1984,* a novel that gave us the terms "Big Brother" and "doublethink."

LINDA PASTAN (1932–   ). As a writer, Pastan has devoted herself almost exclusively to poetry, of which she was an accomplished writer even as a college student. In fact, while still a student at Radcliffe, Pastan won a national poetry-writing contest, beating out Sylvia Plath, who would become one of the twentieth century's greatest poets. Despite her success as a poet in college, Pastan somewhat reluctantly gave up her writing during the early years of her marriage, devoting herself instead to the care of her home and family. Those everyday relationships and activities became the subject of much of her poetry, which often explores the role of domesticity in a woman's life and which in sparse, conversational, and often melancholy language attempts to look deeply into the commonplaces of life.

CHARLES PERRAULT (1628–1703). Perrault was born and educated in Paris. The son of a lawyer, he himself studied the law and passed the bar exam. He practiced for only a short time before becoming disenchanted, though, and, after working as a clerk for his brother, he began a career of public service. He wrote both light verse and more serious poetry and drama, but he is best known for the fairy tales he collected in *Histoires ou contes du temps passé avec des moralitez* [*Tales of Olden Times with Morals*].

MARGE PIERCY (1936–   ). Born in Detroit, Michigan, and educated at the University of Michigan and Northwestern University, poet and novelist Marge Piercy writes from a political and feminist perspective. Influenced by her status as a white child in a poor, largely African American neighborhood in Detroit and having seen the struggles of her poorly educated and hardworking parents, Piercy believes that class, social status, and gender inform much of American life. She has joined a number of political movements: in the 1960s, she was active in the Civil Rights movement and in the Students for a Democratic Society (SDS), and she later became active in the women's movement. Some critics fault Piercy's work as overly political, feminist, and polemical, but Piercy rejects such notions, arguing that all writing is essentially political.

SYLVIA PLATH (1932–1963). Plath was born in Boston, Massachusetts, the daughter of a professor and a teacher. Educated at Smith College, Plath wrote poetry, a well-known novel (*The Bell Jar*), a radio play, and children's stories. Much of her work is autobiographical; it tells of her often troubled relationships with her parents and with her husband, poet Ted Hughes. "Daddy," one of her most famous poems, tells of her ambivalent relationship with her authoritarian German immigrant father, whose death left her feeling alone and betrayed. Her novel, *The Bell Jar,* is often autobiographical as well; it tells the story of a young woman facing a nervous breakdown and attempting suicide. From adolescence onward, Plath herself suffered from bipolar disorder, the manic-depressive illness that caused her to attempt suicide as a college student and, later, to succeed in killing herself. Plath's poetry and her life have earned her critical acclaim and almost a cultlike following among some, especially women. She earned the Pulitzer Prize for poetry in 1982.

EDGAR ALLAN POE (1809–1849). Poe was born in Baltimore, Maryland, the son of a lawyer/actor and an actress, both of whom died when he was a young child. In 1811, he was taken into the household of John Allan, a wealthy tobacco merchant, who sent Poe first to the University of Virginia and, after two years of military service, to West Point. In both cases, however, Poe was forced to leave for financial reasons. After leaving West Point, Poe worked for a time as the editor of *The Southern Literary Messenger* and lived with his aunt and cousin. He later married his thirteen-year-old cousin, who died of tuberculosis only ten years later and who became the subject of some of his poetry. Poe's writings are characterized by a sometimes morbid romantic sentimentality and, especially in his fiction, by an interest in gothic suspense. Poe is known as one of the fathers of modern fiction, especially of the detective story. As in "The Tell-Tale Heart," he often tells his stories from the perspective of the criminal, thus making use of the relatively new field of psychology. Interested in the sounds and structures of art rather than in its moral "lessons," he was also one of the major figures of the "art for art's sake" movement. Poe's own death has some of the mystery characteristic of his fiction: he was found half conscious outside a Baltimore polling place on election day, unable to explain what had happened; never regaining full consciousness, he died four days later.

THEODORE ROETHKE (1908–1963). Born in Saginaw, Michigan, Roethke was educated at the University of Michigan and Harvard University. A poet, essayist, and children's author, he taught English and coached the varsity tennis team at several universities. Roethke was a challenging and popular teacher, given to unusual anecdotes and antics. (In teaching the importance of description, he once asked students to describe his activities as he went out the window and onto a ledge.) The energy and commitment Roethke brought to both his teaching and his writing may in part be responsible for the nervous breakdowns that he suffered and that caused him to be dismissed from his teaching job at Michigan State University. (When a similar attempt was made at the University of Washington, the president of the university defended Roethke—despite his nervous ailments—as an "extraordinarily gifted" asset to the university.) Roethke's poetry, which is often intensively introspective, earned him the Pulitzer Prize for poetry in 1954.

MURIEL RUKEYSER (1913–1980). The writer of biographies, poetry, plays, and children's literature, Rukeyser was born in New York City and attended both Vassar College and Columbia University. A social activist who even as a college student reported on the world's injustices (she reported, for instance, on the infamous Scottsboro trial of nine young black men who were falsely accused of raping two white girls), Rukeyser was also an outspoken activist in a number of global political causes, among them the Spanish Civil War, the Vietnam War, and the attempts to free a South Korean poet who had been sentenced to death. Rukeyser's political interests find expression in much of her poetry, in which she often writes passionately from the position of the underdog. However, her writings are more wide-ranging and optimistic than her political interests might imply. She was also well known for her nonfiction, especially her biographies. Many are the biographies of nonliterary figures, including mathematicians and scientists, illustrating Rukeyser's belief that our culture too often divorces science and literature.

ANNE SEXTON (1928–1974). Born in Newton, Massachusetts, Sexton attended Garland Junior College and then went on to become a fashion model and a high school teacher. Plagued with depression (she spent some time in mental hospitals), Sexton began writing poetry at the suggestion of her therapist. There is often, indeed, a nightmarish, confessional quality to her poetry that critics have responded to with mixed reviews. Some have found the poetry *too* personal, too obsessed with the pains of childhood and with death. Others, however, have found Sexton's autobiographical poems and her retellings of the Grimms' fairy tales (in a book called *Transformations*) both passionate and powerful. Sexton was awarded the Pulitzer Prize for poetry in 1967. She committed suicide in 1974.

WILLIAM SHAKESPEARE (1564–1616). Born in Stratford-on-Avon in England, Shakespeare was the eldest of five children; his father was a prosperous tradesman and his mother the daughter of a gentleman farmer. Given his family's social status, Shakespeare probably studied the Latin and Greek classics. At 18, Shakespeare married Anne Hathaway, a woman who was eight years older than he and who bore him a daughter shortly after their marriage; a few years later, the couple had twins. Little else is known about Shakespeare's marriage; the couple apparently lived apart for much of their married life, but Shakespeare continued to provide for his wife and children even during the years of separation. We do know that Shakespeare eventually joined an acting troupe and wrote plays for it, sometimes taking on as well the role of an actor. The writer of comedies and tragedies, history plays and romances, poems about love and poems about death, Shakespeare writes about such a range of characters and human experiences that it has been said that in his writings lives every kind of person who has ever existed. Few doubt his place as one of the top three or four writers who have ever lived.

LESLIE SILKO (1948–   ). Born in Albuquerque, New Mexico, and raised on the Laguna Pueblo Reservation, Silko graduated from the University of New Mexico and taught for a time there and at Arizona State University. She first came to critical attention with *Ceremony* (1977), a novel about Native American life, beliefs, and rituals and about the importance of story. Silko also writes poetry and short stories that, like "Yellow Woman," weave together the myths and stories of Western European and Native American cultures.

SOPHOCLES (496? B.C.–406 B.C.). The author of more than 120 plays, Sophocles was indisputably one of the three greatest playwrights of what is often called the Greek Golden Age. It is said that in the Greek dramatic contests, at least eighteen of Sophocles' plays won first prize, and all the others won second prize. Oddly enough, the play for which he is probably best known—*Oedipus the King*—did not win first prize. Both *Oedipus* and *Antigone* contain elements common in most Sophoclean plays: both portray a central figure's unwillingness to compromise and the tragedy that results from that unwillingness. In addition to writing plays, Sophocles also served in the Athenian army and in the Senate, as a priest of one of the minor Greek gods, and as a representative of the Athenian state.

WALLACE STEVENS (1879–1955). Stevens was born in Reading, Pennsylvania, the son of a lawyer and a schoolteacher. While attending Harvard University, he worked for and published in two of the school's literary journals, and he won a number of the school's prizes for writers. Unable to complete his studies at Harvard for financial reasons, he took a job as a reporter for a time. Encouraged by his father to pursue a practical career, Stevens enrolled at New York Law School and obtained a law degree. Throughout his adulthood, he worked as an insurance lawyer while writing his poetry, essays, and plays. With William Carlos Williams, Ezra Pound, and others, Stevens became part of the Imagist movement in poetry; his writing often sees in a single perfect image a kind of transcendent reality. Among the recognitions he received during his lifetime were two National Book Awards and a Pulitzer Prize for poetry.

ROBERT LOUIS STEVENSON (1850–1894). Stevenson was born in Edinburgh, Scotland, and attended Edinburgh University. He also studied law and was admitted to the Scottish bar, but he never practiced as a lawyer. Among his better-known writings are *Treasure Island* and *The Strange Case of Dr. Jekyll and Mr. Hyde,* both of which explore the mixture of good and evil inside each of us. Stevenson wrote *Treasure Island* after an afternoon of drawing with his stepson, when he found himself drawing a pirates' map. *Dr. Jekyll and Mr. Hyde* was inspired by a nightmare Stevenson had, and he wrote the story in three days, only to throw it into the fire when his wife said it was too sensational. At her suggestion, he rewrote the story; the version we now have became an immediate bestseller, and, though Stevenson did not think it one of his better works, it remains one of his best known. Toward the end of his life, Stevenson moved his family to Samoa; much of his writing champions Samoan causes, and Stevenson became a popular figure among the Samoans.

JONATHAN SWIFT (1667–1745). Although he was born in Dublin, Ireland, Swift's parents were both English. His father died seven months before he was born, and he was kidnapped by his nurse and taken to England when he was only a year old. He was returned to his mother three years later, but when he was school-aged, he was sent to boarding school in Ireland, and his mother and sister moved to England. Swift earned a degree at Trinity College and an MA at Oxford, and he became an Anglican priest. He is best known as the author of *Gulliver's Travels,* the story of a man who travels to fantastic lands populated by such rare species as talking horses and miniature people. Although in modified versions *Gulliver's Travels* has often been presented as a children's book, it actually contains biting political satire, so much so that Swift claimed to have worried about whether its publication would put him in some danger. "A Modest Proposal," Swift's most famous essay, was equally shocking to Swift's contemporaries, some of whom believed that Swift was seriously proposing the solution of cannibalism. It remains one of the greatest examples of satirical irony in the English language.

DYLAN THOMAS (1914–1953). Born and raised in Wales, Thomas began writing poetry as a child and throughout his life saw himself primarily as a poet, though he also worked for the BBC during World War II and wrote screenplays and short stories. His poetry often reveals his love of words and sensual images, and he was influenced by both the symbolist and surrealist movements of the twentieth century. There is also a romantic strain in his poetry, especially in his use of myth and his emphasis on the importance of emotion, imagination, and intuition. At the same time, it is difficult to put a literary label on Thomas; he clearly saw himself as an individualist and resisted attempts to categorize him. Thomas's reputation as a poet has sometimes been overshadowed by his reputation as a man: he drank heavily and was sometimes rude and behaved inappropriately in social situations. His poetry has received mixed reviews, but poems such as "The Hand That Signed the Paper" and "Do Not Go Gentle" are widely acclaimed, and his short story "A Child's Christmas in Wales" has enjoyed some popularity.

JAMES THURBER (1894–1961). Born in Columbus, Ohio, Thurber graduated from Ohio State University and, with the assistance of writer E. B. White, became a staff writer for *The New Yorker,* for which he wrote a regular column and drew cartoons. Thurber is best known as a humorist who often, as in "The Unicorn in the Garden," took a slightly outlandish look at everyday events and relationships, especially between men and women. But he was surprised to hear his humor called "gentle," and in his later years he developed a pessimism that he said made it almost impossible for him to write comic stories. Nevertheless, he is perhaps best known for his humorous short story "The Secret Life of Walter Mitty," which tells of a husband's vividly imagined acts of heroism and adventure away from the watchful eye of his wife and outside the realm of everyday reality.

JOHN UPDIKE (1932–   ). John Updike was born in Shillington, Pennsylvania, the son of a teacher and an author. After his graduation from Harvard University, he attended the Ruskin School of Drawing and Fine Art at Oxford University. He is perhaps best known for *Rabbit, Run; Rabbit Redux; Rabbit Is Rich;* and *Rabbit at Rest.* These novels chronicle the story of Harry "Rabbit" Angstrom, a middle-class and middle-aged man who faces the everyday difficulties of life. In fact, most of Updike's writing is about the everyday, and some critics have called him a superb stylist who writes about unimportant things. In response to such critics, Updike says that it is in the "middles" of life that the extremes meet and an interesting ambiguity lies. Some critics have also criticized Updike for the sexual amorality in his writing, but most recognize him as one of the most important writers of the twentieth century and see his main characters as heroes of everyday life. It is the examination of that everyday heroism that lies at the heart of Updike's "A & P."

LUIS VALDEZ (1940–   ). The son of migrant farm workers, Valdez was born in the agricultural community of Delano, California, and himself began working in the fields at the age of six. After his graduation from San Jose State University, he spent some time with the San Francisco Mime Troupe, which was well known for its political theater, and then returned to the fields to organize migrant workers. As part of his attempts to unionize migrant workers, he joined and toured with a theater company that staged political dramas on the plight of Chicano workers. This political interest is apparent in much of Valdez's writings, including *Los Vendidos,* though his works also explore the blending of Chicano and Native American cultures. In addition to writing for the theater, Valdez writes screenplays for television and the movies.

ALICE WALKER (1944–   ). Walker was born to poor African American sharecroppers in Eatonton, Georgia. She was an introspective child partly because a childhood accident left her blinded in one eye and slightly disfigured. She was also, though, a bright student; she graduated first in her high school class and then attended Spelman College. She later graduated from Sarah Lawrence College, where her poetry came to the attention of Muriel Rukeyser. Walker's writing is sometimes criticized for its negative portrayals of men, but she has rejected the label of "feminist," preferring to call herself a "womanist," a term that has fewer political connotations. Walker is best known for her story "Everyday Use" and for her novel *The Color Purple*. That novel was turned into a popular movie by Steven Spielberg and earned her a Pulitzer Prize and American Book Award. The author of poetry, short stories, essays, and novels, Walker's most recent writings have generally been nonfiction. She currently lives in San Francisco.

E. B. WHITE (1899–1985). Born in Mount Vernon, New York, and educated at Cornell University, White is perhaps best known for his children's stories, for his coauthorship of a well-regarded style manual (*The Elements of Style*), and for his work on *The New Yorker*. Two of his children's stories, *Charlotte's Web* and *Stuart Little,* have been ranked among the best children's stories, despite the fact that at least one of White's early critics considered *Stuart Little* unfit for children. It is as an essayist, though, that White has most earned his reputation as a writer. A writer for *The New Yorker* almost from its beginnings, White wrote the "Talk of the Town" column; in that column, as in essays such as "Once More to the Lake," his writing—which is generally autobiographical—exhibits a gentle good humor and subtlety that have made him one of the most admired writers and stylists of the twentieth century.

WILLIAM CARLOS WILLIAMS (1883–1963). Born in Rutherford, New Jersey, Williams was raised in a household in which much attention was paid to art and literature. Nevertheless, his own interests inclined toward math and science in high school, and, though he wrote poetry even at that young age, he went on to the University of Pennsylvania to earn his medical degree. During most of his adult life, Williams continued both to write poetry and to practice medicine. He was especially intent on bringing to literature the idiom of American speech; Williams once said that as the child of an English father and a Puerto Rican mother with French, Dutch, Spanish, and Jewish ancestry, he could find a cultural and spiritual home only in America. Although he saw himself as intensely American, he was for a while denied a position with the Library of Congress for what one of its librarians saw as his "communist" tendencies. In addition to its idiomatic language, Williams's poetry is characterized by its visual immediacy. Along with his friend Ezra Pound, Williams was a member of the Imagist movement, and many of his poems focus on a single image from everyday life. Known primarily as a poet, Williams also wrote short stories. "The Use of Force" draws on his medical training and experience.

WILLIAM BUTLER YEATS (1865–1939). Although Yeats spent much of his childhood in London, he was born in Sandymount, Ireland, and he identified himself most fully with his Irish roots and with Irish political causes. While in London, he met and fell in love with Maud Gonne, a woman passionately devoted to the cause of Irish nationalism. Gonne encouraged Yeats to devote himself even more fully to Irish causes, and some of his best poetry has nationalism at its roots. The other major strain in Yeats's poetry, drama, and prose is a mystical one. Interested in the occult from an early age, Yeats became for a time a member of a secret society devoted to ritualistic magic. More important, he also developed a complex occult mythology of his own, which draws on Celtic mythology. Yeats also moved in the public sphere: he became a senator of the Irish Free State when such positions brought some danger and, with the patronage and aid of Lady Gregory, founded and promoted the Irish National Theater. Firmly established as one of the most important poets of the twentieth century, Yeats earned the Nobel Prize for literature in 1923.

Credits

ERNEST JONES Excerpt from "Tragedy and the Mind of the Infant" from *Hamlet and Oedipus* by Ernest Jones. Copyright © 1949 by Ernest Jones, renewed © 1982 by Merwyn Jones. Used by permission of W. W. Norton & Company, Inc. and the estate of Ernest Jones.

ALLISON JOSEPH "Barbie's Little Sister" from *In Every Seam,* by Allison Joseph, © 1997. Reprinted by permission of the University of Pittsburgh Press. First published in the Kenyon Review—New Series, Spring 1996, Volume XVIII, number 2.

JAMES JOYCE "Araby" from *Dubliners* by James Joyce. Copyright © 1916 by B. W. Heubsch. Definitive text copyright © 1967 by the Estate of James Joyce. Used by permission of Viking Penguin, a division of Penguin Putnam Inc.

DAVID KILEY From *Getting the Bugs Out* by David Kiley, published by John Wiley & Sons, 2002. Copyright © 2002 John Wiley & Sons. This material is used by permission of John Wiley & Sons, Inc.

JAMAICA KINCAID Reprinted by permission of Farrar, Straus and Giroux, LLC: "Girl" from *At the Bottom of the River* by Jamaica Kincaid. Copyright © 1983 by Jamaica Kincaid.

FLORENCE KING "A WASP Looks at Lizzie Borden" from *National Review,* August 17, 1992. Copyright © 1992 by National Review, Inc., 215 Lexington Avenue, New York, NY 10016. Reprinted by permission.

YUSEF KOMUNYAKAA "Facing It" from *Dien Cai Dau.* Copyright © 1988 by Yusef Komunyakaa and reprinted by permission of Wesleyan University Press.

D. H. LAWRENCE "Piano" by D. H. Lawrence, from *The Complete Poems of D. H. Lawrence* by D. H. Lawrence, edited by V. de Sola Pinto & F. W. Roberts. Copyright © 1964, 1971 by Angelo Ravagli and C. M. Weekley, Executors of the Estate of Frieda Lawrence Ravagli. "The Rocking-Horse Winner." Copyright © 1933 by the Estate of D. H. Lawrence, renewed © 1961 by Angelo Ravagli and C. M. Weekley, Executors of the Estate of Frieda Lawrence, from *Complete Short Stories of D. H. Lawrence.* Both used by permission of Viking Penguin, a division of Penguin Putnam Inc.

LI-YOUNG LEE "I Ask My Mother to Sing" from *Rose.* Copyright © 1986 by Li-Young Lee. Reprinted with the permission of BOA Editions, Ltd.

TANITH LEE "Wolfland," first published in *The Magazine of Fantasy & Science Fiction,* October 1980. Reprinted by permission of The McCarthy Agency, on behalf of the author.

TOM LEHRER "Oedipus Rex" lyrics. Copyright © 1959 Tom Lehrer. Used by permission.

CAROLYN LEIGH "I Won't Grow Up" from *Peter Pan.* Lyrics by Carolyn Leigh. Music by Mark Charlap. Copyright © 1954 (Renewed) Carolyn Leigh and Mark Charlap. All rights Controlled by Edwin H. Morris & Company, a Division of MPL Communications, Inc. and Carwin Music Inc. All Rights Reserved. Used by permission.

DENISE LEVERTOV "O Taste and See" by Denise Levertov, from *Poems 1960–1967.* Copyright © 1964 by Denise Levertov. "Advent 1966" from *Relearning the Alphabet.* Copyright © 1970 by Denise Levertov. Both reprinted by permission of New Directions Publishing Corp.

ANNE MORROW LINDBERGH "The Unicorn in Captivity" from *The Unicorn and Other Poems* by Anne Morrow Lindbergh. Copyright © 1956 by Anne Morrow Lindbergh, renewed 1984 by Anne Morrow Lindbergh. Used by permission of Pantheon Books, a division of Random House, Inc.

STEPHEN SHU-NING LIU "My Father's Martial Art." Copyright © 1981 by the Antioch Review, Inc. First Appeared in the *Antioch Review,* Vol. 39, No. 3. Reprinted by permission of the Editors.

M. G. LORD "Who is Barbie, Anyway?", pp. 2–17 from *Forever Barbie* by M. G. Lord. Copyright © 1994 by M. G. Lord. Reprinted by permission of HarperCollins Publishers, Inc. Willliam Morrow.

ARCHIBALD MACLEISH "You, Andrew Marvell" from *Collected Poems 1917–1982* by Archibald MacLeish. Copyright © 1985 by The Estate of Archibald MacLeish. Reprinted by permission of Houghton Mifflin Company. All rights reserved.

LOUIS MACNEICE "Rites of War" from *The Collected Poems* by Louis MacNeice. Oxford University Press, 1967. Reprinted by permission of David Higham Associates.

DAVID MAMET From *Oleanna* by David Mamet. Copyright © 1992 by David Mamet. Used by permission of Pantheon Books, a division of Random House, Inc.

KATHERINE MANSFIELD "Her First Ball" from *The Short Stories of Katherine Mansfield* by Katherine Mansfield. Copyright © 1923 by Alfred A. Knopf, a division of Random House, Inc. and renewed 1951 by John Middleton Murry. Used by permission of Alfred A. Knopf, a division of Random House, Inc.

JOHN UPDIKE "A & P" from *Pigeon Feathers and Other Stories* by John Updike. Copyright © 1962 and renewed 1990 by John Updike. Originally appeared in The New Yorker. Used by permission of Alfred A. Knopf, a division of Random House, Inc.

LUIS VALDEZ "Los Vendidos" by Luis Valdez is reprinted with permission from the publisher of Luis Valdez—*Early Works: Actos, Bernabé and Pensamiento Serpentino* (Houston: Arte Público Press—University of Houston, 1990).

P. H. VELLACOTT "The Guilt of Oedipus" from *Greece and Rome,* 1944, Vol. XIII. Reprinted by permission of Oxford University Press.

ALICE WALKER "Everday Use" by Alice Walker from *In Love & Trouble: Stories of Black Women.* Copyright © 1973 by Alice Walker, reprinted by permission of Harcourt, Inc.

MARILYN NELSON WANIEK "Emily Dickinson's Defunct" from *For the Body* by Marilyn Nelson Waniek. Copyright © 1978 by Marilyn Nelson Waniek. Reprinted by permission of Louisiana State University Press.

E. B. WHITE "Once More to the Lake" from *One Man's Meat.* Text copyright © 1941 by E. B. White. Copyright renewed. Reprinted by permission of Tilbury House, Publishers, Gardiner, Maine.

WILLIAM CARLOS WILLIAMS "Raleigh Was Right" from *The Collected Poems: 1939–1962: Volume II.* Copyright © 1944 by William Carlos Williams. "The Use of Force" from *The Collected Stories of William Carlos Williams.* Copyright © 1938 by William Carlos Williams. "Landscape With The Fall of Icarus" from *Collected Poems 1939–1962: Volume II.* Copyright © 1953 by William Carlos Williams. All reprinted by permission of New Directions Publishing Corp.

W. B. YEATS "The Lake of Innisfree" and "The Second Coming" reprinted with the permission of Scribner, an imprint of Simon & Schuster Adult Publishing Group. From *The Collected Works of W. B. Yeats, Volume 1: The Poems, Revised* by Richard J. Finneran. (New York: Scribner, 1997).

RAY A. YOUNG BEAR "Wadasa Nakamoon." First appeared in *TriQuarterly* #59. Reprinted with permission of the author.

Photo Credits

Chapter 1, p. 15: Reprinted from NeuroImage vol. 17, Andrews TJ, Schluppeck D, Homfray D, Matthews P and Blakemore, Activity in the fusiform gyrus predicts conscious perception of Rubin's vase-face illusion, p. 890–901, © 2002, with permission from Elsevier; **Chapter 5,** p. 115: (top) © Castle Rock Entertainment 1996. Photo supplied by Photofest, Inc.; p. 115: (bottom) © 2000 Miramax Films. All rights reserved. Photo supplied by Photofest, Inc. **Chapter 6,** p. 141: © AP Photo/IIHS; p. 142: © Miramax Films; **Chapter 8,** p. 183: © Bettmann/CORBIS; p. 198: © Nancy Ellison. Photo supplied by Photofest, Inc.; p. 210: © Erich Lessing/Art Resource, NY; p. 334: © MGM, 1956. Photo by Jagarts. Photo supplied by Photofest, Inc. **Chapter 9,** p. 423: Pygmalion and Galatea (oil on canvas) by Gerome, Jean Leon (1824-1904)/Bridgeman Art Library; p. 503: © Giraudon/Art Resource, NY; p. 504: The Metropolitan Museum of Art, The Cloisters Collection, Gift of John D. Rockefeller, Jr., 1937. (37.80.6); p. 573: Oleanna © 1994 Bay Kinescope, Inc. The Samuel Goldwyn Company and Channel Four Television Corporation. All rights reserved. Photo supplied by Photofest, Inc. **Chapter 10,** p. 617: © 1993 Bludgeon Riffola Ltd. Manufactured and Marketed by PolyGram Records, Inc. New York, NY. All rights reserved.; p. 655: © Archivo Iconografico, S.A./CORBIS; p. 736: © Jeremy Horner/CORBIS; p. 740: © United States Postal Service, 1999.; p. 771: P.125-1950.pt8 The Lamb: plate 8 from 'Songs of Innocence and of Experience' (copy AA) c.1815–26 (etching, ink and w/c) by Blake, William (1757–1827)/Bridgeman Art Library; p. 773: P.124-1950.pt43 The Tyger: plate 43 from 'Songs of Innocence and of Experience' (copy R) c.1802–08 (etching, ink and w/c) by Blake, William (1757–1827)/Bridgeman Art Library. **Chapter 11,** p. 843: © New York Public Library/Art Resource, NY © 2003 Succession H, Matisse, Paris/Artists Rights Society (ARS), New York; p. 858: © Scala/Art Resource, NY; p. 869: © Erich Lessing/Art Resource, NY © 2003 The Munch Museum/The Munch-Ellingsen Group/Artists Rights Society (ARS), NY; p. 870 (both) © Twentieth Century Fox. Photo supplied by PhotoFest; p. 909: © Lee Teter/Vietnam Veterans of America, Inc. Chapter 172, Toll Free 800-482-VETS; p. 930: © Digital Image © The Museum of Modern Art/Licensed by SCALA/Art Resource, NY. **Chapter 12,** p. 1106: © 1968, Universal Pictures. **Chapter 13,** p. 1318: © Castle Rock Entertainment 1996. Photo supplied by Photofest, Inc. **Chapter 14,** p. 1416: (left) © Classics Illustrated; p. 1416: (right) © Marvel Enterprises, Inc.

Color insert, INS 1: © Castle Rock Entertainment 1996. © Castle Rock Entertainment 1996. Photo supplied by Photofest, Inc. INS 2: © 2000 Miramax Films. All rights reserved. Photo supplied by Photofest, Inc. INS 3: ©

Index of Glossed Words

Index